Frommer

Europe
8th Edition

Here's what the critics say about Frommer's:

"Amazingly easy to use. Very portable, very complete."

—Booklist

"Detailed, accurate, and easy-to-read information for all price ranges."
—Glamour Magazine

"Hotel information is close to encyclopedic."

—Des Moines Sunday Register

"Frommer's Guides have a way of giving you a real feel for a place."
—Knight Ridder Newspapers

Wiley Publishing, Inc.

Published by:

Wiley Publishing, Inc.

111 River St.
Hoboken, NJ 07030-5774

ISBN 0-7645-6891-4

Editors: Alexis Lipsitz Flippin, *with* Elizabeth Albertson, Stephen Bassman, Mike Kelly, Amy Lyons, Marie Morris, and John Vorwald
Production Editor: M. Faunette Johnston
Cartographer: Roberta Stockwell
Photo Editor: Richard Fox
Production by Wiley Indianapolis Composition Services

Front cover photo: Rome: The Forum; woman looking at the Arch of Septimus Severus

Back cover photo: Los Gabrieles Cafe & Bar, Madrid

For information on our other products and services or to obtain technical support, please contact our Customer Care Department within the U.S. at 800/762-2974, outside the U.S. at 317/572-3993 or fax 317/572-4002.

Wiley also publishes its books in a variety of electronic formats. Some content that appears in print may not be available in electronic formats.

Manufactured in the United States of America

5   4   3   2   1

Contents

by Darwin Porter & Danforth Prince

by Darwin Porter & Danforth Prince

by George McDonald

3   The Czech Republic   144

by Hana Mastrini

4   Denmark   192

by Darwin Porter & Danforth Prince

5   England   218

by Darwin Porter & Danforth Prince

6   France   289

by Darwin Porter & Danforth Prince

16   Spain   893

by Sascha Segan & Herbert Bailey Livesey

17   Sweden   975

by Darwin Porter & Danforth Prince

18   Switzerland   1001

by Darwin Porter & Danforth Prince

Index   1045

List of Maps

About the Authors

A team of veteran travel writers, **Darwin Porter** and **Danforth Prince** have produced numerous titles for Frommer's, including best-selling guides to Italy, France, the Caribbean, England, and Germany. Porter, a former bureau chief of the *Miami Herald*, is also a Hollywood biographer. His most recent releases are *The Secret Life of Humphrey Bogart* and *Katharine the Great*, the latter a close-up of the private life of the late Katharine Hepburn. Prince was formerly employed by the Paris bureau of the *New York Times*, and is today president of Blood Moon Productions and other media-related firms.

Suzanne Rowan Kelleher is a freelance travel writer and the former Europe Editor of *Travel Holiday* magazine. She has traveled extensively in Ireland, is married to an Irishman, and currently lives in County Dublin. She is the author of *Frommer's Ireland* and a co-author of *Frommer's Europe from $70 a Day*.

All four of **Joseph S. Lieber**'s grandparents emigrated from Eastern Europe at the turn of the 20th century, settling in New York City, where he was born and raised. Mr. Lieber lived in Hungary for several years in the early 1990s. He presently practices law in Boston and is the co-author of *Frommer's Budapest & the Best of Hungary* and *Frommer's Europe from $70 a Day*.

Herbert Bailey Livesey is the author or co-author of 10 travel guides (including *Frommer's New England, Frommer's Canada,* and *Frommer's Montréal & Québec City*), a novel about deep-sea sportfishing, and several books on education and sociology. His articles have appeared in *Travel + Leisure, Food & Wine,* and *Playboy*.

George McDonald has lived and worked in both Amsterdam and Brussels as deputy editor of the KLM in-flight magazine and as editor-in-chief of the Sabena in-flight magazine. Now a freelance journalist and travel writer, he has written extensively on both the Netherlands and Belgium for magazines and guidebooks. He's the author of *Frommer's Amsterdam, Frommer's Brussels, Bruges, Ghent & Antwerp,* and *Frommer's Belgium, Holland & Luxembourg,* and a co-author of *Frommer's Europe from $70 a Day*.

Sherry Marker's love of Greece began when she majored in classical Greek at Harvard. She has studied at the American School of Classical Studies in Athens and studied ancient history at the University of California at Berkeley. Author or co-author of a number of Frommer's guides to Greece, she has published articles in the *New York Times, Travel + Leisure,* and *Hampshire Life*.

Hana Mastrini is a native of the western Czech spa town of Karlovy Vary who became a veteran of the "Velvet Revolution" as a student in Prague in 1989. She began contributing to Frommer's guides while helping her husband, John, better understand his new home in the Czech Republic.

Sascha Segan, a freelance writer, is a columnist on air travel and destinations for Frommers.com. He is the author of *Frommer's Fly Safe, Fly Smart* and has contributed to many Frommer's guides. In his spare time, he writes about gadgets for technology magazines. He lives in New York City.

Christina Shea served as a Peace Corps volunteer in Hungary and subsequently directed Peace Corps language-training programs in Lithuania and Kyrghyzstan. She's the author of the novel *Moira's Crossing* (St. Martin's) and a co-author of *Frommer's Budapest & the Best of Hungary* and *Frommer's Europe from $70 a Day*.

An Invitation to the Reader

In researching this book, we discovered many wonderful places—hotels, restaurants, shops, and more. We're sure you'll find others. Please tell us about them, so we can share the information with your fellow travelers in upcoming editions. If you were disappointed with a recommendation, we'd love to know that, too. Please write to:

Frommer's Europe, 8th Edition
Wiley Publishing, Inc. • 111 River St. • Hoboken, NJ 07030-5774

An Additional Note

Other Great Guides for Your Trip:

Frommer's Europe from $85 a Day

Frommer's Gay & Lesbian Europe

Europe For Dummies

Hanging Out in Europe

Frommer's Road Atlas Europe

Frommer's Star Ratings, Icons & Abbreviations

Every hotel, restaurant, and attraction listing in this guide has been ranked for quality, value, service, amenities, and special features using a **star-rating system.** In country, state, and regional guides, we also rate towns and regions to help you narrow down your choices and budget your time accordingly. Hotels and restaurants are rated on a scale of zero (recommended) to three stars (exceptional). Attractions, shopping, nightlife, towns, and regions are rated according to the following scale: zero stars (recommended), one star (highly recommended), two stars (very highly recommended), and three stars (must-see).

In addition to the star-rating system, we also use **seven feature icons** that point you to the great deals, in-the-know advice, and unique experiences that separate travelers from tourists. Throughout the book, look for:

Finds	Special finds—those places only insiders know about
Fun Fact	Fun facts—details that make travelers more informed and their trips more fun
Kids	Best bets for kids and advice for the whole family
Moments	Special moments—those experiences that memories are made of
Overrated	Places or experiences not worth your time or money
Tips	Insider tips—great ways to save time and money
Value	Great values—where to get the best deals

The following **abbreviations** are used for credit cards:

AE	American Express	DISC	Discover	V	Visa
DC	Diners Club	MC	MasterCard		

Frommers.com

Now that you have the guidebook to a great trip, visit our website at **www.frommers.com** for travel information on more than 3,000 destinations. With features updated regularly, we give you instant access to the most current trip-planning information available. At Frommers.com, you'll also find the best prices on airfares, accommodations, and car rentals—and you can even book travel online through our travel booking partners. At Frommers.com, you'll also find the following:

- Online updates to our most popular guidebooks
- Vacation sweepstakes and contest giveaways
- Newsletter highlighting the hottest travel trends
- Online travel message boards with featured travel discussions

What's New in Europe

Here are some of the latest developments in Europe.

AUSTRIA Vienna Housing one of the greatest graphics collections in the world, and closed for a decade, the **Albertina** reopened in 2003. It offers more exhibition space than before, a new restaurant, and a four-story graphic-arts collection ranging from the late Gothic era through the present day. It's housed in the neoclassical Albertina Palace, the largest residential palace in Vienna.

BELGIUM Brussels As the Eiffel Tower is the symbol of Paris, the **Atomium** is the symbol of Brussels, and, like Paris's landmark, it was built for a world's fair, the 1958 Brussels World's Fair. Closed for renovation through 2004, it's due to reopen early in 2005. Rising 102m (335 ft.) like a giant plaything of the gods that's fallen to earth, the Atomium is an iron atom magnified 165 billion times.

CZECH REPUBLIC In May 2004, the country was admitted to the European Union.

DENMARK Copenhagen As a sign of changing times, the brand-new **Sonoma California Grille & Lounge** has opened on the site of Den Gyldne Fortun (Golden Fortune) a dining room that since 1796 attracted the likes of Hans Christian Andersen, Jenny Lind, and Henry Wadsworth Longfellow. Copenhagen has rarely seen cuisine like this, heavily influenced by the kitchens of California, Hawaii, Japan, and Mexico, with farm-raised seasonal produce prepared in the healthiest and tastiest of fashion.

Tivoli Gardens' newest attraction, a state-of-the-art **roller coaster,** was scheduled to open in spring 2004 at a cost of 10 million euros. It will be the fastest, tallest roller coaster in Denmark.

FRANCE Paris The Musée d'Orsay is now bigger and better, with the completion in 2004 of new reception facilities, enhanced exhibition space, and a permanent Photography Gallery.

GERMANY Berlin The **Ritz-Carlton**, one of Berlin's most glamorous and prestigious hotels, opened in January 2004 at the Potsdamer Platz. The building evokes the Art Nouveau heyday of the New York City skyscrapers constructed in the 1920s.

GREECE Athens The 2004 Summer Olympics are being held August 13 to August 29 in and around Athens, the first home of the Olympic Games.

HUNGARY Budapest The **Antique Restaurant** is a combination of an antiques shop on the ground floor and a stylish restaurant in the basement, with a fantastic location in the heart of Pest. Every evening live Hungarian music accompanies the delicious dishes.

IRELAND Irish pubs and restaurants became smoke-free zones in March 2004, as a long-awaited smoking ban in public places was finally implemented. Enforcement is a different story, however, and it remains to be seen whether Irish publicans—

especially those in rural areas—will comply with the new law.

ITALY Rome Once hailed as Rome's grandest and best restaurant, Sans Souci faded into history like the Italian lira. Now the good news: The staff has reincarnated the restaurant. It's called **Antico Bottaro,** Passegiata di Ripetta 15 (℗ **06-3236763**), and its classic Franco/Italian cuisine is better than ever.

NETHERLANDS Amsterdam Sometime early in 2005, a new, state-of-the-art concert hall, **Muziekgebouw** (www.muziekgebouw.nl), will open on the waterfront between Centraal Station and the cruise-liner Passenger Terminal Amsterdam.

There's bad news for visitors who come to Amsterdam to admire some of the best of both Dutch and world art. The nation's premier cultural collection, the **Rijksmuseum,** Stadhouderskade 42 (℗ **020/670-7047**), is closed for renovation until sometime in 2008. As a consolation, one wing remains open to display important paintings by the 17th-century Dutch Masters.

NORWAY Bergen The 2005 **Bergen Festival** (www.festspillene.no) is scheduled for May 19–30. The festival features performances by regional, national, and international orchestras, dance ensembles, and theater groups.

PORTUGAL Lisbon The hotel **Lapa Palace** has introduced a new afternoon tea service in the Rio Tejo Bar, with a selection of more than 40 of the finest and rarest tea varieties in the world.

SCOTLAND Edinburgh In April 2003 guided parties were allowed to visit the dwellings in the **Real Mary King's Close,** Writers' Court, off the Royal Mile (℗ **0870/243-0160**) for the first time. Beneath the City Chambers, this warren of hidden streets has been dug out and opened to the public, revealing a place where people lived and worked for centuries.

SPAIN Madrid A massive expansion of the **Prado** is expected to add two new wings in June and October 2004, doubling the size of one of the world's most important art museums and giving it enough room to display a good chunk of its 20,000-work collection.

SWEDEN Stockholm In 2004, the **Nordic Hotel** (℗ **800/337-4685**) was named "The World's Sexiest Hotel" by *Elle UK* magazine. The decor of this resort complex was inspired by both the watery calm of the Nordic Sea and the "post-minimalist luminescence" of the northern lights.

The fastest and cheapest way to go from the airport to Stockholm's Central Station is the high-speed **Arlanda Express** train (www.arlandaexpress. com), which takes only 20 minutes and is covered by the Eurailpass.

Planning Your Trip to Europe

by Darwin Porter & Danforth Prince

The goal of a United States of Europe is still a visionary's dream, in spite of the euro, which binds many nations in a common currency. But even the euro can't link all of the countries of the European Union—"holdouts" remain, such as Denmark, which clings to its kroner, and the British Isles, which is still locked into the traditional pound sterling.

Nonetheless, in a continent where neighbors battled neighbors in two world wars, a great renaissance in art, culture, and economic growth is underway. Most of the nations of Western Europe are cooperating as never before, in spite of the inevitable minor squabble (Italy and Germany, for example, often tussle over cultural issues). Emerging capitals like Stockholm and Prague now lure visitors who once only patronized the classic "grand tour" European haunts, like Paris or Rome. As European cities move deeper into the millennium, new and exciting attractions such as Bilbao in Spain and the Tate Modern in London are challenging such traditional sights as the Tower of London and the Louvre as top tourist destinations.

Of course, you don't visit Europe to fret over their economies and politics. The rich culture and histories in each of its myriad countries and regions have always been the lure, and they remain so today. From the splendor of a walled hill town rising above the verdant Tuscan landscape to the majestic snowcapped peaks of the Alps, from the sound of flamenco in a Madrid *tablaos* (flamenco nightclub) to the blasting of a brass band in Munich's Hofbraühaus—one Europe it may be on the map (and now in the bank books), but on the ground, it's still a Europe of countless facets and proud, distinct, diverse heritages. There's no other place where you can experience such enormous cultural changes by driving from one mountain valley to the next, where in just a few miles or kilometers you're likely to encounter not only a completely different language but also different food, architecture, and culture.

Europe has seen some of the greatest intellectual and artistic developments the world has ever known, and the landscape is dense with museums, cathedrals, palaces, and monuments serving as repositories for much of this past glory. But the good news is that the Continent is still in a dynamic creative mode; artistic and cultural ferment are very much part of the present, and Europe helps set the trends in fashion, industrial design, cinema, technology, music, literature, and science. The dynamic environment is all about life, innovation, entertainment, and food, which exist side by side with the artistic and cultural grandeur of the past.

Europe is also about people. Europeans have seen the best and the worst of times, and a better-educated, more sophisticated younger generation is waiting to welcome you. They're as diverse and fascinating as the lands they come from,

Europe

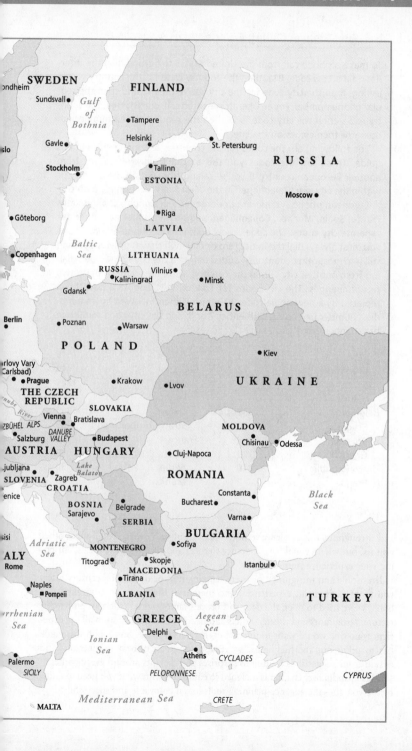

Number, Please: Calling Europe

To make a phone call **from the United States to Europe,** dial the international access code, **011,** then the **country code** for the country you're calling, then the **city code** for the city you're calling, and then the regular phone number. For an operator-assisted call, dial **01,** then the country code, then the city code, and then the regular phone number; an operator then comes on the line.

The following are the codes for the countries and major cities in this guide. These are the codes you use to call from overseas or from another European country. If you're calling from within the country or within the city, see "Telephone" in the "Fast Facts" section for each city.

European phone systems are undergoing a prolonged change. **Italy, France, Spain, Monaco, Copenhagen, and now Portugal no longer use separate city codes.** The code is now built into all phone numbers, and you must always dial the initial zero or nine (which was previously—and still is in most other countries—added before a city code only when dialing from another city within the country). Also, be aware of these two recent changes: The city codes for London (171 and 181) have been replaced by a new single code, 20, which is then followed by an eight-digit number beginning with either 7 or 8; and the city code for Lisbon has changed from 1 to 21.

Austria	3	Denmark	45
Innsbruck	12	England	44
Salzburg	62	Bath	1225
Vienna	1	London	20
Belgium	32	Oxford	1865
Bruges	50	Stratford-upon-Avon	1789
Brussels	2	France	33
Ghent	9	Germany	49
Czech Republic	420	Berlin	30
Prague	2	Munich	89

and throughout this book we've noted places not only where you'll meet other visitors, but where you'll have a chance to meet and chat with the locals, enriching your experience immeasurably.

Irresistible and intriguing, the ever-changing Europe of the 21st century offers you more excitement, experiences, and memories than ever. In compiling this book, we've tried to open the door to Europe's famous cities (their art and architecture, restaurants and theater, hotels and history) and guide you to all the experiences no one would want to miss on even a cursory visit. So though this guide has to point out the highlights, we've also tossed in offbeat destinations and adventurous suggestions leading to surprises and delights around every corner.

This introductory chapter is designed to equip you with what you need to know before you go—the advance-planning tools for an enjoyable and successful trip.

Greece	30	Norway	47
Athens	1	Oslo	22
Delphi	265	Portugal	351
Hungary	36	Scotland	44
Budapest	1	Edinburgh	131
Ireland	353	Spain	34
Dublin	1	Sweden	46
Italy	39	Stockholm	8
Monaco	377	Switzerland	41
Netherlands	31	Bern	31
Amsterdam	20	Geneva	22

The easiest and cheapest way to call home from abroad is with a calling card. On the road, you just dial a local access code (almost always free) and then punch in the number you're calling as well as the calling-card number. If you're in a non–touch-tone country, just wait for an English-speaking operator to put your call through. The "Telephone" entry in the "Fast Facts" for each city gives the AT&T, MCI, and Sprint access codes for that country (your calling card will probably come with a wallet-size list of local access numbers). You can also call any one of those companies' numbers to make a collect call as well; just dial it and wait for the operator.

When it comes to dialing direct, calling from the United States to Europe is much cheaper than the other way around, so whenever possible, have friends and family call you at your hotel rather than you calling them. To dial direct back to the **United States** and **Canada** from Europe, the international access code is often, but not always, **00**; the country code is **1**, and then you punch in the area code and number. For **Australia** and **New Zealand,** the access code is also **00**; the country codes are **61** and **64,** respectively.

1 Visitor Information

TOURIST OFFICES

Start with the **European tourist offices** in your own country; for a complete list, see below. If you aren't sure which countries you want to visit, send for an information-packed free booklet called *Planning Your Trip to Europe,* revised annually by the 31-nation **European Travel Commission,** 1 Rockefeller Plaza, Suite 214, New York, NY 10020

(© 212/218-1200; www.visiteurope.com). Or check out *Europe For Dummies,* available at most bookstores.

AUSTRIAN TOURIST OFFICE, INC.

www.Austria-tourism.com; info@oewnyc.com

IN THE U.S. 120 W. 45th St., New York, NY 10036 (© **212/944-6880;** fax 212/730-4568).

IN THE U.K.　14 Cork St., London W1X 1PF (☏ **020/7629-0461;** fax 020/7499-6038).

BELGIAN TOURIST OFFICE

www.visitbelgium.com or www.belgiumtheplaceto.be; info@visitbelgium.com

IN THE U.S.　220 E. 42nd St., New York, NY 10017 (☏ **212/758-8130;** fax 212/355-7675).

IN CANADA　P.O. Box 760 NDG, Montreal, H4A 342 (☏ **514/457-2888;** fax 514/489-8965).

IN THE U.K.　217 Marsh Wall, London E14 9FJ (☏ **020/7531 0391;** fax 020/7531-0393).

VISIT BRITAIN

www.visitbritain.com or www.travelbritain.org; travelinfo@bta.org.uk

IN THE U.S.　551 Fifth Ave., Suite 701, New York, NY 10176-0799 (☏ **800/462-2748** or 212/986-2266; fax 212/986-1188).

IN AUSTRALIA　Level 16, Gateway, 1 Macquarie Place, Sydney, NSW 2000 (☏ **02/9377-4400;** fax 02/9377-4499).

IN NEW ZEALAND　Fay Richwhite Blvd., 17th Floor, 151 Queen St., Auckland 1 (☏ **09/303-1446;** fax 09/377-6965).

CZECH TOURIST AUTHORITY

www.czechcenter.com or www.czech.cz; travelczech@pop.net

IN THE U.S.　1109 Madison Ave., New York, NY 10028 (☏ **212/288-0830;** fax 212/288-0971).

IN CANADA　401 Bay St. Suite 1510, Toronto, ON M5H 2Y4 (☏ **416/363-9928;** fax 416/363-0239; ctacanada@iprimus.ca).

FRENCH GOVERNMENT TOURIST OFFICE

www.franceguide.com; info@francetourism.com

IN THE U.S.　444 Madison Ave., 16th Floor, New York, NY 10022 (☏ **212/838-7800;** fax 212/838-7855); 875 N. Michigan Ave., Suite 3214, Chicago, IL 60611 (☏ **312/751-7800;** fax 312/337-6339); 9454 Wilshire Blvd., Suite 715, Beverly Hills, CA 90212 (☏ **310/271-6665;** fax 310/276-2835). To request information at any of these offices, call the **France on Call hot line** at ☏ **900/990-0040** (50¢ per min.).

IN CANADA　Maison de la France/French Government Tourist Office, 1981 av. McGill College, Suite 490, Montreal, PQ H3A 2W9 (☏ **514/876-9881;** fax 514/845-4868).

IN THE U.K.　Maison de la France/French Government Tourist Office, 178 Piccadilly, London W1J 9AL (☏ **0906/824-4123;** fax 020/7493-6594).

IN AUSTRALIA　French Tourist Bureau, 25 Bligh St., Sydney, NSW 2000 (☏ **02/9231-5244;** fax 02/9221-8682).

GERMAN NATIONAL TOURIST OFFICE

www.cometogermany.com; gntony@aol.com

IN THE U.S.　122 E. 42nd St., 52nd Floor, New York, NY 10168-0072 (☏ **800/637-1171** or 212/661-7200; fax 212/661-7174).

IN CANADA 480 University Avenue, Suite 1410, Toronto, ON M53 1V2 (☏ **416/968-1685;** fax 416/968-0562).

IN THE U.K.　P.O. Box 2695, London W1A 3TN (☏ **020/7317-0908** or 020/7495-6129).

IN AUSTRALIA　P.O. Box A980, Sydney, NSW 1235 (☏ **02/9267-8148;** fax 02/9267-9035).

GREEK NATIONAL TOURIST ORGANIZATION

www.gnto.gr or www.greektourism.com; info@greektourism.com

IN THE U.S.　645 Fifth Ave., Suite 903, New York, NY 10022 (☏ **212/421-5777;** fax 212/826-6940).

IN CANADA 91 Scollard St., Toronto, ON M5R 1G4 (☏ **416/968-2220;** fax 416/968-6533).

IN THE U.K. 4 Conduit St., London W1S 2DJ (☏ **020/7734-5997;** fax 020/7287-1369).

IN AUSTRALIA 51–57 Pitt St., Sydney, NWS 2000 (☏ **02/9241-1663;** fax 02/9235-2174).

HUNGARIAN NATIONAL TOURIST OFFICE

www.gotohungary.com; info@gotohungary.com

IN THE U.S. & CANADA 150 E. 58th St., 33rd Floor, New York, NY 10155 (☏ **212/355-0240;** fax 212/207-4103).

IN THE U.K. c/o Embassy of the Republic of Hungary, Trade Commission, 46 Eaton Place, London, SW1X 8AL (☏ **020/7823-1032;** fax 020/7823-1459).

IRISH TOURIST BOARD

www.ireland.travel.ie or www.tourismireland.com; info@tourismireland.com

IN THE U.S. 345 Park Ave., New York, NY 10154 (☏ **800/223-6470** or 212/418-0800; fax 212/371-9052).

IN THE U.K. British Visitors Centre, 1 Regents St., London SW1Y 4XT (☏ **0800/039-7000**).

IN AUSTRALIA 36 Carrington St., 5th Floor, Sydney, NSW 2000 (☏ **02/9299-6177;** fax 02/9299-6323).

ITALIAN GOVERNMENT TOURIST BOARD

www.enit.it or www.italiantourism.com; italy@italiantouristboard.com

IN THE U.S. 630 Fifth Ave., Suite 1565, New York, NY 10111 (☏ **212/245-4822;** fax 212/586-9249); 500 N. Michigan Ave., Suite 2240, Chicago, IL 60611 (☏ **312/644-0996;** fax 312/644-3019); 12400 Wilshire Blvd., Suite 550, Los Angeles, CA 90025 (☏ **310/820-1898;** fax 310/820-6357).

IN CANADA 175 Bloor St. E., South Tower, Suite 907, Toronto, ON M4W 3R8 (☏ **416/925-4882;** fax 416/925-4799).

IN THE U.K. 1 Princes St., London W1R 8AY (☏ **020/7408-1254;** fax 020/7399-3567).

MONACO GOVERNMENT TOURIST OFFICE

www.monaco-tourism.com; Monaco@Monaco.co.uk

IN THE U.S. & CANADA 565 Fifth Ave., New York, NY 10017 (☏ **800/753-9696** or 212/286-3330; fax 212/286-9890).

IN THE U.K. 3–8 Chelsea Garden Market, Chelsea Harbour, London, SW10 0XF (☏ **0500/006-114** or 020/7352-9962; fax 020/7352-2103).

NETHERLANDS BOARD OF TOURISM

www.holland.com; info@goholland.com

IN THE U.S. & CANADA 355 Lexington Ave., 19th Floor, New York, NY 10017 (☏ **888/464-6552** or 212/557-3500; fax 212/370-9507).

IN THE U.K. Imperial House, 7th Floor, 15–19 Kingsway, London, WC2B 6UN (☏ **020/7539-7950;** fax 020/7539-7953).

PORTUGUESE TRADE & TOURISM OFFICE

www.portugal.org or www.portugalinsite.com; tourism@portugal.org

IN THE U.S. 590 Fifth Ave., 3rd Floor, New York, NY 10036 (☏ **212/354-4403;** fax 212/575-4737).

IN CANADA 60 Bloor St. W., Suite 1005, Toronto, ON M4W 3B8 (☏ **416/921-7376;** fax 416/921-1353).

IN THE U.K. 22 Sackville St., 2nd Floor, London W1S 3LY (☏ **020/7494-5720;** fax 020/7494-1868).

SCANDINAVIAN TOURIST BOARDS (DENMARK, NORWAY & SWEDEN)

www.goscandinavia.com, www.visitdenmark.com, www.visitnorway.com, or www.visit-sweden.com; usa@nortra.no, info@gosweden.org, dtb.london@dt.dk, or greatbritain@nortra.no

IN THE U.S. & CANADA P.O. Box 4649, Grand Central Station, New York, NY 10163-4649 (© **212/885-9700;** fax 212/885-9710).

IN THE U.K. Danish Tourist Board, 55 Sloane St., London SW1X 9SY (© **020/7259-5959;** fax 020/7259-5955); Norwegian Tourist Board, 5 Regent St., London, SW1Y 4LR (© **020/7839-2650;** fax 020/7839-6014); Swedish Travel & Tourism Council, 5 Upper Montagu St., London W1H 2AG (© **020/7870-5604;** fax 020/7724-5872).

SWITZERLAND TOURISM

www.switzerlandtourism.com; info.uk@switzerland tourism.ch or info.usa@switzerland.com

IN THE U.S. 608 Fifth Ave., New York, NY 10020 (© **877/794-8037** or 212/757-5944; fax 212/262-6116).

IN THE U.K. Swiss Centre, 10 Wardour St., London, W1D 6QF (© **020/7292-1550;** fax 020/7437-4577).

TOURIST OFFICE OF SPAIN

www.okspain.org; oetny@here-i.com

IN THE U.S. 666 Fifth Ave., 35th Floor, New York, NY 10103 (© **212/265-8822;** fax 212/265-8864); 845 N. Michigan Ave., Suite 915E, Chicago, IL 60611 (© **312/642-1992;** fax 312/642-9817); 8383 Wilshire Blvd., Suite 956, Los Angeles, CA 90211 (© **323/658-7188;** fax 323/658-1061); 1221 Brickell Ave., Suite 1850, Miami, FL 33131 (© **305/358-1992;** fax 305/358-8223).

IN CANADA 2 Bloor St. W., 34th Floor, Toronto, ON M5S 1M9 (© **416/961-3131;** fax 416/961-1992).

IN THE U.K. 22–23 Manchester Sq., London W1M 5AP (© **020/7486-8077;** fax 020/7486-8034).

TRAVEL AGENTS

Travel agents can save you plenty of time and money by hunting down the best airfare for your route and arranging for rail passes and rental cars. For now, most travel agents still charge you nothing for their services—they're paid through commissions from the airlines and other agencies they book for you. However, a number of airlines have begun cutting commissions, and increasingly, agents are finding they have to charge you a fee to hold the bottom line (or else unscrupulous agents will offer you only the travel options that bag them the juiciest commissions). Shop around and ask hard questions.

If you decide to use a travel agent, make sure the agent is a member of the **American Society of Travel Agents (ASTA),** 1101 King St., Alexandria, VA 22314 (© **703/739-8739;** www.astanet.com). If you send them a self-addressed stamped envelope, ASTA will mail you the booklet *Avoiding Travel Problems* for free.

2 Entry Requirements & Customs

PASSPORTS

If you don't already have one, you can download a passport application from the websites listed below. Countries covered in this guide do *not* require visas for U.S. or Canadian citizens for stays less than 90 days. Though a valid U.S. state driver's license usually suffices, it's wise to carry an **International Driving Permit** ($10), which you can obtain from any AAA branch if you bring two passport-size photos.

U.S. CITIZENS If you're applying for a first-time passport, you need to do it in person at a U.S. passport office; a federal, state, or probate court; or a major post office (though not all post offices accept applications; call the number below to find the ones that do). You need to present a certified birth certificate as proof of citizenship, and it's wise to bring along your driver's license, state or military ID, and social security card as well. You also need two identical passport-size photos (2 in. by 2 in.), taken at any corner photo shop (not one of the strip photos, however, from a photo-vending machine).

For people over 15, a passport is valid for 10 years and costs $55; for those 15 and under, it's valid for 5 years and costs $40 plus a $30 execution fee. If you're over 15 and have a valid passport that was issued within the past 12 years, you can renew it by mail for $40. Allow plenty of time before your trip to apply; processing normally takes 3 weeks but can take longer during busy periods (especially spring). For general information, call the **National Passport Agency** (© 202/647-0518). To find your regional passport office, either check the U.S. State Department website (http://travel.state.gov) or call the **National Passport Information Center** toll-free number (© 877/487-2778) for automated information.

CANADIAN CITIZENS Canadian passports are valid for 5 years and cost $85. Children under 16 may be included on a parent's passport but need their own to travel unaccompanied by the parent. Applications, which must be accompanied by two identical passport-size photographs and proof of Canadian citizenship, are available at passport offices throughout Canada, at post offices, or from the central **Passport Office, Department of Foreign Affairs and International Trade,** Ottawa, ON K1A 0G3 (© 800/267-6788; www.dfait-maeci.gc.ca). Processing takes 5 to 10 days if you apply in person, or about 3 weeks by mail.

U.K. CITIZENS As a member of the European Union, you need only an identity card, not a passport, to travel to other EU countries. However, if you already possess a passport, it's always useful to carry it. To pick up an application for a regular 10-year passport (the Visitor's Passport has been abolished), visit your nearest passport office, major post office, or travel agency. You can also contact the **United Kingdom Passport Service** at © 0870/521-0410 or search its website at www.ukpa.gov.uk. Passports are £42 for adults and £25 for children under 16.

IRISH CITIZENS You can apply for a 10-year passport, costing €57 at the **Passport Office,** Setanta Centre, Molesworth Street, Dublin 2 (© 01/671-1633; www.irlgov.ie/iveagh). Standard passports are €57. Those under age 18 and over 65 must apply for a 3-year passport costing €12. You can also apply at 1A South Mall, Cork (© 021/494-4700); or over the counter at most main post offices.

AUSTRALIAN CITIZENS Apply at your local post office or passport office or search the government website

---

Tips **Savvy Travel Safeguards**

Safeguard your passport in an inconspicuous, inaccessible place like a money belt. If you lose it, visit the nearest consulate of your native country as soon as possible for a replacement. Before leaving home, make two photocopy collages of your important documents: the first page of your passport (the page with the photo and identifying info), driver's license, and other ID. Leave one copy at home with a family member or friend and carry the other with you (separate from the originals!).

at **www.passports.gov.au**. Passports cost A$148 for adults and A$74 for those under 18. The **Australia State Passport Office** can be reached at (C) **02/131232;** travelers must schedule an interview to submit your passport application materials.

NEW ZEALAND CITIZENS You can pick up a passport application at any travel agency or Link Centre. For more info, contact the **Passport Office,** Department of Internal Affairs, 47 Boulcott House, Wellington ((C) **0800/225-050;** www.passports. govt.nz). Passports are NZ$71 for adults and NZ$36 for those under 16.

CUSTOMS

U.S. CITIZENS Returning **U.S. citizens** who have been away for at least 48 hours are allowed to bring back, once every 30 days, $800 worth of merchandise duty-free. You'll be charged a flat rate of 10% duty on the next $1,000 worth of purchases. Be sure to have your receipts handy. On mailed gifts, the duty-free limit is $200. You cannot bring fresh food-stuffs into the United States; some tinned foods, however, are allowed. For more information, contact **U.S. Customs & Border Protection (CBP),** 1300 Pennsylvania Ave. NW, Washington, DC 20229 ((C) **877/287-8667**) and request the free pamphlet *Know Before You Go.* It's also available on the Web at **www.cbp.gov**. (Click on "Travel," and then click on "Know Before You Go! Online Brochure.")

U.K. CITIZENS If you are **returning from a European Community (EC) country,** you will go through a separate Customs Exit (called the "Blue Exit") especially for EC travelers. In essence, there is no limit on what you can bring back from an EC country, as long as the items are for personal use (this includes gifts), and you have already paid the necessary duty and tax. However, Customs law sets out guidance levels. If you bring

in more than these levels, you may be asked to prove that the goods are for your own use. Guidance levels on goods bought into the EC for your own use are 3,200 cigarettes, 200 cigars, 3 kilograms of smoking tobacco, 10 liters of spirits, 90 liters of wine, and 110 liters of beer. For more information, contact **HM Customs & Excise,** National Advice Service, Dorset House, Stamford St., London SE1 9PY ((C) **0208/929-0152;** or consult their website at www.hmce.gov.uk).

U.K. citizens returning from a non-EC country have a Customs allowance of 200 cigarettes; 50 cigars; 250 grams of smoking tobacco; 2 liters of still table wine; 1 liter of spirits or strong liqueurs (over 22% volume); 2 liters of fortified wine, sparkling wine or other liqueurs; 60cc (ml) of perfume; 250cc (ml) of toilet water; and £145 worth of all other goods, including gifts and souvenirs. People under 17 cannot have the tobacco or alcohol allowance. For more information, contact **HM Customs & Excise** (see above).

CANADIAN CITIZENS For a clear summary of **Canadian** rules, write for the booklet *I Declare,* issued by the **Canada Customs and Revenue Agency** ((C) **800/461-9999** in Canada, or 204/983-3500; www.ccra-adrc.gc. ca). Canada allows its citizens a C$750 exemption, and you're allowed to bring back duty-free 1 carton of cigarettes, 1 can of tobacco, 40 imperial ounces of liquor, and 50 cigars. In addition, you're allowed to mail gifts to Canada valued at less than C$60 a day, provided they're unsolicited and don't contain alcohol or tobacco (write on the package "Unsolicited gift, under $60 value"). All valuables should be declared on the Y-38 form before departure from Canada, including serial numbers of valuables you already own, such as expensive foreign cameras. *Note:* The $750 exemption can only be used once a year and only after an absence of 7 days.

AUSTRALIAN CITIZENS The duty-free allowance in **Australia** is A$400 or, for those under 18, A$200. Upon returning to Australia, citizens can bring in 250 cigarettes or 250 grams of loose tobacco, and 1,125ml of alcohol. If you're returning with valuable goods you already own, such as foreign-made cameras, you should file Form B263. A helpful brochure, available from Australian consulates or Customs offices, is *Know Before You Go*. For more information, contact **Australian Customs Services,** 477 Pitt St., GPO Box 8, Sydney NSW 2000 (© **02/6275-6666** in Australia, or 202/797-3189 in the U.S.), or go to **www.customs.gov.au**.

NEW ZEALAND CITIZENS The duty-free allowance for **New Zealand** is NZ$700. Citizens over 17 can bring in 200 cigarettes, or 50 cigars, or 250 grams of tobacco (or a mixture of all three if their combined weight doesn't exceed 250g); plus 4.5 liters of wine and beer, or 1.125 liters of liquor. New Zealand currency does not carry import or export restrictions. Fill out a certificate of export, listing the valuables you are taking out of the country; that way, you can bring them back without paying duty. Most questions are answered in a free pamphlet available at New Zealand consulates and Customs offices: *New Zealand Customs Guide for Travellers, Notice no. 4.* For more information, contact **New Zealand Customs,** 17–21 Whitmore St., P.O. Box 2218, Wellington, NZ (© **04/473-6099**), or go to www. customs.govt.nz.

3 Money

Traveler's checks, while still the safest way to carry money, are going the way of the dinosaur. The aggressive evolution of international computerized banking and ATM networks has led to the triumph of plastic in Europe— even if cold cash is still the most trusted currency. Odds are you can saunter up to an ATM in the dinkiest Bavarian village with your bank card or PIN-enabled Visa and get some local cash out of it. Never rely on credit cards and ATMs alone, however. Though most hotels and many restaurants around Europe accept plastic, smaller towns and cheaper places are still wary, and occasionally the phone lines and computer networks used to verify your card can go down and render your plastic useless. Always carry some local currency and some traveler's checks for insurance.

Although currency conversions in this guide were accurate at press time, European exchange rates fluctuate. For up-to-date rates, look in the business pages or travel section of any major U.S. newspaper, check online at the **Universal Currency Converter (www.xe.com)**, or call **Thomas Cook** (see "Traveler's Checks," below).

It's more expensive to purchase foreign currency in your own country than once you've reached your destination. But it's a good idea to arrive in Europe with a bit of the local currency—at least enough to get you from the airport to your hotel, so you can avoid the bad rates you get at airport exchanges. Bring along about $30 to $50 in the local currencies—usually euros—of every European city you'll be visiting (call around to the major branches of local banks in your hometown to find the best rate).

While traveling, either withdraw local currency from an ATM (see below) or convert your cash or traveler's checks at a bank whenever possible— banks invariably give better rates than tourist offices, hotels, travel agencies, or exchange booths. You lose money every time you make a transaction, so it's often better to convert large sums at once (especially in flat-fee transactions). The rates for converting traveler's

The World's Greatest Financial Merger: The Euro

On March 1, 2002, the euro officially replaced the legacy currencies as legal tender in the "euro zone," including the countries of Austria, Belgium, Finland, France, Germany, Greece, Ireland, Italy, Luxembourg, the Netherlands, Portugal, and Spain. Britain, Denmark, and Sweden do not fall under the euro umbrella, even though they are members of the EU. The Czech Republic, Hungary, Norway, and Switzerland are not part of the EU.

Euros come in note denominations of 5, 10, 20, 50, 100, 200, and 500, and coin denominations of 1- and 2-euros and 1, 2, 5, 10, 20, and 50 cents. Coins have a common face on one side. The opposite face has a design chosen by the issuing country.

Note: As this book went to press, 1€ was worth approximately $1.15 and gaining in strength, so your dollars might not go as far as you'd expect. For up-to-the-minute exchange rates between the euro and the dollar, check the currency-converter website **www.xe.com**.

checks are usually better than those for cash, but you get the best rates by withdrawing money from an ATM with your bank or credit card.

ATMS

PLUS, Cirrus, and other networks work on many ATMs in Europe, giving you local currency and drawing it directly from your checking account. This is the fastest, easiest, and least expensive way to change money. You take advantage of the bank's bulk exchange rate (better than anything you'll get on your own exchanging cash or traveler's checks) and, unless your home bank charges you for using a nonproprietary ATM, you won't have to pay a commission. Make sure the PINs on your bank and credit cards will work in Europe; you usually need a four-digit code (six digits often won't work). Keep in mind you're usually able to access only your checking account, not savings, from ATMs abroad.

Both the **Cirrus** (© 800/424-7787; www.mastercard.com) and the **PLUS** (© 800/843-7587; www.visa.com) networks have ATM locators listing the banks in each country that accept your

card; alternately, you can just search out any machine with your network's symbol on it. Europe is getting to be like America—with a bank on virtually every corner—and most banks are globally networked. You'll get the best exchange rate if you withdraw money from an ATM, but keep in mind that many banks impose a fee every time a card is used at an ATM in a different city or bank. On top of this, the bank from which you withdraw cash may charge its own fee.

You can also get a cash advance through Visa or MasterCard (contact the issuing bank to enable this feature and get a PIN), but note that the credit card company will begin charging you interest immediately, and many have begun assessing a fee every time. American Express card cash advances are usually available only from Amex offices, which you'll find in every European city.

CREDIT CARDS

Most middle-bracket and virtually all first-class and deluxe hotels, restaurants, and shops in Europe accept major credit cards—American Express,

Diners Club, MasterCard, and Visa (not Discover). Some budget establishments accept plastic; others don't. The most widely accepted cards these days are Visa and MasterCard, but it pays to carry American Express, too. Note that you can now often choose to charge credit card purchases at the price in euros or in the local currency; since most European currencies are now locked together, the dollar amount always comes out the same, but it could help you comparison shop. If you do choose to stick with plastic, keep in mind that your credit card company will likely charge a commission (1% or 2%) on every foreign purchase you make, and that most banks assess a 2% fee for currency conversion on credit charges.

TRAVELER'S CHECKS

Most large banks sell traveler's checks, charging fees of 1% to 2% of the value of the checks. AAA (American Automobile Association) members can buy American Express checks commission-free. Traveler's checks are great travel insurance because if you lose them—and have kept a list of their numbers (and a record of which ones were cashed) in a safe place separate from the checks themselves—you can get them replaced at no charge. Hotels and shops usually accept them, but you get a lousy exchange rate. Use traveler's checks for exchanges for local currency at banks or American Express offices. Personal checks are next to useless in Europe.

American Express (© 800/221-7282; www.americanexpress.com) is one of the largest issuers of traveler's checks, and theirs are the most commonly accepted. They also sell checks to holders of certain types of American Express cards at no commission. **Thomas Cook** (© 800/223-7373 in the U.S. and Canada, or 1733/318-950 collect from other parts of the world; www.thomascook.com) issues MasterCard traveler's checks. **Citicorp**

(© 800/645-6556; www.citibank.com) and many other banks issue checks under their own name or under MasterCard or Visa. Get checks issued in dollar amounts—they're more widely accepted abroad.

WIRE SERVICES

MoneyGram, 7401 W. Mansfield Ave., Englewood, CO 80155 (© 800/926-9400; www.moneygram.com), allows friends back home to wire you money in an emergency in less than 10 minutes. Senders should call to learn the address of the closest outlet that handles MoneyGrams. Cash, credit card, or the occasional personal check (with ID) are acceptable forms of payment. The fee is $19 for the first $500, with a sliding scale for larger sums. The service includes a short telex message and a 3-minute phone call from sender to recipient. The beneficiary must present a photo ID at the outlet where the money is received.

VALUE-ADDED TAX (VAT)

All European countries charge a **value-added tax (VAT)** of 15% to 25% on goods and services—it's like a sales tax that's already included in the price. Rates vary from country to country (as does the name—it's called the IVA in Italy and Spain, the TVA in France, and so on), though the goal in EU countries is to arrive at a uniform rate of about 15%. Citizens of non-EU countries can, as they leave the country, get back most of the tax on purchases (not services) if you spend above a designated amount (usually $80–$200) in a single store.

Regulations vary from country to country, so inquire at the tourist office when you arrive to find out the procedure; ask what percentage of the tax is refunded, and if the refund is given to you at the airport or mailed to you later. Look for a TAX FREE SHOPPING FOR TOURISTS sign posted in participating stores. Ask the storekeeper for the necessary forms, and, if possible, keep the purchases in their original packages. Save all your receipts and VAT forms from each EU country to process all of them at the **"Tax Refund"** desk in the airport of the last country you visit before flying home (allow an extra 30 min. or so at the airport to process forms).

To avoid VAT refund hassles, ask for a Global Refund form ("Shopping Checque") at a store where you make a purchase. When leaving an EU country, have it stamped by customs, after which you take it to the Global Refund counter at more than 700 airports and boarder crossings in Europe. Your money is refunded on the spot. For information, contact **Global Refund** (℃ **800/566-9828;** www. globalrefund.com).

4 When to Go

Europe is a continent for all seasons, offering everything from a bikini beach party on the Riviera in summer to the finest skiing in the world in the Alps in winter.

Europe has a Continental climate with distinct seasons, but there are great variations in temperature from one part to another. Northern Norway is plunged into Arctic darkness in winter, but in sunny Sicily the climate is usually temperate—though snow can fall even on the Greek Islands in winter, and winter nights are cold anywhere. Europe is north of most of the United States, but along the Mediterranean they see weather patterns more along the lines of the U.S. southern states. In general, however, seasonal changes are less extreme than in most of the United States.

The **high season** lasts from mid-May to mid-September, with the most tourists hitting the Continent from mid-June to August. In general, this is the most expensive time to travel, except in Austria and Switzerland, where prices are actually higher in winter during the ski season. And since Scandinavian hotels depend on business clients instead of tourists, lower prices can often be found in the fleeting summer, when business clients vacation and a smaller number of tourists take over.

You'll find smaller crowds, relatively fair weather, and often lower prices at hotels in the **shoulder seasons,** from Easter to mid-May and mid-September

to mid-October. **Off season** (except at ski resorts) is from November to Easter, with the exception of December 25 to January 6. Much of Europe, Italy especially, takes August off, and from August 15 to August 30 is vacation time for many locals, so expect the cities to be devoid of natives but the beaches packed.

WEATHER

BRITAIN & IRELAND   Everyone knows it rains a lot in Britain and Ireland. Winters are rainier than summers; August and from September to mid-October are the sunniest months. Summer daytime temperatures average from the low 60s Fahrenheit (10s Celsius) to the mid-60s (20s Celsius), dropping to the 40s (5s Celsius) on winter nights. Ireland, whose shores are bathed by the Gulf Stream, has a milder climate and the most changeable weather—a dark rainy morning can quickly turn into a sunny afternoon, and vice versa. The Scottish Lowlands have a climate similar to England's, but the Highlands are much colder, with storms and snow in winter.

CENTRAL EUROPE   In Vienna and along the Danube Valley the climate is moderate. Summer daytime temperatures average in the low 70s Fahrenheit (20s Celsius), falling at night to the low 50s (10s Celsius). Winter temperatures are in the 30s Fahrenheit (below 0 Celsius) and 40s (10s Celsius) during the day. In Budapest, temperatures can reach

80°F (25°C) in August and dip to 30°F (0°C) in January. Winter is damp and chilly, spring is mild, and May and June are usually wet. The best weather is in the late summer through October. In Prague and Bohemia, summer months have an average temperature of 65°F (18°C) but are the rainiest, while January and February are usually sunny and clear, with temperatures around freezing.

FRANCE & GERMANY The weather in Paris is approximately the same as in the U.S. mid-Atlantic states, but like most of Europe, there's less extreme variation. In summer, the temperature rarely goes above the mid-70s Fahrenheit (mid-20s Celsius). Summers are fair and can be hot along the Riviera. Winters tend to be mild, in the 40s Fahrenheit (10s Celsius), though it's warmer along the Riviera. Germany's climate ranges from the moderate summers and chilly, damp winters in the north to the mild summers and very cold, sunny winters of the alpine south.

NORTHERN EUROPE In the Netherlands, the weather is never extreme at any time of year. Summer temperatures average around 67°F (20°C) and the winter average is about 40°F (5°C). The climate is rainy, with the driest months from February to May. From mid-April to mid-May, the tulip fields burst into color. The climate of northern Germany is very similar. Belgium's climate is moderate, varying from 73°F (23°C) in July and August to 40°F (5°C) in December and January. It does rain a lot, but the weather is at its finest in July and August.

SCANDINAVIA Summer temperatures above the Arctic Circle average around the mid-50s Fahrenheit (mid-10s Celsius), dropping to around 14°F (–10°C) during the dark winters. In the south, summer temperatures average around 70°F (22°C), dropping to the 20s Fahrenheit (below 0s Celsius) in winter. Fjords and even the ocean are often warm enough for summer swimming, but rain is frequent. The sun shines 24 hours in midsummer above the Arctic Circle, where winter brings semi-permanent twilight. Denmark's climate is relatively mild by comparison. It has moderate summer temperatures and winters that can be damp and foggy, with temperatures just above the mid-30s Fahrenheit (0s Celsius).

SOUTHERN EUROPE Summers are hot in Italy, Spain, and Greece, with temperatures around the high 80s Fahrenheit (30s Celsius) or even higher in some parts of Spain. Along

---

What Time Is It, Anyway?

Based on U.S. Eastern Standard Time, Britain, Ireland, and Portugal are 5 hours ahead of New York City; Greece is 7 hours ahead of New York. The rest of the countries in this book are 6 hours ahead of New York. For instance, when it's noon in New York, it's 5pm in London and Lisbon; 6pm in Paris, Copenhagen, and Amsterdam; and 7pm in Athens. The European countries now observe daylight savings time. The time change doesn't usually occur on the same day or during the same month as in the U.S.

If you plan to travel to Ireland or Continental Europe from Britain, keep in mind that the time will be the same in Ireland and Portugal, 2 hours later in Greece, and 1 hour later in the other countries in this guide.

the Italian Riviera, summer and winter temperatures are mild, and except in the alpine regions, Italian winter temperatures rarely drop below freezing. The area around Madrid is dry and arid, and summers in Spain are coolest along the Atlantic coast, with mild temperatures year-round on the Costa del Sol. Seaside Portugal is very rainy but has temperatures of 50°F to 75°F (10°C–25°C) year-round. In Greece there's sunshine all year, and winters are usually mild, with temperatures around 50°F to 54°F (10°C–12°C). Hot summer temperatures are often helped by cool breezes. The best seasons to visit Greece are from mid-April to June and mid-September to late October, when the wildflowers bloom and the tourists go home.

SWITZERLAND & THE ALPS The alpine climate is shared by Bavaria in southern Germany and the Austrian Tyrol and Italian Dolomites—winters are cold and bright, and spring comes late, with snow flurries well into April. Summers are mild and sunny, though the alpine regions can experience dramatic changes in weather any time of year.

EUROPE CALENDAR OF EVENTS

January

Epiphany celebrations, Italy, nationwide. All cities, towns, and villages in Italy stage Roman Catholic Epiphany observances. One of the most festive celebrations is the Epiphany Fair at Rome's Piazza Navona. January 6, 2005.

February

Carnevale, Venice, Italy. At this riotous time, theatrical presentations and masked balls take place throughout Venice and on the islands in the lagoon. The balls are by invitation only (except the Doge's Ball), but the street events and fireworks are open to everyone. Contact the **Venice Tourist Office,** San Marco, Giardinetti Reali, Palazzo Selva, 30124 Venezia (℃ **041/529-8711**). The week before Ash Wednesday, the start of Lent.

February Basler Fasnacht, Basel, Switzerland. Called "the wildest of carnivals," with a parade of "cliques" (clubs and associations). Call ℃ **061/268-68-68** or visit www.fasnacht.ch for more information. First Monday after Ash Wednesday.

March

Holmenkollen Ski Festival, Oslo, Norway. This is one of Europe's largest ski festivals, with World Cup Nordic skiing and biathlons and international ski-jumping competitions, all held at Holmenkollen Ski Jump on the outskirts of Oslo. To participate or request more information, contact **Skiforeningen,** Kongeveien 5, Holmenkollen, N-0390 Oslo 3 (℃ **22-92-32-00;** www.skiforeningen.no). February 28 to March 14.

St. Patrick's Dublin Festival, Dublin, Ireland. This massive 4-day fest is open, free, and accessible to all. Street theater, carnival acts, music, fireworks, and more culminate in Ireland's grandest parade. Call ℃ **01/676-3205** or go to www.stpatricksday.ie. March 11 to 17.

Budapest Spring Festival, Budapest, Hungary. For 2 weeks, performances of everything from opera to ballet, from classical music to drama, are held in all the major halls and theaters of Budapest. Simultaneously, temporary exhibitions open in many of Budapest's museums. Tickets are available at 1053 Budapest, Egyetem tér 5 (℃ **36/1-486-3311;** www.festivalcity.hu) and at the individual venues. Mid- to late March.

April

Semana Santa (Holy Week), Seville, Spain. Although many of the country's smaller towns stage similar celebrations, the festivities in Seville are by far the most elaborate. From Palm Sunday to Easter Sunday, processions with hooded penitents move to the piercing wail of the *saeta,* a love song to the Virgin or Christ. Call the **Seville Office of Tourism** for details (© **95-422-1404**). Usually the last week of March.

Holy Week observances, Italy, nationwide. Processions and age-old ceremonies—some from pagan days, some from the Middle Ages—are staged. The most notable procession is led by the pope, passing the Colosseum and the Roman Forum up to Palatine Hill; a torch-lit parade caps the observance. 4 days before Easter Sunday; sometimes at the end of March but often in April.

Pasqua (Easter Sunday), Rome, Italy. In an event broadcast around the world, the pope gives his blessing from the balcony of St. Peter's.

Feria de Sevilla (Seville Fair), Seville, Spain. This is the most celebrated week of revelry in all of Spain, with all-night flamenco dancing, entertainment booths, bullfights, flower-decked coaches, and dancing in the streets. Reserve your hotel early. Contact the **Seville Office of Tourism** (© **95-422-1404**). Second week after Easter.

May

Brighton Festival, Brighton, England. The country's largest arts festival features some 400 cultural events. Contact the **Brighton Tourist Information Centre,** 10 Bartholomew Sq., Brighton BN1 1JS (© **0906/711-2255,** 50¢ per minute; www.visitbrighton.com). Most of May.

Prague Spring Music Festival, Prague, Czech Republic. This world-famous 3-week series of classical music and dance performances brings some of the world's best talent to Prague. For details, call © **420/ 25732 0468** or go to www.festival. cz. Mid-May to early June.

Festival International du Film (Cannes Film Festival), Cannes, France. Movie madness transforms this city into a media circus. Reserve early and make a deposit. Admission to the films is by invitation only. There are box-office tickets for the other films, which play 24 hours. Contact the **Festival International du Film (FIF),** 99 bd. Des Malesherbes, 75008 Paris (© **01-45-72-96-45;** www.festivaldufilm deparis.com). Two weeks before the festival, the event's administration moves to the Palais des Festivals, esplanade Georges-Pompidou, 06400 Cannes. May 12 to 23, 2005.

International Music Festival, Vienna, Austria. This traditional highlight of Vienna's concert calendar features top-class international orchestras, conductors, and classical greats. The venue and booking address is **Wiener Musikverein,** Lothringer-Strasse 20, A-1030 Vienna (© **01/242-002;** www. musik.verein.at). Early May through first 3 weeks of June.

Fiesta de San Isidro, Madrid, Spain. Madrileños run wild with a 10-day celebration honoring their city's patron saint. Food fairs, street parades, parties, dances, bullfights, and other events mark the occasion. Expect crowds and traffic. For details, contact the **Oficina Municipal de Información y Turismo** (© **91-580-2311**). Mid-May.

Bath International Music Festival, Bath, England. One of Europe's most prestigious international festivals of music and the arts features as many as 1,000 performers at various venues. Contact the **Bath Festivals Trust,** 5 Broad St., Bath, Somerset

BA1 5LJ (© **01225/462231**; www. bathfestivals.org.uk). Late May to early June.

Bergen Festspill (Bergen International Festival), Bergen, Norway. This world-class music event features artists from Norway and around the world. Many styles of music are presented, but classical music—especially the work of Grieg—is emphasized. This is one of the largest annual musical events in Scandinavia. Contact the **Bergen International Festival**, Vågsallmenningen 1, 5804, Bergen (© **55-21-06-30**; www.fib.no). Mid-May to early June.

Maggio Musicale Fiorentino (Musical May Florentine), Florence, Italy. Italy's oldest and most prestigious music festival emphasizes music from the 14th century to the 20th century but also presents ballet and opera. For schedules and tickets, contact the **Maggio Musicale Fiorentino/Teatro Comunale**, Corso Italia 12, 50123 Firenze (© **055-27-791** or 055-211-158; www.maggiofiorentino.com). Late April to early July.

June

Hellenic Festival (Athens, Lycobettus & Epidaurus festivals), Greece. The three festivals are now organized under the umbrella term of Hellenic Festival. The Athens Festival features superb productions of ancient drama, opera, modern dance, ballet, and more in the Odeum of Herodes Atticus, on the southwest side of the Acropolis. The Lycabettus Festival presents performances at the amphitheater on Mount Lycovitos. The Epidaurus Festival presents classic Greek drama in its famous amphitheater. Call © **210/928-2900** or go to www. hellenicfestival.gr. June to early October.

Festival di Spoleto, Spoleto, Italy. Dating from 1958, this festival was the artistic creation of maestro and world-class composer Gian Carlo Menotti, who still presides over the event. International performers convene for 3 weeks of dance, drama, opera, concerts, and art exhibits in this Umbrian hill town. The main focus is music composed from 1300 to 1799. For tickets and details, contact the **Spoleto Festival**, Piazza della Libertà 12, 06049 Spoleto (© **0743/44700**; www.spoletofestival.it). Late June to mid-July.

Roskilde Festival, Roskilde, Denmark. Europe's biggest rock festival has been going strong for more than 30 years, now bringing about 90,000 revelers each year to the central Zealand town. Besides major rock concerts, scheduled activities include theater and film presentations. Call © **46-36-66-13** or check www.roskilde-festival.dk. June 30 to July 3.

July

Tour de France, France. Europe's most hotly contested bicycle race pits crews of wind-tunnel-tested athletes along an itinerary that detours deep into the Massif Central and ranges across the Alps. The race is decided at a finish line drawn across the Champs-Elysées. Call © **01-41-33-15-00**; www. letour.fr. Month of July.

Karlovy Vary International Film Festival, Karlovy Vary, Czech Republic. This annual 10-day event predates Communism and has regained its "A" rating from the international body governing film festivals, which puts it in the same league as Cannes and Venice but without the star-drawing power of the more glittery stops. For more information, call © **420/221-41-1-011** or check www.iffkv.cz. Early July to mid-July.

Montreux International Jazz Festival, Montreux, Switzerland. More than jazz, this festival features everything from reggae bands to African tribal chanters. Monster dance-fests also break out nightly. The 2½-week festival concludes with a 12-hour marathon of world music. Write to the **Montreux Jazz Festival,** Case Postale Box 97, CH-1820 Montreux, or call © **021/966-44-44;** www.montreuxjazz.com. Early July.

Bastille Day, France, nationwide. Celebrating the birth of modern-day France, the nation's festivities reach their peak in Paris with street fairs, pageants, fireworks, and feasts. In Paris, the day begins with a parade down the Champs-Elysées and ends with fireworks at Montmartre. July 14, 2005.

Around Gotland Race, Sandhamn, Sweden. The biggest and most exciting open-water Scandinavian sailing race starts and finishes at Sandhamn in the Stockholm archipelago. About 450 boats, mainly from Nordic countries, take part. Call the **Stockholm Tourist Center** (© **08/789-24-15**) for information. Two days in mid-July.

Salzburg Festival, Salzburg, Austria. Since the 1920s, this has been one of the premier cultural events of Europe, sparkling with opera, chamber music, plays, concerts, appearances by world-class artists, and many other cultural presentations. Always count on stagings of Mozart operas. For tickets, write several months in advance to the **Salzburg Festival,** Postfach 140, A-5010 Salzburg (© **0662/8045;** www.salzburgfestival.at). July 23 to August 31, 2005.

Il Palio, Siena, Italy. Palio fever grips this Tuscan hill town for a wild and exciting horse race from the Middle Ages. Pageantry, costumes, and the celebrations of the victorious *contrada* (sort of a neighborhood social club) mark the spectacle. For details, contact the **Azienda di Promozione Turistica,** Piazza del Campo 56, 53100 Siena (© **0461-839000**). Early July.

The Proms, London, England. A night at "The Proms"—the annual Henry Wood promenade concerts at Royal Albert Hall—attracts music aficionados from around the world. Staged almost daily (except for a few Sun), these traditional concerts were launched in 1895 and are the principal summer engagements for the BBC Symphony Orchestra. Cheering and clapping, Union Jacks on parade, banners, and balloons—it's great summer fun. Call © **020/7589-8212,** or go to www.bbc.co.uk/proms. Mid-July to mid-September.

Richard Wagner Festival, Bayreuth Festspielhaus, Germany. One of Europe's two or three major opera events, this festival takes place in the composer's Festspielhaus in Bayreuth, the capital of upper Franconia. *Note:* Opera tickets often must be booked years in advance. Contact **Festival Administration,** Bayreuther Festspiele, Am Festspiele, Kartenbüro Postfach 100262, D-95445 Bayreuth (© **0921/7-87-80;** www.festspiele.de). Late July to late August.

Festival d'Avignon, Avignon, France. This world-class festival has a reputation for exposing new talent to critical acclaim. The focus is usually on avant-garde works in theater, dance, and music. Much of the music is presented within the 14th-century courtyard of the Palais de l'Ancien Archeveché (the Old Archbishop's Palace). Make hotel reservations early. For information, call © **04-90-27-66-50** or fax 04-90-27-66-83; www.festival-avignon. com. Last 3 weeks of July.

August

Edinburgh International Festival, Edinburgh, Scotland. Scotland's best-known festival is held for 3 weeks. Called an "arts bonanza," it draws major talent from around the world, with more than a thousand shows presented and a million tickets sold. Book, jazz, and film festivals are also staged at this time. Contact the **Edinburgh International Festival,** The Hub, Castle Hill, Edinburgh EH1 2NE (© **0131/473-2001;** www.eif.co.uk). Three weeks in August.

Fire Festival Regatta, Silkeborg, Denmark. Denmark's oldest and biggest festival features nightly cruises on the lakes, with thousands of candles illuminating the shores. The fireworks display on the last night is the largest and most spectacular in northern Europe. Popular Danish artists provide entertainment at a large fun fair. Contact the **Turistbureau,** Godthåbsuej 4, DK-8600 Silkeborg (© **86-82-19-11**). Early August.

Festas da Senhora da Agonia, Viana do Castelo, north of Porto, Portugal. The most spectacular festival in the north honors "Our Lady of Suffering." A replica of the Virgin is carried through the streets over carpets of flowers. Float-filled parades mark the 3-day-and-a-night event as a time of revelry. A blaze of fireworks ends the festival. Call the **festival office** (© **058/82-1079**) for exact dates, which vary from year to year. Mid-August.

St. Stephen's Day, Hungary. This is Hungary's national day. The country's patron saint is celebrated with cultural events and a dramatic display of fireworks over the Danube at 9pm. Hungarians also ceremoniously welcome the first new bread from the crop of July wheat. August 20.

September

Highland Games & Gathering, Braemar, Scotland. The queen and many members of the royal family often show up for this annual event, with its massed bands, piping and dancing competitions, and performances of great strength by a tribe of gigantic men. Contact the **tourist office** in Braemar, The Mews, Mar Road, Braemar, Aberdeenshire, AB35 5YL (© **01339/741-600;** www.braemargathering.org). First Saturday in September.

Oktoberfest, Munich, Germany. Germany's most famous festival happens mainly in September, not October. Millions show up, and hotels are packed. Most activities are at Theresienwiese, where local breweries sponsor gigantic tents that can hold up to 6,000 beer drinkers. Always reserve hotel rooms well in advance. Contact the **Munich Tourist Office** (© **089/2-33-03-00;** www.muenchen-tourist.de). Mid-September to the first Sunday in October.

October

Autumn Wine Growers' Festival, Lugano, Switzerland. A parade and other festivities mark harvest time. Little girls throw flowers from blossom-covered floats, and oxen pull festooned wagons in a colorful procession. For information call © **091/921-46-64.** Three days in early October.

November

All Saints' Day, Spain, nationwide. This public holiday is reverently celebrated, as relatives and friends lay flowers on the graves of the dead. November 1.

December

La Scala Opera Season, Teatro alla Scala, Milan. At the most famous opera house of them all, the season opens on December 7, the feast day of Milan's patron St. Ambrogio, and runs into July. Even though opening-night tickets are close to impossible to get, it's worth a try; call © **02/7200-3744** for information, or 02/86-0775 for reservations; www.lascala.milano.it.

Nobel Peace Prize Ceremony, Oslo, Norway. This major event on the Oslo calendar attracts world attention. It's held at Oslo City Hall on December 10. Attendance is by invitation only. For details, contact the **Nobel Institute,** Drammensveien 19, N-0255 Oslo 2 (© **22-44-36-80;** www.nobel.se).

5 Active & Other Special-Interest Vacations

CYCLING

Cycling tours are a great way to see Europe at your own pace. Some of the best are conducted by the **CTC** (Cyclists' Tourist Club), Cotterell House, 69 Meadrow, Godalming, Surrey, England GU7 3H5 (© **0870/873-0060;** www.ctc.org.uk). **Hindriks European Bicycle Tours, Inc.,** P.O. Box 6086, Huntington Beach, CA 92615 (© **800/852-3258;** fax 714/593-1710; www.hollandbicyclingtours. com), leads 8-day bicycle tours throughout Europe. **ExperiencePlus!,** 415 Mason Ct., Number 1, Fort Collins, CO 80524 (© **800/685-4565;** fax 970/493-0377; www.experience plus.com), runs bike and walking tours across Europe. **Ciclismo Classico,** 30 Marathon St., Arlington, MA 02474 (© **800/866-7314** or 781/646-3377; fax 781/641-1512; www.ciclismo classico.com), is an excellent outfit running tours of Italy. Florence-based **I Bike Italy, Inc.** ★, P.O. Box 64-3824, Vero Beach, FL (© **772/388-0783;** www.ibikeitaly.com), offers guided single-day rides in the Tuscan countryside.

HIKING

Wilderness Travel, 1102 9th St., Berkeley, CA 94710 (© **800/368-2794** or 510/558-2488; fax 510/558-2489; www.wildernesstravel.com), specializes in walking tours, treks, and inn-to-inn hiking tours of Europe, as well as less strenuous walking tours. **Sherpa Expeditions,** 131A Heston Rd., Hounslow, Middlesex, England TW5 0RF (© **020/8577-2717;** www.sherpa expeditions.com), offers both self-guided and group treks through off-the-beaten-track regions. Two somewhat upscale walking tour companies are **Butterfield & Robinson,** 70 Bond St., Suite 300, Toronto, ON M5B 1X3 (© **800/678-1147** or 416/864-1354; fax 416/864-0541; www.butterfield. com); and **Country Walkers,** P.O. Box 180, Waterbury, VT 05676-0180 (© **800/464-9255** or 802/244-1387; fax 802/244-5661; www.country walkers.com).

Most European countries have associations geared toward aiding hikers and walkers. In England it's the **Ramblers' Association,** 87–90 Albert Embankment; London SE1 7TW, 2nd Floor, Camelford House (© **020/7339-8500;** www.ramblers.org.uk). In Italy, contact the **Club Alpino Italiano,** 6 Via Silvo Pellico, Milan 20121 (© **02/8646-3516;** www.caimilano.it). For Austria, try the **Osterreichischer Alpenverein (Austrian Alpine Club),** Wilhelm-Greil-Strasse 15, A-6010 Innsbruck (© **0512/595470;** fax 0512/575528; www.alpenverein.at). In Norway, it's the **Norwegian Mountain Touring Association,** Dennorske Touristforening, Storgata 3, Box 7 Sentrum 0101 Oslo (© **22-82-28-00;** fax 22-82-28-01; www.turistforeningen.no).

HORSEBACK RIDING

One of the best companies is **Equitour,** P.O. Box 807, Dubois, WY 82513

(© **800/545-0019** or 307/455-3363; fax 307/455-2354; www.ridingtours. com), which offers 5- to 7-day rides through many of Europe's most popular areas, such as Tuscany and the Loire Valley.

EDUCATIONAL TRAVEL

The best (and one of the most expensive) of the escorted tour operators is **Group IST (International Specialty Travel)** (© **212/594-8787;** www. groupist.com), whose tours are first class all the way and accompanied by a certified expert in whatever field the trip focuses on. If you missed out on study abroad in college, the brainy **Smithsonian Journeys** (© **877/EDU-TOUR** or 202/357-4700; fax 202/633-9250; www.smithsonianjourneys. org) may be just the ticket, albeit a pricey one. Study leaders are often world-renowned experts in their field. Journeys are carefully crafted and go to some of the most compelling places in Europe, avoiding tourist traps. Also contact your alma mater or local university to see if it offers summer tours open to the public and guided by a professor specialist.

The **National Registration Center for Studies Abroad (NRCSA),** 207 E. Buffalo St., Milwaukee, WI 53202 (© **414/278-0631** or 202/338-5927; fax 414/271-8884; www.nrcsa.com); and the **American Institute for Foreign Study (AIFS),** River Plaza, 9 W. Broad St., Stamford, CT 06902 (© **800/727-2437** or 203/399-5000; fax 203/399-5590; www.aifs.com), can both help you arrange study programs and summer programs abroad.

The biggest organization dealing with higher education in Europe is the **Institute of International Education (IIE),** with headquarters at 809 United Nations Plaza, New York, NY

10017-3500 (© **212/883-8200;** www. iie.org). A few of its booklets are free, but for $47, plus $6 postage, you can buy the more definitive *Short Term Study Abroad.* To order publications, check out the IIE's online bookstore at www.iiebooks.org.

A clearinghouse for information on European-based language schools is **Lingua Service Worldwide,** 75 Prospect St., Suite 4, Huntington, NY 11743 (© **800/394-LEARN** or 631/424-0777; fax 631/271-3441; www. linguaserviceworldwide.com).

CULINARY SCHOOLS

Cuisine International, P.O. Box 25228, Dallas, TX 75225 (© **214/373-1161;** fax 214/373-1162; www. cuisineinternational.com), brings together some of the top independent cooking schools and teachers based in various European countries so you can book your weeklong culinary dream vacation.

Apicius, Via Guelfa 85, 50129 Florence, Italy (© **055/2658135;** www. apicius.it), is the finest cooking school in Florence, an expert on Tuscan culinary arts. Its monthly programs are taught by local chefs and food experts, with an emphasis on wine appreciation. From May to October, the **International Cooking School of Italian Food and Wine,** 201 E. 28th St., Suite 15B, New York, NY 10016-8538 (© **212/779-1921;** fax 212/779-3248; www.marybethclark.com), offers courses in Bologna, the "gastronomic capital of Italy." **Le Cordon Bleu,** 8 rue Léon-Delhomme, 75015 Paris (© **800/457-2433** in the U.S., or 01-53-68-22-50; www.cordonbleu.edu), was established in 1895 as a means of spreading the tenets of French cuisine to the world at large. It offers many programs outside its flagship Paris school.

6 Health & Insurance

HEALTH

In most of Europe the tap water is generally safe to drink (except on trains and wherever it's marked as nondrinking water), the milk pasteurized, and health services good. You will, however, be eating foods and spices your body isn't used to, so you might want to bring along Pepto-Bismol or Imodium tablets in case indigestion or diarrhea strikes.

In many cases, if you get sick or require emergency treatment on your trip abroad, you may be forced to pay all medical costs upfront and be reimbursed later. If you worry about getting sick away from home, consider **medical travel insurance** (see "Insurance," below).

If you suffer from a chronic illness, consult your doctor before your departure. For conditions like epilepsy, diabetes, or heart problems, wear a **MedicAlert identification tag** (© 888/633-4298; www.medicalert. org), which will immediately alert doctors to your condition and give them access to your records through MedicAlert's 24-hour hot line.

Contact the **International Association for Medical Assistance to Travelers (IAMAT;** © 716/754-4883; www. iamat.org) for tips on travel and health concerns in the countries you're visiting, and for lists of local, English-speaking doctors. The United States **Centers for Disease Control and**

Prevention (© 800/311-3435 or 404/ 639-3534; www.cdc.gov) provides up-to-date information on necessary vaccines and health hazards by region or country (their booklet, *Health Information for International Travel,* is $29 by mail; on the Internet, it's free). Any foreign consulate can provide a list of area doctors who speak English. If you get sick, consider asking your hotel concierge to recommend a local doctor—even his or her own.

INSURANCE

Check your existing insurance policies before you buy travel insurance to cover trip cancellation, lost luggage, medical expenses, or car rental insurance. You're likely to have partial or complete coverage. But if you need some, ask your travel agent about a comprehensive package. The cost of travel insurance varies widely, depending on the cost and length of your trip, your age and overall health, and the type of trip you're taking. More dangerous activities may be excluded from basic policies.

And keep in mind that in the aftermath of the September 11, 2001, terrorist attacks, a number of airlines, cruise lines, and tour operators are no longer covered by insurers. *The bottom line:* Always, always check the fine print before you sign on; more and more policies have built-in exclusions and restrictions that may leave you out in the cold if something does go awry.

Tips A Packing Tip

Pack prescription medications in your carry-on luggage. Carry written prescriptions in generic (not brand-name) form, and dispense all prescription medications from their original labeled vials. This helps foreign pharmacists fill them and Customs officials approve them. If you wear contact lenses, pack an extra pair in case you lose one.

For information, contact one of the following recommended insurers:

- **Access America** (© 866/807-3982; www.accessamerica.com)
- **Travel Guard International** (© 800/826-4919; www.travelguard.com)
- **Travel Insured International** (© 800/243-3174; www.travelinsured.com)
- **Travelex Insurance Services** (© 888/457-4602; www.travelex-insurance.com)

Some credit cards (American Express and certain gold and platinum Visas and MasterCards, for example) offer automatic flight insurance against death or dismemberment in case of an airplane crash if you charged the cost of your ticket.

Medical Insurance For travel overseas, most health plans (including Medicare/Medicaid) do not provide coverage, and the ones that do often require you to pay for services upfront and reimburse you when you return home. Even if your plan does cover overseas treatment, most out-of-country hospitals make you pay your bills up front, and send you a refund after you've returned home and filed the necessary paperwork with your insurance company. As a safety net, you may want to consider purchasing travel medical insurance. *Note:* Members of **Blue Cross/Blue Shield** can now use their cards at selected hospitals in most major cities worldwide

(© **800/810-BLUE** or www.bluecares.com for a list of hospitals).

If you require additional insurance, try one of the following companies:

- **MEDEX Assistance,** 8501 LaSalle Rd., Suite 200, Towson, MD 21286 (© **888/MEDEX-00** or 410/453-6300; fax 410/453-6301; www.medexassist.com)
- **Travel Assistance International** (© **800/821-2828;** www.travelassistance.com), 9200 Keystone Crossing, Suite 300, Indianapolis, IN 46240 (for general information on services, call the company's Worldwide Assistance Services, Inc., at © **800/777-8710**)

Lost-Luggage Insurance On international flights (including U.S. portions of international trips), baggage coverage is limited to approximately $9.05 per pound, up to approximately $635 per checked bag. If you plan to check items more valuable than the standard liability, you may purchase "excess valuation" coverage from the airline, up to $5,000. Lost luggage may also be covered by your homeowner's or renter's policy. Many platinum and gold credit cards cover you as well. If you choose to purchase additional insurance, be sure not to buy more than you need. Buy in advance from the insurer or a trusted agent (prices will be much higher at the airport).

For information on **car renter's insurance,** see "Getting Around," later in this chapter.

7 Specialized Travel Resources

TRAVELERS WITH DISABILITIES

Europe won't win any medals for accessibility for travelers with disabilities, but in the past few years its big cities have made an effort to accommodate them.

Many travel agencies offer customized tours and itineraries for travelers with disabilities. **Flying Wheels**

Travel (© **507/451-5005;** fax 507/451-1685; www.flyingwheelstravel.com) offers escorted tours and cruises that emphasize sports and private tours in minivans with lifts. **Accessible Journeys** (© **800/TINGLES** or 610/521-0339; www.disabilitytravel.com) caters specifically to slow walkers and wheelchair travelers and their families and friends.

Organizations that offer assistance to travelers with disabilities include **Moss-Rehab** (✆ **800/CALL-MOSS;** www.mossresourcenet.org), which provides friendly, helpful phone assistance through its Travel Information Service. **SATH** (Society for Accessible Travel and Hospitality) (✆ **212/447-7284;** fax 212-725-8253; www.sath.org) offers a wealth of travel resources for all types of disabilities and informed recommendations on destinations, access guides, travel agents, tour operators, vehicle rentals, and companion services. Annual membership costs $45 for adults; $30 for seniors and students. **The American Foundation for the Blind (AFB)** (✆ **800/232-5463** or 212/502-7600; www.afb.org) is a referral resource for the blind or visually impaired that includes information on traveling with Seeing Eye dogs.

Among publications, check out **Twin Peaks Press** (✆ **360/694-2462;** http://disabilitybookshop.virtualave.net/blist84.htm), which publishes travel-related books for travelers with special needs. *Open World Magazine,* published by SATH (see above), is full of good resources and information. A year's subscription is $13 ($21 outside the U.S.).

For U.K. Citizens The **Royal Association for Disability and Rehabilitation (RADAR),** Unit 12, 250 City Rd., London EC1V 8AF (✆ **020/7250-3222;** fax 020/7250-0212; www.radar.org.uk) publishes three holiday "fact packs." The first provides general info, including planning and booking a holiday, insurance, finances, and useful organizations and holiday providers; the second outlines transportation and rental equipment options; and the third deals with specialized accommodations. Another good service is the **Holiday Care Service,** Sunley House, 7th Floor, 4 Bedford Park, Croydon, Surrey CR0 2AP (✆ **0845/124-9971;** fax 0845/1124-9972; www.holidaycare.org), a national charity that advises on accessible accommodations for seniors and persons with disabilities. Annual membership is £38.

GAY & LESBIAN TRAVELERS

Much of Europe has grown to accept same-sex couples over the past few decades, and in most countries homosexual sex acts are legal. To be on the safe side, do a bit of research and test the waters for acceptability in any one city or area. As you might expect, smaller towns tend to be less accepting than cities. Gay centers include London, Paris, Amsterdam, Berlin, Milan, Ibiza, Sitges, and the Greek Islands (Mykonos). For coverage of the gay scene in Europe's top destinations, consider purchasing a copy of *Frommer's Gay & Lesbian Europe* (www.frommers.com).

The International Gay and Lesbian Travel Association (IGLTA; ✆ **800/448-8550** or 954/776-2626; fax 954/776-3303; www.iglta.org) links travelers with gay-friendly hoteliers, tour operators, and airline and cruise-line representatives. It offers monthly newsletters, marketing mailings, and a membership directory that's updated once a year. Membership is $200 yearly, plus a $100 administration fee for new members.

Many agencies offer tours and travel itineraries specifically for gay and lesbian travelers. **Above and Beyond Tours** (✆ **800/397-2681** or 760/325-0702; www.abovebeyondtours.com) offers gay and lesbian tours worldwide and is the exclusive gay and lesbian tour operator for United Airlines. **Now, Voyager** (✆ **800/255-6951;** www.nowvoyager.com) is a San Francisco–based gay-owned and -operated travel service. *Out and About* (✆ **800/929-2268;** www.outandabout.com) offers guidebooks and a newsletter ($20/year; 10 issues) packed with solid information on the global gay and lesbian scene.

SENIOR TRAVELERS

Don't be shy about asking for discounts, but always carry some kind of ID, such as a driver's license, showing your date of birth. Also mention that you're a senior when you first make your travel reservations. Many hotels offer seniors discounts, and in most cities, people over age 60 qualify for reduced admission to theaters, museums, and other attractions as well as discounted fares on public transportation.

Members of **AARP** (formerly known as the American Association of Retired Persons), 601 E St. NW, Washington, DC 20049 (© **800/424-3410** or 202/434-2277; www.aarp.org), get discounts on hotels, airfares, and car rentals. AARP offers members a wide range of benefits, including *AARP The Magazine* and a monthly newsletter. Anyone over 50 can join.

Elderhostel (© **877/426-8056;** www.elderhostel.org) arranges study programs for those ages 55 and over (and a spouse or companion of any age) in the U.S. and in more than 80 countries around the world. Most courses last 5 to 7 days in the U.S. (2–4 weeks abroad), and many include airfare, accommodations in university dormitories or modest inns, meals, and tuition.

Recommended publications offering travel resources and discounts for seniors include: the quarterly magazine *Travel 50 & Beyond* (www.travel50andbeyond.com); *Travel Unlimited: Uncommon Adventures for the Mature Traveler* (Avalon); *101 Tips for Mature Travelers,* available from Grand Circle Travel (© **800-221-2610** or 617/350-7500; www.gct.com); *The 50+ Traveler's Guidebook* (St. Martin's Press); and *Unbelievably Good Deals and Great Adventures That You Absolutely Can't Get Unless You're Over 50* (McGraw-Hill), by Joann Rattner Heilman.

FAMILY TRAVEL

Europeans expect to see families traveling together. It's a multigenerational continent, and you'll sometimes see the whole clan traveling around. And Europeans tend to love kids. You'll often find that a child guarantees you an even warmer reception at hotels and restaurants.

At **restaurants,** ask waiters for a half portion to fit junior's appetite. If you're traveling with small children, three- and four-star hotels may be your best bet—**babysitters** are on call so you can take the occasional romantic dinner, and such hotels have a better general ability to help you access the city and its services. But even cheaper hotels can usually find you a sitter. Traveling with a pint-size person usually means pint-size rates. An **extra cot** in the room won't cost more than 30% extra (if anything), and most museums and sights offer **reduced or free admission** for children under a certain age (which can range from 6–18). And kids almost always get discounts on plane and train tickets.

Familyhostel (© **800/733-9753** or 603/862-1147; www.learn.unh.edu/familyhostel) takes the whole family on moderately priced domestic and international learning vacations. All trip details are handled by the program staff, and lectures, field trips, and sightseeing are guided by a team of academics. The trips are for kids ages 8 to 15 accompanied by their parents and/or grandparents.

STUDENT TRAVEL

If you're planning to travel outside the U.S., you'd be wise to arm yourself with an **international student ID card,** which offers substantial savings on rail passes, plane tickets, and entrance fees. It also provides you with basic health and life insurance and a 24-hour help line. The card is available for $22 from **STA Travel** (© **800/781-4040;** www.sta.com or www.statravel.com), the biggest student travel agency in the world. If you're no longer a student but are still under 26, you can get an **International Youth Travel Card (IYTC)** for the same price from the same people, which entitles you to insurance and some discounts (but not on museum admissions).

In Canada, **Travel CUTS** (© **800/ 667-2887** or 416/614-2887; www. travelcuts.com) offers similar services.

The Hanging Out Guides (www. frommers.com/hangingout), published by Frommer's, is the top student travel series for today's students, covering everything from adrenaline sports to the hottest club and music scenes.

8 Planning Your Trip Online

SURFING FOR AIRFARES

The "big three" online travel agencies, **Expedia.com, Travelocity,** and **Orbitz,** sell most of the air tickets bought on the Internet. (Canadian travelers should try expedia.ca and Travelocity.ca; U.K. residents can go for expedia.co.uk and opodo.co.uk.) Each has different business deals with the airlines and may offer different fares on the same flights, so it's wise to shop around. Expedia and Travelocity will also send you **e-mail notification** when a cheap fare becomes available to your favorite destination. Of the smaller travel agency websites, **SideStep** (www.sidestep.com) has gotten the best reviews from Frommer's authors. It's a browser add-on that purports to "search 140 sites at once,"

but in reality only beats competitors' fares as often as other sites do.

Also remember to check **airline websites,** especially those for low-fare carriers such as Southwest, JetBlue, AirTran, WestJet, or Ryanair, whose fares are often misreported or simply missing from travel agency websites. Even with major airlines, you can often shave a few bucks from a fare by booking directly through the airline and avoiding a travel agency's transaction fee. But you'll get these discounts only by **booking online:** Most airlines now offer online-only fares that even their phone agents know nothing about. For the websites of airlines that fly to and from your destination, go to "Getting There," below.

Tips **Vigilance Overseas: Leave the Ten-Gallon Hat at Home**

American citizens around the globe face increased fears they may be targeted for more terrorist attacks. American embassies, companies, museums, and schools, even the American Library in Paris, are on increased alert. Government officials have announced that the threat to U.S. institutions "is particularly high and seems likely to remain so."

Terrorist experts recommend that U.S. citizens traveling abroad forego such traditional garb as cowboy boots or draping symbols of the American flag on their backs or luggage. The American Express in Rome has been so cautious as to install metal detectors in its offices.

The U.S. State Department continues to monitor information about potential threats to Americans overseas, and issues data on the Web at **http://travel.state.gov**. Citizens planning to travel abroad should consult the State Department's announcements, travel warnings, and consular information sheets, all available at this website.

In addition to the Internet, U.S. travelers may hear recorded information by calling the department in Washington at **202/647-5225**.

Great **last-minute deals** are available through free weekly e-mail services provided directly by the airlines. Most of these are announced on Tuesday or Wednesday and must be purchased online. Most are only valid for travel that weekend, but some (such as Southwest's) can be booked weeks or months in advance. Sign up for weekly e-mail alerts at airline websites or check megasites that compile comprehensive lists of last-minute specials, such as **Smarter Living** (http://smarterliving. com). For last-minute trips, **site59. com** in the U.S. and **lastminute.com** in Europe often have better deals than the major-label sites.

If you're willing to give up some control over your flight details, use an **opaque fare service** like **Priceline** (www.priceline.com; www.priceline. co.uk for Europeans) or **Hotwire** (www.hotwire.com). Both offer rock-bottom prices in exchange for travel on a "mystery airline" at a mysterious time of day, often with a mysterious change of planes en route. The mystery airlines are all major, well-known carriers—and the possibility of being sent from Philadelphia to Chicago via Tampa is remote; the airlines' routing computers have gotten a lot better than they used to be. But your chances of getting a 6am or 11pm flight are pretty high. If you're new at this, the helpful folks at **BiddingForTravel** (www.biddingfortravel.com) do a good job of demystifying Priceline's prices. Priceline and Hotwire are great for flights between the U.S. and Europe. But for flights to other parts of the world, consolidators will almost always beat their fares.

In 2004, Priceline added nonopaque service to its roster. You now have the option to pick exact flights, times, and airlines from a list of offers—or opt to bid on opaque fares as before.

For much more about airfares and savvy air-travel tips and advice, pick up a copy of *Frommer's Fly Safe, Fly Smart* (Wiley Publishing, Inc.).

SURFING FOR HOTELS

Shopping online for hotels is much easier in the U.S., Canada, and certain parts of Europe than it is in the rest of the world. Also, many smaller hotels and B&Bs—especially outside the U.S.—don't show up on websites at all. Of the "big three" sites, **Expedia. com** offers a long list of special deals and "virtual tours" or photos of available rooms so you can see what you're paying for (a feature that helps counter the claims that the best rooms are often held back from bargain booking websites). **Travelocity** posts unvarnished customer reviews and ranks its properties according to the AAA rating system. Also reliable are hotel specialist sites **Hotels.com** and **Quikbook.com**. An excellent free program, **TravelAxe** (www.travelaxe. net), helps you search multiple hotel sites at once, even ones you may never have heard of.

SURFING FOR RENTAL CARS

For booking rental cars online, the best deals are usually found at rental-car company websites, although all the major online travel agencies also offer rental-car reservations services. Priceline and Hotwire work well for rental cars, too; the only "mystery" is which

---

Tips **Europe Online**

For country- and city-specific websites, see **"Visitor Information"** sections within each chapter. Also, check individual listings for hotel, restaurant, and attraction websites.

Frommers.com: The Complete Travel Resource

For an excellent travel-planning resource, we highly recommend **Frommers. com** (www.frommers.com), voted Best Travel Site by *PC Magazine*. We're a little biased, of course, but we guarantee that you'll find the travel tips, reviews, monthly vacation giveaways, bookstore, and online-booking capabilities thoroughly indispensable. Among the special features are our popular Destinations section, where you'll get expert travel tips, hotel and dining recommendations, and advice on the sights to see for more than 3,500 destinations around the globe; the **Frommers.com Newsletter**, with the latest deals, travel trends, and money-saving secrets; our **Community** area featuring **Message Boards**, where Frommer's readers post queries and share advice (sometimes even our authors show up to answer questions); and our **Photo Center**, where you can post and share vacation pics. When your research is done, the **Online Reservations System** (www.frommers. com/book_a_trip) takes you to Frommer's preferred online partners for booking your vacation at affordable prices.

---

major rental company you get, and for most travelers the difference between Hertz, Avis, and Budget is negligible.

ONLINE TRAVELER'S TOOLBOX

Veteran travelers usually carry some essential items to make their trips easier. Following is a selection of online tools to bookmark and use.

- **Airplane Seating & Food.** Find out which seats to reserve and which to avoid (and more) on all major domestic airlines at www. seatguru.com. And check out the type of meal (with photos) you'll likely be served on airlines around the world at www.airline meals.com.
- **Subway Navigator** (www.subway navigator). Download subway maps and get savvy advice on using subway systems in dozens of major cities around the world.
- **Time & Date** (www.timeanddate. com). See what time (and day) it is anywhere in the world.
- **Visa ATM Locator** (www.visa. com), for locations of PLUS ATMs worldwide, or **MasterCard ATM Locator** (www.mastercard.com),

for locations of Cirrus ATMs worldwide.

- **Foreign Languages for Travelers** (www.travlang.com). Learn basic terms in more than 70 languages and click on any underlined phrase to hear what it sounds like. *Note:* Free audio software and speakers are required.
- **Intellicast** (www.intellicast.com) and **Weather.com** (www.weather. com). Weather forecasts for all 50 states and for cities around the world.
- **Mapquest** (www.mapquest.com). This best of the mapping sites lets you choose a specific address or destination and, in seconds, it will return a map and detailed directions.
- **Universal Currency Converter** (www.xe.com). See what your dollar or pound is worth in more than 100 other countries.
- **Travel Warnings** (www.travel. state.gov). Reports on places where health concerns or unrest might threaten U.S. travelers. It also lists the locations of U.S. embassies around the world.

9 Getting There

FLYING FROM NORTH AMERICA

Most major airlines charge competitive fares to European cities, but price wars break out regularly and fares can change overnight. Tickets tend to be cheaper if you fly midweek or off season. **High season** on most routes is usually from June to mid-September—the most expensive and most crowded time to travel. **Shoulder season** is from April to May, mid-September to October, and December 15 to December 24. **Low season**—with the cheapest fares—is from November to December 14 and December 25 to March.

MAJOR NORTH AMERICAN AIRLINES North American carriers with frequent service and flights to Europe are **Air Canada** (✆ 888/247-2262; www.aircanada.ca), **American Airlines** (✆ 800/433-7300; www.aa.com), **Continental Airlines** (✆ 800/525-0280; www.continental.com), **Delta Airlines** (✆ 800/221-1212; www.delta.com), **Northwest KLM Airlines** (✆ 800/225-2525; www.nwa.com), and **US Airways** (✆ 800/428-4322; www.usairways.com).

For the latest on airline websites, check **www.itn.com**.

EUROPEAN NATIONAL AIRLINES Not only will the national carriers of European countries offer the greatest number of direct flights from the United States (and can easily book you through to cities beyond the major hubs), but since their entire U.S. market is to fly you to their home country, they often run more competitive deals than most North American carriers. Major national and country-affiliated European airlines include the following:

- **Austria:** Austrian Airlines. In the U.S. and Canada: ✆ 800/843-0002. In the U.K.: ✆ 020/8897-3037. www.flysn.com.

- **Belgium:** SN Brussels Airline. In the U.S. and Canada: ✆ 322/723-2323. In the U.K.: ✆ 0845/601-0933. www.flysn.com.

- **Czech Republic:** CSA Czech Airlines. In the U.S.: ✆ 800/223-2365. In Canada: ✆ 514/844-4200. In the U.K.: ✆ 0870/4443-747. In Australia: ✆ 02/9247-7706. www.csa.cz.

- **France:** Air France. In the U.S.: ✆ 800/237-2747. In Canada: ✆ 800/667-2747. In the U.K.: ✆ 0845/0845-111. In Australia: ✆ 02/9244-2100. In New Zealand: ✆ 064/9308-3352. www.airfrance.com.

- **Germany:** Lufthansa. In the U.S.: ✆ 800/645-3880. In Canada: ✆ 800/399-LUFT. In the U.K.: ✆ 0845/773-7747. In Australia: ✆ 1300-655-727. In New Zealand: ✆ 0800/945220. www.lufthansa-usa.com.

- **Greece:** Olympic Airways. In the U.S.: ✆ 800/223-1226, or 718/269-2200 in New York State. In Canada: ✆ 514/878-3891 in Montreal, or 905/676-4841 in Toronto. In the U.K.: 0870/606-0460. In Australia: ✆ 02/9251-1044. www.olympic-airways.gr.com.

- **Hungary:** Malev Hungarian Airlines. In the U.S.: ✆ 800/223-6884 outside New York, or 212/566-9944 in New York. In Canada: ✆ 800/665-6363. In the U.K.: ✆ 020/7439-0577. In Australia: ✆ 02/9244-2111. In New Zealand: ✆ 09/379-4455. www.hungarianairlines.com.

- **Ireland:** Aer Lingus. In the U.S.: ✆ 866/IRISH-AIR. In the U.K.: ✆ 0845/084-4444. In Australia: ✆ 02/9244-2123. In New Zealand: ✆ 09/308-3351. www.aerlingus.com.

- **Italy:** Alitalia. In the U.S. and Canada: ✆ 800/223-5730. In the

U.K.: ✆ 0870/544-8259. In Australia: ✆ 02/9244-2445. www.alitalia.com.

- **The Netherlands:** Northwest KLM. In the U.S. and Canada: ✆ 800/374-7747. In the U.K.: ✆ 08705/074074. www.klm.com.
- **Portugal:** TAP Air Portugal. In the U.S.: ✆ 800/221-7370. In the U.K.: ✆ 0845/601-0932. www.tap-airportugal.pt.
- **Scandinavia (Denmark, Norway, Sweden):** SAS Scandinavian Airlines. In the U.S.: ✆ 800/221-2350. In the U.K.: ✆ 0870/6072-7727. In Australia: ✆ 1300/727-707. www.scandinavian.net.
- **Spain:** Iberia. In the U.S. and Canada: ✆ 800/772-4642. In the U.K.: ✆ 0845/601-2854. www.iberia.com.
- **Switzerland:** Swiss International Airlines. In the U.S.: ✆ 877/FLY-SWISS. In Canada: ✆ 877/359-7947. In the U.K.: ✆ 0845/601-0956. www.swiss.com.
- **United Kingdom:** (1) British Airways. In the U.S. and Canada: ✆ 800/247-9297. In the U.K.: ✆ 0870/850-9850. In Australia: ✆ 02/8904-8800. www.britishairways.com. (2) Virgin Atlantic Airways. In the U.S. and Canada: ✆ 800/862-8621. In the U.K.: ✆ 01293/450-150. In Australia: ✆ 02/9244-2747. www.virgin-atlantic.com.

PACKAGE TOURS Package tours aren't the same thing as escorted tours. They're simply a way of buying your airfare and accommodations at the same time and getting an excellent rate on both. Your trip is your own. In many cases, a package including airfare, hotel, and transportation to and from the airport costs less than the hotel alone if you booked it yourself. The downside is that many stick you in large international-style hotels (which in Europe are often outside the historic city center). You do get a good rate for that sort of hotel, but with a little more work (and the hotel reviews in this book), you can easily find on your own a midrange pension or friendly B&B for the same price or less and right in the heart of the action.

All major airlines flying to Europe sell vacation packages (see phone numbers and websites, above). The best place to start looking for independent packagers is the travel section of your local Sunday newspaper and national travel magazines. **Vacation Together** (✆ **800/839-9851;** www.vacationtogether.com) allows you to search for and book packages offered by a number of tour operators and airlines. **Liberty Travel** (✆ **888/271-1584;** www.libertytravel.com) is one of the biggest packagers in the Northeast and usually boasts a full-page ad in Sunday papers. **Kemwel** (✆ **800/678-0678;** www.kemwel.com) is a reputable option, too.

FLY/DRIVE TOURS Fly/drive vacations, which combine airfare and car rental, are increasing in popularity and are a lot cheaper than booking both airfare and car rental independently. They're available mainly through major European airlines (see above).

ESCORTED GROUP TOURS With a good escorted group tour, you'll know ahead of time what your trip will cost, and you won't have to worry about transportation, luggage, hotel reservations, communicating in foreign languages, and other basics—an experienced guide will take care of all that and lead you through all the sightseeing. The downside of a guided tour is that you trade much of the freedom and personal free time independent travel grants you and often see only the canned postcard-ready side of Europe through the tinted windows of a giant bus. You get to *see* Europe, but rarely do you get the chance to really *know* it. Consult a

> ⌒Tips **Flying for Less: Tips for Getting the Best Airfares**
>
> Passengers sharing the same airplane cabin rarely pay the same fare. Travelers who need to purchase tickets at the last minute, change their itinerary at a moment's notice, or fly one-way often get stuck paying the premium rate. Here are some ways to keep your airfare costs down.
>
> - Passengers who can book their ticket **long in advance,** who can **stay over Saturday night,** or who **fly midweek** or **at less-trafficked hours** may pay a fraction of the full fare. If your schedule is flexible, say so, and ask if you can secure a cheaper fare by changing your plans.
> - You can also save on airfares by keeping an eye out in local newspapers for **promotional specials** or **fare wars,** when airlines lower prices on their most popular routes. You rarely see fare wars offered for peak travel times, but if you can travel in the off-months, you may snag a bargain.
> - **Search the Internet** for cheap fares. See "Planning Your Trip Online," above.
> - **Consolidators,** also known as bucket shops, are great sources for international tickets. Start by looking in Sunday newspaper travel sections; U.S. travelers should focus on the *New York Times, Los Angeles Times,* and *Miami Herald.* For less-developed destinations, small travel agents who cater to immigrant communities in large cities often have the best deals. *Beware:* Bucket shop tickets are usually nonrefundable or rigged with stiff cancellation penalties, often as high as 50% to 75% of the ticket price, which may leave at inconvenient times and experience delays. Several reliable consolidators are worldwide and available on the Net. **STA Travel** is now the world's leader in student travel, thanks to their purchase of Council Travel. It also offers good fares for travelers of all ages. **ELTExpress (Flights.com)** (© 800/TRAV-800; www.eltexpress.com) started in Europe and has excellent fares worldwide, but particularly to that continent. It also has "local" websites in 12 countries. **FlyCheap** (© 800/FLY-CHEAP; www.1800flycheap.com) is owned by package-holiday megalith MyTravel and so has especially good access to fares for sunny destinations. **Air Tickets Direct** (© 800/778-3447; www.airticketsdirect.com) is based in Montreal and leverages the currently weak Canadian dollar for low fares; it'll also book trips to places that U.S. travel agents won't touch, such as Cuba.
> - For many more tips about air travel, including a rundown of the major frequent-flier credit cards, pick up a copy of *Frommer's Fly Safe, Fly Smart* (Wiley Publishing, Inc.).

good travel agent for the latest offerings and advice.

The two largest tour operators conducting escorted tours of Europe are **Globus/Cosmos** (© 800/338-7092; www.globusandcosmos.com) and **Trafalgar** (www.trafalgartours.com). Both companies have first-class tours that run about $100 a day and budget tours for about $75 a day. The differences are mainly in hotel location and the number of activities. There's little difference in the companies' services, so choose your tour based on the itinerary and preferred date of departure. Brochures are available at travel agencies, and all tours must be booked through travel agents.

GETTING TO THE CONTINENT FROM THE UNITED KINGDOM

BY TRAIN   Many rail passes and discounts are available in the United Kingdom for travel in continental Europe. One of the most complete overviews is available from **Rail Europe Special Services Department,** 10 Leake St., London SE1 7NN (✆ **0870/584-8848**). This organization is particularly well versed in information about discount travel as it applies to persons under 26, full-time or part-time students, and seniors.

The most prevalent option for younger travelers, the **EuroYouth passes,** are available only to travelers under 26 and entitle the pass holder to unlimited second-class rail travel in 26 European countries.

BY CHUNNEL   The Eurostar train shuttles between London and both Paris and Brussels; trip time is under 3 hours (compared to 10 hr. on the traditional train-ferry-train route). **Rail Europe** (✆ **877/272-RAIL;** www.raileurope.com) sells tickets on the Eurostar between London and Paris or Brussels (both $312 one-way).

For Eurostar reservations, call ✆ **800/EUROSTAR** in the U.S., 08705/186-186 in London, or 08-92-35-35-39 in Paris; www.eurostar.com. Eurostar trains arrive at and depart from Waterloo Station in London, Gare du Nord in Paris, and Central Station in Brussels.

BY FERRY & HOVERCRAFT Brittany Ferries (✆ **08703/665-333;** www.brittanyferries.com) is the largest British ferry/drive outfit, sailing from the southern coast of England to five destinations in Spain and France. From Portsmouth, sailings reach St-Malo and Caen; from Poole, Cherbourg. From Plymouth, sailings go to Santander in Spain. **P&O Ferries** (✆ **0870/520-2020;** www.poferries. com) operates car and passenger ferries between Portsmouth and Cherbourg (three departures a day; 5–7 hr.); between Portsmouth and Le Havre, France (three a day; 5 hr.); and between Dover and Calais, France (25 sailings a day; 1¼ hr.).

Unless you're interested in a leisurely sea voyage, passengers without cars might be better off using the quicker, and slightly cheaper, **Hoverspeed** (✆ **0870/5240-241;** www.hoverspeed. com). Hoverspeeds make the 35-minute crossing between Calais and Dover 7 to 15 times per day, with the more curtailed schedule in winter. Prices are £26 adults on foot or £13 children; vehicle fares are £122 to £143. Prices are one-way.

BY CAR   Many car-rental companies won't let you rent a car in Britain and take it to the Continent, so always check ahead. There are many "drive-on/drive-off" car-ferry services across the Channel; see "By Ferry & Hovercraft," above. There are also Chunnel trains that run a drive-on/drive-off service every 15 minutes (once an hour at night) for the 35-minute ride between Ashford and Calais.

BY COACH   Though travel by coach is considerably slower and less comfortable than travel by train, if you're on a budget you might opt for one of Eurolines's regular departures from London's Victoria Coach Station to destinations throughout Europe. Contact **Eurolines** at 52 Grosvenor Gardens, Victoria, London SW1W OAU (✆ **020/7730-8235;** www.eurolines.co.uk).

10 Getting Around

BY TRAIN

In Europe, the shortest—and cheapest—distance between two points is lined with rail tracks. European trains are less expensive than those in the United States, far more advanced in many ways, and certainly more extensive. Modern high-speed trains (130 mph) make the rails faster than the plane for short journeys, and overnight trains get you where you're going without wasting valuable daylight hours—and you save money on lodging to boot.

SOME TRAIN NOTES Many European high-speed trains, including the popular EC (EuroCity), IC (Inter-City), and EN (EuroNight), require you to pay a **supplement** in addition to the regular ticket fare. It's included when you buy tickets but not in any rail pass, so check at the ticket window before boarding; otherwise, the conductor will sell you the supplement on the train—along with a fine. **Seat reservations** ($20–$50 or more, when a meal is included) are required on some high-speed runs—any marked with an R on a printed train schedule. You can usually reserve a seat within a few hours of departure, but be on the safe side and book your seat a few days in advance. You need to reserve any sleeping couchette or sleeping berth, too.

With two exceptions, there's no need to buy individual train tickets or make seat reservations **before you leave the United States.** However, on the high-speed Artesia run (Paris-Turin and Milan) you must buy a supplement, on which you can get a substantial discount if you have a rail pass, but only if you buy the supplement in the United States along with the pass. It's also wise to reserve a seat on the Eurostar, as England's frequent "bank holidays" (long weekends) book the train solid with Londoners taking a short vacation to Paris.

The difference between **first class** and **second class** on European trains is minor—a matter of 1 or 2 inches of extra padding and maybe a bit more elbow room. European **train stations** are usually as clean and efficient as the trains, if a bit chaotic at times. In stations you'll find posters showing the track number and timetables for regularly scheduled runs (departures are often on the yellow poster). Many stations also have tourist offices and hotel reservations desks, banks with ATMs, and newsstands where you can buy phone cards, bus and metro tickets, maps, and local English-language event magazines.

You can get many more details about train travel in Europe and automated schedule information by fax by contacting **Rail Europe** (© **877/272-RAIL;** fax 800/432-1329; www.raileurope. com). If you plan on doing a lot of train travel, consider buying the *Thomas Cook European Timetable* ($29 from travel specialty stores; or order it at © **800/FORSYTH;** www.forsyth. com). Each country's national railway website, which includes schedules and fare information, occasionally in English, is listed at **Mercurio (http://mercurio.iet.unipi.it).**

RAIL PASSES The greatest value in European travel has always been the **rail pass,** a single ticket allowing you unlimited travel (or travel on a certain number of days) within a set time period. If you plan on going all over Europe by train, buying a rail pass will end up being much less expensive than buying individual tickets. Plus, a rail pass gives you the freedom to hop on a train whenever you feel like it, and there's no waiting in ticket lines. For more focused trips, you might want to look into national or regional passes or just buy individual tickets as you go.

Passes Available in the United States
The granddaddy of passes is the **Eurail-pass,** covering 17 countries (most of western Europe except Britain). It has been joined by the **Europass,** covering 5 to 12 countries (depending on which version you buy); this pass is mainly for travelers who are going to stay in the heart of western Europe.

Rail passes are available in either **consecutive-day** or **flexipass** versions (in which you have, say, 2 months in which to use 10 days of train travel). Consecutive-day passes are best for those taking the train frequently (every few days), covering a lot of ground, and making many short train hops. Flexipasses are for folks who want to range far and wide but plan on taking their time over a long trip and intend to stay in each city for a while. If you're under 26, you can opt to buy a regular first-class pass or a second-class youth pass; if you're 26 or over, you're stuck with buying a first-class pass. Passes for kids 4 to 11 are half price, and kids under 4 travel free.

It's best to buy these passes in the United States (they're available from some major European train stations but are up to 10% more expensive). You can get them from most travel agents, but the biggest supplier is **Rail Europe** (*C* **877/272-RAIL;** www.rail europe.com), which also sells most national passes, except for a few minor British ones. The company also publishes a free annual brochure, "Europe on Track," outlining a traveler's various pass and rail options.

The rates below are for 2003; they rise each year, usually after press time, so we can't include rates for 2004 here.

- **Eurailpass:** Consecutive-day Eurailpass at $588 for 15 days, $762 for 21 days, $946 for 1 month, $1,338 for 2 months, or 1,654 for 3 months.
- **Eurail Flexipass:** Good for 2 months of travel at $694 for 10 days (consecutive or not) or $914 for 15 days.
- **Eurail Saverpass:** Good for two to five people traveling together at $498 per person for 15 days, $648 for 21 days, $804 for 1 month, $1,138 for 2 months, or $1,408 for 3 months.
- **Eurail Saver Flexipass:** Good for two to five people traveling together at $592 per person for 10 days within 2 months, or $778 per person for 15 days within 2 months.
- **Eurail Youthpass:** Second-class pass for travelers under 26 at $414 for 15 days, $534 for 21 days, $664 for 1 month, $938 for 2 months, or $1,160 for 3 months.
- **Eurail Youth Flexipass:** Only for travelers under 26 at $488 for 10 days of travel within 2 months or $642 for 15 days within 2 months.
- **Eurail Selectpass:** The pass offers unlimited travel on the national rail networks of any 3, 4, or 5 bordering countries out of the 17 Eurail nations linked by train or ship. Two or more passengers can travel together for big discounts, getting 5, 6, 8, 10, or 15 days of rail travel within any 2-month period on the national rail networks of any 3, 4, or 5 adjoining Eurail countries linked by train or ship. A sample fare: for 5 days in

Countries Honoring Train Passes

Eurail Countries: Austria, Belgium, Denmark, Finland, France, Germany, Greece, Hungary, Ireland, Italy, Luxembourg, the Netherlands, Norway, Portugal, Spain, Sweden, Switzerland.

> ## *Tips* Train Trip Tips
>
> To make your train travels as pleasant as possible, remember a few general rules:
>
> - **Hold on to your train ticket** after it's been marked or punched by the conductor. Some European railroad systems require that you present your ticket when you leave the station platform at your destination.
> - While you sleep—or even nap—**be sure your valuables are in a safe place.** You might temporarily attach a small bell to each bag to warn you if someone attempts to take it. If you've left bags on a rack in the front or back of the car, consider securing them with a small bicycle chain and lock to deter thieves, who consider trains happy hunting grounds.
> - Few European trains have drinking fountains, and the dining car may be closed just when you're at your thirstiest, so **take along a bottle of mineral water.** As you'll soon discover, the experienced European traveler comes loaded with hampers of food and drink and munches away throughout the trip.
> - If you want to leave bags in a train station locker, **don't let anyone help you store them in it.** A favorite trick among thieves is feigned helpfulness, then pocketing the key to your locker while passing you the key to an empty one.

2 months you pay $356 for three countries.

- **EurailDrive Pass:** Mixes train travel and rental cars (through Hertz or Avis) for less money than it would cost to do them separately (and one of the only ways to get around the high daily car-rental rates in Europe when you rent for less than a week). You get 4 rail days and 2 car days within a 2-month period. Prices (per person for one adult/two adults) vary with the class of the car: $452/$409 economy class, $481/$423 compact, and $496/$431 midsize. You can add up to five extra rail and/or car days. Extra rail days are $45 each; car days are $49 each for economy class, $64 compact, and $75 midsize. You have to reserve the first car day a week before leaving the United States but can make other reservations as you go (always subject to availability). If

there are more than two adults, the extra passengers get the car portion free but must buy the 4-day rail pass for $365.

- **Eurail Selectpass Drive:** This is a fine way to visit three to five European countries with great flexibility. You're granted 3 days of unlimited train travel and 2 days of car rental with unlimited mileage from Avis or Hertz. You have 2 months to complete your travel, all of which is first class on the rail. Prices depend on your choice of car. Typical prices range from $291 to $331 per person based on two passengers traveling together.

There are also **national rail passes** of various kinds and **regional passes** like ScanRail (Scandinavia), BritRail (Great Britain), and the European East Pass (Austria, Czech Republic, Slovakia, Hungary, Poland). Some national passes you have to buy in the United States, some you can get on either side of the Atlantic, and still others you must buy in Europe. Remember: Seniors, students, and youths can usually get discounts on European trains—in some countries just by asking, in others by buying a discount card good for a year or for some other period of time. Rail Europe or your travel agent can fill you in on all the details.

If you plan on traveling in Great Britain, then **BritRail** (© 877/677-1066; fax 877/477-1066; www.britrail. com), which specializes in rail passes for use in Great Britain, is your best bet.

Passes Available in the United Kingdom Many rail passes are available in the United Kingdom for travel in Britain and Europe. The most popular ticket is the **Interrail Card,** which is offered for persons who have lived in Europe at least 6 months. It offers unlimited travel in most European countries within 22 days or 1 month and is valid on all normal trains, or else high-speed trains such as TGV if you pay a supplement. The price depends on the trip duration and how many of the eight different "zones" you plan to travel in. Typical zones include Britain or Ireland, Finland, Norway and Sweden, or else combos as Austria, Denmark, Germany, and Switzerland. Typical prices for one zone are 276€ ($317) for 22 days or 258€ ($297) for two zones (good for 1 month).

For help in determining the best option for your trip and to buy tickets, stop in London at the **International Rail Centre** in Victoria Station (© 8705/848-848).

BY CAR

Many rental companies grant discounts if you **reserve in advance** (usually 48 hr.) from your home country. Weekly rentals are almost always less expensive than day rentals. Three or more people traveling together can usually get around cheaper by car than by train (even with rail passes).

When you reserve a car, be sure to ask if the price includes the EU value-added tax (VAT), personal accident insurance (PAI), collision-damage waiver (CDW), and any other insurance options. If not, ask what these extras cost, because at the end of your rental, they can make a big difference in your bottom line. The CDW and other insurance might be covered by your credit card if you use the card to pay for the rental; check with the card issuer to be sure.

If your credit card doesn't cover the CDW (and it probably won't in Ireland), **Travel Guard International,** 1145 Clark St., Stevens Point, WI 54481 (© **800/826-1300** or 715/345-0505; www.travelguard.com), offers it for $7 per day. Avis and Hertz, among other companies, require that you purchase a theft-protection policy in Italy.

The main car-rental companies are **Avis** (© **800/331-1212;** www.avis. com), **Budget** (© **800/472-3325;** www.budget.com), **SIXT** (Dollar in the U.S.; © **800/800-3665;** www. dollar.com), **Hertz** (© **800/654-3131;** www.hertz.com), and **National** (© **800/227-7368;** www.nationalcar. com). U.S.-based companies specializing in European rentals are **Auto Europe** (© **800/223-5555;** www.auto europe.com), **Europe by Car** (© **800/ 223-1516,** or 212/581-3040 in New York; www.europebycar.com), and **Kemwel Holiday Auto** (© **800/678-0678;** www.kemwel.com). Europe by Car, Kemwel, and **Renault USA** (© **800/221-1052;** www.renaultusa. com) also offer a low-cost alternative to renting for longer than 15 days: **short-term leases** in which you technically buy a fresh-from-the-factory car and then sell it back when you return it. All insurance is included, from liability and theft to personal injury and CDW, with no deductible. And unlike at many rental agencies, who won't rent to anyone under 25, the minimum age for a lease is 18.

The **AAA** supplies good maps to its members. **Michelin maps** (© **800/ 423-0485** or 864/458-5619; www. michelin.com) are made for the tourist. The maps rate cities as "uninteresting" (as a tourist destination); "interesting"; "worth a detour"; or "worth an entire journey." They also highlight particularly scenic stretches of road in green, and have symbols pointing out scenic overlooks, ruins, and other sights along the way.

BY PLANE

Though trains remain the cheapest and easiest way to get around in Europe, air transport options have improved drastically in the past few years. Intense competition with rail and ferry companies has slowly forced airfares into the bargain basement. **British Airways** (© **800/AIRWAYS** in the U.S., or 0870/850-9850 in the U.K.; www. britishairways.com) and other scheduled airlines fly regularly from London to Paris for only £107 ($171) round-trip, depending on the season. Lower fares usually apply to midweek flights

and carry advance-purchase requirements of 2 weeks or so.

The biggest airline news in Europe is the rise of the **no-frills airline** modeled on American upstarts like Southwest. By keeping their overheads down through electronic ticketing, forgoing meal service, and flying from less popular airports, these airlines are able to offer low fares. Most round-trip tickets are $40 to $170. This means now you can save lots of time, and even money, over long train hauls, especially from, say, London to Venice or from central Europe out to peripheral countries like Greece and Spain. Budget airlines include **EasyJet** (© **0870/6-000-000** in England; www.easyjet.com); **Ryanair** (© **0870/333-1231** in England; www. ryanair.com) in Ireland; and **Virgin Express** (© **020/7744-0004;** www. virgin-express.com), an offshoot of Virgin Air, in Belgium. Be aware, though, that the names might change because these small airlines are often economically vulnerable and can fail or merge with a big airline. Still, as

---

The Rules of the Road: Driving in Europe

- First off, know that European drivers tend to be more aggressive than their American counterparts.
- Drive on the right except in England, Scotland, and Ireland, where you drive on the left. And *do not drive* in the left lane on a four-lane highway; it is truly only for passing.
- If someone comes up from behind and flashes his lights at you, it's a signal for you to slow down and drive more on the shoulder so he can pass you more easily (2-lane roads here routinely become 3 cars wide).
- Except for the German autobahn, most highways do indeed have speed limits of around 100 to 135kmph (60–80 mph).
- Remember that everything's measured in kilometers here (mileage and speed limits). For a rough conversion, 1 kilometer = .6 miles.
- Be aware that although gas may look reasonably priced, the price is per liter, and 3.8 liters = 1 gallon—so multiply by four to estimate the equivalent per-gallon price.
- Never leave anything of value in the car overnight, and don't leave anything visible any time you leave the car (this goes double in Italy, triple in Naples).

quickly as one disappears, another will take off.

Lower airfares are also available throughout Europe on **charter flights** rather than regularly scheduled ones. Look in local newspapers to find out about them. Consolidators cluster in cities like London and Athens.

Flying across Europe on regularly scheduled airlines can destroy a budget and be superexpensive. Whenever possible, book your total flight on one ticket before leaving. For example, if you're flying from New York to Rome, but also plan to visit Palermo, Florence, and Turin, have the total trip written up on one ticket. Don't arrive in Rome and book separate legs of the journey, which costs far more when it's done piecemeal.

Sometimes national carriers offer remarkable deals to non-European residents, which cuts the cost of flying within Europe. A good example is **Alitalia**'s "Europlus." First, you have to book a transatlantic flight, perhaps from New York to Rome. After that, and for only $315, you can buy a package of three flight coupons entitling you to fly on any three flights anywhere in Europe served by Alitalia (not just Italy). You can also purchase unlimited additional tickets, one-way, for another $100 per ticket.

Another fine deal is offered in London by **Easy Jet** (© **0870/607-6543** in London; www.easyjet.com), a subsidiary of British Airways. The carrier offers 40% off standard round-trip airfares. Sample round-trip air fares from London are as follows: Edinburgh £23, Barcelona £54, Munich £24, Milan £24.

American citizens can contact **Europe by Air** (© **888/387-2479**; www.europebyair.com) for their Europe flight pass serving 30 countries, 30 airlines, and 150 European cities. It costs only $99 to travel one-way between these cities.

Because discount passes are always changing on air routes within Europe, it's best to check in with **Air Travel Advisory Bureau** in London (© **020/7636-5000**; www.atab.co.uk). This bureau offers a free service directory to the public for suppliers of discount airfares from all major U.K. airports.

BY BUS

Bus transportation is readily available throughout Europe; it sometimes is less expensive than train travel and covers a more extensive area but can be slower and much less comfortable. European buses, like the trains, outshine their American counterparts, but they're perhaps best used only to pick up where the extensive train network leaves off. One major bus company serves all the countries of western Europe (no service to Greece): **Eurolines** in London (© **0870/514-3219**; www.eurolines.com), whose staff can check schedules, make reservations, and quote prices.

11 Tips on Accommodations

Traditional European hotels tend to be simpler than American ones and emphasize cleanliness and friendliness over amenities. For example, even in the cheapest American chain motel, free cable is as standard as indoor plumbing. In Europe, however, few hotels below the moderate level even have in-room TVs.

Unless otherwise noted, all hotel rooms in this book have private en-suite bathrooms. However, the standard European hotel bathroom might not look like what you're used to. For example, the European concept of a shower is to stick a nozzle in the bathroom wall and a drain in the floor. Shower curtains are optional. In some cramped private bathrooms, you'll have to relocate the toilet paper outside the bathroom before turning on the shower and drenching the whole room. Another interesting fixture is the "half tub," in which there's only room to sit, rather than lie down. The half tub usually sports a shower nozzle that has nowhere to hang—so your knees get very clean and the floor gets very wet. Hot water may be available only once a day and not on demand—this is especially true with shared bathrooms. Heating water is costly, and many smaller hotels do it only once daily, in the morning.

SAVING ON YOUR HOTEL ROOM

The **rack rate** is the maximum rate that a hotel charges for a room. Hardly anybody pays this price, however, except in high season or on holidays. To lower the cost of your room:

- **Ask about special rates or other discounts.** Always ask whether a room less expensive than the first one quoted is available, or whether any special rates apply to you. You may qualify for corporate, student, military, senior, or other discounts. Mention membership in AAA, AARP, frequent-flier programs, or trade unions, which may entitle you to special deals as well. Find out the hotel policy on children— do kids stay free in the room or is there a special rate?
- **Dial direct.** When booking a room in a chain hotel, you'll often get a better deal by calling the individual hotel's reservation desk rather than the chain's main number.
- **Book online.** Many hotel websites offer Internet-only discounts.

- **Look into group or long-stay discounts.** If you come as part of a large group, you should be able to negotiate a bargain rate, since the hotel can then guarantee occupancy in a number of rooms. Likewise, if you're planning a long stay (at least 5 days), you might qualify for a discount. As a general rule, expect 1 night free after a 7-night stay.
- **Investigate reservations services.** These outfits usually work as consolidators, buying up or reserving rooms in bulk, and then dealing them out to customers at a profit. You can get 10% to 50% off; but remember, these discounts apply to inflated rack rates that savvy travelers rarely end up paying. You may get a decent rate, but always call the hotel as well to see if you can do better. Among the more reputable reservations services, offering both telephone and online bookings, are: **Accommodations Express** (© 800/950-4685; www. acex.net); **Hotels.Com** (© 800/ 715-7666; www.hotels.com or www.180096HOTEL.com); and **Quikbook** (© 800/789-9887; includes fax on demand service; www.quikbook.com). Online, try booking your hotel through **Frommers.com** (www.frommers. com). **Microsoft Expedia** (www. expedia.com) features a "Travel Agent" that will also direct you to affordable lodgings.

Tips **Home Exchanges**

Intervac U.S., 30 Corte San Fernando, Tiburon, CA 94159 (© 800/756-HOME or 415/435-3497; www.intervacus.com), is part of the largest worldwide home-exchange network, with a special emphasis on Europe. It publishes four catalogs a year, listing homes in more than 36 countries. Members contact each other directly. Depending on your type of membership, fees begin at $65.

> **Tips A Traveler's Tip**
>
> If you call a hotel from home to reserve a room, *always follow up with a confirmation fax.* Not only is it what most hotels prefer, but it is also printed proof you've booked a room. Keep the language simple—state your name, number of people, what kind of room (like "double with bathroom and one bed" or "double with bathroom and two beds"), how many nights you'd like to stay, and the starting date for the first night. Remember that Europeans abbreviate dates day/month/year, not month/day/year.

HOTEL BOOKING SERVICES

When you arrive in town, you'll find that a desk in the train station or at the tourist office (or both) acts as a central hotel reservations service for the city. Tell them your price range, where you'd like to be in the city, and sometimes even the style of hotel, and they'll use a computer database to find you a room in town.

The advantages of booking services are that they do all the room-finding work for you—for a nominal fee—and always speak English, while individual hoteliers may not. When every hotel in town seems to be booked up (during a convention or festival or just in high season), they can often find space for you at inns not listed in guidebooks or other main sources. On the downside, hotels in many countries often charge higher rates to people booking through such a service.

1

Austria

by Darwin Porter & Danforth Prince

Austria stands at the crossroads of Europe, as it did in the heyday of the Austro-Hungarian Empire. Its capital, Vienna, stranded during the postwar years on the edge of western Europe, is taking its place again as an important international city. Salzburg, "The City of Mozart," is a world-class cultural destination and a magnet for music lovers.

The country offers plenty to do, from exploring historic castles and palaces to skiing on some of the world's finest alpine slopes.

1 Vienna ⭐⭐⭐

Vienna still retains much of the glory and grandeur of the empire's heady days. Museum treasures from all over Europe, baroque palaces through which Maria Theresa and her brood wandered, Johann Strauss's lively music, Gustav Klimt's paintings, the concert halls, the unparalleled opera—it's all still here, as if the empire were still flourishing.

Tourism is growing as thousands arrive every year to view Vienna's great art and architecture, to feast on lavish Viennese pastries, to explore the Vienna Woods, to sail down the Danube, to attend Vienna's balls, operas, and festivals, and to listen to the "music that never stops."

Visitors today face a newer and brighter Vienna, a city with more joie de vivre and punch than it's had since before the war. There's also a downside: Prices are on the rise—they haven't reached the height of the Ferris wheel at the Prater, but they're climbing there.

ESSENTIALS

GETTING THERE **By Plane** Vienna International Airport (VIE; ⓒ 01/70070; http://english.viennaairport.com) is about 19km (12 miles) southeast of the city center. There's regular bus service between the airport and the **City Air Terminal,** adjacent to the Vienna Hilton and directly across from the **Wien Mitte/Landstrasse** rail station, where you can easily connect with subway and tram lines. Buses run every 20 minutes from 4:30am to 12:30pm, and hourly from midnight to 5am. The trip takes about 20 minutes and costs 6€ ($6.90) per person. Tickets are sold on the bus and must be purchased with Austrian money. There's also bus service between the airport and two railroad stations, the Westbahnhof and the Südbahnhof, leaving every 30 minutes to an hour. Fares are also 6€ ($6.90).

There's also local train service, Schnellbahn (S-Bahn), between the airport and the Wien Nord and Wien Mitte rail stations. Trains run hourly from 4:30am to 9:30pm and leave from the basement of the airport. Trip time is 40 to 45 minutes, and the fare is 3€ ($3.45).

The official **Vienna Tourist Information Office** in the arrival hall of the airport is open daily from 8:30am to 9pm.

By Train Vienna has four principal rail stations, with frequent connections from all Austrian cities and towns and from all major European cities. For train information for all stations, call © **05/1717.**

Westbahnhof (West Railway Station), on Europaplatz, is for trains arriving from western Austria, France, Germany, Switzerland, and some eastern European countries. It has frequent links to major Austrian cities such as Salzburg, which is a 3-hour train ride from Vienna. The Westbahnhof connects with local trains, the U3 and U6 underground lines, and several tram and bus routes.

Südbahnhof (South Railway Station), on Südtirolerplatz, has train service to southern and eastern Austria, Italy, Hungary, Slovenia, and Croatia. It is linked with local rail service and tram and bus routes.

Both of these stations house useful travel agencies **(Österreichisches Verkehrsbüro)** that provide tourist information and help with hotel reservations. In the Westbahnhof the agency is in the upper hall and at the Südbahnhof, in the lower hall.

Other stations in Vienna include **Franz-Josef Bahnhof,** on Franz-Josef-Platz, used mainly by local trains, although connections are made here to Prague and Berlin. You can take the D-tram line to the city's Ringstrasse from here. **Wien Mitte,** at Landstrasser Hauptstrasse 1, is also a terminus for local trains, plus a depot for trains to the Czech Republic and to Vienna International Airport.

By Bus The **City Bus Terminal** is at the Wien Mitte rail station, Landstrasser Hauptstrasse 1. This is the arrival depot for Post buses and Bundesbuses from points all over the country, and also the arrival point for private buses from various European cities. The terminal has lockers, currency-exchange kiosks, and a ticket counter open daily from 6:15am to 6pm. For bus information, call © **05/1717** daily from 6:15am to 6pm.

By Car You can reach Vienna from all directions via major highways *(Autobahnen)* or by secondary highways. The main artery from the west is Autobahn A1, coming in from Munich 468km (291 miles), Salzburg 336km (209 miles), and Linz 187km (116 miles). Autobahn A2 arrives from the south, from Graz 200km (124 miles) and Klagenfurt 309km (192 miles). Autobahn A4 comes in from the east, connecting with Route E58, which runs to Bratislava and Prague.

Vienna

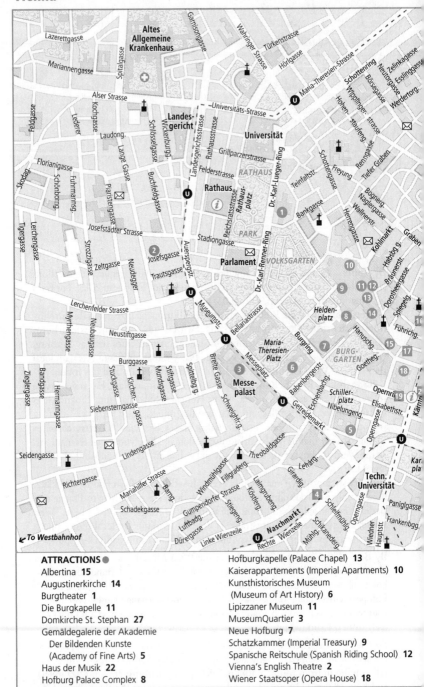

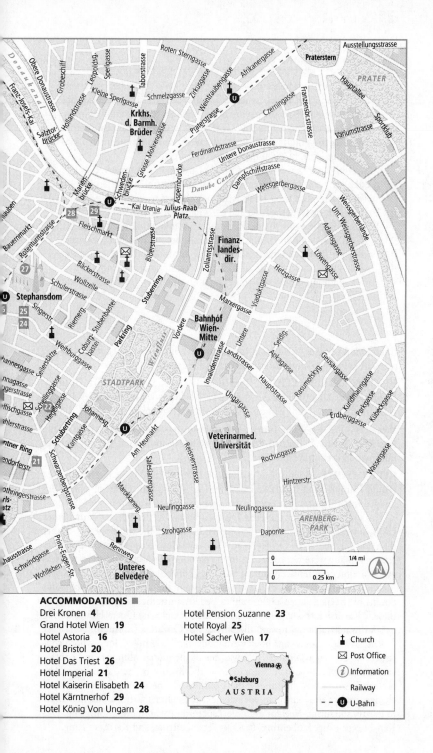

ACCOMMODATIONS ■

Drei Kronen **4**
Grand Hotel Wien **19**
Hotel Astoria **16**
Hotel Bristol **20**
Hotel Das Triest **26**
Hotel Imperial **21**
Hotel Kaiserin Elisabeth **24**
Hotel Kärntnerhof **29**
Hotel König Von Ungarn **28**

Hotel Pension Suzanne **23**
Hotel Royal **25**
Hotel Sacher Wien **17**

† Church
⊠ Post Office
ⓘ Information
— Railway
- - Ⓤ U-Bahn

Vienna ✸
●Salzburg
AUSTRIA

Native Behavior

Get accustomed to hearing *Grüss Gott* (God bless you) when Austrians greet you and *Auf Wiedersehen* when they leave. These greetings are practiced by everybody from your hotel manager to the shoeshine man.

Although no one will kick you off the premises, it is a local custom to dress up for a night at the opera or ballet. You can show up in a jogging suit or jeans but you might feel out of place.

Austria is perhaps the most formal of the countries reviewed in this guide. Yes, some gents nostalgic for the old Austro-Hungarian Empire still bow and click their heels when introduced to a lady. Prepare to shake hands on both meeting and parting. The Austrians are great sticklers for titles, however minor or honorific, including *Doktor* or *Professor.*

If you've never hung out in coffeehouses before, making it your second living room, Austria is a wonderful introduction to this custom. The Viennese especially can sit for hour after hour over a single cup of coffee reading magazines and newspapers or else watching the world parade by.

Autobahn A22 takes traffic from the northwest, and Route E10 connects to the cities and towns of southeastern Austria and Hungary.

VISITOR INFORMATION Tourist Office   The official **Wien Tourist-Information,** Albertinaplatz 7 (© **01/211-14-481;** www.info.wien.at), is open daily from 9am to 7pm. You can make room reservations here.

Websites   Besides **Wien Tourist-Information (www.info.wien.at),** go to the **Austrian National Tourist Office (www.austria-tourism.at/us)** for current information on culture and events.

CITY LAYOUT   Vienna has evolved into one of the largest metropolises of central Europe, with a surface area covering 415 sq. km (160 sq. miles). It's divided into 23 districts *(Bezirke),* each identified by a Roman numeral.

The size and shape of the **First District,** known as the **Innere Stadt (Inner City),** roughly corresponds to the original borders of the medieval city. Other than the Cathedral of St. Stephan, very few Gothic or medieval buildings remain—many were reconstructed in the baroque or neoclassical style, whereas others are modern replacements of buildings bombed during World War II. As Austria's commercial and cultural nerve center, the central district contains dozens of streets devoted exclusively to pedestrian traffic. The most famous of these is **Kärntnerstrasse,** which bypasses the Vienna State Opera House during its southward trajectory toward the province of Carinthia (Kärnten).

Ringstrasse is a circular boulevard about 4km (2½ miles) long whose construction between 1859 and 1888 was one of the most ambitious (and controversial) examples of urban restoration in the history of central Europe. The boulevard surrounds the Inner City. Confusingly, the name of this boulevard changes many times during its encirclement of the Inner City. Names that apply to it carry the suffix *-ring:* for example, Opernring, Schottenring, Burgring, Dr.-Karl-Lueger-Ring, Stubenring, Parkring, Schubertring, and Kärntner Ring.

Surrounding Ringstrasse and the Inner City, in a more or less clockwise direction, are the inner suburban districts (2–9), which contain many hotels and restaurants popular for their close proximity to the city center. The outer districts (10–23) form another concentric ring of suburbs, comprising a variety of neighborhoods from industrial parks to rural villages.

Northeast of the Inner City, beyond the Danube Canal, is the **2nd District,** home to the famous amusement park, the Prater. East of the center, in the **3rd District,** you'll find the art treasures and baroque setting of the Belvedere Palace. West of the center is Schönbrunn Palace.

GETTING AROUND   By Public Transportation   Wiener Verkehrsbetriebe (Vienna Transport), with its network of facilities covering hundreds of miles, can take you where you want to go—by U-Bahn (subway), tram (streetcar), or bus. **Informationdienst der Wiener Verkehrsbetriebe (Vienna Public Transport Information Center)** has five locations: Opernpassage (an underground passageway adjacent to the Wiener Staatsoper), Karlsplatz, Stephansplatz (near Vienna's cathedral), Westbahnhof, and Praterstern. For information about any of these outlets, call © **01/790-9105.**

Vienna maintains a uniform fare that applies to all forms of public transport. A ticket for the bus, subway, or tram will cost 1.50€ ($1.75) if you buy it in advance at a Tabac-Trafiks (a store or kiosk selling tobacco products and newspapers) or 2€ ($2.30) if you buy it on board. Smart Viennese buy their tickets in advance, usually in blocks of at least five at a time, from any of the city's thousands of Tabac-Trafiks or at any of the public transport centers noted above. No matter what vehicle you decide to ride within Vienna, remember that once a ticket has been stamped (validated) by either a machine or a railway attendant, it's valid for one trip in one direction, anywhere in the city, including transfers.

By U-Bahn (Subway)   The U-Bahn consists of five lines labeled as U1, U2, U3, U4, and U6 (there is no U5). Karlsplatz, in the heart of the Inner City, is the most important underground station for visitors, as the U1, U2, and U4 converge here. The U2 traces part of the Ring, the U4 goes to Schönbrunn, and the U1 stops in Stephansplatz. The U3 also stops in Stephansplatz and connects with the Westbahnhof. The U-Bahn runs daily from 6am to midnight.

Value **The Vienna Card**

The **Vienna Card** gives you access to all public modes of transportation (subway, bus, and tram) within Vienna—as well as discounts in city museums, shops, and restaurants—for a single discounted price. A 24-hour network pass costs 5€ and is good for a full day of public transport. A 72-hour network pass sells for 17€ ($19). There's also a green ticket, priced at 24€ ($28), that contains eight individual partitions. Each of these, when stamped, is good for 1 day of unlimited travel. An individual can opt to reserve all eight of the partitions for his or her own use, thereby gaining 8 days of cost-effective travel on the city's transport system. Or the partitions can be subdivided among a group of several riders, allowing—for example—two persons 4 days each of unlimited rides. Vienna Cards are easy to find throughout the capital, or you can buy one outside Vienna by calling © **01/7984-40028** with a credit card.

Vienna Public Transport

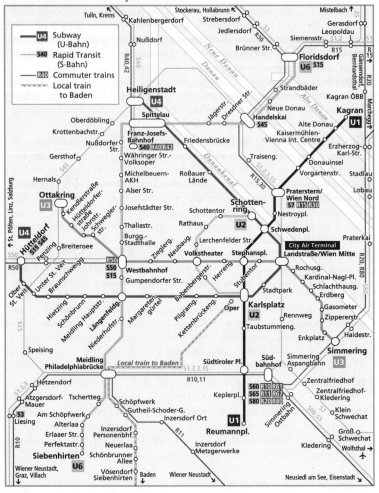

By Bus Buses traverse Vienna in all directions and operate Monday through Saturday from 6am to 10pm and Sunday from 6am to 8pm. Bus nos. 1A, 2A, and 3A will get you around the Inner City. Convenient night buses are available on weekends and holidays starting at 12:15am. They go from Schwedensplatz to the outer suburbs (including Grinzing). Normal tickets are not valid on these late "N" buses. Instead, you pay a special fare of 1.50€ ($1.75) on board.

By Tram Riding the red-and-white trams *(Strassenbahn)* is not only a practical way to get around, it's a great way to see the city. Tram stops are well marked and lines are labeled as numbers or letters. Lines 1 and 2 will bring you to all the major sights on the Ringstrasse. Line D skirts the outer Ring and goes to the Südbahnhof, whereas line 18 goes between the Westbahnhof and the Südbahnhof.

By Taxi Taxi stands are marked by signs, or you can call for a radio cab by phoning ℂ **31300,** 60160, or 40100. Fares are indicated on an officially calibrated taximeter. The basic fare is 2.50€ ($2.90), plus 1.10€ ($1.25) per kilometer. There's an extra charge of 1€ ($1.15) for luggage carried in the trunk. For rides after 11pm, and for trips on Sunday and holidays, there's a surcharge of 1€ ($1.15). There is an additional charge of 2€ ($2.30) if the taxi is ordered by phone.

By Car Major car-rental companies operating in Vienna include **Avis,** Opernring 3–5 (© **800/654-3001** in the U.S., 01/700-732-700 at the Vienna airport, or 01/587-6241 in downtown Vienna; U-Bahn: Karlsplatz); **Budget Rent-a-Car,** Hilton Air Terminal (© **800/472-3325** in the U.S., or 01/714-6565 in Vienna; U-Bahn: Landstrasse/Wien Mitte); and **Hertz,** in the Marriott Hotel, Parkring 12A (© **01/512-8677**).

By Bicycle Vienna has more than 250km (155 miles) of marked bicycle paths within the city limits. In the summer, many Viennese leave their cars in the garage and ride bikes. You can take bicycles on specially marked U-Bahn cars for free, but only Monday through Friday from 9am to 3pm and 6:30pm to midnight. On weekends in July and August bicycles are carried free from 9am to midnight.

Rental stores abound at the Prater and along the banks of the Danube Canal, which is the favorite bike route for most Viennese. One of the best of the many sites specializing in bike rentals is **Pedalpower,** Ausstellungsstrasse 3 (© **01/729-7234;** www.pedalpower.at), which is open March to October from 9am to 7pm. The Vienna Tourist Board can also supply a list of rental shops and more information about bike paths. Bike rentals begin at about 28€ ($32) per day. You are supplied with a map for a self-guided tour.

FAST FACTS: Vienna

American Express The office at Kärntnerstrasse 21–23 (© **01/51540-770**), near Stock-im-Eisenplatz, is open Monday through Friday from 9am to 5:30pm and Saturday from 9am to noon.

Business Hours Most shops are open Monday through Friday from 9am to 6pm and Saturday from 9am to noon, 12:30pm, or 1pm, depending on the store. On the first Saturday of every month, shops customarily remain open until 4:30 or 5pm. The tradition is called *langer Samstag.*

City Code The telephone city code for Vienna is **01.** It is only used when you're calling from outside Vienna.

Currency Exchange During off-hours you can exchange money at *bureaux de change* (exchange bureaus) throughout the Inner City (there's one at the intersection of Kohlmarkt and the Graben), as well as at travel agencies, train stations, and the airport. There's also a 24-hour exchange service at the post office (Hauptpostamt) at Fleischmarkt 19.

Dentists/Doctors For dental problems, call © **01/512-2078.** A list of physicians can be found in the telephone directory under *Arzte.* If you have a medical emergency at night, call © **141** daily from 7pm to 7am.

Drugstores Called *Apotheke,* they're open Monday through Friday from 8am to noon and 2 to 6pm and Saturday from 8am to noon. Each Apotheke posts in its window a list of shops that take turns staying open at night and on Sunday.

Embassies/Consulates   The embassy of the **United States** is at Boltzmanngasse 16, A-1090 Vienna (© **01/31339;** U-Bahn: Stadtpark). The consular section, Gartenbaupromenade 2–4, A-1010 Vienna (© **01/31339**), handles lost passports, tourist emergencies, and other matters. Both are open Monday through Friday from 8:30am to noon and 1 to 2pm.

The embassy of **Canada,** Laurenzerberg 2 (© **01/531-380**), is open Monday through Friday from 8:30am to 12:30pm and 1:30 to 3:30pm. The embassy of the **United Kingdom,** Jauresgasse 12 (© **01/71613-0**), is open Monday through Friday from 10am to noon and 2 to 4pm. The embassy of **Australia,** Mattiellistrasse (© **01/50674**), is open Monday through Friday from 9am to noon and 2 to 4pm. The embassy of **New Zealand,** Springsiedelgasse 28 (© **01/318-8505**), is open Monday through Friday from 8:30am to 5pm, but it's best to call to see if it's actually open. The embassy of **Ireland,** Rotenturn Strasse 16–18 (© **01/715-4246**), is open Monday though Friday from 9:30 to 11:30am and 1:30 to 4pm.

Emergencies   Call © **122** to report a fire, © **133** for the police, or © **144** for an ambulance.

Internet Access   **Café Stein,** Währingerstrasse 6 (© **01/319-72-41**), offers Internet access at the rate of 3€ every half-hour and is open daily from 7am to 2am.

Police   The emergency number is © **133.**

Post Office   Post offices in Vienna can be found in the heart of every district. Addresses for these can be found in the telephone directory under "Post." Post offices are generally open for mail services Monday through Friday from 7am to noon and 2 to 6pm. The central post office (Hauptpostamt), Barbaragasse 2 (© **01/51570**), and most general post offices are open 24 hours a day, 7 days a week.

Safety   In recent years, Vienna has been plagued by purse-snatchers. Small foreign children often approach sympathetic adults and ask for money. As the adult goes for his wallet or her purse, full-grown thieves rush in and grab the money, fleeing with it. Unaccompanied women should hold onto their purses tightly, and never open them in public.

Telephone   The **country code** for Austria is **43.** The **city code** for Vienna is **1;** use this code when you're calling from outside Austria. If you're within Austria, use **01** before the local number (**01** is included in all telephone numbers in this chapter, so it is not necessary to add any other numbers when calling these telephone numbers within Austria).

Hotels add huge surcharges to long-distance calls; go to the post office instead. Consider purchasing a **phone card** at any post office. **International direct dial** numbers include **AT&T** (© **0800-200-280**); **MCI** (© **0800-200-235**); and **Sprint** (© **0800-20-02-36**).

Tipping   A service charge of 10% to 15% is included on hotel and restaurant bills, but it's a good policy to leave something extra for waiters and 1.85€ ($2.15) per day for your hotel maid. Railroad station, airport, and hotel porters get 1.45€ ($1.65) per piece of luggage, plus a .75€ (85¢) tip. Tip your hairdresser 10% of the bill, and give the shampoo person a 1.45€ ($1.65) gratuity. Toilet attendants are usually given .35€ (40¢), and coat-check attendants expect .50€ to 1.10€ (60¢–$1.25).

WHERE TO STAY
INNERE STADT (INNER CITY)
Very Expensive

Grand Hotel Wien ★★★   Some of the most discerning hotel guests in Europe, often music lovers, prefer this seven-story deluxe hotel to the more traditional and famous Imperial or Bristol. Only a block from the Staatsoper, it's a honey, and has been at the hub of Viennese social life since the turn of the 20th century. You enter a world of beveled mirrors, crystal chandeliers, and a grand staircase. The spacious accommodations are posh, with all the modern extras such as heated floors, phones in the marble bathrooms, and even "antifog" mirrors. The more expensive units have more elaborate furnishings and decoration, including delicate stucco work.

Kärnter Ring 9, A-1010 Vienna. © **01/515-800.** Fax 01/515-13-13. www.anagrand.com. 205 units. 370€–450€ ($426–$518) double; from 660€ ($759) suite. AE, DC, MC, V. U-Bahn: Karlsplatz. **Amenities:** 3 restaurants; 2 bars; health club; business center; boutiques; salon; 24-hr. room service; massage; babysitting; laundry service/dry cleaning service; nonsmoking rooms; rooms for those with limited ability. *In room:* A/C, TV, dataport, minibar, coffeemaker, hair dryer, safe, trouser press.

Hotel Bristol ★★★   This six-story landmark is a superb choice—only the Imperial is grander. When it was constructed in 1894 across the street from the State Opera, it was the ultimate in luxury style, but it's been updated to give guests the benefit of black-tiled bathrooms equipped with tub/shower combos and modern conveniences. Rooms are sumptuously appointed. The club floor offers luxurious comfort, enhanced by period furnishings. Corkscrew columns of rare marble grace the **Korso,** Bristol's restaurant, which is one of the best in Vienna.

Kärntner Ring 1, A-1015 Vienna. © **888/625-5144** in the U.S., or 01/515-160. Fax 01/515-16-550. www. westin.com/bristol. 140 units. 225€–445€ ($259–$512) double; from 858€ ($987) suite. AE, DC, MC, V. Parking 28€ ($32). U-Bahn: Karlsplatz. Tram: 1 or 2. **Amenities:** 2 restaurants; bar; business center; fitness center; Jacuzzi; solarium; sauna; 24-hr. room service; babysitting; laundry service/dry cleaning. *In room:* A/C, TV, dataport, minibar, hair dryer, safe.

Hotel Imperial ★★★   This hotel is Vienna's grandest and the most "imperial" looking in Austria, 2 blocks from the State Opera and 1 block from the Musikverein. The hotel was built in 1869 as a private residence and was converted into a private hotel in 1873. Everything is outlined against a background of polished marble, crystal chandeliers, Gobelin tapestries, and fine rugs. Some of the royal suites are palatial, but all rooms are soundproof and generally spacious, with deluxe full bathrooms. The **Hotel Imperial Restaurant** is a fabled turn-of-the-20th-century restaurant.

Kärntner Ring 16, A-1015 Vienna. © **800/325-3589** in the U.S., or 01/501100. Fax 01/5011-0410. www.luxury collection.com/imperial. 138 units. 535€–950€ ($615–$1,093) double; from 1,300€ ($1,495) suite. AE, DC, MC, V. Parking 30€. U-Bahn: Karlsplatz. **Amenities:** 2 restaurants; bar; health club; sauna; 24-hr. room service; massage; babysitting; laundry service/dry cleaning; nonsmoking rooms. *In room:* A/C, TV, dataport, hair dryer, safe.

Hotel Sacher Wien ★★★   Much of the glory of the Hapsburgs is still evoked by the public rooms here, although the hotel, founded in 1876, is no longer the grandest in Vienna, having lost out to the Bristol or Imperial. The red velvet, crystal chandeliers, and brocaded curtains are reminiscent of Old Vienna. The hotel is popular with groups, however, and the heavy traffic is taking a toll. The reception desk is fairly flexible about making arrangements for salons or apartments, or joining two rooms together. Rooms near the top are small with cramped bathrooms, but most accommodations are generous in size and often have sitting areas and midsize marble bathrooms with shower-tub combinations.

Philharmonikerstrasse 4, A-1010 Vienna. ℂ **01/514560.** Fax 01/512-56-810. www.sacher.com. 108 units. 350€–575€ ($403–$661) double; 682€–1,058€ ($784–$1,217) junior suite; from 1,544€ ($1,776) suite. AE, DC, MC, V. Parking 29€ ($33). U-Bahn: Karlsplatz. Tram: 1, 2, 62, 65, D, or J. Bus: 4A. **Amenities:** 2 restaurants; bar; nearby fitness center; 24-hr. room service; massage; babysitting; laundry service/dry cleaning; nonsmoking rooms. *In room:* A/C, TV, dataport, minibar, hair dryer, safe.

Expensive

Hotel Astoria ★   This landmark is for nostalgia buffs who want to recall the grand life of the closing days of the Austro-Hungarian Empire. A first-class hotel, the Astoria has a desirable location on the shopping mall close to St. Stephan's Cathedral and the State Opera. Decorated in a slightly frayed late-19th-century style, the hotel offers well-appointed and traditionally decorated rooms. The interior rooms tend to be too dark, and singles are just too cramped. It was most recently renovated in 1996, but the old style has been respected. Bathrooms are luxurious with dual basins, shower-tub combos, and heated towel racks.

Kärntnerstrasse 32–34, A-1015 Vienna. ℂ **01/515770.** Fax 01/515-7782. www.austria-trend.at. 118 units. 203€–254€ ($233–$292) double; 239€–299€ ($275–$344) suite. Rates include breakfast. AE, DC, MC, V. Parking 22€ ($25). U-Bahn: Stephansplatz. **Amenities:** Restaurant; bar; limited room service; babysitting; laundry service/dry cleaning; nonsmoking rooms. *In room:* TV, dataport, minibar, hair dryer, safe.

Hotel Das Triest ★★ *Finds*   Sir Terence Conran, the famous English architect and designer, has created the interior decoration for this contemporary hotel in the center of Vienna, a 5-minute walk from St. Stephan's Cathedral. Conran has done for Das Triest what Philippe Starck did for New York's Paramount Hotel—created a stylish address in the heart of one of the world's most important cities. An emerging favorite with artists and musicians, this hip hotel has such grace notes as a courtyard garden. Its old cross-vaulted rooms, which give the structure a distinctive flair, have been transformed into lounges and suites. Guest rooms are midsize to spacious, tastefully furnished, and comfortable. The white-tiled bathrooms have heated towel racks, shower-tub combinations, deluxe toiletries, and vanity mirrors. In the afternoon, guests gather for tea in front of the cozy fireplace.

Wiedner Hauptstrasse 12, A-1040 Vienna. ℂ **01/589-18.** Fax 01/589-18-18. www.dastriest.at. 72 units. 245€ ($282) double; from 299€ ($344) suite. Rates include buffet breakfast. AE, DC, MC, V. Parking 21€ ($24). U-Bahn: Karlsplatz. **Amenities:** Restaurant; bar; fitness center; sauna; salon; 24-hr. room service; business center; massage; babysitting; laundry service/dry cleaning; nonsmoking rooms. *In room:* A/C, TV, dataport, minibar, hair dryer, safe.

Hotel König Von Ungarn ★   In a choice site on a narrow street near the cathedral, this hotel has been in the business for more than 4 centuries and is Vienna's oldest continuously operated accommodation. It's an evocative, intimate, and cozy retreat in an early-17th-century building, once a pied-à-terre for Hungarian noble families visiting the Austrian capital. Everywhere you look you'll find low-key luxury, tradition, and modern convenience. Mozart reportedly lived here in 1791. Guest rooms have been remodeled with Biedermeier accents and traditional furnishings. Most bathrooms are generous in size and have dual basins, shower-tub combinations, and tiled walls. The professional staff is highly efficient, keeping the hotel spotless. The hotel restaurant is one of Vienna's finest.

Schulerstrasse 10, A-1010 Vienna. ℂ **01/515840.** Fax 01/515848. www.kvu.at. 33 units. 185€ ($213) double; 216€–296€ ($248–$340) apt. Rates include breakfast. AE, DC, MC, V. U-Bahn: Stephansplatz. **Amenities:** Restaurant; bar; limited room service; babysitting; laundry service/dry cleaning. *In room:* A/C, TV, minibar, hair dryer, safe.

Moderate

Hotel Kaiserin Elisabeth ⭑   This yellow-stoned hotel is conveniently located near the cathedral. The interior is decorated with Oriental rugs on well-maintained marble and wood floors. The small, quiet rooms have been considerably updated since Wolfgang Mozart, Richard Wagner, Franz Liszt, and Edvard Grieg stayed here, and their musical descendants continue to patronize the place. Polished wood, clean linen, and perhaps another Oriental rug grace each guest room. Bathrooms are a bit cramped, but they are tiled and equipped with shower-tub combinations and vanity mirrors.

Weihburggasse 3, A-1010 Vienna. ☏ **01/515260.** Fax 01/515267. www.kaiserinelisabeth.at. 63 units. 200€ ($230) double; 220€ ($253) suite. Rates include buffet breakfast. AE, DC, MC, V. Parking 28€ ($32). U-Bahn: Stephansplatz. **Amenities:** Restaurant; breakfast room; bar; limited room service; laundry service/dry cleaning. *In room:* A/C (in some), TV, dataport, minibar, hair dryer, safe.

Hotel Royal ⭑⭑   The lobby of this hotel less than a block from St. Stephan's contains the piano where Wagner composed *Die Meistersinger von Nürnberg.* Each good-size room is furnished differently, in a style influenced by 19th-century Italy, with some good reproductions of antiques and an occasional original. The entire facility was built in 1960 and reconstructed in 1982. Try for a room with a balcony and a view of the cathedral. Corner rooms with spacious foyers are also desirable, although those facing the street tend to be noisy. Most bathrooms have both tub and shower.

Singerstrasse 3, A-1010 Vienna. ☏ **01/515680.** Fax 01/513-9698. 81 units. 140€–170€ ($161–$196) double; 230€ ($265) suite. Rates include breakfast. AE, DC, MC, V. U-Bahn: Stephansplatz. **Amenities:** 2 restaurants; bar; limited room service; laundry service/dry cleaning; nonsmoking rooms. *In room:* TV, dataport, minibar, hair dryer.

Inexpensive

Drei Kronen ⭑   The celebrated architect Ignaz Drapala designed this splendid Art Nouveau building in a charming section of Vienna close to the famous Naschmarkt. The hotel enjoys one of Vienna's best locations, close to such monuments as the Vienna State Opera and St. Stephan's Cathedral. The midsize to spacious guest rooms are fresh and bright, with comfortable furnishings along with immaculate bathrooms with shower. Some of the rooms are large enough to contain three beds.

Schleifmuehlgasse 25, A-1040 Vienna. ☏ **01/587-3289.** Fax 01/710-1920. www.hotel3kronen.at. 41 units. 72€–101€ ($83–$116) double; 91€–114€ ($105–$131) triple. Rates include breakfast buffet. AE, DC, MC, V. Parking 13€ ($15). U-Bahn: Karlsplatz. **Amenities:** Breakfast room; lounge; nonsmoking rooms. *In room:* TV, safe in some.

Hotel Kärntnerhof ⭑ *Kids*   A 4-minute walk from the cathedral, the Kärntnerhof advertises itself as a family-oriented hotel. The decor of the public areas is tastefully arranged around Oriental rugs, well-upholstered chairs and couches with cabriole legs, and an occasional 19th-century portrait. The midsize rooms are more up-to-date, usually with the original parquet floors and striped or patterned wallpaper set off by curtains. The small private bathrooms glisten with tile walls and floors; about half of them contain shower-tub combinations.

Grashofgasse 4, A-1011 Vienna. ☏ **01/512-1923.** Fax 01/5132-22833. www.karntnerhof.com. 44 units. 100€–146€ ($115–$168) double; 180€–230€ ($207–$265) suite. Rates include buffet breakfast. AE, DC, MC, V. Parking 16€ ($18). U-Bahn: Stephansplatz. **Amenities:** Breakfast room; lounge; limited room service; laundry service/dry cleaning. *In room:* TV.

Hotel Pension Suzanne ⭑ *Kids*   Only a 45-second walk from the opera house, this is a real discovery. Once you get past its postwar facade, the interior warms considerably, brightly decorated in a comfortable, traditional style, with antique beds, plush chairs, and the original molded ceilings. Rooms are midsize and exceedingly well maintained, facing either the busy street or else a courtyard. Families often stay here because some accommodations contain three beds. A number of guest rooms are like small apartments with kitchenettes. Each unit comes with a private bathroom with a shower-tub combination.

Walfischgasse 4, A-1010 Vienna. ℂ 01/513-25-07. Fax 01/513-25-00. www.pension-suzanne.at. 25 units. 90€–102€ ($104–$117) double; 111€ ($128) double with kitchenette; 119€–139€ ($137–$160) triple. Rates include continental breakfast. AE, DC, MC, V. U-Bahn: Karlsplatz. **Amenities:** Breakfast room; lounge; babysitting; nonsmoking rooms. *In room:* TV, dataport, hair dryer.

WHERE TO DINE
INNERE STADT (INNER CITY)
Very Expensive

Drei Husaren ✹✹✹ VIENNESE/INTERNATIONAL Just off Kärntnerstrasse, this enduring favorite—a Viennese landmark since 1935—serves an inventive and classic Viennese cuisine. To the music of Gypsy melodies, you'll dine on such stellar dishes as freshwater salmon with pike soufflé, mussel soup, breast of guinea fowl, an array of sole dishes, and longtime favorites like *Tafelspitz* (boiled beef). The chef specializes in veal, including his deliciously flavored Kalbsbrücken Metternich. The place is justifiably celebrated for its repertoire of more than 35 hors d'oeuvres, which are on four separate carts rolled around the dining room.

Weihburggasse 4. ℂ 01/512-1092. Reservations required. Main courses 21€–33€ ($24–$38); *menu dégustation* (6 courses) 68€ ($78); 4-course fixed-price business lunch 34€ ($39). AE, DC, MC, V. Daily noon–3pm and 6pm–1am. U-Bahn: Stephansplatz.

König von Ungarn (King of Hungary) ✹ VIENNESE/INTERNATIONAL This beautifully decorated restaurant is inside the famous hotel of the same name. Food is well prepared but traditional—not at all experimental. You dine under a vaulted ceiling in an atmosphere of crystal, chandeliers, antiques, and marble columns. If you're in doubt about what to order, try the Tafelspitz, a savory boiled-beef specialty elegantly dispensed from a cart. Other seasonal choices include a ragout of seafood with fresh mushrooms, tournedos of beef with a mustard-and-horseradish sauce, and appetizers like scampi in caviar sauce. The service is superb.

Schulerstrasse 10. ℂ 01/515-840. Reservations required. Main courses 15€–18€ ($17–$21); fixed-price menu 39€ ($4) dinner. AE, DC, MC, V. Daily 6–10:30pm. U-Bahn: Stephansplatz. Bus: 1A.

Korso bei der Oper ✹✹✹ VIENNESE/INTERNATIONAL This chic and glittering choice is decorated with tasteful paneling, sparkling chandeliers, and, flanking either side of a baronial fireplace, two of the most breathtaking baroque columns in Vienna. The kitchen concocts an alluring mixture of traditional and modern cuisine for discriminating palates. Your meal may feature filet of char with a sorrel sauce, saddle of veal with cèpe mushrooms and homemade noodles, or the inevitable *Tafelspitz* (boiled beef). The rack of lamb is excellent, as are the medallions of beef with a shallot-infused butter sauce and Roquefort-flavored noodles. The wine list is extensive.

In the Hotel Bristol, Kärntneering 1. ℂ 01/5151-6546. Reservations required. Main courses 16€–36€ ($18–$41); fixed-price menu 32€–38€ ($37–$44) lunch, 57€–87€ ($66–$100) dinner. AE, DC, MC, V. Sun–Fri noon–2pm; daily 7–11pm. U-Bahn: Karlsplatz. Tram: 1 or 2.

Mörwald ✹✹✹ VIENNESE/INTERNATIONAL In the Hotel Ambassador, this is the most stylish and one of the best restaurants in Vienna. Bankers, diplomats, and what one local food critic called "Helmut Lang–clad hipsters" show up here to see and be seen, but also to enjoy the delectable modern Viennese cuisine of Christian Domschitz. He's shown a genius for giving classic Viennese dishes a modern twist. Prepared with élan and precision, some of his best dishes include saddle of suckling pig with white cabbage dumplings, veal meatloaf with puréed spring onions, and a spicy brook char, one of the better fish offerings. You might start with his velvety-smooth foie gras in Kirschwasser. For dessert, we recommend the diced semolina pancakes.

In the Hotel Ambassador, Kärntner Strasse 22. $\mathcal{C}$ 01/961-61-0. www.ambassador.at. Reservations required. Main courses 23€–32€ ($26–$37). Mon–Sat 11am–3pm and 6:30–11pm. AE, DC, MC, V. U-Bahn: Stephansplatz.

Sacher Hotel Restaurant ★ AUSTRIAN/INTERNATIONAL This is a long-enduring favorite for pre- or postopera dining. It seems as if all celebrities who come to Vienna eventually are seen either in the **Red Bar,** with its adjacent dining room, where live piano music is presented every evening from 7pm to midnight, or in the brown-and-white **Anna Sacher Room,** the site of many a high-powered meal. There's no better place in Vienna to sample the restaurant's most famous dish, Tafelspitz, that's fit for an emperor. The chef serves it with a savory, herb-flavored sauce. Other delectable dishes include fish terrine and veal steak with morels. For dessert, the Sacher torte enjoys world renown. It's primarily a chocolate sponge cake that's sliced in half and filled with apricot jam. This most famous of pastries in Vienna was supposedly created in 1832 by Franz Sacher when he served as Prince Metternich's apprentice.

Philharmonikerstrasse 4. $\mathcal{C}$ 01/514560. Reservations required. Main courses 28€–32€ ($32–$37). AE, DC, MC, V. Daily noon–3pm and 6–11:30pm. U-Bahn: Karlsplatz.

Expensive

Dö & Co ★ CONTINENTAL/INTERNATIONAL Stylish, upscale, and rather expensive, this restaurant is owned by one of Austria's most esoteric food stores. Its location is on the seventh floor of the aggressively ultramodern Haas Haus, which stands in jarring proximity to Vienna's cathedral. Menu items change with the season, but considering the rarefied nature of the organization presenting it, each is appropriately rare, and unusual. Examples include Uruguayan beef; Austrian venison; grilled baby turbot from the coast of Norway; deep-fried monkfish; and carpaccio "Parmigiana," as well as traditional Austrian specialties. There's also a repertoire of Thai dishes, including crispy pork salad, red curried chicken, and sweet-and-sour red snapper. And there's a "wok buffet," wherein you assemble the ingredients for your meal on a plate, then deliver it to a uniformed chef who will quick-sear it for you with whatever sauces you want.

In the Haas Haus, Stephansplatz 12 $\mathcal{C}$ 01/535-3969. Reservations recommended. Main courses 16€–23€ ($18–$26); set menus 45€–52€ ($52–$60). V. Daily noon–3pm and 6pm–midnight. U-Bahn: Stephansplatz.

Plachutta ★ VIENNESE Few restaurants have built such a culinary shrine around one dish: Tafelspitz, the boiled beef dish that was the favorite of Emperor Franz Josef throughout his prolonged reign. Whichever of the 10 versions you order, it will invariably come with sauces and garnishes that perk up what sounds like a dull dish into a delectable culinary traipse through the tastes of yesteryear. The differences between the versions are a function of the cut of beef you request as part of your meal. Regardless of the cut you specify, your meal will be accompanied with hash brown potatoes, chives, and an appealing mixture of horseradish and chopped apples.

Wollzeile 38. $\mathcal{C}$ 01/512-1577. Reservations recommended. Main courses 12€–28€ ($14–$32). AE, DC, MC, V. Daily 11:30am–midnight. U-Bahn: Stubentor.

Wiener Rathauskeller ✿✿ VIENNESE/INTERNATIONAL City halls throughout the Teutonic world have traditionally maintained restaurants in their basements, and Vienna is no exception. In half a dozen richly atmospheric dining rooms, with high vaulted ceilings and stained-glass windows, you can enjoy good and reasonably priced food. The chef's specialty is a Rathauskellerplatte for two, consisting of various cuts of meat, including a veal schnitzel, lamb cutlets, and pork medallions. Beginning at 8pm, live musicians ramble through the world of operetta, waltz, and *Schrammel* (traditional Viennese music), as you dine.

Rathausplatz 1. © 01/4051-2190. Reservations required. Main courses 11€–19€ ($12–$22). AE, DC, MC, V. Mon–Sat 11:30am–3pm and 6–11pm. U-Bahn: Rathaus.

Moderate

Griechenbeisl AUSTRIAN This local favorite opened in 1450 and is still one of Vienna's leading restaurants. It has a labyrinthine collection of dining areas on three floors, all with low vaulted ceilings, smoky paneling, and wrought-iron chandeliers. As you go in, be sure to see the so-called inner sanctum, with signatures of such former patrons as Mozart, Beethoven, and Mark Twain. The food is hearty, ample, and solidly bourgeois. Menu items include deer stew, both Hungarian and Viennese goulash, sauerkraut garni, Wiener schnitzel, and venison steak—in other words, all those favorite recipes from Grandmother's kitchen. As an added treat, the restaurant features nighttime accordion and zither music.

Fleischmarkt 11. © 01/533-1941. Reservations required. Main courses 15€–20€ ($17–$23); fixed-price menu 25€–38€ ($29–$44). AE, DC, MC, V. Daily 11:30am–1am (last orders at 11:30pm). Tram: N, 1, 2, or 21.

Inexpensive

Augustinerkeller AUSTRIAN The beer and wine flow at this Viennese legend. Augustinerkeller, in the basement of the part of the Hofburg complex that shelters the Albertina Collection, has served wine, beer, and food since 1857, although the vaulted ceilings and sense of timelessness evoke an establishment even older than that. It attracts a lively group of patrons from all walks of life, and sometimes they get boisterous, especially when the *Schrammel* music goes late into the night. It's one of the best values for wine tasting in Vienna. Aside from the wine and beer, the establishment serves simple food, including roast chicken on a spit, schnitzel, and Tafelspitz.

Augustinerstrasse 1. © 01/533-1026. Main courses 8€–20€ ($9–$23). AE, DC, MC, V. Daily 11am–midnight. U-Bahn: Stephansplatz.

Buffet Trzésniewski ✿ SANDWICHES Everyone in Vienna knows about this place, from the most hurried office workers to the city's elite hostesses. Its current incarnation is unlike any buffet you may have seen, with six or seven cramped tables and a rapidly moving queue of clients who jostle for space next to the glass countertops. You'll indicate to the waitress the kind of sandwich you want, and if you can't read German signs, just point. Most people come here for the delicious finger sandwiches, which include 18 combinations of cream cheese, egg, onion, salami, mushrooms, herring, green and red peppers, tomatoes, lobster, and many more items. If you order a drink, the cashier will give you a rubber token, which you'll present to the person at the far end of the counter.

Dorotheergasse 1. © 01/512-3291. Reservations not accepted. Sandwiches .90€ ($1.05). No credit cards. Mon–Fri 9:30am–7:30pm; Sat 9am–5pm. U-Bahn: Stephansplatz.

Café Leopold ✿ INTERNATIONAL Critics have defined this restaurant as a postmodern version, in architectural form, of the Viennese Expressionist paintings (including many by Egon Schiele) that are exhibited within the museum that

Coffeehouses & Cafes

One of the best-known cafes in Vienna also pays more attention to its window displays than any of its competitors. The windows of the **Café Demel,** Kohlmarkt 14 (ⓒ **01/533-5516;** U-Bahn: Stephansplatz or Herrengasse), are filled with fanciful tributes to a changing array of themes, some of which have made, in a small-scale way, local history. Depending on the season, you might see spun-sugar and marzipan depictions of Christmas or *Midsummer Night's Dream* characters; depictions of famous Austrain emperors or composers; autumn or spring foliage in the city's parks, even effigies of famous visitors to the city. Inside is a splendidly baroque Viennese landmark with black marble tables, cream-colored embellished plaster walls, and crystal chandeliers covered with white milk-glass globes. Dozens of pastries are offered every day, including cream-filled horns *(Gugelhupfs).* It's open daily 10am to 7pm.

Café Dommayer, Dommayergasse 1 (ⓒ **01/877-5465;** U-Bahn: Schönbrunn), boasts a reputation for courtliness that goes back to 1787. In 1844, Johann Strauss Jr. made his musical debut here, and beginning in 1924, the site became known as *the* place in Vienna for tea dancing. During clement weather, a garden with seats for 300 opens in back. The rest of the year, the venue is restricted to a high-ceilinged black-and-white old-world room. Every Saturday from 2 to 4pm, a pianist and violinist perform; and on the first Saturday of every month, an all-woman orchestra plays mostly Strauss from 2 to 4pm. It's open daily from 7am to midnight.

One of the Ring's great cafes, **Café Landtmann,** Dr.-Karl-Lueger-Ring 4 (ⓒ **01/241-00-111;** tram: 1, 2, or D), dates from the 1880s. Overlooking the Burgtheater and the Rathaus, it has traditionally drawn a mix of politicians, journalists, and actors, and was Freud's favorite. The original chandeliers and the prewar chairs have been refurbished. We highly suggest spending an hour or so here, whether perusing the newspapers, sipping on coffee, or planning the day's itinerary. The cafe is open daily from 7:30am to midnight (meals are served 11:30am–11pm).

contains it. During the day, the place functions as a conventional cafe and restaurant, serving a postmodern blend of *Mitteleuropaïsche* (central European) and Asian food. Three nights a week, however, from around 10pm till at least 2am, any hints of kitsch and coziness are banished as soon as a DJ begins cranking out dance tunes for a hard-drinking denizens-of-the-night crowd.

In the Leopold Museum, Museumsplatz 1. ⓒ 01/523-67-32. Reservations not necessary. Main courses 6.50€–11€ ($7.50–$13) 2-course set-price menu 8.70€ ($10). AE, DC, MC, V. Daily 10am–2am. U-Bahn: Volkstheater or Babenbergstrasse/MuseumsQuartier.

Café Restaurant Halle INTERNATIONAL   Set within the Kunsthalle, this is the direct competitor of the also-recommended Café Leopold. Larger, and with a more sophisticated menu than the Café Leopold's, it's a postmodern, airy, big-windowed quartet of wood-trimmed, cream-colored rooms. The menu will always contain a half-dozen meal-size salads, many garnished with strips of steak, chicken, or shrimp; two daily homemade soups; and a rotating series of platters.

In the Kunsthalle Wien, Museumsplatz 1, in the MuseumsQuartier. ℂ 01/523-7001. Reservations not necessary. Main courses 7€–14€ ($8.05–$16). MC, V. Daily 10am-2am. U-Bahn: MuseumsQuartier.

Gulaschmuseum ⚜ AUSTRIAN/HUNGARIAN If you thought that *Gulasch* (goulash) was available in only one form, think again. This restaurant celebrates at least 15 varieties of it, each of them an authentic survivor of the culinary traditions of Hungary, and each redolent with the taste of that country's most distinctive spice, paprika. You can order versions of goulash based on roast beef, veal, pork, and fried chicken livers. Vegetarians rejoice: Versions made with potatoes, beans, or mushrooms are also available. Boiled potatoes and rough-textured brown or black bread will usually accompany your choice. An excellent beginning is a dish so firmly associated with Hungary that it's been referred to as the Magyar national crepe, *Hortobágyi Palatschinken,* stuffed with minced beef and paprika-flavored cream sauce.

Schulerstrasse 20. ℂ 01/512-1017. Reservations recommended. Main courses 6€–12€ ($6.90–$14). MC, V. Mon–Fri 11:30am–11pm; Sat–Sun 10am–11pm. U-Bahn: Wollzeile or Stephansplatz.

Hansen ⚜ MEDITERRANEAN/INTERNATIONAL Part of the charm of this intriguing and stylish restaurant involves trekking through masses of plants and elaborate garden ornaments on your way to your dining table. Choose from a small but savory menu that changes every week. Excellent examples include a spicy bean salad with strips of chicken breast served in a summer broth; risotto with cheese and sour cherries; and poached *Saibling* (something akin to trout from the cold-water streams of the Austrian Alps) with a potato-and-celery purée and watercress.

In the cellar of the Börsegebäude (Vienna Stock Exchange), Wipplingerstrasse 34 at the Schottenring. ℂ 01/532-05-42. Reservations recommended. Main courses 9.50€–18€ ($11–$21). AE, DC, MC, V. Mon–Fri 9am–8pm (last order); Sat 9am–3pm (last order). U-Bahn: Schottenring.

Palmenhaus AUSTRIAN Architectural grace and marvelous food combine for a happy marriage here. Many architectural critics consider the Jugendstil glass canopy of this greenhouse the most beautiful in Austria. A sophisticated menu changes monthly, and might include perfectly prepared fresh Austrian goat cheese with stewed peppers and zucchini salad; young herring with sour cream, horseradish, and deep-fried beignets stuffed with apples and cabbage; or breast of chicken layered with gooseliver. If you've already eaten, no one will mind if you drop in just for a drink and one of the voluptuous pastries.

In the Burggarten. ℂ 01/533-1033. Reservations recommended for dinner. Main courses 17€–25€ ($20–$29); pastries 3.20€–4.20€ ($3.70–$4.85). AE, DC, MC. V. Daily 10am-2am. U-Bahn: Opera.

Restaurant Salzamt ⚜ AUSTRIAN This is the best restaurant in the neighborhood. It evokes a turn-of-the-20th-century Viennese bistro, replete with Weiner Werkstatte–inspired chairs and lighting fixtures, cream-colored walls, and dark tables and banquettes. Sit within its vaulted interior or—if weather permits—move out to any of the tables on the square, overlooking Vienna's oldest church, St. Ruprecht. Well-prepared items include a terrine of broccoli and artichoke hearts; light-textured pastas; filets of pork with a Gorgonzola-enriched cream sauce; roast beef with wild lettuce salad; several kinds of goulash; and fresh fish. One of the most noteworthy of these is fried filets of *Saibling,* a fish native to the cold-water streams of western Austria, served with lemon or tartar sauce.

Ruprechtsplatz 1. ℂ 01/533-5332. Reservations recommended. Main courses 8€–14€ ($9.20–$16). V. Daily 6pm–midnight. U-Bahn: Schwedenplatz.

Zwölf-Apostelkeller VIENNESE   For those seeking a taste of old Vienna, this is the place. Sections of this old wine tavern's walls predate 1561. Rows of wooden tables stand under vaulted ceilings, with lighting provided partially by streetlights set into the masonry floor. This place is popular with students, partly because of its low prices and because of its proximity to St. Stephan's. In addition to beer and wine, the establishment serves hearty Austrian fare. Specialties include roast pork with dumplings, Hungarian goulash soup, a limited number of vegetarian dishes, and a *Schlachtplatte* (hot black pudding, liverwurst, pork, and pork sausage with a hot bacon-and-cabbage salad).

Sonnenfelsgasse 3. ℂ **01/512-6777.** Main courses 8€–15€ ($9.20–$17). AE, DC, MC, V. Daily 4:30pm–midnight. Tram: 1, 2, 21, D, or N. Bus: 1A. U-Bahn: Stephansplatz.

IN LANDSTRASSE

Steirereck ★★★ VIENNESE/AUSTRIAN/INTERNATIONAL   *Steirereck* means "corner of Styria," which is exactly what Heinz and Margarethe Reitbauer have created in the rustic decor of this intimate restaurant. On the Danube Canal, between Central Station and the Prater, it has been acclaimed by some Viennese as the best restaurant in the city. The Reitbauers offer both traditional Viennese dishes and "New Austrian" selections. You might begin with a caviar-semolina dumpling, roasted turbot with fennel (served as an appetizer), or the most elegant and expensive item of all, gooseliver Steirereck. The menu is wisely limited and well prepared, changing daily depending on the fresh produce available at the market. The restaurant is popular with after-theater diners. The large wine cellar holds some 35,000 bottles.

Rasumofskygasse 2. ℂ **01/713-3168.** Reservations required. Main courses 25€–30€ ($29–$35). 3-course fixed-price lunch 35€ ($40); 5-course fixed-price dinner 70€ ($81). AE, DC, MC, V. Mon–Fri 10:30am–2pm and 7pm–midnight. Closed holidays. Tram: N. Bus: 4.

SEEING THE SIGHTS OF VIENNA

The Inner City (Innere Stadt) is the tangle of streets from which Vienna grew in the Middle Ages. Much of your exploration will be confined to this area, encircled by the boulevards of "The Ring" and the Danube Canal. The main street of the Inner City is **Kärntnerstrasse,** most of which is a pedestrian mall. The heart of Vienna is **Stephansplatz,** the square on which St. Stephan's Cathedral sits.

SIGHTSEEING SUGGESTIONS FOR FIRST-TIME VISITORS

If You Have 1 Day Begin at **St. Stephan's Cathedral,** and from there branch out for a tour of the enveloping Inner City. But first, climb the tower of the cathedral for a panoramic view of the city (you can also take an elevator to the top). Stroll down **Kärntnerstrasse,** the main shopping artery, and enjoy the 11am ritual of coffee in a grand cafe, such as the **Café Imperial.** In the afternoon, visit **Schönbrunn,** seat of the Hapsburg dynasty. Have dinner in a typical Viennese wine tavern.

If You Have 2 Days On the second day, explore other major attractions of Vienna, including the **Hofburg,** the **Imperial Crypts,** and the **Kunsthistorisches Museum.** In the evening, attend an opera performance or some other musical event.

If You Have 3 Days On your third day, try to attend a performance of either the **Spanish Riding School** (Tues–Sat) or the **Vienna Boys' Choir** (singing at Sun Mass). Explore the **Belvedere Palace** and its art galleries; visit the art complex at

MuseumsQuartier; stroll through the **Naschmarkt,** the city's major open-air market; and cap the day with a visit to one or more of Vienna's cabarets, wine bars, or beer cellars.

EXPLORING THE HOFBURG PALACE COMPLEX 🎭🎭🎭

The winter palace of the Hapsburgs, known for its vast, impressive courtyards, the Hofburg sits in the heart of Vienna. To reach it (you can hardly miss it), head up Kohlmarkt to Michaelerplatz 1, Burgring (© **01/587-3666**). You can take the U-Bahn to Stephansplatz, Herrengasse, or Mariahilferstrasse, or else tram 1, 2, D, or J to Burgring.

This complex of imperial edifices, the first of which was constructed in 1279, grew and grew as the empire did, so that today the Hofburg Palace is virtually a city within a city. The palace, which has withstood three major sieges and a great fire, is called simply *die Burg,* or "the palace," by Viennese. Of its more than 2,600 rooms, fewer than two dozen are open to the public.

Schatzkammer (Imperial Treasury) 🎭🎭🎭   This is the greatest treasury in the world. It's divided into two sections: the Imperial Profane and the Sacerdotal Treasuries. One part displays the crown jewels and an assortment of imperial riches; the other exhibits ecclesiastical treasures. The most outstanding exhibit is the imperial crown, dating from 962. It's so big that even though padded, it probably slipped down over the ears of many a Hapsburg at his coronation. Studded with emeralds, sapphires, diamonds, and rubies, this 1,000-year-old symbol of sovereignty is a priceless treasure. Also on display is the imperial crown worn by the Hapsburg rulers from 1804 to the end of the empire. You'll see the saber of Charlemagne and the holy lance. Among great Schatzkammer prizes is the Burgundian Treasure seized in the 15th century, rich in vestments, oil paintings, gems, and robes.

Hofburg, Schweizerhof. © **01/525-24486.** Admission 7.50€ ($8.65) adults; 5.50€ ($6.35) children, seniors, and students; free for children under 6. Wed–Mon 10am–6pm.

Kaiserappartements (Imperial Apartments) 🎭🎭   The Hofburg complex includes the Kaiserappartements, where the emperors and their wives and children lived, on the first floor. To reach these apartments, enter via the rotunda of Michaelerplatz. The apartments are richly decorated with tapestries, many from Aubusson. The Imperial Silver and Porcelain Collection provides an insight into Hapsburg court etiquette. Most of these pieces are from the 18th and 19th centuries. Leopoldinischer Trakt (Leopold's Apartments) dates from the 17th century. These Imperial Apartments are more closely associated with Franz Josef than with any other emperor.

Michaeler Platz 1 (inside the Ring, about a 4-min. walk from Hervengasse; entrance via the Kasertor in the Inneren Burghof). © **01/533-7570.** Admission 7.50€ ($8.65) adults, 5.90€ ($6.80) students under 25, 3.90€ ($4.50) children 6–15, free for children 5 and under. Daily 9am–4:30pm. U-Bahn: U-1 or U-3 to Hervengasse. Tram: 1, 2, or J to Burgring.

Die Burgkapelle (Home of the Vienna Boys' Choir)   Construction of this Gothic chapel began in 1447 during the reign of Emperor Frederick III, but the building was subsequently massively renovated. From 1449, it was the private chapel of the royal family. Today the Burgkapelle is the home of the **Hofmusikkapelle (Court Musicians) 🎭🎭,** an ensemble consisting of the Vienna Boys' Choir and members of the Vienna State Opera chorus and orchestra, which performs works by classical and modern composers. Written applications for reserved seats should be sent at least 8 weeks in advance. Use a credit card; do not send cash or checks. For reservations, write to Verwaltung der Hofmusikkapelle, Hofburg, A-1010 Vienna. If you fail to reserve in advance, you may be lucky enough to secure tickets from a block sold at the Burgkapelle box office every Friday from 11am to 1pm or 3 to 5pm, plus Sunday from 8:15 to 9:15am. The line starts forming at least half an hour before that. If you're willing to settle for standing room, it's free.

Hofburg (entrance on Schweizerhof). ⓒ 01/533-9927. Mass: Seats 5€–29€ ($5.75–$33); standing room free. Masses (performances) held only Jan–June and mid-Sept to Dec, Sun and holidays 9:15am.

Neue Hofburg   The last addition to the Hofburg complex was the Neue Hofburg (New Château). Construction started in 1881 and continued until work was halted in 1913. The palace was the residence of Archduke Franz Ferdinand, the nephew and heir apparent of Franz Josef, whose assassination at Sarajevo set off the chain of events that led to World War I. The **arms and armor collection** 🏵🏵 is second only to that of the Metropolitan Museum of Art in New York. It's in the **Hofjagd and Rüstkammer,** on the second floor of the New Château. On display are crossbows, swords, helmets, pistols, and armor. Another section, the **Musikinstrumentensammlung** 🏵 (ⓒ **01/52524**), is devoted to musical instruments, mainly from the 17th and 18th centuries. In the **Ephesos-Museum (Museum of Ephesian Sculpture),** with an entrance behind the Prince Eugene monument, you'll see high-quality finds from Ephesus in Turkey and the Greek island of Samothrace. Here the prize exhibit is the Parthian monument, the most important relief frieze from Roman times ever found in Asia Minor. It was erected to celebrate Rome's victory in the Parthian wars (A.D. 161–65).

Heldenplatz. ⓒ 01/525-24-484. Admission for each museum 7.50€ ($8.65) adults, 5.50€ ($6.35) children. Wed–Mon 10am–6pm.

Albertina 🏵🏵   Housing one of the greatest graphics collections in the world, and closed for a decade, the Albertina reopened in 2003. It offers more exhibition space than before, a new restaurant, and a four-story graphic-arts collection ranging from the late Gothic era through the present day. It's housed in the neoclassical Albertina Palace, the largest residential palace in Vienna, and it's named for Albert, duke of Saxony-Teschen (1738–1822), who launched the collection. Today it comprises some 65,000 drawings and a million prints that include such old masters Leonardo da Vinci, Michelangelo, Manet, and Rubens. Its most

---

Moments **The Vienna Boys' Choir**

In 1498, the emperor Maximilian I decreed that 12 boys should be included among the official court musicians. Over the next 500 years, this group evolved into the world-renowned Vienna Boys' Choir *(Wiener Sängerknaben).* They perform in Vienna at various venues, including the Staatsoper, the Volksoper, and Schönbrunn Palace. The choir also performs at Sunday and Christmas Masses with the Hofmusikkapelle (Court Musicians) at the Burgkapelle (see review for details). The choir's boarding school is at Augartenpalais, Obere Augartenstrasse. For more information on where they are performing and how to get tickets, go to the choir's website (www.wsk.at).

important collection is the Dürer exhibition; unfortunately, much of the art you see from that master is a copy; the originals, such as *Praying Hands,* are shown only during special exhibitions.

For the first time, visitors can walk through the historic state rooms designed for Archduke Charles (1771–1847), who defeated Napoleon at the Battle of Aspern in 1809. Unknown to many of the Viennese themselves, the Albertina contains a wealth of 20th-century art from Jackson Pollock to Robert Rauschenberg.

The graphics arts on parade here go back to the 14th century. Yes, Poussin; yes, Fragonard; yes, Rembrandt—the list of artists on exhibit seem limitless. Allow at least 3 hours just to skim the surface.

Albertinaplatz 1. ℂ **01/53483.** www.albertina.at. Admission 9€ ($10) adults, 7.50€ ($8.65) seniors, 6.50€ ($7.50) students, free for children under 6. Tues–Sun 10am–6pm.

Augustinerkirche   This church was constructed in the 14th century as part of the Hofburg complex to serve as the parish church of the imperial court. In the latter part of the 18th century it was stripped of its baroque embellishments and returned to the original Gothic features. The Chapel of St. George, dating from 1337, is entered from the right aisle. The **Tomb of Maria Christina** ⋒, the favorite daughter of Maria Theresa, is housed in the main nave near the rear entrance, but there's no body in it. (The princess was actually buried in the Imperial Crypt.) This richly ornamented empty tomb is one of Canova's masterpieces. The royal weddings of Maria Theresa and François of Lorraine (1736), Marie Antoinette and Louis XVI of France (1770), Marie-Louise of Austria to Napoleon (1810, but by proxy—he didn't show up), and Franz Josef and Elizabeth of Bavaria (1854) were all held in the church. The most convenient, and dramatic, time to visit is Sunday at 11am, when a High Mass is celebrated with choir, soloists, and orchestra.

Augustinerstrasse 3. ℂ **01/533-70-99.** Daily 8am–6pm. Free admission. U-Bahn: Stephansplatz.

Spanische Reitschule (Spanish Riding School) ⋒   The Spanish Riding School is in the crystal-chandeliered white ballroom in an 18th-century building of the Hofburg complex. We always marvel at the skill and beauty of the sleek Lipizzaner stallions as their adept trainers put them through their paces in a show that hasn't changed in 4 centuries. These are the world's most famous, classically styled equine performers. Reservations for performances must be made in advance, as early as possible. Order your tickets for the Sunday and Wednesday shows by writing to **Spanische Reitschule,** Hofburg, A-1010 Vienna (fax 01/533-903-240), or through a travel agency in Vienna (tickets for Sat shows can be ordered only through a travel agency). Tickets for training sessions with no advance reservations can be purchased at the entrance.

Michaelerplatz 1, Hofburg. ℂ **01/533-9032.** www.srs.at. Regular performances 35€–160€ ($40–$184) seats, 24€–27€ ($28–$31) standing room. Morning exercise with music 12€ ($13) adults, 5€ ($5.75) for children 3–6 with an adult; children under age 3 not admitted. Training session 12€ ($14) adults, 5€ ($5.75) children. Regular shows Mar–June and Sept to mid-Dec, most Sun at 11am and some Fri at 6pm. Classical dressage with music performances Apr–June and Sept, most Sun at 11am. Training sessions Mar–June, first 2 weeks in Sept, Oct, and Dec, Tues–Sat 10am–noon.

Lipizzaner Museum   The latest attraction at the Hofburg is this museum near the stables of the famous white stallions. The exhibition begins with the historic inception of the Spanish Riding School in the 16th century and extends to the stallions' near destruction in the closing weeks of World War II. Exhibits such as paintings, historic engravings, drawings, photographs, uniforms, and bridles, plus video and film presentations, bring to life the history of the Spanish Riding

School, offering an insight into the breeding and training of these champion horses. Visitors to the museum are able to see through a window into the stallions' stables while they are being fed and saddled.

Reitschulgasse 2. (*) 01/525-24-583. www.lipizzaner.at. Admission 5€ ($5.75) adults, 3.60€ ($4.15) seniors and children, 10€ ($12) family card (2 adults, 3 children). Daily 9am–6pm. U-Bahn: Stephansplatz.

EXPLORING THE MUSEUMSQUARTIER COMPLEX ✪✪✪

With the opening of this long-awaited giant modern-art complex, critics claim that the assemblage of art installed in 18th-century royal stables has tipped the city's cultural center of gravity from Hapsburgian pomp into the new millennium. This massive structure, one of the 10-largest cultural complexes in the world, has been likened to a combination of the Guggenheim Museum and New York's Museum of Modern Art, with the Brooklyn Academy of Music, a children's museum, an architecture and design center, theaters, art galleries, video workshops, and much more thrown in for good measure. There's even an ecology center, architecture museum, and a tobacco museum. For more information, go the MuseumsQuartier website at **www.mqw.at**.

Kunsthalle Wien ✪ Cutting-edge contemporary and classic modern art are showcased here. Exhibits focus on specific subjects and seek to establish a link between modern art and current trends. You'll find works by everyone from Picasso and Juan Miró to Jackson Pollock and Paul Klee, from Wassily Kandinsky to Andy Warhol and, surprise, Yoko Ono. From expressionism to cubism to abstractionism, exhibits reveal the major movements in contemporary art since the mid–20th century. The five floors can be explored in 1 to 2 hours, depending on what interests you.

Museumsplatz 1. (*) 01/521-89-0. Admission 8€ ($9.20) adults; 6.50€ ($7.50) seniors, students, and children. Daily 10am–7pm (Thurs to 10pm).

Leopold Museum ✪✪ This extensive collection of Austrian art includes the world's largest treasure trove of the works of Egon Schiele (1890–1918), who was once forgotten in art history but now takes his place alongside van Gogh and Modigliani in the ranks of great doomed artists. Dying before he was 28, his collection of art at the Leopold includes more than 2,500 drawings and watercolors and 330 oil canvases. Other Austrian modernist masterpieces include paintings by Oskar Kokoschka, the great Gustav Klimt, Anton Romaki, and Richard Gerstl. Major statements in Arts and Crafts from the late 19th and 20th centuries include works by Josef Hoffmann, Kolo Moser, Adolf Loos, and Franz Hagenauer.

Museumsplatz 1. (*) 01/525-70. Admission 9€ ($10) adults, 5.50€ ($6.35) students and children over 7. Mon, Wed–Thurs, and Sat–Sun 10am–7pm; Fri 10am–9pm. Closed Tues.

MUMOK (Museum of Modern Art Ludwig Foundation) ✪ This gallery presents one of the most outstanding collections of contemporary art in Central Europe. It comprises mainly works from American Pop Art mixed with concurrent Continental movements such as the Hyperrealism of the 1960s and 1970s. The museum features five exhibition levels (three of them aboveground and two underground). So that it will be easier to cross and compare a single art movement such as cubism or surrealism, paintings "in the same family" are grouped together. Expect to encounter works by all the fabled names such as Robert Indiana, Jasper Johns, Roy Lichtenstein, Robert Rauschenberg, George Segal, and, of course, Andy Warhol.

Museumsplatz 1. (*) 01/525-00. Admission 8€ ($9.20) adults, 2€ ($2.30) children. Daily 9am–6pm.

OTHER TOP ATTRACTIONS IN THE INNER CITY

Domkirche St. Stephan (St. Stephan's Cathedral) ★★★ The cathedral was founded in the 12th century in what was the town's center. Stephansdom was virtually destroyed in a 1258 fire, and in the early 14th century the ruins of the Romanesque basilica gave way to a Gothic building. It suffered terribly in the Turkish siege of 1683 and from the Russian bombardments of 1945. Reopened in 1948, the cathedral is today one of the greatest Gothic structures in Europe, rich in woodcarvings, altars, sculptures, and paintings. The chief treasure of the cathedral is the carved, wooden **Wiener Neustadt altarpiece** ★★ that dates from 1447. Richly painted and gilded, the altar was discovered in the Virgin's Choir. In the Apostles' Choir look for the curious **Tomb of Emperor Frederick III** ★★. Made of a pinkish Salzburg marble, the carved 17th-century tomb depicts hideous little hobgoblins trying to enter and wake the emperor from his eternal sleep. The steeple, rising some 135m (450 ft.), has come to symbolize the very spirit of Vienna. You can climb the 343-step South Tower, which dominates the Viennese skyline and offers a view of the Vienna Woods. Called Alter Steffl (Old Steve), the tower with its needlelike spire was built between 1350 and 1433. The North Tower (Nordturm), reached by elevator, was never finished, but was crowned in the Renaissance style in 1579. From here you get a panoramic sweep of the city and the Danube.

Stephansplatz 1. ⓒ **01/515-52563.** Cathedral, free admission; tour of catacombs 4€ ($4.60) adults, 1.50€ ($1.75) children under 15. Guided tour of cathedral 4€ ($4.60) adults, 1.50€ ($1.75) children under 15. North Tower 4€ ($4.60) adults, 1.50€ ($1.75) children under 15; South Tower 3€ ($3.45) adults, 1€ ($1.15) students, 1€ ($1.15) children under 15. Evening tours, June-Sept, including tour of the roof, 10€ ($12) adults, 4€ ($4.60) children under 15. Cathedral daily 6am–10pm except times of service. Tour of catacombs Mon–Sat 10, 11, and 11:30am, 12:30, 1:30, 2, 2:30, 3:30, 4, and 4:30pm; Sun 2, 2:30, 3, 3:30, 4, and 4:30pm. Guided tour of cathedral Mon–Sat 10:30am and 3pm; Sun 3pm. Special evening tour Sat 7pm (June–Sept). North Tower Oct–Mar daily 8:30am–5pm; Apr–Sept daily 8:30am–6pm. South Tower daily 9am–5:30pm. Bus: 1A, 2A, or 3A. U-Bahn: Stephansplatz.

Gemäldegalerie der Akademie der Bildenden Kunste (Gallery of Painting and Fine Arts) ★ Visit this painting gallery to see the *Last Judgment* by the incomparable Hieronymus Bosch. In this work, the artist conjured up all the demons of the nether regions for a terrifying view of the suffering and sins of humankind. There are many 15th-century Dutch and Flemish paintings and several works by Lucas Cranach the Elder. The academy is noted for its 17th-century art by Van Dyck, Rembrandt, Botticelli, and a host of others. Rubens is represented here by more than a dozen oil sketches. You can see Rembrandt's *Portrait of a Woman* and scrutinize Guardi's scenes of 18th-century Venice.

Schillerplatz 3. ⓒ **01/58816.** Admission 5€ ($5.75) adults, 3€ ($3.45) students and children. Tues–Sun 10am–4pm. U-Bahn: Karlsplatz.

Haus der Musik ★ Mozart is long gone, but Vienna finally got around to opening a full-scale museum devoted to music. This hands-on museum is high-tech. You can take to the podium and conduct the Vienna Philharmonic. Wandering the halls and niches of this museum, you can encounter nostalgic reminders of the great composers who have lived in Vienna, not only Mozart but Beethoven, Schubert, Brahms, and others. In the rooms you can listen to your favorite renditions of their works and explore their memorabilia. A memorial, *Exodus,* pays tribute to the Viennese musicians driven into exile or murdered by the Nazis. At the **Musicantino Restaurant** on the top floor you can enjoy a panoramic view of the city and some good food. On the ground floor is a coffeehouse.

Seilerstätte 30. ⓒ **01/516-48-51.** Admission 10€ ($12) adults, 8.50€ ($9.80) students and seniors, 5.50€ ($6.35) children. Daily 10am–10pm.

Kunsthistorisches Museum (Museum of Art History) ★★★ Across from the Hofburg, this huge building houses the fabulous art collections gathered by the Hapsburgs. A highlight is the fine collection of ancient Egyptian and Greek art. The museum also has works by many of the greatest European masters, such as Velázquez, Titian, Brueghel the Elder, Van Dyck, Ruben, Rembrandt, and Dürer.

Maria-Theresien-Platz, Burgring 5. (**C**) **01/525-24-405.** Admission 10€ ($12) adults, 7.50€ ($8.65) students and seniors, free for children under 6. Tues–Sun 10am–6pm (Thurs until 9pm). U-Bahn: Mariahilferstrasse. Tram: 1 or 2.

ATTRACTIONS OUTSIDE THE INNER CITY

Schönbrunn Palace ★★★ A Hapsburg palace of 1,441 rooms, Schönbrunn was designed and built between 1696 and 1712 in a grand baroque style meant to surpass that of Versailles. When Maria Theresa became empress in 1740, she changed the original plans, and the Schönbrunn we see today, with its delicate rococo touches, is her conception. It was the imperial summer palace during Maria Theresa's 40-year reign, the scene of great ceremonial balls, lavish banquets, and the fabulous receptions during the Congress of Vienna in 1815. The State Apartments are the most stunning. Much of the interior ornamentation is in 23½-karat gold, and many porcelain tile stoves are in evidence. Of the 40 rooms that you can visit, particularly fascinating is the "Room of Millions" decorated with Indian and Persian miniatures, the grandest rococo salon in the world. On the grounds of the palace, the orangerie or, less frequently, the Schlosstheater, are the sites for occasional presentations of live chamber music, although hours and venues are widely divergent. For information, call (**C**) **01/81113239.**

Schönbrunner Schlossstrasse. (**C**) **01/811130.** www.schoenbrunn.at. Admission 11€ ($12) adults, 5.40€ ($6.20) children 6–15, free for children under 6. Apr–Oct daily 8:30am–5pm (till 6pm during July and Aug); Nov–Mar daily 8:30am–4pm. U-Bahn: Schönbrunn.

Österreichische Galerie Belvedere ★★ The Belvedere Palace was built as a summer home for Prince Eugene of Savoy and consists of two palatial buildings. The pond reflects the sky and palace buildings, which are made up of a series of interlocking cubes, and the interior is dominated by two great, flowing staircases. The Unteres Belvedere (Lower Belvedere), with its entrance at Rennweg 6A, was constructed from 1714 to 1716 and contains the Gold Salon, one of the palace's most beautiful rooms. It also houses the Barockmuseum (Museum of Baroque Art). The original sculptures from the Neuermarkt fountain, the work of Georg Raphael Donner, are displayed here. The Oberes Belvedere (Upper Belvedere) was started in 1721 and completed in 1723. It contains the Gallery of 19th- and 20th-Century Art, with an outstanding collection of the works of Gustav Klimt, including his extraordinary *Judith*. The Museum of Medieval Austrian Art is in the Orangery.

Prinz-Eugen-Strasse 27. (**C**) **01/79557.** www.belvedere.at. Admission 7.50€ ($8.65) adults, free for children 10 and under. Tues–Sun 10am–6pm (last entrance 5:30pm). Tram: D to Schloss Belvedere.

ORGANIZED TOURS

Wiener Rundfahrten (Vienna Sightseeing Tours), Graf Starhemberggasse 25 ((**C**) **01/7124-6830;** www.viennasightseeingtours.com; U-Bahn: Landstrasse Wien Mitte), offers some of the best-organized tours of Vienna and its surroundings. Tours depart from a signposted area in front of the State Opera (U-Bahn: Karlsplatz) and include running commentary in both German and English.

CITY TOURS A **"Historical City Tour,"** which includes visits to Schönbrunn and Belvedere palaces, leaves the Staatsoper daily at 9:45am and 2pm (in summer also at 10:30am) (U-Bahn: Karlsplatz). It lasts about 3 hours and costs

33€ ($38) adults and 15€ ($17) children. It's ideal for visitors who are pressed for time and yet want to be shown the major (and most frequently photographed) monuments of Vienna. It takes you past the historic buildings of Ringstrasse—the State Opera, Hofburg Palace, museums, Parliament, City Hall, the Burgtheater, the University, and the Votive Church—into the heart of Vienna.

Another tour, **"Following Sisi's Footsteps,"** is the same as the "Historical City Tour" except that you also watch the Lipizzaner horses being trained at the Spanish Riding School. These tours leave at 9:45am Tuesday through Saturday. They cost 33€ ($38) adults and 15€ ($17) children, with the entrance fee to the Spanish Riding School (13€/$14) to be paid separately.

TOURS OUTSIDE THE CITY "Vienna Woods—Mayerling," another popular excursion, lasting about 4 hours, leaves from the Staatsoper and takes you to the towns of Perchtoldsdorf and Modling, and also to the Abbey of Heiligenkreuz, a center of Christian culture since medieval times. The tour also takes you for a short walk through Baden, the spa that was once a favorite summer resort of the aristocracy. Tours cost 39€ ($45) adults and 15€ ($17) children.

THE SHOPPING SCENE

Vienna is known for the excellent quality of its works, including petit point, hand-painted porcelain, work by goldsmiths and silversmiths, handmade dolls, ceramics, enamel jewelry, wrought-iron articles, and leather goods. Also popular is loden, a boiled and rolled wool fabric made into overcoats, suits, and hats, as well as knitted sweaters. Popular destinations can be found on **Kärntnerstrasse,** between the Staatsoper and Stock-im-Eisen-Platz; the **Graben,** between Stock-im-Eisen-Platz and Kohlmarkt; **Kohlmarkt,** between the Graben and Michaelplatz; and **Rotensturmstrasse,** between Stephansplatz and Kai. You can also shop on **Mariahilferstrasse,** between Babenbergerstrasse and Schönbrunn, one of the longest streets in Vienna; **Favoritenstrasse,** between Südtiroler Platz and Reumannplatz; and **Landstrasser Hauptstrasse.**

The **Naschmarkt** is a vegetable-and-fruit market with a lively scene every day. It's at Linke and Rechte Wienzeile, south of the opera district.

Albin Denk, Graben 13 (℃ 01/512-4439; www.albindenk.24on.cc; U-Bahn: Stephansplatz), is the oldest continuously operating porcelain store in Vienna, in business since 1702. You'll see thousands of objects from Meissen, Dresden, and other regions.

Opened in 1830 by the Plankl family, **Loden Plankl,** Michaelerplatz 6 (℃ 01/533-8032; www.loden-plankl.at; U-Bahn: Stephansplatz), is the oldest and most reputable outlet in Vienna for traditional Austrian clothing. You'll find Austrian loden coats, shoes, trousers, dirndls, jackets, lederhosen, and suits for men, women, and children. The building, opposite the Hofburg, dates from the 17th century. The three-floor **Ö. W. (Österreichische Werkstatten),** Kärntnerstrasse 6 (℃ 01/512-2418; U-Bahn: Stephansplatz), sells hundreds of handmade art objects from Austria. Some 200 leading artists and craftspeople throughout the country organized this cooperative to showcase their wares. It's easy to find, only half a minute's walk from St. Stephan's Cathedral.

VIENNA AFTER DARK

The best source of information about what's happening on the cultural scene is *Wien Monatsprogramm,* distributed free at tourist information offices and at many hotel reception desks. *Die Presse,* the Viennese daily, publishes a special magazine in its Thursday edition outlining the major cultural events for the coming week. It's in German but might still be helpful.

THE PERFORMING ARTS

OPERA & CLASSICAL MUSIC   Music is at the heart of cultural life in Vienna. This has been true for a couple of centuries or so, and the city continues to lure composers, musicians, and music lovers.

The **Wiener Staatsoper (State Opera),** Opernring 2 (© **01/5144-42250;** www.wiener-staatsoper.at; U-Bahn: Karlsplatz), is one of the three most important opera houses in the world. With the Vienna Philharmonic in the pit, some of the leading opera stars of the world perform here. In their day, Richard Strauss and Gustav Mahler worked as directors. Daily performances are given September through June. Tickets range from 10€ to 178€ ($12–$205). Tours are offered two to five times daily, for 4.50€ ($5.20) per person; times are posted on a board outside the entrance.

Count yourself fortunate if you get to hear a concert at **Musikverein,** Dumbastrasse 3 (© **01/505-8190;** www.musikverein-wien.at; U-Bahn: Karlsplatz). The Golden Hall is regarded as one of the four acoustically best concert halls in the world. Some 600 concerts per season (Sept–June) are presented here. Only 10 to 12 of these are played by the Vienna Philharmonic, and these are subscription concerts, so they're always sold out long in advance. Standing room is available at almost any performance, but you must line up hours before the show. Tickets are 4€ to 7€ ($4.60–$8.05) for standing room; 10€ to 80€ ($12–$92) for seats. The box office is open Monday through Friday from 9am to 7:30pm; Saturday from 9am to 5pm.

Vienna is the home of four major symphony orchestras, including the world-acclaimed Vienna Symphony and the Vienna Philharmonic. In addition to the ÖRF Symphony Orchestra and the Niederöster-reichische Tonkünstler, there are literally dozens of others, ranging from smaller orchestras to chamber orchestras. The orchestras sometimes perform at the **Konzerthaus,** Lothringerstrasse 20 (© **01/242-002;** www.konzerthaus.at; U-Bahn: Stadt-Park), a major concert hall with three auditoriums, and also the venue for chamber music and other programs.

THEATER   For performances in English, head to **Vienna's English Theatre,** Josefsgasse 12 (© **01/402-12600;** www.englishtheatre.at; U-Bahn: Rathaus). The **Burgtheater (National Theater),** Dr.-Karl-Lueger-Ring 2 (© **01/5144-4145;** www.burgtheater.at; tram: 1, 2, D, or J to Burgtheater), produces classical and modern plays. Even if you don't understand German, you might want to attend a performance here, especially if a familiar Shakespeare play is being staged. This is one of Europe's premier repertory theaters. Tickets are 4€ to 178€ ($4.60–$205) for seats, 1.50€ to 3.50€ ($1.75–$4.05) for standing room.

NIGHTCLUBS, CABARETS & BARS

The noteworthy architect Adolf Loos designed the very dark, sometimes mysterious **Loos American Bar,** Kärntnerdurchgang 10 (© **01/512-3283;** U-Bahn: Stephansplatz), in 1908. Today it welcomes singles, couples who tend to be bilingual and very hip, and all manner of clients from the arts and media scenes of Vienna. The mixologist's specialties include six kinds of martinis, plus five kinds of Manhattans. It's open Sunday through Wednesday from noon to 4am, and Thursday through Saturday from noon to 5am.

The most famous jazz pub in Austria, **Jazzland,** Franz-Josefs-Kai 29 (© **01/533-2575;** U-Bahn: Schwedenplatz), is noted for the quality of its U.S.- and

Wine Tasting in the *Heurigen*

Heurigen are Viennese wine taverns, celebrated in operettas, films, and song. They are found on the outskirts of Vienna, principally in Grinzing (the most popular district) and in Sievering, Neustift, Nussdorf, or Heiligenstadt. **Grinzing** (tram: 38) lies at the edge of the Vienna Woods, a 15-minute drive northwest of the center.

Only 20 minutes from Vienna, **Weingut Wolff,** Rathstrasse 50, Neustift (© 01/440-3727; bus: 35), is one of the most durable of Heurigen. Although aficionados claim the best are "deep in the countryside" of Lower Austria, this one comes closest on the borderline of Vienna to offering an authentic experience. In summer, you're welcomed to a flower-decked garden set against a backdrop of ancient vineyards. You can really fill up your platter here, with some of the best wursts (sausages) and roast meats (especially the delectable pork), as well as fresh salads. Find a table under a cluster of grapes and sample the fruity young wines, especially the chardonnay, Sylvaner, and Gruner Veltliner. The tavern is open daily from 11am to 1am with main courses ranging from 7€ to 13€ ($8.05–$15).

Altes Presshaus, Cobenzigasse 15 (© 01/320-0203), was established in 1527, the oldest continuously operating Heurige in Grinzing, with an authentic cellar you might ask to visit. The place has an authentic, smoke-stained character with wood paneling and antique furniture. The garden terrace blossoms throughout the summer. Try such Heurigen-inspired fare as smoked pork shoulder, roast pork shank, sauerkraut, potatoes, and dumplings. Meals cost 10€ to 15€ ($12–$17); 3-course menu 22€ to 28€ ($25–$32); drinks begin at 3€ ($3.45). It's open March to October daily from 4pm to midnight.

central European–based performers. It's in a deep, 200-year-old cellar, of the type the Viennese used to store staples during the city's many sieges. Amid exposed brick walls and dim lighting, you can order drinks or dinner. The place is open Monday to Saturday from 7pm to 1am. Music begins at 9pm, and three sets are performed.

In a surprising location in the Leopold Museum, **Café Leopold,** Museumsplatz 1 (© 01/523-67-32), is all the rage. It has a revolving cycle of DJs, each vying for local fame, and a wide selection of party-colored cocktails, priced from 6.80€ ($7.80). The cafe-and-restaurant section of this place is open Sunday to Wednesday 9am to 2am, and Thursday and Friday 9am to 4am. The disco operates Thursday to Saturday from 10pm to between 2 to 4am, depending on business. There's no cover.

One of the town's newest clubs is **Mirage,** Johannesgasse 27 (© 01/512-8282; U-Bahn: Stadtpark), which plays music from the 1980s up until today, including soul and Latin salsa. There's no cover charge. Hours are Monday to Saturday 9pm to 4am.

Alfi's Goldener Spiegel, Linke Wienzeile 46 (entrance on Stiegengasse; © 01/586-6608; U-Bahn: Kettenbrückengasse), is the most enduring gay restaurant in Vienna and also its most popular gay bar, attracting mostly male clients to its position near Vienna's Naschmarkt. The place is very cruisy. The bar is open Wednesday through Monday from 7pm to 2am.

Frauencafé, Langegasse 11 (📞 **01/406-37-54;** U-Bahn: Volkstheater), is exactly what a translation of its name would imply: a politically conscious cafe for lesbians and (to a lesser degree) heterosexual women who appreciate the company of other women. Established in 1977 in cramped quarters in a century-old building, it's filled with magazines, newspapers, modern paintings, and a clientele of Austrian and foreign women.

2 Salzburg ★★★

A baroque city on the banks of the Salzach River, set against a mountain backdrop, Salzburg is the beautiful capital of the state of Salzburg. The city and the river were named after its early residents who earned their living in the salt mines. In this "heart of the heart of Europe," Mozart was born in 1756, and the composer's association with the city beefs up tourism.

The **Old Town** lies on the left bank of the river, where a monastery and bishopric were founded in 700. From that start, Salzburg grew in power and prestige, becoming an archbishopric in 798. In the heyday of the prince-archbishops, the city became known as the "German Rome." Responsible for much of its architectural grandeur are those masters of the baroque, Fischer von Erlach and Lukas von Hildebrandt.

"The City of Mozart," "Silent Night," and *The Sound of Music*—Salzburg lives essentially off its rich past. It is a front-ranking cultural mecca for classical music year-round. The city is the setting for the Salzburg Festival, a worldrenowned annual event that attracts music lovers, especially Mozart fans, from all over the globe. Salzburg's natural setting among alpine peaks on both banks of the Salzach River gives it the backdrop perpetuating its romantic image.

As one of Europe's greatest tourist capitals, most of Salzburg's day-to-day life spins around promoting its music and its other connections. Although *The Sound of Music* was filmed in 1964, this Julie Andrews blockbuster has become a cult attraction and is definitely alive and well in Salzburg. Ironically, Austria was the only country in the world where the musical failed when it first opened. It played for only a single week in Vienna, closing after audiences dwindled.

Salzburg is only a short distance from the Austrian-German frontier, so it's convenient for exploring many of the attractions of Bavaria (see chapter 7). Situated on the northern slopes of the Alps, the city lies at the intersection of traditional European trade routes and is well served by air, Autobahn, and rail.

ESSENTIALS
GETTING THERE   By Plane   The **Salzburg Airport–W.A. Mozart,** Innsbrucker Bundesstrasse 95 (📞 **0662/8580;** www.salzburg-airport.com), lies 3km (2 miles) southwest of the city center. It has regularly scheduled air service to all Austrian airports, as well as to Frankfurt, Amsterdam, Brussels, Berlin, Dresden, Düsseldorf, Hamburg, London, Paris, and Zurich. Major airlines serving the Salzburg airport are Austrian Airlines (📞 **0662/85-45-11**), Air France (📞 **01/50-2222-403**), Lufthansa (📞 **0800/222240**), and Tyrolean (📞 **0662/85-45-33**).

Bus no. 2 runs between the airport and Salzburg's main rail station. Departures are frequent, and the 20-minute trip costs 3€ ($3.45) one-way. By taxi it's only about 15 minutes, but you'll pay at least 10€ to 15€ ($12–$17).

By Train   Salzburg's main rail station, the **Salzburg Hauptbahnhof,** Südtirolerplatz (📞 **05/1717**), is on the major rail lines of Europe, with frequent arrivals from all the main cities of Austria and from European cities such as Munich. Between 5:05am and 8:05pm, trains arrive every 30 minutes from Vienna (trip time: 3½ hr.); a one-way fare is 37€ ($43). There are eight daily trains from Innsbruck (2 hr.); a one-way fare is 30€ ($35). Trains also arrive every 30 minutes from Munich (2½ hr.), with a one-way ticket costing 26€ ($30).

From the train station, buses depart to various parts of the city, including the Altstadt. Or you can walk to the Altstadt in about 20 minutes. Taxis are also available. The rail station has a currency exchange and storage lockers.

By Car Salzburg is 334km (209 miles) southwest of Vienna and 152km (95 miles) east of Munich. It's reached from all directions by good roads, including Autobahn A8 from the west (Munich), A1 from the east (Vienna), and A10 from the south. Route 20 comes into Salzburg from points north and west, and Route 159 serves towns and cities from the southeast.

VISITOR INFORMATION **Tourist Offices** The **Salzburg Information Office,** Mozartplatz 5 (℃ **0662/88987-330;** www.salzburginfo.at; bus: 5, 6, or 51), is open July through September daily from 9am to 7pm and off season Monday through Saturday from 9am to 6pm. The office makes hotel reservations for a 10% deposit (which will be credited to your hotel bill), plus a 2.20€ ($2.55) booking fee. There's also a **tourist information office** on Platform 2A of the Hauptbahnhof, Südtirolerplatz (℃ **0662/88987-340**).

CITY LAYOUT Most of what visitors come to see lies on the left bank of the Salzach River in the **Altstadt (Old Town).** If you're driving, you must leave your car in the modern part of town—the right bank of the Salzach—and enter the Old Town on foot, as most of it is for pedestrians only.

The heart of the inner city is **Residenzplatz,** which has the largest and finest baroque fountain this side of the Alps. On the western side of the square stands the **Residenz,** palace of the prince-archbishops, and on the southern side of the square is the **Salzburg Cathedral** (or Dom). To the west of the Dom lies **Domplatz,** linked by archways dating from 1658. Squares to the north and south appear totally enclosed. On the southern side of Max-Reinhardt-Platz and Hofstallgasse, edging toward **Mönchsberg,** stands the **Festspielhaus (Festival Theater),** built on the foundations of the 17th-century court stables.

(Value The Salzburg Card

The **Salzburg Card** not only lets you use **unlimited public transportation,** but it acts as an admission ticket to the city's most important **cultural sights.** With the card you can visit Mozart's birthplace, the Hohensalzburg fortress, the Residenz gallery, the world-famous water fountain gardens at Hellbrunn, the Baroque Museum in the Mirabell Gardens, and the gala rooms in the Archbishop's Residence. The card is also good for sights outside of town, including the Hellbrunn Zoo, the open-air museum in Grossingmain, the salt mines of the Dürnberg, and the gondola trip at Untersberg. The card, approximately the size of a credit card, comes with a brochure with maps and sightseeing hints.

Cards are valid for 24, 48, and 72 hours and cost 20€ ($23), 28€ ($32), and 34€ ($39), respectively. Children from 6 to 15 years of age receive a 50% discount. You can buy the pass from Salzburg travel agencies, hotels, tobacconists, and municipal offices.

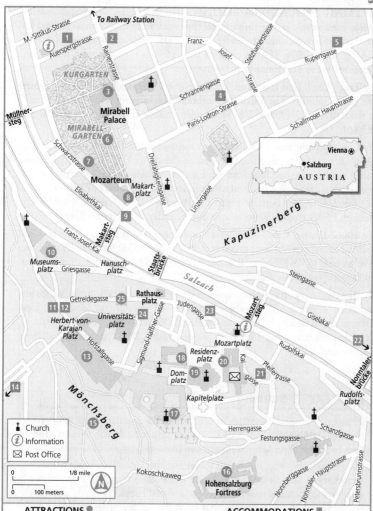

Salzburg

To Railway Station

M-Sittikus-Strasse

Auerspergstrasse

KURGARTEN

Müllner-steg

Mirabell Palace

MIRABELL-GARTEN

Schwarzstrasse

Mozarteum

Makart-platz

Elisabethkai

Franz-Josef-Kai

Makart-steg

Museums-platz

Griesgasse

Hanusch-platz

Staats-brücke

Salzach

Herbert-von-Karajan Platz

Getreidegasse

Rathaus-platz

Universitäts-platz

Judengasse

Mozart-steg

Hofstallgasse

Sigmund-Haffner-Gasse

Mozartplatz

Residenz-platz

Dom-platz

Kapitelplatz

Mönchsberg

Petersfriedhof

Herrengasse

Festungsgasse

Hohensalzburg Fortress

Kokoschkaweg

Franz-Josef-Strasse

Schrannengasse

Paris-Lodron-Strasse

Dreifaltigkeitsgasse

Linzergasse

Stelzhamerstrasse

Rupertgasse

Schallmoser Hauptstrasse

Kapuzinerberg

Steingasse

Giselakai

Rudolfskai

Pfeifergasse

Kai-gasse

Rudolfs-platz

Schanzlgasse

Nonntaler-brücke

Nonnberggasse

Nonntaler Hauptstrasse

Petersbrunnstrasse

Vienna

Salzburg

AUSTRIA

Legend
- † Church
- (i) Information
- ⊠ Post Office

0 — 1/8 mile
0 — 100 meters

N

GETTING AROUND **By Bus/Tram** The city buses and trams provide quick, comfortable service through the city center from the Nonntal parking lot to Sigsmundsplatz, the city-center parking lot. The one-ride fare is 1.70€ ($1.95) adults, .90€ ($1.05) children 6 to 15; those 5 and under travel free. Note that buses stop running at 11pm.

By Taxi You'll find taxi stands scattered at key points all over the city center and in the suburbs. The **Salzburg Funktaxi–Vereinigung** (radio taxis) office is at Rainerstrasse 27 (© **0662/8111** to order a taxi in advance). Fares start at 3€ ($3.45).

By Car Driving a car in Salzburg isn't recommended. However, you'll probably want a car for touring the areas outside the city (such as Land Salzburg), as using public transportation can be time consuming. Arrangements for car rentals are always best if made in advance. Try **Avis** (© **0662/877278**) or **Hertz** (© **0662/876674**), both at Ferdinand-Porsche-Strasse 7 and open Monday through Friday from 8:30am to 6pm and Saturday from 8am to 1pm.

By Horse-Drawn Cab You rent a horse-drawn cab (called a *Fiaker* in German) at Residenzplatz. Four people usually pay 33€ ($38) for 20 to 25 minutes, 45€ to 66€ ($52–$76) for 50 minutes (99€/$114 for 1 hr. and 15 min.). But all fares are subject to negotiation.

By Bicycle City officials have developed a network of bicycle paths, which are indicated on city maps. May through September, you can rent bicycles at **Top-bike,** at the Staatsbrücke or Main Bridge (© **0627/24656**), daily from 9am to 7pm. Rentals cost about 13€ ($15) per day, with a 10% discount for Salzburg Cardholders.

FAST FACTS: Salzburg

American Express The office at Mozartplatz 5–7, adjacent to Residenzplatz (© **0662/8080**; bus: 5 or 6), is open Monday through Friday from 9am to 5:30pm and Saturday from 9am to noon.

Business Hours Most shops and stores are open Monday through Friday from 9am to 6pm and Saturday usually from 9am to noon. Some of the smaller shops shut down at noon for a lunch break. Salzburg observes *langer Samstag,* which means that most stores stay open until 5pm on selected Saturdays. Banks are open Monday through Friday from 8am to noon and 2 to 4:30pm.

Currency Exchange You can exchange money at the Hauptbahnhof on Südtirolerplatz daily from 7am to 10pm, and at the airport daily from 9am to 4pm.

Dentists For an English-speaking dentist, call **Dentistenkammer,** Faberstrasse 2 (© **0662/87-34-66**).

Doctors If you suddenly fall ill, your best source of information for finding a doctor is the reception desk of your hotel. If you want a comprehensive list of doctors and their respective specialties, which you can acquire in Salzburg or even before your arrival, contact **Ärztekammer für Salzburg,** Bergstrasse 14, A-5020 Salzburg (© **0662/87-13-27**). And if your troubles flare up over a weekend, the **Medical Emergency Center of the Austrian**

Red Cross maintains a hot line (© 141), which you can use to describe your problem. A staff member there will either ask you to visit their headquarters at Karl Renner Strasse 7, or send a medical expert to wherever you're staying. This service is available from 5pm on Friday to 8am on Monday, and on public holidays.

Drugstores (Apotheke) Larger pharmacies, especially those in the city center, tend to remain open without a break Monday through Friday from 8am to 6pm and Saturday from 8am to noon. For night service, and service on Saturday afternoon and Sunday, pharmacies display a sign giving the address of the nearest pharmacy that has agreed to remain open over the weekend or throughout the night. A pharmacy that's particularly convenient to Salzburg's commercial center is **Elisabeth-Apotheke,** Elisabethstrasse 1 (© **0662/87-14-84**), north of Rainerstrasse toward the train station.

Embassies/Consulates The consular agency of the **United States,** at Alter Markt 1 (© **0662/84-87-76**), is open Monday, Wednesday, and Thursday 9am to noon to assist U.S. citizens with emergencies. The consulate of **Great Britain,** at Alter Markt 4 (© **0662/84-81-33**), is open Monday through Friday from 9am to noon.

Emergencies Call © **133** for police, © **122** to report a fire, and © **144** for an ambulance.

Internet Access The most convenient cafe with Internet capability is the **Internet Café,** Mozartplatz (© **0662/84-48-22**; bus: 5 or 6), across from the tourist office. It's open daily from 9am to 11pm and charges 9€ per hour of Internet access.

Post Office The main post office is at Residenzplatz 9 (© **0662/844-1210**; bus: 5 or 6). The post office at the main railway station is open Monday to Friday from 7am to 9:30pm, Saturday 7am to 2pm, and Sunday 7am to 6pm.

Telephone The **country code** for Austria is **43.** The **city code** for Salzburg is **662;** use this code when you're calling from outside Austria. If you're within Austria, use **0662.**

WHERE TO STAY
ON THE LEFT BANK (ALTSTADT)
Very Expensive

Altstadt Radisson SAS ★★   This is not your typical Radisson property—in fact, it's a radical departure for the chain in style and charm. Dating from 1377, it's a luxuriously and elegantly converted Altstadt hostelry. Its closest rival in town is the old-world Goldener Hirsch, to which it comes in second. The old and new are blended in perfect harmony here, and the historic facade conceals top-rate comforts and amenities. In a structure of this size, rooms naturally vary greatly in size, but all have a certain charm and sparkle and are exceedingly comfortable with some of the city's best beds, plus luxurious bathrooms with showers.

Rudolfskai 28/Judengasse 15, A-5020 Salzburg. © **800/333-3333** in the U.S., or 0662/848-571. Fax 0662/ 848-571-6. www.austria-trend.at/ass. 62 units. 218€–500€ ($251–$575) double; 413€–615€ ($475–$707) suite. Rates include buffet breakfast. AE, DC, MC, V. Parking 25€ ($29). Bus: 5 or 6. **Amenities:** Restaurant; bar; 24-hr. room service; babysitting; laundry service/dry cleaning; nonsmoking rooms. *In room:* TV, minibar, hair dryer, safe.

Goldener Hirsch ★★★   The award for the finest hotel in Salzburg goes to this place, steeped in legend and with a history dating from 1407. The hotel is built on a small scale yet it absolutely reeks of aristocratic elegance, which is enhanced by the superb staff. Near Mozart's birthplace, the hotel is composed of four medieval town houses, three of which are joined together in a labyrinth of rustic hallways and staircases. The fourth, called "The Coppersmith's House," is across the street and contains 17 charming, spacious rooms. All rooms in the complex are beautifully furnished and maintained, with luxurious full-size bathrooms.

Getreidegasse 37, A-5020 Salzburg. (℃) 800/325-3535 in the U.S., or 0662/8084. Fax 0662/843349. www. goldenerhirsch.com. 69 units. 157€–660€ ($181–$759) double; 395€–1,110€ ($454–$1,277) suite. Higher rates at festival time (the 1st week of Apr and mid-July to Aug). AE, DC, MC, V. You can double-park in front of the Getreidegasse entrance or at the Karajanplatz entrance, and a staff member will take your vehicle to the hotel's garage for 28€ ($32). Bus: 55. **Amenities:** 2 restaurants; bar; 24-hr. room service; babysitting; laundry service/dry cleaning; nonsmoking rooms. *In room:* A/C, TV, dataport, minibar, hair dryer, safe.

Moderate

Altstadthotel Weisse Taube   This hotel is in the pedestrian area of the Old Town a few steps from Mozartplatz, but you can drive up to it to unload baggage. Constructed in 1365, the Weisse Taube has been owned by the Haubner family since 1904. Rooms are, for the most part, renovated and comfortably streamlined, with traditional furnishings, frequently renewed beds, and small but efficiently laid-out bathrooms with shower-tub combinations. The whole place is kept up with spotless housekeeping.

Kaigasse 9, A-5020 Salzburg. (℃) **0662/84-24-04.** Fax 0662/84-17-83. www.weissetaube.at. 31 units. 95€–157€ ($109–$181) double. Rates include breakfast. AE, DC, MC, V. Garage 9€. Bus: 5, 51, or 55. **Amenities:** Breakfast room; lounge. *In room:* TV, minibar, hair dryer, safe.

Hotel Am Nussdorferhof   The only drawback to this hotel is its location in a quiet residential suburb—a 20-minute walk south of Salzburg's historic core. If that isn't a problem for you, it might make a safe and happy refuge for you during your time in Salzburg. Its congenial owners, Herbert and Ilse Kronegger, know the cultural and geographical features of their city in intricate detail and are eager to help newcomers with the city's logistics. About half the guest rooms are outfitted in old-fashioned Teutonic patterns, with touches of wood and alpine references. The other half are conservatively international, with bland 1970s-era furnishings and enough modern comforts to ensure a pleasant overnight stay. Bathrooms are trimmed in tile and in most cases come with shower-tub combinations. On-site are a bar and a cozy Italian restaurant, **Senza Confini,** which features well-prepared versions of pizza, pasta, and (usually) tried-and-true northern Italian cuisine.

Moosstrasse 36, A-5020 Salzburg. (℃) **0662/824838.** Fax 0662/824-8389. www.nussdorferhof.at. 30 units. High season 90€–130€ ($104–$150) double; winter 82€–100€ ($94–$115) double. Rates include breakfast and parking. AE, DC, MC, V. Bus: 15 or 16. **Amenities:** Restaurant; bar; limited room service; Jacuzzi; babysitting. *In room:* TV, dataport, hair dryer, minibar.

Hotel Blaue Gans   Only a short walk from the much more expensive Goldener Hirsch, the much-renovated "Blue Goose" has been functioning as an inn for more than 400 years. The building that houses the inn is probably 700 years old, but the rooms were renovated extensively between 1998 and 2000. All have good beds with firm mattresses and full bathrooms. Those facing the courtyard are quieter and much more desirable. Room nos. 332 and 336 are the most spacious.

Getreidegasse 41-43, A-5020 Salzburg. (℃) **0662/84-13-17.** Fax 0662/84-13-179. www.blauegans.at. 37 units. 109€–185€ ($125–$213) double; 175€–195€ ($201–$224) junior suite. Rates include buffet breakfast. AE, DC, MC, V. Parking 14€ ($16). Bus: 1 or 2. **Amenities:** Restaurant; bar; babysitting; laundry/dry cleaning service. *In room:* TV, minibar, hair dryer, safe.

Hotel Elefant   Near the Old Town Rathaus, in a quiet alley off Getreidegasse, is this well-established, family-run hotel. It, too, is in one of Salzburg's most ancient buildings—more than 700 years old. The well-furnished and high-ceilinged rooms have small bathrooms with shower-tub combinations. Inside the hotel are two restaurants serving Austrian and international cuisine: the vaulted Bürgerstüberl, where high wooden banquettes separate the tables, and the historic Ratsherrnkeller, known as the wine cellar of Salzburg in the 17th century.

Sigmund-Haffner-Gasse 4, A-5020 Salzburg. ✆ 0662/84-33-97. Fax 0662/84-01-0928. www.elefant.at. 31 units. 128€–192€ ($147–$221) double. Rates include buffet breakfast. AE, DC, MC, V. Nearby parking 7.30€ ($8.40). Bus: 1, 2, 5, 6, or 51. **Amenities:** 2 restaurants; bar; limited room service; babysitting; laundry service/dry cleaning; nonsmoking rooms. *In room:* A/C (in some), TV, dataport, minibar, hair dryer, safe.

ON THE RIGHT BANK
Expensive

Sacher Salzburg Osterreichischer Hof ★★★   Only the Goldener Hirsch rivals this charmer. Built as the Hotel d'Autriche in 1866, this hotel has survived the ravages of war and been renovated countless times. A new era began when the Gürtler family, owners of the Hotel Sacher in Vienna, took over in 1988, turning the hotel into a jewel amid the villas on the riverbank. The cheerful rooms are well furnished, quite spacious, and individually decorated; each has a luxurious bathroom equipped with a tub/shower combo. Try to reserve one overlooking the river. The cafe serves Austria's most fabled pastry, the original Sacher torte.

Schwarzstrasse 5–7, A-5020 Salzburg. ✆ 800/223-6800 in the U.S. and Canada, or 0662/889-77. Fax 0662/889-77-551. www.sacher.com. 118 units. 205€–815€ ($236–$937) double; from 560€ ($644) suite. AE, DC, MC, V. Parking 25€ ($29). Bus: 1, 5, 6, 29, or 51. **Amenities:** 2 restaurants; 2 bars; cafe; lounge; fitness center; sauna; limited room service; laundry service/dry cleaning; nonsmoking rooms; 1 room for those with limited mobility. *In room:* TV, dataport, minibar, hair dryer, safe.

Salzburg Sheraton Hotel ★★   One of the crown jewels of the Sheraton chain, this government-rated five-star seven-story hotel opened in 1984 in a desirable location about a 10-minute walk from Mozartplatz. The Austrian architect who designed this place took great pains to incorporate it into its 19th-century neighborhood. Rooms have thick wall-to-wall carpeting and contain beds with built-in headboards. Bathrooms have make-up mirrors and hair dryers. The exclusive junior, queen, and presidential suites are filled with elegant Biedermeier furniture. Half the rooms overlook the Mirabell Gardens.

Auerspergstrasse 4, A-5020 Salzburg. ✆ 800/325-3535 in the U.S., or 0662/88-99-90. Fax 0662/88-17-76. www.sheraton.com. 163 units. 130€–320€ ($150–$368) double; 295€–595€ ($339–$684) junior suite. AE, DC, MC, V. Parking 15€ ($17). Bus: 1. **Amenities:** 2 restaurants; bar; indoor pool; sauna; 24-hr. room service; babysitting; laundry service/dry cleaning; nonsmoking rooms; 1 room for those with limited mobility. *In room:* TV, minibar, hair dryer, safe.

Moderate

Hotel Auersperg ★   With its own sunny gardens, this traditional family run hotel consists of two buildings: a main structure and a less expensive and less desirable annex. There's an old-fashioned look of charm wherever you go, from the reception hall with its molded ceilings to the antiques-filled drawing room to the convivial and informal library bar. The warm, cozy, and large guest rooms are especially inviting, with excellent beds and well-equipped bathrooms with tubs and showers.

Auerspergstrasse 61, A-5027 Salzburg. ✆ 0662/889-44-0. Fax 0662/88-944-55. www.auersperg.at. 51 units. 112€–177€ ($129–$204) double; 175€–375€ ($201–$431) suite. Rates include breakfast. AE, DC, MC, V. Free parking. Bus: 15 from the train station. **Amenities:** Breakfast room; bar; fitness center; sauna; laundry service/dry cleaning; nonsmoking rooms; rooms for those with limited mobility. *In room:* TV, dataport (in some), minibar, hair dryer, safe.

Inexpensive

Altstadthotel Wolf-Dietrich ✪   Two 19th-century town houses were joined together to make this select little hotel. The lobby and ground-floor reception area have a friendly and elegant atmosphere and bright, classical furnishings. The smallish rooms are appealing and comfortably furnished, with excellent beds and tiny bathrooms with shower-tub combinations. The ground-floor cafe, **Weiner Kaffeehaus,** is reminiscent of the extravagant coffeehouses built in the 19th century in Vienna, Budapest, and Prague.

Wolf-Dietrich-Strasse 7, A-5020 Salzburg. ✆ **0662/87-12-75.** Fax 0662/88-23-20. www.salzburg-hotel.at. 27 units. 89€–179€ ($102–$206) double; 134€–209€ ($154–$240) suite. Rates include breakfast. AE, DC, MC, V. Parking 12€ ($14). Restaurant closed Feb to Mar 15. Bus: 1, 2, 5, 6, or 51. **Amenities:** 2 restaurants; bar, cafe; pool; sauna; solarium; limited room service; babysitting; laundry service. *In room:* TV, minibar, hair dryer.

Hotel Gastein ✪   This prosperous-looking Teutonic villa lies amid calm green scenery on the bank of the Salzach River. Only a few minutes from the center of the town's oldest boroughs, the house offers true Salzburg atmosphere. You'll feel like you're staying in an upper-class private home. During the annual music festival the place is filled with musicians, who love the spacious flowering garden for breakfast or afternoon tea. The large guest rooms have furniture crafted by well-known Salzburg artists, firm beds, and private balconies. Bathrooms, though often small, are exceedingly well maintained and equipped with shower-tub combinations.

Ignaz-Rieder-Kai 25, A-5020 Salzburg. ✆ **0662/62-25-65.** Fax 0662/62-25-659. www.hotel-gastein.at. 13 units. 105€–156€ ($121–$179) double; 214€–258€ ($246–$297) suite. Rates include breakfast. AE, DC, MC, V. Free parking. Bus: 49. **Amenities:** Breakfast room; lounge. *In room:* TV, minibar.

Pension Bergland ✪ (Finds)   Cozy, personalized, and substantial, this guesthouse sits in a quiet residential neighborhood. It welcomes visitors in a "music room" where there's a bar serving beer, wine, and coffee, and a collection of guitars and lutes displayed on the walls. Guest rooms are comfortable, minimalist, and modern looking, with larger-than-expected bathrooms containing shower-tub combinations and, in many cases, a piece of furniture handmade by members of the Kuhn family, your hosts. The pension will rent you a bike and dispense information about where to ride.

15 Rupertsgasse, A-5020 Salzburg. ✆ **0662/872318.** Fax 0662/872318-8. www.berglandhotel.at. 17 units. 87€ ($100) double. Rates include buffet breakfast. AE, DC, MC, V. Closed mid-Nov to mid-Dec. Free parking. Bus: 27 or 29. **Amenities:** Breakfast room; lounge; nonsmoking rooms. *In room:* TV, hair dryer.

WHERE TO DINE

Two special desserts you'll want to sample while here are the famous *Salzburger Nockerln,* a light mixture of stiff egg whites, as well as the elaborate confection known as the *Mozart-Kugeln,* with bittersweet chocolate, hazelnut nougat, and marzipan. You'll also want to taste the beer in one of the numerous Salzburg breweries.

ON THE LEFT BANK (OLD TOWN)
Very Expensive

Goldener Hirsch ✪✪✪ AUSTRIAN/VIENNESE   The best restaurant in Salzburg's best hotel attracts the brightest luminaries of the international music and business community. The venue is chic, top-notch, impeccable, and charming, richly sought after during peak season. It's staffed with a superb team of chefs and waiters who preside over an atmosphere of elegant simplicity. The food is so tasty and beautifully served that the kitchen ranks among the top two or

Cafe Society

Café-Restaurant Glockenspiel, Mozartplatz 2 (*©* **0662/84-14-03-0**; bus: 55), is the city's most popular cafe, with about 100 tables with armchairs out front. You might want to spend an afternoon here, particularly when there's live chamber music. Upon entering, you can't miss a glass case filled with every caloric delight west of Vienna. For dinner, you can sit on the balcony and look over Salzburg's famous buildings while enjoying regional and international specialties. Many people, however, come just for the drinks and pastries. Try the Maria Theresia, which contains orange liqueur. In summer, the cafe is open daily from 9am to between 10pm and midnight, and in winter, it's open daily from 9am to between 7 and 8pm, depending on business and the season. Although snacks are available throughout opening hours, warm food is usually available until around 2 hours prior to closing. It's closed the second and third weeks of November and January.

Established in 1705, **Café Tomaselli** ✦, Alter Markt 9 (*©* **0662/ 84-44-88**; bus: 5, 6, or 55), opens onto one of the most charming cobblestone squares of the Altstadt. Aside from the summer chairs placed outdoors, you'll find a high-ceilinged room with many tables. It's a great place to just sit and talk. Another, more formal room to the right of the entrance with oil portraits of well-known 19th-century Salzburgers attracts a haute bourgeois crowd. A waiter will show you a pastry tray filled with 40 different kinds of cakes, which you're free to order or wave away. Other menu items include omelets, wursts, ice cream, and a wide range of drinks. Of course, the pastries and ice cream are all homemade. The cafe is open Monday through Saturday from 7am to midnight and Sunday from 8am to 9pm.

three in Salzburg. Specialties include saddle of farm-raised venison with red cabbage; king prawns in an okra-curry ragout served with perfumed Thai rice; and tenderloin of beef and veal on morel cream sauce with cream potatoes. In season, expect a dish devoted to game, such as venison or roast duckling.

Getreidegasse 37. *©* 0662/80-84-0. Reservations required. Main courses 20€–35€ ($23–$40). 3-course fixed-price lunch or dinner 35€ ($40); 5-course fixed-price dinner 56€ ($64). AE, MC, V. Daily noon–2:30pm and 6:30–9:30pm. Bus: 55.

Purzelbaum ✦ AUSTRIAN/FRENCH   In a residential neighborhood, this restaurant is near a duck pond at the bottom of a steep incline leading up to Salzburg Castle. During the Salzburg Festival you're likely to see the most dedicated music lovers in Europe hanging out here. Menu items change according to the whim of the chef and include such well-prepared dishes as turbot-and-olive casserole; lamb in white-wine sauce with beans and polenta; and the house specialty, scampi Grüstl, composed of fresh shrimp with sliced potatoes baked with herbs in a casserole.

Zugallistrasse 7. *©* 0662/84-88-43. Reservations required. Main courses 22€–29€ ($25–$33); 5-course fixed-price menu 52€–56€ ($60–$64). AE, DC, MC, V. Mon–Sat noon–2pm and 6–11pm. Also open Sun in Aug. Closed July 1–14. Bus: 55.

Moderate

Herzl Tavern ★★ *(Value)* AUSTRIAN/VIENNESE With an entrance on the landmark Karajanplatz, Herzl Tavern lies next door to the glamorous Goldener Hirsch, of which it's a part. Good value attracts both visitors and locals to its pair of cozy rooms, one paneled and timbered. Waitresses in dirndls serve appetizing entrees, which are likely to include roast pork with dumplings, various grills, game stew (in season), and, for the heartiest eaters, a farmer's plate of boiled pork, roast pork, grilled sausages, dumplings, and sauerkraut.

Karajanplatz 7. © 0662/808-4889. Reservations recommended. Main courses 8€–16€ ($9.20–$18). AE, DC, MC, V. Daily 11:30am–10pm. Bus: 55.

Stiftskeller St. Peter (Peterskeller) ★ AUSTRIAN/VIENNESE Legend has it that Mephistopheles met with Faust in this tavern, which isn't that far-fetched, considering it was established by Benedictine monks in A.D. 803. In fact, it's the oldest restaurant in Europe and is housed in the abbey of the church that supposedly brought Christianity to Austria. Aside from a collection of baroque banquet rooms, there's an inner courtyard with rock-cut vaults, a handful of dignified wood-paneled rooms, and a brick-vaulted cellar. In addition to wine from the abbey's own vineyards, the tavern serves good home-style Austrian cooking, including roast pork in gravy with sauerkraut and bread dumplings, and loin of lamb with asparagus. Vegetarian dishes, such as semolina dumplings on noodles in a parsley sauce, are also featured. They are especially known here for their desserts. Try the apple strudel or sweet curd strudel with vanilla sauce or ice cream, and, most definitely, the famed Salzburger Nockerln.

St.-Peter-Bezirk 1–4. © 0662/84-12-680. Reservations recommended. Main courses 10€–23€ ($12–$26); fixed-price menus 18€–45€ ($21–$52). AE, MC, V. Daily 11am–11:45pm. Closed Dec. Bus: 29.

Zum Eulenspiegel ★ AUSTRIAN/VIENNESE Opposite Mozart's birthplace, this restaurant sits at one end of a quiet cobblestone square in the Old Town. Inside, guests have a choice of five rooms on three different levels, all rustically but elegantly decorated. A small and rustic bar area on the ground floor is a pleasant place for predinner drinks. Traditional Austrian cuisine is meticulously adhered to here. The menu features such classic dishes as Tafelspitz, the famous Wiener schnitzel, braised trout with dill-flavored potatoes, pork cutlets with fresh herbs, filet of pork with warm cabbage salad and bacon, and Salzburger Nockerln or peaches with hot fudge and vanilla ice cream for dessert.

Hagenauerplatz 2. © 0662/84-31-80. Reservations required. Main courses 15€–20€ ($17–$23). AE, MC, V. Mon–Sat 11am–2pm and 6–10:30pm. Tram: 2. Bus: 2.

Inexpensive

Festungsrestaurant ★ *(Kids)* SALZBURG/AUSTRIAN Come here and you'll be dining at the former stronghold of the prince-archbishops of Salzburg. The restaurants and gardens are actually in the castle, perched on a huge rock 122m (400 ft.) above the Old Town and the Salzach. The restaurant commands a panoramic view of the city and the surrounding countryside. From Easter to October classical concerts are held nightly in the *Fürstenzimmer,* often featuring the work of Mozart. The kitchen offers local specialties such as a Salzburger *Bierfleisch* (goulash) and Salzburger schnitzel, along with many other dishes. This is good old-fashioned Austrian cooking. In winter, when the restaurant is closed, the *Burgtaverne* inside the castle serves food and drink.

Hohensalzburg, Mönchsberg 34. © 0662/84-17-80. Reservations required July–Aug. Main courses 8.50€–16€ ($9.80–$18). MC, V. Apr–Oct daily 10am–9pm; Dec–Mar daily 10am–5pm. Closed Nov. Funicular from the Old Town.

Krimpelstätter SALZBURGER/AUSTRIAN   This is an enduring Salzburg favorite dating from 1548. In summer, the beer garden, full of roses and trellises, attracts up to 300 visitors at a time. If you want a snack, a beer, or a glass of wine, head for the paneled door marked *Gastezimmer* in the entry corridor. If you're looking for a more formal, less visited area, three cozy antique dining rooms sit atop a flight of narrow stone steps. You'll find tasty and high-quality Land Salzburg regional cuisine featuring wild game dishes. Start with the cream of goose soup or homemade chamois sausage. Traditional main courses include roast pork with dumplings, and fried sausages with sauerkraut and potatoes. Spinach dumplings are topped with a cheese sauce, and marinated beef stew comes with noodles in butter.

Müllner Hauptstrasse 31. ✆ 0662/43-22-74. Reservations recommended. Main courses 6€–12€ ($6.90–$14). No credit cards. Tues–Sat 11am–2pm and 6pm–midnight (also Mon May–Sept). Closed 3 weeks in Jan. Bus: 49 or 95.

Sternbräu AUSTRIAN   This place seems big enough to have fed half the Austro-Hungarian army, with a series of rooms that follow one after the other in varying degrees of formality. The Hofbräustübl is a rustic fantasy. You can also eat in the chestnut-tree-shaded beer garden, usually packed on a summer's night, or under the weathered arcades of an inner courtyard. Daily specials include typical Austrian dishes such as Wiener and chicken schnitzels, trout recipes, cold marinated herring, Hungarian goulash, hearty regional soups, and lots of other *gutbürgerlich* selections. You come here for hearty portions—not for refined cuisine.

Griesgasse 23. ✆ 0662/84-21-40. No reservations. Main courses 8€–15€ ($9.20–$17); fixed-price menu 12€–18€ ($13–$20). AE, MC, V. Daily 9am–11pm. Bus: 2, 5, 12, 49, or 51.

ON THE RIGHT BANK
Expensive
Restaurant Bristol CONTINENTAL   This is the dining counterpart to the upscale restaurant in Salzburg's other top-notch hotel, the Goldener Hirsch. In this case, the venue is a stately, baronial-looking area outfitted in tones of pale orange and accented with large-scale oil paintings. A well-trained staff organizes meals, the best of which include scampi with arugula salad and tomatoes; carpaccio of beef or (in season) venison; Arctic char served with homemade noodles, saffron sauce, and goose liver; roasted lamb served with a gratin of polenta and spinach; and all-vegetarian casseroles.

In the Hotel Bristol, Makartplatz 4. ✆ 0662/873-5577. Reservations recommended. Main courses 21€–28€ ($24–$32). AE, DC, MC, V. Mon–Sat 11am–2pm and 6–10pm. Bus: 1, 5, 29, or 51.

Inexpensive
BIO Wirtshaus Hirschenwirt ★ *Finds* AUSTRIAN   This is a hotel dining room, but a hotel dining room with a difference: All of the ingredients used in its cuisine derive from organically grown ingredients, raised in Austria without chemical fertilizers or insecticides. The setting is a quartet of cozy and traditional-looking dining rooms. Menu items change with the season, but might include a creamy pumpkin soup, carpaccio of Austrian beef, Tafelspitz, several versions of Wiener schnitzel, and about five different vegetarian dishes, the best of which is small spaetzle in a cheese-flavored onion sauce.

In the Hotel zum Hirschen, St. Julien Strasse 23. ✆ 0662/88-13-35. Reservations recommended. Main courses 6.90€–18€ ($7.95–$21). AE, DC, MC, V. Mon–Sat 11am–2pm and 5pm–midnight. Bus: 3 or 6.

Hotel Stadtkrug Restaurant AUSTRIAN/INTERNATIONAL   Across the river from the Altstadt, on the site of a 14th-century farm, this restaurant occupies a structure rebuilt from an older core in 1458. In the 1960s, a modern hotel was added in back. In an antique and artfully rustic setting, you can enjoy hearty, traditional Austrian cuisine, such as cream of potato soup "Old Vienna" style; braised beef with burgundy sauce; or glazed cutlet of pork with caraway seeds, deep-fried potatoes, and French beans with bacon. A dessert specialty is apple strudel.

Linzer Gasse 20. ⓒ **0662/87-35-45.** Reservations recommended. Main courses 15€–24€ ($17–$28). AE, DC, MC, V. Wed–Mon noon–2pm and 6–10:30pm. Bus: 27 or 29.

Zum Fidelen Affen AUSTRIAN   On the eastern edge of the river near the Staatsbrücke, this is the closest thing in Salzburg to a loud, animated, and jovial pub with food service. It's in one of the city's oldest buildings, dating from 1407. Management's policy is to allow only three reserved tables on any particular evening; the remainder are given to whoever happens to show up. It's best to give your name to the maître d'hôtel, then wait at the bar. Menu items are simple, inexpensive, and based on regional culinary traditions. A house specialty is a gratin of green (spinach) noodles in cream sauce with strips of ham. Also popular are Wiener schnitzels, ham goulash with dumplings, casseroles of seasonal meats and mushrooms, and at least three different kinds of main-course dumplings flavored with meats, cheeses, herbs, and various sauces.

Priesterhausgasse 8. ⓒ **0662/877-361.** No reservations. Main courses 8.50€–14€ ($9.80–$16). DC, MC, V. Mon–Sat 5–11:30pm.

SEEING THE SIGHTS IN THE CITY OF MOZART

The Old Town lies between the left bank of the Salzach River and the ridge known as the **Mönchsberg,** which rises to a height of 500m (1,650 ft.) and is the site of Salzburg's gambling casino. The main street of the Altstadt is **Getreidegasse,** a narrow little thoroughfare lined with five- and six-story burghers' buildings. Most of the houses along the street are from the 17th and 18th centuries. Mozart was born at no. 9 (see below). Many lacy-looking wrought-iron signs are displayed, and a lot of the houses have carved windows.

You might begin your tour at **Mozartplatz,** with its outdoor cafes. From here you can walk to the even more expansive Residenzplatz, where torchlight dancing is staged every year, along with outdoor performances.

SIGHTSEEING SUGGESTIONS FOR FIRST-TIME VISITORS

If You Have 1 Day Start slowly with a cup of coffee at the **Café-Restaurant Glockenspiel** on Mozartplatz. Then, from the Altstadt, take the funicular to the **Hohensalzburg Fortress** for a tour. After lunch in an old tavern, visit **Mozart's birthplace** on Getreidegasse, and stroll along the narrow street, most typical in the city. Later, visit the **Residenz.**

If You Have 2 Days In the morning of your second day, explore the **Dom** and the **cemetery of St.**

Peter's, and take a walking tour in the afternoon through the **Altstadt.**

If You Have 3 Days On day 3, visit the many attractions of Salzburg you've missed so far: the **Mönchsberg,** the **Mozart Wohnhaus,** and the **Museum Carolino Augusteum** in the morning. In the afternoon, see the **Mirabell Gardens** and **Mirabell Palace** and at least look at the famous **Festspielhaus (Festival Hall),** dating from 1607; tours are sometimes possible.

THE TOP ATTRACTIONS

Residenz State Rooms/Residenzgalerie Salzburg ★★   This opulent palace, just north of Domplatz in the pedestrian zone, was the seat of the Salzburg prince-archbishops after they no longer needed the protection of the gloomy Hohensalzburg Fortress of Mönchsberg. The Residenz dates from 1120, but work on its series of palaces, which comprised the ecclesiastical complex of the ruling church princes, began in the late 1500s and continued until about 1796. The 17th-century Residenz fountain is one of the largest and most impressive baroque fountains north of the Alps. The child prodigy Mozart often played in the Conference Room for guests. More than a dozen state rooms, each richly decorated, are open to the public via guided tour. On the second floor you can visit the **Residenzgalerie Salzburg** (✆ **0662/84-04-51**, ext. 24), an art gallery containing European paintings from the 16th century to the 19th century.

Residenzplatz 1. ✆ **0662/80-42-26-90** or 0662/84-04-51. Admission to Residenz State Rooms, 5€ ($5.75) adults, 4€ ($4.60) students 16–18 and seniors, 2€ ($2.30) children 6–15, free for children 5 and under. Combined ticket to state rooms and gallery, 7.30€ ($8.40). Residenzgalerie, 5€ ($5.75) adults, 4€ ($4.60) students 16–18 and seniors, 2€ ($2.30) children 6–16. Jan, Mar 26–Oct, and Nov 27–Dec daily 10am–5pm. Bus: 5 or 6.

Glockenspiel (Carillon)   The celebrated glockenspiel with its 35 bells stands across from the Residenz. You can hear this 18th-century carillon at 7am, 11am, and 6pm. At press time, actual visitation of the interior was not allowed. The ideal way to hear the chimes is from one of the cafes lining the edges of the Mozartplatz while sipping your favorite coffee or drink.

Mozartplatz 1. ✆ **0662/80-42-27-84**. Bus: 1, 5, 6, or 51.

Dom (Salzburg Cathedral) ★   Located where Residenzplatz flows into Domplatz, this cathedral is world renowned for its 4,000-pipe organ. Hailed by some critics as the "most perfect" northern Renaissance building, the cathedral has a marble facade and twin symmetrical towers. The mighty bronze doors were created in 1959. The themes are Faith, Hope, and Love. The interior has a rich baroque style with elaborate frescoes, the most important of which, along with the altarpieces, were designed by Mascagni of Florence. In the crypt, traces of the old Romanesque cathedral have been unearthed.

The treasure of the cathedral and the "arts and wonders" the archbishops collected in the 17th century are displayed in the **Dom Museum** entered through the cathedral. The **cathedral excavations** around the corner (left of the Dom entrance), show the ruins of the original foundation.

South side of Residenzplatz. ✆ **0662/84-41-89**. Free admission to cathedral; excavations 2€ ($2.30) adults, .80€ (90¢) children 6–15, free for children 5 and under; museum 5€ ($5.75) adults, 1.50€ ($1.75) children. Cathedral daily 8am–7pm (to 6pm in winter); excavations May–Sept Tues–Sun 9am–5pm (closed mid-Oct to Easter); museum Wed–Sun 10am–5pm, Sun 1–6pm. Closed Nov–Apr. Bus: 1, 3, or 5.

Stiftskirche St. Peter ★★   Founded in A.D. 696 by St. Rupert, whose tomb is here, this is the church of St. Peter's Abbey and Benedictine Monastery. Once a Romanesque basilica with three aisles, it was completely overhauled in the 17th and 18th centuries in elegant baroque style. The west door dates from 1240. The church is richly adorned with art treasures that include altar paintings by Kremser Schmidt.

St.-Peter-Bezirk. ✆ **0662/844-578**. Free admission. Daily 9am–5pm. Bus: 5, 6, or 55.

Petersfriedhof (St. Peter's Cemetery) ★★   This cemetery lies at the stone wall that merges into the Mönchsberg. Many of the aristocratic families of Salzburg lie buried here, as do many other noted persons, including Nannerl

Mozart, sister of Wolfgang Amadeus (4 years older than her better-known brother, Nannerl was also an exceptionally gifted musician). You can see the Romanesque Chapel of the Holy Cross and St. Margaret's Chapel, dating from the 15th century. You can also take a self-guided tour through the early Christian catacombs in the rock above the church cemetery.

St.-Peter-Bezirk. © 0662/84-45-76-0. Free admission to cemetery. Catacombs 1€ ($1.15) adults, .60€ (70¢) children. May–Sept daily 10:30am–5pm; Oct–Apr Wed–Thurs 10:30am–3:30pm, Fri–Sun 10:30am–4pm. Bus: 1.

Hohensalzburg Fortress ★★ *Kids*   The stronghold of the ruling prince-arch-bishops before they moved "downtown" to the Residenz, this fortress towers 120m (400 ft.) above the Salzach River on a rocky dolomite ledge. The massive fortress crowns the Festungsberg and literally dominates Salzburg. Work on Hohensalzburg began in 1077 and wasn't finished until 1681. This is the largest completely preserved castle in central Europe. The elegant state apartments, once the courts of the prince-archbishops, are on display. The **Burgmuseum** contains a collection of medieval art. Plans and prints tracing the growth of Salzburg are on exhibit, as well as instruments of torture and many Gothic arti-facts. The **Rainermuseum** has displays of arms and armor. The beautiful late-Gothic **St. George's Chapel** (1501) is adorned with marble reliefs of the apostles. If you're athletic you can reach the fortress on foot from Kapitelplatz by way of Festungsgasse or from the Mönchsberg via the Schartentor.

Visit Hohensalzburg even if you're not interested in the fortress, just for the view from the terrace. From the Reck watchtower you get a panoramic sweep of the Alps. The Kuenberg bastion has a fine view of Salzburg's domes and towers.

You can see the fortress grounds on your own or take a tour of the interior. Conducted 40- to 50-minute tours go through the fortress daily, but hours and departure times depend on the season: November through March, from 10am to 4pm; April through June, from 9:30am to 5pm; July through August, from 9am to 6pm; and September through October, from 9:30am to 5pm. The con-ducted tour of the fortress and the Rainier Museum costs 3.60€ ($4.15) adults, 2€ ($2.30) children 6 to 15, free for children under 6.

Mönchsberg 34. © 0662/84-24-30-11. Admission (excluding guided tour but including museum) 7.20€ ($8.30) adults, 4€ children 6–19, free for children 5 and under. Family ticket 16€ ($18). Fortress and muse-ums Oct–Mar daily 9:30am–4:30pm; Apr–Sept daily 9:30am–5:30pm.

MORE ATTRACTIONS

Mozart Geburtshaus (Mozart's Birthplace) ★   The house where Wolfgang Amadeus Mozart was born on January 27, 1756, contains exhibition rooms and the apartment of the Mozart family. The main treasures are the valuable paint-ings (such as the well-known *Mozart and the Piano,* by Joseph Lange) and the violin Mozart used as a child; his concert violin; and his viola, fortepiano, and clavichord.

Getreidegasse 9. © 0662/84-43-13. Admission 5.50€ ($6.35) adults, 4.50€ ($5.20) students, 1.50€ ($1.75) children 6–14. Daily 9am–6pm.

Mozart Wohnhaus (Mozart Residence) ★   In 1773, the Mozart family vacated the cramped quarters of Mozart's birthplace, and the young Mozart lived here with his family until 1780. In the rooms of the former Mozart family apartments, a museum documents the history of the house and the life and work of Wolfgang Amadeus. The original house was destroyed by bombing in 1944, was rebuilt, and reopened on the eve of Mozart's birthday in 1996. A mechanized audio tour in six languages with relevant musical samples accompanies the visitor through the rooms of the museum.

Makartplatz 8. ℂ **0662/84-43-13.** Admission 5.50€ ($6.35) adults, 4.45€ ($5.10) students, 1.50€ ($1.75) children 14 and under. Daily 9am–6pm.

Schloss Mirabell (Mirabell Palace) ✯ This palace and its gardens were built as a luxurious private residence called Altenau. Prince-Archbishop Wolf Dietrich had it constructed in 1606 for his mistress and the mother of his children, Salome Alt. Not much remains of the original grand structure. Lukas von Hildebrandt rebuilt the *schloss* in the first quarter of the 18th century, and it was modified after a great fire in 1818. The palace, which is a smaller version of the Tuileries in Paris, today serves as the official residence of the mayor of Salzburg. The ceremonial marble "angel staircase," with its sculptured cherubs, carved by Raphael Doner in 1726, is a stunning piece of architectural fantasy.

Rainerstrasse. ℂ **0662/8072-0.** Free admission. Staircase: daily 8am–6pm. Bus: 1, 5, 6, or 51.

Museum Carolino Augusteum Several collections are brought together under one roof in this museum reflecting Salzburg's cultural history. The archaeological collection contains the well-known Dürnberg beaked pitcher, as well as Roman mosaics. Some 15th-century Salzburg art is on view, and there are many paintings from the Romantic period, as well as works by Hans Makart, born in Salzburg in 1840.

Museumsplatz 1. ℂ **0662/6208-08-111.** Admission 3.50€ ($4.05) adults, 2.70€ ($3.10) seniors over 60, 1.10€ ($1.25) children 6–19, free for children 5 and under. Daily 9am–5pm (until 8pm on Thurs). Bus: 2, 3, or 51.

Mönchsberg ✯✯ This heavily forested ridge extends for some 2km (1½ miles) above the Altstadt and has fortifications dating from the 15th century. A panoramic view of Salzburg is possible from Mönchsberg Terrace just in front of the Grand Café Winkler.

West of the Hohensalzburg Fortress. ℂ **0662/448-06-285.** The elevators leave daily 9am–11pm; round-trip fare is 2.60€ ($3) adults, 1.30€ ($1.50) children 6–15, free for children 5 and under.

Mirabell-Garten (Mirabell Gardens) ✯ Laid out by Fischer von Erlach on the right bank of the river off Makartplatz, these baroque gardens are studded with statuary and reflecting pools, making them a virtual open-air museum. Be sure to visit the bastion with fantastic marble baroque dwarfs and other figures, by the Pegasus Fountains in the lavish garden west of Schloss Mirabell. You'll also find a natural theater. In summer, free brass band concerts are held Wednesday at 8:30pm and Sunday at 10:30am. From the gardens, you have an excellent view of the Hohensalzburg Fortress.

Free admission. Daily 7am–8pm. Bus: 1, 5, 6, or 51.

ORGANIZED TOURS

The best-organized tours are offered by **Salzburg Panorama Tours,** Mirabellplatz (ℂ **0662/88-32-11-0;** www.panoramatours.at), which is the Gray Line company for Salzburg.

The original *"Sound of Music* **Tour"** combines the Salzburg city tour with an excursion to the lake district and other places where the 1965 film with Julie Andrews was shot. The English-speaking guide shows you not only the highlights from the film, but also historical and architectural landmarks in Salzburg and parts of the Salzkammergut countryside. The 4½-hour tour departs daily at 9am and 2pm and costs 33€ ($38).

You must take your passport along for any of the three trips into **Bavaria** in Germany. One of these—called the **"Eagle's Nest Tour"**—takes visitors to Berchtesgaden and on to Obersalzburg, where Hitler and his inner circle had a vacation retreat. The 4½-hour tour departs daily at 9am, May 15 through October 20, and costs 45€ ($52). **"The City & Country Highlights"** tour takes in historic castles and the surrounding Land Salzburg landscape. This 5-hour tour departs daily at 2pm, and costs 45€ ($52). Coffee and pastry at the Castle Fuschl are an added treat.

You can book these tours at the bus terminal at Mirabellplatz/St. Andrä Kirche (© 0662/87-40-29). Tour prices are the same for all ages.

THE SHOPPING SCENE

Good buys in Salzburg include souvenirs of Salzburg state, dirndls, lederhosen, petit point, and all types of sports gear. **Getreidegasse** is a main shopping thoroughfare, but you'll also find some intriguing little shops on **Residenzplatz.**

Opened in 1871, **Drechslerei Lackner,** Badergasse 2 (© 0662/84-23-85; bus: 68 or 81), offers both antique and modern country wood furniture. Among the new items are chests, chessboards, angels, cupboards, crèches, candlesticks, and, most definitely, chairs. **Musikhaus Pühringer,** Getreildegasse 13 (© 0662/84-32-67; bus: 1, 2, 29, or 49), established in 1910, sells all kinds of classical musical instruments, especially those popular in central Europe, as well as a large selection of electronic instruments (including synthesizers and amplifiers). You'll find classical and folk-music CDs and tapes, plus many classical recordings, especially those by Mozart.

Salzburger Heimatwerk, Am Residenzplatz 9 (© 0662/84-41-10; bus: 5 or 55), is one of the best places in town to buy local Austrian handcrafts and original regional clothing.

Wiener Porzellanmanufaktur Augarten Gesellschaft, Alter Markt 11 (© 0662/84-07-14; bus: 2), might very well tempt you to begin a porcelain collection. The origins of this world-class manufacturer go back 275 years. Today, its product is legendary and its patterns, such as *Wiener Rose, Maria Theresia,* and the highly distinctive *Biedermeier,* are well known. The company also produces such historical pieces as the black-and-white demitasse set created by architect/designer Josef Hoffman.

SALZBURG AFTER DARK
THE PERFORMING ARTS

It's said there's a musical event—often a Mozart concert—staged virtually every night in Salzburg. To find the venue, visit the **Salzburg tourist office,** Mozartplatz 5 (© 0662/88987-330). Here you'll be given a free copy of *Offizieller Wochenspiegel,* a monthly pamphlet listing all major and many minor local cultural events. The annual Mozart Week is in January.

Tips **Getting Tickets to the Salzburg Festival**

One of the premier music attractions of Europe, the Salzburg Festival celebrated its 85th season in 2005. Details on the festival are available by contacting **Salzburg Festival,** Hofstallgasse 1, A-5010 Salzburg, Austria (© 0662/8045-579; www.salzburgfestival.at).

The major ticket agency affiliated with the city of Salzburg is located adjacent to Salzburg's main tourist office, at Mozartplatz 5. The **Salzburger Ticket Office** (© **0662/84-03-10**) is open Monday through Friday from 9am to 6pm (to 7pm in midsummer) and Saturday from 9am to noon.

If you don't want to pay a ticket agent's commission, you can go directly to the box office of a theater or concert hall. However, many of the best seats may have already been sold, especially those at the Salzburg Festival.

CONCERTS & OTHER ENTERTAINMENT

The rich collection of concerts that combine every summer to form the Salzburg Festival's program are presented in several different concert halls scattered throughout Salzburg. The largest is the **Festspielhaus,** Hofstallgasse 1 (© **0662/ 8045;** bus: 1, 5, or 6). Within the Festspielhaus complex you'll find the **Felsen-reitschule,** an outdoor auditorium with a makeshift roof. Originally built in 1800 as a riding rink, it's famous as the site where scenes from *The Sound of Music* were filmed. Tickets cost from 15€ to 330€ ($17–$380) (the higher cost for the best seats at the Salzburg Festival); average but good seats run 35€ to 80€ ($40–$92). Instead of going directly to the Festspielhaus, you can purchase tickets in advance at the box office at Waagplatz 1A (© **0662/84-53-46**), close to the tourist office, Monday through Friday from 8am to 6pm.

On the right back of the Salzach River, near the Mirabell Gardens, is the **Mozarteum,** Schwarzstrasse 26 and Mirabellplatz 1 (© **0662/87-31-54;** bus: 1, 5, 6, or 51), the major music and concert hall of Salzburg. All the big orchestra concerts, as well as organ recitals and chamber-music evenings, are offered here. It's also a music school, and you can ask about free events staged by the students. The box office is open Monday through Thursday from 9am to 2pm and Friday from 9am to 4pm with some exceptions. Performances are usually at 11am or 7:30pm. Tickets cost 10€ to 220€ ($112–$253); the best seats run from 90€ to 350€ ($104–$403).

Besides the venues above, you can attend a concert in dramatic surroundings in the Fürstenzimmer (Prince's Chamber) of the **Hohensalzburg Fortress.** You're likely to hear heavy doses of Mozart and, to a lesser degree, works by Schubert, Brahms, and Beethoven. From mid-May to mid-October, performances are generally held at 9am or 8:30pm every night of the week. The rest of the year, they're presented most (but not all) nights, with occasional weeklong breaks, usually at 7:30pm. The box office for the events is at Adlgasser Weg 22 (© **0662/ 82-58-58**). To reach the fortress, take the funicular from Festungsgasse.

BEER GARDENS

Regardless of the season, you'll have one of your most enjoyable and authentic evenings in Salzburg at **Augustiner Bräustübl,** Augustinergasse 4 (© **0662/ 43-12-46;** bus: 27). This Bierstube and Biergarten has been dispensing oceans of beer since it was established in 1622. Depending on the weather, the city's beer-drinking fraternity gathers either within the cavernous interior, where three separate rooms each hold up to 400 people, or in the chestnut-shaded courtyard. You'll find about a dozen kiosks, where you can buy takeout portions of wursts, sandwiches, and pretzels. Farther on, choose a thick stoneware mug from the racks and carry it to the beer tap, paying the cashier as you go. A full liter begins at 4.80€ ($5.50); a half liter costs 2.40€ ($2.75) depending on the type of beer. The place is open Monday through Friday from 3 to 11pm and Saturday and Sunday from 2:30 to 11pm.

Immediately below the Hohensalzburg Fortress and established in the early 1800s, part of the **Stiegelkeller,** Festungsgasse 10 (✆ **0662/84-26-81;** bus: 5, 6, or 55), is carved into the rocks of Mönchsberg. To get here, you'll have to negotiate a steep cobblestone street that drops off on one side to reveal a panoramic view of Salzburg. The cavernous interior is open only in summer, when you can join hundreds of others in drinking beer and eating sausages, schnitzels, and other Bierkeller food.

Sound of Music **dinner shows,** featuring music from the film, are presented in the Stiegelkeller May through September, daily from 7:30 to 10pm. A three-course meal and show cost 45€ ($52). Or you can arrive at 8:15pm to see the show and just have Apfelstrudel and coffee for 28€ ($32). On the first Sunday of the month, a *Fruhschoppen*—a traditional Salzburger music fest—is presented from 10:30pm to midnight. No ticket is necessary—you pay for what you eat and drink. Likewise, no ticket is necessary to attend another musical evening, a *Happing,* staged May through September, every Thursday from 6 to 8pm.

No one in Salzburg is really sure whether to classify **Salzburger Altstadtkeller,** Rudolfskai 26 (✆ **0662/849688**), as a restaurant, an inn, a pub, or a nightclub, since it combines so gracefully elements of all of them. The result is fun and convivial. The setting is a medieval cellar beneath the Altstadt Radisson Hotel, immediately adjacent to the banks of the river. Don't come here expecting fine dining: What you'll get is a short list of Austrian-style platters, and a reverberating roster of musical acts that include swing, Latino, jazz, and blues. Every Thursday, the acts get more nostalgic and folkloric, as the stage is turned over to bands specializing in Austrian or Bavarian "evergreen" music. Music plays from around 9:15pm to 1am, with guests then lingering over their drinks for at least another hour. There's no cover charge, but a half-liter mug of beer costs 3.30€ ($3.80). Main courses cost from 8€ to 10€ ($9.20–$12). Service is Tuesday to Saturday from 7pm to 3am.

3 Innsbruck ✦ & Tyrol

Land of ice and mountains, dark forests and alpine meadows full of spring wildflowers, summer holidays and winter sports—that's Tyrol. Those intrepid tourists, the British, discovered its vacation delights and made it a fashionable destination in the last century. Tyrol is now the most frequented winter playground in Austria, and in summer, the extensive network of mountain paths lures visitors.

Skiers flock here in winter for a ski season that runs from mid-December to the end of March. Many prefer its ski slopes to those of Switzerland. It's been a long time since the eyes of the world focused on Innsbruck at the Winter Olympics in 1964 and 1976, but the legacy lives on in the ski conditions and facilities on some of the world's choicest slopes.

INNSBRUCK

Innsbruck has a particularly lovely medieval town center, and town planners have protected this historic Altstadt. Visitors can take countless excursions in the environs; at Innsbruck's doorstep lie some of the most beautiful drives in Europe. Just take your pick: Head in any direction, up any valley, and you'll be treated to mountains and alpine beauty almost unmatched anywhere else, including Switzerland.

Innsbruck

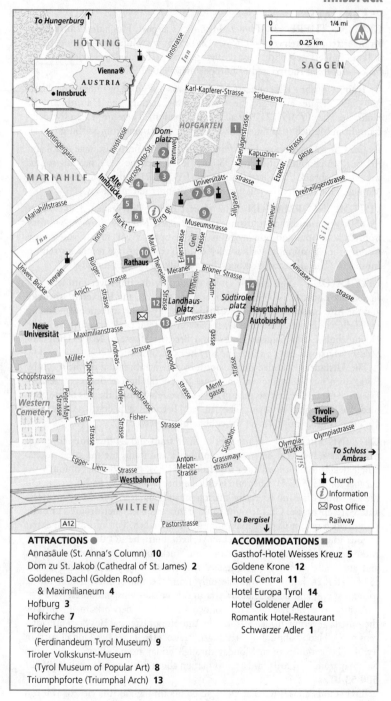

ESSENTIALS

GETTING THERE   By Plane   Innsbruck's airport, **Flughafen Innsbruck-Kranebitten,** Fürstenweg 180 (© **0512/22525;** www.Innsbruck-airport.com), is 3km (2 miles) west of the city. It offers regularly scheduled air service from the major airports of Austria and of Europe's major cities.

By Train   Innsbruck is connected with all parts of Europe by international railway links. Trains arrive at the main railway station, the **Hauptbahnhof,** Südtiroler Platz (© **05/1717** for all rail information). There are at least five daily trains from Munich (trip time: 3 hr.) and eight daily trains from Salzburg (1 hr.).

By Car   If you're **driving** down from Salzburg in the northeast, take Autobahn A8 west, which joins Autobahn A93 (later it becomes the A12), heading southwest to Innsbruck. This latter Autobahn (A93/A12) is the main artery from Munich. From the south, you can take the Brenner toll motorway.

VISITOR INFORMATION   The **tourist office,** Burggraben 3 (© **0512/ 59-850;** www.innsbruck-tourismus.com), is open Monday through Saturday from 8am to 6pm and Sunday from 9am to 6pm. It will supply you with a wealth of information, as well as a list of inexpensive private rooms for rent in Innsbruck. The office can also book bus or walking tours of the city.

CITY LAYOUT   This historic city is divided by the Inn River into left- and right-bank districts. Two major bridges cross the Inn, the **Universittssbrücke** and the **Alte Innsbrücke (Old Inn Bridge).** Many of the attractions, including the Hofkirche and the Goldenes Dachl, are on the right bank. If you arrive at the Hauptbahnhof, take Salurner Strasse and Brixener Strasse to Maria-Theresien-Strasse, which will put you into the very heart of Innsbruck.

The **Altstadt** is bounded on the north by the Inn River and on the south by Burggraben and Marktgrabben. The main street of this historic district is **Herzog-Friedrich-Strasse,** which becomes **Maria-Theresien-Strasse,** the axis of the postmedieval new part of town. The Altstadt becomes a pedestrian zone after 10:30am (wear good shoes on the cobblestone streets).

GETTING AROUND   A network of three **tram** and 25 **bus lines** covers all of Innsbruck and its close environs, and buses and trams use the same tickets. Single tickets in the central area cost 1.60€ ($1.85), and a booklet of four tickets goes for 5€ ($5.75). The tram is called either *Strassenbahn* or *Trambahn.* On the left bank of the Inn River, the main tram and bus arteries are Museumstrasse and Mariahilfstrasse. On the right bank, trams and buses aren't routed into the pedestrian zone but to their main stop in Marktgraben. For information about various routes, call the **Innsbrucker Verkehrsbetriebe** (© **0512/530-7102**). Most tickets can be purchased at the Innsbruck tourist office, tobacco shops, and automated vending machines. A *Tageskarte* **(day pass),** costing 3.30€ ($3.80) for 24 hours, is available only from the tourist information office, tobacco shops, and cafes. It allows you to ride on all trains and buses.

Austria Postal Service buses (one of two different bus networks maintained by the Austria government) leave from the Autobushof (Central Bus Station), adjacent to the Hauptbahnhof on Sterzinger Strasse. Here buses head for all parts of Tyrol. The station is open Monday through Friday from 7:30am to 6pm and Saturday from 7am to 1pm. For information about bus schedules, call © **0512/ 500-53-07.**

Taxi stands are scattered at strategic points throughout the city, or you can call a radio car (© **0512/5311**). For a nostalgic ride, you can hire a horse-drawn carriage *(Fiaker)* from a spot adjacent to the **Tiroler Landestheater,** Rennweg.

If neither the tram nor the carriage options appeal to you, consider renting a **bike** at the Hauptbahnhof. Rentals cost 20€ ($23) per day or 16€ ($18) for 5 hours. You can return these bikes to any rail station in Austria if you don't plan to return to Innsbruck. Rentals are available April through early November only. For more information, call **Sport Neuner** (© **0512/561-501**).

Although you can make a better deal renting a car before you leave North America, it's possible to rent cars in Innsbruck. You might try **Avis,** Salurner Strasse 15 (© **0512/57-17-54**); or **Hertz,** Südtirolerplatz 1 (© **0512/58-29-51**), across from the Hauptbahnhof. Although paperwork and billing errors are harder to resolve whenever you rent from a non-U.S.-based car-rental outfit, you might also check the rates at a local car outfitter, **Ajax,** Amrasserstrasse 6 (© **0512/583-232**).

FAST FACTS: Innsbruck

Currency Exchange Banks are usually open Monday through Thursday from 7:45am to 12:30pm and 2:30 to 4pm; and Friday from 7:45am to 3pm. There are also exchange facilities at Innsbruck's tourist office (see above). The automated currency exchange facilities at the Hauptbahnhof are available 24 hours a day.

Dentists/Doctors Check with the tourist office for a list of private English-speaking dentists and doctors; or contact the **University Clinic,** Anichstrasse 35 (© **0512/504**).

Drugstores In the heart of Innsbruck, **St.-Anna Apotheke,** Maria-Theresien-Strasse 4 (© **0512/58-58-47**), is open Monday to Saturday from 8am to 6pm. The pharmacy posts addresses of other pharmacies open on weekends or at night.

Emergencies In case of trouble, call © **133** for the police, © **122** for a fire, or © **144** for an ambulance.

Internet Access You can check e-mail or access the Internet for a fee of 11€ ($13) an hour at the **Picasso Internet Café,** Maria-Theresien-Strasse 16 (© **0512/58-48-48**; tram: 3). It's open Monday to Saturday from 6:30am to 1am.

Post Office The **Hauptpostamt (Central Post Office),** Maximilianstrasse 2 (© **0512/5000**), is open daily from 8am to 9pm. The post office at the **Hauptbahnhof,** Bruneckstrasse 1–3 (© **0512/5000**), is open Monday through Saturday from 6:30am to 9pm.

Telephone The **country code** for Austria is **43**. The **city code** for Innsbruck is **512**; use this code when you're calling from outside Austria. If you're within Austria, use **0512**.

WHERE TO STAY
Very Expensive

Hotel Europa Tyrol ★★   The town's finest and most elegant hotel stands opposite the rail station, inviting you inside its formal lobby. The spacious rooms and suites are handsomely furnished, with all the modern conveniences and Tyrolean or Biedermeier-style decorations. Each tasteful unit offers a bathroom equipped with a tub/shower combo. The restaurant, **Europastüberl** (p. 93), is the finest in Tyrol.

Südtirolerplatz 2, A-6020 Innsbruck. © **800/223-5652** in the U.S. and Canada, or 0512/5931. Fax 0512/ 58-78-00. www.europatyrol.com. 122 units. 183€–288€ ($210–$331) double; 320€–450€ ($368–$518) suite. Rates include breakfast. AE, DC, MC, V. Parking 15€ ($17). **Amenities:** Restaurant; bar; sauna; solarium; 24-hr. room service; babysitting; laundry service/dry cleaning; 1 nonsmoking room; rooms for those with limited mobility. *In room:* TV, dataport, minibar, hair dryer, safe.

Expensive

Romantik Hotel-Restaurant Schwarzer Adler ★★ This is it for those who like authentic Austrian charm. The hotel's owners, the Ultsch family, have furnished the charming interior with hand-painted regional furniture, antiques, and lots of homey clutter, making for a cozy and inviting ambience. The midsize rooms are virtually one of a kind, each with its special character. Beds are exceedingly comfortable, with some of the thickest mattresses in town and well-stuffed duvets. Bathrooms have dual basins and tub/shower combos with powerful showerheads. We prefer the older accommodations, which are more spacious and have more Tyrolean character.

Kaiserjägerstrasse 2, A-6020 Innsbruck. © **0512/58-71-09.** Fax 0512/56-16-97. www.deradler.com. 39 units. 150€–187€ ($173–$215) double; 275€–445€ ($316–$512) suite. Additional person 46€ ($53). Rates include breakfast. AE, DC, MC, V. Parking 9€ ($10). Tram: 1 or 3. **Amenities:** Restaurant; bar; fitness center; health spa; 24-hr. room service; massage; laundry service/dry cleaning; nonsmoking rooms; rooms for those with limited mobility. *In room:* A/C, TV, dataport (in some), minibar, hair dryer, safe.

Moderate

Hotel Central One of the most unusual hotels in Innsbruck, Hotel Central was originally built in the 1860s, but from its very modern exterior you might not realize it. The comfortable rooms have an Art Deco design that evokes an almost Japanese simplicity. Most rooms are quite spacious with excellent beds. Bathrooms are small, with shower units. In total contrast to the simplicity of the rest of the hotel, the ground floor contains a grand Viennese cafe with marble columns, sculpted ceilings, and large gilt-and-crystal chandeliers.

Gilmstrasse 5, A-6020 Innsbruck. © **0512/59-20.** Fax 0512/58-03-10. www.central.co.at. 85 units. 125€–148€ ($144–$170) double. Rates include breakfast. Additional person 21€ ($24) extra. AE, DC, MC, V. Parking 12€ ($14). Tram: 1 or 3. **Amenities:** Restaurant; bar; fitness center; sauna; limited room service; laundry service/dry cleaning; nonsmoking rooms. *In room:* TV, minibar, hair dryer.

Hotel Goldener Adler ★★ Even the phone booth near the reception desk of this 600-year-old family-run hotel is outfitted in antique style. Famous guests have included Goethe, Mozart, and the violinist Paganini, who cut his name into the windowpane of his room. Rooms are handsomely furnished, and vary in size and decor. Some have decorative Tyrolean architectural features such as beamed ceilings. Others are furnished in a more modern style. The bathroom's size depends on your room assignment; bathrooms can be everything from spacious combination models to cramped rooms with shower stalls.

Herzog-Friedrich-Strasse 6, A-6020 Innsbruck. © **0512/57-11-11.** Fax 0512/58-44-09. www.goldeneradler.com. 35 units. 128€–168€ ($147–$193) double; from 198€ ($228) suite. Rates include breakfast. AE, DC, MC, V. Parking 11€ ($13). Tram: 1 or 3. **Amenities:** Restaurant; bar; limited room service; babysitting; laundry service/ dry cleaning; nonsmoking rooms; 1 room for those with limited mobility. *In room:* TV, minibar, hair dryer, safe.

Inexpensive

Gasthof-Hotel Weisses Kreuz ★ *Value* This atmospheric inn, located in the center of Innsbruck, has not changed much during its lifetime. Rooms are cozy and atmospheric, either small or medium size, with comfortable furnishings. Some have private bathrooms with neatly kept shower units. Hallway bathrooms are adequate and well maintained. In 1769, 13-year-old Wolfgang Mozart and his father, Leopold, stayed here.

Herzog-Friedrich-Strasse 31, A-6020 Innsbruck. (© 0512/594790. Fax 0512/59-47-990. www.weisseskreuz.at. 40 units, 31 with bathroom. 63€–66€ ($72–$76) double without bathroom; 84€–109€ ($97–$125) double with bathroom. Rates include breakfast. AE, MC, V. Parking 9€ ($10). Tram: 3. **Amenities:** Restaurant; bar; limited room service; nonsmoking rooms. *In room:* TV.

Goldene Krone *Value* Near the Triumphal Arch on Innsbruck's main street, this baroque house is one of the city's best budget bets. All rooms are modern, comfortable, well maintained, and, for the most part, spacious with plenty of light. The duvet-covered beds are comfortable, and bathrooms are small but spotless, with shower stalls. The hotel offers a Viennese-inspired coffeehouse/restaurant, the **Art Gallery-Café.**

Maria-Theresien-Strasse 46, A-6020. Innsbruck. (© **0512/58-61-60.** Fax 0512/580-18-96. www.city-crownhotel-innsbruck.com. 39 units. 85€–105€ ($98–$121) double; 110€–142€ ($127–$163) suite. Rates include breakfast. AE, MC, V. Parking 7.50€ ($8.65). Tram: 1. Bus: A, H, K, or N. **Amenities:** Restaurant; bar; cafe; lounge; nonsmoking rooms; rooms for those with limited mobility. *In room:* TV, dataport.

WHERE TO DINE
Expensive

Europastüberl ★★ AUSTRIAN/INTERNATIONAL This distinguished restaurant, with a delightful Tyrolean ambience, is in a hotel that's the finest address in Innsbruck. The chef succeeds beautifully in fashioning creative takes on traditional regional cooking. Diners can choose from both warm and cold appetizers, ranging from iced anglerfish with Chinese tree morels to a small ragout of crayfish in a spicy biscuit with kohlrabi. Some dishes are served only for two people, such as Bresse guinea hen roasted and presented with an herb sauce. Fresh Tyrolean trout almost always appears on the menu, or you may prefer the meat dishes, ranging from red deer ragout to saddle of venison to fried jelly of calf's head Vienna-style with a lamb's tongue salad.

In the Hotel Europa Tyrol, Brixnerstrasse 6. (© 0512/5931. Reservations required. Main courses 11€–25€ ($13–$29); fixed-price 3-course menu 38€ ($44); fixed-price 4-course menu 42€ ($48). AE, DC, MC, V. Daily 11:30am–2:30pm and 6:30–11pm.

Restaurant Goldener Adler ★ AUSTRIAN/TYROLEAN/INTERNA-TIONAL Richly Teutonic and steeped in the decorative traditions of alpine Tyrol, this beautifully decorated restaurant has a deeply entrenched reputation and a loyal following among local residents. The menu includes good, hearty fare inspired by cold-weather outdoor life—the chefs aren't into delicate subtleties. Examples of the cuisine are Tyrolean bacon served with horseradish and farmer's bread; cream of cheese soup with croutons; and Tyroler *Zopfebraten,* a flavorful age-old specialty consisting of strips of veal steak served with herb-enriched cream sauce and spinach dumplings. A well-regarded specialty is a platter known as *Adler Tres.* It contains spinach dumplings, stuffed noodles, and cheese dumplings, all flavorfully tied together with a brown butter sauce and a gratin of mountain cheese.

Herzog-Friedrich-Strasse 6. (© 0512/57-11-11. Reservations recommended. Main courses 14€–21€ ($16–$24); set menus 18€–45€ ($21–$52). AE, DC, MC, V. Daily 11:30am–10:30pm. Tram: 1 or 3.

Restaurant Schwarzer Adler ★★ AUSTRIAN Even if you're not a guest at the richly atmospheric Romantik Hotel, you might appreciate a meal within its historic premises. Among the finest examples of the elaborate cuisine is a salad of wild quail served with lentils, strips of braised gooseliver, and a sauce that's enhanced with apple liqueur. The wine list is long, broad, and impressive, with lots of wines from relatively obscure regions of Austria.

In the Romantik Hotel, Kaiserjägerstrasse 2. (€) 0512/587-109. Reservations recommended. Main courses 18€–25€ ($21–$29). AE, DC, MC, V. Mon–Sat 11am–2pm and 6–10:30pm. Tram: 1 or 3.

Moderate

Hirschen-Stuben INTERNATIONAL   Beneath a vaulted ceiling in a house built in 1631, this restaurant is charming, well established, and welcoming. By its own admission, the establishment is at its best in spring, autumn, and winter, since it lacks a garden or outdoor terrace for alfresco summer dining. Menu items include steaming platters of pasta, fish soup, trout meunière, sliced veal in cream sauce Zurich style, beef Stroganoff, pepper steak, stewed deer with vegetables, and filet of flounder with parsley and potatoes. The kitchen staff is equally familiar with the cuisines of both Austria and Italy.

Kiebachgasse 5. (€) 0512/58-29-79. Reservations recommended. Main courses 6.90€–21€ ($7.95–$24). DC, MC, V. Mon–Sat 6–11pm. Tram: 1 or 3.

Inexpensive

Restaurant Ottoburg ☆ AUSTRIAN/INTERNATIONAL   This historic restaurant, established around 1745, occupies a 13th-century building that some historians say is the oldest in Innsbruck. Inside, four intimate and atmospheric dining rooms—with a decor that is best described as "19th-century neo-Gothic"—lie scattered over two different floors. Hearty dishes include venison stew, "grandmother's mixed grill," and fried trout. In summer, a beer garden operates in the rear, open April to October Tuesday to Sunday from 11am to midnight.

Herzog-Friedrich-Strasse 1. (€) 0512/58-43-38. Reservations recommended. Main courses 9€–21€ ($10–$24). AE, DC, MC, V. Tues–Sun 11am–3pm and 6pm–midnight. Tram: 1 or 3.

Weisses Rössl ☆ AUSTRIAN/TYROLEAN   You'll enter this time-honored place through a stone archway set on one of the Old Town's most famous streets. At the end of a flight of stairs, marked with a very old crucifix, you'll find a trio of dining rooms with red-tile floors and a history of welcoming guests since 1590. At first glance, the menu appears simple, listing such dishes as a Tyroler *Grüstl* (a kind of hash composed of sautéed onions, sliced beef, alpine herbs, and potatoes cooked and served in a frying pan), *Safigoulash* with polenta, several kinds of schnitzels, and a grilled platter *(Alt Insprugg)* for two diners.

Kiebachgasse 8. (€) 0512/58-30-57. Reservations recommended. Main courses 7.20€–16€ ($8.30–$18); 3-course lunch 5€–10€ ($5.75–$12); 3-course dinner 15€–20€ ($17–$23). AE, DC, MC, V. Mon–Sat 11:30am–2:30pm and 6–10pm. Closed 2 weeks after Easter and 2 weeks in Nov. Tram: 1 or 3.

EXPLORING THE TOWN

The Altstadt and the surrounding alpine countryside are Innsbruck's main attractions. Often it's fascinating just to watch the passersby, who are occasionally attired in Tyrolean regional dress.

Maria-Theresien-Strasse ☆, which cuts through the heart of the city from north to south, is the main street and a good place to begin exploring the city. Many 17th- and 18th-century houses line this wide street. On the south end of the street, there's a **Triumphpforte (Triumphal Arch),** modeled after those in Rome. Maria Theresa ordered it built in 1765 to honor her son's marriage and to commemorate the death of her beloved husband, Emperor Franz I. From this arch southward the street is called Leopoldstrasse.

Going north from the arch along Maria-Theresien-Strasse, you'll see **Annasäule** (**St. Anna's Column**) in front of the 19th-century Rathaus (town hall). The column was erected in 1706 to celebrate the withdrawal in 1703 of invading Bavarian armies during the War of the Spanish Succession. Not far north of the Annasäule, the wide street narrows and becomes **Herzog-Friedrich-Strasse,** running through the heart of the medieval quarter. This street is arcaded and flanked by a number of well-maintained burghers' houses with their jumble of turrets and gables; look for the multitude of dormer windows and oriels.

Goldenes Dachl (Golden Roof) & Maximilianeum ★ "The Golden Roof," Innsbruck's greatest tourist attraction and its most characteristic landmark, is a three-story balcony on a house in the Altstadt; the late-Gothic oriels are capped with 2,657 gold-plated tiles. It was constructed for Emperor Maximilian I in the beginning of the 16th century to serve as a royal box where he could sit in luxury and enjoy tournaments in the square below.

A small museum, the **Maximilianeum,** is on the second floor of the municipal building attached to the Goldenes Dachl. Inside are exhibits celebrating the life and accomplishments of the Innsbruck-based Hapsburg emperor, Maximilian I, who bridged the gap between the Middle Ages and the German Renaissance.

You can also visit the **Stadtturm (City Tower),** Herzog-Friedrich-Strasse 21 (© **0512/561-5003**). Formerly a prison cell, the tower dates from the mid-1400s and stands adjacent to the Rathaus. Its top affords a panoramic view of the city rooftops and the mountains beyond. It's open daily from 10am to 5pm (to 8pm July–Aug). Admission is 2.50€ ($2.90) adults and 1€ ($1.15) children 17 and under, 5.50€ ($6.35) family ticket (2 adults, 3 children).

Herzog-Friedrich-Strasse 15. © 0512/581-111. Admission to the Maximilianeum 3.60€ ($4.15) adults, 1.80€ ($2.05) seniors, students, and children 17 and under. No charge for views of the Goldenes Dachl, and no restrictions as to when it can be viewed. Maximilianeum summer daily 10am–6pm; winter Tues–Sun 10am–5pm. Tram: 1 or 3.

Swarovski Kristallwelten (Crystal Worlds) ★★★ *(Kids)* Designed by the Viennese multimedia artist, Andrew Heller, this attraction some 15km (9 miles) from Innsbruck is dedicated to the vision of Daniel Swarovski, founder of the world's leading producer of full crystal. Since it opened in 1995, millions of visitors have descended on the site, and you can easily spend 2 hours here.

After entering the giant head with its glittering eyes and waterfall, you'll immediately see a long wall of crystal with 12 tons of the finest cut stones in the world. In other chambers you can wander into the "Planet of the Crystals," with a 3-D light show. Crystalline works of art on display were designed by everybody from Andy Warhol to Salvador Dalí. In the Crystal Dome you get an idea of what it's like being inside a giant crystal, and in the Crystal Theater a fairy-tale world of color, mystery, and graceful movement unfolds.

Kristallweltenstrasse 1. © 05224/51080. www.kristallwelten.com. Admission 8€ ($9.20), free for children under 12. Daily 9am–6pm. Take the Wattens motorway exit (A 12) and follow signs to Kristallwelten, or take the Wattens bus from the Busbahnhof, next to the Hauptbahnhof.

Hofburg ★ The 15th-century imperial palace of Emperor Maximilian I, flanked by a set of domed towers, was rebuilt in the baroque style (with rococo detailing) during the 18th century on orders of Maria Theresa. It's a fine example of baroque secular architecture, with four wings and a two-story *Riesensaal* (Giant's Hall), painted in white and gold and filled with portraits of the Hapsburgs. Also of compelling interest are the State Rooms, the chapel, and a scattering of private apartments. You can wander at will through the rooms, but if you want to participate in a guided tour, management conducts two a day, at 11am and 2pm, in a multilingual format that includes English. Each tour lasts 30 to 45 minutes and costs 2€ ($2.30).

Rennweg 1. ✆ 0512/58-71-86. Admission 5.45€ ($6.25) adults, 3.65€ ($4.15) students, 1.10€ ($1.25) children under 12. Daily 9am–5pm. Tram: 1 or 3.

Hofkirche The most important treasure in the Hofkirche is the cenotaph of Maximilian I, a great example of German Renaissance style. It has 28 bronze 16th-century statues of Maximilian's real and legendary ancestors surrounding the kneeling emperor.

Universitätsstrasse 2. ✆ 0512/58-43-02. Admission 3€ ($3.45) adults, 2.05€ ($2.35) students or children, free for children 5 and under. Mon–Sat 9am–5pm. Tram: 1 or 3.

Dom zu St. Jakob (Cathedral of St. James) Designed and rebuilt from 1717 to 1724 by Johann Jakob Herkommer, the Dom has a lavishly embellished baroque interior. A chief treasure is Lucas Cranach the Elder's *Maria Hilf (St. Mary of Succor)* on the main altar.

Domplatz 6. ✆ 0512/58-39-02. Free admission. Winter daily 6:30am–6pm; summer daily 7am–7pm. Closed Fri noon–3pm. Tram: 1 or 3.

Tiroler Landesmuseum Ferdinandeum (Ferdinandeum Tyrol Museum) ✦ This celebrated gallery of Flemish and Dutch masters also traces the development of popular art in Tyrol, with highlights from the Gothic period. You'll see the original bas-reliefs used in designing the Goldenes Dachl.

Museumstrasse 15. ✆ 0512/59-489. Admission 8€ ($9.20) adults, 4€ ($4.60) students, 1.50€ children. May–Sept daily 10am–6pm; Oct–Apr Tues–Sat 10am–5pm, Sun 10am–1pm. Tram: 1 or 3.

Tiroler Volkskunst-Museum (Tyrol Museum of Popular Art) ✦✦ This popular art museum is in the Neues Stift (New Abbey) adjoining the Hofkirche on its eastern side. It contains one of the largest and most impressive collections of Tyrolean artifacts, ranging from handcrafts, furniture, Christmas cribs, and national costumes to religious and secular popular art. You'll also find a collection of models of typical Tyrolean houses.

Universitätsstrasse 2. ✆ 0512/58-43-02. Admission 5€ ($5.75) adults, 3.50€ ($4.05) students, 1.50€ ($1.75) children. Tues–Sat 9am–5pm; Sun 9am–noon. Tram: 1 or 3.

ENJOYING THE GREAT OUTDOORS

Five sunny, snow-covered, avalanche-free **ski areas** around the Tyrol are served by five cableways, 44 chairlifts, and ski hoists. The area is also known for bob-sled and toboggan runs and ice-skating rinks.

In summer you can play tennis at a number of courts, and golf on either a 9- or an 18-hole course; or you can go horseback riding, mountaineering, gliding, swimming, hiking, or shooting.

The **Hofgarten,** a public park containing lakes and many shade trees, lies north of Rennweg. Concerts are often presented in the garden during the summer.

THE SHOPPING SCENE

You'll find a large selection of Tyrolean specialties and all sorts of skiing and mountain-climbing equipment for sale in Innsbruck. Stroll around **Maria-Theresien-Strasse, Herzog-Friedrich-Strasse,** and **Museumstrasse,** ducking in and making discoveries of your own. Here are some suggestions.

Lodenbaur, Brixner Strasse 4 (✆ **0512/58-09-11**), is devoted to regional Tyrolean dress, most of which is made in Austria. There's a full array for men, women, and children. **Tiroler Heimatwerk,** Meraner Strasse 2 (✆ **0512/ 58-23-20**), is one of the best stores in Innsbruck for handcrafted sculpture and pewter, carved chests, furniture and lace. Do-it-yourselfers can buy regionally inspired fabrics and dress patterns, and whip up a dirndl (or whatever).

Using old molds discovered in abandoned Tyrolean factories, **Zinnreproduktionen U,** Kiebachgasse 8 (✆ **0512/58-92-24**), offers fine reproductions of century-old regional pewter at reasonable prices. The owner also reproduces rare pewter objects acquired from auctions throughout Europe. Look for a copy of the 18th-century pewter barometer emblazoned with representations of the sun and the four winds.

INNSBRUCK AFTER DARK

THE PERFORMING ARTS   The major venue for the performing arts is the 150-year-old **Landestheater,** Rennweg 2 (✆ **0512/52-074**). The box office is open daily from 9:30am to 7pm, and performances usually begin at 7:30 or 8pm. Ticket prices are 7.50€ to 38€ ($8.65–$44) for most operas or operettas, 6.50€ to 32€ ($7.50–$37) for theater seats. It's also the showcase for musicals and light operetta. For tickets, call ✆ **0512/53-56-30.** Concerts are presented in the Hofgarten in summer.

BARS, CLUBS & FOLK MUSIC   One of Innsbruck's most whimsical discos is **Blue Chip,** Wilhelm-greil-Strasse 17 (✆ **0512/57-04-73**), situated in a modern building in the center of town. The busy dance floor attracts a clientele in the 25-to-40 age range, and music includes an appealing mixture of funk, soul, and "black beat" (their term). Entrance is free, and hours are Tuesday to Saturday 11pm to 4am. One flight up in the same building is **Jimmy's Bar.** There's no dance floor and no live music, but it's something of an Innsbruck cliché that you should begin your evening at Jimmy's with a drink or two before proceeding downstairs to Blue Chip. Jimmy's is open daily 11am to 2am.

If you're looking for the biggest and the best in Innsbruck, head for the **Hofgartencafé,** Rennweg 6 (✆ **0512/58-88-71**), where a lively crowd of young people, mostly in their twenties and thirties, grace the largest beer garden in town. With three massive outdoor bars and a modern indoor decor, this hot spot is the place to be seen. You'll find live music here during the summer. It's open May to September daily from 11am to 3am. In winter, hours are Tuesday through Saturday from 6pm to 3am.

Young people hang out at **Treibhaus,** Angerzellgasse 8 (✆ **0512/58-68-74**), a combination cafe, bar, and social club. Within its battered walls, you can attend a changing roster of art exhibitions, cabaret shows, and protest rallies, Monday through Saturday from 10am to 1am, with live music presented at erratic intervals. Cover for live performances is 10€ to 20€ ($12–$23).

Limerick Bill's, Maria-Theresia-Strasse 9 (✆ **0512/5820111**), is dark and cavelike because of its location in a building without windows, a short walk north of Old Town. It's a genuine Irish pub for Celtic wannabes, and the cellar attracts a dancing crowd on Friday and Saturday nights, especially between December and March, when there's live music from 9pm to midnight. Open daily 4pm to 3am.

Fischerhausel Bar, Herrengasse 8 (✆ **0512/58-35-35**), is a rustic second-floor restaurant and street-level bar open Monday to Saturday 10am to 2am,

Sunday 6pm to 2am. In the Tyrolean style, it's a good, friendly joint for quaffing schnapps or suds. In warm weather, drinkers move out to the garden in back.

ST. ANTON AM ARLBERG ★★★

A modern resort has grown out of this old village on the Arlberg Pass, 99km (62 miles) west of Innsbruck. At St. Anton (1,288m/4,225 ft.), Hannes Schneider developed modern skiing techniques and began teaching tourists how to ski in 1907. Before his death in 1955, Schneider saw his ski school rated as the world's finest. Today the school is still one of the world's largest and best, with about 300 instructors (most of whom speak English). St. Anton am Arlberg in winter is popular with the wealthy and occasional royalty—a more conservative segment of the rich and famous than you'll see at other posh ski resorts.

There's so much emphasis on skiing here that few seem to talk of the summertime attractions. In warm weather, St. Anton is tranquil and bucolic, surrounded by meadowland. A riot of wildflowers blooming in the fields announces the beginning of spring.

ESSENTIALS

GETTING THERE By Train Because of St. Anton's good rail connections to eastern and western Austria, most visitors arrive by train. St. Anton is an express stop on the main lines crossing the Arlberg Pass between Innsbruck and Bregenz. About one train per hour arrives in St. Anton from both directions. Trip time from Innsbruck is 75 to 85 minutes; from Bregenz, around 85 minutes. For rail information, call ✆ **05/1717.**

By Car Motorists should take Route 171 west from Innsbruck.

VISITOR INFORMATION The **tourist office** in the **Arlberghaus** in the town center (✆ **05446/22-690;** www.stantonamarlberg.com) is open Monday through Friday from 8:30am to noon and 2 to 6:30pm, Saturday from 9am to noon and 2 to 6pm, and Sunday from 10am to noon.

WHERE TO STAY

Hotel Schwarzer Adler ★★ Owned and operated by the Tschol family since 1885, this is our preferred stopover at the resort. The beautiful building in the center of St. Anton was constructed as an inn in 1570 and became known for its hospitality to pilgrims crossing the treacherous Arlberg Pass. The 400-year-old frescoes on the exterior were discovered during a restoration. The interior is rustic yet elegant, with blazing fireplaces, painted Tyrolean baroque armoires, and Oriental rugs. There are handsomely furnished and well-equipped guest rooms in the main hotel, plus 13 slightly less-well-furnished (but less expensive) rooms in the annex, which is across the street above the **Café Aquila.** Nearly all bathrooms have big bathtubs, although a few singles offer only showers.

A-6580 St. Anton am Arlberg. ✆ **800/528-1234** in the U.S., or 05446/22-440. Fax 05446/22-44-62. www. schwarzeradler.com. 72 units. Winter 164€–400€ ($189–$460) double; summer 132€–176€ ($152–$202) double. Rates include half board. MC, V. Closed May–June and Sept–Dec 5. **Amenities:** Restaurant (see below); bar; indoor pool; fitness center; sauna; limited room service; massage; babysitting; laundry service/dry cleaning. *In room:* TV, dataport, hair dryer, safe.

WHERE TO DINE

If you're not able to secure a reservation at Raffl-Stube (see below), don't despair. You can get classic Austrian dishes at the historic **Hotel Alte Post Restaurant,** A-6580 St. Anton am Arlberg (✆ **05446/25530**); and at the first-rate **Hotel Kertess Restaurant,** A-6580 St. Anton am Arlberg (✆ **05446/2005**), located high on a slope in the suburb of Oberdorf. For superb international cuisine,

head to the medieval **Hotel Schwarzer Adler Restaurant,** A-6580 St. Anton am
Arlberg (℗ **05446/22440**).

Raffl-Stube ♔ AUSTRIAN   This restaurant didn't exist until 1982, when
members of the Raffl family enclosed a corner of their lobby. The place contains
only eight tables, and in the peak of the season, reservations are imperative, especially if you're not staying here. Overflow diners are offered a seat in a spacious
but less special dining room across the hall. Quality ingredients are always used,
and the kitchen prepares such tempting specialties as roast gooseliver with salad,
cream of parsley soup with sautéed quail eggs, filet of salmon with wild rice,
trout "as you like it," and roast filet of pork, along with the ever-popular fondue
bourguignon.

In the Hotel St. Antoner Hof, St. Anton am Arlberg. ℗ **05446/29-10.** Reservations required. Main courses
19€–28€ ($22–$32). AE, DC, MC, V. Daily 11:30am–2pm and 7–9:30pm. Closed May–Nov.

HITTING THE SLOPES IN ST. ANTON

The snow in this area is perfect for skiers, and the total lack of trees on the slopes
makes the situation ideal. The ski fields of St. Anton stretch over some 16 sq.
km (6 sq. miles). Beginners stick to the slopes down below, and more experienced skiers head to the runs from the **Galzig** and **Valluga** peaks. A cableway
will take you to Galzig (2,092m/6,860 ft.), where there's a self-service restaurant.
You go from here to Vallugagrat (2,649m/8,685 ft.). The peak of the Valluga
(2,812m/9,220 ft.), which commands a panoramic view, is also reached by
cableway.

Other major ski areas include the **Gampen/Kapall,** an advanced-intermedi-
ate network of slopes, whose lifts start just behind St. Anton's railway station;
and the **Rendl,** a relatively new labyrinth of runs to the south of St. Anton that
offers many novice and intermediate slopes.

You'll find many other cold-weather pursuits in St. Anton, including ski
jumping, mountain tours, curling, skating, tobogganing, and sleigh rides, plus
après-ski relaxing.

THE KITZBÜHEL ALPS ♔♔♔

Hard-core skiers and the rich and famous are attracted to this ski region. The
Kitzbühel Alps are covered with such a dense network of lifts that they now form
the largest skiing complex in the country, with a series of superlative runs. The
action centers on the town of Kitzbühel, but there are many satellite resorts that
are much less expensive, including St. Johann in Tyrol. Kitzbühel is, in a sense,
a neighbor of Munich, which lies 130km (81 miles) to the northeast: Most visitors to the Kitzbühel Alps use Munich's international airport.

ESSENTIALS

ARRIVING   By Train   Two and three **trains** per hour (many express) arrive in
Kitzbühel from Innsbruck (trip time: 60 min.) and Salzburg (2½ hr.), respectively.

By Bus   The most useful of these bus lines runs every 30 to 60 minutes
between Kitzbühel and St. Johann in Tyrol (25 min.). In addition, about half a
dozen buses travel every day from Salzburg's main railway station to Kitzbühel
(2¼ hr.). For regional bus information, call ℗ **05356/627-15.**

By Car   Kitzbühel is 449km (279 miles) southwest of Vienna and 100km (62
miles) east of Innsbruck. If you're driving from Innsbruck, take Autobahn A12
east to the junction with Route 312 heading to Ellmau. After bypassing Ellmau,
continue east to the junction with Route 342, which you take south to Kitzbühel.

VISITOR INFORMATION   The **tourist office,** Hinterstadt 18 (© **05356/ 621-55;** www.kitzbuhel.com), is open Monday through Friday from 8:30am to 6pm, Saturday from 8:30am to noon and 4 to 6pm, and Sunday from 10am to noon and 4 to 6pm.

WHERE TO STAY

Hotel Bruggerhof 😊 *Finds*   About 1.6km (1 mile) west of the town center, near the Schwarzsee, is this countryside chalet with a sun terrace. Originally built as a farmhouse in the 1920s, it later gained local fame as a restaurant. The interior has massive ceiling beams and a corner fireplace. Rooms are comfortable and cozy and decorated in an alpine style. All have a well-lived-in look, although housekeeping is attentive. Firm beds are most inviting. Bathrooms, which contain shower-tub combinations, can be a bit cramped.

Reitherstrasse 24, A-6370 Kitzbühel. © **05356/628-06.** Fax 05356/64-47-930. www.bruggerhof-camping.at. 28 units. Winter 154€–210€ ($177–$242) double; summer 110€–140€ ($127–$161) double. Rates include half board. AE, DC, MC, V. Closed Apr and Oct 15–Dec 15. **Amenities:** Restaurant; bar; indoor pool; tennis court; fitness center; Jacuzzi; sauna; solarium; minigolf; limited room service; babysitting; laundry service/dry cleaning; nonsmoking rooms. *In room:* TV, dataport (in some), minibar, hair dryer, safe.

Hotel Zur Tenne 😊   This hotel combines Tyrolean *Gemütlichkeit* with urban style and panache, and the staff shows genuine concern for its clientele. The hotel was created in the 1950s by joining a trio of 700-year-old houses. Rooms are as glamorous as anything in Kitzbühel: wood trim, comfortable beds, eiderdowns, and copies of Tyrolean antiques. Many have working fireplaces and canopied beds for a romantic touch. Bathrooms are generally large, with vanity mirrors and shower-tub combinations. In addition to intimate lounges, niches, and nooks, the hotel sports the most luxurious health complex in town, complete with a tropical fountain, two hot tubs, and a hot-and-cold foot bath.

Vorderstadt 8–10, A-6370 Kitzbühel. © **05356/64-44-40.** Fax 05356/648-03-56. www.zurtenne.at. 50 units. Winter 255€–305€ ($293–$351) double, 313€ ($360) suite for 3; summer 138€–212€ ($159–$244) double, 298€ ($343) suite for 3. Rates include breakfast. Half board 37€ ($43) per person. AE, DC, MC, V. Free parking outdoors; 12€ ($14) in covered garage nearby. **Amenities:** 3 restaurants; bar; lounge; solarium; fitness center; 2 Jacuzzis; sauna; limited room service; massage; babysitting; laundry/dry cleaning service. *In room:* TV, dataport, minibar, hair dryer, safe.

WHERE TO DINE

The Dining Rooms in the Schloss Lebenberg 😊 AUSTRIAN/INTERNATIONAL   Although the Schloss Lebenberg hotel offers comfortable rooms, we actually prefer it for its well-managed restaurant and its sense of history. Originally built in 1548, it was transformed in 1885 into Kitzbühel's first family-run hotel. Always-reliable specialties include cream of tomato soup with gin, Tyroleanstyle calf's liver, Wiener schnitzel, roulade of beef, and many desserts, which often feature mountain berries.

Lebenbergstrasse 17. © **05356/690-10.** Reservations required. Main courses 13€–21€ ($15–$24). AE, DC, MC, V. Daily 7:30–10:30am, noon–2pm, and 6:45–8:45pm.

Restaurant Goldener Greif 😊😊 TYROLEAN   The setting is cozy and warm, and the cuisine is some of the resort's best. The dining room features vaulted ceilings, intricate paneling, ornamental ceramic stoves, 19th-century paintings, and, in some cases, views out over the base of some of Kitzbühel's busy cable cars. Menu items are savory and designed to satisfy appetites heightened by the bracing alpine climate. You might order veal steak with fresh vegetables, pepper steak Madagascar, or venison. Many kinds of grilled steaks are regularly featured. A "Vienna pot" is one of the chef's specials, and fresh Tyrolean trout is offered daily. All the meat, sausages, and smoked meat come from the restaurant's own butcher.

Hinterstadt 24. (℃ **05356/643-11.** Reservations recommended. Main courses 8€–30€ ($9.20–$35). Fixed-price menus 20€–25€ ($23–$29). AE, DC, MC, V. June–Aug daily 10am–2pm and 7–10pm; mid-Dec to May daily 6–10pm. Closed mid-Apr to late May and mid-Oct to mid-Dec.

SEEING THE SIGHTS IN TOWN

The town has two main streets, both pedestrian walkways: **Vorderstadt** and **Hinterstadt.** Along these streets Kitzbühel has preserved its traditional architectural style. You'll see three-story stone houses with oriels and scrollwork around the doors and windows, heavy overhanging eaves, and Gothic gables.

The **Pfarrkirche (Parish Church)** was built from 1435 to 1506 and renovated in the baroque style during the 18th century. The lower part of the **Liebfrauenkirche (Church of Our Lady)** dates from the 13th century, the upper part from 1570. Between these two churches stands the **Ölbergkapelle (Ölberg Chapel)** with a 1450 "lantern of the dead" and frescoes from the latter part of the 16th century.

In the **Heimatmuseum,** Hinterstadt 34 (℃ **05356/645-88**), you'll see artifacts from prehistoric European mining eras and the north alpine Bronze Age, a winter-sports section with trophies of Kitzbüheler skiing greats, and exhibits detailing the town's history. The museum is open year-round Monday through Saturday from 10am to 1pm. Admission is 4.50€ ($5.20) adults, 2.25€ ($2.60) persons under 18.

HITTING THE SLOPES & OTHER OUTDOOR ACTIVITIES

SKIING   In winter the emphasis in Kitzbühel, 702m (2,300 ft.) above sea level, is on skiing, and facilities are offered for everyone from novices to experts. The ski season starts just before Christmas and lasts until late March. With more than 62 lifts, gondolas (cable cars), and mountain railroads on five different mountains, Kitzbühel has two main ski areas, the **Hahnenkamm** (renovated in 1995) and the **Kitzbüheler Horn** ★★. Cable cars (Hahnenkammbahn) are within easy walking distance, even for those in ski boots.

The linking of the lift systems on the Hahnenkamm has created the celebrated **Kitzbühel Ski Circus** ★★★, which makes it possible to ski downhill for more than 80km (50 miles), with runs that suit every stage of proficiency. Numerous championship ski events are held here; the World Cup event each January pits the skills of top-flight skiers against the toughest, fastest downhill course in the world, a stretch of the Hahnenkamm especially designed for maximum speed. Its name, *Die Streif,* is both feared and respected among skiers.

OTHER WINTER ACTIVITIES   There's also curling, ski-bobbing, ski jumping, ice-skating, tobogganing, hiking on cleared trails, and hang gliding, as well as indoor activities like tennis, bowling, and swimming. The children's ski school, **Schi-schule Rote Teufel,** Museumkeller, Hinterstadt (℃ **05356/635-00**), provides training for the very young skier. And don't forget the après-ski, with bars, nightclubs, and dance clubs rocking from teatime until the wee hours.

SUMMER ACTIVITIES   Kitzbühel has summer pastimes, too, such as walking tours, visits to the **Wild Life Park at Aurach** (about 3km/2 miles from Kitzbühel), tennis, horseback riding, golf, squash, brass-band concerts in the town center, cycling, and swimming. For the last, there's an indoor swimming pool, but we recommend going to the **Schwarzsee (Black Lake).** This *See,* about a 15-minute walk northwest of the center of town, is an alpine lake with a peat bottom that keeps the water relatively murky. Covering an area of 6.4 hectares (16 acres), with a depth that doesn't exceed about 8m (25 ft.), it's the site of beaches and **Seiwald Boosverleih,** Schwartzsee (© **05356/623-81**), an outfit that rents rowboats and putt-putt electric-driven engines in case you want to fish or sunbathe from a boat.

One of the region's most exotic collection of alpine flora is clustered into the jagged and rocky confines of the **Alpine Flower Garden Kitzbühel,** where various species of gentian, gorse, heather, and lichens are found on the sunny slopes of the Kitzbüheler Horn. Set at a height of around 1,830m (6,000 ft.) above sea level, the garden—which is owned and maintained by Kitzbühel as an incentive to midsummer tourism—is open from late May to early September, daily from 8:30am to 5:30pm, and is most impressive in June, July, and August. Admission is free. Many visitors see the garden by taking the Seilbahn Kitzbüheler cable car to its uppermost station and then descending on foot via the garden's labyrinth of footpaths to the gondola's middle station. (You can also climb upward within the garden, reversing the order of the gondola stations, although that would require a lot more effort.) The **Seilbahn Kitzbüheler cable car** (© **05356/ 69-51**), 18€ ($21) round-trip, departs from Kitzbühel at half-hour intervals daily throughout the summer and winter. In spring and autumn, it operates Saturday and Sunday only.

2

Belgium

by George McDonald

Modest little Belgium has never been known to boast of its charms, yet its variety of languages, cultures, history, and cuisines would do credit to a country many times its size. Belgium's diversity stems from its location at the cultural crossroads of Europe. The boundary between the Continent's Germanic north and Latin south cuts clear across the nation's middle, leaving Belgium divided into two major ethnic regions: Dutch-speaking Flanders and French-speaking Wallonia.

Although international attention is focused on Brussels as the "capital of Europe," another Belgium is waiting in the wings—a place of Gothic cathedrals, medieval castles, cobblestone streets, and tranquil canals. In a country the size of Maryland, the timeless beauty of Bruges and Ghent are accessible, even to the most hurried visitor. Both of these Flemish cities are showcases of medieval art and architecture. Some of the northern Renaissance's most outstanding paintings hang in their museums and churches. Yet each has a distinctive character that makes visiting them complementary. You can easily visit both in day trips from Brussels, but for a more thorough inspection you'll want to stay overnight.

1 Brussels ✶✶✶

A city with a notable history, Brussels is carving out a bright future. Headquarters of the European Union, it both symbolizes the Continent's vision of unity and is a bastion of officialdom, a breeding ground for the regulations that govern and often exasperate the rest of Europe.

Bruxellois have ambivalent feelings about their city's transformation into a power center. At first, the waves of Eurocrats brought a new cosmopolitan air, but as old neighborhoods were leveled to make way for office towers, people wondered whether Brussels was losing its soul. After all, this city is not just about politics and business. It inspired surrealism and Art Nouveau, worships comic strips, prides itself on handmade lace and chocolate, and serves each one of its craft beers in its own unique glass.

Fortunately, not all of Brussels's individuality has been lost. The city's spirit survives in traditional cafes, bars, bistros, and restaurants. Whether elegantly Art Nouveau or eccentrically festooned with posters, curios, and knickknacks, such centuries-old establishments provide a warm, convivial ambience that is peculiarly Belgian.

ESSENTIALS

GETTING THERE   By Plane   Brussels National Airport (② 0900/70-000 for flight information; www.brusselsairport.be) is 14km (9 miles) northeast of the city. In the arrival hall are currency-exchange offices, ATMs, a tourist information office, car-rental desks from the major international rental companies, bars, restaurants, and shops.

A **train** connects the airport with Brussels's three major railway stations (see below) every 20 minutes daily from 5:30am to 11:30pm; a one-way ride is 2.60€ ($3); trip time to Gare Centrale is 25 minutes (other city stops are just minutes away). The **Airport Line bus,** no. 12, departs from the airport 1 to 4 times an hour to place Schuman (Métro: Schuman) in the center, with stops on the way, and costs 3€ ($3.45); **De Lijn bus** BZ connects the airport hourly with Gare du Nord railway station for the same price. A **taxi** from the airport to the center city is around 30€ ($35); be sure to use only licensed cabs.

By Train   High-speed Eurostar trains from London; Thalys from Paris, Amsterdam, and Cologne; and TGV from France (not Paris) arrive at Gare du Midi, rue de France, south of the city center. Other international trains arrive at Gare du Midi; Gare Centrale, Carrefour de l'Europe, downtown, a few blocks from the Grand-Place; and Gare du Nord, rue du Progrès, north of the city center. For train information, call ℂ **02/528-28-28** or go to www.sncb.be. All three stations are served by Métro, tram, and bus lines and have taxi ranks outside.

Warning: Muggers, attracted by rich pickings from international travelers, haunt the environs of Gare du Midi, which are in the middle of a years-long redevelopment. Pickpockets and bag-snatchers work the interior. To avoid this threat, do not travel to or leave the station on foot—take a taxi or public transportation. Inside, keep a close eye on your possessions.

By Bus   Eurolines (ℂ **02/274-13-50;** www.eurolines.com) buses from London, Paris, Amsterdam, and other cities arrive at the bus station adjoining Gare du Nord railway station.

By Car   Major expressways to Brussels are E19 from Amsterdam and Paris, and E40 from Bruges and Cologne. Avoid if possible the "hell on wheels" R0 Brussels ring road. Then, do yourself a favor: Leave the car at a parking garage.

Native Behavior

Bruxellois are never happier than when they're setting forks and spoons to work on one of their country's proud regional cuisine specialties, and easing its assimilation with a carefully crafted artisanal Belgian beer—or three. If this can be done over an extended lunch, in the boss's time, and at the boss's expense, so much the better. You can join them in spirit, if not on expenses, by making lunch an important part of the day's proceedings.

Then, to really feel like a local, start grousing over the overpaid, underworked, arrogant, dimwitted, probably corrupt, expense-account-toting, comfortably pensioned "Eurocrats" who run the bureaucracy—and boy, is that some bureaucracy—of the gravy train that goes by the name of the European Union and is ensconced like a bloated alien body in their midst. See, it's easy!

Whom do you kiss and how often? Some rules of thumb: After a first formal handshake, people invariably kiss on meeting again, though the kiss is more like a peck on the cheek, or on each cheek; men don't kiss other men until they know them better, when it's fine; and men should kiss all the women (and not return to the start of the line to kiss the prettiest ones again).

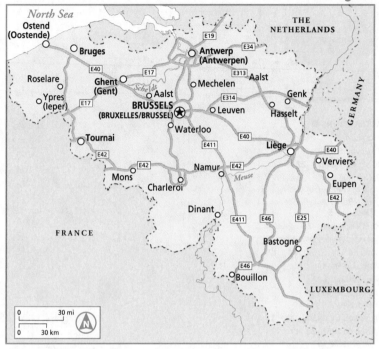

VISITOR INFORMATION **Brussels International Tourism,** Hôtel de Ville, Grand-Place, 1000 Bruxelles (*C* **02/513-89-40;** fax 02/513-83-20; www.brusselsinternational.be; Métro: Gare Centrale), is on the ground floor of the Town Hall. The office is open April to October, daily from 9am to 6pm; November to December, Monday to Saturday from 9am to 6pm, and Sunday from 10am to 2pm; and January to March, Monday to Saturday from 9am to 6pm.

Press For English-speaking visitors, the most useful publication is the weekly magazine *The Bulletin,* published on Thursdays and filled with local news, articles, shopping, and information on cultural events.

Websites A good starting point for exploring Brussels and the Wallonia and Flanders regions of Belgium on the Web are the official tourist office websites **www.brusselsinternational.be**, **www.visitbelgium.com**, **www.opt.be**, and **www.toervl.be**. You might also want to check out the independent **www.trabel.com**. A website in English that covers Belgian news, weather, tourism, and more is **www.xpats.com**. A good website for hotel research, where you can compare prices and see pictures of the rooms, is **www.hotels-belgium.com**. For dining-out pointers, go to **www.resto.be**.

CITY LAYOUT The city center's small, cobbled streets are clustered around the magnificent **Grand-Place.** Two of the most traveled lanes nearby are restaurant-lined **rue des Bouchers** and **Petite rue des Bouchers,** part of an area known as the **Ilôt Sacré.** A block from the Grand-Place is the classical colonnaded Bourse (Stock Exchange). A few blocks north, on **place de la Monnaie,** is the Monnaie opera house and ballet theater, named after the coin mint that

Brussels

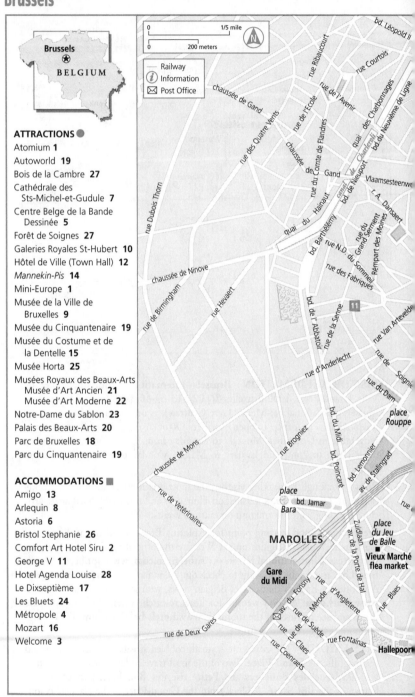

Brussels
⊛
BELGIUM

ATTRACTIONS ●

Atomium **1**
Autoworld **19**
Bois de la Cambre **27**
Cathédrale des
 Sts-Michel-et-Gudule **7**
Centre Belge de la Bande
 Dessinée **5**
Forêt de Soignes **27**
Galeries Royales St-Hubert **10**
Hôtel de Ville (Town Hall) **12**
Mannekin-Pis **14**
Mini-Europe **1**
Musée de la Ville de
 Bruxelles **9**
Musée du Cinquantenaire **19**
Musée du Costume et de
 la Dentelle **15**
Musée Horta **25**
Musées Royaux des Beaux-Arts
 Musée d'Art Ancien **21**
 Musée d'Art Moderne **22**
Notre-Dame du Sablon **23**
Palais des Beaux-Arts **20**
Parc de Bruxelles **18**
Parc du Cinquantenaire **19**

ACCOMMODATIONS ■

Amigo **13**
Arlequin **8**
Astoria **6**
Bristol Stephanie **26**
Comfort Art Hotel Siru **2**
George V **11**
Hotel Agenda Louise **28**
Le Dixseptième **17**
Les Bluets **24**
Métropole **4**
Mozart **16**
Welcome **3**

Railway
ⓘ Information
✉ Post Office

0   1/5 mile
0   200 meters

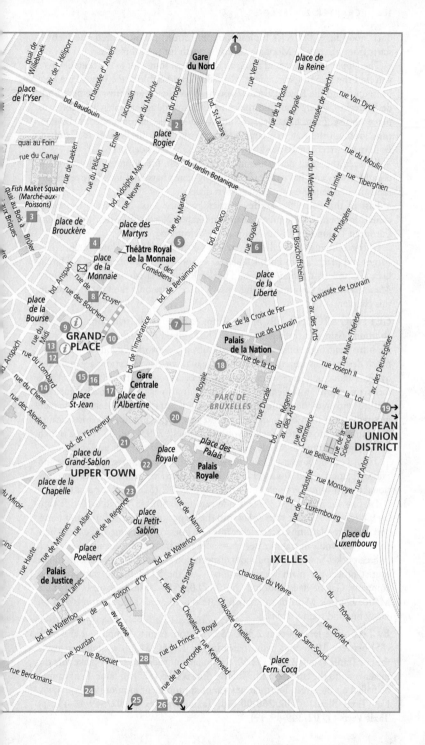

place de
la Reine

Gare
du Nord

place de l'Yser

bd. Baudouin

chaussée d'Anvers

quai de Willebroek

av. de l'Héliport

Jacqmain

rue du Marché

rue du Progrès

bd. St-Lazare

rue Verte

rue de la Poste

rue Royale

chaussée de Haecht

rue Van Dyck

place
Rogier

rue du Moulin

quai au Foin

rue du Canal

rue de Laeken

rue du Pélican

bd. Émile

bd. Adolphe Max

rue Neuve

bd. du Jardin Botanique

rue du Marais

bd. Pacheco

rue Royale

bd. Bischoffsheim

rue la Limite

rue Tiberghien

rue du Méridien

rue Potagère

Fish Maket Square
(Marché-aux-Poissons)

quai au Bois à Brûler

aux Briques

place de
Brouckère

place des
Martyrs

Théâtre Royal
de la Monnaie

place
de la
Monnaie

r. des
Comédiens

bd. de Berlaimont

place
de la
Liberté

chaussée de Louvain

place de
la Bourse

bd. Anspach

rue de l'Écuyer

rue des Bouchers

rue du Midi

GRAND-
PLACE

bd. de l'Impératrice

rue de la Croix de Fer

rue de Louvain

Palais
de la Nation

rue de la Loi

av. des Arts

rue Marie-Thérèse

rue Joseph II

av. des Deux-Églises

rue du Lombard

bd. Anspach

rue du Chêne

rue des Alexiens

place
St-Jean

Gare
Centrale

place de
l'Albertine

rue Royale

PARC DE
BRUXELLES

rue Ducale

rue de la Loi

bd. du Régent
av. des Arts

rue de Commerce

rue de la Science

EUROPEAN
UNION
DISTRICT

rue d'Arlon

bd. de l'Empereur

place du
Grand-Sablon

place
Royale

place des
Palais

Palais
Royale

rue Belliard

rue Montoyer

place de la
Chapelle

UPPER TOWN

rue de l'Industrie

rue du Luxembourg

place du
Luxembourg

du Miroir

rue aux Laines

rue de Mnimes

rue Allard

rue de la Régence

place
du Petit-
Sablon

rue de Namur

bd. de Waterloo

IXELLES

rue Haute

place
Poelaert

Palais
de Justice

av. de la Toison d'Or

r. des

rue de Strassart

chaussée du Wavre

rue du Trône

rue Goffart

bd. de Waterloo

av. Louise

rue du Prince Royal

Chevaliers

rue de la Concorde

rue Keyenveld

chaussée d'Ixelles

rue Sans-Souci

place
Fern. Cocq

rue Berckmans

rue Jourdan

rue Bosquet

107

once stood here. Brussels's busiest shopping street, pedestrianized **rue Neuve,** starts from place de la Monnaie and runs north for several blocks.

The Upper Town is spread along an escarpment southeast of the center, where you find the second great square, **place du Grand-Sablon,** the Royal Fine Arts Museums, and the Royal Palace. If you head southwest and cross the broad **bd. de Waterloo,** where you find the most exclusive designer stores, you come to **place Louise.** From here, Brussels's most fashionable thoroughfare, **av. Louise,** runs south all the way to a large wooded park called the **Bois de la Cambre.** Both main streets are flanked by attractive residential side streets.

Between the Palais de Justice and Gare du Midi, the unpretentious working-class **Marolles** area has cozy cafes, drinking-man's bars, and inexpensive restaurants; its denizens even speak their own dialect.

East of this zone, the **Ixelles** district, near the Free University, has many casual, inexpensive restaurants, bars, and cafes. North of Ixelles, the modern European Union district surrounds **place Schuman.**

In this bilingual city, called *Bruxelles* in French and *Brussel* in Dutch, street names and places are in both languages. Grand-Place is *Grote Markt* in Dutch; Gare Centrale is *Centraal Station;* Théatre Royal de la Monnaie is *Koninklijke Munttheater.* For convenience and to save space, I use only the French names in this chapter.

GETTING AROUND **By Métro, Tram & Bus** Public transportation begins at around 6am and the regular service ends around midnight. After that, there are infrequent night buses. The Métro (subway) network is good for getting to major destinations around and on the edge of town. Métro stations are indicated by signs showing a large white M on a blue background. Trams (streetcars) and buses are yellow; stop them by extending your arm as they approach. Stops are marked with red-and-white signs. Though not as fast as the Métro, trams are generally faster than buses and are a great way to get around, not least because you can view the cityscape while you ride—lines 92, 93, and 94 cover a bunch of key sights along rue Royale, rue de la Régence, and as far as av. Louise.

Tickets can be purchased from the driver on trams and buses, from Métro and railway station ticket counters, and (some tickets) from the Brussels International tourist office. A single ride (a *direct*) is 1.40€ ($1.60). You can also buy a 1-day pass for 3.80€ ($4.35), a 5-ride card for 6.50€ ($7), and a 10-ride card for 9.80€ ($11). Insert your ticket into the orange machines on buses and trams and at Métro platforms. Your ticket must be inserted each time you enter a new vehicle, but you can transfer free from Métro to tram to bus for up to 1 hour.

Free pocket maps of the public transportation network are available from the tourist office, the main Métro stations, and the **STIB** public transportation company, Galerie de la Toison d'Or 20 (© **02/515-20-00;** www.stib.irisnet.be; Métro: Louise). Maps of the network are posted at all Métro stations and on many bus and tram shelters.

By Taxi The fare starts at 2.35€ ($2.70) from 6am to 10pm, and at 4.35€ ($5) between 10pm and 6am, increasing by 1.15€ ($1.30) a kilometer inside the city (tariff 1) and 2.30€ ($2.60) a kilometer outside (tariff 2)—make sure the meter is set to the correct tariff. Waiting time is 22€ ($25) an hour. Taxis cannot be hailed on the street, but there are stands at prominent locations around town. Call **Taxis Bleus** (© **02/268-00-00**), **Taxis Oranges** (© **02/349-43-43**), or **Taxis Verts** (© **02/349-49-49**).

By Car Driving in Brussels is akin to life during the Stone Age: nasty and brutish—though it's rarely short. In some cases (but not always), traffic from the right has the right of way, even if it is coming from a minor road onto a more important one. You can imagine how this plays at multiple-road intersections, particularly since Belgians will relinquish their *priorité de droite* under no known circumstances, cost what it might. If you must drive, all the top international firms rent here: **Avis,** rue de France 2 (✆ **02/527-17-05;** Métro: Gare du Midi); **Budget,** av. Louise 327B (✆ **02/646-51-30;** Métro: Louise); **Europcar,** rue du Page 29 (✆ **02/348-92-12;** tram: 81 or 82); and **Hertz,** bd. Maurice-Lemmonier 8 (✆ **02/717-32-01;** Métro: Anneessens). All of these firms also have desks at the airport. Rates begin at around 45€ ($52) for a small car with unlimited mileage.

Remember: You get the best deal if you arrange the rental before you leave home.

By Bike Brussels's hoggish drivers and biased road laws combine to make this a poor option. If you want to rent a bike anyway, try **Pro Vélo,** rue de Londres 15 (✆ **02/217-01-58;** www.provelo.be; Métro: Porte de Namur). In July and August, it's open daily from 9am to 6pm; September to June, hours are Monday to Friday from 9am to 6pm. Rental is 12€ ($15) for 1 day. They also organize bike tours with a commentary in English.

By Foot There's no better way to explore the historic core of the town than walking, especially around Grand-Place. You'll also enjoy strolling uptown around place du Grand-Sablon. Beyond these areas, you'll want to use public transportation. Don't expect cars to stop for you just because you're crossing at a black-and-white "pedestrian crossing." It's only recently that drivers have been obliged legally to stop at these, and many of them haven't got the message yet.

FAST FACTS: Brussels

American Express The office at bd. du Souverain 100, 1000 Bruxelles (✆ **02/ 676-21-11;** Métro: Horrmann-Debroux), is open Monday to Friday from 9am to 1pm and 2 to 5pm. Call ahead before visiting, as this is an administrative office only, and is out in the suburbs.

Business Hours **Banks** are open Monday to Friday from 9am to 1pm and 2 to 4:30 or 5pm. Open hours for **offices** are Monday to Friday from 9 or 10am to 4 or 5pm. Most **stores** are open Monday to Saturday from 9 or 10am to 6 or 7pm; some stay open on Friday to 8 or 9pm.

Currency Belgium's currency is the euro (€). At press time, $1 = .85€ ($), or 1€ = $1.15.

Currency Exchange Banks give the best rates, and currency-exchange offices in railway stations come close. Hotels and *bureaux de change* (currency-exchange offices), open regular hours plus evenings and weekends, charge a low commission (or none at all) but give a low rate. **Thomas Cook,** Grand-Place 4 (✆ **02/513-28-45;** Métro: Gare Centrale), has fair rates.

You'll find many **ATMs** around town, identified by BANCONTACT and MISTER CASH signs. A convenient bank with an ATM is **CBC,** Grand-Place 5 (✆ **02/ 547-12-11;** Métro: Gare Centrale), open Monday to Friday from 9am to 5pm.

Doctors & Dentists For 24-hour emergency medical service, call ℂ **02/ 479-18-18**; ask for an English-speaking doctor. For emergency dental care, call ℂ **02/426-10-26.**

Drugstores/Pharmacies For both prescription and non-prescription medicines, go to a pharmacy (*pharmacie* in French; *apotheek* in Dutch). Regular pharmacy hours are Monday to Saturday from 9am to 6pm (some close earlier on Sat). Try the centrally located **Grande Pharmacie de Brouckère,** Passage du Nord 10–12 (ℂ **02/218-05-07;** Métro: De Brouckère). All pharmacies post locations of nearby all-night and Sunday pharmacies on the door.

Embassies **United States,** bd. du Régent 25–27 (ℂ **02/508-21-11;** Métro: Arts-Loi), open Monday to Friday from 9am to noon for visas and 1:30 to 4:30pm for assistance. **Canada,** av. de Tervuren 2 (ℂ **02/741-06-11;** Métro: Mérode), open Monday, Wednesday, and Friday from 9am to noon and 2 to 4pm; Tuesday and Thursday from 9am to noon. **United Kingdom,** rue Arlon 85 (ℂ **02/287-62-11;** Métro: Maalbeek), open Monday to Friday from 9:30am to noon. **Ireland,** rue Wiertz 50 (ℂ **02/235-66-76;** Métro: Schuman), open Monday to Friday from 10am to 1pm. **Australia,** rue Guimard 6–8 (ℂ **02/286-05-00;** Métro: Arts-Loi), open Monday to Friday from 9am to 12:30pm and 2 to 4pm. **New Zealand,** Square de Meeûs 1 (ℂ **02/512-10-40;** Métro: Trone), open Monday to Friday from 9am to 1pm and 2 to 3:30pm.

Emergencies For police assistance, call ℂ **101.** For an ambulance or the fire department, call ℂ **100.**

Holidays January 1 (New Year's Day), Easter Monday, May 1 (Labor Day), Ascension, Pentecost Monday, July 21 (Independence Day), August 15 (Assumption), November 1 (All Saints Day), November 11 (Armistice Day), and December 25 (Christmas). The dates of Easter, Ascension, and Pentecost change each year

Hospital **Cliniques Universitaires St-Luc,** av. Hippocrate 10 (ℂ **02/764- 11-11;** Métro: Alma), has an emergency department.

Internet Access In the center, **easyInternetcafé,** place de Brouckère 9–13 (ℂ **02/211-08-20;** www.easyeverything.com; Métro: De Brouckère), is open daily from 8am to 11pm; access begins at 2.50€ ($2.90) per hour.

Mail Most **post offices** are open Monday to Friday from 9am to 5pm. The office at Centre Monnaie, place de la Monnaie (ℂ **02/226-21-11;** Métro: De Brouckère), is open Monday to Friday from 9am to 5pm, Saturday from 9:30am to 3pm. The office at Gare du Midi, av. Fonsny 1E/F (ℂ **02/538- 33-98;** Métro: Gare du Midi), is open 24 hours.

Postage for a postcard or letter to the U.S., Canada, Australia, or New Zealand is .85€ ($1); to the U.K. or Ireland .45€ (50¢).

Police In an emergency, call ℂ **101.** In non-urgent situations, go to the **Brussels Central Police Station,** rue du Marché-au-Charbon 30 (ℂ **02/279- 79-79),** just off of the Grand-Place.

Safety Brussels is generally safe, but there's a rise in crime, in particular pickpocketing, theft from and of cars, and muggings in places such as Métro station foot tunnels. Don't overestimate the risk, but take sensible precautions, particularly in obvious circumstances such as on crowded Métro trains and when taking cash from an ATM at night.

Taxes There's a value-added tax (TVA) of 6% on hotel bills and 21.5% on restaurant bills and on many purchases. For information on how to recover some of the tax on purchases, see "The Shopping Scene," later in this chapter.

Telephone Belgium's **country code** is **32.** Brussels's **city code** is **2;** use the **32-2** code when calling from the United States or any other country outside Belgium. In Belgium, use the **area code 02.** You need to dial the **02** area code both from inside Brussels and from elsewhere in Belgium; you always need to use the area code in Belgium.

A local phone call from a pay phone costs .25€ (30¢) a minute at peak time (Mon–Fri 8am–7pm) and .25€ (30¢) per 2 minutes at off-peak time. An international call, per minute, to the U.S., Canada, the U.K., or Ireland is .35€ (40¢); and to Australia or New Zealand 1€ ($1.15). You can use most pay phones in booths all around town with a plastic Belgacom **telecard,** selling for 5€ ($6), 13€ ($15), and 25€ ($29) at post offices, train ticket counters, and newsstands. Some pay phones take coins of .10€, .20€, .50€, and 1€. On both card and coin phones, watch the digital reading, which tracks your decreasing deposit so you know when to add another card or more coins. For information inside the country, call ① **1207** or **1307;** for international information in English, call ① **1405.**

To charge a call to your calling card, dial **AT&T** (① **0800/100-10**); **MCI** (① **0800/100-12**); **Sprint** (① **0800/100-14**); **Canada Direct** (① **0800/100-19**); or **British Telecom** (① **0800/100-24**).

Tipping The prices on most restaurant menus already include a service charge of 16%, so it's unnecessary to tip. However, if the service is good, it's usual to show appreciation with a tip (5%–10%). Service is included in your hotel bill as well. For taxi drivers, you can round up the fare if you like, but you need not add a tip unless you have received an extra service such as help with luggage.

Toilets Be sure to *pay the person* who sits at the entrance to a *toilette.* He or she has a saucer in which you put your money. If you don't, you might have a visitor in the inner sanctum while you're transacting your business. Even if you have paid, in busy places the attendant may have forgotten your face by the time you emerge and will then pursue you out of the toilet and along the street. It's tiresome, but toilet use is usually only about .50€ (60¢).

WHERE TO STAY

If you arrive in Brussels without a reservation, you should stop by the **Brussels International Tourism** office in the Grand-Place (see "Visitor Information," earlier in this chapter), which makes same-day reservations, if you go in person, for a small fee (deducted by the hotel from its room rate). You can also contact **Belgian Tourist Reservations,** bd. Anspach 111, 1000 Bruxelles (① **02/513-74-84;** fax 02/513-92-77; Métro: Bourse), which reserves hotel rooms throughout Belgium and can often give substantial discounts.

The **Sheraton Brussels Airport** hotel, Brussels National Airport (facing Departures), 1930 Zaventem (① **800/325-3535** in the U.S. and Canada, or

02/725-10-00; fax 02/710-80-80; www.sheraton.com), couldn't be more convenient to the airport without being on the runway. And you have all the comfort you would expect of a top-flight Sheraton. Doubles are 375€ to 395€ ($431–$454) a night.

A cheaper option near the airport is the **Holiday Inn Express Brussels Airport,** Berkenlaan 5 (access road opposite NATO HQ), 1831 Diegem (*℃* **02/ 725-33-80;** fax 02/725-38-10; www.holidayinn.com). Doubles are 125€ to 175€ ($112–$126), and frequently are discounted. You can dine at its big brother Holiday Inn next door. There's free parking and an airport shuttle.

AROUND THE GRAND-PLACE
Very Expensive

Amigo 🏨🏨   In Brussels slang, an *amigo* is a prison, and indeed a prison once stood here. But any resemblance to the former accommodations is purely nominal, as the Amigo is among the city's finest lodgings. Its Spanish Renaissance architecture, stately corridors, and flagstone lobby are right at home in this ancient neighborhood. The rooms are quite spacious and traditionally elegant, but with touches of modern Flemish design to brighten things up—and motifs from the classic comic *Tintin* in the bathrooms to add an element of whimsy. Ask for a room with a view of the Town Hall's Gothic spire.

Rue de l'Amigo 1–3 (off of the Grand-Place), 1000 Bruxelles. *℃* **02/547-47-47.** Fax 02/513-52-77. www. roccofortehotels.com. 174 units. 480€–540€ ($552–$621) double; from 820€ ($943) suite. AE, DC, MC, V. Valet parking 15€ ($17). Métro: Bourse. **Amenities:** Restaurant; bar; lounge; health club; concierge; 24-hr. business center; 24-hr. room service; babysitting; laundry service; same-day dry cleaning; nonsmoking rooms; executive rooms. *In room:* A/C, TV w/pay movies, dataport, minibar, hair dryer, safe.

Expensive

Hotel Métropole 🏨🏨   Even if you're not staying here, the hotel is worth a visit on its own account. An ornate, marble-and-gilt interior distinguishes this late-19th-century hotel several blocks from the Grand-Place. Soaring ceilings, potted palms, and lavishly decorated public rooms add to the Belle Epoque allure. Spacious rooms have classic furnishings and some modern luxuries, including heated towel racks, hair dryers, and trouser presses. An elegant French restaurant, **L'Alban Chambon,** caters to the sophisticated diner, and the Belle Epoque **Café Métropole** to the sophisticated cafe hound.

Place de Brouckère 31 (close to Centre Monnaie), 1000 Bruxelles. *℃* **02/217-23-00.** Fax 02/218-02-20. www.metropolehotel.be. 305 units. 329€–429€ ($378–$493) double; from 450€ ($518) suite. Rates include buffet or continental breakfast. AE, DC, MC, V. Parking 13€ ($15). Métro: De Brouckère. **Amenities:** Restaurant; lounge; sidewalk cafe; health club and spa; concierge; 24-hr. room service; laundry service; dry cleaning. *In room:* TV w/pay movies, minibar, coffeemaker, hair dryer, safe.

Le Dixseptième 🏨🏨 *Value*   This graceful 17th-century house, once the official residence of the Spanish ambassador, stands close to the Grand-Place in a neighborhood of restored dwellings. Guest rooms have wood paneling and marble chimneys, and are as big as the suites in many hotels; some have balconies, and most overlook a tranquil courtyard patio. All are in 18th-century style and are named after Belgian painters from Brueghel to Magritte. Two beautiful lounges are decorated with carved wooden medallions and 18th-century paintings.

Rue de la Madeleine 25 (off place de l'Albertine), 1000 Bruxelles. *℃* **02/502-57-44.** Fax 02/502-64-24. www.ledixseptieme.be. 24 units. 190€ ($219) double; from 260€ ($299) suite. Rates include buffet breakfast. AE, DC, MC, V. Limited street parking. Métro: Gare Centrale. **Amenities:** 2 lounges; laundry service; dry cleaning. *In room:* A/C, TV, minibar, hair dryer, safe.

Moderate

Arlequin ✶ You can't get closer to the heart of the city than this, with the restaurant-lined rue des Bouchers right outside the hotel's back entrance. Then there's the fine views from some rooms of the Town Hall spire in the neighboring Grand-Place (spectacular when lit at night) and of the Old City's rooftops and narrow medieval streets from the top-floor breakfast room. The guest rooms themselves are not quite as spectacular as the views, but all have modern, comfortable furnishings, and most have plenty of natural light.

Rue de la Fourche 17–19 (off rue des Bouchers), 1000 Bruxelles. ✆ **02/514-16-15.** Fax 02/514-22-02. www.arlequin.be. 92 units. 80€–125€ ($92–$144) double. Rates include buffet breakfast. AE, DC, MC, V. No parking. Métro: Bourse. **Amenities:** Limited room service; laundry service; dry cleaning. *In room:* TV w/pay movies, hair dryer.

Inexpensive

Mozart Go up a flight from the busy, cheap-eats street level, and guess which famous composer's music wafts through the lobby? Salmon-colored walls, plants, and old paintings create a warm, intimate ambience that's carried over into the guest rooms. Although furnishings are blandly modern, colorful fabrics and exposed beams lend each room a rustic originality. Several are duplexes with a sitting room underneath the loft bedroom. Top-floor rooms have a great view.

Rue du Marché-aux-Fromages 23 (close to the Grand-Place), 1000 Bruxelles. ✆ **02/502-66-61.** Fax 02/502-77-58. www.hotel-mozart.be. 47 units. 95€ ($109) double. AE, DC, MC, V. No parking. Métro: Gare Centrale. **Amenities:** Lounge; laundry service. *In room:* TV, fridge.

THE LOWER CITY
Moderate

Welcome ✶✶ The name of this gem of a hotel, overlooking the Fish Market, couldn't be more accurate, thanks to the untiring efforts of the husband-and-wife proprietors. You can think of it as a country *auberge* (inn) right in the heart of town. Rooms are furnished and styled on individual, unrelated themes, such as Provence, Tibet, Egypt, Africa, Jules Verne, and Laura Ashley, all to a high standard. The fine in-house seafood restaurant **La Truite d'Argent** closed in 2004, creating space for more rooms, but there's no shortage of good alternatives on the Marché-aux-Poissons. The hotel provides free airport shuttle to and from Brussels National Airport. Book ahead; the Welcome's regular guests are fiercely loyal.

Quai au Bois-à-Brûler 23 (at the Marché-aux-Poissons), 1000 Bruxelles. ✆ **02/219-95-46.** Fax 02/217-18-87. www.hotelwelcome.com. 17 units. 95€–130€ ($109–$150) double; 150€ ($173) suite. AE, DC, MC, V. Parking 10€ ($12). Métro: Ste-Catherine. **Amenities:** Lounge; Internet desk. *In room:* A/C (some rooms), TV, dataport, minibar, hair dryer, safe.

Inexpensive

George V This agreeable little hotel is tucked away in a corner of the city center that looks more down at the heels than it really is and is currently being reborn as a trendy shopping-and-eating area. Situated in a town house from 1859 within easy walking distance of the Grand-Place, the George provides a free shuttle bus to this square and the main museums, and to Gare du Midi. The rooms are plain but clean and have new furnishings, but some of the fittings are in clear need of replacement.

Rue 't Kint 23 (off place du Jardin-aux-Fleurs), 1000 Bruxelles. ✆ **02/513-50-93.** Fax 02/513-44-93. www.george5.com. 16 units. 74€ ($85) double. Rates include continental breakfast. AE, MC, V. Parking 7€ ($8). Métro: Bourse. **Amenities:** Bar; limited room service. *In room:* TV.

THE UPPER CITY
Expensive

Astoria ★★   You're transported to a more elegant age the moment you walk into this fine hotel's Belle Epoque foyer, where the sumptuous surroundings feature Corinthian columns, antique furnishings, and textured marble. Guest rooms, which are somewhat smaller than in other hotels of this category, are attractively and comfortably furnished, though not extravagantly so, in a style that's in keeping with the hotel's character. You can dine at the beautiful French restaurant, **Le Palais Royal,** and have a drink in the ornate **Pullman Bar,** which is based on the restaurant car of the legendary Orient Express train.

Rue Royale 103 (close to Colonne du Congrès), 1000 Bruxelles. ℂ **800/SOFITEL** in the U.S. and Canada, or 02/227-05-05. Fax 02/217-11-50. www.sofitel.com. 118 units. 350€ ($403) double; from 450€ ($518) suite. AE, DC, MC, V. Parking 18€ ($21). Métro: Botanique. **Amenities:** Restaurant; lounge; health club and spa; concierge; 24-hr. room service; laundry service; dry cleaning. *In room:* A/C, TV w/pay movies, minibar, coffeemaker, hair dryer, safe.

AROUND AV. LOUISE
Expensive

Bristol Stephanie ★★   From its lobby fittings to furnishings in the kitchenette suites, every feature of this sleek Norwegian-owned hotel, set on one of the city's toniest shopping streets, is streamlined, functional, and representative of the best in Nordic design. Some rooms have four-poster beds and "antiallergy" hardwood floors; all are quite large, and furnished to a high level of modern style and comfort (though the standard rooms could use a little more Nordic drawer space). Try to get a room in the main building—nothing beats a 24-hour doorman for security. The French restaurant **Le Chalet d'Odin** has a refined menu.

Av. Louise 91–93, 1050 Bruxelles. ℂ **02/543-33-11.** Fax 02/538-03-07. www.bristol.be. 142 units. 350€–390€ ($403–$449) double; from 600€ ($690) suite. AE, DC, MC, V. Parking 20€ ($23). Métro: Louise. **Amenities:** Restaurant; lounge; bar; heated indoor pool; exercise room; Jacuzzi; sauna; concierge; business center; 24-hr. room service; babysitting; laundry service; dry cleaning; nonsmoking rooms; executive rooms. *In room:* A/C, TV w/pay movies, minibar, coffeemaker, hair dryer, iron, safe.

Moderate

Hotel Agenda Louise ★   This exquisite little hotel has modern rooms decorated with light-colored wood furniture and gold and orange curtains and fittings. All have coffeemakers and come with complete kitchens. Ask for a room that overlooks the inner courtyard for the best view.

Rue de Florence 6 (off av. Louise), 1000 Bruxelles. ℂ **02/539-00-31.** Fax 02/539-00-63. www.hotelagenda.com. 37 units. 116€ ($133) double. Rates include buffet breakfast. AE, DC, MC, V. Parking 6€ ($7). Métro: Louise. **Amenities:** Lounge; same-day dry cleaning; nonsmoking rooms. *In room:* TV, minibar, coffeemaker, hair dryer.

Inexpensive

Les Bluets ★   If you're searching for classic European charm or are a fan of American B&Bs, you'll enjoy it here. The town house from 1864 is more comfortable country residence than hotel. You feel as though you're staying with friends when you breakfast in the antiques-filled dining room or in the sunroom. A sweeping stairway (no elevator) leads up to the rooms, several of which have 4m (14-ft.) ceilings and ornate moldings; all have antiques and knickknacks. This is one of the city's few nonsmoking hotels.

Rue Berckmans 124 (off av. Louise), 1060 Bruxelles. ℂ 02/534-39-83. Fax 02/543-09-70. www.geocities.com/les_bluets. 10 units. 53€–81€ ($61–$93) double. Rates include continental breakfast. MC, V. Limited street parking. Métro: Hôtel des Monnaies. *In room:* TV.

AROUND GARE DU NORD
Moderate

Comfort Art Hotel Siru ★★ Set in an area of fancy office towers, this fascinating art-gallery-cum-hotel is not easily forgotten. What sets the Siru apart is that the proprietor persuaded 130 Belgian artists, including some of the country's biggest names, to "decorate" each of the coolly modern, well-equipped rooms and the corridors with a work on the theme of travel. Given the unpredictable nature of reactions to modern art, some clients reserve the same room time after time; others ask to change in the middle of the night.

Place Rogier 1 (opposite Gare du Nord), 1210 Bruxelles. © **800/228-3323** in the U.S. and Canada, or 02/203-35-80. Fax 02/203-33-03. www.comforthotelsiru.com. 101 units. 90€–210€ ($104–$242) double. Rates include buffet breakfast. AE, DC, MC, V. Parking 15€ ($17). Métro: Rogier. **Amenities:** Restaurant; babysitting; laundry service; same-day dry cleaning; nonsmoking rooms; executive rooms. *In room:* TV w/pay movies, dataport, minibar, hair dryer, safe.

WHERE TO DINE

The city's French- and Dutch-speaking residents may have their differences, but they both value a good meal. Indeed, food is a passion in Brussels, and you can always find somewhere to eat well—it's hard to eat badly here—at a reasonable price.

Among the sturdy regional dishes you find on menus around town are: *waterzooï,* fish or chicken stew with a parsley-and-cream sauce; *stoemp,* a purée of vegetables and potatoes with sausage, steak, or chops; *paling in 't groen,* eel in a grass-green sauce; *ballekes,* spicy meatballs; *hochepot,* stew; *lapin à la gueuze,* rabbit with a Brussels beer sauce; and *carbonnades à la flamande,* beef stew with a beer sauce. While most of the city's favorite dishes are based on local products, the famous *moules* (mussels)—prepared in countless ingenious variations and served in tureens—come from Zeeland in neighboring Holland. A selection from Belgium's 300 craft cheeses is a good way to finish off.

If you are a nonsmoker you're mostly out of luck—get ready to consume a garnish of secondhand smoke with your meal. Finally, don't fret if the service is slow: People take their time dining out here.

AROUND THE GRAND-PLACE
Very Expensive

La Maison du Cygne ★★ CLASSIC FRENCH This grande dame of Brussels's internationally recognized restaurants overlooks the Grand-Place from the former guild house of the Butchers Guild—where Karl Marx worked on *The Communist Manifesto* during a 3-year sojourn in Brussels. The service, though a tad stuffy, is as elegant as the polished walnut walls, bronze wall sconces, and green velvet. The menu has haute cuisine Belgian and French classics. Because of its location, the restaurant is usually crowded at lunchtime, but dinner reservations are likely to be available.

Grand-Place 9 (entrance at rue Charles Buls 2). ℂ 02/511-82-44. www.lamaisonducygne.be. Reservations recommended. Main courses 30€–58€ ($35–$67); *menu du jour* 90€ ($104). AE, DC, MC, V. Mon–Fri noon–2pm and 7pm–midnight; Sat 7pm–midnight. Métro: Gare Centrale.

Expensive

De l'Ogenblik ★★ FRENCH/BELGIAN   In the elegant surrounds of the Galeries Royales St-Hubert, this restaurant supplies good taste in a Parisian bistro–style setting that's popular with off-duty actors and audiences from the nearby Gallery theater, among others. It often gets busy, but the ambience in the split-level, wood-and-brass-outfitted dining room, with a sand-strewn floor, is convivial, though a little too tightly packed when it's full. Look for garlicky meat and seafood menu dishes, and expect to pay a smidgen more for atmosphere than might be strictly justified by results on the plate.

Galerie des Princes 1 (in the Galeries Royales St-Hubert). ℂ 02/511-61-51. www.ogenblik.be. Main courses 22€–28€ ($25–$32); *plat du jour* 11.50€ ($13). AE, DC, MC, V. Mon–Thurs noon–2:30pm and 7pm–midnight; Fri–Sat noon–2:30pm and 7pm–12:30am. Métro: De Brouckère.

Moderate

Brasserie de la Roue d'Or ★★ TRADITIONAL BELGIAN   This welcoming Art Nouveau brasserie, with lots of dark wood, mirrors, a high frescoed ceiling, Magritte images on the walls, and marble-topped tables, has a loyal local following. An extensive menu, ranging from grilled meats to seafood, and old Belgian favorites like stoemp, caters to just about any appetite. The beer, wine, and spirits list is long. Jeff De Gelas, the colorful proprietor (he also owns 't Kelderke; see below), is known as the "King of Stoemp."

Rue des Chapeliers 26 (off the Grand-Place). ℂ 02/514-25-54. Main courses 13€–23€ ($14–$26). AE, DC, MC, V. Daily noon–12:30am. Métro: Gare Centrale.

Falstaff Gourmand ★ *Value* BELGIAN/FRENCH   The Falstaff cafe across from the Bourse (see "Brussels After Dark," later in this chapter) is widely renowned as a classic Art Nouveau cafe. Around the corner, its former sister establishment—now operating on its own hook—has a different but equally notable style. Service is attentive, prompt, and friendly. First-class Belgian and French menu dishes include one of the best deals in Brussels: a three-course *menu gourmand,* which includes an aperitif, a glass of wine with a starter, and a small pitcher of wine with the main course.

Rue des Pierres 38 (close to the Bourse). ℂ 02/512-17-61. Main courses 13€–20€ ($15–$23); *menu gourmand* 30€ ($35). AE, DC, MC, V. Tues–Sat noon–3pm and 7–11pm; Sun noon–3pm. Métro: Bourse.

Inexpensive

L'Auberge des Chapeliers ★★ *Value* TRADITIONAL BELGIAN   Behind a beautiful brick facade, in a 17th-century building that was once the headquarters of the hat-makers' guild, these dining rooms are graced with timber beams and paneling and connected by a narrow wooden staircase. Popular with both locals and with visitors for its historic charm and fine food, and modest prices, it can get crowded at the height of lunch hour, so a good idea is to come before noon or after 2pm. The food is typical hearty Belgian fare, with an accent on mussels in season and dishes cooked in beer.

Rue des Chapeliers 3 (off of the Grand-Place). ℂ 02/513-73-38. Reservations recommended on weekends. Main courses 8.50€–18€ ($10–$21); fixed-price menus 15€–21€ ($17–$24). AE, DC, MC, V. Mon–Thurs noon–2pm and 6–11pm; Fri noon–2pm and 6pm–midnight; Sat noon–3pm and 6pm–midnight; Sun noon–3pm and 6–11pm. Métro: Gare Centrale.

Travel Tip: He who finds the best hotel deal has more to spend on facials involving knobbly vegetables.

Hello, the Roaming Gnome here. I've been nabbed from the garden and taken round the world. The people who took me are so terribly clever. They find the best offerings on Travelocity. For very little cha-ching. And that means I get to be pampered and exfoliated till I'm pink as a bunny's doodah.

travelocity®

1-888-TRAVELOCITY / travelocity.com / America Online Keyword: Travel

Plan your vacation

- flights, hotels, car rentals
- cruises & vacation packages
- destination guides
- fare alerts
- go to yahoo.com, click travel

't Kelderke ★★ *(Finds)* TRADITIONAL BELGIAN   The Little Cellar is one of the Grand-Place's most delightful surprises, even if it does have little in the way of frills. It's hidden beneath an ornate guild house, and the entrance isn't easy to spot. But when you descend the steps, you'll find a crowded, lively restaurant in the 17th-century brick-vaulted room at the bottom. As many Bruxellois as tourists throng the long wooden tables. The menu is replete with Belgian favorites like stoemp, served with a pork chop; Flemish beef stew; rabbit in beer; and Zeeland mussels in season, served from an open kitchen.

Grand-Place 15. ℂ **02/513-73-44.** Main courses 9.50€–20€ ($11–$22); *plat du jour* 9.75€ ($11). AE, DC, MC, V. Daily noon–2am. Métro: Gare Centrale.

THE LOWER CITY
Very Expensive
Comme Chez Soi ★★★ CLASSIC FRENCH   A visit to the revered, Art Nouveau "Just Like Home," which sports the maximum three Michelin stars, will surely be the culinary highlight of your trip. Although the food is a long way from being what most people actually eat at home, the welcome from master chef Pierre Wynants is warm, and his standards are high enough for the most rigorous taste buds. Ask for a table in the kitchen, where you can watch the master at work. Book for dinner as far ahead as possible; getting a table at short notice is more likely at lunchtime.

Place Rouppe 23 (at av. de Stalingrad). ℂ **02/512-29-21.** www.commechezsoi.be. Reservations required. Main courses 31€–94€ ($36–$108); fixed-price menus 56€–124€ ($64–$143). AE, DC, MC, V. Tues–Sat noon–1:30pm and 7–9:30pm. Métro: Anneessens.

Expensive
Aux Armes de Bruxelles ★★ TRADITIONAL BELGIAN   In business since 1921, this large, family-run Art Deco restaurant commands universal respect. It has hosted countless celebrities over the years, from Laurel and Hardy to Danny DeVito to Belgian favorites like singer Jacques Brel. The service is gracious and rather formal, but the ambience is totally relaxed. The vast menu—a Belgian cuisine primer in itself—includes local specialties like beef stewed in beer, mussels in a variety of guises, a delicious waterzooï, and shrimp croquettes, all at quite reasonable prices.

Rue des Bouchers 13 (a block from Grand-Place). ℂ **02/511-55-98.** Lunch menu 13€ ($14); main courses 14€–21€ ($16–$24); dinner menu 28€ ($32). AE, DC, MC, V. Tues–Sun noon–11:15pm. Métro: Gare Centrale.

Moderate
La Manufacture ★★ FRENCH/INTERNATIONAL   This was formerly the factory of chic leather-goods maker Delvaux, and even in its former industrial incarnation, style was a primary concern—though the neighborhood is unprepossessing. Fully refurbished, with parquet floors, polished wood, leather

---

Tips A Perfect Brew

Belgian beer is the perfect accompaniment to your meal. The country is renowned for its 450 brands of beer produced by dozens of breweries. Belgium's chefs use beer in their sauces the way French chefs use wine. Beef, chicken, and fish are often bathed in a savory sauce based on the local Brussels *gueze, faro,* and *kriek* brews.

banquettes, and stone tables set amid iron pillars and exposed air ducts, it produces trendy world cuisine with a French foundation for a mostly youthful public. It might at first seem disconcerting to find dim sum, sushi, Moroccan couscous, Lyon sausage, and Belgian waterzooï on the same menu, but don't worry—everything is tasty. There's piano music some evenings.

Rue Notre-Dame du Sommeil 12–22 (off place du Jardin-aux-Fleurs). ℰ 02/502-25-25. Main courses 12€–19€ ($13–$21); *menu du jour* (lunch only) 14€ ($16). AE, DC, MC, V. Mon–Fri noon–2pm and 6–11pm; Sat 6pm–midnight. Métro: Gare Centrale.

Inexpensive

In 't Spinnekopke ★★ *Finds* TRADITIONAL BELGIAN "In the Spider's Web" occupies a coach inn from 1762, just far enough off the beaten track downtown to be frequented mainly by those in the know. You dine in a tilting, tiled-floor building, at plain tables, and more likely than not squeezed into a tight space. This is one of Brussels's most traditional restaurants—so much so, that the menu lists its hardy regional standbys in the old Bruxellois dialect. *Stoemp mi sossisse* is stew with sausage, and *toung ave mei* is sole. The bar stocks a large selection of Belgian beers.

Place du Jardin-aux-Fleurs 1 (off rue Van Artevelde). ℰ 02/511-86-95. www.spinnekopke.be. Main courses 11€–20€ ($12–$22); *plat du jour* 8.15€ ($9). AE, DC, MC, V. Mon–Fri noon–3pm and 6–11pm; Sat 6pm–midnight. Métro: Bourse.

AROUND AV. LOUISE
Expensive

La Quincaillerie ★★ MODERN FRENCH/OYSTER BAR In the Ixelles district, where fine restaurants are as common as streetlights, this spot stands out, even though it may be a little too aware of its own modish good looks and is a shade pricey. The setting is a traditional former hardware store from 1903, with a giant railway station clock, wood paneling, and masses of wooden drawers, designed by students of Art Nouveau master Victor Horta. It's busy enough to get the waitstaff harassed and absent-minded, yet they're always friendly. Seafood dishes predominate on the menu.

Rue du Page 45 (at rue Américaine). ℰ 02/533-98-33. www.quincaillerie.be. Main courses 16€–24€ ($18–$28); fixed-price menus 13€–25€ ($15–$29). AE, DC, MC, V. Mon–Fri noon–2:30pm and 7pm–midnight; Sat–Sun 7pm–midnight. Tram: 81, 82, 91, or 92 to chaussée de Charleroi.

Moderate

L'Amadeus ★★ MODERN BELGIAN The postmodern chic of this restaurant/wine bar/oyster bar in a former sculptor's studio with garden-courtyard terrace makes a refreshing change from traditional Belgian style. Its candlelit interior is so dim you would think they're hiding something, but the cooking is nothing to be ashamed of. The menu includes such vegetarian treats as lasagna and ricotta-and-spinach tortellini; for meat eaters, choices include caramelized spare ribs and several salmon dishes. All are accompanied by delicious home-made nut bread. The Sunday brunch is an all-you-can-eat affair that includes smoked fish, cheese, eggs, bread, cereal, juice, and coffee.

Rue Veydt 13 (off chaussée de Charleroi). ℰ 02/538-34-27. Main courses 15€–23€ ($17–$26); *plat du jour* Mon–Fri 9.50€ ($11); Sun brunch 18€ ($21). AE, DC, MC, V. Tues–Fri and Sun noon–2:30pm and 7pm–1am; Mon and Sat 7pm–1am. Tram: 91 or 92.

SEEING THE SIGHTS

Brussels has such a wide variety of things to see and do. There are more than 75 museums dedicated to just about every special interest under the sun (from cartoons to cars), in addition to impressive public buildings, leafy parks, and interesting squares. History is just around every corner. Fortunately, numerous sidewalk cafes offer respite for weary feet, and there's good public transportation to those attractions beyond walking distance of the compact, heart-shaped city center, which contains many of Brussels's most popular attractions.

SIGHTSEEING SUGGESTIONS FOR FIRST-TIME VISITORS

If You Have 1 Day Beginning in the **Grand-Place,** visit the 15th-century Hôtel de Ville and the Musée de la Ville de Bruxelles, and view the decorated facades of the square's elegant guild houses. Squeeze in a pilgrimage to the nearby *Manneken-Pis* statue before returning to the Grand-Place for lunch at the convivial restaurant 't Kelderke. Shop (or window-shop), at the elegant 19th-century **Galeries Royales St-Hubert,** on the way to the **Cathédrale des Sts-Michel-et-Gudule.** End with the adventures of comic-book heroes at the **Centre Belge de la Bande-Dessinée.** After a dinner that should include mussels, in season, spend the evening checking out one or more of the city's famed cafes.

If You Have 2 Days View Belgian art masterpieces by Brueghel and Rubens at the **Musée d'Art Ancien,** and by Magritte and Delvaux at the **Musée d'Art Moderne** next door. After lunch, take a look at the neoclassical harmony of **place Royale,** the elegant **Palais Royal,** and the adjacent **Parc de Bruxelles.** Buy a bag of handmade chocolates at Wittamer on **place du Grand-Sablon,** then browse the antiques stores around the square. Stroll through the 15th-century church of Notre-Dame du Sablon before heading over to tranquil **place du Petit-Sablon** for a rest.

If You Have 3 Days Get up early and stop by the **Vieux-Marché** flea market on place du Jeu-de-Balle in the Marolles district. Then, head out to **Bruparck,** an attractions park on the city's northern edge that includes Mini-Europe and the Océade water leisure center. Nearby are the giant spheres of the **Atomium** and a panoramic view of the city from its viewing deck. Return to earth by having dinner in one of the guild hall restaurants, like La Maison du Cygne, that overlook the Grand-Place.

If You Have 4 or 5 Days On day 4, compare the old and the new by spending the morning in the city's most ancient quarter, around place Ste-Catherine, and the afternoon at the ultra-modern European District. On day 5, head out of town to critique Napoleon's generalship at the **Waterloo** battlefield, south of Brussels. If military history isn't your thing, explore instead Brussels's Art Nouveau architectural heritage by visiting the **Musée Horta,** and by strolling the side streets off av. Louise and around square Ambiorix.

THE GRAND-PLACE ★★★

Ornamental gables, medieval banners, gilded facades, sunlight flashing off gold-filigreed rooftop sculptures, a general impression of harmony and timelessness—there's a lot to take in all at once when you first enter the historic **Grand-Place** (Métro: Gare Centrale). The city's central square has always been the very heart of Brussels. Characterized by French playwright Jean Cocteau as "a splendid stage," it's the city's theater of life. Some call it the world's most beautiful square.

The Grand-Place has been the center of the city's commercial life and public celebrations since the 12th century. Most of it was destroyed in 1695 by the army of France's Louis XIV and then rebuilt over the next few years. Thanks to the town's close monitoring of later alterations, each building preserves its baroque splendor. Important guilds owned most of these buildings, and each competed to outdo the others with highly ornate facades of gold leaf and statuary, often with emblems of their guilds. Some now house cafes and restaurants. The illuminated square is even more beautiful at night than during the day.

Top honors go to the Gothic **Hôtel de Ville** and the neo-Gothic **Maison du Roi.** You'll also want to admire no. 9, **Le Cygne,** former headquarters of the butchers' guild and now a tony restaurant of the same name; no. 10, **L'Arbre d'Or,** headquarters of the brewers' guild and location of the Brewing Museum; and nos. 13 to 19, an ensemble of seven mansions known as the **Maison des Ducs de Brabant,** adorned with busts of 19 dukes.

Hôtel de Ville ✦✦ The facade of the dazzling Town Hall, from 1402, shows off Gothic intricacy at its best, complete with dozens of arched windows and sculptures—some of these, like the drunken monks, a sleeping Moor and his harem, and St. Michael slaying a female devil, displaying a sense of humor. A 66m (215-ft.) tower sprouts from the middle, yet it's not placed directly in the center. A colorful but untrue legend has it that when the architect realized his "error," he jumped from the summit of the tower.

The building is still the seat of the civic government, and its wedding room is a popular place to tie the knot. You can visit the interior on 40-minute tours, which start in a room full of paintings of the past foreign rulers of Brussels, who have included the Spanish, Austrians, French, and Dutch. In the spectacular Gothic Hall, open for visits when the city's aldermen are not in session—and surrounded by mirrors, presumably so each party can see what underhanded maneuvers the others are up to—you can see baroque decoration. In other chambers are 16th- to 18th-century tapestries. One of these depicts the Spanish

---

A Cool Little Guy

Two blocks south of the Grand-Place, at the intersection of rue de l'Etuve and rue du Chêne, is the **Manneken-Pis** ✦ (Métro: Bourse). A small bronze statue of a urinating child, Brussels's favorite character gleefully does what a little boy's gotta do, generally ogled by a throng of admirers. Children especially enjoy his bravura performance.

No one knows when this child first came into being, but it's clear he dates from quite a few centuries ago—the 8th century, according to one legend. Thieves have made off with the tyke several times in history. One criminal who stole and shattered the statue in 1817 was sentenced to a life of hard labor. The pieces were used to recast another version and that "original" was removed for safekeeping.

King Louis XV of France began the tradition of presenting colorful costumes to "Little Julian," which he wears on special occasions (during Christmas season he dons a Santa suit, complete with white beard), to make amends for Frenchmen having kidnapped the statue in 1747. The vast wardrobe is housed in the Musée de la Ville de Bruxelles in the Grand-Place (see above).

duke of Alba, whose cruel features reflect the brutal oppression he and his Council of Blood imposed on the Low Countries; others show scenes from the life of Clovis, first king of the Franks.

Grand-Place. ✆ **02/279-43-65.** Admission (guided tours only) 3€ ($3.45) adults, 2€ ($2.30) children 5–15, free for children under 5. Guided tours in English: Apr–Sept Tues and Wed 3:15pm, Sun 10:45am and 12:15pm; Oct–Mar Tues and Wed 3:15pm. Closed Jan 1, May 1, Nov 1 and 11, Dec 25. Métro: Gare Centrale.

Musée de la Ville de Bruxelles (Museum of the City of Brussels) ✦
Housed in the 19th-century neo-Gothic Maison du Roi (King's House)—though no king ever lived here—the museum displays a mixed collection associated with the art and history of Brussels. On the ground floor you can admire detailed tapestries from the 16th and 17th centuries, and porcelain, silver, and stone statuary. After climbing a beautiful wooden staircase, you can trace the history of Brussels in old maps, prints, photos, and models. Among the most fascinating exhibits are old paintings and scaled reconstructions of the historic city center, particularly those showing the riverside ambience along the now-vanished River Senne. On the third floor are more than 650 costumes that have been donated to *Manneken-Pis* (see below), including an Elvis costume.

Grand-Place. ✆ **02/279-43-50.** Admission 3€ ($3.45) adults, 2.50€ ($2.90) seniors and students, 1.50€ ($1.75) travelers with limited mobility and children 6–15, free for children under 6. Tues–Fri 10am–5pm; Sat–Sun 11am–5pm. Closed Jan 1, May 1, Nov 1 and 11, Dec 25. Métro: Gare Centrale.

SOME MEMORABLE MUSEUMS

Centre Belge de la Bande Dessinée (Belgian Comic-Strip Center) ✦✦ *Kids*
As you'll soon find out, Belgians are crazy for cartoons. The unique "CéBéBéDé," focuses on Belgium's own popular cartoon characters, like Lucky Luke, Thorgal, and, of course, Tintin, complete with red-and-white-checkered moon rocket, yet it doesn't neglect the likes of Superman, Batman, and the Green Lantern. The building, the Maisons des Waucquez, designed by Art Nouveau architect Victor Horta, is an attraction in itself.

Rue des Sables 20 (off of bd. de Berlaimont). ✆ **02/219-19-80.** www.brusselsbdtour.com. Admission 6.20€ ($7) adults, 5€ ($6) students and seniors, 2.50€ ($2.90) children under 12. Tues–Sun 10am–6pm. Closed Jan 1, Dec 25. Métro: Gare Centrale.

Musée du Costume et de la Dentelle Honoring a once-vital industry—10,000 Bruxellois produced lace in the 18th century—that now operates in a reduced but still notable fashion, this museum shows off particularly fine costumes and lace from 1599 to the present, and mounts frequently changing exhibitions.

Rue de la Violette 6 (near Grand-Place). ✆ **02/213-44-50.** Admission 2.50€ ($2.90) adults, 2€ ($2.30) children 6–16, free for children under 6. Mon–Tues and Thurs–Fri 10am–12:30pm and 1:30–5pm (until 4pm Oct–Mar); Sat–Sun 2–4:30pm. Closed Jan 1, May 1, Nov 1 and 11, Dec 25. Métro: Gare Centrale.

Musée Horta *Finds* Brussels owes much of its rich Art Nouveau heritage to Victor Horta (1861–1947), a resident architect who led the development of the style. His home and adjoining studio in St-Gilles, restored to their original condition, showcase his use of flowing, sinuous shapes and colors, in both interior decoration and architecture.

Rue Américaine 25 (off of chaussée de Charleroi). ✆ **02/543-04-90.** www.hortamuseum.be. Admission 4.95€ ($6) adults, 3.70€ ($4) seniors/students, 2.50€ ($2.90) children 5–18, free for children under 5. Tues–Sun 2–5:30pm. Closed national holidays. Tram: 81, 82, 91, or 92.

Musées Royaux des Beaux-Arts (Royal Museums of Fine Arts) ✦✦✦
In a vast museum of several buildings, this complex combines the **Musée d'Art**

Ancien and the **Musée d'Art Moderne** under one roof, connected by a passage. The collection displays mostly Belgian works, from the 14th century to the 20th century. Included in the historical collection are Hans Memling's portraits from the late 15th century, which are marked by sharp lifelike details; works by Hieronymus Bosch; and Lucas Cranach's *Adam and Eve.* Be sure to see the works of Pieter Brueghel, including his *Adoration of the Magi.* Don't miss his unusual *Fall of the Rebel Angels,* with grotesque faces and beasts. But don't fear—many of Brueghel's paintings, like those depicting Flemish village life, are of a less fiery nature. Later artists represented include Rubens, Van Dyck, Frans Hals, and Rembrandt.

Next door, in a circular building connected to the main entrance, the modern art section has an emphasis on underground works—if only because the museum's eight floors are all below ground level. The overwhelming collection includes works by van Gogh, Matisse, Dalí, Ernst, Chagall, Miró, and local heroes Magritte, Delvaux, De Braekeleer, and Permeke.

Rue de la Régence 3 (at place Royale). (℃ 02/508-32-11. www.fine-arts-museum.be. Admission 5€ ($6) adults, 3.50€ ($4) students, seniors, and travelers with limited mobility, free for children under 12; free for everyone 1st Wed afternoon of the month (except during special exhibits). Tues–Sun 10am–5pm. Closed Jan 1, May 1, Nov 1 and 11, Dec 25. Métro: Parc.

PARC DU CINQUANTENAIRE

Designed to celebrate the half centenary of Belgium's 1830 independence, the Cinquantenaire Park was a work in progress from the 1870s until well into the 20th century. Extensive gardens have at their heart a triumphal arch topped by a bronze four-horse chariot sculpture, representing *Brabant Raising the National Flag,* flanked by several fine museums.

Autoworld *Kids*   Even if you're not a car enthusiast, you'll find this display of 500 historic cars set in the hangarlike Palais Mondial fascinating. The collection starts with early motorized tricycles from 1899 and moves on to a 1911 Model T Ford, a 1924 Renault, a 1938 Cadillac that was the official White House car for FDR and Truman, a 1956 Cadillac used by Kennedy during his June 1963 visit to Berlin, and more.

Parc du Cinquantenaire 11. (℃ 02/736-41-65. www.autoworld.be. Admission 5€ ($6) adults; 3.70€ ($4) students, seniors, and travelers with limited mobility; 2€ ($2.30) children 6–13; free for children under 6. Apr–Sept Mon–Fri 9:30am–6pm, Sat–Sun 10am–6pm; Oct–Mar daily 10am–5pm. Closed Jan 1, Dec 25. Métro: Mérode.

Musée du Cinquantenaire ★   This vast museum shows off an eclectic collection of antiques, decorative arts (tapestries, porcelain, silver, and sculptures), and archaeology. Some highlights are an Assyrian relief from the 9th century B.C., a Greek vase from the 6th century B.C., a tabletop model of imperial Rome in the 4th century A.D., the A.D. 1145 reliquary of Pope Alexander, some exceptional tapestries, and colossal statues from Easter Island.

Parc du Cinquantenaire 10. (℃ 02/741-72-11. www.kmkg-mrah.be. Admission 4€ ($4.60) adults, 2.50€ ($2.90) students and seniors, 1.25€ ($1.45) children 12–18, free for children under 12; free for everyone 1st Wed afternoon of the month (except during special exhibits). Tues–Fri 9:30am–5pm; Sat–Sun and holidays 10am–5pm. Closed Jan 1, May 1, Nov 1 and 11, Dec 25. Métro: Mérode.

BRUPARCK

Built on the site of the 1958 Brussels World's Fair, this attractions park (Métro: Heysel) is home to the **Atomium** and **Mini-Europe** (see below); **The Village,** a collection of restaurants and cafes, including a restaurant in a 1930s railway car

---

---

of the legendary Orient Express; **Océade,** an indoor/outdoor watersports pavilion with water slides, pools, and saunas; a **planetarium;** and **Kinepolis,** a 26-screen movie multiplex. Ask for cheaper combination tickets if you plan to visit more than one Bruparck attraction.

Atomium As the Eiffel Tower is the symbol of Paris, the Atomium is the symbol of Brussels, and, like Paris's landmark, it was built for a world's fair, the 1958 Brussels World's Fair. Closed for renovation through 2004, it's due to reopen early in 2005. Rising 102m (335 ft.) like a giant plaything of the gods that's fallen to earth, the Atomium is an iron atom magnified 165 billion times. Its metal-clad spheres, representing individual atoms, are connected by enclosed escalators and elevators. It's the topmost atom that attracts most people: a restaurant/observation deck that provides a sweeping panorama of the metropolitan area.

Bd. du Centenaire, Heysel. ✆ 02/475-47-77. www.atomium.be. Admission 5.50€ ($6) adults, 4€ ($4.60) children under 13, free for children under 1.2m (4 ft.). Last week Mar–June and Sept daily 9:30am–5pm; July–Aug daily 9:30am–7pm (to 11pm mid-July to mid-Aug); Oct–Dec and New Year holidays 10am–5pm. Métro: Heysel.

Mini-Europe *Kids* Because Brussels is the "capital of Europe," it's fitting that the city is home to a miniature rendering of all the Continent's most notable architectural sights. Even a few natural wonders and technological developments are represented. Built on a scale of ¹⁄₂₅ of the originals, Big Ben, the Leaning Tower of Pisa, the Seville bullring, the Channel Tunnel, the Brandenburg Gate, and more, exhibit remarkable detail. Although children like Mini-Europe the best, adults certainly find it fun.

Bruparck, Heysel. ✆ 02/478-05-50. www.minieurope.com. Admission 12€ ($13) adults, 8.70€ ($10) children under 13, free for children under 1.2m (4 ft.). Apr–June and Sept 9:30am–5pm; July–Aug 9:30am–7pm; mid-July to mid-Aug Fri, Sat, and Sun 9:30am–11pm; Oct–Dec and 1st week Jan 10am–5pm. Closed rest of Jan–Mar. Métro: Heysel.

HISTORIC CHURCHES

Cathédrale des Sts-Michel-et-Gudule Victor Hugo considered this magnificent church, dedicated to the city's patron St. Michael and to St. Gudula, to be the "purest flowering of the Gothic style." Begun in 1226, it was officially consecrated as a cathedral only in 1961. The 16th-century Habsburg Emperor Charles V donated the superb stained-glass windows. Apart from these, the spare interior decoration focuses attention on its soaring columns and arches. The bright exterior stonework makes a fine sight. On Sunday at 10am, the Eucharist is celebrated with a Gregorian choir. In July, August, and September, polyphonic Masses are sung by local and international choirs at 10am. From August to October, chamber music and organ concerts are occasionally performed on weekdays at 8pm. In spring and autumn at 12:30pm, Mass is sung accompanied by instrumental soloists and readings by actors (in French).

Parvis Ste-Gudule (off bd. de l'Impératrice 2 blocks west of Gare Centrale). (℃ **02/217-83-45**. Cathedral, free admission; crypt, treasury, archaeological zone 2.50€ ($2.90). Mon–Fri 8:30am–6pm; Sat–Sun 8am–6pm. Métro: Gare Centrale.

Notre-Dame du Sablon   This late-Gothic 15th-century to 16th-century structure is noted for its four-fold gallery with brightly colored stained-glass windows, illuminated from the inside at night, in striking contrast with the gray-white Gothic arches and walls. Also worth seeing are the two baroque chapels, which are decorated with funeral symbols in white marble.

Rue Bodenbroeck 6 (at place du Grand-Sablon). (℃ **02/511-57-41**. Free admission. Mon–Fri 9am–5pm; Sat–Sun 10am–6:30pm. Tram: 92, 93, or 94.

OTHER HISTORIC SQUARES

Considered classier than the Grand-Place (see above) by the locals, though busy traffic diminishes your enjoyment of its cafe-terraces, **place du Grand-Sablon** ★★ (tram: 92, 93, or 94) is lined with gabled mansions. This is antiques territory, and many of those mansions house antiques stores or private art galleries, with pricey merchandise on display. On Saturday and Sunday an excellent antiques market sets up its stalls in front of Notre-Dame du Sablon Church (see above).

Across rue de la Régence, the Grand-Sablon's little cousin, **place du Petit-Sablon** ★ (tram: 92, 93, or 94), has a small sculptured garden with a fountain and pool at its center. This magical little retreat from the city bustle is surrounded by wrought-iron railings, atop which stand 48 small statues of medieval guildsmen.

At the meeting-point of rue de la Régence and rue Royale (streets on which stand many of the city's premier attractions), **place Royale** ★ (tram: 92, 93, or 94) is graced by an equestrian statue of Duke Godefroid de Bouillon, leader of the First Crusade. Also in place Royale is the neoclassical St-Jacques-sur-Coudenberg Church.

PARKS

The most attractive park in town is the **Parc de Bruxelles** ★★ (Métro: Parc), extending in front of the Palais Royal. Once the property of the dukes of Brabant, this well-designed park with geometrically divided paths running through it—which form the outline of Masonic symbols—became public in 1776. The many benches make it a fine place to stop for a picnic. It's also historic: The first shots in Belgium's 1830 war of independence were fired here. In 2001, the park was restored as closely as possible to its 18th-century look. The refurbished 1840s bandstand hosts regular summer concerts.

The large public park called the **Bois de la Cambre** ★ begins at the top of av. Louise in the southern section of Brussels (tram: 23, 90, 93, or 94). This is the city's lung, and it gets busy on sunny weekends. Its centerpiece is a small lake with an island in its center that you can reach via an electrically operated pontoon. Some busy roads run through the park and traffic moves fast on them, so be careful with children at these points.

Continuing south from the Bois, the **Forêt de Soignes** ★ is no longer a park with playing areas and regularly mown grass, but a forest stretching almost to Waterloo; this is a great place for getting away from it all, particularly in the fall, when the colors are dazzling.

ORGANIZED TOURS

Brussels City Tours, rue de la Colline 8, off Grand-Place (✆ **02/513-77-44;** www.brussels-city-tours.com; Métro: Gare Centrale), operates a guided 2¾-hour "Brussels City Tour" by bus for 20€ ($23) for adults, 18€ ($21) for students and seniors, and 10€ ($12) for children. You can book tours at most hotels, and arrangements can be made for hotel pickup.

From June 15 to September 15, **Le Bus Bavard,** rue des Thuyas 12 (✆ **02/ 673-18-35**), operates a 3-hour daily "chatterbus" tour at 10am from the Galeries Royales St-Hubert (Métro: Gare Centrale), a mall next to rue du Marché-aux-Herbes 90, a few steps off of the Grand-Place. A walking tour covers the historic center, followed by a bus ride through areas the average visitor never sees. You hear about life in Brussels and get a real feel for the city. The price is 8.75€ ($10). You don't need a reservation for this fascinating experience—just be there by 10am.

ARAU, bd. Adolphe-Max 55 (✆ **02/219-33-45;** www.arau.org. Métro: De Brouckère), organizes tours that help you discover not only Brussels's countless treasures but also problems the city faces. It runs 3-hour themed coach tours: "Grand-Place and Its Surroundings," "Brussels 1900—Art Nouveau," "Brussels 1930—Art Deco," "Surprising Parks and Squares," and "Alternative Brussels." You are advised to book ahead. Tours by bus are 15€ ($17), and 12€ ($14) for those under 26; tours by foot are 10€ ($12). Tours take place on Saturday mornings from March to November; private group tours can be arranged year-round.

THE SHOPPING SCENE

Lace is the overwhelming favorite purchase, followed by crystal, jewelry, antiques, and pewter. Chocolate, beer, and other foods are more economical. And in souvenir stores you find replicas of *Manneken-Pis,* so you can bring the little guy home with you.

Don't look for many bargains. As a general rule, Upper Town around av. Louise and Porte de Namur is more expensive than Lower Town around rue Neuve. You can enjoy a stroll along modern shopping promenades, the busiest of which is the pedestrians-only rue Neuve, starting at place de la Monnaie and running north to place Rogier; it's home to boutiques; big department stores like Inno, H&M, and Marks & Spencer; and several malls.

Some of the trendiest boutiques are on rue Antoine-Dansaert, across from the Bourse. An interesting street for window-shopping, rue des Eperonniers, near the Grand-Place, hosts many small stores selling antiques, toys, old books, and clothing.

STORES & OUTDOOR MARKETS

The **Galeries Royales St-Hubert** (Métro: Gare Centrale) is an airy arcade hosting expensive boutiques, cafes with outdoor terraces, and buskers playing classical music. Opened in 1847, architect Pierre Cluysenaer's Italian neo-Renaissance gallery has a touch of class and is well worth a stroll through, even if you have no intention of shopping. The elegant gallery is near the Grand-Place, between rue du Marché-aux-Herbes and rue de l'Ecuyer, and is split by rue des Bouchers.

In a former guild house, **Maison Antoine,** Grand-Place 26 (✆ **02/ 512-48-59;** Métro: Gare Centrale), is one of the best places in town to buy lace. The quality is superb, the service is friendly, and the prices aren't unreasonable.

Visit **De Boe,** rue de Flandre 36 (✆ **02/511-13-73;** Métro: Ste-Catherine), a small store near the Marché-aux-Poissons, for the heavenly aromas of roasted

---

Tips **Tax Saver**

If you spend over 125€ ($144) in some stores, and you are not a resident of the European Union, you can get a tax refund when you leave the EU. Stores that display a TAX-FREE SHOPPING sign provide visitors who are not resident in the European Union the form they need for recovering some of the 21.5% value-added tax (TVA) on purchases. At the airport, show the Customs officials your purchase and receipt and they'll stamp the form. Mail this form back to the Belgian Tax Bureau (the address is on the form) or bring it in directly to the Best Change office at the airport, which charges a small commission but gives you an on-the-spot refund.

---

and blended coffee, a superb selection of wines in all price categories, and an array of specialty teas, spices, and epicurean snacks. **Dandoy,** rue au Beurre 31 (✆ **02/511-03-26;** Métro: Bourse), is where cookie and cake fans can try traditional Belgian specialties like spicy *speculoos* (traditional Belgian cookies made with brown sugar and cinnamon and baked in wooden molds) and *pain à la grecque* (caramelized, sugary flaky pastries).

If you have a sweet tooth, you'll feel you're in heaven when you see Brussels's famous chocolate stores, filled with sumptuous soft-centered pralines, from around 12€ ($14) a kilogram (2¼ lb.). You find some of the best confections at **Chocolatier Mary,** rue Royale 73 (✆ **02/217-45-00;** Métro: Parc), supplier to the royal court; **Neuhaus,** Galerie de la Reine 25 (✆ **02/502-59-14;** Métro: Gare Centrale); **Wittamer,** place du Grand-Sablon 12 (✆ **02/512-37-42;** tram: 92, 93, or 94); and **Léonidas,** bd. Anspach 46 (✆ **02/218-03-63;** Métro: Bourse).

For kids, pick up some Tintin mementos from **Boutique de Tintin,** rue de la Colline 13 (✆ **02/514-45-50;** Métro: Gare Centrale). **Waterstone's,** bd. Adolphe Max 75 (✆ **02/219-27-08;** Métro: Rogier), has English-language books, newspapers, and magazines.

The city's favorite *marché-aux-puces* (flea market) is the **Vieux-Marché (Old Market;** Métro: Porte de Hal), on place du Jeu-de-Balle, a large cobblestone square in the Marolles district, open daily from 7am to 2pm. Every Sunday from 7am to 2pm, hundreds of merchants assemble their wares in a **street market** outside Gare du Midi (Métro: Gare du Midi), and because many of the merchants are of Arab origin, the scene resembles a *casbah.* It has many excellent food bargains, making it a perfect place to gather provisions for a few days. You can also find household items and odds and ends at low cost. Hold on to your wallet, however: The market attracts pickpockets.

BRUSSELS AFTER DARK

Although the city isn't as noted for its nightlife as some other European capitals, it has a full array of things to do. And if the range is narrower than in bigger cities like London and Paris, the quality is not. A listing of upcoming events—opera, classical music, dance, theater, live music, film, and other events—is in the *What's On* guide in the weekly English-language magazine *The Bulletin.*

You can order tickets for performing-arts venues from the **Central Booking Office** (✆ **0800/21-221**), open Monday to Friday from 9am to 7pm, Saturday from 10am to 7pm. The tourist office in the Town Hall on the Grand-Place (see "Visitor Information," earlier in this chapter) can reserve concert/theater tickets for 1€ ($1.15).

THE PERFORMING ARTS

An opera house in the grand style, the **Théâtre Royal de la Monnaie** ★★, place de la Monnaie (② **02/229-12-00;** www.lamonnaie.be; Métro: De Brouckère), is home to the Opéra Royal de la Monnaie, which has been called the best in the French-speaking world, and to the Orchestre Symphonique de la Monnaie. The resident modern dance company, Anne Theresa de Keersmaeker's Group Rosas, is noted for its original moves. The box office is open Tuesday to Saturday from 11am to 6pm. Tickets run 8€ to 148€ ($9–$170); for those age under 28, they're 8€ ($9) and available 5 minutes before a show.

The **Bozar,** rue Ravenstein 23 (② **02/507-82-00;** Métro: Gare Centrale)— formerly the elegantly named Palais des Beaux-Arts until some "bright spark" came up with the idea of trendifying it—is home to the Belgian National Orchestra. The box office is open Monday to Saturday from 11am to 6pm, with tickets running 10€ to 75€ ($12–$86). The **Cirque Royal,** rue de l'Enseigne-ment 81 (② **02/218-20-15;** Métro: Parc), formerly a real circus, now hosts music, opera, and ballet. The box office is open Tuesday to Saturday from 11am to 6pm, with tickets for 8€ to 65€ ($9–$75).

LIVE-MUSIC CLUBS

The jazz café **Marcus Mingus Jazz Spot,** impasse de la Fidelité 10, off rue des Bouchers (② **02/502-02-97;** Métro: Gare Centrale), attracts top local perform-ers and an occasional international name. The Art Deco bar **L'Archiduc,** rue Antoine Dansaert 6 (② **02/512-06-52;** Métro: Bourse), serves up a sophisti-cated program of jazz on weekends.

DANCE CLUBS

Top clubs include the always popular **Le Sparrow,** rue Duquesnoy 16 (② **02/ 512-66-22;** Métro: Gare Centrale); **Le Fuse,** rue Blaes 208 (② **02/511-97-89;** bus: 20 or 48) for techno; and **Griffin's Night Club,** in the Royal Windsor Hotel, rue Duquesnoy 5 (② **02/505-55-55;** Métro: Gare Centrale), fashionable for older hoofers.

GAY & LESBIAN CLUBS

Rue des Riches-Claires and **rue du Marché-au-Charbon** host gay and lesbian bars. **Macho 2,** rue du Marché-au-Charbon 108 (② **02/513-56-67;** Métro: Bourse), a block from rue des Riches-Claires, has a gay men's sauna, pool, steam room, and café. **Le Fuse** and **Le Sparrow** (see above) have gay nights. Cover varies.

⌒Moments Puppet Theater

Traditional Brussels marionette theater is performed at **Théâtre Royal de Toone,** impasse Schuddeveld 6, Petite rue des Bouchers 21 (② **02/217-27-23;** Métro: Gare Centrale). In a tiny theater in the old **Toone VII** café, puppet master José Géal presents adaptations of classic tales like *Faust* and *The Three Musketeers.* Some performances are in English, others are in French, Dutch, German, or the local patois, Bruxellois, with plots and characters so familiar that even if you don't understand a word, you'll be able to follow the action. Performances are Tuesday to Saturday at 8:30pm; tickets are 10€ ($12).

For more information about clubs and gay life in Brussels, contact **Infor Homo,** av. de Roodebeek 57 (© **02/733-10-24;** Métro: Diamant), open Tuesday to Friday 8am to 6pm. Or stop by the gay and lesbian community center, **Telsquels,** rue du Marché-au-Charbon 81 (© **02/512-45-87;** Métro: Bourse), open Saturday to Thursday 5pm to 2am, Friday 8am to 4am.

CAFES & BARS

The city's many watering holes run the gamut from Art Nouveau palaces to plain and convivial. You should linger a few hours in one, preferably savoring one of the incredible beers for which Belgium is famous. It's always satisfying to sit at a sidewalk cafe on the Grand-Place and drink in the beauty of the floodlit golden buildings ringing the square. Drinks on a Grand-Place terrace are more expensive than those in ordinary cafes, but once you've ordered one you can nurse it for hours—or until the waiter's patience wears out and he grabs the glass from you, empty or not.

The city's oldest cafe, in a 1690 building, **Le Roy d'Espagne,** Grand-Place 1 (© **02/513-08-07;** Métro: Gare Centrale), accommodates patrons in several areas. In addition to the outdoor tables, you can drink in a room preserving a 17th-century Flemish interior—a masterpiece of wooden architecture with a wooden walkway, wooden beams above, and a fireplace covered by a black metal hood. The fourth-floor view of the Grand-Place is spectacular. It's open daily from 10am to 1am.

Although its name means "Sudden Death," you'll likely survive **A la Mort Subite,** rue Montagne-aux-Herbes-Potagères 7 (© **02/513-13-18;** Métro: Gare Centrale), a 1911 cafe with stained-glass mirrors, old photographs, paintings, and prints. A good place to enjoy an afternoon coffee or an evening beer, it's open daily from 10am to 1am. A block from the Grand-Place, in a 1642 house, **A l'Imaige de Nostre-Dame,** rue du Marché-aux-Herbes 6–8 (© **02/219-42-49;** Métro: Gare Centrale), is often filled with people of all ages enjoying reasonably priced beer amid wooden ceiling beams and old wooden tables. It's open daily from noon to midnight.

You can still enjoy a drink in the stunning setting of legendary Art Nouveau tavern **Le Falstaff,** rue Henri Maus 17–25 (© **02/511-98-77;** Métro: Bourse), though its cool image has suffered under new owners. It's open daily from 8am to around 3am (4am on weekends). Across the way, at **Le Cirio,** rue de la Bourse 18 (© **02/512-13-95;** Métro: Bourse), you sip your drink in quiet, refined surroundings that make the exercise seem worthwhile. It's open daily from 10am to 1am.

In a 17th-century building, **Le Fleur en Papier Doré,** rue des Alexiens 53, off place de la Chapelle (© **02/511-16-59;** Métro: Bourse), calls itself a "temple of surrealism" because Magritte used to relax here. Despite the grandmotherly decor, the cafe attracts a wide assortment of arty types. On Friday and Saturday from 9 or 10pm, an accordion player pumps out some tunes, and there are occasional poetry readings upstairs. The cafe is open daily from 11am to 11pm.

Gargoyles, devils, and other assorted creatures from the darker recesses of the human mind—the decor at **Halloween,** rue des Grands-Carmes 10 (© **02/514-12-56;** Métro: Bourse)—are enough to give you the creeps. It helps create a memorable ambience in a bar patronized mostly by the young and the hip. It's open Tuesday to Sunday from 7pm to 1am.

In an early-1900s town house on the edge of the city center, **De Ultieme Hallucinatie,** rue Royale 316 (© **02/217-06-14;** Métro: Botanique), has rocky

> **Tips** **Belgian Brews Pack a Punch**
>
> **Be warned:** Belgian beers are stronger than their American counterparts—alcohol content can be as high as 12%. Try a rich, dark Trappist ale brewed by monks from Chimay, Orval, Rochefort, Sint-Benedictus, Westmalle, and Westvleteren monasteries. Brussels is well known for its *lambic* beers, which use naturally occurring yeast for fermentation, are often flavored with fruit, and come in bottles with champagne-type corks. Unlike any other beer, they're more akin to a sweet sparkling wine. *Gueuze,* a blend of young and aged lambic beers, is one of the least sweet. If you prefer something sweeter, try raspberry-flavored *framboise* or cherry-flavored *kriek. Faro* is a low-alcohol beer, sometimes sweetened or lightly spiced.

walls and plants along one side, a long marble-top bar along the other, and a small outdoor cafe area in back. You can choose from beers and wines (a wide selection), coffee, and a few snacks. Downstairs, a futuristic dance club has abstract outer-space art. The bar is open Monday to Friday from 11am to 3am, Saturday and Sunday from 4pm to 3am.

A SIDE TRIP TO WATERLOO ★

Europe's Gettysburg, the battle that ended Napoleon's empire was fought on rolling farmland near **Waterloo,** just south of Brussels. On June 18, 1815, 72,000 British, Dutch, Belgian, and German troops, aided before the day's end by around 40,000 Prussians, defeated the mighty Napoleon Bonaparte and his 76,000 French, leaving 40,000 dead and wounded on the field. Napoleon survived, but his attempt to rebuild his empire was crushed; he was exiled to the island of St. Helena, where he died 6 years later.

From Brussels, bus W departs twice hourly for Waterloo from Gare du Midi (Métro: Gare du Midi). The 18km (11-mile) ride takes 50 minutes and costs 3€ ($3.45). The bus stops at both the Wellington Museum in Waterloo itself and at the battlefield visitor center, south of the town. By **car** from Brussels, take the ring road (R0) to Exit 27 for Waterloo, and N5 south to the battlefield.

The battlefield remains much as it was on that fateful day. Before touring it, you should study a 360-degree **panoramic mural** and see a short audiovisual presentation of the battle, including scenes from Sergei Bondarchuk's epic movie *Waterloo,* at the **Centre du Visiteur,** route du Lion 252–254, Braine l'Alleud (© **02/385-19-12;** www.waterloo1815.be). To survey the battlefield, climb the nearby **Butte du Lion (Lion Mound),** a conical hill surmounted by a bronze lion, behind the center.

These three sites are open daily: April to September 9:30am to 6:30pm and October to March 10am to 5pm; closed Jan 1, Dec 25. Admission to the visitor center is free; the audiovisual presentation is 4.95€ ($6) for adults, 4.20€ ($4.85) for seniors and students, and 3.35€ ($3.85) for children ages 6 to 12; admission to the Lion Mound is 1€ ($1.15) for adults, and .50€ (60¢) for children ages 6 to 12; admission to the panorama is 2.75€ ($3.15) for adults, 2€ ($2.30) for seniors and students, and 1.50€ ($1.70) for children ages 6 to 12; a combination ticket is 7.45€ ($9) for adults, 6.20€ ($7) for seniors and students, and 4.70€ ($5) for children ages 6 to 12; in all cases, free for children under 6.

> **Tips**   Waterloo Redux
>
> The next reenactment of the Battle of Waterloo, a spectacular event that is staged once every 5 years and features thousands of uniformed participants from around the world, is due to take place on June 19, 2005—the Sunday nearest to the battle's June 18 anniversary. *Note:* The date had not been confirmed at this writing, so you should call ahead to the visitor center before going. The previous day, Saturday, when the "troops" are assembling, is also an interesting time to be in Waterloo and at the battlefield.

In Waterloo itself, you can fill in details of the battle at the **Musée Wellington,** chaussée de Bruxelles 147 (© **02/354-78-06;** www.museewellington.com), a former inn that served as Wellington's headquarters. It's open daily, April to September from 9:30am to 6:30pm and October to March from 10:30am to 5pm. Admission, which includes an audio guide (except for children under 6), is 5€ ($6) for adults, 4€ ($4.60) for seniors and students, 1€ ($1.15) for children ages 6 to 12, and free for children under 6.

2 Bruges ★★★

Walking around the almost perfectly preserved city of Bruges is like taking a step back in time. From its 13th-century origins as a cloth-manufacturing town to its current incarnation as a tourism mecca, Bruges seems to have changed little. As in a fairy tale, swans glide down the winding canals and the stone houses look like they're made of gingerbread. Even though glass-fronted stores have taken over the ground floors of ancient buildings, and the swans scatter before tour boats chugging along the canals, Bruges has made the transition from medieval to modern with remarkable grace. The town seems revitalized rather than crushed by the tremendous influx of tourists.

ESSENTIALS
GETTING THERE   By Train   Bruges is 55 minutes from Brussels, and trains depart every hour. Bruges is well connected to Ghent, Antwerp, the North Sea resort of Ostend, and the ferry port of Zeebrugge. Bruges station (look out for BRUGGE, the town's Dutch name, on the destination boards) is on Stationsplein (© **050/38-23-82),** 1.5km (1 mile) from the city center. To get to the center, take a 20-minute walk or a short bus ride—choose any bus labeled CENTRUM and get out at the Markt.

By Bus   Eurolines (© **02/274-13-50;** www.eurolines.com) buses from Brussels, London, Paris, Amsterdam, and other cities arrive at the bus station adjoining Bruges railway station.

By Car   If you're driving from Brussels or Ghent, take A10/E40. Drop off your car at a parking lot or garage (see "Getting Around," below). The network of one-way streets in the center makes driving a trial.

VISITOR INFORMATION   **Toerisme Brugge,** Burg 11, 8000 Brugge (© **050/44-86-86;** fax 050/44-86-00; www.brugge.be), in the center of town. The office, which can make hotel reservations, is open April to September, Monday to Friday from 9:30am to 6:30pm, Saturday, Sunday and holidays from 10am

Bruges

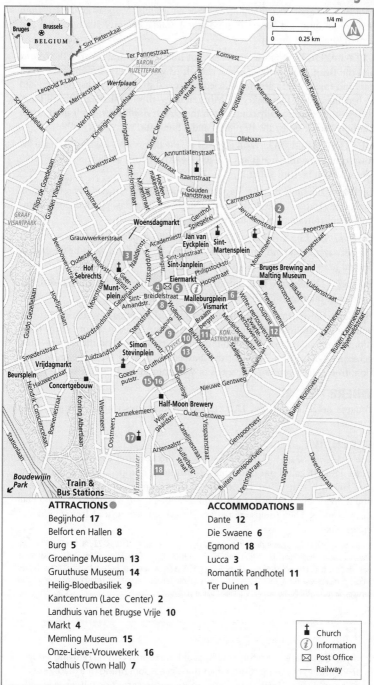

ATTRACTIONS ●
Begijnhof **17**
Belfort en Hallen **8**
Burg **5**
Groeninge Museum **13**
Gruuthuse Museum **14**
Heilig-Bloedbasiliek **9**
Kantcentrum (Lace Center) **2**
Landhuis van het Brugse Vrije **10**
Markt **4**
Memling Museum **15**
Onze-Lieve-Vrouwekerk **16**
Stadhuis (Town Hall) **7**

ACCOMMODATIONS ■
Dante **12**
Die Swaene **6**
Egmond **18**
Lucca **3**
Romantik Pandhotel **11**
Ter Duinen **1**

✝ Church
ⓘ Information
✉ Post Office
...... Railway

to 12:30pm and 2 to 6:30pm; October to March, Monday to Friday from 9:30am to 5pm, and Saturday, Sunday and holidays from 9:30am to 1pm and 2 to 5:30pm.

CITY LAYOUT Narrow streets fan out from two central squares, the **Markt** and the **Burg.** A network of canals threads its way to every section of the small city, and the center is almost encircled by a canal that opens at its southern end to become a swan-filled lake, the **Minnewater**—this translates as Lake of Love, though the name actually comes from the Dutch *Binnen Water,* meaning Inner Harbor—bordered by the Begijnhof and a fine park.

GETTING AROUND Walking is by far the best way to see Bruges, since the town center is traffic-free (but wear good walking shoes, as those charming cobblestones can be hard going).

By Bike Biking is a terrific way to get around town. You can rent a bike from the railway station (© **050/38-58-71**) for 9€ ($10) a day, plus a deposit. Some hotels and stores rent bikes, for 5€ to 9€ ($6–$10) a day.

By Bus De Lijn city buses (© **070/22-02-00**) depart the bus station beside the railway station, and from the big square called 't Zand, west of the Markt. Several bus routes pass through the Markt.

By Taxi There's a taxi rank outside the railway station (© **050/38-46-60**), and another at the Markt (© **050/33-44-44**).

By Car Movement by car through the old center is tightly restricted. Leave your car in your hotel's parking garage, if it has one. You can use one of the large, prominently signposted underground parking garages around the center—these get expensive for long stays—or the inexpensive parking lot at the railway station, from where you can take a bus or walk into the heart of the city.

WHERE TO STAY

Bruges's hotels fill up fast. Don't arrive without a reservation, particularly in summer.

EXPENSIVE

Die Swaene ★★★ This small hotel on the beautiful city-center Groenerei canal has been called one of the most romantic in Europe, thanks in part to the care lavished on it by the Hessels family. The comfortable rooms are elegantly and individually furnished, and the lounge, from 1779, was once the Guild Hall of the Tailors. The in-house restaurant has earned rave reviews from guests and critics alike.

Steenhouwersdijk 1 (across the canal from the Burg), 8000 Brugge. © **050/34-27-98.** Fax 050/33-66-74. www.dieswaene-hotel.com. 32 units. 170€–245€ ($196–$282) double; 320€–420€ ($368–$483) suite. Rates include buffet breakfast. AE, DC, MC, V. Parking 10€ ($12). **Amenities:** Restaurant; lounge; bar; heated indoor pool; exercise room; sauna; concierge; limited room service; babysitting; laundry service; secretarial services. *In room:* A/C (some units), TV, minibar, hair dryer.

Tips Avoid the Tourist Crush

If you don't care much for crowds, avoid the tourist crush by staying away from Bruges in summertime, when the place is something of a madhouse. You could visit Ghent instead. Go to Bruges in spring or fall, or even in winter. (But you'll miss out on a lot of animation, too.)

Romantik Pandhotel ★★ Close to the Markt, this lovely 18th-century mansion surrounded by plane trees is an oasis of tranquillity. Although it provides modern conveniences, its exquisite, old-fashioned furnishings lend special grace to comfortable rooms. Guests praise Mrs. Chris Vanhaecke-Dewaele for her hospitality and attention to detail. You can use an Internet-connected computer in the lobby to send and receive e-mail.

Pandreitje 16 (off Rozenhoedkaai), 8000 Brugge. ℂ **050/34-06-66.** Fax 050/34-05-56. www.pandhotel.com. 24 units. 150€–225€ ($173–$259) double; 225€–325€ ($259–$374) suite. Rates include full breakfast. AE, DC, MC, V. Limited street parking. **Amenities:** Bar; concierge; 24-hr. room service; in-room massage; babysitting; laundry service; dry cleaning; nonsmoking rooms. *In room:* A/C, TV, dataport, minibar, hair dryer.

MODERATE

Dante This ultramodern brick hotel is set alongside a lovely canal, a short walk west from the center of Bruges. It takes its name from a reference to Bruges in the Florentine poet Dante Alighieri's *Divine Comedy*. The hotel is an artful marriage of old Bruges style and modern amenities and fittings. Its spacious guest rooms are restfully decorated in warm colors like peach and furnished with bamboo and rattan beds. Most have a view of the canal at Coupure. The Dante's vegetarian restaurant, **Toermalijn,** is highly regarded locally.

Coupure 30 (close to Gentpoort), 8000 Brugge. ℂ **050/34-01-94.** Fax 050/34-35-39. www.hoteldante.be. 22 units. 106€–193€ ($122–$222) double. Rates include buffet breakfast. AE, DC, MC, V. Limited street parking. **Amenities:** Restaurant; game room; limited room service; laundry service; same-day dry cleaning; nonsmoking rooms. *In room:* TV, minibar, hair dryer.

Egmond ★★ In a rambling mansion next to Minnewater Park, the Egmond has just eight rooms, but the lucky few who stay here will find ample space, plenty of family ambience, abundant local color, and lots of peace and tranquillity. All guest rooms have recently been redecorated and are furnished in an individual style with views of the garden and Minnewater Park. Every afternoon, free coffee and tea are served in the new garden terrace or in the lounge, which has an 18th-century fireplace. At the "honesty bar" you can help yourself to a drink and leave the payment.

Minnewater 15 (at Minnewater Park), 8000 Brugge. ℂ **050/34-14-45.** Fax 050/34-29-40. www.egmond.be. 8 units. 120€ ($138) double. Rates include buffet breakfast. No credit cards. Free parking. *In room:* A/C (some units), TV, dataport, hair dryer, safe.

Ter Duinen ★ This charming hotel is an ideal blend of classical style and modern conveniences. Guest rooms are ample in size and brightly decorated, and have modern furnishings. Some rooms have wooden ceiling beams, and some have a great view overlooking the tranquil Langerei canal, just north of the town center and within easy walking distance. Proprietors Marc and Lieve Bossu-Van Den Heuvel take a justified pride in their hotel and extend a friendly welcome to guests.

Langerei 52 (at Kleine Nieuwstraat), 8000 Brugge. ℂ **050/33-04-37.** Fax 050/34-42-16. www.terduinenhotel.be. 20 units. 98€–148€ ($113–$170) double. Rates include buffet breakfast. AE, DC, MC, V. Limited street parking. **Amenities:** Lounge; limited room service; dry cleaning. *In room:* A/C, TV, hair dryer, safe.

INEXPENSIVE

Lucca ★ *Value* This mansion right in the heart of romantic Bruges was built in the 14th century by a wealthy merchant from Lucca, Italy, and the high ceilings and wide halls convey a sense of luxury. The welcome is warm, and the guest rooms are in excellent condition and sport pine furnishings. Units with bathrooms also have TVs. Breakfast is served in a cozy medieval cellar decorated with antiques.

Naaldenstraat 30 (off Sint-Jakobsstraat), 8000 Brugge. © 050/34-20-67. Fax 050/33-34-64. www.hotellucca.be. 19 units, 14 with bathroom. 50€ ($58) double without bathroom; 62€–82€ ($71–$94) double with bathroom. Rates include buffet breakfast. AE, DC, MC, V. Limited street parking. *In room:* TV (some units).

WHERE TO DINE
VERY EXPENSIVE
De Karmeliet ★★★ BELGIAN/FRENCH In 1996, chef Geert Van Hecke became the first Flemish chef to be awarded three Michelin stars. He has described his award-winning menu as "international cuisine made with local products" that aims to merge French quality with Flemish quantity. The result is outstanding, and the decor in the 1833 town house is as elegant as the cuisine deserves.

Langestraat 19 (off of Hoogstraat). © 050/33-82-59. www.dekarmeliet.be. Reservations required. Main courses 45€–70€ ($52–$81); fixed-price menus 50€–125€ ($58–$144). AE, DC, MC, V. Tues 7–9:30pm; Wed–Sat noon–2pm and 7–9:30pm; Sun noon–2pm.

EXPENSIVE
't Pandreitje ★★ FRENCH/BELGIAN This restaurant is one of the nicest spots in town. It's in the shade of the medieval Market Hall's bell tower, just off the Rozenhoedkaai, one of the most beautiful canal sides in Bruges. The interior of this Renaissance-era private home has been turned into an elegant Louis XVI setting from 1740 for a menu of classic dishes.

Pandreitje 6 (off Rozenhoedkaai). © 050/33-11-90. www.pandreitje.be. Reservations required. Main courses 28€–40€ ($32–$46); gastronomische menu 50€–80€ ($58–$92). AE, DC, MC, V. Mon–Tues and Thurs–Sat noon–2pm and 7–9:30pm.

MODERATE
De Stove ★★ FLEMISH/SEAFOOD This small, family-owned restaurant combines a rustic atmosphere with a more modern style than is the norm in Bruges. The seafood specialties are well worth a try, particularly the Flemish fish stew.

Kleine Sint-Amandsstraat 4 (close to the Markt). © 050/33-78-35. www.restaurantdestove.be. Reservations recommended on weekends. Main courses 17€–30€ ($20–$35); fixed-price menu 42€ ($48). AE, MC, V. Fri 6:30–9:30pm; Sat–Tues noon–1:45pm and 6:30–9:30pm.

Kasteel Minnewater ★★ FRENCH/BELGIAN Old paintings on the walls, chandeliers, and fine table linens complement this château/restaurant's location close to the Begijnhof, with a garden terrace on the Minnewater (Lake of Love). It exudes an unstuffy charm, and though its prices have been edging up, it still provides a good deal considering the setting. Specialties include sole Ostendaise, North Sea shrimp, and lamb cutlet with potatoes gratiné.

Minnewater 4 (at Minnewater Park). © 050/33-42-54. Main courses 14€–23€ ($16–$26); *Markt-menu* 26€ ($30). V. Summer daily 11am–11pm (food at lunch and dinner only); winter Mon–Fri noon–2:30pm and 6:30–11pm, Sat–Sun 11am–11pm (food at lunch and dinner times only).

INEXPENSIVE
Brasserie Erasmus ★ FLEMISH Small but popular, this is a great stop after viewing the cathedral and nearby museums. It serves a large variety of dishes, including a very good waterzooï with fish and rabbit in a beer sauce, and has around 150 different brands of beer.

In the Hotel Erasmus, Wollestraat 35 (close to the Markt). © 050/33-57-81. www.hotelerasmus.com. Main courses 15€–25€ ($17–$29); fixed-price menus 20€–30€ ($23–$35). MC, V. Tues–Sun noon–4pm (summer also Mon) and 6–11pm.

Lotus ⭐ VEGETARIAN Even nonvegetarians will likely enjoy the delicious lunch here. There are just two menu options—but you can choose from small, medium, or large servings—each with a hearty assortment of imaginatively prepared vegetables, served in a tranquil but cheery Scandinavian-style dining room.
Wapenmakersstraat 5 (off of the Burg). ℂ 050/33-10-78. Fixed-price lunch menus 8€–9.50€ ($9–$11). No credit cards. Mon–Sat 11:30am–2pm.

EXPLORING HISTORIC BRUGES
THE MARKT ⭐⭐
Begin at this historic market square, where a **sculpture group** in the middle depicts two Flemish heroes, butcher Jan Breydel and weaver Pieter de Coninck. They led a bloody 1302 uprising against pro-French merchants and nobles who dominated the city, then went on to an against-all-odds victory over French knights later the same year at the Battle of the Golden Spurs. The large neo-Gothic **Provinciaal Hof,** which was constructed in 1887, houses the government of West Flanders province.

Belfort en Hallen (Belfry and Market Halls) ⭐⭐ The 13th-to-16th-century belfry's octagonal tower soars 84m (272 ft.) and has a magnificent 47-bell carillon. If you have enough energy, climb the 366 steps to the summit for a panoramic view of the old town—you can pause for breath at the second-floor Treasury, where the town seal and charters were kept behind multiple wrought-iron grilles. Much of the city's cloth trade and other commerce was conducted in the Hallen in centuries past. Local art dealers now use the building for exhibits.
Markt. ℂ 050/44-87-11. Admission 5€ ($6) adults, 3€ ($3.45) seniors and ages 13–26, free for children under 13. Tues–Sun 9:30am–5pm (also Easter Mon, Pentecost Mon). Closed Jan 1, Ascension Day afternoon, Dec 25.

THE BURG ⭐⭐⭐
An array of beautiful buildings, which adds up to a trip through the history of Bruges architecture, stands in this beautiful square just steps away from the Markt. During the 9th century Count Baldwin "Iron Arm" of Flanders built a castle here at a then tiny riverside settlement that would grow into Bruges.

Heilig-Bloedbasiliek (Basilica of the Holy Blood) ⭐⭐ Since 1150, this richly decorated Romanesque basilica next to the Town Hall has been the repository of a fragment of cloth stained with what's said to be Christ's holy blood, brought to Bruges after the Second Crusade by the count of Flanders. The relic is in the basilica museum, inside a rock-crystal vial that's kept in a magnificent gold-and-silver reliquary, and is exposed frequently for the faithful to kiss. Every Ascension Day, in the Procession of the Holy Blood, the relic is carried through the streets, accompanied by costumed residents acting out biblical scenes.
Burg 10. ℂ 050/33-67-92. Basilica, free admission; museum, 1.50€ ($1.75) adults, .50€ (60¢) children 5–18, free for children under 5. Apr–Sept daily 9:30am–noon and 2–6pm; Oct–Mar Thurs–Tues 10am–noon and 2–4pm, Wed 10am–noon. Closed Jan 1, Nov 1, Dec 25.

Landhuis van het Brugse Vrije (Palace of the Liberty of Bruges) Dating mostly from 1722 to 1727, when it replaced a 16th-century building as the seat of the Liberty of Bruges—the Liberty being the district around Bruges in the Middle Ages. The palace later became a courthouse and now houses the city council's administration. Inside, at no. 11A, is the **Renaissancezaal Brugse Vrije (Renaissance Hall of the Liberty of Bruges)** ⭐⭐, the Liberty's council chamber, which has been restored to its original 16th-century condition. The hall has a superb black-marble fireplace decorated with an alabaster frieze and topped by an oak chimney piece carved with statues of Emperor Charles V, who visited Bruges in 1515, and his grandparents: Emperor Maximilian of Austria, Duchess Mary of Burgundy, King Ferdinand II of Aragon, and Queen Isabella I of Castile.

Burg 11. ✆ 050/44-87-11. Courtyard, free admission; Renaissance Hall (includes admission to Town Hall's Gothic Room), 2.50€ ($2.90) adults, 1.50€ ($1.75) seniors and ages 13–26, free for children under 13. Tues–Sun 9:30am–5pm (also Easter Mon, Pentecost Mon). Closed Jan 1, Ascension Day afternoon, Dec 25.

Stadhuis (Town Hall) ☆ This beautiful Gothic building, from the late 1300s, is Belgium's oldest. Don't miss the upstairs **Gotische Zaal (Gothic Room)** ☆☆, with ornate, oak-carved vaulted ceiling and murals depicting biblical scenes and highlights of the town's history. The statues in the niches on the Town Hall facade are 1980s replacements for the originals, which had been painted by Jan van Eyck and were destroyed by the French in the 1790s.

Burg 12. ✆ 050/44-87-11. Admission (includes admission to Renaissance Hall in the Palace of the Liberty of Bruges) 2.50€ ($2.90) adults, 1.50€ ($1.75) seniors and ages 13–26, free for children under 13. Tues–Sun 9:30am–5pm (also Easter Mon, Pentecost Mon). Closed Jan 1, Ascension Day afternoon, Dec 25.

TOP MUSEUMS & ATTRACTIONS

Groeninge Museum ☆☆☆ This is one of Belgium's leading traditional museums of fine arts, with a collection that covers Low Countries painting from the 15th century to the 20th century. The Flemish Primitives Gallery has 30 works—which seem far from primitive—by such painters as Jan van Eyck (portrait of his wife, Margareta van Eyck), Rogier van der Weyden, Hieronymus Bosch *(The Last Judgment)*, and Hans Memling. Works by Magritte and Delvaux are also on display.

Dijver 12. ✆ 050/44-87-11. Admission (combined ticket with neighboring Arentshuis) 8€ ($9) adults, 5€ ($6) seniors and ages 13–26, free for children under 13. Tues–Sun 9:30am–5pm (also Easter Mon, Pentecost Mon). Closed Jan 1, Ascension Day afternoon, Dec 25.

Gruuthuse Museum ☆ In a courtyard next to the Groeninge Museum is the ornate mansion where Flemish nobleman Lodewijk van Gruuthuse lived in the 1400s. It contains thousands of antiques and antiquities, including paintings, sculptures, tapestries, lace, weapons, glassware, and richly carved furniture.

Dijver 17 (in a courtyard next to the Groeninge Museum). ✆ 050/44-87-11. Admission (combined ticket with nearby Archaeological Museum) 6€ ($7) adults, 4€ ($4.60) seniors and ages 13–26, free for children under 13 Tues–Sun 9:30am–5pm (also Easter Mon, Pentecost Mon). Closed Jan 1, Ascension Day afternoon, Dec 25.

Kantcentrum (Lace Center) ☆ Bruges lace is famous the world over, and there's no lack of stores to tempt you with the opportunity to take some home. The Lace Center, in the 15th-century Jerusalem Almshouse founded by the Adornes family of Genoese merchants, is where the ancient art of lace making is passed on to the next generation. In the afternoon, you get a firsthand look at craftspeople making items for future sale in all the town's lace stores (handmade lace is the best, but it's more expensive than machine-made).

Peperstraat 3A. ✆ 050/33-00-72. Admission 2.50€ ($2.90) adults, 2€ ($2.30) seniors and children 7–18, free for children under 7. Mon–Fri 10am–noon and 2–6pm; Sat 10am–noon and 2–5pm. Closed holidays.

Memling Museum ☆☆ The former Sint-Janshospitaal (Hospital of St. John), where the earliest wards date from the 13th century, houses a magnificent collection of paintings by the German-born artist Hans Memling (ca. 1440–94), who moved to Bruges in 1465. You can view masterpieces like his triptych altarpiece of St. John the Baptist and St. John the Evangelist, which consists of the paintings *The Mystic Marriage of St. Catherine*, the *Shrine of St Ursula*, and the *Virgin with Child and Apple*. A 17th-century apothecary in the cloisters near the hospital entrance is furnished as it was when the building's main function was to care for the sick.

Mariastraat. 𝄜 050/44-87-11. Admission 8€ ($9) adults, 5€ ($6) seniors and ages 13–26, free for children under 13. Tues–Sun 9:30am–5pm (also Easter Mon, Pentecost Mon). Closed Jan 1, Ascension Day afternoon, Dec 25.

SIGHTS OF RELIGIOUS INTEREST

One of the most tranquil spots in Bruges is the **Begijnhof** ✹✹, Wijngaardstraat (𝄜 050/33-00-11). Begijns were religious women, similar to nuns, who accepted vows of chastity and obedience but drew the line at poverty. Today, the begijns are no more, and the Begijnhof is occupied by Benedictine nuns who try to keep the begijn traditions alive. Little whitewashed houses surrounding a lawn with trees make a marvelous place of escape. One of the begijns' houses has been set up as a museum. The house is open March and October to November, daily 10:30am to noon and 1:45 to 5pm; April to September, daily 10am to noon and 1:45 to 5:30pm (6pm Sun); December to February, Wednesday, Thursday, Saturday, Sunday 2:45 to 4:15pm, and Friday 1:45 to 6pm. Admission is 2€ ($2.30) adults, 1€ ($1.15) children ages 5 to 18, and free for children under 5. The Begijnhof itself is permanently open, and admission is free.

Onze-Lieve-Vrouwekerk (Church of Our Lady) ✹✹   It took 2 centuries (the 13th–15th) to build the magnificent Church of Our Lady, and its soaring spire, 122m (396 ft.) high, is visible from a wide area around Bruges. Among its many art treasures are a marvelous marble *Madonna and Child* ✹✹✹ by Michelangelo (one of his few works outside Italy); the *Crucifixion*, a painting by Anthony Van Dyck; and inside the church sanctuary the impressive side-by-side bronze **tomb sculptures** ✹ of Charles the Bold of Burgundy (d. 1477), and his daughter Mary of Burgundy (d. 1482).

Onze-Lieve-Vrouwekerkhof-Zuid (at Mariastraat). 𝄜 050/34-53-14. Church and *Madonna and Child* altar, free admission; sanctuary of Charles and Mary and museum, 2.50€ ($2.90) adults, 1.50€ ($1.75) seniors and ages 13–26, free for children under 13. Tues–Fri 9:30am–12:30pm and 1:30–5pm (also Easter Mon, Pentecost Mon); Sat 9:30am–12:30pm and 1:30–4pm; Sun 1:30–5pm.

BREWERIES

Brugs Brouwerij-Mouterijmuseum (Bruges Brewing and Malting Museum)   The De Gouden Boom Brewery has been operating in this area since 1587. Beer vats and other equipment are still in place in the 1902 malthouse, which houses the museum. Exhibits here feature not just the museum's parent brewery, but also the other 31 breweries that were brewing up a storm in the city at the turn of the 19th century. From here it's but a hop to Langestraat 45, and the **brewery** itself, where you can watch popular De Gouden Boom ales such as Brugs Blond, Brugse Tripel, and Steenbrugge being brought to life, and get to taste some of the finished product. Brewery visits are guided and by prior arrangement only.

Verbrand Nieuwland 10 (at Langestraat). 𝄜 050/33-06-99. Museum, admission 3.50€ ($4) May–Sept Wed–Sun 2–6pm. Brewery, admission 3€ ($3.45) Apr–Sept Wed–Sun 2–6pm.

Brouwerij De Halve Maan (Half-Moon Brewery) ✹   The brewery here was turning out ale at least as long ago as 1546. Today it produces Bruges's famous

Straffe Hendrik beer, a strapping blond ale that can be sampled in the brewery's own brasserie, after a perusal of the facility.

Walplein 26. ⓒ 050/33-26-97. Admission 3.70€ ($4.25). Guided visits Apr–Sept daily on the hour 11am–4pm; Oct–Mar daily 11am–3pm.

ESPECIALLY FOR KIDS

The **Boudewijn Theme Park and Dolfinarium** 👫, De Baeckestraat 12 (ⓒ **050/38-38-38;** www.boudewijnpark.be; bus: 7 or 17), in the southern suburb of Sint-Michiels, is a big favorite with children. For some unfathomable reason, they seem to prefer its rides, paddle boats, dolphins, and orca (killer whale), to Bruges's many historic treasures. Strange but true! The park is open Easter holidays, daily from 11am to 5pm; May to June, daily from 10:30am to 5pm (6pm Sun and holidays); July to August, daily from 10am to 6pm; September, Wednesday and Saturday from 10:30am to 5pm, and Sunday from 10:30am to 6pm. Admission is 19€ ($22) for adults and children over 1m (39 in.), 16€ ($18) for seniors, and free for children under 1m (39 in.).

BOAT TRIPS & OTHER ORGANIZED TOURS

Be sure to take a **boat trip** ★★★ on the canals, onboard one of the open-top tour boats that cruise year-round from five departure points around the center, all marked with an anchor icon on maps available from the tourist office. The boats operate March to November, daily from 10am to 6pm; and December to February, Saturday, Sunday, and school holidays from 10am to 6pm (except if the canals are frozen). A half-hour cruise is 5.20€ ($6) for adults, 2.60€ ($3) for children ages 4 to 11 accompanied by an adult, and free for children under 4.

Another lovely way to tour Bruges is by **horse-drawn carriage.** From March to November, carriages are stationed in the Burg (Wed in the Markt); a 30-minute ride is 28€ ($32), and 14€ ($16) for each extra 15 minutes.

Minivan tours by **Sightseeing Line** (ⓒ 050/35-50-24) last 50 minutes and depart hourly every day from the Markt. The first tour departs at 10am; the last tour departs at 8pm July to September, at 7pm April to June, at 6pm October, at 5pm March, and at 4pm November to February. Fares are 12€ ($13) for adults, 6.25€ ($7) children ages 6 to 12, free for children under 6, and 30€ ($35) for a family of two adults and two children.

If you'd like a qualified guide to accompany you, the tourist office can provide one for 40€ ($46) for the first 2 hours, and 20€ ($23) for each additional hour. In July and August, join a daily guided **walking tour** at 3pm from the tourist office for 5€ ($6), and free for children under 12.

You can ride through Bruges, and get out of town into the West Flanders countryside, on a bicycling tour with **Quasimundo Biketours Bruges** (ⓒ 050/33-07-75; www.quasimundo.com). Call ahead to book; meeting and departure point is the Burg. Tours run from 18€ ($21), 16€ ($18) for ages 8 to 26, and free for children under 8.

BRUGES AFTER DARK

For information on what's on and where, pick up a copy of the free monthly *Exit* brochure from the tourist office.

THE PERFORMING ARTS   Classical music, opera, and ballet are performed at the ultramodern **Concertgebouw,** 't Zand 34 (ⓒ **050/37-69-99;** www. concertgebouw.be), which opened in 2002. The **Koninklijke Stadsschouwburg,** Vlamingstraat 29 (ⓒ **050/44-30-60**), from 1869, continues to feature theater (mainly in Dutch) and dance.

PERIOD THEATER   Step back in time to medieval Bruges, at Brugge Anno 1468, Vlamingstraat 84–86 (© **050/34-75-72**), in a former Jesuit church. Players re-create the wedding of Duke Charles the Bold of Burgundy to Duchess Margaret of York while the audience piles into a period banquet. Performances take place April to October, Friday and Saturday from 7:30 to 10:30pm; and November to March, Saturday from 7:30 to 10:30pm. Tickets are 57€ to 73€ ($65–$83) for adults, 50% of the adult price for children ages 11 to 14, 13€ ($14) for children ages 6 to 10, and free for children under 6.

BARS & TAVERNS   Traditional cafe **'t Brugs Beertje,** Kemelstraat 5 (© **050/33-96-16**), serves more than 300 kinds of beer. **'t Dreupelhuisje,** Kemelstraat 9 (© **050/34-24-21**), does something similar with *jenever* (a gin-like spirit), serving up dozens of craft-produced examples of this deadly art. **Gran Kaffee De Passage,** Dweersstraat 26 (© **050/34-02-32**), is a quiet and elegant spot to sip a drink.

3 Ghent ★★

Austere but more authentic than Bruges, Ghent has been spruced up and has never looked so good. This former seat of the powerful counts of Flanders, at the confluence of the Scheldt and Leie rivers, has plenty of cobblestone streets, meandering canals, and antique Flemish architecture.

ESSENTIALS

GETTING THERE   By Train   Ghent is 32 minutes from Brussels, and trains depart every half-hour or so. The main railway station, **Gent Sint-Pieters,** Maria Hendrikaplein (© **09/222-44-44**), is 1.5km (1 mile) south of the city center. From outside the station, take tram no. 1, 10, 11, or 12 to the center.

By Car   Take A10/E40 from Brussels and Bruges.

VISITOR INFORMATION   Infokantoor, Raadskelder (Belfry Cellar), Botermarkt 17A, 9000 Gent (© **09/266-52-32;** fax 09/224-15-55; www. gent.be), can make hotel reservations for a returnable deposit, and is open April to October daily from 9:30am to 6:30pm; and November to March daily from 9:30am to 4:30pm.

GETTING AROUND   Ghent has an excellent **tram** and **bus** network (© **09/210-94-91**), with many lines converging at Korenmarkt and Sint-Pieters railway station. Walking is the best way to view the center and experience its combination of history and modernity at a human pace. Beyond the center, use public transportation. For a **taxi,** call **V-Tax** (© **09/222-22-22**).

WHERE TO STAY

Erasmus ★   Each room is different in this converted 16th-century house, and all are plush, furnished with antiques and knickknacks. Rooms have high oak-beam ceilings, and bathrooms are modern. Some rooms have leaded-glass windows, some overlook a carefully manicured inner garden, and some have elaborate marble fireplaces. Breakfast is served in an impressive room that would have pleased the counts of Flanders.

Poel 25 (off of Sint-Michielsstraat), 9000 Gent. © **09/224-21-95.** Fax 09/233-42-41. www.hotelerasmus.be. 11 units. 74€–105€ ($85–$121) double; 125€ ($144) suite. Rates include buffet breakfast. AE, MC, V. Limited street parking. **Amenities:** Bar. *In room:* TV, coffeemaker, hair dryer.

Gravensteen ★★ You enter this lovely mansion, built in 1865 as the home of a Ghent textile baron, through the old carriageway (made up of ornamented pillars and an impressive wall niche occupied by a marble statue), which sets the tone for what you find inside. The elegant, high-ceilinged parlor is a sophisticated blend of pastels, gracious modern furnishings, and antiques, with a small bar tucked into one corner. The rooms are attractive and comfortably furnished.

Jan Breydelstraat 35 (close to the Castle of the Counts), 9000 Gent. ✆ **09/225-11-50.** Fax 09/225-18-50. www.gravensteen.be. 49 units. 140€–154€ ($161–$177) double; 197€ ($227) suite. AE, DC, MC, V. Parking 5€ ($6). **Amenities:** Restaurant, bar; laundry service. *In room:* TV, minibar, hair dryer.

WHERE TO DINE

Brasserie Pakhuis ★ FLEMISH/CONTINENTAL In a town where the Middle Ages are *big*, this brasserie is almost modern and certainly hip. In fact, Pakhuis (which means "warehouse" in Dutch) may be a little too conscious of its own sense of style. The oyster and seafood platters are notable, and you won't go wrong with meat-based offerings like baked ham in a mustard sauce, or Flemish favorites like waterzooï and *garnaalkroketten* (shrimp croquettes).

Schuurkenstraat 4 (off Veldstraat). ✆ **09/223-55-55.** www.pakhuis.be. Main courses 9.60€–19€ ($11–$22); fixed-price menus 22€–29€ ($26–$33). AE, DC, MC, V. Mon–Thurs 11:30am–1am; Fri–Sat 11:30am–2am (full meals at lunch and dinner only).

Jan Breydel ★★ SEAFOOD/FLEMISH High honors go to this exquisite restaurant on a quaint street near the Castle of the Counts. Its interior is a garden delight of greenery, white napery, and light woods. Proprietors Louis and Pat Hellebaut see to it that dishes issued from their kitchen are as light as the setting, with delicate sauces and seasonings enhancing fresh ingredients. Seafood and regional specialties like the traditional Ghent fish stew, waterzooï, are all superb.

Jan Breydelstraat 10 (facing the Museum voor Sierkunst en Vormgeving). ✆ **09/225-62-87.** Main courses 18€–32€ ($21–$37); fixed-price menus 31€–48€ ($43–$55). AE, DC, MC, V. Tues–Sat noon–2pm and 7–10pm; Mon 7–10pm.

EXPLORING HISTORIC GHENT

Belfort en Lakenhalle (Belfry and Cloth Hall) ★★ These form a glorious medieval ensemble. From the 14th-century Belfry, great bells have rung out Ghent's civic pride down through the centuries, and a 54-bell carillon does so today. You can get high in the belfry with a guide and the aid of an elevator. The Cloth Hall of 1425 was the gathering place of medieval wool and cloth merchants.

Emile Braunplein. ✆ **09/223-99-22.** Admission 3€ ($3.45) adults, .90€ ($1.05) children under 15. Mid-Mar to mid-Nov daily 10am–1pm and 2–6pm. Free guided tours Easter and May–Sept 2:10, 3:10, and 4:10pm.

Het Gravensteen (Castle of the Counts) ★ Formidable and forbidding, the castle was designed by the counts of Flanders to send a clear message to rebellion-inclined Gentenaars. Surrounded by the waters of the Leie River, the castle begun by Count Philip of Alsace in 1180 has walls 2m (6 ft.) thick, and battlements and turrets. If these failed to intimidate the populace, the counts could always turn to a well-equipped torture chamber; some of its accouterments are on display in a small museum.

Sint-Veerleplein. ✆ **09/225-93-06.** Admission 6.20€ ($7) adults, 1.20€ ($1.40) seniors and ages 12–25, free for children under 12. Apr–Sept daily 9am–6pm; Oct–Mar daily 9am–5pm.

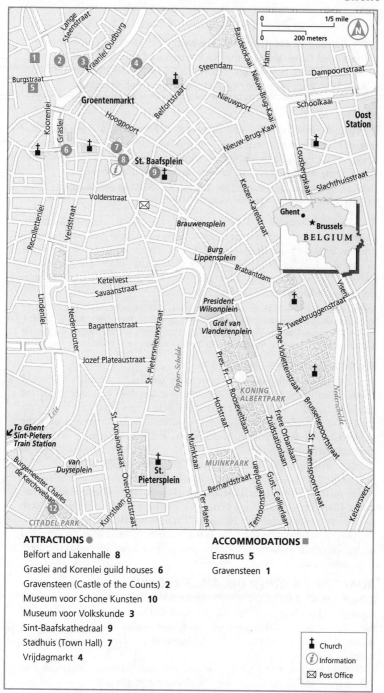

Ghent

| 0 | | 1/5 mile |
| 0 | 200 meters | |

Lange Steenstraat
Kraanlei Oudburg
Burgstraat
Groentenmarkt
Koorenlei
Graslei
Hoogpoort
Belfortstraat
Steendam
Baudelokaai
Nieuw-Brug-Kaai
Ham
Nieuwport
Dampoortstraat
Schoolkaai
Oost Station
Nieuw-Brug-Kaai
St. Baafsplein
Volderstraat
Keizer-Karelstraat
Lousbergskaai
Slachthuisstraat
Brauwensplein
Burg Lippensplein
Brabantdam
Ketelvest
Savaanstraat
President Wilsonplein
Graf van Vlanderenplein
Bagattenstraat
Jozef Plateaustraat
St. Pietersnieuwstraat
Opper-Schelde
Pres. Fr. D. Rooseveltlaan
Lange Violettenstraat
Tweebruggenstraat
Frere Orbanlaan
Zuidstationlaan
Brusselsepoortstraat
St. Lievenspoortstraat
Viserij
Nederschelde
Recolettenlei
Veldstraat
Lindenlei
Nederkouter
Leie
St. Amandstraat
Overpoortstraat
Muinkkaai
Hofstraat
KONING ALBERTPARK
MUINKPARK
Bernardstraat
Ter Platen
Tentoonstellingslaan
Gust. Callierlaan
Keizervest
To Ghent Sint-Pieters Train Station
Burgemeester Charles de Kerchovelaan
van Duyseplein
Kunstlaan
CITADEL PARK
St. Pietersplein

Ghent •
★ Brussels
BELGIUM

ATTRACTIONS ●

Belfort and Lakenhalle **8**
Graslei and Korenlei guild houses **6**
Gravensteen (Castle of the Counts) **2**
Museum voor Schone Kunsten **10**
Museum voor Volkskunde **3**
Sint-Baafskathedraal **9**
Stadhuis (Town Hall) **7**
Vrijdagmarkt **4**

ACCOMMODATIONS ■

Erasmus **5**
Gravensteen **1**

✝ Church
ⓘ Information
✉ Post Office

Tips **Flower Power**

The **Gentse Floraliën (www.floralien.com),** held every 5 years, is among the biggest flower shows in the flower-mad Low Countries. If you're a fan of flowers at all, be sure to hotfoot it to Ghent for the 2005 show, from April 14 to April 24, at the city's Congrescentrum in Citadelpark.

Museum voor Schone Kunsten (Museum of Fine Arts) ⭐   In a park close to Sint-Pieters railway station, this museum is home to old and new master-pieces, including works by Van der Weyden, Brueghel, Rubens, Van Dyck, and Bosch, along with moderns like James Ensor and Constant Permeke.

Citadelpark. ✆ **09/240-07-00.** Admission 2.50€ ($2.90) adults, 1.20€ ($1.40) seniors and ages 12–25, free for children under 12. Tues–Sun 10am–6pm. Closed Jan 1, Dec 25, 26.

Sint-Baafskathedraal (St. Bavo's Cathedral) ⭐⭐⭐   The 14th-century cathedral's plain Gothic exterior belies a splendid baroque interior and some priceless art. A 24-panel altarpiece, *The Adoration of the Mystic Lamb,* completed by Jan van Eyck in 1432, is St. Bavo's showpiece. Other treasures include Rubens' *The Conversion of St. Bavo* (1624), in the Rubens Chapel off the semi-circular ambulatory behind the high altar.

Sint-Baafsplein. ✆ **09/269-20-45.** Free admission to cathedral; *Mystic Lamb* chapel and crypt 2.50€ ($2.90) adults (includes audio guide in English), 1.25€ ($1.45) children 6–12, free children under 6. Cathedral, Apr–Oct daily 8:30am–6pm; Nov–Mar daily 8:30am–5pm. *Mystic Lamb* chapel and crypt, Apr–Oct Mon–Sat 9:30am–4:45pm, Sun 1–4:30pm; Nov–Mar Mon–Sat 10:30am–3:45pm, Sun 1–3:30pm.

MORE PLACES OF INTEREST

A row of gabled **guild houses** ⭐ built along **Graslei** between the 1200s and 1600s, when the waterway was Ghent's harbor, forms an ensemble of colored facades reflected in the Leie River. To view them as a whole, cross the bridge over the Leie to **Korenlei,** and stroll along the bank. These buildings were once the headquarters of the craftsmen, tradespeople, and merchants who formed the city's commercial core.

In the **Vrijdagmarkt,** a statue of Jacob Van Arteveld pays tribute to a rebel hero of the 1300s. This large, lively square hosts a street market every Friday.

The mixed Renaissance and Gothic style of the **Stadhuis (Town Hall),** Boter-markt 1, reflects a construction period that ran from 1518 until the 18th century. In an upstairs chamber called the **Pacificatiezaal** was signed the 1567 Pacification of Ghent, by which the Low Countries repudiated Spanish rule and declared religious freedom. The building can only be visited by guided tour from the tourist office (see above).

BOAT TRIPS & OTHER ORGANIZED TOURS

A **boat trip** ⭐ on the canals (✆ **09/223-88-53**) is a good way to view the city's highlights. Tour boats sail from Graslei April to October, daily from 10am to 6pm; November to March, on weekends from 11am to 4pm. Cruises begin at 4.50€ ($5), and 2.25€ ($2.60) for children under 12, for 40 minutes; longer tours are available.

If you'd like a qualified guide to accompany you, the tourist office can pro-vide one for 50€ ($58) for the first 2 hours, and 25€ ($29) for each additional hour. May to November, you can join a daily guided **walking tour** at 2:30pm

(Apr, weekends only) from the tourist office for 6€ ($7), and free for children under 12.

Easter to October, tours by **horse-drawn carriage** (℅ **09/227-62-46**) depart from Sint-Baafsplein daily from 10am to 6pm. A half-hour ride is 23€ ($26) for a 4- or 5-seat carriage.

GHENT AFTER DARK

THE PERFORMING ARTS   Opera is performed at the 19th-century **Vlaamse Opera,** Schouwburgstraat 3 (℅ **09/225-24-25**).

BARS & TAVERNS   You should have a memorable evening in any one of Ghent's atmospheric cafes. **De Witte Leeuw,** Graslei 6 (℅ **09/233-37-33**), has a 17th-century setting and more than 300 varieties of beer. At **Dulle Griet,** Vrij-dagmarkt 50 (℅ **09/224-24-55**), also known as Bier Academie, you'll be asked to deposit one of your shoes before being given a potent Kwak beer in a too-collectible glass with a wood frame that allows the glass to stand up.

Het Waterhuis aan de Bierkant, Groentenmarkt 9 (℅ **09/225-06-80**), has more than 100 different Belgian beers, including locally made Stopken. A couple of doors along, **'t Dreupelkot,** Groentenmarkt 12 (℅ **09/224-21-20**), specializes in deadly little glasses of *jenever* (a stiff spirit similar to gin), of which it has a hundred varieties. Across the tramlines, the tiny **'t Galgenhuisje,** Groenten-markt 5 (℅ **09/233-42-51**), is popular with students.

3

The Czech Republic

by Hana Mastrini

The Czech Republic, comprising the ancient kingdoms of Bohemia, Moravia, and Silesia, is the westernmost of the former Soviet satellite countries and probably the best place to explore what used to be the other side of the Iron Curtain.

It's certainly one of the most progressive. In May 2004, nearly 15 years after 1989's bloodless "Velvet Revolution" over Communism and over a decade after the peaceful split with the Slovak part of the former Czechoslovakia, the Czechs topped the head of the list of new states admitted to the European Union.

If you have time to visit only one eastern European city, it should be Prague—widely regarded as one of the most beautiful cities in Europe, if not the world. The quirky and compact heart of Bohemia is a jumble of architecture. Gothic bestrides baroque, Renaissance adjoins cubist, with a splash of socialist realism and postmodern kitsch thrown in for good measure. On the hills and plains fronting the River Vltava you will glimpse the triumphs and tragedies of the past 10 centuries spiked with the peculiarity of the post-Communist reconstruction.

But Prague isn't the Czech Republic's only draw. Visitors are flocking to west Bohemia's world-renowned spas, which have been restored to their Victorian-era splendor, and to its many historic castles.

1 Prague ✦✦✦

Prague has stood the test of time, but the floods of August 2002 threatened to ruin centuries of culture and history forever. Happily, the waters were no match for the robust landmarks and iron will of the people of this ancient kingdom, and the city is back, and better than ever.

Here, the last 1,000 years of triumphs in art and architecture have collided, often violently, with power politics and religious conflicts. While Prague's rich collection of Gothic, baroque, and Renaissance buildings has stood stoically through all the strife, the streets and squares fronting the grand halls have often been the stages for tragedy. The well-worn cobblestones have felt the hooves of king's horses, the jackboots of Hitler's armies, the heaving wheels of Soviet tanks, and the shuffling feet of students in passive revolt. Today spaghetti-strand alleys winding through Old Town are jammed with armies of visitors jostling for space to experience the aura of "Golden Prague" only to be bombarded with peddlers trying to make a quick buck or mark (or crown when the home currency is stable).

But while Prague's rebirth and its embrace of capitalism have come with labor pains of inflation, traffic jams (with new Western cars), and the ever-present pounding of construction crews, the stately spires of this living baroque and

medieval museum rise above it all. Despite the furious development and reconstruction popping up all over, the classical monuments remain the city's
bedrock. Prague Castle's reflection in the Vltava or the mellow nighttime glow
of the lanterns around the 18th-century Stavovské Divadlo (Estates' Theater)
gives the city a Mozart-really-was-here feel.

ESSENTIALS

GETTING THERE **By Plane** Newly rebuilt **Ruzyně Airport** (② 220-
111-111) is 19km (12 miles) west of the city center. You'll find a bank for
changing money (usually open daily 7am–11pm), several car-rental offices, and
a few information stands that will also make hotel reservations.

Plenty of official taxis line up in front of the airport. **CEDAZ** (② 220-
114-296; www.aas.cz/cedaz) operates an **airport shuttle bus** from the airport to
náměstí Republiky in central Prague. It leaves the airport daily every 30 minutes
from 5am to 9pm and stops near the náměstí Republiky metro station; shuttles
make the return trip from 5:30am to 9:30pm (every 30 min.). The shuttle costs
90Kč ($3.20) one-way. You can also take city bus no. 119 to the Dejvická Metro
station (Line A) for 12Kč (40¢).

By Train Of the two central rail stations, **Hlavní nádraží,** Wilsonova třída,
Praha 2 (② 224-614-071), is the grander and more popular; however, it's also
seedier. The station's basement holds a left-luggage counter, which is open 24
hours and charges 15Kč (55¢) per bag per day. Though cheaper, the nearby
lockers aren't secure and should be avoided. In the ground-level main hall, there's

---

Tips **Getting a Fair Fare**

Prague's taxi drivers are often arrogant and dishonest. Negotiate the fare
in advance and have it written down; getting an honestly metered ride
from the airport is close to impossible. You should pay no more than
700Kč to 800Kč ($25–$28) for the 20-ride from the airport to the city center.

Prague

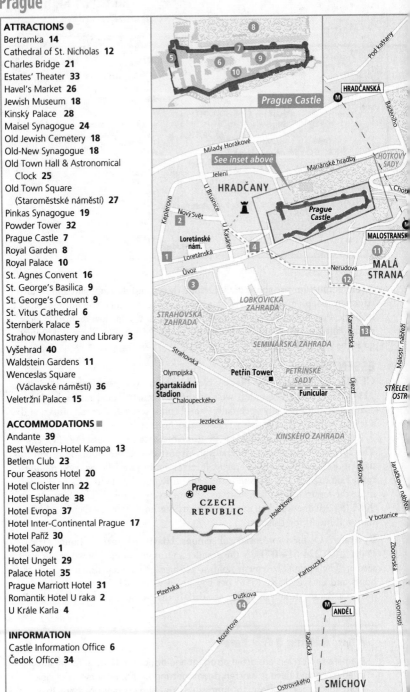

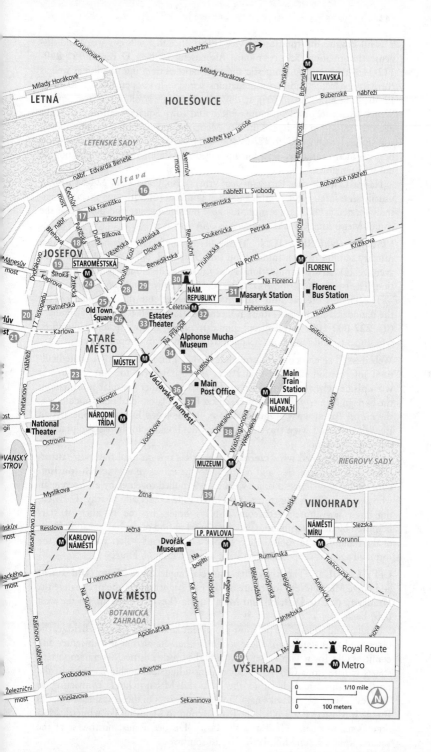

a useful **Prague Information Service (PIS)** office that sells city maps and dispenses information, and restrooms. Also useful is the **ČD center** (© 840-112-113) that provides domestic and international train information as well as currency exchange and accommodations services. It is open daily 3:30am to 12.30am. From the main train station it's a 5-minute stroll to the "top" end of Wenceslas Square or a 15-minute walk to Old Town Square. Metro Line C connects the station to the rest of the city. Metro trains depart from the lower level, and tickets, costing 8Kč to 12Kč (30¢–40¢), are available from the newsstand near the metro entrance. Taxis line up outside the station day and night, but are not recommended.

Nádraží Holešovice, Partyzánská at Vrbenského, Praha 7 (© 224-615-865), usually serves trains from Berlin and other points north. Although it isn't as centrally located as the main station, its more manageable size and position at the end of Metro Line C make it almost as convenient.

VISITOR INFORMATION   Those arriving by train at either of the two primary stations can get information from **AVE Ltd.** (© 224-223-226; www.avetravel.cz), an accommodations agency that also distributes printed information. The two train station AVE offices are open daily from 7am to 9pm.

The city's **Cultural and Information Center,** on the ground floor of the remodeled Municipal House (Obecní dům), náměstí Republiky 5, Praha 1 (© 222-002-100; www.obecni-dum.cz), offers advice, tickets, souvenirs, refreshments, and restrooms. It's open daily from 10am to 6pm.

Websites   The city's own information service, PIS, has regularly updated cultural information in English and acts as a gateway to tourism websites at **www.pis.cz** or **www.prague-info.cz**. For visa and other consular information, the Foreign Ministry site is **www.czech.cz**. For the latest local news updates, try the *Prague Post* at **www.praguepost.com**. Prague-based **E-travel.cz** operates an English website at **www.travel.cz** that provides booking for hotels and practical touring information.

The well-designed **www.czechsite.com** offers tips on local transport, attractions, museums, galleries, and restaurants. The extensive **www.czech-tourism. com** roundup of links to other websites was pulled together by a Net veteran who awards a Czech flag icon to sites he considers especially worthy. The well-organized **www.hotelsczech.com** displays hotels by the number of stars bestowed by the government. Click on a hotel to find prices by date and photos of the buildings and rooms. Reservations aren't instant—after you fill out the form, an agent is supposed to get back to you within 48 hours.

CITY LAYOUT   The River Vltava bisects Prague. **Staré Město (Old Town)** and **Nové Město (New Town)** are on the east (right) side of the river, while the **Hradčany (Castle District)** and **Malá Strana (Lesser Town)** are on the west (left) bank.

Bridges and squares are the most prominent landmarks. **Charles Bridge,** the oldest and most famous of those spanning the Vltava, is at the epicenter and connects Old Town with Lesser Town and the Castle District. Several important streets radiate from Old Town Square, including fashionable Pařížská to the northwest, historic Celetná to the east, and Melantrichova, connecting to Wenceslas Square (Václavské nám.) to the southeast. On the west side of Charles Bridge is Mostecká, a 3-block-long connection to Malostranské náměstí, Malá Strana's main square. Hradčany, the Castle District, is just northwest of the square, while a second hill, Petřín, is just southwest.

Prague Metro

GETTING AROUND   By Metro, Bus & Tram   Prague's public transport network is a vast system of subways, trams, and buses. You can ride a maximum of four stations on the Metro or 15 minutes on a tram or bus, without transfers, for 8Kč (30¢); children 5 and under ride free. This is usually enough for trips in the historic districts. Rides of more than four stops on the Metro, or longer tram or bus rides, with unlimited transfers for up to 1 hour after your ticket is validated, cost 12Kč (45¢). You can buy tickets from coin-operated orange machines in Metro stations or at most newsstands marked TABÁK or TRAFIKA. Hold on to your ticket (which you must validate at the orange or yellow stamp clocks in each tram or bus when you get on board or at the entrance to the Metro) during your ride—you'll need it to prove you've paid if a ticket collector asks.

If you're caught without a valid ticket, you'll be fined on the spot (make sure the collector shows you a very official-looking badge). The fine is 400Kč ($14) on trams and the metro, double that on buses. **Warning:** Oversize luggage (larger than carry-on size) requires a single trip ticket for each piece. You may be fined 50Kč ($1.80) for not having tickets for your luggage.

A **1-day pass** good for unlimited rides is 70Kč ($2.50), a **3-day pass** 200Kč ($7.15), a **7-day pass** 250Kč ($8.90), and a **15-day pass** 280Kč ($10). Note that the city council is considering a hike in the fees as this book goes to press. You can buy the day passes at the "DP" windows at any Metro station.

Tips Reading Maps

When reading maps or searching for addresses, keep in mind that *ulice* (abbreviated ul. or omitted) means "street," *třída* (abbreviated tr.) means "avenue," *náměstí* (abbreviated nám.) is "square" or "plaza," *most* is "bridge," and *nábřeží* is "quay." In Czech, none of these terms are capitalized. In addresses, street numbers follow the street name (like Václavské nám. 25). Each address is followed by a district number, such as Praha 1 (Praha is "Prague" in Czech).

Metro trains operate daily from 5am to midnight and run every 2 to 6 minutes. On the three lettered lines (A, B, and C, color-coded green, yellow, and red, respectively), the most convenient central stations are Můstek, at the foot of Václavské náměstí (Wenceslas Sq.); Staroměstská, for Old Town Square and Charles Bridge; and Malostranská, serving Malá Strana and the Castle District.

The 24 electric tram (streetcar) lines run practically everywhere. You never have to hail trams; they make every stop. The most popular, no. 22 and no. 23 (the "tourist trams" and the "pickpocket express"), run past top sights such as the National Theater and Prague Castle. Regular bus and tram service stops at midnight, after which selected routes run reduced schedules, usually only once per hour. Schedules are posted at stops. If you miss a night connection, expect a long wait for the next.

By Funicular The cog railway makes the scenic run up and down Petřín Hill every 15 minutes or so from 9:15am to 8:45pm, with an intermediate stop at the Nebozízek Restaurant halfway down the hill, which overlooks the city. It requires the same 12Kč (40¢) ticket as other public transport. The funicular departs from a small house in the park just above the middle of Újezd in Malá Strana.

By Taxi Avoid taxis! If you must, hail one in the streets or in front of train stations, large hotels, and popular attractions, but be forewarned that many drivers simply gouge tourists. The best fare you can hope for is 17Kč (55¢) per kilometer, but twice or three times that isn't rare. Rates are usually posted on the dashboard, making it too late to haggle once you're in and on your way. Negotiate a price and have it written down before getting in. Better yet, go on foot or by public transport. Some reputable companies with English-speaking dispatchers are **AAA Taxi** (© **14014** or 221-102-211; www.aaataxi.cz); **ProfiTaxi** (© **14035**); or **SEDOP** (© **271-726-666**). Demand a receipt for the fare before you start, as it'll keep them a little more honest.

By Car Driving in Prague is not worth the money or effort. The roads are frustrating and slow, and parking is minimal and expensive. If you want to rent a car to explore the environs, try **Europcar Czech Rent a Car,** Pařížská 28, Praha 1 (© **224-811-290;** www.europcar.cz), or at Ruzyně Airport, Praha 6 (© 235-364-531). There's also **Hertz,** Karlovo nám. 28, Praha 2 (© **220-102-424;** www.hertz.cz). **Budget** is at Ruzyně Airport (© **220-113-253;** www.budget.cz) and in the Hotel InterContinental, náměstí Curieových, Praha 1 (© 224-889-995).

Local Czech car-rental companies sometimes offer lower rates than the big international firms. Try **SeccoCar,** Přístavní 39, Praha 7 (© **220-800-647;** www.seccocar.cz; Metro: Nádraží Holešovice, then tram 12 or 25).

FAST FACTS: Prague

American Express For travel arrangements, traveler's checks, currency exchange, and other member services, visit the city's sole American Express office at Václavské nám. 56 (Wenceslas Sq.), Praha 1 (© **222-800-237;** Metro: Muzeum). It's open daily from 9am to 7pm. To report lost or stolen cards, call © **222-800-222.**

Business Hours Most **banks** are open Monday through Friday from 8am to 6pm. **Pubs** are usually open daily from 11am to midnight. Most **restaurants** open for lunch from noon to 3pm and for dinner from 6 to 11pm; only a few stay open later. **Stores** are typically open Monday to Friday from 9am to 6pm and Saturday from 9am to 1pm, but those in the tourist center keep longer hours and are open Sunday as well.

Currency The basic unit of currency is the **koruna** (plural, **koruny**) or crown, abbreviated **Kč.** Each koruna is divided into 100 **haléřů** or hellers. At press time, $1 = approximately 28Kč; or 1Kč = 3.5¢. £1 = 45Kč; or 1Kč = £0.02256.

Currency Exchange Banks generally offer the best exchange rates. Don't hesitate to use a credit or a debit card to withdraw cash for the best rates. **Komerční banka** has three convenient Praha 1 locations with ATMs that accept Visa, MasterCard, and American Express: Na Příkopě 33, Národní 32, and Václavské nám. 42 (© **222-432-111,** central switchboard for all branches). The exchange offices are open Monday to Friday from 8am to 5pm, but the ATMs are accessible 24 hours.

Doctors/Dentists If you need a doctor or dentist and your condition isn't life-threatening, you can visit the **Polyclinic at Národní,** Národní 9, Praha 1 (© **222-075-120;** Metro: Můstek), during walk-in hours from 8am to 5pm. Dr. Stránský is an Ivy League–trained straight-talking physician. For **emergency medical aid,** call the **Foreigners' Medical Clinic,** Na Homolce Hospital, Roentgenova 2, Praha 5 (© **257-272-146,** or 257-272-191 after hours; Metro: Anděl, then bus no. 167).

Drugstores The most central pharmacy *(lékárna)* is at Václavské nám. 8, Praha 1 (© **224-227-532;** Metro: Můstek), open Monday through Friday from 8am to 6pm. The nearest emergency (24-hr.) pharmacy is at Palackého 5, Praha 1 (© **224-946-982;** Metro Můstek). If you're in Praha 2, there's an emergency pharmacy on Belgická 37 (© **222-513-396;** Metro: Náměstí Míru).

Embassies The **U.S. Embassy** is at Tržiště 15, Praha 1 (© **257-530-663**). The **Canadian Embassy** is at Mickiewiczova 6, Praha 6 (© **272-101-811**). The **U.K. Embassy** is at Thunovská 14, Praha 1 (© **257-402-111**). You can visit the **Australian Honorary Consul** at Klimentská 10, Praha 1 (© **251-018-350**). The **Irish Embassy** is at Tržiště 13, Praha 1 (© **257-530-061**). The **New Zealand Honorary Consul** is at Dykova 19, Praha 10 (© **222-514-672**).

Emergencies You can reach Prague's **police** at © **158** and **fire** services by dialing © **150** from any phone. To call an **ambulance,** dial © **155.**

Hospitals Particularly welcoming to foreigners is **Nemocnice Na Homolce,** Roentgenova 2, Praha 5 (© **257-272-146,** or 257-272-191 after hours; Metro: Anděl, then bus no. 167). The English-speaking doctors can also make house calls.

Internet Access   One of Prague's trendiest places is the **Globe** ⍟, Pštrossova 6, Praha 1 (✆ **224-916-264**; www.globebookstore.cz), a cafe-cum-bookstore that provides Internet access. You can browse for 1.30Kč per minute. Its new location is open daily from 10am until midnight.

Telephone   The **country code** for the Czech Republic is **420**. As of 2002, *you must dial all nine digits for local Czech calls.* For directory assistance in English and for information on services and rates calling abroad, dial ✆ **1181**.

There are two kinds of **pay phones** in normal use. The first accepts coins and the other operates exclusively with a phone card, available from post offices and news agents in denominations ranging from 50Kč to 500Kč ($1.80–$18). The minimum cost of a local call is 4Kč (15¢). Coin-op phones have displays telling you the minimum price for your call, but they don't make change, so don't load more than you have to. You can add more coins as the display gets near zero. Phone-card telephones automatically deduct the price of your call from the card. These cards are especially handy if you want to call abroad, as you don't have to continuously chuck in the change. If you're calling the States, you'd better get a phone card with plenty of points, as calls run about 20Kč (55¢) per minute; calls to the United Kingdom cost 15Kč (40¢) per minute.

A fast, convenient way to call the United States from Europe is via services like AT&T USA Direct. This bypasses the foreign operator and automatically links you to an operator with your long-distance carrier in your home country. The access number in the Czech Republic for **AT&T USA Direct** is ✆ **00-420-00101**. For **MCI CALL USA**, dial ✆ **00-420-00112**, and for **Sprint Global One**, call ✆ **00-420-87187**. Canadians can connect with **Canada Direct** at ✆ **00-420-00151**, and Brits can connect with **BT Direct** at ✆ **00-420-04401**. From a pay phone in the Czech Republic, your local phone card will be debited only for a local call.

Tipping   At most restaurants and pubs, locals just round the bill up to the nearest few koruny. When you get good service at tablecloth places, a 10% tip is proper (check to see if service is included before leaving a tip). Washroom and cloakroom attendants usually expect a couple of koruny, and porters at airports and train stations usually receive 25Kč (90¢) per bag. Taxi drivers should get about 10%, unless they've already ripped you off.

WHERE TO STAY

Prague's full-service hotels have had to tighten efficiency in the face of heavier international competition, but due to low supply, room rates still top those of many similar or better-quality hotels in western Europe. Pensions with limited services are cheaper than hotels, but compared with similar western European B&Bs, they're pricey. The best budget lodgings are rooms in private homes or apartments.

Several local agencies offer all kinds of private housing. The leader now is Prague-based **E-Travel.cz** (www.travel.cz), which offers all types of accommodations at their main website, or you can tap into their large pictured database of apartments at **www.apartments.cz**. Its office is near the National Theater at Ostrovní 7 (✆ **224-990-983**). Another agency, especially good for those arriving late by train or air, is **AVE Travel Ltd.** (✆ **224-223-226;** www.avetravel.cz). It has outlets at the airport (7am–10pm); at the main train station (6am–10pm); and at the north train station (7am–9pm).

STARÉ MĚSTO (OLD TOWN) & JOSEFOV
Very Expensive

Four Seasons Hotel ★★★   Prague's most prestigious new luxury hotel provides an elegant base for exploring Old Town. Guests can choose from rooms in the neo-Renaissance house with its towering ceilings, or in the neoclassical wing with suites offering marble bathrooms and some of the best views of the bridge and the castle. In the tasteful and lower-priced Art Nouveau wing, rooms are comfortable but the street-side views are much less impressive. All rooms are fitted with fine solid wood furniture, and include such amenities as CD players and bathrobes.

Veleslavínova 2a, Praha 1. ✆ **221-427-000**. Fax 221-426-000. www.fourseasons.com. 162 units. From 6,977Kč ($250) double; from 18,200Kč ($650) suite. AE, DC, MC, V. Metro: Staroměstská. **Amenities:** Restaurant; bar; health club; concierge; business services; 24-hr. room service; laundry; dry cleaning overnight. *In room:* A/C, TV, VCR (in all suites), dataport, minibar, hair dryer, safe.

Hotel InterContinental Prague ★   The upper suites here have hosted luminaries such as Madeleine Albright, and, so legend has it, terrorist Carlos the Jackal. The standard rooms aren't very large but are comfortable, with decent but not exceptional furniture and marble bathrooms. A riverside window might give you a glimpse of the castle or the metronome at the top of Letná Park across the river.

Náměstí Curieových 43/5, Praha 1. ✆ **296-631-111**. Fax 224-810-071. www.interconti.com. 364 units. From 4,980Kč ($178) double; from 10,696Kč ($382) suite. Rates include buffet breakfast. AE, DC, MC, V. Metro: Staroměstská. **Amenities:** 2 restaurants; cafe; indoor swimming pool; fitness center; concierge; car rental; fax and business services; salon; 24-hr. room service; massage; laundry. *In room:* A/C, TV, minibar, hair dryer.

Hotel Paříž ★   At the edge of náměstí Republiky and across from the Municipal House, the Paříž provides a rare glimpse back into the gilded First Republic. Each light fixture, etching, and curve at this Art Nouveau landmark recalls the days when Prague was one of the world's richest cities. For a glimpse of the hotel's atmosphere, rent the film *Mission Impossible;* you can see Tom Cruise plotting his revenge from within one of the fine suites. The rooms are some of the most comfortable in Prague, with modern updates of Art Deco accents.

U Obecního domu 1, Praha 1. ✆ **222-195-195**. Fax 224-225-475. www.hotel-pariz.cz. 94 units, 74 with tub/shower combination, 20 with shower only. 5,600Kč ($200) double; 10,920Kč ($390) suite. AE, DC, MC, V. Metro: Náměstí Republiky. **Amenities:** Restaurant; cafe; concierge; business services; 24-hr. room service; babysitting; laundry; dry cleaning. *In room:* A/C, TV, minibar, hair dryer, safe.

Expensive

Hotel Ungelt ★ *(Value) (Kids)*   It's not very opulent, but the Ungelt—just off Old Town Square—offers airy, spacious suites that are great for families. Each contains a living room, a full kitchen, and a bathroom. Rooms have standard-issue beds; some have hand-painted ceilings.

Štupartská 1, Praha 1. ✆ **224-828-686**. Fax 224-828-181. www.ungelt.cz. 10 units. 4,431Kč ($158) 1-bedroom suite; 5,514Kč ($196) 2-bedroom suite. Rates include breakfast. AE, MC, V. Metro: Staroměstská or line B to Náměstí Republiky. **Amenities:** Bar; tour and activities desk at reception; car rental; business services; laundry; iron. *In room:* TV, minibar, hair dryer.

Native Behavior

The Czechs are the quintessential live-and-let-live people. Simple pleasures are the most important, the main one being the requisite evenings in the local *hospoda* (pub) inhaling liters of the national liquid gold.

Still, for people who spend a disproportionate number of hours in beer joints, Czechs remain proud of their erudite traditions. The highly educated populace has a vast interest in literature, film, theater, and, of course, serious music.

Most Czechs are easygoing with strangers and happy to give advice, and many will even invite complete strangers to their weekend cottages to see how real Bohemians live.

Moderate

Betlem Club *Value* This small hotel offers a great location on a cobblestone square across from where Protestant firebrand Jan Hus once preached. Rooms are bland but comfortable and fairly priced. One great advantage is that if you come by car, the Betlem lets you park in front of the hotel, a rarity in this parking-space-deficient city.

Betlémské nám. 9, Praha 1. © 222-221-575. Fax 222-220-580. www.betlemclub.cz. 22 units, all with tub/shower combination. 3,600Kč ($128) double; 3,900 Kč ($139) suite. Rates include breakfast. No credit cards. Metro: Národní třída. **Amenities:** Babysitting; laundry; safe. *In room:* TV, minibar.

Inexpensive

Hotel Cloister Inn ✪ *Value* Between Old Town Square and the National Theater (a 3-min. walk from the Charles Bridge), the Cloister Inn occupies a building that the secret police once used to hold prisoners. It sounds ominous, but it offers sparse, clean accommodations at an unbeatable price for the location. The hotel's new owner has refurbished the property and installed comfortable Nordic furniture in the guest rooms.

Konviktská 14, Praha 1. © 224-211-020. Fax 224-210-800. www.cloister-inn.cz. 73 units, all with shower only. 4,200Kč ($150) double. Rates include breakfast. AE, DC, MC, V. Metro: Národní třída. **Amenities:** Concierge; tour and activities desk; safe. *In room:* TV, hair dryer, safe.

NOVÉ MĚSTO (NEW TOWN)
Very Expensive

Palace Hotel ✪ Surpassed in comfort only by the Savoy in Hradčany, the Palace is a top, upscale, central-city offering, a block from Wenceslas Square, although if you have a choice, the Paříž has far more character. Rooms are some of the largest and most modern luxury accommodations in Prague; each has a marble bathroom. Two rooms for travelers with disabilities are available.

Panská 12, Praha 1. © 224-093-111. Fax 224-221-240. www.palacehotel.cz. 124 units. From 3,920Kč ($140) double; 9,800Kč ($350) suite. Rates include breakfast. AE, DC, MC, V. Metro: Můstek. **Amenities:** 2 restaurants; lounge; concierge; business services; 24-hr. room service; laundry. *In room:* A/C, TV/VCR, minibar, safe.

Expensive

Hotel Esplanade ✪ Located on a side street opposite the main train station, the Esplanade began life as a bank and the offices of an Italian insurance company. Rooms are bright and airy, some with standard beds, others with French Provincial headboards, and still others with extravagant canopies. Number 101 is over the top with antique wooden chairs, intricate inlaid tables, and a fascinating embossed wall covering. The doorman says the hotel is safe, but we recommend you not to stroll alone in this neighborhood at night.

Washingtonova 19, Praha 1. © **224-501-111.** Fax 224-229-306. www.esplanade.cz. 74 units, 47 with shower only. 4,256Kč–6,356Kč ($152–$227) double; from 6,748Kč ($241) suite. Rates include breakfast. AE, DC, MC, V. Metro: Muzeum. **Amenities:** Restaurant; bar; cafe/lounge; sauna; concierge; car-rental desk; room service; massage; babysitting; laundry; dry cleaning; executive-level rooms. *In room:* TV, dataport, minibar, hair dryer, safe.

Prague Marriott Hotel ★★★ *Kids*   The Marriott provides just what you would expect: a high-standard space with tasteful, homogenized furniture and all of the business amenities and services demanded by the virtual salesperson. The Marriott is right off nám[e]stí Republiky; in an area of Old Town more commercial than attractive. In an effort to attract families, the Marriott offers Sunday family brunches in the Brasserie Praha, where kids are welcome and PC games are available. The hotel's massive fitness center is better equipped than the InterContinental's (see above).

V Celnici 8, Praha 1. © **222-888-888.** Fax 222-888-889. www.marriott.com. 328 units. 5,017Kč ($179) double; 7,369Kč ($263) executive level double; from 9,564Kč ($341) suite. Rates for suites and executive rooms include breakfast. AE, DC, MC, V. Metro: Náměstí Republiky. **Amenities:** Restaurant; cafe; bar; indoor swimming pool; fitness center; saunas; whirlpools; gym; concierge service; fully equipped business center; 24-hr. room service; laundry and dry-cleaning service; valet service with underground parking. *In room:* A/C, TV, dataport, minibar, hair dryer, safe.

Moderate

Andante *Value*   A great value choice, the understated Andante is tucked away on a dark side street, about 2 blocks off the top of Wenceslas Square. Despite its less than appealing neighborhood (women traveling alone might feel more comfortable staying elsewhere), this is the most comfortable property in the moderate range. It lacks the character of the old Hotel Evropa (see below), but is better cared for. With bathrooms in every room and high-grade Scandinavian furniture, you gain in comfort what you lose in adventure.

Ve Smečkách 4, Prague 1. © **222-211-616.** Fax 222-210-591. www.andante.cz. 32 units, some with shower only, some with tub only. 3,444Kč ($123) double; 4,704Kč ($168) suite. Rates include breakfast. AE, MC, V. Metro: Muzeum. **Amenities:** Restaurant; tours arranged with the reception desk; business services; limited room service. *In room:* TV, minibar; hair dryer, iron, safety box available at the reception desk.

Inexpensive

Hotel Evropa   The statue-studded exterior is still one of the most striking landmarks on Wenceslas Square, but unlike other early-20th-century gems, it hasn't been polished and so continues to get duller. Rooms are aging and most don't have bathrooms; some are just plain shabby. The best choice is a room facing the square with a balcony, but all are falling into various levels of disrepair. Still, this is an affordable chance to stay at one of Wenceslas Square's once-grand addresses.

Václavské nám. 25, Praha 1. © **224-215-387.** Fax 224-224-544. 90 units, 20 with bathroom (tub only). 2,210Kč ($78) double without bathroom; 3,390Kč ($121) double with bathroom; from 3,556Kč ($127) suite. Rates include continental breakfast. AE, MC, V. Metro: Můstek or Muzeum. **Amenities:** Restaurant; concierge; safe; luggage storage.

MALÁ STRANA (LESSER TOWN)
Expensive

U Krále Karla ★   This Castle Hill property does so much to drive home its Renaissance roots, King Charles's heirs should be getting royalties. Replete with period-print open-beamed ceilings and stained-glass windows, the atmosphere is almost Disneyesque in its pretense, but it's somehow appropriate for this location at the foot of Prague Castle. This is a fun, comfortable choice, with heavy period furniture and colorful angelic accents everywhere.

Nerudova-Úvoz 4, Prague 1. © **257-532-869.** Fax 257-533-591. www.romantichotels.cz. 19 units, 13 with shower only. 5,500Kč ($196) double; 7,900Kč ($282) suite. Rates include breakfast. AE, MC, V. Tram: 22 or 23 to Malostranské náměstí and then up the hill. **Amenities:** Restaurant; bike or scooter rental; tour and activities desk; private limousine hire; limited room service; babysitting; laundry; dry cleaning. *In room:* TV, minibar, kitchenette, hair dryer, iron, safe.

Moderate

Best Western–Hotel Kampa The Kampa has a choice location on a quiet winding alley off the park, giving you quick access to Malá Strana and Charles Bridge. The rooms smack of Communist chintz, but they're comfortable if you don't expect first-class surroundings. The best rooms boast a park view, so request one when booking or checking in.

Všehrdova 16, Praha 1. © **257-320-404.** Fax 257-320-262. www.euroagentur.cz. 84 units, all with shower only. 5,800Kč ($207) double. Rates include breakfast. AE, DC, MC, V. Metro: Malostranská; then take tram 12, 22, or 23 to the Hellichova stop. **Amenities:** Restaurant with garden; bar; limited room service; laundry service; dry cleaning; wireless Internet access; currency exchange; souvenir shop. *In room:* TV, minibar, hair dryer, safe.

HRADČANY
Very Expensive

Hotel Savoy ★★★ One of Prague's finest hotels, the Savoy attracts a demanding clientele. Behind the massive Foreign Ministry, a few blocks from the castle, it welcomes you with a tastefully modern lobby. The guest rooms are richly decorated and boast spacious marble bathrooms. The beds are huge, in contrast to the customary central European style of two twin beds shoved together. The pleasant staff provides an attention to detail that's a cut above the service at most hotels in town. The Savoy's Hradčany Restaurant is also one of the finest dining rooms in town (see "Where to Dine," below).

Keplerova 6, Praha 1. © **224-302-430.** Fax 224-302-128. www.hotel-savoy.cz. 61 units. From 7,979Kč ($280) double; from 10,466Kč ($370) suite. Rates include breakfast. AE, DC, MC, V. Tram: 22 or 23. **Amenities:** Restaurant; exercise room; sauna; whirlpool; concierge; business services; salon; 24-hr. room service; laundry. *In room:* A/C, TV/VCR, dataport, minibar, hair dryer, safe.

Expensive

Romantik Hotel U Raka ★★ *Finds* Hidden among the stucco houses and cobblestone streets of a pristine medieval neighborhood on the far side of Prague Castle is this most pleasant surprise. In a ravine below the Foreign Ministry gardens, the old-world farmhouse has been lovingly reconstructed. This is the quietest getaway you could imagine in tightly packed Prague. The rustic rooms have heavy wooden furniture, open-beam ceilings, and exposed brick. The much-sought-after suite has a fireplace and adjoins a private garden, making it a favorite of honeymooners.

Černínská 10, Praha 1. © **220-511-100.** Fax 220-510-511. www.romantikhotels.com/Prag. 6 units, 5 with shower only. 6,200Kč ($221) double; 7,900Kč ($282) suite. Rates include breakfast. AE, MC, V. Tram: 22 or 23. **Amenities:** Laundry service. *In room:* A/C, TV, minibar, hair dryer.

WHERE TO DINE

The true Czech dining experience can be summed up in three native words: *vepřo, knedlo, zelo*—pork, dumplings, cabbage. If that's what you want, try most any *hostinec* (Czech pub). Most offer a hearty *guláš* or pork dish with dumplings and cabbage for about 80Kč to 150Kč ($3–$5.70). After you wash it down with Czech beer, you won't care about the taste—or your arteries.

At most restaurants, menu prices include value-added tax (VAT). Tipping has become more commonplace in restaurants where the staff is obviously trying harder; rounding up the bill to about 10% or more is usually adequate.

STARÉ MĚSTO (OLD TOWN) & JOSEFOV
Expensive

Bellevue ★★★ INTERNATIONAL   With its excellent view of Prague Castle, Bellevue is my perennial top choice in town. The intelligent menu boasts choice beef, nouvelle sauces, well-dressed fish and game, delicate pastas, and gorgeous desserts. For an extraordinary treat, try the rack of New Zealand lamb. Al dente pastas share a plate with lobster-and-spinach purée, garlic and herbs, or tomatoes and olives. The consistent food and presentation, and the pleasant and perfectly timed service make dinner at the Bellevue an evening to remember.

Smetanovo nábřeží 18, Praha 1. ⓒ 222-221-443. www.pfd.cz. Reservations recommended. Main courses 390Kč–890Kč ($14–$32); fixed-price menu 1,090Kč–1,990Kč ($39–$71). AE, DC, MC, V. Mon–Sat noon–3pm and 5:30–11pm; Sun 11am–3:30pm (jazz brunch) and 7–11pm (jazz dinner). Metro: Staroměstská.

Vinárna V zátiší ★★ INTERNATIONAL   V zátiší ("still life") has a casual elegance, like the living room of a beachfront Mediterranean villa with cushy, upholstered, wrought-iron chairs and plenty of artfully arranged flora. Here, you'll find several fish and game choices, vegetarian selections, and a scampi that never disappoints. The excellent desserts often echo those at the Bellevue (see above), which is run by the same restaurant group.

Liliová 1, Praha 1. ⓒ 222-221-155. Reservations recommended. Main courses 275Kč–775Kč ($9–$26); fixed-price menus 700Kč–1,275Kč ($23–$42). AE, DC, MC, V. Mon–Sat noon–3pm and 5:30–11pm. Metro: Národní Třída.

Moderate

Kogo ★★ (Value) ITALIAN   This ristorante-pizzeria in the middle of Old Town is very trendy and popular. Fresh and well-prepared salads, pizza, pasta, and Italian specialties are served by an above-average waitstaff in a pleasant atmosphere.

Tips **A Few Dining Warnings**

Beware: Some restaurants gouge customers by charging exorbitant amounts for nuts or other seemingly free pre-meal snacks left on your table. Ask before you eat.

Many places, especially in the evening, tack on an extra 30Kč or 50Kč per person as a cover charge, even if they don't offer live entertainment. If this charge is mentioned at all, it'll be written discreetly on the menu as *couvert*.

Finally, as more Czech restaurants begin to accept credit cards, stories of waiters adding a digit or two to your total have increased. One protection is to write out the total in words on the credit card bill, the way you would on a personal check. Also ask for the carbons and keep a good record of where you've used your card to check against your bank statement to ensure that someone hasn't been using your number. The restaurants we list don't seem to engage in these practices, but be on guard, especially if you veer from these suggested establishments.

Beyond the standard and tasty pasta roster, the roasted veal is a good choice or try the rare (for Prague) and tasty mussels in white wine and garlic. The wine list is extensive, and the tiramisu, if you get it before the nightly supply runs out, is light and sweet.

A second Kogo restaurant is located at Na Příkopě 22, Praha 1 (𝒞 221-451-259; Metro: Můstek).

Havelská 27, Praha 1. 𝒞 224-214-543. www.kogo-prague.cz. Reservations recommended. Main courses 200Kč–400Kč ($7–$14). AE, MC, V. Daily 9am–midnight. Metro: Můstek.

Red Hot & Blues 𝒜 *Kids* AMERICAN/CAJUN/MEXICAN   As a former resident of the region that inspired Red Hot & Blues, my husband was skeptical about this Prague attempt at Creole/Cajun cooking. But while you won't find a crawfish lurking about, the étouffée is excellent and the spicy Cajun shrimp delivers a punch. Tex-Mex regulars, plus burgers and nachos, round out the menu. Sunday brunch, best enjoyed in the small courtyard, includes tangy huevos rancheros on crispy tortillas. From 7 to 10:30pm you can hear live jazz.

Jakubská 12, Praha 1. 𝒞 222-314-639. www.redhotandblues.com. Main courses 139Kč–499Kč ($5–$18). AE, MC, V. Daily 9am–11pm; Sat–Sun brunch 9am–4pm. Metro: Náměstí Republiky.

Inexpensive

Creperie Café Gallery Restaurant FRENCH   This affordable French eatery rests at the foot of Charles Bridge on the Old Town side. Occupying a wing of the St. Francis church complex, the creperie creates the feel of a cozy farmhouse with old wooden chairs and hand-stitched pillows thrown on sturdy benches. The savory galettes are filled with spinach, tangy niva cheese or chicken and make a good light lunch after a heavy morning of trudging. The sweet crepes with chocolate, fruit compote, or whipped cream are good for an afternoon break or for dessert following an evening stroll across the bridge.

Křížovnické nám. 3, Praha 1. 𝒞 221-108-240. Crepes and galettes 75Kč–129Kč ($2.65–$4.60). AE, MC, V. Daily 10am–midnight. Metro: Staroměstská.

Pivnice Radegast CZECH   The raucous Radegast dishes up Prague's best pub guláš in a single narrow vaulted hall, where the namesake Moravian brew seems to never stop flowing from its taps. Around the corner from a bunch of popular bars and close to Old Town Square, the Radegast attracts a good mix of visitors and locals and a young, upwardly mobile crowd.

Templová 2, Praha 1. 𝒞 222-328-237. Main courses 68Kč–240Kč ($2.40–$8.55). AE, MC, V. Daily 11am–midnight. Metro: Můstek or Náměstí Republiky.

Pizzeria Rugantino 𝒜𝒜 *Kids* PIZZA/PASTA   Pizzeria Rugantino serves generous iceberg salads and the best selection of individual pizzas in Prague. Wood-fired stoves and handmade dough result in a crisp and delicate crust. The Diabolo with fresh garlic bits and very hot chiles goes nicely with a salad and Krušovice beer. The constant buzz, a nonsmoking area, heavy childproof wooden tables, and lots of baby chairs make this a family favorite.

Dušní 4, Praha 1. 𝒞 222-318-172. Reservations not necessary. Individual pizzas 100Kč–300Kč ($3.55–$11). No credit cards. Mon–Sat 11am–11pm; Sun 5–11pm. Metro: Staroměstská.

U medvídků 𝒜𝒜 CZECH   Bright and noisy, the House at the Little Bears serves a better-than-average vepřo, knedlo, and zelo with two-color cabbage. The pub, on the right after entering, is much cheaper and livelier than the bar to the left. It's a hangout for locals, German tour groups, and foreign journalists in search of the original Czech Budweiser beer, Budvar. In high season, an oompah band plays in the beer wagon.

Na Perštýně 7, Praha 1. ℂ **224-211-916.** Main courses 90Kč–250Kč ($2.20–$8.90). AE, MC, V. Daily 11am–11pm. Metro: Národní třída.

NOVÉ MĚSTO (NEW TOWN)
Moderate

Restaurant U Čížků ★ *Value* CZECH   One of the city's first private restaurants, this cozy cellar-cum-hunting lodge on Charles Square is still an excellent value. The fare is purely Czech, and the massive portions of game, smoked pork, and other meats will stay with you for a while. The traditional *Staročeský talíř* (local pork meat, dumplings, and cabbage) is about as authentic Czech as it gets.

Karlovo nám. 34, Praha 2. ℂ **222-232-257.** www.restaurantucizku.cz. Reservations recommended. Main courses 75Kč–175Kč ($2.65–$6.25). AE, MC, V. Daily noon–10pm. Metro: Karlovo nám.

Inexpensive

Café-Restaurant Louvre CZECH/INTERNATIONAL   This big, breezy upstairs dining hall in New Town is great for a coffee, an inexpensive pre-theater meal, or an upscale game of pool. A fabulous Art Nouveau interior with huge original chandeliers buzzes with shoppers, businessmen, and students. Main dishes range from trout with horseradish to beans with garlic sauce. Avoid the always-overcooked pastas and stick to the basic meats and fish. In the snazzy billiards parlor in back, you can have drinks or a light meal.

Národní třída 20, Praha 1. ℂ **224-930-949.** Reservations accepted. Main courses 90Kč–300Kč ($3.20–$11). AE, DC, MC, V. Daily 8am–11:30pm. Metro: Národní třída.

Jarmark ★ *Value* CZECH   This is Bohemia's answer to those endless cafeteria lines your parents dragged you through, except this one serves a really tasty variety of meats, sides, and salads, and, of course, beer. And this one is not all-you-can-eat for one price despite its convenient come-and-shove-it-in system. Everyone gets a ticket upon entering, which is validated at each stop you make among the rows of steaming hot tables, veggie carts, and drink dispensers.

Vodičkova 30, Dům "U Nováků." ℂ **224-233-733.** Reservations not accepted. Main courses 70Kč–150Kč ($2.50–$5.35). No credit cards. Daily 11am–10pm; Mon–Fri breakfast 8–10am. Metro: Můstek.

MALÁ STRANA
Expensive

U Malířů ★ FRENCH   The owners of the previously pricy U Malířů have given in to the pressure of competition and now offer a more affordable chance to sample the finer attributes of a Parisian kitchen. Surrounded by Romantic-age murals and gorgeously appointed tables in three intimate dining rooms, you're faced with some tough choices. Creamy scallops ragout swim in light vanilla sauce, rack of lamb is glazed in tarragon, and an exotic set of quail chicks bathe in Armagnac. If you want a truly old-world evening of elegant romance and French specialties, U Malířů is finally worth it.

Maltézské nám. 11, Praha 1. ℂ **257-530-000.** www.umaliru.cz. Reservations necessary. Main courses 520Kč–1,490Kč ($19–$53); fixed-price menus 1,190Kč ($43) and 1,790Kč ($64). AE, DC, MC, V. Daily 7pm–2am. Metro: Malostranská.

Moderate

U modré kachničky CZECH/WILD GAME   The antiques-filled "Blue Duckling," on a narrow Malá Strana street, is our choice for the most innovative attempt at refining standard Czech dishes into true Bohemian haute cuisine.

The menu is loaded with an array of wild game and quirky spins on Czech village favorites. The roast rabbit, one of my mom's favorite dishes, is cooked to tender perfection in a creamy herb sauce with cranberries.

Nebovidská 6, Praha 1. © **257-320-308**. Reservations recommended. Main courses 300Kč–500Kč ($10–$17). AE, MC, V. Daily noon–4pm and 6:30–11:30pm. Metro: Malostranská.

Moments Kavárna Society

Cafe life is back in a big way in Prague. From dissident blues to high society, these are the places where nonpub Praguers spend their afternoons and evenings, sipping coffee and smoking cigarettes while reading, writing, or talking with friends.

The **Kavárna (Cafe) Slavia** ✿, Národní at Smetanovo nábřeží 2, Praha 1 (© **224-218-493**; Metro: Národní třída), reopened in 1997, after a half-decade sleep. The restored crisp Art Deco room recalls the Slavia's 100 years as the meeting place for the city's cultural and intellectual crowd. You'll still find a relatively affordable menu of light fare served with the riverfront views of Prague Castle and the National Theater. It's open daily 8am to midnight.

The quaint **Café Milena,** Staroměstské nám. 22, Praha 1 (© **221-632-602**; Metro: Staroměstská), is managed by the Franz Kafka Society and named for Milena Jesenská, one of the writer's lovers. The draw is a great view of the Orloj, the astronomical clock with the hourly parade of saints on the side of Old Town Square's city hall. It's open daily 10am to 8pm.

Of all the beautifully restored spaces in the Municipal House, the **Kavárna Obecní dům** ✿✿, nám. Republiky 5, Praha 1 (© **222-002-763**; Metro: náměstí Republiky), might be its most spectacular room. Lofty ceilings, marble accents and tables, an altarlike mantle, huge windows, and period chandeliers provide the awesome setting for coffees, teas, and other drinks, along with pastries and light sandwiches. It's open daily 7:30am to 11pm.

In the neighborhood behind the National Theater is **Angel Café** ✿, Opatovická 3, Praha 1 (© **224-930-019**; Metro: Národní třída). This cafe best reflects the light-and-bright 1990s restaurant movement captured by Pret a Manger in Britain. Unlike the cash-and-carry Pret, you can sit comfortably in the relaxing Angel atmosphere and linger over tasty sandwiches served with quality cheeses, spreads, and vegetables on fresh bread. French pastries highlight the breakfast lineup along with properly stiff espressos. Who needs Starbucks?

A New Age alternative to the clatter of the kavárnas is **Dahab** ✿✿, Dlouhá 33, Praha 1 (© **224-827-375**; Metro: nám. Republiky). This tearoom was founded by Prague's king of tea, Luboš Rychvalský, who introduced Prague to Eastern and Arabic tea cultures soon after the 1989 revolution. Here you can choose from about 20 varieties of tea and more than 10 kinds of coffee. Arabic soups, hummus, tahini, couscous, pita, and tempting sweets are also on the menu. It's open daily from noon to midnight.

Inexpensive
Bohemia Bagel ★★ *Value* BAGELS/SANDWICHES   The roster of golden-brown, hand-rolled, stone-baked bagels at this restaurant near the Jewish Quarter, at the base of Petřín Hill, is stellar. Plain, cinnamon raisin, garlic, or onion provides a sturdy but tender frame for Scandinavian lox and cream cheese or jalapeño-cheddar cheese (on which you can lop Tex-Mex chili for the Sloppy Bagel). The cushioned wooden booths in an earthy contemporary setting are comfortable.

Újezd 16, Praha 1. ✆ **257-310-694.** Bagels and sandwiches 25Kč–145Kč (90¢–$5.15). No credit cards. Mon–Fri 7am–midnight; Sat–Sun 8am–midnight. Tram: 6, 9, 12, 22, or 23 to Újezd stop.

HRADČANY
Expensive
Hradčany Restaurant ★ INTERNATIONAL   Matching the crisp English setting of the Savoy Hotel in which it resides, the Hradčany is the most elegant choice this side of the castle. The menu lists a variety of beef, pork, and seafood, including succulent poached salmon and lean sliced veal in herb cream sauce. There are also surprises, such as herb-stuffed tortellini and prawns in avocado mousse. The service sets the standard for Prague, and the new lunch sitting is sure to attract a solid crowd to this jewel beyond the castle gates.

In the Hotel Savoy, Keplerova 6, Praha 1. ✆ **224-302-150.** Reservations recommended. Main courses 590Kč–790Kč ($21–$28). AE, DC, MC, V. Daily noon–3pm and 6–11pm. Tram: 22 or 23, 2 stops past Prague Castle.

Inexpensive
Saté Indonéská Restaurace INDONESIAN   A lunchtime savior near the castle, the Saté has made quite a business out of simple Indonesian dishes at low prices. The unassuming storefront near the Swedish Embassy doesn't stand out, so look closely. The pork satay comes in a peanut sauce along with a hearty *mie goreng* (traditional Indonesian fried noodles). This casual place is a good choice if you've just visited the castle and need to refuel and rest your feet.

Pohořelec 152/3, Praha 1. ✆ **220-514-552.** Main courses 80Kč–200Kč ($2.85–$7.15). No credit cards. Daily 11am–10pm. Tram: 22 or 23.

IN VINOHRADY
Moderate
Ponte *Value* INTERNATIONAL   My favorite choice above Wenceslas Square in Vinohrady, Ponte is one of the best values in Prague. Shun the cold of an autumn or winter evening near the roaring fire in the restaurant's brick cellar dining room. As its name suggests, this place is a bridge between Italian cuisine and other Continental foods. Beyond the penne and pesto, there are several vegetarian and low-calorie, chicken-based selections. Jazz combos play on most nights from a small stage in the corner.

Anglická 15, Praha 2. ✆ **224-221-665.** www.ponte-restaurant. Reservations recommended. Main courses 180Kč–695Kč ($6.45–$25). AE, MC, V. Daily 11:30am–midnight. Metro: I. P. Pavlova or Náměstí Míru.

Inexpensive
Radost FX ★★ VEGETARIAN   In vogue and vegetarian, Radost is a clubhouse for hip New Bohemians that's a short walk from the Main Train Station. The veggie burger is well seasoned and substantial on a grain bun, and the soups, such as lentil and onion, are light and full of flavor. The dining area is a dark rec room of upholstered armchairs, chaise longues, couches from the 1960s, and coffee tables on which you eat. It serves as an art gallery as well.

Bělehradská 120, Praha 2. ✆ **224-254-776.** Reservations not accepted. Main courses 120Kč–250Kč ($4.25–$8.90). MC, V. Daily 10am–5am. Metro: I. P. Pavlova.

SEEING THE SIGHTS

In Prague, you'll get the most enjoyment from a slow, aimless wander through the city's heart. Except for the busy main streets, where you may have to dodge traffic, Prague is ideal for walking—really the only way to explore the city. Most of the city's oldest areas are walking zones, with motor traffic restricted. If you have the time and energy, absorb the grand architecture of Prague Castle and the Old Town skyline (best from Charles Bridge) at sunrise and then at sunset. You'll see two completely different cities.

SIGHTSEEING SUGGESTIONS FOR FIRST-TIME VISITORS

If You Have 1 Day If you have only 1 day, do what visiting kings and potentates do on a short visit: Walk the **Royal Route** from the top of the Hradčany hill (tram nos. 22 or 23 or a taxi are suggested for the ride up unless you're very fit). Tour **Prague Castle,** and then stroll across Charles Bridge on the way to the winding alleys of **Staré Město (Old Town).**

If You Have 2 Days On day 2, explore the varied sights of **Staré Město (Old Town), Malá Strana (Lesser Town),** and **Josefov (the Jewish Quarter).** Wander and browse through numerous shops and galleries offering the finest Bohemian crystal, porcelain, and modern artwork, as well as top boutiques, cafes, and restaurants.

If You Have 3 Days On day 3, visit the **National Art Gallery** at Šternberk Palace and the **Strahov Monastery** with its ornate libraries. Include the **Loreto Palace,** with its peculiar artwork.

If You Have 4 or 5 Days Beyond day 3, tour one of the many other museums or galleries. For a great respite from the crowded city, visit the old southern citadel over the Vltava, **Vyšehrad,** where you get a completely different view of the city you've just explored.

PRAGUE CASTLE & CHARLES BRIDGE

Dating from the 14th century, **Karlův most (Charles Bridge)** ★★★, Prague's most celebrated structure, links Prague Castle to Staré Město. For most of its 600 years, the 518m (1,700-ft.) span has been a pedestrian promenade, although for centuries walkers had to share the concourse with horse-drawn vehicles and trolleys. Today, the bridge is filled with hordes walking among folksy artists and street musicians.

The best times to stroll across the bridge are in early morning and around sunset, when the crowds have thinned and the shadows are more mysterious. You'll be crisscrossing the bridge throughout your stay.

Pražský Hrad (Prague Castle) ★★★ *(Moments* The huge hilltop complex known collectively as Pražský Hrad encompasses dozens of towers, churches, courtyards, and monuments. A visit could easily take an entire day or more. Still, you can see the top sights—St. Vitus Cathedral, the Royal Palace, St. George's Basilica, the Powder Tower, plus Golden Lane—in the space of a morning or an afternoon.

Chrám sv. Víta (St. Vitus Cathedral) ★, constructed in A.D. 926 as the court church of the Premyslid princes, was named for a wealthy 4th-century Sicilian martyr and has long been the center of Prague's religious and political life. The key part of its Gothic construction took place in the 14th century. In the 18th and 19th centuries, subsequent baroque and neo-Gothic additions were made. In 1997, Pope John Paul II visited Prague to honor the 1,000th anniversary of the death of 10th-century Slavic evangelist St. Vojtěch.

Královský palác (the Royal Palace) ✮, in the third courtyard of the castle grounds, served as the residence of kings between the 10th and the 17th centuries. Vaulted Vladislav Hall, the interior's centerpiece, was used for coronations and is still used for inauguration of the Czech presidents and for special occasions. The adjacent Diet was where the king met with advisers and where the supreme court was held. You'll find a good selection of guidebooks, maps, and related information at the entrance.

Kostel sv. Jiří (St. George's Basilica), adjacent to the Royal Palace, is Prague's oldest Romanesque structure, dating from the 10th century. It was also Bohemia's first convent, which now houses a museum of historic Czech art.

Zlatá ulička (Golden Lane) is a picturesque, fairy-tale street of tiny 16th-century servants' houses built into the castle fortifications. The houses now contain shops, galleries, and refreshment bars. In 1917, Franz Kafka lived briefly at no. 22.

Prašná věž, aka Mihulka **(the Powder Tower),** forms part of the northern bastion of the castle complex just off the Golden Lane. Originally a gunpowder storehouse and a cannon tower, it was turned into a laboratory for the 17th-century alchemists serving the court of Emperor Rudolf II.

Tickets are sold at the **Prague Castle Information Center** (✆ **224-373-368**), in the second courtyard after you pass through the main gate from Hradčanské náměstí. The center also arranges tours in various languages and sells tickets for individual concerts and exhibits.

Hradčanské nám., Hradčany, Praha 1. ✆ **224-373-368**. Fax 224-310-896. www.hrad.cz. Grounds free. Combination ticket for tour A to 5 main attractions (St. Vitus Cathedral, Royal Palace, St. George's Basilica, Powder Tower, Golden Lane), without guide, 220Kč ($7.85) adults, 110Kč ($3.90) students; with English-speaking guide, 300Kč ($11) adults, 190Kč ($6.80) students. Tour B (St. Vitus Cathedral, Royal Palace, Golden Lane) 180Kč ($6.40) adults, 90Kč ($3.20) students; Tour C (only Golden Lane) 40Kč ($1.40). For guided tours (group of 5 and more), supplement 80Kč ($2.85) per person (only Tues–Sun 9am–4pm). All tours free for children under 6. Ticket valid 1 day. The Castle is open daily 9am–5pm (to 4pm Nov–Mar). Metro: Malostranská, then tram 22 or 23, up the hill 2 stops.

THE JEWISH MUSEUM

The Jewish Museum manages all the Jewish landmarks in Josefov, which forms the northwest quarter of Old Town. The museum offers English-language guided package tours as part of a comprehensive admission price. The package includes the Ceremonial Hall, Old Jewish Cemetery, Pinkas Synagogue, Klaus Synagogue, Maisel Synagogue, and Spanish Synagogue.

Maisel Synagogue   Maisel Synagogue is used as the exhibition space for the Jewish Museum. Most of Prague's ancient Judaica was destroyed by the Nazis during World War II. Ironically, those same Germans constructed an "exotic museum of an extinct race," thus salvaging thousands of objects, such as the valued Torah covers, books, and silver now displayed here.

Maiselova 10 (between Široká and Jáchymova 3), Praha 1. ✆ **222-317-191**. Fax 222-317-181. www.jewishmuseum.cz. Admission to museum sites listed above is 290Kč ($11) adults, 200Kč ($7.60) students. Apr–Oct tours for groups of 10 or more on the hour starting 9am (last tour 5pm). Nov–Apr tours leave whenever enough people gather in same language, open 9am–4:30pm Sun–Fri. Metro: Staroměstská.

Staronová synagoga (Old-New Synagogue) ✮   First called the New Synagogue to distinguish it from an even older one that no longer exists, the

Old-New Synagogue, built around 1270, is Europe's oldest Jewish house of worship. Jews have prayed here continuously for more than 700 years, carrying on even after a massive 1389 pogrom in Josefov that killed more than 3,000 Jews. Worship was interrupted only between 1941 and 1945, during the Nazi occupation. The synagogue is also one of Prague's largest Gothic buildings, with vaulted ceilings and Renaissance-era columns.

Červená 3. ℭ **222-317-191**. Admission 200Kč ($7.60) adults, 140Kč ($5.30) students. Sun–Thurs 9am–6pm; Fri 9am–5pm. Metro: Staroměstská.

Old Jewish Cemetery (Starý židovský hřbitov) ✮ Just 1 block from the Old-New Synagogue, this is one of Europe's oldest Jewish burial grounds, dating from the mid–15th century. Because the local government of the time didn't allow Jews to bury their dead elsewhere, graves were dug deep enough to hold 12 bodies vertically, with each tombstone placed in front of the last. The result is one of the world's most crowded cemeteries: a 1-block area filled with more than 20,000 graves. Among the most famous persons buried here are the celebrated Rabbi Loew (Löw; d. 1609), who created the legend of Golem (a giant clay "monster" to protect Prague's Jews). The adjoining Ceremonial Hall at the end of the path is worth a look for the heart-wrenching drawings by children held at the Terezín concentration camp during World War II (see "Day Trips from Prague," later in this chapter, for more on Terezín).

U Starého hřbitova 3A. ℭ **222-317-191**. Fax 222-317-181. www.jewishmuseum.cz. Admission to all Jewish Museum sites 290Kč ($11) adults, 200Kč ($7.60) students. Sun–Fri 9am–6pm. Metro: Staroměstská.

THE NATIONAL GALLERY

The national collection of fine art is grouped for display in the series of venues known collectively as the **Národní Galerie** (**National Gallery;** www.ngprague.cz). Remember that this term refers to several locations, not just one gallery.

The most extensive collection of classic European works spanning the 14th to 18th centuries is found at the Archbishop's Palace complex in the **Šternberský palác** across from the main gate to Prague Castle. **Veletržní Palace** houses most of the 20th-century art collection, and now also shows the important national revival works from Czech artists of the 19th century. While much of the national collection is shown at **Kinský Palace** on Old Town Square, Gothic pieces may be seen at **St. George's Convent** at Prague Castle, and 19th-century Czech painters and sculptors are shown at **St. Agnes Convent** near the river in Old Town.

Šternberk palác (Šternberský Palace) ✮ The jewel in the National Gallery crown (also known casually as the European Art Museum), the gallery at Šternberský Palace, adjacent to the main gate of Prague Castle, displays a wide menu of European art throughout the ages. It features 5 centuries of everything from Orthodox icons to Renaissance oils by Dutch masters. Pieces by Rembrandt, El Greco, Goya, and Van Dyck are mixed among numerous pieces by Austrian imperial-court painters.

Hradčanské nám. 15, Praha 1. ℭ **233-090-570**. www.ngprague.cz. Admission 150Kč ($5.35) adults, 70Kč ($2.50) students and children. Tues–Sun 10am–6pm. Metro: Line A to Malostranská or Hradčanská.

Klášter sv. Anežky české (St. Agnes Convent) This complex of early Gothic buildings and churches dates from the 13th century. The convent, tucked in a corner of Staré Město, is appropriately home to a collection of Gothic and Renaissance art.

U milosrdných 17, Praha 1. ℭ **224-810-628**. www.ngprague.cz. Admission 100Kč ($3.65) adults, 50Kč ($1.80) children. Tues–Sun 10am–6pm. Metro: Line A to Staroměstská.

Klášter sv. Jiří na Pražském hradě (St. George's Convent at Prague Castle) Dedicated to displaying traditional Czech art, the castle convent is especially packed with Gothic and baroque Bohemian iconography as well as portraits of patron saints. The most famous among the unique collection of Czech Gothic panel paintings are those by the Master of the Hohenfurth Altarpiece and the Master Theodoricus. There's also a noteworthy collection of Czech mannerist and baroque paintings from the 17th and 18th centuries.

Jiřské nám. 33. (✆ **257-320-536**. www.ngprague.cz. Admission 100Kč ($3.65) adults, 50Kč ($1.80) students, free for children under 6. Tues–Sun 10am–6pm. Metro: Line A to Malostranská or Hradčanská.

Palác Kinských (Kinský Palace) ✪ *Finds* This rococo palace houses graphic works from the National Gallery collection, including pieces by Georges Braque, André Derain, and other modern masters. Pablo Picasso's 1907 *Self-Portrait* is here and has virtually been adopted as the National Gallery's logo.

Staroměstské nám. 12, Praha 1. (✆ **224-810-758**. www.ngprague.cz. Admission is different for each exhibition. Tues–Sun 10am–6pm. Metro: Line A to Staroměstská.

Veletržní Palace (National Gallery) This 1925 constructivist palace, built for trade fairs, holds the bulk of the National Gallery's collection of 20th- and 21st-century works by Czech and other European artists. Three atrium-lit concourses provide a comfortable setting for some catchy and kitschy Czech sculpture and multimedia works. Alas, the best cubist works from Braque and Picasso, Rodin bronzes, and many other primarily French pieces have been relegated to the second floor. In 2000, the museum's 19th-century collection was moved here as well.

Veletržní at Dukelských hrdinů 47, Praha 7. (✆ **224-301-024**. www.ngprague.cz. Admission 250Kč ($8.90) adults, 120Kč ($4.30) students for 4 floors of the palace; 200Kč ($7.15) adults, 100Kč ($3.55) students for 3 floors; 150Kč ($5.35) adults, 70Kč ($2.50) students for 2 floors; 100Kč ($3.55) adults, 50Kč ($1.80) students for 1 floor. Free for children under 6. Tues–Sun 10am–6pm. Metro: Line C to Vltavská. Tram: 17.

FAMOUS SQUARES

The most celebrated square, **Staroměstské náměstí (Old Town Square)** ✪✪✪, is surrounded by baroque buildings and packed with colorful craftspeople, cafes, and entertainers. In ancient days, the site was a major crossroads on central European merchant routes. At its center stands a memorial to Jan Hus, the 15th-century martyr who crusaded against Prague's German-dominated religious and political establishment and the persecution of Czech nationalists. Unveiled in 1915, on the 500th anniversary of Hus's execution, the Art Nouveau monument's most compelling features are the asymmetry of the composition and the fluidity of the figures. Take metro line A to Staroměstská.

The **Orloj (Astronomical Clock)** at Staroměstská radnice (Old Town Hall) performs a glockenspiel spectacle daily on the hour from 8am to 8pm. Originally constructed in 1410, the clock has long been an important symbol of Prague.

Václavské náměstí (Wenceslas Sq.) ✪✪, a former horse market, has thrice been the focal point of riots and revolutions—in 1918, 1968, and 1989. The pedestal of the giant equestrian statue of St. Wenceslas on horseback surrounded by four other saints has become a popular platform for speakers. Take metro line A or B to Můstek.

MORE ATTRACTIONS

Bertramka (W. A. Mozart Museum) Mozart loved Prague, and when he visited he often stayed with the family that owned this villa, the Dušeks. Now a museum, the villa contains displays that include his written work and harpsichord. There's also a lock of Mozart's hair, encased in a cube of glass. Much of the Bertramka villa was destroyed by fire in the 1870s, but Mozart's rooms, where he finished composing *Don Giovanni,* miraculously remained untouched. Chamber concerts are often held here.

Mozartova 169, Praha 5. ℰ 257-318-465. www.bertramka.cz. Admission 90Kč ($3.20) adults, 50Kč ($1.80) students, free for children under 6. Concert tickets 350Kč ($13) adults, 230Kč ($8.20) students. Daily 9:30am–6pm (Nov–Mar till 5pm). Tram: 4, 6, 7, 9, 10, 14, or 16 from Anděl metro station.

Stavovské divadlo (Estates' Theater) ✦ The theater was completed in 1783 by the wealthy Count F. A. Nostitz. There are no daily tours, but tickets for performances—and the chance to sit in one of the elegant private boxes—are usually available. Tour events are occasionally scheduled, and individual tours for this and other major monuments can be arranged through **Pražská informační služba** (ℰ **12-444;** www.pis.cz).

Ovocný trh 1, Praha 1. ℰ **224-901-448.** Metro: Line A or B to Můstek.

Strahovský klášter a knihovna (Strahov Monastery and Library) ✦ The second-oldest monastery in Prague, Strahov was founded high above Malá Strana in 1143 by Vladislav II. It's still home to Premonstratensian monks, a scholarly order closely related to the Jesuits, and their dormitories and refectory are off-limits. What draws visitors are the monastery's ornate libraries, holding more than 125,000 volumes.

Strahovské nádvoří 1, Praha 1. ℰ **220-516-671.** Admission 60Kč ($2.15) adults, 40Kč ($1.40) students. Daily 9am–noon and 1–5pm. Tram: 22 or 23 from Malostranská metro station.

Chrám sv. Mikuláše (Cathedral of St. Nicholas) This church is critically regarded as one of the best examples of the high baroque north of the Alps. K. I. Dienzenhofer's 1711 design was augmented by his son Kryštof's 80m (260-ft.) dome, which has dominated the Malá Strana skyline since its completion in 1752. Prague's smog has played havoc with the building's exterior, but its gilded interior is stunning. Gold-capped marble-veneered columns frame altars packed with statuary and frescoes.

Malostranské nám. 1, Praha 1. Free admission. Tues–Sun 10am–5pm (concerts are usually held at 5pm). Metro: Line A to Malostranská.

PARKS & GARDENS

From **Vyšehrad,** Soběslavova 1 (ℰ **224-920-735;** tram 3 from Karlovo náměstí to Výtoň south of New Town), legend has it that Princess Libuše looked out over the Vltava valley toward the present-day Prague Castle and predicted the founding of a great state and capital city. Vyšehrad was the seat of the first Czech kings of the Premyslid dynasty before the dawn of this millennium. Today,

---

Fun Fact **Mozart in Prague**

Mozart staged the premier of *Don Giovanni* at the Estates' Theater in 1787 because he felt the conservative patrons in Vienna didn't appreciate him or his passionate and often shocking work. "Praguers understand me," Mozart was quoted as saying. Czech director Miloš Forman returned to his native country to film his Oscar-winning *Amadeus,* shooting the scenes of Mozart in Prague with perfect authenticity at the Estates'.

Moments **An Old-Fashioned Tram Ride**

If you're traveling in a large group and want a unique sightseeing experience, why not rent your own classic trolley? With enough people, it really is affordable, thanks to the **Historic Tram Tour (Elektrické dráhy DP)**, Patočkova 4, Praha 6 (𝒞 and fax **233-343-349**).

If you send a fax with details 1 day ahead, the city transport department will arrange a private tour using one of the 19th-century wooden tram cars that actually traveled on regular lines through Prague. Up to 24 people can fit in one car, which sports wood-planked floors, cast-iron conductors' levers, and the "ching-ching" of a proper tram bell. The ride costs 2,940Kč ($105) per hour. Up to 60 people can fit into a double car for 3,780Kč ($135) per hour. You can also order a cold smorgasbord with coffee, beer, or champagne; a waiter to serve them; and an accordion player if you wish. You can choose the route the tram takes—the no. 22 route is best.

---

within the confines of the citadel, lush lawns and gardens are crisscrossed by dozens of paths, leading to historic buildings and cemeteries. From here you'll see one of the city's most panoramic views. The park is open at all times.

Královská zahrada (The Royal Garden) at Prague Castle, once the site of the sovereigns' vineyards, was founded in 1534. Dotted with lemon trees and surrounded by 16th-, 17th-, and 18th-century buildings, the garden is laid out with abundant shrubbery and fountains. Enter from U Prašného mostu (the street north of the castle complex). It's open daily from 10am to 6pm.

In Hradčany, the castle's **Zahrada na Valech (Garden on the Ramparts),** below the castle with a gorgeous city panorama, was reopened in spring 1995 after being thoroughly refurbished. The park is open Tuesday through Sunday from 10am to 6pm. Part of the excitement of **Wallenstein Valdštejnská zahrada (Waldstein Gardens)** is its location, behind a 9m (30-ft.) wall on the back streets of Malá Strana. Inside, elegant, leafy gravel paths, dotted by classical bronze statues and gurgling fountains, fan out in every direction. Recently refurbished sections include the Ledeburská, the Small and Great Pálffyovská, the Kolowratská, and the Small Furstenberská gardens. The gardens are open May to September, daily from 9am to 7pm.

THE SHOPPING SCENE

Czech **porcelain, glass,** and cheap but well-constructed clothing draw hordes of day-trippers from Germany. Blood-red **garnets** are the official Czech national gem, and the ones that you can buy here are among the world's finest, as well as one of the country's top exports. Finally, because beer is a little heavy to carry home and the local wine isn't worth it, take home a bottle of **Becherovka,** the nation's popular herbal liqueur from Karlovy Vary. You'll find the distinctive green decanter in shops around the city, and it costs about 300Kč ($11) per liter.

Private retailers have been allowed to operate here only since late 1989, but many top international retailers have already arrived. Shops lining the main route from Old Town Square to Charles Bridge are also great for browsing. For clothing, porcelain, jewelry, garnets, and glass, stroll around Wenceslas Square and Na Příkopě, connecting Wenceslas Square with náměstí Republiky.

For glass and crystal, try **Moser,** at Na Příkopě 12, Praha 1 (© **224-211-293;** www.moser-glass.com; Metro: Můstek), or at Malé nám. 11, Praha 1 (© **221-611-520;** Metro: Můstek). The Moser family began selling Bohemia's finest crystal in central Prague in 1857, drawing customers from around the world. The store at Na Příkopě is open Monday to Friday from 9am to 8pm, Saturday and Sunday from 10am to 6pm; the Malé náměstí store is open Monday to Friday from 10am to 7pm, Saturday and Sunday from 10am to 6pm.

Celetná Crystal, Celetná 15, Praha 1 (© **223-240-022;** www.czechcrystal. com; Metro: Náměstí Republiky), has a wide selection of world-renowned Czech crystal, china, arts and crafts, and jewelry displayed in a spacious three-floor showroom right in the heart of Prague.

Czechs swear by **Halada,** Na Příkopě 16, Praha 1. (© **224-221-304;** Metro: Můstek), Prague's premier jeweler, for its quality, price, and selection of garnets. There is also an outlet of this store among the displays on the ground floor of Tesco. It's open daily from 9am to 7pm.

On the short, wide street perpendicular to Melantrichova, between Staroměstské náměstí and Václavské náměstí, **Havelský trh (Havel's Market),** Havelská ulice, Praha 1, is an outdoor market (named well before Havel became president) featuring dozens of private vendors selling seasonal home-grown fruits and vegetables at the best prices in the city center. Other goods, including detergent, flowers, and cheese, are also for sale. Open Monday to Friday from 8am to 6pm. Take metro line A or B to Můstek.

PRAGUE AFTER DARK

Prague's nightlife has changed completely since the Velvet Revolution—for the better if you plan to go clubbing, for the worse if you hope to sample the city's classical offerings. Still, seeing *Don Giovanni* in the Estates' Theater, where Mozart first premiered it, is worth the admission cost. Ticket prices, while low by Western standards, have become prohibitively high for the average Czech. You'll find, however, the exact reverse in the rock and jazz scene. Dozens of clubs have opened, and world-class bands are finally adding Prague to their European tours.

Turn to the *Prague Post* (www.praguepost.cz) for listings of cultural events and nightlife around the city; it's available at most newsstands in Old Town and Malá Strana.

Once in Prague, you can buy tickets at theater box offices or from any one of dozens of agencies throughout the city center. Large, centrally located agencies (take the Metro to Můstek for all) are **Prague Tourist Center,** Rytířská 12, Praha 1 (© **224-212-209;** www.ptc.cz), **Bohemia Ticket International,** Na Příkopě 16, Praha 1 (© **224-215-031;** www.ticketsbti.cz); **Čedok,** Na Příkopě 18, Praha 1 (© **800-112-112** toll-free in Prague; www.cedok.cz); and **Ticketpro,** Salvátorská 10, Praha 1 (© **296-329-999;** www.ticketpro.cz).

THE PERFORMING ARTS

Although there's plenty of music year-round, the symphonies and orchestras all come to life during the **Prague Spring Music Festival,** a 3-week series of concerts featuring the country's top performers, as well as noted guest conductors, soloists, and visiting symphony orchestras. The festival runs from May 12 to June 2. Tickets for concerts run from 100Kč to 2,000Kč ($3.55–$71) and should be booked well in advance.

The **Czech Philharmonic Orchestra** performs at the **Rudolfinum,** Alšovo nábřeží 12, Praha 1 (© **227-059-352;** Metro: Staroměstská). It's the traditional voice of the country's national pride, often playing works by Dvořák and Smetana. The **Prague Symphony** performs at the Art Nouveau **Smetana Hall,** náměstí Republiky 5, Praha 1 (© **222-002-430;** Metro: Náměstí Republiky). It focuses more on 20th-century music with occasional forays into Bach. Tickets cost 100Kč to 600Kč ($3.55–$21).

In a city full of spectacularly beautiful theaters, the massive pale-green **Stavovské divadlo (Estates' Theater),** Ovocný trh 1, Praha 1 (© **224-215-001;** Metro: Můstek), is one of the most awesome. Built in 1783 and site of the premiere of Mozart's *Don Giovanni* (conducted by the composer himself), the theater now hosts many of the classic productions of European opera and drama. Simultaneous English translation, transmitted via headphone, is available for most plays. Tickets range from about 300Kč to 1,500Kč ($11–$54) and are often available up to curtain time.

Lavishly constructed in the late-Renaissance style of northern Italy, the gold-crowned **Národní divadlo (National Theater),** Národní třída 2, Praha 1 (© **224-901-448;** www.nd.cz; Metro: Národní Třída), overlooking the Vltava River, is one of Prague's most recognizable landmarks. Completed in 1881, the theater was built to nurture the Czech National Revival—a grassroots movement to replace the dominant German culture with that of native Czechs. Today, classic productions are staged here in a larger setting than at the Estates' Theater, but for about the same ticket prices.

The **National Theater Ballet** performs at the National Theater. The troupe has seen most of its top talent go west since 1989, but it still puts on a good show. Some critics complained that Prague's top company had been performing virtually the same dances for many years, and that they were in serious need of refocusing. Choreographer Libor Vaculík responded with humorous and quirky stagings of off-the-wall ballets such as *Some Like It Hot* and *Psycho.* Tickets are 100Kč to 500Kč ($3.55–$18); call © **224-933-782** for information.

Laterna Magika, Národní třída 4, Praha 1 (© **224-931-482;** Metro: Národní Třída), is a performance-art show in the new wing of the National Theater. The multimedia show, which combines live theater with film and dance, was once considered on the radical edge. The shows are not for those easily offended by nudity. Tickets 500Kč ($18); should be bought in advance.

THE CLUB & MUSIC SCENE

Prague's club and music scene is limited but lively. Local acts still have a garage-band sound but are adding more sophisticated numbers to their gigs. Many venerable jazz groups who toiled in the cellar clubs are finding a new audience in visitors who stumble upon their smoky underground venues. It is no longer a huge shock to see well-known western European bands playing sets in Prague.

JAZZ CLUBS   Upscale by Czech standards, **AghaRTA Jazz Centrum,** Krakovská 5, Praha 1 (© **222-211-275;** www.agharta.cz; Metro: Muzeum), regularly features some of the best music in town, from standard acoustic trios to Dixieland, funk, and fusion. Hot Line, the house band led by AghaRTA part-owner and drummer extraordinaire Michal Hejna, regularly takes the stage with its keyboard-and-sax Crusaders-like sound. Bands usually begin at 9pm. It's open daily from 7pm to midnight. Cover is 100Kč ($3.55). **Reduta Jazz Club,** Národní třída 20, Praha 1 (© **224-933-487;** Metro: Národní Třída), is a smoky subterranean room that looks exactly like a jazz cellar should. An adventurous booking policy, which even included a saxophone gig with a U.S. president in 1994, means that different bands play almost every night. Music usually starts around 9pm. It's open Monday to Saturday from 9pm to midnight; cover is usually 100Kč ($3.55).

PUBS & BARS

For many Czechs, the best nighttime entertainment is boisterous discussion and world-class brew at a noisy pub. You'll experience true Czech after-dark culture in only one kind of place—a smoky local *hospoda* serving some of the world's best beer. Remember to put a cardboard coaster in front of you to show you want a mug, and never wave for service; the typically surly waiter will just ignore you.

Originally a brewery dating back to 1459, **U Fleků,** Křemencova 11, Praha 2 (© **224-915-118;** Metro: Národní Třída), is Prague's most famous beer hall, and one of the only pubs that still brews its own beer. This huge place has a myriad of timber-lined rooms and a large, loud courtyard where an oompah band performs. Tourists come here by the busload, so U Fleků is avoided by disparaging locals who don't like its German atmosphere anyway. The pub's special dark beer is excellent, however, and not available anywhere else. It's open daily from 9am to 11pm.

One of the most famous Czech pubs, **U Zlatého tygra,** Husova 17, Praha 1 (© **222-221-111;** Metro: Staroměstská or Můstek), was a favorite watering hole of former president Václav Havel and the late writer Bohumil Hrabal. Particularly smoky, and not especially tourist friendly, "At the Golden Tiger" is a one-stop education in Czech culture. Václav Havel and Bill Clinton joined Hrabal for a traditional Czech pub evening here during Clinton's 1994 visit to Prague. It's open daily from 3 to 11pm.

DAY TRIPS FROM PRAGUE

KARLŠTEJN CASTLE   By far the most popular day trip from Prague, this medieval castle, 30km (18 miles) southwest of Prague, which has been restored to its original state, was built by Charles IV in the 14th century to safeguard the crown jewels of the Holy Roman Empire. As you approach the castle by train from the Prague, little will prepare you for your first view: a spectacular castle perched high on a hill, surrounded by lush forests and vineyards. The **Holy Rood Chapel** is famous for the more than 2,000 precious and semiprecious inlaid gems that adorn its walls, and the Chapel of St. Catherine was King Karel IV's private oratory. Both the **Audience Hall** and the **Imperial Bedroom** are impressive, despite being stripped of their original furnishings. To see the Holy Rood Chapel you need to make a reservation (© **274-008-154;** www.spusc.cz or www.hradkarlstejn.cz).

Admission for a 50-minute tour costs 200Kč ($7.15) adults, 100Kč ($3.55) students, 20Kč (70¢) children under 6; the 70-minute tour with the Holy Rood Chapel costs 300Kč ($11) adults, 100Kč ($3.55) students, free for children under 6. The castle is open Tuesday to Sunday: May, June, and September 9am to noon and 12:30 to 5pm; July and August 9am to noon and 12:30 to 6pm; April and October 9am to noon and 1 to 4pm; November, December, and March 9am to noon and 1 to 3pm; closed January and February.

Getting There   The best way to get to Karlštejn is by **train** (there's no bus service). Most trains leave from Prague's Hlavní nádraží to the castle on an hourly basis throughout the day (trip time: 43 min.). One-way second-class fare is 46Kč ($1.75). You can also **drive:** Leave Prague on Highway 4 southwest in the direction of Strakonice and take the Karlštejn cutoff, following the signs (and traffic!).

TEREZÍN (THERESIENSTADT)   The name Terezín (Theresienstadt in German) occupies a unique place in the atrocious history of Nazism. This former Austro-Hungarian imperial fortress, turned into a concentration camp, 50km (30 miles) northwest of Prague, witnessed no gas chambers, mass machine-gun executions, or medical testing; it was used instead as a transit camp. About 140,000 people passed though Terezín's gates; many died here, and more than half ended up at the death camps of Auschwitz and Treblinka.

Terezín stands as a memorial to the dead and a monument to human depravity. Once inside the **Major Fortress,** you'll immediately be struck by its drab, plain streets. Just off the main square lies the **Museum of the Ghetto,** chronicling the rise of Nazism and life in the camp. English pamphlets describing the exhibits are provided. It's open daily: October to March from 9am to 5:30pm and April to September from 9am to 6pm. Admission is 160Kč ($5.70) adults and 130Kč ($4.65) children. The **Minor Fortress** is about a 10-minute walk from the Major Fortress over the Ohře River. Just in front of the fortress's main entrance is the **Národní hřbitov (National Cemetery),** where the bodies exhumed from the mass graves were buried. As you enter the main gate, the sign above it, ARBEIT MACHT FREI (Work Sets One Free), sets a gloomy tone. You can walk through the prison barracks, execution grounds, workshops, and isolation cells. A ticket to enter both the **Minor Fortress** and the **Museum of the Ghetto** is 180Kč ($6.40) adults and 140Kč ($5) children. The Minor Fortress is open daily: October to March 8am to 4:30pm and April to September 8am to 6pm.For more information or reservations for guided tours, call ℂ **416-782-225** or head online to **www.pamatnik-terezin.cz.**

Getting There   Terezín is a 45-minute **drive** from Prague, on the main highway north towards Berlin via Dresden. Six **buses** leave daily from Florenc bus station (metro line C). The ride takes about an hour and costs 40Kč ($1.40). Through Prague's **Martin Tour,** Štěpánská 61, Praha 1 (ℂ **224-212-473;** www. martintour.cz), you can visit Terezín with their English-speaking guide. Their bus leaves Wednesday, Friday, and Sunday at 9:30am from Staroměstské náměstí. The 5-hour trip costs 1,100Kč ($39).

2 West Bohemia & the Spas

The Czech Republic is composed of two regions: Bohemia and Moravia. The larger of the two, Bohemia, occupying the central and western areas of the country, has for centuries been caught between a rock (Germany) and a hard place (Austria). Bohemia was almost always at the center of regional conflicts, both secular and religious. But the area also flourished, as witnessed by the wealth of castles that dot the countryside and the spa towns that were once the playgrounds of the rich and famous.

Although Bohemia is historically undivided, there are clear-cut distinctions in the region's geography that make going from town to town easier if you "cut" Bohemia into sections. This section focuses on west Bohemia, home to the country's spa towns. It's also one of the few regions in the Czech Republic where a full-blown tourist infrastructure is already in place. Its main towns—**Karlovy Vary (Carlsbad), Mariánské Lázně (Marienbad),** and to a lesser extent, **Plzeň**—offer a wide array of accommodations, restaurants, and services to meet every visitor's needs and means.

A relatively inexpensive network of trains and buses covers the region, allowing travel between towns and to and from Prague with a minimum of fuss. West

Bohemia is generally rougher terrain, so only serious cyclists should consider seeing the area on two wheels. For those with a car, the highways can range from top-notch, such as the Prague-Plzeň motorway, to an asphalt horror ride such as the Prague–Karlovy Vary route. Roads generally are much slower than in western Europe, so leave yourself plenty of time. Gas stations are constantly springing up, so stops for food and fuel are rarely hard to come by.

Most towns are distant enough that you should drive from one to another. However, if you'd rather stay in one place and make day trips, we recommend staying in Karlovy Vary. The **Kur-Info,** Vřídelní Kolonáda, 360 01 Karlovy Vary (© **353-229-312;** www.karlovyvary.cz/ruzne/kurinfo.htm), can provide information on bus trips to Mariánské Lázně and other regional sights.

KARLOVY VARY (CARLSBAD)

The discovery of Karlovy Vary (Carlsbad), 120km (75 miles) west of Prague, by Charles IV reads something like a 14th-century episode of *The Beverly Hillbillies.* According to local lore, the king was out huntin' for food when up from the ground came a-bubblin' water (though discovered by his dogs, not an errant gunshot). Knowing a good thing when he saw it, Charles immediately set to work building a small castle, naming the town that evolved around it Karlovy Vary (Charles's Boiling Place). The first spa buildings were built in 1522, and before long, notables like Albrecht of Wallenstein, Russian Czar Peter the Great, and later Bach, Beethoven, Freud, Goethe, and Marx, all came to take the waters.

After World War II, East Bloc travelers (following in the footsteps of Marx, no doubt) discovered the town, and Karlovy Vary became a destination for the proletariat. On doctors' orders, most workers enjoyed regular stays of 2 or 3 weeks, letting the mineral waters ranging from 110°F to 162°F (44°C–72°C) from the town's 12 spas heal their tired and broken bodies. Even now, most spa guests are there by doctor's prescription.

Most of the 40-plus years of Communist neglect have been erased by a barrage of renovators bent on restoring the spa's former glory. Gone is the statue of Yuri Gagarin, the Russian cosmonaut. Gone are almost all the crumbling building facades that used to line both sides of the river. In their places now stand restored buildings, cherubs, caryatids, and more.

Today, some 150,000 people, both traditional clientele and newer patrons, travel to the spa resort every year to sip, bathe, and frolic, though most enjoy the "13th spring" (actually a hearty herb-and-mineral liqueur called Becherovka) as much as—if not more than—the 12 nonalcoholic versions. Czechs will tell you that all have medical benefits.

ESSENTIALS

GETTING THERE   By Train   At all costs, *avoid the train from Prague* (trip time: over 4 hr.). If you're arriving from another direction, Karlovy Vary's main train station is connected to the town center by bus no. 11.

By Bus   Frequent express **buses** make it from Prague's Florenc bus station in 2¼ hours at a cost of 130Kč ($4.65). From Karlovy Vary's bus station take a 10-minute walk or local bus no. 4 into the town center. Note that you must have a ticket to board local transport. You can buy tickets for 8Kč (30¢) at the bus station stop or, if you have no change, the kiosk across the street sells tickets during regular business hours. For timetable information go to **www.jizdnirady.cz.**

By Car   The nearly 2-hour **drive** from Prague to Karlovy Vary can be very busy and dangerous due to undisciplined Czech drivers. If you're going by car, take

Highway E48 from the western end of Prague and follow it straight through to Karlovy Vary. This two-lane highway widens in a few spots to let cars pass slow-moving vehicles on hills.

VISITOR INFORMATION   **Kur-Info,** inside the Vřídelní Kolonáda (℄ 353-229-312), provides accommodations services, arranges guided tours and spa treatments, and sells tickets for some events. Be sure to pick up *Promenáda* magazine, a comprehensive collection of events with a small map of the town center.

Infocentrum města Karlovy Vary operates the official town information centers at the main Mlýnská Kolonáda, on Lázeňská 1 (℄ 353-224-097), and at the terminal of the bus and train station on Západní ulice (℄ 353-232-838). The staff will help you with reserving accommodations, getting tickets for entertainment in the city, and so on. All the info centers are open April to October, Monday to Friday from 7am to 5pm and Saturday and Sunday from 9am to 3pm; November to March, Monday to Friday from 7am to 4pm. You'll also find information on **www.karlovyvary.cz.**

SPECIAL EVENTS   The **International Film Festival Karlovy Vary** is one of the few places to see and be seen. Each summer (in early July), film stars and celebrities take part in one of Europe's biggest film festivals. Nine venues screen more than 300 films during the 10-day festival. Go to **www.iffkv.cz** for more information.

Karlovy Vary plays host to several other events, including a **jazz festival** and **beer Olympiad** in May, a **Dvořák singing contest** in June, a **Summer Music Festival** in August, and a **Dvořák Autumn Music Festival** in September and October.

For more information on any of the festivals, contact **Kur-Info** (℄ 353-229-312).

WHERE TO STAY

Private rooms used to be the best places to stay in Karlovy Vary with regard to quality and price. But this is changing as more and more hotels renovate and raise standards . . . as well as prices. Private accommodations can still provide better value, but they take a little extra work. If you want to arrange a room, try the **Infocentrum** (see above). Expect to pay about 1,000Kč ($36) for a single and 1,500Kč ($55) for a double.

Some of the town's major spa hotels accommodate only those who are paying for complete treatment, unless for some reason their occupancy rates are particularly low. The hotels I've listed below accept guests for stays of any length.

Grandhotel Pupp ★★★   Well known as one of Karlovy Vary's best hotels, the Pupp, built in 1701, is also one of Europe's oldest. Its public areas boast the expected splendor and charm, as do the guest rooms, which have been recently renovated. The best rooms tend to be those facing the town center and are located on the upper floors; these have good views and sturdy wooden furniture. The Grand Restaurant serves up as grand a dining room as you'll find, with the food to match (see "Where to Dine," below).

Mírové nám. 2, 360 91, Karlovy Vary. ℄ 353-109-631. Fax 353-226-638. www.pupp.cz. 112 units. 6,600Kč ($220) double deluxe; from 8,400Kč ($280) suite. Breakfast an extra 390Kč ($13). The crown rate for the room fluctuates, based on the latest crown rate against the dollar on the day the payment is made because of the crown's volatility. The dollar rate remains constant for those paying in dollars or by credit card. A daily exchange rate is used for those who want to pay in crowns by cash. AE, DC, MC, V. **Amenities:** 2 restaurants; cafe; 3 bars; golf; Roman spa with sauna; Jacuzzi; concierge; car-rental desk; salon; room service; massage; laundry; dry cleaning; casino. *In room:* A/C (some), TV w/pay movies, minibar, hair dryer, safe.

Moments Spa Cures & Treatments

Most visitors to Karlovy Vary come specifically to get a spa treatment, a therapy that lasts 1 to 3 weeks. After consulting with a spa physician, guests are given a regimen of activities that may include mineral baths, massages, waxings, mudpacks, electrotherapy, and pure oxygen inhalation. After spending the morning at a spa or sanatorium, guests are then usually directed to walk the paths of the town's surrounding forest.

The common denominator of all the cures is an ample daily dose of hot mineral water, which bubbles up from 12 springs. This water definitely has a distinct odor and taste. You'll see people chugging it down, but it doesn't necessarily taste very good. Some thermal springs actually taste and smell like rotten eggs. You might want to take a small sip at first.

You'll also notice that almost everyone in town seems to be carrying "the cup." This funny-looking cup is basically a mug with a built-in straw running through the handle. Young and old alike parade around with their mugs, filling and refilling them at each thermal water tap. You can buy these mugs everywhere for as little as 50Kč ($1.80) or as much as 500Kč ($18); they make a quirky souvenir. *But be warned:* None of the mugs can make the warmer hot springs taste any better.

The minimum spa treatment lasts 1 week and must be arranged in advance. A spa treatment package traditionally includes room, full board, and complete therapy regimen; the cost varies from about $40 to $100 per person per day, depending on season and facilities. Rates are highest from May to September and lowest from November to February. For information and reservations in Prague, contact **Čedok**, at Na Příkopě 18, and also at Václavské nám. 53, Praha 1 (© **224-197-632**; fax 224-213-786). Many hotels also provide spa and health treatments, so ask when you book your room. Most will happily arrange a treatment if they don't provide them directly.

Visitors to Karlovy Vary for just a day or two can experience the waters on an "outpatient" basis. The largest complex in town (and in the Czech Republic) is the **Alžbětiny Lázně-Lázně V,** Smetanovy sady 1145/1 (© **353-222-536;** www.spa5.cz). On their menu are all kinds of treatments, including water cures, massages, a hot-air bath, a steam bath, a whirlpool, and a pearl bath, as well as use of their swimming pool. You can choose packages of different procedures between 90Kč and 895Kč ($3.20 and $32). It's open Monday to Friday 8am to 3pm for spa treatments; the pool is open Saturday and Sunday from 10am to 6pm.

Hotel Dvořák ⭑   Now part of the Vienna International hotel/resort chain, the Dvořák has improved immensely, especially in terms of service. This hotel is within sight of the Pupp, but it's less expensive. The Pupp may have the history and elegance, but the Dvořák has the facilities. The rooms are spacious and the staff is very attentive.

Nová Louka 11, 360 21 Karlovy Vary. *C* **353-102-111.** Fax 353-102-119. www.hotel-dvorak.cz. 106 units. $146 double. The current exchange rate is used for those who want to pay crowns by cash. AE, DC, MC, V. **Amenities:** Restaurant; indoor pool; tennis courts; fitness center; sauna; salon; casino. *In room:* AC, TV, minibar, iron, safe.

Hotel Embassy ★★   On the riverbank across from the Pupp, this family-run hotel offers well-appointed rooms, many with an early-20th-century motif, in a historic house. The staff here really helps make this hotel worthy of consideration, as does the proximity to the pub on the first floor, which serves up some of the best goulash and beer in the city.

Nová Louka 21, 360 01 Karlovy Vary. *C* **353-221-161.** Fax 353-223-146. www.embassy.cz. 20 units. 2,595Kč–3,290Kč ($93–$118) double; 3,415Kč–3,830Kč ($122–$137) suite. AE, V. **Amenities:** Pub. *In room:* TV, minibar, safe.

Parkhotel Pupp ★   Part of the Pupp complex, these are basically rooms in the section of the hotel that doesn't quite measure up to the grand standards of its sister. But they are still nice and functional, if not quite as cozy and elegant as the others. Personally, I'd stay in one of these rooms and use the money I save on a nice meal and a couple of Karlovy Vary kisses (Becherovka in a frozen glass).

Mírové nám. 2, 360 91 Karlovy Vary. *C* **353-109-111.** Fax 353-224-032. 255 units. No rates in local currency; hotel charges at a converted rate upon checkout. $102 double; $138 apt. Breakfast $9. AE, DC, MC, V. **Amenities:** Restaurant; indoor pool; tennis courts; fitness center; sauna; salon; casino. *In room:* TV, minibar, iron, safe.

WHERE TO DINE

Embassy CZECH/CONTINENTAL   On the ground floor of the hotel of the same name, the Embassy restaurant has a pub on one side and an intimate dining room on the other. On a cold day the pub works wonders with a hearty goulash soup. But dining is the Embassy's hidden treasure. Here you'll find many traditional Czech dishes with slight twists that make them interesting. The grilled loin of pork covered with a light, creamy, green-pepper sauce makes a nice change from the regular roast pork served by most Czech restaurants.

Nová Louka 21. *C* **353-221-161.** Reservations recommended. Soups 35Kč–75Kč ($1.25–$2.65); main courses 155Kč–950Kč ($5.55–$34). AE, V. Daily noon–11pm.

Grand Restaurant ★ CONTINENTAL   It's no surprise that the Grandhotel Pupp has the nicest dining room in town: an elegant space with tall ceilings, huge mirrors, and glistening chandeliers. A large menu features equally large portions of salmon, chicken, veal, pork, turkey, and beef in a variety of heavy and heavier sauces. Even the mouthwatering trout with mushrooms is smothered in butter sauce.

In the Grandhotel Pupp, Mírové nám. 2. *C* **353-109-646.** Reservations recommended. Main courses 290Kč–1,090Kč ($10–$39). AE, V. Daily noon–3pm and 6–11pm.

Hospoda U Švejka CZECH   U Švejka plays on the tried-and-true touristy *Good Soldier Svejk* theme. Luckily, the tourist trap goes no further, and once inside, you find a refreshingly unsmoky though thoroughly Czech atmosphere. Locals and tourists alike rub elbows while throwing back some fine lager for 50Kč ($1.95) per half liter, and standard pub favorites such as goulash and beef tenderloin in cream sauce.

Stará Louka 10. *C* **353-232-276.** Main courses 121Kč–279Kč ($4.30–$9.95). MC, V. Daily 11am–11pm.

Promenáda ★ CZECH/CONTINENTAL   This cozy spot may not be as elegant as the Grand, but it remains a local favorite and serves creative meals.

Across from the Vřídelní Kolonáda, the Promenáda offers a wide selection of excellent dishes served in generous portions. The daily menu usually includes well-prepared wild game, but the mixed grill for two and the chateaubriand, both flambéed at the table, are the chef's best dishes. The wine list is extensive.

Tržiště 31. (𝒞 353-225-648. Reservations highly recommended. Main courses 210Kč–699Kč ($7.50–$25). AE, V. Daily noon–11pm.

EXPLORING KARLOVY VARY

The town's slow pace and pedestrian promenades, lined with Art Nouveau buildings, turn strolling into an art form. Nighttime walks take on an even more mystical feel as the sewers, river, and many major cracks in the roads emit steam from the hot springs underneath.

If you're traveling here by train or bus, a good place to start your exploration is the **Hotel Thermal,** I. P. Pavlova 11 (𝒞 359-001-111), at the north end of the old town's center. The 1970s glass, steel, and concrete Thermal, between the town's eastern hills and the Ohře River, sticks out like a sore Communist thumb amid the 19th-century architecture. Nonetheless, you'll find three important places here: its outdoor pool (the only one centrally located); its upper terrace, boasting a spectacular view; and its cinema, Karlovy Vary's largest, which holds many of the film festival's premier events. Look at it, and then turn and walk away. Try not to picture it again.

As you enter the heart of the town on the river's west side, you'll see the renovated ornate white wrought-iron **Sadová Kolonáda** adorning the beautifully manicured park **Dvořákovy sady.** Continue following the river, and about 100m (330 ft.) later you'll encounter the **Mlýnská Kolonáda,** a long, covered walkway housing several Karlovy Vary springs, which you can sample 24 hours a day. Each spring has a plaque beside it telling which mineral elements are present and the temperature of the water. Bring your own cup or buy one just about anywhere to sip the waters, as most are too hot to drink from your hands.

When you hit the river's bend, the majestic **Church of St. Mary Magdalene** sits perched atop a hill, overlooking the **Vřídlo,** the hottest spring in town. Built in 1736, the church is the work of Kilian Ignac Dientzenhofer, who also created two of Prague's more notable churches—both named St. Nicholas. Housing Vřídlo, which blasts water some 15m (50 ft.) into the air, is the glass building where the statue of Soviet astronaut Gagarin once stood. (Gagarin's statue has since made a safe landing at the Karlovy Vary airport.) Now called the **Vřídelní Kolonáda,** the structure, built in 1974, houses several hot springs you can sample for free. The building also holds the Kur-Info information center and several kiosks selling postcards, stone roses, and drinking cups.

Heading away from the Vřídelní Kolonáda are Stará and Nová Louka streets, which line either side of the river. Along **Stará (Old) Louka** you'll find several fine cafes and glass and crystal shops. **Nová (New) Louka** is lined with hotels and the historic **Town's Theater,** just newly reconstructed.

Both streets lead to the **Grandhotel Pupp,** Mírové nám. 2 (𝒞 353-109-631). The Pupp's main entrance and building have just come out of extensive renovations that have more or less erased the effects of 40 years of Communism (the hotel's name had been changed to the Moskva-Pupp). Regardless of capitalism or Communism, the Pupp remains what it always was: the grande dame of hotels in the area. Once catering to nobility from all over central Europe, the Pupp still houses one of the town's finest restaurants, the Grand, while its grounds are a favorite with the hiking crowd.

If you still have the energy, atop the hill behind the Pupp stands the **Diana Lookout Tower.** Footpaths leading through the forests eventually spit you out at the base of the tower, as if to say, "Ha, the trip is only half over." The five-story climb tests your stamina, but the view of the town is more than worth it. For those who aren't up to the climb just to get to the tower, a cable car runs to the tower every 15 minutes or so.

THE SHOPPING SCENE

Crystal and porcelain are Karlovy Vary's other claims to fame. Dozens of shops throughout town sell everything from plates to chandeliers.

Ludvík Moser founded his first glassware shop in 1857 and became one of this country's foremost names in glass. You can visit the **Moser Factory,** kapitána Jaroše 19 (© **353-449-455;** moser@moser-glass.com; bus: 1, 10, or 16), just west of the town center. It's open Monday to Friday from 9am to 1pm; its glass museum is open Monday to Friday 8am to 5:30pm and Saturday 9am to 3pm. There's also a **Moser Store,** on Tržiště 7 (© **353-235-303**), right in the heart of new town; it's open Monday to Sunday from 10am to 7pm (Sat, Sun till 6pm).

ČESKÝ KRUMLOV

If you have time for only one day-trip, consider making it **Český Krumlov** , 155km (96 miles) south of Prague. One of Bohemia's prettiest towns, Krumlov is a living gallery of elegant Renaissance-era buildings housing charming cafes, pubs, restaurants, shops, and galleries. In 1992, UNESCO named Český Krumlov a World Heritage Site for its historic importance and physical beauty.

Bustling since medieval times, the town, after centuries of embellishment, is exquisitely beautiful. In 1302, the Rožmberk family inherited the castle and moved in, using it as their main residence for nearly 300 years. You'll feel that time has stopped as you look from the Lazebnický Bridge and see the waters of the Vltava below snaking past the castle's gray stone. At night, by the castle lights, the view becomes even more dramatic.

Few dared change the appearance of Český Krumlov over the years, not even the Schwarzenbergs, who had a flair for opulence. At the turn of the 19th century, several facades of houses in the town's outer section were built, as were inner courtyards. Thankfully, economic stagnation in the area under Communism meant little money for "development," so no glass-and-steel edifices, like the Hotel Thermal in Karlovy Vary, jut out to spoil the architectural beauty. Instead, a medieval sense reigns supreme, now augmented by the many festivals and renovations that keep the town's spirit alive.

ESSENTIALS

GETTING THERE   The only way to reach Český Krumlov by **train** from Prague is via České Budějovice, a slow ride that deposits you at a station relatively

---

Tips **Traveler's Tip**

Consider yourself warned: Word has spread about Český Krumlov. Summer season can be unbearable, as thousands of visitors blanket its medieval streets. If possible, try to visit in the off season—we suggest autumn to take advantage of the colorful surrounding hills—when the crowds recede, the prices decrease, and the town's charm can really shine. Who knows? You might even hear some Czech!

far from the town center (trip time: 3 hr. 50 min.). Six trains leave daily from Prague's Hlavní nádraží; the fare is 336Kč ($12) first class, 224Kč ($8) second class.

The nearly 3-hour **bus** ride from Prague usually involves a transfer in České Budějovice. The fare is 150Kč ($5.35), and the bus station in Český Krumlov is a 15-minute walk from the town's main square.

From Prague, it's a 2½-hour **drive** along E-55.

VISITOR INFORMATION   Right on the main square, the **Information Centrum,** náměstí Svornosti 2, 381 01 Český Krumlov (© **380-704-621;** www.ckrumlov.cz), provides a complete array of services, from booking accommodations to reserving tickets for events, as well as a phone and fax service. It's open daily from 9am to 5pm (until 8pm in summer).

SPECIAL EVENTS   After being banned during Communism, the **Slavnost pětilisté růže (Festival of the Five-Petaled Rose)** has made a triumphant comeback. It's held each year during the summer solstice. Residents of Český Krumlov dress up in Renaissance costume and parade through the streets. Afterward, the streets become a stage for chess games with people dressed as pieces, music, plays, and even duels "to the death."

Český Krumlov also plays host to a 2-week **International Music Festival** every August, attracting performers from all over the world. Performances are held in nine spectacular venues. For details or ticket reservations, contact the festival organizer, **Auviex,** at Perlitová 1820, 140 00, Praha 4 (© **241-445-404**); or in Český Krumlov at Latrán 37 (© **380-711-453;** www.auviex.cz).

WHERE TO STAY

With the rise of free enterprise after the fall of Communism, many hotels have sprouted up or are getting a "new" old look. PENSION and ZIMMER FREI signs line Horní and Rooseveltova streets and offer some of the best values in town. For a comprehensive list of area hotels and help with bookings, call or write to the Information Centrum listed above.

Expensive

Hotel Růže (Rose Hotel) ✦   Once a Jesuit seminary, this stunning Italian Renaissance building has been turned into a well-appointed hotel. Comfortable in a big-city kind of way, it's packed with amenities and is one of the top places to stay in Český Krumlov. This well-reconstructed hotel will allow you to enjoy all the conveniences of our age in a historical setting.

Horní 154, 381 01 Český Krumlov. © **380-772-100.** Fax 380-713-146. www.hotelruze.cz. 71 units. $121–$228 double; $171–$307 suite. Rates, which are calculated in U.S. dollars and then converted into crowns, include breakfast. AE, MC, V. **Amenities:** Restaurant; bar; Internet cafe; indoor pool; fitness center; sauna; bike rental; rafting; concierge; tour desk; courtesy minibus; limited room service; laundry. *In room:* TV, minibar, hair dryer.

Inexpensive

Hotel Konvice   The rooms at the Konvice are on the small side and have rustic furniture. The real lure here is the view. Ask for a room with a view out the back—as you gaze at the river and the castle on the opposite bank, you'll wonder why anyone would stay at the Růže just a few doors up.

Horní ul. 144. 381 01 Český Krumlov. © **380-711-611.** Fax 380-711-327. www.boehmerwaldhotels.cz. 10 units. 1,300Kč–1,600Kč ($46–$57) double; 1,700Kč–2,600Kč ($60–$92) suite. Rates include breakfast. No credit cards. **Amenities:** Restaurant. *In room:* TV.

Pension Anna ✦ *Kids*   Along "pension alley," this is a comfortable and rustic place. What makes the pension a favorite are the friendly management and

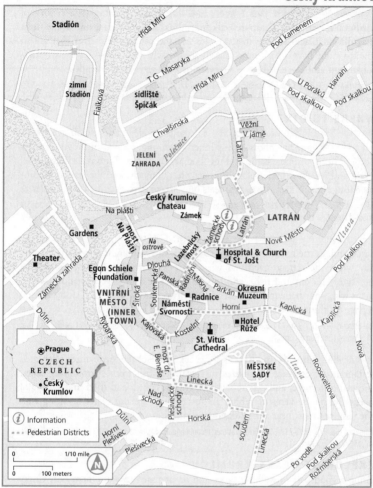

homey feeling you get as you walk up to your room. Forget hotels—this is the kind of place where you can relax. The owners even let you buy drinks and snacks at the bar downstairs and take them to your room. The suites, with four beds and a living room, are great for families and groups.

Rooseveltova 41, 381 01 Český Krumlov. © **380-711-692.** 8 units. 1,200Kč–1,500Kč ($42–$53) double; 1,500Kč–2,100Kč ($53–$75) suite. Rates include breakfast. No credit cards. **Amenities:** Bar. *In room:* TV.

Pension Na louži ⭐ Smack-dab in the heart of the Inner Town, the small Na louži, decorated with early-20th-century wooden furniture, is full of charm. If the person at reception starts mentioning names without apparent reason, don't worry; it's not a language problem. Management has given the rooms human names instead of numbers. The only drawback is that the beds can be a little short for tall people.

Kájovská 66, 381 01 Český Krumlov. © and fax **380-711-280.** www.nalouzi.cz. 7 units. 1,100Kč ($39) double; 1,350Kč ($48) triple; 1,700Kč ($60) suite. No credit cards. **Amenities:** Restaurant/bar.

Pension Ve Věži (In the Tower) ★★ A private pension in a renovated medieval tower just a 5-minute walk from the castle, Ve Věži is one of the most magnificent places to stay in town. It's not the rooms themselves that are so grand—none have a bathroom and all are sparsely decorated—it's the wonderful ancient ambience. Advance reservations are always recommended.

Pivovarská 28, 381 01 Český Krumlov. ⓒ 380-711-742. 4 units, all with shared bathroom. May–Sept 1,200Kč ($42) double, 1,800Kč ($64) quad. Rates include breakfast. No credit cards.

WHERE TO DINE

Hospoda Na louži *Value* CZECH The large wooden tables encourage you to get to know your neighbors at this Inner Town pub, located in a 15th-century house. The atmosphere is fun and the food above average. If no table is available, stand and have a drink; tables turn over pretty quickly, and the staff is accommodating. In summer, the terrace seats only six, so dash over if a seat empties.

Kájovská 66. ⓒ **380-711-280.** Main courses 55Kč–129Kč ($1.95–$4.60). No credit cards. Mon–Sat 10am–11pm; Sun 10am–10pm.

Restaurace Na Ostrově (On the Island) CZECH In the shadow of the castle and, as the name implies, on an island, this restaurant is best on a sunny day when the terrace overflows with flowers, hearty Czech food (including plenty of chicken and fish), and lots of beer. The staff is very friendly, which helps with your patience since usually only two waiters work each shift, making service on the slow side. A great place to relax and enjoy the view.

Na ostrově 171. ⓒ 380-711-326. Main courses 69Kč–250Kč ($2.45–$8.90). No credit cards. Mon–Sat 11:30am–11pm; Sun till 6pm.

Rybářská Bašta Jakuba Krčína CZECH One of the town's most celebrated restaurants, this place specializes in freshwater fish from surrounding lakes. Trout, perch, pike, and eel are sautéed, grilled, baked, and fried in a variety of herbs and spices. Venison, rabbit, and other game are also available, along with the requisite roast beef and pork cutlet dinners.

Kájovská 54. ⓒ 380-712-692. Reservations recommended. Main courses 94Kč–335Kč ($3.35–$12). AE, MC, V. Daily 11am–11pm.

EXPLORING ČESKÝ KRUMLOV

Bring a good pair of walking shoes and be prepared to wear them out. Český Krumlov's hills and alleyways cry out for hours of exploration, but if you push the pace you can see everything in 1 day. No cars, thank goodness, are allowed in the historic town, and the cobblestones keep most other vehicles at bay. The town is split into two parts—the **Inner Town** and **Latrán,** which houses the castle. They're best tackled separately, so you won't have to crisscross the bridges several times.

Begin at the **Okresní Muzeum (Regional Museum;** ⓒ **380-711-674)** at the top of Horní ulice. Once a Jesuit seminary, the three-story museum now contains artifacts and displays relating to Český Krumlov's 1,000-year history. The highlight of this mass of folk art, clothing, furniture, and statues is a giant model of the town that offers a bird's-eye view of the buildings. Admission is 50Kč ($1.80). The museum is open May to September, daily 10am to 5pm (till 6pm in July and Aug); October to December, Tuesday to Friday 9am to 4pm; and March and April, Saturday and Sunday 1 to 4pm.

Across the street is the **Hotel Růže (Hotel Rose),** which was once a Jesuit student house. Built in the late 16th century, the hotel and the prelature next to it show the development of architecture; Gothic, Renaissance, and rococo influences are all present. If you're not staying at the hotel, don't be afraid to walk around and even ask questions at the reception desk.

Continue down the street to the impressive late Gothic **St. Vitus Cathedral.** Be sure to climb the church tower, which offers one of the most spectacular views of both the Inner Town and the castle across the river.

As you continue down the street, you'll come to **náměstí Svornosti.** The town's main square is a little disappointing, as few buildings here show any character. The **Radnice (Town Hall),** at náměstí Svornosti 1, is one of the few exceptions. Open daily from 9am to 6pm, its Gothic arcades and Renaissance vault inside are exceptionally beautiful in this otherwise run-down area. From the square, streets fan out in all directions. Take some time to wander through the streets.

When you get closer to the river, you still can see the high-water marks on some of the quirky bank-side houses, which were devastated by the floods of 2002. A few places have taken the opportunity to make a fresh start after massive reconstruction. **Krumlovský Mlýn (The Krumlov Mill),** Široká 80 (© **380-712-293;** www.krumlovskymlyn.cz), is a combination restaurant, gallery, antiques shop, and exhibition space. For an additional treat, stroll through the exhibition of historical motorcycles. Open daily 10am to 10pm.

One of Český Krumlov's most famous residents was Austrian-born 20th-century artist Egon Schiele. He was a bit of an eccentric who, on more than one occasion, raised the ire of the town's residents (many were distraught with his use of their young women as his nude models); his stay was cut short when residents' patience ran out. But the town readopted the artist in 1993, setting up the **Egon Schiele Foundation and the Egon Schiele Centrum** in Inner Town, Široká 70–72, 381 01, Český Krumlov (© **380-704-011**). Back across the river from the castle, it documents his life and work, housing a permanent selection of his paintings as well as exhibitions of other 20th-century artists. Admission depends on the exhibitions being displayed. The center is open daily from 10am to 6pm.

For a different perspective on the town, take the stairs from the **Městské divadlo (Town Theater)** on Horní ulice down to the riverfront and rent a rowboat from **Maleček Boat Rentals** (© **380-712-508;** www.malecek.cz) at 300Kč ($11) for a half-hour trip (400Kč/$14 in July and Aug).

You might want to grab a light lunch at one of the many cafes in Inner Town before crossing the river.

As you cross the bridge and head toward the castle, you'll see immediately to your right the former **hospital and church of St. Jošt.** Founded at the beginning of the 14th century, it has since been turned into apartments. Feel free to snoop around, but don't enter the building.

EXPLORING THE ČESKÝ KRUMLOV CHÂTEAU ✍

Reputedly the second-largest castle in Bohemia (after Prague Castle), **Český Krumlov Château** was constructed in the 13th century as part of a private estate. Throughout the ages, it has been passed on to a variety of private owners, including the Rožmberk family, Bohemia's largest landholders, and the Schwarzenbergs, the Bohemian equivalent of the TV show *Dynasty*'s Carrington family.

Follow the path for the long climb up to the **castle.** Greeting you is a round 12th-century **tower,** with its Renaissance balcony. You'll pass over the moat, now occupied by two brown bears. Next is the **Dolní Hrad (Lower Castle)** and then the **Horní Hrad (Upper Castle).**

Perched high atop a rocky hill, the château is open only from April to October, exclusively by guided tour. Visits begin in the rococo **Chapel of St. George,** continue through the portrait-packed **Renaissance Hall,** and end in the **Royal Family Apartments,** outfitted with ornate furnishings that include Flemish wall tapestries and European paintings.

Tours last 1 hour and depart frequently. The tour costs 140Kč ($5) for adults and 70Kč ($2.50) for students and children. The castle hours are Tuesday to Sunday: June to August from 9am to noon and 1 to 4pm; April, May, September, and October from 9am to noon and 1 to 5pm. The last entrance is 1 hour before closing. For more information, call ✆ **380-704-721** or go to **www.castle. ckrumlov.cz.**

Once past the main castle building, you can see one of the more stunning views of Český Krumlov from **Most Na Plášti,** a walkway that doubles as a belvedere to the Inner Town. Even farther up the hill lie the castle's riding school and gardens.

Most visitors don't realize that beyond this part of the castle, you can have one of the Czech Republic's finest dining experiences at **Krčma Markéta** (✪, Latrán 67 (✆ **380-711-453**). To get there, walk all the way up the hill through the castle, past the Upper Castle and past the Castle Theater. Walk through the raised walkway and into the Zámecká zahrada (Castle Garden), where you'll eventually find this Renaissance pub. Going inside is like leaving this century. There's no need for plates here, as meals are served on wooden blocks. Drinks come in pewter mugs. Although owners have come and gone, the atmosphere and good times are still the same. There's no menu—just go up to the spit and see what's roasting; usually there's a wide variety of meat, including succulent pork cutlets, rabbit, chickens, and pork knees, a Czech delicacy. The waiter/cook will bring bread and a slab of spiced pork fat (considered a good base for drinking), but don't worry—refusing to eat it won't raise anyone's ire. Instead, wait until the entree comes. Yes, that obligatory smattering of cabbage is all the vegetables you're going to get. Vegetarians need not apply. Before the night is over, you'll probably find yourself talking to someone else at the pub's large wooden tables. Time seems to stand still in this place. Krčma Markéta is open daily from 6 to 11pm. Reservations are recommended. Soup costs 20Kč (70¢), and main courses are 80Kč to 235Kč ($2.85–$8.40). No credit cards are accepted.

MARIÁNSKÉ LÁZNĚ (MARIENBAD)

When Thomas Alva Edison visited Mariánské Lázně in the late 1800s, he proclaimed, "There is no more beautiful spa in all the world." The town is 47km (29 miles) southwest of Karlovy Vary and 160km (100 miles) west of Prague.

Mariánské Lázně now stands in the shadow of the Czech Republic's most famous spa town, Karlovy Vary, but it wasn't always that way. First noted in 1528, the town's mineral waters gained prominence at the end of the 18th and beginning of the 19th centuries. Nestled among forested hills and packed with romantic and elegant pastel hotels and spa houses, the town, commonly known by its German name, Marienbad, has played host to such luminaries as Goethe (this is where his love for Ulrika von Levetzow took root), Mark Twain, Chopin, Strauss, Wagner, Freud, and Kafka. England's Edward VII found the spa resort so enchanting that he visited nine times and even commissioned the building of the country's first golf club.

ESSENTIALS

GETTING THERE There are five express **trains** from Prague's main station for 224Kč ($8) (trip time: 2 hr. 50 min.). Mariánské Lázně train station, Nádražní nám. 292, is south of the town center; take bus no. 5 into town. If getting here from Karlovy Vary, there are about ten trains daily; Trip time ranges from 1 hour 30 minutes to 2 hours 30 minutes, and the fare is 76Kč ($2.70). For timetables, go to **www.jizdnirady.cz**.

The **bus** from Prague takes about 3 hours and costs about 120Kč ($4.30). The Mariánské Lázně bus station is adjacent to the train station on Nádražní náměstí; take bus no. 5 into town.

Driving from Prague, take Highway E50 through Plzeň to Stříbro—about 22km (14 miles) past Plzeň—and head northwest on Highway 21. The clearly marked route can take up to 2 hours.

VISITOR INFORMATION   Along the main strip lies the **Infocentrum,** Hlavní 47, 353 01, Mariánské Lázně (© **354-622-474**). In addition to dispensing advice, the staff sells maps and concert tickets and can arrange accommodations. It's open daily 9am to noon and 12:30 to 6pm. Though not directly run by the city information office, the website, **www.marienbad.cz** has plenty of good information and tips about what's going on each day.

SPECIAL EVENTS   Mariánské Lázně honors one of its frequent visitors, Chopin, with a yearly festival devoted to the Polish composer and his works. The **Chopin Festival** usually runs for 8 to 10 days near the end of August. Tickets range from 150Kč to 1,500Kč ($5.35–$53).

Each June, the town also plays host to a **classical music festival** featuring many of the Czech Republic's finest musicians, as well as those from around the world. For more information or ticket reservations for either event, contact Infocentrum (see "Visitor Information," above).

Patriotic Americans can show up on **July 4th** for a little down-home fun, including a parade and other flag-waving special events commemorating the town's liberation by U.S. soldiers in World War II.

WHERE TO STAY

The main strip along Hlavní třída is lined with hotels, many with rooms facing the Kolonáda. If you feel comfortable about doing this, I suggest walking the street and shopping around for a room. Most hotels charge from 2,000Kč to 4,000Kč ($71–$142) for a double from May to September. Off-season prices can fall by as much as half.

For private accommodations, try **Palackého ulice,** running south of the main spa area.

Hotel Koliba *Value*   Away from the main strip but still only a 7-minute walk from the Kolonáda, the Koliba is a rustic hunting lodge set in the hills on Dusíkova, the road leading to the golf course and Karlovy Vary. The rooms are warm and inviting, with the wooden furnishings giving the hotel the feel of a country cottage. The Koliba provides a wide array of spa and health treatments, which cost extra.

Dusíkova 592, 353 01 Mariánské Lázně. © **354-625-169.** 15 units. 1,350Kč–1,500Kč ($48–$53) double. AE, MC, V. **Amenities:** Restaurant/bar; spa. *In room:* TV, minibar.

Hotel Palace *★★*   The 1920s Palace is a beautiful Art Nouveau hotel 90m (300 ft.) from the Kolonáda. The rooms are tastefully decorated and extremely comfortable, with high ceilings and large bay windows lending an airy effect. The hotel has a good Bohemian restaurant with a lovely terrace.

Hlavní třída 67, 353 01 Mariánské Lázně. © **354-685-111.** Fax 354-624-262. 45 units. 2,184Kč–3,192Kč ($78–$114) double; 2,688Kč–4,368Kč ($96–$156) suite. AE, DC, MC, V. **Amenities:** Restaurant; bar; cafe; wine room; spa. *In room:* TV, minibar, hair dryer, iron, safe.

Hotel Villa Butterfly ⓐ The Butterfly has upgraded its rather ordinary rooms into 94 first-rate, spacious living quarters. Oddly enough, the renovations have had a reverse effect on the hotel's prices, now a good 15% lower. An English-speaking staff is an added bonus. The Fontaine is a quiet place to eat top-rate Czech and international cuisine, and the bar mixes a good cocktail.

Hlavní třída 72, 353 01 Mariánské Lázně. ⓒ 354-654-111. Fax 354-654-200. www.marienbad.cz. 94 units. 3,780Kč ($126) double; 5,950Kč ($198) suite; 7,910Kč ($263) apt. Rates include breakfast. AE, DC, MC, V. **Amenities:** Restaurant; cafe; bar; fitness center; tour guide; room service; babysitting. *In room:* TV, minibar, hair dryer.

Hotel Zvon Next door to the Palace, the Zvon lacks a bit of the panache of its smaller neighbor, but it still ranks as one of the town's nicer hotels, and sits in a prime spot directly across from the Kolonáda. Ask for a room facing the Kolonáda. Not only is the view spectacular, but rooms on this side tend to be larger and brighter.

Hlavní třída 68, 353 01 Mariánské Lázně. ⓒ 354-622-015. Fax 354-623-245. 79 units. 1,720Kč–4,720Kč ($57–$157) double; 2,370Kč–8,460Kč ($79–$282) suite. AE, DC, MC, V. **Amenities:** Cafe restaurant; bar; spa. *In room:* TV, minibar.

Parkhotel Golf ⓐ One of the more luxurious hotels, the Golf isn't actually in town but across from the golf course about 3km (2 miles) down the road leading to Karlovy Vary. This hotel is busy, so reservations are recommended. The English-speaking staff delivers on its pledge to cater to every wish. Rooms are bright and spacious, and there's an excellent restaurant and terrace on the first floor. Not surprisingly, the staff can help arrange a quick 18 holes across the street. In the winter, the golf course is used freely by cross-country skiers.

Zádub 580, 353 01 Mariánské Lázně. ⓒ 354-622-651. Fax 354-622-655. 28 units. 2,479Kč–3,922Kč ($82–$130) double; 4,699Kč–6,068Kč ($156–$202) suite. Rates include breakfast. AE, DC, MC, V. **Amenities:** Restaurant; cafe; indoor pool; golf; spa. *In room:* TV, minibar.

WHERE TO DINE

Churchill Club Restaurant ⓐ CZECH Don't let the name fool you—the food is traditional Czech, not British, with few surprises. A lively bar with a good selection of local and imported beer makes the Churchill one of the few fun places to be after dark in this quiet town. Try the Winston steak platter if you're really hungry.

Hlavní třída 121. ⓒ 354-622-705. Main courses 90Kč–550Kč ($3.20–$18). AE, MC, V. Daily 11am–11pm.

Hotel Koliba Restaurant ⓐ CZECH This bucolic hotel dining room, centered on an open fire grill, boasts a hearty rustic atmosphere that goes perfectly with the restaurant's strength: wild game. Check the daily menu to see what's new, or choose from the wide assortment of specialties *na roštu* (from the grill), including wild boar and venison. The Koliba also has an excellent selection of Moravian wines that you can order with your meal. The wine bar has dancing to a Gypsy band from 7pm to midnight Tuesday to Sunday.

Dusíkova 592. ⓒ 354-625-169. Reservations recommended. Main courses 99Kč–425Kč ($3.55–$15). No credit cards. Daily 11am–midnight.

Restaurant Fontaine CZECH/INTERNATIONAL The dining room is very large but remains quiet, though a little too well lit. The Fontaine is one of the more formal gastronomical experiences you will find in town. Bow-tied waiters serve traditional Bohemian specialties such as succulent roast duck, broiled trout, and chateaubriand, as well as some inventive variations.

In the Villa Butterfly, Hlavní třída 72. ⓒ 354-654-111. Main courses 120Kč–390Kč ($4.30–$14). AE, DC, MC, V. Daily 6–11pm.

TAKING THE WATERS AT MARIÁNSKÉ LÁZNĚ

When walking through the town, it's almost impossible to miss the **Lázeňská Kolonáda,** just off Skalníkovy sady. From Hlavní třída, walk east on Vrchlick-ého ulice. Recently restored to its former glory, the eye-catching cast-iron and glass colonnade is adorned with ceiling frescoes and Corinthian columns. Built in 1889, it connects a half-dozen major springs in the town center; this is the focal point of those partaking in the ritual. Bring a cup to fill or, if you want to fit in with the thousands of guests who are serious about their spa water, buy one of the porcelain mugs with a built-in straw that are offered just about every-where. Do keep in mind that the waters are used to treat internal disorders, so the minerals may act to cleanse the body thoroughly. You can wander the colon-nade any time; water is distributed daily from 6am to noon and 4 to 6pm.

MORE TO SEE & DO

There's not much town history, since Mariánské Lázně officially came into existence only in 1808, but engaging brevity is what makes the two-story **Městské Muzeum (City Museum),** Goethovo nám. 11 (© **354-622-740**), recommendable. Chrono-logically arranged displays include photos and documents of famous visitors. Goethe slept in the upstairs rooms in 1823, when he was 74 years old. If you ask nicely, the museum guards will play an English-language tape that describes the contents of each of the rooms. You can also request to see the museum's English-language film about the town. Admission is 20Kč (70¢), and it's open Wednesday to Sunday from 9am to noon and 1 to 4pm (July–Sept until 5pm).

You can also take a walk in the woods. The surrounding **Slavkovský les (Slavkov Forest)** has about 70km (43 miles) of marked footpaths and trails through the area's gentle hills.

The **Mariánské Lázně Golf Club** (© **354-624-300;** www.golfml.cz), a par-72 championship course, lies on the edge of town. The club takes pay-as-you-play golfers, with a fully equipped pro shop that rents clubs. Greens fees are 1,300Kč to 1,500Kč ($46–$53) and club rental is 400Kč ($14). Reservations are recommended on weekends.

ČESKÉ BUDĚJOVICE

This fortress town was born in 1265, when Otakar II decided that the intersec-tion point of the Vltava and Malše rivers would be the perfect site to protect the approaches to southern Bohemia. Although Otakar was killed at the Battle of the Moravian Field in 1278, and the town was subsequently ravaged by the rival Vítkovic family, the construction of České Budějovice continued, eventually taking the shape originally envisaged.

Today, České Budějovice, hometown of the original Budweiser brand beer, is more a bastion for the beer drinker than a protector of Bohemia. But its slow pace, relaxed atmosphere, and interesting architecture make it a worthy stop, especially as a base for exploring southern Bohemia or for those heading on to Austria.

The Spa Treatment

For a relaxing mineral bubble bath or massage, make reservations through the **Marienbad Kur & Spa Hotels Information Service,** Masarykova 22, 353 29 (© **354-655-550;** www.marienbad.cz). Also ask at your hotel, as most provide spa treatments and massages or can arrange them. Treatments begin at 350Kč ($13).

ESSENTIALS

GETTING THERE **By Train** Ten express trains from Prague's Hlavní nádraží make the trip to České Budějovice in about 2½ hours. The fare is 306Kč ($11) first class or 204Kč ($7.30) second class.

Several express **buses** run from Prague's Florenc station each day and take 2 hours; tickets cost 118Kč ($4.20).

If you're **driving,** leave Prague to the south via the main D1 expressway and take the cutoff for Highway E55, which runs straight to České Budějovice. The trip takes about 1½ hours.

VISITOR INFORMATION **Tourist Infocentrum,** náměstí Přemysla Otakara II. 2 (② **386-359-480**), provides maps and guidebooks and finds lodging. A good website with information on the city can be found at **www.mesto. budweb.cz**.

SPECIAL EVENTS Each August, České Budějovice hosts the largest **International Agricultural Show** (think "state fair") in the country.

WHERE TO STAY

Several agencies can locate reasonably priced private rooms. Expect to pay about 500Kč ($17) per person, in cash. Tourist Infocentrum (see "Visitor Information," above) can point you toward a wide selection of conveniently located rooms and pensions.

Grandhotel Zvon Location is everything for the city's most elegant hotel, which occupies several historic buildings on the main square. Upper-floor rooms have been renovated and tend to be more expensive, especially those with a view of the square—they're not only brighter, they're larger and nicer, too. Others are relatively plain and functional. Try to avoid the smaller rooms, usually reserved for tour groups. There's no elevator, but if you don't mind the climb, stay on the fourth floor. One of the biggest changes here in recent years has been the staff, which seems to be learning that guests deserve respect and quality treatment.

Náměstí Přemysla Otakara II. 28, 370 42 České Budějovice. ② **387-311-385.** Fax 386-358-929. www. hotel-zvon.cz. 75 units. 1,980Kč–3,080Kč ($70–$110) double; 2,420Kč–3,720Kč ($86–$132) suite. AE, DC, MC, V. **Amenities:** Restaurant; cafe; bar. *In room:* TV.

Hotel Malý Pivovar (Small Brewery) ★★ Around the corner from the Zvon (see above), a renovated 16th-century microbrewery combines the charms of a B&B with the amenities of a modern hotel. The kind of management found here is a rarity in the Czech tourism industry—they work hard to help out. Rooms are bright and cheery, with antique-style wooden furniture. Exposed wooden ceiling beams lend a farmhouse feel. The hotel is definitely worth consideration if being only 30m (100 ft.) from the square isn't a problem.

Ulice Karla IV. 8–10, 370 01 České Budějovice. ② **386-360-471.** Fax 386-360-473. www.budvar.cz. 29 units. 1,990Kč–2,500Kč ($71–$89) double; 2,190Kč–2,900Kč ($78–$103) suite. Rates include breakfast. AE, DC, MC, V. **Amenities:** Restaurant/pub; wine bar. *In room:* TV, minibar.

WHERE TO DINE

Masné Krámy (Meat Shops) ★ CZECH If you've pledged not to go to any "tourist traps," you might make an exception for this one housed in a historic building. Just northwest of náměstí Přemysla Otakara II, labyrinthine Masné Krámy occupies a series of drinking rooms on either side of a long hall, and is a must for any serious pub goer. The inexpensive and filling food is pure Bohemian, including several pork, duck, and trout dishes. Come for the boisterous atmosphere, or for what's possibly the best goulash in the Czech Republic.

Krajinská 29. ✆ **387-318-609.** Main courses 79Kč–195Kč ($2.80–$6.95). No credit cards. Daily 10am–11pm.

U paní Emy CZECH/INTERNATIONAL   Usually crowded, U paní Emy has a good selection at reasonable prices. The chicken and fish dishes are the most popular. The pan-fried trout tastes very light, not oily as most Czech restaurants tend to make it. A wine bar here stays open until the wee hours.

Široká 25. ✆ **387-312-846.** Main courses 79Kč–205Kč ($2.80–$7.30). No credit cards. Daily 10am–3am.

EXPLORING THE TOWN

You can comfortably see České Budějovice in a day. At its center is one of central Europe's largest squares, the cobblestone **náměstí Přemysla Otakara II.** The square contains the ornate **Fountain of Sampson,** an 18th-century water well that was once the town's principal water supply, plus a mishmash of baroque and Renaissance buildings. On the southwest corner is the **town hall,** an elegant baroque structure built by Martinelli between 1727 and 1730. On top of the town hall, the larger-than-life statues by Dietrich represent the civic virtues: justice, bravery, wisdom, and diligence.

One block northwest of the square is the **Černá věž (Black Tower),** visible from almost every point in the city. Its 360 steps are worth the climb to get a bird's-eye view in all directions. The most famous symbol of České Budějovice, the 70m (232-ft.) 16th-century tower was built as a belfry for the adjacent **St. Nicholas Church.** This 13th-century church, one of the town's most important sights, was a bastion of Roman Catholicism during the 15th-century Hussite rebellion. You shouldn't miss the flamboyant white-and-cream 17th-century baroque interior. The tower is open Tuesday to Sunday from 10am to 6pm; admission is 20Kč (70¢). The church is open daily from 9am to 8pm.

TOURING A BEER SHRINE

On the town's northern edge sits a shrine to those who pray to the gods of the amber nectar. This is where **Budějovický Budvar,** the original brewer of Budweiser beer, has its one and only factory. Established in 1895, Budvar draws on more than 700 years of the area's brewing tradition to produce one of the world's best beers.

Four trolleybuses—nos. 2, 4, 6, and 8—stop by the brewery; this is how the brewery ensures that its workers and visitors reach the plant safely each day. The trolley ride to the brewery costs 8Kč (30¢). You can also hop a cab from the town square for about 120Kč ($4.30).

Tours can be arranged by phoning ahead, but only for groups. Contact Budvar n.p., Karolíny Světlé 4, České Budějovice (✆ **387-705-341;** www.budvar.cz). If you're traveling alone or with only one or two other people, ask a hotel concierge at one of the bigger hotels (we suggest the Zvon or Hotel Malý Pivovar) if he or she can put you with an already-scheduled group. Failing that, you may want to take a chance and head up to the brewery where, if a group has arrived, another person or two won't be noticed.

CHEB (EGER) & FRANTIŠKOVY LÁZNĚ (FRANZENSBAD)

As with Plzeň, few people who travel through **Cheb,** 170km (105 miles) west of Prague and 40km (25 miles) southwest of Karlovy Vary, actually stop and look around. From the outside, that's understandable, but it's too bad. The center of Cheb is one of the more architecturally interesting places in west Bohemia, and its history is fascinating as well.

A former stronghold for the Holy Roman Empire on its eastern flank, Eger, as it was then known, became part of Bohemia in 1322. Cheb stayed under Bohemian rule until it was handed over to Germany as part of the 1938 Munich Pact. Soon after the end of World War II, it was returned to Czech hands, when most of the area's native Germans, known as Sudeten Germans, were expelled for their open encouragement of the invading Nazi army. You can see this bilingual, bicultural heritage in the main square, which can be mistaken for being on either side of the border if it weren't for the Czech writing on windows. These

---

Moments **Visiting Plzeň, the Birthplace of Beer**

České Budějovice may be the home of Budweiser, but the town of **Plzeň (Pilsen)** is the self-proclaimed birthplace of beer. Founded in 1295 by Václav II, Plzeň was and remains western Bohemia's administrative center. The king's real gift to the town, however, was granting it brewing rights. Some 400 years ago, a group of men formed Plzeň's first beer-drinking guild, and in 1842, the brewers combined their expertise to produce a superior brew through what became known as the Pilsner brewing method. Today, beer is probably the only reason you'll want to stop at this otherwise industrial town.

Plzeňský Prazdroj (Pilsner Breweries), at U Prazdroje 7, will interest anyone who wants to learn more about the brewing process. It's actually made up of several breweries, pumping out brands like Pilsner Urquell and Gambrinus, the most widely consumed beer in the Czech Republic. The 1-hour tour of the factory includes a 15-minute film and visits to the fermentation cellars and brewing rooms. The tour starts at 12:30pm daily (Apr–Sept), Monday through Friday from October to March; the tour is also offered at 2pm in July and August. It costs 120Kč ($4); the price includes a tasting of freshly brewed beer. (For details on other tours available, call ✆ **377-062-888** or e-mail visit@pilsner-urquell.com.)

If you didn't get your fill of beer facts at the brewery, the **Pivovarské Muzeum (Beer Museum;** ✆ **377-224-955)** is 1 block away on Veleslavínova 6. Inside this former 15th-century house, you'll learn everything there is to know about beer but were afraid to ask. Rooms display a wide collection of pub artifacts, brewing equipment, and mugs. Most displays have English captions, but ask for a more detailed museum description in English when you enter. Admission is 60Kč ($2), and hours are Tuesday through Sunday from 10am to 6pm (to 5pm in winter months).

The best way to get to Plzeň is by **train**. A number of fast trains from Prague whisks travelers to Plzeň in just under 2 hours. The train costs 210Kč ($7.50) first class or 140Kč ($5) second class. To get from the train station to town, walk out the main entrance and take Americká Street across the river; turn right onto Jungmannova, which leads to the main square. The **City Information Center Plzeň**, náměstí Republiky 41, 301 16 Plzeň (✆ **378-035-330**; www.plzen-city.cz), is packed with literature to answer your questions.

days, the Germans have returned as tourists; many indulge in the town's thriving sex trade and cheap alcohol. Don't be surprised to see women plying their trade around almost every corner. Still, Cheb is worth exploring for its mélange of architectural styles, the eerie Jewish Quarter Špalíček, and the enormous Romanesque Chebský Hrad (Cheb Castle).

Only about 20 minutes up the road from Cheb is the smallest of the three major Bohemian spa towns, **Františkovy Lázně.** Though it pales in comparison to Karlovy Vary and Mariánské Lázně, Františkovy Lázně has taken great strides in the past few years to erase the decline it experienced under Communism. There's not much to see save for the **Spa Museum,** which holds an interesting display of bathing artifacts, but it's a much quieter and cleaner place to spend the night than Cheb. Listed below are places to stay in both Cheb and Františkovy Lázně.

ESSENTIALS

GETTING THERE   Cheb is located on the E48, one of the main highways leading to Germany. If you're **driving** from Prague, take the same route you would to Karlovy Vary, which eventually brings you to Cheb. The drive takes about 2 hours.

To get to Františkovy Lázně from Cheb by car, take Highway E49. The trip takes about 20 minutes.

Express **trains** from Prague usually stop in Cheb, as do several trains daily from Karlovy Vary. Cheb is on a main train route of the Czech Republic, so it's easy to catch many international connections here. The train takes 3½ hours and costs 375Kč ($13) first class and 250Kč ($8.90) second class.

Cheb is a long **bus** ride from Prague, and I suggest avoiding it if possible. It's more manageable to take the bus from Karlovy Vary or Mariánské Lázně.

VISITOR INFORMATION   You'll find maps, guidebooks, and lodging at the **Informační Centrum,** náměstí Krále Jiřího z Poděbrad 33 (© **354-422-705;** www.cheb-etc.cz).

WHERE TO STAY
In Cheb

Hotel Hvězda (Hotel Star)   Overlooking the rather noisy main square, the Hvězda is a lone star in the Cheb hotel universe. The rooms are small, but most overlook the square, and the staff tries to make your stay comfortable. If you can't stay in Františkovy Lázně and don't want to drive farther, this is really the only recommended hotel in town.

Náměstí Krále Jiřího z Poděbrad 4, 350 01 Cheb. © **354-422-549.** Fax 354-422-546. 40 units. 900Kč–1,500Kč ($32–$53) double. AE, MC, V. *In room:* TV.

In Františkovy Lázně

Hotel Tři Lilie (Three Lilies Hotel)   The Three Lilies is worth the extra money since it's the only luxury hotel in the area. Cheb needs a nice hotel like this. At night, you can relax, blocking out noise in your spotless, spacious room that's outfitted with satellite television. The staff is very attentive and can arrange spa treatments, massages, and other health services. On the main floor is a nice, though pricey, bar and restaurant.

Národní 3, 351 01 Františkovy Lázně. © **354-208-900.** Fax 354-208-995. 32 units. 2,300Kč ($82) double; 3,000Kč ($107) suite. AE, MC, V. **Amenities:** Restaurant; bar; cafe. *In room:* TV, minibar.

WHERE TO DINE

Restaurace Fortuna CZECH   If you're craving a schnitzel, this is as good a place as any. Most Czech specialties are served, and the goulash's slightly piquant sauce is a pleasant surprise. It's one of the only restaurants open late, and a terrace right on the main square lends to its appeal.

Náměstí Krále Jiřího z Poděbrad 29. ©︎ 354-422-110. Main courses 79Kč–185Kč ($2.80–$6.60). No credit cards. Daily 10am–2am.

Staročeská Restaurace CZECH/CHINESE   This restaurant serves much the same fare as all of the other restaurants on or around the square, but what catches the eye are a few Chinese dishes. The *kuře kung-pao* (kung pao chicken) is a good spicy alternative to the customary sausages and meat with dumplings. The chicken with mushrooms is also a nice light choice if you've had your fill of heavy meals.

Kamenná 1. No phone. Main courses 69Kč–260Kč ($2.45–$9.30). No credit cards. Daily 10am–10pm.

EXPLORING CHEB

The main square, **náměstí Krále Jiřího z Poděbrad,** attracts most of the attention and is a good place to begin a stroll of the Old Town. Though it has been overrun with tourist shops and cafes that serve mediocre German fare, the square still shines with Gothic burgher houses and the baroque **Old Town Hall (Stará radnice).** At its south end, the **statue of Kašna Roland,** built in 1591 and a former symbol of capital punishment, reminds people of the strength wielded by justice. At the other end of the square stands the **Kašna Herkules,** a monument to the town's former strength and power. Next to it is a cluster of 11 timber houses, called **Špalíček.** These used to be owned by Jews in the early 14th century, but a fervently anti-Semitic clergy in the area incited such hatred that the Jews were forced up Židská ulice (Jews St.) and into an alleyway called ulička Zavražděných (Murder Victim's Lane), where they were unceremoniously slaughtered in 1350.

Across from Špalíček is the **Cheb Museum** (©︎ 354-422-246), where another murder took place almost 300 years later—that of Albrecht von Wallenstein in 1634. On the upper level, a display vividly depicts the assassination. The museum's first floor displays many 20th-century paintings, from which you can trace the town's slow demise. Admission is 30Kč ($1.05). Hours are March to December, Tuesday to Sunday from 9am to 12:30pm and 1 to 5pm; it's open daily in July and August.

The old town is also packed with churches. The most interesting is **St. Nicholas,** around the corner from the museum. It's a hodgepodge of architectural styles: Its Romanesque heritage is reflected in the tower windows, while a Gothic portal and baroque interior round out the renovations over the years. The church is open daily from 9am to 6pm.

TOURING CHEB CASTLE

An excellent example of Romanesque architecture in the northeast part of the Old Town is **Cheb Castle.** Overlooking the Elbe River, the castle, built in the late 12th century, is one of central Europe's largest Romanesque structures.

The castle's main draws are its **Chapel of Sts. Erhard and Ursala** and the **Černá věž (Black Tower).** The two-tiered, early Gothic chapel has a somber first floor where the proletariat would congregate, while the emperor and his family went to the much cheerier and brighter second floor with its Gothic windows.

Across the courtyard from the chapel stands the Černá věž (Black Tower). From its 18m (60-ft.) high lookout, you'll have the best views of the town. The tower seems dusty and smeared with pollution; its color is black because the blocks from which it is made are lava rocks taken from the nearby Komorní Hůrka volcano (now dormant).

Alas, there are no tours of the castle, and the English text provided at the entrance does little to inform you. Admission is 50Kč ($1.80). It's open Tuesday to Sunday: June to August from 9am to noon and 1 to 6pm, May and September from 9am to noon and 1 to 5pm, and April and October from 9am to noon and 1 to 4pm.

Denmark

by Darwin Porter & Danforth Prince

In this chapter, we concentrate on Copenhagen, Denmark's capital, and have added a few important side trips you can take in a day or two. Copenhagen got its name from the word *københavn,* meaning "merchants' harbor." This city grew in size and importance because of its position on the *Øresund* (the Sound) between Denmark and Sweden, guarding the entrance to the Baltic. From its humble beginnings, Copenhagen has become the largest city in Scandinavia, home to 1.7 million people.

If you'd like to tie in a visit to Copenhagen with the châteaux country of Sweden, it's as easy as crossing a bridge: In 2000 Denmark was linked to Sweden by the 16km (10-mile) Øresund Bridge. The two cities of Copenhagen and Malmö, Sweden, are the hubs of the Øresund Region, northern Europe's largest domestic market, larger than Stockholm and equal in size to Berlin, Hamburg, and Amsterdam. The bridge is the longest combined rail-and-road bridge in the world.

1 Copenhagen

Copenhagen is a city with much charm, as reflected in its canals, narrow streets, and old houses. Its most famous resident was the writer Hans Christian Andersen, whose memory still lives on here. Another of Copenhagen's world-renowned inhabitants was Søren Kierkegaard, who used to take long morning strolls in the city, planning his next essay; his completed writings eventually earned him the title "father of existentialism."

But few modern Copenhageners are reading Kierkegaard today, and neither are they as melancholy as Hamlet. Most of them are out having too much fun. Copenhagen epitomizes the Nordic joie de vivre, and the city is filled with a lively atmosphere, good times (none better than at the Tivoli Gardens), sex shows, countless outdoor cafes, and all-night dance clubs. Of course, if you come in winter, the fierce realities of living above the 55th parallel set in. That's when Copenhageners retreat inside their smoky jazz clubs and beer taverns.

Modern Copenhagen still retains some of the characteristics of a village. If you forget the suburbs, you can cover most of the central belt on foot, which makes it a great tourist spot. It's almost as if the city were designed for pedestrians, as reflected by its **Strøget** (strolling street), Europe's longest and oldest walking street.

ESSENTIALS

GETTING THERE   By Plane   SAS (© 800/221-2350; www.scandinavian. net) is the major carrier to Copenhagen. **Finnair** (© 800/950-4768; www.finnair.com) offers flights through Helsinki from New York, and Miami. **Icelandair** (© 800/223-5500; www.icelandair.com) has service through Reykjavik from several North American cities.

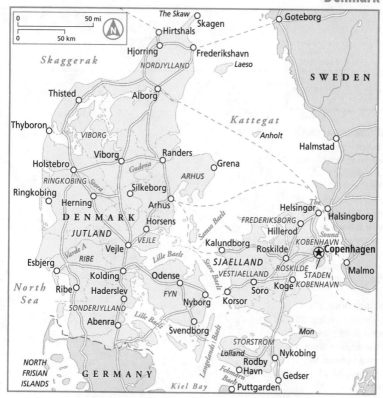

You arrive at **Kastrup Airport** (© **45/3231-3231**), 12km (7¼ miles) from the center of Copenhagen. Since 1998, air rail trains have linked the airport with Copenhagen's Central Railway Station, in the center of the hotel zone, and the whole affair now takes a mere 11 minutes and costs 23DKK ($3.60). The Air Rail Terminal is underneath the airport's arrivals and departure halls, just a short escalator ride from the gates. You can also take an SAS bus to the city terminal; the fare is 23DKK ($3.60). A taxi to the city center costs around 160DKK ($25). Yet another option is a local bus, no. 250S, which leaves from the international arrivals terminal every 15 or 20 minutes for Town Hall Square in central Copenhagen and costs 23DKK ($3.60).

By Train Trains from the Continent arrive at the **Hoved Banegård (Central Railroad Station),** in the very center of Copenhagen, near the Tivoli and the Rådhuspladsen. For **rail information,** call © **33-14-17-01.** The station operates a luggage-checking service, but room bookings are available only at the tourist office (see "Visitor Information," below). You can also exchange money at the **Den Danske Bank** branch on-site, open daily from 7am to 8pm.

From the Central Railroad Station, you can connect with **S-tog,** the local subway, with trains leaving from platforms in the terminus itself. To find out which train you should board to reach your destination, inquire at the information desk near Tracks 9 and 12.

Copenhagen

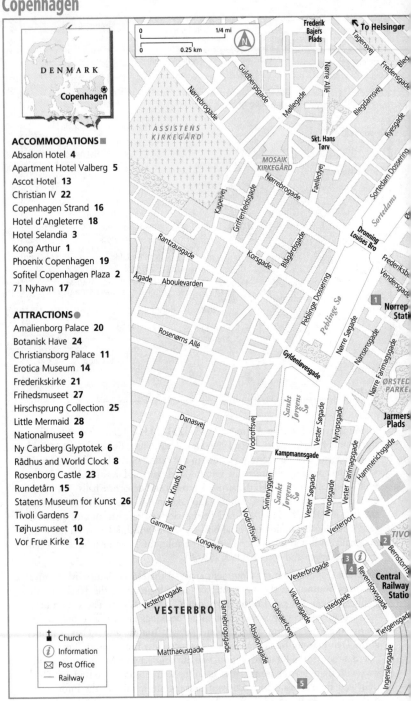

ACCOMMODATIONS ■
Absalon Hotel **4**
Apartment Hotel Valberg **5**
Ascot Hotel **13**
Christian IV **22**
Copenhagen Strand **16**
Hotel d'Angleterre **18**
Hotel Selandia **3**
Kong Arthur **1**
Phoenix Copenhagen **19**
Sofitel Copenhagen Plaza **2**
71 Nyhavn **17**

ATTRACTIONS ●
Amalienborg Palace **20**
Botanisk Have **24**
Christiansborg Palace **11**
Erotica Museum **14**
Frederikskirke **21**
Frihedsmuseet **27**
Hirschsprung Collection **25**
Little Mermaid **28**
Nationalmuseet **9**
Ny Carlsberg Glyptotek **6**
Rådhus and World Clock **8**
Rosenborg Castle **23**
Rundetårn **15**
Statens Museum for Kunst **26**
Tivoli Gardens **7**
Tøjhusmuseet **10**
Vor Frue Kirke **12**

† Church
ⓘ Information
⊠ Post Office
— Railway

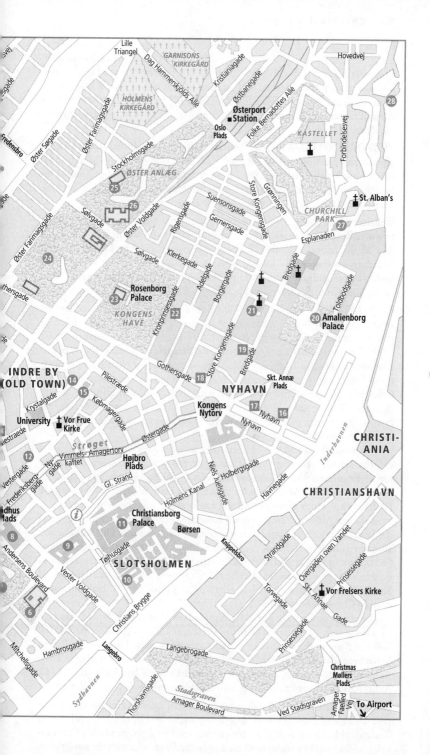

By Car If you're driving from Germany, a car-ferry will take you from Travemünde to Gedser in southern Denmark. From Gedser, get on E-55 north, an express highway that will deliver you to the southern outskirts of Copenhagen. If you're coming from Sweden and crossing at Helsingborg, you'll land on the Danish side at Helsingør. Take express highway E-55 south to the northern outskirts of Copenhagen. If you're coming from Malmö, Sweden, you can cross on the Øresund Bridge.

VISITOR INFORMATION Tourist Office Wonderful Copenhagen Tourist Information, Bernstorffsgade 1 (© 33-25-38-44; see website below), across from Tivoli's main entrance, is open September to October Monday to Saturday 9am to 4pm; November to April Saturday 9am to 2pm; May and June daily 9am to 8pm; July and August daily 8am to 11pm.

Websites The Wonderful Copenhagen Tourist Information Center website (www.visitcopenhagen.dk) takes a while to load but is worth the wait; you'll find all the basics on dining, lodging, and attractions. The **Danish Tourist Board** (www.visitdenmark.com) offers a wide-ranging website where you'll find late news and transportation tips; the accommodations choices range from castles and manor houses to farm holidays.

CITY LAYOUT The heart of **Old Copenhagen** is a maze of pedestrian streets, formed by Nørreport Station to the north, Town Hall Square (Rådhuspladsen) to the west, Kongens Nytorv to the east, and the Inderhavnen (Inner Harbor) to the south. One continuous route, **Strøget,** the world's longest pedestrian street, goes east from Town Hall Square to Kongens Nytorv and is made up of five streets: Frederiksberggade, Nygade, Vimmelskaftet, Amagertorv, and Østergade. Strøget is lined with shops, bars, restaurants, and sidewalk cafes in summer. **Pistolstraede,** a narrow street a 3-minute walk west of Kongens Nytorv, is a maze of galleries, restaurants, and boutiques, all housed in restored 18th-century buildings.

Fiolstræde (Violet St.), a dignified street with antiques shops and bookshops, cuts through the university (Latin Quarter). If you turn into Rosengaarden at the top of Fiolstræde, you'll come to **Kultorvet (Coal Sq.)** just before you reach Nørreport Station. Here you join the third main pedestrian street, **Købmagergade (Butcher St.),** which winds around and finally meets Strøget on Amagertorv.

At the end of Strøget you approach **Kongens Nytorv (King's Sq.),** the site of the Royal Theater and Magasin, the largest department store. This will put you at the beginning of **Nyhavn,** the former seamen's quarter that has been gentrified into an upmarket area of expensive restaurants, apartments, cafes, and boutiques. The government of Denmark is centered on the small island of **Slotsholmen,** connected to the center by eight bridges. Several museums, notably Christiansborg Castle, are found here.

The center of Copenhagen is **Rådhuspladsen (Town Hall Sq.).** From here it's a short walk to the Tivoli Gardens, the major attraction, and to the Central Railroad Station, the main railroad and subway terminus. The wide boulevard, **Vesterbrogade,** passes by Tivoli until it reaches the Central Railroad Station. Another major street is named after Denmark's most famous writer; **H. C. Andersens Boulevard** runs along Rådhuspladsen and the Tivoli Gardens.

GETTING AROUND A joint zone-fare system includes Copenhagen Transport buses and State Railway and S-tog trains in Copenhagen and North Zealand, plus some private rail routes within a 40km (25-mile) radius of the capital, enabling you to transfer from train to bus and vice versa with the same ticket.

> **Value** **Traveling for Less**
>
> The **Copenhagen Card** entitles you to free and unlimited travel by bus
> and rail throughout the metropolitan area (including North Zealand),
> 25% to 50% discounts on crossings to and from Sweden, and free admis-
> sion to many sights and museums. The card is available for 3 days and
> costs 395DKK ($62) adults, 225DKK ($35) children between 10 and 15
> years old. For more information, contact the Copenhagen Tourist Infor-
> mation Center (see above).

A *grundbillet* (basic ticket) for both buses and trains costs 15DKK ($2.35).
You can buy 10 tickets for 95DKK ($15). Children under 12 ride for half fare;
those under 5 travel free on local trains, and those under 7 free on buses. You
can purchase a ticket allowing 24-hour bus and train travel through nearly half
of Zealand for 90DKK ($14); half price for children 7 to 11; free for children
under 7.

Students who have an **International Student Identity Card (ISIC)** are entitled to a number of travel breaks. You can buy a card in the United States at **STA
Travel** (© **800/781-4040;** www.statravel.com).

For information about low-cost train and plane trips, go to **Waastels,**
Skoubogade 6 (© **33-14-46-33**). Hours are Monday through Friday from 9am
to 5pm. Waastels specializes in inexpensive travel by plane within Europe, and
they also are the experts on special youth fares.

Eurailpasses and Nordturist Pass tickets are accepted on local trains.

By Bus   Copenhagen's well-maintained buses are the least expensive method of
getting around. Most buses leave from Rådhuspladsen. A basic ticket allows 1
hour of travel and unlimited transfers within the zone where you started your
trip. For information, call © **36-13-14-15.**

By S-tog (Subway)   The S-tog connects heartland Copenhagen with its suburbs. Use of the tickets is the same as on buses (above). You can transfer from a
bus line to an S-train on the same ticket. Eurailpass holders generally ride free.
For more information, call © **33-14-17-01** at any time.

By Metro   In 2001 Copenhagen launched its first Metro line, taking passengers from east to west across the city and vice versa. Operating around the clock,
the Metro runs as far west as Vanløse and as far south as Vestamager. Nørreport
is the transfer station to the S-tog system, the commuter rail link to the suburbs.
Metro trains run every 2 minutes during rush hours and every 15 minutes at
night. Fares are integrated into the existing zone system (see "By Bus," above).

By Car   It's best to park your car in any of the dozens of city parking lots, then
retrieve it when you're ready to explore the capital's environs. Many parking lots
are open 24 hours; a few others tend to close between 1 and 7am. Some close
on Saturday afternoon and on Sunday during non-peak business hours when
traffic is presumably lighter. Costs tend to be about 24DKK ($3.75) per hour or
240DKK ($37) per 24 hours. One of the most central parking lots is **Indus-
triens Hus,** H. C. Andersens Blvd. 18 (© **33-91-21-75**), open Monday
through Friday from 7am to 12:15am and Saturday and Sunday from 9am to
12:45am.

By Taxi   Watch for the FRI (free) sign or green light to hail a taxi. Be sure the taxis are metered. **Københavns Taxa** (© 35-35-35-35) operates the largest fleet of cabs. *Note:* Tips are included in the meter price: 23DKK ($3.60) at the drop of the flag and 11DKK ($1.70) per kilometer thereafter, Monday through Friday from 6am to 6pm. From 6pm to 6am and all day and night on Saturday and Sunday, the cost is 15DKK ($1.95) per kilometer. Basic drop-of-the-flag costs remain the same, however. Many drivers speak English.

By Bicycle   To reduce pollution from cars, Copenhageners ride bicycles. For 75DKK ($12) per day, plus a 500DKK ($78) deposit, you can rent a bike at **Københavns Cykler,** Reventlowsgade 11 (© 33-33-86-13). Hours are Monday through Friday from 8am to 5pm, Saturday from 9am to 1pm, and Sunday from 10am to 1pm (July 1–Sept 1).

FAST FACTS: Copenhagen

American Express   American Express is represented throughout Denmark by **Neiman & Schultz,** Nansens (© **33-13-11-81**), with a branch in Terminal 3 of the Copenhagen Airport. Fulfilling all the functions of American Express except foreign-exchange services, the main office is open Monday through Thursday from 8:30am to 4:30pm, and Friday from 8:30am to 4pm. The airport office remains open till 8:30pm Monday through Friday. On weekends, and overnight on weekdays, a recorded message, in English, will deliver the phone number of a 24-hour Amex service in Stockholm. This is useful for anyone who has lost a card or traveler's checks. As for foreign exchange, you'll find Neiman & Schultz offices scattered throughout Copenhagen, including a branch that's open 24 hours a day at the railway station.

Business Hours   Most **banks** are open from Monday through Friday from 9:30am to 4pm (Thurs to 6pm). **Stores** are generally open Monday through Thursday from 9am to 6pm, Friday from 9am to 7 or 8pm, and Saturday from 9am to 3pm; most are closed Sunday.

Currency   The Danish currency is the **krone (crown),** or DKK, made up of 100 øre. The rate of exchange used in this chapter is $1 = 6.35DKK, or 1DKK = 15 U.S. cents. At press time, £1 = 10.6DKK (or 1DKK = 9 pence). Note that in contrast to the fiscal policies of most of western Europe, Denmark opted not to convert its monetary system to the euro in January of 2001, despite its membership in the EU. Therefore, at least as of this writing, the euro is not the legal tender of Denmark.

Currency Exchange   Banks are generally your best bet to exchange currency. When banks are closed, you can exchange money at **Forex** (© **33-11-22-20**; S-tog: Central Station) in the Central Railroad Station, open daily from 8am to 9pm, or at the **Change Group** (© **33-93-04-55**; bus: 1, 6, or 9, Metro: Kongens Nytorv), Østergade 61, open Monday through Saturday from 8:30am to 10pm and Sunday from 10am to 6pm.

Dentists/Doctors   For emergency dental treatment, go to **Tandlaegevagten,** Oslo Plads 14 (© **35-38-02-51**; S-tog: Østerport), near Østerport Station and the U.S. Embassy. It's open Monday through Friday from 8am to 9:30pm and Saturday, Sunday, and holidays from 10am to noon. Be prepared to pay in cash. To reach a doctor, dial ℂ **70-13-00-41** Monday through Friday from 8am to 4pm or ℂ **38-88-60-41** after hours. The doctor's fee is payable in cash. Virtually every doctor speaks English.

Drugstores An *apotek* (pharmacy) open 24 hours a day in central Copenhagen is **Steno Apotek,** Vesterbrogade 6C (ℂ **33-14-82-66;** bus: 6).

Embassies All embassies are in Copenhagen. The embassy of the **United States** is at Dag Hammärskjölds Allé 24, DK-2100 København 0 (ℂ 35-55-31-44). Other embassies are the **United Kingdom,** Kastelsvej 36-40, DK-2100 København (ℂ 35-44-52-00); **Canada,** Kristen Berniskows Gade 1, DK-1105 København (ℂ 33-48-32-00); **Australia,** Dampfaergeveg 26, DK-2100 København (ℂ 70-26-36-76); and **Ireland,** Østbanegade 21, DK-2100 København (ℂ 35-42-32-33).

Emergencies Dial ℂ **112** for the fire department, the police, or an ambulance; or to report a sea or air accident.

Internet Access To check your e-mail or to send messages, go to **Copenhagen Hovebibliotek,** Krystalgade 15 (ℂ 33-73-60-60; bus: 14 or 16), open Monday through Friday from 10am to 7pm, Saturday from10am to 2pm. Access is free.

Post Office For information about the Copenhagen post office, call ℂ **33-41-56-00.** The main post office is at Tietgensgade 35–39, DK-1570 København (ℂ **31-41-56-00;** S-tog: Central Station), open Monday through Friday from 9am to 6:30pm, Saturday from 9:30am to 2pm. The post office at the Central Railroad Station is open Monday through Friday from 8am to 10pm, Saturday from 9am to 4pm, and Sunday from 10am to 4pm.

Taxes The 25% VAT (value-added tax) on goods and services is known in Denmark as *moms* (pronounced "mumps"). Special tax-free exports are possible, and many stores will mail goods home to you, circumventing *moms.* If you want to take your purchases with you, look for shops displaying Danish tax-free shopping notices. Such shops offer tourists' tax refunds for personal export. This refund applies to purchases of at least 300DKK ($39) for U.S. and Canadian visitors. Your tax-free invoice must be stamped by Danish Customs when you leave the country. You can receive your refund at Copenhagen's Kastrup International Airport when you depart. If you go by land or sea, you can receive your refund by mail. Mail requests for refunds to Danish Tax-Free Shopping A/S, H. J. Holstvej 5A, DK-2605 Brøndby, Denmark. You'll be reimbursed by check, cash, or credit or charge card credit in the currency you want. Service and handling fees are deducted from the total, so actual refunds come to about 18%.

A 25% *moms* is included in hotel and restaurant bills, service charges, entrance fees, and repair bills for foreign-registered cars. No refunds are possible on these items.

Telephone The country code for Denmark is **45.** It should precede any call made to Denmark from another country.

Danish phones are fully automatic. Dial the eight-digit number; there are no city area codes. Don't insert any coins until your party answers. At public telephone booths, use two 50-øre coins or a 1-krone or 5-krone coin only. You can make more than one call on the same payment if your time hasn't run out. Remember that calling direct from your hotel room can be expensive. Emergency calls are free. You can reach a U.S. operator with an **AT&T** calling card by dialing ⓒ **800/CALL-ATT**. For **MCI** dial ⓒ **800/888-8000**.

Tipping Tips are seldom expected, but when they are, you should give only 1DKK or 2DKK. Porters charge fixed prices, and tipping is not customary for hairdressers or barbers. Service is built into the system, and hotels, restaurants, and even taxis include a 15% service charge in their rates. Because of the service charge, plus the 25% *moms*, you'll probably have to pay an additional 40% for some services!

Consider tipping only for special services—some Danes would feel insulted if you offered them a tip.

WHERE TO STAY
NEAR KONGENS NYTROV & NYHAVN
Very Expensive

Hotel d'Angleterre ✮✮✮   If you've made it, stay here. At the top of Nyhavn, this seven-story hotel, built in 1755 and extensively renovated, is the premier choice for Denmark (though it's a bit staid and stodgy). The rooms are beautifully furnished with art objects and the occasional antique. They vary in size, but each has a grand bed that has sheltered notables ranging from Hans Christian Andersen to Madonna and Ricky Martin. The bathrooms come with phones and scales.

Kongens Nytorv 34, DK-1021 København. ⓒ **800/44-UTELL** in the U.S., or 33-12-00-95. Fax 33-12-11-18. www.remmen.dk. 123 units. 2,470DKK–3,470DKK ($385–$541) double; from 4,470DKK ($697) suite. AE, DC, MC, V. Parking 175DKK ($27). Bus: 1A, 5, 15, or 18. **Amenities:** Restaurant; bar; indoor pool; fitness center; spa; sauna; 24-hr. room service; babysitting; laundry service/dry cleaning, nonsmoking rooms. *In room:* A/C, TV, dataport, minibar, hair dryer, safe.

Phoenix Copenhagen ✮✮   More than any other hotel, this top-of-the-line lodging poses a challenge to the discreet grandeur of the nearby d'Angleterre. Opened in 1991, the Phoenix was a royal guesthouse, originally built in 1780 to accommodate the aristocratic courtiers of Amalienborg Palace. The spacious rooms are tastefully elegant and decorated with discreet Louis XVI reproductions. The large beds sport fine linens, and the bathrooms are state-of-the-art. The very best units also have faxes, bathrobes, and phones in the bathrooms.

Bredgade 37, DK-1260 København. ⓒ **33-95-95-00**. Fax 33-33-98-33. 213 units. 1,990DKK–2,890DKK ($310–$451) double; from 3,500DKK ($546) suite. AE, DC, MC, V. Parking 100DKK ($16). Bus: 1, 6A, 15, or 19. **Amenities:** Restaurant; bar; room service (6:30am–10pm); babysitting; laundry service/dry cleaning, non-smoking rooms. *In room:* A/C, TV, dataport, minibar, hair dryer, safe.

Expensive

71 Nyhavn ✮✮   On the corner between Copenhagen harbor and Nyhavn Canal, this hotel is housed in a restored old warehouse from 1804, and was thoroughly renovated in 1997. Most of the rooms have a harbor and canal view. The rooms have a nautical decor, with exposed brick, dark woods, and crisscrossing timbers. Bathrooms are rather small; most have a stall shower. The best rooms are equipped with faxes and bathrobes, and computer plugs are available at the reception desk.

Nyhavn 71, DK-1051 København. ⓒ **33-43-62-00**. Fax 33-43-62-01. www.71nyhavnhotelcopenhagen.dk. 150 units. Mon–Thurs 1,650DKK–2,350DKK ($257–$367) double, 3,000DKK–5,000DKK ($468–$780) suite;

Fri–Sun 1,290DKK–1,790DKK ($201–$279) double, 2,190DKK–3,800DKK ($342–$593) suite. AE, DC, MC, V. Free parking. Bus: 1A, 6A, 29, or 650-S. Metro: Kongens Nytorf. **Amenities:** Restaurant; bar; room service (noon–10:30pm); babysitting; laundry service/dry cleaning, nonsmoking rooms. *In room:* A/C (in some), TV, dataport, minibar, hair dryer, iron/ironing board (in some), safe, trouser press (in some).

Moderate

Christian IV　This small, cozy hotel enjoys one of the most desirable locations in Copenhagen. Dating from 1958, the hotel takes its name from Christian IV, who constructed Rosenburg Castle lying adjacent to the hotel. The hotel provides a "bridge" linking King's Garden, the castle, and the more modern structures in the neighborhood. Enjoying a lot of repeat business, it offers attractively decorated bedrooms with a modern Danish design, along with immaculately kept private bathrooms with tub and shower.

Dronningens Tvaergade 45, DK-1302 København. ⓒ **33-32-10-44.** Fax 33-32-07-06. www.arp-hansen.dk/christian/christianol.html. 42 units. 720DKK–1,525DKK ($112–$238) double. Rates include breakfast. AE, DC, MC, V. Bus: 26. **Amenities:** Breakfast room; bar; laundry service (Mon–Fri); 1 room for those with limited mobility. *In room:* TV.

Copenhagen Strand ⚑　One of the city's most modern hotels, opened in 2000, lies within a pair of former brick-and-timber factories. The savvy architects retained as many of the old-fashioned details as they could. The medium-size rooms are filled with comfortable, contemporary-looking furnishings. The hotel is rated three stars by the Danish government, but frankly, all that it lacks for elevation into four-star status is a full-fledged restaurant.

Havnegade 37, DK-1058 København K. ⓒ **33-48-99-00.** Fax 33-48-99-01. www.copenhagenstrand.dk. 174 units. 1,595DKK ($249) double; 2,795DKK–3,195DKK ($436–$498) suite. AE, DC, MC, V. Parking 113DKK ($18). Metro: Kongens Nytorv. **Amenities:** Bar; business center; 24-hr. room service; babysitting; laundry service/dry cleaning; rooms for those with limited mobility; nonsmoking rooms. *In room:* TV, minibar, hair dryer.

NEAR RÅDHUSPLADSEN & TIVOLI
Expensive

Sofitel Copenhagen Plaza ⚑　This successful overhaul of an older hotel near the rail station combines first-class comfort and antique furnishings. Opposite the Tivoli Gardens, the hotel was commissioned by King Frederik VIII in 1913 and has entertained its share of celebrities and royalty. Rooms vary greatly in size and resemble what you might find in an English country house—but with all the modern amenities. The antiques, double-glazed windows, and views from many rooms make this a good choice. Bathrooms are generous in size. The **Library Bar** is one of Copenhagen's most charming.

Bernstorffsgade 4, DK-1577 København. ⓒ **800/223-5652** or 33-14-92-62. Fax 33-93-93-62. www.sofitel.com. 93 units. 1,999DKK ($312) double; 2,999DKK–6,499DKK ($468–$1,014) suite. AE, DC, MC, V. Parking 165DKK ($26). Bus: 2A, 5A, 150S, or 46. Metro: Norreport. **Amenities:** Restaurant; bar; fitness center; 24-hr. room service; babysitting; laundry service/dry cleaning, nonsmoking rooms. *In room:* A/C, TV, dataport, minibar, hair dryer, safe.

Moderate

Absalon Hotel ⚑ *Value*　Since 1938 the Nedergaard family has been welcoming guests to their hotel, which has grown and expanded over the years in the neighborhood near the rail station. Today the hotel comprises a government-rated three-star hotel with private bathrooms, and a one-star annex without private bathrooms, the two hotels sharing the same entrance and reception. You can stay here in comparative luxury or at budget prices, depending on your choice of accommodations. Most bedrooms are medium in size or even somewhat cramped, but all are comfortably furnished and well maintained. If you want to stay here luxuriously, opt for one of the large and elegantly furnished top-floor rooms in a classical English or French Louis XIV style.

Helgolandsgade 15, DK-1653. København. © **33-24-22-11.** Fax 33-24-34-11. www.absalon-hotel.dk. 166 units. Absalon Hotel (with private bathroom): May–Sept 1,235DKK–1,700DKK ($193–$265) double; Oct–Apr 995DKK–1,525DKK ($155–$238) double. Annex (without private bathroom): May–Sept 725DKK ($113) double; Oct–Apr 600DKK ($94) double. Rates include breakfast. AE, DC, MC, V. Closed Dec 19–Jan 2. Bus: 6, 10, 16, 27, or 28. **Amenities:** Breakfast room; lounge; laundry service/dry cleaning; nonsmoking rooms. In room: TV, dataport (in some), fridge (in some), hair dryer (in some), safe (in some), trouser press (in some).

Ascot Hotel ⭑ ⟨Value⟩   On a side street, 180m (600 ft.) from the Tivoli and a 2-minute walk from Town Hall Square, sits one of Copenhagen's best small hotels. The Ascot was built in 1902 and enlarged and modernized in 1994. The furniture is standard but very comfortable, and a few of the units offer a kitchenette. The finest rooms open onto the street, though the rooms in the rear get better air circulation and more light. Bathrooms are large and tidily maintained.

Studiestræde 61, DK-1554 København. © **33-12-60-00.** Fax 33-14-60-40. www.ascothotel.dk. 165 units. 1,280DKK–1,480DKK ($200–$231) double; 1,695DKK–2,560DKK ($264–$399) suite. Rates include buffet breakfast. Winter discounts available. AE, DC, MC, V. Free parking. Bus: 2, 6, 8, 11, 14, 28, 29, 30, 34, 67, 68, 69, 150S, or 250S. Metro: Norreport. **Amenities:** Breakfast room; bar; fitness center; room service (7am–9pm); babysitting; laundry service/dry cleaning. In room: TV, hair dryer, kitchenette, safe.

Hotel Selandia   One of the better hotels behind the railroad station, this solidly built structure has been receiving guests since 1928, and has been renovated many times since. A longtime favorite of budget-conscious travelers, it is well-maintained, with comfortable, immaculately kept bedrooms. The furnishings in the midsize bedrooms are contemporary Scandinavian modern, and all units come with tidy bathrooms with shower/tub combinations. A good Danish breakfast is served in a ground-floor room.

Helgolandsgade 12, DK-1653 København. © **33-31-46-10.** Fax 33-31-4 6-10. Fax 33-31-46-09. www.hotelselandia.dk. 87 units, 57 with bathroom. 540DKK–650DKK ($84–$101) double without bathroom; 740DKK–1,150DKK ($115–$179) double with bathroom. Rates include breakfast. AE, DC, MC, V. Closed Dec 15–Jan 5. Bus 10 or 26. **Amenities:** Breakfast room; babysitting; laundry service/dry cleaning. In room: TV, minibar in some, hair dryer in some.

Kong Arthur ⭑ ⟨Value⟩   An orphanage when it was built in 1882, this hotel sits behind a private courtyard next to the tree-lined Peblinge Lake. Today it's an antiques-filled mansion of old-world charm. It's been completely renovated into a contemporary hostelry, and a recent expansion offers more spacious rooms, including 30 for nonsmokers. Bathrooms are medium-size.

Nørre Søgade 11, DK-1370 København. © **33-11-12-12.** Fax 33-32-61-30. www.kongarthur.dk. 107 units. 1,400DKK–1,600DKK ($218–$250) double; from 2,900DKK ($452) suite. Rates include buffet breakfast. AE, DC, MC, V. Free parking. Bus: 5, 8, 14, 42, or 43. **Amenities:** 3 restaurants; bar; sauna; 24-hr. room service; babysitting; laundry service/dry cleaning; nonsmoking rooms. In room: TV, dataport, minibar, hair dryer, safe, trouser press.

Inexpensive

Apartment Hotel Valberg   Simple but well kept, this five-story hotel in a charming building from 1903, is about a 10-minute walk from the Central Railroad Station. It was renovated in 2003 into apartment-style rooms, with each unit now featuring a kitchenette and bathroom. Breakfast is the only meal served.

Sønder Blvd. 53, DK-1720 København V. © **33-25-25-19.** Fax 33-25-25-83. www.valberg.dk. 15 units. 1,100DKK ($172) double. Extra bed 200DKK ($31). Rates include breakfast. DC, DISC, MC, V. Bus: 10. **Amenities:** Lounge. In room: TV, kitchenette, hair dryer.

WHERE TO DINE

That national institution, the smørrebrød (open-faced sandwich), is introduced at lunch. Literally, this means "bread and butter," but the Danes stack this sandwich as if it were the Leaning Tower of Pisa—then they throw in a slice of curled cucumber and bits of parsley or perhaps sliced peaches or a mushroom for added color.

NEAR KONGENS NYTORV & NYHAVN
Very Expensive

Era Ora ✿✿✿ ITALIAN This reminder of the "Golden Age" is on virtually everyone's list as the best Italian restaurant in Denmark, and is one of the consistently best restaurants of any kind within Copenhagen. Established in 1982 by Tuscan-born partners Alessandro and Elvio, it offers an antique-looking dining room. Enjoy a cuisine based on Tuscan and Umbrian models, with sophisticated variations inspired by Denmark's superb array of fresh seafood and produce. Traditional favorites include a platter of 10 types of antipasti. All pastas are freshly made every day. Depending on the season and the inspiration of the chef, main courses include succulent veal dishes, rack of venison with balsamic vinegar and chanterelles, and ultrafresh fish.

Overgaden Neden Vandet 33B. © **32-54-06-93.** Reservations required. Fixed-price menus 570DKK–690DKK ($89–$108). AE, DC, MC, V. Mon–Sat 6:30pm–midnight. Bus: 2, 8, or 48.

Godt ✿✿✿ INTERNATIONAL This small-scale favorite is known to everyone in the neighborhood, including the queen of Denmark. Despite its fame, there's an appealing lack of pretentiousness here. Food is prepared fresh every day, based on ingredients that are the best at the market. The repertoire served here is splendid and the atmosphere so special it is worth reserving for your final night in Copenhagen. Some exciting new dishes on the menu include quail stuffed with foie gras served with a salad of apple and celery; venison with a sauce of wild mushrooms; or fresh fish marinated in black currant served with a sauce of almonds, vanilla, and fresh berries.

Gothersgade 38. © **33-15-21-22.** Reservations required. Fixed-price menus 480DKK–600DKK ($75–$94). DC, MC, V. Tues–Sat 6–10pm. Closed July and Dec 23–Jan 3. Bus: 6, 10, or 14.

Kommandanten ✿✿ DANISH/FRENCH Built in 1698 as the residence of the city's military commander, this deluxe restaurant is the epitome of Danish chic and charm. The menu offers a mouthwatering array of classical dishes mixed with innovative selections, a medley of strong yet subtle flavors. The finest seasonal ingredients are used, and the menu changes every 2 weeks. You might be offered the grilled catch of the day, Danish deer with a Jerusalem artichoke fricassee, grilled turbot with olive sauce, or gratiné of shellfish. The service is the best in Copenhagen.

Ny Adelgade 7. © **33-12-09-90.** Reservations required. Main courses 310DKK–330DKK ($48–$51); 3-course menu 690DKK ($108). AE, DC, MC, V. Mon–Fri noon–2pm; Mon–Sat 6–10pm. Bus: 1, 2, 5, or 6.

Kong Hans Kaelder ✿✿✿ MODERN DANISH/INTERNATIONAL Housed in the oldest building in the city that's still in commercial use, this vaulted Gothic cellar may be the best restaurant in Denmark. Its most serious competition comes from Kommandanten, which many discriminating palates hail as the best. On "the oldest corner of Copenhagen," the restaurant has been carefully restored and is now a Relais Gourmand. A typical three-course dinner would include smoked salmon from the restaurant's smokehouse, breast of duck with *bigarade* (sour orange) sauce, and plum ice cream with Armagnac. If you dine here, prepare for innovation and delightful taste sensations, as evoked by slightly smoked scallops with a side of Sevruga caviar. Another signature dish is sautéed lobster with Jerusalem artichokes in a soy-ginger butter. These dishes can be served as either a starter or a main course.

Vingårdsstræde 6. (*C*) **33-11-68-68.** Reservations required. Main courses 225DKK–450DKK ($35–$70); fixed-price menus 700DKK–800DKK ($109–$125). AE, DC, DISC, MC, V. Mon–Sat 6pm–10pm. Closed July 20–Aug 4, Dec 24–26. Bus: 1, 6, or 9.

Moderate

Café Lumskebugten ★ *Finds* DANISH   This restaurant is a well-managed bastion of Danish charm, with an unpretentious elegance. Now-legendary matriarch Karen Marguerita Krog established it in 1854 as a rowdy tavern for sailors. A tastefully gentrified version of the original beef hash is still served. Two glistening-white dining rooms are decorated with antique ships' models, oil paintings, and pinewood floors. The food and service are excellent. Specialties include tartar of salmon with herbs, Danish fish cakes with mustard sauce and minced beet root, sugar-marinated salmon with mustard-cream sauce, and a symphony of fish with saffron sauce and new potatoes. A filling lunch platter of assorted house specialties is offered for 225DKK ($35).

Esplanaden 21. (*C*) **33-15-60-29.** Reservations recommended. Main courses 195DKK–250DKK ($30–$39); 3-course fixed-price lunch 395DKK ($62); 4-course fixed-price dinner 595DKK ($93). AE, DC, MC, V. Mon–Fri 11am–10:30pm; Sat 4–10:30pm. Bus: 1, 6, or 8.

Restaurant Els DANISH/FRENCH   With its original 1854 decor and murals by the famous 19th-century Danish artist, Christian Hitsch, this is one of the most respected and traditional restaurants of Copenhagen, attracting such clients as Hans Christian Andersen. If you're dropping in for lunch, you might make an entire meal out of those delectable open-faced Danish sandwiches, but in the evening the market-fresh menu is based on an expanded, mainly French-inspired repertoire. You'll feast on dishes made with prime ingredients, including breast of wild duck with blackberry sauce and other tasty delights.

Store Strandstraede 3, off Kongens Nytorv. (*C*) **33-14-13-41.** Reservations recommended. Main courses 45DKK–115DKK ($7–$18) lunch, 178DKK–225DKK ($28–$35) dinner. AE, DC, MC, V. Mon–Sat noon–3pm; daily 5:30–10pm. Bus: 1, 6, or 10.

Inexpensive

Ida Davidsen ★ *Kids* SANDWICHES   This restaurant has flourished since 1888, when the forebears of its present owner, Ida Davidsen, established a sandwich shop. Today, five generations later, the matriarch and namesake is known as the "smørrebrød queen of Copenhagen." Her restaurant sells a greater variety of open-faced sandwiches (250 kinds) than any other in Denmark. The fare has even been featured at royal buffets at Amalienborg Castle. You select by pointing to your choice in a glass-fronted display case; a staff member carries it to your table. The vast selection includes salmon, lobster, smoked duck with braised cabbage and horseradish, liver pâté, ham, and boiled egg. Two of them, perhaps with a slice of cheese, make a worthy lunch. If in doubt, a member of the service team, or perhaps Ida's charming husband, Adam Siesbye, will offer suggestions.

Store Kongensgade 70. (*C*) **33-91-36-55.** Reservations recommended. Sandwiches 35DKK–250DKK ($5.45–$39). AE, DC, MC, V. Mon–Fri 10am–4pm. Bus: 6, 9, or 15.

NEAR RÅDHUSPLADSEN & TIVOLI
Moderate

Copenhagen Corner *Kids* SCANDINAVIAN   In the very heart of Copenhagen, this restaurant opens onto Rådhuspladsen, around the corner from the Tivoli Gardens. It offers well-prepared, unpretentious, and reasonably priced meals. The menu features the Danes' favorite dishes, beginning with three kinds of herring or freshly peeled shrimp with dill and lemon. The fish is fresh and beautifully prepared, especially the steamed Norwegian salmon with a "lasagna" of potatoes, and baked halibut with artichokes. Meat and poultry courses, although not always equal to the fish, are tasty and tender, especially the veal liver Provençal.

H. C. Andersens Blvd. 1A. 🕐 **33-91-45-45**. Reservations recommended. Main courses 89DKK–289DKK ($14–$45); 3-course fixed-price menu 298DKK ($46). AE, DC, MC, V. Daily 11:30am–11pm. Bus: 1, 6, or 8.

Søren K ⭐ MODERN/EUROPEAN   Named after Denmark's most celebrated philosopher, this is an artfully minimalist dining room that's on the ground floor of the newest addition to the Royal Library. Opened in 1999, it has big-windowed views that stretch out over the sea. Menu items change frequently, but might include carpaccio of veal, foie gras, oyster soup, and main courses such as veal chops served with lobster sauce and a half-lobster, and venison roasted with nuts and seasonal berries and a marinade of green tomatoes. The restaurant virtually never cooks with butter, cream, or high-cholesterol cheeses, making a meal here a dietetic as well as a savory experience.

On the ground floor of the Royal Library's Black Diamond Wing, 1 Søren Kierkegaards Plads. 🕐 **33-47-49-49**. Reservations recommended. Main courses 75DKK–130DKK ($12–$20) lunch, 195€ ($224) dinner. 2-course fixed price dinner 215DKK ($34); 3-course fixed-price dinner 350DKK ($55). AE, DC, MC, V. Mon–Sat noon–midnight. Bus: 8.

Inexpensive

Axelborg Bodega DANISH   Across from the Benneweis Circus and near Scala and the Tivoli, this 1912 cafe has outdoor tables where you can enjoy a brisk Scandinavian evening. Order the *dagens ret* (daily special). Typical Danish dishes are featured, including *frikadeller* (meatballs) and pork chops. A wide selection of club sandwiches is also available for 65DKK to 82DKK ($10–$13) each. Although the atmosphere is somewhat impersonal, this is a local favorite; diners enjoy recipes that seem drawn from Grandma's kitchen.

Axeltorv 1. 🕐 **33-11-06-38**. Reservations recommended. Main courses 74DKK–135DKK ($9.70–$18). AE, DC, MC, V. Daily 11:30am–8:45pm; bar daily 10am–2am. Bus: 1 or 6.

Domhus Kælderen DANISH/INTERNATIONAL   The good food at this bustling, old-fashioned emporium of Danish cuisine draws a mixed crowd from City Hall's courtrooms across the square as well as visiting foreigners. The half-cellar room holds memorabilia from its 50 years as a restaurant (before that, it was a butcher shop). Lunch tends to be more conservative and more Danish than dinner. It might include *frikadeller* (meatballs) and heaping platters of herring, cheeses, smoked meats and fish, and salads. Dinner could be pickled salmon; prime rib of beef with horseradish; and fine cuts of beef, served with béarnaise or pepper sauce. Also look for the catch of the day, prepared just about any way you like. You get no culinary surprises here, but you're rarely disappointed.

Nytorv 5. 🕐 **33-14-84-55**. Reservations recommended. Main courses 38DKK–128DKK ($5.95–$20) lunch, 158DKK–188DKK ($25–$29) dinner. AE, DC, MC, V. Daily 11am–4pm and 5:30–10:30pm. Bus: 8.

NEAR ROSENBORG SLOT
Very Expensive

Skt. Gertruds Kloster ⭐ INTERNATIONAL   Near Nørreport Station and south of Rosenborg Castle, this is the most romantic restaurant in town. There's no electricity in the labyrinth of 14th-century underground vaults, and the 1,500 flickering candles, open grill, iron sconces, and rough-hewn furniture create an elegant medieval ambience. The food is equally impressive. Try the fresh homemade foie gras with black truffles; lobster served in turbot bouillon; scallops sautéed with herbs in sauterne; venison with green asparagus and truffle sauce; or fish and shellfish terrine studded with chunks of lobster and salmon.

Hauser Plads 32. ⓒ 33-14-66-30. Reservations required. Main courses 198DKK–248DKK ($31–$39); 3-course dinner 398DKK ($62); 6-course dinner 608DKK ($95). AE, DC, MC, V. Daily 4pm–midnight (close at 11pm on Sun). Closed Dec 25–Jan 1. Bus: 14 or 16. Metro: Norreport.

AT GRÅBRØDRETORV
Moderate

Bøf & Ost DANISH/FRENCH   "Beef & Cheese" is housed in a 1728 building, and its cellars come from a medieval monastery. In summer, a pleasant outdoor terrace overlooks Gray Friars Square. Although the menu changes monthly, specialties can include lobster soup, fresh Danish bay strips, a cheese plate with six selections, and some of the best grilled tenderloin in town. One local diner confided: "The food is not worthy of God's own table, but it's so good I come here once a week."

Gråbrødretorv 13. ⓒ 33-11-99-11. Reservations required. Main courses 165DKK–195DKK ($26–$30); fixed-price lunch 89DKK–188DKK ($14–$29). DC, MC, V. Mon–Sat 11:30am–10:30pm. Closed Jan 1, Dec 24–25. Bus: 5.

Peder Oxe's Restaurant/Vinkælder Wine Bar DANISH/ASIAN   This romantic building dates from the 1700s, with its original wooden floors and Portuguese tiles, and the crowd is young, fun, and value conscious. The salad bar is 20DKK ($3.10) when accompanied by a main course. It's so tempting that many prefer to enjoy it alone for 56DKK ($8.75) per person. Dishes include lobster soup, Danish bay shrimp, fresh asparagus, open-faced sandwiches, hamburgers, and fresh fish. Specialties influenced by Asia have recently been added to the menu, including such delights as tuna tartare with avocado and mango.

Gråbrødretorv 11. ⓒ 33-11-00-77. Reservations recommended. Main courses 85DKK–189DKK ($13–$29); fixed-price lunches 80DKK–118DKK ($12–$18). DC, MC, V. Daily 11:30am–midnight. Bus: 5.

Inexpensive

Pasta Basta *Value* ITALIAN/INTERNATIONAL   This restaurant's main attraction is an enormous buffet (sometimes called the "Pasta Basta Table") loaded with cold antipasti and salads. With more than nine selections, it's one of the best deals in town at 69DKK ($11). The restaurant is divided into half a dozen cozy dining rooms decorated in the style of ancient Pompeii, with faded frescoes patterned after originals from Italy. It's on a historic cobblestone street off the main shopping street, Strøget. Menu choices include at least 15 kinds of pasta (all made fresh on the premises); a platter with three kinds of Danish caviar (whitefish, speckled trout, and vendace, served with chopped onions, lemon, toast, and butter); fresh mussels cooked in dry white wine with pasta and creamy saffron sauce; thinly sliced salmon with a cream-based sauce of salmon roe; and sliced Danish suckling lamb with fried spring onions and tarragon.

Valkendorfsgade 22. ⓒ 33-11-21-31. Reservations recommended. Main courses 70DKK–165DKK ($11–$26). DC, MC, V. Sun–Thurs 11:30am–3am; Fri–Sat 11:30am–5:30am. Bus: 5.

AT CHRISTIANSBORG
Very Expensive

Krogs Fiskerestaurant ⭐ SEAFOOD A short walk from Christiansborg Castle, the most famous restaurant in the district was built in 1789 as a fish shop. The canal-side plaza where fishers once moored their boats is now the site of the restaurant's outdoor dining terrace. The restaurant serves fresh seafood in a single large room decorated in antique style, with old oil paintings. The well-chosen menu includes lobster soup, bouillabaisse, oysters, mussels steamed in white wine, and poached salmon trout with saffron sauce. Each dish is impeccably prepared and flavorful. A selection of meat dishes is available, but the fish is better.

Gammel Strand 38. ℂ **33-15-89-15.** Reservations required. Main courses 315DKK–635DKK ($49–$99); 5-course fixed-price menu 735DKK ($115). AE, DC, MC, V. Mon–Sat noon–4pm and 6-10:30pm. Bus: 1, 2, 10, 16, or 29.

Expensive

Sonoma California Grille & Lounge ⭐ *Finds* CALIFORNIAN/PACIFIC RIM As a sign of changing times, this brand-new restaurant has opened on the site of Den Gyldne Fortun (Golden Fortune) a dining room that since 1796 attracted the likes of Hans Christian Andersen, Jenny Lind, and Henry Wadsworth Longfellow. Copenhagen has rarely seen cuisine like this, heavily influenced by the kitchens of California, Hawaii, Japan, and Mexico, with farm-raised seasonal produce prepared in the healthiest and tastiest of fashion. Even the desserts are unusual for this Danish city: passionfruit soufflé or, get this, a grilled pineapple lasagna. Naturally, California wines are heavily featured on on the menu.

Ved Stranden 18. ℂ **33-12-20-11.** Reservations recommended. Main courses 176DKK–205DKK ($27–$32); 4-course fixed-price menu 369DKK ($58). AE, DC, MC, V. Daily 11am–midnight. Bus: 1, 6, or 10.

Inexpensive

Cafeen Nikolaj DANISH This place makes no pretense of being more than it is: a simple cafe that prepares good-tasting food with fresh ingredients at fair prices. The cafe, which evokes Greenwich Village in the 1950s, lies on the site where Hans Tausen, a father of the Danish Reformation, delivered thundering sermons in the 16th century. No one is thundering now—they're ordering an array of typical Danish lunches, including a tasty variety of open-faced sandwiches and homemade soups. You can always count on various types of herring. Danish sliced ham on good homemade bread is a perennial favorite, and there is also a selection of Danish cheeses.

Nikolaj Plads 12. ℂ **70-26-64-64.** Main courses 60DKK–130DKK ($9.35–$20). 3-course meal 190DKK ($30). AE, DC, MC, V. Mon–Sat 11:30am–5pm. Bus: 2, 6, 8, or 10.

IN TIVOLI

Food prices inside Tivoli are about 30% higher than elsewhere. Try skipping dessert at a restaurant and picking up a less expensive treat at one of the many stands. Take bus no. 1, 6, 8, 16, 29, 30, 32, or 33 to reach the park and either of the following restaurants. *Note:* These restaurants are only open from May to mid-September.

Very Expensive

La Crevette ⭐⭐ SEAFOOD/CONTINENTAL For one really big splurge meal before you leave Copenhagen, reserve a table at this classic restaurant housed in a 1909 pavilion with an outdoor terrace in the middle of the Tivoli

Gardens. Some of the freshest and best seafood in Copenhagen is served at this restaurant by chefs who dare to be innovative while still adhering to classic culinary principles. Most dishes here are "sure bets," including such Danish delights as marinated slices of salmon with oyster flan and egg cream with chives or grilled sea bass and scampi on crispy spinach and sautéed eggplant.

Vesterbrogade 3, Tivoli Gardens. © **33-14-68-47.** Reservations required. Main courses 225DKK–315DKK ($34–$47); 4-course, fixed-price dinner 445DKK ($67). AE, DC, MC, V. Daily noon–10pm.

Moderate

Færgekroen DANISH   In a cluster of trees at the edge of the lake, this restaurant resembles a pink half-timbered Danish cottage. In warm weather, try to sit on the outside terrace. The menu offers drinks, snacks, and full meals. Meals might include omelets, beef with horseradish, fried plaice (a flounderlike fish) with melted butter, pork chops with red cabbage, curried chicken, or fried meatballs. If you like honest and straightforward fare, without fancy trimmings, and don't like to spend a lot of money, this is the place for you. A pianist provides singalong music every evening starting at 8pm.

Vesterbrogade 3, Tivoli. © **33-12-94-12.** Main courses 95DKK–195DKK ($15–$30); fixed-price lunch 125DKK–140DKK ($20–$22). AE, DC, MC, V. Daily 11am–midnight (hot food until 9:45pm).

EXPLORING COPENHAGEN

SIGHTSEEING SUGGESTIONS FOR FIRST-TIME VISITORS

If You Have 1 Day Take a walking tour through the heart of the old city, which will give you time to recover from jet lag. Spend the late afternoon at **Christiansborg Palace** on Slotsholmen Island, where the queen of Denmark receives guests. Early in the evening, head to the Tivoli.

If You Have 2 Days On day 2, visit **Amalienborg Palace,** the queen's residence. Try to time your visit to witness the changing of the guard. Continue beyond the palace to *The Little Mermaid* statue. In the afternoon, see the **art treasures** of Ny Carlsberg Glyptotek. At night, seek out a local tavern.

If You Have 3 Days On the morning of the third day, journey to **Rosenborg Castle,** summer palace of King Christian IV, then wander through the park and gardens. Have lunch at one of the restaurants lining the canal at Nyhavn, the traditional seamans' quarter of Copenhagen. In the afternoon, go to **Rundetårn (Round Tower)** for a panoramic view of the city, and if time remains, stop in at the **National Museum** and **Denmark's Fight for Freedom Museum.**

If You Have 4 Days Head north to **Louisiana,** the modern-art museum, and continue on to Helsingør to visit **Kronborg Castle,** famously associated with Shakespeare's *Hamlet.* Return by train to Copenhagen in time for a stroll along the Strøget, Europe's longest walking street. For dinner, visit the village of Dragør.

If You Have 5 Days On the fifth day, visit **Frilandsmuseet,** at Lyngby, a half-hour train ride from Copenhagen. Have lunch at the park. Return to Copenhagen and take a walking tour along its canals. If time remains, tour the **Carlsberg brewery.** Pay a final visit to the Tivoli to cap your adventure in the Danish capital.

Copenhagen's *Little Mermaid*

The one statue *everybody* wants to see is the life-size bronze of **Den Lille Havfrue** ⚓, inspired by Hans Christian Andersen's "The Little Mermaid," one of the world's most famous fairy tales. The statue, unveiled in 1913, was sculpted by Edvard Eriksen and rests on rocks right off the shore. The mermaid has been attacked more than once, losing an arm in one misadventure, decapitated as recently as January 6, 1998. The latest attack occurred in the early morning hours in September 2003 when explosives may have been used to topple the statue from its stone base. The much-abused statue is based on a mythical sea king's mermaid daughter who, according to the Hans Christian Andersen tale, falls in love with a prince and must wait 300 years to become human.

All year, a 2½-hour **City and Harbor Tour** of Copenhagen makes a significant stop at the *Little Mermaid* and costs 180DKK ($28) adults, 90DKK ($14) children. For more information, call Copenhagen Excursions at ℭ **32-54-06-06**. In summer, a special "Mermaid Bus" leaves from Rådhuspladsen (Vester Voldgade) at 9am and then at half-hour intervals until 5:30pm. On the "Langelinie" bus there's a 20-minute stop at *The Little Mermaid.* If you want more time, take bus no. 1, 6, or 9.

THE TIVOLI GARDENS

Tivoli Gardens ★★ Since it opened in 1843, this 8-hectare (20-acre) garden and amusement park in the center of Copenhagen has been a resounding success, with its thousands of flowers, a merry-go-round of tiny Viking ships, games of chance and skill (pinball arcades, slot machines, shooting galleries), and a Ferris wheel of hot-air balloons and cabin seats. There's even a playground.

An Arabian-style fantasy palace, with towers and arches, houses more than two dozen restaurants in all price ranges, from a lakeside inn to a beer garden. Take a walk around the edge of the tiny lake, with its ducks, swans, and boats.

Tivoli's newest attraction, a state-of-the-art **roller coaster,** was scheduled to open in spring 2004 at a cost of 10,000,000€. It will be the fastest, tallest roller coaster in Denmark.

A parade of the red-uniformed Tivoli Boys Guard takes place on weekends at 5:30 and 7:30pm, and their regimental band gives concerts Saturday at 3pm on the open-air stage. The oldest building at Tivoli, the Chinese-style Pantomime Theater, with its peacock curtain, stages pantomimes in the evening.

Vesterbrogade 3. ℭ **33-15-10-01**. Admission 55DKK–65DKK ($8.60–$10) adults, 30DKK–35DKK ($4.70–$5.45) children under 14; combination ticket including admission and all rides 190DKK ($30). May to mid-Sept daily 11am–midnight. Partial Christmastime opening from mid-Nov until Christmas Eve (reduced admission). Closed mid-Sept to Apr. Bus: 1 or 16.

THE TOP MUSEUMS

Don't worry about not understanding the explanations in the museums; virtually all have write-ups in English.

Ny Carlsberg Glyptotek ★★★ The Glyptotek, behind the Tivoli, is one of Scandinavia's most important art museums. Founded by 19th-century art collector Carl Jacobsen, the museum holds modern art and antiquities. The modern section has both French and Danish art, mainly from the 19th century; sculpture, including works by Rodin; and works of the Impressionists and related artists, including van Gogh's *Landscape from St-Rémy*. Antiquities include Egyptian, Greek, Roman, and Etruscan works. The Egyptian collection is outstanding; the prize is a prehistoric rendering of a hippopotamus. A favorite of ours is the Etruscan art display. In 1996, the Ny Glyptotek added a French Masters' wing, where you'll find an extensive collection of masterpieces.

Dantes Plads 7. (℃) **33-41-81-41.** Admission 40DKK ($6.25) adults, free for children; free for all Wed and Sun. Tues–Sun 10am–4pm. Bus: 1, 2, 5, 6, 8, or 10.

Statens Museum for Kunst (Royal Museum of Fine Arts) ★★ This well-stocked museum, one of the best in Scandinavia, houses painting and sculpture from the 13th century to the present. There are Dutch golden-age landscapes and marine paintings by Rubens, plus portraits by Frans Hals and Rembrandt. Eckersberg, Købke, and Hansen represent the Danish golden age. French 20th-century art includes 20 works by Matisse. In the Royal Print Room are 300,000 drawings, prints, lithographs, and other works by such artists as Dürer, Rembrandt, Matisse, and Picasso.

A major expansion in 1998 added a concert hall, a Children's Art Museum, and a glass wing designed for temporary exhibits.

Sølvgade 48–50. (℃) **33-74-84-94.** Admission 30DKK–60DKK ($4.70–$9.35) adults, 25DKK–45DKK ($3.90–$7) students, free for children under 16. Higher admission for special exhibitions only. Tues and Thurs–Sun 10am–5pm; Wed 10am–8pm. Bus: 6, 8, 10, 14, 40, 42, 43, 184, or 185.

Den Hirschsprungske Samling (The Hirschsprung Collection) This collection of 19th- and early-20th-century Danish art is in Ostre Anlaeg, a park in the city center. Tobacco merchant Heinrich Hirschsprung (1836–1908) created the collection, and it has been growing ever since. The emphasis is on the Danish golden age, with such artists as Eckersberg, Købke, and Lundbye, and on the Skagen painters, P. S. Krøyer, and Anna and Michael Ancher. Some furnishings from the artists' homes are exhibited.

Stockholmsgade 20. (℃) **35-42-03-36.** Admission 35DKK ($5.45) adults, free for children under 16. Wed–Mon 11am–4pm. Bus: 14, 40, 42, 43, 150, or 184.

Nationalmuseet (National Museum) ★★★ A gigantic repository of anthropological artifacts, this museum features objects from prehistory, the Middle Ages, and the Renaissance in Denmark, including Viking stones, helmets, and fragments of battle gear. Especially interesting are the "lur" horn, a Bronze Age musical instrument among the oldest in Europe, and the world-famous Sun Chariot, an elegant Bronze Age piece of pagan art. The Royal Collection of Coins and Medals contains various coins from antiquity. There are also outstanding collections of Egyptian and Classical antiquities.

Ny Vestergade 10. (℃) **33-13-44-11.** Admission 50DKK ($7.80) adults, 40DKK ($6.25) students, free for children under 16. Tues–Sun 10am–5pm. Closed Dec 24, 25, and 31. Bus: 1, 5, 6, 8, or 10.

Frihedsmuseet (Museum of Danish Resistance, 1940–45) The horrors of the Nazi occupation of Denmark live on here. On display are relics of torture and concentration camps, the equipment used by the Danish resistance for forbidden wireless communications and the production of illegal propaganda films, British propaganda leaflets, satirical caricatures of Hitler, information about both Danish Jews and Danish Nazis, and the paralyzing nationwide strikes. Also look for an armed car used for drive-by shootings of Danish Nazi informers and collaborators.

Churchillparken. ℂ **33-13-77-14**. Admission 40DKK ($6.25) adults, free for children under 16. May–Sept 15 Tues–Sat 10am–4pm, Sun 10am–5pm; Sept 16 to Apr Tues–Sat 11am–3pm, Sun 11am–4pm. Bus: 1 or 6.

Frilandsmuseet (Open-Air Museum) ⭐
This reconstructed village in Lyngby, on the fringe of Copenhagen, captures Denmark's one-time rural character. The "museum" is nearly 36 hectares (90 acres); a 3.2km (2-mile) walk around the compound reveals a dozen authentic buildings—farmsteads, windmills, fishers' cottages. Exhibits include a half-timbered 18th-century farmstead from one of the tiny windswept Danish islands, a primitive longhouse from the remote Faroe Islands, thatched fishers' huts from Jutland, tower windmills, and a mid-19th-century potter's workshop.

Kongevejen 100. ℂ **33-13-44-11**. Admission 50DKK ($7.80) adults, 40DKK ($6.25) students and seniors, free for children under 16. Easter–Sept Tues–Sun 10am–5pm; Oct 1–18 Tues–Sun 10am–4pm. Closed Oct 19–Easter. S-tog: Copenhagen Central Station to Sorgenfri (trains leave every 20 min.). Bus: 184 or 194.

Erotica Museum ⭐
This is the only museum in the world where you can learn about the sex lives of Freud, Marilyn Monroe, Hugh Hefner, Nietzsche, and Duke Ellington. Founded by Ole Ege, a well-known Danish photographer of nudes, it's within walking distance of the Tivoli and the Central Railroad Station. In addition to revealing a glimpse into the sex lives of the famous, it presents a survey of erotica around the world and through the ages. The exhibits range from Etruscan drawings and Chinese paintings to Greek vases depicting sexual activity.

Købmagergade 24. ℂ **33-12-03-11**. Admission 79DKK ($12) without museum catalog, 99DKK ($15) with catalog. May–Sept daily 10am–11pm; Oct–Apr Mon–Thurs 11am–8pm, Fri-Sat 10am–10pm, Sun 11am–8pm. S-tog: Nørreport. Those ages 16–18 must be accompanied by an adult. No one under 16 admitted.

Tøjhusmuseet (Royal Arsenal Museum)
This museum features a fantastic display of weapons used for hunting and warfare. On the ground floor is the Canon Hall, the longest vaulted Renaissance hall in Europe, stocked with artillery equipment dating from 1500 up to the present day. Above the Canon Hall is the impressive Armory Hall, which houses one of the world's finest collections of small arms, colors, and armor.

Tøjhusgade 3. ℂ **33-11-60-37**. Admission 40DKK ($6.25) adults, 20DKK ($3.10) students and seniors, free for children under 15. Tues–Sun noon–4pm. Closed Jan 1, Dec 23–26 and 31. Bus: 1, 2, 5, 6, 8, 10, 28, 29, 30, 32, 33, or 42.

Amalienborg Palace ⭐⭐
These four 18th-century French-inspired rococo mansions are the home of the Danish royal family, a position they have held since 1794, when the original royal palace burned. Visitors flock to witness the changing of the guard at noon when the royal family is in residence. A swallow-tail flag at mast signifies that the queen is in Copenhagen. The Royal Life Guard in black bearskin busbies leaves Rosenborg Castle at 11:30am and marches to Amalienborg. After the event, the guard, still accompanied by the band, returns to Rosenborg Castle.

In 1994, some of the official and private rooms in Amalienborg were opened to the public for the first time. The rooms, reconstructed to reflect the period 1863 to 1947, belonged to members of the reigning royal family, the Glücksborgs, who ascended the throne in 1863. The highlight is the period devoted to the long reign (1863–1906) of King Christian IX and Queen Louise.

Native Behavior

If you want to be taken for a real Copenhagener, rent a bike and pedal your way around the city, up and down its streets and along its canals. It's estimated that half the population does the same.

After all that exercise, do as the Danes do and order your fill of smørrebrød for lunch. Sold all over the city, these are open-faced sandwiches on which Danes are known to pile almost anything edible. Our favorite is a mound of baby shrimp, although roast beef topped with pickle is another tasty offering. And to top off the native experience, order aquavit (also called snaps in Denmark) with your lunch, though less reliable stomachs may opt instead for a Carlsberg or Tuborg beer.

Whatever you do, though, don't tell any Dane that you eat pancakes for breakfast. In Denmark, a pancake is strictly a dessert.

And finally, greet everyone you encounter with a *"God dag"* ("Good day"). If you do, you'll no doubt end up having one yourself.

Christian VIII's Palace. ℭ **33-12-21-86.** Admission 45DKK ($7) adults, 25DKK ($3.90) students and seniors, 10DKK ($1.55) children 5–12, free for children under 5. Oct–May Tues–Sun 11am–4pm; June–Aug daily 7am–4pm; Sept daily 11am–4pm. Closed Dec 14–25. Bus: 1, 6, 9, or 10.

Christiansborg Palace ✦ This granite-and-copper palace on the Slotsholmen—a small island that has been the center of political power in Denmark for more than 800 years—houses the Danish parliament, the Supreme Court, the prime minister's offices, and the Royal Reception Rooms. A guide will lead you through richly decorated rooms, including the Throne Room, banqueting hall, and Queen's Library. Before entering, you'll be asked to put on soft overshoes to protect the floors. Under the palace, visit the well-preserved ruins of the 1167 castle of Bishop Absalon, founder of Copenhagen.

Christiansborg Slotsplads. ℭ **33-92-64-92.** Royal Reception Rooms 45DKK ($7) adults, 10DKK ($1.55) children; parliament free; castle ruins 20DKK ($3.10) adults, 5DKK ($.80) children. Reception rooms guided tours May–Sept daily at 11am, 1pm, and 3pm; Oct–Apr Tues–Thurs and Sat–Sun at 3pm. Parliament English-language tours daily 3pm year-round. Ruins May–Sept daily 10am–4pm; Oct–Apr Tues–Sun 10am–4pm.

Rosenborg Castle ✦✦✦ This redbrick Renaissance-style castle houses everything from narwhal-tusk and ivory coronation chairs to Frederik VII's baby shoes—all from the Danish royal family. Its biggest draws are the dazzling crown jewels and regalia in the basement Treasury, where a lavishly decorated coronation saddle from 1596 is also shown. Try to see the Knights Hall (room no. 21), with its coronation seat, three silver lions, and relics from the 1700s. Room no. 3 was used by founding father Christian IV, who died in this bedroom decorated with Asian lacquer art and a stucco ceiling.

Øster Voldgade 4A. ℭ **33-15-32-86.** Admission 60DKK ($9.35) adults, 30DKK ($4.70) students and seniors, 10DKK ($1.55) children 5–12, free for children 4 and under. Palace and treasury (royal jewels), June–Aug daily 10am–5pm; May and Sept to mid-Oct daily 10am–4pm; mid-Oct to Apr Tues–Sun 11am–3pm. S-tog: Nørreport. Bus: 5, 10, 14, 16, 31, 42, 43, 184, or 185. Metro: Norreport.

CHURCHES & OTHER ATTRACTIONS

Frederikskirke This 2-centuries-old church, with its green copper dome—one of the largest in the world—is a short walk from Amalienborg Palace. After an unsuccessful start during the neoclassical revival of the 1750s in Denmark, the church was finally completed in Roman baroque style in 1894. In many ways, it's more impressive than Copenhagen's cathedral.

Frederiksgade 4. ☎ **33-15-37-63.** Free admission to church; dome 20DKK ($3.10) adults, 10DKK ($1.55) children. Church Mon, Tues, Thurs 10am–5pm; Wed 10am–6pm; Fri–Sun noon–5pm. Dome June–Sept 1 daily 1–3pm; Sept 2–May Sat–Sun 1–3pm. Bus: 1, 6, or 9.

Vor Frue Kirke (Copenhagen Cathedral)   This early-19th-century Greek Revival–style church, near Copenhagen University, features Bertel Thorvaldsen's white marble neoclassical works, including *Christ and the Apostles.* The funeral of H. C. Andersen took place here in 1875, and that of Søren Kierkegaard in 1855.

Nørregade 8. ☎ **33-15-10-78.** Free admission. Mon–Thurs 8:30am-5pm; Fri 8:30am–10:30am and noon–5pm; Sat 8:30am–5pm; Sun noon–4:30pm. Bus: 5.

Rådhus (Town Hall) and World Clock ✦   Built in 1905, the Town Hall has impressive statues of H. C. Andersen and Niels Bohr, the Nobel Prize–winning physicist. Jens Olsen's famous **World Clock** is open for viewing Monday through Friday from 10am to 4pm and Saturday at noon. The clockwork is so exact that the variation over 300 years is 0.4 seconds. Climb the tower for an impressive view.

Rådhuspladsen. ☎ **33-66-25-82.** Rådhus 30DKK ($4.70); clock 10DKK ($1.55) adults, 5DKK (80¢) children. Guided tour: 30DKK ($4.70) adults or children. Rådhus Mon–Fri 3pm; tower Mon–Sat noon. Bus: 1, 6, or 8.

Rundetårn (Round Tower) ✦   This 17th-century public observatory, attached to a church, is visited by thousands who climb the spiral ramp (no steps) for a panoramic view of Copenhagen. The tower is one of the crowning architectural achievements of the Christian IV era. Peter the Great, in Denmark on a state visit, galloped up the ramp on horseback.

Købmagergade 52A. ☎ **33-73-03-73.** Admission 20DKK ($3.10) adults, 5DKK ($.80) children. Tower June–Aug Mon–Sat 10am–8pm, Sun noon–8pm; Sept–May Mon–Sat 10am–5pm, Sun noon–5pm. Observatory Oct 15–Mar 20 Tues–Wed 7–10pm. Bus: 5, 14, 16, or 42. Metro: Norreport.

Botanisk Have (Botanical Gardens)   Planted from 1871 to 1874, the Botanical Gardens, across from Rosenborg Castle, are on a lake that was once part of the city's defensive moat. Special features include a cactus house and a palm house, all of which appear even more exotic in the far northern country of Denmark. An alpine garden contains mountain plants from all over the world.

Gothersgade 128. ☎ **35-32-22-40.** Free admission. May–Sept daily 8:30am–6pm; Oct–Apr Tues–Sun 8:30am–4pm. S-tog: Nørreport. Bus: 5, 7, 14, 16, or 24.

ORGANIZED TOURS

BUS & BOAT TOURS   For orientation, try the 1½-hour **City Tour** (2½ hr. with a visit to a brewery) that covers major scenic highlights like *The Little Mermaid,* Rosenborg Castle, and Amalienborg Palace. On workdays, tours also visit the Carlsberg brewery. Tours depart daily at 1pm from May 30 to September 30 and cost 130DKK ($20) adults and 65DKK ($10) children.

The **City and Harbor Tour,** a 2½-hour trip by launch and bus, departs from Town Hall Square. The boat tours the city's main canals, passing *The Little Mermaid* and the Old Fish Market. It operates from May 30 to September 13. Tours cost 175DKK ($27) adults and 65DKK ($10) children under 12.

Shakespeare buffs will be interested in an afternoon excursion to the castles of North Zealand. The 7-hour English-language tour explores the area north of Copenhagen, including a visit to Kronborg (Hamlet's Castle); a brief trip to Fredensborg, the queen's residence; and a stopover at Frederiksborg Castle and the

National Historical Museum. Tours depart from the Town Hall Square May 2 through October 16, Wednesday, Saturday, and Sunday at 9:30am; November to April Wednesday to Sunday 9:30am. The cost is 400DKK ($62) adults, half price for children.

For more information about these tours, contact **Copenhagen Excursions** (© **32-54-06-06;** www.cex.dk).

GUIDED WALKS THROUGH COPENHAGEN   Staff members of the Copenhagen Tourist Information Office conduct 2-hour guided walking tours of the city Monday through Saturday at 10:30am, between May and September. The price is 100DKK ($16) for adults, 30DKK ($4.70) for children. For information, contact **Wonderful Copenhagen Tourist Information,** Bernstorffsgade 1 (© **33-25-38-44;** www.woco.dk).

THE SHOPPING SCENE

Royal Copenhagen, Amagertorv 6 (© **33-13-71-81;** www.royalcopenhagen.com; bus: 1, 2, 6, 8, 28, 29, or 41 for the retail outlet, 1 or 15 for the factory), was founded in 1775. Royal Copenhagen's trademark, three wavy blue lines, has come to symbolize quality in porcelain throughout the world.

In the Royal Copenhagen retail center, legendary **Georg Jensen,** Amagertorv 6 (© **33-11-40-80;** www.georgjensen.com; bus: 1, 6, 8, 9, or 10), is known for its fine silver. For the connoisseur, there's no better address—this is the largest and best collection of Jensen holloware in Europe. Jewelry in traditional and modern design is also featured. One department specializes in seconds produced by various porcelain and glassware manufacturers.

Customers refer to the two owners of **The Amber Specialist,** Frederiksberggade 28 (© **33-11-88-03;** bus: 28, 29, or 41), as "The Amber Twins." These blonde-haired ladies specialize in "the gold of the north." This stone—really petrified resin—originated in the large coniferous forests that covered Denmark some 35 million years ago.

The elegant **Magasin,** Kongens Nytorv 13 (© **33-11-44-33;** bus: 1, 6, 9, or 10), is the biggest department store in Scandinavia. It offers an assortment of Danish designer fashion, glass and porcelain, and souvenirs. Goods are shipped abroad tax-free.

COPENHAGEN AFTER DARK

In Copenhagen, a good night means a late night. On warm weekends hundreds of rowdy revelers crowd Strøget until sunrise, and jazz clubs, traditional beer houses, and wine cellars are routinely packed. The city has a more serious cultural side as well, exemplified by excellent theaters, operas, and ballets. **Halfprice tickets** for some concerts and theater productions are available the day of the performance from the ticket kiosk opposite the Nørreport rail station, at Nørrevoldgade and Fiolstræde; it's open Monday through Friday from noon to 7pm and Saturday from noon to 3pm. On summer evenings outdoor concerts are held in Faelled Park near the entrance, near Frederik V's Vej; inquire about dates and times at the Copenhagen tourist office.

THE PERFORMING ARTS

Det Kongelige Teater (Royal Theater), Kongens Nytorv (© **33-69-69-69;** www.kgl-teater.dk; bus: 1, 6, 9, or 10), which dates from 1748, is home to the world-renowned **Royal Danish Ballet** and the **Royal Danish Opera.** Because the arts are state subsidized in Denmark, ticket prices are comparatively low, and some seats may be available at the box office the day before a performance. We recommend making reservations in advance. The season runs from August to May. Tickets are 30DKK to 645DKK ($4.70–$101), half price for seniors 67 and over and those under 26 (1 week before a show begins). The box office is open Monday through Saturday from 1 to 8pm; phone hours are Monday through Friday 1 to 8pm, Saturday from 10am to 8pm, and Sunday 3 hours before a performance (performances are usually at 3pm).

LIVE-MUSIC CLUBS

In the very heart of the city, **Cat Walk,** H. C. Andersens Blvd. 7 (℗ **33-12-20-32;** bus: 28 or 30), with its lively atmosphere, is a good place for people-watching and dancing. If you can stand the scrutiny, you'll be admitted only after being inspected through a peephole. The club is open Friday and Saturday from 9pm to 8am. There's a 60DKK ($9.35) cover.

Copenhagen JazzHouse, Niels Hammingsensgade 10 (℗ **33-15-26-00;** S-tog: Nørreport), plays host to more non-Danish jazz artists than just about any other jazz bar in town. Live music tends to begin around 8:30pm and usually finishes reasonably early. Around midnight on Thursday, Friday, and Saturday, the venue shifts from a live concert hall into a dance club. Cover is 70DKK to 300DKK ($11–$47); closed Monday.

Mojo Blues Bar, Løngangsstraede 21C (℗ **33-11-64-53;** bus: 2, 8, or 30), is a candlelit drinking spot that offers blues music, mostly performed by Scandinavian groups. It's open daily from 8pm to 5am. There's no cover from Sunday to Thursday, a cover of 50DKK ($7.80) Friday and Saturday.

BARS & CELLARS

Det Lille Apotek, Stor Kannikestraede 15 (℗ **33-12-56-06;** bus: 2, 5, 8, or 30), is a good spot for English-speaking foreign students to meet their Danish contemporaries. Though the menu varies, keep an eye out for the prawn cocktail and tenderloin. The main courses run about 89DKK to 148DKK ($14–$23) at dinner. It's open daily from 11am to midnight.

Frequented by celebrities and royalty, the **Library Bar,** in the Hotel Plaza, Bernstorffsgade 4 (℗ **33-14-92-62;** bus: 6), was rated by the late Malcolm Forbes as one of the top five bars in the world. In a setting of antique books and works of art, you can order everything from a cappuccino to a cocktail. It's open daily 4pm to midnight.

Nyhavn 17, Nyhavn 17 (℗ **33-12-54-19;** bus: 1, 6, 27, or 29; Metro: Kongens Nytorv), is the last of the honky-tonks that used to make up the former sailors' quarter. This cafe is a short walk from the Kongens Nytorv and d'Angleterre hotels. In summer you can sit outside. In the evening there's free entertainment from a solo guitarist or guitar duet. The cafe is open Sunday through Thursday from 10am to 2am and Friday and Saturday until 3am. Built in 1670, **Hvids Vinstue,** Kongens Nytorv 19 (℗ **33-15-10-64;** bus: 1, 6, 9, or 10), is a wine cellar that's a dimly lit safe haven for an eclectic crowd, many patrons—both theatergoers and actors and dancers—drawn from the Royal Theater across the way. It's open daily from 10am to 1am.

A leading nightlife venue, popular with gay men and women, is **Oscar Bar & Café,** 77 Radhuspladsen (℗ **33-12-09-99**), which operates a good restaurant serving an international cuisine and also has a cruisy bar. It's an all-around rendezvous point for many of the capital's gay men and women, also attracting foreign visitors looking for action. The crowd is trendy and hip, and the bar is also frequented by straight people for its music and atmosphere. The bar and cafe is open daily from noon to 2am, the restaurant daily from noon to 10pm.

2 Day Trips from Copenhagen

DRAGØR ★★

Visit the past in this old seafaring town on the island of Amager, 5km (3 miles) south of Copenhagen's Kastrup Airport. It's filled with well-preserved, half-timbered, ocher-and-pink 18th-century cottages with steep red-tile or thatch roofs, many of them under the protection of the National Trust.

Dragør (pronounced *Drah-wer*) was a busy port on the herring-rich Baltic Sea in the early Middle Ages, but when fishing fell off, it became just another sleepy waterfront village. After 1520, Amager Island and its villages—Dragør and Store Magleby—were inhabited by the Dutch, who brought their own customs, Low-German language, and agricultural expertise, especially their love of bulb flowers. In Copenhagen, you still see wooden-shoed Amager islanders selling their hyacinths, tulips, daffodils, and lilies in the streets.

A rich trove of historic treasures is in the **Amager Museum,** Hovedgaden 4–12, Store Magleby (✆ **32-53-93-07;** bus: 30, 33, or 350S), outside Dragør. The exhibits reveal the affluence achieved by the Amager Dutch, with rich textiles, fine embroidery, and amenities like carved silver buckles and buttons. The interiors of a Dutch house are especially interesting. Admission is 30DKK ($4.70) adults, 10DKK ($1.55) children. The museum is open April through September Tuesday through Sunday from noon to 4pm; October through March, Wednesday and Sunday from noon to 4pm.

The exhibits at the harborfront **Dragør Museum,** Havnepladsen 2–4 (✆ **32-53-41-06;** bus: 30 or 350S), show how the Amager Dutch lived from prehistoric times to the 20th century. Farming, goose breeding, seafaring, fishing, ship piloting, and ship salvage are delineated through pictures and artifacts. Admission is 20DKK ($3.10) adults, 10DKK ($1.55) for children under 14 years old. It's open May through September Tuesday through Sunday from noon to 4pm; closed October through April.

LOUISIANA

Established in 1958, the **Louisiana Museum of Modern Art** ★★★, Gl. Strandvej 13 (✆ **49-19-07-19;** www.louisiana.dk), is idyllically situated in a 19th-century mansion on the Danish Riviera, surrounded by a sculpture park opening directly onto the Øresund. Paintings and sculptures by modern masters, such as Giacometti and Henry Moore, as well as the best and most controversial works of modern art, are displayed. The museum's name came from the estate's first owner, Alexander Brun, who had three wives, each named Louise. Admission is 72DKK ($11) adults, 65DKK ($10) students, 20DKK ($3.10) children 4 to 16, and free for children under 4. It's open Thursday through Tuesday from 10am to 5pm, Wednesday from 10am to 10pm; closed December 24, 25, and 31.

Getting There   Humlebaek, the nearest town to Louisiana, may be reached by train from Copenhagen (København-Helsingør). Two trains an hour leave from the main station in Copenhagen (trip time: 40 min.). Once you're at Humlebaek, follow signs to the museum, a 15-minute walk.

HELSINGØR (ELSINORE) ★

Helsingør is visited chiefly for "Hamlet's Castle." Aside from its literary associations, the town has a certain charm: a quiet market square, medieval lanes, and old half-timbered and brick buildings, remains of its once-prosperous shipping industry. The **Tourist Office,** Havnepladsen 3 (*©* **49-21-13-33**), is open September to April Monday through Friday from 9am to 4pm and Saturday from 10am to 1pm; May to August Monday to Thursday 9am to 5pm, Friday 9am to 6pm, and Saturday 10am to 3pm.

There's no evidence Shakespeare ever saw this sandstone-and-copper Dutch Renaissance–style castle, full of intriguing secret passages and casemates, but he made **Kronborg Slot** ★★★, Kronborg (*©* **49-21-30-78**), famous in *Hamlet.* According to 12th-century historian Saxo Grammaticus, though, if Hamlet had really existed, he would have lived centuries before Kronborg was erected (1574–85). Over the years, some famous productions of *Hamlet* have been staged here, the castle's bleak atmosphere providing a good foil to the drama.

During its history, the castle has been looted, bombarded, gutted by fire, and used as a barracks (1785–1922). The starkly furnished Great Hall is the largest in northern Europe. The church with its original oak furnishings and the royal chambers are also worth exploring. Admission to the castle is 40DKK ($6.25) adults, 15DKK ($2.35) children 6 to 14. May through September, it's open daily from 10:30am to 5pm; October and April, hours are Tuesday through Sunday from 11am to 4pm; November through March, it's open Tuesday through Sunday from 11am to 3pm (closed Christmas). The castle is 1km (½ mile) from the rail station.

Getting There   Once you reach Helsingør, 40km (25 miles) north of Copenhagen, you'll be deposited in the center of town and can cover all the major attractions on foot. There are frequent trains from Copenhagen, taking 50 minutes. A one-way ticket is 52DKK ($8.10). Buses leave Copenhagen daily via the town of Klampenorg for the 90-minute trip to Helsingør.

5

England

by Darwin Porter & Danforth Prince

London is the most happening city in Europe—lively, fast paced, and teeming with action. London touts its fascinating contradictions: It's both an overwhelming jumble of antiquity and a world leader in the latest music, fashion, and food (the cuisine is better than ever). As stimulating as the city is, however, you'll want to tear yourself away to visit legendary Stonehenge, Oxford University, and the classic city of Bath.

1 London

Samuel Johnson said, "When a man is tired of London, he is tired of life; for there's in London all that life can afford." We'll survey a segment of that life: ancient monuments, literary shrines, museums, walking tours, Parliament debates, royal castles, waxworks, palaces, cathedrals, and parks.

ESSENTIALS

GETTING THERE   By Plane   Heathrow Airport (✆ **0870/000-0123**) is divided into four terminals, each relatively self-contained. The 24km (15-mile) trip from Heathrow to the center of London takes 35 to 40 minutes via the London subway, the **Underground (Tube);** the fare is £5.40 ($10). A **taxi** is likely to cost from £40 to £55 ($74–$102). For more information about Tube or bus connections, call ✆ **020/7222-1234.**

The British Airport Authority now operates **Heathrow Express** (✆ **0845/ 600-1515** or 877/677-1066; www.heathrowexpress.com), a 160kmph (100-mph) train service running every 15 minutes daily from 5:10am until 11:40pm between Heathrow and Paddington Station in the center of London. Trips cost £13 ($24) each way in economy class, rising to £21 ($39) in first class. Children under 15 go for free (when accompanied by an adult). You can save £1 ($1.85) by booking online or by phone. The trip takes 15 minutes each way between Paddington and Terminals 1, 2, and 3; 23 minutes to or from Terminal 4. The trains have special areas for wheelchairs. From Paddington, passengers can connect to other trains and the Underground, or you can hail a taxi. You can buy tickets on the train or at self-service machines at Heathrow Airport (also available from travel agents).

At Paddington, a bus link, **Hotel Express,** takes passengers to a number of hotels in central London. The cost is £3 ($5.55) for adults, £2 ($3.70) for children 5 to 15, free for children under 5. The service has revolutionized travel to and from the airport, much to the regret of London cabbies. Hotel Express buses are clearly designated outside the station, with frequent departures throughout the day.

By Train   Each of London's train stations is connected to the city's vast bus and Underground network, and each has phones, restaurants, pubs, luggage storage areas, and London Transport Travel Information Centres.

If you're coming from France, the fastest way to get to London is by the **HoverSpeed** connection between Calais and Dover, where you can get a BritRail train into London. For one-stop travel, you can take the Chunnel train direct from Paris to Waterloo Station in London.

By Car   If you're taking a car across the Channel, you can quickly connect by motorway (superhighway) into London. London is encircled by a ring road. Determine which part of the city you wish to enter, and follow the signs. You should confine your driving in London to the *bare minimum;* before you arrive, call your hotel for advice on where to park. Be warned—parking is scarce and expensive. The most important tip for driving in England: *Remember to drive on the left.*

VISITOR INFORMATION   Tourist Offices   The **Britain and London Visitor Centre,** 1 Regent St., Piccadilly Circus, London W1 (Tube: Piccadilly Circus), caters to walk-in visitors who need information about all parts of Britain. Telephone service has been suspended; you must show up in person and often wait in a lengthy line. On the premises, you'll find a British Rail ticket office, travel and theater ticket agencies, a hotel-booking service, a bookshop, and a souvenir shop. The center is open Monday through Friday from 9:30am to 6:30pm, and Saturday and Sunday from 10am to 4pm, with extended hours on Saturday from June to September.

London Tourist Board's Visit London, 1 Warwick Row, SW1 E5ER (walk-ins only; no phone; Tube: Victoria Station), can help you with almost anything. The center deals chiefly with accommodations in all price categories and can handle the whole spectrum of travelers' questions. It also arranges tour ticket sales and theater reservations, and offers a wide selection of books and souvenirs. From Easter to October, the center is open daily from 8am to 7pm; from November to Easter, it's open Monday through Saturday from 8am to 6pm and Sunday from 9am to 4pm.

The London Tourist Board also has tourist information centers at Heathrow Terminals 1, 2, and 3; on the Underground concourse at Liverpool Street Railway Station; and at the Arrivals Hall at the Waterloo International train terminal.

Websites   The British Tourist Authority's site expressly for U.S. travelers (**www.visitbritain.com**) lets you order brochures, provides trip-planning hints, and even allows e-mail questions for prompt answers. The outstanding Automobile Association site (**www.theaa.co.uk**) provides a route-planning service similar to its U.S. counterpart. It also lists lodgings, ranked by price and quality; many accept online bookings. The extensive London Theatre Guide (**www.officiallondontheatre.co.uk**) carries not only information on half-price tickets and what's on but also casting news, upcoming openings, and "last chance to see" shows. The official site from the British monarchy (**www.royal. gov.uk**) offers history, images, and descriptions of the "working palace" and "visitors' palace."

CITY LAYOUT   For our purposes, London begins at **Chelsea,** on the north bank of the Thames, and stretches north through Kensington to **Hampstead,** then east and south to **Tower Bridge.** Within this area, you'll find all the hotels and restaurants and nearly all the sights that are usually of interest to visitors.

The logical, though not geographical, center of this area is **Trafalgar Square.** Stand here facing the steps of the imposing National Gallery; you're looking northwest. That's the direction of **Piccadilly Circus**—the real core of tourist London—and the maze of streets that makes up **Soho.** Farther north runs **Oxford Street,** London's gift to moderately priced shopping, and still farther northwest lie Regent's Park and the zoo.

At your back (south from Trafalgar Square) runs **Whitehall,** which houses or skirts nearly every British government building, including the official residence of the prime minister at **10 Downing Street.** A bit farther south stand the Houses of Parliament and Westminster Abbey. Flowing southwest from Trafalgar Square is the table-smooth **Mall,** flanked by parks and mansions and leading to Buckingham Palace, the queen's residence. Farther along in the same direction lie **Belgravia** and **Knightsbridge,** the city's plushest residential areas; and south of them are chic **Chelsea** and **King's Road** (an upscale boulevard for shopping).

Due west from Trafalgar Square stretches the superb and high-priced shopping area bordered by **Regent Street** and **Piccadilly.** Farther west lie the equally elegant shops and even more elegant homes of **Mayfair.** Then comes **Park Lane,** with its deluxe hotels. Beyond is **Hyde Park,** the biggest park in central London and one of the largest in the world.

Charing Cross Road runs north from Trafalgar Square, past **Leicester Square,** and intersects with **Shaftesbury Avenue.** This is London's Theaterland. A bit farther along, Charing Cross Road turns into a browser's paradise, lined with shops selling new and secondhand books. At last, it funnels into **St. Giles Circus.** Beyond is **Bloomsbury,** site of the University of London, the British

Museum, and erstwhile stamping ground of the famed "Bloomsbury group," led by Virginia Woolf. Northeast from Trafalgar Square lies **Covent Garden,** known for its Royal Opera House; today it's a major shopping, restaurant, and cafe district.

Follow **The Strand** eastward from Trafalgar Square and you'll come to **Fleet Street.** From the 19th century through most of the 20th century, this area was the most concentrated newspaper district in the world. **Temple Bar** stands where The Strand becomes Fleet Street, and only here do you enter the actual City of London, or "the City." Its focal point and shrine is the Bank of England on **Threadneedle Street,** with the Stock Exchange next door and the Royal Exchange across the street. In the midst of all the hustle and bustle rises **St. Paul's Cathedral,** Sir Christopher Wren's monument to beauty and tranquillity. At the far eastern fringe of the City looms the **Tower of London,** shrouded in legend, blood, and history and permanently besieged by battalions of visitors.

GETTING AROUND   By Public Transportation   The London Underground subway, known locally as "the Tube," and the city buses are operated by **London Transport** (© 020/7222-1234; www.londontransport.co.uk) on a

---

Discount Passes for Public Transportation

If you plan to use public transportation a lot, investigate the range of fare discounts available. **Travelcards** offer unlimited use of buses, Underground, and British Rail services in greater London for any period ranging from a day to a year. Travelcards are available from Underground ticket offices, Travel Information Centres, main post offices in the London area, and some newsstands. You need to bring a passport-size photo to purchase a Travelcard; you can take a photo at any of the instant photo booths in London's train stations. Children under age 5 generally travel free on the Tube and buses.

The **1-Day Travelcard** allows you to go anywhere throughout Greater London. For travel anywhere within zones 1 and 2, the cost is £5.30 ($9.80) for adults or £2.60 ($4.80) for children 5 to 15. The **Off-Peak 1-Day Travelcard,** which isn't valid until after 9:30am on weekdays (or on night buses), is even cheaper. For travel within zones 1 and 2, the cost is £4.30 ($7.95) for adults and £2 ($3.70) for children 5 to 15.

Weekend Travelcards are valid for 1 weekend, plus Monday if it's a national holiday. They're not valid on night buses. Travel anywhere within zones 1 and 2 all weekend costs £6.40 ($12) for adults, £2 ($3.70) for kids 5 to 15.

1-Week Travelcards cost adults £17 ($31) and children £7 ($13) for travel in zones 1 and 2.

The 1-day **Family Travelcard** allows as many journeys as you want on the Tube, on buses (excluding night buses) displaying the London Transport bus sign, and even on the Docklands Light Railway or any rail service within the travel zones designated on your ticket. The family card is valid Monday through Friday after 9:30am and all day on weekends and public holidays. It's available for families as small as two (one adult and one child) and as large as six (two adults and four children). The cost is £2.80 ($5.20) per adult and 80p ($1.50) per child.

system of six fare zones that radiate out in rings from the central Zone 1, which is where most visitors spend the majority of their time. It covers an area from Aldgate East and Tower Gateway in the east to Notting Hill in the west, and from Waterloo in the south to Baker Street, Euston, and King's Cross in the north. To travel beyond these boundaries, you need at least a two-zone ticket. Note that all one-way, round-trip, and 1-day-pass tickets are valid only on the day of purchase. **London Transport Travel Information Centres** are at several major Tube stations: Euston, King's Cross, Oxford Circus, St. James's Park, Liverpool Street Station, and Piccadilly Circus, as well as the British Rail stations at Euston and Victoria and each terminal at Heathrow Airport. Most are open daily (some close Sun) from at least 9am to 5pm.

All stations in the **Underground** are clearly marked with a red circle and blue crossbar. Fares are based on zones. The flat fare for one trip within Zone 1 is £2 ($3.70). Trips from Zone 1 to destinations in the suburbs generally range from £2.20 to £3.80 ($4.05–$7.05). Be sure to keep your ticket, as it must be presented when you exit at your destination.

The **bus system** is almost as good as the Underground, and you'll have a better view of the city. As with the Underground, fares vary according to distance traveled. Generally, bus fares are slightly less than Tube fares, £1 ($1.85) adults, 40p (75¢) children; a 1-day pass costs £2.50 ($4.65) adults, £1 ($1.85) children. It's also possible to purchase weekly passes for £9.50 ($18) adults or £4 ($7.40) children. To find out about current routes, pick up a free bus map at any Underground station or at one of the London Transport Travel Information Centres listed above.

By Taxi London cabs are among the most comfortable and best designed in the world. You can pick one up either by heading for a cab stand or by hailing one in the street (the taxi is available if the yellow taxi sign on the roof is lighted); once it has stopped for you, a taxi is obliged to take you anywhere you want within 9.5km (6 miles) of the pickup point, provided it's within the metropolitan area. To **call a cab,** phone ℂ **020/7272-0272** or 020/7253-5000.

The meter starts at £3.80 ($7.05), with increments of £3.40 ($6.30) per mile thereafter, based on distance or time. Each additional passenger is charged 40p (75¢). Passengers pay 10p (20¢) for each piece of luggage in the driver's compartment and any other item more than .6m (2 ft.) long. Surcharges are imposed after 8pm and on weekends and public holidays. All these tariffs include VAT. Fares usually increase annually. It's recommended that you tip 10% to 15% of the fare.

If you call for a cab, the meter starts running when the taxi receives instructions from the dispatcher, so you could find that the meter already reads a few pounds more than the initial drop of £3.80 ($7.05) when you climb inside.

By Car Rent a car only if you plan to take excursions into the environs. Because of traffic and parking difficulties, it's virtually impossible to see London by car.

By Bicycle One of the most popular bike-rental shops is **On Your Bike,** 52–54 Tooley St., London Bridge, SE1 (ℂ **020/7378-6669;** Tube: London Bridge), open Monday through Friday from 8am to 7pm, and Saturday from 10am to 6pm, Sunday 11am to 5pm. The first-class mountain bikes, with high seats and low-slung handlebars, cost £12 ($22) per day, £25 ($46) per weekend, or £60 ($111) per week, and require a £200 ($370) deposit on a credit card.

FAST FACTS: London

American Express The main office is at 30–31 Haymarket, SW1 (© 020/ 7484-9600; Tube: Piccadilly Circus). Full services are available Monday through Saturday from 9am to 6pm; foreign-exchange only is open Sunday from 10am to 5pm.

Business Hours **Banks** are usually open Monday through Friday from 9:30am to 3:30pm. **Pubs and bars** are open Monday through Saturday from 11am to 11pm and Sunday from noon to 10:30pm; some pubs close Sunday from 3 to 7pm. **Stores** are generally open daily from 9am to 5:30pm, to 7pm Wednesday or Thursday. Most central shops close Saturday around 1pm.

Currency The basic unit of currency is the **pound sterling** (£), which is divided into 100 pence (p). The rate of exchange used in this chapter is £1 = $1.85.

Dentists/Doctors For dental emergencies, call **Eastman Dental Hospital** (© 020/7915-1000; Tube: King's Cross). Some hotels have doctors on call. **Medical Express,** 117A Harley St., W1 (© **020/7499-1991;** Tube: Regent's Park), is a private British clinic that's not part of the free British medical establishment. It's open Monday through Friday from 9:30am to 5:30pm.

Drugstores In Britain, they're called "chemists." Every police station in the country has a list of emergency chemists. Dial "0" (zero) and ask the operator for the local police, who will give you the name of the chemist nearest you.

Embassies & High Commissions

- The embassy of the **United States** is at 24 Grosvenor St., W1 (© **020/ 7499-9000;** www.usembassy.org.uk; Tube: Bond St.); hours are Monday through Friday from 8:30am to 5:30pm. For passport and visa information, go to the U.S. Passport and Citizenship Unit, 55–56 Upper Brook St., London, W1 (© 020/7499-9000, ext. 2563 or 2564; Tube: Marble Arch or Bond St.), Monday through Friday from 8:30am to 11:30am and from 2 to 4pm on Monday and Friday only.
- The high commission of **Canada,** MacDonald House, 38 Grosvenor St., W1 (© **020/7258-6600;** www.dfait-maeci.gc.ca/canadaeuropa/united_ kingdom; Tube: Bond St.), is open Monday through Friday from 8am to 4pm; 8 to 11am for immigration services.
- The high commission of **Australia,** Australia House, Strand, WC2 (© 020/ 7379-4334; www.australia.org.uk; Tube: Charing Cross or Aldwych), is open Monday through Friday from 9am to 5:20pm; 9 to 11am for immigration services; passports 9:30am to 3:30pm.
- The high commission of **New Zealand,** New Zealand House, 80 Haymarket at Pall Mall, SW1 (© 020/7930-8422; www.nzembassy.com; Tube: Charing Cross or Piccadilly Circus), is open Monday through Friday from 10am to 4pm.
- The embassy of **Ireland,** 17 Grosvenor Place, SW1 (© **020/7235-2171;** http://ireland.embassyhomepage.com; Tube: Hyde Park Corner), is open Monday through Friday from 9:30am to 1pm and 2 to 5pm.
- The high commission of **South Africa,** South Africa House, Trafalgar Square, WC2N 5DP (© **020/7925-8900;** www.southafricahouse.com; Tube: Westminster), is open Monday through Friday from 9am to 5pm.

Emergencies In London, for police, fire, or an ambulance, dial ⓒ **999**.

Hospitals Emergency care 24 hours a day, with the first treatment free under the National Health Service, is offered by **Royal Free Hospital,** Pond Street, NW10 (ⓒ **020/7794-0500**; Tube: Belsize Park); and by **University College Hospital,** Grafton Way, WC1E 3DB (ⓒ **020/7387-9300**; Tube: Warren St.).

Internet Access You can send e-mails or check your messages at **Cyberia,** 39 Whitfield St. (ⓒ **020/7209-0984**; www.cyberiacafe.net).

Post Office The **Main Post Office,** 24–28 William IV St., WC2N 4DL (ⓒ **020/ 7484-9307**; Tube: Charing Cross), operates as three separate businesses: inland and international postal service and banking; philatelic postage stamp sales; and the post shop, selling greeting cards and stationery. All are open Monday through Friday from 8:30am to 6:30pm and Saturday 9am to 5:30pm.

Safety Stay in well-lit areas and out of questionable neighborhoods, especially at night. In Britain, most of the crime perpetrated against tourists is pickpocketing and mugging. These attacks usually occur in such cities as London, Birmingham, or Manchester. Most villages are safe.

Taxes To encourage energy conservation, the British government levies a 25% tax on gasoline (petrol). There is also a 17.5% national value-added tax (VAT) that is added to all hotel and restaurant bills and is included in the price of many items you purchase. This can be refunded if you shop at stores that participate in the Retail Export Scheme (signs are posted in the window). For information on getting your VAT refund, go to the "Money" section of the "Planning Your Trip to Europe" chapter.

A departure tax is included in the price of your travel ticket.

Telephone The country code for the United Kingdom is **44**. London's city code is **020**.

For **directory assistance** in London, dial **142**; for the rest of Britain, **192**.

There are three types of public pay phones: those taking only coins, those accepting only phone cards (called Cardphones), and those taking both phone cards and credit cards. At coin-operated phones, insert your coins before dialing. The minimum charge is 10p (20¢).

Phone cards are available in four values: £2 ($3.70), £4 ($7.40), £10 ($19), and £20 ($37)—and are reusable until the total value has expired. Cards can be purchased from newsstands and post offices.

To make an international call from Britain, dial the international access code **(00)**, then the country code, then the area code, and finally the local number. Or call through one of the following long-distance access codes: **AT&T Direct Service** (ⓒ 0800/890011), **Canada Direct** (ⓒ 0800/890016), **Australia** (ⓒ 0800/890061), and **New Zealand** (ⓒ 0800/890064). Common country codes are: USA and Canada, **1**; Australia, **61**; New Zealand, **64**; and South Africa, **27**.

Tipping For cab drivers, add about 10% to 15% to the fare on the meter. If the driver loads or unloads your luggage, add something extra.

In hotels, porters receive 75p ($1.40) per bag, even if you have only one small suitcase. Hall porters are tipped only for special services. Maids receive £1 ($1.85) per day. In top-ranking hotels, the concierge will often submit a separate bill showing charges for newspapers and other items; if he or she has been particularly helpful, tip extra.

Hotels often add a service charge of 10% to 15% to bills. In smaller bed-and-breakfasts, the tip is not likely to be included. Therefore, tip those who perform special services, such as the waiter who serves you breakfast. If several people have served you in a bed-and-breakfast, you may ask that 10% to 15% be added to the bill and divided among the staff.

In both restaurants and nightclubs, a 15% service charge is added to the bill, which is distributed among all the help. To that, add another 3% to 5%, depending on the service. Waiters in deluxe restaurants and nightclubs are accustomed to the extra 5%. Sommeliers (wine stewards) get about £1 ($1.85) per bottle of wine served. Tipping in pubs isn't common, but in wine bars, the server usually gets about 75p ($1.40) per round of drinks.

WHERE TO STAY
MAYFAIR

At press time, the venerable **Hotel May Fair** had been bought by Radisson Edwardian Hotels, which plans an extensive restoration of the 1927 property located in the heart of Mayfair. In the meantime, Radisson is offering special introductory room rates. For information, go to **www.radissonedwardian.com**.

Very Expensive

Brown's Hotel ⭐⭐⭐ Almost every year a new hotel attempts to evoke an English country-house ambience with Chippendale furniture and chintz, but this quintessential town-house hotel always comes out on top. Created by a former manservant to Lord Byron, Brown's opened its doors in 1837, the same year Queen Victoria took the throne. Today, Brown's occupies 14 historic houses off Berkeley Square. The guest rooms show stately, restrained taste—even the washbasins are tasteful antiques. Accommodations have such extras as voice mail, dual phone lines, and dataports, and bathrooms are equipped with robes, cosmetics, tubs, and showers. In keeping with the atmosphere of the rest of the hotel, the lounges pay homage to the past: They include the Roosevelt Room (TR honeymooned here in 1886), the Rudyard Kipling Room (the author was a frequent visitor), and the paneled St. George's Bar.

30 Albemarle St., London W1S 4BP. ⓒ 020/7493-6020. Fax 020/7493-9381. www.brownshotel.com. 118 units. £239–£345 ($442–$638) double; from £403 ($746) suite. AE, DC, MC, V. Off-site parking £40 ($74). Tube: Green Park. **Amenities:** 3 restaurants; bar; health club; concierge; business center; 24-hr. room service; laundry service; same-day dry cleaning; nonsmoking rooms. *In room:* A/C, TV/VCR, dataport, minibar, hair dryer, safe.

Sheraton Park Lane Hotel ⭐⭐ Since 1924, this has been the most traditional of the Park Lane mansions. The hotel was sold in 1996 to the Sheraton Corporation, which continues to upgrade it but maintains its quintessential British style. Its Silver Entrance remains an Art Deco marvel that has been used as a backdrop in many films, including the classic BBC miniseries *Brideshead Revisited*. Overlooking Green Park, the hotel offers luxurious accommodations that are a good deal—well, at least for pricey Park Lane, where anything under

London Accommodations

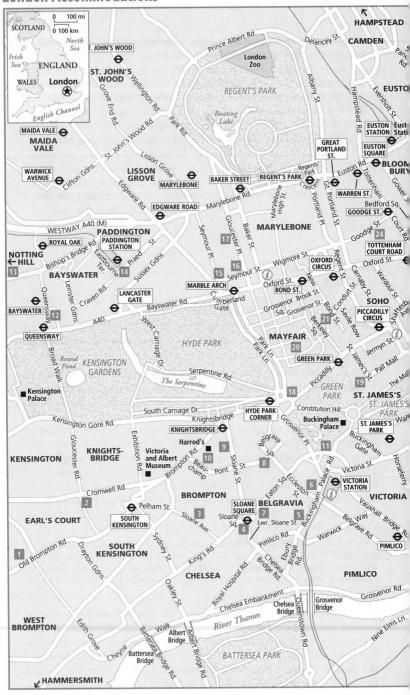

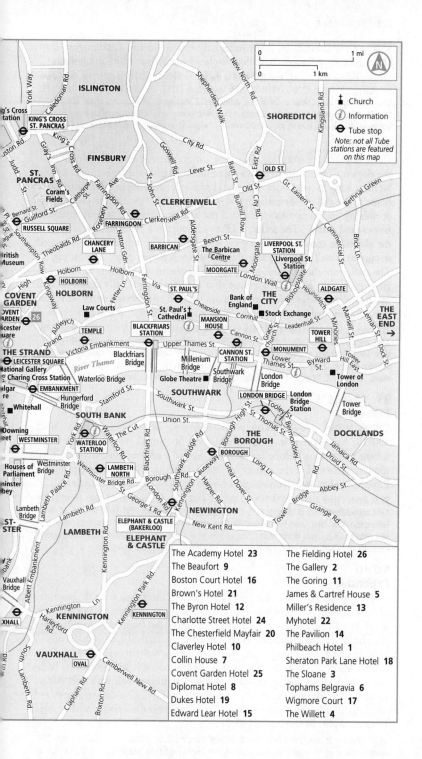

The Academy Hotel **23**	The Fielding Hotel **26**
The Beaufort **9**	The Gallery **2**
Boston Court Hotel **16**	The Goring **11**
Brown's Hotel **21**	James & Cartref House **5**
The Byron Hotel **12**	Miller's Residence **13**
Charlotte Street Hotel **24**	Myhotel **22**
The Chesterfield Mayfair **20**	The Pavilion **14**
Claverley Hotel **10**	Philbeach Hotel **1**
Collin House **7**	Sheraton Park Lane Hotel **18**
Covent Garden Hotel **25**	The Sloane **3**
Diplomat Hotel **8**	Tophams Belgravia **6**
Dukes Hotel **19**	Wigmore Court **17**
Edward Lear Hotel **15**	The Willett **4**

$500 a night is a bargain. Many suites have marble fireplaces and original marble bathrooms. All rooms have double-glazed windows to block out noise.

Piccadilly, London W1J 7BX. © **800/325-3535** in the U.S., or 020/7499-6321. Fax 020/7499-1965. www.sheraton.com. 307 units. £270–£310 ($500–$574) double; from £429 ($794) suite. AE, DC, MC, V. Parking £35 ($65). Tube: Hyde Park Corner or Green Park. **Amenities:** 2 restaurants; afternoon tea in the fabled 1920s Palm Court; bar; health club; concierge; business center; 24-hr. room service; laundry service; same-day dry cleaning; nonsmoking rooms. *In room:* A/C (in most rooms), TV w/pay movies, dataport, minibar, hair dryer, iron, safe.

Expensive

The Chesterfield Mayfair 🌟🌟   Just a short distance from Berkeley Square, the elegant Chesterfield serves up a traditional English atmosphere and offers a lot more bang for your buck than most hotels in pricey Mayfair. The hotel, once home to the earl of Chesterfield, still sports venerable features that evoke an air of nobility, including richly decorated public rooms featuring woods, antiques, fabrics, and marble. The secluded Library Lounge is a great place to relax, and the glassed-in conservatory is a good spot for tea. The sumptuously decorated restaurant is well regarded, as is the bar, where a pianist plays on most nights. The staff, from the reception clerks to the chambermaids, couldn't be nicer. The guest rooms are generally not huge, but they are dramatically decorated and make excellent use of space—there's a ton of closet and counter space—and feature such unusual amenities as complimentary bottled waters and jelly beans.

35 Charles St., London W1J 5EB. © **877/955-1515** in the U.S. and Canada, or 020/7491-2622. Fax 020/7491-4793. www.chesterfieldmayfair.com. 110 units. £190–£260 ($352–$481) double; £250–£595 ($463–$1,101) suite. Special packages available. AE, DC, MC, V. Tube: Green Park. **Amenities:** 2 restaurants; bar; concierge; business services; 24-hr. room service; babysitting; laundry service; same-day dry cleaning; nonsmoking rooms. *In room:* A/C, TV w/pay movies, dataport, coffeemaker, hair dryer, iron, safe.

ST. JAMES'S
Expensive

Dukes Hotel 🌟🌟🌟   Dukes provides elegance without ostentation. Since 1908, it has stood in a quiet courtyard off St. James's Street. It attracts the urbane guest who's looking for charm, style, and tradition. Each well-furnished room is decorated in the style of a particular period, ranging from Regency to Edwardian. The well-maintained bathrooms contain tub/shower combos.

35 St. James's Place, London SW1A 1NY. © **800/381-4702** in the U.S., or 020/7491-4840. Fax 020/7493-1264. www.dukeshotel.co.uk. 89 units. £225–£260 ($416–$481) double; from £350 ($648) suite. AE, DC, MC, V. Parking £54 ($86). Tube: Green Park. **Amenities:** Restaurant; bar; health club; spa; concierge; tour desk; business services; 24-hr. room service; babysitting; laundry service; same-day dry cleaning; nonsmoking rooms; rooms for those with limited mobility. *In room:* A/C, TV, dataport, minibar, hair dryer, safe.

SOHO
Expensive

Charlotte Street Hotel 🌟🌟   In North Soho, a short walk from the heartbeat of Soho Square, this town house has been luxuriously converted into a high-end hotel that is London chic at its finest, with everything from a Los Angeles–style juice bar to a private screening room. The latter has made it a hit with the movie, fashion, and media crowd, many of whom had never ventured to North Soho before. Midsize to spacious rooms have fresh modern English interiors. Bathrooms are state of the art, designed in solid granite and oak with twin basins, tubs, walk-in showers, even TVs. Guests relax in the elegant drawing room and library with a log-burning fireplace. The decor evokes memories of the fabled Bloomsbury set of Virginia Woolf.

15–17 Charlotte St., London W1T 1RJ. © **800/553-6674** in the U.S., or 020/7806-2000. Fax 020/7806-2002. www.firmdale.com. 52 units. £220–£310 ($407–$574) double; from £340 ($629) suite. AE, DC, MC, V. Tube:

Tottenham Court. **Amenities:** Restaurant and long pewter bar; exercise room; concierge; 24-hr. room service; laundry service; same-day dry cleaning; nonsmoking rooms; rooms for those with limited mobility. *In room:* A/C, TV/DVD, fax, dataport, minibar, hair dryer, safe.

BAKER STREET
Inexpensive

Wigmore Court *Value*   A convenient family hotel, this inn lies near the street made famous as the fictional address of Sherlock Holmes. It is close to Marble Arch, Oxford Street, and Madame Tussauds. A somber Victorian structure, it has been tastefully converted into a fine B&B suitable only for serious stair climbers, as there is no elevator. Rooms, many quite spacious, are comfortably furnished. Most contain double or twin beds. About half of the small bathrooms have tub/shower combos. Request a room in the rear if you're bothered by the noise from the traffic outside.

23 Gloucester Place, London W1U 8HS. © **020/7935-0928.** Fax 020/7487-4254. 18 units. £75 ($139) double; £90 ($167) triple. MC, V. Tube: Marble Arch. **Amenities:** Guest kitchen; coin-op washers and dryers. *In room:* TV, dataport, coffeemaker.

BLOOMSBURY
Expensive

The Academy Hotel *★*   The Academy is in the heart of London's publishing district. Looking out your window, you'll see where members of the literary Bloomsbury Group used to pass by. Many original architectural grace notes were preserved when these three 1776 Georgian row houses were joined. The hotel was substantially upgraded in the 1990s, with a bathroom added to every guest room (whether there was space or not). With their overstuffed armchairs and half-canopied beds, rooms here evoke English country-house living, but that of the poorer relations. The beds, so they say, were built to "American specifications." True or not, they assure you of a restful night's sleep. **Warning:** If you have a problem with stairs, this may not be the place for you—there are no elevators rising to the four floors.

21 Gower St., London WC1E 6HG. © **020/7631-4115.** Fax 020/7636-3442. www.etontownhouse.com. 49 units. £163–£189 ($302–$350) double; £215 ($398) suite. AE, DC, MC, V. Tube: Tottenham Court Rd., Goodge St., or Russell Sq. **Amenities:** Bar; limited room service; laundry service; same-day dry cleaning; nonsmoking rooms. *In room:* A/C, TV, dataport, minibar, beverage maker, hair dryer, iron/ironing board, safe, trouser press.

Myhotel *★* *Finds*   Creating shock waves among staid Bloomsbury hoteliers, Myhotel is a London row house on the outside with an Asian moderne-style interior. It is designed according to feng shui principles—the ancient Chinese art of placement that analyzes the flow of energy in a space. The rooms have mirrors, but they're positioned so that you don't see yourself when you first wake up—feng shui rule no. 1 (probably a good rule, feng shui or not). Rooms are havens of comfort, taste, and tranquillity. Excellent sleep-inducing beds are found in all units, along with a small bathroom with a shower stall. Tipping is discouraged, and each guest is assigned a personal assistant responsible for that guest's happiness. Aimed at today's young, hip traveler, Myhotel lies within a short walk of Covent Garden and the British Museum.

11–13 Bayley St., Bedford Sq., London WC1B 3HD. © **020/7667-6000.** Fax 020/7667-6001. www.myhotels. co.uk. 78 units. £185–£250 ($342–$463) double; from £330 ($611) suite. AE, DC, MC, V. Tube: Tottenham Court Rd. **Amenities:** Restaurant; bar; exercise room; spa; car at discounted rate; 24-hr. room service; massage; babysitting; laundry service; same-day dry cleaning; nonsmoking rooms. *In room:* A/C, TV w/pay movies, dataport, hair dryer, safe.

COVENT GARDEN
Very Expensive
Covent Garden Hotel ★★★   This former hospital building lay neglected for years until it was reconfigured in 1996 by hot hoteliers Tim and Kit Kemp—whose flair for interior design is legendary—into one of London's most charming boutique hotels in one of the West End's hippest shopping neighborhoods. *Travel & Leisure* called this hotel one of the 25 hottest places to stay in the *world*. It remains so. The hotel has a welcoming lobby outfitted with elaborate inlaid furniture and elegant draperies. Upstairs, accessible via a dramatic stone staircase, soundproof bedrooms are furnished in English style with Asian fabrics and contain such luxurious amenities as two phone lines with voice mail, full marble bathrooms with double vanities, and deep soaking tubs.

10 Monmouth St., London WC2H 9HB. © 800/553-6674 in the U.S., or 020/7806-1000. Fax 020/7806-1100. www.firmdale.com. 58 units. £245–£295 ($453–$546) double; £350–£795 ($648–$1,471) suite. AE, MC, V. Tube: Covent Garden or Leicester Sq. **Amenities:** Restaurant; bar; small exercise room; concierge; tour desk; business services; 24-hr. room service; massage; babysitting; laundry service; same-day dry cleaning; video library; nonsmoking rooms. *In room:* A/C, TV/VCR, dataport, minibar, hair dryer, safe.

Moderate
The Fielding Hotel ★ *Finds*   One of London's more eccentric hotels, the Fielding is cramped, quirky, and quaint, and an enduring favorite. Luring media types, the hotel is named after novelist Henry Fielding of *Tom Jones* fame, who lived in Broad Court. It lies on a pedestrian street still lined with 19th-century gas lamps. The Royal Opera House is across the street; and the pubs, shops, and restaurants of lively Covent Garden are just beyond the front door. Rooms are small, but charmingly old-fashioned. Some units are "touched up" every year, though floors dip and sway, and the furnishings and fabrics, though clean, have known better times. But with a location like this, in the heart of London, the Fielding keeps guests coming back; in fact, many love the hotel's rickety charm.

4 Broad Ct., Bow St., London WC2B 5QZ. © 020/7836-8305. Fax 020/7497-0064. www.the-fielding-hotel. co.uk. 24 units. £100–£115 ($185–$213) double; £130 ($241) suite. AE, DC, MC, V. Tube: Covent Garden. **Amenities:** Bar; laundry service; nonsmoking rooms. *In room:* TV, dataport, coffeemaker.

VICTORIA
Very Expensive
The Goring ★★★   For tradition and location, the Goring is our first choice in Westminster. Just behind Buckingham Palace, it lies within easy reach of the royal parks, Victoria Station, Westminster Abbey, and the Houses of Parliament. It also offers the finest personal service of all its nearby competitors. Built in 1910, this was the first hotel in the world to have central heating and a private bathroom in every room. Today's guest rooms still offer all the comforts, including luxurious refurbished bathrooms with extralong tubs, red marble walls, dual pedestal basins, bidets, deluxe toiletries, and power shower heads. Rooms overlooking the garden are best. The charm of a traditional English country hotel is conjured up in the paneled drawing room, where fires crackle in the ornate fireplaces on nippy evenings. The adjoining bar overlooks the rear gardens.

15 Beeston Place, Grosvenor Gardens, London SW1W OJW. © 020/7396-9000. Fax 020/7834-4393. www. goringhotel.co.uk. 74 units. £255–£340 ($472–$629) double; from £340 ($629) suite. AE, DC, MC, V. Parking £30 ($56). Tube: Victoria. **Amenities:** Grand afternoon tea in the drawing room; classic restaurant; bar; free use of nearby health club; concierge; 24-hr. room service; babysitting; laundry service; same-day dry cleaning; nonsmoking rooms; rooms for those with limited mobility. *In room:* A/C, TV w/pay movies, dataport, hair dryer, safe.

Moderate

Tophams Belgravia ⭐ Tophams came into being in 1937, when five small row houses were interconnected. With its flower-filled window boxes, the place has a bucolic flavor. All guest rooms are tastefully furnished, and the best are appointed with four-poster beds and private bathrooms equipped with shower-tub combinations. Not all rooms have private bathrooms. The restaurant offers traditional and modern English cooking for lunch and dinner. And the location is ideal, especially if you plan to cover a lot of ground by Tube or train: It's only a 3-minute walk to Victoria Station.

28 Ebury St., London SW1W 0LU. © 020/7730-8147. Fax 020/7823-5966. www.tophams.co.uk. 40 units, 34 with bathroom. £110 ($204) double without bathroom; £130–£170 ($241–$315) double with bathroom; £170 ($315) triple with bathroom. AE, DC, MC, V. Tube: Victoria. **Amenities:** Restaurant; bar; access to nearby health club; limited room service; babysitting; laundry service; same-day dry cleaning. *In room:* TV, dataport, coffeemaker, hair dryer, iron.

Inexpensive

Collin House ⭐ This B&B emerges as a winner on a street lined with the finest Victoria Station–area B&Bs. William IV had just begun his reign when this house was constructed in 1830. Private, shower-only bathrooms have been discreetly installed, and everything works efficiently. For rooms without bathrooms, there are adequate hallway facilities, some of which are shared by only two rooms. Outside traffic in this area of London is heavy, and the front windows are not soundproof, so be warned if you're a light sleeper. Year after year, the owners continually make improvements, and all guest rooms are comfortably furnished and well maintained. A generous breakfast awaits you each morning in the basement of this nonsmoking facility.

104 Ebury St., London SW1W 9QD. © and fax **020/7730-8031**. www.collinhouse.co.uk. 12 units, 8 with bathroom (shower only). £68 ($126) double without bathroom; £82 ($152) double with bathroom; £95 ($176) triple without bathroom. Rates include English breakfast. MC, V. Tube: Victoria. *In room:* TV in most, hair dryer available, safe, no phone.

James & Cartref House *Kids* Hailed by many publications as one of the top 10 B&B choices in London, James House and Cartref House (across the street from each other) deserve their accolades. *Warning:* Whether or not you like this nonsmoking hotel will depend on your room assignment. Some accommodations are fine but several rooms are hardly large enough to move around in. This is especially true of some third-floor units. Some "bathrooms" reminded us of those found on small oceangoing freighters. On the plus side, each room is individually designed, and those with bunk beds make nice family choices. The English breakfast is so generous that you may end up skipping lunch—and you're just a stone's throw from Buckingham Palace should the queen invite you over for tea.

108 and 129 Ebury St., London SW1W 9QD. James House © 020/7730-7338; Cartref House © 020/7730-6176. Fax 020/7730-7338. www.jamesandcartref.co.uk. 19 units, 12 with bathroom. £70 ($130) double without bathroom; £85 ($157) double with bathroom; £135 ($250) quad with bathroom. Rates include English breakfast. AE, MC, V. Tube: Victoria. *In room:* TV, coffeemaker, hair dryer, no phone.

KNIGHTSBRIDGE
Expensive

The Beaufort ⭐⭐ If you'd like to stay at one of London's finest boutique hotels, offering personal service in an elegant, tranquil town-house atmosphere just 200 yards from Harrods, head here. Owner Diana Wallis, a television producer, combined a pair of adjacent houses from the 1870s, ripped out the old decor, and created a stylish hotel that has the feeling of a private house. Each guest room is individually decorated in a modern color scheme and adorned with well-chosen paintings by London artists. Rooms come with earphone radios, flowers, and a selection of books. Included in the rates are a 24-hour free bar, continental breakfast, and light meals from room service, plus English cream teas each afternoon, and brandy, chocolates, and shortbread in each room. Junior suites include complimentary limo to or from the airport.

33 Beaufort Gardens, London SW3 1PP. © 020/7584-5252. Fax 020/7589-2834. www.thebeaufort.co.uk. 28 units. £195–£260 ($361–$481) double; £310 ($574) junior suite. Rates include continental breakfast, bar, light meals, and afternoon tea. AE, DC, MC, V. Tube: Knightsbridge. **Amenities:** Bar; access to nearby health club; 24-hr. room service; babysitting; laundry service; same-day dry cleaning. *In room:* A/C, TV, dataport, hair dryer, iron.

Moderate

Claverley Hotel ★   Located on a quiet cul-de-sac, this tasteful hotel, one of the neighborhood's very best (and winner of the Spencer Trophy for the Best Bed & Breakfast Hotel in Central London), is just a few blocks from Harrods. It's a small, cozy place accented with Georgian-era accessories. The lounge has the atmosphere of a country house. Most rooms have wall-to-wall carpeting and comfortably upholstered armchairs. Recently refurbished rooms have a marble bathrooms and "power showers."

13–14 Beaufort Gardens, London SW3 1PS. © 800/747-0398 in the U.S., or 020/7589-8541. Fax 020/7584-3410. www.claverleyhotel.co.uk. 29 units. £120–£190 ($222–$352) double; £190–£215 ($352–$398) junior suite. Rates include English breakfast. AE, DC, MC, V. Free parking on Sun; £21 ($39) during the week. Tube: Knightsbridge. **Amenities:** Same-day dry cleaning. *In room:* TV, dataport, hair dryer, safe.

BELGRAVIA
Moderate

Diplomat Hotel ★ *Finds*   Part of the Diplomat's charm is that it is a small, reasonably priced hotel located in an otherwise prohibitively expensive neighborhood. Only minutes from Harrods, it was built in 1882 as a private residence by noted architect Thomas Cubbitt. It's very well appointed and was completely overhauled in 2002 and 2003. The registration desk is framed by the sweep of a partially gilded circular staircase. The staff is helpful, well mannered, and discreet. The high-ceilinged guest rooms are tastefully done in Victorian style. You get good—not grand—comfort here.

2 Chesham St., London SW1X 8DT. © 020/7235-1544. Fax 020/7259-6153. www.btinternet.com/~diplomat. hotel. 26 units. £125–£170 ($231–$315) double. Rates include English buffet breakfast. AE, DC, MC, V. Tube: Sloane Sq. or Knightsbridge. **Amenities:** Snack bar; nearby health club; business services; laundry service; same-day dry cleaning; rooms for those with limited mobility. *In room:* TV, dataport, coffeemaker, hair dryer, iron.

CHELSEA
Expensive

The Sloane ★★   This "toff" (dandy) address, a redbrick Victorian-era town house that has been tastefully renovated in recent years, is located in Chelsea near Sloane Square. It combines valuable 19th-century antiques with modern comforts. Our favorite spot here is the rooftop terrace; with views opening onto Chelsea, it's ideal for a relaxing breakfast or drink. Guest rooms range from small to spacious, but all are opulently furnished with flouncy draperies, tasteful fabrics, and sumptuous beds. The deluxe bathrooms have chrome power showers, wall-width mirrors (in most rooms), and luxurious toiletries.

29 Draycott Place, London SW3 2SH. © 800/324-9960 in the U.S., or 020/7581-5757. Fax 020/7584-1348. www.sloanehotel.com. 22 units. £215–£250 ($398–$463) double; £250 ($463) suite. AE, DC, MC, V. Tube: Sloane Sq. **Amenities:** Airport transportation (by prior arrangement); business services; 24-hr. room service; laundry service; same-day dry cleaning. *In room:* A/C, TV/VCR w/pay movies, dataport, hair dryer, safe.

Moderate

The Willett ⭐ *Value*   On a tree-lined street leading off Sloane Square, this restored town house lies in the heart of Chelsea. It evokes the days when King Edward was on the throne; stained glass and chandeliers reflect the opulence of that age. Under a mansard roof with projecting bay windows, the hotel is just a 5-minute walk from the shopping mecca of King's Road and close to such stores as Peter Jones, Harrods, and Harvey Nichols. Individually decorated guest rooms come in a wide range of sizes. Some are first class, but a few of the standard twins are best left for Lilliputians.

32 Sloane Gardens, London SW1 8DJ. © 800-270-9206 in the U.S., or 020/7824-8415. Fax 020/7730-4830. www.eeh.co.uk. 19 units. £100–£170 ($185–$315) double. Rates include English breakfast. AE, DC, MC, V. Tube: Sloane Sq. **Amenities:** Concierge; limited room service; babysitting; laundry service; same-day dry cleaning; nonsmoking rooms. *In room:* A/C in most, TV/VCR, dataport, minibar in suites, coffeemaker, hair dryer, iron.

SOUTH KENSINGTON
Moderate

The Gallery ⭐ *Finds*   This is the place to go if you want to stay in an exclusive little town-house hotel but don't want to pay £300 ($475) a night for the privilege. Two splendid Georgian residences have been restored and converted into this remarkable and relatively unknown hotel. The location is ideal, near the Victoria and Albert Museum, Royal Albert Hall, Harrods, Knightsbridge, and King's Road. Guest rooms are decorated in Laura Ashley style, with half-canopied beds and marble-tiled bathrooms with brass fittings and tub-and-shower combos. The junior suites have private roof terraces, minibars, Jacuzzis, and air-conditioning. A team of butlers takes care of everything. The lounge, with its mahogany paneling and deep colors, has the ambience of a private club.

8–10 Queensberry Place, London SW7 2EA. © 800-270-9206 in the U.S., or 020/7915-0000. Fax 020/7915-4400. www.eeh.co.uk. 36 units. £130–£170 ($241–$315) double; from £250 ($463) junior suite. Rates include English breakfast. AE, DC, MC, V. Tube: South Kensington. **Amenities:** Bar; access to nearby health club; courtesy car; business center; babysitting; laundry service; same-day dry cleaning; 24-hr. butler service; nonsmoking rooms. *In room:* TV, dataport, coffeemaker, hair dryer, safe.

PADDINGTON
Moderate

The Pavilion *Finds*   Until the early 1990s, this was a rather ordinary-looking B&B. Then, a team of entrepreneurs with ties to the fashion industry took over and redecorated the rooms with sometimes-wacky themes. The result is a theatrical and often outrageous decor that's appreciated by the many fashion models and music-industry folks who regularly make this their temporary home in London. Rooms are, regrettably, rather small, but each has a distinctive style. Examples include a kitschy 1970s room ("Honky-Tonk Afro") and an Asian bordello–themed room ("Enter the Dragon").

34–36 Sussex Gardens, London W2 1UL. © 020/7262-0905. Fax 020/7262-1324. www.pavilionhoteluk.com. 29 units. £100 ($185) double; £120 ($222) triple. Rates include continental breakfast. AE, DC, MC, V. Parking £5 ($9.25). Tube: Paddington Station. **Amenities:** Same-day dry cleaning; laundry service. *In room:* TV, dataport, coffeemaker.

MARYLEBONE
Inexpensive

Boston Court Hotel   Upper Berkeley is a classic street of B&Bs. In days of yore, it was home to Elizabeth Montagu (1720–1800), the "queen of the blue-stockings" (a pejorative term for the women's literary clubs that sprang up in the

18th c.). She defended Shakespeare against attacks by Voltaire, who was fond of saying such things as: "Shakespeare is a savage with sparks of genius which shine in a horrible night." Today, it's a good, safe retreat at an affordable price. The simply decorated hotel offers accommodations in a centrally located Victorian-era building within walking distance of Oxford Street shopping and Hyde Park. The small, basic rooms have been refurbished and redecorated with a no-nonsense decor. Guest rooms come with well-kept bathrooms with private showers.

26 Upper Berkeley St., Marble Arch, London W1H 7PF. © 020/7723-1445. Fax 020/7262-8823. www.bostoncourthotel.co.uk. 15 units, 7 with shower only. £69 ($128) double with shower only; £75–£79 ($139–$146) double with bathroom; £85–£89 ($157–$165) triple with bathroom. Rates include continental breakfast. MC, V. Tube: Marble Arch. **Amenities:** Laundry service; nonsmoking rooms. *In room:* TV w/pay movies, dataport, fridge, coffeemaker, hair dryer.

Edward Lear Hotel   This popular hotel, situated a block from Marble Arch, is made all the more desirable by the bouquets of fresh flowers in its public rooms. It occupies a pair of brick town houses dating from 1780. The western house was the London home of 19th-century artist and poet Edward Lear, famous for his nonsense verse, and his illustrated limericks adorn the walls of one of the sitting rooms. Steep stairs lead up to cozy rooms which range from spacious to broom-closet size. Things are a bit tattered here and there, but with this location and price level, few can complain, as this is an area of £400-a-night ($740) mammoths. If you're looking for classiness, know that the bacon on your plate came from the same butcher used by the queen. One major drawback to the hotel: This is a very noisy part of town; rear rooms are quieter. Bathrooms are tidy and well maintained, each with a shower and tub.

28–30 Seymour St., London W1H 7JB. © 020/7402-5401. Fax 020/7706-3766. www.edlear.com. 31 units, 12 with bathroom. £67 ($124) double without bathroom; £74 ($137) double with bathroom; £79 ($146) suite. Rates include English breakfast. MC, V. Tube: Marble Arch. *In room:* TV w/pay movies, dataport, coffeemaker.

BAYSWATER
Expensive
Miller's Residence ★ (Finds)   Staying here is like spending a night in Charles Dickens's *Old Curiosity Shop*. Others say that the little hotel looks like a set of *La Traviata*. Miller's calls itself an 18th-century rooming house, and there's nothing quite like it in London. A roaring log fire blazes in the large book-lined drawing room in winter. The individually designed rooms are named after Romantic poets. They vary in shape and size, but all are luxuriously furnished with antiques, prints, and tasteful curios. Each guest room includes a small bathroom with a shower and tub. For guests who are staying longer than a week, Miller's offers sumptuous apartments with multiple bedrooms, a drawing room, and a kitchen.

111A Westbourne Grove, London W2 4UW. © 020/7243-1024. Fax 020/7243-1064. www.millersuk.com. 8 units. £150–£185 ($278–$342) double; £230 ($426) suite; from £1,600 ($2,960) per week apt. Rates include continental breakfast. AE, DISC, MC, V. Tube: Bayswater or Notting Hill Gate. **Amenities:** Limited business services; babysitting; laundry service; same-day dry cleaning. *In room:* TV/VCR, dataport.

Moderate
The Byron Hotel (Value)   A mostly American clientele appreciates this family-run hotel, just north of Kensington Gardens, for its country-house atmosphere, its helpful staff (who spend extra time with guests to make their stay in London special), and the good value it offers. The interior was recently redesigned and refurbished, and the rooms are better than ever, with ample closets and tile

bathrooms with good showers. An elevator services all floors, and breakfast is served in a bright and cheery room.

36–38 Queensborough Terrace, London W2 3SH. ℂ **020/7243-0987**. Fax 020/7792-1957. www.capricornhotels. co.uk. 45 units. £120 ($222) double; £150–£180 ($278–$333) suite. Rates include English/continental breakfast. AE, DC, MC, V. Tube: Bayswater or Queensway. **Amenities:** 24-hr. room service; laundry service; same-day dry cleaning. *In room:* A/C, TV, dataport, coffeemaker, hair dryer, iron, safe.

A GAY HOTEL

Philbeach Hotel   One of Europe's largest gay hotels, the Philbeach is a Victorian row house on a wide crescent behind the Earl's Court Exhibition Centre, open to both men and women. It offers standard budget-hotel rooms; the showers are tiny, but the shared bathrooms are clean. Room no. 8A, a double with a shower-only bathroom, has a balcony overlooking the small back garden.

30–31 Philbeach Gardens, London SW5 9EB. ℂ **020/7373-1244**. Fax 020/7244-0149. www.philbeachhotel. freeserve.co.uk. 40 units, 16 with bathroom. £70 ($130) double without bathroom; £90 ($167) double with bathroom. Rates include continental breakfast. AE, DC, MC, V. Tube: Earl's Court. **Amenities:** Restaurant; gay bar (Jimmies); laundry service; same-day dry cleaning. *In room:* TV.

WHERE TO DINE

All restaurants and cafes in Britain are required to display the prices of their food and drink in a place that the customer can see before entering the eating area. Charges for service and any minimum charge or cover must also be made clear. Most restaurants add a 10% to 15% service charge to your bill, but if nothing has been added, leave a 12% to 15% tip.

MAYFAIR
Very Expensive

Gordon Ramsay at Claridge's ★★★ EUROPEAN   Gordon Ramsay, the volatile and outspoken Scotsman who once played soccer for the Glasgow Rangers, is the hottest high-octane chef in London today. Ramsay now rules at the staid, traditional Claridge's hotel. The famed Art Deco dining room retains many of its original architectural features, but the cuisine is hardly the same. In "bad boy" Ramsay's own words, he got "rid of the dribble mats and the waltzing."

We were recently dazzled by the lunch set menu, which is relatively reasonably priced and which included roast monkfish tails served on a bed of lobster and crushed potatoes with a creamy coriander-laced lemon-grass sauce; and pot-roasted belly of pork with an eggplant caviar and baby spinach. A three-course dinner featured such delights as filet of sea bass wrapped in fresh basil leaves and served with a caviar sauce; and roast Scottish baby lobster cooked slowly in lime butter and served with tomato couscous. The desserts are among our favorite in London, including a bread-and-butter brioche pudding with clotted-cream ice cream.

Brook St., W1. ℂ **020/7499-0099**. Reservations required as far in advance as possible. Fixed-price lunch £30 ($56); a la carte menu £55 ($102); 6-course fixed-price dinner £65 ($120). Early bird fixed-price menu (5:45–6:30pm) £30 ($56). AE, DC, MC, V. Daily noon–3pm; Mon–Sat 5:45–11pm, Sun 5:45–10:30pm. Tube: Bond St.

Le Gavroche ★★★ FRENCH   Although challengers come and go, this luxe dining room remains the number one choice in London for classical French cuisine, although not of the "essentially old-fashioned bourgeois repertoire" as some critics suggest. The service is faultless and the ambience is chic without being stuffy. Try some of the signatures: soufflé Suissesse, papillote of smoked salmon, or whole Bresse chicken with truffles and a Madeira cream sauce. Other menu options include an herb-seasoned cassoulet of snails with frog thighs, mousseline of lobster in champagne sauce, pavé of braised turbot with red Provençal wine and smoked bacon, and filet of red snapper with caviar and oyster-stuffed tortellini. Lighter, more modern dishes include red mullet with a cockle risotto, and poached lobster flavored with star anise.

43 Upper Brook St., W1. ℂ 020/7408-0881. Fax 020/7491-4387. Reservations required as far in advance as possible. Main courses £24–£45 ($44–$83); fixed-price lunch £42 ($78); *menu exceptionnel* for entire table £82 ($152) per person. AE, MC, V. Mon–Fri noon–2pm and 7–11pm; Sat 7–11pm. Tube: Marble Arch.

Petrus ✹✹ FRENCH Clubby and not at all stuffy, this is the domain of Marcus Wareing, a former boxer from Lancashire. Here in a sleek, opulent setting, you get reasonably priced food that is prepared with a technical precision but also a touch of whimsy. It's best to order the chef's six-course tasting menu to appreciate his culinary ambitions. You're likely to be dazzled with everything from marinated foie gras to an apple and artichoke salad, from Bresse pigeon in a truffle confit to a Valhrona chocolate fondant. We've delighted in all the dishes sampled here, from the eggplant caviar to crisp roast sea bass paired with caramelized endive and plump oysters.

33 St. James's St., SW1. ℂ 020/7930-4272. Reservations required. Fixed-price menu £26–£56 ($48–$104) for 3 courses, £60 ($111) for 6-course tasting menu. AE, DC, MC, V. Mon–Fri noon–2:30pm; Mon–Sat 6:45–10:45pm. Tube: Green Park.

Expensive

L'Oranger ✹ FRENCH This bistro-cum-brasserie manages to elevate a Gallic brasserie into an artfully upscale dining experience for a clientele that has been described as "people who have made it." The set-price menus are likely to include foie gras poached in a red Pessac wine sauce; and pan-fried filet of sea bass with zucchini, tomatoes, basil, and a black-olive vinaigrette. Other delectable staples may be crispy cod filets with bouillabaisse sauce and new potatoes; or braised leg of rabbit in Madeira sauce with whole cloves of yellow garlic *en confit* and braised cabbage.

5 St. James's St., SW1A. ℂ 020/7839-3774. Reservations recommended. Fixed-price lunch £24–£28 ($44–$52); fixed-price dinner £12–£32 ($22–$59). AE, DC, MC, V. Mon–Fri noon–2pm; Mon–Sat 6:30–11pm. Tube: Green Park.

PICCADILLY & LEICESTER SQUARE
Expensive

J. Sheekey ✹ SEAFOOD British culinary tradition lives on in this restored fish joint, long a favorite of West End actors. The same jellied eels that delighted Laurence Olivier and Vivien Leigh are still here, along with an array of fresh oysters from the coasts of Ireland and Brittany, plus that Victorian favorite, fried whitebait. Sheekey's fish pie is still on the menu, as is a delightful Dover sole, even a Cornish fish stew that's quite savory. The old "mushy" vegetables still appear but the chefs get experimental and occasionally more daring and offer the likes of steamed organic sea beet. The double chocolate pudding soufflé is a delight. But look for something daring every now and then—perhaps fried plum ravioli with yogurt ice cream.

28–32 St. Martin's Court, WC2. ℂ 020/7240-2565. Reservations recommended. Main courses £10–£31 ($19–$57). AE, DC, MC, V. Mon–Sat noon–3pm and 5:30pm–midnight; Sun noon–3:30pm and 6pm–midnight. Tube: Leicester Square.

Moderate

Atlantic Bar & Grill ✪✪ MODERN BRITISH   A titanic restaurant in a former Art Deco ballroom off Piccadilly Circus, this cosmopolitan locale draws a trendy crowd to London's heart. Chef Steve Carter is doing much to recapture the restaurant's mid-1990s chic, with emphasis on organic and homegrown produce, seafood, and meats. Many dishes are quite complex and taste as good as they sound: swordfish dumplings with a salsa of plum tomatoes, fresh cilantro, sautéed shiitake, soy-infused ginger, and fresh wilted spinach; or the loin of yellowfin tuna served with a wild parsley-and-eggplant relish and a pesto made of roasted red bell peppers.

20 Glasshouse St., W1. © 020/7734-4888. Reservations required. Main courses £13–£22 ($24–$41); fixed-price 3-course lunch £16 ($30). AE, DC, MC, V. Mon–Fri noon–3pm; Mon–Sat 6pm–3am; Sun 6–10:30pm. Tube: Piccadilly Circus.

The Criterion Brasserie ✪ MODERN BRITISH/FRENCH   Designed by Thomas Verity in the 1870s, this palatial neo-Byzantine mirrored marble hall is a glamorous backdrop for superb cuisine, served under a golden ceiling with peacock-blue draperies, by a mainly French staff. The menu is wide ranging, offering everything from Paris brasserie food to "nouvelle-classical," a combination of classic French cooking techniques with some of the lighter, more experimental leanings of modern French cuisine. The food is excellent, but falls short of sublime. The roast skate wing with deep-fried snails is delectable, as is the roast saddle of lamb stuffed with mushrooms and spinach.

224 Piccadilly, W1. © 020/7930-0488. Main courses £14–£23 ($26–$43). Fixed-price 2-course lunch £15 ($28); fixed-price 3-course lunch £18 ($33). AE, MC, V. Daily noon–2:30pm and 5:30–11:30pm. Tube: Piccadilly Circus.

SOHO
Expensive

Spoon+ ✪ AMERICAN/INTERNATIONAL   Housed in Ian Schrager's hot Sanderson Hotel, this is a branch of the Spoon restaurant in Paris where master chef Alain Ducasse cooks for *tout Paris*. It's Monsieur Ducasse's take on American fusion cuisine. And who can beat Spoon+ when it comes to dishing up the best bubble-gum ice cream in London? We don't mean to make a caricature of the food, but some items seemed designed to shock. This is the only place you can go in London to eat a French version of that American classic: macaroni and cheese. Of course, there's also lobster in banana leaves if you want to go native. Much of what is offered, though, is really good, especially the crab ceviche, and the iced tomato soup. Spoon+ chefs allow you to compose your own meal or at least pair ingredients—perhaps a beautiful sole with a crushed lemon confit, or do you prefer it with satay sauce? On our last visit, we found the restaurant ridiculously overpriced, but reconsidered when the entertainment of the evening arrived. Our fellow diners turned out to be none other than Madonna and her husband, Guy Ritchie.

50 Berners St., W1. © 020/7300-1400. Reservations required. Main courses £21–£30 ($39–$56). AE, DC, MC, V. Daily noon–3pm and 6–11:30pm (until 10:30pm Sun). Tube: Leicester Sq. or Covent Garden.

Moderate

The Ivy ✪✪ MODERN BRITISH/INTERNATIONAL   Effervescent and sophisticated, The Ivy is the dining choice of visiting theatrical luminaries. It has been intimately associated with the theater district ever since it opened in 1911. With its ersatz 1930s look and tiny bar near the entrance, this place is fun and hums with the energy of London's glamour scene. The kitchen has a solid appreciation for fresh ingredients. Our favorite dishes include white asparagus with sea kale and truffle butter; seared scallops with spinach, sorrel, and bacon; and salmon fish cakes.

1–5 West St., WC2. ✆ **020/7836-4751.** Reservations required. Main courses £9–£35 ($17–$65); Sat–Sun fixed-price 3-course lunch £20 ($36). AE, DC, MC, V. Mon–Sat noon–3pm and daily 5:30pm–midnight (last order); Sun noon–3:30pm. Tube: Leicester Sq.

Mezzo EUROPEAN/ASIAN   This 750-seat, blockbuster Soho spot—the creation of Sir Terence Conran—is the biggest restaurant in London. The mammoth space is the former site of rock's legendary Marquee club. Mezzo is actually composed of several restaurants: **Mezzonine** upstairs, serving Thai/Asian cuisine with a European flair; swankier **Mezzo** downstairs, offering modern European cuisine in a 1930s Hollywood atmosphere; and **Mezzo Cafe,** where you can stop in for a simple sandwich and a drink.

The food is at its most ambitious downstairs at Mezzo, where 100 chefs work behind glass to feed up to 400 diners at a time. This is dinner-as-theater. Not surprisingly for a restaurant of this size, the cuisine tends to be uneven. We suggest the rotisserie rib of beef with red wine and creamed horseradish, or the roast cod, which is crisp-skinned and cooked to perfection. A live jazz band entertains after 10pm from Wednesday to Saturday.

100 Wardour St., W1. ✆ **020/7314-4000.** Reservations recommended. Mezzo 3-course fixed-price dinner £17 ($31); Mezzonine 3-course dinner £15 ($28); Mezzo Cafe main courses £5–£10 ($9.25–$19). AE, DC, MC, V. Mezzo: Wed–Fri noon–3pm; Sun 12:30–3pm; Mon–Thurs 6pm–1am; Fri–Sat 6pm–3am; Sun 6–11pm. Mezzonine: Mon–Fri noon–3pm; Sat noon–4pm; Mon–Thurs 5:30pm–1am; Fri–Sat 5:30pm–3am. Mezzo Cafe: Mon–Sat 8am–11pm. Tube: Piccadilly Circus.

Rasa Samundra ✿ *(Value)* INDIAN   Whereas most Indian restaurants in London specialize in the cuisine of the north, Rasa Samundra features the cooking of the southern state of Kerala, whose specialties are plucked from the sea. Try *malslam pattichathu* (king fish cooked in fresh spices, with green chile and coconut paste), *para konju nirachathu* (lobster cooked with black pepper, garlic, and Indian shallots and served with whole lemon and beet curry), *masala dosa* (paper-thin rice and black graham pancake filled with potato and ginger masala), and *moru kachlathu* (green bananas and mangoes cooked in a yogurt sauce with turmeric and onions).

5 Charlotte St., W1. ✆ **020/7637-0222.** Reservations required. Main courses £10–£30 ($19–$56); fixed-price lunch £20 ($37); fixed-price dinner £30 ($56). AE, DC, MC, V. Daily noon–11pm. Tube: Tottenham Court Rd.

BLOOMSBURY
Moderate

Townhouse Brasserie ✿ FRENCH/INTERNATIONAL   Near the British Museum, this old Georgian town house is one of the most up-and-coming restaurants in Bloomsbury. The ground floor is enhanced with contemporary art, and upstairs is a traditional old English dining room, except for an infusion of Peruvian art. The menu is a culinary tour de force, drawing inspiration from around the world. Launch your repast with the cream of leek soup or sweet-potato soup with basil. Then it's on to a delectable charcoal-grilled duck breast with an Asian-style salad. Especially pleasing is a fresh seafood pasta flavored with chives, thick cream, and white wine. It's worth it to save up room for one of the tempting desserts, made fresh daily.

24 Coptic St., WC1. ✆ **020/7636-2731.** Reservations recommended. Main courses £11–£18 ($20–$33). AE, DC, MC, V. Mon–Sat 11am–11pm; Sun 10am–6pm. Tube: Tottenham Court Rd. or Holborn.

Villandry ✪ INTERNATIONAL/CONTINENTAL   Food lovers and gourmands flock to this combination food store, florist, delicatessen, and restaurant. The setting is an oversize Edwardian-style storefront north of Oxford Circus. Inside, ingredients change so frequently the menu is revamped and rewritten twice a day. You're likely to face such perfectly crafted dishes as breast of duck with fresh spinach and a gratin of baby onions; boiled haunch of pork with blood sausages, mashed potatoes, kale, and mustard sauce; filet of black codfish with prosciutto, radicchio, and creamed lentils; and pan-fried turbot with deep-fried celery, artichoke hearts, and hollandaise sauce.

170 Great Portland St., W1. ✆ 020/7631-3131. Reservations recommended. Main courses £16–£21 ($30–$39). AE, DC, MC, V. Restaurant: Mon–Sat noon–3pm and 6–10:30pm. Food store: Mon–Sat 8am–10pm; Sun 11am–4pm. Tube: Great Portland St.

Inexpensive

Wagamama JAPANESE   This noodle joint, in a basement just off New Oxford Street, is noisy and overly crowded, and you'll have to wait in line for a table. The fast-serve, fast-out concept calls itself a "nondestination food station" and caters to some 1,200 customers a day. All dishes are built around ramen noodles with your choice of chicken, beef, or salmon served with gyoza, a light pancake filled with vegetables. Vegetarian dishes are available, but skip the so-called "Korean-style" dishes.

4 Streatham St., WC1. ✆ 020/7323-9223. Reservations not accepted. Main courses £5.50–£11 ($10–$20). AE, MC, V. Mon–Sat noon–11pm; Sun 12:30–10pm. Tube: Tottenham Court Rd.

COVENT GARDEN & THE STRAND
Expensive

Rules ✪ TRADITIONAL BRITISH   If you're looking for London's most quintessentially British restaurant, eat here. London's oldest restaurant was established in 1798 as an oyster bar; today, the antler-filled Edwardian dining rooms exude nostalgia. You can order such classic dishes as Irish or Scottish oysters, jugged hare, and mussels. Game dishes are offered from mid-August to February or March, including wild Scottish salmon; wild sea trout; wild Highland red deer; and game birds such as grouse, snipe, partridge, pheasant, and woodcock. As a finale, the "great puddings" continue to impress.

35 Maiden Lane, WC2. ✆ 020/7836-5314. Reservations recommended. Main courses £15–£21 ($28–$39). AE, DC, MC, V. Daily noon–11:30pm. Tube: Covent Garden.

Moderate

Porter's English Restaurant ✪✪ *Kids* TRADITIONAL BRITISH   The seventh earl of Bradford serves "real English food at affordable prices" at this restaurant. He succeeds notably—and not just because Lady Bradford turned over her carefully guarded recipe for banana-and-ginger pudding. This comfortable, two-story restaurant is family friendly, informal, and lively. Porter's specializes in classic English pies, including Old English fish pie; lamb and apricot pie; and ham, leek, and cheese pie. Bangers and mash is another popular dish. Main courses are so generous—and accompanied by vegetables and side dishes—that you hardly need to start with appetizers. A traditional English tea is served from 2:30 to 5:30pm for £4.75 ($8.80) per person.

17 Henrietta St., WC2. ✆ 020/7836-6466. Reservations recommended. Main courses £8.95–£13 ($17–$24); fixed-price menu £20 ($37). AE, DC, MC, V. Daily noon–11:30pm (until 10:30pm Sun). Tube: Covent Garden or Leicester Sq.

Sarastro ⭐ TURKISH/CYPRIOT   The setting makes you feel like you're in a prop room of an opera house. This is a fun place, especially after a show in Theaterland. The restaurant takes its name from a character in Mozart's *The Magic Flute*. The cuisine celebrates the bounty of the Mediterranean, particularly Turkey and Cyprus. Launch yourself with such delights as asparagus in red-wine sauce or fresh grilled sardines. Market-fresh fish is usually the way to go, especially river trout or grilled halibut. A zesty favorite is lamb Anatolian style (that is, with eggplant and zucchini). We're also fond of the well-seasoned lamb meatballs. A good-tasting specialty is chicken Sarastro with walnuts and raisins.

126 Drury Lane, WC2. ⓒ 020/7836-0101. Reservations required. Main courses £8.50–£15 ($16–$28); fixed-price menu £10–£20 ($19–$37); pretheater menu £10 ($19). AE, DC, MC, V. Daily noon–midnight. Tube: Covent Garden.

FLEET STREET
Inexpensive
Ye Olde Cheshire Cheese TRADITIONAL BRITISH   Dating from the 13th century, this is the most famous of the old city chophouses (restaurants) and pubs. It claims to be the spot where Samuel Johnson entertained admirers. Later, many of the ink-stained journalists and scandalmongers of Fleet Street made its four-story premises their "local." Within, you'll find six bars and two dining rooms. The house specialties include "Ye Famous Pudding"—steak, kidney, mushrooms, and game—and Scottish roast beef with Yorkshire pudding and horseradish sauce.

Wine Office Court, 145 Fleet St., EC4. ⓒ 020/7353-6170. Main courses £7.50–£10 ($14–$19). AE, DC, MC, V. Meals Mon–Fri noon–9:30pm; Sat noon–2:30pm and 6–9:30pm; Sun noon–2:30pm. Drinks and bar snacks Mon–Fri 11:30am–11pm. Tube: St. Paul's or Blackfriars.

WESTMINSTER
Moderate
Tate Britain Restaurant ⭐⭐ *Value* MODERN BRITISH   Located in the Tate Britain gallery (see later in this chapter), this restaurant is particularly attractive to wine fanciers. It offers what may be the best bargains for superior wines anywhere in Britain. Bordeaux and burgundies are in abundance, and the management keeps the markup between 40% and 65%, rather than the 100% to 200% added in most restaurants. In fact, the prices here are lower than they are in most wine shops. Wine begins at £15 ($28) per bottle, or £3.95 ($7.30) per glass. Oenophiles frequently come for lunch. The restaurant offers an English menu that changes about every month. Dishes may include pheasant casserole, pan-fried skate with black butter and capers, and a selection of vegetarian dishes. One critic found the staff and diners as traditional "as a Gainsborough landscape." Access to the restaurant is through the museum's main entrance on Millbank.

Millbank, SW1. ⓒ 020/7887-8825. Reservations recommended. Main courses £11–£18 ($20–$33). Fixed-price lunch £18 ($33) 2 courses; £21 ($39) 3 courses. AE, DC, MC, V. Mon–Sat noon–3pm; Sun noon–4pm. Tube: Pimlico.

KNIGHTSBRIDGE
Very Expensive
Zafferano ⭐⭐ ITALIAN   There's something honest and satisfying about this restaurant, where decor consists of little more than ocher-colored walls, immaculate linens, and a bevy of diligent staff members. A quick review of past clients includes Margaret Thatcher, Richard Gere, and Eric Clapton. The modernized

Moments   Where to Have a Cuppa Tea

The lounge at **Brown's Hotel,** 29–34 Albemarle St., W1 (© 020/7518-4108; Tube: Green Park), is decorated with English antiques, oil paintings, and floral chintz, much like an English country estate. Give your name to the concierge upon arrival (reservations aren't accepted); arrangements will be made for you to be seated on clusters of sofas and settees or at low tables. Served daily from 2 to 5:30pm, the regular afternoon tea (£25/$46) includes a choice of 12 teas, plus sandwiches, scones, and pastries. The teatime rituals at **Claridge's,** Brook Street, W1 (© 020/7629-8860; Tube: Bond St.), have managed to persevere through the years with as much pomp and circumstance as the empire itself. A portrait of Lady Claridge gazes beneficently from the paneled walls as a choice of 17 teas is served ever so politely each day from 3 to 6pm. Reservations are recommended, and jackets are required for men. It's served Monday through Friday for £26 ($48); and on Saturday and Sunday for £35 ($65), including champagne.

A flood of visitors is somehow gracefully herded into the high-volume but nevertheless elegant **Georgian Restaurant,** on the fourth floor of Harrods, 87–135 Brompton Rd., SW1 (© 020/7255-6800; Tube: Knightsbridge), in a room so long its staff refers to its shape and size as the "Mississippi River." The list of teas available—at least 50—is sometimes so esoteric the experience might remind you of choosing among vintages in a sophisticated wine cellar. Served Monday through Saturday from 3:15 to 5:30pm (last order), high tea runs £19 ($35) per person; reservations are recommended. **The Orangery,** in the gardens just north of Kensington Palace, W8 (© 020/7376-0239; Tube: High St. Kensington or Queensway), occupies a long and narrow garden pavilion built in 1704 by Queen Anne as a site for her tea parties. Tea is still served (daily 10am–6pm) amid rows of potted orange trees basking in sunlight from soaring windows. Reservations are not accepted. A pot of tea costs £1.75 to £1.95 ($3.25–$3.60), and summer cakes and puddings run £2.95 to £3.95 ($5.45–$7.30).

interpretation of Italian cuisine features such dishes as ravioli of pheasant with black truffles, wild pigeon with garlic purée, sea bream with spinach and balsamic vinegar, and monkfish with almonds. Joan Collins claimed that the chefs produce culinary fireworks, but found the bright lighting far too harsh.

15 Lowndes St., SW1. © 020/7235-5800. Reservations required. Set menus £29–£35 ($54–$65). AE, MC, V. Daily noon–2:30pm and 7–11pm. Tube: Knightsbridge.

Expensive

English Garden ★ TRADITIONAL BRITISH   This is a metropolitan restaurant par excellence. The decor in this historic town house is pretty and lighthearted: The Garden Room is whitewashed brick with a domed conservatory roof; vivid florals, rattan chairs, banks of plants, and candy-pink linens to complete the scene. Every component of the meal is carried out perfectly. Some of the dishes sound as if they were copied directly from an English cookbook of the Middle Ages—and are they ever good. For a main course, opt for such delights as roast baron of rabbit with oven-dried tomato, prunes, and olive oil mash; or saddle of venison with potted cabbage. Desserts, especially the rhubarb and cinnamon ice cream, and the candied orange tart with orange syrup, would've pleased Miss Marple.

10 Lincoln St., SW3. ✆ 020/7584-7272. Reservations required. Fixed-price lunch £24 ($44); 3-course dinner £29 ($54). AE, DC, MC, V. Mon–Sat noon–3pm; Sun 12:30–2pm; daily 6:30–10:30pm. Tube: Sloane Sq.

KENSINGTON
Moderate

Pasha MOROCCAN Few ethnic restaurants equal the zest and stylishness of this re-created Marrakech palace. Within a duet of dining rooms outfitted with flickering candles, belly-dancing music, and artifacts from the sub-Sahara, you'll enjoy regional and time-honored specialties. The best examples include a crispy lamb salad with pomegranate and mint; grilled sea bass with warm hummus and a parsley salad; chicken *tagine* with fennel, olives, and preserved lemon; and charcoal-grilled skewered chicken with green-chile salsa. And if you like couscous, you'll have at least three kinds from which to choose.

1 Gloucester Rd., SW7. ✆ 020/7589-7969. Reservations recommended. Main courses £9.75–£17 ($18–$31). AE, DC, MC, V. Mon–Sat noon–3pm and 6–11pm; Sun 5:30–10pm. Tube: Gloucester Rd.

SOUTH KENSINGTON
Expensive

Greens Restaurant & Oyster Bar SEAFOOD/TRADITIONAL BRITISH Critics say it's a triumph of tradition over taste, but as far as seafood in London goes, this is a tried-and-true favorite, thanks to an excellent menu with moderately priced dishes, a central location, and a charming staff. This place has a cluttered entrance leading to a crowded bar where you can sip fine wines and, from September to April, enjoy oysters. In the faux-Dickensian dining room, you can choose from a long menu of fresh seafood dishes, which changes monthly depending on what is in season. The standard menu ranges from fish cakes with leaf spinach to whole Scottish lobster. Desserts include bread-and-butter pudding. *Note:* London has two different Duke streets. Greens is on the one in St. James's.

36 Duke St., St. James's, SW1. ✆ 020/7930-4566. Reservations recommended. Main courses £12–£38 ($22–$70). AE, DC, MC, V. Restaurant daily 11:30am–3pm; Mon–Sat 5:30–11pm. Oyster Bar Mon–Sat 11:30am–3pm and 5:30–11pm; Sun noon–3pm and 5:30–9pm. Tube: Green Park.

CHELSEA
Moderate

Admiral Codrington ★ (Finds) MODERN BRITISH/CONTINENTAL Once a lowly pub, this stylish bar and restaurant is all the rage nowadays. The old "Cod," as it is affectionately known, offers plush dining with a revitalized decor by Nina Campbell, and a glass roof that rolls back on sunny days. The bartenders still offer a traditional pint, but the sophisticated menu features such delectable fare as homemade tortellini of pumpkin and Parmesan cheese, or caramelized breast of duckling with sweet potato. A real palate pleaser is the monkfish spring roll with fresh herbs and thyme salsa. Stars of the menu are the grilled breast-of-chicken salad with bean sprouts, apple slices, and cashews; and the grilled tuna with a couscous salad and eggplant "caviar."

17 Mossop St., SW3. ✆ 020/7581-0005. Reservations recommended. Main courses £10–£15 ($19–$28). MC, V. Mon–Sat 11:30am–midnight; Sun noon–10:30pm. Tube: South Kensington.

MARYLEBONE
Expensive

Orrey ⭐⭐ INTERNATIONAL/FRENCH   This is one of London's classic French restaurants. Sea bass from the shores of Montpellier, olive oil from Maussane-les-Alpilles, mushrooms from the fields of Calais, and poultry from Bresse—it all turns up on this highly refined menu, the creation of chef Andre Garret. On the first floor of The Conran Shop in Marylebone, the restaurant changes its menu seasonally to take advantage of the best produce. Our favorites are tagine of pigeon with a saffron-flavored couscous; Barbary duck with foie gras; and seared scallops with pieces of pork belly and cauliflower. A wild mushroom consommé arrives with a medley of such fungi as *pieds de bleu*, *pieds de mouton*, chanterelles, and *trompettes de morte*, all from French forests. Lazy summer evenings are to be enjoyed on a fourth-floor terrace, where you can drink and order light fare from the bar menu.

55 Marylebone High St., W1. ℭ 020/7616-8000. Reservations required. Main courses £17–£30 ($31–$56); fixed-price menu £24 ($44) 3 courses, £50 ($93) 5 courses. AE, DC, MC, V. Daily noon–3pm; Mon–Sat 7–11pm; Sun 7–10:30pm. Tube: Baker St. or Regency Park.

Moderate

Caldesi ITALIAN   Good food, reasonable prices, fresh ingredients, and authentic Tuscan family recipes attract a never-ending stream of diners to this eatery. The extensive menu includes a wide array of pasta, antipasti, fish, and meat dishes. Start with an excellent *insalata Caldesi*, made with tomatoes slow roasted in garlic and rosemary oil and served with mozzarella flown in from Tuscany. Pasta dishes include an especially flavor-filled homemade tortellini stuffed with salmon and ricotta and served with a creamy spinach sauce. Monkfish and prawns are flavored with wild fennel and fresh basil, or you might sample the tender duck breast a l'orange, steeped in white wine, honey, thyme, and rosemary.

15–17 Marylebone Lane, W1. ℭ 020/7935-9226. Reservations required. Main courses £9–£20 ($17–$37). AE, MC, V. Mon–Fri noon–2:30pm; Mon–Sat 6–11pm. Tube: Bond St.

NOTTING HILL GATE
Expensive

Pharmacy Restaurant and Bar ⭐ EUROPEAN   The theme of this medical-chic restaurant evokes all sorts of drug-related venues, from a harmless small-town pharmacy to a drug lord's secret stash of mind-altering pills. This ambiguity is appreciated by the arts-conscious crowd that flocks here, partly because they're interested in what Damien Hirst (*enfant terrible* of London's art world) has created, and partly because the place can be a lot of fun. A drink menu lists lots of highly palatable martinis as well as a somewhat icky concoction known as a Cough Syrup (cherry liqueur, honey, and vodka that's shaken, not stirred, over ice). Bottles of pills; bar stools with seats shaped like aspirins; and painted representations of fire, water, air, and earth decorate the bar area. Upstairs in the restaurant, the pharmaceutical theme is less pronounced but subtly omnipresent. Menu items include trendy but comforting food items such as carpaccio of whitefish, chargrilled lamb, pan-fried cod in red wine with Jerusalem artichokes and shallots, and roast saddle of hare in pear sauce.

150 Notting Hill Gate, W11. ℭ 020/7221-2442. Reservations required Fri–Sat, strongly recommended other nights. Main courses £14–£20 ($26–$37). AE, DISC, MC, V. Daily noon–3pm and 7–10:30pm. Tube: Notting Hill Gate.

THE CITY
Expensive

Prism ★★ MODERN BRITISH/CONTINENTAL   In the financial district, called "The City," this restaurant attracts London's movers and shakers. In the former Bank of New York, Harvey Nichols—known for his chic department store in Knightsbridge—took this 1920s neo-Grecian hall and installed Mies van der Rohe chairs in chrome and lipstick-red leather. In such a setting, traditional English dishes from the north are given a light touch—try the tempura of Whitby cod or cream of Jerusalem artichoke soup with roasted scallops and truffle oil. For a first course, you may opt for a small seared calf's liver with a mushroom risotto, or else a salad composed of flecks of Parmesan cheese seasoning a Savoy cabbage salad and Parma ham.

147 Leadenhall St., EC3. ℭ 020/7256-3888. Reservations required. Main courses £16–£25 ($30–$46). AE, DC, DISC, MC, V. Mon–Fri noon–3pm and 6–10pm. Tube: Bank.

SEEING THE SIGHTS
LONDON ATTRACTIONS

London isn't a city to visit hurriedly. It is so vast, so stocked with treasures, that it would take a lifetime to explore it thoroughly. But even a quick visit will give you a chance to see what's creating the hottest buzz in shopping and nightlife as well as the city's time-tested treasures.

SIGHTSEEING SUGGESTIONS FOR FIRST-TIME VISITORS

If You Have 1 Day No first-time visitor should leave London without visiting **Westminster Abbey.** See **Big Ben** and the **Houses of Parliament,** then walk over to see the **Changing of the Guard** at Buckingham Palace if it's being held. Have dinner in **Covent Garden,** perhaps at Porter's English Restaurant. For your nightcap, head over to the **Red Lion,** 2 Duke of York St. (ℭ **020/7930-2030**), in Mayfair, quite a Victorian pub.

If You Have 2 Days Devote a good part of your second day to exploring the **British Museum,** one of the world's largest and best museums. Spend the afternoon visiting the **Tower of London** and seeing the crown jewels (but expect slow-moving lines). Cap your day by boarding one of the London Launches to experience the city from the river. Go to one of London's landmark restaurants such as **Rules,** 35 Maiden Lane.

If You Have 3 Days In the morning of your third day, go to the **National Gallery** on Trafalgar Square. Then enjoy an afternoon at **Madame Tussauds.** Take some time to stroll through **St. James's** and try to catch a cultural performance at the South Bank Centre, site of the Royal Festival Hall, or a play or musical in the West End.

If You Have 4 Days In the morning of your fourth day, head for the **City,** the financial district. Tour **St. Paul's Cathedral.** Spend a few hours strolling the City and visit a few of its many attractions. In the late afternoon, head down **King's Road** in Chelsea to shop the many and varied boutiques.

If You Have 5 Days On your fifth day, explore the **Victoria and Albert Museum** in the morning, then head to the **Tate Britain Restaurant** for lunch. Finally, see where history was made during the dark days of World War II in the **Cabinet War Rooms** at Clive Steps, where Churchill directed the British operations against the Nazis. In the evening, attend the theater.

THE TOP ATTRACTIONS

Tower of London ★★★   This ancient fortress continues to pack in visitors because of its macabre associations with legendary figures who were imprisoned and/or executed here (Sir Walter Raleigh, Anne Boleyn and her daughter Elizabeth, Lady Jane Grey). The finest structure is the White Tower. Here you can view the Royal Armouries collection of armor and weapons. Instruments of torture and execution are on view in Bowyer Tower. In summer, go early in the day to see the **Crown Jewels** because long lines often form. Uniformed Yeoman Warders (also known as "Beefeaters") give 1-hour tours at frequent intervals, starting at 9:30am from the Middle Tower near the main entrance. The tour includes the Chapel Royal of St. Peter ad Vincula (St. Peter in Chains). The last guided walk starts at about 3:30pm in summer, 2:30pm in winter.

Insider's tip: The secret of avoiding the Tower's notoriously long lines is to buy your ticket in a kiosk inside the Tube station before emerging aboveground. Also, go early in the morning. Avoid Sunday between noon and 2pm if you can—crowds are at their worst then.

Tower Hill, EC3. ℂ 0870/756-6060. www.tower-of-london.org.uk. Admission £14 ($25) adults, £11 ($19) students and seniors, £9 ($17) children, free for children under 5, £38 ($69) family of 5 (but no more than 2 adults). Mar–Oct Mon–Sat 9am–6pm, Sun 10am–6pm; Nov–Feb Tues–Sat 9am–5pm, Sun and Mon 10am–5pm. Tube: Tower Hill.

Westminster Abbey ★★★   In 1065, the Saxon king, Edward the Confessor, founded a Benedictine abbey on this spot overlooking Parliament Square. The first king crowned in the abbey was Harold in 1066. The coronation tradition has continued to the present day, broken only twice (Edward V and Edward VIII). The abbey is the site of state occasions, including the September 1997 funeral of Diana, princess of Wales. The Gothic structure existing today owes more to Henry III's plans than to those of any other sovereign, although many architects, including Wren, have contributed to the abbey. Henry VII Chapel is one of the loveliest in Europe, with its fan vaulting, Knights of Bath banners, and Torrigiani-designed tomb of the king. You can also visit the most hallowed spot in the abbey, the shrine of Edward the Confessor (canonized in the 12th c.). In the saint's chapel is the Coronation Chair, made at the command of Edward I in 1300 to display the Stone of Scone. Another noted spot is the Poets' Corner, to the right of the entrance to the Royal Chapel, with monuments to Chaucer, Shakespeare, "O Rare Ben Johnson" (his name misspelled), Samuel Johnson, the Brontë sisters, Thackeray, Dickens, Tennyson, Kipling, even the American Longfellow.

On Sunday, the Royal Chapels are closed, but the rest of the church is open unless a service is being conducted. For times of services, phone the **Chapter Office** (ℂ 020/7654-4832). The College Garden is open Tuesday through Thursday, April through September from 10am to 6pm and October through March from 10am to 4pm.

Broad Sanctuary, SW1. ℂ 020/7654-4900. www.westminster-abbey.org. Admission £7.50 ($14) adults; £5 ($9.25) for students, seniors, and children 11–18; free for children under 11; £15 ($28) family. Mon–Tues and Thurs–Fri 9:30am–3:45pm; Wed 9:30am–7pm; Sat 9am–1:45pm. Tube: Westminster or St. James's Park.

Houses of Parliament ★★   These Houses are the stronghold of Britain's democracy. Both Houses (Commons and Lords) are situated in the former royal Palace of Westminster, the king's residence until Henry VIII moved to Whitehall. The present Houses of Parliament were built in 1840, but the Commons chamber was bombed and destroyed by the Luftwaffe in 1941. The 98m (320-ft.)

London Attractions

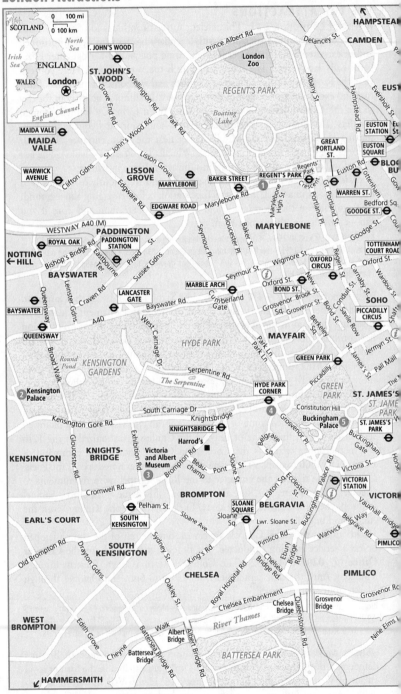

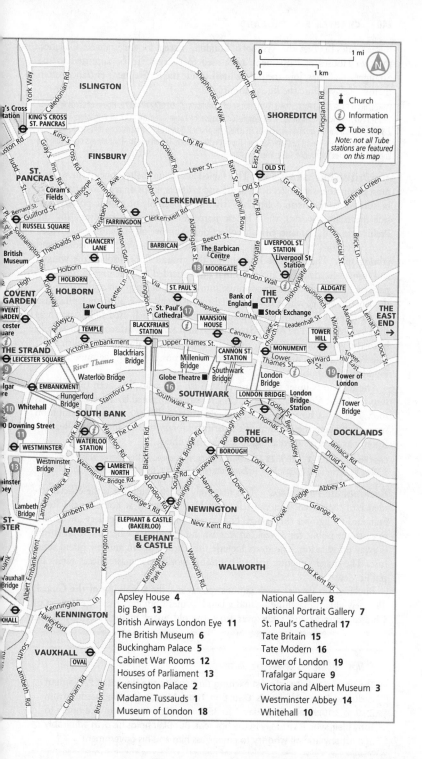

ISLINGTON

SHOREDITCH

King's Cross
Station

KING'S CROSS
ST. PANCRAS

York Way

Caledonian Rd.

New North Rd.

Shepherdess Walk

Kingsland Rd.

✝ Church

ⓘ Information

Ⓔ Tube stop

Note: not all Tube
stations are featured
on this map

FINSBURY

ST.
PANCRAS

Gray's Inn Rd.

King's Cross Rd.

Calthorpe St.

Goswell Rd.

City Rd.

Lever St.

Bath St.

Old St.

East Rd.

OLD ST.

Gt. Eastern St.

Commercial St.

Bethnal Green

Brick Ln.

Coram's
Fields

Bernard St.
Guilford St.

Theobald's Rd.

Southampton Row

RUSSELL SQUARE

Rosebery Ave.

Farringdon Rd.

St. John St.

CLERKENWELL

Clerkenwell Rd.

Bunhill Row

City Rd.

FARRINGDON

CHANCERY
LANE

Hatton Gdn.

BARBICAN

Beech St.

Aldersgate St.

The Barbican
Centre

LIVERPOOL ST.
STATION

Liverpool St.
Station

Bishopsgate

Hounsditch

ALDGATE

THE
EAST
END

British
Museum

High

Kingsway

Holborn

HOLBORN

Holborn

HOLBORN

Fetter Ln.

Farringdon St.

Via.

ST. PAUL'S

Cheapside

Moorgate

London Wall

MOORGATE 18

Bank of
England

THE CITY

Cornhill

Stock Exchange

Leadenhall St.

Grace Church St.

Minories

Leman St.

Mansell St.

COVENT
GARDEN

COVENT
GARDEN

Leicester
Square

Aldwych

Strand

Law Courts

TEMPLE

St. Paul's
Cathedral 17

MANSION
HOUSE

CANNON ST.
STATION

MONUMENT

Lower
Thames St.

TOWER
HILL

Byward
St.

Tower
Hill East

Dock St.

THE STRAND

LEICESTER SQUARE

Victoria Embankment

BLACKFRIARS
STATION

Upper Thames St.

Cannon St.

TOWER
HILL

Tower of
London 19

Tower
of
London

Trafalgar
Square

EMBANKMENT

Blackfriars
Bridge

River Thames

Waterloo Bridge

Millenium
Bridge

Globe Theatre 16

Southwark
Bridge

London
Bridge

LONDON BRIDGE

London
Bridge
Station

Tower
Bridge

DOCKLANDS

Whitehall

Hungerford
Bridge

Stamford St.

SOUTH BANK

SOUTHWARK

Southwark St.

Union St.

SOUTHWARK

St. Thomas St.

Tooley St.

Bermondsey St.

Jamaica Rd.

Druid St.

10 Downing Street

WESTMINSTER

WATERLOO
STATION

York Rd.

Waterloo Rd.

The Cut

THE BOROUGH

BOROUGH

Long Ln.

Abbey St.

Westminster
Bridge

Westminster
Abbey

LAMBETH
NORTH

Westminster Bridge Rd.

St. George's Rd.

London Rd.

Borough Rd.

Borough High St.

Kennington Causeway

Great Dover St.

Harper Rd.

Tower Bridge Rd.

Grange Rd.

Lambeth
Bridge

Lambeth Palace Rd.

Lambeth Rd.

LAMBETH

Kennington Rd.

ELEPHANT & CASTLE
(BAKERLOO)

ELEPHANT
& CASTLE

NEWINGTON

New Kent Rd.

Albert Embankment

Vauxhall
Bridge

VAUXHALL

OVAL

VAUXHALL

Kennington Ln.

Harleyford Rd.

KENNINGTON

Kennington Park Rd.

Walworth Rd.

WALWORTH

Old Kent Rd.

Clapham Rd.

Brixton Rd.

South Lambeth Rd.

Apsley House 4
Big Ben 13
British Airways London Eye 11
The British Museum 6
Buckingham Palace 5
Cabinet War Rooms 12
Houses of Parliament 13
Kensington Palace 2
Madame Tussauds 1
Museum of London 18

National Gallery 8
National Portrait Gallery 7
St. Paul's Cathedral 17
Tate Britain 15
Tate Modern 16
Tower of London 19
Trafalgar Square 9
Victoria and Albert Museum 3
Westminster Abbey 14
Whitehall 10

tower houses Big Ben, the "symbol of London." Except for the Strangers' Galleries, the two Houses of Parliament are closed to tourists. To be admitted to the Strangers' Galleries, join the public line outside the St. Stephen's entrance; often there's a delay before the line is admitted.

Westminster Palace, Old Palace Yard, SW1. House of Commons (©) 020/7219-4272. House of Lords (©) 020/7219-3107. www.parliament.uk. Free admission. House of Lords open mid-Oct to Aug Mon–Wed from 2:30pm, Thurs from 11am, and sometimes Fri (check by phone). House of Commons open mid-Oct to Aug Mon 2:30–10:30pm, Tues–Wed 11:30am–7:30pm, Thurs 11:30am–6pm, Fri call ahead—not always open. Join the line at St. Stephen's entrance. Tube: Westminster.

The British Museum This fabled attraction shelters one of the world's most comprehensive collections of art and artifacts. Even on a cursory first visit, be sure to see the Asian collections (the finest assembly of Islamic pottery outside the Islamic world), the Chinese porcelain, the Indian sculpture, and the Prehistoric and Romano-British collections. The overall storehouse is divided into collections of antiquities; prints and drawings; coins and medals; and ethnography. The Assyrian Transept on the ground floor displays the winged and human-headed bulls and lions that once guarded the gateways to the kings' palaces. From here, you can continue into the hall of Egyptian sculpture to see the Rosetta Stone, whose discovery led to the deciphering of hieroglyphs. Also on the ground floor are the Parthenon Sculptures, which used to be known as the Elgin Marbles. The Anglo-Saxon burial ship *Sutton Hoo* discovered in Suffolk is, in the words of an expert, "the richest treasure ever dug from English soil." The Portland Vase, one of the most celebrated possessions of the museum, was found in 1582 outside Rome.

The museum's inner courtyard, hidden for 150 years, has been transformed into the Great Court, a 1-hectare (2-acre) square spanned by a spectacular glass roof. The court houses a center for education, galleries, and more exhibition space. Following the removal of the British Library to St. Pancras, the Reading Room has been restored as a public reference library.

Great Russell St., WC1. (©) 020/7323-8299. www.thebritishmuseum.ac.uk. Free admission. Sat–Wed 10am–5:30pm; Thurs–Fri 10am–8:30pm. Tube: Holborn, Tottenham Court Rd., Goodge St., or Russell Sq.

Buckingham Palace This massively graceful building is the official residence of the queen. You can tell when Her Majesty is at home by the Royal Standard flying over the palace. The staterooms and picture gallery are usually open to the public for 8 weeks in August and September, when the royal family is away on vacation. The tours include the Throne Room and the grand staircase. The queen's picture gallery has some world-class masterpieces rarely on public view.

Buckingham Palace's most famous spectacle is the **Changing of the Guard.** The new guard, marching behind a band, comes from either the Wellington or Chelsea Barracks and takes over from the old guard in the forecourt of the

Tips **Blair in the Hot Seat**

The hottest ticket and most exciting time to visit the Houses of Parliament is during **Prime Minister's Question Time,** Monday to Wednesday from 2:30 to 3:10pm and Thursday 3 to 3:30pm, which must seem like hours to Tony Blair, who is virtually in the hot seat. But Blair holds his own admirably against any and all who try to embarrass him and his government.

palace. When this martial ceremony occurs is the subject of mass confusion—*when* it happens, it begins at 11:30am. In theory, that is supposed to be from mid-April to July and on alternate days the rest of the year. It can be canceled in bad weather and during major state events. Call ahead to find out whether this world-famous military ritual is likely to be staged during your visit.

At end of The Mall (on the road running from Trafalgar Sq.). ℂ **020/7170-4299** or 020/7321-2233. www.royal.gov.uk. Palace tours £13 ($23) adults, £11 ($19) seniors, £6.50 ($12) children under 17. Changing of the Guard free. Palace open for tours Aug 1–Sept 26 daily 9:30am–4:15pm. Changing of the Guard daily Apr–July at 11:30am, and every other day for the rest of the year at 11am. Tube: St. James's Park, Green Park, or Victoria.

The Saatchi Gallery ★★
Ex-adman Charles Saatchi has amassed one of the largest independent collections of modern British and international art in the world. On London's South Bank, the gallery stands right between the sites of the two Tate galleries. Devoted to modern, often very controversial and headline-grabbing art, the gallery focuses on the work of younger British artists, such as Damien Hirst. *Note:* At press time, a devastating warehouse fire destroyed a number of important pieces in Saatchi's collection of 1990s "Brit Art."

County Hall, Southbank. ℂ **020/7823-2363.** www.saatchi-gallery.co.uk. Admission £8.75 ($16) adults, £6.75 ($12) concessions, £5.25 ($9.50) prebooked groups, £26 ($47) family ticket. Sun–Thurs 10am–8pm; Fri–Sat 1am–10pm. Tube: Charing Cross, Embankment, Lambeth North, Waterloo, or Westminster.

Madame Tussauds ★ Kids
In 1770, an exhibition of life-size wax figures was opened in Paris by Dr. Curtius. He was soon joined by his niece, Strasbourg-born Marie Tussaud, who learned the secret of making lifelike replicas of the famous and the infamous. During the French Revolution, the head of almost every distinguished victim of the guillotine was molded by Madame Tussaud or her uncle. An enlarged Grand Hall continues to house years of old favorites, as well as many of today's heads of state and political leaders. In the Chamber of Horrors, you can have the vicarious thrill of walking through a Victorian London street where special effects include the shadowy terror of Jack the Ripper. Planetarium shows begin at 10:20am daily and are presented every 40 minutes.

Marylebone Rd., NW1. ℂ **0870/400-3000.** www.madame-tussauds.co.uk. Admission £18 ($33) adults, £15 ($28) seniors, £14 ($26) children ages 5–16, free for children under 5. Mon–Fri 9:30am–5:30pm; Sat–Sun 9am–6pm. Tube: Baker St.

Tate Britain ★★★
What's now known as Tate Britain was known as the Tate Gallery before the modern works in its collection were moved to the Tate Modern (see below). Fronting the Thames near Vauxhall bridge in Pimlico, the gallery houses the national collection of British art from the 16th century to the present. The works include some of the best of Gainsborough, Reynolds, Stubbs, Blake, Constable, and Hogarth (particularly his satirical *O the Roast beef of Old England,* known as *The Gate of Calais*). The illustrations of William Blake, the incomparable mystical poet, for such classic works as *The Book of Job, The Divine Comedy,* and *Paradise Lost* are here. The collection of works by J. M. W. Turner is its largest by a single artist; Turner himself willed most of the paintings and watercolors here to the nation. Also on display are the works of many major 19th- and 20th-century painters, including Paul Nash.

Millbank, SW1. ℂ **020/7887-8000.** www.tate.org.uk. Free admission; special exhibitions £3–£8.50 ($5.55–$16). Daily 10am–5:50pm. Tube: Pimlico.

Tate Modern ★★★
In a transformed Bankside Power Station in Southwark, this museum draws some two million visitors a year to see the greatest collection

of international 20th-century art in Britain. As such, it is one of the three or four most important modern art galleries in the world. Tate Modern is viewer friendly with eye-level hangings. All the big painting stars are here, a whole galaxy ranging from Dalí to Matisse to Rothko to Warhol. The Modern is also a gallery of new and exciting art. Instead of exhibiting art chronologically and by school, the Tate Modern, in a radical break from tradition, takes a thematic approach. This allows displays to cut across movements. You can cross the reopened Millennium Bridge, a pedestrian-only walk from the steps of St. Paul's, over the Thames to the new gallery.

Bankside, SE1. ⟨℃⟩ 020/7887-8008. www.tate.org.uk. Free admission. Sun–Thurs 10am–6pm; Fri–Sat 10am–10pm. Tube: Southwark.

National Gallery ✵✵✵   This museum houses a comprehensive collection of Western paintings, representing all the major schools from the 13th century to the early 20th century. Of the early Gothic works, the *Wilton Diptych* is the rarest treasure; it depicts Richard II being introduced to the Madonna and Child by John the Baptist and the Saxon king, Edward the Confessor. The 16th-century Venetian masters and the northern European painters are well represented.

North side of Trafalgar Sq., WC2. ⟨℃⟩ 020/7747-2885. www.nationalgallery.org.uk. Free admission. Thurs–Tues 10am–6pm; Wed 10am–9pm. Tube: Charing Cross, Embankment, Leicester Sq., or Piccadilly Circus.

St. Paul's Cathedral ✵✵✵   It was during the Great Fire of 1666 that the old St. Paul's was destroyed, making way for a baroque structure designed by Sir Christopher Wren and built between 1675 and 1710. The dome of St. Paul's dominates the City's square mile. The cathedral houses few art treasures but has many monuments, including a memorial chapel to American service personnel who lost their lives in World War II. Encircling the dome is the Whispering Gallery, where vocal discretion is advised. Wren lies in the crypt, along with the duke of Wellington and Lord Nelson. Of course, this was where Prince Charles married Lady Diana Spencer in 1981.

St. Paul's Churchyard, EC4. ⟨℃⟩ 020/7236-4128. www.stpauls.co.uk. Cathedral and galleries £6 ($11) adults, £3 ($5.55) children 6–16. Guided tours £2.50 ($4.65) adults, £2 ($3.70) students and seniors, £1 ($1.85) children; recorded tours £3.50 ($6.50). Free for children 5 and under. Sightseeing Mon–Sat 8:30am–4pm. No sightseeing Sun (services only). Tube: St. Paul's.

Victoria and Albert Museum ✵✵✵   On display here are fine and decorative arts, the world's greatest collection. Medieval holdings include many treasures, such as the Eltenberg Reliquary; the Early English Gloucester Candlestick; the Byzantine Veroli Casket, with its ivory panels based on Greek plays; and the Syon Cope, an English embroidery from the early 14th century. Islamic art includes the 16th-century Persian Ardabil carpet. The V&A has the largest collection of Renaissance sculpture outside Italy, including a Donatello marble relief. Raphael's cartoons for tapestries for the Sistine Chapel, owned by the queen, can also be seen here.

In 2001, V&A opened 15 new galleries—called the **British Galleries** ✵✵✵ —unfolding the story of British design from 1500 to 1900. From Chippendale to Morris, all of the top British designers are featured. Star exhibits range from the 5m (17-ft.) high Melville Bed (1697), with its red silk velvet hangings, to the wedding suite of James II and one of the most prized possessions, the "Great Bed of Ware," mentioned in Shakespeare's *Twelfth Night*.

Cromwell Rd., SW7. ⟨℃⟩ 020/7942-2000. www.vam.ac.uk. Free admission. Daily 10am–5:45pm (Wed until 10pm). Tube: South Kensington.

Kensington Palace This mansion dates from 1605 but was redesigned by Sir Christopher Wren in 1689. Since the end of the 18th century, it has been home to various members of the royal family, and the State Apartments are open for tours. The palace was the London home of the late Princess Margaret and was once the home of Diana, princess of Wales, and her two sons. Newly restored, the State Apartments and Ceremonial Dress Collection display trompe l'oeil murals by William Kent and ceremonial robes belonging to Queen Mary and George V. Visitors are guided through a series of theme rooms, including a tailor shop stocked with materials used in court dress. Of the 30 rooms, 15, including the restored King's Gallery and the Cupola Room, where Queen Victoria was baptized, are permanently open to the public. In the northwestern corner of Kensington Gardens (see below) is the **Princess Diana Memorial Playground,** dedicated to the late princess in 2000.

The Broad Walk, Kensington Gardens, W8. © **0870/751-5170.** Admission £11 ($19) adults, £7 ($13) seniors and students, £6.50 ($12) children, free for children under 5; £31 ($57) family. Mar–Oct daily 10am–7pm; Nov–Feb daily 10am–6pm. Tube: Queensway or Notting Hill Gate; High St. Kensington on south side of gardens.

Cabinet War Rooms **Whitehall**, the seat of the British government, extends south from Trafalgar Square to Parliament Square. Along it you'll find the Home Office, the Old Admiralty Building, and the Ministry of Defense. Visitors today can see the Cabinet War Rooms, a bombproof bunker suite of rooms, just as they were left by Winston Churchill at the end of World War II. You can see the Map Room with its huge wall maps; the Atlantic map is a mass of pinholes (each hole represents at least one convoy). Next door is Churchill's bedroom-cum-office, which has two BBC microphones on the desk for his broadcasts of those famous speeches that stirred the nation.

Clive Steps at the end of King Charles St., SW1, off Whitehall near Big Ben. © **020/7930-6961.** www.iwm.org.uk/cabinet. Admission £7.50 ($14) adults, £6 ($11) seniors and students, free for children under 16. Apr–Sept daily 9:30am–6pm (last admission 5:15pm); Oct–Mar daily 10am–6pm (last admission 5:15pm). Closed Christmas holidays. Tube: Westminster or St. James's.

MUSEUMS

Apsley House This former town house of the duke of Wellington (1769–1852), who defeated Napoleon at the Battle of Waterloo and later became prime minister, was opened as a public museum in 1952. The building was designed by Robert Adam and constructed from 1771 to 1778.

Hyde Park Corner, W1. © **020/7499-5676.** www.apsleyhouse.org.uk. Admission £4.50 ($8.35) adults, £3 ($5.55) students, free for children under 18 and seniors over 60. Tues–Sun 11am–5pm. Tube: Hyde Park Corner.

Museum of London In the Barbican near St. Paul's, the museum traces London's history from prehistoric times through relics, costumes, household effects, maps, and models. Anglo-Saxons, Vikings, Normans—they're all here, displayed on two floors around a central courtyard.

150 London Wall, EC2. © **020/7600-3699.** www.museumoflondon.org.uk. Free admission. Mon–Sat 10am–5:50pm; Sun noon– 5:50pm. Tube: St. Paul's or Barbican.

National Portrait Gallery This museum was founded in 1856 to collect the likenesses of famous British men and women. Today the collection is the most comprehensive of its kind in the world and constitutes a unique record of those who created the history and culture of the nation. A few paintings will catch your eye, including Sir Joshua Reynolds's portrait of Samuel Johnson ("a man of most dreadful appearance"). You'll also see a portrait of William Shakespeare,

Wheeling Around

The world's largest observation wheel, the **British Airways London Eye** ★, Millennium Jubilee Gardens (② 0870/500-0600; www.londoneye.com), opened in February 2000. The fourth-tallest structure in London, it offers panoramic views that extend for some 40km (25 miles) if the weather's clear. Passengers are carried in 32 "pods" that make a complete revolution every half-hour. Along the way you see some of London's landmarks from a bird's-eye point of view. Some two million visitors are expected to ride the eye every year.

Tickets for the ride are £12 ($21) for adults, £9 ($17) for seniors and students, and £5.75 ($11) for children 5 to 15. In May and September, hours are Monday through Thursday from 9:30am to 8pm, Friday through Sunday from 9:30am to 10pm; in June, Monday through Thursday 9:30am to 9pm, Friday through Sunday from 9:30am to 10pm; in July and August, daily from 9:30am to 10pm; and from October to April, daily from 9:30am to 8pm. Tube: Embankment or Waterloo.

---

which is claimed to be the most "authentic contemporary likeness" of its subject, and the portrait of the Brontë sisters, painted by their brother Branwell. The most recent additions to the gallery include portraits of British sports figures, a tribute to athletic icons from the *Chariots of Fire* athletes of the 1920s to the superstars of today.

In 2000, Queen Elizabeth opened the Ondaatje Wing of the gallery, granting the gallery more than 50% more exhibition space. The most intriguing part of the additional space is the splendid Tudor Gallery, with portraits of Richard III and Henry II, his conqueror in the Battle of Bosworth in 1485, as well as a portrait of Shakespeare first acquired by the gallery in 1856.

St. Martin's Place, WC2. ② 020/7306-0055. www.npg.org.uk. Free admission; fee charged for certain temporary exhibitions. Mon–Wed 10am–6pm; Thurs–Fri 10am–9pm; Sat–Sun 10am–6pm. Tube: Charing Cross or Leicester Sq.

LONDON'S PARKS

London's parklands easily rate as the greatest "green lung" system of any large city. One of the largest is **Hyde Park** ★. With the adjoining Kensington Gardens, it covers 257 hectares (636 acres) of central London with velvety lawn interspersed with ponds, flower beds, and trees. **Kensington Gardens** are home to the celebrated statue of Peter Pan (with the bronze rabbits that toddlers are always trying to kidnap) and to the **Princess Diana Memorial Playground.** East of Hyde Park, across Piccadilly, stretch **Green Park** ★ and **St. James's Park** ★, forming an almost unbroken chain of landscaped beauty. This is an ideal area for picnics. You'll find it hard to believe this was once a festering piece of swamp near the leper hospital. **Regent's Park,** north of Baker Street and Marylebone Road, was designed by the 18th-century genius John Nash to surround a palace that never materialized. The **open-air theater** and the **London Zoo** ★★ are in this most classically beautiful of London's parks.

In July 2000, a 11km (7-mile) **walk commemorating the life of Princess Diana** opened. The walk passes through four of London's royal parks—St. James's Park, Green Park, Hyde Park, and Kensington Gardens. A **memorial fountain** to Diana was expected to be in place next to the Serpentine in Hyde Park by the summer of 2004.

ORGANIZED TOURS

For the first-timer, the quickest and most economical way to bring the big city into focus is to take a bus tour. One of the most popular is **The Original London Sightseeing Tour,** which passes all the major sights in just about 1½ hours. The tour, which uses a traditional double-decker bus with live commentary by a guide, costs £15 ($28) for adults, £10 ($19) for children under 16, free for those under 5. The tour allows you to hop on or off the bus at any point in the tour at no extra charge. The tour plus admission to Madame Tussauds is £28 ($52) for adults, £20 ($37) for children.

Departures are from convenient points within the city; you can choose your departure point when you buy your ticket. Tickets can be purchased on the bus or at a discount from any London Transport or London Tourist Board Information Centre. Most hotel concierges also sell tickets. For information or phone purchases, call © **020/8877-1722.** It's also possible to book online at **www. theoriginaltour.com**.

Touring boats operate on the Thames year-round and can take you to various places within Greater London and beyond. Main embarkation points are Westminster Pier, Charing Cross Pier, and Tower Pier, a system that enables you, for instance, to take a "water taxi" from the Tower of London to Westminster Abbey, or a more leisurely cruise from Westminster to Hampton Court Palace or Kew Gardens. Several companies operate motor launches offering panoramic views en route. For information and reservations, contact the **Westminster-Greenwich Thames Passenger Boat Service,** Westminster Pier, Victoria Embankment, SW1 (© **020/7930-4097;** www.westminsterpier.co.uk).

The Original London Walks, 87 Messina Ave., P.O. Box 1708, London NW6 4LW (© **020/7624-3978;** http://london.walks.com), the oldest established walking-tour company in London, is run by an Anglo-American journalist/actor couple, David and Mary Tucker. Their hallmarks are variety, reliability, reasonably sized groups, and—above all—superb guides. The renowned crime historian Donald Rumbelow, the leading authority on Jack the Ripper and author of the classic guidebook *London Walks,* is a regular guide, as are several prominent actors (including classical actor Edward Petherbridge). Walks are regularly scheduled daily and cost £5 ($9.25) for adults, £4 ($7.40) for students and seniors; children under 15 go free. Call for a schedule; no reservations are needed.

THE SHOPPING SCENE
THE TOP SHOPPING STREETS & NEIGHBORHOODS

THE WEST END   As a neighborhood, the West End includes Mayfair and is home to the core of London's big-name shopping. Most of the department stores, designer shops, and chain stores have their flagships in this area.

The key streets are **Oxford Street** for affordable shopping (Tube: Bond St.), and **Regent Street,** which intersects Oxford Street at Oxford Circus (Tube: Oxford Circus). **Marks & Spencer**'s Marble Arch store (on Oxford St.) is their flagship and worth shopping at for their high-quality goods; a grocery store is in the basement and a home furnishings department is upstairs. Regent Street has fancier shops—more upscale department stores (including the famed **Liberty of London**), chain stores (**Laura Ashley**), and specialty dealers—and leads all the way to Piccadilly.

In between the two, parallel to Regent Street, is **Bond Street.** Divided into New and Old, Bond Street (Tube: Bond St.) also connects Piccadilly with Oxford Street and is synonymous with the luxury trade. Bond Street has had a recent revival and is the hot address for international designers. **Burlington Arcade** (Tube: Piccadilly Circus), the famous glass-roofed, Regency-style passage leading off Piccadilly, is lined with intriguing shops and boutiques specializing in fashion, jewelry, Irish linen, cashmere, and more.

Just off Regent Street, **Carnaby Street** (Tube: Oxford Circus) might sound like a tired name from the Swinging '60s, but it's still alive and flourishing. The area includes surrounding streets as well: Newburg, Ganton, Marlborough Court, Lowndes Court, Marshall, Beak, Kingly, and Foubert's Place. Each of these streets has new and exciting shops along with trendy cafes and bars. New retailers are moving in all the time, including a concept by Levi's to sell its vintage clothing under the label "Red." You can expect the unexpected here, and innovative boutiques come and go virtually every week. The entire district is also a place to hang out at such bars as JUS Cafe, on Foubert's Place, the most fashionable juice bar in London.

For a total contrast, check out **Jermyn Street,** on the far side of Piccadilly, a tiny 2-block-long street devoted to high-end men's haberdashers and toiletries shops; many have been doing business for centuries. Several hold royal warrants, including **Turnbull & Asser,** where HRH Prince Charles has his pj's made.

The West End also includes the theater district, so there are two more shopping areas: the still-not-ready-for-prime-time **Soho,** where sex shops are slowly being turned into cutting-edge designer shops; and **Covent Garden,** which is a masterpiece unto itself. The original marketplace has taken over the surrounding neighborhood so that even though the streets run a little higgledy-piggledy and you can easily get lost, it's fun to just wander and shop. Covent Garden is especially mobbed on Sundays (Tube: Covent Garden).

KNIGHTSBRIDGE & CHELSEA   This is the second-most-famous retail district because it's the home of **Harrods** (Tube: Knightsbridge). Harrods is London's—indeed Europe's—top department store. The sheer range, variety, and quality of merchandise are dazzling; be sure not to miss the delicatessen and food halls. A small street nearby, Sloane Street, is chockablock with designer shops; and another street in the opposite direction, **Cheval Place,** is lined with designer resale shops.

Walk toward Museum Row and you'll soon find **Beauchamp Place** (pronounced *Bee*-cham). The street is only a block long, but it features the kinds of shops where young British aristos buy their clothing. Head out at the **Harvey Nichols** ("Harvey Nicks") end of Knightsbridge, away from Harrods, and shop your way through the designer stores on Sloane Street (**Hermès, Armani, Prada,** and the like), then walk past Sloane Square and you're in an altogether different neighborhood: Chelsea.

King's Road (Tube: Sloane Sq.), the main street of Chelsea, which starts at Sloane Square, will forever remain a symbol of London in the Swinging '60s. More and more, King's Road is a lineup of markets and "multistores," large or small conglomerations of indoor stands, stalls, and booths within one building or enclosure. Chelsea doesn't begin and end with King's Road. If you choose to walk in the other direction from Harrods, you connect to a part of Chelsea called **Brompton Cross,** another hip and hot area for designer shops made popular when Michelin House was rehabbed by Sir Terence Conran for **The Conran Shop.**

Also, seek out **Walton Street,** a tiny little snake of a street running off Brompton Cross. About 2 blocks are devoted to fairy-tale shops where a *lady* buys aromatherapy, needlepoint, or costume jewelry, or meets with her interior designer. Finally, don't forget all those museums right there in the corner of the shopping streets. They have great gift shops.

KENSINGTON & NOTTING HILL   **Kensington High Street** (Tube: High St. Kensington) is the most recent hangout of the classier breed of teens, who have graduated from Carnaby Street and are ready for street chic. While a few staples of basic British fashion can be found on this strip, most of the stores feature items that stretch, are very, very short, or are very, very tight.

From Kensington High Street, you can walk up **Kensington Church Street,** which, like Portobello Road, is one of the city's main shopping avenues for antiques. Kensington Church Street dead-ends into the Notting Hill Gate Tube station, which is where you would arrive for shopping in **Portobello Road.** The weekend market is 2 blocks beyond.

THE TOP MARKETS

THE WEST END   The most famous market in all of England, **Covent Garden Market** (Tube: Covent Garden), offers several different markets daily from 9am to 6pm (we think it's most fun to come on Sun). **Apple Market** is the fun, bustling market in the courtyard, where traders sell, well, everything. Many of the items are what the English call collectible nostalgia; they include a wide array of glassware and ceramics, leather goods, toys, clothes, hats, and jewelry. Some of the merchandise is truly unusual. This becomes an antiques market on Monday. Meanwhile, out back is **Jubilee Market,** which is also an antiques market on Monday. Every other day of the week, it's sort of a fancy hippie-ish market with cheap clothes and books. Out front are a few tents of cheap stuff, except again on Monday, when antiques dealers take over here, too.

St. Martin-in-the-Fields Market (Tube: Charing Cross) is good for teens and hipsters who don't want to trek all the way to Camden Market and can be satisfied with imports from India and South America, crafts, and local football souvenirs. It's near Trafalgar Square and Covent Garden; hours are Monday through Saturday from 11am to 5pm, Sunday from noon to 5pm.

NOTTING HILL   The area has become synonymous with the Julia Roberts and Hugh Grant movie, but Londoners already know that no matter what you may collect, you'll find it at the **Portobello Market** (Tube: Notting Hill Gate). It's mainly a Saturday happening from 6am to 5pm. You needn't be here at the crack of dawn; 9am is fine. You just want to beat the motor-coach crowd. Once known mainly for fruit and vegetables (still sold here throughout the week), Portobello in the past 4 decades has become synonymous with antiques. But don't take the stall holder's word for it that the fiddle he's holding is a genuine Stradivarius left to him in the will of his Italian great-uncle; it might just as well have been nicked from an East End pawnshop.

The market is divided into three major sections. The most crowded is the antiques section, running between Colville Road and Chepstow Villas to the south. (*Warning:* There's a great concentration of pickpockets in this area.) The second section (and the oldest part) is the "fruit and veg" market, lying between Westway and Colville Road. In the third and final section, there's a flea market, where Londoners sell bric-a-brac and lots of secondhand goods they didn't really want in the first place. Looking around makes for interesting fun.

LONDON AFTER DARK

Weekly publications such as *Time Out* and *Where,* available at newsstands, give full entertainment listings and contain information on restaurants, nightclubs, and theaters. You'll also find listings in daily newspapers, notably *The Times* and *The Telegraph*.

THE PERFORMING ARTS

To see specific shows, especially hits, purchase your tickets in advance. The best method is to buy your tickets from the theater's box office, which you can do over the phone using a credit card. You'll pay the theater price and pick up the tickets the day of the show. You can also go to a reliable ticket agent (the greatest cluster is in Covent Garden), but you'll pay a fee, which varies depending on the show. You can also make theater reservations through ticket agents. In the case of hit shows, only brokers may be able to get you a seat, but you'll pay for the privilege. For tickets and information before you go, try **Global Tickets,** 234 West 44th St., Suite 1000, New York, NY 10036 (© **800/223-6108** or 212/398-1468; www.keithprowse.com). They also have offices in London at the **British Visitors Center,** 1 Regents St., W1 V1PJ (© **020/7014-8550**); and at the **Harrods** ticket desk, 87–135 Brompton Rd. (© **020/7589-9109**), located on the lower-ground floor opposite the British Airways desk. They'll mail tickets to your home, or fax you a confirmation and leave your tickets at the box office. Instant confirmations are available with special "overseas" rates for most shows. A booking and handling fee of up to 20% is added to the ticket price.

THEATER   Occupying a prime site on the South Bank of the River Thames is the flagship of British theater, the **Royal National Theatre,** South Bank, SE1 (© **020/7452-3000;** www.nt-online.org; Tube: Waterloo, Embankment, or Charing Cross). The National houses three theaters. Tickets are £11 to £40 ($20–$74).

   Barbican Theatre–Royal Shakespeare Company, Barbican Centre, Silk Street, Barbican, EC2 (© **0870/609-1110;** www.rsc.org.uk; Tube: Barbican or Moorgate), is one of the world's finest theater companies. The core of the company's work remains the plays of William Shakespeare, but it also presents a wide-ranging program. There are three different productions each week in the Barbican Theatre, the main auditorium, and the Pit, a small studio space where much of the company's new writing is presented. Barbican Theatre tickets are £5 to £40 ($9.25–$74); the Pit, £7 to £24 ($13–$44).

   A recent addition to London's theater scene is the replica of **Shakespeare's Globe Theatre,** New Globe Walk, Bankside, SE1 (© **020/7902-1400;** www. shakespeares-globe.org; Tube: Mansion House or Blackfriars). Performances are staged, on the theater's original site, as they were in Elizabethan times: without lighting, scenery, or such luxuries as cushioned seats or a roof over the audience. From May to September, the company intends to hold performances Tuesday through Saturday at 2 and 7pm. There will be a limited winter schedule. In any season, the schedule may be affected by weather, because this is an outdoor theater. Tickets are £5 ($9.25) for groundlings (patrons who stand in the uncovered yard around the stage), £11 to £29 ($20–$54) for gallery seats.

   Sadler's Wells Theatre, Rosebery Avenue, EC1 (© **020/7863-8198;** www.sadlers-wells.com; Tube: Angel), is London's premier venue for dance. The theater, rebuilt from the detritus of a bulldozed 18th-century theater and reopened in 1998, can change its interior shape, size, mood, and even color for almost any performance. The program for Sadler's for each year is approximately 25 weeks of dance and 10 to 12 weeks of opera. The remaining time will offer a medley of visual theater. The box office is open Monday through Saturday from 10am to 8pm. Tickets are £11 to £50 ($19–$92).

Tips **Fringe Benefits**

Some of the best theater in London is performed on the "fringe"—at the dozens of so-called fringe theaters that usually attempt more adventurous productions than the established West End theaters; they're also dramatically lower in price and staged in more intimate surroundings. Check *Time Out* for schedules and show times.

CLASSICAL MUSIC & OPERA   The **Royal Opera** and **Royal Ballet** are back at the newly restored **Royal Opera House,** Bow St., Covent Garden, WC2 (© **020/7304-4000** or 020/7212-9123; www.royalopera.org; Tube: Covent Garden), which reopened in 1999 after a massive restoration and modernization.

Opera performances are usually sung in the original language with English subtitles; tickets are £15 to £170 ($28–$315). The Royal Ballet performs a repertory with a tilt toward the classics, including works by its earlier choreographer-director, Sir Frederick Ashton, and Sir Kenneth MacMillan; tickets are £44 to £77 ($81–$142).

London Coliseum, St. Martin's Lane, WC2 (© **020/7632-8300;** www.eno. org; Tube: Leicester Sq.), is London's largest and most splendid theater. **English National Opera** performs a wide range of works in English, from great classics to Gilbert and Sullivan to new and experimental works, staged with flair and imagination. Tickets are £5 to £78 ($9.25–$144). About 100 discount balcony tickets are sold from 10am on the day of performance.

Royal Albert Hall, Kensington Gore, SW7 (© **020/7589-8212;** www. royalalberthall.com; Tube: South Kensington), is the annual setting for the BBC Henry Wood Promenade Concerts ("The Proms") from mid-July to mid-September. A British tradition since 1895, the programs are outstanding, often presenting newly commissioned works for the first time. Tickets are £18 to £52 ($33–$96).

Across Waterloo Bridge rises **Royal Festival Hall,** South Bank, SE1 (© **0870/ 401-8181;** www.rfh.org.uk; Tube: Waterloo or Embankment). Here are three of the most comfortable and acoustically perfect concert halls in the world: Royal Festival Hall, Queen Elizabeth Hall, and the Purcell Room. Within their precincts, more than 1,200 performances a year are presented. Tickets are £6 to £55 ($11–$102).

THE CLUB & MUSIC SCENE

ROCK   A long-established venue for rock 'n' roll, blues, and indie bands, **The Rock Garden,** 6–7 The Piazza, Covent Garden (© **020/7836-4052;** Tube: Covent Garden), maintains a bar and a stage in the cellar and a restaurant on the street level. The cellar area, known as The Venue, has hosted such bands as Dire Straits, The Police, and U2 before they became famous. It's open Monday through Thursday from 5pm to 3am; Friday and Saturday from 5pm to 4am; and Sunday from 5pm to 2am. Cover is £5 to £15 ($9.25–$28); diners enter free.

JAZZ & BLUES   The reasonably priced **100 Club,** 100 Oxford St., W1 (© **020/ 7636-0933;** Tube: Tottenham Court Rd. or Oxford Circus), is a serious rival to the city's upscale jazz clubs. Its cavalcade of bands includes the best British jazz musicians, as well as many touring Americans. Rock, R&B, and blues are also presented. It's open Monday through Wednesday from 7:30 to 11:30pm; Thursday and Friday from noon to 3pm and 8pm to 12:30am; Saturday from 7:30pm to 1am; and Sunday from 7:30 to 11:30pm. Cover is £7 to £12 ($13–$22); discounts available for club members.

Mention the word "jazz" in London and people immediately think of **Ronnie Scott's Club,** 47 Frith St., W1 (© **020/7439-0747;** Tube: Leicester Sq. or Piccadilly Circus), long the citadel of modern jazz in Europe, where the best English and American groups are booked. Featured on almost every bill is an American band, often with a top-notch singer. In the Main Room, you can

---

(*Moments* **The Pub Crawl, London Style**

Dropping into the local pub for a pint of real ale or bitter is the best way to soak up the character of the different villages that make up London. You'll hear the accents and slang and see first-hand how far removed upper-crust Kensington is from blue-collar Wapping. Catch the local gossip or football talk—and, of course, enjoy some of the finest ales, stouts, ciders, and malt whiskeys in the world.

Central London is awash with wonderful historic pubs as rich and varied as the city itself. The **Cittie of Yorke,** 22 High Holborn, WC1 (© **020/7242-7670;** Tube: Holborn or Chancery Lane), boasts the longest bar in Britain, rafters ascending to the heavens, and a long row of immense wine vats, all of which give it the air of a great medieval hall—appropriate since a pub has existed at this location since 1430. Samuel Smiths is on tap, and the bar offers novelties such as chocolate-orange-flavored vodka.

Dickens once hung out in the **Lamb & Flag,** 33 Rose St., off Garrick Street, WC2 (© **020/7497-9504;** Tube: Leicester Sq.), and the room itself is little changed from the days when he prowled this neighborhood. The pub has an amazing and somewhat scandalous history. John Dryden was almost killed by a band of thugs outside its doors in December 1679; the pub gained the nickname the "Bucket of Blood" during the Regency era (1811–20) because of the routine bare-knuckled prizefights that broke out. Tap beers include Courage Best, Courage Directors, Old Speckled Hen, John Smith's, and Wadworth 6X.

The **Nag's Head** (10 James St., WC2; © **020/7836-4678;** Tube: Covent Garden) is one of London's most famous Edwardian pubs. In days of yore, patrons had to make their way through lorries of fruit and flowers to drink here. But when the market moved, 300 years of British tradition faded away. Today, the pub is patronized mainly by young people. The draft Guinness is very good. Lunch is typical pub grub: sandwiches, salads, pork cooked in cider, and garlic prawns. Snacks are available in the afternoon.

The snug little **Dog & Duck** (18 Bateman St., corner of Frith St., W1; © **020/7494-0697**), a Soho landmark, is the most intimate pub in London. One former patron was author George Orwell, who came here to celebrate his sales of *Animal Farm* in the United States. A wide mixture of patrons of all ages and persuasions flock here, chatting amiably while ordering the delights of Tetleys or Timothy Taylor Landlord. If business warrants it, the cozy upstairs bar is opened.

either stand at the bar to watch the show or sit at a table, where you can order dinner. The Downstairs Bar is more intimate. On weekends, the separate Upstairs Room has a disco called Club Latino. It's open Monday through Saturday from 8:30pm to 3am. Cover for nonmembers is £15 ($28) on Monday through Thursday and £25 ($46) on Friday and Saturday; for members, it's £5 ($9.25) during the week and £10 ($19) on Friday and Saturday.

DANCE CLUBS   **Bar Rumba,** 36 Shaftesbury Ave., W1 (© **020/7287-6933;** Tube: Piccadilly Circus), is a Latin bar and club that could be featured in a book on "Underground London" in spite of its location on Shaftesbury Avenue. It leans toward radical jazz fusion on some nights, funk on other occasions. It boasts two full bars and a different musical theme every night. Tuesday and Wednesday are the only nights you won't have to queue at the door. Monday's "That's How It Is" showcase features jazz, hip-hop, and drum and bass; and Saturday's "Garage City" buzzes with house and garage. On weeknights, you have to be 18 or older; on Saturday and Sunday, nobody under 21 is allowed in. The club is open Monday from 9pm to 3:30am; Tuesday, Thursday, and Friday from 6pm to 3:30am; Saturday from 7pm to 6am; and Wednesday and Sunday from 8pm to 3:30am. Cover is £3 to £12 ($5.55–$22).

Equinox, Leicester Square, WC2 (© **020/7437-1446;** Tube: Leicester Sq.), has nine bars, the largest dance floor in London, and a restaurant modeled along the lines of an American diner from the 1950s. Virtually every kind of dance music, save "rave," is featured here. It's open Monday through Thursday from 9pm to 3am, and Friday and Saturday from 9pm to 3:30am. Cover is £6 to £12 ($11–$22).

Hippodrome, Leicester Square, WC2 (© **020/7437-4311;** Tube: Leicester Sq.), is one of London's greatest discos, an enormous place where light and sound envelop you from all directions. Revolving speakers even descend from the roof to deafen you in patches, and you can watch yourself on closed-circuit video. It's open Monday through Friday from 9pm to 3am, Saturday from 9pm to 3:30am. Cover is £8 to £11 ($15–$20).

THE GAY & LESBIAN SCENE

The most reliable source of information on gay clubs and activities is the (always busy) 24-hour **Gay and Lesbian Switchboard** at © **020/7837-7324.**

Adjacent to one of Covent Garden's best-known traffic junctions, **The Box,** at Seven Dials, 32–34 Monmouth St., WC2 (© **020/7240-5828;** Tube: Covent Garden or Leicester Sq.), is a Mediterranean-style bar. Gay men outnumber lesbians, though the venue is sophisticated and blasé about sexual definition. Year-round, the place defines itself as a "summer bar," throwing open its doors and windows to a cluster of outdoor tables that attracts a crowd at the slightest hint of warmth. It's open Monday through Saturday from 11am to 11pm and Sunday from noon to 10:30pm. No cover.

First Out, 52 St. Giles High St., WC2 (© **020/7240-8042;** Tube: Tottenham Court Rd.), prides itself on being the first (est. 1986) all-gay coffee shop in London. Set in a 19th-century building whose venerable wood panels have been painted all colors of the rainbow, it maintains two intimate floors (read: not particularly cruisy) where menu items are exclusively vegetarian. Don't expect raucousness; some clients have even brought their grandmothers here. First Out is open Monday through Saturday from 10am to 11pm and Sunday from 11am to 10:30pm.

THE BAR SCENE

At the **American Bar,** in The Savoy, The Strand, WC2 (© **020/7836-4343;** Tube: Embankment, Charing Cross, or Covent Garden), still one of the most sophisticated gathering places in London, the bartender is known for such special concoctions as the "Savoy Affair" and the "Prince of Wales," as well as for pouring the best martini in town. The bar is open Monday through Saturday from 11am to 11pm; jazz piano music begins at 7pm.

The owners spent millions of pounds outfitting the **Zoo Bar** (13-18 Bear St., WC2; © 020/7839-4188; Tube: Leicester Sq.), and the result is a bar with the slickest, flashiest, and most psychedelic decor in London. Zoo Bar upstairs is a menagerie of mosaic animals beneath a glassed-in ceiling dome. Downstairs the music is intrusive enough to make conversation futile. Clients range from 18 to 35, and androgyny is the look of choice. The bar is open Monday through Friday from 4pm to 3:30am, Saturday 1pm to 3:30am, and Sunday 4pm to 12:30am.

DAY TRIPS FROM LONDON

HAMPTON COURT PALACE ✴✴✴   On the north side of the Thames, 21km (13 miles) west of London in East Molesey, Surrey, this 16th-century palace of Cardinal Wolsey can teach us a lesson: Don't try to outdo your boss, particularly if he happens to be Henry VIII. The rich cardinal did just that. He eventually lost his fortune, power, and prestige—and he ended up giving his lavish palace to the Tudor monarch. Although the palace enjoyed prestige and pomp in Elizabethan days, it owes much of its present look to William and Mary—or rather to Sir Christopher Wren, who designed and built the Northern or Lion Gates. You can parade through the apartments today, filled as they are with porcelain, furniture, paintings, and tapestries. The Renaissance Gallery is graced with paintings by old masters on loan from Queen Elizabeth II.

Hampton Court (© **0870/752-7777;** www.hampton-court-palace.org.uk) is easily accessible. Frequent trains run from Waterloo Station (Network Southeast) to **Hampton Court Station** (© **08457/484-950** or 01603/764776). **London Transport** (© **020/7730-3466**) bus nos. 11, 131, 216, 267, and 461 make the trip from Victoria Coach Station on Buckingham Palace Road (just southwest of Victoria Station). If you're driving from London, take the A308 to the junction with the A309 on the north side of Kingston Bridge over the Thames.

Admission to Hampton Court is £11.50 ($21) adults, £8.50 ($16) students and seniors, £7.50 ($14) children 5 to 15, free for children under 5, £34 ($63) family. Gardens are open year-round daily from 7am to dusk (no later than 9pm); admission is free to all except Privy Garden (admission £3/$5.55 adults, £2/$3.70 children) without a palace ticket during summer months. Cloisters, courtyards, state apartments, the great kitchen, cellars, and Hampton Court exhibition are open March 28 through October 25, Monday from 10:15am to 6pm, Tuesday through Sunday from 9:30am to 6pm (last entry 5:15pm); October 26 through March 27, Monday from 10:15am to 4:30pm, Tuesday through Sunday from 9:30am to 4:30pm (last entry 5:15pm).

WINDSOR CASTLE ✴✴✴   When William the Conqueror ordered a castle built on this spot, he began a legend and a link with English sovereignty that has known many vicissitudes, the most recent being a 1992 fire. The state apartments display many works of art, porcelain, armor, furniture, three Verrio ceilings, and several 17th-century Gibbons carvings. Several works by Rubens adorn the King's Drawing Rooms. Of the apartments, the grand reception room, with its Gobelin tapestries, is the most spectacular.

Queen Mary's Doll's House is a palace in perfect miniature. It was given to Queen Mary in 1923 as a symbol of national goodwill. The house, designed by Sir Edwin Lutyens, was created on a scale of 1 to 12. It took 3 years to complete and involved the work of 1,500 tradespeople and artists.

St. George's Chapel is a gem of the Perpendicular style, sharing the distinction with Westminster Abbey as a pantheon of English monarchs (Victoria is a notable exception). The present St. George's was founded in the late 15th century by Edward IV on the site of the original Chapel of the Order of the Garter (from 1348).

Lying 34km (21 miles) west of London, Windsor Castle (℃ **020/7321-2233;** www.royalresidences.com) can be reached in 50 minutes by train from Paddington Station. Admission is £12 ($22) adults, £6 ($11) children 16 and under, £30 ($56) family of four. The castle at Castle Hill is open March through October daily from 9:45am to 5:15pm and November through February daily from 9:45am to 4:15pm.

2 Oxford & Stratford-upon-Avon

TOWN & GOWN: OXFORD ★★

Oxford is a city of business and commerce, home to several industries; it's much more of a real city than Cambridge. Oxford isn't entirely dominated by its university, although the college spires are the reason the hordes, including tour buses, flock here. The fast-flowing pedestrian traffic may cause you to think you've been transported back to London instead of delivered to not-so-sleepy Oxford.

At any time of the year, you can tour the colleges, many of which represent a peak in England's architectural kingdom, as well as a valley of Victorian contributions. The Oxford Tourist Information Centre (see below) offers guided walking tours daily year-round. Just don't mention the other place (Cambridge), and you shouldn't have any trouble. Comparisons between the two universities are inevitable of course, Oxford being better known for the arts and Cambridge more for the sciences.

The city predates the university—in fact, it was a Saxon town in the early part of the 10th century. By the 12th century, Oxford was already growing in reputation as a seat of learning, at the expense of Paris. The first colleges were founded in the 13th century. The story of Oxford is filled with local conflicts: The relationship between town and gown wasn't as peaceful as it is today, and riots often flared over the rights of the university versus the town. Nowadays, the young people of Oxford take out their aggressions in sporting competitions.

Ultimately, the test of a great university lies in the caliber of the people it turns out. Oxford can name-drop a mouthful: Roger Bacon, Sir Walter Raleigh, John Donne, Sir Christopher Wren, Samuel Johnson, William Penn, Lewis Carroll, Harold Macmillan, Graham Greene, T. E. Lawrence, just to name a select few.

ESSENTIALS

GETTING THERE   Oxford is 87km (54 miles) northwest from London.

By Train   Trains from London's Paddington Station depart hourly for Oxford (trip time: 1½ hr.). A cheap, same-day round-trip ticket costs £17 ($31); call ℃ **0845/748-4950** or visit www.railtrack.co.uk for information.

By Bus   **The Oxford Express** (operated by the Oxford Bus Company) provides coach service from London's Victoria Station (℃ **0870/580-8080;** www. oxfordbus.co.uk) to the Oxford bus station. Coaches usually depart about every

30 minutes during the day (trip time: about 1¾ hr.). A same-day round-trip ticket costs £11 ($20) adults, £5.50 ($10) children.

By Car Take M-40 west from London and follow the signs. Traffic and parking are a disaster in Oxford; you may want to use one of the four "Park and Ride" lots just outside the city.

VISITOR INFORMATION The **Oxford Tourist Information Centre,** at 15–16 Broad St., Gloucester Green (© **01865/726871;** www.visitoxford.org), sells maps, brochures, and souvenirs, as well as the famous Oxford University T-shirt. It also provides hotel booking services for £3 ($5.55). Guided walking tours leave from the center daily (see "Walking Around the Colleges," below). It's open Monday through Saturday from 9:30am to 5pm and Sunday and bank holidays in summer from 10am to 3:30pm.

GETTING AROUND Competition thrives in Oxford transportation, and the public benefits with swift, clean service by two companies. The **Oxford Bus Company,** 395 Cowley Rd. (© **01865/785400;** www.oxfordbus.co.uk), has green Park and Ride buses that leave from four parking lots in the city using the north-south or east-west routes. A round-trip ticket costs £1.80 ($3.35). Their blue CityLink buses travel to London, Heathrow, and Gatwick. The company's red CityLink buses cover 15 routes in all suburbs; a day pass allows unlimited travel for £2.90 ($5.35). Weekly and monthly passes are available.

The competition, **Stagecoach of Oxfordshire,** Unit 4, Horsepath, Cowley (© **01865/772250;** www.stagecoach-oxford.co.uk), uses blue-and-cream minibuses and tricolored red, blue, and orange coaches. City buses leave from Queen Street in Oxford's city center. Stagecoach's Explorer Pass (£5.50/$10) is a 1-day unlimited pass for travel in central and southeast England. Abington Road buses are marked WANTAGE and Iffley Road buses are labeled ROSE HILL.

WHERE TO STAY

Oxford Tourist Information Centre, Gloucester Green, opposite the bus station (© **01865/726871**), operates a year-round room-booking service for a fee of £3 ($5.55), plus a refundable deposit. The center has a list of accommodations, maps, and guidebooks.

Expensive

Eastgate Hotel ✦ The Eastgate, built on the site of a 1600s structure, stands within walking distance of Oxford College and the city center. Recently refurbished, it offers modern facilities while somewhat retaining the atmosphere of an English country house. The guest rooms are well worn but still cozy, and range in size from small to medium. The bathrooms have minimum space, but are equipped with shower-tub combinations.

23 Merton St., The High St., Oxford, Oxfordshire, OX1 4BE. © 0870/400-8201. Fax 01865/791681. www.macdonaldhotels.co.uk. 64 units. £160 ($296) double; £180 ($333) suite. AE, DC, MC, V. Bus: 3, 4, 7, or 52. **Amenities:** Restaurant; bar; limited room service; babysitting; laundry/dry-cleaning service; nonsmoking rooms. *In room:* A/C, TV, dataport, coffeemaker, hair dryer, trouser press.

Old Bank Hotel ✦✦✦ Located on Oxford's main street and surrounded by some of its oldest colleges and sights, the building dates from the 18th century and was once a bank. The first hotel created in the center of Oxford in 135 years, it opened late in 1999, immediately surpassing the traditional favorite, the Randolph, in style and luxuries. The guest rooms are comfortably and elegantly appointed, often opening onto views. Linen bedcovers trimmed in velvet and shantung silk give the accommodations added style. Each unit includes a well-kept bathroom with terra-cotta or marble tiles and a shower-tub combination.

92–94 High St., Oxford OX1 4BN. ✆ **01865/799599.** Fax 01865/799598. www.oxford-hotels-restaurants.co.uk. 42 units. £160–£235 ($296–$435) double; from £265–£320 ($490–$592) suite. AE, DC, MC, V. Bus: 7. **Amenities:** Restaurant; bar; concierge; 24-hr. room service; babysitting; laundry/dry-cleaning service; nonsmoking rooms. *In room:* A/C, TV, CD player, dataport, coffeemaker, hair dryer, safe.

Old Parsonage Hotel ✦✦   This extensively renovated hotel, near St. Giles Church and Keble College, is so old it looks like an extension of one of the ancient colleges. Originally a 13th-century hospital, it was restored in the early 17th century. In the 20th century, a modern wing was added, and in 1991 it was completely renovated and made into a first-rate hotel. This intimate old hotel is filled with hidden charms such as tiny gardens in its courtyard and on its roof terrace. In this tranquil area of Oxford, you feel like you're living at one of the colleges yourself. The rooms (all nonsmoking) are individually designed but not large, each opening onto the private gardens. All have bathrooms with shower-tub combinations.

1 Banbury Rd., Oxford OX2 6NN. ✆ **01865/310210.** Fax 01865/311262. www.oxford-hotels-restaurants.co.uk. 30 units. £135–£170 ($250–$315) double; £195 ($361) suite. AE, DC, MC, V. Bus: 7. **Amenities:** Restaurant; bar; 24-hr. room service; laundry/dry-cleaning service. *In room:* TV, dataport, hair dryer, safe, trouser press.

The Randolph ✦   Since 1864, the Randolph has overlooked St. Giles, the Ashmolean Museum, and the Cornmarket. The hotel is an example of how historic surroundings can be combined with modern conveniences to make for elegant accommodations. The lounges, though modernized, are cavernous enough for dozens of separate and intimate conversational groupings. The furnishings are traditional. Some rooms are quite large; others are a bit cramped. All units come equipped with well-maintained bathrooms containing shower-tub combinations. The double-glazing on the windows seems inadequate to keep out the noise of midtown traffic. In this price range, we'd opt first for the more stylish and intimate Old Parsonage.

Beaumont St., Oxford, Oxfordshire OX1 2LN. ✆ **0870/400-8200.** Fax 01865/791678. www.macdonaldhotels. co.uk. 114 units. £120–£195 ($222–$361) double; from £355–£600 ($657–$1,110) suite. AE, DC, MC, V. Parking £22 ($41). Bus: 7. **Amenities:** Restaurant; 2 bars; concierge; 24-hr. room service; babysitting; laundry/dry-cleaning service; nonsmoking rooms. *In room:* TV, dataport, coffeemaker, hair dryer, trouser press.

Inexpensive

Tilbury Lodge Private Hotel *(Kids)*   On a quiet country lane about 3km (2 miles) west of the center of Oxford, this small hotel is less than a mile from the railway station, where hotel staff will pick you up to save you the walk. Eddie and Eileen Trafford accommodate guests in their comfortable, well-furnished rooms. The most expensive room has a four-poster bed. Rooms (all nonsmoking) vary in size, but most are cozy with adequate space. Bathrooms, although tiny, are well kept, usually with a shower stall. The guesthouse also has a Jacuzzi and welcomes children.

5 Tilbury Lane, Eynsham Rd., Botley, Oxford, Oxfordshire OX2 9NB. ✆ **01865/862138.** Fax 01865/863700. 9 units. £66–£75 ($122–$139) double. Rates include English breakfast. MC, V. Bus: 4A, 4B, or 100. **Amenities:** Jacuzzi. *In room:* TV, coffeemaker, hair dryer.

WHERE TO DINE
Very Expensive

Cherwell Boathouse Restaurant ✦ FRENCH/MODERN ENGLISH
An Oxford landmark on the River Cherwell, this restaurant is owned by

Anthony Verdin, assisted by a young crew. The cooks change the fixed-price menu every 2 weeks to take advantage of the availability of fresh vegetables, fish, and meat. The kitchen is often cited for its "sensible combinations" of ingredients, as reflected quite well by its cream of artichoke and celery soup for a starter, or its shellfish terrine with a velvety chive-flavored crème fraîche. The success of the main dishes is founded on savory treats such as a pink and juicy breast of pigeon matched with a salad of smoked bacon on which tantalizing dribbles of raspberry dressing have been dropped. The tender and flavorful pork is perfectly married to an apple-and-prune compote. In summer, the restaurant also serves meals on the terrace.

Bardwell Rd. © **01865/552746.** www.cherwellboathouse.co.uk. Reservations recommended. Fixed-price dinner from £23 ($43); Sun lunch £22 ($41); Mon–Fri lunch £20 ($37). AE, DC, MC, V. Mon–Sun 12:30–2pm and 6:30–9pm. Closed Dec 24–30. Bus: Banbury Road.

Le Manoir aux Quat' Saisons ⊀⊀ FRENCH (MODERN) Some 19km (12 miles) southeast of Oxford, Le Manoir aux Quat' Saisons offers the finest cuisine in the Midlands. The gray- and honey-colored stone manor house was originally built by a Norman nobleman in the early 1300s, and over the years has attracted many famous visitors. Today, the restaurant's connection with France has been masterfully revived by the Gallic owner and chef, Raymond Blanc. His reputation for comfort and cuisine attracts guests from as far away as London. You can enjoy such creative treats as roasted squab and foie gras ravioli with wild mushrooms; roasted grouse in a blackberry and red-wine sauce; or a truly delicious roasted breast of Barbary hen duck with figs and fennel seeds and a pan-fried foie gras. Each dish is an exercise in studied perfection.

Accommodations are also available here. The gabled house was built in the 1500s and improved and enlarged in 1908. An outdoor swimming pool was added much later. Each very pricey room—rates are £275 to £485 ($509–$897) for a double, £490 to £875 ($907–$1,619) for a suite—is decorated boudoir-style with luxurious beds and linens, ruffled canopies, and high-quality antique reproductions.

Church Rd., Great Milton, Oxford, Oxfordshire OX44 7PD. © **800/845-4274** in the U.S., or 01844/278881. Fax 01844/278847. www.manoir.com. Reservations required. Main courses £26–£38 ($48–$70); lunch *menu du jour* £45 ($83); lunch or dinner *menu gourmand* £95 ($176). AE, DC, MC, V. Daily noon–2:30pm and 7–9:45pm. Take Exit 7 off M40 and continue on A329 toward Wallingford; look for signs for Great American Milton Manor about 1.6km (1 mile) down the road.

Expensive

Restaurant Elizabeth ⊀ FRENCH/CONTINENTAL The restaurant was named after its original owner, a matriarch who founded this stone-sided house opposite Christ Church College in the 1930s. Today, you're likely to find a well-trained staff from Spain, serving beautifully presented dishes in the French style. The larger of the two dining rooms displays reproductions of paintings by Goya and Velázquez and exudes a restrained dignity; the smaller room is devoted to *Alice in Wonderland* designs inspired by Lewis Carroll. Dishes are based on the use of fine produce prepared with skilled culinary technique, as exemplified by filet of salmon sautéed in butter and cooked with a white-wine sauce, or the grilled filet steak in a Madeira-flavored mushroom sauce. Breast of chicken is cooked in butter and delectably served in a creamy sauce of cognac and white wine.

82 St. Aldate's St. © **01865/242230.** Reservations recommended. Main courses £14–£33 ($26–$61); fixed-price lunch £16 ($30). AE, DC, MC, V. Tues–Sat 12:30–2:30pm and 6:30–11pm; Sun 7–10:30pm. Closed Good Friday and Christmas week. Bus: 7.

Moderate

Gee's Restaurant ⋆ MEDITERRANEAN/INTERNATIONAL   This restaurant, in a spacious Victorian glass conservatory, was converted from what for 80 years was the leading florist of Oxford. Its original features were retained by the owners, the Old Parsonage Hotel (see above), who have turned it into one of the most nostalgic and delightful places to dine in the city. Around since 1984, it has come more into fashion under a new chef. From students to professors, clients are mixed, but all enjoy a well-chosen list of offerings that ranges from succulent pastas to chargrilled steaks, from fresh fish to crisp salads. The grilled halibut steak with a lemon-and-thyme butter is predictable but nonetheless fine in every way. The confit of duck is a savory choice, enhanced by Savoy cabbage, smoked bacon, and herb-roasted potatoes. Count on a freshly made soup and Mediterranean-inspired salads with roast pepper, French beans, and olives. Always reliable is Scottish prime rib-eye steak with mushrooms and shoestring "chips."

61 Banbury Rd. © **01865/553540.** www.oxford-hotels-restaurants.co.uk. Reservations recommended. Main courses £11–£20 ($20–$37). Fixed-price lunch £13–£17 ($24–$31). AE, MC, V. Mon–Sat noon–2:30pm and 6–11pm; Sun noon–11pm.

Inexpensive

Al-Salam ⋆ *Value* LEBANESE   Some Oxford students think this place offers the best food value in the city, and we tend to agree. You'll dine within one of three sand-colored dining rooms, each separated from the other with antique (and very solid) wooden doors. Ironically, the newest of the three rooms, added in 2002, looks as if it's the oldest, thanks to stone-built arches and a commitment to the kinds of raw materials (wood and masonry) that would have been available in Lebanon a century ago. The menu depends on what's available in the marketplace, and the chef's skill is reflected in such dishes as king prawns sautéed with a garlic and tomato sauce, or spicy lamb with a chile and onion sauce. Long lines can form at the door, especially on Friday and Saturday.

6 Park End St. © **01865/245710.** Reservations recommended. Main courses £7.50–£12 ($14–$22). MC, V. Daily noon–midnight.

WALKING AROUND THE COLLEGES

The best way to get a running commentary on the important sights is to take a 2-hour **walking tour** through the city and the major colleges. The tours leave daily from the Oxford Tourist Information Centre at 11am and 2pm. Tours costs £6.50 ($12) for adults and £3 ($5.55) for children; the tours do not include New College or Christ Church.

AN OVERVIEW   For a bird's-eye view of the city and colleges, climb **Carfax Tower** ⋆, located in the center of the city. This structure is distinguished by its clock and figures that strike on the quarter-hour. Carfax Tower is all that remains from St. Martin's Church, where William Shakespeare once stood as godfather for William Davenant, who also became a successful playwright. A church stood on this site from 1032 until 1896. The tower used to be higher, but after 1340 it was lowered, following complaints from the university to Edward III that townspeople threw stones and fired arrows at students during town-and-gown disputes. Admission is £1.50 ($2.80) for adults, 60p ($1.10) for children. The tower is open year-round, except from Christmas Eve to January 1. April through October, its hours are from 10am to 5pm daily. Off-season hours are Monday through Saturday from 10am to 3:30pm. Children under 5 are not admitted. For information, call © **01865/792653.**

CHRIST CHURCH ★★   Begun by Cardinal Wolsey as Cardinal College in 1525, Christ Church (© **01865/276150;** www.chch.ox.ac.uk), known as the House, was founded by Henry VIII in 1546. Facing St. Aldate's Street, Christ Church has the largest quadrangle of any college in Oxford. Tom Tower houses Great Tom, an 18,000-pound bell. It rings at 9:05pm nightly, signaling the closing of the college gates. The 101 times it peals originally signified the number of students in residence at the time of the founding of the college.

The college chapel was constructed over a period of centuries, beginning in the 12th century. The cathedral's most distinguishing features are its Norman pillars and the vaulting of the choir, dating from the 15th century. In the center of the great quadrangle is a statue of Mercury mounted in the center of a fishpond. The college and cathedral can be visited daily from 9am to 5:30pm, though times vary (1–5:30pm on Sun, for example). It's best to call before you visit. The entrance fee is £4 ($7.40) adults and £3 ($5.55) children.

MAGDALEN COLLEGE ★★   Magdalen (pronounced *Maud*-lin) College, High Street (© **01865/276000;** www.magd.ox.ac.uk), was founded in 1458 by William of Waynflete, bishop of Winchester and later chancellor of England. Its alumni range from Wolsey to Wilde. Opposite the botanic garden, the oldest in England, is the bell tower, where the choristers sing in Latin at dawn on May Day. The reflection of the 15th-century tower is cast in the waters of the Cherwell below. On a not-so-happy day, Charles I—with his days numbered—watched the oncoming Roundheads from this tower. Visit the 15th-century chapel, in spite of many of its latter-day trappings. Ask when the hall and other places of special interest are open. The grounds of Magdalen are the most extensive of any Oxford college; there's even a deer park. You can visit year-round from 1pm to dusk daily. Admission is £3 ($5.55).

MERTON COLLEGE ★★   Founded in 1264, Merton College, Merton Street (© **01865/276310;** www.merton.ox.ac.uk), is among the three oldest colleges at the university. It stands near Corpus Christi College on Merton Street, the sole survivor of Oxford's medieval cobbled streets. Its library, built between 1371 and 1379, is said to be the oldest college library in England. The library has practiced a tradition of keeping some of its most valuable books chained; now only one book is so secured, to illustrate that historical custom. One treasure of the library is an astrolabe (an astronomical instrument used for measuring the altitude of the sun and stars) thought to have belonged to Chaucer. You pay £1 ($1.85) to visit the ancient library, as well as the Max Beerbohm Room (the satirical English caricaturist who died in 1956). The library and college are open Monday through Friday from 2 to 4pm and Saturday from 10am to 4pm (closed for 1 week at Easter, 1 week at Christmas, and on winter weekends).

THE SHOPPING SCENE

In its way, **Alice's Shop,** 83 St. Aldate's (© **01865/723793**), might have played a more important role in English literature than any other shop in Britain. Set in a 15th-century building, it functioned as a general store (brooms, hardware, and so on) during the period that Lewis Carroll, at the time a professor of mathematics at Christ Church College, was composing *Alice in Wonderland.* As such, it is believed to have been the model for important settings in the book. Today, the place is a favorite stop of Lewis Carroll fans, who gobble up commemorative pencils, chess sets, party favors, bookmarks, and, in rare cases, original editions of some of Carroll's works.

Calling on Churchill at Blenheim Palace

Just 13km (8 miles) northwest of Oxford stands the extravagantly baroque **Blenheim Palace** ★★★ (© **01993/811091**; www.blenheim palace.com), England's answer to Versailles. Blenheim is the home of the 11th duke of Marlborough, a descendant of John Churchill, the first duke, who was an on-again, off-again favorite of Queen Anne's. In his day (1650–1722), the first duke became the supreme military figure in Europe. Fighting on the Danube near a village named Blenheim, Churchill defeated the forces of Louis XIV, and the lavish palace of Blenheim was built for the duke as a gift from the queen. It was designed by Sir John Vanbrugh; the landscaping was created by the famous 18th-century landscape gardener, Capability Brown. You may recognize Blenheim because it was used as the setting for Kenneth Branagh's *Hamlet*.

The palace is loaded with riches: antiques, porcelain, oil paintings, tapestries, and chinoiserie. North Americans know Blenheim as the birthplace of Sir Winston Churchill. His birth room is included in the palace tour, as is the Churchill exhibition, four rooms of letters, books, photographs, and other relics. Today, the former prime minister lies buried in Bladon Churchyard, near the palace.

Blenheim Palace is open from mid-February to mid-December daily from 10:30am to 5:30pm. Admission is £13 ($23) adults, £10 ($19) seniors/students, and £7 ($13) children 5 to 15; free for children under 5. If you're driving, take the A-44 from Oxford; otherwise, the no. 20 Gloucester Green bus (© **01865/772250**) leaves Oxford about every 30 minutes during the day for the half-hour trip.

Bodleian Library Shop, Old School's Quadrangle, Radcliffe Square, Broad Street (© **01865/277216**), specializes in Oxford-derived souvenirs. There are more than 2,000 objects inventoried here, including books describing the history of the university and its various colleges, paperweights made of pewter and crystal, and Oxford banners and coffee mugs.

Castell & Son (The Varsity Shop), 13 Broad St. (© **01865/244000;** www. varsityshop.co.uk), is the best outlet for clothing emblazoned with the Oxford logo or heraldic symbol. Objects include both whimsical and dead-on-serious neckties, hats, T-shirts, sweatshirts, pens, bookmarks, beer and coffee mugs, and cuff links.

STRATFORD-UPON-AVON ★★

Stratford is virtually overrun by visitors in the summer months; the crowds dwindle in winter, allowing you at least to walk on the streets and seek out the places of genuine historic interest. Stratford is 146km (91 miles) northwest of London and 64km (40 miles) northwest of Oxford.

William Shakespeare, of course, was born here. Little is known about his early life, and many of the stories connected with Shakespeare's days in Stratford are largely fanciful, invented to amuse the vast number of literary fans who make the pilgrimage. David Garrick, the actor, really launched the shrine in 1769 when he organized the first of the Bard's commemorative birthday celebrations.

Tourist magnets include the Royal Shakespeare Theatre, where the Royal Shakespeare Company performs for 11 months each year. Visitors often rush back to London after a performance. Despite the crowds, Stratford's literary pilgrimage sights merit your interest. The town today aggressively hustles the Shakespeare connection, a bit suffocatingly so; everybody seems in business to make a buck off the Bard.

ESSENTIALS
GETTING THERE   By Train   The journey from London's Paddington Station to Stratford-upon-Avon takes about 2 hours and a round-trip ticket costs £23 ($43). For schedules and information, call © **0845/748-4950.** The train station at Stratford is on Alcester Road. On Sundays from October to May, it is closed, so you'll have to rely on the bus.

By Bus   Eight **National Express** buses a day leave from London's Victoria Station, with a trip time of 3¼ hours. A single-day round-trip ticket costs £13 ($24) except on Friday, when the price is £20 ($37). For schedules and information, call © **0870/580-8080.**

By Car   If you're driving from London, take the M40 toward Oxford and continue to Stratford-upon-Avon on the A34.

VISITOR INFORMATION   The **Tourist Information Centre,** Bridgefoot (© **01789/293127;** www.shakespeare-country.co.uk), will provide any details you may want to know about the Shakespeare houses, theater, and other attractions, and will assist you in booking rooms. It's open April 1 through October, Monday through Saturday from 9am to 6pm and Sunday from 10:30am to 4:30pm; November through March, Monday through Saturday from 9am to 5pm and Sunday from 10am to 4pm.

WHERE TO STAY
Very Expensive
Menzies Welcombe Hotel & Golf Course 🟊🟊🟊   For a formal, historic hotel, there's none better in Stratford, and that includes Alveston Manor. One of England's great Jacobean country houses, this hotel is a 10-minute ride from the heart of Stratford. It is surrounded by 64 hectares (157 acres) of grounds. The public areas are heroic in size, with high windows providing views of the park. Rooms—some big enough for tennis matches—are luxuriously furnished; those in the garden wing, although comfortable, are small. Bathrooms come with a tub/shower combo.

Warwick Rd., Stratford-upon-Avon, Warwickshire CV37 0NR. © 01789/295252. Fax 01789/414666. www.welcombe.co.uk. 78 units. £150–£250 ($278–$463) double; £275–£450 ($509–$833) suite. Rates include English breakfast. AE, DC, MC, V. Take A439 2km (1½ miles) northeast of the town center. **Amenities:** Restaurant; bar; golf course; tennis court; 24-hr. room service; laundry/dry-cleaning service. *In room:* TV, hair dryer, iron.

Expensive
Alveston Manor Hotel 🟊🟊   This black-and-white timbered manor is perfect for theatergoers; it's just a 2-minute walk from the River Avon. The Welcombe and Ettington Park may have cornered the deluxe trade, but the Alveston, along with the Shakespeare (see below), are the most atmospheric choices in town. The hotel has everything from an Elizabethan gazebo to Queen Anne windows. Mentioned in the *Domesday Book,* the building predates the arrival of William the Conqueror. The 19 rooms in the manor house will appeal to those who appreciate old slanted floors, overhead beams, and antique furnishings; some have half-tester beds. Other accommodations—full of tour groups—are in a 30-year-old motel-like wing. The

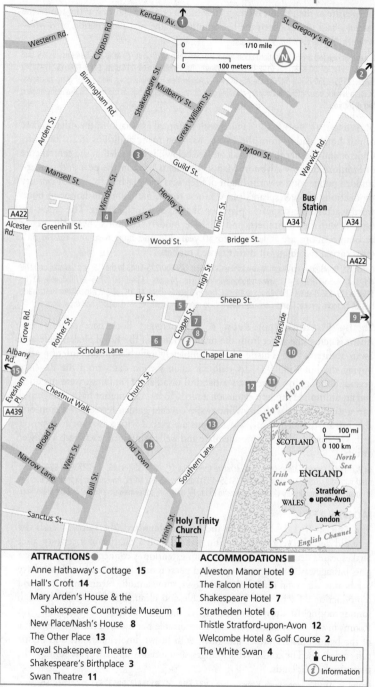

Stratford-upon-Avon

0 1/10 mile
0 100 meters

Kendall Av. **1**

Western Rd.
St. Gregory's Rd.
Clopton Rd.
Birmingham Rd.
Shakespeare St.
Mulberry St.
Great William St.

2

Arden St.
Mansell St.
Windsor St.
Henley St.
Payton St.
Warwick Rd.

3
Guild St.

Meer St.
Union St.

Bus Station
A34   A34

A422
Alcester Rd.
Greenhill St.
4
Wood St.
Bridge St.

A422

High St.
Ely St.
Sheep St.
5
Chapel St.
7
8
Waterside
9

Grove Rd.
Rother St.
Scholars Lane
6
Chapel Lane
10

Albany Rd.
15
Eversham Pl.
Church St.
11
12
River Avon

A439
Chestnut Walk
13

Broad St.
West St.
Bull St.
Old Town
14

Narrow Lane
Southern Lane

Sanctus St.
Trinity St.
Holy Trinity Church

0 100 mi
0 100 km
SCOTLAND
North Sea
Irish Sea
ENGLAND
Stratford-upon-Avon
WALES
London
English Channel

ATTRACTIONS ●
Anne Hathaway's Cottage **15**
Hall's Croft **14**
Mary Arden's House & the
    Shakespeare Countryside Museum **1**
New Place/Nash's House **8**
The Other Place **13**
Royal Shakespeare Theatre **10**
Shakespeare's Birthplace **3**
Swan Theatre **11**

ACCOMMODATIONS ■
Alveston Manor Hotel **9**
The Falcon Hotel **5**
Shakespeare Hotel **7**
Stratheden Hotel **6**
Thistle Stratford-upon-Avon **12**
Welcombe Hotel & Golf Course **2**
The White Swan **4**

✝ Church
ⓘ Information

lounges are in the manor; there's a view of the centuries-old tree at the top of the garden—said to have been the background for the first presentation of *A Midsummer Night's Dream.*

Clopton Bridge (off B4066), Stratford-upon-Avon, Warwickshire CV37 7HP. ℂ 800/225-5843 in the U.S. and Canada, or 0870/400-8181. Fax 01789/414095. www.heritage-hotels.co.uk. 114 units. £125–£160 ($231–$296) double; £195–£230 ($361–$426) suite. AE, DC, MC, V. **Amenities:** Restaurant; bar; indoor pool; gym; sauna; 24-hr. room service; babysitting; laundry/dry-cleaning service; nonsmoking rooms. *In room:* TV, minibar, coffeemaker, hair dryer, iron.

Shakespeare Hotel ★★   Filled with historical associations, the original core of this hotel, dating from the 1400s, has seen many additions in its long life. Quieter and plusher than the Falcon (see below), it is equaled in the central core of Stratford only by Alveston Manor. Residents relax in the post-and-timber–studded public rooms, within sight of fireplaces and playbills from 19th-century productions of Shakespeare's plays. Guest rooms are named in honor of noteworthy actors, Shakespeare's plays, or Shakespearean characters. The oldest are capped with hewn timbers, and all have modern comforts. Even the newer accommodations are at least 40 to 50 years old and have rose-and-thistle patterns carved into many of their exposed timbers.

Chapel St., Stratford-upon-Avon, Warwickshire CV37 6ER. ℂ 800/225-5843 in the U.S. and Canada, or 0870/400-8182. Fax 01789/415411. www.macdonaldhotels.co.uk. 74 units. £138–£150 ($255–$278) double; £178–£190 ($329–$352) suite. Children up to 16 stay free in parent's room. AE, DC, MC, V. **Amenities:** Restaurant; bar; 24-hr. room service; laundry service; nonsmoking rooms. *In room:* AC, TV, dataport, hair dryer, iron.

Thistle Stratford-upon-Avon ★   Theatergoers flock here because The Arden is across the street from the main entrance of the Royal Shakespeare and Swan theaters. The Thistle chain completely refurbished the interior after buying the hotel in 1993. Its redbrick main section dates from the Regency period, although over the years a handful of adjacent buildings were included and an uninspired modern extension added. Today, the interior has a lounge and bar; a dining room with bay windows; a covered garden terrace; and comfortable but narrow bedrooms. Most rooms are graced with a two- or four-poster bed. The small bathrooms are adequate and well maintained, each with a shower or tub.

44 Waterside, Stratford-upon-Avon, Warwickshire CV37 6BA. ℂ 0870/333-9146. Fax 0870/333-9246. www.stratfordthistle.co.uk. 63 units. £73–£179 ($135–$331) double. AE, DC, MC, V. **Amenities:** Restaurant; bar; 24-hr. room service; laundry/dry-cleaning service. *In room:* TV, dataport, coffeemaker, hair dryer, trouser press, iron.

MODERATE

The Falcon Hotel   Located in the heart of Stratford, the Falcon blends the very old and the very new. The inn was licensed a quarter of a century after Shakespeare's death. A 1970s guest-room extension is connected to its rear by a glass passageway. The recently upgraded guest rooms in the mellowed part have oak beams, diamond leaded-glass windows, some antique furnishings, and good reproductions. Each room is comfortable and clean, but there is not enough soundproofing to drown out the BBC on your next-door neighbor's telly. Rooms in the newer section are also comfortable but more sterile in tone. Some of the bathrooms are rather unsightly, with brown linoleum floors and plastic tub enclosures. The comfortable lounges, also recently upgraded, are some of the finest in the Midlands.

Chapel St., Stratford-upon-Avon, Warwickshire CV37 6HA. ℂ 01789/279953. Fax 01789/414260. www.corushotels.com/thefalcon. 84 units. £80–£125 ($148–$231) double; from £140 ($259) suite. AE, DC, MC, V. **Amenities:** Restaurant; 3 bars; 24-hr. room service. *In room:* TV, dataport, coffeemaker, hair dryer.

Inexpensive

Stratheden Hotel   A short walk north of the Royal Shakespeare Theatre, the Stratheden Hotel is tucked away in a desirable location. Built in 1673, and currently the oldest remaining brick building in the town center, it has a tiny rear garden and top-floor rooms with slanted, beamed ceilings. Under the ownership of the Wells family for the past quarter century, it has improved again in both decor and comfort with the addition of fresh paint, new curtains, and good beds. Most of the small bathrooms have shower stalls, although a few have bathtubs.

5 Chapel St., Stratford-upon-Avon, Warwickshire CV37 6EP. ℭ/fax **01789/297119.** www.ukstay.com/warwick/ stratheden. 9 units. £66–£72 ($122–$133) double. Rates include full English breakfast. AE, MC, V. **Amenities:** Breakfast room. *In room:* TV.

The White Swan ⋆   This cozy, intimate hotel is one of the most atmospheric in Stratford and is, in fact, the oldest building here. In business for more than a century before Shakespeare appeared on the scene, it competes successfully with the Falcon in offering an ancient atmosphere. The gabled medieval front would present the Bard with no surprises, but the modern comforts inside would surely astonish him, even though many of the rooms have been preserved. Guest rooms are comfortable but generally lack style. Except for an occasional four-poster or half-canopy bed, most are twins or doubles.

Rother St., Stratford-upon-Avon, Warwickshire CV37 6NH. ℭ **01789/297022.** Fax 01789/268773. www.e-travel guide.info/whiteswan. 41 units. £80 ($148) double. Rates include English breakfast. AE, DC, MC, V. **Amenities:** Restaurant; bar; limited room service. *In room:* TV, coffeemaker, hair dryer, trouser press.

WHERE TO DINE

The Quarto's Restaurant ⋆ FRENCH/ITALIAN/ENGLISH   This restaurant enjoys the best location in town—in the theater itself, with glass walls providing an unobstructed view of swans on the Avon. You can purchase an intermission snack feast of smoked salmon and champagne, or dine by flickering candlelight after the performance. Many dishes, such as apple-and-parsnip soup, are definitely old English; others reflect a Continental touch, such as fried polenta with filets of pigeon and bacon. For your main course, you may select Dover sole, pheasant supreme, or roast loin of pork. Homemade crème brûlée is an old-time favorite. The theater lobby has a special phone for reservations.

In the Royal Shakespeare Theatre, Waterside. ℭ **01789/403415.** Reservations required. Matinee lunch £18 ($33); dinner £16–£22 ($30–$41). AE, MC, V. Thurs and Sat noon–2:30pm; Mon–Sat 5:30pm–midnight. Closed when theater is shut down.

Thai Boathouse ⋆ THAI   The only restaurant set on the Avon, this charming choice is reached by crossing Clopton Bridge toward Oxford and Banbury. The second-floor dining room opens onto vistas of the river. This restaurant, originally established 4 decades ago in Bangkok, has brought spice and zest to Stratford's lazy restaurant scene. The decor comes from Thailand itself, with elephants, woodcarvings, and Buddhas. Seasonal specialties such as wild duck and pheasant are special features of the menu. Fresh produce, great skill in the kitchen, and exquisite presentations are the hallmarks of this restaurant. Sample a selection of authentic Thai appetizers before going on to such delectable main courses as fresh sea bass in lemon grass or lime leaves wrapped in banana leaf and grilled over charcoal, or a salmon stir-fried with curry sauce and coconut cream, enhanced by the use of Thai herbs. One of our favorites is their lamb in a yellow curry with potatoes, onions, and cashew nuts.

Swan's Nest Lane. ℭ **01789/297733.** Reservations recommended. Main courses £5.50–£12 ($10–$22); fixed-price menus £21–£27 ($39–$50). MC, V. Daily noon–2:30pm and 5:30–10:30pm.

PUBS

The Black Swan ("The Dirty Duck") ★★ ENGLISH   Affectionately known as The Dirty Duck, this has been a popular hangout for Stratford players since the 18th century. The wall is lined with autographed photos of its many famous patrons. The front lounge and bar crackle with intense conversation. Typical English grills, among other dishes, are featured in the Dirty Duck Grill Room, though no one has ever accused it of serving the best food in Stratford. You'll have a choice of a dozen appetizers, most of which would make a meal in themselves. In fair weather, you can have drinks in the front garden and watch the swans glide by on the Avon.

Waterside. ℂ 01789/297312. Reservations required for dining. Main courses £8–£16 ($15–$30); bar snacks £5–£7.25 ($9.25–$13). AE, DC, MC, V (in the restaurant only). Daily 11am–11pm (no dinner Sun).

The Garrick Inn ENGLISH   Near Harvard House, this black-and-white timbered Elizabethan pub has an unpretentious charm. The front bar is decorated with tapestry-covered settles, an old oak refectory table, and an open fireplace that attracts the locals. The back bar has a circular fireplace with a copper hood and mementos of the triumphs of the English stage. The specialty is homemade pies such as steak and kidney or chicken and mushroom.

25 High St. ℂ 01789/292186. Main courses £6.50–£13 ($12–$24). MC, V. Meals daily noon–9pm. Pub Mon–Sat 11am–11pm; Sun noon–10:30pm.

THEATER

Royal Shakespeare Company has a major showcase at the Royal Shakespeare Theatre, Waterside, Stratford-upon-Avon CV37 6BB (ℂ **01789/403403;** www. rsc.org.uk), on the banks of the Avon. Plays, including on average five by Shakespeare each season, are staged at the 1,500-seat Royal Shakespeare and the 430-seat Swan Theatre as well as at 170-seat **The Other Place,** a smaller, more experimental venue.

You usually need **ticket reservations,** with two successive booking periods, each one opening about 2 months in advance. You can pick these up from a North American or English travel agent. A small number of tickets are always held for sale on the day of a performance, but it may be too late to get a good seat if you wait until you arrive in Stratford. Tickets can be booked, with a service charge, through **Keith Prowse** (ℂ **800/223-6108** in North America, or 020/7014-8550 in London; www.keithprowse.com).

You can also call the **theater box office** directly (ℂ **0870/609-1110**) and charge your tickets. The box office is open Monday through Saturday from 9am to 8pm, although it closes at 6pm on days when there are no performances. Seat prices range from £8 to £50 ($15–$93). You can make a credit card reservation and pick up your tickets on the performance day, but you must cancel at least 2 full weeks in advance to get a refund.

SHAKESPEARE PILGRIMAGE SIGHTS

Besides the attractions on the periphery of Stratford, there are many Elizabethan and Jacobean buildings in town, many of them administered by the Shakespeare Birthplace Trust. One combination ticket—costing £13 ($24) adults, £12 ($22) seniors and students, and £6.50 ($12) children—lets you visit the five most important sights: Shakespeare's Birthplace, Anne Hathaway's Cottage, Mary Arden's House & the Shakespeare Countryside Museum, Hall's Croft, and New Place/Nash's House. You can also buy a family ticket to all five sights (good for two adults and three children) for £29 ($54)—a good deal. You can buy tickets at any of the Trust properties.

Anne Hathaway's Cottage ⚒ In the hamlet of Shottery, 1.6km (1 mile) from Stratford, is the thatched, wattle-and-daub cottage where Anne Hathaway lived before her marriage to Shakespeare. It's the most interesting of the Trust properties, and the most unchanged. The Hathaways were yeoman farmers, and the cottage provides a rare insight into the life of a family of Shakespeare's day. Many original furnishings, including the courting settle and utensils, are preserved inside the house, which was occupied by descendants of Shakespeare's wife's family until 1892.

Cottage Lane, Shottery. ℂ **01789/292100**. Admission £5.20 ($9.60) adults, £2 ($3.70) children. Nov–Mar daily 10am–4pm; Apr–May Mon–Sat 9:30am–5pm, Sun 10am–5pm; June–Aug Mon–Sat 9am–5pm, Sun 9:30am–5pm; Sept–Oct Mon–Sat 9:30am–5pm, Sun 10am–5pm. Closed Dec 23–26. Take a bus from Bridge St. or walk via a marked pathway from Evesham Place in Stratford across the meadow to Shottery.

Hall's Croft It was here that Shakespeare's daughter Susanna probably lived with her husband, Dr. John Hall. Furnished in the style of a middle-class home of the time, Hall's Croft is an outstanding Tudor house with a beautiful walled garden. Dr. Hall was widely respected and built up a large medical practice in the area, and exhibits illustrating the theory and practice of medicine in Dr. Hall's time are on view. You're welcome to use the adjoining Hall's Croft Club, which serves morning coffee, lunch, and afternoon tea.

Old Town (near Holy Trinity Church). ℂ **01789/292107**. Admission £3.50 ($6.50) adults, £1.70 ($3.15) children. Nov–Mar daily 11am–4pm; Apr–May daily 11am–5pm; June–Aug Mon–Sat 9:30am–5pm, Sun 10am–5pm; Sept–Oct daily 11am–5pm. Closed Dec 23–26. To reach Hall's Croft, walk west from High St., which becomes Chapel St. and Church St.; at the intersection with Old Town, go left.

Mary Arden's House & the Shakespeare Countryside Museum ★ So what if millions of visitors have been tricked into thinking this timber-framed farmhouse with its old stone dovecote and various outbuildings was the girlhood home of Shakespeare's mother, Mary Arden? It's still one of the most intriguing sights outside Stratford, even if the local historian Dr. Nat Alcock discovered in 2000 that the actual childhood home of Arden was the dull-looking brick-built farmhouse, Glebe Farm, next door. It was all the trick of an 18th-century tour guide, John Jordan, who decided Glebe Farm was too unimpressive to be the home of the Bard's mother, so he told tourists it was this farmstead instead. The so-called Mary Arden's House wasn't actually constructed until the late 16th century, a little late to be her home. Nonetheless, visit it anyway as it contains country furniture and domestic utensils. In the barns, stable, cow shed, and farmyard is an extensive collection of farming implements illustrating life and work in the local countryside from Shakespeare's time to the present.

Wilmcote. ℂ **01789/204016**. Admission £5.70 ($11) adults, £5 ($9.25) students and seniors, and £2.50 ($4.65) children. Nov–Mar Mon–Sat 10am–4pm, Sun 10:30am–4pm; Apr and May Mon–Sat 10am–5pm, Sun 10:30am–5pm; June–Aug Mon–Sat 9:30am–5pm, Sun 10am–5pm; Sept–Oct Mon–Sat 10am–5pm, Sun 10:30am–5pm. Closed Dec 23–26. Take A3400 (Birmingham) for 5.5km (3½ miles).

New Place/Nash's House This is the site where Shakespeare retired in 1610, a prosperous man. He died 6 years later, at the age of 52. Regrettably, his former home was torn down, and only the site remains. You enter the gardens through Nash's House (Thomas Nash married a granddaughter of the poet). The house has 16th-century period rooms and an exhibition illustrating the history of Stratford. The delightful Knott Garden adjoins the site and represents the style of a fashionable Elizabethan garden. New Place has its own great garden, which once belonged to Shakespeare.

Chapel St. Ⓒ **01789/204016**. Admission £3.50 ($6.50) adults, £3 ($5.55) seniors and students, £1.70 ($3.15) children. Nov–Mar daily 11am–4pm; Apr and May daily 11am–5pm; June–Aug Mon–Sat 9:30am–5pm, Sun 10am–5pm; Sept and Oct daily 11am–5pm. Closed Dec 23–26. Walk west down High St.; Chapel St. is a continuation of High St.

Shakespeare's Birthplace 🐾 The son of a glover and whittawer (leather worker), the Bard was born here on St. George's Day (Apr 23) in 1564 and died 52 years later on the exact same date. Filled with Shakespeare memorabilia, including a portrait and furnishings of the writer's time, the Trust property is a half-timbered structure, dating from the first part of the 16th century. The house, bought by public donors in 1847, is preserved as a national shrine. You can visit the oak-beamed living room, the bedroom where Shakespeare was probably born, a fully equipped kitchen of the period (look for the "baby-minder"), and a Shakespeare Museum, illustrating his life and times.

Henley St. (in the town center near the post office, close to Union St.). Ⓒ **01789/204016**. Admission £6.50 ($12) adults, £5.50 ($10) students and seniors, £2.60 ($4.80) children. Nov–Mar Mon–Sat 10am–4pm, Sun 10:30am–4pm; Apr–May Mon–Sat 10am–4pm, Sun 10:30am–5pm; June–Aug Mon–Sat 9am–5pm, Sun 9:30am–5pm; Sept–Oct Mon–Sat 10am–5pm, Sun 10:30am–5pm. Closed Dec 23–26.

A Visit to Warwick Castle

Perched on a rocky cliff above the Avon River in the town center, **Warwick Castle** 🐾🐾🐾 is a stately late-17th-century–style mansion surrounded by a magnificent 14th-century fortress. The first significant fortifications were built by Ethelfleda, daughter of Alfred the Great, in 914. Two years after the Norman Conquest in 1068, William the Conqueror ordered the construction of a "motte and bailey" castle. The mound is all that remains today of the Norman castle.

The Beauchamp family, earls of Warwick, is responsible for the appearance of the castle today, and much of the external structure remains unchanged from the mid–14th century. The staterooms and Great Hall house fine collections of paintings, furniture, arms, and armor. The armory, dungeon, torture chamber, ghost tower, clock tower, and Guy's tower create a vivid picture of the castle's turbulent past and its important role in the history of England.

Sir Walter Scott described Warwick Castle in 1828 as "that fairest monument of ancient and chivalrous splendor which yet remains uninjured by time." Visitors can also see the Victorian rose garden, a re-creation of an original design from 1868 by Robert Marnock. On Castle Hill, Warwick Castle (Ⓒ **0870/442-2000**; www.warwick-castle.co.uk) is open April through September daily from 10am to 6pm; October through March daily from 10am to 5pm; closed Christmas Day. Admission is £13 ($24) adults, £9 ($17) seniors, £7.50 ($14) children 4 to 16, free for children 4 and under, and £32 ($59) family.

Trains run frequently between Stratford-upon-Avon and Warwick. Call Ⓒ **0845/748-4950** for schedules and information. One **Stagecoach** bus per hour departs Stratford-upon-Avon during the day. The trip takes 15 to 20 minutes. Call the Tourist Information Centre (Ⓒ **01789/293127**) for schedules. Motorists should take the A46 from Stratford-upon-Avon.

ORGANIZED TOURS

Guided tours of Stratford-upon-Avon are conducted by **City Sightseeing,** Civic Hall, Rother Street (www.city-sightseeing.com). In summer, open-top double-decker buses depart every 15 minutes daily from 9am to 6pm. You can take a 1-hour ride without stops, or you can get off at any or all of the town's five Shakespeare properties. Though the bus stops are clearly marked along the historic route, the most logical starting point is the sidewalk in front of the Pen & Parchment Pub, at the bottom of Bridge Street. Tour tickets are valid all day, so you can hop on and off the buses as many times as you want. The tours cost £8.50 ($16) for adults, £6 ($11) for seniors or students, and £3.50 ($6.50) for children under 12. A family ticket sells for £20 ($36), and children under 5 go free.

THE SHOPPING SCENE

At the **National Trust Shop,** 45 Wood St. (© **01789/262197**), you'll find textbooks and guidebooks describing esoteric places in the environs of Stratford, descriptions of National Trust properties throughout England, stationery, books, china, pewter, and toiletries, each inscribed, embossed, or painted with logos that evoke some aspect of English tastes and traditions.

Set in an antique house that lies across from Shakespeare's Birthplace, the **Shakespeare Bookshop,** 39 Henley St. (© **01789/292176**), is the region's premier source for textbooks and academic treatises on the Bard and his works. It specializes in books conceived for every level of expertise, from picture books for junior high school students to weighty tomes geared toward anyone pursuing a Ph.D. in literature.

3 Stonehenge & Bath

Many visitors with very limited time head for the West Country, where they explore its two major attractions: Stonehenge—the most important prehistoric monument in Britain—and Bath, England's most elegant city, famed for its architecture and its hot springs. If you have the time, you may also want to visit Salisbury Cathedral and the other prehistoric sites in the area, at Avebury and Old Sarum.

STONEHENGE ✦✦✦

At the junction of A-303 and A-344/A-360, 3km (2 miles) west of Amesbury and about 15km (9 miles) north of Salisbury, stands the renowned monument of Stonehenge, a stone circle believed to be approximately 5,000 years old. This circle of lintels and megalithic pillars is the most important prehistoric monument in Britain.

ESSENTIALS

GETTING THERE   By Car   To reach Stonehenge from London, head in the direction of Salisbury (see below), 145km (90 miles) to the southwest. Take the M-3 to the end of the run, continuing the rest of the way on A-30. Once at Salisbury, after stopping to view its cathedral (see below), head north on Castle Road. At the first roundabout (traffic circle), take the exit toward Amesbury (A-345) and Old Sarum. Continue along this route for 13km (8 miles) and then turn left onto A-303 in the direction of Exeter. Stonehenge is signposted, leading you up the A-344 to the right. In all, it's about 19km (12 miles) from Salisbury.

By Train or Bus   A **Network Express** train departs hourly from Waterloo Station bound for Salisbury (trip time: 1½ hr.). Call **0845/748-4950** or visit www.railtrack.co.uk for information. Buses also depart four or five times per day from

---

> **⌒Finds⌐ Biking to Stonehenge**
>
> If you'd like to bike out to Stonehenge, go to **Hayball's Cycle Shop,** 26–30 Winchester St. (✆ **01722/411378**), which rents mountain bikes for £10 ($19) per day. For an extra £2.50 ($4.65), you can keep the bike overnight. A £25 ($46) deposit is required. A 7-day rental is £65 ($120). Hours are daily from 9am to 5:30pm.

Victoria Station heading for Salisbury (2½ hr.). Once at Salisbury, take a **Wilts & Dorset bus** (✆ **01722/336855** for schedules), which runs several vehicles daily, depending on demand, from Salisbury to Stonehenge. This company's buses depart from the train station at Salisbury, heading directly to Stonehenge (40 min.). Round-trip fare is £6 ($11) adults, £3 ($5.55) children ages 5 to 14 (4 and under ride free). Use Salisbury as a refueling stop.

EXPLORING STONEHENGE

Despite its familiarity, visitors cannot help but be impressed when they first see Stonehenge, an astonishing engineering feat. The boulders, the bluestones in particular, were moved many miles, possibly from as far away as southern Wales, to this site.

The widely held view of the 18th- and 19-century Romantics that Stonehenge was the work of the druids is without foundation. The boulders, many weighing several tons, are believed to have predated the arrival in Britain of the Celtic druidic cult. Recent excavations continue to bring new evidence to bear on the origin and purpose of the prehistoric circle; controversy has surrounded the site, especially since the publication of *Stonehenge Decoded* by Gerald S. Hawkins and John B. White, which maintains that Stonehenge was an astronomical observatory— that is, a Neolithic calendar capable of predicting eclipses.

The site is now surrounded by a fence to protect it from vandals and souvenir hunters. Your ticket permits you to go inside the fence, all the way up to a short rope barrier about 15m (50 ft.) from the stones. You can make a full circular tour around Stonehenge; a modular walkway has been introduced to cross the archaeologically important area that runs between the Heel Stone and the main circle of stones. This lets you complete a full circuit of the stones, an excellent addition to the well-received audio tour.

Admission to Stonehenge (✆ **01980/623108**) is £5 ($9.25) adults, £3.80 ($7.05) students and seniors, and £2.50 ($4.65) children; a family ticket is £12.50 ($23). It's open March 16 through May and September through October 15 daily from 9am to 5pm; June through August daily from 9am to 7pm; and October 16 through March 15 daily from 9:30am to 4pm.

AVEBURY 👁👁

Avebury, one of Europe's largest prehistoric sites, lies 32km (20 miles) north of Stonehenge on the Kennet River, 11km (7 miles) west of Marlborough. The small village actually lies within the vast stone circle. Unlike Stonehenge, you can walk around the 11-hectare (28-acre) site, winding in and out of the circle of more than 100 stones, some of which weigh up to 50 tons. The stones are made of sarsen, a sandstone found in Wiltshire. Inside this large circle are two smaller ones, each with about 30 stones standing upright. Native Neolithic tribes are believed to have built these circles.

GETTING THERE Avebury is on A-361 between Swindon and Devizes and 1.6km (1 mile) from the A-4 London-Bath road. The closest rail station is at Swindon, some 19km (12 miles) away, which is served by the main rail line from London to Bath. A limited bus service (no. 49) runs from Swindon to Devizes through Avebury.

You can also reach Avebury by bus from Salisbury by taking one of two buses (nos. 5 and 6) run by **Wilts & Dorset** (© 01722/336855). The buses leave five times a day from Monday to Saturday and three times on Sunday (trip time: 1 hr., 40 min.). Round-trip tickets are £6 ($11) for adults, £4.20 ($7.75) seniors, £11.50 ($21) family ticket, and £3 ($5.55) for children ages 5 to 14 (4 and under ride free).

AN ARCHAEOLOGICAL MUSEUM

The **Alexander Keiller Museum** (© 01672/539250) houses one of Britain's most important archaeological collections. It began with material from excavations at Windmill Hill and Avebury, and now includes artifacts from other prehistoric digs at West Kennet, Long Barrow, Silbury Hill, West Kennet Avenue, and the Sanctuary. Admission is £4.20 ($7.75) adults, £2.10 ($3.90) children, and £10 ($19) family. The museum is open April through October, daily from 10am to 6pm; November through March, daily from 10am to 4pm.

SALISBURY ★★

Long before you enter Salisbury, the spire of the cathedral comes into view, just as John Constable painted it many times. Salisbury lies in the Avon River Valley, and is a fine place to stop for lunch and a look at the cathedral on your way to Stonehenge.

ESSENTIALS

GETTING THERE **By Train** **Network Express trains** depart for Salisbury hourly from Waterloo Station in London; the trip takes 1½ hours. Sprinter trains offer fast, efficient service every hour from Portsmouth, Bristol, and South Wales. Direct rail service is also available from Exeter, Plymouth, Brighton, and Reading. For information, call © 0845/748-4950 in the United Kingdom.

By Bus Three **National Express buses** per day run from London's Victoria Coach Station to Salisbury, Monday through Friday. On Saturday and Sunday, three buses depart daily. The trip takes 2½ hours. Call © 0870/580-8080 for schedules and information.

By Car If you're driving from London, head west on the M3 to the end of the run, continuing the rest of the way on the A30.

VISITOR INFORMATION The **Tourist Information Centre** at Fish Row (© 01722/334956) is open October through April, Monday through Saturday from 9:30am to 5pm; in May, Monday through Saturday from 9:30am to 5pm and Sunday from 10:30am to 4:30pm; June through September, Monday through Saturday from 9:30am to 6pm and Sunday from 10:30am to 4:30pm.

WHERE TO STAY

The Beadles ★★ *finds* A traditional modern Georgian house with antique furnishings and a view of the cathedral, The Beadles offers unobstructed views of the beautiful Wiltshire countryside from its .4-hectare (1-acre) gardens. It's situated in a small, unspoiled English village, 13km (8 miles) from Salisbury, which offers excellent access to Stonehenge, Wilton House, the New Forest, and the rambling moors of Thomas Hardy country. Even the road to Winchester is an ancient Roman byway. Furnished tastefully, this nonsmoking household contains rooms with twins or doubles, each with a full private bathroom. Owners David and Anne-Marie Yuille-Baddeley delight in providing information on the area.

Middleton, Middle Winterslow, near Salisbury, Wiltshire SP5 1QS. ℂ **01980/862922.** Fax 01980/863565. www.guestaccom.co.uk/754.htm. 3 units. £60 ($111) double. Rates include English breakfast. MC, V. Turn off A30 at Pheasant Inn to Middle Winterslow. Enter the village, make the 1st right, turn right again, and it's the 1st right after TREVANO. **Amenities:** Dining room; tour services. *In room:* TV, coffeemaker, hair dryer, iron.

The Rose and Crown 𝕮𝕮𝕮   This half-timbered, 13th-century gem stands with its feet almost in the River Avon; beyond the water, you can see the tall spire of the cathedral. Because of its tranquil location, it's our top choice. From here, you can easily walk over the arched stone bridge to the center of Salisbury in 10 minutes. Old trees shade the lawns and gardens between the inn and the river, and chairs are set out so that you can enjoy the view and count the swans. The inn has both a new and an old wing. The newer wing is modern, but the old wing is more appealing, with sloping ceilings and antique fireplaces and furniture. Guest rooms in the new wing are more spacious and better designed than those in the main house. Bathrooms include a shower-and-tub combination.

Harnham Rd., Salisbury, Wiltshire SP2 8JQ. ℂ **01722/399955.** Fax 01722/339816. 28 units. £118 ($218) double. AE, DC, MC, V. Take A3094 2.5km (1½ miles) from the center of town. **Amenities:** Restaurant; 2 bars; 24-hr. room service; laundry/dry cleaning. *In room:* TV, hair dryer, iron, trouser press.

WHERE TO DINE

Harper's Restaurant ENGLISH/INTERNATIONAL   The chef-owner of this place prides himself on specializing in "real food," homemade and wholesome. The pleasantly decorated restaurant is on the second floor of a redbrick building at the back end of Salisbury's largest parking lot, in the center of town. In the same all-purpose dining room, you can order from two different menus, one with affordable bistro-style platters, including beefsteak casserole with "herbey dumplings." A longer menu, listing items that take a bit more time to prepare, includes all-vegetarian pasta diavolo, or spareribs with french fries and rice.

6–7 Ox Row, Market Sq. ℂ **01722/333118.** Reservations recommended. Main courses £6.20–£13 ($11–$24); 2-course fixed-price meal £7.50–£8.50 ($14–$16) at lunch and dinner. AE, DC, MC, V. Mon–Sat noon–2pm; daily 6–9:30pm (until 10pm on Sat). Closed Sun Oct–May.

Howard's House Hotel Restaurant 𝕮 INTERNATIONAL   If you'd like to dine in one of the loveliest places in the area, and enjoy a refined cuisine at the same time, leave Salisbury and head for this hotel restaurant. It's a 14km (9-mile) drive to Teffort Evias but well worth the trip. The village itself is one of the most beautiful in Wiltshire. The elegantly appointed restaurant, with flower arrangements, showcases a finely honed cuisine prepared with first-class ingredients such as mallard duck or local pheasant. The menu changes daily but is likely to feature such delights as home-smoked filet of salmon in a saffron sauce with a side dish of steamed leeks. Desserts include white peach ice cream with an orange coulis, or chilled mango mousse with marinated strawberries.

Teffont Evias, near Salisbury. ℂ **01722/716392.** www.howardshousehotel.co.uk. Reservations required. Main courses £18–£23 ($33–$43); fixed-price menu £24 ($44). AE, DC, MC, V. Mon–Sat 12:30–2pm and 7:30–9pm; Sun noon–2pm. Leave Salisbury on the A36 until you reach a roundabout. Take the 1st left leading to the A30. On the A30, continue for 5km (3 miles) coming to the turnoff (B3089) for Barford Saint-Martin. Continue for 6.5km (4 miles) on this secondary road to the town of Teffont Evias, where the hotel is signposted.

Salisbury Haunch of Venison ENGLISH   Right in the heart of Salisbury, this creaky-timbered 1320 restaurant serves excellent dishes, especially English roasts and grills. Stick to what it's known for, and you'll rarely go wrong. Begin perhaps with tasty grilled venison sausages in a Dijon mustard sauce, then follow with the time-honored house specialty: roast haunch of venison with gin and juniper berries. Many other classic English dishes are served, such as a medley of fish and shellfish or else grilled Barnsley lamb chops with "bubble and squeak" (cabbage and potatoes).

1 Minster St. ⓒ **01722/322024.** Main courses £8.25–£16 ($15–$30); bar platters for lunches, light suppers, and snacks £4–£8 ($7.40–$15). MC, V. Daily noon–2pm; Mon–Sat 6–9pm. Pub Mon–Sat 11am–11pm; Sun noon–3pm and 7–10:30pm. Closed Christmas and Easter.

ATTRACTIONS IN & AROUND SALISBURY

Salisbury Cathedral 𝆑𝆑𝆑 You can search all of England, but you'll find no better example of early English or pointed style than Salisbury Cathedral. Construction began as early as 1220 and took 38 years to complete; this was rather fast since it was customary in those days for a cathedral building to require at least 3 centuries. The soaring spire was completed at the end of the 13th century. Despite an ill-conceived attempt at renovation in the 18th century, the architectural integrity of the cathedral has been retained.

The 13th-century octagonal chapter house (note the fine sculpture), which is especially attractive, possesses one of the four surviving original texts of the Magna Carta, along with treasures from the diocese of Salisbury and manuscripts and artifacts belonging to the cathedral. The cloisters enhance the beauty of the cathedral, and the exceptionally large close, with at least 75 buildings in its compound (some from the early 18th c., others earlier), sets off the cathedral most effectively.

The Close, Salisbury. ⓒ **01722/555120.** www.salisburycathedral.org.uk. Suggested donation £3.80 ($7.05) adults, £3.30 ($6.10) students and seniors, £2 ($3.70) children, £8.50 ($16) family. Jan–May and Sept–Dec Mon–Sat 7:15am–6:15pm; June–Aug Mon–Sat 7:15am–7:15pm. Year-round Sun 7:15am–6:15pm.

Old Sarum 𝆑 This relic from antiquity is believed to have been an Iron Age fortification. The earthworks were known to the Romans as *Sorbiodunum.* Much later, Saxons also used the fortification. The Normans built a cathedral and a castle here in what was then a Middle Ages walled town. Parts of the old cathedral were taken down to build the city of New Sarum (Salisbury).

3km (2 miles) north of Salisbury off A345 on Castle Rd. ⓒ **01722/335398.** Admission £2.50 ($4.65) adults, £1.90 ($3.50) seniors, £1.30 ($2.40) children. Apr–Sept daily 10am–5pm; Oct daily 10am–5pm; Nov–Mar daily 11am–3pm. Bus nos. 3, 5, 6, 7, 8, and 9 run every 30 min. during the day from the Salisbury bus station.

Wilton House 𝆑𝆑 This home of the earls of Pembroke is in the town of Wilton. It dates from the 16th century but has undergone numerous alterations, most recently in Victoria's day, and is noted for its 17th-century staterooms, designed by celebrated architect Inigo Jones. Shakespeare's troupe is said to have entertained here, and Eisenhower and his advisers prepared here for the D-Day landings at Normandy, with only the Van Dyck paintings as silent witnesses.

The house is filled with beautifully maintained furnishings and world-class art, including paintings by Rubens, Brueghel, and Reynolds. You can visit a reconstructed Tudor kitchen and Victorian laundry plus "The Wareham Bears," a unique collection of some 200 miniature dressed teddy bears.

On the 8.4-hectare (21-acre) estate are giant cedars of Lebanon trees, the oldest of which were planted in 1630, as well as rose and water gardens, riverside and woodland walks, and a huge adventure playground for children.

5km (3 miles) west of Salisbury on A36. ⓒ **01722/746720.** www.wiltonhouse.com. Admission £9.75 ($18) adults, £8 ($15) seniors, £5 ($9.25) children 5–15, £24 ($44) family, free for children under 5. Price inclusive of grounds. Easter–Oct Tues–Sun 10:30am–5:30pm (last entrance at 4:30pm). Grounds only open Mon.

BATH ✦✦✦

The city of Bath has had two lives. Originally, it was a Roman spa known as Aquae Sulis. The foreign legions founded their baths here (which may be visited today) to ease their rheumatism in the curative mineral springs. In 1702, Queen Anne made the trek from London, 185km (115 miles) west to the mineral springs of Bath, thereby launching a fad that was to make the city England's most celebrated spa.

The most famous personage connected with Bath's growing popularity was the 18th-century dandy Beau Nash. The master of ceremonies of Bath, Nash cut a striking figure. In all the plumage of a bird of paradise, he was carted around in a sedan chair, dispensing (at a price) trinkets to courtiers and aspirant gentlemen. This polished arbiter of taste and manners succeeded in making dueling déclassé.

The 18th-century architects John Wood the Elder and his son envisioned a proper backdrop for Nash's activities. They designed a city of honey-colored stone from the nearby hills, a feat so substantial and lasting that Bath today is the most harmoniously laid-out city in England. The city attracted leading political and literary figures, such as Dickens, Thackeray, Nelson, Pitt, and, most important, of course, Jane Austen. Canadians may already know that General Wolfe lived on Trim Street, and Australians may want to visit the house at 19 Bennett St. where their founding father, Admiral Phillip, lived.

Remarkable restoration and careful planning have ensured that Bath retains its handsome look today. It has somewhat of a museum appearance, with the attendant gift shops. Prices, stimulated by massive tourist invasion, tend to be high. But Bath remains one of the high points of the West Country.

ESSENTIALS

GETTING THERE   By Train   Trains leave London's Paddington Station bound for Bath once every half-hour during the day. The trip takes about 1½ hours. For rail information, call ℭ **0845/748-4950.**

By Bus   A **National Express** coach leaves London's Victoria Coach Station every 1½ hours during the day. The trip takes 3½ hours. Coaches also leave Bristol bound for Bath and make the trip in 40 minutes. For schedules and information, call ℭ **0870/580-8080.**

By Car   Drive west on the M4 to the junction with the A4, on which you continue west to Bath.

VISITOR INFORMATION   The **Bath Tourist Information Centre,** at Abbey Chambers, Abbey Church Yard (ℭ **01225/477101;** www.visitbath.co.uk), next to Bath Abbey, is open June through September, Monday through Saturday from 9:30am to 6pm, Sunday from 10am to 4pm; off season, Monday through Saturday from 9:30am to 5pm, Sunday from 10am to 4pm.

SPECIAL EVENTS   For 17 days in late May and early June, the city is filled with more than 1,000 performers—orchestras, soloists, and artists from all over the world. The **Bath International Music Festival** focuses on classical music, jazz, new music, and opening-night celebrations with fireworks. There's also all the best in walks, tours, and talks, plus free street entertainment. For more information, contact the **Bath Festivals Box Office,** 2 Church St., Abbey Green, Bath BA1 1NL (ℭ **01225/463362;** www.bathmusicfest.org.uk).

GETTING AROUND   One of the best ways to explore Bath is by bike. Rentals are available at **The Bath & Dundas Canal Company,** Brass Knocker Basin at Monkton Combe (ℭ **01225/722292;** www.bathcanal.com). Daily rentals go for £14 ($26).

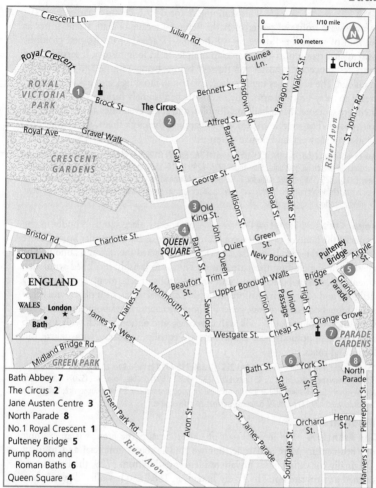

Map Legend:
- Bath Abbey **7**
- The Circus **2**
- Jane Austen Centre **3**
- North Parade **8**
- No.1 Royal Crescent **1**
- Pulteney Bridge **5**
- Pump Room and Roman Baths **6**
- Queen Square **4**

WHERE TO STAY
Expensive

Bath Priory ★★★   Converted from one of Bath's Georgian houses in 1969, the Priory is situated on .8 hectares (2 acres) of formal and award-winning gardens with manicured lawns and flower beds. The hotel reopened in the spring of 1997, vastly refurbished and more inviting than ever. The rooms are furnished with antiques; our personal favorite is Clivia (all rooms are named after flowers or shrubs), a nicely appointed duplex in a circular turret. Rooms range from medium in size to spacious deluxe units, the latter with views, large sitting areas, and generous dressing areas. Each has a lovely old English bed, often a half-tester; bathrooms are beautifully kept and come with a set of deluxe toiletries.

Weston Rd., Bath, Somerset BA1 2XT. ℂ **01225/331922.** Fax 01225/448276. www.thebathpriory.co.uk. 28 units. £245 ($453) standard double; £360 ($666) deluxe room. Rates include English breakfast. AE, DC, MC, V. **Amenities:** Restaurant; bar; 2 pools; croquet lawn; health club; Jacuzzi; sauna; concierge; limited room service; babysitting; laundry/dry cleaning; nonsmoking rooms. *In room:* A/C, TV, hair dryer.

Bath Spa Hotel ★★★   This stunning restored 19th-century mansion is a 10-minute walk from the center of Bath. Behind a facade of Bath stone, it lies at the end of a tree-lined drive on 2.8 hectares (7 acres) of landscaped grounds, with a Victorian grotto and a Grecian temple. In its long history, it served many purposes (once as a hostel for nurses) before being returned to its original grandeur. The hotel uses log fireplaces, elaborate moldings, and oak paneling to create country-house charm. The rooms are handsomely furnished, and most of them are spacious. Most beds are doubles, and some even offer an old-fashioned four-poster. The marble bathrooms are among the city's finest, with long tubs, hand-held showers, and deluxe toiletries.

Sydney Rd. (east of the city, off A36), Bath, Somerset BA2 6JF. © **01225/444424.** Fax 01225/444006. www. macdonaldhotels.co.uk. 102 units. Sun–Thurs £225–£290 ($416–$537) double; Fri–Sat £300 ($555) double. Daily £315–£425 ($583–$786) suite for 2. AE, DC, MC, V. **Amenities:** 2 restaurants; bar; pool; tennis court; health spa; children's nursery; 24-hr. room service; salon; laundry service; valet; nonsmoking rooms. *In room:* TV, minibar, coffeemaker, hair dryer, safe, trouser press.

Royal Crescent Hotel ★★★ *Finds*   This special place stands proudly in the center of the famed Royal Crescent. Long regarded as Bath's premier hotel (before the arrival of the even better Bath Spa), it has attracted the rich and famous. The guest rooms, including the Jane Austen Suite, are lavishly furnished with such amenities as four-poster beds and marble tubs. Each room is individually designed and offers such comforts as bottled mineral water, fruit plates, and other special touches. Guest rooms, generally quite spacious, are elaborately decked out with thick wool carpeting, silk wall coverings, and antiques, each with a superb and rather sumptuous bed. Bathrooms are equally luxurious, with deluxe toiletries and robes.

15–16 Royal Crescent, Bath, Somerset BA1 2LS. © **888/295-4710** in the U.S., or 01225/823333. Fax 01225/339401. www.royalcrescent.co.uk. 45 units. £207–£377 ($383–$697) double; from £382 ($707) suite. AE, DC, MC, V. **Amenities:** Restaurant; bar; health club; indoor pool; steam room; 24-hr. room service; babysitting; laundry/dry cleaning. *In room:* TV, dataport, minibar, hair dryer, safe.

Moderate

The Francis ★   An integral part of Queen Square, the Francis is an example of 18th-century taste and style, but we find it too commercial and touristy. Originally consisting of six private residences dating from 1729, the Francis was opened as a private hotel by Emily Francis in 1884 and has offered guests first-class service for more than 100 years. Many of the well-furnished and traditionally styled guest rooms overlook Queen Square, named in honor of George II's consort, Caroline. Rooms range in size from rather small to medium, with either twin or double beds. Accommodations in the older building have more charm, especially the upper floor. Bathrooms are small but equipped with heated towel racks, plus a combination tub and shower.

Queen Sq., Bath, Somerset BA1 2HH. © **888/892-0038** in the U.S. and Canada, or 0870/400-8223. Fax 01225/319715. www.macdonaldhotels.co.uk. 95 units. £150 ($278) double; £210 ($389) suite. AE, DC, MC, V. **Amenities:** Restaurant; bar; 24-hr. room service; laundry/dry cleaning; nonsmoking rooms. *In room:* TV, dataport, hair dryer, iron.

Pratt's Hotel ★   Once the home of Sir Walter Scott, Pratt's dates from the heady days of Beau Nash. Functioning as a hotel since 1791, it has become part of the legend and lore of Bath. Several elegant terraced Georgian town houses were joined together to form this complex with a very traditional British atmosphere. Rooms are individually designed, and as is typical of a converted private home, they range from small to spacious (the larger ones are on the lower floors).

Regardless of their dimensions, the rooms are furnished in a comfortable though utilitarian style, with small but efficiently organized shower-only bathrooms.

S. Parade, Bath, Somerset BA2 4AB. © **01225/460441**. Fax 01225/448807. www.prattshotel.com. 46 units. £130–£160 ($241–$296) double. Children under 14 sharing a room with 2 adults stay free. Rates include English breakfast. AE, DC, MC, V. Parking £10 ($19). **Amenities:** Restaurant; bar; 24-hr. room service; laundry/dry cleaning. *In room:* TV, coffeemaker, hair dryer, iron, trouser press.

The Queensberry Hotel 🌶 A gem of a hotel, this early Georgian-era town house has been beautifully restored by Stephen and Penny Ross. In our view, it is now among the finest places to stay in a city where the competition for restored town-house hotels is fierce. The marquis of Queensberry commissioned John Wood the Younger to build this house in 1772. Rooms—often spacious but usually medium in size—are delightful, each tastefully decorated with antique furniture and such thoughtful extras as fresh flowers. Bathrooms are well kept and equipped with good showers.

Russel St., Bath, Somerset BA1 2QF. © **01225/447928**. Fax 01225/446065. www.thequeensberry.co.uk. 29 units. £100–£195 ($185–$359) double. Rates include continental breakfast. AE, MC, V. Free parking. **Amenities:** Restaurant; bar; 24-hr. room service; babysitting; laundry/dry cleaning. *In room:* TV, hair dryer, iron.

Inexpensive

Apsley House Hotel 🌶🌶 *(Finds)* This charming and stately building, just 1.5km (1 mile) west of the center of Bath, dates from 1830, during the reign of William IV. In 1994, new owners refurbished the hotel, filling it with country-house chintzes and a collection of antiques borrowed from the showrooms of an antiques store they own. (Some furniture in the hotel is for sale; inquire further about details.) Style and comfort are the keynote here, and all the relatively spacious guest rooms are inviting, appointed with plush beds.

141 Newbridge Hill, Bath, Somerset BA1 3PT. © **01225/336966**. Fax 01225/425462. www.apsley-house. co.uk. 9 units. £70–£140 ($130–$259) double; £100–£160 ($185–$296) suite. Rates include English breakfast. AE, MC, V. Take A4 to Upper Bristol Rd., fork right at the traffic signals into Newbridge Hill, and turn left at Apsley Rd. **Amenities:** Bar; limited room service; babysitting; laundry/dry cleaning service; nonsmoking rooms. *In room:* TV, dataport, coffeemaker, hair dryer, iron.

Duke's Hotel A short walk from the heart of Bath, this 1780 building is fresher than ever following a complete restoration in 2001. Many of the original Georgian features, including cornices and moldings, have been retained. Rooms, ranging from small to medium, are exceedingly comfortable. All of the bathrooms are small but efficiently arranged and sport shower-tub combinations and bathrobes. Guests can relax in a refined drawing room or patronize the cozy bar overlooking a garden. The entire setting has been called a "perfect *Masterpiece Theatre* take on Britain," with a fire burning in the grate. A traditional English menu is also offered.

53–54 Great Pulteney St., Bath, Somerset BA2 4DN. © **01225/787960**. Fax 01225/787961. www.dukesbath. co.uk. 18 units. £85–£155 ($157–$287) double; £115 ($213) family unit. Rates include English breakfast. MC, V. **Amenities:** Restaurant; bar; limited room service; babysitting; laundry; dry cleaning. *In room:* TV, hair dryer.

In Nearby Ston Easton

Ston-Easton Park 🌶🌶🌶 *(Finds)* This is one of the great country hotels of England. From the moment you pass a group of stone outbuildings and century-old beeches set on a 12-hectare (30-acre) park—up the road from Farrington Gurney—you know you've come to a very special place. The mansion was created in the mid-1700s from the shell of an Elizabethan house; in 1793, Sir Humphry Repton designed the landscape. In 1977, after many years of neglect, Peter and Christine Smedley acquired the property and poured money, love, and labor into its restoration. The tasteful rooms are filled with flowers and antiques, and feature spacious, sumptuous beds. A gardener's cottage was artfully upgraded from a utilitarian building to contain a pair of intensely decorated and very glamorous suites. In addition to the cottage suite, plus the "standard and deluxe" rooms of the main house, you'll find half a dozen "state rooms," four of which have four-poster beds, and all of which contain lavish but genteel decor. Bathrooms are equally luxurious, with deluxe toiletries and shower-tub combinations.

Ston Easton, Somerset BA3 4DF. © **01761/241631.** Fax 01761/241377. www.stoneaston.co.uk. 24 units, 1 cottage suite, 7 state rooms. £150–£335 ($278–$620) double; from £605 ($1,119) 3-room cottage suite; £335 ($620) state room. AE, DC, MC, V. Lies 19km (12 miles) south of Bath; follow A39 south to the signposted turnoff to the hamlet of Ston Easton. **Amenities:** Restaurant; tennis court; croquet; billiard room; limited room service; babysitting; laundry/dry cleaning. *In room:* TV, dataport, hair dryer, safe, iron.

WHERE TO DINE
Expensive

The Moody Goose ★★★ ENGLISH   In a highly competitive city, this "bird" serves the finest and most refined cuisine. In an elegant and landmarked Georgian terrace in the center of the city, the restaurant has two cozy dining rooms and a little bar. The kitchen has an absolute passion for fresh ingredients and food cooked to order, and the chefs believe in using produce grown as near home as possible, though the Angus beef comes in from Scotland, fresh fish from the coasts of Cornwall and Devon. Natural flavors are appreciated here and not smothered in sauces. Even the breads, ice creams, and petits fours are homemade.

Launch your repast with such temptations as pan-fried veal sweetbreads with a salad of pink grapefruit and walnuts, or a brown trout confit in puff pastry. For a main dish, be dazzled with whole roasted quail with braised chicory and roasted apple, roasted rump of lamb, or poached filet of halibut with fresh clams. We're especially fond of the desserts, particularly a fresh rhubarb cheesecake.

7A Kingsmead Sq. © **01225/466688.** Reservations required. Main courses £18–£20 ($33–$37); fixed-price lunch £18 ($33), dinner £25 ($46). AE, DC, MC, V. Mon–Sat noon–1:30pm and 6–9:30pm.

Popjoy's Restaurant MODERN BRITISH/CONTINENTAL   Two sprawling dining rooms on separate floors are in this Georgian home (ca. 1720) where Beau Nash and his mistress, Julianna Popjoy, once entertained friends and set the fashions of the day. Inventiveness and solid technique go into many of the dishes. The food is unpretentious and generally quite satisfying. The starters are always imaginative and good tasting, as exemplified by the guinea fowl and wood-pigeon terrine with cranberry jam and brandy-soaked prunes. Equally excellent is the smoked-fish plate with oak-smoked salmon, tuna, trout, and egg with fresh horseradish served with a glass of iced Smirnoff Black Label. A certain exoticism appears in the oven-roasted Barbary duck breast with a wild bramble and cherry marmalade, or the stir-fried shiitake mushrooms, bok choy, zucchini, and roasted almonds on sun-dried tomato blinis with spicy sour cream and chickpeas.

Sawclose. © **01225/460494.** www.popjoys.co.uk. Reservations recommended. Main courses £18–£22 ($33–$41); 3-course fixed-price lunch £16 ($30). AE, DC, MC, V. Mon–Sat noon–2pm and 6–11pm.

Moderate

Beaujolais *Kids* FRENCH   This is the best-known bistro in Bath, maintaining its regulars while attracting new admirers every year. Diners are drawn to the honest fare and good value. The house wines are modestly priced. Begin with grilled monkfish served with a creamy white sauce, and follow it with roast partridge or duck confit. Also served is a wide variety of vegetarian dishes, one of them a mushroom-and-spinach combination. One area of the restaurant is reserved for nonsmokers. Persons with disabilities will appreciate the wheelchair access, and parents can order special helpings for children.

5 Chapel Row, Queen Sq. (℃) **01225/423417.** Reservations recommended. Main courses £12–£18 ($22–$33); 2- and 3-course lunches £13–£17 ($24–$31). AE, MC, V. Mon–Sat noon–2:30pm; daily 6–10pm.

The Olive Tree MODERN ENGLISH/MEDITERRANEAN Stephen and Penny Ross operate one of the most sophisticated little restaurants in Bath. Stephen uses the best local produce, with an emphasis on freshness. The menu is changed to reflect the season, with game and fish being the specialties. You may begin with grilled scallops with noodles and pine nuts, or Provençal fish soup with rouille and croutons. Proceed with roast squab pigeon, salsify purée, and crispy parsnip; or grilled Aberdeen Angus rump filet, creamed onions, and rosemary in a red-wine-and-peppercorn jus. Stephen is also known for his desserts, which are likely to include such treats as a hot chocolate soufflé or an apricot and almond tart.

In the Queensberry Hotel, Russel St. (℃) **01225/447928.** Reservations highly recommended. Main courses £17–£18 ($31–$33). 3-course fixed-price lunch £16 ($30), dinner £26 ($48). MC, V. Tues–Sat noon–2pm and 7–10pm; Sun 7–9:30pm.

Inexpensive

The Moon and Sixpence INTERNATIONAL One of the leading restaurants and wine bars of Bath, The Moon and Sixpence occupies a stone structure east of Queen Square. The food may not be as good as that served at more acclaimed choices, including The Hole in the Wall, but the value is unbeatable. At lunch, a large cold buffet with a selection of hot dishes is featured in the wine bar section. In the upstairs restaurant overlooking the bar, full service is offered. Main courses may include filet of lamb with caramelized garlic or roast breast of duck with Chinese vegetables. Look for the daily specials on the Continental menu.

6A Broad St. (℃) **01225/460962.** Reservations recommended. Main courses £13–£15 ($24–$28); fixed-price lunch £7.95 ($15). AE, MC, V. Daily noon–2:30pm; Mon–Thurs 5:30–10:30pm; Fri–Sat 5:30–11pm; Sun 6–10:30pm.

Woods *Value* MODERN ENGLISH/FRENCH/ASIAN Named after John Wood the Younger, architect of Bath's famous Assembly Room across the street, this restaurant is run by horse-racing enthusiast David Price and his French-born wife, Claude. A fixed-price menu is printed on paper, whereas the seasonal array of a la carte items is chalked onto a frequently changing blackboard. Good bets include the pear and parsnip soup or chicken cooked with mushrooms, red wine, and tarragon.

9–13 Alfred St. (℃) **01225/314812.** Reservations recommended. Main courses £9.50–£18 ($18–$33). Fixed-price lunch £9.50 ($18), dinner £13–£25 ($24–$46). MC, V. Mon–Sat noon–2:30pm and 6–10:30pm; Sun noon–2pm.

EXPLORING BATH

Stroll around to see some of the buildings, crescents, and squares in town. The **North Parade** (where Goldsmith lived) and the **South Parade** (where English novelist and diarist Frances Burney once resided) represent harmony, as well as the work of John Wood the Elder, who also designed beautiful **Queen Square,** where both Jane Austen and Wordsworth once lived. Also of interest is **The Circus** 🌟🌟🌟, built in 1754, as well as the shop-lined **Pulteney Bridge,** designed by Robert Adam and often compared to the Ponte Vecchio of Florence.

The younger John Wood designed the **Royal Crescent** 🌟🌟🌟, an elegant half-moon row of town houses (copied by Astor architects for their colonnade in New

York City in the 1830s). At **No. 1 Royal Crescent** (© **01225/428126**), the interior has been redecorated and furnished by the Bath Preservation Trust to look as it might have toward the end of the 18th century. The house is located at one end of Bath's most magnificent crescents, west of the Circus. Admission is £4 ($7.40) for adults and £3.50 ($6.50) for children, seniors, and students; a family ticket is £12 ($22). The house is open from mid-February to October, Tuesday through Sunday from 10:30am to 5pm, and in November, Tuesday through Sunday from 10:30am to 4pm (last admission 30 min. before closing); closed Good Friday.

The **Jane Austen Centre,** 40 Gay St. (© **01225/443000**), is located in a Georgian town house on an elegant street where Miss Austen once lived. Exhibits and a video convey a sense of life in Bath during the Regency period. The center is open Monday through Saturday from 10am to 5:30pm and Sunday from 10:30am to 5:30pm. Admission is £4.65 ($8.60) for adults, £3.95 ($7.30) students, and £2.50 ($4.65) children; a family ticket is £12.50 ($23).

American Museum   Some 4km (2½ miles) from Bath is the first American museum established outside the United States. In a Greek Revival house

Two More Magnificent Houses: Longleat House & Stourhead

Between Bath and Salisbury, 6.5km (4 miles) southwest of Warminster and 7km (4¼ miles) southeast of Frome on A-362, is **Longleat House** ★★★, Warminster, Wiltshire (© **01985/844400**; www.longleat. co.uk), owned by the seventh marquess of Bath. The first view of this Elizabethan house, built in the early Renaissance style, is romantic enough, but the wealth of paintings and furnishings in its lofty rooms is dazzling. From the Elizabethan Great Hall to the library, state rooms, and grand staircase, the house is filled with fine tapestries and paintings. The library contains the finest private collection in the country. The Victorian kitchens are open, and various exhibitions are mounted in the stable yard.

Admission to Longleat House is £9 ($17) adults, £7 ($13) children. The house is open daily from 10am to 5:30pm. A separate safari park is open April through November 2, daily from 10am to 6pm (last cars admitted at 5pm or sunset).

After a visit to Longleat, you can drive 10km (6¼ miles) down B-3092 to Stourton, a village just off the highway 5km (3 miles) northwest of Mere (A-303). A Palladian house, **Stourhead** ★★★ (© **01747/ 841152**) was built in the 18th century by the banking family of Hoare. The fabulous gardens, blending art and nature, became known as *le jardin anglais*. Set around an artificial lake, the grounds are decorated with temples, bridges, islands, and grottoes, as well as statuary. From March to October, admission to the gardens and house is £9.40 ($17) adults, £4.50 ($8.35) children; admission to the gardens or house alone is £5.40 ($10) adults, £3 ($5.55) children. Off season, the admission is to the gardens only: £4.10 ($7.60) adults, £2 ($3.70) children. The Stourhead house and gardens are open Friday through Tuesday from 9am to 7pm (or until dusk). Last admission is at 4:30pm.

(Claverton Manor), the museum sits on extensive grounds high above the Avon valley. Authentic exhibits of pioneer days have been shipped over from the States. On the grounds are a copy of Washington's flower garden at Mount Vernon and an American arboretum. A permanent exhibition in the New Gallery displays the Dallas Pratt Collection of Historical Maps.

Claverton Manor, Bathwick Hill. (C) **01225/460503.** www.americanmuseum.org. Admission £6.50 ($12) adults, £5.50 ($10) students and seniors, £3.50 ($6.50) children 5–16, free for ages 4 and under; £18 ($32) family. Late Mar to Nov Tues–Sun 2–5pm for the museum; Tues–Fri 1–6pm and Sat–Sun noon–6pm for the garden.

Bath Abbey 🔎 Built on the site of a much larger Norman cathedral, the present-day abbey is a fine example of the late Perpendicular style. When Queen Elizabeth I came to Bath in 1574, she ordered a national fund set up to restore the abbey. The interior and its many windows plainly illustrate why the abbey is called the "Lantern of the West." Note the superb fan vaulting, with its scalloped effect. Beau Nash was buried in the nave and is honored by a simple monument totally out of keeping with his flamboyant character. In 1994, the Bath Abbey Heritage Vaults opened on the south side of the abbey. This subterranean exhibition traces the history of Christianity at the abbey site since Saxon times.

Orange Grove. (C) **01225/422462.** www.bathabbey.org. £2.50 ($4.65) donation requested. Admission to the Heritage Vaults £2.50 ($4.65) adults; £1.50 ($2.80) students, children, and seniors. Abbey Apr–Oct Mon–Sat 9am–6pm; Nov–Mar Mon–Sat 9am–4:30pm; year-round Sun 1–2:30pm and 4:30–5:30pm. The Heritage Vaults year-round Mon–Sat 10am–3:30pm (last entrance).

Pump Room 🔎 **and Roman Baths** 🔎🔎 Founded in A.D. 75 by the Romans, the baths were dedicated to the goddess Sulis Minerva; in their day they were an engineering feat. Today, still fed by Britain's most famous hot-spring water, they're among the finest Roman remains in the country. After centuries of decay, the original baths were rediscovered during Queen Victoria's reign. The site of the Temple of Sulis Minerva has been excavated and is now open to view. The museum displays many interesting objects from Victorian and recent digs (look for the head of Minerva). Coffee, lunch, and tea, usually with music from the Pump Room Trio, can be enjoyed in the 18th-century pump room, overlooking the hot springs. There's also a drinking fountain with hot mineral water that tastes horrible but is supposedly beneficial.

In the Bath Abbey churchyard. (C) **01225/477785.** www.romanbaths.co.uk. Admission £9 ($17) adults, £5 ($9.25) children, £24 ($44) family. Apr–Sept daily 9am–6pm; Oct–Mar Mon–Sat 9am–5pm.

ORGANIZED TOURS

Free 1¾-hour walking tours are conducted throughout the year by the **Mayor's Honorary Society** ((C) **01225/477786**). Tours depart from outside the Roman Baths Sunday through Friday at 10:30am and 2pm, Saturday at 10:30am; May through September, another tour is added on Tuesday, Friday, and Saturday at 7pm. To tour Bath by bus, you can choose among several tour companies. One of the best is **Patrick Driscoll,** Elmsleigh, Bathampton ((C) **01225/462010**), with tours that are more personalized than most.

   River Avon boat cruises depart from a pier adjacent to the Pulteney Bridge (directly across the water from the Parade Gardens). Cruises last 50 minutes and are £5 ($9.25) for adults, £2.50 ($4.65) for children. They run from Easter to October via two boats maintained by **The Boating Station** ((C) **01225/466407**).

THE SHOPPING SCENE

Bath has the finest shopping possibilities outside of London. Here is a sampling to get you started. The four floors of merchandise at **Rossiter's,** 38–41 Broad St.

(✆ **01225/462227**), may remind you of a very English version of a department store. They'll ship any of the Royal Doulton, Wedgwood, or Spode to anywhere in the world. Look especially for the displays of ginger jars, vases, and clocks manufactured by Moorcroft, and perfumes by London-based Floris.

The most charming and unusual emporium in Bath, **Whittard of Chelsea,** 14 Union Passage (✆ **01225/483529**), supplies everything you'll need to duplicate the dearly held tea-drinking ritual. Ask for Monkey-Picked Oolong, a Chinese tea from plants so difficult to reach that leaves can be gathered only by trained monkeys.

The most important gallery of contemporary art in Bath, **Beaux Arts Gallery,** 13 York St. (✆ **01225/464850**), specializes in well-known British artists. The gallery occupies a pair of interconnected, stone-fronted Georgian houses, set close to Bath Abbey.

BATH AFTER DARK

To gain a very different perspective of Bath, you may want to take the **Bizarre Bath Walking Tour** (✆ **01225/335124**), a 1½-hour improvisational tour of the streets during which the tour guides pull pranks, tell jokes, and behave in a humorously annoying manner toward tour-goers and unsuspecting residents. Running nightly at 8pm from Easter to October, it requires no reservations; just show up, ready for anything, at the Huntsman Inn at North Parade Passage. The tour costs £5 ($9.25) for adults, £4.50 ($8.35) for students and children.

After your walk, you may want to check out the local club scene. At **The Bell,** 103 Walcot St. (✆ **01225/460426**), music ranges from jazz and country to reggae and blues on Monday and Wednesday nights and Sunday at lunch. On music nights, the band performs in the center of the long, narrow, 400-year-old room. The two-story **Hat and Feather,** 14 London St. (✆ **01225/425672**), has live musicians or DJs playing funk, reggae, or dance music nightly.

France

by Darwin Porter & Danforth Prince

Though France covers only 342,513 sq. km (212,741 sq. miles), making it slightly smaller than Texas, no other country has such a diversity of sights and scenery in such a compact area. A visitor can travel to Paris, one of the world's great cities; drive among the Loire Valley's green hills; or head south to sunny Provence and the French Riviera. Discover the attractions (and transport, lodging, and dining offerings) in each of these regions in this chapter.

1 Paris ★★★

Discovering the City of Light and making it your own has always been the most compelling reason to visit Paris. If you've been away for a while, expect changes: Taxi drivers may no longer correct your fractured French but address you in English—tantamount to a revolution. Paris, aware of its role in a united Europe, is an international city. Parisians are attracted to foreign music, videos, and films, especially from America. Security is tighter than ever. Expect to see police in bulletproof vests at all transport hubs and government buildings, as well as at high-profile sites such as the Eiffel Tower.

As Paris and the country itself move deeper into the new millennium, the French fear a loss of identity. France continues to attract record numbers of immigrants from its former colonies. Though Paris is in flux culturally and socially, it lures travelers for the same reasons it always has. You'll still find classic sights like the Eiffel Tower, Notre-Dame, the Arc de Triomphe, Sacré-Coeur, and all those atmospheric cafes, as well as trendy new projects like the Grand Arche de La Défense, the Cité des Sciences et de l'Industrie, and the Cité de la Musique. And don't forget the parks, gardens, and squares; the Champs-Elysées and other grand boulevards; the River Seine and its quays. Paris's beauty is still overwhelming, especially at night, when it truly is the City of Light.

ESSENTIALS

GETTING THERE   By Plane   Paris has two international airports: Aéroport Roissy-Charles de Gaulle, 23km (14 miles) northeast of the city; and Aéroport d'Orly, 14km (8½ miles) south. A shuttle (16€/$18) makes the 50- to 75-minute journey between the two airports about every half-hour.

At **Charles de Gaulle Airport** (© 01-48-62-22-80), foreign carriers use Aérogare 1, Air France Aérogare 2. From Aérogare 1, you take a moving walkway to the passport checkpoint and the Customs area. A *navette* (shuttle bus) links the two terminals.

The shuttle also transports you to the **Roissy rail station,** from which fast RER (Réseau Express Régional) trains leave every 15 minutes for Métro stations including Gare du Nord, Châtelet, Luxembourg, Port-Royal, and Denfert-Rochereau. A typical fare from Roissy to any point in central Paris is 12€ ($14) in first class, 7.75€ ($8.90) in second class.

You can also take an **Air France shuttle bus** (10€/$12) to central Paris. It stops at the Palais des Congrès (Port Maillot) and continues to place Charles-de-Gaulle-Etoile, where subway lines can carry you to any point in Paris. That ride, depending on traffic, takes 45 to 55 minutes. The shuttle departs about every 12 minutes between 5:40am and 11pm.

Another option is the **Roissybus** (© 01-58-76-10-10), departing the airport daily from 5:45am to 11pm and costing 4.20€ ($4.85) for the 45- to 50-minute ride. Departures are about every 15 minutes, and the bus will leave you near the corner of rue Scribe and place de l'Opéra in the heart of Paris.

A **taxi** from Roissy into the city will cost about 45€ ($52); from 8pm to 7am the fare is 40% higher. Long lines for taxis form outside each of the airport's terminals and are surprisingly orderly.

Orly Airport (© 01-49-75-15-15) has two terminals—Orly *Sud* (south) for international flights and Orly *Ouest* (west) for domestic flights. A free shuttle bus (trip time: 15 min.) connects them.

Air France buses leave from Exit E of Orly Sud and from Exit F of Orly Ouest every 12 minutes between 5:45am and 11pm for Gare des Invalides; the fare is 7.50€ ($8.60). Returning to the airport (about 30 min.), buses leave the Invalides terminal for Orly Sud or Orly Ouest every 15 minutes.

Another way to get to central Paris is on the free **shuttle bus** that leaves both of Orly's terminals about every 15 minutes for the nearby Métro and RER train station (Pont-de-Rungis/Aéroport-d'Orly). RER trains take 35 minutes for rides into the city center. A trip to Les Invalides, for example, is 3.20€ ($3.60).

A **taxi** from Orly to central Paris costs about 30€ ($35), more at night. Don't take a meterless taxi from Orly—it's much safer (and usually cheaper) to hire one of the metered cabs, which are under the scrutiny of a police officer.

By Train Paris has six major stations: **Gare d'Austerlitz,** 55 quai d'Austerlitz, 13e (serving the southwest with trains to and from the Loire Valley, Bordeaux, the Pyrénées, and Spain); **Gare de l'Est,** place du 11-Novembre-1918, 10e (serving the east with trains to and from Strasbourg, Reims, and beyond, to Zurich and Austria); **Gare de Lyon,** 20 bd. Diderot, 12e (serving the southeast, with trains to and from the Côte d'Azur [Nice, Cannes, St-Tropez], Provence, and beyond, to Geneva and Italy); **Gare Montparnasse,** 17 bd. Vaugirard, 15e (serving the west, with trains to and from Brittany); **Gare du Nord,** 18 rue de Dunkerque, 15e (serving the north, with trains to and from London, Holland, Denmark, and northern Germany); and **Gare St-Lazare,** 13 rue d'Amsterdam, 8e (serving the northwest, with trains to and from Normandy). Buses operate

---

⟨Tips⟩ The Paris Airport Shuttle

Cheaper than a taxi for one or two people but more expensive than airport buses and trains, the **Bee Shuttle** (© 01-53-11-01-25; fax 01-43-21-35-68; www.paris-anglo.com/clients/ashuttle.html) will pick you up in a minivan at Charles de Gaulle or Orly and take you to your hotel for 24€ ($28) for one person or 15€ ($17) per person for parties of two or more. It'll take you to the airports from your hotel for the same price. The **Paris Airport Service** (© 01-58-34-01-26; fax 01-58-34-09-88) offers a similar service. It charges 20€ ($23) for one person or 14€ ($16) per person in larger parties going to Charles de Gaulle or Orly. Both companies accept Visa and MasterCard, with 1-day advance reservations required.

between the stations. Each has a Métro stop. For train information and to make reservations, call ℂ **08-92-35-35-35** between 7am and 8pm daily. A one-way ticket to Tours costs 35€ ($40); one-way to Strasbourg, 20€ ($23).

Warning: The stations and surrounding areas are usually seedy and frequented by pickpockets, hustlers, hookers, and addicts. Be alert, especially at night.

By Bus   Most buses arrive at the **Eurolines France** station, 28 av. du Général-de-Gaulle, Bagnolet (no phone; fax 01-49-72-51-61; Métro: Gallieni).

By Car   Driving in Paris is *not* recommended. Parking is difficult and traffic dense. If you drive, remember that Paris is encircled by a ring road, the *périphérique*. Always obtain detailed directions to your destination, including the name of the exit on the *périphérique* (exits aren't numbered). Avoid rush hours.

The major highways into Paris are A1 from the north; A13 from Rouen, Normandy, and other points northwest; A10 from Spain and the southwest; A6 and A7 from the French Alps, the Riviera, and Italy; and A4 from eastern France.

VISITOR INFORMATION   The **Paris Convention and Visitors Bureau** (ℂ **01-92-68-30-00;** .35€/40¢ per minute; www.paris-touristoffice.com) has offices throughout the city, with the main headquarters at 25–27 rue des Pyramides, 1er (Métro: Pyramides). It's open April through October daily from 9am to 8pm, off season daily from 11am to 6pm. Branch offices include **Opéra-Grands Magasins,** 11 rue Scribe, 9e (Métro: Opéra), open Monday through Saturday from 9am to 6:30pm; **Gare de Lyon,** 20 bd. Diderot, 12e (Métro:

Gare de Lyon), open Monday through Saturday from 8am to 6pm; **Gare du Nord**, 18 rue de Dunkerque, 10e (Métro: Gare du Nord), open daily from 12:30 to 8pm; **Montmartre Tourist Office,** 21 place du Tertre, 18e (Métro: Abbesses), daily from 10am to 7pm. The branches will make hotel reservations; the service charge is free for hostels, 2€ ($2.30) for government-rated one-star hotels, 4€ ($4.60) for two-star hotels, and 6€ ($6.90) for three-star hotels. The offices are very busy in summer, so be prepared to wait in line.

Websites Surf these recommended websites for information on the City of Light: Bonjour Paris, **www.bparis.com**, is one of the most comprehensive and fun sites about life in Paris, written from an American expatriate point of view. Paris Digest, **www.parisdigest.com**, is an independent website containing articles that link to restaurants, hotels, museums, monuments, parks, and activities. It includes city history and tips for getting around. Paris France Guide, **www. parisfranceguide.com**, has lots of useful information, such as articles and current listings for nightlife, events, theater, and music. Paris Tourist Office, **www. paris-touristoffice.com**, offers information on city events arranged by week, month, favorites, and year, plus the closest Métro stops for museums, lodgings, restaurants, and nightlife.

CITY LAYOUT Paris is surprisingly compact. Occupying 696 sq. km (432 sq. miles), it's home to more than 10 million people. The River Seine divides Paris into the *Rive Droite* **(Right Bank)** to the north and the *Rive Gauche* **(Left Bank)** to the south. These designations make sense when you stand on a bridge and face downstream (west)—to your right is the north bank, to your left is the south. A total of 32 bridges link the Right Bank and the Left Bank. Some provide access to the two islands at the heart of the city—**Ile de la Cité,** the city's birthplace and site of Notre-Dame; and **Ile St-Louis,** a moat-guarded oasis of 17th-century mansions.

The "main street" on the Right Bank is **avenue des Champs-Elysées,** beginning at the Arc de Triomphe and running to place de la Concorde. Avenue des Champs-Elysées and 11 other avenues radiate like the arms of an asterisk from the Arc de Triomphe, giving it its original name, place de l'Etoile (*étoile* means "star"). It was renamed place Charles-de-Gaulle following the general's death; today, it's often referred to as place Charles-de-Gaulle-Etoile.

Maps If you're staying more than 2 or 3 days, purchase an inexpensive pocketsize book called *Paris par arrondissement* at a newsstand or bookshop; prices start at 6.10€ ($7). This guide provides you with a Métro map, a foldout map of the city, and maps of each arrondissement, with all streets listed and keyed.

Arrondissements in Brief The heart of medieval Paris was the **Ile de la Cité** and the areas immediately surrounding it. As Paris grew, it absorbed many of the once-distant villages, and today each of these *arrondissements* (districts) retains a distinct character. They're numbered 1 to 20 starting at the center and progressing in a clockwise spiral. The key to finding any address in Paris is to look for the arrondissement number, rendered as a number followed by "er" or "e" (1er, 2e, and so on). If the address is written out more formally, you can tell what arrondissement it's in by looking at the postal code. For example, the address may be written with the street name, then "75014 Paris." The last two digits, 14, indicate that the address is in the 14th arrondissement, Montparnasse.

On the Right Bank, the **1er** is home to the Louvre, place Vendôme, rues de Rivoli and St-Honoré, Palais Royal, and Comédie-Française—an area filled with grand institutions and grand stores. At the center of the **2e,** the city's financial center, is the Bourse (Stock Exchange). Most of the **3e** and the **4e** is referred to as the Marais, the old Jewish quarter that in the 17th century was home to the aristocracy. Today it's a trendy area of boutiques and restored mansions as well as the center of Paris's gay and lesbian community. On the Left Bank, the **5e** is known as the Latin Quarter, home to the Sorbonne and associated with the intellectual life that thrived in the 1920s and 1930s. The **6e,** known as St-Germain-des-Prés, stretches from the Seine to boulevard du Montparnasse. It is associated with the 1920s and 1930s and known as a center for art and antiques; it boasts the Palais and Jardin du Luxembourg. The **7e,** containing both the Eiffel Tower and Hôtel des Invalides, is a residential district for the well heeled.

Back on the Right Bank, the **8e** epitomizes monumental Paris, with the triumphal avenue des Champs-Elysées, the Elysées Palace, and the fashion houses along avenue Montaigne and the Faubourg St-Honoré. The **18e** is home to Sacré-Coeur and Montmartre and all that the name conjures of the bohemian life painted most notably by Toulouse-Lautrec. The **14e** incorporates most of Montparnasse, including its cemetery. The **20e** is where the city's famous lie buried in Père-Lachaise and where today recent immigrants from North Africa live. Beyond the arrondissements stretch the vast *banlieue,* or suburbs, of Greater Paris, where the majority of Parisians live.

GETTING AROUND   Paris is a city for strollers, whose greatest joy is rambling through unexpected alleys and squares. Given a choice of conveyance, try to make it on your own two feet whenever possible.

By Metro (Subway)   The **Métro** (© 08-92-68-77-14) is the fastest, most efficient means of transportation in Paris. All lines are numbered, and the final destination of each line is clearly marked on subway maps, in the underground passageways, and on the train cars. The Métro runs daily from 5:30am to 1:15am. It's reasonably safe at any hour, but beware of pickpockets.

To familiarize yourself with Paris's Métro, check out the **color map** on the inside front cover of this book.

To make sure you catch the correct train, find your destination on the map, then follow the rail line it's on to the end of the route and note the name of the final destination—this final stop is the direction. In the station, follow the signs for your direction in the passageways until you see the label on a train.

Transfer stations are *correspondances*—some require long walks; Châtelet is the most difficult—but most trips require only one transfer. When transferring, follow the orange CORRESPONDANCE signs to the proper platform. Don't follow a SORTIE (exit) sign or you'll have to pay again to get back on the train.

Many of the larger stations have maps with push-button indicators that light up your route when you press the button for your destination.

By Bus Buses are much slower than the Métro. Most run from 7am to 8:30pm (a few operate until 12:30am, and 10 operate during early-morning hours). Service is limited on Sunday and holidays. Bus and Métro fares are the same; you can use the same tickets on both. Most bus rides require one ticket, but some destinations require two (never more than two within the city limits).

At certain stops, signs list the destinations and numbers of the buses serving that point. Destinations are usually listed north to south and east to west. Most stops are also posted on the sides of the buses. During rush hours, you may have to take a ticket from a dispensing machine, indicating your position in the line at the stop.

If you intend to use the buses a lot, pick up an RATP bus map at the office on place de la Madeleine, 8e, or at the tourist offices at RATP headquarters, 53 bis quai des Grands-Augustins, 6e. For detailed recorded information (in English) on bus and Métro routes, call © **08-92-68-77-14.**

The same organization that runs the Métro and the buses, **RATP** (© **08-92-68-77-14**), also operates the **Balabus,** big-windowed orange-and-white motor coaches that run during limited hours: Sunday and national holidays from noon to 9pm, from April 15 to the end of September. Itineraries run in both directions between Gare de Lyon and the Grande Arche de La Défense, encompassing some of the city's most beautiful vistas. It's a great deal—three Métro tickets carry you the entire route. You'll recognize the bus and the route it follows by the *Bb* symbol emblazoned on each bus's side and on signs posted beside the route it follows.

By Taxi It's impossible to get one at rush hour, so don't even try. Taxi drivers are organized into a lobby that limits their number to 15,000.

Watch out for common rip-offs. Always check the meter to make sure you're not paying the previous passenger's fare. Beware of cabs without meters, which often wait outside nightclubs for tipsy patrons, or settle the tab in advance. You can hail regular cabs on the street when their signs read LIBRE. Taxis are easier to find at the many stands near Métro stations.

The flag drops at 4.25€ ($4.90), and from 7am to 7pm you pay 1€ ($1.15) per kilometer. From 7pm to 7am, you pay 1.20€ ($1.40) per kilometer. On airport trips, you're not required to pay for the driver's empty return ride.

You're allowed several pieces of luggage free if they're transported inside and are less than 5 kilograms (11 lb.). Heavier suitcases carried in the trunk cost 1.50€ ($1.70) apiece. Tip 12% to 15%—the latter usually elicits a *merci.* For radio cabs, call © **08-25-16-10-10** or 01-47-39-47-39—but note that you'll be charged from the point where the taxi begins the drive to pick you up.

By Car Don't even consider driving in Paris. The streets are narrow and parking is next to impossible.

By Bicycle In recent years, the city has added many miles of right-hand lanes designated for cyclists as well as hundreds of bike racks. Cycling is especially popular in the larger parks and gardens.

Paris-Vélos, 2 rue du Fer-à-Moulin, 5e (℃ **01-43-37-59-22;** Métro: Censier-Daubenton), rents bicycles by the day (15€–26€/$17–$30), weekend (27€–35€/$31–$40), or week (72€–98€/$83–$113). You must leave a 400€ ($460) deposit. It's open Monday through Saturday from 10am to 12:30pm and 2 to 7pm.

By Boat   The **Batobus** (℃ **01-44-11-33-99**) is a 150-passenger ferry with big windows. Every day between April and November, the boats operate along the Seine, stopping at points of interest: the **Eiffel Tower,** the **Musée d'Orsay,** the **Louvre, Notre-Dame,** and the **Hôtel de Ville.** Transit from one stop to another is 2.50€ ($2.90), and departures are every 15 to 25 minutes from 10am to 7pm. The views are panoramic, but the Batobus isn't really a sightseeing tour (there's no recorded commentary); it simply offers a way to move from one attraction to another.

FAST FACTS: Paris

American Express   The busy office is at 11 rue Scribe, 9e (℃ **01-47-14-50-00;** Métro: Opéra, Chaussée-d'Antin, or Havre-Caumartin; RER: Auber). It's open Monday through Friday from 9am to 6pm. On Saturday the bank is open from 8am to 5:30pm, but the mail-pickup window is closed.

Area Code   All French telephone numbers consist of 10 digits, the first two of which are like an area code. If you're calling anywhere in France from within France, just dial all 10 digits—no additional codes are needed. If you're calling from the United States, drop the initial 0 (zero).

Currency   France fell under the euro (€) umbrella in 2002. At press time, 1€ = $1.15, or $1 = .85€.

Currency Exchange   American Express can fill most banking needs. Most banks in Paris are open Monday through Friday from 9am to 4:30pm, and a few are open Saturday; ask at your hotel for the location of the one nearest you. For the best exchange rate, cash your traveler's checks at banks or foreign-exchange offices, not at shops and hotels. Most post offices will change traveler's checks or convert currency. Currency exchanges are also at Paris airports and train stations and along most of the major boulevards. They charge a small commission.

Dentists   For emergency dental service, call **S.O.S. Dentaire,** 87 bd. du Port-Royal, 13e (℃ **01-43-37-51-00;** Métro: Port-Royal), Monday through Friday from 8pm to midnight and Saturday and Sunday from 9:30am to midnight. You can also call or visit the **American Hospital** (see "Doctors," below).

Doctors   Some large hotels have a doctor on staff. You can also try the **American Hospital,** 63 bd. Victor-Hugo, in the suburb of Neuilly-sur-Seine (℃ **01-46-41-25-25;** Métro: Pont-de-Levallois or Pont-de-Neuilly; bus: 82), which operates a 24-hour emergency service. The bilingual staff accepts Blue Cross and other American insurance plans.

Drugstores   After regular hours, have your concierge contact the Commissariat de Police for the nearest 24-hour pharmacy. French law requires one pharmacy in any given neighborhood to stay open 24 hours. You'll find the address posted on the doors or windows of all other drugstores.

Embassies & Consulates Call before you go; offices often keep strange hours and observe both French and home-country holidays. The embassy of the **United States,** 2 av. Gabriel, 8e (℃ **01-43-12-22-22;** Métro: Concorde), is open Monday through Friday from 9am to 6pm. The embassy of **Canada,** 35 av. Montaigne, 8e (℃ **01-44-43-29-00;** Métro: Franklin-D- Roosevelt or Alma-Marceau), is open Monday through Friday from 9am to noon and 2 to 5pm. The embassy and consulate of the **United Kingdom,** 35 rue du Faubourg St-Honoré, 8e (℃ **01-44-51-31-00;** Métro: Concorde or Madeleine), is open Monday through Friday from 9:30am to 12:30pm and 2:30 to 5pm. The embassy of **Australia,** 4 rue Jean-Rey, 15e (℃ **01-40-59-33-00;** Métro: Bir Hakeim), is open Monday through Friday from 9:15am to noon and 2 to 4:30pm. The embassy of **New Zealand,** 7 ter rue Léonard-de-Vinci, 16e (℃ **01-45-00-24-11;** Métro: Victor Hugo), is open Monday through Friday from 9am to 1pm and 2:30 to 6pm. The embassy of **Ireland,** 4 rue Rude, 16e (℃ **01-44-17-67-00;** Métro: Charles-de-Gaulle-Etoile), is open Monday through Friday from 9:30am to noon and 2:30 to 5:30pm. The embassy of **South Africa** is at 59 quai d'Orsay, 7e (℃ **01-53-59-23-23;** Métro: Invalides). Hours are Monday through Friday from 9am to noon.

Emergencies For the police, call ℃ **17;** to report a fire, call ℃ **18.** For an ambulance, call the fire department at ℃ **01-45-78-74-52;** a fire vehicle rushes cases to the nearest emergency room. **S.A.M.U.** is an independently operated, privately owned ambulance company; call ℃ **15.**

Police In an emergency, call ℃ **17.** For nonemergency situations, the principal préfecture is at 9 bd. du Palais, 4e (℃ **01-53-73-53-73;** Métro: Cité).

Post Office The **Bureau de Poste,** 52 rue du Louvre, 75001 Paris (℃ **01-40-28-76-00;** Métro: Louvre-Rivoli), is open 24 hours a day for the sale of stamps and expedition of faxes and telegrams. For other financial services such as the sale of money orders, hours are Monday through Friday from 8am to 5pm and Saturday from 8am to noon. Your mail can be sent to this post office *poste restante* (general delivery) for a small fee. Take an ID such as a passport. Airmail letters to North America cost .65€ (75¢); to other European countries .45€ (50¢); to Australia and New Zealand .80€ (90¢).

Safety Beware of child pickpockets, who prey on visitors around sites such as the Louvre, Eiffel Tower, Notre-Dame, and Montmartre, and who like to pick pockets in the Métro, often blocking the entrance and exit to the escalator. Women should hang on to their purses.

Telephones The country code for France is **33.** All phone numbers in France have 10 digits, including the **area code** (or regional prefix). For example, the phone number for the Paris police, 01-53-73-53-73, contains the area code **(01)** for Paris and the Ile de France. To make a **long-distance call within France,** dial the 10-digit number. **When calling from outside France,** dial the international prefix for your country (**011** for the United States and Canada), the country code for France, and then the last 9 digits of the number, dropping the 0 (zero) from the regional prefix.

Public phone booths are in cafes, restaurants, Métro stations, post offices, airports, and train stations, and sometimes on the street. The French use a *télécarte,* a prepaid calling card available at rail stations, post offices, and other places. Sold in two versions, it allows you to use either

50 or 120 charge units (depending on the card) by inserting the card into the slot of most public phones. Depending on the type of card you buy, the cost is 7.45€ to 15€ ($8.50–$17).

A relatively inexpensive way to call home is to use USA Direct/AT&T WorldConnect. From within France, dial ☎ **08-00-99-00-11,** -10-11, -11-11, or -12-11. Follow the instructions, which will ask you to punch in the number of your AT&T credit card or a MasterCard or Visa. The countries that participate in the system include the U.S., Canada, the United Kingdom, Ireland, Australia, New Zealand, and South Africa. By dialing the number you want in any of these countries, you'll avoid hotel surcharges. The country code for the U.S. and Canada is **1.** Great Britain is **44;** Ireland is **353;** Australia is **61;** New Zealand is **64;** South Africa is **27.**

Tipping By law, all bills say *service compris,* which means the tip is included; additional gratuities are customarily given as follows: For **hotel staff,** tip the porter 1.05€ to 1.50€ ($1.20–$1.70) per item of baggage, and tip the chambermaid 1.50€ ($1.70) per day. You're not obligated to tip the concierge, doorman, or anyone else unless you use his or her services. In **cafes** and **restaurants,** waiter service is usually included, though you can leave a couple of francs. Tip **taxi drivers** 12% to 15% of the amount on the meter.

WHERE TO STAY

Although Paris hotels are quite expensive, there is some good news. Scores of lackluster lodgings have been renovated and offer much better value in the moderate-to-inexpensive price range. The most outstanding example is in the **7th arrondissement,** where several good-value hotels have blossomed from dives.

Hot weather doesn't last long in Paris, so most hotels (except the deluxe ones) don't provide air-conditioning. To avoid the noise problem when you have to open windows, request a room in the back when making a reservation.

Most hotels offer a continental breakfast of coffee, tea, or hot chocolate; a freshly baked croissant and roll; and limited quantities of butter and jam or jelly. The word *breakfast* in the following entries refers to this continental version.

Rates quoted include service and value-added tax, unless otherwise specified. Unless otherwise specified, all hotel rooms have a private bathroom.

RIGHT BANK: 1ST ARRONDISSEMENT
Very Expensive

Hôtel Ritz ★★★   The Ritz is Europe's greatest hotel, an enduring symbol of elegance on one of Paris's most beautiful and historic squares. César Ritz, the "little shepherd boy from Niederwald," converted the Hôtel de Lazun into a luxury hotel in 1898. With the help of the culinary master Escoffier, he made the Ritz a miracle of luxury. In 1979, the Ritz family sold the hotel to Mohammed al Fayed, who refurbished it and added a cooking school. The hotel annexed two town houses, joined by an arcade lined with display cases representing 125 of Paris's leading boutiques. Each guest room is uniquely decorated, most with Louis XIV or XV reproductions; all have fine rugs, marble fireplaces, tapestries, brass beds, and more. The spacious bathrooms are the city's most luxurious.

15 place Vendôme, 75001 Paris. ☎ **800/223-6800** in the U.S. and Canada, or 01-43-16-30-30. Fax 01-43-16-36-68. www.ritzparis.com. 175 units. 590€–750€ ($678–$862) double; from 1,180€ ($1,357)

Paris Accommodations

Information
Post Office
Railway

Moulin Rouge
bd. de Clichy
MONTMARTRE
bd. de la Chapelle
place Pigalle
bd. de Rochechouart
rue Pigalle
rue Blanche
rue N.D. de Lorette
Ste-Trinité
sino Paris
av. Trudaine
Gare du Nord
bd. de Magenta
rue de Dunkerque
rue La Fayette
St-Joseph
rue Condorcet
rue du Faubourg St-Martin
av. Jean Jaurès
rue Armand Carrel
avenue Secrétan
St-Georges
place du Colonel Fabien
PARC DES BUTTES-CHAUMONT
St-Vincent de Paul
rue de Chabrol
Gare de l'Est
Notre-Dame de Lorette
Folies Bergère
rue de Paradis
rue du Faubourg Poissonnière
rue du Faubourg St-Denis
rue du Faubourg St-Martin
St-Laurent
quai de Jemmapes
quai de Valmy
rue de Grange
rue St-Maur
bd. de la Villette
d. Haussmann
Opéra Garnier
place de l'Opéra
bd. des Italiens
bd. Montmartre
rue du 4 Septembre
Bourse des Valeurs
rue de Richelieu
rue du Mail
rue de Cléry
rue d'Aboukir
rue Réaumur
bd. de Bonne Nouvelle
bd. de Strasbourg
bd. St-Denis
bd. St-Martin
Conservatoire des Arts et Métiers
place de la République
rue du Faubourg du Temple
St-Joseph
avenue de la République
St-Roch
rue St-Augustin
rue des Petits Champs
dôme
Palais Royal
place A. Malraux
LERIES
rue de Valois
 8
rue du Louvre
Bourse du Commerce
rue Étienne Marcel
rue de Turbigo
rue du Temple
bd. du Temple
bd. Voltaire
St-Ambroise
place du Carrousel
Musée du Louvre
rue de Rivoli
Forum des Halles
rue St-Martin
rue Beaubourg
rue des Archives
rue de Turenne
LE MARAIS
quai des Tuileries
pont des Arts
Théâtre du Châtelet
23
St-Merri
22
Archives Nationales
St-Denis
rue du Chemin Vert
Ecole Nationale des Beaux-Arts
9
Seine
pont au Change
pont N. Dame
Hôtel de Ville
rue St-Antoine
St-Gervais
place des Vosges
bd. Beaumarchais
rue de la Roquette
Théâtre de la Bastille
ST-GERMAIN-DES-PRÉS
10 11
St-Germain
12
13
quai des Grands Augustins
quai de Conti
pont Neuf
ILE DE LA CITÉ
Cloître N.Dame
quai de l'Hôtel de Ville
St-Paul
21
place de la Bastille
rue du Faubourg St-Antoine
St-Sulpice
14
quai St-Michel
Notre-Dame
18
ILE ST-LOUIS
St-Louis
20
Opéra Bastille
bd. Henry IV
rue de Charenton
avenue Daumesnil
Palais du Luxembourg
15
Sorbonne
rue Saint Jacques
rue des Écoles
bd. St-Germain
Institut du Monde Arabe
19
pont de Sully
quai Henry IV
quai Saint Bernard
bd. Bourdon
rue de Lyon
av. L. Rollin
bd. Diderot
JARDIN DU LUXEMBOURG
QUARTIER LATIN
16
Panthéon
Université Paris VII
Gare de Lyon
de Vaugirard
rue d'Assas
Université Paris V
bd. St-Michel
rue Gay Lussac
rue d'Ulm
JARDIN DES PLANTES
pont d'Austerlitz
quai de Bercy
du Montparnasse
17
Mosquée
St-Médard
rue Claude Bernard
rue Buffon
rue Censier
Université Paris III
Gare d'Austerlitz
Seine
quai d'Austerlitz
quai de la Rapée

suite. AE, DC, MC, V. Parking 44€ ($51). Métro: Opéra, Concorde, or Madeleine. **Amenities:** 2 restaurants; 3 bars; indoor pool; health club; sauna; 24-hr. room service; in-room massage; babysitting; laundry service; dry cleaning; cooking school. *In room:* A/C, TV, dataport, minibar, hair dryer, iron, safe.

Moderate

Hôtel Britannique *Value*   Conservatively modern and plush, this is a much-renovated 19th-century hotel near Les Halles and Notre-Dame. The place is not only British in name, but seems to cultivate an English graciousness. The guest rooms are small but immaculate and soundproof, with comfortable beds and well-maintained bathrooms with shower-tub combinations. A satellite receiver gets U.S. and U.K. television shows. The reading room is a cozy retreat.

20 av. Victoria, 75001 Paris. © 01-42-33-74-59. Fax 01-42-33-82-65. www.hotel-britannic.com. 39 units. 157€–180€ ($181–$207) double; 280€ ($322) suite. AE, DC, MC, V. Parking 20€ ($23). Métro: Châtelet. **Amenities:** Limited room service; laundry service; dry cleaning. *In room:* A/C, TV, dataport, minibar, hair dryer, safe.

Hôtel Burgundy *★ Value*   The Burgundy is one of the best values in this expensive area. The frequently renovated building was constructed in the 1830s as two adjacent town houses—one a pension where Baudelaire wrote poetry in the 1860s, the other a bordello. British-born managers who insisted on using the English name linked the houses. Renovated in 1992, with improvements in 2001, the hotel hosts many North and South Americans and features conservatively decorated rooms, each with a bathroom with full tub and shower.

8 rue Duphot, 75001 Paris. © 01-42-60-34-12. Fax 01-47-03-95-20. www.burgundyhotel.com. 89 units. 165€–195€ ($190–$224) double; 300€ ($345) suite. AE, DC, MC, V. Métro: Madeleine or Concorde. **Amenities:** Restaurant; bar; limited room service; babysitting; laundry service; dry cleaning. *In room:* TV, dataport, minibar, hair dryer.

Inexpensive

Timhôtel Louvre *Kids*   This hotel and its sibling in the 2e, the Timhôtel Palais-Royal, are part of a new breed of two-star family friendly hotels cropping up in France. These Timhôtels share the same manager and temperament. Though the rooms at the Palais-Royal branch are a bit larger than the ones here, this branch is so close to the Louvre that it's almost irresistible. The ambience is modern, with monochromatic rooms and wall-to-wall carpeting. Each bathroom holds a tub and shower.

4 rue Croix des Petits-Champs, 75001 Paris. © 01-42-60-34-86. Fax 01-42-60-10-39. www.timhotel.fr. 56 units. 125€–150€ ($144–$173) double. Children under 12 stay free in parent's room. AE, DC, MC, V. Métro: Palais Royal. The 56-unit **Timhôtel Palais-Royal** is at 3 rue de la Banque, 75002 Paris (© 01-42-61-53-90; fax 01-42-60-05-39; Métro: Bourse). **Amenities:** Limited room service; babysitting; laundry service; dry cleaning. *In room:* A/C, TV, dataport.

RIGHT BANK: 3RD, 4TH & 8TH ARRONDISSEMENTS
Very Expensive

Four Seasons Hotel George V *★★★*   In its latest incarnation, with all its glitz and glamour, this hotel is one of the best in the world. It opened in 1928 in honor of George V of England. During the liberation of Paris, it housed Dwight D. Eisenhower. After its acquisition by Saudi Prince Al Waleed and a 2-year renovation, it reopened under the banner of Toronto-based Four Seasons. The guest rooms are about as close as you'll come to residency in a private home where teams of decorators have lavished vast amounts of attention and money. It's deluxe all the way. The renovation reduced the number of units from 300 to 245, which come in three sizes. The largest are magnificent; the smallest are, in the words of a spokesperson, "très agreeable." Security is tight—a fact appreciated by the sometimes-notorious guests.

31 av. George V, 75008 Paris. ℂ **800/332-3442** in the U.S. and Canada, or 01-49-52-70-00. Fax 01-49-52-70-10. www.fourseasons.com. 245 units. 670€–890€ ($771–$1,024) double; 1,250€ ($1,438) suite. AE, DC, MC, V. Parking 40€ ($46). Métro: George-V. **Amenities:** Restaurant; bar; indoor pool; fitness center; spa; sauna; 24-hr. room service; babysitting; laundry service; dry cleaning. *In room:* A/C, TV, dataport, minibar, hair dryer, safe.

Hotel Pershing Hall 🌟🌟🌟   On a hyperstylish street that parallels the avenue Montaigne, this hotel was created when one of France's most celebrated modern designers, Andrée Putnam, radically altered a late-19th-century town house. Admittedly, she had fascinating raw materials: The five-story town house was built in 1890 by the comte de Paris, at the time the heir apparent to the French monarchy had it been fully restored, as a home for his mistress. During World War I, it was the Paris headquarters of American Gen. John Pershing. Today, the walls of the soaring courtyard are draped in lush tropical plants from Southeast Asia that thrive in the microclimate of the courtyard. Inside, don't expect homage to the imperial days of the French monarchy, but rather the warm, artfully spartan and rectilinear style favored by Putnam.

49 rue Pierre Charron, 75008 Paris. ℂ **01-58-36-58-00.** Fax 01-58-36-58-01. www.pershing-hall.com. 26 units. 330€–390€ ($380–$449) double; 850€–1,000€ ($978–$1,150) suite. AE, DC, MC, V. Metro: Georges V. **Amenities:** Restaurant; bar; health club; sauna; babysitting; laundry service; dry cleaning. *In room:* A/C, TV, dataport, minibar, hair dryer, safe.

Expensive

Hôtel du Jeu de Paume 🌟   This small-scale hotel encompasses a pair of 17th-century town houses accessible through a timbered passageway from the street outside. The rooms are a bit larger than those of some nearby competitors. Originally, the hotel was a clubhouse for members of the court of Louis XIII, who amused themselves with *les jeux de paume* (an early form of tennis) nearby. Public areas are outfitted in a simple version of Art Deco. Guest rooms are freshly decorated in sleek contemporary style, with elegant materials such as oaken floors, and fine craftsmanship. All contain well-maintained bathrooms with tub-shower combinations.

54 rue St-Louis en l'Ile, 75004 Paris. ℂ 01-43-26-14-18. Fax 01-40-46-02-76. www.jeudepaumehotel.com. 30 units. 215€–285€ ($247–$328) double; 465€ ($535) suite. AE, DC, MC, V. Métro: Pont Marie. **Amenities:** Bar; gym; sauna; limited room service; babysitting; laundry service; dry cleaning. *In room:* TV, dataport, minibar, hair dryer, safe.

Hôtel Saint-Louis 🌟 *Value*   Proprietors Guy and Andrée Record maintain a charming family atmosphere at this antiques-filled hotel in a 17th-century town house. It represents an incredible value considering its prime location on Ile St-Louis. Expect cozy, slightly cramped rooms, each with a small bathroom containing a shower-tub combination. With mansard roofs and old-fashioned moldings, the top-floor units sport tiny balconies that afford sweeping views. The breakfast room is in the cellar, which has 17th-century stone vaulting.

75 rue St-Louis-en-l'Ile, 75004 Paris. ℂ 01-46-34-04-80. Fax 01-46-34-02-13. www.hotelsaintlouis.com. 19 units. 130€–210€ ($150–$242) double. MC, V. Métro: Pont Marie or St-Michel. **Amenities:** Limited room service; babysitting. *In room:* TV, dataport, minibar, hair dryer, safe.

Moderate

Galileo Hotel 🌟 *Finds*   This is one of the 8th's most charming hotels, run by Roland and Elisabeth Buffat. A short walk from the Champs-Elysées, the town house is the epitome of French elegance and charm. The medium-size rooms are decorated in understated cocoa and beige. Beautifully kept bathrooms hold a tub or shower. The most spacious rooms are nos. 100, 200, 501, and 502, with a glass-covered veranda you can use even in winter.

54 rue Galilée, 75008 Paris. © **01-47-20-66-06.** Fax 01-47-20-67-17. 27 units. 153€ ($176) double. AE, DC, MC, V. Parking 23€ ($26). Métro: Charles-de-Gaulle-Etoile or George-V. **Amenities:** Limited room service; laundry service; dry cleaning. *In room:* A/C, TV, minibar, hair dryer, safe.

Hôtel Saint-Merry ★ *Finds* The rebirth of this once-notorious brothel as a charming, upscale hotel is an example of how the area has been gentrified. It contains only a dozen rooms, each relatively small, but accented with neo-Gothic detail, exposed stone, 18th-century ceiling beams, and lots of quirky architecture. Suites, much larger than doubles, have upgraded furnishings. All units contain tiled bathrooms with shower-tub combinations. According to the staff, the clientele here is about 50% gay males; the other half is straight and involved in the neighborhood arts scene.

78 rue de la Verrerie, 75004 Paris. © **01-42-78-14-15.** Fax 01-40-29-06-82. www.hotelmarais.com. 12 units. 130€–230€ ($150–$265) double; 335€ ($385) suite. MC, V. Metro: Hôtel de Ville or Châtelet. **Amenities:** Breakfast lounge; limited room service; babysitting; laundry service; dry cleaning. *In room:* Hair dryer, safe.

Inexpensive

Hôtel de la Place des Vosges ★ *Value* Built about 350 years ago, during the same era as the majestic square for which it's named (a 2-min. walk away), this well-managed, small-scale property has reasonable prices and lots of charm. The structure was once a stable for the mules of Henri IV. Many of the small guest rooms have beamed ceilings, tiled bathrooms (with tub or shower), small TVs hanging from the ceiling, and a sense of cozy, well-ordered efficiency. The most desirable and expensive accommodation is top-floor room no. 60, overlooking the city rooftops, with a luxurious bathroom.

12 rue de Birague, 75004 Paris. © **01-42-72-60-46.** Fax 01-42-72-02-64. 16 units. 120€–140€ ($138–$161) double. AE, MC, V. Métro: Bastille. **Amenities:** Limited room service. *In room:* TV, dataport, hair dryer, minibar, safe.

Hôtel du 7e Art The hotel occupies one of the many 17th-century buildings in this neighborhood classified as historic monuments. Don't expect luxury: Guest rooms are cramped and outfitted with the simplest of furniture, relieved by 1950s-era movie posters. Each unit has white walls, and some—including those under the sloping mansard-style roof—have exposed ceiling beams. All have small bathrooms with a tub or shower. The five-story hotel has a lobby bar and breakfast room, but no elevator. The "7th Art" is a reference to filmmaking.

20 rue St-Paul, 75004 Paris. © **01-44-54-85-00.** Fax 01-42-77-69-10. 23 units. 75€–130€ ($86–$150) double. AE, DC, MC, V. Métro: St-Paul. **Amenities:** Bar; health club; coin laundry. *In room:* TV, dataport, hair dryer, safe.

RIGHT BANK: 16TH ARRONDISSEMENT
Expensive

Hôtel Sofitel Trocadero Dokhan's ★★ If not for the porters walking through its public areas carrying luggage, you might suspect that this well-accessorized hotel is a private home. It's in a stately 19th-century building vaguely inspired by Palladio, and contains accessories like antique paneling, Regency-era armchairs, and chandeliers. Each guest room has a different style, with antiques or good reproductions, lots of personalized touches, triple-glazed windows, and beautifully maintained bathrooms with shower-tub combinations.

117 rue Lauriston, 75116 Paris. © **01-53-65-66-99.** Fax 01-53-65-66-88. www.sofitel.com. 45 units. 400€–480€ ($460–$552) double; 820€ ($943) suite. AE, DC, MC, V. Parking 20€ ($23). Métro: Trocadero. **Amenities:** Restaurant (lunch only); champagne bar; babysitting; laundry service; dry cleaning. *In room:* A/C, TV, fax, minibar, hair dryer, safe.

LEFT BANK: 5TH ARRONDISSEMENT
Moderate

Hôtel-Résidence Saint-Christophe   This hotel, in one of the Latin Quarter's undiscovered areas, has a gracious English-speaking staff. It was created in 1987 when an older hotel was connected to a butcher shop. All the small- to medium-size rooms were renovated in 1998, with Louis XV–style furniture and carpeting. Half of the bathrooms have tubs in addition to showers.

17 rue Lacépède, 75005 Paris. 🕐 **01-43-31-81-54.** Fax 01-43-31-12-54. www.charme-hotel-paris.com. 31 units. 100€–125€ ($115–$144) double. AE, DC, MC, V. Métro: Place Monge. **Amenities:** Limited room service. *In room:* TV, dataport, minibar, hair dryer.

Inexpensive

Familia-Hôtel   As the name implies, this hotel has been family run for decades. Many personal touches make the place unique. Finely executed sepia-colored frescoes of Parisian scenes grace the walls of 14 rooms. Eight units have restored stone walls, and seven boast balconies with delightful views over the Latin Quarter. Half of the bathrooms come with tubs as well as showers. Thanks to the dynamic owners, the guest rooms are renovated as often as needed to maintain a high level of comfort.

11 rue des Ecoles, 75005 Paris. 🕐 **01-43-54-55-27.** Fax 01-43-29-61-77. www.hotel-paris.familia.com. 30 units. 79€–109€ ($91–$125) double. AE, DC, MC, V. Métro: Jussieu or Maubert-Mutualité. **Amenities:** Car-rental desk; limited room service. *In room:* TV, minibar, hair dryer.

LEFT BANK: 6TH ARRONDISSEMENT
Very Expensive

Relais Christine 🌟🌟   This hotel welcomes you into a former 16th-century Augustinian cloister. From a cobblestone street, enter a symmetrical courtyard to find an elegant reception area with Renaissance antiques. Each room is uniquely decorated with wooden beams and Louis XIII–style furnishings. Extras include mirrored closets, plush carpets, and thermostats. Bed configurations vary, but all mattresses are on the soft side, offering comfort with quality linens. Some units have balconies facing the courtyard. The least attractive rooms are those in the interior.

3 rue Christine, 75006 Paris. 🕐 **01-40-51-60-80.** Fax 01-40-51-60-81. www.relais-christine.com. 51 units. 335€–430€ ($385–$495) double; 480€–730€ ($552–$840) duplex or suite. AE, DC, MC, V. Free parking. Métro: Odéon or St-Michel. **Amenities:** Honor bar in lobby; gym; 24-hr. room service; massage; babysitting; laundry service; dry cleaning. *In room:* A/C, TV, dataport, minibar, hair dryer, iron, safe.

Expensive

Hôtel de Fleurie 🌟 *Kids*   Off boulevard St-Germain on a colorful little street, the Fleurie is one of the best of the "new" old hotels; its statuary-studded facade recaptures 17th-century elegance, and the stone walls have been exposed in the salon. Many of the well-maintained guest rooms have elaborate draperies and antique reproductions. Because some rooms are larger than others and contain an extra bed for kids, the hotel has long been a family favorite.

32–34 rue Grégoire-de-Tours, 75006 Paris. 🕐 **01-53-73-70-00.** Fax 01-53-73-70-20. www.hotel-de-fleurie.tm.fr. 29 units. 165€–185€ ($190–$213) double; 290€–325€ ($334–$374) family room. Children under 13 stay free in parent's room. AE, DC, MC, V. Métro: Odéon or Mabillon. **Amenities:** Bar; car rental; limited room service; laundry service; dry cleaning. *In room:* A/C, TV, dataport, minibar, hair dryer, safe.

L'Hôtel 🌟   Ranking just a notch below the Relais Christine, this is one of the Left Bank's most charming boutique hotels. It was once a 19th-century fleabag whose major distinction was that Oscar Wilde died here. But today's guests aren't anywhere near destitution. In 2000, the superstar aesthete Jacques Garcia redecorated the hotel, retaining its Victorian-baroque sense. Guest rooms vary in size, style, and price; all have nonworking fireplaces and fabric-covered walls. Room themes reflect China, Russia, Japan, India, or high-camp Victorian. About half the bathrooms are small, tubless nooks. All the sumptuous beds have tasteful fabrics and crisp linens.

13 rue des Beaux-Arts, 75006 Paris. ℰ **01-44-41-99-00.** Fax 01-43-25-64-81. www.l-hotel.com. 20 units. 248€–721€ ($285–$829) double; from 721€ ($829) suite. AE, DC, MC, V. Métro: St-Germain-des-Prés. **Amenities:** Restaurant; bar; indoor pool; steam room; limited room service; babysitting; laundry service; dry cleaning. *In room:* A/C, TV, dataport, minibar, hair dryer, safe.

Moderate

Hôtel Le Clos Médicis   The location of this hotel across from the Jardin du Luxembourg is a major advantage. You'll find a garden with lattices and stone walls, a lobby with modern spotlights and simple furniture, and a multilingual staff. The warmly colored rooms, small to medium in size, are comfortable, and each comes with a neatly tiled bathroom with combination tub and shower. Book one of the multilevel suites with spacious living areas and tasteful furnishings.

56 rue Monsieur-le-Prince, 75006 Paris. ℰ **01-43-29-10-80.** Fax 01-43-54-26-90. www.closmedicis.com. 38 units. 170€–210€ ($196–$242) double; 250€ ($288) duplex suite. AE, DC, MC, V. Parking 23€ ($26). Métro: Odéon. RER: Luxembourg. **Amenities:** Bar; limited room service; laundry service; dry cleaning. *In room:* A/C, TV, dataport, minibar, hair dryer, safe.

Inexpensive

Hôtel du Globe   This 17th-century building is on an evocative street; inside you'll find most of the original stonework and dozens of original timbers and beams. There's no elevator (and a very narrow antique staircase) and no breakfast area (trays are brought to your room). Each guest room is decorated with old-fashioned flair. The rooms with tubs are almost twice as large as those with shower stalls. The largest and most desirable are nos. 1, 12 (with a canopy bed), 14, 15, and 16. The room without a bathroom is a single that goes for 50€ ($58).

15 rue des Quatre-Vents, 75006 Paris. ℰ **01-46-33-62-69.** Fax 01-46-33-62-69. 15 units. 70€–105€ ($81–$121) double. MC, V. Closed Aug. Métro: Mabillon, Odéon, or St-Sulpice. **Amenities:** Limited room service. *In room:* TV.

LEFT BANK: 7TH ARRONDISSEMENT
Very Expensive

Hôtel Montalembert 🏵🏵   Unusually elegant for the Left Bank, the beaux-arts Montalembert dates from 1926. Its decor borrows elements of Bauhaus and postmodern design. The guest rooms are spacious, except for some standard doubles, which are small unless you're a very thin model. Frette linens decorate roomy beds topped with cabana-stripe duvets crowning deluxe mattresses. Bathrooms are luxurious, with deep tubs, Cascais marble, and tall pivoting mirrors.

3 rue de Montalembert, 75007 Paris. ℰ **800/786-6397** in the U.S. and Canada, or 01-45-49-68-68. Fax 01-45-49-69-49. www.montalembert.com. 56 units. 340€–430€ ($391–$495) double; 560€–750€ ($644–$863) suite. AE, DC, MC, V. Parking 25€ ($29). Métro: Rue du Bac. **Amenities:** Restaurant; bar; access to nearby health club; 24-hr. room service; laundry service; dry cleaning. *In room:* A/C, TV, dataport, minibar, hair dryer, safe.

Moderate

Hôtel de l'Université 🏵   Long favored by well-heeled parents of North American students studying in Paris, this 300-year-old, antiques-filled town house sits in a discreetly upscale neighborhood. Room no. 54 is a favorite, containing a rattan bed and period pieces. Another charmer is room no. 35, which has a fireplace and opens onto a courtyard with a fountain. The most expensive unit has a small terrace overlooking the surrounding rooftops. You'll sleep well here on comfortable beds.

22 rue de l'Université, 75007 Paris. ℂ 01-42-61-09-39. Fax 01-42-60-40-84. www.hoteluniversite.com. 27 units. 160€–205€ ($184–$236) double. AE, DC, MC, V. Métro: St-Germain-des-Prés. **Amenities:** Limited room service. *In room:* A/C, TV, dataport, hair dryer, minibar, safe.

Inexpensive

Hôtel du Quai Voltaire   Built in the 1600s as an abbey, then transformed into a hotel in 1856, the Quai Voltaire is best known for its illustrious guests, like Wilde, Wagner, and Baudelaire, who occupied room nos. 47, 55, and 56, respectively. Pissarro painted Le Pont Royal from the window of his fourth-floor room. Many guest rooms in this modest inn have been renovated; most overlook the bookstalls and boats of the Seine.

19 quai Voltaire, 75007 Paris. ℂ **01-42-61-50-91**. Fax 01-42-61-62-26. www.quaivoltaire.fr. 33 units. 118€–125€ ($136–$144) double. AE, DC, MC, V. Parking 20€ ($23) nearby. Métro: Musée d'Orsay or Rue du Bac. **Amenities:** Bar; limited room service; laundry service. *In room:* TV, hair dryer.

WHERE TO DINE

Our best piece of advice—even if your budget is lean—is to splurge on one grand French meal. (And make reservations well in advance!) A meal at a place such as **La Tour d'Argent** ✹✹✹, **Taillevent** ✹✹✹, **Alain Ducasse** ✹✹✹, or **Carré des Fevillants** ✹✹✹ will be an eternal memory.

In the past, suits and ties were a given, and women always wore smart dresses or suits. Well, you can kiss your suits *au revoir*. Except in first-class and deluxe places, attire is more relaxed. Relaxed doesn't mean sloppy jeans and workout clothes! Parisians still value style, even when dressing informally.

Restaurants are required by law to post their menus outside, so peruse them carefully. The prix-fixe menu remains a solid choice if you want to have some idea of what your bill will be when it's presented by the waiter (whom you call *monsieur,* not *garçon*).

RIGHT BANK: 1ST ARRONDISSEMENT
Very Expensive

Carré des Feuillants ✹✹✹ MODERN FRENCH   This is a bastion of perfection, an enclave of haute gastronomy between the place Vendôme and the Tuileries. When chef Alain Dutournier turned this 17th-century convent into a restaurant, it was an overnight success. The interior is like an early-1900s bourgeois house, with several salons opening onto a sky-lit courtyard, across from a glass-enclosed kitchen. You'll find a sophisticated reinterpretation of cuisine from France's southwest, using seasonal ingredients and lots of know-how. Examples are roasted veal kidneys cooked in their own fat, and grilled wood pigeon with chutney and polenta. Lighter dishes are scallops wrapped in parsley-infused puff pastry served with cabbage and truffles, and mullet-studded risotto with lettuce. For dessert, try pistachio cream cake with candied tangerines.

14 rue de Castiglione. ℂ 01-42-86-82-82. Fax 01-42-86-07-71. Reservations required far in advance. Main courses 54€–55€ ($62–$63); fixed-price lunch 140€ ($161). AE, DC, MC, V. Mon–Fri noon–2:30pm and 7:30–10pm. Closed Aug. Métro: Tuileries, Concorde, Opéra, or Madeleine.

Expensive

Goumard ✹✹✹ SEAFOOD   Opened in 1872, this landmark is one of Paris's leading seafood restaurants. It's so devoted to the fine art of preparing fish that other food is banned from the menu (the staff will verbally present a limited roster of meat dishes). The decor consists of a collection of Lalique crystal fish in artificial aquariums. Even more unusual are the men's and women's restrooms, classified as historic monuments; the Art Nouveau master cabinetmaker designed the commodes Majorelle in the early 1900s. Much of the seafood is flown in from Brittany daily. Examples are *craquant* (crisp-cooked) crayfish in herb salad, lobster soup with coconut, and grilled turbot salad on a bed of artichokes with tarragon. In all these dishes, nothing (no excess butter, spices, or salt) is allowed to interfere with the natural flavor of the sea. Be prepared for some unusual food—the staff will help translate the menu items for you.

9 rue Duphot. © 01-42-60-36-07. Fax 01-42-60-04-54. www.goumard.com. Reservations required far in advance. Main courses 29€–75€ ($33–$86); fixed-price menu 40€ ($46). AE, DC, MC, V. Daily noon–2:30pm and 7:30–10:30pm. Closed 2 weeks in Aug. Métro: Madeleine or Concorde.

Moderate

Il Cortile ★★ ITALIAN/MEDITERRANEAN Flanking the verdant courtyard of a small hotel, this much-talked-about restaurant serves the best Italian food in Paris. The cuisine is fresh, inventive, and seasonal. Dishes are from throughout Italy, with emphasis on the north. Look for items like farfalle pasta with squid ink and fresh shellfish, and an award-winning guinea fowl (spit-roasted and served with artfully shaped slices of the bird's gizzard, heart, and liver). The service is flawless: The Italian-speaking staff is diplomatic and good-humored. If you want to see what's cooking, ask for a seat in the dining room with a view of the rotisserie, where hens and guinea fowl slowly spin. In warm weather, tables fill an enclosed patio—a luxury in this congested neighborhood.

In the Hôtel Castille, 37 rue Cambon. © 01-44-58-45-67. Reservations recommended. Main courses 17€–35€ ($20–$40); fixed-price menu 40€ ($46). AE, DC, DISC, MC, V. Mon–Fri noon–2:30pm and 7:30–10:30pm. Métro: Concorde or Madeleine.

Inexpensive

La Fermette du Sud-Ouest ★ SOUTHWESTERN FRENCH This restaurant, which occupies the site of a 1500s convent, is in the heart of one of Paris's oldest neighborhoods. After the Revolution, the convent was converted into a coaching inn, preserving the original stonework and massive beams. La Fermette prepares rich, savory stews and confits celebrating agrarian France, and serves them on the ground floor and on a mezzanine resembling a choir loft. Menu items include ever-popular magret of duckling with flap mushrooms, *andouillette* (chitterling sausages), and a sometimes startling array of *cochonailles* (pork products and by-products) you probably need to be French to appreciate. Cassoulet and pot-au-feu are enduring specialties.

31 rue Coquillière. © 01-42-36-73-55. Reservations recommended. Main courses 15€–22€ ($17–$24); fixed-price lunch 16€ ($18); set menu 25€ ($29) MC, V. Mon–Sat noon–2pm and 7:30–10pm. Métro: Les Halles.

RIGHT BANK: 3RD ARRONDISSEMENT (LE MARAIS)
Inexpensive

L'Ambassade d'Auvergne ★ AUVERGNAT/FRENCH You enter this rustic tavern through a bar with heavy oak beams, hanging hams, and ceramic plates. It showcases the culinary bounty of France's most isolated region, the Auvergne, whose pork products are widely celebrated. Try chicory salad with apples and pieces of country ham; pork braised with cabbage, turnips, and white beans; or grilled tripe sausages with mashed potatoes and cantal cheese with garlic. Nonpork specialties are pan-fried duck liver with gingerbread, perch steamed in verbena tea, and roasted rack of lamb with wild mushrooms. Dessert might be a poached pear with crispy almonds and caramel sauce.

22 rue de Grenier St-Lazare. © 01-42-72-31-22. Reservations recommended. Main courses 16€–19€ ($18–$22); fixed-price menu 27€ ($31). AE, MC, V. Daily noon–2pm and 7:30–11pm. Métro: Rambuteau.

RIGHT BANK: 4TH ARRONDISSEMENT
Moderate

Bofinger ☞ ALSATIAN/FRENCH   Opened in the 1860s, Bofinger is the oldest Alsatian brasserie in town and one of the best. It's a Belle Epoque dining palace, resplendent with brass and stained glass. Weather permitting, you can dine on an outdoor terrace. Affiliated with La Coupole, Julien, and Brasserie Flo, the restaurant has updated its menu, retaining the most popular traditional dishes, like sauerkraut and sole meunière. Recent additions include roasted leg of lamb with fondant of artichoke hearts and parsley purée; grilled turbot with *brandade* of fennel; and stingray with chives and burnt-butter sauce. Shellfish, including fresh oysters and lobster, is almost always available in season.

5–7 rue de la Bastille. ✆ 01-42-72-87-82. Reservations recommended. Main courses 15€–35€ ($17–$40). AE, DC, MC, V. Mon–Fri noon–3pm and 6:30pm–1am; Sat–Sun noon–1am. Métro: Bastille.

Inexpensive

Chez Jo Goldenberg ☞ JEWISH/CENTRAL EUROPEAN   This is the best-known restaurant on the "Street of the Rose Bushes." Albert Goldenberg, the doyen of Jewish restaurateurs in Paris, moved to choicer surroundings (69 av. de Wagram, 17e), but his brother, Joseph, has remained. Dining is on two levels, one for nonsmokers. Look for the collection of samovars, the fantail pigeon in a wicker cage, and the paintings. *Carpe farcie* (stuffed carp) is a preferred selection, and beef goulash is also good. We like eggplant moussaka and pastrami. The menu offers Israeli wines, but M. Goldenberg admits they're not as good as French wines. Live Yiddish music begins every night at 9pm, and special menus are offered during Jewish holidays—reservations are a must.

7 rue des Rosiers. ✆ 01-48-87-20-16. Reservations required. Main courses 13€–18€ ($15–$21). AE, MC, V. Daily 11am–midnight. Métro: St-Paul.

RIGHT BANK: 8TH ARRONDISSEMENT
Very Expensive

Pierre Gagnaire ✰✰✰ MODERN FRENCH   If you're able to get a reservation, it's worth the effort. The menus are seasonal to take advantage of France's rich bounty; owner Pierre Gagnaire demands perfection, and the chef has a dazzling way with flavors and textures. Stellar examples are crayfish cooked tempura style with thinly sliced flash-seared vegetables and sweet-and-sour sauce; and turbot cooked in a bag and served with fennel and Provençal lemons. Chicken with truffles comes in two stages—first the breast in wine-based aspic, then the thighs chopped into roughly textured pieces. For dessert, try chocolate soufflé served with a frozen parfait and pistachios.

6 rue Balzac. ✆ 01-58-36-12-50. Fax 01-58-36-12-51. Reservations imperative and difficult to get. Main courses 65€–120€ ($75–$138); fixed-price menu 90€ ($104) lunch, 195€ ($224) dinner. AE, DC, MC, V. Mon–Fri noon–1:30pm and 7–10pm; Sun 7:30-10pm. Métro: George-V.

Restaurant Plaza Athénée (Alain Ducasse) ✰✰✰ MODERN & TRADITIONAL FRENCH   Few other chefs have been catapulted to international fame as quickly as Alain Ducasse. There's a lot of marketing involved, but what you'll find in this world-renowned hotel is a lobby-level hideaway that top-notch decorator Patrick Jouin transformed with layers of pearl-gray paint and yards of translucent organdy. The five-star Michelin chef divides his time between Paris and Monaco, though he insists he doesn't repeat himself in either of his famous eateries. He makes wonderful use of produce from every corner of France—rare local vegetables, fish from the coasts. Dishes incorporate cardoons, turnips, celery, turbot, cuttlefish, and Bresse fowl. Though many dishes are light, Ducasse isn't afraid of lard, as he proves with thick, oozing slabs of pork grilled to a crisp.

In the Hotel Plaza Athénée, 25 av. Montaigne. ℂ **01-53-67-66-65** or 01-53-67-65-00. Fax 01-53-67-66-66. Reservations required 6–8 weeks in advance. Main courses 70€–105€ ($81–$121); fixed-price menus 190€–300€ ($218–$345). AE, DC, MC, V. Thurs–Fri noon–2pm; Mon–Fri 8–10:30pm. Closed mid-July to Aug 29 and Dec 17–31. Metro: Alma-Marceau.

Taillevent ★★★ MODERN & TRADITIONAL FRENCH   This is the Parisian *ne plus ultra* of gastronomy. Taillevent opened in 1946 and has climbed steadily in excellence; today it ranks as Paris's outstanding all-around restaurant, challenged only by Lucas-Carton and Pierre Gagnaire. It's in a grand 19th-century town house off the Champs-Elysées, with paneled rooms and crystal chandeliers. The place is small, which permits the owner to give personal attention to every facet of the operation and maintain a discreet atmosphere. You might begin with *boudin* (sausage) of Breton lobster a la Nage, cream of watercress soup with sevruga caviar, or duck liver with spice bread and ginger. Main courses include red snapper with black olives, Scottish salmon cooked in sea salt with a sauce of olive oil and lemons, and cassoulet of crayfish.

15 rue Lamennais. ℂ **01-44-95-15-01.** Fax 01-42-25-95-18. Reservations required 4–6 weeks in advance. Main courses 34€–90€ ($39–$103); *menu dégustation* (tasting menu) 130€ ($150). AE, DC, MC, V. Mon–Fri noon–2:30pm and 7–10pm. Closed Aug. Métro: George-V.

Expensive

Buddha Bar ★ FRENCH/PACIFIC RIM   This place remains Paris's restaurant of the moment, even though it's been around for a while. A location near the Champs-Elysées and place de la Concorde, and an allegiance to a fusion of French, Asian, and Californian cuisines, attract trendy diners devoted to the whims of fashion. A giant Buddha presides over the vast dining room, and the culinary theme combines Japanese sashimi, Vietnamese spring rolls, lacquered duck, sautéed shrimp with black-bean sauce, grilled chicken skewers with orange sauce, sweet-and-sour spareribs, and crackling squab a l'orange. There are two seatings for dinner: 7 to 9pm and 10:30pm to 12:30am. Many come here just for a drink in the lacquered bar, upstairs from the street-level dining room.

8 rue Boissy d'Anglas. ℂ **01-53-05-90-00.** Reservations required far in advance. Main courses 70€–80€ ($81–$103). AE, MC, V. Mon–Fri noon–3pm; daily 7pm–12:30am. Métro: Concorde.

L'Angle du Faubourg ★★ FRENCH   Throughout the 1980s and early 1990s, a reservation at the Restaurant Taillevent was sought after by diplomats, billionaires, and *demi-mondains* from around Europe. In 2001, the owner and chef, M. Vrinat, opened a cost-conscious bistro that capitalized on Taillevent's reputation, but at much lower prices. Lunches here tend to be efficient, relatively quick, and businesslike, while dinners are more leisurely, even romantic. The restaurant has an ultra-modern dining room, additional seating in the cellar, and a menu that simplifies Taillevant's lofty culinary ideas. The best examples include cream of beet soup; marinated salmon; risotto with ingredients that change weekly; and a grilled, low-fat version of *daurade,* served with a sweet-and-sour sauce, appreciated by the many diet-conscious *photo-modèles* who stop in between bouts of shopping. Dessert might be old-fashioned rice pudding.

195 rue du Faubourg St-Honoré. ℂ **01-40-74-20-20.** Reservations required. Main courses 18€–28€ ($21–$32); fixed-price menu 35€–60€ ($40–$69). AE, DC, MC, V. Mon–Fri noon–2:30pm and 7–10:30pm. Métro: Terme.

Spoon, Food & Wine ★ INTERNATIONAL   This hypermodern venture by star chef Alain Ducasse is hailed as a "restaurant for the millennium" and condemned by some as surreal and a bit absurd. Despite that, there can be a 2-week wait for a dinner reservation. This upscale but relatively affordable restaurant might be the least pretentious and most hip of Ducasse's ventures. The decor of the somewhat claustrophobic dining room has both Parisian and Californian references, and the cuisine—the menu changes every 2 months—roams the world. Examples include grilled tuna steak with satay sauce; deliberately undercooked grilled squid (part of it evokes sushi) with curry sauce; and roasted pigeon with an Italian *dolce-forte* (sweet-and-sour) sauce. Vegetarians appreciate stir-fried dishes in which you can mix and match up to 15 ingredients. Desserts feature Parisian versions of such U.S.-inspired dishes as cheesecake and doughnuts drenched with bitter chocolate.

In the Hôtel Marignan-Elysée, 14 rue Marignan. ✆ 01-40-76-34-44. Reservations recommended 2 weeks in advance. Main courses 25€–40€ ($23–$46). AE, DC, V. Mon–Fri noon–2pm and 7–11pm. Métro: Franklin-D-Roosevelt.

RIGHT BANK: 9TH, 10TH & 12TH ARRONDISSEMENTS
Expensive
Au Trou Gascon ★★★ GASCONY One of Paris's most acclaimed chefs, Alain Dutournier lures fashionable palates to an un-chic area. His parents mortgaged their Gascony inn to allow Dutournier to open an early-1900s bistro in a little-known part of the 12th. Word spread of a savant in the kitchen who practiced authentic *cuisine moderne*. Dutournier's wife, Nicole, is the welcoming hostess. You can start with duck foie gras cooked in a terrine, or Gascony-cured ham. The best main courses include fresh tuna with braised cabbage, superb cassoulet, and chicken from the Chalosse region of Landes, which Dutournier roasts and serves in its own drippings.

40 rue Taine, 12e. ✆ 01-43-44-34-26. Reservations required far in advance. Main courses 28€–35€ ($32–$40); fixed-price lunch 36€ ($41). AE, DC, MC, V. Mon–Fri noon–2pm; Mon–Sat 7:30–10pm. Closed Aug. Métro: Daumesnil.

Moderate
Brasserie Flo ★ ALSATIAN This remote restaurant is hard to find, but once you arrive (after walking through passageway after passageway), you'll see that *fin-de-siècle* Paris lives on. The restaurant opened in 1860 and has changed its decor very little. The specialty is *la formidable choucroute* (a mound of sauerkraut with boiled ham, bacon, and sausage) for two. Onion soup and sole meunière are always good, as are warm foie gras and guinea hen with lentils. Look for the *plats du jour,* ranging from roast pigeon to veal fricassee with sorrel.

7 cour des Petites-Ecuries, 10e. ✆ 01-47-70-13-59. Reservations recommended. Main courses 15€–27€ ($17–$31). Fixed-price menus 26€ ($30) lunch, 31€ ($36) dinner. AE, DC, MC, V. Daily noon–3pm and 7pm–1:30am. Métro: Château d'Eau or Strasbourg-St-Denis.

RIGHT BANK: 17TH ARRONDISSEMENT
Very Expensive
Guy Savoy ★★★ TRADITIONAL FRENCH One of the hottest chefs in Europe, Guy Savoy serves the kind of food he likes to eat, prepared with consummate skill. Although the superb meals comprise as many as nine courses, portions are small; you won't necessarily be satiated at the end. The menu changes with the seasons and may include cream soup of lentils and crayfish; duckling foie gras with aspic and gray salt; or sea bass grilled in a salt shell and served with a sauce of sweet herbs. If you come in the right season, you may have a chance to order game. Savoy is fascinated with mushrooms, serving, for example, a delectable pan-fried combination of mussels and wild mushrooms.

18 rue Troyon. ☎ **01-43-80-40-61.** Fax 01-46-22-43-09. Reservations required 1 week in advance. Main courses 72€–160€ ($83–$184); *menu dégustation* (tasting menu) 200€–250€ ($230–$288). AE, DC, MC, V. Tues–Fri noon–2pm; Tues–Sat 7:30–10:30pm. Métro: Charles-de-Gaulle-Etoile or Ternes.

LEFT BANK: 5TH ARRONDISSEMENT
Very Expensive
La Tour d'Argent ✿✿✿ TRADITIONAL FRENCH   This penthouse restaurant, a national institution, enjoys a panoramic view over the Seine and Notre-Dame. Although its reputation as the best in Paris has been eclipsed, dining here remains an unsurpassed event. A restaurant has stood on this site since 1582: Mme de Sévigné refers to a cafe here in her letters, and Dumas used it in one of his novels. The fame of La Tour d'Argent spread during its ownership by Frédéric Delair, who started the practice of issuing certificates to diners who ordered *caneton* (pressed duckling). The birds are numbered: The first was served to Edward VII in 1890, and now they number over one million! Under the sharp eye of owner Claude Terrail, the cooking is superb and the service impeccable. Start with pheasant consommé or pike-perch quenelles André Terrail; follow with ravioli with foie gras or filet of sole Cardinal with shrimp sauce.

15–17 quai de la Tournelle. ☎ **01-43-54-23-31.** Fax 01-44-07-12-04. Reservations required far in advance. Main courses 60€–70€ ($69–$81); fixed-price lunch 70€ ($81). AE, DC, MC, V. Wed–Sun noon–1:15pm; Tues–Sun 7:30–9pm. Métro: St-Michel or Pont Marie.

Moderate
Marty ✿ *(Finds* MODERN FRENCH   Charming, with a stone-trimmed decor that's authentic to the era (1913) when it was established, this restaurant has been "discovered" by new generations of restaurant-goers. Named after its founders, Etienne and Marthe Marty, its fame now extends beyond the 5th arrondissement. Food is savory, satisfying, and unfussy. Views from the hideaway tables on the mezzanine sweep over the entire human comedy unfolding above and below you. Begin your meal with tartare of sea bream flavored with anise and lime; lobster ravioli with sherry vinegar; or fresh oysters. Continue with *suprême* of guinea fowl with vegetable moussaka; a platter that combines grilled squid with grilled strips of red mullet; or perhaps brochette of hake and salmon, served with a mustard-flavored olive tapenade. Dessert might be soup of red fruit with orange-flavored liqueur.

20 av. des Gobelins. ☎ **01-43-31-39-51.** Main courses 19€–27€ ($22–$31); set menu 36€ ($42). AE, DC, MC, V. Daily noon–midnight. Métro: Les Gobelins.

Inexpensive
Coco de Mer ✿ *(Finds* SEYCHELLE ISLANDS   The theme of this restaurant tugs at the emotions of Parisians who have spent their holidays on the beaches of the Seychelles in the Indian Ocean. It contains several dining rooms, one of which is outfitted like a beach, with a sand-covered floor, replicas of palm trees, and a scattering of conch shells. Menu items feature such exotic dishes as tartare of tuna flavored with ginger, olive oil, salt, and pepper; and smoked swordfish, served as carpaccio or in thin slices with mango mousse and a spicy sauce. Main courses focus on fish, including a species of red snapper *(boirzoes)* imported from the Seychelles. Dessert might be a crème de banana gratiné.

34 bd. St-Marcel. ☎ **01-47-07-06-64.** Reservations recommended. Main courses 14€–20€ ($16–$23); set menus 23€–30€ ($26–$35). AE, DC, MC, V. Tues–Sat noon–3pm; Mon–Sat 7:30pm–midnight. Métro: Les Gobelins or St-Marcel.

LEFT BANK: 6TH ARRONDISSEMENT
Expensive

Restaurant d'Hélène/Salon d'Hélène ★★★ SOUTHWESTERN
FRENCH   Hélène d'Arroze is the most famous female chef in Paris, a Basque-
born wunderkind whose southwestern French cuisine is a superb modern take
on a classic. Be very clear about what you want before you enter: The upstairs
dining room (Le Restaurant d'Hélène, with elaborately set round tables) is more
formal, expensive, and sedate than the bistro (Le Salon d'Hélène). In both areas,
expect bright, pop-influenced decor and relatively slow service. Upstairs, menus
are artfully composed and presented as part of fixed-price meals that contain,
among others, confit of foie gras with grilled apples; salad of white beans and
clams; and roast wild duck stuffed with foie gras and truffles. On street level,
food focuses on an array of plats du jour (skate Grenobloise with lemon and
capers) and tapas, which might include raw marinated tuna with Basque-derived
red-pepper sauce, or cannelloni gratinéed with Basque sheep's-milk cheese and
smoked Basque ham.

4 rue d'Assas. © 01-42-22-00-11. Reservations required. Restaurant fixed-price menus 150€–195€ ($173–
$224). Salon fixed-price lunch 61€ ($70); tapas 7€–15€ ($8–$17). AE, MC, V. Tues–Sat 12:30–2:15pm and
7:30–10pm. Métro: Sèvres-Babylone.

Moderate

Ze Kitchen Galerie ★ *Finds* FRENCH/INTERNATIONAL   The owner and
head chef of this restaurant trained in *haute* Parisian gastronomy under culinary
czar Guy Savoy. Since William Ledeuil established the place in 2001, he's
attracted the likes of First Lady Laura Bush, who dined here in 2002. The setting is a colorful loft space in an antique building, with an open-to-view showcase kitchen. Main courses are divided into meats and fish that are usually
cooked *a la plancha* (on a flat-top grill). The best examples include platters of
oysters, mussels, and sea urchins served with herb sauce and crostini; and grilled
shoulder of wild boar with tamarind sauce.

4 rue des Grands-Augustins. © 01-44-32-00-32. Reservations recommended. Main courses 21€–25€
($25–$29); fixed-price lunch with wine 21€–32€ ($24–$37). AE, DC, MC, V. Mon–Fri noon–2:30pm;
Mon–Sat 7–11pm. Closed Sun. Metro: Saint-Michel.

Inexpensive

Crémerie-Restaurant Polidor ★ *Kids* TRADITIONAL FRENCH
Crémerie Polidor is the most traditional bistro in the Odéon area, serving
cuisine familiale (home cooking). Its name dates from the early 1900s, when it
specialized in frosted cream desserts, but the restaurant can trace its history to
1845. The Crémerie was André Gide's favorite, and Joyce, Hemingway, Valéry,
Artaud, and Kerouac also dined here. The place still attracts students and artists,
who head for the rear. Peer beyond the lace curtains and brass hat racks to
see drawers where repeat customers lock up their cloth napkins. Overworked
but smiling waitresses serve the 19th-century cuisine. Try pumpkin soup
followed by boeuf bourguignon, Basque-style chicken, or *blanquette de veau*
(traditional veal stew). For dessert, order a chocolate, raspberry, or lemon tart—
the best in Paris.

41 rue Monsieur-le-Prince. © 01-43-26-95-34. Main courses 8€–15€ ($9–$17); fixed-price menu
(Mon–Fri) 9€ ($10) lunch, 18€–26€ ($21–$30) dinner. No credit cards. Daily noon–2:30pm; Mon–Sat
7pm–12:30am; Sun 7–11pm. Métro: Odéon.

LEFT BANK: 7TH & 14TH ARRONDISSEMENTS
Very Expensive

L'Arpège ★★★ MODERN FRENCH L'Arpège is best known for Alain Passard's specialties—no restaurant in the 7th serves better food. Surrounded by etched glass, burnished steel, monochromatic oil paintings, and pearwood paneling, you can enjoy specialties like couscous of vegetables and shellfish; lobster braised in the yellow wine of the Jura; pigeon roasted with almonds and honey-flavored mead; and carpaccio of crayfish with caviar-flavored cream sauce. While Passard is loath to include red meat on his menus, it does appear from time to time, in Kobe beef and (during late autumn and early winter) venison. But he focuses on fish, shellfish, poultry, and—his current passion—vegetables. These he elevates to levels unequalled by any other chef in Paris. The signature dessert is a candied tomato stuffed with 12 kinds of dried and fresh fruit, served with anise-flavored ice cream.

84 rue de Varenne, 7e. ✆ **01-47-05-09-06.** Fax 01-44-18-98-39. Reservations required far in advance. Main courses 74€–200€ ($85–$230); *menu dégustation* (tasting menu) 320€ ($368). AE, DC, MC, V. Mon–Fri 12:30–2:30pm and 8–10pm. Métro: Varenne.

Expensive

Le Violon d'Ingres ★★★ FRENCH This restaurant is Paris's pièce de résistance. Chef-owner Christian Constant is "the new Robuchon." Those fortunate enough to dine in Violon's warm atmosphere rave about the artistic dishes. They range from pan-fried foie gras with gingerbread and spinach salad to more

---

The Top Cafes

Whatever your pleasure—reading, meeting a lover, writing your memoirs, or drinking yourself into oblivion—you can do it at a French cafe.

Across from the Centre Pompidou, avant-garde **Café Beaubourg,** 100 rue St-Martin, 4e (✆ **01-48-87-63-96;** Métro: Rambuteau or Hôtel-de-Ville), boasts soaring concrete columns and minimalist decor by the architect Christian de Portzamparc. In summer, tables spill onto the sprawling terrace. The cafe is open Sunday through Thursday from 8am to 1am and Friday and Saturday from 8am to 2am.

The legendary **Deux Magots,** 6 place St-Germain-des-Prés, 6e (✆ **01-45-48-55-25;** Métro: St-Germain-des-Prés), is still the hangout for sophisticates and a tourist favorite in summer. Inside are two Asian statues that give the cafe its name. It's open daily from 7:30am to 1:30am.

Fouquet's, 99 av. des Champs-Elysées, 8e (✆ **01-47-23-50-00;** Métro: George-V), is the premier cafe on the Champs-Elysées. Outside, a barricade of potted flowers separates cafe tables from the sidewalk. Inside are a grill room and a restaurant. Both are open daily from 8am to 2am; the restaurant is open daily from noon to 3pm and 7pm to midnight.

At **La Coupole,** 102 bd. Montparnasse, 14e (✆ **01-43-20-14-20;** Métro: Vavin), the crowd ranges from artists' models to young men dressed like Rasputin. Perhaps order a coffee or cognac VSOP at one of the sidewalk tables. The dining room serves food that is sometimes good, sometimes indifferent. But people really come here to see and be seen. Open daily from 8:30am to 1am (buffet breakfast Mon–Fri 8:30–10:30am).

elegant main courses like lobster ravioli with crushed vine-ripened tomatoes; roasted veal in light, creamy milk sauce served with tender spring vegetables; and even a selection from the rotisserie, like spit-roasted leg of lamb rubbed with fresh garlic and thyme. A well-chosen selection of wine is offered. The service is charming and discreet.

135 rue St-Dominique, 7e. ⊙ **01-45-55-15-05.** Fax 01-45-55-48-42. Reservations required at least 4–5 days in advance. Main courses 40€–46€ ($46–$53); *menu dégustation* (tasting menu) 110€ ($126). AE, MC, V. Tues–Sat noon–2:30pm and 7–11:30pm.

SEEING THE SIGHTS IN THE CITY OF LIGHT

The best way to discover Paris is on foot. Walk along the grand avenue des Champs-Elysées, tour the quays of the Seine, wander around Ile de la Cité and Ile St-Louis, browse through the countless shops and stalls, wander through the famous squares and parks. Each turn will open a new vista.

SIGHTSEEING SUGGESTIONS FOR FIRST-TIME VISITORS

If You Have 1 Day Get up early and find a cafe for a typical Parisian breakfast of coffee and croissants. The two most popular museums are the **Louvre** and the **Musée d'Orsay;** the three most enduring monuments are the **Eiffel Tower,** the **Arc de Triomphe,** and **Notre-Dame.** If it's a toss-up between the Louvre and the d'Orsay, we'd choose the Louvre if you're a first-timer; if it's a toss-up between monuments, we'd make it the Eiffel Tower, for the view of the city. If your day is too short to visit museums, then spend your time strolling—the streets of Paris are live theater. The most elegant place for a walk is Ile St-Louis, filled with 17th-century mansions. On the **Left Bank,** wander St-Germain-des-Prés or place St-Michel, the heart of the student quarter. As the sun sets over Paris, head for **Notre-Dame** along the banks of the Seine, and watch the shadows fall over Paris and the lights come on.

If You Have 2 Days Spend your second day taking in the Right Bank. Begin at the **Arc de Triomphe** and stroll down the **Champs-Elysées,** the main boulevard of Paris, until you reach the Egyptian obelisk at **place de la Concorde.** Some of France's most notable figures met the guillotine here; it

affords terrific views of the **Madeleine,** the **Palais Bourbon,** the Arc de Triomphe, and the Louvre. Then we'd suggest a rest stop in the **Jardin de Tuileries,** or lunch in a Right Bank bistro. After exploring the heart of elegant, monumental Paris, why not go for a walk on the seedy side? Our favorite is a stroll along rue des Rosiers in the **Marais,** the heart of the Jewish community. After a rest, follow Hemingway's footsteps and head down to **Mont-parnasse** for a lively dinner.

If You Have 3 Days This is the day to follow your special interests. Many will want to visit the **Centre Pompi-dou.** You might explore the **Musée Picasso** as well, along with some of the galleries of the Marais. At mid-day, head for lunch in Paris's most charming square, **place des Vosges.** Reserve the afternoon for the **Ile de la Cité;** you can see the **Concierg-erie,** where Marie Antoinette and others were held prisoner, and the **Sainte-Chapelle** in the Palais de Justice, with its stunning stained glass. For dinner, we suggest a bistro in Le Marais.

If You Have 4 or 5 Days On your fourth day, go on your own or take an organized tour to **Versailles.** Then head back to the city for dinner and

Paris Attractions

Arc de Triomphe **5**
Basilique du Sacré-Coeur **24**
Bois de Boulogne **2**
Cathédrale Notre-Dame **17**
Centre Pompidou **20**
Cemetière du Père-Lachaise **22**
Conciergerie **19**

Eiffel Tower **3**
Hôtel des Invalides **1**
Jardin des Tuileries **8**
Jardin du Luxembourg **12**
Latin Quarter **14**
Montmartre **23**
Musée National d'Art Moderne **4**

Musée d'Orsay **9**
Musée du Louvre **10**
Musée National du Moyen
   Age/Musée de Cluny **11**
Musée Picasso **21**
Panthéon **13**
Parc Monceau **6**

Place de la Bastille **15**
Place de la Concorde **7**
Place des Vosges **16**
Sainte-Chapelle **18**

ⓘ Information
⊠ Post Office
— Railway

an evening stroll in the **Latin Quarter.** On your fifth day, devote at least a morning to **Montmarte,** on top of the highest of Paris's seven hills. Visit the **Basilica du Sacré-Coeur,** for the view if nothing else.

THE TOP MUSEUMS

Musée du Louvre ★★★   The Louvre is one of the world's largest and greatest museums. The $1.2 billion Grand Louvre Project, a 15-year undertaking, is officially complete, but refurbishment of individual galleries and paintings continues. For up-to-the-minute data on what is open or about to open, you can check out the website (www.louvre.fr).

The collection is staggering. You'll have to resign yourself to missing some masterpieces, because you simply can't see everything. People on one of those "Paris-in-a-day" tours race to glimpse the *Mona Lisa* and the *Venus de Milo.* Those with an extra 5 minutes go in pursuit of *Winged Victory.* The good news is that after 2 centuries here, the *Mona Lisa* has her own special room. To enter the Louvre, you pass through the 21m (71-ft.) **I. M. Pei glass pyramid** in the courtyard.

Tips on tickets: If you don't want to wait in line at the entrance of the pyramid or use the automatic ticket machines, you can order tickets over the phone (see below) with a credit card. You can also order advance tickets (and take a virtual tour) at the website. Tickets can be mailed to you in the U.S., or you can pick them up at any FNAC store location in Paris.

Pressed for time? Take a **guided tour** (in English), which lasts about 90 minutes. These start under the pyramid at the station marked ACCEIL DES GROUPES.

The collections are divided into seven departments: Asian antiquities; Egyptian antiquities; Greek, Etruscan, and Roman antiquities; sculpture; paintings; prints and drawings; and objets d'art. **The Grand Galerie,** a 180m (600-ft.) hall opening onto the Seine, is dedicated to mostly Italian paintings from the 1400s to the 1700s, including works by Raphael and Leonardo da Vinci.

The **Richelieu Wing** houses northern European and French paintings, decorative arts, French sculpture, Asian antiquities (a rich collection of Islamic art), and the grand salons of Napoleon III. Of the Greek and Roman antiquities, the most notable (aside from *Venus* and *Winged Victory*) are fragments of the Parthenon's frieze.

When you tire of strolling the galleries, you might like a pick-me-up at the Richelieu Wing's **Café Richelieu** or at **Café Marly,** 93 rue de Rivoli, 1er (☏ **01-49-26-06-60**). Boasting Napoleon III opulence, the Marly offers a perfect oasis. Try a cafe crème, a club sandwich, a pastry, or something from the bistro menu.

34–36 quai du Louvre, 1er. Main entrance in the glass pyramid, cour Napoléon. ☏ 01-40-20-53-17, 01-40-20-51-51 for recorded message, 08-92-68-46-94 for advance credit-card sales. www.louvre.fr. Admission 8.50€ ($9.75) before 3pm. Free for children under 18 Sun; free to all 1st Sun of every month. Mon and Wed 9am–9:30pm; Thurs–Sun 9am–6pm. Parts of museum begin to close at 5:30pm. 1½-hr. English-language tours Mon (short tour only) and Wed–Sat 3.50€ ($4), free for children under 13 with museum ticket. Métro: Palais Royal–Musée du Louvre.

Musée d'Orsay ★★★   The neoclassical Gare d'Orsay train station has been transformed into one of the world's great museums—and is now even bigger and better, with the completion in 2004 of new reception facilities, enhanced exhibition space, and a permanent Photography Gallery. It contains an important collection devoted to the pivotal years from 1848 to 1914. Across the Seine from the Louvre and the Tuileries, it is a repository of works by the Impressionists as well as the Symbolists, Pointillists, Realists, and late Romantics. Artists represented include van Gogh, Manet, Monet, Degas, and Renoir. It houses thousands of sculptures and paintings across 80 galleries, plus Belle Epoque furniture, photographs, objets d'art, architectural models, and a cinema.

One of Renoir's most joyous paintings is here: *Moulin de la Galette* (1876). Another celebrated work is by James McNeill Whistler—*Arrangement in Gray and Black: Portrait of the Painter's Mother.* The most famous piece in the museum is Manet's 1863 *Déjeuner sur l'herbe* (Picnic on the Grass).

1 rue de Bellechasse or 62 rue de Lille, 7e. (C) **01-40-49-48-14.** www.musee-orsay.fr. Admission 7€ ($8.05) adults, 5€ ($5.75) seniors and ages 18–24, free for children under 18. Tues–Wed and Fri–Sat 10am–6pm; Thurs 10am–9:45pm (June 20–Sept 20 9am–6pm); Sun 9am–6:30pm. Métro: Solférino. RER: Musée d'Orsay.

Musée Picasso ★★★   This museum offers an unparalleled view of the artist's career, including his fabled gaunt blue figures and harlequins. The world's greatest Picasso collection, acquired by the state in lieu of $50 million in inheritance taxes, consists of 203 paintings, 158 sculptures, 16 collages, 19 bas-reliefs, 88 ceramics, and more than 1,500 sketches and 1,600 engravings, plus 30 notebooks. These works span some 75 years of Picasso's life and changing styles. Paintings include a 1901 self-portrait and such masterpieces as *Le Baiser* (The Kiss). Another masterpiece is *Reclining Nude and the Man with a Guitar.*

In the Hôtel Salé, 5 rue de Thorigny, 3e. (C) **01-42-71-25-21.** www.paris.org/Musees/Picasso. Admission 5.50€ ($6.25) adults, 3€ ($3.45) seniors and ages 17–25, free for children under 19. Wed–Mon 9:30am–5:30pm. Métro: St-Paul, Filles du Calvaire, or Chemin Vert.

Centre Pompidou ★★★   This center for 20th-century art, designed by Richard Rogers and Renzo Piano, opened in 1977 and became the focus of controversy. Its bold exoskeletal architecture and the brightly painted pipes and ducts crisscrossing its transparent facade (green for water, red for heat, blue for air, and yellow for electricity) were jarring in the old Beaubourg neighborhood. The Centre Pompidou encompasses four separate attractions. The **Musée National d'Art Moderne (National Museum of Modern Art)** offers a large collection of 20th-century art. With some 40,000 works, this is the big draw, although only some 850 works can be displayed at one time. If you want to view some real charmers, see Alexander Calder's 1926 *Josephine Baker,* one of his earlier versions of the mobile, an art form he invented. Marcel Duchamp's *Valise* is a collection of miniature reproductions of his fabled Dada sculptures and drawings; they're displayed in a carrying case.

You can visit a re-creation of **l'Atelier Brancusi,** the Jazz Age studio of the Romanian sculptor; it's configured as a mini-museum slightly separate from the rest of the action.

Place Georges-Pompidou, 4e. (C) **01-44-78-12-33.** www.centrepompidou.fr. Admission 7€ ($8.05) adults, 5€ ($5.75) students, free for children under 18. Special exhibits 9€ ($10) adults, 7€ ($8.05) students, free for children under 13. Wed–Mon 11am–10pm. Métro: Rambuteau, Hôtel de Ville, or Châtelet–Les Halles.

ON THE CHAMPS-ELYSEES

Arc de Triomphe ★★★   At the western end of the Champs-Elysées, the Arc de Triomphe is the largest triumphal arch in the world, about 49m (163 ft.) high and 44m (147 ft.) wide. Don't cross the square to reach it! With a dozen streets radiating from the "Star," the traffic circle is vehicular roulette. Take the underground passage. Commissioned by Napoleon in 1806 to commemorate his Grande Armée's victories, the arch wasn't completed until 1836, under Louis-Philippe. Of the sculptures decorating the monument, the best known is Rude's *Marseillaise,* also called *The Departure of the Volunteers.* J. P. Cortot's *Triumph of Napoléon in 1810,* along with the *Resistance of 1814* and *Peace of 1815,* both by

Etex, also adorn the facade. The arch is engraved with the names of hundreds of generals who commanded troops in Napoleonic victories. You can take an elevator or climb the stairway to the top, where there's an exhibition hall with lithographs and photos depicting the arch throughout its history. From the observation deck, you have a panoramic view of the Champs-Elysées as well as such landmarks as the Louvre, the Eiffel Tower, and Sacré-Coeur.

Place Charles de Gaulle-Etoile, 16e. (© 01-55-37-73-77. www.monum.fr. Admission 7€ ($8.05) adults, 4.50€ ($5) ages 18–25, free for children under 18. Apr–Sept daily 10am–11pm; Oct–Mar daily 10am–10:30pm. Métro: Charles de Gaulle–Etoile. Bus: 22, 30, 31, 52, 73, or 92.

ILE DE LA CITE: WHERE PARIS WAS BORN

Medieval Paris, that architectural blending of grotesquerie and Gothic beauty, began on this island in the Seine. Explore as much of it as you can, but if you're in a hurry, try to visit at least Notre-Dame, the Sainte-Chapelle, and the Conciergerie.

Notre-Dame ★★★   For 6 centuries, it has stood as a Gothic masterpiece of the Middle Ages. You'll have to walk around the entire structure to appreciate this "vast symphony of stone" with its classic flying buttresses. Better yet, cross the bridge to the Left Bank and view it from the quay. From the square parvis (the courtyard in front), you can view the trio of 13th-century sculpted portals. On the left, the Portal of the Virgin depicts the signs of the zodiac and the Virgin's coronation. The central Portal of the Last Judgment is in three levels: the first shows Vices and Virtues; the second, Christ and his Apostles; and the third, Christ in triumph after the Resurrection. On the right is the Portal of Ste-Anne, depicting such scenes as the Virgin enthroned with Child. It's Notre-Dame's most perfect piece of sculpture. Over the central portal is a remarkable rose window, 9m (31 ft.) in diameter, forming a showcase for a statue of the Virgin and Child. Equally interesting is the Cloister Portal (around on the left), with its 13th-century Virgin, a unique survivor of many that originally adorned the facade. (Unfortunately, the child she's holding is decapitated.) In the **treasury** are displayed vestments and gold objects, including crowns.

If possible, view the interior at sunset. Of the three giant medallions that warm the austere cathedral, the north rose window in the transept, from the mid–13th century, is best. To visit the gargoyles immortalized by Victor Hugo (where Quasimodo lurked), you have to scale steps leading to the twin square towers, rising to a height of 68m (225 ft.). Once here, you can inspect those devils (some sticking out their tongues), hobgoblins, and birds of prey.

Approached through a garden behind Notre-Dame is the **Memorial des Martyrs Français de la Déportation.** This memorial honors the French martyrs of World War II, deported to camps like Auschwitz and Buchenwald. In blood red are the words (in French): "Forgive, but don't forget." It's open Monday through Friday from 8:30am to 9:45pm, Saturday and Sunday from 9am to 9:45pm. Admission is free.

6 place du parvis Notre-Dame, 4e. (© 01-42-34-56-10. www.paris.org/Monuments/NDame. Admission free to cathedral; towers 6.10€ ($7) adults, 4.10€ ($4.75) seniors and ages 18–25, free for children under 18; treasury 3€ ($3.45) adults, 2€ ($2.30) ages 12–25 and seniors, free for children under 12. Cathedral year-round daily 8am–6:45pm. Towers and crypt Apr–Sept daily 9:30am–6pm; Oct–Mar daily 10am–5:15pm. Museum Sat–Sun 2–5pm. Treasury Mon–Sat 9:30am–6pm. Métro: Cité or St-Michel. RER: St-Michel.

Sainte-Chapelle ★★★   Come here if for no other reason than to see one of the world's greatest examples of Flamboyant Gothic architecture—"the pearl among them all," as Proust called it—and brilliant stained-glass windows with a lacelike delicacy. Sainte-Chapelle is Paris's second-most important monument of the Middle Ages (after Notre-Dame); it was erected to enshrine relics from the First Crusade, including the Crown of Thorns, two pieces from the True Cross, and the Roman lance that pierced the side of Christ.

Viewed on a bright day, the 15 stained-glass windows depicting Bible scenes seem to glow ruby red and Chartres blue. The walls consist almost entirely of the glass. Built in only 5 years, beginning in 1246, the chapel has two levels. You enter through the lower chapel, supported by flying buttresses and ornamented with fleurs-de-lis. The servants of the palace used the lower chapel, and the upper chamber was for the king and his courtiers; the latter is reached by ascending a narrow spiral staircase. Sainte-Chapelle stages **concerts** in summer, with tickets at 19€ to 25€ ($22–$29). Call (C 01-42-77-65-65 from 11am to 6pm daily for details.

Palais de Justice, 4 bd. du Palais, 1er. (C 01-53-73-78-50. www.monum.fr. Free admission. Apr–Sept daily 9:30am–6:30pm; Oct–Mar daily 10am–5pm. Métro: Cité, St-Michel, or Châtelet–Les Halles. RER: St-Michel.

THE EIFFEL TOWER & ENVIRONS ★★★

From place du Trocadéro, you can step between the wings of the Palais de Chaillot and gaze out on a panoramic view. At your feet lie the Jardins du Trocadéro. Directly in front of you, the Pont d'Iéna spans the Seine, leading to the Eiffel Tower. Beyond, stretching as far as your eye can see, is the Champ-de-Mars, a garden with arches, grottoes, lakes, and cascades.

Eiffel Tower ★★★   This may be the single most recognizable structure in the world—it's the symbol of Paris. Gustave-Alexandre Eiffel built it for the Universal Exhibition of 1889. The tower, including its 17m (55-ft.) TV antenna, is 317m (1,056 ft.) tall. Its open-framework construction ushered in the almost-unlimited possibilities of steel construction, paving the way for skyscrapers.

You can visit the tower in three stages: Taking the elevator to the first landing, you'll have a view over the rooftops of Paris. There are a cinema, museum, restaurants, and a bar open year-round. The second landing provides a panoramic look at the city (on this level is Le Jules Verne restaurant). The third landing offers the best view, allowing you to identify monuments and buildings. To get to **Le Jules Verne** ((C 01-45-55-61-44), take the private south foundation elevator. You can enjoy an aperitif in the piano bar, then take a seat at one of the dining room's tables, all of which provide an inspiring view. Reservations are recommended. *Insider tip:* The least expensive way to see the tower is to walk up the first two floors for 3.20€ ($3.60). You bypass the long lines for the elevator.

Champ de Mars, 7e. (C 01-44-11-23-23. www.tour-eiffel.fr. Admission to 1st landing 3.70€ ($4.25), 2nd landing 7€ ($8.05), 3rd landing 10€ ($12). Stairs to 2nd floor 3€ ($3.45). Sept–May daily 9:30am–11pm; June–Aug daily 9am–midnight. Fall and winter, stairs open only to 6:30pm. Métro: Trocadéro, Ecole Militaire, or Bir Hakeim. RER: Champ de Mars–Tour Eiffel.

Hôtel des Invalides (Napoléon's Tomb) ★★★   The glory of the French military lives on in the **Musée de l'Armée.** Included in the collections (begun in 1794) are Viking swords, Burgundian basinets, 14th-century blunderbusses, Balkan khandjars, American Browning machine guns, war pitchforks, salamander-engraved Renaissance serpentines, musketoons, and grenadiers. As a sardonic touch, there's even Gen. Daumesnil's wooden leg. There are suits of armor worn by kings and dignitaries. The famous "armor suit of the lion" was made for François I. The displays of swords are among the world's finest.

Crossing the Cour d'Honneur (Court of Honor), you'll come to **Eglise du Dôme,** designed by Hardouin-Mansart for Louis XIV. He began work on the church in 1677, though he died before its completion. In the Napoléon Chapel is the hearse used at the emperor's funeral on May 9, 1821. To accommodate the Tomb of Napoléon—made of red porphyry, with a green granite base—the architect Visconti had to redesign the high altar. First buried at St. Helena, Napoleon's remains were returned to Paris in 1840.

Place des Invalides, 7e. (℃ **01-44-42-37-72.** Admission to Musée de l'Armée, Napoléon's Tomb, and Musée des Plans-Reliefs (a museum in the Hôtel des Invalides containing scale models of French fortresses and fortified towns of the 17th and 18th c.) 7€ ($8.05) adults, 5€ ($5.75) students, free for children under 19. Oct–Mar daily 10am–5pm; Apr–May and Sept daily 10am–6pm; June–Aug daily 10am–7pm. Closed Jan 1, May 1, Nov 1, Dec 25. Métro: Latour-Maubourg, Varenne, or Invalides.

IN MONTMARTRE ✫✫✫

From the 1880s to just before World War I, Montmartre enjoyed its golden age as the world's best-known art colony, where *la vie de bohème* reigned supreme.

Before its discovery, Montmartre was a sleepy farming community, with windmills dotting the landscape. Those who find the trek up to Paris's highest elevations too much of a climb may prefer to ride **Le Petit Train de Montmartre,** which passes all the major landmarks; it seats 55 and offers English commentary. Board at place Blanche (near the Moulin Rouge); the fare is 5.50€ ($6.25) adults, 3.50€ ($4) children under 13. From June to September, trains run daily from 10am to 10pm; off season, daily from 10am to 6pm. For information, contact **Promotrain,** 131 rue de Clignancourt, 18e (℃ **01-42-62-24-00**).

The simplest way to reach Montmartre is to take the Métro to Anvers, then walk up rue du Steinkerque to the funicular, which runs to the precincts of Sacré-Coeur every day from 5:30am to 12:30am. Except for Sacré-Coeur, Montmartre has only minor attractions; it's the architecture and the atmosphere that are compelling.

Specific attractions to look for include the **Bateau-Lavoir (Boat Warehouse),** on place Emile-Goudeau. Although gutted by fire in 1970, it has been reconstructed. Picasso once lived here and, in the winter of 1905–06, painted one of the world's most famous portraits, *The Third Rose* (Gertrude Stein).

Espace Montmartre Salvadore-Dalí, 11 rue Poulbot, 18e (℃ **01-42-64-40-10**), presents Dalí's phantasmagorical world with 330 original works, including his 1956 *Don Quixote* lithograph. It's open daily from 10am to 6:30pm (until 9pm July–Aug); admission is 7€ ($8.05) for adults, 6€ ($6.90) for seniors, and 5€ ($5.75) for ages 8 to 26. It's free for children under 8.

Basilique du Sacré-Coeur ✫✫✫   Montmartre's crowning achievement is Sacré-Coeur, though its view of Paris takes precedence over the basilica itself. Its gleaming white domes and campanile tower over Paris like a Byzantine church of the 12th century. But it's not that old: After France's defeat by the Prussians in 1870, the basilica was planned as an offering to cure the country's misfortunes; rich and poor alike contributed. Construction began in 1873, but the church wasn't consecrated until 1919. The interior is decorated with mosaics, the most striking of which are the ceiling depiction of Christ and the mural of the Passion at the back of the altar. The crypt contains what some believe is a piece of the sacred heart of Christ—hence the church's name. On a clear day, the vista from the dome can extend for 56km (35 miles).

Place St-Pierre, 18e. (℃ **01-53-41-89-00.** www.paris.org/Monuments/Sacre.Coeur. Free admission to basilica; joint ticket to dome and crypt 5€ ($5.75) adults. Basilica daily 6am–11pm; dome and crypt daily 9am–6pm. Métro: Abbesses; take the elevator to the surface and follow the signs to the funicular, which goes up to the church for the price of a Métro ticket.

Cimetière de Montmartre ✦ Novelist Alexandre Dumas and Russian dancer Vaslav Nijinsky are just a few of the famous composers, writers, and artists interred here. The remains of the great Stendhal are here, along with Hector Berlioz, Heinrich Heine, Edgar Degas, Jacques Offenbach, and even François Truffaut.

20 av. Rachel (west of the Butte Montmartre and north of bd. de Clichy), 18e. ✆ **01-53-42-36-30.** Sun–Fri 8am–6pm; Sat 8:30am–6pm (closes at 5:30pm in winter). Métro: La Fourche.

IN THE LATIN QUARTER ✦✦
This is the Left Bank precinct of the **University of Paris (the Sorbonne).** Rabelais called it the *Quartier Latin* because of the students and professors who spoke Latin in the classrooms and on the streets. The sector teems with belly dancers, restaurants from Vietnamese to Balkan, sidewalk cafes, bookstalls, and clubs in smoky cellars.

A good starting point is **place St-Michel** (Métro: St-Michel), where the young Balzac got water from the fountain. The quarter centers around **boulevard St-Michel,** to the south (the students call it "Boul Mich").

Musée National du Moyen Age (Musée de Cluny) ✦✦ There are two reasons to come here: the world's finest collection of art from the Middle Ages, including jewelry and tapestries; and the well-preserved manor house, built atop Roman baths, that holds the collection. The Cluny was the mansion of a 15th-century abbot. By 1515, it was the home of Mary Tudor, the widow of Louis XII and daughter of Henry VII of England and Elizabeth of York. Most people come to see the **Unicorn Tapestries** ✦✦✦, discovered a century ago in the Château de Boussac in the Auvergne. Five seem to deal with the senses (one depicts a unicorn looking into a mirror held by a maiden). The sixth shows a woman under an elaborate tent, her pet dog resting on an embroidered cushion beside her. The lovable unicorn and its friendly companion, a lion, hold back the flaps. Downstairs are the ruins of the Roman baths, dating from around A.D. 200.

Insider tip: The garden represents a return to the Middle Ages. It was inspired by the luxuriant detail of the museum's most fabled treasure, the 15th-century tapestry of *The Lady of the Unicorn.* It's small, but richly planted.

In the Hôtel de Cluny, 6 place Paul-Painlevé, 5e. ✆ **01-53-73-78-15.** Admission 5.50€ ($6.25) adults, 4€ ($4.60) ages 18–25, free for children under 18. Wed–Mon 9:15am–5:45pm. Métro: Cluny–La Sorbonne.

HISTORIC GARDENS & SQUARES
GARDENS Bordering place de la Concorde, the statue-studded **Jardin des Tuileries** ✦✦, 1er (✆ **01-44-50-75-01;** Métro: Tuileries), are as much a part of Paris as the Seine. Le Nôtre, Louis XIV's gardener and planner of the Versailles grounds, was the designer. **Jardin du Luxembourg** ✦✦, 6e (✆ **01-44-61-20-89;** Métro: Odéon; RER: Luxembourg), has always been associated with artists; students from the Sorbonne and children predominate nowadays. The gardens are the best on the Left Bank (if not in all of Paris).

SQUARES In **place de la Bastille** ✦, 3e, on July 14, 1789, a mob of Parisians attacked the Bastille and sparked the French Revolution. Nothing remains of the historic Bastille, built in 1369. Many prisoners were kept within its walls, the best known being the "Man in the Iron Mask." Bastille Day is celebrated with great festivity on July 14. In the center of the square is the Colonne de Juillet (July Column), but it doesn't commemorate the revolution. It honors the victims of the 1830 July revolution, which put Louis-Philippe on the throne.

Place des Vosges ✦✦✦, 4e (Métro: St-Paul or Chemin Vert), is Paris's oldest square and once its most fashionable. In the heart of the Marais, it was called the Palais Royal in the days of Henri IV, who planned to live here—but his assassin, Ravaillac, had other ideas. Henry II was killed while jousting on the square in 1559. Its *grand siècle* redbrick houses are ornamented with white stone. Its covered arcades allowed people to shop at all times, even in the rain—an innovation at the time.

The Champs-Elysées begins at **place de la Concorde** ★★★, an octagonal traffic hub built in 1757 to honor Louis XV and one of the world's grandest squares. The statue of the king was torn down in 1792 and the name of the square changed to place de la Révolution. Floodlit at night, it's dominated by an Egyptian obelisk from Luxor, the oldest man-made object in Paris; it was carved around 1200 B.C. and presented to France in 1829 by the viceroy of Egypt. During the Reign of Terror, Dr. Guillotin's little invention was erected on this spot and claimed thousands of lives.

For a spectacular sight, look down the Champs-Elysées—the view is framed by Coustou's Marly horses, which once graced the gardens at Louis XIV's Château de Marly (these are copies—the originals are in the Louvre).

HISTORIC PARKS & A CEMETERY

PARKS   One of the most spectacular parks in Europe is the **Bois de Boulogne** ★★★, Porte Dauphine, 16e (© **01-40-67-90-82;** Métro: Les-Sablons, Porte-Maillot, or Porte-Dauphine). Horse-drawn carriages traverse it, but you can also drive through. Many of its hidden pathways, however, must be discovered by walking. The park was once a forest for royal hunts. When Napoleon III gave the grounds to the city in 1852, Baron Haussmann developed them. Separating Lac Inférieur from Lac Supérieur is the Carrefour des Cascades (you can stroll under its waterfall). The Lower Lake contains two islands connected by a footbridge.

Parc Monceau ★, 17e (© **01-42-27-39-56;** Métro: Monceau or Villiers), is ringed with 18th- and 19th-century mansions, some evoking Proust's *Remembrance of Things Past*. It was built in 1778 by the duc d'Orléans (or Philippe-Egalité, as he became known). Parc Monceau was laid out with an Egyptian-style obelisk, a thatched alpine farmhouse, a Chinese pagoda, a Roman temple, an enchanted grotto, various chinoiseries, and a waterfall. The park was opened to the public during Napoleon III's Second Empire.

A CEMETERY   Cemetière du Père-Lachaise ★★, 16 rue de Repos, 20e (© **01-55-25-82-10;** Métro: Père-Lachaise), contains more illustrious dead than any other cemetery. When it comes to name-dropping, this cemetery knows no peer—it's been called the "grandest address in Paris." Everybody from Sarah Bernhardt to Oscar Wilde is buried here. So are Balzac, Delacroix, and Bizet. Colette's body was taken here in 1954, and her black granite slab always bears flowers (legend has it that cats replenish the red roses). In time, the "little sparrow," Edith Piaf, followed. Marcel Proust's black tombstone rarely lacks a bunch of violets. Some tombs are sentimental favorites—Jim Morrison's reportedly draws the most visitors. Another stone is marked Gertrude Stein on one side and Alice B. Toklas on the other. The cemetery is open Monday through Friday from 8am to 6pm, Saturday from 8:30am to 6pm, and Sunday from 9am to 6pm (closes at 5:30pm Nov to early Mar).

ORGANIZED TOURS

BY BUS   Cityrama, 149 rue St-Honoré, 1er (© **01-44-55-61-00;** Métro: Palais-Royal–Musée-du-Louvre), offers the most popular get-acquainted tour. A double-decker bus takes you on a 2-hour ride through the city. You don't go inside any attractions, but you get a look at the outside of Notre-Dame and the Eiffel Tower, among other sights. There's commentary in 10 languages on earphones. Tours depart daily at 10am, 11am, 2pm, and 3pm. There are additional tours Saturday and Sunday at 11:30am, and between March and October, there are tours every day at 3:30 and 4:30pm. A 2-hour orientation tour is 24€ ($28). A morning tour with interior visits to Notre-Dame and the Louvre costs 48€ ($55). A tour of the nighttime illuminations leaves daily at 10pm in summer, 7pm in winter, and costs 24€ ($28); it tends to be touristy.

The **RATP** (© **08-92-68-77-14**) operates the **Balabus,** a fleet of orange-and-white big-windowed motor coaches, on Sunday and national holidays only. For information, see "Getting Around: By Bus," earlier in this chapter.

BY BOAT   Bateaux-Mouche (© **01-40-76-99-99;** Métro: Alma-Marceau) cruises depart from the Right Bank of the Seine, adjacent to Pont de l'Alma, and last about 75 minutes. Tours leave daily at 20- to 30-minute intervals from 10:15am to 11pm between May and October. Between November and April, there are at least nine departures daily between 11am and 9pm, with a schedule that changes according to demand and the weather. Fares are 7€ ($8.05) for adults and 4€ ($4.60) for children under 13. Dinner cruises depart Tuesday to Saturday at 8:30pm, last 3 hours, and cost 125€ ($144). On dinner cruises, jackets and ties are required for men.

Batobus (© **01-44-11-33-99**) boats are 150-passenger ferries with big windows. See "Getting Around: By Boat," earlier in this chapter, for information.

THE SHOPPING SCENE

The City of Light is one of the rare places in the world where you don't go anywhere in particular to shop—shopping surrounds you on almost every street. You don't have to buy anything—just peer in the *vitrines* (display windows), absorb cutting-edge ideas, witness trends—and take home an education in style.

Shops are usually open Monday through Saturday from 10am to 7pm, but hours vary, and Paris doesn't run at full throttle on Monday morning. Small shops sometimes take a 2-hour lunch break. Thursday is the best day for late-night shopping, with stores open until 9 or 10pm.

THE BEST BUYS

Perfumes and **cosmetics,** including such famous brands as Guerlain, Chanel, Schiaparelli, and Jean Patou, are almost always cheaper in Paris than in the United States. Paris is also a good place to buy Lalique and Baccarat **crystal.** They're expensive but still priced below international market value.

From Chanel to Yves Saint Laurent, Nina Ricci to Sonia Rykiel, the city overflows with **fashion** boutiques, ranging from haute couture to the truly outlandish. Accessories, such as those by Louis Vuitton and Céline, are among the finest in the world. Smart Parisians know how to dress in style without mortgaging their condos: They head for discount and resale shops. **Anna Lowe,** 104 rue du Faubourg St-Honoré, 8e (© **01-42-66-11-32;** Métro: Miromesnil), is one of the top boutiques for women who wish to purchase a Chanel or a Versace at a discount, *bien sur.* Many clothes are runway samples; some have been gently worn. French film stars often shop at **Défilé des Marques,** 171 rue de Grenelles, 7e (© **01-45-55-63-47;** Métro: Latour-Maubourg), but anyone can pick up discounted Laurent, Dior, Lacroix, Prada, Chanel, Versace, Hermès, and others.

Lingerie is another great French export. All the top lingerie designers are represented in boutiques as well as in the major department stores, Galeries Lafayette and Le Printemps.

Chocolate lovers will find much to tempt them in Paris. **Christian Constant,** 37 rue d'Assas, 6e ((**C** **01-53-63-15-15;** Métro: St-Placide), produces some of Paris's most sinfully delicious chocolates. Racks and racks of chocolates are priced individually or by the kilo at **Maison du Chocolat,** 225 rue du Faubourg St-Honoré, 8e ((**C** **01-42-27-39-44;** Métro: Ternes), though it'll cost you about 92€ ($106) for a kilo (2.2 lb.). There are five other branches around Paris.

GREAT SHOPPING AREAS

1er & 8e   Because these two adjoin each other and form the heart of Paris's best Right Bank shopping, they function as one shopping neighborhood. This area includes the famed **rue du Faubourg St-Honoré,** where the big designer houses are, and **avenue des Champs-Elysées,** where the mass-market and teen scenes are hot.

At one end of the 1st is the **Palais Royal,** where an arcade of boutiques flanks the garden of the former palace. At the other side of town, at the end of the 8th, lies **avenue Montaigne** (Métro: Franklin-D-Roosevelt or Alma-Marceau), 2 blocks of the fanciest shops in the world, where you float from big name to big name. You'll find fabulous perfumes at **Parfums Caron** ((**C** **01-47-23-40-82**), 34 av. Montaigne, which was founded in 1904.

3e & 4e   The difference between these two arrondissements gets fuzzy, especially around **place des Vosges,** center stage of Le Marais. Even so, they offer several dramatically different shopping experiences.

On the surface, the shopping includes the real-people stretch of **rue de Rivoli** (which becomes **rue St-Antoine**). Two department stores are in this area. **La Samaritaine,** 19 rue de la Monnaie ((**C** **01-40-41-20-20;** Métro: Pont Neuf), occupies four architecturally noteworthy buildings erected between 1870 and 1927. Of special interest are the annual sales in October and November, when much, but not all, of the merchandise is reduced by 20% to 40%. **BHV (Bazar de l'Hôtel de Ville),** which opened in 1856, has seven floors loaded with merchandise. It lies adjacent to Paris's City Hall at 52–64 rue de Rivoli ((**C** **01-42-74-90-00;** Métro: Hôtel de Ville).

In the Marais is a medieval warren of tiny twisting streets chockablock with cutting-edge designers and up-to-the-minute fashions and trends. Start by walking around place des Vosges to see art galleries, designer shops, and fabulous little finds, then dive in and get lost in the area leading to the Musée Picasso.

Place de la Bastille—an up-and-coming area for artists and galleries—is in the 4th arrondissement (leading to the 12th), as is the Ile St-Louis. The **Viaduc des Arts,** 9–147 av. Daumesnil, 12e ((**C** **01-44-75-80-66**), begins at the Opéra Bastille and stretches to the 12th arrondissement. This is a complex of boutiques and craft workshops, occupying the vaulted spaces beneath one of the 19th-century railway access routes into the Gare de Lyon.

6e & 7e   While the 6th arrondissement is one of the most famous shopping districts—it's the soul of the Left Bank—a lot of the good stuff is hidden in the zone that becomes the wealthy 7th. **Rue du Bac,** stretching from the 6th to the 7th in a few blocks, stands for all that wealth and glamour can buy. The street is jammed with art galleries, home-decorating stores, and gourmet-food shops.

9e   To add to the fun of shopping the Right Bank, the 9th arrondissement sneaks in behind the 1st, so if you don't choose to walk toward the Champs-Elysées and the 8th, you can head to the big department stores in a row along **boulevard Haussmann** in the 9th. These stores include not only the mammoth French icons, **Au Printemps,** 64 bd. Haussmann, 9e (© **01-42-82-50-00;** Métro: Havre-Caumartin; RER: Auber), and **Galeries Lafayette,** 40 bd. Hauss-mann, 9e (© **01-42-82-34-56;** Métro: Chausée d'Antin–La Fayette; RER: Auber), but a large branch of Britain's **Marks & Spencer,** 35 bd. Haussmann, 9e (© **01-47-42-42-91;** Métro: Chausée d'Antin; RER: Auber).

PARIS AFTER DARK
THE PERFORMING ARTS

Announcements of shows, concerts, and operas are on kiosks all over town. You can find listings in *Pariscope,* a weekly entertainment guide, and the English-language *Boulevard,* a bimonthly magazine.

There are many ticket agencies in Paris, but most are near the Right Bank hotels. *Avoid them if possible.* You can buy the cheapest tickets at the theater box office. Tip the usher who shows you to your seat in a theater or movie house.

Several agencies sell tickets for cultural events and plays at discounts of up to 50%. One is the **Kiosque Théâtre,** 15 place de la Madeleine, 8e (no phone; Métro: Madeleine), offering leftover tickets for about half price on the day of performance. Tickets for evening performances are sold Tuesday through Friday from 12:30 to 8pm and Saturday from 2 to 8pm. For matinees, tickets are sold Saturday from 12:30 to 2pm and Sunday from 12:30 to 4pm.

For easy access to tickets for festivals, concerts, and the theater, try one of two locations of the **FNAC** department-store chain: 136 rue de Rennes, 6e (© **01-49-54-30-00;** Métro: St. Placide), or in the Forum des Halles, 1–7 rue Pierre-Lescot, 1er (© **01-40-41-40-00;** Métro: Châtelet–Les-Halles).

Even those with only a modest understanding of French can delight in a sparkling production of Molière at the **Comédie-Française,** 2 rue de Richelieu, 1er (© **01-44-58-15-15;** www.comedie-francaise.fr; Métro: Palais-Royal–Musée-du-Louvre), established to keep the classics alive and to promote important contemporary authors. The box office is open daily from 11am to 6pm; the hall is dark from July 21 to September 5. The Left Bank annex is the **Comédie-Française-Théâtre du Vieux-Colombier,** 21 rue du Vieux-Colombier, 4e (© **01-44-39-87-00;** Métro: Sèvres-Babylone or Saint-Sulpice). Although its repertoire can vary, it's known for presenting some of the most serious French dramas in town.

The **Opéra Bastille,** place de la Bastille, 120 rue de Lyon, 12e (© **08-92-89-90-90;** Métro: Bastille), was inaugurated in July 1989, for the Revolution's bicentennial. Since its much-publicized opening, the opera house has presented works like Mozart's *Marriage of Figaro* and Tchaikovsky's *Queen of Spades.* The main hall is the largest French opera house, with 2,700 seats, but music critics have lambasted the acoustics. The building contains two additional concert halls, including an intimate room seating 250, usually used for chamber music. Both traditional opera performances and symphony concerts are presented here. There are sometimes free concerts on French holidays; call before your visit.

Opéra Garnier, place de l'Opéra, 9e (② **08-92-89-90-90;** Métro: Opéra), is the premier stage for dance and opera. Because of the competition from the Opéra Bastille, the original opera has made great efforts to present more up-to-date works. Charles Garnier designed this rococo wonder in the heyday of the empire. The facade is adorned with marble and sculpture, including *The Dance* by Carpeaux. Restoration has returned the Garnier to its former glory, the ceiling (painted by Marc Chagall) has been cleaned, and air-conditioning has been added. The box office is open Monday through Saturday from 11am to 6:30pm.

Conceived by the Mitterrand administration, **Cité de la Musique,** 221 av. Jean-Jaurès, 19e (② **01-44-84-45-00,** or 01-44-84-44-84 for tickets and information; Métro: Porte-de-Pantin), has been widely applauded. At the city's northeastern edge in what used to be a run-down neighborhood, the $120 million stone-and-glass structure, designed by Christian de Portzamparc, incorporates a network of concert halls, a library and research center, and a museum. The complex stages a variety of concerts, ranging from Renaissance to 20th-century programs.

For the best orchestra performances in France, try **Maison de Radio France,** 116 av. du Président-Kennedy, 16e (② **01-56-40-15-16;** Métro: Passy-Ranelagh), which offers top-notch concerts with guest conductors. It's the home of the Orchestre Philharmonique de Radio France and the Orchestre National de France. The box office is open Monday through Saturday from 11am to 6pm.

NIGHTCLUBS & CABARETS

Folies-Bergère Folies-Bergère is a Paris institution; foreigners have flocked here since 1886. Josephine Baker became "the toast of Paris" here. Since the naughty Belle Epoque days when the cancan was likely to be performed by women who didn't necessarily wear underpants, Folies-Bergère has witnessed many changes, many modernizations, and an attempt in the mid-1990s to become a "legitimate" dramatic theater. (It didn't work particularly well—audiences preferred the cabaret revues that had made the place famous.)

In 2002, Folies-Bergère reverted to its original role, mounting 2-hour revues in a state-of-the-art 1,600-seat theater that showcase an appreciation for the (partially unclothed) elegance and allure of *la femme.* Be prepared for G-strings and brassieres, which management refers to as *léger, léger* (very light), lots of feathers and sequins, and all the ooh-la-la razzmatazz you'd expect. Each show includes two female singers performing in a mixture of French and English, a juggler, and lots of mostly female flesh. Shows are usually presented Tuesday through Sunday at 9pm. 34 rue Richer, 9e. ② 01-44-79-98-98. www.foliesbergere.com. Tickets 34€–52€ ($39–$60); fixed-price dinner (includes access to show) 90€ ($104). Metro: Grands Boulevards or Cadet.

Moulin Rouge This is a camp classic. The establishment that Toulouse-Lautrec immortalized is still here, but the artist would probably have a hard time recognizing it. Colette created a scandal here by offering an on-stage kiss to Mme de Morny, but shows today have a harder time shocking audiences. Try to get a table—the view is much better on the main floor than from the bar. What's the theme? Strip routines and the saucy sexiness of *la Belle Epoque,* and permissive Paris between the wars. Handsome men and girls, girls, girls, virtually all topless, keep the place going. Dance finales usually include two dozen of the belles ripping loose with a topless cancan. Revues begin nightly at 9 and 11pm. Place Blanche, 18e. ② 01-53-09-82-82. Cover including champagne 82€–90€ ($94–$104); 7pm dinner and show 130€–160€ ($150–$184); cover for seats at the bar (including 2 drinks) 63€ ($72); 7pm dinner and show 125€ ($144). Métro: Blanche.

LIVE MUSIC & DANCING

JAZZ   The great jazz revival is still going strong here. Most clubs are on the Left Bank near the Seine, between rue Bonaparte and rue St-Jacques. For the latest details, see *Jazz Hot, Jazz Magazine,* or *Pariscope.* **Au Duc des Lombards,** 42 rue des Lombards, 1er (© **01-42-33-22-88;** Métro: Châtelet), is comfortable and appealing. Performers begin playing nightly at 9pm and continue (with breaks) for 5 hours, touching on everything from free jazz to more traditional forms like hard bop. Cover is 19€ to 23€ ($22–$26). **Le Bilboquet,** 13 rue St-Benoît, 6e (© **01-45-48-81-84;** Métro: St-Germain-des-Prés), schedules some of the best music in the city. Jazz is featured on the upper level in a wood-paneled room with a copper ceiling, brass-trimmed bar, and Victorian candelabra. The classic French menu is limited; dinner costs 55€ ($63). There's no cover. Hours are Tuesday through Saturday from 8pm to 2am; jazz music 9:30pm to 1:30am.

DANCE CLUBS   The area around the Eglise St-Germain-des-Prés is full of dance clubs. For the most up-to-date information, see *Time Out, Pariscope,* or *L'Officiel des Spectacles.* **Batofar,** facing 11 quai François Mauriac, 13e (© **01-56-29-10-33;** Métro: Quai de la Gare), is proud of its status as a club that everybody views as hip. It sits on a converted barge that floats on the Seine, sometimes with hundreds of gyrating dancers, most of whom are in their 20s and 30s. House, garage, techno, and live jazz by groups that hail from (among other places) Morocco, Senegal, and Germany sometimes add to the mix. Come here for an insight into late-night Paris at its most raffish and countercultural. The cover ranges from 8€ to 15€ ($9–$17). Tapas prices start at 4€ ($4.60) and beer costs around 7€ ($8.05) a bottle. Hours are Tuesday through Saturday from 6pm to 3 or 4am, depending on business. It's closed November through March.

ROCK   **Bus Palladium,** 6 rue Fontaine, 9e (© **01-53-21-07-33;** Métro: Blanche or Pigalle), is a single room with a long bar, a rock 'n' roll temple with

---

Native Behavior

Call adult males *Monsieur* ("sir"). Addressing women isn't so easy. When the English say "Mrs.," the French say *Madame.* If you're talking to an unmarried woman, call her *Mademoiselle.* When in doubt, go with Madame.

After you get to know someone, if only briefly, kisses (called *bises* in French) are freely exchanged. Women kiss women and men kiss women, and often men kiss each other, one kiss for each cheek. If you're not at the kissing stage, handshaking will do.

The French believe that "going Dutch"—that is, splitting the bill—is best left for the Dutch. If you invite someone for drinks or dinner, you are expected to pay the bill. Don't ask the waiter to split the tab. The French would view that as barbaric.

If invited to someone's home, bring a gift. Wine will do, but not a cheap bottle. Flowers are also good to carry along, but never chrysanthemums: They're reserved for paying respects to the dead.

If you can, do as the Parisians do and avoid Paris in summer. As Catherine Deneuve once noted, "That is the time we turn the city over to American tourists and pickpockets."

varnished hardwoods and fabric-covered walls that barely absorb the reverberations of nonstop recorded music. It appeals to hard-core, mostly heterosexual, rock wannabes ages 25 to 35. Alcoholic drinks cost 10€ to 13€ ($12–$15) except for women on Tuesday, when they drink free. The cover is 20€ ($23) all the time for men, and Friday and Saturday only for women.

GAY & LESBIAN BARS   Gay life centers on Les Halles and Le Marais, with the greatest concentration of establishments between the Hôtel-de-Ville and Rambuteau Métro stops.

Banana Café, 13 rue de la Ferronnerie, 1er (© **01-42-33-35-31;** Métro: Châtelet–Les Halles), is the most popular gay bar in the Marais. On two floors of a 19th-century building, it has dim lighting and a well-publicized policy of raising the price of drinks after 10pm. There's a street-level bar and a dance floor in the cellar featuring a live pianist and recorded music. On many nights, go-go dancers perform on spotlit platforms.

Le Pulp, 25 bd. Poissonnière, 2e (© **01-40-26-01-93;** Métro: Grand Blvd.), is one of the most popular lesbian discos in Paris. The decor, evoking a burgundy-colored 19th-century French music hall, makes its seedy past a distant memory. Today it's fun, trendy, and chic. It's best to show up before midnight. The venue, as the French like to say, is very cool, with all types of cutting-edge music in a setting that just happens to discourage the presence of men.

DAY TRIPS FROM PARIS: THE ILE DE FRANCE

VERSAILLES 🌟🌟🌟   Within 50 years the **Château de Versailles** (© **01-30-83-78-00;** www.chateauversailles.fr) was transformed from Louis XIII's simple hunting lodge into an extravagant palace. What you see today is the greatest living museum of a vanished way of life. Begun in 1661, the construction of the château involved 32,000 to 45,000 workmen, some of whom had to drain marshes—often at the cost of their lives—and move forests. Louis XIV set out to create a palace that would awe all Europe, and the result was a symbol of pomp and opulence that has been copied yet never duplicated.

The six magnificent **Grands Appartements** 🌟🌟🌟 are in the Louis XIV style; each takes its name from the allegorical painting on its ceiling. The most famous room is the 72m (236-ft.) **Hall of Mirrors** 🌟🌟🌟. Begun by Mansart in 1678 in the Louis XIV style, it was decorated by Le Brun with 17 arched windows matched by beveled mirrors in simulated arcades.

Spread across 100 hectares (250 acres), the **Gardens of Versailles** 🌟🌟🌟 were laid out by the great landscape artist André Le Nôtre. A long walk across the park will take you to the **Grand Trianon** 🌟🌟🌟, in pink-and-white marble, designed by Hardouin-Mansart for Louis XIV in 1687. Traditionally it's been a place where France has lodged important guests. Gabriel, the designer of place de la Concorde in Paris, built the **Petit Trianon** 🌟🌟 in 1768 for Louis XV; its construction was inspired by Mme de Pompadour, who died before it was completed. In time, Marie Antoinette adopted it as her favorite residence.

Three main avenues radiate from place d'Armes in front of the palace. The **tourist office** is at 2 bis av. de Paris, 78000 Versailles (© **01-39-24-88-88**).

The château is open from May 2 to September 30, Tuesday through Sunday from 9am to 6:30pm (5:30pm the rest of the year). It's closed December 25 and January 1. Call or visit the website for a complete schedule of fees, which vary depending on which attractions you visit. The grounds are open daily from dawn to dusk. The individual attractions may have earlier opening and closing times.

Getting There   To get to Versailles, catch the **RER** line C at the Gare d'Auster-litz, St-Michel, Musée d'Orsay, Invalides, Pont de l'Alma, Champ de Mars, or Javel stop and take it to the Versailles Rive Gauche station, from which there's a shuttle bus to the château. A round-trip ticket costs 5.20€ ($6), and the trip takes 35 to 40 minutes. Eurailpass holders travel free on the RER, but you'll need to show your Eurailpass at the kiosk near any RER entrance for a ticket.

Alternatively, you can take one of the frequent **SNCF trains** from Gare St-Lazare or Gare Montparnasse. Trains departing from Gare St-Lazare arrive at the Versailles Rive Droite station; trains departing from Gare Montparnasse arrive at Versailles Chantiers. Both are a 10-minute walk from the château, and we highly recommend the walk as a means of orienting yourself to the town, its geography, its scale, and its architecture. You can also take bus B, bus H, or (in midsummer) a shuttle bus marked CHATEAU from any of the three stations to the château for 2.50€ to 3€ ($2.85–$3.45). The vagaries of the bus schedules are another reason we highly recommend the walk. Directions to the château are clearly marked from each of the three railway stations. If you're **driving,** exit the *périphérique* on N10 (av. du Général-Leclerc), and park on the place d'Armes in front of the château.

CHARTRES ✫✫✫   The architectural aspirations of the Middle Ages reached their highest expression in the **Cathédrale Notre-Dame de Chartres,** 16 Cloître Notre-Dame (© **02-37-21-59-08**). A mystical light seems to stream through this stained glass, which gave the world a new color—Chartres blue. One of the world's greatest high Gothic cathedrals, Chartres contains some of the oldest (some created as early as the 12th c.) and most beautiful medieval stained glass anywhere. It was spared in both World Wars; the glass was removed piece by piece for storage and safekeeping.

The cathedral you see today dates principally from the 13th century. It was the first to use flying buttresses, giving it a higher and lighter construction. French sculpture in the 12th century broke into full bloom when the **Royal Portal** was added; the sculptured bodies are elongated and formalized, but the faces are amazingly lifelike. Admission is free; the cathedral is open daily from 8:30am to 7:30pm. If you feel fit enough, climb to the top of the **tower.** Open daily from 8:30am to noon and 2 to 7:30pm, it costs 4€ ($4.60) for adults, 3€ ($3.45) for students. The **crypt** can only be visited on a guided tour (in French), costing 1.65€ ($1.90).

Getting There   From Paris's Gare Montparnasse, **trains** run directly to Chartres in under an hour. A round-trip ticket costs 23.60€ ($27). **By car,** take A10/A11 southwest from the *périphérique* and follow the signs to Le Mans and Chartres.

Visitor Information   The **tourist office** is on place de la Cathédrale (© **02-37-18-26-26**).

2 The Loire Valley Châteaux ✫✫✫

Bordered by vineyards, the Loire Valley cuts through the land of castles in France's heart. When royalty and nobility built châteaux throughout this valley during the Renaissance, sumptuousness was uppermost in their minds. An era of excessive pomp reigned until Henri IV moved his court to Paris.

The Loire is blessed with abundant attractions—there's even the castle that inspired the fairy tale *Sleeping Beauty.* Tours is the traditional gateway; from there you can explore east or west, depending on your interests. From Paris, you can reach Tours by autoroute (take A10 southwest).

In general, Loire Valley **tourist offices** are open October through March, Monday through Saturday from 9am to 6:30pm and Sunday from 10am to noon; the rest of the year, hours are Monday through Saturday from 9am to 7pm and Sunday from 9:30am to 12:30pm.

TOURS

Tours, 232km (144 miles) southwest of Paris and 113km (70 miles) southwest of Orléans, is at the junction of the Loire and Cher rivers. The devout en route to Santiago de Compostela in northwest Spain once stopped here to pay homage to St. Martin, the Apostle of Gaul, bishop of Tours in the 4th century. Tours is the traditional place to begin your exploration of the medieval Loire Valley.

ESSENTIALS

GETTING THERE **Trains** to Tours depart Paris from the Gare Montparnasse and the Gare d'Austerlitz. The quickest are usually from Gare Montparnasse, departure point for up to 10 TGV (very fast) trains per day, charging 46€ ($53) or the 70-minute transit. Most conventional trains to Tours depart from the Gare d'Austerlitz. Taking about 2¼ hours for the trip, they cost from 31€ to 40€ ($36–$46), based on the time and day. Trains arrive at place du Maréchal-Leclerc, 3 rue Edouard-Vaillant (© **08-91-35-35-35** for information). If you're **driving,** take Highway A10 to Tours.

GETTING AROUND It's easy to **walk** from one end of central Tours to the other. For taxi service, call **Taxi Radio** (© **02-47-20-30-40**). There are several car rental offices in or near the train station, including **Avis,** inside the station (© **02-47-20-53-27**), open daily from 8am to noon and 1:15 to 7pm; and **Hertz,** 57 rue Marcel-Tribut (© **02-47-75-50-00**), open daily from 8am to noon and 2 to 7pm. You can rent a bike at **Vélomania,** 109 rue Colbert (© **02-47-05-10-11**) for 15€ ($17) a day. It's open Monday from 3:30 to 7:30pm, Tuesday through Friday from 10:30am to 1:30pm and 2:30 to 7:30pm, and Saturday and Sunday from 10:30am to 7:30pm.

VISITOR INFORMATION The **Office de Tourisme** is at 78 rue Bernard-Palissy (© **02-47-70-37-37**).

WHERE TO STAY

Best Western Le Central *Value* This old-fashioned hotel is within walking distance of the river and cathedral, surrounded by gardens, lawns, and trees. Built in 1850, it is a modest, economical choice. The Tremouilles family offers comfortable rooms at reasonable rates. Accommodations come in a variety of shapes and sizes; a renovation in 2003 improved them and updated the plumbing in the small bathrooms.

21 rue Berthelot, 37000 Tours. © **800/528-1234** in the U.S. and Canada, or 02-47-05-46-44. Fax 02-47-66-10-26. www.tours-online-com/central-hotel. 39 units. 75€–122€ ($86–$139) double. AE, DC, MC, V. Parking 8.50€ ($9.75). Bus: 1, 4, or 5. **Amenities:** Bar; limited room service; babysitting; laundry service; dry cleaning. *In room:* A/C, TV, dataport, minibar, hair dryer.

Clarion Hôtel de l'Univers This hotel was erected in 1853, making it the oldest in town. It has been upgraded to a government-rated four-star status, with its midsize rooms redecorated and made more upscale. Bathrooms with shower and tub have also been renewed. On weekdays, it's filled with business travelers; on weekends, it hosts many area brides and grooms.

5 bd. Heurteloup, 37000 Tours. © **02-47-05-37-12.** Fax 02-47-61-51-80. www.hotel-univers-loirevalley.com. 85 units. 185€–255€ double ($213–$293). AE, DC, MC, V. Parking 10€ ($12). Bus: 1, 4, or 5. **Amenities:** Limited room service; laundry service; dry cleaning. *In room:* A/C, TV, minibar, hair dryer.

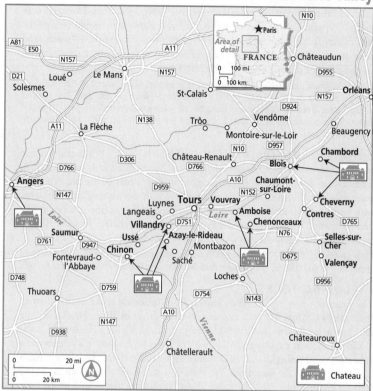

Hôtel du Manoir   On a quiet street with shops and restaurants, this 19th-century residence provides guests with a comfortable place to stay. The cheerful reception area is an indication of the quality of the rooms. Though small to average in size, all units have windows that let in lots of light and afford views of the neighborhood or the hotel's courtyard.

2 rue Traversière, 37000 Tours. ☎ **02-47-05-37-37.** Fax 02-47-05-16-00. manoir37@aol.com. 20 units. 46€–53€ ($53–$61) double. AE, DC, MC, V. Parking 3€ ($3.45). Bus: 3 or 70. *In room:* A/C, TV.

WHERE TO DINE

Château Belmont (Jean Bardet) ✦ MODERN FRENCH   In three rooms of a 19th-century château, this restaurant is the creation of the Michelin two-star chef Jean Bardet, who considers all meals here "an orchestration of wines, alcohol, food, and cigars." That's not to say that you must partake of all four to have one of the best meals in the region. Specialties include lobster ragout, sliced sea bass with confit of tomatoes and artichoke hearts, and scallops with a purée of shallots and truffle cream. The duck giblets and lobster accompanied by a red-wine and orange sauce is reason enough to visit.

57 rue Groison. ☎ **02-47-41-41-11.** www.jeanbardet.com. Reservations recommended. Main courses 37€–60€ ($43–$69); set-price menus 54€–190€ ($62–$218). AE, DC, MC, V. Apr–Nov Tues–Sun noon–2pm, daily 7:30–9:30pm; Dec–Mar Tues–Sun noon–2pm, Tues–Sat 7:30–9:30pm.

La Roche le Roy ✦✦ MODERN FRENCH   One of the hottest chefs in town, Alain Couturier blends new and old techniques in a 15th-century manor south of the town center. Couturier's repertoire includes scalloped foie gras with lentils, cod with saffron cream, and pan-fried scallops with truffle vinaigrette. His masterpiece is suprême of pigeon with "roughly textured" sauce, and matelote of eel with Chinon or Bourgeuil wine. For dessert, try a slice of warm orange-flavored chocolate served with coffee-flavored sherbet.

55 rte. St-Avertin. ℂ 02-47-27-22-00. Reservations recommended. Main courses 22€–32€ ($25–$37); fixed-price menu (lunch only) 29€ ($33). AE, MC, V. Tues–Sat noon–1:45pm and 7:30–10pm. Closed 3 weeks in Aug, 1 week in Feb. From the center of town, take av. Grammont south (follow signs to St-Avertin–Vierzon). The road crosses a bridge but doesn't change name. The restaurant is beside that road, on the southern periphery of Tours.

Les Tuffeaux *Value* TRADITIONAL FRENCH This 18th-century house contains one of the best restaurants in Tours. Menu items change about three times a year, depending on the inspiration of chef Gildas Marsollier, who prepares a roster of classics but also experiments with noisettes of roasted rabbit with bacon and almonds, fricassee of chicken livers with raspberry vinegar, and braised turbot with a gratinéed *viennoise* of Comté cheese. Roasted filet of pigeon with pink grapefruit is an enduring favorite.

19 rue Lavoisier. ℂ 02-47-47-19-89. Reservations required. Main courses 18€–23€ ($21–$26); fixed-price menu 19€–35€ ($22–$40). AE, MC, V. Tues and Thurs–Sun noon–2pm; Mon–Sat 7:30–9:30pm. Bus: 1, 4, or 5.

EXPLORING TOURS

The heart of town is **place Jean-Jaurès. Rue Nationale** is the principal street (the valley's Champs-Elysées), running north to the Loire River. Head along rue du Commerce and rue du Grand-Marché to reach La Vieille Ville, the old town.

One of the best ways to get an overview of Tours (in English) is a ride aboard a rubber-wheeled **train** that operates between Easter and mid-October, daily at 10am and 11am and on the hour from 2 to 6pm. It costs 5€ ($5.75) for adults, 2.50€ ($3) for children under 12. Rides last about 50 minutes, depart and return from in front of the tourist office, 78–82 rue Bernard Palissy (ℂ **02-47-70-37-37**), and incorporate the city's historic core. Buy tickets at the tourist office or aboard the train.

Cathédrale St-Gatien The cathedral's flamboyant Gothic facade is flanked by towers with bases from the 12th century, though the lanterns are Renaissance. The choir is from the 13th century, and each century through the 16th saw new additions. Some of the glorious stained-glass windows are from the 13th century.

5 place de la Cathédrale. ℂ 02-47-70-21-00. Free admission. Daily 9am–7pm.

Musée des Beaux-Arts This fine provincial museum is in the Palais des Archevêques. It's worth visiting for its lovely rooms and gardens. There are works by Degas, Delacroix, Rembrandt, and Boucher, and sculpture by Houdon and Bourdelle.

18 place François-Sicard. ℂ 02-47-05-68-73. Museum 4€ ($4.60) adults, 2€ ($2.30) seniors and students, free for children under 13. Gardens free admission. Museum Wed–Mon 9am–12:45pm and 2–6pm. Gardens daily 7am–8:30pm. Bus: 3.

VILLANDRY ✶✶✶

The extravagant 16th-century-style gardens of the Renaissance **Château de Villandry,** 37510 Villandry (ℂ **02-47-50-02-09**), are celebrated throughout the Touraine. Forming a trio of superimposed cloisters, with a water garden on the highest level, the gardens were purchased in a decaying state and restored by Spanish doctor and scientist Joachim Carvallo, the present owner's great-grandfather.

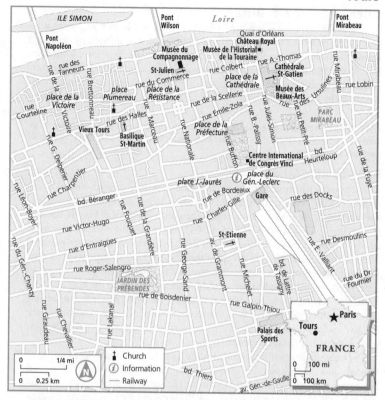

The grounds contain 17km (10½ miles) of boxwood sculpture, which the gardeners must cut to style in only 2 weeks in September. Every square of the gardens seems like a geometric mosaic. The borders represent the many faces of love: for example, tender, tragic (with daggers), or crazy (with a labyrinth that doesn't get you anywhere).

A feudal castle stood at Villandry, but in 1536 Jean Lebreton, the chancellor of François I, built the present château; the buildings form a U and are surrounded by a two-sided moat.

Admission to the gardens with a guided tour of the château costs 7.50€ ($8.50) for adults, 5€ ($5.75) for ages 8 to 18, and free for children under 8. Visiting the gardens separately, without a guide, costs 5€ ($5.75) for adults, 3.50€ ($4) for ages 8 to 18, and free for children under 8. Year-round, the gardens are open daily from 9am to between 5:30 and 7:30pm, depending on the hour of sunset; the château is open daily year-round from 9am to between 5 and 6:30pm, depending on a complicated seasonal schedule. Tours are conducted in French with leaflets in English.

ESSENTIALS

GETTING THERE There is no train service to Villandry. The nearest connection from Tours is at the town of Savonnières. From Savonnières, you can walk along the Loire for 4km (2½ miles) to reach Villandry, rent a **bike** at the station, or take a **taxi.** You can also **drive,** following D7 from Tours.

WHERE TO STAY & DINE

Le Cheval Rouge MODERN FRENCH   This well-known lunch stopover near the château has a sometimes difficult staff. Set in a conservatively decorated dining room about 90m (300 ft.) from the banks of the Cher, it won't offer you your most memorable meal in the Loire Valley. Specialties include lobster thermidor, and medallions of veal with morels. The inn also rents 18 rooms, all with private bathroom and telephone. A double is 47€ to 52€ ($54–$60). Parking is free.

37510 Villandry. © **02-47-50-02-07.** Fax 02-47-50-08-77. www.lecheval-rouge.com. Reservations recommended. Main courses 10€–18€ ($12–$21); fixed-price menus 16€–29€ ($18–$33). AE, DC, MC, V. Daily noon–2pm and 7:30–9pm.

AZAY-LE-RIDEAU 🏸🏸

This château's machicolated towers and blue-slate roof pierced with dormers shimmer in the moat, creating a reflection like a Monet painting. But the defensive medieval look is all for show; the Renaissance **Château d'Azay-le-Rideau,** 37190 Azay-le-Rideau (© **02-47-45-42-04**), was created during as a residence at an idyllic spot on the Indre River. Gilles Berthelot, François I's finance minister, commissioned the castle, and his spendthrift wife, Philippa, supervised its construction. So elegant was the creation that the Chevalier King grew jealous. In time, Berthelot was forced to flee, and the château reverted to the king.

Before entering, circle the château, enjoying the perfect proportions of this crowning achievement of the Renaissance in Touraine. Its most fanciful feature is a bay enclosing a grand stairway with a straight flight of steps. The Renaissance interior is a virtual museum.

The château is open daily July and August from 9:30am to 7pm; April through June and September through October from 9:30am to 6pm; and November through March from 9:30am to 12:30pm and 2 to 5:30pm. Admission is 6.10€ ($7) for adults, 4.10€ ($4.75) for ages 18 to 25, free for children under 18. Allow 2 hours for a visit. From May to July, *son et lumière* (sound-and-light) performances, about an hour in length, with recorded music and lights beaming on the exterior of the château, begin at 10:30pm; during August they begin at 10pm; and in September at 9:30pm. Tickets are 9€ ($10) for adults, 5€ ($5.75) for ages 18 to 25, free for children under 18.

ESSENTIALS

GETTING THERE   To reach Azay-le-Rideau, take the **train** from Tours or Chinon. Trip time is about 30 minutes; the one-way fare is 4.40€ ($5.10). Both Tours and Chinon have express service to Paris. For SNCF bus and rail schedules to Azay-le-Rideau, call © **08-91-35-35-35.** If you're **driving** from Tours, take D759 southwest to Azay-le-Rideau.

VISITOR INFORMATION   The **Syndicat d'Initiative** (tourist office) is on place de l'Europe (© **02-47-45-44-40**).

WHERE TO DINE

L'Aigle d'Or 🏸 TRADITIONAL FRENCH   Owners Jean-Luc and Ghislaine Fèvre work in the kitchens and dining room of this century-old house, the best restaurant in town for nearly 2 decades. The restaurant is in the village center, about .3km (¼ mile) from the château. The service is professional, the welcome charming, and the food the best in Azay. In a dining room accented with ceiling beams, a fireplace, and pastel colors, you'll enjoy dishes including crayfish with foie gras, and a *blanquette* (stew) of Loire Valley whitefish prepared with one of the region's white wines. Desserts are made fresh daily. In summer, the party expands onto an outdoor terrace.

10 av. Adélaïde-Riché. (✆ **02-47-45-24-58.** Reservations recommended. Main courses 25€–40€ ($29–$46); fixed-price lunch 40€–56€ ($46–$64); children's menu 10€ ($12). V. Thurs–Tues noon–2pm and 7:30–9:30pm. Closed Sun night year-round and Tues night off season.

AMBOISE ✮✮✮

On the banks of the Loire, Amboise is in the center of vineyards known as Touraine-Amboise. Leonardo da Vinci spent his last years here. Dominating the town is the **Château d'Amboise** ✮✮ (✆ 02-47-57-00-98), the first in France to reflect the Italian Renaissance. A combination of both Gothic and Renaissance, this 15th-century château is mainly associated with Charles VIII.

You enter on a ramp, opening onto a panoramic terrace fronting the river. At one time, buildings surrounded this terrace, and fêtes were staged in the enclosed courtyard. After the revolution, the castle declined, and only about a quarter of the once-sprawling edifice remains. First you come to the Flamboyant Gothic Chapelle St-Hubert, distinguished by its lacelike tracery. Tapestries cover the walls of the château's grandly furnished rooms. The *Logis du Roi* (king's apartment) is open to visitors.

The château is open daily, July and August from 9am to 7pm; April through June from 9am to 6:30pm; September and October from 9am to 6pm; November 1 to November 15 from 9am to 5:30pm; November 16 through January from 9am to noon and 2 to 4:45pm; and February through March from 9am to noon and 1:30 to 5:30pm. Admission is 7.50€ ($8.50) adults, 6.50€ ($7.30) students, 4.20€ ($4.80) children ages 7 to 14, free for children under 7.

You might also wish to visit **Clos-Lucé** ✮, 2 rue du Clos-Lucé (✆ **02-45-57-00-73**), a 15th-century manor that contains a museum devoted to Leonardo da Vinci. In what had been an oratory for Anne de Bretagne, François I installed "the great master in all forms of art and science," Leonardo da Vinci. Venerated by the Chevalier King, Leonardo lived here for 3 years, dying at the manor in 1519. (The paintings of Leonardo dying in François's arms are symbolic; the king was supposedly away at the time.) The manor contains furniture from his era, sketches, and models for his flying machines, bridges, cannon, and even a primitive example of a machine gun. Clos-Lucé is open daily in January from 9am to 5pm; February and March and November and December from 9am to 6pm; April through June and September and October from 9am to 7pm; July and August from 9am to 8pm. Admission is 9€ to 11€ ($10–$13) adults, 7.30€ to 9€ ($8.25–$10) students, 4€ ($4.60) children 6 to 15, free for children under 6.

ESSENTIALS

GETTING THERE Amboise is on the Paris–Blois–Tours rail line, with 14 **trains** per day from both Tours and Blois. The trip from Tours takes 23 minutes and costs 4.40€ ($5) one-way; from Blois, it takes 22 minutes and costs 5.50€ ($6.25). Five conventional trains a day leave from Paris's Gare d'Austerlitz (trip time: 3 hr.), and several high-speed TGV trains (2¼ hr.) depart from the Gare Montparnasse for St-Pierre-des-Corps, less than a kilometer from Tours. From St-Pierre-des-Corps, you can transfer to a conventional train for Amboise. Fares from Paris to Amboise start at 34€ ($39). For information, call (✆ **08-91-35-35-35.**

If you prefer to travel by bus, **Autocars de Touraine** (✆ 02-47-57-00-44), which operates out of the Gare Routière in Tours, just across from the town's railway station, runs about six **buses** every day between Tours and Amboise. The trip takes about 40 minutes and costs 3.25€ ($3.65) one-way.

If you're **driving** from Tours, take N152 east to D32 and then turn south, following the signs to Amboise.

VISITOR INFORMATION The **Office de Tourisme** is on quai du Général-de-Gaulle (© 02-47-57-09-28).

WHERE TO STAY

Le Choiseul ✦✦✦   There's no better address in Amboise and no better place for cuisine than this 18th-century hotel, in the valley between a hillside and the Loire. Guest rooms, 25 of which are air-conditioned, are luxurious; though modernized, they've retained their old-world charm. The small bathrooms contain combination tub-showers. The formal dining room has a view of the Loire and welcomes nonguests who phone ahead. The cuisine is better than that in Tours or the surrounding area; it is deluxe, international, classic French, and regional, utilizing the freshest ingredients. On the grounds is a garden with flowering terraces.

36 quai Charles-Guinot, 37400 Amboise. © 02-47-30-45-45. Fax 02-47-30-46-10. www.le-choiseul.com. 32 units. 125€–270€ ($144–$310) double; 280€–335€ ($322–$408) suite. AE, DC, MC, V. Closed Dec 20–Feb 6. **Amenities:** Restaurant; bar; outdoor pool; tennis court; limited room service; babysitting; laundry service; dry cleaning. *In room:* A/C, TV, minibar, hair dryer.

Le Vieux Manoir ✦✦ *Finds*   Gloria and Bob Belknap, an American couple, fell in love with France and this 18th-century manor, which they restored and turned into an elegant B&B. Their beautifully furnished guest rooms have country antiques, exposed oak beams, stone walls, and tile floors; a glass conservatory overlooks a garden. Guests are also housed in a 17th-century structure with old oak beams and exposed stone walls. This latter accommodation, with its fully equipped kitchen, is ideal for families. Locally made tiles line the bathrooms, the finest in Amboise, with heavy German fixtures and tub-shower combinations. Accommodations are named after various legends, from Georges Sand and Colette to Joséphine and Mme du Barry.

13 rue Rabelais, 37400 Amboise. © 02-47-30-41-27. Fax 02-47-30-41-27. www.le-vieux-manoir.com. 6 units, 2-bedroom cottage. 125€–175€ ($144–$201) double; 250€–335€ ($288–$408) cottage for 4. Rates include breakfast. No credit cards. *In room:* TV.

WHERE TO DINE

The finest dining choice is **Le Choiseul** (see "Where to Stay," above).

Brasserie de l'Hotel de Ville *Kids* FRENCH   In the town's historic core, a short walk from the château, this bustling Paris-style brasserie has enjoyed a solid reputation since the early 1990s. It attracts local office workers and art lovers visiting the historic sites during the day, and boisterous groups of friends at night. Expect a noisy environment, hassled waiters, and steaming platters that emerge relatively quickly from the overworked kitchen. Menu items include a full range of old-fashioned cuisine that many locals remember from childhood. Examples include such staples as sole meunière, grilled beefsteak with french fries, pot-au-feu, calves' liver, and a scattering of dishes from France's Southwest, including a savory version of cassoulet.

1–3 rue François 1er. tel] 02-47-57-26-30. Reservations recommended. Main courses 11€–15€ ($13–$17); set-price menus 14€ ($16); children's menu 7.40€ ($8.50). MC, V. Daily 10am–3pm and 6-11pm.

BLOIS ✦✦

This town of 55,000 receives half a million visitors yearly. It rises on the right bank of the Loire, its skyline dominated by its château, where the duc de Guise was assassinated on December 23, 1588, on orders of his archrival, Henri III. Several French kings lived here, and the town has a rich architectural history.

The murder of the duc de Guise is only one of the events associated with the **Château de Blois** ★★★ (☎ 02-54-90-33-33), begun in the 13th century by the comtes de Blois. Blois reached the apex of its power in 1515, when François I moved to the château. For that reason, Blois is often called the "Versailles of the Renaissance," the second capital of France, and the "city of kings."

Blois was also a palace of banishment. Louis XIII got rid of his interfering mother, Marie de Médici, by sending her here, but the plump matron escaped by sliding into the moat down a mound of dirt left by the builders.

If you stand in the courtyard, you'll find that the château is like an illustrated storybook of French architecture. The Hall of the Estates-General is a 13th-century work; the Charles d'Orléans gallery was built by Louis XII from 1498 to 1501, as was the Louis XII wing. Mansart constructed the Gaston d'Orléans wing between 1635 and 1638. Most remarkable is the François I wing, a masterpiece of the French Renaissance, containing a spiral staircase with elaborately ornamented balustrades and the king's symbol, the salamander.

The château is open daily in July and August from 9am to 7pm; mid-March through June and September from 9am to 6pm; and October through mid-March from 9am to noon and 2 to 5:30pm. Admission is 6€ ($6.90) adults, 4€ ($4.60) students 12 to 20, 2€ ($2.30) children 6 to 11, free for children under 6. A *son-et-lumière* presentation takes place nightly May through September, beginning between 9:30 and 10:30pm. The show costs 9.50€ ($11) for adults, 4.50€ ($5.25) for children 7 to 15, free for children under 7.

ESSENTIALS

GETTING THERE   The Paris-Austerlitz line via Orléans runs six **trains** per day from Paris (trip time: 2 hr.), costing 21€ ($24) one-way; from Tours, five trains arrive per day (trip time: 40 min.), at a cost of 8.30€ ($9.50) one-way. For information, call ☎ 08-91-35-35-35. The station is at place de la Gare. Once here, you can take a **bus** (☎ 02-54-90-41-41) to tour various châteaux, including Chambord, Chaumont, Chenonceau, and Amboise. Buses depart from the train station from June to September only. If you're **driving** from Tours, take RN152 east to Blois. If you'd like to explore the area by **bike,** go to **Cycles Le Blond,** 44 levée des Tuileries (☎ 02-54-74-30-13), where rentals cost 6€ to 13€ ($6.90–$15) per day, depending on the model. You have to leave your passport, a credit card, a driver's license, or a 250€ ($288) deposit.

VISITOR INFORMATION   The **Office de Tourisme** is in the Pavillon Anne-de-Bretagne, 3 av. Jean-Laigret (☎ 02-54-90-41-41; www.loiredeschateaux.com).

WHERE TO STAY

Hôtel le Savoie   This modern 1930s-era hotel is both inviting and livable, from its courteous staff to its guest rooms, which are small but quiet and cozy. They were last renovated in 2002. Bathrooms are small but have sufficient shelf space; each has a shower. In the morning, a breakfast buffet is set up in the bright dining room.

6–8 rue du Docteur-Ducoux, 41000 Blois. ☎ 02-54-74-32-21. Fax 02-54-74-29-58. www.citoel.com. 25 units. 42€–49€ ($48–$56) double. MC, V. **Amenities:** Bar; limited room service; babysitting; laundry service. *In room:* TV.

Mercure Centre ★   This is the best-located hotel in Blois—three stories of reinforced concrete and big windows beside the quays of the Loire, a 5-minute walk from the château. Rooms never rise above the chain-style format and road-side-motel look, but they are roomy and soundproof. Bathrooms come with a combination tub-shower.

28 quai St-Jean, 41000 Blois. ✆ **02-54-56-66-66.** Fax 02-54-56-67-00. www.mercure.com. 96 units. 102€–111€ ($117–$128) double. AE, DC, MC, V. Bus: Quayside marked PISCINE. **Amenities:** Restaurant; bar; indoor pool; Jacuzzi; sauna; limited room service; babysitting; laundry service; dry cleaning. *In room:* A/C, TV, dataport, minibar, hair dryer.

WHERE TO DINE

Le Médicis ✿ TRADITIONAL FRENCH   Christian and Annick Garanger maintain one of the most sophisticated inns in Blois—ideal for a gourmet meal or an overnight stop. Fresh fish is the specialty. Typical main courses are asparagus in mousseline sauce, scampi ravioli with saffron sauce, and *suprême* of perch with morels. Chocolate in many manifestations is the dessert specialty.

2 allée François-1er, 41000 Blois. ✆ **02-54-43-94-04.** Fax 02-54-42-04-05. www.le-medicis.com. Reservations required. Main courses 22€–32€ ($25–$37); fixed-price menus 29€–69€ ($33–$79). AE, MC, V. Daily noon–2pm and 7–9pm. Closed Jan and Sun night Nov–Mar. Bus: 2.

L'Orangerie du Château ✿✿✿ TOURAINE   Next to the château sits the grandest and best restaurant in the area. You approach through a gated courtyard, which sets the elegant tone. Chef Jean-Marc Molveaux dazzles with an intriguing array of specialties. His faithful customers, along with the most discerning foodies visiting Blois, delight in his filet mignon with truffles. You can also sample his lovely medley of shellfish and nuts in cream sauce, or perfectly roasted monkfish flavored with fresh thyme. Everything tastes better with a Sauvignon de Touraine. For dessert, our special favorite is melted chocolate and pistachio with crème fraîche. Prepare to make an evening of it if you dine here.

1 av. Jean-Laigret. ✆ **02-54-78-05-36.** Reservations required. Main courses 22€–34€ ($25–$39). Fixed-price menus Mon–Fri 30€ ($35) and daily 42€–62€ ($48–$71). Children's menu 14€ ($16). MC, V. Thurs–Tues noon–1:45pm and 7:15–9:15pm. Closed Sun night and mid-Feb to mid-Mar.

CHAMBORD

When François I used to say, "Come on up to my place," he meant the **Château de Chambord** ✿✿✿, 41250 Bracieux (✆ **02-54-50-40-00**). Some 2,000 workers began to piece together "the pile" in 1519. What emerged after 20 years was the pinnacle of the French Renaissance, the largest château in the Loire Valley. It was ready for the visit of Charles V of Germany, who was welcomed by nymphets in transparent veils gently tossing wildflowers in his path. French monarchs like Henri II and Catherine de Médici, Louis XIV, and Henri III came and went from Chambord.

The château is set in a park of more than 5,200 hectares (13,000 acres), enclosed by a wall stretching some 32km (20 miles). Looking out a window in one of the 440 rooms, François is said to have carved these words on a pane with a diamond ring: "A woman is a creature of change; to trust her is to play the fool." Four huge towers dominate Chambord's facade. The keep has a spectacular terrace on which the ladies used to stand to watch for the return of their men from the hunt.

The château is open daily (except Jan 1, May 1, and Dec 25) from 9am to 6:30pm (last entrance at 5:45pm). Admission is 7€ ($8) for adults, 4.50€ ($5) for ages 18 to 25, and free for children under 18. At the tourist office, you can pick up tickets for the summer *son-et-lumière* presentation, *Jours et Siècles* (Days and Centuries). The price is 12€ ($14).

ESSENTIALS

GETTING THERE   It's best to **drive** to Chambord. Take the D951 northeast from Blois to Ménars, turning onto the rural road to Chambord. You can also rent a **bicycle** in Blois and ride the 18km (11 miles) to Chambord, or take a

tour to Chambord from Blois in summer. From June 15 to September 15, **Transports du Loir et Cher** (© 02-54-58-55-61) operates bus service to Chambord, leaving Blois at 9am and 1:30pm, with returns at 1 and 6pm.

VISITOR INFORMATION   The **Office de Tourisme** on place St-Michel (© 02-54-33-39-16) is open only from April to September.

WHERE TO STAY & DINE

Hôtel du Grand-St-Michel   Across from the château, and originally built as a kennel for the royal hounds, this inn is the only one of any substance in town. Try for a front room overlooking the château, which is dramatic when floodlit at night. Accommodations are plain but comfortable, with provincial decor and shower-only private bathrooms. The regional dishes are complemented by a collection of Loire wines so good they almost overshadow the cooking. High points include a stew of wild boar (in late autumn and winter), breast of duckling in green-peppercorn sauce, and several local pâtés and terrines, including the coarsely textured and very flavorful rillettes of regional pork.

103 place St-Michel, 41250 Chambord, near Bracieux. © 02-54-20-31-31. Fax 02-54-20-36-40. 39 units. 49€–79€ ($56–$91) double. MC, V. Free parking. Closed mid-Nov to mid-Dec. **Amenities:** Restaurant; tennis court. *In room:* TV.

CHEVERNY

The *haut monde* still come to the Sologne area for the hunt as if the 17th century had never ended. However, 20th-century realities, like taxes, are *formidable* here—and the **Château de Cheverny** ★★★ (© 02-54-79-96-29) must open some of its rooms to visitors.

Unlike most of the Loire châteaux, Cheverny is the residence of the descendants of the original owner, the vicomte de Sigalas. The family's lineage can be traced back to Henri Hurault, the son of the chancellor of Henri III and Henri IV, who built the original château here in 1634. Designed in classic Louis XIII style, it boasts square pavilions flanking the central pile.

The furnishings, tapestries, decorations, and objets d'art are impressive. A 17th-century artist, Jean Mosnier, decorated the fireplace with motifs from the legend of Adonis. In the Guards' Room is a collection of medieval armor. Most impressive is the stone stairway of carved fruit and flowers.

The château is open daily in July and August from 9:15am to 6:45pm; April through June and September from 9:15am to 6:15pm; March and October from 9:30am to noon and 2:15 to 5:30pm; and November through February from 9:30am to noon and 2:15 to 5pm. Admission is 5.90€ ($6.75) for adults, 2.80€ ($3.25) for children 7 to 14, free for children under 7.

ESSENTIALS

GETTING THERE   Cheverny is 19km (12 miles) south of Blois, along D765. It's best reached by **car** or on a **bus tour** from Blois with **Transports du Loir et Cher** (© 02-54-58-55-61). From the railway station at Blois, a bus departs for Cheverny once a day at noon, returning to Blois 4 hours later, according to an oft-changing schedule. Most visitors find it a lot easier to take their own car or a **taxi** from the railway station at Blois.

WHERE TO STAY & DINE

Les Trois Marchands TRADITIONAL FRENCH   This coaching inn, more comfortable than St-Hubert, has been handed down for many generations. Today, Jean-Jacques Bricault owns the three-story building with awnings, a mansard roof, a glassed-in courtyard, and sidewalk tables under umbrellas. In the tavern-style dining room, the menu might include foie gras, lobster salad, frogs' legs, fresh asparagus in mousseline sauce, or fish in a salt crust. The inn rents 24 well-furnished, comfortable rooms for 42€ to 55€ ($48–$63) double.

Place de l'Eglise, 41700 Cour-Cheverny. ⓒ 02-54-79-96-44. Fax 02-54-79-25-60. Main courses 16€–30€ ($18–$35); fixed-price menu 21€–35€ ($24–$40). AE, DC, MC, V. Tues–Sun noon–2:15pm and 7:30–9:15pm. Closed Feb 1–Mar 15. **Amenities:** 2 restaurants; limited room service. *In room:* TV.

St-Hubert TRADITIONAL FRENCH   About 450m (1,500 ft.) from the château, this inn was built in the 1950s in the provincial style. The least expensive menu might include terrine of quail, pike-perch with beurre blanc, cheeses, and a fruit tart. The most expensive may offer an aiguillette of duckling prepared with grapes, salmon braised in white wine, a casserole of seafood with shellfish sauce, or, in season, thigh of roebuck in pepper sauce. The St-Hubert offers 20 conservatively decorated rooms with bathroom, for 44€ to 54€ ($51–$62) double.

Rte. Nationale, 41700 Cour-Cheverny. ⓒ 02-54-79-96-60. Fax 02-54-79-21-17. Main courses 14€–21€ ($16–$24); fixed-price menu 13€–37€ ($15–$43). AE, MC, V. Daily 12:15–2pm and 7:30–9:30pm. Closed Jan, Sun night off season.

CHENONCEAUX

A Renaissance masterpiece, the **Château de Chenonceau** ★★★ (ⓒ 02-47-23-90-07) is best known for the *dames de Chenonceau* who have occupied it. (Note that the village is spelled with a final x, but the château is not.) In 1547, Henri II gave Chenonceau to his mistress, Diane de Poitiers. For a time this remarkable woman was virtually queen of France, infuriating Henri's dour wife, Catherine de Médici. When Henri died, Catherine forced Diane to abandon her beloved home.

Many of the château's walls are covered with Gobelin tapestries, including one depicting a woman pouring water over the back of an angry dragon. The chapel contains a marble *Virgin and Child,* plus portraits of Catherine de Médici in her traditional black and white. There's even a portrait of stern Catherine in the former bedroom of her rival, Diane de Poitiers. In François I's Renaissance bedchamber, the most interesting portrait is that of Diane as the huntress Diana.

The history of Chenonceau is related in 15 tableaux in the **Musée de Cire** (wax museum), located in a Renaissance-era annex a few steps from the château. Open the same hours as the château, it charges a general admission fee of 3€. Diane de Poitiers, who, among other things, introduced the artichoke to France, is depicted in three tableaux. One portrays Catherine de Médici tossing out her husband's mistress.

From mid-March to mid-September, it's open daily from 9am to 7pm. The rest of the year, it's open daily from 9am to between 5 and 6pm. Admission is 8€ ($9.20) for adults, 6.50€ ($7.50) for students and children 7 to 15. A *son-et-lumière* show, *The Era of the Ladies of Chenonceaux,* starts at 10:15pm daily in July and August; admission is 5€ ($5.75), free for children under 7. Allow 2 hours to see this château.

ESSENTIALS
GETTING THERE   There are four daily **trains** from Tours to Chenonceaux (trip time: 30 min.), costing 5.75€ ($6.50) one-way. The train deposits you at the base of the château; from there, you can walk or take a taxi.

VISITOR INFORMATION   The **Syndicat d'Initiative** (tourist office) is at 1 rue Bretonneau (ⓒ 02-47-23-94-45), open year-round on a frequently changing schedule.

WHERE TO STAY

Hôtel du Bon-Laboureur et du Château ★★   This inn is your best bet for a comfortable night's sleep and some of the best cuisine in the Loire Valley. Founded in 1786, the hotel maintains the flavor of that era, thanks to thick walls, solid masonry, and a scattering of antiques. Most guest rooms are small, especially on the upper floors; each comes with a private bathroom with shower or tub. The rear garden has a guesthouse and formally planted roses. The place is noted for its restaurant. In fair weather, tables are set up in the courtyard, amid trees and flowering shrubs. Fixed-price menus are 29€ to 69€ ($33–$79).

6 rue du Dr. Bretonneau, Chenonceaux, 37150 Bléré. © **02-47-23-90-02.** Fax 02-47-23-82-01. www.amboise. com/laboureur. 27 units. 70€–125€ ($81–$144) double; 145€–175€ ($167–$201) suite. AE, DC, MC, V. Closed Nov 15–Dec 20. **Amenities:** Restaurant; bar; outdoor pool; limited room service; babysitting; laundry service; dry cleaning. *In room:* A/C, TV, kitchenette, hair dryer, safe.

La Roseraie ★ *Value*   La Roseraie is the most charming hotel in Chenonceaux, with individually decorated rooms and well-kept gardens. Each unit contains a small bathroom with shower. In the 1940s, its guests included Winston Churchill, Eleanor Roosevelt, and Harry Truman. The inn is operated by the exceptionally charming Laurent and Sophie Fiorito, who have banned smoking from their excellent dining room. Our favorites include house-style foie gras; magret of duckling with pears and cherries; and an unusual and delicious invention—*emincée* (a dish made with braised meat) of rump steak with wine-marinated pears.

7 rue du Dr. Bretonneau, Chenonceaux, 37150 Bléré. © **02-47-23-90-09.** Fax 02-47-23-91-59. www.charming roseraie.com. 17 units. 53€–95€ ($61–$109) double; 90€–120€ ($104–$138) for 4; 170€ ($196) apt. MC, V. Closed mid-Nov to Feb. **Amenities:** Restaurant; bar; outdoor pool; laundry service; dry cleaning. *In room:* TV.

WHERE TO DINE

Note that **La Renaudière,** 24 rue du Dr. Bretonneau (© **02-47-23-90-04**), and **La Roseraie** (see above) operate very good restaurants.

Au Gateau Breton TRADITIONAL FRENCH   The terrace in back of this Breton-type inn, a short walk from the château, is a refreshing place for dinner or tea. Gravel paths run among beds of pink geraniums and lilacs, and bright umbrellas adorn the red tables. In cool months, meals are served in the rustic dining rooms. Make a meal of the home cooking and cherry liqueur, a regional specialty. Worthwhile dishes include small chitterling sausages of Tours, chicken with Armagnac sauce, and coq au vin. Tasty pastries are sold in the front room.

16 rue du Dr. Bretonneau. © **02-47-23-90-14.** Fax 02-47-23-92-57. Reservations required July–Aug. Fixed-price menu 11€–22€ ($13–$25). AE, MC, V. Mar–Oct daily noon–2:30pm, Thurs–Mon 7–10pm; Nov–Feb Thurs–Tues noon–2:30pm.

CHINON ★★

In the film *Joan of Arc,* Ingrid Bergman sought out the dauphin as he tried to conceal himself among his courtiers—an action whose real-life equivalent took place at the Château de Chinon. Charles VII, mockingly known as the king of Bourges, centered his government at Chinon from 1429 to 1450. In 1429, with the English besieging Orléans, the Maid of Orléans, that "messenger from God," prevailed on the weak dauphin to give her an army. The rest is history. The seat of French power stayed at Chinon until the Hundred Years' War ended.

Chinon retains a medieval atmosphere. It consists of winding streets and turreted houses, many built in the 15th and 16th centuries. For the best view, drive across the river, turning right onto quai Danton. From that vantage point, you'll have the best perspective, seeing the castle in relation to the village and the river.

The most typical street is **rue Voltaire,** lined with 15th- and 16th-century town houses. This is one of the most medieval-looking streets in the entire Loire Valley. At no. 44, Richard the Lion-Hearted died on April 6, 1199, after being wounded while besieging Chalus in Limousin. In the heart of Chinon, the **Grand Carroi** lies at the intersection of an ancient Roman road that was later joined by a medieval road. The village of Chinon evolved from this crossroad.

The most famous son of Chinon, François Rabelais, the earthy and often bawdy Renaissance writer, lived on the rue de la Lamproie; today a plaque marks the spot where his father practiced law and maintained a prosperous home and office. The cottage 6km (3½ miles) west of Chinon where he was born is the site of the **Musée de la Devinière** (② 02-47-95-91-18). Admission is 3.80€ ($4.35) adults, 2.70€ ($3) students, 2€ ($2.30) children 7 to 18, free for children under 7. It's open daily, January 1 through March 13 and October 1 through December 31, from 9:30am to 12:30pm and 2 to 5pm; March 15 through April 30 daily 9:30am to 12:30am and 2 to 6pm; May 1 through September 14 daily 10am to 7pm. To reach it from Chinon, follow the road signs pointing to Saumur and the D117.

Château de Chinon ⋆⋆ (② 02-47-93-13-45) consists of three separate strongholds, once badly ruined. Two of the buildings, the Château du Milieu and the Château du Coudray, have been restored but still lack roofs. Some of the grim walls from other edifices remain, though many of the buildings—including the Great Hall where Joan of Arc sought out the dauphin—have been torn down. The restored Château du Milieu dates from the 11th to the 15th centuries; it contains the keep and the clock tower, which houses the Musée Jeanne d'Arc. The Château du Coudray contains the Tour du Coudray, where Joan of Arc once stayed. In the 14th century the Knights Templar were imprisoned here before meeting violent deaths.

The château is open daily April through September from 9am to 7pm, October through March from 9:30am to 5pm. Admission is 5.50€ ($6.25) adults, 3.50€ ($4) students, 3€ ($3.45) ages 7 to 18, and free for children under 7.

ESSENTIALS

GETTING THERE   The SNCF runs about 10 **trains** and four **buses** every day to Chinon from Tours (trip time: about 1 hr.). Call ② **08-91-35-35-35** for information. Both buses and trains arrive at the train station, which lies at the edge of the very small town. If you're **driving** from Tours, take D759 southwest through Azay-le-Rideau to Chinon.

VISITOR INFORMATION   The **Office de Tourisme** is at place Hoffheim (② **02-47-93-17-85**).

WHERE TO STAY

Hostellerie Gargantua ⋆   This 15th-century mansion has a terrace with a château view. The building was once a courthouse where in the 15th century the father of François Rabelais worked as a lawyer. Art historians admire its early Renaissance staircase, its chiseled-stone details, and its allegiance to its original grandeur, despite its reasonable lodging prices. Try to stop here for a meal, served in a medieval hall. You can sample Loire *sandre* (pikeperch fish) prepared with Chinon wine, or duckling with dried pears and smoked lard, followed by a medley of seasonal red fruits in puff pastry. Guest rooms are traditional, although they were renovated as recently as 2000. Bathrooms are old-fashioned but in working order; half of them contain tubs.

73 rue Voltaire, 37500 Chinon. © **02-47-93-04-71.** Fax 02-47-93-08-02. www.hostelleriegargantua.com.
8 units. 45€–90€ ($52–$104) double. MC, V. Free parking. Closed mid-Nov to mid-Dec. **Amenities:** Restaurant; bar; limited room service; babysitting; laundry service. *In room:* TV, hair dryer.

WHERE TO DINE

Au Plaisir Gourmand ★★ TRADITIONAL FRENCH   This is the premier restaurant in the area, owned by Jean-Claude Rigollet. The 18th-century building contains a small dining room. Menu items are likely to include roast rabbit in aspic with foie gras sauce, oxtail in Chinon red-wine sauce, and sautéed crayfish with a spicy salad. For dessert, try prunes stuffed in puff pastry.

2 rue Parmentier. © **02-47-93-20-48.** Reservations required. Main courses 14€–25€ ($16–$29); tasting menus 27€ ($31) and 59€ ($68). AE, V. Wed–Sun noon–3:30pm; Tues–Sat 7:30–8:30pm. Closed mid-Feb to mid-Mar.

ANGERS ★★★

Once the capital of Anjou, Angers straddles the Maine River. Although it suffered extensive damage in World War II, it has been considerably restored, blending provincial charm with the suggestion of sophistication. The town is often used as a base for exploring the château district to the west.

The moated 9th-century **Château d'Angers** ★★★ (© **02-41-87-43-47**) was once the home of the comtes d'Anjou. After the castle was destroyed, St. Louis reconstructed it. From 1230 to 1238 the outer walls and 17 massive towers were built, creating a fortress to withstand invaders. The château was favored by "Good" King René; until he was forced to surrender Anjou to Louis XI, a brilliant court life flourished. Louis XIV turned the château into a prison. During World War II, the Nazis used it as a munitions depot. Allied planes bombed it in 1944.

The castle displays the **Apocalypse Tapestries** ★★★, masterpieces of medieval art. (This series of tapestries wasn't always so highly regarded; they once served as a canopy to protect orange trees from unfavorable weather, and at another time to cover the damaged walls of a church.) Master weaver Nicolas Bataille created the tapestries. The series illustrates the Book of St. John in 77 pieces that stretch 100m (335 ft.). One scene is called *La Grande prostituée,* and another shows Babylon invaded by demons.

You can tour the fortress, including the courtyard of the nobles, prison cells, ramparts, windmill tower, 15th-century chapel, and royal apartments. The château and its tapestries can be visited daily from May through August 9:30am to 6:30pm, September to April 10am to 5:30pm.

Admission to the château and exhibits is 5.45€ ($6.25) adults, 3.50€ ($4) seniors and students 19 to 25, free for children under 19. Once you've paid, you can take a guided tour on the architecture and history of the château. They depart every day from May through August at 10am, 11:30am, 1:15pm, 2:30pm, and 3:30pm, and on a reduced schedule in the off season. The 90-minute tours are in French, with foreign-language leaflets (in English and seven other languages) available.

ESSENTIALS

GETTING THERE   Three **trains** per day make the 1½-hour trip from Paris's Gare de Montparnasse; the cost is 52€ ($60) one-way. From Tours, seven trains per day make the 1-hour trip; a one-way ticket is 13€ ($15). The Angers train station, at place de la Gare, is a convenient walk from the château. For train information, call © **08-91-35-35-35.** From Saumur, there are three **bus** connections a day from Monday to Saturday (1½ hr.). Buses arrive at place de la République. Call © **02-41-33-64-64** for schedules. If you're **driving** from Tours, take N152 southwest to Saumur and turn west on D952.

VISITOR INFORMATION The **Office de Tourisme,** 7 place du Président-Kennedy (© **02-41-23-50-00**), is opposite the entrance to the château.

WHERE TO STAY

Hôtel d'Anjou Beside a park, this hotel is the best choice for overnighting in the area. Although comparable in price to the Quality Hôtel de France, it has more upscale appointments and amenities, along with a better restaurant (see "Where to Dine," below). The guest rooms closer to the ground have higher ceilings and are more spacious.

1 bd. Foch, 49100 Angers. © **800/528-1234** in the U.S. and Canada, or 02-41-21-12-11. Fax 02-41-87-22-21. 53 units. 75€–152€ ($86–$174) double. AE, DC, MC, V. Parking 8€ ($9.20). **Amenities:** Restaurant; bar; laundry service; dry cleaning. *In room:* TV, minibar.

Quality Hôtel de France This 19th-century hotel, one of the most respected in town, has been run by the Bouyers since 1893. It's the best choice near the railway station. Rooms are soundproof, and many were renovated in the late 1990s. Bathrooms are very small and hold tubs.

8 place de la Gare, 49100 Angers. © **02-41-88-49-42.** Fax 02-41-86-76-70. www.destination-anjou.com/hoteldefrance. 55 units. 85€–115€ ($98–$132) double. AE, DC, MC, V. Parking 7€ ($8.05). **Amenities:** 2 restaurants; bar; limited room service; laundry service; dry cleaning. *In room:* A/C, TV, minibar, hair dryer.

WHERE TO DINE

Le Salamandre ⊛ CLASSIC FRENCH Any educated French person can tell you that the salamander was the symbol of King François I, and in this formal and elegant restaurant you'll see portraits of, and references to, that strategist everywhere. Beneath massive ceiling beams, beside a large wooden fireplace, you'll enjoy the most impeccable service and the best food in town. Shining examples include filet of red snapper in lime-flavored cream sauce; scallops in mushroom cream sauce; and squid stuffed with crayfish and served with shellfish-flavored cream sauce.

In the Hôtel d'Anjou, 1 bd. Foch. © **02-41-88-99-55.** Reservations recommended. Main courses 20€–25€ ($23–$29); fixed-price menu 23€–41€ ($26–$47) lunch, 31€–41€ ($36–$47) dinner. AE, DC, MC, V. Mon–Sat noon–2pm and 7:30–9:30pm.

3 Provence & the Côte d'Azur

Provence has been called a bridge between the past and the present, which blend in a quiet, often melancholy way. Peter Mayle's *A Year in Provence* and its sequels have played a large role in the popularity of this sunny corner of France.

The Greeks and Romans filled the landscape with cities boasting baths, theaters, and arches. Romanesque fortresses and Gothic cathedrals followed. In the 19th century, the light and landscapes attracted painters like Cézanne and van Gogh.

Provence has its own language and customs. The region is bounded on the north by the Dauphine, the west by the Rhône, the east by the Alps, and the south by the Mediterranean. We cover the northern area of this region, what's traditionally thought of as Provence, and then head to the southern part, the Côte d'Azur, or French Riviera.

The Riviera has been called the world's most exciting stretch of beach and "a sunny place for shady people." Each resort—be it Beaulieu by the sea or eagle's-nest Eze—has a unique flavor and special merits. Glitterati and eccentrics have always

been drawn to this narrow strip of fabled real estate. A trail of modern artists, attracted to the brilliant light, have left a rich heritage: Matisse in his chapel at Vence, Cocteau at Menton and Villefranche, Picasso at Antibes and seemingly everywhere else, Léger at Biot, Renoir at Cagnes, and Bonnard at Le Cannet. The best art collection of all is at the Maeght Foundation in St-Paul-de-Vence.

The Riviera's high season used to be winter and spring. With changing tastes, July and August have become the most crowded months, and reservations are imperative. The average summer temperature is 75°F (24°C); the average winter temperature, 49°F (10°C).

The Corniches of the Riviera, featured in countless films, stretch from Nice to Menton. The Alps drop into the Mediterranean, and roads were carved along the way. The lower road, about 32km (20 miles) long, is the **Corniche Inférieure.** Along this road are Villefranche, Cap-Ferrat, Beaulieu, and Cap-Martin. Built between World War I and the start of World War II, the **Moyenne Corniche (Middle Road),** 30km (19 miles) long, also runs from Nice to Menton, winding in and out of tunnels and through mountains. The highlight is at Eze. Napoleon ordered the construction of the **Grande Corniche**—the most panoramic—in 1806. La Turbie and Le Vistaero are the principal towns along the 32km (20-mile) stretch, which reaches more than 488m (1,600 ft.) high at Col d'Eze.

In general, **tourist offices** in Provence are open from April to September, Monday through Friday from 9am to 1pm and 2 to 6pm, and Saturday and Sunday from 9am to 1pm and 2 to 5pm (closed Sun the rest of the year).

AVIGNON ★★★

In the 14th century, Avignon was the capital of Christendom. The pope lived here during what the Romans called the Babylonian Captivity. The legacy left by that court makes Avignon one of the most beautiful of Europe's medieval cities.

Today, this walled city of some 100,000 residents is increasingly known as a cultural center. Artists and painters have been moving here; experimental theaters, galleries, and cinemas have brought diversity to the inner city.

ESSENTIALS

GETTING THERE   The fastest and easiest way to get here is to fly from Paris's Orly Airport to **Aéroport Avignon–Caumont** (© **04-90-81-51-51**), 8km (5 miles) southeast of Avignon (trip time: 1 hr.). Taxis from the airport to the center cost 18€ to 20€ ($21–$23). From Paris, TGV **trains** from Gare de Lyon take 2 hours and 38 minutes. The one-way fare is 114€ ($131) in first class, 83€ ($95) in second class. Trains arrive frequently from Marseille, taking 70 minutes and costing 23€ ($26); and from Arles, taking 30 minutes and costing 5.70€ ($6.50). For train information and reservations, call © **08-92-35-35-39.**

If you're **driving** from Paris, take A6 south to Lyon, then A7 south to Avignon. If you'd like to explore the area by **bike,** go to **Cycles Peugeot,** 80 rue Guillaume-Puy (© **04-90-86-32-49**), which rents all sorts of bikes, including 10-speed road bikes and mountain bikes, for around 13€ ($15) per day. A deposit of 190€ ($218) in cash or a credit card imprint is required.

VISITOR INFORMATION   The **Office de Tourisme** is at 41 cours Jean-Jaurès (© **04-32-74-32-74**; www. ot-avignon.fr).

WHERE TO STAY

Hotel Clarion Cloître St-Louis ★   This hotel is in a former Jesuit school built in the 1580s. Much of the original premises remain, including the baroque facade, the wraparound arcades, and the soaring ceiling vaults. Guest rooms are rather dull as a result of renovations. Rooms range from medium to spacious, and some have sliding glass doors overlooking the patio. Each unit has modern decor without a lot of extras; all but three have a combination tub-shower.

20 rue Portail Boquier, 84000 Avignon. © **800/CLARION** in the U.S., or 04-90-27-55-55. Fax 04-90-82-24-01. www.cloitre-saint-louis.com. 80 units. 100€–250€ ($115–$288) double; 220€–315€ ($253–$362) suite. AE, MC, V. Parking 10€–12€ ($12–$14). **Amenities:** Restaurant; bar; outdoor pool; limited room service. *In room:* A/C, TV, dataport, minibar, hair dryer, safe.

Hôtel d'Angleterre   This three-story Art Deco structure in the heart of Avignon is the city's best budget hotel, with the advantage of being located inside the city ramparts. It was built in 1929 of gray stone, emulating the style that local builders imagined was characteristic of most English houses. The rooms are on the small side, but they are comfortably furnished. All except one come with a compact shower-only bathroom. Breakfast is the only meal served.

29 bd. Raspail, 84000 Avignon. © **04-90-86-34-31.** Fax 04-90-86-86-74. www.hoteldangleterre.fr. 39 units. 40€–68€ ($46–$78) double. MC, V. Parking 7€ ($8.05). Closed Dec 20–Jan 20. **Amenities:** Laundry service; dry cleaning. *In room:* TV.

La Mirande ★★★   In the heart of Avignon (behind the Palais des Papes), this 700-year-old town house is one of France's grand little luxuries. In 1987, Achim and Hannelore Stein transformed this place into a citadel of opulence. The hotel treats you to 2 centuries of decorative art: from the 1700s Salon Chinois to the Salon Rouge, with its striped walls in Rothschild red. Room no. 20 is the most

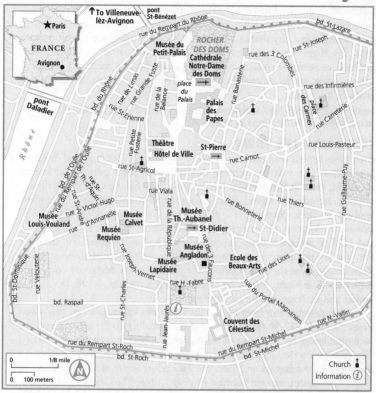

sought-after—its lavish premises open onto the garden. All the rooms are stunning, with exquisite decor, hand-printed fabrics on the walls, antiques, bedside controls, and huge bathtubs. The restaurant, among the finest in Avignon, deserves its one Michelin star.

4 place de la Mirande, 84000 Avignon. ⓒ **04-90-85-93-93.** Fax 04-90-86-26-85. www.la-mirande.fr. 20 units. 300€–430€ ($345–$495) double; 614€–875€ ($706–$1,006) suite. AE, DC, V. Parking 15€ ($17). **Amenities:** Restaurant; bar; limited room service; babysitting; laundry service; dry cleaning. *In room:* A/C, TV, dataport, minibar, hair dryer, safe.

WHERE TO DINE

Christian Etienne ★★★ PROVENÇAL   The stone house containing this restaurant was built in 1180, around the same time as the Palais des Papes (next door). Owner Christian Etienne continues to reach new culinary heights. His dining room contains period frescoes honoring the marriage of Anne de Bretagne to the French king in 1491. Several of the fixed-price menus feature themes: Two present seasonal tomatoes, mushrooms, or vegetables; one offers preparations of lobster; and the priciest *(menu confiance)* relies on the chef's imagination. A la carte specialties include filet of red snapper with black-olive coulis, and a dessert of fennel sorbet with saffron-flavored English cream sauce. The vegetable menus aren't completely vegetarian; they're flavored with meat, fish, or sometimes meat drippings.

10 rue Mons. ⓒ **04-90-86-16-50.** Reservations required. Main courses 15€–32€ ($17–$37); fixed-price menus 50€–92€ ($58–$106). AE, DC, MC, V. Tues–Sat noon–2:30pm and 8–10pm.

La Fourchette (Value) FRENCH   This bistro offers creative cooking at a moderate price, although it shuts down on the weekend. There are two dining rooms, bright and airy thanks to large bay windows that flood the inside with light. You might begin with fresh sardines flavored with citrus, ravioli filled with haddock, or parfait of chicken livers with spinach flan and confit of onions. For a main course, we recommend monkfish stew with endive, or daube of beef with gratin of macaroni.

7 rue Racine. ℂ 04-90-85-20-93. Fixed-price lunch 22€ ($25); fixed-price dinner 27€ ($31). MC, V. Mon–Fri noon–2:30pm and 7:30–10pm. Closed Jan 30–Feb 5. Bus: 11.

EXPLORING THE TOWN

Even more famous than the papal residency is the ditty "Sur le pont d'Avignon, l'on y danse, l'on y danse," echoing through every French nursery and around the world. **Pont St-Bénézet** ★★ was far too narrow for the *danse* of the rhyme, inspired, according to legend, by a vision a shepherd named Bénézet had while tending his flock. Spanning the Rhône and connecting Avignon with Villeneuve-lèz-Avignon, the bridge is now a fragmented ruin. Built between 1177 and 1185, it suffered various disasters; in 1669 half of it toppled into the river. On one of the piers is the two-story Chapelle St-Nicolas—one story in Romanesque style, the other Gothic. The remains of the bridge are open daily from 9am to 6:30pm. Admission is 4€ ($4.60) for adults, 3.30€ ($3.75) for seniors and students, free for children under 8.

Dominating Avignon from a hill is the **Palais des Papes,** place du Palais-des-Papes (ℂ 04-90-27-50-00). The guided tour usually lasts 50 minutes and can be monotonous, because most of the rooms have been stripped of their finery. The exception is the Chapelle St-Jean, known for its frescoes of scenes from the lives of John the Baptist and John the Evangelist, attributed to the school of Matteo Giovanetti, painted between 1345 and 1348. The Grand Tinel, or banquet hall, is about 41m (135 ft.) long and 9m (30 ft.) wide; the pope's table stood on the south side. The pope's bedroom is on the first floor of the Tour des Anges. It's open daily, November through March from 9:30am to 5:45pm; April through June and August through October from 9am to 7pm; July from 9am to 8pm. Admission (including tour with guide or cassette) is 9.50€ ($11) adults, 7.50€ ($8.50) seniors and students, free for children under 8.

Near the palace is the 12th-century **Cathédrale Notre-Dame,** place du Palais-des-Papes (ℂ 04-90-86-81-01), containing the Flamboyant Gothic tomb of some of the apostate popes. The cathedral's hours vary, but generally it's open daily from 9am to noon and 2 to 6pm; admission is free. From the cathedral, enter the promenade du Rocher-des-Doms to stroll through its garden and enjoy the view to Villeneuve-lèz-Avignon.

ST-REMY-DE-PROVENCE ★

Nostradamus, the physician, astrologer, and author of over 600 obscure verses, was born here in 1503. In 1922, Gertrude Stein and Alice B. Toklas found St-Rémy after "wandering around everywhere a bit," as Stein wrote to Cocteau. But St-Rémy is mainly associated with van Gogh, who committed himself to an asylum here in 1889 after cutting off his left ear. Between moods of despair, he painted such works as *Olive Trees* and *Cypresses* here. The town lies 26km (16 miles) northeast of Arles and 13km (8 miles) north of Les Baux.

ESSENTIALS

GETTING THERE   Local **buses** from Avignon (between four and nine per day) take 40 minutes and cost around 6€ ($7) one-way. In St-Rémy, buses pull

into the place de la République, in the town center. For bus information, call
© **04-90-82-07-35.** If you're **driving,** head south from Avignon along D571.

VISITOR INFORMATION   The **Office de Tourisme** is on place Jean-Jaurès
(© **04-90-92-05-22**).

WHERE TO STAY

Château de Roussan ★★ *Finds*   Although other château hotels are more stylish, this one is more evocative of another time. Its most famous resident, the psychic Nostradamus, lived in an outbuilding a few steps from the front door. Today,
you'll pass beneath an archway of 300-year-old trees leading to the neoclassical
facade, built in 1701. Most rooms are spacious. Expect old-fashioned plumbing
with combination tub-showers. History will envelop you as you wander the
grounds, especially when you come upon the sculptures lining a basin, fed by a
stream. The staff can be off-putting, but the sense of mysticism and the historical
importance of this place usually compensate for any crabbiness.

Rte. de Tarascon, 13210 St-Rémy-de-Provence. © **04-90-92-11-63.** Fax 04-90-92-50-59. www.chateau-de-
roussan.com. 21 units. 71€–122€ ($82–$140) double. Half board 35€ ($40). AE, DC, MC, V. From the cen-
ter, head in the direction of Tarascon (D99) for 2km (1¼ miles). **Amenities:** Restaurant; bar; limited room
service; laundry service.

WHERE TO DINE

La Maison Jaune ★★ FRENCH/PROVENÇAL   One of the most enduringly
popular restaurants in St-Rémy is in the former residence of an 18th-century merchant. In a pair of dining rooms occupying two floors, you'll appreciate cuisine
prepared and served with flair by François and Catherine Perraud. In nice weather,
additional seats are on a terrace overlooking the Hôtel de Sade. Menu items
include pigeon roasted in wine from Les Baux; grilled sardines served with candied
lemon and raw fennel; artichoke hearts marinated in white wine and served with
tomatoes; and a succulent version of roasted rack of lamb served with tapenade of
black olives and anchovies.

15 rue Carnot. © **04-90-92-56-14.** Reservations required. Fixed-price menus 30€–55€ ($35–$63). Apr–Dec
noon–1:30pm and 7–9:30pm. Closed Jan–Feb.

EXPLORING ST-REMY & ENVIRONS

One interesting activity is visiting the cloisters of the asylum van Gogh made
famous in his paintings at the 12th-century **Monastère de St-Paul-de-Mausole.**
Now a psychiatric hospital for women, the former monastery is east of D5, a
short drive north of Glanum (see below). You can't visit the cell in which van
Gogh was confined, but it's still worth a visit to explore the Romanesque chapel
and cloisters with circular arches and columns. On your way to the church,
you'll see a bust of van Gogh. The cloisters are open daily April through October from 9:30am to 7pm, November through March 11am to 5pm. Admission
is 2€ ($2.30) adults, 1€ ($1.15) students and children 12 to 16, free for children under 12. There's no public number for the monastery, but you can call the
nearby clinic (© **04-90-92-77-00**) for information.

Just south of St-Rémy on D5 is **Ruines de Glanum** ★, avenue Vincent-van-
Gogh (© **04-90-92-23-79**), a Gallo-Roman city. Its monuments include an Arc
Municipal (a triumphal arch dating from the time of Julius Caesar) and a cenotaph called the Mausolée des Jules. Garlanded with sculptured fruits and flowers, the arch dates from 20 B.C. and is the oldest in Provence. The mausoleum
was raised to honor the grandsons of Augustus and is the only extant monument
of its type. In the area are entire streets and foundations of private residences
from the 1st-century town. Some remains are from a Gallo-Greek town dating

from the 2nd century B.C. Admission is 6.10€ ($7) adults, 4.10€ ($4.75) students and ages 12 to 25, free for children under 12. The excavations are open April through September daily from 9am to 7pm, October through March Tuesday to Sunday 10:30am to 5pm. From the town center, follow the signs to Les Antiques.

LES BAUX ★★★

What Cardinal Richelieu called "a nesting place for eagles" lies 19km (12 miles) north of Arles and 81km (50 miles) north of Marseille and the Mediterranean. Once it was the citadel of iron-fisted seigneurs; today, in its lonely position on a windswept plateau overlooking the southern Alpilles, Les Baux is a ghost of its former self. Still, there is no more dramatically situated town in Provence than this one, nestled in a valley surrounded by mysterious, shadowy rock formations.

ESSENTIALS

GETTING THERE   Les Baux is best reached by car; there is no rail service. Most **train** passengers get off at Arles. Bus service has been discontinued. Taxis in Arles (✆ **06-80-27-60-92**) will take you to Les Baux for around 30€, but fares must be agreed upon in advance.

VISITOR INFORMATION   The **Office de Tourisme** (✆ **04-90-54-34-39**) is on Maison du Roy, near the northern entrance to the old city.

WHERE TO STAY & DINE

Oustau de Baumanière ★★★   This Relais & Châteaux member is one of southern France's legendary hotels. Raymond Thuilier bought the farmhouse in 1945, and by the 1950s, it was a rendezvous for the glitterati. Today, managed by its founder's grandson, it's not as glitzy, but the three stone houses, draped in flowering vines, are still charming. The plush rooms evoke the 16th and 17th centuries. All units contain large sitting areas, and no two are alike. If there's no vacancy in the main building, the hotel will assign you to one of the annexes. In this case, request Le Manor, the most appealing. The spacious bathrooms contain tub-showers. In the stone-vaulted dining room, the chef serves specialties like ravioli of truffles with leeks, *rossini* (stuffed with foie gras) of veal with fresh truffles, and roast duckling with olives. The award-winning *gigot d'agneau* (lamb) en croûte has become this place's trademark.

Les Baux, 13520 Maussane-les-Alpilles. ✆ **04-90-54-33-07.** Fax 04-90-54-40-46. 30 units. 250€–450€ ($288–$517) double; 405€–450€ ($462–$517) suite. AE, DC, MC, V. Closed Jan 6–Mar 5. Restaurant closed Wed Oct–Apr 1. **Amenities:** Restaurant; outdoor pool; limited room service; babysitting; laundry service. *In room:* A/C, TV, dataport, minibar, hair dryer, iron, safe.

EXPLORING LES BAUX

Some one million visitors a year flock here to wander the feudal ruins, inspect the foundation of a demolished castle, and explore the facades of restored Renaissance homes. The **Château des Baux** (✆ **04-90-54-55-56**) is carved out of the rocky mountain peak; the site of the former castle covers an area at least five times that of Les Baux itself. As you stand here, you can look out over the **Val d'Enfer (Valley of Hell).** At the castle you can enjoy the panorama from the Sarazen Tower (Tour Sarrazin). Admission to the castle is 7€ ($8.05) for adults, 5.50€ ($6.25) for students, and 3.50€ ($4) for children 7 to 17, free for children under 7. The site is open daily in July and August from 9am to 8:30pm; March and September through October from 9am to 6:30pm; and November through February from 9am to 5pm.

ARLES ✶✶✶

Arles, 35km (22 miles) southwest of Avignon and 89km (55 miles) northwest of Marseille, has been called "the soul of Provence." This town on the Rhône attracts art lovers, archaeologists, and historians alike. Van Gogh left Paris for Arles in 1888 and painted some of his most celebrated works here—*Starry Night, The Bridge at Arles, Sunflowers,* and *L'Arlésienne,* among others. Many of these luminous scenes remain to delight visitors today.

Arles isn't quite as charming as Aix-en-Provence, but it has first-rate museums, excellent restaurants, and summer festivals. Though not as lovely as it was when Picasso came here, Arles has enough antique Provençal flavor to keep its appeal alive.

ESSENTIALS

GETTING THERE   **Trains** leave from Paris's Gare de Lyon and arrive at Arles's **Gare SNCF** (av. Paulin-Talabot), a short walk from the town center. One high-speed direct TGV travels from Paris to Arles each day (4½ hr.; 107€/$123 1st class, 72€/$83 2nd). For other trains, you must change in Avignon. There are hourly connections between Arles and Avignon (15 min.; 8.60€/$10 1st class, 5.70€/$6.50 2nd), Marseille (1 hr.; 17€/$20 1st class, 12€/$12 2nd), and Aix-en-Provence (1¾ hr., change in Marseille; 23€/$26 1st class, 15€/$18 2nd). For rail schedules and information, call ☎ **08-92-35-35-35.** There are about four **buses** per day from Aix-en-Provence (trip time: 1¾ hr.). For bus information, call ☎ **04-90-93-74-90.** If you're **driving,** head south along D570 from Avignon.

VISITOR INFORMATION   The **Office de Tourisme** is on esplanade Charles-de-Gaulle (☎ **04-90-18-41-20;** www.tourisme-ville-orles.fr).

WHERE TO STAY

Hôtel Jules César et Restaurant Lou Marquês ✶✶✶   This 17th-century Carmelite convent is now a country hotel with the best restaurant in town. Although it's in a noisy neighborhood, most rooms face the cloister. You'll wake to the scent of roses and the sounds of birds singing. Throughout, you'll find a blend of antique neoclassic architecture and modern amenities. The decor is luxurious, with antique Provençal furnishings. The interior rooms are the most tranquil and also the darkest, though enlivened by bright fabrics. Most of the downstairs units are spacious, and although the upstairs rooms are small, they have a certain old-world charm. The rooms in the modern extensions are comfortable but lack character.

9 bd. des Lices, 13631 Arles CEDEX. ☎ 04-90-52-52-52. Fax 04-90-52-52-53. www.hotel-julescesar.fr. 58 units. 129€–215€ ($148–$247) double; 271€–382€ ($312–$439) suite. AE, DC, MC, V. Parking 12€ ($14). Closed Nov 12–Dec 24. **Amenities:** Restaurant; bar; limited room service; babysitting; laundry service; dry cleaning. *In room:* TV, dataport, minibar, hair dryer, safe.

WHERE TO DINE

Chez Gigi *Value* PROVENÇAL   A few steps from the Arena, this popular neighborhood restaurant offers home cooking at reasonable prices. The setting is casual, with several generations of families squeezed next to young dating couples. The menu is heavy on regional specialties, using Provençal herbs, and prepared with care. Noteworthy dishes are *soupe des poissons* (fish soup served with crusty breads and cheese) and authentic *dorade Provençal* (an ocean fish grilled with Provençal herbs). For dessert, there's a lovely crème brûlée.

49 rue des Arènes. ☎ 04-90-96-68-59. Reservations recommended. Main courses 9.50€–13€ ($11–$14). MC, V. Wed–Sun noon–2pm (by reservation only) and 7:30pm–12:30am.

EXPLORING ARLES

At the tourist office (see "Essentials," above), buy a ***billet global*** ⍟, a pass that admits you to the town's museums, Roman monuments, and major attractions; it costs 14€ ($16) adults, 12€ ($14) students and children under 19.

The town is full of Roman monuments. The vicinity of the old Roman forum is occupied by **place du Forum,** shaded by plane trees. The Café de Nuit, immortalized by van Gogh, once stood on this square. Two Corinthian columns and pediment fragments from a temple are visible at the corner of the Hôtel Nord-Pinus. South of here is **place de la République** (also known as the place de l'Hôtel de Ville), the principal plaza, dominated by a 15m (50-ft.) blue porphyry obelisk. On the north is the impressive Hôtel-de-Ville (town hall) from 1673, built to Mansart's plans and surmounted by a Renaissance belfry.

On the east side of place de la République is the **Eglise St-Trophime** ⍟ (② **04-90-49-33-53**), noted for its 12th-century portal, one of the finest achievements of southern Romanesque style in all of France. In the pediment, Christ is surrounded by the symbols of the Evangelists. The cloister, designed in both the Gothic and Romanesque styles, is noted for its medieval carvings. Admission to the church is free; for the cloister, it's 3.50€ ($4) adults, 2.60€ ($3) students and ages 12 to 18, free for children under 12. The church is open daily from 8:30am to 6:30pm; the cloister daily from May through September 9am to 6:30pm, with shorter hours in the off season.

The city's two great classical monuments are the **Théâtre Antique** ⍟⍟, rue du Cloître (② **04-90-49-36-25**), and the Amphitheater (see below). The Roman theater begun by Augustus in the 1st century was mostly destroyed, and only two Corinthian columns remain. Now rebuilt, the theater is the setting for an annual drama festival in July. The theater was where the Venus of Arles was discovered in 1651. Take rue de la Calade from city hall. The theater is open daily May through September from 9am to 6pm; March, April, and October from 9 to 11:30pm and 2 to 5:30pm; and November through February from 10 to 11:30am and 2 to 4:30pm. Admission is 3€ ($3.45) for adults, 2.20€ ($2.50) for students and ages 12 to 18, free for children under 12.

Nearby, the **Amphitheater** ⍟⍟, Rond-Pont des Arènes (② **04-90-49-36-36**), also built in the 1st century, seats almost 25,000 and still hosts bullfights in summer. The government warns you to visit the old monument at your own risk, because of the worn and uneven masonry. For a good view, you can climb the three towers that remain from medieval times, when the amphitheater was turned into a fortress. Hours are daily May through September from 9am to 7pm; March, April, and October from 9am to 6pm; and November through February from 10am to 4:30pm. Admission costs 4€ ($4.60) for adults, 3€ ($3.45) for students and children under 19.

Perhaps the most memorable sight in Arles is **Les Alyscamps** ⍟, rue Pierre-Renaudel (② **04-90-49-36-87**), once a necropolis established by the Romans, converted into a Christian burial ground in the 4th century. It became a setting for legends in epic medieval poetry and was mentioned in Dante's *Inferno.* Today, it's lined with poplars and surviving sarcophagi: a cool oasis in hot weather. Hours are the same as for the Théâtre Antique (see above). Admission is 3.50€ ($4) adults, 2.60€ ($3) ages 12 to 18, free for children under 12.

AIX-EN-PROVENCE ⍟⍟

Founded in 122 B.C. by Roman general Caius Sextius Calvinus, who named it Aquae Sextiae after himself, Aix evolved from a Roman military outpost to a

> ## *Moments* Aix Through the Eyes of Cézanne
>
> The best experience in Aix is a walk along the *route de Cézanne* (D17), which winds eastward through the countryside toward Ste-Victoire. From the east end of cours Mirabeau, take rue du Maréchal-Joffre across boulevard Carnot to boulevard des Poilus, which becomes avenue des Ecoles-Militaires and finally D17. The stretch between Aix and the hamlet of Le Tholonet is full of twists and turns where Cézanne often set up his easel to paint. The entire route is a lovely 5.5km (3½-mile) stroll. Le Tholonet has a cafe or two where you can refresh yourself while waiting for one of the frequent buses back to Aix.

provincial administrative capital, the seat of an archbishop, and the official residence of the medieval comtes de Provence.

The celebrated son of this faded university town is Paul Cézanne. Montagne Ste-Victoire looms over the town today as it did in Cézanne's time, though a string of high-rises has cropped up. Aix is 81km (50 miles) southeast of Avignon and 32km (20 miles) north of Marseille.

ESSENTIALS

GETTING THERE   The city is easily accessible, with 21 trains arriving daily from Marseille. The trip takes 35 minutes and costs 7€ ($8) one-way. Eight trains arrive from Nice; the trip takes 3 to 4 hours and costs 29€ ($33) one-way. There are eight trains per day from Cannes (3½ hr.), costing 26€ ($20) one-way. High-speed TGV trains arrive at Vitroll, 5.5km (3½ miles) west of Aix. Bus links to the center of Aix cost 3.60€ ($4.10) one-way. For more information, call © **08-92-36-35-35.** Buses from Marseille arrive every 10 minutes, from Avignon five times a day, from Nice twice a day. For more information, call © **04-42-91-26-80.** If you're **driving** to Aix from Avignon or other points north, take A7 south to RN7 and follow it into town. From Marseilles or other points south, take A51 north into town.

VISITOR INFORMATION   The **Office de Tourisme** is at 2 place du Général-de-Gaulle (© **04-42-16-11-61;** www.aixenprovencetourism.com).

WHERE TO STAY

Hôtel Cardinal *Value*   Not everything is state-of-the-art here, but for many travelers, the Cardinal is the best value in Aix. Lying on the other side of the cours in the Mazarin quarter, it is distinguished by a lingering air of fragility and nostalgia. Guests stay in simply furnished rooms either in the main building or in the high-ceilinged 18th-century annex up the street. This building holds most of the suites, each of which has a kitchenette. Bathrooms tend to be small but have good showers.

54 rue Cardinale, 13100 Aix-en-Provence. © **04-42-38-32-30.** Fax 04-42-26-39-05. 29 units. 50€–68€ ($58–$78) double; 73€ ($84) suite. MC, V. **Amenities:** Limited room service. *In room:* A/C, TV, hair dryer.

La Villa Gallici ★★★   This elegant, relentlessly chic inn is the most stylish hotel in town. The rooms, richly infused with local decorative traditions, are subtle and charming. Some units boast a private terrace or garden, and each comes with a combination tub-shower. The villa sits in a large enclosed garden in the heart of Aix, close to one of the best restaurants, Le Clos de la Violette (see "Where to Dine," below). It's a 5-minute walk to the town center.

Av. de la Violette (impasse des Grands Pins), 13100 Aix-en-Provence. ☎ **04-42-23-29-23.** Fax 04-42-96-30-45. www.villagallici.com. 22 units. 280€–550€ ($322–$632) double; 550€–600€ ($632–$690) suite. AE, DC, MC, V. **Amenities:** Restaurant; bar; pool; 24-hr. room service; babysitting; laundry service; dry cleaning. *In room:* A/C, TV, dataport, minibar, hair dryer, safe.

WHERE TO DINE

Le Bistro Latin ★★ *Value* PROVENÇAL   The best little bistro in Aix-en-Provence (for the price) is run by Gilles Holtz, who prides himself on his fixed-price menus. Guests dine in two intimate rooms: a street-level space and another in the cellar, decorated in Greco-Latin style. The staff is young and enthusiastic. Try chartreuse of mussels, a meat dish with spinach-and-saffron cream sauce, scampi risotto, or crepe of hare with basil sauce. We've enjoyed the classic cuisine on all our visits.

18 rue de la Couronne. ☎ 04-42-38-22-88. Reservations recommended. Main courses 14€–17€ ($16–$20); fixed-price menus 16€ ($18) lunch, 21€–32€ ($25–$37) dinner. MC, V. Tues–Sat noon–2pm; Mon–Sat 7–10:30pm.

Le Clos de la Violette ★★★ MODERN FRENCH   This innovative restaurant is a few steps from La Villa Gallici (see "Where to Stay," above), in an elegant neighborhood that most visitors reach by taxi. The Provençal villa has an octagonal reception area and several dining rooms. Menu items are stylish and seasonal, and include a medley of dishes highlighting the flavors of Provence. Examples include mousseline of potatoes with sea urchins and fish roe; braised sea wolf with crisp fried shallots and a "cappuccino" of spicy Spanish sausages; and rack of suckling lamb stuffed with carrots and chickpeas. An absolutely superb dessert is a "celebration" of Provençal figs—an artfully arranged platter containing a galette of figs, a tart of figs, a parfait of figs, and a sorbet of figs.

10 av. de la Violette. ☎ 04-42-23-30-71. Reservations required. Main courses 30€–35€ ($35–$40); fixed-price lunch 54€ ($62); tasting menu 117€ ($135). AE, V. Apr–Oct Tues and Thurs–Sat noon–1:30pm, Tues–Sat 7:30–9:30pm; Nov–Mar Tues–Sat noon–2:30pm and 7:30–10pm. Closed 2 weeks in Feb, 3 weeks in Aug.

EXPLORING THE CITY

The main street, **cours Mirabeau** ★★, is one of the most beautiful in Europe. Plane trees act like umbrellas, shading the street from the sun and filtering the light into shadows that play on the rococo fountains. On one side are shops and sidewalk cafes, on the other embellished sandstone *hôtels particuliers* (mansions) from the 17th and 18th centuries. The street, which honors Mirabeau, the revolutionary and statesman, begins at the 1860 fountain on place de la Libération.

Outside town, at 9 av. Paul-Cézanne, is the **Atelier de Cézanne** (☎ **04-42-21-06-53**), the studio of the painter who was the major forerunner of Cubism. Surrounded by a wall, the house was restored by American admirers. Repaired again in 1970, it remains much as Cézanne left it in 1906. It's open daily from 10am to noon and 2:30 to 6pm (2–5pm Oct–May). Admission is 5.50€ ($6.25) adults, 2€ ($2.30) students and children.

ST-TROPEZ ★★

Sun-kissed lasciviousness is rampant in this carnival town, 76km (47 miles) southwest of Cannes, but "we can be classy, too," one native insisted. Creative people in the arts and ordinary folk create a compelling mixture.

Colette lived here for many years. Diarist Anaïs Nin posed on the beach in 1939 in a Dorothy Lamour–style bathing suit. Earlier, St-Tropez was known to Maupassant, Matisse, and Bonnard. Today, artists, composers, novelists, and the film colony come to St-Tropez in summer. Trailing them is a line of humanity unmatched anywhere else on the Riviera for sheer flamboyance.

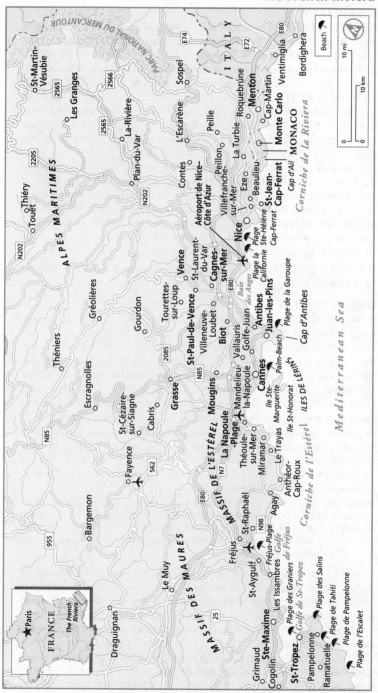

The French Riviera

PARC NATIONAL DU MERCANTOUR

I T A L Y

St-Martin-Vésubie

Les Granges

2565

2566

La-Rivière

Plan-du-Var

2565

2205

Thiéry

Touët

Théniers

ALPES MARITIMES

N202

N202

Sospel

L'Escarène

Peille

Contes

Peillon

La Turbie

Eze

Roquebrune

Menton

Cap-Martin

Ventimiglia

Monte Carlo

MONACO

Cap d'Ail

Bordighera

E74

E80

E72

Beach

10 mi

10 km

0

0

Corniche de la Riviera

St-Jean-

Cap-Ferrat

Cap-Ferrat

Beaulieu

Ste-Hélène

Villefranche-sur-Mer

Aéroport de Nice-Côte d'Azur

Nice

Plage

Gréolières

Vence

St-Laurent-du-Var

Cagnes-sur-Mer

Tourettes-sur-Loup

St-Paul-de-Vence

Villeneuve-Loubet

Biot

Vallauris

Golfe-Juan

Antibes

Juan-les-Pins

Plage la Californie

Baie des Anges

Plage la Garoupe

Cap d'Antibes

Plage de la Garoupe

Gourdon

Escragnolles

St-Cézaire-sur-Siagne

Cabris

Grasse

Mougins

Mandelieu-la-Napoule

Cannes

Palm-Beach

Ile Ste-Marguerite

Ile St-Honorat

ILES DE LÉRINS

La Napoule-Plage

Théoule-sur-Mer

Le Trayas

Miramar

Anthéor-Cap-Roux

Corniche de l'Estérel

MASSIF DE L'ESTÉREL

N7

Fayence

Bargemon

562

N85

2085

N85

E80

Corniche de l'Estérel

Mediterranean Sea

St-Raphaël

St-Aygulf

Agay

Fréjus

Fréjus-Plage

Golfe de Fréjus

N98

Le Muy

MASSIF DES MAURES

25

Draguignan

FRANCE

Paris

The French Riviera

955

Les Issambres

Ste-Maxime

Plage des Graniers de St-Tropez

Golfe de St-Tropez

Grimaud

Cogolin

St-Tropez

Pampelonne

Ramatuelle

Plage des Salins

Plage de Tahiti

Plage de Pampelonne

Plage de l'Escalet

355

ESSENTIALS

GETTING THERE   The nearest **rail** station is in St-Raphaël, a neighboring resort. At the Vieux Port, four or five **boats** per day between April and October leave the **Gare Maritime de St-Raphaël,** rue Pierre-Auble (© **04-94-95-17-46**), for St-Tropez (trip time: 50 min.), at a cost of 10€ ($12) each way. Year-round, 10 to 15 Sodetrav **buses** per day leave from the Gare Routière in St-Raphaël (© **04-94-97-88-51**) for St-Tropez, taking 1½ to 2¼ hours, depending on the bus and the traffic, which during midsummer is usually horrendous. A one-way ticket costs 8.70€ ($10). Buses run directly to St-Tropez from Toulon and Hyères. Buses also run directly to St-Tropez from the nearest airport, at Toulon-Hyères, 56km (35 miles) away.

If you **drive,** note that parking in St-Tropez is very difficult. You can park in the **Parc des Lices** (© **04-94-97-34-46**), beneath place des Lices; enter on avenue Paul-Roussel. This lot charges 2€ ($2.30) per hour. Many visitors prefer it, because it's more secure than any other lot. If you don't use it, you'll have to squeeze your car into tiny parking spaces wherever you find them. To get here from **Cannes,** drive southwest along the coastal highway (RD98), turning east when you see the signs to St-Tropez.

VISITOR INFORMATION   The **Office de Tourisme** is on quai Jean-Jaurès (© **04-94-97-45-21;** www.saint-tropez.st).

WHERE TO STAY

Hôtel Byblos ★★★   The builder said he created "an anti-hotel, a place like home." That's true if your home resembles a palace in Beirut with salons decorated with Phoenician gold statues from 3000 B.C. On a hill above the harbor, this complex boasts intimate patios and courtyards and retreats filled with antiques and objects like polychrome carved woodwork, marquetry floors, and a Persian-rug ceiling. Every room is unique and might feature a fireplace on a raised hearth or a bed recessed on a dais. The rooms range from medium to spacious, often with high ceilings and antiques or reproductions and each with an elegant bed. Le Hameau contains 10 duplex suites built around a small courtyard with an outdoor spa. Some rooms have balconies overlooking an inner courtyard; others open onto a terrace. You can dine by the pool, enjoying Provençal food. Later, you can dance on a circular floor surrounded by bas-relief columns in the nightclub, **Caves du Roy.**

Av. Paul-Signac, 83990 St-Tropez. © **04-94-56-68-00.** Fax 04-94-56-68-01. www.byblos.com. 98 units, 10 duplex suites. 360€–690€ ($414–$793) double; 585€–1,700€ ($673–$1,955) suite. AE, DC, MC, V. Parking 30€ ($35) in garage. Closed Oct 15 to mid-Apr. **Amenities:** 2 restaurants; 2 bars; nightclub; outdoor pool; gym; spa; sauna; salon; limited room service; massage; babysitting; laundry service; dry cleaning. *In room:* A/C, TV, dataport, minibar, hair dryer, safe.

Hôtel La Ponche ★★   The same family has run this homey hotel overlooking the port for more than half a century. It's filled with the original airy paintings of Jacques Cordier, which add to the atmosphere. The recently redecorated rooms are well equipped and open onto sea views. Each floor holds two or three rooms. The beds are elegantly appointed with linen and quality mattresses, and the bathrooms are midsize to large.

Port des Pêcheurs, 83990 St-Tropez. © **04-94-97-02-53.** Fax 04-94-97-78-61. www.laponche.com. 18 units. 135€–385€ ($155–$443) double; 205€–505€ ($235–$580) suite. AE, MC, V. Parking 21€ ($24). Closed Nov to mid-Feb. **Amenities:** Restaurant; bar; limited room service; babysitting; laundry service; dry cleaning. *In room:* A/C, TV, dataport, minibar, hair dryer, safe.

WHERE TO DINE

Chez Maggi ★★ PROVENÇAL/ITALIAN   This is St. Tropez's most flamboyant gay restaurant and bar, but it draws straight diners and drinkers as well. At least half its space is devoted to a bar, where patrons range in age from 20 to 60. There are no tables in front. Consequently, cruising at Chez Maggi, in the words of loyal patrons, is *très crazée*. Meals are served in an adjoining dining room. Menu items include chicken salad with ginger, goat-cheese salad, *petits farcis provençaux* (vegetables stuffed with minced meat and herbs), and chicken curry with coconut milk, capers, and cucumbers.

7 rue Sibille. ✆ 04-94-97-16-12. Reservations recommended. Main courses 15€–29€ ($17–$33); fixed-price menu 31€ ($36). MC, V. Restaurant daily 7pm–midnight; bar daily 7pm–3am. Closed Oct to mid-Mar.

Leï Mouscardins ★★★ FRENCH/PROVENÇAL   This restaurant has won awards for culinary perfection. The dining room is in formal Provençal style with an adjoining sunroom under a canopy. We recommend *moules* (mussels) *marinières* for an appetizer. On the menu are a celebrated Côte d'Azur fish stew, *bourride Provençale*, and an unusual main-course specialty, crushed chestnuts garnished with morels, crayfish, and truffles. The fish dishes are excellent, particularly sauté of monkfish, wild mushrooms, and green beans. The dessert specialties are soufflés made with Grand Marnier or Cointreau.

1 rue Portalet. ✆ 04-94-97-29-00. Reservations required. Main courses 40€–58€ ($46–$67); fixed-price menus 65€ ($75) lunch, 65€–120€ ($75–$138) dinner. AE, DC, MC, V. June–Sept daily noon–2pm and 7:30–10pm; Oct–May Wed–Mon noon–2pm and 7:30–9:30pm. Closed Jan 10–Feb 15.

Spoon Byblos ★★ FRENCH/INTERNATIONAL   This is one of the latest statements of Alain Ducasse, considered by some the world's greatest chef—or at least the most acclaimed. Originally launched in Paris, Spoon has traveled everywhere from London to the Riviera. Here it serves the cuisines of many cultures with produce mainly from the Mediterranean. It draws special inspiration from the food of Catalonia, Andalusia, and Morocco, and offers more than 300 wines from around the world. The restaurant opens onto a circular bar of blue-tinted glass and stainless steel. Dig into shrimp and squid consommé with a hint of jasmine and orange, or spicy king prawns on a skewer. Then try delectable lamb couscous or spit-roasted John Dory. You might top off a meal with the chef's favorite cheesecake.

In the Hotel Byblos, av. Paul-Signac. ✆ 04-94-56-68-00. Reservations required. Main courses 29€–38€ ($33–$44). Daily summer 8pm–12:30am; off season 8–11pm.

EXPLORING ST-TROPEZ & ENVIRONS

Near the harbor is the **Musée de l'Annonciade (Musée St-Tropez),** at place Grammont (✆ **04-94-97-04-01**), in the former chapel of the Annonciade. It boasts one of the Riviera's finest modern art collections. Many of the artists, including Paul Signac, depicted the port of St-Tropez. The collection includes such works as Van Dongen's *Women of the Balustrade* and paintings and sculpture by Bonnard, Matisse, Braque, Utrillo, Seurat, Derain, and Maillol. The museum is open from June to September, Wednesday through Monday from 10am to noon and 3 to 7pm; October and December through May, Wednesday through Monday from 10am to noon and 2 to 6pm. It's closed in November. Admission is 5.50€ ($6.25) adults, 3.50€ ($4) children under 12.

HITTING THE BEACH & OTHER OUTDOOR ACTIVITIES

BEACHES   St-Tropez has the Riviera's best beaches. The best for families are those closest to the town center, including the amusingly named **Bouillabaisse**

and **Plage des Graniers.** More daring are the 9.5km (6-mile) sandy crescents at **Plage des Salins** and **Plage de Pampelonne,** beginning some 3km (2 miles) from the town center and best reached by bike if you're not driving. If you ever wanted to go topless, this is the place!

BOATING The highly recommended **Suncap Company,** 15 quai de Suffren (✆ **04-94-97-11-23**), rents boats from 5.5m to 12m (18 ft.–40 ft.) long. The smallest can be rented to qualified sailors without a captain, but the larger ones come with a captain at the helm. Prices begin at 1,200€ ($1,380) per day.

SCUBA DIVING A team of dive enthusiasts will show you the azure-colored depths off the coast of St-Tropez from the *Octopussy I* and *II.* Both are aluminum-sided, yellow-painted dive boats. They're based year-round in St-Tropez's Nouveau Port. Experienced divers pay 30€ to 44€ ($35–$51) for a one-tank "exploration" dive, depending on how much of their own equipment they use; novices pay 50€ ($58) for a *baptême* that includes one-on-one supervision and descent to a depth of around 5m (15 ft.). For the *baptême,* you must show strong swimming skills in advance; you must have a license to participate in the conventional dives. For reservations and information, contact *Les Octopussys,* quartier de Bertaud, Gassin, 83900 St-Tropez (✆ **04-94-56-53-10;** fax 04-94-56-46-59).

TENNIS Anyone who phones in advance can use the eight courts (both artificial grass and "Quick," a form of concrete) at the **Tennis-Club de St-Tropez,** route des Plages, St-Claude (✆ **04-94-97-80-76**), about half a mile from the resort's center. Open year-round, the courts rent for 16€ ($18) per hour for green set, 23€ ($29) per hour for clay set, from 8am to 9pm.

ST-TROPEZ AFTER DARK

On the lobby level of the Hôtel Byblos, **Les Caves du Roy,** avenue Paul-Signac (✆ **04-94-97-16-02**), is the most self-consciously chic nightclub in St-Tropez. Entrance is free, but drink prices begin at a whopping 18€ ($21). It's open nightly from 11:30pm till dawn, from May to late September.

Le Papagayo, in the Résidence du Nouveau-Port, rue Gambetta (✆ **04-94-97-76-70**), is one of the largest nightclubs in town. The decor was inspired by the psychedelic 1960s. Entrance is 17€ ($20) and includes the first drink. Next to Le Papagayo is **Le VIP Room,** in the Résidence du Port (✆ **04-94-97-14-70**), where patrons pay about 12€ ($14) per cocktail for the chance to (demurely or not) whoop it up. Expect an active bar, a dance floor, and the kind of posturing that can be amusing or not depending on your point of view.

Le Pigeonnier, 13 rue de la Ponche (✆ **04-94-97-84-26**), rocks, rolls, and welcomes a crowd that's mostly gay, male, and between the ages of 20 and 50. Most of the socializing revolves around the long, narrow bar, where men from all over Europe seem to enjoy chitchat. There's also a dance floor.

CANNES ★★★

When Coco Chanel came here and got a suntan, returning to Paris bronzed, she startled the milk-white society ladies. They quickly began copying her. Today the bronzed bodies—clad in nearly nonexistent swimsuits—that line the beaches of this chic resort continue to copy the late fashion designer.

Something is always happening at Cannes, except in November, traditionally a dead month. Popular with celebrities, Cannes is at its most frenzied in late May during the **International Film Festival** at the Palais des Festivals on promenade de la Croisette.

Cannes, sheltered by hills, lies 26km (16 miles) southwest of Nice. For many it consists of only one street, **promenade de la Croisette,** curving along the coast and split by islands of palms and flowers. Hotels, apartment houses, and boutiques line the seafront. Many of the bigger hotels claim parts of the beaches for guests' private use; there are also public areas.

ESSENTIALS

GETTING THERE   **Trains** arrive frequently throughout the day. Cannes is 15 minutes by train from Antibes and 35 minutes from Nice. The TGV from Paris via Marseille reaches Cannes in about 6 breathless hours. For rail information and schedules, call ✆ **08-92-35-35-35.**

The **Nice international airport** (✆ **08-20-42-33-33**) is a 20-minute drive northeast. **Buses** pick up passengers at the airport every 40 minutes during the day, delivering them to the Gare Routière, place de l'Hôtel de Ville (✆ **04-93-45-20-08**). Bus service from Antibes operates every half-hour.

By **car** from Marseille, take A51 north to Aix-en-Provence, continuing along A8 east to Cannes. From Nice, follow A8 southwest to Cannes.

VISITOR INFORMATION   The **Office de Tourisme** is in the Palais des Festivals, esplanade Georges-Pompidou (✆ **04-93-39-24-53;** www.cannes.fr).

WHERE TO STAY

Although some hotels in Cannes have e-mail addresses, a shared e-mail address reaches all hotels in the city: infos@cannes.hotel.com.

Hôtel Carlton Inter-Continental ★★★   Cynics say that one of the most amusing sights in Cannes is the view from under the grand gate of the Carlton. Here you'll see vehicles of every description dropping off huge amounts of baggage and numbers of fashionable (and sometimes not-so-fashionable) guests. It's the epitome of luxury and has become such a part of the city's heartbeat that to ignore it would be to miss the resort's spirit. The twin gray domes at either end of the facade are often the first things recognized by starlets planning their grand entrances, grand exits, and grand scenes in the hotel's public and private rooms.

Built in 1912, the Carlton once attracted the most prominent members of Europe's *haut monde.* Today the hotel is more democratic, hosting conventions and motor-coach tour groups; however, in summer (especially during the film festival) the public rooms still fill with all the voyeuristic and exhibitionistic fervor that seems so much a part of the Riviera. Guest rooms are plush and a bit airier than you might expect. The most spacious rooms are in the west wing, and many upper-floor rooms open onto waterfront balconies.

58 bd. de la Croisette, 06400 Cannes. ✆ **04-93-06-40-06.** Fax 04-93-06-40-25. http://cannes.interconti.com. 326 units. 280€–790€ ($322–$908) double; from 790€ ($908) suite. AE, DC, MC, V. Parking 30€ ($35). **Amenities:** 3 summer restaurants; 1 winter restaurant; 2 bars; health club; sauna; business center; 24-hr. room service; laundry service; dry cleaning; casino. *In room:* A/C, TV, dataport, minibar, hair dryer, safe.

Hôtel Gray-d'Albion ★★   The smallest of the major hotels isn't on La Croisette. Some consider the Gray-d'Albion among the most luxurious hotels in France. Groups form a large part of its clientele, but it also caters to the individual. All rooms are medium in size, blending contemporary and traditional furnishings; the generous-size bathrooms have tub-shower combinations. Each unit has a balcony, but the views aren't notable, except from rooms on the eighth and ninth floors, which overlook the Mediterranean.

38 rue des Serbes, 06400 Cannes. ✆ **04-92-99-79-79.** Fax 04-93-99-26-10. www.lucienbarriere.com. 199 units. 160€–285€ ($184–$328) double; from 650€ ($748) suite. AE, DC, MC, V. **Amenities:** Restaurant; bar;

salon; 24-hr. room service in summer (limited in winter); babysitting; laundry service; dry cleaning. *In room:* A/C, TV, dataport, minibar, hair dryer, safe.

Hôtel le Fouquet's ★ *Finds*   This intimate hotel draws discreet patrons, often from Paris, who'd never think of patronizing the grand hotels. Very "Riviera French" in design and decor, it's several blocks from the beach. Each of the cozy guest rooms is outfitted just a bit differently from its neighbor. Each has pastel colors and contemporary furniture. The owner is often on-site, making the hotel feel a bit like an intimate B&B. Bathrooms, though small, are efficiently organized, with showers and tubs.

2 rond-point Duboys-d'Angers, 06400 Cannes. ✆ **04-92-59-25-00.** Fax 04-92-98-03-39. www.le-fouquets.com. 10 units. 135€–200€ ($155–$230) double. AE, DC, MC, V. Parking 12€ ($14). Closed Nov to mid-Mar. Bus: 1. **Amenities:** Limited room service; babysitting; laundry service; dry cleaning. *In room:* A/C, TV, dataport, minibar, hair dryer, safe.

Hotel Splendid ★ *Value*   Opened in 1871, this is a favorite of scholars, politicians, actors, and musicians. The Splendid's ornate white building with wrought-iron accents looks out onto the sea, the old port, and a park. The rooms boast antique furniture and paintings as well as videos; about half have kitchenettes. Each comes with a good bed and a small but efficient bathroom with a combination tub-shower. The more expensive rooms have sea views.

Rue Félix-Faure, 06400 Cannes. ✆ **04-97-06-22-22.** Fax 04-93-99-55-02. www.splendid-hotel-cannes.fr. 62 units. 119€–246€ ($137–$283) double; 199€–250€ ($230–$288) suite. AE, MC, V. Parking 10€ ($12). **Amenities:** Limited room service; babysitting. *In room:* A/C, TV, dataport, hair dryer, safe.

Hôtel Villa de l'Olivier *Finds*   Charming and personal, this is a hideaway with a low-key style. In the 1930s, it was a villa; in the 1960s it became a hotel with a six-unit annex in the garden. Today, you'll find buildings with lots of glass overlooking a pool, and decor combining the French colonial tropics with the late 19th century and Provence. Rooms have upholstered walls, each in a different color and pattern, and lots of Provençal accessories. Bathrooms come in a variety of sizes, each with a combination tub-shower.

5 rue des Tambourinaires, 06400 Cannes. ✆ **04-93-39-53-28.** Fax 04-93-39-55-85. www.hotelolivier.com. 24 units. 97€–125€ ($112–$144) double; 244€ ($280) suite. AE, DC, MC, V. Parking 10€ ($12). Closed 3 weeks in Dec. **Amenities:** Bar; outdoor pool; limited room service; laundry service; dry cleaning. *In room:* A/C, TV, dataport, hair dryer.

WHERE TO DINE

La Palme d'Or ★★★ MODERN FRENCH   Movie stars on the see-and-be-seen circuit head here during the film festival. It's a sophisticated rendezvous that also serves some of the Riviera's finest hotel cuisine. The light wood–paneled Art Deco marvel has bay windows, a winter garden theme, and terraces overlooking the pool, the sea, and La Croisette. Menu items change with the seasons but are likely to include warm foie gras with fondue of rhubarb; filets of fried red mullet with a beignet of potatoes, zucchini, and olive-cream sauce; and a medley of crayfish, clams, and squid marinated in peppered citrus sauce. A modernized version of a Niçoise staple includes three parts of a rabbit with rosemary sauce, fresh vegetables, and chickpea rosettes. The most appealing dessert is wild strawberries from Carros, with Grand Marnier–flavored *nage* and "cream sauce of frozen milk." The service is worldly without being stiff.

In the Hôtel Martinez, 73 bd. de la Croisette. ✆ **04-92-98-74-14.** Reservations required. Main courses 52€–160€ ($60–$184); fixed-price menus 55€–140€ ($63–$160) lunch Wed–Sat, 70€–140€ ($81–$161) dinner. AE, DC, MC, V. Tues–Sat 12:30–2pm and 8–10pm (Tues 7:30–10:30pm mid-June to mid-Sept). Closed Apr 12–27 and Nov 15–Dec 20.

Le Monaco *Value* FRENCH/ITALIAN/PROVENÇAL   Restaurant tabs on La Croisette often resemble the GNP of a small country. But pricey Cannes has working people who have to eat, and they go to Le Monaco, a blue-collar eatery with great food served bistro style. Menu choices include osso buco with sauerkraut, paella, couscous, roast rabbit with mustard sauce, mussels, trout with almonds, and daube Provençal. Another specialty is grilled sardines, which many restaurants won't serve, considering them too messy and old-fashioned. Dessert might be a slice of orange tart.

15 rue du 24-Août. (© **04-93-38-37-76.** Reservations required. Main courses 7€–14€ ($8.05–$16); fixed-price menu 14€–25€ ($16–$29). AE, MC, V. Mon–Sat noon–3pm and 7–10:30pm.

EXPLORING CANNES

Above the harbor, the old town of Cannes sits on Suquet Hill, where you'll see a 14th-century tower that the English dubbed the **Lord's Tower.**

The **Musée de la Castre** ✿, in the Château de la Castre, Le Suquet (© **04-93-38-55-26**), contains paintings, sculpture, decorative arts, and a section on ethnography, which includes objects from all over, including Peruvian and Maya pottery. There's also a gallery devoted to relics of Mediterranean civilizations, from the Greeks to the Romans, from the Cypriots to the Egyptians. Five rooms are devoted to 19th-century paintings. The museum is open Tuesday to Sunday June to August 10am to 1pm and 3 to 7pm; April, May, and September 10am to 1pm and 2 to 6pm; and October to March 10am to 1pm and 2 to 5pm. Admission is 2€ ($2.30)

HITTING THE BEACH & OTHER OUTDOOR PURSUITS

BEACHES   Looking for a free public beach? Head for **Plage du Midi,** just west of the Vieux Port (© **04-93-39-92-74**); or **Plage Gazagnaire,** just east of the Port Canto (no phone). Here you'll find greater numbers of families with children and lots of caravan-type vehicles parked nearby. Between these two public beaches are many private ones where you can gain entrance by paying a fee that includes a mattress and parasol.

BICYCLING & MOTOR-SCOOTERING   Despite the roaring traffic, the flat landscapes between Cannes and satellite resorts like La Napoule are well suited for riding a bike or motor scooter. At **Cycles Daniel,** 2 rue du Pont Romain (© **04-93-99-90-30**), *vélos tout terrain* (mountain bikes) cost 11€ ($13) a day. Motorized bikes and scooters cost 26€ ($30) per day, and renters must be at least 14 years old. For larger scooters, renters must present a valid driver's license. Another purveyor of bikes is **Mistral Location,** 4 rue Georges Clémenceau (© **04-93-39-33-60**), which charges 11€ ($13) per day.

BOATING   Several companies can rent you a boat of any size, with or without a crew, for a day, a week, or a month. An outfit known for short-term rentals

---

Finds Provençal Olives for Sale

A charming old-fashioned shop, **Cannolive,** 16–20 rue Vénizelos (© **04-93-39-08-19**), is owned by the Raynaud family, who founded the place in 1880. It sells Provençal olives and their by-products—*tapenades* (pastes) that connoisseurs refer to as "Provençal caviar," black "olives de Nice," and green "olives de Provence," as well as olive oil from regional producers. Oils and food products are at no. 16; gift items (fabrics, porcelain, and Provençal souvenirs) are sold next door.

of small craft, including motorboats, sailboats, and canoes, is **Elco Marine,** 110 bd. du Midi (✆ **04-93-47-55-54**). For larger boats, including motor-driven and sailing yachts and craft suitable for deep-sea fishing, try **MS Yachts,** 57 La Croisette (✆ **04-93-99-03-51**), or **Mediterranée Courtage** (Agence Y.P.), 22 quai St-Pierre (✆ **04-93-38-30-40**).

CANNES AFTER DARK

Cannes has a pair of world-class casinos. The better established is the **Casino Croisette,** in the Palais des Festivals, 1 jetée Albert-Edouard (✆ **04-92-98-78-00**). A well-respected fixture in town since the 1950s, it's a competitor of the newer **Palm Beach Casino,** place F-D. Roosevelt, Pointe de la Croisette (✆ **04-97-06-36-90**), on the southeast edge of La Croisette. Originally inaugurated in 1933 and rebuilt in 2002, it features three restaurants and Art Deco decor. It's glossier, newer, and a bit hungrier for new business. Both casinos offer slot machines that operate daily from 11am to 5am. Suites of rooms devoted to *les grands jeux* (blackjack, roulette, and chemin de fer) open nightly from 8pm to 5am. Both casinos charge 11€ ($13) and require a passport or ID card for access to *les grands jeux.*

JUAN-LES-PINS ★★

This suburb of Antibes is a resort developed in the 1920s. In the 1930s Juan-les-Pins drew a chic winter crowd. Today it attracts young Europeans from many economic backgrounds, in pursuit of sex, sun, and sea, in that order.

Juan-les-Pins is often called the "Coney Island of the Riviera," but anyone who calls it that hasn't seen Coney Island in a long time. One writer said that Juan-les-Pins is "for the young and noisy." Even F. Scott Fitzgerald decried it as a "constant carnival." If he could see it now, he'd know he was a prophet.

The town has some of the best nightlife on the Riviera, and the action reaches its frenzied height during the **Festival International de Jazz,** which takes place in mid-July for 10 to 12 days. For more information on the festival, contact the tourist office. The pines sweep down to a good beach, crowded with summer sunbathers, most often in skimpy swimwear.

ESSENTIALS

GETTING THERE Juan-les-Pins is connected by **rail** and bus to most other coastal resorts, notably Nice (trip time: 30 min.). For rail information, call ✆ **08-92-35-35-35. Buses** arrive from Nice and its airport at 40-minute intervals throughout the day. A bus leaves for Juan-les-Pins from Antibes at place Guynemer (✆ **04-93-34-37-60**) daily every 20 minutes and costs 1.10€ ($1.25) one-way (trip time: 10 min.). To **drive** to Juan-les-Pins from Nice, take N7 south; from Cannes, follow the signposted roads. Juan-les-Pins is just outside of Cannes.

VISITOR INFORMATION The **Office de Tourisme** is at 51 bd. Charles-Guillaumont (✆ **04-92-90-53-05;** www.antibesjuanlespins.com).

WHERE TO STAY

Hôtel Cecil *(Value* A stone's throw from the beach, this well-kept small hotel is one of the best bargains in Juan-les-Pins. It originated in 1929 when a 19th-century villa was enlarged with another story and transformed into a hotel. The traditionally furnished rooms are well worn yet well maintained, ranging from small to midsize, each with a compact tiled bathroom with shower. Owner-chef Michel Courtois provides a courteous welcome and good meals. In summer, you can enjoy his food on a patio.

Rue Jonnard, 06160 Juan-les-Pins. ℂ **04-93-61-05-12.** Fax 04-93-67-09-14. www.hotelcecilfrance.com. 21 units. Feb–Oct 50€–87€ ($58–$100) double. AE, DC, MC, V. Parking 8€ ($9.20). Closed Nov–Jan. **Amenities:** Restaurant; limited room service; babysitting. *In room:* A/C, TV, dataport, hair dryer.

Hôtel des Belles-Rives ⭐⭐⭐   This is one of the Riviera's fabled addresses. Once it was a holiday villa occupied by Zelda and F. Scott Fitzgerald. It has played host to the illustrious, like the duke and duchess of Windsor, Josephine Baker, and Edith Piaf. A 1930s aura lingers through recent renovations. Double-glazing and air-conditioning help a lot. As befits a hotel of this age, rooms come in a variety of shapes and sizes, from small to spacious; each has a luxurious bathroom with a combination tub-shower. The lower terraces hold garden dining rooms, an aquatic club with a snack bar and lounge, and a jetty. The beach is private. Dinners are served in the romantic **La Terrasse** with a panoramic bay view.

33 bd. Baudoin, 06160 Juan-les-Pins. ℂ **04-93-61-02-79.** Fax 04-93-67-43-51. www.bellesrives.com. 44 units. 225€–660€ double ($259–$759); 450€–1,210€ ($517–$1,392) suite. AE, DC, MC, V. Free parking. Closed Jan to mid-Feb. **Amenities:** 2 summer restaurants; 1 winter restaurant; 2 bars; courtesy car; limited room service; babysitting; laundry service; dry cleaning; dock. *In room:* A/C, TV, dataport, minibar, hair dryer, safe.

WHERE TO DINE

La Terrasse ⭐⭐⭐ FRENCH/MEDITERRANEAN   Chefs here cook with a light, precise, and creative hand, and the cuisine is among the finest along the Riviera. The setting is lively and sophisticated, overlooking the garden and a glassed-in terrace whose roof opens for ventilation and a view of the stars. Menu items are steeped in the flavors of Provence. Examples include clam-filled cannelloni in black squid ink with shellfish juice and fresh basil leaves; and saddle of Pauillac lamb baked in a clay casserole, stuffed with zucchini flowers, and flavored with thyme flower juice. Dessert might be a napoleon of wild strawberries with mascarpone cream sauce.

In the Hôtel Juana, La Pinède, av. Gallice. ℂ **04-93-61-20-37.** Reservations required. Main courses 38€–85€ ($44–$98). Fixed-price menus 48€ ($55) lunch, 92€–135€ ($106–$155) dinner. AE, MC, V. Apr–Sept daily 12:30–2pm and 7:30–10:30pm; Oct–Mar Thurs–Mon 12:30–2pm and 7:30–10:30pm.

ANTIBES & CAP D'ANTIBES ⭐⭐

On the other side of the Baie des Anges (Bay of Angels), across from Nice, is the port of Antibes. The town has a quiet charm unique on the Côte d'Azur. Its harbor is filled with fishing boats and yachts, and in recent years it has emerged as a hot spot. The marketplaces are full of flowers. If you're in Antibes in the evening, you can watch fishers playing the popular Riviera game of *boule.*

Spiritually, Antibes is totally divorced from Cap d'Antibes, a peninsula studded with the villas of the superrich. In *Tender Is the Night,* Fitzgerald described it as a place where "old villas rotted like water lilies among the massed pines."

ESSENTIALS

GETTING THERE   Trains from Cannes arrive at the rail station, on place Pierre-Semard, every 20 minutes (trip time: 10 min.); the one-way fare is 3€ ($3.45). Trains from Nice arrive every 30 minutes (trip time: 18 min.), and the one-way fare is around 4€ ($4.60). For information, call ℂ **08-92-35-35-35.** The **bus** station, La Gare Routière, place Guynemer (ℂ **04-93-34-37-60**), receives buses from throughout Provence.

If you're **driving,** follow E1 east from Cannes and take the turnoff to the south for Antibes. From Nice, take E1 west until you come to the turnoff for Antibes. From the center of Antibes, follow the coastal road, boulevard Leclerc, south until you come to Cap d'Antibes.

VISITOR INFORMATION The **Office de Tourisme** is at 11 place du Général-de-Gaulle (© **04-92-90-53-00;** fax 04-92-90-53-01; www.Antibes juanlespins.com).

WHERE TO STAY

Auberge de la Gardiole ★   This is a country inn run with a personal touch. The large villa, surrounded by gardens, is in an area of private estates. The charming rooms are on the upper floors of the inn and in the little buildings in the garden; they come in a variety of shapes and sizes, each furnished with a certain charm and an eye on comfort. Half the units come with showers, half with combination tub-showers. Fifteen have air-conditioning. The cheerful dining room serves French and Provençal cuisine; in good weather you can dine under a wisteria-covered trellis.

Chemin de la Garoupe, 06160 Cap d'Antibes. © **04-93-61-35-03.** Fax 04-93-67-61-87. www.hotel-lagaroupe-gardiole.com. 20 units. Summer 95€–150€ ($109–$173) double, 170€–200€ ($195–$230) suite; off season 75€–130€ ($86–$150) double, 145€–165€ ($167–$190) suite. AE, MC, V. Closed Nov–Mar. Bus: A2. **Amenities:** Restaurant; bar; pool; limited room service; laundry service. *In room:* TV, minibar, safe.

Castel Garoupe *(Value)*   We highly recommend this Mediterranean villa, which was built in 1968 on a private lane in the center of the cape. It offers tastefully furnished, spacious rooms with fine beds and compact bathrooms with showers and tubs. Many rooms have private balconies, and each has shuttered windows. Some units have air-conditioning, and some have TVs. There's a tranquil garden on the premises.

959 bd. de la Garoupe, 06160 Cap d'Antibes. © **04-93-61-36-51.** Fax 04-93-67-74-88. www.castel-garoupe. com. 28 units. 115€–146€ ($132–$168) double; 139€–179€ ($160–$206) studio apt with kitchenette. Rates include breakfast. AE, MC, V. Closed Nov to mid-Mar. Bus: A2. **Amenities:** 2 bars; outdoor pool; exercise room; limited room service; babysitting; laundry service; dry cleaning. *In room:* Dataport, kitchenette, minibar, hair dryer, safe.

Hôtel du Cap-Eden Roc ★★★   Legendary for the glamour of its setting and its clientele, this Second Empire hotel, opened in 1870, is surrounded by gardens. It's like a country estate, with spacious public rooms, marble fireplaces, and chandeliers. The guest rooms are among the most sumptuous on the Riviera, with deluxe beds. Bathrooms are spacious, with tub-shower combinations. Even though the guests snoozing by the pool, which was blasted out of the cliff side at enormous expense, might appear undraped during the day, evenings are upscale, with lots of emphasis on clothing and style. The famous Pavillon Eden Roc, near a rock garden apart from the hotel, has a panoramic sea view. Venetian chandeliers, Louis XV chairs, and elegant draperies add to the drama. Lunch is served on a terrace, under umbrellas and an arbor.

Bd. J.-F.-Kennedy, 06600 Cap d'Antibes. © **04-93-61-39-01.** Fax 04-93-67-13-83. www.edenroc-hotel.fr. 140 units. 360€–550€ ($414–$632) double; 810€–1,200€ ($932–$1,380) suite. No credit cards. Closed mid-Oct to Apr. Bus: A2. **Amenities:** Restaurant; 2 bars; outdoor pool; gym; sauna; secretarial service; limited room service; massage; babysitting; laundry service; dry cleaning. *In room:* A/C, TV (on request), hair dryer, safe.

WHERE TO DINE

La Taverne du Saffranier *(Value)* PROVENÇAL   Earthy and irreverent, this brasserie in a century-old building serves a medley of savory local specialties. Portions are generous. Examples are a platter of *petits farcis* (stuffed vegetables); ceviche, the cold raw fish in hot sauce that's refreshing on a hot day; and a medley of grilled fish (including sardines) served with a dash of fresh lemon. The kitchen can prepare bouillabaisse if you give a day's notice.

Place du Saffranier. (**04-93-34-80-50**. Reservations recommended. Main courses 15€–30€ ($17–$35); fixed-price menu 13€ ($15). No credit cards. Tues–Sun noon–2:30pm; Tues–Sat 7–10:30pm.

Restaurant de Bacon ★★★ SEAFOOD   The Eden Roc restaurant at the Hôtel du Cap is more elegant, but Bacon serves the best seafood around. This restaurant on a rocky peninsula offers a panoramic coast view. Bouillabaisse aficionados claim that Bacon offers the best in France. In its deluxe version, saltwater crayfish float atop the savory brew; we prefer the simple version—a waiter adds the finishing touches at your table. If bouillabaisse isn't to your liking, try fish soup with garlicky *rouille* sauce, fish terrine, or something from a collection of fish unknown in North America. These include sar, pageot, and denti.

Bd. de Bacon. (**04-93-61-50-02**. Reservations required. Main courses 17€–115€ ($20–$132); fixed-price menu 44€–67€ ($51–$77). AE, MC, V. Wed–Sun noon–2pm; Tues–Sun 8–10pm. Closed Oct–Jan.

A MUSEUM WORTH VISITING

On the ramparts above the port is the Château Grimaldi, once the home of the princes of Antibes of the Grimaldi family, who ruled the city from 1385 to 1608. Today it houses the **Musée Picasso** ★★, place du Mariejol ((**04-92-90-54-20**), one of the world's great Picasso collections. Picasso came to town after the war and stayed in a small hotel at Golfe-Juan until the museum director at Antibes invited him to work and live at the museum. He spent 1946 painting here. When he departed, he gave the museum all the work he'd done: 24 paintings, 80 pieces of ceramics, 44 drawings, 32 lithographs, 11 oils on paper, 2 sculptures, and 5 tapestries. The gallery of contemporary art exhibits Léger, Miró, Ernst, and Calder, among others. Admission is 5€ ($5.75) adults, free for children under 16. The museum is open from October to May, Tuesday through Sunday from 10am to noon and 2 to 6pm (June–Sept Tues–Sun 10am–6pm).

ST-PAUL-DE-VENCE ★★

Of all the perched villages of the Riviera, St-Paul-de-Vence is the best known. It was popularized in the 1920s when many artists lived here, occupying the 16th-century houses flanking the cobblestone streets. Its ramparts (allow about 30 min. to circle them) overlook a setting of flowers and olive and orange trees. They haven't changed much since they were constructed from 1537 to 1547 by order of François I. From the north ramparts you can look out on Baou de St-Jeannet, a sphinx-shaped rock that was painted into the landscape of Poussin's *Polyphème*.

ESSENTIALS

GETTING THERE   The nearest **rail** station is in Cagnes-sur-Mer. Some 20 **buses** per day leave from Nice's Gare Routière, dropping passengers off in St-Paul-de-Vence, then in Vence. For information, call the Société SAP ((**04-93-58-37-60**). If you're **driving** from Nice, take the coastal A8 highway east, turn inland at Cagnes-sur-Mer, and follow signs north to St-Paul-de-Vence.

VISITOR INFORMATION   The **Office de Tourisme** is at Maison Tour, 2 rue Grande ((**04-93-32-86-95;** www.stpaulweb.com).

EXPLORING ST-PAUL-DE-VENCE

The tourist office has created a 1-hour tour of the town's historic center. The price (8€/$9.05) includes admission to the Musée d'Histoire de St-Paul.

Fondation Maeght ★★★   On a hill in pine-studded woods, Fondation Maeght ((**04-93-32-81-63**) is like Shangri-La. Nature and the creations of men and women blend harmoniously in this unique achievement of the architect José Luis Sert. Its white concrete arcs give the impression of a giant pagoda.

A stark Calder rises on the lawn. In a courtyard, the bronze works of Giacometti form a surrealistic garden. Sculpture is displayed inside, but the museum is at its best in a natural setting of terraces and gardens. It's built on several levels, its many glass walls providing an indoor-outdoor vista. The foundation, a gift "to the people" from Aimé and Marguerite Maeght, also provides a showcase for new talent. Everywhere you look, you see 20th-century art: mosaics by Chagall and Braque, Miró ceramics in the "labyrinth," and Ubac and Braque stained glass in the chapel. Bonnard, Kandinsky, Léger, Matisse, Barbara Hepworth, and many other artists are well represented.

Fondation Maeght is open daily from July to September from 10am to 7pm, from October to June 10am to 12:30pm and 2:30 to 6pm. Admission is 11€ ($13) adults, 9€ ($10) students and ages 10 to 25, free for children under 10.

North of St-Paul-de-Vence, you can visit the sleepy old town of **Vence** ⚐, with its **Vieille Ville (Old Town).** If you're wearing comfortable shoes, the narrow, steep streets are worth exploring. The **cathedral** on place Godeau is unremarkable except for some 15th-century choir stalls. If it's the right day of the week, however, most visitors pass through the narrow gates of this once-fortified walled town on their way to the **Chapelle du Rosaire** ⚐⚐, av. Henri-Matisse (© **04-93-58-03-26**), created by Henri Matisse. Matisse was 77 when he set out to design this masterpiece, which he called "the culmination of a whole life dedicated to the search for truth." From the front you might find the chapel of the Dominican nuns of Monteils unremarkable—until you spot a 12m (40-ft.) crescent-adorned cross rising from a blue-tile roof. The light inside picks up the coloring in the simply rendered leaf forms and abstract patterns: sapphire blue, aquamarine, and lemon yellow. In black-and-white ceramics, St. Dominic is depicted in a few lines. The Stations of the Cross are also black-and-white tile, with Matisse's self-styled "tormented and passionate" figures. The chapel is open December through September Monday through Thursday and Saturday from 2 to 5:30pm, and on Tuesday and Thursday from 10 to 11:30am. Admission is 2.50€ ($3) for adults, 1€ ($1.15) for children under 17; contributions to maintain the chapel are welcome.

NICE ⚐⚐⚐

Nice is the capital of the Riviera. It's also one of the country's most ancient cities, founded by the Greeks, who called it Nike (Victory). By the 19th century, the Victorian upper class and tsarist aristocrats flocked here. These days it's not as chichi and expensive, especially compared to Cannes. Of all the major resorts of France, Nice is the most affordable. It's also the best place to base yourself on the Riviera, especially if you're dependent on public transportation. From the Nice airport, the second largest in France, you can travel by train or bus along the entire coast. Because of its brilliant sunshine and relaxed living, Nice has attracted artists and writers, among them Matisse, Dumas, Nietzsche, Flaubert, Hugo, Sand, and Stendhal.

ESSENTIALS
GETTING THERE **Trains** arrive at Gare Nice-Ville, avenue Thiers (© **08-92-35-35-35**). From there you can take trains to Cannes, Monaco, and Antibes, with easy connections to anywhere else along the Mediterranean coast. There's a small tourist center at the train station, open Monday through Saturday from

---

Value **Bus Passes for Easy Travel**

If you plan on using the city's buses, consider buying a **Sun Pass,** available from tobacco stands and newspaper kiosks throughout the city. Valid for 1, 5, or 7 days, the pass allows unlimited transit on any municipal bus. The price is 4€ ($4.60) for a 1-day pass, 13€ ($15) for a 5-day pass, 17€ ($19) for a 7-day pass. For additional information, call **Société SunBus** (© **04-92-17-52-52**).

8am to 6:30pm and Sunday from 8am to noon and 2 to 5:30pm. If you face a long delay, you can eat at the cafeteria and even shower at the station.

Transatlantic and intercontinental flights land at **Aéroport Nice–Côte d'Azur** (© **08-20-42-33-33**). From here, municipal bus nos. 23 and 99 depart at 20-minute intervals from the airport for the bus station or **Gare Routière,** 5 bd. Jean-Jaurès (© **04-93-85-61-81**); the one-way fare is 3.50€ ($4). A more luxurious mode of transport involves a yellow-sided shuttle bus *(la navette de l'aéroport)* that charges 4.50€ ($5.25) for a ride between the airport and Nice's main bus station. A **taxi** ride from the airport into the city center will cost at least 25€ to 30€ ($29–$35) each way. Trip time is about 30 minutes.

GETTING AROUND   Most local buses serve the **Station Central,** 10 av. Félix-Faure (© **04-93-13-53-13**), a very short walk from the place Masséna. Municipal buses charge 1.30€ ($1.50) for a ride within Greater Nice. To save money, consider buying a 14-ticket *carnet* for 16€ ($18). Bus nos. 2 and 12 make frequent trips to the beach. Long-distance buses making the trek, say, between Nice and such destinations as Monaco, Cannes, St-Tropez, and other parts of France and Europe depart from the **Gare Routière,** 5 bd. Jean-Jaurès (© **04-93-85-61-81**).

The best place to rent bikes and mopeds in Nice is **Cycles Arnaud,** 5 rue François 1e (© **04-93-87-88-55**), just behind the place Grimaldi. Open Monday through Friday from 9am to noon and 2 to 7pm, it charges 15€ ($17) per day for a bike or moped, and requires a deposit of at least 300€ ($345), depending on the value of the machine you rent. Somewhat less appealing, but useful when Cycles Arnaud is closed, is **Nicea Rent,** 12 rue de Belgique (© **04-93-82-42-71,** or 06-12-44-15-37 for somewhat erratic mobile phone service). It charges about the same rates but the staff isn't always on the premises.

WHERE TO STAY
Very Expensive
Hôtel Negresco ★★★   The Negresco is one of the Riviera's super-glamorous hotels. This Victorian wedding-cake hotel is named after its founder, Henry Negresco, a Romanian who died franc-less in Paris in 1920. It was built on the seafront, in the French château style, with a mansard roof and domed tower. Its decorators scoured Europe to gather antiques, tapestries, and art. Some of the guest rooms are outfitted in homage to the personalities who stayed here: the Coco Chanel Room, for example. Suites and public areas are even grander; they include the Louis XIV salon, reminiscent of the Sun King, and the Napoleon III suite, where swagged walls, a leopard-skin carpet, and a half-crowned canopy create a sense of majesty. The most expensive rooms with balconies face the Mediterranean. The staff wears 18th-century costumes. The beach is private. The featured restaurant—one of the Riviera's greatest—is **Chantecler** (see below).

37 promenade des Anglais, 06007 Nice CEDEX. ℂ **04-93-16-64-00.** Fax 04-93-88-35-68. www.hotel-negresco-nice.com. 150 units. 225€–280€ ($259–$322) double; 584€–1,500€ ($672–$1,725) suite. AE, DC, MC, V. Free parking. **Amenities:** 2 restaurants; bar; fitness center; secretarial service; 24-hr. room service; massage; babysitting; laundry service; dry cleaning. *In room:* A/C, TV, dataport, minibar, hair dryer.

Expensive

La Pérouse ★ *(Finds)* Once a prison, La Pérouse is a unique Riviera hotel. Set on a cliff, it's built right in the gardens of an ancient château-fort. No hotel affords a better view over both the old city and the Baie des Anges. Many people stay here for the view alone. The hotel is like an old Provençal home, with low ceilings, white walls, and antiques. Most of the lovely rooms have loggias overlooking the bay. The spacious rooms are beautifully furnished, often with Provençal fabrics. The bathrooms are large and done in Boticino marble.

11 quai Rauba-Capéu, 06300 Nice. ℂ **04-93-62-34-63.** Fax 04-93-62-59-41. www.hroy.com/la-perouse. 62 units. 150€–405€ ($173–$465) double; 600€–800€ ($690–$920) suite. AE, DC, MC, V. Parking 15€ ($17). **Amenities:** Restaurant (mid-May to mid-Sept); bar; outdoor pool; exercise room; Jacuzzi; sauna; limited room service; babysitting; laundry service. *In room:* A/C, TV, dataport, minibar, hair dryer, safe.

Moderate

Château des Ollières ★ *(Finds)* This appealing, unusual hotel made its debut in 1996. It's within a 5-minute walk of the Negresco and the promenade des Anglais. The setting is one of the largest tracts of privately owned land in Nice—an 8-hectare (20-acre) park. The centerpiece is a beaux-arts villa built in the 1870s by a Russian prince. The high-ceilinged guest rooms are outfitted in the same ornate style as the public areas. Bathrooms are quite luxurious. The restaurant occupies the original dining room and a garden wing. Menus change according to the inspiration of the chef and the availability of fresh ingredients.

39 av. des Baumettes, 06000 Nice. ℂ **04-92-15-77-99.** Fax 04-92-15-77-98. www.chateaudesollieres.com. 9 units. 140€–370€ ($161–$425) double; 350€–500€ ($402–$575) suite. AE, MC, V. Bus: 38. **Amenities:** Restaurant; bar; limited room service; babysitting; laundry service; dry cleaning. *In room:* A/C, TV, dataport, minibar, hair dryer.

Inexpensive

Hôtel de la Mer *(Value)* In the center of Old Nice, this place was built around 1910, transformed into a hotel in 1947, and renovated in 1993. Despite that, it manages to keep prices low. Ms. Feri Forouzan, the owner, welcomes you with personal charm. Most guest rooms are of good size, each with a small bathroom with shower. It's a 2-minute walk to the promenade des Anglais and the seafront. Breakfast is served in one of the public salons or in your room.

4 place Masséna, 06000 Nice. ℂ **04-93-92-09-10.** Fax 04-93-85-00-64. hotel-mer@wanadoo.fr. 12 units. 50€–75€ ($58–$86) double. AE, MC, V. Bus: 1, 2, 5, 15, or 17. **Amenities:** Limited room service; massage. *In room:* A/C, TV, minibars in some rooms.

WHERE TO DINE

Chantecler ★★★ TRADITIONAL/MODERN FRENCH This is Nice's most prestigious and best restaurant. Panels removed from a château in Puilly-Fussé cover the walls, and a Regency-style salon serves before- and after-dinner drinks. A much-respected chef, Alain Llorca, revised the menu to include the most sophisticated and creative dishes in Nice. They change almost weekly but may include turbot filet served with purée of broad beans, sun-dried tomatoes, and asparagus; roasted suckling lamb served with beignets of fresh vegetables and ricotta-stuffed ravioli; and a melt-in-your-mouth fantasy of marbled hot chocolate drenched in almond-flavored cream sauce.

In the Hôtel Negresco, 37 promenade des Anglais. © **04-93-16-64-00.** Reservations required. Main courses 33€–100€ ($38–$115); fixed-price menus 45€–55€ ($52–$63) lunch, 90€–130€ ($104–$150) dinner. AE, MC, V. Daily 12:30–2pm and 8–10pm. Closed mid-Nov to mid-Dec. Bus: 8, 9, 10, or 11.

La Merenda ★★ *Finds* NIÇOISE   Because there's no phone, you have to go by this place twice: once to make a reservation and once to dine. It's worth the effort. Forsaking his chef's crown at Chantecler (above), Dominique Le Stanc opened this tiny bistro serving sublime cuisine. Though he was born in Alsace, his heart and soul belong to the Mediterranean, the land of black truffles, wild morels, sea bass, and asparagus. His food is a lullaby of gastronomic unity, with texture, crunch, richness, and balance. Look for specials on a chalkboard. Perhaps you'll find stuffed cabbage, fried zucchini flowers, or oxtail flavored with fresh oranges. Lamb from the Sisteron is cooked until it practically falls from the bone. Raw artichokes are paired with a salad of mâche. Service is discreet and personable. We wish we could dine here every day.

4 rue Terrasse. No phone. Reservations required. Main courses 30€–42€ ($35–$48). No credit cards. Mon–Fri noon–2pm and 7–9:30pm. Closed Feb 16–22, Aug 4–18, Dec 24–Jan 4. Bus: 8.

La Zucca Magica ★ *Finds* VEGETARIAN/ITALIAN   The chef at this popular harborside restaurant has been named best Italian chef in Nice. That this honor should go to a vegetarian restaurant was the most startling part of the news. Chef Marco certainly has a fine pedigree—he's a relative of Luciano Pavarotti. He serves refined, creative cuisine at reasonable prices, using recipes from Italy's Piedmont region and updating them with no meat or fish. You'll have to trust Marco, because everyone is served the same meal. You can count on savory cuisine using lots of herbs, Italian cheeses, beans, and pasta.

4 bis quai Papacino. © **04-93-56-25-27.** Reservations recommended. Menus 17€ ($20) lunch, 27€ ($31) dinner. No credit cards. Tues–Sat noon–2pm and 7–10pm.

IN & AROUND NICE

The wide **promenade des Anglais** fronts the bay. Split by "islands" of palms and flowers, it stretches for about 6.5km (4 miles). Fronting the beach are rows of grand cafes, the Musée Masséna, villas, and hotels—some good, others decaying.

In the east, the promenade becomes **quai des Etats-Unis,** lined with some of the best restaurants in Nice, all specializing in bouillabaisse. Rising sharply on a rock is the site known as **Le Château,** where the ducs de Savoie built their castle, torn down in 1706. The hill has been turned into a garden of pines and exotic flowers. To reach the site, you can take an elevator; many people take the elevator up, then walk down. The park is open daily from 8am to dusk.

The center of Nice is **place Masséna,** with pink buildings in the 17th-century Genoese style and the **Fontaine du Soleil (Fountain of the Sun)** by Janoit. Stretching from the main square to the promenade is the **Jardin Albert-1er,** with an open-air terrace and a Triton Fountain. Palms and exotic flowers make this the most relaxing oasis at the resort.

A PAIR OF MUSEUMS WORTH A LOOK

Musée des Beaux-Arts ★★   The collection is housed in the former residence of the Ukrainian Princess Kotchubey. There's a gallery devoted to the masters of the Second Empire and the Belle Epoque. The gallery of sculptures includes works by J. B. Carpeaux, Rude, and Rodin. Note the important collection by a dynasty of painters, the Dutch Vanloo family. One of its best-known members, Carle Vanloo, born in Nice in 1705, was Louis XV's premier *peintre*. A fine collection of 19th- and 20th-century art includes works by Ziem, Raffaelli, Boudin, Renoir, Monet, Guillaumin, and Sisley.

33 av. des Baumettes. © **04-92-15-28-28.** Admission 4€ ($4.60) adults, 2.50€ ($3) students, free for children under 18. Tues–Sun 10am–6pm. Bus: 3, 9, 12, 22, 24, 38, 60, or 62.

Musée International d'Art Naïf Anatole-Jakovsky (Museum of Naïve Art) ⭐ This museum is in the Château Ste-Hélène in the Fabron district. The museum's namesake, for years one of the world's leading art critics, once owned the collection. His 600 drawings and canvases were turned over to the institution and made accessible to the public. Artists from more than two dozen countries are represented here—from primitive painting to 20th-century works.

Château St-Héléne, av. de Fabron. © **04-93-71-78-33.** Admission 4€ ($4.60) adults, 2.50€ ($3) seniors and students, free for children under 19. Wed–Mon 10am–6pm. Bus: 8, 9, 10, 11, 11B, 12, 23, 34, or 60; 10-min. walk.

A MUSEUM IN NEARBY CIMIEZ ⭐⭐

Founded by the Romans, who called it Cemenelum, Cimiez, a hilltop suburb 5km (3 miles) north of Nice, was the capital of the Maritime Alps province. Take bus no. 15 or 17 from place Masséna.

Musée Matisse ⭐ This museum honors the artist, who died in Nice in 1954. Seeing his nude sketches today, you'll wonder how early critics could have denounced them as "the female animal in all her shame and horror." The museum has several permanent collections. These include *Nude in an Armchair with a Green Plant* (1937), *Nymph in the Forest* (1935–42), and a chronologically arranged series of paintings from 1890 to 1919. The most famous of these is *Portrait of Madame Matisse* (1905), usually displayed near a 1900 portrait of the artist's wife by Marquet. There's also an ensemble of drawings and designs *(Flowers and Fruits)* he prepared as practice sketches for the Matisse Chapel at Vence. The most famous works are *The Créole Dancer* (1951), *Blue Nude IV* (1952), and around 50 dance-related sketches he did between 1930 and 1931.

In the Villa des Arènes-de-Cimiez, 164 av. des Arènes-de-Cimiez. © **04-93-53-40-53.** Admission 4€ ($4.60) adults, 2.50€ ($3) students, free for children under 19. Wed–Mon 10am–6pm. Closed Jan 1, May 1, and Dec 25. Bus: 15, 17, 20, 22, or 25.

HITTING THE LINKS & OTHER OUTDOOR PURSUITS

GOLF The oldest golf course on the Riviera is about 16km (10 miles) from Nice: **Golf Bastide du Roi** (also known as the Golf de Biot), avenue Michard Pellissier, Biot (© **04-93-65-08-48**). Open daily, this is a flat, not particularly challenging sea-fronting course. (Golfers must cross a highway midway through to complete 18 holes.) Tee times are from 8am to 6pm; you can play until sunset. Reservations aren't necessary, though on weekends you should expect a delay. Greens fees are 40€ ($46) Monday to Friday, 45€ ($52) on weekends.

SCUBA DIVING The best outfit is the **Centre International de Plongée de Nice,** 2 ruelle des Moulins (© **06-09-52-55-57** or 04-93-55-59-50), adjacent to the city's old port, between quai des Docks and boulevard Stalingrad. A *baptême* (dive for first-timers) costs 29€ ($33). A one-tank dive for experienced divers, equipment included, is 34€ ($39); a license is required.

TENNIS The oldest tennis club in Nice is the **Nice Lawn Tennis Club,** Parc Impérial, 5 av. Suzanne-Lenglen (© **04-92-15-58-00**). It's open daily from 9am to 8pm (mid-Oct to mid-Apr) and charges 20€ ($23) per person for 2 hours of court time, or 60€ ($69) per person for unlimited access to the courts for 1 week. The club has a cooperative staff, loyal clientele, 13 clay courts, and six hard-surfaced courts. Reserve a court the night before.

NICE AFTER DARK

Nice has some of the most active nightlife along the Riviera; pick up a copy of *La Semaine de Spectacles,* which outlines the week's diversions. The major cultural center is the **Opéra de Nice,** 4 rue St-François-de-Paule (© 04-92-17-40-40). It presents a full repertoire, with emphasis on serious, often large-scale operas. The opera hall is also the major venue for concerts and recitals. Tickets are available a day or two prior to any performance. You can show up at the box office (Mon–Sat 10am–5:30pm, Sun 10am–6pm) or buy tickets in advance with a major credit card by phoning © 04-92-17-40-40. Tickets run 8€ ($9.20) for nosebleed (and we mean it) seats to 80€ ($92) for front-and-center seats on opening night.

ST-JEAN-CAP-FERRAT ★★

Of all the oases along the Côte d'Azur, no other place has the snob appeal of Cap-Ferrat. It's a 15km (9-mile) promontory sprinkled with luxurious villas, outlined by sheltered bays, beaches, and coves. The vegetation is lush. In the port of St-Jean, the harbor accommodates yachts and fishing boats.

The cape is home to the **Musée Ile-de-France** ★★, avenue Denis-Séméria (© 04-93-01-33-09), in one of the Côte d'Azur's legendary villas. Its owner, Baronne Ephrussi de Rothschild, died in 1934, leaving the Italianate building and its gardens to the Institut de France. The wealth of her collection is preserved: 18th-century furniture; Tiepolo ceilings; Savonnerie carpets; screens and panels from the Far East; tapestries from Gobelin, Aubusson, and Beauvais; Fragonard drawings; canvases by Boucher; Sèvres porcelain; and more. The sprawling gardens contain fragments of statuary from churches, monasteries, and palaces. An entire section is planted with cacti. Admission is 8.50€ ($9) adults, 6€ ($6.90) students and children 7 to 18. The museum is open from March to October, daily from 10am to 6pm; November to February, Monday through Friday from 2 to 6pm, Saturday and Sunday from 10am to 6pm.

ESSENTIALS

GETTING THERE   Most visitors drive or take a **bus** or **taxi** from the rail station at nearby Beaulieu. Buses at Beaulieu depart hourly for Cap-Ferrat. There's also bus service from Nice. For bus information, call © 04-93-85-64-44. By car, St-Jean-Cap-Ferrat is best reached from Nice along N7 east.

VISITOR INFORMATION   The **Office de Tourisme** is on avenue Denis-Séméria (© 04-93-76-08-90; www.riviera.fr/tourisme.htm).

WHERE TO STAY

Grand Hôtel du Cap-Ferrat ★★★   This early-1900s palace is at the tip of the peninsula in the midst of a 5.6-hectare (14-acre) garden. It has been the retreat of the international elite since 1908. Parts of the exterior have open loggias and big arched windows; you can also enjoy the views from the flowering terrace over the sea. Accommodations are generally spacious and open to sea views, and most have a sumptuous bathroom. Rates include admission to the pool, Club Dauphin. The beach is accessible by funicular from the main building.

71 bd. du Général-de-Gaulle, 06230 St-Jean-Cap-Ferrat. © 04-93-76-50-52. Fax 04-93-76-04-52. www. grand-hotel-cap-ferrat.com. 53 units. 355€–1,100€ ($408–$1,265) double; from 1,070€ ($1,230) suite. Rates include breakfast. AE, MC, V. Indoor parking 80€ ($92); outdoor parking free. Closed Jan–Feb. **Amenities:** 2 restaurants; 2 bars; outdoor Olympic-size heated pool; 2 tennis courts; sauna; bicycles; 24-hr. room service; babysitting; laundry service; dry cleaning. *In room:* A/C, TV, dataport, minibar, hair dryer, safe.

Hôtel Clair Logis *Value*   This B&B was created by the grandmother of the present owners when she added two outbuildings to the grounds of her early-1900s villa, about a 10-minute walk from the beach. The hotel's most famous guest was de Gaulle, who stayed in a room called *Strelitzias* (Bird of Paradise). The pleasant rooms, each named after a flower, are scattered over three buildings in the confines of the garden. The most romantic and spacious are in the main building; the seven in the annex are the most modern but have the least character and tend to be smaller and cheaper.

12 av. Centrale, 06230 St-Jean-Cap-Ferrat. ℂ 04-93-76-51-81. Fax 04-93-76-51-82. www.hotel-clair-logis.fr. 18 units. 95€–155€ ($109–$178) double. AE, DC, MC, V. Closed Jan 10 to mid-Mar and Nov–Dec 15. **Amenities:** Limited room service; laundry service. *In room:* TV, dataport, minibar, hair dryer.

WHERE TO DINE
Le Provençal ✦ FRENCH/PROVENÇAL   Near the top of Nice's highest peak, this grand restaurant boasts a panoramic view. Many of the menu items are credited to the inspiration of "the Provençal." Selections include marinated artichoke hearts beside half a lobster, *tarte fine* of potatoes with deliberately undercooked foie gras, rack of lamb with local herbs and tarragon sauce, and crayfish with asparagus and black-olive tapenade. The dessert sampler, *les cinq desserts du Provençal,* consists of five desserts that usually include macaroons with chocolate and crème brûlée. The cooking seems more inspired than ever.

2 av. Denis-Séméria. ℂ 04-93-76-03-97. Reservations required. Main courses 35€–45€ ($40–$52); fixed-price menu 69€ ($79). AE, MC, V. Apr–Sept daily noon–2:30pm and 7:30–11pm; Oct–Mar Wed–Sun noon–2:30pm and 7:30–11pm.

MONACO ✦✦✦
Monaco—or rather its capital, Monte Carlo—has for a century been a symbol of glamour. The 1956 marriage of Prince Rainier III to American actress Grace Kelly enhanced its status. Although not always happy in her role, Princess Grace soon won the respect and adoration of her people. The Monégasques still mourn her death in a 1982 car accident.

Monaco became a property of the Grimaldi clan, a Genoese family, as early as 1297. With shifting loyalties, it has maintained something resembling independence ever since. In a fit of impatience, the French annexed it in 1793, but the ruling family recovered it in 1814, though the prince at the time couldn't bear to tear himself away from the pleasures of Paris for "dreary old Monaco."

ESSENTIALS
GETTING THERE   Monaco has rail, bus, and highway connections from other coastal cities, especially Nice. **Trains** arrive every 30 minutes from Cannes, Nice, Menton, and Antibes. For information, call ℂ **08-92-35-35-35.** Monaco's railway station (Gare SNCF) is on avenue Prince Pierre. It's a long walk uphill from the station to Monte Carlo. If you'd rather take a **taxi,** call ℂ **93-15-01-01.** There are no border formalities when entering Monaco from mainland France. If you're on the Riviera, **drive** from Nice along N7 northeast. It's only 19km (12 miles), but with traffic, the drive can take 30 minutes.

VISITOR INFORMATION   The **Direction du Tourisme** is at 2A bd. des Moulins (ℂ **92-16-61-16;** www.monaco-tourisme.com).

To call Monaco from France, dial **00** (the international access code), followed by Monaco's country code, **377,** then the eight-digit local phone number.

WHERE TO STAY
Columbus Monaco Hotel ✦✦ *Value*   In the Fontvieille sector of Monaco, this stylish, contemporary hotel faces Princess Grace's rose garden and the sea. Guest rooms are done in a style that evokes both Miami and London. Details include

Monaco

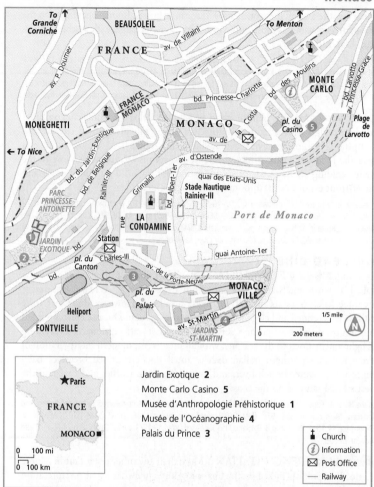

Jardin Exotique **2**
Monte Carlo Casino **5**
Musée d'Anthropologie Préhistorique **1**
Musée de l'Océanographie **4**
Palais du Prince **3**

✝ Church
ⓘ Information
✉ Post Office
— Railway

deluxe bed linens and Frette bathrobes. Each unit comes with a first-class tiled bathroom with tub and shower. The hotel is in a condo complex whose residents share the pool. A boat carries guests to a tranquil sandy beach nearby.

The brasserie serves a fabulous antipasto buffet and savory pastas and pizzas; the lively bar, **Downstairs,** attracts a hip crowd, including Prince Albert.

23 av. des Papalins, 98000 Monaco. ⓒ **92-05-90-00.** Fax 92-05-91-67. www.columbushotels.com. 181 units. 220€–270€ ($253–$310) double; 370€–470€ ($425–$540) suite. AE, MC, V. Parking 23€ ($26). Closed Nov–Mar. **Amenities:** Restaurant; bar; outdoor pool; fitness room; business center; salon/barber; 24-hr. room service; babysitting; laundry service; dry cleaning. *In room:* A/C, TV, dataport, minibar, hair dryer, iron, safe.

Hôtel de Paris ✸✸✸ On the resort's main plaza, opposite the casino, this is one of the world's most famous hotels. The facade has marble pillars, and the lounge has an Art Nouveau rose window at the peak of the dome. The decor includes marble pillars, statues, crystal chandeliers, Louis XVI chairs, and a wall-size mural. The guest rooms come in a variety of styles, with period or contemporary furnishings. Some are enormous. Elegant fabrics, rich carpeting, and classic accessories make this a favorite among the world's most discerning guests. Rooms opening onto the sea aren't as spacious as those in the rear. Bathrooms are large, with marble and elegant brass fittings.

Place du Casino, 98007 Monaco. ✆ **92-16-30-30**. Fax 92-16-26-26. www.montecarloresort.com. 197 units. 385€–1,150€ ($443–$1,322) double; from 2,000€ ($2,300) suite. AE, DC, MC, V. Parking 25€ ($29). **Amenities:** 3 restaurants; bar; large indoor pool; fitness center; Thermes Marins spa; 2 saunas; concierge; salon; 24-hr. room service; babysitting; laundry service; dry cleaning. *In room:* A/C, TV, dataport, minibar, hair dryer, safe.

Hôtel Mirabeau ✦✦ In the heart of Monte Carlo, the Mirabeau combines modern design with a refined atmosphere. Large mirrors, lighted closets, and sumptuous beds make staying here idyllic; many rooms have terraces with views over the Mediterranean. Although the newest rooms are as fine as those in the main building, many guests prefer older ones for their old-fashioned decor and street-front exposures. Bathrooms are well appointed.

1 av. Princesse-Grace, 98000 Monaco. ✆ **92-16-65-65**. Fax 93-50-84-85. www.montecarloresort.com. 87 units. 265€–375€ ($305–$431) double; 430€–860€ ($495–$989) suite. AE, DC, MC, V. Parking 25€ ($29). **Amenities:** Restaurant; bar; outdoor pool; gym; sauna; limited room service; babysitting; laundry service; dry cleaning. *In room:* A/C, TV, dataport, minibar, hair dryer, safe, robes.

WHERE TO DINE

Le Louis XV ✦✦✦ FRENCH/ITALIAN The Louis XV offers what one critic called "down-home Riviera cooking within a Fabergé egg." When it lost one of its three Michelin stars in 2001, it made headlines. However, don't fear—the cuisine is as refined and elegant as always. Star chef Alain Ducasse creates refined but not overly adorned cuisine, served by the finest staff in Monaco. Everything is light and attuned to the seasons, with an intelligent, modern interpretation of Provençal and northern Italian dishes. You'll find chargrilled breast of baby pigeon with sautéed duck liver, and everything from truffles and caviar to the best stewed salt cod on the coast.

In the Hôtel de Paris, place du Casino. ✆ **92-16-30-01**. Reservations recommended. Jacket and tie required for men. Main courses 80€–92€ ($92–$104); fixed-price menus 160€–180€ ($184–$207). AE, MC, V. Thurs–Mon 12:15–1:45pm and 8–9:45pm. Also June–Sept Wed 12:15–1:45pm. Closed Feb 24-Mar 10 and Nov 30–Dec 29.

Rampoldi ✦ FRENCH/ITALIAN More than any other restaurant in Monte Carlo, Rampoldi is linked to the charming but somewhat dated interpretation of *La Dolce Vita*. Opened in the 1950s at the edge of the Casino Gardens and staffed with a mix of old and new, it's more Italian than French in spirit. It also serves some of the best cuisine in Monte Carlo. Menu items include an array of such pastas as tortelloni with cream and white-truffle sauce; sea bass roasted in a salt crust; ravioli stuffed with crayfish; and veal kidneys in Madeira sauce. Crêpes suzette makes a spectacular finish.

3 av. des Spélugues. ✆ **93-30-70-65**. Reservations required. Main courses 30€–42€ ($35–$48). AE, MC, V. Daily 12:15–2:30pm and 7:30–11:30pm.

EXPLORING MONACO

The second-smallest state in Europe (Vatican City is the tiniest), Monaco consists of four parts. The old town, **Monaco-Ville,** is on a promontory, "the Rock," 60m (200 ft.) high, and is the seat of the royal palace and the government building, as well as the home of the Oceanographic Museum. West of the bay, **La Condamine,** the 19th-century home of the Monégasques, is at the foot of the old town, forming its harbor and port sector. Up from the port (walking is steep in Monaco) is **Monte Carlo,** once the playground of European royalty and still the center for the wintering wealthy; it's the setting for the casino and its gardens and the deluxe hotels. The fourth part, **Fontvieille,** is a neat industrial suburb.

Monte-Carlo Beach, at the far frontier, is on French soil. It attracts a chic crowd, including movie stars.

The home of Monaco's royal family, the **Palais du Prince** ⚘, dominates the principality. On a tour of **Les Grands Appartements du Palais,** place du Palais (© **93-25-18-31**), you see the Throne Room and some of the art collection, including Brueghels and Holbeins, as well as Princess Grace's state portrait. The palace was built in the 13th century, and part of it is from the Renaissance. The ideal time to arrive is 11:55am, to watch the 10-minute changing of the guard. A combination ticket including admission to the **Musée du Palais du Prince (Souvenirs Napoléoniens et Collection d'Archives)** is 6€ ($6.90) adults, 3€ ($3.45) children 8 to 14, free for children under 8. The palace is open daily June to September from 9:30am to 6pm and in October from 10am to 5pm. It's closed to visitors from November to May. The museum keeps the same hours in high season and is also open on a reduced schedule in early November and from mid-December through May.

Jardin Exotique ⚘⚘, boulevard du Jardin-Exotique (© **93-15-29-80**), was built on the side of a rock and is known for its cactus collection. The gardens were begun by Prince Albert I, who was both a naturalist and a scientist. He spotted some succulents growing in the palace gardens and created the garden from them. You can also explore the grottoes here, as well as the **Musée d'Anthropologie Préhistorique** (© **93-15-80-06**), which is surrounded by the gardens. The view of the principality is splendid. Admission to the complex costs 6.70€ ($7.60) adults, 3.60€ ($4.10) children 6 to 18, free for children under 6. The gardens and museum are open daily from mid-May through mid-September from 9am to 7pm; mid-September through mid-May from 9am to 6pm. Closed November 15 to December 15.

Musée de l'Océanographie ⚘⚘, avenue St-Martin (© **93-15-36-00**), was founded by Albert I, great-grandfather of the present prince. In the main rotunda is a statue of Albert dressed as a sea captain. Displayed are specimens he collected during 30 years of oceanographic expeditions. The aquarium, one of the finest in Europe, has more than 90 tanks, including Le Lagoon, a large holding tank for sharks. Hours are daily April through June and September from 9am to 7pm; July and August from 9am to 8pm; and October through March from 10am to 6pm. Admission is 11€ ($13) adults, 6€ ($6.90) children 6 to 18, free for children under 6.

TAKING A DIP & OTHER OUTDOOR ACTIVITIES

BEACHES/SWIMMING   Monaco offers swimming and sunbathing at the **Plage de Larvotto,** off avenue Princesse-Grace (© **93-30-63-84**). There's no charge to enter this strip of beach, whose surface is frequently replenished with sand hauled in by barge. It is open to the public at all hours.

You can also try the **Monte-Carlo Beach Club,** adjoining the Monte-Carlo Beach Hotel, 22 av. Princesse-Grace (© **04-93-28-66-66**). The beach club has thrived for years as an integral part of Monaco's social life. The sand is replenished at regular intervals, and you'll find two large pools (one for children), cabanas, a restaurant, a cafe, and a bar. As the temperature drops in late August, it closes for the winter. The admission charge of 50€ to 75€ ($58–$86) grants you access to the changing rooms, toilets, restaurants, and bar, and includes use of a mattress for sunbathing. A day's use of a cubicle, where you can lock up your street clothes, costs an extra 16€ to 23€ ($18–$25). A fee of 147€ ($169) will get you a day's use of a private cabana. Most socializing occurs around the pool's edges. Topless is de rigueur, but bottomless isn't.

GOLF The prestigious **Monte Carlo Golf Club,** route N7, La Turbie (✆ 04-92-41-50-70), on French soil, is a par-72 course with scenic panoramas. Certain perks (including use of electric carts) are reserved for members. In order to play, nonmembers are asked to show proof of membership in another club and provide evidence of their handicap. Greens fees for 18 holes are 90€ ($104) Monday through Friday and 110€ ($126) Saturday and Sunday. Clubs can be rented for 20€ ($23). The course is open daily from 8am to sunset.

SPA TREATMENTS In 1908, the Société des Bains de Mer launched a seawater (thalassotherapy) spa in Monte Carlo. It was bombed during World War II and didn't reopen until 1996. **Les Thermes Marins de Monte-Carlo,** 2 av. de Monte-Carlo (✆ 92-16-40-40), is one of the largest spas in Europe. Spread over four floors are a pool, a Turkish *haman,* a diet restaurant, a juice bar, two tanning booths, a fitness center, a beauty center, and private treatment rooms. A day pass, giving access to the sauna, steam rooms, fitness facilities, and pools, costs 65€ ($75). Massages cost 57€ ($66) for a 30-minute session, 95€ ($109) for a 60-minute session.

GAMBLING & OTHER AFTER-DARK DIVERSIONS

CASINOS **Sun Casino,** in the Monte Carlo Grand Hôtel, 12 av. des Spélugues (✆ 93-50-65-00), is a huge room filled with one-armed bandits. It also features blackjack, craps, and American roulette. Additional slot machines are available on the roof starting at 11am. The rooms with slot machines open daily from 11am to 4am, and gaming tables are open daily from 5pm to 4am. Admission is free.

A speculator, François Blanc, developed the **Monte-Carlo Casino,** place du Casino (✆ 92-16-21-21), into the most famous in the world. The architect of Paris's Opéra Garnier, Charles Garnier, built the oldest part of the casino, and it remains an example of the 19th century's most opulent architecture. It consists of an area devoted to the casino and other areas for different kinds of entertainment, including a theater presenting opera and ballet. Baccarat, roulette, and chemin de fer are the most popular games, though you can play *le craps* and blackjack as well. Admission is 10€ to 20€ ($12–$23).

Salle Américaine, containing only slot machines, opens at noon, as do doors for roulette and *trente-quarente.* A section for roulette and chemin de fer opens at 3pm. Most of the facilities are operational by 4pm, when additional rooms open with more roulette, craps, and blackjack. The gambling continues until very late or early, depending on the crowd. The casino classifies its "private rooms" as the more demure, nonelectronic areas devoid of slot machines. To enter the casino, you must carry a passport, be at least 21, and pay an admission of 10€ to 20€ ($12–$23), depending on where you want to go. In lieu of a passport, an ID card or driver's license will suffice. After 9pm, the staff will insist that gentlemen wear jackets and neckties for entrance to the private rooms.

The premises also contain a **Cabaret** in the Casino Gardens, where a well-rehearsed orchestra plays before the show. A cabaret featuring feathers, glitter, jazz dance, ballet, and Riviera-style seminudity is presented at 10:30pm Wednesday through Sunday, mid-September through June. For reservations, call ✆ 92-16-36-36. Entrance to the cabaret costs 10€ to 15€ ($12–$17) and includes a first drink.

Theoretically, the **Opéra de Monte-Carlo,** whose patron is Prince Rainier, is headquartered in the lavish Belle Epoque **Salle Garnier** of the casino. It is closed for renovations until sometime in 2005. Meanwhile, venues for concerts, ballets, and operas are the **Salle du Canton,** Les Terrasses, avenue de Fontvieille (© **92-16-22-99** for tickets and information), or the **Grimaldi Forum,** 10 av. Princesse-Grace (© **99-99-30-00** for tickets and information). At both the Salle du Canton and the Grimaldi Forum, tickets to ballets cost 8€ to 26€ ($9.20–$30); tickets to concerts cost 15€ to 30€ ($17–$35); and tickets to operas cost 30€ to 115€ ($35–$132).

7

Germany

by Darwin Porter & Danforth Prince

The rebuilding of Berlin in the 21st century comes at a rapid pace as the city solidifies its position as the capital of a unified Germany. What was once the city's biggest tourist attraction, the Berlin Wall, is now a bicycle path where Berliners push baby strollers. Restored baroque Munich, in the south, known as Germany's "secret capital," is the gateway to the Bavarian Alps and colorful alpine villages. For a taste of medieval Germany, explore the untouched towns of the Romantic Road and Ludwig II's fairy-tale castle of Neuschwanstein.

1 Berlin ★★★

When Heinrich Heine arrived in Berlin in 1819, he exclaimed, "Isn't the present splendid!" Were he to arrive today, he might make the same remark. Visitors who come by plane to Berlin see a splendid panorama. Few metropolitan areas are blessed with as many lakes, woodlands, and parks—these cover one-third of the city's area, and small farms with fields and meadows still exist in the city limits.

Berlin today is an almost completely modern city. Regrettably, Berlin is hardly the architectural gem that old-time visitors remember from the pre-Nazi era; it wasn't rebuilt with the same kind of care lavished on Munich and Cologne. But in spite of its decades-long "quadripartite status," it's a vibrant city, always receptive to new ideas, a major economic and cultural center, and a leader in development and research. Because of its excellent facilities, it is a favored site for trade fairs, congresses, and conventions.

Berlin today is shedding its dark history and reinventing itself as Europe's "capital of cool." Suddenly, it's hip to claim, "Ich bin ein Berliner." Nothing dramatizes the change more than the once dreary Potsdamer Platz, the so-called Times Square of Berlin. No longer a Cold War relic, it has blossomed into a showcase of modern architecture, dominated by the 25-story DaimlerChrysler building, whose viewing platform can be reached in only 20 seconds from the ground.

"No city on earth has gone through such a roller-coaster ride—from villain to victim, from horrors to heroics," said Richard Holbrooke, former U.S. ambassador to Germany. Today Berlin is the fourth-most-popular tourist destination in Europe, having surged past Madrid.

ESSENTIALS

GETTING THERE **By Plane** **Tegel Airport** is the city's busiest, serving most flights from the west. Historic **Tempelhof Airport,** made famous as the city's lifeline during the Berlin Airlift, has declined in importance. **Schönefeld,** the airport in the eastern sector, is used primarily by Russian and eastern European airlines. Private bus shuttles among the three airports operate constantly so you

can make connecting flights at different airports. Buses from each airport will also take you into the city center. For information on all three airports, call ℂ **0180/500-01-86** or visit www.berlin-airport.de.

By Train   Frankfurt and Hamburg, among other cities, have good rail connections to Berlin. From Frankfurt to Berlin takes about 4 hours. Hamburg is now closer than ever, thanks to a high-speed InterCity Express train running between the two cities nonstop in 2 hours and 8 minutes. Eurailpass and GermanRail passes are valid. Most arrivals from western European and western German cities are at the **Bahnhof Zoologischer Garten** (ℂ **030/250-025** for tourist information), the main train station, called "Bahnhof Zoo," in western Berlin. In the center of the city, close to the Kurfürstendamm, it's well connected for public transportation. Facilities include a tourist information counter dispensing free maps and tourist brochures, open daily from 10am to 7pm. The staff will make same-day hotel reservations for 3€ ($3.45).

Berlin has four other train stations, the **Berlin Hauptbahnhof, Berlin Lichtenberg Lehrterbahnhof,** and **Berlin Spandaubahnhof.** Call the railway information number at ℂ **0800/150-70-90** or visit http://bahn.hafas.de for information.

By Bus   The operations center for several independent bus operators is headquartered within a central arrivals and departures point, the **ZOB Omnibusbahnhof am Funkturm,** Messedamm 6 (ℂ **030/301-03-80**). Call for departure times and fare information for routes to and from other parts of Europe.

Western Berlin

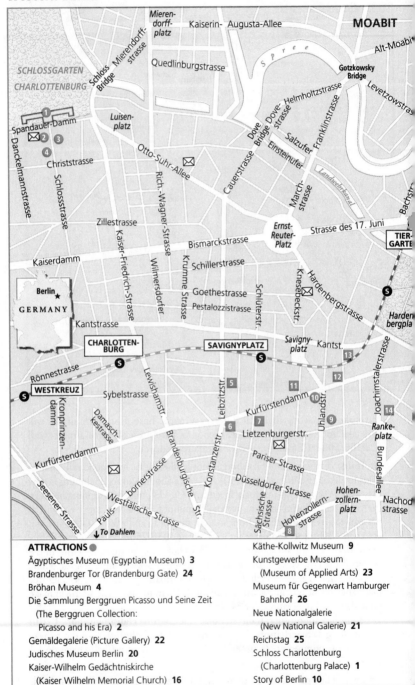

ATTRACTIONS ●

Ägyptisches Museum (Egyptian Museum) **3**

Brandenburger Tor (Brandenburg Gate) **24**

Bröhan Museum **4**

Die Sammlung Berggruen Picasso und Seine Zeit
(The Berggruen Collection:
Picasso and his Era) **2**

Gemäldegalerie (Picture Gallery) **22**

Judisches Museum Berlin **20**

Kaiser-Wilhelm Gedächtniskirche
(Kaiser Wilhelm Memorial Church) **16**

Käthe-Kollwitz Museum **9**

Kunstgewerbe Museum
(Museum of Applied Arts) **23**

Museum für Gegenwart Hamburger
Bahnhof **26**

Neue Nationalgalerie
(New National Galerie) **21**

Reichstag **25**

Schloss Charlottenburg
(Charlottenburg Palace) **1**

Story of Berlin **10**

ACCOMMODATIONS

Art Nouveau **5**
Bleibtreu Hotel **7**
Brandenburger Hof Relais & Châteaux **15**
Grand Hotel Esplanade **19**
Hecker's Hotel **11**
Hotel-Pension Bregenz **6**
Hotel Sylter Hof Berlin **18**
Kempinski Hotel Bristol Berlin **12**
Palace Berlin **17**
Pension München **8**
Savoy **13**
Sorat Art'otel **14**

Post Office ⊠
S-Bahn stop **S**

By Car From Frankfurt, take A-66 to Bad Herzfeld, and either go east on A-4 to pick up A-9 to Berlin, or continue on A-7 to Braunschweig and east on A-2 toward Berlin. North of Nürnberg, A-9 leads to Berlin. From Leipzig, take A-14 in the direction of Halle; at the intersection of A-9, head northeast into Berlin. From Dresden, head northeast on A-13 into Berlin. Expect heavy traffic delays on *Autobahnen,* especially on weekends and sunny days when everyone is out touring.

VISITOR INFORMATION **Tourist Office** For tourist information and hotel bookings, head for the **Berlin Tourist Information Center,** in the Europa-Center near the Memorial Church, entrance on the Budapesterstrasse side (© **030/25-00-25;** www.berlin-tourism.de), open Monday through Saturday from 10am to 7pm and Sunday from 10am to 6pm.

Websites Visit **www.berlin-info.de** for a virtual tour of Berlin's sights, but be aware that some of the links go to German-only pages. The site **www.hotelstravel.com/germany.html** not only provides detailed listings for hotels in Germany but also has links to related sites, like Ritz-Carlton and Relais & Châteaux, that offer lodging and general travel info. The definitive dining guide **www.eat-germany.net** lets you search the site for restaurants or view its top 10 for each city. The restaurants are selected by users who rate them, giving an aura of objectivity. With lots of detail about type of food, hours, locations, and kinds of patrons, searches can be narrowed by nation, state, or city.

CITY LAYOUT The center of activity in the western part of Berlin is the 3km (1¾-mile) long **Kurfürstendamm,** called the Ku'damm by Berliners. Along this wide boulevard you'll find the best hotels, restaurants, theaters, cafes, nightclubs, shops, and department stores. The huge **Tiergarten,** the city's largest park, is crossed by Strasse des 17 Juni, which leads to the famed **Brandenburg Gate (Brandenburger Tor);** just north is the Reichstag. On the southwestern fringe of the Tiergarten is the **Zoologischer Garten (Berlin Zoo).** From the Ku'damm you can take Hardenbergstrasse, crossing Bismarckstrasse and traversing Otto-Suhr-Allee, which leads to **Schloss Charlottenburg,** one of your major sight-seeing goals. The **Dahlem Museums** are on the southwestern fringe, often reached by going along Hohenzollerndamm.

The Brandenburg Gate is the start of Berlin's most celebrated street, **Unter den Linden,** the cultural heart of Berlin before World War II. The famous street runs from west to east, cutting a path through the city. It leads to **Museumsinsel (Museum Island),** where the most outstanding museums of eastern Berlin, including the Pergamon, are situated. As it courses along, Unter den Linden crosses another major Berlin artery, **Friedrichstrasse.** If you continue south along Friedrichstrasse, you'll reach the former location of **Checkpoint Charlie,** the famous border-crossing site of the Cold War days.

⌐*Value* **The Welcome Card**

If you're going to be in Berlin for 3 days, you can purchase a **WelcomeCard** for 19€ ($22), entitling holders to 72 free hours on public transportation in Berlin and Brandenburg. You also get free admission or price reductions up to 50% on sightseeing tours, museums, and other attractions. Reductions of 25% are granted at 10 of the city's theaters as well. It's valid for one adult and up to three children 13 or younger.

Unter den Linden continues east until it reaches **Alexanderplatz,** the center of eastern Berlin, with its TV tower (Fernsehturm). A short walk away is the restored **Nikolaiviertel (Nikolai Quarter),** a neighborhood of bars, restaurants, and shops that evoke life in the prewar days.

GETTING AROUND   By Public Transportation   The Berlin transport system consists of buses, trams, and U-Bahn and S-Bahn trains. The network is run by the **BVG** (*©* **030/1-94-49;** www.bvg.de), which operates an information booth outside the Bahnhof Zoo on Hardenbergplatz, open daily from 6am to 10pm. The staff will provide details about which U-Bahn (underground) or S-Bahn (elevated railway) line to take to various locations and the ticket options. You can also purchase tickets, including discount cards.

The **BVG standard ticket** *(Einzelfahrschein)* is 2.20€ to 3.30€ ($2.55–$3.80) and is valid for 2 hours of transportation in all directions, transfers included. Also available at counters and vending machines is a 24-hour ticket; the price is 5.60€ to 6.50€ ($6.45–$7.50). On buses, only standard tickets can be purchased, and tram tickets must be purchased in advance. Tickets should be kept until the end of the journey; otherwise, you'll be liable for a fine of 40€ ($46).

By Taxi   Taxis are available throughout Berlin. The meter starts at 2.50€ ($2.90), plus 1.50€ ($1.75) per kilometer after that. After 7km, the fare is 1€ ($1.15) per kilometer. Visitors can flag down taxis that have a T-sign illuminated. For a taxi, call *©* **21-02-02,** 26-10-25, or 44-33-22.

By Car   Touring Berlin by car isn't recommended. Free parking places are difficult to come by.

FAST FACTS: Berlin

American Express   Reiseland American Express offices are at Bayreuther Strasse 37 (*©* **030/21-49-830;** U-Bahn: Wittenbergplatz); open Monday to Friday 9am to 7pm and Saturday 10am to 1pm; and Friedrichstrasse 172 (*©* **030/20-17-400;** U-Bahn: Friedrichstrasse or Stadtmitte), are all open Monday through Friday from 9am to 6pm and Saturday 10am to 1pm.

Business Hours   Most **banks** are open Monday through Friday from 9am to 1 or 3pm. Most other **businesses** and **stores** are open Monday through Friday from 9 or 10am to 6:30pm and Saturday from 9am to 4pm. On *langer Samstag,* the first Saturday of the month, shops stay open until 4 or 6pm. Some stores observe late closing on Thursday, usually at 8:30pm.

Currency   The long-standing German mark faded into history on January 1, 2002, giving way to the euro. Currently, the U.S. dollar and the European euro are trading a 1€=US$1.15, with slight daily fluctuations.

Currency Exchange   You can exchange money at all airports, major department stores, any bank, and the American Express offices (above).

Dentists/Doctors   The Berlin tourist office in the Europa-Center (see "Visitor Information," p. 382) keeps a list of English-speaking dentists and doctors in Berlin. In case of a medical emergency, call *©* **030/31-00-31** or Dental Emergency Service *©* **030/8900-4333.**

Drugstores   If you need a pharmacy *(Apotheke)* at night, go to one on any corner. There you'll find a sign in the window giving the address of the nearest drugstore open at night; such posting is required by law. A central pharmacy is **Europa-Apotheke,** Osnabrücker Strasse 4 (© **030/3-44-56-56;** U-Bahn: Kurfürstendamm). It's open Monday through Friday from 9am to 8pm and Saturday to 6pm.

Embassies & Consulates The embassy of the **United States** is at Neustaedtische Kirchstrasse 4–5 (© **030/2-38-51-74;** U-Bahn: Friedrichstrasse), and a consulate at Clayallee 170 (© **030/8-32-92-33;** U-Bahn: Hüttenweg). Hours are Monday through Friday from 8:30am to 4pm. The embassy of the **United Kingdom** is at Wilhelmstrasse 70 (© **030/20-45-70;** U-Bahn: Friedrichstrasse). Hours are Monday through Friday from 9am to noon and 2 to 4pm. The embassy of **Australia** is at Wall Strasse 376–379 (© **030/ 8-80-08-80;** U-Bahn: Märkisches Museum). Hours are Monday through Friday from 9am to noon. **Canada** maintains a consulate at Friedrichstrasse 95 (© **030/20-31-20;** U-Bahn: Friedrichstrasse). Hours are Monday through Friday from 9am to noon and 1:30 to 4pm by appointment. The embassy of **New Zealand** is at Friedrichstrasse 60 (© **030/20-62-10;** U-Bahn: Friedrichstrasse). Hours are Monday through Friday from 9am to 1pm and 2 to 5:30pm. The consulate of **Ireland** is at Friedrichstrasse 200 (© **030/ 22-07-20;** U-Bahn: Friedrichstrasse). Hours are Monday through Friday from 9:30am to 12:30pm and 2:30 to 4:45pm.

Emergencies Call the police at © **110;** dial © **112** to report a fire or to call an ambulance.

Internet Access If you're feeling out of touch, visit **Easy Internet Café,** Kurfürstendamm 224 (© **030/88-70-79-70;** U-Bahn: Kurfürstendamm, bus: 109 or 129). Open Monday to Saturday 6:30am to 2am.

Post Office You'll find post offices scattered throughout Berlin, with particularly large branches positioned at Bahnhof Zoo, Hardenbergplatz (U-Bahn: Zoologischer Garten); at both Tel and Schönefeld airports, the main railway station (Hauptbahnhof), and in the town center at Joachimstalerstrasse 10. With a limited number of exceptions, most post offices in Germany are open Monday to Friday from 8am to 6pm and Saturday from 8am to 1pm. None of them receive direct telephone calls from the public, but if you're interested in postal rates and procedures, click on either www.deutschepost.de or www.kindenservice@deutschepost.de, or © **0180/ 23-333** for information about postal procedures throughout Germany. Know in advance that unlike the old days, German post offices no longer offer the use of pay telephones for long-distance calls, and no longer send international telegrams. (A limited number, however, offer telegram service for destinations within Germany.) When you enter a German post office, know in advance that the yellow-painted windows are for issues about the mail; and that the blue-painted windows are for issues associated with money orders and banking rituals. If you just want to buy a stamp for mailing a letter, it's usually more convenient to buy it at any of thousands of small stores, newsstands, or tobacco shops throughout the country that stock them.

Safety Germany is a reasonably safe country in which to travel, although neo-Nazi skinheads have sometimes attacked black or Asian travelers, especially in the eastern part of the country. One of the most dangerous places, especially at night, is around the large railway stations of large cities, such as Berlin. Some beer halls get rowdy late at night.

Taxes As a member of the European Union, Germany imposes a tax on most goods and services known as the **value-added tax (VAT)** or, in German, *Mehrwertsteuer.* Nearly everything is taxed at 16%, including vital necessities such as gas or luxury items like jewelry. VAT is included in the price of restaurants and hotels. Note that goods for sale, such as cameras, also have the 16% tax already factored into the price; but the listed prices of services, such as having a mechanic fix your car, don't include VAT, so an extra 16% will be tacked on to your bill. Stores that display a TAX FREE sticker will issue you a Tax-Free Shopping Check at the time of purchase. You can then get a refund at one of the Tax-Free Shopping Service offices in the major airports and many train stations (and some of the bigger ferry terminals). Otherwise, send checks to Tax-Free Shopping Service, Mengstrasse 19, 23552 Lübeck, Germany.

Telephone The **country code** for Germany is **49**; the **city code** for Berlin is **30** for calls from outside Germany or **030** if you're calling within the country.

If you're going to make a lot of phone calls or wish to make an international call from a phone booth, you'll probably want to purchase a **phone card.** Phone cards are sold at post offices and newsstands. The 6.15€ ($7.05) card offers about 40 minutes, and the 26€ ($30) card is useful for long-distance calls. Simply insert them into the telephone slot. Phone cards are becoming so popular in Germany that many public phones no longer accept coins.

To make a **collect or calling-card call,** dial one of the following access numbers to reach an operator or an English-language voice prompt: **AT&T** (© **0130-0010**), **MCI** (© **0130-0012**), or **Sprint** (© **0130-0013**). To call the U.S. direct, dial **001** followed by the area code and phone number.

Tipping If a restaurant bill says *Bedienung,* that means a service charge has already been added, so just round up to the nearest euro. If not, add 10% to 15%. Round up to the nearest euro for taxis. Bellhops get 1€ ($1.15) per bag, as does the doorperson at your hotel, restaurant, or nightclub. Room cleaning staffs get small tips in Germany, as do concierges who perform some special favors such as obtaining hard-to-get theater or opera tickets. Tip hairdressers or barbers 5% to 10%.

WHERE TO STAY
ON OR NEAR THE KURFÜRSTENDAMM
Very Expensive

Grand Hotel Esplanade ★★★ The Esplanade rivals the Kempinski for supremacy in Berlin. Rooms are spacious, bright, and cheerfully decorated, with sound insulation. Beds are large with quality linens and duvets. Bathrooms, which contain tub/shower combos, are among the city's most luxurious. When reserving, ask for one of the corner rooms, as they're the biggest and have the best views. Even if you don't stay here, stop in for a drink at the elegant **Harry's New York Bar,** or go native at the traditional German **EckKneipe.**

Lützowufer 15, 10785 Berlin. © **030/25-47-80.** Fax 030/254-78-82-22. www.esplanade.de. 386 units. 170€–306€ ($196–$352) double; from 480€ ($552) suite. AE, DC, MC, V. Parking 16€ ($18). U-Bahn:

Berlin U-Bahn & S-Bahn

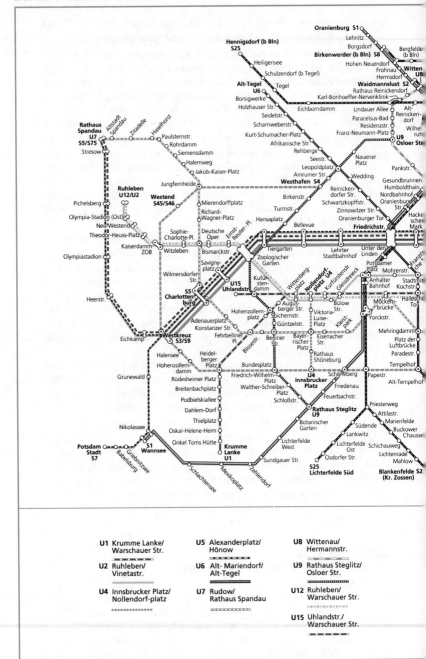

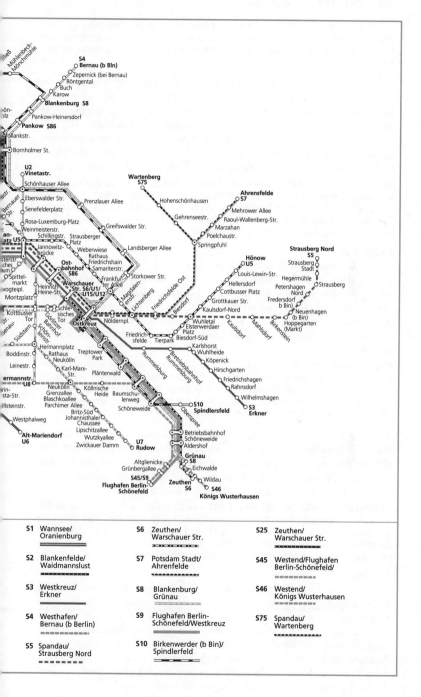

S1	Wannsee/ Oranienburg	S6	Zeuthen/ Warschauer Str.	S25	Zeuthen/ Warschauer Str.
S2	Blankenfelde/ Waidmannslust	S7	Potsdam Stadt/ Ahrenfelde	S45	Westend/Flughafen Berlin-Schönefeld/
S3	Westkreuz/ Erkner	S8	Blankenburg/ Grünau	S46	Westend/ Königs Wusterhausen
S4	Westhafen/ Bernau (b Berlin)	S9	Flughafen Berlin- Schönefeld/Westkreuz	S75	Spandau/ Wartenberg
S5	Spandau/ Strausberg Nord	S10	Birkenwerder (b Bin)/ Spindlerfeld		

Kurfürstenstrasse, Nollendorfplatz, or Wittenbergplatz. **Amenities:** 3 restaurants; 2 bars; indoor pool; sauna; whirlpool; solarium; 24-hr. room service; babysitting; laundry service/dry cleaning; nonsmoking rooms; rooms for those with limited mobility. *In room:* A/C, TV, ISDN modems, kitchenettes in some, minibar, hair dryer, bathrobes.

Kempinski Hotel Bristol Berlin ★★★ The legendary Kempinski, or "Kempi," is matched in style only by the Grand Hotel Esplanade. Rooms range in size from medium to spacious. Furnishings are elegant and the mattresses firm. The cheapest (and smallest) rooms are called the Berlin rooms. The high category Bristol rooms are larger and better appointed, and the finest accommodations of all are refined Kempinski rooms. Each room has a spacious bathroom with tub/shower combos, dual basins, scales, shoehorns, and deluxe toiletries.

Kurfürstendamm 27, 10719 Berlin. ☎ 800/426-3135 in the U.S., or 030/88-43-40. Fax 030/88-360-75. www. kempinski.com. 301 units. 211€–312€ ($243–$359) double; from 400€ ($460) suite. AE, DC, MC, V. Parking 21€ ($24). U-Bahn: Kurfürstendamm. **Amenities:** 2 restaurants; bar; indoor pool; fitness room; sauna; solarium; 24-hr. room service; massage; babysitting; laundry service/dry cleaning; nonsmoking rooms; rooms for those with limited mobility. *In room:* A/C, TV, dataport, minibar, hair dryer, safe.

Expensive

Brandenburger Hof Relais & Châteaux ★★★ Rooms at this white-fronted classic, though perhaps too severe and minimalist for some tastes, are among the most stylish in the city. This is authentic Bauhaus—torchier lamps, black leather upholstery, and platform beds. French doors open to small balconies, but not on the top floors. Bathrooms are spacious, with large tub/shower combos. Housekeeping is among the finest in Berlin, and there's state-of-the-art security.

Eislebener Strasse 14, 10789 Berlin. ☎ 030/21-40-50. Fax 030/21-40-51-00. www.brandenburger-hof.com. 82 units. 240€–280€ ($276–$322) double; from 450€ ($518) suite. Rates include breakfast buffet. AE, DC, MC, V. Parking 18€ ($21). U-Bahn: Kurfürstendamm or Augsburger Strasse. S-Bahn: Zoologischer Garten. **Amenities:** 2 restaurants; piano bar; 24-hr. room service; massage; sauna; babysitting; laundry service/valet/dry cleaning. *In room:* TV, dataport, minibar, hair dryer.

Savoy ★ If you don't demand the full-service facilities of the grander choices, this is the hotel for you. In general, rooms are a bit small but they are comfortable nonetheless, with such amenities as double-glazed windows and fine furnishings. Bathrooms are decent sizes, are maintained spotlessly, and contain tub/shower combos. For a nightcap, try the cozy **Times Bar.**

Fasanenstrasse 9–10, 10623 Berlin. ☎ 800/223-5652 in the U.S. and Canada, or 030/3-11-0-30. Fax 030/3-11-03-333. www.savoy-hotels.com. 125 units. 112€–192€ ($129–$221) double; 212€–302€ ($244–$347) suite. Children under 12 stay free in parent's room. AE, DC, MC, V. Parking 10€ ($12). U-Bahn: Kurfürstendamm. **Amenities:** Restaurant; bar; sauna; theater ticket desk; car rental; limited room service; babysitting; laundry service/dry cleaning; nonsmoking rooms. *In room:* TV, dataport in some, minibar, hair dryer, safe, trouser press.

Moderate

Art Nouveau On the fourth floor of an Art Nouveau apartment house, this little-known hotel is an atmospheric choice. Even the elevator is a historic gem of the upmarket and desirable neighborhood. Art Nouveau was fully renovated in 1998. The comfortable midsize rooms are pleasantly decorated and high ceilinged, with excellent beds and bathrooms with shower-tub combinations. Rooms in the rear are more tranquil except when the schoolyard is full of children. There's an honor bar in the lobby where guests keep track of their own drinks. A generous breakfast is the only meal served.

Leibnizstrasse 59, 10629 Berlin. ☎ 030/3-27-74-40. Fax 030/327-744-40. www.hotelartnouveau.de. 20 units. 110€–165€ ($127–$190) double; 175€–230€ ($201–$265) suite. AE, MC, V. Rates include breakfast. Parking 4€ ($4.60). U-Bahn: Adenauerplatz. **Amenities:** Laundry service/dry cleaning; all nonsmoking rooms. *In room:* TV, dataport, hair dryer.

Bleibtreu Hotel ⭐   Hidden away from the bustle of Berlin, this is a trend-conscious choice. Its tiny lobby is accessible via an alleyway that leads past a garden and a big-windowed set of dining and drinking facilities. The setting is the labyrinthine premises of what was built long ago as a Jugendstil-era apartment house. Rooms are small, minimalist, and furnished in carefully chosen natural materials. Bathrooms are cramped but well designed with tub/shower combos.

Bleibtreustrasse 31, 10707 Berlin (1 block south of the Kurfürstendamm). ℰ 800/223-5652 for reservations in the U.S. and Canada, or 030/88474-0. Fax 030/88474-444. www.bleibtreu.com. 60 units. 182€–262€ ($209–$301) double. AE, DC, MC, V. U-Bahn: Uhlandstrasse. **Amenities:** Restaurant; bar; limited room service; steam bath; laundry service/dry cleaning; nonsmoking rooms; rooms for those with limited mobility. *In room:* TV, minibar, hair dryer, safe.

Inexpensive

Hotel-Pension Bregenz   This dignified pension occupies the fourth and sunniest floor of a four-story apartment building, accessible by elevator. The owner, Mr. Zimmermann, works hard to maintain the cleanliness and charm of his comfortably furnished, relatively large rooms. Double doors help minimize noise from the public corridors outside. A continental breakfast is served each morning in a small dining area. The staff assists guests in reserving tickets for shows and tours.

Bregenzer Strasse 5, 10707 Berlin. ℰ 030/8-81-43-07. Fax 030/8-82-40-09. 14 units, 11 with bathroom (shower only). 66€ ($76) double without bathroom; 67€–82€ ($77–$94) double with bathroom. Rates include breakfast. MC, V. Parking 3€ ($3.45). S-Bahn: Savignyplatz. U-Bahn: Adenauerplatz. **Amenities:** All nonsmoking rooms. *In room:* TV, dataport, minibar, hair dryer, safe.

Pension München   This pension occupies only part of the third floor of a massive four-story building (with an elevator) erected as an apartment house in 1908. It offers a simple but tasteful decor of modern furnishings accented with fresh flowers. The small rooms are clean and color-coordinated, with bathrooms containing shower stalls, contemporary furnishings, and prints and engravings by local artists. Look for sculptures by the owner, an artist, in some of the public areas as well. Note that if no rooms are available at this place, you're likely to be recommended to a similar pension.

Guntzelstrasse 62 (close to Bayerischer Platz), 10717 Berlin. ℰ 030/8-57-91-20. Fax 030/85-79-12-22. 8 units. 65€–80€ ($75–$92) double. AE, DC, MC, V. Parking is available on the street. U-Bahn: Guntzelstrasse. *In room:* TV.

NEAR THE MEMORIAL CHURCH & ZOO
Expensive

Palace Berlin ⭐   The stylish and comfortable Palace is much improved over recent years. However, in some rooms, the double-glazing on the windows is unable to deafen the noise from the adjacent Europa-Center. Rooms range from medium to spacious, each with deluxe bed. The best are in the more recent Casino Wing. Bathrooms are medium-size, most often with tub/shower combo (sometimes with shower only).

In the Europa-Center, Budapesterstrasse 45, 10787 Berlin. ℰ 800/457-4000 in the U.S., or 030/2-50-20. Fax 030/2502-1161. www.palace.de. 282 units. 200€–355€ ($230–$408) double; from 455€ ($523) suite. AE, DC, MC, V. Parking 21€ ($24). U-Bahn: Zoologischer Garten. **Amenities:** 2 restaurants (see First Floor, "Where to Dine," p. 394); 2 bars; indoor pool; large health club; fitness center; solarium; massage; sauna; 24-hr. room service; nonsmoking rooms; 1 room for those with limited mobility. *In room:* A/C, TV, minibar, hair dryer, safe, trouser press.

Sorat Art'otel ⭐   Those partial to the more famous and highly regarded Brandenburger Hof (above) also like this tasteful, discreet hotel. Chic and avant-garde, the Sorat is unlike any other hotel in Berlin. Rooms, all medium-size, are minimalist, with a touch of industrial design. Although they will not please clients seeking a traditional Berlin hotel, modernists will be at home with the pedestal tables evoking cable spools and chrome-legged furnishings, and everyone will appreciate the large beds. Bathrooms are generously proportioned with showers.

Joachimstalerstrasse 29, 10719 Berlin. ⓒ 030/88-44-70. Fax 030/88-44-77-00. www.sorat-hotels.com. 133 units. 89€–267€ ($102–$307) double. Rates include buffet breakfast with champagne. Parking 11€ ($13). AE, DC, MC, V. U-Bahn: Kurfürstendamm. **Amenities:** Breakfast room; laundry service/dry cleaning; nonsmoking rooms. *In room:* A/C, TV, dataport in some, minibar, hair dryer.

Moderate

Hecker's Hotel   This hotel is near the Ku'damm and the many bars, cafes, and restaurants around the Savignyplatz. Rooms range from small to medium, but are fairly routine despite good beds. There's a sterility here but also up-to-date comfort and top-notch maintenance. Bathrooms are small, with shower units.

Grolmanstrasse 35, 10623 Berlin. ⓒ 030/8-89-00. Fax 030/8-89-02-60. www.heckers-hotel.de. 69 units. 150€–200€ ($173–$230) double; 280€–480€ ($322–$552) suite. AE, DC, MC, V. Parking 12€ ($14). U-Bahn: Uhlandstrasse. Bus: 109 from Tegel Airport to Uhlandstrasse or 119 from Tempelhof Airport. **Amenities:** Small restaurant; bar (roof dining in summer); 24-hr. room service; laundry service; nonsmoking rooms; 1 room for those with limited mobility. *In room:* TV, dataport, minibar, hair dryer, safe.

Hotel Sylter Hof Berlin   This hotel offers rich trappings at good prices. The main lounges are warmly decorated in old-world style. The well-maintained rooms, most of which are singles, may be too small for most tastes, but the staff pay special attention to your comfort. Bathrooms are cramped but efficiently arranged, with tub/shower combos.

Kurfürstenstrasse 116, 10787 Berlin. ⓒ 030/2-12-00. Fax 030/214-28-26. www.sylterhof-berlin.de. 161 units. 125€–140€ ($144–$161) double; from 175€ ($201) suite. Rates include buffet breakfast. AE, DC, MC, V. Parking 10€–50€ ($12–$58). U-Bahn: Wittenbergplatz. Bus: 119, 129, 146, or 185. **Amenities:** Restaurant; bar; coffee bar; nightclub next door; laundry service/dry cleaning. *In room:* TV, dataport in some, minibar, hair dryer.

IN BERLIN-MITTE
Very Expensive

Hotel Adlon 🏵🏵🏵   Only steps from the Brandenburg Gate, this hotel is one of Berlin's premier addresses and is famous among celebrities. The large, beautifully appointed rooms contain king-size or twin beds. Bathrooms are spacious with tub/shower combos, deluxe toiletries, and a phone.

Unter den Linden 77, 10117 Berlin. ⓒ 800/426-3135 in the U.S., or 030/22-61-0. Fax 030/22-61-11-16. www.hotel-adlon.de. 337 units. 330€–490€ ($380–$564) double; 440€–850€ ($506–$978) junior suite. AE, DC, MC, V. Parking 23€ ($26). S-Bahn: Unter den Linden. **Amenities:** 3 restaurants; bar; indoor pool; health club; spa; 24-hr. room service; babysitting; laundry service/dry cleaning; nonsmoking rooms; rooms for those with limited mobility. *In room:* A/C, TV, CD player, dataport, minibar, hair dryer, safe.

The Ritz-Carlton 🏵🏵🏵   One of Berlin's most glamorous and prestigious hotels opened in January 2004 at the Potsdamer Platz. The building evokes the Art Nouveau heyday of the New York City skyscrapers constructed in the 1920s. The club-level rooms and the suites are, of course, the most luxurious way to stay here, but even the standard guest rooms are luxuriously furnished and decorated. The hotel is full of grace notes, such as afternoon tea in the lobby lounge by an open fireplace, live jazz or blues in the hotel bar, the Curtain Club, and an indoor pool. The dining facilities are among the finest in town.

Potsdamer Platz 3, 10785 Berlin. ⓒ 030/33-77-77. Fax 030/777-55-55. www.ritzcarlton.com/hotels/berlin. 302 rooms. 250€–530€ ($288–$610) double; 390€–610€ ($448–$700) junior suite; 1,800€ ($2,070) suite.

Amenities: 2 restaurants; indoor pool; fitness center; spa; Jacuzzi; sauna; 24-hr. room service; laundry service/dry cleaning; nonsmoking rooms; rooms for those with limited mobility. *In room:* A/C, TV, dataport, minibar, hair dryer, safe.

Westin Grand ★★★ Many hotels call themselves grand—this one truly is, rivaled only by the Kempinski. Since taking over, Westin has spent a fortune in making the rooms among the finest in the city. All are spacious and tastefully decorated. Bathrooms are also large and state-of-the-art with tub/shower combos and deluxe toiletries.

Friedrichstrasse 158–164, 10117 Berlin. ℂ 888/625-5144 in the U.S., or 030/2-02-70. Fax 030/20-27-33-62. www.westin.com/berlin. 358 units. 134€–320€ ($154–$368) double; from 289€ ($332) junior suite; from 427€ ($491) apt suite. AE, DC, MC, V. Parking 20€ ($23). U-Bahn: Französische Strasse. S-Bahn: Friedrichstrasse. **Amenities:** 3 restaurants; bar; indoor pool; fitness club; Jacuzzi; sauna; solarium; salon; 24-hr. room service; massage; babysitting; laundry service/dry cleaning; nonsmoking rooms; rooms for those with limited mobility. *In room:* A/C, TV, dataport, minibar, hair dryer.

Expensive

Four Seasons ★★★ One of Berlin's most opulent hotels was built in 1996 on the site of a bombed-out parking lot about a block from the Gendarmenmarkt. From the look of things, you'd never realize the venue is new, as everything about the place evokes Versailles and an undeniable sense of well-established and very plush prosperity. Rooms are furnished with timeless taste and elegance, with very large bathrooms that have walk-in showers, deep tubs, and a selection of toiletries.

Charlottenstrasse 49, 10117 Berlin. ℂ 800/332-3442 in the U.S., or 030/2-03-38. Fax 030/203-36-119. www.fourseasons.com. 204 units. 265€–365€ ($305–$420) double; from 550€ ($633) suite. AE, DC, MC, V. Parking 21€ ($24). U-Bahn: Französische Strasse. **Amenities:** Restaurant; bar; health club; spa services; Jacuzzi; sauna; 24-hr. room service; massage; babysitting; laundry service/dry cleaning; nonsmoking rooms; rooms for those with limited mobility. *In room:* A/C, TV, dataport, minibar, hair dryer, safe.

Moderate

Hotel Hackescher Markt ★ You'd never know this nugget of charm had been built in 1998, as everything about it evokes a late-19th-century landmark. Rooms are soothing, partially oak-paneled, and outfitted with comfortable and practical furniture. Standard singles tend to be just a bit small—a better bet might be one of the more upscale doubles. Bathrooms have heated floors and almost all contain tub/shower combos. Some guests appreciate the romantic overtones of bedrooms on the uppermost floor, whose walls are angled thanks to the building's mansard roof.

Grosse Präsidentenstrasse 8, 10178 Berlin. ℂ 030/28-00-30. Fax 030/28-00-31-11. www.hackescher-markt. com. 31 units. 185€–205€ ($213–$236) double; 195€–225€ ($224–$259) suite. AE, DC, MC, V. S-Bahn: Hackescher Markt. **Amenities:** Bar; 24-hr. room service; laundry service/dry cleaning; nonsmoking rooms. *In room:* TV, dataport, minibar, hair dryer, safe.

Hotel Künstlerheium Luise ★ *(Finds)* This discovery is a select boutique hotel where every accommodation was designed and individually furnished by a different German artist. Under historical preservation, the hotel is installed in a restored 1825 city palace. Clients from the arts, media, and even the political and business worlds are drawn to this unusual hostelry. Each room is decorated by a different artist. Some units evoke modern minimalism, whereas others are much more quirky.

Luisenstrasse 19, 10119 Berlin. ℂ 030/284-480. Fax 030/2844-84-48. 46 units. www.kuenstlerheim-luise.de. 94€ ($108) double without bathroom; 135€ ($155) double with bathroom; 144€ ($166) suite. Rates include breakfast. AE, DC, MC, V. U-Bahn: Friedrichstrasse. **Amenities:** Restaurant/bar next door; laundry service/dry cleaning. *In room:* A/C in some units, TV, minibar in suites, safe in suites.

Hotel Luisenhof ⭐ One of the most desirable small hotels in Berlin's eastern district, the Luisenhof occupies a dignified 1822 house. Five floors of high-ceilinged rooms will appeal to those desiring to escape modern Berlin's sterility. Rooms range greatly in size, but each is equipped with good queen-size or twin beds. Bathrooms, though small, are beautifully appointed, with shower stalls (often with a large tub).

Köpenicker Strasse 92, 10179 Berlin. ☎ **030/2-41-59-06**. Fax 030/2-79-29-83. www.luisenhof.de. 27 units. 120€–135€ ($138–$155) double; 150€–250€ ($173–$288) suite. Rates include breakfast. AE, DC, MC, V. U-Bahn: Märkisches Museum. **Amenities:** Restaurant; bar; room service (6am–midnight); laundry service/dry cleaning; nonsmoking rooms; 1 room for those with limited mobility. *In room:* TV, dataport, minibar, hair dryer.

WHERE TO DINE

For food on the run, try one of the dozens of kabob stalls *(Imbisse)* that dot the streets. Some 200,000 Turks live in Berlin, and the food that they've introduced— meat- or *Scharfskäse-* (sheep's cheese, virtually identical to feta) stuffed pitas— make a filling, cheap meal, but watch out for the cascades of cabbage. Good sit-down Turkish restaurants are harder to find, but one of the best is **Hitit,** Knobelsdorffstrasse 35 (☎ **030/322-45-57**), near Charlottenburg Schloss, with a full array of Turkish specialties, some 150 dishes in all. It's open daily 8am to midnight.

ON OR NEAR THE KURFÜRSTENDAMM
Expensive

Harlekin ⭐⭐ FRENCH/INTERNATIONAL Chefs at traditional favorite restaurants were chagrined at this spot's success. The menu is perfectly balanced between tradition and innovation. Appetizers are likely to include such dishes as calves' consommé with crayfish or osso buco consommé with lobster spaetzle. For your main course, you might be won over by the saddle of lamb baked in a spring roll or turbot roasted with mixed root vegetables.

In the Grand Hotel Esplanade, Lützowufer. ☎ **030/254-78-858**. Reservations recommended. Main courses 22€–32€ ($25–$37); 3- to 5-course fixed-price menu 48€–72€ ($55–$83). AE, DC, MC, V. Tues–Sat 6:30–11pm. Closed 3½ weeks in July (dates vary). U-Bahn: Nollendorfplatz or Wittenbergplatz.

Paris Bar ⭐ FRENCH This French bistro has been a local favorite since the postwar years, when two Frenchmen established the restaurant to bring a little Parisian cheer to the dismal gray of bombed-out Berlin. The place is just as crowded with elbow-to-elbow tables as a Montmartre tourist trap, but you'll find it a genuinely pleasing little eatery. It's a true restaurant on the see-and-be-seen circuit between Savignyplatz and Gedächtniskiche. The food is invariably fresh and well prepared but not particularly innovative.

Kantstrasse 152. ☎ **030/313-80-52**. Reservations recommended. Main courses 19€–25€ ($21–$28). AE. Daily noon–2am. U-Bahn: Uhlandstrasse.

Moderate

Marjellchen ⭐ EAST PRUSSIAN This is the only restaurant in Berlin spe-cializing in the cuisine of Germany's long-lost province of East Prussia, along with the cuisines of Pomerania and Silesia. Amid a Bismarckian ambience of still lifes, vested waiters, and oil lamps, you can enjoy a savory version of red-beet soup with strips of beef, East Prussian potato soup with crabmeat and bacon, *falscher Gänsebraten* (pork spareribs stuffed with prunes and bread crumbs), and *mecklenburger Kümmelfleisch* (lamb with chives and onions).

Mommsenstrasse 9. ☎ **030/883-26-76**. Reservations required. Main courses 10€–20€ ($12–$23). AE, DC, MC, V. Mon–Sat 5pm–midnight. Closed Dec 23, 24, and 31. U-Bahn: Adenauerplatz or Uhlandstrasse. Bus: 109, 119, or 129.

Cafe Society

The family-owned **Café/Bistro Leysieffer,** Kurfürstendamm 218 (© 030/ 885-74-80; U-Bahn: Kurfürstendamm), opened in the early 1980s within what had been the Chinese embassy. The street level contains a pastry and candy shop, but most clients climb the flight of stairs to a marble- and wood-sheathed cafe with a balcony overlooking the busy Ku'damm. The breakfast menu is one of the most elegant in town: Parma ham, smoked salmon, a fresh baguette, French butter, and—to round it off— champagne. Hours are Sunday through Thursday from 10am to 8pm, Friday and Saturday from 10am to 9pm.

Restaurant Mario NORTHERN ITALIAN Named for its owner, this restaurant serves some of the most imaginative northern Italian food in Berlin. It was created by an East Berliner who'd never been to Italy but wanted to "cook Italian," nevertheless. Today the chefs are fully grounded in the repertoire of Italy. The innovative and refreshing dishes might include platters of the most delectable antipasti in town or else carpaccio. At least two different kinds of pastas are offered nightly, including a favorite made with a green-pepper pesto. Savory ravioli and rigatoni appear several different ways.

Carmerstrasse 2. © 030/312-31-15. Reservations recommended. Main courses 11€–20€ ($13–$23); fixed-price menus 21€–40€ ($24–$46). AE, DC, MC, V. Mon–Fri noon–midnight; Sat 4pm–midnight. S-Bahn: Savignyplatz.

YVA Suite ★ *Finds* INTERNATIONAL There's an excellent restaurant associated with this club, a meeting place for the hip denizens of Berlin's inner sanctum of writers, artists, and cultural icons. The setting is on the ground floor of a building near the Savignyplatz, within a decor that's high-ceilinged, stylish, and almost surgically minimalist. Expect walls almost entirely sheathed in slabs of volcanic lava rock, elegant table settings, well-prepared food that includes selections for both hearty and delicate appetites, and a formidable tradition of welcoming stars and starlets from Germany's world of high fashion, sports, and the arts. Menu items vary with the season and the inspiration of the chefs, but are likely to include lemon-coconut soup with chicken satay; terrine of goose-liver; various forms of carpaccio; curried breast of duck with chorizo sausages; and Thai-style bouillabaisse.

Schlüterstrasse 52. © 030/88-72-55-73. Reservations recommended. Main courses 12€–19€ ($14–$22). AE, MC, V. Bar and full menu daily 6pm–midnight; bar and limited menu daily midnight–3 or 4am. S-Bahn: Savignyplatz.

Inexpensive

Hard Rock Cafe AMERICAN This is the local branch of the familiar worldwide chain that mingles rock 'n' roll nostalgia with American food. Menu choices range from a veggie burger to a "pig" sandwich (hickory smoked pork barbecue) that you might find in rural Georgia. The food is unexceptional, but service is friendly.

Meinekestrasse 21. © 030/88-46-20. Reservations accepted for groups of 10 or more. Main courses 7.75€–17€ ($8.90–$20). AE, MC, V. Sun–Thurs noon–11pm; Fri–Sat noon–1am. U-Bahn: Kurfürstendamm.

Lubitsch CONTINENTAL Its conservative chic reputation was enhanced in 1999 when Chancellor Schröder dropped in for lunch and a photo-op, causing ripples of energy to reverberate through the neighborhood. Menu items include lots of cafe drinks and steaming pots of afternoon tea, but if you drop in for a meal, expect platters of chicken curry salad with roasted potatoes; Berlin-style potato soup; braised chicken with salad and fresh vegetables; a roulade of suckling pig; and Nürnberger-style wursts. Expect brusque service, a black-and-white decor with Thonet-style chairs, and a somewhat arrogant environment that, despite its drawbacks, is very, very *Berliner.*

Bleibtreustrasse 47. ℭ **030/882-37-56.** Main courses 6€–15€ ($6.90–$17); business lunch 10€ ($12). AE, DC, MC, V. Mon–Sat 10am–midnight; Sun 6pm–1am. U-Bahn: Kurfürstendamm.

NEAR THE MEMORIAL CHURCH & ZOO
Very Expensive
First Floor ★★ REGIONAL GERMAN/FRENCH   This is the showcase restaurant within one of the most spectacular hotels ever built near the Tiergarten. Set one floor above street level, it features a perfectly orchestrated service and setting that revolve around the cuisine of a master chef. Winning our praise are such dishes as a terrine of veal with arugula-flavored butter; sophisticated variations of Bresse chicken; guinea fowl stuffed with foie gras and served with a truffle vinaigrette sauce; a cassoulet of lobster and broad beans in a style vaguely influenced by the culinary precepts of southwestern France; filet of sole with champagne sauce; and a mascarpone mousse with lavender-scented honey.

In the Palace Berlin, Budapesterstrasse 42. ℭ **030/25-02-10-20.** Reservations recommended. Main courses 34€–36€ ($39–$41). Set menus 40€ ($46) at lunch only, 68€–105€ ($78–$121) at lunch and dinner. AE, DC, MC, V. Daily noon–2pm and 6–11pm. U-Bahn: Zoologischer Garten.

TIERGARTEN
Expensive
Paris-Moskau INTERNATIONAL   The grand days of the 19th century are alive and well at this restaurant in the beautiful Tiergarten area, where good dining spots are scarce. Menu items are both classic and more cutting-edge. The fresh tomato soup is excellent. Some of the dishes are mundane—the grilled filet of beef in mushroom sauce comes to mind—but other, lighter dishes with delicate seasonings are delightful. We recommend the grilled North Sea salmon with herbs accompanied by basil-flavored noodles. The chef should market his recipe for saffron sauce, which accompanies several dishes. You'll receive attentive service from the formally dressed staff.

Alt-Moabit 141. ℭ **030/3-94-20-81.** Reservations recommended. Main courses 18€–25€ ($21–$29); fixed-price menus 58€–82€ ($67–$94). No credit cards. Daily 6–11:30pm. S-Bahn: Auhalter Bahnhof.

IN & AROUND CHARLOTTENBURG
Expensive
Alt-Luxemburg ★★ CONTINENTAL/FRENCH/GERMAN   Bamberger Reiter may be the leader among Berlin restaurants, but the Alt-Luxemburg is nipping at its heels. Chef Karl Wannemacher is one of the most outstanding chefs in eastern Germany. Known for his quality and market-fresh ingredients, he prepares a seductively sensual plate. Everything shows his flawless technique, especially the stuffed veal or the saddle of venison with elderberry sauce. Taste his excellent lacquered duck breast with honey sauce or saddle of lamb with stewed peppers. Alt-Luxemburg offers a finely balanced wine list, and service is both unpretentious and gracious.

Windscheidstrasse 31. ℭ **030/323-87-30.** Reservations required. Fixed-price 4-course menu 65€ ($75); fixed-price 5-course menu 72€ ($83). AE, DC, MC, V. Mon–Sat 5–11pm. U-Bahn: Sophie-Charlotteplatz.

Moderate

Bierhaus Luisen-Bräu GERMAN   Luisen-Bräu brewery established this restaurant in 1987. The decor includes enormous stainless-steel vats of the fermenting brew, from which the waiters refill your mug. There's no subtlety of cuisine here; it's robust and hearty fare. You serve yourself from a long buffet table. The seating is indoor or outdoor, depending on the season, at long picnic tables that encourage a sense of beer-hall *Bruderschaft* (camaraderie).

Luisenplatz 1, Charlottenburg (close to Charlottenburg Castle). ✆ 030/3-41-93-88. Reservations recommended on weekends. Main courses 11€–22€ ($12–$25). AE, MC, V. Sun–Thurs 9am–1am; Fri–Sat 9am–2am. U-Bahn: Richard-Wagner-Platz.

IN BERLIN-MITTE
Expensive

Margaux ✹✹✹ CONTINENTAL   Chef Michael Hoffmann will dazzle your palate with his seductive, inventive dishes and his brilliant wine cellar. Several 21st-century food magazines have named his the "best gourmet restaurant in Berlin." Only a few steps from the Brandenburg Gate, the restaurant has a stunning modern interior, designed by the noted architect Johanne Nalbach. The exceptional food is made from only the highest-quality ingredients. Our party of four recently launched our repast with such perfectly prepared starters as marinated duck liver and Breton lobster, which appears with curry and, surprisingly, watermelon. Hoffmann's star shines brightest with his fish, such as John Dory with a Mediterranean "aroma" that turned out to be anchovies, olives, tomatoes, and pepper. Frogs' legs are delectably perfumed with parsley and garlic.

Unter den Linden 78. ✆ 030/22-65-26-11. www.margaux-berlin.de. Reservations required. Main courses 20€–40€ ($23–$46). Set-lunch menus 52€–120€ ($60–$138); fixed-price dinner 75€ ($86). AE, DC, MC, V. Mon–Sat noon–2pm and 7–11pm. S-Bahn: Unter den Linden.

Restaurant VAU ✹✹ INTERNATIONAL   This restaurant is the culinary showcase of master chef Kolja Kleeberg. Choices include terrine of salmon and morels with rocket salad; aspic of suckling pig with sauerkraut; salad with marinated red mullet, mint, and almonds; crisp-fried duck with marjoram; ribs of suckling lamb with thyme-flavored polenta; and desserts such as woodruff soup with champagne-flavored ice cream. The wine list is international and well chosen.

Jägerstrasse 54-55 (near the Four Seasons Hotel and the Gendamenmarkt). ✆ 030/202-9730. Reservations recommended. Main courses 20€–35€ ($23–$40). Set-price lunches 48€–52€ ($55–$60); set-price dinners 75€–100€ ($86–$115). AE, DC, MC, V. Mon–Sat noon–2:30pm and 7–10:30pm. U-Bahn: Hausvoigteiplatz.

Schwarzengraben ✹ ITALIAN   "Black Crows" (its English name) evokes a SoHo-style restaurant in New York. This is the watering hole of the Berlin *Schickeria,* or chic crowd. One Berlin paper defined these trendies as "media honchos and their overblond dates." The see-and-be-seen scene might be more important than the cuisine, but two Italian brothers, Ivo and Rudolf Girolo, succeed admirably with super-fresh ingredients that are well prepared. Sea bass is baked between slices of eggplant, and it's a most credible dish, as is the Italian gnocchi with sausage and green olives. Remarkably, the kitchen is prepared to make on short notice some 300 pasta dishes. Our dining companion for the evening hailed the gnocchi with rabbit ragout and truffles as "orgasmic." We're fond of the duck and rabbit *pastele.* The main dining is upstairs; downstairs is for whiskey and cigars.

Neue Schonhauswer Schonhauser Strasse 13. ✆ 030/2839-1698. Reservations recommended. Main courses 19€–25€ ($22–$29). AE, MC, V. Mon–Sat 10am–3:30pm and 6:30pm–midnight. U-Bahn: Weinmeister.

Moderate

Guy ✦ INTERNATIONAL   At this top-notch restaurant, anticipate a strong sense of gastronomy as theater. Proceed to any of three separate balconies, each supporting at least one row of artfully decorated tables. The overall effect can be compared to the balconies and private boxes of an old-fashioned opera house. The cuisine is very haute, even to the point of seeming experimental. Examples change frequently, but might include a medley of marinated quail and goose liver; mussels served on a purée of arugula; lobster and sweetbreads cooked in puff pastry with tarragon-flavored cream sauce; and braised breast of goose with a roulade of potatoes and herbs.

Jägerstrasse 59–60. ℂ 030/20-94-26-00. Reservations recommended. Main courses 21€–25€ ($24–$29). Set-price lunches 15€–20€ ($17–$23); set-price dinners 51€–74€ ($59–$85). AE, MC, V. Mon–Fri noon–3pm and 6pm–1am; Sat 6pm–1am. U-Bahn: Stadtmitte or Französischer Strasse.

Restaurant Borchardt *Value* INTERNATIONAL   This restaurant is elegant, lighthearted, and fashionable among the city's artistic movers and shakers. You can order anything from a simple salad (as supermodel Claudia Schiffer often does) to the more substantial cream of potato soup with bacon and croutons; filet of carp prepared with Riesling and herbs and finished with champagne; foie gras served with caramelized apples; chicken stuffed with morels and served with cream-and-herb sauce; and a pistachio mousse garnished with essence of fresh fruit.

Französische Strasse 47. ℂ 030/2038-7110. Reservations recommended. Daily special menu 9€ ($10); main courses 9.50€–20€ ($11–$22). AE, V. Daily noon–2am (kitchen closes at midnight). U-Bahn: Französische Strasse.

Inexpensive

Dressler CONTINENTAL   No other bistro along Unter den Linden so successfully re-creates Berlin's pre-war decor and style. Designed to resemble an arts conscious bistro of the sort that might have amused and entertained tuxedo-clad clients in the 1920s, it's outfitted with leather banquettes, tile floors, mirrors, and film memorabilia from the great days of early German cinema. Waiters scurry around, carrying trays of everything from caviar to strudel, as well as three kinds of oysters and hefty portions of lobster salad. Substantial menu items include perfectly prepared turbot with champagne vinaigrette; pheasant breast with Riesling sauce; local salmon trout with white-wine sauce and braised endive; stuffed breast of veal; and calves' liver with apples.

Unter den Linden 39. ℂ 030/204-44-22. Reservations recommended. Main courses 12€–22€ ($14–$25). AE, DC, MC, V. Daily 8am–midnight. S-Bahn: Unter den Linden.

La Gaiola ITALIAN   It's crowded, it's hip, and its decor evokes the 1930s allure of what might have been a coffee plantation in the highlands of Africa. Many clients come here just for its bar scene, but if you're hungry, the food is firmly based on what's cooking in the area that stretches between North Germany and southern Austria, and is served in generous portions. Come here for a chance to meet unattached residents of the surrounding neighborhood, a dialogue with a hip Berliner or two, and good-tasting food items that include beef filet with braised arugula; all manner of fresh fish; homemade salmon with apples, roasted potatoes, and horseradish; and drinks that include raspberry daiquiris.

Monbijouplatz 11–12. ℂ 030/28-53-98-90. Reservations recommended. Main courses 8€–20€ ($9.20–$23). AE, MC, V. Mon–Sat 6pm–midnight. U-Bahn: Hackescher Markt.

Mutter Hoppe GERMAN   This cozy, wood-paneled restaurant still serves the solid Teutonic cuisine favored by a quasi-legendary matriarch (Mother Hoppe) who used to churn out vast amounts of *gütbergerlich* cuisine to members of her extended family and entourage. Within a quartet of old-fashioned dining rooms, you'll enjoy heaping portions of such rib-sticking fare as sauerbraten with roasted potatoes; creamy goulash with wild mushrooms; filets of zander with dill-flavored cream sauce; and braised filets of pork in mushroom-flavored cream sauce. Wine is available, but most guests opt for at least one foaming mug of beer.

Rathausstrasse 21, Nikolaiviertel. ⓒ 030/241-56-25. Reservations recommended. Main courses 8€–25€ ($9.20–$29). DC, MC, V. Daily 11:30am–midnight. U- and S-Bahn: Alexanderplatz.

StäV ★ *Finds* RHENISH   For years, this upscale tavern entertained the politicians and journalists whose business involved the day-to-day running of the German government from Germany's former capital of Bonn. Although its owners at first opposed the reinauguration of Berlin as the German capital, when the switch was made, they valiantly pulled out of the Rhineland and followed their clientele to new digs within a 5-minute walk of the Brandenburg Gate near the Friedrichstrasse Bahnhof. The only beer served is Kölsch, a brew more closely associated with the Rhineland than any other beer. Rhenish food items include a mass of apples, onions, and blood sausage known as *Himmel und Ärd* ("heaven and hell"); braised beef with pumpernickel and raisin sauce; and Rhineland sauerbraten with noodles. Other items, many influenced by the culinary traditions of Berlin, include braised liver with bacon and onions; a crisp version of Alsatian pizza known as *Flammenküche;* and a potato cake topped with apples and shredded beets or with smoked salmon and sour cream.

8 Schiffbauerdamm. ⓒ 030/282-3965. Reservations recommended. Main courses 3.60€–9.80€ ($4.15–$11). AE, DC, MC, V. Daily 10am–1am. U-Bahn: Friedrichstrasse.

SEEING THE SIGHTS

SIGHTSEEING SUGGESTIONS FOR FIRST-TIME VISITORS

If You Have 1 Day Get up early and visit the **Brandenburg Gate,** symbol of Berlin, then walk down **Unter den Linden** and have coffee and pastry at the Operncafé. Visit the **Gemäldegalerie** to see some of the world's greatest masterpieces. Afterward, go to **Charlottenburg** to view the celebrated bust of Queen Nefertiti in the **Egyptian Museum.** In the evening, walk along the Kurfürstendamm, visit the **Kaiser Wilhelm Memorial Church,** and dine in a local restaurant.

If You Have 2 Days On day 2, visit the **Pergamon Museum** on Museum Island, seeing the Pergamon Altar. Explore the **National Gallery,** then head for Alexanderplatz. Take the elevator up for a view from its TV tower, before exploring the **Nikolai Quarter** on foot. Spend an hour in the evening walking around the rebuilt **Potsdamer Platz.**

If You Have 3 Days On day 3, go to **Potsdam** (see "Day Trips from Berlin," p. 410).

If You Have 4 or 5 Days On day 4, visit the **Judisches Museum Berlin.** In the afternoon return to Charlottenburg Palace and explore the **Historical Apartments,** and in the evening visit the **Europa-Center** for drinks and dinner. On day 5, see some of the sights you might have missed. Take some walks through Berlin and stop at the Cold War's **Checkpoint Charlie,** with its museum. If time remains, visit the **Berlin Zoo,** stroll through the **Tiergarten,** and attend a cabaret in the evening.

THE TOP MUSEUMS
In the Tiergarten

Gemäldegalerie ★★★   This is one of Germany's greatest painting galleries. Several rooms are devoted to early German masters, with altarpieces dating from the 13th to 15th centuries. Note the panel of *The Virgin Enthroned with Child* (1350), surrounded by angels that resemble the demons so popular in the later works of Hieronymus Bosch. Eight paintings make up the Dürer collection in adjacent rooms.

Another gallery is given over to Italian painting. Here are five Raphael Madonnas; and works by Titian *(The Girl with a Bowl of Fruit),* Fra Filippo Lippi, Botticelli, and Correggio *(Leda with the Swan).* There are also early Netherlandish paintings from the 15th and 16th centuries (van Eyck, Van der Weyden, Bosch, and Bruegel). Several galleries are devoted to Flemish and Dutch masters of the 17th century, with no fewer than 20 works by Rembrandt, including the *Head of Christ.*

Stauffenbergstrasse (entrance is at Mattäiskirchplatz 4). ℂ 030/20-90-55-55. www.smb.spk-berlin.de/gg/ e/s.html. Admission 6€ ($6.90) adults, 3€ ($3.45) children. Tues–Sun 10am–6pm (Thurs to 10pm). U-Bahn: Potsdamer Platz, then bus 148. Bus: 129 from Ku'damm (plus a 4-min. walk).

Neue Nationalgalerie (New National Gallery) ★   In its modern glass-and-steel home designed by Ludwig Mies van der Rohe, the Neue Nationalgalerie is a sequel of sorts to the art at Dahlem. It contains a continually growing collection of modern European and American art. Here you'll find works of 19th-century artists, with a stellar concentration on French Impressionists. German art starts with Adolph von Menzel's paintings from about 1850. The 20th-century collection includes works by Max Beckmann, Edvard Munch, and E. L. Kirchner *(Brandenburger Tor),* as well as a few paintings by "the usual suspects," Bacon, Picasso, Ernst, Klee, and American artists such as Barnett Newman. There's food service in the cafe on the ground floor. Hot meals are served from 11am to 5pm.

Potsdamer strasse 50 (just south of the Tiergarten). ℂ 030/2-66-26-62. www.smb.spk-berlin.de/nng/ e/s.html. Permanent collection, 6€ ($6.90) adults, 3€ ($3.45) children; temporary exhibitions, 3€ ($3.45). Tues–Wed and Fri 10am–6pm; Thurs-Sat 10am–10pm. (Opening times vary according to new exhibitions.) U-Bahn: Mendelssohn-Bartholdy-Park. S-Bahn: Potsdamer Platz.

Museumsinsel (Museum Island)

Pergamon Museum ★★★   The Pergamon Museum houses several departments, but if you have time for only one exhibit, go to the central hall of the U-shaped building to see the **Pergamon Altar** ★★★. This Greek altar (180–160 B.C.) has a huge room all to itself. Some 27 steps lead up to the colonnade. Most fascinating is the frieze around the base, tediously pieced together over a 20-year period. Depicting the struggle of the Olympian gods against the Titans as told in Hesiod's *Theogony,* the relief is strikingly alive, with figures projecting as much as a foot from the background. This, however, is only part of the collection of Greek and Roman antiquities, housed in the north and east wings. You'll also find a Roman market gate discovered in Miletus, and sculptures from many Greek and Roman cities, including a statue of a goddess holding a pomegranate (575 B.C.), found in southern Attica. The **Near East Museum** ★, in the

Native Behavior

Traditional Germans enjoy their big meal at noon and, in the evening, satisfy hunger with deli cold cuts, open-faced sandwiches, sour pickles, and liver sausage, among other food. To be truly native, you'll begin your *Mittagessen* (main noonday meal) with *Leberknodel-suppe* (liver dumpling).

Germany is a land that welcomes all serious beer drinkers. The country is home to about 40% of the world's breweries, the largest concentration found in Bavaria. The best and most plentiful beer gardens and beer halls are in Munich (see the box "What's Brewing at the Beer Halls?," p. 433).

In general the German people are rather candid, especially if they don't agree with something. Whereas this might appear argumentative to foreigners, locals might counterclaim that they are "merely being honest, not hypocritical."

Many young Germans seem obsessed with all things Yankee; yet, almost in contradiction, they possess deeply felt anti-American sentiments. You must wander carefully through the maze of politics, if the subject comes up at all.

As a rule, expect more formality in Germany than in America or even Britain. By all means, if you have an appointment, show up on time!

south wing, contains one of the largest collections anywhere of antiquities discovered in the lands of ancient Babylonia, Persia, and Assyria. Among the exhibits is the Processional Way of Babylon with the Ishtar Gate (580 B.C.).

Bodestrasse 1–3. ✆ 030/2090-55-77. Admission 6€ ($6.90) adults, 3€ ($3.45) children; free the 1st Sun of the month. Tues–Wed and Fri–Sun 10am–6pm; Thurs 10am–10pm. U-Bahn/S-Bahn: Friedrichstrasse. Tram: 1, 2, 3, 4, 5, 13, 15, or 53.

Altes Museum ✮ Karl Friedrich Schinkel, the city's greatest architect, designed this structure, which resembles a Greek Corinthian temple, in 1822. On its main floor is the **Antikensammlung** or Museum of Greek and Roman Antiquities. This great collection of world-famous works of antique decorative art was inaugurated in 1960. It's rich in pottery; Greek, Etruscan, and Roman bronze statuettes and implements; ivory carvings, glassware, objects in precious stone, and jewelry of the Mediterranean region, as well as gold and silver treasures; mummy portraits from Roman Egypt; wood and stone sarcophagi; and a few marble sculptures. The collection includes some of the finest Greek vases of the black- and red-figures style dating from the 6th century to the 4th century B.C. The best known is a large Athenian wine jar (amphora) found in Vulci, Etruria, dating from 490 B.C., which shows a satyr with a lyre and the god Hermes.

Museumsinsel am Lustgarten. ✆ 030/20-90-55-55. Admission 6€ ($6.90) adults, 3€ ($3.45) children. Tues–Sun 10am–6pm; closes at 10pm on Thurs. U-Bahn/S-Bahn: Friedrichstrasse. Bus: 100 to Lustgarten, 147, 157, or 358.

Alte Nationalgalerie ✮ This museum is known for its collection of 19th-century German art as well as for its French Impressionists. A feature of the museum is the world's largest collection of the works of one of the best known of all Berlin artists, Adolph von Menzel (1815–1905). We especially like his *Das Balkonzimmer*. Other paintings include a galaxy of art representing the romantic and classical movements as well as the Biedermeier era. Allow at least an hour and a half to take in canvasses by everybody from Pissarro to Cézanne, from Delacroix to Degas, and from van Gogh to Monet. We are especially fond of the works of Max Liebermann and Max Beckmann. The collection would have been far greater than it is had not the Nazis either sold or destroyed so many early-20th-century works they viewed as "degenerate."

Bodestrasse 1–3. ⓒ 030/20905555. Admission 6€ ($6.90) adults, 3€ ($3.45) children. Tues, Wed, and Fri 10am–6pm; Thurs 10am–10pm; Sat–Sun 11am–6pm. S-Bahn: Hackescher Markt or Friedrichstrasse. Tram: 12, 3, 4, 5, 13, 15, or 53. Bus: 100, 157, or 378.

In Charlottenburg

Charlottenburg is the quarter of Berlin just west of the Tiergarten. In addition to viewing the exhaustive collections in Charlottenburg Palace, you can enjoy a relaxing ramble through Schlossgarten Charlottenburg. The gardens have been restored and landscaped much as they were in the days of Friedrich Wilhelm II.

Schloss Charlottenburg (Charlottenburg Palace) ★★ Napoleon exaggerated a bit in comparing Schloss Charlottenburg to Versailles when he invaded Berlin in 1806, but in its heyday this palace was the most elegant residence for Prussian rulers outside the castle in Potsdam. Begun in 1695 as a summer palace for the Electress Sophie Charlotte, patron of philosophy and the arts and wife of King Frederick I (Elector Frederick III), the little residence got out of hand until it grew into the massive structure you see today. The main wing contains the apartments of Frederick I and his "philosopher queen." The **new wing,** known as the Knobelsdorff-Flügel and built from 1740 to 1746, shelters the apartments of Frederick the Great, which now houses a collection of paintings, many of which were either collected or commissioned by the king.

Luisenplatz. ⓒ 030/320-91-275. Combined ticket for all buildings and historical rooms 12€ ($14) adults, 9€ ($10) children under 14 and students. Palace Tues–Fri 9am–4pm, Sat–Sun 10am–4pm; museum Tues–Fri 10am–6pm; gardens (free admission) daily 6:30am–8pm. Closes at 6pm Nov–Feb. U-Bahn: Richard-Wagner-Platz. Bus: 145 or 204.

Ägyptisches Museum (Egyptian Museum) ★ The western Berlin branch of the Egyptian Museum is housed in the east guardhouse built for the king's bodyguard. It's worth the trip just to see the famous colored bust of **Queen Nefertiti** ★★★, dating from about 1340 B.C. The bust, stunning in every way, is all by itself in a dark first-floor room, illuminated by a spotlight. It is believed that the bust never left the studio in which it was created but served as a model for other portraits of the queen. The left eye was never drawn in. In addition, look for the head of Queen Tiy and the world-famous head of a priest in green stone. The monumental Kalabasha Gateway was built by Emperor Augustus around 30 B.C. Other displays feature jewelry, papyrus, tools, and weapons, as well as objects relating to the Egyptian belief in the afterlife.

Schlossstrasse 70. ⓒ 030/34-35-73-11. Admission 6€ ($6.90) adults, 3€ ($3.45) children; free admission 1st Sun of each month. Tues–Sun 10am–6pm. U-Bahn: Sophie-Charlotte-Platz or Richard-Wagner-Platz. Bus: 109, 145, 210, or X21.

Die Sammlung Berggruen: Picasso und Seine Zeit (The Berggruen Collection: Picasso and his Era) ★ *Finds* One of the most unusual private museums in Berlin has accumulated the awesome collection of respected art and antiques dealer Heinz Berggruen. A native of Berlin who fled the Nazis in 1936,

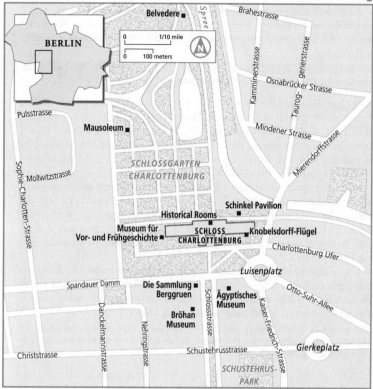

he later established antiques dealerships in Paris and California before returning, with his collection, to his native home in 1996. The setting is a renovated former army barracks designed by noted architect August Stüler in 1859. Although most of the collection is devoted to Picasso; there are also works by Cézanne, Braque, Klee, and van Gogh. Some 60 or more works in all, the Picasso collection alone is worth the trip, ranging from his teenage efforts to all of his major periods.

Schlossstrasse 1. *©* 030/326-95815. Admission 6€ ($6.90) adults, 3€ ($3.45) students and children. Tues–Sun 10am–6pm. U-Bahn: Richard-Wagner-Platz, followed by a 10-min. walk. Bus: 129, 145, or 210.

Bröhan Museum   This wonderful museum specializes in decorative objects of the Art Nouveau (*Jugendstil* in German) and Art Deco periods (1889–1939), with exquisite vases, glass, furniture, silver, paintings of artists belonging to the Berlin Secession, and other works of art arranged in drawing-room fashion, including an outstanding porcelain collection.

Schlossstrasse 1a. *©* 030/3269-0600. Admission 4€ ($4.60) adults, 3€ ($3.45) students/children. Tues–Sun 10am–6pm. U-Bahn: Sophie-Charlotte-Platz. Bus: 109 or 145 to Luisenplatz/Schloss Charlottenburg.

OTHER MUSEUMS

Deutsche Guggenheim Berlin ✪   This state-of-the-art museum is devoted to organizing and presenting exhibitions of modern and contemporary art. The Guggenheim Foundation conceives, organizes, and installs several exhibitions annually, and also presents exhibitions of newly commissioned works created specifically for this space by world-renowned artists. In addition to contemporary artists, exhibition subjects in the past have ranged from Picasso and Cézanne to Andy Warhol.

Unter den Linden 13–15. (C) 030/2020-930. Admission 3€ ($3.45) adults, 2€ ($2.30) children. Free on Mon. Daily 11am–8pm (Thurs to 10pm). S-Bahn: Unter den Linden.

Judisches Museum Berlin ★★   The most talked-about museum in Berlin, the Jewish Museum is housed in a building that is one of the most spectacular in Berlin. Called "the silver lightning bolt," it was designed by architect Daniel Libeskind. To some viewers, the building suggests a shattered Star of David by its building plan and the scarring in the zinc-plated facade. Odd-shaped windows are haphazardly embedded in the building's exterior.

Inside, the spaces are designed to make the visitor uneasy and disoriented, simulating the feeling of those who were exiled. A vast hollow cuts through the museum to mark what is gone. When the exhibits reach the rise of the Third Reich, the hall's walls, ceiling, and floor close in as the visitor proceeds. A chillingly hollow Holocaust Void, a dark, windowless chamber, evokes much that was lost.

The exhibits concentrate on three themes: Judaism and Jewish life, the devastating effects of the Holocaust, and the post–World War II rebuilding of Jewish life in Germany. The on-site Liebermanns Restaurant features world cuisine, with an emphasis on Jewish recipes—all strictly kosher.

Lindenstrasse 9–14. (C) 030/25-99-33. Admission 5€ ($5.75); free for kids 6 and under. Family ticket 10€ ($12) for 2 adults, and up to 4 children. Mon 10am–10pm; Tues–Sun 10am–8pm. U-Bahn: Hallesches Tor or Kochstrasse. Bus: 129, 240, or 341.

Käthe-Kollwitz Museum ★   More than any other museum in Germany, this one reflects the individual sorrow of the artist whose work it contains. Some visitors call it a personalized revolt against the agonies of war, as well as a welcome change from the commercialism of the nearby Ku'damm. Established in 1986, it was inspired by Berlin-born Käthe Kollwitz, an ardent socialist, feminist, and pacifist whose stormy social commentary led to the eventual banning of her works by the Nazis. Many Kollwitz works show the agonies of wartime separation of mother and child, inspired in part by her loss of a son in Flanders during World War I and a grandson during World War II.

Fasanenstrasse 24. (C) 030/882-52-10. Admission 5€ ($5.75) adults, 2.50€ ($2.90) children and students. Wed–Mon 11am–6pm. U-Bahn: Uhlandstrasse or Kurfürstendamm. Bus: 109, 119, 129, or 219.

Märkisches Museum   The full cultural history of Berlin is displayed in one of the most prominent buildings on the banks of the Spree; 42 rooms contain collections of artifacts from excavations, plus such art treasures as Slav silver items and Bronze Age finds. You can learn about Berlin's theaters and literature, the arts in Berlin and Brandenburg, and the life and work of Berlin artists. Most visitors like the array of mechanical musical instruments that can be played Sunday from 11am to 2pm, for an extra euro.

Am Köllnischen Park 5. (C) 030/30-86-60. Admission 4€ ($4.60) adults, 2€ ($2.30) children. Tues–Sun 9am–5pm. U-Bahn: Märkisches Museum. Bus: 147, 240, or 265.

Museum für Gegenwart Hamburger Bahnhof   This Museum of Contemporary Art opened in 1996 north of the Spree in the old Hamburger Bahnhof. The structure was the terminus for trains from Hamburg. Today, the station no longer receives trains but is a premier storehouse of postwar art, a sort of Musée d'Orsay of Berlin. Traces of its former function are still evident in the building, including the high roof designed for steam engines. The modern art on display is some of the finest in Germany, the nucleus of the collection, a donation from the Berlin collector Erich Marx (no relation to Karl Marx). A multimedia event, you can view everything from Andy Warhol's now legendary *Mao* to an audiovisual Joseph Beuys archive. The museum houses one of the best collections of Cy Twombly. Other works on display are by Rauschenberg, Lichtenstein, and Dan Flavin. The conceptual artist Beuys is also represented by 450 drawings.

Invalidenstrasse 50–51. (*) 030/39-78-34-12. Admission 6€ ($6.90) adults, 3€ ($3.45) children. Tues–Fri 10am–6pm; Sat–Sun 11am–6pm. U-Bahn: Zinnowitzer Strasse. S-Bahn: Lehrter Bahnhof. Bus: 157, 245, 248, or 340.

Museum Haus am Checkpoint Charlie   This small building houses exhibits depicting the tragic events leading up to and following the erection of the former Berlin Wall. You can see some of the instruments of escape used by East Germans. Photos document the construction of the wall, escape tunnels, and the postwar history of both parts of Berlin from 1945 until today, including the airlift of 1948 and 1949. One of the most moving exhibits is the display on the staircase of drawings by schoolchildren who, in 1961 and 1962, were asked to depict both halves of Germany in one picture.

Friedrichstrasse 43-45. (*) 030/253-72-50. Admission 7.50€ ($8.65) adults, 4.50€ ($5.20) children. Daily 9am–10pm. U-Bahn: Kochstrasse or Stadtmitte. Bus: 129.

Kunstgewerbe Museum (Museum of Applied Arts)   This museum, next to the Gemäldegalerie in a modern redbrick edifice built for the collection, is devoted to European applied arts from the early Middle Ages to the present, including the Renaissance, baroque, rococo, Jugendstil (German Art Nouveau), and Art Deco periods. Displayed are glassware, porcelain, silver, furniture, jewelry, and clothing. The collection of medieval goldsmiths' works is outstanding, as are the displays of Venetian glass, early Meissen and KPM porcelain, and Jugendstil vases, porcelain, furniture, and objects.

Matthäiskirchplatz. (*) 030/2662-902. Admission 3€ ($3.45) adults, 1.50€ ($1.75) students/children. Tues–Fri 10am–6pm; Sat–Sun 11am–6pm. U-Bahn/S-Bahn: Potsdamer Platz. Bus: 129 from Ku'damm to Potsdamer Brücke, also buses 142, 148, 248, 346, or 348.

The Story of Berlin   This multimedia extravaganza portrays 8 centuries of the city's history through photos, films, sounds, and colorful displays. Beginning with the founding of Berlin in 1237, it chronicles the plague, the Thirty Years' War, Frederick the Great's reign, military life, the Industrial Revolution and the working poor, the Golden 1920s, World War II, divided Berlin during the Cold War, and the fall of the Wall. Lights flash in a media blitz as you enter the display on the fall of the Wall, making you feel like one of the first East Berliners to wonderingly cross to the West. Conclude your tour on the 14th floor with a panoramic view over today's Berlin. Though the displays are a bit jarring and the historical information is too jumbled to be truly educational, the museum does leave a lasting impression. Allow at least 2 hours.

Ku'damm-Karree, Kurfürstendamm 207–208 (at the corner of Uhlandstrasse). (*) 01805/99-20-10. Admission 9.30€ ($11) adults, 7.50€ ($8.65) students/seniors/children, 21€ ($24) families. Daily 10am–8pm (you must enter by 6pm). U-Bahn: Uhlandstrasse.

HIGHLIGHTS OF BERLIN-MITTE

Reichstag (Parliament)   On the night of February 17, 1933, a fire broke out in the seat of the German parliament, the Reichstag. It was obviously set by the Nazis, but the German Communist Party was blamed. That was all the excuse Hitler's troops needed to begin mass arrests of "dissidents and enemies of the lawful government." During World War II, the Reichstag faced massive Allied bombardment. Today it's once again the home of Germany's parliament. A glass dome, designed by English architect Sir Norman Foster, now crowns the neo-Renaissance structure originally built in 1894. You can go through the west gate for an elevator ride up to the dome, where a sweeping vista of Berlin opens before you. There's both an observation platform and a rooftop restaurant (the view is better than the food).

Platz der Republik 1. ⓒ 030/2273-2152. Free admission. Daily 8am–midnight (last entrance at 10pm). S-Bahn: Unter den Linden. Bus: 100.

Brandenburger Tor (Brandenburg Gate) ★★   This triumphal arch stood for many years next to the Wall, symbolizing the divided city. Today it represents the reunited German capital. Six Doric columns hold up an entablature inspired by the Propylaea of the Parthenon at Athens. Surrounded by the famous and much photographed Quadriga of Gottfried Schadow from 1793, the gate was designed by Carl Gotthard Langhans in 1789. Napoleon liked the original Quadriga so much he ordered them taken down and shipped to Paris, but they were returned to Berlin in 1814. In Berlin's heyday before World War II, the gate marked the grand western extremity of the "main street," Unter den Linden. In the Room of Silence, visitors still gather to meditate and reflect on Germany's past.

Pariser Platz. Free admission. Room of Silence daily 11am–6pm. S-Bahn: Unter den Linden. Bus: 100.

A PARK & A ZOO

Tiergarten ★   Tiergarten, the largest green space in central Berlin, covers just under 2.5 sq. km (1½ sq. miles), with more than 23km (14 miles) of meandering walkways. Late in the 19th century, partially to placate growing civic unrest, it was opened to the public, with a layout formalized by one of the leading landscape architects of the era, Peter Josef Lenné. The park was devastated during World War II, and the few trees that remained were chopped down for fuel as Berlin shuddered through the winter of 1945 and 1946. Beginning in 1955, trees were replanted and alleyways, canals, ponds, and flower beds rearranged in their original patterns through the cooperative efforts of many landscape architects.

The park's largest monuments include the Berlin Zoo, described below, and the **Siegessäule (Victory Column),** which perches atop a soaring red-granite pedestal from a position in the center of the wide boulevard (Strasse des 17 Juni) that neatly bisects the Tiergarten into roughly equivalent sections.

From the Bahnhof Zoo to the Brandenburger Tor. Bus: 100, 141, or 341 to Grosser Stern.

Zoologischer Garten Berlin (Berlin Zoo) ★ *Kids*   Occupying most of the southwest corner of Tiergarten is Germany's oldest and finest zoo. Founded in 1844, it's a short walk north from the Ku'damm. Until World War II, the zoo boasted thousands of animals of every imaginable species and description—many familiar to Berliners by nicknames. The tragedy of the war struck here as well, and by the end of 1945, only 91 animals remained. Since the war, the city has

Berlin-Mitte

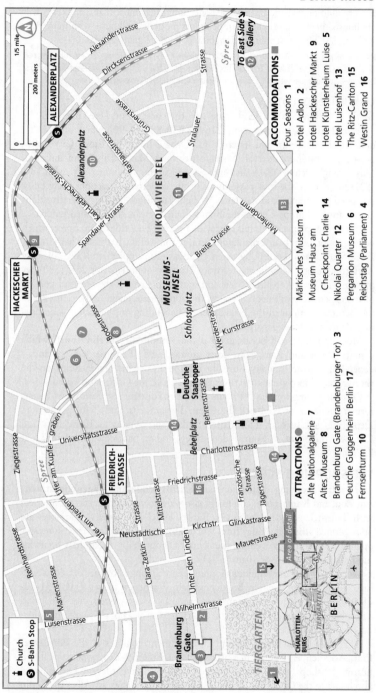

ACCOMMODATIONS ■

Four Seasons **1**
Hotel Adlon **2**
Hotel Hackescher Markt **9**
Hotel Künstlerheium Luise **5**
Hotel Luisenhof **13**
The Ritz-Carlton **15**
Westin Grand **16**

Märkisches Museum **11**
Museum Haus am
  Checkpoint Charlie **14**
Nikolai Quarter **12**
Pergamon Museum **6**
Reichstag (Parliament) **4**

ATTRACTIONS ●

Alte Nationalgalerie **7**
Altes Museum **8**
Brandenburg Gate (Brandenburger Tor) **3**
Deutche Guggenheim Berlin **17**
Fernsehturm **10**

† Church
Ⓢ S-Bahn Stop

0 ___ 1/5 mile
0 ___ 200 meters

been rebuilding its large and unique collection; today more than 13,000 animals are housed here. The zoo has Europe's most modern birdhouse, with more than 550 species. The most valuable inhabitants here are giant pandas.

Hardenbergplatz 8. (€) 030/25-40-10. Zoo, 9€ ($10) adults, 4.5€ ($5.20) children. Zoo and aquarium, 14€ ($16) adults, 7€ ($8.05) children. Zoo daily Nov–Feb 9am–5pm; Mar 9am–5:30pm; Apr–Sept 9am–6:30pm; Oct 9am–6pm. Aquarium year-round, daily 9am–6pm. S-Bahn/U-Bahn: Zoologischer Garten.

ORGANIZED TOURS

BUS & BOAT TOURS Some of the best tours are operated by **Severin+Kühn,** Kurfürstendamm 216 ((€) **030/880-41-90**), which offers half a dozen tours of Berlin and its environs. Their 2-hour **"14 Stops City Tour"** departs at 30-minute intervals November through March daily 10am and 3pm, May through October 10am and 4pm (every 15 min. in summer). Priced at 18€ ($21) per person, the tour passes most of the important attractions using buses equipped with taped commentaries in eight languages. Among the attractions visited are the Europa-Center, the Brandenburg Gate, and Unter den Linden.

You can supplement this bus tour with a 1-hour boat ride on the Spree, which will carry you past the riverbanks and among some of the backwater harbors that are difficult to access except by water. The boat-tour supplement is available only April to October, with departures from 10am to 4pm daily for 26€ ($30) per person. The Severin+Kühn drivers and staff, at the end of the bus tour portion of the experience, will deposit you at the appropriate quays (either adjacent to the Berliner Dom or in the Nicolaiviertel, depending on the day of your visit) in time for the boat's departure.

More appealing and personalized is the 3-hour **"Big Berlin Tour,"** which departs 10am and 2pm daily, costs around 22€ ($25) per person, and— depending on the itinerary—usually incorporates sights not included on the shorter tour. Among the attractions is a section of the Grünewald Forest.

One interesting tour lasts 4 hours and visits Potsdam and Sans Souci Palace, former residence of Frederick the Great. The price is 35€ ($40) per person. Departures are Tuesday, Thursday, Saturday, and Sunday at 10am; May and October, there are additional departures Friday, Saturday, and Sunday at 2:15pm.

THE SHOPPING SCENE

The central shopping destinations are **Kurfürstendamm, Tauentzienstrasse, Am Zoo,** and **Kantstrasse.** You might also want to walk up streets that intersect with Tauentzienstrasse: Marburger, Ranke, and Nürnberger. Most stores are open Monday through Friday from 9 or 10am to 6 or 6:30pm. Many stores stay open late on Thursday evening, usually until about 8:30pm. Saturday hours for most stores are from 9 or 10am to 2pm.

One of Berlin's largest indoor shopping centers, topped by the Mercedes-Benz logo, is the **Europa-Center,** Breitscheidplatz Tauentzienstrasse ((€) **030/31-80-08-00;** U-Bahn: Kurfürstendamm), in the heart of the western city. You'll find a number of restaurants and cafes, in addition to an array of shops offering wide-ranging merchandise.

The city's largest shopping and entertainment complex is the **Potsdamer Platz Arkaden,** Alte Potsdamer Strasse 7 ((€) **030/2559-270**), where you'll find nearly 150 shops, cafes, and restaurants on three different levels. The square is also home to the Grand Hyatt Berlin and a movie complex as well as the Berlin casino.

TWO STORES WORTH A LOOK

Known popularly as KaDeWe (pronounced kah-*day*-vay), **Kaufhaus des Westens,** Wittenbergplatz (© **030/21-21-0;** www.kadewe.de; U-Bahn: Wittenbergplatz), is about 2 blocks from the Kurfürstendamm. The huge luxury store, whose name means "department store of the west," was established some 75 years ago. Displaying extravagant items, it's known mainly for its sixth-floor food department. It's been called the greatest food emporium in the world. More than 1,000 varieties of German sausages are displayed, and delicacies from all over the world are shipped in.

Despite its abbreviated name, **KPM,** Wegelystrasse 1 (© **030/39-00-90;** S-Bahn: Tiergarten), is one of Europe's most prestigious emporiums of luxury dinnerware. Königliche Porzellan Manufaktur was founded in 1763 when Frederick the Great invested his personal funds in a lackluster porcelain factory and elevated it to royal status. Each item is hand painted, hand decorated, and hand packed in almost unbreakable formats that can be shipped virtually anywhere.

BERLIN AFTER DARK

The German *Zitty* and *Tip* include some listings in English, and keep you informed about various nightlife and cultural venues. Both *Berlin Programm* and *Kultur!news* also contain theater listings and other diversions. Performance arts are also covered in *Berlin,* a quarterly published in both English and German. These pamphlets and magazines are available at news kiosks.

THE PERFORMING ARTS

The **Berliner Philharmonisches Orchester (Berlin Philharmonic)** is one of the world's premier orchestras. Its home, **the Philharmonie,** in the Kulturforum, Herbert-von-Karajan Strasse 1 (© **030/254-88-0;** www.berlin-philharmonic. com; U-Bahn: Potsdamer Platz), is a significant piece of modern architecture; you may want to visit even if you do not attend a performance. None of the 2,218 seats are more than 30m (100 ft.) from the rostrum. The box office is open Monday through Friday from 3 to 6pm and Saturday and Sunday from 11am to 2pm. You can place orders by phone at © **030/25-48-89-99.** If you're staying in a first-class or deluxe hotel, you can usually get the concierge to obtain seats for you. Tickets are 18€ to 83€ ($21–$95), special concerts 45€ to 110€ ($52–$127).

The famed **Deutsche Oper Berlin (Berlin Opera),** Bismarckstrasse 35 (© **030/34-384-01;** www.deutscheoperberlin.de; U-Bahn: Deutsche Oper, S-Bahn: Charlottenburg), performs in one of the world's great opera houses, built on the site of the prewar opera house in Charlottenburg. A ballet company performs once a week. Concerts, including *Lieder* evenings, are also presented on the opera stage. Tickets are 15€ to 102€ ($17–$117).

Deutsche Staatsoper (German State Opera), Unter den Linden 7 (© **030/20-35-45-55;** www.staatsoperberlin.de; U-Bahn: Französische Strasse), presents some of the finest opera in the world, along with a regular repertoire of ballet and concerts. Its home was rebuilt within the walls of the original 1740s Staatsoper, destroyed in World War II. The box office generally is open Monday through Friday from 11am to 7pm and Saturday and Sunday from 2pm to 7pm. Concert tickets are 5€ to 38€ ($5.75–$44); opera tickets are 7€ to 63€ ($8.05–$72). The opera closes from late June to the end of August.

Komische Oper Berlin, Behrensstrasse 55–57 (© **030/20-26-00;** www. komische-oper-berlin.de; U-Bahn: Französische Strasse, S-Bahn: Friedrichstrasse or Unter den Linden), lies in the middle of the city near Brandenburger Tor. Over the years, it has become one of the most innovative theater ensembles in Europe, presenting many avant-garde productions. The box office is open Monday through Saturday from 11am to 7pm and Sunday from 1pm until 1½ hours before the performance. Tickets are 8€ to 62€ ($9.20–$71).

LIVE-MUSIC CLUBS

A-Trane, Pestalozzistrasse 105 (© 030/313-25-50; S-Bahn: Savignyplatz), is a small and smoky jazz house where virtually everyone seems to have a working familiarity with great names from the jazz world's past and present. The name is a hybrid of the old Duke Ellington standard, "Take the 'A' Train," with the "ane" in "Trane" derived from the legendary John Coltrane's name. It's open daily at 9pm; music begins around 10pm. Closing hours vary. Cover is 7.65€ to 15€ ($8.80–$17), depending on who's playing.

With its kitschy knickknacks, colored lights, and wine-red walls, **Wild at Heart,** Wienerstrasse 20 (© 030-6-11-92-31; U-Bahn: Görlitzer Bahnhof), is dedicated to the rowdier side of rock. Hard-core punk, rock, and rockabilly bands from Germany and elsewhere are featured. Live performances take place

---

Moments Come to the Cabaret!

If you know how to sing "Life is a cabaret, old chum," in German no less, you may enjoy an evening in this postwar "Porcupine." Like its namesake, **Die Stachelschweine,** Tauentzienstrasse and Budapester Strasse (in the basement of the Europa-Center; © 030/261-47-95; U-Bahn: Kurfürstendamm), pokes prickly fun at German, and often American, politicians. Get a ticket early, because the Berliners love this one. The box office is open Tuesday through Friday from 11am to 2pm and 3 to 7:30pm, and Saturday from 10am to 2pm and 3 to 8:45pm. Shows are presented from Tuesday to Friday at 8pm and Saturday at 6 and 9pm. Cover is 11€ to 23€ ($12–$26). The cabaret is closed during July.

Opened in 1893 as one of the most popular purveyors of vaudeville in Europe, the **Wintergarten,** Potsdamer Strasse 96 (© 030/230-88-230; U-Bahn: Kurfürstenstrasse), operated in fits and starts throughout the war years, until it was demolished in 1944 by Allied bombers. In 1992, a modernized design reopened. Today, it's the largest and most nostalgic Berlin cabaret, laden with schmaltzy reminders of yesteryear and staffed with chorus girls; magicians from America, Britain, and countries of the former Soviet bloc; circus acrobats; political satirists; and musician/dancer combos. Shows begin at 8pm Monday through Friday, at 6pm and 10pm Saturday, and at 6pm Sunday. Shows last around 2¼ hours. The box office is open Monday to Saturday 10am to 6pm and Sunday 2 to 6pm. Cover Friday and Saturday is 29€ to 53€ ($33–$61), Sunday through Thursday 18€ to 43€ ($21–$49), depending on the seat. The price including a two-course meal is 63€ ($72). On Friday and Saturday, the price including a two-course meal is 73€ ($84). The price includes your first drink.

from Wednesday to Saturday nights. It's open Monday through Friday from 8pm to 3am, and Saturday and Sunday from 8pm to 10am (yes, you may miss breakfast). Cover is 8€ ($9.20).

Hypertrendy **Oxymoron,** in the courtyard at Rosenthaler Strasse 40–41 (© **030/283-91-88-6;** S-Bahn: Hackenschen Höfe), is a lot of fun on most nights. The setting is a high-ceilinged room with old-fashioned proportions and enough battered kitsch to remind you of a century-old coffeehouse in Franz-Josef's Vienna. Local wits refer to it as a *Gesamtkunstwerk*—a self-obsessed, self-sustaining work of art that might have been appreciated by Wagner. On Friday and Saturday after around 11pm, a slightly claustrophobic, much-used annex room—all black with ghostly flares of neon—opens as a disco, usually with a clientele that's about 75% hetero and 100% iconoclastic. If live bands appear at all, it will usually be on Thursday. The restaurant is open daily from 11am to 2am. Cover is 5.10€ to 10€ ($5.85–$12).

Knaack-Klub, Greifswalderstrasse 224 (© **030/442-7060;** S-Bahn: Alexanderplatz), is a household name to an army of young clubgoers in Berlin, thanks partly to the fact that its prices are cheaper than any other club in the city, and because of its sprawling premises that incorporate four floors, seven bars, a roiling mass of clients, and a huge variety of musical styles. Painted a strident shade of red, it was originally built as a slaughterhouse in the 19th century, with a small part of its echoing interior transformed into a nightclub in 1952. Expect a very loud medley of, among others, "alternative hard-core punk," heavy metal, indie, rock, and disco from the '70s and '80s. There's even a tuckaway bar devoted to karaoke. Some of the bars within this place open nightly at 6pm; and by 9pm, the whole place is usually a full swing, staying open till at least 2am, and sometimes later. Performances by live bands are interspersed with the recorded tunes every Wednesday, Friday, and Saturday. Depending on what time of night you arrive, the cover charge ranges from 2.50€ to 5€ ($2.90–$5.75).

The premises that contain **Opernschänke,** in the Opernpalais, Unter den Linden 5 (© **030/20-26-83;** U-Bahn: Friedrichstrasse), were built in 1762, a fact that seems to add a certain importance to a setting that's undeniably historic, and to the artists who perform their music live. For the most part, this is a restaurant serving Continental food every day from noon to midnight, with the last order accepted at 11:30pm. Main courses cost 10€ to 18€ ($12–$21). The food is augmented with live music, usually jazz, Thursday, Friday, and Saturday nights from 6pm to 1am, as well as Sunday afternoon from 11am to 2pm, as part of set-price "Jazz Brunch" costing 26€ ($30). After the end of the jazz brunch, the restaurant remains open till 7pm for food and drink.

DANCE CLUBS

Gays, straights, and everybody in between show up at **SO 36,** Oranienstrasse 190 (© **030/61-40-13-06;** U-Bahn: Görlitzer Bahnhof), for wild action and frantic dancing into the wee hours. A young, vibrant Kreuzberg crowd is attracted to this joint where the scene changes nightly. On Wednesday it's strictly gay and lesbian disco. On Friday and Saturday the parties "get really wild, man," as the bartender accurately promised. Some nights are devoted to themes such as James Bond where you can show up looking like a Cold War spy. Wednesdays and Sundays are generally all gay. Hours are Wednesday through Saturday from 10pm until "we feel like closing," and Sunday from 5 to 11pm. Cover ranges from 4€ to 21€ ($4.60–$24), depending on the venue.

Metropole, Nollendorfplatz 5, Schöneberg (© **030/217-36-80;** U-Bahn: Nollendorfplatz), one of the leading dance clubs in Berlin, opens only on weekends and attracts patrons ages 18 to 38. Built as a theater around a century ago, Metropole hosts live concerts and special events. It's open Friday 9pm to 6am and Saturday 10pm to 6am. Cover is 8€ ($9.20).

Cilli-Bom, in The Metropole, Nollendorfplatz 5 (© **030/217-36-80**), is where gay men and women sweat, dance, flirt, and groove but only on Friday from 9pm to 6am and Saturday 10pm to 6am. Dark and shadowy, with flashing strobes and a busy bar activity, it charges an 8€ ($9.20) entrance fee. Know in advance that Cilli-Bom and Metropole (see above) are different clubs within the same building, and entrance into one does not allow entrance into the other.

DAY TRIPS FROM BERLIN

POTSDAM ✦✦✦   Of all the tours possible from Berlin, the best attraction is the baroque town of Potsdam, 24km (15 miles) southwest of Berlin on the Havel River, often called Germany's Versailles. From the beginning of the 18th century it was the residence and garrison town of the Prussian kings. World attention focused on Potsdam from July 17 to August 2, 1945, when the Potsdam Conference shaped postwar Europe.

West of the historic core lies **Sans Souci Park,** with its palaces and gardens. Northwest of Sans Souci are the New Garden and the Cecilienhof Palace, on the Heiliger See.

Getting There   There are 29 daily connections by rail from Bahnhof Zoo (trip time: 23 min.) and Berliner Hauptbahnhof (54 min.). For rail information in Potsdam, call © **018/05-99-66-33.** Potsdam can also be reached by S-Bahn (30 min.). Car access is via the E-30 Autobahn east and west or the E-53 north and south.

Visitor Information   The organization known as **Tourist-Information der Stadt Potsdam** maintains two offices in Potsdam, one at Friedrich-Ebert-Strasse 5 and another at the **Neuer Markt** (© for both branches is **0331/275-58-50**). Both branches are open April to October Monday to Friday 9am to 7pm, Saturday and Sunday 9am to 4pm; November to March Monday to Friday 10am to 6pm, Saturday and Sunday 10am to 4pm.

Exploring Potsdam   In the 18th century, Prussia's answer to Paris' Château de Versailles was clustered within the **Sans Souci Park** ✦✦✦, whose gardens and fountains represented the finest and most elegant aspect of north Germany during the Age of Enlightenment. Covering about a square mile of terraced, statue-dotted grounds, a very short walk west of Potsdam's center, it's the destination of many locals, who stroll around its precincts, perhaps reflecting on another era of German history. You can enter from many points around the perimeter of the park, but the main entrance, and the one closest to the park's major monument, is in **Zur Historisches Mühle,** inside of which you'll find the Welcome Station (Besucher Zentrum; © **0331/96-94-200**). Whereas you can visit the park's buildings only during the hours noted below, you can stroll within most areas of the park at any hour.

Frederick II ("the Great") chose Potsdam rather than Berlin as his permanent residence. The style of the buildings he ordered erected is called Potsdam rococo, an achievement primarily of Georg Wenzeslaus von Knobelsdorff. Knobelsdorff built **Sans Souci Palace** ✦✦✦, with its terraces and gardens, as a summer residence for Frederick II. The palace, inaugurated in 1747, is a long one-story building crowned by a dome and flanked by round pavilions. The music salon

---

Tips A Fabulous Place to Dine in Potsdam

In 1878, a courtier in the service of the Prussian monarch built an elegant villa on the shore of the Heiliger See. During the 1920s, author Bernhardt Kellerman wrote some of his best work here. After a Cold War stint as a base for Russian officers, it now functions as the most talked-about restaurant in Potsdam: **Villa Kellerman,** Mangerstrasse 33–36 (© **0331/ 29-15-72;** bus: 695). The classical Italian cuisine might include marinated carpaccio of whitefish; a mixed platter of antipasti; spaghetti with scampi, herbs, and garlic; or John Dory in butter-and-caper sauce. Reservations are recommended. American Express and Visa are accepted. It's open Tuesday to Sunday noon to 10pm.

---

is the supreme example of the rococo style, and the elliptical Marble Hall is the largest in the palace. As a guest of the king, Voltaire visited in 1750.

The Palace of Sans Souci is open April to October daily 9am to 5pm; November to March Tuesday to Sunday 9am to 4pm. You'll have to visit its interior as part of a guided, 40-minute tour that's conducted mostly in German, and which costs 8€ ($9.20) for adults and 5€ ($5.75) for children under 18. Entrance is free for children under 6.

Schloss Charlottenhof ✦, south of Okonomieweg (© **0331/969-42-00;** tram: 1 or 4), was designed by Karl Friedrich Schinkel, the great neoclassical master, and built between 1826 and 1829. He erected the palace in the style of a villa and designed most of the furniture inside. It's open only between May and October, every Tuesday to Sunday from 10am to 5pm, and completely closed the rest of the year. Guided tours, mostly in German, depart at 30-minute intervals throughout opening hours, and are priced at 4€ ($4.60) for adults, 3€ ($3.45) for persons under 18. Participation is free for children under 6.

North of the 80-hectare (200-acre) park, the **Cecilienhof Palace** ✦, Im Neuer Garten (© **0331/969-42-44;** tram: 92 or 95, then bus 692), was built in the style of an English country house by Kaiser Wilhelm II between 1913 and 1917. The 176-room mansion became the new residence of Crown Prince Wilhelm of Hohenzollern. It was occupied as a royal residence until March 1945, when the crown prince and his family fled to the West, taking many of their possessions. Cecilienhof was the headquarters of the 1945 Potsdam Conference. It's open year-round, Tuesday through Sunday, as follows: April through October from 9am to 5pm; November through March from 9am to 4pm. Between November and March, adults pay 4€ ($4.60), and children under 7 and students pay 3€ ($3.45); visitors must visit the palace as part of a guided tour, which is included in the entrance price. Between April and October, adults pay 5€ ($5.75), and children under 7 and students pay 4€ ($4.60). During that period (Apr–Nov), if visitors opt not to participate in the guided tour, they're free to visit the palace on their own. In that event, they pay only 4€ ($4.60) for adults and 3€ ($3.45) for students.

2 Munich ✦✦✦ & the Bavarian Alps ✦✦

Sprawling Munich, home of some 1.3 million people and such industrial giants as Siemens and BMW, is the pulsating capital and cultural center of Bavaria. One of Germany's most festive cities, Munich exudes a hearty Bavarian *Gemütlichkeit.*

Munich

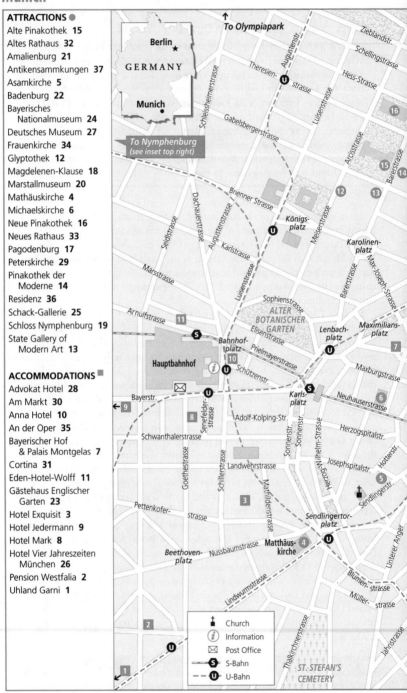

To Olympiapark

Berlin ★

GERMANY

Munich ●

To Nymphenburg
(see inset top right)

Zieblandstr.
Schellingstrasse
Hess-Strasse
Theresien-strasse
Augustenstr.
Schleißheimerstrasse
Gabelsbergerstrasse
Luisenstrasse
Arcisstrasse
Barerstrasse
Brienner Strasse
Dachauerstrasse
Augustenstrasse
Königs-platz
Meiserstrasse
Karolinen-platz
Seidlstrasse
Karlstrasse
Luisenstrasse
Barerstrasse
Max-Joseph-Strasse
Marsstrasse
Sophienstrasse
ALTER BOTANISCHER GARTEN
Elisenstrasse
Lenbach-platz
Maximilians-platz
Arnulfstrasse
Bahnhof-platz
Prielmayerstrasse
Maxburgstrasse
Hauptbahnhof
Schützenstr.
Karls-platz
Neuhauserstrasse
Bayerstr.
Senefelder-strasse
Adolf-Kolping-Str.
Sonnenstrasse
Herzog-Wilhelm-Strasse
Herzogspitalstr.
Hottestr.
Schwanthalerstrasse
Goethestrasse
Schillerstrasse
Landwehrstrasse
Mathildenstrasse
Josephspitalstr.
Pettenkofer-strasse
Sendlingerstr.
Sendlingertor-platz
Beethoven-platz
Nussbaumstrasse
Matthäus-kirche
Lindwurmstrasse
Blümen-strasse
Müller-strasse
Unter Anger
Thalkirchnerstrasse
Jahnstrasse
ST. STEFAN'S CEMETERY

† Church
ⓘ Information
✉ Post Office
Ⓢ S-Bahn
Ⓤ U-Bahn

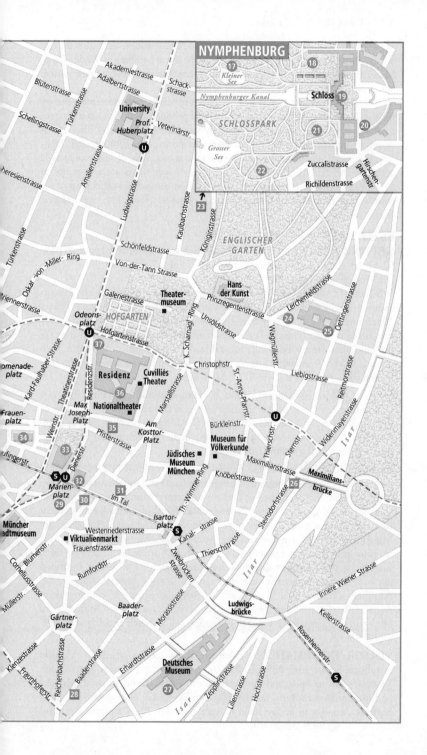

NYMPHENBURG

Kleiner See

Nymphenburger Kanal

SCHLOSSPARK

Grosser See

Schloss

Zuccalistrasse

Richildenstrasse

Akademiestrasse

Blütenstrasse

Adalbertstrasse

Schack-strasse

Schellingstrasse

Türkenstrasse

University

Prof.-Huberplatz

Veterinärstr.

Theresienstrasse

Amalienstrasse

Ludwigstrasse

Kaulbachstrasse

Königinstrasse

ENGLISCHER GARTEN

Türkenstrasse

Oskar -von -Miller- Ring

Schönfeldstrasse

Von-der-Tann Strasse

Brienerstrasse

Galeriestrasse

Theater-museum

Hans der Kunst

Prinzregentenstrasse

Lerchenfeldstrasse

Oettingenstrasse

Odeons-platz

HOFGARTEN

Hofgartenstrasse

K. Scharnagl -Ring

Unsöldstrasse

Wagmüllerstr.

Promenade-platz

Kard-Faulhaber-Strasse

Theatinerstrasse

Residenzstr.

Residenz

Cuvilliés Theater

Christophstr.

St.-Anna-Parstr.

Liebigstrasse

Reitmorstrasse

Frauen-platz

Weinstr.

Max Joseph-Platz

Nationaltheater

Marstallstrasse

Am Kosttor-Platz

Bürkleinstr.

Thierschstr.

Sternstr.

Widenmayerstrasse

Isar

Dienerstr.

Prsterstrasse

Museum für Völkerkunde

Maximilianstrasse

Maximilians-brücke

ufingerstr.

Marien-platz

Jüdisches Museum München

Im Tal

Th.-Wimmer-Ring

Knöbelstrasse

Steinsdorfstrasse

Müncher adtmuseum

Westenriederstrasse

Viktualienmarkt

Frauenstrasse

Isartor-platz

Kanal- strasse

Thierschstrasse

Innere Wiener Strasse

Corneliusstrasse

Blumenstr.

Rumfordstr.

Zweibrücken strasse

Morassistrasse

Isar

Ludwigs-brücke

Kellerstrasse

Müllerstr.

Gärtner-platz

Baader-platz

Rosenheimerstr

Klenzestrasse

Fraunhoferstr.

Reichenbachstrasse

Baaderstrasse

Erhardtstrasse

Deutsches Museum

Zeppelinstrasse

Lilienstrasse

Hochstrasse

Isar

Longtime resident Thomas Mann wrote: "Munich sparkles." Although the city he described was swept away by some of the most severe bombing of World War II, Munich continues to sparkle, as it introduces itself to thousands of new visitors annually.

The Munich cliché as a beer-drinking town of folkloric charm is marketed by the city itself. Despite a roaring gross national product, Munich likes to present itself as a large, agrarian village peopled by jolly beer drinkers who cling to rustic origins despite the presence on all sides of symbols of the computer age, high-tech industries, a sophisticated business scene, a good deal of Hollywood-style glamour, and fairly hip night action. Bavarians themselves are a minority in Munich—more than two-thirds of the population comes from other parts of the country or from outside Germany—but everybody buys into the folkloric charm and schmaltz.

ESSENTIALS

GETTING THERE   **By Plane**   The **Munich International Airport** (© 089/ 97-52-13-13;** www.munich-airport.de) lies 27km (17 miles) northeast of central Munich at Erdinger Moos.

S-Bahn (© 089/41-42-43-44) trains connect the airport with the Hauptbahnhof (main railroad station) in downtown Munich, with departures every 20 minutes for the 40-minute trip. The fare is 9€ ($10); Eurailpass holders ride free. A taxi into the center costs about 50€ to 60€ ($58–$69). You can also take the Lufthansa Airport Bus which runs directly into the heart of Munich, with just one stop in Schwabing. The trip takes 35 to 50 minutes, depending on traffic and costs 9€ to 15€ ($10–$17) round-trip.

By Train   Munich's main rail station, the **Hauptbahnhof,** on Bahnhofplatz, is one of Europe's largest. Near the city center, it contains a hotel, restaurants, shopping, car parking, and banking facilities. All major German cities are connected to this station, most with service every hour. For information about long-distance trains, call © **0800/150-70-90.**

By Bus   Munich is one of the biggest metropolitan areas in Europe, and as such, receives dozens of buses that congregate here from other parts of Europe. A few of them, including the bus that services central Munich from the airport, stops in the town center, at the **Zentraler BusBahnhof,** immediately adjacent (on the western end) of the city's main railway station (Hauptbanhhof München), with an entrance on the Arnulfstrasse. Note, however, that the majority of long-distance buses pulling into Munich arrive in the city's northern suburbs, at the **Fröttmanning Bus Terminal,** about 7 km (about 4¼ miles) north of the Marienplatz, beside the highway running between Munich and Nürnberg. (From central Munich, take U-Bahn line 6 for a 15-minute ride to reach it). For information about most bus services coming into Munich from other parts of Germany and the rest of Europe, call **Deutsch Touring** at © 089/ 88-98-95-13.

VISITOR INFORMATION   There are three tourist offices in Munich: Sendlinger Strasse 1 (© **089/233-03-00**), open Monday to Friday 8am to 8pm, Saturday 9am to 8pm, and Sunday 10am to 6pm; Bahnhofplatz 2, Monday to Saturday 9am to 8pm, Sunday 10am to 6pm; and Marienplatz in Neuen Rathaus, Monday to Friday 10am to 8pm, Saturday 10am to 4pm. For information call © **089/233-03-00.**

Websites   Updated for each year's Oktoberfest, **www.munich-tourist.de** from the Munich Tourist Office includes a program of events, a guide to various beer tents, and images from past festivals. Descriptions of hotel packages and discount voucher packages are added. All things Bavarian are touched on at **www. bavaria.com,** such as Mad King Ludwig's castle and an Oktoberfest beer and music raft ride down the river Isar. There's advice on shopping, getting around, and enjoying the Alps, among many other nuggets.

CITY LAYOUT   Munich's Hauptbahnhof lies just west of the town center and opens onto Bahnhofplatz. From the square, you can take Schützenstrasse to **Karlsplatz** (nicknamed Stachus), one of the major centers of Munich. Many tram lines converge on this square. From Karlsplatz, you can continue east along the pedestrians-only Neuhauserstrasse and Kaufingerstrasse until you reach Marienplatz, where you'll be deep in the Altstadt (Old Town) of Munich.

From **Marienplatz,** the center and heart of the city, you can head north on Dienerstrasse, which will lead you to Residenzstrasse and finally to **Max-Joseph-Platz,** a landmark square, with the National Theater and the former royal palace, the Residenz. East of this square runs **Maximilianstrasse,** the most fashionable shopping and dining street of Munich. Between Marienplatz and the National Theater is the **Platzl** quarter, where you'll want to head for nighttime diversions, as it's the seat of some of the finest (and some of the worst) restaurants in Munich, along with the landmark Hofbräuhaus, the most famous beer hall in Europe.

North of the old town is **Schwabing,** the university and former Bohemian section whose main street is Leopoldstrasse. The large, sprawling municipal park grounds, the Englischer Garten, are found due east of Schwabing.

GETTING AROUND   By Public Transportation   The city's efficient rapid-transit system is the **U-Bahn,** or Untergrundbahn, one of the most modern subway systems in Europe. The **S-Bahn** rapid-transit system, a 420km (260-mile) network of tracks, provides service to various city districts and outlying suburbs. The city is also served by a network of **trams** and **buses.** The same ticket entitles you to ride the U-Bahn, the S-Bahn, trams, and buses. For more information, call © **089/41-42-43-44** or go to www.mvv.de.

A single-journey ticket for a ride within the city's central zone—a large area that few tourists ever leave—costs 2€ ($2.30). If you go to the outermost zones of the subway system, your ride could cost as much as 8€ ($9.20). One of the best things about Munich's transit system is that you can make as many free transfers between subways, buses, and trams as you need to reach your destination.

More economical than single-journey tickets is the *Streifencarte,* a strip-ticket that contains 10 units, two of which are annulled for each zone of the system you travel through. A Streifencarte costs 9€ ($10). Children ages 6 to 14 can purchase a *Kinderstreifencarte* for 3.80€ ($4.35). With this type of ticket, you can travel in one continuous direction during any 2-hour time period with unlimited transfers. You can also use it for multiple passengers (for two people to ride two zones, simply stamp four strips).

⟨*Value* **A Money-Saving Tip**

Munich's S-Bahn is covered by Eurail, so if you have a rail pass, don't buy a separate ticket.

An even better deal may be the *Tageskarte* (day ticket), which for 4.50€ ($5.20) gives you unlimited access within the central zone for a full day. Double the price for access to all of Greater Munich—an 80km (50-mile) radius.

By Taxi Cabs are relatively expensive—you'll pay 3.70€ ($4.25) when you get inside, plus 1.25€ ($1.45) per kilometer; add 1€ if you call for pickup. In an emergency, call © **089/2161-0** or 089/194-10 for a radio-dispatched taxi.

By Car Driving in the city, which has an excellent public transportation system, is not advised. The streets around Marienplatz in the Altstadt are pedestrian-only. If you are interested in renting a car locally, try **Sixt Autovermietung,** Einsteinstrasse 106 (© **1805/25-25-25**), or look under *Autovermietung* in the Munich yellow pages.

By Foot & Bicycle Of course, the best way to explore Munich is by foot, since it has a vast pedestrian zone in the center. Many of its attractions can, in fact, be reached only by foot. Pick up a good map and set out.

The tourist office sells a pamphlet that outlines itineraries for touring Munich by bicycle called *Radl-Touren für unsere Gäste,* costing .40€ (45¢). One of the most convenient places to rent a bike is **Radius Bikes** (© **089/59-61-13**), at the far end of the Hauptbahnhof, near lockers opposite tracks 27 and 36. The charge is 12€ to 16€ ($14–$18) up to 4 hours, or else 14€ to 18€ ($16–$21) from 10am to 6pm. Mountain bikes are rented for about 25% more. A deposit of 51€ ($59) is assessed; students and Eurailpass holders are granted a 10% discount. The store is open May through early October daily from 10am to 6pm; it's closed November to April.

FAST FACTS: Munich

American Express The American Express Foreign Exchange Service, Kaufingerstrasse 24 (© **089/228-013-87**), is open Monday through Friday from 9:30am to 6:30pm, Saturday from 10am to 3pm. Reisland American Express, Promenadeplatz 6 (© **089/290-900;** U-Bahn: Marienplatz), is open for mail pickup and check cashing Monday through Friday from 9am to 6pm, Saturday from 9:30am to 12:30pm.

Business Hours Most **banks** are open Monday through Friday from 8:30am to 12:30pm and 1:30 to 3:30pm (many stay open until 5:30pm on Thurs). Most **businesses** and **stores** are open Monday through Friday from 9am to 6pm and Saturday from 9am to 2pm. On *langer Samstag* (1st Sat of the month), stores remain open until 6pm. Many observe an 8 or 9pm closing on Thursday.

Consulates There's a **United States** consulate at Känigstrasse 4–5 (© **089/ 288-80;** U-Bahn: Universität); hours are Monday through Friday from 8 to 11am. The Consulate General Office for the **United Kingdom** at Bürkleinstrasse 10 (© **089/21-10-90;** U-Bahn: Isartor) is open Monday through Friday 8:30am to noon and 1 to 3:30pm. The consulate of **Canada** at Tal Strasse 29 (© **089/219-95-70;** U-Bahn: Marienplatz) is open Monday to Thursday 9am to noon and 2 to 5pm, Friday from 9am to noon and 2 to 3:30pm. The governments of Australia and New Zealand do not maintain offices in Munich.

Currency See "Fast Facts: Berlin," p. 383.

Currency Exchange You can get a better rate at a bank than at your hotel. On weekends or at night, you can exchange money at the Hauptbahnhof exchange, open daily from 6am to 11:30pm.

Dentists/Doctors For an English-speaking dentist, go to **Klinik und Poliklinik für Kieferchirurgie der Universität München**, Lindwurmstrasse 2A (☎ **089/51-60-00**; U-Bahn: Goetheplatz); it deals with emergency cases and is always open. The American, British, and Canadian consulates keep a list of recommended English-speaking physicians. For dental or medical emergencies, call **Notfallpraxis**, Elisenstrasse 3 (☎ **089/55-17-71**; bus: 69). It's open Monday, Tuesday, and Thursday from 7 to 11pm; Wednesday and Friday from 2 to 11pm; and Saturday, Sunday, and holidays from 8am to 11pm.

Drugstores For an international drugstore where English is spoken, go to **Bahnhof Apotheke**, Bahnhofplatz 2 (☎ **089/59-41-19**; U-Bahn/S-Bahn: Hauptbahnhof), open Monday to Friday from 8am to 6:30pm and Saturday from 8am to 2pm. If you need a prescription filled during off-hours, call ☎ **089/55-76-61** for information about what's open. The information is recorded and in German only, so you may need to get someone from your hotel staff to assist you.

Emergencies Call the police at ☎ **110**.

Internet Access You can send e-mails or check your messages at the **Easy Internet Café**, Bahnhofplatz 1; U-Bahn: Hauptbahnhof. It's open daily from 7:30am to 11:45pm.

Post Office The most central post office is found at Bahnhofplatz (U-Bahn/S-Bahn: Hauptbahnhof), opposite the main train station exit. It's open Monday through Friday from 7am to 8pm, Saturday from 9am to 4pm, and Sunday from 10am to 3pm. You can have your mail sent here Poste Restante (general delivery), but include the zip code 80335. You'll need a passport to reclaim mail, and you can't call for information but have to show up in person.

Telephone The **country code** for Germany is **49**. The **city code** for Munich is **89**. Use this code when you're calling from outside Germany; if you're within Germany, use **089**. For more information on making calls from Germany, see "Fast Facts: Berlin," p. 385.

WHERE TO STAY
VERY EXPENSIVE

Bayerischer Hof & Palais Montgelas ★★★   A Bavarian version of New York's Waldorf-Astoria, this hotel is in a swank location, opening onto a little tree-filled square. Rooms range from medium to extremely spacious, each with plush duvets; many beds are four-posters. Decor ranges from Bavarian provincial to British country-house chintz. The large bathrooms have tub/shower combos, private phones, and state-of-the-art luxuries.

Promenadeplatz 2–6, 80333 München. ☎ **800/223-6800** in the U.S., or 089/2-12-00. Fax 089/21-20-906. www.bayerischerhof.de. 395 units. 279€–416€ ($321–$478) double; 1,126€–1,491€ ($1,295–$1,715) suite. AE, DC, MC, V. Parking 21€ ($24). Tram: 19. **Amenities:** 3 restaurants; 5 bars; nightclub; rooftop pool and garden; gym; sauna; limited room service; massage; babysitting; laundry service/dry cleaning; nonsmoking rooms; 1 room for those with limited mobility; sun terrace. *In room:* TV, dataport, minibar, hair dryer, safe.

Hotel Vier Jahreszeiten München ★★★ This grand hotel, with a tradition dating from 1858, is the most elegant place to stay in Munich. Rooms range from medium to very spacious. Bedside controls, luxury furnishings, and Oriental rugs, plus spacious bathrooms with showers, will keep any guest comfortable. The restaurant is one of the most esteemed in Germany.

Maximilianstrasse 17, 80539 München. ⓒ **800/426-3135** in the U.S., or 089/212-50. Fax 089/21-25-20-00. www.kempinski-vierjahreszeiten.de. 316 units. 345€–495€ ($397–$569) double; from 700€ ($805) junior suite. AE, DC, MC, V. Parking 20€ ($23). Tram: 19. **Amenities:** Restaurant; bistro; indoor pool; sauna; solarium; 24-hr. room service; babysitting; laundry service/dry cleaning; sun terrace. *In room:* A/C, TV, dataport, minibar, hair dryer, safe, bathrobe.

EXPENSIVE

Eden-Hotel-Wolff ★ If you must stay near the train station, this is your best bet, a hotel that lies directly across the street from the Munich terminus of the Lufthansa Airport Bus. With some exceptions, most rooms are spacious, their styles ranging from modern to rustic Bavarian. Rooms have luxurious appointments and double-glazed windows; and the large bathrooms have tub/shower combos. Some rooms are hypoallergenic with special beds and a private ventilation system.

Arnulfstrasse 4–8, 80335 München. ⓒ **089/55-11-50.** Fax 089/551-15-555. www.ehw.de. 216 units. 169€–261€ ($194–$300) double; 256€–358€ ($294–$412) suite. 1 child up to age 6 stays free in parent's room. Rates include buffet breakfast. AE, DC, MC, V. Parking 14€ ($16). U-Bahn/S-Bahn: Hauptbahnhof. **Amenities:** Restaurant; bar; limited room service; babysitting; laundry service; nonsmoking rooms. *In room:* TV, dataport, minibar, hair dryer, safe.

MODERATE

Advokat Hotel This hotel occupies a 1930s apartment house. Its streamlined interior borrows in discreet ways from Bauhaus and minimalist models. The rooms look as if Philippe Starck had gone on a shopping binge at Ikea. All come with neatly kept bathrooms with tub/shower combination. The result is an aggressively simple, clean-lined, and artfully spartan hotel with very few extras and facilities.

Baaderstrasse 1, 80469 München. ⓒ **089/21-63-10.** Fax 089/21-63-190. www.hotel-advokat.de. 50 units. 150€–190€ ($173–$219) double. Rates include breakfast. AE, DC, MC, V. S-Bahn: Isartor. **Amenities:** Breakfast room; nonsmoking rooms. *In room:* TV, dataport, minibar, hair dryer.

An der Oper ★ Just off Maximilianstrasse, near Marienplatz, this is a superb choice for sightseeing or shopping in the traffic-free malls, just steps from the Bavarian National Theater. Built in the 1970s, it's one of the best-run hotels in this price category. Recently renovated rooms, which range from small to medium, have such amenities as double-glazed windows, firm beds, a small sitting area, and a table for those who want breakfast in their rooms. Bathrooms are medium in size and beautifully maintained, with tub/shower combos.

Falkenturmstrasse 11, 80331 München. ⓒ **089/290-02-70.** Fax 089/290-02-729. www.hotelanderoper.de. 68 units. 150€–235€ ($173–$270) double; 220€–350€ ($253–$403) apts. Rates include buffet breakfast. AE, MC, V. Tram: 19. **Amenities:** Nonsmoking rooms; rooms for those with limited mobility. *In room:* TV, minibar, hair dryer.

Anna Hotel In 1900 this building was a four-story office block, but in 2002 it was converted into a stylish and streamlined hotel. This clean, charming, well-managed hotel has a minimalist and stylish decor that's loaded with wood paneling and warm tones of ocher and russet, with touches of yellow and black marble in all the bathrooms. A collection of postmodern sculptures in the lobby

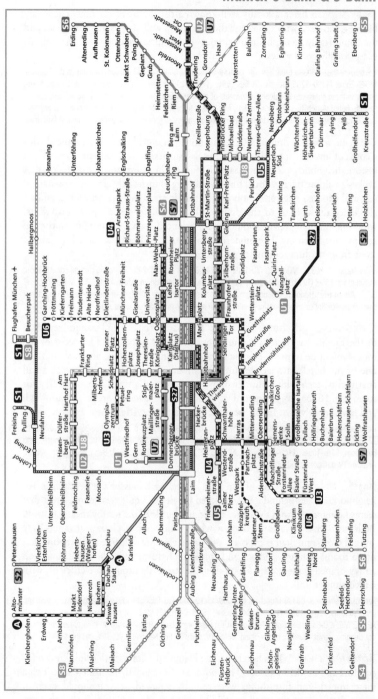

are by Stephan Ester, a locally well-known artist. Many of the hotel clients are business travelers, who appreciate the stylish and well-choreographed service and the comfortably secure bedrooms. Four of the suites are in a tower that affords exceptionally good views.

1 Schützenstrasse, 80335 München. ℂ **089/59-99-40.** Fax 089/55-99-43-33. www.annahotel.de. 56 units. 165€–205€ ($190–$236) double; 205€–255€ ($236–$293) tower rooms. Rates include breakfast and access, without charge, to nonalcoholic contents of minibar. MC, V. Parking: 15€ ($17). U-Bahn: Karlsplatz or Hauptbahnhof. **Amenities:** Restaurant; bar; free access to health club and sauna at the Anna's sister hotel, the Könighof; laundry service/dry cleaning; nonsmoking rooms. *In room:* A/C, TV, dataport, minibar, hair dryer.

Cortiina ★ *Finds* Built in 2001, this hotel has quickly gained a foothold with a corps of loyal business clients. It rises five stories above a centrally located and historic neighborhood in the heart of Munich, in a cozy and warm design that evokes an alpine retreat. You'll find a sheathing of intricately crafted dark-stained oak and exposed flagstones in both the public areas and the bedrooms, and an allegiance throughout to the design principles of feng shui, wherein objects, windows, traffic patterns, and doors are balanced for a maximum of emotional and psychic harmony. The modern bathrooms are partially sheathed in slabs of stone from the Jura mountains of France.

Lederstrasse 8, 80331 München. ℂ **089/242-24-90.** Fax 089/242249-100. www.cortiina.com. S-Bahn: Marienplatz. 186€ ($214) double; 206€ ($237) studio. Rates include breakfast. AE, DC, MC, V. Parking: 13€ ($15). **Amenities:** Honor bar/lounge; breakfast room; room service (7–11am and 6pm–1am); babysitting; laundry service/dry cleaning; nonsmoking rooms. *In room:* TV, minibar, hair dryer, safe.

Gästehaus Englischer Garten ★ This oasis of charm and tranquillity, close to the Englischer Garten, is one of our preferred stopovers. The decor of the rooms might be termed "Bavarian grandmother." Bathrooms are small and not one of the hotel's stronger features. In an annex across the street are 15 small apartments, each with a shower-only bathroom and a tiny kitchenette. Try for room nos. 16, 23, 26, or especially 20; all are more spacious, are better furnished, and have better views. In fair weather, breakfast is served in a rear garden.

Liebergesellstrasse 8, 80802 München-Schwabing. ℂ **089/38-39-41-0.** Fax 089/38-39-41-33. 28 units, 22 with bathroom. 68€–78€ ($78–$90) double without bathroom; 94€–115€ ($108–$132) double with bathroom; 94€–105€ ($108–$121) apt. AE, DC, MC, V. Parking 8€ ($9.20). U-Bahn: Münchner Freiheit. *In room:* TV, dataport, minibar.

Hotel Exquisit ★ One of the most appealing hotels in the Sendlinger Tot neighborhood lies behind a wine-colored facade on a quiet residential street that seems far removed from the heavy traffic and bustle of the nearby theater district. Built in 1988, it has a paneled lobby whose focal point is a lounge that gets busy around 6 or 7pm. Staff is pleasant, offering a genuine welcome and ushering you up to rooms that are spacious and comfortably furnished. About half overlook an ivy-draped garden, others look over the street. Bathrooms are efficient, with a tiled shower unit.

Pettenkoferstrasse 3, 80336 München. ℂ **089/55-19-900.** Fax 089/199-499. www.augustiner-restaurant. com. 50 units. 110€–195€ ($127–$224) double; 150€–240€ ($173–$276) suite. Rates include breakfast. AE, DC, MC, V. U-Bahn: Sendlinger Tor. **Amenities:** Restaurant; bar; sauna; 24-hr. room service; laundry service/ dry cleaning; private garden; nonsmoking rooms. *In room:* TV, minibar, hair dryer, safe, dataport.

Hotel Mark *Value* This hotel near the Hauptbahnhof's south exit is known for comfort and moderate prices. The rooms are functionally furnished, although a bit cramped, and furnishings were recently renewed, so you should sleep in peace. Bathrooms are small but tidily maintained, each with a shower unit. Breakfast is the only meal served.

Senefelderstrasse 12, 80336 München. ✆ **089/55-98-20.** Fax 089/559-82-333. www.heh.de. 95 units. 107€–177€ ($123–$204) double. Rates include buffet breakfast. AE, DC, MC, V. Parking 9.50€ ($11). U-Bahn/S-Bahn: Hauptbahnhof. **Amenities:** Laundry service/dry cleaning; nonsmoking rooms. *In room:* TV, dataport (in some), minibar, hair dryer, safe.

INEXPENSIVE

Am Markt   This popular but basic Bavarian hotel stands in the heart of the older section. You're likely to find yourself surrounded by opera and concert artists who stay here to be close to where they perform. The rooms are trim, neat, and small—space to store your stuff is at a minimum. Private bathrooms are also small, and corridor bathrooms are kept quite fresh; all with shower units.

Heiliggeistrasse 6, 80331 München. ✆ **089/22-50-14.** Fax 089/22-40-17. 32 units, 16 with bathroom (shower only). 66€–68€ ($76–$78) double without bathroom; 87€–92€ ($100–$106) double with bathroom. Rates include continental breakfast. MC, V. Parking 8€. U-Bahn/S-Bahn: Marienplatz. *In room:* TV.

Hotel Jedermann *Value*   This pleasant spot's central location and value make it a good choice. It's especially good for families, as both cribs and cots are available. Rooms are generally small and old-fashioned, but are cozy and comfortable. Private bathrooms with shower stalls are also small. A generous breakfast buffet is served in a charming room.

Bayerstrasse 95, 80335 München. ✆ **089/54-32-40.** Fax 089/54-32-41-11. www.hotel-jedermann.de. 55 units. 57€–149€ ($66–$171) double; 100€–180€ ($115–$207) triple. Rates include buffet breakfast. MC, V. Parking 10€ ($12). U-Bahn/S-Bahn: Hauptbahnhof. *In room:* TV, dataport, hair dryer, private safe (in most units).

Pension Westfalia   Facing the meadow where the annual Oktoberfest takes place, this 19th-century town house near Goetheplatz is another of Munich's top pensions. Rooms range from small to medium, but the owner takes great pride in seeing that they are well maintained and comfortable. Private bathrooms with shower stalls are small, and corridor bathrooms are well maintained and do the job just as well.

Mozartstrasse 23, 80336 München. ✆ **089/53-03-77.** Fax 089/54-39-120. www.pension-westfalia.de. 19 units, 14 with bathroom (shower only). 50€–55€ ($58–$63) double without bathroom; 65€–70€ ($75–$81) double with bathroom. Rates include buffet breakfast. AE, MC, V. Parking, when available, is free on the street. U-Bahn: Goetheplatz. Bus: 58. **Amenities:** Nonsmoking rooms. *In room:* TV.

Uhland Garni   In a residential area, just a 10-minute walk from the Hauptbahnhof, the Uhland could easily become your home in Munich. It offers friendly, personal service. The stately town mansion, built in Art Nouveau style, stands in its own small garden. Its rooms are soundproof, traditional, and cozy. The bathrooms contain shower units. Only breakfast is served.

Uhlandstrasse 1, 80336 München. ✆ **089/54-33-50.** Fax 089/54-33-52-50. www.hotel-uhland.de. 30 units. 77€–165€ ($89–$190) double. Rates include buffet breakfast. AE, DC, MC, V. Free parking. U-Bahn/S-Bahn: Theresienwiese. Bus: 58. *In room:* TV, minibar, hair dryer, safe.

WHERE TO DINE

For beer halls serving plenty of low-priced food, see the box "What's Brewing at the Beer Halls?" on p. 433.

VERY EXPENSIVE

Boettner's ✦ INTERNATIONAL   The restaurant today is housed in Orlandohaus, a Renaissance structure in the very heart of Munich. Culinary fans from yesterday will recognize its wood-paneled interior, which was dismantled from a previous site and moved here. The cookery is lighter and more refined, and seems better than ever. Try the lobster stew in a cream sauce and almost any dish with white truffles. Pike balls appear delectably in a Chablis herb sauce, and succulent lamb or venison appear enticingly in a woodsy morel sauce. Desserts are as sumptuous as ever. The French influence is very evident, as are many traditional Bavarian recipes.

Pfisterstrasse 9. ℰ **089/22-12-10**. Reservations required. Main courses 25€–46€ ($29–$53). AE, DC, MC, V. Summer Mon–Fri 11:30am–3pm and 6–10pm; Oct–May Mon–Sat 11:30am–10pm. U-Bahn/S-Bahn: Marienplatz.

Ederer 🎔🎔 MODERN INTERNATIONAL   Noted as one of the most posh and immediately desirable addresses in Munich, and the culinary domain of celebrity chef Karl Ederer, this restaurant occupies an antique building with huge windows, very high ceilings, several blazing fireplaces, and an appealing collection of paintings. Inspiration for the menu items covers the gamut of cuisines from Bavaria, France, Italy, the New World, and the Pacific Rim, and as such, the restaurant has received raves in the German press. The menu changes with the seasons and the whim of the kitchen staff but might include such starters as marinated sweet-and-sour pumpkin served with shiitake mushrooms, parsley roots, and lukewarm chunks of octopus; and terrine of duckling foie gras with a very fresh brioche and a dollop of pumpkin jelly. Main courses might include a roasted breast of duckling with stuffing, glazed baby white cabbage, mashed potatoes, and gooseliver sauce; or pan-fried anglerfish with a sauce made from olive oil, lemon grass, and thyme.

Kardinal Faulhaber Strasse 10. ℰ **089/24-23-13-11**. Reservations recommended. Main courses 20€–26€ ($23–$30). Set-price 2-course lunch 20€ ($23); set-price 10-course dinner 70€ ($81). AE, DC, MC, V. Mon–Sat noon–2pm and 6:30–10pm. U-Bahn: Marienplatz or Odéonplatz.

Restaurant Königshof 🎔🎔 INTERNATIONAL/FRENCH   On the top floor of this deluxe hotel, this is Munich's best shot at hotel dining. You're rewarded not only with a fine cuisine, but with a view of the city. Appetizers are sometimes pleasantly startling in their originality, as exemplified by the delicately diminutive rib and loin chops, liver, and rolled duck in a sweet-and-sour ice wine, the flavor enhanced by a pumpkin vinaigrette. Instead of the typical lasagna, you get a pasta layered with morels and crayfish, a real delicacy. The city's best veal dishes are served here; veal sweetbreads rest on a bed of fresh vegetables, including beets and green beans. The wine list is one of the finest in Germany, though it may take you a good hour just to read it.

In the Hotel Königshof, Karlsplatz 25 (Am Stachus). ℰ **089/55-13-60**. Reservations required. Main courses 22€–38€ ($25–$44); fixed-price menus 78€–118€ ($90–$136). AE, DC, MC, V. Tues–Sat noon–2:30pm and 7–10pm. S-Bahn: Karlsplatz. Tram: 19, 20, or 21.

Tantris 🎔🎔🎔 FRENCH/INTERNATIONAL   Tantris serves Munich's finest cuisine. Hans Haas was voted the top chef in Germany in 1994, and, if anything, he has refined and sharpened his culinary technique since. Once inside, you're transported into an ultramodern atmosphere with fine service. The food is a treat to the eye as well as to the palate. You might begin with a terrine of smoked fish served with green cucumber sauce, then follow with classic roast duck on mustard-seed sauce, or perhaps a delightful concoction of lobster medallions on black noodles. These dishes show a refinement and attention to detail that you find nowhere else in Munich. And just when you think you've had the perfect meal, the dessert arrives, and you're hungry again as you sample the gingerbread soufflé with chestnut sorbet.

Johann-Fichte-Strasse 7, Schwabing. ℰ **089/3-61-95-90**. Reservations required. Fixed-price 5-course lunch 85€ ($98); fixed-price dinner 128€ ($147) for 8 courses, 110€ ($127) for 5 courses. AE, DC, MC, V. Tues–Sat noon–2pm and 6:30–10:30pm. Closed public holidays, annual holidays in Jan and May. U-Bahn: Dietlindenstrasse.

EXPENSIVE

Alois Dallmayr ✿ CONTINENTAL   One of the city's most historic and famous dining spots was established in 1700 as a food shop. Today, you'll find one of the city's most prestigious delicatessens on the street level, and a rather grand restaurant upstairs, where you'll find a subtle German version of Continental cuisine that owes many of its inspirations to France. The food array is rich, varied, and sophisticated, including the best herring and sausages we've ever tasted, very fresh fish, meats, and game dishes. Partially thanks to its dual role as a delicatessen with products imported from around the world, you'll find such rare treats as vine-ripened tomatoes flown in from Morocco, splendid papayas from Brazil, and the famous French hens, *poulets de Bresse,* believed by many gourmets to be the world's finest.

Dienerstrasse 14–15. ✆ **089/213-51-00.** Reservations recommended. Main courses 20€–25€ ($23–$29); set-price menus 33€–45€ ($38–$52). AE, DC, MC, V. Mon–Fri 11:30am–7pm; Sat 9am–4pm. Tram: 19.

Spatenhaus ✿ BAVARIAN/INTERNATIONAL   One of Munich's best-known beer restaurants has wide windows overlooking the opera house on Max-Joseph-Platz. Of course, to be loyal, you should accompany your meal with the restaurant's own beer, Spaten-Franziskaner-Bier. You can sit in an intimate, semiprivate dining nook or at a big table. The Spatenhaus has old traditions, offers typical Bavarian food, and is known for generous portions and reasonable prices. If you want to know what all this fabled Bavarian gluttony is about, order the "Bavarian plate," which is loaded down with various meats, including lots of pork and sausages.

Residenzstrasse 12. ✆ **089/290-70-60.** Reservations recommended. Main courses 14€–22€ ($16–$25). AE, MC, V. Daily 11:30am–11:30pm. U-Bahn: Odeonsplatz or Marienplatz.

MODERATE

Buon Gusto (Talamonti) ✿ ITALIAN   Some of Munich's best Italian food is served here in the rustic-looking bistro, or in the more formal and more upscale-looking dining room. Menu items and prices are identical in both. Owned and managed by an extended family, the Talamontis, the restaurant emphasizes fresh ingredients, strong and savory flavors, and food items inspired by the Italian Marches and Tuscany. Stellar examples include ravioli stuffed with mushrooms and herbs, roasted lamb with potatoes, lots of scaloppine, and fresh fish that seems to taste best when served simply, with oil or butter and lemon. Especially appealing are the array of risottos whose ingredients change with the seasons. During Oktoberfest and trade fairs, the place is mobbed.

Hochbruckenstrasse 3. ✆ **089/296-383.** Reservations recommended. Main courses 18€–21€ ($21–$24). AE, MC, V. Mon–Sat 11am–1am. Closed Dec 23–Jan 3. U-Bahn/S-Bahn: Marienplatz.

Hunsiger's Pacific ✿ SEAFOOD   Despite the name, don't expect the menu to be devoted exclusively to Pacific Rim cuisine. Fish is the premier item here. Preparation is based on classic French-inspired methods, but the innovative flavors come from Malaysia (coconut milk), Japan (wasabi), Thailand (lemon grass), and India (curry). You could begin with a tuna carpaccio with sliced plum, fresh ginger, and lime. Main courses include a succulent version of bouillabaisse with aioli, which you might follow with cold melon soup garnished with a dollop of tarragon-flavored granita. Fried monkfish in the Malaysian style and turbot in chile-and-ginger sauce are evocative of Hawaii. Prices here are relatively low compared to those of its competitors.

Maximiliansplatz 5 (entrance on Max-Joseph-Strasse). ✆ **089/5502-9741.** Main courses 19€–27€ ($22–$31). AE, DC, MC, V. Mon–Sat noon–2:30pm and 6–11pm. Closed Sun May–Sept. U-Bahn: Stachus/Odeonsplatz.

Lenbach CONTINENTAL/ASIAN   Aggressively hip and aesthetically striking, this restaurant has some of the most sought-after tables in Munich. It occupies a landmark brick-and-stone building erected in 1887. Today, it owes its look to the design input of British-born entrepreneur Sir Terence Conran. An unusual blend of hypermodern and Renaissance motifs greets clients here, whose path to their table is along a slightly elevated "catwalk."

Menu items include a salad of foie gras with sweet roasted peppers; a selection of seven appetizers (they call them "the seven sins") piled high on one plate; red snapper with coriander-flavored pesto; grilled scampi with fresh herbs; roasted lamb with lentils and polenta; mussels with a truffle-flavored spinach sauce; and Thai-style curry with tiger prawns and rice.

Ottostrasse 6. ℭ **089/549-13-00.** Reservations recommended. Lunch main courses 8€–13€ ($9.20–$15); dinner main courses 9€–26€ ($10–$30). Set-price lunch (3 courses) 15€ ($17); set-price dinner (4–5 courses) 40€–50€ ($46–$58). AE, DC, MC, V. Mon–Sat 11:30am–2:30pm and 6pm–midnight. U-Bahn: Stachus.

Pfistermühle BAVARIAN   The country comes right into the heart of Munich at this authentic and old-fashioned place. A warm welcome and a refreshing cuisine await you here. Many of the dishes would be familiar to your Bavarian grandmother, and portions are generous and most satisfying. Come here for some of the most perfectly prepared roasts in the city. You can also opt for a fine array of fresh fish from the lakes and rivers of Bavaria, especially the delectable salmon trout or brown trout. Most fish dishes come with chive-flecked sour cream and a potato pancake. The fish is also simply prepared, such as pikeperch sautéed in butter. Finish with a pyramid of vanilla custard served with a fresh berry sauce, followed by a glass of wild cherry schnapps.

In the Platz Hotel, Pfistermühle 4. ℭ **089/2370-3865.** Reservations recommended. Main courses 11€–19€ ($12–$22); set menus 35€–45€ ($40–$52). AE, DC, MC, V. Mon–Sat 11:30am–midnight. U-Bahn: Marienplatz.

Ratskeller München BAVARIAN   Go here for the old Bavarian ambience at one of the best town hall cellars in the country. The decor is typical: lots of dark wood and carved chairs. The most interesting tables, the ones staked out by in-the-know locals, are the semiprivate dining nooks in the rear, under the vaulted painted ceilings. Bavarian music adds to the ambience. The menu, a showcase of regional fare, includes many vegetarian choices, which is unusual for a rathskeller. Some of the dishes are a little heavy and too porky, but you can find lighter fare if you search the menu.

Im Rathaus, Marienplatz 8. ℭ **089/219-98-90.** Reservations required. Main courses 6.90€–18€ ($7.95–$20). AE, MC, V. Daily 10am–midnight. U-Bahn/S-Bahn: Marienplatz.

INEXPENSIVE

Andechser am Dom GERMAN/BAVARIAN   Set on two floors of a postwar building erected adjacent to the back side of the Frauenkirche, this restaurant and beer hall serves copious amounts of a beer brewed in a monastery near Munich (Andechser) as well as generous portions of German food. Order a snack, a full meal, or just a beer, and enjoy the frothy fun of it all. Menu items include such dishes as veal schnitzels, steaks, turkey croquettes, roasted lamb, fish, and several kinds of sausages that taste best with tangy mustard. During clement weather, tables are set up on the building's roof and on the sidewalk in front, both of which overlook the back of one of the city's most evocative churches.

Weinstrasse 7A. ℭ **089/29-84-81.** Reservations recommended. Main courses 6.50€–15€ ($7.50–$17). AE, DC, MC, V. Daily 10am–1am. U-Bahn/S-Bahn: Marienplatz.

Donisl ✦ *Value* BAVARIAN/INTERNATIONAL   This is one of Munich's oldest beer halls, dating from 1715. The seating capacity of this relaxed and comfortable restaurant is about 550, and in summer you can enjoy the hum and bustle of Marienplatz while dining in the garden area out front. The standard menu offers traditional Bavarian food, as well as a weekly changing specials menu. The little white sausages, Weisswürst, are a decades-long tradition here.

Weinstrasse 1. ✆ **089/22-01-84.** Reservations recommended. Main courses 5.60€–6.50€ ($6.45–$7.50.) AE, DC, MC, V. Daily 9am–midnight. U-Bahn/S-Bahn: Marienplatz.

Hundskugel BAVARIAN   The city's oldest tavern, Hundskugel dates from 1440, and apparently serves the same food as it did back then. If it was good a long time ago, why mess with the menu? Built in an alpine style, the tavern is within easy walking distance of Marienplatz. Perhaps half the residents of Munich have at one time or another made their way here to enjoy the honest Bavarian cookery that has no pretensions. Although the chef specializes in *Spanferkel* (roast suckling pig with potato noodles), you might prefer *Tafelspitz* (boiled beef) in dill sauce, or roast veal stuffed with goose liver.

Hotterstrasse 18. ✆ **089/26-42-72.** Reservations required. Main courses 15€–20€ ($17–$23). No credit cards. Daily 11am–midnight. U-Bahn/S-Bahn: Marienplatz.

Nürnberger Bratwurst Glöckl Am Dom *Value* BAVARIAN   In the coziest and warmest of Munich's local restaurants, the chairs look as if they were made by some Black Forest woodcarver, and the place is full of memorabilia—pictures, prints, pewter, and beer steins. Upstairs through a hidden stairway is a dining room decorated with reproductions of Dürer prints. The restaurant has a strict policy of shared tables, and service is on tin plates. The homesick Nürnberger comes here just for one dish: *Nürnberger Schweinwurstl mit Kraut* (little sausages with kraut). Last food orders go in at midnight. If you're with a party of between four and eight, consider ordering one of the house specialties, a *pfanne* (large frying pan) that's loaded with a mixed grill of chops, wursts, and cutlets interspersed with potatoes and vegetables. Many groups of travelers opt for this, helping themselves to the contents as it's perched in the center of your table grouping. The cost per pfanne is 104€ ($120).

Frauenplatz 9. ✆ **089/29-52-64.** Reservations recommended. Main courses 10€–21€ ($12–$24). MC, V. Daily 10am–1am. U-Bahn/S-Bahn: Marienplatz.

SEEING THE SIGHTS

SIGHTSEEING SUGGESTIONS FOR FIRST-TIME VISITORS

If You Have 1 Day Local tourist tradition calls for a morning breakfast of Weisswürst; head for **Donisl** (above). A true Münchener downs them with a mug of beer. Then walk to **Marienplatz,** with its glockenspiel and **Altes Rathaus (Old Town Hall).** Later, stroll along **Maximilianstrasse,** one of Europe's great shopping streets. In the afternoon, visit the **Neue Pinakothek** and see at least some exhibits at the **Deutsches Museum.**

Cap the evening with a night of Bavarian food, beer, and music at the **Hofbräuhaus am Platzl.**

If You Have 2 Days In the morning of day 2, visit the **Bayerisches Nationalmuseum (Bavarian National Museum),** with three vast floors devoted to Bavaria's artistic and historical riches. If the weather's right, plan a lunch in one of the beer gardens of the **Englischer Garten.** In the afternoon, visit the

Nymphenburg Palace, summer residence of the Wittelsbach dynasty, longtime rulers of Bavaria.

If You Have 3 Days Pass your third day exploring the sights you've missed so far: the **Residenz,** the **Antikensammlungen (Museum of Antiquities),** and the **Glyptothek.** If you have any more time, return to the Deutsches Museum. Enjoy dinner or at least a drink at **Olympiapark,** along with a panoramic view of the Alps.

If You Have 4 or More Days As fascinating as Munich is, tear yourself away on day 4 for an excursion to the **Royal Castles** once occupied by the "mad king" Ludwig II (see "Organized Tours," p. 430, and "The Romantic Road," p. 444). On day 5, take an excursion to **Dachau,** the notorious World War II concentration camp, and in the afternoon visit **Mittenwald** for a taste of the Bavarian Alps.

EXPLORING THE ALTSTADT (OLD TOWN)

Marienplatz, dedicated to the patron of the city whose statue stands on a huge column in the center of the square, is the heart of the Altstadt. On its north side is the **Neues Rathaus (New City Hall)** built in 19th-century Gothic style. Each day at 11am, and also at noon and 5pm in the summer, the **Glockenspiel** on the facade performs a miniature tournament, with enameled copper figures moving in and out of the archways. Since you're already at the Rathaus, you may wish to climb the 55 steps to the top of its tower (an elevator is available if you're conserving energy) for a good overall view of the city center. The **Altes Rathaus (Old City Hall),** with its plain Gothic tower, is to the right. It was reconstructed in the 15th century, after being destroyed by fire.

MUSEUMS & PALACES

Alte Pinakothek ✸✸✸   This is one of the most significant art museums in Europe. The paintings represent the greatest European artists of the 14th through the 18th centuries. Begun as a small court collection by the royal Wittelsbach family in the early 1500s, the collection has grown and grown. There are two floors with exhibits, but the museum is immense. Albrecht Altdorfer, landscape painter par excellence of the Danube school, is represented by no fewer than six monumental works. Albrecht Dürer's works include his greatest—and final—*Self-Portrait* (1500). Here the artist has portrayed himself with almost Christ-like solemnity. Also displayed is the last great painting by the artist, his two-paneled work called *The Four Apostles* (1526).

Barer Strasse 27. ✆ 089/238-052-16. Admission 5€ ($5.75) adults, 3.50€ ($4.05) students, free for children 15 and under; free entrance on Sun. Combination ticket to Neue Pinakothek, Alte Pinakothek, Pinakothek der Moderne, and Schack-Galerie, 12€ ($14) adults, 7€ ($8.05) students and seniors, free for children 15 and under. Tues 10am–8pm; Wed–Sun 10am–5pm. U-Bahn: Theresienstrasse. Tram: 27. Bus: 53.

Bayerisches Nationalmuseum (Bavarian National Museum) ✸✸
Three vast floors of sculpture, painting, folk art, ceramics, furniture, textiles, and scientific instruments demonstrate Bavaria's artistic and historical riches. Entering the museum, turn to the right and go into the first large gallery, called the **Wessobrunn Room.** Devoted to early church art from the 5th century to the 13th century, this room holds some of the oldest and most valuable works. The desk case contains ancient and medieval ivories, including the so-called Munich ivory, from about A.D. 400. The **Riemenschneider Room** is devoted to the works of the great sculptor Tilman Riemenschneider (ca. 1460–1531) and his

contemporaries. The second floor contains a fine collection of stained and painted glass—an art in which medieval Germany excelled—baroque ivory carvings, Meissen porcelain, and ceramics.

Prinzregentenstrasse 3. ✆ 089/211-2401. Admission 3€ ($3.45) adults, 2€ ($2.30) students and seniors, free for children under 15. Free on Sun. Tues–Sun 10am–5pm; Thurs 10am–8pm. U-Bahn: Lehel. Tram: 17. Bus: 53.

Deutsches Museum (German Museum of Masterpieces of Science and Technology) ★★★ On an island in the Isar River is the largest technological museum of its kind in the world. Its huge collection of priceless artifacts and historic originals includes the first electric dynamo (Siemens, 1866), the first automobile (Benz, 1886), the first diesel engine (1897), and the laboratory bench at which the atom was first split (Hahn, Strassmann, 1938). There are hundreds of buttons to push, levers to crank, and gears to turn, as well as a knowledgeable staff to answer questions and demonstrate how steam engines, pumps, or historical musical instruments work. Among the most popular displays are those on mining, with a series of model coal, salt, and iron mines, as well as the electrical power hall, with high-voltage displays that actually produce lightning. There are many other exhibits, covering the whole range of science and technology.

Museumsinsel 1. ✆ 089/2-17-91. Admission 7.50€ ($8.65) adults, 5€ ($5.75) seniors, 3€ ($3.45) students, free for children 6 and under. Daily 9am–5pm. Closed major holidays. S-Bahn: Isartor. Tram: 18. U-Bahn: Fraunhoferstrasse.

Glyptothek ★ The Glyptothek supplements the pottery and smaller pieces of the main museum with an excellent collection of ancient Greek and Roman sculpture. Included are the famous pediments from the temple of Aegina, two marvelous statues of *kouroi* (youths) from the 6th century B.C., the colossal figure of a *Sleeping Satyr* from the Hellenistic period, and a splendid collection of Roman portraits.

Königsplatz 3. ✆ 089/28-61-00. Admission 3€ ($3.45) adults, 2€ ($2.30) students and seniors, 2€ ($2.30) children. Combination ticket to the Museum of Antiquities and the Glyptothek, 5.10€ ($5.85) adults, 2.55€ ($2.95) students and children, free for children under 14. Tues–Sun 10am–5pm; Thurs 10am–8pm. U-Bahn: Königsplatz.

Neue Pinakothek ★★ This gallery is a showcase of Munich's most valuable 18th- and 19th-century art, an artistic period that was hardly the Renaissance but has its artistic devotees nonetheless. Across Theresienstrasse from the Alte Pinakothek, the museum has paintings by Gainsborough, Goya, David, Manet, van Gogh, and Monet. Among the more popular German artists represented are Wilhelm Leibl and Gustav Klimt. Note particularly the genre paintings by Carl Spitzweg.

Barer Strasse 29. ✆ 089/23-80-51-95. Admission 5€ ($5.75) adults, 3.50€ ($4.05) students and seniors, free for children 15 and under. Combination ticket to Neue Pinakothek, Alte Pinakothek, Pinakothek der Moderne, and Schack-Galerie 12€ ($14) adults, 7€ ($8.05) students and seniors, free for children 15 and under. Thurs–Mon 10am–5pm; Wed 10am–8pm. U-Bahn: Theresienstrasse. Tram: 27. Bus: 53.

Pinakothek der Moderne ★★ In 2002, one of the world's largest museums devoted to the visual arts of the 19th and 20th centuries opened in Munich, just minutes from the Alte and Neue Pinakothek. Four major collections have been brought together under one roof, making this the most vast display of fine and applied arts in the country. It's Munich's version of the Tate Gallery in London or the Pompidou in Paris.

Wander where your interest dictates: the **Staatsgalerie Moderner Kunst (State Gallery of Modern Art)** ★★★, with paintings, sculpture, photography, and video; **Die Neue Sammlung,** which constitutes the national museum of applied art featuring design and craftwork; the **Architekturmuseum der Technischen Universität (University of Architecture Museum),** with architectural drawings, photographs, and models; and the **Staatliche Grapische Sammlung,** with its outstanding collection of prints and drawings.

Whenever we visit, we spend most of our time in the modern art collection, lost in a world of some of our favorite artists: Picasso, Magritte, Klee, Kandinsky, even Francis Bacon, de Kooning, and Warhol. The museum also owns 400,000 drawings and prints from Leonardo da Vinci to Cézanne up to contemporary artists. They are presented as alternating exhibits.

The architectural galleries hold the largest specialist collection of its kind in Germany, comprising some 350,000 drawings, 100,000 photographs, and 500 models. The applied arts section features more than 50,000 items. You go from the beginnings of the Industrial Revolution up to today's computer culture, with exhibitions of Art Nouveau and Bauhaus along the way.

Barerstrasse 40. ℂ **089/23805-360.** Admission 9€ ($10) adults, 5€ ($5.75) students and ages 17 and under. Fri–Sun and Wed 10am–5pm; Thurs 10am–8pm. Combination ticket to Neue Pinakothek, Alte Pinakothek, Pinakothek der Moderne, and Schack-Galerie 12€ ($14) adults, 7€ ($8.05) students and seniors, free for children 15 and under. U-Bahn: Odeonsplatz.

Residenz ✮ The official residence of Bavaria's rulers from 1385 to 1918, the complex is a conglomerate of various styles of art and architecture. Depending on how you approach the Residenz, you might first see a German Renaissance hall (the western facade), a Palladian palace (on the north), or a Florentine Renaissance palace (on the south facing Max-Joseph-Platz). The Residenz has been completely restored since its almost total destruction in World War II and now houses the Residenz Museum, a concert hall, the Cuvilliés Theater, and the Residenz Treasure House.

Residenzmuseum comprises the southwestern section of the palace, some 120 rooms of art and furnishings collected by centuries of Wittelsbachs. There are two guided tours, one in the morning and the other in the afternoon, or you may visit the rooms on your own.

If you have time to view only one item in the **Schatzkammer (Treasure House)** ✮✮, make it the 16th-century Renaissance statue of *St. George Slaying the Dragon.* The equestrian statue is made of gold, but you can barely see the precious metal for the thousands of diamonds, rubies, emeralds, sapphires, and semiprecious stones embedded in it.

From the Brunnenhof, you can visit the **Cuvilliés Theater** ✮, whose rococo tiers of boxes are supported by seven bacchants. The huge box, where the family sat, is in the center. In summer, this theater is the scene of frequent concert and opera performances. Mozart's *Idomeneo* was first performed here in 1781.

Max-Joseph-Platz 3. ℂ **089/29-06-71.** Combination ticket for Residenzmuseum and Schatzkammer 9€ ($10) adults, 4.50€ ($5.20) students/seniors, free for ages 15 and under. Ticket for either Schatzkammer or Residenzmuseum 6€ ($6.90) adults, 3€ ($3.45) seniors/students, free for ages 16 and under. Daily 9am–4pm. U-Bahn: Odeonsplatz.

Schack-Galerie To appreciate this florid and romantic overdose of sentimental German paintings of the 19th century, you've got to enjoy fauns and elves at play in picturesque, even magical, landscapes. Such art has its devotees. Obviously, if you're a Picasso Cubist, you'd be better off going elsewhere. But this once-private collection adheres to the baroque tastes of Count Adolf Friedrich von Schack of Schwerin (1815–94), who spent a rich life acquiring works by the likes of Spitzweg, Schwind, Fuerbach, and others, many others, some of whom frankly should have been assigned to the dustbin of art history. Still, in all, we find a visit here fun, at least on a rainy, gray day. It's like wandering back to a lost world and getting absorbed in the taste of yesterday.

Prinzregentenstrasse 9. Ⓒ **089/23805-224.** Admission 2.50€ ($2.90) adults, 2€ ($2.30) children. Combination ticket to Neue Pinakothek, Alte Pinakothek, Pinakothek der Moderne, and Schack-Galerie 12€ ($14) adults, 7€ ($8.05) students and seniors, free for children 15 and under. Daily except Tues 10am–5pm. U-Bahn: U4 and U5 to Lehel.

Schloss Nymphenburg ★★   In summer, the Wittelsbachs would pack up their bags and head for their country house, Schloss Nymphenburg. A more complete, more sophisticated palace than the Residenz, it was begun in 1664 in Italian villa style and went through several architectural changes before completion.

The main building's great hall, decorated in rococo colors and stuccos with frescoes by Zimmermann (1756), was used for both banquets and concerts. Concerts are still presented here in summer. From the main building, turn left and head for the arcaded gallery connecting the northern pavilions. The first room in the arcade is the Great Gallery of Beauties. More provocative, however, is Ludwig I's Gallery of Beauties in the south pavilion (the apartments of Queen Caroline). Ludwig commissioned no fewer than 36 portraits of the most beautiful women of his day. The paintings by J. Stieler include the *Schöne Münchnerin (Lovely Munich Girl)* and a portrait of Lola Montez, the dancer whose "friendship" with Ludwig I caused a scandal that factored into the revolution of 1848.

To the south of the palace buildings, in the rectangular block of low structures that once housed the court stables, is the **Marstallmuseum.** In the first hall, look for the glass coronation coach of Elector Karl Albrecht, built in Paris in 1740. From the same period comes the elaborate hunting sleigh of Electress Amalia, adorned with a statue of Diana, goddess of the hunt; even the sleigh's runners are decorated with shellwork and hunting trophies. The coaches and sleighs of Ludwig II are displayed in the third hall.

One of Nymphenburg's greatest attractions is the **park** ★. Stretching for 200 hectares (500 acres) in front of the palace, it's divided into two sections by the canal that runs from the pool at the foot of the staircase to the cascade at the far end of the English-style gardens.

Within the park are a number of pavilions. The guided tour begins with **Amalienburg** ★★, whose plain exterior belies the rococo decoration inside. Built as a hunting lodge for Electress Amalia (in 1734), the pavilion carries the hunting theme through the first few rooms and then bursts into salons of flamboyant colors, rich carvings, and wall paintings. The most impressive room is the Hall of Mirrors, a symphony of silver ornaments on a faint blue background.

Other attractions include the **Porzellansammlung,** or museum of porcelain, which is above the stables of the Marstallmuseum. Some of the finest pieces of porcelain in the world, executed in the 18th century, are displayed here, along with an absolute gem—extraordinarily detailed miniature porcelain reproductions of some of the grand masterpieces in the Old Pinakothek, each commissioned by Ludwig I.

The **Botanischer Garten (Botanical Gardens)** ★★ is among the most richly planted in Europe. It's worth a spring trip to Munich for garden lovers to see this great mass of vegetation burst into bloom.

Schloss Nymphenburg 1. Ⓒ **089/17-908-668.** Admission to all attractions 5.60€ ($6.45) adults, free for children 6 and under. Separate admissions: 3.50€ ($4.05) Schloss Nymphenburg or 3€ ($3.45) to either Marstallmuseum, Amalienburg, or Porzellansammlung; free for children 15 and under. Oct–Mar daily 10am–4pm; Apr–Sept daily 9am–6pm. Parking beside the Marstallmuseum. U-Bahn: Rotkreuzplatz, then tram 17 to Botanischergarten. Bus: 41.

CHURCHES

When the smoke cleared from the 1945 bombings, only a fragile shell remained of Munich's largest church, the **Frauenkirche (Cathedral of Our Lady)** ✹, Frauenplatz 1 (© **089/290-08-20;** U-Bahn/S-Bahn: Marienplatz). Workers and architects who restored the 15th-century Gothic cathedral used whatever remains they could find in the rubble, along with modern innovations. The overall effect of the rebuilt Frauenkirche is strikingly simple yet dignified. The twin towers, which remained intact, have been a city landmark since 1525. Instead of the typical flying buttresses, huge props on the inside that separate the side chapels support the edifice. The Gothic vaulting over the nave and chancel is borne by 22 simple octagonal pillars. Except for the tall chancel window, when you enter the main doors at the west end, you don't notice windows; they're hidden by the enormous pillars. According to legend, the devil laughed at the notion of hidden windows and stamped in glee at the stupidity of the architect—you can still see the strange footlike mark called "the devil's step" in the entrance hall.

    Peterskirche (St. Peter's Church), Rindermarkt 1 (© **089/260-48-28;** U-Bahn/S-Bahn: Marienplatz), is Munich's oldest church (1180). Its tall steeple is worth the climb in clear weather for a view as far as the Alps. In its gilded baroque interior are murals by Johann Baptist Zimmermann. The **Asamkirche** ✹, Sendlinger Strasse (U-Bahn/S-Bahn: Sendlingertor), is a remarkable example of rococo, designed by the Asam brothers, Cosmas Damian and Edgar Quirin, from 1733 to 1746. The **Michaelskirche,** Neuhauser Strasse 6 (U-Bahn/S-Bahn: Karlsplatz), has the distinction of being the largest Renaissance church north of the Alps. The lovely **Theatinerkirche,** Theatinerstrasse 22 (U-Bahn/S-Bahn: Odeonsplatz), with its graceful fluted columns and arched ceilings, is the work of the court architect, François Cuvilliés and his son.

ORGANIZED TOURS

The easiest, and fastest, way to gain an overview of Munich is on a guided tour. One of the largest organizers of these is **Panorama Tours,** Arnulfstrasse 8 (© **089/ 550-28995;** U-Bahn/S-Bahn: Hauptbahnhof), just north of the Hauptbahnhof. At least a half dozen touring options are available, ranging from a quickie 1-hour overview of the city to full-day excursions to such outlying sites as Berchtesgaden, Oberammergau, and Hohenschwangau, site of three of Bavaria's most stunning palaces.

    City tours encompass aspects of both modern and medieval Munich, and depart from the main railway station. Departures, depending on the season and the tour, occur between two and eight times a day, and tours are conducted in both German and English.

    Depending on the tour, adults pay 11€ to 23€ ($13–$26); children under 14 pay 6€ to 12€ ($6.90–$14), for experiences that last between 1 and 2½ hours, depending on the tour. Advance reservations for most city tours aren't required, and you can buy your ticket from the bus driver at the time you board. The company also offers a 4½-hour "Munich by Night" tour that costs 60€ ($69) per person and departs several nights a week at 7:30pm, and which hauls its participants in and out of a series of cabarets and beerhalls at a lukewarm, and ultimately not particularly happy encounter that has "I am a tourist" permeating almost every aspect of the experience.

    If you want to participate in any tour that covers attractions outside the city limits, advance reservations are required, especially if you want the bus to pick you up at any of Munich's hotels. Travel agents in Munich, as well as the concierge or reception staff at your hotel, can book any of these tours, but if you want to contact Panorama Tours directly, they're open year-round Monday to Friday 9am to 6pm and Saturday 9am to 1pm.

Pedal pushers will want to try Mike Lasher's **Mike's Bike Tour** (© 089/651-4275; www.mikesbiketours.com). His bike rentals for 12€ to 18€ ($14–$21) include maps and locks, child and infant seats, and helmets at no extra charge. English and bilingual tours of central Munich run from March to November, leaving daily at 10:30am (call to confirm). The cost of the tour is included in the rental fee.

THE SHOPPING SCENE

The most interesting shops are concentrated on Munich's pedestrians-only streets between **Karlsplatz** and **Marienplatz.**

Handmade crafts can be found on the fourth floor of Munich's major department store, **Ludwig Beck am Rathauseck,** Am Marienplatz 11 (© **089/236-910;** U-Bahn/S-Bahn: Marienplatz). **Wallach,** Residenzstrasse 3 (© **089/22-08-71;** U-Bahn/S-Bahn: Odeonplatz), is a fine place to obtain handcrafts and folk art, both new and antique. Shop here for a memorable object to remind you of your trip. You'll find antique churns, old hand-painted wooden boxes and trays, painted porcelain clocks, and many other items.

On the grounds of Schloss Nymphenburg at Nördliches Schlossrondell 8, you'll find **Nymphenburger Porzellan-manufaktur** (© **089/17-91-970;** U-Bahn: Rotkreuzplatz, then tram no. 17 toward Amalienburgstrasse; bus: 41), one of Germany's most famous porcelain makers. You can visit the exhibition and sales rooms; shipments can be arranged if you make purchases. There's also a branch in Munich's center, at Odeonsplatz 1 (© **089/28-24-28;** U-Bahn/S-Bahn: Odeonplatz).

MUNICH AFTER DARK

To find out what's happening in the Bavarian capital, go to the tourist office and buy a copy of "Monats-programm." This pamphlet contains complete information about what's going on in Munich and how to purchase tickets.

THE PERFORMING ARTS

Nowhere else in Europe, other than London and Paris, will you find so many musical and theatrical performances. And the good news is the low cost of the seats—you'll get good tickets if you're willing to pay anywhere from 10€ to 45€ ($12–$52).

A part of the Residenz (see "Museums & Palaces," p. 426), **Altes Residenztheater (Cuvilliés Theater),** Residenzstrasse 1 (© **089/2185-19-40;** U-Bahn: Odeonsplatz), is a sightseeing attraction in its own right, and Germany's most outstanding example of a rococo tier-boxed theater. During World War II, the interior was dismantled and stored. You can tour it Tuesday through Friday from 2 to 4pm and Sunday from 11am to 5pm. **Bavarian State Opera** and the **Bayerisches Staatsschauspiel (State Theater Company;** © **089/2185-1920)** perform smaller works here in keeping with the tiny theater's intimate character. Box-office hours are Monday through Friday from 10am to 6pm, plus 1 hour before performances; Saturday from 10am to 1pm only. Opera tickets are 13€ to 160€ ($14–$184); theater tickets 13€ to 40€ ($15–$46); building tours 5€ ($5.75).

The regular season of the **Deutsches Theater,** Schwanthalerstrasse 13 (© **089/552-34-444;** www.deutsches-theater.de; U-Bahn: Karlsplatz/Stachus), lasts year-round. Musicals, operettas, ballets, and international shows are performed here. During carnival season (Jan–Feb) the theater becomes a ballroom for more than 2,000 guests. Tickets are 16€ to 44€ ($18–$51), higher for special events.

Gasteig München GmbH, Rosenheimer Strasse 5 (© **089/48-09-80;** www. gasteig.de; S-Bahn: Rosenheimerplatz; tram: 18; bus: 51), is the home of the **Münchner Philharmoniker** (www.muenchnerphilharmoniker.de), founded in 1893. Its present home opened in 1985 and shelters the Richard Strauss Conservatory and the Munich Municipal Library. The orchestra performs in Philharmonic Hall. Purchase tickets Monday through Friday from 9am to 6pm, Saturday from 9am to 2pm, for 10€ to 51€ ($12–$59). The Philharmonic season runs mid-September to July.

Practically any night of the year, except from August to mid-September, you'll find a performance at the **Nationaltheater,** Max-Joseph-Platz 2 (© **089/21-85-01;** www.staatstheater.bayern.de; U-Bahn/S-Bahn: Marienplatz or Odeonsplatz), home of the **Bavarian State Opera,** one of the world's great opera companies. The productions are beautifully mounted and presented, and sung by famous singers. Hard-to-get tickets may be purchased Monday through Friday from 10am to 6pm, plus 1 hour before performance; Saturday from 10am to 1pm. The Nationaltheater is also home to the **Bavarian State Ballet.** Opera tickets are 13€ to 240€ ($15–$276); ballet tickets, 7.65€ to 66€ ($8.80–$76).

THE CLUB & MUSIC SCENE

You'll find some of Munich's most sophisticated entertainment at **Bayerischer Hof Night Club,** in the Hotel Bayerischer Hof, Promenadeplatz 2–6 (© **089/ 212-00;** tram: 19). Within one very large room is a piano bar where a musician plays melodies every night except Monday from 11am to 2am. Behind a partition that disappears at 10pm, there's a bandstand for live orchestras, which play to a crowd of dancing patrons until 3 or 4am. The piano bar is free, but there's a nightclub cover charge of 5€ to 50€ ($5.75–$58). Daily happy hour is from 7 to 8:30pm in the piano bar.

Jazzclub Unterfahrt, Einsteinstrasse 42 (© **089/448-27-94;** U-Bahn/S-Bahn: Ostbahnhof), is Munich's leading jazz club, lying near the Ostbahnhof in the Haidhausen district. The club presents live music Tuesday through Sunday from 8:30pm to 1am (it opens at 8pm). Wine, small snacks, beer, and drinks are sold as well. Sunday night there's a special jam session for improvisation. Cover from Tuesday to Saturday is 9.20€ to 14€ ($11–$16), Sunday jam session 15€ ($17). Club members pay half the regular cover. Small, dark, and popular with blues and jazz aficionados, **Mister B's,** Herzog-Heinrichstrasse 38 (© **089/ 534901;** U-Bahn: Goetheplatz), hosts a slightly older, mellower crowd than the rock and dance clubs. It's open Tuesday through Sunday from 8pm to 3am. Blues, jazz, and rhythm-and-blues combos take the stage Thursday through Saturday. Cover is 5.50€ to 8.50€ ($6.35–$9.80.)

Set in a huge factory warehouse, **Nachtwerk,** Landesbergerstrasse 185 (© **089/ 578-3800;** S-Bahn: Donnersbergerbrücke), is a cavernous mostly straight dance club that also books bands. It's a festive place that's not nearly as pretentious as other more "exclusive" discos (the doorman won't send you away for wearing the wrong shoes or pants). The club is open Thursday from 10pm to 4am; Friday and Saturday from 10:30pm. Cover is 6€ to 8€ ($6.90–$9.20).

Parkcafé, Sophienstrasse 7 (© **089/59-83-13;** U-Bahn: Lebachplatz), contains three distinct subdivisions, each catering to the food, beverage, and socializing

What's Brewing at the Beer Halls?

The world's most famous beer hall, **Hofbraühaus am Platzl,** Am Platzl 9 (✆ **089/22-16-76;** U-Bahn/S-Bahn: Marienplatz), is a legend. Visitors with only 1 night in Munich usually target the Hofbräuhaus as their top nighttime destination. Owned by the state, the present Hofbräuhaus was built at the end of the 19th century, but the tradition of a beer house on this spot dates from 1589. In the 19th century it attracted artists, students, and civil servants and was known as the Blue Hall because of its dim lights and smoky atmosphere. When it grew too small to contain everybody, architects designed another in 1897. This one was the 1920 setting for the notorious meeting of Hitler's newly launched German Workers Party. Today, 4,500 beer drinkers can crowd in on a given night. Several rooms are spread over three floors, including a top-floor room for dancing. The ground floor, with its brass band (which starts playing at 11am), is exactly what you'd expect of a beer hall—here it's eternal Oktoberfest. It's open daily from 10am to midnight.

In a century-old house northwest of Schwabing at the edge of Luit-pold Park, **Bamberger Haus,** Brunnerstrasse 2 (✆ **089/308-89-66;** U-Bahn: Scheidplatz), is named after the city most noted for the quantity of beer its residents drink. Bavarian and international specialties served in the street-level restaurant include well-seasoned soups, grilled steak, veal, pork, and sausages. If you only want to drink, visit the rowdier and less expensive beer hall in the cellar, where a large beer is 2.60€ ($3). The restaurant is open daily noon to midnight and the beer hall daily 5pm to 1am; in summer, weather permitting, a beer garden is open daily from 11am to 11pm.

Englischer Garten, the park between the Isar River and Schwabing, is the biggest city-owned park in Europe. It has a main restaurant and several beer gardens, of which the **Biergärten Chinesischer Turm,** Englischer Garten 3 (✆ **089/38-38-73-27;** U-Bahn: Giselastrasse), is our favorite. It takes its name from its location at the foot of a pagoda-like tower. Plenty of beer and cheap Bavarian food are what you get here. A large glass or mug of beer (ask for *ein mass Bier*), enough to bathe in, costs 5.80€ to 6€ ($6.65–$6.90). Homemade dumplings are a specialty, as are all kinds of tasty sausage. Oompah bands often play. It's open daily from 10am to midnight (closed Jan 11–Feb 5).

On the principal pedestrian-only street of Munich, **Augustinerbrau,** Neuhäuserstrasse 27 (✆ **089/260-4106;** U-Bahn/S-Bahn: Stachus), offers generous helpings of food, good beer, and a mellow atmosphere. It's been around for a little less than a century, but beer was first brewed on this spot in 1328. The cuisine is not for dieters: It's hearty, heavy, and starchy, but it sure soaks up that beer. Hours are daily from 9am to midnight. **Waldwirtschaft Grosshesslohe,** George-Kalb-Strasse 3 (✆ **089/74-99-4030;** tram: 7), is a popular summertime rendezvous seating some 2,000 drinkers. The gardens are open daily from 10am to 11pm (they have to close early because neighborhood residents complain). Music ranges from Dixieland to English jazz to Polish bands. Entrance is free and you bring your own food. It's above the Isar River in the vicinity of the zoo.

needs of the young, the restless, and the occasionally cutting-edge residents of Munich. Come here for a drink, snack, or coffee at the **Parkcafé,** and perhaps extend the venue into a full meal at the immediately adjacent premises of the **Parkcafé Kitchen.** Both establishments are open daily 10am to midnight for food (until 1am for drinks). And if you're in the mood to dance, surrounded by nocturnal denizens of Munich who might be dressed in Teutonic punk or leather and perhaps heavily pierced, come here every night of the week from 11pm to 4am for access to the **Parkcafé Club,** where hipster music blares and entrance costs from 8€ to 11€ ($9.20–$13), depending on the night of the week.

THE BAR & CAFE SCENE
Once a literary cafe, **Alter Simpl,** Türkenstrasse 57 (© **089/272-30-83;** U-Bahn: University), attracts a diverse crowd of locals, including young people. The real fun begins after 11pm, when the iconoclastic artistic ferment becomes more reminiscent of Berlin than Bavaria. It's open Sunday through Thursday from 11am to 3am, Friday and Saturday from 11am to 4am.

Nachtcafé, Maximilianplatz 5 (© **089/59-59-00;** tram: 19), hums, thrives, and captures the nocturnal imagination of everyone—no other nightspot in Munich attracts such an array of soccer stars, film celebrities, literary figures, and, as one employee put it, "ordinary people, but only the most sympathetically crazy ones." Waves of patrons appear at different times of the evening: at 11pm, when live concerts begin; at 2am, when the restaurants close; and at 4am, when die-hard revelers seek a final drink in the predawn hours. The music is jazz, blues, funk, and soul, and the decor is updated 1950s. There's a cover only rarely and for special entertainment. It's open daily from 9pm to 6am.

Schumann's, Odensplatz 6–7 (© **089/22-90-60**), doesn't waste any money on decor—it depends on the local beau monde to keep it looking chic. In warm weather the terrace spills onto the street. Schumann's is known as a "thinking man's bar." Charles Schumann, author of three bar books, wanted a bar that would be an artistic, literary, and communicative social focus of the metropolis. Popular with the film, advertising, and publishing worlds, his place is said to have contributed to a remarkable renaissance of bar culture in the city. It's open Sunday from 6pm to 3am, Monday through Friday from 9am to 3am; closed on Saturday.

GAY & LESBIAN CLUBS
Much of Munich's gay and lesbian scene takes place in the blocks between the Viktualienmarkt and Gärtnerplatz, particularly on Hans-Sachs-Strasse.

A virtual communications center of hip Munich, the **Stadtcafe,** St. Jakobsplatz 1 (© **089/266-949;** U-Bahn: Marienplatz), attracts creative people, often in the arts. By Munich nightlife standards, it closes relatively early; night owls drift on to other late-night venues. Expect lots of chitchat from table to table, and there's sure to be someone scribbling away at his or her unfinished story (or unfinished novel). It's open Sunday through Thursday from 11am to midnight, Friday and Saturday from 11am to 1am, and Sunday from 10:30am to midnight. **Soul City,** Maximilianplatz 5 (© **089/595272;** U-Bahn: Karlsplatz), is *the* gay dance club in Munich. Scattered nooks allow conversation sheltered from one of the best sound systems in the city, as well as offer a brief respite from the throng on the dance floor and at the bar. The 6€ ($6.90) cover charge on Thursday and Friday includes free drinks, and on Saturday you get discounted drink coupons. The club is open Thursday through Saturday from 10pm to 6am.

DAY TRIPS FROM MUNICH
HERRENCHIEMSEE ✶ & NEUES SCHLOSS ✶✶ Known as the "Bavarian Sea," Chiemsee is one of the Bavarian Alps' most beautiful lakes in a serene landscape. Its main attraction lies on the island of Herrenchiemsee, where "Mad" King Ludwig II built one of his fantastic castles.

Neues Schloss, begun in 1878, was never completed because of the king's death in 1886. The castle was to have been a replica of the grand palace of Versailles that Ludwig so admired. One of the architects was Julius Hofmann, whom the king had also employed for the construction of his alpine castle, Neuschwanstein. When work was halted in 1886, only the center of the enormous palace had been completed. The palace and its formal gardens remain one of the most fascinating of Ludwig's adventures, in spite of their unfinished state.

The splendid Great Hall of Mirrors most authentically replicates Versailles. The 17 door panels contain enormous mirrors reflecting the 33 crystal chandeliers and the 44 gilded candelabra. The vaulted ceiling is covered with 25 paintings depicting the life of Louis XIV. The dining room is a popular attraction because of "the little table that lays itself." A mechanism in the floor permitted the table to go down to the room below to be cleared and relaid between courses.

You can visit Herrenchiemsee at any time of the year. April through September, tours are given daily from 9am to 6pm; off season, from 10am to 4:15pm. Admission—in addition to the 5.70€ ($6.55) for the round-trip boat fare—is 6.50€ ($7.50) adults, 5.50€ ($6.35) students, and free for children under 17.

Getting There Take the train to Prien am Chiemsee (trip time: 1 hr.). For information, call © **08001/50-70-90.** There's also regional bus service offered by **RVO Regionalver-kehr Oberbayern** (© **08652/944-80**). Access by car is via A-8 Autobahn.

From Prien, lake steamers make the trip to Herrenchiemsee. They are operated by **Chiemsee-Schiffahrt Ludwig Fessler** (© **08051/60-90**). The round-trip fare is 5.70€ ($6.55). For visitor information, contact the **Kur und Verkehrsamt,** Alte Rathausstrasse 11, in Prien am Chiemsee (© **08051/9050**), open September to March Monday to Friday from 8:30am to 5pm. April to August, the office is also open on Saturday from 8:30am to 6pm.

GARMISCH-PARTENKIRCHEN ✶✶✶
In spite of its urban flair, Garmisch-Partenkirchen, Germany's top alpine resort, has maintained the charm of an ancient village. Even today, you occasionally see country folk in traditional costumes, and you may be held up in traffic while the cattle are led from their mountain grazing grounds down through the streets of town. Garmisch is about 88km (55 miles) southwest of Munich.

ESSENTIALS
GETTING THERE   By Train The **Garmisch-Partenkirchen Bahnhof** lies on the major Munich-Weilheim-Garmisch-Mittenwald-Innsbruck rail line with frequent connections in all directions. Twenty trains per day arrive from Munich (trip time: 1 hr. 22 min.). For rail information and schedules, call © **0800/ 1-50-70-90.**

By Bus Both long-distance and regional buses through the Bavarian Alps are provided by **RVO Regionalverkehr Oberbayern** in Garmisch-Partenkirchen (© **08821/948-274** for information).

By Car Access is via A-95 Autobahn from Munich; exit at Eschenlohe.

Outdoors in the Bavarian Alps

HITTING THE SLOPES & OTHER WINTER ACTIVITIES The winter **skiing** here is the best in Germany. Winter snowfall in January and February measures 30 centimeters to 50 centimeters (12 in.–20 in.), which in practical terms means about 2m (6 ft.) of snow in the areas served by ski lifts. The great **Zugspitzplatt** snowfield can be reached in spring or autumn by a rack railway. The Zugspitze, at 2,960m (9,720 ft.), is the tallest mountain peak in Germany. Ski slopes begin at a height of 2,650m (8,700 ft.).

The second great ski district in the Alps is **Berchtesgadener Land,** with alpine skiing centered on Jenner, Rossfeld, Götschen, and Hochschwarzeck, and consistently good snow conditions until March. Here you'll find a cross-country skiing center and many miles of tracks kept in first-class condition, natural toboggan runs, one artificial ice run for toboggan and skibob runs, artificial ice skating, and ice-curling rinks. Call the local "Snow-Telefon" at © 08652/9670 for current snow conditions.

From October to February, you can use the world-class **ice-skating** rink in Berchtesgaden (the Eisstadion). Less reliable, but more evocative of Bavaria's wild open spaces, it involves skating on the surface of the Hintersee Lake once it's sufficiently frozen. Rarer is an ice-skating experience on the Königsee, whose surface freezes to the degree that you can skate on average only once every 10 winters. A particularly cozy way to spend a winter's night is to huddle with a companion in the back of a **horse-drawn sled.** For a fee of 50€ to 80€ ($58–$92) per hour, this can be arranged by calling © 08652/1760.

HIKING & OTHER SUMMER ACTIVITIES In summer, **alpine hiking** is a major attraction. Hikers are able at times to observe endangered species firsthand. One of the best areas for hiking is the 1,237m (4,060-ft.) **Eckbauer** lying on the southern fringe of Partenkirchen (the tourist office at Garmisch-Partenkirchen will supply maps and details). Many visitors come to the Alps in summer just to hike through the **Berchtesgaden National Park,** bordering the Austrian province of Salzburg. The 2,466m (8,091-ft.) Watzmann Mountain, the Königssee (Germany's cleanest, clearest lake), and parts of the Jenner—the pride of Berchtesgaden's four ski areas—are within the boundaries of the national park, which has well-mapped trails cut through protected areas. Information about hiking in the park is provided by the **Nationale Parkverwaltung,** Franciscanalplatz 7, 83471 Berchtesgaden (© 08652/64343). It's open daily from 9am to 5pm.

From Garmisch-Partenkirchen, serious hikers can embark on full-day or, if they're more ambitious, overnight alpine treks, following clearly marked footpaths and staying in isolated mountain huts maintained by the German Alpine Association (Deutscher Alpenverein/DAV). Some huts are staffed and serve meals. For the truly remote unsupervised huts, you'll be provided with information on how to gain access and your responsibility in leaving them tidy after your visit. For information, inquire at the local tourist office or write to the **German Alpine Association,** Am Franciscanalplatz 7, 83471, Berchtesgaden (© 08652/64343). The GAA can also route you to staff members of a privately owned tour operator, the

Summit Club, an outfit devoted to the organization of high-altitude expeditions throughout Europe and the world.

If you're a true outdoors person, you'll briefly savor the somewhat touristy facilities of Garmisch-Partenkirchen, and then use it as a base for exploring the rugged **Berchtesgaden National Park,** which is within an easy commute of Garmisch. You can also stay at one of the inns in Mittenwald or Oberammergau and take advantage of a wide roster of sporting diversions within the wild open spaces. Any of the outfitters below will provide directions and link-ups with their sports programs from wherever you decide to stay. Street maps of Berchtesgaden and its environs are usually available for free from the **Kurdirektion** (the local tourist office) at Berchtesgaden (© 08652/967-0), and more intricately detailed maps of the surrounding alpine topography are available for a fee.

In addition to hill climbing and rock climbing, summertime activities include **ballooning,** which can be arranged through **Outdoor Club Berchtesgaden,** Am Gmundberg (© 08652/9776-0), open from Monday through Friday from 8am to 6pm. Local enthusiasts warn that ballooning is not a sport for the timid or anyone who suffers unduly in the cold. The seasonal heyday for ballooning is from December to February. A local variation of **curling** (*Eisstock*) can usually be arranged even when ice and snows have melted on the surrounding slopes at the town's biggest ice rink, **Berchtesgaden Eisstadion,** An der Schiessstätte (© 08652/61405). A kiosk (© 08652/3384) within the ice stadium rents a wide spectrum of ice skates in all sizes for around 3.50€ ($4.05) adults, 3€ ($3.45) children per hour.

Cycling and **mountain biking,** available through the rental facilities of **Para-Taxi,** Maximilianstrasse 16 (© 08652/948450), give outdoor enthusiasts an opportunity to enjoy the outdoors and exercise their leg muscles simultaneously. It's open Monday through Friday from 9am to 12:30pm and 2 to 6pm, Saturday from 9am to 12:30pm.

Anglers will find plenty of **fishing** opportunities (especially salmon, pikeperch, and trout) at Lake Hintersee and the rivers Ramsauer Ache and Königsseer Ache, although in most cases it's best to obtain a fishing permit. To acquire one, contact the Kurdirektion (tourist office) at Berchtesgaden, which will direct you to any of four different authorities, based on where you want to fish. For fishing specifically within the Hintersee, contact officials at the **Kurverwaltung,** Im Tal 2 (© 08657/98-89-20) at Ramsau, 12km (7½ miles) from Berchtesgaden.

Despite its obvious dangers, **hang gliding** or **paragliding** from the vertiginous slopes of Mount Jenner can be thrilling. To arrange it, contact **Para-Taxi,** Maximilianstrasse 15 (© 08652/948450). The headquarters for a loosely allied group of parasailing enthusiasts, the **Berchtesgaden Gleitschirmflieger** (© 08652/23-63) sometimes arranges communal paragliding excursions to which qualified newcomers are invited. Practice your **kayaking** or **white-water rafting** techniques on one of the many rivers in the area, such as the Ramsauer, Königisser, Bischofswiesener, and Berchtesgadener Aches. For information and options, contact the above-mentioned **Outdoor Club Berchtesgaden.**

VISITOR INFORMATION For tourist information, contact the **Kurverwaltung und Verkehrsamt,** Richard-Strauss-Platz (✆ **08821/180-700**), open Monday through Saturday from 8am to 6pm, Sunday from 10am to noon.

GETTING AROUND An unnumbered municipal bus services the town, depositing passengers at Marienplatz or the Bahnhof, from where you can walk to all central hotels. This free bus runs every 15 minutes.

WHERE TO STAY

Gästehaus Trenkler *Value* For a number of years, Frau Trenkler has made travelers feel well cared for in her quiet, centrally located guesthouse. She rents four doubles, each with shower and sink. Each duvet-covered bed is equipped with a good mattress. Rooms range from small to medium, and corridor bathrooms are adequate and tidily maintained.

Kreuzstrasse 20, 82467 Garmisch-Partenkirchen. ✆ 08821/34-39. Fax 08821/15-67. www.gaestehaus-trenkler.de. 4 units with shower. 60€ ($69) double. Rates include continental breakfast. No credit cards. Free parking. Bus: Eibsee no. 1. *In room:* No phone.

Post-Hotel Partenkirchen ✦ This is one of the town's most prestigious hotels, especially with the asset of its unusually fine restaurant (see "Where to Dine," below). The U-shaped and handsomely furnished rooms are generally medium size. Duvets rest on comfortable beds, mostly doubles or twins. Bathrooms are handsomely maintained with tub/shower combos and deluxe toiletries. The balconies overlook a garden and offer a view of the Alps.

Ludwigstrasse 49, 82467 Garmisch-Partenkirchen. ✆ 08821/9363-0. Fax 08821/9363-2222. www.post-hotel.de. 59 units. 95€–150€ ($109–$173) double; 140€–200€ ($161–$230) suite. Rates include buffet breakfast. AE, DC, MC, V. **Amenities:** 2 restaurants; 4 dining rooms; bar; nearby golf, mountain climbing; laundry service/dry cleaning. *In room:* TV, minibar, hair dryer, safe.

Reindl's Partenkirchner Hof ✦✦ This special Bavarian retreat maintains a high level of luxury and hospitality. The annexes have balconies, and the main building has wraparound verandas, giving each room an unobstructed view of the mountains and town. All rooms have a cozy charm. The best are suites opening onto panoramic views of mountains or the garden. Rustic pine furniture adds to the allure of this place. Bathrooms are spacious with a tub/shower combo.

Bahnhofstrasse 15, 82467 Garmisch-Partenkirchen. ✆ 08821/943870. Fax 08821/9438-7250. www.reindls.de. 63 units. 100€–140€ ($115–$161) double; 170€–220€ ($196–$253) suite. AE, DC, MC, V. Parking 8€ ($9.20). Closed Nov 15–Dec 15. **Amenities:** Restaurant (see "Where to Dine," below); 2 bars; indoor covered pool; health club; Jacuzzi; sauna; massage; limited room service; laundry service; sunroom; solariums; open terrace; 2 gardens. *In room:* TV, dataport, minibar, hair dryer, safe.

Romantik-Hotel Clausing's Posthotel ✦ This hotel in the heart of town was originally built in 1512 as a tavern and has retained its *gemütlich* antique charm. In the early 1990s, it was radically upgraded. Rooms range from rather small and cozy Bavarian nests to spacious. The owners have installed comfortable furnishings, and bathrooms are beautifully kept and have tub/shower combos.

Marienplatz 12, 82467 Garmisch-Partenkirchen. ✆ 08821/7090. Fax 08821/70-92-05. www.clausings-posthotel.de. 47 units. 95€–205€ ($109–$236) double. DC, MC, V. Free parking. **Amenities:** 2 restaurants; historic tavern; bar; room service. *In room:* TV, minibar, hair dryer.

WHERE TO DINE

Flösserstuben INTERNATIONAL Regardless of the season, a bit of the Bavarian Alps always seems to flower amid the wood-trimmed nostalgia of this intimate restaurant close to the town center. You can select a seat at a colorful wooden table or on an ox yoke–inspired stool in front of the spliced saplings that decorate the bar. Moussaka and souvlakia, as well as sauerbraten and all kinds of Bavarian dishes, are abundantly available. You can also order Mexican tacos and tortillas or even *Tafelspitz* (boiled beef) from the Austrian kitchen. The menu isn't imaginative but is soul satisfying, especially on a cold night.

Schmiedstrasse 2. (✆ **08821/28-88**. Reservations recommended. Main courses 5€–17€ ($5.75–$20). AE, MC, V. Daily 11:30am–2:30pm and 5–10pm. Town bus.

Post-Hotel Partenkirchen ⭐ BAVARIAN   This hotel dining room is renowned for its distinguished cuisine. The interior rooms are rustic, with lots of mellow, old-fashioned atmosphere. You could imagine meeting Dürer here. Everything seems comfortably subdued, including the guests. The best way to dine is to order one of the fixed-price menus, which change daily, depending on the availability of seasonal produce. The a la carte menu is extensive, featuring game in the autumn. The Wiener schnitzel served with a large salad is the best we've had in the resort.

Ludwigstrasse 49. (✆ **08821/5-93-630**. Reservations required. Main courses 10€–25€ ($12–$29); fixed-price menus 20€–25€ ($23–$29). AE, DC, MC, V. Daily noon–2pm and 6–10pm.

Reindl's Restaurant ⭐ CONTINENTAL   Reindl's is first class all the way. Chic, charming, cozy, and alpine, it's filled with Teutonic antiques and the scent of sophisticated, freshly cooked food. It has aquariums for both salt- and fresh-water fish, for the storage of live lobsters, and live freshwater alpine fish, including trout. Menu items change seasonally and to some extent, daily, but enduring specialties include roasted rack of venison with forest mushrooms; zander with Riesling; and roasted saddle of lamb with garlic and herbs, and green beans and potatoes dauphnoise. About two-thirds of the 80-or-so seats are in an elegant main dining room; the remainder are within a richly paneled and very cozy *stube* that evokes alpine and Bavarian *gemütlichkeit*.

In the Partenkirchner Hof, Bahnhofstrasse 15. (✆ **08821/5-80-25**. Reservations required. Main courses 12€–24€ ($14–$28); fixed-price menus 15€–45€ ($17–$52). AE, DC, MC, V. Daily noon–3pm and 6:30pm–midnight. Closed Nov 10–Dec 15.

SEEING THE SIGHTS IN TOWN

The symbol of the city's growth and modernity is the **Olympic Ice Stadium,** Spiridon-Louis-Ring (✆ **089/30-67-21-50;** U-Bahn: 3 to Olympia-Zentrum), built for the 1936 Winter Olympics and capable of holding nearly 12,000 people. On the slopes at the edge of town is the much larger **Ski Stadium,** with two ski jumps and a slalom course. In 1936 more than 100,000 people watched the events in this stadium. Today it's still an integral part of winter life in Garmisch—the World Cup Ski Jump is held here every New Year.

Garmisch-Partenkirchen is a center for winter sports, summer hiking, and mountain climbing. In addition, the town environs offer some of the most panoramic views and colorful buildings in Bavaria. The **Philosopher's Walk** in the park surrounding the pink-and-silver 18th-century pilgrimage **Chapel of St. Anton** is a delightful spot to enjoy the views of the mountains around the low-lying town.

Exploring the Environs

One of the most beautiful of the alpine regions around Garmisch is the **Alpspitz region,** which hikers and hill climbers consider uplifting and healing for both body and soul. Here, you'll find alpine meadows, masses of seasonal wildflowers, and a rocky and primordial geology whose savage panoramas might strike you as Wagnerian. Ranging in altitude from 1,200m to 1,800m (4,000 ft.–6,000 ft.) above sea level, the Alps around Garmisch-Partenkirchen are accessible via more than 30 ski lifts and funiculars, many of which run year-round.

The most appealing and panoramic of the lot includes the Alpspitz (Oster-felderkopf) cable car that runs uphill from the center of Garmisch to the top of the Osterfelderkopf peak, at a height of 1,980m (6,500 ft.). It makes its 9-minute ascent at least every hour, year-round, from 8am to 5pm. The round-trip cost for nonskiers is 19€ ($22) adults, 14€ ($16) persons ages 15 to 17, and 9€ ($10) children ages 6 to 14. After admiring the view at the top, you can either return directly to Garmisch, or continue your journey into the mountains via other cable cars. If you opt to continue, take the Hochalm cable car across the high-altitude plateaus above Garmisch. At its terminus, you'll have two options, both across clearly marked alpine trails. The 20-minute trek will take you to the uppermost station of the Kreuzbergbahn, which will carry you back to Garmisch. The 75-minute trek will carry you to the upper terminus of the Hausbergbahn, which will also carry you back to Garmisch.

Another of the many cable-car options within Garmisch involves an eastward ascent from the center of Partenkirchen to the top of the 1,780m (5,850-ft.) Wank via the Wankbahn, for a round-trip price of 16€ ($18) adults, 11€ ($13) persons ages 16 to 18, and 9.50€ ($11) children. From here, you'll get a sweeping view of the plateau upon which the twin villages of Garmisch and Partenkirchen sit. With minor exceptions, the Wankbahn is open only between mid-April and early October. But during clement weather, the top of the Wank is a favorite with the patrons of Garmisch's spa facilities because the plentiful sunshine makes it ideal for the *Liegekur* (deck-chair cure).

If you plan on pursuing any of these options, it's to your advantage to invest in a day pass, the **Classic Garmisch Pass,** with which you'll be able to ride most of the cable cars in the region (including those to the above-recommended Alpspitz, Kreuzeck, and Wank, as well as several others that fan out over the Eckbauer and the Ausberg) as many times as you like within the same day. Priced at 34€ ($39) per person, the pass is available from any of the town's cable car stations. For information on all the cable car schedules and itineraries within the region, call © **08821/7970.**

Another option for exploring the environs of Garmisch involves an ascent to the top of the **Zugspitze,** at 2,960m (9,720 ft.) the tallest mountain in Germany, with a base set astride the Austrian frontier. Ski slopes begin at 2,650m (8,700 ft.). For a panoramic view over both the Bavarian and Tyrolean Alps, go to the summit. The first stage begins in the center of Garmisch by taking the cog railway to an intermediary alpine plateau (Zugspitzplatz). Trains depart hourly throughout the year from 7:39am to 2:15pm, although we recommend that you begin by 1:15pm (and preferably earlier) and not wait until the cog railway's final ascent from Garmisch. At Zugspitzplatz, you can continue uphill on the same cog railway to the debut of a high-speed, 4-minute ride aboard the Gletscherbahn cable car, the high-altitude conveyance you'll ride to the top of the Zugspitz peak. And if you absolutely want to glut yourself in alpine panoramas for a day, consider buying a round-trip ticket that will incorporate transit from the center of Garmisch via a network of cog railways and cable cars, to the summits of both the Zugspitze (the region's highest peak) and the nearby Alpspitze. The combination will provide views that stretch far into neighboring

Austria, depending on the cloud cover, and will require a full day's outing. The price of such an excursion will cost 44€ ($51) adults, 31€ ($36) persons 16 to 17, and 27€ ($31) children 5 to 15. Children under 4 ride free. For more information, call © **08821/720-688** or click on www.zugspitze.de.

MITTENWALD ⭑

Seeming straight out of *The Sound of Music,* the year-round resort of Mittenwald lies in a pass in the Karwendel Range, 18km (11 miles) southeast of Garmisch-Partenkirchen. Especially noteworthy and photogenic are the painted Bavarian houses with overhanging eaves. Even the baroque church tower is covered with frescoes. On the square stands a monument to Mathias Klotz, who introduced violin making to Mittenwald in 1684. The town is a major international center for this highly specialized craft.

ESSENTIALS
GETTING THERE   By Train   Mittenwald lies on the express rail line between Munich and Innsbruck and can be reached by almost hourly train service from Munich (trip time: 1½–2 hr.). Call © **0800/1-50-70-90** for information.

By Bus   Regional bus service from Garmisch-Partenkirchen and nearby towns is frequent; call **RVO Regionalverkehr Oberbayern** at Garmisch (© **08821/94-82-74** for information).

By Car   Access by car is via A-95 Autobahn from Munich.

VISITOR INFORMATION   Contact the **Kurverwaltung und Verkehrsamt,** Dammkarstrasse 3 (© **08823/3-39-81**), open Monday through Friday from 8:30am to noon and 1 to 5pm, Saturday from 9am to noon.

WHERE TO STAY
Die Alpenrose   In the village center at the foot of a rugged mountain, this inn is covered with decorative designs and window boxes holding flowering vines. The main building, a former 14th-century monastery, is much more desirable than the more functionally furnished annex, the Bichlerhof. Rooms in the main building are very charming, with their old-fashioned farmhouse cupboards and dark wood paneling. The private bathrooms are well kept but a bit small, with shower stalls.

Obermarkt 1, 82481 Mittenwald. © **08823/92-700.** Fax 08823/37-20. www.hotel-alpenrose-mittenwald.de. 19 units. 66€–85€ ($76–$98) double. Rates include buffet breakfast. AE, DC, MC, V. Free parking. **Amenities:** Restaurant; bar; limited room service. *In room:* TV, minibar, hair dryer.

Gästehaus Franziska 🅥alue   The Kufler family labors to make this the most personalized guesthouse in town. Each small room is comfortably furnished and beautifully maintained—first-rate beds feature crisp linen duvets. All have balconies with mountain views. Bathrooms are a bit small but inviting and tidy, with shower stalls. Breakfast is the only meal served. It's extremely difficult to obtain bookings from June 20 to October 2.

Innsbrucker-Strasse 24, 82481 Mittenwald. © **08823/92030.** Fax 08823/3893. 19 units. 74€–80€ ($85–$92) double; 82€–92€ ($94–$106) suite. Rates include buffet breakfast. AE, MC, V. Free parking. Closed Nov–Dec 15. *In room:* TV, dataport, minibar, tea/coffeemaker (suites only), safe.

Hotel Post ⭑   Dating from 1632, this hotel remains Mittenwald's finest address. A delightful breakfast is served on the sun terrace, with a view of the Alps; in cool weather you can enjoy a beer in the snug lounge-bar with its open fireplace. Rooms are comfortable but standard. Beds (twin or double) and mattresses are among the best in town. Bathrooms are small and contain shower stalls. The maids are especially helpful if you need something extra.

Obermarkt 9, 82481 Mittenwald. (℃) **08823/938-2333.** Fax 08823/938-2999. www.posthotel-mittenwald.de. 90 units. 86€–140€ ($99–$161) double; 140€–160€ ($161–$184) suite. Rates include buffet breakfast. MC, V. Free parking. **Amenities:** Wine tavern/restaurant; bar/lounge; indoor pool; sauna; massage; non-smoking rooms. *In room:* TV, dataport, minibar, hair dryer, safe.

WHERE TO DINE

Restaurant Arnspitze BAVARIAN   Housed in a modern chalet hotel on the outskirts, this is the finest dining room in town. The restaurant is decorated in the old style; the cuisine is solid, satisfying, and wholesome. You might order sole with homemade noodles or veal steak in creamy smooth sauce, then finish with one of the freshly made desserts. There's an excellent fixed-price lunch.

Innsbruckerstrasse 68. (℃) **08823/24-25.** Reservations required. Main courses 16€–21€ ($18–$24); fixed-price lunch 20€ ($23); fixed-price dinner 38€ ($44). AE. Thurs–Mon noon–2pm; Wed–Mon 6–9pm; closed Tues all day and Wed for lunch. Closed Oct 25–Dec 15.

SEEING THE SIGHTS

The town's museum has exhibits devoted to the evolution of violins and other string instruments. The **Geigenbau-und Heimatmuseum,** Ballenhausgasse 3 (℃ **08823/25-11**), is open Tuesday through Friday from 10am to 1pm and 3 to 6pm, Saturday and Sunday from 10am to 1pm. Admission is 2.50€ ($2.90) adults and 1.50€ ($1.75) children. The museum is closed from November 1 to December 20.

In the countryside, you are constantly exposed to the changing scenery of the Wetterstein and Karwendel ranges. Horse and carriage trips are available as well as coach tours from Mittenwald to nearby villages. In the evening there's typical Bavarian entertainment, often consisting of folk dancing and singing, zither playing, and yodeling, but you also have your choice of concerts, dance bands, discos, and bars. Mittenwald has good spa facilities, in large gardens landscaped with tree-lined streams and trout pools. Concerts during the summer are held in the music pavilion.

OUTDOOR ACTIVITIES

In winter, the town is a skiing center, but it remains equally active throughout the summer. Some 130km (80 miles) of paths wind up and down the mountains around the village, with chairlifts making the hiking trails readily accessible. Of course, where there are trails, there's mountain biking. A biking map is available from the tourist office (see above), and mountain-climbing expeditions are also available. You can always go swimming to cool off on a hot summer's day—the Lautersee and Ferchensee are brisk waters that, even in summer, might be for-feited by the fainthearted for the heated adventure pool in Mittenwald.

OBERAMMERGAU ✦

A visit to Oberammergau, 19km (12 miles) north of Garmisch-Partenkirchen, is ideal in summer or winter. It stands in a wide valley surrounded by forests and mountains, with sunny slopes and meadows. The world-famous **Passion Play** is presented here, usually every 10 years; the next one is scheduled for 2010. It has also long been known for the skill of its woodcarvers. Here in this village right under the Kofel, farms are still intact, and tradition prevails.

ESSENTIALS

GETTING THERE   By Train   The Oberammergau Bahnhof is on the Murnau–Bad Kohlgrum–Oberammergau rail line, with frequent connections in all directions. Murnau has connections to all major German cities. Daily trains from Munich take 2 hours. For information, call ✆ **0800/1-50-70-90.**

By Bus Regional bus service to nearby towns is offered by **RVO Regionalverkehr Oberbayern** in Garmisch-Partenkirchen (✆ **08821/948-274**). An unnumbered bus travels between Oberammergau and Garmisch-Partenkirchen.

By Car Take A-95 Munich-Garmisch-Partenkirchen Autobahn and exit at Eschenlohe (trip time: 1½ hr.).

VISITOR INFORMATION Contact the **Oberammergau Tourist Information Office,** Eugen-Papst-Strasse 9A (✆ **08822/92310**), open Monday through Friday from 8:30am to 6pm, Saturday from 9am to noon and 1 to 5pm.

SEEING THE SIGHTS

Oberammergau's most respected citizens include an unusual group, the woodcarvers, many of whom have been trained in the village's woodcarver's school. In the **Pilatushaus,** Ludwigthomstrasse (✆ **08822/92310**), you can watch local artists at work, including woodcarvers, painters, sculptors, and potters. Hours are May through October, Monday through Friday from 1 to 5pm. You'll see many examples of these art forms throughout the town, on the painted cottages and inns and in the churchyard. Also worth seeing when strolling through the village are the houses with 18th-century frescoes by Franz Zwink that are named after fairy-tale characters, such as "Hansel and Gretel House" and the "Little Red Riding Hood House."

Heimatmuseum, Dorfstrasse 8 (✆ **08822/94136**), has a notable collection of Christmas crèches, all hand carved and painted, dating from the 18th century through the 20th century. It's open mid-April to mid-October, Tuesday through Saturday from 2 to 6pm; off season, only on Saturday from 2 to 6pm. Admission is 2.50€ ($2.90) adults and 1.50€ ($1.75) children.

NEARBY ATTRACTIONS The Ammer Valley, with Oberammergau in the (almost) center, offers easy access to many nearby attractions. **Schloss Linderhof** ★★ (✆ **08822/920321**), designed as a French rococo palace, the smallest of Ludwig II's constructions, is open year-round. This is in many ways the most successful of his palaces. The gardens and smaller buildings here are even more elaborate than the two-story main structure. Especially outstanding is a Hall of Mirrors, set in white and gold panels, decorated with gilded woodcarvings. The king's bedchamber overlooks a Fountain of Neptune and the cascades of the garden. The palace is open daily April through September from 9am to 5:30pm, October through March from 10am to 4pm. Admission is 4.50€ to 7€ ($5.20–$8.05), free for children under 17. Buses arrive from Garmisch-Partenkirchen throughout the day. Motorists can leave Oberammergau following the road signs to Ettal, 5km (3 miles) away. From Ettal, follow the signs for another 5km (3 miles) to Draswang, at which point the road into Schloss Linderhof is signposted.

OUTDOOR ACTIVITIES

Numerous **hiking trails** lead through the mountains around Oberammergau to hikers' inns such as the **Kolbenalm** and the **Romanshohe.** You can, however, simply go up to the mountaintops on the Laber cable railway or the Kolben chairlift. Oberammergau also offers opportunities to tennis buffs, minigolf players, cyclists, swimmers, hang-gliding enthusiasts, and canoeists. The recreation center **Wellenberg,** with its large alpine swimming complex with open-air pools, hot water and fountains, sauna, solarium, and restaurant, is one of the Alps' most beautiful recreation centers.

WHERE TO STAY & DINE

Alte Post   This provincial inn in the village center with a wide overhanging roof, green-shuttered windows, and tables set on a sidewalk under a long awning, is the village social hub. The interior has storybook charm, with a ceiling-high green ceramic stove, alpine chairs, and shelves of pewter plates. Most of the rustic rooms have views. Wide, comfortable beds with giant posts range in size from cozy to spacious. Bathrooms are medium-size with a shower stall. Nonresidents are welcome to the thriving and excellent Bavarian restaurant.

Dorfstrasse 19, 82487 Oberammergau. ℂ **08822/91-00**. Fax 08822/910-100. 32 units. 55€–95€ ($63–$109) double. Rates include buffet breakfast. AE, DC, MC, V. Free parking. **Amenities:** Restaurant; nonsmoking rooms. *In room:* TV.

Hotel Café–Restaurant Friedenshöhe (*Value*)   This 1906 villa enjoys a beautiful location and is among the town's best bargains. Well-maintained rooms range from rather small singles to spacious doubles. Corner rooms are bigger, but bathrooms tend to be small, each with a shower stall. Even nonresidents join the townspeople who head for one of the four dining rooms, which has both indoor and outdoor terraces opening onto panoramic views, and serves Bavarian favorites.

König-Ludwig-Strasse 31, 82487 Oberammergau. ℂ **08822/35-98**. Fax 08822/43-45. www.friedenshöhe.com. 16 units. 60€–92€ ($69–$106) double. Rates include buffet breakfast. AE, DC, MC, V. Closed Nov–Dec 14. **Amenities:** Restaurant; bar. *In room:* TV on request.

Hotel Restaurant Böld   A stone's throw from the river, this well-designed chalet hotel is one of the town's premier choices. Rooms in both the main building and the annex have equally good beds, usually doubles or twins. Most rooms open onto balconies. The spotless bathrooms are medium-size with shower stalls. A tranquil atmosphere and attentive service await you here. The restaurant serves Bavarian and international fare.

König-Ludwig-Strasse 10, 82487 Oberammergau. ℂ **08822/91-20**. Fax 08822/71-02. 57 units. 82€–130€ ($94–$150) double. Rates include continental breakfast. AE, MC, V. Free outside parking; 5.50€ ($6.30) in the garage. **Amenities:** Restaurant; bar; sauna; solarium; whirlpool; limited room service; laundry service; nonsmoking rooms; rooms for those with limited mobility. *In room:* TV, minibar, hair dryer.

3 The Romantic Road ★ ★

No area of Germany is more aptly named than the Romantische Strasse. Stretching 290km (180 miles) from Würzburg to Füssen in the foothills of the Bavarian Alps, it passes through untouched medieval villages and 2,000-year-old towns.

The best way to see the Romantic Road is by car, stopping whenever the mood strikes you and then driving on through vineyards and over streams until you arrive at the alpine passes in the south. Frankfurt and Munich are convenient gateways. Access is by A-7 Autobahn from north and south, or A-3 Autobahn from east and west; A-81 Autobahn has links from the southwest. You can also explore the Romantic Road by train or bus, or by organized tour.

ROTHENBURG OB DER TAUBER ★ ★ ★

This city was first mentioned in written records in 804 as Rotinbure, a settlement *ob* (above) the Tauber River that grew to be a free imperial city, reaching its apex of prosperity under a famous Burgermeister, Heinrich Toppler, in the 14th century.

The place is such a gem and so well known that its popularity is its chief disadvantage—tourist hordes march through here, especially in summer, and the

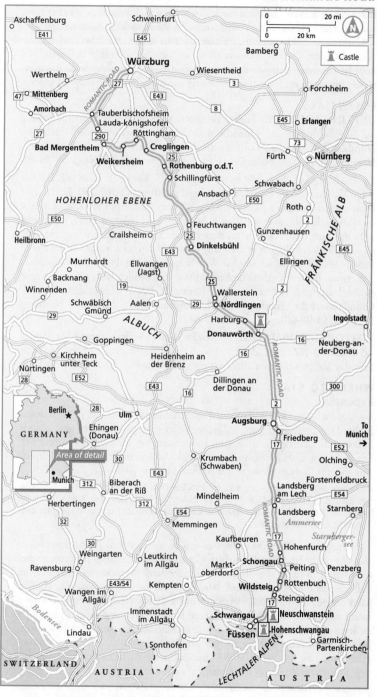

The Romantic Road

concomitant souvenir peddlers hawk kitsch. Even so, if your time is limited and you can visit only one town on the Romantic Road, make it Rothenburg.

Contemporary life and industry have made an impact, and if you arrive at the railroad station, the first things you'll see are factories and office buildings. But don't be discouraged. Inside those undamaged 13th-century city walls is a completely preserved medieval town, relatively untouched by the passage of time.

ESSENTIALS
GETTING THERE **By Train** Rothenburg lies on the Steinach-Rothenburg rail line, with frequent connections to all major German cities, including Nürnberg and Stuttgart. Daily trains arrive from Frankfurt (trip time: 3 hr.), Hamburg (5½ hr.), or Berlin (7 hr.). For information, call © 0800/1-50-70-90.

By Bus The bus that traverses the length of the Romantic Road is EB189 or EB189E, operated by **Deutsche Touring Frankfurt** (© 069/790-3261). Two buses operate along this route every day, but only from April to October. Know in advance that although you'll see a lot of romantic color en route, travel time to Rothenburg from Frankfurt via these buses is 5 hours because of frequent stops en route. Any travel agent in Germany or abroad can book you a seat on any of these buses, each of which stops at Würzburg, Augsburg, Füssen, and Munich.

Regional bus service that's limited to towns and hamlets within the vicinity of Rothenburg and the rest of the Romantic Road is provided by **OVF Omnibusverkehr Franken GmbH,** Kopernikusplatz 5, 90459 Nürnberg (© 0911/43-90-60).

VISITOR INFORMATION Contact **Stadt Verkehrsamt,** Marktplatz (© 09861/40-492), open Monday through Friday from 9am to noon and 1 to 6pm, Saturday and Sunday from 10am to 3pm (Nov–Mar it closes at 5pm weekdays).

WHERE TO STAY
Expensive
Burg Hotel ★ This old-fashioned timbered house at the end of a cul-de-sac is out of the Brothers Grimm. Its Tauber Valley view, picket fences, and window boxes exude German charm. Rooms are spread across three floors (no elevator). Extras include spacious bathrooms with tub/shower combos and large mirrors. Any room is likely to please, but if you want a view, ask for no. 7, 12, or 25.

Klostergasse 1–3, 91541 Rothenburg o.d.T. © 09861/94-89-0. Fax 09861/94-89-40. www.burghotel. rothenburg.de. 15 units. 120€–160€ ($138–$184) double; from 160€ ($184) suite. Rates include buffet breakfast. MC, V. Parking 7.50€ ($8.65). **Amenities:** Nonsmoking rooms; rooms for those with limited mobility. *In room:* TV, minibar, hair dryer, safe.

Eisenhut ★★ The most celebrated inn on the Romantic Road, Eisenhut is also one of the finest small hotels in Germany. Four medieval patrician houses were joined to make this distinctive inn. Demand for rooms is great, and the staff appears forever overworked. No two rooms are alike—yours may contain hand-carved, monumental pieces or have a 1940s Hollywood touch with a tufted satin headboard. All are enhanced by comforters and pillows piled high on state-of-the-art German beds. Extras include bedside controls, and spacious bathrooms outfitted with tub/shower combos and twin basins. The three-story galleried dining hall is one of the most distinctive in Germany, with a multi-tiered flagstone terrace on the Tauber.

Herrngasse 3–5, 91541 Rothenburg o.d.T. © 09861/70-50. Fax 09861/70-545. www.eisenhut.com. 79 units. 155€–205€ ($178–$236) double; 280€–340€ ($322–$391) suite. AE, DC, MC, V. Parking 9€ ($10). Closed Jan 3–Feb 28. **Amenities:** Restaurant; piano bar; Bavarian beer garden; limited room service; laundry service/dry cleaning; nonsmoking rooms. *In room:* TV, dataport, minibar, hair dryer.

Hotel Tilman Riemenschneider ⭐ This hotel's half-timbered facade rises directly above one of Rothenburg's busy historic streets. Its rear courtyard, adorned with geraniums, offers a cool and calm oasis from the heavy pedestrian traffic in front. Most rooms are medium-size though a few are small. All have well-kept bathrooms with tub/shower combos.

Georgengasse 11–13, 91541, Rothenburg o.d.T. ✆ **09861/9790.** Fax 09861/29-79. www.tilman-riemen schneider.de. 59 units. 105€–205€ ($121–$236) double. Rates include buffet breakfast. AE, DC, MC, V. Parking 6€ ($6.90). **Amenities:** Restaurant (see "Where to Dine," p. 449); lounge; fitness center; sauna; solarium; tanning bed; 2 whirlpools; limited room service; laundry service/dry cleaning; rooms for those with limited mobility. *In room:* TV, dataport, hair dryer.

Romantik Hotel Markusturm ⭐⭐ This is one of the charming nuggets of Rothenburg, without the facilities and physical plant of the Eisenhut, but a winner in its own right. When this hotel was constructed in 1264, one of Rothenburg's defensive walls was incorporated into the building. Some rooms have four-poster beds, and about half the bathrooms have tubs and showers. Many guests request room no. 30, a cozy attic retreat. The hotel employs one of the most helpful staffs in town.

Rödergasse 1, 91541 Rothenburg o.d.T. ✆ **09861/9-42-80.** Fax 09861/9-42-81-13. www.markusturm.de. 25 units. 125€–190€ ($144–$219) double. Rates include buffet breakfast. AE, DC, MC, V. Free parking. **Amenities:** Limited room service; babysitting; laundry service/dry cleaning; nonsmoking rooms. *In room:* TV, dataport, hair dryer.

Moderate

Hotel Gasthof Glocke *Value* South of the town center off Wenggasse, this hotel does not have the charm and style of the premier inns, but it's a good choice for those who want plain, simple, affordable rooms; a family atmosphere; and good food. The small rooms, though a bit institutional, are nonetheless comfortable and a good value for pricey Rothenburg. Bathrooms are exceedingly small, each with a shower stall.

Am Plönlein 1, 91541 Rothenburg o.d.T. ✆ **09861/95899-0.** Fax 09861/95899-22. 24 units. 89€–105€ ($102–$121) double. Rates include continental breakfast. AE, DC, MC, V. Parking 4.50€ ($5.20). Closed Dec 23–Jan 7. **Amenities:** Restaurant (see "Where to Dine," p. 448). **Amenities:** Nonsmoking rooms. *In room:* TV, hair dryer, safe.

Hotel Reichs-Küchenmeister ⭐ We consider this hotel, one of Rothenburg's oldest structures, near St. Jakobskirche, comparable with Tilman Riemenschneider and the Goldener Hirsch. The owners take special care with the guests' comfort. Rooms are nicely furnished with painted wooden furniture. Bathrooms are a bit small, each with a shower stall. An extra 25 rooms are available in the duller annex across the street.

Kirchplatz 8, 91541 Rothenburg o.d.T. ✆ **09861/9700.** Fax 09861/86-965. www.reichskuechenmeister.com. 45 units. 73€–110€ ($84–$127) double; 155€ ($178) suite for 2; 250€ ($288) suite for 5. Rates include buffet breakfast. AE, DC, MC, V. Parking 5€ ($5.75) in lot, 6.50€ ($7.50) in garage. **Amenities:** Restaurant (see "Where to Dine," below); wine bar; sauna; solarium; Turkish bath; whirlpool; nonsmoking rooms. *In room:* TV, dataport.

Inexpensive

Bayerischer Hof This little place, midway between the Bahnhof and the medieval walled city, doesn't even try to compete with the grand inns. And why should it? It's found a niche as a B&B, and although the outside looks rather sterile, many cozy warm Bavarian touches grace the interior. Beds are comfortable, and rooms are small; bathrooms come with shower stalls. Housekeeping is excellent, and the staff is most hospitable.

Ansbacherstrasse 21, 91541 Rothenburg o.d.T. ✆ **09861/60-63.** Fax 09861/86-56-1. www.bayerischer hof.com. 9 units. 60€–84€ ($69–$97) double. Rates include breakfast. MC, V. Free parking. Closed Jan. **Amenities:** Restaurant/bar. *In room:* TV.

WHERE TO DINE
Expensive

Louvre ✦ NEW GERMAN   Chef Bernhard Reiser is a man of multiple talents, and he has brought a lighter touch to the kitchens of Rothenburg with his *Neuer Küche* (new cuisine) style of cookery. His appetizers are dazzling, especially roasted cheesecake with spinach and red-wine sauce, or our favorite, orange-flavored pumpkin soup with grilled mussels. For a main course, try the perfectly cooked halibut with a potato sauce or else the roulade of guinea fowl with herb-infused cabbage and white-flour dumplings. The elegant cuisine is served against a mainly black decor with high-tech lighting and paintings on display. The wine list, for the most part, is good and fairly priced.

Klingengasse 15. © 09861/87809. Reservations required. Main courses 25€–28€ ($29–$32); fixed-price menu 49€–85€ ($56–$98). AE, MC, V. Daily 6pm–1am.

Moderate

Baumeisterhaus ✦ FRANCONIAN   Right off Marktplatz, the Baumeisterhaus is housed in an antique patrician residence, built in 1596. It has Rothenburg's most beautiful courtyard (which only guests can visit), with colorful murals, serenely draped by vines. Frankly, although the menu is good, the romantic setting is better. The food, for the most part, is rib-sticking fare beloved of Bavarians, including roast suckling pig with potato dumplings, and one of the chef's best dishes, *sauerbraten* (braised beef marinated in vinegar), served with *spaetzle* (small flour dumplings).

Obere Schmiedgasse 3. © **09861/94-700.** Reservations required for courtyard tables. Main courses 10€–18€ ($12–$21). AE, DC, MC, V. Wed–Mon 11am–7:30pm. Closed mid-Nov and mid-Mar.

Ratsstube FRANCONIAN   This restaurant enjoys a position right on the market square, one of the most photographed spots in Germany. It's a bustling center of activity throughout the day—a day that begins when practically every Rothenburger stops by for coffee. Inside, a true tavern atmosphere prevails with hardwood chairs and tables, vaulted ceilings, and pierced copper lanterns. Downstairs you'll find a wine bar offering live music nightly. The a la carte menu of Franconian wines and dishes includes sauerbraten and venison, both served with fresh vegetables and potatoes. For dessert, you can order homemade Italian ice cream and espresso. This is a longtime favorite of those who prefer typical Franconian cookery without a lot of fuss and bother. If you arrive at 9am, the staff will serve you an American breakfast.

Marktplatz 6. © **09861/55-11.** Reservations recommended. Main courses 10€–15€ ($12–$17). MC, V. Mon–Sat 9am–10pm; Sun 9am–6pm.

Reichs-Küchenmeister FRANCONIAN   The main dishes served here are the type Bavarians have loved for years, including sauerbraten, or pork tenderloin; white herring and broiled salmon are also available. The *Lebensknodel* (liver dumpling) or goulash soup is perfect for cold days. The chef makes one of the best Wiener schnitzels in town. The restaurant is near St. Jakobskirche and has a typical Weinstube decor, along with a garden terrace and a *Konditorei* (cake shop). Service is warm and efficient.

Kirchplatz 8. © 09861/9700. Reservations required. Main courses 11€–19€ ($12–$22). AE, DC, MC, V. Daily 7:30am–10pm.

Inexpensive

Hotel Gasthof Glocke FRANCONIAN   This traditional hotel and guesthouse serves good-tasting regional specialties along with a vast selection of local wine. Meals emphasize seasonal dishes and range from a simple vegetarian plate to lobster. If your expectations aren't too high, you'll probably enjoy this good regional cookery. Service is polite and attentive.

Am Plönlein 1. ℂ 09861/958-990. Reservations recommended. Main courses 6.90€–19€ ($7.95–$22). AE, DC, MC, V. Daily 11am–2pm; Mon–Sat 6–9:30pm. Closed Dec 24–Jan 6.

Tilman Riemenschneider FRANCONIAN   This traditional old Weinstube is housed in one of Rothenburg's finest hotels. The old-fashioned cookery is served in generous portions. You might begin with air-dried beef or smoked filet of trout, then follow it with poached eel, halibut steak, or loin of pork. Everything is served in generous portions with good results.

Georgengasse 11. ℂ 09861/9790. Main courses 8.50€–25€ ($9.80–$29); fixed-price menu 15€–21€ ($17–$24). AE, DC, MC, V. Daily 11:30am–2pm and 6–9pm.

EXPLORING THE MEDIEVAL TOWN

The **Rathaus (Town Hall)** ⭐ on the Marktplatz (ℂ 09861/404-92), along with the Jakobskirche, are the outstanding attractions, along with the medieval walls. The town hall consists of two sections: The older, Gothic section dates from 1240. From the 50m (165-ft.) tower of the Gothic hall, you get an overview of the town. The belfry has quite a history—in 1501, fire destroyed part of the building, and after that the belfry became a fire watchtower. Guards had to ring the bell every quarter-hour to prove they were awake and on the job. The newer Renaissance section, built in 1572, is decorated with intricate friezes, an oriel extending the building's full height, and a large stone portico opening onto the square. The octagonal tower at the center of the side facing the square contains a grand staircase leading to the upper hall. On the main floor is the large courtroom.

Admission to the tower is 1€ ($1.15) adults, .50€ (60¢) children. The Rathaus is open Monday through Friday from 8am to 6pm. The tower is open April through October, daily from 9:30am to 12:30pm and 1 to 5pm; November through March, Saturday, Sunday, and holidays only, from noon to 3pm.

St. Jakobskirche (Church of St. James), Klostergasse 15 (ℂ 09861/70-06-20), contains the famous *Altar of the Holy Blood* ⭐⭐ (west gallery), a masterpiece of the Würzburg sculptor and woodcarver Tilman Riemenschneider (1460–1531). The Rothenburg Council commissioned the work in 1499 to provide a worthy setting for the *Reliquary of the Holy Blood.* The relic is contained in a rock-crystal capsule set in the reliquary cross (about 1270) in the center of the shrine, and beneath it the scene of *The Last Supper* makes an immediate impact on the viewer—Jesus is giving Judas the morsel of bread, marking him as the traitor. The altar wings show (left) the *Entry of Christ into Jerusalem* and (right) *Christ Praying in the Garden of Gethsemane.*

The vertical Gothic church has three naves. The choir, dating from 1336, is the oldest section and has fine late Gothic painted-glass windows. To the left is the tabernacle (1390–1400), which was recognized as a "free place," a sanctuary for condemned criminals where they could not be touched. It's open April through October, Monday through Saturday from 9am to 5:30pm, Sunday from 11am to 5:30pm. In December, it's open daily from 10am to 5pm. In November and January through March, it's open daily from 10am to noon and 2 to 4pm. Admission costs 1.55€ ($1.80) adults, and .50€ (60¢) children under 6 and students of any age.

Also of interest is the **Reichsstadtmuseum** ⭐, Klosterhof 5 (ℂ 09861/939-043). This is Rothenburg's historical collection, housed in a 13th-century

Dominican nunnery with well-preserved cloisters. You'll find on display here an enormous tankard that holds 3.5 liters (3½ qt.), whose story has echoes all over the city. In 1631, during the Thirty Years' War, the Protestant city of Rothenburg was captured by General Tilly, commander of the armies of the Catholic League. He promised to spare the town from destruction if one of the town burghers would drink the huge tankard full of wine in one draft. Burgermeister Nusch accepted the challenge and succeeded, and so saved Rothenburg. There's a festival every spring at Whitsuntide to celebrate this event. Among the exhibits is the 1494 *Rothenburg Passion* series, 12 pictures by Martinus Schwartz, and works by English painter Arthur Wasse (1854–1930), whose pictures managed to capture in a romantic way the many moods of the city. Admission to the museum is 3€ ($3.45) adults, 2€ ($2.30) children; a family card costs 5.50€ ($6.35). The museum is open daily April through October from 9:30am to 5:30pm, November through March from 1 to 4pm.

Kriminal Museum, Burggasse 3 (© **09861/53-59**), is the only one of its kind in Europe. The museum's four floors display 10 centuries of legal history and provide insight into the life, laws, and punishments of medieval days. You'll see chastity belts, shame masks, a shame flute for bad musicians, and a cage for bakers who baked bread too small or too light. It's open daily April through October from 9:30am to 6pm; November and January through February from 2 to 4pm; and December and March from 10am to 4pm. Admission is 3.50€ ($4.05) adults and 1.90€ ($2.20) children 6 and older.

DINKELSBÜHL ⭑

Still surrounded by medieval walls and towers, Dinkelsbühl is straight out of a Brothers Grimm story, even down to the gingerbread, which is one of its main products. Behind the ancient 10th-century walls is a town that retains its quiet, provincial ambience in spite of the many tourists who come here. The cobblestone streets are lined with fine 16th-century houses, many with carvings and paintings depicting biblical and mythological themes. In the center of town, on Marktplatz, is the late Gothic **Georgenkirche** (1448–99). It contains a carved Holy Cross Altar and pillar sculptures.

ESSENTIALS
GETTING THERE **By Train** The nearest train station is in Ansbach, which has several trains arriving daily from Munich and Frankfurt (trip time: 2½–3 hr.), Nürnberg, and Stuttgart. From Ansbach, Dinkelsbühl can be reached by bus. For information, call © **0800/1-50-70-90.**

By Bus For long-distance bus service along the Romantic Road, see "Rothenburg ob der Tauber," earlier in this chapter. Regional buses link Dinkelsbühl with local towns. There are three to five buses a day to Rothenburg and five or six to Nördlingen.

By Car Take B-25 south from Rothenburg.

VISITOR INFORMATION Contact **Stadt Verkehrsamt,** Marktplatz (© **09851/9-02-40**). April through October, hours are Monday to Friday from 9am to 6pm, Saturday from 10am to 4pm, and Sunday from 10am to noon. November to March, it's open Monday to Friday 10am to noon and 1 to 5pm, Saturday 10am to noon.

SPECIAL EVENTS The **Kinderzeche (Children's Festival),** held for 10 days in July, commemorates the saving of the village by its children in 1632. According to the story, the children pleaded with conquering Swedish troops to leave their town without pillaging and destroying it—and got their wish. The pageant includes concerts given by the local boys' band dressed in historic military costumes.

WHERE TO STAY & DINE

Blauer Hecht   The inn is the best of a lackluster lot. The elegant pale beige facade 17th-century building was once a brewery tavern, and the owners still brew in the backyard. The midsize rooms are tranquil and sunny. Most rooms have bedside controls. Bathrooms are routine but well maintained, each with a shower stall. Good regional meals are served in the hotel restaurant/bar open to nonresidents.

Schweinemarkt 1, 91150 Dinkelsbühl. © 09851/5810. Fax 09851/581170. www.hotel-blauer-hecht.de. 43 units. 85€–115€ ($98–$132) double. Rates include continental breakfast. AE, DC, MC, V. Free parking. **Amenities:** Restaurant/bar; laundry service; indoor pool; sauna; steam bath; nonsmoking rooms. *In room:* TV, minibar, safe.

Deutsches Haus   The facade of Deutsches Haus, which dates from 1440, is rich in painted designs and festive woodcarvings. Rooms are unique; you may find yourself in one with a ceramic stove or in another with a Biedermeier desk. For the tradition minded, there're no finer rooms in town. Bathrooms are spotless, often with a tub/shower combo. The Altdeutsches Restaurant, one of the finest in Dinkelsbühl, is intimate and convivial, serving regional dishes.

Weinmarkt 3, 91550 Dinkelsbühl. © 09851/60-58. Fax 09851/79-11. www.deutsches-haus-dkb.de. 10 units. 115€ ($132) double; 135€ ($155) suite. Rates include continental breakfast. AE, MC, V. Parking 8€ ($9). Closed Jan 8–Feb 1. **Amenities:** Restaurant. *In room:* TV, minibar, hair dryer.

Eisenkrug   This is a hit-or-miss choice, letting you stay in traditional style or sterile modernity. The stylish rooms are filled with engaging old furniture. A newer wing contains the most contemporary rooms, all rather standard and modern, each medium in size. The older rooms offer more charm, although some tend to be smaller. Some beds are canopied, and housekeeping and maintenance are top-notch. Bathrooms vary from small to spacious; all but one have a shower instead of a tub. Consider Mediterrano for your dining choice even if you're a nonresident. The chef invents his own recipes and carefully selects ingredients that go into his market-fresh cuisine. His is an indigenous Franconian-Swabian approach, with many innovative touches. The superior wine cellar has some really unusual vintages.

Dr.-Martin-Luther-Strasse 1, 91550 Dinkelsbühl. © 09851/57700. Fax 09851/577070. www.hotel-eisenkrug.de. 13 units. 81€–100€ ($93–$115) double. Rates include continental breakfast. MC, V. Free parking. **Amenities:** 2 restaurants. *In room:* TV, minibar, hair dryer.

Goldene Rose *(Value)*   A landmark in the heart of this village since 1450, the intricately timbered Goldene Rose rises three stories, with a steeply pitched roof and overflowing window boxes. Although it doesn't match the impressive standards of the Eisenkrug, it is one of Dinkelsbühl's best values. The small- to medium-size rooms have been modernized in a style more institutional and functional than traditional Bavarian. The more expensive rooms offer more charm. Bathrooms are rather small, but 10 have full tub and shower. The dining rooms are country-inn style. The a la carte menu (in English) offers such tempting items as tenderloin of wild hare flavored with hazelnuts, and rump steak. This is another good choice to consider even if you're a nonresident.

Marktplatz 4, 91550 Dinkelsbühl. © 09851/57-750. Fax 09851/57-75-75. www.hotel-goldene-rose.com. 63 units. 68€–126€ ($78–$145) double. Rates include continental breakfast. AE, DC, MC, V. Parking 4€ ($4.60) in lot, 8€ ($9.20) in garage. **Amenities:** Restaurant, bar. *In room:* TV, minibar, hair dryer.

NÖRDLINGEN ✿

One of the most irresistible and perfectly preserved medieval towns along the Romantic Road, Nördlingen is still completely encircled by its well-preserved 14th- to 15th-century **city fortifications.** You can walk around the town on the covered parapet, which passes 11 towers and five fortified gates set into the walls.

Things are rather peaceful around Nördlingen today, and the city still employs sentries to sound the message, *"So G'sell so"* ("All is well"), as they did in the Middle Ages. However, events around here weren't always so peaceful. The valley sits in a gigantic crater, the Ries. The Ries was once thought to be the crater of an extinct volcano; it is now known that a large meteorite was responsible. It hit the ground at more than 100,000 mph, the impact having the destructive force of 250,000 atomic bombs. Debris was hurled as far as Slovakia, and all plant and animal life within a radius of 160km (100 miles) was destroyed. This momentous event took place some 15 million years ago. Today it is the best-preserved and most scientifically researched meteorite crater on earth. The American Apollo 14 and 17 astronauts had their field training in the Ries in 1970.

ESSENTIALS

GETTING THERE   By Train   Nördlingen lies on the main Nördlingen-Aalen-Stuttgart line, with frequent connections in all directions (trip time: 2 hr. from Stuttgart and Nürnberg, 1 hr. from Augsburg). Call ✆ **0800/1-50-70-90** for information.

By Bus   The long-distance bus that operates along the Romantic Road includes Nördlingen; see "Rothenburg ob der Tauber," p. 444.

By Car   Take B-25 south from Dinkelsbühl.

VISITOR INFORMATION   Contact the **Verkehrsamt,** Marktplatz 2 (✆ **09081/43-80**). The office is open Easter through October, Monday through Thursday from 9am to 5pm and Friday from 9am to 3:30pm. The rest of the year, hours are Monday through Thursday from 9am to 6pm, Friday from 9am to 4:30pm, and Saturday from 9:30am to 1pm.

WHERE TO STAY

Astron Hotel Klösterle ✿   This is the best place to stay in town. In 1991, this 13th-century former monastery was renovated, a new wing added, and the entire complex transformed into the town's most luxurious hotel. Rated four stars by the government, it offers elevator access and a hardworking, polite staff. Rooms have excellent furnishings, lots of electronic extras, and large bathrooms with tub/shower combos and deluxe toiletries.

Am Klösterle 1, 86720 Nördlingen. ✆ **09081/88-054.** Fax 09081/870-8100. 97 units. 90€–145€ ($104–$167) double; 110€–160€ ($127–$184) suite. Rates include breakfast. AE, DC, MC, V. Parking 7.70€ ($8.85). **Amenities:** Restaurant; bar; fitness center; solarium; sauna; limited room service; laundry. *In room:* TV, dataport, minibar, hair dryer, safe.

Kaiser Hotel Sonne ✿   Next to the cathedral and the Rathaus is the Sonne, an inn since 1405. Among its guests have been Frederick III, Maximilian I, Charles V, and, in more recent times, the American Apollo astronauts. Many of the midsize rooms contain hand-painted four-posters to bring out the romantic in you. Others are regular doubles or twins. Goethe may have complained of the lack of comfort he found here, but you'll fare well. Bathrooms are fresh and immaculate, with tub/shower combos.

Marktplatz 3, 86720 Nördlingen. ✆ **09081/50-67.** Fax 09081/23-999. 43 units, 35 with bathroom. 86€ ($99) double without bathroom; 110€ ($127) double with bathroom; 140€ ($161) suite. Rates include breakfast and parking. AE, DC, MC, V. **Amenities:** Restaurant; bar; limited room service; babysitting; laundry/dry cleaning. *In room:* TV, minibar, hair dryer.

WHERE TO DINE

Meyer's Keller CONTINENTAL   The conservative, modern decor here seems a suitable setting for the restrained *neue Küche* of talented chef and owner Joachim Kaiser, adroit with both rustic and refined cuisine. The menu changes according to availability of ingredients and the chef's inspiration; typical selections are likely to include roulade of sea wolf and salmon with baby spinach and wild rice, or—a perfect delight—John Dory with champagne-flavored tomato sauce. The wine list is impressive, with many bottles quite reasonably priced.

Marienhöhe 8. (C) 09081/44-93. Reservations required. Main courses 16€–24€ ($18–$28); fixed-price meals 38€–65€ ($44–$75). AE, MC, V. Wed–Sun 11am–2pm; Tues–Sun 6–10pm. Local bus to Marktplatz.

SEEING THE SIGHTS

At the center of the circular Altstadt within the walls is **Rübenmarkt.** If you stand in this square on market day, you'll be swept into a world of the past—the country people have preserved many traditional customs and costumes here, which, along with the ancient houses, create a living medieval city. Around the square stand a number of buildings, including the Gothic **Rathaus.** An antiquities collection is displayed in the **Stadtmuseum,** Vordere Gerbergasse 1 (**(C) 09081/273-8230**), open Tuesday through Sunday from 1:30 to 4:30pm; closed November through February. Admission is 2.55€ ($2.95) adults and 1.55€ ($1.80) children.

The 15th-century Hallenkirche, the **Church of St. George,** on the square's northern side, is the town's most interesting sight and one of its oldest buildings. Plaques and epitaphs commemorating the town's more illustrious 16th- and 17th-century residents decorate the fan-vaulted interior. Although the original Gothic altarpiece by Friedrich Herlin (1470) is now in the Reichsstadt Museum, a portion of it, depicting the crucifixion, remains in the church. Above the high altar today stands a more elaborate baroque altarpiece. The church's most prominent feature, however, is the 90m (295-ft.) French Gothic tower, called the "Daniel." At night, the town watchman calls out from the steeple, his voice ringing through the streets. The tower is open daily April through October from 9am to 8pm. Admission is 1.55€ ($1.80) adults and 1€ ($1.15) children.

Rieskrater-Museum, Hintere Gerbergasse (**(C) 09081/273-8220**), documents the impact of the stone meteorite that created the Ries. Examine fossils from Ries Lake deposits and learn about the fascinating evolution of this geological wonder. Hours are Tuesday through Sunday from 10am to noon and from 1:30 to 4:30pm. Admission is 3€ ($3.45) adults; 1.50€ ($1.75) students, seniors, and large groups. Tours of the crater are possible through the museum.

EN ROUTE TO AUGSBURG

After Nördlingen, B-25 heads south to Augsburg. After a 19km (12-mile) ride you can stop to visit **Schloss Harburg** 🌟 (it's signposted), one of the best-preserved medieval castles in Germany. It once belonged to the Hohenstaufen emperors and contains treasures collected by the family over the centuries. It is open mid-March through September, Tuesday through Sunday from 10am to 5pm; October, Tuesday through Sunday from 10am to 4pm. Admission is 4.50€ ($5.20) adults and 3€ ($3.45) children, including a guided tour. For information call (**C) 09080/96860.**

After exploring the castle, continue 11km (6¾ miles) south to the walled town of **Donauwörth** 🌟, where you can stop to walk through the oldest part of

454 CHAPTER 7 · GERMANY

the town, on an island in the river, connected by a wooden bridge. Here the Danube is only a narrow, placid stream. The town's original walls overlook its second river, the Woernitz.

After a brief stopover, continue your southward trek for 48km (30 miles) to Augsburg, the largest city on the Romantic Road.

AUGSBURG ★★

Augsburg is near the center of the Romantic Road and the gateway to the Alps and the south. Founded 2,000 years ago by the Roman emperor Augustus, for whom it was named, it once was the richest city in Europe. Little remains from the early Roman period. However, the wealth of Renaissance art and architecture is staggering. Over the years, Augsburg has boasted an array of famous native sons, including painters Hans Holbein the Elder and Hans Holbein the Younger, and playwright Bertolt Brecht. It was here in 1518 that Martin Luther was summoned to recant his 95 theses before a papal emissary. Only 15% of the city was left standing after World War II, but there's still much here to intrigue. Today, Augsburg is an important industrial center on the Frankfurt–Salzburg Autobahn, and Bavaria's third-largest city after Munich and Nürnberg.

ESSENTIALS

GETTING THERE   By Train   About 90 Euro and InterCity trains arrive here daily from all major German cities. For information, call ℂ **0800/1-50-70-90.** There are 60 trains a day from Munich (trip time: 30–50 min.), and 35 from Frankfurt (3–4½ hr.).

By Bus   Long-distance buses (lines EB190 and 190A, plus line 189) service the Romantic Road. The buses are operated by **Deutsche Touring GmbH** at Am Römerhof in Frankfurt (ℂ **069/790-350** for reservations and information).

VISITOR INFORMATION   Contact **Tourist-Information,** Bahnhofstrasse (ℂ **0821/50-20-70**), Monday through Friday from 9am to 5pm, Saturday at Rathausplatz from 10am to 2pm; closed Sunday.

GETTING AROUND   The public transportation system in Augsburg consists of four tram and 31 bus lines covering the inner city and reaching into the suburbs. Public transportation operates daily from 5am to midnight.

WHERE TO STAY
Very Expensive

Steigenberger Drei Mohren ★★   This is one of the premier choices for a stopover along the Romantic Road and one of the top inns if you didn't book into the Eisenhut at Rothenburg. The original hotel, dating from 1723, was renowned in Germany before its destruction in an air raid. In 1956, it was rebuilt in a modern style. Decorators worked hard to create a decor that was both comfortable and inviting, with thick carpets, subdued lighting, and double-glazing at the windows. Rooms vary in size and appointments, however, ranging from some economy specials that are a bit small with narrow twin beds and showers (no tubs) to spacious, luxurious rooms with full shower and tub. Many rooms are smoke free, and most bathrooms are fairly spacious.

Maximilianstrasse 40, 86150 Augsburg. ℂ **800/223-5652** in the U.S. and Canada, or 0821/5-03-60. Fax 0821/15-78-64. www.augsburg.steigenberger.de. 106 units. 143€–165€ ($164–$190) double; 280€–650€ ($322–$748) suite. AE, DC, MC, V. Parking 12€ ($14). Tram: 1. **Amenities:** Restaurant; bar; golf by arrangement; sauna (in suites only); 24-hr. room service; babysitting; laundry service/dry cleaning; nonsmoking rooms. *In room:* TV, dataport, minibar, hair dryer, trouser press (in suites only).

Moderate

Dom Hotel   Although it may not have the decorative flair of the more expensive hotels such as Drei Mohren, the low rates and an indoor pool make this one of the most appealing choices in town. The hotel is a half-timbered structure, next to Augsburg's famous cathedral, and was built in the 15th century. Rooms on most floors are medium-size and nicely appointed, although we prefer the smaller attic accommodations where you can rest under a beamed ceiling and enjoy a panoramic sweep of the rooftops of the city. Bathrooms are small, with tub and shower combos. Only breakfast is served but it's a treat in a garden beside the town's medieval fortifications.

Frauentorstrasse 8, 86152 Augsburg. ℂ **0821/34-39-30.** Fax 0821/34-39-32-00. www.domhotel-augsburg.de. 52 units. 73€–121€ ($84–$139) double; 99€–134€ ($114–$154) suite. Rates include buffet breakfast. AE, DC, MC, V. Free street parking or 6€ ($6.90) garage. Tram: 2. **Amenities:** Indoor pool; sauna; solarium; laundry service; nonsmoking rooms. *In room:* TV, dataport, minibar, hair dryer, safe.

Hotel Am Rathaus *Value*   Many repeat guests consider this hotel's location just behind the town hall to be its best asset. Built in a three-story contemporary format in 1986, it offers comfortable, midsize rooms but small bathrooms with well-maintained showers. The hotel serves a very generous breakfast buffet. It may be short on style but it's long on value.

Am Hinteren Perlachberg 1, 86150 Augsburg. ℂ **0821/34-64-90.** Fax 0821/346-49-99. www.hotel-am-rathaus-augsburg.de. 32 units. 90€–110€ ($104–$127) double. Rates include breakfast. AE, DC, MC, V. Parking 9€ ($10). Tram: 1. **Amenities:** Bar; nonsmoking rooms. *In room:* TV, minibar, hair dryer.

Romantik Hotel Augsburger Hof ★★   Its main competitor, the Drei Mohren, still has more flair, but this hotel enjoys a comfortable runner-up slot. Originally built in 1767 in a solid, thick-walled design with exposed beams and timbers, the hotel was carefully restored in 1988. In the town center, it's a favorite for its traditional atmosphere and excellent food. In spite of the Renaissance interior, the rooms are completely up to date and not as romantic as the name of the hotel suggests. They range from cozy to spacious, each with a fine bed. Those overlooking the calm inner courtyard are more expensive than ones facing the street. Some bathrooms seemed crowded in as an afterthought, but each is beautifully maintained, containing a shower stall.

Auf dem Kreuz 2, 86152 Augsburg. ℂ **0821/34-30-50.** Fax 0821/343-0555. www.augsburger-hof.de. 36 units. 80€–130€ ($92–$150) double. Rates include buffet breakfast. AE, DC, MC, V. Parking 6€ ($6.90). Tram: 2. **Amenities:** Restaurant; lounge; sauna; limited room service; dry cleaning/laundry service; nonsmoking rooms. *In room:* TV, minibar, hair dryer.

Inexpensive

Hotel Garni Weinberger *Value*   One of the best budget accommodations in the area lies about 3km (1¾ miles) from the center along Augsburgerstrasse in the western sector. Rooms are small but well kept with good beds. The bathrooms are rather cramped with shower stalls, but housekeeping is excellent. The place is well patronized by bargain-hunting Germans.

Bismarckstrasse 55, 86391 Stadtbergen. ℂ **0821/24-39-10.** Fax 0821/43-88-31. 31 units. 60€ ($69) double. Rates include buffet breakfast. AE, MC, V. Closed Aug 15–30. Tram: 3. **Amenities:** Nonsmoking rooms. *In room:* Clock radio.

WHERE TO DINE

Die Ecke ★   FRENCH/SWABIAN   Dripping with atmosphere, this place seemingly dates from the Last Supper. Well, almost. At least it was founded in the year Columbus sighted the New World, and its guests have included Hans

Holbein the Elder, Wolfgang Amadeus Mozart, and, in more contemporary times, Bertolt Brecht, whose sharp-tongued irreverence tended to irritate diners of more conservative political leanings. The Weinstube ambience belies the skilled cuisine of the chef, which wins us over year after year. Breast of duckling might be preceded by pâté, and the filet of sole in Riesling is deservedly a classic. Venison dishes in season are a specialty—the best in town.

Elias-Holl-Platz 2. ✆ 0821/51-06-00. Reservations required. Main courses 14€–30€ ($16–$35); fixed-price dinner 38€ ($44) for 4 courses, 59€ ($68) for 6 courses. AE, DC, MC, V. Daily 11am–2pm and 5:30–10pm. Tram: 2.

Fuggerei Stube GERMAN/SWABIAN   Not as atmospheric as Die Ecke, this is nonetheless a local and enduring favorite with good food and decent prices. The large dining room, suitable for 60 persons, has welcomed diners since 1946, with very little change in the menu, the decor, or the ambience. Expect generous portions of well-prepared food such as sauerbraten, roasted pork, and pork schnitzel; game dishes such as venison, pheasant, and rabbit; and fish such as filet of sole served with boiled potatoes and parsley. The beer foaming out of the taps here is Storchenbräu, and most visitors find that it goes wonderfully with the conservative German specialties.

Jakoberstrasse 26. ✆ 0821/3-08-70. Reservations recommended. Main courses 8€–19€ ($9.20–$21); set-price menu 18€ ($20). AE, MC, V. Tues–Sun 12:30pm–2:30pm; Tues–Sat 5:30–11:30pm.

SEEING THE SIGHTS IN TOWN

Rathaus   In 1805 and 1809, Napoleon visited the Rathaus, built by Elias Holl in 1620. Regrettably, it was also visited by an air raid in 1944, leaving a mere shell of the building that had once been a palatial eight-story monument to the glory of the Renaissance. Its celebrated "golden chamber" was left in shambles. Now, after costly restoration, the Rathaus is open to the public.

Am Rathausplatz 2. ✆ 0821/3249-180. Admission 1.55€ ($1.80) adults, .75€ (85¢) children 7–14. Daily 10am–6pm. Tram: 1.

Dom St. Maria   The cathedral of Augsburg has the distinction of containing the oldest stained-glass windows in the world. Those in the south transept, dating from the 12th century, depict Old Testament prophets in a severe but colorful style. They are younger than the cathedral itself, which was begun in 944. You'll find the ruins of the original basilica in the crypt beneath the west chancel. Partially Gothicized in the 14th century, the church stands on the edge of the park, which also fronts the **Episcopal Palace,** where the basic Lutheran creed was presented at the Diet of Augsburg in 1530. The 11th-century bronze doors, leading into the three-aisle nave, are adorned with bas-reliefs of biblical and mythological characters. The cathedral's interior, restored in 1934, contains side altars with altarpieces by Hans Holbein the Elder and Christoph Amberger.

Hoher Weg. ✆ 0821/31-66-353. Free admission. Mon–Sat 7am–5pm; Sun noon–5pm. Tram: 1.

Church of St. Ulrich and St. Afra ✪   This is the most attractive church in Augsburg. It was constructed between 1476 and 1500 on the site of a Roman temple. The church and the dom, one Protestant, one Catholic, stand side by side, a tribute to the 1555 Peace of Augsburg, which recognized the two denominations, Roman Catholic and Lutheran. Many of the church's furnishings, including the three altars representing the birth and resurrection of Christ and the baptism of the church by the Holy Spirit, are baroque. In the crypt are the tombs of the Swabian saints, Ulrich and Afra.

Ulrichplatz 19. ✆ 0821/34-55-60. Free admission. Daily 9am–5pm. Tram: 1.

Schaezlerpalais   Facing the Hercules Fountain is the Schaezlerpalais, home to the city's art galleries. Constructed as a 60-room mansion between 1765 and 1770, it was willed to Augsburg after World War II. Most of the paintings are Renaissance and baroque. One of the most famous is Dürer's portrait of Jakob Fugger the Rich, founder of the dynasty that was once powerful enough to influence the elections of the Holy Roman emperors. Other works are by local artists Hans Burgkmair and Hans Holbein the Elder; Rubens, Veronese, and Tiepolo are also represented.

Maximilianstrasse 46. ℂ 0821/324-4125. Admission 3€ ($3.45) adults, 1.50€ ($1.75) children. Wed–Sun 10am–4pm. Tram: 1.

NEUSCHWANSTEIN ✰✰✰ & HOHENSCHWANGAU ✰✰: THE ROYAL CASTLES

The 19th century saw a great classical revival in Germany, especially in Bavaria, mainly because of the enthusiasm of Bavarian kings for ancient art forms. Beginning with Ludwig I (1786–1868), who was responsible for many Greek Revival buildings in Munich, this royal house ran the gamut of ancient architecture in just 3 short decades. It culminated in the remarkable flights of fancy of "Mad" King Ludwig II, who died under mysterious circumstances in 1886. In spite of his rather lonely life and controversial alliances, both personal and political, he was a great patron of the arts.

Although the name "Royal Castles" is limited to Hohenschwangau (built by Ludwig's father, Maximilian II) and Neuschwanstein, the extravagant king was responsible for the creation of two other magnificent castles, Linderhof (near Oberammergau) and Herrenchiemsee (on an island in Chiemsee).

In 1868, after a visit to the great castle of Wartburg, Ludwig wrote to his good friend, composer Richard Wagner: "I have the intention to rebuild the ancient castle ruins of Hohenschwangau in the true style of the ancient German knight's castle." The following year, construction began on the first of a series of fantastic edifices, a series that stopped only with Ludwig's death in 1886, only 5 days after he was deposed because of alleged insanity.

The nearest towns to the castles are **Füssen**, 3km (1¾ miles) away at the very end of the Romantic Road, and **Schwangau**, where accommodations can be found.

ESSENTIALS

GETTING THERE   By Train   There're frequent trains from Munich (trip time: 2½ hr.) and Augsburg (3 hr.) to Füssen. For information, call ℂ **01805/99-66-33.** Frequent buses travel to the castles.

By Bus   Long-distance bus service into Füssen from other parts of the Romantic Road, including Würzburg, Augsburg, and Munich, is provided by the **Deutsche Touring GmbH** bus EB189 or EB190A. For information and reservations, call ℂ **069/790-30** in Frankfurt, or look on the Web at www.deutsche-touring.com. Regional service to villages around Füssen is provided by **RVA Regionalverkehr Allgau GmbH** in Füssen (ℂ **08362/939-0505**). Its most important routing, at least for visitors to Füssen, includes about 14 orange, yellow, or white-sided buses that depart every day from Füssen's railway station for the village of Hohenschwangau, site of both Hohenschwangau Palace and Neuschwanstein Palace, a 10-minute ride. The cost of a one-way ticket to the village or to either of the two palaces is 1.45€ ($1.65). For more information, contact the Füssen tourist office.

By Car   Take B-17 south to Füssen, then head east from Füssen on B-17.

VISITOR INFORMATION   For information about the castles and the region in general, contact the **Kurverwaltung,** Kaiser-Maximilian-Platz 1, Füssen (② 08362/938-50), open Monday through Friday from 8am to noon and 2 to 5pm, Saturday from 10am to noon. Information is also available at the Kurverwaltung, Rathaus, Münchenerstrasse 2, Schwangau (② 08362/8-19-80). It's open Monday through Friday from 8am to 12:30pm and 1:30 to 5pm.

WHERE TO STAY
In Hohenschwangau

Hotel Müller Hohenschwangau   As if the yellow walls, green shutters, and gabled alpine detailing of this hospitable inn weren't incentive enough, its location near the foundation of Neuschwanstein Castle makes it even more alluring. Mid-size rooms are inviting and have a bit of Bavarian charm, each with a good bed. The shower-only bathrooms are spotless. Nature lovers usually enjoy hiking the short distance to nearby Hohenschwangau Castle. All rooms are nonsmoking.

Alpseestrasse 16, 87645 Hohenschwangau. ② **08362/8-19-90.** Fax 08362/81-99-13. www.hotel-mueller.de. 41 units. 120€–160€ ($138–$184) double; 230€ ($265) suite. Rates include buffet breakfast. AE, DC, MC, V. Free parking. Closed Jan–Feb. **Amenities:** 4 restaurants; bar; limited room service . *In room:* TV, hair dryer, minibar (in some).

Schlosshotel Lisl and Jägerhaus   This graciously styled villa and its annex across the street sit in a narrow valley, surrounded by their own gardens. Most rooms have a view of at least one of the two royal castles, and some rooms open onto views of both. We prefer the rooms in the main building to the more sterile annex, but all are comfortable and have good furnishings. Bathrooms, though small, are adequate, with shower stalls.

Neuschwansteinstrasse 1–3, 87645 Hohenschwangau. ② **08362/88-70.** Fax 08362/81-107. www.neuschwanstein-hotels.de. 47 units. 110€–160€ ($127–$184) double; 200€ ($230) suite. AE, DC, MC, V. Free parking. Closed Dec 21–26. **Amenities:** 2 restaurants; bar; nonsmoking rooms. *In room:* TV, minibar, safe (in some).

In or Near Füssen

AlstadHotel Zum Hechten   Family owners have maintained this impeccable guesthouse for generations—it's one of the oldest (and most comfortable) in town. In spring, you'll open your window to a flower box of geraniums, and feel like Gretel (or Hansel) getting ready to milk the cows. Rooms are small to medium-size; the bathrooms are spotless but a bit cramped, containing shower stalls. Corridor bathrooms are adequate and well maintained.

Ritterstrasse 6, 87629 Füssen. ② **08362/91-600.** Fax 08362/91-6099. www.hotel-hechten.com. 35 units, 33 with bathroom. 60€–65€ ($69–$75) double without bathroom; 78€–85€ ($90–$98) double with bathroom. Rates include buffet breakfast. AE, V. Free parking. **Amenities:** 2 restaurants. *In room:* TV.

Hotel Christine   The Christine, 5 minutes by taxi from the train station in Füssen, is one of the best local choices for accommodations. The staff spends the winter months refurbishing the rooms so they'll be fresh and sparkling for spring visitors. A Bavarian charm pervades the hotel, and rooms are cozy, though hardly fit for King Ludwig. Each is well maintained and supplied with decent furnishings. The shower-only bathrooms are a bit cramped. Breakfast, the only meal offered, is served on beautiful regional china as classical music plays in the background.

Weidachstrasse 31, 87629 Füssen. ② **08362/72-29.** Fax 08362/94-05-54. 13 units. 95€–130€ ($109–$150) double. Rates include breakfast. V. Closed Jan 15–Feb 15. *In room:* TV, minibar.

Steig Mühle ✿ *Value*   Owners and hosts Gunter and Nedwig Buhmann like things to be cozy, and their chaletlike guesthouse is almost a cliché of Bavarian charm. The rooms open onto views of the lake or the mountains, and many have their own balconies. Each room has been outfitted with double or twin beds. Private bathrooms (shower only) are well kept. There aren't a lot of frills, but the place offers one of the most exceptional hotel values in the area.

Alte Steige 3, 87629 Weissensee-Oberkirch. © 08362/91-76-0. Fax 08362/31-48. www.steigmuehle.de. 24 units. 52€–58€ ($60–$67) double. Rates include buffet breakfast. No credit cards. Free outside parking; 3€ ($3.45) in garage. From Füssen, take Rte. B310 north toward Kempten, a 5-min. drive. *In room:* TV.

WHERE TO DINE

Fischerhütte SEAFOOD   In Hopfen am See, at the edge of the lake within sight of dramatic mountain scenery 5km (3 miles) northwest of Füssen, lie four old-fashioned dining rooms, plus a terrace in summer. As the name "Fisherman's Cottage" suggests, the establishment specializes in an array of international fish dishes: half an Alaskan salmon (for two); a garlicky version of French bouillabaisse; fresh alpine trout, pan-fried or with aromatic herbs in the style of Provence; North Atlantic lobster; and grilled halibut. A few meat dishes are also offered, as well as tempting desserts. The food is well prepared and top rate.

Uferstrasse 16, Hopfen am See. © 08362/91-97-0. Reservations recommended. Main courses 14€–26€ ($16–$30). AE, DC, MC, V. Daily 10am–10:30pm.

Zum Schwanen SWABIAN/BAVARIAN   This small, old-fashioned restaurant serves a conservative yet flavor-filled blend of Swabian and Bavarian specialties. Good-tasting and hearty specialties include homemade sausage, roast pork, lamb, and venison. Expect robust flavors and a crowd of cheery diners who don't believe in the Weight Watchers packaged dinner.

Brotmarkt 4, Füssen. © 08362/61-74. Reservations required. Main courses 6€–14€ ($6.90–$16). MC, V. Tues–Sun 11:30am–2pm; Tues–Sat 5:30–9pm. Closed Nov.

VISITING THE ROYAL CASTLES

There are often very long lines in summer, especially in August. With 25,000 people a day visiting, the wait in peak summer months can be as long as 4 or 5 hours for a 20-minute tour. For more information on Neuschwanstein, call © 08362/8-10-35 or visit the website at **www.neuschwanstein.com**. For information on Hohenschwangau, call © 08362/8-11-27 or visit the website at **www.hohenschwangau.de**.

Neuschwanstein ✦✦✦

This is the fairy-tale castle of Ludwig II. Construction went on for 17 years, until the king's death, when all work stopped, leaving a part of the interior uncompleted. Ludwig lived here on and off for about 6 months from 1884 to 1886.

The doorway off the left side of the vestibule leads to the king's apartments. The study, like most of the rooms, is decorated with wall paintings showing scenes from the Nordic legends (which inspired Wagner's operas). The theme of the study is the Tannhäuser saga, painted by J. Aigner. The curtains and chair coverings are in hand-embroidered silk, designed with the Bavarian coat of arms.

From the vestibule, you enter the throne room through the doorway at the opposite end. This hall, designed in Byzantine style by J. Hofmann, was never completed. The floor, a mosaic design, depicts the animals of the world. The columns in the main hall are the deep copper red of porphyry.

The king's bedroom is the most richly carved and decorated in the entire castle— it took 4½ years to complete. Aside from the mural showing the legend of Tristan and Isolde, the walls are decorated with panels carved to look like Gothic windows. In the center is a large wooden pillar completely encircled with gilded brass sconces. The ornate bed is on a raised platform with an elaborately carved canopy.

The fourth floor of the castle is almost entirely given over to the **Singer's Hall,** the pride of Ludwig II and all of Bavaria. Modeled after the hall at Wartburg, where the legendary song contest of Tannhäuser supposedly took place, this hall is decorated with marble columns and elaborately painted designs interspersed with frescoes depicting the life of Parsifal.

The castle is open year-round, and in September, visitors have the additional treat of hearing Wagnerian concerts and other music in the Singer's Hall. For information and reservations, contact the tourist office in Schwangau, **Verkehrsamt,** at the Rathaus (℗ **08362/93-85-23**). The castle, which is seen by guided tour, is open daily April through September from 9am to 6pm, October through March from 10am to 4pm. Admission is 8€ ($9.20) adults, 7€ ($8.05) students and seniors over 65, free for children under 14.

Reaching Neuschwanstein involves a steep 1km (½-mile) climb from the parking lot of Hohenschwangau Castle—about a 25-minute walk for the energetic, an eternity for anybody else. To cut down on the climb, you can take a bus to Marienbrücke, a bridge that crosses over the Pollat Gorge at a height of 93m (305 ft.). From that vantage you, like Ludwig, can stand and meditate on the glories of the castle and its panoramic surroundings. If you want to photograph the castle, don't wait until you reach the top, where you'll be too close. It costs 3€ ($3.45) for the bus ride up to the bridge or 1€ ($1.15) if you'd like to take the bus back down the hill. From the Marienbrücke Bridge it's a 10-minute walk to Neuschwanstein over a very steep footpath that is not easy to negotiate for anyone who has trouble walking up or down precipitous hills.

The most colorful way to reach Neuschwanstein is by horse-drawn carriage, costing 6.50€ ($7.50) for the ascent, 2.50€ ($2.90) for the descent. However, some readers have objected to the rides, complaining that too many people are crowded in.

Hohenschwangau ★★

Not as glamorous or spectacular as Neuschwanstein, the neo-Gothic Hohenschwangau Castle nevertheless has a much richer history. The original structure dates back to the 12th-century knights of Schwangau. When the knights faded away, the castle began to do so too, helped along by the Napoleonic Wars. When Ludwig II's father, Crown Prince Maximilian (later Maximilian II), saw the castle in 1832, he purchased it and 4 years later had completely restored it. Ludwig II spent the first 17 years of his life here and later received Richard Wagner in its chambers, although Wagner never visited Neuschwanstein on the hill above.

The rooms of Hohenschwangau are styled and furnished in a much heavier Gothic mode than those in Ludwig's castle and are typical of the halls of medieval knights' castles. Also unlike Neuschwanstein, this castle has a comfortable look about it, as if it actually were a home, not just a museum. The small chapel, once a reception hall, still hosts Sunday Mass. The suits of armor and the Gothic arches set the stage. Among the most attractive chambers is the **Hall of the Swan Knight,** named for the wall paintings that tell the saga of Lohengrin.

Hohenschwangau is open April 1 to September from 8:30am to 5:30pm, off season from 9:30am to 4pm. Admission is 8€ ($9.20) adults, 7€ ($8.05) children 12 to 15 and seniors over 65, free for children under 12. Several parking lots nearby enable you to leave your car while visiting both castles. For ticket information for either castle, call ℗ **08362/930-830.**

Greece

by Sherry Marker

It doesn't take something special like the 2004 Summer Olympics in and around Athens to bring visitors to Greece, the first home of the Olympic Games. The "glory that was Greece" continues to lure visitors year-round, to such attractions as Olympia, where the games began; Delphi, with the magnificent temple of Apollo; Mycenae, where Agamemnon met his bloody death when he returned home from Troy; Epidauros, with its astonishingly well-preserved ancient theater—and, of course, the best-known symbol of Greece: the Acropolis in Athens. There's also a profusion of less well-known ancient sites such as Nemea, home to a carefully restored stadium and a handsome 4th-century-B.C. temple, several of whose columns were recently restored and re-erected. Greece also has a wealth of Byzantine monuments, including the churches of Daphni, just outside Athens, and Osios Loukas, near Delphi. But myths and monuments are only one aspect of the country's allure: Greece is also the quintessential vacationland of glorious beaches and towering mountain ranges. After sightseeing, you can laze the day away on a perfect beach— and then dance the night away in a cafe at the foot of the Acropolis or on one of the breathtakingly beautiful "isles of Greece."

1 Athens

Athens is the city that Greeks love to hate. They complain that it's too expensive, too crowded, and too polluted. The city does seem to be bursting at the seams: Some 40% of Greece's population lives here, with five million inhabitants, a rumored 17,000 taxis, and streets so congested you'll suspect that each of those five million Athenians has a car. Hopes are high that when the Metro subway system is completely finished, Athens's perpetual gridlock and endemic *nefos* (smog) will be substantially alleviated. A serendipitous by-product of the Metro excavations are handsome small museums in the Syntagma and Acropolis stations featuring antiquities unearthed during the dig. Throughout central Athens, pedestrians are enjoying the new network of walkways that will eventually link the major archaeological sites—although pedestrianizing important roads such as Dionyssiou Areopagitou has increased congestion on once-tranquil side streets. In short, as always in Athens, things are in a state of flux. So, why are you here? Because you, too, will probably soon develop a love-hate relationship with the city. You'll snarl at the traffic and resent the construction, all the while marveling at the view of the Acropolis as you stroll on Dionyssiou Areopagitou. You may find yourself fuming at a taxi driver who tries to overcharge you, and only moments later thanking the stranger who realizes you're lost and walks several blocks out of his way to take you where you're going.

Tips **Olympics Alert!**

If you plan to visit Greece around the time of the Athens Summer Olympics from August 13 to August 29, 2004, be forewarned: Hotel rooms in and around Athens for the Olympics were booked months before the games. In addition, many hotel rooms have been booked for several weeks before and after the games. In addition, 2004 is not shaping up to be a good year for a budget trip to Greece—*all* prices, including transportation, hotel, restaurant, and even museum and archaeological sites, are likely to be in considerable flux during and after the Olympics. The price hikes occasioned by the Olympics—rises of more than 100% are common—may be in place for some time to come. Nonetheless, some hotels and restaurants are braced to lower their prices if the Olympics do not bring the expected tourism boon to Greece. It remains to be seen if costs will return to pre-Olympics levels in 2005.

Allow yourself some time to make haste slowly in Athens. Your best moments may come at a small cafe, sipping a tiny cup of the sweet sludge that Greeks call coffee, or in the Plaka, getting hopelessly lost—only to find yourself in the shady courtyard of an old church. With a little planning, you should enjoy a comfortable stay in a good hotel, eat well in convivial restaurants, and leave Athens expecting to return, as the Greeks say, *tou chronou:* next year.

ESSENTIALS

BY PLANE   Athens International Airport Eleftherios Venizelos (© 210/353-0000; www.aia.gr), 27km (17 miles) northeast of Athens at Spata, opened in 2001. The good news is that this is a large, modern facility, with ample restrooms, interesting shops, and acceptable restaurants. The bad news is that unlike Hellinikon airport, which was virtually in Athens, the new airport is a serious slog from Athens. Although both the direct six-lane link road to Athens and the ring road that links up with the National Highway into the Peloponnese at Eleusis are officially complete, not all exits, entrances, and feeder roads are in place, nor are they accurately signposted. At present, allow at least an hour for the journey from the airport to Athens (and vice-versa) by bus or taxi; you may be pleasantly surprised that you need less time, but you may find yourself glad you allowed the full hour. A taxi into central Athens usually costs from 20€ to 30€ ($23–$35), depending on the time of day and traffic. Bus service to Syntagma Square or to Piraeus costs about 4€ ($4.60). Officially, there's one bus to Syntagma and one to Piraeus every 20 minutes. Bus and taxi stations are signposted at the airport. Keep in mind that the airport's website and official publications cannot always be relied on for accurate, up-to-date information. The airport has shops (including a good bookstore and stores carrying attractively priced perfumes and colognes) and restaurants—including the inevitable McDonald's.

When planning your carry-on luggage for the Athens airport, keep in mind that you may have quite a trek from your arrival point to the baggage-claim area. Tourist information, currency exchange, a post office, baggage storage (left luggage), and car rentals are available at the Arrivals level of the Main Terminal. ATMs, telephones, toilets, and luggage carts (1€/$1.15) are available at the baggage-claim area. There are also several free phones from which you can call for a porter. *Note:* Porters' fees are highly negotiable.

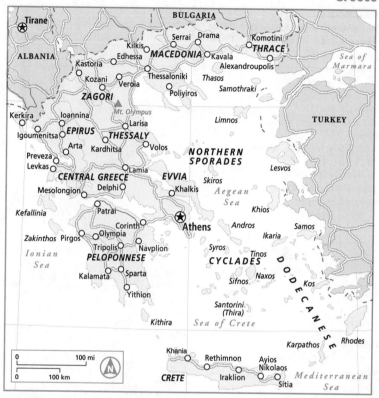

There have been frequent complaints that adequate information on arrivals, departures, cancellations, delays, and gate changes is not always posted on the flight information screens. Nonetheless, it is important to check these screens and at the information desks, as there are currently no flight announcements. Arrive at your gate as early as possible; gates are sometimes changed at the last minute, necessitating a considerable scramble to reach the new gate in time.

Note: Rumors continue to circulate that Olympic Airways will announce bankruptcy. Olympic has managed to pull itself back from the brink thus far, but it has had to cut back significantly on scheduled flights. Virgin Atlantic Airways has closed its Athens office, which has led to increased fares by other carriers that fly the London-Athens route.

Tips **Taxi Savvy**

If you decide to take a taxi, ask an airline official or a policeman what the fare should be, and let the taxi driver know you've been told the official rate before you begin your journey. If you're taking a taxi to the airport, try to have the desk clerk at your hotel order it for you well in advance of your departure. Many taxis refuse to go to the airport, fearing that they'll have a long wait before they get a return fare.

Athens

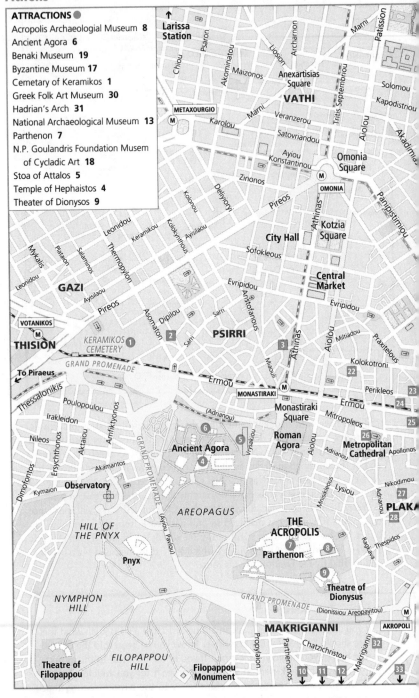

↑
Larissa Station

Chiou
Psaron
Akominatou
Maizonos

METAXOURGIO
Ⓜ
Karolou

Marni
Liosion
Archarnon
Marni
Patission

Anexartisias Square

VATHI

Solomou
Kapodistriou

Tritis Septembriou
Aiolou
Akadimias

Veranzerou
Satovriandou

Ayiou Konstantinou

Zinonos

Omonia Square

Ⓜ
OMONIA

Pireos
Athinas

Kotzia Square

Panipistimiou

City Hall

Sofokleous

Central Market

Leonidou
Keramikou
Kolokynthous
Ayisilaou
Deliyiori
Kolonou

Leonidou
Mykalis
Plataion
Salaminos
Thermopylon

Evripidou
Aristofanous

Evripidou

GAZI

Ayisilaou
Pireos

Asomaton
Dipilou
Sarri

Miaouli
Athinas
Aiolou
Miltiadou
Praxitelous

Kolokotroni

VOTANIKOS
Ⓜ

THISION

KERAMIKOS CEMETERY ①

② **PSIRRI**

③
22

To Piraeus
←

GRAND PROMENADE

Sarri

Ermou

Perikleos
23

Thessalonikis

MONASTIRAKI
Ⓜ

Ermou
24

Poulopoulou
Irakleidon

(Adrianou)

Monastiraki Square

Mitropoleos
25

Nileos
Ersychthonos
Aktaiou
Amfiktyonos

6
5

Roman Agora

Aiolou
Adrianou

26

Apollonos

Ancient Agora
4

Akamantos

Metropolitan Cathedral

Dimofontos
Kymaion

Observatory

GRAND PROMENADE (Ayiou Pavlou)

AREOPAGUS

Minsikleous
Lysiou

Nikodimou

27

Adrianou
PLAKA
28

HILL OF THE PNYX

THE ACROPOLIS

Pnyx

7 **8**
Parthenon

Ragkava
Thespidos

9

NYMPHON HILL

GRAND PROMENADE

Theatre of Dionysus
(Dionissiou Areopayitou)

Ⓜ
AKROPOLI

MAKRIGIANNI

Theatre of Filopappou

FILOPAPPOU HILL

Filopappou Monument

Propylaion
Parthenonos
Chatzichristou
Makrigianni

32

10 **11** **12**
↓ ↓ ↓

33
↓

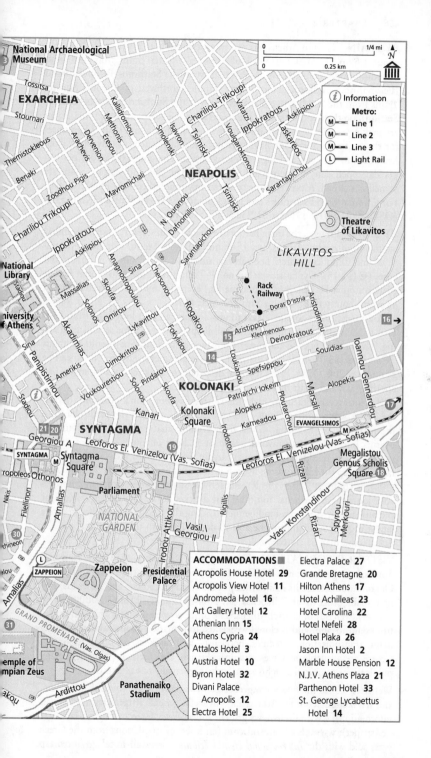

ACCOMMODATIONS ■
Acropolis House Hotel **29**
Acropolis View Hotel **11**
Andromeda Hotel **16**
Art Gallery Hotel **12**
Athenian Inn **15**
Athens Cypria **24**
Attalos Hotel **3**
Austria Hotel **10**
Byron Hotel **32**
Divani Palace
  Acropolis **12**
Electra Hotel **25**

Electra Palace **27**
Grande Bretagne **20**
Hilton Athens **17**
Hotel Achilleas **23**
Hotel Carolina **22**
Hotel Nefeli **28**
Hotel Plaka **26**
Jason Inn Hotel **2**
Marble House Pension **12**
N.J.V. Athens Plaza **21**
Parthenon Hotel **33**
St. George Lycabettus
  Hotel **14**

BY TRAIN Central Athens has two train stations; both are just off Dilyianni, about 1.5km (1 mile) northwest of Omonia Square. Trains from the west, including Eurail connections via Patra, arrive at the **Stathmos Peloponnissou (Peloponnese Station),** about 1.5km (1 mile) northwest of Omonia Square. Trains from the north arrive 3 blocks north at the **Stathmos Larissis (Larissa Station),** on the opposite side of the tracks from the Peloponnese Station. If you are making connections from one station to the other, allow 10 to 15 minutes for the walk. Both stations have currency-exchange offices usually open daily from 8am to 9:15pm; and luggage-storage offices charging 4€ ($4.60) per bag per day, open daily from 6:30am to 9:30pm. The cafe and waiting room are sometimes closed. A **taxi** into the center of town should cost about 6€ ($6.90). For information on schedules and fares, contact the **Greek Railroad Company (OSE;** ⓒ **210/512-4913** or 210/529-7777; www.ose.gr).

BY BOAT **Piraeus,** the main harbor of Athens's main seaport, 11km (6¾ miles) southwest of central Athens, is a 15-minute subway (Metro) ride from Monastiraki and Omonia squares. The subway runs from about 5am to midnight and costs 1€ ($1.15). The far-slower bus no. 040 runs from Piraeus to central Athens (with a stop at Filellinon off Syntagma Sq.) every 15 minutes between 5am and 1am and hourly from 1am to 5am, for .50€ (55¢).

You might prefer to take a **taxi** to avoid what can be a long hike from your boat to the bus stop or subway terminal. Be prepared for some serious bargaining. The normal fare on the meter from Piraeus to Syntagma should be about 7€ to 12€ ($8.05–$14), but many drivers simply offer a flat fare, which can be as much as 20€ ($23). Pay it if you're desperate, or walk to a nearby street, hail another taxi, and insist that the meter be turned on.

If you travel to Piraeus by hydrofoil *(Flying Dolphin),* you'll probably arrive at the **Zea Marina** harbor, about a dozen blocks south across the peninsula from the main harbor. Even our Greek friends admit that getting a taxi from Zea Marina into Athens can involve a wait of an hour or more—and that drivers usually drive a hard (and exorbitant) bargain. To avoid both the wait and the big fare, walk up the hill from the hydrofoil station and catch bus no. 905 for .50€ (50¢); it connects Zea to the Piraeus subway station, where you can complete your journey into Athens. You must buy a ticket at the small ticket stand near the bus stop or at a newsstand before boarding the bus. *Warning:* If you arrive late at night, you might not be able to do this, as both the newsstand and the ticket stand may be closed.

VISITOR INFORMATION **Tourist Office** In 2003, the **Greek National Tourism Organization (GNTO** or **EOT,** also known as the Hellenic Tourism Organization) closed its main office just off Syntagma Square at 2 Amerikis. The new main office is at 7 Tsochas St., Ambelokipi (ⓒ **210/870-0000;** www. gnto.gr), well out of central Athens. The office is open Monday through Friday from 8am to 3pm and is closed weekends. Information about Athens, free city maps, transportation schedules, hotel lists, and booklets on other regions of Greece are available in Greek, English, French, and German, although many publications on popular sights seem to be perpetually out of print.

Websites Sites include **www.greece.gr, www.culture.gr, www.phantis.com,** and **www.ellada.com** for Athens and Greece in general; **http://city.net** (Athens information); **www.athensnews.gr** (*The Athens News,* Greece's English-language newspaper); **www.eKathimerini.com** (an insert of translations from the Greek press sold with the *International Herald Tribune*); **www.all-hotels.gr/intro.asp**

> ### ⟮Tips⟯ Personal Safety
>
> In June 2003, The "Personal Safety Survey" done annually by the Mercer Human Resource Consulting Group listed Athens as the 10th worst-rated holiday destination in terms of personal safety. Pickpocketing, especially in the Plaka area, and even on the Acropolis, has become a real problem. Visitors to Greece—long one of the world's safest destinations—are now advised to exercise all the usual precautions of only carrying their passport, large sums of money, or credit cards with them on the street if these valuables are in a secure place.

(information on hotels); **www.dilos.com** (travel information, including discounted hotel prices); **www.gtp.gr** (information on ferry service); **www.greekislands.gr** (information on the islands); **www.greektravel.com** (a helpful site on all aspects of Greece run by American Matt Barrett); **www.ancientgreece.com** and **www.perseus.tufts.edu** (an excellent source about ancient Greece); and **www. greekbooks.com**, **www.book.culture.gr**, and **www.greekbooks.gr** (useful sites for information on books on many aspects of Greece). For information on the Olympics, check out **www.athens2004.com** and **www.cultural-olympiad.gr**.

CITY LAYOUT   If you, like the Greek mathematician Euclid, find it easy to imagine geometric forms, it will help you to think of central Athens as an almost perfect equilateral triangle, with its points at **Syntagma (Constitution) Square, Omonia (Harmony) Square,** and **Monastiraki (Little Monastery) Square,** near the **Acropolis.** In government jargon, the area bounded by Syntagma, Omonia, and Monastiraki squares is defined as the commercial center, from which cars are banned (in theory, if not in practice) except for several cross streets. Most Greeks consider Omonia the city center, but visitors usually get their bearings from Syntagma, where the House of Parliament is. Few Athenians were enchanted with Omonia's "facelift" in honor of the Olympics. Twenty-seven months and two million euros later, it is now possible to walk across Omonia Square—on lots of cement; the promised trees, at least at press time, had not appeared. Syntagma Square was also redesigned, losing several lanes of traffic— and becoming increasingly congested—as well as several fountains and some greenery. Omonia and Syntagma squares are connected by the parallel **Stadiou Street** and **Panepistimiou Street,** also called **Eleftheriou Venizelou.** West from Syntagma Square, ancient **Ermou Street** and broader **Mitropoleos Street** lead slightly downhill to **Monastiraki Square.** Here you'll find the **flea market,** the **Ancient Agora (Market)** below the Acropolis, and the **Plaka,** the oldest neighborhood, with many street names and a scattering of monuments from antiquity. A special bonus: **Adrianou,** the main drag in Plaka, which once teemed with traffic, is now pedestrianized. From Monastiraki Square, **Athinas Street** leads north past the modern market (the Central Market) to Omonia Square. Bustling with shoppers in the daytime, Athinas Street is less savory and best avoided at night, when prostitutes and drug dealers tend to hang out here.

In general, finding your way around Athens is easy, except in the Plaka, at the foot of the Acropolis. This labyrinth of narrow, winding streets can challenge even the best navigators. Don't panic: The area is small enough that you can't go far astray, and its side streets, with small houses and neighborhood churches, are so charming that you won't mind being lost. One excellent map may help: the

Greek Archaeological Service's **Historical Map of Athens,** which includes the Plaka and the city center and shows the major archaeological sites. The map costs about 4€ ($4.60) and is sold at many bookstores, museums, ancient sites, and newspaper kiosks.

GETTING AROUND   By Public Transportation   The **blue-and-white buses** run regular routes in Athens and its suburbs every 15 minutes daily from 5am to midnight. The **orange electric trolley buses** serve areas in the city center daily from 5am to midnight. The **green buses** run between the city center and Piraeus every 20 minutes daily from 6am to midnight, then hourly to 6am. At press time, tickets cost .50€ (55¢) and must be bought in advance, usually in groups of 10, from any news kiosk or special bus ticket kiosks at the main stations. When you board, validate your ticket in the automatic machine. Hold onto it: Uniformed and plainclothes inspectors periodically check tickets and can levy a basic fine of 5€ ($5.75) or a more punitive fine of 20€ ($23), on the spot.

The major bus stations in Athens are: **Suburban bus terminal** at Areos Park; **Long Distance Bus Terminal A,** 100 Kiffissou (reached by bus no. 051 from Zinonos and Menandrou sts., off Omonia Sq.); and **Long Distance Bus Terminal B,** 260 Liossion (reached by bus no. 024 from Amalias Ave., Syntagma Sq.). *Note:* Confusingly, the number of the bus (usually displayed prominently) serving any individual route often changes without advance warning—and fares are certain to increase around the Olympics.

The original **Metro** line links Piraeus, Athens's seaport; central Athens itself; and Kifissia, an upscale northern suburb. A second line, with its main station in Syntagma Square, links the Defense Ministry on Mesogheion Avenue with central Athens and the northwest suburb of Sepolia. Original plans for the entire 21-station Metro to be running by the end of 2002 were changed to target the August 2004 Summer Olympics (now if only someone would just figure out how to build adequate parking lots near the new Metro stops so that commuters can leave their cars there rather than park them on every available inch of the sidewalks). In the city center, the main stops are **Syntagma, Acropolis, Monastiraki, Omonia,** and **Viktorias (Victoria).** Trains run about every 5 to 15 minutes daily from 5am to midnight. At present, tickets on the old line cost .60€ (65¢); tickets on the new line cost .75€ (80¢); and a day pass costs 3€ ($3.45)—but don't be surprised if these prices have gone up by the time you arrive. Validate your ticket in the machine as you enter the waiting platform, or risk a fine. Metro and bus tickets are not interchangeable.

By Taxi   Supposedly there are 17,000 taxis in Athens, but finding one empty is almost never easy. Especially if you have travel connections to make, it's a good idea to pay the 2€ ($2.30) surcharge and reserve a radio taxi. The minimum fare in a taxi is 2€ ($2.30). Some radio taxi companies and phone numbers are: **Athina** ⓒ210/921-7942; **Express** ⓒ 210/993-4812; **Parthenon** ⓒ 210/532-3300; **Piraeus** ⓒ 210/418-2333. Most hotels and restaurants will call a radio taxi for you without charge.

(Tips   **Ride the Metro & View Artifacts**

Allow a little extra time when you catch the Metro in central Athens. Two stations—**Syntagma Square** and **Acropolis**—handsomely display finds from the subway excavations in what amounts to Athens's newest small museums. For more on the Athens Metro, go to **www.ametro.gr**.

> **Tips** **A Taxi Warning**
>
> Increasing numbers of unlicensed cab drivers ply their trade in Athens and Piraeus. Usually, these pirate cabbies (many from eastern Europe) drive not the standard gray Athens taxi but a gray car you might mistake for an Athens cab. It's always a good idea to make sure your cab driver has a meter and a photo ID. Many of the unlicensed cab drivers are uninsured and unfamiliar with the metropolitan area.

When you get into a taxi, check to see that the meter is turned on and set on "1" rather than "2"; it should be set on "2" (double fare) only from midnight to 5am or if you take a taxi outside the city limits. (If you plan to take a cab out of town, it is best to negotiate a flat rate in advance.) Unless your cab is caught in very heavy traffic, a trip to the center of town from the airport between 5am and midnight shouldn't cost more than 20€ to 30€ ($23–$35). Don't be surprised if your driver picks up other passengers en route; he'll work out everyone's share, and probably the worst that will happen is you'll get less of a break on the shared fare than you would if you spoke Greek. Most Greek passengers at least round out the fare—for example, from 2.90€ to 3€ ($3.35–$3.45)—and some give a bit more of a tip.

If you suspect you've been overcharged, ask for help at your hotel or other destination before you pay the fare. Keep in mind that your driver may have difficulty understanding your pronunciation of your destination. If you are taking a taxi from your hotel, a staff member can tell the driver your destination or write down the address for you to show to the driver. If you carry a business card from your hotel, you can show it to the driver when you return. Most restaurants will call for a taxi at no charge.

By Car   Parking is so difficult and traffic so heavy in Athens that you should use a car only for trips outside the city. Keep in mind that on any day trip (to Sounion or Daphni, for example), you'll spend at least several hours leaving and reentering central Athens.

Car-rental agencies in the Syntagma Square area include **Avis,** 48 Amalias Ave. (© **800/331-1084** in the U.S., or 210/322-4951); **Auto Europe,** 29 Hatzihristou, right off Syngrou (© **800/223-5555** in the U.S., or 210/924-2206); and **Budget,** 8 Syngrou Ave. (© **800/527-0700** in the U.S., or 210/921-4711). *Remember:* You almost always get the best deal if you arrange the rental before you leave home. You will usually get the worst possible deal if you arrive in Athens and want a car for only 1 day. In season, prices for rentals from well-known international companies range from about 40€ to 100€ ($46–$115).

Warning: Sign up for full insurance and be sure that the price you're quoted includes everything. Often the price quoted doesn't include all taxes, a drop-off fee, gasoline charges, and so on. Be particularly vigilant if you intend to collect or return your car at an airport: Many companies charge—but do not mention it when you reserve your car—a hefty fee for this.

By Foot   Most of what you probably want to see and do in Athens is in the city center, allowing you to sightsee mostly on foot. The pedestrian zones in sections of the Plaka, the commercial center, and Kolonaki make strolling, window-shopping, and sightseeing infinitely more pleasant than on other, traffic-clogged streets. Nonetheless, visitors should keep in mind that here, as in many busy cities, a red traffic light or stop sign is no guarantee that cars will stop for pedestrians.

FAST FACTS: Athens

American Express The office at 2 Ermou, near the southwest corner of Syntagma Square (© 210/324-4975; fax 210/322-7893), offers currency exchange and other services weekdays from 8:30am to 4pm and Saturday from 8:30am to 1:30pm.

Business Hours **Banks** are generally open Monday through Thursday from 8am to 2pm and Friday from 8am to 1:30pm. In winter, shops are generally open Monday and Wednesday from 9am to 5pm; Tuesday, Thursday, and Friday from 10am to 7pm; and Saturday from 8:30am to 3:30pm. In summer, shops are generally open Monday, Wednesday, and Saturday from 8am to 3pm; and Tuesday, Thursday, and Friday from 8am to 1:30pm and 5:30 to 10pm. Note that many shops geared to visitors keep especially long hours, but some close from about 2 to 5pm. Most **food stores** and the **Central Market** are open Monday and Wednesday from 9am to 4:30pm, Tuesday from 9am to 6pm, Thursday from 9:30am to 6:30pm, Friday from 9:30am to 7pm, and Saturday from 8:30am to 4:30pm.

Currency On January 1, 2002, the monetary unit in Greece became the euro €. At press time, 1€ = $1.15, or $1 = .85€.

Currency Exchange Most banks have currency-exchange counters that use the rates set daily by the government, which are usually more favorable than those offered at unofficial exchange bureaus. It's worth doing a little comparison shopping for the best rate of exchange; for example, many hotels offer rates (usually only for cash) that are better than the official bank rates. ATM cash dispensers are increasingly common in Athens, and the National Bank of Greece operates a 24-hour ATM next to the tourist information office on Syntagma Square. It's not a good idea to rely on using ATMs exclusively in Athens because the machines are sometimes out of service on holidays or during bank strikes.

Dentists & Doctors If you need an English-speaking doctor or dentist, call your embassy for advice; or try **SOS Doctor** (© **210/331-0310** or 210/331-0311). The English-language *Athens News* lists some American- and British-trained doctors and hospitals offering emergency services. Most of the larger hotels have doctors whom they can call for you in an emergency.

Drugstores *Pharmakia,* identified by green crosses, are scattered throughout Athens. Hours are usually from 8am to 2pm on weekdays. In the evening and on weekends most are closed, but they usually post a notice listing the names and addresses of pharmacies that are open or will open in an emergency. The English-language *Athens News* (published on Fri) often lists pharmacies open outside regular hours.

Embassies/Consulates These may be found at the following locations: **United States,** 91 Leoforos Vas. Sofias (© 210/721-2951; emergency number 210/729-4301); **Canada,** 4 Ioannou Yenadiou (© 210/727-3400 or 210/725-4011); **United Kingdom,** 1 Ploutarchou (© 210/723-6211); **Ireland,** 7 Vas. Konstantinou (© 210/723-2771); **Australia,** 37 Leoforos Dimitriou Soutsou (© 210/645-0404-5); **New Zealand,** 24 Xenias, Ambelokipi (© 210/771-0112); **South Africa,** 60 Kifissias, Maroussi (© 210/680-6645). Be sure to phone ahead before you go to any embassy. Most are only open for business Monday through Friday from 9am to noon and are usually closed on their own country's holidays as well as Greek holidays.

Emergencies In an emergency, dial 🕿 **100** for fast police assistance and 🕿 **171** for the **Tourist Police**. Dial 🕿 **199** to report a **fire** and 🕿 **166** for an **ambulance** and **hospital**.

Internet Access Most cybercafes charge about 6€ ($6.90) an hour. The very efficient and helpful **Sofokleous.com Internet C@fe** ✧, 5 Stadiou, a block off Syntagma Square (🕿 and fax **210/324-8105**), is open daily from 10am to 10pm. The **Astor Internet Cafe**, 27 Patission, a block off Omonia Square (🕿 **210/523-8546**), is open Monday through Saturday 10am to 10pm and Sunday from 10am to 4pm. Across from the National Archaeological Museum is the **Museum Internet Cafe**, 28 Octobriou (the street is also called Patission; 🕿 **210/883-3418**; www.museumcafe.gr), open daily from 9am to 11pm. In the Plaka, **Plaka Internet World**, 29 Pandrossou, Monastiraki, is usually open from 11am to 11pm.

Post Office The main **post offices** in central Athens are at 100 Eolou, just south of Omonia Square, and in Syntagma Square on the corner of Mitropoleos Street. They're open Monday through Friday from 7:30am to 8pm, Saturday from 7:30am to 2pm, and Sunday from 9am to 1pm. All the post offices can accept small parcels. The **parcel post office**, 4 Stadiou, inside the arcade (🕿 **210/322-8940**), is open Monday through Friday from 7:30am to 8pm. Parcels must be open for inspection before you seal them (bring your own tape and string) at the post office.

Telephone/Telegrams/Faxes The country code for Greece is **30**. The city code for Athens is **210**.

Many of the city's public phones now accept only **phone cards,** available at newsstands and OTE offices in several denominations starting at 5€. Some kiosks still have **metered phones;** you pay what the meter records. Local phone calls cost about .05€. North Americans can phone home directly by contacting **AT&T** at 🕿 00-800-1311, **MCI** at 🕿 00-800-1211, or **Sprint** at 🕿 00-800-1411; calls can be collect or billed to your phone charge card. You can send a telegram or fax from offices of the **Telecommunications Organization of Greece (OTE)**. The three main OTE offices in central Athens are at 15 Stadiou, near Syntagma; Omonia Square; and Victoria Square at 85 Patission.

Tipping Restaurants include a service charge in the bill, but many visitors add a 10% tip. Most Greeks don't give a percentage tip to taxi drivers but round the fare up to the nearest euro, adding more for a higher fare.

Country & City Codes

Greek telephone codes have changed several times in the past few years. To dial a number in Athens from outside Greece, dial 011-30 (Greece) plus 210 (Athens) and then the 7-digit Athens number. To dial Athens from within Greece, dial 210 plus the 7-digit Athens number. To dial a number outside Athens from outside Greece, dial 011-30 (Greece) plus the local area code plus the local number. To dial a number outside of Athens from within Greece, dial the local area code plus the local number. *Remember:* When you are in Greece, you must use the area code even if you are phoning within the same area—even if you are just phoning across the street!

WHERE TO STAY

Virtually all Greek hotels are clean and comfortable; few are charming, elegant, or memorable. Most, in fact, are monotonous, with one guest room a bit larger, another a bit smaller—and few have any individual touch to warm the traveler's heart. (I've noted those hotels that are truly distinctive in the listings below.) Keep in mind that, in the absence of clearly distinguishing characteristics, location is often the most important factor in choosing your hotel.

A few suggestions: If shower and tub facilities are important to you, be sure to have a look at the bathroom. Many Greek tubs are tiny, and the showers are hand held. Don't assume that just because a hotel says it has air-conditioning, the air-conditioning is working—and be sure to see if the hotel has adequately functioning central heating in the winter.

Although many guidebooks do, I don't recommend staying in any of the luxury hotels on Syngrou Avenue. Sure, the Metropolitan, the Leda Marriott, and the Athenaem-Intercontinental have all the creature comforts, but Syngrou Avenue is ugly, noisy, and away from everything you want to see in Athens. In short, the Syngrou hotels are just fine for the businesspeople here for conferences who never leave their hotels—but not for visitors here to see the sights.

Warning: Hotel prices were accurate at press time, but massive price hikes are rumored for the Olympics; in addition, many hoteliers hope to maintain the high prices that—in theory—were to be in effect *only* for the 2004 Summer Olympics.

IN PLAKA
Expensive

Electra Palace ★★   Just a few blocks southwest of Syntagma Square, the Electra is the most modern and stylish Plaka hotel; it even has a decent restaurant, and the rooftop pool is a real bonus. Rooms are a good size and have balconies. The top floors (5–7) are where you want to be, both for the Acropolis view and to escape traffic noise. And that's the problem: the Electra won't guarantee you a top-floor room when you reserve, and if you sit on your balcony on one of the lower floors, you'll inhale lots of fumes, hear lots of traffic noise, and have a view of the building across the street. Still, you can always retreat to the rooftop pool and take in the Acropolis view there.

18 Nikodimou, Plaka, 105 57 Athens. (210/324-1401 or 210/324-1407. Fax 210/324-1875. 106 units. 210€–300€ ($242–$345) double. Rates include breakfast. AE, DC, MC, V. **Amenities:** Restaurant; bar; rooftop pool. *In room:* A/C, TV, minibar, hair dryer.

Moderate

Acropolis House Hotel   Location is almost everything in this venerable small hotel in a renovated 150-year-old villa with minimalist furnishings in the bedrooms. Try to get room no. 401 or 402 for an Acropolis view. The relatively quiet pedestrianized Plaka side street is a real plus, although motorcycles can be a problem. The newer wing (only 65 years old) isn't architecturally special, and the toilets (one for each room) are across the hall. There's a washing machine (for a small fee; free after a 4-day stay). If the Acropolis House is full, try the less appealing Adonis or (still less appealing) Kouros.

6–8 Kodrou, 105 58 Athens. (210/322-2344. Fax 210/324-4143. 25 units, 15 with bathroom. 70€ ($79) double without bathroom; 85€ ($98) double with bathroom. 10€ ($12) surcharge for A/C. Rates include continental breakfast. V. Walk 2 blocks out of Syntagma Sq. on Mitropoleos and turn left on Voulis, which becomes pedestrianized Kodrou. *In room:* A/C.

Byron Hotel   Every year I come close to eliminating the Byron, where the indifferent-at-best service is a real drawback. Still, it offers one real plus: the relatively quiet central Plaka location just off recently pedestrianized Dionyssiou Areopagitou Street. The price is fair (and often highly negotiable). That said, if you don't remember the dingy Byron before its remodeling 4 years ago, the new decor, which lacks charm, might not impress you. I've also had reports that the air-conditioning is temperamental at best. Alas, the same can be said for the service, which is usually haphazard and often curt.

19 Vyronos, 105 58 Athens. ⓒ **210/325-3554.** Fax 210/323-0327. 20 units. 85€–95€ ($98–$109) double. Rates include breakfast. No credit cards. From Syntagma Sq., walk south on Amalias Ave. past Hadrian's Arch, stay right, and turn right on Dionyssiou Areopagitou; Vyronos ("Byron" in Greek) is the 2nd street on the right, and the hotel (with a portrait of Lord Byron by the door) is on the right. **Amenities:** Bar. *In room:* A/C.

Hotel Nefeli ⭐   The little Nefeli, just steps from the main Plaka shopping and restaurant streets, was completely redecorated in 1999, with new beds and furniture. The rooms are small but comfortable, the quietest overlooking pedestrianized Angelikis Hatzimihali Street (although illegal motorcycle traffic can be a problem at night). I've found the staff courteous and helpful, and friends who've stayed here say the same. I was, therefore, surprised by one reader's report of curt service, sleep interrupted by a noisy tour group, and a grubby bathroom.

16 Iperidou, 105 58 Athens. ⓒ **210/322-8044.** Fax 210/322-5800. 18 units, 5 with shower only. 85€–95€ ($98–$109) double. Rates include continental breakfast. AE, V. Walk 2 blocks west from Syntagma Sq. on Mitropoleos, turn left on Voulis, cross Nikodimou, and turn right on Iperidou. **Amenities:** Breakfast room. *In room:* A/C, TV.

Hotel Plaka ⭐⭐   This 10-year-old hotel—popular with Greeks, who prefer its modern conveniences to the old-fashioned charms of most other hotels in the Plaka area—has a terrific location and fair prices. Many rooms have balconies. Fifth- and sixth-floor rooms in the rear (where it's usually quieter) have views of the Plaka and the Acropolis, also splendidly visible from the roof-garden bar (open in summer). Friends who stayed here recently weren't charmed by the service but loved the Plaka's central and relatively quiet location. Rates here are usually considerably cheaper off season.

Mitropoleos and 7 Kapnikareas, 105 56 Athens. ⓒ **210/322-2096.** Fax 210/322-2412. plaka@tourhotel.gr. 67 units, 38 with shower only. 100€–125€ ($115–$144) double. Rates include breakfast. AE, MC, V. Follow Mitropoleos out of Syntagma Sq. past the cathedral and turn left onto Kapnikareas. **Amenities:** Bar; roof garden. *In room:* A/C, TV, minibar, hair dryer.

NEAR MONASTIRAKI SQUARE
Moderate

Attalos Hotel ⭐   The six-story Attalos is well situated for those wanting to take in the exuberant daytime street life of the nearby Central Market and the exuberant nighttime scene at the cafes and restaurants of the Psirri district. The rooms here are plain, but not gloomy; 40 have balconies and 12 have Acropolis views. Unusual for Greece, nonsmoking rooms are available, and all rooms have lock boxes. The roof garden offers fine views of the city and the Acropolis. The Attalos often gives a 10% discount to Frommer's readers. *One caution:* Drug dealing and prostitution are not unknown on Athinas Street.

29 Athinas, 105 54 Athens. ⓒ **210/391-2801.** Fax 210/324-3124. ww.attalos.grr. 80 units. 150€–270€ ($173–$311) double. Rates include buffet breakfast. AE, MC, V. From Monastiraki Sq., walk about 1½ blocks north on Athinas. **Amenities:** Luggage storage. *In room:* A/C, TV, hair dryer (most rooms).

Jason Inn Hotel ⭐⭐ *(Value)*   If you don't mind walking a few extra blocks to Syntagma, this is one of the best values in Athens, with a staff that's usually very helpful. You're just out of the Plaka, around the corner from the newly fashionable Psirri district and steps from bustling Athinas Street. The hotel is redecorated on a regular basis and has bright, attractive, decent-size rooms with modern amenities and double-paned windows to keep out traffic noise. If the Jason Inn is full, the staff may be able to find you a room in one of its other hotels: the similarly priced Adrian, in the Plaka; or the slightly less expensive King Jason or Jason, both a few blocks from Omonia Square.

12 Ayion Assomaton, 105 53 Athens. © 210/325-1106. Fax 210/324-3123 or 210/523-4786. Douros@ hotelnet.gr. 57 units. 95€–155€ ($109–$178) double. Rates include American buffet breakfast. AE, MC, V. From Monastiraki Sq., head west on Ermou, turn right at Thisio Metro station, pass the small below-ground-level church, and bear left. *In room:* A/C, TV, minibar.

ON & AROUND SYNTAGMA SQUARE
Very Expensive

Hotel Grande Bretagne ★★★   The legendary Grande Bretagne, one of Athens's most distinguished 19th-century buildings, reopened in 2003 after a $70 million renovation. The exquisite beaux-arts lobby has been preserved, and indoor and outdoor swimming pools and a spa (with some treatments attributed to the theories of the 5th-c.-B.C. physician Hippocrates!) have been added. Bedrooms that were once grand—and then rather dingy for too many years—are once again very grand indeed. If you decide to stay at the hotel where everyone from Winston Churchill to Sting has been a guest, be sure to insist on a room (or a suite, if you can swing it) with a balcony overlooking Syntagma Square, the Parliament building, and the Acropolis.

Syntagma Sq., 105 64 Athens. © 210/333-000. Fax 210/333-0160. www.grandebretagne.gr. 327 units. 350€–800€ ($402–$920) double/suite. AE, DC, MC, V. **Amenities:** 2 restaurants; 2 bars; indoor and outdoor swimming pools; health club with spa and Jacuzzi; airport pickup arranged; business center; shopping arcade; salon; 24-hr. room service; same-day laundry/dry cleaning services; nonsmoking rooms. *In room:* AC, TV, minibar, hair dryer.

N. J. V. Athens Plaza ★   The Athens Plaza, managed by the Grecotel group, reopened its glitzy doors in March 1998 after a complete remodeling. Many of the guest rooms—most with two king-size beds, armchairs, a desk, and a table—are larger than substantial living rooms, and many have balconies overlooking Syntagma Square. In short, this is a modern, up-to-date hotel with a superb location, good restaurants, a congenial bar, and an expansive lobby. That said, the service, while professional, is devoid of any personal touch.

Syntagma Sq., 105 64 Athens. © 210/325-5301. Fax 210/323-5856. 207 units. 350€–475€ ($402–$546) double. AE, DC, MC, V. **Amenities:** 2 restaurants; 2 bars; exercise room; concierge; business center; 24-hr. room service; same-day dry cleaning/laundry. *In room:* A/C, TV, minibar, hair dryer.

Expensive

Electra Hotel ★ (Value)   If Ermou Street remains pedestrianized and the Electra sticks to its present rates, this hotel, whose off-season rates are often excellent value, is an excellent choice. The location is central (steps from Syntagma Sq.) and quiet (despite the presence of lots of tour groups). Although not large, most rooms come with comfortable armchairs, large windows, and modern bathrooms; about half have balconies. The front desk is sometimes understaffed, but the service is generally acceptable.

5 Ermou, 105 63 Athens. © 210/322-3223. Fax 210/322-0310. electrahotel@ath.forthnet.gr. 110 units. 150€–200€ ($173–$230) double . Rates include buffet breakfast. AE, DC, MC, V. The Electra is about 2 blocks down on the left as you walk along Ermou with Syntagma Sq. behind you. **Amenities:** Restaurant; bar. *In room:* A/C, TV, minibar, hair dryer.

Moderate

Athens Cypria ★★ After extensive renovations, the former Diomia Hotel was reborn in 2000 as the Athens Cypria. Gone are the Diomia's gloomy lobby and rooms, but the very convenient central location on a street with (usually) no traffic and the splendid Acropolis views from room nos. 603 to 607 remain (as do the less-than-enchanting views of walls and rooftops from other rooms). The breakfast buffet offers hot and cold dishes from 7 to 10am in a mirrored dining room. One criticism: Responses to requests for information and reservations are often sluggish.

5 Diomias, 105 62 Athens. ℂ **210/323-8034.** Fax 210/324-8792. 71 units. 130€–150€ ($150–$173) double. Reductions possible off season. Rates include buffet breakfast. AE, MC, V. Take Karayioryi Servias out of Syntagma Sq.; Diomias is on the left, after Lekka. **Amenities:** Bar and snack bar; luggage storage. *In room:* A/C, TV, minibar, hair dryer.

Hotel Achilleas The Achilleas (Achilles) has a great location on a relatively quiet side street steps from Syntagma Square and was completely renovated in 2001. Guest rooms here are sometimes heavily discounted off season. Rooms are a good size and light. Some rear ones have small balconies. Several rooms on the fifth floor can be used as interconnecting family suites. The very central location and fair prices make this hotel a good choice, and the breakfast room is pleasant.

21 Lekka, 105 62 Athens. ℂ **210/323-3197.** Fax 210/322-2412. www.achilleashotel.gr. 34 units. 155€ ($178) double. Rates include breakfast. AE, DC, MC, V. With Hotel Grande Bretagne on your right, walk 2 blocks out of Syntagma Sq. on Karayioryi Servias and turn right into Lekka. **Amenities:** Snack bar. *In room:* A/C, TV, minibar; hair dryer and safe in most units.

Inexpensive

Hotel Carolina ★★ The family-owned and -operated Carolina, on the outskirts of the Plaka, a brisk 5-minute walk from Syntagma, has always been popular with students. In the last few years, the hotel undertook extensive remodelings and now attracts a wide range of frugal travelers, who enjoy its casual atmosphere. Guest rooms have double-glazed windows against street noise and air-conditioning; many, like room nos. 407 and 308, have large balconies. Several rooms, such as no. 308, have four or five beds, which makes them popular with families and students.

55 Kolokotroni, 105 60 Athens. ℂ **210/324-3551.** Fax 210/324-3350. hotelcarolina@galaxtnet.gr. 31 units. 75€–110€ ($86–$126) double; breakfast 5€. MC, V. Take Stadiou out of Syntagma Sq. to Kolokotroni St. (on left). **Amenities:** Breakfast room. *In room:* A/C, TV.

IN KOLONAKI
Very Expensive

Saint George Lycabettus Hotel ★★ Kolonaki is a fashionable residential and shopping neighborhood northeast of Syntagma at the foot of Mount Likavitos. The rooftop pool is a real plus, as are the two excellent restaurants, and the hotel is just steps from the chic Kolonaki restaurants and shops—but keep in mind that when you head back to the hotel, those steps are steeply uphill. The distinctively appointed rooms (different floors have different decorative motifs, from baroque to Italian modern) look toward Mount Likavitos or a small park. Some have views of both Likavitos and the Acropolis. In short, this is a distinctive and classy hotel (much-used by wealthy Greeks for private events), although the surrounding street traffic keeps it from being an absolute oasis of calm.

2 Kleomenous, 106 75 Athens. ℂ **210/729-0711.** Fax 210/721-0439. www.sglycabettus.gr. 167 units. 235€–375€ ($270–$430) double. Breakfast 20€ ($23). AE, DC, MC, V. From Kolonaki Sq., take Patriarchou Ioachim to Loukianou; follow Loukianou uphill to Kleomenous; turn left on Kleomenous; the hotel overlooks Dexamini Park. **Amenities:** 2 restaurants; 2 bars; pool; concierge; 24-hr. room service. *In room:* A/C, TV, minibar.

Moderate

Athenian Inn ⭐ The Athenian Inn is on a relatively quiet side street 3 blocks from Kolonaki Square's cafes, restaurants, and shops. Between stays, I tend to forget how small the rooms are here, which suggests to me that the staff is doing a good job of making guests (including many academics) feel comfortable. A quote from the guest book: "At last the ideal Athens hotel, good and modest in scale but perfect in service and goodwill." Breakfast is served in the small ground-floor lounge, which has a TV. Keep in mind that if you stay here, you will do a good deal of walking (some of it fairly steep) to get to and from the central attractions. Neighborhood doves coo vigorously at night, a sound you will probably find either soothing or infuriating.

22 Haritos, Kolonaki, 106 75 Athens. ℂ **210/723-8097**. Fax 210/724-2268. 28 units. 135€–150€ ($155–$173) double. Rates include breakfast. AE, DC, V. From Syntagma Sq., go east on Vasilissis Sofias Ave. to Loukianou; turn left on Loukianou and take it 6 blocks uphill to Haritos. **Amenities:** Breakfast room. *In room:* A/C.

IN THE EMBASSY DISTRICT
Very Expensive

Andromeda Hotel ⭐⭐⭐ The city's only boutique hotel is easily the most charming in Athens, with a staff that makes you feel that this is your ideal home away from home, on a quiet residential street by the American ambassador's garden, not far from the Megaron Musikis (Athens Concert Hall). Most rooms are quite large, all are elegantly decorated, the service is superb, and the breakfast buffets are lavish. The only drawbacks: It's a serious hike (20–30 min.) or a 10-minute taxi ride to Syntagma; and there are relatively few restaurants in this residential neighborhood, although the superb Vlassis is just around the corner. If you're planning a long stay in Athens, check out the Andromeda's new (and very lovely) service apartments just across the street.

22 Timoleontos Vassou (off Plateia Mavili), 115 21 Athens. ℂ **210/641-5000**. Fax 210/646-6361. Reservations@ andromedaathens.gr. 42 units. 455€–600€ ($523–$690) double/suite/service apts. Rates include breakfast. Discounts sometimes available. AE, DC, MC, V. **Amenities:** Restaurant; breakfast room; bar. *In room:* A/C, TV, dataport, minibar, hair dryer, safe.

Hilton Athens ⭐⭐⭐ When the Hilton opened in 1963, it was the most modern hotel in town—and the tallest building on the horizon. In 2001, it closed for a long-overdue renovation, and 3 years and 96 million euros later it reopened. Furnishings are fresh and spanking new, with bedrooms decorated in the generic (but very comfortable) international Hilton style, with Greek touches. The Plaza Executive floor offers a separate business center and complimentary breakfast buffet and cocktails (with generous hors d'ouevres). The rooftop **Galaxy Bar** has a spectacular view over Athens, and the pool is the largest hotel pool in town. The Hilton sometimes runs promotions, so ask about special rates before booking. *Note:* The entire hotel is booked by the International Olympics Committee for the 2004 games.

46 Leoforos Vas. Sofias, 111528 Athens. ℂ **800/445-8667** in the U.S., or 210/728-1111. www.hilton.com. 350€–700€ ($402–$805) double. AE, DC, MC, V. **Amenities:** 4 restaurants; 3 bars; outdoor freshwater pool; health club and spa with Jacuzzi; game room; concierge; tour desk; car-rental desk; airport pickup arranged; business center; secretarial services; shopping arcade; salon; 24-hr. room service; babysitting; same-day laundry/dry-cleaning services; nonsmoking rooms; rooms for those with limited mobility. *In room:* A/C, TV, dataport, minibar, hair dryer, safe.

NEAR THE ACROPOLIS (MAKRIYANNI & KOUKAKI DISTRICTS)

Very Expensive

Divani Palace Acropolis ★★ Just 3 blocks south of the Acropolis, in a quiet residential neighborhood (there's a handy SPAR supermarket a block away at 4 Parthenonos, as well as a shop at 7 Parthenonos that sells American and English newspapers), the Divani Palace Acropolis does a brisk tour business but welcomes independent travelers. The blandly decorated rooms are large and comfortable, with generously sized bathrooms. (The breakfast buffet is more than generous.) A section of Athens's 5th-century B.C. defense wall is preserved behind glass in the basement. The same hotel group operates the **Divani Caravel Hotel,** near the National Art Gallery and Hilton Hotel at 2 Vas. Alexandrou Ave. (© 210/725-3725; fax 210-723-6683).

19–25 Parthenonos, Makriyanni, 117 42 Athens. © **210/928-0100.** Fax 210/921-4993. www.divanicaravel.gr. 253 units. 225€–375€ ($259–$431) double. AE, DC, MC, V. From Syntagma Sq., take Amalias Ave. to pedestrianized Dionyssiou Areopagitou; turn left into Parthenonos; the hotel is on your left after about 3 blocks. **Amenities:** Restaurant; 2 bars; small pool; concierge; business center; 24-hr. room service; roof garden. *In room:* A/C, TV, minibar, hair dryer.

Moderate

Acropolis View Hotel ★ The Acropolis View is located in a generally quiet neighborhood, not far from the Herodes Atticus theater, at the base of Philopappos Hill, a 10- to 15-minute walk from the heart of the Plaka. Rooms (most freshly painted each year) are small but clean and pleasant, with good bathrooms; 16 have balconies. Some, like no. 405, overlook Philopappos Hill, and others, like no. 407, face the Acropolis.

Robertou Galli and 10 Webster, 117 42 Athens. © 210/921-7303. Fax 210/923-0705. www.acropolisview.gr. 32 units. 135€ ($155) double. Rates include buffet breakfast. Substantial reductions Nov–Apr 1. AE, MC, V. From Syntagma Sq. take Amalias Ave. to Dionyssiou Areopagitou; head west past Herodes Atticus theater to Robertou Galli. Webster (Gouemster on some maps) is the little street intersecting Robertou Galli between Propilion and Garibaldi. **Amenities:** Breakfast room; bar. *In room:* A/C, TV, minibar.

Art Gallery Hotel ★ As you might expect, this small hotel—in a half-century-old house that has been home to several artists—has an artistic flair (and a nice old-fashioned cage elevator). Customers tend to be loyal, many of them on repeat visits, greeting old friends and cordial to newcomers. Rooms are small and plain but comfortable, some with ceiling fans, although all now have air-conditioning. There's a nice Victorian-style breakfast room on the fourth floor.

5 Erechthiou, Koukaki, 117 42 Athens. © 210/923-8376. Fax 210/923-3025. ecotec@otenet.gr. 22 units. 60€–90€ ($69–$104) double. Rates include generous breakfast. Hotel sometimes closed Nov–Mar; when open then, prices reduced. AE, MC, V. *In room:* A/C, TV.

Austria Hotel ★ This very well maintained hotel at the base of wooded Philopappos Hill is operated by a Greek-Austrian family, who can point you to local sights (including a convenient neighborhood laundry!). The Austria's guest rooms and bathrooms are rather spartan but more than acceptable—and the very efficient staff is a real plus. It offers a great view over Athens and out to sea (I could see the island of Aegina) from the rooftop, where you can sun or sit under an awning.

7 Mousson, Filopappou, 117 42 Athens. © 210/923-5151. Fax 210/924-7350. www.austriahotel.com. 36 units, 11 with shower only. 135€ ($155) double. Rates include breakfast. AE, DC, MC, V. Follow Dionyssiou Areopagitou around south side of Acropolis to where it meets Robertou Galli; take Garibaldi around base of Filopappou Hill until you reach Mousson. **Amenities:** Breakfast room; rooftop terrace. *In room:* A/C, dataport, hair dryer, safe deposit box.

Parthenon Hotel   This recently redecorated hotel has an excellent location just steps from the Plaka and the Acropolis. The Parthenon is one of the AirOtel group of four Athenian hotels; if it's full, the management will try to get you a room at the Christina, a few blocks away, or at the Riva or Alexandros, near the Megaron (Athens Concert Hall). One warning: On occasion I've found the desk staff less than helpful and infuriatingly vague about room prices.

6 Makri, 115 27 Athens. ☎ 210/923-4594. Fax 210/644-1084. 79 units. 115€–125€ ($132–$144) double. MC, V. From Syntagma, take Amalias into Dionyssiou Areopagitou; Makri is the 2nd street on the left. **Amenities:** Restaurant; bar; garden. *In room:* A/C, TV.

Inexpensive

Marble House Pension ★★   Named for its marble facade, usually covered by bougainvillea, this small hotel, whose front rooms offer balconies overlooking quiet Zinni Street, is popular with budget travelers (including many teachers). Over the last several years, the pension has been remodeled and redecorated, gaining all-new bathrooms and guest room furniture. There are two easy-access ground-floor guest rooms, two guest rooms with kitchenettes, and nine guest rooms with air-conditioning. If you're spending more than a few days in Athens and don't mind being out of the center, this is a homey base. We have had one worrying report recently of a decline in the service here—let us know what you think.

35 A. Zinni, Koukaki, 117 41 Athens. ☎ 210/923-4058. Fax 210/922-6461. 16 units, 12 with bathroom. 60€ double without bathroom; 75€ ($86) double with bathroom. 10€ ($12) supplement for A/C. Monthly rates available off season. No credit cards. From Syntagma Sq. take Amalias Ave. to Syngrou Ave; turn right onto Zinni; the hotel is in the cul-de-sac beside the small church. **Amenities:** Luggage storage. *In room:* TV, minibar.

WHERE TO DINE

Athens has an astonishing number of restaurants and tavernas (and a growing number of fast-food joints) offering everything from good, cheap Greek food in plain surroundings to fine Greek, French, Asian, and other international cuisines served in luxurious surroundings.

Most restaurants have menus in Greek and English, but many don't keep their printed (or handwritten) menus up to date. If a menu is not in English, there's almost always someone working at the restaurant who can either translate or rattle off suggestions for you in English. That may mean you'll be offered some fairly repetitive suggestions because restaurant staff members tend to suggest what most tourists request. In Athens, that means *moussaka* (baked eggplant casserole, usually with ground meat), *souvlakia* (chunks of beef, chicken, pork, or lamb grilled on a skewer), *pastitsio* (baked pasta, usually with ground meat and béchamel sauce), or *dolmadakia* (grape leaves, stuffed usually with rice and ground meat). Although all these dishes can be delicious, all too often restaurants catering to tourists serve profoundly dull moussaka and unpleasantly chewy souvlakia.

Tips Don't Count on Credit Cards

One of my most humiliating travel moments happened a number of years ago when I was taking Athenian friends out to dinner—and planning to pay with a credit card. The restaurant took only cash, and my friends ended up having to take me to dinner. Much has changed in Athens since then—but, amazingly, my friends are still speaking to me. One thing that has not changed is that many Athenian restaurants still do not accept credit cards. Consider yourself warned.

Mezedes (appetizers served with bread) are one of the great delights of Greek cuisine, and often can be enjoyed in lieu of a main course. Some perennial favorites include *tzatziki* (garlic, cucumber, dill, and yogurt dip), *melitzanosalata* (eggplant dip), *skordalia* (garlic sauce), *taramosalata* (fish roe dip), *keftedes* (crispy meatballs), *kalamaria* (squid), *gigantes* (large white beans in tomato sauce), *loukanika* (little sausages), and *oktopodi* (octopus).

If you're wondering what to use to wash all this down with, the best-known Greek table wine is **retsina.** It's usually white, although sometime rosé or red, and flavored with pine resin. In theory, the European Union now controls the amount of resin added, so you're less likely to come across the harsh retsina that some compare to turpentine. If you don't like the taste of retsina, try *aretsinato* (wine without resin).

To find out more about the wide range of excellent Greek wines, pick up a copy of Dimitri Hadjinicolaou's *The A to Z Guide of Greek Wines* (Oenos O Agapitos Publisher). This handy pocket-size Greek/English guide has illustrations of labels and information on vintages, and sells for about 10€ ($12).

When it comes time for dessert or a midafternoon infusion of sugar, Greeks usually head to a *zaharoplastion* (sweet shop). Consequently, most restaurants don't offer a wide variety of desserts. Almost all do serve fruit (stewed in winter, fresh in season), and, increasingly, many serve sweets such as *baklava* (pastry and ground nuts with honey), *halva* (sesame, chopped nuts, and honey), and *kataifi* (shredded wheat with chopped nuts and lots of honey). All these sweets are seriously sweet. If you want coffee with your dessert, keep in mind that for Greeks, regular coffee usually includes a mere teaspoon of sugar. Sweet coffee seems to be about a fifty-fifty mixture of coffee and sugar. Watch out for the grounds in the bottom of the cup—and try to get a Greek to show you how to tell your fortune from the grounds.

Greek **brandy** is a popular after-dinner drink (although—you guessed it—it's a bit sweet for non-Greek tastes), but the most popular Greek hard drink is *ouzo.* The anise-flavored liqueur is taken either straight or with water, which turns it cloudy white. You may see Greek men drinking quarter- and even half-bottles of ouzo with their lunch; if you do the same, you'll find out why the after-lunch siesta is so popular. There are many cafes *(ouzeri)* where ouzo, wine, and a selection of mezedes are served from breakfast to bedtime.

IN THE PLAKA

Some of the most charming old restaurants in Athens are in the Plaka—as are some of the worst tourist traps. Here are a few things to keep in mind when you head off for a meal.

Some Plaka restaurants station waiters outside who don't just urge you to come in and sit down, but virtually pursue you down the street with an unrelenting sales pitch. The hard sell is almost always a giveaway that the place caters to tourists. In general, it's a good idea to avoid places with floor shows; many charge outrageous amounts (and levy surcharges not always openly stated on menus) for drinks and food. If you get burned, and the proprietor is insistent, stand your ground, phone the **Tourist Police** (© 171), and pay nothing before they arrive. Often the mere mention of the Tourist Police has the miraculous effect of causing a bill to be lowered. And remember: Prices during the August 2004 Olympics are predicted to be sky-high.

Tips **Eating Well**

To avoid the ubiquitous favorites-for-foreigners, tell your waiter you'd like to have a look at the food display case, often positioned just outside the kitchen, and then point to what you'd like to order. Many restaurants are perfectly happy to have you take a look in the kitchen itself, but it's not a good idea to do this without checking first. Not surprisingly, you'll get the best value and the tastiest food at establishments serving a predominantly Greek, rather than a transient tourist, clientele.

Expensive

Daphne's ✸✸✸ ELEGANT GREEK/NOUVELLE   This lovingly restored neoclassical 1830s town house has frescoes on the walls and a shady garden with bits of ancient marble found when the restaurant was built. The menu employs familiar ingredients in innovative ways (delicious hot pepper and feta cheese dip, zesty eggplant salad). I could cheerfully just eat the hors d'oeuvres all night, but I have also enjoyed the *stifado* (stew) of rabbit in *mavrodaphne* (sweet wine) sauce and the tasty prawns with toasted almonds. Most nights, a pair of strolling musicians entertains with a repertoire that ranges from Greek favorites to "My Darling Clementine." The staff is attentive, encouraging, endearing, and beyond excellent.

4 Lysikratous. ✆ and fax **210/322-7971.** Reservations recommended. Main courses 16€–25€ ($18–$29), with some fish priced by the kilo. AE, DC, MC, V. Daily 8pm–1am. Closed Dec 20–Jan 15. From Syntagma Sq., head south on Amalias to Lysikratous (across from Hadrian's Gate).

Moderate

Eden Vegetarian Restaurant ✸ VEGETARIAN   You can find vegetarian dishes at almost every Greek restaurant, but if you want to experience organically grown products, soy (rather than eggplant) moussaka, mushroom pie with a whole-wheat crust, freshly squeezed juices, and salads with bean sprouts, join the young Athenians and Europeans who patronize the Eden. The prices are reasonable, if not cheap, and the decor is engaging, with 1920s-style prints and mirrors and wrought-iron lamps.

12 Lissiou. ✆ and fax **210/324-8858.** Main courses 8€–15€ ($9.20–$17). AE, MC, V. Daily noon–midnight. Closed Tues and usually closed Aug. From Syntagma Sq., head south on Filellinon or Nikis to Kidathineon, which intersects Adrianou; turn right on Adrianou and take Mnissikleos up 2 blocks toward the Acropolis to Lissiou.

Platanos Taverna ✸✸ TRADITIONAL GREEK   This taverna on a quiet pedestrian square has tables outdoors in good weather beneath a spreading plane tree (*Platanos* means "plane tree"). Inside, where locals congregate to escape the summer sun at midday and the tourists in the evening, you can enjoy looking at the old paintings and photos on the walls. The Platanos has been serving good *spitiko fageto* (home cooking) since 1932 and has managed to keep steady customers happy while enchanting visitors. If artichokes or spinach with lamb are on the menu, you're in luck: They're delicious. The house wine is tasty, and there's a wide choice of bottled wines from many regions of Greece.

4 Dioyenous. ✆ **210/322-0666.** Fax 210/322-8624. Main courses 7€–15€ ($8.05–$17). No credit cards. Mon–Sat noon–4:30pm and 8pm–midnight; Mar–May and Sept–Oct Sun noon–4:30pm. From Syntagma Sq., head south on Filellinon or Nikis to Kidathineon; turn right on Adrianou, and take Mnissikleos up 1 block toward the Acropolis; turn right on Dioyenous.

Taverna Xinos ✿ TRADITIONAL GREEK   Despite the forgivable spelling lapse, Xinos's business card says it best: "In the heart of old Athens there is still a flace [sic] where the traditional Greek way of cooking is upheld." In summer, you can dine at tables in the courtyard; in winter, you can warm yourself by the coal-burning stove. While the strolling musicians may not be as good as the Three Tenors, they do sing wonderful Greek golden oldies, accompanying themselves on the guitar and bouzouki. (If you're serenaded, you may want to give the musicians a tip. If you want to hear the theme from *Never on Sunday*, ask for "Ena Zorbas.") Most evenings, tourists predominate until after 10pm, when locals begin to arrive.

4 Geronta. 𝄡 210/322-1065. Main courses 7€–15€ ($8.05–$17). No credit cards. Daily 8–11pm or later. Sometimes closed Sun, usually closed part of July and Aug. From Syntagma Sq., head south on Filellinon or Nikis to Kidathineon; turn right on Geronta and look for the sign for Xinos in the cul-de-sac.

Inexpensive

Damigos (The Bakaliarakia) ✿✿✿ GREEK/CODFISH   Since 1865, Damigos has been serving delicious deep-fried codfish and eggplant, as well as chops and stews for inveterate meat-eaters. This basement taverna serves wine from family vineyards. (If you wish, you can usually buy a bottle to take away.) There are few pleasures greater than sipping the white or rosé retsina while watching the cook turn out unending meals in his absurdly small kitchen. Don't miss the delicious *skordalia* (garlic sauce), equally good with cod, eggplant, bread— well, you get the idea.

41 Kidathineon. 𝄡 210/322-5084. Main courses 5€–10€ ($8.05–$17). No credit cards. Daily 7–11pm or later. Usually closed June–Sept. From Syntagma Sq., head south on Filellinon or Nikis to Kidathineon; Damigos is downstairs on the left just before Adrianou.

Kouklis Ouzeri (To Yerani) ✿ GREEK/MEZEDES   Besides Kouklis Ouzeri and To Yerani, Greeks call this popular old favorite with its winding staircase to the second floor the "Skolario" because of the nearby school. Sit down at one of the small tables and a waiter will present a large tray with about a dozen plates of *mezedes*—appetizer portions of fried fish, beans, grilled eggplant, taramosalata, cucumber-and-tomato salad, olives, fried cheese, sausages, and other seasonal specialties. If you don't choose all 12, you can enjoy a tasty and inexpensive meal, washed down with the house *krasi* (wine). No prices are posted, but the waiter will tell you what everything costs if you ask. Now if only the staff could be just a bit more patient when foreigners are trying to decide what to order.

14 Tripodon. 𝄡 210/324-7605. Appetizers 3€–12€ ($3.45–$14). No credit cards. Daily 11am–2am. From Syntagma Sq., head south on Filellinon or Nikis to Kidathineon; take Kidathineon across Adrianou to Thespidos and climb toward Acropolis; Tripodon is the 1st street on the right after Adrianou.

NEAR MONASTIRAKI SQUARE
Moderate

Taverna Sigalas ✿ TRADITIONAL GREEK   This longtime family- owned and -run Plaka taverna, housed in a vintage 1879 commercial building, boasts that it's open 365 days a year. The decor includes massive old retsina kegs and dozens of black-and-white photos of Greek movie stars. After 8pm nightly, there's Greek Muzak. At all hours, Greeks and tourists wolf down large portions of stews, moussaka, grilled meatballs, baked tomatoes, gyros, and other hearty dishes, washed down with the house red and white retsinas.

Plateia Monastiraki 2. 𝄡 210/321-3036. Main courses 5€–16€ ($5.75–$18). AE, DC, MC, V. Daily 7pm–2am. Across Monastiraki Sq. from the Metro station.

Inexpensive

Diporto *Finds* GREEK   This little place, sandwiched between olive shops, serves up salads, stews, and delicious *revithia* (chickpeas), a Greek winter dish popular among stall owners, shoppers, and Athenians who make their way to the market for cheap and delicious food. If you like Diporto, try Papandreou, also in the Central Market, and famous for its restorative tripe soup, a Greek remedy for hangovers.

Athens Central Market. No phone. Dishes 4€–9€ ($4.60–$10). No credit cards. Mon–Sat 6am–6pm. From Syntagma Sq., follow Hermou to Athinas; the Central Market is on the right side of the street.

Thanasis ★★ *Value* GREEK/SOUVLAKIA   Thanasis serves individual souvlakia, souvlakia and pita sandwiches, and plates heaped with sliced gyro (grilled lamb) and exceptionally good fries, both to go and at its outdoor and indoor tables; as always, the prices are higher if you sit down. On weekends, it often takes the strength and determination of an Olympic athlete to get through the door and place an order. It's worth the effort: This is both a great budget choice and a great place to take in the local scene, which often includes a fair sprinkling of Gypsies, including some cute and very determined child beggars.

69 Mitropoleos. ✆ 210/324-4705. Main courses 3€–10€ ($3.45–$12). No credit cards. Daily 9am–2am. On northeast corner of Monastiraki Sq. Hermou leads directly from Syntagma Sq. to Monastiraki Sq.

NEAR SYNTAGMA SQUARE
Expensive

Aigli ★★ INTERNATIONAL   When the bistro in the Zappeion Gardens closed in the 1970s, it was sorely missed. Now it's back, along with a cinema and fine restaurant. Once more, chic Athenian families head here for foie gras, oysters, Chinese ravioli, rich profiteroles, and delicious yogurt crème brûlée. You can sit at tables indoors, or outdoors by the trees, where you can relax with a morning cup of coffee and watch the balloon sellers tempt families with their wares. In the evening, take in a movie at the open-air cinema here before dinner, or have a drink and snack at one of several cafes. In short, this is a wonderful spot to while away an afternoon or evening.

Zappeion Gardens (adjacent to the National Gardens fronting Vas. Amalias Blvd.). ✆ 210/336-9363. Reservations recommended. Main courses 16€–28€ ($18–$32). Daily 10am–midnight. Sometimes closed in Aug.

Inexpensive

Neon ★ *Value* GREEK/INTERNATIONAL   If you're tired of practicing your restaurant Greek, the Neon restaurants are good places to eat, since most items are self-service. This centrally located member of the chain is convenient, albeit not as pleasant as the original on Omonia Square. There is also a very handy Neon a block north of Kolonaki Square at Tsakalof and Iraklitou. You're sure to find something to your taste—maybe a Mexican omelet, spaghetti bolognese, a salad bar, or sweets ranging from Black Forest cake to tiramisu.

3 Mitropoleos (on the southwest corner of Syntagma Sq.). ✆ 210/322-8155. Snacks 2€–5€ ($2.30–$5.75); sandwiches 4€–8€ ($4.60–$9.20); main courses 5€–20€ ($5.75–$23). No credit cards. Daily 9am–midnight.

IN KOLONAKI
Expensive

To Kafeneio ★★ GREEK/INTERNATIONAL   This is hardly a typical *kafeneio* (coffee shop/cafe). If you relax, you can easily run up a substantial tab (50€/$58 for lunch or dinner for two is easy), but you can also eat more modestly and equally elegantly. If you have something light, like the artichokes a la polita, leeks in crème fraîche, or onion pie (one, not all three!), accompanied by draft beer or the house wine, you can finish with profiteroles and not put too big a dent in your budget. I've always found this an especially congenial spot when I'm eating alone (perhaps because I love people-watching and profiteroles).

26 Loukianou. ⓒ 210/722-9056. Reservations recommended. Main courses 6€–25€ ($6.90–$29). No credit cards. Mon–Sat 11am–midnight or later. Closed Sun and most of Aug. From Kolonaki Sq., follow Patriarkou Ioakim several blocks uphill to Loukianou and turn right on Loukianou.

Moderate

Filipou ⭐ TRADITIONAL GREEK   This longtime Athenian favorite almost never disappoints. The traditional dishes such as stuffed cabbage, stuffed vine leaves, vegetable stews, and fresh salads are consistently good. In the heart of Kolonaki, near the very fashionable George Lykabettus Hotel, this is a place to head for when you want good *spitiko* (home) cooking in the company of the Greeks and resident expatriates who prize the food here.

19 Xenokratous. ⓒ 210/721-6390. Main courses 7€–15€ ($8.05–$17). No credit cards. Mon–Fri 8:30pm–midnight; Sat lunch (call for hours); closed Sun. From Kolonaki Sq., take Patriarch Ioakim to Ploutarchou, turn left on Ploutarchou, and then turn right on Xenokratous.

Rhodia ⭐ TRADITIONAL GREEK   This respected taverna in a handsome old Kolonaki house has tables in its small garden in good weather—although the interior, with its tile floor and old prints, is so charming that you might be tempted to eat indoors. The Rhodia is a favorite of visiting archaeologists from the nearby British and American Schools of Classical Studies, as well as of Kolonaki residents. It may not sound like just what you'd always hoped to have for dinner, but the octopus in mustard sauce is terrific, as are the veal and *dolmades* (stuffed grape leaves) in egg-lemon sauce. The house wine is excellent, as is the halva, which manages to be both creamy and crunchy.

44 Aristipou. ⓒ 210/722-9883. Main courses 7.50€–16€ ($8.60–$18). No credit cards. Mon–Sat 8pm–2am. From Kolonaki Sq., take Patriarkou Ioakim uphill to Loukianou; turn left on Loukianou, climb steeply uphill to Aristipou, and turn right.

To Ouzadiko ⭐⭐ GREEK/MEZEDES   This ouzo bar has at least 40 kinds of ouzo and as many *mezedes,* including fluffy *keftedes* (meatballs) that make all others taste leaden. To Ouzadiko is very popular with Athenians young and old who come to see and be seen while having a snack or a full meal, often after concerts and plays. A serious foodie friend of mine comes here especially for the wide variety of *horta* (greens), which she says are the best she's ever tasted. If you see someone at a nearby table eating something you want and aren't sure which of the bean or eggplant dishes it is, ask your waiter, and it will appear for you—sometimes after a bit of a wait, as the staff here is often seriously overworked.

25–29 Karneadou (in the Lemos International Shopping Center), Kolonaki. ⓒ 210/729-5484. Reservations recommended. Mezedes and main courses 7€–18€ ($8.05–$21). No credit cards. Tues–Sat 1pm–12:30am. From Kolonaki Sq., take Kapsali across Irodotou into Karneadou. The Lemos Center is the mini-skyscraper on your left.

To Prytaneion ⭐ GREEK/INTERNATIONAL   The trendy bare stone walls here are decorated with movie posters and illuminated by baby spotlights. Waiters with cellphones serve customers with cellphones tempting plates of some of Athens's most expensive and eclectic *mezedes,* including beef carpaccio, bruschetta, and shrimp in fresh cream, as well as that international favorite, the hamburger. This place is so drop-dead chic that it comes as a pleasant surprise to learn that it functioned as a neighborhood hangout during the 1999 earthquake and the 2001 snowstorm that shut down Athens.

7 Milioni, Kolonaki. (C) **210-364-3353** or 210/364-3354. Reservations recommended. Mezedes and snacks 7€–28€ ($8.05–$32). No credit cards. Mon–Sat 10am–3am. From Kolonaki Sq., head downhill a (pedestrianized) block or 2 until you hit Milioni on your right. To Prytaneion is on your left.

AROUND OMONIA SQUARE & THE NATIONAL ARCHAEOLOGICAL MUSEUM
Moderate

Athinaikon ★★ GREEK/OUZERI   Not many tourists come to this favorite haunt of lawyers and businesspeople working in the Omonia Square area. You can have just some appetizers (technically, this is an *ouzeri*) or a full meal. Obviously, the way to have a reasonably priced snack is to stick to the appetizers, including delicious *loukanika* (sausages) and *keftedes* (meatballs), and pass on the pricier grilled shrimp or seafood paella. Whatever you have, you'll enjoy taking in the old photos on the walls, the handsome tiled floor, the marble-topped tables and bentwood chairs, and the regular customers, who combine serious eating with animated conversation.

2 Themistokleous. (C) **210/383-8485**. Appetizers and main courses 4€–16€ ($4.60–$18). No credit cards. Mon–Sat 11am–midnight. Closed Sun and usually in Aug. From Omonia Sq., take Panepistimou a block to Themistokleous; the Athinaikon is almost immediately on your right.

Ideal ★ GREEK TRADITIONAL   The oldest restaurant in the heart of Athens, today's Ideal has an Art Deco decor and lots of old favorites, from egg-lemon soup to stuffed peppers, pork with celery, and lamb with spinach. This is a favorite of businesspeople, and the service is usually brisk, especially at lunchtime. It may not be the place for a quiet rendezvous, but it's definitely the spot for good, hearty Greek cooking.

46 Panepistimiou. (C) **210/330-3000**. Reservations recommended. Main courses 8€–16€ ($9.20–$18). AE, DC, MC, V. Mon–Sat noon–midnight. From Omonia or Syntagma, take Panepistimiou (the Ideal is just outside Omonia Sq.).

NEAR THE ACROPOLIS
Expensive

Symbosio ★★ ELEGANT GREEK/CONTINENTAL   This lovingly cared-for 1920s Makriyanni town house with its own garden is a very pretty place to eat. Initially, we thought the food here was delicious but a tad fussy, with a bit too much lily gilding and use of sauces. The last few times we have been here, however, we've been swept away by the *mezedes,* the quality of the fish, the delicate seasonings used in meat dishes, the fresh veggies, and the excellent wine list.

46 Erechthiou. (C) **210/922-5321**. Fax 210/923-2780. Main courses 14€–30€ ($16–$35); fish priced by the kilo. AE, MC, V. Mon–Sat about 8pm–midnight. Usually closed 2nd half of Aug; sometimes closed in Jan.

Moderate

Socrates' Prison/Samaria ★ GREEK/CONTINENTAL   This longtime visitors' favorite has moved around the corner to a new location (and a new name that not everyone uses), where it remains an excellent place to head when you want good food near the Plaka but want to avoid the frenzy of the central Plaka. The new place has a roof garden with an Acropolis view, a real plus for summer evenings. Greeks, as well as American and European expats living in Athens, love this place, with its tables outdoors in good weather and in the pleasant rooms year-round. In addition to the usual Greek meat dishes, the menu includes tasty veggie croquettes, *salade niçoise* and—for those who can't decide between veggies and meat—vegetable-stuffed pork roll. The retsina is excellent, and there's a wide choice of bottled wines and beers.

17 Robertou Galli. © 210/922-3434. Main courses 10€–17€ ($12–$20). AE, DC, MC, V. Mon–Sat 11am–4pm and 7pm–1am. Closed Aug. From Syntagma Sq., take Amalias Ave. to pedestrianized Dionyssiou Areopagitou, walk away from Temple of Zeus on the side of Dionyssiou Areopagitou across from Acropolis, and turn left onto Mitseon and right onto Robertou Galli.

Strofi ✰ GREEK   The rooftop terrace here has a drop-dead view of the Acropolis and the Herodes Atticus theater. After performances, actors and members of the audience cross the street to Strofi to dine on grills, stews, good salads, and *horta* (greens). The cooking can be a bit rough and ready and the waiters a bit rushed, but the Acropolis view makes this place pretty irresistible.

25 Robertou Galli, Makriyianni (across from the Herodes Atticus theater). © 210/921-4130. Main courses 8€–20€ ($9.20–$23). DC, MC, V. Mon–Sat 8pm–1am. Closed Sun. From Syntagma Sq., take Amalias Ave. to pedestrianized Dionyssiou Areopagitou, walk away from Temple of Zeus on the side of Dionyssiou Areopagitou across from Acropolis, and turn left onto Mitseon and right onto Robertou Galli.

HERE & THERE
Very Expensive
Varoulko ✰✰✰ SEAFOOD/NOUVELLE   In an unlikely location on a side street in Piraeus, chef-owner Lefteris Lazarou has created what many consider not just the city's finest seafood restaurant, but the finest restaurant in the greater Athens area. I had one of the best meals in my life here—smoked eel; artichokes with fish roe; crayfish with sun-dried tomatoes; monkfish livers with soy sauce, honey, and balsamic vinegar—and the best sea bass and monkfish I have ever eaten. The bare-brick walls of the restaurant are softened with artwork, and the food is beautifully presented and absolutely delicious.

14 Deligeorgi, Piraeus. © 210/411-2043. Fax 210/422-1283. Reservations necessary (arrange several days in advance). Dinner for 2 from about 125€ ($144); fish priced by the kilo. No credit cards. Mon–Sat about 8pm–midnight. Closed Sun and most of June–Sept, when it often relocates outdoors at the Peace and Friendship Stadium. We recommend taking a taxi to this restaurant, which is hard to find and not in central Piraeus.

Expensive
Boschetto ✰✰ ITALIAN/INTERNATIONAL   Tucked away in the garden below the Evangelismos Hospital, just across from the Hilton Hotel, Boschetto serves up some of the best Italian cuisine in Athens. If you don't want shrimp cannelloni or any of the other pastas, there's fresh fish (sea bass is usually on the menu) and squid, duck, sweetbreads, and excellent beef dishes. This surprisingly tranquil spot just feet from the hubbub of central Athens often attracts an almost entirely Athenian clientele that appreciates the excellent food, careful service, and indoor/outdoor dining here. There's an excellent wine list.

Alsos Evangelismos (Garden of Evangelismos Hospital). © 210/721-0893. Reservations recommended. Main courses 18€–32€ ($21–$37); fish priced by the kilo. AE, V. Mon–Sat 8pm–midnight. Usually closed in Aug. From Syntagma, take Vas. Sophias Blvd. to the Evangelismos Garden. If you come to Gennadiou, you've gone too far.

Spondi ✰✰✰ GREEK   *Athinorama*, the weekly review of the Athenian scene, has chosen Spondi several years running as the best place in town. The menu offers light dishes—the fresh fish, especially the salmon, is superb—as well as a number of heavier dishes that you will find either delightful or a bit cloying (roast pork with *myzithra* cheese and a fig-and-yogurt sauce). The setting, a handsome 19th-century town house with a courtyard, is lovely, the wine list is extensive, the service is excellent, and the desserts are divine. You'll probably want to take a cab here: Pyrronos runs between Empedokleous and Dikearchou, behind the Olympic Stadium.

5 Pyrronos, Pangrati. ℭ 210/752-0658. Reservations recommended. Main courses 20€–35€ ($23–$40). No credit cards. Mon–Sat 8pm–1am.

Moderate

Vlassis ★★★ TRADITIONAL GREEK   Greeks call this kind of food *paradisiako:* traditional, but paradisiacal is just as good a description. This very reasonably priced food is fit for the gods: delicious fluffy vegetable croquettes, eggplant salad that tastes like no other, hauntingly tender lamb in egg-lemon sauce. It's a sign of Vlassis's popularity with Athenians—each time I eat here, I seem to be the only obvious foreigner—that there's not even a discreet sign announcing its presence in a small apartment building on hard-to-find Paster. Figure the price of a taxi (no more than 10€/$12) into your meal tab; you may feel so giddy with delight after eating you won't mind the half-hour walk back to Syntagma.

8 Paster (off Plateia Mavili). ℭ 210/646-3060. Reservations recommended. Main courses 8€–20€ ($9.20–$23). No credit cards. Mon–Sat 8pm–1am. Closed much of June–Sept. From Syntagma Sq., take Vasilissis Sophias Ave. to Plateia Mavili, and follow D. Tsoustou out of Plateia Mavili to Chatzikosta; Paster is the cul-de-sac on the left after you turn right onto Chatzikosta.

Rising Stars in the Psirri District

These days, it's hard to keep up with the cafes, bars, restaurants, and galleries opening in the newly fashionable Psirri district, between Ermou and Athinas. Only 5 years ago this was a neighborhood largely noted for its derelict warehouses and tumbledown houses. The low rents prompted young would-be restaurateurs and gallery owners to renovate neglected buildings. You'll see lots of bare brick walls, minimalist decor, and *tons* of yuppies here, especially after dark.

At **Taki 13,** 13 Taki (ℭ 210/325-4707), the food is less the thing than the bar, the music, and the stylish young Athenians who gather here. **Zeidoron,** 10 Taki and Ayios Anaryiron (ℭ 210/321-5368), is basically a *mezedopolio* (hors d'oeuvres place), although it also serves entrees. The *mezedes* are also delicious at **To Krasopoulio tou Kokkora,** Karaiskaki and 4 Aisopou (ℭ 210/321-1565), where you can dine indoors or out. During the summer at **Couzina Cine-Psyrri,** 40 Sarri (ℭ 210/321-5534), you can watch a movie on an outdoor screen while you dine.

Many of Psirri's galleries stay open late, which means that you can eat and browse—or browse and eat. **Epistrofi,** 6–8 Taki (ℭ 210/321-8640; www.epistrofi.gr), is worth a visit just to see the handsomely restored early-19th-century town house it occupies; it sometimes hosts concerts as well as art exhibitions. **Stigma,** 20–22 Agios Anargyros (ℭ 210/322-1675), features frequent shows of local artists.

When you tire of Psirri, you can strike out for neighboring **Gazi,** a once-desolate wasteland dominated by the gasworks, now on the verge of becoming chic. You could do worse than try a meal at **Mamacas,** 41 Persephoni (ℭ 210/346-4984), an upmarket taverna that was one of the first of the new wave of restaurants here.

SEEING THE SIGHTS

SIGHTSEEING SUGGESTIONS FOR FIRST-TIME VISITORS

If You Have 1 Day Try to be at the **Acropolis** as soon as it opens (or in the hour before it closes) so that you can take in the site and enjoy seeing the **Parthenon** and the **Acropolis Museum** with as few people around as possible. Afterward, walk downhill to visit the **Ancient Agora** and then head into **Monastiraki** and the **Plaka,** where you can window-shop and relax over lunch or dinner. Keep an eye out for the Plaka **tram.** The half-hour ride begins in Palia Agora Square, loops through the Plaka, and passes the Acropolis on Dionyssiou Areopagitou Boulevard before heading back into the Plaka (10am–10pm in summer; 5€/ $5.75). It's a great (and relaxing) way to get a sense of what you may want to explore on foot in the Plaka.

If You Have 2 Days It's worth spending several hours of day 2 at the **National Archaeological Museum**—but call to make sure it's open during your visit. The museum closed for renovations in 2002; was slated to reopen in May 2004 in time for the August 2004 Summer Olympics—and there were rumors that it might close again thereafter for additional work. Try to arrive the minute it opens to beat the crowds; or choose the hour before it closes, when there are fewer visitors. If the archaeological museum is closed, check out some of Athens's smaller museums, or, if you prefer a change of pace, head up **Mount Likavitos** on the funicular that leaves from the top of Ploutarchou Street (4€/ $4.60), 10am to midnight, about every 20 minutes in summer. If the *nefos* (smog) isn't too bad, you'll have a wonderful view of Athens, Piraeus, and the Saronic Gulf. If you have an extra hour, stroll down one of the paths from the summit, enjoying the scent of pine trees and the changing views of the city.

If You Have 3 Days or More For the rest of your stay, visit more of the museums listed below, or consider a day trip to one of the great sights of antiquity, such as Delphi or **Sounion;** or a day excursion to **Corinth, Mycenae,** and **Epidauros** (best done on a bus tour). If you don't want to go home without seeing one of the "isles of Greece," take a day trip by boat from Piraeus to one of the islands of the Saronic Gulf. **Aegina (Egina), Poros,** and **Hydra (Idra)** are all feasible day trips—but they are best not done the day before you leave Athens, lest bad weather strands you on an island.

THE TREASURES OF ANTIQUITY

The Acropolis ★★★ **Note:** The monuments of the Acropolis underwent extensive renovation in honor of the 2004 Summer Olympics. At press time, these renovations had not been completed. The Temple of Nike, which had been entirely dismantled for restoration, was partially reerected. The Propylaia and Parthenon were encased in scaffolding. What follows is an attempt to describe what you should see when the renovations are completed.

When you climb up the Acropolis—the heights above the city—you'll realize why people seem to have lived here as long ago as 5000 B.C. The sheer sides of the Acropolis make it a superb natural defense, just the place to avoid enemies and to be able to see invaders coming across the sea or the plains of Attica. And,

---

Tips **The Ups & Downs of Ticket Prices**

At press time, ticket prices for many monuments and museums were in flux. The prices listed in this guide are based on the prices available at press time and "guesstimates" offered by some museums. As if that is not sufficiently confusing, keep in mind that virtually all the major attractions plan to raise their admission fees "soon." Because there is—surprise!—no fixed policy on cheaper tickets for students and seniors, be sure to ask about a discounted ticket if you are a senior or a student, and be prepared to show your ID.

---

of course, it helped that in antiquity there was a spring here, ensuring a steady supply of water.

In classical times, when Athens's population had grown to around 250,000, people lived on the slopes below the Acropolis, which had become the city's most important religious center. Athens's civic and business center, the Agora, and its cultural center, with several theaters and concert halls, bracketed the Acropolis; when you peer over the sides of the Acropolis at the houses in the Plaka and the remains of the ancient **Agora** and the **Theater of Dionysos,** you'll see the layout of the ancient city. Syntagma and Omonia squares, the heart of today's Athens, were well out of the ancient city center.

Even the Acropolis's height couldn't protect it from the Persian invasion of 480 B.C., when most of its monuments were burned and destroyed. You may notice some immense column drums built into the Acropolis's walls. When the great Athenian statesman Pericles ordered the monuments rebuilt, he had the drums from the destroyed Parthenon built into the walls lest Athenians forget what had happened—and so they would remember that they had rebuilt what they had lost. Pericles' rebuilding program began about 448 B.C.; the new Parthenon was dedicated 10 years later, but work on other monuments continued for a century.

The **Parthenon** ✹✹✹—dedicated to Athena Parthenos (the Virgin), patron goddess of Athens—was the most important religious monument, but there were shrines to many other gods and goddesses on the Acropolis's broad summit. As you climb up, you pass through first the **Beule Gate,** built by the Romans and now known by the name of the French archaeologist who discovered it in 1852. Next comes the **Propylaia** ✹, the monumental 5th-century-B.C. entranceway. You'll notice the little **Temple of Athena Nike (Athena of Victory)** ✹ perched above the Propylaia; the beautifully proportioned Ionic temple was built in 424 B.C. Off to the left of the Parthenon is the **Erechtheion** ✹✹, which the Athenians honored as the tomb of Erechtheus, a legendary king of Athens. A hole in the ceiling and floor of the northern porch indicates the spot where Poseidon's trident struck to make a spring (symbolizing control of the sea) gush forth during his contest with Athena to be the city's chief deity. Athena countered with an olive tree (symbolizing control of the rich Attic plain); the olive tree planted beside the Erechtheion reminds visitors of her victory. Give yourself a little time to enjoy the delicate carving on the Erechtheion, and be sure to see the original **caryatids** (the monumental female figures who served as columns on the Erechtheion's porch) in the Acropolis Museum.

However charmed you are by these elegant little temples, you're probably still heading resolutely toward the **Parthenon,** and you may be disappointed to realize

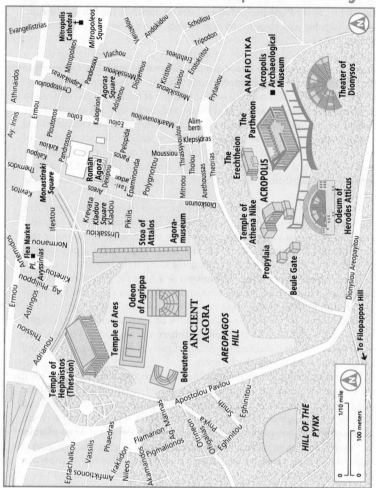

that visitors are not allowed inside, both to protect the monument and to allow any ongoing restoration work to proceed safely. If you find this frustrating, keep in mind that in antiquity only priests and honored visitors were allowed in to see the monumental 11m (36-ft.) statue of Athena designed by the great Phidias, who supervised Pericles's building program. Nothing of the huge gold-and-ivory statue remains, but there's a small Roman copy in the National Archaeological Museum—and horrific renditions on souvenirs ranging from T-shirts to ouzo bottles.

The Parthenon's entire roof and much of the interior were blown to smithereens in 1687, when a party of Venetians attempted to take the Acropolis from the Turks. A shell fired from nearby Mouseion Hill struck the Parthenon—where the Turks were storing gunpowder and munitions—and caused appalling damage to the building and its sculptures. Most of the remaining sculptures were carted off to London by Lord Elgin in the first decade of the 19th century. Those surviving sculptures—known to most of the world as **Elgin Marbles,** but known here as the **Parthenon Marbles**—are on display in the British Museum, causing ongoing pain to generations of Greeks, who continue to press for their return.

The Parthenon originally had sculpture in both its pediments, as well as a frieze running around the entire temple. Alternating **triglyphs** (panels with three incised grooves) and **metopes** (sculptured panels) made up the frieze. The message of most of this sculpture was the triumph of knowledge and civilization (read: Athens) over the forces of darkness and barbarians. An interior frieze showed scenes from the Panathenaic Festival each August, when citizens walked in procession through the streets, bringing a new *peplos* (tunic) for the statue of Athena. Only a few fragments of any of the sculptures remain in place, and every visitor will have to decide whether it's a good or a bad thing that Lord Elgin removed so much before the smog spread over Athens and ate away at the remaining sculpture.

If you're lucky enough to visit the Acropolis on a smog-free and sunny day, you'll see the golden and cream tones of the Parthenon's handsome Pentelic marble at their most subtle. It may come as something of a shock to realize that the Parthenon, like most other monuments here, was painted in antiquity, with gay colors that have since faded, revealing the tones of the marble.

The **Acropolis Archaeological Museum** ✫✫ hugs the ground to detract as little as possible from the ancient monuments. Inside, you'll see the four original caryatids from the Erechtheion that are still in Athens (one disappeared during the Ottoman occupation, and one is in the British Museum). Other delights here include sculpture from the original Parthenon burned by the Persians, statues of *korai* (maidens) dedicated to Athena, figures of *kouroi* (young men), and a wide range of finds from the Acropolis.

Those interested in learning more about the Acropolis should check to see if the **Center for Acropolis Studies,** on Makriyanni Street just southeast of the Acropolis (✆ **210/923-9381**), has reopened. If so, it will be open daily from 9am to 2:30pm; admission is free. Items on display should include artifacts, reconstructions, photographs, drawings, and plaster casts of the Elgin Marbles (see above). A museum is being built here to house the marbles when (if) they're returned to Athens. Construction has been slowed by the discovery of important Byzantine remains here.

You'll probably want to spend half a day on the Acropolis.

Dionyssiou Areopagitou. ✆ 210/321-0219. Admission 12€ ($14) adults. Free Sun. This ticket, which is valid for 1 week, includes admission to the Acropolis, Acropolis Museum, Ancient Agora, Theater of Dionysos, Karameikos Cemetery, Roman Forum, Tower of the Winds, and Temple of Olympian Zeus. It is still possible to buy individual tickets at the other sites. The Acropolis is usually open summer daily 8am–7pm, winter daily 8:30am–2:30pm. The Acropolis Museum usually closes at least half an hour earlier than the Acropolis. From Syntagma Sq., take Amalias Ave. into pedestrianized Dionyssiou Areopagitou, and follow the marble path up to the Acropolis. The ticket booth, along with a small post office and a snack bar, are slightly below the Acropolis entrance.

Ancient Agora ✫✫ The Agora was Athens's commercial and civic center, with buildings used for a wide range of political, educational, philosophical, theatrical, and athletic purposes—which may be why what remains seems such a jumble. This is a nice place to wander and enjoy the views up toward the Acropolis; take in the herb garden and flowers planted around the 5th-century B.C. **Theseion (Temple of Hephaistos);** peek into the heavily restored 11th-century church of **Ayii Apostoli (Holy Apostles);** and admire the 2nd-century B.C. **Stoa of Attalos,** totally reconstructed in the 1950s.

The museum in the Stoa's ground floor has finds from 5,000 years of Athenian history, including sculpture and pottery, as well as a voting machine and a child's potty seat, all with labels in English. The museum (which, by the way, has excellent toilet facilities) closes 15 minutes before the site.

You'll want to spend at least 2 hours here.

Below the Acropolis on the edge of Monastiraki (entrance on Adrianou, near Ayiou Philippou Sq., east of Monastiraki Sq. and on Ay. Apostoli, the road leading down into Plaka from the Acropolis). ℂ 210/321-0185. Admission (includes museum) 4€ ($4.60).

Cemetery of Keramikos   This ancient cemetery, where **Pericles** gave his famous funeral oration, is a short walk from the Ancient Agora and not far from the presumed site of **Plato's Academy.** There are a number of well-preserved funerary monuments and the remains of the colossal **Dipylon Gate,** the main entrance to the ancient city of Athens. In 2002, the well-preserved marble figure of a *kouros* (youth) was found in excavations here, a hint of what treasures remain to be found. For now, you can see the substantial remains of the 5th-century-B.C. fortifications known as the "Long Walls" that ran from Athens to Piraeus. The Keramikos is seldom crowded, which makes it a pleasant spot to sit and read. If you like cemeteries, be sure to take in Athens's enormous **First Cemetery,** near the Athens Stadium, where notables such as former prime minister George Panandreou are buried beneath elaborate monuments. Both cemeteries are pleasant spots in which to spend a few hours.

148 Ermou. ℂ 210/346-3553. Admission 2€ ($2.30). Tues–Sun 8:30am–3pm. Walk west from Monastiraki Sq. on Ermou past Thisio Metro station; cemetery is on the right.

THE TOP MUSEUMS

The National Archaeological Museum ★★★   *Note:* The museum closed for renovations in 2002 and was scheduled to reopen in May 2004 in time for the August 2004 Summer Olympics. The second floor of the museum, where most of the extensive collection of Greek vases was housed, had already been closed since 1999, when an earthquake shook Athens. It was not known at press time where objects would be displayed; therefore, for now, we can only detail the museum's main attractions, not where they will be displayed. Be sure to check ahead for updated opening times and prices.

This is an enormous and enormously popular museum; try to arrive as soon as it opens (or the hour before it closes) so that you can see the exhibits and not just the other visitors' backs. The collection includes objects from the Neolithic to the Roman eras. Don't miss the stunning gold masks, cups, dishes, and jewelry unearthed from the site of Mycenae by Heinrich Schliemann in 1876; the elegant marble Cycladic figurines (ca. 2000 B.C.); and the famous marble and bronze statues. The museum's extensive collection of black-and-red figure vases is, not surprisingly, the finest in the world. The museum shop has reproductions and books on aspects of the collection. You'll probably want to spend a minimum of 3 hours here—and wish you'd spent more.

44 Patission. ℂ 210/821-7717. protocol@eam.culture.gr. Admission 6€ ($6.90). Mon 12:30–6pm; Tues–Fri 8am–6pm; Sat–Sun and holidays 8:30am–3pm. From Omonia Sq., walk about .5km (½ mile) or 10 min. north on the road officially named 28 Oktovriou (October 28) Ave. but usually called Patission.

N. P. Goulandris Foundation Museum of Cycladic Art ★★★   This handsome museum houses the largest collection of Cycladic art outside the National Archaeological Museum. See if you agree with those who have compared the faces of the Cycladic figurines to the works of the Italian painter Modigliani. Be

---

Tips **Online Museum Updates**

Information on most Greek museums and archaeological sites—and updates on any price hikes—should be available on **www.culture.gr**.

---

sure to go through the courtyard into the museum's newest acquisition: an elegant 19th-century house with some of its original furnishings and visiting exhibits. The museum shop has a wide variety of books and reproductions—and a resolutely unhelpful staff. You'll want to spend at least 3 hours here; be sure to take a break in the garden cafe.

4 Neophytou Douka. ✆ **210/722-8321.** www.cycladic-m.gr. Admission 4€ ($4.60). Mon and Wed–Fri 10am–4pm; Sat 10am–3pm. From Syntagma Sq., walk 7 blocks east along Vasilissis Sofias Ave., then ½ block north on Neophytou Douka.

Benaki Museum ★★   This stunning private collection includes treasures from the Neolithic era to the 20th century. The folk art collection (including magnificent costumes and icons) is superb, as are the two entire rooms from 18th-century northern Greek mansions, ancient Greek bronzes, gold cups, Fayum portraits, and rare early Christian textiles. A new wing doubles the exhibition space of the original 20th-century neoclassical town house that belonged to the wealthy Benaki family. The museum shop is excellent, and new galleries have special exhibitions. Dine with a spectacular view over Athens at the excellent rooftop cafe, which offers a buffet supper (30€/$35) Thursday evenings, when the museum remains open until midnight. This is a very pleasant place to spend several hours—or days.

Koumbari 1 (at Leoforos Vasilissis Sofias, Kolonaki, 5 blocks east of Syntagma Sq.). ✆ **210/367-1000.** www.benaki.gr. Admission 6€ ($6.90); free on Thurs. Mon, Wed, Fri, Sat 9am–5pm; Thurs 9am–midnight; Sun 9am–3pm; closed Tues.

Byzantine Museum ★   If you love icons (paintings, usually of saints, usually on wood) or want to find out about them, this is the place to go. As its name makes clear, this museum, in a 19th-century Florentine-style villa, is devoted to the art and history of the Byzantine era (roughly 4th–15th c. A.D.). Selections from Greece's most important collection of icons and religious art—along with sculptures, altars, mosaics, religious vestments, Bibles, and a small-scale reconstruction of an early Christian basilica—are exhibited on several floors around a courtyard. Allow at least an hour for your visit; 2 hours is better. If there is a special exhibit, try to allow 3 hours or more.

22 Vasilissis Sofias Ave. ✆ **210/723-1570** or 210/721-1027. Admission 4€ ($4.60). Tues–Sun 8:30am–3pm. From Syntagma Sq., walk along Queen Sophias Ave. for about 15 min. The museum is on your right. If you come to the Hilton Hotel, you have gone too far.

Greek Folk Art Museum ★★ *(Kids)*   This endearing small museum has dazzling embroideries and costumes, carved wooden furniture and tools, and ceramic and copper utensils from all over the country, plus a small room with zany frescoes of gods and heroes done by eccentric artist Theofilos Hadjimichael, who painted in the early part of the 20th century. Lots of Greek schoolchildren visit here, and sometimes puppet shows are offered. It's a great place to spend several hours.

17 Kidathineon, Plaka. ✆ **210/322-9031.** Admission 2€ ($2.30). Tues–Sun 10am–2pm. From Syntagma, take Filellinon to Kidathineon.

Museum of Greek Popular Musical Instruments ★★   Photographs show the musicians, while recordings let you listen to the tamborines, Cretan lyres, lutes, pottery drums, and clarinets on display. In addition, this museum is just steps from the excellent Platanos taverna, so you can alternate the pleasures of food, drink, and music. On a recent visit, an elderly Greek gentleman listened to some music, transcribed it, stepped out into the courtyard, and played it on his own violin! The shop has a wide selection of CDs and cassettes.

1–3 Dioyenous (around the corner from the Tower of the Winds). ✆ 01-325-0198. Free admission. Tues and Thurs–Sun 10am–2pm; Wed noon–6pm. Dioyenous 1–3 (around the corner from the Tower of the Winds). ✆ 01-325-0198. Free admission. Tues and Thurs–Sun 10am–2pm; Wed noon–6pm. Metro: Acropolis or Monastiraki.

Ilias Lalaounis Jewelry Museum ★★   The 3,000 pieces on display here are so spectacular that even those who don't care about jewelry will enjoy this small, glitzy museum, founded by one of Greece's most successful jewelry designers. The first floor has a boutique stocking 2,000 items and a small workshop. The second and third floors display pieces inspired by ancient, Byzantine, and Cycladic designs, as well as by flora and fauna. The museum has frequent special exhibits and a cafe. Many of the exhibits are small and detailed, so you'll probably want to spend several hours here.

12 Kalisperi (at Karyatidon). ✆ 210/922-1044. Fax 210/923-7358. www.lalaounis-jewelrymuseum.gr. Admission 4€ ($4.60). Mon and Thurs–Sat 9am–4pm; Wed 9am–9pm (free after 3pm); Sun 10am–4pm. Walk 1 block south of the Acropolis between Theater of Dionysos and Odeum of Herodes Atticus.

GALLERIES

One of the great (usually free) pleasures of visiting Athens is browsing in its small art galleries. Very occasionally a gallery will have an admission fee for a special exhibit, but usually there is no charge. This is a wonderful way to get a sense of the contemporary Greek art scene and possibly buy something to take home. Openings are usually not by invitation only, so if you see a notice of an opening, feel free to stop by. A good way to check on what's on is to pick up a free copy of the quarterlies *Art and the City* and *The Athens Contemporary Art Map.* Both are free, bilingual in Greek and English, and usually available in hotels in galleries. In case you do not immediately find a copy of either quarterly, here are some galleries to keep an eye out for in central Athens. The **Epistrofi Gallery,** 6 Taki (✆ 210/321-8640), in trendy **Psirri** (so trendy that it has its own website: www.psiri.gr/english), has occasional concerts as well as shows; the **Epikentro Gallery,** 10 Armodiou (✆ 210/331-2187), stages frequent exhibits in its improbable location in the Athens Central Market; the **Rebecca Kamhi Gallery,** Sophokleous 23 (✆ 210/321-0448), not far from the Central Market, and one of Athens's best-known galleries, is open by appointment only in August; **Bernier/Eliades Gallery,** 11 Eptachalkou, Theseion (✆ 210/341-3935), stages group exhibitions, as does **Kappatos,** Agias Irenes 6 (✆ 210/321-7931). There are also frequent shows at the **Melina Mercouri Cultural Center,** Iraklidon and Thessalonikis 66 (✆ 210/345-2150), not far from the Theseion and at the Melina Mercouri Foundation, Polygnotou 9–11 (✆ 210/331-5601), in the Plaka. The fashionable Kolonaki district is chockablock with galleries: the **Athens Art Center,** 4 Glyconos, Dexameni (✆ 210/721-3938); **Photohoros,** Tsakalof 44 (✆ 210/321-0448); and **Medussa,** Xenokratous 7 (✆ 210/724-4552), are three to look for. The **Athens Arts and Technology School** (✆ 210/381-3700) usually stages shows around Athens in July and August when many galleries close or move out of town. One just-out-of-town suburban gallery that's open year-round and well worth a visit (in part for its great cafe and shop) is **The Deste Foundation for Contemporary Art,** Omirou 8, Nea Psychico (© **210/672-9460;** www.deste.gr), a 20-minute cab ride from Syntagma.

ORGANIZED TOURS

You can book tours of Athens through most hotels or any travel agency. A half-day tour of city highlights costs from 50€ to 150€ ($58–$173), with more expensive tours including a full meal. Night tours can include a sound-and-light show, Greek folk dancing at the Dora Stratou Dance Theater, or dinner and Greek dancing. Since many Athenian nightclubs are clip joints, the safety-in-numbers aspect of a visit with a tour group may appeal to you.

   Educational Tours & Cruises, 9 Irving, Medford, MA 02111 (© **800/275-4109;** edtours@ars.nep.gr), and 1 Artemídos, Glyfáda 16674, Athens (© **210/898-1741**), can arrange tours in Athens and throughout Greece, including individual tours with an emphasis on Greek culture. **CHAT Tours,** 9 Xenofondos (Syntagma, 4th floor; © **210/322-3137;** fax 210/323-5270; chat@chatours.gr); and **Key Tours,** 4 Kalliroïs (© **210/923-3166;** fax 210/923-2008), are reliable, established companies that offer tours of Athens and various day trips. Destinations include the temple of Apollo at Sounion, Delphi (day trip or overnight visit), and the Peloponnese (day trip usually taking in Corinth, Mycenae, and Epidauros; 3-day trips of the major sites; and a 5-day trip, usually including Delphi).

THE SHOPPING SCENE

You may find a copy of the monthly magazines *Athens Today* and *Now in Athens,* both of which have a shopping section, in your hotel room; sometimes copies are also available at the **Greek National Tourism Organization,** 2 Amerikis. *Note:* Keep in mind that most of the restaurants and shops featured pay for the privilege. This is not true of places featured in the excellent English-language magazine *Odyssey.*

   You're in luck shopping in Athens, because almost everything you'll probably want to buy can be found in the central city, bounded by Omonia, Syntagma, and Monastiraki squares. This is where you'll find most of the shops frequented by Athenians, including a number of large **department stores.**

   Monastiraki has its famous **flea market,** which is especially lively on Sundays. Although it has a vast amount of ticky-tacky stuff for sale here, it also has some real finds, including retro clothes and old copper. Many Athenians furnishing new homes head here to try to pick up old treasures.

   The **Plaka** has pretty much cornered the market on souvenir shops, with enough T-shirts, reproductions of antiquities (including obscene playing cards, drink coasters, bottle openers, and more), fishermen's sweaters (increasingly made in the Far East), and jewelry (often not real gold) to circle the globe.

   In the Plaka-Monastiraki area, several shops worth seeking out amid the endlessly repetitive souvenir shops include **Stavros Melissinos,** the Poet-Sandalmaker of Athens, 89 Pandrossou (© **210/321-9247**); **Iphanta,** the weaving workshop, 6 Selleu (© **210/322-3628**); **Emanuel Masmanidis' Gold Rose Jewelry Shop,** 85 Pandrossou (© **210/321-5662**); the **Center of Hellenic Tradition,** 59 Mitropoleos and 36 Pandrossou (© **210/321-3023**), which sells arts and crafts; and the **National Welfare Organization,** 6 Ipatias and Apollonos, Plaka (© **210/325-0524**), where a portion of the proceeds from everything sold (including handsome woven and embroidered carpets) goes to the National Welfare Organization, which encourages traditional crafts. Two shops in Monastiraki have impressive selections of traditional Greek musical instruments, including bouzoukis, tambourines, and lyres: **Vasilios Kevorkian,** 6 Ifestou (© 210/321-0024), and **Xannis Samouelian's Musical Instruments,** 36 Ifestou (© 210/321-2433).

Kolonaki, up on the slopes of Mount Likavitos, is boutique heaven—but it's a better place to window-shop than to buy, since much of what you see is imported and heavily taxed. If you're here during the January or August sales, you may find some bargains. If not, it's still a lot of fun to work your way up pedestrian Voukourestiou, along Tsakalof and Anagnostopoulou (with perhaps the most expensive boutiques in Athens), before collapsing at a cafe by one of the pedestrian shopping streets in Kolonaki Square—perhaps the very fashionable Milioni. Then you can engage in the other really serious business of Kolonaki: people-watching. Give yourself about 15 minutes to discern the season's must-have accessory.

ATHENS AFTER DARK

Greeks enjoy their nightlife so much that they take an afternoon nap to rest up for it. The evening often begins with a leisurely *volta* (stroll); you'll see it in most neighborhoods, including the Plaka and Kolonaki Square. Most Greeks don't think of dinner until at least 9pm—when there's still no hurry. Around midnight the party may move on to a club for music and dancing. Feel free to try places on your own, although you may feel like the odd man out because Greeks seldom go anywhere alone. If you're a woman on your own and want to be left alone, you'll probably find hitting the bars and dance clubs uncongenial.

Check the daily *Kathimerini* insert in the *International Herald-Tribune* or the *Athens News,* both sold at most major newsstands, for current cultural and entertainment events, including films, lectures, theater, music, and dance. The weekly *Hellenic Times* and *Athenscope* and the monthly *Now in Athens* list nightspots, restaurants, movies, theater, and much more. The weekly Greek publication *Athinorama* has comprehensive listings of events.

Best of all, if you have a Greek friend, ask for pointers on what's currently on. If you ask a taxi driver, he's likely to take you to either his cousin George's joint or the place that gives him a kickback for bringing you. Be especially wary of heading out of the city to the places that spring up each summer on the airport road; these spots are usually overpriced and often unsavory. That said, the Asteria Club (© 210/894-4558) and the Bio-Bio Club (© 210/894-1300) in

---

Open in August

A great many popular after-dark spots close in August, when much of Athens flees to the country to escape the summer heat. Among the places that stay open are a number of bars, cafes, *ouzeries,* and tavernas on the pedestrian **Iraklion Walkway** near the Theseion. **Stavlos,** the restaurant, bar, and disco popular with all ages, remains open on August weekends. Nearby, the **Berlin Club,** which caters to a young crowd and specializes in rock 'n' roll, is open most nights; **Ambibagio** has quite genuine Greek music. The sweet shop **Aistisis** has great views of the Acropolis and stays open as late as the nearby bars.

Glyfada were popular during the summer of 2003, as was **Riba's** (© **210/ 965-5555**) in Varkiza and **Gefira** (© **210/940-9221**) at 26–28 Posidonos, Tzitzifies. In Athens itself, Kolonaki's **Haritos** has a number of popular bars, as does the **Psirri district** and the **Thission district.** Expect to pay about 20€ ($23) for one or two drinks after paying an entrance charge of at least that much at all these live-music joints. (Also see below under "Live-Music Clubs.")

THE PERFORMING ARTS

Tickets for the **Athens, Lycabettus,** and **Epidauros festivals** are available at the **Hellenic Festival Box Office,** 39 Panepistimiou in the arcade (© **210/322- 1459**). Advance booking for the Athens and Epidauros festivals starts 3 weeks before each performance; 10 days before each event for the Lycabettus Festival. Tickets (if available) are also on sale at the box offices at each theater 2 hours before each performance.

Additional information on the Hellenic Festival, including the Athens, Epidauros, and Lycabettus festivals, is available at the websites **www. hellenicfestival.gr, www.cultureguide.gr,** and **www.greektourism.com.** Many of these events, and others, are sponsored by the **Cultural Olympiad** (www. cultural-olympiad.gr), which was part of the buildup to the 2004 Summer Olympics.

The **Athens Festival** at the **Odeon of Herodes Atticus** features famous Greek and foreign artists performing music, plays, opera, and ballet from the beginning of June to the beginning of October in a beautiful open-air setting. The only drawbacks are that the stone seats are hard, with thin foam cushions, and that there are no backrests. Find out what's being presented through the English-language press or at the **Hellenic Festival Box Office,** 39 Panepis- timiou in the arcade (© **210/322-1459,** 210/322-3111, or 210/322-3110, ext. 137). The office is open Monday through Saturday from 8:30am to 2pm and 5 to 7pm, and Sunday from 10am to 1pm. Tickets usually cost about 15€ to 50€ ($17–$58). If they're available—and that's a big "if"—tickets can also be purchased at the **Odeon** (© **210/323-2771**) several hours before a performance.

Information on performances (often of pop music) at the Lycabettus Festival, staged in a modern amphitheater on the slopes of Mount Lycabettus each sum- mer, is available from the Hellenic Festival Box Office (see above).

Information on performances (primarily of ancient Greek drama, usually translated into modern Greek) in the ancient theater of Epidauros at the Epidauros Festival take place each summer; information is available from the Hellenic Festival Box Office (see above) and, if available, at the theater in Epidauros on the day of performances.

The acoustically marvelous new **Megaron Mousikis Concert Hall,** 89 Vasilissis Sofias Ave. (© **210/729-0391** or 210/728-2333), hosts a wide range of classical music programs that include chamber music, operas in concert, sym- phonic concerts, and recitals. The box office is usually open weekdays from 10am to 6pm, Saturday from 10am to 2pm, and Sunday from 6 to 10:30pm on per- formance nights only. Tickets, usually costing about 5€ to 50€ ($5.75–$58), are also sold weekdays from 10am to 5pm in the Megaron's convenient downtown kiosk in the Spiromillios Arcade, 4 Stadiou (the arcade is in the courtyard off Stadiou). The Megaron has a limited summer season but is in full swing the rest of the year.

Most major jazz and rock concerts, as well as some classical performances, take place at the **Pallas Theater,** 1 Voukourestiou (© **210/322-8275**).

English-language theater and American-style music are performed at the **Hellenic American Union Auditorium,** 22 Massalias, between Kolonaki and Omonia squares (© **210/362-9886**); you can usually get a ticket from around 10€ ($11.50). Arrive early and check out the art show or photo exhibition at the adjacent gallery. The **Greek National Opera** performs at the **Olympia Theater,** 59 Akadimias, at Mavromihali (© **210/361-2461**).

The **Dora Stratou Folk Dance Theater,** which performs May through October on Philopappos Hill, is the best known of the traditional dance troupes. For several years there have been rumors of the company's closing, but thus far regional dances continue to be performed in costume with appropriate (if overamplified) musical accompaniment nightly at 10:15pm, with additional shows at 8:15pm on Wednesday and Sunday (no performances on Mon). You can buy tickets from about 10€ to 20€ ($12–$23) from 8am to 2pm at the box office, 8 Scholio, Plaka (© **210/924-4395,** or 210/921-4650 after 5:30pm).

Sound-and-light shows, seen from the Pnyx, the hill across Dionyssiou Areopagitou Street from the Acropolis, illuminate (sorry) Athens's history by focusing on the history of the Acropolis. Try to sit away from the (very) loud speakers, so you won't be deafened by the booming historical narrative and all-too-stirring music and can concentrate instead on the play of lights on the monuments of the Acropolis. Shows are held April through October. Performances in English begin at 9pm and last 45 minutes. Tickets can be purchased at the **Hellenic Festival Box Office,** 39 Panepistimiou in the arcade (© **210/322-1459**); or at the entrance to the sound-and-light show (© **210/922-6210**), which is signposted on the Pnyx. Ticket prices had not been set at press time, but should be about 10€ ($12).

LIVE-MUSIC CLUBS

Walk the streets of the Plaka on any night and you'll find lots of tavernas offering pseudo-traditional live music (usually at clip-joint prices) and a few offering the real thing. **Taverna Mostrou,** 22 Mnissikleos (© **210/324-2441**), is one of the largest, oldest, and best known for traditional Greek music and dancing. Shows begin about 11pm and usually last to 2am. The cover charge (from about 30€/$35) includes a fixed-price supper; a la carte fare is available but expensive. Nearby, **Palia Taverna Kritikou,** 24 Mnissikleos (© **210/322-2809**), is another lively open-air taverna with music and dancing. Other reliable tavernas with live traditional music are **Nefeli,** 24 Panos (© **210/321-2475**); **Dioyenis,** 3 Sellei (© **210/324-7933**); **Stamatopoulou,** 26 Lissiou (© **210/322-8722**); and **Xinou,** 4 Geronta (© **210/322-1065**).

Those interested in authentic *rebetika* (music of the urban poor and dispossessed) should consult their hotel receptionist or the current issue of *Athenscope* or *Athinorama* (in Greek) to see which clubs are featuring the best performers. Shows usually don't start until nearly midnight, and although there's usually no cover, a 25€ ($29) charge per drink isn't uncommon. Most clubs are closed in summer, and many are far from the town center, so budget at least another 30€ to 50€ ($35–$58) for round-trip taxi fare.

One of the more central clubs is the **Stoa Athanaton,** 19 Sofokleous, in the Central Meat Market (© **210/321-4362**), which has live rebetika Monday through Saturday from 3 to 6pm and after midnight and serves good food; the minimum charge is 10€ ($12), but is scheduled to go up at least 5€ ($5.75) during the 2004 Olympics; many of the places below plan to follow suit. **Taximi,** 29 Isavron, Exarchia (© **210/363-9919**), is consistently popular, with drinks costing about 10€ ($11.50). It's closed Sunday and July and August. **Frangosyriani,** 57 Arachovis, Exarchia (© **210/360-0693**), specializes in the music of rebetika legend Markos Vamvakaris; it's closed Tuesday and Wednesday. The downscale, smoke-filled **Rebetiki Istoria,** in a neoclassical building at 181 Ippokratous (© **210/642-4937**), features old-style rebetika music, played to a mixed crowd of older regulars and younger students and intellectuals. The music usually starts at 11pm, but arrive earlier to get a seat. The legendary Maryo I Thessaloniki (Maryo from Thessaloniki), sometimes described as the Bessie Smith of Greece, has often sung rebetika at **Perivoli t'Ouranou,** 19 Lysikratous in the Plaka (© **210/323-5517** or 210/322-2048); admission is around 25€ ($29).

A number of clubs and cafes specialize in jazz but also offer everything from Indian sitar music to rock and punk. **The Café Asante,** 78 Damareos in Pangrati (© **210/756-0102**), has music most nights from 11pm. As at most of these clubs and cafes, admission varies, but count on spending around at least 35€ ($40) at the Café Asante if you have a couple of drinks. The very popular **Half Note Jazz Club,** 17 Trivonianou, Mets (© **210/921-3310**), offers up everything from medieval music to jazz nightly. Performance times vary from 8 to 11pm and later; admission is usually around 15€ to 20€ ($17–$23). At **The House of Art,** 4 Sahtouri and Sari (© **210/321-7678**), and at **Pinakothiki,** 5 Agias Theklas (© **210/324-7741**), both in newly fashionable Psyrri, you can often hear jazz from 11pm; admission is around 20€ ($23), including the first drink. **The Rodon Club,** 24 Marni, west of Omonia Square (© **210/523-6293**), also has jazz and pop concerts many nights from 10pm; admission is usually from 20€ ($23). Again, keep in mind that these press-time prices were all rumored to go up some 10% to 20%.

GAY & LESBIAN BARS

The scene is fairly low key; get-togethers are sometimes advertised in the English-language press. Information is also available from the Greek national gay and lesbian organization **AKOE-AMPHI,** P.O. Box 26002, 10022 Athens.

The friendliest bar is **Aleko's Island,** 42 Tsakalof, Kolonaki (no phone), a fun place where you can actually have a conversation. **Granazi,** 20 Lembesi (© **210/325-3979**), attracts a loud and lively young crowd. The disco **Lambda,** 15 Lembesi and 9 Syngrou Ave. (© **210/922-4202**), is hip and trendy with the young locals. In Kolonaki, **Alexander's,** 44 Anagnostopoulou (© **210/364-6660**), is more sedate, with more variety. **Porta,** 10 Phalirou (© **210/924-3858**), and **Fairytale,** 25 Kolleti (© **210/330-1763**), are well-established lesbian bars.

DANCE CLUBS

Hidden on the outskirts of the Plaka, **Booze,** 57 Kolokotroni, second floor (© **210/324-0944**), blasts danceable rock to a hip student crowd. There's art on every wall, gelled stage lights, and two bars. If it's disco you're craving, head east to **Absolut,** 23 Filellinon (no phone); **Q Base,** 49 Evripidou, Omonia (© **210/321-8256**); or **R-Load,** 161 Ermou (© **210/345-6187**). If you feel a bit too old there, head north to Panepistimiou Street, where the **Wild Rose,** in the arcade at 10 Panepistimiou (© **210/364-2160**), and **Mercedes Rex,** at 48 Panepistimiou (© **210/361-4591**), usually have varied programs. Admission at all these clubs usually begins at around 15€ ($17).

2 Delphi & the Northern Peloponnese

With the exception of the Acropolis in Athens, the most famous and beautiful ancient sites in Greece bracket the Gulf of Corinth. Apollo's sanctuary at Delphi is on the mainland north of the gulf, and Agamemnon's palace at Mycenae, the Mycenaean fortress of Tiryns, the spectacular 4th-century B.C. theater of Epidauros, and Olympia, the birthplace of the Olympic Games, are south of the gulf in the northern Peloponnese.

EXPLORING THE REGION BY CAR   Thanks to the excellent road linking Athens and the Peloponnese at Corinth, and the new Rio-Antio Rio bridge across the Gulf of Corinth (much speedier than the old ferry service), it's easy to combine a visit to Delphi with a tour of the most important ancient sites in the Peloponnese. Try to allow at least 4 days (spending 2 nights at Nafplion and 1 night each at Olympia and Delphi).

If traffic is light (and it almost never is), you can drive the 88km (55 miles) from Athens to Corinth on the National Road in an hour. After you take a look at the Corinth Canal and the sprawling site of ancient Corinth, an hour's drive (less if you take the new National Road to Argos and double back) through the farmland of Corinthia and Argolis will take you to Mycenae, 114km (70 miles) southwest of Athens. From Mycenae, an hour's drive will easily get you to Nafplion, 145km (90 miles) southwest of Athens. Generally considered the prettiest town in the Peloponnese, Nafplion is the perfect spot to spend the night before visiting Epidauros.

Although it's only 32km (20 miles) from Nafplion to Epidauros, the road is usually clogged with tour buses, especially when there are performances at the ancient theater; allow at least an hour for the drive. From Nafplion and Epidauros, two routes lead across the Peloponnese to Olympia. You can return to Corinth and join the National Road, which runs as far as Patras, where you take the good coast road on to Olympia. (Although there are signs in Patras pointing you toward Olympia, the heavy traffic in Patras means that you can easily spend an hour getting across town.)

Tips **Driving Tips**

Keep in mind that although most Greek roads are quite good, much of your journey to and around the Peloponnese will be on beautiful, but sometimes vertiginous, winding mountain and coastal roads that make distances deceptive. Plus, severe rains and flooding in the winter of 2003–04 damaged many roads; in spring 2004, road repairs were still in progress. Check road conditions with your rental-car agency in Athens when you pick up the car, or contact the **Greek Automobile Association (ELPA;** Athens Tower, 2–4 Mossogion, Athens 115 27; *©* **210/779-1615),** which has a reciprocity arrangement with many foreign auto clubs. The ELPA emergency number is *©* **104.** I've indicated how long you should expect each part of the trip to take, rather than give you a false sense of how quickly you can travel by just telling you how much distance you'll cover. Also keep in mind that only Portugal has more traffic fatalities each year than Greece, so buckle up and be careful out there!

If you want to avoid Patras, you can join the National Road at Argos and drive through the Arcadian mountains via Tripolis to Olympia, 320km (199 miles) west of Athens. Either way, expect to spend at least 4 hours en route—and try to spend more, so that you can enjoy the coastal scenery or the mountain villages of Arcadia. Then, to reach Delphi from Olympia, simply head to Rio, just north of Patras, and take the new **Rio-AntiRio bridge** (www.gefyra.gr) across the Gulf. With a 2,252m (7,200-ft.) fully suspended continuous deck and 40km (25 miles) of cables, this is the longest cable-stayed bridge in the world, built to withstand both earthquakes and bombs. From the north shore of the Gulf, a good road runs all the way to Delphi, 177km (110 miles) west of Athens. With a coffee break or two, the trip from Olympia to Delphi is about 5 hours; the Athens to Delphi journey takes about 3 hours, except on winter weekends, when skiers heading for Mt. Parnassus clog the road.

THE NORTHERN PELOPONNESE & THE CLASSICAL SITES

One of the delights of visiting the northern Peloponnese is that it's relatively uncrowded when many of the Aegean islands are sagging under the weight of tourists each summer. That doesn't mean you'll have famous spots like Mycenae, Epidauros, and Olympia to yourself if you arrive at high noon in August. It does mean that if you arrive just as they open or just before they close, you may have an hour under the pine trees at Olympia or Epidauros virtually alone, and be able to stand in Mycenae's Treasury of Atreus with swallows as your only companions.

Because even the most avid tourists do not live by culture alone, it's good to know that one of the great delights of spending time in the northern Peloponnese comes from quiet hours spent in shady *plateias* (squares), watching fishers mend their nets while local families settle down for a leisurely meal. An hour in a seaside cafe watching the locals watching you watch them is the ideal way to unwind after a day's sightseeing.

Warning: If you visit here in the winter, make sure your hotel has functioning heating.

CORINTH

Corinth exported its pottery around the Mediterranean and dominated trade in Greece for much of the 8th century and 7th century B.C. It experienced a second golden age under the Romans in the 2nd century A.D. Today, as in antiquity, Corinth and Patras are the two major gateways to the Peloponnese. As you pause here, you'll want to leave the main highway (look for the turnoff for the Canal Tourist Area) to take a look at the Corinth Canal and visit ancient Corinth before heading deeper into the northern Peloponnese.

Essentials

GETTING THERE **By Train** Several trains a day run from Athens's Stathmos Peloponnisou to the Corinth station off Demokratias (© **27410/22-522**).

Tips **Tourist Office Switchover**

Many of the rural Greek National tourist offices (EOT) are being turned over to local authorities. In most cases, the office remains at the same address, with the same phone and work hours—but be sure to check before you go.

The trains are almost invariably late, often taking 3 hours or more. Refreshments sometimes are available on board. For information on schedules and fares, contact **OSE** (© 210/512-4913 in Athens; www.ose.gr).

By Bus At least 15 buses a day run to Corinth from the Stathmos Leoforia Peloponnisou, 100 Kifissou in Athens. For schedule and fare information, call © 210/512-8233 in Athens. Buses to and from Athens come and go from the **bus station** at Ermou and Koliatsou streets (© 27410/25-645). Buses for Ancient Corinth sometimes leave from this station or from another bus stop on Koliatsou. Inquire upon arrival and allow 20 minutes for the bus ride to Archaia Korinthos (Ancient Corinth); buses usually run once an hour from about 8am to 8pm. Buses from Corinth for the Peloponnese leave from the station at the corner of Konstantinou and Aratou streets (© 27410/24-403).

By Car Corinth is 88km (54 miles) west of Athens on the National Highway; the toll is 2€ ($2.30). The highway continues past the Corinth Canal; just after the canal, you'll see signs for Ancient Corinth (the splendid archaeological site), Epidauros, and Corinth (the architecturally uninteresting modern town).

FAST FACTS You can find **ATMs** and exchange currency at the **National Bank of Greece,** 7 Ethniki Antistaseos, and several banks on Leoforos Vas. Konstantinos. The **hospital** (© 27410/25-711) is clearly signposted in town. The **police** (© 100 or 27410/22-143) and the **tourist police** (© 27410/23-282) are both at 51 Ermou, near the Athens bus station. The **telephone office (OTE),** 33 Kolokotroni (open 6am–midnight), and the **post office,** by the park on Adimantou (open Mon–Fri 7:30am–2pm), are both signposted.

The Corinth Canal

When the main road ran directly past the restaurants and cafes on either side of the canal, almost everyone used to stop here for a coffee, a souvlakia, and a look at the canal that separates the Peloponnese from the mainland. Now buses, trucks, and most cars stay on the new highway, but you can still take the exit for the Canal and Tourist Area to see the canal and have a snack. There's a small post office at the canal and a kiosk with postcards and English-language newspapers. Most of the large souvlakia places have surprisingly clean toilet facilities (and very tough souvlakia).

The French engineers who built the Corinth Canal between 1881 and 1893 used lots of dynamite, blasting through 87m (285 ft.) of sheer rock to make this 6km (3¾-mile) long, 27m (89-ft.) wide passageway. The canal utterly revolutionized shipping in the Mediterranean; vessels that previously had spent days making their way around Cape Matapan, at the southern tip of the Peloponnese, could dart through the canal in hours.

Exploring Ancient Corinth

To reach Ancient Corinth, follow the signs after the Corinth Canal for Ancient and Old Corinth. It's a 20-minute bus ride from the train station or 10 minutes by taxi. A number of small restaurants and cafes are adjacent to the ancient site; frankly, we have had bad or mediocre meals at most of them. There is one exception: **Marinos Rooms** (© 27410/31-209), a 5-minute walk from the excavations, has very simple rooms and very good food. If you are heading on to Nafplion, you will be able to get excellent accommodations and food there.

Ancient Corinth ★★ Although Corinth's greatest period of prosperity was between the 8th and 5th centuries B.C., most of the ancient remains here are from the Roman period. Razed and destroyed when the Romans conquered Greece in 146 B.C., Corinth was refounded by Julius Caesar in 44 B.C. and began a second period of wealth and prosperity. When Paul visited here in A.D. 52, he found it all too sophisticated and chastised the Corinthians for their wanton ways.

By the 2nd century A.D., Corinth was much larger and more powerful than Athens. During the next hundred years, a series of barbarian invasions and attacks undermined Corinth's prosperity. Thereafter, although the long series of invaders fought for control of the strategic citadel of Acrocorinth, Corinth itself was a provincial backwater with a glorious past.

The most conspicuous—and the most handsome—surviving building at Ancient Corinth is clearly the 6th-century B.C. **Temple of Apollo,** which stands on a low hill overlooking the extensive remains of the **Roman Agora** (forum or marketplace). Only seven of the temple's 38 monolithic Doric columns are standing, the others having long since been toppled by earthquakes.

Ancient Corinth's main drag, the 12m (40-ft.) wide marble-paved road that ran from the port of Lechaion into the heart of the marketplace, is clearly visible from the temple. Along the road, and throughout the Agora, are the foundations of hundreds of the stores that once stocked everything from spices imported from Asia Minor to jugs of wine made from Corinth's excellent grapes.

Two spots in the Agora are especially famous—the **Fountain of Peirene** and the **Bema.** In the 2nd century A.D., the famous Roman traveler Philhellene and benefactor Herodes Atticus is thought to have encased the modest Greek fountain in an elaborate two-story building with arches, arcades, and a 5-sq.-m (50-sq.-ft.) courtyard. Later benefactors further beautified the fountain, which honored Peirene, a woman who wept so hard when her son died that she dissolved into the spring that still flows here. As for the Bema (public platform), this was where Paul had to plead his case when the Corinthians, irritated by his constant criticisms, hauled him in front of the Roman governor Gallo in A.D. 52.

If you visit here in the summer, you may see archaeologists at work excavating more of Ancient Corinth. They are usually willing to be observed, less willing to chat. Work continues on an extensive Roman villa unearthed near the ancient Agora/forum and on the considerable remains of medieval Corinth.

Old Corinth. (C) 27410/31-207. Admission to archaeological site and museum 6€ ($6.90). Summer Mon–Fri 8am–7pm; Sat–Sun 8am–3pm. Winter Mon–Fri 8:45am–3pm; Sat–Sun 8:30am–3pm.

Archaeological Museum ✯   As you'd expect, this museum just inside the site entrance has a particularly fine collection of the famous Corinthian pottery, which is often decorated with charming red-and-black figures of birds and animals. There are also a number of statues of Roman worthies and several mosaics, including one in which Pan is shown piping away to a clutch of cows. The museum courtyard is a shady spot in which to sit and read up on the ancient site, which has virtually no shade. When you visit, be sure to see the handsome sculpture and vases stolen from the museum in 1990, found in Miami, Florida, in 1998, and officially handed over to Greece in 2001, some of which is again on display.

Ancient Corinth, in the town of Old Corinth. (C) 27410/31-207. Admission to museum and archaeological site 6€ ($6.90). Summer Mon–Sun 8am–7pm; winter Mon–Sun 8am–5pm.

Acrocorinth ✯✯ *Moments*   It's hard to say what's more impressive here: the superb fortifications or the spectacular view across the plain of Corinth to the

Gulf and beyond into central Greece. A winding dirt road runs from the site of Ancient Corinth to the summit of Acrocorinth, the rugged limestone sugarloaf mountain topped by centuries of fortifications that dominates the plain of Corinth. A superb natural acropolis, Acrocorinth was fortified first by the Greeks and later by the Byzantines, Franks, Venetians, and Turks. Extensive remains of the centuries of walls, turrets, and towers built here still remain. After you roam around enjoying the seemingly endless view over the rich plain below, you can relax at the small cafe just outside the site entrance.

Old Corinth. Free admission. Summer daily 8am–7pm; winter daily 8am–5pm.

NAFPLION ✦✦

With two hilltop Venetian fortresses, shady parks, an interesting assortment of small museums, and better-than-average hotels, restaurants, and shops—and even a miniature castle (the Bourtzi) in the harbor—this port town on the northeast coast of the Gulf of Argos is almost everyone's first choice as the most charming town in the Peloponnese. A good deal of Nafplion's appeal comes from the fact that for several years after the Greek War of Independence (1821–28), this was the country's first capital. Although the palace of Greece's young King Otto—a mail-order monarch from Bavaria—burned down in the 19th century, an impressive number of handsome neoclassical civic buildings and private houses have survived, as have a scattering of Turkish fountains and several mosques.

Essentials

GETTING THERE **By Bus**   At least a dozen buses a day run to Nafplion from the **Stathmos Leoforia Peloponnisou,** 100 Kifissou, Athens (© 210/513-4110 or 210/513-4588). The trip takes about 4 hours because the bus goes into Corinth and Argos before reaching Nafplion.

By Boat   *Flying Dolphin* hydrofoil service runs from Marina Zea, Piraeus, to Nafplion, Monday through Saturday, weather permitting. The hydrofoil makes a number of stops and takes almost as long as the bus to reach Nafplion. For fare and schedule information, call © **210/324-2281** or 210/453-6107 in Athens.

By Car   From Athens, head south to the Corinth Canal. Take the new Corinth-Tripolis road to the Argos exit and follow signs into Argos and Nafplion. You'll almost certainly get lost at least once in Argos, which has an abysmal system of directional signs. Allow at least 3 hours for the drive from Athens to Nafplion. When you reach Nafplion, park in the large, free municipal lot by the harbor. If you want to stop at Mycenae or Nemea, take the winding old road to Nafplion. If you want to stop at Epidauros, take the signposted turn for Epidauros just after the canal.

VISITOR INFORMATION   The tourist information office (the former **Greek National Tourist Organization [EOT]** office) is at 16 Photomara (© 27520/28-131), cater-cornered across from the bus station in Plateia Nikitara. It's usually open weekdays from 9am to 2pm, but seems to have frequent unscheduled closings. The helpful brochure "Nafplion Day and Night" is sometimes available here, in shops, and in hotels.

FAST FACTS   The **post office** is open weekdays from 8am to 2pm, and the **OTE** telephone and telegraph office is open weekdays from 8am to 7pm. Both are signposted from the bus station. The **National Bank of Greece** has a branch on the main square, Syntagma Square. There are a number of **travel agencies** in Nafplion, including **Staikos Travel,** by the harbor (© 27520/27-950). The best place to swim is at the **beach** beneath the Palamidi, a 15-minute walk (with the sea on your right) from the harborside cafes.

Where to Stay

Byron Hotel ⭐ The Byron was one of the first hotels here to attempt to add individual charm and creature comfort to a pleasant location. Word has gotten out about the Byron's charm, and it's almost impossible to stay here in July or August without a reservation, especially on weekends, when the entire hotel can be taken over by Athenians. The hotel is in a quiet, breezy location overlooking the Church of Agiou Spiridona, a short but steep hike up from the main *plateia* (square). It has nice bits of Victoriana in the sitting rooms and guest rooms, as well as modern conveniences. The cheapest rooms are quite small and have no view; so it is worth it to pay more and get a view of Nafplion—and enough space that you won't feel the burden of togetherness with your roommate.

2 Platonos, Plateia Agiou Spiridona, 211 00 Nafplion. ⓒ **27520/22-351**. Fax 27520/26-338. byronhotel@ otenet.gr. 17 units. 70€–95€ ($81–$109) double. AE, MC, V. **Amenities:** Breakfast room; terrace. *In room:* A/C, TV, minibar, hair dryer.

Hotel Nafsimedon ⭐ This "boutique" hotel in a handsome mid-19th-century neoclassical house is a welcome addition to Nafplion's hotels. It's set back from the street and overlooks relatively quiet Kolokotronis Park. The exterior is a warm peach color, and the interior walls are peach and apricot (fashionably sponge-painted, of course). Rooms are attractively furnished, some with bits of Victoriana and four-poster beds; most are larger than those in most Greek hotels. The service was rather casual for a "boutique" hotel when we visited, but several letters from travelers praised the service, ambience, and comfort.

9 Sideras Merarhias (on Kolokotronis Park), 211 00 Nafplion. ⓒ **27520/25-060**. Fax 27520/26-913. www.nafsimedon.gr. 13 units. 80€–110€ ($92–$126) double. Reductions possible off season. No credit cards. **Amenities:** Breakfast room; bar; garden. *In room:* A/C, TV.

King Otho ⭐ This longtime favorite (we first stayed here in the early 1960s) was somewhat down at the heels before its complete and completely successful renovation in 2000. In 2002, the owners bought and restored another wonderful town house a few blocks up the hill on Staikopoulou. Now Nafplion has two small hotels contending for the honor of having the most breathtaking curved staircase in the Pelopponese. Both hotels have high ceilings (some with frescoes); wood floors; period furniture; and all the modern amenities. The new Otho is more expensive, because every room is a room with a view (of Nafplion and of the harbor). Each hotel has a garden, a real plus for breakfast or a quiet hour's reading.

Original hotel: 4 Farmakapoulou, 211 00 Nafplion. ⓒ **27520/27-585**. Fax 27520/27-595. 12 units. 85€ ($98) double. Rates include continental breakfast. No credit cards. **Amenities:** Breakfast room. *In room:* A/C, TV. New hotel: 21 Staikopoulou, Nafplion 21100. ⓒ **27520/27-595**. Fax 27520/27-595. 10 units. 100€ ($115) double. Rates include continental breakfast. **Amenities:** Breakfast room. *In room:* A/C, TV.

Nafplia Palace *Overrated* When this was built as the Xenia Palace Hotel in the 1970s, the disco, minibars, and in-bathroom telephones made it a relentlessly modern provincial hotel. By the 1990s, the hotel was sadly down at the heels (once when I opened my bathroom door, it came off the wall!) and soon thereafter underwent a thorough renovation. Unfortunately, when I last visited, service was lax, the food was indifferent, the decor was bland, and there was no toilet paper in the restroom off the restaurant. Still, to its credit, this hotel has large guest rooms and the best views in town of the harbor and Bourtzi. We look forward to hearing from any readers who stay here.

Acronafplia, 210 00 Nafplion. ✆ **27520/28-981** or 27520/752-99-555. Fax 27520/28-783. palace@nafplionhotels.gr. 51 units, 54 bungalows. 225€ ($259) double with demi-pensione; 175€ ($200) bungalow. Significant off-season reductions possible. AE, DC, MC, V. **Amenities:** Restaurant; bar; pool. *In room:* A/C, TV, minibar.

Omorfi Poli Pension 🏠🏠 What a lovely place! This small pension/hotel above the charming cafe by the same name (Beautiful City) has gone all out, giving guests the sense that you're staying in a Nafplion home—but with your own privacy. There's nothing to fault here—the beds are good, and the tile floors and prints on the walls are handsome. This makes a very pleasant base for touring the area. Families will like the rooms with fridges and sleeping lofts for children (80€/$92), and the breakfasts with freshly baked bread.

Sofroni 5, 211 00 Nafplion. ✆ **27520/21-565.** Fax 27520/29-014. sofroni5@otenet.gr. 9 units, all with shower only. 65€ ($75) double; 80€ ($92) family suite for up to 5. Rates include breakfast. **Amenities:** Cafe. *In room:* A/C, TV, fridge.

Where to Dine

Oddly enough, the restaurants in and just off Syntagma Square are not the tourist traps you'd expect. Furthermore, you'll see a good number of Greeks at the big harborside cafes on Akti Miaoulis. In short, Nafplion has lots of good restaurants, and any number of ice-cream parlors selling elaborate gooey confections.

Antica Gelateria di Roma 🏠🏠🏠 SWEETS/ICE CREAM/COFFEES/DRINKS What a wonderful addition to Nafplion! Marcello and Claudia Raffo make and sell the best ice creams and ices in the entire Peloponnese. You can have anything from a banana split to a tiny cup with just a taste. Flavors not to miss are hazelnut, lemon, mango, strawberry, chocolate—well, you get the idea. If you tire of ice cream, you can always have a freshly made *panini* (sandwich) with tomato and mozzarella and finish with a real espresso.

3 Pharmakopoulou and Komninou. ✆ **27520/23-520.** spyde@tri.forthnet.gr. Sweets and sandwiches 2€–10€ ($2.30–$12). Open most days 10am–midnight.

Hellas Restaurant 🏠 GREEK Kostas, the omnipresent host of the Hellas, says that there's been a restaurant here for more than 100 years. Shady trees and awnings make this a cool spot to eat outdoors; there's also an inside dining room, where locals tend to congregate year-round. Excellent dolmades with egg-lemon sauce are usually on the menu, as well as stuffed tomatoes and peppers in season. Just about everyone in town passes through Syntagma Square, so this is a great spot to people-watch.

Syntagma Sq. ✆ **27520/27-278.** Main courses 6€–12€ ($6.90–$14). AE, MC, V. Daily 9am–midnight.

Karamanlis 🏠 GREEK This pleasantly old-fashioned harbor-front taverna several blocks east of the cluster of harbor-front cafes tends to get fewer tourists (and a good number of local businesspeople, lawyers, and civil servants) than most of the places in town. It serves good grills and several kinds of meatballs (*keftedes, sousoutakia,* and *yiouvarlakia*). If you like the food here, you'll probably enjoy the Kanares Taverna and the Hundalos Taverna, both also on Bouboulinas.

1 Leoforos Bouboulinas. ✆ **27520/27-668.** Main courses 5€–12€ ($5.75–$14); fish priced daily by the kilo. AE, MC, V. Daily 11am–midnight.

Paleo Archontiko ★★ GREEK   This excellent restaurant in a nicely restored town house serves up tasty *stifado* (beef stew with onions), chops, and a wide range of popular favorites—but usually only in the evening. Live music is often offered here on Friday and Saturday, when half the customers may be Athenians down for the weekend; there's also often music on summer evenings. In good weather, tables are set up in the pedestrianized street outside the restaurant; in winter, the rooms indoors are cozy and congenial.

Corner of Siokou and Ipsilantou sts. ⓒ 27520/27-704. Reservations recommended weekends. Main courses 6€–14€ ($6.90–$16). No credit cards. Hours irregular; usually open for dinner 8pm–midnight.

Savouras Psarotaverna ★★ SEAFOOD   This harborside restaurant has been here more than 20 years, and its fresh fish attracts Greek day-trippers from Tripolis and even Athens. What you eat depends on what was caught that day—and it's always a good idea to check the price before ordering. Expect to pay at least 50€ ($58) (and easily more) for two fish dinners, a salad, and some house wine. On summer weekends this restaurant can be terribly crowded.

79 Leoforos Bouboulinas. ⓒ 27520/27-704. Fish priced daily by the kilo. AE, MC, V. Daily noon–11pm.

Sokaki ★ CREPES/SWEETS/BREAKFASTS/COFFEE   In the morning, tourists tuck into the full American breakfast here, while locals toy with a tiny cup of Greek coffee. In the evening, young men lounge here, some eyeing the women who pass by, others eyeing the men. This is a nice place to take a break and watch people watching people. The yogurt with honey and fresh fruit is delicious and the serving so generous that it is a meal in itself.

Corner of Eth. Antistaseos and Nafpleo sts. ⓒ 27520/26-032. Drinks and snacks 2€–12€ ($2.30–$14). Daily 9am–midnight (to about 8pm in winter).

Stathmos Cafe ★ *Moments* DRINKS/SNACKS   This is a nice shady spot in which to sit and take a break from touring Nafplion, perhaps after visiting the Museum of Childhood next door. The old train station is decorated with a splendid painting of an old steam engine, and has elaborate wooden gingerbread trim, comfortable chairs under shady trees, and a cozy inside room for cold weather.

The old railroad station, Kapodistras Park. No phone. Soda 2€ ($2.30); assorted *mezedes* from 4€ ($4.60). No credit cards. Daily about 9am–midnight.

Exploring the Town

Nafplion is a stroller's delight, and one of the great pleasures here is simply walking through the parks, up and down the stepped side streets, and along the harbor. Don't make the mistake of stopping your harborside stroll when you come to the last of the large seaside cafes by the Hotel Agamemnon. If you continue, you can watch fishing boats putting in at the pier and explore several cliff-side chapels. Nafplion is so small that you can't get seriously lost, so have fun exploring. Here are some suggestions on how to take in the official sights after you've had your initial stroll.

ACRONAFPLIA & THE PALAMIDI   Nafplion's two massive fortresses, Acronafplia and the Palamidi, dominate the skyline. There's no charge to visit the cliffs known as **Acronafplia,** where there are considerable remains of Greek, Frankish, and Venetian fortresses, as well as two modern hotels, undergoing renovations at press time (see the Nafplia Palace, above). This is not an easy walk if it is hot, and you may prefer to take a taxi up for 6€ ($6.90) and walk down. If you do walk up, follow signs in the lower town to the **Church of Saint Spyridon,** one of whose walls has the mark left by one of the bullets that killed Ianni

Kapodistria, the first governor of modern Greece. From Saint Spyridon, follow the signs farther uphill to the **Catholic Church of the Metamorphosis.**

This church is as good a symbol as any for Nafplion's vexed history. Built by the Venetians, it was converted into a mosque by the Turks and then reconsecrated as a church after the War of Independence. Inside, an ornamental doorway has an inscription listing Philhellenes who died for Greece, including nephews of Lord Byron and George Washington. As you continue to climb to Acronafplia, keep an eye out for several carvings of the winged lion that was the symbol of Mark, the patron saint of Venice.

Similarly, if you're not in the mood to climb the 800-plus steps to the summit of the **Palamidi** ⚔, you can take a taxi up and then walk down. The Venetians spent 3 years building the Palamidi, only to have it conquered the next year (1715) by the Turks. You'll enter the fortress the way the Turkish attackers did, through the main gate to the east. Once inside, you can trace the course of the massive wall that encircled the entire summit and wander through the considerable remains of the five fortresses that failed to stop the Turkish attack. In June, concerts are sometimes held here in the evening. The Palamidi is open weekdays from 8am to 7pm in summer, from 8:30am to 5pm in winter. Admission is 3€ ($3.45).

NAFPLION'S MUSEUMS   All four of Nafplion's museums are within easy walking distance of one another. Almost as soon as it opened in 1981, the **Folk Art Museum** ⚔⚔, also called the **Peloponnesian Folklore Foundation** (1 V. Alexandros; © **27520/28-947;** fax 27520/27-960; pff@otenet.gr), with its superb collection of Greek costumes, won the European Museum of the Year Award. The display highlights "The Best of the Peloponnesian Folk Foundation," with exhibits from its more than 25,000-object collection, which includes coins, ceramics, furniture, and farm implements as well as all those costumes. The museum occupies three floors in an elegant 18th-century house with a shady courtyard and a welcome snack bar. Throughout, labels are in English as well as Greek, and a number of dioramas (my favorite shows nine elegant matrons in a 19th-c. parlor) help visitors imagine life in Greece, especially during the 19th century when the Western world impinged on the Greek world. The small gift shop is excellent, with fine ceramic and copper reproductions. This is a wonderful place to get an idea of life in Greece in the "good old days"—which still exist in many villages. It's open Wednesday through Monday from 9am to 3pm; closed Tuesday and the month of February. Admission is 4€ ($4.60).

The **Museum of Childhood,** Stathmos, Kolokotronis Park, an offshoot of the Folk Art Museum, has an eclectic collection of dolls, baby clothes, and toys. In theory, it's open year-round, Tuesday through Saturday from 10am to 2pm, Sunday from 11am to 2pm, but there are frequent unscheduled closings. Admission is 1.50€ ($1.80).

The **Nafplion Archaeological Museum,** Syntagma Square (© **27520/ 27-502**), is housed in the handsome 18th-century Venetian arsenal that dominates Syntagma Square. The thick walls make it a deliciously cool place to visit on even the hottest day. Displays are from sites in the area and include pottery, jewelry, and some horrific Mycenaean terra-cotta idols, as well as a handsome bronze Mycenaean suit of armor. The museum is open Tuesday through Sunday from 8:30am to 1pm; admission is 2€ ($2.30). **Note:** At press time, the museum was closed for renovations, but was scheduled to reopen "soon."

A Day Trip from Nafplion: Tiryns

Tiryns ✦✦ is 5km (3 miles) outside Nafplion on the Argos road; if possible, visit Tiryns and Mycenae (see below) together, to get the best sense of Greece's two best-known Mycenaean sites. From the moment you see it, you'll understand why Homer called this **citadel**, which may have been Mycenae's port, "well walled." Tiryns stands on a rocky outcropping 27m (87 ft.) high and about 302m (990 ft.) long, girdled by the massive walls that so impressed Homer—but that didn't keep Tiryns from being destroyed around 1200 B.C. Later Greeks thought that only the giants known as Cyclopes could have hefted the 14-ton red limestone blocks into place for the walls that archaeologists still call "Cyclopean." Even today, Tiryns's walls stand more than 9m (30 ft.) high; originally, they were twice as tall—and as much as 17m (57 ft.) thick. The citadel is crowned by the palace, whose **megaron** (great hall) has a well-preserved circular hearth and the base of a throne. This room would have been gaily decorated with frescoes (the surviving frescoes are now in the National Archaeological Museum in Athens).

The site is officially open daily, from 8am to 7pm in the summer, from 8am to 5pm in the winter. Admission is 2€ ($2.30). Visitors without cars can reach Tiryns from Nafplion by taxi (expect to pay about 20€/$23 for a 1-hr. round-trip) or by the frequent (about every half-hour) Nafplion-Argos-Nafplion bus (about 2€/$2.30; tell the driver you want to get off at Tiryns).

MYCENAE ✦✦✦

Greek legend and the poet Homer tell us that King Agamemnon of Mycenae was the most powerful leader in Greece at the time of the Trojan War. In about 1250 B.C., Homer says, Agamemnon led the Greeks from Mycenae to Troy, where they fought for 10 years to reclaim fair Helen, the wife of Agamemnon's brother Menelaus, from the Trojan prince Paris. The German archaeologist Heinrich Schliemann, who found and excavated Troy, began to dig at Mycenae in 1874. Did Schliemann's excavations here prove that what Homer wrote was based on an actual event, not myth and legend? Scholars are suspicious, although most admit that Mycenae could have been built to order from Homer's descriptions of its palaces.

Essentials

GETTING THERE   By Bus   Buses run frequently from Athens's **Stathmos Leoforia Peloponnisou,** 100 Kifissou (© **210/513-4100**), to Corinth, Argos, and Nafplion. Allow 3 to 4 hours. From any of those places, allow an hour for the trip to Mycenae.

By Car   Mycenae is 114km (70 miles) southwest of Athens and 50km (31 miles) south of Corinth. From Corinth, take the old Corinth–Argos highway south for about 48km (30 miles), and then take the left turn to Mycenae, which is about 8km (5 miles) down the road. (There is also a poorly signposted side road for Mycenae not far after the Corinth-Argos highway crosses the railroad tracks.) From Nafplion, take the road out of town toward Argos. When you reach the Corinth-Argos highway, turn right and then, after about 16km (10 miles), turn right again at the sign for Mycenae.

FAST FACTS   You can buy stamps and change money at the mobile **post office** at the ancient site weekdays from 8am to 2pm. This office is sometimes open on weekends and after 2pm, but don't count on it.

Where to Stay & Dine

Most of the restaurants specialize in serving set-price meals to groups. If you eat at one of the big, impersonal roadside restaurants, you're likely to be served a bland, lukewarm "European-style" meal of overcooked roast veal, underripe tomatoes and, even in summer, canned vegetables. You'll have better luck at the smaller restaurants at the hotels listed below.

La Belle Helene The real reason to stay here is to add your name to those of Schliemann and other luminaries in the guest book and take in the photos of the archaeologists who rediscovered Agamemnon's palace. Tradition aside, this small hotel is usually quiet (although it sometimes does a brisk business with tour groups in its large restaurant), and the simple rooms are clean and comfortable. If you stay here, be sure to drive or walk up to the ancient site at night, especially if is a full moon—it's magical.

Mycenae, 212 00 Argolis. ⓒ **27510/76-225.** Fax 27510/76-179. 8 units, none with bathroom. 35€–65€ ($40–$75) double. Rates include breakfast. Off-season discounts sometimes available. DC, V. On the main road to Mycenae, on the left as you approach the site. **Amenities:** Restaurant.

La Petite Planete The bright, good-size rooms would make this a nice place to stay even without its swimming pool, which is irresistible after a hot day's trek around Mycenae. We've found it quieter here than at La Belle Helene, and friends who stayed here recently praised the restaurant (in the evening, not at lunch, which is aimed at tour groups) and enjoyed the view from their window over the hills.

Mycenae, 212 00 Argolis. ⓒ **27510/76-240.** Fax 27510/76-610. 30 units. 70€–80€ ($81–$92) double. Rates include breakfast. Usually closed Dec–Apr. Off-season discounts sometimes available. AE, V. The hotel is on the main road to Mycenae, on the left as you approach the site. **Amenities:** Restaurant; bar; pool. *In room:* A/C.

Exploring Ancient Mycenae

The long-awaited **Archaeological Museum of Mycenae** ★★★ (ⓒ **27510/ 76-585**) opened in 2003 and tells the story of the excavations here and of Mycenaean civilization through its displays of objects found at Mycenae and in the surrounding countryside. If possible, visit the museum before the site, as its exhibits put flesh on the bones of the excavations. The museum is situated on the northern side of the archaeological site, at the foot of the Mycenae acropolis. At press time, tickets for the museum, as well as its excellent guidebook, were sold at the site's main entrance (entrance 6€/$6.90; guidebook 5€/$5.75; hours identical to site). Throughout the museum, exhibits are labeled in Greek and English, and there are very welcome toilet facilities.

The Citadel & the Treasury of Atreus ★★★ As you walk uphill to Mycenae, you begin to get an idea of why people settled here as long ago as 5000 B.C. Mycenae straddles a low bluff between two protecting mountains and is a superb natural citadel overlooking one of the richest plains in Greece. By the time of the classical era, almost all memory of the Mycenaeans had been lost, and Greeks speculated that places like Mycenae and Tiryns had been built by the Cyclopes. Only such enormous giants, people reasoned, could have moved the huge rocks used to build the ancient citadels' defense walls.

You enter Mycenae through just such a wall, passing under the massive Lion Gate, whose two lions probably symbolized Mycenae's strength. The door itself (missing, like the lions' heads) probably was made of wood and covered with bronze for additional protection; cuttings for the doorjambs and pivots are clearly visible in the lintel. Soldiers stationed in the round **tower** on your right would have shot arrows down at any attackers who tried to storm the citadel.

One of the most famous spots at Mycenae is immediately ahead of the Lion Gate—the so-called **Grave Circle A,** where Schliemann found the gold jewelry now on display at the National Archaeological Museum in Athens. When archaeologist Heinrich Schliemann opened the tombs and found some 14 kilograms (30 lb.) of gold here, including several solid-gold face masks, he concluded he had found the grave of Agamemnon himself. However, recent scholars have concluded that Schliemann was wrong, and that the kings buried here died long before Agamemnon was born.

From the grave circle, head uphill past the low remains of a number of houses. Mycenae was not merely a palace, but a small village, with administrative buildings and homes on the slopes below the **palace.** The palace had reception rooms, bedrooms, a throne room, and a large megaron (ceremonial hall). You can see the imprint of the four columns that held up the roof in the megaron, as well as the outline of a circular altar on the floor.

If you're not claustrophobic, head to the northeast corner of the citadel and climb down the flight of stairs to have a look at Mycenae's enormous **cistern.** (You may find someone here selling candles, but it's a good idea to bring your own flashlight.) Along with Mycenae's great walls, this cistern, which held a water supply channeled from a spring 450m (1,500 ft.) away, helped make the citadel impregnable for several centuries.

There's one more thing to see before you leave Mycenae. The massive tomb known as the **Treasury of Atreus** is the largest of the tholos tombs (circular marble structures) found here. You'll see signs for the Treasury of Atreus on your right as you head down the modern road away from Mycenae. The Treasury of Atreus may have been built around 1300 B.C., at about the same time as the Lion Gate, in the last century of Mycenae's real greatness. The enormous tomb, with its 118-ton lintel, is 13m (43 ft.) high and 14m (47 ft.) wide. To build the tomb, workers first cut the 35m (115-ft.) passageway into the hill and faced it with stone blocks. Then the tholos chamber itself was built, by placing slightly overlapping courses of stone one on top of the other until a capstone could close the final course. As you look up toward the ceiling of the tomb, you'll see why these are called "beehive tombs." Once your eyes get accustomed to the poor light, you can make out the bronze nails that once held hundreds of bronze rosettes in place in the ceiling. This tomb was robbed even in antiquity, so we'll never know exactly what it contained, although the contents of Grave Circle A give an idea of what riches must have been here. If this was the family vault of Atreus, it's entirely possible that Agamemnon himself was buried here.

There's a good deal of up-and-down walking here, much on slippery terrain; give yourself at least 3 hours to absorb this magnificent and mysterious site.

ⓒ 27510/76-585. Admission 6€ ($6.90). Summer Mon–Fri 8am–7:30pm; Sat–Sun 8am–3pm. Winter Mon–Fri 8am–5pm; Sat–Sun 8:30am–3pm.

EPIDAUROS ⭒⭒

Epidauros, dedicated to the healing god Asclepios, was one of the most famous shrines in ancient Greece. Greeks came to the shrine of Asclepios in antiquity as they go to the shrine of the Virgin on the island of Tinos today, to give thanks for good health and in hopes of finding cures for their ailments. While at Epidauros, patients and their families could "take the waters" at any one of a number of healing springs and in the superb baths. Visitors could also take in a performance in the theater, just as you can today.

Essentials

GETTING THERE   By Bus   Two buses a day run from the **Stathmos Leoforia Peloponnisou,** 100 Kifissou, Athens (© **210/513-4100**). The trip takes about 3 hours. There are three buses a day to Epidauros from the Nafplion bus station, off Plateia Kapodistrias (© **27530/27-323**), with extra buses when there are performances at the Theater of Epidauros. The trip takes about an hour.

By Car   Epidauros is 63km (39 miles) south of Corinth and 32km (20 miles) east of Nafplion. If you're coming from Athens or Corinth, turn left at the sign for Epidauros immediately after the Corinth Canal and take the coast road to the Theatro (ancient theater), not to Nea Epidauros or Palaia Epidauros. From Nafplion, follow the signs for Epidauros. If you drive to Epidauros from Nafplion for a performance, be alert; the road will be clogged with tour buses and other tourists who are driving the road for the first time.

THEATER PERFORMANCES   Performances are often held at the ancient theater on Saturday and Sunday from June to September. Many are given by the National Theater of Greece, some by foreign companies. For information and ticket prices, in Athens contact the **Hellenic Festival Box Office,** 39 Panepis-timiou in the arcade (© **210/322-1459**); in Epidaurus, contact the **Epidaurus Festival Box Office** (© 27530/22-006). Most of the travel agencies in Nafplion sell tickets, as does the theater itself, from 5pm on the day of a performance. The performance starts around 9pm. The ancient tragedies are usually performed in classical or modern Greek; programs cost 3€ ($3.45) and usually have a full translation or a synopsis of the play. The excellent Odyssey bookstore on Syntagma Square in Nafplion often has English translations of the plays being performed at Epidauros.

   If you are in Epidauros in July, check out the **Musical July Festival** at the Little Theater of Ancient Epidauros. Performances in the past have ranged from chamber music to flamenco. Information on ticket prices and bus transportation from Athens is usually available from the **Megaron Mousikis (Athens Concert Hall),** 1 Kokkali and Vas, Sophias (© **210/728-2000**) from early June or from the **Municipality of Palea Epidaurus** (©27530/41-250).

Where to Stay & Dine

If you are not attending a performance at the theater, you may wish to take a look at the small hotels springing up in nearby Palea Epidauros, which is on the coast; the **Christina** (© 27530/41-451) and the **Verdelis Inn** (© 27530/41-332) are good choices. Keep in mind that Palea Epidauros (like many seaside resorts) can be quite noisy, especially on summer weekends.

Epidauros Xenia Hotel   Although the location beside the ancient site is charming, the hotel is not. Still, the convenience of staying here (especially if you are attending a performance at the theater) makes this (admittedly gloomy) hotel your best choice. Once everyone leaves, this is a lovely, quiet spot, in a pine grove beside the ancient site. The bungalow-like units (which could use some serious sprucing up and redecoration) go quickly, so reserve well in advance if you plan to be here the night of a performance (the closer it is to a performance, the higher room prices tend to be). The restaurant serves bland but acceptable food, so you may want to try the **Leonidas Restaurant** (© 27520/22-115) in the village of Epidauros; it's usually packed (often with actors) after perform-ances at the ancient theater.

Ligourio, Nafplias, Peloponnese. © **27530/22-003-5**. 26 units, 12 with bathroom. From 75€ ($86) double. Rates include breakfast. Off-season discounts sometimes available. No credit cards. **Amenities:** Restaurant.

Exploring the Ancient Site

The **excavation museum** at the entrance to the site helps put some flesh on the bones of the confusing remains of the Sanctuary of Asclepios. The museum has an extensive collection of architectural fragments from the sanctuary, including lovely acanthus flowers from the mysterious tholos, which you'll see when you visit the site. Also on view are an impressive number of votive offerings from pilgrims: The terra-cotta body parts show precisely what part of the anatomy was cured. The display of surgical implements will send you away grateful that you didn't have to go under the knife here, although hundreds of inscriptions record the gratitude of satisfied patients.

It's pleasant to wander through the shady **Sanctuary of Asclepios,** but it's not at all easy to decipher the scant remains. The Asclepion had accommodations for visitors, several large bathhouses, civic buildings, a stadium and gymnasium, and several temples and shrines. The remains are so meager that you might have to take this on faith. Try to find the round tholos, which you'll pass about halfway into the sanctuary. The famous 4th-century B.C. architect Polykleitos, who built similar round buildings at Olympia and Delphi, was the designer here. If you wonder why the inner foundations of the tholos are so convoluted and labyrinthine, you're in good company—scholars aren't sure what went on here, although some suspect that Asclepios's healing serpents lived in the labyrinth.

The museum and archaeological site (© **27530/23-009**) are open in summer, weekdays from 8am to 7pm and Saturday and Sunday from 8:30am to 3:15pm; in winter, weekdays from 8am to 5pm and Saturday and Sunday from 8:30am to 3:15pm. Admission (also covering the theater; see below) is 6€ ($6.90). Several kiosks sell snacks and cold drinks near the ticket booth.

The Theater

If you found the remains of the ancient sanctuary a bit of a letdown, don't worry—the **Theater of Epidauros** is one of the most impressive sights in Greece. Probably built in the 4th century B.C., possibly by Polykleitos, the architect of the tholos, the theater seats some 14,000 spectators. Unlike so many ancient buildings, and almost everything at the Sanctuary of Asclepios, the theater was not pillaged for building blocks in antiquity. As a result, it's astonishingly well preserved, and restorations have been minimal and tactful.

If you climb to the top, you can look down over the seats, divided into a lower section of 34 rows and an upper section with 21 rows. The upper seats were added when the original theater was enlarged in the 2nd century B.C. The theater's acoustics are famous; you'll almost certainly see someone demonstrating that a whisper can be heard all the way from the orchestra to the topmost row of seats. Just as the stadium at Olympia brings out the sprinter in many visitors, the theater at Epidauros tempts many to step center stage and recite poetry, declaim the opening of the Gettysburg Address, or burst into song. It's always a magical moment when a performance begins, as the sun sinks behind the orchestra and the first actor steps onto the stage.

The 6€ ($6.90) admission to the museum and archaeological site (see above) includes the theater; they keep the same hours.

OLYMPIA ✦✦✦

With its shady groves of pine, olive, and oak trees, the considerable remains of two temples, and the stadium where the first Olympic races were run in 776 B.C., Olympia is the most beautiful major site in the Peloponnese. The archaeological museum is one of the finest in Greece, and you can easily spend a full day or more here. The straggling modern village of Olympia (confusingly known as Ancient Olympia) is bisected by its one main street, Leoforos Kondili. The town has the usual assortment of tourist shops as well as more than a dozen hotels and restaurants. The ancient site of Olympia lies a 15-minute walk south of the modern village, but if you have a car, you might as well drive; the road teems with tour buses, and the walk is less than relaxing.

Essentials

GETTING THERE **By Train** Several trains a day run from Athens to Pirgos, where you change to the train for Olympia. Information on schedules and fares is available from the **Stathmos Peloponnisou** (railroad station for the Peloponnese) in Athens (© **210/513-1601;** www.ose.gr).

By Bus Three buses a day run to Olympia from the Stathmos Leoforia Peloponnisou, 100 Kifissou, Athens (© **210/513-4110**). There are also frequent buses from Patras to Pirgos, with connecting service to Olympia. In Patras, **KTEL** buses leave from the intersection of Zaimi and Othonos streets (© **2610/273-694**).

By Car Olympia, 320km (198 miles) from Athens, is at least a 6-hour drive whether you take the coast road that links Athens to Corinth, Patras, and Olympia or head inland to Tripolis and Olympia on the new Corinth-Tripolis road. Heavy traffic in Patras, 159km (99 miles) south, means that the drive from Patras to Olympia can easily take 2 hours.

VISITOR INFORMATION The tourist information office (the former **Greek National Tourist Organization [EOT]** office) is on the way to the ancient site near the south end of Leoforos Kondili, the main street (© **26240/23-100** or 26240/23-125). It's usually open daily, from 9am to 10pm in the summer and from 11am to 6pm in the winter. That said, when I spent time in Olympia in both June and October 2003, the office had an OPEN sign in its window, but in fact was closed.

FAST FACTS Everything you want is on or off the main drag, and most things are signposted. The **OTE telephone and telegraph office** on Praxitelous is open weekdays from 7:30am to 10pm. The **train station** is at the north end of town, one street off Leoforos Kondili. You can call © **26240/22-580** for a **taxi.**

Where to Stay

Olympia has more than 20 hotels, which means you can almost always find a room, although if you arrive without a reservation in July or August, you might not get your first choice. In the winter, many hotels are closed. If you're here in winter, check to see if the hotel you choose has functioning central heating.

Hotel Europa ★★ The Europa is the best hotel in town—and one of the best in the Peloponnese. Part of the Best Western chain, it's a few minutes' drive out of town on a hill overlooking both the modern village and the ancient site. Most rooms overlook a large pool and garden, and several have views of a bit of the ancient site. Rooms are large, with extrafirm mattresses and sliding glass doors opening onto generous balconies. One drawback, pointed out to us by a visitor on crutches: Although there is an elevator, you have to use the stairs to get to the pool and the breakfast room.

270 65 Ancient Olympia, Peloponnese. © **800/528-1234** in the U.S., 26240/22-650, or 26240/22-700. Fax 26240/23-166. 80 units. 125€ ($144) double. Considerable reductions off season. Rates include breakfast. AE, DC, MC, V. **Amenities:** Restaurant; bar; pool. *In room:* A/C, TV, unstocked minifridge, hair dryer.

Hotel Neda With a pleasant rooftop cafe, a comfortable lobby, a serviceable restaurant, and a distinctive red-and-white facade, the Neda (off the noisy main drag) offers good value. Rooms are large, with good bedside reading lamps. Some of the doubles have double beds, but most have twins, so specify which you want. Each room has a good-size balcony, and the bathrooms are better than those usually found in hotels in this price category (thanks to the presence of shower curtains, which help you avoid spraying the entire room). Rooms here are usually quieter than those in hotels on the main street.

Praxiteles, 270 65 Ancient Olympia, Peloponnese. ☎ **26240/22-563**. Fax 26240/22-206. 43 units. 55€–60€ ($63–$69) double. AE, V. **Amenities:** Restaurant; rooftop cafe bar; breakfast room.

Hotel Olympia Palace ⭑⭑ Back for a return engagement (for many years this was the Altis Hotel), the completely remodeled Olympia Palace is an excellent choice if you want to be poised on Olympia's main street to investigate the village. If you don't want to venture out, the hotel has its own restaurant and plans to open several shops in the lobby. Rooms in the front can be noisy; rooms in the back have views over the countryside. The good-size guest rooms (each with a balcony) are very tastefully decorated (with nice rugs on the floor and attractive furniture); the bathrooms are modern and spacious. This hotel avoids the pallid anonymous colors so beloved of most Greek hotels.

2 Praxiteleous Kondili, 270 65 Ancient Olympia, Peloponnese. ☎ **26240/23-101**. Fax 26240/22-525. 60 units. 90€–120€ ($104–$144) double. AE, MC, V. **Amenities:** 2 restaurants; bar; shops. *In room:* A/C, TV, minibar, hair dryer.

Where to Dine

There are almost as many restaurants as hotels in Olympia. The ones on and just off the main street with large signs in English and German tend to have indifferent food and service; it's possible to get a decent snack of yogurt and honey or *tiropites* (cheese pies) in most of the cafes and several of the local bakeries.

Taverna Ambrosia GREEK This large restaurant with a pleasant outside veranda continues to attract locals, although it does a brisk business with tour groups. You'll find the usual grilled chops and souvlakia here, but the vegetable dishes (especially the vegetable casserole usually called *briam*) are unusually good, as is the lamb stew with lots of garlic and oregano. If you like rabbit, try the tasty stew with onions.

Behind the train station. ☎ **26240/23-414**. Main courses 5€–12€ ($5.75–$14). AE, MC, V. Daily 8–11pm. Lunch served every weekend noon–3pm.

Taverna Kladeos ⭑⭑ GREEK The charming Kladeos, a hearteningly traditional taverna in the midst of Olympia's growing throng of blah tourist places, has the best food in town, with a menu that changes seasonally. You'll likely find lots of locals here. In good weather, tables are set up under canvas awnings and roofs made of rushes. The lightly grilled green peppers, zucchini, and eggplant are especially delicious. The house wine, a light rosé, is heavenly. If you want to buy a bottle to take away with you, give your empty water bottle to the waiter and ask him to fill it with *krasi* (wine).

Best approached by the road past the Ambrosia Taverna. ☎ **26240/23-322**. Main courses 6€–15€ ($6.90–$17). MC, V. Daily 1:30–3pm and 6pm–1am. Usually closed Nov–Apr.

The Museums & the Ancient Site ⭑⭑⭑

Archaeological Museum Even though you'll be eager to see the ancient site, it's a good idea to begin your visit with the museum, whose collection makes clear Olympia's astonishing wealth and importance in antiquity. Every victorious city and almost every victorious athlete dedicated a bronze or marble statue here. Nothing but the best was good enough for Olympia, and many of the superb works of art found since excavations began here more than 150 years ago are on view in the museum. The museum was closed for renovations and reinstallation in honor of the 2004 Olympics, and had not reopened at press time, so our description is based on what we have been told visitors will see when the museum is open. Most of the exhibits are in galleries on either side of the main entrance and follow a chronological sequence, from severe Neolithic vases to baroque Roman imperial statues. The museum's superstars are in the central galleries directly ahead of the entrance.

The monumental images from the **Temple of Zeus** are probably the finest surviving examples of archaic Greek sculpture. The sculpture from the west pediment shows the battle of the Lapiths and Centaurs raging around the magisterial figure of Apollo. On the east pediment, Zeus oversees the chariot race between Oinomaos, king of Pisa, and Pelops, the legendary figure who wooed and won Oinomaos's daughter by the unsporting expedient of loosening his opponent's chariot pins. On either end of the room, sculptured metopes show scenes from the labors of Hercules, including the one he performed at Olympia: cleaning the Augean stables.

Just beyond the sculpture from the Temple of Zeus are the 5th-century B.C. **Winged Victory** done by the artist Paionios and the 4th-century B.C. figure of Hermes and the infant Dionysios known as the **Hermes of Praxiteles.** The Hermes has a room to itself—or would, if tourists didn't make a beeline to admire Hermes smiling with amused tolerance at his chubby half-brother Dionysios. In addition to several cases of glorious bronze heads of snarling griffins and the lovely terra-cotta of a resolute Zeus carrying off the youthful Ganymede, the museum has a good deal of **athletic paraphernalia** from the ancient games. You'll see stone and bronze weights used for balance by long jumpers, bronze and stone discuses, and even an enormous stone with an inscription boasting that a weight lifter raised it over his head with only one hand.

You can easily spend a day at Olympia, wandering back and forth between the site and the museum, with a break for lunch.

Ⓒ and fax **26240/22-529.** www.culture.gr. Admission 6€ ($6.90); museum and site 9€ ($10). Summer Mon noon–7pm; Tues–Sun 8am–7pm. Winter Mon noon–5pm; Tues–Fri 8am–5pm; Sat–Sun 8:30am–5pm. The museum is directly across the road from the Ancient Site (see below).

Ancient Site   Olympia's setting is magical—pine trees shade the little valley, dominated by the conical Hill of Kronos that lies between the Alphios and Kladeos rivers. Since the 1980s, excavations have concentrated on Roman Olympia, especially in the southern area of the site. Although considerable progress has been made, neither the main entrance nor the route of the ceremonial way during Roman times is yet known. The handsome temples and the famous stadium are not at once apparent as you enter the site. Immediately to the left are the unimpressive low walls that are all that remain of the **Roman baths** where athletes and spectators could enjoy hot and cold plunge baths; some recently restored mosaics are on view. The considerably more impressive remains with the slender columns on your right mark the **gymnasium** and **palestra,** where athletes practiced their footracing and boxing skills. The enormous gymnasium had one roofed track, precisely twice the length of the stadium, where athletes could practice in bad weather. Also on the right are the fairly meager remains of a number of structures, including a swimming pool and the large square **Leonidaion,** which served as a hotel for visiting dignitaries until a Roman governor decided it would do nicely as his villa. If you want, you can continue around the outskirts of the site, identifying other civic buildings, but you'll probably want to enter the sanctuary itself.

The religious sanctuary is dominated by two shrines: the good-size **Temple of Hera** and the massive **Temple of Zeus.** The Temple of Hera, with its three standing columns, is the older of the two, built around 600 B.C. If you look closely, you'll see that the temple's column capitals and drums are not uniform. That's because this temple was originally built with wooden columns, and as each column decayed, it was replaced; inevitably, each new column had slight variations. The Hermes of Praxiteles was found here, buried under the mud that covered Olympia for so long, caused by the repeated flooding of the rivers. The Temple of Zeus, which once had a veritable thicket of 34 stocky Doric columns, was built around 456 B.C. The entire temple—so austere and gray today—was anything but plain in antiquity. Gold, red, and blue paint was everywhere, and inside the temple stood an enormous gold-and-ivory statue of Zeus seated on an ivory-and-ebony throne. The statue was so ornate that it was considered one of the Seven Wonders of the Ancient World—and so large that people joked that if the Zeus stood up, his head would go through the temple's roof. In fact, the antiquarian Philo of Byzantium suggested that Zeus had created elephants simply so that the sculptor Phidias would have the ivory to make his statue.

Not only do we know that Phidias made the 13m (42-ft.) statue, we know where he made it: **The Workshop of Phidias** was on the site of the well-preserved brick building clearly visible west of the temple outside the sanctuary. How do we know that this was Phidias's workshop? Because a cup with "I belong to Phidias" on it and artist's tools were found here. Between the Temples of Zeus and Hera you can make out the low foundations of a round building: This is all that remains of the **shrine** that Philip of Macedon, never modest, built here to pat himself on the back after conquering Greece in 338 B.C. Beyond the two temples, built up against the Hill of Kronos, are the curved remains of a once-elegant **Roman fountain** and the foundations of 11 **treasuries** where Greek cities stored votive offerings and money. In front of the treasuries are the low bases of a series of bronze statues of Zeus dedicated not by victorious athletes but by those caught cheating in the stadium. The statues would have been the last thing competitors saw before they ran through the vaulted tunnel into the stadium.

Note: In 2000, restoration work began on several columns of the Zeus Temple and on the Echo Colonnade and the Treasury of Gela.

Admission 6€; site and museum 9€ ($10). Summer Mon–Fri 7:30am–7pm; Sat–Sun 8:30am–3pm. Winter Mon–Fri 8am–5pm; Sat–Sun 8:30am–3pm.

Museum of the Olympic Games   When you head back to town, try to set aside half an hour or so to visit the Museum of the Olympic Games. At press time, the museum had not yet installed a planned exhibit of memorabilia from the 2004 Olympics. Not many tourists come here, and the guards are often glad to show visitors around. Displays include victors' medals, commemorative stamps, and photos of winning athletes, such as former King Constantine of Greece and the great American athlete Jesse Owens. This is a pleasant place to spend an hour.

📞 26420/22-544. Admission 2€ ($2.30). Mon–Sat 8am–3:30pm; Sun and holidays 9am–2:30pm.

DELPHI ★★★

Delphi, which the ancient Greeks believed was the center of the world, is the big enchilada of Greek sites. Even more than Olympia, it has everything: a long and glorious history as the scene of Apollo's famous oracle and the Pythian games; spectacular ancient remains, including the Temple of Apollo and the well-preserved stadium where the ancient games took place; a superb museum; and a heart-achingly beautiful location on the slopes of Mount Parnassus. Look up and you see the cliffs and crags of Parnassus; look down at Greece's most beautiful plain of olive trees stretching as far as the eye can see toward the town of Itea on the Gulf of Corinth.

Many tour groups offer day trips to Delphi, stopping at the Byzantine monastery of Osios Loukas (see "Organized Tours," earlier in this chapter). In the summer, tour groups clog Delphi's few streets by day, but many head elsewhere for the night, which means that hotel rooms are usually available—although often all the cheap rooms are gone by midmorning. In the winter, thousands of Greeks head here each weekend, not for the archaeological site, but for the excellent skiing on Mount Parnassus. Getting a room in the once-sleepy nearby hamlet of Arachova is virtually impossible without a reservation on winter weekends, and Delphi itself is often full.

Every summer (usually in June), the European Cultural Center of Delphi sponsors the **Festival of Delphi,** featuring ancient Greek drama and works inspired by ancient pieces. Tickets and schedules are usually available at the Center's Athens office at 9 Frynihou, Plaka (*©* **210/331-2798**), and at the Center's Delphi office (*©* **22650/82-733**). Budget travelers take note: Tickets are sometimes substantially discounted or even free close to performance time.

ESSENTIALS

GETTING THERE   By Bus   Depending on the season, as many as five daily buses make the 3-hour trip to Delphi from the **Athens station,** 260 Liossion (*©* **210/831-7096**), north of Omnia Square.

By Car   Take the Athens-Corinth National Highway 74km (46 miles) west of Athens to the Thebes turnoff and continue 40km (25 miles) west to Levadia. If you want to stop at the monastery of Osios Loukas, take the Distomo turnoff for 9km (5½ miles). Return to Distomo and continue via Arachova for 26km (16 miles) to Delphi or via the seaside town of Itea for 64km (40 miles) to Delphi. The approach from Itea on a steeply climbing road with views back to the sea is well worth the time if you aren't in a hurry—and don't mind hairpin curves.

VISITOR INFORMATION   The tourist information office (the former **Greek National Tourism Organization [GNTO]** Office) (*©* **22650/82-900**) ll on the main street (Frederikis) is usually open from 8am to 3pm (sometimes later in summer)—and sometimes mysteriously closed.

FAST FACTS   Most services are available on Frederikis Street. The **post office** is usually open from 8am to 4pm, and sometimes Sunday from 9am to 1pm. The **OTE telephone and telegraph office** is open Monday through Saturday from 7:30am to 3pm and Sunday from 9am to 1pm. Both banks on Frederikis Street have **ATMs** (not always in service).

GETTING AROUND   The village of Delphi, with its handful of long, parallel streets connected by stepped side streets, is small enough that most visitors find it easiest to abandon their cars and explore on foot. If you have to drive to the site rather than make the 5- to 10-minute walk from town, be sure to set off early to get one of the few parking places. Whether you walk or drive, keep an eye out for the enormous tour buses that barrel down the center of the road—and for the not-terribly-well-marked one-way streets in the village.

WHERE TO STAY

There's no shortage of hotels in Delphi, and you can usually get a room even in July and August. Still, if you want a room in a specific price category or with a view, it's best to make a reservation. Finally, in summer (but not in winter when the skiers take over this hamlet), consider staying in nearby **Arachova,** where the hotels are usually less crowded (see "A Day Trip from Delphi," below). Be sure to check whether your hotel has functioning heating if you visit in the winter.

Hotel Varonos ★ *Value*   This small, family owned hotel has very clean, spare rooms (completely remodeled every few years) with fine views out over the olive plain. If you can, take in the rooftop view. This is usually a very welcoming place: we once arrived here with an ailing gardenia plant, and the entire family pitched in to make sure that it was well taken care of during our stay. If you want to have an early breakfast, mention it at the desk the night before. Be sure to check out the owners' shop next door, with local produce and crafts.

25 Vasileos Pavlou and Frederikis, 330 54 Delphi. ℂ and fax 22650/82-345. 11 units, 10 with shower, 1 with shower/tub. 75€–90€ ($86–$104) double. Rates include breakfast (although room without breakfast sometimes possible). Inquire about the 20% discount sometimes available. MC, V. **Amenities:** Breakfast room; lounge with fireplace. *In room:* A/C, TV.

Hotel Vouzas ★   The Vouzas has a cozy fireplace in the lobby, spectacular views from most rooms, and a wraparound veranda. It's a short walk from everything you've come to see—and it's the hotel closest to ancient Delphi itself. Guest rooms and bathrooms are very comfortable, and the balconies have not only a table and chairs but also, when we stayed there, a welcoming pot of basil. That said, on a recent visit the desk staff had no record of our reservation and, when that was sorted out, was supremely uninterested that our TV did not work—but with the view at Delphi, it's borderline criminal to watch TV.

1 Frederikis (at Vasileos Pavlou), 330 54 Delphi. ℂ 22650/82-232. Fax 22650/82-033. 59 units. 125€–150€ double ($144–$173). AE, DC, MC, V. **Amenities:** Restaurant; bar. *In room:* A/C, TV.

WHERE TO DINE

You won't starve in Delphi, but there's no really outstanding restaurant, so you may prefer to head to the village of Arachova, 10km (6¼ miles) to the north (see "A Day Trip from Delphi," below). That said, in Delphi you might try **Topiki Gefsi,** Pavlou and 19 Frederikis (ℂ 22650/82-480); the **Taverna Vakchos,** 31 Apollonos (ℂ 22650/82-448); or the family run **Taverna Lekaria,** 33 Apollonos (ℂ 22650/82-864). Its main street location, periodic live music, and fine views probably make Topiki Gefsi the most expensive of the three (about 20€ ($23) per person). I've often enjoyed the simple food (and tasty toasted bread, sometimes topped with garlic and cheese) at the Lekaria, but this is not a good place to come to if you are in a hurry.

EXPLORING THE SITE

If possible, begin your visit when the site and museum open in the morning (both are sometimes relatively uncrowded in the hour before closing, too). If you begin your visit at the museum, you'll arrive at the site already familiar with many of the works of art that once decorated the sanctuary. As with Olympia, it's easy to spend a whole day here, taking in the site and museum, with a break for lunch.

Delphi Archaeological Museum ★★★   *Note:* At press time, the partly renovated, expanded, and reinstalled museum announced it would reopen in time for the 2004 Athens Summer Olympics and close indefinitely thereafter. Our description is based on what we have been told visitors will see. Each of the museum's rooms has a specific focus: sculpture from the elegant Siphnian treasury in one room, finds from the Temple of Apollo in two rooms, discoveries from the Roman period (including the Parian marble statue of the epicene youth Antinous, the beloved of the emperor Hadrian) in another. Keep an eye out for the impressively large 4th-century B.C. marble egg, a symbol of Delphi's position as the center of the world. According to legend, when Zeus wanted to determine the earth's center, he released two eagles from Mount Olympus. When the eagles met over Delphi, Zeus had his answer. (You can still see eagles in the sky above Delphi, but as often as not, the large birds circling overhead are the less distinguished Egyptian vultures.)

The star of the museum, with a room to himself, is the famous 5th-century B.C. **Charioteer of Delphi,** a larger-than-life bronze figure that was part of a group that originally included a four-horse chariot. It's an irresistible statue—don't miss the handsome youth's delicate eyelashes shading wide enamel and stone eyes or the realistic veins that stand out in his hands and feet.

Although the charioteer is the star of the collection, he's in good company. Delphi was chockablock with superb works of art given by wealthy patrons, such as King Croesus of Lydia, who contributed the massive silver bull that's on display. Many of the finest exhibits are quite small, such as the elegant bronzes in the museum's last room, including one that shows Odysseus clinging to the belly of a ram. According to Homer, this is how the wily hero escaped from the cave of the ferocious (but nearsighted) monster Cyclops.

© 22650/82-312. Admission (which includes the site) 6€ ($6.90). Summer Mon noon–5:30pm; Tues–Fri 7:30am–6:30pm; Sat–Sun 8:30am–3pm. Winter usually daily 8:30am–3pm.

Sanctuary of Apollo, Castalian Spring & Sanctuary of Athena Pronaia
As you enter the **Sanctuary of Apollo,** just past the museum, you'll be on the marble **Sacred Way,** following the route that visitors to Delphi have taken for thousands of years. The Sacred Way twists uphill past the remains of Roman **stoas** (porticoes) and a number of **Greek treasuries** (including the Siphnian and Athenian treasuries, whose sculpture is in the museum). Take a close look at the treasury walls: You'll see not only beautiful dry-wall masonry, but countless inscriptions. The ancient Greeks were never shy about using the walls of their buildings as bulletin boards. Alas, so many contemporary visitors have added their own names to the ancient inscriptions that the Greek Archaeological Service no longer allows visitors inside the massive 4th-century B.C. **Temple of Apollo,** which was built here after several earlier temples were destroyed.

From the temple, it's a fairly steep uphill climb to the remarkably well preserved 4th-century B.C. theater and the stadium, extensively remodeled by the Romans. In antiquity, contests in the Pythian festivals took place in both venues. Today the theater and stadium are used most summers for the Festival of Delphi—which, on occasion, has featured exceptionally nonclassical pop music.

Keep your ticket as you leave the Sanctuary of Apollo and begin the 10-minute walk along the Arachova-Delphi road to the Sanctuary of Athena (also called the

Marmaria, which refers to all the marble found here). En route, you'll pass the famous **Castalian Spring,** where Apollo planted a laurel. Above are the rose-colored cliffs known as the Phaedriades (the Bright Ones), famous for the way they reflect the sun's rays. Drinking from the Castalian Spring has inspired legions of poets; however, poets now have to find their inspiration elsewhere because the spring is off-limits to allow repairs to the Roman fountain facade. Poets, be warned: Once an antiquity is closed in Greece, it often stays closed for quite a while.

A path descends from the main road to the **Sanctuary of Athena Pronaia,** goddess of wisdom, who shared the honors at Delphi with Apollo. The remains here are quite fragmentary, except for the large 4th-century B.C. gymnasium, and you might choose simply to wander about and enjoy the site without trying too hard to figure out what's what. The round 4th-century B.C. tholos with its three graceful standing Doric columns is easy to spot—but no one knows why the building was constructed, why it was so lavishly decorated, or what went on inside. Again, the oracle is silent.

© 22650/82-313. Admission (which includes the museum) 6€ ($6.90). Summer Mon–Fri 7:30am–6:30pm; Sat, Sun, holidays 8:30am–3pm. Winter usually daily 8:30am–3pm.

A DAY TRIP FROM DELPHI

ARACHOVA   The mountain village of Arachova, 10km (6¼ miles) north of Delphi, clings to Mount Parnassus some 945m (3,100 ft.) above sea level. Arachova is famous for its hand-loomed *tagari* shoulder bags, heavy blankets, and fluffy *flokakia* rugs. When several tour buses stop here during the daytime, the tiny village can be seriously crowded. Don't despair—come in the evening, when the shops are still open and the cafes and restaurants allow you to escape from the tourist world of Delphi to the village world of Greece—except, of course, in winter, when Athenian skiers in full après-ski outfits roam the village. Year-round, in decent weather, there's usually an energetic evening *volta* (stroll) on the main street, and if you climb the steep stairs to the upper town, you'll find your-self on quiet neighborhood streets where children play and families sit in front of their homes.

On the main street, a string of shops offer local weavings and crafts, repro-ductions of antiques, and local cheeses. For lunch or dinner, try one of the restau-rants strung along the main street with its lovely freshwater springs and cafes: **Taverna Karathanassi** (© 22670/31-360), **Taverna Dasargyri** (also known as Barba Iannis; © 22670/31-391), or **Taverna Kaplanis** (© 22670/31-891). The Dasargyri has tasty *loukanika* (sausages) and delicious *kokoretsi,* the stuffed entrails that are perhaps not to every traveler's taste. No credit cards are accepted; all are open daily approximately from noon to midnight but sometimes close from about 4 to 7pm. Dinner for two costs about 20€ to 30€ ($23–$35) at all these restaurants; in winter, prices are higher.

If you want to stay in Arachova, the **Xenia Hotel** (© **22670/31-230;** fax 22670/32-175) has 44 rooms, each with a balcony (but charmless decor); dou-bles are 80€ ($92). The very pleasant **Anemolia** (© **22670/31-640;** fax 22670/31-642), situated on a hill just outside Arachova above the Delphi road, was originally a member of the Best Western chain, and its 52 rooms are large and comfortable. The 44-room **Arachova** Inn, with a cozy fireplace in the lobby, is just out of town and has its own restaurant. Tentative prices for all three for 2004 are 85€ ($98) for a double (sometimes as much as 20€–50€/$23–$58 higher on the weekend).

3 The Cyclades

When most people think of the "Isles of Greece," they're thinking of the Cyclades, the rugged (even barren) chain of Aegean islands whose villages of dazzling white houses look from a distance like so many sugar cubes. The Cyclades got their name from the ancient Greek word meaning "to circle," or surround, because the island chain encircles the sacred island of Delos. Today, especially in the summer, it's the visitors who circle these islands, taking advantage of the swift island boats and hydrofoils that link them.

Mykonos, with its dazzling architecture, superb tradition of weaving, and poverty—all of which made it susceptible to the tourist trade—was the first of the islands to become popular in the 1960s. Although the Beautiful People may have moved on, Mykonos remains a favorite, although expensive, island— especially in the summer, when reservations are imperative. The crescent of **Santorini (Thira),** with its black-sand beaches and blood-red cliffs, is all that remains of the island that was blown apart in antiquity by a volcano that still steams and hisses today. Santorini's exceptional physical beauty, dazzling relics, and elegant restaurants and boutiques cause people to call it "sophisticated." Unfortunately, Santorini's charms draw so many day-trippers from cruise ships that the island almost sinks under the weight of tourists each summer. **Tinos,** whose hills are dotted with elaborate dovecotes, is the most important destination in all Greece for religious pilgrims, yet it remains one of the least commercialized islands of the Cyclades—and a joy to visit for that reason.

The Cyclades are usually crowded and expensive in the high season, roughly from mid-June to mid-September—and the season seems to get longer every year. If this doesn't appeal to you, visit the Cyclades in the off season; the best times are in the autumn (mid-Sept to Oct) or in the spring (Apr to early June, which can still be chilly in these islands). Although the restaurant you'd hoped to eat at may be closed and some of the chic shops shuttered in the off season, you'll be able to enjoy the islands without feeling that you're surrounded by other visitors—and pay much less for your hotel room. Should you visit in winter, keep in mind that many island hotels have minimal heating; make sure that your hotel conforms to your expectations for heating before you check in. And should you visit during the summer of 2004, keep in mind that the islands are expected to be very crowded with visitors who come to see the Olympics but also want to visit at least one Greek island.

On most of these islands, the capital town has the name of the island itself. It's also sometimes called "Hora," or "Chora," a term meaning "the place" that's commonly used for the most important regional town.

GETTING TO THE CYCLADES
BY AIR   **Olympic Airways** (© **210/966-6666,** or 210/936-9111 in Athens) has frequent daily service from Athens to Mykonos and Santorini; there's service several times a week from Mykonos or Santorini to Thessaloniki, Iraklio, Crete, and Rhodes. In addition, an increasing number of charter flights from all over Europe fly into the various islands. Several small, private Greek airlines serving the islands have gone in (and out) of business in recent years; you might check to see if **Aegean Air** (© **0801-2000;** www.aegeanair.com) is in service when you are traveling. *Note:* In the past, Aegean Air has offered 20% discounts for students and for travelers over 60.

BY SEA   Ferries leave daily from Athens's main port of Piraeus and from Rafina, the port east of Athens; contact the Piraeus Port Authority (© **210/ 451-1310** or 210/451-1311) or the Rafina Port Police (© **22940/22-300**) for schedules. The speedy **Seajet** (© **210/414-1250**) catamaran service also departs from Rafina and zips between Andros, Syros, Tinos, Mykonos, Paros, Naxos, and Santorini (Thira). **Ilio Lines** (© **210/422-4772** in Athens, or 22940/ 22-888 in Rafina) offers regular **hydrofoil** service from Rafina to a number of destinations.

It can take an hour for the 27km (17-mile) bus ride from Athens to Rafina (the most convenient port for Mykonos and Tinos), but you save about an hour of sailing time and usually about 20% on the fare. Buses leave every 30 minutes from 6am to 10pm from 29 Mavromateon (© **210/821-0872**), near Areos Park north of the National Archaeological Museum (indicated on most city maps).

In the summer there's regular ferry service to Iraklio, Crete, from Piraeus, the port of Athens. There are also ferry and hydrofoil connections several times a week between Mykonos and Kos and Rhodes; twice a week between Mykonos and Skyros, Skiathos, and Thessaloniki; daily between Tinos and Paros and Syros, and two or three times a week between Syros and the Dodecanese.

Warning: In September 2000, the ferry *Express Samina* sank, with a loss of 82 lives, when it hit rocks entering the harbor at Paros. The subsequent investigation disclosed many oversights in safety precautions on the Samina and other Greek ferries. *A word to the wise:* When you travel by ferry, make sure you know where the exits are and where the lifeboats and life jackets are—and do not board any ferry that appears overcrowded. If you book a cabin, make sure that it is not located below the cargo deck. The excellent Thomas Cook guide *Island Hopping* (published annually) is a useful guide to the safety rating of Greek ferryboats.

Remember: Many of the rural Greek National tourist offices (EOT) are being turned over to local authorities. In most cases, the office remains at the same address, with the same phone and work hours; but call in advance to make sure.

GETTING AROUND THE CYCLADES

You are advised to double-check all ferry information in Greece. Although there is frequent ferry service between most of the islands, schedules can be erratic, and service diminishes suddenly at the end of the season. Changes in the line that serves an island can occur with little advance warning. Smaller excursion vessels are easily affected by high winds. To further complicate matters, a line

---

⟨Tips The Wind & the Sea

The winds frequently complicate sea travel on the Aegean. For this reason, plan to arrive back in Athens from the islands **at least** 24 hours before you have to make any critical air or sea connections. In July the strong winds known as the *meltemi* usually kick up, often playing havoc with hydrofoil schedules. The larger ferries still run—although if you're prone to seasickness, take precautions. In the winter the strong north winds *(vorias)* frequently make sea travel impossible for days at a time. That said, this is one of the best ways to travel and enjoy Greece—but, perhaps, as we say in Greece: *siga, siga* (slowly, slowly)—with all the more time to enjoy the moment.

The Cyclades

ATTICA

ANDROS
Gavrio
Batsi

Aegean Sea

GREECE
Athens
The Cyclades

KEA
Gyaros
Kea

TINOS
Koumaros
Falatados
Tinos

MYKONOS
Ayios
Stephanos
Platis Yialos

SYROS
Ano Syros
Ermoupolis
Possidon
DELOS

Kythnos
KYTHNOS

SERIFOS
Serfopoula
Serifos
Livadi

SIFNOS
Artemona
Kastro
Kamares
Apollonia
Platís Yialos
Antiparos

Naoussa
Aliki
PAROS

Naxos
(Hora)
Ay. Anna
Ay. Prokopios
NAXOS

Apollonas
Koronos
DONOUSSA
Donoussa

Koufonissi
Karos
Iraklia

Milos
Apolionia
Adamas
MILOS
Folegandros

Hora
Yialos
IOS

Lefkes
AMORGOS

Ia
SANTORINI
(THIRA)
Fira
Kamari
Emborio
Perissa
Anafi

Ferry Route

will sometimes authorize only one agent to sell tickets or limit the number of tickets available to an agency, giving other agents little incentive to tout its service. You may want to visit several agents or inquire at the port authority. (For specifics, see "Getting There," under "Essentials," for each island.)

The easiest, most comfortable, and most expensive way to island-hop is on a **chartered yacht cruise;** you don't have to worry about ferry connections, hotel reservations, and most meals. **Viking Star Cruises,** 1 Artemidos, Glyfada, 166 74 Athens (© 210/898-0729; fax 210/894-0952; vikings@forum.ars.net.gr or bjgh44a@prodigy.com), offers 7-day cruises beginning every Friday, from April to early November. The cruises stop at Tinos, Ios, Santorini, Paros, Naxos, Mykonos, and Delos. Last-minute discount fares are occasionally available.

If you want to cruise around the Cyclades (or elsewhere in Greece) for a week or two, and don't want to travel with strangers, put together your own group and contact **Ari Drivas Yachting** (© 210/411-3194; fax 210/411-4459; drivasy@ ath.forthnet.gr). Choose among a stunning array of motor yachts and sailing vessels with from 2 to 24 cabins. Drivas prides itself on its superbly trained crews, which include excellent cooks.

For more information on cruises, contact the **Greek National Tourist Organization** (© **212/421-5777** in New York, 020/7734-5997 in London, or 210/331-0437 or 210/331-0562 in Athens) or the **Greek Island Cruise Center** (© **800/342-3030** in the U.S.). **Sea Cloud Cruises** (© **888/732-2568** in the U.S.) uses a four-masted private yacht that takes up to 60 passengers on Aegean cruises.

MYKONOS

What makes this small (about 16km/10 miles long; pop. 15,000), arid island so popular? At least initially, it was the exceptionally handsome Cycladic architecture—and the fact that many on the poor island were more than eager to rent their houses to visitors. First came the jet-setters, artists, and expatriates (including a number of sophisticated gay visitors), as well as the mainland Greeks who opened many of the chic shops and restaurants—all followed by a curious mixture of jet-set wannabes and backpackers. Now, with cruise ships lined up in the harbor all summer and as many as 10 flights each day from Athens, it's easier to say who *doesn't* come to Mykonos than who does. That's why it's very important not to arrive here without reservations in July and August (when it can feel as if every one of the island's annual 800,000 visitors is here), unless you enjoy sleeping outdoors—and don't mind being moved from your sleeping spot by the police, who are not always charmed to find foreigners alfresco.

ESSENTIALS

GETTING THERE   By Air   Olympic Airways has as many as 10 flights daily between Athens and Mykonos. In addition, there's usually one flight daily between Mykonos and Iraklio (Crete), Rhodes, and Santorini, and three flights a week between Mykonos and Ios, Lesvos, and Samos. It's difficult to get a seat on any of these flights, so make reservations early and reconfirm them at the office in Athens (© **210/966-6666** or 210/936-9111) or Mykonos (© **22890/22-490** or 22890/22-237).

By Sea   From Piraeus, **Ventouris Lines** (© **210/482-5815** or 210/482-8001) has departures at least once daily, usually at 8am, with a second on summer afternoons. From Rafina, **Strintzis Lines** has daily ferry service; schedules can be checked with the **Port Police** (© **22940/28-888**). There are usually daily ferry connections between Mykonos and Andros, Paros, Syros, and Tinos; five to seven trips a week to Ios; four a week to Iraklio, Crete; several a week to Kos and Rhodes; and two a week to Ikaria, Samos, Skiathos, Skyros, and Thessaloniki. **Hellas Flying Dolphins** offers service from **Piraeus** (© **210/451-1311;** booking@mfd.gr) in summer.

On Mykonos, your best bet for getting boat information is to check at individual agents, or check if the **Port Authority** (© **22890/22-218;** by National Bank), **Tourist Police** (© **22890/22-482;** at the north end of the harbor), or **tourist office** (© **22890/23-990;** fax 22890/22-229; also on the harbor) has an up-to-date list of sailings.

Hydrofoil service to Crete, Ios, Paros, and Santorini is often irregular. For information, check at the **Port Authority** in Piraeus (© **210/451-1311**), Rafina (© **22940/23-300**), or Mykonos (© **22890/22-218**).

Note: Check each travel agent's current schedule, because most ferry tickets are not interchangeable. Reputable agents on the main square in Mykonos (Hora) town include: **Delia Travel** (© **22890/22-490;** fax 22890/24-440); **Sea & Sky Travel** (© **22890/22-853;** fax 22890/24-753); and the **Veronis Agency** (© **22890/22-687;** fax 22890/23-763).

VISITOR INFORMATION The **Mykonos Accommodations Center,** at the corner of Enoplon Dhinameon and Malamatenias (© **22890/23-160;** mac@mac.myk.forthnet.gr), helps visitors find accommodations. It also functions as a tourist information center. **Windmills Travel** (© **22890/23-877;** www.windmills-travel.com) has an office at Fabrica Square where you can get general information, book accommodations (often at substantial discounts), arrange excursions, and rent a car or moped (also usually at an excellent price). If you travel on to Tinos, be sure to use the amazingly efficient Windmills branch there (see "Tinos: Visitor Information," below). The free *Mykonos Summertime* magazine is available in cafes, shops, and hotels throughout the island.

TOWN LAYOUT Legend has it that the streets of Mykonos town—which locals call Hora—were designed to confuse pirates, so your own confusion will be understandable. As you get off the ferry, you can see the main square south across the harbor beyond the small town beach and a cluster of buildings; we refer to it as **Taxi Square,** although it's officially called Plateia Manto Mavroyenous, after a local heroine. Here you'll find several travel agents, kiosks, snack bars, and, of course, the town's taxi stand. The map published by **Stamatis Bozinakis** is sold at most kiosks for 2€ ($2.30) and is quite decent; the excellent **Mykonos Sky Map** is free at some hotels and shops.

The main street, **Matoyanni,** leads south off Taxi Square behind the church; it's narrow, but you can hardly miss the bars, boutiques, and restaurants. Several "blocks" along it you'll find a "major" cross street, **Kaloyera,** and by turning right, you'll find several of the hotels and restaurants we recommend. If you get lost—and you will—remember that in Mykonos that's part of the fun.

GETTING AROUND **By Foot** One of Hora's greatest assets is the government decree that made the town an architectural landmark and prohibited motorized traffic on its streets. If you don't arrive with your donkey or bicycle, you can walk around town. Much of the rest of the island is served by local buses.

By Bus Mykonos has one of the best bus systems in the Greek islands; the buses run frequently and on schedule. Depending on your destination, a ticket costs about .50€ to 3.50€ (55¢–$4). There are two bus stations in Hora: one near the archaeological museum and one near the Olympic Airways office (follow the helpful blue signs). Check at the tourist office to see which station the bus you want leaves from, or look for one of the schedules sometimes available in hotels. Bus information in English is sometimes available from the office of Greece's long-distance bus service, **KTEL** (© **22890/23-360).**

Tips **Finding an Address**

Although some shops hand out a map of Mykonos town, you'll probably do better finding restaurants, hotels, and attractions by asking people to point you in the right direction. Many streets do not have their names posted, and the map leaves off most of the small, twisting, streets—and Mykonos has almost nothing but small, twisting, streets!

By Boat Weather permitting, excursion boats to **Delos** depart every day at 9am from the west side of the harbor near the tourist office. For more information, see "An Excursion to the Island of Delos," later in this chapter, or consult a travel agent; guided tours are available. Caiques (sailboats) to the beaches of **Super Paradise, Agrari,** and **Elia** depart from the town harbor every morning, weather permitting. Caiques to **Paradise, Super Paradise, Agrari,** and **Elia** also leave from **Plati Yialos** every morning, weather permitting. (Caique service is almost continuous during the high season, when boats also depart from **Ornos Bay.**)

By Car & Moped Rental cars and Jeeps are available from travel agents for about 60€ ($69) per day, including full insurance, during the high season, and for substantially less at other times if you bargain. Mopeds can be a fun way to get around if you know how to handle one and can negotiate the sometimes treacherous roads. Mopeds (around 15€–30€/$17–$35 a day) are available from shops near both bus stations.

Note: If you park in town or in a no-parking area, the police will remove your license plates, and you, not the rental office, will have to find the police station and pay a steep fine to get them back.

By Taxi Getting a taxi in Hora is easy; walk to Taxi Square, near the statue, and get in line; a notice board gives rates for each destination for both high and low seasons. You can also phone (✆ **22890/22-400,** or 22890/23-700 for late-hour and out-of-town service). You'll be charged the fare from Hora to your pickup point plus the fare to your destination, so before calling, try to find an empty taxi returning to Hora or flag one down along the road. You can also take a moped taxi in Mykonos town, but only if you like to live dangerously.

FAST FACTS: **Mykonos**

Banks The Commercial Bank and the National Bank of Greece are on the harbor a couple of blocks west of Taxi Square. Both are open weekdays from 8am to 2pm. The ATMs usually (but not always) function after hours. Traveler's checks can be cashed at the post office and at many travel agents and hotels, usually at a less favorable rate than at banks.

Hospital The **Mykonos Health Center** (✆ **22890/23-994** or 22890/23-996) handles routine medical complaints; serious cases are usually airlifted to the mainland.

Internet Access Using the Internet is expensive on Mykonos. The **Mykonos Cyber Café,** 26 M. Axioti, on the road between the south bus station and the windmills (✆ **22890/27-684**), is usually open daily from 9am to 10pm and charges 15€ ($17) per hour or 4€ ($4.60) or 15 minutes. **Angelo's Internet Café,** on the same road (✆ **22890/24-106**), may have lower rates.

Police The **Tourist Police** office (✆ **22890/22-482**) is on the west side of the port near the ferries to Delos. The **Port Police** office (✆ **22890/22-218**) is on the east side of the harbor front near the post office. The local **police office** (✆ **22890/22-235**) is behind the grammar school.

Post Office The post office (✆ **22890/22-238**), on the east side of the harbor near the Port Police, is open weekdays from 7:30am to 2pm.

Telephone The **OTE telephone office** (© **22890/22-499**), on the east side of the harbor beyond the Hotel Leto, is usually open daily from 7:30am to 10pm.

WHERE TO STAY

In summer, if you arrive by ferry, you're met by a throng of people hawking rooms, some in small hotels, others in private homes. If you don't have a hotel reservation, one of these rooms may be very welcome. If you're pretty sure that won't suit your needs, be sure you have reserved a room 1 to 3 months in advance of your visit (see information on the Mykonos Accommodations Center, above, under "Visitor Information"). Many hotels are fully booked all summer by tour groups or regular patrons. Keep in mind that Mykonos is an easier, more pleasant place to visit in the late spring or early fall, and that off-season hotel rates are sometimes half the quoted high-season rate. Also keep in mind that many small hotels (and restaurants and shops) close in winter, especially if business is slow.

In & Around Hora

Belvedere Hotel ⭐   The spiffy Belvedere, in part occupying a handsome and handsomely restored 1850s town house on the main road into town, has stunning views over the town and harbor, a few minutes' walk away. Rooms are nicely, if not distinctively, furnished. This is the place to stay if you want the creature comforts of Mykonos's beach resorts but prefer to be within walking distance of Hora. The in-house **Remvi** restaurant has a cellar with 5,000 bottles of wine, and is both excellent and pricey; there's also a sushi bar. In season, the hotel offers massage, hairdresser, and barber services. Off season, the hotel often has excellent specials, including a free Jeep for a day if you stay 4 nights, or a 5th night free after a 4-night stay.

Hora, School of Fine Arts District, 846 00 Mykonos. © **22890/25-122**. Fax 22890/25-126. belvedere@mykonos-accomodations.com. 48 units. 160€–270€ ($184–$310) double. Rates include American buffet breakfast. Considerable off-season reductions usually available. AE, MC, V. **Amenities:** 2 restaurants; bar; pool; fitness center; Jacuzzi; sauna. *In room:* A/C, TV, dataport (10 rooms), minibar, hair dryer.

Cavo Tagoo ⭐⭐   This elegant hotel set into a cliff with spectacular views over Mykonos town is hard to resist—and consistently makes it into *Odyssey* magazine's list of the 10 best Greek hotels. Cavo Tagoo's island-style architecture has won awards, and its gleaming marble floors, nicely crafted wooden furniture, queen- and king-size beds, and local-style weavings are a genuine pleasure. It's only a 15-minute walk to Hora's harbor, although you may find it hard to budge: A (saltwater) pool and a good restaurant are right here.

Hora, 846 00 Mykonos. © **22890/23-692**, 22890/23-693, or 22890/23-694. Fax 22890/24-923. cavotagoo@mykonos-accomodation.com. 72 units. 190€–360€ ($218–$414) double. Rates include buffet breakfast. AE, MC, V. Closed Nov–Mar. **Amenities:** Restaurant; bar; pool. *In room:* A/C, TV, minibar, hair dryer.

Matina Hotel ⭐   This small hotel set in a large garden is surprisingly quiet, given its central location. If you want to avoid the large, isolated hotels and enjoy the comings and goings in a Hora neighborhood, this may be the place for you. Rooms are a bit on the small side but are modern and comfortable, and the owner has been described by several readers as "very helpful." We agree.

3 Fournakion, Hora, 846 00 Mykonos. © **22890/22-387**. Fax 22890/24-501. www.matina.gr. 19 units. 100€ ($115) double. Rates include buffet breakfast. AE, MC, V. Closed Nov–Mar. **Amenities:** Breakfast room; garden.

Philippi Hotel   Each room in this homey little hotel in the heart of Mykonos town is different, so you might want to have a look at several before choosing yours. The owner tends a lush garden that often provides flowers for her son's restaurant, the elegant **Philippi** (see "Where to Dine," below), which can be reached through the garden.

25 Kaloyera, Hora, 846 00 Mykonos. ℂ **22890/22-294.** Fax 22890/24-680. 13 units. 75€ ($86) double. No credit cards. **Amenities:** Restaurant; breakfast room.

Around the Island

Although most visitors prefer to stay in Hora and commute to the beaches, there are hotels near many of the more popular island beaches.

There are private studios and simple pensions at Paradise and Super Paradise beaches, but rooms are almost impossible to get, and prices more than double in July and August. Contact the **Mykonos Accommodations Center** (ℂ **22890/ 23-160**)—or, for Super Paradise, **GATS Travel** (ℂ **22890/22-404**)—for information on the properties they represent. The tavernas at each beach may also have suggestions.

AT KALAFATI   The sprawling **Aphrodite Hotel** (ℂ **22890/71-367**) has a large pool, two restaurants, and 150 rooms. It's a good value in May, June, and October, when a double costs from 100€ ($115). This place is popular with tour groups and Greek families.

AT ORNOS BAY ★★   The elegant **Kivotos Club Hotel,** Ornos Bay, 846 00 Mykonos (ℂ **22890/25-795;** fax 22890/22-844; www.kivotosclubhotel.gr), is a small luxury hotel where most of its 45 distinctively decorated units overlook the Bay of Ornos. If you don't want to walk that far for a swim, head for the salt-water pool, or for the Jacuzzi and sauna. Kivotos Clubhouse is small enough to be intimate and tranquil; the service (including frozen towels to cool poolside guests on hot days) gets raves from guests. Small wonder that this popular honeymoon destination has appeared on *Odyssey* magazine's annual list of the best hotels in Greece. If you ever want to leave (and you may not—it has several restaurants and bars), the hotel minibus will whisk you into town. Doubles cost from 400€ ($460); suites are priced as high as 1,000€ ($1,150).

AT PLATI YIALOS   The 82 units at the **Hotel Petassos Bay,** Plati Yialos, 846 00 Mykonos (ℂ **22890/23-737;** fax 22890/24-101), all have air-conditioning and minibars, and are large and comfortable. Doubles rent for about 180€ ($207). Each has a balcony overlooking the (relatively secluded) beach, which is less than 36m (120 ft.) away. The hotel has a good-size pool, sun deck, Jacuzzi, gym, and sauna, and offers free round-trip transportation from the harbor or airport, safety boxes, and laundry service. The new seaside restaurant has a great view and serves a big buffet breakfast (not included in the room rate).

AT AYIOS STEPHANOS   This popular resort, about 4km (2½ miles) north of Hora, has a number of hotels. The 38-unit **Princess of Mykonos,** Ayios Stephanos, 846 00 Mykonos (ℂ **22890/23-806;** fax 22890/23031), is the most elegant. The Princess has bungalows, a gym, a pool, and an excellent beach; doubles cost from 200€ ($230). The **Hotel Artemis,** Ayios Stephanos, 846 00 Mykonos (ℂ **22890/22-345**), near the beach and bus stop, offers 23 units with bathroom from 125€ ($144) with breakfast included. The small **Hotel Mina,** Ayios Stephanos, 846 00 Mykonos (ℂ **22890/23-024**), uphill behind the Artemis, has 15 doubles with bathroom that go from 80€ ($92). All these hotels are usually closed November through March.

AT PSARROU BEACH   **Grecotel Mykonos Blu,** Psarrou Beach, 846 00 Mykonos (© **22890/27-900;** fax 22890/27-783; www.grecotel.gr), is another of the island's serious luxury hotels, with award-winning Cyclades-inspired architecture. Like Cavo Tagoo and Kivotos, this place is popular with wealthy Greeks, honeymooners, and jet-setters. The private beach, large pool, and in-house Poets of the Aegean restaurant allow guests to be just as lazy as you wish (although there is a fitness club and spa for the energetic). Doubles (many with private terraces and balconies) cost from 250€ to 500€ ($288–$575).

WHERE TO DINE

Unfortunately, most restaurants here know that you're probably just passing through—hardly an incentive to offer the best in food or service. Restaurants also come and go, so if possible, check with other travelers or locals as to what's just opened and is getting good reviews.

As usual on the islands, most of the harborside tavernas are expensive and mediocre, although **Kounelas** 🍴 on the harbor (no phone; no credit cards) is still a good value for fresh fish—as the presence of locals dining here attests. Elsewhere, expect to pay dearly for fish (not always fresh, but always pricey).

Antonini's GREEK   Antonini's is one of the oldest of Mykonos's restaurants, and it serves consistently decent stews, chops, and mezedes. Locals still eat here, although in summer they tend to leave the place to tourists.

Plateia Manto, Hora. © **22890/22-319.** Main courses 10€–18€ ($12–$21). No credit cards. Daily noon–3pm and 7pm–1am in summer. Usually closed Nov–Mar.

Edem 🍴 GREEK/CONTINENTAL   This restaurant beside a pool in a garden has a quiet location—unless you have the bad luck to arrive here, as I once did, just before a raucous tour group occupied all the other tables. If that happens, console yourself with the food: the excellent appetizers, lots of tasty (and very pricey) seafood (usually including baked shrimp, something of a house spe-cialty), and lamb stews with delicate seasonings that visitors have enjoyed here for more than 30 years.

Signposted off Matoyanni (near the church). © **22890/22-855.** Reservations recommended July–Aug. Main courses 11€–30€ ($13–$35); fish priced by the kilo. AE, DC, MC, V. Daily noon–3pm and 7pm–midnight in summer (hours are flexible; sometimes open in winter).

Philippi 🍴🍴 GREEK/CONTINENTAL   This restaurant in the garden of the Hotel Philippi is a nice place in which to escape the hurly-burly of the harbor. Old Greek favorites share space on the menu with French dishes and a more than impressive wine list.

32 Kalogera, off Matoyanni. © **22890/22-294.** Reservations recommended July–Aug. Main courses 11€–28€ ($13–$33). AE, MC, V. Daily 7pm–1am. Walk up the main street, past Kaloyera, and you'll find it on the right.

Sea Satin Market 🍴🍴 GREEK/SEAFOOD   Restaurants open and close on Mykonos, but this quite new (1999) place on the sea by Hora's famous cluster of windmills looks like a success. First, there's the location: a perfect spot to take in the sunset by the sea. And the food is more than tasty, specializing in fish, grills, and decent salads and vegetables.

On the beach below the windmills, Hora. © **22890/24-676.** Main courses 9€–38€ ($10–$44); fish priced by the kilo. AE, V. Daily 6:30pm–12:30am.

EXPLORING THE ISLAND

Even if you're here for the beaches or to visit the island of Delos, you'll probably want to spend some time exploring Hora, enjoy the twists and turns of the narrow streets, and admire the harborfront's resident pelican. Try to remember to make haste slowly, and enjoy the unexpected sights you'll see when you (inevitably!) get lost in Hora's maze of streets.

The **Archaeological Museum** (☎ 22890/22-325), near the harbor, has finds from Delos; it's open Monday and Wednesday through Saturday from 9am to 3:30pm, Sunday and holidays from 10am to 3pm. Admission is 3€ ($3.45); free on Sunday. The **Nautical Museum of the Aegean** (☎ 22890/22-700), across from the park on Enoplon Dinameon Street, has just what you'd expect, including some handsome ship models. It's open daily from 10:30am to 1pm and 7 to 9pm; admission is 2€ ($2.30). The **Museum of Folklore** (☎ 22890/25-591), in a 19th-century sea captain's mansion near the quay, has examples of local crafts and furnishings and a re-created 19th-century island kitchen. It's usually open Monday through Saturday from 4 to 8pm; admission is free.

Hora also has the remains of a small **Venetian Kastro** (fortress) and the island's most famous church, the **Panagia Paraportiani (Our Lady of the Postern Gate),** a thickly whitewashed asymmetrical edifice made up of four small chapels. Beyond the Panagia Paraportiani is the Alefkandra quarter, better known as **Little Venice** ✿✿, for its cluster of homes built overhanging the sea. Many buildings here have been converted into fashionable bars prized for their sunset views; you can sip a margarita and listen to Mozart most nights at the Montparnasse or Kastro bars (see "Mykonos After Dark," below).

Another nearby watering spot is at the famous **Tria Pigadia (Three Wells)** ✿✿. Local legend says that if a virgin drinks from all three she is sure to find a husband, but it's probably not a good idea to test this hypothesis by drinking the brackish well water. After you visit the Tria Pigadia, you may want to take in the famous **windmills** of **Kato Myli** and enjoy the views back toward Little Venice.

THE SHOPS   Mykonos has a lot of shops, mostly selling overpriced souvenirs, clothing, and jewelry. The finest jewelry shop is **Lalaounis,** 14 Polykandrioti (☎ 22890/22-444), associated with the famous Lalaounis museum and shops in Athens. It has superb reproductions of ancient and Byzantine jewelry as well as original designs. If you want to see some serious works of art, try the **Scala Gallery,** 48 Matoyianni (☎ 22890/23-407; fax 22890/26-993), which represents a wide range of contemporary Greek artists and frequently has exhibitions. When you finish your shopping, treat yourself to a local delicacy, almond biscuits from **Efthemios,** 4 Florou Zouganeli (☎ 22890/22-281), off the harborfront.

THE BEACHES   If you've come to Mykonos to find a secluded beach, you have made a serious mistake. People come to Mykonos to see and be seen, whether in their best togs at cafes or naked on nudist beaches. If you want to hit the "in" beaches, take a little time to ask around, because beaches go in and out of favor quickly. Then catch the bus or a caique to the beach of your choice. If you want a quick swim, the closest beach to Hora is **Megali Ammos (Big Sand),** about a 10-minute walk south of town, and usually very crowded. A better but still-crowded beach is 4km (2½ miles) farther north of Megali Ammos at **Ayios Stephanos,** a major resort center with watersports.

Plati Yialos is another favorite. It's served by a bus that runs every 15 minutes from 8am to 8pm, then every 30 minutes until midnight during the summer. If Plati Yialos is too crowded, you can catch a caique there for the more distant beaches of Paradise, Super Paradise, Agrari, and Elia. **Paradise,** the island's most famous nude beach, remains beautiful, despite the crowds and activity, with especially clear water. Paradise is also easily reached by local bus or taxi.

Plindri (Super Paradise) is accessible only by a very poor road, footpath, or caique, so it's less crowded. It's predominantly gay and nude, but clothed sun-bathing by heterosexuals is tolerated. Farther east across the little peninsula is **Agrari,** a lovely cove (about to undergo serious overdevelopment) with good shade and a good little taverna.

Elia, a 45-minute caique ride from Plati Yialos, is one of the island's best and largest beaches, attracting many nudists, gays—and, thanks to a **Watermania,** a theme park with a water slide—families with children (open daily in season 9am–midnight; 12€/$14 adults, 6€/$7 children under 12).

The next major beach, **Kalo Livadi (Good Pasture),** a beautiful spot in an idyllic farming valley, is accessible by a scramble over the peninsula east from Elia and by bus from the north station in the summer. There's even a nice restaurant.

The last resort area on the southern coast accessible by bus from the north sta-tion is at **Kalafati,** a fishing village that was once the port for the ancient citadel of Mykonos. It's now dominated by the large Aphrodite Beach Hotel complex. Several miles farther east, accessible by a fairly good road from Kalafati, is **Lia,** which has fine sand, clear water, bamboo windbreaks, and a small taverna.

Beaches to avoid on Mykonos because of pollution, noise, and crowds include **Tourlos** and **Korfos Bay.**

MYKONOS AFTER DARK

Mykonos has the liveliest, most abundant (and expensive), and most chameleon-like nightlife—especially gay nightlife—in the Aegean. New places open and shut here every season. Here I try to suggest a few durable favorites and some new places. I've given phone numbers where available; if you dial one of these places and get no reply, don't assume it's closed—when business is brisk, phones are often not answered.

Watching the sunset is a popular sport at the sophisticated bars in Little Venice. The **Kastro** (© 22890/23-072), near the Paraportiani Church, is famous for classical music and frozen daiquiris. This is a great spot to watch (or join in with) handsome young men flirting with each other. If you find it too crowded or tame, sashay up the block on Scarpa to **Le Caprice,** which also has a seaside perch; or **Porta** (© 22890/27-807), a popular gay cruising spot. The **Mont-parnasse** (© 22890/23-719), on the same lane, is cozier, with classical music and Toulouse-Lautrec posters. The **Veranda** (© 22890/23-290), in an old man-sion overlooking the water with a good view of the windmills, is as relaxing as its name implies. **Galeraki** (© 22890/27-118) has a wide variety of exotic cock-tails (and customers) and an in-house art gallery that gives this popular spot its name ("little gallery").

The decibel level is considerably higher along the harbor, where **Pierro's** (© 22890/22-177), popular with gay visitors, rocks all night long to American and European music; the adjacent **Icarus** is best known for its drag shows. The **Anchor** plays blues, jazz, and classic rock for its 30-something clients, as does **Argo. Stavros Irish Bar** and the **Scandinavian Bar-Disco** draw customers from Ireland, Scandinavia, and, quite possibly, as far away as Antarctica. If you'd like to sample some Greek music and dancing, try **Thalami** (© 22890/23-291), a small club underneath the town hall. If you'd like to relax at a movie, head for **Cinemanto** (© 22890/27-190), which shows films nightly around 9pm. Many films are American; most Greek films have English subtitles.

How much are you going to spend going out on the town for a drink at a chic spot on Mykonos? As little as 10€ ($12)—and after that, the sky really is the limit here!

AN EXCURSION TO THE ISLAND OF DELOS ★★★

According to legend, Delos is the spot where Leto gave birth to the twins Artemis and Apollo. Why did Leto pick this tiny—less than 5 sq. km (3 sq. miles)—barren island as her nursery? Because she hoped to escape her lover Zeus's jealous spouse Hera by hiding on the smallest and least conspicuous of the Cycladic islands. Although remote and tiny, Delos had an excellent harbor (long since silted up) that made it a vital way station for ancient ships plying the Aegean. The island was also a significant religious shrine in the cult of Apollo, with an oracle second in importance only to Delphi. When the Greeks banded together after defeating the Persians in 478 B.C., they called their association, with its headquarters at Delos, the Delian League. The Delian Festival held here every year was one of the most important ancient festivals, drawing visitors from across the Greek world. Less endearingly, in Roman times Delos was the most important slave market in the Aegean; there are reports of as many as 10,000 slaves being sold here in a single day. Today, the extensive ruins on Delos make the island rival Delphi and Olympia as one of the most impressive ancient sites in all Greece—although you'll long for the shady pine trees of Delphi and Olympia when you visit virtually shadeless Delos.

Although your entrance ticket usually comes with an excellent map of the archaeological site, you will probably want to buy one of the many helpful site guides on sale both on Mykonos and Delos.

GETTING THERE   Delos can be visited only by sea, and many days the sea is too rough for boats to put in here. The site is usually open from 8:30am to 3pm and is always closed on Monday. Spending the night is not allowed. Most people visit on excursion boats from nearby Mykonos, although there are excursions from other neighboring islands (including Tinos; see below). Delos is also is a customary stop for cruise ships and yachts. From Mykonos, organized guided and unguided excursions leave about four times a day from Tuesday to Sunday from the west end of the harbor; the trip takes about 40 minutes and costs about 12€ ($14) round-trip for transportation alone (departure from Mykonos around 8:30am; return to Mykonos around 3pm). **Yiannakis Tours** (© 22890/22-089) offers guided tours for about 30€ ($35) that depart at 9 or 10am and return at 12:30 or 2pm.

Note: High seas can prevent boats going to Delos at any time of the year, so if you want to visit, don't put it off, as the weather can change unexpectedly. When you go, try to leave as early as possible in the morning, especially in the summer, when both the afternoon heat and the crowds are intense. Be sure to wear sunscreen, sturdy shoes, a hat, and bring water and a snack. (There's a cafe near the museum, but the prices are high and the quality is poor.)

SANTORINI (THIRA) ★★★

Especially if you arrive by sea, you won't confuse Santorini with any of the other Cyclades—although you might be confused to learn that it's also known as Thira. Small ships arrive at Santorini (pop. 7,000; 240km/130 nautical miles southeast of Piraeus) in Skala, a spectacular harbor that's part of the enormous caldera (crater) formed when a volcano blew out the island's center around 1450 B.C. To this day, some scholars speculate that the destruction gave birth to the myth of the lost continent of Atlantis.

Your first choice upon disembarking at Skala will be to decide whether you want to ride the funicular (5€/$5.75) or a donkey (5€/$5.75) the 335m (1,100 ft.) up the sheer sides of the caldera to the island's capital, Fira. If you arrive on a large ship, you'll be spared this choice, as you'll dock at the new harbor at Athinios and grab a cab costing about 9€ ($10) into Fira. Once there, you may decide to reward yourself with a glass of the island's rosé wine before you explore the shops and restaurants of Fira, swim at the black volcanic beach of Kamari, or visit the dazzling site of Akrotiri, an Aegean Pompeii destroyed when the volcano erupted. In case you were wondering, the volcano is now officially dormant, so you don't have to fret about the plumes of steam you might see around the islands of Kamenes in the harbor.

ESSENTIALS

GETTING THERE   By Air   Olympic Airways has several (six in the high season) daily flights between Athens and the airport at Monolithos (© **22860/ 31-525**), which also receives European charters. There are also daily connections with Mykonos; three or four a week with Rhodes; two or three a week with Iraklion, Crete; and three a week during the high season with Thessaloniki. For schedule information and reservations, check with the Olympic Airways office on Ayiou Athanassiou Street (© **22860/22-493,** 210/961-6161, or 210/966-6666 in Athens). **Aegean Airlines** (© **210/998-2888** in Athens), with an office at the Monolithos airport (© **22860/28-500**), also has several flights daily between Athens and Santorini.

By Sea   Several companies operate **ferry service** at least twice daily from Piraeus; the trip takes 10 to 12 hours and costs from 25€ ($29) one-way (deck). If you can book a day sailing, you'll see many of the Cyclades en route to Santorini. In summer, there are often daily ferry connections from Santorini to Ios, Mykonos, and Paros. **Excursion boats** go to and from Iraklion, Crete, almost daily. The fare is from 20€ ($23) one-way. Because this is an open-sea route, the trip can be an ordeal in bad weather. Check the schedules with the **Tourist Police** in Athens (© **171**) or with the **Port Authority** in Piraeus (© **210/ 451-1311**) or Santorini (© **22860/22-239**).

High-speed **hydrofoils** connect Santorini with Ios, Paros, Mykonos, and Iraklio, Crete, almost daily in the high season and three times weekly in the low season, if the winds aren't too strong.

VISITOR INFORMATION   There's no official government tourist office, but there are a number of travel agencies. Several travelers have written of good experiences dealing with **Kamari Tours,** 2 blocks south of the main square on the right (© **22860/31-390;** fax 22860/31-497; kamaritours@san.forthnet.gr). **Maria Tours** (© **22860/24-701;** fax 22860/23-848) often seems to offer car rentals and island tours at especially good prices. Other agencies include **Joint Travel Service** (© **22860/24-900;** fax 22860/24992; joint@otenet.gr), next to the Olympic Airways office in Fira; and **Nomikos Travel** (© **22860/23-660**), with offices in Fira, Karterados, and Perissa. Any of these agencies should be able to help you find accommodations, rent a car, get boat tickets, or book a tour. Expect to pay about 28€ ($32) to join a bus tour to Akrotiri or Ancient Thira.

GETTING AROUND   By Bus   Santorini has very good bus service. The island's central bus station is just south of the main square in Fira. Schedules and prices are posted on the wall of the office above it; most routes are serviced every half-hour from 7am to 11pm in the summer, less frequently in the off season.

By Car   Most travel agents can help you rent a car. You might find that a local company such as **Zeus** (© **22860/24-013**) offers better prices than the big names, although the quality might be a bit lower. Of the better-known agencies, try **Budget Rent-A-Car,** a block below the bus stop square in Fira (© **22860/ 22-900;** fax 22860/22-887), where a small car should cost from 50€ ($58) a day, with unlimited mileage. If you reserve in advance through Budget in the United States (© **800/527-0700**), you should be able to beat that price.

By Moped   The roads on the island are notoriously treacherous, narrow, and winding; add local drivers who take the roads at high speed and visiting drivers who aren't sure where they're going, and you'll understand the island's high accident rate. If you're determined to use two-wheeled transportation, expect to pay 25€ ($29) a day (less off season)—and be sure to ask for a helmet.

By Taxi   The taxi station is just south of the main square. In high season, you should book ahead by phone (© **22860/22-555** or 22860/23-951) if you want a taxi for an excursion; prices are standard from point to point. If possible, ask your hotel to make the booking for you. If you call for a taxi outside Fira, you'll be charged a pickup fee of at least 1.50€ ($1.85). The fare from Ia to Akrotiri, for example, is about 17€ ($20), not including additional charges for luggage, pickup, or late-night travel. If you call for a taxi outside Fira, you're required to pay the fare from there to your pickup point, although you can sometimes find a taxi that has dropped off a passenger. All bus service usually shuts down at midnight, so it's a good idea to book a taxi in advance if you need it after midnight. If you find yourself walking home, keep in mind that lots of drivers on the roads are newcomers to the island and may not know every twist and turn.

FAST FACTS: Santorini

Area Code   The telephone area code for Santorini is **22860**.

Banks   The **National Bank** (open weekdays 8am–2pm; ATM) is a block south from the main square on the right near the taxi station. Many travel agents also change money; most are open daily from 8am to 9:30pm.

Hospital   The **health clinic** (© **22860/22-237**) is near the main Olympic Airways office.

Internet Access   The **PC World Club** (© **22860/25-551**) is in the main square, Fira. It's usually open Monday through Saturday from 9am to 2pm and 5 to 8pm; 4€ ($5) per hour for use.

Police   The police station is on Dekigala Street (© **22860/22-649**), several blocks south of the main square, on the left. The Port Authority can be reached at © **22860/22-239**.

Post Office   The post office (© **22860/22-238;** fax 22860/22-698) is off to the right of the bus station. It's open weekdays from 8am to 1pm.

Telephone   The **OTE telephone office** is just off Ypapantis Street, up from the post office. It's usually open Monday through Friday from 8am to 4pm.

WHERE TO STAY

Despite its growing number of hotels, efficiency apartments, and rooms-to-rent, Santorini is packed in July and August—and increasingly crowded year-round.

If you plan a summer visit, make a reservation with a deposit at least 2 months in advance or be prepared to accept potluck. Don't accept rooms offered (sight unseen) at the port unless you're exhausted and don't care where you wake up—possibly in a small room in a village in Santorini's interior plain, quite a distance from what you've come here to see. If you come between April and mid-June or in September or October, when the island is less crowded and far more pleasant, the rates can be considerably less than the high-season rates we quote. Keep in mind that during the off season many of the hotels, restaurants, shops, and bars here are closed. Most of the hotels recommended below don't have air-conditioning, but with cool breezes blowing through, you won't need it; if you take a room here in the winter, make sure that it offers working central heat or a serviceable room heater.

Two youth hostels, near Thira's main square, the **Thira Youth Hostel** (© 22860/22-387) and the **International Youth Hostel** (© 222860/24-472), usually offer the island's cheapest accommodations, at around 15€ ($17.25) per person. You don't have to be young to stay at these hostels, but it helps to be young-at-heart and very relaxed about shared facilities and noise. About 2km (1¼ miles) outside Fira, the village of Karterados is in the throes of development. It has one budget choice that's worth a stay: the 20-unit **Pension George** ★ (www.pensiongeorge.com), with a small pool; simple, attractive, and reasonably priced accommodations; and very helpful owners, George and Helen Halaris. Doubles run from about 40€ to 80€ ($46–$92).

Astra Apartments ★★★   Perched on a cliff side, with spectacular views, this is one of the nicest places to stay in all of Greece—in fact, friends who stayed here recently say that this was the highlight of their entire holiday! The Astra Apartments look like a tiny, whitewashed village (with an elegant pool) set in the village of Imerovigli, which is still much less crowded than Fira or Oia. Every detail here is perfect. Best of all, although each unit has its own kitchenette, breakfast is served on your private terrace or balcony, and you can order delicious salads and sandwiches from the bar day and night. The superb manager, George Karayiannis, is always at the ready to arrange car rentals, recommend a wonderful beach or restaurant—or even help you plan your wedding and honeymoon here. My only problem when I stayed here: I didn't want to budge from my terrace, especially at sunset, when the view over the offshore islands is dazzling. You may want to go whole hog, as it were, and book one of the new apartments or suites, two with private Jacuzzis, two with private pools.

Imerovigli, 847 00 Santorini. © **22860/23-641.** Fax 22860/24-765. www.astra.gr. 25 units. 220€–310€ ($253–$356) standard double apt; 370€–590€ ($426–$679) suite. AE, MC, V. **Amenities:** Bar; pool. *In room:* A/C, TV, minibar, hair dryer, radio.

Katikies ★★   If you find a more spectacular pool anywhere on the island, let us know: This one runs virtually to the side of the caldera, so that you can paddle around and enjoy an endless view. (There's also a smaller pool intended for the use of guests who have suites.) The hotel's island-style architecture incorporates twists and turns, secluded patios, beamed ceilings, and antiques. If the people in the next room like to sing in the shower, you might hear them—but most people who stay here treasure the tranquillity. The top-of-the-line honeymoon suite has its own Jacuzzi, just in case you can't be bothered going to either outdoor pool. The **White Cave** restaurant has only three tables, so be sure to book ahead! We welcome comments on the service here, about which we have had mixed notices.

Oia, 847 02 Santorini. © **22860/71-401.** Fax 22860/71-129. www.katikies.com. 22 units. 175€–260€ ($201–$299) double; 210€–350€ ($241–$402) superior; 235€–1,050€ ($270–$1,207) suite. Rates include breakfast. MC, V. **Amenities:** 2 restaurants; bar; 2 pools. *In room:* A/C, TV, minibar, hair dryer.

Loucas Hotel ⭐ This is one of the oldest and best hotels on the caldera, with barrel-ceilinged "caves" built to prevent collapse during an earthquake. Rooms are recently renovated; some were enlarged and have arched ceilings and shared patios overlooking the pool and the caldera. The hotel is an excellent value for the location, amenities, and view, although it's sufficiently in the heart of things in Fira that it can be noisy here at night.

Fira, 847 00 Santorini. ℂ **22860/22-480** or 22860/22-680. Fax 22860/24-882. loucas@ath.forthnet.gr. 22 units. 150€–175€ ($173–$201) double. Rates include breakfast. MC, V. **Amenities:** Restaurant, bar; pool. *In room:* A/C, TV, minibar.

WHERE TO DINE

Camille Stephani GREEK/INTERNATIONAL Even if you're not staying at Kamari, this restaurant on the north end of the beach, 460m (1,500 ft.) from the bus stop, will make the trip worthwhile. The house specialty is a tender beef filet with green pepper in Madeira sauce. You can take a moonlight stroll along the beach after dinner.

Kamari Beach. ℂ **22860/31-716.** Reservations recommended July–Sept. Main courses 15€–30€ ($17–$35). AE, DC, MC, V. Daily 1–4pm and 6:30pm–midnight (but often open all day; often closed off season).

Katina Fish–Taverna ⭐ *(Moments* SEAFOOD One of the best places to eat in Oia isn't in town but down in the port of Ammoudi, which is best reached by donkey (ask in the village about hiring a donkey), or you can walk or take a taxi. Katina Pagoni is considered one of the very best local cooks, and the setting beside the glittering Aegean is romantic.

Port of Oia (Ammoudi). ℂ **22860/71-280.** Fish priced daily by the kilo. No credit cards. Daily 11am–1am.

Koukoumavolos ⭐⭐ NOUVELLE GREEK This elegant restaurant was for many years in Oia, but it now overlooks the caldera in Fira. There's delicious fresh fish (wonderful monkfish!) and an adventurous menu of "nouvelle Greek" cuisine (dishes are lighter and less oil-saturated than is customary in Greece), and a wide selection of island and off-island wines and cheeses. The view over the caldera is fantastic—and so is the panna cotta with yogurt and cherry sauce.

Fira (below the Atlantis Hotel). ℂ **22860/23-807.** Reservations recommended for dinner. Fish priced daily by the kilo. Main courses 18€–23€ ($21–$26). AE, MC, V. Daily noon–3pm and 8pm–midnight.

Selene ⭐⭐⭐ TRADITIONAL GREEK The best restaurant on Santorini— and one of the best in all Greece—Selene uses local produce to highlight what owners Evelyn and George Hatziyiannakis call the "creative nature of Greek cuisine." The appetizers, including a delicious eggplant salad with octopus and tomato, mushrooms with crabmeat and cheese, and fluffy fava balls with caper sauce, are deservedly famous. Entrees include sea bass grilled with pink peppers or saddle of lamb with yogurt and mint sauce. If you eat only one meal on Santorini, eat it here, in a truly distinguished restaurant with distinctive local architecture—and be sure to try the enormous local capers.

Fira (in the passageway between the Atlantis and Aressana hotels). ℂ **22860/22-249.** Fax 22860/24-395. Reservations recommended. Main courses 18€–28€ ($21–$32). AE, MC, V. Mid-Apr to early Oct daily 7pm–midnight. Closed late Oct to early Apr.

EXPLORING THE ISLAND

FIRA If you're staying overnight on Santorini, take advantage of the fact that almost all the day-trippers from cruise ships leave in the late afternoon, and explore the capital in the evening. As you stroll, you may be surprised to discover that Fira has a Roman Catholic cathedral and convent in addition to the predictable Greek Orthodox cathedral, a legacy from the days when the Venetians controlled much of the Aegean. The name Santorini, in fact, is a Latinate corruption of the Greek for "Saint Irene." The **Megaron Gyzi Museum** (© **22860/22-244**), by the cathedral, has church and local memorabilia, including some before-and-after photographs of the island at the time of the devastating earthquake of 1956. It's open Monday through Saturday from 10:30am to 1pm and 5 to 8pm, and Sunday from 10:30am to 4:30pm; admission is 3€ ($3.45). The small **Archaeological Museum** (© **22860/22-217**) has both Minoan and classical finds. It's open Tuesday through Sunday from 8:30am to 3pm; admission is 3€ ($3.45). You might find it almost deserted, as most visitors head directly for Thira's shops. Before you do the same, stop at the **Thera Foundation** (© **22860/230-16**), near the cable car station en route to Firostephani, to have a look at the spectacular reproductions and re-creations of the frescoes from Akrotiri. It's usually open Tuesday through Sunday from 8:30am to 3pm; admission is 3€ ($3.45). The **Museum of Prehistoric Thira** near the bus station has a small, but excellent, collection of finds (mainly from Ancient Akrotiri). It's open Tuesday through Sunday from 8:30am to 3pm; admission is free.

VILLAGES   Two island villages well worth visiting are **Pirgos (Tower),** the oldest and highest settlement on the island, and **Oia** (also spelled **Ia**), on a cliff above the caldera. Badly damaged in a massive earthquake in 1956, Oia was virtually a ghost town until it was rebuilt in the 1960s and 1970s and resettled. Now its chic shops (check out the **Art Gallery** and **Art Gallery Oia** on Oia's meandering main drag) and gorgeous sunsets make it an increasingly popular place to stay or to visit—especially with those who find Fira too frenetic. The **Naval Museum** (© **22860/71-156;** open Wed–Mon 12:30–4pm and 5–8:30pm; 2€/$2.30), in a restored neoclassical museum, showcases the island's long intimate relationship with seafaring. If you travel to either village (local buses run here from Fira, or you can take a taxi), keep a lookout for some of the island's cave dwellings (homes hollowed out of Santorini's soft volcanic stone).

BEACHES   Santorini does not have the soft sand beaches of Mykonos, but the black volcanic sand and pebble beach make **Kamari** a very nice place to swim, especially in the morning, before the all-day sunbathers arrive (and before the black sand gets seriously hot). Kamari also has the **Volcano Diving Center** (© **22860/33-177;** www.scubagreece.com), which offers guided snorkel swims for around 20€ ($23) and scuba lessons from around 65€ ($75). On the way to or from Kamari from or to Fira by local bus or taxi, you can stop at the Antoniou, Roussos, or Boutari vintners to see how wine is made, have a free sample, and perhaps buy a bottle or two to sample later. *Be warned:* Vino Santo, Santorini's sweet wine, is *very* sweet. **Boutari,** Megalohori (© **22860/81-011**), is the island's largest vintner. For about 6€ ($6.90) you can see the wine press, sample the wines, and snack on mezedes. The **Antoniou winery** (run by the

---

Tips **Submerged Santorini**

There's a new way to explore Santorini: a 1-hour submarine ride under the surface of the caldera. Sink to 30m (100 ft.) below the surface and get a glimpse of the submerged volcanic crater. The trip costs 50€ ($58); information is available at © **22860/28-900** or at most local travel agencies.

same family who has the Antoniou jewelry in Fira) is especially charming, with the old wine press and barrels on display.

ANCIENT THIRA & AKROTIRI   Above Kamari beach on a rocky promontory are the ruins of **Ancient Thira** (✆ **02860/22-217** or 02860/22-366), settled in the 9th century B.C., although most of the scattered remains date from the Hellenistic era. At press time, it was open Tuesday through Friday from 8am to 2:30pm, Sunday and holidays from 8am to 2:30pm; it was also sometimes open on Saturday from 8am to 2:30pm. Admission is 6€ ($6.90). A good but alarmingly narrow road now runs almost to the summit, which can also be reached on foot or by donkey (for hire from some travel agents) by a path. The hilltop site is very fine, but if you have to choose between Ancient Thira and Akrotiri, head for Akrotiri.

The excavations at **Akrotiri,** the Minoan settlement destroyed when the volcano erupted around 1450 B.C., have unearthed buildings three stories tall that were lavishly decorated with frescoes. It's breathtaking to visit the Akrotiri site and walk down the streets and peek in the windows of houses in a town whose life was extinguished in a torrent of lava and ash so long ago. Most of the frescoes discovered were taken to the National Archaeological Museum in Athens. At press time, it was uncertain whether they would be on display when the museum reopens in 2004 or returned to Thira. At present, you can see several frescoes from Akrotiri in the Museum of Prehistoric Thera in Fira. The **site** (✆ **22860/81-366**) is open Tuesday through Sunday from 8:30am to 3pm; admission is 6€ ($6.90). Akrotiri can be reached by public bus, taxi, or one of the bus tours available from island travel agents.

SANTORINI AFTER DARK

Most people will want to start the evening with a drink on the caldera watching the sunset. **Franco's** (✆ **22860/22-881**) is the most famous place for this magic hour, but drinks are expensive; the nearby **Tropical** (no phone) has almost as good a view and charges less. **Archipelago** (✆ **22860/23-673**) and the **Canava Cafe** (✆ **22860/22-565**) also have good views. For more reasonable prices and the same fantastic view, continue past the Loucas Hotel to the **Renaissance Bar** (✆ **22860/22-880**).

Most of the action is north and west of the main square. Underneath the square, the **Kirathira Bar** plays jazz at a level that permits conversation. The **Town Club** appeals to clean-cut rockers, while the **Two Brothers** pulls in the biggest, chummiest crowd on the island. For Greek music, find the **Apocalypse Club,** or **Bar 33** for bouzouki. Discos come and go; follow your ears to find them. The **Koo Club** is the biggest (with some five individual bars), and **Enigma** is popular with those interested in good dance music. In Oia, **Melissa's Piano Bar** and **Zorba's** are good spots for a drink at sunset.

(*Tips* Santorini Swings

The height of the tourist season is also the height of the music season in Santorini: If you are here in July, you may want to take in the annual **Santorini Jazz Festival** (www.jazzfestival.gr), which has been bringing several dozen international jazz bands and artists here every summer since 1997. Many performances are on Kamari beach.

None of the places recommended above have specific street addresses; it's best just to ask someone for directions. ***Remember:*** At virtually all of these places, you'll probably pay at least 10€ ($12) for one drink.

TINOS

Unlike Santorini and Mykonos—where foreigners often outnumber locals—**Tinos** is one Cycladic island where you are likely to hear more Greek spoken than German or French. Tinos (pop. 3,500; 161km/87 nautical miles southeast of Piraeus) is the most important destination in Greece for religious pilgrims, yet it remains one of the least commercialized islands of the Cyclades. That makes Tinos a real joy to visit—as do its lovely villages, uncrowded beaches, green hills crossed by stone walls and dotted with the elaborate *peristerionades* (**dovecotes**) for which the island is famous, and excellent restaurants that serve the thousands of year-round Greek pilgrims who come here to visit the **Panayia Evanyelistria** ("Our Lady of Good Tidings"), sometimes called the "Lourdes of Greece."

From well out to sea, the Panayia Evanyelistria—illuminated at night—is visible atop a hill overlooking Tinos town, which the inhabitants call "Hora." Like a number of the Cyclades, Tinos had a Venetian occupation, and a number of fine, old Venetian mansions (locally known as *pallada,* the name also used for the harborfront) still stand on the side streets off the harbor. **Megalocharis** is the long, steep street that leads from the harbor to the red-carpeted steps that are the final approach to the cathedral; some devout pilgrims make the entire journey on their knees. Adjacent pedestrianized **Evangelistria** is a market street, as well as a pilgrimage route, with many shops selling candles and icons. It's important to remember that Tinos *is* a pilgrimage place: It is considered disrespectful to wear shorts, short skirts, halters, or sleeveless shirts in the precincts of the Evanyelistria (or any other church, for that matter). And taking snapshots of the pilgrims, especially those approaching the shrine on hands and knees, is not appreciated.

The inland villages of Tinos are some of the most beautiful in the Cyclades. Many of the most picturesque are nestled into the slopes of **Exobourgo,** the rocky pinnacle visible from the port, connected by a network of walking paths that make this island a hiker's paradise. In these villages and dotting the countryside, you'll see the elaborately carved marble lintels, door jambs, and fan windows on village houses, and ornately decorated medieval dovecotes . The island's beaches may not be the best in the Cyclades, but they are plentiful and uncrowded throughout the summer. All this may change if an airport is built here—all the more reason to visit Tinos now.

ESSENTIALS

GETTING THERE   There are several ferries to Tinos daily from Piraeus (5 hr.) and usually catamaran (1½ hr.) and ferry service (4 hr.) daily in summer from Rafina. Schedules should be checked with the Athens **GNTO** (✆ **210/331-0562),** the **Port Authority in Piraeus** (✆ **210/459-3223** or 210/422-6000; phone seldom answered), or the **Rafina Port Authority** (✆ **22940/22-300**). Several times a day, boats connect Tinos with nearby Mykonos (15–40 min.). Boats to Siros (20–50 min.) and hydrofoils to Santorini (4–6 hr.), Paros (1½ hr.), and Naxos (2 hr.) are regular in summer and somewhat less frequent during the winter months (though there is a daily boat to Siros, and Tinos has more winter connections than most Cycladic isles because of its religious tourism, which

---

⌒ *Tips* **When *Not* to Visit Tinos**

Don't even think about arriving on Tinos without a reservation around **August 15,** when thousands of pilgrims travel here to celebrate the Feast of the Assumption of the Virgin. **March 25** (Feast of the Annunciation) is the second-most important feast day here, but it draws fewer pilgrims because traveling by sea in March is less easy. Pilgrims also come here on July 23 (the anniversary of St. Pelagia's vision of the icon) and January 30 (the anniversary of the finding of the icon). In addition, it's not a good idea to show up here without a reservation on a weekend, when Greek families bring their babies for baptism..

---

continues year-round). In summer, a day excursion to Delos and Mykonos usually departs from the old pier in Tinos harbor at 10am Tuesday through Sunday, returning to Tinos at 7pm; the fare is 25€ ($29) for adults and 9€ ($10) for children under 11.

Warning: Tinos harbor has three docking points. Be sure to find out from which pier your ship will depart; most ferries, the small catamarans (Seajet, Flying Cat, and Jet One), as well as the excursion boat to Delos/Mykonos, still dock at the old pier in the town center; some use the new pier to the north, on the side of town in the direction of Kionia. The **Tinos Port Authority** (not guaranteed to be helpful) can be reached at ⓒ **22830/22-348.**

VISITOR INFORMATION   For information on accommodations, car rentals, island tours, and Tinos in general, head to **Windmills Travel** 🌟🌟🌟 (ⓒ **22830/23-398;** fax 22830/23-327; www.windmills-travel.com), on the harbor by the new port, next to St Anthony's Catholic church. The office has a large painting of a windmill's round, spoked pinwheel on its exterior. Sharon Turner is the friendly, amazingly helpful and efficient manager, with unparalleled knowledge of Tinos and its neighboring islands. What's more, Turner can get you substantial discounts on island accommodations, transportation, and tours.

FAST FACTS: Tinos

Banks Several **banks** are located the harbor and are open Monday through Thursday from 8am to 2pm and Friday from 8am to 1:30pm; all have ATMs.

First Aid The **first-aid center** can be reached at ⓒ **22830/22-210.**

Police The police (ⓒ **22830/22-348**) are just beyond the new pier, past the Lito Hotel and Windmills Travel.

Post office The post office (ⓒ **22830/22-247**), open Monday through Friday from 7:30am to 2pm, is at the south end of the harbor next to the Tinion Hotel.

Telephone office (OTE) The OTE (ⓒ **22830/22-399**), on the main street leading to the church of Panayia Evanyelistria, about halfway up on the right, is open Monday through Friday from 7:30am to 12:30pm.

GETTING AROUND **By Bus** The **bus station** (© 22830/22-440) is on the harbor, opposite the National Bank of Greece. Schedules are usually posted or available here. There are frequent daily buses to most island villages.

By Car & Moped Rental agencies in Tinos town include two just off the harbor on Trion Ierarchon, the street where taxis hang out. **Vidalis** (© 22830/23-995) and **Dimitris Rental** (© 22830/23-585) are next door; both have car rentals from 25€ ($29) and mopeds from 12€ ($14).

By Taxi Taxis hang out on Trion Ierarchon, which runs uphill from the harbor just before the Palamaris supermarket and the Hotel Tinion.

WHERE TO STAY

Sharon Turner of **Windmills Travel** (see "Visitor Information," under "Essentials," above) can get substantial discounts on island accommodations, transportation, and tours. In addition to hotel accommodations, Windmills has houses for rent in several villages—a great way to see more of the island and get a taste for village life. The weekly cost is from 1,000€ ($1,150) for a one-bedroom house, including car rental.

Oceanis Hotel ✦ This 10-year old harborfront hotel is a bit out of the center; hence, it's somewhat quieter than the other hotels on the harbor. Because the hotel is often taken over by Greek groups visiting the island's religious shrines, the independent traveler may feel a bit odd man out—or simply make new friends! The rooms are simply furnished (with small balconies); the bathrooms are decent sized. The Oceanis stays open all year and usually has reliable heat in the winter.

Akti G. Drossou, Hora, 84200 Tinos. © 22830/22-452. Fax 22830/25-402. 47 units. 70€–80€ ($81–$92) double. No credit cards. From the old harbor, walk south (right) along the paralia until you come to the Oceanis, whose large sign is clearly visible from the harbor. **Amenities:** Restaurant; bar. *In room:* A/C, TV.

Porto Tango ✦ At present, this is the island's one serious resort hotel, with all the frills (sauna, health club) that one expects at a resort hotel—a but without that all-important beachfront location. The hotel overlooks a good beach, has its own pool, but is a 10-minute walk from the sea. Many rooms have balconies or terraces; some have both. Rooms in the "green" section have the best views. Unfortunately, when we visited in 2003, extensive renovations were underway, and this presumably tranquil and comfortable place had all the charm of a construction site. A friend who visited when the renovation was finished had high praise for everything except the restaurant, which was perfectly okay, but not memorable—and very expensive.

Porto, 84200 Tinos. ((© 22830/24-411. Fax 22830/24-416. www.portotango.gr. 61 units. 120€–150€ ($138–$173) double; 250€ ($287) suite. Breakfast buffet included. AE, MC, V. **Amenities:** 2 restaurants; bar; pool; health club and spa. *In-room:* A/C, TV, minibar, hair dryer.

Tinos Beach Hotel ✦ *Kids* Despite a somewhat impersonal character and substantially faded 1960s elegance, this is the best choice in a beachfront hotel near Hora. The rooms all have balconies, most with views of sea and pool (the view affects the room price). Especially pleasant are the suites: Large sitting rooms open onto poolside balconies. Rooms located in a cluster of bungalows built to resemble a Cycladic village are similar in size and furnishings; all have shaded terraces, and most offer a view toward the sea. The pool is the longest on the island, and there's a separate children's pool as well. Umbrellas are set out on the stretch of sand and cobble beach fronting the hotel; paddle boats and canoes are available for rent.

Kionia (4km/2½ miles west of Tinos town on the coast road), 84200 Tinos. ⓒ **22830/22-626** or 22830/22-627. Fax 22830/23-153. 180 units. 120€–150€ ($138–$173) double. Rates include breakfast. Children 7 and under stay free in parent's room. AE, DC, MC, V. Closed Nov–Mar. **Amenities:** Restaurant, snack bar, piano bar, tavern; 2 pools, tennis court, card room, table tennis. *In room:* A/C, TV, fridge, balcony.

WHERE TO DINE

As in many other Greek coastal towns, it's a good idea to avoid most harborfront joints, where the food is generally inferior and service can be rushed. That said, we've had perfectly tasty souvlaki in congenial surroundings while other diners played leisurely games of *tavoli* (backgammon) at **Karkavelas** (ⓒ **22830/23-122**).

To Koutouki tis Eleni ★★ GREEK   Known in town simply as Koutouki, this excellent small taverna doesn't usually have a menu. What it does have are good, basic ingredients cooked up into simple meals that remind you how delightful Greek food can be. Local cheese and wine, fresh fish and meats, delicious vegetables—these are the staples that come together so well in this taverna, which demonstrates that you don't have to pay a fortune to experience good *paradisiako* (traditional) home cooking.

Paralia, Hora. ⓒ **22830/24-857.** Main courses 5€–15€ ($5.75–$17). No credit cards. Daily noon–midnight. From the harbor turn onto Evanyelistria, the market street; take the 1st right up a narrow lane with 3 tavernas; Koutouki is the 1st on the left.

Metaxi Mas ★★★ GREEK   A long-time American resident of Tinos took us here, and we can't wait to go back. This family-run restaurant calls itself a *mezedopoleio* (hors d'oeuvres place). A cozy interior dining room has a fireplace for when it's chilly, and tables are set outside in the pedestrianized lane when the weather's warm. More important, the mezedes are irresistible: vegetable croquettes, fried sun-dried tomatoes, piquant fried cheeses, succulent octopus, and lots, lots more. If you still want an entrée, the cabbage dolmades are memorable, and old standbys like veal or goat *stifado* (stew) are very tasty. And did we mention the desserts? Try the heavenly *galatovouriko* (a cholesterol bomb of milk and butter nestled between the filo leaves used in baklava). No wonder the same Greek families we'd seen earlier in the day at the Evangelistria Church showed up here to dine—Greeks take their food seriously when they travel.

Kontoyioryi, Paralia, Hora. ⓒ **22830/24-857.** Main courses 6€–15€ ($6.90–$17). No credit cards. Daily noon–midnight. Off the harbor, in a lane between the old and new harbors. Look for the sign over the door, sometimes also a Metaxi Mas banner strung across the lane.

Palaia Pallada ★★★ GREEK   The same longtime American resident of Tinos who suggested Metaxi Mas also recommended Palaia Pallada—pointing out, quite accurately, that it may be a bit more down-home and less inventive than Metaxi Mas—but equally good. Once again, she got it right: You'll find fewer ruffles and flourishes here, but the food (grills, stews, salads) in this family-run place is excellent, as is the local wine. You can eat indoors or outside in the lane.

Kontoyioryi, Paralia, Hora. ⓒ **22830/23-516.** Main courses 5€–12€ ($5.75–$14). No credit cards. Daily noon–midnight. Off the harbor, in a lane between the old and new harbors. Look for the sign over the door, and the sign that overhangs the lane.

Xynari ★★ GREEK   Good food in lovely surroundings in a distinguished 19th-century house are the trademarks of what for years has been considered the town's most upmarket restaurant. This place has been known for grills that make you realize how poorly many places do meat and eggplant dishes (the latter perky and piquant here). Xynari has new owners, but the initial reports have been good. In warm weather, tables are set up on the balcony, but the interior rooms are charming. There's often live music on weekends, and the location, just off the harbor on Evangelistra, guarantees great people-watching.

13 Evangelistria, Hora. ℭ 22830/23-665. Main courses 6€–25€ ($6.90–$29). AE, MC, V. Daily 7pm–midnight.

EXPLORING THE ISLAND

TINOS TOWN　The **Church of Panagia Evangelistria (Our Lady of Good Tidings)** ★★★ and its museums are usually open from about 7am to 5pm in winter, later in summer. In 1822, a local nun, Pelagia, had a vision that a miraculous icon of the Virgin Mary would be found here; it was, and the church was erected to house the icon, which the faithful believe was painted by Saint Luke. The church is made of gleaming marble from Paros and Tinos, with a tall, slender bell tower and handsome black-and-white pebble mosaics in the exterior courtyard. Inside, hundreds of gold and silver hanging lamps illuminate the icon, which is almost entirely hidden by the votive offerings of gold, silver, diamonds, and other precious jewels, dedicated by the faithful. Even those who do not make a lavish gift customarily make a small offering and light a candle. Beneath the church is the crypt with the chapel of the Zoodochos Pigi, where the icon was found, and several smaller chapels; the crypt is often crowded with Greek parents and children in white, waiting to be baptized with water from the font, or to fill vials with holy water from the spring.

Note: To enter the church, men must wear long pants and shirts with sleeves, and women must wear dresses or skirts and blouses with sleeves. If there is a church service while you are here, you will hear the beautiful, resonant chanting that typifies a Greek Orthodox service—but remember that it's not appropriate to explore the church during a service. There is usually a service in the early morning and periodically throughout the day.

Within the high walls that surround the church are various **museums and galleries,** each of which is worth a quick visit. The gallery of 14th- through 19th-century religious art has icons and church garments and vessels; the gallery of Tinian artists is just that; the picture gallery has the private collection of a local collector of Greek paintings of the 19th and 20th centuries; the sculpture museum has works by former and current island sculptors, many of whom studied with the help of the cathedral charitable foundation. Admission is sometimes charged at these collections, which keep irregular hours.

Exobourgo ★★, a mountain eminence crowned by the remains of a Venetian *kastro* (castle), is some 15 km (9¼ miles) outside of Hora, from which it is visible. The fortress is surrounded by sheer rock walls on three sides; the only path to the summit starts behind a Catholic church at the base of the rock, on the road between Mesi and Koumaros. As you make the 15-minute ascent, you'll pass several lines of fortification—the whole hill is riddled with walls and hollow with chambers. As you might expect, the view over the Cyclades is superb from the summit (565m/1,800 ft.).

SHOPPING IN TINOS TOWN

Shops and stalls lining Evangelistria street sell icons, incense, candles, medallions, and *tamata* (tin, silver, and gold votives). You'll also find local embroidery, weavings, and the delicious local nougat, as well as *loukoumia* (Turkish delight) from Siros. There's also a fish and a farmer's market weekdays in the square by the docks. Keep an eye out for the rather pink-plumed pelican who, reasonably enough, hangs out by the fish market.

There are two fine jewelry shops side by side on Evanyelistria: **Artemis,** 18 Evangelistria (© **2830/23-781**) and **Harris Prassas Ostria-Tinos,** 20 Evangelistria (© **22830/23-893;** fax 22830/24-568). Near the top of Evangelistria, on the left in a neoclassical building, the small **Evangelismos Biotechni Shop** (the outlet of a local weaving school; © **22830/22-894**) sells reasonably priced table and bed linens, as well as rugs.

Authentic hand-painted icons (from around 200€/$130) are sold in the small shop of **Maria Vryoni,** the first left from the port off Leoforos Megaloharis, the second shop on the left. Cross over to 16 Megaloharis to the shop of the **local agricultural cooperative,** where you can buy pungent capers, creamy cheeses, olive oil, and the fiery local *tsiporo* liqueur (© **22830/21-184**). Several shops along the harbor sell international newspapers and local guidebooks and maps.

VILLAGES

Most visitors to Tinos think that **Pirgos** ★★, at the western end of the island, is its most beautiful village. It has an enchanting small plateia with trees, a marble fountain, several cafes, and a taverna, usually open for lunch and dinner in summer, less regularly off season. Renowned for its school of fine arts, Pirgos is a center for marble sculpting, and many of the finest sculptors of Greece have trained here. The **Dellatos Marble Sculpture School** (© **22830/23-164;** www.tinosmarble.com), just outside the village by the police station, offers 1- and 2-week workshops for would-be marble workers. The **Museum of Yiannoulis Chalepas** and the **Museum of Panormian Artists** occupy adjacent houses, and give visitors a chance not only to see sculpture by local artists, but to step into an island house. The museums are located near the bus station, on the main lane leading toward the village; both are open Tuesday through Sunday from 11am to 1:30pm and 5:30 to 6:30pm; admission 2€ ($2.30).

Other especially attractive Tinian villages include **Loutra** ★, which has a number of *stegasti,* streets occupying tunnels beneath the projecting second-floor rooms of village houses. **Volax** is situated in a remote valley known for a bizarre lunar landscape of rotund granite boulders—the villagers have recently constructed a stone amphitheater for theatrical productions, so be sure to ask at Windmills Travel (© and fax **22830/23-398**) for a schedule of performances (most occur in Aug). Volax is also known for its local basket weavers and attractive town spring. **Koumaros** is a beautiful small village on the road between Volax and Mesi, both of which have many *stegasti.*

Tips **Affordable & Portable Tinian Folk Art**

In a small hardware shop across from Pirgos's two museums, **Nikolaos Panorios** ★★★ makes and sells whimsical tin funnels, boxes, spoon holders, and dustpans, as well as dovecotes, windmills, and sailing ships. Each item is made of tin salvaged from containers like those that hold olive oil; each one is different, some with scenes of Pallas Athena, others with friezes of sunflowers, olive gatherers, or fruits and vegetables. All are delightful (from 10€/$12). Eugenia and Nikolaos Panoriou are usually in their shop mornings (© **22830/32-263**) from 9am to 1pm.

BEACHES

Tinos is not best known for its beaches, but you'll find a decent fine-sand beach 3km (1¾ miles) west of Tinos town at **Kionia,** and another 2km (1¼ miles) east of town at busy **Ayios Fokas.** From Tinos, there's bus service on the south beach road (usually four times a day) to the resort of **Porto,** 8km (5 miles) to the east. Porto offers several long stretches of uncrowded sand, a few hotel complexes, and numerous tavernas, several at or near the beach. The beach at **Ayios Ioannis,** facing the town of Porto, is okay, but you'd be better off walking west across the small headland to a longer, less populous beach, extending from this headland to the church or Ayios Sostis at its western extremity; you can also get there by driving or taking the bus to Ayios Sostis. **Kolimbithres** has two beaches on the north side of the island, easily accessed by car, although protection from the *meltemi* winds can be a problem—the second is the best, with fine sand in a small rocky cove and two tavernas. Just beyond Pirgos, the beach at **Panormou** is in the throes of development as a holiday resort. Finally, a series of hairpin paved and unpaved roads leads down—and we mean "way down"—to beaches at **Ayiou Petrou, Kalivia,** and **Giannaki,** west of Tinos town.

WALKING

Tinos has a good network of paths and remote interior regions waiting to be explored. Some of the best walks are in the vicinity of Exobourgo—paths connect the cluster of villages circling this craggy fortress, offering great views and many places to stop for refreshment along the way. There isn't currently an English-language guide to walks in Tinos, but you can ask for information at **Windmills Travel** (© and fax **22830/23-398**) in Tinos town; the office is planning to arrange walking tours in the future and may be able to offer information on organized walks or routes for you to explore on your own.

9

Hungary

by Joseph S. Lieber & Christina Shea

The dramatic political changes of 1989 irreversibly altered life in Hungary. Awakened after its long slumber behind the Iron Curtain, Hungary is now one of Europe's hottest destinations. Poised between East and West, both geographically and culturally, it's at the center of the region's rebirth.

To best understand and appreciate Hungary, go beyond its stately capital, Budapest. Get to know the great river that runs through the country's heart. Take a slow boat (or a fast hydrofoil) up the Danube to the "Bend" towns of Szentendre, Esztergom, or Visegrád.

1 Budapest

Budapest came of age in the 19th century, at the start of which the two towns of Buda and Pest were little more than provincial outposts on the Danube. In 1867, Hungary finally came to terms with Austrian domination, agreeing to the formation of the Austro-Hungarian empire. The dawning of a modern Hungarian identity spawned the city's neoclassical development. The great post-1867 boom coincided with the rise of an eclectic style of architecture, and most of the historic inner city was created at this time. Indeed, Budapest, notwithstanding its long and tattered history of Roman, Mongol, and Turkish conquest, is very much a late-19th-century city, with its characteristic coffeehouse and music hall culture. The decades after World War I and the fall of the Hapsburg monarchy weren't kind to Hungary's charming capital, and Budapest's glory seemed irretrievably lost. However, the city has undergone a post–Cold War renaissance and is once again attracting visitors from far and wide at the start of the new century.

Budapest retains an exotic atmosphere seldom experienced in the better-known capitals of Europe. Explore it fully. Turn off any of the main boulevards and you'll quickly find yourself in a quiet residential neighborhood. The rich scent of a hearty *gulyás* (beef stew) wafts from a kitchen window, salamis hang in the window of the little grocer's shop, and cigarette smoke fogs the cavelike entry of the corner pub.

ESSENTIALS

GETTING THERE   By Plane   All flights arrive at **Ferihegy II** (© 1/296-7155 general info, 1/296-5052 arrivals, or 1/296-5883 departures), located in the XVIII district in southeastern Pest.

The easiest way into the city is probably the **Airport Minibus** (© 1/296-8555; fax 1/296-8993), a public service of the LRI (Budapest Airport Authority). The minibus, which leaves every 10 or 15 minutes throughout the day, takes you directly to any address in the city. From either terminal, it costs 2,100 Ft ($9.45); the price includes luggage transport. The trip takes from 30 minutes to an hour, depending on how many stops are made. The Airport Minibus desk

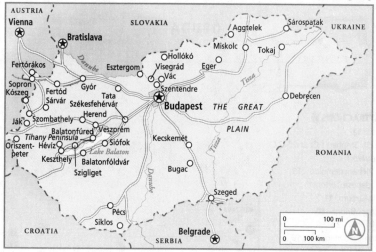

is easily found in the main hall. Minibuses also provide the same efficient service returning to the airport; arrange for your pickup from your hotel *1 full day in advance* by calling the number above.

Note: We strongly discourage the use of cabs from the **Airport Taxi** fleet (© 1/296-6534), which are notoriously overpriced. A ride downtown in one of these cabs could cost as much as twice the fare of a ride in a reasonably priced taxi. Alas, for reasons no one has been able to explain to us with a straight face, cabs from the Airport Taxi fleet are the only cabs permitted to wait for fares on the airport grounds. However, dozens of cabs from the cheaper fleets that we recommend are at all times stationed at roadside pullouts just off the airport property, a stone's throw from the terminal, waiting for radio calls from their dispatchers. You can phone any of these fleets from the terminal and a cab will be there for you in a few minutes. (See "By Taxi," in the "Getting Around" section, below, for other taxi fleet phone numbers.) For two or more people traveling together, a taxi from a recommended fleet to the city will generally be cheaper than the combined minibus fares, at about 4,500 Ft ($20). A taxi from the airport to downtown takes about 20 to 30 minutes.

It's also possible (and very cheap) to get to the city by public transportation; the bus-to-Metro-to-town trip takes about 1 hour total. Take the red-lettered **bus no. 93** to the last stop, Kőbánya-Kispest. From there, the Blue Metro line runs to the Inner City of Pest. The cost is two transit tickets, which are 250 Ft ($1.10) all together; tickets can be bought from the automated vending machine at the bus stop (coins only) or from any newsstand in the airport.

By Train Budapest has three major train stations: Keleti pályaudvar (Eastern Station), Nyugati pályaudvar (Western Station), and Déli pályaudvar (Southern Station). The stations' names, curiously, correspond neither to their geographical location in the city nor to the origins or destinations of the trains serving them. Each has a Metro station beneath it and an array of accommodations offices, currency-exchange booths, and other services.

Most international trains pull into bustling **Keleti Station** (© 1/314-5010; Metro: Keleti pu.), a classic steel-girded European train station located in Pest's

Budapest

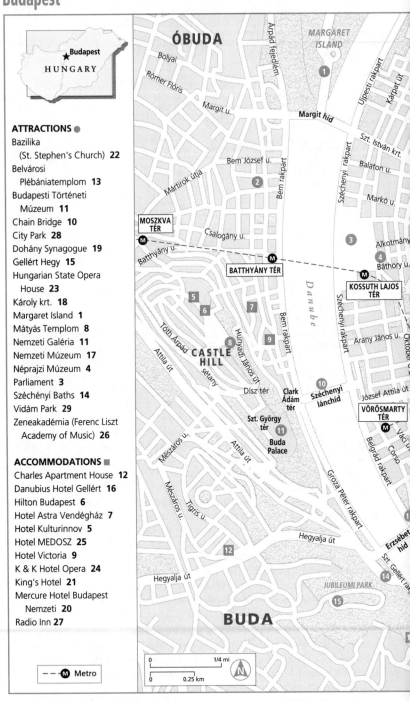

seedy Baross tér. The Red line of the metro is below the station; numerous bus, tram, and trolleybus lines serve Baross tér as well. Some international trains arrive at **Nyugati Station** (© 1/349-0115; Metro: Nyugati pu.), another classic of a station designed by the Eiffel company and built in the 1870s. Numerous tram and bus lines serve busy Nyugati tér, which is located on the Outer Ring. Few international trains arrive at **Déli Station** (© 1/375-6293; Metro: Déli pu.), an ugly modern building in central Buda; the terminus of the Red metro line is here.

Train-station phone numbers are good from 8pm to 6am. During the day, obtain **domestic train information** over the phone by dialing © 1/461-5400 and **international train information** at © 1/461-5500. Purchase tickets at train station ticket windows or from the MÁV Service Office, VI. Andrássy út 35 (© 1/322-80482), open Monday through Friday 9am to 6pm in summer, 9am to 5pm in winter. You need at least half an hour before departure time to make a reservation.

MÁV operates a minibus that will take you from any of the three stations to the airport for 2,100 Ft ($9.45) per person, or between stations for 1,200 Ft ($5.40) per person. To order the minibus, call © 1/353-2722. Often, however, a taxi fare will be cheaper, especially for groups of two or more travelers (see p. 554 for reliable taxi companies).

By Bus   The Népliget Bus Station is the city's recently opened modern main bus terminal on the Red metro line at the **Népstadion stop.** The Blue line goes to the much smaller **Árpád híd bus station** that caters to domestic bus service only.

By Car   Several major highways link Hungary to nearby European capitals. The recently modernized **E60** (or M1) connects Budapest with Vienna and points west; it is a toll road from the Austrian border to the city of Györ. The **E65** connects Budapest with Prague and points north.

The **border crossings** from Austria and Slovakia (from which countries most Westerners enter Hungary) are hassle-free. In addition to your passport, you may be requested to present your driver's license, vehicle registration, and proof of insurance (the number plate and symbol indicating country of origin are acceptable proof). A green card is required of vehicles bearing license plates of Bulgaria, France, the former USSR, Greece, Poland, Italy, Romania, and Israel. Hungary no longer requires the International Driver's License. Cars entering Hungary are required to have a decal indicating country of registration, a first-aid kit, and an emergency triangle.

By Hydrofoil   The Hungarian state shipping company **MAHART** operates hydrofoils on the Danube between Vienna and Budapest (sometimes with a stop in Bratislava) in spring and summer. It's an extremely popular route, so book your tickets well in advance. To book, contact your local Austrian National Tourist Board. In Vienna, contact MAHART, Handelskai 265 (© 0043/729-2 161; fax 0043/729-2163). The Budapest office of **MAHART** is at V. Belgrád rakpart (© 1/318-1880). Boats and hydrofoils from Vienna arrive at the international boat station next door to the MAHART office on the **Belgrád rakpart,** which is on the Pest side of the Danube, between the Szabadság and Erzsébet bridges.

VISITOR INFORMATION   Tourist Offices   The best information source in the city is **Tourinform** (© 1/317-9800 or 1/317-8992; www.hungarytourism. hu), the office of the Hungarian Tourist Board. Centrally located at V. Sütő u.

2, just off Deák tér (reached by all three metro lines) in Pest, the main office is open daily from 8am to 8pm. There is now another Tourinform office in the bustling entertainment district of Liszt Ferenc tér, open daily from 9am to 7pm (Liszt Ferenc tér is just down the street from Oktogon, reached by yellow line of the metro or tram no. 4 or 6).

Another very useful information source is **Vista Visitor Center** at V. Paulay Ede u. 7 (© **1/267-8603;** www.vista.hu), a 5-minute walk from Deák tér (reached by all three metro lines) in Pest. This travel agency/cafe is open Monday through Friday from 9am to 8pm, and Saturday and Sunday from 10am to 4pm. This place is best used as an in-country travel resource.

Websites The site **www.gotohungary.com** has a wealth of tourist information, as does **www.hungarytourism.hu.** Current local news, entertainment listings, and the like can be found at either **www.budapestsun.com** or **www. budapestweek.com**.

CITY LAYOUT The city of Budapest came into being in 1873, the result of a union of three separate cities: **Buda, Pest,** and **Óbuda.** Budapest, like Hungary itself, is defined by the **River Danube (Duna),** along which many historic sites are found. Eight bridges join the two banks; five of them are in the city center.

On the right bank of the Danube lies Pest, flat as a *palacsinta* (pancake), spreading far into the distance. Pest is the commercial and administrative center not just of the capital, but of all Hungary. Central Pest, the term used in this guide, is that part of the city between the Danube and the semicircular **Outer Ring boulevard (Nagykörút),** stretches of which are named after former Austro-Hungarian monarchs: Ferenc körút, József körút, Erzsébet körút, Teréz körút, and Szent István körút. The Outer Ring begins at the Pest side of the Petőfi Bridge in the south and wraps itself around the center, ending at the Margit Bridge in the north. Several of Pest's busiest squares are found along the Outer Ring, and Pest's major east-west avenues bisect the Ring at these squares.

Central Pest is further defined by the **Inner Ring (Kiskörút),** which lies within the Outer Ring. It starts at Szabadság híd (Freedom Bridge) in the south and is alternately named Vámház körút, Múzeum körút, Károly körút, Bajcsy-Zsilinszky út, and József Attila utca before ending at the Chain Bridge. Inside this ring is the **Belváros,** the historic Inner City of Pest.

Váci utca (distinct from Váci út) is a popular pedestrian-only shopping street between the Inner Ring and the Danube. It spills into **Vörösmarty tér,** one of the area's best-known squares. The **Dunakorzó (Danube Promenade),** a popular evening strolling spot, runs along the river in Pest between the Chain Bridge and the Erzsébet Bridge. The historic Jewish district of Pest is in the **Erzsébetváros (Elizabeth Town),** between the two ring boulevards.

On the left bank is **Buda;** to its north, beyond the city center, lies **Óbuda.** Buda is as hilly as Pest is flat. Buda's **Castle Hill** is widely considered the most

Tips **A Note on Addresses**

Budapest is divided into 22 districts called **kerülets** (abbreviated ker.). A Roman numeral followed by a period precedes every written address in Budapest, signifying the kerület; for example, XII. Csörsz utca 9 is in the 12th kerület. Because many street names are repeated in different parts of the city, it's important to know which kerület a certain address is in.

beautiful part of Budapest. A number of steep paths, staircases, and small streets go up to Castle Hill, but no major roads come this way. The easiest access is from **Clark Ádám tér** (at the head of the Chain Bridge) by funicular, or from **Várfok utca** (near Moszkva tér) by foot or bus. Castle Hill consists of the royal palace itself, home to numerous museums, and the so-called **Castle District,** a lovely neighborhood of small, winding streets, centered on the Gothic Matthias Church. Below Castle Hill, along the Danube, is a long, narrow neighborhood, historically populated by fishermen and other river workers, known as the **Víziváros (Watertown). Central Buda** is a collection of low-lying neighborhoods below Castle Hill. The main square is **Moszkva tér,** just north of Castle Hill. Beyond Central Buda, mainly to the east, are the Buda Hills.

Óbuda is also on the left bank of the Danube, north of Buda. Although the greater part of Óbuda is modern and drab, it features a beautiful old city center and impressive Roman ruins.

GETTING AROUND   Budapest has an extensive and inexpensive public transportation system. However, except for 17 well-traveled bus and tram routes, all forms of transport shut down nightly at around 11:30pm; certain areas of the city, most notably the Buda Hills, are beyond the reach of the limited night service, so you'll have to take a taxi if you're out late. Be on the alert for pickpockets when on crowded public transportation. Keep your money and valuables inside your clothing in a money belt.

All forms of public transportation (metro, bus, tram, trolleybus, some HÉV railway lines, and cogwheel railway) in Budapest require the **self-validation of prepurchased tickets** *(vonaljegy),* which cost 125 Ft (55¢) apiece (children under 6 travel free); single tickets can be bought at metro ticket windows, newspaper kiosks, and the occasional tobacco shop. There are also automated machines in most Metro stations and at major transportation hubs. We recommend that you buy a handful of tickets in advance so that you can avoid the trouble of constantly having to replenish your stock with the appropriate coins for the vending machines. For 1,100 Ft ($4.95) you can get a 10-pack *(tizes csomag),* and for 2,150 Ft ($9.70), you can get a 20-pack *(huszas csomag).*

Your best bet is to buy a day pass or multiday pass. Passes are inexpensive and only need to be validated once. A pass will probably save you some money too, as you're likely to be getting on and off public transportation all day long. **Day passes** *(napijegy)* cost 975 Ft ($4.35) and are valid until midnight of the day of purchase; **3-day passes** *(turistajegy)* cost 1,950 Ft ($8.80); and **7-day passes** *(hétibérlet)* cost 2,350 Ft ($11). You can buy these passes from Metro ticket windows; the clerk will validate the pass at the time of purchase.

Uniformed inspectors frequently come around checking for valid tickets, particularly at the top or bottom of the escalators to Metro platforms. On-the-spot fines of 1,500 Ft ($6.75) are assessed to fare dodgers. All public transportation operates on rough schedules, posted at bus and tram shelters and in Metro stations. The Budapest Transport Authority (BKV térkép) produces a detailed transportation map, available at most Metro ticket windows for 380 Ft ($1.70).

By Metro   The Metro is clean and efficient, with trains running every 3 to 5 minutes from about 4:30am until about 11:30pm. The three lines are universally known by color—Yellow, Red, and Blue. Officially they have numbers as well (1, 2, and 3 respectively), but all signs are color-coded. All three lines converge at the **Deák tér** station, the only point where any lines meet. Each station has two separate entrances, one for each direction.

The **Yellow (1) line** is the oldest metro on the European continent. Built in 1894 as part of the Hungarian millennial celebration, it has been refurbished and restored to its original splendor. The Yellow line runs from Vörösmarty tér, site of Gerbeaud's Cukrászda in the heart of central Pest, out the length of Andrássy út, past the Városliget (City Park), ending at Mexikói út, in a trendy residential part of Pest known as Zugló. The **Red (2)** and **Blue (3) lines** are modern Metros, deep underground and accessible by escalator. The Red line runs from Örs vezér tere in eastern Pest, through the center, and across the Danube to Batthyány tér, Moszkva tér, and finally Déli Station. Keleti Station is also along the Red line. The Blue line runs from Kőbánya-Kispest, in southeastern Pest, through the center, and out to Újpest-Központ in northern Pest. Nyugati Station is along the Blue line.

Tickets must be validated at the automated time-stamp boxes before you descend the escalator. When changing lines at Deák tér, you must validate a new ticket at the orange machines in the hallway between lines.

By Bus   Many parts of the city, most notably the Buda Hills, are best accessed by bus *(busz)*. With the exception of night buses, most lines are in service from about 4:30am to about 11:30pm, with less frequent (or nonexistent) weekend service on some. A few buses run all night long (an *É*—with an accent—signifies *éjszaka,* meaning that the bus runs all night). This information is both on the reverse of the BKV transportation map and on the schedules posted at every bus stop.

Black-numbered local buses constitute the majority of the bus fleet. Rednumbered buses are express. If the red number on the bus is followed by an *E,* the bus is express, so it follows the same routes as the local bus but skips several stops (however, remember that an *É*—with an accent—signifies *éjszaka,* meaning that the bus runs all night). A few buses are labeled by something other than a number; one you'll probably use is the **Várbusz (Palace Bus),** a minibus that runs between Várfok utca, off Buda's Moszkva tér, and the Castle District.

You must validate your bus ticket on board at the mechanical red box found by each door. Tickets for Budapest buses cannot be purchased from the driver (though in smaller cities and towns the drivers generally do sell tickets). You can board the bus by any door.

By Tram   You'll find Budapest's bright-yellow trams (known as *villamos* in Hungarian) very useful, particularly the nos. **4** and **6,** which travel along the Outer Ring (Nagykörút) and the nos. **47** and **49,** which run along the Inner Ring. You must validate your ticket on board. As with buses, tickets are valid for one ride, not for the line itself. Trams stop at every station, and all doors open, regardless of whether anyone is waiting to get on. *Important:* The buttons near the tram doors are for emergency stops, not stop requests.

By Trolleybus   There are 14 trolleybus lines in Budapest, all in Pest. Of particular interest to train travelers is no. 73, the fastest route between Keleti Station and Nyugati Station. All the information in the "By Bus" section above regarding boarding, ticket validation, and stop-skipping applies to trolleybuses as well.

By HÉV   The HÉV is a suburban railway network that connects Budapest to various points along the city's outskirts. There are four HÉV lines; only one, the **Szentendre line,** is of serious interest to tourists. The terminus for the Szentendre HÉV line is Buda's Batthyány tér, also a station of the Metro Red line. Most hotels, restaurants, and sights in northern Buda and Óbuda are best reached by the HÉV. To reach Óbuda's Fő tér (Main Sq.), get off at the Árpád híd (Árpád Bridge) stop. The HÉV runs regularly between 4am and 11:30pm. For trips within the city limits, the cost is one transit ticket, self-validated as on a bus or tram. HÉV tickets to destinations beyond the city limits are available at HÉV ticket windows at the Batthyány tér station, at the Margit híd station, or from the conductor onboard (no penalty assessed for such purchase).

By Taxi Budapest taxis are largely unregulated, so fares vary tremendously. The best rates are invariably those of the larger fleet companies. We particularly recommended Fő Taxi (℃ 1/222-2222). Other reliable fleets include Volántaxi (℃ 1/466-6666), City Taxi (℃ 1/211-1111), Tele5 (℃ 1/355-5555), and 6×6 (℃ 1/266-6666).

By Car We don't recommend using a car for sightseeing in Budapest. You may, however, want to rent one for trips outside the capital. We recommend **Fox Auto Rental,** XVI. Vegyesz u. 17-25, 1116 Budapest (℃ **1/382-9000;** fax 1/382-9003), which rents the Fiat Seicento for 29€ ($33) per day for a rental of 1 to 6 days, and 174€ ($200) for a week, insurance and mileage included. Fox will deliver the car to you at your hotel without charge between 8am to 6pm. The more expensive **Denzel Europcar InterRent,** VIII. Üllői út 60–62, 1082 Budapest (℃ **1/477-1080;** fax 1/477-1099), offers the Opel Corza or Fiat Punto for 95€ ($109) per day (insurance included), or 70€ ($81) per day for 3 to 4 days. They also have a rental counter at the airport (℃ **1/296-6610**), but here you pay an additional 12% airport tax.

FAST FACTS: Budapest

American Express Budapest's Amex office is between Vörösmarty tér and Deák tér in central Pest, at V. Deák Ferenc u. 10, 1052 Budapest (℃ 1/235-4330 or 1/235-4300; fax 1/267-2028; Metro: Deák tér). It's open year-round on weekdays from 9am to 5:30pm and Saturday from 9am to 2pm. There is an American Express ATM on the street in front.

Business Hours Most **stores** are open Monday through Friday from 10am to 6pm and Saturday from 9 or 10am to 1 or 2pm. Some shops close for an hour at lunchtime, and most stores are closed Sunday, except those in the central tourist areas. Some shop owners and restaurateurs also close for 2 weeks in August. **Banks** are usually open Monday through Thursday from 8am to 3pm and Friday from 8am to 2pm. **Museums** in Budapest are usually open Tuesday through Sunday from 10am to 6pm.

Currency As of this writing, the rate of exchange is $1 = 230 Ft (or 100 Ft = 43¢), and this is the rate used to calculate all the U.S. dollar prices in this book. Of course, exchange rates fluctuate over time.

Note: Several hotels and pensions in Budapest list their prices in U.S. dollars, while most list prices in euros. This is done predominantly as a hedge against forint inflation; Hungary is a member of the European Union as of May 2004 but is not planning to introduce the euro until 2007. All hotels in Budapest accept payment in Hungarian forints as well as in most foreign currencies.

Currency Exchange Exchange booths are located throughout the city center, in train stations, and in most luxury hotels, and they almost always offer lower rates than banks. This is particularly true of one chain called Inter Change, which offers a rate up to 20% lower than the going bank rate, depending on the amount you exchange. ATMs are found throughout the city. You may withdraw forints at the daily exchange rate from your home account through the Cirrus and PLUS networks.

Doctors & Dentists We recommend the **American Clinic,** in a modern building across from the Mammut shopping center at I. Hattyu u. 14 (© **1/224-9090;** Metro: Moszkva tér); a private outpatient clinic with two U.S. board–certified physicians and several English-speaking Hungarian doctors. Check with Vista Visitor Center for discount coupons. For dental work, we recommend **Dr. Susan Linder,** II. Vihorlat u. 23 (© **1/335-5245;** bus: 5 or 29), the dentist for the U.S. and British embassies. Her hours are Monday, Tuesday, and Thursday from 8am to 6pm by appointment; she is also available for emergencies, except on weekends. In a pinch, you can also try **S.O.S. Dent Kft,** a 24-hour emergency dental clinic at VII. Király u. 14 (© **1/269-6010**), just a few minutes by foot from Deák tér (all three metro lines).

Embassies The embassy of **Australia** is at XII. Királyhágó tér 8–9 (© **1/457-9777**); the embassy of **Canada** is at XII. Budakeszi út 32 (© **1/392-3360**); the embassy of the **Republic of Ireland** is at V. Szabadság tér 7 (© **1/302-9600**); the embassy of the **United Kingdom** is at V. Harmincad u. 6 (© **1/266-2888**); and the embassy of the **United States** is at V. Szabadság tér 12 (© **1/475-4400**). New Zealand does not have an embassy in Budapest, but the U.K. embassy can handle matters for New Zealand citizens.

Emergencies Dial © **104** for an ambulance, © **105** for the fire department, or © **107** for the police. © **1/438-8080** is a newly established 24-hour hot line in English for reporting crime.

Internet Access The best place in town at press time is the 24-hour **Internet Café,** VI. Andrássy út 46 (© **1/331-9102**). They provide full service, including Internet access (minimum time is 15 min. for 200 Ft/90¢). We also frequent **Vista Visitor Center,** at V. Paulay Ede u. 7 (© **1/267-8603;** Metro: Deák tér, all three metro lines), which has about 10 terminals in a small mezzanine area. The cost is 5 Ft (2¢) per minute. It's open Monday through Saturday from 10am to 10pm, and Sunday from 10am to 8pm. Another option, with less of a wait, is **Internet Café,** V. Kecskeméti u. 5 (© **1/328-0292**), near Kálvin tér (Blue line), open daily from 10am to 10pm. The cost is 900 Ft ($4.05) for an hour, with pricing by 30-minute intervals (except 10 min. or less, which costs 150 Ft/70¢).

Pharmacies The Hungarian word for "pharmacy" is *gyógyszertár* or *patika.* Generally, pharmacies carry only prescription drugs. There are a number of 24-hour pharmacies in the city—every pharmacy posts the address of the nearest one in its window, in case the one that you've gone to is not open at the time. Your best bet for 24-hour service throughout the year is **Oktogon Patika** on Teréz körút, next to Hotel Béke Radisson (off Oktogon Sq.; Metro: Yellow line; tram: 4 or 6). If you are looking for basics like pantyhose, lip balm, and so on, you'll want to find a drugstore rather than a pharmacy. A number of European drug store chains have set up shop in Budapest; look for the Drogerie Mart, know as DM.

Post Office The main branch of the Magyar Posta (Hungarian Postal Service) is at V. Petőfi Sándor u. 17–19, 1052 Budapest, Hungary (© 36/1-318-3947 or 36/1-487-1100; Metro: Deák tér). This rather confusing office is open Monday through Saturday from 7am to 9pm. The post office at VIII. Baross tér 11/c (© 36/1-322-9013; Metro: Keleti pu.) is open Monday through Saturday from 7am to 9pm. The post office at VI. Teréz krt. 51 (© 36/1-312-1480; Metro: Nyugati pu.) is open Monday through Friday from 7am to 9pm and Saturday from 8am to 8pm. At press time, an airmail postcard costs 150 Ft (70¢), and an airmail letter 230 Ft ($1) and up, depending on size of envelope and weight.

Restrooms The word for toilet in Hungarian is *WC* (pronounced vay-tsay). *Női* means "women's"; *férfi* means "men's."

Safety By U.S. standards, Budapest is a relatively safe city—muggings and violent attacks are rare. Though they're clearly less of a threat now than a few years ago, teams of professional pickpockets still plague Budapest, operating on crowded trams, Metros, and buses. Be particularly careful on bus no. 26 (Margaret Island) and tram nos. 4 and 6, or in any other crowded setting. Avoid being victimized by wearing a money belt under your clothes instead of wearing a fanny pack or carrying a wallet or purse. No valuables should be kept in the outer pockets of a backpack.

Telephone The **country code** for Hungary is **36**. The **city code** for Budapest is **1**; use this code when you're calling from outside Hungary. If you're within Hungary but not in Budapest, first dial **06**; when you hear a tone, dial the city code and phone number. If you're calling within Budapest, simply leave off the code and dial only the regular seven-digit phone number.

Be aware that some Budapest phone numbers may change as MATÁV continues to upgrade its system. Note, for instance, that any number beginning with a "1" has been changed; try replacing the 1 with a 3 or 4. Usually, if the number you're dialing has changed, you'll get a recording first in Hungarian and then in English, indicating the new number. If further information is needed, dial © **198** for domestic directory assistance and **199** for international queries.

The Hungarian phone company MATÁV provides much better service than in the past, but it still falls significantly short of Western standards. For best results, dial slowly and don't be too quick to trust a busy signal—try again.

Numbers beginning with **06-20, 06-30,** or **06-70,** followed by a seven-digit number, are **mobile phone numbers.** Mobile phones are extremely popular and some of the listings in this chapter are mobile phone numbers. Be aware that all phone calls made to a mobile phone are charged as long distance calls, regardless of the location of the caller or the receiver.

Public **pay phones** charge varying amounts for local calls depending on the time of day you place your call. It's cheapest to call late in the evenings and on weekends. Public phones operate with 20, 50, and 100 Ft coins or with phone cards (in 50 or 120 units), which can be purchased from post offices, tobacco shops, supermarkets, travel agencies, and any MATÁV customer service office (MATÁV Pont).

You can reach the **AT&T** operator at © **00/800-01111**, the **MCI** operator at © **00/800-01411**, and the **Sprint** operator at © **00/800-01877**.

Tipping Tipping is generally 10%. Among those who welcome tips are waiters, taxi drivers, hotel employees, barbers, cloakroom attendants, toilet attendants, masseuses, and tour guides. If a restaurant bill includes a service fee, as most restaurants do, there is no need to tip. However, be aware that newer restaurants have started not including a service charge in the bill; waiters at these places are likely to remind you if this is the case.

WHERE TO STAY

Budapest's accommodations range from beautiful, historic turn-of-the-20th-century gems to drab, utilitarian establishments that are products of the city's Warsaw Pact days. Although the most notable establishments—among them the stunning Art Nouveau Hotel Gellért, the Hotel Béke Radisson, and Castle Hill's distinctive Hilton Hotel—are among the city's priciest lodgings, accommodations rates in Budapest remain among the lowest of any European capital.

Despite the many new hotels and pensions (small inn-like hotels) that have opened in recent years, Budapest retains its reputation as a city without enough guest beds. Indeed, in high season it can be quite difficult to secure a hotel or pension room or a hostel bed (although private rooms in private apartments are always available), so make reservations and get written confirmation well in advance of your stay if possible.

Many hotels and pensions in Budapest list their prices in euros or U.S. dollars. This is done as a hedge against forint inflation; all hotels in Budapest accept payment in Hungarian forints as well as foreign currencies. We have listed lodging prices either in forints or euros and give the conversion to U.S. dollars.

Although there is an unfortunate dearth of recommendable budget hotels in Budapest, travelers can take advantage of the wealth of good alternative accommodations. Small pensions, rooms in private homes, and a number of good youth hostels make the city inviting to travelers on any budget. An attractive accommodation alternative in Hungary is a room in a **private apartment.** Typically, you share the bathroom with the hosts or with other guests. Breakfast isn't officially included, but the host will often offer a continental breakfast for 550 Ft to 850 Ft ($2.50–$3.80). You may have limited kitchen privileges (ask in advance). Some hosts will greet you when you arrive, give you a key, and seemingly disappear; others will want to befriend you, show you around, and cook for you. Most rooms are adequate, some are even memorable, but any number of reasons may cause you to dislike yours: Noisy neighborhoods, tiny bathrooms, and bad coffee are among the complaints we've heard. The great majority of visitors, though, appear to be very satisfied. Plus, staying in a private room provides a window into everyday Hungarian life that you might otherwise miss.

The most established agencies for hotel, pension, and apartment reservations are the former state-owned travel agents **Ibusz, Cooptourist, MÁV Tours,** and **Budapest Tourist.** Although newer, private agencies have proliferated, the older ones tend to have the greatest number of rooms listed. There are agencies at the airport, at all three major train stations, throughout central Pest, and along the main roads into Budapest for travelers arriving by car. The main **Ibusz reservations office** is at Ferenciek tere 10 (© **1/485-2700;** fax 1/318-2805;

Native Behavior

When you are first introduced to someone, make sure to call him or her by the appropriate title (such as Dr., Mr., Mrs.) followed by the last name. When in doubt in Hungary, opt for formality in addressing people. Also remember that handshakes are common gestures of greeting, no matter how well you know someone.

On business cards and the like, the last name precedes the first name.

Expect to be offered plenty of food and drink when you enter someone's home. Always accept at least a modest serving of whatever is offered.

www.ibusz.hu; Metro: Ferenciek tere), open year-round Monday through Friday from 8:15am to 5pm. All major credit cards are accepted. **Cooptourist,** Nyugati Station (© 36/1-458-6200), is open from 9am to 4:30pm Monday through Friday and does not accept credit cards. **Budapest Tourist,** Nyugati Station (© 36/1-318-6552), is open 9am to 5pm Monday through Friday and 9am to noon Saturday. The agency does not accept credit cards. **MÁV Tours,** Keleti Station (© 36/1-382-9011), is open 9am to 5pm Monday through Friday and does not accept credit cards.

When booking, keep in mind that if you want a room with a double bed, you should specifically request it; otherwise, you are likely to get a room with twin beds. Single rooms are generally available, as are extra beds or cots. Hungarian hotels often use the word *apartment* to describe connected rooms without a kitchen. In these listings, we have referred to such rooms as "suites," reserving the term *apartment* for accommodations with kitchen facilities.

IN THE INNER CITY & CENTRAL PEST
Expensive
K & K Hotel Opera ★★★ *(Value* Operated by the Austrian K & K hotel chain, this tasteful, elegant establishment opened in 1994 and expanded in 1997. Directly across the street from the Opera House in central Pest, the hotel blends nicely with its surroundings. The interior is pleasing and the staff is uniformly friendly and helpful.

VI. Révay u. 24, 1065 Budapest. © 1/269-0222. Fax 1/269-0230. www.kkhotels.com. 205 units. 143€ ($164) double. Rates 5% lower in low season. Rates include breakfast. AE, DC, MC, V. Parking 10€ ($12). Metro: Opera (Yellow line). **Amenities:** Exercise room; sauna; business center; nonsmoking rooms. *In room:* A/C, TV, minibar, coffeemaker, hair dryer, safe.

Mercure Hotel Budapest Nemzeti ★★★ *(Finds* Turn-of-the-20th-century Hotel Nemzeti, just off Blaha Lujza Square, underwent a 1987 restoration that reinstated much of the hotel's Art Nouveau splendor. This is perhaps Pest's most handsome and historic hotel. Its biggest drawback is its location; though very centrally located, the hotel directly overlooks what is perhaps the busiest square on the Outer Ring. Half the rooms face the heavily trafficked street (and the soundproofing does not mask the noise), while the other half face a lovely interior courtyard (request one of these!). The rooms have wonderful high ceilings and spacious bathrooms. The rooms on the top (5th) floor (there is an elevator) are the most interesting, with slanted ceilings and funky windows. There is a non-smoking floor. The hotel has a restaurant that was recently restored to its formal elegance and is one of Budapest's most fashionable eateries.

VIII. József krt. 4, 1088 Budapest. © 1/477-2000. Fax 1/477-2001. www.mercure-nemzeti.hu. 76 units. 112€ ($129) double. Rates include breakfast. Rates 20% lower in low season. AE, DC, MC, V. Parking available in neighborhood garage for 3,000 Ft ($14) per day. Metro: Blaha Lujza tér (Red line). **Amenities:** Restaurant; bar; car-rental desk; 24-hr. room service; laundry service. *In room:* A/C, TV, dataport, minibar, hair dryer, safe.

Moderate

King's Hotel ★★ *Finds* King's Hotel opened for business in 1995 in a beautifully renovated and restored fin de siècle building in the heart of Pest's Jewish district. The reception is friendly and helpful. Despite the somewhat drab modern furnishings, rooms retain a 19th-century atmosphere, many boasting small balconies overlooking the quiet residential street. Most, but not all, have a private bathroom. The kosher hotel restaurant is the only one of its kind in Budapest. *Note:* Meals are served on weekends and Jewish holidays in the hotel's restaurant by prior arrangement only.

VII. Nagydiófa u. 25–27 Budapest. © and fax 1/352-7675. kingsbudapest.4t.com. 80 units. 60€–80€ ($69–$92) double; 140€ ($161) suite. Rates include breakfast. AE, DC, MC, V. Parking available on street for 1,150 Ft ($5) per day. Metro: Astoria (Red line). **Amenities:** Restaurant (kosher). *In room:* A/C, TV, safe.

Inexpensive

Hotel MEDOSZ ★ *Value* The MEDOSZ was formerly a trade-union hotel for agricultural workers. It is located on sleepy Jókai tér, in the heart of Pest's theater district, just across the street from the bustling Liszt Ferenc tér, Pest's most recent nightlife hub, a couple of blocks from the Opera House. This is as good as it gets off the river in central Pest. Although the hotel has not been renovated since privatization, it remains a great value given its location. The rooms are simple but clean. Next door to Hotel MEDOSZ is one of Budapest's special treats for children: a puppet theater *(bábszínház)*.

VI. Jókai tér 9, 1061 Budapest. © 1/374-3000. Fax 1/332-4316. www.medoszhotel.hu. 67 units. 55€ ($63) double; 42€ ($48) single. Rates are 20% lower in low season. Rates include breakfast. No credit cards. Metered on-street parking difficult in neighborhood; there is an indoor garage in nearby Aradi utca. Metro: Oktogon (Yellow line). **Amenities:** Restaurant; bar; laundry service. *In room:* TV.

JUST BEYOND CENTRAL PEST
Inexpensive

Radio Inn ★★ *Value* As the official guesthouse of Hungarian National Radio, the Radio Inn houses many visiting dignitaries and offers apartments to individual tourists. The inn is in an exclusive embassy neighborhood (next door to the Chinese embassy), a stone's throw from City Park, and a block from Pest's

---

Tips High, Mid- & Low Season in Budapest

Most hotels and pensions in Budapest divide the year into three seasons. **High season** is roughly from March or April to September or October, the week between Christmas and New Year's, the week of Easter, and the period of the Budapest Spring Festival (mid- to late March). **Midseason** is usually considered March, and October and/or November. **Low season** is roughly from November to February, except Christmas week. Some hotels discount as much as 30% in low season, while others offer no winter discount. Be sure to inquire.

grand Andrássy út. The Metro's Yellow line takes you into the center of Pest in 5 minutes; alternatively, it's a 30-minute walk. Behind the building, there's an enormous private courtyard full of flowers. The huge apartments (all with fully equipped, spacious kitchens) are comfortably furnished and painstakingly clean. Note that the toilets and bathrooms are separate, European style. The management is somewhat old-system (read: begrudging with information, slightly suspicious of foreigners), yet cordial enough.

VI. Benczúr u. 19, 1068 Budapest. 📞 1/342-8347 or 1/322-8284. Fax 1/322-8284. www.hotels.hu/radio_inn_budapest. 36 units. High season 43€ ($49), 65€ ($75), and 84€ ($97) for 1, 2, and 3-person apts; low season 43€ ($49), 48€ ($55), and 61€ ($70) for 1, 2, and 3-person apts. Breakfast 5€ ($5.75) extra. MC, AE, MC, V. Parking available on street, but parking meter is 100 Ft (45¢) per hour 8am–6pm weekdays. Metro: Bajza utca/Yellow line. **Amenities:** Restaurant; bar; 24-hr. room service; laundry service; nonsmoking rooms. *In room:* TV, kitchen, minibar.

THE CASTLE DISTRICT
Very Expensive

Hilton Budapest ★★★ Overlooking the river and Pest beyond, the Hilton, built in 1977, is widely considered the city's classiest hotel. Its location, on Hess András tér, next door to Matthias Church and the Fisherman's Bastion, is no less than spectacular. The award-winning design incorporates the ruins of a 13th-century Dominican church and the baroque facade of a 17th-century Jesuit college (the main entrance). More expensive rooms have views over the Danube, with a full Pest skyline; rooms on the other side of the hotel overlook the delightful streets of the Castle District.

I I. Hess András tér 1–3, 1014 Budapest. 📞 1/488-6600. Fax 1/488-6644. www.hilton.com. 322 units. 270€–350€ ($311–$403) double; 350€–1,900€ ($403–$2185) suite. Rates about 10% lower in low season. Children stay free in parent's room. Breakfast 19€ ($22) extra. AE, DC, MC, V. Parking 28€ ($32) per day in garage. Bus: "Várbusz" from Moszkva tér or 16 from Deák tér. **Amenities:** 4 restaurants, 2 bars; exercise room; concierge; tour desk; free airport minibus; full business center; salon; 24-hr. room service; babysitting; laundry service; nonsmoking rooms. *In room:* A/C, TV w/pay movies, dataport, minibar, hair dryer, safe.

Moderate

Hotel Kulturinnov ★★ *Finds* There are three main reasons to stay here: location, location, location. Hotel Kulturinnov is right in the middle of Buda's lovely Castle District. This is the guesthouse of the Hungarian Culture Foundation, dedicated to forging ties with ethnic Hungarians in neighboring countries. It's open to the public, but few travelers know about it. The rooms are small and simple. The hotel can be a bit hard to find; the entrance is unassuming and practically unmarked. Go through the iron grille door and pass through an exhibition hall, continuing up the grand red-carpeted staircase to the right.

I. Szentháromság tér 6, 1014 Budapest. 📞 1/355-0122 or 1/375-1651. Fax 1/375-1886. 16 units. 70€ ($81) double. Rates almost 50% lower in low season. Rates include breakfast. AE, DC, MC, V. Bus: "Várbusz" from Moszkva tér or 16 from Deák tér. **Amenities:** 2 restaurants; 2 bars. *In room:* Fridge.

CENTRAL BUDA
Very Expensive

Danubius Hotel Gellért ★★★ *Kids* This splendid, sprawling Art Nouveau hotel first opened in 1918 and has not seen any renovations since 1970. It's pretty run-down now, but it's still one of the most charming hotels in Budapest. Located at the base of Gellért Hill in Buda, on the bank of the Danube, the Gellért is one of several thermal-bath hotels in Budapest that are managed or owned by Danubius Hotels. The quality and size of the rooms vary greatly—it seems to be hit or miss. Some rooms with balconies offer great views over the Danube, but these can be noisy—the hotel fronts busy Gellért Square. Although most visitors don't come for the official spa treatment, a number of spa-related facilities are available to guests free of charge, including the **Art Nouveau Gellért Baths,** perhaps the most popular of Budapest's thermal baths.

XI. Gellért tér 1, 1111 Budapest. ✆ 1/889-5500. Fax 1/889-5505. www.danubiusgroup.com. 234 units. 190€–205€ ($219–$236) double; 250€–275€ ($288–$316) suite. Rates include breakfast and spa packages. AE, DC, MC, V. Parking 5€ ($5.75) per night. Tram: 47 or 49 from Deák tér. **Amenities:** 3 restaurants; bar; 2 swimming pools (1 indoor and 1 outdoor) and thermal pools; sauna; tour desk; business center; 24-hr. room service; massage; babysitting; laundry service. *In room:* A/C (some rooms), TV, minibar.

Expensive

Hotel Astra Vendégház ★★ *Finds* This little gem of a hotel opened in 1996 inside a renovated 300-year-old building on a quiet side street in Buda's lovely Watertown neighborhood. The rooms are large, with wood floors and classic Hungarian-style furniture; the overall effect is a far more homey and pleasant space than that found in most Budapest hotel rooms. The staff are friendly. Some rooms overlook the inner courtyard, while others face the street.

Vám u. 6, 1011 Budapest. ✆ 1/214-1906. Fax 1/214-1907. www.hotelastra.hu. 12 units. 106€ ($122) double. Rates include breakfast. Rates 10% lower in low season. Only meter parking is available on street. Metro: Batthyány tér (Red line). **Amenities:** Restaurant, bar; car-rental desk; babysitting (on request). *In room:* A/C, TV, minibar.

Hotel Victoria ★★ The Hotel Victoria, located in Buda's lovely Watertown district, is separated from the Danube bank by the busy road that runs alongside the river. The narrow building has three rooms on each of its nine floors. Two-thirds are corner rooms with large double windows providing great views over the river to Pest. Rooms are quite large, with spacious bathrooms. Middle rooms, though smaller than corner ones, also have windows facing the river. Unfortunately, noise from the road beneath your window may disturb you.

I. Bem rakpart 11, 1011 Budapest. ✆ 1/457-8080. Fax 1/457-8088. www.victoria.hu. 27 units. 102€ ($117) double. Rates include breakfast. Rates 25% lower in low season. AE, DC, MC, V. Parking in garage 9€ ($10). Tram: 19 from Batthyány tér to the 1st stop. **Amenities:** Bar; sauna; limited room service; laundry service. *In room:* A/C, TV, dataport, minibar, hair dryer, safe.

Inexpensive

Charles Apartment House ★ *Value* Owner Károly Szombati has amassed 70 apartments in a group of apartment buildings in a dull but convenient Buda neighborhood (near the Hotel Novotel). All are average Budapest apartments with full kitchens, but the furnishings are comfortable and clean. Hegyalja út is a very busy street, but only a few of the apartments it; the rest are in the interior of the buildings or on side streets. A nearby park has tennis courts and a track.

I. Hegyalja út 23, 1016 Budapest. ✆ 1/212-9169. Fax 1/202-2984. www.charleshotel.hu. 70 units. 48€–136€ ($55–156) apt for 1–4. Rates include breakfast. Rates approximately 5% lower in low season. AE, DC, MC, V. Parking 2,000 Ft ($9) per day. Bus: 78 from Keleti pu. to Mészáros utca. **Amenities:** Restaurant; bar; bike rental; tour desk; business center; babysitting; laundry service. *In room:* A/C, TV, kitchen, minibar, hair dryer, safe.

IN THE BUDA HILLS
Inexpensive

Gizella Panzió ★ This fine pension in the Buda Hills is a 10-minute walk from the tram station. Built on the side of a hill, it has a lovely view and a series of terraced gardens leading down to the swimming pool. The pension also features a solarium. Guest rooms are all unique but uniformly quaint and sunny.

Owner Gizella Varga has good taste. A sightseeing car and driver can be arranged for guests upon request.

XII. Arató u. 42/b, 1121 Budapest. ℂ and fax 1/249-2281. gazelle@axelero.hu. 9 units. 65€ ($75) double; 75€ ($86) suite. Rates include breakfast. Rates lower in low season. DC, MC, V. Free parking. Tram: 59 from Moszkva tér to the last stop. Pets welcome. **Amenities:** Bar; outdoor pool; exercise room; sauna; limited room service; massage; babysitting; laundry service; dry cleaning. *In room:* TV, minibar.

WHERE TO DINE

Budapest is gaining a reputation for good dining at reasonable prices, so live it up.

Étterem is the most common Hungarian word for restaurant and is used for everything from cafeteria-style eateries to first-class restaurants. A *vendéglő,* or guesthouse, is a smaller, more intimate restaurant, often with a Hungarian folk motif; a *csárda* is a countryside vendéglő. An *étkezde* is an informal lunchroom open only in the daytime. An *őnkiszolgáló* is a self-service cafeteria, typically open only for lunch. Stand-up *büfés* (snack counters) are often found in bus stations and near busy transport hubs. A *cukrászda* or *kávéház* is a classic central European coffeehouse, where lingering has developed into an art form. A *borozó* is a wine bar, and a *söröző* is a beer bar; sandwiches are usually available at both. Finally, a *kocsma* is a sort of roadside tavern; the Buda Hills are filled with them. Most kocsmas serve full (if greasy) dinners, but their kitchens close very early.

IN THE INNER CITY & CENTRAL PEST
Very Expensive

Antique Restaurant ★★ HUNGARIAN This new establishment, a combination of an antiques shop on the ground floor and a stylish restaurant in the basement, has a fantastic location in the heart of Pest. Every evening live Hungarian music accompanies the delicious dishes, which are always made from fresh organic ingredients. The house is so confident of its cuisine that there is a standing offer to cook up any exquisite meal requested to satisfy even the most sophisticated connoisseur's palate. The elegant dining area only seats 30 people, so make reservations.

V. Bárczy István u. 3-5. ℂ 1/266-4993. Reservations recommended. Soups 900 Ft–1,200 Ft ($4.05–$5.40); main dishes 2,500 Ft–7,000 Ft ($11–$32). AE, MC, V (cash is preferred). Mon–Fri noon–3pm; Mon–Sat 7pm–midnight. Metro: Deák tér (all lines).

Expensive

Articsóka ★★ INTERNATIONAL An exceptionally well designed establishment, Articsóka is a welcome addition to Budapest's classy nightlife scene. The Moorish interior has a careful, harmonious design that is evident in every detail, from the quality of paper used for the menu to the type of lighting. The menu has been planned with great care; the variety is impressive, including Hungarian as well as vegetarian and international delicacies. Try the cold goose liver with celery-and-apple salad or the roasted goose liver in an apple-walnut Calvados sauce. If you feel like something lighter, check out the filet of salmon with creamed spinach. You should not leave without tasting the divine chocolate-and-pistachio parfait, definitely the best in town (and a reasonable 850 Ft/$3.80).

VI. Zichy Jenő u. 17. ℂ 1/302-7757. Reservations recommended, especially for the roof terrace. Appetizers 760 Ft–2,300 Ft ($3.40–$10); soup 640 Ft–720 Ft ($2.90–$3.25); main courses 1,250 Ft–5,200 Ft ($5.65–$23). MC, V. Daily 11am–midnight. Metro: Opera (Yellow line).

Moderate

Marquis de Salade ★★★ RUSSIAN/MIDDLE EASTERN Vegetarians will jump for joy here. On the edge of Pest's theater district, this recently renovated restaurant employs an eclectic team of eight cooks from five different areas

> ### *Tips* The Etiquette of Paying & Tipping
>
> In most restaurants, you'll have to initiate the paying and tipping ritual by summoning the waiter. The waiter usually brings the bill, nestled in a small booklet, to your table. Occasionally you'll be asked to confirm what you ordered. If you think your bill is incorrect, don't be embarrassed to call it into question; waiters readily correct bills when challenged. After handing over the bill, in most restaurants, the waiter will disappear. The tip (generally about 10%) should be included in the amount you place in the booklet. In smaller, less formal lunchroom-type places, waiters will often remain at your table after delivering the bill, waiting patiently for payment. In these face-to-face encounters, state the full amount you are paying (bill plus tip) and the waiter will make change. Hungarians never leave tips on the table.

(Russia, Bangladesh, Hungary, Italy, and the Caucasus Mountains), who turn out an amazing assortment of exceptional dishes from a number of cuisines. The offerings are sophisticated yet earthy. Try the lamb with rice (Azerbaijan) or the borscht soup (Russian). A nonsmoking area is available.

VI. Hajós u. 43. ✆ 1/302-4086. Appetizers 900 Ft–3,500 Ft ($4.05–$16); main courses 1,600 Ft–3,000 Ft ($7.20–$14). V. Daily 11am–midnight. Metro: Arany János u. (Blue line).

Inexpensive

Kádár Étkezde ★★★ *Finds* HUNGARIAN   By 11:45am, Uncle Kádár's, in the heart of the Jewish district, is filled with regulars—from paint-spattered workers to elderly Jewish couples. Uncle Kádár, a neighborhood legend, personally greets them as they file in. From the outside, the only indication of the restaurant is a very small red sign saying KÁDÁR ÉTKEZDE. The place is no more than a lunchroom, but it has a great atmosphere: high ceilings, wood-paneled walls with photos (many autographed) of actors and athletes, and old-fashioned seltzer bottles on every table. The food is simple but hearty, and the service is friendly. Table sharing is the norm. Try the soup.

VII. Klauzál tér 9. ✆ 1/321-3622. Soup 300 Ft ($1.35); main courses 500 Ft–750 Ft ($2.25–$3.40). No credit cards. Tues–Sat 11:30am–3:30pm. Metro: Astoria (Red line) or Deák tér (all lines).

JUST BEYOND CENTRAL PEST
Very Expensive

Gundel ★★ *Moments* HUNGARIAN/INTERNATIONAL   Budapest's fanciest and most famous historic restaurant, Gundel was reopened in 1992 by the well-known restaurateur George Lang, owner of New York's Café des Artistes. Located in City Park, Gundel has an opulent dining room and a large, carefully groomed garden. Lamb and wild-game entrees are house specialties. The menu highlights fruits and vegetables in season. In late spring, don't miss out on the asparagus served in hollandaise with grilled salmon. Gundel has an extensive wine list, and the waiters are well versed in its offerings. Homemade fruit ice cream served in the shape of the fruit makes for a delectable dessert, as does the famous Gundel torta, a decadently rich chocolate layer cake.

XIV. Állatkerti út 2. ✆ 1/468-4040. www.gundel.hu. Reservations highly recommended. Soup 1,090 Ft–1,680 Ft ($4.90–$7.55); main courses 4,500 Ft–8,900 Ft ($20–$40); prix-fixe menu 8,400 Ft–15,500 Ft ($38–$70); Sun brunch 4,700 Ft ($21). 10% service charge included. AE, DC, MC, V. Daily noon–4pm and 6:30pm–midnight. Metro: Hősök tere (Yellow line).

IN CENTRAL BUDA
Expensive

Kacsa Vendéglő ★ HUNGARIAN Kacsa (meaning "duck") is located on the main street of Watertown, the Buda neighborhood that lies between Castle Hill and the Danube. Here you'll find an intimate, elegant dining atmosphere, though the service seems overly attentive and ceremonious. Enticing main courses include roast duck with Morello cherries and haunch of venison with grapes. The vegetarian plate is the best we've had anywhere in town.

Fő u. 75. ℂ 1/201-9992. Reservations recommended. Soup 600 Ft–1,300 Ft ($2.70–$5.85); main courses 2,700 Ft–5,900 Ft ($12–$27). MC, V. Daily noon–3pm and 6pm–1am. Metro: Batthyány tér (Red line).

Moderate

Le Jardin de Paris ★★ FRENCH This wonderful little French bistro is in the heart of Buda's Watertown, fittingly located just across the street from the Institut Français. A cozy cellar space, it's decorated with an eclectic collection of graphic arts. A jazz trio entertains diners from 7 to 11pm daily. The menu contains nouvelle French specialties, and the wine list features French as well as Hungarian vintages. The presentation is impeccable and the service is excellent. In summer there's outdoor seating in a garden area.

I. Fő u. 20. ℂ 1/201-0047. Reservations recommended. Soup 600 Ft–1,200 Ft ($2.70–$5.40); appetizers 800 Ft–1,800 Ft ($3.60–$8.10); main courses 1,200 Ft–4,000 Ft ($5.40–$18). AE, DC, MC, V. Daily noon–midnight. Metro: Batthyány tér (Red line).

IN THE BUDA HILLS
Expensive

Náncsi Néni Vendéglője ★★ *Finds* HUNGARIAN Decorated with photographs of early 1900s Budapest, this popular but remote restaurant is located high in the Buda Hills. There's outdoor garden dining in the summer, with live guitar music at night. The menu features classic Hungarian fare, prepared with great care. The cottage-cheese dumplings are the very best in town.

II. Ördögárok út 80. ℂ 1/397-2742. Reservations recommended for dinner. Soup 680 Ft–980 Ft ($3.05–$4.40); main courses 1,650 Ft–3,780 Ft ($7.40–$17). MC, V. Daily noon–11pm. Tram: 56 from Moszkva tér to the last stop, then change to bus no. 63 to Széchenyi utca.

Coffeehouse Culture

Imperial Budapest, like Vienna, was famous for its coffeehouse culture. Literary movements and political circles alike were identified in large part by which coffeehouse they met in. You can still go to several classic coffeehouses, all of which offer delicious pastries, coffee, and more in an atmosphere of splendor. Table sharing is common.

The best are **Gerbeaud's** ★★★, in the Inner City at V. Vörösmarty tér 7 (ℂ 1/429-9000; Metro: Vörösmarty tér/Yellow line); **Művész Kávéház** ★, across the street from the Opera House at VI. Andrássy út 29 (ℂ 1/352-1337; Metro: Opera); **Central**, at V. Károlyi Mihály u. 9 (ℂ 1/266-2110; Metro: Ferenciek tere/Blue line); **Ruszwurm Cukrászda** ★, in the Castle District at I. Szentháromság u. 7 (ℂ 1/375-5284; Várbusz [Castle Bus] from Moszva tér); and **Angelika Cukrászda** ★★, also in Buda, at I. Batthyány tér 7 (ℂ 1/212-3784; Metro: Batthyány tér).

Moderate

Szép Ilona ★★ HUNGARIAN This cheerful, unassuming restaurant serves a mostly local crowd. There's a good selection of Hungarian specialties: Try the *borjúpaprikás galuskával* (veal paprika) served with *galuska* (a typical central European style of dumpling). There's a small sidewalk garden for summer dining. After your meal, take a stroll through the tree-lined streets in this area.

II. Budakeszi út 1–3. ✆ 1/275-1392. Soup 350 Ft–720 Ft ($1.55–$3.25); main courses 600 Ft–3,200 Ft ($2.70–$14). No credit cards. Daily 11:30am–10pm. Bus: 158 from Moszkva tér (departs from Csaba utca, at the top of the stairs, near the stop from which the Várbusz departs for the Castle District).

IN NORTHERN BUDA & ÓBUDA
Expensive

Kis Buda Gyöngye ★★ *Finds* HUNGARIAN/INTERNATIONAL On a quiet side street in a residential Óbuda neighborhood, Kis Buda Gyöngye ("Little Pearl of Buda") serves impeccably prepared Hungarian standards. This cheerful place features an interior garden shaded by a wonderful old gnarly tree. Inside, an eccentric violinist entertains diners. Consider the goose plate, a rich combination platter including a roast goose leg, goose cracklings, and goose liver.

III. Kenyeres u. 34. ✆ 1/368-6402 or 1/368-9246. Reservations highly recommended. Soup 820 Ft–980 Ft ($3.70–$4.40); main courses 1,800 Ft–3,200 Ft ($8.10–$14). AE, DC, MC, V. Mon–Sat noon–midnight. Tram: 17 from Margit híd (Buda side).

SEEING THE SIGHTS

SIGHTSEEING SUGGESTIONS FOR FIRST-TIME VISITORS

If You Have 1 Day Spend a few hours in the morning exploring the **Inner City** and **central Pest.** Stroll along the Danube as far as the neo-Gothic **Parliament,** noting the **Chain Bridge** and **Gresham Palace** along the way. In the afternoon, visit the major sites of **Castle Hill** and meander the cobblestone streets of the **Castle District.**

If You Have 2 Days On your first day, see **Pest,** saving the Castle District for day 2. Walk the **Outer Ring Boulevard,** noting Nyugati Railway Station and the **New York Palace.** Stop for coffee and a slice of *dobos torta* (layer cake) in the newly renovated Lukács Cukrászda, just a block away from Oktogon on grand Andrássy út. Later, head to Buda's

Gellért Hotel and unwind in the medicinal **spa** waters there. Refreshed, hike up the stairs of Gellért Hill to see the **Liberation Monument** and get an unparalleled panorama of the city.

If You Have 3 Days or More On day 3, take a boat up the Danube to visit **Szentendre,** a charming riverside town. On days 4 and 5, visit some of the central sites you may have missed, and after lunch cross the Chain Bridge to **Watertown** to explore Buda's historic riverside neighborhood. See **St. Anne's Church,** the **Capuchin Church,** and the **Király Bathrooms.** Check out Pest's indoor **market halls** and visit **Margaret Island.**

THE TOP MUSEUMS
In Pest

Nemzeti Múzeum (Hungarian National Museum) ★★ This enormous neoclassical structure, built from 1837 to 1847, played a major role in the beginning of the Hungarian Revolution of 1848 and 1849. On its wide steps, on

March 15, 1848, poet Sándor Petőfi and other young radicals are said to have exhorted the people of Pest to revolt against the Hapsburgs. The two main museum exhibits on view are *The History of the Peoples of Hungary from the Paleolithic Age to the Magyar Conquest* and *The History of the Hungarian People from the Magyar Conquest to 1989.* The museum's main attraction is the replica of the so-called crown of St. Stephen (King Stephen ruled 1000–38).

VIII. Múzeum krt. 14. ℂ 1/338-2122. Admission 600 Ft ($2.70). Tues–Sun 10am–6pm (to 5pm in winter). Metro: Kálvin tér (Blue line).

Néprajzi Múzeum (Ethnographical Museum) Directly across from Parliament, the vast Ethnographical Museum features an ornate interior equal to that of the Opera House. A ceiling fresco of Justitia, the goddess of justice, by artist Károly Lotz, dominates the lobby. Although a third of the museum's holdings are from outside Hungary, most exhibits concentrate on the items from Hungarian ethnography. The fascinating permanent exhibition, *From Ancient Times to Civilization,* features everything from drinking jugs to clothing.

V. Kossuth tér 12. ℂ 1/473-2440. Admission 500 Ft ($2.25). Tues–Sun 10am–6pm. Metro: Kossuth tér (Red line).

In Buda

Budapesti Történeti Múzeum (Budapest History Museum) This museum, also known as the Castle Museum, is the best place to get a sense of the once-great medieval Buda. Even though the museum's descriptions are written in English, it's probably worth splurging for a guided tour—the history of the palace's repeated cycles of destruction and reconstruction is so arcane that it's difficult to understand what you're seeing without a guide.

I. In Buda Palace, Wing E, on Castle Hill. ℂ 1/225-7815. Admission 700 Ft ($3.15). Guided tours by qualified staff in English for serious history buffs, at a whopping 6,000 Ft ($27), are available upon advance request. May 15–Sept 15 Wed–Mon 10am–6pm; Sept 16–May 14 Wed–Mon 10am–4pm. Bus: Várbusz from Moszkva tér or no.16 from Deák tér to Castle Hill. Funicular: From Clark Ádám tér to Castle Hill.

Nemzeti Galéria (Hungarian National Gallery) ★ Hungary has produced some fine artists, particularly in the late 19th century, and this is the place to view their work. The giants of the time are the brilliant but moody Mihály Munkácsy; László Paál, a painter of village scenes; Károly Ferenczy, a master of light; and Pál Szinyei Merse, a plein-air artist whose own artistic developments paralleled those of the early French Impressionists.

I. In Buda Palace, Wings B, C, and D, on Castle Hill. ℂ 1/375-5567. Admission 600 Ft ($2.70). Tues–Sun 10am–6pm. Bus: Várbusz from Moszkva tér or no. 16 from Deák tér to Castle Hill. Funicular: From Clark Ádám tér to Castle Hill.

HISTORIC SQUARES & BUILDINGS

Hősök tere (Heroes' Square) ★★ *Kids* Situated at the end of Pest's great boulevard, Andrássy út, and at the entrance to its most famous park, City Park (Városliget), the wide open plaza of Hősök tere (Heroes' Square) is one of the symbols of the city. Two of Budapest's major museums, the Museum of Fine Arts and the Exhibition Hall, flank Heroes' Square.

Take the metro to Hősök tere (Yellow line).

Magyar Állami Operaház (Hungarian State Opera House) ★★ Completed in 1884, Budapest's Opera House boasts a fantastically ornate interior featuring frescoes by two of the best-known Hungarian artists of the day, Bertalan

Székely and Károly Lotz. Home to both the State Opera and the State Ballet, the Opera House has a rich and evocative history.

VI. Andrássy út 22. © 1/331-2550. Tour 1,500 Ft ($6.75). Tours given daily at 3 and 4pm (available in English). Metro: Opera (Yellow line).

Parliament   Budapest's great Parliament, an eclectically designed building, mixing the predominant neo-Gothic style with a neo-Renaissance dome, was completed in 1902. Standing proudly on the Danube bank, visible from almost any riverside point, it has from the outset been one of Budapest's symbols, though until 1989, a democratically elected government had convened here only once (just after World War II, before the Communist takeover). The main cupola is decorated with statues of Hungarian kings. On either side of the cupola are waiting rooms leading into the respective houses of Parliament. The ceiling frescoes are by Károly Lotz, Hungary's best-known artist of that genre. Note the purportedly largest handmade carpet in Europe, from the small Hungarian village of Békésszentandrás. The Parliament is also home to the legendary crown jewels of St. Stephen, which were moved here from the National Museum in 2000.

V. Kossuth tér. © 1/441-4415. Admission (by guided tour only): 30-min. tour in English 1,700 Ft ($7.65), 800 Ft ($3.60) students. Tickets are available at Gate X, enter at Gate XII. Tours are given Mon–Fri 10am and 2pm (but not on days in which Parliament is in session, which is usually Tues–Wed); and on Sat at 4pm and Sun at 2pm. Metro: Kossuth tér (Red line).

CHURCHES & SYNAGOGUES

Bazilika (St. Stephen's Church)   It may not be a basilica in the technical sense of the word, but Hungarians like to call St. Stephen's "the Basilica" in honor of its sheer size: It's the largest church in the country. It took more than 50 years to build (the 1868 collapse of the dome caused significant delay) and was finally completed in 1906. Szent István Square, a once-sleepy square in front of the church, was recently converted into an elegant pedestrian-only zone. In the Chapel of the Holy Right (Szent Jobb Kápolna), you can see Hungarian Catholicism's most cherished—and bizarre—holy relic: the right hand of Hungary's first Christian king, Stephen I.

V. Szent István tér 33. © 1/317-2859. Church free; treasury 200 Ft (90¢); tower 400 Ft ($1.80). Church daily 7am–7pm, except during services; treasury daily 9am–5pm (10am–4pm in winter); Szent Jobb Chapel Mon–Sat 9am–5pm (10am–4pm in winter), Sun 1–5pm; tower Apr–Oct Mon–Sat 10am–6pm (closed Nov–Mar). Metro: Arany János utca (Blue line) or Bajcsy-Zsilinszky út (Yellow line).

Dohány Synagogue ★   Built in 1859, this is Europe's largest synagogue and the world's second-largest synagogue. Budapest's Jewish community still uses it. The architecture has striking Byzantine and Moorish elements; the interior is vast and ornate, with two balconies and the unusual presence of an organ. There's a Jewish museum next door devoted to the long history of Jews in Hungary. Displays include ritual and everyday artifacts.

VII. Dohány u. 2–8. © 1/342-8949. Admission 600 Ft ($2.70). Tues–Thurs 10am–5pm; Fri 10am–2pm; Sun 10am–2pm. Services are held Fri 6pm and Sat 9am. Metro: Astoria (Red line) or Deák tér (all lines).

Mátyás Templom (Matthias Church) ★★★   Officially named the Church of Our Lady, this symbol of Buda's Castle District is popularly known as Matthias Church after the 15th-century king who was twice married here. Though it dates from the mid–13th century, like other old churches in Budapest it has an interesting history of destruction and reconstruction, always being refashioned in the architectural style of the time. Organ concerts are held here every other Friday evening in July and August at 8pm. Daily Mass is held at 8:30am, 12:30pm, and 6pm; Sunday Mass at 8:30am, 9:30am, noon, and 6pm.

I. Szentháromság tér 2. ⓒ 1/355-5657. Admission 400 Ft ($1.80). Daily 9am–6pm. Bus: Várbusz from Moszkva tér or no. 16 from Deák tér Castle Hill. Funicular: From Clark Ádám tér to Castle Hill.

PARKS & PANORAMAS

Gellért Hegy (Gellért Hill), towering 230m (750 ft.) above the Danube, offers the city's single best panorama. It's named after the Italian Bishop Gellért, who assisted Hungary's first Christian king, Stephen I, in converting the Magyars. Gellért became a martyr when vengeful pagans, outraged at the forced and violent nature of Stephen's proselytizing, killed the bishop by rolling him in a barrel down the side of the hill on which his enormous statue now stands. On top of Gellért Hill you'll find the Liberation Monument, built in 1947 to commemorate the Red Army's liberation of Budapest from Nazi occupation. Also atop the hill is the Citadella, built by the Austrians shortly after they crushed the Hungarian War of Independence (1848–49). To get here, take bus no. 27 from Móricz Zsigmond körtér or hike up on any of the various paved pathways that originate at the base of the hill.

Margit-sziget (Margaret Island) ★★ has been a public park since 1908 (bus: 26 from Nyugati tér; tram: 4 or 6, which stop at the entrance to the island midway across the Margaret Bridge). The long, narrow island, connected to both Buda and Pest by the Margaret and Árpád bridges, is barred to most vehicular traffic. Facilities on the island include the Palatinus Strand open-air baths, which draw upon the famous thermal waters under Margaret Island; the Alfréd Hajós Sport Pool; and the Open-Air Theater. Sunbathers line the steep embankments along the river, and bicycles are available for rent. Despite its popularity, Margaret Island is a quiet, tranquil place.

Városliget (City Park) ★ is an equally popular place to spend a summer day (Metro: Hósök tere/Heroes' Square and Széchenyi Fürdó). Heroes' Square, at the end of Andrássy út, is the most logical starting point for a walk in City Park. The lake behind the square is used for boating in summer and ice-skating in winter. The park's Zoo Boulevard (Állatkerti körút), the favorite street of generations of Hungarian children, is where the **zoo,** the **circus,** and the **amusement park** are all found. **Gundel,** Budapest's most famous restaurant, is also here, as are the **Széchenyi Baths.**

Károly kert (Charles Garden) ★★★, a little enclosed park in the southern half of the Inner City (Metro: Astoria/Red line), houses Budapest's most charming playground. To enter the park, you must pass through a gigantic wrought-iron gate. The equipment here might not be as modern or as varied as that of some of the city's other playgrounds, but this place has a distinct old-world charm and its location in the Inner City makes it a convenient destination.

FOR KIDS

Vidám Park (Amusement Park) ★★★ *Kids* This is a must if you're traveling with kids, and two rides in particular aren't to be missed (even if you're not traveling with kids). The 100-year-old **Merry-Go-Round (Körhinta),** constructed almost entirely of wood, was recently restored to its original grandeur. Riders must actively pump to keep the horses rocking, and authentic Würlitzer music plays. The **Ferris wheel (Óriáskerék)** is also wonderful. A gangly bright-yellow structure, it rotates at a liltingly slow pace, gently lifting you high for a remarkable view. The Vidám Park also features Europe's longest wooden roller coaster.

XIV. Állatkerti krt. 14–16. (℮ 1/343-0996. Admission 300 Ft ($1.35) adults; free for children under 120cm tall (about 4 ft.); rides 150 Ft–600 Ft (70¢–$2.70); your best bet is to buy a stack of 20 tickets (plus 2 "free" extra tickets) on entry for 3,000 Ft ($14). Apr–Sept Mon–Fri 10am–7pm, Sat–Sun to 8pm; Oct–Mar Mon–Fri noon–6pm, Sat–Sun 10am–6:30pm. Metro: Széchenyi fürdő (Yellow line).

ORGANIZED TOURS

BUS & BOAT TOURS Ibusz (℮ 1/485-2700; fax 1/318-2805; www.ibusz.hu), with decades of experience, offers 11 different boat and bus tours, ranging from basic city tours to special folklore-oriented tours. Unfortunately, the tours are pretty sterile and boring, and we actually think you're better off taking a walking tour or a different boat tour (see below). Ibusz operates year-round, with an abbreviated schedule in the off season. All buses are air-conditioned, and all guides speak English. There's a free hotel pickup service that will pick you up 30 minutes before departure time. For a full list of tours, pick up the Ibusz *Budapest Sightseeing* catalog, available at all Ibusz offices, Tourinform, and most hotels.

A boat tour is a great way to absorb the scope and scale of the Hungarian capital, and a majority of the city's grand sights can be seen from the river. The Hungarian state company **MAHART,** V. Belgrád rakpart (℮ 1/318-1704 or 1/489-4013), operates daily sightseeing cruises on the Danube. Boats depart frequently from Vigadó tér on weekends and holidays in spring and every day in summer.

WALKING TOURS We recommend "The Absolute Walking Tour in Budapest" offered by a company called **Absolute Walking Tours** ★★ (℮ 06-30/ 211-8861; www.absolutetours.com). Tours last anywhere from 3½ to 5 hours, depending on the mood of the group, and take you throughout both central Pest and central Buda. **Budapest Walks** (℮ 1/340-4232) is another company offering walking tours. It features four tours: "Highlights of Pest," "Gems of Buda Castle," "Music Budapest," and "Fine Arts Museum and the City Park." For both of these companies, call for times and prices, and to find out where the tour begins.

THE SHOPPING SCENE

Year-round, shoppers fill the pedestrian-only street **Váci utca,** from the stately Vörösmarty tér, in the center of Pest, across the roaring busy street of Kossuth Lajos utca, all the way to Vámház krt (Yellow line). The **Castle District** in Buda, with many folk-art boutiques and galleries, is another popular area for souvenir hunters. Locals (and budget travelers) might window-shop in these two neighborhoods, but they do their serious shopping elsewhere. One popular street is Pest's **Nagykörút (Outer Ring);** another bustling shopping street is Pest's **Kossuth Lajos utca,** off the Erzsébet Bridge, and its continuation **Rákóczi út,** extending all the way out to Keleti Station. **Andrássy út,** from Deák tér to Oktogon, is also a popular, though much more upscale, shopping street.

BEST BUYS   Folkloric Objects Folklore objects are the most popular souvenirs among travelers visiting Budapest. A chain called **Folkart Háziipar** has shops (one is called Népművészeti bolt, another is called Háziipari bolt) that boast great selections of handmade goods at unbeatable prices. Popular items include pillowcases, pottery, porcelain, dolls, dresses, skirts, and sheepskin vests. The main store, **Folkart Centrum,** now relocated in the upper end of the mall, is at V. Váci u. 58 (© **1/318-5840**), and is open daily from 10am to 7pm (until 9pm July–Aug). One outstanding private shop on Váci utca is **Vali Folklór,** in the courtyard of V. Váci u. 23 (© **1/337-6301**). This cluttered shop is run by a soft-spoken man named Bálint Ács who travels the villages of Hungary and neighboring countries in search of authentic folk items. **Holló Folkart Gallery,** at V. Vitkovics Mihály u. 12 (© **1/317-8103**), is an unusual gallery selling hand-crafted reproductions of folk-art pieces from various regions of the country.

Porcelain & Pottery Porcelain, particularly from the country's two best-known producers, Herend and Zsolnay, is very popular. Although both brands are available in the West, you'll find a better selection here and prices are about 50% lower. You'll find world-renowned hand-painted Herend porcelain (www.herend.com), which was first produced in 1826 in the town of Herend near Veszprém in western Hungary, at the **Herend Shop,** V. József nádor tér 11 (© **1/317-2622**). This shop has the widest Herend selection in the capital, and can arrange overseas shipping. If the formal Herend porcelain isn't within your price range, you'll find lovely casual pottery at **Herend Village Pottery,** II. Fő utca 61 © **1/356-7899**). Delightfully gaudy Zsolnay porcelain from the southern city of Pécs is Hungary's second-most celebrated brand of porcelain; you'll find it at **Zsolnay Márkabolt,** V. Kígyó u. 4 (© **1/318-3712**).

Hungarian Foods Connoisseurs generally agree that **Pick Salami,** from the southeastern city of Szeged, is the best of the world-renowned Hungarian salamis (though some people have reported difficulty in clearing U.S. Customs with salami). Chestnut paste *(gesztenye püré),* found in a tin or a block wrapped in foil, is rare abroad and used primarily as a pastry filling, but it can also top desserts and ice cream. Paprika paste *(pirosarany)* is also hard to find outside Hungary; it comes in a bright-red tube in hot *(csípős),* deli-style *(csemege),* and sweet *(édes)* varieties. All of the items mentioned above can be found in grocery stores *(élelmiszer)* and delicatessens *(csemege).*

Hungarian Wines Fine, affordable Hungarian wines from the Szekszárd, Villány, Tokaj, and Eger regions are abundant. The most renowned red wines come from the region around Villány, a town to the south of Pécs by the Croatian border. The country's best white wines are generally believed to be those from the Lake Balaton region, though some Hungarians insist that white wines from the Sopron region (by the Austrian border) are better. *Tokaj* wines, especially *Szamorodni* and *Aszu*—both *száraz* (dry) or *édes* (sweet)—are popular as aperitifs and dessert wines.

MARKETS Budapest has a handful of **vásárcsarnok (vintage market halls),** wonders of steel and glass, built in the 1890s in the ambitious grandiose style of the time. Three are still in use and provide a measure of local color you won't find in the grocery store. The **Központi Vásárcsarnok (Central Market Hall),** on IX. Vámház körút, is the largest and most spectacular market hall. In the Inner Ring (Kiskörút), on the Pest side of the Szabadság Bridge, this tri-level hall was impeccably reconstructed in 1995. Other vintage market halls include the **Belvárosi Vásárcsarnok (Inner City Market Hall),** on V. Hold utca, behind Szabadság tér in central Pest; and the **Rákóczi téri Vásárcsarnok,** on VIII. Rákóczi tér. The **Fehérvári úti Vásárcsarnok,** at XI. Fehérvári út 22 (© **1/381-0355**), in front of the Buda Skála department store, is the latest classic food market in Budapest to be renovated. Some of the charm is lost, but such is progress. Another lively market is **Fény utca Piac,** on II. Fény utca, just off Moszkva tér in Buda.

BUDAPEST AFTER DARK

The most complete schedule of mainstream performing arts events is found in the free bimonthly *Koncert Kalendárium* at the Central Philharmonic Ticket Office in Vörösmarty tér. *Koncert Kalendárium* lists events in English. The *Budapest Sun* and the *Visitors' Guide* also have comprehensive events calendars.

Színházak Központi Jegyiroda (Central Theater Ticket Office), VI. Andrássy út 18 (© 1/267-1267; Metro: Opera), sells tickets to just about everything, from theater and operetta to sports events and rock concerts; it's open Monday through Friday from 10am to 6pm. For **classical performances,** go to the National Philharmonic Ticket Office (Filharmónia Nemzeti Jegyiroda), VII. Madách utca 3 (© 1/321-4199), open Monday through Thursday from 10am to 5:30pm, and Friday from 10am to 5pm. For **opera and ballet,** go to the Hungarian State Opera Ticket Office (Magyar Állami Opera Jegyiroda), VI. Andrássy út 20 (entrance inside the courtyard; © 1/332-7914; Metro: Opera), open Monday through Friday 11am to 5pm, or simply visit www.ticketexpress.hu. For events during the **Spring Festival,** go to the Festival Ticket Service, V. 1081 Rákóczi út 65 (© 1/486-3300; Metro: Blaha Lujza tér/Red line). For **rock and jazz concert** tickets, try Ticket Express, VI. Jókai u. 40 (© 1/353-0692; Metro: Opera/Yellow line).

THE PERFORMING ARTS

Completed in 1884, the **Magyar Állami Operaház (Hungarian State Opera House),** VI. Andrássy út 22 (© 1/331-2550; Metro: Opera), is Budapest's most famous performance hall and a tourist attraction in its own right. Hungarians adore opera, and a large percentage of seats are sold on a subscription basis; buy

---

Moments   Music for a Summer Evening

During the summer, you'll find several special places to enjoy classical music. Tickets for all summer-program venues are available at the **National Philharmonic Ticket Office,** VII. Madách utca 3 (© 1/321-4199), open Monday through Thursday 10am to 5:30pm and Friday 10am to 5pm.

The historic outdoor Dominican Courtyard, inside the Castle District's Hilton Hotel, I. Hess András tér 1–3 (© 1/488-6600; Metro: Moszkva tér, then bus "Várbusz"; or Deák tér, then bus no. 16), is the site of a series of classical recitals during the summer. The beautiful **Mátyás Templom (Matthias Church),** next door at I. Szentháromság tér 2, holds a regular Tuesday- and Friday-night series of organ concerts from June to September. Concerts start at 8pm. You can buy tickets at the National Philharmonic Ticket Office, during the day in the church (9am–7pm), or just before the performance on-site.

Organ concerts are also held Monday evenings at 7pm during July and August at **Bazilica (St. Stephen's Church),** Hungary's largest church, V. Szent István tér 33 (© 1/317-2859; Metro: Arany János utca or Bajcsy-Zsilinszky út). All tickets cost 1,200 Ft ($5.40) and can be purchased before the performance at the church entry or at the National Philharmonic Ticket Office.

your tickets a few days ahead, if possible. The box office is open Monday through Friday from 11am to 6pm. Ticket prices range from 600 Ft to 8,700 Ft ($2.70–$39).

The Nagyterem (Great Hall) of the **Zeneakadémia (Ferenc Liszt Academy of Music),** VI. Liszt Ferenc tér 8 (© **1/341-4788;** Metro: Oktogon), is the city's premier music hall. The academy has the best acoustics in the city. Box-office hours are from 2pm to show time on the day of performance. Tickets range from 1,000 Ft to 8,000 Ft ($4.50–$36).

LIVE MUSIC CLUBS

Because the club scene in Budapest is always changing, you'd be wise to check **Pesti Est** or **Visitors' Guide** (available in tourist offices and at newsstands) or ask a local for the latest club information.

Fat Mo's Music Club is *the* place to be, at V. Nyári Pál u. 11 (© **1/267-3199;** Metro: Kálvin tér/Blue line). Live jazz concerts start at 9pm and dancing starts at 11pm. The best night is definitely Monday, with Hot Jazz Band performing in the style of the 1920s and 1930s. Make sure you book a table if you wish to enjoy the superb food, including the best succulent steaks in town. The **Fél 10 Jazz Klub,** VIII. Baross u. 30 (no phone; Metro: Kálvin tér), features live jazz performances nightly, while techno-free dance parties get going in the wee hours from Thursday to Saturday. It's open Monday through Friday from noon to 4am and Saturday and Sunday from 7pm to 4am. **Old Man's,** VIII. Akácfa u. 13 (© **1/322-7645;** Metro: Blaha Luzja tér), is the place to take in the best jazz and blues in Hungary. Hobo, the legendary figure of Hungarian beat music since the late 1960s, regularly plays here with his blues band. This very hip spot is open daily from 3pm to 3am.

TRAFO, XI. Liliom u. 41 (© **1/215-1600;** tram: 4 or 6 to Üllöi út), is an old electric power station that has been renovated and transformed into a cultural center for young alternative artists. It hosts the hippest disco in town.

BARS

The **Irish Cat Pub,** V. Múzeum krt. 41 (© **1/266-4085;** Metro: Kálvin tér), is an Irish-style pub with Guinness on tap and a whiskey bar. It's a popular meeting place for expatriates and travelers, serving a full menu, and is open Monday through Saturday from 10am to 2am and Sunday from 5pm to 2am. **Morrison's Music Pub,** VI. Révay u. 25 (© **1/269-4060;** Metro: Opera), is a casual place packed by an almost-20-something crowd. There's a small dance floor, an eclectic variety of loud live music, and a number of beers on tap. It's open Monday through Saturday 8:30pm to 4am.

HUNGARIAN DANCE HOUSES

Recent years have seen the growth of an urban-centered folk revival movement known as the *táncház* (dance house). This interactive evening of **folk music** and **folk dancing,** held in community centers around town, is one of the best cultural experiences you can have in Hungary. The format usually consists of about an hour of dance-step instruction, followed by several hours of dancing accompanied by a live band, which might include some of Hungary's best folk musicians, in an authentic, casual atmosphere.

The leading Hungarian folk band, Muzsikás, hosts an excellent táncház for children every Thursday (except July–Aug) at 8pm at the **Marczibányi Square Cultural House (Marczibányi tér Művelődési Ház),** II. Marczibányi tér 5/a (© **1/212-0803**). The cost is 300 Ft ($1.35). **FMH Cultural House**

(Szakszervezetek Fővárosi Művelődési Ház), XI. Fehérvári út 47 (© **1/203-3868;** tram: 47 to Deák tér), hosts a táncház for kids every Tuesday (except July–Aug) from 5 to 6:30pm for 200 Ft (90¢). Folk bands that perform on traditional instruments play every Thursday or Friday evening, September through May, for 400 Ft ($1.80). The evening kicks off with a táncház hour at 7pm. Also at the FMH Cultural House, *csángó táncház,* the oldest and most authentic type of traditional Hungarian folk dance, is danced Friday or Saturday from 7 to 11pm, for 400 Ft ($1.80). On the first Saturday of each month, you can enjoy the best klezmer bands in town.

DAY TRIPS ALONG THE DANUBE BEND

The delightful towns along the Bend—Szentendre, Esztergom, and Visegrád—are easy day trips from Budapest. The great natural beauty of the area, with forested hills looming over the river, makes it a welcome departure for the city weary.

GETTING THERE By Boat & Hydrofoil From April to September, boats run between Budapest and the towns of the Danube Bend. All boats leave Budapest's Vigadó tér boat landing, which is located in Pest between Erzsébet Bridge and Szabadság Bridge, stopping to pick up passengers 5 minutes later at Buda's Batthyány tér landing, which is in Buda and is also a Red line metro stop, before continuing up the river.

Schedules and towns served are complicated, so contact **MAHART,** the state shipping company, at the Vigadó tér landing (© **1/318-1704;** www.mahart passnave.hu, click on the British flag) for information. You can also get MAHART information from Tourinform.

Round-trip prices are 1,330 Ft ($6) to Szentendre, 1,390 Ft ($6.25) to Visegrád, and 1,460 Ft ($6.60) to Esztergom. Children up to age 14 receive a 50% discount, and children under 4 can travel free if they don't require their own seats. The approximate travel time from Budapest is 2 hours to Szentendre, 3½ hours to Visegrád, and 5 hours to Esztergom. If time is tight, consider the train or bus (both of which are also considerably cheaper).

By Train To Szentendre: The HÉV suburban railroad connects Budapest's Batthyány tér with Szentendre. Trains leave daily, year-round, every 20 minutes or so from 4am to 11:30pm. One-way fare is 320 Ft ($1.45); subtract 125 Ft (55¢) if you have a valid Budapest public transportation pass. The trip takes 45 minutes.

To Visegrád: There's no direct train service to Visegrád. Instead, take the train departing from Nyugati Station to Nagymaros. The trip takes 1 hour, and there are 20 daily trains. From Nagymaros, take a **ferry** (RÉV, © **06/80/ 406-611**) across the river to Visegrád. The ferry dock is a 5-minute walk from the train station. A ferry leaves every hour throughout the day. The train ticket to Nagymaros costs 436 Ft ($1.95); the ferry ticket to Visegrád costs 200 Ft (90¢).

To Esztergom: Seventeen trains daily make the run between Budapest's Nyugati Station and Esztergom. The trip takes about 1¼ hours. Train tickets cost 436 Ft ($1.95).

SZENTENDRE Occupied in medieval times by Serbian settlers, Szentendre (pronounced *Sen*-ten-dreh), 21km (13 miles) north of Budapest, counts half a dozen Serbian churches among its rich collection of historical buildings. Since the turn of the 20th century, Szentendre has been home to an artist's colony and has a wealth of museums and galleries. The town is an extremely popular destination.

Visitor Information One of Szentendre's information offices, **Tourinform,** is at Dumtsa Jenő u. 22 (℃ **26/317-965**), with maps of Szentendre (and the Danube Bend region), as well as concert and exhibition schedules. The office can also provide accommodations information. The office is open April through October Monday to Friday from 9am to 7pm, and weekends from 9am to 2pm; the office is closed on weekends in the off season but is open weekdays from 9am to 5pm. **The Ibusz** office is located on the corner of Bogdányi út and Gőzhajó utca (℃ **26/310-181**) and is open April to October Monday through Friday from 9am to 5pm and weekends 10am to 2pm. From November to March, it's open weekdays only, 9am to 4pm. Another good source of information, particularly if you are planning to stay in the region more than a day, is **Jági Utazás,** at Kucsera F. u. 15 (℃ and fax **26/310-030**).

Exploring the Museums & Churches The **Margit Kovács Museum** ★★★, Vastagh György u. 1 (℃ **26/310-244**), is a must-see, displaying the exceptional and highly original work of Hungary's best-known ceramic artist. Her sculptures of elderly women and friezes of village life are particularly moving. The museum is open April through October Tuesday through Sunday from 9am to 5pm (Nov–Mar 10am–4pm). Admission is 600 Ft ($2.70). The Serbian Orthodox **Blagovestenska church** at Fő tér 4 dates from 1752. A rococo iconostasis features paintings by Mihailo Zivkovic—notice that the eyes of all the icons are on you. Next door at Fő tér 6 (℃ **26/310-244**) is the **Ferenczy Museum** ★★, dedicated to the art of the prodigious Ferenczy family. The paintings of Károly Ferenczy, one of Hungary's leading Impressionists, are featured. It's open Wednesday through Sunday 10am to 5pm. The **Ámos and Anna Muzeum,** Bogdány u. 10 (℃ **26/310-790**), was the former home of artist couple Imre Ámos and Margit Anna, whose work represents the beginning of expressionist painting in Hungary. This is Szentendre's best-kept secret. It's open daily 10am to 6pm (in winter 1–5pm), and admission is 500 Ft ($2.25).

Where to Dine If you get hungry, **Aranysárkány Vendéglő (Golden Dragon Inn)** ★, Alkotmány u. 1/a (℃ **26/301-479**), just east of Fő tér on Hunyadi utca, is always crowded, often with locals (definitely a good sign in a tourist town like Szentendre). Choose from such enticing offerings as alpine lamb, roast leg of goose, spinach cream, and venison ragout. A very tasty vegetarian plate is also offered. Various traditional Hungarian beers are on draft. If you walk directly south from Fő tér, you'll find **Régimódi,** Futó u. 3 (℃ **26/311-105**). This elegant restaurant is in a former private home and serves Hungarian specialties, with an emphasis on game dishes. Be sure to stop at the **Nosztalgia Café in the Dobos Museum** ★, Bogdányi u. 2, for a slice of authentic *dobos torta,* a sumptuously rich layer cake named after pastry chef József Dobos, who experimented with butter frostings in the 19th century, and was appointed the Hapsburg emperor's official baker because of his success.

VISEGRÁD Halfway between Szentendre and Esztergom, Visegrád (pronounced *Vee*-sheh-grod) is a sparsely populated, sleepy riverside village, which makes its history all the more fascinating and hard to believe: The Romans built a fort here, which was still standing when Slovak settlers gave the town its present name (meaning "High Castle") in the 9th or 10th century. After the Mongol invasion (1241–42), construction began on both the present ruined hilltop citadel and the former riverside palace. Eventually, Visegrád boasted one of the finest royal palaces ever built in Hungary. Only one king, Charles Robert (1307–42), actually used it as his primary residence, but monarchs from Béla IV,

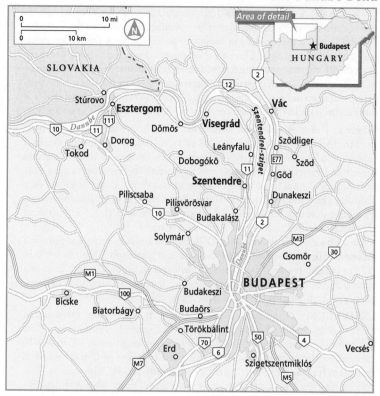

in the 13th century, through Matthias Corvinus, in the late 15th century, spent time in Visegrád and contributed to its development, the latter expanding the palace into a great Renaissance center known throughout Europe.

Visitor Information   **Visegrád Tours,** RÉV u. 15 (② **26/398-160**), is located across the road from the RÉV ferryboat landing (not to be confused with the MAHART boat landing, just down the road). It is open April through October, daily from 9am to 6pm; November through March, weekdays from 10am to 4pm.

Each summer on the second weekend in July, Visegrád hosts the **International Palace Tournament,** an authentic medieval festival replete with dueling knights on horseback, early music, and dance. If you cannot make it to this fabulous event, you can enjoy a tournament on a smaller scale combined with a medieval dinner at 6pm on Thursdays in July and August, at the Renaissance Restaurant (see below). For information, contact Visegrád Tours (see above).

Exploring the Palace & the Citadel   The **Royal Palace** covered much of the area where the MAHART boat landing and Fő utca (Main St.) are now found. Indeed, the entrance to its open-air ruins, called the **King Matthias Museum** ★★, is at Fő u. 27 (② **26/398-026**). Admission is 400 Ft ($1.80). The museum is open Tuesday through Sunday from 9am to 4:30pm. The buried ruins of the palace, having achieved a near-mythical status, were not discovered until this century. Almost all of what you see is the result of ongoing reconstruction, which has been rigorous in recent years. Because of the under-construction aspect of the place, you need to keep a close eye on the kids here.

The **Citadel** ✫✫✫ (© **26/398-101**), on the hilltop above Visegrád, affords one of the finest views you'll find over the Danube. Admission to the Citadel is 400 Ft ($1.80). It is open daily in summer 9am to 6pm, in winter on weekends only from 9:30am to 6pm. There are three buses a day to the Citadel, departing from the RÉV ferryboat terminal at 9:26am, 12:26pm, and 3:26pm. Otherwise, "City Bus," a van taxi that awaits passengers outside Visegrád Tours, takes people up the steep hill for the steep fare of 2,500 Ft ($11) apiece. Note that it is not a casual walk to the Citadel; consider it a day hike and pack accordingly.

Where to Dine   **Renaissance Restaurant,** at Fő u. 11, across the street from the MAHART boat landing (© **26/398-081**), specializes in authentic medieval cuisine. Food is served in clay crockery without silverware (only a wooden spoon), and guests are offered paper crowns to wear. The restaurant is open daily from noon to 10pm. If you're big on the medieval theme, come for dinner on a Thursday (July–Aug), when a six-course "Royal Feast" is celebrated following a 45-minute duel between knights. No vegetarians, please! Tickets for this special evening are handled by Visegrád Tours (see above).

Don Vito Pizzeria ✫, Fő u. 83 (© **26/397-230**), serves very good pizza in a pleasant, relaxed atmosphere. Individual pan-size pizzas cost 600 Ft to 1,400 Ft ($2.70–$6.30). Try the "Don Vito," a delicious mushroom, goose-liver, and apple pizza; or the equally tempting "Albino," a vegetarian pizza with a ricotta, garlic, and herb topping. Beer and wine are served.

ESZTERGOM   Formerly a Roman settlement, Esztergom (pronounced *Ess*-tair-gome), 46km (29 miles) northwest of Budapest, was the seat of the Hungarian kingdom for 300 years. Hungary's first king, István I (Stephen I), crowned by the pope in A.D. 1000, converted Hungary to Catholicism, and Esztergom became the country's center of the early church. Although its glory days are long gone, the quiet town remains the seat of the archbishop-primate— the "Hungarian Rome."

Visitor Information   **Gran Tours,** Széchenyi tér 25 (© **33/502-001**), is the best source of information. Summer hours are Monday through Friday from 8am to 4pm and Saturday from 9am to noon; winter hours are Monday through Friday from 8am to 4pm.

Exploring the Town   The massive, neoclassical **Esztergom Cathedral** (© **33/411-895**), in Szent István tér on Castle Hill, is Esztergom's most popular attraction and one of Hungary's most impressive buildings. It was built in the last century to replace the cathedral ruined during the Turkish occupation. The cathedral **Kincstár (Treasury)** ✫ contains a stunning array of ecclesiastical jewels and gold works. Since Cardinal Mindszenty's body was moved to the crypt in 1991 (he died in exile in 1975), it has been a place of pilgrimage for Hungarians. If you brave the ascent of the cupola, you'll be rewarded at the top with unparalleled views of Esztergom and the surrounding Hungarian and Slovak countryside. The cathedral, treasury, crypt, and cupola are open daily in summer from 9am to 6pm, winter daily 11 am to 4pm (the cathedral itself is closed Jan–Feb). Admission to the cathedral and the crypt are free, but it costs 350 Ft ($1.60) to see the treasury and 250 Ft ($1.10) to see the cupola.

It's definitely worthwhile to take a break from the crowds at the cathedral and stroll through the quiet cobblestone streets of **Víziváros (Watertown).** There you'll find the **Keresztény Múzeum (Christian Museum),** Mindszenty tér 2 (© **33/413-880**), in the neoclassical former primate's palace. It houses Hungary's largest collection of religious art and the largest collection of medieval art outside the National Gallery. Hours are Tuesday through Sunday from 10am to 6pm (closed Jan–Feb), and admission is 350 Ft ($1.60).

Where to Dine   The food at **Szalma Csárda** ★★★, Nagy-Duna sétány 2 (© **33/315-336**), is absolutely first-rate, with everything made to order and served piping hot. The excellent house soups—fish soup *(halászlé)*, goulash *(gulyásleves)*, and bean soup *(babgulyás)*—constitute meals in themselves. It's open daily from noon to 10pm in summer, and Monday through Friday noon to 8pm and Saturday and Sunday 10am to 10pm in winter. They don't accept credit cards.

10

Ireland

by Suzanne Rowan Kelleher

Which Ireland do you imagine in your mind's eye? The Emerald Isle of thatched cottages, craggy seascapes, and pubs that smell of polished mahogany and Guinness? Or do you imagine the hip, urban country of trendy bistros, sushi bars, and modern-art galleries? Truth is, you can find plenty of both in today's Ireland.

Old Ireland lingers and, to be sure, the country remains a land of breathtaking beauty, whose people possess more than their share of wit and welcoming charm. But today's Ireland is no longer a poor, ramshackle cousin to wealthy European nations. The 1990s heralded an economic boom known as the "Celtic Tiger," a renaissance that has made the country richer, more self-confident, and more sophisticated than before.

Though the pace of that boom has slowed of late, Ireland remains one of the most prosperous and savvy spots in Europe. Unfortunately, it's also now one of the priciest. Inflation is the dark cloud behind the Celtic Tiger's silver lining. But regardless of whether you're looking for the old or new Ireland, you'll be joining six million annual visitors, many of whom come a long way to see it for themselves.

1 Dublin

"Seedy elegance" may have aptly described much, if not most, of Dublin until the mid-1990s, when the city's transformation from endearingly frumpy to cutting-edge cool began. The change was remarkably swift: In 1997 *Fortune* magazine named Dublin the number one European city in which to do business—an accolade fueled, no doubt, by its reputation as the "Silicon Valley" of Europe and strategic Euro-headquarters for computer giants like Microsoft, Dell, Intel, and Sun Microsystems. Then, in 1998, Dublin became the fifth-most-visited city in Europe—nudging ahead of traditional tourist powerhouses like Rome and Amsterdam. More recently, in 2000 an annual survey of world cities ranked Dublin among the world's top-10 most livable cities—above New York, Boston, and Washington, D.C.

Unsurprisingly, the actor Colin Farrell never misses an opportunity to proclaim that his hometown is a great place to visit, and he's often seen around town between movie shoots. The River Liffey may never be potable, but otherwise the sky seems to be the limit here. New hotels and restaurants continue to sprout up in the race to keep up with demand. Dublin is "ground zero" for the new Ireland, the lair of the "Celtic Tiger," and uncontestably the hottest spot on the island.

ESSENTIALS

GETTING THERE   By Plane   Dublin International Airport (© **01/814-1111;** www.dublin-airport.com) is 11km (6¾ miles) north of the city center. A travel information desk located in the Arrivals Concourse provides information on public bus and rail services throughout the country.

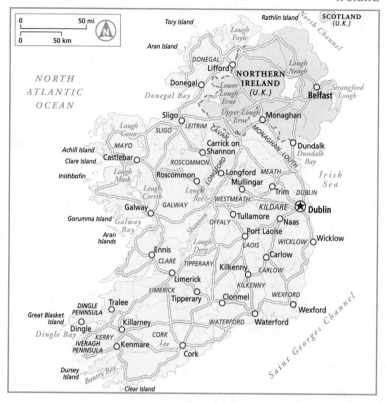

An excellent airport-to-city bus service called **AirCoach** operates 24 hours a day, making runs at 15-minute intervals. AirCoach runs direct from the airport to Dublin's city center and south side, servicing O'Connell Street, St. Stephen's Green, Fitzwilliam Square, Merrion Square, Ballsbridge, and Donnybrook—that is, all the key hotel and business districts. The one-way fare is €6 ($6.90) (round-trip costs €12/$14); you buy your ticket from the driver. AirCoach is more expensive than the Dublin Bus (see below), but it is faster because it makes fewer intermediary stops and brings you right into the hotel districts. To confirm AirCoach departures and arrivals, call 🕾 **01/844-7118** or find it on the Web at **www.aircoach.ie**.

If you need to connect with the Irish bus or rail service, the **Airlink Express Coach** (🕾 **01/873-4222;** www.dublinbus.ie) provides express coach service from the airport to the city's central bus station, **Busaras,** on Store Street, and on to the two main rail stations, **Connolly** and **Heuston.** Service runs daily from 7am until 11pm (till 8:30pm Sun), with departures every 20 to 30 minutes. The one-way fare is €5 ($5.75) for adults and €2 ($2.30) for children under age 12.

Finally, the main **Dublin Bus** (🕾 **01/873-4222;** www.dublinbus.ie) service runs several routes between the airport and the city center from 6am to 11:30pm. The one-way trip takes about 30 minutes, and the fare is €5 ($5.75). Numbers 16a, 33, 41, 41a, 41b, 41c, 46x, 58x, 746, 747, and 748 all serve the city center from Dublin Airport.

Dublin

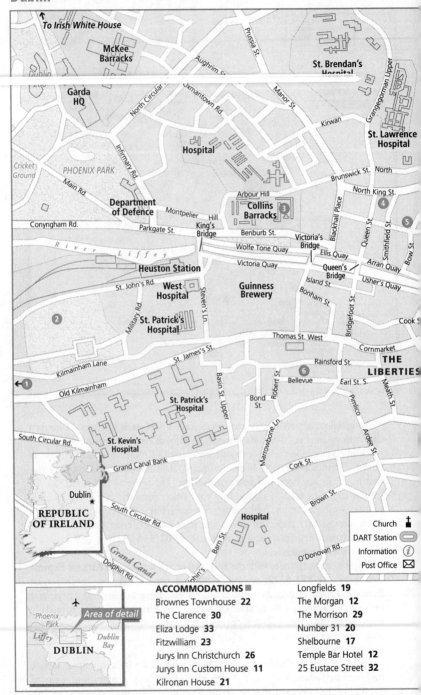

To Irish White House

McKee Barracks

Dublin Zoo

Garda HQ

Prussia St.

Aughrim St.

North Circular

Oxmantown Rd.

Manor St.

St. Brendan's Hospital

Grangegorman Upper

Kirwan

St. Lawrence Hospital

Cricket Ground

PHOENIX PARK

Main Rd.

Infirmary Rd.

Hospital

Brunswick St. North

North King St. ④

⑤

Arbour Hill

Collins Barracks ③

Blackhall Place

Queen St.

Smithfield St.

Bow St.

Department of Defence

Montpelier Hill

King's Bridge

Benburb St.

Victoria's Bridge

Ellis Quay

Arran Quay

Conyngham Rd.

Parkgate St.

Wolfe Tone Quay

Queen's Bridge

Usher's Quay

River Liffey

Victoria Quay

Island St.

Heuston Station

St. John's Rd.

West Hospital

Steven's Ln.

Guinness Brewery

Bonham St.

Bridgefoot St.

Cook St

②

Military Rd.

St. Patrick's Hospital

Thomas St. West

Cornmarket

THE LIBERTIES

Kilmainham Lane

St. James's St.

Rainsford St.

⑥

Bellevue

Earl St. S.

Meath St.

←①

Old Kilmainham

Basin St. Upper

Bond St.

Robert St.

Pimlico

Ardee St.

South Circular Rd.

St. Patrick's Hospital

Marrowbone Ln.

Cork St.

St. Kevin's Hospital

Grand Canal Bank

Dublin ★

REPUBLIC OF IRELAND

South Circular Rd.

Brown St.

Hospital

Barn St.

O'Donovan Rd.

Grand Canal

Dolphin Rd.

Church ✝
DART Station 🚉
Information ⓘ
Post Office ✉

ACCOMMODATIONS ■

Brownes Townhouse **22**
The Clarence **30**
Eliza Lodge **33**
Fitzwilliam **23**
Jurys Inn Christchurch **26**
Jurys Inn Custom House **11**
Kilronan House **21**

Longfields **19**
The Morgan **12**
The Morrison **29**
Number 31 **20**
Shelbourne **17**
Temple Bar Hotel **12**
25 Eustace Street **32**

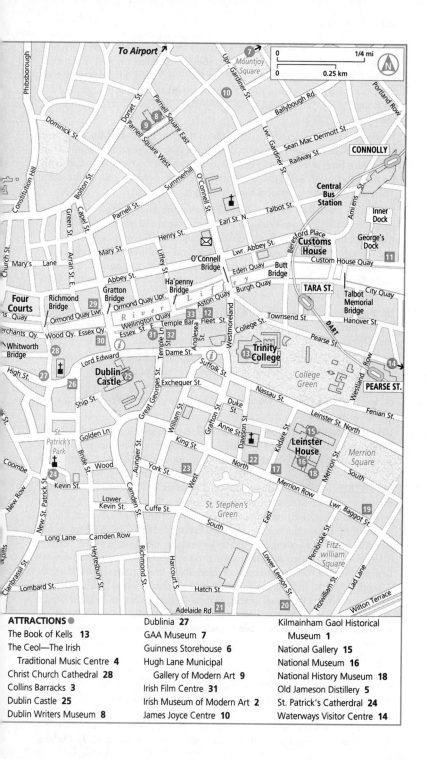

ATTRACTIONS ●

The Book of Kells **13**
The Ceol—The Irish
    Traditional Music Centre **4**
Christ Church Cathedral **28**
Collins Barracks **3**
Dublin Castle **25**
Dublin Writers Museum **8**

Dublinia **27**
GAA Museum **7**
Guinness Storehouse **6**
Hugh Lane Municipal
    Gallery of Modern Art **9**
Irish Film Centre **31**
Irish Museum of Modern Art **2**
James Joyce Centre **10**

Kilmainham Gaol Historical
    Museum **1**
National Gallery **15**
National Museum **16**
National History Museum **18**
Old Jameson Distillery **5**
St. Patrick's Cathedral **24**
Waterways Visitor Centre **14**

581

For speed and ease—especially if you have a lot of luggage—a **taxi** is the best way to get directly to your hotel or guesthouse. Depending on your destination in Dublin, fares average between €15 and €20 ($17–$23). Depending on traffic, a cab should take from 20 to 45 minutes to get into the city center. A 10% tip is standard. Taxis are lined up on a first-come, first-served taxi stand outside the arrivals terminal.

By Ferry   Passenger/car ferries from Britain arrive at the **Dublin Ferryport** (© **01/855-2222**), on the eastern end of the North Docks; and at the **Dun Laoghaire Ferryport,** about 16km (10 miles) south of the city center. Call **Irish Ferries** (© **01/661-0511;** www.irishferries.ie) for bookings and information. There are bus and taxi services from both ports.

By Train   Irish Rail (© **01/836-6222;** www.irishrail.ie) operates daily train service into Dublin from Belfast in Northern Ireland and all major cities in the Irish Republic, including Cork, Galway, Limerick, Killarney, Sligo, Wexford, and Waterford. Trains from the south, west, and southwest arrive at **Heuston Station,** Kingsbridge, off St. John's Road; from the north and northwest at **Connolly Station,** Amiens Street; and from the southeast at **Pearse Station,** Westland Row, Tara Street.

By Bus   Bus Eireann (© **01/836-6111;** www.buseireann.ie) operates daily express coach and local bus services from all major cities and towns in Ireland into Dublin's central bus station, Busaras, on Store Street.

By Car   If you are arriving by car from other parts of Ireland or via car ferry from Britain, all main roads lead into the heart of Dublin and are well signposted to An Lar (City Centre). To bypass the city center, the East Link (toll bridge €1.50/$1.75) and West Link are signposted, and the M50 circuits the city on three sides.

VISITOR INFORMATION   Tourist Offices   Dublin Tourism (© **01/605-7700;** www.visitdublin.com) operates six year-round walk-in visitor centers in greater Dublin. The principal center is in the former Church of St. Andrew, on Suffolk Street, Dublin 2, open June through August Monday through Saturday from 8:30am to 6:30pm, Sunday and bank holidays from 10:30am to 3pm, and the rest of the year Monday through Saturday from 9am to 5:30pm. For accommodations reservations throughout Ireland by credit card, contact Dublin Tourism; for other information call **Bord Failte** (© **1850/230330** from within Ireland; www.travel.ireland.ie). Other services at the Suffolk Street Dublin Tourism office include a currency-exchange counter, an American Express services desk, a car-rental counter, bus and rail information desks, a gift shop, and a cafe. The other five Dublin Tourism centers are at the Arrivals Hall of **Dublin Airport;** Exclusively Irish, **O'Connell Street,** Dublin 1; **Baggot Street Bridge,** Baggot Street, Dublin 2; **The Square Towncentre,** Tallaght, Dublin 24; and the new ferry terminal, **Dun Laoghaire Harbor** (all telephone inquiries should be directed to the number listed above). All centers are open year-round with at least the following hours: Monday through Friday from 10am to 5pm.

In addition, an independent center offers details on concerts, exhibits, and other arts events in the **Temple Bar** section at 18 Eustace St., Temple Bar, Dublin 2 (© **01/677-2255;** www.temple-bar.ie), open year-round Monday through Friday from 9:30am to 5:30pm, and Saturday from 10am to 5pm.

At any of these centers you can pick up the free *Tourism News* or the free *Event Guide,* a biweekly entertainment guide (www.eventguide.ie). *In Dublin,* a biweekly arts-and-entertainment magazine selling for €3.70 ($4.25), is available at most newsstands.

Websites   Your first stop should be **Dublin Tourism**'s **www.visitdublin.com**. To tap into a nearly overwhelming breadth of listings, try **www.goireland.com**, which offers more than 11,000 lodging listings (many with pictures) and thousands of restaurants (some with menus), although in some cases the info is pretty thin. Use the well-designed **www.ireland.travel.ie** for tips on getting around, places to stay, and things to do. Visit **www.shamrock.org** to learn about package vacations and find some special deals, such as off-peak fares on Aer Lingus.

CITY LAYOUT   Compared with other European capitals, Dublin is a relatively small metropolis; it's easy to get to know and easily traversed. The city center—identified in Irish as An Lar—is bisected by the River Liffey flowing west to east into Dublin Bay, with 15 bridges linking the north and south banks. Canals ring the city center; the Royal Canal forms a skirt through the north half, and the Grand Canal the south half. True Dubliners, it is said, live between the two canals. North-side suburbs include Drumcondra, Glasnevin, Howth, Clontarf, and Malahide. Southside suburbs include Ballsbridge, Blackrock, Dun Laoghaire, Dalkey, Killiney, Rathgar, and Rathmines.

GETTING AROUND   By Bus   Dublin Bus operates a fleet of green double-decker buses, frequent single-deck buses, and minibuses (called "imps") throughout the city and its suburbs. Most buses originate on or near **O'Connell Street, Abbey Street,** or **Eden Quay** on the north side, and from **Aston Quay, College Street,** or **Fleet Street** on the south side. Destinations and bus numbers are posted above the front windows; buses destined for the city center are marked with the Irish Gaelic words **An Lar.**

Bus service runs daily throughout the city, starting around 6am (10am on Sun), with the last bus at 11:30pm on most routes; on Thursday, Friday, and Saturday nights, the NiteLink service from city center to the suburbs extends bus hours to 3am. Schedules are posted on revolving notice boards at each bus stop. City bus fares are calculated on the distances traveled and run from a base fare of €.85 ($1) to €1.75 ($2). The NiteLink fare is a flat €4 ($4.60). Tickets should be purchased from a ticket machine as you enter the bus; exact change is welcomed but not required on most buses, but only coins are accepted. One-day, 4-day, and weekly passes are available at reduced rates. For more information, contact **Dublin Bus,** 59 Upper O'Connell St. (© **01/872-1000;** www.dublinbus.ie).

By DART   Although Dublin has no subway in the strict sense, there is an electrified-train rapid-transit system, known as the **DART (Dublin Area Rapid Transit),** Pearse Station, Dublin 2 (© **01/836-6222;** www.irishrail.ie). It links the city-center stations at **Connolly Station, Tara Street, Pearse Street,** and **Amiens Street** with suburbs and seaside communities as far as Balbriggan to the north and Greystones to the south. Service operates roughly every 10 to 20 minutes Monday through Saturday from 7am to midnight and Sunday from 9:30am to 11pm. The minimum fare is €1.25 ($1.45). One-day, 4-day, and weekly passes, as well as family tickets, are available at reduced rates.

By Tram   The newest addition to Dublin's public transportation network is the sleek light-rail tram known as **LUAS,** due for completion at the end of 2004 and the answer, many hope, to Dublin's congestion problems. Traveling at a maximum speed of 70kmph (45 mph) and departing every 5 minutes in peak hours, LUAS brings the city's transportation into the 21st century. Three lines will link the city center at **Connolly Station** and **St. Stephen's Green** with the suburbs of Tallaght in the southwest and Dundrum and Sandyford to the south. Fares were not yet set at press time. For more information, contact **LUAS** (✆ **01/703-2029;** www.luas.ie).

By Taxi It's very difficult to hail a taxi on the street; instead, taxis line up at stands located outside all the leading hotels, at bus and train stations, and on prime thoroughfares such as Upper O'Connell Street, College Green, and the north side of St. Stephen's Green. You can also phone for a taxi. Some of the companies that operate a 24-hour radio-call service are **Co-Op** (✆ **01/676-6666**), **Shamrock Radio Cabs** (✆ **01/855-5444**), and **VIP Taxis** (✆ **01/478-3333**). (If you need a wake-up call, VIP even offers that service, along with especially courteous dependability.) Taxi rates are fixed by law and posted in each taxi. The minimum fare in central Dublin is €2.75 ($3.15) for the first .9km (½ mile); after that, it's €.15 for each additional .2km (⅕ mile). There's an additional charge for each extra passenger and for each suitcase of €.50 (60 ¢), up to a maximum of two pieces of luggage. It costs an extra €1.50 ($1.75) for a dispatched pick-up. Some hotel or guesthouse staff, when asked to arrange for a taxi, tack on as much as €5 ($5.75) for their services, although this practice violates city taxi regulations.

By Bicycle Riding a bike in Dublin isn't recommended. Traffic is very heavy, the streets are narrow, and pedestrians crowd every corner. For those determined to take to the streets on wheels, bicycle rental averages €20 ($23) per day, €70 ($81) per week, with a €65 ($75) deposit. In the downtown area, bicycles can be rented from **Raleigh Ireland,** Kylemore Road, Dublin 10 (✆ **01/626-1333;** Raleigh@iol.ie).

By Car Unless you plan to do a lot of driving from Dublin to neighboring counties, it's not practical or affordable to rent a car. In fact, getting around the city and its environs is much easier without a car. If you must drive in Dublin, remember to keep to the *left-hand side of the road,* and don't drive in bus lanes. The most reliable and safest places to park are at surface parking lots or in multistory car parks in central locations, such as Kildare Street, Lower Abbey Street, Marlborough Street, and St. Stephen's Green West. The speed limit in the city is 46kmph (30 mph), and seat belts must be worn at all times by driver and passengers.

By Foot Small and compact, Dublin is ideal for walking, but be careful to look right and then left for oncoming traffic and to obey traffic signals. Each traffic light has timed WALK/DON'T WALK signals for pedestrians. Pedestrians have the right of way at specially marked, zebra-striped crossings; as a warning, there are usually two flashing lights at these intersections. For walking-tour suggestions, see "Organized Tours," under "Seeing the Sights," later in this chapter.

FAST FACTS: Dublin

American Express The Dublin office offers currency exchange, traveler's checks, and (for members) mail-holding. It's located opposite the Dublin Tourism Office, formerly the Church of St. Andrew, on Suffolk Street (✆ **01/605-7709**). In an emergency, traveler's checks can be reported lost or stolen by dialing toll-free ✆ **1890/706706.**

Business Hours Nearly all banks are open Monday through Friday from 10am to 4pm (to 5pm Thurs) and have ATMs that accept Cirrus network cards as well as MasterCard and Visa. **Post offices** (known as **An Post**) are open from 9am to 5:30pm Monday through Friday and from 9am to 1:30pm Saturday. The GPO on O'Connell Street is open from 8am to 8pm Monday through Saturday, and from 10:30am to 6:30pm Sunday (for stamps only). **Museums** and **attractions** are generally open from 10am to 5pm Tuesday through Saturday, and from 2 to 5pm Sunday. **Shops** generally open from 9am to 6pm, Monday through Friday, with late openings on Thursday until 7pm or 8pm. In the city center, most department stores and many shops are open from noon to 6pm Sunday.

Currency The official currency of Ireland is the **euro** (€). At press time, the rate of exchange (and the rate used in this chapter) was $1 = 87p (or €1 = $1.15).

Currency Exchange Currency-exchange services, signposted as BUREAU DE CHANGE, are in all banks and at many branches of the Irish post office system, known as **An Post.** A bureau de change operates daily during flight arrival and departure times at Dublin airport; a foreign currency note-exchanger machine is also available on a 24-hour basis in the main arrivals hall. Some hotels and travel agencies offer bureau de change services, although the best rate of exchange usually results when you use your bank card at an ATM.

Dentist & Doctor For medical or dental emergencies, contact the **Eastern Health Board Headquarters,** Dr. Steevens Hospital, Dublin 8 (© 01/679-0700), or try **Molesworth Clinic,** 2 Molesworth Place, Dublin 2 (© 01/661-5544). See also "Dental Surgeons" in the Golden Pages (Yellow Pages) of the telephone book. The American Embassy (see "Embassies," below) can provide a list of dentists in the city and surrounding areas. Expect to be charged upfront for services.

Drugstores Centrally located drugstores, known locally as pharmacies or chemist shops, include **Hamilton Long & Co.,** 5 Lower O'Connell St. (© 01/874-8456); and **Dame Street Pharmacy,** 16 Dame St., Dublin 2 (© 01/670-4523). A late-night chemist shop is **Byrne's Pharmacy,** 4 Merrion Rd., Dublin 4 (© 01/668-3287). It closes at 9pm on weekdays, 6pm on Saturday, and 1pm on Sunday.

Embassies The embassy of the **United States** is at 42 Elgin Rd., Ballsbridge, Dublin 4 (© 01/668-8777); the embassy of **Canada** is at 65/68 St. Stephen's Green, Dublin 2 (© 01/417-4100); the embassy of the **United Kingdom** is at 29 Merrion Rd., Dublin 2 (© 01/205-3700); and the embassy of **Australia** is at Fitzwilton House, Wilton Terrace, Dublin 2 (© 01/676-1517). Call for hours.

Emergencies For the **Garda** (police), fire, or other emergencies, dial © **999.**

Hospitals For emergency care, two of the most modern health-care facilities are **St. Vincent's Hospital,** Elm Park (© 01/269-4533), on the south side of the city; and **Beaumont Hospital,** Beaumont Road, Dublin 9 (© 01/837-7755 or 01/809-3000), on the north side.

Internet Access In cyber-savvy Dublin, public access terminals are no longer hard to find, appearing in shopping malls, hotels, and hostels throughout the city center. Like all of Dublin's public libraries, the **Central**

Library, in the ILAC Centre, off Henry Street, Dublin 1 (✆ **01/873-4333**), has a bank of PCs with free Internet access. Three centrally located cyber-cafes are the **Central Cybercafe**, 6 Grafton St., Dublin 2 (✆ **677-8298**), **Planet Cyber Café**, 13 St. Andrews St., Dublin 2 (✆ **01/670-5182**), and **The Connect Point**, 33 Dorset St. Lower, Dublin 1 (✆ 01/834-9821). A half-hour online averages €3.50 ($4).

Post Office The **General Post Office (GPO)** is located on O'Connell Street, Dublin 1 (✆ **01/705-7000**). Hours are Monday through Saturday from 8am to 8pm, Sunday and holidays from 10:30am to 6:30pm. Branch offices, identified by the sign OIFIG AN POST/POST OFFICE, are open Monday through Friday from 9am to 5:30pm and Saturday from 9am to 1:30pm.

Taxes Sales tax is called VAT (value-added tax) and is often already included in the price quoted to you or shown on price tags. VAT rates vary—for hotels, restaurants, and car rentals, it's 13.5%; for souvenirs and gifts, it's 21%. If you're not a citizen of an EU country, you're entitled to have this money refunded. You can get your money back through **Global Refund** (✆ **800/566-9828**; www.globalrefund.ie), the world's largest pri-vate company offering VAT refunds. If a shop isn't part of the Global Refund network, get a full receipt at the time of purchase that shows the shop's name, address, and VAT paid. When you're ready to depart Ireland, go to the Customs office at the airport or ferry port and have your receipts stamped; then send the stamped receipts back to the store where you made your purchase, which will then mail you a VAT refund check.

Telephone The **country code** for the Republic of Ireland is **353**. The **city code** for Dublin is **01**. If you're calling from outside Ireland, drop the ini-tial 0 (zero) from the city code. Thus, to call from the United States, you would dial ✆ 011-353-1, followed by the 7-digit local number. For direct-dial calls to the United States, dial the international access code (**00** from Ireland), and then the U.S. country code (**1**), followed by area code and number. To place a collect call to the United States from Ireland, dial ✆ **1-800/550-000** for USA Direct service. The toll-free international access codes are: **AT&T** ✆ **1-800-550-000**, **Sprint** ✆ **1-800-552-001**, and **MCI** ✆ **1-800-551-001**.

Local calls from a phone booth require a **Callcard,** a prepaid computer-ized card that you insert into the phone instead of coins. Callcards can be purchased in a range of denominations at phone company offices, post offices, and many retail outlets (such as newsstands). There's a local and international phone center at the General Post Office on O'Connell Street. If you have difficulty reaching a party, the Irish toll-free number for **direc-tory assistance** is ✆ 11811.

Tipping Most hotels and guesthouses add a service charge to the bill, usually 12.5% to 15%, although some smaller places add only 10% or nothing at all. If you feel the service charge is sufficient, there is no need for more gratuities. If, however, staff members have provided exceptional service, by all means tip them extra. For taxi drivers, tip as you would at home, 10% to 15%. For restaurants, the policy is usually printed on the menu—either a gratuity of 10% to 15% is automatically added to your bill or it's left up to you (always ask if you are in doubt). As a rule, bartenders do not expect a tip, except when table service is provided.

WHERE TO STAY
HISTORIC OLD CITY & TEMPLE BAR/TRINITY COLLEGE AREA
Very Expensive

The Clarence ★★★   So what if the place is partly owned by members of the rock band U2? Don't dismiss it as merely a glitzy, see-and-be-seen haunt for celebrities (Robert DeNiro, Gwyneth Paltrow, and Mick Jagger are fans)—the Clarence is one of the finest and truly stylish hotels in Dublin. Situated beside the Liffey in Temple Bar, this mid-19th-century, Regency-style hotel was totally overhauled in 1996 to offer larger rooms and luxurious suites. In the process it traded antique charm for contemporary elegance. Each room features a rich color—crimson, royal blue, eggplant, chocolate, or gold—against cream walls and light Shaker-style oak furniture, including exceptionally firm beds. Twin rooms are available, but most doubles feature king-size beds. Suites and deluxe rooms have balconies, some overlooking the Liffey. The Clarence's elegant **Tea Room** restaurant, in what was once the ballroom, is one of the best places in town to dine on contemporary Irish cuisine. For drinks and lighter fare there's the hip **Octagon Bar** or the **Study,** which has the feel of a gentlemen's club and is a relaxing hangout for guests.

6–8 Wellington Quay, Dublin 2. ℂ 01/670-9000. Fax 01/407-0820. www.theclarence.ie. 50 units. €315 ($362) double; €640 ($736) 1-bedroom suite; €780 (897) 2-bedroom suite. Full Irish breakfast €25 ($29). AE, DC, MC, V. Valet parking/service (fee charged). Bus: 51B, 51C, 68, 69, or 79. **Amenities:** Restaurant; bar; study; concierge; salon; 24-hr. room service; babysitting; laundry/dry cleaning; nonsmoking rooms; foreign-currency exchange; video library. *In room:* A/C, TV, DVD, dataport, minibar, hair dryer, safe.

Moderate

Eliza Lodge ★   This hotel opened a few years ago right beside the Liffey and embodies all the exuberance and zest of Temple Bar. Rooms are very attractive, done up in neutral creams and blond woods, with big floor-to-ceiling windows— the better to take in the riverside vistas. At the top end, executive rooms have Jacuzzi tubs and mod, round bay windows perched over the quay. But better value are the smaller penthouse doubles, which have balconies overlooking the river and are a comparative steal at €150 ($173) to €190 ($219).

23 Wellington Quay, Dublin 2. ℂ **01/671-8044.** Fax 01/671-8362. www.dublinlodge.com. 18 units. €130–€177 ($150–$204) double; €190–€228 ($219–$262) executive rooms. AE, MC, V. Bus: 51B, 51C, 68, 69, or 79. **Amenities:** Restaurant; bar; nonsmoking rooms. *In room:* A/C, TV, tea/coffeemaker, hair dryer, iron.

The Morgan ★★   If you love Temple Bar but can't afford to stay at the Clarence, this is a fabulous consolation prize. In just a few short years, this styl-ized little boutique hotel has developed a cult following among folks in fashion and music. Rooms are airy and minimalist, featuring light beechwood furnish-ings and crisp, white bedspreads against creamy neutral tones, with a smattering of modern artworks adding visual punch. The overall effect is understated ele-gance, with a modern, luxurious twist. But the attraction here goes beyond mere good looks. Every detail—from the classy cutlery to the way the staff is unobtru-sively attentive—hits just the right note. Though it sounds like a contradiction in

---

A Parking Note

The majority of Dublin hotels do not offer parking; if you have a car, you'll have to find (and pay for) street parking. In this section, we've provided parking information only for the few hotels that do offer parking arrangements or discounts for guests.

Tips Room Booking Savvy

In general, rates for Dublin hotels don't vary as greatly with the seasons as they do in the Irish countryside. Hotels often charge higher prices, however, during special events, such as the Dublin Horse Show. For the best deals, try to reserve for more than a single night. Many Dublin hotels cut their rates drastically for midweek and weekend multinight stays. Significant reductions are often available when you book online, so check online booking sites and the hotel's website for special offers.

---

terms, this place manages to be both trendy and a classic at the same time. Check the website for online booking specials.

10 Fleet St., Dublin 2. © **01/679-3939.** Fax 01/679-3946. www.themorgan.com. 66 units. €140–€200 ($161–$230) double. AE, DC, MC, V. Bus: 78A or 78B. **Amenities:** Cafe; bar; fitness center; limited room service; aromatherapy/masseuse; babysitting; laundry/dry cleaning; nonsmoking rooms; video/CD library. *In room:* TV/VCR, CD player, dataport, tea/coffeemaker, iron, garment press, safe, voice mail.

Temple Bar Hotel ★   It's twice as big and half as stylish as the Morgan, but still a solid pick if the Morgan is sold out. This five-story hotel was developed from a former bank building, with great care taken to preserve the brick facade and Victorian mansard roof. The Art Deco lobby features a cast-iron fireplace and lots of greenery. Guest rooms feature traditional mahogany furnishings and an autumnal russet-and-green color palette, with a very comfortable level of amenities. The double-size orthopedic beds are blissfully firm, though they make the rooms fairly cramped. The hotel has a skylit, garden-style **Terrace Restaurant** serving light fare (sandwiches and pasta) and an Old Dublin–theme pub, **Buskers.**

Fleet St., Temple Bar, Dublin 2. © **800/44-UTELL** in the U.S., or 01/677-3333. Fax 01/677-3088. www.temple barhotel.com. 130 units. €130–€160 ($150–$184) double. Rates include full Irish breakfast. AE, DC, MC, V. DART: Tara St. Bus: 78A or 78B. **Amenities:** Restaurant; bar; access to a nearby health club; concierge; room service; babysitting; nonsmoking rooms; foreign-currency exchange. *In room:* TV, tea/coffeemaker, hair dryer, garment press.

Moderate/Inexpensive

Jurys Inn Christchurch ★ *Value*   A good location in Old City, facing Christ Church cathedral, makes this a solid choice in the budget category. Totally refurbished in 1998, the rooms are larger than you'd expect and bright, though the decor has the same floral bedspreads and framed watercolors you see in nearly every other chain hotel. Make your reservations early and request a fifth-floor room facing west for a memorable view of Christ Church. *Tip:* Room nos. 501, 507, and 419 are especially spacious.

Christ Church Place, Dublin 8. © **800/44-UTELL** in the U.S., or 01/454-0000. Fax 01/454-0012. www.jurys.com. 182 units. €87–€108 ($100–$124) double. Breakfast €10 ($12). Service charge included. AE, MC, V. Discounted parking available at adjacent lot. Bus: 21A, 50, 50A, 78, 78A, or 78B. **Amenities:** Restaurant (Continental); pub; babysitting; laundry/dry cleaning; nonsmoking rooms. *In room:* A/C, TV, coffeemaker, hair dryer.

Self-Catering

25 Eustace Street ★★   This wonderfully restored Georgian town house has an enviable location smack in the heart of Temple Bar. It's truly a privilege to stay here for even 1 night. The house has been faithfully reinstated to the gracious, slightly sober atmosphere of a house of its period, with its superb timber-paneled staircase, fireplaces in every room, mainly mahogany furniture, and brass beds. You have the run of three entire floors of the house, including a huge drawing room with a baby grand piano, a dining room, an equipped galley kitchen, and three bedrooms (a double, a twin, and a triple). There are two bathrooms, one of which is enormous with an extraroomy cast-iron claw-foot tub placed dead center. All this, and Temple Bar at your doorstep.

25 Eustace St., Dublin 2. Contact the Irish Landmark Trust Ⓒ 01/670-4733. Fax 01/670-4887. www.irishlandmark. com. €285 ($328) per night; €1,320 ($1,518) per week. **Amenities:** Full kitchen. *In room:* No phone.

ST. STEPHEN'S GREEN/GRAFTON STREET AREA
Very Expensive

Fitzwilliam ⟨★⟩ Take an unbeatable location with stunning views over the Green, a fabulous restaurant, and cool, contemporary design by Terence Conran, and you have the makings of the Fitzwilliam. Conran has a knack for understated luxury, using clean lines and neutral colors throughout. Rooms are beautifully appointed and very relaxing. The **Citron** restaurant is downstairs, and you can also dine at the stylish **Inn on the Green** bar. If staying somewhere fashionable is important to you, this gets the nod over the Shelbourne (see below). Always check the website for deals, which can be as low as €149 ($171) per night for a double.

109 St. Stephen's Green, Dublin 2. Ⓒ **01/478-7000.** Fax 01/478-7878. www.fitzwilliam-hotel.com. 130 units. €240–€290 ($276–$334) double. AE, DC, MC, V. DART: Pearse. Bus: 10, 11A, 11B, 13, or 20B. **Amenities:** Restaurant; bar; concierge; room service; babysitting; laundry/dry cleaning; roof garden; nonsmoking rooms. *In room:* A/C, TV/VCR, fax, CD player, dataport, minibar, tea/coffeemaker, hair dryer, garment press, voice mail.

Shelbourne ⟨★⟩ While the Fitzwilliam is all about cutting-edge style, the Shelbourne is all about tradition. This is Dublin's answer to the Grand Hotel, and nothing—not even getting swallowed up by the Meridien Group—has changed its status. The hotel played a significant role in Irish history—the constitution was drafted here in 1922, in room no. 112. Rooms vary in size, but all are beautifully appointed with antiques and period pieces. Ask for one that overlooks bucolic St. Stephen's Green. The public areas, replete with glowing fireplaces, Waterford chandeliers, and original artworks, are popular rendezvous spots for Dublin's movers and shakers. Service is impeccable, and you get to experience a slice of Irish heritage to boot. Booking online can deliver rates as low as €169 ($194) for a double.

27 St. Stephen's Green, Dublin 2. Ⓒ **800/225-5843** in the U.S., or 01/663-4500. Fax 01/661-6006. www. shelbourne.ie. 190 units. €240–€360 ($276–$414) double. Service charge 15%. AE, DC, MC, V. Limited free parking. DART: Pearse. Bus: 10, 11A, 11B, 13, or 20B. **Amenities:** 2 restaurants; 2 bars; tearoom; fitness center; concierge; room service; babysitting; laundry/dry cleaning. *In room:* A/C, TV, radio, minibar.

Expensive

Brownes Townhouse ⟨★⟩ If you love luxury but hate big chain hotels, look no further than this sumptuously restored, award-winning Georgian town house with an unbeatable location on St. Stephen's Green. Downstairs is all Georgian splendor: comfy wingback chairs, rich upholsteries, and ornate ceiling plasterwork. The dozen guest rooms come in all shapes and sizes, but all are sumptuously decorated with period furnishings, four-poster king-size beds (some of them 2.4m/8 ft. wide!), marble bathrooms, and unique architectural details. When you book, voice your decor preferences, as rooms vary drastically according to masculine, feminine, classic, or eccentric tastes. If you splurge on the Thomas Leighton suite, you'll sleep on a magnificent king-size mahogany Murphy bed that once belonged to Marilyn Monroe. Downstairs, the elegant **Brasserie** serves up excellent traditional French fare.

22 St. Stephen's Green, Dublin 2. © **01/638-3939.** Fax 01/638-3900. www.brownesdublin.com. 12 units. €210–€240 ($242–$276) double. No service charge. Rates include full breakfast. MC, V. DART: Pearse. Bus: 10, 11A, 11B, 13, or 20B. **Amenities:** Restaurant. *In room:* A/C, TV, fax, dataport, tea/coffeemaker, hair dryer.

Expensive/Moderate

Number 31 ⭐ A plaque placed discreetly at an elegant gated entrance in the heart of Georgian Dublin is your only clue that what lies beyond is an award-winning town-house B&B. The house is actually two beautifully renovated coach houses, featuring a striking sunken fireside seating area with mosaic tiles in the main lounge. In the main house, rooms range from grand, high-ceilinged affairs to cozier nests. The smaller coach house has lower ceilings, but some rooms have their own patios. All the rooms are a triumph of quiet good taste, decorated with fine fabrics against a cream backdrop. Breakfast is truly magnificent—think mushroom frittatas, cranberry bread, and scrumptious little potato cakes.

31 Leeson Close, Lower Leeson St., Dublin 2. © **01/676-5011.** Fax 01/676-2929. www.number31.ie. 20 units. €140–€230 ($161–$265) double. Rates include breakfast. AE, MC, V. Bus: 11, 11A, 11B, 13, 13A, or 13B. **Amenities:** Lounge; bar; conservatory. *In room:* TV, hair dryer.

FITZWILLIAM/MERRION SQUARE AREA
Expensive/Moderate

Longfields ⭐⭐ Created from two 18th-century Georgian town houses, this award-winning hotel is a small, elegant alternative to the large upscale hotels in this area. The hotel is named after Richard Longfield (also known as Viscount Longueville), who originally owned this site and was a member of the Irish Parliament 2 centuries ago. Totally restored and refurbished, it combines Georgian decor and reproduction-period furnishings of dark woods and brass trim. Though some of the standard rooms are smallish, the superior doubles (at €210/$242) are noticeably more spacious; and the best doubles (at €230/$265) are even larger and feature four-poster beds. Longfields is centrally located yet remarkably quiet, an elegant yet unpretentious getaway 5 minutes' walk from St. Stephen's Green. The restaurant, simply known as **Number 10,** is beloved by foodies. The website sometimes offers deals as low as €99 ($114) per double.

10 Lower Fitzwilliam St., Dublin 2. © **01/676-1367.** Fax 01/676-1542. www.longfields.ie. 26 units. €165–€230 ($190–$265). No service charge. Rates include full breakfast. AE, DC, MC, V. No parking available. DART: Pearse. Bus: 10. **Amenities:** Restaurant; concierge; room service; babysitting; laundry/dry cleaning; foreign-currency exchange. *In room:* TV, clock radio, hair dryer.

Moderate

Kilronan House ⭐ This extremely comfortable B&B is set on a peaceful, leafy road just 5 minutes' walk from St. Stephen's Green. Much of the Georgian character remains, in the ceiling corniging, hardwood parquet floors, and the fine staircase. The sitting room on the ground floor is particularly intimate, with a fire glowing through the cold months of the year. Rooms are brightly inviting in white and yellow, and those facing the front have commodious bay windows. There's no elevator, so consider requesting a room on a lower floor. The front rooms, facing Adelaide Street, are preferable to those in back, which face office buildings and a parking lot. Breakfast here is especially good, featuring homemade breads. You can sometimes land rooms as low as €96 ($111) per double by booking online at the website below.

70 Adelaide Rd., Dublin 2. © **01/475-5266.** Fax 01/478-2841. www.dublinn.com/kilronan.htm. 15 units, 13 with private bathroom (shower only). €152–€170 ($175–$196) double. Rates include full breakfast. AE, MC, V. Free private parking. Bus: 14, 15, 19, 20, or 46A. *In room:* TV, tea/coffeemaker, hair dryer.

O'CONNELL STREET AREA
Very Expensive

The Morrison ★★ Just when it seemed that everything chic and hip happened south of the Liffey, the Hong Kong–born, Irish designer John Rocha opened the Morrison and pow!—the central Northside ain't so shabby after all. This stunning contemporary hotel is a 5-minute walk from O'Connell Street and across the river from Temple Bar. Rocha used clean minimalist lines, neutral colors, and natural elements to evoke a sensuous, luxurious feeling of space and relaxation. **Halo,** the atrium-style main restaurant, is one of the most exciting eateries in town. The upshot: The Morrison is just as stylish as the Clarence (Temple Bar) and the Fitzwilliam (St. Stephen's Green), with the sky-high rates to prove it. Booking via the hotel's website can sometimes land you a double for just €145 ($167) midweek or €220 ($253) on the weekend.

Lower Ormond Quay, Dublin 1. ℂ 01/887-2400. Fax 01/878-3185. www.morrisonhotel.ie. 93 units. €270–€445 ($311–$512) double. Rates include VAT and service charge. AE, DC, MC, V. DART: Connolly. Bus: 70 or 80. **Amenities:** 2 restaurants; 2 bars; concierge; room service; babysitting; dry cleaning; video/CD library. *In room:* A/C, CD player, dataport, minibar, hair dryer, safe, voice mail.

Inexpensive

Jurys Inn Custom House ★★ *Value* Ensconced in the grandiose new financial-services district and facing the quays, this Jurys Inn follows the successful formula of affordable comfort without frills. Single rooms have a double bed and a pullout sofa, while double rooms offer both a double and a twin bed. Request one of the 22 especially spacious rooms, which, if available, cost nothing extra. Rooms facing the quays also enjoy vistas of the Dublin hills, but those facing the financial district are quieter. Occupancy runs at 100% from May to September and at roughly 95% for the rest of the year, so be sure to book well in advance.

Custom House Quay, Dublin 1. ℂ 800/44-UTELL in the U.S., or 01/607-5000. Fax 01/829-0400. www.jurys. com. 239 units. €87–€112 ($100–$129) double. Rates include service charge. Full Irish breakfast €10 ($12). AE, DC, MC, V. Discounted parking available at adjacent lot. DART: Tara Street. Bus: 27A, 27B, or 53A. **Amenities:** Restaurant; bar; laundry/dry cleaning; nonsmoking rooms. *In room:* TV, dataport, tea/coffeemaker, hair dryer.

BALLSBRIDGE/EMBASSY ROW AREA

Situated south of the Grand Canal, this is the most prestigious part of town, known for its embassies, tree-lined streets, and historic buildings. If you're coming to Dublin specifically for a conference at the RDS show grounds or a match at the Lansdowne Rugby Ground, this neighborhood will put you right in the thick of things. The downside is that it's a good 20- to 30-minute walk to get into the city's best sightseeing and shopping areas.

Very Expensive

Four Seasons ★★ If money is no object, the drop-dead gorgeous Four Seasons blows Dublin's other luxury hotels out of the water in terms of services and leisure facilities. The health club is state of the art. The public areas and guest rooms share a smart and very plush look, thanks to the liberal use of natural elements and fine fabrics. This is a fabulous place for families, with a babysitting service, complimentary cribs, childproof bedrooms, and a roster of children's activities to keep the kids occupied while you kick back and get some head space. Check the website for year-round deals as low as €245 ($282) for a double.

Simmonscourt Rd., Ballsbridge, Dublin 4. ℂ 800/819-5053 in the U.S., or 01/665-4000. Fax 01/665-4099. www.fourseasons.com. 259 units. €355–€795 ($408–$914) double/suite. AE, DC, MC, V. Valet parking. DART: Sandymount (5-min. walk). Bus: 7, 7A, 7X, 8, or 45. **Amenities:** 2 restaurants; bar; lobby lounge; indoor pool; health club/spa; whirlpool; children's programs; concierge; 24-hr. room and concierge service; babysitting;

laundry/dry cleaning; nonsmoking rooms; conservatory. *In room:* TV/VCR, radio, CD player available, dataport, minibar, hair dryer, safe, voice mail.

Expensive

Butlers Town House ⭐ This beautifully restored and expanded Victorian town-house B&B feels like a gracious family home into which you are lucky enough to be welcomed. The atmosphere is semiformal yet invitingly elegant, class without the starched collar. Rooms are richly furnished with four-poster or half-tester beds. It's hard to elude comfort here—you're pampered by two-fold Egyptian cotton sheets, heavenly water pressure, and an especially solicitous staff. A bonus is the **Glendalough Room** restaurant, which requires early booking. The hotel offers free tea and coffee all day. Breakfast, afternoon tea, and high tea are served in the atrium dining room.

44 Lansdowne Rd., Ballsbridge, Dublin 4. **℃ 800/44-UTELL** in the U.S., or 01/667-4022. Fax 01/667-3960. www.butlers-hotel.com. 20 units. €190–€220 ($219–$253) double. Rates include full breakfast. AE, DC, MC, V. Closed Dec 23–Jan 8. DART: Lansdowne Rd. Bus: 7, 7A, 8, or 45. **Amenities:** Breakfast room; room service; babysitting; laundry/dry cleaning. *In room:* A/C, TV, dataport, hair dryer.

Moderate/Inexpensive

Waterloo House These two adjacent Georgian town houses make up one of the most popular B&Bs in Dublin. Perhaps it's because Evelyn Corcoran and her staff take such good care of you, in a friendly but unobtrusive manner. The place is charming in an old-world kind of way, with classical music wafting through the lobby, and an elegant, high-ceilinged drawing room. Rooms are comfortable and large (a few have two double beds), but some might find the traditional red-patterned carpet and box-pleated bedspreads a tad dated. The varied breakfast menu is a high point. This is a nonsmoking house.

8–10 Waterloo Rd., Ballsbridge, Dublin 4. **℃ 01/660-1888.** Fax 01/667-1955. www.waterloohouse.ie. 17 units. €74–€164 ($85–$189) double. Rates include full breakfast. MC, V. Closed Christmas week. DART: Lansdowne Rd. Bus: 5, 7, or 8. **Amenities:** Drawing room; breakfast room; nonsmoking house. *In room:* TV, tea/coffeemaker, hair dryer, garment press.

Inexpensive

Bewley's Hotel *Value* Bewley's occupies what was once a 19th-century brick Masonic school building adjacent to the RDS show grounds and next to the British Embassy. A modern wing harmonizes well with the old structure and is indistinguishable in the interior. All the rooms are studios with a writing desk, an armchair, and a large double bed. An additional room contains a foldout couch, a table (seats six), a pullout kitchenette/bar hidden in a cabinet, and an additional bathroom (shower only). The basement restaurant (**O'Connell's**) is run by the Allen family of Ballymaloe fame and offers very good food at reasonable prices; there's also an informal Bewley's tearoom. The hotel is an excellent value for families, but the big downside is its location outside the city center.

Merrion Rd., Ballsbridge, Dublin 4. **℃ 01/668-1111.** Fax 01/668-1999. www.bewleyshotels.com. 300 units. €99 ($114) studio double. Rates include service charge and taxes. AE, DC, MC, V. DART: Sandymount (5-min. walk). Bus: 7, 7A, 7X, 8, or 45. **Amenities:** Restaurant; tearoom; nonsmoking rooms. *In room:* TV, dataport, kitchenette, tea/coffeemaker, hair dryer, safe, garment press.

WHERE TO DINE

HISTORIC OLD CITY & TEMPLE BAR/TRINITY COLLEGE AREA

Very Expensive

The Tea Room ⭐⭐⭐ INTERNATIONAL This ultrasmart restaurant, ensconced in the very hip Clarence hotel, is virtually guaranteed to deliver one of your most memorable meals in Ireland. This gorgeous dining room's soaring yet understated lines are the perfect backdrop for Antony Ely's complex but controlled cooking. A classic such as beef filet with red-wine jus is downright zingy when served with arugula on a Dijon-infused potato-and-onion mash. Likewise, the saucisson of salmon becomes up-to-date and elegant astride teeny risoni pasta and chive dressing. Desserts, such as the caramelized peach with rice pudding pie, are heaven-sent. Bono and the Edge of U2 are part-owners of the hotel, so the potential celebrity-spotting quotient is always high.

In the Clarence, 6–8 Wellington Quay, Dublin 2. (© 01/670-9000. Reservations required. Fixed-price 1-course dinner €31 ($36), 2-course dinner €41 ($47), 3-course dinner €53 ($61). AE, MC, V. Mon–Fri 12:30–2pm; Mon–Sun 6:30–9:45pm. Bus: 51B, 51C, 68, 69, or 79.

Expensive

Jacob's Ladder ★★★ *Value* MODERN IRISH When a talented, confident chef knows what to do with exceptional-quality Irish produce, the results can be superb. Inspired cooking by chef-owner Adrian Roche and a stylish dining room with great views over Trinity College make this one of the most consistently packed places in town. Roche's forte is taking old Irish stalwarts and updating them into sublime signature dishes. His Dublin Coddle is a soupy seafood stew of onions, potatoes, mussels, clams, Dublin bay prawns, salmon, carrots, and turnips. He serves his excellent braised wood pigeon with colcannon—an old Irish favorite of potatoes and cabbage mashed together with plenty of butter— a version that is fluffier and more refined than that found anywhere else on the island. You get great value for your money—this is one of the few upscale restaurants that hasn't upped its prices in the past year.

4–5 Nassau St., Dublin 2. (© 01/670-3865. www.jacobsladder.ie. Reservations required. Main courses €17–€24 ($20–$28); early-bird menu 6–7pm €18 ($21); fixed-price dinner €32 ($37). AE, DC, MC, V. Mon–Fri 12:30–2:30pm; Tues–Fri 6–10pm; Sat 7–10pm. Closed Dec 24–Jan 4. DART: Pearse. Bus: 7, 8, 10, 11, or 46A.

Mermaid Café ★★★ MODERN The Mermaid Café—known to locals as simply the Mermaid—has attained cult status in Dublin. And justifiably so, since Chef Temple Garner's cooking is downright terrific—think classic cooking with a fresh, eclectic twist. Start with the orange, feta, and watercress salad with beet and mild chile dressing or, if you're appetite is bigger, the Mermaid antipasti combined with a dangerously appealing assortment of freshly baked breads. The New England crab cakes, grilled swordfish with mango relish, roast duck breast on curried noodles, and chargrilled monkfish are all flawlessly prepared and quite memorable. On top of all that, the wine list is one of the best in Ireland, and the desserts—especially the pecan pie—are divine.

70 Dame St., Dublin 2. (© 01/670-8236. www.mermaid.ie. Reservations required. Dinner main courses €19–€30 ($22–$35). Sun brunch €9–€15 ($10–$17). MC, V. Mon–Sat 12:30–2:30pm and 6–11pm; Sun brunch 12:30–3:30pm and dinner 6–9pm. Bus: 50, 50A, 54, 56A, 77, 77A, or 77B.

Moderate

Elephant & Castle ★★ AMERICAN You'd be forgiven for thinking you can find this kind of food—burgers, chicken wings, omelets—at any old Yankee-style

---

Down in Smoke

Irish pubs and restaurants became smoke-free zones in March 2004, as a long-awaited smoking ban in public places was finally implemented. Enforcement is a different story, however, and it remains to be seen whether Irish publicans—especially those in rural areas—will comply with the new law.

joint, but give it a chance and you won't be disappointed: Noel Alexander works a stove as if he was brought up in American diners. His chicken wings are scrumptious, his burgers out of this world, and his omelets "spot on," as the Irish would say. It's a buzzing, immensely popular place for breakfast, brunch, lunch, afternoon nibble, dinner, or late dinner.

18 Temple Bar, Dublin 2. ⑦ **01/679-3121**. www.elephantandcastle.com. Main courses €8–€22 ($9–$25). AE, MC, V. Mon–Fri 8am–11:30pm; Sat 10:30am–11:30pm; Sun noon–11:30pm. Bus: 51B, 51C, 68, 69, or 79.

Inexpensive

Juice ⋆⋆ VEGETARIAN   Uh-oh. The V word. Don't worry, this place isn't about suffering for a higher principle. The menu is so interesting and the food so downright fabulous, it's almost a bonus that everything on the menu is organic, healthy, and fresh. And what a hip room: Lofty, 30-foot ceilings are softened by a suspended sailcloth and muted lighting. One entire wall is painted claret, with a net of tiny white fairy lights twinkling in the distance. Weekend brunch offers perennial faves like pancakes and French toast topped with fresh fruit and organic maple syrup, but the menu takes you around the world. Sample the homemade dips—hummus, baba ghanouj, tapenade, roasted carrot pâté, smoked pimento pâté—served tapas-style with crudités and warm pita bread strips. True to its name, Juice has around 30 kinds of juices and smoothies on offer, all whipped up frothy and festive. You can easily eat well here for under €20 ($23), proving that V is for value, too.

Castle House, 73 S. Great Georges St., Dublin 2. ⑦ **01/475-7856**. Reservations recommended Fri–Sat. Main courses €6–€10 ($6.90–$12); early-bird 3-course dinner (Mon–Fri 5–7pm) €14 ($16). AE, MC, V. Daily 11am–11pm. Bus: 50, 50A, 54, 56, or 77.

Leo Burdock's FISH & CHIPS   Every visitor should go to a Dublin takeout "chipper" at least once, and you might as well do it at the best in town. Established in 1913 across from Christ Church, this quintessential Irish takeout shop remains a cherished Dublin institution, despite a devastating fire in 1998. Rebuilt from the ground up, Burdock's is back. Cabinet ministers, university students, and businesspeople alike can be found in the queue. There's no seating, but you can stroll down to the park at St. Patrick's Cathedral.

2 Werburgh St., Dublin 8. ⑦ **01/454-0306**. Main courses €4–€7 ($4.60–$8.05). No credit cards. Mon–Sat noon–midnight; Sun 4pm–midnight. Bus: 21A, 50, 50A, 78, 78A, or 78B.

ST. STEPHEN'S GREEN/GRAFTON STREET AREA
Very Expensive

One Pico ⋆⋆⋆ MODERN EUROPEAN   About a 5-minute walk from Stephen's Green, on a wee lane off Dawson Street, is one of the city's most coveted restaurants. Talented chef-owner Eamonn O'Reilly has become a celebrity chef in no time flat, and getting a table here can be a feat in itself. This is a sophisticated, grown-up, classy place, with excellent service and fantastic food. Favorite dishes include a starter of seared foie gras with pineapple tatin; memorable main dishes include scallops with baby beets and lime, confit of duck with fig tatin, and beef with Roquefort ravioli. For dessert, a caramelized lemon tart is the end to a near-perfect meal.

5–6 Moleworth Place, Schoolhouse Lane, Dublin 2. ⑦ **01/676-0300**. www.onepico.com. Reservations required. Fixed-price 2-course lunch €22 ($25), 3-course lunch €26 ($30); dinner main courses €20–€27 ($23–$31). AE, DC, MC, V. Mon–Sat 12:30–2pm and 6–10:30pm. DART: Pearse. Bus: 10, 11A, 11B, 13, or 20B.

Moderate

Aya @ Brown Thomas ⋆⋆ JAPANESE   This buzzy annex to "B.T.," Ireland's poshest department store, is a good-time destination for chilled-out devotees of

Japanese food. Aya opened a few years ago as Ireland's first conveyor-belt sushi bar, but it's gone on to develop a loyal clientele because, beyond the trendiness, the food here is damn good. Table service comes with a pricier, more elaborate menu, so take a seat at the horseshoe bar; besides saving money, you'll have a heck of a lot more fun. Chefs prepare the sushi in open view while you select from a never-ending production line of *nigiri* (sushi strapped with seaweed onto a rice bed), *norimaki* (sushi and rice wrapped into a seaweed roll), *temaki* (sushi wrapped in a seaweed cone), green salads with carrot-and-ginger dressing, and spring rolls. Prices are rock bottom during "Happy Time" (Mon–Fri 2–7pm and 9–10pm; Sat 3–7pm and 9–11pm; Sun 1–5pm and 9–10pm), when you can choose five plates from the belt for €12 ($14), accompanied by as much *gari* (pickled ginger), wasabi (hot radish paste), and complimentary cups of *konacha* (green tea) as you like. You'll leave feeling well fed and thoroughly feted.

49–52 Clarendon St., Dublin 2. © 01/677-1544. Reservations recommended for dinner. Lunch averages €12 ($14); dinner averages €32 ($37). AE, DC, MC, V. Mon–Sat 10:30am–11pm; Sun noon–10pm. DART: Tara St. Bus: 16A, 19A, 22A, 55, or 83.

Mimo ★★ *Value* INTERNATIONAL   Take a shopping break at this chic little cafe in the tony Powerscourt Townhouse minimall. It's a wonderfully classy and surprisingly budget-minded place to stop for terrific salads, pasta dishes, and inventive sandwiches. Against the old-world backdrop of a skylit Georgian town-house courtyard—one of Dublin's most attractive conversions—Mimo exudes contemporary chic, with leather banquettes the color of espresso, enormous vases of orchids, and wooden tables and bars buffed to a high sheen. Sink into an armchair and order the tasty salad of marinated flat mushrooms, piled high atop a bed of crisp green beans and Parmesan shavings with lemon-and-thyme dressing, and served with toasted ciabatta. Or go for the warm goat's cheese crostini with caramelized figs, wild honey, and beet dressing. A piano player is a civilized touch on Thursday and Friday afternoons.

Powerscourt Townhouse, Dublin 2. © 01/674-6712. Main courses €8–€10 ($9.20–$12). MC, V. Mon–Sun noon–5:30pm. Bus: Any city-center bus.

Inexpensive

Bewley's Café TRADITIONAL CAFE/TEAROOM   Bewley's, a three-story landmark on Grafton Street, has been a staple of Dublin life since 1840, with a traditional interior of dark woods, amber glass, and deep red velvet banquettes. Go once, because Bewley's is a quintessential hit of real Dublin and the people-watching is great. But stick to coffee and tea, since the food can be mediocre. Most Bewley's establishments are self-service cafeterias, but Bewley's of Grafton Street also has several full-service tearooms. Other locations are at 11 Westmoreland St., Dublin 2; 13 S. Great George's St., Dublin 2; 40 Mary St., Dublin 1 (near the ILAC shopping center north of the Liffey); shopping centers in Dundrum, Stillorgan, and Tallaght; and Dublin Airport.

78–79 Grafton St., Dublin 2. © 01/677-6761. Homemade soup €3 ($3.45); lunch main courses €4–€9 ($4.60–$10) and specials from €7 ($8.05); dinner main courses from €15 ($17). AE, DC, MC, V. Sun–Thurs 7:30am–11pm; Fri–Sat 7:30am–1am (continuous service for breakfast, hot food, and snacks). Bus: Any city-center bus.

Caifé Trí-D ★★ *Value* SANDWICHES   This unpretentious, eclectic little cafe just steps from the wrought-iron rails of the Trinity College campus is a great find on a street known for booksellers. The menu half-written *as gaeilge* is your clue that Caifé Trí-D is that Dublin rarity: a heart-on-its-sleeve Irish-language hangout. Lunches draw a workaday crowd from nearby businesses and shops, while in the evenings the place comes into its own as a gathering place for trendy young Dubs in search of some Irish conversation. *Ceapairí* and *fillteáin* (sandwiches and wraps) tempt with simple but interesting ingredients, like the winning combination of sharp Dubliner cheese, tomato relish, lettuce, and tomato. Try Brie and cranberry sauce on toasted brown bread, and you'll be plotting a recreation in your own kitchen. You'll love how the soup of the day (maybe mushroom and spinach or carrot and coriander) comes with a chunky slab of homemade soda bread and butter. And how iced tea arrives in an ice-cream-parlor-style goblet, with a little silver teapot alongside with enough tea for two refills. Simply perfect.

3 Dawson St., Dublin 2. © 01/474-1054. Soups, sandwiches, and wraps for €5 ($5.75) and under. Mon–Sat 9am–7pm. DART: Pearse. Bus: 10, 11A, 11B, 13, or 20B.

FITZWILLIAM/MERRION SQUARE AREA
Very Expensive

L'Ecrivain ✦✦ FRENCH   This is one of Dublin's truly exceptional restaurants, from start to finish. The atmosphere is relaxed, welcoming, and unpretentious, and chef Derry Clarke's food is extraordinary in its attention to detail. Each course consists of traditional "best of Irish" ingredients, prepared without dense sauces. The roast monkfish with citrus ravioli and the entrecôte with caramelized onion are not only perfectly prepared, but elegantly presented. For dessert, the crème brûlée here may be the best outside of France.

109 Lower Baggot St., Dublin 2. © 01/661-1919. www.lecrivain.com. Reservations required Fixed-price 2-course lunch €22 ($25), 3-course lunch €35 ($40). Fixed-price 4-course dinner €58 ($67). Main courses €38–€40 ($44–$46). 10% service charge. AE, DC, MC, V. Mon–Fri 12:30–2pm; Mon–Thurs 6:30–10:30pm; Fri–Sat 7–11pm. Bus: 10.

Restaurant Patrick Guilbaud ✦ FRENCH   Ireland's most lauded restaurant has a glowing Michelin-star reputation for fine food and artful service. The menu features such dishes as roasted West Cork turbot, veal sweetbreads with black truffles, wild sea bass with ragout of mussels, and a casserole of winter vegetables with wild mushrooms. Start with the open ravioli of lobster with coconut cream, follow with the sole and duck confit flavored with walnut liqueur, and finish with the *assiette gourmande au chocolat* (five small hot and cold chocolate desserts).

In the Merrion Hotel, 21 Upper Merrion St., Dublin 2. © 01/676-4192. Reservations required. Fixed-price lunch €30 ($35); dinner main courses from €46 ($53). AE, DC, MC, V. Tues–Sat 12:30–2:15pm and 7–10:15pm. DART: Westland Row. Bus: 10, 11A, 11B, 13, or 20B.

Expensive/Moderate

L'Aubergine ✦✦✦ FRENCH   In a very short while, Mark Ussher has become one of Dublin's most talked-about chefs and made L'Aubergine one of the most in-demand restaurants. Ussher's cooking is that perfect balance between classic and imaginative, serving up dishes where the ingredient combinations can be daring but never foolhardy. Ussher understands that God is in the details, especially with modern, precision cooking. Start with something zingy like the twice-cooked Roquefort soufflé flavored with mesclun and hazelnut pesto. Fish is a strong point of the menu, so you won't go wrong with a main course of filet of red mullet with escabèche or seared hake with roast root vegetables. Save room for dessert, but don't overindulge on the overpriced wines.

112 Lower Baggot St., Dublin 2. © 01/676-7617. www.laubergine.com. Reservations necessary. Dinner main courses €16–€23 ($18–$26). MC, V. Mon–Fri 12:30–2:30pm; Tues–Sat 6:30–10:30pm. Bus: 10.

Inexpensive

National Gallery of Ireland Restaurant ✦✦ CAFETERIA   There's something inherently civilized about dining in an art museum, especially one with an elegant address on Dublin's best-preserved Georgian square. Under the soaring atrium roof of the National Gallery's new Millennium Wing, this restaurant is minimalist, with cream-colored stone floors and walls and blond wood furnishings accented with jet-black seats. A two-course set lunch lets you choose from five entrees and five tempting salads made fresh that day, all for under €10 ($12). The operation is self-service, but this ain't no cafeteria food. The salmon filet is marinated in a balsamic vinaigrette, then pan-fried until its crust is light and crispy, and served cold with cherry tomatoes and hazelnut dressing. Then there's the scrumptiously gooey sweet-potato, leek, and Brie frittata, one of those seemingly impossible combinations that comes up trumps. A raft of small but elegant touches—weighty silverware, a big dollop of hand-whipped cream in your coffee, and a bud vase on every table holding a single, perfect yellow freesia—deliver as close to an upscale experience as you'll get without a waiter.

National Gallery of Ireland Restaurant, Merrion Square West, Dublin 2. ℃ **01/475-7856.** Free admission to gallery. 2-course set lunch €9–€10 ($10–$12). MC, V. Tues–Sat 10am–5pm; Sun 2–5pm. Bus: 7, 7A, 8, 10, 11, or 13.

O'CONNELL STREET AREA
Expensive

Halo ☆☆ FUSION   This is easily the hippest, hottest, coolest, most stylish place to eat in Dublin right now—so book your table before you leave home. Eating at Halo is an intense experience for all of your senses. Chef Jean-Michel Poulot's cooking is fusion at its best—snazzy, mind-blowing combinations of taste and texture that are elegant and not simply out there. Consider the curried king scallops with lime potato, fennel, mizuna, and ginger vinaigrette. Or the baked goat's cheese wrapped in Parma ham with mizuna salad.

In the Morrison Hotel, Ormond Quay, Dublin 1. ℃ **01/878-2999.** Reservations required. Lunch €25 ($29); dinner €45 ($52). AE, MC, V. Daily 12:30–2pm and 7–10:30pm. DART: Connolly. Bus: 70 or 80.

Inexpensive

Epicurean Food Hall ☆☆ GOURMET FOOD COURT   This wonderful food hall houses a wide variety of artisan produce, local Irish delicacies, and regional specialties. Favorites include: **Caviston's,** Dublin's premier deli, for smoked salmon and seafood; **Itsabagel,** for its delicious bagels, imported from H&H Bagels in New York City; **Crème de la Crème,** for its French-style pastries and cakes; **Missy and Mandy's,** for its American-style ice cream; **Nectar,** for its plethora of healthy juice drinks; and **Aroma Bistro,** for Italian paninis. There is limited seating, and this place gets uncomfortably jammed during lunchtime midweek, so go midmorning or afternoon.

Middle Abbey St., Dublin 1. No phone. All items €2–€12 ($2.30–$14). No credit cards. Mon–Sat 10am–6pm. Bus: 70 or 80.

Soup Dragon ☆☆ SOUPS   Soup has become the healthy, hip alternative to stodgy sandwiches and fast food, and the Soup Dragon leads the way for cheap and cheerful chow-downs in Dublin. This place may be tiny, with less than a dozen stools alongside a bar, but it's big on drama: Think blue walls, black and red mirrors, orange slices and spice sticks flowing out of giant jugs, and huge flower-filled vases. The menu changes daily, but usually features a few traditional choices (potato and leek, carrot and coriander) as well as the more exotic (curried parsnip and *sag aloo,* a spicy Indian spinach and potato concoction). It's also a good place for dessert. Try the bread-and-butter pudding.

168 Capel St., Dublin 1. ℃ **01/872-3277.** All items €3–€8 ($3.45–$9.20). MC, V. Mon–Sat 9:30am–6pm; Sun 1–6pm. Bus: 70 or 80.

BALLSBRIDGE/EMBASSY ROW AREA
Expensive
Dish 🏵🏵 INTERNATIONAL   This is deservedly one of the city's most popular and consistently buzzy restaurants. The chic, contemporary surroundings work well with the ambitious, eclectic cooking that awaits you. Chef Gerard Foote believes in fresh, organic ingredients and is a master at combining unlikely flavors and coming up with tantalizing results. The griddled scallops with mousseline potatoes and garlic butter are perfect, as is the grilled salmon with avocado, papaya and tequila-lime dressing. The desserts—including a meltaway vanilla panna cotta and amaretti chocolate cheesecake—are nothing short of sensational.

146 Upper Leeson St., Dublin 4. ℂ 01/664-2135. Reservations recommended. Fixed-price lunch €20 ($23); dinner main courses €16–€26 ($18–$30). AE, DC, MC, V. Daily noon–11:30pm. DART: Tara St. Bus: 21A, 46A, 46B, 51B, 51C, 68, 69, or 86.

Moderate
The French Paradox 🏵🏵 Value WINE BAR   Just what tony Dublin 4 needed: a price-conscious, darling little bistro-cum-*bar de vin* that's endeared itself to everyone in the city. The wine's the thing here, so relax with a bottle of bordeaux or Côte du Rhone and whatever nibbles you like from the menu. There's a lovely cheese plate named for West Cork cheese maker Bill Hogan, superb Iberico hams from Spain, and, if you're more hungry, the delicious bistro stalwart of confit of duck with vegetables. Simply delicious.

53 Shelbourne Rd., Dublin 4. ℂ 01/660-4068. www.thefrenchparadox.com. Reservations recommended. All items €6–€15 ($6.90–$17). Main dishes come with glass of wine. AE, MC, V. Mon–Sat noon–3pm and 2 evening sittings at 6 and 9pm. DART: Lansdowne Rd. Bus: 5, 6, 7, 8, 18, or 45.

Roly's Bistro 🏵🏵 IRISH/INTERNATIONAL   This shop-front restaurant has been a beloved Dublin institution for over a decade. Chef Paul Cartwright cooks the kind of excellent, tummy-warming food you never get tired of: confit of duck with garlic mash, chicken-and-bean-sprout spring roll, pan-fried Dublin Bay prawns, wild mushroom risotto. The main dining room, an airy affair with lots of windows, can be noisy when the house is full, but the nonsmoking section has an enclave of booths laid out in an intimate Orient Express style.

7 Ballsbridge Terrace, Dublin 4. ℂ 01/668-2611. Reservations required. Main courses €15–€20 ($17–$23). Fixed 2-course lunch €18 ($21). AE, DC, MC, V. Daily noon–3pm and 6–10pm. DART to Lansdowne Rd. Station. Bus: 5, 6, 7, 8, 18, or 45.

SEEING THE SIGHTS
SIGHTSEEING SUGGESTIONS FOR FIRST-TIME VISITORS
If You Have 1 Day Start at the beginning—Dublin's medieval quarter, the area around **Christ Church** and **St. Patrick's Cathedral.** Tour these great churches and then walk the cobblestone streets and inspect the nearby old city walls at **High Street.** From Old Dublin, take a turn eastward and see **Dublin Castle** and then **Trinity College** with the famous Book of Kells. Cross over the River Liffey to **O'Connell Street,** Dublin's main thoroughfare. Walk up this wide street, passing the landmark General Post Office (GPO), to Parnell Square and the picturesque Garden of Remembrance. If time permits, visit the **Dublin Writers Museum,** and then hop on a double-decker bus heading to the south bank of the Liffey for a relaxing stroll amid the greenery of **St. Stephen's Green.** Cap the day with a show at the **Abbey Theatre** and maybe a drink or two at a nearby pub.

If You Have 2 Days On your first day, get oriented with a sightseeing tour—the most fun is the amphibious **Viking Splash Tour,** though the **Dublin City Tour** gives a broader overview of the city, plus it goes to some of the leading sights on the edge of the city, such as the **Guinness Brewery,** the **Royal Hospital,** and **Phoenix Park.** Later in the day, head for **Grafton Street** for some shopping. If time allows, stroll around **St. Stephen's Green** and **Merrion Square** for a sampling of the best of Dublin's Georgian architecture. Spend the evening in Temple Bar and end up with a few pints in a pub. On your second day, follow the 1-day itinerary, above.

If You Have 3 Days Make day 3 a day for Dublin's artistic and cultural attractions—visit the **National Museum** and **National Gallery,** the **Guinness Hop Store,** or a special-interest museum, such as the **Writers Museum.** Save time to walk around **Temple Bar** by day, when the city's Left Bank district is all about art galleries and film studios, interesting secondhand shops, and casual eateries.

If You Have 4 Days On day 4, take a ride aboard DART to one of the southern suburbs, either **Dun Laoghaire** or medieval **Dalkey.** DART follows the rim of Dublin Bay, so you'll enjoy a scenic ride and get to spend some time in an Irish coastal village. Or take a trip to the **Boyne Valley** in nearby County Meath to visit the burial mounds at Newgrange, the site of the Battle of the Boyne, and King William's Glen. This trip is also worthwhile for the glimpses of Irish countryside it affords.

DUBLIN'S TOP ATTRACTIONS

Áras an Uachtaráin (The Irish White House) ★ Áras an Uachtaráin (Irish for "House of the President") was once the Viceregal Lodge, the summer retreat of the British viceroy, whose ordinary digs were in Dublin Castle. From what were never humble beginnings, the original 1751 country house was expanded several times. President Mary McAleese recently opened her home to visitors; guided tours originate at the Phoenix Park Visitor Centre every Saturday. After an introductory historical film, a bus brings visitors to and from Áras an Uachtaráin. The focus of the 1-hour tour is the state reception rooms. Only 525 tickets are given out, first-come, first-served; arrive before 1:30pm, especially in summer.

Note: For security reasons, no backpacks, travel bags, strollers, buggies, cameras, or mobile phones are allowed on the tour. No smoking, eating, or drinking are permitted, and no visitor toilets are available once the tour begins.

In Phoenix Park, Dublin 7. ℂ **01/670-9155.** www.irlgov.ie/aras. Free admission. Summer Sat 10am–5pm; winter 10:30am–4pm. Closed Dec 24–26. Same-day tickets issued at Phoenix Park Visitor Centre (see later in this chapter). Bus: 10, 37, or 39.

The Book of Kells ★★★ The jewel in Ireland's tourism crown is the Book of Kells, a magnificent manuscript of the four Gospels, around A.D. 800, with elaborate scripting and illumination. This famous treasure and other early Christian manuscripts are on permanent public view at Trinity College, in the Colonnades, an exhibition area on the ground floor of the Old Library. Also housed in the Old Library is the **Dublin Experience,** an excellent multimedia introduction to the history and people of Dublin. The oldest university in Ireland, Trinity was founded in 1592 by Queen Elizabeth I. It occupies a beautiful 16-hectare (40-acre) site just south of the River Liffey, with cobbled squares, gardens, a picturesque quadrangle, and buildings dating from the 17th to the 20th centuries.

College Green, Dublin 2. 🕜 **01/608-2320**. www.tcd.ie/Library/Visitors/kells.htm . Free admission to college grounds. €6 ($6.90) adults, €5 ($5.75) seniors/students, €11 ($13) families, free for children under 12. Combination tickets for the Library and Dublin Experience also available. Mon–Sat 9:30am–5pm; Sun noon–4:30pm (opens at 9:30am June–Sept).

Christ Church Cathedral ★★
Standing on high ground in the oldest part of the city, this cathedral is one of Dublin's finest historic buildings. It dates from 1038, when Sitric, Danish king of Dublin, built the first wooden Christ Church here. In 1171, the original simple foundation was extended into a cruciform and rebuilt in stone by Strongbow. The present structure dates mainly from 1871 to 1878, when a huge restoration took place. Highlights of the interior include magnificent stonework and graceful pointed arches, with delicately chiseled supporting columns. This is the mother church for the diocese of Dublin and Glendalough of the Church of Ireland. The Treasury in the crypt is open to the public, and you can hear bells pealing in the belfry.

Christ Church Place, Dublin 8. 🕜 **01/677-8099**. cccdub@indigo.ie. Suggested donation €5 ($5.75) adults, €2.50 ($2.90) students and children under 15. Daily 10am–5:30pm. Closed Dec 26. Bus: 21A, 50, 50A, 78, 78A, or 78B.

Collins Barracks
Officially part of the National Museum, Collins Barracks is the oldest military barracks in Europe. Even if it were empty, it would be well worth a visit for the structure itself, a splendidly restored early-18th-century masterwork by Colonel Thomas Burgh, Ireland's chief engineer and surveyor general under Queen Anne. The collection housed here focuses on the decorative arts. Most notable is the extraordinary display of Irish silver and furniture. Until the acquisition of this vast space, only a fraction of the National Museum's collection could be displayed, but that is changing, and more and more treasures find their way here. It is a prime site for touring exhibitions, so consult *The Event Guide* for details. A cafe and gift shop are on the premises.

Benburb St., Dublin 7. 🕜 **01/677-7444**. Free admission. Tours (hours vary) €1.50 ($1.75) adults, free for seniors and children. Tues–Sat 10am–5pm; Sun 2–5pm. Bus: 34, 70, or 80.

Dublin Castle ★★
Built between 1208 and 1220, this complex represents some of the oldest surviving architecture in the city. It was the center of British power in Ireland for more than 7 centuries, until the new Irish government took it over in 1922. Film buffs might recognize the castle's courtyard as a setting in the Neil Jordan film *Michael Collins*. Highlights include the 13th-century Record Tower; the State Apartments, once the residence of English viceroys; and the Chapel Royal, a 19th-century Gothic building with particularly fine plaster decoration and carved oak gallery fronts and fittings. The newest developments are the Undercroft, an excavated site on the grounds where an early Viking fortress stood, and the Treasury, built between 1712 and 1715 and believed to be the oldest surviving office building in Ireland. Also here are a crafts shop, a heritage center, and a restaurant.

Palace St. (off Dame St.), Dublin 2. 🕜 **01/677-7129**. dublincastle@eircom.net. Admission €4.25 ($4.90) adults, €3.25 ($3.75) seniors and students, €1.75 ($2) children under 12. No credit cards. Mon–Fri 10am–5pm; Sat–Sun and holidays 2–5pm. Guided tours every 20–25 min. Bus: 50, 50A, 54, 56A, 77, 77A, or 77B.

Dublin Writers Museum ★★
Housed in a stunning 18th-century Georgian mansion with splendid plasterwork and stained glass, the museum is itself an impressive reminder of the grandeur of the Irish literary tradition. A fine collection of personal manuscripts and mementos that belonged to Yeats, Joyce, Beckett, Behan, Shaw, Wilde, Swift, and Sheridan are among the items that celebrate the written word. One of the museum's rooms is devoted to children's literature.

18–19 Parnell Sq. N., Dublin 1. © 01/475-0854. Admission €6 ($6.90) adults, €5 ($5.75) seniors, students and children, €17 ($19) families (2 adults and up to 4 children). AE, DC, MC, V. Mon–Sat 10am–5pm (6pm June–Aug); Sun and holidays 11am–5pm. DART to Connolly Station. Bus: 11, 13, 16, 16A, 22, or 22A.

Dublinia ★   What was Dublin like in medieval times? This historically accurate presentation of the Old City from 1170 to 1540 is re-created through a series of theme exhibits and experiences. Highlights include an illuminated Medieval Maze, complete with visual effects, sounds, and aromas that lead you on a journey through time from the arrival of the Anglo-Normans in 1170 to the closure of the monasteries in the 1530s. The medieval Fayre displays the wares of merchants from all over Europe. You can try on a flattering new robe, or, if you're feeling vulnerable, stop in at the armorer's and get fitted for chain mail.

St. Michael's Hill, Christ Church, Dublin 8. © 01/679-4611. www.dublinia.ie. Admission €5.75 ($6.60) adults; €4.50 ($5.20) seniors, students, and children; €15 ($17) family. AE, MC, V. Apr–Sept daily 10am–5pm; Oct–Mar Mon–Sat 11am–4pm, Sun 10am–4:30pm. Bus: 50, 78A, or 123.

Hugh Lane Municipal Gallery of Modern Art ★   This gallery is housed in a finely restored 18th-century building known as Charlemont House, next to the Dublin Writers Museum. It is named after Hugh Lane, an Irish art connoisseur who was killed during the sinking of the *Lusitania* in 1915 and who willed his collection (including works by Courbet, Manet, Monet, and Corot) to be shared between the government of Ireland and the National Gallery of London. With the Lane collection as its nucleus, this gallery also contains Impressionist and post-Impressionist paintings, sculptures by Rodin, stained glass, and works by modern Irish artists. In 2001 the museum opened the reconstructed studio of Irish painter Francis Bacon. The bookshop is considered the best art bookshop in the city.

Parnell Sq. N., Dublin 1. © 01/874-1903. Fax 01/872-2182. www.hughlane.ie. Free admission to museum; Francis Bacon studio €7 ($8.05) adults, €3.50 ($4) students. MC, V. Tues–Thurs 9:30am–6pm; Fri–Sat 9:30am–5pm; Sun 11am–5pm. DART to Connolly or Tara stations. Bus: 3, 10, 11, 13, 16, or 19.

Kilmainham Gaol Historical Museum ★   This is a key sight for anyone interested in Ireland's struggle for independence from British rule. Within these walls political prisoners were incarcerated, tortured, and killed from 1796 until 1924, when President Eamon de Valera left as its final prisoner. To walk along these corridors, through the exercise yard, or into the main compound is a moving experience that lingers hauntingly in the memory. *Note:* The **War Memorial Gardens** (© **01/677-0236**), along the banks of the Liffey, are a 5-minute walk from Kilmainham Gaol. The gardens were designed by the famous British architect Sir Edwin Lutyens (1869–1944). They continue to present a moving testimony to Ireland's war dead. They're open weekdays 8am to dark, Saturday 10am to dark.

Kilmainham, Dublin 8. © 01/453-5984. www.heritageireland.ie. Guided tour €5 ($5.75) adults, €3.50 ($4) seniors, €2 ($2.30) children, €11 ($13) family. AE, MC, V. Apr–Sept daily 9:30am–4:45pm; Oct–Mar Mon–Fri 9:30am–4pm, Sun 10am–4:45pm. Bus: 51B, 78A, or 79 at O'Connell Bridge.

National Gallery ★★★   This museum houses Ireland's national art collection, as well as a superb collection of 14th- to 20th-century European art. Every major European school of painting is represented, including fine selections by Italian Renaissance artists, French Impressionists, and Dutch 17th-century masters. The Millennium Wing houses various temporary exhibitions as well as the Irish collection, which includes many mesmerizing works of Jack B. Yeats, brother of the poet William Butler Yeats. All public areas are wheelchair accessible. The museum has a fine gallery shop and an excellent self-service restaurant (see review in "Where to Dine," above).

Merrion Sq. W., Dublin 2. © **01/661-5133.** Fax 01/661-5372. www.nationalgallery.ie. Free admission. Mon–Sat 9:30am–5:30pm (Thurs–8:30pm); Sun noon–5pm. Free guided tours (meet in the Shaw Room) Sat 3pm, Sun 2, 3, and 4pm. Closed Good Friday and Dec. 24–26. DART: Pearse. Bus: 5, 6, 7, 7A, 8, 10, 44, 47, 47B, 48A, or 62.

National Museum *★★★*   Established in 1890, this museum is a reflection of Ireland's archaeological and historical heritage from 2000 B.C. to the present. It is the home of many of the country's greatest historical finds, including the Ardagh Chalice, Tara Brooch, and Cross of Cong. Other highlights range from the artifacts from the Wood Quay excavations of the Old Dublin Settlements to "Or," an extensive exhibition of Irish Bronze Age gold ornaments dating from 2200 to 700 B.C. The museum has a shop and a cafe. *Note:* The National Museum encompasses two other attractions, **Collins Barracks** and the **Natural History Museum;** see their separate listings.

Kildare and Merrion sts., Dublin 2. © **01/677-7444.** Free admission. Tours (hours vary) €1.50 ($1.70) adults, free for seniors and children. MC, V. Tues–Sat 10am–5pm; Sun 2–5pm. DART: Pearse. Bus: 7, 7A, 8, 10, 11, or 13.

MORE ATTRACTIONS

GAA Museum   On the grounds of Croke Park, principal stadium of the Gaelic Athletic Association, this museum dramatically presents the athletic heritage of Ireland. The Gaelic Games (Gaelic football, hurling, handball, and camogie) have long been held on an annual basis between teams representing the various regions of Ireland. Test your skills with interactive exhibits, and peruse the extensive video archive of football finals dating back to 1931. The 12-minute film *A Sunday in September* captures admirably the hysteria of the final match. *Note:* The museum is open only to those holding tickets in the new stands on match days.

Croke Park, Dublin 3. © **01/855-8176.** Fax 01/855-8104. www.gaa.ie. Admission €5 ($5.75) adults, €3.50 ($4) students, €3 ($3.45) children, €13 ($15) family. May–Sept daily 9:30am–5pm; Oct–Apr Tues–Sat 10am–5pm, Sun noon–5pm. Bus: 3, 11, 11A, 16, 16A, 51A, or 123.

Guinness Storehouse   Founded in 1759, the Guinness Brewery is one of the world's largest breweries, producing the distinctive dark beer called stout, famous for its thick, creamy head. Although tours of the brewery are no longer allowed, visitors are welcome to explore the adjacent Guinness Storehouse, a converted 19th-century four-story building. It houses the World of Guinness Exhibition, an audiovisual presentation showing how the stout is made, and a bar where visitors can sample a glass. The brewery recently became home to the largest glass of stout in the world, roughly 60m (200 ft.) tall, whose head is in fact an observatory restaurant offering spectacular views of the city.

St. James's Gate, Dublin 8. © **01/408-4800.** www.guinness.com. Admission €14 ($16) adults, €12 ($14) seniors, €9 ($10) students, €3 ($3.45) children 6-12, €28 ($32) family. AE, MC, V. Mon–Sun 9:30am–5pm. Guided tours every half-hour. Bus: 51B, 78A, or 123.

James Joyce Centre *★*   Near Parnell Square and the Dublin Writers Museum, the Joyce center is in a restored 1784 Georgian town house, once the home of Denis J. Maginni, a dancing instructor who appears briefly in *Ulysses.* The Ulysses Portrait Gallery on the second floor has a fascinating collection of photographs and drawings of characters from *Ulysses* who had a life outside the novel. The Paul Leon Exhibition Room holds the writing table used by Joyce in Paris when he was working on *Finnegans Wake.* There are talks and audiovisual

Native Behavior: The Art of Pouring Guinness

No trip to Ireland is complete without sampling the national beverage, whether you call it Guinness or simply "the black stuff." Despite its thick-as-pitch color, don't be afraid of it; Guinness isn't a heavy beer, only 11 calories per ounce or about 150 calories per pint, about the same as domestic beer. Draft Guinness is actually lower in alcohol than Coors Light. To the Irish, it's a classic "session beer," one with low alcohol and a great taste that can be enjoyed without leaving you feeling bloated. There are plenty of hops thrown in to give it a robust taste, and the Irish will vouch for the old advertising slogan that "Guinness is good for you."

Yet the Guinness ritual doesn't begin in the drinking; it starts in the pouring. And pouring the perfect pint is, as any respectable Irish barman will tell you, an art form known as the "two-shot pour." Watch as he quickly fills the pint glass three-quarters of the way with swirling stout, then sets the glass on the counter for about a minute and a half so that the gas can break out. It's the 75% nitrogen to 25% carbon dioxide mix that builds the famous Guinness head. Next, the barman tops up the pint, and serves it while a sepia-colored storm brews inside. Patience, patience: No sipping until the pint has settled into a distinct line between the black stout and the honey-colored head. Classically, the head should stand "proud," just slightly above the rim of the glass and quite thick and moussey. And with a "Cheers!" or "Slainte!" (pronounced slahn-chuh, Irish for "To your health!") you're finally ready to enjoy your pint.

presentations daily. Guided walking tours through the neighborhood streets of "Joyce Country" in Dublin's north inner city are offered daily.

35 N. Great George's St., Dublin 1. ✆ 01/878-8547. www.jamesjoyce.ie. Admission €4.50 ($5.20) adults; €3.50 ($4) seniors, students, and children under 10; €13 ($14) family. Separate fees for walking tours and events. AE, MC, V. Mon–Sat 9:30am–5pm; Sun 12:30–5pm. Closed Dec 24–26. DART: Connolly. Bus: 3, 10, 11, 11A, 13, 16, 16A, 19, 19A, 22, or 22A.

The Joyce Tower Museum ✪   Sitting on the edge of Dublin Bay about 10km (6¼ miles) south of the city center, this 12m (40-ft.) granite monument is one of a series of Martello towers built in 1804 to withstand an invasion threatened by Napoleon. The tower's great claim to fame is that James Joyce lived here in 1904. He was the guest of Oliver Gogarty, who had rented the tower from the Army for an annual fee of £8. Joyce, in turn, made the tower the setting for the first chapter of *Ulysses,* and it has been known as Joyce's Tower ever since. Its collection of Joycean memorabilia includes letters, documents, first and rare editions, personal possessions, and photographs.

Sandycove, County Dublin. ✆ 01/280-9265. Admission €6 ($6.90) adults; €5 ($5.75) seniors, students, and children; €17 ($19) family. Apr–Oct Mon–Sat 10am–1pm and 2–5pm; Sun 2–6pm. Closed Nov–Mar. DART: Sandycove. Bus: 8.

Natural History Museum   A division of the National Museum of Ireland, the recently renovated Natural History Museum is considered one of the finest traditional Victorian-style museums in the world. In addition to presenting the zoological history of Ireland, it contains examples of major animal groups from around the world, including many that are rare or extinct. The Blaschka glass models of marine animals are a big attraction.

Merrion St., Dublin 2. C 01/677-7444. Free admission. Tues–Sat 10am–5pm; Sun 2–5pm. DART: Pearse. Bus: 7, 7A, 8, or 13A.

Irish Film Centre ★   This art-house film institute is a hip hangout in Dublin's artsy Temple Bar district. The Irish Film Centre houses two cinemas, the Irish Film Archive, a library, a bookshop and cafe, and eight film-related organizations. Follow a movie with lunch in the cafe for a perfect midday outing.

6 Eustace St., Dublin 2. C 01/679-5744 or 01/679-3477 for cinema box office. Free admission; cinema tickets €6 ($6.90). Centre open daily 10am–11pm; cinemas daily 2–11pm; cinema box office daily 1:30–9pm. Bus: 21A, 78A, or 78B.

Irish Museum of Modern Art (IMMA) ★ *Kids*   Housed in the splendidly restored 17th-century Royal Hospital, IMMA is a showcase of Irish and international art from the latter half of the 20th century. The buildings and grounds also provide a venue for theatrical and musical events. The galleries contain the work of Irish and international artists from the small but impressive permanent collection, with numerous temporary exhibitions. There's even a drawing room, where kids and parents can record their impressions of the museum with crayons. The formal gardens, an important early feature of this magnificent structure, are open to the public during museum hours. A new bookshop and a cafe are located in the former vaults of the building.

Military Rd., Kilmainham. C 01/612-9900. www.modernart.ie. Free admission. Tues–Sat 10am–5:30pm; Sun noon–5:30pm. Bus: 79 or 90.

Old Jameson Distillery   This museum illustrates the history of Irish whiskey, known in Irish as *uisce beathectare* ("the water of life"). Housed in a former distillery warehouse, it consists of a short introductory audiovisual presentation, an exhibition area, and a whiskey-making demonstration. At the end of the tour, visitors can sample whiskey at an in-house pub, where an array of fixed-price menus (for lunch, tea, or dinner) is available. An added attraction here at Smithfield Village is **"The Chimney,"** a ride to the top of a 56m (185-ft.) brick chimney built in 1895 and converted to support an observation chamber from which you'll enjoy unparalleled views of the city.

Bow St., Smithfield Village, Dublin 7. C 01/807-2355. Admission €7 ($8.05) adults, €5.75 ($6.60) students and seniors, €3 ($3.45) children, €18 ($21) family. Daily 9:30am–6pm (last tour at 5pm). Mon–Sat 10am–6pm; Sun 11am–7pm. Bus: 67, 67A, 68, 69, 79, or 90.

St. Patrick's Cathedral   It is said that St. Patrick baptized converts on this site, and consequently a church has stood here since A.D. 450, making it the oldest Christian site in Dublin. The present cathedral dates from 1190, but because of a fire and 14th-century rebuilding, not much of the original remains. It's mainly early English in style, with a square medieval tower that houses the largest ringing peal bells in Ireland and an 18th-century spire. The 90m (300-ft.) interior makes it the longest church in the country. Jonathan Swift was dean from 1713 to 1745, and his tomb lies in the south aisle. St. Patrick's is the national cathedral of the Church of Ireland.

21–50 Patrick's Close, Patrick St., Dublin 8. C 01/475-4817. Fax 01/454-6374. www.stpatrickscathedral.ie. Admission €4 ($4.60) adults, €3 ($3.45) students and seniors, €9 ($10) family. MC, V. Mon–Fri 9am–6pm year-round; Nov–Feb Sat 9am–5pm, Sun 9am–3pm. Closed except for services Dec 24–26 and Jan 1. Bus: 65, 65B, 50, 50A, 54, 54A, 56A, or 77.

Waterways Visitor Centre Heading south from Dublin on the DART, you'll see the tiny Waterways Visitor Centre, a brilliant white cube floating on the Grand Canal Basin amid massive derelict brick warehouses. This intriguing modern building is home to a fascinating exhibit describing the history of Ireland's inland waterways, a network of canals connecting Dublin westward and northward to the Shannon watershed. A series of displays describe aspects of canal design, and several interactive models attempt to demonstrate dynamically the daily operations of the canals. No longer used for transporting goods, the canals of Ireland are now popular among boaters and hikers, and the Visitor Centre offers information for those interested in these activities.

Grand Canal Quay, Ringsend Rd., Dublin 2. ℂ 01/677-7510. Admission €2.50 ($2.90) adults, €1.90 ($2.20) seniors, €1.20 ($1.40) students, €1.50 ($1.40) children, €6.35 ($7.30) family. No credit cards. June–Sept daily 9:30am–5:30pm; Oct–May Wed–Sun 12:30–5pm. DART: Pearse. Bus: 1 or 3.

PARKS & ZOOS

St. Stephen's Green ✿ Preserved as an open space for Dubliners since 1690 and a short walk from most city-center locations, this large park is popular for picnics, reading, a quiet stroll, and summertime concerts. While you're here, be sure to visit the **Iveagh Gardens** ✿, a small garden hidden behind the National Concert Hall. Largely neglected by visitors, this is something of a hidden treasure within the city center. The main entrance is from Clonmel Street, off Harcourt Street, less than 5 minutes from Stephen's Green. The hours are the same as those for St. Stephen's Green.

St. Stephen's Green, Dublin 2. Mon–Sat 8am–dark; Sun 10am–dark. DART: Pearse. Bus: 10, 11A, 11B, 13, or 20B.

Phoenix Park ✿ Dublin's 712-hectare (1,760-acre) playground (Europe's largest enclosed urban park) opened in 1747. Situated 3km (1¾ miles) west of the city center, it is traversed by a network of roads and quiet pedestrian walkways and is informally landscaped with ornamental gardens, nature trails, and broad expanses of grassland separated by avenues of trees, including oak, beech, pine, chestnut, and lime. The residences of the Irish president (see earlier in this chapter) and the U.S. ambassador are on its grounds. Livestock graze peacefully on pasturelands, deer roam the forested areas, and horses romp on polo fields. The Phoenix Park Visitor Centre, adjacent to Ashtown Castle, offers exhibitions and an audiovisual presentation on the park's history. The cafe/restaurant is open from 10am to 5pm weekdays, from 10am to 6pm weekends. A shuttle bus runs on Saturday only from the visitor center, with stops throughout the park. One-day hop-on, hop-off service is €1.50 ($1.75) per person. On Saturdays only, free tickets are issued at the visitor center for tours of **Áras an Uachtaráin (The President's Residence;** ℂ **01/670-9155)** (see earlier in this chapter).

The **Dublin Zoo** (ℂ **01/677-1425;** www.dublinzoo.ie), also located here in Phoenix Park, was established in 1830 and is the third-oldest zoo in the world (after those in London and Paris). In the past few years, the zoo has doubled in size to about 25 hectares (60 acres) and provides a naturally landscaped habitat for more than 235 species of wild animals and tropical birds. Highlights for youngsters include the Children's Pets' Corner and a train ride around the zoo. There are playgrounds interspersed throughout the zoo, as well as several restaurants, coffee shops, and gift shops.

Phoenix Park, Dublin 8. ℂ 01/677-0095. www.heritageireland.ie. Visitor Centre: Admission €2.75 ($3.15) adults, €2 ($2.30) seniors and students, €1.25 ($1.45) children, €9 ($10) families. June–Sept 10am–6pm (call for off-season hours). Bus: 37, 38, or 39. Zoo: Admission €11 ($13) adults, €7 ($8.05) seniors and children 3–16, free for children under 3, €29–€34 ($33–$39) family, depending on number of children. V. Summer Mon–Sat 9:30am–6pm, Sun 10:30am–6pm. Bus: 10, 25, or 26.

National Botanic Gardens Remember this quiet, lovely haven when you suddenly crave refuge from the bustle of the city. Established by the Royal Dublin Society in 1795 on a rolling 20-hectare (50-acre) expanse of land north of the city center, this is Dublin's horticultural showcase. The attractions include more than 20,000 different plants and cultivars, a Great Yew Walk, a bog garden, a water garden, a rose garden, and an herb garden. A variety of Victorian-style glass houses are filled with tropical plants and exotic species. All but the rose garden are wheelchair accessible.

Botanic Rd., Glasnevin, Dublin 9. (℃ 01/837-7596. Free admission. Guided tour €2 ($2.30). Apr–Oct Mon–Sat 9am–6pm, Sun 11am–6pm; Nov–Mar Mon–Sat 10am–4:30pm, Sun 11am–4:30pm. Bus: 13, 19, or 134.

ORGANIZED TOURS

BUS TOURS If you want to get a general feel for the city, **Dublin Bus** (℃ **01/873-4222;** www.dublinbus.ie) operates a very good, 75-minute hop-on, hop-off **Dublin City Tour** that connects 10 major points of interest, including museums, art galleries, churches and cathedrals, libraries, and historic sites. It departs from the Dublin Bus office at 59 Upper O'Connell St., Dublin 1, daily from 9:30am to 6:30pm. Free pickup from many hotels is available for morning tours. Fares are €13 ($14) adults, €6 ($6.90) children under 14, €17 ($20) for a family of four. You can buy your ticket from the bus driver or book in advance at the Dublin Bus office or at the Dublin Tourism ticket desk on Suffolk Street.

Gray Line (℃ **01/605-7705;** www.guidefriday.com) operates its own hop-on, hop-off city tour, covering the same major sights as the Dublin Bus's Dublin City Tour. The tours are identical, so there's no reason to pay more for Gray Line. The first tours leave at 10am from 14 Upper O'Connell St., and at 10am from the Dublin Tourism Center on Suffolk Street, Dublin 2, and run every 10 to 15 minutes thereafter. The last departures are at 4pm from Suffolk Street, 4:30pm from O'Connell Street. You can also join the tour at any of a number of pickup points along the route and buy your ticket from the driver. Gray Line's Dublin City Tour costs €14 ($16) adults, €12 ($14) seniors and students, €5 ($5.75) children, €32 ($37) family.

WALKING TOURS You can set out on your own with a map, but the best way to avoid any hassles or missed sights is to follow one of the four signposted and themed **"tourist trails":** Old City Trail for historic sights; Georgian Trail for the landmark buildings, streets, squares, terraces, and parks; a "Rock 'n Stroll Guide" for a walking tour with a music theme; and Cultural Heritage Trail for a circuit of the top literary sites, museums, galleries, theaters, and churches. Each trail is mapped out with commentary in a handy booklet available at the tourist office or as a free printable guide from Dublin Tourism's website (www.visitdublin.com).

A number of firms offer guided tours led by knowledgeable locals. Tour times and charges vary, but many last about 2 hours and cost between €9 ($10) and €10 ($12). A complete listing of walking tours is available from Dublin Tourism, but here are some of the best:

Historical Walking Tours of Dublin (℃ **01/878-0227;** €10/$12) delivers your best introductory walk, an award-winning 2-hour primer on Dublin's historic landmarks, from medieval walls and Viking remains around Wood Quay to Christ Church, Dublin Castle, City Hall, and Trinity College. Guides are history graduates of Trinity College, and participants are encouraged to ask questions.

If you prefer an evening tour, there's the **Literary Pub Crawl** (℃ **01/670-5602;** €10/$12), a winner of the "Living Dublin Award." The tour follows in the footsteps of Joyce, Behan, Beckett, Shaw, Kavanagh, and other Irish literary greats to local pubs, with actors providing humorous performances and commentary between stops. Throughout the night, there is a Literary Quiz with prizes for the winners.

Zosimus Ghostly Experience (© 01/661-8646; €9/$10) is the latest rage on the walking-tour circuit. Its creators describe it as a "cocktail mix" of ghosts, murderous tales, horror stories, humor, circus, history, street theater, and whatever's left, all set in medieval Dublin. Your storyteller is the blind and aging Zosimus, and you help guide him down the austere alleyways. It's essential to book this tour in advance, when you'll receive the where (gate of Dublin Castle, opposite the Olympia Theatre) and the when (7pm in winter, 9pm in summer). The experience lasts approximately 1½ hours.

HORSE-DRAWN CARRIAGE TOURS   If you don't mind being conspicuous, you can tour Dublin in style in a handsomely outfitted horse-drawn carriage while your driver points out the sights. To arrange a ride, consult with one of the drivers stationed with carriages on the Grafton Street side of St. Stephen's Green. Rides range from a short swing around the Green to an extensive half-hour Georgian tour or an hour-long Old City tour. Rides are available on a first-come, first-served basis from April to October (weather permitting) and cost anywhere from €15 to €50 ($17–$58) for one to four passengers, depending on the duration of the ride.

LAND & WATER TOURS   The immensely popular **Viking Splash Tour** ★★ (© 01/855-3000; www.vikingsplashtours.com) brings you aboard a reconditioned World War II amphibious landing craft, or "duck." The tour begins on land (from Bull Alley St. beside St. Patrick's Cathedral) and eventually splashes into the Grand Canal. Passengers wear horned Viking helmets (a reference to the original settlers of the Dublin area) and are encouraged to issue war cries at appropriate moments. Tours last 75 minutes and depart roughly every half-hour Monday through Saturday from 10am to 5pm and Sunday from 11am to 6:30pm. It costs €14 ($16) for adults, €7.95 ($9) for children under 12, and €47 ($54) for a family of five. To book with a credit card by phone, call © 086/828-3773.

THE SHOPPING SCENE

The hub of shopping south of the Liffey is the pedestrians-only **Grafton Street,** crowned by the city's most fashionable department store, Brown Thomas (known simply as BT), and most exclusive jeweler, Weirs. Sadly, many Irish specialty shops on Grafton Street have been displaced over the years by British chain shops (Principles, Jigsaw, Monsoon, Oasis, A–Wear, Next, Boots, Mothercare), so that it now resembles the average High Street in England. Pedestrianized Grafton Street tends to have a festive atmosphere thanks to street performers and sidewalk artists. But you'll find better shopping on the smaller streets radiating out from Grafton—Duke, Dawson, Nassau, and Wicklow—which have more Irish shops that specialize in small books, handcrafts, jewelry, gifts, and clothing. Two upscale shopping malls, the **Powerscourt Townhouse Centre** and **St. Stephen's Green Centre,** are examples of Dublin's ongoing renovation and gentrification.

A 2-minute walk northwest toward the river brings you to **Temple Bar,** the hub of Dublin's colorful, bohemian district and the setting for art and music shops, vintage-clothing stores, and a host of other increasingly fine and interesting boutiques, cafes, and restaurants. Dublin's latest "it" shopping district is **Old City,** located just west of Temple Bar and roughly comprising the area between Castle Street and Fishamble Street. Though still under development, it already has a good mix of hip fashion, modern interior design, crafts, and leisure shops.

The center of the action is a cobbled, pedestrianized street called Cow's Lane, which links Lord Edward Street with Essex Street West.

North of the Liffey, the **O'Connell Street** area is the main inner-city shopping nucleus, along with its nearby offshoots—Abbey Street for crafts, Moore Street for its open-air market, and, most notably, Henry Street, a pedestrian-only strip of chain stores, department stores, and indoor malls such as the ILAC Centre and the Jervis Shopping Centre.

BOOKS   This city of literary legends has quite a few good bookstores. For fine new and used books, including first editions of works by famous Irish authors, try **Hodges Figgis,** 57 Dawson St., Dublin 2 (© 01/677-4754); more affordable used books can be found at **Greene's Bookshop,** 16 Clare St., Dublin 2 (© 01/676-2554) and the **Winding Stair,** 40 Lower Ormond Quay, Dublin 1 (© 01/873-3292).

CHINA & CRYSTAL   China Showrooms, 32/33 Abbey St. (© 01/878-6211; www.chinashowrooms.ie), is a one-stop source of fine china such as Belleek, Aynsley, and Royal Doulton, and hand-cut crystal from Waterford, Tipperary, and Tyrone. The **Dublin Crystal Glass Company,** Brookfield Terrace, Carysfort Avenue, Blackrock (© 01/288-7932; www.dublincrystal.ie), is Dublin's own distinctive hand-cut crystal business, founded in 1764 and revived in 1968. Dublin Crystal is a 15-minute walk from the Blackrock DART station.

CRAFTS & GIFTS   Whichcraft, 5 Castlegate, Lord Edward St. (© 01/670-9371), is an essential stop for finding out what the best contemporary artisans from all over Ireland are doing. All kinds of crafts are represented, from wooden bowls to basketry to rocking horses to pottery to jewelry to batiks. A second Whichcraft shop is on Cow's Lane in the burgeoning Old City.

FASHION   Alias Tom, Duke House, Duke St. (© 01/671-5443), is Dublin's best small, men's designer shop. The emphasis is on Italian (Gucci, Prada, Armani) labels, but chic designers from the rest of Europe and America are also represented. **Claire Garvey,** 6 Cow's Lane (© 01/671-7287), is a Dublin native with a talent for creating romantic, dramatic, and feminine clothing with Celtic flair. A favorite designer of Irish divas Enya and Sinead O'Connor, Garvey transforms hand-dyed velvet and silk into sumptuous garments that beg to be worn on special occasions. Her one-of-a-kind bijou handbags are a white-hot fashion accessory. **Design Centre,** Powerscourt Townhouse (© 01/679-4144), is the city's best one-stop shop for finding apparel from Ireland's hottest contemporary designers—including Louise Kennedy, Mary Gregory, Karen Millen, Mary Grant, and Sharon Hoey. Prices are generally high, but good bargains can be had during sale seasons and on the seconds rack.

HERALDRY   Heraldic Artists, 3 Nassau St. (© 01/679-7020), has been known for helping visitors celebrate their family roots for over 20 years. In addition to tracing surnames, it also sells all the usual heraldic items, from parchments and mahogany wall plaques to crests, scrolls, and books on researching ancestry.

KNITWEAR   Blarney Woollen Mills, 21–23 Nassau St. (© 01/671-0068), known for its competitive prices, stocks a wide range of woolen knitwear made at its home base in Blarney, as well as crystal, china, pottery, and souvenirs. **Brown Thomas,** 88–95 Grafton St. (© 01/605-6666), is the only place in town to find Dubliner Lainey Keogh's creative and sensuous knitwear—a far cry from the chunky Aran sweaters you see everywhere else. What *Vogue* magazine calls "amazingly organic knitwear" is a staple in the closets of such Hollywood celebrities as Demi Moore and Isabella Rossellini. Keogh works mostly with cashmere, and her pieces are predominantly made by expert hand-knitters, so prices are high. **Dublin Woollen Mills,** 41 Lower Ormond Quay (© **01/677-0301**), is on the north side of the River Liffey next to the Ha'penny Bridge, a leading source of Aran hand-knit sweaters as well as vests, hats, jackets, and tweeds. For cashmere, go to **Monaghan's,** 15–17 Grafton Arcade, Grafton Street (© **01/677-0823**), which has the best selection of colors, sizes, and styles for both men and women anywhere in Ireland. It's also located at 4–5 Royal Hibernian Way, off Dawson Street (© **01/679-4451**).

DUBLIN AFTER DARK

One general fact to keep in mind concerning Dublin's nightlife is that there are very few fixed points. Apart from a handful of established institutions, venues come and go, change character, open their doors to ballet one night and cabaret the next. Two publications, *In Dublin* and *The Event Guide,* offer the most thorough and up-to-date listings of what's happening in town. They can be found at any newsstand.

The award-winning website of the *Irish Times* (**www.ireland.com**) offers a "what's on" daily guide to cinema, theater, music, and whatever else you're up for. The **Dublin Events Guide,** at www.dublinevents.com, also provides a comprehensive listing of the week's entertainment possibilities. *Time Out* now covers Dublin as well; check out their website at **www.timeout.com/dublin/**.

Advance bookings for most large concerts, plays, and so forth can be made through **Ticketmaster Ireland** (© **01/677-9409**; www.ticketmaster.ie), with ticket centers in most HMV stores, as well as at the Dublin Tourism Centre, Suffolk Street, Dublin 2.

THE PERFORMING ARTS
Concert & Performance Halls

National Concert Hall, Earlsfort Terrace, Dublin 2 (© **01/475-1572**; www. nch.ie), is home to the National Symphony Orchestra and Concert Orchestra, and is host to an array of international orchestras and performing artists. In addition to classical music, there are evenings of Gilbert and Sullivan, opera, jazz, and recitals. The box office is open Monday through Saturday from 10am

---

Traditional Irish Entertainment

Culturlann Na hEireann, 32 Belgrave Sq., Monkstown (© **01/280-0295**; www.comhaltas.com), is the home of Comhaltas Ceoltoiri Eireann, an Irish cultural organization that has been the prime mover in encouraging the renewal of Irish traditional music. An authentic fully costumed show featuring traditional music, song, and dance is staged mid-June through early September, Monday through Thursday at 9pm. No reservations are necessary. Year-round, ceili dances are performed Friday from 9pm to midnight; informal music sessions are held Wednesday, Friday, and Saturday at 9pm. Tickets for ceilis are €6 ($6.90); informal music sessions €2 ($2.30) from Friday to Saturday, free Wednesday; stage shows €8 ($9.20).

Jury's Irish Cabaret, Pembroke Road, Ballsbridge (© **01/660-5000**), Ireland's longest-running show (over 30 years), offers a mix of traditional Irish music and Broadway classics, set dancing, humorous monologues, and audience participation. Shows take place May through October, Tuesday through Sunday, with dinner at 7:15pm and the show at 8pm. Dinner and show are €50 ($58); show with two drinks €35 ($40).

to 3pm and from 6pm to the concert's close. Tickets are €10 to €32 ($12–$37). Lunchtime concerts are €5 ($5.75).

For more than 90 years, the **Abbey Theatre,** Lower Abbey St., Dublin 1 (℗ **01/878-7222;** www.abbeytheatre.ie), has been the national theater of Ireland. The Abbey's artistic reputation within Ireland has risen and fallen many times and is at present reasonably strong. The box office is open Monday through Saturday from 10:30am to 7pm; performances begin at 8 or 8:15pm. Tickets are €15 to €26 ($17–$30).

The Gate, 1 Cavendish Row, Dublin 1 (℗ **01/874-4368;** fax 01/874-5373), just north of O'Connell Street off Parnell Square, was founded in 1928 by Hilton Edwards and Michael MacLiammoir to provide a showing for a broad range of plays. This policy prevails today, with a program that includes a blend of modern works and the classics. Although less well known by visitors, the Gate is easily as distinguished as the Abbey. The box office is open Monday through Saturday from 10am to 7pm. Tickets are €21 to €25 ($24–$29).

The **Andrews Lane Theatre,** 12–16 Andrews Lane, Dublin 2 (℗ **01/679-5720**), has a growing reputation for fine theater. It consists of a main theater where contemporary works from home and abroad are presented, and a studio geared for experimental productions. The box office is open Monday through Saturday from 10:30am to 7pm. Tickets are €13 to €20 ($15–$23).

With a seating capacity of 3,000, **The Point Depot,** East Link Bridge, North Wall Quay (℗ **01/836-3633**), is one of Dublin's larger indoor theater/concert venues, attracting top Broadway-caliber shows and international stars such as Neil Young and Justin Timberlake. The box office is open Monday through Saturday from 10am to 6pm. Tickets are €13 to €65 ($15–$75).

THE PUB SCENE
Pubs for Conversation & Atmosphere
The brass-filled and lantern-lit **Brazen Head,** 20 Lower Bridge St. (℗ **01/679-5186**), has atmosphere in spades. It's a tad touristy, which isn't surprising when you consider that it's the city's oldest pub—licensed in 1661 and occupying the site of an earlier tavern dating from 1198. On the south bank of the River Liffey, it's at the end of a cobblestone courtyard and was once the meeting place of Irish freedom fighters such as Robert Emmet and Wolfe Tone.

Try for one of the comfy booths in the back of the **Mercantile,** Dame Street (℗ **01/679-0522**), an ultratrendy watering hole that draws a mixed crowd of locals and in-the-know out-of-towners. Despite being very big, it's always buzzing and tends to get overjammed on weekends, so midweek nights are the best. U2 members The Edge and Larry Mullen are regulars. Converted from an old merchant's warehouse, the **River Club,** in the Ha'penny Theatre, 48 Wellington Quay (℗ **01/677-2382**), is a wine bar–cum–supper club with soaring ceilings, an enviable position overlooking the river, and contemporary furnishings for an overall feeling of easygoing sophistication. It's a favorite of Ireland's film glitterati for a late drink, so don't be surprised to spy author-screenwriter Roddy Doyle, Pierce Brosnan, or director Jim Sheridan.

Referred to as a "moral pub" by James Joyce in *Ulysses,* **Davy Byrnes,** 21 Duke St., just off Grafton Street (℗ **01/677-5217**), has drawn poets, writers, and lovers of literature ever since. Davy Byrnes first opened the doors in 1873; he presided here for more than 50 years and visitors today can still see his likeness on one of the turn-of-the-20th-century murals hanging over the bar.

Flannery's Temple Bar, 47–48 Temple Bar (℗ **01/497-4766**), in the heart of the trendy Temple Bar district on the corner of Temple Lane, was established in 1840. The decor is an interesting mix of crackling fireplaces, globe ceiling lights, old pictures on the walls, and shelves filled with local memorabilia. Tucked into a busy commercial street, **The Long Hall,** 51 S. Great George's St. (© **01/475-1590**), is one of the city's most photographed pubs, with a beautiful Victorian decor of filigree-edged mirrors, polished dark woods, and traditional snugs. The hand-carved bar is said to be the longest counter in the city.

Adjacent to the back door of the Gaiety Theatre, **Neary's,** 1 Chatham St., Dublin 2 (© **01/677-7371**), is a favorite with stage folk and theatergoers. Trademarks here are the pink-and-gray marble bar and the brass hands that support the globe lanterns adorning the entrance. Three generations of the Ryan family have contributed to the success of **J. W. Ryan,** 28 Parkgate St. (© **01/677-6097**), on the north side of the Liffey near Phoenix Park. The pub is a Victorian gem featuring a pressed tin ceiling and domed skylight, etched glass, brass lamp holders, a mahogany bar, and four old-style snugs.

Pubs with Traditional & Folk Music

Tucked between St. Stephen's Green and Merrion Street, **O'Donoghue's,** 15 Merrion Row, Dublin 2 (© **01/660-7194**), is a much-touristed, smoke-filled, kingpin of traditional music pubs. The Dubliners, one of Ireland's favorite traditional bands, got their start here, and impromptu music sessions are held almost every night. Situated in the heart of Temple Bar and named for one of Ireland's literary greats, **Oliver St. John Gogarty,** 57–58 Fleet St. (© **01/671-1822**), has an inviting old-world atmosphere, with shelves of empty bottles, stacks of dusty books, a horseshoe-shaped bar, and old barrels for seats. There are traditional music sessions every night from 9 to 11pm. A Saturday session is at 4:30pm, and a Sunday session from noon to 2pm.

THE CLUB & MUSIC SCENE

The club and music scene in Dublin is confoundingly complex and changeable. Jazz, blues, folk, country, traditional, rock, and comedy move from venue to venue, night by night. The same club could be a gay fetish scene one night and a traditional music hot spot the next, so you have to stay on your toes to find what you want. The first rule is to get the very latest listings and see what's on and where (see the introduction to "Dublin After Dark," above, for suggested resources). Keeping all this in mind, a few low-risk generalizations might prove helpful to give you a sense of what to expect.

One fact unlikely to change is that the after-hours scene in Dublin is definitively young, averaging about 25. The hottest clubs have a "strict" (read: unfriendly) door policy of admitting only "regulars." It helps if you're a celebrity or a supermodel—or just look like one. But barring that, your chances of getting past the door increase if you go in smallish groups, and if you wear your hippest clothes and your coolest attitude.

Dozens of clubs and pubs all over town feature rock, folk, jazz, and traditional Irish music. This includes the so-called "late-night pubs"—pubs with an exemption allowing them to remain open past the usual closing time, mandated by law (11pm in winter, 11:30pm in summer). Check *In Dublin* magazine or *The Event Guide* for club schedules. One of the most popular rock clubs is **Whelan's,** 25 Wexford St., Dublin 2 (© **01/478-0766**); you should also visit the new **Hot Press Irish Music Hall of Fame,** 57 Middle Abbey St., Dublin 1 (© **01/878-3345**), with music from Celtic to rock most nights; and the second-oldest pub in Dublin, **Bleeding Horse,** 24–25 Camden St., Dublin 2 (© **01/475-2705**). Other venues especially popular with the over-30 late crowd include: **Bad Bob's**

Backstage Bar, East Essex Street, Dublin 2 (© **01/677-5482**); **Major Tom's,** South King Street, Dublin 2 (© **01/478-3266**); the **Baggot Inn,** Baggot Street, Dublin 4 (© **01/676-1430**); and **Sinnotts,** South King Street, Dublin 2 (© **01/478-4698**). All are open daily, with live music most nights. When there is a cover charge, it's usually €5 to €10 ($5.75–$12).

The city's largest gay bar is the **George,** 89 S. Great George's St., Dublin 2 (© **01/478-2983**), a two-story venue where both the decor and clientele tend toward camp. It's open daily from 12:30pm to 2:30am; check listings magazines for theme nights, which start around 10pm.

2 Kerry & the Dingle Peninsula

For many first-time travelers to this island, Kerry is the Ireland they'd envisioned and hoped to encounter. For starters, it's picture-postcard gorgeous, with spectacular coastal vistas and vibrant towns. Spend a bit of time here, and you'll also see that Kerry is a place of disorienting contrasts, where the crassest tourist attractions coexist with some of Ireland's most spectacular scenic wonders. It's a rugged place for the most part, some of it so rugged that it's seldom visited and remains quite pristine; Ireland's two highest mountains, Carrantuohill and Mount Brandon, are examples of such places. You could be driving along—say, on the famous and much-trafficked Ring of Kerry, which traces the shores of the Iveragh Peninsula—make one little detour from the main road, and be in true wilderness. The transition can be startling.

Like many of Ireland's western counties, County Kerry has always been an outpost of Gaelic culture. Poetry and music are intrinsic to the lifestyle, as is a love of the outdoors and sports. Gaelic football is an obsession in this county, and "The Kingdom" wins more than their share of the national championships. You'll also find some of Ireland's best golf courses, and the fishing for salmon and trout is equally hard to resist.

GETTING TO COUNTY KERRY   **By Train**   Irish Rail (© **01/836-6222;** www.irishrail.ie) operates daily train service from Dublin, Limerick, Cork, and Galway to the **Killarney Railway Station** (© **064/31067**) on Railway Road, off East Avenue Road.

By Bus   Bus Eireann (© **01/836-6111;** www.buseireann.ie) operates daily express coach and local bus services to Killarney from Dublin and other parts of Ireland. The bus depot (© **064/34777**) is adjacent to the train station at Railway Road, off East Avenue Road. Once you're there, there's also limited daily service from Killarney to Caherciveen, Waterville, Kenmare, and other towns on the Ring of Kerry. Some private, Killarney-based companies offer daily sightseeing tours of the Ring of Kerry by bus.

By Car   Roads leading into Kerry include N6 from Dublin, N21 and N23 from Limerick, and N22 from Cork. The best way to do the Ring of Kerry (comprising the N70 and N71) is by car.

KILLARNEY TOWN

Killarney is the busiest beehive of tourism in Ireland, the Grand Central Station of the southwest, with all the positive and negative connotations that this implies. The town becomes one giant traffic jam of battling tour buses every summer and a mecca for pushy jaunting-car (horse-and-buggy) drivers. Tourism is more in-your-face here than perhaps anywhere else in Ireland, with generic souvenir shops and overpriced restaurants chockablock. If this doesn't sound like

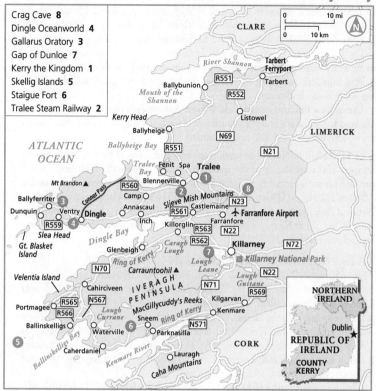

Crag Cave **8**
Dingle Oceanworld **4**
Gallarus Oratory **3**
Gap of Dunloe **7**
Kerry the Kingdom **1**
Skellig Islands **5**
Staigue Fort **6**
Tralee Steam Railway **2**

your bag, then resist Killarney's gravitational pull and base yourself in the incredibly scenic hinterlands that border the town on all sides. Then you can sneak into town at some point to sample the best of what this tourist megalopolis has to offer without experiencing the tourist trap in full gear.

It's important to remember that the reason Killarney draws millions of visitors a year has nothing to do with the town. It's all about the valley in which the town is nestled, a landscape of lakes and mountains that's so truly spectacular that Brendan Behan once said, "Even an ad man would be ashamed to eulogize it." And entering these wonders is ever so easy. Walk from the town car park toward the cathedral, and turn left into the national park (see below). During the summer, the evenings are long, the twilight is often indescribable, and you needn't share the lanes. Apart from deer and locals, the park is all yours until dark.

The lakes and the surrounding woodlands are part of the 65-sq.-km (25-sq.-mile) **Killarney National Park.** The ground is a soft carpet of moss and the air is fragrant with wildflowers. Cars are banned from most of the ferny trails, so take a hike or hire a "jarvey," an old-fashioned horse-and-buggy that's a holdover from the days when the Victorians waxed poetically about Killarney and brought it to the attention of the world.

ESSENTIALS

VISITOR INFORMATION County Kerry's official tourism website is **www.kerry-tourism.com**. The **Killarney Tourist Office,** Aras Fáilte, is located at the Town Centre Car Park, Beech Road, Killarney (© **064/31633**). It's open

October to April, Monday to Saturday 9:15am to 1pm and 2:15 to 5:30pm; May, Monday to Saturday 9:15am to 5:30pm; June, Monday to Saturday 9am to 6pm, Sunday 10am to 1pm and 2 to 6pm; July and August, Monday to Saturday 9am to 8pm, Sunday 10am to 1pm and 2 to 6pm; September, Monday to Saturday 9am to 6pm, Sunday 10am to 1pm and 2:15 to 6pm. It offers many helpful booklets, including the *Tourist Trail* walking-tour guide and the *Killarney Area Guide,* with maps.

Useful local publications include **Where: Killarney,** a quarterly magazine distributed free at hotels and guesthouses. It is packed with current information on tours, activities, events, and entertainment.

GETTING AROUND The town is so small and compact that it's best traversed on foot. Taxi cabs line up at the stand on **College Square** (© 064/31331). You can also phone for a taxi from **John Burke** (© 064/32448), **Dero's Taxi Service** (© 064/31251), or **O'Connell Taxi** (© 064/31654). You can drive to Killarney National Park (but not through it), or go by **jaunting car.** The horse-drawn jaunting cars line up at Kenmare Place, offering rides to Killarney National Park sites and other scenic areas.

KILLARNEY NATIONAL PARK ★★★

This is Killarney's centerpiece: a 10,000-hectare (25,000-acre) area of natural beauty. The park's three lakes are Killarney's main attraction. The first, the Lower Lake, is sometimes called "Lough Leane" or "Lough Lein," which means "the lake of learning." It's the largest, more than 6.5km (4 miles) long, and is dotted with 30 small islands. The second lake is aptly called the "Middle Lake" or "Muckross Lake," and the third simply "Upper Lake." Upper Lake, the smallest, is full of storybook islands covered with a variety of trees—evergreens, cedars of Lebanon, juniper, holly, and mountain ash.

The most noteworthy of Killarney's islands is **Innisfallen,** or "Fallen's Island," which seems to float peacefully in the Lower Lake. You can reach it by rowboat, available for rental at Ross Castle. St. Fallen founded a monastery here in the 7th century, and it flourished for 1,000 years. It's said that Brian Boru, the great Irish chieftain, and St. Brendan the Navigator were educated here. From 950 to 1320, the *Annals of Innisfallen,* a chronicle of early Irish history, was written at the monastery; it's now in the Bodleian Library at Oxford University. Traces of an 11th-century church and a 12th-century priory can still be seen today.

Found within the park's limits are two major demesnes, or estates, **Muckross** and **Knockreer,** and the remains of major medieval abbeys and castles. A profusion of foliage, such as rhododendrons, azaleas, magnolias, camellias, hydrangeas, and tropical ferns, blossoms in season. At almost every turn, you'll see Killarney's own botanical wonder, the arbutus, or strawberry tree, plus eucalyptus, redwoods, and native oak.

The park also contains a large variety of wildlife, including a rare herd of red deer. You can't drive through the park (parking lots are available, however, if you want to drive *to* it), so touring is best done on foot, bicycle, or horse-drawn jaunting car. The park offers four signposted walking and nature trails along the lakeshore.

Access to the park is available from several points along the Kenmare road (N71), with the main entrance being at Muckross House, where a new visitor center features background exhibits on the park and a 20-minute film titled *Mountain, Wood, Water.* Admission is free, and the park is open year-round during daylight hours.

VIEWS & VISTAS   The journey through the **Gap of Dunloe** ☆☆ is a must. The winding and rocky mountain pass is situated amid mountains and lakelands about 10km (6¼ miles) west of Killarney. The route through the gap passes a kaleidoscope of craggy rocks, massive cliffs, meandering streams, and deep valleys. The route through the gap ends at Upper Lake. One of the best ways to explore the gap is by bicycle. Horse fanciers may want to take one of the excursions offered by **Castlelough Tours,** 7 High St. (© **064/31115**); **Corcoran's Tours,** Kilcummin (© **064/36666**); **Dero's Tours,** 22 Main St. (© **064/31251** or 064/31567); or **Tangney Tours,** Kinvara House, Muckross Road (© **064/ 33358**). Combination horse/boat tours cost €37 ($43). If you'd rather have someone else handle the horse, you can take an 11km (6¾-mile) jaunting-car tour. Excursions go from Kate Kearney's Cottage through the Gap of Dunloe to Lord Brandon's Cottage and back.

Aghadoe Heights ☆, on the Tralee Road (off N22), is a spectacular viewing point over the lakes and town. To your left is the ruin of the 13th-century Castle of Parkvonear, erected by Norman invaders and well worth a visit. In the nearby churchyard are the remains of a stone church and round tower dating from 1027.

MORE ATTRACTIONS

Muckross House and Gardens ☆☆   This estate is the focal point of the Middle Lake and, in many ways, of the entire national park. It's often called "the jewel of Killarney." The property consists of a gracious ivy-covered Victorian mansion and its elegant surrounding gardens. Dating from 1843, the 20-room Muckross House has been converted into a museum of County Kerry folk life, showcasing locally carved furniture, prints, maps, paintings, and needlework. Imported treasures like Oriental screens, Venetian mirrors, Chippendale chairs, Turkish carpets, and curtains woven in Brussels are on display. The cellars have been converted into craft shops where local artisans demonstrate traditional trades such as bookbinding, weaving, and pottery. The adjacent mature gardens, known for their fine collection of rhododendrons and azaleas, are also worth exploring.

The ruin of the 15th-century **Muckross Abbey,** founded about 1448 and burned by Cromwell's troops in 1652, is also near the house. The abbey's central feature is a vaulted cloister around a courtyard that contains a huge yew tree, said to be as old as the abbey itself. A combination ticket includes Muckross Traditional Farms (see below).

Kenmare Rd. (N71), Killarney, County Kerry. © **064/31440.** www.muckross-house.ie. Admission €5.50 ($6.35) adults, €4.25 ($4.90) seniors, €2.25 ($2.60) students and children, €14 ($16) family. July–Aug daily 9am–7pm; Nov–June and Sept–Oct daily 9am–6pm.

Muckross Traditional Farms ☆   Located just across from Muckross House, this 28-hectare (70-acre) park is home to displays of traditional farm life and artisans' shops so authentically detailed that visitors feel they are dropping in on working farms and lived-in houses. It's a fascinating place, especially for families with children. You'll be able to watch sowing and harvesting or potato picking and hay making, depending on the season. Farmhands work in the fields and tend the animals, while the blacksmith, carpenter, and wheelwright ply their trades in the old manner. Women draw water from wells and cook meals in traditional kitchens with authentic household items. *Note:* A combination ticket allows you to visit Muckross House for €2.50 ($2.90) extra per person.

Kenmare Rd. (N71), Killarney, County Kerry. © **064/31440.** www.muckross-house.ie. Admission €5.50 ($6.35) adults, €4.25 ($4.90) seniors, €2.25 ($2.60) students and children, €14 ($16) family. Combination ticket with Muckross House €8.25 ($9.50) adults, €6.25 ($7.20) seniors, €3.75 ($4.30) students and children, €21 ($24) family. Mid-Mar to Apr and Oct Sat–Sun 1–6pm; May daily 1–6pm; June–Sept daily 10am–7pm. Closed Nov to mid-Mar.

Ross Castle   This 15th-century restored fortress sits on the edge of the Lower Lake, 3km (1¾ miles) outside Killarney Town. Built by the O'Donoghue chieftains, this castle distinguished itself in 1652 as the last stronghold in Munster to surrender to Cromwell's forces. All that remains today is a tower house, surrounded by a fortified bawn (enclosure) with rounded turrets. The tower has been furnished in the style of the late 16th and early 17th centuries and offers a magnificent view of the lakes and islands from its top. Access is by guided tour only. A lovely lakeshore walk stretches for 1.6km (1 mile) between Killarney and the castle. Lake cruises are run from the castle (see "Boat Tours," below), including boats to **Innisfallen Island,** which has the ruins of a 7th-century monastery and a 12th-century oratory.

Ross Rd., off Kenmare rd. (N71), Killarney, County Kerry. ℂ 064/35851. Admission €5 ($5.75) adults, €3.50 ($4) seniors, €2 ($2.30) students and children, €11 ($13) family. Apr daily 10am–5pm; May and Sept daily 10am–6pm; June–Aug daily 9am–6:30pm; Oct Tues–Sun 10am–5pm. Last admission 45 min. before closing. Closed Nov–Mar.

SIGHTSEEING TOURS

BUS TOURS   **Dero's Tours,** 7 Main St., Killarney (ℂ **064/31251** or 064/31567; www.derostours.com), offers a 3-hour tour showing off Killarney's lakes from the best vantage points, including Aghadoe, the Gap of Dunloe, Ross Castle, Muckross House and Gardens, and Torc Waterfall. The tour is offered May through September daily at 10:30am, but schedules vary, so check in advance. It costs €15 ($17).

Castlelough Tours, 7 High St., Killarney (ℂ **064/31115;** www.castleloughtours.com), offers a tour through the spectacularly scenic Gap of Dunloe that includes a boat tour of the Killarney lakes for €18 ($21). It's offered May through September; call for current hours and bookings.

In addition to Killarney's main sights, some bus tours also venture into the two prime scenic areas nearby: the Ring of Kerry and Dingle Peninsula. From May to September, tours are offered daily; prices average €18 ($21) per person. Check the following companies if that's the kind of tour for you: **Bus Eireann,** Bus Depot, Railway Road, off East Avenue Road (ℂ **064/34777;** www.bus eireann.ie); **Castlelough Tours,** 7 High St. (ℂ **064/31115**); **Corcoran's Tours,** 10 College St. (ℂ **064/36666;** www.corcorantours.com); and **Dero's Tours,** 22 Main St. (ℂ **064/31251** or 064/31567; www.derostours.com).

JAUNTING-CAR TOURS   If you prefer walking or bicycling, just say no to the numerous jaunting-car drivers who will inevitably offer their services as you make your way around the Killarney lakes. These quaint horse-driven buggies are one of the main features of the landscape here, and if at some point you decide to give one a try, keep in mind that jaunting-car rates are set and carefully monitored by the Killarney Urban District Council. Current rates, all based on four persons to a jaunting car, run roughly from €35 to €55 ($40–$63) per jaunting car, for up to four persons, depending on destinations that may include Ross Castle, Muckross House and Gardens, Torc Waterfall, Muckross Abbey, Dinis Island, and Kate Kearney's Cottage, gateway to the Gap of Dunloe. To arrange a tour in advance, contact Kinvara House, Muckross Road, Killarney (ℂ **064/33358**).

BOAT TOURS   There is nothing quite like seeing the sights from a boat on the Lakes of Killarney. Two companies operate regular boating excursions, with full commentary. **MV *Pride of the Lakes* Tours,** Scotts Gardens, Killarney (*©* **064/32638**), sails daily in an enclosed boat from the pier at Ross Castle from April to October at 11am, 12:30pm, 2:30pm, 4pm, and 5:15pm. The trip lasts just over an hour, and reservations are suggested. The cost is €8 ($9.20) adults, €4 ($4.60) children. **MV *Lily of Killarney* Tours,** 3 High St., Killarney (*©* **064/ 31068**), sails from April to October at 10:30am, noon, 1:45pm, 3:15pm, and 4:30pm for €8 ($9.20) adults, €4 ($4.60) children, €20 ($23) family.

ENJOYING THE GREAT OUTDOORS

BICYCLING   **Killarney National Park,** with its many lakeside and forest pathways, trails, and byways, is a paradise for bikers. Various vehicles are available for rent, from 21-speed touring bikes and mountain bikes to tandems. Rental charges average €12 ($14) per day, €70 ($81) per week. Bicycles can be rented from **David O'Sullivan's Cycles,** Bishop Lane, New Street (*©* **064/31282**). Most shops are open year-round daily 9am to 6pm, until 8 or 9pm in the summer.

One great ride beginning in Killarney takes you through the Gap of Dunloe along a dirt forest road, where you'll see some of the best mountain scenery in the area; it can be made into a 56km (35-mile) loop if you return on N71.

FISHING   Fishing for salmon and brown trout in Killarney's unpolluted lakes and rivers is a big attraction. Brown trout fishing is free on the lakes, but a permit is necessary for the rivers Flesk and Laune. A trout permit costs €4 to €14 ($4.60–$16) per day.

Salmon fishing anywhere in Ireland requires a license; the cost is €10 ($12) per day, €20 ($23) for 21 days. In addition, some rivers also require a salmon permit, which costs €10 to €14 ($12–$16) per day. Permits and licenses can be obtained at the Fishery Office at the **Knockreer Estate Office,** New Street (*©* **064/31246**).

For fishing tackle, bait, rod rental, and other fishing gear, as well as permits and licenses, try **O'Neill's,** 6 Plunkett St. (*©* **064/31970**). The shop also arranges the hire of boats and ghillies (fishing guides) for €80 ($92) per day on the Killarney Lakes, leaving from Ross Castle.

GOLF   Visitors are always welcome at the twin 18-hole championship courses of the **Killarney Golf & Fishing Club,** Killorglin Road, Fossa (*©* **064/31034;** www.killarney-golf.com), 4.8km (2¾ miles) west of the town center. Widely praised as one of the most scenic golf settings in the world, these courses, known as "Killeen" and "Mahony's Point," are surrounded by lake and mountain vistas. Greens fees are €70 ($81) weekdays and €75 ($86) weekends.

HORSEBACK RIDING   Many trails in the Killarney area are suitable for horseback riding. Hiring a horse costs about €20 ($23) per hour at **Killarney Riding Stables,** N72, Ballydowney (*©* **064/31686**), and **Rocklands Stables,** Rockfield, Tralee Road (*©* **064/32592**). Lessons and weeklong trail rides can also be arranged.

WALKING   Killarney is ideal for hiking. On the outskirts of town, the **Killarney National Park** offers four signposted nature trails. The **Mossy Woods Nature Trail** starts near Muckross House, by Muckross Lake, and rambles 2.4km (1½ miles) through yew woods along low cliffs. **Old Boat House Nature Trail** begins at the 19th-century boathouse below Muckross Gardens and leads half a mile around a small peninsula by Muckross Lake. **Arthur Young's Walk**

(4.8km/2¾ miles) starts on the road to Dinis, traverses natural yew woods, and then follows a 200-year-old road on the Muckross Peninsula. The **Blue Pool Nature Trail** (2.4km/1½ miles) goes from Muckross village through woodlands and past a small lake known as the Blue Pool. Leaflets with maps of the four trails are available at the park visitor center.

THE SHOPPING SCENE: KERRY GLASS & MORE

Shopping hours are normally Monday through Saturday from 9am to 6pm, but May through September most shops stay open to 9 or 10pm. Although there are more souvenir and crafts shops in Killarney than you can shake a stick (or shillelagh) at, here are a few of the best.

Blarney Woollen Mills, 10 Main St. (© **064/33222;** www.blarneywoollen mills.ie), a branch of the highly successful County Cork–based enterprise, occupies a beautiful shop front on the corner of Plunkett Street in the center of town. The wares range from hand-knit or hand-loomed sweaters to tweeds, china, pottery, and souvenirs of all sizes, shapes, and prices. **Quill's Woolen Market,** 1 High St. (© **064/32277**), is one of the best shops in town for hand-knit sweaters of all kinds, as well as tweeds, mohair, and sheepskins.

The **Mucros Craft Centre,** on the grounds of Muckross House (© **064-3144;** www.muckross-house.ie), is a studio-cum-shop carrying on many County Kerry craft traditions that features an on-premises weaver's workshop as well as a working pottery. There is also a wide selection of quality crafts from all over Ireland, and a skylit cafeteria overlooking the walled garden area. In town, **Serendipity,** 15 College St. (© **064/31056**), offers a wide range of unusual crafts from local artisans, such as hand-thrown pottery from the likes of Nicholas Mosse and Stephen Pearce, Jerpoint glass, and handcrafted jewelry.

WHERE TO STAY
Very Expensive

Killarney Park Hotel ✦ Voted by the Jameson Guide as "Hotel of the Year" for 2002, this handsome, neo-Georgian property is on the eastern edge of town, near the railway station. Public areas are posh and spacious and evoke a distinguished Victorian country house, with oil paintings, open fireplaces, and a sunlit conservatory-style lounge overlooking the gardens. Rooms have a traditional, conservative style, with quality provincial furnishings, designer fabrics, and marble-finished bathrooms.

Kenmare Place, Killarney, County Kerry. © 064/35555. Fax 064/35266. www.killarneyparkhotel.ie. 75 units. €240–€360 ($276–$414) double; €340–€700 ($391–$805) suite. No service charge. Rates include full breakfast. AE, DC, MC, V. **Amenities:** Restaurant; bar; indoor swimming pool; gym; Jacuzzi; sauna/steam room; concierge; room service; massage; babysitting; laundry service; library. *In room:* TV, minibar, hair dryer, garment press.

Moderate

Earl's Court House ✦ Award-winning Earl's Court, a 5-minute walk from the town center, is among Killarney's most attractive guesthouses. On arrival, you'll be greeted with tea and scones in a lovely lounge. Rooms are spacious and stylishly furnished with Irish antiques. Some have half-tester beds, others have sitting areas, and nearly all have balconies. Rooms on the second floor have the best views of the mountains. The copious breakfast can be enjoyed in the gracious, formal dining room or, by request, in your room.

Signposted off N71, Woodlawn Junction, Muckross Rd., Killarney, County Kerry. © 064/34009. Fax 064/34366. www.killarney-earlscourt.ie. 11 units, 1 single with shower only. €90–€150 ($104–$173) double. Rates include full Irish breakfast and service charge. MC, V. Closed Nov 6–Feb. Free parking. **Amenities:** Limited room service; nonsmoking rooms. *In room:* TV, radio, dataport, hair dryer.

Kathleen's Country House   Of the many guesthouses in the area, this one stands out. About 1.5km (1 mile) north of town on 1.2 hectares (3 acres) of gardens next to a dairy farm, it's a two-story contemporary stone house with a modern mansard-style roof and many picture windows. Enthusiastic, efficient hostess Kathleen O'Regan-Sheppard offers totally refurbished guest rooms with antique pine furniture and light floral paisley fabrics, complemented by Kathleen's collection of contemporary pastels and paintings. Smoking is permitted only in the enclosed front foyer.

Madam's Height, Tralee Rd. (N22), Killarney, County Kerry. © 064/32810. Fax 064/32340. www.kathleens. net. 17 units. €95–€130 ($109–$150) double. No service charge. Rates include full breakfast. AE, MC, V. Closed mid-Nov to early Mar. Free parking. **Amenities:** Nonsmoking rooms; drawing room; sunroom. *In room:* TV, tea/coffeemaker, hair dryer, garment press.

Killarney Great Southern ★★   Set amid 15 hectares (36 acres) of gardens on the eastern edge of town, this ivy-covered mansion is the grande dame of Killarney hotels. It was built around the time of Queen Victoria's visit to Killarney and has since welcomed presidents, princes, and personalities from all over the world. The public areas hearken to yesteryear, with high ceilings, glowing fireplaces, and Waterford chandeliers. Rooms have a traditional decor and are spacious and comfortable. Train and bus terminals are opposite the hotel.

Railway Rd., off E. Avenue Rd., Killarney, County Kerry. © 800/44-UTELL in the U.S., or 064/31262. Fax 064/ 31642. www.gsh.ie. 180 units. €150–€170 ($173–$196) double. Rates include full breakfast. AE, DC, MC, V. Street parking only. **Amenities:** 2 restaurants; bar; lounge; indoor heated swimming pool; 2 tennis courts; gym; Jacuzzi; sauna/steam room; concierge; salon; room service; laundry; dry cleaning. *In room:* TV, hair dryer, garment press.

Randles Court   A former rectory, this attractive yellow gabled house is located just outside Killarney on the road to Muckross House. Since it opened as a hotel more than a decade ago, the Randle family has turned this into one of the most charming places to stay in Killarney. The public areas are rich with marble floors, fireplaces, chandeliers, gilt mirrors, tapestries, and old prints. Three of the rooms are in the original building and the rest are in a new wing. All have distinctive furnishings, including armoires, antique desks, or vanities.

Muckross Rd. (N71), Killarney, County Kerry. © 800/4-CHOICE in the U.S., or 064/35333. Fax 064/35206. www.randleshotels.com. 37 units. €140–€180 ($161–$207) double. Rates include full breakfast and service charge. AE, DC, MC, V. Free parking. **Amenities:** Restaurant; bar; fitness center; limited room service; babysitting; laundry service. *In room:* TV, hair dryer.

Inexpensive/Moderate

Gleann Fia Country House ★   Although it's just a mile from town, this Victorian-style guesthouse feels pleasantly secluded, tucked away in 4 hectares (1¾ acres) of lawns and woodlands. Conor and Bridget O'Connell are thoughtful hosts whose presence makes this a highly personable place. The house has an airy conservatory with tea-making facilities, a guest lounge, and an unusually extensive breakfast menu. There is a nature walk along the stream by one side of the house.

Deerpark, Killarney, County Kerry. © 064/35035. Fax 064/35000. www.gleannfia.com. 17 units. €70–€126 ($81–$145) double. Rates include full breakfast. AE, MC, V. Closed Dec–Feb. Free parking. **Amenities:** Lounge; nonsmoking rooms; conservatory. *In room:* TV, hair dryer.

WHERE TO DINE
Expensive

Gaby's Seafood Restaurant ★★ SEAFOOD   One of Killarney's longest-established restaurants, this nautically themed place is a mecca for seafood lovers. Its walls are adorned with commendations and awards, which could be a tacky turnoff if the food weren't so good. Gaby's is known for its succulent lobster, served grilled or in a house sauce of cognac, wine, cream, and spices. Other choices include haddock in wine, a delectable tempura of prawns, and a giant Kerry shellfish platter—a veritable feast of prawns, scallops, mussels, lobster, and oysters.

27 High St., Killarney, County Kerry. ℂ **064/32519**. Reservations recommended. Main courses €25–€30 ($29–$35). AE, DC, MC, V. Mon–Sat 6–10pm. Closed late Feb to mid-Mar and Christmas week.

Moderate

Bricín ⭐ TRADITIONAL IRISH   Old-time Kerry boxty dishes (potato pancakes with various fillings, such as chicken, seafood, curried lamb, or vegetables) are the trademark of this restaurant above a very good crafts shop and bookshop. The menu also offers a variety of fresh seafood, pastas, and Irish stew. Specials might include filet of pork with sage and apricot stuffing, and chicken Bricín (breast of chicken in red-currant and raspberry sauce). Bricín is in one of Killarney's oldest buildings, dating from the 1830s. It sports original stone walls, pine furniture, turf fireplaces, and—very rare in Ireland—a completely nonsmoking room that seats 40. Snacks and light fare are served during the day.

26 High St., Killarney, County Kerry. ℂ **064/34902**. Reservations recommended for dinner. Fixed-price 2-course dinner €19 ($22); dinner main courses €17–€23 ($20–$26). AE, DC, MC, V. Year-round Tues–Sat 10am–4:30pm; Easter–Oct Mon–Sat 6–9:30pm.

Coopers Café and Restaurant ⭐⭐ MODERN CONTINENTAL   Coopers has clearly broken the mold here in Killarney, with its chic, urban, nightclub decor, making the most of glass, stone, aluminum, and sharp black-and-white contrasts. Overhead, the many-tendrilled wire-sculpture chandeliers with flower-cup lights cast a magical fairylike illumination. Menu options include wild pheasant cooked in Irish cream liqueur; escallop of venison; filet of wild pigeon; grilled swordfish and salmon; wild filet of sea trout; and baked cod Provençal. The alluring array of desserts includes crumbles, tarts, homemade ice creams, meringues, crème brûlées, and a dark chocolate and pistachio mousse.

Old Market Lane, off High St. (at New St.), Killarney, County Kerry. ℂ **064/37716**. Reservations recommended. Main courses €14–€22 ($16–$25). MC, V. Mon–Sat 12:30–3pm; Mon–Thurs 6:30–9:30pm; Fri–Sat 6:30–10pm; Sun 4–9:30pm.

IVERAGH PENINSULA/THE RING OF KERRY

For the majority of the literally millions of annual tourists to County Kerry, whose explorations follow the turn of a bus driver's wheel, the Iveragh Peninsula is synonymous with the Ring of Kerry. It's important to realize, however, that the Ring is a two-lane strip of tarmac measuring roughly 178km (110 miles), tracing the peninsula's shores and missing its tip altogether, while the Iveragh Peninsula itself is nearly 1,820 sq. km (700 sq. miles) of wild splendor, which you'll notice once you get off the tourist strip. Admittedly, almost everyone who gets this far feels compelled to "do" the Ring of Kerry; so, once it's done, why not take an unplanned turn, get truly lost, and let serendipity lead you to the unexpected and the unspoiled?

ESSENTIALS

MAKING THE DRIVE   By Bus   Bus Eireann (ℂ **064/34777**) provides limited daily service from Killarney to Caherciveen, Waterville, Kenmare, and other towns on the Ring of Kerry.

By Car   This is by far the best way to get around the Ring. For the most part, the route follows N70.

VISITOR INFORMATION   Stop in at the **Killarney Tourist Office,** Aras Fáilte, at the Town Centre Car Park, Beech Road, Killarney (✆ **064/31633**), before you explore the area. For hours, see "Visitor Information," under "Killarney Town," earlier in this chapter. The **Kenmare Tourist Office,** Market Square, Kenmare (✆ **064/41233**), is open daily Easter through September, 9:15am to 5:30pm, with extended hours in July and August. The rest of the year (Oct–Easter), it's open Monday to Saturday.

EXPLORING THE RING

Although it's possible to circle the peninsula in as little as 4 hours, the only way to get a feel for the area and the people is to leave the main road, get out of your car, and explore some of the inland and coastal towns. **Portmagee** is a lovely seaside town, connected by a bridge to **Valentia Island,** which houses the informative Skellig Heritage Centre. **Caherdaniel** has a museum devoted to Daniel O'Connell, one of Ireland's great historical figures.

The most memorable and magical site to visit on the Iveragh Peninsula is **Skellig Michael,** a rocky pinnacle towering over the sea, where medieval monks built their monastery in ascetic isolation. The crossing to the island can be rough, so you'll want to visit on as clear and calm a day as possible. Seabirds nest here in abundance, and more than 20,000 pairs of gannets inhabit neighboring Little Skellig during the summer nesting season.

Kenmare is by far the most enchanting town on the Ring of Kerry route. Originally called Neidin (pronounced *Nay-deen,* meaning "little nest" in Irish), Kenmare is indeed a little nest of verdant foliage tucked between the River Roughty and Kenmare Bay. It's an ideal base for Kerry sightseeing, as it is well laid out and immaculately maintained—flower boxes in the windows, litter-free sidewalks—and full of excellent restaurants and places to stay.

From Kenmare to **Killarney,** the Ring road takes you through a scenic mountain stretch known as **Moll's Gap.** Killarney is best known for the natural beauty surrounding the town, and in particular for the spectacular **Killarney National Park,** which includes the famous **Killarney Lakes** and the scenic **Gap of Dunloe.** The town itself, while colorful and bustling, has become a victim of its own success in recent years.

Departing Killarney, follow the signs for **Killorglin.** When you reach this little town, you're on N70. You might want to stop and walk around Killorglin, a spot that's widely known for its annual mid-August horse, sheep, and cattle fair. It's officially called the **Puck Fair,** because local residents capture a wild goat (symbolizing the *puka* or *puki,* a mischievous sprite) from the mountains and enthrone it in the center of town as a sign of unrestricted merrymaking.

Continue on N70, and vistas of Dingle Bay will soon appear on your right. **Carrantuohill,** at 1,024m (3,414 ft.) Ireland's tallest mountain, is to your left. The open bog land constantly comes into view. From it, the local residents dig pieces of peat, or turf, to burn in their fireplaces. Formed thousands of years ago, the bog lands are mainly composed of decayed trees. They tend to be bumpy if you attempt to drive over them too speedily, so do be cautious.

The Ring winds around cliffs and the edges of mountains, with nothing but the sea below—another reason you will probably average only 48kmph (30 mph), at best. As you go along, you'll notice the remains of many abandoned cottages. They date from the famine years, in the mid-1840s, when the Irish potato crop failed and millions of people starved to death or were forced to emigrate. This peninsula alone lost three-fourths of its population.

The next town on the Ring is **Glenbeigh,** a palm tree–lined fishing resort with a lovely duned beach called Rossbeigh Strand. You might want to stop here or continue the sweep through the mountains and along the sea's edge to **Cahirciveen.** From Cahirciveen, you can make a slight detour to see **Valentia** (which you may also see spelled "Valencia"). The offshore island is 11km (6¾ miles) long and one of Europe's westernmost points. Connected to the mainland by a bridge at Portmagee, this was the site from which the first telegraph cable was laid across the Atlantic in 1866. In the 18th century, the Valentia harbor was famous as a refuge for smugglers and privateers; it's said that John Paul Jones, the Scottish-born American naval officer in the War of Independence, often anchored here.

Head next for **Waterville,** an idyllic spot wedged between Lough Currane and Ballinskelligs Bay off the Atlantic. For years, it was known as the favorite retreat of Charlie Chaplin; today it's the home of the only Irish branch of Club Med.

If you follow the sea road north of town out to the Irish-speaking village of **Ballinskelligs,** at the mouth of the bay, you can catch a glimpse of the two Skellig Rocks. Continuing on N70, the next point of interest is **Derrynane,** at **Caherdaniel,** the home of Daniel O'Connell, remembered as "the Liberator" who freed Irish Catholics from the last of the English Penal Laws in 1829. Derrynane is a national monument and park and a major center of Gaelic culture.

Watch for signs to **Staigue Fort,** about 3km (1¾ miles) off the main road. One of the best preserved of all ancient Irish structures, this circular fort is constructed of rough stones without mortar of any kind. The walls are 4m (13 ft.) thick at the base, and the diameter is about 27m (90 ft.). Not much is known of its history, but experts think it probably dates from around 1000 B.C.

Sneem, the next village on the circuit, is a colorful little hamlet with twin parklets. Its houses are painted in vibrant shades of blue, pink, yellow, purple, and orange, like a little touch of the Mediterranean plunked down in Ireland.

As you continue on the Ring, the foliage becomes lusher, thanks to the warming waters and winds of the Gulf Stream. When you begin to see lots of palm trees and other subtropical vegetation, you'll know you are in **Parknasilla,** once a favorite haunt of George Bernard Shaw.

WHERE TO STAY AROUND THE RING
Very Expensive
The Park Hotel Kenmare ★★★   Ensconced in palm tree–lined gardens beside Kenmare Bay, this imposing limestone building was built at the end of the 19th century by the Great Southern Railway as a hotel for train travelers. The interior is rich in high-ceilinged sitting rooms and lounges, crackling open fireplaces, original oil paintings, tapestries, plush furnishings, and museum-worthy antiques (including an eye-catching cistern decorated with mythological figures and supported by gilded sea horses and dolphins).

The individually decorated guest rooms are decked out in a mix of Georgian and Victorian furnishings and rich upholsteries. Many have four-poster or canopy beds, hand-carved armoires, china lamps, curios, and luxurious extras like telephones in the bathroom and heated towel rails. Most rooms offer river and mountain vistas. Amid all the elegance, this hotel exudes an intrinsically welcoming atmosphere, and service is top-notch without being stuffy. The elegant dining room, with romantic views of the water and gardens, is one of the most acclaimed hotel restaurants in Ireland, meriting a Michelin star.

Kenmare, County Kerry. ✆ 800/323-5463 in the U.S., or 064/41200. Fax 064/41402. www.parkkenmare.com. 49 units. €366–€726 ($421–$835) double. No service charge. Rates include full breakfast. AE, DC, MC, V.

Closed Nov–Dec 22 and Jan 3–Mar. **Amenities:** Restaurant; bar; 18-hole golf course; joggers' trail; tennis court; croquet lawn; salmon fishing; concierge; limited room service; babysitting; laundry service; nonsmoking rooms; drawing room. *In room:* TV, CD player, minibar, hair dryer, garment press.

Sheen Falls Lodge ★★★   Everything at Sheen Falls conspires to make you feel stress-free and pampered—the fabulous service, the faultless attention to detail—which is why it's a favorite getaway for Irish and Hollywood celebrities and *Condé Nast Traveler* magazine voted it the third-best hotel in Europe. Originally the 18th-century home of the Earl of Kerry, this salubrious resort sits beside a natural waterfall on 120 hectares (300 acres) of lawns and semitropical gardens where the River Sheen meets the Kenmare Bay estuary. The public areas are graceful, with pillars and columns, polished woodwork, open fireplaces, traditional furnishings, and original oil paintings. The staff make an effort to address guests by name, the bar feels like a drawing room, and the 1,000-volume library, with its green leather sofas and floor-to-ceiling bookshelves, hearkens back to a fine gentlemen's club. The guest rooms are spacious, decorated in elegant, contemporary style; each overlooks the falls (stunning when floodlit at night) or the bay. It all comes at a price, but Sheen Falls has the perfect Irish country-house atmosphere: elegant yet relaxed.

Kenmare, County Kerry. © 800/537-8483 in the U.S., or 064/41600. Fax 064/41386. www.sheenfallslodge.ie. 61 units. €260–€395 ($299–$454) double; €395–€1,500 ($454–$1,725) suite. No service charge. AE, DC, MC, V. Closed Dec 24–Feb 1. **Amenities:** 2 restaurants; bar; indoor swimming pool; private salmon fishing; horseback riding; tennis; croquet; billiard room; gym; Jacuzzi; sauna/steam room; health and beauty treatments; concierge; room service; laundry/dry cleaning; library; helicopter pad. *In room:* A/C, TV/VCR, radio, minibar, hair dryer, garment press.

Moderate

Iskeroon ★★ *Value*   This is as good as it gets for this price. David and Geraldine Hare's wonderfully light B&B has an arrestingly beautiful setting in a 1.8-hectare (4½-acre) tropical garden overlooking the sailboats of Derrynane Harbour and the Skelligs beyond. And if the views don't convince you, just step inside. The Hares have renovated their circa-1930s villa in a modern, fresh, Cape Cod style: Think stone floors, a sea-blue and sand palette, baskets and assorted objets d'art. It's got the best of both worlds: The setting is tranquil and yet just a short walk away from the beach or a lovely pub or the pier, for island cruises. Breakfasts are excellent here, too. With only three rooms, this place gets sold out long in advance, so book early.

Bunavalla (near pier), Caherdaniel, County Kerry. © 066/947-5119. Fax 066/947-5488. www.iskeroon.com. 3 units, all with private bathroom. €110 ($127) double. Rates include full Irish breakfast and service charge. MC, V. Closed early Oct to mid-Apr. **Amenities:** Restaurant; lounge; outdoor swimming pool; tennis court; gym; sauna/steam room. *In room:* TV.

Sallyport House ★★   This wonderful country house B&B won the Irish Automobile Association's "Guest Accommodation of the Year" award in 2000. It's got a great location, just 2 minutes on foot into Kenmare, yet set on extensive, well-kept grounds that run down to the Kenmare River. After spending years refurbishing her brother's B&B in California, Janey Arthur returned to Kenmare and did up her own handsome manor splendidly with a sophisticated, uncluttered, and luxurious feel. The spacious, individually decorated guest rooms are furnished with well-chosen antiques, including very large beds and exceptionally grand bathrooms. Each room has a striking feature—extradeep window seats that beg you to take in mountain views, an enormous king-size four-poster bed, or perhaps a lovely river view.

Glengarriff Rd., Kenmare, County Kerry. ⓒ **064/42066**. Fax 0646/42067. www.sallyporthouse.com. 5 units. €120–€140 ($138–$161) double. Rates include full breakfast and service charge. No credit cards. Closed Nov to mid-Apr. **Amenities:** Lounge; nonsmoking rooms. *In room:* TV, hair dryer.

Shelburne Lodge ⟨★⟩   Yet another fabulous, reasonably priced place to ink into your travel journal. This time, it's a Georgian farmhouse that the owners Maura and Tom Foley have transformed into one of the most original, stylish, and comfortable B&Bs on the island. Every room in the house has polished wood parquet floors, truly beautiful (and beautifully arranged) antique furnishings, contemporary artwork, and boldly colored walls that go pow. The guest rooms are all large and gorgeously appointed, with particularly sumptuous bathrooms (heated towel rails and handmade mirrors). The breakfasts are nothing short of decadent, and Maura and Tom really take care of you throughout your stay.

Killowen, Cork Rd., Kenmare, County Kerry. ⓒ **064/41013**. Fax 0646/42135. 9 units. €95–€120 ($109–$138) double. Rates include full breakfast and service charge. MC, V. Closed Nov–Mar. **Amenities:** Tennis court; drawing room. *In room:* TV.

Inexpensive

Hawthorn House ⟨★⟩ ⟨*Value*⟩   On a quiet side street in Kenmare, this excellent-value town-house B&B has attracted a huge following over the years. Mary O'Brien is a congenial, gifted hostess, and her hospitality sets the tone for your stay. Her guest rooms all have a pretty, feminine feel, with floral bedspreads and pastel walls. Rooms here may be slightly smaller than you'd find at rural B&Bs that were built for this purpose, but they are certainly comfortable. Breakfasts are bountiful and delicious.

Shelbourne St., Kenmare, County Kerry. ⓒ **064/41035**. Fax 064/41932. www.hawthornhousekenmare. com. 8 units. €70 ($81) double. Rates include full breakfast and service charge. MC, V. Closed Christmas. **Amenities:** Sitting room. *In room:* TV, hair dryer.

WHERE TO DINE AROUND THE RING

Café Indigo ⟨★★⟩ MODERN CONTINENTAL/SEAFOOD   Vanessa Falvey is one of Ireland's hottest young chefs. Her cooking is a model of sophistication and simplicity, using a combination of fresh, local ingredients to bring one strong flavor to the fore. She's especially good with fish and seafood, with dishes like oven-baked salmon complemented by sun-dried-tomato tapenade, or celeriac purée with perfectly grilled sea scallops. The dining room is understated, the food is classy and memorable, and the crowd is happy.

The Square (above Square Pint pub), Kenmare, County Kerry. ⓒ **064/42356**. Reservations recommended. Main courses €18–€23 ($21–$26); main courses, grill menu €12–€15 ($14–$17). AE, DC, MC, V. Wed–Mon 7–11pm. Closed mid-Jan to mid-Mar.

d'Arcy's ⟨★★⟩ CONTINENTAL   In a two-story stone house at the top end of Kenmare, this restaurant has a homey atmosphere with a big open fireplace. The owner, Pat Gath, and head chef, James Mulchrone, make a great team, and this place is a standout even in this restaurant-rich town. Using fresh local ingredients, the menu includes classics such as peppered filet of beef with crispy onions and baked salmon with rosemary butter. Mulchrone's penchant for Mediterranean flavors is evident in dishes like the goat's cheese starter with olive-and-tomato sauce or the rack of lamb main course that comes stuffed with garlic and sun-dried tomatoes. The homemade breads and desserts are also excellent.

Main St., Kenmare, County Kerry. ⓒ **064/41589**. Reservations recommended. Main courses €20–€28 ($23–$32). MC, V. Daily 6:30–10pm. Closed Jan to mid-Mar.

Mulcahy's ★★★ MODERN/FUSION   This place is a wonderful example of why Kenmare has become one of Ireland's premier foodie towns. Bruce Mulcahy's restaurant is an out-of-the-box experience, from the moment you walk into the postmodern, avant-garde interior through the meal itself, a celebration of imaginative, but serious, fusion cooking. This is that rare combination of style and substance. Starters might include anything from pea soup to sushi. Zingy Asian influences may come to bear on European classics, but everything is done with just the right amount of restraint. For dessert, try the lemon tart with Amaretto cream. Good service, buzzing clientele, fabulous dining experience.

16 Henry St., Kenmare, County Kerry. ✆ 064/42383. Reservations recommended. Main courses €18–€23 ($21–$32). MC, V. Wed–Mon 6:30–10:30pm. Closed 2 weeks in mid-Jan and Nov.

Packie's ★★ BISTRO   If you're looking for a stylish place to have a great meal that won't break the bank, this little place is it. There's always a buzz here, and the smart crowd fits in perfectly with the bistro look—colorful window boxes, slate floor, stone walls filled with contemporary art, and dark oak tables and chairs. Everyone comes for the food, and chef-owner Maura Foley is known for never serving a bad meal. Her menu includes tried-and-true favorites such as Irish stew, delicious potato pancakes, mint-infused rack of lamb, and crab claws in garlic butter. But there are also more creative combinations, such as gratin of crab and prawns, beef braised in Guinness with mushrooms, and curry sabayon with Castletownberre prawns. Desserts are terrific, too.

Henry St., Kenmare, County Kerry. ✆ 064/41508. Reservations recommended. Main courses €14–€25 ($16–$29). MC, V. Easter to mid-Nov Tues–Sat 6–10pm.

Purple Heather ★★ (Finds) IRISH   This lovely little eatery is *the* place to lunch in Kenmare. The food is all about tearoom classics with a gourmet twist—wild smoked salmon or prawn salad, smoked trout pâté, vegetarian omelets, and Irish cheese platters, as well as homemade soups.

Henry St., Kenmare, County Kerry. ✆ 064/41016. All items €4–€17 ($4.60–$20). No credit cards. Mon–Sat 11am–7pm. Closed Christmas week.

SHOPPING IN KENMARE

The Green Note, 18 Henry St. (✆ 064/41212), is a traditional Irish-music store selling banjos, harps, and tin whistles. The **Kenmare Bookshop,** Shelburne St. (✆ 064/41578), specializes in books on Ireland, particularly Irish biographies and books by Irish writers, as well as maps and guides to the surrounding area, including ordinance survey maps, walking and specialist guides, and marine charts. **Nostalgia Linen and Lace,** 27 Henry St. (✆ 064/41389), specializes in Irish linens and sells lace by the meter. **Cleo,** Shelburne Road (✆ 064/41410), a branch of the long-established Dublin store of the same name, is a trendy women's-wear shop known for its beautiful, vibrantly colored tweed and linen fashions, as well as specialty items such as Kinsale cloaks. Perched in a most scenic setting, **Avoca Handweavers at Moll's Gap,** N71 (✆ 064/34720), is a branch of the famous tweed makers of County Wicklow. This outlet is set on a high mountain pass between Killarney and Kenmare. The wares range from colorful hand-woven capes, jackets, throws, and knitwear to pottery and jewelry. Oh, and it has an excellent coffee shop to boot.

TRALEE

Tralee is the commercial center of County Kerry; with its population of 22,000, it's three times the size of Killarney. This is more a functioning town than a tourist center, and locals outnumber visitors, except during the ever-popular **Rose of Tralee festival** in August (for more information, go to the website **www. roseoftralee.ie**). The town is the permanent home of the National Folk Theatre of Ireland, Siamsa Tíre, which operates year-round but is most active in July and August.

ESSENTIALS

GETTING THERE   By Air   Aer Lingus operates daily nonstop flights from Dublin into **Kerry County Airport,** Farranfore, County Kerry (✆ **066/976-4644**), about 24km (15 miles) south of Tralee.

By Bus   Buses from all parts of Ireland arrive daily at the **Bus Eireann Depot,** John Joe Sheehy Road (✆ **066/712-3566;** www.buseireann.ie).

By Train   Trains from major cities arrive at the **Irish Rail Station,** John Joe Sheehy Road (✆ **066/712-3522;** www.irishrail.ie).

By Car   Four major national roads converge on Tralee: N69 and N21 from Limerick and the north, N70 from the Ring of Kerry and points south, and N22 from Killarney, Cork, and the east.

VISITOR INFORMATION   The **Tralee Tourist Office,** Ashe Memorial Hall, Denny Street (✆ **066/712-1288**), offers information on Tralee and the Dingle Peninsula. It is open weekdays 9am to 1pm and 2 to 5pm, with weekend and extended hours in the spring and summer. There is also a first-rate cafe on the premises. For Tralee tourist information on the Web, explore **www. tralee-insight.com**.

SEEING THE SIGHTS

Believed to be more than a million years old, the limestone **Crag Cave** ✸, 24km (15 miles) north of Killarney off N21, Castleisland (✆ **066/41244;** www.crag cave.com), was discovered in 1983. Guides accompany you 3,750m (12,510 ft.) into the passage on a well-lit tour revealing some of the largest stalactites in Europe. A crafts shop and a restaurant are on the premises. Admission is €5 ($5.75) adults, €3.80 ($4.35) seniors and students, €2.50 ($2.90) children ages 6 to 17, €15 ($17) family (up to four children, children under 6 free). It's open daily mid-March through June and September through October from 10am to 6pm, July through August from 10am to 7pm.

Europe's westernmost railway, the restored **Tralee Steam Railway** ✸✸ train, Ballyard Station, Tralee (✆ **066/712-1064**), offers narrated, scenic 3km (1¾-mile) trips from Tralee to Blennerville. It uses equipment that was once part of the Tralee and Dingle Light Railway (1891–1953), one of the world's most famous narrow-gauge railways. Round-trip fare costs €5 ($5.75) adults, €3.50 ($4) students and seniors, €2.50 ($2.90) children, and €12 ($14) family. Trains run daily from May to October.

One of Ireland's largest indoor heritage centers, **Kerry the Kingdom** ✸, Ashe Memorial Hall, Denny Street, Tralee (✆ **066/712-7777**), offers three separate attractions that give an in-depth look at 7,000 years of life in County Kerry. A 10-minute video, *Kerry in Colour,* presents the seascapes and landscapes of Kerry; the Kerry County Museum chronologically examines the county's music, history, legends, and archaeology through interactive and hands-on exhibits; and the exhibit on Gaelic football is unique. Complete with lighting effects and aromas, a theme-park-style ride called "Geraldine Tralee" takes you through a re-creation of Tralee's streets, houses, and abbeys during the Middle Ages. Admission is €8 ($9.20) adults, €6.50 ($7.50) students, €5 ($5.75) children,

€22 ($25) family. The center is open daily mid-March through July from 10am to 6pm, August from 10am to 7pm, September through October from 10am to 6pm, and November through December 22 from noon to 5pm.

WHERE TO STAY

Abbey Gate Hotel ★ This relatively new three-story hotel brings much-needed quality lodging and a broader dimension of social activity to the center of Tralee town. The hotel is ideally located near Tralee's prime attractions, shops, and pubs. Guest rooms, like the public areas, are furnished with reproductions, and fabrics, art, and accessories convey an air of Georgian and Victorian Tralee.

Maine St., Tralee, County Kerry. ℂ 066/712-9888. Fax 066/712-9821. www.abbeygatehotel.com. 100 units. €110–€160 ($127–$184) double. No service charge. AE, DC, MC, V. Limited parking. **Amenities:** 2 restaurants; bar; limited room service; nonsmoking rooms. *In room:* TV, tea/coffeemaker, hair dryer.

Ballyseede Castle Hotel ★ Ballyseede Castle, a 15th-century castle complete with a live-in ghost, was once the chief garrison of the legendary Fitzgeralds, the earls of Desmond. The Blennerhassett family occupied it until 1966 and in 1985 turned it into a hotel. The lobby has Doric columns and a hand-carved oak staircase. Two drawing rooms are decorated with cornices of ornamental plasterwork and warmed by marble fireplaces. Guest rooms are spacious and elegantly appointed with period furnishings. The castle is 3.2km (2 miles) east of Tralee, on 12 hectares (30 acres) of parkland.

Tralee-Killarney rd., Tralee, County Kerry. ℂ 066/712-5799. Fax 066/712-5287. www.ballyseedecastle.com. 12 units. €130–€190 ($150–$219) double. MC, V. **Amenities:** Restaurant; piano lounge; library. *In room:* TV, hair dryer, garment press.

The Shores ★ *Value* This is a modern house, tastefully done over about 5 years ago, on the south side of Brandon Bay. It commands wonderful views of Tralee Bay and Mount Brandon. Annette O'Mahoney is an avid interior decorator and has extended a Victorian theme and a feeling of luxury throughout the house. Furnishings are lavish, with a canopy bed in one room and writing desks in three rooms. A downstairs room has a private entrance and a fireplace. All rooms have orthopedic beds, with crisp white cotton and cream lace linen. There's a sun deck and a beach for when the heavens are kind, and a guest library and video rentals for when they are not. Breakfast options are particularly extensive, with smoked salmon and waffles as alternatives to the standard fry.

.8km (½ mile) west of Stradbally on the Conor Pass Rd., Cappatigue, Castlegregory, County Kerry. ℂ 066/713-9196. 6 units. €70 ($81) double. Rates include full breakfast. MC, V. Closed Dec–Jan. **Amenities:** Nonsmoking rooms. *In room:* TV, tea/coffeemaker.

WHERE TO DINE

In addition to the recommendations below, you can get excellent pub grub, especially steaks, at **Kirby's Olde Brogue Inn,** Rock Street, Tralee (ℂ **066/712-3357**). This pub has a barnlike layout, with an interior that incorporates farming memorabilia and rush-work tables and chairs. Sometimes traditional music and folk ballads are served up as well.

Larkin's ★ *Value* SEAFOOD This bright, welcoming, Irish-country restaurant with antique pine furnishings is conveniently located and widely acclaimed for its catch of the day and roast rack of Irish lamb. The offerings are modestly priced and immodestly tasty. Proprietor Michael Fitzgibbon greets guests personally and generously provides information on the area.

Princes St., Tralee, County Kerry. ℂ 066/976-7217. Reservations recommended. Main courses €12–€21 ($14–$24); set-price menu €19 ($22). DC, MC, V. Mon–Fri 12:30–2pm and 6:30–9:30pm; Sat 6:30–9:30pm.

Restaurant David Norris ★★ MODERN CONTINENTAL   One of the best things to have happened to Tralee in the past few years is the return of David Norris to his hometown. Set in the pretty upstairs of Ivy House in the middle of Tralee, his restaurant has caused quite a stir in food circles since it opened. Come here for the kind of modern comfort food that never gets old: homemade fettuccine with wild mushrooms, chile-roasted pineapple and duck confit, and a luscious slab of Kerry beef with colcannon. Everything is made with precision and care. Service is good, desserts are worth saving room for—in short, it's the destination restaurant Tralee needed all those years.

Ivy House, Ivy Terrace, Tralee, County Kerry. ℂ 066/718-5654. Reservations necessary. Main courses €15–€22 ($17–$25). AE, MC, V. Tues–Sat 6:30–10pm.

The Tankard SEAFOOD   This is one of the few restaurants in the area that capitalizes on sweeping views of Tralee Bay. Situated on the water's edge, it has wide picture windows and sleek contemporary decor. The straightforward menu features local shellfish and seafood, such as lobster, scallops, prawns, and black sole. It also includes rack of lamb, duck, quail, and steak. This restaurant is at its best in the early evening, especially at sunset.

10km (6¼ miles) northwest of Tralee, Kilfenora, Fenit, County Kerry. ℂ 066/713-6164. Reservations recommended. Main courses €11–€20 ($13–$23). AE, DC, MC, V. Bar food daily 12:30–10pm; restaurant daily 6–10pm.

TRALEE AFTER DARK

Siamsa Tire, the National Folk Theatre of Ireland, is located at Town Park, Tralee (ℂ 066/712-3055; www.siamsatire.com). Founded in 1974, Siamsa (pronounced *Sheem*-sha) offers a mixture of music, dance, and mime. The scenes depict old folk tales and farmyard activities such as thatching a cottage roof, flailing sheaves of corn, and twisting a sugan (straw) rope. Siamsa also presents a full program of drama and musical concerts (from traditional to classical) performed by visiting amateur and professional companies. Admission is €16 ($18) adults; €14 ($16) seniors, students, and children. The schedule is Monday through Saturday from April to mid-October; curtain time is 8:30pm.

PUBS   Tralee pubs can be a little crowded and impersonal. **Olde Macs,** the Mall (ℂ 066/712-1572), is an exception. From the delightful flowers in the hanging baskets outside to the dark-wood interior, the pub exudes atmosphere. Conversation is lighthearted, and the regulars are extremely friendly. The nicest location of any pub in the Tralee area belongs to the **Oyster Tavern,** Fenit Road (ℂ 066/713-6102), 5km (3 miles) west of town overlooking Tralee Bay. The pub grub available includes seafood soups and platters.

THE DINGLE PENINSULA

Like the Iveragh Peninsula, Dingle has a spectacularly scenic peripheral road, and a substantially tacky tourist trade has blossomed along it. But as soon as you veer off the main roads or penetrate to such hinterlands of the peninsula as the Blasket Islands or Brandon Head, you'll discover extraordinary desolate beauty, seemingly worlds away from the tour buses and shamrock-filled shops. Dingle Town itself is definitely touristy, but it's smaller and less congested than Killarney and retains more traces of being a real, year-round town with an identity beyond the tourist trade. While the Dingle Peninsula is an ideal drive, it also makes a fine bicycling tour. Dingle village is a delightful place to stay (see below) while you explore the peninsula.

Don't miss **Slea Head,** at the southwestern extremity of the peninsula. It's a place of pristine beaches, great walks, and fascinating archaeological remains. The village of **Dunquin,** stunningly situated between Slea Head and Clogher Head, is home to the Blasket Centre. **Dunbeg Fort** sits on a rocky promontory just south of Slea Head, its walls rising from the cliff edge. Although much of the fort has fallen into the sea, the place is well worth a visit at the bargain-basement rate of €2 ($2.30) per person. From Slea Head, the Dingle Way continues east to Dingle Town (24km/15 miles) or north along the coast toward Ballyferriter.

Just offshore from Dunquin are the seven **Blasket Islands;** a ferry (© 066/915-6455) connects Great Blasket with the mainland when the weather permits. Alternatively, you can take a 3-hour cruise around the islands with **Blasket Island Tours** (© 066/915-6422), leaving from Dunquin Pier. The islands were abandoned by the last permanent residents in 1953 and now are inhabited only by a few summer visitors who share the place with the seals and seabirds. A magnificent 13km (8-mile) walk goes to the west end of Great Blasket and back, passing sea cliffs and ivory beaches; you can stop along the way at the only cafe on the island, which serves lunch and dinner.

DINGLE TOWN

With a charter dating back many centuries, Dingle was Kerry's principal harbor in medieval times. Even though it's just a small town (pop. 1,500), Dingle has more fine restaurants than many of Ireland's major cities, and is known for the traditional Irish music in its pubs.

EXPLORING THE TOWN

Despite the big-sounding name, **Dingle's Oceanworld Aquarium,** Dingle Harbour (© 066/915-2111; www.dingle-oceanworld.ie), is a relatively small aquarium with little to see to justify the ticket price: Admission costs €8 ($9.20) adults, €6 ($6.90) seniors and students, €5 ($5.75) children, €22 ($25) family. Various sea critters swim behind glass in the aquarium's 29 tanks, and young staffers carry around live marine creatures and introduce them up close to visitors. This compact, hands-on, interactive place gets bonus points for effort, but in the end it doesn't provide the wow factor of many other aquariums. It's open September and June from 9:30am to 7pm; July through August from 9:30am to 8:30pm; and October through May from 9:30am to 6pm.

Forget Flipper. In Dingle, the name to know is Fungie the Dolphin. Every day, **Fungie the Dolphin Tours** ★★, the Pier, Dingle (© 066/915-2626), ferry visitors out into the nearby waters to see the famous village mascot. Trips cost €10 ($12) for adults and €5 ($5.75) for children under 12. They last about 1 hour and depart regularly, roughly every 2 hours off season and as frequently as every half-hour in high season. Fungie really does swim up to the boat, and the boatmen stay out long enough for ample sightings—and long, wonderful eyefuls of the gorgeous bay. If you want to get up close and personal with Fungie, you can also arrange an early-morning dolphin swim. Although Fungie can swim about 25 mph, he enjoys human company and is usually willing to slow down and swim with his new acquaintances. To arrange a dolphin encounter, contact John Brosnan (© 066/915-1967), almost any day from 8am to 8pm. You book a swim the day before, when you rent your gear (semi-dry suit, mask, snorkel, boots, and fins, all in one duffel). The full overnight outfitting cost is €20 ($23) per person. Then you show up in your gear early the next morning to be brought out by boat to your aquatic rendezvous. The 2-hour escorted swim costs an additional €15 ($17). If you prefer, you can use your rented outfit and swim out on your own. Fungie also welcomes drop-ins. This outing is for teenagers on up, although smaller children will certainly enjoy watching.

ENJOYING THE GREAT OUTDOORS

BEACHES   The Dingle Peninsula has some of the most dramatic beaches in Ireland. The most famous is **Inch Strand,** a 5km (3-mile) long dune-covered sandy spit—one of the largest dune fields in Ireland. Scenes from *Ryan's Daughter,* the 1969 David Lean production with Robert Mitchum and Sarah Miles, were filmed here.

If you've never seen a boulder beach, then **Kilmurray Bay at Minard** is a Lilliputian dream come to life. Here in the shadow of Minard Castle, giant sausage-shaped sandstone boulders form a beach unlike anything you've ever seen. If you want drama, **Trabeg Beach** features exquisite wave-sculptured maroon sandstone statues, sheer rock cliffs, and small sea caves lined with veins of crystalline quartz.

Some of the calmest beaches for swimming in this area are east of Castlegregory, on the west side of Tralee Bay. The beach at **Maherabeg** has a coveted European Blue Flag, and the beaches of **Brandon Bay** are exceptionally scenic and good for walking and swimming.

BICYCLING   Mountain bikes can be rented at the **Mountain Man,** Strand Street, Dingle (*©* **066/915-2400**), for €10 ($12) per day or €50 ($58) per week. Mike Shea knows the area well, and can suggest a number of 1-day or overnight touring options on the Dingle Peninsula. Touring and mountain bikes are also available year-round from **Foxy John Moriarty,** Main Street, Dingle (*©* **066/915-1316**).

SAILING   The **Dingle Sailing Club,** c/o The Wood, Dingle (*©* **066/ 915-1629**), offers an array of courses taught by experienced, certified instructors. Summer courses run from €130 to €150 ($150–$173).

SEA ANGLING   For sea-angling packages and day trips, contact Nicholas O'Connor at **Angler's Rest,** Ventry (*©* **066/915-9947**); or Seán O'Conchúir (*©* **066/915-5429**), representing the **Kerry Angling Association.**

WALKING   The **Dingle Way** begins in Tralee and circles the peninsula, covering 153km (95 miles) of gorgeous mountain and coastal landscape. The most rugged section is along Brandon Head, where the trail passes between Mount Brandon and the ocean; the views are tremendous, but the walk is long (about 24km/15 miles or 9 hr.) and strenuous, and should be attempted only when the sky is clear. The section between Dunquin and Ballyferriter follows an especially lovely stretch of coast. For more information, see *The Dingle Way Map Guide,* available in local tourist offices and shops.

WHERE TO STAY

Benners Hotel ★★ *Value*   One of the few hotels out here that stay open year-round, Benners is a good-value choice with character that's right in the heart of town. The lovely Georgian doorway with a fanlight at the front entrance sets the tone. Dating from more than 250 years ago, the hotel blends old-world charm and modern comforts, thanks to a recent refurbishment. It's furnished with Irish antique pine furniture, including four-poster beds and armoires in the guest rooms. Special 2- and 3-night rates are available on the hotel's website.

Main St., Dingle, County Kerry. *©* 066/915-1638. Fax 066/915-1412. www.bennershotel.com. 52 units. €134–€204 ($154–$235) double. Rates include full Irish breakfast and service charge. AE, DC, MC, V. **Amenities:** Restaurant; 2 bars. *In room:* TV, tea/coffeemaker, hair dryer.

The Captain's House ⭐ *Value* You won't get better value-for-money in Dingle. Jim and Mary Milhench own and run this friendly, dapper little B&B smack in the middle of Dingle. The name is inspired by Jim's former life as a sea captain. Everything here is done with an eye for orderly, shipshape detail. When you arrive, you're offered tea with scones or a slice of rich porter cake (don't decline—it's wonderful) and made to feel genuinely welcome. As in many town houses, rooms were built to a smallish scale, but the whole place is done up so delightfully that the overall effect is cozy rather than cramped. Returning guests often request room 10, which is tucked under the gables and has a sloping ceiling. Mary's breakfasts are excellent.

The Mall, Dingle, County Kerry. ℂ 066/915-1531. Fax 066/915-1079. 9 units. €80–€90 ($92–$104) double. No service charge. Rates include full breakfast. AE, MC, V. Closed Dec–Jan. **Amenities:** Sitting room. *In room:* TV.

Doyle's Townhouse ⭐⭐ Sister to the successful Doyle's Seafood Restaurant next door, this three-story guesthouse is a favorite Dingle hideaway. It has a lovely Victorian fireplace in the drawing room area, and many of the antique fixtures date from 250 years ago or more. Period pieces and country pine predominate in the guest rooms, although they're totally up-to-date with firm beds and good-size Italian marble bathrooms with towel warmers. Most are so spacious that they have a pullout couch that can accommodate a third person. Front rooms look out onto the town, and back rooms have a balcony or patio and face a garden, with mountain vistas in the background. Two ground-floor rooms are perfect for folks who have difficulty with stairs. Just down the road, off a little courtyard, there are four little town houses—each with its own entrance and a sitting room downstairs, with a bedroom and bathroom on the upper level.

5 John St., Dingle, County Kerry. ℂ 800/223-6510 in the U.S., or 066/915-1174. Fax 066/915-1816. www.doylesofdingle.com. 12 units. €112–€124 ($129–$143) double. Rates include full breakfast. DC, MC, V. Closed Christmas and mid-Jan to mid-Feb. **Amenities:** Drawing room. *In room:* TV, hair dryer.

Greenmount House ⭐ Perched on a hill overlooking Dingle Bay and the town, this modern bungalow-style bed-and-breakfast home is a standout in its category. It has all the comforts of a hotel at bargain prices, including spacious guest rooms, each with its own sitting area and large bathroom. Breakfasts, ranging from smoked salmon omelets to ham-and-pineapple toasties, have won awards for proprietors Mary and John Curran.

John St., Dingle, County Kerry. ℂ 066/915-1414. Fax 066/915-1974. www.greenmounthouse.com. 12 units. €85–€120 ($98–$138) double. No service charge. Rates include full breakfast. MC, V. Closed Dec 20–26. **Amenities:** Nonsmoking rooms; conservatory; sitting room. *In room:* TV, tea/coffeemaker.

Milltown House ⭐⭐ You couldn't wish for a more picturesque setting than this bayside haven with a privileged location just minutes from Dingle Town. The simple white-and-black 19th-century exterior conceals a fine family-run guesthouse that incorporates the amenities of a hotel with the informal warmth of a B&B. The spacious guest rooms—each uniquely designed—have sitting areas and firm, orthopedic beds. Half have sea views and nearly all have patios. Two are wheelchair accessible. The nonsmoking sitting room—all easy chairs and open fires—is elegant and comfortable, while the conservatory breakfast room (where you'll enjoy a lavish breakfast menu) looks out on Dingle Bay. Room no. 2 is where Robert Mitchum stayed while filming *Ryan's Daughter*.

Milltown (off Ventry Rd), Dingle, County Kerry. ℂ 066/915-1372. Fax 066/915-1095. http://indigo.ie/~milltown. 10 units. €110–€140 ($127–$161). Rates include full breakfast. MC, V. **Amenities:** Conservatory; sitting room. *In room:* TV, tea/coffeemaker, hair dryer.

WHERE TO DINE

Beginish ★★ SEAFOOD   Mrs. Pat Moore runs this delightful small restaurant, and she's managed to achieve an atmosphere of quiet elegance, unassuming and comfortable. A lovely conservatory overlooks the garden in back, with room for outdoor tables in summer. Although lamb and beef dishes and a vegetarian special are offered each night, the emphasis is on fish—the cooking is simple, traditional, and always delightful. Among the starters, the smoked salmon with shallots, capers, and horseradish cream is exquisite—nothing fancy, just excellent ingredients combined in perfect proportions. You can't go wrong with any of the fish entrees, such as monkfish with Provençal sauce or cod on thyme-scented potatoes and sweet red peppers. For dessert, chef Pat Moore's hot rhubarb soufflé tart is legendary in these parts.

Green St., Dingle, County Kerry. © 066/915-1321. Reservations recommended. Dinner main courses €22–€30 ($25–$35). MC, V. Tues–Sun noon–2pm and 6–10pm. Closed Jan.

The Chart House ★★ MODERN COUNTRY   For several years now, this has been the hottest table in Dingle—in fact, it's quickly become a destination restaurant that draws folks from outside Kerry—so book ahead and prepare to enjoy. As the *Sunday Tribune* food critic gushed, "The food, the service, and the buzz all conspire to set this place apart." There's the ubiquitously inviting bistro-like atmosphere—complete with country half-door and chunky pine furniture—but everyone comes for Laura Boyce's confident, simple cooking. Think wonderful comfort food with a flair—filet of beef with garlicky mashed spuds; herb-marinated John Dory on a bed of citrus-infused couscous; roast monkfish with zucchini (called courgette in Ireland) and mustard sauce; home-smoked pork with apple frittatas. It's the kind of food you never tire of. And the service is, as the Irish would say, "spot on."

The Mall, Dingle, County Kerry. © 066/915-2255. Reservations required. Dinner main courses €15–€29 ($17–$33). MC, V. Daily 6:30 –10pm. Closed Jan 8–Feb 12.

Doyle's Seafood Bar ★ SEAFOOD   John Doyle meets the fishing boats each morning to select the best of the day's catch. The atmosphere is homey, with stone walls and floors, tweedy place mats, and old Dingle sketches. All the ingredients come from the sea, the Doyles' gardens, or nearby farms—and the Doyles even smoke their own salmon. Specialties include baked filet of lemon sole with prawn sauce; salmon filet in puff pastry with sorrel sauce; and a signature platter of seafood (sole, salmon, lobster, oysters, and crab claws).

4 John St., Dingle, County Kerry. © 066/915-1174. www.doylesofdingle.com. Reservations required. Main courses €19–€30 ($22–$35). MC, V. Mon–Sat 6–10pm. Closed mid-Dec to mid-Feb.

DINGLE AFTER DARK

At night virtually every pub in Dingle offers live music from 9pm on. **An Droichead Beag/The Small Bridge,** Lower Main Street (© 066/915-1723), is one of Dingle's most atmospheric pubs. It has a dark, cavernous interior that's filled with banter and laughter. Traditional Irish music takes place every night at 9pm. But be warned: It's popular, so get there early if you want a seat.

Although Richard "Dick" Mack died a few years ago, his family keeps up the traditions at **Dick Mack's "Haberdashery,"** Green Street (© 066/915-1070), where Dick handcrafted leather boots, belts, and other items in between pub chores. Corridors lined with old pictures and mugs lead into snug bars where locals and visitors stand around sipping stout and exchanging gossip. It's been a favorite pub with such celebrities as Robert Mitchum, Timothy Dalton, and Paul Simon, whose names are now commemorated with stars on the sidewalk outside.

Italy

by Darwin Porter & Danforth Prince

Italy is a feast for the senses and the intellect. Any mention of Italy calls up visions of Pompeii, the Renaissance, and Italy's rich treasury of art and architecture. But some of the country's best experiences can involve the simple act of living in the Italian style, eating the regional cuisines, and enjoying the countryside.

1 Rome ★★★

The city of Rome is simultaneously strident, romantic, and sensual. And although the romantic poets would probably be horrified at today's traffic, pollution, overcrowding, crime, political discontent, and barely controlled chaos of modern Rome, the city endures and thrives in a way that is called "eternal."

It would take a lifetime to know a city filled with 27 centuries of artistic achievement. A cradle of Western civilization, Rome is timeless with its ancient history, art, and architecture, containing more treasures per square foot than any other city in the world. Caesar was assassinated here, Charlemagne crowned, and the list of the major events goes on and on.

In between all that absorption of culture and history, take time to relax and meet the Romans. Savor their succulent pastas while enjoying a fine glass of wine on one of the city's splendid squares where one of the reigning Caesars might have gone before you, or perhaps Michelangelo or Raphael.

ESSENTIALS

GETTING THERE   By Plane   Chances are that you'll arrive in Italy at Rome's **Leonardo da Vinci International Airport** (© 06-65951, or 06-65953640 for information; www.adr.it), popularly known as **Fiumicino,** 30km (19 miles) from the city center. Domestic flights arrive at one terminal, international ones at the other. If you're flying by charter, you might arrive at Ciampino Airport.

To get into the city, there's a **shuttle service** known as the Leonardo Express that takes you directly from Fiumicino to Stazione Termini, the main train station. Upon leaving Customs, follow the signs marked TRENI. Trains go back and forth between the airport and the rail station daily from 7:07am to 11:37pm. A one-way ticket costs 9€ ($10). There's also a local train departing every 20 minutes and taking 45 minutes to reach the Tiburtina station. The cost is 4.75€ ($5.45) each way. But you'll have to change at the Piramide Metro stop, catching the B line into Termini for .75€ (85¢). If you have luggage, this is a more awkward transit but cheaper, of course.

Taxis from Fiumicino to the city center are expensive—43€ ($50) and up, plus another 3€ ($3.45) or so for your luggage.

Should you arrive on a charter flight at **Ciampino Airport** (© 06-794941; www.adr.it), take a COTRAL bus, departing every 20 minutes or so, which will deliver you to the Anagnina stop of Metropolitana (subway) line A. The one-way cost is 1€ ($1.15). At Anagnina you can take Metro line A to Stazione Termini, where you can make your final connections. The trip takes about 45 minutes and costs .75€ (85¢).

By Train Trains arrive in the center of old Rome at **Stazione Termini,** Piazza dei Cinquecento (℗ **1848-88088;** www.romatermini.it), the train and subway transportation hub for the city. For information and timetables, contact **FS** (℗ **848-888088;** www.trenitalia.it). Many hotels lie near the station, and you can walk to your hotel if you don't have too much luggage. Otherwise, an array of taxi, bus, and subway lines awaits you.

If you're taking the **Metropolitana** (subway), follow the illuminated M sign in red that points the way. To catch a bus, go straight through the outer hall of the Termini and enter the sprawling bus lot of Piazza dei Cinquecento. Taxis are also found here.

By Bus Arrivals are at the **Stazione Termini** (see "By Train," above).

By Car From the north, the main access route is **A-1 (Autostrada del Sole),** cutting through Milan and Florence; or you can take the coastal route, SSI Aurelia, from Genoa. If you're driving north from Naples, take the southern lap of the **Autostrada del Sole (A-2).** All these autostradas join with the **Grande Raccordo Anulare,** a ring road that encircles Rome, channeling traffic into the city.

VISITOR INFORMATION   Tourist Offices Information is available at three locations maintained by the **Azienda Provinciale di Turismo (APT):** a kiosk at **Leonardo da Vinci International Airport** (℗ 06-6595-6074), a kiosk at Stazione Termini, and the **administrative headquarters** at Via Parigi 5 (℗ **06-6595-6074;** www.romaturismo.it). The Via Parigi 5 location is open Monday through Friday from 8:15am to 7:15pm, Saturday to 2pm. The airport and Stazione Termini kiosk are open daily from 8:15am to 7:15pm, but we've never found these locations to be great resources.

More helpful, stocking maps and brochures, are the offices maintained by the **Comune di Roma** at half a dozen sights around the city. You can identify them by their red-and-orange or yellow-and-black signs saying COMUNE DI ROMA— PUNTI DI INFORMAZIONE TURISTICA. The offices are staffed daily from 9am to 6pm and can be found in Piazza Pia, near the Castello Sant'Angelo (℗ 06-68809707); in Piazza San Giovanni in Laterano (℗ 06-77203598); along Largo Carlo Goldoni, near the intersection of Via del Corso and Via Condotti (℗ 06-68136061); on Via Nazionale, near the Palazzo delle Esposizioni (℗ 06-47824525); on Largo Corrado Ricci, near the Colosseum (℗ 06-69924307); and in Trastevere on Piazza Sonnino (℗ 06-58333457). The Stazione Termini office (℗ 06-48906300) is open daily from 8am to 9pm. Other offices have also opened, including Piazza 5 Lune, near Piazza Navona (℗ 06-68809240); Piazza Santa Maria Maggiore (℗ 06-4740955); and Piazza dei 500, outside Stazione Termini (℗ 06-47825194).

Websites Rome's official site, **www.romaturismo.it,** has a fair amount of info on most aspects of the Rome experience. Maintained by a private company, **www.enjoyrome.com** fills you in on useful information for visiting the city (they, after all, pen the official tourist office's "Info for Tourists" pamphlet) while promoting its walking tours in Rome, Florence, and Venice as well as guided trips to Pompeii.

The extensive **www.initaly.com** helps you find all sorts of accommodations (country villas, historic residences, convents, and farmhouses) and includes tips

on shopping, dining, driving, and viewing works of art. Check out **www.italy tour.com** for coverage of the arts, culture, business, tours, entertainment, restaurants, lodging, media, shopping, sports, and major Italian cities. To stay up to date on trends in modern Italian culture, go to **www.dolcevita.com**, the self-proclaimed "insider's guide to Italy." It's all about style—as it pertains to fashion, cuisine, design, and travel.

CITY LAYOUT The drive into the city from the airport is rather uneventful until you pass through the still remarkably intact **Great Aurelian Wall,** begun in A.D. 271 to calm Rome's barbarian jitters. Suddenly, ruins of imperial baths loom on one side and great monuments can be seen in the middle of blocks.

Stazione Termini, the modern railroad station, faces the huge **Piazza dei Cinquecento,** named after 500 Italians who died heroically in a 19th-century battle in Africa.

The bulk of ancient, Renaissance, and baroque Rome lies on the east side of the **Fiume Tevere (Tiber River),** which meanders between 19th-century stone embankments. However, several important monuments are on the other side: **St. Peter's Basilica** and the **Vatican,** the **Castel Sant' Angelo** (formerly the tomb of the emperor Hadrian), and the colorful section known as **Trastevere.** The city's various quarters are linked by boulevards mostly laid out since the late 19th century.

Major streets fan out from **Piazza Venezia** in front of the **Vittorio Emmanuele monument,** a highly controversial pile of snow-white Brescian marble. Running north to **Piazza del Popolo** and the city wall is **Via del Corso,** one of Rome's main streets. Called simply "Il Corso," it's noisy, congested, and always crowded with buses and shoppers. Going west across the Tiber toward St. Peter's is **Corso Vittorio Emanuele.** Running toward the Colosseum is **Via dei Fori Imperiali,** named for the excavated ruins of the imperial forums that flank this avenue. **Via Quattro Novembre** runs east and becomes **Via Nazionale** before terminating at **Piazza della Repubblica.**

GETTING AROUND   Much of the inner core of Rome is traffic-free—so you'll need to walk whether you like it or not. However, walking in many parts of the city is hazardous and uncomfortable because of overcrowding, heavy traffic, and very narrow and uneven sidewalks.

By Subway   The **Metropolitana,** or **Metro** for short, is the fastest means of transportation in Rome. It has two underground lines: **A** and **B.** A big red letter M indicates the subway entrance. The fare is .75€ (85¢). Tickets are available from vending machines at all stations. Ticket booklets are available at *tabacchi* (tobacco) shops and in some terminals. *Tip:* Avoid riding the trains when the Romans are going to or from work or you'll be mashed flatter than fettuccine.

By Bus/Tram   Roman buses are operated by **ATAC (Azienda Tramvie e Autobus del Comune di Roma),** Via Volturno 65 (② **06-46951** for information). The service is quite good and you can ride to most parts of Rome for only .75€ (85¢). The ticket is valid for 1¼ hours, and you can get on as many buses during that time period as you want, using the same ticket; you can also transfer free between the Metro and the bus within the 75 minutes of validity. Bus service runs from 5:30am to midnight and the night service is from 12:10 to 5:30am; an N after the line number defines buses running at night. A 2-hour bus tour of the city is offered by bus no. 110, leaving from Stazione Termini daily at 2:30pm.

By Taxi   Don't count on hailing a taxi on the street or even getting one at a stand. If you're going out, have your hotel call one. At a restaurant, ask the waiter or cashier to dial for you. If you want to call yourself, try one of these numbers: ② **06-6645,** 06-3570, or 06-4994. The meter begins at 2.25€ ($2.50) for the first 3km, then .65€ (75¢) per kilometer. On Sunday, a 1€ ($1.15) supplement is assessed, plus another 2.50€ ($2.75) supplement from 10pm to 7am. There's yet another 1€ ($1.15) supplement for every suitcase. The driver will expect a 10% tip.

By Car   You can rent a car from **Hertz,** near the parking lot of the Villa Borghese, Via Veneto 156 (② **06-3216831**); **Italy by Car,** Via Ludovisi 60 (② **06-4870010**); the local Italian company **Maggiore,** Via di Tor Cervara 225 (② **06-22935356**); or **Avis** at Stazione Termini (② **06-4814373**).

Value **Traveler's Tip**

At the Stazione Termini, you can buy a special **tourist bus and subway pass,** which costs 3€ ($3.45) for 1 day or 12€ ($14) for a week.

By Bicycle   You can rent bicycles at many places throughout Rome. Ask at your hotel for the nearest rental location, or else go to **I Bike Rome,** Via Veneto 156 (℡ **06-3225240**), which rents bicycles from the underground parking garage at the Villa Borghese. Most bikes cost 2€ ($2.30) per hour or 5€ ($5.75) per day. It's open daily from 9am to 7pm. Bring an ID card with you.

FAST FACTS: Rome

American Express   The Rome offices are at Piazza di Spagna 38 (℡ **06-67641;** Metro: Spagna). The travel service is open Monday through Friday from 9am to 5pm, and Saturday from 9am to 12:30pm. Hours for the financial and mail services are Monday through Friday from 9am to 5pm. The tour desk is open during the same hours as those for travel services and also Saturday from 2 to 2:30pm (May–Oct).

Business Hours   In general, **banks** are open Monday through Friday from 8:30am to 1:30pm and 3 to 4pm. Most **stores** are open generally Monday 3:30 to 7:30pm and Tuesday through Saturday 9:30 or 10am to 1pm and 3:30 to 7 or 7:30pm. Some shops are open on Monday mornings, however, and some shops don't close for the afternoon break.

Currency   On January 1, 2002, the euro (€), the new European currency, became the legal tender in place of the lira. At press time, 1€ = $1.15, or $1 = .85€.

Currency Exchange   There are **exchange offices** throughout the city and at all major rail and air terminals, including Stazione Termini, where the **cambio** beside the rail information booth is open daily from 8am to 8pm. At some cambi, you'll have to pay commissions, often 1.5%. Likewise, banks often charge commissions. **Automated teller machines (ATMs)**—with both the **Cirrus** (℡ **800/424-7787;** www.mastercard.com) and the **PLUS** (℡ **800/843-7587;** www.visa.com) networks represented—are prevalent in all Italian cities and even in smaller towns, and often offer a good exchange rate.

Dentists   There is a 24-hour **G. Eastman Dental Hospital,** Viale Regina Elena 287B (℡ **06-844831;** Metro: Policlinico).

Doctors/Hospitals   Call the U.S. embassy at ℡ **06-46741** for a list of doctors who speak English. All big hospitals have a 24-hour first-aid service (go to the emergency room, *Pronto Soccorso*). You'll find English-speaking doctors at the privately run **Salvator Mundi International Hospital,** Viale delle Mura Gianicolensi 67 (℡ **06-588961;** bus: 44). For medical assistance, the **International Medical Center** is on 24-hour duty at Via Firenze 47 (℡ **06-4882371;** Metro: Razza Repubblica). You can also contact the **Rome American Hospital,** Via Emilio Longoni 69 (℡ **06-22551**), where English-speaking doctors are on duty 24 hours.

Drugstores/Pharmacies   A reliable pharmacy is **Farmacia Internazionale,** Piazza Barberini 49 (℡ **06-4825456;** Metro: Barberini), open day and night. Most pharmacies are open from 8:30am to 1pm and 4 to 7:30pm. In general, pharmacies follow a rotation system, so several are always open on Sunday.

Embassies/Consulates   The embassy of the **United States,** Via Vittorio Veneto 119A (℡ **06-46741;** Metro: Barberini), is open Monday through Friday from

8:30am to 5:30pm. Consular and passport services for **Canada,** Via Zara 30
(© **06-445981;** Metro: Policlinico; bus: 36), are open Monday through Friday
from 10am to 12:30pm; the embassy of Canada is at Via G. B. De Rossi 27
(© **06-445981;** bus: 36 or 60). The embassy of the **United Kingdom,** Via XX
Settembre 80A (© **06-42200001;** Metro: Barberini), is open Monday through
Friday from 9:15am to 1:30pm. The embassy of **Australia,** Via Alessandria 215
(© **06-852721;** Metro: Policlinico; bus: 36 or 60), is open Monday through
Thursday from 8:30am to noon and 1:30 to 5pm and Friday from 9am to
noon; the consulate of Australia is at Corso Trieste 25 (© **06-852721;** bus: 36
or 60), and is open Monday through Friday from 8:30am to noon and 1:30 to
4:15pm. The embassy of **New Zealand,** Via Zara 28 (© **06-4417171;** Metro:
Policlinico; bus: 36 or 60), is open Monday through Friday from 8:30am to
12:45pm and 1:45 to 5pm. The embassy of **Ireland** is at Piazza di Campitelli 3
(© **06-697912;** Metro: Circo Massimo; bus: 46); for consular queries call © **06-
69791211** (call for hours). In an **emergency,** embassies have a 24-hour referral service.

Emergencies Dial © **113** for an ambulance or to call the police; to report
a fire, call © **115.**

Internet Access You can log onto the Web in central Rome at **Thenetgate,**
Piazza Firenze 25 (© **06-87406008;** bus: 116). Summer hours are Monday
through Saturday from 6am to noon and 3:30pm to midnight, and winter
hours are daily from 10:40am to 8:30pm. A 20-minute visit costs 3€
($3.45), and 1 hour costs 5€ ($5.75). Access is free on Saturday from 10:30
to 11am and 2 to 2:30pm.

Mail It's easiest just to buy stamps and mail letters and postcards at your
hotel's front desk. Stamps *(francobolli)* can also be bought at tabacchi.
You can buy special stamps at the **Vatican City Post Office,** adjacent to the
information office in St. Peter's Square; it's open Monday through Friday
from 8:30am to 7pm and Saturday from 8:30am to 6pm. Letters mailed at
Vatican City reach North America far more quickly than mail sent from
within Rome for the same cost.

Safety Pickpocketing is the most common problem. Men should keep
their wallets in their front pocket or inside jacket pocket. Purse snatching
is also commonplace, with young men on Vespas who ride past you and
grab your purse. To avoid trouble, stay away from the curb; keep your
purse on the wall side of your body and place the strap across your chest.
Don't place anything valuable on tables or chairs, where it can be
grabbed. Gypsy children have long been a particular menace, although
the problem isn't as severe as in years past. If they completely surround
you, you'll often literally have to fight them off. They might approach you
with pieces of cardboard hiding their stealing hands. Just keep repeating
a firm *"No!"*

Telephone The **country code** for Italy is **39.** The **city code** for Rome is **06,**
which is the code you'll use every time you dial a party located within
Rome, regardless of whether you're within the city limits or not. To call
from one city code to another within Italy, dial the city code, complete
with the initial zero, then the local number. To **dial direct internationally,**
dial **00,** then the country code for the country you are calling, then the

area or city code, and then the local number. Direct-dial calls from the United States to Italy are usually cheaper than calls placed from an Italian hotel to most phones in North America, so if possible, try to arrange for friends and acquaintances to call you at your hotel at prearranged times.

To ring national **telephone information** (in Italian) in Italy, dial **12**. International information is available at **176**, but costs .60€ (70¢) per request.

To make a **collect or calling-card call** from a public phone, drop in .10€ or insert a prepaid phone card (available from most tabacchi) and dial one of the following access numbers to reach an American operator or an English-language voice prompt: **AT&T** ☎ **172-10-11** (if calling a country other than the United States, after the access code dial 01, the country code of country you are calling, city code, and local number); **MCI** ☎ **172-10-22**; and **Sprint** ☎ **172-18-77**.

Tipping More and more restaurants automatically add a 15% service charge to your bill. Ask when you receive the bill; otherwise you might end up tipping twice. Add 15% if service is not included. It's customary to leave another .75€ (80¢) or so on the table. Tip taxi drivers 10%.

WHERE TO STAY
NEAR STAZIONE TERMINI
Expensive
Hotel Mediterraneo ★ A recent influx of cash has returned this golden oldie to some of its former glory. Located on the triumphant passageway through Rome, the hotel sports vivid Italian Art Deco styling. Its height, coupled with its position on one of Rome's hills, provides panoramic views from the most expensive rooms on the highest floors (some with lovely terraces) and from its roof garden/bar (open in May and especially charming at night).

Via Cavour 15, 00184 Roma. ☎ 06-4884051. Fax 06-4744105. www.bettojahotels.it. 267 units. 306€ ($352) double; from 675€ ($776) suite. Rates include buffet breakfast. AE, DC, MC, V. Parking 21€–26€ ($24–$30). Metro: Termini. **Amenities:** 2 restaurants; bar; car-rental desk; room service (6:30am–1am); babysitting; laundry service; dry cleaning. *In room:* A/C, TV, dataport, minibar, hair dryer, safe.

Moderate
Aberdeen Hotel This completely renovated hotel near the Opera is centrally located for most landmarks and for rail and bus connections. It lies in front of the Ministry of Defense, in a rather quiet and fairly safe area of Rome. The recently renovated rooms are furnished in a modern style and sport neatly kept bathrooms with tub/shower combo. All rooms are nonsmoking.

Via Firenze 48, 00184 Roma. ☎ 06-4823920. Fax 06-4821092. www.travel.it/roma/aberdeen. 36 units, 20 with shower only. 140€–160€ ($161–$184) double; 150€–210€ ($173–$242) suite. Rates include buffet breakfast. AE, DC, MC, V. Parking 21€ ($24). Metro: Repubblica. Bus: 64 or 170. **Amenities:** Laundry service; dry cleaning ; 1 room for those with limited mobility. *In room:* A/C, TV, dataport, minibar, hair dryer, iron, safe.

Hotel Columbia ★★ *(Finds* This is one of the newest hotels in the neighborhood, with a hardworking multilingual staff. A government-rated three-star choice, originally built around 1900, it underwent a successful, radical renovation in 1997. The interior contains Murano chandeliers and conservatively modern furniture. The compact and cozy guest rooms compare well against the accommodations in the best hotels nearby. The appealing roof garden has a view over the surrounding rooftops.

Rome Accommodations

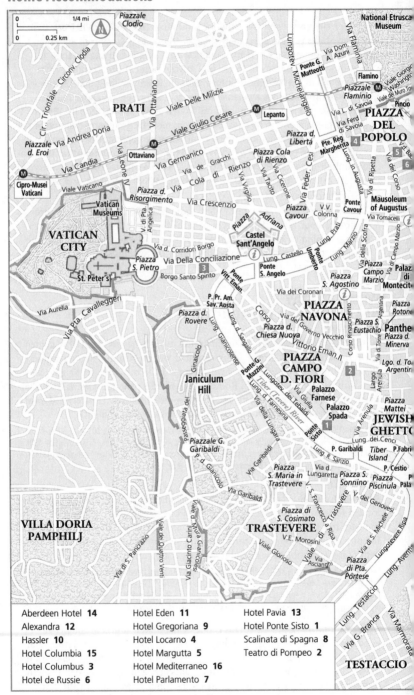

Aberdeen Hotel **14**	Hotel Eden **11**	Hotel Pavia **13**
Alexandra **12**	Hotel Gregoriana **9**	Hotel Ponte Sisto **1**
Hassler **10**	Hotel Locarno **4**	Scalinata di Spagna **8**
Hotel Columbia **15**	Hotel Margutta **5**	Teatro di Pompeo **2**
Hotel Columbus **3**	Hotel Mediterraneo **16**	
Hotel de Russie **6**	Hotel Parlamento **7**	

Via del Viminale 15, 00184 Roma. © 06-4744289 or 06-4883509. Fax 06-4740209. www.venere.it/roma/ columbia. 45 units. 38€–154€ ($159–$177) double. Rates include buffet breakfast. AE, DC, MC, V. Parking nearby 20€ ($23). Metro: Termini. **Amenities:** Bar; room service (7am–11pm); laundry service; nonsmoking rooms. *In room:* A/C, TV, dataport, minibar, hair dryer, safe.

Inexpensive

Hotel Pavia ★ This is a popular choice on this quiet street near the gardens of the Baths of Diocletian. Established in the 1980s, it occupies a much-renovated century-old building. The front rooms tend to be noisy, but that's the curse of all Termini hotels. Nevertheless, the rooms are comfortable and fairly attractive, and were last renovated in 1998. Each comes with a neatly tiled shower bathroom.

Via Gaeta 83, 00185 Roma. © 06-483801. Fax 06-4819090. www.hotelpavia.com. 20 units, showers only. 100€–190€ ($115–$219) double. Rates include breakfast. AE, DC, MC, V. Parking 11€ ($13). Metro: Termini. **Amenities:** Bar; limited room service. *In room:* A/C, TV, minibar, hair dryer, safe.

NEAR VIA VENETO & PIAZZA BARBERINI
Very Expensive

Hotel Eden ★★★ During the heyday of this ornate hotel, all the big names—Hemingway, Maria Callas, Ingrid Bergman, Fellini—checked in here. In 1994, it reopened after a 2-year (and $20 million) radical renovation that enhanced its original fin de siècle grandeur and added the modern amenities its government-rated five-star status calls for. Its hilltop position guarantees a panoramic city view from most rooms. Understated elegance is the rule.

Via Ludovisi 49, 00187 Roma. © 06-478121. Fax 06-4821584. www.hotel-eden.it. 121 units. 645€–745€ ($742–$857) double; from 1,800€–2,800€ ($2,070–$3,220) suite. AE, DC, DISC, MC, V. Parking 52€ ($60). Metro: Piazza Barberini. **Amenities:** Restaurant; bar; health club; room service (24-hr.); babysitting; laundry service; dry cleaning; nonsmoking rooms. *In room:* A/C, TV, dataport, minibar, hair dryer, safe.

Moderate

Alexandra ★ *Finds* Here's where you can stay on Via Veneto without going broke. Set in what was originally a 19th-century private mansion, this hotel offers comfortable, well-kept accommodations filled with antique furniture and modern conveniences such as private bathrooms, some with shower and some with tub and shower. Rooms facing front are exposed to roaring traffic and animated street life; those in back are quieter but have less of a view. Breakfast is the only meal served. The garden-inspired breakfast room designed by Paolo Portoghesi is especially appealing.

Via Vittorio Veneto 18, 00187 Roma. © 06-4881943. Fax 06-4871804. www.hotelalexandraroma.com. 60 units, some with shower only. 230€ ($265) double; 350€ ($403) suite. Rates include buffet breakfast. AE, DC, MC, V. Parking 26€–31€ ($30–$36). Metro: Piazza Barberini. **Amenities:** Room service (7am–10pm); laundry service; dry cleaning; nonsmoking rooms; rooms for those with limited mobility. *In room:* A/C, TV, dataport (in some), minibar, hair dryer, iron, safe.

AROUND THE SPANISH STEPS & PIAZZA DEL POPOLO
Very Expensive

The Hassler ★★★ The only deluxe hotel in this old part of Rome, it uses the Spanish Steps as its grand entrance. The crown worn by the Hassler is still in place after all these years; the hostelry has such a mystique that it prospers and endures in spite of high prices. Rooms, some of which are small, have a personalized look, with French windows, comfortable beds, and—the nicest touch of all—bowls of fresh flowers. Some have balconies with views of the city.

Piazza Trinità dei Monti 6, 00187 Roma. © 800/223-6800 in the U.S., or 06-699340. Fax 06-6789991. www.hotelhasslerroma.com. 100 units. 566€–860€ ($651–$989) double; from 1,950€ ($2,243) suite. AE,

DC, MC, V. Parking 30€ ($35). Metro: Piazza di Spagna. **Amenities:** Restaurant; bar; gym; free use of bicycles; room service (6:30am–midnight); massage; babysitting; laundry service; dry cleaning; 1 room for those with limited mobility. *In room:* A/C, TV, dataport, minibar, hair dryer, safe.

Hotel de Russie ★★★   This government-rated five-star deluxe hotel lies just off Piazza del Popolo. Lovers of *luxe* are deserting such traditional favorites as the Hassler to stay here. In one of the choicest platinum locations in Rome, it is lavishly furnished and was once a favorite of Russian dignitaries (hence, its name) and of such artists as Jean Cocteau, Picasso, and Stravinsky. In World War II, it was the spy center for Italy. About 30% of the spacious rooms are traditionally furnished, the others more minimalist with a strikingly contemporary motif. Bathrooms are elegantly tiled, with tub and shower.

Via del Babuino 9, 00187 Roma. ✆ **800/323-7500** in North America, or 06-328881. Fax 06-3288888. www. roccofortehotels.com. 125 units. 580€–700€ ($667–$805) double; from 1,000€ ($1,150) suite. AE, DC, MC, V. Metro: Flaminia. **Amenities:** Lovely restaurant and bar; gym; spa; children's programs; salon; limited room service, nonsmoking rooms; rooms for those with limited mobility. *In room:* A/C, TV, dataport, minibar, hair dryer, safe.

Expensive

Hotel Locarno ★ *Finds*   This little charmer near Piazza del Popolo is said to be haunted by the imperial ghost of Nero, although that isn't expected to disturb your night's sleep. You can count on Rome's heavy traffic to do that. The hotel's most winning feature is its large roof terrace where you can take your breakfast while enjoying some of the major sights of Rome's skyline. If you'd like to go exploring, the Locarno will provide you with a bike. A 1920s aura pervades the hotel, as evoked by the wrought-iron elevator cage or the marble-topped walnut bar with its Tiffany-style lamp. Guest rooms and bathrooms with a tub/shower combo are completely up-to-date.

Via della Penna 25, 00186 Roma. ✆ **06-3610841.** Fax 06-3215249. www.hotellocarno.com. 72 units. 190€–310€ ($219–$357) double; 510€ ($587) suite. Rates include breakfast. AE, DC, MC, V. Parking 30€–40€ ($35–$46). Metro: Flaminio. Bus: 116 or 117. **Amenities:** Bar; lunch buffet; 24-hr. room service; laundry service; dry cleaning; nonsmoking rooms; 1 room for those with limited mobility. *In room:* A/C, TV, dataport, minibar, safe.

Scalinata di Spagna ★★   This upscale B&B near the Spanish Steps has always been one of the most sought-after in Rome. It's right at the top of the steps, directly across the small piazza from the deluxe Hassler. Decor varies radically from one room to the next; some have low beamed ceilings and ancient-looking wood furniture, others offer loftier ceilings and more average appointments. All rooms were renovated and upgraded in 1998, bathrooms—each with a tub and shower—receiving special attention. In season, breakfast is served on the rooftop garden terrace with its sweeping view of the dome of St. Peter's across the Tiber.

Piazza Trinità dei Monti 17, 00187 Roma. ✆ **06-6793006.** Fax 06-69940598. www.hotelscalinata.com. 16 units, tubs only. 200€–350€ ($230–$403) double; 340€–400€ ($391–$460) triple. Rates include breakfast. AE, MC, V. Parking 40€ ($46). Metro: Piazza di Spagna. **Amenities:** Bar; babysitting; laundry service/dry cleaning; nonsmoking rooms. *In room:* A/C, TV, dataport, minibar, hair dryer, safe.

Moderate

Hotel Gregoriana ★   Although surrounded by much more expensive neighbors like the pricey Hassler, the small Gregoriana in a former 17th-century convent has its fans—mainly members of the Italian fashion industry. Rooms are small but comfortable, each with a small, neatly organized private bathroom with tub and shower combo. The elevator cage is a black-and-gold Art Deco fantasy, and the door to each room has a reproduction of an Erté print whose fanciful characters indicate the letter designating that room.

Via Gregoriana 18, 00187 Roma. ✆ **06-6794269.** Fax 06-6784258. 20 units. 217€ ($250) double. Rates include breakfast. No credit cards. Parking 25€ ($29). Metro: Spagna. **Amenities:** Room service; babysitting; laundry service; dry cleaning. *In room:* A/C, TV, minibar, hair dryer, safe.

Inexpensive

Hotel Margutta Located on a cobblestone street near Piazza del Popolo, this hotel offers attractively decorated but exceedingly small rooms and cramped bathrooms, some with shower, some with a tub and shower combo. Its helpful staff makes it an enduring favorite, nonetheless. The best rooms are on the top floor; two of these share a terrace, and another larger room has a private terrace.

Via Laurina 34, 00187 Roma. ✆ **06-3223674.** Fax 06-3200395. 24 units, shower only. 104€–125€ ($120–$144) double; 150€–160€ ($173–$184) triple. Rates include breakfast. AE, DC, MC, V. Metro: Flaminio. **Amenities:** Room service (7am–4pm). *In room:* A/C, TV, hair dryer.

Hotel Parlamento The Parlamento has a four-star government rating at two-star prices. Expect a friendly pensione-style reception. The furnishings are antiques or reproductions, and the firm beds are backed by carved wood or wrought-iron headboards. Fifteen rooms are air-conditioned, and the bathrooms were recently redone with heated towel racks, phones, and (in a few) even marble sinks. Rooms are different in style; the best are no. 82, with its original 1800s furniture, and nos. 104, 106, and 107, which open onto the roof garden.

Via delle Convertite 5 (at the intersection with Via del Corso), 00187 Roma. ✆ **06-6792082.** Fax 06-69921000. www.hotelparlamento.it. 23 units. 109€–125€ ($125–$144) double. Rates include breakfast. AE, DC, MC, V. Parking 26€ ($30). Metro: Spagna. **Amenities:** Bar. *In room:* A/C (some), TV, hair dryer, safe.

NEAR CAMPO DE' FIORI
Moderate

Teatro di Pompeo ★ *Finds* Built on the top of the ruins of the Theater of Pompey, which dates from about 55 B.C., this small charmer lies near the spot where Julius Caesar met his fate. Intimate and refined, it's on a quiet piazzetta near the Palazzo Farnese and Campo de' Fiori. Rooms, all doubles, are decorated in an old-fashioned Italian style with hand-painted tiles, and the beamed ceilings date from the days of Michelangelo. The tiled bathrooms are neatly kept, some with shower and some with a tub/shower combo. There's no restaurant, but breakfast is served.

Largo del Pallaro 8, 00186 Roma. ✆ **06-68300170.** Fax 06-68805531. www.hotelteatrodipompeo.it. 13 units, shower only. 180€–190€ ($207–$219) double. Rates include breakfast. AE, DC, MC, V. Bus: 46, 62, or 64. **Amenities:** Bar; limited room service; babysitting; laundry service; dry cleaning. *In room:* A/C, TV, minibar, hair dryer, safe.

NEAR VATICAN CITY
Expensive

Hotel Columbus ★ In an impressive 15th-century palace, Hotel Columbus lies a few minutes' walk from St. Peter's. It was once the private home of a wealthy cardinal who later became Pope Julius II and had Michelangelo paint the Sistine Chapel. Rooms are considerably simpler than the tiled and tapestried salons. All are spacious; a few are enormous and still have such original details as decorated wood ceilings and frescoed walls. All units come with a well-organized private bathroom with tub/shower combo.

Via della Conciliazione 33, 00193 Roma. ✆ **06-6865435.** Fax 06-6864874. www.hotelcolumbus.net. 92 units. 307€ ($353) double; 414€ ($476) suite. Rates include buffet breakfast. AE, DC, MC, V. Bus: 40, 62, or 64. **Amenities:** Restaurant; bar; 24-hr. room service; babysitting; laundry service; dry cleaning. *In room:* A/C, TV, dataport (in some), minibar, hair dryer, safe.

IN TRASTEVERE
Expensive

Hotel Ponte Sisto ★ *Finds*   Just steps from the River Tiber, this hotel lies on the most exclusive residential street in historic Rome at the gateway to Trastevere. The hotel is imbued with a bright, fresh look in contrast to some of the timeworn buildings surrounding it. Your windows will look out on the monumental core of Renaissance and baroque Rome. The 18th-century structure has been totally renovated with a certain class and elegance. Cool chic is achieved by the use of light pastels and marble floors, and the walls are highlighted with strips of black marble. If you can live in the small bedrooms (the singles are really cramped), you'll enjoy this choice address, with its cherrywood furnishings.

Via dei Pettinari 64, 00186 Roma. € 06-6863100. Fax 06-68301712. www.hotelpontesisto.it. 103 units. 310€ ($357) double; 420€ ($483) suite. Rates include breakfast. AE, DC, MC, V. Parking: 26€ ($30). Tram 8. **Amenities:** Restaurant for guests only; breakfast-only room service; laundry service; dry cleaning; garden; rooms for those with limited mobility. *In room:* A/C, TV, dataport, minibar.

WHERE TO DINE
NEAR STAZIONE TERMINI
Very Expensive

Agata e Romeo ★★ NEW ROMAN   One of the most charming places near the Vittorio Emanuele Monument is this striking duplex restaurant in turn-of-the-20th-century Liberty style. You'll enjoy the creative cuisine of Romeo Caraccio (who manages the dining room) and his wife, Agata (who prepares her own version of sophisticated Roman food). Look for pasta garnished with broccoli and cauliflower and served in skate broth, as well as a crisp *sformato* (a type of soufflé) loaded with eggplant, Parmesan, mozzarella, and fresh Italian herbs. There's a charming wine cellar with a wide choice of international and domestic wines. One of their most enduring dessert specialties is their own version of *millefoglie*—chantilly cream laced with liqueur and served in puff pastry.

Via Carlo Alberto 45. € 06-4466115. Reservations recommended. Main courses 18€–26€ ($21–$30). AE, DC, MC, V. Mon–Fri 1–2:30pm and 8–10:30pm. Metro: Vittorio Emanuele.

Moderate

Alvaro al Circo Massimo ★ ITALIAN   Located at the edge of the Circus Maximus, Alvaro is the closest thing you'll find in Rome to a genuine provincial inn, right down to the hanging corncobs and rolls of fat sausages. The antipasti and pastas are fine, the meat courses are even better, and the fresh fish is never overcooked. Other specialties are tagliolini with mushrooms and truffles or briny roasted turbot with potatoes. Look for exotic seasonal mushrooms, including black truffles rivaling the ones you'd find in Spoleto. A basket of fresh fruit rounds out the meal. The atmosphere is comfortable and mellow.

Via dei Cerchi 53. € 06-6786112. Reservations required. Main courses 30€ ($35). AE, DC, MC, V. Tues–Sat 12:30–3:30pm and 7:30–11pm; Sun 12:30–3:30pm. Closed Aug. Metro: Circo Massimo.

NEAR VIA VENETO & PIAZZA BARBERINI
Moderate

Césarina EMILIANA-ROMAGNOLA/ROMAN   This restaurant perpetuates the culinary traditions of the late Césarina Masi in a newer manifestation of the original hole-in-the-wall. Today, with three dining rooms and more than 200 seats, the restaurant serves excellent versions of *bollito misto* (an array of well-seasoned boiled meats), rolled from table to table on a cart; and *misto Césarina*—three kinds of pasta, each handmade and served with a different

The Cafe Scene

Caffè de Paris, Via Vittorio Veneto 90 ((✆) **06-4885284;** Metro: Barberini), rises and falls in popularity depending on the decade. In the 1950s, it was a haven for the fashionable and now it's a popular restaurant in summer where the tables spill out onto the sidewalk filled with patrons. It's open Wednesday through Monday from 8am to 1am. **Canova Café,** Piazza del Popolo 16 ((✆) **06-3612231;** Metro: Flaminio), has a sidewalk terrace for people-watching, plus a snack bar, a restaurant, and a wine shop inside. In summer you'll have access to a courtyard with ivy-covered walls. Meals cost 18€ ($21) and up. It's open daily from 8am to midnight or later, depending on the crowd.

Since 1760, **Antico Caffè Greco,** Via Condotti 86 ((✆) **06-6791700;** Metro: Spagna), has been Rome's most posh and fashionable coffee bar. It has for years enjoyed a reputation as the gathering place of the literati. In the front is a wooden bar, and beyond that a series of small salons, decorated in a 19th-century style. It's open daily from 8am to 8:30pm. **Caffè Sant'Eustachio,** Piazza Sant'Eustachio 82 ((✆) **06-6861309;** bus: 116), is one of the city's most celebrated espresso shops, on a small square near the Pantheon. The water supply comes from a source outside Rome, which the emperor Augustus funneled into the city with an aqueduct in 19 B.C. Rome's most experienced espresso judges claim that the water plays an important part in the coffee's flavor. The cafe is open daily from 8:30am to 1:30pm.

sauce. Equally appealing is *saltimbocca* (veal with ham) and *cotoletta alla bolognese* (veal cutlet baked with ham and cheese).

Via Piemonte 109. (✆) **06-4880828.** Reservations recommended. Main courses 7€–25€ ($8.05–$29). AE, DC, MC, V. Mon–Sat 12:30–3pm and 7:30–11pm. Metro: Barberini. Bus: 52, 53, 63, or 80.

Colline Emiliane (☆) EMILIANA-ROMAGNOLA   This small restaurant right off Piazza Barberini serves *classica cucina bolognese.* It's a family-run place where everybody helps out. The owner is the cook and his wife makes the pasta, which, incidentally, is about the best you'll encounter in Rome. The house specialty is an inspired *tortellini alla panna* (cream sauce) with truffles. An excellent main course is *braciola di maiale*—boneless rolled pork cutlets that have been stuffed with ham and cheese, breaded, and sautéed. *Bollito misto* (mixed boiled meats) is another specialty.

Via Avignonesi 22 (off Piazza Barberini). (✆) **06-4817538.** Reservations highly recommended. Main courses 11€–15€ ($13–$17). MC, V. Sat–Thurs 12:45–2:45pm and 7:45–10:45pm. Closed Aug. Metro: Barberini.

NEAR THE SPANISH STEPS & PIAZZA DEL POPOLO
Expensive

El Toulà (☆) ROMAN/VENETIAN   This luxe restaurant offers quintessential Roman haute cuisine with creative flair in an elegant setting of vaulted ceilings and large archways. One menu section is devoted exclusively to culinary specialties of Venice, including Venice's classic dish, *fegato* (liver) *alla Veneziana;* calamari stuffed with vegetables; *baccalà* (codfish) mousse with polenta; and another Venetian classic, *broetto* (soup made with monkfish and clams). There's a charming bar. El Toulà usually isn't crowded at lunchtime.

Via della Lupa 29B. © 06-6873498. Reservations required for dinner. Main courses 20€–25€ ($23–$29); 4-course *menu veneto* 57€ ($66); 5-course *menu degustazione* 68€ ($78). AE, DC, MC, V. Tues–Fri noon–3pm; Mon–Sat 7:30–11pm. Closed Aug. Bus: 81, 90, 90b, 628, or 913.

Moderate

Dal Bolognese ★ BOLOGNESE   If *La Dolce Vita* were being filmed now, this restaurant would be used as a backdrop, its patrons photographed in their latest Fendi drag. It's one of those rare dining spots that's not only chic, but noted for its food as well. To begin your meal, we suggest *misto di pasta*—four pastas, each flavored with a different sauce, arranged on the same plate. For your main course, specialties include *lasagne verdi, tagliatelle alla bolognese,* and a most recommendable *cotoletta alla bolognese* (veal cutlet topped with cheese). Although almond cake is the house specialty, it's hard to resist the fresh strawberry tart.

Piazza del Popolo 1–2. © 06-3611426. Reservations required. Main courses 10€–39€ ($12–$45). AE, DC, MC, V. Tues–Sun 12:30–3pm and 8:15pm–midnight (last dinner order at 11:15pm). Closed 20 days in Aug. Metro: Flaminio.

Inexpensive

Macceroni ROMAN   In the heart of Rome you can dine in a rustic tavern enjoying food that you often have to go to the Latium countryside to enjoy. The chef shops wisely for his bevy of regional dishes, and backs up his menu with a well-chosen wine list that includes the house chianti. Pasta is the house specialty, and it's never better than in the spaghetti flavored with bacon and onion. You can also order gnocchi, ravioli, and fettuccine with various sauces.

Piazza della Copelle 44. © 06-68-30-78-95. Reservations recommended. Main courses 8€–13€ ($9.20–$15). AE, MC, V. Daily noon–3pm and 8pm–midnight. Open year-round. Metro: Spagna. Bus: 64, 70, 75, or 116.

NEAR CAMPO DE' FIORI & THE JEWISH GHETTO
Moderate

Da Giggetto ROMAN   Da Giggetto, in the old ghetto, is a short walk from the Theater of Marcellus. Romans flock to this bustling trattoria for their special traditional dishes. None are more typical than *carciofi alla giudea,* baby-tender fried artichokes. This is a true delicacy! The cheese concoction, mozzarella in carrozza, is another good choice, as are the zucchini flowers stuffed with mozzarella and anchovies, even the dried salted cod filet. Also sample shrimp sautéed in garlic and olive oil.

Via del Portico d'Ottavia 21/A. © 06-6861105. Reservations recommended. Main courses 11€–17€ ($12–$20). AE, DC, MC, V. Tues–Sun 12:30–3pm and 7:30–11pm. Closed last week of July, 1st week of Aug. Bus: 62, 64, 75, 90, or 170.

Inexpensive

Le Maschere ★★ *(Finds* CALABRESE   This trattoria specializes in the fragrant, often-fiery cooking of Calabria's Costa Viola, with lots of fresh garlic and wake-up-your-mouth red peppers. Begin with a selection of *antipasti calabresi*. For your first course, try one of the many preparations of eggplant or a pasta— perhaps with broccoli or with devilish red peppers, garlic, bread crumbs, and more than a touch of anchovy. The chef also grills meats and fresh swordfish caught off the Calabrian coast—and does so exceedingly well.

Via Monte della Farina 29 (near Largo Argentina). © 06-6879444. Reservations recommended. Main courses 6€–15€ ($6.90–$17). AE, DC, MC, V. Tues–Sun 7:30–11pm. Closed Aug. Bus: 46, 62, or 64.

NEAR PIAZZA NAVONA & THE PANTHEON
Expensive

Il Convivio ✿✿✿ ROMAN/INTERNATIONAL   This is one of the most acclaimed restaurants in Rome, and one of the very few to be granted a coveted Michelin star. The Troiano brothers turn out an inspired cuisine based on shopping for the best and freshest ingredients at the market. To launch yourself, order their giant shrimp tossed with fresh greens. Among the pasta selections, their gnocchi stuffed with zucchini and dribbled with a well-seasoned seafood sauce delights, as does one of the chef's specialties—*petto di faraona*, stuffed chicken spiced up with fresh olives.

Vicolo dei Soldati 31. ℰ **06-6869432**. Reservations required. All main courses 29€–31€ ($33–$36). AE, DC, MC, V. Mon–Sat 1–2:30pm and 8–11pm. Bus: 40 or 64.

Moderate

Osteria dell'Antiquario ✿ *Finds* INTERNATIONAL/ROMAN   Virtually undiscovered, this little Roman osteria lies a few blocks down the Via dei Coronari as you leave the Piazza Navona and head toward St. Peter's. It has three dining rooms and a terrace for fair-weather dining. We prefer to begin with a delectable appetizer of sautéed shellfish (usually mussels and clams), although you might opt for the risotto with porcini mushrooms. For a main course, you can go experimental with the filet of ostrich covered by a slice of ham and grated Parmesan, or else opt for shellfish flavored with saffron. The fish soup with fried bread is excellent, as is an array of freshly made soups and pastas. Veal rolls Roman style and turbot flavored with fresh tomatoes and basil are other excellent choices. This is dining in the classic Roman style.

Piazzetta di S. Simeone 26/27, Via dei Coronari. ℰ **06-6879694**. Reservations recommended. Main courses 10€–23€ ($12–$26). AE, DC, MC, V. Mon–Sat 8–11pm. Closed 15 days in mid-Aug, Christmas, and Jan 1–15. Bus: 70, 87, or 90.

Inexpensive

Il Miraggio ROMAN/SARDINIAN/SEAFOOD   You might want to escape the roar of traffic along Via del Corso by ducking into this informal spot on a crooked side street (about midway between Piazza Venezia and Piazza Colonna). It's a cozy neighborhood setting where every dish has a rich and savory flavor. The risotto with scampi or the fettuccine with porcini mushrooms will have you begging for more. The grilled scampi is done to perfection, or you might prefer a steaming kettle of mussels flavored with olive oil, lemon juice, and fresh parsley. We're especially fond of the house specialty, spaghetti *alla bottarga* (with roe sauce), especially if it's followed by *spigola alla vernaccia* (sea bass sautéed in butter and Vernaccia wine from Tuscany).

Vicolo Sciarra 59. ℰ **06-6780226**. Reservations recommended. Main courses 8€–16€ ($9.20–$18). AE, MC, V. Thurs–Tues 12:30–3:30pm and 7:30–11pm. Closed Jan 6–30. Metro: Barberini. Bus: 56, 60, 62, 81, 85, 95, 160, 175, 492, or 628.

Pizzeria Baffetto ✿ *Kids* PIZZA   Our Roman friends always take out-of-towners here when they request the best pizza in Rome. Arguably, Pizzeria Baffetto fills the bill and has done so admirably for the past 80 years. Pizzas are sold as *piccolo* (small), *media* (medium), or *grande* (large). Most pizza aficionados order the Margherita, the simplest version with mozzarella and a delectable tomato sauce, but a wide range of toppings is served. The chef is preening proud of his pizza Baffetto, the house specialty. It comes with a topping of tomato sauce, mozzarella, mushrooms, onions, sausages, roasted peppers, and eggs. The pizza crusts are delightfully thin, and the pies are served piping hot from the intense heat of the ancient ovens.

Via del Governo Vecchio 114. ℰ **06-6861617.** Reservations not accepted. Pizza 3.50€–7.50€ ($4.05–$8.65). No credit cards. Daily 6:30pm–1am. Closed last 2 weeks in Aug. Bus: 46, 62, or 64.

NEAR VATICAN CITY
Moderate

Cesare ROMAN/TUSCAN   Cesare is a fine old-world dining room known for its deft handling of fresh ingredients. You can select your fresh fish from the refrigerated glass case at the entrance. We come here for the tender seafood salad, brimming with cuttlefish, shrimp, squid, mussels, and octopus, and dressed with olive oil, fresh parsley, and lemon. Our table was blessed with an order of *spaghetti all'amatriciana*—the spicy tomato sauce flavored with hot peppers and tiny bits of salt pork. The *saltimbocca alla romana,* that classic Roman dish, is a masterpiece as served here—butter-tender veal slices topped with prosciutto and fresh sage and sautéed in white wine.

Via Crescenzio 13, near Piazza Cavour. ℰ **06-6861227.** Reservations recommended. Main courses 13€–25€ ($15–$29). AE, DC, MC, V. June 15–Aug 7 Mon–Sat 12:30–3pm and 7–11:30pm. Off season Tues–Sat 12:30–3pm and 7–11:30pm; Sun 12:30–3pm. Closed 3 weeks Aug. Metro: Lepanto or Ottaviano. Bus: 23, 34, or 49.

Inexpensive

Ristorante Giardinaccio ITALIAN/MOLISIAN/ROMAN   This popular restaurant is only 180m (600 ft.) from St. Peter's. Unusual for Rome, it offers specialties from the provincial Molise region in southeast Italy, and is appropriately decorated in rustic country-tavern style. Flaming grills provide succulent versions of perfectly done quail, goat, and other dishes, but you might want to be adventurous and try the mutton goulash. Many pastas are featured, including *taconelle,* a homemade pasta with lamb sauce. Vegetarians and others will like the large self-service selection of antipasti.

Via Aurelia 53. ℰ **06-631367.** Reservations recommended, especially on weekends. Main courses 9€–20€ ($10.35–$23); fixed-price menus 8€–20€ ($9.20–$23). AE, DC, MC, V. Daily 12:15–3:15pm and 7:15–11:15pm. Bus: 46, 62, or 98.

IN ANCIENT ROME
Expensive

Trattoria San Teodoro ⚜ (Kids ROMAN   At last there's a good place to eat in the former gastronomic wasteland near the Roman Forum and Palatine Hill. The helpful staff welcomes you to a shady terrace or to a dimly lit dining room. The chef specializes in seafood, and does such exceedingly well, as reflected by his minisize baby squid sautéed with Roman artichokes. His signature dish is seafood carpaccio made with tuna, turbot, or sea bass. Succulent meats such as medallions of veal in a nutmeg-enhanced cream sauce round out the menu at this family-friendly place. All the pastas are homemade.

Via dei Fienili 49–51. ℰ **06-6780933.** Reservations recommended. Main courses 15€–25€ ($17–$29). AE, MC, V. Mon–Sat 12:30–3:30pm and 7:30pm–midnight. Closed Jan 15–Feb 15. Metro: Circo Massimo.

Moderate

F.I.S.H. ⚜ (Finds SEAFOOD   If you've got a dinner date with Madonna and Guy Ritchie, take them here. It's one of Rome's hottest restaurants, managing to be both chic and good. Its initials stand for "Fine International Seafood House," and the restaurant lives up to its self-billing. It's tiny but choice, and count yourself lucky if you can get a table. The decor is sleek and minimalist, but with a touch of elegance. In the bar you can study the creatures in the tropical aquarium, perhaps contemplating one for your dinner.

Via dei Serpenti 16. © 06-47824962. Reservations imperative. Main courses 12€–20€ ($14–$23). AE, DC, MC, V. Tues–Sun noon–3pm and 7:45pm–1am. Closed Aug 7–26 and Dec 24–25. Metro: Colosseo.

Inexpensive

Hostaria Nerone ⭐ ROMAN/ITALIAN   Built atop the ruins of the Golden House of Nero, this trattoria is run by the energetic de Santis family, which cooks, serves, and handles the large crowds of hungry locals and visitors. Opened in 1929 at the edge of the Colle Oppio Park, it contains two compact dining rooms, plus a terrace lined with flowering shrubs that offers a view over the Colosseum and the Bath of Trajan. The copious antipasti buffet represents the bounty of Italy's fields and seas. The pastas include savory spaghetti with clams and, our favorite, pasta *fagioli* (with beans). You can also order grilled crayfish and swordfish or Italian sausages with polenta. Roman-style tripe is a local favorite, but maybe you'll skip it for the osso buco (braised veal shanks) with mashed potatoes and seasonal mushrooms. The wide list of some of the best Italian wines is reasonably priced.

Via Terme di Tito 96. © 06-4817952. Reservations recommended. Main courses 7.50€–13€ ($8.65–$15). AE, DC, MC, V. Mon–Sat noon–3pm and 7–11pm. Metro: Colosseo. Bus: 75, 85, 87, 117, or 175.

IN TRASTEVERE
Expensive

Alberto Ciarla ⭐⭐ SEAFOOD   Alberto Ciarla is the best and most expensive restaurant in Trastevere, although it's not as chic as it was in the 1980s. It serves some of the most elegant fish dishes in the city. Specialties include a handful of ancient recipes subtly improved by Signor Ciarla, such as soup of pasta and beans with seafood. Original dishes include a delectable salmon Marcel Trompier with lobster sauce, as well as well-flavored sushi, a full array of shellfish, and filet of sea bass prepared in at least three different ways, including an award-winning version with almonds.

Piazza San Cosimato 40. © 06-5818668. Reservations required. Main courses 16€–30€ ($18–$35); fixed-price menus 40€–70€ ($46–$81). AE, DC, MC, V. Mon–Sat 8:30pm–12:30am. Closed 1 week in Jan and 1 week in Aug. Bus: 44, 75, 170, 280, or 718.

Moderate

La Cisterna ROMAN   This trattoria lies deep in the heart of Trastevere. For more than half a century it has been run by the Simmi family, which is genuinely interested in serving only the best as well as providing a good time for all guests. If you like traditional cookery based on the best of regional produce, come here. In summer you can inspect the antipasti—a mixed selection of hors d'oeuvres—right out on the street before going in. House specialties include Roman-style suckling lamb *(abbacchio)*, rigatoni *all'amatriciana* (with diced bacon, olive oil, garlic, tomatoes, red peppers, and onions), and fresh fish—especially sea bass baked with herbs.

Via della Cisterna 13. © 06-5812543. Reservations recommended. Main courses 7€–15€ ($8.05–$17). AE, MC, V. Mon–Sat 7pm–1:30am. Bus: 44, 75, 170, 280, or 710.

EXPLORING THE ETERNAL CITY

Rome is studded with ancient monuments that silently evoke its history as one of the greatest centers of Western civilization—once all roads led to Rome, with good reason. It was the first cosmopolitan city in Europe, importing everything from slaves and gladiators to great art from the far corners of the empire. With all its carnage and mismanagement, it left a legacy of law and order and an uncanny lesson in how to conquer enemies by absorbing their cultures. But ancient Rome is only part of the spectacle. The Vatican also made the city a center of the world in art as well as religion. And although Vatican architects rifled much of the glory of the past for their projects, they also created the great Renaissance treasures we come to see today.

SIGHTSEEING SUGGESTIONS FOR FIRST-TIME VISITORS

If You Have 1 Day Rome wasn't built in a day and you aren't likely to see it in a day either, but make the most of your limited time. You'll basically have to decide on the legacy of **Imperial Rome**—the Roman Forum, the Imperial Forum, and the Colosseum—or else St. Peter's and the **Vatican.** Walk along the **Spanish Steps** at sunset. At night go to **Piazza del Campidoglio** for a fantastic view of the Forum below. Have a nightcap on **Via Veneto**, which, although past its prime, is still appealing. Toss a coin in the **Trevi fountain** and promise yourself you'll return.

If You Have 2 Days If you elected to see the Roman Forum and the Colosseum on your first day, then spend the second day exploring St. Peter's and the **Vatican Museums** (or vice versa). Have dinner in a restaurant in **Trastevere.**

If You Have 3 Days In the morning go to the **Pantheon** in the heart of Old Rome; then, after lunch, explore the **Castel Sant'Angelo** and the **Etruscan Museum.** Have dinner at a restaurant in or around **Piazza Navona.**

If You Have 4 or 5 Days On day 4 head for the environs, notably **Tivoli,** where you can see the Villa d'Este and Hadrian's Villa. On Day 5 explore the ruins of **Ostia Antica,** return to Rome for lunch, and visit the **Capitoline Museum** and **Basilica di San Giovanni in Laterano** in the afternoon.

ST. PETER'S & THE VATICAN

Basilica di San Pietro (St. Peter's Basilica) ★★★ As you stand in Bernini's **Piazza San Pietro (St. Peter's Square),** you'll be in the arms of an ellipse; like a loving parent, the Doric-pillared colonnade reaches out to embrace the faithful. Holding 300,000 is no problem for this square. Inside, the size of this famous church is awe-inspiring—though its dimensions (about two football fields long) are not apparent at first. St. Peter's is said to have been built over the tomb of the crucified saint. The original church was erected on the order of Constantine, but the present structure is Renaissance and baroque; it showcases the talents of some of Italy's greatest artists.

In such a grand church, don't expect subtlety. But the basilica is rich in art. Under Michelangelo's dome is the celebrated **baldacchino** ★★★ by Bernini. In

---

Tips **A St. Peter's Warning**

St. Peter's has a strict dress code: no shorts, no skirts above the knee, and no bare shoulders. You will not get in if you don't come dressed appropriately. In a pinch, men and women alike can buy a big cheap scarf from a nearby souvenir stand and wrap it around their legs as a long skirt or throw it over their shoulders as a shawl.

Rome Attractions

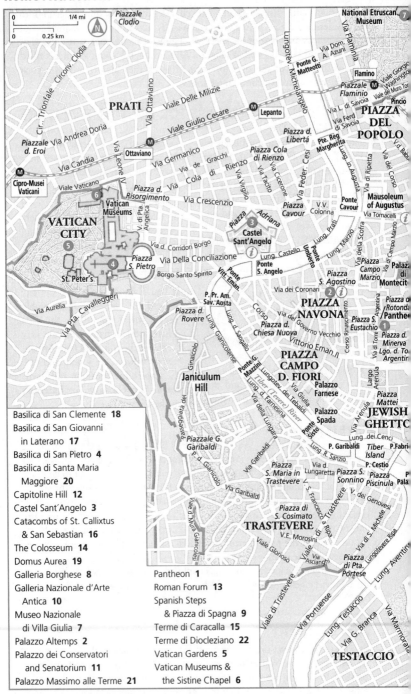

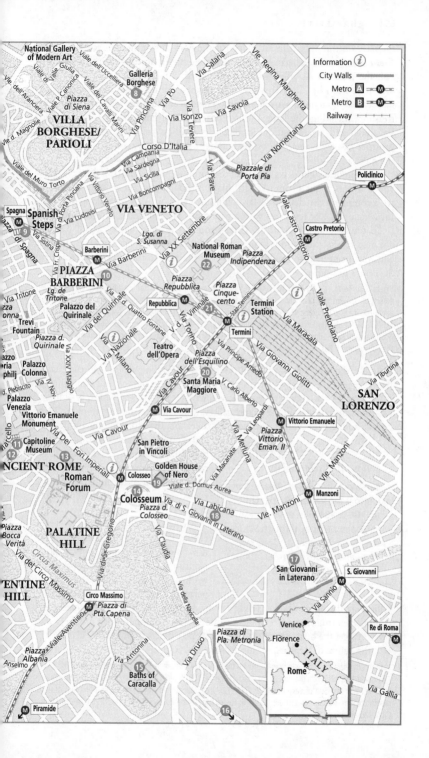

National Gallery
of Modern Art

Viale dell'Uccelliera

Viale di Valle Giulia

Galleria
Borghese

8

Via Po

Via Salaria

Vle. Regina Margherita

Vle. dell'Arancera

Viale P. Canonica

Viale dei Cavalli Marini

Piazza
di Siena

Via Pinciana

Via Isonzo

Via Savoia

Vle. di Magnolie

VILLA
BORGHESE/
PARIOLI

Corso D'Italia

Via Nomentana

Viale del Muro Torto

Via Campania

Via Sardegna

Via Sicilia

Via Piave

Piazzale di
Porta Pia

Viale Castro Pretorio

Policlinico

M

Spagna

M

Spanish
Steps

9

Via Sistina

Via di Porta Pinciana

Via Vittorio Veneto

Via Ludovisi

VIA VENETO

Lgo. di
S. Susanna

Via XX Settembre

National Roman
Museum

22

Piazza
Indipendenza

Castro Pretorio

M

Piazza di Spagna

Barberini

M

Via Fr. Crispi

Via Barberini

i

Via Tritone

PIAZZA
BARBERINI

10

Lg. de
Tritone

Piazza
Repubblica

Piazza
Cinque-
cento

Termini
Station

i

Viale Pretoriano

zza
onna

Palazzo del
Quirinale

Via del Quirinale

Via d. Quattro Fontane

Repubblica

M

Via Viminale

Staz. Termini

Termini

M

Via Marsala

Trevi
Fountain

Piazza d.
Quirinale

i

Via Nazionale

Via Milano

Teatro
dell'Opera

Piazza
dell'Esquilino

Via Principe Amedeo

Via Giovanni Giolitti

Via Tiburtina

azzo
ria
philj

Palazzo
Colonna

Via XXIV Maggio

20

Santa Maria
Maggiore

V. Carlo Alberto

SAN
LORENZO

J. Plebiscito

Via Nov.

Palazzo
Venezia

Vittorio Emanuele
Monument

Via Cavour

Via Cavour

M

Via Cavour

Via Leopardi

Via Merulana

Vittorio Emanuele

M

Piazza
Vittorio
Eman. II

Vle. Manzoni

rcello

Capitoline
Museum

11

Via Dei Fori Imperiali

San Pietro
in Vincoli

12

NCIENT ROME

Roman
Forum

13

i

Colosseo

M

19

Golden House
of Nero

Viale d. Domus Aurea

Via Macanate

Manzoni

M

14

Colosseum

Via di S. Giovanni in Laterano

Via Labicana

Vle. Manzoni

Piazza d.
Colosseo

18

Via della Navicella

Via Claudia

Via di S. Gregorio

Piazza
Bocca
Verità

PALATINE
HILL

17

San Giovanni
in Laterano

S. Giovanni

M

ENTINE
HILL

Via del Circo Massimo

Circus Maximus

Circo Massimo

M

Piazza di
Pta. Capena

Via Antonina

Via Druso

Piazza di
Pla. Metronia

Via Sannio

Re di Roma

M

Piazza
Albania

Anselmo

Vle. Aventino

15

Baths of
Caracalla

Venice

Florence

ITALY

Rome

M

Piramide

16

Via Gallia

Information i
City Walls
Metro A M
Metro B M
Railway

the nave on the right (the 1st chapel) is the best-known piece of sculpture, the **Pietà** ✮✮✮ that Michelangelo sculpted while still in his early twenties. You can visit the **treasury** ✮, filled with jewel-studded chalices, reliquaries, and copes. One robe worn by Pius XII strikes a simple note in these halls of elegance. The sacristy now contains a **Museo Storico (Historical Museum)** displaying Vatican treasures, including the large 1400s bronze tomb of Pope Sixtus V by Antonio Pollaiuolo and several antique chalices. In addition you can visit the **Vatican grottoes** ✮✮ with their tombs, both ancient and modern (Pope John XXII gets the most adulation).

The grandest sight is yet to come: the climb to **Michelangelo's dome** ✮✮✮, which towers about 115m (375 ft.) high. Although you can walk up the steps, we recommend the elevator as far as it'll carry you. You can walk along the roof, for which you'll be rewarded with a panoramic view of Rome and the Vatican.

To tour the area around **St. Peter's tomb,** you must apply several days in advance to the excavations office (✆ **06-69885318**), open Monday through Saturday from 9am to 3:30pm. Pass under the arch to the left of the facade of St. Peter's to find it.

Piazza San Pietro. ✆ 06-69881662 (for information on celebrations). Basilica (including grottoes) free admission. Guided tour of excavations around St. Peter's tomb 9€ ($10); children younger than 15 are not admitted. Stairs to the dome 4€ ($4.60); elevator to the dome 4€ ($4.60); Sacristy (with Historical Museum) 5€ ($5.75). Basilica (including the sacristy and treasury) Oct–Mar daily 9am–6pm; Apr–Sept daily 9am–7pm. Grottoes daily 8am–5pm. Dome Oct–Mar daily 8am–5pm; Apr–Sept 8am–6pm. Metro: Ottaviano/San Pietro, then a long stroll. Bus: 46.

Vatican Museums & the Sistine Chapel ✮✮✮   The Vatican Museums contain a gigantic repository of treasures. You can follow one of four itineraries—A, B, C, or D—according to the time you have (1½–5 hr.) and your special interests. You can choose from the picture gallery, which houses paintings from the 11th century to the 19th century, the Egyptian collection, the Etruscan museum, Greek and Roman sculpture, and, of course, the **Sistine Chapel.** Consult the large panels at the entrance, then follow the letter and color of the itinerary chosen. Facilities for persons with disabilities are available.

Michelangelo labored for 4 years (1508–12) over the epic Sistine Chapel, now restored, although not without controversy, to its original glory. The work was so physically taxing that it permanently damaged his eyesight.

> **Tips   A Vatican Tip**
>
> On the left side of Piazza San Pietro is the **Vatican Tourist Office** (✆ **06-69884866**; www.vatican. va), open Monday through Saturday from 8:30am to 7pm with maps and guides and reservations for Vatican Gardens tours.

Glorifying the human body as only a sculptor could, Michelangelo painted nine panels taken from the pages of Genesis, and surrounded them with prophets and sibyls. To get the best view of the Sistine Chapel's frescoes, bring binoculars. Also, visit the Stanze di Raphael, rooms decorated by Raphael when still a young man.

Vatican City, Viale Vaticano (a long walk around the Vatican walls from St. Peter's Square). ✆ 06-69883333. Admission 10€ ($12); children under 14 years of age 7€ ($8.05); free for children under 6. Mid-Nov to Feb Mon–Sat and first Sun of each month 8:45am–12:20pm. Mar to mid-Nov Mon–Sat and first Sun of each month 8:45am–3:20pm. Closed: Jan 1 and 6, Easter, May 1 and 20, Nov 1, and Dec 8 and 24–25. Metro: Cipro-Musei Vaticani.

THE FORUM, THE COLOSSEUM & THE HIGHLIGHTS OF ANCIENT ROME

Foro Romano (Roman Forum) ★★★   The Roman Forum was built in the marshy land between the Palatine and the Capitoline hills. It flourished as the center of Roman life in the days of the Republic, before it gradually lost prestige to the Imperial Forum. By day the columns of now-vanished temples and the stones from which long-forgotten orators spoke are mere shells. But at night, when the Forum is silent in the moonlight, it isn't difficult to imagine that Vestal Virgins still guard the sacred temple fire.

If you want the stones to have some meaning, you'll have to purchase a detailed plan, as the temples can be hard to locate. The best of the lot is the handsomely adorned **Temple of Castor and Pollux** ★★★, erected in the 5th century B.C. in honor of a battle triumph. The **Temple of Faustina** ★★, with its lovely columns and frieze (griffins and candelabra), was converted into the San Lorenzo in Miranda Church. The **Temple of the Vestal Virgins** ★★★ is a popular attraction; some of the statuary, mostly headless, remains.

A long walk up from the Roman Forum leads to the **Palatine Hill** ★★★, one of the seven hills of Rome; your ticket from the Forum will admit you to this attraction (it's open the same hours). The Palatine, tradition tells us, was the spot on which the first settlers built their huts, under the direction of Romulus. In later years, the hill became a patrician residential district that attracted citizens like Cicero. It's worth the climb for the panoramic, sweeping view of both the Roman and Imperial forums, as well as the Capitoline Hill and the Colosseum. Of the ruins that remain, none is finer than the so-called **House of Livia** ★★ (the "abominable grandmother" of Robert Graves's *I, Claudius*).

When the glory that was Rome has completely overwhelmed you, you can enjoy a respite in the cooling **Farnese Gardens** ★, laid out in the 16th century, which incorporate some of Michelangelo's designs.

Largo Romolo e Remo. ✆ 06-6990110. Forum free admission; Palatine Hill 8€ ($9.20). Apr–Sept daily 9am–7pm; Oct–Mar daily 9am–3:30pm. Last admission 1 hr. before closing. Closed holidays. Metro: Colosseo. Bus: 81, 85, 87, or 186.

Colosseo (Colosseum) ★★★   In spite of the fact that it's a mere shell, the Colosseum remains the greatest architectural inheritance from ancient Rome. It was inaugurated by Titus in A.D. 80 with a weeks-long bloody combat between gladiators and wild beasts. At its peak, the Colosseum could seat 50,000 spectators; exotic animals—humans also—were shipped in from the far corners of the empire to satisfy their jaded tastes. Many historians now believe that one of the most enduring legends linked to the Colosseum—that Christians were fed to the lions here—is unfounded.

Next to the Colosseum is the **Arch of Constantine** ★★★, erected in honor of Constantine's defeat of the pagan Maxentius (A.D. 306).

Piazzale del Colosseo, Via dei Fori Imperiali. ✆ 06-7004261. Admission 10€ ($12) all levels. Oct–Jan 15 daily 9am–3pm; Jan 16–Feb 15 daily 9am–4pm; Feb 16–Mar 17 daily 9am–4:30pm; Mar 18–Apr 16 daily 9am–5pm; Apr 17–Sept daily 9am–7pm. Guided tours in English with an archaeologist daily 6 times per day (9:30am, 10:15am, 11:15am, 12:30pm, 1:45pm, 3pm) 3.50€ ($4.05). Admission to Colosseo includes visit at Palatine Hill.

Domus Aurea (Golden House of Nero) ★   Nero's fabulous Golden House reopened in 1999 after a 15-year restoration. In A.D. 64, Rome was swept by a disastrous fire—contrary to gossip it has never been proven that Nero set the fire. The emperor did, however, seize more than 80 hectares (200 acres) of the burned-out historic core to create one of the most sumptuous palaces in history. Subsequent emperors, seeking to distance themselves from their unpopular predecessor, destroyed much of the place by using its vast network of rooms and walls as a foundation for new construction. Out of its original 250 rooms, 30 are now open to the public, decorated with some of the sculptures, mosaics, and frescoes that have survived the past 2,000 years. When Nero moved in, he shouted, "At last I can start living like a human being!"

Via della Domus Aurea. ⓒ **06-39967700.** Admission 5€ ($5.75), plus 1€ ($1.15) for a reservation. Wed–Mon 9am–7:45pm. Last admission 1 hr. before closing. Metro: Colosseo.

Campidoglio (Capitoline Hill) ★★★ Of the Seven Hills of Rome, the Campidoglio is the most sacred—its origins stretch way back into antiquity (an Etruscan temple to Jupiter once stood on this spot). The approach to the Capitoline Hill is dramatic—climbing the long, sloping steps designed by Michelangelo. At the top is a perfectly proportioned square, Piazza del Campidoglio, also laid out by the Florentine artist.

One side of the piazza is open; the others are bounded by the **Senatorium (Town Council)** ★★, the statuary-filled **Palazzo dei Conservatori** ★★★, and the **Museo Capitolino (Capitoline Museum)** ★★ (see "More Attractions," below). The Campidoglio is dramatic at night (walk around to the back for a regal view of the floodlit Roman Forum).

Piazza del Campidoglio. Bus: 44, 89, 92, 94, or 716.

Castel Sant'Angelo ★★★ This overpowering structure, in a landmark position on the Tiber just east of Vatican City, was originally built in the 2nd century A.D. as a tomb for the emperor Hadrian; it continued as an imperial mausoleum until the time of Caracalla. It's an imposing and grim castle with thick walls and a cylindrical shape. If it looks like a fortress, it should, as that was its function in the Middle Ages. In the 14th century it became a papal residence. Its legend rests largely on its link with Pope Alexander VI, whose mistress bore him two children—Cesare and Lucrezia Borgia. Today the highlight of the castle is a trip through the Renaissance apartments with their coffered ceilings and lush decoration. Their walls have witnessed plots and intrigues that make up some of the arch-treachery of the High Renaissance. You can climb to the top terrace for another one of those dazzling views of the Eternal City.

Lungotevere Castello 50.ⓒ **06-6819111.** Admission 5€ ($5.75). Tues–Sun 9am–7pm. Metro: Ottaviano, then a long stroll. Bus: 23, 46, 49, 62, 87, 98, 280, or 910.

Pantheon ★★★ Of all the great buildings of ancient Rome, only the Pantheon (All the Gods) remains intact today. It was built in 27 B.C. by Marcus Agrippa, and later reconstructed by the emperor Hadrian in the first part of the 2nd century A.D. This remarkable building is among the architectural wonders of the world because of its dome and its concept of space. The Pantheon was once ringed with niches containing white marble statues of Roman gods. Animals were sacrificed and burned in the center, and the smoke escaped through the only means of light, an opening at the top 8m (27 ft.) in diameter. Michelangelo came here to study the dome before designing the cupola of St. Peter's, whose dome is only .5m (2 ft.) smaller than the Pantheon's.

Piazza della Rotonda. ⓒ **06-68300230.** Free admission. Mon–Sat 8:30am–7:30pm; Sun 9am–6pm. Bus: 46, 62, 64, 170, or 492 to Largo di Torre.

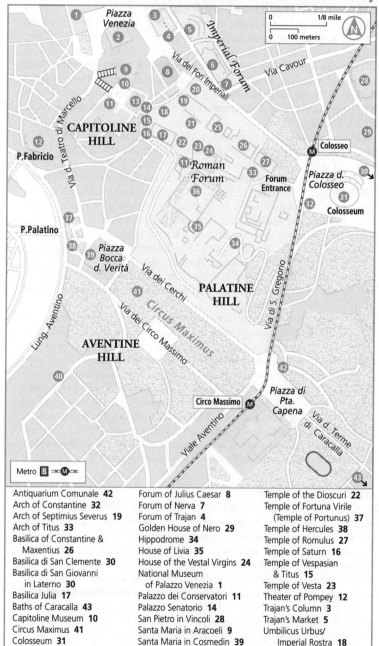

Ancient Rome & Attractions Nearby

Piazza Venezia

Imperial Forum

Via dei Fori Imperiali

Via Cavour

0   1/8 mile
0   100 meters

CAPITOLINE HILL

P.Fabricio

Via d. Teatro di Marcello

Roman Forum

Colosseo

Forum Entrance

Piazza d. Colosseo

Colosseum

P.Palatino

Piazza Bocca d. Verità

Via dei Cerchi

PALATINE HILL

Via di S. Gregorio

Circus Maximus

Via dei Circo Massimo

AVENTINE HILL

Lung. Aventino

Piazza di Pta. Capena

Via d. Terme di Caracalla

Circo Massimo

Viale Aventino

Metro B — M —

THE CATACOMBS OF THE APPIAN WAY

Of all the roads that led to Rome, Via Appia Antica—built in 312 B.C.—was the leader. It eventually stretched all the way from Rome to the seaport of Brindisi, through which trade with the colonies in Greece and the East was funneled.

Along the Appian Way the patrician Romans built great monuments above the ground, whereas Christians met in the catacombs beneath. The remains of both can be visited today. In some dank, dark grottoes (never stray too far from either your party or one of the exposed light bulbs), you can still discover traces of early Christian art.

Of the catacombs open to the public, those of St. Callixtus and of St. Sebastian are the most important. Both can be reached by bus no. 118, which leaves from near the Colosseo Metro station.

Catacombe di San Sebastiano ★★★ are at Via Appia Antica 136 (© **06-7887035;** bus: 118). Today the tomb of the martyr is in the basilica, but it was originally in the catacomb under the building. From the reign of Valerian to that of Constantine, the bodies of Sts. Peter and Paul were hidden in these catacombs. The tunnels, if stretched out, would reach a length of 11km (6¾ miles). Admission is 4€ ($4.60) adults, 2€ ($2.30) children 6 to 15, free for children 5 and under. The catacombs are open April through October Monday through Saturday from 9am to noon and 2:30 to 5:30pm; January through March Monday through Saturday from 8:30am to noon and 2:30 to 5pm. They are closed from November 13 to December 11.

Catacombe di San Callisto (St. Callixtus) ★★★, Via Appia Antica 110 (© **06-51301580;** www.catacombe.roma.it; bus: 118), comprise the first cemetery of the Christian community of Rome, burial place of 16 popes in the 3rd century. The catacombs bear the name of St. Callixtus, the deacon whom the pope St. Zephyrinus put in charge of them. Callixtus himself was later elected pope (217–22). The cemetery complex is made up of a network of galleries stretching for nearly 19km (12 miles), structured in five different levels, reaching a depth of about 20m (65 ft.). Admission is 4€ ($4.60) adults, 2€ ($2.30) children 6 to 15, free for children 5 and under. Hours are March through October Thursday through Tuesday from 8:30am to noon and 2:30 to 5:30pm; November through January Thursday through Tuesday from 8:30am to noon and 2:30 to 5pm; closed in February.

MORE ATTRACTIONS

Scalinata di Spagna (Spanish Steps) ★★★   The steps—filled in spring with azaleas and other flowers, flower vendors, jewelry dealers, and photographers snapping pictures of visitors—and the square take their names from the Spanish Embassy, which used to be headquartered here. Designed by Italian architect Francesco de Sanctis and built from 1723 to 1725, they were funded almost entirely by the French as a preface to Trinità dei Monti at the top. At the foot of the steps is a boat-shaped fountain designed by Pietro Bernini (not to be confused with his son, Giovanni Lorenzo Bernini, a far greater sculptor). The steps and the piazza below are always packed with a crowd: strolling, reading in the sun, browsing the vendors' carts, and people-watching.

Piazza di Spagna. Metro: Spagna.

Terme di Caracalla (Baths of Caracalla) ★★★   Named for the emperor Caracalla, the baths were completed in the early part of the 3rd century. The richness of decoration has faded and the lushness can only be judged from the shell of brick ruins that remain.

Via delle Terme di Caracalla 52. © **06-5758626**. Admission 5€ ($5.75). Oct–Mar 1 daily 9am–3:30pm; Mar 2–Mar 30 daily 9am–5pm; Apr–Sept 30 daily 9am–6pm (every Mon 9am–1pm). Last admission 1 hr. before closing. Closed holidays. Bus: 628.

Basilica di San Clemente ★★ From the Colosseum, head up Via di San Giovanni in Laterano, which leads to the Basilica of Saint Clement. In this church-upon-a-church, centuries of history peel away: A 4th-century church was built over a secular house from the 1st century A.D., beside which stood a pagan temple dedicated to Mithras; Normans destroyed the lower church, and a new one was built in the 12th century. Down in the eerie grottoes (which you can explore on your own—unlike the catacombs on the Appian Way), you'll discover well-preserved frescoes from the 1st to the 3rd centuries.

Via San Giovanni in Laterano at Piazza San Clemente. © **06-7740021**. Basilica free admission; excavations 3€ ($3.45). Mon–Sat 9am–12:30pm and 3–6pm; Sun 10am–12:30pm and 3–6pm. Metro: Colosseo. Bus: 85, 87, or 850.

Basilica di San Giovanni in Laterano ★★★ This church—not St. Peter's—is the cathedral of the diocese of Rome. Catholics all over the world refer to it as their "mother church." Originally built in A.D. 314 by Constantine, the cathedral has suffered many vicissitudes and was forced to rebuild many times. The present structure is characterized by its 18th-century facade by Alessandro Galilei (statues of Christ and the Apostles ring the top). Borromini gets the credit—some say blame—for the interior, built for Innocent X.

The most unusual sight is across the street at the "Palace of the Holy Steps," called the **Santuario della Scala Santa** ★, Piazza San Giovanni in Laterano (© **06-7726641**). It's alleged that these were the actual steps that Christ climbed when he was brought before Pilate. These steps are supposed to be climbed only on your knees, which you're likely to see the faithful doing throughout the day. Visiting hours are daily from 6:15am to noon and 3:30 to 6:30pm. Admission is free.

Piazza San Giovanni in Laterano 4. © **06-69886433**. Basilica free admission; cloisters 2€ ($2.30). Summer daily 9am–6:45pm (off season to 6pm). Metro: San Giovanni. Bus: 4, 16, 30, 85, 87, or 174.

Basilica di Santa Maria Maggiore (Saint Mary the Great) ★★★ This great church was originally founded by Pope Liberius in A.D. 358 but was rebuilt by Pope Sixtus III from 432 to 440. Its campanile, erected in the 14th century, is the loftiest in the city. Much doctored in the 18th century, the facade is not an accurate reflection of the treasures inside. The basilica is especially noted for the 5th-century Roman mosaics in its nave, as well as for its coffered ceiling, said to have been gilded with gold brought from the New World. In the 16th century Domenico Fontana built a now-restored "Sistine Chapel." The church contains the tomb of Bernini, Italy's most important architect during the flowering of the baroque in the 17th century.

Piazza Santa Maria Maggiore. © **06-483195**. Free admission. Daily 7am–7pm. Metro: Termini.

Museo Capitolino ★★ and **Palazzo dei Conservatori** ★★★ The Capitoline Museum was built in the 17th century, based on an architectural sketch by Michelangelo. In the first room is *The Dying Gaul,* a work of majestic skill; in a special gallery all her own is *The Capitoline Venus,* who demurely covers herself—this statue (a Roman copy of the Greek original) has been a symbol of feminine beauty and charm down through the centuries. The famous statue of *Marcus Aurelius* is the only bronze equestrian statue to have survived from ancient Rome. It was retrieved from the Tiber where it had been tossed by marauding barbarians. For centuries it was thought to be a statue of Constantine the Great; this mistake protected it further, since papal Rome respected the memory of the first Christian emperor.

The Palazzo dei Conservatori, across the way, is rich in classical sculpture and paintings. In the courtyard are fragments of a colossal statue of Constantine. One of the most notable bronzes is the *Spinario* (little boy picking a thorn from his foot), a Greek classic from the 1st century B.C. In addition, you'll find *Lupa Capitolina* (Capitoline She-Wolf), a rare Etruscan bronze possibly from the 5th century B.C. (Romulus and Remus, the legendary twins that the she-wolf suckled, were added at a later date.)

Piazza del Campidoglio 1. © 06-67102071. Admission (to both) 7.80€ ($8.95). Tues–Sun 9am–8pm. Bus: 44, 81, 95, 160, 170, 715, or 780.

Galleria Borghese ★★★   Closed for 14 years, this jewel-box collection of masterworks is back in all its fabulous glory. The bad news is that it may be hard to get in because of limited access. This treasure trove of art in what was once the Borghese's summer residence includes such masterpieces as Bernini's *David, The Rape of Persephone,* and his *Apollo and Daphne;* Titian's *Sacred and Profane Love;* Raphael's *Deposition;* even Caravaggio's *Jerome.* One of the most viewed pieces of sculpture in today's gallery is Canova's life-size sculpture of Napoleon's sister, Pauline, in the pose of "Venus Victorious." When Pauline was asked if she felt uncomfortable about posing in the nude, she replied, "Why should I? The studio was heated."

Piazza Scipione Borghese 5 (off Via Pinciano). © 06-32810 for information. Admission 8.50€ ($9.80). Tues–Sun 9am–7pm. Bus: 5 or 910.

Galleria Nazionale d'Arte Antica ★★   The Palazzo Barberini, right off Piazza Barberini, is one of Rome's most magnificent baroque palaces. It was begun by Carlo Maderno in 1627 and completed in 1633 by Bernini, whose lavishly decorated rococo apartments are on view. The palace houses the Galleria Nazionale. The splendid array of paintings includes 13th- to 16th-century works by Simone Martini, Filippo Lippi, Andrea Solario, Francesco Francia, Il Sodoma, and Raphael. Since 1998, you can visit a restored 18th-century apartment decorated with frescoes from the school of Barberini. Admission is 1€ ($1.15), and hours are Tuesday through Sunday from 9am to 7pm.

Via delle Quattro Fontane 13. © 06-4814430. Admission 5€ ($5.75). Tues–Sun 9am–7pm. Metro: Barberini.

Museo Nazionale di Villa Giulia (Etruscan) ★★★   A 16th-century papal palace in the Villa Borghese shelters this priceless collection of art and artifacts of the mysterious Etruscans, who predated the Romans, and of whom little is known except for their sophisticated art and design. If you have time only for the masterpieces, head for Sala 7, which has a remarkable *Apollo* from Veio from the end of the 6th century B.C. (clothed, for a change). Two other widely acclaimed pieces of statuary in this gallery are *Dea con Bambino (Goddess with a Baby)* and a greatly mutilated, but still powerful, *Hercules* with a stag. In the adjoining Sala 8, you'll see the lions' sarcophagus from the mid–6th century B.C., which was excavated at Cerveteri, north of Rome. Finally, in Sala 9, is one of the world's most important Etruscan art treasures, the bride and bridegroom coffin from the 6th century B.C., also from Cerveteri.

Piazzale di Villa Giulia 9. © 06-3201951. Admission 4€ ($4.60). Tues–Sat 8:30am–7pm. Metro: Flaminio. Tram: 225.

MUSEO NAZIONALE ROMANO

Originally the museum occupied only the Diocletian Baths; today it's divided into four sections: Palazzo Massimo alle Terme; Terme di Diocleziano (Diocletian

Baths); the Octagonal Hall annex; and Palazzo Altemps. A ticket including entry into any of the four sections is 7.50€ ($8.65).

Palazzo Massimo alle Terme ✴ If you'd like to go wandering in a virtual garden of classical statues, head for this 19th-century palazzo built to resemble the patrician palaces from the baroque period. If you ever wanted to know what emperors looked like, this museum will make them live again, togas and all. In the central hall are works representing the political and social life of Rome at the time of Augustus. Other works include an altar from Ostia Antica, the ancient port of Rome, plus a statue of a wounded Niobid from 440 B.C. that is a masterwork of expression and character. Upstairs, stand in awe at frescoes, stuccoes, and mosaics from the 1st century B.C. to the Imperial Age. The most celebrated mosaic is of the Four Charioteers. In the basement are a rare numismatic collection and an extensive collection of Roman jewelry.

Largo di Villa Peretti 67. ✆ 06-48903500. Admission 6€ ($6.90). Tues–Sun 9am–7:45pm. Last admission 1 hr. before closing. Metro: Termini.

Palazzo Altemps ✴ This branch of the National Roman Museum is housed in a 15th-century palace only a few steps from the Piazza Navona. It is home to the fabled Ludovisi Collection of Greek and Roman sculpture. Among the masterpieces of the Roman Renaissance, you'll find the *Ares Ludovisi*, a Roman copy of the original dated 330 B.C. and restored by Bernini. In the *Sala delle Storie di Mosè* is *Ludovisi's Throne*, representing the birth of Venus. The *Sala delle Feste* (The Celebrations Hall) is dominated by *Grande Ludovisi*, a sarcophagus depicting the Romans fighting against the Ostrogoth Barbarians from the 2nd century A.D. Other outstanding art includes a 1st-century B.C. copy of Phidias's celebrated Athena that once stood in the Parthenon.

Piazza San Apollinare 8, near the Piazza Navona. ✆ 06-6833759. Admission 5€ ($5.75). Tues–Sun 9am–7:45pm. Closed Mon. Last admission 1 hr. before closing. Bus: 70, 81, 87, or 492.

Terme di Diocleziano (Diocletian Baths) and Aula Ottagona (Octagonal Hall) ✴ This museum occupies part of the 3rd-century A.D. baths of Diocletian and part of a convent that may have been designed by Michelangelo. The Diocletian baths were the biggest thermal baths in the world. Nowadays they host a marvelous collection of funereal art and decorations from the Aurelian period. The Octagonal Hall occupies the southwest corner of the central building. Here you can see the *Lyceum Apollo*. This statue was found in the area surrounding the Trajan Baths. Worthy of a note is the *Aphrodite of Cyrene*, discovered in Cyrene, Libya.

Viale E. di Nicola 79. ✆ 06-4880530. Admission to the Baths 5€ ($5.75); Octagonal Hall free admission. Baths Tues–Sun 9am–7pm. Aula Ottagona Tues–Sat 9am–2pm; Sun 9am–1pm. Last admission 1 hr. before closing. Metro: Termini.

ORGANIZED TOURS

One of the leading tour operators (among the zillions of possibilities) is **American Express,** Piazza di Spagna 38 (✆ **06-67641;** Metro: Spagna), open Monday through Friday from 9am to 5:30pm and Saturday from 9am to 12:30pm. One popular tour is a 4-hour orientation tour of Rome and the Vatican, which departs most mornings at 9:30am and costs 40€ ($46) per person. Another 4-hour tour focuses on ancient Rome (including visits to the Colosseum, the Roman Forum, the Imperial Palace, and the Church of San Pietro in Vincoli); it's 38€ ($44). Outside Rome, a popular excursion from April to October is a 5-hour bus tour to Tivoli, where visits are conducted of the Villa d'Este and its spectacular gardens and the ruins of the Villa Adriana, all for 45€ ($52) per person.

If your time in Italy is rigidly limited, you might opt for 1-day excursions to points farther afield on tours that are marketed (but not conducted) by American Express. A series of 1-day tours is offered to Pompeii and Sorrento for 100€ ($115) per person; to Florence for 105€ ($121); and to Capri and Sorrento for 115€ ($132). These trips, which include lunch, depart from Rome around 7am and return to your hotel sometime after 9 or 10pm.

THE SHOPPING SCENE

The posh shopping streets **Via Borgognona** and **Via Condotti** begin near Piazza di Spagna. For the most part, the merchandise on both is chic and very, very expensive. **Via Frattina** runs parallel to Via Condotti, its more famous sibling. **Via del Corso** doesn't have the image or the high prices of Via Condotti or Via Borgognona; the styles here are aimed at younger consumers. There are, however, some gems scattered amid the shops selling jeans and sporting equipment. The most interesting shops are on the section of the street nearest the fashionable cafes of Piazza del Popolo.

Beginning at the top of the Spanish Steps, **Via Sistina** runs to Piazza Barberini. The shops are small, stylish, and based on the personalities of their owners. The pedestrian traffic is less dense than on other major streets. Most shoppers reach **Via Francesco Crispi** by following Via Sistina 1 long block from the top of the Spanish Steps. Near the intersection of these streets are several shops full of unusual and less expensive gifts. Evocative of *La Dolce Vita,* **Via Veneto** is filled these days with expensive hotels and cafes and an array of relatively expensive stores selling shoes, gloves, and leather goods.

Traffic-clogged **Via Nazionale**—just crossing the street is no small feat—begins at Piazza della Repubblica and runs down almost to Piazza Venezia. Here you'll find an abundance of leather stores—more reasonable in price than those in many other parts of Rome—and a welcome handful of stylish boutiques.

Via dei Coronari, a good street for antiques, is buried in a colorful section of the Campus Martius and is an antiquer's dream, literally lined with magnificent vases, urns, chandeliers, breakfronts, chaises, refectory tables, and candelabra. To find the entrance to the street, turn left out of the north end of Piazza Navona, and pass the excavated ruins of Domitian's Stadium; the street will be just ahead of you. There are more than 40 antiques stores in the next 4 blocks.

A STORE WORTH SEEKING OUT

La Rinascente, Via del Corso 189 at the Piazza Colonna (© **06-6797691;** Metro: Barberini or Spagna), is Rome's most famous department store. Rather upscale, it has a little bit of everything: clothing, hosiery, perfume, cosmetics, housewares, and even furniture, plus its own line of clothing (Ellerre) for men, women, and children.

ROME AFTER DARK

There are few evening diversions quite as pleasurable as a stroll past the solemn pillars of old temples or the cascading torrents of Renaissance fountains glowing under the blue-black sky. Of the **fountains,** the Naiads (Piazza della Repubblica), the Tortoises (Piazza Mattei) and, of course, the Trevi are particularly beautiful at night. The **Capitoline Hill** is magnificently lit after dark, with its Renaissance facades glowing like jewel boxes. Behind the Senatorial Palace is a fine view of the **Roman Forum.** If you're staying across the Tiber, **Piazza San Pietro,** in front of St. Peter's Basilica, is impressive at night without tour buses and crowds. And a combination of illuminated architecture, Renaissance fountains, and frequent sidewalk shows and art expositions is at **Piazza Navona.** If you're ambitious and have a good sense of direction, try exploring the streets to the west of Piazza Navona, which look like a stage set when lit at night.

The mini-magazines *Metropolitan* and *Wanted in Rome* have listings of jazz, rock, and such and give an interesting look at expatriate Rome. The daily *Il Messaggero* lists current cultural news, especially in its Thursday magazine supplement, *Metro.* And *Un Ospite a Roma,* available free from the concierge desks of top hotels, is full of details on what's happening. Even if you don't speak Italian, you can generally follow the listings featured in *TrovaRoma,* a special weekly entertainment supplement published in the newspaper *La Repubblica* on Thursday.

THE PERFORMING ARTS

If you're in the capital for the opera season, usually from December to June, you can attend a performance at the historic **Teatro dell'Opera (Rome Opera House),** located off Via Nazionale, at Piazza Beniamino Gigli 1 (*(C)* **06-481601;** Metro: Repubblica). In the summer the venue switches to Piazza di Siena. The **Rome Opera Ballet** also performs at the Teatro dell'Opera. Look for announcements of classical concerts that take place in churches and other venues.

THE CLUB & MUSIC SCENE

Clubs are generally open Monday through Saturday from 9 or 10pm to 2 to 4am.

NIGHTCLUBS Arciliuto, Piazza Monte Vecchio 5 (*(C)* **06-6879419;** bus: 70, 81, or 87), reputedly the former studio of Raphael, is one of the most romantic candlelit spots in Rome. From 10pm to 2am, Monday through Saturday, guests enjoy a musical salon ambience, listening to a guitarist, a pianist, and a violinist. The evening's presentation also includes live Neapolitan songs and new Italian madrigals, even current hits from Broadway or London's West End. Cover (including one drink) is 18€ ($21). Closed from July 20 to September 6.

One of Rome's largest and most energetic clubs, **Alpheus,** Via del Commercio 36 (*(C)* **06-5747826;** bus: 23 or 716), contains three sprawling rooms, each with a different musical sound and an ample number of bars. You'll find areas devoted to Latin music, rock, jazz, house, commercial, 1980s, whatever. Some Friday nights are devoted to hip-hop or gay-themed parties. It's open Thursday through Sunday from 10pm to 4am; cover is 5€ to 13€ ($5.75–$15).

JAZZ, SOUL & FUNK Every night but Sunday **Alexanderplatz,** Via Ostia 9 (*(C)* **06-39742171;** Metro: Ottaviano), features live jazz. There's also a good restaurant here that serves everything from gnocchi alla romana to Japanese cuisine. A 1-month membership costs 6€ ($6.90). **Big Mama,** Vicolo San Francesco a Ripa 18 (*(C)* **06-5812551;** bus: 75 or 170), is a hangout for jazz and blues musicians; you're likely to meet the up-and-coming jazz stars of tomorrow. Sometimes the big names appear as well. It's closed from June to September. There's no cover for minor shows; cover for big acts is 10€ to 20€ ($12–$23), plus 10€ ($12) for a seasonal membership.

Gilda, Via Mario dei Fiori 97 (*(C)* **06-6784838;** Metro: Spagna), is an adventurous combination of nightclub, disco, and restaurant known for the glamorous acts it books. The artistic direction assures first-class shows, a well-run restaurant, and disco music played between the live musical acts. The restaurant opens at 9:30pm and occasionally presents shows. International cuisine is featured as well,

---

> *Finds* **A Chic Bar**
>
> A former favorite haunt in the historic district of Rome, Hemingway's Pub, has been transformed into the sleek **Riccioli Café**, Piazza delle Coppelle 10A (© **06-68210313;** bus: 64), an oyster and champagne bar. In elegant yet informal surroundings, you can order drinks, of course, but also oysters on the half shell. Many come here to see and be seen. But you can find ample and good-tasting food as well, including sea bass with mango and roast beef with green apples. The loftlike wine cellar competes with the deluxe restaurants of Rome.

---

with meals beginning at 23€ ($26). The nightclub, opening at midnight, presents music of the 1960s as well as modern recordings. Cover (including one drink) is 20€ ($23).

L'Alibi, Via Monte Testaccio 44 (© **06-5743448;** bus: 95), is a year-round venue on many a gay man's agenda, and is one of the hottest clubs in Rome. The crowd, however, tends to be mixed, both Roman and international, straight and gay, male and female. Music ranges from garage to 1970s disco. One room is devoted to dancing. It's open Wednesday through Sunday from 11pm to 4am. Cover is 13€ ($15) Saturday, 7.50€ ($8.65) Friday; otherwise free.

SIDE TRIPS FROM ROME

TIVOLI Tivoli, known as Tibur to the ancient Romans, was the playground of emperors. Today its reputation continues unabated: It's the most popular half-day jaunt from Rome.

While the **Villa d'Este,** Piazza Trento, Viale delle Cento Fontane (© **0774-312070**), is just a dank Renaissance palace with second-rate paintings that's hardly worth the trek from Rome, its **gardens** ★★★—designed by Pirro Ligorio—dim the luster of Versailles. Visitors descend a cypress-studded slope, and on their way are rewarded with everything from lilies to gargoyles spouting water, torrential streams, and waterfalls. The loveliest fountain—on this there's some agreement—is the **Fontana dell'Ovato,** designed by Ligorio. But nearby is the most spectacular achievement, the **hydraulic organ fountain,** dazzling visitors with its water jets in front of a baroque chapel, with four maidens who look tipsy. The best walk is along the promenade, which has 100 spraying fountains. Admission is 4.15€ ($4.75). The villa opens from Tuesday to Sunday at 9am; closing times vary according to the season (1 hr. before sunset). From November to January it closes at 4pm; closing times may be as late as 6:45pm in high season.

Whereas the Villa d'Este dazzles with artificial glamour, **Villa Gregoriana** ★, Largo Sant'Angelo (© **0774-311249**), relies more on nature. The gardens were built by Pope Gregory XVI in the 19th century. At one point on the circuitous walk carved along a slope, visitors stand and look out onto Tivoli's most panoramic waterfall (Aniene). The trek to the bottom on the banks of the Anio is studded with grottoes and balconies that open onto the chasm. From one belvedere, there's a panoramic view of the Temple of Vesta on the hill. Admission is 2.50€ ($2.90). It's open May through August daily from 10am to 7:30pm; September daily from 9:30am to 6:30pm; October through March daily from 9:30am to 4:30pm; and April daily from 9:30am to 6pm.

Of all the Roman emperors dedicated to *la dolce vita,* the globetrotting Hadrian spent the last 3 years of his life in the grandest style. Less than 6.5km

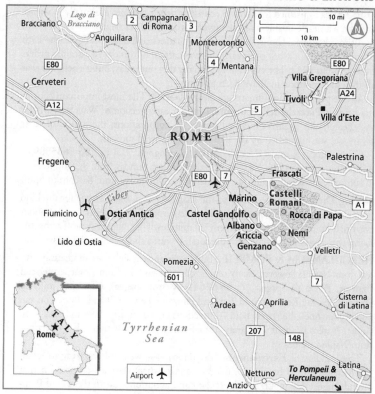

(4 miles) from Tivoli he built his great estate—the **Villa Adriana (Hadrian's Villa)** ⊛⊛⊛, Via di Villa Adriana (© **0774-530203**)—and filled acre after acre with some of the architectural wonders he'd seen on his many trips. Hadrian directed the construction of much more than a villa—it's a self-contained world for a vast royal entourage, the guards required to protect them, and the hundreds of servants needed to bathe them, feed them, and satisfy their libidos. On the estate were theaters, baths, temples, fountains, gardens, and canals bordered with statuary. For a glimpse of what the villa once was, see the plastic reconstruction at the entrance. Admission is 6€ ($6.90). Hours are daily from 9am to 3:15pm (until about 6pm in summer).

Getting There The town of Tivoli is 32km (20 miles) east of Rome on Via Tiburtina—about an hour's drive with traffic. You can also take public transportation: A bus marked TIVOLI leaves every 15 to 20 minutes during the day from Via Gaeta (west of Via Volturno), near the Stazione Termini. Buses also leave from the Rebibbia Metro station.

OSTIA ANTICA ⊛⊛ This major attraction is particularly interesting to those who can't make it to Pompeii. At the mouth of the Tiber, it was the port of ancient Rome. Through it were funneled riches from the far corners of the empire. It was founded in the 4th century B.C., and became a major port and naval base primarily under the emperors Claudius and Trajan. A thriving, prosperous city developed, full of temples, bathrooms, theaters, and patrician homes.

Ostia Antica flourished for about 8 centuries before it began eventually to wither and the wholesale business of carting off its art treasures began.

Although a papal-sponsored commission launched a series of digs in the 19th century, the major work of unearthing was carried out under Mussolini's orders from 1938 to 1942. The city is only partially dug out today, but it's believed that all the chief monuments have been uncovered.

All the principal monuments are clearly labeled. The most important spot in the ruins is **Piazzale delle Corporazioni,** an early version of Wall Street. Near the theater, this square contained nearly 75 corporations; the nature of their businesses was identified by the patterns of preserved mosaics.

Ostia Antica is entered on Viale dei Romagnoli 717 (© **06-56358099**). Admission is 4€ ($4.60). It's open Tuesday through Sunday from 8:30am to 6pm in summer; off-season hours are Tuesday through Sunday from 8:30am to 5pm.

Getting There Take the Metro to the Magliana stop, then change for the Lido train to Ostia Antica, about 26km (16 miles) from Rome. Departures are about every half-hour, and the trip takes only 20 minutes. The train lets you off across the highway that connects Rome with the coast. It's just a short walk to the excavations.

HERCULANEUM & POMPEII Both these ancient sights are more easily visited from Naples; however, many organized tours go here from Rome. **American Express,** Piazza di Spagna (© **06-67641**; Metro: Spagna), offers day tours to Pompeii, leaving Rome around 7am and returning between 9 and 10pm. You can also explore one—but rarely both—attractions on a day's drive here and back from Rome. Naples is about 2½ hours from Rome by frequent trains. For directions from Naples, see below.

The builders of **Herculaneum (Ercolano)** ✿✿ were still working to repair the damage caused by an A.D. 62 earthquake when Vesuvius erupted on that fateful August day in A.D. 79. Herculaneum, about one-fourth the size of Pompeii, didn't start to come to light again until 1709, when Prince Elbeuf launched the unfortunate fashion of tunneling through it for treasures. The prince was more intent on profiting from the sale of objets d'art than in uncovering a dead Roman town. Subsequent excavations at the site, **Ufficio Scavi di Ercolano,** Corso Resina, Ercolano (© **081-7390963**), have been slow. Herculaneum is not completely dug out today.

All the streets and buildings of Herculaneum hold interest, especially the baths *(terme),* divided between those at the forum and those on the outskirts (Terme Suburbane, near the more elegant villas). The municipal baths, which segregated the sexes, are larger, but the ones at the edge of town are more lavishly adorned. Important private homes to see include the **House of the Bicentenary** ✿, the **House of the Wooden Cabinet** ✿✿, and the **House of Poseidon (Neptune) and Amphitrite** ✿✿, the last containing what is the best-known mosaic discovered in the ruins. The finest example of how the aristocracy lived is provided by a visit to the **Casa dei Cervi** ✿✿, named the House of the Stags because of sculpture found inside.

The ruins may be visited daily April through October from 8:30am to 6pm, November through March from 8:30am to 3:30pm. Admission is 8€ ($9.20). To reach them, take the Circumvesuviana train from Stazione Centrale in Naples leaving about every half-hour from Corso Garibaldi 387 for the 20-minute ride; or take bus no. 255 from Piazza Municipio. The excavations are a short walk from the train station. Otherwise, it's a 7km (4¼-mile) drive on the autostrada to Salerno (turn off at Ercolano).

When Vesuvius erupted in A.D. 79, Pliny the Younger, who later recorded the event, thought the end of the world had come. Lying 24km (15 miles) south of Naples, the ruined Roman city of **Pompeii (Pompei)** ★★★ has been dug out from the inundation of volcanic ash and pumice stone. At the excavations, the life of 19 centuries ago is vividly experienced.

The **Ufficio Scavi di Pompei** is entered at Piazza Esedra (ⓒ **081-8610744**). The most elegant of the patrician villas, the **House of Vettii** ★★★ has a courtyard, statuary (such as a two-faced Janus), paintings, and a black-and-red Pompeiian dining room frescoed with cupids. The second important villa, the **Villa dei Misteri (House of Mysteries)** ★★★ near the Porto Ercolano (Herculaneum Gate), lies outside the walls. What makes the villa exceptional are its remarkable frescoes. The **Casa del Fauno (House of the Faun)** ★★, so called because of a bronze statue of a dancing faun found there, takes up a city block and has four different dining rooms and two spacious peristyle gardens. In the center of town is the **Forum** ★★★—although rather small, it was the heart of Pompeiian life.

Pompeii's ruins may be visited daily from 9am to 3:30pm. Admission is 8€ ($9.20). From Stazione Centrale in Naples, take the Sorrento-bound Circumvesuviana train leaving about every half-hour and get off at the Pompei Scavi station; the excavations are across from the station. *Note:* Make sure your train is going to "Pompei Scavi," not "Pompei." Trains bound for Pompei stop at the modern town, not at the ruins.

2 Florence ★★★

No other city in Europe, with the exception of Venice, lives off its past the way Florence does. The Renaissance began here. Florence is a bit foreboding and architecturally severe; many of its *palazzi* (palaces), as was the Medici style, look like fortresses. But you must remember that when these structures were built, the aim was to keep foreign enemies at bay. And these facades guard treasures within, as the thousands of visitors who overrun the narrow streets know and appreciate.

Since the 19th century, Florence has been visited by seemingly half the world—the city has impressed some hard-to-impress people, including Mark Twain, who found it overwhelmed with "tides of color that make all the sharp lines dim and faint and turn the old city to a city of dreams."

It may appear that Florence is caught in a time warp—a Medici returning to the city from the past would have no trouble finding his way around. But Florence virtually pulsates with modern life. Students racing to and from the university quarter add vibrancy to the city, and it's amusing to watch the way many local businesspeople avoid the city's impossible traffic today, whizzing by on Vespas past cars stalled in traffic.

Florentines like to present *una bella figura* (a good appearance) to the rest of the world and are incredibly upset when that appearance is attacked, as in the case of the May 1993 bombing of the Uffizi. The entire city rallied to re-open this treasure trove of Renaissance art.

Try to visit this city, even on the most rushed of European itineraries. There's nothing like it anywhere else. Venice and Rome are too different from Florence to invite meaningful comparisons. Florence is also an ideal base from which to explore Tuscany. Though increasingly built up, Tuscany has enough old hill towns and rolling hills studded with olives and grapevines to attract the romantic. Florence and Siena are the chief drawing cards, but Fiesole and Pisa also have their allure.

Florence

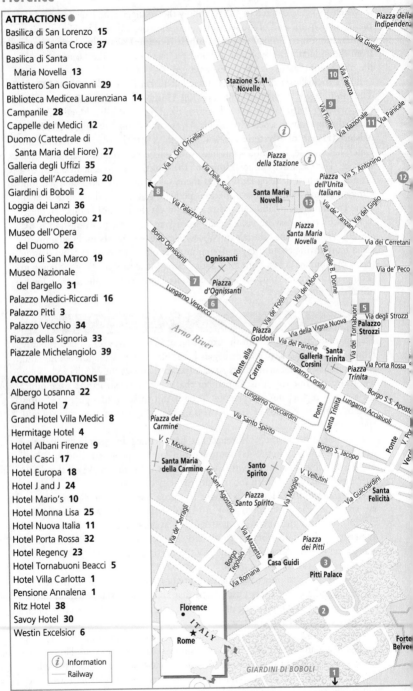

(i) Information
— Railway

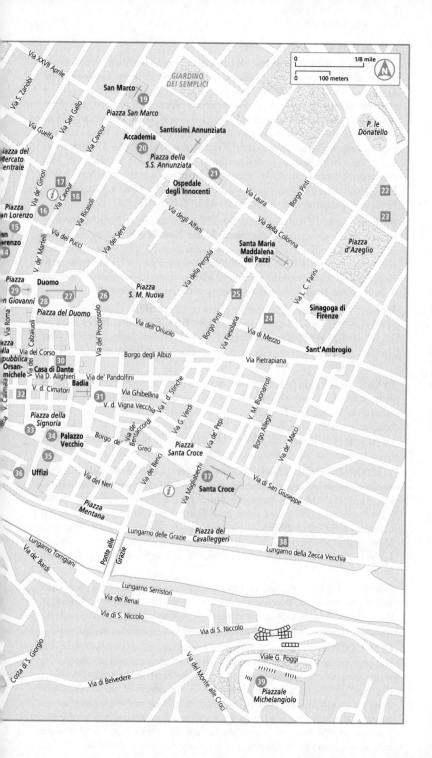

ESSENTIALS

GETTING THERE   By Plane   If you're flying from New York, a much-flown route is to Rome, where you can board a domestic flight to the **Galileo Galilei Airport** at Pisa (© **050-500707;** www.pisa-airport.com), 93km (58 miles) west of Florence. **Alitalia** (© **050-20221** for the airport office; www.alitalia.it) also offers two flights a day from New York to Pisa with one stop in Rome. You can take an express train for the hour-long trip to Florence. There's also a small domestic airport, **Amerigo Vespucci,** on Via del Termine, near A-11 (© **055-373498;** www. airport.florence.it), 6km (3¾ miles) northwest of Florence, a 15-minute drive. This airport can be reached by ATAF bus no. 62, departing from the main Santa Maria Novella rail terminal. Domestic air service is provided by **Alitalia,** with offices in Florence at Lungarno degli Acciaiuoli 10–12R (© **055-27881**).

By Train   If you're coming north from Rome, count on a 2- to 3-hour trip, depending on your connection. **Santa Maria Novella rail station,** in Piazza della Stazione, adjoins Piazza di Santa Maria Novella. For information and timetables, contact **FS** (© **848-888088;** www.trenitalia.it). Some trains into Florence stop at the **Stazione Campo di Marte,** on the eastern side of Florence. A 24-hour bus service (no. 91) runs between the two rail terminals.

By Bus   Long-distance buses service Florence, run by **SITA,** Viale Cadorna 105 (© **055-47821;** www.sita-on-line.it), and by **Lazzi Eurolines,** Piazza Stazione 3R (© **055-215155;** www.eurolines.it). Both SITA and Lazzi Eurolines offer transfers from Florence to Pisa. A one-way ticket from Florence to Pisa costs 5.60€ ($6.45).

By Car   **Autostrada A-1** connects Florence with both the north and the south of Italy. It takes about an hour to reach Florence from Bologna and about 3 hours from Rome. The Tyrrhenian coast is only an hour from Florence on **A-11** heading west. Florence lies 277km (172 miles) north of Rome, 105km (65 miles) west of Bologna, and 298km (185 miles) south of Milan. Use a car only to get to Florence. Don't even contemplate its use once here.

VISITOR INFORMATION   Tourist Offices   Contact the **Azienda Promozione Turistica,** Via A. Manzoni 16 (© **055-23320;** www.firenze.turismo. toscana.it), open Monday through Saturday from 8:30am to 1:30pm. Another helpful office, handling data about both Florence and Tuscany, is **APT** at Via Cavour 1R (© **055-290832**). Hours here are March through November Monday through Saturday from 8:15am to 7:15pm, Sunday from 8:15am to 1:45pm; December through February Monday through Saturday from 8:15am to 1:45pm.

Websites   Updated weekly for news and notices about concerts and dance recitals, **www.mega.it/florence** also lets you explore the art scene by clicking on the museum map. Switch to the monument version for both the city and surrounding regions, including Chianti.

CITY LAYOUT   The city is split by the **Arno River,** which usually looks serene and peaceful but can turn ferocious with floodwaters on rare occasions. The major monumental and historical core lies on the "right" (north) side of the river. But the "left" side—called the **Oltrarno**—is not devoid of attractions. Many longtime visitors frequent the Oltrarno for its tantalizing trattoria meals; they also maintain that the shopping here is less expensive. Even the most hurried visitor will want to cross over the Arno to see the Pitti Palace with its many art treasures and to walk through the Giardini di Boboli, a series of formal gardens.

The Arno is spanned by eight bridges, of which the **Ponte Vecchio,** lined with jewelry stores, is the most celebrated. **Ponte S. Trinità** is the second-most important bridge spanning the Arno. After crossing it you can continue along **Via dei Tornabuoni,** the most important right-bank shopping street. At the Ponte Vecchio you can walk, again on the right bank, along **Via Por Santa Maria,** which will become Calimala. This will lead you into **Piazza della Repubblica,** a commercial district known for its cafes.

From here, you can take **Via Roma,** which leads directly into **Piazza di San Giovanni.** Here you'll find the baptistery and its neighboring sibling, the larger **Piazza del Duomo,** with the world-famous cathedral and bell tower by Giotto. From the far western edge of Piazza del Duomo, **Via del Proconsolo** heads south to **Piazza della Signoria,** sight of the landmark Palazzo Vecchio and its sculpture-filled Loggia dei Lanzi.

GETTING AROUND   By Foot   Because Florence is so compact, the ideal way to get around town is by foot—at times it's the only way, because there're so many pedestrian zones. In theory at least, pedestrians have the right of way at uncontrolled zebra crossings, but don't count on that should you encounter a speeding Vespa.

By Bus   You must purchase your bus ticket before boarding one of the public vehicles. For 1€ ($1.15), you can ride on any public bus in the city for a total of 60 minutes. A 3-hour pass costs 2€ ($2.30), and a 24-hour pass costs 4€ ($4.60). Bus tickets can be purchased from *tabacchi* (tobacconists' shops, marked by a white T) and news vendors. The local **bus station** (which serves as the terminal for ATAF city buses) is at Piazza della Stazione (© **055-56501**). Bus routes are posted at bus stops.

By Taxi   Taxis can be found at stands at nearly all the major squares in Florence. If you need a radio taxi, call © **055-4390** or 055-4798.

By Car   You'll need a car to explore the countryside of Tuscany in any depth. Cars are available at **Avis,** Borgo Ognissanti 128R (© **055-213629**); **Italy by Car,** Borgo Ognissanti 134R (© **055-287161**); and **Hertz,** Via del Termine 1 (© **055-307370**).

By Bicycle or Motor Scooter   **Alinari** is near the rail station at Via Guelfa 85R (© **055-280500**). Depending on the model of bike you rent, it will cost 2€ to 2.50€ ($2.30–$2.75) per hour or 10€ to 15€ ($12–$17) per day. If you want to rent a scooter, it costs 7.50€ ($8.50) per hour, 25€ ($29) for 5 hours, 40€ ($46) per day. The shop is open Monday through Saturday from 9:30am to 1pm and 3 to 7:30pm, Sunday from 10am to 1pm and 3 to 7pm. November through February, the Sunday hours are 10am to 5pm.

FAST FACTS: Florence

American Express   The office is at Via Dante Alighieri 22R (© **055-50981**); it's open Monday through Friday from 9am to 5:30pm and Saturday from 9am to 12:30pm.

Business Hours   Most **banks** are open Monday through Friday from 8:30am to 1:30pm and 2:45 to 3:45pm. **Shops** are generally open Monday from 4 to 7:30pm and Tuesday through Saturday from 9 or 10am to 1pm and 3:30 or 4 to 7:30pm. During the summer some shops are open Monday mornings. However, don't be surprised if shops close for several weeks in August, if not for the entire month.

Consulates The **United States** consulate is at Lungarno Amerigo Vespucci 38 (© 055-2398276), open Monday through Friday from 9am to 12:30pm and 2 to 3:30pm. The **United Kingdom** consulate is at Lungarno Corsini 2 (© 055-284133), near Piazza Santa Trinità, open Monday through Friday from 9:30am to 12:30pm and 2:30 to 4:30pm. Citizens of other English-speaking countries, including **Canada, Australia,** and **New Zealand,** should contact their diplomatic representatives in Rome (see "Fast Facts: Rome," earlier in this chapter).

Currency Exchange Local banks have the best rates, and most are open Monday through Friday from 8:30am to 1:30pm and 2:45 to 3:45pm. The tourist office (see "Visitor Information," under "Essentials," above) exchanges money at official rates when banks are closed and on holidays, but a commission is often charged. You can also go to the Ufficio Informazione booth at the rail station, open daily from 7:30am to 7:40pm. American Express (above) also exchanges money. One of the best places to exchange currency is the post office (below).

Dentists/Doctors For a list of English-speaking doctors or dentists, consult your consulate (above) or contact **Tourist Medical Service,** Via Lorenzo il Magnifico 59 (© 055-475411). Visits without an appointment are possible only Monday through Friday from 11am to noon and 5 to 6pm. After hours, an answering service gives names and phone numbers of dentists and doctors who are on duty.

Emergencies For fire, call © **115;** for an ambulance, call © **118;** for the police, call © **113;** and for road service, call © **116.**

Hospitals Call the **General Hospital** of Santa Maria Nuova, Piazza Santa Maria Nuova 1 (© 055-27581).

Internet Access You can check your messages or send e-mail at **Internet Train,** Via dell'Orivolo 40R (© 055-2638968; www.internettrain.it).

Pharmacies The **Farmacia Molteni,** Via Calzaiuoli 7R (© 055-215472), is open 24 hours.

Police Dial © **113** in an emergency. English-speaking foreigners who want to see and talk to the police should go to the **Ufficio Stranieri station,** Via Zara 2 (© 055-49771), where English-speaking personnel are available daily from 9am to 2pm.

Post Office The **Central Post Office** is at Via Pellicceria 3, off Piazza della Repubblica (© 055-27361 for English-speaking operators), open Monday through Saturday from 8:15am to 7pm. You can buy stamps and telephone cards at window nos. 21 and 22. A foreign exchange office is open Monday through Friday from 8:15am to 6pm. If you want to send packages of up to 20 kilograms (44 lb.), go to the rear of the building and enter at Piazza Davantati 4.

Safety Violent crimes are rare in Florence; most crime consists of pickpockets who frequent crowded tourist centers, such as corridors of the Uffizi Galleries. Members of group tours who cluster together are often singled out as victims. Car thefts are relatively common: Don't leave your luggage in an unguarded car, even if it's locked in the trunk. Women should be especially careful in avoiding purse-snatchers, some of whom grab a purse while whizzing by on a Vespa, often knocking the woman down. Documents such as passports and extra money are better stored in safes at your hotel, if available.

Telephone The **country code** for Italy is **39**. The **city code** for Florence is **055;** use this code when calling from *anywhere* outside or inside Italy— even within Florence itself (and you must now include the 0 every time, even when calling from abroad). See "Fast Facts: Rome," earlier in this chapter, for details on how to call Italy, how to place calls within Italy, and how to call home once you're in Italy.

You can place **long-distance and international calls** at the Telecom office north of the Duomo at Via Cavour 21R (open daily 8am–9:45pm).

WHERE TO STAY
NEAR THE DUOMO
Very Expensive

Savoy Hotel ✮✮✮   Everything is fresh again at Florence's most legendary hotel, which opened in 1896. Completely restored, it now takes its place just under the Excelsior and Grand in luxury. Refined Italian elegance is the hallmark of this landmark monument, which experienced years of decline after World War II. Rooms are decorated sumptuously. Bathrooms are beautifully tiled (some with shower only).

Piazza della Repubblica 7, 50123 Firenze. ✆ **055-27351.** Fax 055-2735888. www.roccofortehotels.com. 107 units, some with shower only. 407€–803€ ($468–$923) double; from 1,122€ ($1,290) suite. AE, DC, MC, V. Parking 35€–50€ ($40–$58). Bus: 22, 36, or 37. **Amenities:** Restaurant; bar; 24-hr. room service; children's program; gym; babysitting; laundry service; dry cleaning; nonsmoking rooms; rooms for those with limited mobility. *In room:* A/C, TV, dataport, minibar, hair dryer, safe.

Expensive

Hotel J and J ✮   This charming hotel, built in the 16th century as a monastery, lies a 5-minute walk from the church of Santa Croce. You'll find a flagstone-covered courtyard and a salon with vaulted ceilings and several preserved ceiling frescoes. Rooms combine an unusual mixture of modern furniture with the monastery's original beamed ceilings. Suites usually contain sleeping lofts and, in some cases, rooftop balconies overlooking the historic core. All units are filled with modern tiled bathrooms with tub/shower combos.

Via di Mezzo 20, 50121 Firenze. ✆ **055-26312.** Fax 055-240282. www.jandjhotel.com. 20 units. 282€–315€ ($324–$362) double; 370€ ($426) junior suite; 430€–460€ ($495–$529) suite. Rates include buffet breakfast. AE, DC, MC, V. Parking 30€ ($35). Bus: A. **Amenities:** Bar; room service (7am–midnight); babysitting; laundry service; dry cleaning. *In room:* A/C, TV, dataport, minibar, hair dryer.

Hotel Monna Lisa ✮   This privately owned Renaissance palazzo is 4 blocks east of the Duomo. Most of the great old rooms overlook either an inner patio or a modest rear garden. Each of the salons is handsomely furnished. Rooms vary greatly—some are quite large, though no two are alike, and each comes with a tiled bathroom with tub/shower combos.

Borgo Pinti 27, 50121 Firenze. ✆ **055-2479751.** Fax 055-2479755. www.monnalisa.it. 45 units. 182€–350€ ($209–$403) double; 235€–415€ ($270–$477) triple. Rates include breakfast. AE, DC, MC, V. Parking 15€

($17). Bus: A, 6, 31, or 32. **Amenities:** Breakfast-only room service; babysitting; laundry service; dry cleaning; nonsmoking rooms; rooms for those with limited mobility. *In room:* A/C, TV, dataport, minibar, hair dryer, safe.

Hotel Porta Rossa ⭐ Reportedly, this is the second-oldest hotel in Italy, dating from 1386. The place is a bit dark, but on a hot Tuscan summer day you welcome that in lieu of air-conditioning. Since it isn't as well known or publicized as some of its competitors such as the Hermitage or Tornabuoni, you stand a better chance of getting a reservation. In spite of its antiquity, the hotel has kept abreast of the times, installing modern conveniences, good beds, and ample bathrooms, some with shower, others with tub. The managers have resisted making two new rooms out of one of the old spacious ones from centuries ago. Breakfast is the only meal served, and a little terrace offers a panoramic view.

Via Porta Rossa 19, 50123 Firenze. © 055-287551. Fax 055-282179. 79 units, some with shower only, some with tub only. 175€ ($201) double. Rates include breakfast. AE, DC, MC, V. Parking 20€–33€ ($23–$38). Bus: A. **Amenities:** Bar; laundry service; dry cleaning; nonsmoking rooms; rooms for those with limited mobility. *In room:* A/C, TV, minibar, hair dryer, safe.

NEAR THE PONTE VECCHIO
Moderate
Hermitage Hotel ⭐ The offbeat, intimate Hermitage is a charming place, with a sun terrace on the roof providing a view. You can take your breakfast under a leafy arbor surrounded by potted roses and geraniums. The small rooms are pleasantly furnished. Bathrooms are superb and contain lots of gadgets; some units come with shower, others with tub. Some recently restored ones have hydro-massage tubs. Those rooms overlooking the Arno offer the most scenic view, and they've been fitted with double-glazed windows.

Vicolo Marzio 1, Piazza del Pesce I, 50122 Firenze. © 055-287216. Fax 055-212208. www.hermitagehotel. com. 28 units. 195€–245€ ($224–$282) double; 230€–275€ ($265–$316) triple; 245€–299€ ($282–$344) family room. Rates include breakfast. MC, V. Parking 20€–40€ ($23–$46). Bus: B. **Amenities:** Bar; tour desk; breakfast-only room service; babysitting; laundry service; dry cleaning; nonsmoking rooms; rooms for those with limited mobility. *In room:* A/C, TV, dataport, hair dryer, safe.

NEAR PIAZZA SANTA TRINITÀ
Moderate
Hotel Tornabuoni Beacci Near the Arno and Piazza S. Trinità, on the principal shopping street, this pensione occupies the top three floors of a 14th-century palazzo. The renovated hotel still bears an air of old-fashioned gentility. The rooms are moderately well furnished, each with a tub and shower combination. The roof terrace is for breakfast or late-afternoon drinks. The view of the nearby churches, towers, and rooftops is worth experiencing.

Via Tornabuoni 3, 50123 Firenze. © 055-212645. Fax 055-283594. www.bthotel.it. 28 units. 185€–240€ ($213–$276) double; 280€–350€ ($322–$403) suite. Rates include buffet breakfast. AE, DC, MC, V. Parking 24€–30€ ($28–$35). Bus: B, 6, 11, or 36. **Amenities:** Restaurant; bar; room service (8am–9pm); babysitting; laundry service; dry cleaning. *In room:* A/C, TV, minibar, hair dryer, safe in suites.

NEAR PIAZZA SAN LORENZO & THE MERCATO CENTRALE
Inexpensive
Hotel Casci Casci is a well-run little hotel, near the Piazza del Duomo and the main rail station. The building dates from the 14th century, and some of the public rooms feature frescoes. The hotel is both traditional and modern, and the English-speaking reception staff is attentive. Rooms are comfortably furnished, and each year four or five are upgraded and renovated. The small bathrooms come with tub/shower combo or shower only.

Via Cavour 13, 50129 Firenze. ℂ **055-211686.** Fax 055-2396461. www.hotelcasci.com. 25 units. 90€–140€ ($104–$161) double; 120€–180€ ($138–$207) triple; 150€–220€ ($173–$253) quad. Rates include buffet breakfast. AE, DC, MC, V. Parking 15€–25€ ($17–$29). Bus: 1, 7, 25, or 33. **Amenities:** Bar; tour desk; babysitting; laundry service/dry cleaning; nonsmoking rooms; 1 room for those with limited mobility. *In room:* A/C, TV, dataport, minibar, hair dryer, safe.

Hotel Europa Two long blocks north of the Duomo, this hotel in a 16th-century building has functioned as a family-run hotel since 1925. Homey touches remind newcomers of its ongoing administration by members of the Gassim family. All but four rooms overlook the back and usually open onto a view of the campanile and dome of the Duomo. Those that face the street are noisier but benefit from double-glazing. Each unit comes with a tub/shower combo.

Via Cavour 14, 50129 Firenze. ℂ **055-2396715.** Fax 055-210361. www.webhoteleuropa.com. 20 units, shower only. 90€–140€ ($104–$161) double; 190€–220€ ($219–$253) triple. Rates include buffet breakfast. AE, MC, V. Parking 20€ ($23) in nearby garage. Bus: 1, 7, 25, or 33. **Amenities:** Bar; babysitting; laundry service; dry cleaning; nonsmoking rooms; rooms for those with limited mobility. *In room:* A/C, TV, dataport, hair dryer, safe.

NEAR PIAZZA SANTA MARIA NOVELLA & THE TRAIN STATION
Very Expensive

Grand Hotel Villa Medici ★★ This old-time favorite occupies an 18th-century Medici palace 2 blocks southwest of the train station. Of all the government-rated five-star hotels of Florence, it is the only one with its own pool and health club. It generally appeals more to Europeans than to Americans, who might want more up-to-date facilities, although it was renovated in 2001 (when the guest rooms were spruced up and given such extras as electronic safes). Most rooms have twin beds. The most peaceful rooms front the garden, but during the day there's noise from the convent school next door.

Via il Prato 42, 50123 Firenze. ℂ **055-2381331.** Fax 055-2381336. www.villamedicihotel.com. 103 units. 450€–560€ ($518–$644) double; 950€–1,400€ ($1,093–$1,610) suite. AE, DC, MC, V. Parking 30€–50€ ($35–$58). Bus: 1, 9, 14, 17, 23, 36, or 37. **Amenities:** Restaurant (including a romantic dining room and outdoor dining in summer); elegant piano bar; outdoor pool; fitness center with sauna; 24-hr. room service; babysitting; laundry service; dry cleaning, rooms for those with limited mobility. *In room:* A/C, TV, dataport, minibar, hair dryer, safe.

Expensive

Hotel Albani Firenze ★ In 1993, a respected nationwide chain transformed a run-down pensione, a 10-minute walk from the Duomo and close to the train station, into one of Florence's most appealing luxury hotels, set in a structure that was built around 1900 as a private villa. Today, you'll find up-to-date comforts, artwork, and architectural embellishments. The high-ceilinged interiors, outfitted in tones of soft terra cottas and browns, sometimes verge on the theatrical but are never forbidding. The guest rooms, ranging from medium to spacious, possess style and grace, with mahogany beds.

Via Fiume 12, 50123 Firenze. ℂ **055-26030.** Fax 055-211045. www.hotelalbani.it. 100 units. 325€–345€ ($374–$397) double; from 680€ ($782) suite. Rates include breakfast. AE, DC, MC, V. Valet parking 20€ ($23). Bus: 10, 12, 25, 31, or 32. **Amenities:** Restaurant; bar; room service; babysitting; laundry/dry cleaning. *In room:* A/C, TV, minibar, hair dryer, safe.

Moderate

Hotel Mario's ★ *Value* Two blocks from the rail station, this is a winning choice. It's on the first floor of an old building that has been a hotel since 1872, when the *Room with a View* crowd started arriving in search of the glory of the Renaissance. Mario Noce is the gracious host, and he and his staff speak English. Although you'll find cheaper inns in Florence, the service and hospitality make Mario's worth your euros. The guest rooms aren't very large but are furnished with taste; wrought-iron headboards frame firm beds. Several rooms open onto a small private garden.

Via Faenza 89, 50123 Firenze. © 055-216801. Fax 055-212039. www.hotelmarios.com. 16 units, shower only. 95€–165€ ($109–$190) double; 125€–220€ ($144–$253) triple. Rates include breakfast. AE, DC, MC, V. Valet parking 20€–25€ ($23–$29). Bus: 10, 13, or 17. **Amenities:** Bar; laundry service; dry cleaning. *In room:* A/C, TV, hair dryer, safe.

Inexpensive

Hotel Nuova Italia ★ *Finds* This little hotel has been welcoming Frommer's readers since 1958, when folks arrived with their dog-eared copies of *Europe on $5 a Day*. A Canadian guest, Eileen, met and fell in love with Luciano Viti, then a bellhop. Today they own the hotel and are grandparents with a new generation of Vitis waiting to take over one day. The guest rooms are pleasantly furnished and decorated with paintings and posters. The Vitis, who serve a fantastic cappuccino, will help you figure out how to get around Florence and offer tips on where to shop and what to do.

Via Faenza 26, 50123 Firenze. © 055-287508. Fax 055-210941. www.hotelnuovaitalia.com. 20 units, shower only. 125€ ($144) double; 145€ ($167) triple. Rates include breakfast. AE, MC, V. Parking 20€ ($23) nearby. Bus: 10, 12, 25, 31, 32, or 91. **Amenities:** Bike rentals; tour desk; car-rental desk; babysitting; laundry service; dry cleaning. *In room:* A/C, TV.

ON PIAZZA OGNISSANTI

Piazza Ognissanti is a fashionable but car-clogged Renaissance square opening onto the Arno. It's home to two of the most legendary hotels in the city.

Very Expensive

Grand Hotel ★★★ The Grand is a bastion of luxury, although neither it nor the Excelsior are as exclusive as the Regency. A hotel of history and tradition, the Grand is known for its halls and salons. Rooms and suites have a refined elegance, and the most desirable overlook the Arno. Each comes with a luxurious bathroom with tub/shower combos. A highlight of the hotel is the Winter Garden, an enclosed court lined with arches where regional and international dishes are served.

Piazza Ognissanti 1, 50123 Firenze. © 800/325-3589 in the U.S. and Canada, or 055-288781. Fax 055-217400. www.luxurycollection.com/grandflorence. 107 units. 555€–620€ ($638–$713) double; 1,099€–1,273€ ($1,264–$1,464) suite. AE, DC, MC, V. Parking from 30€ ($35). Bus: 6 or 17. **Amenities:** Restaurant; 2 bars; valet; 24-hr. room service; babysitting; laundry service; dry cleaning; nonsmoking rooms. *In room:* A/C, TV, minibar, hair dryer, safe.

Westin Excelsior ★★★ The Excelsior, a former patrician mansion, is the ultimate in luxury. Cosmopolitan and sophisticated, it has the best-trained staff in town. If you like glamour and glitz, stay here. The opulent rooms have 19th-century Florentine antiques and sumptuous fabrics. Some of the more desirable rooms open onto views of the Arno. In these old palaces, expect the accommodations to come in a variety of configurations. All contain luxurious bathrooms with tub/shower combos.

Piazza Ognissanti 3, 50123 Firenze. © 888/625-5144 in the U.S. and Canada, or 055-264201. Fax 055-210278. www.starwood.com. 171 units. 546€–790€ ($628–$909) double; from 1,306€ ($1,502) junior suite. AE, DC, MC, V. Parking 30€ ($35). Bus: 6 or 17. **Amenities:** Restaurant; bar; children's program; valet; business center; 24-hr. room service; in-room massages; babysitting; laundry service/dry cleaning; nonsmoking rooms; rooms for those with limited mobility. *In room:* A/C, TV, dataport, minibar, hair dryer, safe.

ON OR NEAR PIAZZA MASSIMO D'AZEGLIO

Piazza Massimo d'Azeglio is a 12-minute walk northeast of the historic core of Florence.

Very Expensive

Hotel Regency ★★★   The Regency is an intimate villa of taste and exclusivity. This well-built old-style villa, a member of Relais & Châteaux, has its own garden across from a park in a residential area. It's a luxurious hideaway, and offers exquisitely furnished rooms with state-of-the-art bathrooms with tub/shower combos. The dining room, Relais le Jardin, is renowned for its *alta cucina*.

Piazza Massimo d'Azeglio 3, 50121 Firenze. (C) **055-245247.** Fax 055-2346735. www.regency-hotel.com. 34 units. 300€–400€ ($345–$460) double; 610€–800€ ($702–$920) suite. Rates include buffet breakfast. AE, DC, MC, V. Parking 26€ ($30). Bus: 6, 31, or 32. **Amenities:** Restaurant; bar; tour desk; 24-hr. room service; in-room massages; babysitting; laundry service; dry cleaning; nonsmoking rooms. *In room:* A/C, TV, dataport, minibar, hair dryer, safe.

Inexpensive

Albergo Losanna   A good choice, Albergo Losanna is a tiny family-run place off Viale Antonio Gramsci, between Piazzale Donatello and Piazza Massimo d'Azeglio. It offers utter simplicity and cleanliness. Rooms are homey and well kept, but the furnishings are simple and a bit tired. Each unit comes with a small bathroom with shower.

Via Vittorio Alfieri 9, 50121 Firenze. (C)/fax **055-245840.** www.albergolosanna.com. 8 units, 3 with bathroom, shower only. 52€ ($60) double without bathroom; 68€ ($78) double with bathroom. Rates include breakfast. AE, MC, V. Parking 18€ ($21). Bus: 6, 31, or 32. *In room:* No phone.

ALONG THE ARNO
Moderate

Ritz Hotel ★ *(Finds)*   Don't be misled by the name "Ritz" and grab to hold onto your wallet. The Ritz of Florence has nothing to do with the *luxe* palaces of London, Paris, or Madrid. The local Ritz is a family-run hotel whose youthful owners have upgraded it and turned it into a reasonably priced alternative in a lethally priced city. They offer well-furnished, medium-size rooms. Some bathrooms have a tub/shower combo, others have a shower. A visit here is like a call on your favorite Florentine aunt back in 1870 but with more modern amenities than she had. Breakfast is the only meal served.

Lugarno Zeccia Vecchia 24, 50122 Firenze. (C) **055-2340650.** Fax 055-240863. www.florenceitaly.net/ritz/index.html. 32 units, some with shower only. 110€–180€ ($127–$207) double; 170€–280€ ($196–$322) suite. Rates include breakfast. AE, DC, MC, V. Bus: 23. **Amenities:** Bar; breakfast only room service; babysitting; laundry service; dry cleaning. *In room:* A/C, TV, minibar, hair dryer, safe.

ACROSS THE ARNO
Expensive

Hotel Villa Carlotta ★ *(Finds)*   This hotel from the Edwardian age was built as a villa and bought in the 1950s by Carlotta Schulmann. Her lavish renovations have transformed it into one of Florence's most charming smaller hotels. It's still very homey and stands in a residential neighborhood. Rooms have silk wallpaper and bedspreads, reproduction antiques, safes, and crystal chandeliers; each has a view of the garden. The bathrooms are exceedingly well maintained. The hotel is only a 10-minute walk from the Ponte Vecchio; by taxi, it's a 5-minute ride.

Via Michele di Lando 3, 50125 Firenze. (C) **055-220530.** Fax 055-2336147. www.hotelvillacarlotta.it. 32 units, some with shower only. 150€–195€ ($173–$224) double; 170€–305€ ($196–$351) triple. Rates include buffet breakfast. AE, DC, MC, V. Free parking. Bus: 11, 36, or 37. **Amenities:** Restaurant; bar; lounge; car-rental desk; 24-hr. room service; babysitting; laundry service; dry cleaning; nonsmoking rooms; rooms for those with limited mobility. *In room:* A/C, TV, dataport, minibar, hair dryer, safe.

Moderate

Pensione Annalena ★ *(Finds)*   Most of the simply furnished rooms in this historic hotel overlook a secret garden; five face an open-air galleria on the loggia, evoking an idyllic landscape that might have been painted by Gozzoli. Don't be put off by the lack of air-conditioning; the high ceilings and thick masonry walls almost guarantee a relatively comfortable temperature in summer. The bathrooms are small but have adequate shelf space. The pensione is about a 5-minute walk from the Pitti and 10 minutes from the Ponte Vecchio.

Via Romana 34, 50125 Firenze. ℂ 055-222402. Fax 055-222403. www.hotelannalena.it. 20 units. 126€–166€ ($145–$191) double. Rates include breakfast. AE, DC, MC, V. Parking 21€ ($24). Bus: C, 11, 36, or 37. **Amenities:** Lounge; room service; laundry/dry cleaning. *In room:* TV, hair dryer.

WHERE TO DINE
NEAR THE DUOMO
Moderate

Il Cavallino TUSCAN/ITALIAN   A local favorite since the 1930s, Il Cavallino is the kind of discreetly famous restaurant where Florentines invariably go to be with one another. It's on a tiny street (which probably won't even be on your map) that leads off Piazza della Signoria at its northern end, not far from the equestrian statue. Menu items are typical hearty Tuscan fare, including an assortment of boiled meats in green herb sauce, grilled filet of steak, breast of chicken Medici style, and the inevitable Florentine spinach.

Via della Farine 6R. ℂ 055-215818. Reservations recommended. Main courses 10€–16€ ($12–$18). AE, DC, MC, V. Mar–Oct daily noon–3pm and 7–10:30pm; off season Thurs–Tues noon–3pm, Thurs–Mon 7–10:30pm. Bus: B.

Paoli ✦ TUSCAN/ITALIAN   Paoli, between the Duomo and Piazza della Signoria, is one of Florence's finest restaurants. It turns out a host of specialties, but could be recommended almost solely for its medieval-tavern atmosphere. All pastas are homemade, and the fettuccine alla Paoli is served piping hot and full of flavor. The chef also does a superb *rognoncino trifolato* (thinly sliced kidney cooked with oil, garlic, and parsley) and sole meunière. A recommendable side dish is *piselli* (garden peas) in the Florentine style.

Via dei Tavolini 12R. ℂ 055-216215. Reservations required. Main courses 11€–19€ ($13–$22). AE, DC, MC, V. Wed–Mon noon–2:30pm and 7–10:30pm. Closed 3 weeks in Aug. Bus: A.

NEAR THE PONTE VECCHIO
Inexpensive

Buca dell'Orafo ✦ *Finds* FLORENTINE   This little dive is one of many cellars or *buca*-type establishments beloved by Florentines. The trattoria is usually stuffed with regulars so if you want a seat, go early. Over the years the chef has made little concession to the foreign palate, turning out genuine Florentine specialties, like tripe and mixed boiled meats with a green sauce, and *stracotto e fagioli* (beef braised in a sauce of chopped vegetables and red wine), served with beans in a tomato sauce.

Via Volta dei Girolami 28R. ℂ 055-213619. Main courses 10€–18€ ($12–$21). No credit cards. Tues–Sat 12:30–2:30pm and 7:30–10:30pm. Closed Aug and 2 weeks in Dec. Bus: B.

NEAR PIAZZA SAN LORENZO & THE MERCATO CENTRALE
Inexpensive

Le Fonticine TUSCAN/BOLOGNESE   Owner Silvano Bruci took this former convent and its adjoining garden and turned it into one of the most hospitable restaurants in Florence. He and his wife use recipes she collected from her childhood in Bologna. The food, served in copious portions, is both traditional and delectable. Begin with a platter of fresh antipasti, then enjoy samplings of three of the most excellent pasta dishes of the day. This might be followed by veal scaloppini, or stewed wild boar.

Via Nazionale 79R. ℂ 055-282106. Reservations recommended for dinner. Main courses 8.50€–19€ ($9.80–$22). AE, DC, MC, V. Tues–Sat 12:30–2:30pm and 7–10pm. Closed 2 weeks at Christmas and Aug. Bus: 7, 10, 11, 12, 25, 31, 33, or 70.

Trattoria Antellesi ⚜ *Finds* TUSCAN   On the ground floor of a 15th-century historic monument, a few steps from the Medici Chapel, this restaurant is devoted almost exclusively to Tuscan recipes that have stood the test of time. The restaurant prepares at least seven *piatti del giorno* that change according to the availability of the ingredients. Menu items may include tagliatelle with porcini mushrooms or with braised arugula, *crespelle alla fiorentina* (a Tuscan Renaissance cheesy spinach crepe), market-fresh fish (generally on Fri), and delicious Valdostana chicken.

Via Faenza 9R. ℂ 055-216990. Reservations recommended. Main courses 10€–16€ ($12–$18). AE, DC, MC, V. Daily noon–3pm and 7–10:30pm. Closed Tues Dec–Apr. Bus: 1, 6, 7, 11, 17, 33, 67, or 68.

NEAR PIAZZA SANTA MARIA NOVELLA & THE TRAIN STATION
Moderate

Buca Lapi ⚜ TUSCAN   Buca Lapi, a cellar restaurant under the Palazzo Antinori, is big on glamour, good food, and the enthusiasm of fellow diners. Its decor alone makes it fun: Vaulted ceilings are covered with travel posters from all over the world. The cooks know how to turn out the most classic dishes of the Tuscan kitchen with superb finesse. Specialties include pâté, cannelloni, *scampi giganti alla griglia* (a supersize shrimp), and *bistecca alla fiorentina* (local beefsteak), still cooked over coals in the old-fashioned way. In season, the *fagioli toscani all'olio* (Tuscan beans in the native olive oil) are a delicacy. Owner and chef Luciano Ghinasi's cookbook, available in English, reveals some of his secrets in preparing succulent Tuscan dishes.

Via del Trebbio 1R. ℂ 055-213768. Reservations required for dinner. Main courses 19€–23€ ($22–$26). AE, DC, MC, V. Mon–Sat 7–11pm. Closed 2 weeks in Aug. Bus: 6, 11, 36, or 37.

Don Chisciotte ⚜ ITALIAN/SEAFOOD   This restaurant is known for its creative cuisine and changing array of very fresh fish. Creative menu items are produced with a flourish from the kitchens. Examples include red taglierini with clams, pesto, and cheese; risotto of broccoli and baby squid; and black ravioli colored with squid ink and stuffed with a puree of shrimp and crayfish. Chefs also prepare one of the city's most flavor-filled Florentine steaks along with a succulent medley of boiled meats with fresh herb seasonings.

Via Ridolfi 4R. ℂ 055-475430. Reservations recommended. Main courses 18€–25€ ($21–$29); tasting menu 52€ ($60). AE, DC, MC, V. Mon 5–10:30pm; Tues–Sat 1–2:30pm and 8–10:30pm. Bus: 20.

Sabatini ⚜ FLORENTINE   Despite its location near the rail station, Sabatini has long been extolled by Florentines and visitors alike as the finest of the restaurants characteristic of the city. To celebrate our return visit every year, we order the same main course—boiled Valdarno chicken with savory green sauce. Other main courses are also delicious, especially the veal scaloppini with artichokes. Of course, you can always order a good sole meunière and the classic beefsteak Florentine.

Via de'Panzani 9A. ℂ 055-211559. Reservations recommended. Main courses 11€–30€ ($13–$35). AE, DC, MC, V. Tues–Sun 12:30–2:30pm and 7:30–10:30pm. Bus: 1, 6, 14, 17, or 22.

Inexpensive

Sostanza ★ *Finds* FLORENTINE   Sostanza is a tucked-away little trattoria where working people have gone since 1869 to get excellent, reasonably priced food. It's the city's oldest and most revered trattoria. The small dining room has crowded family tables. The rear kitchen is open, its secrets exposed to diners. Specialties include breaded chicken breast and a succulent T-bone steak. You might also want to try tripe the Florentine way—cut into strips and baked in a casserole with tomatoes, onions, and Parmesan.

Via del Porcellana 25R. ℂ 055-212691. Reservations recommended. Main courses 7.50€–18€ ($8.65–$21). No credit cards. Mon–Fri 12:30–2:10pm and 7:30–10:45pm. Closed Aug and 2 weeks at Christmas. Bus: 12.

NEAR PIAZZA GOLDONI
Moderate

Harry's Bar ★ INTERNATIONAL/ITALIAN   Harry's Bar, in a prime position on the Arno, is an enclave of expatriate and well-heeled visiting Yankees that deserves its reputation. A specialty is risotto or tagliatelle with ham, onions, and cheese. Harry has created his own *tortellini* (stuffed pasta), but Harry's hamburger and his club sandwich are the most popular items. The chef also prepares about a dozen specialties every day, like breast of chicken "our way," grilled giant-size scampi, and lean broiled sirloin.

Lungarno Vespucci 22R. ℂ 055-2396700. Reservations required. Main courses 18€–30€ ($21–$35). AE, MC, V. Mon–Sat noon–3pm and 7–11pm. Closed Feb 9–22. Bus B.

NEAR PIAZZA SANTA CROCE
Expensive

Cibrèo ★ *Finds* MEDITERRANEAN   Cibrèo is one of the largest eateries in the neighborhood, with both a formal restaurant and a less expensive trattoria on-site. The *New York Times* called the chef and owner, Fabio Picchi, a poet for how he talks and a magician for how he cooks. The kitchens are noteworthy for not containing a grill and not serving pastas. They specialize in foodstuffs cooked in a wood-burning oven and cold marinated dishes, especially vegetables. Menu items include *sformato* (soufflé made from potatoes and ricotta, served with Parmesan and tomato sauce) and flan of Parmesan, veal tongue, and artichokes. A favorite dish of the chef is roast pigeon flavored with a fruity mustard. Among his classic recipes are *zuppa di cavolo* (cabbage soup), *polenta alle erbe* (polenta flavored with seasonal herbs), and *insalata di fave* (fava bean salad with Parmesan flakes).

Via Verrocchio 8R. ℂ 055-2341100. Reservations recommended in the restaurant but not accepted in the trattoria. Main courses 18€–34€ ($21–$39) in the restaurant, 5€–13€ ($5.75–$15) in the trattoria. AE, DC, MC, V (restaurant only). Tues–Sat 12:50–2:30pm and 7–11pm. Closed late July to early Sept. Bus: B or 14.

Moderate/Inexpensive

Osteria del Caffè Italiano ★ *Value* WINE BAR/TUSCAN   Housed in the 13th-century Palazzo Salviati, this wine bar/trattoria is the brainchild of Umberto Montano. Beneath a wrought-iron chandelier hanging from the vaulted 6m (20-ft.) ceiling, you can sample delicious choices from the short menu. Look for the fresh *mozzarella di bufala,* specially couriered from a private supplier in Naples (not available June–Aug). Stop by any time the restaurant isn't serving meals for a by-the-glass introduction to Montano's renowned wine cellar and an assortment of Tuscan *salumi.* Or come back in the evening to dine in the elegant restaurant in the back room and splurge on excellently prepared entrees from the grill and a more serious sampling of wine.

Via Isola delle Stinche 11–13R (2 blocks west of Piazza Santa Croce). 🕐 **055-289368**. Reservations for restaurant (not wine bar) suggested. Wine bar: Small plates 8€–15€ ($9.20–$17). Restaurant main courses 15€–25€ ($17–$29). DC, MC, V. Tues–Sun noon–1am. Bus: A or 14.

EXPLORING THE RENAISSANCE CITY

Florence was the fountainhead of the Renaissance, the city of Dante and Boccaccio. Florentines are noted for their cunning, as represented by Machiavelli; however, they're not noted for their religious zeal, as evoked by Savonarola, who might have found a better reception in Geneva. For 3 centuries, Florence was dominated by the Medici family, patrons of the arts and masters of assassination. But it's chiefly through its artists that we know of the apogee of the Renaissance: Ghiberti, Fra Angelico, Donatello, Brunelleschi, Botticelli, and the incomparable Leonardo da Vinci and Michelangelo.

Piazza della Signoria ✪✪✪, though never completed, is one of the most beautiful in Italy. On the square is the Fountain of Neptune. Nearby is the spot where Savonarola walked his last mile. This zealous monk was a fire-and-brimstone reformer who rivaled Dante in conjuring up the punishment hell would inflict on sinners. For centuries Michelangelo's *David* stood in this piazza before it was moved to the Accademia. The work you see here today is a copy.

On the piazza, the 14th-century **Loggia dei Lanzi** ✪✪ (sometimes called the Loggia della Signoria) is a gallery of sculpture that often depicts fierce, violent scenes. The best piece is a rare work by Benvenuto Cellini, the goldsmith and tell-all autobiographer. Critics have said that his exquisite *Perseus,* who holds the severed head of Medusa, is the most significant Florentine sculpture since Michelangelo's *Night* and *Day.*

For a view of the wonders of Florence below and Fiesole above, climb aboard bus no. 13 from the central station and head for **Piazzale Michelangelo** ✪, a 19th-century belvedere with a view seen in many a Renaissance painting. It's best at dusk, when the purple-fringed Tuscan hills form a frame for Giotto's bell tower, Brunelleschi's dome, and the towering stones sticking up from the Palazzo Vecchio. Another copy of Michelangelo's *David* dominates the square.

SIGHTSEEING SUGGESTIONS FOR FIRST-TIME VISITORS

If You Have 1 Day You'll have to accept the inevitable—you can only visit a small fraction of Florence's stellar attractions. Go to the **Uffizi Galleries** as soon as they open and concentrate only on some of the masterpieces or your favorite artists. Have lunch on **Piazza della Signoria,** dominated by the Palazzo Vecchio, and admire the statues in the Loggia dei Lanzi. After lunch, visit the **Duomo** and **Baptistery,** before continuing north to see Michelangelo's *David* at the **Accademia.** Next, head back south toward the Arno and the Ponte Vecchio. On the way do a little shopping at the fabled **Mercato Nuovo (Straw Market).** Sunset should find you at the landmark **Ponte Vecchio.** Finish your very busy day with a hearty Tuscan dinner in one of Florence's many *bucas* (cellar restaurants).

If You Have 2 Days On day 2, you can spend the morning visiting the **Bargello** to see some of the Renaissance, including another version of Michelangelo's *David.* A short walk will take you to the **Palazzo Vecchio,** where you can explore the Hall of the 500 to see the Vasari Renaissance frescoes. Then, in the afternoon, visit the **Pitti Palace,** on the other side of the Arno, and wander through the Galleria Palatina, with its 16th- and 17th-century masterpieces, including 11 works by Raphael alone. After a visit, stroll through the adjoining **Boboli Gardens.** At sunset, go again to the Duomo and the Baptistery for a much better look.

If You Have 3 Days In the morning of day 3, head for the **Medici Chapels** adjacent to the Basilica of San Lorenzo. Look especially for Michelangelo's figures of *Dawn* and *Dusk.* Later in the morning you can go to the **Museo di San Marco,** a small museum that's a monument to the work of Fra Angelico. After lunch, visit the **Museo dell'Opera del Duomo,** with its sculptural masterpieces from the Duomo, including Donatello's *Mary Magdalene.*

If You Have 4 Days or More On day 4, begin with a morning visit to the **Palazzo Medici-Riccardi,** near the Duomo, to view the mid-15th-century frescoes by Benozzo Gozzoli in the Medici Chapel. Later that morning pop into **Santa Maria Novella,** one of Florence's most distinguished churches, with its Gondi Chapel containing Brunelleschi's wooden Christ on the Cross. Before it closes at 6:30pm, call at the **Basilica di Santa Croce,** with its two restored chapels by Giotto. On day 5, leave Florence, as fascinating as it is, and head south to yet another fascinating art city, **Siena,** the most important of the Tuscan hill towns.

THE TOP MUSEUMS

Galleria degli Uffizi ★★★ This is one of the world's outstanding museums and Italy's finest collection of art. The Uffizi is nicely grouped into periods or schools to show the progress of Italian and European art. The Botticelli rooms contain his finest works, including *The Birth of Venus.* In another room you'll see Leonardo da Vinci's unfinished but brilliant *Adoration of the Magi* and Verrocchio's *Baptism of Christ,* not a very important painting but noted because Leonardo painted one of the angels when he was 14. Also in this salon hangs Leonardo's *Annunciation.* In the rooms that follow are works by Perugino, Dürer, Mantegna, Bellini, Giorgione, and Correggio. Finally, you can view Michelangelo's *Holy Family,* as well as Raphael's *Madonna of the Goldfinch.*

Piazzale degli Uffizi 6. ⓒ **055-23885.** www.uffizi.firenze.it. Admission 8.50€ ($9.80). Tues–Sun 8:15am–7pm (last entrance 45 min. before closing). Bus: A, B, 14, or 23.

Galleria dell'Accademia ★★ This museum boasts many paintings and sculptures, but they're completely overshadowed by one work: Michelangelo's colossal ***David*** ★★★, unveiled in 1504. It first stood in Piazza della Signoria but was moved to the Accademia in 1873 and placed beneath the rotunda of a

---

Tips **Reserving Tickets for the Uffizi & Other Museums**

Finally, you can bypass the hours-long ticket line at the **Uffizi Galleries** by reserving a ticket and an entry time in advance for a 1.50€ ($1.70) fee by calling ⓒ **055-294883** or going to **www.arca.net/uffizi.** By March, entry times can already be booked up over a week in advance. You can also reserve for the **Accademia Gallery** (another interminable line), as well as the **Galleria Palatina** in the Pitti Palace and the **Bargello** (you don't really need it for those last two) and several others. There's a nominal fee (worth every penny).

room built exclusively for its display. When he began work, Michelangelo was just 29. In the connecting picture gallery is a collection of Tuscan masters, such as Botticelli, and Umbrian works by Perugino (teacher of Raphael).

Via Ricasoll 60. ✆ **055-2388609**. Admission 8.50€ ($9.80). Tues–Sun 8:15am–6:20pm. Bus: B, D, or 12.

Palazzo Pitti and Giardini di Boboli (Boboli Gardens) ★★ The Pitti,
built in the mid–15th century (Brunelleschi was the original architect), was once the residence of the powerful Medici family. Today it contains several museums, the most important of which is the **Galleria Palatina** ★★, a repository of old masters. This gallery houses one of Europe's great art collections, with masterpieces hung one on top of the other, as in the days of the Enlightenment. In the **Sala di Saturno,** look for Raphael's *Madonna of the Canopy* and *Madonna of the Chair,* his best-known interpretation of the Virgin.

Other museums are the **Appartamenti Reali,** which the Medici family once called home; the **Museo degli Argenti** (✆ **055-294883**), 16 rooms devoted to displays of the "loot" acquired by the Medici dukes; the **Coach and Carriage Museum;** the **Galleria d'Arte Moderna** (✆ **055-2388601**); the **Museo delle Porcellane** (porcelain); and the **Galleria del Costume.**

Behind the Pitti Palace are the **Boboli Gardens** ★, Piazza de'Pitti 1 (✆ **055-2651838**), through which the Medici romped. The gardens were laid out in the 16th century by the great landscape artist, Triboli. The Boboli is ever popular for a promenade or an idyllic interlude in a pleasant setting. The gardens are filled with fountains and statuary, such as a Giambologna *Venus* in the "Grotto" of Buontalenti. You can climb to the top of the Fortezza di Belvedere for a dazzling city view.

Piazza Pitti, across the Arno. ✆ **055-2388611**. Palatina 6.50€ ($7.50); Modern Art Gallery 5€ ($5.75); 4€ ($4.60) for both Argenti and Boboli Gardens. Galleria Palatina and Appartamenti Reali Tues–Sun 8:15am–6:45pm. Museo degli Argenti and Modern Art Gallery daily 8:30am–1:30pm; closed the 1st, 3rd, and 5th Mon and the 2nd and 4th Sun of each month. Boboli Gardens June–Aug daily 8:30am–7:45pm; Apr–May and Sept–Oct daily 8:30am–6:30pm; Nov–Feb daily 8:15am–4:30pm; closed the 1st and last Mon of each month. Ticket office closes 1 hr. before the gardens. Bus: D, 11, 36, 37, or 68.

Cappelle dei Medici (Medici Chapels) ★★ The Medici tombs are adjacent
to the Basilica of San Lorenzo (see "Other Churches," below). Working from 1521 to 1534, Michelangelo created the Medici tomb in a style that foreshadowed the baroque. Lorenzo the Magnificent was buried near Michelangelo's uncompleted *Madonna and Child* group. Ironically, the finest groups of sculpture were reserved for two Medici "clan" members, who (in the words of Mary McCarthy) "would better have been forgotten." They're represented as armored, idealized princes. The other two figures on Lorenzo's tomb are most often called *Dawn* (represented as woman) and *Dusk* (as man). The best-known figures are *Night* (chiseled as a woman in troubled sleep) and *Day* (a man of strength awakening to a foreboding world) at the feet of Giuliano, the duke of Nemours.

Piazza Madonna degli Aldobrandini 6. ✆ **055-2388602**. Admission 6€ ($6.90). Mon–Sat 8:15am–4:30pm; Sun 8:30am–1:50pm. Closed 2nd and 4th Sun, and 1st, 3rd, and 5th Mon of each month. Bus: 1, 6, 7, 11, 17, 33, 67, or 68.

Museo Nazionale del Bargello ★★★ The National Museum, a short walk
from Piazza della Signoria, is a 13th-century fortress palace whose dark underground chambers once resounded with the cries of the tortured. Today it's a vast repository of some of the most important Renaissance sculpture, including works by Michelangelo and Donatello. Here you'll see another Michelangelo

David (formerly referred to as *Apollo*), chiseled perhaps 25 to 30 years after the figure in the Accademia. The Bargello *David* is totally different—even effete when compared to its stronger brother. Among the more significant sculptures is Giambologna's *Winged Mercury.* The Bargello displays two versions of Donatello's *John the Baptist.* Look for two more *Davids*—Donatello's and Verrocchio's. The Bargello contains a large number of terra-cotta works by the della Robbia clan.

Via del Proconsolo 4. © 055-294883. Admission 5€ ($5.75). Daily 8:30am–1:50pm; 2nd and 4th Sun and 1st, 3rd, and 5th Mon of the month 8:30am–1:50pm. Closed Jan 1, May 1, and Christmas. Bus: A, 14, or 23.

Museo di San Marco ★★★ This state museum is a handsome Renaissance palace whose cell walls are decorated with 15th-century frescoes by the mystical Fra Angelico. In the days of Cosimo dei Medici, San Marco was built as a Dominican convent. It originally contained bleak, bare cells, which Angelico and his students then brightened considerably. One of his better-known paintings here is *The Last Judgment,* which depicts people with angels on the left dancing in a circle and lordly saints towering overhead. On the second floor—at the top of the hall—is Angelico's masterpiece, *The Annunciation.*

Piazza San Marco 1. © 055-294883. Admission 4.15€ ($4.75). Tues–Fri 8:30am–1:50pm; Sat 8:15am–6:50pm. 2nd and 4th and 1st, 3rd, and 5th Mon of the month 8:15am–1:50pm. Ticket office closes 30 min. before the museum. Closed 2nd and 4th Mon of the month; and 1st, 3rd, and 5th Sun of the month; Jan 1, May 1, and Christmas. Bus: 1, 6, 7, 10, 11, 17, or 20.

THE DUOMO, CAMPANILE & BAPTISTERY

Cattedrale di Santa Maria del Fiore (Duomo) ★★★ The Duomo, graced by Brunelleschi's dome, is the crowning glory of Florence. But don't rush inside too quickly, as the view of the exterior, with its geometrically patterned bands of white, pink, and green marble, is, along with the dome, the best feature. One of the world's largest churches, the Duomo represents the flowering of the "Florentine Gothic" style. Begun in 1296, it was finally consecrated in 1436, yet finishing touches on the facade were applied as late as the 19th century.

Inside, the overall effect is bleak, except when you stand under the cupola, frescoed in part by Vasari. Some of the stained-glass windows in the dome were based on designs by Donatello (Brunelleschi's friend) and Ghiberti (Brunelleschi's rival). If you resist scaling Giotto's bell tower (below), you may want to climb Brunelleschi's ribbed dome. The view is well worth the trek.

Piazza del Duomo. © 055-2302885. Cathedral free admission; excavations 3€ ($3.45); cupola 6€ ($6.90). Mon–Fri 8:30am–6:30pm; Sat 8:30am–5pm. Bus: 1, 6, 17.

Campanile (Giotto's Bell Tower) ★★★ Giotto left to posterity the most beautiful campanile (bell tower) in Europe, rhythmic in line and form. The 84m (274-ft.) tower, a "Tuscanized" Gothic, with bands of colored marble, can be scaled for a panorama of the sienna-colored city. The view will surely rank among your most memorable—it encompasses the enveloping hills and Medici villas.

Piazza del Duomo. © 055-2302885. Admission 6€ ($6.90). Daily 8:30am–6:50pm. Closed Jan 1, Easter, Sept 8, and Christmas. Bus: 1 or 3.

Battistero San Giovanni (Baptistery) ★★★ Named after the city's patron saint, Giovanni (John the Baptist), the present octagonal Battistero dates from the 11th and 12th centuries. The oldest structure in Florence, the baptistery is a highly original interpretation of the Romanesque style, with its bands of pink, white, and green marble. Visitors from all over the world come to gape at its three sets of bronze doors. The east door is a copy; the other two are originals.

In his work on two sets of doors, Lorenzo Ghiberti reached the pinnacle of his artistry in *quattrocento* Florence. The gilt panels—representing scenes from the New Testament, including the *Annunciation,* the *Adoration,* and Christ debating the elders in the temple—make up a flowing, rhythmic narration in bronze.

Piazza San Giovanni. ✆ **055-2302885.** Admission 3€ ($3.45). Oct–June daily 8:30am–7pm; July–Sept daily 12:30–1:30pm. Bus: 1 or 3.

OTHER CHURCHES

Basilica di San Lorenzo ★★★ This is Brunelleschi's 15th-century Renaissance church, where the Medici used to attend services from their nearby palace on Via Larga, now Via Camillo Cavour. Most visitors flock to see Michelangelo's Medici Chapels (see "The Top Museums," above), but Brunelleschi's handiwork deserves some time, too. Built in the style of a Latin cross, the church is distinguished by harmonious grays and rows of Corinthian columns.

  Biblioteca Medicea Laurenziana ★★ (✆ **055-210760**) is entered separately at Piazza San Lorenzo 9 and was designed by Michelangelo to shelter the expanding library of the Medici. Beautiful in design and concept, and approached by exquisite stairs, the library is filled with some of Italy's greatest manuscripts—many of which are handsomely illustrated. Hours are Monday through Saturday from 9am to 1pm. Admission is free; the only time you'll be charged is if there's a special exhibition.

Piazza San Lorenzo. ✆ **055-216634.** Free admission; 2.60€ ($3) for special exhibitions. Fri–Mon 10am–5pm; Tues–Thurs 10am–5pm. Bus: 1, 6, 7, 11, 17, 33, 67, or 68.

Basilica di Santa Croce ★★ The Pantheon of Florence, this church shelters tombs or monuments of everyone from Michelangelo to Machiavelli, from Dante to Galileo. Santa Croce was the church of the Franciscans. In the right nave (1st tomb) is the Vasari-executed monument to Michelangelo, whose body was smuggled back to his native Florence from its original burial place in Rome. The Trecento frescoes are reason enough for visiting Santa Croce—especially those by Giotto to the right of the main chapel.

Piazza Santa Croce 16. ✆ **055-244619.** Church free admission; cloisters and church museum 4€ ($4.60). Church Mon–Sat 9am–5:30pm; Sun 1–5:30pm. Museum and cloisters Thurs–Tues 9am–5:30pm. Bus: B, 13, 23, or 71.

Basilica di Santa Maria Novella ★★ Near the railway station is one of Florence's most distinguished churches, begun in 1278 for the Dominicans. Its geometric facade, with bands of white and green marble, was designed in the late 15th century by Leon Battista Alberti, an aristocrat and true Renaissance man. The church borrows from and harmonizes the Romanesque, Gothic, and Renaissance styles. In the left nave as you enter (the 3rd large painting) is Masaccio's *Trinity,* a curious work that has the architectural form of a Renaissance stage setting, but whose figures—in perfect perspective—are like actors in a Greek tragedy. Head straight up the left nave to the Gondi Chapel for a look at Brunelleschi's wooden *Christ on the Cross,* said to have been carved to compete with Donatello's same subject in Santa Croce.

Piazza Santa Maria Novella. ✆ **055-215918.** Church free admission; Spanish Chapel and cloisters 2.60€ ($3). Church Mon–Thurs 9:30am–5pm; Fri 1–5pm. Spanish Chapel and cloisters Sat–Thurs 8am–2pm. Bus: A, 6, 9, 11, 36, 37, or 68.

PALACES

Palazzo Vecchio ★★★ The secular "Old Palace" is without doubt the most famous and imposing palace in Florence. It dates from the closing years of the

13th century. Its remarkable architectural feature is its 94m (308-ft.) tower. Once home to the Medici, the Palazzo Vecchio is occupied today by city employees, but much of it is open to the public. The 16th-century Dei Cinquecento (Hall of the 500), the most outstanding part of the palace, is filled with Vasari and Co. frescoes as well as sculpture. As you enter the hall, look for Michelangelo's *Victory.* Later you can stroll through the apartments and main halls. You can also visit the private apartments of Eleanor of Toledo, wife of Cosimo I, and a chapel that was begun in 1540 and frescoed by Bronzino.

Piazza della Signoria. ✆ 055-2768465. Admission 6€ ($6.90). Sept 16–July 14 Mon–Wed and Fri–Sat 9am–7pm; Thurs 9am–2pm; Sun 9am–7pm. July 15–Sept 15 Mon and Fri 9am–11pm. Ticket office closes 1 hr. before palace. Bus: A, B, 23, or 71.

Palazzo Medici-Riccardi ★★ A short walk from the Duomo, this 15th-century palace was the home of Cosimo dei Medici before he took his household to the Palazzo Vecchio. The brown stone building was also the scene, at times, of the court of Lorenzo the Magnificent. Art lovers visit today chiefly to see the Chapel of the Magi with its mid-15th-century frescoes by Benozzo Gozzoli, which depict the *Journey of the Magi.*

Via Camillo Cavour 1. ✆ 055-2760340. Admission 4€ ($4.60). Thurs–Tues 9am–7pm. Bus: 1, 6, 7, 11, 17, 67, or 68.

OTHER MUSEUMS

Museo Archeologico ★★ The Archaeological Museum, a short walk from Piazza della Santissima Annunziata, houses one of Europe's most outstanding Egyptian and Etruscan collections. Egyptian mummies and sarcophagi are on the first floor, along with Etruscan works. Pause to look at the lid of the coffin of a fat Etruscan. Look for the bronze Chimera, a lion with a goat sticking out of its back, a masterpiece of Etruscan art.

Via della Colonna 38. ✆ 055-23575. Admission 4.15€ ($4.75). Nov–Aug Mon 2–7pm; Tues and Thurs 8:30am–7pm; Wed and Fri–Sun 8:30am–2pm. Sept also Sat 9pm–midnight; Oct also Sun 9am–8pm. Bus: 6, 31, or 32.

Museo dell'Opera del Duomo ★★ Museo dell'Opera del Duomo, behind the cathedral, is beloved by connoisseurs of Renaissance sculptural works. It shelters the sculpture removed from the campanile and the Duomo. A major attraction of this museum is Michelangelo's unfinished *Pietà,* carved between 1548 and 1555 when the artist was in his seventies. Also look for the marble choirs *(cantorie)* of Donatello and Luca della Robbia. The Luca della Robbia choir is more restrained, but it still "praises the Lord" in marble—with clashing cymbals and sounding brass that constitute a reaffirmation of life.

Piazza del Duomo 9. ✆ 055-2302885. Admission 5€ ($5.75). Mon–Sat 9:30am–6:30pm; Sun 9am–1pm.

THE SHOPPING SCENE

Skilled craftsmanship and traditional design unchanged since the days of the Medici have made Florence a destination for serious shoppers. Florence is noted for its hand-tooled **leather goods** and its **straw merchandise,** as well as superbly crafted **gold jewelry.** Its reputation for fashionable custom-made clothes is no longer what it was, having lost its position of supremacy to Milan.

Florence is not a city for bargain shopping. Most visitors interested in gold or silver jewelry head for the **Ponte Vecchio** and its tiny shops. It's difficult to tell one from the other, but you really don't need to since the merchandise is similar. If you're looking for a charm or souvenir, these shops are fine. But the heyday of finding gold jewelry bargains on the Ponte Vecchio is long gone.

The street for antiques in Florence is **Via Maggio;** some of the furnishings and objets d'art here are from the 16th century. Another major area for antiques shopping is **Borgo Ognissanti.**

Florence's Fifth Avenue is **Via dei Tornabuoni.** This is the place to head for the best-quality leather goods, the best clothing boutiques, and stylish but costly shoes. Here you'll find everyone from Armani to Ferragamo. You'll find better shops on **Via Vigna Nuova, Via Porta Rossa,** and **Via degli Strozzi,** too. You might also stroll on the Lungarno along the Arno. For some of the best buys in leather, check out **Via del Parione,** a short narrow street of Tornabuoni.

FLORENCE'S FAMOUS MARKETS

After checking into their hotels, the most intrepid shoppers head for **Piazza del Mercato Nuovo (Straw Market),** called "Il Porcellino" by the Italians because of the bronze statue of a reclining wild boar here. Tourists pet its snout (which is well worn) for good luck. The market stands in the monumental heart of Florence, an easy stroll from the Palazzo Vecchio. It sells not only straw items but leather goods as well, along with an array of typically Florentine merchandise—frames, trays, hand embroidery, table linens, and hand-sprayed and painted boxes in traditional designs. Market hours are Monday through Saturday from 9am to 7pm.

However, even better bargains await those who make their way through push-carts to the stalls of the open-air **Mercato Centrale** (also called the Mercato San Lorenzo), in and around Borgo San Lorenzo, near the train station. If you don't mind bargaining, which is imperative here, you'll find an array of merchandise, including raffia bags, Florentine leather purses, salt-and-pepper shakers, straw handbags, and art reproductions.

FLORENCE AFTER DARK

For theatrical and concert listings, pick up a free copy of *Welcome to Florence,* available at the tourist office. This helpful publication contains information on recitals, concerts, theatrical productions, and other cultural presentations.

Many cultural presentations are performed in churches. These might include open-air concerts in the cloisters of the Badia Fiesolana in Fiesole (the hill town above Florence) or at the Ospedale degli Innocenti, the foundling "hospital of the innocents" (on summer evenings only).

THE PERFORMING ARTS

Teatro Comunale di Firenze, Corso Italia 16 (© **055-211158;** bus: B), is the main theater in Florence, with an opera and ballet season presented from September to December, and a concert season from January until April. This is also the venue for the **Maggio Musicale Fiorentino** (www.maggiofiorentino.com), Italy's oldest and most prestigious festival. It takes place from May to July and offers opera, ballet, concerts, recitals, and cinema productions. The box office is open Tuesday through Friday from 10am to 4:30pm, Saturday from 10am to 1pm, and 1 hour before curtain. Tickets are 20€ to 80€ ($23–$9.20). During the Maggio Musicale, tickets usually range from 23€ to 100€ ($26–$115).

You'll have to understand Italian to appreciate most of the plays presented at **Teatro della Pergola,** Via della Pergola 18 (© **055-2479651;** bus: 6, 14, or 23). Plays are performed year-round except during the Maggio Musicale, when the theater becomes the setting for the many musical presentations of the festival. Performances are Tuesday through Saturday at 8:45pm and Sunday at 3:45pm. The box office is open October through June Tuesday through Saturday from

9:30am to 1pm and 3:30 to 6:45pm, Sunday from 10am to 12:15pm. In July, it's open Tuesday through Friday from 9:30am to 1pm and 4 to 7pm, Saturday from 10am to 12:30pm, Sunday from 10am to 12:15pm. It's closed in August. Tickets are 12€ to 25€ ($14–$29).

MUSIC & DANCE CLUBS

Contained in the cellar of an antique building in the historic heart of town, the well-known **Full-Up,** Via della Vigna Vecchia 23–25R (© **055-293006;** bus: A or 14), attracts college students from the city's many universities, although older clients usually feel at ease, too. One section contains a smallish dance floor and recorded dance music; another is devoted to the somewhat more restrained ambience of a piano bar. Full-Up is open Tuesday through Saturday from 11pm to 4am; no cover.

PUBS & BARS

If you ask whether **Dublin Pub,** Via Faenza 27R (© **055-293049;** bus: 7, 10, 11, 12, 25, 31, or 70), is an Italian pub, the all-Italian staff will respond rather grandly that such a concept doesn't exist, and that pubs are by definition Irish. And once you get beyond the fact that virtually no one on the staff here has ever been outside of Tuscany, and that there's very little to do here except drink and perhaps practice your Italian, you might settle down and have a rollicking old (very Latin) time. Beers, at least, are appropriately Celtic, and include Harp, Guinness, Kilkenny, and Strong's on tap. The pub is near the Santa Maria Novella train station and is open daily from 5pm to 2am (closed 2 weeks in Aug). After an initial success in Rome, **Fiddler's Elbow,** Piazza Santa Maria Novella 7R (© **055-215056;** bus: A), also located near the train station, has now invaded the city of Donatello and Michelangelo. It has quickly become one of the most popular bars in Florence. It's open Monday through Friday from 5pm to 1am, Saturday and Sunday from 2pm to 2am.

ArciGay/Lesbica (aka Azione Gay e Lesbica), Italy's largest and oldest gay organization, has a center in Florence at Via Manara 12 (© **055-671298;** www.azionegayelesbica.it). It's open Monday through Thursday from 6 to 8pm.

A SIDE TRIP TO FIESOLE ⊛

This town, once an Etruscan settlement, is the most popular outing from Florence. Bus no. 7, which leaves from Piazza San Marco, brings you here in 25 minutes and gives you a panoramic view along the way. You'll pass fountains, statuary, and gardens strung out over the hills like pieces of a scrambled jigsaw puzzle.

You won't find anything as dazzling here as the Renaissance treasures of Florence—the charms of Fiesole are more subtle. Fortunately, all major sights branch out within walking distance of the main piazza, beginning with the **Cattedrale di San Romolo** ⊛. Dating from 1000, it was much altered during the Renaissance. In the Salutati Chapel are important sculptural works by Mino da Fiesole. It's open daily from 7:30am to noon and 4 to 7pm.

The ecclesiastical **Bandini Museum,** Via Dupre 1 (© **055-59477**), around to the side of the Duomo, belongs to the Fiesole Cathedral Chapter. On the ground floor are della Robbia terra-cotta works, as well as art by Michelangelo. March through October, hours are daily from 9:30am to 7pm; November through February, Wednesday through Monday from 9:30am to 5pm. Admission is 6€ ($6.90). The ticket is valid 24 hours and includes admission to the Teatro Romano e Museo Civico (see below).

The hardest task you'll have in Fiesole is to take the steep goat-climb up to the **Museo Missionario Francescano Fiesole,** Via San Francesco 13 (© **055-59175**). The church was consecrated in 1516. Inside are many paintings by well-known Florentine artists. In the basement is the ethnological museum. Begun in 1906, the collection has a large section of Chinese artifacts, including ancient bronzes, as well as Etruscan, Roman, and Egyptian objects. Admission is free (donation expected). It's open Tuesday through Friday from 10am to noon and 3 to 5:30pm, Saturday and Sunday from 3 to 7pm in summer (closes at 6pm off season).

On the site of the **Teatro Romano e Museo Civico,** Via Portigiani 1 (© **055-59477**), is the major surviving evidence that Fiesole was an Etruscan city 6 centuries before Christ, then later a Roman town. In the 1st century B.C., a theater was built, the restored remains of which you can see today. Near the theater are the skeleton-like ruins of the baths, which may have been built at the same time. The Etruscan-Roman museum contains many interesting finds that date from the days when Fiesole, not Florence, was supreme (a guide is on hand to show you through). For admission and hours, see the Bandini Museum above.

3 Highlights of the Tuscan & Umbrian Countryside

Rome may rule Italy, but **Tuscany** presides over its heart. The Tuscan landscapes, little changed since the days of the Medicis, look just like Renaissance paintings, with cypress trees, olive groves, evocative hill towns, and those fabled Chianti vineyards.

Tuscany was the place where the Etruscans first appeared in Italy. The Romans followed, absorbing and conquering them, and by the 11th century, the region had evolved into a collection of independent city-states, such as Florence and Siena, each trying to dominate the other. Although the Renaissance was immensely popular in Florence, it was slow to spread into the surrounding region.

When the Renaissance did arrive, however, with its titans of art, like Giotto, Michelangelo, and Leonardo, critics claim that Western civilization was "rediscovered" in Tuscany. According to D. H. Lawrence, Tuscany became "the perfect center of man's universe." Art flourished under the patronage of the powerful Medicis, and the legacy remains through Masaccio, della Francesca, Signorelli, Raphael, Donatello, Botticelli, and countless others. Tuscany also became known for its men of letters, like Dante, Petrarch, and Boccaccio (who wrote in the vernacular rather than in Latin).

Umbria, a small region at the heart of the Italian peninsula, is associated mainly with saints, like St. Francis of Assisi, founder of the Franciscan order, but Umbrian painters (such as Il Perugino) also contributed to the glory of the Renaissance. The landscape is as alluring as that of Tuscany, with fertile plains of olive groves and vineyards.

Tips Tuscan Tours

If you love to walk or bike, **I Bike Italy** (© 055-2342371 Mon–Fri; www.ibikeitaly.com) books guided bike rides through the countryside from March to November. **Country Walks in Italy** can be booked with the same outfit year-round. If you want to see Italy as did the Romans and the Renaissance *condottieri,* you can book a horseback trek through **Equitours** (© 800/545-0019 in the U.S.; www.ridingtours.com).

Tuscany & Umbria

SIENA ★★★

In Rome you see classicism and the baroque; in Florence, the Renaissance; but in the walled city of Siena you stand solidly planted in the Middle Ages. On three sienna-colored hills in the center of Tuscany, Sena Vetus lies in Chianti country, 34km (21 miles) south of Florence. Preserving its original character more markedly than any other Italian city, it's a showplace of the Italian Gothic.

ESSENTIALS

GETTING THERE Trains arrive hourly from both Florence and Pisa. **TRA-IN,** Piazza San Domenico 1 (② **0577-204245**), in Siena, offers bus service to all of Tuscany, with air-conditioned coaches. The one-way fare between Florence and Siena is 6€ ($6.90). Motorists can head south from Florence along the Firenze-Siena autostrada, a superhighway through Poggibonsi linking the cities.

VISITOR INFORMATION The **tourist information office** is at Piazza del Campo 56 (② **0577-280551**), open Monday through Saturday from 8:30am to 7:30pm, Sunday from 9am to 3pm. November through March, hours are Monday through Saturday from 8:30am to 1pm and 3 to 7pm.

WHERE TO DINE

Al Marsili (Ristorante Enoteca Gallo Nero) ★ SIENESE/ITALIAN The beautiful Al Marsili is the best in Siena, standing between the Duomo and Via della Città. You dine beneath crisscrossed ceiling vaults whose russet-colored brickwork was designed centuries ago. Specialties include roast boar with tomatoes and herbs, *ribollita* (savory vegetable soup in the Sienese style), spaghetti with a sauce of seasonal mushrooms, and veal scaloppini with tarragon and tomato sauce.

Via del Castoro 3. ✆ **0577-47154.** Reservations recommended. Main courses 12€–18€ ($14–$21). AE, DC, MC, V. Tues–Sun 12:30–2:30pm and 7:30–10:30pm. Bus: A.

EXPLORING SIENA

Start in the heart of Siena, the shell-shaped **Piazza del Campo (Il Campo)** ★★★, described by Montaigne as "the finest of any city in the world." Pause to enjoy the Fonte Gaia, with embellishments by Jacopo della Quercia (the present sculptured works are reproductions; the badly battered original ones are found in the town hall).

Museo Civico and Torre del Mangia ★★★   The Palazzo Pubblico dates from 1288 to 1309 and is filled with important art works by some of the leaders in the Sienese school of painting and sculpture. Upstairs in the Museo Civico is the **Sala della Pace,** painted from 1337 to 1339 by Ambrogio Lorenzetti, whose allegorical frescoes show the idealized effects of good and bad government. Accessible from the courtyard of the palazzo is the 102m (335-ft.) **Torre del Mangia,** from the 14th century. If you climb the tower, you'll be rewarded with a drop-dead view of the city skyline and Tuscan landscape.

In the Palazzo Pubblico, Piazza del Campo. ✆ **0577-292263.** Admission 6€ ($6.90). Museo and Torre: Apr–Oct daily 10am–7pm; Nov–Mar daily 10am–6:30pm. Bus: A, B, or N.

Il Duomo ★★★   With its bands of colored marble, the Sienese cathedral is an original and exciting building, erected in the Romanesque and Italian Gothic styles during the 12th century. The dramatic facade—designed in part by Giovanni Pisano—dates from the 13th century, as does the Romanesque bell tower. The zebralike interior, with its black-and-white stripes, is equally stunning. The floor consists of various embedded works of art, many of which are roped off to preserve the richness in design, depicting both biblical and mythological subjects. The octagonal 13th-century pulpit is by Nicola Pisano (Giovanni's father), who was one of the most significant Italian sculptors before the dawn of the Renaissance (see his pulpit in the baptistery at Pisa). The Siena pulpit is his masterpiece; it reveals in relief such scenes as the slaughter of the innocents and the Crucifixion.

Piazza del Duomo 17. ✆ **050-560547.** Admission 2€ ($2.30). Nov–Feb Mon–Sat 10am–12:45pm and 3–4:30pm, Sun 1–4:30pm; Oct and Mar Mon–Sat 10am–5:30pm, Sun 1–5:30pm; Apr–Sept Mon–Sat 10am–7:30pm, Sun 1–7pm. Sightseeing visits are discouraged during Masses and religious rites. Bus: A or 3.

Battistero (Baptistery) ★   The Gothic facade of the Baptistery, left unfinished by Domenico di Agostino, dates from the 14th century. But you don't come to see that—you come to see the lavish frescoes inside. In the center of the interior is the star of the place, a baptismal font by Jacopo della Quercia that contains some bas-reliefs by Donatello and Ghiberti.

Piazza del Duomo. ✆ **050-560547.** Admission 5€ ($5.75). Nov–Feb daily 9am–4:30pm; Mar and Oct daily 9am–5:30pm; Apr–Sept daily 8am–7:30pm. Closed Dec 25–Jan 1. Bus: A or 3.

Pinacoteca Nazionale (Picture Gallery) ★★   Housed in the 14th-century Palazzo Buonsignori, the Pinacoteca contains a collection of the Sienese school of painting, which once rivaled that of Florence. Displayed are some of the giants of the pre-Renaissance. The principal treasures are on the second floor, where

Siena

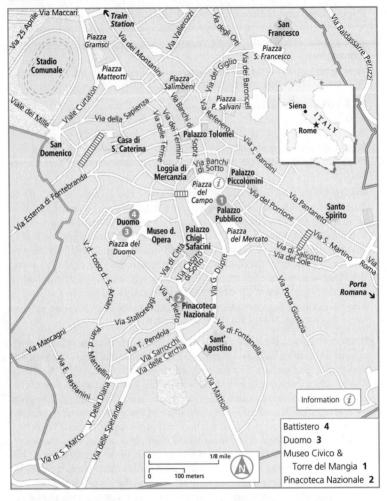

Battistero **4**
Duomo **3**
Museo Civico & Torre del Mangia **1**
Pinacoteca Nazionale **2**

you'll contemplate the artistry of Duccio. The gallery is rich in the art of the 14th-century Lorenzetti brothers, Ambrogio and Pietro. Ambrogio is represented by an *Annunciation* and a *Crucifix,* but one of his most celebrated works is an almond-eyed *Madonna and Bambino* surrounded by saints and angels. Pietro's most important entry is an altarpiece—*The Madonna of the Carmine*—made for a church in Siena in 1329. Simone Martini's *Madonna and Child* is damaged but still one of the best-known paintings here.

In the Palazzo Buonsignori, Via San Pietro 29. © **0577-281161.** Admission 4€ ($4.60). Mon 8:30am–1:30pm; Tues–Sat 8:30am–7pm; Sun 8:30am–1:30pm. Bus: A.

PISA ★★★

Few buildings in the world have captured imaginations as much as the **Leaning Tower of Pisa,** one of the most instantly recognizable buildings in the world. The Leaning Tower is a landmark powerful enough to entice visitors to call at Pisa, and once here, they find many other sights to explore as well.

ESSENTIALS

GETTING THERE   Trains link Pisa and Florence every hour (trip time: 1 hr.); one-way fare is 4.15€ ($4.75). From Florence, motorists take the autostrada west (A-11) to the intersection (A-12) going south to Pisa.

VISITOR INFORMATION   The **tourist information office** is at Via Carlo Cammeo 2 (© **050-560464**), open March through October Monday through Saturday from 9am to 7pm; off season, Monday through Saturday from 9am to 6pm. There's another office at Piazza della Stazione (© **050-42291**), open daily from 9am to 7pm.

WHERE TO DINE

Al Ristoro dei Vecchi Macelli ✦ INTERNATIONAL/PISAN   Near Piazzetta di Vecchi Macelli is the best restaurant in Pisa. After selecting from a choice of two dozen varieties of seafood antipasti, you can enjoy a homemade pasta with scallops and zucchini or fish-stuffed ravioli in shrimp sauce. Other dishes are gnocchi with pesto and shrimp, and roast veal with a velvety truffle-flavored cream sauce.

Via Volturno 49. © **050-20424.** Reservations required. Main courses 10€–15€ ($12–$17); fixed-price menu 45€ ($52) and 65€ ($75). AE, DC, MC, V. Thurs–Sun noon–3pm and 8–10:30pm. Bus: 1.

SEEING THE SIGHTS

In the Middle Ages, Pisa reached the apex of its power as a maritime republic before it eventually fell to its rivals, Florence and Genoa. Its greatest legacy remains at **Piazza del Duomo** ✦✦✦, which D'Annunzio labeled Piazza dei Miracoli (miracles). Here you'll find an ensemble of the top three attractions—original "Pisan-Romanesque" buildings, including the Duomo, the Baptistery, and the Leaning Tower itself.

La Torre di Pisa (Leaning Tower) ✦✦✦   Construction of this eight-story campanile began in 1174 by Bonanno, and a persistent legend is that the architect deliberately intended the bell tower to lean (that claim is undocumented). Another legend is that Galileo let objects of different weights fall from the tower, then timed their descent to prove his theories on bodies in motion. The tower floats on a sandy base of water-soaked clay; it leans at least 5m (16 ft.) from perpendicular. If it stood up straight, the tower would measure about 56m (185 ft.) tall. In 1990, the government closed the Tower and began measures to keep it from falling. The tower was reopened in 2001 to guided tours (see "Climbing the Leaning Tower," below).

Piazza del Duomo 17. © **050-560547.** Fax 050-560505. www.duomo.pisa.it. Admission 15€ ($17). Only a group of 40 admitted at a time. Children under age 8 not admitted. Winter daily 9am–5:50pm; summer 8am–8pm. Bus: A or 3

Tips **Climbing the Leaning Tower**

Late in 2001, the **Leaning Tower** reopened to guided tours of up to 30 visitors each. The 40-minute tour takes you up a narrow, winding, 294-step staircase to the summit. As the number of visitors is strictly limited, it is strongly suggested you purchase tickets in advance. Reservations are available via e-mail (primaziale@sirius.pisa.it) and may be available through the Tower's website (http://torre.duomo.pisa.it). For up-to-date information, check with the **Italian Government Tourist Board (www.italiantourism.com), www. pisaonline.it,** or the very useful Unofficial Leaning Tower of Pisa website (www.endex.com/gf/buildings/ltpisa/ltpisa.html).

Il Duomo ★★ Dating from 1063, the Duomo was designed by Buschetto, though Rainaldo in the 13th century erected the unusual facade with its four layers of open-air arches that diminish in size as they ascend. The cathedral is marked by three bronze doors—rhythmic in line—that replaced those destroyed in a fire in 1596. In the restored interior, the chief art treasure is the pulpit by Giovanni Pisano, finished in 1310. There are other treasures, too: Galileo's lamp (according to unreliable tradition, the Pisa-born astronomer used the chandelier to formulate his laws of the pendulum); mosaics in the apse said to have been designed by Cimabue; the tomb of Henry VII of Luxembourg; *St. Agnes* by Andrea del Sarto; *Descent from the Cross* by Il Sodoma; and a Crucifix by Giambologna.

Piazza del Duomo 17. © 050-560547. Admission 2€ ($2.30) Nov–Feb Mon–Sat 10am–12:45pm and 3–4:30pm, Sun 1–4:30pm; Oct and Mar Mon–Sat 10am–5:30pm, Sun 1–5:30pm; Apr–Sept Mon–Sat 10am–7:30pm, Sun 1–7pm. Sightseeing visits are discouraged during Masses and religious rites. Bus: A or 3.

Battistero (Baptistery) ★★★ Begun in 1153, the Baptistery is like a Romanesque crown. Although it's most beautiful on the exterior, with its arches and columns, venture inside to see the hexagonal pulpit made by Nicola Pisano in 1260. Supported by pillars resting on the backs of three marble lions, the pulpit contains bas-reliefs of the Crucifixion, the Adoration of the Magi, the Presentation of the Christ Child at the Temple, and the Last Judgment (many angels have lost their heads over the years).

Piazza del Duomo. © 050-560547. Admission 5€ ($5.75). Apr–Sept daily 8am–8pm; Oct–Mar daily 9am–5pm. Closed Dec 25–Jan 1. Bus: 1.

Museo Nazionale di San Matteo ★★ Near Piazza Mazzini, the National Museum contains a good assortment of paintings and sculpture, many dating from the 13th century to the 16th century. In the museum are statues by Giovanni Pisano; Simone Martini's *Madonna and Child with Saints,* a polyptych; Nino Pisano's *Madonna de Latte,* a marble sculpture; Masaccio's *St. Paul,* painted in 1426; Domenico Ghirlandaio's two *Madonna and Saints* depictions; works by Strozzi and Alessandro Magnasco; and old copies of works by Jan and Pieter Bruegel.

Piazzetta San Matteo 1 (near Piazza Mazzini). © 050-541865. Admission 4€ ($4.60). Tues–Sat 8:30am–7:30pm; Sun 8:30am–1pm. Closed Dec 25, Jan 1, May 1, and Aug 15. Bus: 2, 7, or 13.

SAN GIMIGNANO ★★★

The golden lily of the Middle Ages is called the Manhattan of Tuscany since it preserves 13 of its noble towers, giving it a skyscraper skyline. It lies 42km (26 miles) northwest of Siena and 55km (34 miles) southwest of Florence. Since you'll want to spend as much time here as possible, an overnight stay is recommended.

ESSENTIALS

GETTING THERE Poggibonsi, serviced by regular trains from Florence and Siena, is the **rail** station nearest to San Gimignano. At Poggibonsi, buses depart from in front of the station at frequent intervals to the center of San Gimignano. For information, call © 0577-204111. **Buses** operated by **TRA-IN** (© 0577-204111) service San Gimignano from Florence with a change at Poggibonsi (trip time: 75 min.). The same company also operates service from Siena, with a change at Poggibonsi (50 min.). In San Gimignano, buses stop at Piazzale Montemaggio, outside Porta San Giovanni, the southern gate. You'll have to walk into the center, as vehicles aren't allowed in most of the town's core.

If you've got a **car,** leave Florence (trip time: 1½ hr.) or Siena (1¼ hr.) by the Firenze–Siena autostrada and drive to Poggibonsi, where you'll need to cut west along a secondary route (S324) to San Gimignano.

VISITOR INFORMATION Go to **Associazione Pro Loco,** Piazza del Duomo 1 (© **0577-940008;** www.sangimignano.com), open November through February daily from 9am to 1pm and 2 to 6pm (Mar–Oct to 7pm).

WHERE TO STAY

Hotel Bel Soggiorno *Value* Though it's no longer the town's best, this hotel is still a good affordable alternative. The Gigli family has run it since 1886 (there's not as much antique charm as you'd think, though). The rear guest rooms and dining room open onto the lower pastureland and the bottom of the village. The medium-size rooms have beds verging on the oversoft, but the management is quite friendly. The best 10 rooms are those with private balconies. All the tiled bathrooms have tub/shower combos. In summer you'll be asked to have your meals at the hotel (the cuisine is excellent). Medieval in style, the dining room boasts murals depicting a wild boat hunt (see "Where to Dine," below).

Via San Giovanni 91, 53037 San Gimignano. © 0577-940375. Fax 0577-907521. www.hotelbelsoggiorno. it. 22 units. 94€ ($108) double; 170€ ($196) suite. AE, DC, MC, V. Parking 10€ ($12). Closed Jan–Feb. **Amenities:** Restaurant; bar; wine cellar; laundry service. *In room:* A/C, TV, minibar, hair dryer.

Relais Santa Chiara *★* This solid, comfortable hotel lies in a residential neighborhood about a 10-minute walk south of the medieval ramparts. It's the most prestigious place to stay. It's surrounded with elegant gardens and a pool, and its spacious public rooms contain Florentine terra-cotta floors and mosaics. Though the hotel is relatively new, the furnishings and ambience blend harmoniously with the Tuscan countryside. Each unit comes with a well-organized private bathroom with tub and shower.

Via Matteotti 15, 53037 San Gimignano. © 0577-940701. Fax 0577-942096. www.rsc.it. 41 units, some with shower only. 134€–215€ ($154–$247) double; 190€–265€ ($219–$305) suite. Rates include buffet breakfast. AE, DC, MC, V. Free parking. **Amenities:** Bar; outdoor pool; gym; sauna; 24-hr. room service; babysitting; laundry service; dry cleaning; rooms for those with limited mobility. *In room:* A/C, TV, minibar, hair dryer, safe.

WHERE TO DINE

Ristorante Bel Soggiorno TUSCAN Thanks to windows overlooking the countryside and a devoted use of fresh ingredients from nearby farms, you'll get a strong sense of Tuscany's agrarian bounty here. Two of the most appealing specialties (available only late summer to late winter) are roasted wild boar with red wine and mixed vegetables, and pappardelle pasta garnished with a savory ragout of pheasant.

In the Hotel Bel Soggiorno, Via San Giovanni 91. © 0577-940375. Reservations recommended. Main courses 14€–16€ ($16–$18); fixed-price menu 50€ ($58). AE, DC, MC, V. Thurs–Tues 7:30–10pm.

Ristorante Le Terrazze TUSCAN The newer of this restaurant's two dining rooms has large windows overlooking the old town and the Val d'Elsa. The setting is one of a country inn, and the food features an assortment of produce from the surrounding farms. Soups and pastas make fine beginnings, and specialties of the house include delectable items like sliced filet of wild boar with polenta and Chianti, breast of goose with walnut sauce, *vitello alla Cisterna* (veal with buttered beans), and Florence-style steaks.

In La Cisterna, Piazza della Cisterna 24. © 0577-940328. Reservations required. Main courses 13€–19€ ($15–$22). AE, DC, MC, V. Wed 7:30–10pm; Thurs–Mon 12:30–2:30pm and 7:30–9:30pm. Nov 1–Jan 6 open only Mon and Wed–Sat 7:30–9:30pm. Closed Jan 7–Mar 10.

EXPLORING THE TOWN

In the town center is the palazzo-flanked **Piazza della Cisterna** ⭐⭐, so named because of the 13th-century cistern in its heart. Connected with the irregularly shaped square is its satellite, **Piazza del Duomo** ⭐⭐, whose medieval architecture—towers and palaces—is almost unchanged. It's the most beautiful spot in town. On the square, the **Palazzo del Popolo's Torre Grossa** ⭐, at 54m (178 ft.), is believed to have been the tallest "skyscraper" in town.

Note: A combination ticket, available at any of the sites below, allows admission to all of them for 10€ ($12).

Duomo Collegiata o Basilica di Santa Maria Assunta ⭐   Residents of San Gimignano still call this a Duomo (cathedral), even though it was demoted to a "Collegiata" once the town lost its bishop. Plain and austere on the outside, it's richly decorated inside. Retreat inside to a world of tiger-striped arches and a galaxy of gold stars. Head for the north aisle, where in the 1360s Bartolo di Fredi depicted scenes from the Old Testament. Two memorable ones are *The Trials of Job* and *Noah with the Animals*. In the right aisle, panels trace scenes from the life of Christ—the Kiss of Judas, the Last Supper, the Flagellation, and the Crucifixion. The chief attraction is the **Chapel of Santa Fina,** designed by Giuliano and Benedetto da Maiano. Michelangelo's fresco teacher, Domenico Ghirlandaio, frescoed it with scenes from the life of a local girl, Fina, who became the town's patron saint.

Piazza del Duomo. ⓒ **0577-283048.** Duomo free admission; library 1.50€ ($1.75). Duomo Nov–Mar 15 daily 8am–1pm and 2:30–5pm (Mar 16–Oct to 7:30pm). Library Mar 15–Oct 31 daily 9am–7:30pm; Nov 1–Mar 14 daily 10am–1pm and 2:30–5pm. Closed Sun mornings, Jan 1, and Dec 25. Bus: A.

Museo Civico (Civic Museum) ⭐   This museum is installed upstairs in the Palazzo del Popolo (town hall). Most notable is the **Sala di Dante,** where the White Guelph–supporting poet spoke out for his cause in 1300. Look for one of the masterpieces of San Gimignano—the *Maestà* (Madonna enthroned) by Lippo Memmi (later touched up by Gozzoli). The first large room upstairs contains another masterpiece: a *Madonna in Glory,* with Sts. Gregory and Benedict, painted by Pinturicchio. On the other side of it are two depictions of the *Annunciation* by Filippino Lippi.

Passing through the Museo Civico, you can scale the **Torre Grossa** and be rewarded with a bird's-eye view of this most remarkable town. The tower, the only one in town you can climb, is open March through October daily from 9:30am to 7:30pm; off season, daily from 10am to 5:30pm. Admission is 4€ ($4.60).

In the Palazzo Faina, Piazza del Duomo 29. ⓒ **0763-341511.** Admission 4.50€ ($5.20) adults; 3€ ($3.45) students, seniors, and children 7–12. Apr 1–Sept 30 daily 9:30am–6pm; Oct 1–Mar 31 Tues–Sun 10am–5pm.

ASSISI ⭐⭐⭐

Ideally placed on the rise to Mount Subasio, watched over by the medieval **Rocca Maggiore,** this purple-fringed Umbrian hill town retains a mystical air. The site of many a pilgrimage, Assisi is forever linked in legend with its native son, St. Francis. The gentle saint founded the Franciscan order and shares honors with St. Catherine of Siena as the patron saint of Italy. But he's remembered by many, even non-Christians, as a lover of nature (his preaching to an audience of birds is one of the legends of his life). Dante compared him to John the Baptist. St. Francis put Assisi on the map, and making a pilgrimage here is one of the highlights of a visit to Umbria.

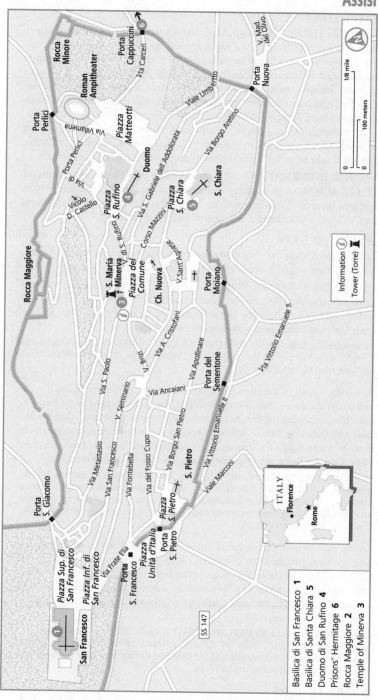

Assisti

Basilica di San Francesco **1**
Basilica di Santa Chiara **5**
Duomo di San Rufino **4**
Prisons' Hermitage **6**
Rocca Maggiore **2**
Temple of Minerva **3**

Information (i)
Tower (Torre) 🔔

ITALY
• Florence
★ Rome

SS 147

ESSENTIALS

GETTING THERE   Although there's no rail station in Assisi, the town, which lies 177km (110 miles) north of Rome and 24km (15 miles) southeast of Perugia, is but a 30-minute bus or taxi ride from the nearby Santa Maria degli Angeli rail station. Buses depart at 30-minute intervals for Piazza Matteotti, in the heart of Assisi. **Trains** between Florence and Assisi usually require a transfer at Terontola. Frequent **buses** connect Perugia with Assisi (trip time: 1 hr.). One bus a day arrives from Rome. Two buses pull in from Florence (2½ hr.).

If you have a **car,** you can be in Assisi in 30 minutes from Perugia by taking S3 southwest. At the junction of Route 147, just follow the signs toward Assisi. But you'll have to park outside the town's core, as it's usually closed to traffic.

VISITOR INFORMATION   The **tourist office** is at Piazza del Comune 12 (℗ 075-812534), open Monday through Friday from 8am to 2pm and 3:30 to 6:30pm, Saturday from 9am to 1pm and 3:30 to 6:30pm, and Sunday from 9am to 1pm. The office is closed December 25 and January 1.

WHERE TO STAY

Space in Assisi tends to be tight, so reservations are vital. For such a small town, however, it has a good number of accommodations.

Albergo Ristorante del Viaggiatore *Value*   This ancient town house is among the tops for value. It's been totally renovated, though the stone walls and arched entryways of the lobby hint at its age. The high-ceilinged rooms are spacious and very contemporary, with shower-only bathrooms.

Via San Antonio 14, 06081 Assisi. ℗ **075-816297** or 075-812424. Fax 075-813051. 12 units, shower only. 71€ ($82) double. Half board 52€ ($60) per person. Rates include breakfast. DC, MC, V. **Amenities:** Restaurant; bar. *In room:* A/C, TV, hair dryer.

Hotel dei Priori   Opened in 1923, this hotel keeps up with the times. It occupies one of the town's most historic buildings, the 17th-century Palazzo Nepis. A homelike, somewhat old-fashioned Umbrian atmosphere prevails. Marble staircases and floors, terra-cotta vaulted ceilings, and stone-arched doorways remain from its seigniorial palazzo heyday. Many of the rooms are a bit small, however. Most of the tiled private bathrooms contain tubs; others have showers.

Corso Mazzini 15, 06081 Assisi. ℗ **075-812237.** Fax 075-816804. www.assisi-hotel.com. 34 units. 105€–190€ ($121–$219) double; 150€–190€ ($173–$219) suite. Rates include breakfast. AE, DC, MC, V. Parking 10€ ($12) nearby. **Amenities:** Restaurant (only for hotel guests; closed Nov–Mar); bar; 24-hr. room service; babysitting; laundry service; dry cleaning; nonsmoking rooms; rooms for those with limited mobility. *In room:* A/C, TV, minibar, hair dryer, safe.

Hotel Sole   For Umbrian hospitality and a general down-home feeling, the Sole is a winner in the heart of medieval Assisi—comfortable but traditional, a bit tattered but affordable. Rooms are rather basic and feature aging bathrooms, half with tub, half with shower. We prefer the rooms in the 15th-century palazzo as opposed to those in the more sterile and nondescript annex, although the latter is serviced by an elevator.

Corso Mazzini 35, 06081 Assisi. ℗ **075-812373** or 075-812922. Fax 075-813706. www.assisihotelsole.com. 38 units, shower only. 62€ ($71) double; 83€ ($95) triple. Half board (Apr–Nov) 50€ ($58) per person. AE, DC, MC, V. **Amenities:** Well-recommended restaurant (closed Dec–Mar); bar; breakfast-only room service; 1 room for those with limited mobility. *In room:* TV, safe.

WHERE TO DINE

Il Medioevo ✦ UMBRIAN/INTERNATIONAL   Assisi's best restaurant is an authentic medieval gem. Alberto Falsinotti and his family prepare superb versions of Umbrian recipes whose origins are as old as Assisi itself. Specialties are *tortel-loni* (a kind of dumpling) stuffed with minced turkey, veal, and beef and served with butter and Parmigiano Reggiano; gnocchi stuffed with ricotta and spinach and sprinkled with Parmigiano Reggiano; roasted rabbit with red-wine sauce and truffles; roast lamb with rosemary, potatoes, and herbs; homemade pasta stuffed with black truffles; and grilled filet of veal with herb sauce.

Via Arco dei Priori 4B. ⓒ **075-813068.** Reservations recommended. Main courses 9€–14€ ($10–$16); fixed-price menu 18€ ($21). AE, DC, MC, V. Thurs–Tues noon–2:30pm and 7:30–10pm. Closed Jan 7–Feb 7 and July 1–20.

Ristorante Buca di San Francesco UMBRIAN/ITALIAN Hospitable and evocative of the Middle Ages, this restaurant occupies a cave near the foundation of a 12th-century palace. There're about 100 seats in the dining room and another 60 in the garden, overlooking Assisi's historic center. Menu items change frequently, but what you're likely to find are spaghetti *alla buca* (with exotic mushrooms and meat sauce); *umbricelli* (big noodles) with asparagus sauce; *cannelloni* (stuffed pasta tubes baked in the oven) with ricotta, spinach, and tomatoes; *car-lacca* (baked crepes stuffed with cheese, prosciutto, and roasted veal); and *piccione alla sisana* (roasted pigeon with olive oil, capers, and aromatic herbs).

Via Brizi 1. ⓒ **075-812204.** Reservations recommended. Main courses 8.50€–16€ ($9.80–$18). AE, DC, MC, V. Tues–Sun noon–2:30pm and 7–10pm. Closed July 1–20.

EXPLORING THE TOWN

In the heart of Assisi, **Piazza del Comune** ★ is a dream for a lover of architecture from the 12th century to the 14th century. On the square is a pagan structure, with six Corinthian columns, called the **Tempio di Minerva (Temple of Minerva)** ★, from the 1st century B.C. With Minerva-like wisdom, the people of Assisi turned it into a baroque church inside so as not to offend the devout. Adjoining the temple is the 13th-century **Torre (Tower),** built by Ghibelline supporters. The site is open daily from 7am to noon and 2:30pm to dusk. In the wake of the earthquakes, the tower can no longer be visited.

Basilica di San Francesco ★★ This Gothic church was finished in the 14th century for the Franciscans. Inside is a Piero della Francesca masterpiece, a restored fresco cycle called *Legend of the True Cross* ★★★. His frescoes are remarkable for their grace, clearness, dramatic light effects, well-chosen colors, and ascetic severity. Vasari credited della Francesca as a master of the laws of geometry and perspective, and Sir Kenneth Clark called Piero's frescoes "the most perfect morning light in all Renaissance painting." The frescoes depict the burial of Adam, Solomon receiving the queen of Sheba at the court (the most memorable scene), the dream of Constantine with the descent of an angel, and the triumph of the Holy Cross with Heraclius, among other subjects.

Piazza San Francesco. ⓒ **0575-20630,** or 0575-900404 for reservations. Free admission. Daily 8:30am–noon and 2–6pm. Guided 30-min. visits to the frescoes 5€ ($5.75). Mon–Sat 9:30–11:30am and 3–5pm; Sun 3–5pm.

Eremo delle Carceri (Prisons' Hermitage) ★★ Eremo delle Carceri dates from the 14th and 15th centuries. The "prison" isn't a penal institution but rather a spiritual retreat. It's believed that St. Francis retired to this spot for meditation and prayer. Out back is a moss-covered gnarled ilex (live oak) more than 1,000 years old, where St. Francis is believed to have blessed the birds, after which they flew in the four major compass directions to symbolize that Franciscans, in coming centuries, would spread from Assisi all over the world. The friary contains some faded frescoes. One of the handful of friars who still inhabit the retreat will show you through.

About 4km (2½ miles) east of Assisi (out Via Eremo delle Carceri), on Via Eremo delle Carceri. © 075-812301. Free admission (donations accepted). Apr–Oct daily 6:30am–7pm; Nov–Mar daily 6:30am–6pm.

Basilica di Santa Chiara (Clare) ★★ This basilica is dedicated to "the little plant of Blessed Francis," as St. Clare liked to describe herself. Born in 1193 into one of the noblest families of Assisi, Clare gave all her wealth to the poor and founded, together with St. Francis, the Order of the Poor Clares. She was canonized by Pope Alexander IV in 1255, and Pope Pius XII declared her Patroness of Television in 1958. She merited that last designation because, in her later years, when she was too infirm to attend Mass, she reportedly saw an image of the service broadcast on a wall in her room. Though many of the frescoes that once adorned the basilica have been completely or partially destroyed, much remains that's worthy of note. The basilica also houses the remains of St. Clare as well as the crucifix under which St. Francis received his command from above.

Piazza di Santa Chiara 1. © 075-812282. Free admission. Nov–Mar daily 6:30am–noon and 2–6:30pm; Apr–Oct daily 6:30am–noon and 2–7pm.

4 Venice ★★★

Venice is a preposterous monument to both the folly and the obstinacy of humankind. It shouldn't exist, but it does, much to the delight of thousands of tourists, gondoliers, lace makers, hoteliers, restaurateurs, and glassblowers.

Fleeing the barbarians centuries ago, Venetians left dry-dock and drifted out to a flotilla of "uninhabitable" islands in the lagoon. Survival was difficult enough, but no Venetian has ever settled for mere survival. The remote ancestors of today's inhabitants created the world's most beautiful and unusual city.

However, it's sinking at a rate of about 6cm (2½ in.) per decade, and it's estimated that one-third of the city's art will have deteriorated hopelessly within the next few decades if action isn't taken to save it. Clearly, Venice is in peril, under assault by uncontrolled tides, pollution, atmospheric acid, and old age.

This is one of the most enchantingly evocative cities on earth, but you must pay a price for all this beauty. In the sultry heat of the Adriatic in summer, the canals become a smelly stew. Steamy, overcrowded July and August are the worst times to visit; May and June or September and October are much more ideal.

ESSENTIALS
GETTING THERE All roads lead not necessarily to Rome but, in this case, to the docks of mainland Venice. The arrival scene at the unattractive Piazzale Roma is filled with nervous expectation, and even the most veteran traveler can become confused. Whether you arrive by train, bus, car, or airport limousine, there's one common denominator—everyone walks to the nearby docks to select a method of transport to his or her hotel. The cheapest way is by vaporetto, the more expensive by gondola or motor launch.

By Plane You'll land at Mestre, with its **Marco Polo Aeroporto** (© 041-2606111; www.veniceairport.it). **Boats** depart every hour directly from the airport, taking you to a terminal near Piazza San Marco. The fare is 9.50€ ($11).

It's less expensive to take a **bus** from the airport to Piazzale Roma (© 041-5287886), a trip of less than 8km (5 miles); one-way fare is 2€ ($2.30). Departures are usually every 30 minutes (trip time: 30 min.). Once at Piazzale Roma, you can make transportation connections to most parts of Venice, including the Lido.

Tips **Finding an Address**

The system of addresses in Venice is so confusing it's probably known only to the postman, if that. The best thing to do is to arm yourself with a good map, such as the **Falk** map of Venice, which is pocket size and available in many kiosks and bookstores.

By Train   Trains pull into the **Stazione di Santa Lucia,** at Piazzale Roma, from Rome (trip time: 5¼ hr.), Milan (3½ hr.), Florence (4 hr.), and Bologna (2 hr.). For information and timetables, contact **FS** (© 848-888088; www.trenitalia.it). The best and least expensive way to get from the station to the rest of town is to take a vaporetto, which departs near the main entrance to the station.

By Bus   Buses arrive from points on the mainland of Italy at **Piazzale Roma.** For information about schedules, contact **ACTV** at Piazzale Roma (© 041-5287886; www.actv.it). If you're coming from a distant city in Italy, it's better to take the train.

By Car   Venice has autostrada links with the rest of Italy, with direct routes from such cities as Trieste (driving time: 1½ hr.), Milan (3 hr.), and Bologna (2 hr.). Bologna is 151km (94 miles) southwest of Venice; Milan, 265km (165 miles) west of Venice; and Trieste, 156km (97 miles) east. Rome is 526km (327 miles) to the southwest.

If you arrive by car, there're several multi-tiered parking areas at the terminus where the roads end and the canals begin. One of the most visible is the **Garage San Marco,** Piazzale Roma (© 041-5235101), near the vaporetto, gondola, and motor-launch docks. You'll be charged 18€ ($21) for 12 hours, 24€ ($28) for 24 hours.

VISITOR INFORMATION   You can get information at the **Azienda di Promozione Turistica,** Castello 4421 (© 041-5298711; www.turismovenezia.it). There's another office at Santa Lucia railway station. Both are open daily from 9am to 1pm and 1:30 to 5pm.

CITY LAYOUT   Venice, 4km (2½ miles) from the Italian mainland and 2km (1¼ miles) from the Adriatic, is an archipelago of some 117 islands. Most visitors, however, concern themselves only with **Piazza San Marco** and its vicinity. In fact, the entire city has only one piazza: San Marco. Venice is divided into six quarters that locals call *sestieri.* These include the most frequented, San Marco, but also Santa Croce, San Polo, Castello, Cannaregio, and Dorsoduro, the last of which has been compared to New York's Greenwich Village.

Many of the so-called streets of Venice are actually **canals,** some 150 in all. A canal is called a *rio,* and a total of 400 bridges span these canals. If Venice has a main street, it's the **Grand Canal,** which is spanned by three bridges: the Rialto, the Academy Bridge, and the stone Railway Bridge. The canal splits Venice into two unequal parts.

South of the section called Dorsoduro, which is south of the Grand Canal, is the **Canale della Giudecca,** a major channel separating Dorsoduro from the large island of La Giudecca. At the point where the Canale della Giudecca meets the Canale di San Marco, you'll spot the little **Isola di San Giorgio Maggiore,** with a church by Palladio. The most visited islands in the lagoon, aside from the **Lido,** are **Murano, Burano,** and **Torcello.**

Once you land and explore Piazza San Marco and its satellite, Piazzetta San Marco, you can head down **Riva degli Schiavoni,** with its deluxe and first-class

Venice

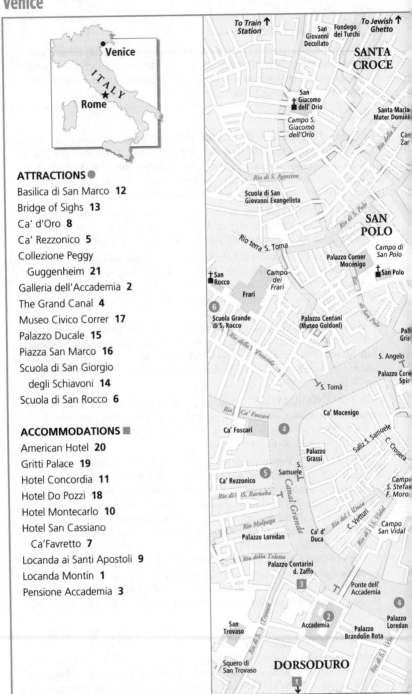

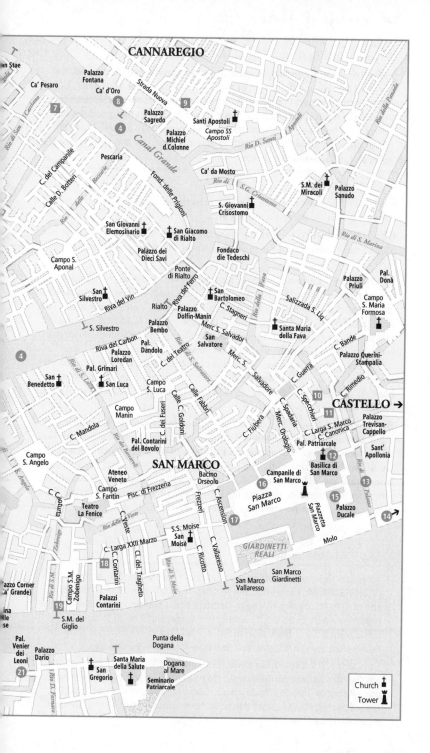

Tips Getting Around by Gondola

When riding in a **gondola,** two major agreements have to be reached: the price of the ride and the length of the trip. The official rate is 60€ ($69), but virtually no one pays that amount; prices really start at about 75€ ($86) for up to 50 minutes. Two major stations at which you can hire gondolas are Piazza San Marco (© **041-5200685**) and the Ponte Rialto (© **041-5224904**). Both organize gondola tours, lasting about 50 minutes and costing from 60€ to 75€ ($69–$86) per person.

---

hotels, or follow the signs along the **Mercerie,** the major shopping artery, which leads to the Rialto, site of the market area.

GETTING AROUND   Walking is the only way to explore Venice unless you plan to see it from a boat on the Grand Canal. Everybody walks in Venice—there's no other way.

By Vaporetto   The motorboats, or *vaporetti,* of Venice provide inexpensive and frequent, if not always fast, transportation in this canal-riddled city. An *accelerato* is a vessel that makes every stop and a *diretto* makes only express stops. The average fare is 3€ ($3.45). In summer, the vaporetti are often fiercely crowded. Pick up a map of the system from the tourist office. There's frequent service daily from 7am to midnight, then hourly from midnight to 7am.

Visitors to Venice may avail yourselves of discount passes, which must be validated before use and shown together with the matrix (the last ticket of the booklet). An all-day ticket costs 9€ ($10) and goes up to 18€ ($21) for 3 days, or 30€ ($35) for 1 week.

By Water Taxi/Motor Launch   The city's many private motor launches are called *taxi acquei.* You may or may not have the cabin of one of these sleek vessels to yourself, since the captains fill their boats with as many passengers as the law allows before taking off. The price of a transit by water taxi from Piazzale Roma (the road and rail terminus) to Piazza San Marco begins at 40€ ($46) for one to six passengers, or else 70€ ($81) from the airport. You can also call for a taxi acquei—try **Cooperativa San Marco** at © **041-5222303.**

FAST FACTS: Venice

American Express   The office is at Salizzada San Moisè, San Marco 1471 (© **041-5200844;** vaporetto: San Marco). The staff can arrange city tours and mail handling. From May to October, hours are Monday through Saturday from 8am to 8pm for currency exchange, and 9am to 5:30pm for all other transactions; from November to April, hours are Monday through Friday from 9am to 5:30pm, and Saturday from 9am to 12:30pm.

Consulates   The **United Kingdom** consulate is at Dorsoduro 1051, at the foot of the Accademia Bridge (© **041-5227207;** vaporetto: Accademia), open Monday through Friday from 10am to noon and 2 to 3pm. The **United States, Canada,** and **Australia** have consulates in Milan, about 3 hours away by train.

Currency Exchange There are many banks in Venice where you can exchange money. You might try the **Banco Commerciale Italiana,** Via XXII Marzo, San Marco 2188 (☎ **041-5296811;** vaporetto: San Marco), or **Banco San Marco,** Calle Larga San Marco, San Marco 383 (☎ **041-5293711;** vaporetto: San Marco). Hours are Monday through Friday from 8:30am to 1:30pm and 2:45 to 4pm.

Dentist/Doctor Your best bet is to have your hotel set up an appointment with an English-speaking dentist or doctor. The American Express office and the British consulate also have lists. Also see "Hospitals," below.

Drugstores If you need a drugstore in the middle of the night, call ☎ **192** for information about which one is open (pharmacies take turns staying open late). A well-recommended central one is **International Pharmacy,** Via XXII Marzo, San Marco 2067 (☎ **041-5222311;** vaporetto: San Marco).

Emergencies Call ☎ **113** for the police, ☎ **118** for an ambulance, or ☎ **115** to report a fire.

Hospitals Contact the **Ospedale Civile Santi Giovanni e Paolo,** Campo Santi Giovanni e Paolo in Castello (☎ **041-785111;** vaporetto: San Toma), staffed with English-speaking doctors 24 hours a day.

Post Office The main post office is at Fondaco dei Tedeschi (☎ **041-2717111;** vaporetto: Rialto), near the Rialto Bridge. It's open Monday through Saturday from 8:15am to 5pm. For information call ☎ **160.**

Safety The curse of Venice is the pickpocket. Violent crime is rare, but because of the overcrowding on vaporetti and even on the small, narrow streets, it's easy to pick pockets. Purse snatchings are commonplace as well. Secure your valuables, and if your hotel has safes, keep them locked there when not needed.

Telephones The **country code** for Italy is **39.** The **city code** for Venice is **041,** which is the code you'll use every time you dial a party located within Venice, regardless of whether you're within the city limits or not. We emphasize that newly imposed technologies will require the use of the "0" and then "41" for calls to parties in Venice, regardless of whether you're within the city limits of Venice or not. For additional information, see "Fast Facts: Rome," earlier in this chapter.

WHERE TO STAY
NEAR PIAZZA SAN MARCO
Very Expensive

Gritti Palace ✦✦✦ In a stately setting on the Grand Canal, Gritti Palace is the renovated palazzo of the 15th-century doge Andrea Gritti. It's a bit starchy but is topped only by the Cipriani in terms of prestige. "Our home in Venice" to Ernest Hemingway, it has for years drawn a clientele of theatrical, literary, political, and royal figures. The range and variety of the rooms seem almost limitless, from elaborate suites to relatively small singles. But in every case the stamp of glamour is evident. For a splurge, ask for Hemingway's old suite or the Doge Suite, once occupied by Somerset Maugham. All accommodations come with luxurious bathrooms with tub/shower combos.

Campo Santa Maria del Giglio, San Marco 2467, 30124 Venezia. ☎ **800/325-3535** in the U.S., or 041-794611. Fax 041-5200942. www.hotelgrittivenice.com. 91 units. 756€–819€ ($869–$942) double; from 1,892€

($2,176) suite. Rates include breakfast. AE, DC, MC, V. Vaporetto: Santa Maria del Giglio. **Amenities:** Elegant restaurant and bar; 24-hr. concierge and butler service; private boat launches and sightseeing tours; salon; 24-hr. room service; babysitting; laundry service; dry cleaning; nonsmoking rooms. *In room:* A/C, TV, minibar, hair dryer, safe.

Expensive

Hotel Concordia ★　The Concordia is the only hotel in Venice that has rooms overlooking St. Mark's Square. A series of gold-plated marble steps takes you to the lobby, where you'll find a comfortable bar area. All rooms are decorated in a Venetian antique style and contain hand-painted furnishings and small Murano chandeliers, plus small bathrooms with tubs.

Calle Larga, San Marco 367, 30124 Venezia. ℂ 041-5206866. Fax 041-5206775. 57 units, some with shower only. 400€–500€ ($460–$575) double; 500€–600€ ($575–$690) suite. Rates include buffet breakfast. AE, DC, MC, V. Vaporetto: San Marco. **Amenities:** Restaurant; bar; 24-hr. room service; babysitting; laundry service; dry cleaning; nonsmoking rooms. *In room:* A/C, TV, dataport, minibar, hair dryer, safe.

Moderate

Hotel Do Pozzi　Small, modernized, and centrally located just a short stroll from the Grand Canal and Piazza San Marco, this place is more like a country tavern than a hotel. Its original structure is 200 years old, and it opens onto a paved front courtyard with potted greenery. The sitting and dining rooms are furnished with antiques (and near antiques) mixed with utilitarian modern decor. A major refurbishing has given everything a fresh touch, including the shower-only bathrooms.

Via XXII Marzo, 2373 San Marco, 30124 Venezia. ℂ 041-5207855. Fax 041-5229413. www.hoteldopozzi.it. 35 units, some with shower only. 130€–210€ ($150–$242) double. Rates include breakfast. AE, DC, MC, V. Vaporetto: Santa Maria del Giglio. **Amenities:** Dining room; bar; babysitting; laundry service; dry cleaning. *In room:* A/C, TV, minibar, hair dryer.

Hotel Montecarlo　Although still unremarkable, this hotel is in a vastly improved 17th-century building, just 2 minutes from Piazza San Marco. The upper halls are lined with paintings by Venetian artists. The guest rooms are decorated with Venetian-style furniture and Venetian-glass chandeliers. Some are quite dark, the curse of many Venetian hotels. All have well-kept bathrooms.

Calle dei Specchieri, San Marco 463, 30124 Venezia. ℂ 041-5207144. Fax 041-5207789. www.venicehotel montecarlo.com. 48 units. 108€–300€ ($124–$345) standard double; 400€ ($460) deluxe double. Rates include buffet breakfast. AE, DC, MC, V. Vaporetto: San Marco. **Amenities:** Restaurant; bar; room service (7am–10pm); babysitting; laundry service; nonsmoking rooms. *In room:* A/C, TV, hair dryer, safe.

IN THE DORSODURO
Moderate

American Hotel ★ 🄫ᵥₐₗᵤₑ　Set on a small waterway, the American Hotel (there's nothing American about it) is one of your best budget bets. The modest lobby is filled with murals, warm colors, and antiques, and the location is perfect for anyone wanting to avoid the crowds that descend in summer. Rooms are comfortably furnished in a Venetian style, but vary in size; some of the smaller ones are a bit cramped. Many rooms with private terraces face the canal. Each contains a small bathroom with tub. On the second floor is a beautiful terrace where guests relax over drinks.

Campo San Vio, Accademia 628, 30123 Venezia. ℂ 041-5204733. Fax 041-5204048. www.hotelamerican. com. 30 units. 100€–300€ ($115–$345) double; 150€–310€ ($173–$357) triple; 160€–350€ ($184–$403) suite. Rates include buffet breakfast. AE, MC, V. Vaporetto: Accademia. **Amenities:** Breakfast room; lounge; 24-hr. room service; babysitting; laundry service; dry cleaning; nonsmoking rooms. *In room:* A/C, TV, dataport, hair dryer, safe.

Pensione Accademia ★ (*Value*)   This is the most patrician of the pensioni, in a villa whose garden extends into the angle created by the junction of two canals. Iron fences, twisting vines, and neoclassical sculpture are a part of the setting. There's an upstairs sitting room and a formal rose garden that's visible from the breakfast room. The recently renovated rooms are spacious and decorated with 19th-century furniture. The small tiled bathrooms contain showers.

Fondamenta Bollani, Dorsoduro 1058, 30123 Venezia. (✆) 041-5237846. Fax 041-5239152. www.pensione accademia.it. 27 units, shower only. 130€–233€ ($150–$268) double. Rates include breakfast. AE, DC, MC, V. Vaporetto: Accademia. **Amenities:** Bar; breakfast-only room service; babysitting; laundry service; dry cleaning. *In room:* A/C, TV, hair dryer, safe.

Inexpensive

Locanda Montin ★ (*Finds*)   The well-recommended Locanda Montin is an old-fashioned Venetian inn whose adjoining restaurant is one of the most loved in the area. The hotel is officially listed as a fourth-class hotel because of its lack of in-room amenities aside from a phone, but the accommodations are considerably larger and better than that rating suggests. Reservations are virtually mandatory, because of the reputation of this locanda. Marked only by a small carriage lamp etched with the name of the establishment, the inn is a little difficult to locate but worth the search.

Fondamenta di Borgo, Dorsoduro 1147, 31000 Venezia. (✆) **041-5227151.** Fax 041-5200255. www.locanda montin.com. 11 units, 5 with bathroom. 110€ ($127) double without bathroom; 140€ ($161) double with bathroom. AE, DC, MC, V. Vaporetto: Accademia. **Amenities:** Restaurant; bar.

IN SANTA CROCE
Moderate

Hotel San Cassiano Ca'Favretto ★   San Cassiano Ca'Favretto was once the studio of 19th-century painter Giacomo Favretto. The views from the hotel's gondola pier and from the dining room's porch encompass the lacy facade of the Ca' d'Oro, the most beautiful building in Venice. The hotel was constructed in the 14th century as a palace. The present owner has worked closely with Venetian authorities to preserve the original details. Fifteen of the conservatively decorated rooms overlook one of two canals, and each comes with a neatly kept bathroom with tub.

Calle della Rosa, Santa Croce 2232, 30135 Venezia. (✆) **041-5241768.** Fax 041-721033. www.sancassiano.it. 35 units. 200€–310€ ($230–$357) double. Rates include breakfast. AE, DC, MC, V. Vaporetto: San Stae. **Amenities:** Dining room; bar; room service; babysitting. *In room:* A/C, TV, hair dryer, safe.

IN CANNAREGIO
Expensive

Locanda ai Santi Apostoli ★   If you can't afford the Gritti Palace (and few can), but still fantasize about living in a palazzo overlooking the Grande Canal, near the Rialto, here is a possibility. The Locanda knows the advantage of its location, however, and doesn't come cheap. But it's a lot less expensive than the grand palaces nearby. It's situated on the top floor of a 15th-century building, and the rooms, although simple, are rather inviting. Naturally, the two rooms actually opening onto the Grand Canal are the most requested. Even if you don't have one of these, there's a view from the main salon. All rooms come with a tiled bathroom with shower. Breakfast is the only meal served.

Strada Nuova, Cannaregio 4391, 30131 Venezia. (✆) **041-5212612.** Fax 041-5212611. www.veneziaweb. com/santiapostoli. 11 units, shower only. 180€–230€ ($207–$265) double; 290€–320€ ($334–$368) double with Grand Canal view; 360€–405€ ($414–$466) suite. Rates include breakfast. AE, DC, MC, V. Vaporetto: Ca d'Oro. **Amenities:** Lounge; babysitting; laundry; dry cleaning; nonsmoking rooms. *In room:* A/C, TV, minibar, hair dryer.

WHERE TO DINE
NEAR PIAZZA SAN MARCO
Very Expensive

Harry's Bar ✿✿✿ VENETIAN   Harry's Bar serves the best food in Venice, though Quadri and the Antico Martini (see below) have more elegant atmospheres. Its fame was spread by Ernest Hemingway. A. E. Hotchner, in *Papa Hemingway*, quoted the writer as saying, "We can't eat straight hamburger in a Renaissance palazzo on the Grand Canal." So he ordered a 5-pound "tin of beluga caviar" to, as he said, "take the curse off it." Hemingway would skip the place today, fleeing from the foreign visitors, and the prices would come as a shock even to him. You can have your choice of dining in the bar downstairs or in the room with a view upstairs. We recommend the Venetian fish soup, followed by scampi thermidor with rice pilaf or seafood ravioli.

Calle Vallaresso, San Marco 1323. © **041-5285777**. Reservations required. Main courses 50€–100€ ($58–$115). AE, DC, MC, V. Daily 10:30am–1am. Vaporetto: San Marco.

Expensive

Antico Martini ✿✿✿ VENETIAN/INTERNATIONAL   As the city's leading traditional restaurant, Antico Martini, located near La Fenice, elevates Venetian cuisine to its highest level. The courtyard is favored in summer. An excellent beginning to your meal is the *risotto di frutti di mare*, creamy Venetian-style risotto with plenty of fresh seafood. For a main dish, try the *fegato alla Veneziana*, which is tender liver fried with onions and served with polenta, a yellow cornmeal mush. The chefs are better at regional dishes than they are with those of the international kitchen.

Campo San Fantin, San Marco 1983. © **041-5224121**. Reservations required. Main courses 24€–55€ ($28–$63); 4-course fixed-price menu 46€–51€ ($53–$59); 6-course menu degustazione 79€ ($91). AE, DC, MC, V. Wed 7–11:30pm; Thurs–Mon noon–2:30pm and 7–11:30pm. Vaporetto: San Marco or Santa Maria del Giglio.

Da Ivo ✿ TUSCAN/VENETIAN   Da Ivo has such a faithful clientele that you'll think at first you're in a semiprivate club. The rustic atmosphere is both cozy and relaxing, with candles on the well-set tables. Homesick Florentines go

The Cafe Scene

Venice's most famous cafe is the **Florian,** Piazza San Marco, San Marco 56–59 (© **041-5205641**; vaporetto: San Marco). It was built in 1720 and remains romantically and elegantly decorated—pure Venetian salons with red plush banquettes, elaborate murals under glass, and Art Nouveau lighting and lamps. Hours are Thursday through Tuesday from 9:30am to midnight. It's closed the first week of December and the first week of January.

    Quadri, Piazza San Marco, San Marco 120–124 (© **041-5222105**; vaporetto: San Marco), stands opposite the Florian. Founded in 1638, it's elegantly decorated in an antique style. Wagner used to drop in for a drink when he was working on *Tristan und Isolde.* The restaurant on the second floor offers refined Venetian cuisine. It's open April through October daily from 9am to midnight; off season, Tuesday through Sunday from 9am to midnight.

here for fine Tuscan cookery; regional Venetian dishes are also served. In season, game, according to an ancient tradition, is cooked over an open charcoal grill. On one cold day, our hearts and plates were warmed when we ordered home-made tagliatelle. It came topped with slivers of tartufi bianchi, the pungent white truffle from the Piedmont district that's unforgettable to the palate. You'll also find delicacies like giant scampi with cherry tomatoes and black pepper, or beef carpaccio covered with arugula and Parmesan flakes.

Calle dei Fuseri, San Marco 1809. © 041-5285004. Reservations required. Main courses 30€–40€ ($35–$46). AE, DC, MC, V. Mon–Sat noon–2:30pm and 7–11:15pm. Closed Jan 6–31. Vaporetto: San Marco.

Quadri ✸✸✸ VENETIAN/INTERNATIONAL   One of Europe's famous restaurants, the deluxe Quadri evokes the world of its former patrons, Marcel Proust and Stendhal. Many diners come here just for the setting and are often surprised when they're treated to high-quality cuisine and impeccable service. You pay for all this nostalgia, however. The Venetian cuisine has been acclaimed—at least by one food critic—as "befitting a doge," though we doubt if those old doges ate as well. The chef is likely to tempt you with such dishes as octopus in fresh tomato sauce, salt codfish with polenta, or sea bass with crab sauce. Try the "baked" ice cream for dessert.

Piazza San Marco, San Marco 121. © 041-5289299. Reservations required. Main courses 23€–43€ ($26–$49). AE, DC, MC, V. Tues–Sun 12:30–2:30pm (except July–Aug) and 7:30–10:30pm. Vaporetto: San Marco.

Moderate

Ristorante da Raffaele ✸ *Value* ITALIAN/VENETIAN   This place is a 5-minute walk from Piazza San Marco and a minute from the Grand Canal. It has long been a favorite canal-side stop. It's often overrun with tourists, but the vet-eran kitchen staff holds up well. The food is excellent, beginning with a choice of tasty antipasti or well-prepared pastas. Seafood specialties include scampi, squid, or a platter of deep-fried fish from the Adriatic. The grilled meats are also succulent and can be followed by rich, tempting desserts.

Calle Larga XXII Marzo (Fondamenta delle Ostreghe), San Marco 2347. © 041-5232317. Reservations rec-ommended Sat–Sun. Main courses 12€–24€ ($14–$28). AE, DC, MC, V. Fri–Wed noon–3pm and 7–10:30pm. Closed Dec 10–Feb. Vaporetto: San Marco or Santa Maria del Giglio.

Taverna la Fenice ✸✸ ITALIAN/VENETIAN   Opened in 1907, when Venetians were flocking in record numbers to hear the *bel canto* performances in the opera house nearby, this restaurant is one of Venice's most romantic dining spots. The interior is suitably elegant, but the preferred spot in clement weather is out beneath a canopy, a few steps from the burned Teatro La Fenice. The serv-ice is smooth and efficient. You might enjoy risotto with scampi and arugula, or freshly made tagliatelle with cream and exotic mushrooms. Among the wide selection of fresh fish, you may be tempted by the exquisite simplicity of the sea bream garnished with seasonal herbs. For pasta lovers the choice ranges from tra-ditional black tagliolini with squid ink and crabmeat, to the more creative tagli-atelle with a combination of scampi and artichokes.

Campiello de la Fenice, San Marco 1938. © 041-5223856. Reservations required. Main courses 19€–35€ ($22–$40). AE, DC, MC, V. Tues–Sun 7–11pm. Vaporetto: San Marco.

Trattoria La Colomba ✸ VENETIAN/INTERNATIONAL   This is one of the most distinctive and popular trattorie in town, with a history going back at least a century. Menu items are likely to include at least five daily specials based exclusively on the time-honored cuisine of Venice. Otherwise, you can order *risotto di funghi del Montello* (risotto with mushrooms from the local hills of Montello) or *baccalà alla vicentina* (milk-simmered dry cod seasoned with onions, anchovies, and cinnamon, then served with polenta). If you're a meat fan, try the chateaubriand accompanied by steamed vegetables and almost a dozen different sauces.

Piscina Frezzeria, San Marco 1665. ② **041-5221175.** Reservations recommended. Main courses 23€–40€ ($26–$46). AE, DC, MC, V. Daily noon–3pm and 7–11pm. Closed Wed Nov–Apr. Vaporetto: San Marco or Rialto.

Vini da Arturo ⭐ *Finds* VENETIAN   Vini da Arturo attracts many devoted regulars, including artists and writers. Here you get some of the most delectable local cooking—and not just the standard cliché Venetian dishes, and not seafood, which may be unique for a Venetian restaurant. Instead of ordering plain pasta, try a tantalizing dish called spaghetti alla Gorgonzola. The beef is also good, especially when prepared with a cream sauce flavored with mustard and freshly ground pepper. The salads are made with crisp, fresh ingredients, often in unusual combinations. The place is small and contains only seven tables; it's between the Fenice Opera House and St. Mark's Square.

Calle degli Assassini, San Marco 3656. ② **041-5286974.** Reservations recommended. Main courses 12€–34€ ($14–$39). No credit cards. Mon–Sat noon–2:30pm and 7–10:30pm. Closed Aug. Vaporetto: San Marco or Rialto.

Inexpensive

Da Bruno VENETIAN   Da Bruno is like a country tavern in the center of Venice. On a narrow street about halfway between the Rialto Bridge and Piazza San Marco, this restaurant attracts its crowds by grilling meats on an open-hearth fire. Get your antipasti at the counter and watch your prosciutto being prepared—paper-thin slices of spicy flavored ham wrapped around breadsticks (*grissini*). In the right season, da Bruno does some of the finest game specialty dishes in Venice. If it's featured, try *capriolo* (roebuck) or *fagiano* (pheasant). Another great dish is veal scaloppini with wild mushrooms. If you feel more in a pasta mood, try the "black spaghetti" with tomato sauce.

Calle del Paradiso San Lio, Castello 5731. ② **041-5221480.** Main courses 8€–18€ ($9.20–$21); fixed-price menu 14€ ($16). AE, DC, MC, V. Daily noon–3pm and 7–11pm. Vaporetto: San Marco or Rialto.

Sempione VENETIAN   This century-old restaurant does an admirable job of feeding local residents and visitors. Set adjacent to a canal near St. Mark's Square, it contains three dining rooms outfitted in a soothingly traditional style, a well-trained staff, and a kitchen that focuses on preparations of traditional Venetian cuisine. Examples include grilled fish, spaghetti with crabmeat, risotto with fish, fish soup, and a timeless and delectable version of Venetian calves' liver. If you like surprises, try spaghetti with crabmeat flavored with a mysterious sauce whose ingredients the chef doesn't want to reveal. Try for a table by the window so you can watch the gondolas slide by.

Ponte Beretteri, San Marco 578. ② **041-5226022.** Reservations recommended. Main courses 8€–17€ ($9.20–$20). AE, DC, MC, V. Wed–Mon 11:30am–3pm and 6:30–10pm. Closed Thurs Nov–Dec. Vaporetto: Rialto.

Trattoria alla Madonna VENETIAN   This restaurant, opened in 1954 and named after *another* famous Madonna, is one of the most popular and characteristic trattorie of Venice, specializing in traditional recipes and an array of grilled fresh fish. A suitable beginning may be the antipasto *frutti di mare*. Pastas, polentas, risottos, meats (including *fegato alla Veneziana,* liver with onions), and many kinds of irreproachably fresh fish are widely available.

Calle della Madonna, San Polo 594. ⓒ **041-5223824.** Reservations recommended but not always accepted. Main courses 10€–14€ ($12–$16). AE, MC, V. Thurs–Tues noon–3pm and 7:15–10pm. Closed Dec 24–Jan and Aug 4–17. Vaporetto: Rialto.

EAST OF PIAZZA SAN MARCO
Moderate

Ristorante Corte Sconta SEAFOOD   This restaurant lies on a narrow alley, whose name is shared by at least three other streets in Venice (this particular one is near Campo Bandiere Moro and San Giovanni in Bragora). The modest restaurant has become well known as a sophisticated gathering place for artists, writers, and filmmakers. It serves a variety of flawlessly grilled fish (much of the "catch" is largely unknown in North America). It's also flawlessly fresh—the gamberi, for example, is placed live on the grill. Begin with marinated salmon with arugula and pomegranate seeds in rich olive oil. If you don't like fish, a tender filet of beef is available.

Calle del Pestrin, Castello 3886. ⓒ **041-5227024.** Reservations required. Main courses 15€–30€ ($17–$35); fixed-price menu 65€ ($75). MC, V. Tues–Sat 12:30–2pm and 7:30–9:30pm. Closed Jan 7–Feb 7 and July 15–Aug 15. Vaporetto: Arsenale or San Zaccaria.

Inexpensive

Nuova Rivetta *Value* SEAFOOD   Nuova Rivetta is an old-fashioned Venetian trattoria where you eat well without having to pay a lot. The restaurant stands in the monumental heart of the old city. Many find it best for lunch during a stroll around Venice. The most representative dish to order is *frittura di pesce*, a mixed fish fry from the Adriatic, which includes squid or various other "sea creatures" that turned up at the market that day. Other specialties are gnocchi stuffed with Adriatic spider crab, pasticcio of fish (a main course), and spaghetti flavored with squid ink.

Campo San Filippo, Castello 4625. ⓒ **041-5287302.** Reservations required. Main courses 8.50€–15€ ($9.80–$17). AE, MC, V. Tues–Sun noon–10pm. Closed July 15–Aug 20. Vaporetto: San Zaccaria.

NEAR THE PONTE DI RIALTO
Moderate

Il Sole Sulla Vecia Cavana ⭑ *Finds* SEAFOOD   This restaurant is off the tourist circuit and well worth the trek through the winding streets. A *cavana* is a place where gondolas are parked, a sort of liquid garage, and the site of this restaurant was such a place in the Middle Ages. When you enter, you'll be greeted by brick arches, stone columns, terra-cotta floors, framed modern paintings, and a photo of 19th-century fishermen relaxing after a day's work. The menu specializes in seafood, such as a mixed grill from the Adriatic, fried scampi, fresh sole, squid, and three types of risotto. The food is authentic and seems prepared for the Venetian palate—not necessarily for the visitor's.

Rio Terà SS. Apostoli, Cannaregio 4624. ⓒ **041-5287106.** Reservations recommended. Main courses 16€–22€ ($18–$25); fixed-price menu 20€ ($23). AE, MC, V. Tues–Sun 12:30–2:30pm and 7:30–10:30pm. Vaporetto: Ca' d'Oro.

Poste Vechie ⭑ SEAFOOD   This is one of Venice's most charming restaurants near the Rialto fish market and connected to the rest of the city by a small, privately owned bridge. It was established in the early 1500s as the local post office—food was served to the mail carriers to fortify them for their deliveries. Today, it's one of the oldest restaurants in town. Menu items include a super fresh array of fish from the nearby markets; a salad of shellfish and exotic mushrooms; a spicy soup of Adriatic fish; tagliolini flavored with squid ink, crabmeat, and fish sauce; and the restaurant's pièce de résistance, *seppie* (cuttlefish) *alla Veneziana* with polenta. If you don't like fish, calves' liver or veal shank with ham and cheese are also well prepared. The desserts come rolling to your table on a trolley and are usually sumptuous.

Pescheria Rialto, San Polo 1608. ℭ 041-721822. Reservations recommended. Main courses 12€–24€ ($14–$28). AE, DC, MC, V. Wed–Mon noon–3:30pm and 7–10:30pm. Vaporetto: Rialto.

IN SAN POLO
Expensive

Osteria da Fiore ⊛ *(Finds)* SEAFOOD   This restaurant serves only fish, and has done so since 1910. You'll find everything from scampi (a sweet Adriatic prawn, cooked in as many different ways as there are chefs) to granzeola, a type of spider crab. Try such dishes as *capelunghe alla griglio* (razor clams opened on the grill), *masenette* (tiny green crabs that you eat shell and all), and *canoce* (mantis shrimp). For your wine, we suggest Prosecco, which has a distinctive golden-yellow color and a bouquet that's refreshing and fruity.

Calle del Scaleter, San Polo 2202. ℭ 041-721308. Reservations required. Main courses 22€–43€ ($25–$49). AE, DC, MC, V. Tues–Sat 12:30–2:30pm and 8–10:30pm. Closed 3 weeks in Aug and Dec 25–Jan 14. Vaporetto: San Tomà or San Silvestro.

IN THE DORSODURO
Expensive

La Furatola SEAFOOD   La Furatola (an old Venetian word meaning "restaurant") is very much a Dorsoduro neighborhood hangout, but it has captured the imagination of local foodies. You'll need a good map and a lot of patience to find it. The specialty is fish brought to your table in a wicker basket so you can judge its size and freshness by its bright eyes and red gills. A display of seafood antipasti is set out near the entrance. A standout is the baby octopus boiled and eaten with a drop of red-wine vinegar.

Calle Lunga San Barnaba, Dorsoduro 2870A. ℭ 041-5208594. Reservations required. Main courses 25€–30€ ($29–$35). AE, DC, MC, V. Fri–Sun 12:30–2:30pm and Fri–Mon 7:30–10:30pm. Closed Aug and Jan. Vaporetto: Ca' Rezzonico.

Inexpensive

Locanda Montin ⊛ INTERNATIONAL/ITALIAN   Since this restaurant opened just after World War II, its famous patrons have included Ezra Pound, Jackson Pollock, Mark Rothko, and Peggy Guggenheim's artist friends. The inn is owned and run by the Carretins. Today the arbor-covered garden courtyard of this 17th-century building is filled with regulars. The menu includes a variety of salads, grilled meats, and fish caught in the Adriatic. Specialties include fresh crab with virgin olive oil and lemon, *tortelloni* (a kind of dumpling) stuffed with artichokes and covered in a scampi cream sauce, and seasonal fish often served in a Barolo red wine sauce.

Fondamenta di Borgo, Dorsoduro 1147. ℭ 041-5227151. Reservations recommended. Main courses 14€–20€ ($16–$23). AE, DC, MC, V. Thurs–Tues 12:30–2:30pm; Thurs–Mon 7:30–10pm. Closed 10 days in mid-Aug and 20 days in Jan. Vaporetto: Accademia

SEEING THE SIGHTS IN VENICE
Unlike Florence, Venice would reward you with treasures even if you never ducked inside a museum or church. In the city on the islands, the frame eternally competes with the picture inside.

SIGHTSEEING SUGGESTIONS FOR FIRST-TIME VISITORS

If You Have 1 Day Get up early and watch the sun rise over **Piazza San Marco,** as the city wakes up. The pigeons will already be here to greet you. Have an early morning cappuccino on the square, then visit the **Basilica of San Marco** and the **Palazzo Ducale.** We recommend a lunch stop at **Poste Vecchie,** at Pescheria Rialto, San Polo 1608 (© **041-721822;** vaporetto: Rialto). This restaurant near the fish market is the oldest in Venice, open Wednesday through Monday from noon to 3pm and 7 to 10:30pm. Ride the **Grand Canal** in a gondola 2 hours before sunset and spend the rest of the evening wandering the narrow streets of this strangely unreal and most fascinating city. Apologize to yourself for such a short visit and promise to return.

If You Have 2 Days On day 2 it's time for more concentrated sightseeing. Begin at Piazza San Marco (viewing it should be a daily ritual, regardless of how many days you have in Venice), then head for the **Accademia,** in the morning. In the afternoon, visit the **Collezione** **Peggy Guggenheim** (modern art) and perhaps the **Ca' d'Oro** and **Ca' Rezzonico.**

If You Have 3 Days Begin day 3 by having a cappuccino on Piazza San Marco, then inspect the **Campanile di San Marco.** Later in the morning visit the **Museo Correr.** In the afternoon, go to the **Scuola Grande di San Rocco** to see the works of Tintoretto. Spend the rest of the day strolling the streets of Venice and ducking into shops that capture your imagination. Even if you get lost, you'll eventually return to a familiar landmark, and you can't help but see the signs pointing you back to Piazza San Marco. Have dinner in one of the most typical of Venetian trattorie, such as **Locanda Montin.**

If You Have 4 or 5 Days On day 4 plan to visit the islands of the lagoon, including **Murano, Burano,** and **Torcello.** All three can be covered, at least briefly, on 1 busy day. On day 5, relax and stroll the streets; serendipity may await around the corner.

THE GRAND CANAL ★★★

Peoria may have its Main Street, Paris its Champs-Elysées—but Venice, for uniqueness, tops them all with its **Canal Grande (Grand Canal).** Lined with *palazzi* (palaces)—many in elegant Venetian-Gothic style—this great road of water is today filled with vaporetti, motorboats, and gondolas. Along the canal, the boat moorings are like peppermint sticks. It begins at Piazzetta San Marco on one side and Longhena's Salute Church on the opposite bank. At midpoint it's spanned by the Rialto Bridge. Eventually the canal winds its serpentine course to the railway station. We can guarantee that there's not a dull sight en route.

THE BASILICA, DOGES' PALACE & CAMPANILE

Piazza San Marco (St. Mark's Square) ★★★ was the heartbeat of La Serenissima (the Serene Republic) in the heyday of its glory as a seafaring state, the crystallization of its dreams and aspirations. If you have only 1 day for Venice, you need not leave the square, as the city's major attractions, such as the Basilica of St. Mark and the Doges' Palace, are centered here or nearby. Thanks to

Napoleon, the square was unified architecturally. The emperor added the Fabbrica Nuova, thus bridging the Old and New Procuratie. Flanked with medieval-looking palaces, Sansovino's Library, elegant shops, and colonnades, the square is now finished—unlike Piazza della Signoria in Florence.

If Piazza San Marco is the drawing room of Europe, then its satellite, **Piazzetta San Marco** ★★, is the antechamber. Hedged in by the Doges' Palace, Sansovino's Library, and a side of St. Mark's Basilica, the tiny square faces the Grand Canal. One of the two tall granite columns in the piazzetta is surmounted by a winged lion, which represents St. Mark. The other is topped by a statue of a man taming a dragon, supposedly the dethroned patron saint Theodore. Both columns came from the East in the 12th century.

Basilica di San Marco ★★★ This so-called "Church of Gold" dominates Piazza San Marco, and is one of the world's greatest and most richly embellished churches—in fact, it looks as if it had been moved intact from Istanbul. The basilica is a conglomeration of styles, yet it's particularly indebted to Byzantium. It incorporates other schools of design, such as Romanesque and Gothic, with freewheeling abandon. Like Venice itself, it's adorned with booty from every corner of the city's once far-flung mercantile empire—capitals from Sicily, columns from Alexandria, porphyry from Syria, sculpture from Constantinople. The basilica is capped by a dome that, like a spider plant, sends off shoots, in this case, a quartet of smaller-scale cupolas. Spanning the facade is a loggia, surmounted by replicas of the four famous St. Mark's horses—the *Triumphal Quadriga.*

If you look back at the aperture over the entryway, you can see a mosaic, the dance of Salome in front of Herod and his court. Wearing a star-studded russet-red dress and three white fox tails, Salome dances under a platter holding John's head. Her glassy face is that of a Madonna, not an enchantress. Proceed up the right nave to the doorway to the *tesoro* **(treasury).** The entrance to the **presbytery** is nearby. On the high altar, the alleged sarcophagus of St. Mark rests under a green marble blanket and is held up by four sculptured alabaster Corinthian columns. The Byzantine-style **Pala d'Oro,** from Constantinople, is the rarest treasure at St. Mark's—made of gold and studded with precious stones.

On leaving the basilica, head up the stairs in the atrium for the **Marciano Museum** and the Loggia dei Cavalli. The star attraction of the museum is the world-famous *Quadriga,* four horses looted from Constantinople by Venetian crusaders in the sack of that city in 1204. This is the only quadriga (a quartet of horses yoked together) to have survived from the classical era.

Piazza San Marco. ⓒ **041-5225205.** Basilica free admission; treasury 2€ ($2.30); presbytery 1.50€ ($1.70); Marciano Museum 1.50€ ($1.70). Basilica and presbytery Apr–Sept Mon–Sat 9:30am–5:30pm, Sun 2–5:30pm; Oct–Mar Mon–Sat 10am–4:30pm, Sun 2–4:30pm. Treasury Mon–Sat 9:30am–5pm; Sun 2–5pm. Marciano Museum Apr–Sept Mon–Sat 10am–5:30pm, Sun 2–4:30pm; Oct–Mar Mon–Sat 10am–4:30pm, Sun 2–4:30pm. Vaporetto: San Marco.

Palazzo Ducale ★★★ You enter the Palace of the Doges through the magnificent 15th-century Porta della Carta on the piazzetta. It's somewhat like a frosted birthday cake in pinkish red marble and white Istrian stone. The Venetian–Gothic palazzo—with all the architectural intricacies of a doily—gleams in the tremulous Venetian light. The grandest civic structure in Italy, it dates back to 1309, though a fire in 1577 destroyed much of the original.

After climbing the Sansovino stairway of gold, proceed to the Anti-Collegio salon, which houses the palace's greatest artworks—notably Veronese's *Rape of*

Europa, to the far left on the right wall. Tintoretto is well represented with his *Three Graces* and *Bacchus and Ariadne.* Some critics consider the latter his supreme achievement.

Now trek downstairs through the once-private apartments of the doges to the grand Maggior Consiglio, with its allegorical *Triumph of Venice* on the ceiling, painted by Veronese. What makes the room outstanding, however, is Tintoretto's *Paradise,* over the Grand Council chamber—said to be the largest oil painting in the world.

Re-enter the Maggior Consiglio and follow the arrows on their trail across the **Bridge of Sighs** ✶, linking the Doges' Palace with the Palazzo delle Prigioni, where the cellblocks are found, the ones that lodged the prisoners who felt the quick justice of the Terrible Ten. The "sighs" in the bridge's name stemmed from the sad laments of the numerous victims led across it to certain torture and possible death.

Piazzetta San Marco. ℂ **041-5224951.** Admission 9.50€ ($11) adults. Apr–Oct daily 9am–7pm; Nov–Mar daily 9am–5pm. Closed Dec 25 and Jan 1. Vaporetto: San Marco.

Campanile di San Marco ✶✶   One summer night back in 1902, the bell tower of the Basilica of St. Mark on Piazza San Marco, which was suffering from years of rheumatism in the damp Venetian climate, gave out a warning sound that sent the fashionable crowd scurrying from the Florian Caffè in a dash for their lives. But the campanile gracefully waited until the next morning, July 14, before it tumbled into the piazza. The Venetians rebuilt their belfry, and it's now safe to ascend. A modern elevator takes you up for a pigeon's view of the city. It's a particularly good vantage point for viewing the cupolas of St. Mark's Basilica.

Piazza San Marco. ℂ **041-5224064.** Admission 6€ ($6.90). Oct–Feb daily 9:30am–4pm; Mar–June daily 9am–7pm; July–Sept daily 9am–9pm. Closed Jan 7–31. Vaporetto: San Marco.

MUSEUMS & GALLERIES

Galleria dell'Accademia ✶✶✶   The pomp and circumstance, the glory that was Venice, lives on in this remarkable collection of paintings spanning the 14th century to the 18th century. The hallmark of the Venetian school is color and more color. From Giorgione to Veronese, from Titian to Tintoretto, with a Carpaccio cycle thrown in, the Accademia has samples—often their best—of its most famous sons.

You'll first see works by such 14th-century artists as Paolo and Lorenzo Veneziano, who bridged the gap from Byzantine art to Gothic (see the latter's *Annunciation*). Next, you'll view Giovanni Bellini's *Madonna and Saint* (poor Sebastian, not another arrow), and Carpaccio's fascinating yet gruesome work of mass crucifixion. Two of the most important works with secular themes are Mantegna's armored *St. George,* with the dragon slain at his feet, and Hans Memling's 15th-century portrait of a young man. Giorgione's *Tempest* is the most famous painting at the Accademia.

Campo della Carità, Dorsoduro. ℂ **041-5222247.** Admission 6.50€ ($7.50). Mon 8:15am–2pm; Tues–Sun 8am–7:15pm. Vaporetto: Accademia.

Collezione Peggy Guggenheim ✶✶✶   This is one of the most comprehensive and brilliant modern-art collections in the Western world, and it reveals the foresight and critical judgment of its founder. The collection is housed in an unfinished palazzo, the former home of Peggy Guggenheim. In the tradition of her family, Guggenheim was a lifelong patron of contemporary painters and sculptors. As her private collection increased, she decided to find a larger showcase and selected Venice. Displayed here are works not only by Pollock and Ernst but also by Picasso (see his cubist *The Poet* of 1911), Duchamp, Chagall, Mondrian, Brancusi, Delvaux, and Dalí, plus a garden of modern sculpture that includes works by Giacometti.

In the Palazzo Venier dei Leoni, Calle Venier dei Leoni, Dorsoduro 701. ⓒ **041-2405411.** Admission 8€ ($9.20) adults, 5€ ($5.75) children and students, free for children under 9. Wed–Mon 10am–6pm. Vaporetto: Accademia.

Ca' d'Oro ✸✸✸ This is one of the most handsomely embellished palaces along the Grand Canal. Although it contains the important **Galleria Giorgio Franchetti,** the House of Gold (so named because its facade was once gilded) competes with its own paintings. Built in the first part of the 15th century in the ogival style, it has a lacy look. Baron Franchetti, who restored the palace and filled it with his collection of paintings, sculpture, and furniture, presented it to Italy during World War I. In a special niche reserved for the masterpiece of the Franchetti collection is Andrea Mantegna's icy-cold *St. Sebastian,* the central figure of which is riddled with what must be a record number of arrows.

Cannaregio 3931–3932. ⓒ **041-5238790.** Admission 5€ ($5.75). Tues–Sun 8:15am–7:15pm. Closed Jan 1, May 1, and Dec 25. Vaporetto: Ca' d'Oro.

Museo Civico Correr ✸✸ This museum traces the development of Venetian painting from the 14th century to the 16th century. On the second floor are the red and maroon robes once worn by the doges, plus some fabulous street lanterns. There's also an illustrated copy of *Marco Polo in Tartaria.* You can see Cosmé Tura's *La Pietà,* a miniature of renown from the genius in the Ferrara School. This is one of his more gruesome works, depicting a bony, gnarled Christ sprawled on the lap of the Madonna. Farther on, search out a Schiavone *Madonna and Child* (no. 545), our candidate for ugliest bambino ever depicted on canvas (no wonder the mother looks askance). One of the most important rooms at the CorS is filled with three masterpieces: Antonello da Messina's *Pietà,* Hugo van der Goes's *Crucifixion,* and Dieric Bouts's *Madonna and Child.* The star attraction of the Correr is the Bellini salon, which includes works by founding padre Jacopo and his son, Gentile. But the real master of the household was the other son, Giovanni.

Fondamenta Rezzonico, Dorsoduro 3136. ⓒ **041-2410100.** Admission 6.50€ ($7.50). Nov–Mar Wed–Mon 10am–5pm; Apr–Oct Wed–Mon 10am–6pm. Vaporetto: Ca' Rezzonico. Closed Jan 1, May 1, and Dec 25.

Ca' Rezzonico ✸✸ This 17th- and 18th-century palace along the Grand Canal is where Robert Browning set up his bachelor headquarters. Pope Clement XIII also stayed here. It's a virtual treasure house, known for its baroque paintings and furniture. You first enter the Grand Ballroom with its allegorical ceiling, then proceed through lavishly embellished rooms with Venetian chandeliers, brocaded walls, portraits of patricians, tapestries, gilded furnishings, and touches of chinoiserie. At the end of the first walk is the Throne Room, with its allegorical ceilings by Giovanni Battista Tiepolo.

Upstairs you'll find a survey of 18th-century Venetian art. Head for the first salon on your right (facing the canal) that contains paintings from the brush of Pietro Longhi. His most famous work, *The Lady and the Hairdresser,* is the first canvas to the right on the entrance wall.

Fondamenta Rezzonico, Dorsoduro 3136. ⓒ **041-2410100.** Admission 6.50€ ($7.50). Nov–Mar Wed–Mon 10am–5pm; Apr–Oct Wed–Mon 10am–6pm. Vaporetto: Ca' Rezzonico. Closed Jan 1, May 1, and Dec 25.

THE SCUOLE

Scuola di San Rocco ★★★   Of Venice's *scuole* (in the Renaissance, scuole were centers used by social and religious organizations affiliated with the local parish), none are as richly embellished as the Scuola di San Rocco, filled with epic canvases by Tintoretto. By a clever trick, he won the competition to decorate the darkly illuminated early-16th-century building. He began painting in 1564 and the work stretched on until his powers as an artist waned. The paintings sweep across the upper and lower halls, mesmerizing the viewer with a kind of passion play. In the grand hallway, they depict New Testament scenes, devoted largely to episodes in the life of Mary (*Flight into Egypt* is among the best). In the top gallery are works illustrating the Old and New Testaments, the most renowned devoted to the life of Christ. In a separate room is Tintoretto's masterpiece—a mammoth *Crucifixion*, one of the world's most celebrated paintings.

Campo San Rocco, San Polo. ⟨℃⟩ **041-5234864.** Admission 5.50€ ($6.30) adults, 1.50€ ($1.70) children. Mar 28–Nov 2 daily 9am–5:30pm; Nov 3–30 and Mar 1–27 daily 10am–4pm; Dec–Feb Mon–Sat 7:30am–12:30pm, Sun 7:30am–12:30pm and 2–4pm. Closed Easter and Dec 25–Jan 1. Ticket office closes 30 min. before last entrance. Vaporetto: San Tomà.

Scuola di San Giorgio degli Schiavoni ★★   At the Fondamenta dei Furlani (St. Antonino Bridge) is the second important scuola to visit in Venice. Between 1502 and 1509, Vittore Carpaccio painted a pictorial cycle here of exceptional merit and interest. Of enduring fame are his works of St. George and the dragon—these are our favorite pieces of art in all of Venice and certainly the most delightful. In one frame, St. George charges the dragon on a field littered with half-eaten bodies and skulls. Gruesome? Not at all. Any moment you expect the director to call "Cut!"

Calle dei Furiani, Castello. ⟨℃⟩ **041-5228828.** Admission 3€ ($3.45). Nov–Mar Tues–Sat 10am–12:30pm and 3–6pm; Sun 10am–12:30pm; Apr–Oct Tues–Sat 9:30am–12:30pm and 3:30–6:30pm; Sun 9:30am–12:30pm. Last entrance 30 min. before closing. Vaporetto: San Zaccaria.

ORGANIZED TOURS

Daily at 9:10am, **American Express,** San Marco 1471 (⟨℃⟩ **041-5200844;** vaporetto: San Marco), offers a 2-hour guided tour of the city costing 23€ ($26). Sights include St. Mark's Square, the basilica, the Doges' Palace, the prison, the bell tower, and, in some cases, a demonstration of the art of Venetian glass blowing. Monday through Saturday at 3pm, a 2-hour guided tour incorporates visits to the exteriors of several palaces along Campo San Benetto and other sights of the city. The tour eventually crosses the Grand Canal to visit the Church of Santa Maria dei Frari, which contains an *Assumption* by Titian. The tour continues by gondola down the canal to visit the Ca' d'Oro and ends at the Rialto Bridge. The cost of the afternoon tour is 29€ ($33).

The **Evening Serenade Tour,** at 30€ ($35) per person, allows a nocturnal view of Venice accompanied by the sound of singing musicians in gondolas. From April to October there are two daily departures, at 7:30pm and 8:30pm, leaving from Campo Santa Maria del Giglio, but from November to March there's just one departure at 3:30pm. Five to six occupants fit in each gondola as a singer and a handful of musicians perform throughout the Venetian evening. The experience lasts 50 minutes.

The **Islands Tour** is a 3-hour tour of Murano, Burano, and Torcello for 15€ ($17) per person. Departures are at 2:30pm year-round and also at 9:30am from March 15 to October.

THE SHOPPING SCENE

Venetian **glass** and **lace** are known throughout the world. However, selecting quality products in either craft requires a shrewd eye, as there's much that is tawdry and shoddily crafted. Some of the glassware hawked isn't worth the cost of shipping it home. Yet other pieces represent some of the world's finest artistic and ornamental glass. Murano is famous for its handmade glass, but you can find little glass animal souvenirs in shops all over Venice. If you're looking for an heirloom, stick to such award-winning houses as **Pauly & Co.** or **Venini** (see below).

For lace, head to Burano, where the last of a long line of women put in painstaking hours to produce some of the finest lace in the world. *The* name in Venetian lace is **Jesurum** (see below), which has stood for quality since the last century.

SHOPPING STROLLS   All the main shopping streets of Venice, even the side streets, are touristy and overrun. The greatest concentration of shops is around Piazza San Marco and around the Rialto Bridge. Prices are much higher at San Marco, but the quality of merchandise is better. There are two major shopping strolls in Venice. First, from Piazza San Marco you can stroll through Venice toward the spacious square of **Campo Morosini.** You just follow one shop-lined street all the way to its end (although the name will change several times along the way). You begin at Salizzada San Moisè, which becomes Via 22 Marzo and then Calle delle Ostreghe before it opens onto Campo Santa Maria Zobenigo. The street then narrows again and changes its name to Calle Zaguri before widening once more into Campo San Maurizio, finally becoming Calle Piovan before it reaches Campo Morosini. The only deviation from this tour is a detour down Calle Vallaressa, between San Moisè and the Grand Canal, which is one of the major shopping arteries with some of the biggest designer names in the business.

The other great shopping stroll in Venice wanders from Piazza San Marco to the Rialto in a succession of streets collectively known as **The Mercerie.** It's virtually impossible to get lost because each street name is preceded by the word *merceria,* such as Merceria dell'Orologio, which begins near the clock tower in Piazza San Marco. Many commercial establishments, mainly shops, line the Mercerie before it reaches the Rialto, which then explodes into one vast shopping emporium.

SOME SHOPS WORTH A LOOK

At **Pauly & Co.,** Ponte Consorzi, San Marco (© **041-5209899;** www.pauly glassfactory.com; vaporetto: San Zaccaria), you can wander through 21 salons, enjoy an exhibition of artistic glassware, and later see a furnace in full action. Pauly's production, which is mainly made-to-order, consists of continually renewed patterns, subject to change and alteration based on customer desire. The Venetian glass of **Venini,** Piazzetta Leoncini, San Marco 314 (© **041-5224045;** vaporetto: San Zaccaria), has won collector fans all over the globe. The store sells lamps, bottles, and vases, but not ordinary ones. Many are works of art, representing the best of Venetian craftsmanship. Their best-known glass has a distinctive swirl pattern in several colors, which is called a *venature.*

The elegant **Jesurum,** Mercerie del Capitello, San Marco 4857 (© **041-5206177;** www.jesurum.it; vaporetto: Rialto), the best place in Venice for serious lace purchases, has been in a 12th-century church since 1868. You'll find Venetian hand- or machine-made lace and embroidery on table, bed, and bath linens; and hand-printed bathing suits. **Laboratorio Artigiano Maschere,** Barbaria delle Tole, Castello 6657 (© **041-5223110;** vaporetto: Rialto), is one of the best places to purchase carnival masks handcrafted in papier-mâché or leather. The masks carry names and symbols, the best known being the birdlike luck bringer, called *Buonaventura* in Italian.

VENICE AFTER DARK

The tourist office distributes a free pamphlet (part in English, part in Italian), called *Un Ospite di Venezia.* A section of this useful publication lists events, including any music and opera or theatrical presentations, along with art exhibitions and local special events.

In addition, classical concerts are often at various churches, such as the Chiesa di Vivaldi. To see if any **church concerts** are being presented at the time of your visit, call **Kele and Teo Travel Agency** (© 041-5208722) for information.

THE PERFORMING ARTS

The city's main venue for performing arts, the fabled **La Fenice** at Campo San Fantin, has been a blackened shell since 1996. However, you can still see performances of the Orchestra and Caro della Fenice in a temporary venue, **PalaFenice,** in the Tronchetto parking facilities near Piazzale Roma (© 041-786500 for information; www.teatrolafenice.it; vaporetto: Tronchetto). Tickets for most events range from 15€ to 100€ ($17–$115), but this can vary. The **box office** is open Monday through Friday from 8:30am to 1:30pm and 1 hour before the performance (© 041-5210161).

Teatro Goldoni, Calle Goldoni, near Campo San Luca (© **041-2402011;** vaporetto: Rialto), close to the Ponte Rialto in the San Marco district, honors Carlo Goldoni (1707–93), the most prolific—critics say the best—Italian playwright. The theater presents a changing repertoire of productions, often plays in Italian, but musical presentations as well. The box office is open Monday through Saturday from 10am to 1pm and 4:30 to 7pm. Tickets are 13€ to 25€ ($15–$29).

PIANO BARS & DANCE CLUBS

The pub **Il Piccolo Mondo,** Calle Contarini Corfu 1056A (© 041-5200371; vaporetto: Accademia), near the Accademia, is open during the day, and at night features disco dancing and organized parties. The crowd is often young, and dance music prevails. Hours are daily 10pm to 4am, but the action doesn't begin until after midnight. Cover (including the first drink) ranges from 6€ to 9€ ($6.90–$10).

Martini Scala Club, Campo San Fantin, San Marco 1980 (© **041-5224121;** vaporetto: San Marco or Santa Maria del Giglio), is an elegant restaurant with a piano bar that has functioned as some kind of an inn since 1724. You can enjoy its food and wine until 2am—it's the only kitchen in Venice that stays open late. After 10pm, you can come here to enjoy the piano bar. The restaurant is open March through November, Wednesday through Monday from 7 to 11:30pm; December through February, Wednesday through Monday from noon to 2:30pm and 7 to 11:30pm. The bar, which offers a piano bar and food, is open every day but Tuesday from 10pm to 3am, and is closed in July and August.

DAY TRIPS FROM VENICE

MURANO ★★   On this island, **glass blowers** have for centuries performed oral gymnastics to turn out those fantastic chandeliers that Victorian ladies used to prize so highly. They also produce heavily ornamented glasses so ruby red or so indigo blue you can't tell if you're drinking blackberry juice or pure wood grain. Happily, the glass blowers are still plying their trade, though increasing competition, notably from Sweden, has compelled a greater degree of sophistication in design. You can combine a tour of Murano with a trip along the lagoon. To reach it, take vaporetto 5 at Riva degli Schiavoni, a short walk from Piazzetta San Marco. The boat docks at the landing platform at Murano, where the first furnace conveniently awaits. It's best to go Monday through Friday from 10am to noon if you want to see glass-blowing action.

BURANO ✹✹   Burano became world famous as a center of **lace making,** a craft that reached its pinnacle in the 18th century. If you can spare a morning to visit this island, you'll be rewarded with a charming little fishing village far removed in spirit from the grandeur of Venice, but lying only half an hour away by ferry. Boats leave from Fondamente Nuove, overlooking the Venetian graveyard (which is well worth the trip all on its own). Take vaporetto 12 or 52 from Riva degli Schiavoni, get off at Fondamente Nuove, and catch boat 12, marked BURANO.

Once at Burano, you'll discover that the houses of the islanders come in varied colors—sienna, robin's-egg or cobalt blue, barn-red, butterscotch, grass green. **Scuola Merietti** stands in the center of the fishing village on Piazza Baldassare Galuppi. The Burano School of Lace was founded in 1872 as part of a resurgence movement aimed at restoring the age-old craft that had earlier declined, giving way to such other lace-making centers as Chantilly and Bruges. By going up to the second floor you can see the lace makers, mostly young women, at painstaking work and can purchase hand-embroidered or handmade lace items.

After visiting the lace school, you can walk across the square to the **Duomo** and its leaning campanile (inside, look for a *Crucifixion* by Tiepolo). However, walk quickly; the bell tower is leaning so precariously it looks as if it may topple at any moment.

TORCELLO ✹✹   Of all the islands of the lagoon, Torcello—the so-called Mother of Venice—offers the most charm. If Burano is behind the times, Torcello is positively antediluvian. You can follow in the footsteps of Hemingway and stroll across a grassy meadow, traverse an ancient stone bridge, and step back into that time when the Venetians first fled from invading barbarians to create a city of Neptune in the lagoon. To reach Torcello, take vaporetto 12 from Fondamenta Nuova on Murano. The trip takes about 45 minutes.

Cattedrale di Torcello, also called the Church of Santa Maria Assunta Isola di Torcello (© 041-730119), was founded in A.D. 639 and was subsequently rebuilt. It stands in a lonely, grassy meadow beside a campanile dating from the 11th century. It's visited chiefly because of its Byzantine mosaics. Clutching her child, the weeping Madonna in the apse is a magnificent sight, whereas on the opposite wall is a powerful *Last Judgment.* It's open daily April through October from 10:30am to 6; November through March from 10am to 5pm. Admission is 2.50€ ($2.85).

While on the island, you can dine in Venice's most idyllic luncheon stopover, **Locanda Cipriani** ✹✹, Piazza San Fosca 29 (© 041-730150), operated by Bonifacio Brass, nephew of Harry Cipriani of Hotel Cipriani and Harry's Bar fame. This low-key, deliberately rustic locanda serves an authentic Venetian cuisine, everything from a succulent risotto made from fresh vegetables and herbs from the family garden to filet of John Dory in the style of Carla, a late and much-revered matriarch here (the fish is flavored with tomatoes and capers). Main courses run from 15€ to 25€ ($17–$29). Hours are Wednesday through Monday from noon to 3pm and Saturday from 7 to 10pm; closed from January 15 to February 15. American Express, Diners Club, MasterCard, and Visa are accepted.

12

The Netherlands

by George McDonald

Like an Atlantis in reverse, Holland has emerged from the sea. Much of the country was once underwater, or precariously separated from rivers, lakes, and the sea by dikes and dunes. As the centuries rolled past, the land was recovered and stitched together through a combination of Dutch ingenuity and hard work. The result is a flat, green-and-silver Mondrian of a country, with nearly half its land and two-thirds of its 16 million people below sea level.

Easygoing, prosperous Amsterdam, full of canals, bridges, and world-class museums, and enveloped in the afterglow of its 17th-century golden age, is the natural focus of a visit to the Netherlands. From here you can make day trips to various nearby places: historic Haarlem; brash Zandvoort on the North Sea coast; the pretty conservation village of Zaanse Schans; and the traditional IJsselmeer lakeside villages of Volendam and Marken.

Also, you should aim to make time for Delft, famous for its Dutch royal connections and blue-and-white porcelain, and Leiden, known for its associations with the Pilgrim Fathers.

1 Amsterdam

The Dutch capital has never entirely shed its twofold reputation as a hippie haven and a tulips-and-windmills landmark, even with an economy that has moved far beyond these clichés. Powered more by business than by the combustion of semilegal exotic plants, prosperity has settled like a North Sea mist around the graceful cityscape of canals and 17th-century town houses.

The historic center recalls Amsterdam's Golden Age as the command post of a vast trading network and colonial empire, when wealthy merchants constructed gabled residences along neatly laid-out canals.

A delicious irony is that the placid old structures also host brothels, smoke shops, and some extravagant nightlife. The city's inhabitants, proud of their live-and-let-live attitude, which is based on pragmatism as much as a long history of tolerance, have decided to control what they cannot effectively outlaw. They permit licensed prostitution in the Red Light District and the sale of hashish and marijuana in designated "coffee shops."

But don't think Amsterdammers drift around town in a drug-induced haze. They are too busy whizzing around on bikes, jogging through Vondelpark, feasting on arrays of ethnic dishes, or simply watching the parade of street life from a sidewalk cafe. A new generation of entrepreneurs has revitalized old neighborhoods like the Jordaan, turning some of the distinctive houses into offbeat stores and bustling cafes, hotels, and restaurants.

Between dips into Amsterdam's artistic and historical treasures, be sure to take time out to absorb the freewheeling spirit of Europe's most vibrant city.

ESSENTIALS

GETTING THERE   By Plane   If you fly into Amsterdam, you arrive at the efficient, single-terminal **Amsterdam Airport Schiphol** (℅ **0900/0141** for flight information; www.schiphol.nl), 13km (8 miles) southwest of the center city. You exit from Customs into Schiphol Plaza, a combined arrivals hall and mall, with currency-exchange offices, ATMs, bars, restaurants, and stores. You can get questions answered and make hotel reservations at the **Holland Tourist Information** desk, open daily from 7am to 10pm.

A **train** from Schiphol Station, a floor below Schiphol Plaza, connects the airport with Amsterdam's Centraal Station. The fare is 2.95€ ($3.40) one-way and takes 20 minutes. Frequency ranges from six trains an hour at peak times to one an hour at night.

The **Connexxion Hotel Bus** (℅ **0900/9292**) shuttles between the airport and the city center on a circular route directly connecting 16 top hotels that are close to many others. A bus leaves from in front of Schiphol Plaza every 20 minutes from 7am to 5pm, every 30 minutes from 5 to 7pm, and every hour from 7 to 9pm. The fare is 8.50€ to 11€ ($10–$12) one-way. Bus no. 197 connects the airport and the center city every half-hour and costs 3.40€ ($3.90) one-way. A **taxi** from the airport to the city center is around 45€ ($52).

By Train   Whether you arrive by Thalys high-speed train from Brussels or Paris, by ordinary international train, or by a train from elsewhere in the Netherlands,

Amsterdam

ⓘ Information   – – – Ferry route
⊠ Post Office   ——— Railway

THE JORDAAN

THE CANAL BELT

THE MUSEUMPLEIN AREA

Concertgebouw

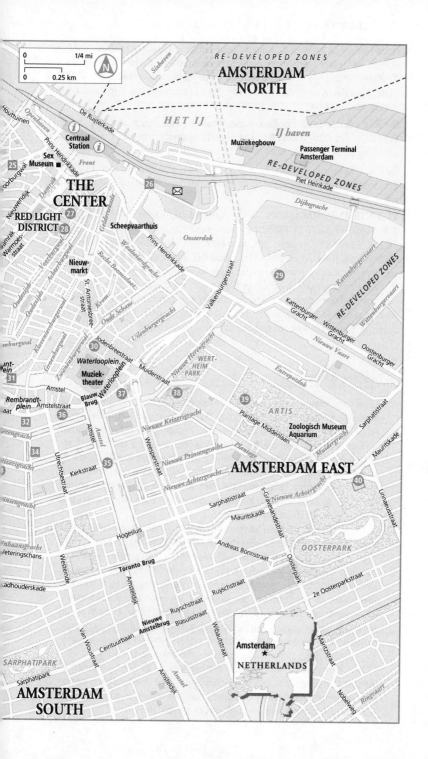

you'll likely find yourself deposited in the center at **Centraal Station.** For information on trains (and other public transportation) in the Netherlands, call ℂ **0900/9292** or go to **www.9292ov.nl.** For international trains, call ℂ **0900/ 9296.** Right in front of the station is an array of tram and bus stops, and a Metro station (downstairs).

By Bus Buses from London, Paris, Brussels, and other cities, operated by **Eurolines** (ℂ **020/560-8788;** www.eurolines.com), arrive at the bus station adjoining Amstel railway station (Metro: Amstel) in the south of the city.

By Car European expressways E19, E35, E231, and E22 converge on Amsterdam from France and Belgium to the south and from Germany to the north and east.

VISITOR INFORMATION **VVV Amsterdam,** Stationsplein 10 (ℂ **0900/ 400-4040;** fax 020/625-2869; www.visitamsterdam.nl; tram: 1, 2, 4, 5, 6, 9, 13, 16, 17, 24, or 25), in front of Centraal Station. The office is open daily from 9am to 5pm (to 4:30pm Nov–Mar). Another office, on Platform 2 in the railway station, is open Monday to Saturday from 8am to 8pm and Sunday from 8:30am to 4:30pm. Both offices provide maps, brochures, and details about the city, reserve hotels and tours, and sell theater and concert tickets. A VVV information center at Leidseplein 1 (tram: 1, 2, 5, 6, 7, or 10) is open Monday to Saturday from 9am to 8pm and Sunday from 9am to 5pm.

Native Behavior

Look for someplace *gezellig,* and treasure it. *Gezelligheid* (the state of being *gezellig*) underlines everyday Dutch life. It's an imprecise, enigmatic, untranslatable-in-a-single-word concept that defines a mood and an attitude, the special *something* that makes a place comfortable, congenial, cozy, familiar, friendly, intimate, memorable, tolerant, warm, and welcoming. Dutch, in fact. You find it all over—in a "brown" cafe; in a candlelit restaurant with a view of a softly illuminated canal; even onboard a packed-to-bursting tram where everyone sees the funny side of the situation.

The bicycle might have been invented with Amsterdam in mind, and there are reckoned to be anywhere from 600,000 and up bikes in the city. To get close to the Amsterdam experience, you positively have to get into the saddle and ride. It takes a while to get used to moving smoothly and safely through the whirl of trams, cars, buses, trucks, fellow bikers, and pedestrians, particularly if you're on a typically ancient, one-speed, much-battered *stadfiets* (city bike), also known as an *omafiets* (grandmother bike)—the only kind that makes economic sense here, since anything fancier will attract a crowd of people wanting to steal it. It's better to develop your street smarts slowly.

Not every local council in the Netherlands is as liberal-minded as Amsterdam when it comes to smoking pot—and Amsterdam is not so tolerant that you should just light up on the street, in cafes, and on trams and trains (though enough dopey people do).

Be sure to pick up a copy of *Amsterdam Day by Day* for 1.50€ ($1.75). This monthly magazine is full of details about art exhibits, concerts, and theater performances, and lists bars, dance clubs, and restaurants.

For more details on cultural events and to reserve and purchase tickets for almost every venue in the city, stop by the **Amsterdam Uit Buro (AUB),** on the corner of Leidseplein and Marnixstraat (© **020/621-1211;** tram: 1, 2, 5, 6, 7, or 10), open Monday to Saturday from 10am to 6pm.

Websites The official website of the **Netherlands Board of Tourism (www. visitholland.com)** has useful advice for upcoming events, bicycling, and culture—and it even lets you know when the tulips bloom. Amsterdam's most comprehensive website, **www.visitamsterdam.nl,** lays out the details on sightseeing, walking routes, wining and dining, shopping for antiques, and current events. For information on many of Amsterdam's more than 40 museums, go to **www. hollandmuseums.nl.** To book a hotel online, visit **www.go-amsterdam.org.** One of the best virtual tours on the Net is **www.channels.nl**—the images are clear, you can direct your own tour, and you can chat with others about Amsterdam. Visitors give their impressions of restaurants, hotels, museums, and hash houses. At **www.amsterdamhotspots.nl,** they mean "hot." Here are *the* places to fill your nights, from eating and drinking to where to toke, what the top gay bars are, and where to see those famous working girls on display behind picture windows. Good eating-out info is available from **www.dinner-in-amsterdam.nl.**

CITY LAYOUT Although Amsterdam center is small enough that residents think of it as a village, it can be confusing until you get the hang of it. A map like the handy VVV Amsterdam Map, available from VVV tourist offices for 3.50€ ($4), is essential.

When you step out of Centraal Station's main entrance, you're facing south toward the center. From here the **Old City** is laid out along five concentric semi-circles of canals: **Singel, Herengracht, Keizersgracht, Prinsengracht,** and **Sin-gelgracht** (*gracht* means "canal"). Along this necklace of man-made waterways, wealthy 17th-century merchants built their elegant homes, most of which are still standing. Within these canals are many smaller canals and connecting streets, radiating from the center.

Damrak, a busy tourist street, leads from Centraal Station to the **Dam,** once the location of the original dam on the Amstel River that gave the city its name and now a large open square on which stands the Royal Palace. To the left is the famous **Red Light District,** where government-licensed prostitutes sit in their windows, waiting for customers. A block to the right of Damrak is **Nieuwendijk** (which becomes **Kalverstraat** when it crosses the Dam), a pedestrianized shopping street. If you follow Kalverstraat to the end, you'll be at **Muntplein** (*plein* means "square"), identified by the old Mint Tower. Cross Singel and continue in the same direction to reach **Rembrandtplein,** one of the main nightlife areas. Beyond Rembrandtplein is **Waterlooplein,** which hosts the Muziektheater and a great flea market.

At the heart of another important nightlife zone is **Leidseplein,** on Singel-gracht. Leidseplein is at the end of Leidsestraat, a pedestrians-only shopping street. **Museumplein,** where you find Amsterdam's three most famous muse-ums—the Rijksmuseum, Van Gogh Museum, and Stedelijk Museum (the latter rehoused temporarily to near Centraal Station)—is a short walk along Singel-gracht from Leidseplein.

The **Jordaan,** a fast-developing old neighborhood now filled with inexpensive restaurants, unusual stores, and small galleries, lies between Prinsengracht, Brouwersgracht, Singelgracht, and Rozengracht. Turn right off Damrak at any point between Centraal Station and the Dam, and when you cross Prinsengracht, you're in the Jordaan.

GETTING AROUND   In looking at a map of Amsterdam, you might think the city is too large to explore by foot. This isn't true: It's possible to see almost every important sight in the Old City on a 4-hour walk.

By Tram, Bus & Metro   Public transportation begins around 6am and the regular service ends around midnight. After that, there are infrequent night buses. Riding the distinctive yellow **trams** (streetcars) is the most convenient means of getting around; they're fast, cheap, and fun, and provide a great view of the sights. Of 16 tram routes in the city, 11 begin and end at Centraal Station.

An extensive **bus** network complements the trams and reaches many points the trams don't cover.

The city's four **Metro** (subway) lines don't serve most areas you'll want to visit, being used mainly to get people to and from the suburbs, but from Centraal Station you can use Metro trains to reach Nieuwmarkt and Waterlooplein, both stops in the central zone.

Maps showing the transportation network and fare zones are posted at most tram/bus shelters and all Metro stations. A detailed map is available from VVV tourist offices and the **GVB Amsterdam Tickets & Info** office (*②* **0900/9292**) on Stationsplein in front of Centraal Station.

You can buy tickets from drivers, conductors, ticket dispensers, GVB Amsterdam Tickets & Info office, VVV tourist offices, and many news vendors. An *enkeltje* (single-journey ticket) costs 1.60€ ($1.85) for one zone and 2.40€ ($2.75) for two zones. Tourists rarely travel outside the central zone.

A *dagkaart* (day ticket) is good for unlimited travel in all city zones for up to 9 days. A 1-day card is 6.30€ ($7) from the GVB Amsterdam Tickets & Info office. Also available are day tickets valid for 2 and 3 days, for 10€ ($12) and 13€ ($15).

A flexible option is to buy a *strippenkaart* (strip card) that you can use throughout your stay. You can buy an eight-strip card for 6.40€ ($7) from drivers and conductors, or the more cost-effective 15-strip card, also for 6.40€ ($7) and the 45-strip card for 19€ ($22) from the locations referred to above. Before boarding a tram or bus, determine how many zones you'll be traversing. Fold your strip card so that one more box than the number of zones is facing up, and stick this end into the yellow box near the door as you enter. The machine stamps your card (some trams have a conductor who stamps the card). On buses, have the driver stamp your card. The ticket includes transfers to other tram, bus, and Metro lines within 1 hour of the time stamped.

Keep in mind that inspectors, sometimes undercover, may demand to see your ticket at any time. If you haven't paid the proper fare, you'll be fined 30€ ($35) plus the fare for the ride.

By Bike   Follow the Dutch example and pedal. A bike is one of the best ways of getting around in this flat city where too many cars clog the narrow streets. You see children barely old enough to walk, their great-grandparents, and even businesswomen in high heels pedaling through the city in any kind of weather. Sunday, when the city is quiet, is a good day to pedal through the parks and to practice riding on cobblestones and dealing with trams before venturing into a rush-hour fray.

Warning: Watch out for unpredictable car drivers, and always lock your bike and its front wheel to something fixed and solid—theft is common.

Bike-rental averages 7€ ($8) per day or 30€ ($35) per week, with a deposit required. The following outfits are located in the city center and have good rates and service: **Take a Bike,** in the basement of Centraal Station, to the right of the main entrance as you face the station (℗ **020/624-8391;** tram: 1, 2, 4, 5, 9, 13, 16, 17, 24, or 25); **Damstraat Rent-a-Bike,** Damstraat 22–24 (℗ **020/625-5029;** tram: 4, 9, 14, 16, 24, or 25); **MacBike,** Mr. Visserplein 2 (℗ **020/620-0985;** tram: 4, 9, or 14); **MacBike Too,** Marnixstraat 220 (℗ **020/626-6964;** tram: 10 or 17); and **Bike City,** Bloemgracht 70 (℗ **020/626-3721;** tram: 13, 14, or 17).

By Taxi   Officially, you can't simply hail a cab, but they'll often stop if you do. You can get a taxi in front of any major hotel and at Centraal Station, the Dam, Leidseplein, Rembrandtplein, and other locations. To phone for a cab, call **Taxi Centrale** (℗ **020/677-7777**). Fares start at 2.90€ ($3.35) and increase by 1.80€ ($2.05) a kilometer, or about 2.90€ ($3.35) a mile; waiting time is 32€ ($36) an hour.

By Boat   The **Museumboot** (℗ **020/530-1090;** www.lovers.nl) operates canal buses near virtually all Amsterdam's museums and attractions. The boats leave from in front of Centraal Station every 30 minutes daily from 10am to 5pm. Tickets are available at the Lovers Canal Cruises counter near the dock. A day ticket is 14€ ($16) for adults, 9.50€ ($11) for children ages 4 to 12, and free for children under 4; after 1pm, tickets are, respectively, 13€ ($14) and 7.25€ ($8). The ticket allows reduced admission to most of the museums and attractions on the route.

The **Canal Bus** (℗ **020/623-9886;** www.canal.nl) boats operate daily from 10am to around 6:30pm on three fixed routes—Green, Red, and Blue—that connect important museums and shopping and entertainment districts, with two buses an hour at peak times. A day pass, valid until noon the next day and including a museum admission discount, is 15€ ($17) for adults and 7.95€ ($9) for children ages 4 to 12, and free for children under 4.

A water taxi, from a dock outside Centraal Station, takes up to eight passengers, at 60€ ($69) per half-hour and with a 25€ ($29) pickup charge. If you feel like a splurge, call **Watertaxi** (℗ **020/535-6363**).

By Rental Car   Don't drive in Amsterdam. The city is a jumble of one-way streets, narrow bridges, and trams and cyclists darting every which way. Tough measures are in place to make driving as difficult as possible. No-parking zones are rigorously enforced and the limited parking spaces are expensive. Car break-ins are common.

Outside the city, driving is a different story and you may want to rent a car to see the nearby countryside. All the top international firms rent here: **Avis,** Nassaukade 380 (℗ **020/683-6061;** tram: 1 or 6); **Budget,** Overtoom 121 (℗ **020/612-6066;** tram: 1 or 6); **Europcar,** Overtoom 197 (℗ **020/683-2123;** tram: 1 or 6); and **Hertz,** Overtoom 333 (℗ **020/201-5312;** tram: 1, 6). All of these firms also have desks at the airport. Rates begin at around 45€ ($52) for a small car with unlimited mileage.

Remember: You get the best deal if you arrange the rental before leaving home.

FAST FACTS: **Amsterdam**

American Express The offices at Damrak 66 (℡ **020/504-7777**; tram: 4, 9, 14, 16, 24, or 25) and Van Baerlestraat 39 (℡ **020/673-8550**; tram: 2, 3, 5, or 12) are open Monday to Friday from 9am to 5pm and Saturday from 9am to noon. The Damrak office provides currency exchange and books tours; the Van Baerlestraat office only books tours.

Business Hours **Banks** are open Monday to Friday from 9am to 4 or 5pm, and some to 7pm on Thursday. Hours for **offices** are Monday to Friday from 9 or 10am to 4 or 5pm. Regular **shopping** hours are Monday from 10 or 11am to 6pm; Tuesday, Wednesday, and Friday from 9am to 6pm; Thursday from 9am to 9pm; and Saturday from 9am to 5pm. Some stores are open Sunday from noon to 5pm.

Currency The Netherlands uses the **euro** (€).

Currency Exchange The best options for changing money are the VVV tourist offices, banks, and, if you carry American Express traveler's checks, **American Express** (see above). Other fair-dealing options are **Thomas Cook,** Damrak 125 (℡ **020/620-3236**; tram: 4, 9, 14, 16, 29, 24, or 25), Dam 23–25 (℡ **020/625-0922**; tram: 4, 9, 14, 16, 29, 24, or 25), and Leidseplein 31A (℡ **020/626-7000**; tram: 1, 2, 5, 6, 7, or 10); and the **Grenswisselkantoor (GWK)** exchange at Centraal Station (℡ **020/627-2731**).

Some centrally located bank branches with **automated teller machines (ATMs)** are **ABN-AMRO Bank,** Dam 2 (tram: 4, 9, 14, 16, 24, or 25), and at Leidsestraat 1 (tram: 1, 2, or 5) at Leidseplein; **Rabobank,** Dam 16 (tram: 4, 9, 14, 16, 24, or 25); and **Fortis Bank,** Singel 548 (tram: 4, 9, 14, 16, 24, or 25), at the Flower Market.

Dentists/Doctors Call the **Central Medical Service** (℡ **020/592-3434**).

Drugstores/Pharmacies For both prescription and nonprescription medicines, go to an *apotheek* (pharmacy). Regular pharmacy hours are Monday to Saturday 9am to 5:30pm. Try **Dam Apotheek,** Damstraat 2 (℡ **020/624-4331**; tram: 4, 9, 14, 16, 24, or 25). All pharmacies post locations of nearby all-night and Sunday pharmacies on the door.

Embassies & Consulates **U.S. Consulate:** Museumplein 19 (℡ **020/575-5309**; tram: 3, 5, 12, or 16), open Monday to Friday 8:30am to noon and 1:30 to 3:30pm; **U.K. Consulate-General:** Koningslaan 44 (℡ **020/676-4343**; tram: 2), open Monday to Friday 9am to noon and 2 to 4pm.

Embassies are in The Hague (Den Haag): **U.S.:** Lange Voorhout 102 (℡ **070/310-9209**); **Canada:** Sophialaan 7 (℡ **070/311-1600**); **U.K.:** Lange Voorhout 10 (℡ **070/427-0427**); **Ireland:** Dr. Kuyperstraat 9 (℡ **070/363-0993**); **Australia:** Carnegielaan 4 (℡ **070/310-8200**); **New Zealand:** Carnegielaan 10 (℡ **070/346-9324**).

Emergencies For police assistance, an ambulance, or the fire department, call ℡ **112.**

Holidays The following holidays are observed in Amsterdam: January 1 (New Year's Day); Good Friday; Easter Monday; April 30 (Queen's Day/ *Koninginnedag*); Ascension Day; Pentecost Monday; December 25 (Christmas Day) and December 26. The dates for Easter, Ascension, and Pentecost change each year.

Hospitals Two hospitals with emergency services are the **Onze-Lieve-Vrouwe Gasthuis,** Eerste Oosterparkstraat 179 (© **020/599-9111**; tram: 3, 7, or 10), in Amsterdam Oost; and the giant **Academisch Medisch Centrum (AMC),** Meibergdreef 9 (© **020/566-3333**; Metro: Holendrecht), in Amsterdam Zuidoost.

Internet Access In the city center, **easyInternetcafé** (www.easyInternetcafe.com) has two locations: Damrak 33 (© **020/320-8082**; tram: 1, 2, 4, 5, 9, 13, 16, 17, 24, or 25); and Reguliersbreestraat 22 (© **020/320-6291**; tram: 4, 9, or 14). Both are open 24 hours a day, and access begins at 1.50€ ($1.75) an hour. A less-crowded choice is the **Internet Café,** Martelaarsgracht 11 (© **020/627-1052**; info@internetcafe.nl; tram: 1, 2, 5, 13, or 17), open Sunday to Thursday from 9am to 1am, Friday to Saturday from 9am to 3am; access is 2.75€ ($3.15) an hour.

Mail Most **post offices** are open Monday to Friday from 9am to 5pm. The office at Singel 256, at the corner of Raadhuisstraat (tram: 13, 14, or 17), is open Monday to Friday from 9am to 6pm (to 8pm Thurs), Saturday from 9am to 3pm. Postage for a postcard or ordinary letter to the U.S., Canada, Australia, and New Zealand is .75€ (85¢); to the U.K. or Ireland it's .45€ (50¢).

Police In an emergency, call © **112**. In nonurgent situations, go to the **Police Headquarters,** Elandsgracht 117 © **020/559-9111.**

Safety Random violent crime is not common in Amsterdam, though it does happen. Nonviolent crimes like pickpocketing and theft from cars are common; tourists in particular are targets. Muggings are more rare, but you still need to watch out in some places and circumstances, like strolling through the Red Light District or along a deserted canal side at night.

Taxes A **value-added tax (BTW)** of 6% is levied on hotel and restaurant bills (19% on beer, wine, and liquor), and 6% or 19% (the amount depends on the product) on purchases. For information on how to recover some of the 19% rate of tax on purchases, see "The Shopping Scene," later in this chapter.

Telephone The **country code** for the Netherlands is **31**. The **city code** for Amsterdam is **20**; use this code when you're calling from outside the Netherlands. If you're within the Netherlands but not in Amsterdam, use **020**. If you're calling within Amsterdam, simply leave off the code and dial only the regular seven-digit phone number.

Both local and long-distance calls from a pay phone are .30€ (35¢) per minute. International calls, per minute, are: **U.S.** and **Canada** .30€ (35¢); **U.K.** and **Ireland** .35€ (40¢); **Australia** and **New Zealand** .40€ (45¢). You can use pay phones in booths all around town with a KPN *telekaart* (phone card), selling for 5€ ($6), 13€ ($15), and 25€ ($29) from post offices, train ticket counters, and newsstands. Some pay phones take coins of .10€, .20€, .50€, and 1€. For information inside the Netherlands, call © **0900/8008**; for international information, call © **0900/8418.**

To charge a call to your calling card, dial AT&T (© **0800/022-9111**); MCI (© **0800/022-9122**); Sprint (© **0800/022-9119**); Canada Direct (© **0800/022-9116**); or British Telecom (© **0800/022-9944**).

Tipping A 15% service is included in the price of the meals at almost all restaurants (if it isn't, it will generally say so on the menu), so it's not necessary to leave a tip. But waitstaff do appreciate tips, and if the service is good you might want to leave a small one by rounding up in cash, not on a credit card slip, to the nearest euro or the nearest 5€ ($6), depending on the price of the meal (in an expensive restaurant you might feel obliged to go up to the nearest 10€ ($12). Taxi fares are high and include a service charge; though drivers appreciate a tip, it's not really necessary to give one unless you want to.

WHERE TO STAY

Booking ahead is always advised. The Dutch hotel industry runs a free hotel-booking service, the **Netherlands Reservation Center,** P.O. Box 404, 2260 AK Leidschendam (© **070/419-5500;** fax 070/419-5519; or book online at www.hotelres.nl). If you arrive in Amsterdam without a reservation, consult the **VVV tourist offices** (see "Visitor Information," earlier in this chapter). Or contact the VVV's **Amsterdam Reservation Center** (© **0777/000-888;** reservations@amsterdamtourist.nl). In summer, it's imperative you look for a room early in the day—by late afternoon many hotels are already full.

If you need to stay close to the airport, try the **Sheraton Amsterdam Airport,** Schiphol Blvd. 101, 1118 BG Schiphol Airport (© **800/325-3535** in the U.S. and Canada, or 020/316-4300; fax 020/316-4399; www.starwood.com/sheraton/search/hotel_detail.html?propertyID=301). You will have all the comfort you would expect from a top-flight Sheraton. Doubles cost 325€ to 395€ ($374–$454). A less expensive option is the **Dorint Schiphol Amsterdam,** Sloterweg 299, 1171 VB Badhoevedorp (© **020/658-8111;** fax 020/658-8100; www.dorint.de). Doubles cost 175€ to 210€ ($201–$242).

AROUND THE DAM & CENTRAAL STATION
Expensive

Die Port van Cleve ★★ Oozing history and class, one of the city's oldest hotels began its life in 1864 as the first Heineken brewery. Behind the ornamental facade, complete with turrets and alcoves, the recently renovated rooms, though on the small side, are comfortably furnished in modern yet cozy style. You won't eat better Dutch food than in the hotel's character-rich restaurant **Brasserie De Poort,** and you can drink in the equally notable bar **De Blauwe Parade,** which is watched over by Delft Blue tiles.

Nieuwezijds Voorburgwal 176–180 (behind the Royal Palace), 1012 SJ Amsterdam. © **020/622-6429.** Fax 020/622-0240. www.dieportvancleve.com. 120 units. 215€–350€ ($247–$403) double; 350€–525€ ($403–$604) suite; add 5% city tax. AE, DC, MC, V. No parking. Tram: 1, 2, 5, 6, 13, 14, or 17 to the Dam. **Amenities:** Restaurant; bar; cafe; concierge; business center; limited room service; executive rooms; nonsmoking rooms. *In room:* TV w/pay movies, hair dryer, safe.

Moderate

Avenue Hotel ★ About 2 minutes from Centraal Station, this recently renovated and expanded establishment has some of the style and amenities of its neighbor, the Crowne Plaza (see below), at less than half the price. Part of the premises is a converted warehouse from the city's golden age that belonged to the V.O.C., the United East India Company. The rooms aren't huge, but they are bright and have clean furnishings and good-size bathrooms, some with a double sink.

Nieuwezijds Voorburgwal 33 (near Centraal Station), 1012 RD Amsterdam. ✆ 020/530-9530. Fax 020/530-9599. www.avenue-hotel.nl. 78 units. 150€–180€ ($173–$207) double. Rates include buffet breakfast. AE, DC, MC, V. Limited street parking. Tram: 1, 2, 5, 6, 13, or 17 to Nieuwezijds Kolk. **Amenities:** Bar/brasserie; bike rental; dry cleaning. *In room:* TV w/pay movies, dataport, hair dryer.

Inexpensive

Amstel Botel ⭐ Where better to experience a city built on water than on a moored boat-hotel? Built in 1993, Amsterdam's only floating hotel has become quite popular, largely because of its location, seemingly adventurous nature, and rates. The rooms, on four decks connected by an elevator, are furnished in a no-nonsense but comfortable modern style; the showers are small. To get here, leave the station and turn left, passing the bike rental—the Botel is painted white and is directly in front of you. Be sure to ask for a room with a view on the water-side, not on the uninspiring quay side.

Oosterdokskade 2–4 (at Centraal Station), 1011 AE Amsterdam. ✆ 020/626-4247. Fax 020/639-1952. www.amstelbotel.com. 175 units. 87€–92€ ($100–$106) double. AE, DC, MC, V. Limited parking on quay. Tram: 1, 2, 4, 5, 6, 9, 13, 16, 17, 24, or 25 to Centraal Station. *In room:* TV.

ALONG THE CANAL BELT
Expensive

Ambassade ⭐⭐ Perhaps more than any other hotel in Amsterdam, this one, in 10 17th- and 18th-century canal houses on the Herengracht and Singel canals, re-creates the feeling of living in an elegant canal house. The pastel-toned rooms are individually styled, their size and shape varying according to the char-acter of the individual houses. Everyone who stays at the Ambassade enjoys the view each morning with breakfast in the bi-level, chandeliered breakfast room or each evening in the adjoining parlor, with Persian rugs and a stately grandfather clock ticking away.

Herengracht 341 (near Spui), 1016 AZ Amsterdam. ✆ 020/555-0222. Fax 020/555-0277. www.ambassade-hotel.nl. 59 units. 188€ ($216) double; 260€–325€ ($299–$374) suite. AE, DC, MC, V. Limited street parking. Tram: 1, 2, or 5 to Spui. **Amenities:** Bike rental; 24-hr. room service; massage at nearby float center; babysitting; laundry service; dry cleaning. *In room:* TV, hair dryer, safe.

Moderate

Amsterdam Wiechmann ⭐ It takes only a moment to feel at home in this hotel's antiques-adorned lobby. Owned for years by American T. Boddy and his Dutch wife, Nicky, the Wiechmann, which has no elevator, is comfortable and casual. Like a good wine, it gets better with age, and the location is one of the best you'll find in this or any price range. Most rooms are furnished in modern style, with twin or double beds, and some have big bay windows. Higher-priced doubles have antique furnishings, and many have a canal view.

Prinsengracht 328–332 (at Looiersgracht), 1016 HX Amsterdam. ✆ 020/626-3321. Fax 020/626-8962. www.hotelwiechmann.nl. 38 units. 120€–140€ ($138–$161) double. Rates include continental breakfast. MC, V. Limited street parking. Tram: 1, 2, or 5 to Prinsengracht. **Amenities:** Bar. *In room:* TV, safe.

Canal House ⭐⭐ A contemporary approach to reestablishing the elegant canal-house atmosphere has been taken by the owner of this small hotel, in an effort to create a home away from home. Three adjoining houses dating from 1630 were rebuilt to provide private bathrooms, and then filled with antiques, quilts, and Chinese rugs. Room no. 26 has a panoramic view of the canal. The beds, some with drapes, have new and comfortable mattresses on antique frames.

An elegant breakfast room, seemingly unchanged since the 17th century, overlooks the back garden, and there's a cozy Victorian-style saloon.

Keizersgracht 148 (near Leliegracht), 1015 CX Amsterdam. ✆ **020/622-5182.** Fax 020/624-1317. www.canalhouse.nl. 26 units. 140€–190€ ($161–$219) double. Rates include continental breakfast. DC, MC, V. Limited street parking. Tram: 6, 13, 14, or 17 to Westermarkt. **Amenities:** Lounge; limited room service. *In room:* Hair dryer.

Hotel Estheréa ★★ If you like to stay at elegant, not-too-big hotels, you'll be pleased by the Estheréa. It's been owned by the same family since its beginnings and, like so many hotels in Amsterdam, was built anew within the walls of a group of neighboring 17th-century canal houses. The family touch shows in careful attention to detail and a breezy but professional approach. While the hotel may look dated to some, the wood bedsteads and dresser-desks in fact lend warmth to recently renovated and upgraded rooms. The room sizes vary considerably according to their location in the canal houses, and a few are quite small.

Singel 305 (near Spui), 1012 WJ Amsterdam. ✆ **020/624-5146.** Fax 020/623-9001. www.estherea.nl. 70 units. 166€–280€ ($191–$322) double; add 5% city tax. AE, DC, MC, V. Limited street parking. Tram: 1, 2, or 5 to Spui. **Amenities:** Bar; lounge; bike rental; concierge; limited room service; babysitting; laundry service; dry cleaning; nonsmoking rooms. *In room:* TV, minibar, hair dryer, safe.

Inexpensive

Hoksbergen ★ *(Kids)* At a tranquil point on the historic Singel canal, this inexpensive hotel in a 300-year-old canal house is neither flashy nor elegant, but it's bright and fresh, which makes it appealing to budget-conscious travelers who don't want to swap creature comforts for euros. Its central location makes it easy to get to all the surrounding sights and attractions. Rooms at the front have canal views. There's no elevator.

Singel 301 (near Spui), 1012 WH Amsterdam. ✆ **020/626-6043.** Fax 020/638-3479. www.hotelhoksbergen.com. 14 units. 80€–104€ ($92–$120) double. Rates include continental breakfast. AE, DC, MC, V. Limited street parking. Tram: 1, 2, or 5 to Spui. *In room:* TV.

IN THE JORDAAN
Inexpensive

Acacia ★ Not on one of the major canals, but in Jordaan, facing a small canal and just a block from the Prinsengracht, the Acacia is run by a friendly couple who are justifiably proud of their welcoming and well-kept hotel. Simple, clean, and comfortable, the rooms have recently been equipped with new beds, writing tables, and chairs, and all have canal views. Two houseboats for guests on nearby Lijnbaansgracht add an authentic local touch. There's no elevator.

Lindengracht 251 (at Lijnbaansgracht), 1015 KH, Amsterdam. ✆ **020/622-1460.** Fax 020/638-0748. www.hotelacacia.nl. 18 units (including houseboats). 80€–90€ ($92–$104) double; 95€–110€ ($110–$127) houseboat double. Rates include continental breakfast. MC, V (5% surcharge). Limited street parking. Tram: 3 or 10 to Marnixplein. *In room:* TV.

Tips A Canal-House Warning

Be prepared to climb hard-to-navigate stairways if you want to save money on lodging in Amsterdam by staying in a canal house. Narrow and steep as ladders, these stairways were designed to conserve space in the narrow houses along the canals. If you have difficulty climbing stairs, ask for a room on a lower floor.

AROUND LEIDSEPLEIN
Very Expensive

Crowne Plaza Amsterdam–American ★★★   A fanciful, castlelike mix of Venetian Gothic and Art Nouveau, the American has been both a prominent landmark and a popular meeting place for Amsterdammers since 1900. While the exterior must always remain a protected architectural treasure of turrets, arches, and balconies, the interior (except that of the cafe, which is also protected) is modern and chic, though at times a bit gaudy. Rooms are subdued, refined, and superbly furnished, and while some have a view of the Singelgracht, others overlook kaleidoscopic Leidseplein.

Leidsekade 97 (at Leidseplein), 1017 PN Amsterdam. © 800/227-6963 in the U.S. and Canada, or 020/556-3000. Fax 020/556-3001. www.amsterdam-american.crowneplaza.com. 174 units. 220€–405€ ($253–$466) double; 385€–470€ ($443–$541) suite; add 5% city tax. AE, DC, MC, V. No parking. Tram: 1, 2, 5, 6, 7, or 10 to Leidseplein. **Amenities:** Restaurant; bar; exercise room; sauna; concierge; 24-hr. room service; in-room massage; laundry service; same-day dry cleaning. *In room:* A/C, TV w/pay movies, dataport, minibar, coffeemaker, hair dryer, iron, safe.

AROUND REMBRANDTPLEIN
Very Expensive

Hôtel de l'Europe ★★★   On a stretch of prime riverside real estate in the city center, this elegant old establishment is a member of the Leading Hotels of the World. Its red-and-white facade, at the point where the Amstel River flows into the city's canal network, is an iconic element in the classic view of the city. Built in 1896, the de l'Europe has a grand style and a sense of ease, a smooth combination of aged dignity and modern comforts. Guest rooms and bathrooms are spacious and bright, furnished with classic good taste. Some rooms have minibalconies overlooking the river, and all boast marble bathrooms.

Nieuwe Doelenstraat 2–8 (facing Muntplein), 1012 CP Amsterdam. © 800/223-6800 in the U.S. and Canada, or 020/531-1777. Fax 020/531-1778. www.leurope.nl. 100 units. 350€–435€ ($403–$500) double; from 455€ ($523) suite; add 5% city tax. AE, DC, MC, V. Valet and self-parking 40€ ($46). Tram: 4, 9, 14, 16, 24, or 25 to De Munt. **Amenities:** 2 restaurants; 2 bars; heated indoor pool; health club; sauna; concierge; 24-hr. room service; massage; babysitting; laundry service; dry cleaning; nonsmoking rooms. *In room:* A/C, TV w/pay movies, dataport, minibar, hair dryer, safe.

Expensive

NH Schiller Hotel ★★   An Amsterdam gem from 1912, now fully restored, this hotel boasts a blend of Art Nouveau and Art Deco in its public spaces, a theme that is reflected in the tasteful furnishings in the rooms. Its sculpted facade, wrought-iron balconies, and stained-glass windows stand out on the often brash Rembrandtplein. **Brasserie Schiller** is a gracious, oak-paneled dining room, and **Café Schiller** is one of Amsterdam's few permanent sidewalk cafes.

Rembrandtplein 26–36, 1017 CV Amsterdam. © 020/554-0700. Fax 020/626-6831. www.nh-hoteles.com. 93 units. 250€ ($288) double; from 290€ ($334) suite. AE, DC, MC, V. Limited street parking. Tram: 4, 9, or 14 to Rembrandtplein. **Amenities:** Restaurant, 2 bars; health club; 24-hr. room service; babysitting; laundry service; dry cleaning. *In room:* TV, minibar, coffeemaker, hair dryer.

Moderate

Seven Bridges ★★   Each huge room at this fine hotel is unique, with antique furnishings, plush carpets, and reproductions of modern art; one room even has a bathroom with a skylight and wooden walls similar to those in a sauna. Decor includes handmade Italian drapes, hand-painted tiles, and wood-tiled floors. Some attic rooms have sloped ceilings and exposed beams. There's no elevator. The front rooms overlook a small canal, and the rear rooms overlook a garden. Proprietors Pierre Keulers and Gunter Glaner are extremely helpful.

Reguliersgracht 31 (at Keizersgracht), 1017 LK Amsterdam. ✆ 020/623-1329. No fax. 8 units. 120€–220€ ($138–$253) double. Rates include full breakfast. AE, MC, V. Limited street parking. Tram: 4 to Keizersgracht. *In room:* TV, hair dryer.

AROUND MUSEUMPLEIN
Expensive
Bilderberg Hotel Jan Luyken ★★   In a residential neighborhood 1 block from Pieter Cornelisz Hooftstraat's classy stores, this is best described as a small hotel with many of the amenities and facilities of a big one. Rooms are classically furnished, bathrooms modern. The owners are proud of the setting they've created and are constantly improving the hotel's facilities.

Jan Luijkenstraat 58 (near the Rijksmuseum), 1071 CS Amsterdam. ✆ 800/641-0300 in the U.S. and Canada, or 020/573-0730. Fax 020/676-3841. www.janluyken.nl. 62 units. 220€–295€ ($253–$340) double; add 5% city tax. AE, DC, MC, V. Limited street parking. Tram: 2 or 5 to Hobbemastraat. **Amenities:** Wine bar; spa; concierge; 24-hr. room service; in-room massage; babysitting; laundry service; dry cleaning; nonsmoking rooms. *In room:* A/C, TV, dataport, minibar, hair dryer, iron, safe.

Moderate
De Filosoof ★★   On a quiet street of brick houses near Vondelpark, this extraordinary, elegant hotel should at least make you think. One of the owners, a philosophy professor, has decorated rooms with posters, framed quotes, and unusual objects chosen to represent philosophical and cultural themes. Ponder the meaning of life in rooms dedicated to thinkers like Goethe, Wittgenstein, Nietzsche, Marx, and Einstein, or motifs like Eros, the Renaissance, or astrology. You can even consult your private bookshelf of philosophical works or join in a weekly philosophy debate. The rooms in an annex across the street are larger; some open onto a private terrace.

Anna van den Vondelstraat 6 (off Overtoom, at Vondelpark), 1054 GZ Amsterdam. ✆ 020/683-3013. Fax 020/685-3750. www.hotelfilosoof.nl. 38 units. 115€–138€ ($132–$159) double. Rates include buffet breakfast. AE, MC, V. Limited street parking. Tram: 1 or 6 to Jan Pieter Heijestraat. **Amenities:** Lounge. *In room:* TV, hair dryer, safe.

Inexpensive
Piet Hein ★   Occupying a villa close to the city's most important museums, the Piet Hein is named after a Dutch folk hero, a 17th-century admiral who captured a Spanish silver shipment. Rooms are spacious and well furnished, and the staff friendly and professional. Half the rooms overlook the park; two second-floor doubles have semicircular balconies; and a honeymoon suite has a waterbed. Lower-priced rooms are in an annex.

Vossiusstraat 52–53 (off of Van Baerlestraat), 1071 AK Amsterdam. ✆ 020/662-7205. Fax 020/662-1526. www.hotelpiethein.com. 65 units. 118€–160€ ($136–$184) double. Rates include buffet breakfast. AE, DC, MC, V. Limited street parking. Tram: 3, 5, or 12 to Van Baerlestraat. **Amenities:** Bar; concierge; limited room service; laundry service; dry cleaning; nonsmoking rooms. *In room:* TV w/pay movies.

IN AMSTERDAM SOUTH
Inexpensive
Van Ostade Bicycle Hotel ★★   The young proprietors of this establishment have hit on an interesting idea: They cater to visitors who wish to explore Amsterdam on bikes and can help you plan biking routes through and around the city. You can rent bikes for 5€ ($5.75) daily, no deposit, and stable your trusty steed indoors. The recently renovated rooms have new carpets and plain but

comfortable modern furnishings; some have kitchenettes and small balconies, and there are large rooms for families. There's no elevator.

Van Ostadestraat 123 (off of Ferdinand Bolstraat), Amsterdam 1072 SV. ⓒ 020/679-3452. Fax 020/ 671-5213. www.bicyclehotel.com. 16 units, 8 with bathroom. 70€–99€ ($81–$114) double with bathroom; 61€–70€ ($70–$81) double without bathroom. Rates include continental breakfast. AE, MC, V. Parking 17€ ($20). Tram: 3, 12, or 25 to Ceintuurbaan-Ferdinand Bolstraat. **Amenities:** Bike rental. *In room:* TV.

WHERE TO DINE

As a trading and gateway city that positively revels in its status as a melting pot, Amsterdam has absorbed culinary influences from far and wide. You find dozens of ethnic eateries serving everything from Argentine to Yugoslavian food. Indonesian food is extremely popular, notably the *rijsttafel* (see "Spice of Life," below). Many of these ethnic places serve hearty and delicious meals at very reasonable prices. And you'll find plenty of traditional Dutch restaurants.

AROUND CENTRAAL STATION
Expensive

De Silveren Spiegel ⭐ TRADITIONAL DUTCH/CLASSICAL FRENCH The two houses forming the premises were constructed in 1614 for wealthy soap maker Laurens Jansz Spieghel. It's typically Old Dutch inside, with the bar downstairs and more dining rooms where the bedrooms used to be. There's a garden in back, and the place emanates a traditional Dutch tidiness that's very welcoming. The updated menu has finely prepared seafood and meat dishes like baked sole filets with wild spinach, and Texel lamb with ratatouille; traditional Zaanse mustard is always available.

Kattengat 4–6 (off Singel). ⓒ **020/624-6589.** Main courses 25€–30€ ($29–$35); fixed-price menus 38€–45€ ($44–$52). AE, MC, V. Daily 6–11pm. Tram: 1, 2, 5, 6, 13, or 17 to Martelaarsgracht.

ALONG THE CANAL BELT
Expensive

Christophe ⭐⭐ MODERN FRENCH The star of this show is owner and chef Jean-Christophe Royer, who offers sensuous, sophisticated food served up in an elegant setting that features dark cherrywood paneling, thick carpets, ricepaper lamp shades, stately cacti by the windows, and floral paintings by the contemporary Dutch artist Martin van Vreden. The food is similarly refined, using traditional Mediterranean ingredients—figs, truffles, olives, and saffron—in exciting new ways. Try the roasted milk-fed Pyrenean lamb, or roasted turbot in a light curry sauce, and finish with a light tart of prunes in Armagnac.

Leliegracht 46 (between Prinsengracht and Keizersgracht). ⓒ **020/625-0807.** www.christophe.nl. Main courses 31€–56€ ($36–$64); fixed-price menus 67€–75€ ($77–$86). AE, DC, MC, V. Tues–Sat 6:30–10:30pm. Tram: 6, 13, 14, or 17 to Westermarkt.

Moderate

Bolhoed ⭐ VEGETARIAN Forget the wholesome, dull, corn-sheaf-and-brown-rice image of vegetarian dining—Bolhoed adds a touch of spice to its health food formula with its Latin style, world music background, candlelight in the evenings, and fine view of the canal from its twin rooms beside the Prinsengracht. Service is zestful and friendly. Try such veggie delights as the *ragoût croissant* (pastry filled with leeks, tofu, seaweed, and curry sauce), or *zarzuela*. If you want to go whole hog, so to speak, and eat vegan, most of Bolhoed's dishes can be so prepared on request, and in any case most are made with organically grown produce.

Prinsengracht 60–62 (near Noordermarkt). ⓒ **020/626-1803.** Main courses 12€–15€ ($14–$17). No credit cards. Sun–Fri noon–11pm; Sat 11am–11pm. Tram: 6, 13, 14, or 17 to Westermarkt.

Moments Spice of Life

You haven't really eaten in Amsterdam until you've had an **Indonesian**
rijsttafel. This traditional "rice table" banquet consists of as many as 20
succulent and spicy foods served in tiny bowls. Pick and choose from
among the bowls and add your choice to the pile of rice on your plate.
It's almost impossible to eat all the food set on your table, but give it a
shot—it's delicious and a true taste of multicultural Amsterdam. For an
abbreviated version served on one plate, try *nasi rames.* At lunch, the
standard Indonesian fare is *nasi goreng* (fried rice with meat and vegetables) or *bami goreng* (fried noodles prepared in the same way).

De Belhamel ★★ *Finds* CONTINENTAL   Classical music complements Art
Nouveau in a graceful setting overlooking the Herengracht and Brouwersgracht
canals. The menu changes seasonally, and game is a specialty. You can expect
such menu dishes as puffed pastries layered with salmon, shellfish, crayfish tails,
and chervil beurre-blanc to start; and beef tenderloin in Madeira sauce with zucchini rösti and puffed garlic for a main course. Vegetarian dishes are also offered.

Brouwersgracht 60 (at Herengracht). ✆ 020/622-1095. Main courses 19€–20€ ($21–$23); fixed-price menu
32€ ($37). AE, MC, V. Sun–Thurs 6–10pm; Fri–Sat 6–10:30pm. Tram: 1, 2, 5, 6, 13, or 17 to Martelaarsgracht.

Tempo Doeloe ★★★ INDONESIAN   For authentic Indonesian cuisine, from
Java, Sumatra, and Bali—which doesn't leave out much—this place is hard to
beat. Though its local reputation goes up and down with the tide, it's invariably
busy. You dine in a batik ambience that's Indonesian but restrained, and a long
way short of being kitsch. The attractive decor and the fine china are unexpected
pluses. Try the many little meat, fish, and vegetable dishes of the three different
rijsttafel (rice table) options, from the 15-plate vegetarian rijsttafel sayoeran and
the 15-plate rijsttafel stimoelan to the sumptuous 25-plate rijsttafel istemewa.

Utrechtsestraat 75 (between Prinsengracht and Keizersgracht). ✆ 020/625-6718. www.tempodoeloerestaurant.
nl. Reservations recommended on weekends. Main courses 18€–23€ ($21–$26); rijsttafel 24€–32€ ($28–$36);
fixed-price menu 27€–43€ ($31–$49). AE, DC, MC, V. Mon–Sat 6–11:30pm. Tram: 4 to Keizersgracht.

Inexpensive

De Prins ★★ *Value* MODERN DUTCH/CONTINENTAL   In a 17th-cen-
tury canal house, this companionable brown cafe/restaurant opposite the Anne
Frankhuis serves the kind of food you'd expect from a much more expensive
place. The clientele is loyal, so the relatively few tables fill up quickly. It's a quiet
neighborhood restaurant—nothing fancy or trendy, but quite appealing, with
the bar on a slightly lower level than the restaurant and a sidewalk terrace for
drinks in summer.

Prinsengracht 124 (at Egelantiersgracht). ✆ 020/624-9382. Main courses 7.50€–15€ ($9–$17); dish of
the day 9.90€ ($12); specials 11€–15€ ($13–$17). AE, DC, MC, V. Daily 10am–1 or 2am (kitchen to 10pm).
Tram: 6, 13, 14, or 17 to Westermarkt.

Pancake Bakery ★ *Kids* PANCAKES   In a 17th-century canal warehouse is
this two-story restaurant with winding staircases and exposed beams, serving
some of the most delicious and unusual pancakes you'll ever taste. There are several dozen varieties, almost all of which make for a full meal. Choices include
salami and cheese, cheese and ginger, honey nuts and whipped cream, and ice

cream and *advokaat* (a Dutch eggnoglike cocktail). One of the bestsellers is what they call the American pancake: with fried chicken, sweet corn, peppers, carrots, Cajun sauce, and salad.

Prinsengracht 191 (at Prinsenstraat). ☎ 020/625-1333. www.pancake.nl. Reservations required for large groups. Pancakes 4€–10€ ($4.60–$12). AE, MC, V. Daily noon–9:30pm. Tram: 6, 13, 14, or 17 to Westermarkt.

AROUND SPUI
Expensive
D'Vijff Vlieghen ★ MODERN DUTCH   Touristy? Yes, but the "Five Flies" is one of Amsterdam's most famous restaurants, and the food is authentic stick-to-the-ribs Dutch fare. The chef is passionate about an updated form of Dutch cuisine he calls "the new Dutch kitchen." The menu has a selection of seasonal fish and game often marinated with fresh herbs and served with unusual vegetables like chard, wild spinach, and Brussels sprouts. If you're feeling adventurous, try the wild boar with sweet chestnuts and a sauce made with jenever (liquor flavored with juniper berries). The restaurant is a kind of Dutch theme park, with seven dining rooms in five canal houses decorated with artifacts from Holland's golden age. Don't miss the four original Rembrandt etchings in the Rembrandt Room and the collection of handmade glass in the Glass Room.

Spuistraat 294–302 (at Spui). ☎ 020/530-4060. www.thefiveflies.com. Reservations recommended on weekends. Main courses 21€–30€ ($24–$35); seasonal menu 32€–53€ ($36–$60). AE, DC, MC, V. Daily 5:30–10pm. Tram: 1, 2, or 5 to Spui.

Moderate
Haesje Claes TRADITIONAL DUTCH   If you're yearning for a cozy Old Dutch environment and hearty Dutch food at moderate prices, this is the place to go. It's inviting and intimate, with lots of nooks and crannies and with brocaded benches and traditional Dutch hanging lamps. The menu covers a lot of ground, ranging from canapés to caviar, but you'll be happiest with such Dutch stalwarts as tournedos, *hutspot* (stew), *stampot* (mashed potatoes and cabbage), or various fish stews, including those with IJsselmeer *paling* (eel).

Spuistraat 273–275 (at Spui). ☎ 020/624-9998. www.haesjeclaes.nl. Main courses 13€–20€ ($15–$23); tourist menu 19€ ($22). AE, DC, MC, V. Daily noon–10pm. Tram: 1, 2, or 5 to Spui.

Kantjil en de Tijger ★ INDONESIAN   Unlike Indonesian restaurants that wear their ethnic origins on their sleeve, the "Antelope and the Tiger" is modern and cool. Two bestsellers here are *nasi goreng Kantjil* (fried rice with pork kabobs, stewed beef, pickled cucumbers, and mixed vegetables) and the 20-item *rijsttafel* (rice with meat, seafood, and vegetables) for two. Other choices are stewed chicken in soy sauce, tofu omelet, shrimp with coconut dressing, Indonesian pumpkin, and mixed steamed vegetables with peanut-butter sauce. Finish with the cinnamon layer cake or the coffee with ginger liqueur and whipped cream.

Spuistraat 291–293 (beside Spui). ☎ 020/620-0994. www.kantjil.nl. Reservations recommended on weekends. Main courses 11€–15€ ($13–$17); rijsttafel 40€–50€ ($46–$58) for 2. AE, DC, MC, V. Daily 4:30–11pm. Tram: 1, 2, or 5 to Spui.

Inexpensive
Café Luxembourg ★★ INTERNATIONAL   "One of the world's great cafes," wrote the *New York Times* about this stylish, grand cafe. Unlike other cafes in Amsterdam, which often draw a distinctive clientele, the Luxembourg attracts all kinds of people with its amazingly large portions of food at reasonable prices. Soups, sandwiches, and such dishes as meatloaf are available. A special

attraction: You may find such exotica as Chinese dim sum and *satay ajam* (Indonesian grilled chicken in a peanut sauce) on the menu.

Spui 24 (at Spui). ℂ **020/620-6264.** Salads and specials 8.50€–11€ ($10–$13); lunch 4€–8.50€ ($4.60–$10); main courses 8€–18€ ($9–$21). AE, DC, MC, V. Sun–Thurs 9am–1am; Fri–Sat 9am–2am. Tram: 1, 2, or 5 to Spui.

AROUND LEIDSEPLEIN
Expensive

De Oesterbar SEAFOOD   De Oesterbar, which is more than 50 years old, is the best-known and most popular fish restaurant in Amsterdam. Its seafood is delivered fresh twice daily. The decor is a delight: all white tiles with fish tanks bubbling at your elbows on the street level, and Victorian brocades and etched glass in the more formal dining room upstairs. The menu is a directory of Dutch seafood dishes, but it also includes a few meat selections. Choices include sole Danoise with tiny Dutch shrimps; sole Véronique with Muscadet grapes; stewed eel in wine sauce; and the assorted fish plate of turbot, halibut, and fresh salmon.

Leidseplein 10. ℂ **020/623-2988.** Main courses 25€–34€ ($28–$39). AE, DC, MC, V. Daily noon–1am. Tram: 1, 2, 5, 6, 7, or 10 to Leidseplein.

Moderate

Café Américain ✿ INTERNATIONAL   This is a national monument of Dutch Jugendstil and Art Deco. Mata Hari held her wedding reception here in her pre-espionage days, and since its 1900 opening, this has been a haven for Dutch and international artists, writers, dancers, and actors. Leaded windows, newspaper-littered reading tables, bargello-patterned velvet upholstery, frosted-glass chandeliers from the 1920s, and tall, carved columns are all part of the dusky sit-and-chat setting. Menu dishes include monkfish, perch, rack of Irish lamb, and rosé breast of duck with creamed potatoes. Jazz lovers can dine to good music at a Sunday jazz brunch.

In the American Hotel, Leidsekade 97 (at Leidseplein). ℂ **020/556-3232.** www.amsterdam-american. crowneplaza.com Main courses 16€–21€ ($18–$24). AE, DC, MC, V. Daily 10:30am–midnight. Tram: 1, 2, 5, 6, 7, or 10 to Leidseplein.

AROUND REMBRANDTPLEIN
Inexpensive

Golden Temple ✿ VEGETARIAN   In its fourth decade of tickling meat-shunning palates, this temple of taste is still one of the best vegetarian (and vegan) options in town. The first thing you notice when you enter is that you can actually *see* the place—the veil of cigarette smoke that obscures most Amsterdam restaurants has been lifted here by a nonsmoking policy that adds a heavenly touch all on its own. If anything, the limpid atmosphere is a tad too hallowed, an effect enhanced by a Zen-like absence of decorative flourishes. The menu livens things up, however, with an unlikely roster of Indian, Middle Eastern, and Mexican dishes, and the multiple-choice platters are a good way to go.

Utrechtsestraat 126 (close to Frederiksplein). ℂ **020/626-8560.** www.restaurantgoldentemple.nl. Main courses 6.50€–9.50€ ($7–$11); mixed platter 12€ ($14). MC, V. Daily 5–10pm. Tram: 4 to Prinsengracht.

IN AMSTERDAM WEST
Moderate

Amsterdam ✿✿✿ *Finds* CONTINENTAL   Think of it as *Amsterdam: The Restaurant,* because it's quite a performance. Based in a century-old water-pumping station, complete with diesel-powered engine, this cafe-restaurant has taken this monument of Victorian industrial good taste and made of it a model

---

Tips Sweet Talk

If you have a sweet tooth, be sure to try some traditional Dutch desserts, such as *poffertjes* (miniature pancakes), *oliebollen* (like powdered sugar–covered doughnut holes), or pancakes. All these come with various fillings or toppings, many of which contain a liqueur of some sort. Traditional *poffertje* snack bars are garish affairs that look as though they're part of a circus. There's one on Weteringcircuit west of Leidseplein.

---

of contemporary good eats. Service is friendly, and the food is good and moderately priced. If you're feeling flush, spring for a double starter of half a lobster with six Zeeland oysters. The Amsterdam is a little bit out from the city center, but is easily worth the tram ride.

Watertorenplein 6 (off Haarlemmerweg). ℂ 020/682-2666. www.cradam.nl. Reservations recommended on weekends. Main courses 9.85€–18€ ($11–$21). AE, DC, MC, V. Daily 11am–midnight. Tram: 10 to Van Hallstraat.

IN AMSTERDAM EAST
Moderate

Gare de l'Est ★★ *Value* TRADITIONAL FRENCH/MEDITERRANEAN
The detached, distinctive house, with a recently added conservatory and a large sidewalk terrace, was originally a coffeehouse for workers at the Eastern Dock. Service is both relaxed and knowledgeable, and the fixed-price menu is excellent value for money, so any surprises appear on your plate rather than on the check. The strict five-course formula (starter, salad, main course of meat or fish, cheese, and dessert) leaves no room for choice—except for the main course. How does this sound—*pulpo stofado* with *risotto nero* (inkfish stew with black risotto) as a starter, and roast lamb with gazpacho sauce and farfalle pasta as a main course?

Cruquiusweg 9 (at the East Harbor). ℂ 020/463-0620. www.garedelest.nl. Reservations recommended on weekends. Fixed-price menu 30€ ($35). No credit cards. Daily 6–11pm. Tram: 7 or 10 to Zeeburgerdijk.

IN AMSTERDAM SOUTH
Moderate

De Kas ★★ CONTINENTAL   A converted 1926 greenhouse with a smokestack on open ground is the setting for this bright, spacious new place to see and be seen, with an atmosphere that's maybe a tad too precious. You get just a couple of variations on a three-course, daily-changing, fixed menu, with cheese board extra. Mediterranean-style greens and herbs come fresh from an adjacent working hothouse and the restaurant's own farm, and meat is sourced daily from nearby animal-friendly eco-producers. Service is attentive enough that the waitstaff seems to be acquainted personally with every item on your plate.

Kamerlingh Onneslaan 3 (close to Amstel Station). ℂ 020/462-4562. www.restaurantdekas.nl. Reservations required. Fixed-price lunch 32€ ($37); fixed-price dinner 44€ ($50). AE, DC, MC, V. Mon–Fri noon–3pm and 6:30–10pm; Sat 6:30–10pm. Tram: 9 to Hogeweg.

SEEING THE SIGHTS

Amsterdam has an almost bewildering embarrassment of riches. There are 160 canals to cruise, with a combined length of 76km (47 miles), spanned by 1,281 bridges; hundreds of narrow streets to wander; almost 8,000 historic buildings to see in the city center; more than 40 museums of all types to visit; diamond cutters and craftspeople to watch as they practice generations-old skills . . . the list is as long as every visitor's individual interests—and then some.

SIGHTSEEING SUGGESTIONS FOR FIRST-TIME VISITORS

If You Have 1 Day For the perfect introduction to the city, take a **canal cruise** and admire the many gabled merchants' houses and almost 1,200 bridges. In the afternoon, stroll through **Vondelpark** and return to the center through lively **Leidseplein.** In the evening, dine at a traditional restaurant or opt for an Indonesian rijsttafel, and end your day by dropping into a **brown cafe** (a traditional Amsterdam bar).

If You Have 2 Days Begin by going early to the **Anne Frank House.** Then, stroll along the central canals until lunchtime. In the afternoon, continue exploring the historic center on foot, visiting the **Dam** and the **Royal Palace** and ending up at bustling **Rembrandtplein.** In the evening, attend a concert at the nearby **Concertgebouw,** or opera or dance at the **Muziektheater.**

If You Have 3 or More Days Visit the **Van Gogh Museum** in the morning. Relax over coffee at the **Café Américain** on Leidseplein, with its stunning Art Nouveau interior. Look into some **street markets,** either the Albert Cuyp market, the floating Flower Market, or the Waterlooplein flea market. In the evening, take a walk in the **Red Light District** (if this isn't your idea of an edifying experience, consider instead the alternative dining option from day 1).

If You Have 4 or 5 Days Broaden your experience by mixing a focused perusal of interesting areas of Amsterdam with short out-of-town trips. For example, one morning you can tour **De Wallen,** the oldest part of the city, which includes the Red Light District (a far different kind of place during the daylight hours), before going by bus to **Volendam** and **Marken** on the IJsselmeer lake. On the other day, tour the **Jordaan** district in the morning (taking in a street market if you go on Mon or Sat), and take a breath of sea air at **Zandvoort** in the afternoon.

THREE KEY MUSEUMS

Rijksmuseum ★★★   Holland's premier museum, at Museumplein, is closed for renovations until mid-2008, and most of the museum's complete collection will be "invisible" to visitors for some time to come. During this period, however, key paintings from the magnificent 17th-century Dutch golden age collection can be viewed in the museum's own Philips Wing. Other elements of the collection likely will be on view at other venues in the city. The three-star rating given here is an indicator of the Rijksmuseum's importance when it is fully open. During the renovation period, you can find a complete review of the Rijksmuseum at **www.frommers.com**.

Stadhouderskade 42 (at Museumplein,). ℂ 020/647-7000. www.rijksmuseum.com. Admission 8.50€ ($10) adults, free for under 18. Daily 10am–5pm. Closed Jan 1. Tram: 2 or 5 to Hobbemastraat; 6, 7, or 10 to Weteringschans.

Van Gogh Museum ★★★   Anyone who has ever responded to van Gogh's vibrant colors and vivid landscapes will find walking through the rooms of this rather stark contemporary building a moving experience. The museum displays, in chronological order, more than 200 van Gogh paintings. As you move through the rooms, the canvases reflect the artist's changing environment and much of

---

⌒ **Value** Passport to Amsterdam

One of the best discounts in town is the **Amsterdam Pass,** available at VVV tourist offices for 31€ ($36) for 1 day, 41€ ($47) for 2 days, and 51€ ($59) for 3 days. It provides up to 150€ ($173) in savings, offering free or discounted admission to 38 museums and attractions (including the Rijksmuseum, Rembrandthuis, and Oude Kerk), a free canal cruise, and discounts on selected restaurants and stores. A free 1-, 2-, or 3-day transport ticket is included.

---

his inner life, so that gradually van Gogh himself becomes almost a tangible presence standing at your elbow. By the time you reach the vaguely threatening painting of a flock of black crows rising from a waving cornfield, you can almost feel the artist's mounting inner pain.

In addition to the paintings, nearly 600 drawings by van Gogh are on display in the museum's new wing, a free-standing, multistory, half-oval structure designed by the Japanese architect Kisho Kurokawa. It's constructed in a bold combination of titanium and gray-brown stone, and is connected to the main building by a subterranean walkway.

Note: Lines at the museum can be very long, especially in summer—try going on a weekday morning. Allow 2 to 4 hours to get around once you're inside.

Paulus Potterstraat 7 (at Museumplein). ℂ 020/570-5200. www.vangoghmuseum.nl. Admission 9€ ($10) adults, 2.50€ ($2.90) children 13–17, free for children under 13. Daily 10am–6pm. Closed Jan 1. Tram: 2, 3, 5, or 12 to Van Baerlestraat.

Anne Frankhuis ★★ A teenage Jewish girl, Anne Frank wrote her famous diary here while she and seven other Jewish refugees hid from the Nazis in a secret annex at the back of this large canal house. On July 6, 1942, the Franks and another Jewish family went into hiding to avoid being deported to Nazi concentration camps. Anne, the youngest Frank daughter, had been given a diary for her 13th birthday in 1942. With the eyes of a child and the writing skills of a girl who hoped one day to be a writer, she chronicled the almost-silent life in hiding of the *onderduikers* (divers or hiders), the continued persecution of Jews by Hitler, the progress of the war, and her personal growth as a young woman. Anne achieved her dream of being a famous writer: Today more than 13 million copies of *The Diary of Anne Frank* have been sold, in 50 languages.

The cramped, gloomy hiding place, where they were forced to maintain nearly total silence, kept them safe for more than 2 years until they were betrayed and pro-German Dutch police raided their refuge on August 4, 1944. Anne died of typhus in March 1945 at Bergen-Belsen, tragically close to the war's end; six of the others also died in concentration camps. Although the rooms contain no furniture and are as bare as they were when Anne's father, Otto, the only survivor, returned, the exhibits, including a year-by-year chronology of Anne's life, fill in the missing details. This lack of distraction allows you to project yourself into Anne's claustrophobic, fear-filled world.

Note: Lines here can be very long, especially in summer—try going on a weekday morning. This advice isn't as useful as it once was, because everybody is both giving it and heeding it, but it should still save you some waiting time. An alternative strategy if you're in town from April to August, when the museum is open to 9pm, is to go in the evening; it is invariably quiet then—till now at any rate. Once you're inside, an hour should do it, though many people linger.

Prinsengracht 263 (at Westermarkt). (C) 020/556-7100. www.annefrank.nl. Admission 7.50€ ($9) adults, 3.50€ ($4.05) children 10–17, free for children under 10. Apr–Aug daily 9am–9pm; Sept–Mar daily 9am–7pm; Jan 1 and Dec 25 noon–7pm. Closed Yom Kippur. Tram: 6, 13, 14, or 17 to Westermarkt.

MORE TOP MUSEUMS & GALLERIES

Amsterdams Historisch Museum ★★ In a huge 17th-century former orphanage, now housing exhibits covering nearly 700 years of the city's history, this fascinating museum gives you a better understanding of everything you see as you explore the city. Gallery by gallery, century by century, you learn how a fishing village became a major world trading center. The main focus is on the city's 17th-century golden age, a period when Amsterdam was the richest city in the world, and some of the most interesting exhibits are of the trades that made it rich. You can also view many famous paintings by Dutch masters. Next to the museum is the **Schuttersgalerij (Civic Guard Gallery),** a narrow, skylit chamber bedecked with 17th-century group portraits of militiamen. The hours are the same as for the museum, and admission is free.

Kalverstraat 92, Nieuwezijds Voorburgwal 357, and Sint-Luciënsteeg 27 (next to the Begijnhof). (C) 020/523-1822. www.ahm.nl. Admission 6€ ($7) adults, 4.50€ ($5) seniors/children 6–16, free for children under 6. Mon–Fri 10am–5pm; Sat–Sun and holidays 11am–5pm. Closed Jan 1, Apr 30, Dec 25. Tram: 1, 2, 4, 5, 9, 14, 16, 24, or 25 to Spui.

Joods Historisch Museum ★ Housed in the four restored 17th- and 18th-century synagogues of the beautiful Ashkenazi Synagogue complex, the Jewish Historical Museum tells the intertwining stories of Jewish identity, religion, culture, and history of the Jewish Dutch community. Inside are objects, photographs, artworks, and interactive displays. Jewish religious artifacts are a major focus. An exhibit covers the persecution of Jews in the Netherlands and throughout Europe under Hitler. The synagogues stand at the heart of a neighborhood that was the Jewish quarter for 300 years until the Nazi occupation during World War II emptied the city of its Jewish population. The oldest of the four, built in 1670, is the oldest public synagogue in western Europe; the newest dates from 1752.

Jonas Daniël Meijerplein 2–4 (at Waterlooplein). (C) 020/625-4229. www.jhm.nl. Admission 6.50€ ($7) adults, 4€ ($4.60) seniors/students, 3€ ($3.45) children 13–17, 2€ ($2.30) children 6–12, free for children under 6. Daily 11am–5pm. Closed Yom Kippur. Tram: 9 or 14 to Waterlooplein.

Museum Amstelkring Although Amsterdam has been known as a tolerant city for many centuries, just after the Protestant Reformation, Roman Catholics fell into disfavor. Forced to worship in secret, they devised ingenious ways of gathering for Sunday services. In an otherwise ordinary-looking 17th-century canal house in the middle of the Red Light District is the most amazing of these clandestine churches, known to the general public as "Our Lord in the Attic." Built in the 1660s by a wealthy Catholic merchant, the three houses making up this museum were designed specifically to house a church. Today they're furnished much as they would have been in the mid–18th century. Nothing prepares you for the mini-cathedral you come upon when you climb the last flight of stairs into the attic. A large baroque altar, religious statuary, pews to seat 150, an 18th-century organ, and an upper gallery complete this miniature church.

Oudezijds Voorburgwal 40 (near the Oude Kerk). (C) 020/624-6604. www.museumamstelkring.nl. Admission 7€ ($8) adults, 5€ ($6) students, 1€ ($1.15) children under 18. Mon–Sat 10am–5pm; Sun and holidays 1–5pm. Closed Jan 1, Apr 30. Tram: 1, 2, 4, 5, 6, 9, 13, 16, 17, 24, or 25 to Centraal Station.

Museum Het Rembrandthuis ⚜ When Rembrandt van Rijn moved into this three-story house in 1639, he was already a well-established wealthy artist. However, the cost of buying and furnishing the house led to his financial downfall in 1656. The museum houses a nearly complete collection of Rembrandt's etchings, and the artist's printing press. Of the 300 prints he made, 250 are here, with around half hanging on the walls at any one time. Rembrandt's prints show amazing detail, and you can see his use of shadow and light for dramatic effect. Wizened patriarchs, emaciated beggars, children at play, Rembrandt himself in numerous self-portraits, and Dutch landscapes are the subjects you'll long remember after a visit here. Temporary exhibits are mounted in an adjacent house that belonged to Rembrandt's wife, Saskia.

Jodenbreestraat 4 (at Waterlooplein). ℭ 020/520-0400. www.rembrandthuis.nl. Admission 7€ ($8) adults, 5€ ($6) students, 1.50€ ($1.75) children 6–15, free for children under 6. Mon–Sat 10am–5pm; Sun and holidays 1–5pm. Closed Jan 1. Tram: 9 or 14 to Waterlooplein.

Museum Van Loon   This magnificent patrician house from 1672 was owned by the van Loon family from 1884 to 1945. On its walls hang more than 80 family portraits, including those of Willem van Loon, one of the founders of the Dutch United East India Company; Nicolaes Ruychaver, who liberated Amsterdam from the Spanish in 1578; and another Willem van Loon, who became mayor in 1686. A marble staircase with an ornately curlicued brass balustrade leads up through the house, connecting restored period rooms that are filled with richly decorated paneling, stucco work, mirrors, fireplaces, furnishings, porcelain, medallions, chandeliers, rugs, and more. In the garden are carefully tended hedges and a coach house modeled on a Greek temple.

Keizersgracht 672 (near Vijzelstraat). ℭ 020/624-5255. www.museumvanloon.nl. Admission 5€ ($6) adults, 4€ ($4.60) students/children 5–18, free for children under 5. Sept–June Fri–Mon 11am–5pm; July–Aug daily 11am–5pm. Tram: 16, 24, or 25 to Keizersgracht.

Museum Willet-Holthuysen   For a glimpse of what life was like for Amsterdam's wealthy merchants during the 18th and 19th centuries, pay a visit to this elegant canal-house museum. Each room is furnished much as it would have been 200 years ago. In addition, there's an extensive collection of ceramics, china, glass, and silver. Of particular interest are the large old kitchen and the formal garden in back.

Herengracht 605 (at the Amstel). ℭ 020/523-1870. www.willetholthuysen.nl. Admission 4€ ($4.60) adults, 2€ ($2.30) seniors/children 6–15, free for children under 6. Mon–Fri 10am–5pm; Sat–Sun and holidays 11am–5pm. Closed Jan 1, Apr 30, Dec 25. Tram: 4, 9, or 14 to Rembrandtplein.

Scheepvaartmuseum (Maritime Museum) ⚜⚜ A bonanza for anyone who loves the sea, the Netherlands Maritime Museum is housed in a former arsenal of the Amsterdam Admiralty dating from 1656 and appropriately overlooks the busy harbor. Around the inner courtyard are 25 rooms with exhibits: ship models, charts, instruments, maps, prints, and paintings—a chronicle of Holland's abiding ties to the sea through commerce, fishing, yachting, navigational development, and war. Old maps include a 15th-century Ptolemaic atlas and a sumptuously bound edition of the *Great Atlas* by Jan Blaeu, master cartographer of Holland's golden age. Among the historic papers on display are several pertaining to Nieuwe Amsterdam (New York City) and Nieuwe Nederland (New York State).

A full-size replica of the Dutch East India Company *Amsterdam*, which in 1749 foundered off Hastings on her maiden voyage to the fabled Spice Islands

(Indonesia), is moored at the museum's wharf, as is a recently completed replica of the *Stad Amsterdam,* a three-masted iron clipper from 1854. Other ships include a steam icebreaker, a motor lifeboat, and a herring lugger. You can reach this museum by taking a 20-minute walk along the historical waterfront, the Nautisch Kwartier (Nautical Quarter).

Kattenburgerplein 1 (in the Eastern Dock). ℗ 020/523-2222. www.scheepvaartmuseum.nl. Admission 7.50€ ($9) adults, 6€ ($7) seniors, 5.60€ ($6) students, 4€ ($4.60) children 6–17, free for children under 6. Tues–Sat 10am–5pm (also Mon during school vacations); Sun noon–5pm. Bus: 22 or 32 to Kattenburgerplein.

Stedelijk Museum ⚹ *Note:* As of this writing, the Stedelijk Museum's premises on Paulus Potterstraat was closed until mid-2006 for renovation and expansion. The collection was scheduled to move sometime in 2004 to temporary quarters, most likely the TPG building beside Centraal Station. Admirers of modern art should check the Stedelijk website or contact the VVV Amsterdam tourist office for the latest news. The following review stands as a guide to the collection, and the practical details reflect probabilities at the time of writing.

The city's modern-art museum is the place to see works by such Dutch painters as Karel Appel, Willem de Kooning, and Piet Mondrian, alongside works by the French artists Chagall, Cézanne, Picasso, Renoir, Monet, and Manet and by the Americans Calder, Oldenburg, Rosenquist, and Warhol. The Stedelijk centers its collection around the De Stijl, Cobra, post-Cobra, Nouveau Réalisme, pop art, color-field painting, zero, minimalist, and conceptual schools of modern art. It houses the largest collection outside Russia of the abstract paintings of Kasimir Malevich. In the museum cafe is a giant Appel mural. Mondrian is represented by, among other works, his *Composition in Red, Black, Blue, Yellow, and Gray* (1920) and, by way of variation, *Composition in Blue, Red, Black, and Yellow* (1922)—the gray's still there, in fact, but he chose not to mention it in the title.

Temporary address: Oosterdokskade 3–5. ℗ 020/573-2737. www.stedelijk.nl. Admission 7€ ($8) adults, 3.50€ ($4.05) seniors/children 7–17, free for children under 7. Daily 11am–5pm. Closed Jan 1. Tram: 1, 2, 4, 5, 6, 9, 13, 16, 17, 24, or 25 to Centraal Station.

Tropenmuseum (Tropical Museum) ⚹ *Kids* One of Amsterdam's most interesting museums, the Tropical Museum is dedicated to presenting the tropics to people living in a far different climate. Although founded in the 19th century by the Royal Tropical Institute as a monument to the nation's colonial empire, in particular the Dutch East Indies, today's Indonesia, the museum now focuses on contemporary culture and problems in tropical areas.

On the three floors surrounding the spacious main hall are numerous life-size tableaux depicting life in tropical countries. There are displays of beautiful handicrafts and antiquities from these regions, but the main focus is the life of the people today. There are hovels from the ghettoes of Calcutta and Bombay, and mud-walled houses from the villages of rural India. Bamboo huts from Indonesia and crowded little stores no bigger than closets show you how people live in such areas as Southeast Asia, Latin America, and Africa. Sound effects play over hidden speakers: dogs bark, children scream, car horns blare, frogs croak, and vendors call out their wares.

In the **Kindermuseum (Children's Museum) TM Junior,** youngsters 6 to 12 can explore and participate in all sorts of activities (one adult is allowed to accompany each child).

Linnaeusstraat 2 (at Mauritskade). ℗ 020/568-8215. www.tropenmuseum.nl. Admission 7.50€ ($9) adults, 5€ ($6) seniors/students, 3.75€ ($4.30) children 6–17, free for children under 6. Daily 10am–5pm (3pm Dec 5, 24, 31). Closed Jan 1, Apr 30, May 5, Dec 25. Tram: 7, 9, 10, or 14 to Mauritskade.

Finds **Gay Remembrance**

The *Homomonument,* Westermarkt (tram: 13, 14, or 17), a sculpture group of three pink granite triangles near the Anne Frankhuis, is dedicated to the memory of gays and lesbians killed during World War II, or as a result of oppression and persecution because of their sexuality. People also visit to remember those who have died of AIDS.

HISTORIC BUILDINGS & MONUMENTS

Only steps from busy shopping streets, the **Begijnhof** ★, at Spui (tram: 1, 2, or 5), is the city's most tranquil spot. Hidden behind a nondescript facade is a 14th-century courtyard with a central garden ringed with restored almshouses formerly occupied by *begijns,* pious laywomen of the order of the Beguines. Most of the tiny 17th- and 18th-century buildings house elderly widows, and you should respect their privacy, especially after sunset. In the southwest corner of the cloister, at no. 34, stands **Het Huyten Huys,** one of Amsterdam's pair of surviving timber houses, built around 1425. (The authorities prohibited construction of timber houses in 1452 after a series of disastrous fires.) The complex includes a clandestine Roman Catholic church and the former Beguine church from 1419, donated by the city's Protestant rulers to Scottish Presbyterian exiles in 1607, and now misnamed slightly as the Engelse Kerk (English Church). Allow an hour.

Koninklijk Paleis (Royal Palace) The 17th-century neoclassical Royal Palace, built on top of 13,659 wooden pilings to prevent it from sinking into the soft Amsterdam soil, was Amsterdam's town hall for 153 years. It was first used as a palace during Napoleon's rule in the early 19th century, when from 1806 to 1810 the French emperor's brother Louis Bonaparte was king of the Netherlands. You can visit its high-ceilinged Citizens' Hall, Burgomasters' Chambers, and Council Room, as well as the Vierschaar—a marble tribunal where in the 17th century death sentences were pronounced. Although this is the monarch's official palace, Queen Beatrix rarely uses it for more than occasional receptions or official ceremonies.

Dam. ⓒ 020/620-4060. www.koninklijkhuis.nl. Admission 4.50€ ($5) adults, 3.60€ ($4.15) seniors/students/children 6–16, free for children under 6. Easter holidays and June–Aug, daily 11am–5pm; Sept to mid-Dec and mid-Feb to May (except Easter holidays), generally Tues–Thurs 12:30–5pm (open days and hours vary; check before going). Free guided tours usually Wed 2 pm; Closed during periods of royal residence and state receptions. Tram: 1, 2, 4, 5, 6, 9, 13, 14, 16, 17, 24, or 25 to the Dam.

HISTORIC CHURCHES

Nieuwe Kerk This church across from the Royal Palace is new in name only. Construction on this late-Gothic structure began about 1400, but much of the interior, including the organ, dates from the 17th century. Since 1815, all Dutch kings and queens have been crowned here. Today the church is used primarily as a cultural center where special art exhibits are held. Regular performances on the church's huge organ are held in summer.

Dam (next to the Royal Palace). ⓒ 020/638-6909. www.nieuwekerk.nl. Daily 10am–6pm (Thurs to 10pm during exhibits). Admission varies with different events; free when there's no exhibit. Tram: 1, 2, 4, 5, 6, 9, 13, 14, 16, 17, 24, or 25 to the Dam.

Oude Kerk ★ This Gothic church from the 13th century is the city's oldest, and its many stained-glass windows are particularly beautiful. It now stands smack dab in the middle of the Red Light District, surrounded by old almshouses turned into prostitutes' rooms. Inside are monumental tombs, including that of Rembrandt's wife, Saskia van Uylenburg. The organ, built in 1724, is played regularly in summer; many connoisseurs believe it has the best tone of any organ in the world. During summer, you can climb the 70m (230-ft.) tower for an excellent view of old Amsterdam.

Oudekerksplein (at Oudezijds Voorburgwal). ✆ 020/625-8284. www.oudekerk.nl. Admission 4€ ($4.60) adults, 3.20€ ($3.70) seniors/students, free for children under 12; rates may vary for special exhibits. Church: Mon–Sat 11am–5pm; Sun 1–5pm. Tower: June–Sept Wed–Sun 2–4pm; Sept–Apr Sun–Fri 1–5pm, Sat 11–5pm. Tram: 1, 2, 4, 5, 6, 9, 13, 14, 16, 17, 24, or 25 to the Dam.

Westerkerk ✿ Built between 1620 and 1630, this church is a masterpiece of Dutch Renaissance style. At the top of the 84m (275-ft.) tower, the highest, most beautiful tower in Amsterdam, is a giant replica of the imperial crown of Maximilian of Austria. Somewhere in this church (no one knows where) is Rembrandt's grave. During summer, regular organ concerts are played on a 300-year-old instrument. You can climb the tower or go by elevator to the top for a great view.

Westermarkt. ✆ 020/624-7766. Church: Free admission. Apr–June and Sept Mon–Fri 11am–3pm; July–Aug Mon–Sat 11am–3pm. Tower: Admission 3€ ($3.45). June–Sept Mon–Sat 10am–5pm. Tram: 6, 13, 14, or 17 to Westermarkt.

OTHER SIGHTS & ATTRACTIONS

Heineken Experience The experience, such as it is, unfolds inside the former Heineken brewing facilities, which date from 1867 to 1988. You "meet" Dr. Elion, the 19th-century chemist who isolated the renowned Heineken "A" yeast, which gives the beer its taste. In one amusing attraction, you stand on a moving floor, facing a large video screen, and get to see and feel what it's like to be a Heineken beer bottle—one of a half-million every hour—careening on a conveyor belt through a modern Heineken bottling plant. Best of all, in another touchy-feely presentation, you "sit" aboard an old brewery dray-wagon, "pulled" by a pair of big Shire horses on the video-screen in front of you, that shakes, rattles, and rolls on a mini-tour of Amsterdam. The admission is steep, though, even if you do get two "free" glasses of Heineken beer and a "free" Heineken glass for a souvenir.

Stadhouderskade 78 (at Ferdinand Bolstraat). ✆ 020/523-9666. www.heinekenexperience.com. Admission 7.50€ ($9); under 18 not admitted. Tues–Sun 10am–6pm. Closed Jan 1, Dec 25. Tram: 16, 24, or 25 to Stadhouderskade.

Hortus Botanicus ✿ Established in 1682, Amsterdam's Botanical Garden is a medley of color and scent, containing 250,000 flowers and 115,000 plants and trees from 8,000 different varieties. It owes its origins to the treasure trove of tropical plants the Dutch found in their colonies—Indonesia, Surinam, and the Antilles—and its popularity to the Dutch love affair with flowers. Among highlights are the **Semicircle,** which reconstructs part of the original design from 1682; the **Mexico–California Desert House; Palm House,** with one of the world's oldest palm trees; and the **Tri-Climate House,** which displays tropical, subtropical, and desert plants.

Plantage Middenlaan 2A (close to Artis Zoo). ✆ 020/625-9021. www.dehortus.nl. Admission 6€ ($7) adults, 3€ ($3.45) children 5–14, free for children under 5. Feb–Nov Mon–Fri 9am–5pm, Sat–Sun 10am–5pm; Dec–Jan Mon–Fri 9am–4pm, Sat–Sun 10am–4pm. Closed Jan 1, Dec 25. Tram: 9 or 14 to Plantage Middenlaan.

ESPECIALLY FOR KIDS

Artis ★★ *Kids*   If you're at a loss for what to do with the kids, Artis is a safe bet—1.2 million visitors a year agree. Established in 1838, the oldest zoo in the Netherlands houses 6,000 animals from 1,400 species. Of course, you'll find the usual tigers, lions, giraffes, wolves, leopards, elephants, camels, monkeys, penguins, and peacocks no self-respecting zoo can do without. The African residents even stroll around on a miniature savanna. Yet Artis has much more, for no extra charge, like the excellent Planetarium (closed Mon morning), and a Geological and Zoological Museum. The refurbished Aquarium, built in 1882, is superbly presented, particularly the sections on the Amazon River, coral reefs, and Amsterdam's own canals with their fish populations and burden of wrecked cars, rusted bikes, and other urban detritus. Finally, in the children's farm kids can stroke and help tend to the needs of resident Dutch species, including moorland sheep, long-haired Veluwe goats, and tufted ducks. You can rest for a while and have a snack or lunch at **Artis Restaurant.**

Plantage Kerklaan 38–40 (at Plantage Middenlaan). ℂ 020/523-3400. www.artis.nl. Admission 15€ ($17) adults, 11€ ($13) children 3–9, free for children under 3. Daily 9am–5pm. Tram: 9 or 14 to Plantage Kerklaan, 6 to Plantage Doklaan.

PARKS

When the sun shines in Amsterdam, people head for the parks. The most popular and conveniently located of Amsterdam's 20 parks is the 49-hectare (122-acre) **Vondelpark** ★★ (tram: 1, 2, 3, 5, 6, 7, 10, or 12), home to skateboarding, Frisbee-flipping, in-line skating, model-boat sailing, soccer, softball, basketball, open-air concerts and theater, smooching in the undergrowth, parties, picnics, crafts stalls, topless sunbathing—you name it. Its lakes, ponds, and streams are surrounded by meadows, trees, and colorful flowers. Vondelpark lies generally southwest of Leidseplein and has entrances all around; the most popular is adjacent to Leidseplein, on Stadhouderskade. Beware the tasty-looking "gâteau" sold

Checking Out the Red Light District

You might want to study the quaint gabled architecture along the narrow canals of De Wallen (The Walls), the oldest part of the city. And, oh yes, you might also notice certain ladies watching the world go by through their red-fringed windows.

The warren of streets east of the Dam, around Oudezijds Achterburgwal and Oudezijds Voorburgwal, is the *Rosse Buurt* (Red Light District), one of the most famous features of Amsterdam sightseeing (Metro: Nieuwmarkt). It's extraordinary to see women of all nationalities dressed in exotic underwear and perched in windows waiting for customers. With radios and TVs blaring, they knit, brush their hair, or just slink enticingly in their seats.

The Red Light District has now become a major attraction, not only for customers of storefront sex but also for sightseers. If you do choose to look around, you need to exercise some caution. Watch out for pickpockets. In a neighborhood where anything seems permissible, the one no-no is taking pictures. Violate this rule and your camera could be removed from you and broken.

here, or you might find yourself floating above the trees: Drug-laced "space cake" is an acquired taste. This park, open daily from 8am to sunset, is extremely popular in summer with young people from all over the world; admission is free.

To enjoy scenery and fresh air, head out to the giant **Amsterdamse Bos** (tram: 16 or 24 to Stadionplein, and then any bus, except the no. 23, south on Amstelveenseweg to the main entrance), in the Amstelveen southern suburb. Nature on the city's doorstep, the park was laid out during the Depression years as a public works project. By now the trees, birds, insects, and small animals are firmly established. From the entrance, follow a path to the **Roeibaan,** a rowing course 2km (1¼ miles) long. Beyond its western end, at the **Bosmuseum** (© **020/676-2152**), you can trace the park's history and learn about its wildlife. The museum is open daily from 10am to 5pm; admission is free. Nearby is a big pond called the **Grote Vijver,** where you can rent boats (© **020/644-5119**), and the **Openluchttheater (Open-Air Theater),** which often has performances on summer evenings. In 2000, the **Kersenbloesempark (Cherry Blossom Park)** opened in the Amsterdamse Bos. Its 400 cherry trees, donated by the Japan Women's Club, marked 400 years of cultural ties between the Netherlands and Japan. The Bos is open 24 hours; admission is free.

ORGANIZED TOURS

Although you could see most of Amsterdam's important sights in one long walking tour, it's best to break the city into shorter walks. Luckily, the **VVV Amsterdam** tourist office has done that. For 1.80€ ($2.05), you can buy a brochure outlining one of four walking tours: *Voyage of Discovery Through Amsterdam, A Walk Through Jewish Amsterdam, A Walk Through the Jordaan,* and *A Walk Through Maritime Amsterdam.*

A **canal-boat cruise** ★★ is the best way to view the old houses and warehouses. If you have to choose among a walking tour, a bus tour, and a boat tour, definitely take a boat. This is a city built on the shipping trade, so it's only fitting you should see it from the water, just as the golden age merchants saw their city. There are several canal-boat jetties, all of which have signs stating the time of the next tour. The greatest concentration of canal-boat operators is along Damrak and Rokin from Centraal Station; another cluster is on Singelgracht, near Leidseplein. Most tours last 1 hour and are around 8.50€ ($10) for adults, 5.75€ ($7) for children ages 4 to 12, and free for children under 4 (prices may vary a little from company to company). Since the tours are all basically the same, simply pick the one that's most convenient for you. Some cruises include snacks and drinks, with floating candlelit dinners extra.

You can take a self-guided, self-powered tour on a **water bike.** These small pedal boats for two to four are available from **Canal Bike** (© **020/626-5574**) at Leidseplein near the Rijksmuseum (tram: 1, 2, 5, 6, 7, or 10), at Westerkerk (tram: 13, 14, or 17), and on Keizersgracht near Leidsestraat (tram: 1, 2, or 5).

Finds **Ferry Tale**

Free ferries connect the city center with Amsterdam Noord (North). The short crossings for foot passengers and bikes make ideal minicruises for the cash-strapped and provide a good view of the harbor. Ferries depart from piers along De Ruyterkade behind Centraal Station every 10 to 15 minutes from 6:30am to 6pm.

Canal bikes are available daily from 10am to 4pm in spring and autumn (to 10pm in summer). The hourly rate is 8€ ($9) a head for one or two people and 7€ ($8) a head for three or four. There's a 50€ ($58) refundable deposit. You can pick one up at one jetty and drop it off at another.

A 2½-hour **bus tour** of the city is around 18€ ($21). Children 4 to 13 are usually charged half price, and children under 4 are free. Tour companies include **The Best of Holland,** Damrak 34 (🕾 **020/623-1539**); **Holland International Excursions,** Dam 6 (🕾 **020/551-2800**); **Holland Keytours,** Dam 19 (🕾 **020/624-7304**); and **Lindbergh Excursions,** Damrak 26 (🕾 **020/622-2766**).

THE SHOPPING SCENE

Strolling Amsterdam's streets, you could get the impression the city is one giant outdoor mall. Everywhere you look are stores ranging in price and variety from the Jordaan's used-clothing stores and bookstores to Pieter Cornelisz Hooftstraat's designer boutiques. Alas, most stores have little in the way of bargains. However, many typically Dutch souvenirs and gift items might appeal to you and can be real bargains if you shop around.

Best buys in Amsterdam include special items produced by the Dutch to perfection, or produced to perfection in the past and that now retail as antiques—Delftware, pewter, crystal, and old-fashioned clocks—or commodities in which they have significantly cornered a market, such as diamonds. If cost is an important consideration, remember the Dutch also produce inexpensive specialties such as cheese, flower bulbs, and chocolate.

For jewelry, trendy clothing, and athletic gear, try the department stores and specialized stores around the Dam. On the long, pedestrianized Nieuwendijk-Kalverstraat shopping street and on Leidsestraat, you find inexpensive clothing stores and souvenir stores. For designer boutiques and upscale fashion and accessories, shop on Pieter Cornelisz Hooftstraat and Van Baerlestraat. Pricey antiques and art dealers congregate on Nieuwe Spiegelstraat. For fashion boutiques and funky little specialty stores, or a good browse through a flea market or secondhand store, roam the streets of the Jordaan. The Red Light District specializes in stores selling erotic clothing, sex aids and accessories, and pornographic books and magazines.

STORES WORTH A VISIT

The city's top department store, with the best selection of goods and a great cafe, is **De Bijenkorf,** Dam 1 (🕾 **020/621-8080;** tram: 4, 9, 14, 16, 24, or 25). You can find almost everything there is to buy in Amsterdam at **Magna Plaza** (tram: 1, 2, 5, 13, 14, or 17), a splendid three-story mall in the old main post office building, behind the Dam at the corner of Nieuwezijds Voorburgwal and Raadhuisstraat.

Focke & Meltzer, Gelderlandplein 149, Buitenveldert (🕾 **020/644-4429;** tram: 5 or 51), is the best one-stop store for authentic Delft Blue and Makkumware porcelain, Hummel figurines, Leerdam crystal, and a world of other fine china, porcelain, silver, glass, and crystal. Unless you simply must have brand-name articles, you can save considerably on hand-painted pottery at **Heinen,** Prinsengracht 440, off Leidsestraat (🕾 **020/627-8299;** tram: 1, 2, or 5), and even watch the product being made. Also recommendable is **Delftware,** Nieuwendijk 24 (🕾 **020/627-3974;** tram: 1, 2, 4, 5, 6, 9, 13, 16, 17, 24, or 25).

Tips Tax Saver

Watch for the TAX-FREE SHOPPING sign in some store windows. These stores provide visitors who are not resident in the European Union the check they need for recovering the **value-added tax** (BTW) when they leave the EU. This refund amounts to 13.5% of the total cost of purchases of more than 137€ ($158) in a participating store. When you're leaving by air, present the check to Customs, along with your purchases and receipts; they will stamp it and you can get an immediate refund from the ABN-AMRO bank at Schiphol Airport.

Diamond showrooms offering free individual and small-group tours of their diamond-cutting and -polishing facilities include: **Amsterdam Diamond Center,** Rokin 1 (© **020/624-5787;** tram: 4, 9, 14, 16, 24, or 25), just off the Dam; **Coster Diamonds,** Paulus Potterstraat 2–6 (© **020/676-2222;** tram: 2 or 5), near the Rijksmuseum; and **Van Moppes Diamonds,** Albert Cuypstraat 2–6 (© **020/676-1242;** tram: 4), at the street market.

MARKETS

Buying flowers at the **Bloemenmarkt (Flower Market)** ★★, on a row of barges permanently moored along Singel between Muntplein and Leidsestraat (tram: 1, 2, 4, 5, 9, 14, 16, 24, or 25), is an Amsterdam ritual. The market is open Monday to Saturday from 9am to 5pm.

You can still find a few antiques and near-antiques at the **Waterlooplein flea market** (Tram: 9 or 14), on the square around the Muziektheater, but most of what's for sale these days is used and cheap clothing. The open-air **Albert Cuyp market,** Albert Cuypstraat (Tram: 4, 16, 24, or 25), has more cheap clothing, plus fresh fish and flowers, Asian vegetables, textiles, electronics, cosmetics, and more. Both markets are open Monday to Saturday 9am to 5pm. There's also a **flea market** on Noordermarkt in the Jordaan (Tram: 1, 2, 5, 6, 13, or 17) on Monday morning 8am until midday, and a market for **organic food** on Saturday 10am to 4pm.

Spread through several old warehouses along the Jordaan canals, **Kunst & Antiekcentrum de Looier,** Elandsgracht 109 (© **020/624-9038;** tram: 6, 7, 10, or 17), is a big art and antiques market. Individual dealers rent booths and corners to show their best wares in antique jewelry, prints, and engravings.

AMSTERDAM AFTER DARK

Nightlife centers on Leidseplein and Rembrandtplein, and you'll find dozens of bars, nightclubs, cafes, dance clubs, and movie theaters around these two squares. More cultured evening entertainment can be found in other parts of the city.

For listings of performances, consult the monthly magazine *Amsterdam Day by Day,* available for 1.50€ ($1.75) from VVV Amsterdam tourist offices. *De Uitkrant,* a free monthly magazine in Dutch, has an even more thorough listing of events (which is not hard for English speakers to follow) and is available from performance venues, clubs, and VVV offices.

For tickets to theatrical and musical events (including rock concerts), contact **Amsterdam Uit Buro (AUB) Ticketshop,** Leidseplein 26 (© **0900/0191;** amsterdam.aub.nl); tram 1, 2, 5, 6, 7, or 10), which can reserve tickets for almost every venue in town, for 2€ ($2.30) per ticket. VVV offices also reserve tickets, for a 2.50€ ($2.90) fee.

THE PERFORMING ARTS

CLASSICAL MUSIC   The renowned **Royal Concertgebouw Orchestra** is based at the **Concertgebouw** ★★, Concertgebouwplein 2–6 (*©* **020/671-8345;** www.concertgebouw.nl; tram: 3, 5, 12, or 16), which has an ornate Greek Revival facade and some of the best acoustics of any hall in the world. Performances, by this and other orchestras, are held almost every night in the building's two halls. There are free half-hour rehearsal concerts on Wednesdays at 12:30pm. The box office is open daily from 10am to 7pm (to 8:15pm for same-day tickets), with tickets from 12€ to 90€ ($14–$104).

The **Netherlands Philharmonic Orchestra** (the "NedPho") and the **Netherlands Chamber Orchestra** both perform at the impressive **Beurs van Berlage,** Damrak 243 (*©* **020/627-0466;** www.beursvanberlage.nl; tram: 4, 9, 14, 16, 24, or 25), which was once the Amsterdam stock exchange and now houses two concert halls for symphonies and chamber music. The box office is open Tuesday to Friday from 12:30 to 6pm and Saturday from noon to 5pm, with tickets at 7.50€ to 25€ ($9–$29).

OPERA & DANCE   The **Netherlands Opera** and the **National Ballet** both perform regularly at the modern **Muziektheater,** Waterlooplein (*©* **020/625-5455;** www.muziektheater.nl; tram: 9 or 14); the innovative **Netherlands Dance Theater** company from The Hague is a frequent visitor. The box office is open Monday to Saturday from 10am to 8pm, and Sunday and holidays from 11:30am to 6pm, with tickets from 15€ to 60€ ($17–$69). Music and dance performances are occasionally held at the **Stadsschouwburg** (see "Theater," below).

THEATER   The **Koninklijk Theater Carré,** Amstel 115–125 (*©* **020/622-5225;** Metro: Weesperplein), a huge old domed former circus-theater on the Amstel River near the Magere Brug (Skinny Bridge), occasionally presents touring shows from New York's Broadway or London's West End. The box office is open Monday to Saturday from 10am to 7pm and Sunday from 1 to 7pm, and tickets go for 12€ to 53€ ($14–$61). At the Dutch Renaissance **Stadsschouwburg,** Leidseplein 26 (*©* **020/624-2311;** tram: 1, 2, 5, 6, 7, or 10), from 1894, performances include plays in Dutch and, occasionally, English, plus music and dance performances by international companies. The box office is open daily 10am to 6pm, with tickets at 7€ to 35€ ($8–$40).

Compared by *Time* magazine to Chicago's famous Second City troupe, **Boom Chicago Theater,** Leidsepleintheater, Leidseplein 12 (*©* **020/423-0101;** www.boomchicago.nl; tram: 1, 2, 5, 6, 7, or 10), puts on great improvisational comedy, and Dutch audiences have no problem with the English sketches. You can have dinner and a drink while enjoying the show at a candlelit table. It's open daily in summer, closed Sunday in winter. Cover is 11€ to 32€ ($13–$36) (doesn't include dinner).

THE LIVE-MUSIC SCENE

Amsterdam's biggest and most popular clubs book up-and-coming acts and always charge admission. Plenty of smaller clubs in cafes showcase local bands and charge no admission.

Housed in an old canal-side warehouse, **BIMhuis** ★, Oude Schans 73–77 (*©* **020/623-3373;** Metro: Nieuwmarkt), is Amsterdam's premier jazz club. Music workshops are on Tuesday at 8pm (participants only). During the rest of the week jazz musicians from all over Europe, and occasionally from the States, perform. It's open Wednesday to Sunday from 8pm to 1am, with a 10€ to 15€

($12–$17) cover. You can impress your ears with a never-routine mix of electronic music, avant-garde jazz, and anything else that goes out on a musical limb, in the small concert hall at **De IJsbreker,** Weesperzijde 23 (© 020/ 668-1805; Metro: Weesperplein), a pleasant cafe with an outdoor terrace on the banks of the Amstel. Cover is 7€ to 12€ ($8–$14).

Note: Sometime early in 2005, both BIMhuis and De IJsbreker are due to pack up their music and instruments and decamp to a new, state-of-the-art **Muziekgebouw** (www.muziekgebouw.nl) on the waterfront. At this writing, the concert hall is under construction in the old harbor, between Centraal Station and the cruise-liner Passenger Terminal Amsterdam.

A regular crowd frequents the small, intimate **Alto Jazz Café,** Korte Leidsedwarsstraat 115 (© 020/626-3249), for nightly performances by both regular and guest combos. Check out also the **Bamboo Bar,** Lange Leidsedwarsstraat 64 (© 020/624-3993), and funky **Bourbon Street,** Leidsekruisstraat 6–8 (© 020/ 623-3440), for late-night blues and rock. All three bars are near Leidseplein, reached by tram 1, 2, 5, 6, 7, or 10.

THE BAR SCENE

There are countless bars—or cafes, as they're called here—in the city, many around **Leidseplein** and **Rembrandtplein.** Many of them don't start to get busy until at least 8pm, but they usually open at noon and stay open all day. The most popular drink is draft Pilsener served in small glasses with two fingers of head on top. Also popular is *jenever* (Dutch gin) available in *jonge* (young) and *oude* (old) varieties—oude is stronger, more refined in taste, and higher in alcoholic content.

BROWN CAFES   Particularly old and traditional bars often earn the appellation of *bruine kroeg* (brown cafe), a name said to have been derived as much from the preponderance of wood furnishings as from the browning of the walls from years of dense tobacco smoke. Some have been around since Rembrandt's time. At these warm and friendly (and smoky) cafes you can sit and sip a glass of beer or a mixed drink; at some you can even get a cheap meal.

Papeneiland, Prinsengracht 2, at the corner of Brouwersgracht (© 020/ 624-1989; tram: 1, 2, 5, 6, 13, or 17), is Amsterdam's oldest cafe: Since 1600 or thereabouts, folks have been dropping by for shots of jenever and glasses of beer. Originally a tasting house where people could try liqueurs distilled and aged on the premises, **De Drie Fleschjes,** Gravenstraat 18, between the Nieuwe Kerk and Nieuwendijk (© 020/624-8443; tram: 1, 2, 4, 5, 6, 9, 13, 14, 16, 17, 24, or 25), has been in business for more than 300 years. It's popular with businesspeople and journalists, who stop by to sample the wide variety of jenevers.

The dark walls, low ceilings, and old wooden furniture at **Hoppe,** Spui 18–20 (© 020/420-4420; tram: 1, 2, or 5), one of Amsterdam's oldest and most popular brown cafes, have literally remained unchanged since the cafe opened in 1670. It has become a tourist attraction, but locals love it too, often stopping for a drink on their way home. There's usually standing room only and the crowds overflow onto the sidewalk.

Said to be where the builders of the Westerkerk were paid, **Café Chris,** Bloemstraat 42 (© 020/624-5942; tram: 6, 13, 14, or 17), opened in 1624 and has some curious old features, including a toilet that flushes from outside the bathroom door. In a medieval alley, wood-paneled **In de Wildeman,** Kolksteeg 3 (© 020/638-2348; tram: 1, 2, 5, 6, 13, or 17), serves more than 200 kinds of beer. The tile floor and rows of bottles and jars behind the counters are remnants from its early days as a distillery's retail store.

MODERN CAFES   Flea-market tables, armchairs left over from the 1970s, and rotating exhibits of rather puzzling artwork have made **Café Schuim,** Spuistraat 189 (© 020/638-9357; tram: 1, 2, or 5), the cafe of the moment in the Dam area. The rumpled surroundings attract an assortment of creative types who debate and discuss during the week and try to avoid being crushed by mobs on weekends.

Other notable hangouts are **Café Dante,** Spuistraat 320 (© 020/638-8839; tram 1, 2, or 5), where a different modern-art exhibit is mounted every month; and **Café Schiller,** Rembrandtplein 26 (© 020/624-9846; tram: 4, 9, or 14), which has a bright, glassed-in terrace on the square and a finely carved Art Deco interior; it's popular with artists and writers.

The concept of the Grand Cafe—combining drinks and food in elegant surroundings—has taken Amsterdam by storm. One of the best is **Café Luxembourg,** Spuistraat 24 (© 020/620-6264; tram 1, 2, or 5), a chic rendezvous that takes some of its menu dishes from top eateries around town. Whether you're in jeans or theater attire, you'll feel comfortable at **Royal Café De Kroon,** Rembrandtplein 15 (© 020/625-2011; tram: 4, 9, or 14), with fine views on the square through the big picture windows upstairs, amid a decor that's rigorously modern.

On summer evenings, trendies head to the terrace of **Café Vertigo,** Vondelpark 3 (© 020/612-3021; tram: 2 or 5), in Vondelpark, for one of the liveliest scenes in town. The low, arched ceilings, subtle lighting, and unobtrusive music set a mood of casual sophistication.

THE GAY & LESBIAN SCENE

Amsterdam bills itself as the gay capital of Europe, proud of its open and tolerant attitude toward homosexuality. To find out more about the gay and lesbian scenes, stop by **COC,** Rozenstraat 14 (© 020/623-4079; tram: 6, 13, 14, or 17), 2 blocks off Westerkerk. It houses a cafe open Monday to Saturday from 11pm to 4am as well as a dance club. The dance club is primarily for men on Fridays and primarily for women on Saturdays. Sundays attract a mixed crowd. You can also call the **Gay and Lesbian Switchboard** at © 020/623-6565, open daily from 10am to 10pm.

Gay News Amsterdam, a new monthly newspaper in English, is available free in gay establishments throughout Amsterdam. Of course, you find the best coverage of the Gay Capital of Europe in *Frommer's Gay & Lesbian Europe.*

Some of the more popular spots for men are **April,** Reguliersdwarsstraat 37 (© 020/625-9572; tram: 1, 2, or 5), a sleek modern bar that will feel familiar to any American barfly; **Exit,** Reguliersdwarsstraat 42 (© 020/624-7778; tram: 1, 2, or 5), a dance club that attracts a younger crowd; **iT,** Amstelstraat 24 (© 020/625-0111; tram: 4, 9, or 14), Amsterdam's most famous and flamboyant dance club with a mixed gay and straight crowd; **Cockring,** Warmoesstraat 96 (© 020/623-9604; tram: 4, 9, 14, 16, 24, or 25), a popular dance club; **Argos,** Warmoesstraat 95 (© 020/622-6572; tram: 4, 9, 14, 16, 24, or 25), Europe's oldest leather bar; and **Cosmo,** Kerkstraat 42 (© 020/624-7778; tram: 1, 2, or 5), a late-night bar.

The city has plenty of bars and dance clubs for gay men, but far fewer for lesbians. Generally you find the trendier places around **Rembrandtplein** and on **Reguliersdwarsstraat** (immediately off Leidsestraat, a block south of Singel), a more casual atmosphere on **Kerkstraat** near Leidseplein, and leather bars on **Warmoesstraat. Vive la Vie,** Amstelstraat 7 (© 020/624-0114; tram: 4, 9, or 14), on the edge of Rembrandtplein, is the city's only lesbian bar; this convivial

---

Tips **Toker Talk**

Don't buy on the street. You stand a fair chance of being ripped off, the quality is doubtful, and there may be unpleasant additives.

---

little corner spot on Rembrandtplein hosts periodic parties. **Saarein,** Elandsstraat 119 (© **020/623-4901;** tram: 6, 7, 10, or 17), near Leidseplein, is a women-only bar/cafe that's not exclusively lesbian but has a large following.

DANCE CLUBS

You find dozens of large and small clubs around **Leidseplein** and **Rembrandtplein.** They tend to rise and fall in popularity, so ask someone in a cafe what the current favorites are. Drinks can be expensive—a beer or Coke averages 5€ ($6), and a whiskey or cocktail 7.50€ ($9). Most dance clubs are open Thursday to Sunday 9 or 10pm to 2 or 3am.

Popular clubs include **Arena,** Gravesandestraat 51 (© **020/625-8788;** tram 7 or 10); **Escape,** Rembrandtplein 11 (© **020/625-2011;** tram: 4, 9, or 14); **West Pacific,** Haarlemmerweg 8–10 (© **020/488-7778;** tram: 10); **Odeon,** Singel 460 (© **020/624-9711;** tram: 1, 2, or 5); **Paradiso,** Weteringschans 6–8 (© **020/626-4521;** tram: 1, 2, 5, 6, 7, or 10); **Akhnaton,** Nieuwezijds Kolk 25 (© **020/624-3396;** tram: 1, 2, 5, 6, 13, or 17); and **Melkweg** ⚘, Lijnbaansgracht 234A (© **020/624-1777;** tram: 1, 2, 5, 6, 7, or 10). Cover and music varies.

"COFFEE SHOPS"

Amsterdam is a mecca for the marijuana smoker and seems likely to remain that way. Visitors often get confused about "smoking" coffee shops and how they differ from "nonsmoking" ones. Well, to begin with, "smoking" and "nonsmoking" don't refer to cigarettes—they refer to cannabis. "Smoking" coffee shops not only sell cannabis, most commonly in the form of hashish, but also provide somewhere patrons can sit and smoke it all day if they so choose. Generally, these smoking coffee shops are the only places in Amsterdam called "coffee shops"— regular cafes are called *cafes* or *eetcafes.*

You are allowed to buy only 5 grams (⅕ oz.) of soft drugs at a time for personal use, but you're allowed to be in possession of 30 grams (1⅕ oz.) for personal use.

Coffee shops are not allowed to sell alcohol, so they sell coffee, tea, and fruit juices. You won't be able to get any food (except maybe drug-laced "space cake"), so don't expect to grab a quick bite. You're even allowed to smoke your own stuff in the coffee shop, as long as you buy a drink.

Some of the most popular smoking coffee shops are **The Rookies,** Korte Leidsedwarsstraat 145–147 (© **020/694-2353;** tram: 1, 2, 5, 6, 7, or 10); **Borderline,** Amstelstraat 37 (© **020/622-0540;** tram: 9 or 14); and, with tourists, the shops of the **Bulldog** chain, which has branches around the city. The **Bulldog Palace** is at Leidseplein 15 (© **020/627-1908;** tram: 1, 2, 5, 6, 7, or 10).

2 Environs of Amsterdam

If Amsterdam is your only stop in the Netherlands, try to make at least one excursion into the countryside. Dikes, windmills, and some of Holland's quaintest villages await you just beyond the city limits. And you don't need to travel much farther to reach one of the many historic art towns.

HAARLEM ✦✦

Just 20km (12 miles) west of Amsterdam, Haarlem is a graceful town of wind-ing canals and medieval neighborhoods that also holds several fine museums. The best time to visit is Saturday, for the market on the Grote Markt, or in tulip season (Mar to mid-May), when the city explodes with flowers.

ESSENTIALS

GETTING THERE   Haarlem is 15 minutes from Amsterdam by **train,** and two or three depart every hour from Centraal Station. A round-trip ticket is 5.25€ ($6). There are frequent **buses** from outside Centraal Station. By **car,** take N5 and then A5 west.

VISITOR INFORMATION   VVV **Haarlem,** Stationsplein 1, 2011 Haarlem (✆ **0900/61-61-600;** fax 023/534-0537; www.vvvzk.nl), just outside the rail-way station. The office is open Monday to Friday from 9:30am to 5:30pm, and Saturday from 10am to 2pm.

SEEING THE SIGHTS

Haarlem is where Frans Hals, Jacob van Ruysdael, and Pieter Saenredam were living and painting their famous portraits, landscapes, and church interiors while Rembrandt was living and working in Amsterdam.

Handel and Mozart made special visits just to play the magnificent organ of **Sint-Bavokerk (St. Bavo's Church),** also known as the **Grote Kerk** ✦, Oude Groenmarkt 23 (✆ **023/532-4399**). Look for the tombstone of painter Frans Hals (ca. 1580–1666) and for a cannonball that has been embedded in the church's wall ever since it came flying through a window during the 1572 to 1573 siege of Haar-lem. And, of course, don't miss seeing the famous **Christian Müller Organ,** built in 1738. You can hear it at one of the free concerts given on Tuesday and Thurs-day from April to October. It has 5,068 pipes and is nearly 30m (98 ft.) tall. The woodwork was done by Jan van Logteren. Mozart played the organ in 1766 when he was just 10 years old. St Bavo's is open Monday to Saturday from 10am to 4pm. Admission is 1.50€ ($1.75) for adults, 1€ ($1.15) for children under 15.

From St. Bavo's, it's a short walk to the **Frans Halsmuseum** ✦✦, Groot Heiligland 62 (✆ **023/511-5775**; www.franshalsmuseum.nl), where the gal-leries are the halls and furnished chambers of a former pensioners' home, and famous paintings by the masters of the Haarlem school hang in settings that look like the 17th-century homes they were intended to adorn. The museum is open Tuesday to Saturday from 11am to 5pm, Sunday and holidays from noon to 5pm; closed January 1 and December 25. Admission is 5.40€ ($6) for adults, 4€ ($4.60) for seniors, and free for visitors under 19.

The oldest and perhaps the most unusual museum in the Netherlands, the **Teylers Museum,** Spaarne 16 (✆ **023/531-9010;** www.teylersmuseum.nl), contains a curious collection. There are drawings by Michelangelo, Raphael, and Rembrandt; fossils, minerals, and skeletons; instruments of physics; and an odd assortment of inventions, including a 19th-century radarscope. The museum is open Tuesday to Saturday from 10am to 5pm, and Sunday and holidays from noon to 5pm; closed January 1 and December 25. Admission is 5.50€ ($6) for adults, 1€ ($1.15) for children ages 5 to 18, and free for children under 5.

An ideal way to tour the city is by **canalboat cruise,** operated by **Woltheus Cruises** (✆ **023/535-7723**), from their Spaarne River jetty, Gravensteenbrug. Cruises run from April to October at 10:30am, noon, 1:30, 3, and 4:30pm (during some months the 1st and last tours are on request only), and are 6.50€ ($7) for adults, 4€ ($4.60) for children ages 3 to 11, and free for children under 3.

WHERE TO DINE

De Pêcherie Haarlem aan Zee ✦ SEAFOOD   You can just about smell the fresh North Sea breeze at this fine seafood restaurant facing Haarlem's Grote Kerk. The nautical decor—fishing nets, brass navigation lamps, rope cables—may not be very original, but sitting on old-fashioned, high-backed wicker windbreaker beach chairs only enhances the seacoast ambience and creates a feeling of seclusion. The menu features oysters, crab, prawns, and various fish dishes, all of which go well with the crisp house white wine. Wait times for some courses can be lengthy, in particular at busy times.

Oude Groenmarkt 10 (next to the Grote Kerk). ✆ 023/531-4848. Main courses 15€–22€ ($17–$25); fixed-price menus 20€–45€ ($22). MC, V. Mon–Sat noon–midnight; Sun 5pm–midnight.

Jacobus Pieck ✦ DUTCH/INTERNATIONAL   This popular cafe-restaurant has a lovely shaded terrace in the garden for fine-weather days, while inside is bustling but crisply stylish. Friendly service and good food for reasonable prices draw in a local clientele. Main dinner courses range from wholesome Dutch standards to pastas and Middle Eastern dishes.

Warmoesstraat 18. ✆ 023/532-6144. Main courses 7.50€–15€ ($9–$17). AE, MC, V. Mon–Sat 10am–11pm; Sun noon–11pm.

ZANDVOORT

Should you feel like getting a breath of sea air, do what Amsterdammers do: Head for **Zandvoort,** 26km (16 miles) west of Amsterdam, on the North Sea coast. Zandvoort is 30 minutes from Amsterdam by train, and one leaves Amsterdam Centraal Station every hour. Usually you need to transfer at Haarlem, but during summertime extra trains go direct. Journey time is 30 minutes and a round-trip ticket is 6.75€ ($8). There are also frequent buses from outside Centraal Station. You can go by car via Haarlem on N5, then on A5, but the summer often brings long traffic lines.

There's not much more to Zandvoort than its **beach** ✦, but what a beach. Seemingly endless sands are lined in summertime with beach cafes and discos, and the conditions are good for windsurfing. Down from the mainstream beaches are gay and nudist beaches.

You'll find tranquillity in the **Kennemer Duinen** and **Amsterdamse Waterleiding Duinen,** protected zones of sand dune and vegetation that play an important role in sea defense. Stroll along paths through woods on the eastern side and across dunes leading west toward the sea.

One of 10 legal casinos in the Netherlands, **Holland Casino Zandvoort,** Badhuisplein 7 (✆ 023/574-0574), has roulette, blackjack and more. Dress code is "correct" (collar and tie for men), the minimum age is 18, and you need your passport. It's open daily (except May 4, Dec 31) from 1:30pm to 3am. Admission is 3€ ($3.45).

The town offers plenty of eating and drinking possibilities.

VOLENDAM & MARKEN

Volendam and Marken have long been combined on bus-tour itineraries from Amsterdam as a kind of "packaged Holland and costumes to go." Nonetheless, it's possible to have a delightful day in the bracing air of these two communities on the IJsselmeer lake, where a few residents (fewer with each passing year) may be seen going about their daily business in traditional dress.

There are separate, hourly **buses** to Volendam and Marken from outside Amsterdam's Centraal Station. The fare is 4€ ($4.60) round-trip; the ride takes 35 minutes to Volendam and 45 minutes to Marken.

The IJsselmeer

Only in the Netherlands could you say, "This used to be a sea." The IJsselmeer (pronounced "*Eye*-sselmeer"), a large freshwater lake on Amsterdam's doorstep, actually was once a sea, the Zuiderzee, until the Dutch decided they didn't want a sea any longer, because it was always threatening to flood Amsterdam (and Amsterdammers don't like water in their jenever).

So in the 1930s, workers blocked off the mouth of the Zuiderzee with a massive dike, the Afsluitdijk (Enclosing Dike), from Noord-Holland to Friesland, and that was that. The IJsselmeer is (usually) well behaved, and a tour of its long shoreline, called the "Golden Circle," makes a scenic excursion from Amsterdam.

Geared for tourism, **Volendam,** 18km (11 miles) northeast of Amsterdam, has souvenir stores, boutiques, and restaurants. Its boat-filled harbor, tiny streets, and traditional houses have an undeniable charm. If you want a snapshot of yourself surrounded by fishermen wearing little caps and balloon-legged pants, Volendammers will gladly pose. They understand that the traditional costume is worth preserving, as is the economy of a small town that lost most of its fishing industry when the Zuiderzee enclosure dam cut it off from the North Sea. You can visit attractions like the fish auction, a diamond cutter, a clog maker, and a house with a room entirely wallpapered in cigar bands.

A causeway now connects the onetime island of **Marken** ⍟, 16km (10 miles) northeast of Amsterdam, with the mainland, but it remains as insular as ever. Quieter than Volendam, with a village of green-painted houses on stilts around a tiny harbor, it is also more rural. Clusters of farmhouses dot the *polders* (the reclaimed land from the sea that makes up two-thirds of the Netherlands), and a candy-striped lighthouse stands on the IJsselmeer shore.

Marken does not gush over tourists, but it will feed and water them, and let them wander around its pretty streets. Villagers wear traditional costume, as much to preserve the custom as to appease the tourists who pour in daily. The **Marker Museum,** Kerkbuurt 44–47 (© **0299/601-904**), is a typical house open as a museum May to October, Monday to Saturday from 10am to 4:30pm and Sunday from noon to 4:30pm. Admission is 2€ ($2.30) for adults and 1€ ($1.15) for children.

3 Delft ⍟⍟

Yes, Delft, 54km (34 miles) southwest of Amsterdam, is the town of the famous blue-and-white porcelain. And, yes, you can visit the factory of Koninklijke Porceleyne Fles. But don't let Delftware be your only reason to visit. Not only is this one of the prettiest small cities in the Netherlands, but Delft is also important as a cradle of the Dutch Republic and the traditional burial place of the royal family. Plus, it was the birthplace, and inspiration, of the 17th-century master of light and subtle emotion, painter Jan Vermeer. Delft remains a quiet little town, with flowers in its flower boxes and linden trees bending over its gracious canals.

ESSENTIALS

GETTING THERE   There are several **trains** an hour from Amsterdam's Centraal Station to Delft Station, which is southwest of the center. The trip takes about 1 hour and is 15€ ($17) round-trip. If you go by car, take A4/E19 and then A13/E19 past Den Haag (The Hague) and look for the Delft exit.

VISITOR INFORMATION **Tourist Information Delft,** Hippolytusbuurt 4, 2611 HN Delft (© **015/215-4051;** www.delft.nl), is in the center of town. The office is open Sunday and Monday from 10am to 4pm, Tuesday to Friday from 9am to 6pm, and Saturday from 9am to 5pm.

SEEING THE SIGHTS

Vermeer's house is long gone from Delft, as are his paintings. Instead, you can visit the **Oude Kerk** ✦, Roland Holstlaan 753 (© **015/212-3015**), where he's buried. You might want to visit also the **Nieuwe Kerk** ✦✦, Markt (© **015/ 212-3025**), where Prince William of Orange and other members of the House of Orange–Nassau are buried, and to climb its tower, which is 109m (357 ft.) high. Both churches are open April to October, Monday to Saturday from 9am to 6pm; November to March, Monday to Friday from 11am to 4pm, Saturday from 11am to 5pm. Separate admission to each is 3€ ($3.45) for adults, 1.50€ ($1.75) for children ages 5 to 14, and free for children under 5; separate admission to the Nieuwe Kerk tower is 2€ ($2.30) for adults, 1€ ($1.15) for children ages 5 to 14, and free for children under 5.

The **Prinsenhof Museum** ✦, Sint-Agathaplein 1 (© **015/260-2358**), on the nearby Oude Delft canal, is where William I of Orange (William the Silent) lived and had his headquarters in the years during which he helped found the Dutch Republic. It's also where he was assassinated in 1584 (you can still see the musket-ball holes in the stairwell). Today the Prinsenhof is a museum of paintings, tapestries, silverware, and pottery. It's open Tuesday to Saturday from 10am to 5pm, and Sunday from 1 to 5pm; closed January 1 and December 25. Admission is 5€ ($6) for adults, 4€ ($4.60) for children ages 12 to 16, and free for children under 12.

In the same neighborhood you can see a fine collection of old Delft tiles displayed in the wood-paneled setting of a 19th-century mansion museum called **Lambert van Meerten,** Oude Delft 199 (© **015/260-2358**). It's open Tuesday to Saturday from 10am to 5pm, and Sunday from 1 to 5pm; closed January 1 and December 25. Admission is 3.50€ ($4) for adults, 3€ ($3.45) for children ages 12 to 16, and free for children under 12.

To see a demonstration of the traditional art of making and hand-painting Delftware, visit the factory and showroom of **Koninklijke Porceleyne Fles** ✦, Rotterdamseweg 196 (© **015/251-2030;** bus: 63, 121, or 129 to Jaffalaan), founded in 1653. It's open April to October, Monday to Saturday from 9am to 5pm, and Sunday from 9:30am to 4pm; November to March, Monday to Saturday from 9am to 5pm; closed December 25 to January 1. Admission is 2.50€ ($2.90), and free for children under 13.

WHERE TO DINE

Spijshuis de Dis ✦ DUTCH   Fine Dutch cooking that's traditional at heart but given a modern accent is served up at this atmospheric old restaurant. Among the top dishes are *bakke pot*—a stew made from beef, chicken, and rabbit; V.O.C. mussels (named after the Dutch initials for the East India Company), prepared with garlic, ginger, and curry; and asparagus in season (May–June). The steaks and the pork and lamb filet dishes are great. Don't miss the homemade mushroom soup.

Beestenmarkt 36 (off the Markt). © 015/213-1782. Main courses 13€–23€ ($15–$26); fixed-price menu 27€ ($30). AE, DC, MC, V. Thurs–Tues 5–10:30pm.

Stadsherberg De Mol TRADITIONAL DUTCH   Food is served here in the medieval manner—in wooden bowls from which you eat with your hands. Prices are moderate and quantities copious, and there is fun, too, with live music and dancing.

Molslaan 104 (off Beestenmarkt). © 015/212-1343. www.stadsherbergdemol.nl. Fixed-price menu 65€ ($75). MC, V. Tues–Sun 6–11pm.

4 Leiden ✶✶

Students of U.S. history may know that the Pilgrim Fathers lived in this town, 36km (23 miles) southwest of Amsterdam, for 11 years before sailing for North America on the *Mayflower*. Leiden's proudest homegrown moment came in 1574, when it was the only Dutch town to withstand a full-blown siege by the Spanish invaders. This was the birthplace of the Dutch tulip trade, and of the painters Rembrandt and Jan Steen, and it is the home of the oldest university in the Netherlands. Finally, with 14 museums, covering subjects ranging from antiquities, natural history, and anatomy to clay pipes and coins, Leiden seems perfectly justified in calling itself *Museum Stad* (Museum City).

ESSENTIALS

GETTING THERE   There are several trains an hour from Amsterdam Centraal Station to Leiden Station, which is northwest of the town center (about a 10-min. walk). If you go by car, take A4/E19 in the direction of The Hague and watch for the Leiden exit.

VISITOR INFORMATION   VVV Leiden, Stationsweg 2D, 2312 AV, Leiden (© **0900/222-2333;** fax 071/516-1227; www.leidenpromotie.nl), is situated outside the railway station. The office is open Monday from 11am to 5:30pm, Tuesday to Friday from 9:30am to 6pm, and Saturday from 10am to 4:30pm.

SEEING THE SIGHTS

Among the spectacular antiquities housed at the **Rijksmuseum van Oudheden** ✶✶, Rapenburg 28 (© **071/516-3163;** www.rmo.nl), is the 1st-century-A.D. Temple of Taffeh, presented by the Egyptian government as a gift to the Dutch nation for its assistance in saving monuments prior to the construction of the Aswan High Dam. The museum is open Tuesday to Friday from 10am to 5pm, Saturday, Sunday and holidays (also Easter Monday and Pentecost Monday) from noon to 5pm; closed January 1, October 3, and December 25. Admission is 6€ ($7) for adults, 5.50€ ($6) for children ages 6 to 18, and free for children under 6.

Also noteworthy is the university's **Hortus Botanicus (Botanical Gardens),** Rapenburg 73 (© **071/527-7249;** www.hortus.leidenuniv.nl), from 1587. In 1592, botanist Carolus Clusius brought the first-ever tulip bulbs to Holland and planted them here, but he never got to see them flower because they were stolen by rivals. The gardens are open May to September daily from 10am to 6pm and October to April daily from 10am to 4pm; closed last week in December and January 1. Admission is 4€ ($4.60) for adults, 2€ ($2.30) for children ages 4 to 12, and free for children under 4.

To touch base with those courageous but humble Pilgrim Fathers, pick up the VVV tourist office's brochure *A Pilgrimage Through Leiden: A Walk in the Footsteps of the Pilgrim Fathers.* The walk starts at the **Lodewijkskerk,** which was used as a meeting place by the cloth guild. William Bradford, who later became governor of New Plymouth, was a member of this guild. The walk takes you past the house on William Brewstersteeg (formerly Herensteeg) where William Brewster's Pilgrim Press published the religious views that angered the Church of England. Plaques at **Sint-Pieterskerk** (in a small square off Kloksteeg) memorialize the Pilgrims, in particular Rev. Jon Robinson, who was forced to stay behind because of illness and is buried in this church (an almshouse, the Jean Pesijnhofje, in Kloksteeg, now occupies the house in which he died). Special Thanksgiving Day services are held each year in honor of the little band of refugees who worshipped here.

At the **Leiden American Pilgrim Museum** *, Beschuitsteeg 9 (© 071/512-2413), you can hear a recorded commentary on the Pilgrims and see photocopies of documents relating to their 11-year residence in Leiden. The museum is open Wednesday to Saturday from 1 to 5pm. Admission is 2€ ($2.30), and free for children under 6.

On the other side of town, visit the **Stedelijk Museum de Lakenhal** *, Oude Singel 28–32 (© 071/516-5360; www.lakenhal.nl), to view works by local heroes Rembrandt and Jan Steen, and others, plus period rooms from the 17th to 19th centuries. Also on parade is Leiden's pride and joy: a copper stew pot said to have been retrieved by a small boy who crawled through a chink in the city wall just minutes after the lifting of the Spanish siege. He found this very pot full of boiling stew in the enemy's camp and brought it back to feed the starving inhabitants. Ever since, stew has been a national dish and is still traditionally prepared for the Leiden city holiday, October 3, which is the anniversary of its liberation. Each year on this day *haring en witte brood* (herring and white bread) are distributed, just as they were in 1574. The museum is open Tuesday to Friday from 10am to 5pm, and Saturday, Sunday, and holidays from noon to 5pm; closed January 1 and December 25. Admission is 4€ ($4.60) for adults, 2.50€ ($2.90) for seniors, and free for children under 18.

WHERE TO DINE

Annie's Verjaardag DUTCH/CONTINENTAL This lively, water-level restaurant has vaulted cellars that are a favorite eating spot for both students and locals, who spill out onto the canal-side terrace (and occasionally *into* the canal) in fine weather. When the canals are frozen, the view is enchanting, as skaters practice their turns. The dinner menu is simple but wholesome, and during the day you can snack on sandwiches and tapas.

Oude Rijn 1A. © 071/512-6358. Main courses 8.75€–16€ ($10–$18). No credit cards. Sun–Thurs 10am–1am; Fri–Sat 10am–2am.

Stadscafé van der Werff * FRENCH/BELGIAN This relaxed cafe-restaurant in a grand 1930s villa on the edge of the old town is popular with the town's students and ordinary citizens alike. Even if you're not having dinner, and enjoying dishes like a basic Indonesian satay or their surf and turf *kalfsbiefstukje met gebakken gambas en een kreeftensaus* (beef steak with fried prawns in a lobster sauce), you can still while away the evening just having a drink and reading a paper.

Steenstraat 2. © 071/513-0335. Main courses 8.95€–17€ ($10–$20); fixed-price menu 16€ ($18). AE, DC, MC, V. Daily 9am–10pm (cafe to 1am).

Norway

by Darwin Porter & Danforth Prince

Norway is a land of tradition, as exemplified by its rustic stave churches—look for these mysterious, dark structures with steep gables surmounted by dragons' heads and pointed steeples—and folk dances stepped to the airs of a fiddler. But Norway is also modern, a technologically advanced nation that's rich in petroleum and hydroelectric energy. One of the world's last great natural frontiers, Norway is a land of astonishing beauty; its steep and jagged fjords, salmon-rich rivers, glaciers, mountains, and meadows invite exploration. In winter, the shimmering northern lights beckon; in summer, the midnight sun shines late and warm.

1 Oslo

After World War II, Oslo grew to 450 sq. km (175 sq. miles), making it one of the 10 largest capitals in the world in sheer area, if not in urban buildup. The city is one of the most heavily forested on earth, and fewer than half a million Norwegians live and work here.

One of the oldest Scandinavian capital cities, founded in the mid–11th century, Oslo has never been a mainstream tourist site. But the city is culturally rich with many diversions—enough to fill at least 3 or 4 busy days. It's also the center for many easy excursions along the Oslofjord or to towns and villages in its environs, both north and south.

In recent years Oslo has grown from what even the Scandinavians viewed as a Nordic backwater to one of Europe's happening cities. Restaurants, nightclubs, cafes, shopping complexes, and other venues keep on opening. A kind of Nordic joie de vivre permeates the city; the only drawback is that all this fun is going to cost you—Oslo ranks as one of Europe's most expensive cities.

ESSENTIALS

GETTING THERE   By Plane   Since the closing of a small-scale, relatively outmoded airport named Fornebu, Oslo has learned to cope with all of its air traffic being funneled into the **Oslo International Airport** in Gardermoen (© 81-55-02-50), about 50km (31 miles) east of downtown Oslo, a 45-minute drive from the center. All domestic and international flights coming into Oslo arrive through this much-upgraded airport, including aircraft belonging to SAS, British Airways, and Icelandair.

There's frequent bus service, departing every 20 minutes throughout the day, into downtown Oslo. It's maintained by both SAS (whose buses deliver passengers to the Central Railway station and to most of the SAS hotels within Oslo) and the **Norwegian Bus Express** (© 81-54-44-44), whose buses head for the main railway station. Both companies charge 110NOK ($16) per person, each way. There's also 20-minute high-speed railway service between Gardermoen and Oslo's main railway station, priced at 180NOK ($26) per person each way.

If you want to take a taxi, be prepared for a lethally high charge of around 500NOK ($71) for up to four passengers plus their luggage. If you need a "maxi-taxi," a minivan that's suitable for between 5 and 15 passengers, plus their luggage, you'll be assessed 800NOK ($114).

By Train The first high-speed train between Oslo and Stockholm has reduced travel time to 4 hours and 50 minutes between these two once remotely linked Scandinavian capitals. Depending on the day, there are two to three trains daily in each direction. This high-speed train now competes directly with air travel. Trains from the Continent, Sweden, and Denmark arrive at **Oslo Sentralstasjon (Central Station)**, Jernbanetorget 1 (© **81-50-08-88** for train information). It's at the beginning of Karl Johans Gate, in the center of the city. The station is open daily from 9am to 1am. From the Central Station, trains leave for Bergen, Stavanger, Trondheim, Bodø, and all other rail links in Norway. You can also take trams to all major parts of Oslo.

By Car If you're driving from mainland Europe, the fastest way to reach Oslo is to take the car-ferry from Frederikshavn, Denmark (see below). You can also take a car-ferry from Copenhagen (see below) or drive from Copenhagen by crossing over to Helsingborg, Sweden, from Helsingør, Denmark. Once at Helsingborg, take E-6 north all the way to Stockholm. If you're driving from Stockholm to Oslo, follow E-18 west all the way (trip time: 7 hr.). Once you near the outskirts of Oslo from any direction, follow the signs into the SENTRUM, or city center.

By Ferry Ferries from Europe arrive at the Oslo port, a 15-minute walk (or a short taxi ride) from the city center. From Denmark, Scandinavia's link with the Continent, ferries depart for Oslo from Copenhagen, Hirtshals, and Frederikshavn.

From Strømstad, Sweden, in the summer, the daily crossing to Sandefjord, Norway, takes 2½ hours; from Sandefjord, it's an easy drive or train ride north to Oslo.

VISITOR INFORMATION Assistance and information for visitors are available at the **Tourist Information Office**, Roald Amundsen St., Oslo (© **24-14-77-00;** bus: 27). Free maps, brochures, sightseeing tickets, and guide services are available. The office is open June through August, daily from 9am to 7pm; May and September, Monday through Saturday from 9am to 5pm; October through April, Monday through Friday from 9am to 4pm.

There's also an Oslo-only **information office** at the Oslo Sentralstasjon (Central Station), Jernbanetorget 1, at the beginning of Karl Johans Gate (no phone), open Monday to Saturday from 8am to 5pm.

For information online, try the Norwegian Tourist Board (**www.visitnorway. com**) or Virtual Oslo (**www.oslorightnow.com**).

CITY LAYOUT Oslo is at the mouth of the 95km (60-mile) Oslofjord. Opening onto the harbor is **Rådhusplassen (City Hall Square),** dominated by the modern City Hall, a major attraction. Guided bus tours leave from this square, and the launches that cruise the fjords depart from the pier facing the municipal building. (You can catch ferries to the Bygdøy Peninsula from the quay at Rådhusplassen.)

Out on a promontory to the east is the **Akershus Castle.** At **Bygdøy,** the much larger peninsula that juts out to the west, are four of Oslo's major attractions: the Viking ships, the Polar Ship *Fram* Museum, the *Kon-Tiki* Museum, and the Folk Museum.

Karl Johans Gate, Oslo's main street (especially for shopping and strolling) is north of City Hall Square. This boulevard begins at Oslo **Sentralstasjon (Central Station)** and stretches all the way to the 19th-century **Royal Palace** at the western end. A short walk from the palace is the famed **Student's Grove** (the University of Oslo is nearby), where everybody gathers on a summer day to socialize. Dominating this area is the **National Theater.** South of the theater and near the harbor is **Stortingsgaten,** another shopping street.

The main city square is **Stortorvet,** although it's no longer the center of city life, which has now shifted to Karl Johans Gate.

At a subway stop near the National Theater you can catch an electric train to **Tryvannstårnet,** the loftiest lookout in Scandinavia, and to the **Holmenkollen Ski Jump.**

GETTING AROUND The **Oslo Card (Oslo-Kortet)** can help you become acquainted with the city at a fraction of the usual price. It allows free travel on public transportation, free admission to museums and other top sights, discounts on sightseeing buses and boats, a rebate on your car rental, and special treats in restaurants. You can buy the card at hotels, fine stores, and tourist offices; from travel agents; and in the branches of Sparebanken Oslo Akershus.

Oslo

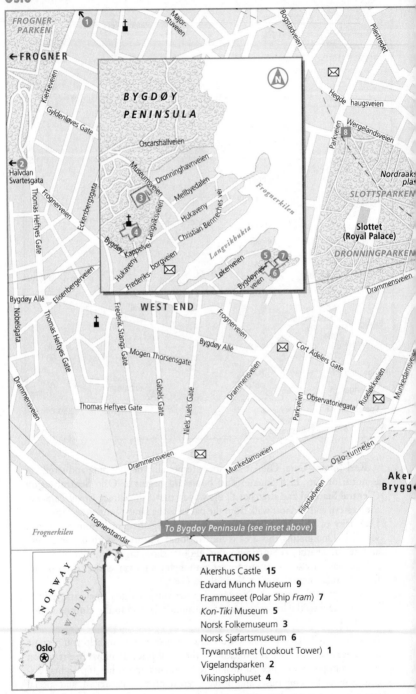

ATTRACTIONS ●

Akershus Castle **15**
Edvard Munch Museum **9**
Frammuseet (Polar Ship *Fram*) **7**
Kon-Tiki Museum **5**
Norsk Folkemuseum **3**
Norsk Sjøfartsmuseum **6**
Tryvannstårnet (Lookout Tower) **1**
Vigelandsparken **2**
Vikingskiphuset **4**

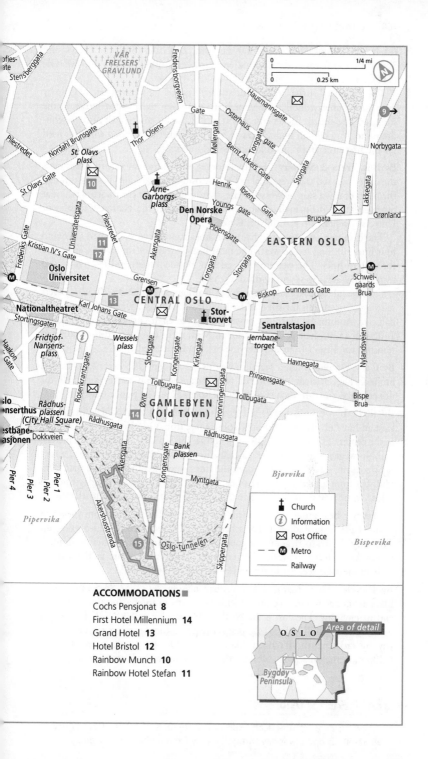

ACCOMMODATIONS ■
Cochs Pensjonat **8**
First Hotel Millennium **14**
Grand Hotel **13**
Hotel Bristol **12**
Rainbow Munch **10**
Rainbow Hotel Stefan **11**

Adults pay 190NOK ($27) for a 1-day card, 280NOK ($40) for 2 days, and 370NOK ($53) for 3 days. Children's cards cost 60NOK ($8.50), 80NOK ($11), and 110NOK ($16).

The 24-hour **Tourist Ticket (Turistkort)** lets you travel anywhere in Oslo by bus, tram, subway, local railway, or boat, including the Bygdøy ferries in the summer. The Tourist Ticket costs 60NOK ($8.50) for adults, half price for children 4 to 15; children under 4 travel free. The ticket is stamped when it's used for the first time and is good for the next 24 hours.

By Bus, Tram & Subway **Jernbanetorget,** in front of the Central Station, is the major bus and tram terminal in Oslo. Most buses and trams passing through the heart of town stop at Wessels Plass, next to the Parliament (Stortinget), or at Stortorvet, the main marketplace. Many also stop at the National Theater or University Square on Karl Johans Gate.

The **T-banen** (subway) has five main lines running to the east of Oslo and four lines running to the west. The most heavily traveled routes by tourists are the eastern lines. The western lines take in Holmenkollen and residential and recreational areas west and north of the city.

For schedule and fare information, call **Trafikanten** (✆ 22-05-70-37). Drivers sell single-trip tickets for 20NOK to 30NOK ($2.85–$4.25); children travel for half fare. Automated machines cancel tickets. An eight-coupon Maxi card costs 140NOK ($20), half price for children. Maxi cards can be used for unlimited transfers for 1 hour from the time the ticket was stamped.

By Car Driving is not a practical way to get around Oslo because parking is limited. The efficient network of public transportation makes a private car unnecessary. You can reach even the most isolated areas by public transportation.

By Taxi If you need a taxi, call ✆ 22-38-80-70, 24 hours a day. Reserve at least an hour in advance. The approximate fare from Oslo International Airport to the center of Oslo is 575NOK to 775NOK ($82–$110). All taxis have meters, and Norwegian cab drivers are generally honest. When a cab is available, a roof light goes on. Taxis can be hailed on the street, provided they're more than 90m (300 ft.) from a taxi stand. The worst times to hail a taxi are Monday through Friday from 8:30 to 10am and 3 to 5pm, and Saturday from 8:30 to 10am.

By Ferry Beginning in mid-April, ferries depart for Bygdøy from Pier 3 in front of the Oslo Rådhuset. For schedules, call **Båtservice** (✆ 23-35-68-90). The ferry or bus to Bygdøy is a good choice, because parking there is limited. Other ferries leave for various parts of the Oslofjord. Inquire at the **Tourist Information Office,** Roald Amundsen St. (✆ 24-14-77-00).

By Bicycle **Den Rustne Eike,** Vestbaneplassen 2 (✆ 22-83-52-08), rents bikes at moderate rates, complete with free maps of interesting routes in Oslo and its environs. The cost is 265NOK ($38) per day or 800NOK ($114) per week, with a 1,000NOK ($142) deposit required (no deposit is required if you pay by credit card). It's open May through October, daily from 10am to 6:30pm; in the off season, Monday through Friday from 10am to 6pm.

FAST FACTS: Oslo

American Express **American Express Reisebyrå,** Karl Johans Gate (✆ 22-98-37-00), is open Monday through Friday from 8:30am to 5:30pm.

Business Hours Most **banks** are open Monday through Friday from 8:30am to 3:30pm (Thurs to 5pm). Most **businesses** are open Monday through Friday from 9am to 4pm. **Stores** are generally open Monday through Friday from 9am to 5pm (many stay open late on Thurs to 6 or 7pm) and Saturday from 9am to 1 or 2pm. Sunday closings are observed.

Currency You'll pay your way in Norway with Norwegian kroner or crowns, which are universally abbreviated NOK. There are 100 øre in 1 krone. The exchange rate used in this chapter is US$1 = 7NOK (or 1NOK = 14¢). At press time, £1 = approximately 11.7NOK (or 1NOK = 8.4 pence). Note that Norway is not a member of the EU.

Currency Exchange **Banks** will exchange most foreign currencies or cash traveler's checks. Bring your passport for identification. If banks are closed, try automated machines at the Oslo Sentralstasjon to exchange currency. You can also exchange currency at the **Bureau de Change** at the main Oslo post office, Kirkegt 20 (✆ **22-97-60-00**).

Dentists/Doctors For a dental emergency, contact the **Tøyen Senter**, Kolstadgate 18 (✆ **22-67-30-00**; T-banen: Groønen), open daily from 11am to 2pm and 7 to 10pm. For private dentists, look under *Tannleger* ("tooth doctors") in volume 1B of the telephone directory; there's rarely a language barrier.

Some larger hotels have arrangements with doctors in case a guest becomes ill. You can also try the 24-hour **Oslo Kommunale Legavakten**, Storgata 40 (✆ **22-93-22-93**). A privately funded alternative is **Oslo Akutten**, Nedre Vollgate 8 (✆ **22-00-81-60**). For more routine medical assistance, you can contact the biggest hospital in Oslo, **Ullaval**, Kirkeveien 166 (✆ **22-11-80-80**). To consult a private doctor (nearly all of whom speak English), check the telephone directory or ask at your hotel for a recommendation.

Drugstores A 24-hour pharmacy is **Jernbanetorvets Apotek**, Jernbanetorget 4B (✆ **22-41-24-82**; T-banen: Jernbanetorget).

Embassies & Consulates The embassy of the **United States** is at Drammensveien 18, N-0244 Oslo (✆ **22-44-85-50**; T-banen: Nationaltheatret). The embassy of the **United Kingdom** is at Thomas Heftyes Gate 8, N-0264 Oslo 2 (✆ **23-13-27-00**; T-banen: Nationaltheatret). The embassy of **Canada** is at Wergelandsveien 7, N-0244 Oslo (✆ **22-99-53-00**; T-banen: Nationaltheatret). Visitors from Ireland and New Zealand should contact the British embassy. Australians should contact the Canadian embassy. Call for hours.

Emergencies Dial the Oslo **police** at ✆ **112**; report a **fire** at ✆ **110**; call an **ambulance** at ✆ **113**.

Internet Access You can tap in free at the **Oslo Public Library (Deichmanske Bibliotek)** (✆ **23-43-29-00**). Hours are May through September, Monday through Friday from 10am to 8pm and Saturday from 9am to 3pm.

Post Office The **Oslo General Post Office** is at Dronningensgatan 15 (✆ **23-14-90-00** for information). Enter at the corner of Prinsensgate. It's open Monday through Friday from 9am to 5pm, Saturday from 9am to 2pm; closed Sunday and public holidays. You can arrange for mail to be sent to the main post office c/o General Delivery. The address is Poste Restante, P.O. Box 1181-Sentrum, Dronningensgatan 15, N-0101 Oslo, Norway. You must show your passport to collect it.

Safety Of the four Scandinavian capitals, Oslo is widely considered the safest. However, don't be lulled into a false sense of security. Oslovians no longer leave their doors unlocked. Be careful, and don't carry your wallet visibly exposed or sling your purse over your shoulder.

Taxes Oslo has no special city taxes. Norway imposes a 19.4% value-added tax (VAT) on most goods and services, which is figured into your final bill. If you buy goods in any store bearing the tax-free sign, you're entitled to a cash refund of up to 18.5% on purchases costing over 310NOK ($44). Ask the shop assistant for a tax-free shopping check, and show your passport to indicate that you're not a resident of Scandinavia. You may not use the articles purchased before leaving Norway, and they must be taken out of the country within 3 months of purchase. Complete the information requested on the back of the check you're given at the store; at your point of departure, report to an area marked by the tax-free sign, not at Customs. Your refund check will be exchanged there in *kroner* for the amount due you. Refunds are available at airports, ferry and cruise-ship terminals, borders, and train stations.

Telephone The country code for Norway is **47,** and the city code for Oslo is **22** (in some rare cases, **23**). For operator assistance in English, dial 🕿 **115.**

Toll-free international access codes are: **AT&T** (🕿 **800/CALL-ATT**), **MCI** (🕿 **800/888-8000**).

Tipping Hotels add a 10% to 15% service charge to your bill, which is sufficient unless someone has performed a special service. Most bellhops get at least 10NOK ($1.40) per suitcase. Nearly all restaurants add a service charge of up to 15% to your bill. Barbers and hairdressers usually aren't tipped, but toilet attendants and hatcheck people expect at least 3NOK (45¢). Don't tip theater ushers. Taxi drivers don't expect tips unless they handle heavy luggage.

WHERE TO STAY
VERY EXPENSIVE

Grand Hotel ★★★ Norway's leading hostelry is on the wide boulevard that leads to the Royal Palace. The stone-walled hotel with its mansard gables and copper tower has been an integral part of Oslo life since 1874. Famous guests have included Arctic explorer Roald Amundsen, Edvard Munch, Gen. Dwight Eisenhower, Charlie Chaplin, Henry Ford, and Henrik Ibsen. Frankly, although it's still the grande dame of Norway hotels, we feel the Grand's stuffiness has cost it its cutting edge. The guest rooms are in the 19th-century core or in one of the modern additions. Newer rooms contain plush facilities and electronic extras, but many guests prefer the old-fashioned accommodations in the older section, which have also been modernized. Most of the old-fashioned bathrooms are done in marble or tile and have shower-tub combinations. Among the hotel's restaurants, the **Grand Café** (see below) is the most famous in Oslo.

Karl Johans Gate 31, N-0159 Oslo. 🕿 **800/223-5652** in the U.S., or 23-21-20-00. Fax 23-21-21-00. www. grand.no. 289 units. Summer 1,250NOK ($178) double, from 2,300NOK ($327) suite. Fall, winter, spring

2,290NOK ($325) double, from 3,516NOK ($499) suite. Rates include buffet breakfast. AE, DC, MC, V. Parking 260NOK ($37). T-banen: Stortinget. **Amenities:** 3 restaurants; 3 bars; nightclub; pool; health club; sauna; boutiques; massage; room service (8am–11pm); laundry service/dry cleaning; nonsmoking rooms; rooms for those with limited mobility. *In room:* A/C, TV, dataport, minibar, hair dryer.

EXPENSIVE

Hotel Bristol ★★★   Loaded with character, and the source of many entertaining anecdotes, this 1920s-era hotel competes aggressively and gracefully with other historic hotel "dragons" of Oslo, including the Grand (see above) and the Continental. Of the three, the Bristol consistently emerges as the most liberal, the hippest, and the most accessible. Set in the commercial core of Oslo, a block north of Karl Johans Gate, it's warm, inviting, rich with tradition, and comfortable. It's becoming the preferred hotel of the media, arts, and show-biz communities, with a sense of playfulness that's unmatched by either of its more formal rivals.

In 2001, the hotel almost doubled its room count, thanks to the annexation and conversion of an office building next door. Guest rooms are comfortable and dignified, each with a tiled or marble bathroom with a tub/shower combination. Lavish public areas evoke the Moorish-inspired Art Deco style in which they were built. There's enormous life and energy in this hotel, thanks to active restaurants, piano bars, and a sense of elegant yet unpretentious conviviality.

Kristian IV's Gate 7, N-0164 Oslo 1. ✆ **22-82-60-00.** Fax 22-82-60-01. www.bristol.no. 252 units. Mon–Thurs 1,350NOK–1,990NOK ($192–$283) double. Fri–Sun year-round and late June to early Aug 1,195NOK ($170) double. Year-round 4,000NOK–8,000NOK ($568–$1,136) suite. AE, DC, MC, V. T-banen: Nationaltheater. Tram: 10, 11, 17, or 18. **Amenities:** Restaurant; 2 bars; live pianist in the lobby; nightclub/dance bar; small-scale exercise room and health club; room service (7am–11pm); babysitting; laundry service/dry cleaning; nonsmoking rooms; rooms for those with limited mobility. *In room:* TV, dataport, minibar, hair dryer, trouser press, safe.

MODERATE

First Hotel Millennium ★ *Finds*   One of Oslo's newest large-scale hotels is housed in what was originally a 12-floor 1930s Art Deco office building. This is one of the "personality" hotels of Oslo, known for its atmosphere and character, and noted for a stylish kind of functional minimalism. It's within walking distance of virtually everything in central Oslo. Rooms are among the most spacious in town, with many Art Deco touches. Extras include two phone lines and large bathrooms with both tub and shower. The top floor offers a dozen rooms with their own large balconies. **Primo Ciaou-Ciaou** is one of Oslo's best restaurants.

Tollbugate 25, N-0157 Oslo. ✆ **21-02-28-00.** Fax 21-02-28-30. www.firsthotels.com. 112 units. Mon–Thurs 1,099NOK–1,499NOK ($156–$213) double; Fri–Sun 769NOK–948NOK ($109–$135) double. AE, DC, MC, V. Metro: Stortingeg. Tram: 12, 15, or 19. **Amenities:** Restaurant; bar; room service (6:30am–10pm); babysitting; laundry service/dry cleaning; nonsmoking rooms; 1 room for those with limited mobility. *In room:* TV, dataport, minibar, coffeemaker, hair dryer.

Rainbow Hotel Stefan   In an excellent location in the center of the city, this hotel is comfortable and unpretentious. Built in 1952, it has been modernized and much improved. Rooms are traditional in style and well furnished and maintained, with small but adequate bathrooms with showers. From May to September 1, weekend rates are granted only to those who make reservations less than 48 hours before arrival. The restaurant is known for its Norwegian buffets for lunch.

Rosenkrantzgate 1, N-0159 Oslo 1. ✆ **23-31-55-00.** Fax 23-31-55-55. www.rainbow-hotels.no. 139 units. Sun–Thurs 1,250NOK ($178) double; Fri–Sat 940NOK ($133) double. Rates include breakfast. AE, DC, MC, V. Parking 180NOK ($26). Tram: 10, 11, 17, or 18. **Amenities:** Restaurant; bar; limited room service; babysitting; laundry service/dry cleaning; 1 room for those with limited mobility. *In room:* TV, minibar, hair dryer, safe.

Rainbow Munch   This hotel is somewhat like a bed-and-breakfast, and it's just 5 minutes north of Karl Johans Gate. Built in 1983, the solid, nine-floor hotel offers comfortably furnished, well-maintained guest rooms, decorated with reproductions of Edvard Munch's paintings. Although not overly large, the rooms are cozy and comfortable. The bathrooms are tiny but come equipped with shower-tub combinations. If you don't plan to spend a lot of time in your room, this is an adequate choice, charging a fair price for what it offers.

Munchsgaten 5, N-0130 Oslo. ⓒ 23-21-96-00. Fax 23-21-96-01. www.rainbow-hotels.no. 180 units. Mon–Thurs 1,145NOK ($163) double; Fri–Sun 790NOK ($112) double. Rates include breakfast. AE, DC, MC, V. Parking 140NOK ($20). T-banen: Stortinget. Tram: 8, 10, 11, or 17. Bus: 37. **Amenities:** Lounge; laundry service/ dry cleaning; rooms for those with limited mobility. *In room:* TV, minibar, hair dryer, safe.

INEXPENSIVE

Cochs Pensjonat *Value*   Built more than a century ago, with an ornate facade that curves around a bend in a boulevard that flanks the northern edge of the Royal Palace, this clean, well-conceived, inexpensive hotel represents excellent value. In 2002, major renovations added a postmodern gloss to many of the guest rooms. The result is a comfortable but simple lodging whose newer rooms have high ceilings and birch furniture, and a spartan but pleasant appearance. Expect very few, if any, amenities and services at this hotel—none of the rooms have a telephone, and no meals are served, but because of the in-room kitchens and a nearby restaurant that offers hotel guests a 25% discount on meals, no one really seems to mind.

Parkveien 25, N-0350 Oslo. ⓒ 23-33-24-00. Fax 23-33-24-10. booking@cochs.no. 88 units, 78 with bathroom and kitchenette. Rooms with bathroom and kitchenette 620NOK–680NOK ($88–$97) double, 765–825NOK ($109–$117) triple, 900NOK ($128) quad. Rooms without kitchenette and without private bathroom 520NOK ($74) double, 645NOK ($92) triple, 780NOK ($111) quad. AE, DC, MC, V. Tram: 11 or 18. *In room:* TV, no phone.

WHERE TO DINE

Norwegians are as fond of smørbrød (smorgasbord) as the Danes (you'll see it offered everywhere for lunch), except they spell it differently. Basically, this is an open-faced sandwich that can be stacked with virtually anything, including ham with a peach slice resting on top or perhaps a mound of dill-flavored shrimp.

VERY EXPENSIVE

Restaurant Julius Fritzner ☆☆☆ NORWEGIAN/CONTINENTAL   This is one of the best and most impressive restaurants in Oslo. It opened in 1995 to rave reviews, and the accolades keep coming. It's one floor above street level in Norway's most prestigious hotel. The venue is appropriately conservative, with a battalion of impeccably trained waiters who maintain their humor and personal touch despite the sophisticated setting. The dishes, all made with the finest Scandinavian ingredients, change with the season and the chef's inspiration. Examples include pan-fried turbot, lobster and caviar sauce, crispy fried cod with sautéed vegetables, poached halibut with vermouth sauce, filet of veal with crispy fried sweetbreads, and roast saddle of lamb with rosemary. The restaurant, incidentally, is named after the controversial entrepreneur who established the Grand Hotel in 1874.

In the Grand Hotel, Karl Johans Gate 31. ⓒ 23-21-20-00. Reservations recommended. Main courses 260NOK–335NOK ($37–$48); 3-course fixed-price menu 525NOK ($75); 4-course fixed-price menu 625NOK ($89); 5-course fixed price menu 715NOK ($102); 6-course fixed-price menu 795NOK ($113). AE, DC, MC, V. Mon–Sat 5–10:30pm. Closed July–Aug 5. T-banen: Stortinget.

EXPENSIVE

Babette's Gjestehus *Finds* ⚡ SCANDINAVIAN/FRENCH   Named for the heroine of the film *Babette's Feast*—which almost every Scandinavian has seen at least once—this restaurant is decorated in the style of a turn-of-the-20th-century Norwegian home. Walls are blue, antiques are genuine, curtains are lace, and there's a scattering of old paintings. Menu items are authentic as well, with such time-tested favorites as filet of reindeer with lingonberries, breast of pheasant with mushroom sauce, and pan-fried breast of duck with creamed cabbage. The masterful chefs use seasonal products to produce reliable, good-tasting food all year.

Rådhuspassasjen, Roald Amundsensgate 6. ℂ **22-41-64-64.** Reservations recommended. Main courses 255NOK–278NOK ($36–$39). AE, DC, MC, V. Mon–Sat 5–11pm. T-banen: Centrum.

MODERATE

A Touch of France ⚡ FRENCH   This aptly named place is one of Oslo's best French bistros. In summer tables spill out onto the sidewalk. The decor is that of a typical French brasserie, the kind you find alongside the road in Alsace. A Touch of France is known for serving the freshest oysters in town. On our most recent visit, we opted for the traditional salt-baked leg of duck that was served in a beautifully made garlic sauce. On other occasions we've enjoyed classic calves' liver with mushrooms, spinach, and bacon. Bouillabaisse is a specialty but that grand dish loses something in translation this far north. The dessert cart is loaded with such temptations as crème brûlée or a chocolate and almond cake.

Øvre Slottsgate 16. ℂ **23-10-01-60.** Reservations recommended. Main courses 185NOK–299NOK ($26–$42). AE, DC, MC, V. Sept–Apr Mon–Fri 4:30–11:30pm, Sat noon–11:30pm; May–Aug Mon–Sat noon–11:30pm. Bus: 27, 29, 30, 41, or 61.

Grand Café ⚡⚡ NORWEGIAN   This traditional cafe is an Oslo legend. A large mural on one wall depicts Ibsen (a fan of whale steaks), Edvard Munch, and many other patrons. A postcard sold at the reception desk identifies the mural's subjects. You can order everything from a napoleon with coffee to a full meal with reindeer steaks. Sandwiches are available for 80NOK ($11) and up. The atmosphere and tradition here are sometimes more compelling than the cuisine. The menu, nonetheless, relies on Norwegian country traditions. (How many places still serve elk stew?) If you like solid, honest flavors, this is the place to visit.

In the Grand Hotel, Karl Johans Gate 31. ℂ **24-14-53-00.** Reservations recommended. Main courses 185NOK–285NOK ($26–$40). AE, DC, MC, V. Daily 6–10am and 11am–11pm. T-banen: Stortinget.

Lipp INTERNATIONAL   Stylish and lighthearted, this restored brasserie is the Oslovian version of Paris in the 1920s. Painted a canary yellow, it employs a traditionally dressed, bistro-style, black-vested staff. On our last visit the dish of the day was roasted grouse served with a wild mushroom pie with crisp bacon. The menu changes about every 5 weeks and is seasonally adjusted, using the finest of produce from the field, not to mention river and lake. You might face a savory salmon in a white-wine sauce or reindeer in a mushroom sauce. Lighter fare is offered as well—perhaps an array of freshly made salads or grilled fish dishes.

In the Hotel Continental, Stortingsgaten 24. ℂ **22-82-40-00.** Reservations recommended. Main courses 186NOK–298NOK ($26–$42). AE, DC, MC, V. Tues–Sat 4–11:30pm. T-banen: Nationaltheatret.

INEXPENSIVE

Engebret Café NORWEGIAN   A favorite since 1857, this restaurant is directly north of Akershus Castle in two landmark buildings. It has an old-fashioned atmosphere—it was formerly a bohemian literati haunt—and good food. During lunch, a tempting selection of open-faced sandwiches is available. The evening menu is more elaborate; you might begin with a terrine of game with blackberry port-wine sauce, or Engebret's fish soup. Main dishes include red wild boar with whortleberry sauce, Norwegian reindeer, salmon Christiania, or Engebret's big fish pot. For dessert, try the cloudberry parfait.

Bankplassen 1. ℭ **22-33-66-94**. Reservations recommended. Main courses 205NOK–345NOK ($29–$49). AE, DC, MC, V. Mon–Sat 11am–11pm. Bus: 27, 29, or 30.

Mamma Rosa *Kids* ITALIAN   Established by two Tuscan brothers, this trattoria enjoys a popularity that's a good indication of Norwegians' changing tastes. The second-floor dining room is decorated in "reproduction rococo." You can order 15 kinds of pizza, fried scampi and squid, rigatoni, pasta Mamma Rosa (three kinds of pasta with three sauces), grilled steaks, and gelato. Frankly, some of the dishes have lost a bit of flavor on the trip this far north, but Mamma Rosa is nonetheless a marvelous change of taste and texture.

Øvre Slottsgate 12. ℭ **22-42-01-30**. Main courses 98NOK–225NOK ($14–$32); pizzas from 103NOK ($15). DC, MC, V. Daily 2–11pm; Sat open at noon. T-banen: Stortinget.

SEEING THE SIGHTS
IN THE BYGDØY PENINSULA

Vikingskiphuset (Viking Ship Museum) ★★★   Displayed here are three Viking burial vessels that were excavated on the shores of the Oslofjord and preserved in clay. The most spectacular find is the 9th-century *Oseberg* ★, discovered near Norway's oldest town. This 20m (64-ft.) dragon ship features a wealth of ornaments and is the burial chamber of a Viking queen and her slave. The *Gokstad* find is an outstanding example of Viking vessels because it's so well preserved. The smaller *Tune* ship was never restored. Look for the *Oseberg* animal-head post, the elegantly carved sleigh used by Viking royalty, and the *Oseberg* four-wheeled cart.

Huk Aveny 35, Bygdøy. ℭ **22-43-83-79**. Admission 40NOK ($5.70) adults, 20NOK ($2.85) children 8–16 years old. Oct–May daily 11am–4pm; June–Sept daily 9am–6pm. Ferry: From Pier 3 facing the Rådhuset (summer only). Bus: 30 from the National Theater.

Polar Ship Fram (Frammuseet)   A long walk from the Viking ships, the Frammuseet contains the sturdy polar exploration ship *Fram*, which Fridtjof Nansen sailed across the Arctic (1893–96). The vessel was later used by Norwegian explorer Roald Amundsen, the first man to reach the South Pole (1911).

Bygdøynesveien. ℭ **23-28-29-50**. Admission 30NOK ($4.25) adults, 15NOK ($2.15) children. Mar–Apr Mon–Sun 11am–3:45pm; May 1–15 and Sept daily 10am–4:45pm; May 16–Aug daily 9am–5:45pm; Oct–Nov Mon–Fri 11am–2:45pm, Sat–Sun 11am–3:45pm; Dec–Feb Sat–Sun 11am–3:45pm. Ferry: From Pier 3 facing the Rådhuset (summer only). Bus: 30 from the National Theater.

Kon-Tiki Museum   *Kon-Tiki* is the world-famed balsa-log raft in which the young Norwegian scientist Thor Heyerdahl and his five comrades sailed for 7,000km (4,300 miles) in 1947—all the way from Callao, Peru, to Raroia, Polynesia. Besides the raft, there are exhibits from Heyerdahl's subsequent visit to Easter Island, including an Easter Island family cave, with a collection of sacred lava figurines.

Bygdøynesveien 36. ℭ **23-08-67-67**. www.kon-tiki.no. Admission 35NOK ($4.95) adults, 20NOK ($2.85) children, 90NOK ($13) family ticket. Apr–May and Sept daily 10:30am–4pm; June–Aug daily 9:30am–5:45pm; Oct–Mar daily 10:30am–4pm. Ferry: From Pier 3 facing the Rådhuset (summer only). Bus: 30 from the National Theater.

Norsk Sjøfartsmuseum (Norwegian Maritime Museum)   This museum, which contains a complete ship's deck with helm and chart house, and a three-deck-high section of the passenger steamer *Sandnaes,* chronicles the maritime history and culture of Norway. The Boat Hall features a fine collection of original small craft. The fully restored polar vessel *Gjoa,* used by Roald Amundsen in his search for America's Northwest Passage, is also on display. The three-masted 1916 schooner *Svanen (Swan)* now belongs to the museum and is used as a training vessel.

Bygdøynesveien 37. ✆ **24-11-41-50.** www.norsksjofartsmuseum.no. Admission to museum and boat hall 40NOK ($5.70) adults, free for children up to age 16. May–Sept daily 10am–6pm; Oct–Apr Mon-Wed and Fri–Sat 10:30am–4pm, Thurs 10:30am–6pm. Ferry: From Pier 3 facing the Rådhuset (summer only). Bus: 30 from the National Theater.

Norsk Folkemuseum ★★   From all over Norway, 140 original buildings have been transported and reassembled on 14 hectares (35 acres) on the Bygdøy Peninsula. This open-air folk museum includes a number of medieval buildings, such as the Raulandstua, one of the oldest wooden dwellings still standing in Norway, and a stave church from about 1200. The rural buildings are grouped together by region of origin, while the urban houses have been laid out in the form of an old town.

Museumsveien 10. ✆ **22-12-37-00.** www.norskfolke.museum.no. Admission 75NOK ($11) adults, 20NOK ($2.85) children under 17. Sept 15–May 14 Mon–Fri 11am–3pm, Sat-Sun 11am–4pm; May 15–Sept 14 daily 10am–6pm. Ferry: From Pier 3 facing the Rådhuset (summer only). Bus: 30 from the National Theater.

IN WESTERN OLSO

Vigeland Museet og Parken (Museum and Park) ★★   The lifetime work of Gustav Vigeland, Norway's greatest sculptor, is displayed inside the museum as well as throughout the nearby 80-hectare (197-acre) Frogner Park in western Oslo. Nearly 212 sculptures in granite, bronze, and iron can be admired. See in particular his four granite columns, symbolizing the fight between humanity and evil (a dragon, the embodiment of evil, embraces a woman). *The Angry Boy* is the most photographed statue in the park, but the really celebrated work is the 16m (52-ft.) monolith, composed of 121 figures of colossal size—all carved into one piece of stone.

Frogner Park, Nobelsgate 32. ✆ **22-54-25-30.** Free admission to park. Museum, 40NOK ($5.70) adults, 20NOK ($2.85) children. Park, daily 24 hr. Museum May–Sept Tues–Sat 10am–6pm, Sun noon–7pm; Oct–Apr Tues–Sat noon–4pm, Sun noon–4pm. Tram: 12 or 15. Bus: 20 or 45.

IN EASTERN OSLO

Munch Museum   Devoted exclusively to the works of Edvard Munch (1863–1944), Scandinavia's leading painter, this exhibit (Munch's gift to the city), traces his work from early realism to his latter-day expressionism. The collection comprises 1,100 paintings, some 4,500 drawings, around 18,000 prints, numerous graphic plates, six sculptures, and important documentary material.

Tøyengate 53. ✆ **23-24-14-00.** http://museumsnett.no/munchmuseet. Admission 60NOK ($8.50) adults, 30NOK ($4.25) children. June to mid-Sept daily 10am–6pm; mid-Sept to May Tues–Sun 10am–5pm. T-banen: Tøyen. Bus: 20.

IN THE CITY CENTER

Akershus Castle   One of the oldest historical monuments in Oslo, Akershus Castle was built in 1300 by King Haakon V Magnusson. It was a fortress and a royal residence for several centuries. A fire in 1527 devastated the northern wing, and the castle was rebuilt and transformed into a Renaissance palace under the Danish-Norwegian king Christian IV. Now it's used for state occasions. A few rooms, including the chapel, are open to the public. In the rectangular court, markings show where the massive medieval keep used to stand. You can wander through two large halls (Olav's and Christian IV's), which occupy the top floor of the north and south wings, respectively. For many, the most interesting part is the dungeon, which includes an "escape-proof room" built for a prisoner, Ole Pedersewn Hoyland. After he was placed in the chamber and realized there was no way he could ever escape, he killed himself.

Festnings-Plassen. ⓒ **22-41-25-21.** Admission 40NOK ($5.70) adults, 10NOK ($1.40) children, 20NOK ($2.85) students and seniors, 70NOK ($9.95) family. May 2–Sept 15 Mon–Sat 10am–4pm, Sun 12:30–4pm. Closed Sept 16–May 1. Tram: 15 or 12. Bus: 60.

ATTRACTIONS NEARBY

Tryvannstårnet (Lookout Tower) This is the loftiest lookout tower in Scandinavia—the gallery is approximately 580m (1,900 ft.) above sea level and offers a view of the Oslofjord with Sweden to the east. A walk down the hill takes you to the famous restaurant Frognerseteren. You can take another 20-minute walk down the hill to the Holmenkollen ski jump, the site of the 1952 Olympic competitions, as well as the Holmenkollen Ski Festival, when skiers compete in downhill, slalom, giant slalom, cross-country ski races, and jumping.

Voksenkollen. ⓒ **22-14-67-11.** Admission 40NOK ($5.70) adults, 20NOK ($2.85) children. May and Sept daily 10am–5pm; June daily 10am–7pm; July–Aug daily 9am–8pm; Oct–Apr Mon–Sun 10am–4pm. T-banen: Frognerseteren SST Line 1 from near the National Theater to Voksenkollen (30-min. ride), then an uphill 15-min. walk.

Henie-Onstad Kunstsenter (Henie-Onstad Art Center) ★★ On a site beside the Oslofjord 11km (6¾ miles) west of Oslo, the ex-movie star and skating champion Sonja Henie and her husband, Niels Onstad, a shipping tycoon, opened a museum to display their art collection. This especially good 20th-century collection includes some 1,800 works by Munch, Picasso, Matisse, Léger, Bonnard, and Miró. Henie's Trophy Room is impressive, with 600 trophies and medals, including three Olympic gold medals—she was the star at the 1936 competition—and 10 world skating championships.

Høkvikodden, Baerum. ⓒ **67-80-48-80.** www.hok.no. Admission 75NOK ($11) adults, 45NOK ($6.40) ages 17–25, free for children 16 and under. Tues–Thurs 11am–7pm; Fri–Sun 11am–6pm. Bus: 151, 152, 251, or 261.

ORGANIZED TOURS

H. M. Kristiansens Automobilbyrå, Hegdehaugsveien 4 (ⓒ **22-20-82-06**), has been showing visitors around Oslo for more than a century. Both of their bus tours are offered daily year-round. The 3-hour "Oslo Highlights" tour is offered at 10am and 1pm. It costs 250NOK ($36) for adults, 130NOK ($18) for children. The 2-hour "Oslo Panorama" tour costs 170NOK ($24) for adults, 90NOK ($13) for children. It departs at 10am and noon. The starting point is in front of the National Theater, Vestbaneplassen 1; arrive 15 minutes before departure. Tours are conducted in English by trained guides.

THE SHOPPING SCENE

Near the marketplace and the Oslo Domkirche (cathedral), **Den Norske Husfliden,** Møllergata 4 (ⓒ **24-14-12-80;** T-banen: Stortinget; tram: 17)— or Husfliden, as it's called—is the display and retail center for the Norwegian Association of Home Arts and Crafts, founded in 1891. Today it's almost eight times larger than any of its competitors, with two floors displaying the very finest of Norwegian design in ceramics, glassware, furniture, and woodworking.

You can also purchase souvenirs, gifts, textiles, rugs, knotted Rya rugs, embroidery, wrought iron, and fabrics by the yard. Goods are shipped all over the world.

Norway's largest department store, **Steen & Strøm,** Kongensgate 23 (© 22-00-40-00; T-banen: Stortinget), is a treasure house with hundreds of Nordic items spread through 58 individual departments. Look for hand-knit sweaters and caps, hand-painted wooden dishes reflecting traditional Norwegian art, and pewter dinner plates made from old molds. **Heimen Husflid,** Rosenkrantzgate 8 (© 22-41-40-50; T-banen: Nationaltheatret), about a block from Karl Johans Gate, carries folk costumes, antiques, and reproductions. Hand-knit sweaters in traditional Norwegian patterns are a special item, as are pewter and brass items.

William Schmidt, Fridtjof Nansens Plass 9 (© 22-42-02-88; T-banen: Stortinget), established in 1853, is a leading purveyor of unique souvenirs, including pewter items (everything from Viking ships to beer goblets), Norwegian dolls in national costumes, woodcarvings (the troll collection is the most outstanding in Oslo), and sealskin moccasins. The shop specializes in hand-knit cardigans, pullovers, gloves, and caps; sweaters are made from mothproofed 100% Norwegian wool.

OSLO AFTER DARK

To find out what's happening when you're visiting, pick up *What's On in Oslo,* which details concerts and theaters and other useful information.

Theater, ballet, and opera tickets are sold at various box offices and also at **Billettsentralen,** Karl Johans Gate 35 (© 81-53-31-33; T-banen: Stortinget)— although this service costs quite a bit more than your typical box office. Tickets to sports and cultural events can now be purchased easily and more cheaply via computer linkup at any post office in the city, so when you buy a stamp you can also buy a voucher for a ticket to the ballet, theater, or hockey game.

THE PERFORMING ARTS

Home to the National Theater Company, the **National Theater,** Johanne Dybwads Plass 1 (© 81-50-08-11; T-banen: Nationaltheatret), opens in late August, so it may be of interest to off-season drama lovers who want to hear Ibsen and Bjørnson in the original. Avant-garde productions go on up at the **Amfiscenen,** in the same building. There are no performances in July and August. Guest companies often perform plays in English. Tickets range from 180NOK to 300NOK ($26–$43) adults, 100NOK to 230NOK ($14–$33) students and seniors.

Two blocks from the National Theater, **Oslo Konserthus,** Munkedamsveien 14 (© 23-11-31-11; T-banen: Stortinget), is the home of the widely acclaimed Oslo Philharmonic. Performances are given from autumn to spring, on Thursday and Friday. Guest companies from around the world often appear on other nights. The hall is closed from June 20 until mid-August, except for occasional performances by folkloric groups. Tickets run from 200NOK to 500NOK ($28–$71).

Originally a movie theater, the 1931 building at Storgaten 23 was adapted for better acoustics and dedicated in 1959 to the **Den Norske Opera** (© 23-31-50-00; T-banen: Jernbanetorget). It's also the leading venue for ballet—the companies alternate performances. About 10 different operas and operettas are staged every year. There are no performances from mid-June to August. Tickets are generally available to nonsubscribers; seats can be reserved in advance and paid for with a credit card. Tickets range from 170NOK to 300NOK ($24–$43) except for galas.

Norwegian Folk Museum, Museumsveien 10, Bygdøy (© **22-12-37-00**), often presents folk-dance performances by its own ensemble on summer Sunday afternoons at the museum's open-air theater. Admission to the museum includes admission to the dance performance; 55NOK ($7.80) adults, 35NOK ($4.95) students and seniors, 20NOK ($2.85) children.

THE CLUB & MUSIC SCENE
Smuget, Rosenkrantzgate 22 (© **22-42-52-62**; T-banen: Nationaltheatret), is the most talked-about nightlife joint in the city, and has the long lines (especially on weekends) to prove it. It's in a 19th-century building in back of the City Hall and has a restaurant, an active dance floor, and a stage where live bands perform. It's open Monday through Saturday from 7pm to 4am; the cover ranges from 60NOK to 100NOK ($8.50–$14).

Blå, Brennerivn 9C (© **22-20-91-81**), is the leading jazz club of Oslo. Dark and industrial with lots of wrought iron and mellow lighting, the place books some of the best jazz acts in Scandinavia. The crowd is a mix of young and old, dressed in casual but sophisticated attire. The weeknights focus strictly on jazz, with Friday and Saturday providing more of a disco atmosphere, when DJs brought in from all over the world spin the best in techno and house music. Open Monday to Thursday and Sunday 8pm to 1am, and Friday and Saturday 8pm to 3:30am. Cover ranges from 70NOK to 120NOK ($9.95–$17); T-Banen: Jernbanetorget.

DAY TRIPS FROM OSLO
The best 1-day excursion from Oslo includes visits to Fredrikstad and Tønsberg, which gives you a chance to explore the scenic highlights of the Oslofjord. A trip to Fredrikstad, in Østfold on the east bank of the Oslofjord, can easily be combined in 1 day with a visit to the port of Tønsberg on the west bank, by crossing over on the ferry from Moss to Horten, then heading south.

Getting There   To reach the first stop, Fredrikstad, take E-6 south from Oslo toward Moss. Continue past Moss until you reach the junction of Route 110, which is signposted south of Fredrikstad. About six buses per day depart for the town from the Central Station in Oslo. Trains from Oslo's Central Station depart from Fredrikstad about every 2 hours during the day (trip time: 30 min.).

FREDRIKSTAD ✿
In recent years Fredrikstad, 95km (60 miles) south of Oslo, has become a major tourist center, thanks to its Old Town and 17th-century fortress. Across the river on the west is a modern industrial section, and although a bridge links the two sections, the best way to reach Old Town is by ferry, which costs 6NOK (85¢). The

---

Tips **Native Behavior**

Although Norwegians love their beer, note that buying a round is virtually unheard of in a Norwegian pub. In this independent country, both men and women pay for their own libations. During the week, never ask someone you meet "out for a drink." He or she will think you're a drunk. On Friday or Saturday night, it's different. Anything goes. Beer taverns are wild and riotous, and few patrons are satisfied with a mere 10 beers.

departure point is about 4 blocks from the Fredrikstad railroad station—simply follow the crowd out the main door of the station, make an obvious left turn, and continue down to the shore of the river. It's also possible to travel between the two areas by bus no. 360 or 362, although most pedestrians opt for the ferry.

Seeing the Sights

Visitor Information   Fredrikstad Turistkontor is on Turistsenteret, Østre Brohode in Gamle Fredrikstad (© **69-30-46-00**). From June to September, it's open Monday through Friday from 9am to 6pm and Saturday from 10am to 4pm; from October to May, it's open Monday through Friday from 9am to 4pm.

Fredrikstad was founded in 1567 as a marketplace at the mouth of the River Glomma. **Gamlebyen (Old Town)** became a fortress in 1663 and continued in that role until 1903, boasting some 200 guns in its heyday. It still serves as a military camp. The main guardroom and old convict prison are now the **Fredrikstad Museum,** Mindre Alvsvei 5 (© **69-30-68-75**), open from May to September, Tuesday through Friday from noon to 5pm, Saturday from 11am to 5pm, and Sunday from noon to 5pm. Admission is 30NOK ($4.25) adults and 10NOK ($1.40) children.

Outside the gates of Old Town is **Kongsten Fort,** on what was first called Gallows Hill, an execution site. When Fredrikstad Fortress was built, it was provisionally fortified in 1677, becoming known as Svenskeskremme (Swede Scarer). Present-day Kongsten Fort with its 20 cannons, underground chambers, passages, and countermines, eventually replaced it.

Since Fredrikstad's heyday as a trading port and merchant base, Old Town has attracted craftspeople and artisans, many of whom create their products in the Old Town's historic houses and barns. Many of these glass blowers, ceramic artists, and silversmiths choose not to display or sell their products at their studios, preferring instead to leave the sales aspect to local shops.

En Route to Tønsberg   You can drive back north from Fredrikstad to the town of Moss, where you can take a ferry to Horten. Once at Horten, signs will point the way south for the short drive to Tønsberg. Tønsberg is about 1½ hours from Oslo, with some 20 trains arriving daily.

TØNSBERG ⭐

Bordering the western bank of the Oslofjord, Tønsberg, 100km (64 miles) south of Oslo, is Norway's oldest town. It's divided into a historic area, filled with old clapboard-sided houses, and the commercial center, where the marketplace is located.

Seeing the Sights

Visitor Information   Tourist Information is at Nedre Langgate 36, N-3126 Tønsberg (© **33-35-45-20**). It's open in July daily from 10am to 5:30pm; from August to June, Monday through Friday from 9:30am to 3:30pm.

Tønsberg was founded a year before King Harald Fairhair united parts of the country in 872, and this Viking town became a royal coronation site. Svend Foyn, who invented modern whaling and seal hunting, was born here.

Slottsfjellet, a huge hill fortress directly ahead of the train station, is touted as "the Acropolis of Norway." But it has only some meager ruins, and people mostly come here for the view from the lookout tower. Built in 1888, the **Slottsfjelltårnet** (© **33-31-18-72**) is open from May 18 to June 23, Monday through Friday from 10am to 3pm; from June 24 to August 18, daily from 11am to 6pm; from August 19 to September 15, Saturday and Sunday from noon to 5pm; and from September 16 to September 29, Saturday and Sunday from noon to 3pm. Admission is 20NOK ($2.85) adults and 10NOK ($1.40) children.

Nordbyen is the old and scenic part of town, with well-preserved houses. **Haugar** cemetery, at Møllebakken, is right in the town center, with the Viking graves of King Harald's sons, Olav and Sigrød.

Sem Church, Hageveien 32 (© **33-36-93-99**), the oldest in Vestfold, was built of stone in the Romanesque style around 1100. It's open Tuesday through Friday from 9am to 2pm; ask at the vestry. Admission is free.

You should also see **Fjerdingen,** a street of charming restored houses. Tønsberg was also a Hanseatic town during the Middle Ages, and some houses have been redone in typical Hanseatic style.

In the **Vestfold Folk Museum** ✦, Frammannsveien 30 (© **33-31-29-19**), there are many Viking and whaling treasures. One of the biggest thrills is the skeleton of a blue whale. A real Viking ship is displayed, the *Klastad* from Tjolling, built about A.D. 800. Admission is 40NOK ($5.70) adults, 20NOK ($2.85) children. It's open from mid-May to mid-September, Monday through Saturday from 10am to 5pm, Sunday and holidays from noon to 5pm; mid-September through mid-May Monday to Friday 10am to 2pm and Sunday noon to 5pm.

2 Bergen & the Fjords

In western Norway the landscape takes on an awesome beauty, with iridescent glaciers; deep fjords that slash into rugged, snowcapped mountains; roaring waterfalls; and secluded valleys that lie at the end of corkscrew-twisting roads. From Bergen the most beautiful fjords to visit are the **Hardanger** (best at blossom time, May and early June), to the south; the **Sogne,** Norway's longest fjord, immediately to the north; and the **Nordfjord,** north of that. A popular excursion on the Nordfjord takes visitors from Loen to Olden along rivers and lakes to the Brixdal Glacier.

If you have time, on the Hardangerfjord you can stop over at one of the fjord resorts, such as Ulvik or Lofthus. The Folgefonn Glacier, Norway's second-largest ice field, which spans more than 250 sq. km (100 sq. miles), can be seen from many vantage points.

Bergen, with its many sightseeing attractions; good hotels and restaurants; and excellent boat, rail, and coach connections, is the best center for touring the fjord district. This ancient city looms large in Viking sagas. Until the 14th century, it was the seat of the medieval kingdom of Norway. The Hanseatic merchants established a major trading post here, holding sway until the 18th century.

BERGEN: GATEWAY TO THE FJORDS
ESSENTIALS
GETTING THERE By Plane The **Bergen Airport** at Flesland, 19km (12 miles) south of the city, offers frequent flights to Copenhagen and London, through which most international flights are routed.

There is frequent airport bus service from the airport to the SAS Royal Hotel, Braathens airlines' office at the Hotel Norge, and the city bus station. Buses depart every 15 minutes from Monday to Friday and every 30 minutes Saturday and Sunday. The one-way fare is 60NOK ($8.50). Taxis are readily available at the airport, or call © **33-30-11-11.** A ride to the city center costs 262NOK ($37).

By Train Day and night trains arrive from Oslo (trip time: 6–8½ hr.). For information, call the Bergen train station at © **55-96-69-00.**

By Bus Express buses travel to Bergen from Oslo in 11 hours. For long-distance bus information, call © **55-55-90-70.**

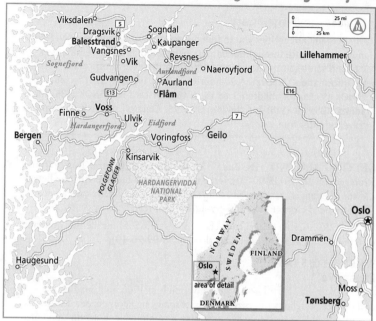

By Car A toll is charged on all vehicles driven into the city center Monday through Friday from 6am to 10pm. A single ticket costs 10NOK ($1.40); a book of 20 tickets, 180NOK ($26).

The trip from Oslo to Bergen is a mountainous drive filled with dramatic scenery. Because mountains split the country, there's no direct road. The southern route, E76, takes you through mountain passes until the junction with Route 47; then you head north to Kinsarvik and make the ferry crossing to E16 leading to Bergen. It's quickest to take the northern route following E16 west. For the first time it's possible to make a ferry-free road connection to Bergen. In 2001 the world's longest tunnel opened, going as deep as 1,470m (4,900 ft.) beneath one of Norway's most scenic mountain areas beginning 300km (185 miles) northwest of Oslo. The 40km (25-mile) Laerdal Tunnel surpasses the 17km (11-mile) St. Gothard Tunnel in the Swiss Alps. It takes 20 minutes to go through the tunnel.

To reduce driving time, motorists can use a tunnel—almost 11km (6¾ miles), the longest in northern Europe—that goes between Flåm and Gudvangen. From Gudvangen, follow E16 southwest to Bergen.

VISITOR INFORMATION **Tourist Information,** Bryggen 7 (© **55-32-14-80;** www.visitbergen.com), provides information, maps, and brochures about Bergen and the rest of the region. It's open from June to August daily from 8:30am to 10pm; May and September daily from 9am to 8pm; from October to April Monday through Saturday from 9am to 4pm.

SPECIAL EVENTS The annual **Bergen Festival,** generally held the last 2 weeks in May (the 2005 festival is scheduled for May 19–30), features performances by regional, national, and international orchestras, dance ensembles, and theater groups. The complete festival schedule is usually available by February of each year. For festival and ticket information, contact the **Bergen Festival Office** (© **55-21-06-30;** www.festspillene.no).

Value The Bergen Card

The **Bergen Card** entitles you to free bus transportation and (usually) free museum entrance throughout Bergen, plus discounts on car rentals, parking, and some cultural activities. Ask for it at the tourist office (see "Visitor Information," above). A 24-hour card costs 165NOK ($23) for adults, 70NOK ($9.95) for children 3 to 15. A 48-hour card is 245NOK ($35) for adults, 105NOK ($15) for children 3 to 15. Children under 3 generally travel or enter free.

GETTING AROUND **By Bus** The **Bystasjonen (Central Bus Station)**, Strømgaten 8 (© **55-55-90-70**), is the terminal for all buses serving the Bergen and the Hardanger area, as well as the airport bus. Gaia Traffic runs a network of yellow-sided **city buses** (© **55-55-44-00**) that serve the city center.

By Taxi Sightseeing by taxi costs about 390NOK ($55) for the first hour and then 300NOK ($43) per hour after that (© **55-99-70-10**).

WHERE TO STAY
Expensive

Clarion Admiral Hotel ✸ When it was built in 1906, this building was one of the largest warehouses in Bergen, with six sprawling floors peppered with massive trusses and beams. In 1987, it became a comfortable, tastefully appointed hotel, and in 1998, it was enlarged and renovated into the bustling establishment you'll see today. Rooms are a bit smaller than you might hope (with small bathrooms equipped with shower-tub combinations), but they are comfortable and have excellent beds. Many rooms lack water views, but the ones that open onto flower-bedecked balconies have the best harbor views in town.

Christian Sundts Gate 9, N-5004 Bergen. © **55-23-64-00**. Fax 55-23-64-64. www.admiral.no. 211 units. Mon–Thurs 1,800NOK–2,000NOK ($256–$284) double, 2,600NOK–4,200NOK ($369–$596) suite (same price every night). Fri–Sun 1,300NOK–1,500NOK ($185–$213) double. AE, DC, MC, V. Bus: 2, 4, or 11. **Amenities:** 2 restaurants; bar; limited room service; laundry service/dry cleaning; nonsmoking rooms; rooms for those with limited mobility. *In room:* TV, minibar, hair dryer.

First Hotel Marin ✸✸ In the heart of Bergen, this first-class hotel is one of Bergen's most modern and streamlined. The brown brick building is set on a steep hillside. The bedrooms are moderate to spacious in size, and each is handsomely furnished in functional, stylish Nordic modern, with immaculately kept tiled bathrooms equipped with shower-tub combinations. For Bergen, the hotel offers a large number of suites—34 deluxe ones in all—the best of which are a trio of penthouse units with views so panoramic they encompass all seven mountains surrounding Bergen. Many accommodations are reserved for nonsmokers, and the finest units are in front, overlooking the harbor.

Rosenkrantzgaten 8, N-5003 Bergen. © **53-05-15-00**. Fax 53-05-15-01. www.firsthotels.com. 131 units. 1,599NOK–2,499NOK ($227–$355) double; 2,499NOK–3,999NOK ($355–$568) suite. AE, DC, MC, V. Bus: 5, 6, 9, 30, or 90. **Amenities:** Restaurant; bar; fitness center; sauna; room service (7am–noon, 4:30–11pm); laundry service/dry cleaning; nonsmoking rooms; rooms for those with limited mobility. *In room:* TV, dataport, minibar, hair dryer (in some).

Moderate

Augustin Hotel ✸ *Finds* The Augustin has one of the best locations in Bergen—right in the harbor's shopping district—with front rooms that have terrific harbor views. Constructed in 1909 in the Jugend or Art Nouveau style, Augustin has been in the same family for four generations. In 1995 it more than doubled in size by adding a new wing, with modern new rooms designed by award-winning Bergen architect Aud Hunskår. Bathrooms in both sections have both showers and tubs. The hotel is decorated with lots of art, many pieces from well-known contemporary Norwegian artists. Special accommodations are available for nonsmokers, wheelchair users, and allergy sufferers.

Carl Sundts Gate 24, N-5004 Bergen. © 55-30-40-40. Fax 55-30-40-10. www.augustin.no. 109 units. Mon–Thurs 1,550NOK ($220) double, 1,890NOK ($268) suite. Fri–Sun 830NOK ($118) double, 1,290NOK ($183) suite. AE, DC, MC, V. Bus: 2. **Amenities:** Restaurant; bar; laundry service/dry cleaning; nonsmoking rooms; rooms for those with limited mobility. *In room:* TV, dataport, minibar, hair dryer.

Victoria Hotel (★ (Value)   Set behind a graceful, bay-fronted facade, this hotel—one of the oldest in town—today operates as one of only two members of the Best Western chain in Bergen. Smaller and more personalized than many equivalently priced hotels in Bergen, and noted for relatively reasonable rates, it's cozy, staffed with concerned employees, and loaded with worthwhile, sometimes rather valuable, art—a result of almost 50 years of collecting on the part of the well-traveled owners. Guest rooms are clean and bright, outfitted with contemporary birch-veneer furniture and lots of contemporary art. Bathrooms are tiled and modern, each with shower but without bathtub.

Kong Oscarsgt 29, N-5017 Bergen. © 800/528-1234 or 55-21-23-00. Fax 55-21-23-50. www.victoriahotel.no. 43 units. Mid-May to mid-Sept 1,090NOK ($155) double; mid-Sept to mid-May Mon–Thurs 940NOK ($133) double, Fri–Sun 830NOK ($118) double. Rates include breakfast. AE, DC, MC, V. Parking 130NOK ($18). Bus: 2 or 31. **Amenities:** Restaurant (under separate ownership); bar; babysitting; laundry service/dry cleaning; nonsmoking rooms. *In room:* TV, dataport, minibar, coffeemaker (in some), hair dryer.

Inexpensive

Hotel Park (★   This converted 1890 town house is in an attractive university area near Grieghall and Nygård Park. The rooms are traditionally furnished, often with antiques. Accommodations vary in size but all have good beds and adequate bathrooms equipped with shower-tub combinations. In the summer, a neighboring building (furnished in the same style) accommodates overflow guests. A delicious Norwegian breakfast is served in the dining room; later in the day, sandwiches, small hot dishes, and wine and beer are available there. In the summer, reserve well in advance. The Park is a 10-minute walk from the train and bus stations.

Harald Hårfagresgaten 35 and Allegaten 20, N-5007 Bergen. © 55-54-44-00. Fax 55-54-44-44. www. parkhotel.no. 33 units. 1,400NOK ($199) double. Rates include breakfast. AE, DC, MC, V. Parking 50NOK ($7.10). Bus: 80 or 90. **Amenities:** Lounge; breakfast room; nonsmoking rooms. *In room:* TV, hair dryer.

Steens Hotel (Value)   Owned and operated by the same family since 1950, this stylish 1890 town house offers great accommodations at most reasonable prices. The modern guest rooms are moderate in size and comfortable, and the bathrooms, though small, are beautifully maintained. The public rooms have plenty of atmosphere. The best rooms are in front and open onto a park. Within a short walk are the bus and railway stations and attractions in the center of town. All doubles have a private bathroom with a shower unit. Coffee and light meals are served. All rooms are nonsmoking.

22 Parkveien, N-5007 Bergen. © 55-31-40-50. Fax 55-32-61-22. 21 units, 16 with private shower. 790NOK ($112) double without bathroom; 980NOK ($139) double with shower. Extra bed 200NOK ($28). Rates include Norwegian breakfast. AE, MC, V. Bus: 1 or 5. **Amenities:** Lounge; breakfast room . *In room:* TV.

WHERE TO DINE
Expensive

Kafe Krystall ★★★ *Finds* CONTINENTAL   Thanks to Jugenstil accessories, the decor of this intimate restaurant evokes Vienna in the era of Sigmund Freud. Billie Holliday music might be playing softly in the cool gray-green parlor. Old-fashioned table settings and the quiet ministrations of a single server (Bergen-born owner Vibeke Bjørvik) create the feeling you're in a dignified private home. Menu listings change every 3 weeks. Our party recently sampled a menu that began delectably with spiced and pan-seared red snapper, accompanied by a shellfish guacamole and mussels sauce, followed by a divine, creamed champagne soup topped with curried, marinated scallops. The rest of the menu items displayed well-balanced flavors, such as the baked sole with fresh tomato and green herbs, served with a fennel and potato purée, and the filet of lamb with caponata. For dessert, our hearts were won over by the vanilla and whiskey *panna cotta* topped with chocolate sauce and a serving of lime-marinated raspberries.

16 Kong Oscargate. ✆ 55-32-10-84. www.krystall.no. Reservations recommended. 3-course fixed-price menu 450NOK ($64); 6-course fixed-price menu 650NOK ($92). AE, DC, MC, V. Mon–Sat 6–10pm. Bus: 20, 21, 22, 23, 50, 70, 71, 80, or 90.

To Kokker ★ FRENCH/NORWEGIAN   To Kokker ("Two Cooks") is a favorite with celebrities, including Britain's prince. Savvy local diners gravitate here for the chef's well-considered juxtaposition of flavors and textures. Menu items include such time-tested favorites as lobster soup; whitebait roe with chopped onions, sour cream, and fresh-baked bread; reindeer with lingonberry sauce; and filet of lamb with mustard sauce and pommes (potatoes) Provençal. The 1703 building is adjacent to the oldest piers and wharves in Bergen. The dining room, one floor above street level, has scarlet walls, old paintings, and a solid staff that works competently under pressure, albeit without a lot of flair.

Enhjørninggården. ✆ 55-32-28-16. Reservations required. Main courses 265NOK–295NOK ($38–$42); 3-course menu 495NOK ($70); 5-course menu 595NOK ($84); 7-course menu 695NOK ($99). AE, DC, MC, V. Mon–Sat 5–10pm. Bus: 1, 5, 9, 70, or 80.

Inexpensive

Bryggeloftet and Stuene ★ NORWEGIAN   The Bryggeloftet and Stuene is the best-established restaurant along the harbor. At street level, the Stuene has low-beamed ceilings, carved banquettes, and 19th-century murals of old Bergen, along with dozens of clipper-ship models. For a more formal meal, head upstairs to the Bryggeloftet, with its high ceilings and wood paneling. Dinner in either section might include fried *porbeagle* (a form of whitefish) served with shrimp, mussels, and white-wine sauce; roast reindeer with cream sauce; or pepper steak with a salad. Several different preparations of salmon and herring are featured, along with grilled filet of reindeer with a creamy wild game sauce. This is a quintessential Norwegian place—come here if you're seeking authentic flavors.

Bryggen 11. ✆ 55-31-06-30. www.bryggeloftet.no. Reservations recommended. Main courses 159NOK–275NOK ($23–$39); lunch smørbrød 89NOK–149NOK ($13–$21). AE, DC, MC, V. Mon–Sat 11am–11:30pm; Sun 1–11:30pm. Bus: 1, 5, 9, 22, or 80.

SEEING THE SIGHTS

In addition to the sights below, take a stroll around **Bryggen (the Quay)** ★★★. This row of Hanseatic timbered houses, rebuilt along the waterfront after the disastrous fire of 1702, is what remains of medieval Bergen. The northern half burned to the ground as recently as 1955. Bryggen is on UNESCO's World

Heritage List as one of the world's most significant cultural and historical re-creations of a medieval settlement. It's a center for arts and crafts, where painters, weavers, and craftspeople have their workshops.

Det Hanseatiske Museum ✪ In one of the best-preserved wooden build-ings at Bryggen, this museum illustrates Bergen's commercial life on the wharf centuries ago. German merchants, representatives of the Hanseatic League cen-tered in Lübeck, lived in these medieval houses built in long rows up from the harbor. The museum is furnished with authentic articles dating from 1704.

Finnegårdsgaten 1A, Bryggen. ✆ **55-31-41-89.** May–Sept admission 45NOK ($6.40) adults; Oct–Apr admis-sion 30NOK ($4.25) adults; free for children. June–Aug daily 9am–5pm; Sept–May daily 11am–2pm. Bus: 1, 5, or 9.

Mariakirke (St. Mary's Church) ✪ The oldest building in Bergen (its exact date is unknown, but perhaps from the mid–12th c.) is this Romanesque church, one of the most beautiful in Norway. Its altar is the oldest ornament in the church, and there's a baroque pulpit, donated by Hanseatic merchants, with carved figures depicting everything from Chastity to Naked Truth. Church-music concerts are given several nights a week from May to August.

Dreggen. ✆ **55-31-59-60.** Admission 10NOK ($1.40) adults, free for children; free to all Sept 10–May 17. May 18–Sept 9 Mon–Fri 11am–4pm; Sept 10–May 17 Tues–Fri noon–1:30pm. Bus: 5, 9, 20, 21, or 22.

Fløibanen A short walk from the fish market is the station where the funic-ular heads up to Fløien, the most famous of Bergen's seven hills, reached after an 8-minute ride. At 320m (1,050 ft.), the view of the city, the neighboring hills, and the harbor is worth every øre.

Vetrlidsalm 23A. ✆ **55-33-68-00.** Round-trip 60NOK ($8.50) adults, 25NOK ($3.55) children 4-16 years old. May 25–Aug Mon–Fri 7:30am–midnight, Sat 8am–11:30pm, Sun 9am–midnight; Sept–May 24 Mon–Thurs 8am–11pm, Fri–Sat 8am–11:30pm, Sun 9am–11pm. Bus: 6.

Gamle Bergen ✪ At Elsesro and Sandviken is a collection of houses from the 18th and 19th centuries set in a park. Old Town is complete with streets, an open square, and narrow alleyways. Some of the interiors are exceptional, including a merchant's living room in the typical style of the 1870s—padded sofas, heavy curtains, potted plants—a perfect setting for Ibsen's *A Doll's House.*

Elsesro and Sandviken. ✆ **55-39-43-00.** Admission 60NOK ($8.50) adults, 30NOK ($4.25) children and stu-dents. Houses mid-May to Aug only, guided tours daily on the hour 10am–5pm. Park and restaurant daily noon–6pm. Bus: 9, 20, 21, 22, or 50.

Troldhaugen (Troll's Hill) ✪ This Victorian house, in beautiful rural sur-roundings at Hop, near Bergen, was the summer villa of composer Edvard Grieg. The house contains Grieg's own furniture, paintings, and mementos. His Steinway grand piano is frequently used at concerts given in the house during the annual Bergen festival, as well as at Troldhaugen's own summer concerts. Grieg and his wife, Nina, are buried in a cliff grotto on the estate.

Troldhaugveien 65, N-5232. ✆ **55-92-29-92.** www.troldhaugen.com. Admission 50NOK ($7.10) adults, 20NOK ($2.85) students, free for children. Jan–Mar Mon–Fri 10am–2pm; Apr and Oct–Nov Mon–Fri 10am–2pm, Sat–Sun noon–4pm; May–Sept daily 9am–6pm. Bus: To Hop from the Bergen bus station (plat-forms 18–20), exit, turn right, walk about 180m (600 ft.), turn left at Hopsvegen, and follow signs. Hop is about 5km (3 miles) from Bergen.

ORGANIZED TOURS

For information about and tickets to tours, contact **Tourist Information,** Bryggen 7 (✆ **55-32-14-80**). The most popular and most highly recommended tour of Bergen is the 3-hour city bus tour. It departs daily at 10am and covers the major attractions, including Troldhaugen and "Old Bergen." It operates from May to September and costs 250NOK ($36) for adults, 160NOK ($23) for children.

THE SHOPPING SCENE

Bargain hunters head to the **Torget (Marketplace).** Many local handicrafts from the western fjord district, including rugs and handmade tablecloths, are displayed. This is one of the few places in Norway where bargaining is welcomed. The market keeps no set hours, but is best visited between 8am and noon. Take bus no. 1, 5, or 9. You'll find the widest selection of national handcrafts in and around **Bryggen Brukskunst,** the restored Old Town near the wharf, where many craftspeople have taken over old houses and ply ancient Norwegian trades. Crafts boutiques often display Bergen souvenirs, many based on designs 300 to 1,500 years old. For example, we purchased a reproduction of a Romanesque-style cruciform pilgrim's badge. Other attractive items are likely to include sheepskin-lined booties and exquisitely styled hand-woven wool dresses. The leading outlet for glassware and ceramics, **Prydkunst-Hjertholm,** Olav Kyrres Gate 7 (© **55-31-70-27**), purchases much of its merchandise directly from the studios of Norwegian and other Scandinavian artisans who turn out quality goods not only in glass and ceramics, but also in pewter, brass, wood, and textiles.

BERGEN AFTER DARK

The modern **Grieghallen (Grieg Hall),** Lars Hillesgate 3A (© **55-21-61-50**), is Bergen's monumental showcase for music, drama, and a host of other cultural events. The **Bergen Symphony Orchestra,** founded in 1765, performs here from August to May on Thursday at 7:30pm and Saturday at 12:30pm.

Norway's oldest theater performs from September to June at **Den National Scene,** Engen 1 (© **55-54-97-10**). Its repertoire consists of classical Norwegian and international drama and contemporary plays, as well as visiting productions of opera and ballet in conjunction with the annual Bergen Festival. Performances are held from Monday to Saturday.

In summer, the **Bergen Folklore dancing troupe** (© **55-55-20-00**) arranges a 1-hour folklore program at the Bryggens Museum on Tuesday and Thursday at 9pm. Tickets, which cost 100NOK ($14), are on sale at the tourist information center or at the door.

The most-frequented pub in the city center, **Kontoret Pub,** Ole Bulls Plass 8–10 (© **55-36-31-33**), lies adjacent to the Hotel Norge next to the Dickens restaurant/pub. Drinkers can wander freely between the two places, since they're connected. In the Kontoret you can order the same food served at Dickens, though most people seem to come here to drink. The pub is open Sunday through Thursday from 4pm to 1am, Friday 4pm to 2am, and Saturday from noon to 2am.

EXPLORING THE FJORDS

Norway's fjords can be explored from both Oslo and Bergen by ship and car or by a scenic train ride. Here are the details.

BY CAR FROM BERGEN

Bergen is the best departure point for trips to the fjords: To the south lies the famous **Hardangerfjord** ★★ and to the north the **Sognefjord** ★★★, cutting

180km (111 miles) inland. We've outlined a driving tour of the fjords, starting in Bergen and heading east on Route 7 to Ulvik, a distance of 150km (93 miles).

ULVIK Ulvik is that rarity: an unspoiled resort. It lies like a fist at the end of an arm of the Hardangerfjord that's surrounded in summer by misty peaks and fruit farms. The village's 1858 church is attractively decorated in the style of the region. It's open June through August, daily from 9am to 5pm, and presents concerts.

From Ulvik, you can explore the **Eidfjord** district, which is the northern tip of the Hardangerfjord, home to some 1,000 people and a paradise for hikers. Anglers are attracted to the area because of its mountain trout.

The district contains nearly one-quarter of **Hardangervidda National Park** ✿, which is on Europe's largest high-mountain plateau. It's home to 20,000 wild reindeer. Well-marked hiking trails connect a series of 15 tourist huts.

Several canyons, including the renowned **Måbø Valley,** lead down from the plateau to the fjords. Here, you'll see the famous 170m (550-ft.) **Voringfoss** ✿ waterfall. The **Valurefoss** in **Hjømo Valley** has a free fall of almost 245m (800 ft.).

Part of the 1,000-year-old road across Norway, traversing the Måbø Valley, has been restored for hardy hikers.

En Route to Voss From Ulvik, take Highway 20 to Route 13. Follow Route 13 to Voss, 40km (25 miles) west of Ulvik and 100km (63 miles) east of Bergen.

VOSS Between the Sogne and Hardanger fjords, Voss is a famous year-round resort, also known for its folklore and as the birthplace of football hero Knute Rockne. Maybe the trolls don't strike fear into the hearts of farm children anymore, but they're still called out of hiding to give visitors a little fun.

Voss is a natural base for exploring the two largest fjords in Norway, the Sognefjord to the north and the Hardangerfjord to the south. In and around Voss are glaciers, mountains, fjords, waterfalls, orchards, rivers, and lakes.

A ride on the **Hangursbanen cable car** (© 55-20-20-20) offers panoramic views of Voss and the environs. The hardy can take the cable car up, then spend the rest of the afternoon strolling down the mountain. A round-trip ride costs 70NOK ($9.95) adults, 35NOK ($4.95) children 8 to 16, and free for children 7 and under. The cable-car entrance is on a hillside that's a 1-hour walk north of the town center. It's open in summer and winter.

Built in 1277, the **Vangskyrkje,** Vangsgata 3 (© 56-52-38-80), with a timbered tower, contains a striking Renaissance pulpit, a stone altar and triptych, fine woodcarvings, and a painted ceiling. It's a 5-minute walk east of the railroad station. We recommend that you call in advance to reserve an English-speaking guide. Admission is 15NOK ($2.15); free for children 17 and under. The church is open only June through August, daily from 10am to 4pm.

Voss Folkemuseum, Mølster (© 56-51-15-11), is a collection of authentically furnished houses that shows what early farm life was like. Lying just north of Voss on a hillside overlooking the town, the museum consists of more than a dozen farmhouses and other buildings, ranging in age from the 1500s to around 1870. Admission is 35NOK ($4.65) adults, free for children. It's open May to September daily from 10am to 5pm; and from October to April Monday through Friday from 10am to 3pm.

A little west of Voss in Finne, **Finnesloftet** (© 56-51-16-75) is one of Norway's oldest timbered houses, dating from the mid–13th century. It's a 15-minute walk west of the railway station. Admission is 20NOK ($2.85) adults and

10NOK ($1.40) children. It's open Tuesday through Sunday from 10am to 4pm from June 15 to August 15.

BALESTRAND   Long known for its arts and crafts, Balestrand lies on the northern rim of the Sognefjord, at the junction of the Vetlefjord, the Esefjord, and the Fjaerlandsfjord.

Kaiser Wilhelm II, a frequent visitor to Balestrand, presented the district with two statues of old Norse heroes, King Bele and Fridtjof the Bold, which stand in the town center.

You can explore by setting out in nearly any direction, on scenic country lanes with little traffic, or a wide choice of marked trails and upland farm tracks. A touring map may be purchased at the **tourist office** in the town center (© 57-69-12-55 in summer; 57-69-16-17 in winter). There's good sea fishing, as well as lake and river trout fishing. Fishing tackle, rowboats, and bicycles can all be rented in the area.

En Route to Flåm   From Balestrand, follow Route 55 east along the Sognefjord, crossing the fjord via ferry at Dragsvik and by bridge at Sogndal. At Sogndal, drive east to Kaupanger, where you'll cross the Ardalsfjord by ferry, south to Revsnes. In Revsnes, pick up Route 11 heading southeast. Drive east until you connect with a secondary road heading southwest through Kvigno and Aurland. When you arrive in Aurland, take Route 601 southwest to the town of Flåm, 95km (60 miles) southeast of Balestrand and 165km (103 miles) east of Bergen.

FLÅM ✦   Flåm (pronounced *Flawm*) lies on the Aurlandsfjord, a tip of the more famous Sognefjord. In the village you can visit the old church dating from 1667, with painted walls done in typical Norwegian country style.

Flåm is an excellent starting point for excursions by car or boat to other well-known centers on the Sognefjord, Europe's longest and deepest fjord. Worth exploring are two of the wildest and most beautiful fingers of the Sognefjord: Nærøyfjord and Aurlandfjord. Ask at the **tourist office,** near the rail station (© 57-63-21-06), about a cruise from Flåm, when you can experience the dramatic scenery of both of these fjords. From Flåm by boat, you can disembark either in Gudvangen or Aurland and continue the tour by coach. Alternatively, you can return to Flåm by train.

There are also a number of easy walks in the Flåm district. The tourist office has a map detailing these walks.

BY SHIP/TOUR FROM BERGEN

There are several ways to visit Sognefjord, Norway's longest fjord, from Bergen. One way is to cross the fjord on an express steamer that travels from Bergen to **Gudvangen.** From Gudvangen, passengers go to Myrdal, and from Myrdal a train runs back to Bergen. You can go by boat, bus, and then train for 1,026NOK ($146) round-trip. Details about this and other tours are available from **Bergen Visitor Information** in Bergen, Bryggen 7 (© 55-32-14-80).

If you have more than a day to see the fjords in the environs of Bergen, you can take the grandest fjord cruise in the world, a **coastal steamer** going to the North Cape and beyond. The coastal steamers are elegantly appointed ships that cruise the western coast of Norway from Bergen to Kirkenes, carrying passengers and cargo to 34 ports along the Norwegian coast. Eleven ships in all make the journey year-round. The ships sail through Norway's more obscure fjords, providing panoramic scenery and numerous opportunities for adventure. Along the way, sightseeing excursions to the surrounding mountains and glaciers are offered, as well as sails on smaller vessels through some of the more obscure fjords.

The chief operator of these coastal cruises is the **Norwegian Coastal Voyage/ Bergen Line,** 405 Park Ave., New York, NY 10022 (© **800/323-7436** or 212/ 319-1300 in the U.S.; www.coastalvoyage.com). Tours may be booked heading north from Bergen, or south from Kirkenes. The 12-day northbound journey costs 774NOK to 3,059NOK ($110–$434) per person double occupancy, including meals, taxes, and port charges.

14

Portugal

by Darwin Porter & Danforth Prince

Lisbon is growing and evolving, and the city is considerably more sophisticated than it once was, no doubt due in part to Portugal's joining the European Union (EU). The smallest capital of Europe is no longer a backwater at the far corner of Iberia. Some 1.6 million people now live in Lisbon. Lisbon presides over a country with one of the fastest-growing economies in Europe, much of it fueled by investments that have poured in since Portugal joined the EU.

About 260km (160 miles) south of Lisbon, the maritime region of the Algarve, often called the "garden of Portugal," is the southwesternmost part of Europe. Its coastline stretches 160km (100 miles) and is dotted with hundreds of beaches—the finest in the country.

1 Lisbon & Environs

Europe's smallest capital is no longer a backwater at the far edge of Iberia. Lisbon has blossomed into a cosmopolitan city. Sections of Avenida da Liberdade, the main street, evoke Paris in miniature. Some of the formerly clogged streets of the downtown Baixa district have been closed to traffic, and cobblestone pedestrian malls have been created. Sidewalk portrait painters offer to sketch your likeness, and vendors peddle jewelry and handcrafts ranging from embroidery to leatherwork. In the cooler months, smoke billows from charcoal braziers roasting chestnuts.

The world dropped in on this city of seven hills as it celebrated EXPO '98, marking the 500th anniversary of Vasco da Gama's journey to India. Although Portugal has since stubbed its toe on its way to greater prosperity, many of its attractions and facilities were left behind after the exhibition, including the Oceanarium, the largest aquarium in Europe, indoor stadiums, convention centers, and a marina that can moor between 700 and 900 leisure craft.

Some 1.6 million people now call Lisbon home, and many Lisboetas, having drifted in from the distant corners of the former empire, don't even speak Portuguese. Consider an off-season visit, when the city is at its most glorious, before or after the hot and humid days of July and August. Lisbon isn't infested with visitors during spring and fall, and prices for lodgings are significantly lower than in summer.

ESSENTIALS

GETTING THERE   By Plane   Foreign and domestic flights land at Lisbon's Aeroporto de Lisboa (© **21/841-35-00**), about 6.5km (4 miles) from the heart of the city. An AERO-BUS runs between the airport and the Cais do Sodré train station every 20 minutes from 7am to 9pm. The fare is 2.45€ ($2.80). It makes

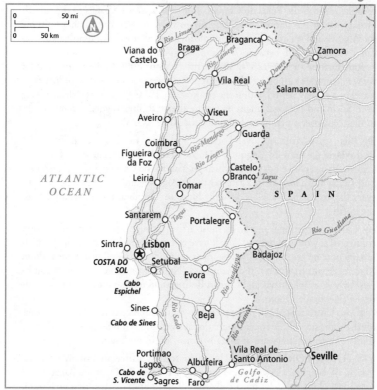

10 intermediate stops, including Praça dos Restauradores and Praça do Comércio. There's no charge for luggage. Taxi passengers line up in a usually well-organized queue at the sidewalk in front of the airport, or you can call **Radiotaxi** at © **21/793-27-56.** The average taxi fare from the airport to central Lisbon is 10€ ($12). Each piece of luggage is 1.50€ ($1.70) extra.

For ticket sales, flight reservations, and information about the city and the country, you can get in touch with the Lisboa personnel of **TAP Air Portugal,** Loja Gare do Oriente, Edificio Estação do Oriente, Avenida de Berlim, 1998 Lisboa (© **707/205-700,** or 21/841-50-00 for reservations; www.tap-airportugal.pt).

By Train Most international rail passengers from Madrid and Paris arrive at the **Estação da Santa Apolónia,** Avenida Infante Dom Henrique, the major terminal. It's by the Tagus near the Alfama district. Two daily trains make the 10-hour run from Madrid to Lisbon. Rail lines from northern and eastern Portugal also arrive at this station. EXPO '98 brought a new, modern terminal to Lisbon. Gare de Oriente at Expo Urbe—connected to the Metro system—opened in 1998 and is the hub for some long-distance and suburban trains, including service to such destinations as Porto, Sintra, the Beiras, Minho, and the Douro. At the **Estação do Rossio,** between Praça dos Restauradores and Praça de Dom Pedro IV, you can get trains to Sintra. The **Estação do Cais do Sodré,** just beyond the south end of Rua Alecrim, east of Praça do Comércio, handles trains to Cascais and Estoril on the Costa do Sol. Finally, you can catch a ferry at Sul e Sueste, next to the Praça do Comércio. It runs across the Tagus to the suburb of Barreiro; at the station there, Estação do Barreiro, you can catch a train for the Algarve and Alentejo. For all rail information, at any of the terminals above, call Ⓒ **808/208-208** between 7am and 11pm daily.

Rail Europe (Ⓒ **877/257-2887** in the U.S., or 800/361-RAIL in Canada; www.raileurope.com) offers a **Portuguese Railpass,** good for 4 days of first-class travel in a 15-day period within the country, for 105€ ($117). Travelers visiting both Spain and Portugal might prefer the **Iberic Railpass,** good for any 3 days in first class over a period of 2 months, for 205€ ($235).

By Bus Buses from all over Portugal, including the Algarve, arrive at the **Rodoviária da Arco do Cego** (Ⓒ **21/358-14-81**). If your hotel is in Estoril or Cascais, you can take bus no. 1, which goes on to the Cais do Sodré. At least six buses a day leave for Lagos, a gateway to the Algarve, and nine buses head north every day to Porto. There are 14 daily buses to Coimbra, the university city to the north

By Car International motorists must arrive through Spain, the only nation connected to Portugal by road. You'll have to cross Spanish border points, which usually pose no great difficulty. The roads are moderately well maintained. From Madrid, if you head west, the main road (N620) from Tordesillas goes southwest by way of Salamanca and Ciudad Rodrigo and reaches the Portuguese frontier at Fuentes de Onoro.

If you have a rented car, make sure that your insurance covers Portugal. Drive on the right side of the road; international signs and symbols are used. Most of the 15 border crossings are open daily from 7am to midnight.

VISITOR INFORMATION The main **tourist office** in Lisbon is at the Palácio da Foz, Praça dos Restauradores (Ⓒ **21/346-63-07**), at the Baixa end of Avenida da Liberdade. It's open daily from 9am to 8pm (Metro: Restauradores). It sells the **Lisbon Card,** which provides free city transportation and entrance fees to museums and other attractions, plus discounts on admission to events. For adults, a 1-day pass costs 12€ ($14), a 2-day pass costs 21€ ($24), and a 3-day pass costs 27€ ($31). Children 5 to 11 pay 5.70€ ($6.50) for a 1-day pass, 8.55€ ($9.80) for a 2-day pass, and 11€ ($13) for a 3-day pass.

Websites In addition to the tourist office's website, **www.portugalvirtual.pt** offers an extensive collection of links for exploring Portugal in depth. Other possibilities are **www.portugal.sunscale.com**, **www.portugal-info.net**, and **www.portugal-insite.pt**.

CITY LAYOUT The best orientation to Lisbon is obtained by locating yourself in its waterside gateway, **Praça do Comércio (aka Black Horse Sq.),** bordering the River Tejo. A majestic square that regained its dignity when parking was banned, it's the site of the Stock Exchange and various government ministries. One block west stands the late-19th-century City Hall, fronting Praça do Município.

Castelo São Jorge tops the hill up to the right, and the steep slopes below are crowded with the medieval quarter called the **Alfama.** As you walk north from Praça do Comércio through the grid of the **Baixa** shopping district, the high ground to the left contains the **Chiado** district and the **Bairro Alto,** a neighborhood almost as old as the Alfama.

Continuing north, you'll enter the bustling **Praça Dom Pedro IV,** known to all as the "Rossio." A long reclamation project was recently completed, and the

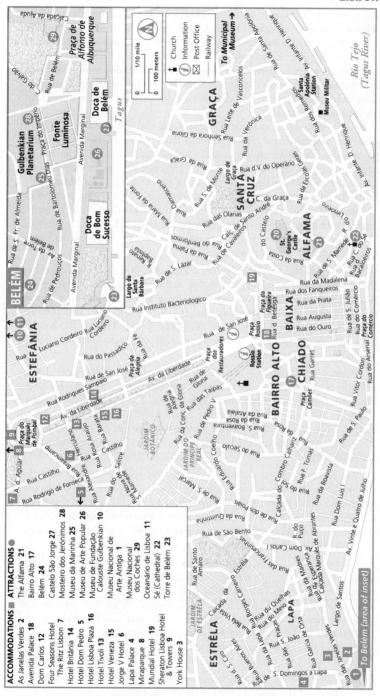

Lisbon

ACCOMMODATIONS ■

As Janelas Verdes **2**
Avenida Palace **18**
Dom Carlos **12**
Four Seasons Hotel
  The Ritz Lisbon **7**
Hotel Britânia **14**
Hotel Dom Pedro **5**
Hotel Lisboa Plaza **16**
Hotel Tivoli **13**
Hotel Veneza **15**
Jorge V Hotel **6**
Lapa Palace **4**
Miraparque **8**
Mundial Hotel **19**
Sheraton Lisboa Hotel
  & Towers **9**
York House **3**

ATTRACTIONS ●

The Alfama **21**
Bairro Alto **17**
Belém **24**
Castelo São Jorge **27**
Mosteiro dos Jerónimos **28**
Museu da Marinha **25**
Museu de Arte Popular **26**
Museu de Fundação
  Calouste Gulbenkian **10**
Museu Nacional de
  Arte Antiga **1**
Museu Nacional
  dos Coches **29**
Oceanário de Lisboa **11**
Sé (Cathedral) **22**
Torre de Belém **23**

square looks better than it has in living memory. The visual undulation of the sidewalks, set with irregular black and white cubes, has led to the appellation "the dizzy praça." Facing the Rossio is the Teatro Nacional Dona Maria II. A block to its left is the **Estação do Rossio,** whose exuberant Manueline architecture is worth seeing. Separating the Rossio from Avenida da Liberdade is **Praça dos Restauradores,** named in honor of the Restoration, when the Portuguese chose their own king and freed themselves from 60 years of Spanish rule. An obelisk marks the event.

Lisbon's main street, **Avenida da Liberdade,** dating from 1880 and once called the "antechamber of Lisbon," is a mile-long concourse with shade trees and promenades. Flanking it are branches of upmarket international clothing chains, headquarters for many major airlines, travel agents, coffeehouses with sidewalk tables, and several large hotels. At the top of the avenue is **Praça Marquês de Pombal,** with a statue erected in honor of Pombal, the 18th-century prime minister credited with Lisbon's reconstruction in the aftermath of the 1755 earthquake. Proceeding north, you'll enter **Parque Eduardo VII,** named in honor of Queen Victoria's son, who paid a state visit to Lisbon. In the park is the Estufa Fria, a greenhouse that's well worth a visit.

GETTING AROUND   CARRIS (② 21/361-30-30; www.carris.pt) operates the network of funiculars, trains, subways, and buses in Lisbon. The company sells a *bilhete de assinatura turístico* (tourist ticket) that's good for 4 days of unlimited travel on its network. It costs 9.95€ ($11). A 1-day pass goes for 2.75€ ($3.15); a 7-day pass costs 14€ ($16). Passes are sold in CARRIS booths, open from 9am to 5pm daily, in most Metro stations and network train stations. You must show a passport to buy a pass.

By Metro   Metro (subway) stations are designated by large "M" signs. Trains run daily from 6:30am to 1am. A single ticket costs .65€ (.75¢) per ride. A 10-trip ticket, called a *cademeta,* costs 5.10€ ($5.90). The 1-day unlimited pass is 1.40€ ($1.60), and the 7-day unlimited pass is 4.80€ ($5.60). For more information, call ② 21/355-8457 or visit **www.metrolisboa.pt**. Single-ride, round-trip, and 10-day tickets can also be purchased at automatic vending machines in Metro stations.

By Bus & Tram   These are among the cheapest public buses and trams in Europe. Electric trams *(electricos)* make the steep run up to the Bairro Alto and Alfama and out to Belém. You pay a flat fare of 1€ ($1.15) on a bus if you buy the ticket from the driver. The transportation system within the city limits is divided into zones ranging from 1 to 5, and your fare depends on how many zones you traverse. Buses and electricos run daily from 6am to 1am.

By Electric Train   Lisbon is connected to all the towns and villages along the Portuguese Riviera by a smooth-running modern electric train system. You can board at the waterfront **Cais do Sordre** station in Lisbon and head up the coast all the way to Cascais. Only one class of seating is offered, and the rides are cheap and generally comfortable. Sintra can't be reached by the electric train. You must go to the **Estação do Rossio,** opening onto Praça Dom Pedro IV, where frequent connections can be made. The one-way fare from Lisbon to Cascais, Estoril, or Sintra is 1.25€ to 2.50€ ($1.45–$2.90) per person.

By Taxi   Newer, beige Mercedes taxis have all but replaced the older green-and-black versions. If the green roof lights are on, the taxi is occupied. The initial charge at flag drop is 1.80€ ($2.10). Fares in the city average 4.50€ ($5.20), with an extra 20% supplement from 10pm to 6am. The driver is allowed by law to tack on another 50% if your luggage weighs more than 30 kilograms (66 lb.). Portuguese tip about 10%. Verify that the meter has indeed been activated the moment you step into a cab. To **radio a taxi,** call ℂ **21/815-5061** or 21/793-2756.

By Car   Car-rental kiosks at the airport and in the city center include **Avis,** Avenida Praia da Vitoria 12C (ℂ **21/351-4560**); **Hertz,** Qto. Frangelha Baixio (ℂ **21/849-2722**); and **Budget,** rue Castillo Cas 167R (ℂ **21/994-0443**). That said, be advised that driving in congested Lisbon is extremely difficult and potentially dangerous; the city has an alarmingly high accident rate, and parking is all but impossible. It's a good idea to rent a car only for excursions into the countryside.

FAST FACTS: Lisbon

American Express   Amex is represented by Top Tours, Avenida Duque de Loule 108 (ℂ **21/315-5872;** Metro: Restauradores). It's open Monday through Friday from 9:30am to 1pm and 2:30 to 6:30pm.

Business Hours   Typically, **shops** are open Monday through Friday from 9am to 1pm and 3 to 7pm (some stay open through lunch) and Saturday from 9am to 1pm; some are also open Saturday afternoon. **Banks** are open Monday through Friday from 8:30am to 3pm; some offer a foreign-exchange service Monday through Saturday from 6 to 11pm.

   ATMs (called *caíxas automáticos*) are widely available, including machines in the arrivals lobby of the airport terminal—look for the sign MULTIBANCO. You can get cash with major credit cards or with Cirrus or PLUS network debit cards.

Dentists/Doctors   Contact **Clinica Medical Espanha,** Rua Dom Luis de Noroha 32 (ℂ **21/796-7457;** Metro: Plaça Espanha), where some dentists speak English. Virtually every hotel maintains a list of doctors and dentists who can be called upon in emergencies.

Drugstores   A central and well-stocked drugstore is **Farmácia Vall,** Avenida Visconde Valmor 60A (ℂ **21/797-3043;** Metro: Saldanha). Pharmacies that are closed post a notice indicating the nearest one that's open.

Embassies/Consulates   If you lose your passport or have some other pressing problem, you'll need to get in touch with the embassy of the **United States,** Avenida das Forcas Armadas (Sete Rios), 1600 Lisboa (ℂ **21/727-3300;** Metro: Entre Campos). Hours are Monday through Friday from 8am to 12:30pm and 1:30 to 5pm. If you've lost a passport, the embassy can take photos for you and help you obtain the proof of citizenship needed to get a replacement. The embassy of **Canada** is at Avenida da Liberdade 144, 1269-121 Lisboa (ℂ **21/316-4600;** Metro: Avenida); hours are Monday through Friday from 9:30am to 12:30pm and 1:30 to 5pm (July–Aug, the embassy closes at 1pm on Fri). The embassy of the **United Kingdom,** Rua São Bernardo 33, 1249-082 Lisboa (ℂ **21/392-4000;** Metro: Avenida), is open Monday through Friday from 9:30am to 12:30pm and 3 to 4:30pm. The British embassy also services citizens of **Australia** and **New Zealand.**

The embassy of the **Republic of Ireland,** Rua de Imprensa à Estrêla 1, 1249-082 Lisboa (© **21/392-9440;** Metro: Rossio), is open Monday through Friday from 9:30am to noon and 2:30 to 4:30pm.

Emergencies For the **police** or an **ambulance** in Lisbon, call © **112.** In case of **fire,** call © **21/342-2222.**

Hospitals In case of a medical emergency, inquire at your hotel or call your embassy and ask the staff there to recommend an English-speaking physician. You can also try the **British Hospital,** Rua Saraiva de Carvalho 49 (© **21/395-5067;** bus: 7, 40, 49, or 60), where the telephone operator, staff, and doctors all speak English.

Post Office The general post office is on Praça dos Restauradores 58 (© **21/394-31-00;** Metro: Restauradoes), open Monday through Friday from 8am to 10pm, and Saturday, Sunday, and holidays from 9am to 6pm.

Safety Portugal remains one of the safest countries in western Europe, but crime rose dramatically in the 1990s, sparked by the flood of homeless and penniless immigrants from the faraway countries of the former Portuguese empire. Lisbon is the most dangerous city, followed by the tourist-infested Algarve, where many hustlers prey on travelers. Pickpocketing remains the major crime against tourists; violent attacks are relatively rare. Take special care on crowded buses or trains, and leave your valuables at the hotel.

Taxes Portugal imposes a value-added tax (VAT) on most purchases made within its borders ranging from 8% to 30%. Known in Portugal as the **IVA,** the amount is almost always written into the bottom line of the bill for any purchase a foreign visitor makes. To get an IVA refund on purchases that qualify, present your passport to the salesperson and ask for the special stamped form. Present the form with your purchases at the booth marked for IVA tax refunds at the airport. You'll get your money refunded right at the booth.

Hotel and restaurant bills are taxed at 17.5%. Car rentals are subject to an additional 17.5% tax. Such deluxe goods as jewelry, furs, and expensive imported liquors include a 30% built-in tax.

Telephone The **country code** for Portugal is **351.** The **city code** for Lisbon is now **21;** use this code when calling from anywhere outside or inside Portugal—even within Lisbon itself.

You can make a **local call** in Lisbon in one of the many telephone booths. For most **long-distance calls,** particularly transatlantic calls, go to the central post office (see above). Give an assistant there the number you wish, and he or she will make the call, billing you at the end. Some phones are equipped to use calling cards, including American Express and Visa. You can also purchase phone cards at the post office; they can be used at any public phone in Portugal. Phone debit cards are used only in public phones in public places. These cards bear one of two different names: TLP or CrediFone. Both are sold at the cashier's desk of most hotels as well as at post offices.

To make an international call using your calling card, thereby bypassing many of the added-on charges imposed by your hotel, dial the appropriate access number to reach a North American operator or an English-language voice prompt. For **AT&T**, call © **05-017-1288**; for **MCI**, call © **05-017-1234**; for **Sprint**, call © **05-017-1877**.

Time For the local time in Lisbon, phone © **15**.

Tipping Most service personnel expect a good tip. Hotels add a service charge (known as *serviço*), which is divided among the entire staff, but individual tipping is also expected. Tip .50€ (.60¢) to the bellhop; .50€ to 1€ (.60¢–$1.15) to the porter hailing you a cab; and 1.50€ ($1.70) to the chambermaid. Tip cab drivers 15% to 20% of the total fare. Restaurants and nightclubs include a service charge and government taxes of 17.5%, which are distributed among the entire staff—not to mention the waiter's mistress and the owner's grandfather—so extra tipping is customary, about 5% in a moderately priced restaurant and 10% in a deluxe establishment.

Transit Information For airport information, call © **21/841-35-00**. For train information, dial © **808/208-208**. **TAP Air Portugal** is at Avenida Do Berlin 1998 (© **21/841-50-00**).

Weather To find out about the weather, call © **12150** (available only in Portuguese). If you don't speak Portuguese, ask someone at your hotel desk to translate one of the weather reports that appear daily in the leading newspapers.

WHERE TO STAY
IN THE CENTER
Very Expensive

Four Seasons Hotel The Ritz Lisbon ✦✦✦   The 10-floor Ritz, built by the dictator Salazar in the late 1950s, is now operated by Four Seasons. Its suites boast the finest decoration you'll see in any major Portuguese hotel: slender mahogany canopied beds with fringed swags, marquetry desks, satinwood dressing tables, and plush carpeting. Some of the soundproofed, spacious, modern rooms have terraces opening onto Edward VII Park; each boasts a marble bathroom with a double basin and a shower-tub combination. The least desirable rooms are the even-numbered ones facing the street. The odd-numbered accommodations, opening onto views of the park, are the best. Some studios with double beds are rented as singles, attracting business travelers. The fifth floor is reserved for nonsmokers.

Rua Rodrigo de Fonseca 88, 1099-039 Lisboa. © **800/332-3442** in the U.S., or 21/383-20-20. Fax 21/383-17-83. www.fourseasons.com. 284 units. 380€–415€ ($437–$477) double; from 710€ ($817) suite. AE, DC, MC, V. Free parking. Metro: Rotunda. Bus: 1, 2, 9, or 32. **Amenities:** Restaurant; bar; pool; health spa; sauna; 24-hr. room service; massage; babysitting; laundry service; dry cleaning. *In room:* A/C, TV, minibar, hair dryer, safe.

Hotel Dom Pedro ✦✦   Rated five stars by the Portuguese government and associated with some of the most glamorous hotels of the Algarve and Madeira, this bastion of luxury is in the central Amoreiras district, across from one of the city's biggest shopping centers. A hypermodern sheathing of reflective glass covers its 21 stories. The interior is as conservative and rich-looking as the exterior is futuristic. The good-size guest rooms are richly furnished, usually with heraldic symbols or medallions woven subtly through the fabrics and wallpapers.

Rooms also contain immaculately kept bathrooms with shower-tub combinations. There are 48 nonsmoking rooms for guests and also several rooms for those with limited mobility.

Av. Engenheiro Duarte Pacheco 24, 1070-109 Lisboa. (✆ 21/389-66-00. Fax 21/389-66-01. www.dompedro. com. 263 units. 300€–332€ ($345–$382) double; from 660€ ($759) suite. AE, DC, MC, V. Parking 15€ ($17). Metro: Marquês de Pombal. **Amenities:** 2 restaurants; 2 bars; car rental; business center; 24-hr. room service; babysitting; laundry; dry cleaning; rooms for those with limited mobility. *In room:* A/C, TV, dataport, minibar, hair dryer, safe.

Sheraton Lisboa Hotel & Towers 🌟🌟🌟   Built in 1972, this deluxe hotel is sheltered in a 25-floor skyscraper lying at a traffic-clogged intersection a bit removed from the center of the action, a few blocks north of Praça do Marquês de Pombal. Most of the guests are business travelers. The impressive pink-marble lobby features chandeliers and fancy carpeting. The guest rooms don't match the grandeur of the public spaces, but they're generally spacious. The understated decor includes thick wool carpeting, print fabrics, traditional (if a bit chunky) wood furniture, and excellent beds. The marble bathrooms are a highlight, with shower-tub combinations. Six rooms are available for those with limited mobility. The most desirable rooms are in the tower, opening onto views of the Vasco da Gama bridge, the Tagus, or the city. There's also a private lounge and bar, and you can enjoy drinks on the 26th floor, with a panoramic view of Lisbon and dancing to live music nightly.

Rua Latino Coelho 1, 1069-025 Lisboa. (✆ 800/325-3535 in the U.S., or 21/357-57-57. Fax 21/354-71-64. www.Sheraton.com/lisboa. 381 units. 320€ ($368) double; from 635€ ($730) suite. AE, DC, MC, V. Parking 12€ ($14). Bus: 1, 36, 44, or 45. **Amenities:** 2 restaurants; 2 bars; pool; health club; sauna; car rental; 24-hr. room service; massage; babysitting; laundry service; dry cleaning. *In room:* A/C, TV, dataport, minibar, hair dryer, safe.

Expensive

Avenida Palace 🌟   Built in 1892, Avenida Palace is the grandest old-fashioned hotel in Lisbon, an antiques-filled link to the past. Its extremely convenient location right at the Rossio is terribly noisy, but once inside, it is another world entirely. It underwent a massive overhaul in the late 1990s. Still the grand dame of Lisbon hotels, it retains its 19th-century aura and elegance, with a marble staircase, beautiful salons, and silk brocades. The Belle Epoque–style Palace offers all the modern comforts, especially in its restored guest rooms. They're soundproofed and elegantly furnished, often in 17th- or 18th-century style. The marble bathrooms come equipped with shower-tub combinations.

Rua 1er Dezembro 123, 1200-359 Lisboa. (✆ 21/321-81-00. Fax 21/342-28-84. hotel.av.palace@mail. telepac.pt. 82 units. 165€–200€ ($190–$230) double; 240€ ($276) junior suite; 350€–375€ ($403–$431) suite. Rates include breakfast. AE, DC, MC, V. Free parking. Metro: Restauradores. Tram: 35. **Amenities:** Breakfast room; bar; lounge; room service (7am–midnight); babysitting; laundry service; dry cleaning. *In room:* A/C, TV, dataport, minibar, hair dryer, safe.

Hotel Lisboa Plaza 🌟🌟   Hotel Lisboa Plaza, in the heart of the city, is a charmer. A family owned and operated government-rated four-star hotel, it has many appealing Art Nouveau touches, including the facade. The hotel was built in 1953 and has been frequently overhauled and modernized since. A well-known Portuguese designer, Graca Viterbo, decorated it in contemporary classic style. The midsize guest rooms—with well-stocked marble bathrooms with shower-tub combinations—are well styled and comfortable. There are 49 rooms for nonsmoking guests. Seek a unit in the rear, looking out over the botanical gardens. Windows are double-glazed.

Travessa do Salitre 7, Av. da Liberdade, 1269-066 Lisboa. (C) 21/321-82-18. Fax 21/347-16-30. www.heritage.pt. 112 units. 148€–225€ ($170–$259) double; 250€–370€ ($288–$426) suite. Children under 13 stay free in parent's room. AE, DC, MC, V. Parking 9€ ($10) nearby. Metro: Avenida. Bus: 1, 2, 36, or 44. **Amenities:** Restaurant; bar; car rental; 24-hr. room service; babysitting; laundry service; dry cleaning. *In room:* A/C, TV, dataport, minibar, hair dryer, safe.

Hotel Tivoli ★★ In spite of increased competition among upmarket hotels, this enduring favorite continues to hold its own, luring guests with such enticing features as the only hotel pool in central Lisbon. Right on the main boulevard, it has extensive facilities, but its prices are not extravagant, considering the luxuries. The two-story reception lobby has an encircling mezzanine lounge that's almost arena-size, with comfortable islands of furniture arranged on Oriental rugs. Adjoining the O Terraço restaurant is a homey salon with a wood-burning fireplace.

The guest rooms contain a mixture of modern and traditional furniture. The first floor is entirely nonsmoking rooms. The larger and best rooms face the front, although those in the rear are quieter. For some reason, rooms ending in the number 50 have the most spacious bathrooms, all of which contain neatly kept shower-tub combinations. There are two rooms for those with limited mobility. Unlike the climate control in many Lisbon hotels, the air-conditioning here actually seems to work. The Tivoli Jardim, next door, is under the same ownership but is inferior to the Hotel Tivoli.

Av. da Liberdade 185, 1269-050 Lisboa Codex. (C) 21/319-89-00. Fax 21/319-89-50. www.tivolihotels.com. 329 units. 195€–255€ ($224–$293) double; from 402€ ($462) suite. Rates include continental breakfast. AE, DC, MC, V. Parking 15€ ($17). Metro: Avenida. Bus: 1, 2, 9, or 32. **Amenities:** 2 restaurants; 2 bars; pool; tennis court; health club; solarium; 24-hr. room service; babysitting; laundry service; dry cleaning. *In room:* A/C, TV, dataport, minibar, hair dryer, safe.

Moderate

Dom Carlos *Value* This central hotel lies just off Praça do Marquês de Pombal. The reason to stay here is economy: The Dom Carlos charges only a fraction of what its rivals in the neighborhood get. The curvy facade is all glass, lending an outdoorsy feeling reinforced by trees and beds of orange and red canna. The good-size guest rooms are paneled in reddish Portuguese wood; even so, they're rather uninspired and functional. An occasional hand-carved cherub softens the Nordic-inspired furnishings. All units come equipped with well-maintained bathrooms containing shower-tub combinations. The hotel faces a triangular park dedicated to Camilo Castelo Branco, a 19th-century poet. The lobby lounge is satisfactory; more inviting is the mezzanine salon, where sofas and chairs face the park.

Av. Duque de Loulé 121, 1050-089 Lisboa. (C) 21/351-25-90. Fax 21/352-07-28. hdcarlos@mail.telepac.pt. 76 units. 118€ ($136) double; 135€ ($157) triple; 150€ ($173) suite. Rates include buffet breakfast. AE, DC, MC, V. Metro: Marquês de Pombal. Bus: 1, 36, 44, or 45. **Amenities:** Restaurant; bar; 24-hr. room service; babysitting; laundry service; dry cleaning. *In room:* A/C, TV, minibar, hair dryer, safe.

Hotel Britânia ★ In its own way, the Britânia is one of the most traditional hotels in Lisbon. The well-known Portuguese architect Cassiano Branco designed the Art Deco building in 1942. Located about a block from Avenida da Liberdade, it boasts a distinguished, loyal clientele and an old-fashioned, almost courtly, staff. In 1995, the six-story hotel was refurbished, making the exceedingly spacious rooms more comfortable. Each has a well-maintained bathroom equipped with a shower-tub combination.

Rua Rodrigues Sampaio 17, 1150-278 Lisboa. © **21/315-50-16.** Fax 21/315-50-21. www.heritage.pt. 30 units. 148€–225€ ($170–$259) double. AE, DC, MC, V. Metro: Avenida. Bus: 1, 2, 11, or 21. **Amenities:** Bar; lounge; 24-hr. room service; laundry service; dry cleaning. *In room:* A/C, TV, dataport, minibar, hair dryer, safe.

Hotel Veneza ★ *Finds*   The Veneza, which opened in 1990, occupies one of the few remaining 19th-century palaces that once lined Avenida da Liberdade. A grand staircase leads to the three upper floors. The well-appointed midsize guest rooms are furnished in soothing modern style and are equipped with well-kept bathrooms containing shower-tub combinations. The Veneza has a bar and serves only breakfast. Guests have access to the facilities at the better-equipped Hotel Tivoli (see above).

Av. da Liberdade 189, 1250-141 Lisboa. © **21/352-26-18.** Fax 21/352-66-78. www.3khoteis.com. 37 units. 130€–150€ ($150–$173) double. Rates include continental breakfast. AE, DC, MC, V. Parking 11€ ($13). Metro: Avenida. **Amenities:** Bar; limited room service; laundry service; dry cleaning. *In room:* A/C, TV, minibar, hair dryer, safe.

Mundial Hotel   One block from the Rossio, the recently expanded Mundial is in the heart of everything. The hotel is high on the list of many European business travelers. The location is both good and bad—the colorful street out front is a bit sleazy, especially at night, but theaters and shops are nearby. The rooms are comfortable, spacious, and restrained in decor. Units in the rear are much quieter than the front rooms, which can be noisy. Seven rooms are available for those with limited mobility. The tiled bathrooms have bidets, shower-tub combinations, and plenty of mirrors and shelf space.

Rua Dom Duarte 4, 1100-198 Lisboa. © **21/884-20-00.** Fax 21/884-21-10. www.hotel-mundial.pt. 262 units. 120€–151€ ($138–$174) double; 180€ ($207) suite. Rates include buffet breakfast. AE, DC, MC, V. Metro: Rossio or Martimonis. **Amenities:** 2 restaurants; bar; car rental; 24-hr. room service; babysitting; laundry service; dry cleaning. *In room:* A/C, TV, minibar, hair dryer, safe.

Inexpensive

Jorge V Hotel   The Jorge V is a neat little hotel with a 1960s design. It boasts a choice location a block off the noisy Avenida da Liberdade. Its facade contains rows of balconies roomy enough for guests to have breakfast or afternoon refreshments. A tiny elevator runs to a variety of aging rooms, which aren't generous in size but are comfortable; all have small tile bathrooms with well-kept showers. There are seven nonsmoking rooms. Guests particularly enjoy the regional-style combination bar and breakfast room.

Rua Mouzinho da Silveira 3, 1250-165 Lisboa. © **21/356-25-25.** Fax 21/315-03-19. www.hoteljorgev.com. 49 units. 79€–92€ ($91–$106) double; 84€–110€ ($97–$106) suite. Rates include continental breakfast. AE, DC, MC, V. Parking 10€ ($12). Metro: Avenida or Marquês de Pombal. **Amenities:** Bar; lounge; limited room service; laundry service; dry cleaning. *In room:* A/C, TV, minibar, hair dryer, safe.

Miraparque   Miraparque lies on a secluded, quiet street opposite Edward VII Park. The small guest rooms haven't been called modern since the 1960s, but they're well maintained. All come equipped with tidily kept bathrooms containing shower-tub combinations. The hotel is a little worn but still recommendable because of its central location and low prices. The wood-paneled lounges are furnished in simulated brown leather.

Av. Sidónio Pais 12, 1050-214 Lisboa. © **21/352-42-86.** Fax 21/357-89-20. www.miraparque.com. 100 units. 67€–91€ ($77–$105) double; 82€–115€ ($94–$132) triple. Rates include buffet breakfast. AE, DC, MC, V. Metro: Parque. Bus: 91. **Amenities:** Restaurant; bar; limited room service; laundry service; dry cleaning. *In room:* A/C, TV, minibar, hair dryer, safe.

WEST OF THE CENTER
Very Expensive

As Janelas Verdes ★★ *Finds* This aristocratic 18th-century mansion near the Museum of Ancient Art was the home of the late Portuguese novelist Eça de Queiroz. It was an annex to York House before becoming a historic hotel. The large, luxurious, marvelously restored rooms have abundant closet space, excellent beds, and generous tile bathrooms equipped with shower-tub combinations. The predominantly red lounge evokes turn-of-the-20th-century Lisbon. The inn has 14 nonsmoking rooms and 1 room for those with limited mobility.

Rua das Janelas Verdes 47, 1200-690 Lisboa. ✆ 21/396-81-43. Fax 21/396-81-44. www.heritage.pt. 29 units. 165€–245€ ($190–$282) double; 190€–315€ ($219–$362) triple. AE, DC, MC, V. Bus: 27, 40, 49, or 60. **Amenities:** Bar; lounge; 24-hr. room service; babysitting; laundry service; dry cleaning. *In room:* A/C, TV, dataport, hair dryer, safe.

Lapa Palace ★★★ In a palace built in 1870 for the count of Valença, this government-rated five-star hotel, purchased by Orient Express in 1998, is the most talked-about accommodation in Lisbon. We never thought we'd see a hotel replace the Four Seasons Hotel The Ritz as the city's premier address, but Lapa has done just that. In 1910, the de Valença family sold the villa and its enormous gardens to a wealthy, untitled family that retained it until 1988. After more than 4 years of renovation, it opened in 1992 amid a flurry of publicity. Its lushly manicured gardens lie close to the Tagus, south of the city center.

All but about 20 of the rooms are in a modern six-story wing. The spacious guest rooms in both sections contain amply proportioned marble surfaces, reproductions of French and English furniture, and a classic design inspired by a late 18th-century model. The marble bathrooms are among the city's most elegant, often adorned with bas-relief and containing shower-tub combinations and, in some cases, whirlpool baths. Each unit opens onto a balcony. The older rooms have more charm and grace; many of the newer ones open onto panoramic vistas of Lisbon. The public areas have multicolored ceiling frescoes and richly patterned marble floors. The hotel has introduced a new afternoon tea service in the **Rio Tejo Bar,** with a selection of more than 40 of the finest and rarest tea varieties in the world.

Rua do Pau de Bandeira 4, 1249-021 Lisboa. ✆ 21/394-94-94. Fax 21/395-06-65. www.orient-express hotels.com. 109 units. 300€–500€ ($345–$575) double; 575€ ($661) junior suite; from 675€ ($776) suite. Rates include breakfast. AE, DC, MC, V. Free parking. Bus: 13 or 27. **Amenities:** 2 restaurants; bar; pool; health club; sauna; 24-hr. room service; massage; babysitting; laundry service; dry cleaning. *In room:* A/C, TV, dataport, minibar, hair dryer, safe.

Moderate

York House ★★ Once a 17th-century convent, York House lies outside the center of traffic-filled Lisbon, attracting those who desire peace and tranquillity. It has long been known to the English and to diplomats, artists, writers, poets, and professors. Book well in advance. Near the National Art Gallery, it sits high

---

Tips **Stateside Booking**

You can make reservations for As Janelas Verdes and many other Lisbon hotels, as well as all the country's rural *pousadas* (inns), through **Marketing Ahead,** 381 Park Ave. S., Suite 718, New York, NY 10016 (✆ **800/223-1356** or 212/686-9213; www.marketingahead.com).

on a hillside overlooking the Tagus and is surrounded by a garden. A distinguished Lisbon designer selected the tasteful furnishings. Guest rooms vary in size; all have antique beds, bathrooms equipped with shower-tub combinations, and 18th- and 19th-century bric-a-brac. The lack of air-conditioning can be a problem in summer. The public rooms boast inlaid chests, coats of armor, carved ecclesiastical figures, and ornate ceramics. The former monks' dining hall has deep-set windows, large niches for antiques, and—best of all—French-Portuguese cuisine.

Rua das Janelas Verdes 32, 1200-691 Lisboa. ℂ 21/396-24-35. Fax 21/397-27-93. 34 units. 140€–200€ ($161–$230) double. AE, DC, MC, V. Nearby parking 7€ ($8.05). Bus: 27, 40, 49, 54, or 60. **Amenities:** Restaurant; bar; 24-hr. room service; babysitting; laundry service; dry cleaning. *In room:* A/C, TV, hair dryer, safe.

WHERE TO DINE
IN THE CENTER
Very Expensive
Gambrinus ✿✿ SEAFOOD   One of the city's premier restaurants, Gambrinus is the top choice for fish and shellfish. It's in the congested heart of the city, off the Rossio near the rail station on a little square behind the National Theater. The dining room is resolutely macho, with leather chairs under a beamed cathedral ceiling, but you can also select a little table beside a fireplace on the raised end of the room.

Gambrinus offers a diverse a la carte menu and specialties of the day. The shades and nuances of the cuisine definitely appeal to the cultivated palate. The soups, especially the shellfish bisque, are good. The most expensive items are shrimp and lobster dishes. However, you might try conch with shellfish thermidor or sea bass *minhota,* cooked in tomato sauce with onions, white wine, and ham. If you don't fancy fish but do like your dishes hot, ask for chicken *piri-piri* (served with blazing chiles). Desserts are elaborate. Coffee with a 30-year-old brandy is the perfect end to a sumptuous meal here.

Rua das Portas de Santo Antão 25. ℂ 21/342-14-66. Reservations required. Main courses 18€–35€ ($21–$40). AE, MC, V. Daily noon–1:30am. Metro: Rossio.

Expensive
Clara ✿✿✿ PORTUGUESE/INTERNATIONAL   On a hillside amid decaying villas and city squares, this green-tile house owned by Zelia Pimpista contains an elegant restaurant. You can enjoy a drink under the ornate ceiling of the bar. Soft piano music accompanies dinner. At night, an indoor seat— perhaps near the large marble fireplace—is especially appealing. During lunch, however, you might prefer a seat near the garden terrace's plants and fountain. Specialties include tournedos Clara, stuffed rabbit with red-wine sauce, four kinds of pasta, codfish Clara, filet of sole with orange, pheasant with grapes, and Valencian paella. Again, as in too many of Lisbon's top-rated restaurants, these dishes aren't creative and innovative in any way, but they're often prepared flawlessly. As one of the staff told us, "When a dish has stood the test of time, why change it?" Perhaps you'll agree.

Campo dos Mártires da Pátria 49. ℂ 21/885-30-53. Reservations required. Main courses 17€–22€ ($20–$25). AE, DC, MC, V. Mon–Fri noon–3:30pm and 7–10:30pm; Sat 7–10:30pm. Closed Aug 1–15. Metro: Avenida.

Escorial ✿ SPANISH/INTERNATIONAL   In the heart of Lisbon's restaurant district, near Praça dos Restauradores, this Spanish-owned restaurant combines classic Spanish dishes with an inviting ambience. The dining room walls are paneled in rosewood, with frosted-globe lighting. You can have a before-dinner drink in the Art Room cocktail lounge, which exhibits work by contemporary Portuguese artists. A menu is printed in English (always look for the course of the day). A selection of the chef's carefully crafted specialties is likely to include barbecued baby goat, beef Stroganoff, paella, mixed shellfish grill, or partridge casserole. In spite of the neighborhood, which grows increasingly sleazy at night, Escorial has stood the test of time and remains an enduring, if not incredibly innovative, favorite. The ingredients are fresh, and the food and service continue to be remarkable for their elegance and professionalism.

Rua das Portas de Santo Antão 47. ✆ 21/346-44-29. Reservations recommended. Main courses 10€–30€ ($12–$35). AE, DC, MC, V. Daily noon–4pm and 7pm–midnight. Metro: Rossio or Restauradores.

Moderate

Restaurant 33 ★ *Finds* PORTUGUESE/INTERNATIONAL   Restaurant 33 is a treasure. Decorated in a style evocative of an English hunting lodge, it lies near many recommended hotels, including the Four Seasons Hotel The Ritz Lisbon. It specializes in succulent seafood dishes, including shellfish rice served in a crab shell, smoked salmon, and lobster Tour d'Argent; it also features tender, well-flavored pepper steak. One reader from New Rochelle, New York, found her meal here "flawless." A pianist performs during dinner. You can enjoy a glass of port in the small bar at the entrance or in the private garden.

Rua Alexandre Herculano 33A. ✆ 21/354-60-79. Reservations recommended. Main courses 14€–18€ ($16–$21). AE, DC, MC, V. Mon–Fri noon–3:30pm; Mon–Sat 8–10:30pm. Metro: Marquês Do Pombal. Bus: 6 or 9.

Inexpensive

Bonjardim *Value* *Kids* PORTUGUESE   Bonjardim rightly deserves this enthusiastic endorsement of a traveler from Boston: "I was given the names of eight inexpensive restaurants to try in Lisbon during my 5-day stay. I ended up trying only two, as I took the rest of my meals at Bonjardim, sampling a different dish for lunch and dinner every day." The restaurant caters mostly to families, providing wholesome meals that fit most budgets. The operation has been so successful that it has taken over a building across the street, where the same menu is offered. The restaurant is just east of Avenida da Liberdade near the grimy Praça dos Restauradores.

In the main restaurant, the air-conditioned, sun-flooded second-floor dining room is designed in rustic Portuguese style, with a beamed ceiling. The street-floor dining room, with an adjoining bar for before-meal drinks, has walls of decorative tiles. During dinner, the aroma of plump chickens roasting on the charcoal spit is likely to prompt you to try one. An order of this house specialty, *frango no espeto,* is adequate for two, with a side dish of french fries. The cook also bakes hake in the Portuguese style, or try pork fried with clams. For dessert, you can order a cassate. If you want to be daring, order chicken with *piri-piri,* a fiery chile sauce.

Bonjardim also has a self-service cafeteria nearby, at Travessa de Santo Antão II (✆ 21/342-43-89). It serves Portuguese dishes, including seafood soup; half a roast chicken with trimmings; grilled fish of the day (the chef's specialty); and velvety chocolate mousse.

Travessa de Santo Antão 10. ✆ 21/342-74-24. Main courses 9€–16€ ($10–$18). AE, DC, MC, V. Daily noon–11pm. Metro: Restauradores.

Cervejaria Brilhante SEAFOOD/PORTUGUESE   Lisboans from every walk of life stop here for a stein of beer and *mariscos* (seafood). The tavern is decorated with stone arches, wood-paneled walls, and pictorial tiles of sea life. The front window is packed with an appetizing array of king crabs, oysters, lobsters, baby clams, shrimp, and even barnacles. The price changes every day, depending on the market, and you pay by the kilo. This is hearty, robust eating, although attracting a waiter's attention is a challenge.

Rua das Portas de Santo Antão 105 (opposite the Coliseu). ℃ **21/346-14-07**. Main courses 10€–18€ ($12–$21); tourist menu 14€ ($16). AE, DC, MC, V. Daily noon–midnight. Metro: Rossio. Bus: 1, 2, 36, 44, or 45.

Cervejaria Ribadoura SEAFOOD   Cervejaria Ribadoura is one of the typical shellfish-and-beer eateries in central Lisbon, located midway along the city's major boulevard. The decor in this tavern-style restaurant is simple—the emphasis is on the fish. Try the *bacalhau* (codfish) à Bras. You can dine lightly, particularly at lunch, on such plates as a shrimp omelet. Many diners follow their fish with a meat dish. However, only those raised on the most mouth-wilting Indian curries should try the sautéed pork cutlets with *piri-piri*, made with red-hot peppers from Angola. A wedge of Portuguese cheese "from the hills" finishes the meal nicely. Although we've always found fish on our 25-odd visits here, some readers have reported that occasionally the fish market was bare.

Av. da Liberdade 155 (at Rua do Salitre). ℃ **21/354-94-11**. Main courses 8€–26€ ($9.20–$30). AE, DC, MC, V. Daily noon–1:30am. Metro: Avenida. Bus: 1, 2, 44, or 45.

IN CHIADO & BAIRRO ALTO
Expensive

Restaurante Tavares ✸✸✸ PORTUGUESE/CONTINENTAL   The oldest restaurant in Lisbon, once known for serving the best food in the city, Tavares still surfaces near the top. It serves well-prepared food with flawless service and continues to attract many diplomats and government heads as well as the literati. White- and gold-paneled walls, three chandeliers, and Louis XV armchairs keep the spirit of the 18th century intact. Drinks are served in the petite front salon.

Your meal might begin with *crepes de marisco* (seafood crepes). A main-course selection might be sole in champagne, stuffed crab, clams Bulhão Pato (clams cooked in white wine and garlic), or tournedos Grand Duc. Many Continental dishes are scattered throughout the menu, including the classic scallops of veal viennoise. The restaurant nearly always serves such basic Portuguese dishes as sardines and salted codfish. To complete your meal, try the chef's dessert specialty, a high-rise soufflé, followed by a *café filtro* (filtered coffee).

Originally a cafe, Tavares was founded in 1784. When the two Tavares brothers died in the 19th century, six waiters formed a partnership and took it over; it's still owned by a group of waiters, who maintain its high standards.

Rua da Misericórdia 37. ℃ **21/342-11-12**. Reservations required. Main courses 20€–30€ ($23–$35). AE, DC, MC, V. Mon–Fri 12:30–3pm; Sun–Fri 7:30–11pm. Bus: 15.

Moderate

Bachus ✸✸ INTERNATIONAL   Amusing murals cover the wood-paneled facade of this deluxe restaurant; inside the decor is elaborate and sophisticated. The ambience is a mixture of a private salon in a Russian palace, a turn-of-the-20th-century English club, and a stylized Manhattan bistro. A brass staircase winds around a column of illuminated glass to the dining room. Menu specialties change frequently, depending on what ingredients are available. Full meals might include mixed grill Bachus, chateaubriand with béarnaise, mountain goat, beef Stroganoff, shrimp Bachus, or other daily specials. The chef has a conservative approach, and perhaps because of this, he reportedly rarely gets complaints. The wine list is extensive.

Largo da Trindade 9. ℃ **21/342-28-28**. Reservations recommended. Main courses 15€–20€ ($17–$23). AE, DC, MC, V. Tues–Fri noon–3pm; Tues–Sun 7pm–midnight. Metro: Chiado. Bus: 58.

Conventual 🐸🐸 PORTUGUESE Many admirers (including the prime minister of Portugal) rank Conventual as the single finest place to dine out in Lisbon today—even though its prices are about 25% less than those at many of its competitors. Conventual is on one of the loveliest residential squares in town, behind a plain wooden door. Inside you'll see a display of old panels from baroque churches, religious statues, and bric-a-brac. Delectably flavored dishes include creamy coriander soup, stewed partridge in port, duck in rich champagne sauce, grilled monkfish in herb-flavored cream sauce, frogs' legs in buttery garlic, and— one of our favorites—stewed clams in a sauce of red peppers, onions, and cream.

Praça das Flores 45. 🕐 **21/390-91-96.** Reservations required. Main courses 15€–22€ ($17–$25). AE, DC, MC, V. Mon–Fri 12:30–3:30pm; Mon–Sat 7:30–11:30pm. Closed Aug. Metro: Avenida. Bus: 100.

Doca Peixe 🐸🐸 SEAFOOD This restaurant, whose Portuguese name means "Fish Dock," stands virtually under the Ponte do 25 de Abril (25th of April Bridge). The best views of the Tagus are from one of the tables upstairs. The fresh fish served here is among the best quality offered in the markets of Lisbon. Every variety of fish and shellfish seems to be swimming in the small aquarium as you enter. If you don't want your fish charcoal grilled, you can order it cooked in salt or baked. Codfish is a specialty, appearing cooked with clams and flavored with fresh coriander, or you can order the grilled platter of shellfish, one of the true delights. For the meat fancier, there are succulent sirloin steaks, among other winning choices.

Doca de Santo Amaro, Armazem 14. 🕐 **21/397-35-65.** Reservations recommended. Main courses 15€–40€ ($17–$46). AE, MC, V. Tues–Sun noon–3pm and 9:30pm–1am. Bus: 15 or 38.

Inexpensive

A Brasileira SANDWICHES/PASTRIES One of Lisbon's oldest coffeehouses, A Brasileira was once a gathering place of Lisbon literati. Patrons sit at small tables on chairs made of tooled leather, amid mirrored walls and marble pilasters. The restaurant here serves basic fare like omelets, steaks, and fish. Note that you'll pay more for sandwiches and pastries in the restaurant and at the outdoor tables than in the coffee bar.

Rua Garrett 120. 🕐 **21/346-9541.** Sandwiches and pastries 1.45€–4.95€ ($1.70–$5.70); meals in restaurant 7€–28€ ($8.05–$32). AE, MC, V (restaurant only). Daily 7am–11pm. Metro: Rossio.

Cervejaria Trindade PORTUGUESE Cervejaria Trindade is a combination German beer hall and Portuguese tavern. In operation since 1836, it's the oldest tavern in Lisbon, owned by the brewers of Sagres beer. It was built on the foundations of the 13th-century Convento dos Frades Tinos, which was destroyed by the 1755 earthquake. Surrounded by walls tiled with Portuguese scenes, you can order tasty little steaks and heaps of crisp french-fried potatoes. Many Portuguese diners prefer *bife na frigideira* (steak with mustard sauce and a fried egg, served in a clay frying pan). The tavern features shellfish; the house specialties are *ameijoas* (clams) à Trindade and giant prawns. A small stein of beer goes nicely with the main courses. For dessert, try a slice of *queijo da serra* (cheese from the mountains) and coffee. Meals are served in the inner courtyard on sunny days.

Rua Nova de Trindade 20C. 🕐 **21/342-35-06.** Main courses 10€–15€ ($12–$17). AE, DC, MC, V. Daily noon–2am. Metro: Chiado. Bus: 15, 20, 51, or 100.

WEST OF THE CENTER
Expensive

Café Alcântara FRENCH/PORTUGUESE Established in 1989, this is one of the city's most fun dining-and-entertainment complexes. Entertainment is provided by some of the best DJs in Portugal. It lies within the solid walls of a

600-year-old timber warehouse and attracts a hip, attractive, fun-loving young crowd. Today the vast building has forest-green and Bordeaux walls, exposed marble, ceiling fans, plants, and simple wooden tables and chairs. The varied clientele includes resident Brazilian, British, and American expatriates. Chefs make the most of regional foodstuffs and prepare hearty fare that is filled with flavor and plenty of spices—maybe too much for some palates. Menu items include rillettes of salmon, fresh fish, lacquered duck, steak tartare, and a Portuguese platter of the day, which might include fried *bacalhau* (codfish) or a hearty *feijoada*, a bean-and-meat stew inspired by the traditions of Trás-os-Montes.

Rua Maria Luisa Holstein 15. ℂ **21/363-71-76.** Reservations recommended. Main courses 16€–25€ ($18–$29). AE, DC, MC, V. Daily 8pm–1am. Bar daily 9pm–3am. Bus: 20 or 38.

Restaurante Cipriani INTERNATIONAL/PORTUGUESE   This is the most upscale and most highly recommended restaurant in Lisbon's major government-rated five-star hotel, the Lapa Palace (reviewed earlier in this chapter). The dignified, elegant dining room has a view of one of the most lavish gardens in this exclusive neighborhood. This restaurant is a favorite with diplomats from the many embassies and consulates nearby. A la carte items available at lunch and dinner vary with the season. They might include fresh salmon fried with sage, lamb chops with mint sauce, a succulent version of a traditional Portuguese *feijoada* (meat stew), and perfectly prepared duck breast baked with pears. This is a perfect spot to retreat to when you want an elegant meal in a refined atmosphere.

In the Lapa Palace Hotel, Rua do Pau de Bandeira 4. ℂ **21/394-94-01.** Reservations recommended. Main courses 17€–29€ ($20–$33). AE, DC, MC, V. Daily 12:30–3:30pm and 7:30–10:30pm. Tram: 25 or 28. Bus: 13 or 17.

Sua Excelência ℛ *Finds* PORTUGUESE   Sua Excelência is the creation of Francisco Queiroz, a travel agent in Angola before settling in Portugal. His restaurant feels like a fashionable drawing room, with colorful tables in intimate Portuguese provincial decor. Some dishes served are uncommon in Portugal, such as Angolan chicken Moamba. Sure-to-please specialties include prawns *piri-piri* (not unreasonably hot), *lulas à moda da casa* (squid stewed in white wine, crème fraîche, and cognac), rollmop sardines, the self-proclaimed best smoked swordfish in Portugal, and clams prepared five different ways. One unusual specialty is "little jacks," a small fish eaten whole, served with a well-flavored paste made from 2-day-old bread. The restaurant is just a block up the hill from the entrance to the National Art Gallery; it could be part of a museum-luncheon adventure, although its ambience is more charming in the evening. Over the years it has remained popular with our readers. We were the first guidebook to discover it, but today it seems to be on everybody's list.

Rua do Conde 34. ℂ **21/390-36-14.** Reservations required. Main courses 13€–19€ ($15–$22). AE, MC, V. Mon–Tues and Thurs–Fri 1–3pm; Thurs–Sun 8–10:30pm. Closed Sept. Tram: 25. Bus: 27, 49, or 60.

ON THE WATERFRONT
Moderate

Espalha Brasas *Finds* TAPAS/GRILLS   This is our favorite of the many shoulder-to-shoulder restaurants lined up at the Alcântara Docks, although part of your evening's entertainment will involve picking whichever of the 20 or so cheek-by-jowl restaurants you actually prefer. You'll enter a high-ceilinged room whose centerpiece is a weather-beaten wooden statue of a nude male beside stairs leading to an upstairs balcony with additional tables. The setting is comfortably cluttered and amiable, with candlelit tables and a display of whatever fresh seafood and meats can be grilled to your preference. The finest menu items include every

Native Behavior

Machismo reigns in Portugal, as in most Latin countries, but it is of a gentler, often wistful variety. Over shots of cherry *ginginha,* a man is less likely to boast of his amorous accomplishments in the bedroom last night than of the prodigious amounts of food he ingested in the dining room. While he is proud of the work he does, he concedes that the true working-class heroes are fishermen, and deep inside he thinks that fishing is what a man *should* do. And, of course, in the Portuguese *tourada*—bullfight—not only does the animal leave the ring alive, but he is encouraged to charge repeatedly into a line of men with no weapons but their bravado.

A strain of nostalgia coupled with fatalism runs deep in Portuguese culture. There is a special word for it—*saudade*—which is, as always seems true of such words, not easily translated into English. It concerns a longing melancholy, for a place, a person, a spirit, even a practice now lost. Hardly unusual for a nation of seafarers and explorers and reluctant emigrants, who are gone from their homes and loves for years or forever, it is expressed in the musical art form called *fado* (see "The Quintessential Lisbon Experience: Fado," later in this chapter). Fado is a mournful wail about loss, and ordinary people, not just professional performers, are still known to break into the sobbing lament in clubs, at fiestas, and even on street corners.

imaginable kind of meat or fish, grilled the way you prefer, as well as daily specials that include rice studded with either turbot and prawns or marinated duck meat, baked haunch of pork, and codfish stuffed with prawns and spinach.

Doca de Santa Amaro, Armazem 12. Alcântara. ☎ 21/396-20-59. Reservations recommended for dinner Fri–Sat night only. Main courses 9€–22€ ($10–$25). AE, MC, V. Sept–July daily noon–1am; Aug daily 7:30pm–1am. Tram: 15 or 18. Bus: 57.

31 de Armada PORTUGUESE   Set directly across the street from the headquarters of the Portuguese navy, this is a well-respected and very traditional restaurant. You'll recognize it by the masses of bougainvillea that cascade over the doorways. Inside, a pair of dining rooms—each interconnected only through the kitchen, but accessible to the street through separate doorways—have beamed ceilings, tiled floors, hardworking and matriarchal-looking waitresses, and an allegiance to the culinary principals of Old Portugal. Your well-prepared meal might begin with soup or a salad, such as cold grilled octopus in vinaigrette, followed with pork or veal cutlets, grilled tuna salads, beefsteaks, and all manner of grilled fish.

Praça de Armada 31. ☎ 21/397-63-30. Reservations recommended for dinner Fri–Sat night only. Main courses 7€–15€ ($8.05–$17). AE, DC, MC, V. Daily noon–3pm and 7:30–10:30pm. Tram: 15. Bus: 27, 49, or 60.

SEEING THE SIGHTS

SIGHTSEEING SUGGESTIONS FOR FIRST-TIME VISITORS

If You Have 1 Day This is just enough time to take a walking tour of the **Alfama,** Lisbon's most colorful district. Visit the 12th-century **Sé (Cathedral)** and take in a view of the city and the River Tejo from the **Santa Luzia Belvedere.** Climb up to the **Castelo São Jorge (St. George's Castle).** Later, take a taxi or tram to **Belém** to see the **Mosteiro dos Jerónimos (Jerónimos Monastery)** and the **Torre de Belém (Tower of Belém).** Back in Lisbon proper, end your day at a **fado cafe** in the **Bairro Alto.**

If You Have 2 Days Spend the morning of day 2 at the **Museu Calouste Gulbenkian,** one of Europe's artistic treasure troves. Have lunch at a *típico* restaurant in the Bairro Alto. In the afternoon see the **Fundação Ricardo Esprito Santo (Museum of Decorative Art)** and the **Museu Nacional de Art Antiga (National Museum of Ancient Art).** At the day's end, wander through **Parque Eduardo VII.** That night, explore the dance clubs and bars of the waterfront.

If You Have 3 Days On day 3, head for **Sintra,** the single most visited sight in the environs—Byron called it a "glorious Eden." Spend the day here, exploring the castle and other palaces in the area. Must-sees are the **Palácio Nacional de Sintra** and the **Palácio Nacional da Pena.** Return to Lisbon for dinner.

If You Have 4 or 5 Days On day 4, take an excursion from Lisbon (perhaps an organized tour) to visit the fishing village of **Nazaré** and the walled city of **Óbidos.** On your final day, slow your pace a bit with a morning at the beach at **Estoril** on Portugal's Costa do Sol. Then continue along the coast to **Cascais** for lunch. After lunch, wander around this old fishing village, which is now a major resort. Go to **Guincho,** 6km (3¾ miles) along the coast from Cascais, which is near the westernmost point on the European continent and has panoramic views.

NEIGHBORHOODS

The Alfama ★★ Ancient Lisbon lives on in this hillside district. A wall built by the Visigoths and incorporated into some of the houses is testimony to its past. The Alfama was the Saracen sector centuries before its conquest by the Christians. Some of the buildings were spared from the devastating 1755 earthquake, and the Alfama has retained much of its original aspect—narrow cobblestone streets, cages of warbling canaries hung outside windows, housewives dropping baskets on ropes from upper stories to take delivery of food, strings of garlic and pepper beside doorways of *típico* taverns, street markets, and flower-decked balconies.

One of the best views is from the belvedere of **Largo das Portas do Sol,** near the Museum of Decorative Art. It's a balcony opening onto the sea, overlooking the tiled-front houses that sweep down to the River Tejo. One of the older churches is **Santo Estevão (St. Stephen),** at Largo de Santo Estevão. It was first built in the 13th century; the present marble structure dates from the 18th. Also of medieval origin is the **Church of São Miguel (St. Michael),** at Largo de São Miguel, deep in the Alfama on a palm-shaded square. **Rua da Judiaria (Street of the Jews)** is another reminder of the past. It was settled largely by Jewish refugees fleeing Spain's Inquisition.

Bairro Alto ★ Like the Alfama, the Bairro Alto (Upper Quarter) preserves the characteristics of an older Lisbon. It was once called the heart of the city, probably for both its location and its inhabitants. Many of its buildings survived the 1755 earthquake. Today it's the home of the most notable fado cafes and many bars and restaurants, both humble and elevated, making it a center of nightlife. The quarter is also an intriguing place to visit during the day, when its

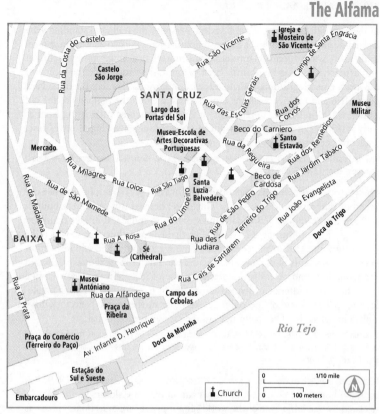

narrow cobblestone streets and alleys, lined with aged buildings, can be appreciated in the warm light coming off the sea.

From the windows and balconies, laundry hangs out to dry, and beside the windows are cages containing canaries, parrots, parakeets, and other birds. In the morning, the street scene is made up of housewives emerging from their homes to shop, following the cries of the *varinas* (fishmongers) and other food vendors.

Belém ★★ At Belém, the most southwestern district of Lisbon, the River Tejo meets the sea. From here, the caravels that charted the unknown oceans were launched on their missions: Vasco da Gama to India, Ferdinand Magellan to circumnavigate the globe, and Bartolomeu Dias to round the Cape of Good Hope. From these explorations, wealth flowed into Belém, especially from the spice trade with the Far East. Belém emerged from the Restelo, the point of land from which the ships set sail across the so-called Sea of Darkness. In time, the royal family established a summer palace here. Wealthy Lisboetas began moving out of the city center and building town houses, establishing the character of the district. For many years Belém was a separate municipality, but it is now incorporated into Lisbon as a parish.

THE TOP ATTRACTIONS

Castelo São Jorge ★★★ Believed to have predated the Romans, this fortress on a hilltop was used to guard the River Tejo and the settlement below. Beginning in the 5th century A.D., the site was a Visigothic fortification; it fell in the early 8th century to Arab invaders. Many of the walls still standing were erected during the centuries of Moorish domination. The Moors were in control until 1147, when Afonso Henríques, the country's first king, pushed them out and extended his kingdom south. Even before Lisbon was made the capital of the newly emerging nation, the site was used as a royal palace. For the finest view of the Tejo and the city, walk the esplanades and climb the ramparts of the old castle, named in commemoration of an Anglo-Portuguese pact dating from as early as 1371. On the grounds, you can stroll through a setting of olive, pine, and cork trees, graced by swans and rare white peacocks.

Rua da Costa do Castelo. ℭ **21/887-72-44.** Free admission. Apr–Sept daily 9am–9pm; Oct–Mar daily 9am–6pm. Tram: 12 or 28. Bus: 37.

Mosteiro dos Jerónimos (Jerónimos Monastery) ★★★   In an expansive mood of celebration, Manuel I, the Fortunate, ordered this monastery built in 1502 to commemorate Vasco da Gama's voyage to India and to give thanks to the Virgin Mary for its success. Manueline, the style of architecture to which the king contributed his name, combines Flamboyant Gothic and Moorish influences with elements of the nascent Renaissance. The 1755 earthquake damaged the monastery, and extensive restoration, some of it ill conceived, was carried out. The church interior is divided into a trio of naves, noted for their fragile-looking pillars. Some of the ceilings, like those in the monks' refectory, have ribbed barrel vaults. The "palm tree" in the sacristy is exceptional.

Praça do Império. ℭ **21/362-00-34.** Admission: Church free; cloisters 3€ ($3.45) adults, free for seniors 65 and over and children under 12. May–Sept Tues–Sun 10am–6pm; Oct–Apr Tues–Sun 10am–5pm. Tram: 15. Bus: 27, 28, 29, 43, or 49.

Museu de Fundação Calouste Gulbenkian ★★★   Opened in 1969, this museum houses the collection of Armenian oil tycoon Calouste Gulbenkian—declared by one critic "one of the world's finest private art collections." It covers Egyptian, Greek, and Roman antiquities; remarkable Islamic art; and vases, prints, and lacquerwork from China and Japan. European works include medieval illuminated manuscripts and ivories, 15th- to 19th-century painting and sculpture, 18th-century French decorative works, French Impressionist painting, and Lalique jewelry and glassware. Notable are two Rembrandts, Rubens's *Portrait of Hélène Fourment,* and Renoir's *Portrait of Madame Claude Monet.*

Av. de Berna 45. ℭ **21/782-30-00.** Admission 3€ ($3.45), free for seniors (65 and over) and students and teachers. Free to all Sun. Wed–Sun 10am–6pm. Metro: Sebastião. Bus: 16, 26, 31, 41, 46, or 56.

Museu Nacional de Arte Antiga (National Museum of Ancient Art) ★   This museum has a number of notable paintings, including the famous 15th-century polyptych from St. Vincent's monastery attributed to Nuno Gonçalves. Outstanding works are Hieronymus Bosch's triptych *The Temptation of St. Anthony;* Hans Memling's *Mother and Child;* Albrecht Dürer's *St. Jerome;* and paintings by Velázquez, Zurbarán, Poussin, and Courbet. Paintings from the 15th through the 19th centuries trace the development of Portuguese art. The museum also exhibits a remarkable collection of gold- and silversmiths' work.

Rua das Janelas Verdes 95. ℭ **21/391-28-00.** Admission 3€ ($3.45) adults, 1.50€ ($1.75) students, free for children under 14. Tues 2–6pm; Wed–Sun 10am–6pm. Tram: 15 or 18. Bus: 7, 27, 40, 49, or 60.

Museu Nacional dos Coches (Coach Museum) ★★   This famous collection of hundreds of aristocratic coaches and sedan chairs is ensconced, appropriately, in a former royal riding school. Some of the carriages are as long as railroad cars, decorated in a mind-boggling, excessive manner, with lashings of gilt, swags of velvet, and swirls of carvings. The oldest dates from 1581; Elisabeth II of Great Britain used the most recent, from 1824, during her 1958 state visit.

Praça de Afonso de Albuquerque. ⒸⒸ **21/361-08-50.** Admission 3€ ($3.45) adults, 1.50€ ($1.75) students 14–25, free for children under 14. Tues–Sun 10am–5:30pm. Closed holidays. Tram: 15. Bus: 14, 27, 28, 29, 43, 49, or 51.

Oceanário de Lisboa ★★ *Kids* This world-class aquarium remains the most enduring and impressive achievement of EXPO '98 (the EXPO site has been renamed the Parque das Nações). Described as the second-biggest aquarium in the world, exceeded in size only by a facility in Osaka, Japan, it's contained within a stone and glass building whose centerpiece is a 5-million-liter (1.3-million-gallon) holding tank. Its waters are divided into four distinct ecosystems replicating the Atlantic, Pacific, Indian, and Antarctic oceans. Each is supplemented with land portions on which birds, amphibians, and reptiles flourish. Look for otters in the Pacific, penguins in the Antarctic, Polynesian trees and flowers in the Indian, and puffins, terns, and seagulls in the Atlantic.

Esplanada d. Carlos I. ⒸⒸ **21/891-70-02.** Admission 9€ ($10) adults, 4.60€ ($5.30) students and children under 13. Daily 10am–7pm. Metro: Estação do Oriente.

ELSEWHERE IN LISBON

Monumento dos Descobrimentos (Monument of the Discoveries) Like the prow of a caravel from the Age of Discovery, this exploration memorial stands on the Tejo, looking as if it's ready to strike out across the Sea of Darkness. Memorable explorers, chiefly Vasco da Gama, are immortalized in stone along the ramps. At the point where the two ramps meet is a representation of Henry the Navigator, whose genius opened up new worlds. One of the stone figures is that of a kneeling Philippa of Lancaster, Henry's English mother; other figures symbolize Crusaders, navigators, monks, cartographers, and cosmographers. Beneath the heroic representations of figures crucial to the country's history, the monument contains a permanent exhibition on the role of the Portuguese in exploring the world, as well as a temporary exhibition related to the Portuguese experience.

Avenida Brasilia, Belém. ⒸⒸ **21/303-1950.** Admission 2€ ($2.30) adults, free for children under 12. Tues–Sun 9:30am–6pm. Tram: 15. Bus: 28, 29, 43, or 51.

Museu da Marinha (Maritime Museum) ★ The pageant and the glory that characterized Portugal's domination of the high seas is evoked for posterity at the Maritime Museum. Appropriately, it's installed in the west wing of the Mosteiro dos Jerónimos, which was built in celebration of Vasco da Gama's voyage. These royal galleys re-create an age of opulence that never feared excess, as exemplified by dragons' heads dripping with gilt and sea monsters coiling with abandon. The museum contains hundreds of models, from 15th-century sailing ships to 20th-century warships. In a special room is a model of the queen's stateroom on the royal yacht of Carlos I, the Bragança king who was assassinated at Praça do Comércio in 1908.

Praça do Império. ⒸⒸ **21/362-00-19.** Admission 3€ ($3.45) adults, 1.50€ ($1.75) students and children ages 6–17, free for seniors (65 and over) and children under 6. Apr–Sept Tues–Sun 10am–6pm; Oct–Mar Tues–Sun 10am–5pm. Bus: 27, 28, 29, 43, 49, or 51.

Museu de Arte Popular (Folk Art Museum) This is the most dramatic exhibition of the folk arts and customs of the Portuguese. The walls of the building were painted by contemporary artists, including Carlos Botelho, Eduardo Ana-hory, Estréla Faria, Manuel Lapa, Paulo Ferreira, and Tomás de Melo. The 1948 opening of the Folk Art Museum was the result of António Ferro's campaign for ethnic revival. The collections—including ceramics, furniture, wickerwork, clothes, farm implements, and paintings—are displayed in five rooms that correspond more or less to the provinces, each of which maintains its distinct personality.

Avenida Brasília. © 21/301-1282. 1.80€ ($2.10) adults, free for children 12 and under. Tues–Sun 10am–12:30pm and 2–5pm. Closed holidays. Tram: 15. Bus: 27, 28, 29, 43, 49, or 51.

Sé (Cathedral) ★ Characterized by twin towers flanking its entrance, the Sé represents an architectural wedding of Romanesque and Gothic styles, with a facade resembling a medieval fortress. When Christian Crusaders, led by Portugal's first king, Afonso Henríques, captured the city early in the 12th century, the Sé became the first church in Lisbon. It was damaged in the earthquakes of 1344 and 1755. Inside the rough exterior are many treasures, including the font where St. Anthony of Padua is said to have been christened in 1195. The cloister, built in the 14th century by King Dinis, is of Gothic ogival construction, with garlands, a Romanesque wrought-iron grille, and tombs with inscription stones. In the sacristy and Treasury Museum, you'll find marbles, relics, valuable images, and ecclesiastical treasures from the 15th and 16th centuries.

Largo da Sé. © 21/886-67-52. Admission: Cathedral free; cloister 1.50€ ($1.75). Tues–Sat 9am–7pm; Sun–Mon 9am–5pm. Tram: 28 (Graça). Bus: 37.

Torre de Belém The quadrangular Tower of Belém is a monument to Portugal's Age of Discovery. Erected between 1515 and 1520, the tower is Portugal's classic landmark. It stands near the spot where the caravels once set out to sea on their courageous exploratory voyages. Its architect, Francisco de Arruda, blended Gothic and Moorish elements in what became known as the Manueline style, using such details as twisting ropes carved in stone. The coat-of-arms of Manuel I rests above the loggia, and balconies grace three sides. Along the balustrade of the loggias, stone crosses symbolize the Portuguese crusaders.

Praça do Império, Avenida de Brasília. © 21/362-00-34. Admission 3€ ($3.45) adults, 1.50€ ($1.75) children, free for seniors (65 and over), Sun free until 2pm. Tues–Sun 10am–5pm. Tram: 15 or 17. Bus: 27, 28, 43, 49, or 51.

ORGANIZED TOURS

BY TRAM Along its entire route, **tram 28** passes through Lisbon's most picturesque neighborhoods—the Bairro Alto, Alfama, and Graça. With its swoops and sudden swift turns, it is almost as much fun as an amusement park ride.

Since 1901, trams have negotiated the intimate alleys and tight corners of Lisbon's old quarters, and they're still going strong. The city's public transport company, **CARRIS** (© 21/358-2334; www.carris.pt), offers a 1½-hour tram tour of historic districts and monuments, with guides and interpreters aboard. The tour departs from Praça do Comércio four times daily in July and August, twice daily in June. Tickets (sold on board) are 15€ ($17) adults and 8€ ($9.20) ages 4 to 10; those 3 and under ride free.

CARRIS also offers two tours on **double-decker buses,** allowing passengers to get on and off at any of the 16 to 18 stops along the Tejo circuit from Baixa to Belém or the Oriente circuit from the center to the Parque das Nações. Tickets cost 13€ ($15) adults and 6.50€ ($7.50) children 4 to 10. They're good for a full day (hang onto your ticket), and you can buy them on board. The buses leave Praça do Comércio hourly from 11:30am to 5:30pm March through October; and at 11:30am, 1:30pm, and 3:30pm November through February. Private companies offering tours in Lisbon (and to such regional destinations as Sintra, Estoril, and Queluz) are **Gray Line** (*©* **21/352-2594**), **Cityrama** (*©* **21/319-1091**), and **Portugal Tours** (*©* **21/352-2902**).

THE SHOPPING SCENE

Baixa, a grid of streets dating from the 18th-century restoration of central Lisbon, is a major shopping area between the Rossio and the River Tejo. **Rua do Ouro (Street of Gold), Rua da Prata,** and **Rua Augusta** are the principal streets. Another major upscale shopping artery is **Rua Garrett,** in Chiado, the district on the hill due west of Baixa. You used to be able to reach the area by the Elevador Santa Justa, but the bridge connection is closed indefinitely. A walk up steep Rua do Carmo is now an access, along with the series of escalators that rise from the Metro station at the west end of Rua Vitoria to Rua Garret.

At the **Feira da Ladra,** an open-air flea market, vendors peddle their wares on Tuesday and Saturday; haggling is expected. Portable stalls and dropcloth displays are lined up in Campo de Santa Clara behind the Igreja São Vicente. Take bus no. 12 from the Santa Apolónia station.

For many browsers, the desirable buys are *azulejos*—hand-painted glazed tiles—and pottery from all over Portugal. Ceramics from Barcelos, decorated with brightly colored roosters, are legendary, as is the ubiquitous blue-and-white pottery made in Coimbra. From Caldas da Rainha come yellow-and-green dishes in the shapes of vegetables, fruits, and animals. Vila Real is known for its black pottery, polychrome pieces come from Aceiro, and the red-clay pots from the Alentejo region are based on designs that go back to the Etruscans.

Founded in 1741 in the Chiado district, **Sant'Anna,** Rua do Alecrim 95–97 (*©* **21/342-2537;** Metro: Estação do Cais do Sodré), is a leading ceramics center, famous for its hand-painted glazed tiles. The showroom is on Rua do Alecrim, but you can also visit the factory at Calçada da Boa Hora 96; make an appointment by calling *©* **21/363-3117. Vista Alegre,** Largo do Chiado 18 (*©* **21/347-5481;** Metro: Chiado), turns out some of the finest porcelain dinner services in the country, along with objets d'art and limited-edition porcelain for collectors and a range of practical day-to-day tableware.

Another good buy in Portugal is gold. Gold is strictly regulated by the government, which requires jewelers to put a minimum of 19¼ karats in the jewelry they sell. Filigree jewelry, made of fine gold or silver wire, is an art that dates from ancient times. **W. A. Sarmento,** Rua Aurea 251 (*©* **21/347-0783;** Metro: Rossio or Chiado), is the most distinguished silver- and goldsmith in Portugal, specializing in lacy filigree jewelry, including charm bracelets. Well on its way to being a century old, the **Joalharia do Carmo,** Rua do Carmo 87B (*©* **21/342-4200;** Metro: Rossio), is an important shop for gold filigree work.

MORE SELECT SHOPS   In the same building as the Hotel Avenida Palace, **Casa Bordados da Madeira,** Rua 1 de Dezembro 137 (*©* **21/342-1447;** Metro: Restauradores), offers handmade embroideries from Madeira and Viana. If you wish to place an order, the staff will mail it to you. **Madeira House,** Rua Augusta 131–135 (*©* **21/342-6813;** Metro: Chiado), specializes in high-quality regional cottons, linens, and gift items.

Adelia Almeida has the finest collection of linens in Lisbon at **Lavandaria,** 11–13 Rua Augusto Rosa (*©* **21/887-5691;** tram: 12 or 28). Much of her stock comes from Guimarães in northern Portugal, where hand weavers still work at home. Other linens are copies of 18th-century designs, including tablecloths. Look for the green-and-yellow embroidery of mimosa flowers on many of the linens.

LISBON AFTER DARK

Consult the official biweekly guide, *Follow Me Lisboa,* available at most newsstands, for the latest entertainment listings (in English). A local newspaper, *Diário de Notícias,* also carries cultural listings, but in Portuguese. Few discount tickets are offered, but students get 50% off tickets purchased for the national theater. Also of interest is *Agenda Cultural,* an English- and Portuguese-language seasonal periodical that's often available without charge at cafes, at hotels, and at the Portuguese tourist office. In it, you'll find an abbreviated listing of musical, theatrical, and cultural choices available throughout the city.

THE PERFORMING ARTS

Teatro Nacional de São Carlos, Rua Serpa Pinto 9 (© 21/325-30-30; Tram: 6, 28, or 28B, Bus: 46), attracts opera and ballet aficionados to performances by top companies from around the world at this 18th-century theater. The season begins in mid-September and extends through July. The box office is open daily from 1 to 7pm. Tickets run from about 25€ to 63€ ($29–$72), depending upon seat location and attraction.

A full menu of jazz, dance, light opera, and chamber concerts is presented at the **Centro Cultural de Belém,** Praça do Império (© 21/361-2400; www. ccb.pt; tram: 15; bus: 27, 28, 29, or 43.). Check locally to see what's happening when you're in town. Admission to the center is free but prices vary for tickets to temporary exhibitions.

Originally built in the 1840s and restored after a disastrous fire in 1964, the **Teatro Nacional Doña Maria II,** Plaza Dom Piedro IV (Rossio; © 21/342-22-10; Metro: Rossio; bus: 21, 31, 36, or 41), ranks along with the Teatro São Carlos as one of the most important cultural venues in Lisbon. Despite being funded by the Ministry of Culture, it does not limit its repertoire to just Portuguese-language productions, although those are the most common. Tickets run 2.50€ to 15€ ($2.90–$17). Students up to 25 years old (with valid ID) are given a 50% discount.

From October to June, jazz and other concerts, plus recitals and occasional ballet shows, are performed at the **Museu de Fundação Calouste Gulbenkian,** Avenida de Berna 45 (© 21/782-3000; Metro: Sebastião; bus: 16, 18, 26, 31, 42, 46, or 56). Inquire locally about what is happening at the time of your visit. Admission is 3€ ($3.45); free for seniors (65 and over) and students and teachers.

BARS

Bachus (p. 804), Largo da Trindade 9 (© 21/342-2828; bus: 58 or 100), is both a restaurant and a convivial watering spot. Amid Oriental carpets, fine hardwoods, bronze statues, and intimate lighting, mingle with some of Lisbon's stylish people. The array of drinks is international, starting at 3.50€ ($4.05). Bachus is open daily from noon to midnight. There's no cover.

A longtime favorite of journalists, politicians, and actors, the once-innovative **Procópio Bar,** Alto de San Francisco 21A (© 21/385-28-51; bus: 9), has become a tried-and-true staple. It might easily become your favorite bar—if you can find it. It lies just off Rua de João Penha, which itself is near the landmark

Moments **The Quintessential Lisbon Experience: Fado**

Fado is Portugal's most vivid folkloric art form. No visit to Lisbon is complete without at least one experience in one of the taverns where this traditional music is heard. Fado is typically sung by women, called *fadistas,* accompanied by guitar and viola. The songs express romantic longing and melancholy—*saudade,* the Portuguese sense of nostalgia for the past.

Adega Machado, Rua do Norte 91 (℃ **21/347-05-50;** bus: 58 or 100), is still one of Portugal's favored fado clubs. Alternating with the fadistas are folk dancers in costume whirling, clapping, and singing. Dinner is a la carte, and the cuisine is Portuguese, featuring regional dishes. Expect to spend at least about 50€ ($58) for a complete meal. The dinner hour starts at 8:30pm, the first show starts at 9:15pm, and doors don't close until 3am. Cover (including 2 drinks) 16€ ($18). The club is open from Tuesday to Sunday.

Every night at **A Severa,** Rua das Gaveas 51 (℃ **21/346-4006;** bus: 20 or 24), male and female singers, alternating with folk dancers, perform. In a niche is a statue honoring the club's namesake, Maria Severa, the legendary 19th-century Gypsy fadista who made fado famous. The kitchen turns out regional dishes based on recipes from the north of Portugal. Expect to spend from at least 35€ ($40) per person for a meal with wine. Cover (including two drinks) is 18€ ($20), and the club is open Friday through Wednesday from 8pm to 3:30am.

Seemingly every fadista worth her shawl has sung at the old-time **Parreirinha da Alfama,** Beco do Espirito Santo 1 (℃ **21/886-8209;** bus: 39 or 46), just a minute's walk from the docks of the Alfama. It's fado only here, open daily from 8pm to 1am; music begins at 9:30pm. In the first part of the program, fadistas get all the popular songs out of the way, then settle into their more classic favorites. Cover (credited toward drinks) 10€ ($12).

Praça das Amoreiras. It's open Monday through Saturday from 6pm to 3am. Mixed drinks cost 5€ ($5.75) and up; beer costs 3€ ($3.45) and up. There's no cover. It's open Monday through Friday from 6pm to 3am, Saturday from 9pm to 3am; closed August 1 to 15.

It would take an appraiser years to catalog the stuff filling the walls and ceilings of the **Pavilhão Chines Bar,** Dom Pedro V 89 (℃ **21/342-4729;** tram: 28). An often-kitschy collection of toys, collectibles, and oddities packs several rooms. The main bar has a lovely marquetry top, a touch of class amid the rows of souvenir plates, armies of tin soldiers, bronze Cupids, cartoons of the Great War antagonists, gobs and gaggles of Victoriana, cases of Toby jugs, ceramics of Buddha, Hussars . . . and Popeye. Martini olives are skewered with hand-carved toothpicks. There are two billiard tables and another bar in a rear room. It's open Monday through Friday from 5pm to 2am, Saturday from 6pm to 2am.

Panorama Bar, Rua Latino Coelho 1 (℃ **21/357-5757;** Metro: Picos), occupies the top floor of the Hotel Lisboa Sheraton. The view sweeps across the old and new cities, the River Tejo, and the towns on the river's far bank. A polite uniformed staff serves you amid a decor of chiseled stone and stained glass. Mixed drinks cost 8.50€ to 10€ ($9.80–$12). The bar is open daily from 6pm to 2am.

Many people come to the bar at **Café Alcântara,** Rua Maria Luisa Holstein 15 (© **21/363-7176;** bus: 12 or 18), which is also a restaurant (p. 805). Long and curvy, it has a full-size replica of the *Winged Victory of Samothrace* rearing above it. It's open nightly from 8pm to 3am; there is no cover.

PORT WINE TASTING   A bar devoted exclusively to the drinking and enjoyment of port in all its known types, **Solar do Vinho do Porto,** Rua de São Pedro de Alcântara 45 (© **21/347-5707;** bus: 58 or 100), is at the edge of the Bairro Alto. Owned by the Port Wine Institute, the facility displays many artifacts related to the industry. But the real reason for dropping in is its *lista de vinhos*—there are more than 200 wines from which to choose. Solar is across the street from the upper terminus of the Gloria funicular. It's open Monday through Saturday from 2pm to midnight. A glass of wine costs on average from 1€ to 23€ ($1.15–$26).

LIVE-MUSIC CLUBS

Fusion jazz and mainstream are featured at the appropriately named **Hot Clube de Portugal,** Praça da Alegria 39 (© **21/346-7369;** Metro: Avenida), a smoky subterranean dive. This is one of the city's best jazz clubs, attracting a wide age group from 18 to 50. A beer costs 2.50€ ($2.90), and the cover is 2.50€ to 8€ ($2.90–$9.20).

Havana, Doca de Santo Amaro, Armazem 5 (© **21/397-9893;** Metro: Alcântara), brings the Cuban music craze sweeping Europe to Lisbon. Decorated accordingly, it is both a bar and a restaurant. Of course it plays salsa, but it also plays pop and dance tunes. Palm trees and ceiling fans evoke the Havana of Hemingway days. Most of the patrons are in the 25-to-40 age range. The food is pretty good. Havana is open daily from noon to 2am (bar daily midnight–4am). There's no cover.

Salsa Latina, Gare Maritima de Alcântara, Docas (© **21/395-0550;** bus: 12 and 20), rocks with Latino rhythms, everything from its namesake salsa to the tango and mambo that evoke 1940s movies starring Carmen Miranda. Some nights the music is recorded; at other times the club vibrates to the sound of live acts. The cover for the bar is 8€ to 12€ ($9.20–$14)). The restaurant is open Tuesday through Saturday from 8 to 11:30pm, the bar the same days from 10:30pm to 6:30am.

THE PORTUGUESE RIVIERA: EXCURSIONS ALONG THE COSTA DO SOL

Lisbon's environs are most appealing, and at least 2 or 3 days should be budgeted to take them in. At minimum, your tour should incorporate the former fishing port of Cascais, the headlands at Guincho, and Lord Byron's "glorious Eden" of Sintra. If you have more time, add in the wonders of the pink rococo palace at Queluz or check out the casino or golf at Estoril.

The **Costa do Sol** 🌟🌟🌟 is the string of beach resorts that forms the Portuguese Riviera, along the northern bank of the mouth of the Tejo, west of Lisbon. Many visitors choose to stay in seaside hotels in Estoril or Cascais, near enough to Lisbon to dart in and out of the capital to see the sights or visit the fado clubs. An inexpensive electric train leaving from the Cais do Sodré in Lisbon makes the trip frequently throughout the day and evening, ending its run in Cascais.

Do ride out on the train, even if you don't plan to stay there. Along the way, you'll pass pastel-washed houses with tile roofs and facades of antique blue-and-white *azulejos;* miles of modern apartment blocks; rows of pine, mimosa, and eucalyptus; and, in the background, green hills studded with villas, chalets, and housing developments. The "Sun Coast" is sometimes known as the Costa dos Reis, the "Coast of Kings," because of all the members of Europe's deposed royalty who settled here over the last 60 years—exiled kings, pretenders, marquesses from Italy, princesses from Russia, baronesses from Germany.

ESTORIL 🐟 The first stop is 24km (15 miles) west of Lisbon. This once-chic resort has long basked in its reputation as a playground of monarchs. The **Parque Estoril,** in the town center, is a well-manicured piece of landscaping, a subtropical setting with plants and stands of palm swaying in the breeze. At night, when it's floodlit, you can go for a stroll. At the top of the park sits the **casino,** which offers not only gambling but international floor shows, dancing, and movies.

Across the railroad tracks is the **beach,** where fashionable men and women sun themselves on peppermint-striped canvas chairs along the Tamariz Esplanade. The atmosphere is cosmopolitan and the beach is sandy, unlike the pebbly strand found at Nice. If you don't want to swim in the polluted ocean, you can check in at an oceanfront pool for a plunge.

CASCAIS 🐟 Just 6km (3¾ miles) west of Estoril and 30km (19 miles) west of Lisbon, Cascais has more of a Portuguese atmosphere than Estoril, even though it has been increasingly overbuilt. Apartment houses, new hotels, and some of the best restaurants along the Costa do Sol draw a never-ending stream of visitors every year.

Even so, commercial fishermen still set out in their boats each day and return to the beach with their catches. Auctions of their bounty, called *lotas,* take place on the main square, though a modern hotel has sprouted up in the background. In the small harbor, rainbow-colored fishing boats share space with pleasure craft owned by an international set that flocks to Cascais from early spring until autumn.

The most popular excursion outside Cascais is to the **Boca de Inferno (Mouth of Hell)** 🐟. Reached by heading out on the highway to Guincho, then turning left toward the sea, the Boca deserves its ferocious reputation. Thundering waves sweep in with such power that they long ago carved a wide hole in the cliffs. However, if you should arrive when the sea is calm, you'll certainly wonder why it's called the Mouth of Hell. This place can be a windswept roaring attraction if you don't stumble over too many souvenir hawkers.

The three sandy **beaches** at Cascais are almost as overcrowded as those at Estoril, but the waters here are said to be less polluted. Still, hotel pools remain the safer choice. Though there's a dangerous undertow, the best beach—at least from the standpoint of lying on the sand—is Praia do Guincho, around Cabo da Roca, right outside Cascais. The beach has dunes, and is relatively uncrowded and pollution-free. The continental winds make it a favorite of surfers.

QUELUZ 🐟🐟 From the Estação Rossio in Lisbon, take the Sintra-line train 15km (9¼ miles) northwest to Queluz. Trains depart every 15 minutes (trip time: 30 min.). After leaving the train station in Queluz, take a left turn and follow the signs to the **Palácio de Queluz** 🐟, Largo do Palácio (© **21/435-0039**), a brilliant example of the rococo style in Portugal. Pedro III ordered its construction in 1747, and the work dragged on until 1787. What you see now isn't exactly what you would have seen in the 18th century. Queluz suffered a lot during the French invasions, and almost all of its belongings were transported to Brazil with the royal family. A 1934 fire destroyed a great deal of Queluz, but tasteful reconstruction has restored the lighthearted aura of the 18th century. Inside, you can wander through the queen's dressing room, lined with painted panels depicting a children's romp; the Don Quixote Chamber (Dom Pedro was born here and returned from Brazil to die in the same bed); the Music Room, complete with a French grand pianoforte and an 18th-century English harpsichord; and the mirrored Throne Room adorned with crystal chandeliers. The palace is open Wednesday through Monday (except holidays) from 10am to 5pm. Admission is 4€ ($4.60). It's always free for anyone under 12, and there's free general admission every Sunday morning.

SINTRA ★★★   Sintra, 29km (18 miles) northwest of Lisbon, is a 45-minute train ride from the Estação Rossio in Lisbon. Lord Byron called it a "glorious Eden," and so it remains. Visitors flock here not only to absorb the town's beauty and scenic setting but also to visit two major sights.

Opening onto the central town square, the **Palácio Nacional de Sintra** ★★, Largo da Rainha D. Amélia (*(C)* 21/923-0085), was a royal palace until 1910. Much of it was constructed in the days of Manuel the Fortunate. The palace's two conical chimney towers are the most distinctive landmarks on the Sintra skyline. The Swan Room was a favorite of João I, one of the founding kings of the Aviz dynasty, father of Henry the Navigator, and husband of Philippa of Lancaster. The Room of the Sirens or Mermaids is one of the most elegant in the palace. In the Heraldic or Stag Room, coats-of-arms of aristocratic Portuguese families and hunting scenes are depicted. The palace is rich in paintings and Iberian and Flemish tapestries. But it's at its best when you wander into the tree- and plant-shaded patio and listen to the fountain. Admission is 4€ ($4.60) adults, half price for children 6 to 16, free for children under 6. The palace is open Thursday through Tuesday from 10am to 1pm and 2 to 5pm.

Towering over Sintra, the **Palácio Nacional da Pena** ★★, Estrada de Pena (*(C)* 21/923-0227), sits on a plateau about 450m (1,500 ft.) above sea level. At the top, the castle is a soaring agglomeration of towers, cupolas, and battlements. Crossing a drawbridge, you'll enter the palace proper, whose last royal occupant was Queen Amélia in 1910. Pena has remained much as Amélia left it, which is part of its fascination; it emerges as a rare record of European royal life in the halcyon days preceding World War I. Admission is 4€ ($4.60), free for children under 15. The palace is open October through May, Tuesday through Sunday from 10am to 5:30pm (last admittance at 5pm); June through September, Tuesday through Sunday from 10am to 6:30pm (last admittance 6pm).

2 The Algarve

The Algarve region, at the southwesternmost corner of Europe, is the nation's foremost resort destination. Its coast stretches 160km (100 miles)—all the way from Henry the Navigator's Cape St. Vincent to the border town of Vila Real de Santo António. The varied shore contains sluggish estuaries, sheltered lagoons, low-lying areas where the cluck of the marsh hen can be heard, long sandy spits, and promontories jutting into the whitecapped ocean. Called Al-Gharb by the Moors, the land south of the *serras* (hills) of Monchique and Caldeirão remains a spectacular anomaly that seems more like a transplanted section of North Africa. Inland, nudging the heavily developed shore, the countryside is heavily cultivated with groves of almonds, lemons, oranges, carobs, pomegranates, and figs.

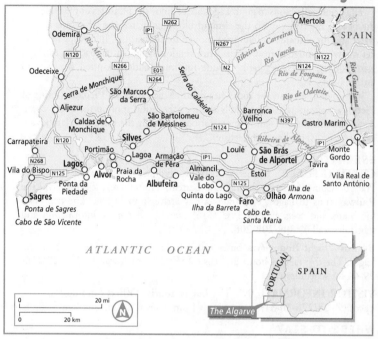

Phoenicians, Greeks, Romans, Visigoths, Moors, and Christians all touched this land. A distinct Arabic flavor prevails in the region's fretwork chimneys, mosquelike cupolas, and whitewashed houses, and some Moorish and even Roman ruins remain. However, much of the historic flavor is gone forever, swallowed by the swarms of dreary high-rise apartment blocks surrounding most towns. Many former fishing villages, now summer resorts, dot the Algarvian coast: Carvoeiro, Albufeira, Olhão, and Portimão. The Atlantic and nearby Mediterranean remain primary sources of life, as they always have been. The marketplaces in the villages sell mats made of *esparto* (a long, coarse grass), copperwork, pottery, and almond and fig sweets that are sometimes shaped like birds and fish.

Both Lagos and Faro make logical home bases, with ample lodging choices, railroad and air connections with Lisbon, and an easy driving range to all the likely destinations along the coast. From Lagos, the road 34km (21 miles) west to Sagres (N-125) generally has minor traffic, while a limited-access highway, the IP1, runs across two-thirds of the region to the Spanish border near Monte Gordo.

LAGOS

Known to the Lusitanians and Romans as Locobriga and to the Moors as Zawaia, Lagos developed as a town dedicated to shipbuilding during the time of Henry the Navigator. Edged by the Costa do Ouro (Golden Coast), the Bay of Sagres at one point in its epic history was big enough to allow 407 warships to maneuver with ease. A port city that has traced its origins back to the Carthaginians, 3 centuries before the birth of Christ, Lagos was well known by the sailors of Admiral Nelson's fleet.

The principal reasons to go to Lagos are to enjoy the pleasures of the table and the beach. Even in winter, the almond blossoms match the whitecaps on the water and the climate is often warm enough for sunbathing. In town, a flea market sprawls through narrow streets, with vendors selling rattan baskets, earthenware pottery, fruits, vegetables, crude furniture, cutlery, knitted shawls, and leather boots.

Just down the coast, the rocky headland of the **Ponta da Piedade (Point of Piety)** ✦ appears. This is arguably the most beautiful spot on the entire coast. Amid the colorful cliffs and secret grottoes carved by the waves are flamboyant examples of Manueline architecture.

ESSENTIALS

GETTING THERE   By Ferry & Train   From Lisbon, take the ferry from Praça do Comércio across the Tagus to Barreiro. From there, the **Southern Line Railway** runs to Lagos. Five trains a day arrive from Lisbon. The trip takes 5½ hours and costs at least 14€ ($16) one-way. For more information and schedules, call ℭ **808/208-208.**

By Bus   Eight **Rodoviária** buses a day make the run between Lisbon and Lagos. The trip takes 4 hours and costs 15€ ($17) each way. Call ℭ **28/276-29-44** for schedules.

VISITOR INFORMATION   The **Lagos Tourist Office,** Sitio de São Joao, Lágos (ℭ **28/276-30-31**), is open daily from 9:30am to 1pm and 2 to 5:30pm.

WHERE TO STAY

Tivoli Lagos ✦   This is a 20th-century castle of Moorish and Portuguese design, with its own ramparts and moats. Standing at the eastern side of the old town, far removed from the beach, this first-class hotel is spread over a hilltop overlooking Lagos. Recently purchased by the Tivoli chain of Lisbon, it will presumably be upgraded over the coming year or two. In the meantime, every room has a view, even if it's of a courtyard with semitropical greenery. Some rooms have ground-level patios, but most are on the upper six floors. The hotel has its own beach club a mile away.

Rua Antonio Crisógono Santos, 8600-678 Lagos. ℭ 28/279-00-79. Fax 28/279-03-45. www.tivolihotels. com. 324 units. 63€–165€ ($72–$190) double; 88€–218€ ($101–$251) suite. Rates include breakfast. AE, DC, MC, V. Free parking outside, 5€ ($5.75) in garage. **Amenities:** 3 restaurants; 2 bars; 3 pools; 3 tennis courts; health club; game room; 24-hr. room service; babysitting; laundry service; dry cleaning. In room: A/C, TV, minibar, hair dryer, safe.

WHERE TO DINE

A Lagosteira PORTUGUESE   A Lagosteira has long been a mecca for knowledgeable diners. Its decor is simple, and there's a small bar on one side. From the a la carte menu, the best openers for a big meal are classic Algarvian fish soup and savory clams Lagosteira style. After the fishy beginning, you might happily move on to a tender sirloin steak grilled over an open fire. Lobster is also a specialty. The selection of vintage wines complements the food.

Rua do 1 de Maio 20. ℭ 28/276-24-86. Reservations recommended. Main courses 7€–14€ ($8–$16). AE, DC, MC, V. Mon–Fri 12:30–3pm and daily 6:30–11pm. Closed Jan 10–Feb 10.

Don Sebastião ✦ PORTUGUESE   This rustically decorated tavern on the main pedestrian street is one of the finest dining choices in Lagos. Portuguese-owned and -operated, it offers a varied menu of local specialties. Options include lip-smacking pork chops with figs, succulent shellfish dishes like clams and shrimp cooked with savory spices, and grills. Live lobsters are kept on the premises. One of the best selections of Portuguese vintage wines in town accompanies the filling, tasty meals. In summer, outdoor dining is available.

Rua do 25 de Abril 20. ℰ **28/276-27-95.** Reservations recommended. Main courses 7€–25€ ($8–$29). Daily noon–10pm. Closed Dec 24–26 and Dec 31—Jan 2.

SEEING THE SIGHTS

Antigo Mercado de Escravos (Old Customs House)   The Old Customs House, now in ruins, stands as a painful reminder of the age of exploration. The arcaded slave market, the only one of its kind in Europe, looks peaceful today, but under its four Romanesque arches captives taken from their homelands were sold to the highest bidders. The house opens onto a peaceful square dominated by a statue of Henry the Navigator.

Praça do Infante Dom Henríques. Free admission. Daily 24 hr.

Igreja de Santo António (Church of St. Anthony) ⭑   Just off the waterfront sits this 18th-century church. Of special note are the rococo gilt carvings of the altar. They were damaged in the 1755 earthquake but subsequently restored. What you see represents the work of many artisans—at times, each apparently pursuing a different theme.

Rua General Alberto Carlos Silveira. ℰ **28/276-23-01.** Free admission. Tues–Sun 9:30am–12:30pm and 2–5pm.

Museu Municipal Dr. José Formosinho (Municipal Museum)   Replicas of the fret-cut chimneys of the Algarve are on view, along with three-dimensional cork carvings, 16th-century vestments, ceramics, 17th-century embroidery, ecclesiastical sculpture, a painting gallery, weapons, minerals, and a coin collection. In the archaeological wing are Neolithic artifacts, as well as Roman mosaics found at Boca do Rio near Budens, fragments of statuary and columns, and other remains of antiquity from excavations along the Algarve.

Rua General Alberto Carlos Silveira. ℰ **28/276-23-01.** Admission 2€ ($2.30) adults, children 11–14 1€ ($1.15). Tues–Sun 9:30am–noon and 2–5pm. Closed holidays.

PLAYING GOLF

Parque da Floresta, Budens, Vale do Poco, 8650 Vila do Bispo (ℰ **282-69-0054**), lies 16km (10 miles) west of Lagos, just inland from the fishing hamlet of Salema. Designed by Spanish architect Pepe Gancedo and built as the centerpiece of a complex of holiday villas, it offers sweeping views. Some shots must be driven over vineyards and others over ravines, creeks, and gardens. Critics of the course have cited its rough grading and rocky terrain. Greens fees are 24€ to 42€ ($28–$48) for 9 holes, and 40€ to 70€ ($46–$81) for 18. Some 4km (2½ miles) west of Lagos is the par-71 **Palmares** course (ℰ **28/276-2961**), designed by Frank Pennink with many differences in altitude. Some fairways require driving a ball across railroad tracks, over small ravines, or around groves of palm, fig, and almond trees. The view from the 17th green is among the most dramatic of any golf course on the Algarve. Greens fees are 48€ to 75€ ($55–$86), depending on the season.

SAGRES ⭑⭑: "THE END OF THE WORLD"

At the extreme southwestern corner of Europe—once called *o fim do mundo* (the end of the world)—Sagres is a rocky escarpment jutting into the Atlantic Ocean. From here, Henry the Navigator, the Infante of Sagres, launched Portugal and the rest of Europe on the seas of exploration. Here he established his school of navigation, where Magellan, Diaz, Cabral, and Vasco da Gama apprenticed. A virtual ascetic, Henry brought together the best navigators, cartographers, geographers, scholars, sailors, and builders; infused them with his rigorous devotion; and methodically set Portuguese caravels upon the Sea of Darkness.

ESSENTIALS
GETTING THERE   **By Ferry & Train**   From Lisbon's Praça do Comércio, you can take a ferry across the Tagus to Barreiro. From there, take the Southern Line Railway to Lagos. For information and schedules, call ℂ **21/888-40-25.** From Lagos, buses go to Sagres.

By Bus   Ten Rodoviária buses (ℂ **28/276-29-44**) run hourly from Lagos to Sagres each day. The trip time is 1 hour, and a one-way ticket costs 2.60€ ($3).

By Car   From Lagos, drive west on Route 125 to Vila do Bispo, and then head south along Route 268 to Sagres

VISITOR INFORMATION   The **Sagres Tourist Office,** Plaza da Republica, Sagres (ℂ **28/262-00-03**), is open Tuesday through Saturday from 10am to 12:30pm and 1:30 to 6:30pm.

WHERE TO STAY
Moderate
Hotel da Baleeira   In a ship's-bow position, Hotel da Baleeira is designed like a first-class *baleeira* (whaleboat) and spread out above the fishing port, lying 50m (164 ft.) from a good beach. The largest hotel on this land projection, it offers guest rooms with sea-view balconies and a private beach. The number of its rooms has nearly doubled in recent years; the older ones are quite small, and some have linoleum floors. The bathrooms are also tiny and equipped with shower-tub combinations.

Sítio da Baleeira, Sagres, 8650 Vila do Bispo. ℂ **28/262-42-12.** Fax 28/262-44-25. www.sagres.net/sagres/ baleeira/index.htm. 122 units. 60€–122€ ($69–$140) double. Rates include breakfast. AE, DC, MC, V. Free parking. **Amenities:** Restaurant; snack bar; bar; saltwater pool; tennis court; car rental; limited room service; babysitting; laundry service. *In room:* TV, safe.

Pousada do Infante ★★   Pousada do Infante, the best address in Sagres, seems like a monastery built by ascetic monks who wanted to commune with nature. You'll be charmed by the rugged beauty of the rocky cliffs, the pounding surf, and the sense of the ocean's infinity. Built in 1960, the glistening white government-owned tourist inn spreads along the edge of a cliff that projects rather daringly over the sea. It boasts a long colonnade of arches with an extended stone terrace set with garden furniture, plus a second floor of accommodations with private balconies. Each midsize guest room is furnished with traditional pieces. Room nos. 1 to 12 are the most desirable. All are equipped with neatly kept bathrooms containing shower-tub combinations.

The public rooms are generously proportioned, gleaming with marble and decorated with fine tapestries depicting the exploits of Henry the Navigator. Large velvet couches flank the fireplace. An official annex, the Fortaleza do Beliche (see "Where to Dine," below), offers less luxurious rooms.

Ponta da Atalaia, 8650-385 Sagres. ℂ **28/262-02-40.** Fax 28/262-42-25. www.pousadas.pt. 39 units. Sun–Thurs 97€–139€ ($112–$160) double, Fri–Sat 107€–152€ ($123–$175) double; Sun–Thurs 135€–184€ ($155–$212) suite, Fri–Sat 148€–204€ ($170–$235) suite. Rates include breakfast. AE, DC, MC, V. Free parking. **Amenities:** Restaurant; bar; tennis court; riding stables; car rental; limited room service; babysitting; laundry service. *In room:* A/C, TV, minibar, hair dryer, safe.

WHERE TO DINE

Fortaleza do Beliche ★ PORTUGUESE/INTERNATIONAL   This establishment occupies the much-restored remnants of a medieval fortress built around the heyday of Henry the Navigator. It's on a sandy, rocky stretch of the coastal road between Sagres and the southwesternmost tip of Portugal, Cabo de São Vicente. All four dining rooms enjoy partial, or angled, views of the nearby sea, but one offers a wider panorama. The menu offerings are simple, straightforward, and flavorful. They include *caldo verde* (soup with ham hocks, greens, and potatoes); tasty fish soup; fried or grilled squid; grilled swordfish; well-prepared but uncomplicated versions of veal, pork, and beef; and whatever fresh fish is available from the local market.

In addition to its restaurant, the establishment maintains four guest rooms, each with TV and telephone. Doubles cost 90€ ($104) Sunday through Thursday and 102€ ($117) Friday and Saturday, including breakfast. The place is an official annex of the more expensive, more luxurious Pousada do Infante (see "Where to Stay," above). Parking is free.

Fortaleza do Beliche, Vila do Bispo, 8650 Sagres. ☎ **28/262-41-24.** Main courses 10€–14€ ($12–$16); fixed-price menu 22€ ($25). AE, MC, V. Daily 1–2:30pm and 7:30–9:30pm. Closed Nov 15–Feb 15. From Sagres, drive west for 5km (3 miles) along the coastal road, following signs to Cabo de São Vicente.

EXPLORING THE AREA

Both the Cabo de São Vicente and Sagres (especially from the terrace of the Pousada) offer unobstructed views of sunsets over the Atlantic. To the ancient world, the cape was the last explored point, although in time the Phoenicians pushed beyond it. Many mariners thought that when the sun sank beyond the cape, it plunged over the edge of the world, and thus to venture around the promontory was to face the demons of the unknown.

Today, at the reconstructed site of Henry's windswept fortress on Europe's land's end, is a huge stone compass dial, Venta de Rosa, that Henry is alleged to have used in the naval studies pursued at Sagres. Housed in the fortress is a small museum of minor interest that documents some of the area's history. Admission is 1.35€ ($1.55), and it's open Tuesday through Sunday from 10am to noon and 2 to 6pm. At a simple chapel, restored in 1960, sailors are said to have prayed for help before setting out into uncharted waters. The chapel is closed to the public.

The promontory of **Cabo de São Vicente** ★★ is 5km (3 miles) away. According to legend, the body of St. Vincent arrived mysteriously here on a boat guided by ravens, hence the name. Others claim that the body of the patron saint, murdered at Valencia, Spain, washed up on Lisbon's shore. A lighthouse, the second most powerful in Europe, beams light 100km (60 miles) across the ocean. It's generally open daily from 8am to noon and 2 to 9pm, but you must get permission from the gatekeeper to climb it. Here, seagulls glide on the air currents, and on the approach, a few goats graze on a hill where even the trees are bent from the gusty winds.

No buses connect the cape with Sagres. You must go by car.

OUTDOOR ACTIVITIES

BEACHES   Many beaches fringe the peninsula—some attracting nude bathers. **Mareta,** at the bottom of the road leading from the center of town toward the water, is not only the best, but the most popular. Rock formations can be seen jutting far out into the Atlantic. East of town is **Tonel,** also a good sandy beach. The beaches west of town, **Praia de Baleeira** and **Praia de Martinhal,** are better for windsurfing than for swimming.

EXPLORING   If you'd like to rent a **bike** to explore the cape, go to **Turinfo,** Praça da República, Sagres (© **28/262-00-03**). The charge is 6€ ($6.90) for 4 hours and 9.50€ ($11) for a full day. Turinfo's **Jeep tours** of the natural preserve of the cape, including lunch, cost 38€ ($44).

PRAIA DA ROCHA

En route to Praia da Rocha, off N-125 between Lagos and Portimão, 18km (11 miles) away, you'll find several good beaches and rocky coves, particularly at **Praia dos Três Irmãos** and **Alvor.** But the most popular seaside resort on the Algarve is the creamy yellow beach of Praia da Rocha. At the outbreak of World War II there were only two small hotels on the Red Coast, but nowadays Praia da Rocha is booming, as many have been enchanted by the spell cast by its shoreline and climate.

The area is named Praia da Rocha, the "Beach of the Rock," because of its sculptural rock formations. At the end of the mussel-encrusted cliff, where the Arcade flows into the sea, are the ruins of the **Fort of St. Catarina,** whose location offers many views of Ferragudo (the village adjacent to Portimão) and of the bay.

To reach Praia da Rocha from Portimão, you can catch a bus for the 2.5km (1½-mile) trip south. Service is frequent. Algarve buses aren't numbered but are marked by their final destination, such as PRAIA DA ROCHA.

WHERE TO STAY

Algarve Hotel Casino ★★★   The leading hotel at the resort is strictly for those who love glitter and glamour and don't object to the prices. With a vast staff at your beck and call, you'll be well provided for in this elongated block of rooms poised securely on the top ledge of a cliff.

The midsize to spacious guest rooms have white walls, colored ceilings, intricate tile floors, mirrored entryways, indirect lighting, balconies with garden furniture, and bathrooms with separate shower-tub combinations. Many are vaguely Moorish in design, and many have terraces opening onto the sea. The Yachting, Oriental, Presidential, and Miradouro suites are decorative tours de force. There are 24 nonsmoking rooms and 10 rooms for those with limited mobility.

Av. Tomás Cabreira, Praia da Rocha, 8500-802 Portimão. © **28/240-20-00.** Fax 28/240-20-99. www. solverde.pt. 209 units. 117€–264€ ($135–$304) double; 183€–488€ ($210–$561) suite. Rates include breakfast. AE, DC, MC, V. Free parking on street, 5€ ($5.75) in garage. **Amenities:** 3 restaurants; 5 bars; 2 pools; 2 tennis courts; sauna; watersports; salon; barber shop; boutiques; 24-hr. room service; babysitting; laundry; dry cleaning; 10 rooms for those with limited mobility. *In room:* A/C, TV, dataport, minibar, hair dryer, safe.

Bela Vista ★ *Finds*   Bela Vista is an old Moorish-style mansion built in 1916 as a wealthy family's summer home. It has a minaret-type tower at one end and a statue of the Virgin set into one of the building's corners. Since 1934, it has been a special kind of hotel, ideal for those who respond to the architecture of the past; you'll need to make a reservation way in advance. The guest rooms facing the sea, the former master bedrooms, are the most desirable. All come with neatly kept bathrooms equipped with shower-tub combinations. Decorations vary from crystal sconces to an inset tile shrine to the Virgin Mary. The hotel is on the ocean, atop its own palisade, with access to a sandy cove where you can swim. The villa is white with a terra-cotta tile roof, a landmark for fishermen bringing in their boats at sundown. It's flanked by the owner's home and a simple cliff-edge annex shaded by palm trees.

Av. Tomás Cabreira, Praia da Rocha, 8500-802 Portimão. © **28/245-04-80.** Fax 28/241-53-69. 14 units. 50€–115€ ($58–$132) double; 75€–170€ ($86–$196) suite. Rates include breakfast. AE, DC, MC, V. Free parking. **Amenities:** Breakfast room; bar; limited room service; laundry service. *In room:* TV, minibar, safe.

WHERE TO DINE

Titanic ★★ INTERNATIONAL   Complete with gilt and crystal, the 100-seat air-conditioned Titanic is the most elegant restaurant in town. Its open kitchen serves the best food in Praia da Rocha, including shellfish and flambé dishes. Despite the name, it's not on —or in, thank goodness—the water, but in a modern residential complex. You can dine very well here on such appealing dishes as the fish of the day, pork filet with mushrooms, prawns *a la plancha* (grilled), Chinese fondue, or excellent sole Algarve. Service is among the best at the resort.

In the Edifício Colúmbia, Rua Eng. Francisco Bivar. ℂ **28/242-23-71.** Reservations recommended, especially in summer. Main courses 9€–24€ ($10–$28). AE, DC, MC, V. Daily 7pm–midnight. Closed Nov 27–Dec 27.

PLAYING GOLF

Vale de Pinta (Pestana Golf), Praia do Carvoeiro (ℂ **28/234-0900),** are twin par-72 courses, sharing a clubhouse and staff. They're set amid a landscape of tawny rocks and arid hillocks, and they route their players through groves of twisted olive, almond, carob, and fig trees. Views from the fairways, designed in 1992 by Californian Ronald Fream, sweep over the low masses of the Monchique mountains, close to the beach resort of Carvoeiro. Experts cite the layouts of these two courses as some of the most varied sets of challenges in the competitive world of Portuguese golf. Clusters of bunkers, barrier walls, and abrupt changes in elevation make the course complicated. Greens fees are 50€ to 90€ ($58–$104).

PRAIA DOS TRÊS IRMÃOS & ALVOR ★★

You can visit **Praia dos Três Irmãos (Beach of the Three Brothers)** for its beach, even if you prefer not to stay overnight. It's just a 5km (3-mile) drive southwest of Portimão, or you can reach it (or the tourist development at Alvor) by bus. Service is frequent throughout the day. At Praia dos Três Irmãos, you'll find 14km (8¾ miles) of golden sand, broken only by an occasional crag riddled with arched passages. Snorkelers and scuba divers have discovered this beach and enjoy exploring its undersea grottoes and shore-side cave.

Praia dos Três Irmãos's neighbor is the whitewashed fishing village of **Alvor,** where Portuguese and Moorish arts and traditions have mingled since the Arabs gave up their 500 years of occupation. Alvor was a favorite coastal haunt of João II. The summer hordes descend on the long strip of sandy beach here. It's not the best beach in the area, but at least you'll have ample space.

WHERE TO STAY

Le Meridien Penina ★★★   The first deluxe hotel on the Algarve between Portimão and Lagos continues to be a major sporting mecca. Most rooms contain picture windows and honeycomb balconies, with views of the golf course and pool or vistas of the Monchique hills. Standard rooms are spacious and contain good-size Portuguese provincial spool beds; the so-called attic rooms have the most charm, with French doors opening onto terraces. Facilities include three championship golf courses (one 18-hole and two 9-hole) and a private beach.

Estrada Nacional 125, 8501-952 Portimão. ℂ **800/225-5843** in the U.S., or 28/242-02-00. Fax 28/242-03-00. www.lemeridien-penina.com. 196 units. 145€–325€ ($167–$374) double; 275€–715€ ($316–$822) suite. 1 child 3–11 stays free in parent's room. Rates include breakfast. AE, DC, MC, V. Free parking. **Amenities:** 4 restaurants; 2 bars; pool; 3 golf courses; 6 tennis courts; sauna; watersports; nursery for children; salon; limited room service; babysitting; laundry service. *In room:* A/C, TV, dataport, minibar, hair dryer, safe.

Pestana Carlton Alvor ★★   On a landscaped hillcrest, this citadel of hedonism is so self-contained that you may never stray from the premises. Rooms are decorated in a classically modern style, and most contain oversize beds. Many have private balconies where guests can eat breakfast with a view of the Bay of Lagos. Avoid those in the rear with so-so views, small balconies, and Murphy beds. The bi-level main dining room boasts three glass walls so every guest has an ocean view. The beach is accessible by elevator. Horseback riding and water-skiing are just some of the offered activities.

Praia dos Três Irmãos, Alvor, 8501-904 Portimão. (℃ 28/240-09-00. Fax 28/240-09-99. www.pestana.com. 198 units. 239€–299€ ($275–$344) double; 381€–449€ ($438–$516) suite. Rates include buffet breakfast. AE, DC, MC, V. Free parking. **Amenities:** 3 restaurants; 2 bars; 3 pools; 7 tennis courts; health club; sauna; solarium; water-skiing; horseback riding; salon; 24-hr. room service; babysitting; laundry service. *In room:* A/C, TV, dataport, minibar, hair dryer, safe.

WHERE TO DINE

O Búzio ★ INTERNATIONAL   Restaurante O Búzio stands at the end of a road encircling a resort development dotted with private condos and exotic shrubbery. In summer, so many cars line the narrow blacktop road that you'll probably need to park near the resort's entrance and then walk downhill to the restaurant.

Dinner is served in a room whose blue curtains reflect the shimmering ocean at the bottom of the cliffs. Your meal might include excellent fish soup, refreshing gazpacho, or *carre de borrego Serra de Estrêla* (gratiné of roast rack of lamb with garlic, butter, and mustard). Other good choices are Italian pasta dishes, boiled or grilled fish of the day, flavorful pepper steak, and lamb kabobs with saffron-flavored rice. There's seating for 50 inside and for almost as many on the sea-view terrace. There's an extensive wine cellar.

Aldeamento da Prainha, Praia dos Três Irmãos. (℃ 28/245-87-72. Reservations recommended. Main courses 9.25€–21€ ($11–$24). AE, DC, MC, V. Daily 7–10:30pm. Closed Dec. 15–Jan 7.

PLAYING GOLF

Penina, Apartado 146 (℃ 28/242-0200), lies 5km (3 miles) west of Portimão, farther west than many of the other great golf courses of the Algarve. Completed in 1966, it was one of the first courses built in the area. It is the acknowledged masterpiece of British designer Sir Henry Cotton. It occupies what was once a network of marshy rice paddies, on level terrain that critics said was unsuited for anything except wetlands. The solution involved planting groves of eucalyptus (350,000 trees in all), which grew quickly in the muddy soil, eventually drying it out enough to bulldoze dozens of water traps and a labyrinth of fairways and greens. The course wraps itself around a luxury hotel (Le Meridien Penina, reviewed above). Greens fees for the 18-hole course are 60€ to 70€ ($69–$81); for either of the 9-hole courses, they're 35€ ($40).

ALBUFEIRA ★

This cliff-side town, once a fishing village, is the St-Tropez of the Algarve. Sunshine, beaches, and the lazy days they inspire make it a haven for young people and artists, though local old-timers still regard the tourist invasion that began in the late 1960s with ambivalence. Some residents open the doors of their cottages to those seeking a place to stay. Travelers without the money often sleep in tents on the cliff or under the sky.

The big, bustling resort has the characteristics of a North African seaside community. Its streets are steep, and villas are staggered up and down the hillside. Albufeira rises above a sickle-shaped beach that shines in the sunlight. A rocky, grotto-filled bluff separates the strip used by the sunbathers from the working beach, where brightly painted fishing boats are drawn up on the sand. Beach access is through a passageway tunneled through the rock.

ESSENTIALS

GETTING THERE **By Train** Trains run between Albufeira and Faro (see below), which has good connections to Lisbon. For schedule information, call ② **28/957-26-91.** The train station lies 6.5km (4 miles) from the center. Buses from the station to the resort run every 30 minutes; the fare is 1€ ($1.15) one-way.

By Bus Buses run between Albufeira and Faro every hour. Trip time is 1 hour, and a one-way ticket costs 3.30€ ($3.80). Seven buses per day make the 1-hour trip from Portimão to Albufeira. It costs 3.50€ ($4) one-way. For information and schedules, call ② **28/958-97-55.**

By Car From east or west, take the main coastal route, N125. Albufeira also lies near the point where the express highway from the north, N264, feeds into the Algarve. The town is well signposted in all directions. Take Route 595 to reach Albufeira and the water.

VISITOR INFORMATION The **Tourist Information Office** is at Rua do 5 de Outubro (② **28/958-52-79**). From July to September, hours are daily from 9:30am to 7pm; October to June, they're from 10am to 5:30pm.

WHERE TO STAY

Hotel BoaVista Built in the Algarvian style, the Residence of the Good View sits high above the sea outside the center, some 450m (1,476 ft.) from a good beach. The units open onto balconies, some of which afford views over orange-tile-roofed whitewashed cottages to the bay below. Traditional wicker-wood decor matches the carpets and ceramics, and bathrooms contain shower-tub combinations.

Rua Samora Barros 20, Albufeira. ② **28/958-91-75.** Fax 28/958-91-80. www.hotelboavista.pt. 85 units. 57€–133€ ($66–$153) double; 101€–230€ ($116–$265) suite. Rates include breakfast. AE, DC, MC, V. Limited free parking on street. **Amenities:** 2 restaurants; 2 bars; pool; sauna; car rental; limited room service; babysitting; laundry service. *In room:* A/C, TV, minibar, safe.

Hotel Montechoro ✦ The leading choice at Montechoro, just more than 3km (1¾ miles) northeast of the center of Albufeira, looks like a hotel you might encounter in North Africa. It's a fully equipped, self-contained, government-rated four-star resort complex, with such ample facilities that you might get lost—which is just as well because the one thing it lacks is a beach. The spacious rooms afford views of the countryside and are generally done in modern style, with excellent beds and tidily kept bathrooms equipped with shower-tub combinations.

Rua Alexandre O'Neill (Apdo. 928), 8201-912 Albufeira. ② **28/958-94-23.** Fax 28/958-99-47. hotel@grupomontechoro.com. 362 units. 83€–171€ ($95–$197) double; 124€–256€ ($143–$294) suite. Rates include buffet breakfast. AE, DC, MC, V. Free parking. **Amenities:** 2 restaurants; 2 bars; pool; 8 tennis courts; 2 squash courts; sauna; car rental; 24-hr. room service; babysitting; laundry service; dry cleaning. *In room:* A/C, TV, dataport, hair dryer, safe.

WHERE TO DINE

O Cabaz da Praia ✦ FRENCH/PORTUGUESE The Beach Basket, near the Hotel Sol e Mar, sits on a colorful little square near the Church of São Sebastião. In a former fishermen's cottage, the restaurant has an inviting ambience and good food. It has a large, sheltered terrace and a view over the main Albufeira beach. Main courses, including such justifiable favorites as cassoulet of seafood, salade océane, monkfish with mango sauce, and beef filet with garlic and white-wine sauce, are served with a selection of fresh vegetables. The restaurant is renowned for its lemon meringue pie and soufflés.

Praça Miguel Bombarda 7. ☎ 28/951-21-37. Reservations recommended. Main courses 19€–24€ ($22–$28). AE, MC, V. Fri–Wed noon–2pm and 7:30–11pm.

VALE DO LOBO ✦

Almancil, 13km (8 miles) west of Faro and 24km (15 miles) east along N-125 from Albufeira, is a small market town of little interest, yet it's a center for two of the most exclusive tourist developments along the Algarve: **Vale do Lobo,** 6km (3¾ miles) southeast of Almancil, and **Quinta do Lago,** 10km (6¼ miles) southeast of town. Both are golfers' paradises.

WHERE TO STAY

Le Méridien Dona Filipa ★★★ *Kids* A citadel of ostentatious living, Dona Filipa is a deluxe golf hotel with such touches as gold-painted palms holding up the ceiling. The grounds are impressive, embracing 180 hectares (445 acres) of rugged coastline with steep cliffs, inlets, and sandy bays. The hotel's exterior is comparatively uninspired, but Duarte Pinto Coelho lavished the interior with green silk banquettes, marble fireplaces, Portuguese ceramic lamps, and old prints over baroque-style love seats. The midsize to spacious guest rooms are handsomely decorated with antiques, rustic accessories, and handmade rugs. Most have balconies and twin beds. Bathrooms have dual basins, shower-tub combinations, and robes.

Vale do Lobo, 8135-901 Almancil. ☎ 28/935-72-00. Fax 28/935-72-00. www.lemeridien-donafilipa.com. 154 units. 296€–414€ ($340–$476) double; 446€–626€ ($513–$720) junior suite; 610€–930€ ($702–$1,070) deluxe suite. Rates include breakfast. AE, DC, MC, V. Free parking. **Amenities:** 2 restaurants; bar; 2 pools; golf nearby; 3 tennis courts; "village" for children; salon; 24-hr. room service; babysitting; laundry service. *In room:* A/C, TV, dataport, minibar, hair dryer, safe.

Quinta do Lago ★★★ A pocket of the high life since 1986, Quinta do Lago is a sprawling 800-hectare (1,976-acre) estate that contains some private plots beside the Ria Formosa estuary. The hotel is an investment by Prince Faisal of Saudi Arabia, who has wisely turned over management to the Orient Express hotel chain. Its riding center and 27-hole golf course are among the best in Europe.

The estate's contemporary Mediterranean-style buildings rise three to six floors. The luxurious hotel rooms overlook a saltwater lake and feature modern comforts. Decorated with thick carpeting and pastel fabrics, the guest rooms are generally spacious, with tile or marble bathrooms equipped with shower-tub combinations. Rooms are decorated with contemporary art and light-wood furniture, and the balconies open onto views of the estuary. There are 70 nonsmoking rooms and 2 rooms for those with limited mobility.

Quinta do Lago, 8135-024 Almancil. ☎ 800/223-6800 in the U.S., or 28/935-03-50. Fax 28/939-49-05. www.quintadolagohotel.com. 141 units. 190€–510€ ($219–$587) double; 295€–565€ ($339–$650) junior suite. Rates include breakfast. AE, DC, MC, V. Free parking. **Amenities:** 2 restaurants; bar; 2 pools; 2 tennis courts; health club; sauna; concierge; car rental; business center; 24-hr. room service; massage; babysitting; laundry service. *In room:* A/C, TV, dataport, minibar, hair dryer, safe.

WHERE TO DINE

Casa Velha ★★★ FRENCH Casa Velha, an excellent dining choice, is not part of the nearby Quinta do Lago resort. On a hillside behind its massive neighbor, it overlooks the resort's lake from the premises of a century-old farmhouse that has functioned as a restaurant since the early 1960s. The cuisine is mainly

French, with a scattering of Portuguese and international dishes. Start with foie gras or marinated lobster salad. Specialties include a salad of chicken livers and gizzards with leeks and vinaigrette, and lobster salad flavored with an infusion of vanilla. Other choices are carefully flavored preparations of sea bass, filet of sole, and breast of duck with 12 spices.

Quinta do Lago. (© **28/939-49-83**. Reservations recommended. Main courses 15€–28€ ($17–$32). AE, MC, V. Mon–Sat 7:30–10:30pm.

Ermitage ★ ITALIAN/SWISS/INTERNATIONAL   Surrounded by gardens and flowering vines, the 18th-century farmhouse housing this homey restaurant has fireplaces for winter and a dining terrace for warm days. This is serious food, with such starters as goose-liver terrine with blackberry sauce and shrimp, and spinach-stuffed ravioli surrounded with four other pastas and sauces. Main courses include grilled fish of the day with hollandaise and filet of monkfish with prawn-and-curry sauce.

Estrada Almancil-Vale do Lobo. (© **28/939-43-29**. Reservations recommended. Main courses 26€–32€ ($30–$37); fixed-price menus 65€ ($75). AE, MC, V. Tues–Sun 7–10:30pm. Closed 2 weeks in Jan and 3 weeks in Dec. Drive about 3km (1¾ miles) from Almancil, following signs to Vale do Lobo.

PLAYING GOLF

Visit www.algarvegolf.net for more information on courses in the Algarve region. **Vale do Lobo,** 8135 Almancil (© **28/939-3939**), has played an important role in establishing Portugal's image as a golfer's mecca. Its name, which means Valley of the Wolf, suggests some forlorn spot set amid bleak terrain, but this course is hardly that. Originally designed by British golfer Henry Cotton as three 9-hole courses, the courses have been reconfigured into the 18-hole Oceanfront Course and the 18-hole Royal Course. Some of the long shots along both of these courses require driving the ball over ravines, where variable winds make a straight shot difficult. Greens fees, depending on the day of the week and other factors, range from 55€ to 69€ ($63–$79) for 9 holes to 115€ to 135€ ($132–$155) for 18 holes. From Almancil, drive 4km (2½ miles) south of town, following signs to Vale do Lobo.

Since opening in 1991, **Vila Sol,** Alto do Semino (© **28/930-0505**), has been judged as having the best fairways and the boldest and most inventive contours of any course in the Algarve. Designed by English architect Donald Steel, it's part of a 145-hectare (362-acre) residential estate. Great care was taken in allowing the terrain's natural contours to determine the layout of the fairways and greens. Golfers especially praise the configuration of holes 6, 8, and 14, which collectively manage to funnel golf balls around and over ponds, creek beds, and pine groves in nerve-racking order. Par is 72. Greens fees are 35€ to 115€ ($40–$132).

The most famous and sought-after of these three golf courses is the **Vilam-oura Old Course,** sometimes called Vilamoura I (© **28/931-0341**), laid out in 1969 by noted English architect Frank Pennink. Its design, texture, and conception are the most English of south Portugal's golf courses. The course is invariably cited for its beauty, its lushness, and the maturity of its trees and shrubberies. Though some of its holes are almost annoyingly difficult (four of them are par-5s), the course is among the most consistently crowded on the Algarve. Par is 73, and greens fees are 110€ ($127).

Quinta do Lago resort (p. 828) also has superb facilities and is one of the most elegant "tourist estates" on the Algarve. This pine-covered beachfront property has been *the* retreat for everybody from movie stars to European presidents. The resort's 27 superb holes of golf are a potent lure.

Of the four golf courses that undulate across the massive Quinta do Lago development, the par-72 **São Lourenço** ⊛⊛ (© **28/939-6522**) is the most challenging and prestigious. Set amid the grassy wetlands of the Rio Formosa Nature Reserve, home to millions of waterfowl, its contours were crafted by American golf designers William (Rocky) Roquemore and Joe Lee. In 1997, *Golf World* magazine voted it the second-most-desirable course in continental Europe. Although the course lies within the confines of Quinta do Logo, it's closely associated with Le Meridien Dona Felipa Hotel in Vale do Lobo, 7km (4¼ miles) to the west. Many long drives, especially those aimed at the 17th and 18th holes, soar over the waters of a saltwater lagoon. Greens fees are 75€ ($86) for 9 holes and 150€ ($173) for 18 holes.

FARO ⊛

Loved by the Romans and later by the Moors, Faro is the principal city of the Algarve. Since Afonso III drove out the Moors for the last time in 1266, Faro has been Portuguese. On its outskirts, an international jet airport brings in thousands of visitors every summer. The airport, currently being expanded, with new access roads, has done more than anything else to speed tourism not only to Faro but also to the entire Algarve.

ESSENTIALS
GETTING THERE   By Plane   Jet service makes it possible to reach Faro from Lisbon in 30 minutes. For flight information, call the **Faro airport** (© **28/ 980-08-01** or 28/980-08-00). You can take bus no. 14 or 16 from the airport to the railway station in Faro for 1.10€ ($1.25). The bus operates every 35 minutes daily from 7:10am to 7:45pm.

By Train   Trains arrive from Lisbon five times a day. The trip takes 5 hours and costs 14€ ($16) one-way. For rail information in Faro, call the train station at Largo da Estação (© **28/980-30-89**). For information in Lisbon, dial © **808/ 208-208.**

By Bus   Buses arrive every 5 hours from Lisbon. The journey takes 3½ hours. The bus station is on Avenida da República 5 (© **28/989-97-61**); a one-way ticket costs 15€ ($17).

By Car   From the west, Route 125 runs into Faro and beyond. From the Spanish border, pick up N125 west.

VISITOR INFORMATION   The **Tourist Office** is at Rua da Misericórdia 8–12 (© **28/980-36-04**) or at the airport © **28/981-85-82.**

WHERE TO STAY
Eva ⊛   Eva dominates the harbor like a fortress. It's a modern, eight-story hotel that occupies an entire side of the yacht-clogged harbor. The hotel was beginning to look worn, but a rejuvenation in 1996 perked it up. There are direct sea views from most of the midsize guest rooms, which are furnished in a restrained, even austere style. The better rooms have large balconies and open onto the water. All units are equipped with well-maintained bathrooms containing shower-tub combinations. Three rooms are available for those with limited mobility. Eva's best features are its penthouse restaurant and rooftop pool, supported on 16 posts, with sun terraces and a bar.

Av. da República, 8000-078 Faro. © 28/900-10-00. Fax 28/900-10-02. 148 units. 90€–133€ ($104–$153) double; 133€–213€ ($153–$245) suite. Rates include breakfast. AE, DC, MC, V. Limited free parking available on street. **Amenities:** 2 restaurants; 3 bars; pool; salon; 24-hr. room service; babysitting; laundry service. *In room:* A/C, TV, minibar, hair dryer, safe.

WHERE TO DINE

Adega Nortenha *Value* PORTUGUESE   It's hardly a deluxe choice, but if you gravitate to simple regional food served at an affordable price, check out this little eatery. It offers one of the town's best food values. Fresh tuna steak is a delicious choice, as is the roast lamb, which is herb flavored and perfumed with garlic. A mixture of bits of seafood cooked with chunks of pork makes for a savory cataplana casserole. The service is friendly and efficient, and locals swear by this one. The decoration is in the typical Algarvian style with a balcony.

Praça Ferreira de Almeida 25. © 28/982-27-09. Main courses 5.50€–11€ ($6.35–$12). AE, DC, MC, V. Daily noon–3pm and 7–10pm.

Dois Irmãos PORTUGUESE   This popular bistro, founded in 1925, offers a no-nonsense atmosphere and has many devotees. The menu is as modest as the establishment and its prices, but you get a good choice of fresh grilled fish and shellfish dishes. Ignore the paper napkins and concentrate on the fine kettle of fish before you. Clams in savory sauce are a justifiable favorite, and sole is regularly featured—but, of course, everything depends on the catch of the day. Service is slow but amiable.

Largo do Terreiro do Bispo 13–15. © 28/982-33-37. Reservations recommended. Main courses 10€–20€ ($12–$23). AE, DC, MC, V. Daily noon–4pm and 6–11pm.

SEEING THE SIGHTS

The most bizarre attraction in Faro is the **Capela d'Ossos (Chapel of Bones)** ⟨★⟩, entered via a courtyard from the rear of the Igreja (Church) de Nossa Senhora do Monte do Carmo do Faro, on Largo do Carmo. Erected in the 19th century, this chapel is completely lined with human skulls and bones, an extraordinarily bizarre display. It's estimated that there are 1,245 skulls. The chapel is open Monday through Friday from 10am to 1pm and 2:30 to 5pm, Saturday from 10am to 1pm. Entrance is free to the church, but 1.35€ ($1.55) to the chapel.

Other religious monuments include the old Sé (cathedral), **Largo da Sé,** merging Gothic and Renaissance styles. A Muslim mosque once stood on this site but was razed for this church, a common practice in Iberia. Another church, the **Igreja de São Francisco,** Largo de São Francisco (© 28/982-36-96), is the other church of note. Its facade doesn't even begin to hint at the baroque richness inside. Panels of glazed earthenware tiles in milk-white and Dutch blue depict the life of the patron saint, St. Francis. One chapel is richly gilded. Open hours are Monday through Friday from 8 to 9:30am and 5:30 to 7pm (but in the sleepy Algarve, you might sometimes find it closed).

But most visitors don't come to Faro to look at churches. Rather, they take the harbor ferry to the wide white-sand beaches called the **Praia de Faro,** on an islet. The ride is available only in summer. The beach is also connected to the mainland by bridge, a distance of 6km (3¾ miles) from the town center. Once here, you can water-ski and fish or just rent a deck chair and umbrella and lounge in the sun.

DAY TRIPS FROM FARO

OLHÃO ⟨★⟩   Described as the living re-creation of a Georges Braque collage, Olhão is the famed cubist town of the Algarve, so long beloved by painters. In its heart, white blocks stacked one on the other, with flat red-tile roofs and exterior stairs on the stark walls, evoke the casbahs of Africa. But don't imagine too romantic a portrait. Some readers have found it disappointing—dirty, dusty, and too commercial.

If you do go here, try to attend the **fish market** near the waterfront when a *lota* (auction) is underway. Olhão is also known for its bullfights of the sea, in which fishermen wrestle with struggling tuna trapped in nets and headed for the smelly warehouses along the harbor.

For the best view, climb **Cabeça Hill,** its grottoes punctured with stalagmites and stalactites, or **St. Michael's Mount,** offering a panorama of the casbahlike Barreta. Finally, for a visit to what is one of the most idyllic beaches on the Algarve, take a 10-minute motorboat ride to the **Ilha de Armona,** a nautical mile away. Olhão is 10km (6¼ miles) west of Faro and is reached by going east on N-125.

SÃO BRAS DE ALPORTEL   Traveling north from Faro for 20km (13 miles), you'll pass through groves of figs, almonds, and oranges, and through pine woods where resin collects in wooden cups on the tree trunks. At the end of the run is isolated São Bras de Alportel, one of the Algarve's most charming and least-known spots.

Far from the crowded beaches, it attracts those wanting pure air, peace, and quiet—a bucolic setting filled with flowers pushing through nutmeg-colored soil. Northeast of Loulé, this whitewashed, tile-roofed town rarely gets lively except on market days. Like its neighbor, Faro, it's noted for its perforated plaster chimneys. Lying at the foot of the Serra do Caldeirão, the whole area has been called one vast garden.

A change of pace from seaside accommodations is offered at **Pousada de São Brás** ⚜, Estrada de Lisboa, N2, 8150 São Brás de Alportel (© **28/984-2305**). This government-owned inn, built in 1942, is a hilltop villa, with fret-cut limestone chimneys and a hawk's-eye view of the surrounding *serras.* Many visitors arrive just for lunch or dinner (daily 12:30–3pm and 7:30–10pm). In the dining room, rustic mountain-tavern chairs and tables rest on hand-woven rugs. The 22€ ($25) table d'hôte dinner offers soup, a fish course, a meat dish, vegetables, and dessert. The cuisine is plain but good. After dinner, you might want to retire to the sitting room to watch the embers of the evening's fire die down. The 22 guest rooms contain private bathrooms and phones. Doubles cost 140€ ($161) Friday and Saturday, and 130€ ($150) Sunday through Thursday, including breakfast. Amenities include an outdoor swimming pool, laundry service, and room service (until 10pm). Parking is free, and most major credit cards are accepted.

VILA REAL DE SANT ANTÓNIO/MONTE GORDO

Twenty years after the marquês de Pombal rebuilt Lisbon, which had been destroyed in the 1755 earthquake, he sent architects and builders to Vila Real de Santo António, where they re-established the frontier town on the bank opposite Spain. It took only 5 months. Pombal's motivation was jealousy of Spain. Much has changed, of course, though Praça de Pombal remains. An obelisk stands in the center of the square, which is paved with inlays of black-and-white tiles radiating like rays of the sun. Separated from its Iberian neighbor by the Guadiana River, a car ferry connects Vila Real de Santo António with Ayamonte, Spain.

Today, Vila Real is a mostly residential and industrial community that prides itself on its royal and antique associations as a border town. Adjacent to Vila Real is Monte Gordo, a town whose buildings mostly date from the 1920s and later. Set 3km (1¾ miles) to the east, it's the site of most of the region's tourist facilities and hotels, with easier access to the sandy beaches that attract tourists every summer from as far away as northern Europe.

ESSENTIALS
GETTING THERE **By Train** The bus (see below) is a better option for travelers from Faro. Eighteen trains per day arrive from Faro. The trip takes 1 hour and 20 minutes and costs 1.50€ ($1.75) one-way. Four trains make the 4½-hour trip from Lagos; a one-way ticket costs 5.25€ ($4.75). The station is located on Rua dos Caminho de Serro; for information and schedules, call ℭ **808/208-208.** To make connections with trains from Spain (1 hr. ahead of Portuguese time in summer), take a ferry from Vila Real de Santo António to Ayamonte (for ferry information, see below). From Ayamonte, buses from the main square will deliver you to the station at Huelva or Sevilla.

By Bus From Faro to Vila Real, the bus is better than the train. Buses run each day to the Vila Real bus station on Avenida da República. They take 1 hour and 45 minutes and cost 3.50€ ($4.05) one-way. Eight buses make the 4-hour journey from Lagos, which costs 5.50€ ($6.35) one-way. For information and schedules, call ℭ **28/151-18-07.**

BY FERRY In summer, ferries run between Ayamonte, Spain, and Vila Real daily from 9am to 7pm. The fare is 1.20€ ($1.40) per passenger or 4€ ($4.60) per car. Ferries depart from the station on Avenida da República; call ℭ **28/154-31-52** for more information.

VISITOR INFORMATION The **tourist office** is on Avenida Infante Dom Henríque, 8900 Monte Gordo (ℭ **28/154-44-95**). It's open Monday through Friday from 9:30am to 5:30pm October through April, and Tuesday through Thursday 9:30am to 7pm and Friday through Monday 9:30am to 5:30pm May through September.

WHERE TO STAY
In Vila Real
Hotel Apolo This hotel lies on the western edge of town. Near the beach and the river, it attracts vacationers as well as travelers who don't want to cross the Spanish border at night. The hotel is a marginal choice, with a spacious marble-floored lobby leading into a large bar scattered with comfortable sofas and flooded with sunlight. Each small, simply furnished guest room has a private balcony and a neatly kept bathroom equipped with a shower-tub combination. It's not the classiest stopover on the Algarve, but it's certainly adequate for an overnight stay.

Av. dos Bombeiros Portugueses, 8900-209 Vila Real de Santo António. ℭ 28/151-24-48. Fax 28/151-24-50. www.apolo-hotel.com. 42 units. 41€–100€ ($47–$115) double. Rates include breakfast. AE, DC, MC, V. Free parking. **Amenities:** Bar; pool; laundry. *In room:* A/C, TV, hair dryer, safe.

In Monte Gordo
Hotel Alcázar This hotel is the best in town, but that isn't saying much. Curved expanses of white balconies punctuate its palm-fringed brick facade. A free-form pool is built on terraces into the retaining walls that shelter it from the wind and extend the high season far into autumn. The vaguely Arab-style interior design incorporates many arches and vaults that create niches that are imaginatively lit at night. Each rather austere midsize room contains its own sun terrace. Beds, usually twins, are excellent. All units contain neatly kept bathrooms with shower-tub combinations.

Rua de Ceuta 9, Monte Gordo, 8900-474 Vila Real de Santo António. ℭ 28/151-01-40. Fax 28/151-01-49. 119 units. 48€–104€ ($55–$120) double; 60€–124€ ($69–$143) suite. Rates include breakfast. AE, DC, MC, V. **Amenities:** Restaurant; bar; pool; tennis court; room service; laundry service. *In room:* A/C, TV, safe.

Hotel dos Navegadores   The sign in front of this large hotel is so discreet that you might mistake it for an apartment house. The establishment is popular with vacationing Portuguese and British families, who congregate under the dome covering the atrium's swimming pool, near the reception desk. You'll find a bar that serves fruit-laden drinks, and semitropical plants throughout the public rooms. About three quarters of the guest rooms have private balconies. The hotel remains a group tour favorite. Rooms are comfortable but standard, without any flair. All units are equipped with well-maintained bathrooms containing shower-tub combinations. The beach is a 5-minute walk away.

Monte Gordo, 8900-474 Vila Real de Santo António. ℰ 28/151-08-60. Fax 28/151-08-79. 344 units. 64€–160€ ($74–$184) double; 88€–210€ ($101–$242) suite. Rates include breakfast. AE, DC, MC, V. Free parking. **Amenities:** Restaurant; 3 bars; pool; gym; sauna; salon; 24-hr. room service; laundry service. *In room:* A/C, TV, dataport, minibar, hair dryer, safe (only in suites).

Hotel Vasco da Gama   The entrepreneurs here know what their northern guests seek: lots of sunbathing and swimming. Although the hotel sits on a long, wide sandy beach, it also offers an Olympic-size pool with a high-dive board and about .5 hectares (1¼ acres) of flagstone sun terrace. All the spartan, rather small guest rooms are furnished conservatively and come equipped with neatly kept bathrooms containing shower-tub combinations. Glass doors open onto balconies.

Av. Infante Dom Henrique, Monte Gordo, 8900-412 Vila Real de Santo António. ℰ 28/151-09-00. Fax 28/151-09-01. 182 units. 54€–153€ ($62–$176) double; 64€–164€ ($74–$189) triple. Rates include breakfast. AE, DC, MC, V. Free parking. **Amenities:** Restaurant; bar; snack bar; pool; room service; babysitting; laundry service. *In room:* A/C, TV, minibar, hair dryer, safe.

WHERE TO DINE

Edmundo PORTUGUESE   The most popular restaurant in Vila Real, Edmundo overlooks the river and Spain across the water—try to get a sidewalk table. It's a longtime favorite with Spaniards who visit the Algarve for the day. The people who run this place are friendly and justifiably proud of their local cuisine, especially fresh fish. You might begin with shrimp cocktail and then follow with fried sole, crayfish, or delightful sautéed red mullet. Meat dishes such as lamb cutlets and veal filet are also available.

Av. da República 55. ℰ 28/154-46-89. Reservations recommended. Main courses 6€–12€ ($6.90–$14). AE, DC, MC, V. Mon–Sat noon–3pm; daily 7–10pm.

EXPLORING VILA REAL

A long esplanade, **Avenida da República,** borders the river. Often, more Spanish than Portuguese is heard along the promenade, for this is a popular day trip for Spaniards looking for bargains. Gaily painted **horse-drawn carriages** take visitors sightseeing past the shipyards and the lighthouse.

A short drive north on the road to Mertola will bring you to the gray castle-fortress of **Castro Marim,** a legacy of the old border wars between Spain and Portugal. The ramparts and walls peer across the river at the former enemy. Afonso III, who expelled the Moors from this region, founded the original fortress, which was leveled by the 1755 earthquake. Inside the walls are the ruins of the **Church of São Tiago,** dedicated to St. James.

Directly southwest of Vila Real is the emerging resort of **Monte Gordo,** which has the greatest concentration of hotels in the eastern Algarve after Faro. Monte Gordo is the last in a long line of Algarvian resorts, located 3km (1¾ miles) southwest of the frontier town of Vila Real de Santo António at the mouth of the Guadiana River. Pine-studded lowlands back the resort's wide beach, one of the finest along the southern coast of Portugal. This was once a sleepy little fishing village. Now young men work in hotels instead of on the sea, fishing for tips instead of tuna. Monte Gordo has succumbed to high-rises, attracting Spaniards from across the border. It has many good hotels, and a number of Europeans use it as their place in the Algarvian sun.

15

Scotland

by Darwin Porter & Danforth Prince

Whether you go to Scotland to seek out your ancestral roots, explore ancient castles, drive the Malt Whisky Trail, or partake in the internationally acclaimed Edinburgh Festival, you'll find a country rich in history, legend, and romance. If it's the outdoors you love, Scotland offers great salmon fishing, peaceful walks in heather-covered Highland hills, and some of the best (and oldest) golf courses.

1 Edinburgh & Environs

Called one of Europe's fairest cities, the "Athens of the North" is the second-most-visited city in Britain after London. In contrast to industrialized bastions like Aberdeen and Glasgow, it's a white-collar city. Home of the Royal Mile, Princes Street, and the popular Edinburgh Festival, with its action-packed list of cultural events, Edinburgh is both hip and historic. John Knox, Mary Queen of Scots, Robert Louis Stevenson, Sir Arthur Conan Doyle, Alexander Graham Bell, Sir Walter Scott, Bonnie Prince Charlie, and Deacon Brodie are all part of the city's past; you can walk in their footsteps and explore sights associated with them.

ESSENTIALS

GETTING THERE **By Plane** Edinburgh is about an hour's flying time from London, 633km (393 miles) south. **Edinburgh Airport** (© **0131/333-1000**) is 10km (6¼ miles) west of the center, receiving flights from within the British Isles and the rest of Europe. Before heading into town, you might want to stop at the **information and accommodation desk** (© **0131/473-3800**); it's open Monday to Saturday 8am to 8pm and Sunday 9am to 4:30pm. A double-decker Airlink bus makes the trip from the airport to the city center every 15 minutes, letting you off near Waverley Bridge, between the Old Town and the New Town; the fare is £3.30 ($6) one-way or £5 ($9.25) round-trip, and the trip takes about 25 minutes. A taxi into the city will cost £12 ($22) or more, depending on traffic, and the ride will be about 25 minutes.

By Train InterCity trains link London with Edinburgh and are fast and efficient, providing both restaurant and bar service as well as air-conditioning. Trains from London's King's Cross Station arrive in Edinburgh at **Waverley Station,** at the east end of Princes Street (© **08457/484950** in London for rail information). Trains depart London every hour or so, taking about 4½ hours and costing £41 to £91 ($75–$167) one-way. Overnight trains have a sleeper berth, which you can rent for an extra £35 ($65). Taxis and buses are right outside the station in Edinburgh.

By Bus The least expensive way to go from London to Edinburgh is by bus, but it's an 8-hour journey. Nevertheless, it'll get you there for only about £27

($50) one-way or £38 ($70) round-trip. **Scottish Citylink** (© **0141/332-9644;** www.citylink.co.uk) coaches depart from London's Victoria Coach Station, delivering you to Edinburgh's **St. Andrew Square Bus Station,** St. Andrew Square (© **8705/808080** for information).

By Car   Edinburgh is 74km (46 miles) east of Glasgow and 169km (105 miles) north of Newcastle-upon-Tyne in England. No express motorway links London and Edinburgh. The M1 from London takes you part of the way north, but you'll have to come into Edinburgh along secondary roads: A68 or A7 from the southeast, A1 from the east, or A702 from the north. The A71 or A8 comes in from the west, A8 connecting with M8 just west of Edinburgh; A90 comes down from the north over the Forth Road Bridge. Allow 8 hours or more for the drive north from London.

VISITOR INFORMATION   Tourist Offices   Edinburgh & Scotland Information Centre, Fairways Business Park, Deer Park Road, at the corner of Princes Street and Waverley Bridge (© **0131/473-3800;** fax 0131/473-3881; www.edinburgh.org; bus: 3, 331, or 69), can give you sightseeing information and also help find lodgings. The center sells bus tours, theater tickets, and souvenirs of Edinburgh. It's open year-round, Monday through Saturday from 9am to 8pm. There's also an information and accommodations desk at Edinburgh Airport.

Edinburgh

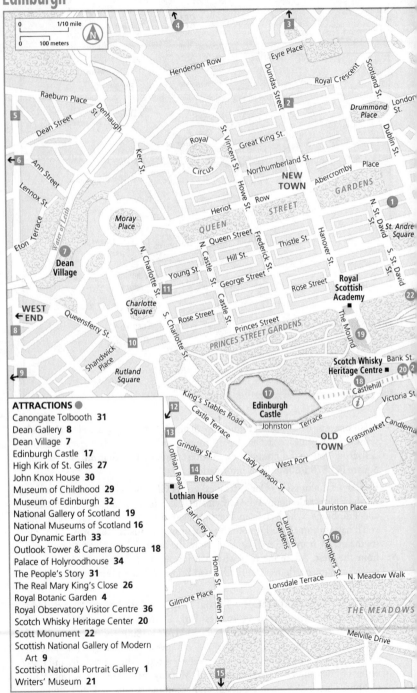

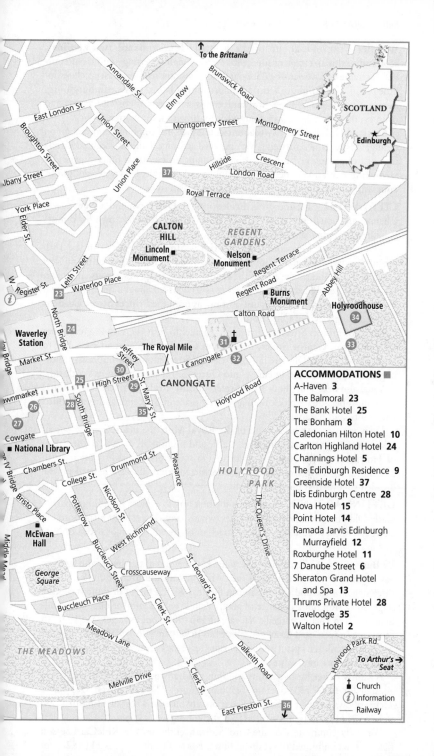

ACCOMMODATIONS ■

A-Haven **3**
The Balmoral **23**
The Bank Hotel **25**
The Bonham **8**
Caledonian Hilton Hotel **10**
Carlton Highland Hotel **24**
Channings Hotel **5**
The Edinburgh Residence **9**
Greenside Hotel **37**
Ibis Edinburgh Centre **28**
Nova Hotel **15**
Point Hotel **14**
Ramada Jarvis Edinburgh
  Murrayfield **12**
Roxburghe Hotel **11**
7 Danube Street **6**
Sheraton Grand Hotel
  and Spa **13**
Thrums Private Hotel **28**
Travelodge **35**
Walton Hotel **2**

✝ Church
ⓘ Information
---- Railway

Websites   The official site of the **Scottish Tourist Board** (**www.holiday. scotland.net**) is an excellent source for events, lodging, getting around, and outdoor activities. However, the "Special Offers" section requires a lot of clicks for little payoff. The **Edinburgh and Lothians Tourist Board** (**www.edinburgh.org**) discusses what's new, travel tips, and events and festivals for city, coast, and country; they include a page about what to do with kids, written *by* kids.

Scotland Holiday Net (**www.aboutscotland.co.uk**) combines information on dining, lodging, and sightseeing with personal accounts. Curious about Scotland's top 20 free attractions? Interested in restaurant reviews from other diners? Try **www.travelscotland.co.uk**. Listing locations and greens fees, **www.uk-golfguide. com** will help you find a course wherever you plan to be.

CITY LAYOUT   Edinburgh is divided into an **Old Town** and a **New Town.** Chances are, you'll find lodgings in New Town and visit Old Town for dining, drinking, shopping, and sightseeing.

New Town, with its world-famous **Princes Street,** came about in the 18th century in the "Golden Age" of Edinburgh. The first building went up in New Town in 1767, and by the end of the century, classical squares, streets, and town houses had been added. Princes Street runs straight for about a mile; it's known for its shopping and for its beauty, as it opens onto the **Princes Street Gardens** with stunning views of Old Town.

North of Princes Street, and running parallel to it, is the second great street of New Town, **George Street.** It begins at Charlotte Square and runs east to St. Andrew Square. Directly north of George Street is another impressive thoroughfare, **Queen Street,** opening onto Queen Street Gardens on its north side.

You'll also hear a lot about **Rose Street,** directly north of Princes Street. It has more pubs per square block than any other place in Scotland, and is also filled with shops and restaurants.

Everyone seems to have heard of the **Royal Mile,** the main thoroughfare of Old Town, beginning at Edinburgh Castle and running all the way to the Palace of Holyroodhouse. A famous street to the south of the castle (you have to descend to it) is **Grassmarket,** where convicted criminals were hanged on the dreaded gallows that once stood here.

GETTING AROUND   Walking is the best way to explore Edinburgh, particularly Old Town, with its narrow lanes, wynds, and closes. Most attractions are along the Royal Mile, along Princes Street, or on one of the major streets of New Town.

By Bus   The bus will probably be your chief method of transport. The fare you pay depends on the distance you ride, with the **minimum fare** 80p ($1.50) for three stages or less and the **maximum fare** £1 ($1.85) for 44 or more stages. (A stage isn't a stop but a distance of about ½ mile with a number of stops.) Children ages 5 to 15 are charged a flat rate of 50p (90¢), but teenagers age 13 to 15 must carry a **teen card** (available where bus tickets are sold—see below) as proof of age, and children ages 4 and under ride free. Exact change is required if you're paying your fare on the bus.

A **family ticket** for two adults and four children goes for £6 ($11) a day, and another for £1.60 ($3) operates 6:30pm onward. The **Edinburgh Day Saver Ticket** allows 1 day of unlimited travel on city buses at a cost of £1.80 to £2.50 ($3.35–$4.60) adults and £1.80 ($3.35) children.

For daily commuters or die-hard Scottish enthusiasts, a **RideCard** season ticket allows unlimited travel on all buses. For adults, the price is £11 ($20) for

1 week and £33 ($61) for 4 weeks; tickets for children cost £7 ($13) for 1 week and £21 ($39) for 4 weeks. Travel must begin on Sunday.

You can get these tickets and further information in the city center at the **Waverley Bridge Transport Office,** Waverley Bridge (© **0131/554-4494;** bus: 3 or 31), open Monday to Saturday 8:30am to 6pm and Sunday 9:30am to 5pm, or at the Hanover Street office (bus: 3 or 31), open Monday to Saturday 8:30am to 6pm. For details on timetables, call © **0131/555-6363.**

By Taxi   You can hail a taxi or pick one up at a taxi stand. Meters begin at £2 ($3.70) and increase £2 ($3.70) every kilometer (½ mile). Taxi stands are at Hanover Street, North St. Andrew Street, Waverley Station, Haymarket Station, and Lauriston Place. Fares are displayed in the front of the taxi and charges posted, including extra charges for night drivers or destinations outside the city limits, and a call-out is charged at 60p ($1.10). You can also call a taxi. Try **City Cabs** at © **0131/228-1211** or **Central Radio Taxis** at © **0131/229-2468.**

By Car   Car rentals are relatively expensive, and driving in Edinburgh is a tricky business. The city is a warren of one-way streets, with parking spots at a premium. A car is convenient, however, and sometimes a must, for touring the countryside. Most companies will accept your U.S. or Canadian driver's license, provided you have held it for more than a year and are over 21. At the Edinburgh airport, try **Avis** (© **0131/333-1866**), **Hertz** (© **0131/333-1019**), or **Europcar** (© **0131/333-2588**).

By Bicycle   Biking isn't a good idea for most visitors because the city is constructed on a series of high ridges and terraces. You may, however, want to rent a bike for exploring the flatter countryside around the city. Try **Central Cycle Hire,** 13 Lochrin Place (© **0131/228-6333;** bus: 10), off Home Street in Tollcross, near the Cameo Cinema. Depending on the type of bike, charges run from £15 ($28) and up per day. A deposit of £100 ($185) is imposed. June to September, the shop is open Monday to Saturday 9:30am to 6pm and Sunday noon to 7pm; October to May, hours are Monday to Saturday 10am to 5:30pm.

FAST FACTS: **Edinburgh**

American Express The office is at 139 Princes St. (© **0131/225-7881;** Bus: 3, 39, or 69), 5 blocks from Waverley Station. It's open Monday through Friday from 9am to 5:30pm and Saturday from 9am to 4pm; on Thursday, the office opens at 9:30am.

Business Hours In Edinburgh, banks are usually open Monday through Wednesday from 9:30am to 3:45pm and Thursday and Friday from 9:30am to 5 or 5:30pm. Shops are generally open Monday through Saturday from 10am to 5:30 or 6pm; on Thursday, stores are open to 8pm. Offices are open Monday through Friday from 9am to 5pm.

Currency The basic unit of currency is the **pound sterling** (£), which is divided into 100 **pence** (p). The exchange rate at press time is £1 = $1.85. Note that though the United Kingdom is part of the EU, it does not plan to switch to the euro at this time.

Currency Exchange There's a **Bureau de Change** of the Clydesdale Bank at 20 Hanover St. (© **08457/826-302**).

Dentists/Doctors For a dental emergency, go to the **Edinburgh Dental Institute,** 39 Lauriston Place (ⓒ **0131/536-4900;** bus: 23 or 41), open Monday through Friday from 9am to 3pm. In a medical emergency, you can seek help from the **Edinburgh Royal Infirmary,** 1 Lauriston Place (ⓒ **0131/536-1000;** bus: 23 or 41). Medical attention is available 24 hours.

Drugstores There are no 24-hour drugstores ("chemists" or "pharmacies") in Edinburgh. The major drugstore is **Boots,** 48 Shandwick Place (ⓒ **0131/225-6757;** bus: 3 or 31), open Monday through Friday from 8am to 8pm, Saturday from 8am to 6pm, and Sunday from 10am to 4pm.

Embassies/Consulates The consulate of the **United States** is at 3 Regent Terrace (ⓒ **0131/556-8315;** bus: 26, 85, or 86), which is an extension of Princes Street beyond Nelson's Monument. All the other embassies are in London.

Emergencies Call ⓒ **999** in an emergency to summon the police, an ambulance, or firefighters.

Hospital The best and most convenient is the **Edinburgh Royal Infirmary,** 1 Lauriston Place (ⓒ **0131/536-1000;** bus: 23 or 41).

Internet Access You can check your e-mail or send messages at the **International Telecom Centre,** 52 High St. (ⓒ **0131/559-7114;** bus: 1 or 6), along the Royal Mile. The rate is £1 ($1.85) for 15 minutes. The center is open daily from 9am to 10pm.

Post Office The Edinburgh Branch **Post Office,** St. James's Centre (ⓒ **0845/722-3344;** bus: 23 or 41), is open Monday through Friday from 9am to 5:30pm and Saturday from 9am to noon.

Telephones The United Kingdom's **country code** is **44.** The city code for **Edinburgh** is **0131.** If you're calling from inside the United Kingdom but outside the city code area, dial the complete area code; if you're calling from outside the United Kingdom, drop the zero. If you're calling from inside the code area, dial just the seven-digit number.

Public phones cost 10p (15¢) for the first 3 minutes and accept coins of various denominations. You can also buy a phone card for use in special phones at post offices and newsstands. You can receive U.S. rates for collect or credit card calls by dialing toll-free **AT&T** (ⓒ **0800/890011), World Phone** (ⓒ **0800/890222),** or **Sprint** (ⓒ **0800/890877).**

Tipping In most restaurants, tax and service charge are included, so it's unnecessary to leave a tip. If a service charge hasn't been included in the bill, the standard tip is 10%. Taxi drivers also expect a 10% tip.

WHERE TO STAY
IN THE CENTER
Very Expensive

The Balmoral ★★★   This legendary establishment was opened in 1902 as the largest, grandest, and most impressive hotel in the north of Britain. Its soaring clock tower is a city landmark. Rooms are distinguished, conservative, and rather large, a graceful reminder of Edwardian sprawl with a contemporary twist. Many benefit from rounded or oversize windows and the many Victorian/ Edwardian quirks that were originally designed as part of its charm.

1 Princes St., Edinburgh, Lothian EH2 2EQ. ✆ **0131/556-2414.** Fax 0131/557-3747. www.roccofortehotels.com. 188 units. Apr–Oct £280–£330 ($518–$610) double; from £450 ($832) suite. Off season £220–£240 ($407–$444) double; from £450 ($832) suite. AE, DC, MC, V. Parking £15 ($28). Bus: 16 or 34. **Amenities:** 2 restaurants (see "Where to Dine," later in this chapter); bar; pool; heath club; 24-hr. room service; nonsmoking rooms; rooms for those with limited mobility. *In room:* A/C, TV, dataport, minibar, hair dryer.

Caledonian Hilton Hotel ★★★   "The Caley," built in 1903, is Edinburgh's most visible hotel, with commanding views over Edinburgh Castle and the Princes Street Gardens. The pastel-colored public areas are reminiscent of Edwardian splendor. Rooms are conservatively but individually styled, and are often exceptionally spacious. Fifth-floor rooms are the smallest. Although the accommodations are comparable to other first-class hotels in Edinburgh, the Caledonian lacks the leisure facilities of its major competitor, the Balmoral.

Princes St., Edinburgh EH1 2AB. ✆ **0131/222-8888.** Fax 0131/222-8889. www.hilton.com. 251 units. £150–£290 ($277–$536) double; £250–£450 ($462–$832) suite. Children 15 and under stay free in parent's room. AE, DC, DISC, MC, V. Parking £9.50 ($18). Bus: 3, 12, 25, 44, or 66. **Amenities:** 2 restaurants; 4 bars; pool; gym; business center; 24-hr. room service; laundry service; dry cleaning; nonsmoking rooms; rooms for those with limited mobility. *In room:* TV, dataport, minibar, coffeemaker, hair dryer, safe, trouser press.

Expensive

The Bonham ★★   One of Edinburgh's most stylish hotels occupies a trio of Regency town houses. Rooms are outfitted in an urban and very hip blend of old and new. The decor combines ancient vases, Art Nouveau objects, marble busts, contemporary art—an eclectic but tasteful mix. Each unit has a TV with a keyboard hooked up to a barrage of facilities on the Internet, the first setup of its kind in Scotland.

35 Drumsheugh Gardens, Edinburgh EH3 7RN. ✆ **0131/623-6060.** Fax 0131/226-6080. www.thebonham. com. 48 units. £127–£245 ($235–$453) double; £221–£333 ($409–$616) suite. AE, DC, MC, V. Bus: 41 or 42. **Amenities:** Restaurant; bar; 24-hr. room service; babysitting; laundry service; dry cleaning; nonsmoking rooms; 1 room for those with limited mobility. *In room:* TV, dataport, minibar, coffeemaker, hair dryer, iron.

Carlton Highland Hotel ★★   The Victorian turrets, Flemish gables, and severe gray stonework rise imposingly from a street corner on the Royal Mile, a few steps from Waverley Station. The former department store has been converted into a bright and airy milieu full of modern conveniences. Rooms have a kind of Scandinavian simplicity. Bathrooms tend to be small. To relax, enjoy the sounds of a pianist in the lounge area, or stop by the cafe, **Central Perk,** based on the same coffee bar as the one on the TV show *Friends.* Although the hotel doesn't have the style and grandeur of the Caledonian, it has more facilities.

19 N. Bridge, Edinburgh, Lothian EH1 1SD. ✆ **0131/556-7277.** Fax 0131/556-2691. www.paramount-hotels. co.uk. 189 units. £280 ($518) executive double. Children 14 and under stay free in parent's room. AE, DC, MC, V. Valet parking £15 ($28). Bus: 3, 31, or 33. **Amenities:** Restaurant; bar; pool; gym; aerobics studio; 2 squash courts; solarium; whirlpool; sauna; limited room service; babysitting; laundry service; rooms for those with limited mobility, nonsmoking rooms. *In room:* A/C, TV, dataport, coffeemaker, hair dryer, safe, trouser press.

Channings Hotel ★★   Five Edwardian terrace houses were combined to create this hotel 7 blocks north of Dean Village in a tranquil residential area. It maintains the atmosphere of a Scottish country house. Rooms are outfitted in a modern yet elegant style. Front units have views of a cobblestone street. Back rooms are quieter, and standard accommodations are a bit cheaper but are much smaller. The most desirable rooms are labeled "Executive," and have bay windows and wingback chairs.

S. Learmonth Gardens 15, Edinburgh EH4 1EZ. © 0131/332-3232. Fax 0131/332-9631. www.channings. co.uk. 46 units. £98–£195 ($181–$361) double; £120–£240 ($222–$444) suite. Rates include breakfast. Children 14 and under stay free in parent's room. AE, DC, MC, V. Bus: 41. **Amenities:** 2 restaurants; bar; 24-hr. room service; babysitting; laundry service; dry cleaning, nonsmoking rooms. *In room:* TV, dataport, coffeemaker, hair dryer, trouser press.

The Edinburgh Residence ✮✮✮ If Robert Burns, who liked his luxuries, were checking into a hotel in Edinburgh today, he no doubt would be booked in here. It's one of the finest luxury hotels in Scotland, a series of elegant townhouse suites installed in a trio of architecturally beautiful and sensitively restored Georgian buildings. As you enter, grand staircases and classic wood paneling greet you. A stay here is like finding lodging in an elegant town house from long ago, albeit with all the modern conveniences. This hotel is as good as or better than its siblings, the Howard, Bonham, and Channings. Accommodations are the ultimate in local comfort. A trio of classic suites have private entrances. All units are spacious—even the smallest is the size of a tennis court—and all are nonsmoking.

7 Rothesay Terrace, Edinburgh EH3 7RY. © 0131/226-3380. Fax 0131/226-3381. www.theedinburghresidence. com. 29 units. £150–£295 ($278–$546) suite; £295–£395 ($546–$731) apt. AE, MC, V. Free parking. Bus: 37. Rates include continental breakfast. **Amenities:** Meals (24-hr. room service only); honesty bar in the drawing room; 1 room for those with limited mobility. *In room:* TV, dataport, minibar, hair dryer.

Point Hotel ✮ With one of the most dramatic contemporary interiors of any hotel in Edinburgh, this is a stylish place in the shadow of Edinburgh Castle. The decor has appeared in a book detailing the 50 premier hotel designs in the world, with a great emphasis on color and innovation, including a black stone floor at the front that's marked by "dusty footprints." In one area, an optical fantasy is created when blue walls are brilliantly lighted by red neon. For a dramatic minimalist effect, a lone armchair and sofa will occupy 93 sq. m (1,000 sq. ft.) of space. Guest rooms are spacious and attractively furnished. Most of the guest rooms open onto views of the castle; however, those in the rear do not, so be duly warned. If you like stainless steel, laser projections, and chrome instead of Scottish antiques, this might be an address for you. Standard rooms are a bit small, the premium rooms more comfortable and spacious.

34 Bread St., Edinburgh EH3 9AF. © 0131/221-5555. Fax 0131/221-9929. www.point-hotel.co.uk. 140 units. Summer £105–£160 ($194–$296) double; £350 ($648) suite. Off season £60–£80 ($111–$148) double; £200–£300 ($370–$555) suite. Rates include English breakfast. AE, DC, MC, V. Bus: 16 or 35. **Amenities:** Restaurant; bar; limited room service; babysitting; laundry service; dry cleaning; nonsmoking rooms; 1 room for those with limited mobility. *In room:* TV, dataport, hair dryer, iron.

Roxburghe Hotel ✮ Originally a stately Robert Adam town house, the hotel stands on a tree-filled square a short walk from Princes Street. In 1999, it opened another wing, more than doubling the original size of the hotel. The old wing maintains a traditional atmosphere with ornate ceilings and woodwork, antique furnishings, and tall, arched windows. The more modern wing offers government-rated four-star hotel comfort, completely contemporary styling, and up-to-date furnishings.

38 Charlotte St., Edinburgh EH2 4HG. © 0131/240-5500. Fax 0131/240-5555. www.macdonaldhotels. co.uk. 197 units. £99–£220 ($183–$407) double; from £190 ($352) suite. Children 13 and under stay free in parent's room. AE, DC, MC, V. Parking (very limited) £8.50 ($16). Bus: 100. **Amenities:** 2 restaurants; 2 bars; pool; gym; sauna; 24-hr. room service; babysitting; laundry service; dry cleaning; nonsmoking rooms; rooms for those with limited mobility. *In room:* TV, minibar, coffeemaker, hair dryer, iron/ironing board, trouser press.

Sheraton Grand Hotel and Spa ★★   This elegant hotel, in a postmodern complex on a former railway siding a short walk from Princes Street, is the most appealing modern hotel in the capital. If you seek Victorian grandeur, make it the Caledonian. But if you'd like to be situated in the "new Edinburgh" (a financial center called The Exchange), then make it the Sheraton Grand. The hotel has more of international flavor than its rival, the Balmoral. Rooms may lack character, but they are exceedingly comfortable. The best units are called "Castle View," and they are on the top three floors.

1 Festival Sq., Edinburgh, Lothian EH3 9SR. © **888/625-5144** in the U.S. and Canada, or 0131/229-9131. Fax 0131/228-4510. www.sheraton.com. 278 units. June–Sept £115–£270 ($213–$500) double; from £450 ($833) suite. Off season £105–£270 ($194–$500) double; £450 ($833) suite. Children 16 and under stay free in parent's room. AE, DC, MC, V. Bus: 4, 15, or 44. **Amenities:** 3 restaurants; 2 bars; indoor heated pool; gym; spa; 24-hr. room service; babysitting; laundry service; dry cleaning; nonsmoking rooms; rooms for those with limited mobility. *In room:* A/C, TV, dataport, minibar, coffeemaker, hair dryer, iron/ironing board.

Moderate

The Bank Hotel *(Value)*   This modest hotel in a 1923 building offers better value than many of its competitors in this congested neighborhood beside the Royal Mile. Until around 1990 it was a branch of the Royal Bank of Scotland, and the past is still evident in its bulky, no-nonsense design. Upstairs, high ceilings, simple furnishings, and king-size beds provide comfort in the clean guest rooms. Each comes with a shower-only bathroom.

Royal Mile at 1 S. Bridge St., Edinburgh EH1 1LL. © **0131/622-6800.** Fax 0131/622-6822. www.festival-inns. co.uk. 9 units. £100–£130 ($185–$240) double. Rates include breakfast. AE, DC, MC, V. Nearby parking £6 ($11). Bus: 4, 15, 31, or 100. **Amenities:** Bar; nonsmoking rooms. *In room:* TV, coffeemaker, hair dryer, safe (in some), trouser press.

Ibis Edinburgh Centre *(Value)*   For sheer location off the Royal Mile and for good value, this hotel is a winner. With a chain-hotel format and bandboxy accommodations, the Ibis may be short on charm, but it's situated within walking distance of the major attractions of Old Town. It is a workable choice in a very expensive city, with comfortable, bright, and practical rooms and attractive well-maintained furnishings, including efficient private bathrooms with shower. Rooms in the rear are quieter. Breakfast is self-service.

6 Hunter Square, Edinburgh EH1 1QW. © **0131/2407000.** Fax 0131/2407007. www.accorhotels.com. 99 units. £50–£70 ($92–$129) double. AE, DC, MC, V. Parking £5 ($9.25). Bus: 7, 8, 30, 31, or 33. **Amenities:** Breakfast room; bar; laundry service; nonsmoking rooms; units for those with limited mobility. *In room:* TV, dataport, beverage maker, iron/ironing board.

7 Danube Street ★   This B&B is in Stockbridge, a quiet, stylish residential neighborhood a 10-minute walk north of the center. It's the 1825 home of Fiona Mitchell-Rose and her husband, Colin. The establishment is proud of its charmingly decorated rooms that reflect Fiona's experience as a decorator in London. Rooms look out onto the sloping garden. The most desirable has a four-poster bed and direct garden access. Bathrooms are shower-only. You're likely to meet your hosts and other guests in the formal dining room in the morning, where the breakfast is inspired by Scotland's old-fashioned agrarian tradition. All rooms are nonsmoking.

7 Danube St., Edinburgh EH4 1NN. © **0131/332-2755.** Fax 0131/343-3648. www.aboutedinburgh.com/ danube.html. 5 units. £110–£130 ($204–$240) double. Rates include breakfast. MC, V. Free parking nearby. Bus: 28. **Amenities:** Dining room. *In room:* TV, dataport, coffeemaker, hair dryer, iron.

Travelodge *(Kids)*   Off the Royal Mile in Old Town, this modern seven-floor chain hotel offers few frills but a lot of comfort—all at a good price. Lying in the vicinity of the Dynamic Earth Museum, it has an ideal location for sight-seers, lying a 7-minute walk from the train station and all city buses. The rooms are fairly spacious and well-equipped, everything done in smart styling. The lodge is suitable for both business travelers and families and is well maintained and efficiently run. Each accommodation comes with an efficiently organized private bathroom with tub and shower. Many of the units can easily house two adults and two children. Just don't come here seeking excitement or Old Town ambience: Similar chain accommodations can be found all along the roadways of Britain. In other words, you won't feel you're in Edinburgh.

33 St. Mary's St., Edinburgh EH1 1TA. © 0131/1911637. Fax 0131/5573681. www.travelodge.co.uk. 193 units. £50–£70 ($92–$129) double. Parking £5 ($9.25). Bus: 1 or 6. **Amenities:** Cafe; bar; nonsmoking rooms; units for those with limited mobility. *In room:* TV, beverage maker.

Inexpensive

A-Haven　This semidetached 1862 Victorian house is a 15-minute walk or 5-minute bus ride north of the rail station. Rooms are of various sizes (the biggest on the 2nd floor). Some in back overlook the Firth of Forth, and those in the front open onto views of Arthur's Seat. David Kay extends a Scottish welcome in this family-type place, and often advises guests about sightseeing.

180 Ferry Rd., Edinburgh EH6 4NS. © 0131/554-6559. Fax 0131/554-5252. www.a-haven.co.uk. 14 units. £30–£50 ($55–$92) double per person. Rates include breakfast. AE, MC, V. Free parking. Bus: 7, 11, or 14. **Amenities:** Restaurant; bar. *In room:* TV, dataport, coffeemaker, hair dryer, iron, trouser press.

Greenside Hotel　This 1820 Georgian house is furnished with antiques to give it the right spirit. There are singles, doubles, twins, and three family rooms, all centrally heated and all with private bathrooms with showers. Rooms, refurbished in 1998, open onto views of a private garden or the Firth of Forth and are so large that 10 of them contain a double bed and two singles.

9 Royal Terrace, Edinburgh EH7 5AB. © and fax 0131/557-0022. www.townhousehotels.co.uk. 15 units. £50–£70 ($92–$130) double. Rates include breakfast. AE, DC, MC, V. Bus: 4, 15, or 44. **Amenities:** Meals arranged; bar; lounge area; nonsmoking rooms; 1 room for those with limited mobility. *In room:* TV, coffeemaker, hair dryer, iron/ironing board.

Walton Hotel ★ *Finds*　A real discovery, this little hotel lies right in the heart of Edinburgh in a restored 200-year-old town house. A complete refurbishment and renovation have maintained the essential Georgian character and elegant features, but have revitalized and modernized the entire hotel. Guest rooms are midsize, cozy, comfortable, and tranquil. In the morning you're served a fine breakfast. The location is only a few minutes' walk to Princes Street. All rooms are nonsmoking.

79 Dundas St., Edinburgh EH3 6SD. © 0131/556-1137. Fax 0131/557-8367. www.waltonhotel.com. 10 units. Summer £99 ($183) double; off season £88 ($163) double. Rates include breakfast. MC, V. Bus: 23, 24, or 27. **Amenities:** Breakfast lounge. *In room:* TV, beverage maker, fridge (in some), hair dryer.

WEST OF THE CENTER

Ramada Jarvis Edinburgh Murrayfield ★　Standing in walled gardens, this three-story Edwardian country house offers the privacy of a home. It's in a dignified west-end residential section near the Murrayfield rugby grounds, about a 5-minute ride from the center, a distance of 3.2km (2 miles), and is one of Edinburgh's best moderately priced hotels. The well-equipped rooms vary in size and are in either the main house or a less desirable annex. After recent refurbishments, the hotel is better than ever, and service is first class.

4 Ellersly Rd., Edinburgh EH12 6HZ. © 0131/337-6888. Fax 0131/313-2543. www.ramadajarvis.co.uk. 57 units. £145 ($268) double; £165 ($305) suite. AE, DC, MC, V. Free parking. Take A-8 4km (2½ miles) west of

the city center. **Bus:** 12, 21, 26, 31, or 36. **Amenities:** Restaurant; 24-hr. room service; laundry service; wine cellar; nonsmoking rooms; rooms for those with limited mobility. *In room:* TV, dataport, beverage maker, hair dryer.

SOUTH OF THE CENTER

Thrums Private Hotel   Situated 1.6km (1 mile) south of Princes Street, Thrums is a pair of connected antique buildings, one a two-story 1820 Georgian and the other a small inn from around 1900. The hotel contains recently refurbished high-ceilinged rooms with contemporary furnishings (in the inn) or reproduction antique furnishings (in the Georgian). Each unit comes with a tidy midsize private bathroom with shower. The bistro-inspired Thrums restaurant serves set-price menus of British food, and there's also a bar and a peaceful garden.

14–15 Minto St., Edinburgh EH9 1RQ. © 0131/667-5545. Fax 0131/667-8707. www.thrumshoteledinburgh. com. 15 units. £70–£80 ($130–$148) double; £75–£120 ($139–$222) family room. Rates include breakfast. MC, V. Free parking. **Bus:** 3, 7, 8, 31, 81, or 87. **Amenities:** Restaurant; bar; laundry service; nonsmoking rooms. *In room:* TV, coffeemaker, hair dryer, trouser press.

WHERE TO DINE
IN THE CENTER—NEW TOWN
Expensive

The Atrium 🏵 MODERN SCOTTISH/INTERNATIONAL   Since 1993, this is one of the most emulated restaurants in Edinburgh. The "deliberately moody" atmosphere is a fusion of Argentine hacienda and stylish Beverly Hills

---

Native Behavior

The quickest way to brand yourself a tourist is to ask a kilt-wearing Scotsman what he wears underneath the kilt. A true Scotsman—and, of course, many a Scottish lass—already knows the answer to that one. A guard at Edinburgh Castle told us, "I must get asked that question at least 10 times a day."

It takes more than the swirl of tartan to make you blend in with the Scots. It also helps to perk up your ears at the skirl of pipes and to claim membership in a clan, the more ancient the better. If you're a big man, the ability to toss a giant caber (tree trunk) will get you a free round of brew at the local pub.

When talking with Scots, it helps if you express a firm belief in the existence of the Loch Ness monster and refer to her as "Nessie." If you really want to show your familiarity with the creature, call her "Beastie," as the locals do who actually live on the loch. To report an actual sighting will endear you even more to the Scots.

If you're invited to a Scottish home, you'll immediately be offered tea no matter what time of day. As a local told us, "It's always tea time in Scotland." In the Lowlands it's called "a fly cup"—that is, a quick cup between meals. In the Highlands, it's called "a wee strupach," which means the same thing.

And finally, on the subject of drink, it's wise to drink only Scottish whisky (spelled without the "e") and to express your loathing of such "hogwash" as American, Canadian, or Irish whiskey with an "e."

bistro. Flickering oil lamps create shadows on the dark walls while patrons enjoy dishes prepared by chef Alan Metheison. Our favorites include grilled salmon and roasted sea bass. Whether it's game or lamb from the Scottish Highlands, dishes have taste, style, and flair. The desserts are equally superb, especially the lemon tart with berry coulis and crème fraîche.

10 Cambridge St. (beneath Saltire Court). ℂ **0131/228-8882**. Reservations recommended. Main courses £10–£21 ($19–$39) lunch, £16–£21 ($30–$39) dinner. AE, DC, MC, V. Mon–Fri noon–2pm and 6–10pm; Sat 6:30–10pm. Closed 1 week at Christmas.

No. 1 Princes Street ✦ SCOTTISH/CONTINENTAL   This intimate, crimson-colored enclave is the premier restaurant in the Balmoral Hotel. The walls are studded with Scottish memorabilia in formal yet sporting patterns. You can sample the likes of pan-seared Isle of Skye monkfish with saffron mussel broth; roulade of Dover sole with langoustine, oyster, and scallop garnish; or grilled filet of Scottish beef served with bourguignon sauce. For dessert you can have a variety of sorbets or British cheeses, or something more exotic such as mulled wine parfait with a cinnamon sauce. The restaurant also has a separate vegetarian menu and a wide-ranging wine list with celestial tariffs.

In the Balmoral Hotel, 1 Princes St. ℂ **0131/556-2414**. Reservations recommended. Main courses £21–£24 ($39–$44). Fixed-price dinners £41 ($76) 3 courses, £55 ($102) 6 courses, £85 ($157) 6 courses with wine. AE, DC, MC, V. Daily 7–9:30pm.

Moderate

Café Saint-Honoré FRENCH/SCOTTISH   Between Frederick and Hanover streets, this is a French-inspired bistro with a dinner format that's much more formal and expensive than its deliberately rapid lunchtime venue. An upbeat and usually enthusiastic staff serves a combination of Scottish and French cuisine that includes venison with juniper berries and wild mushrooms; local pheasant in wine and garlic sauce; and lamb kidneys with broad beans inspired by the cuisine of the region around Toulouse. Fish is very fresh.

34 NW Thistle St. Lane. ℂ **0131/226-2211**. Reservations recommended. Main courses £7.75–£20 ($14–$36) lunch, £16–£21 ($30–$39) dinner; pretheater fixed-price meal £15–£26 ($28–$48) 2 courses, £30 ($55) 3 courses. AE, DC, MC, V. Mon–Fri noon–2:15pm and pretheater meal 5–7pm; Mon–Sat 7–10 or 11pm. Bus: 3, 16, 17, 23, 27, or 31.

Duck's at Le Marché Noir ✦ SCOTTISH/FRENCH   The cuisine here is more stylish and more tuned to the culinary sophistication of London than the cuisine at many other restaurants in Edinburgh. Set within a wood house whose outside and inside are decorated in dark green, it honors the traditions of Scotland with a handful of dishes. (An example is their baked haggis in phyllo pastry on a bed of turnip purée and red-wine sauce.) More modern dishes include a boudin of chicken and foie gras served with wilted spinach and applesauce; seared salmon with leeks, asparagus, zucchini, and a pickled ginger and sesame salad; roasted rack of lamb with thyme juice and roasted vegetables; and grilled red snapper with wild rice and lime-marinated sweet-potato pickles.

2/4 Eyre Place. ℂ **0131/558-1608**. www.ducks.co.uk. Reservations recommended. Set-price 3-course lunch £13.50 ($25); dinner main courses £9.50–£21 ($18–$38). AE, DC, MC, V. Tues–Fri noon–3pm and 6–10pm; Sun–Mon 6–10pm. Bus: 16 or 23.

Haldanes Restaurant ✦ SCOTTISH   Set in the cellar of the Albany Hotel building, within a pair of royal blue and gold-tinted dining rooms, Haldanes features the cuisine of George Kelso. During clement weather, the venue moves out to the building's verdant garden. Our recent party of Scottish friends dug into such delights as braised shank of Scottish lamb with Puy lentils; pan-fried breast of guinea fowl stuffed with a leek mousse; and baked filet of Scottish salmon topped with a chive crème fraîche. If you want to go truly local, order the Highland venison with black pudding and beets in a rosemary sauce.

39A Albany St. © 0131/556-8407. Reservations recommended. Dinner main courses £17–£25 ($31–$46). AE, DC, MC, V. Daily 6–9:30pm. Bus: 15.

The Tower ⭐⭐ SEAFOOD/MODERN BRITISH   This is a hot dining ticket set at the top of the Museum of Scotland. The inventive kitchen will regale you with hearty portions of some of the finest steaks and roast beef, along with excellent and freshly caught seafood. Dig into an array of oysters or lobsters, or try a platter of mixed seafood. We still remember fondly the smoked haddock risotto with a poached egg and shavings of Parmesan cheese. Sea bass is perfectly seasoned and grilled, and there's even sushi on the menu. Scottish loin of lamb is given a modern twist with a side dish of minted couscous.

In the Museum of Scotland, Chambers St. © 0131/225-3003. Reservations required. Set-price lunch £9.95 ($18) 2 courses; £8.95–£19 ($17–$34) lunch main courses; £13–£20 ($24–$37) dinner main courses. AE, DC, MC, V. Daily noon–4:30pm and 5–11pm. Closed Dec 25–26. Bus: 3, 7, 21, 30, 31, 53, 69, or 80.

Inexpensive

Henderson's Salad Table ⭐ *Value* VEGETARIAN   This is a Shangri-la for health-food lovers. Hot dishes such as peppers stuffed with rice and pimiento are served on request, and a vegetarian twist on the national dish of Scotland, haggis, is usually available. Other well-prepared dishes filled with flavor include cheese and onion potato croquette, vegetable lasagna, and a broccoli and cheese crumble. The homemade desserts include a fresh fruit salad and a cake with double-whipped cream and chocolate sauce. The wine cellar offers 30 wines. Live music, ranging from classical to jazz to folk, is played every evening.

94 Hanover St. © 0131/225-2131. Main courses £4.95–£5.25 ($9–$10); fixed-price lunch £7.75 ($14); fixed-price dinner £8.50 ($16). AE, MC, V. Mon–Sat 8am–10:30pm. Bus: 23 or 27.

Valvona & Crolla INTERNATIONAL   In 1872, a recent arrival from Italy opened this restaurant, and it's still going strong. It shares space with a delicatessen and food emporium. A few steps down from the main shopping area, this cafe and lunch restaurant serves very fresh food at refreshingly low prices. Here, you can order three kinds of breakfast (continental, Scottish, or vegetarian) for a fixed price of £4.95 ($9.15); or you can order platters of pasta, mixed sausages, cold cuts, crostini, risottos, or omelets. Don't expect leisurely dining, as the place caters to office workers and shoppers who appreciate the informality, low prices, and freshness of the food.

19 Elm Row. © 0131/556-6066. Breakfast £4.95 ($9.15); pizzas, pastas, or platters £3–£10 ($5.55–$19). AE, DC, MC, V. Cafe with limited food service Mon–Sat 8:30am–5:30pm; full lunch service Mon–Sat noon–2:30pm. Bus: 7, 10, 11, 12, or 14.

IN THE CENTER—OLD TOWN
Moderate

Dubh Prais SCOTTISH   Dubh Prais (Gaelic for "The Black Pot") conjures up an image of an old-fashioned Scottish recipe bubbling away in a stewpot above a fireplace. Menu items are time-tested and not at all experimental, but flavorful nonetheless. Examples include smoked salmon; ragout of wild mushrooms and Ayrshire bacon served with garlic sauce; saddle of venison with juniper sauce; and a supreme of salmon with grapefruit-flavored butter sauce.

123B High St., Royal Mile. © 0131/557-5732. Reservations recommended. Lunch main courses £6.50–£9.50 ($12–$18); dinner main courses £13–£17 ($23–$31). AE, MC, V. Tues–Fri noon–2pm; Tues–Sat 6–10:30pm. Bus: 11.

Inexpensive

Baked Potato Shop *Value* VEGETARIAN/WHOLE FOOD   This is the least expensive restaurant in a very glamorous neighborhood, and it attracts mobs of office workers every day. Many carry their food away. Only free-range eggs, whole foods, and vegetarian cheeses are used. Vegan cakes are a specialty.

56 Cockburn St. © 0131/225-7572. Reservations not accepted. Food items 60p–£3.20 ($1.10–$5.90). No credit cards. Daily 9am–9pm (to 10pm in summer). Bus: 5.

LEITH

In the northern regions of Edinburgh, Leith is the old port town, opening onto the Firth of Forth. Once it was a city in its own right until it was slowly absorbed into Edinburgh.

Expensive

Martin Wishart ★★★ MODERN FRENCH   Several gourmet associations rate this as one of the finest restaurants in all of Scotland. The chef/owner Martin Wishart takes it all in stride and continues to improve the quality of his cuisine in a fashionable part of the Leith docklands. With white walls and modern art, the decor is minimalist. The menu is short but sweet and ever changing. Many dishes are simply prepared, the natural flavors coming through. Others show a touch of elegance and fantasy, including partridge breast with black truffle and foie gras, and lobster ravioli with a light shellfish cream. After you eat the glazed lemon tart with praline ice cream on which white raspberry coulis has been dribbled, the day is yours.

54 The Shore, Leith. © 0131/553-35571. Reservations required. Main courses £21–£25 ($38–$45); set lunch £19 ($34) (3 courses). AE, MC, V. Tues–Fri noon–2pm; Tues–Thurs 6:30–10pm; Fri–Sat 6:30–10:30pm. Bus: 22.

Moderate

Vintner's Room ★ *Finds* FRENCH/SCOTTISH   Join locals and visitors down by the waterfront in Leith. Chances are they are heading to this restaurant. Near the entrance, beneath a venerable ceiling of oaken beams, a wine bar serves platters and drinks beside a large stone fireplace. Most diners, however, head for the small but elegant dining room, illuminated by flickering candles. Fresh ingredients are used in a vast array of specialties. You might begin with such appetizers as pear-and-watercress soup or pigeon-and-juniper terrine. The baked halibut with lobster bisque makes a tasty main course, as does the saddle of hare with brandy and grapes. Game delights are the thyme-flavored roast partridge with Marsala or the noisettes of venison with heather honey and red currants. Finish off with grilled apricots flavored with Amaretto and served with a basil-flavored ice.

The Vaults, 87 Giles St., Leith. © 0131/554-6767. Reservations recommended. Table d'hôte lunch £13–£17 ($24–$31); dinner main courses £15–£19 ($28–$35). AE, MC, V. Tues–Sat noon–2pm and 7–10pm; Sun noon–2pm. Closed 2 weeks in Jan. Bus: 7, 10, or 22.

SEEING THE SIGHTS

SIGHTSEEING SUGGESTIONS FOR FIRST-TIME VISITORS

If You Have 1 Day Visit **Edinburgh Castle** as soon as it opens in the morning, then walk the **Royal Mile** to the Palace of **Holyroodhouse,** former abode of Mary, Queen of Scots. Look out over the city from the vantage point of **Arthur's Seat.** Stroll through **Princes Street Gardens,** capping your day with a walk along the major shopping thoroughfare, **Princes Street.**

If You Have 2 Days In the morning of your second day, head for Old Town again, but this time explore its narrow streets, wynds, and closes, and visit the **John Knox House,** the **High Kirk of St. Giles,** and the small museums. After lunch, climb the **Scott Monument** for a good view of Old Town and the Princes Street Gardens. Spend the rest of the afternoon exploring the **National Gallery of Scotland.**

If You Have 3 Days Spend day 3 getting acquainted with the major attractions of New Town, including the **National Museum of Scotland, National Portrait Gallery, Georgian House,** and **Royal Botanic Garden.**

If You Have 4 or 5 Days On the fourth day, take a trip west to **Stirling Castle** and see some of the dramatic scenery of the **Trossachs.** On the fifth day you'll feel like a native, so seek out some of the city's minor but interesting attractions, such as the **Camera Obscura,** the **Scotch Whisky Heritage Centre,** and **Dean Village.**

THE ROYAL MILE ★★

The Royal Mile (bus: 1, 6, 23, 27, 30, 34, 35, or 36) stretches from Edinburgh Castle all the way to the Palace of Holyroodhouse. Walking along it, you'll see some of the most interesting old structures in Edinburgh, with turrets, gables, and towering chimneys.

High Kirk of St. Giles   Built in 1120, a short walk downhill from Edinburgh Castle, this church is one of the most important architectural landmarks along the Royal Mile. It combines a dark and brooding stone exterior with surprisingly graceful and delicate flying buttresses. One of its outstanding features is its **Thistle Chapel,** housing beautiful stalls and notable heraldic stained-glass windows. Cathedral guides are available at all times to conduct tours.

High St. ℂ 0131/225-9442. Free admission, but £1 ($1.85) donation suggested. Easter–Sept Mon–Fri 9am–7pm, Sat 9am–5pm, Sun 1–5pm; Oct–Easter Mon–Sat 9am–5pm, Sun 1–5pm. Sun services at 8, 10, and 11:30am and 6 and 8pm.

Writers' Museum   This 1622 house takes its name, Lady Stair's House, from a former owner, Elizabeth, the dowager countess of Stair. Today it's a treasure trove of portraits, relics, and manuscripts relating to three of Scotland's greatest men of letters. The Robert Burns collection includes his writing desk, rare manuscripts, portraits, and many other items. Also on display are some of Sir Walter Scott's possessions, including his pipe, chess set, and original manuscripts. The museum holds one of the most significant Robert Louis Stevenson collections anywhere, including personal belongings, paintings, photographs, and early editions.

In Lady Stair's House, off Lawnmarket. ℂ 0131/529-4901. www.cac.org.uk. Free admission. Mon–Sat 10am–4:45pm.

Museum of Childhood *Kids*   The world's first museum devoted solely to the history of childhood stands just opposite John Knox's House. Contents of its four floors range from antique toys to games to exhibits on health, education, and costumes, plus video presentations and an activity area. Because of the youthful crowd it naturally attracts, it ranks as the noisiest museum in town.

42 High St. ℂ 0131/529-4142. www.cac.org.uk. Free admission. Mon–Sat 10am–5pm; July–Aug, also Sun 2–5pm.

The Real Mary King's Close *Finds*   Beneath the City Chambers on the Royal Mile lies Old Town's deepest secret, a warren of hidden streets where people lived and worked for centuries. This attraction allows you to go back into the turbulent days of plague-ridden Edinburgh in the 17th century. Today's visitors can see a number of underground "closes," originally very narrow walkways with houses on either side, some dating back centuries. When the Royal Exchange (now the City Chambers) was constructed in 1753, the top floors of the buildings of the close were torn down, although the lower sections were used as the foundations of the new building, leaving a number of dark and mysterious passages intact. In April 2003, guided parties were allowed to visit these dwellings for the first time. Subtle lighting and audio effects add to the experience. You can visit everything from a gravedigger's family stricken with the plague to a grand 16th-century town house. The haunted **Shrine Room** is the best surviving 17th-century house in Scotland.

Writers' Court, off the Royal Mile. © 0870/243-0160. Admission £7 ($13) adults, £5 ($9.25) children, £21 ($39) family. Bus: 1 or 6.

The People's Story   If you continue walking downhill along Canongate toward Holyroodhouse, you'll see one of the handsomest buildings on the Royal Mile. Built in 1591, the **Canongate Tolbooth** was once the courthouse, prison, and center of municipal affairs for the burgh of Canongate. Now it contains a museum celebrating the social history of the inhabitants of Edinburgh from the late 18th century to the present, with lots of emphasis on the cultural displacements of the Industrial Revolution.

163 Canongate. © 0131/529-4057. www.cac.org.uk. Free admission. Mon–Sat 10am–5pm. Bus: 1.

Museum of Edinburgh   Across from the Canongate Tolbooth is this fine example of a restored 16th-century mansion. Today it functions as Edinburgh's principal museum of local history. The interior contains faithfully crafted reproductions of rooms inspired by the city's traditional industries, including exhibits devoted to glassmaking, pottery, wool processing, and cabinetry, always with a focus on the stamina and struggles of the workers who labored within.

142 Canongate. © 0131/529-4143. www.cac.org.uk. Free admission. Mon–Sat 10am–5pm; during the Edinburgh Festival, also Sun 2–5pm. Bus: 1.

Scotch Whisky Heritage Centre   This center is privately funded by a conglomeration of Scotland's biggest distillers. It highlights the economic effect of whisky on both Scotland and the world and illuminates the centuries-old traditions associated with whisky making, showing the science and art of distilling. There's a 7-minute audiovisual show and an electric car ride past 13 sets showing historic moments in the whisky industry. A tour entitling you to sample five whiskies and take away a miniature bottle is £12 ($22) per person.

354 Castlehill. © 0131/220-0441. www.whisky-heritage.co.uk. Admission £7.50 ($14) adults, £5.50 ($10) seniors and students with ID, £3.95 ($7.30) ages 5–17, free for children 4 and under. Oct–Apr daily 10am–5pm; May–Sept 9:30am–6:30pm.

HISTORIC SITES

Edinburgh Castle 🟊🟊   Although its early history is vague, it's believed that Edinburgh was built on the dead volcano, Castle Rock. It's known that in the 11th century Malcolm III (Canmore) and his Saxon queen, later venerated as St. Margaret, founded a castle on this same spot. The only fragment left of their original castle—in fact the oldest structure in Edinburgh—is **St. Margaret's**

Moments **For Mr. Hyde Fans**

Near Gladstone's Land is **Brodie's Close**, a stone-floored alleyway. You can wander into the alley for a view of old stone houses that'll make you think you've stepped into a scene from a BBC production of a Dickens novel. It was named in honor of the notorious Deacon Brodie, a respectable councilor by day and a thief by night (he was the inspiration for Robert Louis Stevenson's *The Strange Case of Dr. Jekyll and Mr. Hyde*, though Stevenson set his story in foggy London town, not in Edinburgh). Brodie was hanged in 1788, and the mechanism used for the hangman's scaffolding had previously been improved by Brodie himself—for use on others, of course. Across the street is the most famous pub along the Royal Mile: **Deacon Brodie's Tavern** (see later in this chapter).

Chapel. Built in the Norman style, the oblong structure dates principally from the 12th century.

Inside the castle you can visit the **State Apartments,** particularly Queen Mary's bedroom, where Mary, Queen of Scots, gave birth to James VI of Scotland (later James I of England). The highlight is the Crown Chamber, which houses the Honours of Scotland (Scottish Crown Jewels), used at the coronation of James VI, along with the scepter and the sword of state of Scotland.

You can also view the **Stone of Scone,** or "Stone of Destiny," on which Scottish kings had been crowned since time immemorial. Edward I of England carried the stone off to Westminster Abbey in 1296, where it rested under the British coronation chair. It was finally returned to its rightful home in Scotland in November 1996, where it was welcomed with much pomp and circumstance.

Castlehill. © **0131/225-9846.** Admission £8.50 ($16) adults, £2 ($3.70) children ages 15 and under. Apr–Sept daily 9:30am–5:15pm; Oct–Mar daily 9:30am–4:15pm. Bus: 1 or 6.

Palace of Holyroodhouse ★★   This palace was built adjacent to an Augustinian abbey established by David I in the 12th century. The nave, now in ruins, remains today. James IV founded the palace nearby in the early part of the 16th century, but only the north tower is left. Much of what you see today was ordered built by Charles II.

The most dramatic incident in the history of Holyroodhouse occurred in the old wing when Mary, Queen of Scots, was in residence. Her Italian secretary, David Rizzio, was murdered (with 56 stab wounds) in the audience chamber by Mary's husband, Lord Darnley, and his accomplices. The palace suffered long periods of neglect, although it basked in glory at the ball thrown by Bonnie Prince Charlie in the mid–18th century. The present queen and Prince Philip live at Holyroodhouse whenever they visit Edinburgh. When they're not in residence, the palace is open to visitors.

Canongate, at the eastern end of the Royal Mile. © **0131/556-7371.** Admission £7.50 ($14) adults, £6 ($11) seniors, £4 ($7.40) children ages 15 and under, £19 ($35) families (up to 2 adults and 2 children). Daily 9:30am–5:15pm. Closed 2 weeks in May and 3 weeks in late June and early July (dates vary). Bus: 1 or 6.

MORE ATTRACTIONS

Scott Monument ★   Completed in the mid–19th century, the Gothic-inspired Scott Monument is the most famous landmark of Edinburgh. Sir Walter Scott's heroes are carved as small figures in the monument, and you can climb to the top. You can also see the first-ever **floral clock,** which was constructed in 1904, in the West Princes Street Gardens.

In the East Princes St. Gardens. ℂ **0131/529-4068.** Admission £2.50 ($4.60). Mar–May and Oct Mon–Sat 9am–6pm, Sun 10am–6pm; June–Sept Mon–Sat 9am–8pm, Sun 10am–6pm; Nov–Feb Mon–Sat 9am–4pm, Sun 10am–4pm. Bus: 1 or 6.

National Gallery of Scotland ★★★

This museum is located in the center of Princes Street Gardens. The gallery is rather small, but the collection was chosen with great care. The duke of Sutherland has lent the museum some paintings, including two Raphaels, Titian's two Diana canvases and his *Venus Rising from the Sea,* and the *Seven Sacraments,* a work of the great 17th-century Frenchman Nicolas Poussin. The Spanish masters are represented as well. You can also see excellent examples of English painting: Gainsborough's *The Hon. Mrs. Graham* and Constable's *Dedham Vale,* along with works by Turner, Reynolds, and Hogarth. Naturally, the work of Scottish painters is prominent, including Alexander Naysmith and Henry Raeburn, whose most famous work, *The Reverend Walker,* can be seen here.

2 The Mound. ℂ **0131/624-6200.** www.natgalscot.ac.uk. Free admission. Mon–Sat 10am–5pm; Sun noon–5pm (during the festival, Mon–Sat 10am–6pm, Sun 11am–6pm). Bus: 13.

Our Dynamic Earth ★ Kids

The Millennium Dome at Greenwich outside London may have been a bust, but the millennium museum for Scotland is still packing in the crowds. Not far from the Palace of Holyroodhouse, Our Dynamic Earth tells the story of Earth in all its diversity. You can push buttons to simulate earthquakes, meteor showers, and views of outer space. You can see replicas of the slimy green primordial soup where life began. Time capsules wind their way back through the eons, and a series of specialized aquariums re-create primordial life forms. That's not all; there is so much more, ranging from simulated terrains of polar ice caps to tropical rainforests with plenty of creepy-crawlies. All 11 galleries have stunning special effects.

Holyrood Rd. ℂ **0131/550-7800.** www.dynamicearth.co.uk. Admission £8.95 ($15) adults; £6.50 ($12) students, £5.45 ($10) seniors, £6.50 ($12) children ages 5–15; free for children under 5; £17–£29 ($30–$53) family. Apr–Aug daily 10am–6pm; Sept–Oct daily 10am–5pm; Nov–Mar Wed–Sun 10am–5pm. Bus: 35 or 64.

Outlook Tower & Camera Obscura

The 1853 periscope is at the top of the Outlook Tower, from which you can view a panorama of the surrounding city. Trained guides point out the landmarks and talk about Edinburgh's fascinating history. In addition, there are several entertaining exhibits, all with an optical theme, and a well-stocked shop selling books, crafts, and compact discs.

Castlehill. ℂ **0131/226-3709.** Admission £5.75 ($11) adults, £4.60 ($8.50) seniors, £3.70 ($6.90) children. Apr–Oct Mon–Fri 9:30am–6pm, Sat–Sun 10am–6pm (until 7:30pm in July and 7pm in Aug); Nov–Mar daily 10am–5pm. Bus: 1 or 6.

National Museums of Scotland (NMS) ★★★

In 1998, two long-established museums, the Royal Museum of Scotland and the National Museum of Antiquities, were united into this single institution 2 blocks south of the Royal Mile. The museum showcases exhibits in the decorative arts, ethnography, natural history, geology, archaeology, technology, and science. Six modern galleries distill billions of years of Scottish history, a total of 12,000 items ranging from rocks found on the island of South Uist dating back 2.9 billion years to a Hillman Imp, one of the last 500 cars manufactured at the Linwood plant near Glasgow before it closed in 1981. One gallery is devoted to Scotland's role as an independent nation before it merged with the United Kingdom in 1707. Another gallery, devoted to industry and empire from 1707 to 1914, includes exhibits on shipbuilding, whisky distilling, the railways, and such textiles as the tartan and paisley.

Chambers St. ⓒ 0131/247-4422. www.nms.ac.uk. Free admission. Mon and Wed–Sat 10am–5pm; Tues 10am–8pm; Sun noon–5pm. Walk south from Waverley Station for 10 min. to reach Chambers St. or take bus no. 27, 35, 41, 42, or 45.

Scottish National Gallery of Modern Art ★★   Scotland's national collection of 20th-century art is set on 5.5 hectares (12 acres) of grounds, just a 15-minute walk from the west end of Princes Street. The collection is international in scope and high in quality despite its modest size. Major sculptures outside the building include pieces by Henry Moore and Barbara Hepworth. Inside, the

---

Britannia: The People's Yacht

In case the queen never invited you for a sail on her 125m (412-ft.) yacht, there's still a chance to go aboard this world-famous vessel. Launched on April 16, 1953, the luxury yacht was decommissioned December 11, 1997. Today, the yacht—technically a Royal Navy ship—which has sailed more than a million miles, rests at anchor in the port of Leith, 3km (1¾ miles) from the center of Edinburgh. The gangplank is now lowered for the public, whereas it once was lowered for such world leaders as Mahatma Gandhi, Tony Blair, and Nelson Mandela.

British taxpayers spent £160 million maintaining the yacht throughout most of the 1990s. Even a major refit would have prolonged the vessel's life for only a few more years. Because of budgetary constraints, a decision was made to put it in dry dock. The public reaches the vessel by going through a visitor center designed by Sir Terence Conran. At its centerpiece is the yacht's 12m (41-ft.) tender floating in a pool.

Once on board, you're guided around all five decks by an audio tour. You can also visit the drawing room and the Royal Apartments, once occupied by the likes of not only the queen, but Prince Philip and princes William, Harry, Edward, and Andrew, as well as princesses Anne and Margaret. Even the engine room, the galleys, and the captain's cabin can be visited.

All tickets should be booked as far in advance as possible by calling ⓒ 0131/555-5566. You can also get the latest up-to-date information by going to the website www.royalyachtbritannia.co.uk. The yacht is open daily October to March with tours starting at 10am and ending at 3:30pm, and April to September with tours starting at 9:30am and ending at 4:30pm. Lasting 90 to 120 minutes, each tour is self-guided with the use of a headset lent to participants. Adults pay £8.50 ($16), seniors £6.50 ($12), and children ages 5 to 17 £4.50 ($8.50); those ages 4 and under visit for free. A family ticket, good for two adults and up to two children, is £23 ($43). From Waverley Bridge, take either city bus (Lothian Transport) X50 or the Guide Friday tour bus, which has the words BRITANNIA marked all over its sides.

collection ranges from a fauve Derain and cubist Braque and Picasso to recent works by Paolozzi. There's a strong representation of English and Scottish artists—William Turner, John Constable, Henry Raeburn, and David Wilkie, to name a few. Works by Matisse, Miró, Kirchner, Kokoschka, Ernst, Ben Nicholson, Nevelson, Balthus, Lichtenstein, Kitaj, and Hockney are also on view.

Belford Rd. © 0131/556-8921. www.natgalscot.ac.uk. Free admission, except for some temporary exhibits. Daily 10am–5pm. Bus: 13 stops by the gallery but is infrequent; nos. 18, 20, and 41 pass along Queensferry Rd., a 5-min. walk up Queensferry Terrace and Belford Rd. from the gallery.

Dean Gallery ★ *Finds* Across from the Scottish National Gallery of Modern Art, Dean Gallery houses the Modern Art's extensive collections of Dada and Surrealism. For those of us who are fascinated by these art movements, there's nothing better in Scotland. All of our favorite artists—and maybe yours too— are here, from Max Ernst to Joan Miró and, of course, Salvador Dalí. The major exhibit here consists of a large part of the works of Sir Eduardo Paolozzi, a hip modern Scottish sculptor. The collection of prints, drawings, plaster maquettes (models), molds, and contents of his studio are housed in the gallery.

73 Belford Rd. © 0131/624-6200. www.natgalscot.ac.uk. Free admission to permanent collection; variable prices to special exhibitions. Mon–Sat 10am–5pm; Sun noon–5pm. Bus 13.

Scottish National Portrait Gallery Housed in a red stone Victorian Gothic building by Rowand Anderson, this portrait gallery gives you a chance to see what the famous people of Scottish history looked like. The portraits, several by Ramsay and Raeburn, include everybody from Mary, Queen of Scots, to Sean Connery, and from Flora Macdonald to Irvine Welsh.

1 Queen St. © 0131/624-6200. www.natgalscot.ac.uk. Free admission, except for some temporary exhibits. Mon–Wed and Fri–Sun 10am–5pm; Thurs 10am–7pm. Bus: 18, 20, or 41.

A GARDEN

Gardeners and nature lovers will be attracted to the **Royal Botanic Garden,** Inverleith Row (© **0131/552-7171**). Main areas of interest are the Exhibition Hall, Alpine House, Demonstration Garden, annual and herbaceous borders (summer only), copse, Woodland Garden, Wild Garden, Arboretum, Peat Garden, Rock Garden, Heath Garden, and pond. Admission is by voluntary donation. It's open April through September from 10am to 7pm, March and October from 10am to 6pm, and November through February from 10am to 4pm.

Moments **A Step Back in Time at Historic Dean Village**

The village is one of the most photographed sights in the city. Set in a valley about 30m (100 ft.) below the level of the rest of Edinburgh, it's full of nostalgic charm. The settlement dates from the 12th century, and for many centuries it was a grain-milling center. The current residents worked hard to restore the old buildings—many of which were converted into flats and houses—and managed to maintain all of the original Brigadoon-like charm. A few minutes from the West End, it's located at the end of Bell's Brae, off Queensferry Street, on the Water of Leith. You can enjoy a celebrated view by looking downstream under the high arches of Dean Bridge, designed by Telford in 1833. The most scenic walk is along the water in the direction of St. Bernard's Well.

ORGANIZED TOURS

For a quick introduction to the principal attractions in and around Edinburgh, consider the tours offered from April to late October by **Lothian Region Transport,** 14 Queen St. (℗ **0131/555-6363;** www.lothianbuses.co.uk). You can see most of the major sights of Edinburgh, including the Royal Mile, the Palace of Holyroodhouse, Princes Street, and Edinburgh Castle, by double-decker motor coach for £7.50 ($14) adults, £6 ($11) seniors and students, and £2.50 ($4.60) children. This ticket is valid all day on any **LRT Edinburgh Classic Tour bus,** which allows passengers to get on and off at any of the 15 stops along its routes. Buses start from Waverley Bridge daily beginning at 9:40am, departing every 15 minutes in summer and about every 30 minutes in winter, then embark on a circuit of Edinburgh, which takes about 1 hour if you stay on the bus without ever getting off. Commentary is offered along the way.

Tickets for any of these tours can be bought at LRT offices at Waverley Bridge, or at 14 Queen St., or at the tourist information center in Waverley Market. Advance reservations are a good idea. For more information, call ℗ **0131/555-6363,** 24 hours a day.

The **Edinburgh Literary Pub Tour** (℗ **0131/226-6665;** http://home.btconnect.com/sltc) follows in the footsteps of such literary greats as Robert Burns, Robert Louis Stevenson, and Sir Walter Scott. The *Edinburgh Evening News* has hailed this tour (and we concur) as "vivid, erudite, and entertaining." The tour goes into the city's famous or infamous taverns and *howffs* highlighting such literary legends as the adventures of Dr. Jekyll and Mr. Hyde or the erotic love poetry of Burns. Tours depart from the Beehive Inn on the Grassmarket in the Old Town, going along the Royal Mile. The 2-hour tour costs £8 ($15) for adults and £6 ($11) for children. From June to September tours leave nightly at 7:30pm; April, May, and October Thursday to Sunday at 7:30pm, and November to March Friday at 7:30pm.

The **Witchery Tours** (℗ **0131/225-6745;** www.witcherytours.com) are filled with ghosts, gore, and witchcraft, enlivened by "jumper-outers"—actors who jump out to scare you. Two tours—Ghost & Gore and Murder & Mystery—are a bit similar and overlap in parts. Scenes of many horrific tortures, murders, and supernatural happenings in the historic Old Town are visited, all under the cloak of darkness. The ghost tour departs daily at 7pm and 7:30pm, with the murder tour leaving daily at 9pm and again at 10pm year-round. Tours last 1 hour and 15 minutes, costing £7 ($13) and £4 ($7.40) for children. Departures are from outside the Witchery Restaurant on Castlehill.

Mercat Tours (℗ **0131/557-9933;** www.mercattours.com) conducts the best walking tours of Edinburgh, covering a wide range of interests from "Secrets of the Royal Mile" to a "Haunted Underground Experience." Tours meet outside the Tourist Office on Princes Street. The Secrets of the Royal Mile Tour leaves daily at 10:30am, with a Grand Tour departing at 10am daily. The Hidden Vaults tour runs hourly from May to September 11am to 4pm; off season daily at noon, 2pm, and 4pm. The cost of these tours begins at £6 ($11) for adults and £4 ($7.40) for children. Most tours last 1½ hours.

Guide Friday (℗ **0131/556-2244;** www.guidefriday.com) is good for a quick overview. You can later follow up with more in-depth visits. You're taken around the city in one of the company's fleet of open-top, double-decker buses, with informed and often amusing running commentaries. Highlights include the Royal Mile, Princes Street, Holyroodhouse Palace, and Edinburgh Castle, as well as the New Town. Tours run between 9:20am and dusk, costing £8.50

($16) for adults and £2.50 ($4.60) for kids 5 to 15. Departures are from Waverly Bridge, with tours lasting 1 hour.

THE SHOPPING SCENE

The best buys are tartans and woolens, along with bone china and Scottish crystal. Princes Street, George Street, and the Royal Mile are the major shopping arteries. Here are a few suggestions.

Looking for a knitted memento? Moira-Anne Leask, owner of the **Shetland Connection,** 491 Lawnmarket (© **0131/225-3525;** bus: 28), promotes the skills of the Shetland knitter, and her shop is packed with sweaters, hats, and gloves in colorful Fair Isle designs. She also offers hand-knitted mohair, Aran, and Icelandic sweaters. Items range from fine-ply cobweb shawls to chunky ski sweaters handcrafted by skilled knitters in top-quality wool.

If you've ever suspected that you might be Scottish, **Tartan Gift Shops,** 54 High St. (© **0131/558-3187;** bus: 35), has a chart indicating the place of origin, in Scotland, of your family name. You'll then be faced with a bewildering array of hunt-and-dress tartans. The high-quality wool is sold by the yard as well as in the form of kilts for both men and women.

Clan Tartan Centre, 70–74 Bangor Rd., Leith (© **0131/553-5161;** bus: 7 or 10), is one of the leading tartan specialists in Edinburgh, regardless of which clan you claim as your own. If you want help in identifying a particular tartan, the staff at this shop will assist you. At the same location is the **James Pringle Woollen Mill** (© **0131/553-5161**), which produces a large variety of top-quality wool items, including a range of Scottish knitwear—cashmere sweaters, tartan and tweed ties, travel rugs, tweed hats, and tam-o'-shanters. In addition, the mill has the only Clan Tartan Centre in Scotland, where more than 2,500 sets and trade designs are accessible through their research facilities.

The two best department stores in Edinburgh are **Debenhams,** 109–112 Princes St. (© **0131/2251320;** www.debenhams.com; bus: 3 or 31), and **Jenners,** 48 Princes St. (© **0131/2252442;** www.jenners.com; bus: 3, 26, 31, or 44). Both stock Scottish and international merchandise.

Another Scottish shopping venue worth checking out is **Old Town Weaving Company,** 555 Castlehill (© **0131/226-4162;** bus: 23 or 27), where you can converse with craftspeople and purchase their work. If you're interested in old-fashioned Scottish crafts, this is the place. Established in 1866, **Hamilton & Inches,** 87 George St. (© **0131/225-4898;** bus: 41 or 42), is a gold- and silversmith with both modern and antique designs. It has a stunning late-Georgian interior as well.

EDINBURGH AFTER DARK

For a thorough list of entertainment options during your stay, pick up a copy of *The List,* a biweekly entertainment paper available free at the Edinburgh & Scotland Information Centre.

FESTIVALS

The highlight of Edinburgh's year—some would say the only time the real Edinburgh emerges—comes in the last weeks of August during the **Edinburgh International Festival.** Since 1947, the festival has attracted artists and companies of the highest international standard in all fields of the arts, including music, opera, dance, theater, exhibition, poetry, and prose, and "Auld Reekie" takes on a cosmopolitan air.

During the festival, one of the most exciting spectacles is the Military Tattoo on the floodlit esplanade in front of Edinburgh Castle, high on its rock above the city. Vast audiences watch the precision marching of Scottish regiments and military units from all parts of the world, and of course the stirring skirl of the bagpipes and the swirl of the kilt.

Less predictable in quality but greater in quantity is the **Edinburgh Festival Fringe** (180 High St., Edinburgh EH1 1BW; ✆ **0131/226-5257;** www.edfringe.com), an opportunity for anybody—professional or nonprofessional, an individual, a group of friends, or a whole company of performers—to put on a show wherever they can find an empty stage or street corner. Late-night reviews, outrageous and irreverent contemporary drama, university theater presentations, maybe even a full-length opera—Edinburgh gives them all free rein. A **Film Festival, Jazz Festival, Television Festival,** and **Book Festival** (every 2nd year) overlap in August.

Ticket prices for the various festivals range from £4 ($7.40) up to about £63 ($117) per seat. (The Fringe festival's **Fringe Sun,** on the 2nd weekend of the festival, is a free open-air showcase for hundreds of festival acts.) Information can be obtained at **Edinburgh International Festival,** The Hub, Castle Hill, Edinburgh EH1 7ND (✆ **0131/473-2000;** fax 0131/473-2003; www.eif.co.uk). The office is open Monday through Friday from 9:30am to 5:30pm.

Other sources of event information include **Edinburgh Book Festival,** 137 Dundee St., Edinburgh EH11 1BG (✆ **0131/228-5444;** www.edbookfest.co.uk); **Edinburgh International Film Festival,** 88 Lothian Rd., Edinburgh EH3 9BZ (✆ **0131/228-4051;** www.edfilmfest.org.uk); and **Edinburgh Military Tattoo,** 32 Market St., Edinburgh EH1 1QB (✆ **0131/225-1188;** www.edintattoo.co.uk).

THEATER

Edinburgh has a lively theater scene. In 1994, the **Festival Theatre,** 13–29 Nicolson St. (✆ **0131/662-1112** for administration, or 0131/529-6000 for tickets during festival times; 0131/473-2000 operational during the Aug festival; bus: 3, 31, or 33), opened in time for some aspects of the Edinburgh Festival. Set on the eastern edge of Edinburgh, near the old campus of the University of Edinburgh, it has since been called "Britain's de facto Dance House" because of its sprung floor, its enormous stage (the largest in Britain), and its suitability for opera presentations of all kinds. Tickets are £6 to £60 ($11–$111).

Another major theater is the **King's Theatre,** 2 Leven St. (✆ **0131/529-6000;** bus: 10 or 11), a 1,600-seat Victorian venue offering a wide repertoire of classical entertainment, including ballet, opera, and West End productions. The **Netherbow Arts Centre,** 43 High St. (✆ **0131/556-9579;** bus: 1), has been called "informal," and productions here are often experimental and delightful—new Scottish theater at its best.

The resident company of **Royal Lyceum Theatre,** Grindlay Street (✆ **0131/248-4848;** bus: 11 or 15), also has an enviable reputation; its presentations range from the works of Shakespeare to new Scottish playwrights. The **Traverse Theatre,** Cambridge Street (✆ **0131/228-1404;** bus: 11 or 15), is one of the few theaters in Britain funded solely to present new plays by British writers and first translations into English of international works. In a modern location, it now offers two theaters under one roof: Traverse 1 seats 250 and Traverse 2 seats 100.

BALLET, OPERA & CLASSICAL MUSIC

The **Scottish Ballet** and the **Scottish Opera** perform at the **Playhouse Theatre,** 18–22 Greenside Place (② **0131/7839-4401;** bus: 7 or 14). With 3,100 seats, it's the town's largest theater. The **Scottish Chamber Orchestra** makes its home at the **Queen's Hall,** Clerk Street (② **0131/668-3456;** bus: 3, 33, or 31), also a major venue for the Edinburgh International Festival.

FOLK MUSIC & CEILIDHS

Folk music is presented in many clubs and pubs in Edinburgh, but these strolling players tend to be somewhat erratic in their appearances. Ceilidhs (pronounced *kay*-lee) are large gatherings where traditional music and folk dancing are featured. It's best to read notices in pubs and talk to the tourist office to see where the ceilidh will be on the night of your visit.

Some hotels regularly feature traditional Scottish music in the evenings. You might check with the **George Hotel** at 19–21 George St. (② **0131/225-1251;** bus: 3, 31, or 33). "Jamie's Scottish Evening" is presented at the **King James Hotel** on Leith Street (② **0131/556-0111;** bus: 7 or 14), April through October daily at 7pm, November Wednesday only; the four-course dinner with wine and show costs £44 ($80).

PUBS & BARS

Edinburgh's most famous pub, **Café Royal Circle Bar,** 17 W. Register St. (② **0131/556-1884;** bus: 3, 31, or 33), is a long-enduring favorite. Part of it is now occupied by the Oyster Bar of the Café Royal, but life in the Circle Bar continues at its old pace. The opulent trappings of the Victorian era are still to be seen. Go up to the serving counter, which stands like an island in a sea of drinkers, and place your order.

The Abbotsford, 3 Rose St. (② **0131/225-5276;** bus: 3, 31, or 33), is near the eastern end of Rose Street, a short walk from Princes Street. This pub has served stiff drinks and oceans of beer since it was founded in 1887. Inside, the gaslight era is alive and thriving, thanks to a careful preservation of the original dark paneling, long battered tables, and ornate plaster ceiling. The inventories of beer on tap change about once a week, supplementing a roster of single-malt Scotches. Platters of food, priced from £3.25 to £11 ($6–$21), are dispensed from the bar. Established in 1806, **Deacon Brodie's Tavern,** 435 Lawnmarket (② **0131/225-6531;** bus: 1), is the neighborhood pub along the Royal Mile. It

---

Moments   A Wee Dram for Fans of Malt Whisky

It requires a bit of an effort to reach it (take bus no. 10A, 16, or 17 from Princes St. to Leith), but for fans of malt whisky, the **Scotch Malt Whisky Society** has been called "The Top of the Whisky Pyramid" by distillery-industry magazines in Britain. It's on the second floor of a 16th-century warehouse at 87 Giles St., Leith (② **0131/554-3451**), and was originally designed to store bordeaux and port wines from France and Portugal. All you can order are single-malt whiskies, served neat, usually in a dram (unless you want yours watered down with branch water) and selected from a staggering choice of whiskies from more than 100 distilleries throughout Scotland. Hours are Monday and Tuesday from 10am to 5pm, Wednesday through Saturday 10am to 11pm, Sunday 11am to 10pm; bus: 22.

perpetuates the memory of Deacon Brodie, good citizen by day, robber by night (see earlier in this chapter). The tavern and wine cellars contain a restaurant and lounge bar.

DAY TRIPS FROM EDINBURGH

LINLITHGOW   In this royal burgh, a county town in West Lothian, 29km (18 miles) west of Edinburgh, Mary, Queen of Scots, was born in 1542. Her birthplace, the roofless **Linlithgow Palace** (✆ **01506/842-896**), can still be explored today, even if it's but a shell of its former self. The queen's suite was in the north quarter but was rebuilt for the homecoming of James VI (James I of England) in 1620. The palace burned to the ground in 1746. The Great Hall is on the first floor, and a small display shows some of the more interesting architectural relics. The ruined palace is 1km (½ mile) from Linlithgow Station. Admission is £3 ($5.50) adults, £2.30 ($4.25) seniors, £1 ($1.85) children. Hours are Monday through Saturday from 9:30am to 4pm, Sunday from 2 to 4pm.

South of the palace stands the medieval kirk of **St. Michael's Parish Church** (✆ **01506/842188**), open only May through September from 10am to 4:30pm. Many a Scottish monarch has worshiped here since its consecration in 1242. Despite being ravaged by the disciples of John Knox and transformed into a stable by Cromwell, it's one of Scotland's best examples of a parish church.

In the midst of beautifully landscaped grounds, laid out along the lines of Versailles, sits **Hopetoun House** (✆ **0131/331-2451**), 16km (10 miles) from Edinburgh. This is Scotland's greatest Adam mansion, and a fine example of 18th-century architecture. The splendid reception rooms are filled with 18th-century furniture, paintings, statuary, and other artworks. From a rooftop platform you see a panoramic view of the Firth of Forth. You can take the nature trail, explore the deer parks, investigate the Stables Museum, or stroll through the formal gardens, all on the grounds. The house is 3km (1¾ miles) from the Forth Road Bridge near South Queensferry, off A-904. If you don't have a car, take a cab from the rail station in Dalmeny for about £3.50 ($6.50). Admission is £6 ($11) adults, £5 ($9.25) seniors, £3 ($5.50) children, £16 ($30) family (up to six). Hours are from 10am to 5:30pm (last admission 4:30pm), daily May through September, Easter weekend, and weekends in October.

Getting There   From Edinburgh, direct **trains** (✆ **0345/484950**) run every 15 minutes during the day to Linlithgow (trip time: 20 min.). Round-trip fare is £6 ($11) adults, £3 ($5.50) children. **Buses** also leave from St. Andrew's Square in Edinburgh (✆ **01324/613-777** for schedules), every 20 minutes (trip time: 1 hr.). Round-trip fare is £4.60 ($8.50) adults, £2.30 ($4.25) children. **Motorists** can take A902 to Corstorphine, then A8 to M9, getting off at the signposted junction (no. 3) to Linlithgow.

DIRLETON   This little town, a preservation village, vies for the title of "prettiest village in Scotland." The town plan, drafted in the early 16th century, is essentially unchanged today. Dirleton has two greens shaped like triangles, with a pub opposite Dirleton Castle, placed at right angles to a group of cottages.

A rose-tinted 13th-century castle with surrounding gardens, once the seat of the wealthy Anglo-Norman de Vaux family, **Dirleton Castle** (✆ **01620/ 850-330**) looks like a fairy-tale fortification, with its towers, arched entries, and oak ramp. Ruins of the Great Hall and kitchen can be seen, as well as what's left of the lord's chamber where the de Vaux family lived. The 16th-century main gate has a hole through which boiling tar or water could be poured to discourage unwanted visitors. The castle's country garden and bowling green are still in use. Admission is £3 ($5.50) adults, £2.30 ($4.25) seniors, £1 ($1.85) children. You can tour the castle April through September daily from 9:30am to 6pm; October through March Monday through Saturday from 9:30am to 4pm, Sunday from 2 to 4pm.

Getting There   Dirleton is on the Edinburgh–North Berwick road (A-198), 8km (5 miles) west of North Berwick and 3km (1¾ miles) east of Edinburgh. **Buses** (© 0870/872-7271) leave from the West Maitlend Street station in Edinburgh at 20 past and 45 till the hour (trip time: 1 hr.). The last bus departs at 10:30pm. One-way fare is £2.35 ($4.35) adults, £1.15 ($2.15) children.

2 Glasgow ★★★

Glasgow is just 64.5km (40 miles) west of Edinburgh, but the contrast between the two cities is striking. Scotland's economic powerhouse and its largest city (Britain's third-largest), up-and-coming Glasgow is now the country's cultural capital and home to half its population. It has long been famous for ironworks and steelworks; the local shipbuilding industry produced the *Queen Mary,* the *Queen Elizabeth,* and other fabled ocean liners.

Once polluted by industry and plagued with some of the worst slums in Europe, Glasgow has been transformed. Urban development and the decision to locate the Scottish Exhibition and Conference Centre here have brought great changes: Industrial grime is being sandblasted away, overcrowding has been reduced, and more open space and less traffic congestion mean cleaner air. Glasgow also boasts a vibrant and even edgy arts scene; it's now one of the cultural capitals of Europe.

In the process, the splendor of the city has reemerged. The planners of the 19th century thought on a grand scale when they designed the terraces and villas west and south of the center, and John Betjeman and other critics have hailed Glasgow as "the greatest surviving example of a Victorian city."

Glasgow's origins are ancient, making Edinburgh, for all its wealth of history, seem comparatively young. The village that grew up beside a fjord 32km (20 miles) from the mouth of the River Clyde as a medieval ecclesiastical center began its commercial prosperity in the 17th century. As it grew, the city engulfed the smaller medieval towns of Ardrie, Renfrew, Rutherglen, and Paisley.

ESSENTIALS
GETTING THERE   By Plane   The **Glasgow Airport** is at Abbotsinch (© 0141/887-1111), 16km (10 miles) west of the city via M8. You can use the regular Glasgow CityLink bus service to get to the city center. From bus stop no. 2, take bus no. 901 or 905 to the Buchanan Street Bus Station in the center of town. The ride takes about 20 minutes and costs £3.30 ($6). A taxi to the city center costs about £17 ($32). You can reach Edinburgh by taking a bus from Glasgow Airport to Queens Station and then changing to a bus for Edinburgh. The entire journey, including the change, should take about 2 hours and costs £6.30 ($12) one-way or £9.50 ($18) round-trip.

Monday to Friday, British Airways runs almost hourly shuttle service from London's Heathrow Airport to Glasgow. The first flight departs London at 7:15am and the last at 8:35pm; service is reduced on weekends, depending on volume. For flight schedules and fares, call British Airways in London at © 0870/850-9850.

From mid-May through October, **American Airlines** (© 800/433-7300; www.aa.com) offers a daily nonstop flight to Glasgow from Chicago; the rest of the year, you'll make at least one transfer. **Northwest Airlines** (© **800/225-2525;** www.nwa.com) operates nonstop flights between Boston and Glasgow daily in summer, somewhat less frequently in winter.

British Midland (© **0870/607-0555)** flies from Heathrow to Glasgow. **Aer Lingus** (© **800/223-6537,** or 01/844-4711 in Ireland; www.aerlingus.ie) flies daily from Dublin to Glasgow.

By Train   Headquarters for British Rail is at Glasgow's Central Station and Queen Street Station. For **National Rail Enquiries,** call © **08457/484-950.** The **Queen Street Station** serves the north and east of Scotland, with trains arriving from Edinburgh every 30 minutes during the day; the one-way trip between the two cities costs £7.80 ($15) and takes 50 minutes. You'll also be able to travel to such Highland destinations as Inverness and Fort William from here.

The **Central Station** serves southern Scotland, England, and Wales, with trains arriving from London's Euston and King's Cross stations (call © **08457/484-950** in London for schedules) frequently throughout the day (trip time is about 5½ hr.). The trains leave Euston Monday to Saturday from 6:15am until 6:25pm, and then the night train departs at 11:45pm, getting into Glasgow at 11:28am. From Glasgow, trains leave for London every hour from 6:15am to 5pm; a night train leaves at 11:45pm. Try to avoid Sunday travel—the frequency of trains is considerably reduced and the duration of the trip lengthened to at least 7 hours because of more stopovers en route.

By Bus   The **Buchanan Street Bus Station** is two blocks north of the Queen Street Station on North Hanover Street (© **08706/082-608). National Express** runs daily coaches from London's Victoria Coach Station to Buchanan frequently throughout the day. Buses from London take 8 hours and 40 minutes to reach Glasgow, depending on the number of stops en route. Call National Express Enquiries at © **08605/808080** for more information or go to **www.nationalexpress.com.**

Scottish Citylink (© **0141/332-9644;** www.citylink.co.uk) also has frequent bus service out of the Buchanan bus station to and from Edinburgh, with a one-way ticket costing £7.25 ($14).

By Car   Glasgow is 64.5km (40 miles) west of Edinburgh, 356km (221 miles) north of Manchester, and 625km (388 miles) north of London. From England in the south, Glasgow is reached by M74, a continuation of M8 that goes right into the city, making an S curve. Call your hotel and find out what exit you should take. M8, another express motorway, links Glasgow and Edinburgh.

Other major routes into the city are A77 northeast from Prestwick and Ayr and A8 from the west (this becomes M8 around the port of Glasgow). A82

Tips **A Bargain Ticket for First-Day Touring**

For only £2.10 ($3.90), you're given a FirstDay Tourist Ticket allowing you to hop on and off buses and to be granted discounts for such select attractions as the House for an Art Lover. A pocket-size ciy map is also provided, and the ticket is valid daily from 9:30am to midnight. It's available at tourist information centers, underground or bus stations, and at certain attractions. For more information, check **www.seeglasgow.com.**

comes in from the northwest (the Highlands) on the north bank of the Clyde, and A80 also goes into the city. (This route is the southwestern section of M80 and M9 from Stirling.)

VISITOR INFORMATION

The **Greater Glasgow and Clyde Valley Tourist Board,** 11 George Sq. (© **0141/ 204-4400;** Underground: Buchanan St.), is the country's most helpful office. It's open Easter to May Monday to Saturday 9am to 6pm and Sunday 10am to 6pm; June Monday to Saturday 9am to 7pm and Sunday 10am to 6pm; July to August Monday to Saturday 9am to 8pm and Sunday 10am to 6pm; September Monday to Saturday 9am to 7pm and Sunday 10am to 6pm; October and January to Easter Monday to Saturday 9am to 6pm; November Monday to Saturday 9am to 6pm; December Monday to Saturday 9am to 7pm.

GETTING AROUND   The best way to explore Glasgow in on foot. The center is laid out on a grid system, which makes map reading relatively easy. However, many of the major attractions, such as the Burrell Collection, are in the surrounding environs, and for those you'll need to rely on public transportation.

Remember: Cars drive on the left, so when you cross streets make certain to look both ways.

By Bus   Glasgow is serviced by **First Glasgow Bus Company.** The buses come in a variety of colors, the lighter ones (blue and yellow) tending to serve the Kelvin Central and Strathclyde rural areas, with the darker ones covering the urban zones. Service is frequent throughout the day, but after 11pm service is greatly curtailed. The major bus station is the **Buchanan Street Bus Station,** Killermont Street (call © **0141/333-3708** for schedules), 2 blocks north of the Queen Station. Fares are between 65p and £1.25 ($1.20–$2.30), but you must have exact change. A special round-trip bus ticket (All Day Ticket) for £2.20 ($4) operates from 9:30am to 11:59pm (the overnight price of £2.50/$4.60 is from midnight to 9:29am).

By Underground   Called the "Clockwork Orange" (because of the vivid orange of the trains) by Glaswegians, a 15-stop subway services the city. Most Underground trains operate from these stops every 4 minutes during peak time, every 6 minutes during the day and every 8 minutes during the evening, with longer intervals between trains on Sunday and at night. The fare is 90p ($1.70). Service is Monday to Saturday 6:30am to 10pm and Sunday 11am to 6pm.

The **Travel Centre** at St. Enoch Square (© **0870/608-2608**), 2 blocks from the Central Station, is open Monday to Saturday 6:30am to 9:30pm and Sunday 7am to 9:30pm. Of the several types of tickets on offer, a Discovery Ticket grants unlimited travel for 1 day and is valid Monday to Saturday after 9:30am and all day Sunday (£1.70/$3.15 for adults and children). A 7-day ticket available at any time sells for £8 ($15) for adults and £4.50 ($8.30) for children.

By Taxi   Taxis are the same excellent ones found in Edinburgh or London. You can hail them on the street or call **TOA Taxis** at © **0141/429-7070.** Fares are displayed on a meter next to the driver. When a taxi is available on the street, a taxi sign on the roof is lit a bright yellow. Most taxi trips within the city cost £4 to £6 ($7.40–$11). The taxi meter starts at £1.80 ($3.35) and increases by 20p (35¢) every 61m (200 ft.), with an extra 10p (20¢) assessed for each additional passenger after the first two. A 80p ($1.50) surcharge is imposed midnight to 6am. Tip at least 10% of the fare shown on the meter.

By Car   Driving around Glasgow is a tricky business, even for locals. You're better off with public transportation. The city is a warren of one-way streets, and parking is expensive and difficult to find. Metered parking is available, but you'll need 20p (35¢) coins, entitling you to only 20 minutes. Be on the lookout for zealous traffic wardens issuing tickets. Some zones are marked PERMIT HOLDERS ONLY—your vehicle will be towed if you have no permit. A yellow line along the curb indicates no parking. Multistory parking lots (car parks), open 24 hours a day, are found at Anderston Cross and Cambridge, George, Mitchell, Oswald, and Waterloo streets.

If you want to rent a car to explore the countryside, it's best to arrange the rental before leaving home. But if you want to rent a car locally, most companies will accept your American or Canadian driver's license. All the major rental agencies are represented at the airport. In addition, **Avis Rent-a-Car** is at 70 Lancefield St. (© **0141/221-2827;** bus: 6A), **Budget Rent-a-Car** at Glasgow Airport (© **0141/221-9241;** bus: 38, 45, 48, or 57), and **Europcar** at 38 Anderson Quay (© **0141/248-8788;** bus: 38, 45, 48, or 57).

By Bicycle   Parts of Glasgow are fine for biking, or you might want to rent a bike and explore the surrounding countryside. For what the Scots call "cycle hire," head to a well-recommended shop about 1km (½) mile west of the town center, just off Great Western Road: **Western End Cycles,** 16–18 Chancellor St., in the Hillhead district (© **0141/357-1344;** Underground: Kelvin Bridge or Hillhead). It rents 21-speed trail and mountain bikes that conform well to the hilly terrain of Glasgow and its surroundings. The cost of £12 ($22) per day must be accompanied by a cash deposit of £100 ($185) or the imprint of a valid credit card.

FAST FACTS: Glasgow

American Express   The office is at 115 Hope St. (© **0870/600-1060;** bus: 38, 45, 48, or 57), and is open Monday to Friday 9am to 5:30pm and Saturday 9am to 5pm.

Business Hours   Most **offices** are open Monday to Friday 9am to 5 or 5:30pm. Most **banks** are open Monday to Wednesday and Friday 9:30am to 4pm, Thursday 9:30am to 5:30pm, and Saturday 10am to 7pm. Opening times can vary slightly from bank to bank. **Shops** are generally open Monday to Saturday 10am to 5:30 or 6pm. On Thursday, stores remain open until 7pm.

Currency Exchange   The tourist office and the American Express office (see above) will exchange most major foreign currencies. City-center banks operate *bureaux de change,* and nearly all will cash traveler's checks if you have the proper ID. You can also go to **Thomas Cook** at 15 Gordon St. (© **0141/201-7200;** Underground: Buchanan St.), open Monday to Saturday 9am to 5:30pm and Sunday noon to 5pm.

Dentists   If you have an emergency, go to the Accident and Emergency Department of **Glasgow Dental Hospital & School NHS Trust,** 378 Sauchiehall St. (© **0141/211-9600;** bus: 57). Its hours are Monday to Friday 9:15am to 5pm and Sunday and public holidays 10:30am to noon.

Doctors   The major hospital is the **Royal Infirmary,** 86 Castle St. (© **0141/211-4000;** bus: 2 or 2A).

Emergencies Call © **999** in an emergency to summon the police, an ambulance, or firefighters.

Internet Access You can send or read e-mail and surf the Net at **Easy Everything Internet Café,** 57–61 St. Vincent St. (© **0141/222-2365**). This outlet offers 400 computers and good rates. Only £1 ($1.85) will buy 40 minutes or even 3 hours, depending on demand. Open daily 7am to 10:30pm.

Pharmacies The best is **Boots,** 200 Sauchiehall St. (© **0141/332-1925;** bus: 57), open Monday to Saturday 8:30am to 6pm (closing at 7pm on Thursday), and Sunday 11am to 5pm.

Post Office The main branch is at 47 St. Vincent's St. (© **0141/204-3689;** Underground: Buchanan St.; bus: 6, 8, or 16). It's open Monday to Friday 8:30am to 5:45pm and Saturday 9am to 5:30pm.

WHERE TO STAY

It's important to reserve your room well in advance (say, 2 months beforehand), especially in late July and August. Glasgow's rates are generally higher than those in Edinburgh, but many business hotels offer bargains on weekends. The airport and the downtown branches of Glasgow's tourist office offer an **Advance Reservations Service**—with 2 weeks' notice, you can book your hotel by calling © **0141/221-0049.** The cost for this service is £3 ($5.55).

CENTRAL GLASGOW
Very Expensive

Hilton Glasgow Hotel ★★★ *Kids*   Glasgow's only government-rated five-star hotel occupies Scotland's tallest building (20 floors). Dignified and modern, it rises in the heart of the city's business district, near the northern end of Argyle Street and exit 18 (Charing Cross) of M8. The good-size guest rooms—plush and conservative, popular with both vacationers and business travelers—offer fine views as far as the Clyde dockyards. The executive floors enjoy the enhanced facilities of a semiprivate club. The youthful staff is alert and helpful.

1 William St., Glasgow G3 8HT. © 800/445-8667 in the U.S. and Canada, or 0141/204-5555. Fax 0141/204-5004. www.hilton.com. 319 units. £125–£165 ($231–$305) double; from £410 ($759) suite. Weekend discounts often available. AE, DC, MC, V. Parking £5 ($9.25). Bus: 62. **Amenities:** 3 restaurants; 2 bars; lounge; pool; tennis court; gym; sauna; boutiques; salon; 24-hr. room service; massage; babysitting; laundry service; dry cleaning; nonsmoking rooms; rooms for those with limited mobility. *In room:* A/C, TV, dataport, minibar, coffeemaker, hair dryer, iron/ironing board, safe, trouser press.

Millennium Hotel Glasgow ★★★   Following a $5 million upgrade, this striking landmark, the original Copthorne from 1810, is now better than ever. It stands near Queen Street Station where trains depart for the north of Scotland. When its high-ceilinged public rooms were renovated, designers searched out antiques and glistening marble panels to give it the aura of the Victorian era.

Even though the building is old, it has been completely modernized with all the amenities and services you'd expect of such a highly rated hotel. The decor is lighter and more comfortable than ever before. Bedrooms are among the finest in Glasgow, with new furnishings and first-class bathrooms with tub and shower. The best accommodations are at the front of the building facing St. George Square; the less desirable ones are those in the rear with no view.

George Square, Glasgow G2 1DS. © 0141/332-6711. Fax 0141/332-4264. www.millenniumhotels.com. 117 units. £110–£275 ($204–$509) double; £225–£235 ($686–$435) suite. AE, DC, MC, V. Parking: £6 ($11).

Underground: Buchanan St. **Amenities:** Restaurant; wine bar; cocktail lounge; 24-hr. room service; babysitting; laundry service; dry cleaning; nonsmoking rooms; 1 room for those with limited mobility. *In room:* A/C, TV, dataport, minibar, beverage maker, hair dryer, trouser press, iron/ironing board, safe.

Expensive

Langs ★ *Finds* If you're looking for Victorian Glasgow, head elsewhere—nothing here is evocative of the city in any way. But if you gravitate to a minimalist Japanese style, check in at this trendy and exceedingly contemporary hotel close to the Buchanan Galleries Shopping Mall and the Glasgow Royal Concert Hall. A diverse medley of bedrooms in various shapes, sizes, and configurations awaits you, each with a certain flair. Nothing is overly adorned here, yet comfort and style, along with a mix of colors and textures, make every unit a winner. The smallest are the studios, but you can also rent a duplex, a theme suite, or a very large suite. Beautifully kept bathrooms contain such extras as power showers with body jets, with flowing and curving interiors. To emphasize the Asian theme all the more, Japanese body treatments are offered in the on-site **Oshi Spa.** Of the two on-site restaurants, one serves up Mediterranean cuisine, and other an array of light fusion foods, including sushi.

2 Port Dundas, Glasgow G2 3LD. ℂ **0141/333-1500.** Fax 0141/333-5700. www.langshotels.com. 100 units. £110–£140 ($204–$259) double; £140–£210 ($259–$389) suite. AE, DC, MC, V. Underground: Queen St. **Amenities:** 2 restaurants; bar; sauna; gym; spa; 24-hr. room service; laundry service; dry cleaning; nonsmoking rooms; rooms for those with limited mobility. *In room:* TV, hair dryer, iron.

Malmaison ★★ *Finds* This place beats out all competitors in having the best contemporary interior. The hip Malmaison opened in 1994 in a historically important building constructed in the 1830s as a Greek Orthodox church. In 1997, an annex with additional bedrooms was added, designed to preserve the architectural character of the church's exterior. Inside, few of the original details remain—the decor is sleek and ultramodern. Bedrooms vary in size from smallish to average but are chic and appointed with extras like CD players, specially commissioned art, and top-of-the-line toiletries.

278 W. George St., Glasgow G2 4LL. ℂ **0141/572-1000.** Fax 0141/572-1002. www.malmaison.com. 72 units. £125 ($231) double; from £145 ($268) suite. AE, DC, MC, V. Parking nearby £9.50 ($18). Underground: Cowcaddens. Bus: 11. **Amenities:** Restaurant; bar; gym; 24-hr. room service; babysitting; laundry service; dry cleaning; nonsmoking rooms; rooms for those with limited mobility. *In room:* A/C, TV, dataport, CD player, minibar, coffeemaker, hair dryer, iron/ironing board, safe.

Moderate

The ArtHouse ★★ *Finds* Acclaimed for its contemporary interior, this 1911 Edwardian building, 6 blocks northwest of Central Station, originally housed school board offices. Today, its conversion to a hotel is one of the most striking in Glasgow, with dramatic colors and textures blending in perfectly with the structure's older features. Commissioned art and period pieces evoke some of the original Edwardian splendor, although everything has been given a modern overlay with rich, bold tones. Sleek furniture and state-of-the-art bathrooms with a combination tub/shower are grace notes. The **ArtHouse Grill** restaurant is one of the city's finest.

129 Bath St., Glasgow G2 2SY. ℂ **0141/221-6789.** Fax 0141/221-6789. www.arthousehotel.com 63 units. £75–£110 ($83–$204) double; £125–£180 ($231–$333) junior suite. AE, DC, MC, V. Underground: St. Enoch. **Amenities:** 2 restaurants; 2 bars; salon; 24-hr. room service; laundry service; dry cleaning; rooms for those with limited mobility; nonsmoking rooms. *In room:* TV, dataport, minibar, hair dryer.

Brunswick Hotel ★ *Finds* In the Merchant City area, this structure stands in dramatic contrast between two old warehouses, each 5 centuries old. A trendy, minimalist design prevails, from the leather-walled restaurant to the sleek-looking bedrooms. The rooms are soothing and inviting with neutral tones, comfortable furnishings, and tiny but adequate bathrooms (most with both tub and shower). The most stunning accommodation is a three-bedroom penthouse nesting under a copper curved roof.

106–108 Brunswick St., Glasgow G1 ITF. © **0141/552-0001.** Fax 0141/552-1551. www.brunswickhotel. co.uk. 18 units. £55–£95 ($102–$110) double; £395 ($731) penthouse suite for 6. Rates include continental breakfast. AE, MC, V. Underground: Buchanan St. **Amenities:** Restaurant; bar; limited room service; laundry service; dry cleaning; nonsmoking rooms; rooms for those with limited mobility. *In room:* TV, dataport, coffeemaker.

Saint Jude's Opened in July 1999, Saint Jude's is hip and modern. Centrally located and 15 minutes from the airport, this two-story town house offers comfortable, well-maintained rooms and friendly service. The hotel attracts a young crowd of artists, musicians, writers, and celebs. Saint Jude's is named after the patron saint of sinners, which sets the tone. All rooms have bathrooms (some with showers, some with tubs) and warm, contemporary furnishings.

190 Bath St., Glasgow, G2 4HG. © **0141/352-8800.** Fax 0141/352-8801. www.saintjudes.com 6 units. £115 ($213) double; £185 ($342) suite. Rates include continental breakfast and newspaper. AE, MC, V. Metered parking. Underground: Cow Caddens. **Amenities:** Restaurant; bar; limited room service; laundry service; dry cleaning. *In room:* TV, dataport, minibar, coffeemaker, hair dryer, trouser press.

Inexpensive

Babbity Bowster *(Value)* In Merchant City, this small but delightful Robert Adam–designed hotel doubles as an art gallery. The guest rooms vary in size but are all attractive, with Victorian reproductions and white-lace bedding (some with shower only). The hotel attracts students and faculty from Strathclyde University and displays the work of Glaswegian artists (most are for sale). In summer, there's an outdoor barbecue area.

16–18 Blackfriars St., Glasgow G1 1PE. © **0141/552-5055.** Fax 0141/552-7774. 6 units. £50 ($93) double. AE, MC, V. Free parking. Underground: Buchanan St. **Amenities:** Restaurant; bar. *In room:* Hair dryer.

The Corus Hotel *(Value)* Location, location, location is what sells this property. Two blocks west of the central rail depot, this contemporary seven-story hotel is surrounded by dreary commercial buildings but is a viable option in the center of Glasgow. Upstairs, the rooms are inviting—although they are small. Massively renovated, it is better than ever.

377 Argyle St. (opposite Cadogan Sq.), Glasgow G2 8LL. © **0141/248-2355.** Fax 0141/221-1014. www. corushotels.com. 121 units. £70–£95 ($130–$176) double. AE, DC, MC, V. Underground: St. Enoch. **Amenities:** Restaurant; bar; limited room service; laundry service; dry cleaning; nonsmoking rooms; 1 room for those with limited mobility. *In room:* TV, hair dryer, coffeemaker, trouser press.

Kirkland House On a quiet street about a 10-minute walk from the Glasgow Art Gallery and Museum, the university, and the Scottish Exhibition Centre, the Kirkland is an impeccably maintained 1832 Victorian crescent house. A mix of antiques and reproductions is used in the large guest rooms, each equipped with a shower bathroom. The owners are keen admirers of American swing music and display a collection of 78 rpm gramophone records, old photographs, and pictures. All rooms are nonsmoking.

42 St. Vincent Crescent, Glasgow G3 8NG. © **0141/248-3458.** Fax 0141/221-5174. www.kirkland.net43. co.uk. 5 units. £55–£65 ($102–$120) double. Rates include continental breakfast. No credit cards. Free parking. Underground: Exhibition Centre. **Amenities:** 1 room for those with limited mobility. *In room:* TV, coffeemaker, hair dryer.

THE WEST END
Very Expensive

One Devonshire Gardens ★★★   This hotel tops even perfection, beating out the Hilton and all others as the most glamorous, most elegant, and most tranquil hotel in Scotland. It also boasts a restaurant, **House Five,** that serves a finer cuisine than that found in any other major Glasgow restaurant. In the Hyndland district just west of the center, the house at no. 1 was built in 1880 and is now even more elegant than it was in its heyday. At the ring of the door-bell, a pair of Edwardian chambermaids with frilly aprons and dust bonnets appear to welcome you. Each of the eight guest rooms in this building is furnished in period style, with lots of luxurious accessories. The success of no. 1 led to the acquisition of nos. 2 and 3. The newer rooms have the same elegant touches and high price tags.

1 Devonshire Gardens, Glasgow G12 0UX. © **0141/339-2001.** Fax 0141/337-1663. www.onedevonshire gardens.com. 37 units. £125–£185 ($231–$342) double; £345–£475 ($638–$879) suite. AE, DC, MC, V. Free parking. Underground: Hillhead. **Amenities:** 2 restaurants; bar; 24-hr. room service; laundry service; dry cleaning. *In room:* TV, dataport, minibar, hair dryer, iron/ironing board, safe.

Moderate

The Kelvin Park Lorne Hotel ★ *Finds*   In the heart of the residential West End, this is a discreet hotel whose public rooms are in the style of early-1900s Scottish designer Charles Rennie Mackintosh. Although it was built 40 years ago, after his death, its bar (**Newberys,** honoring Frances Newbery, Mackintosh's mentor) was designed according to Mackintosh's theories. The hotel consists of an early-19th-century building (four floors) and a later five-story structure. The guest rooms were renovated in 1995, resulting in a kind of neutral contemporary comfort; they vary in size, the older ones being noticeably larger. Most contain combination tub and showers.

923 Sauchiehall St., Glasgow G3 7TE. © **0141/314-9955.** Fax 0141/337-1659. www.regalhotels.co.uk. 100 units. £100 ($185) double; £120 ($222) suite. AE, DC, MC, V. Free parking. Underground: Kelvin Hall. **Amenities:** Restaurant; bar; 24-hr. room service; laundry service; dry cleaning; nonsmoking rooms. *In room:* TV, dataport, coffeemaker, hair dryer, trouser press.

The Town House ★★ *Value*   This is one of the most upmarket and charming of the B&Bs of Glasgow. The stone-built Victorian terraced house has been successfully converted to receive guests to its tranquil little cul-de-sac tucked away in the West End, with a tennis club in the back and a rugby club to the front. As a curiosity note, there remains an air-raid shelter in the garden. The place justifiably wins praise from its many repeat visitors. The hospitality, the comfort level, and the atmosphere are first rate. All the large bedrooms have been faithfully restored and fitted with very good furnishings, along with top-notch private bathrooms with showers. Each room is individually decorated, often with many traditional wooden pieces against a palette of blue or yellow. Guests meet in the living room, with its many books and coal-burning fireplace.

4 Hughenden Terrace, Glasgow G12 9XR. © **0141/357-0862.** Fax 0141/339-9605. www.thetownhouseglasgow. com. 10 units. £72 ($133) double; £82 ($152) triple. Rates include Scottish breakfast. MC, V. Underground: Hillhead. **Amenities:** Breakfast room; bar; limited room service; babysitting; laundry service. *In room:* TV, data-port (in some), beverage maker, hair dryer, iron.

Inexpensive

Albion Hotel   This unpretentious hotel was formed by connecting two nearly identical beige-sandstone row houses in the heart of Glasgow's West End. It offers high-ceilinged guest rooms with modern furniture, some with both tub and shower. If your hotel needs are simple, you'll likely be happy here.

405–407 N. Woodside Rd., Glasgow G20 6NN. (*C*) **0141/339-8620.** Fax 0141/334-8159. www. glasgowhotelsandapartments.co.uk. 16 units. £50–£59 ($93–$109) double. Rates include breakfast. AE, DC, MC, V. Free parking. Underground: Kelvin Bridge. **Amenities:** Breakfast room; lounge; bar; laundry service; nonsmoking rooms; 1 room for those with limited mobility. *In room:* TV, coffeemaker, hair dryer, iron, safe, trouser press.

Ambassador Hotel ✦ (*Value*) Across from the Botanic Garden, this small hotel in an Edwardian town house (ca. 1900) is one of the better B&Bs in Glasgow and was refurbished in 2002. The good-size guest rooms are furnished with modern pieces, each with a combination tub/shower. The hotel is well situated for exploring the West End, with several galleries and many good local restaurants nearby.

7 Kelvin Dr., Glasgow G20 8QG. (*C*) **0141/946-1018.** Fax 0141/945-5377. www.glasgowhotelsandapartments. co.uk. 16 units. £58 ($107) double without breakfast; £66 ($122) double with breakfast. AE, DC, MC, V. Free parking. Underground: Hillhead. **Amenities:** Bar; dining room; lounge; laundry service. *In room:* TV, dataport, coffeemaker, hair dryer, iron/ironing board, trouser press.

WHERE TO DINE
CENTRAL GLASGOW
Expensive

The Belfry ✦ SCOTTISH/FRENCH The pews, pulpits, and stained glass that adorn this place are from a church in northern England. It's the only restaurant in Glasgow where you can contemplate Christ in Majesty while you enjoy a pint of ale. The kitchen produces daily specials like steak pie with roast potatoes; roast rack of lamb with rosemary, thyme, and caramelized shallots; and the Belfry mussel bowl with shallots. The cook is well known for making clever use of fresh Scottish produce.

In the basement of the Buttery restaurant and lounge, 652 Argyle St. (*C*) **0141/221-0630.** Reservations recommended. Table d'hôte £34 ($63) 2 courses, £38 ($70) 3 courses. AE, MC, V. Tues–Fri noon–2pm; Tues–Sat 6–9:30pm. Underground: St. Enoch.

Cameron's ✦✦ MODERN SCOTTISH This is the most glamorous restaurant in Glasgow's best hotel, outfitted like a baronial hunting lodge in the wilds of the Highlands. The chef's conservative menu holds few surprises but is a deftly prepared celebration of market-fresh ingredients. Small slip-ups sometimes mar the effect of a dish or two, but we have always come away pleased. Your best bet when ordering is to stay Scottish. Go with whisky-cured Isle of Arran salmon, confit of Highland duck, or Firth of Lorne sea scallops—and that's only the appetizers. For a main course, try rack of Scottish lamb with a crust of whisky-steeped oatmeal and Arran mustard.

In the Hilton Glasgow Hotel, 1 William St. (*C*) **0141/204-5555.** Reservations recommended. Main courses £18–£38 ($32–$70). AE, DC, MC, V. Mon–Fri noon–1:45pm and 7–9:45pm; Sat 7–9:45pm. Bus: 6A, 16, or 62.

Rogano ✦✦ SEAFOOD Rogano boasts a perfectly preserved Art Deco interior from 1935, when Messrs. Rogers and Anderson combined their talents and names to create a restaurant that has hosted virtually every star of the British film industry. You can enjoy dinner amid lapis-lazuli clocks, etched mirrors, ceiling fans, semicircular banquettes, and potted palms. The menu always emphasizes seafood, such as halibut in champagne-and-oyster sauce and lobster grilled or Thermidor.

A less expensive menu is offered down in the **Cafe Rogano,** where main courses begin at £8.50 ($16).

11 Exchange Place. ✆ 0141/248-4055. Reservations recommended. Main courses £15–£35 ($28–$65); fixed-price lunch £17 ($30). AE, DC, MC, V. Restaurant daily noon–2:30pm and 6:30–10:30pm; cafe Mon–Thurs noon–11pm, Fri–Sat noon–midnight, Sun noon–11pm. Underground: Buchanan St.

Moderate

Café Cossachok ★ *Finds* RUSSIAN   Before the opening of this restaurant near the Tron Theatre, Glasgow was about the last place you'd look for Russian cuisine consumed with lots of vodka. A favorite with actors appearing at the theater nearby, this inviting oasis has beautiful and authentic Russian decor, including plenty of mahogany pieces and much use of the color red. A little art gallery upstairs is a showcase for Russian art and culture. Every Sunday, live music features singers performing in both Russian and English.

The chefs concentrate mainly on Russian fare but are also adept at turning out a selection of Armenian, Georgian, and Ukrainian dishes. Come here to feast on such Russian classics as borscht, savory blinis, and beef Stroganoff. The latter, served with fried straw potatoes, is the finest we've had in Scotland. Chicken Vladimir is another excellent offering, a breaded breast of chicken with a mushroom sauce resting under a cheese topping.

10 King St., Merchant City. ✆ 0141/553-0733. Reservations recommended. Main courses £6.65–£13 ($12–$24); pre-theater 2-course dinner (5–7pm) £9.95 ($19). MC, V. Tues–Wed 11:30am–3pm and 6–11pm; Thurs–Sat 11:30am–11pm; Sun 4–11pm. Underground: St. Enoch.

City Merchant SCOTTISH/INTERNATIONAL   This cozy restaurant in the heart of the city offers friendly service and an extensive menu, and serves throughout the day. The cuisine is more reliable than stunning, but it delivers quite an array of well-prepared fresh food at a good price. Try the roast breast of duck, rack of lamb, or escalope of venison. Also tempting are the fast-seared scallops and classic smoked haddock. Some of the desserts evoke old-time Scotland, such as the clootie dumpling, made with flour, spices, and fried fruit and served with home-churned butter.

97–99 Candlebiggs. ✆ 0141/553-1577. Reservations recommended. Main courses £8.95–£26 ($17–$48); fixed-price lunch £9.50–£12 ($17–$22); 3-course lunch or dinner £27 ($49). AE, DC, MC, V. Mon–Sat noon–10:30pm. Underground: St. Enoch.

Ho Wong Restaurant ★ CANTONESE   Jimmy Ho and David Wong opened this remote outpost of their Hong Kong establishment 2 blocks from the Central Station. It's now one of the city's finest Chinese restaurants. The menu features at least eight duck dishes, along with four types of fresh lobster and some sizzling platters.

82 York St. ✆ 0141/221-3550. Reservations required. Main courses £16–£25 ($27–$46); fixed-price 2-course lunch £9.50 ($18); fixed-price banquet £27 ($50) (5 courses). AE, DC, MC, V. Mon–Sat noon–2pm and 6–11:30pm; Sun 6–11:30pm. Underground: Central Station.

Two Fat Ladies ★ MODERN BRITISH/SEAFOOD   This ranks high on the list of everybody's favorite restaurants, especially for irreverent diners who appreciate the unexpected. The "Two Fat Ladies" are its street number—a nickname for the number 88 in Scotland's church-sponsored bingo games. The restaurant packs in crowds for specialties like pan-fried squid salad with coriander-flavored yogurt sauce, grilled chicken salad with apple chutney, and charcoal-grilled king scallops with tomato-basil sauce. The best dessert is the Pavlova (a chewy meringue) with summer berries and Drambuie sauce.

88 Dumbarton Rd. ℂ 0141/339-1944. Reservations recommended. Fixed-price lunch £11–£13 ($20–$24); fixed-price pretheater supper (5:30–7pm) £11–£13 ($20–$24); main courses £9–£16 ($17–$30). MC, V. Mon–Sat noon–3pm and 5:30–10:50pm; Sun 5:30–10:30pm. Bus: 16, 42, or 57.

Inexpensive

Cafe Gandolfi *Kids* SCOTTISH/FRENCH   Many students and young professionals will tell you this popular place in Merchant City is their favorite caff— you may sometimes have to wait for a table. A remake of a Victorian pub, it boasts rustic wooden floors, benches, and stools. If you don't fill up on soups and salads, try smoked venison with gratin dauphinois or smoked pheasant with an onion tartlet in winter. Vegetarians will also find solace here.

64 Albion St. ℂ 0141/552-6813. Reservations recommended on weekends. Main courses £8.50–£14 ($16–$25). MC, V. Mon–Sat 9am–11:30pm; Sun noon–11:30pm. Underground: St. Enoch/Cannon St.

THE WEST END
Expensive

Ubiquitous Chip ⭐ SCOTTISH   This restaurant is set inside the rough-textured stone walls of a former stable; its glass-covered courtyard boasts masses of climbing vines. Upstairs is a pub where simple platters are served with pints of lager and drams of whisky; these may include chicken, leek, and white-wine casserole or finnan haddies with bacon (but no fish and chips, as you might think from the name). The bistro-style restaurant might feature free-range chicken, shellfish with crispy seaweed snaps, or wild rabbit. Vegetarians are catered to at both places.

12 Ashton Lane, off Byres Rd. ℂ 0141/334-5007. Reservations recommended. Restaurant fixed-price lunch £22 ($40) for 2 courses, £27 ($49) for 3 courses; fixed-price dinner £33 ($61) for 2 courses, £38 ($70) for 3 courses; bar meals £2.15–£15 ($4–$28) at lunch or dinner. AE, DC, MC, V. Restaurant Mon–Sat noon–2:30pm and daily 5:30–11pm; bar Sun 12:30pm–midnight. Underground: Kelvinhall.

Moderate

Stravaigin ⭐⭐ GLOBAL   We've never seen any restaurant like this in Glasgow. The chef and owner truly roams the globe for inspiration. Although some of his ideas might come from as far away as China or the Caribbean, he also knows how to use the finest of the regional bounty of Scotland. Expect concoctions such as marinated venison filet, served with butter-bean and parsley mash, roast baby eggplant, and pomegranate sauce. Rabbit is perfectly cooked and served with tomato essence, while mullet is roasted and served with crisp Parmesan polenta, caponata, and roast pimento sauce. Many locals finish with a selection of Scottish cheeses with red-grape and hazelnut chutney.

28 Gibson St., Hillhead. ℂ 0141/334-2665. Reservations required. Fixed-price menus (lunch or dinner) £23–£29 ($43–$54). AE, DC, MC, V. Fri–Sun noon–2:30pm; Tues–Sun 5–11pm. Underground: Kelvinbridge.

Inexpensive

Ashoka West End ⭐ INDIAN/PUNJABI   This is a culinary landmark in Glasgow, serving the finest cuisine of the subcontinent. Many generations of Glaswegians learned to "eat Indian" at this very restaurant. The eclectic decor features rugs, brass objects, murals, and greenery. The dishes are full of flavor and arrive at your table with fragrant and most pleasing aromas. You might launch your repast with *pakora,* deep-fried chicken, mushrooms, or fish fritters. From here you can order *jalandhri,* a potent fusion of ginger, garlic, onions, peppers, coconut cream, and fresh herbs that can be served with a choice of chicken, lamb, or mixed vegetables. Most dishes are priced at the lower end of the scale.

1284 Argyle St. (**©** 0141/339-3371. Reservations required Fri–Sat. Main courses £6.95–£13 ($13–$24). AE, DC, MC, V. Sun–Thurs 5pm–12:30am; Fri–Sat 5pm–1am; Wed–Thurs noon–2pm. Underground: Kelvin Hall.

SEEING THE SIGHTS

Burrell Collection ★★★   This museum houses the mind-boggling treasures left to Glasgow by Sir William Burrell, a wealthy ship owner who had a lifelong passion for art. Burrell started collecting when he was 14, his passion continuing until 1958 when he died at the age of 96. His tastes were eclectic: Chinese ceramics, French paintings from the 1800s, tapestries, stained-glass windows from churches, even stone doorways from the Middle Ages. It is said that the collector "liked about everything," including one of the very few original bronze casts of Rodin's *Thinker*. He did find some art to his distaste, including avant-garde works ("Monet was just too impressionistic"). You can see a vast aggregation of furniture, textiles, ceramics, stained glass, silver, art objects, and pictures in the dining room, hall, and drawing room reconstructed from Sir William's home, Hutton Castle at Berwick-upon-Tweed. Ancient artifacts, Asian art, and European decorative arts and paintings are featured. There is a restaurant on-site, and you can roam through the surrounding park, 5km (3 miles) south of Glasgow Bridge.

Pollok Country Park, 2060 Pollokshaws Rd. (**©** 0141/287-2550. Free admission. Mon–Sat 10am–5pm; Sun 11am–5pm. Closed Jan 1 and Dec 25. Bus: 45, 48, or 57.

Glasgow Science Centre ★★★ *Kids*   Opened in 2001, this is Britain's most successful millennium project. It lies in the heart of the city, on the banks of the River Clyde and opposite the Scottish Exhibition and Conference Centre. The center is the focal point of Glasgow's drive to become one of Europe's major high-tech locales. Situated in three landmark buildings, the center features the first titanium-clad structures in the United Kingdom, including Scotland's only Space Theatre. Other features include innovative laboratories, multimedia and science theaters, interactive exhibits, and the only 360-degree rotating tower in the world. The overall theme is that of the challenges facing Scotland in the 21st century. The center is also a showcase depicting Glasgow's contribution to science and technology in the past, present, and future.

Children will love the hands-on activities. They'll be able to make their own soundtrack and animation, do a 3-D head scan and rearrange their own features, or star in their own digital video. At special shows and workshops, you'll see a glass smashed by sound, "catch" shadows, experience a million volts of indoor lighting, see liquid nitrogen, view bacteria that lurk on you, and build a lie detector.

The IMAX Theatre, a first for Glasgow and Scotland, uses a film with a frame size 10 times larger than the standard 35mm film. It projects a picture onto the screen that's the size of a five-story tenement block. Some 150 IMAX films are currently available to take viewers into all kinds of experiences—to explore the hidden secrets of natural wonders like the Grand Canyon, perhaps, or even the inside of an atom, and certainly the magic of space. The theater charges separate admission: £5.95 ($11) for adults or £4.95 ($9.15) for students and children, with a family ticket ranging from £19 ($35).

50 Pacific Quay. (**©** 0141/420-5010. www.gsc.org.uk. Admission £6.95 ($13) adults; £4.95 ($9.15) students and seniors; £19 ($35) family pass. Daily 10am–6pm. Underground: Buchan St. to Cessnock, from which there's a 10-min. walk.

Hunterian Art Gallery ☆☆   This gallery owns the artistic estate of James McNeill Whistler, with some 60 of his paintings bestowed by his sister-in-law. It also boasts a Charles Rennie Mackintosh collection, including the architect's home (with his own furniture) on three levels, decorated in the original style. The main gallery exhibits 17th- and 18th-century paintings (Rembrandt to Rubens) and 19th- and 20th-century Scottish works. Temporary exhibits, selected from Scotland's largest collection of prints, are presented in the print gallery, which also houses a permanent display of print-making techniques.

University of Glasgow, Hillhead St. ℂ 0141/330-5431. Free admission. Mon–Sat 9:30am–5pm (Mackintosh House closed 12:30–1:30pm). Underground: Hillhead.

McLellan Galleries ☆ (Finds)   This used to be an unimportant and little-visited gallery. Today that's all changed. Even though it hardly rivals the Burrell Collection, McLellan came into prominence in 2003 with the closing down of the Glasgow Art Gallery and Museum for a major restoration slated to be completed in 2006. Since the Glasgow Art Gallery was the repository of many of the city's greatest artworks, a decision was made to transfer some of its most important pieces, including oil paintings and sculpture, to the heretofore unimportant McLellan.

The McLellan was already the repository of an impressive collection of Italian works from the 16th and 17th centuries, and it is also a showcase for modern art. Many of its temporary exhibits on loan from the Glasgow Art Gallery include a superb collection of Dutch and Italian Old Masters, featuring Giorgione and Rembrandt. Such international artists as Botticelli are also represented. Perhaps you'll get to see Whistler's *Arrangement in Grey and Black no 2: Portrait of Thomas Carlyle,* the first Whistler work to be hung in a British gallery. Expect a rotating series of art.

270 Sauchiehall St. ℂ 0141/331-1854. Free admission. Mon–Thurs and Sat 10am–5pm; Fri–Sun 11am–5pm. Underground: Queen St.

Museum of Transport ☆☆   This museum contains a fascinating collection of all forms of transportation and related technology. Displays include a simulated 1938 Glasgow street with period shop fronts, appropriate vehicles, and a reconstruction of one of the Glasgow Underground stations. The superb and varied ship models in the Clyde Room reflect the significance of Glasgow and the River Clyde as one of the world's foremost areas of shipbuilding and engineering.

1 Bunhouse Rd., Kelvin Hall. ℂ 0141/287-2720. Free admission. Mon–Sat 10am–5pm; Sun and Fri 11am–5pm. Closed Jan 1 and Dec 25. Underground: Kelvin Hall.

Cathedral of St. Kentigern ☆☆☆   Also known as St. Mungo's, this cathedral was consecrated in 1136, burned down in 1192, and rebuilt soon after; the Laigh Kirk (lower church), whose vaulted crypt is said to be the finest in Europe, remains to this day. Visit the tomb of St. Mungo in the crypt, where a light always burns. The edifice is mainland Scotland's only complete medieval cathedral from the 12th and 13th centuries. It was once a place of pilgrimage, but 16th-century zeal purged it of all monuments of idolatry.

Highlights of the interior include the 1400s nave, with a stone screen (unique in Scotland) showing the seven deadly sins. Both the choir and the lower church are in the mid-1200s First Pointed style. The church, though a bit austere, is filled with intricate details left by long-ago craftspeople—note the tinctured bosses of the ambulatory vaulting in the back of the main altar. The lower church, reached via a set of steps north of the pulpit, is where Gothic reigns supreme, with an array of pointed arches and piers. Seek out, in particular, the **Chapel of the Knights,** with its intricate net vaulting and bosses carved with fine detailing. The **Blacader Aisle** projecting from the south transept was the latest addition, a two-story extension of which only the lower part was completed in the late Gothic style.

For the best view of the cathedral, cross the Bridge of Sighs into the **Glasgow Necropolis** (© 0141/287-3961; bus: 2 or 27), the graveyard containing almost every type of architecture in the world. Built on a rocky hill and dominated by a statue of John Knox, this fascinating graveyard was opened in 1832. Typical of the mixing of all groups in this tolerant cosmopolitan city, the first person to be buried here was a Jew, Joseph Levi.

Cathedral Square, Castle St. © 0141/552-6891. Free admission. Apr–Sept Mon–Sat 9:30am–6pm, Sun 1–5pm; Oct–Mar Mon–Sat 9:30am–4pm, Sun 1–4pm. Sun services at 11am and 6:30pm. Underground: Queen St. Station.

St. Mungo Museum of Religious Life and Art ★ (Finds)   Opened in 1993, this eclectic and often controversial museum lies close to the Glasgow Cathedral. It embraces a collection that spans the centuries and highlights various religious groups that have lived in Glasgow and the surrounding area over the years. The museum is hailed as unique in the world in that Buddha, Ganesha, Shiva, and all the "gang" are represented. The most controversial exhibit is the infamous painting of *Christ of St. John the Cross,* a work of the surrealistic Salvador Dalí (1904–89). Also on display is the Chinese robe worn in the film *The Last Emporer,* by Bernardo Bertolucci. In back of the museum is the U.K.'s only Japanese Zen garden.

2 Castle St. © 141/553-2557. Free admission. Apr–Sept Mon–Thurs and Sat 10am–5pm; Oct–Mar Mon–Thurs and Sat 11am–5pm. Bus: 2.

The Tall Ship at Glasgow Harbour   Here's a rare chance to explore one of the last remaining Clyde-built tall ships, the SV *Glenlee,* built in 1896, a vessel that circumnavigated Cape Horn 15 times. Restored in 1999, *Glenlee* is one of only five Clyde-built sailing ships that remain afloat. You can explore the ship and take in an onboard exhibition detailing the vessel's cargo-trading history. On the dock, the **Victorian Pumphouse Centre** contains a restaurant and a nautical gift shop along with exhibition galleries.

100 Stobcross Rd. ©0141/222-2513. Admission £4.50 ($8.35) adults, £3.25 ($6) seniors and students, £2.50 ($4.65) children. Daily 10am–5pm. Train station: SECC.

ORGANIZED TOURS

The *Waverley* is the world's last seagoing paddle steamer, and from the last week of June to the end of August (depending on weather conditions), the Paddle Steamer Preservation Society conducts 1-day trips from Anderston Quay in Glasgow to historic and scenic places beyond the Firth of Clyde. As you sail along, you can take in what were once vast shipyards, turning out more than half the earth's tonnage of oceangoing liners. You're allowed to bring your own sandwiches for a picnic aboard, or you can enjoy lunch in the Waverley Restaurant. Boat tours cost £12 to £35 ($22–$65). For details, contact **Waverley Excursions,** Waverley Terminal, Anderston Quay, Broomielaw (© 0141/221-8152).

There's also regular ferry service run by **Caledonian MacBrayne** (© 01475/650-100) in Gourock on the banks of the Clyde. The ferry stands close to the station in Gourock, connected to Glasgow Central Station by trains that leave every hour and take 30 to 45 minutes. The ferry service, which can take cars, runs every hour to the attractive seaside resort of Dunoon at the mouth of the Clyde. The journey takes about 20 minutes, and ferries run every hour from 6:20am to 8:20pm, April to October 16; in winter the service is less frequent and visitors are advised to check beforehand as it's liable to change. The round-trip costs £4.45 to £5 ($8.25–$9.25) adults and £2.20 to £2.50 ($4–$4.65) seniors and children.

The best Glasgow tours are run by **Scotguide Tourist Services (City Sighting Glasgow),** operated from 153 Queen Street at George Square (© **0141/ 204-0444;** Underground: Buchanan St.). From April 1 to October 31, departures are every 15 minutes 9:30am to 4pm. The price is £8 ($15) adults, £6 ($11) students and seniors, and £3 ($5.55) children ages 5 to 14.

Mercat Glasgow (© **0141/586-5378;** www.mercat-glasgow.co.uk) focuses on a ghostly, ghoulish Glasgow. Historians instead of actors re-create macabre Glasgow, a parade of goons that include hangmen, ghosts, murderers, and body snatchers. Tours leave from the tourist information center on George Square at 7 and 8pm daily, costing £8.50 ($16) adults and £6.50 ($12) seniors, students, and children, with a family ticket going for £20 ($37). The tours take 1½ hours.

THE SHOPPING SCENE

A warren of tiny shops stands in a slightly claustrophobic cluster called **Victorian Village,** 93 W. Regent St. (© **0141/332-0808;** bus: 23, 38, 45, 48, or 57). Much of the merchandise isn't particularly noteworthy, but you can find many exceptional pieces if you're willing to go hunting. Several of the owners stock reasonably priced 19th-century articles; others sell old jewelry and clothing, a helter-skelter of artifacts.

The work of some of the finest craftspeople in Scotland is highlighted at **Scottish Craft Centre** ⋆⋆, Princes Square Mall, 48 Buchanan St. (© **0141/ 248-2885;** Underground: St. Enoch; bus 9, 12, 44, 66, or 75). Most of the items are exquisitely crafted in porcelain, metal, glass, and wood. You can select from such items as metal candle holders, hand-carved wooden boxes, exquisite glasses and china, porcelain vases, and other choice items.

Frasers department store, Buchanan St. (© **0141/221-3880;** Underground: St. Enoch), is Glasgow's version of Harrods. A soaring Victorian-era glass arcade rises four stories, and inside you'll find everything from clothing to Oriental rugs, crystal to handmade local artifacts of all kinds.

The tiny **Mackintosh Shop** ⋆⋆⋆, 167 Renfrew St. (© **0141/353-4526;** Underground: Cowcaddens), prides itself on its stock of books, cards, stationery, coffee and beer mugs, glassware, and sterling-and-enamel jewelry created from the original designs of Mackintosh. The Mackintosh Shop is in the foyer of the Glasgow School of Art.

Drop in the **National Trust for Scotland Shop** ⋆, Hutcheson's Hall, 158 Ingram St. (© **0141/552-8391;** Underground: Buchanan St.), for maps, calendars, postcards, pictures, dish towels, and kitchenware. Some of the crockery is in Mackintosh-design styles. The neoclassical building, constructed as a charity and hospice in 1806, is on the site of a larger hospice built in 1641.

GLASGOW AFTER DARK
OPERA & CLASSICAL MUSIC

The **Theatre Royal,** Hope Street and Cowcaddens Road (© **0141/332-9000;** Underground: Cowcaddens; bus: 23, 48, or 57), is the home of the **Scottish Opera** as well as of the **Scottish Ballet.** The theater also hosts visiting companies from around the world. Called "the most beautiful opera theatre in the kingdom" by the *Daily Telegraph,* it offers splendid Victorian Italian Renaissance plasterwork, glittering chandeliers, and 1,547 comfortable seats, plus spacious bars and buffets on all four levels. However, it's not the decor but the ambitious repertoire that attracts operagoers. Ballet tickets run £4.80 to £33 ($9.90–$61) and opera tickets cost £4.50 to £57 ($8.35–$106). On performance days, the box office is open Monday to Saturday 10am to 8pm; on nonperformance days, hours are Monday to Saturday 10am to 6pm.

In winter, the **Royal Scottish National Orchestra** offers Saturday-evening concerts at the **Glasgow Royal Concert Hall,** 2 Sauchiehall St. (© **0141/332-6633;** Underground: Buchanan St.). The **BBC Scottish Symphony Orchestra** presents Friday-evening concerts at the **BBC Broadcasting House,** Queen Margaret Drive (Underground: St. Enoch), or at **City Halls,** Albion Street (Underground: St. Enoch). In summer, the Scottish National Orchestra has a short Promenade season (dates and venues are announced in the papers). Tickets can only be purchased at individual venues.

THEATER

Although hardly competition for London, Glasgow's theater scene is certainly the equal of Edinburgh's. Young Scottish playwrights often make their debuts here, and you're likely to see anything from Steinbeck's *The Grapes of Wrath* to Wilde's *Salome* to *Romeo and Juliet* done in Edwardian dress.

The prime symbol of Glasgow's verve remains the **Citizens Theatre,** Gorbals and Ballater streets (© **0141/429-0022;** bus: 12 or 66), founded after World War II by James Bridie, a famous Glaswegian whose plays are still produced on occasion there. It's home to a repertory company, with tickets at £4 to £12 ($7.40–$22). The box office hours are Monday to Saturday 10am to 6pm, and 10am to 9pm on performance nights. The company is usually closed from June to the first week in August.

THE CLUB & MUSIC SCENE

Barrowland, Gallowgate 244 (© **0141/552-4601;** Underground: St. Enoch; bus: 61 or 62), seats 2,000 and is open only on nights shows are booked. July and August are the quiet months, as most shows are geared toward a student audience. The cover runs highest when the hall hosts popular bands like White Zombie or the Breeders and ranges from £8 to £25 ($15–$46).

The 13th Note, 50–60 King St. (© **0141/553-1638;** bus: 21, 23, or 38), has moved away from jazz in the past couple of years and now books mainly heavy rock bands on Tuesday, Wednesday, and Thursday nights. On Friday, Saturday, and Sunday, the night is dedicated to ambient and alternative music. Hours are daily noon to midnight.

Most of the crowd at **Fury Murry's,** 96 Maxwell St. (© **07802/538-550;** Underground: St. Enoch), is made up of students looking for nothing more complicated than a good, sometimes rowdy, time listening to disco music that's upbeat but not ultra-trendy. It's situated in a cellar, a 2-minute walk from the very central St. Enoch Shopping Centre. It has a very busy bar, a dance floor, and ample opportunities to meet the best and brightest in Scotland's university system. Jeans and T-shirts are the right garb. It's open Thursday to Sunday 11pm to 3am. Thursday and Friday feature live bands starting at 8:30pm, and other nights are strictly for dancing or can be reserved for private parties. Cover charges range from £3 to £6 ($4.95–$9.90).

FAVORITE PUBS

The amiably battered **Bon Accord,** 153 North St. (© **0141/248-4427;** bus: 6, 8, or 16), is a longtime favorite. It has an array of hand-pumps—a dozen devoted to real British ales, the rest to beers and stouts from the Czech Republic, Belgium, Germany, Ireland, and Holland. The pub is likely to satisfy your taste in malt whisky as well, and offers affordable bar snacks. It's open Monday to Saturday noon to midnight, Sunday noon to 11pm.

The **Cask and Still,** 154 Hope St. (© **0141/333-0980;** bus: 21, 23, or 38), is the best place for sampling malt whisky. You can taste from a selection of more than 350 single malts, at a variety of strengths (perhaps not on the same night) and maturities (that is, years spent in casks). Many prefer the malt whisky that has been aged in a sherry cask. There's good bar food at lunch, including cold meat salads and sandwiches. It's open Monday to Thursday noon to 11pm, Friday and Saturday 11am to midnight.

Opposite the Central Station, the **Corn Exchange,** 88 Gordon St. (© **0141/248-5380;** bus: 21, 23, or 38), was really the Corn Exchange in the mid–19th century but is now of Glasgow's most popular pubs. Amid dark paneling and high ceilings, you can enjoy a pint of lager to 11pm Monday to Thursday, until midnight Friday to Saturday. Affordable pub grub is served daily noon to 9pm.

3 Tayside & Grampian

Tayside and Grampian, two history-rich sections in northeast Scotland, offer a vast array of sightseeing in what are relatively small areas. Tayside, for example, is about 137km (85 miles) east to west, and some 97km (60 miles) south to north. The two regions share the North Sea coast between the Firth of Tay in the south and the Firth of Moray farther north. The so-called Highland Line separating the Lowlands in the south from the Highlands in the north crosses both regions. The Grampians, the highest mountain range in Scotland, are to the west of this line.

Carved out of the old counties of Perth and Angus, **Tayside** is named for its major river, the 190km (119-mile) Tay. The region is easy to explore, and its tributaries and dozens of lochs and Highland streams are among the best salmon and trout waters in Europe. One of the loveliest regions of Scotland, Tayside is filled with heather-clad Highland hills, long blue lochs under tree-lined banks, and miles and miles of walking trails. Tayside provided the backdrop for many novels by Sir Walter Scott, including *The Fair Maid of Perth, Waverley,* and *The Abbot.* Its golf courses are world famous, especially the trio of 18-hole courses at Gleneagles.

The **Grampian** region has Braemar, site of the most famous of the Highland gatherings. The queen herself comes here to holiday at Balmoral Castle, her private residence, a tradition dating back to the days of Queen Victoria and her consort, Prince Albert. As you journey on the scenic roads of Scotland's northeast, you'll pass heather-covered moorland and peaty lochs, wood glens and salmon-filled rivers, granite-stone villages and ancient castles, and fishing harbors as well as North Sea beach resorts.

GLENEAGLES

This famous golfing center and sports complex is on a moor between Strathearn and Strath Allan. Gleneagles has three **18-hole golf courses:** King's Course, the longest one; Queen's Course, next in length; and the PGA Centenary Course, the newest of the trio. They're among the best in Scotland, and the sports complex is one of the best equipped in Europe.

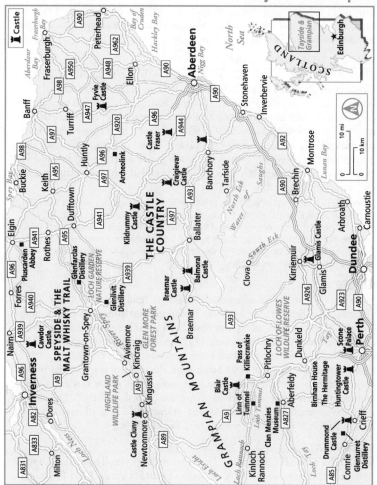

ESSENTIALS

GETTING THERE   By Train   The 15-minute ride from Perth costs £4.10 ($6.75). The trip from Edinburgh takes 1 hour and 30 minutes and costs £8.90 ($15). For information, call ☎ **08457/484950** or visit **www.nationalrail.co.uk**.

By Bus   The only service departs from Glasgow. The trip takes slightly more than an hour and costs £8 ($15). For information and schedules, call ☎ **0870/608-2608**.

By Car   Gleneagles is on A-9, about halfway between Perth and Stirling, a short distance from the village of Auchterarder. It lies 88km (55 miles) from Edinburgh and 72km (45 miles) from Glasgow.

VISITOR INFORMATION   The year-round **tourist center** is at 90 High St., Auchterarder (☎ **01764/663450**). It's open November through March, Monday and Wednesday to Saturday from 10am to 2pm; April through June, Monday through Saturday from 9:30am to 5:30pm, Sunday from 11am to 4pm; July and

August, Monday through Saturday from 9am to 7pm, Sunday from 11am to 6pm; and September and October, Monday through Saturday from 9:30am to 5:30pm, Sunday from 11am to 4pm.

WHERE TO STAY & DINE

Gleneagles Hotel ★★★ Britain's greatest golf hotel stands on its own 344-hectare (850-acre) estate. When it was built in isolated grandeur in 1924, it was Scotland's only five-star hotel. It's a true resort and has tried to keep ahead of the times by offering spa treatments. Rooms vary greatly in size. The best and most spacious choices are in the 60- to 90-block series; these have recently been refurbished. The less desirable rooms, called courtyard units, are a bit small and equipped with shower-only bathrooms. A new building has been added, and 54 more rooms welcome guests. As for cuisine, the golfers rarely complain, but no one dines here to collect recipes.

Auchterarder PH3 1NF. ℭ **01764/662231.** Fax 01764/662134. www.gleneagles.com. 265 units. £325–£445 ($601–$823) double; £740–£910 ($1,369–$1,684) suite. Rates include Scottish breakfast. AE, DC, MC, V. Free parking. Take A-9 2.4km (1½ miles) southwest of Auchterarder. **Amenities:** 3 restaurants; 2 bars; 2 indoor swimming pools; tennis; health club; spa; equestrian center; fishing; hunting excursions; Turkish bath; 24-hr. room service; babysitting; laundry service; dry cleaning; rooms for those with limited mobility. *In room:* TV, dataport, minibar, coffeemaker, hair dryer, iron, safe.

CRIEFF

From Perth, 70km (44 miles) north of Edinburgh, head west on A-85 for 29km (18 miles) to Crieff. At the edge of the Perthshire Highlands, with good fishing and golf, Crieff makes a pleasant stopover. This small burgh was the seat of the court of the earls of Strathearn until 1747, and the gallows in its marketplace was once used to execute Highland cattle rustlers.

You can take a "day trail" into **Strathearn,** the valley of the River Earn, the very center of Scotland. Here highland mountains meet gentle Lowland slopes, and moorland mingles with rich green pastures. North of Crieff, the road to Aberfeldy passes through the narrow pass of the **Sma' Glen,** a famous spot of beauty, with hills rising on either side to 600m (2,000 ft.).

ESSENTIALS

GETTING THERE **By Train** There's no direct service. The nearest rail stations are at Gleneagles, 14km (8¾ miles) away, and at Perth, 29km (18 miles) away. Call ℭ **08457/484950** or visit **www.nationalrail.co.uk** for information.

By Bus Once you arrive in Perth, you'll find regular connecting bus service hourly during the day. For information and schedules, call **Stagecoach** at ℭ **01738/629339.** Round-trip tickets for adults are £4.40 ($8.15) and £2.20 ($4) for children. The bus service from Gleneagles is too poor to recommend.

By Taxi From Gleneagles, a taxi will cost £15 to £25 ($28–$46).

VISITOR INFORMATION The year-round **tourist information office** is in the Town Hall on High Street (ℭ **01764/652578**). It's open November through March, Monday through Saturday from 9:30am to 4:30pm; April through June, Monday through Saturday from 9:30am to 5:30pm; July and August, Monday through Saturday from 9am to 6pm, Sunday from 10am to 5pm; and September and October, Monday through Saturday from 9:30am to 4:30pm, Sunday from 11am to 4pm.

WHERE TO STAY & DINE

Murraypark Hotel This stone-fronted house lies in a residential neighborhood about a 10-minute walk from Crieff's center and close to a golf course. In

1993, a new wing was opened, enlarging the public areas and the number of well-furnished rooms. The property has been considerably upgraded. Rooms in this 19th-century former sea captain's house vary in size and shape, but most open onto views. Although rooms in the new wing are more comfortable, they're hardly as evocative as those in the older wing, with its traditional Victorian aura.

Connaught Terrace, Crieff PH7 3DJ. ☎ **01764/653731.** Fax 01764/655311. www.murraypark.com. 20 units. £75 ($139) double or suite. Rates include Scottish breakfast. AE, DC, MC, V. Free parking. **Amenities:** Restaurant; bar; limited room service; babysitting; rooms for those with limited mobility. *In room:* TV, coffeemaker, hair dryer.

SEEING THE SIGHTS

Glenturret Distillery Ltd   Scotland's oldest distillery, Glenturret was established in 1775 on the banks of the River Turret. Visitors can see the milling of malt, mashing, fermentation, distillation, and cask filling, followed by a free "wee dram" dispensed at the end of the tour. Guided tours take about 50 minutes and leave at frequent intervals—sometimes as often as every 10 minutes when there's a demand for it. The tour can be followed or preceded by a 20-minute video, *The Water of Life,* presented adjacent to a small museum devoted to the implements of the whisky trade.

Hwy. A-85, Glenturret. ☎ **01764/656565.** www.famousgrouse.co.uk. Guided tours £5.95 ($11) adults, £4.95 ($9.15) seniors, £3 ($5.55) persons 5–17, £16 ($30) family, free for children 5 and under. Daily 9:30am–6pm. Closed Dec 25–26. Take A-85 toward Comrie; 1.5km (1 mile) from Crieff, turn right at the crossroads; the distillery is .5km (½ mile) up the road.

Drummond Castle Gardens ★   The gardens of Drummond Castle, first laid out in the early 17th century by John Drummond, second earl of Perth, are among the finest formal gardens in Europe. There's a panoramic view from the upper terrace, overlooking an example of an early Victorian parterre in the form of St. Andrew's Cross. The multifaceted sundial by John Mylne, master mason to Charles I, has been the centerpiece since 1630.

Muthill, Crieff. ☎ **01764/681257.** Admission £3.50 ($6.50) adults, £2.50 ($4.65) seniors, £1.50 ($2.80) children. May–Oct daily 2–5pm; Easter weekend 1–6pm. Closed Nov–Apr. Take A-822 for 5km (3 miles) south of Crieff.

PLAYING GOLF

Crieff Golf Club (☎ **01764/652909**) has two courses—both with panoramic views and excellent facilities. The most challenging is the 18-hole Fern Tower, a par-71 course with three par-5 holes. The Dornock is a 64-par, 9-hole course with three par-3 holes. It's not quite as difficult as the Fern Tower, but a test nonetheless. Greens fees for the Fern Tower are £25 ($46) per round Monday through Friday, and £27 ($50) weekends. Greens fees for the Dornock are £9 ($17) for 9 holes and £14 ($26) for 18 holes. Carts cost £15 ($28) per round. April through October, the golf club is open from 8am to 7:30pm; November through March, it's open daily from 9am to 5pm.

ABERFELDY ★

The "Birks o' Aberfeldy" are among the beauty spots made famous by the poet Robert Burns. Once a Pictish center, this small town makes a fine base for touring Perthshire's glens and lochs. Loch Tay lies 10km (6¼ miles) to the west; Glen Lyon, 24km (15 miles) west; and Kinloch Rannoch, 29km (18 miles) northwest. The town's shops offer good buys in tweeds and tartans, plus other items of Highland dress.

ESSENTIALS

GETTING THERE   By Train   There's no direct service into Aberfeldy. You can take a train to either Perth or Pitlochry, then continue the rest of the way by bus. Call *© 08457/484950* or visit **www.nationalrail.co.uk** for information.

By Bus   Connecting buses at either Perth or Pitlochry make the final journey to Aberfeldy. The private bus line **Stagecoach** (*© 01738/629339*) handles much of the bus travel to the smaller towns and villages in the area.

By Car   From Crieff, take A-822 on a winding road north to Aberfeldy. The 48km (30-mile) drive from Perth takes 30 to 45 minutes.

VISITOR INFORMATION   The **tourist office** is at The Square (*© 01887/ 820276*). Hours are July and August, daily from 9:30am to 6:30pm; April through June, September, and October, Monday to Saturday from 9am to 5:30pm and Sunday 11am to 3pm; and October through March, Monday through Saturday from 9:30am to 4:30pm.

WHERE TO STAY & DINE

Farleyer House Hotel ⭐   A tranquil oasis, this hotel of character stands on 33 hectares (70 acres) of grounds in the Tay Valley. Although restored and altered over the years, the building dates from the 1500s. The staff entertains guests as if you are in a private home. The public areas are immaculate and beautifully furnished, and the guest rooms are well maintained and comfortable.

Hwy. B-846, Aberfeldy PH15 2JE. *© 01887/820332.* Fax 01887/829879. www.farleyer.com. 19 units. £85–£120 ($157–$222) double; £145–£175 ($268–$324) family suite. Rates include breakfast. AE, DC, MC, V. Take B-846 3.2km (2 miles) west of Aberfeldy. **Amenities:** 2 restaurants; 2 bars; limited room service; babysitting; laundry service; dry cleaning; nonsmoking rooms; 1 room for those with limited mobility. *In room:* TV, coffeemaker, hair dryer, safe.

PLAYING GOLF

Aberfeldy Golf Club, at Aberfeldy (*© 01887/820535*), is a flatland course located on the banks of the River Tay. It's an 18-hole par 68 that is viewed as a "challenge" by the local pro. The River Tay comes into play on several holes, and if you're not careful, you'll be making trips back to the Pro Shop for more balls. Greens fees are £18 ($33) for 18 holes (£23/$43 on weekends), and pull-cart fees are £2 ($3.70) per round. April through October, the club is open daily from 8am to 11pm. During other months, call first to see if they're open; it depends on the weather.

DUNDEE & GLAMIS CASTLE ⭐⭐

This royal burgh and old seaport is an industrial city on the north shore of the Firth of Tay. When steamers took over the whaling industry from sailing vessels, Dundee became the leading home port for ships from the 1860s until World War I. Long known for its jute and flax operations, we think today of the Dundee fruitcakes, marmalades, and jams. This was also the home of the man who invented stick-on postage stamps, James Chalmers. Dundee has a raffish charm and serves well as a base for a trip to Glamis Castle.

Spanning the Firth of Tay is the **Tay Railway Bridge,** opened in 1888. Constructed over the tidal estuary, the bridge is some 3km (1¾ miles) long, one of the longest in Europe. There's also a road bridge 2km (1¼ miles) long, with four traffic lanes and a walkway in the center.

ESSENTIALS

GETTING THERE   By Train   **ScotRail** offers frequent service between Perth, Dundee, and Aberdeen. One-way fare from Perth to Dundee is £4.80 ($8.90), from Aberdeen £18 ($34). Call them at ℂ **08457/484950** or visit **www. nationalrail.co.uk** for information.

By Bus Citylink buses offer frequent bus service from Edinburgh and Glasgow. Call ℂ **08705/505050** for information.

By Car The fastest way to reach Dundee is to cut south back to Perth along A-9 and link up with A-972 going east.

VISITOR INFORMATION The **tourist information office** is at 21 Castle St. (ℂ **01382/527-527**). Hours are April through September, Monday through Saturday from 9am to 6pm, Sunday from noon to 4pm; October through March, Monday through Saturday from 9am to 5pm.

WHERE TO STAY

Hilton Dundee ⭑ This chain hotel helps rejuvenate the once-seedy waterfront of Dundee. Built in a severe modern style, the five-story block takes its name from a famous English tea, which most often accompanies marmalade and Dundee fruitcakes, the city's two most famous products. Some of the wellfurnished rooms overlook the Firth, the river, or the Tay Bridge. Both the business and the leisure traveler will find solace here in rooms with bright floral upholstery and draperies, blond wood furnishings, and small bathrooms.

Earl Grey Place, Dundee DD1 4DE. ℂ **01382/229271.** Fax 01382/200072. www.hilton.co.uk. 129 units. £80–£170 ($148–$520) double; from £245 ($453) suite. AE, DC, MC, V. Free parking. Bus: 1A, 1B, or 20. **Amenities:** Restaurant; bar; pool; health club; 24-hr. room service; babysitting; laundry service/dry cleaning; nonsmoking rooms; rooms for those with limited mobility. *In room:* TV, coffeemaker, hair dryer, trouser press, dataport.

Invercarse Hotel In landscaped gardens overlooking the River Tay, this privately owned hotel lies 5km (3 miles) west of the heart of Dundee. Many prefer it for its fresh air, tranquil location, and Victorian country-house aura. Wellmaintained rooms come in a variety of sizes and open onto views across the Tay to the hills of the Kingdom of Fife.

371 Perth Rd., Dundee DD2 1PG. ℂ **01382/669231.** Fax 01382/644112. 44 units. £90 ($167) double. Rates include Scottish breakfast. AE, DC, MC, V. Free parking. **Amenities:** Restaurant; bar; limited room service; laundry service; dry cleaning; nonsmoking rooms; rooms for those with limited mobility. *In room:* TV, coffeemaker, hair dryer.

WHERE TO DINE

Jahangir Tandoori INDIAN Built around an indoor fishpond in a dining room draped with the soft folds of an embroidered tent, this is one of the most exotic restaurants in the region. Meals are prepared with fresh ingredients and cover the gamut of recipes from both north and south India. Some preparations are slow-cooked in clay pots (tandoori) and seasoned to the degree of spiciness you prefer. Both meat and meatless dishes are available.

1 Sessions St. (at the corner of Hawk Hill). ℂ **01382/202022.** Reservations recommended. Main courses £9–£16 ($17–$30). AE, MC, V. Daily 3pm–midnight.

SEEING THE SIGHTS

For a panoramic view of Dundee, the Tay bridges across to Fife, and mountains to the north, go to **Dundee Law,** a 175m (572-ft.) hill just north of the city. The hill is an ancient volcanic plug.

HM Frigate *Unicorn* ⭑ *Kids* This 46-gun wooden ship of war commissioned in 1824 by the Royal Navy, now the oldest British-built ship afloat, has been restored and visitors can explore all four decks: the quarterdeck with 32-pound cannonades, the gun deck with its battery of 18-pound cannons and the captain's quarters, the berth deck with officers' cabins and crews' hammocks, and the orlop deck and hold. Displays portraying life in the sailing navy and the history of the *Unicorn* make this a rewarding visit.

Victoria Dock. 🕿 **01382/200900.** Admission £3.50 ($6.50) adults, £2.50 ($4.65) seniors and children, £7.50–£9.50 ($14–$18) family ticket. Easter–Oct daily 10am–5pm; Nov–Easter Wed–Fri noon–4pm, Sat–Sun 10am–4pm. Bus: 31.

Broughty Castle   This 15th-century estuary fort lies about 6km (3¾ miles) east of the city center on the seafront, at Broughty Ferry, a little fishing hamlet and once the terminus for ferries crossing the Firth of Tay before the bridges were built. Besieged by the English in the 16th century, and attacked by Cromwell's army under General Monk in the 17th century, it was eventually restored as part of Britain's coastal defenses in 1861. Its gun battery was dismantled in 1956, and it's now a museum with displays on local history, arms and armor, and Dundee's whaling story. The observation area at the top of the castle provides fine views of the Tay estuary and northeast Fife.

Castle Green, Broughty Ferry. 🕿 **01382/436916.** Free admission. Apr–Sept Mon–Sat 10am–4pm, Sun 12:30–4pm; Oct–Mar Tues–Sat 10am–4pm, Sun 12:30–4pm. Bus: 75 or 76.

PLAYING GOLF

Caird Park, at Dundee (🕿 **01382/438-871**), is an 18-hole, par-72 course that presents most golfers with an average challenge. The course is quite flat, but there are more than a few bunkers to navigate. There's also a restaurant and bar on the premises. Greens fees are £18 ($33) for 18 holes, or £26 ($48) for a day ticket. No carts of any sort are allowed on the course, and there's no particular dress code. The park is open April through October daily from 7:30am to 8pm.

A DAY TRIP TO GLAMIS

The little village of Glamis (pronounced without the "i") grew up around **Glamis Castle** ★★, Castle Office (🕿 **01307/840393**). Next to Balmoral Castle, visitors to Scotland most want to see Glamis Castle for its link with the crown. For 6 centuries it has been connected to members of the British royal family. The Queen Mother was brought up here; and Princess Margaret was born here, becoming the first royal princess born in Scotland in 3 centuries. The present owner is the queen's great-nephew. The castle contains Duncan's Hall—the Victorians claimed this was where Macbeth murdered King Duncan, but in the play, the murder takes place at Macbeth's castle near Inverness. In fact, Shakespeare was erroneous, as well—he had Macbeth named Thane of Glamis, but Glamis wasn't made a thaneship (a sphere of influence in medieval Scotland) until years after the play takes place.

The present Glamis Castle dates from the early 15th century, but there are records of a castle having been in existence in the 11th century. Glamis Castle has been in the possession of the Lyon family since 1372, and it contains some fine plaster ceilings, furniture, and paintings.

The castle is open to the public, with access to the Royal Apartments and many other rooms, as well as the fine gardens, from the end of March to the end of October only, daily from 10am to 6pm. Admission to the castle and gardens is £6.80 ($12) adults, £3.70 ($6.90) children, £19 ($35) family. If you wish to visit the grounds only, the charge is £3.50 ($6.50) adults, £2.50 ($4.65) children. Buses run between Dundee and Glamis. The 35-minute ride costs £4 ($12) round-trip. *Note:* Buses don't run on Sunday, and they don't stop in front of the castle, which lies 1.6km (1 mile) from the bus stop.

Playing the World's Oldest Course

At **St. Andrew's**, 23km (14 miles) southeast of Dundee and 82km (51 miles) northeast of Edinburgh, the rules of golf in Britain and the world were codified and arbitrated. Golf was played for the first time in the 1400s, probably on the site of St. Andrew's Old Course, and enjoyed by Mary, Queen of Scots, there in 1567. All six of St. Andrew's golf courses are open to the public on a more-or-less democratic basis—ballots are polled 1 day in advance. To participate in the balloting, you first must be staying in St. Andrews for a minimum of 2 days, and you must be able to present a current handicap certificate issued by the governing golf body of your home country. If you meet those requirements, you can enter the ballot in person at the golf course, or by phone at © **01334/466666**, before 1:45pm on the day before the one on which you wish to play. At 2pm each day, the balloting is drawn, and the following day's players are announced at 4pm. Bear in mind that your wait to play will most likely be from 4 to 6 days; however, some lucky players get on the course the next day. Players who call the golf course several weeks in advance to make reservations can often circumvent the balloting system, depending on demand.

The **Old Course**, St. Andrews, Golf Place, St. Andrew's, Fife (© **01334/466666**), is a 6,000m (6,566-yard) 18-hole course billed as "the Home of Golf." Greens fees are £110 ($203) per round from April to September or £72 ($133) otherwise. A caddy will cost £35 ($65) plus tip. Golf clubs rent for £20 to £30 ($37–$56) per round. Electric carts are not allowed, and you can rent a cart only on afternoons from May to September for £3 ($5.55). The course is a par 72.

To reach St. Andrews from Edinburgh, travel along the A90 north to Dunfermline. From there, continue northeast along A910, which becomes A915 at Leven. From Leven, drive northeast on A915 directly to St. Andrews (trip time: 1 hr.).

Where to Stay

Castleton House ★ *(Finds)* This Victorian hotel is run with love and care by its owners, Anthony and Sheila Lilly. In cool weather you're greeted by welcoming coal fires in the public lounge. The youthful staff is the most considerate we've encountered in the area. Rooms of various sizes are furnished with reproductions of antiques. The most superior and most beautiful accommodation is a Regency four-poster bedroom. One of the reasons to stay here is to enjoy the cuisine, among the finest in the area. Some of the produce comes from the hotel's own vegetable garden, including fresh fruits such as strawberries and raspberries. All rooms are nonsmoking.

Eassie by Glamis, Forfar, Tayside DD8 1SJ. © 01307/840340. Fax 01307/840506. www.castletonglamis. co.uk. 6 units. £125 ($230) double; £165 ($305) suite. Children 14 and under stay free in parent's room. Rates include Scottish breakfast. AE, MC, V. Drive 5km (3 miles) west of Glamis on A-94. **Amenities:** 2 restaurants; bar; limited room service; laundry service; dry cleaning. *In room:* TV, dataport, coffeemaker, hair dryer.

Where to Dine

Strathomore Arms CONTINENTAL/SCOTTISH Try this place near the castle for one of the best lunches in the area. You might begin with freshly made soup of the day or the fresh prawns. Regularly featured dishes might include steak pie or venison. For something a little more exotic there's the Indian chicken breast, marinated in yogurt and spices; and for vegetarians, phyllo parcels stuffed with asparagus and cauliflower.

The Square Glamis. ℂ 01307/840248. Reservations recommended. Main courses £7–£15 ($13–$46). MC, V. Daily noon–2pm and 5–9pm.

BRAEMAR

In the heart of some of Grampian's most beautiful scenery, Braemar is not only known for its own castle, but it makes a good center from which to explore Balmoral Castle (see "Ballater & Balmoral Castle," below). In this Highland village, set against a massive backdrop of hills covered with heather in summer, Clunie Water joins the River Dee. The massive **Cairn Toul** towers over Braemar, reaching a height of 1,293m (4,241 ft.).

ESSENTIALS

GETTING THERE **By Train** Take the train to Aberdeen, then continue the rest of the way by bus. For information, call ℂ **08457/484950** or visit **www.nationalrail.co.uk**.

By Bus Buses run daily from Aberdeen to Braemar at the rate of six per day (trip time: 2 hr.). One-way fare is £8 ($15). The bus and train stations in Aberdeen are next to each other on Guild Street (ℂ **01224/212266** for information about schedules).

By Car To reach Braemar from Dundee, return west toward Perth, then head north along A-93, following the signs into Braemar. The 113km (70-mile) drive will take 70 to 90 minutes.

VISITOR INFORMATION The year-round **Braemar Tourist Office** is in The Mews, Mar Road (ℂ **013397/41600**). In June, hours are daily from 9:30am to 6pm; July and August, daily from 9am to 6:30pm; and September, daily from 10am to 1pm and 2 to 6pm. November to January, hours are daily 11am to 4:30pm; February Monday to Saturday 10:30am to 4:30pm, Sunday noon to 4:30pm; March to May daily 10am to 5:30pm.

SPECIAL EVENTS The spectacular **Royal Highland Gathering** takes place annually the first Saturday in September in the Princess Royal and Duke of Fife Memorial Park. The queen herself often attends the gathering. These ancient games are thought to have been originated by King Malcolm Canmore, a chieftain who ruled much of Scotland at the time of the Norman conquest of England. He selected his hardiest warriors from all the clans for a "keen and fair contest."

Call the tourist office (see "Visitor Information," above) for more information. Braemar is overrun with visitors during the gathering—anyone thinking of attending would be wise to reserve accommodations anywhere within a 32km (20-mile) radius of Braemar no later than early April.

WHERE TO STAY & DINE

Braemar Lodge Hotel 𝘒𝘪𝘥𝘴 This hotel, popular with skiers who frequent the nearby Glenshee slopes, is set on 1 hectare (2 acres) of grounds at the head of Glen Clunie. Units vary in shape and size, but each is comfortable and well equipped, containing a well-maintained bathroom with tub and shower. Rooms are bright and airy, with soothing color schemes. Two rooms are large enough for families. On cool evenings, you're greeted by log fires. The hotel is on the road to the Glenshee ski slopes near the cottage where Robert Louis Stevenson wrote *Treasure Island.* On the grounds, three log cabins have been recently built. Fully equipped with all modern conveniences, they can sleep up to six persons.

6 Glenshee Rd., Braemar AB35 5YQ. ℂ and fax 013397/41627. 7 units. £85–£90 ($157–$166) double; from £200 ($370) log cabin. Rates include Scottish breakfast. MC, V. Free parking. Closed Nov. **Amenities:** Restaurant; laundry service; dry cleaning. *In room:* TV, hair dryer.

Invercauld Arms Thistle Hotel ✷   This is the leading inn of the town, with superior amenities and greater comfort than Braemar Lodge. The oldest part of this old granite building dates from the 18th century. In cool weather there's a roaring log fire on the hearth. You can go hill walking and see deer, golden eagles, and other wildlife. Fishing and winter skiing are other pursuits in the nearby area. Rooms are comfortably furnished. Although they lack any style or glamour, they serve their purpose well, and come in a wide range of sizes. In the pub close by, you'll meet the "ghilles" and "stalkers" (hunting and fishing guides).

Braemar AB35 5YR. ℂ 013397/41605. Fax 013397/41428. 66 units. £70–£90 ($130–$276) double. Rates include Scottish breakfast. MC, V. Free parking. Bus: 201. **Amenities:** Restaurant; bar; nonsmoking rooms; rooms for those with limited mobility. *In room:* TV, coffeemaker, hair dryer.

SEEING THE SIGHTS

If you're a Royal Family watcher, you might be able to spot members of the family, even the queen, at **Crathie Church,** 14km (8¾ miles) east of Braemar on A-93 (ℂ **013397/42208**), where they attend Sunday services when in residence. Services are at 11:30am; otherwise, the church is open for viewing April through October, Monday through Saturday from 9:30am to 5pm and Sunday from 1:45 to 5pm.

Nature lovers may want to drive to the **Linn of Dee,** 10km (6¼ miles) west of Braemar, a narrow chasm on the River Dee, which is a local beauty spot. Other beauty spots include Glen Muick, Loch Muick, and Lochnagar. A **Scottish Wildlife Trust Visitor Centre,** reached by a minor road, is located in this Highland glen, off the South Deeside road. An access road joins B-976 at a point 26km (16 miles) east of Braemar. The tourist office (see above) will give you a map pinpointing these beauty spots.

Braemar Castle ✷   This romantic 17th-century castle is a fully furnished private residence with architectural grace, scenic charm, and historical interest. The castle has barrel-vaulted ceilings and an underground prison and is known for its remarkable star-shaped defensive curtain wall.

On the Aberdeen-Ballater-Perth Rd. (A-93). ℂ **013397/41219.** Admission £4 ($7.40) adults, £3.50 ($6.50) seniors and students, £1.50 ($2.80) ages 5–15, free for ages 4 and under. Mon after Easter to Oct Sat–Thurs 10am–5pm. Closed Nov–Easter. Take A93 .5km (½ mile) northeast of Braemar.

PLAYING GOLF

Braemar Golf Course, at Braemar (ℂ **013397/41618**), is the highest golf course in the country. The green of the second hole is 380m (1,250 ft.) above sea level—this is the trickiest hole on the course. Pro golf commentator Peter Alliss has deemed it "the hardest par 4 in all of Scotland." Set on a plateau, the hole is bordered on the right by the River Clunie and lined on the left by rough. Greens fees are as follows: Monday through Friday £20 ($37) for 18 holes and £25 ($46) for a day ticket; Saturday and Sunday £23 ($43) for 18 holes and £28 ($52) for a day ticket. Pull-carts can be rented for £2 ($3.70) per day, and sets of clubs can be borrowed for £10 ($19) per day. The only dress code is "Be reasonable." The course is open daily from April to October only (call in advance; hours can vary).

BALLATER & BALMORAL CASTLE ★★

Ballater is a vacation resort center on the Dee River, with the Grampian Mountains in the background. The town is still centered around its Station Square, where the Royal Family used to be photographed as they arrived to spend vacations. The railway is now closed.

ESSENTIALS

GETTING THERE **By Train** Go to Aberdeen and continue the rest of the way by connecting bus. For information, call © **08457/484950** or visit **www.nationalrail.co.uk**.

By Bus Buses run hourly from Aberdeen to Ballater. The bus and train stations in Aberdeen are next to each other on Guild Street (© **01224/212266** for information). Bus no. 201 from Braemar runs to Ballater (trip time: 1¼ hr.). The fare is £3 ($5.55).

By Car From Braemar, go east along A-93.

VISITOR INFORMATION The **tourist information office** is at Station Square (© **013397/55306**). Hours are May to September, daily from 9am to 6pm; October to April, daily 10am to 5pm.

WHERE TO STAY

Hilton Craigendarroch Hotel ★ This hotel, built in the Scottish baronial style, is set amid old trees on a 13-hectare (28-acre) estate. Modern comforts have been added, but the owners have tried to maintain a 19th-century aura. The public rooms include a regal oaken staircase and a large sitting room. The fair-size rooms open onto views of the village of Ballater and the River Dee. Each is furnished in individual style, with private bathrooms (showers only). Public facilities are luxurious, especially the oak-paneled study with a log fire and book-lined shelves. All rooms are nonsmoking.

Braemar Rd., Ballater AB35 5XA. © 013397/55858. Fax 013397/55447. www.hilton.com. 45 units. £119 ($220) double; £199 ($368) suite. Rates include Scottish breakfast. Half board £92 ($170) extra per person. AE, DC, MC, V. **Amenities:** 2 restaurants; bar; tennis courts; solarium; salon; 24-hr. room service; babysitting; laundry service; dry cleaning. *In room:* TV, dataport, coffeemaker, hair dryer, trouser press.

Monaltrie Hotel _Kids_ This 1835 hotel, the first in the region, was built of Aberdeen granite to accommodate the clients of a now-defunct spa. Today it bustles with a clientele who come for the live music in its pub and for the savory food served, the most unusual of which is a Thai cuisine. Each of the fair-size rooms has comfortable beds along with neatly maintained bathrooms with shower stalls. The hotel lies a 3-minute walk east of the center of town and opens onto the banks of the River Dee. All rooms are nonsmoking.

5 Bridge Sq., Ballater AB35 5QJ. © 013397/55417. Fax 013397/55180. www.monaltriehotel.co.uk. 24 units. £40–£80 ($74–$148) double. Rates include Scottish breakfast. AE, DC, MC, V. Free parking. **Amenities:** Restaurant; bar; fishing; golf; other sports arranged; children's play area. *In room:* TV, radio, beverage maker, hair dryer.

WHERE TO DINE

Green Inn SCOTTISH/MODERN BRITISH In the heart of town, what was once a temperance hotel is now one of the finest dining rooms in town, especially for traditional Scottish dishes. The chef places emphasis on local produce, including homegrown vegetables when available. In season, loin of venison is served with a bramble sauce, and you can always count on fresh salmon and the best of Angus beef. Three very simply furnished double rooms are rented here, all with private bathrooms (with showers) and TV. Half board costs £65 ($120) per person and bed-and-breakfast is £30 ($56) per person.

9 Victoria Rd., Ballater AB35 5QQ. ℂ and fax **013397/55701**. Reservations required. Fixed-price menu £29 ($53) for 2 courses, £34 ($62) for 3 courses. AE, DC, MC, V. Mar–Oct daily 7–9pm; Nov–Feb Tues–Sat 7–9pm.

Oaks Restaurant BRITISH   The most glamorous restaurant in the region, the Oaks is in the century-old mansion that was originally built by the "marmalade kings" of Britain, the Keiller family. (The company's marmalade is still a household word throughout the United Kingdom.) This is the most upscale of the three restaurants in a resort complex that includes hotel rooms, timeshare villas, and access to a nearby golf course. To start, try the venison and duck terrine flavored with orange and brandy and served with a warm black conch vinaigrette. Other main courses are roast rack of lamb, breast of Grampian chicken, loin of venison, and filet of Aberdeen Angus beef.

In the Hilton Craigendarroch Hotel, Braemar Rd. ℂ **013397/55858**. Reservations strongly recommended. Fixed-price dinners £28 ($52) 3 courses, £25 ($46) 2 courses. AE, DC, MC, V. Daily 6:30–9:15pm.

THE CASTLE

Balmoral Castle   "This dear paradise" is how Queen Victoria described Balmoral Castle, rebuilt in the Scottish baronial style by her "beloved" Albert and completed in 1855. Today Balmoral, 13km (8 miles) west of Ballater, is still a private residence of the British sovereign. Its principal feature is a 30m (100-ft.) tower. On the grounds are many memorials to the royal family. In addition to the gardens there are country walks, pony trekking, souvenir shops, and a refreshments room. Of the actual castle, only the ballroom is open to the public; it houses an exhibition of pictures, porcelain, and works of art.

Balmoral, Ballater. ℂ **013397/42534**. Admission £5 ($9.25) adults, £4 ($7.40) seniors, £1 ($1.85) children 5–16, free for ages 4 and under. Apr 1–July 31 daily 10am–5pm. Crathie bus from Aberdeen to the Crathie station; Balmoral Castle is signposted from there (a short walk).

PLAYING GOLF

Ballater Golf Club, at Ballater (ℂ **013397/55567**), is one of the more scenic courses in the area. Set in a bowl of mountains and situated on the banks of the River Dee, this is a 5,155m (5,638-yard), par-67 course. Greens fees are as follows: Monday through Friday, £21 ($39) for 18 holes or £30 ($56) for a day ticket; Saturday and Sunday, £25 ($46) for 18 holes or £35 ($65) for a day ticket. There are no electric carts for hire; pull-carts rent for £2 ($3.70) per day. Dress should be smart but casual. The course is open daily April through September from 8am to sunset. October through March, hours are daily from 9am to sunset but only if the weather permits.

SPEYSIDE ✷ & THE MALT WHISKY TRAIL ✷

Much of the Speyside region covered in this section is in the Moray district, on the southern shore of the Moray Firth, a great inlet cutting into the northeastern coast of Scotland. The district stretches in a triangular shape south from the coast to the wild heart of the Cairngorm Mountains near Aviemore. It's a land steeped in history, as its many castles, battle sites, and ancient monuments testify. It's also a good place to fish and, of course, play golf. Golfers can purchase a 5-day ticket from tourist information centers that will allow you to play at more than 11 courses in the area.

One of the best of these courses is **Boat of Garten,** Speyside (ℂ **01479/ 831282**). Relatively difficult, the almost 5,500m (6,000-yard) course is dotted with many bunkers and wooded areas. April through October, greens fees are £29 to £34 ($54–$63) Monday through Friday from 9:30am to 6pm. On Saturday, greens fees are £34 to £39 ($63–$72), from 10am to 4pm. In winter, call to see if the course is open. Greens fees are then reduced to £12 ($22). Pull-carts can be rented for £2.50 ($4.65) and electric carts are available for £15 ($28). Dress reasonably; blue jeans are not acceptable.

The valley of the second-largest river in Scotland, the Spey, lies north and south of Aviemore. It's a land of great natural beauty. The Spey is born in the Highlands above Loch Laggan, which lies 64km (40 miles) south of Inverness. Little more than a creek at its inception, it gains in force, fed by the many "burns" that drain water from the surrounding hills. One of Scotland's great rivers for salmon fishing, it runs between the towering Cairngorms on the east and the Monadhliath Mountains on the west. Its major center is Grantown-on-Spey.

The major tourist attraction in the area is the **Malt Whisky Trail,** 113km (70 miles) long, running through the glens of Speyside. Here distilleries, many of which can be visited, are known for their production of *uisge beatha,* or "water of life." "Whisky" is its more familiar name.

Spotting Nessie

Sir Peter Scott's *Nessitera rhombopteryx* continues to elude her pursuers. "Nessie," as she's more familiarly known, has captured the imagination of the world, drawing thousands of visitors yearly to Loch Ness. The Loch Ness monster has been described as one of the world's greatest mysteries. Half a century ago, A82 was built alongside the western banks of the loch. Since that time, many more sightings have been recorded.

All types of high-tech underwater contraptions have searched for the Loch Ness monster, but no one can find her. Dr. Robert Rines and his associates at the Academy of Applied Science in Massachusetts maintain a year-round watch with sonar-triggered cameras and strobe lights suspended from a raft in Urquhart Bay.

The loch is 39km (24 miles) long, 1.6km (1 mile) wide, and some 230m (755 ft.) deep. Even if the monster doesn't put in an appearance, you can enjoy the loch seascape. In summer, you can take boat cruises across Loch Ness from both Fort Augustus and Inverness.

Buses from either Fort Augustus or Inverness traverse A82, taking you to Drumnadrochit. Call ✆ **08705/808-080** for schedules and more information. The bucolic hamlet of Drumnadrochit lies a mile from Loch Ness at the entrance to Glen Urquhart. It's the nearest village to the part of the loch from which sightings of the monster have been reported most frequently.

From Grantown-on-Spey, take A938 west until you merge with northwest-bound E15/A9, which leads to Inverness, on the north tip of Loch Ness. From Inverness, travel on the A82 south, which runs the length of the western shoreline. The eastern shoreline can be traveled by following signposted rural roads from Inverness.

Half the malt distilleries in the country lie along the River Spey and its tributaries. Here peat smoke and Highland water are used to turn out single-malt (unblended) whisky. There're five malt distilleries in the area: **Glenlivet, Glenfiddich, Glenfarclas, Strathisla,** and **Tamdhu.** Allow about an hour each to visit them.

The best way to reach Speyside from Aberdeen is to take A-96 northwest, signposted ELGIN. If you're traveling north on the A-9 road from Perth and Pitlochry, your first stop might be Dalwhinnie, which has the highest whisky distillery in the world at 575m (1,888 ft.). It's not in the Spey Valley but is at the northeastern end of Loch Ericht, with views of lochs and forests.

KEITH

Keith, 18km (11 miles) northwest of Huntly, grew up because of its strategic location, where the main road and rail routes between Inverness and Aberdeen cross the River Isla. It has an ancient history, but owes its present look to the "town planning" of the late 18th and early 19th centuries. Today it's a major stopover along the Malt Whisky Trail.

The oldest operating distillery in the Scottish Highlands, the **Strathisla Distillery,** on Seafield Avenue (℃ **01542/783044**), was established in 1786. Hours are Easter through October, Monday through Friday from 10am to 4pm; closed November to Easter. Admission is £5 ($9.25) adults, free for ages 8 to 18; children under 8 are not admitted. *Note:* Tours of this distillery are self-guided.

DUFFTOWN

James Duff, the fourth earl of Fife, founded this town in 1817. The four main streets of town converge at the battlemented **clock tower,** which is also the tourist information center. A center of the whisky-distilling industry, Dufftown is surrounded by seven malt distilleries. The family-owned **Glenfiddich Distillery** is on A-941, just north of Dufftown (℃ **01340/820373**). It's open Monday through Friday from 9:30am to 4:30pm; Easter through mid-October it's also open on Saturday from 9:30am to 4:30pm and on Sunday from noon to 4:30pm. Guides in kilts show visitors around the plant and explain the process of distilling. A film of the history of distilling is also shown. At the finish of the tour, you're given a dram of malt whisky to sample. The tour is free, but there's a souvenir shop where the owners hope you'll spend a few pounds.

Other sights include **Balvenie Castle,** along A-941 (℃ **01340/820121**), the ruins of a moated stronghold from the 14th century on the south side of the Glenfiddich Distillery. During her northern campaign against the earl of Huntly, Mary, Queen of Scots, spent 2 nights here. It's open April through September, daily from 9:30am to 6:30pm. Admission is £1.80 ($3.35) adults, £1.30 ($2.40) seniors, and 50p (85¢) children under 16.

Mortlach Parish Church in Dufftown is one of the oldest places of Christian worship in the country. It's reputed to have been founded in 566 by St. Moluag. A Pictish cross stands in the graveyard. The present church was reconstructed in 1931 and incorporates portions of an older building.

Where to Dine

Taste of Speyside ⚑ SCOTTISH   True to its name, this restaurant in the town center, just off the main square, avidly promotes a Speyside cuisine as well as malt whiskies. In the bar you can buy the product of each of Speyside's 46 distilleries. A platter including a slice of smoked salmon, smoked venison, smoked trout, pâté flavored with malt whisky, locally made cheese (cow or goat), salads, and homemade oat cakes is offered at noon and at night. Nourishing soup is made fresh daily and is served with homemade bread. There's also a choice of meat pies, including venison with red wine and herbs, or rabbit. For dessert, try Scotch Mist, which contains fresh cream, malt whisky, and crumbled meringue.

10 Balvenie St. © 01340/820860. Reservations recommended in the evening. Main courses £12–£16 ($21–$30); Speyside platter £14 ($26) at lunch, £14 ($26) at dinner. AE, MC, V. Mon–Sat 12:30–9pm. Closed Nov–Feb.

GLENLIVET

As you leave Grantown-on-Spey and head east along A-95, drive to the junction with B-9008; drive south and you won't miss the **Glenlivet Distillery.** The location of the **Glenlivet Reception Centre** (© **01542/783220**) is 16km (10 miles) north of the nearest town, Tomintoul. Near the River Livet, a Spey tributary, this distillery is one of the most famous in Scotland. It's open April through October, Monday through Saturday from 10am to 4pm and Sunday from 12:30 to 4pm. Admission is free.

Back on A-95, you can visit the **Glenfarclas Distillery** at Ballindalloch (© **01807/500245**), one of the few malt whisky distilleries that's still independent of the giants. Founded in 1836, Glenfarclas is managed by the fifth generation of the Grant family. It's open October to March, Monday through Friday from 10am to 4pm; April to September Monday to Friday 10am to 5pm; June through September, it's also open Saturday from 10am to 5pm. There's a small crafts shop, and each visitor is offered a dram of Glenfarclas Malt Whisky. The admission of £3.50 ($6.50) is for visitors over 18, and there's a discount of £1 ($1.85) on any purchase of £10 ($19) or more.

Where to Stay

Minmore House Hotel ★ Standing on 1.6 hectares (4 acres) of private grounds adjacent to the Glenlivet Distillery, this is an impressive country house. It was the home of the distillery owners before becoming a hotel. The drawing room opens onto views of the plush Ladder Hills. Well-furnished rooms have basic amenities, and the oak-paneled lounge bar has an open log fire on chilly nights. All rooms are nonsmoking.

Glenlivet, Ballindalloch AB37 9DB. © **01807/590378.** Fax 01807/590472. www.minmorehousehotel.com. 10 units. £98 ($181) per person double; £55 ($102) per person bed-and-breakfast. Double room rates include breakfast, afternoon tea, and 4-course dinner. MC, V. Closed Feb. **Amenities:** Dining room; bar; pool. *In room:* Coffeemaker, hair dryer.

16

Spain

by Sascha Segan & Herbert Bailey Livesey

For a nation with such a rich, storied past, Spain has a remarkable verve for the present. Still a land of sun-washed beaches, terraced vineyards, tranquil hill towns, and dazzling Moorish palaces, Spain has grown into a new-found prosperity after two decades of working to catch up with the rest of Europe. Cultural innovations, high-tech ventures, and contemporary art abound in the new Spain, and even the millennia-old siesta is no longer sacred. This mix of old and new, of "castles in Spain" and cutting-edge cuisine, is making Spain a place that can hold its national head high in the 21st century.

1 Madrid ★★★

Madrid was built to rule, established on a broad, flat plateau in the geographical center of the Iberian peninsula to bring Spain's many fractious regions together. It's no wonder, then, that Madrid is Spain's melting pot. Native *Madrileños* are joined here not only by Basques, Galicians, Catalonians, and Andalusians, but by new immigrants from Africa and South America. Far from the sea and lacking the multimillennial history of Barcelona or Seville, Madrid can still claim more than its fair share of world-class attractions: its impressive royal palace, handsome parks, wealth of art museums, and passionate and diverse population. Madrileños work hard and party hard, dining at midnight and dancing till dawn in throbbing, multilevel nightclubs or whiling away the evening in smoky, atmospheric tapas bars.

Renovation and reconstruction is everywhere in Madrid, whether invisible in the lifted gloom of the Chueca neighborhood, once a dangerous, crime-ridden area and now the city's hottest nightlife district, or thrillingly obvious in the new wings of the Prado, Thyssen, and Reina Sofía museums, three of Spain's greatest temples of art. The result of all this work is a city of comfortable, well-lighted plazas and winding yet approachable streets, and a population that looks to the future with power and pride.

ESSENTIALS

GETTING THERE   By Plane   Aeropuerto Madrid Barajas (© **91-305-8343;** www.aena.es), Madrid's international airport, is 14km (8¾ miles) east of the city center and has three terminals. Most international flights arrive at Terminal 1. The cheapest ride (1.10€/$1.25) into town is on the new **Metro line no. 8.** Its disadvantages are that the station is near Terminal 3, a long trek on moving walkways from Terminal 1, where most international flights arrive, and you have to make at least one line change at Nuevos Ministerios, with more walking. It's a speedy trip, though: Expect to be downtown about half an hour after you enter the system. For 2.40€ ($2.75), the line no. 89 **airport bus** runs daily 4:45am to 1:30am (departures every 10–15 min. 6am–10pm, less often at other times) between the airport and Plaza de Colón in the center of town. A **taxi** costs about 18€ ($21) plus tip and supplemental charges, and the journey takes 30 to 45 minutes, although during rush hours it can take up to an hour. Avoid unmetered limousines.

By Train   Madrid has three major railway stations: **Atocha,** Avenida Ciudad de Barcelona (Metro: Atocha RENFE), for trains to and from Lisbon, Toledo, Andalusia, and Extremadura; **Chamartín,** in the northern suburbs at Augustín de Foxá (Metro: Chamartín), for trains to Barcelona, Asturias, Cantabria, Castilla y León, the Basque country, Aragón, Catalonia, Levante (Valencia), Murcia, and the French border; and **Estación Príncipe Pío** or Norte, Paseo del Rey 30 (Metro: Principe Pío), for trains to northwest Spain (Salamanca and Galicia). Many trains to Atocha run through to Chamartín and vice versa— good to know because the old part of town is much closer to Atocha than to Chamartín.

For information about connections from any of these stations, contact **RENFE,** the Spanish railway company (© **90-224-0202** daily 7am–11pm; www.renfe.es). For tickets, go to the principal office of RENFE, Alcalá 44 (Metro: Banco de España), open Monday through Friday from 9:30am to 8pm; or go to any of the three main stations listed above.

In the United States, **Rail Europe** sells a variety of **rail passes** valid for use throughout Europe or in one or more specific countries, including Spain. For details, call © **888/382-7245** or visit www.raileurope.com.

By Bus   Madrid has at least eight major bus terminals, including the large **Estación Sur de Autobuses,** Calle Méndez Alvaro (© **91-468-4200;** Metro: Alvaro). Most buses pass through or arrive at this station.

By Car   The following are the major highways into Madrid, with driving distances to the city: Route NI from Irún, 507km (314 miles); NII from Barcelona, 626km (389 miles); NIII from Valencia, 349km (217 miles); NIV from Cádiz, 624km (388 miles); NV from Badajoz, 409km (254 miles); and NVI from Galicia, 602km (374 miles).

VISITOR INFORMATION   The **regional government's tourist office** is at Duque de Medinaceli 2 (© **90-235-3570;** www.Madrid.org; Metro: Banco de España). It's open Monday through Saturday from 9am to 7pm and Sunday and holidays from 9am to 3pm. The **city information office,** at **Plaza Mayor 3** (© **91-366-5477;** www.munimadrid.es; Metro: Sol), is open Monday to Saturday from 9am to 7pm and Sundays 10am to 3pm. This office is primarily a distribution center for brochures and maps, although attendants can answer questions.

Websites   The Tourist Office of Spain (**www.okspain.org**) can help you plan your trip with listings of lodging options, attractions, tour operators, and packages, plus handy tips on getting around. For the viewpoints of individual travelers, check **www.tripadvisor.com** and **www.virtualtourist.com**. The highly personal **www.madridman.com** has a home page that looks frivolous but provides a surprising amount of info, especially on cheap hostals.

CITY LAYOUT   The old city of Madrid sits like a small, dense walnut in the middle of new Madrid's vast sprawl. The **Gran Vía** is the major east-west artery of the old town, beginning at **Plaza de España,** with one of Europe's tallest skyscrapers, Edificio España. Great numbers of shops, hotels, restaurants, and

cinemas are concentrated on this principal avenue. Gran Vía ends at Calle de Alcalá, and at this juncture lies **Plaza de la Cibeles,** with its fountain to Cybele, "the mother of the gods," and what has become known as "the cathedral of post offices." From Cibeles northward, the wide **Paseo de Recoletos** begins a short run to **Plaza de Colón.** From this latter square, the majestic **Paseo de la Castellana** heads north through new Madrid, flanked by expensive shops, apartment buildings, luxury hotels, and foreign embassies. Parallel to the Paseo de la Castellana, **Calle de Serrano** is a prominent shopping street that forms the spine of the prosperous Salamanca neighborhood.

Heading south from Cibeles is **Paseo del Prado,** home to the eponymous **Museo del Prado,** as well as the **Jardín Botánica (Botanical Garden).** The paseo continues on to the Atocha Station, at the southern border of the old town. To the east of the Prado lies the **Parque del Retiro,** once reserved for royalty, with restaurants, nightclubs, a rose garden, and two lakes.

South of Gran Vía is the central **Puerta del Sol,** a half-moon-shaped plaza. All road distances in Spain are measured from here, and it is an important hub for buses and the Metro. Here, **Calle de Alcalá** begins and runs east for 4km (2½ miles).

A couple of blocks west is the **Plaza Mayor,** the heart of Old Madrid, and an attraction in itself with its mix of French and Georgian architecture.

GETTING AROUND   The tourist office (see above) provides a street map that includes a schematic of the public transit system. The bus and expanding Metro networks are efficient and extensive, and taxis are abundant. Since traffic is nearly always heavy, though, plan to cover distances under 10 blocks by walking.

By Metro (Subway)   The **Metro** (*①* **90-244-4403;** www.metromadrid.es) is complex, but clean, speedy, and convenient—often more convenient than

Madrid Metro

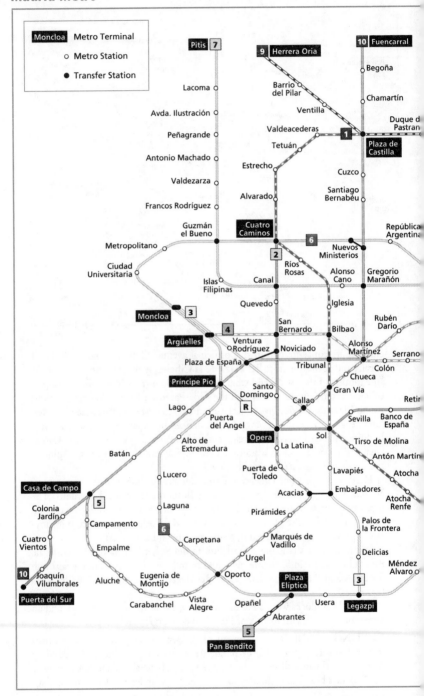

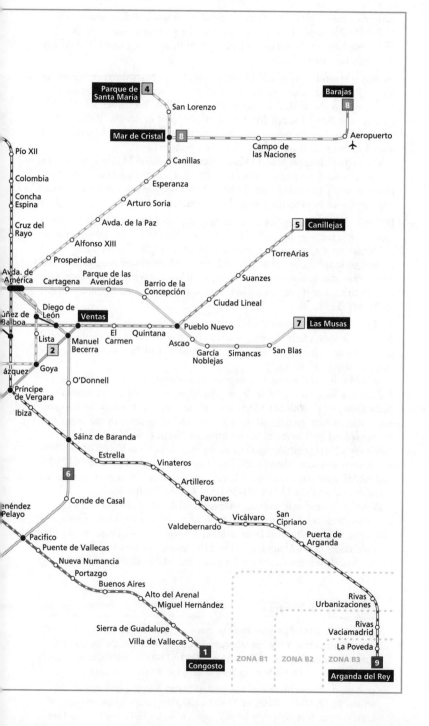

navigating the tangle of streets in the old town. A **single ticket** *(una sencilla)* is 1.10€ ($1.25) and a **10-trip pass** *(metrobús)* a more economical 5.20€ ($6). Ticket machines in the stations accept coins, bills, and credit cards. The subway runs daily 6am to 1:30am.

By Bus Madrid's bus system can be perplexing, as buses travel on circuitous routes. Prices and tickets are the same as on the Metro. Route information is available from the **E.M.T. kiosks** in Plaza de Callao, Puerta del Sol, Plaza de Cibeles, and Atocha (open Mon–Fri 8am–8:15pm) or on the Web at www. emtmadrid.es. Regular buses run 6am to midnight. A limited night service runs every half-hour 12:30am to 2am, then every hour to 6am.

The hop-off, hop-on **Madrid Vision Bus** (© 91-767-1743) lets you travel a full day around three tourist loops for 9.60€ ($11). Each loop lasts 75 minutes, provided that you don't get off the bus. Otherwise, you can opt for an unlimited number of stops, getting on and off at your leisure.

By Taxi When you flag down a taxi, the meter should read 1.45€ ($1.65) and increase by a rate varying from .65€ (75¢) to .95€ ($1.10) per kilometer, with the higher rates applying on weekends and late at night. There's a long list of authorized supplements for trips to and from the bullfighting ring, airport, and bus or rail stations; if you're curious, they're all listed at www.radiotelefono-taxi. com/es/tarifas.asp. It's customary to tip about 10% of the fare. To call a taxi, dial © **91-447-3232.**

By Car Driving is nightmarish and potentially dangerous in very congested Madrid—it always feels like rush hour. It's not a good idea to maintain a rental car while staying in the city. It's nearly impossible to park, and rental cars are the frequent targets of thieves.

Should you want to rent a car to tour the environs, however, you'll have several choices. Save money before leaving for Spain by making arrangements with **Auto Europe** (© **800/223-5555;** www.autoeurope.com), which brokers economical rates with established firms abroad, including some of the companies mentioned below. The major in-city firms are **Hertz,** Gran Via 88 (© **91-542-5805;** www.hertz.com; Metro: Plaza de España); **Avis,** Gran Vía 60 (© **91-548-4204;** www.avis.com; Metro: Gran Vía); **Europcar,** Av. del Partenón 16 (© **91-722-6226;** www.europcar.com; Metro: Campo de las Naciones) and **Atesa,** Paseo de la Castellana 130 (© **91-564-5379;** Metro: Serrano).

Note: You'll need only your state or provincial driver's license to rent a car, but if you're in an accident or stopped on the road by police, a recent regulation stipulates you must produce an **International Drivers Permit.** These are available at AAA offices in the States for $10 to $15. Know, too, that stiff fines are collected when drivers are caught speaking on a hand-held cellphone while driving.

FAST FACTS: Madrid

American Express For your mail or banking needs, you can go to the Amex office at the corner of Marqués de Cubas and Plaza de las Cortes 2, across the street from the Palace Hotel (© **91-572-0303;** Metro: Sevilla). It's open Monday to Friday 9am to 7:30pm and Saturday 10am-2pm.

Consulates The consulate of the **United States** is in the embassy at Calle Serrano 75 (© **91-587-2240,** or 91-587-2200 after hours; www.embusa.es/ indexbis.html; Metro: Núñez Bilbao), open Monday to Friday 9am to 1pm and 3 to 5:30pm. The consulate of **Canada** is in the embassy at Núñez de Balboa 35 (© **91-423-3250;** Metro: Velázquez), open Monday to Thursday 8:30am to 2pm and 3 to 5:30pm (to 4pm in Aug), Friday 8:30am to 2pm. The consulate of the **United Kingdom** is at Paseo de Recoletos 7/9 (© **91-524-9700;** www.ukinspain.com; Metro: Banco de España), open Monday to Friday roughly 8:30am to 2pm. Hours vary depending on the time of year, so call ahead. The consulate of **Ireland** is at Paseo de la Castellana 46 (© **91-436-4093;** Metro: Serrano), open Monday to Friday 10am to 2pm. The consulate of **Australia** is at Plaza Descubridor Diego de Ordás 3 (© **91-441-6025;** Metro: Ríos Rosas), open Monday to Thursday 8:30am to 1:30pm and 2:30 to 4:45pm and Friday 8:30am to 2:15pm. The embassy of **New Zealand** is at Plaza de la Lealtad 2 (© **91-523-0226;** www.nzembassy. com/home.cfm?c=27; Metro: Banco de España), open Monday to Friday 9am to 2pm and 3 to 5:30pm. In July and August, it's open Monday to Friday 8:30am to 1pm and 1:30pm to 4:30pm.

Currency The Spanish peseta gave way to the **euro** on March 1, 2002. At press time, 1€ = $1.15, or $1 = .85€.

Dentist/Doctor For an English-speaking dentist or doctor, contact the U.S. embassy, Calle Serrano 75 (© **91-587-2240**), which maintains a list of dentists and doctors who have offered their services to Americans abroad. Also, hotel concierges *(conserjes)* usually have lists of available doctors and dentists.

Drugstores For a late-night pharmacy, dial © **098** or look in the daily newspaper under *"Farmacias de Guardia"* to learn what drugstores are open after 8pm. Another way to find an open pharmacy is to go to any pharmacy, even if it's closed—it will have posted a list of nearby pharmacies that are open late.

Emergencies In an emergency, call © **080** to report a **fire,** © **091** to reach the **police,** or © **91-588-4400** to request an **ambulance.**

Hospitals/Clinics The **Hospital La Paz,** Castellana 261 (© **91-358-2600;** Metro: Begoña), is on the north side of town; in the city center, a 24-hour **first-aid clinic** *(casa de socorro)* is at Navas de Tolosa 10 (© **91-521-0025;** Metro: Sol). For a medical emergency, call © **91-588-4400** for an ambulance.

Post Office If you don't want to receive your mail at your hotel or the American Express office, direct it to *Lista de Correos* at the central post office in Madrid. To pick up mail, go to the window marked LISTA, where you'll be asked to show your passport. Madrid's central office is the **Palacio de Comunicaciones** at Plaza de Cibeles (© **91-536-0111;** Metro: Banco de España). An airmail letter or postcard to the United States is .75€ (85¢).

Safety Leave valuables in a hotel safe or other secure place when going out. You may need your passport, however, as the police sometimes stop foreigners for identification checks. Carry only enough cash for the day's needs. Pickpockets and purse snatchers work major tourist sites, trains, restaurants, and ATMs. Criminals often work in pairs, grabbing purses from pedestrians, cyclists, even cars. Several scams are meant to divert the victim's attention, such as spilling something on his or her clothing, or thrusting maps or newspapers into his or her face.

Taxes The internal sales tax (known in Spain as IVA) ranges between 7% and 33%, depending on the commodity being sold. Food, wine, and basic necessities are taxed at 7%; most goods and services (including car rentals) at 13%; luxury items (jewelry, all tobacco, imported liquors) at 33%; and hotels at 7%.

If you are not a European Union resident and make purchases in Spain worth more than 90€ ($104), you can get a tax refund. To get the refund, you must complete three copies of a form that the store will give you, detailing the nature of your purchase and its value. Citizens of non–EU countries show the purchase and the form to the Spanish Customs Office. The shop is then supposed to refund the amount due to you. Discuss in what currency your refund will arrive.

Telephone The country code for Spain is **34** and the city code for Madrid is **91**. All numbers in Spain are now nine digits, starting with the two- or-three-digit city code. You must dial all nine digits, no matter where you're calling from or to. Telephone centers are called *locutorios*. The minimum charge for **local telephone calls** is .25€ (30¢). Many pay phones accept major credit cards as well as phone cards you can buy at tobacconists' and post offices.

Tipping Customary tips are somewhat less than you'd see in the U.S. or the U.K. In restaurants, tip 5% to 10%, depending on the quality of the service. Tip the hotel porter 1€ ($1.15) for carrying your bags, the doorman .60€ (70¢) if he's truly helpful, and the hotel maid 1€ ($1.15) per day. Tip cab drivers 10% of the fare.

WHERE TO STAY
ALONG THE PASEO DE LA CASTELLANA
Very Expensive

Hesperia Madrid ★★★ A member of the Leading Hotels of the World, the sleek, five-star Hesperia fits in perfectly with this upscale business neighborhood. The hotel's signature restaurant, **Santceloni,** found itself at the pinnacle of the capital's gastronomic pyramid almost as soon as it opened its doors (so reserve well in advance). A less rarefied but thoroughly competent dining room, **La Manzana,** is on the main floor. Guest rooms are of sufficient size, with exceedingly comfortable beds and such extras as fax machines, terry robes, and fresh flowers. High-speed wireless Internet access is available in the lobby and some rooms. While the hotel is distant from most of the major sights, it is closer to the airport than city-center hotels.

Paseo de la Castellana 57, 28046 Madrid. ℂ **91-210-8800.** Fax 91-210-8899. www.hesperia-madrid.com. 171 units. 165€–415€ ($190–$477) double; from 399€ ($458) suite. AE, DC, MC, V. Parking 10€ ($12). Metro: Gregorio Marañón. **Amenities:** 2 restaurants; bar; concierge; car-rental desk; business center; 24-hr. room service; babysitting; same-day laundry service and dry cleaning. *In room:* A/C, TV w/pay movies, data-port, minibar, hair dryer.

Ritz Madrid ★★★ At the heart of Madrid near the Prado, this remains Madrid's most prestigious address, a bastion of glamour and an enduring relic of the Edwardian Age. Its grand public areas, with their soaring ceilings and graceful columns, were built in 1908 at the request of Alfonso XIII, who was embarrassed that his capital didn't have suitable accommodations for visiting royals.

Rooms are spacious, elegantly furnished, and filled with fresh flowers. Each is equipped with a well-accessorized bathroom. The restaurant, which receives good reviews, has tables that spill onto a garden terrace in warm months.

Plaza de la Lealtad 5, 28014 Madrid. ⊘ **800/225-5843** in the U.S. and Canada, or 91-701-6767. Fax 91-701-6776. www.ritz.es. 167 units. 320€–580€ ($368–$667) double; from 865€ ($995) suite. AE, DC, MC, V. Metro: Banco de España. **Amenities:** 2 restaurants; bar; health club with sauna; concierge; 24-hr. room service; babysitting; same-day laundry service and dry cleaning. *In room:* A/C, TV, dataport, minibar, coffeemaker, hair dryer.

The Westin Palace ★★★ An ornate 1912 structure that captures the pre–World War I grand hotel style, the Palace faces the Prado and Neptune Fountain. When it first opened, it was the largest hotel in Europe. Everyone from Dalí to Picasso, from Sarah Bernhardt to Sophia Loren, has spent the night here. Nevertheless, the Westin Palace hasn't achieved the cachet of its sibling, the Ritz, across the Paseo de Castellana, perhaps because the Westin is so much larger. Rooms are traditional, with plenty of space, containing large marble bathrooms with all the amenities. Do have a drink under the great stained-glass dome at the back of the main floor.

Plaza de las Cortes 7, 28014 Madrid. ⊘ **800/325-3535** in the U.S., 800/325-3589 in Canada, or 91-360-8000 in Spain. Fax 91-360-8100. www.westin.com. 417 units. 240€–550€ ($276–$632) double; from 659€ ($758) suite. AE, DC, MC, V. Metro: Banco de España. **Amenities:** 2 restaurants; bar; well-equipped health club; concierge; 24-hr. room service; babysitting; same-day laundry service and dry cleaning. *In room:* A/C, TV, dataport, minibar, hair dryer, safe.

Inexpensive

Mora ★ *Value* Long one of Madrid's top budget choices, even with recent rate jumps, the Mora is still an excellent choice. The spacious lobby with chandeliers sets the tone. The narrow but bright halls lead to rooms of varied configuration, but all are sufficiently furnished in muted tones, with carpeting. English is spoken by the helpful people at the front desk. The adjacent restaurant, **Bango** (separate management), attracts a polished crowd for low-cost meals.

Paseo del Prado 32, 28014 Madrid. ⊘ **91-420-1569.** Fax 91-420-0564. 62 units. 57€ ($66) single; 75 ($86) double. AE, DC, MC, V. Metro: Atocha. **Amenities:** Restaurant; bar. *In room:* A/C, TV, safe.

NEAR THE ROYAL PALACE
Moderate

Opera ★ A couple of blocks from the royal palace and opposite the opera house, this hotel offers first-rate comfort and a warm welcome from the English-speaking staff. Rooms range from medium to surprisingly spacious, some with balconies, and each is furnished with twin or double beds with quality mattresses. Bathrooms are excellent, some with whirlpools.

Cuesta de Santo Domingo 2, 28013 Madrid. ⊘ **91-541-2800.** Fax 91-541-6923. www.hotelopera.com. 79 units. 90€ ($104) single; 120€ ($138) double. AE, DC, MC, V. Metro: Opera. **Amenities:** Restaurant; bar; limited room service; babysitting; laundry service; dry cleaning. *In room:* A/C, TV, minibar, hair dryer, safe.

Inexpensive

HH Campomanes ★ *Finds* Up a quiet side street from the opera house is a row of attached houses that were scooped out and rebuilt to house this spiffy hotel. Contemporary and minimalist, the colors here are black, white, and pearl gray. However, the surroundings are cozy, not chilly. There are two "minisuites," which are really just large doubles. Singles are relatively large and offer full-size beds. At this moment, hardly anyone knows about this hotel, so get there before they do.

Campomanes 4 (near Arrieta), 28013 Madrid. ⊘ **91-548-8548.** Fax 91-559-1288. 30 units. 99€ ($114) double. Rates include breakfast. AE, MC, V. Metro: Opera. **Amenities:** Bar; laundry service; dry cleaning. *In room:* A/C, TV, minibar, safe.

Madrid

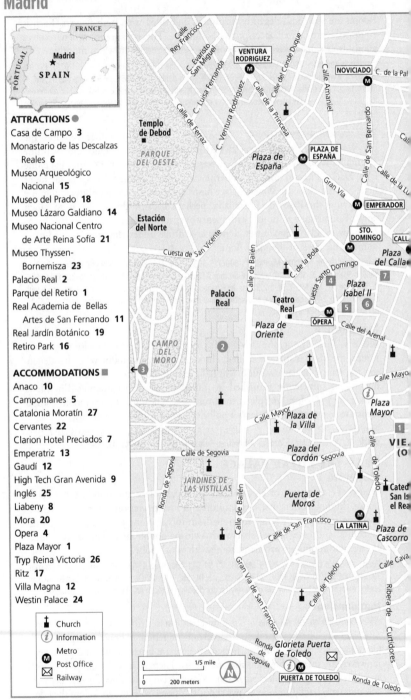

✝ Church
ⓘ Information
Ⓜ Metro
☒ Post Office
☒ Railway

0 — 1/5 mile
0 — 200 meters

ON OR NEAR THE GRAN VIA
Expensive

Gaudí ★★ A majestic early-1900s building at the end of the Gran Vía was gutted to be transformed into this near-luxury hotel. Plaza Mayor and the Prado and Thyssen museums are within walking distance. A siesta-time retreat to these quiet teak-lined quarters is restorative. The weekend rates include an extensive breakfast buffet with hot and cold items, which otherwise costs 12€ ($15) during the week.

Gran Vía 9, 28013 Madrid. ℭ **91-531-2222.** Fax 91-531-5469. www.hoteles-catalonia.es. 185 units. Published rates 198€ ($240) double, but rates can be as low as 80€ ($98) for advance bookings. AE, DC, MC, V. Metro: Gran Vía. **Amenities:** Restaurant; bar; exercise room with sauna/whirlpool; 24-hr. room service; same-day laundry service and dry cleaning. *In room:* A/C, TV, dataport, minibar, hair dryer, safe.

Moderate

Best Western Arosa ★★ Following extensive renovations completed in 2001, the Arosa gained the government's four-star rating. The broad side of this late-19th-century building occupies a block in the middle of the Gran Vía, but double-paned glass keeps the street noise out. Rooms vary significantly in size and layout, but with this many, if you're unhappy with the room you get, a better one is nearly always available. An airport shuttle van runs hourly and costs 6€ ($6.90).

Salud 21, 28013 Madrid. ℭ **91-532-1600.** Fax 91-531-3127. www.bestwestern.com/thisco/bw/92043/ 92043_b.html. 139 units. 100€–155€ ($115–$179) double. AE, DC, MC, V. Metro: Gran Vía. **Amenities:** Restaurant; bar; limited room service; same-day laundry service and dry cleaning. *In room:* A/C, TV, dataport, minibar, hair dryer, safe.

Clarion Hotel Preciados ★★ *Kids* A beautiful mingling of old and new has resulted in this gorgeous hotel in an 1861 building. The original architecture remains, but the rooms are new, sparkling, and breathtakingly well kept, with spacious bathrooms. Light wood furnishings give the rooms a clean, airy feel; hardwood and marble floors recall its classic past. Wireless Internet access gives the hotel a 21st-century touch. The hotel staff are welcoming to kids. One floor is nonsmoking, and another is for women only. The **Varela** restaurant downstairs serves innovative Spanish cuisine.

Preciados 37, 28013 Madrid. ℭ **91-454-4400.** Fax 91-454-4401. www.preciadoshotel.com. 73 units. 117€–129€ ($135–$148) double. AE, DC, MC, V. Metro: Santo Domingo or Callao. **Amenities:** Restaurant; bar; 24 hr. room service; babysitting; laundry service and dry cleaning. *In room:* A/C, TV, dataport, minibar, hair dryer, iron, safe.

High Tech Gran Avenida ★ *Value* This new, swiftly proliferating chain (at press time 12 hotels and counting, split between the High Tech and Petit Palace brands) focuses mostly on bringing older properties up to modern standards. This one opened in September 2003. Dark wood fixtures predominate in the comfortable doubles here, but the real value is in the four-person "family rooms." The multinozzle "hydro showers" in some rooms are also great fun. The best rooms are on the third floor. Room no. 316, which commands a premium, is vast, with a panoramic view of the Gran Via. Sure, it's noisy, but it gives an unparalleled sense of the pulse of Madrid.

Mesonero Romanos 14, 28013 Madrid. ℭ **91-532-7107.** Fax 91-532-7106. www.hthoteles.com. 44 units. 115€–165€ ($132–$190) double. AE, DC, MC, V. Metro: Callao. **Amenities:** Business center; same-day laundry service and dry cleaning. *In room:* A/C, TV, minibar, safe, trouser press (in some rooms).

Liabeny This hotel, named after the original owner (pronounced, more or less, *Ya-bay-nee*) is on a busy plaza midway between the Gran Vía and the Puerta del Sol—the pedestrian shopping district containing the main branch of El Corte Inglés is down a short hill. The contemporary-styled rooms are newly redecorated. Personalized attention from the staff adds to the comfort of your stay. The hotel has its own secure garage. Prices jumped a bit after the latest renovations, but in its category, this hotel is still solid value.

Salud 3, 28013 Madrid. © **91-531-9000**. Fax 91-532-7421. www.hotelliabeny.com. 222 units. 129€ ($148) double. AE, MC, V. Parking 12€ ($14). Metro: Puerta del Sol, Callao, or Gran Vía. **Amenities:** Restaurant; 2 bars; concierge; limited room service; babysitting; same-day laundry service and dry cleaning. *In room:* A/C, TV, minibar, hair dryer, safe.

Inexpensive

Anaco It may not quite sparkle, but the Anaco is a fine place to stay. The first five floors of this popular hotel have been renovated with witty alternating red-and-green color schemes, right down to the towels. Double-glazed windows provide blessed silence. The whole second floor is designated nonsmoking. Off the lobby, the busy *cafetería* offers a 7€ ($8.05) *menú del día* and stays open from 7:30am to 2am every day.

Tres Cruces 3 (at Plaza del Carmen), 28013 Madrid. © **91-522-4604**. Fax 91-531-6484. www.anacohotel. com. 40 units. 92€–97€ ($106–$111) double. AE, DC, MC, V. Metro: Gran Vía. **Amenities:** Restaurant; bar; laundry service; dry cleaning. *In room:* A/C, TV, hair dryer, safe.

AROUND PLAZA SANTA ANA & PLAZA MAYOR
Expensive

Catalonia Moratín ☆ The Catalonia chain rescued a neglected 18th-century mansion and in 2002 turned it into this first-class hotel for both business and leisure travelers. The great granite blocks in its entryway and a marvelous grand staircase are some of the majestic features. The cellar here was used as a bomb shelter during the Civil War and was said to be connected by tunnel to the Royal Palace. Heritage aside, the guest rooms are sizable, many with foldout sleeping sofas and king-size beds. The Puerta del Sol and Plaza Mayor are both 5 minutes away.

Atocha 23, 28012 Madrid. © **91-369-7171**. Fax 91-360-1231. www.hoteles-catalonia.es. 156 units. 122€–198€ ($140–$228) double. AE, DC, MC, V. Metro: Sol or Tirso de Molina. **Amenities:** Restaurant; bar; concierge; limited room service; same-day laundry service and dry cleaning. *In room:* A/C, TV, dataport, minibar, hair dryer, safe.

Tryp Reina Victoria ☆ Staying in a place that faces Madrid's best plaza for tapas has pluses and minuses: You're never far from excellent beer and food, but things get crowded and noisy on weekends. Fortunately, the rooms are comfortable, soundproof, and recently renovated. This first-class hotel, a Sol Meliá property, is situated smack in the center of Old Madrid and very popular; you should reserve well in advance, and make sure to check the website for specials.

Plaza de Santa Ana 14, 28012 Madrid. © **888/95-MELIA** in the U.S., or 91-531-4500 in Spain. Fax 91-522-0307. www.trypreinavictoria.solmelia.com. 201 units. 178€ ($205) double (online specials as low as 90€/$104). AE, DC, MC, V. Parking 11€ ($13). Metro: Tirso de Molina or Puerta del Sol. **Amenities:** Restaurant; bar; concierge; limited room service; babysitting; same-day laundry service and dry cleaning. *In room:* A/C, TV, minibar, hair dryer, safe.

Inexpensive

Inglés A large ship model in the front window alerts you to this popular little hotel. Enter the lobby, with its comfy sofas and armchairs, and you'll find that little has changed in recent years, including the room rates and the too-often dour gents at the front desk. Just beyond the TV lounge is the bar/cafeteria where breakfast is served. Many rooms have sitting areas. Nearby Plaza Santa

Ana and Calle de las Huertas are brimming with tapas and music bars. A parking garage has 25 spaces for guests. Note that only about half of the hotel is air-conditioned, so ask for an air-conditioned room in summer.

Echegaray 8, 28014 Madrid. © **91-429-6551.** Fax 91-420-2423. 51 units. 100€ ($115) double. AE, DC, MC, V. Parking 12€ ($14). Metro: Sol. **Amenities:** Restaurant; bar; exercise room; limited room service. *In room:* TV, safe.

Plaza Mayor ★ A crisp new hotel in the shell of a 19th-century church, this is a welcome addition to Madrid's often dreary budget lodgings. Despite its name, the brick-red building wedges into Plaza Santa Cruz, slightly east of Plaza Mayor. A new entrance has been carved out of the ground floor *taberna.* The bright, contemporary (though often oddly shaped) rooms are of sufficient size, with double-thick windows sealing off traffic noise; four have double beds. The corner rooms offer light and extra space. English is spoken.

Atocha 2, 28012 Madrid. © **91-360-0606** or 91-360-0828. Fax 91-360-0610. www.h-plazamayor.com. 20 units. 70€–80€ ($80–$92) double. Rates include breakfast. AE, MC, V. Metro: Sol. **Amenities:** Restaurant; bar. *In room:* A/C, TV, safe.

NEAR SALAMANCA

Very Expensive

Park Hyatt Villa Magna ★★★ Villa Magna, one of Madrid's most luxurious business hotels, is set behind a bank of pines and laurels bordering the Paseo de la Castellana. Expensive cars purr and growl in the driveway. The hotel surpassed the Westin Palace as soon as it opened, and is equaled in luxury, class, and exquisitely anticipatory service only by the Ritz. This contemporary palace offers plush, dignified rooms decorated in Louis XVI, English Regency, or Italian provincial styles. The hotel is known for its summer terraces set amid gardens.

Paseo de la Castellana 22, 28046 Madrid. © **800/223-1234** in the U.S. and Canada, or 91-587-1234. Fax 91-431-2286. villamagna.park.hyatt.com. 182 units. 250€–475€ ($287–$546) double; from 490€ ($564) suite. AE, DC, MC, V. Parking 20€ ($23). Metro: Rubén Darío. **Amenities:** 2 restaurants; 2 bars; health club with sauna; concierge; car-rental desk; salon; 24-hr. room service; babysitting; same-day laundry service and dry cleaning. *In room:* A/C, TV, dataport, minibar, coffeemaker, hair dryer, safe.

Expensive

Emperatriz ★ This hotel is just off the Paseo de Castellana, in the orbit of some of Madrid's most deluxe hotels and restaurants, but with relatively more reasonable rates than surrounding hotels. Guest rooms, once decked in gloomy earth tones, have been lightened up with both traditional and modern furniture. They're easier on the eye than the somewhat unimaginative public areas. Ask for a seventh-floor room, where you'll get a private terrace at no extra charge, and if you're going for all-out luxe, ask for a suite with a whirlpool and/or saunas.

López de Hoyos 4, 28006 Madrid. © **91-563-80-88.** Fax 91-563-98-04. www.hotel-emperatriz.com. 158 units. 265€–279€ ($305–$320) double; from 365€ ($420) suite. AE, DC, MC, V. Metro: Rubén Darío. **Amenities:** Restaurant; bar; concierge; salon; 24-hr. room service; in-room massage; babysitting; same-day laundry service and dry cleaning. *In room:* A/C, TV, dataport, minibar, hair dryer, safe.

NEAR BARAJAS AIRPORT

Moderate

La Casa Grande ★★ Despite the small number of rooms (all on the 3rd floor with no elevator access), this hotel is conveniently located in a large gated complex near the airport, containing a tavern, a garage, wine *bodegas,* and a 16th-century main building that has served as royal farmhouse and Jesuit monastery. Rooms are small but sumptuously furnished. Meals are served in the regal dining room or on the star-lit terrace, where a singer-guitarist performs nightly in season. Check out the basement gallery's remarkable collection of Russian icons.

28850 Torrejón de Ardoz (19km/12 miles east of Madrid on the Carretera de Barcelona, a few min. from the airport). ℂ **91-675-3900.** Fax 91-675-0691. www.lacasagrande.es. 8 units. 130€ ($150) double. Rates include breakfast and unlimited use of minibar. AE, MC, V. Closed Aug. **Amenities:** 2 restaurants; 2 bars; sauna; 24-hr. room service; same-day laundry service and dry cleaning. *In room:* A/C, TV, fax, minibar, hair dryer, safe.

WHERE TO DINE
ON OR NEAR THE GRAN VIA
Moderate

La Barraca ⋆ REGIONAL SPANISH   On a narrow side street parallel to the Gran Vía, this place has acquired its folkloric atmosphere of lace curtains, ceramic pitchers, and hanging plates over a span of 68 years. The kitchen excels in *arroces*—the rice dishes of southeastern Spain's Valencia, ranging from one dish flavored with squid ink to one that substitutes thin noodles for rice *(fideua marinera).* If it's your first Spanish rice dish, you might want to order the *paella mixta,* with bits of chicken, sausage, shrimp, mussels, pork, and squid. Expect some time to pass before being served—everything is prepared to order. A smooth liver pâté with good bread is an inexpensive appetite-calmer as you await the main event.

Reina 29. ℂ **91-532-7154.** Main courses 12€–20€ ($14–$23). AE, DC, MC, V. Daily 1–4pm and 8:30pm–midnight. Metro: Gran Vía or Banco de España.

Suite INTERNATIONAL   Beginning life a couple of years ago as the "Mad Cafe Club," this hip restaurant/bar remains a popular haunt for the young and fashionable. There's a garden where patrons relax on hot summer nights and a disco that cranks up at midnight. About half of the starters are salads, which are a good choice, since main courses are comprised almost entirely of meat. Preparations are attractive, if decidedly minimalist, as is the case with the three small sea bass filets touched with trout-roe-flavored butter sauce and served with a few chunks of boiled potato scattered around one edge of the plate.

Virgin de los Peligros 4 (between Alcalá and Gran Vía). ℂ **91-532-6228.** Reservations recommended. Main courses 11€–16€ ($13–$18); *menú del día* 10€–14€ ($12–$16) (lunch only). AE, DC, MC, V. Mon–Sat 1–4pm and 9:30pm–3am. Dinner served until 12:30am. Metro: Sevilla, Gran Vía.

NEAR THE PUERTA DEL SOL
Expensive

Lhardy SPANISH/INTERNATIONAL   A Madrileño legend since it opened in 1839, this restaurant's street-level room contains what might be the most elegant snack bar in town. Cups of steaming consommé are self-dispensed from silver samovars into delicate porcelain cups, accompaniments to tasty tapas that run along the lines of creamy-centered croquettes. Early evening is the fashionable time for a stop here. Although it is a gathering place for some of the city's older literati and politicians, food in the formal restaurant upstairs is pricey and rarely better than mediocre; downstairs is the place to go, and is far less expensive.

Carrera de San Jerónimo 8 (east of Puerta del Sol). ℂ **91-521-3385.** Reservations recommended in the upstairs dining room. Main courses (downstairs) 13€–21€ ($15–$24). AE, DC, MC, V. Daily 1–3:30pm and 8:30–11:30pm. Closed Aug. Metro: Puerta del Sol or Sevilla.

Tapa to Tapa to Tapa

No need to go hungry waiting around for the traditional Madrid dinner hour—10pm or later. Throughout the city you'll find bars—variously known as *mesónes, tascas,* and *tabernas*—that set out platters of tempting hot and cold appetizers known as *tapas:* mushrooms, salads, baby eels, shrimp, lobster, mussels, sausages, ham, and, in one establishment at least, bull testicles. Described below are some favorite tapas bars out of hundreds. *Tip:* You can often save money by eating at the bar rather than occupying a table.

La Trucha, Núñez de Arce 6 (**©** **91-532-0882**; Metro: Sol), serves trout as its signature dish. One version is *trucha a La Trucha*—the whole fish is split open, filled with chopped ham and garlic, then sautéed. Most tapas and larger dishes are cooked to order. This is a favorite stop on the tapas circuit, partly because the men behind the counter make new patrons feel like old friends. There's a larger but similar La Trucha at Manuel Fernández y González 3 (**©** 91-429-5833; Metro: Sol).

Casa Mingo, Paseo de la Florida 2 (**©** **91-547-7918**; Metro: Norte), has been known for decades for its cider, both still and bubbly. The perfect accompanying tidbit is a piece of Asturian *cabrales* (goat cheese), but the roast chicken is the specialty of the house. Patrons share big tables under the vaulted ceiling of the dining room; in summer, the staff sets tables out on the sidewalk. Hemingway and the bullfighter Luís Miguel Dominguín used to frequent the casual **Cervecería Alemania,** Plaza de Santa Ana 6 (**©** **91-429-7033**; Metro: Alonso Martín or Tirso de Molina), which earned its name because of its long-ago German clients. Opening onto one of the liveliest plazas in Madrid, it clings to its early-1900s traditions. To accompany your *caña* (a short beer), try the fried sardines or a wedge of *tortilla,* a firm potato-and-egg omelet served at room temperature.

Unique in Madrid, the **Cervecería Santa Bárbara,** Plaza de Santa Bárbara 8 (**©** **91-319-04-49**; Metro: Alonzo Martínez; bus: 3, 7, or 21), is an outlet for a beer factory, and the management has spent a lot to make it modern and inviting. Globe lights and spinning ceiling fans hang above the black-and-white marble floor. You come here for beer, of course: *cerveza negra* (black beer) or *cerveza dorada* (golden beer). Brews are best accompanied by the very pricey shrimp, the lobster, or the ugly but tasty goose barnacles called *percebes.* It's open daily from 11:30am to midnight. Many Madrileños begin their nightly *tapeo* at **Toscana,** Manuel Fernandez y Gonzales 10 (**©** **91-429-6031**; Metro: Puerta del Sol or Sevilla). They sit on crude stools, under sausages, peppers, and sheaves of golden wheat hung from the dark beams, as a man behind the bar ladles out bowls of the nightly specials—kidneys in sherry sauce, perhaps, or veal stew.

Inexpensive

Cornucopia 𝒦𝒦 ECLECTIC   This triumphantly funky, always surprising little joint is crammed into the corner of a 19th-century house opposite the Monasteria de Descalzas Reales. The hostess, an American actress who appears on a Spanish soap opera, co-owns the restaurant with a Frenchman and a Spaniard. The two rooms in ocher and brick, with intricately patterned wood floors and amusing semi-abstract paintings, perfectly suit the international artistic (or at least bohemian) 30-ish crowd. It's all enough for an entertaining evening, but the food's pretty good, too. A simple salad of roasted red peppers and cheese is warm and comforting. Meatballs arrive blanketed by a riot of mashed sweet potatoes; a mushroom crepe is both stuffed with mushrooms and covered in mushroom sauce.

Flora 1 (west of Plaza Descalzas). (✆ 91-547-6465. www.restaurantecornucopia.com. Reservations advised for dinner. Main courses 11€–16€ ($12–$18); *menú del día* 10€ ($12). AE, DC, MC, V. Tues–Sat 1:30–4pm and 9pm–midnight. Metro: Sol.

La Finca de Susana ⭐ *Value* MEDITERRANEAN A concern for light, healthy eating is far from a priority in most Spanish restaurants. But maybe they'll think again after they see the business this newcomer is doing. It's housed in a space that looks like a former bank, with potted palms and a long wall of windows. You'll find a choice of five vegetable dishes and a similar number of low-calorie options. The manager even declares that the specialty of the house is grilled vegetables. That doesn't mean that all diners go the green and leafy route. There's plenty of fish, chicken, and pork on the menu, but prepared with less oil, fat, and salt than at most other restaurants. All classes of age, profession, and society show up, partly because they'd have to go out of their way to spend more than 12€ ($14) per person, with wine. Reservations aren't accepted.

Arlaban 4. (✆ 91-369-3557. Main courses 5.50€–9€ ($6.20–$10). Lunch menu 7€ ($8.05). MC, V. Daily 1–3:45pm and 8:30–11:45pm. Metro: Sevilla.

NEAR PLAZA SANTA ANA
Moderate

Champagnería Gala ⭐ SPANISH Recent price rises have, alas, pushed this restaurant out of the budget category. The front room has blood-orange walls with painted vines coupled with a glassed-over courtyard containing real and artificial plants and a Venetian chandelier. *Arroces* (rice dishes) are featured. Italian risottos have joined the paellas and *fideuàs* (a similar dish with thin noodles instead of rice) and come with a choice of 16 components, from cheese and bull's tail to rabbit and fish. Included in the menu are do-it-yourself *pa amb tomaquet* (Catalan bread rubbed with garlic and tomato pulp and drizzled with oil), a seasonal salad, wine, aioli and *romesco* sauces, dessert, and coffee. Avoid the crowded Sunday afternoons or reserve the day before.

Moratín 22 (west of Paseo del Prado). (✆ 91-429-2562. Main courses 13€–18€ ($15–$21). No credit cards. Daily 1:30–4:30pm and 9pm–2am. Metro: Atocha.

Inexpensive

La Moderna SPANISH/TAPAS Some of the best tapas around the plaza are served at this upscale tavern—no small feat, given the fierce competition. But look first to the inviting cheese and wine selections. A chalkboard tells of the rotated six or seven pressings available by the glass, which go wonderfully with the many regional cheeses. Each glass also comes with a little minitapa, such as a sardine tail on tomato-rubbed bread. Rations of smoked fish, hams, or sausages cost 6.10€ to 13€ ($7–$15).

Plaza de Santa Ana 12 (near the Hotel Reina Victoria). (✆ 91-420-1582. Tapas and *raciones* 3€–14€ ($3.45–$16). MC, V. Daily noon–3am. Metro: Sol.

La Creazione ⭐ ITALIAN On one of Madrid's favorite restaurant streets, this trattoria gratifies several needs. You'll be asked "restaurant or pizzeria?" The "restaurant" has tablecloths, while the tables in the pizzeria are cheerful glass-topped displays of pasta and beans. Both pastas and pizzas are made on the premises and prepared to order. The big stars are the 25 or so pizza variations, each with a thin, crunchy, airy crust and improbable mixes of toppings (bacon, oregano, pine nuts, and currants) that are actually startlingly good. The restaurant menu features sophisticated seafood dishes. Most food is available *para llevar*—for takeout.

Ventura de la Vega 9 (near Carrera de San Jerónimo). ⓒ **91-429-0387**. Main courses 13€–16€ ($15–$18); pizzas and pastas 10€–15€ ($12–$17); *menú turístico* 15€ ($17). AE, DC, MC, V. Tues–Sat 1:30–4:30pm and 9pm–12:30am; Sun 1:30–4:30pm. Metro: Sol.

NEAR THE ROYAL PALACE
Expensive/Moderate

Café de Oriente FRENCH/SPANISH   Bordering on one of Madrid's most historic and royal squares, the Oriente offers bistro informality in the main-floor cafe (inexpensive); grand dining (very expensive) in the 17th-century cellar called the Horno de Leña; and an adjoining tapas bar, La Botillería. Expect members of high-powered corporate groups downstairs, while the cafe is filled with a workaday crowd during the day and fashionable night owls in the evening. All patrons appreciate the generous array of tapas.

Plaza de Oriente 2. ⓒ **91-541-3974**. Reservations recommended (restaurant only). www.grupolezama.com. In cafe and bar tapas 5.20€–10€ ($6–$12). In restaurant, main courses 18€–22€ ($20–$25). AE, DC, MC, V. Cafe daily 8:30am–1:30am. Restaurant daily 1–4pm and 9pm–midnight. Metro: Opera.

Inexpensive

La Bola REGIONAL SPANISH   Easily spotted by its crimson exterior, La Bola has been on the scene since 1870. Hemingway and Ava Gardner were patrons, as attested to by photos above the carved wainscoting. Ask about the restaurant's history and you'll get a leaflet. The big menu item is *cocido madrileño,* the traditional Castilian Sunday boiled dinner: Several kinds of meat and vegetables are slow-cooked together for hours and the rich broth is then strained off and tiny noodles are dropped in as a first course. This course is followed by the vegetables (potatoes, chickpeas, cabbage) and the meats (usually chicken, chorizo, beef, and pork). Fish dishes are well suited to smaller appetites.

Bola 5 (2 blocks north of the Teatro Real). ⓒ **91-547-6930**. Main courses 14€–19€ ($16–$22); *menú del día* 16€ ($18). No credit cards. Mon–Sat 1:30–4pm; daily 8:30–11pm. Metro: Santo Domingo.

NEAR RETIRO & SALAMANCA
Expensive

Alkalde BASQUE/INTERNATIONAL   Alkalde affects a humble, countrified mien, with a barn-like *típico* tavern upstairs and a maze of stone-sided cellars downstairs that are pleasantly cool in summer. You might begin with the fish soup, followed by one of the five different preparations of *merluza* (hake), chicken cutlets, or *cigalas* (crayfish). Other recommended dishes are trout, stuffed peppers, and chicken steak.

Jorge Juan 10 (near Claudio Coello). ⓒ **91-576-3359**. www.alkalderestaurante.com. Reservations advised. Main courses 13€–29€ ($15–$33); *menú del día* 36€ ($41). AE, DC, MC, V. Daily noon–midnight. Metro: Serrano. Bus: 8, 21, 29, or 53.

El Amparo ★★ BASQUE   This superior gastronomic enclave hides with four other restaurants behind a curtain of vines at the end of a mews. The multi-tiered space is defined by rough-hewn beams, and is illuminated by sunlight through the long skylight. The innovative offerings have included cod cheeks in a red-pepper puree, and ravioli with crayfish. A battalion of correct, unobtrusive waiters bring two different *aperitivos* to stoke the appetite, then serve such main courses as cold marinated salmon with tomato sorbet, *lubina* (sea bass), bisque of shellfish with Armagnac, pigs' feet stuffed with morels, and platters of steamed fish of the day.

Callejón de Puígcerdá 8 (at the corner of Jorge Juan). ℭ **91-431-6456.** Reservations required. Main courses 23€–30€ ($26–$35). AE, MC, V. Mon–Fri 1:30–3:30pm and 9–11:30pm; Sat 9:30–11:30pm. Closed the week before Easter and 1 week in Aug. Metro: Goya. Bus: 21 or 53.

Horcher ⭐⭐ GERMAN/INTERNATIONAL   Berlin was the first home of this legendary luxury restaurant, which opened in 1904. Prompted by a tip from a high-ranking officer that Germany was losing World War II, Herr Horcher moved his restaurant to neutral Madrid in 1943. Ever since, the restaurant has continued its grand European traditions, including service by knowledgeable waiters and uniformed doormen. Among the tempting possibilities are shrimp tartare and a distinctive warm hake salad. The venison stew in green pepper with orange peel, and the crayfish with parsley and cucumber, are examples of the elegant fare, served with impeccable style. The kitchen does well with wild boar, veal, and sea bass, as well.

Alfonso XII 6 (near Valenzuela). ℭ **91-532-3596.** Reservations required. Jackets and ties required for men. Main courses 36€–60€ ($41–$69). AE, DC, MC, V. Mon–Fri 1:30–4pm and 8:30pm–midnight; Sat 8:30pm–midnight. Metro: Retiro.

Viridiana ⭐ INTERNATIONAL   Long praised as one of Madrid's most notable restaurants, Viridiana is named after the 1961 Luís Buñuel film classic. As soon as patrons are settled, the captain launches into a lengthy recitation of the day's specials, from salads to desserts. Among these are contemporary takes on traditional recipes, often with Asian touches. Past examples have included tuna tartare, salads of exotic greens with smoked fish, steak filet with truffles, guinea fowl stuffed with herbs and wild mushrooms, baby squid with curry on a bed of lentils, and roast lamb in puff pastry with fresh basil. While rarely as brilliant as it was perceived to be 2 decades ago, the food here is never predictable—you'll find an exciting twist or two in every dish.

Juan de Mena 14 (west of Alfonso XII). ℭ **91-523-4478.** Reservations recommended. Main courses 28€–48€ ($32–$55). V. Mon–Sat 1:30–4pm and 9pm–midnight. Closed Aug and 1 week at Easter. Metro: Retiro Bancode España.

Moderate

El Espejo ⭐ INTERNATIONAL   You'll find good-tasting food and one of the most perfectly crafted Art Nouveau interiors in Madrid at this restaurant. There's an attractive cafe/bar, a neo-Victorian glass pavilion out on the promenade, and outdoor tables and chairs nearby. A piano player often performs on warm nights. Menu items include grouper ragout with clams, steak tartare, guinea fowl with Armagnac, and duck with pineapple.

Paseo de Recoletos 31 (near Zurbarán). ℭ **91-308-2347.** Reservations required. *Menú del día* 12€ ($14) (lunch Mon–Fri at the pavilion), 22€ ($25) (dinner in the cafe). AE, DC, MC, V. Sun–Fri 1–4pm and 9pm–midnight; Sat 9pm–1am. Metro: Banco de España or Colón. Bus: 27.

La Gamella ⭐⭐ FUSION   For more than 30 years, Illinois-born chef-owner Dick Stephens has taken it upon himself to introduce Madrileños to the creative American cuisine developed over that time. His latest venue is near the Puerta de Alcalá, its interior abloom with vibrant colors, as if Matisse had a hand in the decor. Stephens' vegetable and couscous soup is a cheery yet gentle starter, followed by such delectables as hake dressed with white truffles and garlic, beef in mustard sauce, or chicken stewed with almonds and saffron. Homesick Yanks may prefer what has been called "the only edible hamburger in Madrid." It's delicious, even albeit costly, at 15€ ($17).

Alfonso XII 4. 📞 **91-532-4509**. www.lagamella.com. Reservations advised. Main courses 11€–19€ ($12–$22). AE, DC, MC, V. Mon–Fri 1:30–4pm and 9pm–midnight; Sat 9pm–midnight. Closed 2 weeks around Easter and 2 weeks in Aug. Metro: Retiro.

CHAMBERI
Very Expensive

Jockey ✿✿ INTERNATIONAL   On the scene for more than 55 years, this was Madrid's premier restaurant during the Franco era. The food here is more classic than adventurous, but it remains a favorite of international celebrities and executives. The chef prides himself on coming up with creative twists on old-fashioned dishes featuring ingredients that justify the steep prices, such as lobster ragout with fresh pasta showered with grated truffle. The cold melon soup with shrimp is soothing on a hot day, especially when followed by roasted pigeon from Talavera cooked in its own juice or monkfish en papillote with Mantua sauce. Dress up for your meal.

Amador de los Ríos 6. 📞 **91-319-2435**. Reservations required. Main courses 29€–36€ ($33–$41). AE, DC, MC, V. Daily 1–4pm and 9pm–midnight. Closed Aug. Metro: Colón or Serrano.

NEAR PLAZA MAYOR
Moderate

Botín ✿ SPANISH   According to the Guinness Book of World Records, this is the oldest continually operating restaurant in the world. It opened in 1725, and Goya supposedly worked here before becoming a painter. About a hundred years later, Ernest Hemingway helped make this place famous when he had Jake Barnes invite Lady Brett here for dinner. They had the house specialty, roast suckling pig, washed down with Rioja. You'll see an open kitchen with a charcoal hearth, hanging copper pots, an 18th-century tile oven for roasting suckling pig, and a big pot of regional soup whose aroma drifts across the room. Roast lamb is also good. Yes, it's packed with tourists, but don't let that stop you.

Cuchilleros 17 (off southwest corner of Plaza Mayor). 📞 **91-366-4217**. Menu image at www.gomadrid. com/images/botin-menu.jpg. Reservations required. Main courses 7.15€–21€ ($8.15–$24); menú del día 30€ ($34). AE, DC, MC, V. Daily 1–4pm and 8pm–midnight. Closed Christmas. Metro: Puerta del Sol or Tirso de Molina.

Julián de Tolosa ✿ STEAK   This is a Basque version of a steakhouse. The menu is simplicity itself and hasn't changed in over 20 years. Appetizers are fish soup, and hearts of lettuce or unadorned spears of fat white asparagus, mayo on the side. A nice lady comes to announce the night's possibilities, shifting easily into English if you look perplexed. There are two meats, two fish. Have the steak. You'll get a small, tender kernel of filet. Just as you're feeling virtuous for not overindulging, the rest of the slab of meat appears. With coffee, you get an icy cranberry-and-anise liqueur.

Cava Baja 18 (south of Plaza de Puerta Cerrada). 📞 **91-365-8210**. Reservations advised on weekends. Main courses 16€–24€ ($18–$28). AE, DC, MC, V. Mon–Sat 1:30–6pm and 9pm–midnight; Sun 1:30–6pm. Metro: Sol.

CHAMARTÍN
Very Expensive

Zalacaín ✿✿ INTERNATIONAL   Outstanding in food, decor, and service, Zalacaín occupies the apex of Madrid's gastronomical pyramid, although younger challengers are crowding it. When it opened in 1973, it introduced nouvelle cuisine to Madrid. The menu features dishes of French and Basque origin subjected to a great deal of experimentation. The chefs might offer a superb sole in a green sauce, but they also know the glory of grilled pigs' feet. Among other recommendable dishes are roast duck with peppers and cherries, crepes stuffed with smoked fish, and bouillabaisse. One quibble is the restaurant's inclination to stick with one set of menu items for too long, not justifiable at these prices. Men must wear jackets and ties.

Alvarez de Baena 4 (north of María de Molina). ⓒ **91-561-4840.** Reservations required. Main courses 29€–58€ ($33–$67); *menu degustación* 82€ ($94). AE, DC, MC, V. Mon–Fri 1:30–4pm; Mon–Sat 9pm–midnight. Closed Holy Week and Aug. Metro: Rubén Darío.

Expensive

El Olivo ⓐ ★ MEDITERRANEAN   French-born chef-owner Jean Pierre Vandelle makes no bones about his enthusiasm for olive oil, exemplified by the live olive tree at the entrance. No matter what you order in the dining room, a cart of olive oils and vinegars will be wheeled over with an invitation to shake a few drops on whatever dish sits before you. Menus often include a medallion of marinated and grilled *rape* (monkfish) over a tangy compote of fresh tomatoes, quail in their reduced juices with a cube of foie gras on the side, or four preparations of cod—an always featured ingredient—arranged on a single platter and served with a spicy *pil-pil* sauce. With a selection of over 100 sherries at the bar (another of the chef's enthusiasms), you might try a dry *oloroso* as an aperitif.

General Gallegos 1 (near Padre Damián). ⓒ **91-359-1535.** Reservations recommended. Main courses 19€–27€ ($21–$32); *menú del día* 40€–50€ ($46–$58). AE, DC, MC, V. Tues–Sat 1–4pm and 9pm–midnight. Closed Aug 15–31 and 4 days around Easter. Metro: Plaza de Castilla.

SEEING THE SIGHTS

Madrid has something to amuse and enlighten everyone. As the capital of Spain since the 16th century, Madrid is where kings and conquistadors deposited the booty and brilliance of a globe-girdling empire. The city has more than 50 museums and one of the world's grandest palaces. Elegant public parks have been developed from imperial hunting grounds.

SIGHTSEEING SUGGESTIONS FOR FIRST-TIME VISITORS

If You Have 1 Day Spend the morning at the **Prado,** one of the world's great art museums. It's best to arrive when it opens at 9am (remember, it's closed Mon). Have lunch and then visit the **Palacio Real (Royal Palace),** on the other side of the city. Have an early dinner near Plaza Mayor.

If You Have 2 Days On day 2 visit the **Thyssen-Bornemisza Museum** in the morning, stroll around Madrid's medieval area, and visit the **Museo Nacional Centro de Arte Reina Sofía** in the late afternoon or early evening (it closes at 9pm most nights). Here you can see Picasso's *Guernica* and other great art of the 20th century. Have dinner once again at one of the many restaurants off Plaza Mayor.

If You Have 3 Days On your third day take a trip to **Toledo,** where you can visit the cathedral, the Santa Cruz Museum, and the Alcázar. Return to Madrid in the evening.

If You Have 4 Days On day 4 take a 1-hour train ride to the **Monastery of San Lorenzo de El Escorial,** in the foothills of the Sierra de Guadarrama. Return to Madrid in the evening.

THE TOP SIGHTS

Museo del Prado ★★★   With more than 20,000 paintings and other art-works, the Prado is one of the most important repositories of art in the world. The Prado has no equal when it comes to paintings from the Spanish school, so on your first visit, concentrate on the Spanish masters. You'll find a treasure trove of works by El Greco, the Crete-born artist who lived much of his life in Toledo. Look for *Las Meninas,* the museum's most famous painting, and other works by the incomparable Diego Velázquez. The Francisco de Goya collection includes the artist's unflattering portraits of his patron, Charles IV, and his family, as well as the *Clothed Maja,* the *Naked Maja* and pictures from his black period. Look also for paintings by Zurbarán and Murillo, and be sure to search out Flemish genius Hieronymus Bosch's best-known work, *The Garden of Earthly Delights.* (Confusingly, the Spanish call Bosch "El Bosco.") A massive expansion of the Prado will add two new wings in June and October 2004, doubling the size of one of the world's most important art museums and giving it enough room to display a good chunk of its 20,000-work collection.

Paseo del Prado s/n. **© 91-330-2800.** http://museoprado.mcu.es. Admission 3€ ($3.45) adults, 1.50€ ($1.75) students; free for seniors and children, and free for everyone Sat after 2:30pm and Sun. Tues–Sat 9am–7pm; Sun 9am–2pm. Metro: Atocha or Banco de España. Bus: 1, 2, 9, 10, 14, 19, 27, 34, 37, or 45.

Museo Thyssen-Bornemisza ★★★   On display in the late-18th-century Palacio de Villahermosa and a brand-new extension that opened in March 2004 are the works gathered by three generations of the Thyssen-Bornemisza family (pronounced *Tees*-ahn Bore-noh-*mees*-uh). The quirky collection of paintings is like taking a class in art history, with an image or two covering practically every major style and period from the late 13th century to the present. The collection of 19th- and 20th-century paintings is especially strong—certainly the strongest of any Madrid museum. The nucleus of the collection consists of 700 world-class paintings, including works by El Greco, Velázquez, Dürer, and Rembrandt, as well as art from the Impressionist period. Works from the American Abstract Expressionist movement and related movements are also featured.

Paseo del Prado 8. **© 91-369-0151.** www.museothyssen.org. Admission to permanent collection 4.80€ ($5.50) adults, 3€ ($3.45) seniors/students, free for under 12; to temporary exhibits 3.60€ ($4.15) adults, 2.40€ ($2.75) seniors/students, free for under 12. Tues–Sun 10am–7pm. Metro: Banco de España. Bus: 1, 2, 5, 9, 10, 14, 15, 20, 27, 34, 45, 51, 52, 53, 74, 146, or 150.

Museo Nacional Centro de Arte Reina Sofía ★   This 19th-century hospital was converted into a museum that serves as a repository of 20th-century art. Unfortunately, the collection remains sparse and unbalanced. To date, its successes have usually been temporary exhibits rather than highlights from its permanent collection. A new wing devoted entirely to temporary exhibits will open in June 2004, so check the museum's website to see what's up. One guaranteed winner, though, is Picasso's fabled *Guernica* ★★★, now the museum's centerpiece. Largely second-rank works by Spanish artists like **Dalí, Miró, Gris,** and **Solana** supplement Picasso's masterwork. For the moment, the center's most interesting element (outside of *Guernica*) might be the former 18th-century hospital itself.

Santa Isabel 52 (at the corner of Atocha). **© 91-467-5062.** http://museoreinasofia.mcu.es. Admission 3€ ($3.45) adults, 1.50€ ($1.75) students/children under 12; free for everyone Sat after 2:30, free for seniors/children Sun. Mon and Wed–Sat 10am–9pm; Sun 10am–2:30pm. Metro: Atocha.

Palacio Real (Royal Palace) ★★   This opulent palace was begun in 1738 for Felipe V on the site of the Alcázar, a fortified castle that burned in 1734. The decor is a mix of baroque and neoclassical styles. Some of the palace's 2,800 rooms are open to the public, while others are still used for state business. The multilingual guided tour includes the reception room, the state apartments, the royal pharmacy, and the stunning state dining room. The rooms are filled with art treasures and antiques—salon after salon of monumental grandeur, with no apologies for the damask, mosaics, stucco, Tiepolo ceilings, gilt and bronze, chandeliers, and paintings. In the Armory, a collection of weaponry includes scaled-down suits of armor for the royal toddlers.

Plaza de Oriente, Calle de Bailén 2. (②) 91-454-8800. www.patrimonionacional.es. Admission 8€ ($9.20) adults, 3.50€ ($4.05) seniors/students/children under 12; 1€ ($1.15) extra for guided tours; additional fees for temporary exhibits. Mon–Sat 9:30am–5:30pm; Sun and holidays 9am–3pm. Metro: Opera. Bus: 3, 25, 39, or 148.

MORE ATTRACTIONS

Monasterio de las Descalzas Reales   In the heart of old Madrid, near the Puerta del Sol, this richly endowed royal convent was founded in the mid–16th century in the palace where Juana of Austria, Felipe II's sister, was born. She used it as a retreat and brought the Poor Clare nuns here. For many years, the convent sheltered only royal women. Typically, the daughters of aristocrats were sequestered here until they were old enough for arranged marriages. The girls didn't live a spartan existence, though, judging from the wealth of religious artwork that surrounded them, including tapestries, sculptures, and paintings by **Rubens, Brueghel the Elder,** and **Titian.** The main staircase features trompel'oeil paintings and frescoes, and you can view 16 of the 32 lavishly decorated chapels. Compulsory tours for groups of 25 or fewer are conducted in Spanish by guides who hasten visitors from canvas to tapestry to chapel. Try to slow their pace, for there's much to savor. There are frequent alterations to the visiting hours noted below.

Plaza de las Descalzas 3. (②) **91-454-8800.** www.patrimonionacional.es. Admission 5€ ($5.75) adults, 2.50€ ($2.90) seniors/students/children under 13; free to all Wed. Tues–Thurs and Sat 10:30am–12:45pm and 4–5:45pm; Fri 10:30am–12:45pm; Sun and holidays 11am–1:45pm. From Plaza del Callao, off Gran Vía, walk down Postigo de San Martín to Plaza de las Descalzas Reales; the convent is on the left.

Museo Arqueológico Nacional ★★   Reopened after a couple of years of renovations, this underrated museum is in the same vast building as the National Library (which has a separate entrance on Paseo de Recoletos). It houses antiquities from prehistory to the Middle Ages. Most of the artifacts are related specifically to the development of the Iberian Peninsula, although there are some Egyptian and Greek objects. Most illuminating are the rooms devoted to the Iberian period, before Christ and the waves of sequential conquerors, and those rooms containing relics of the Visigoths, who left relatively little behind, rendering these objects of even greater interest. A particular treasure is the *Dama de Elche* ★★, a resplendent example of 4th-century B.C. Iberian sculpture, easily equal to the better-known works produced in Greece at the same time.

Serrano 13 (facing Calle Serrano). (②) **91-577-7912.** www.man.es. Admission 3€ ($3.45) adults; 1.50€ ($1.75) seniors/students; free for seniors/students/children under 12, and for everyone Sat after 2:30pm. Tues–Sat 9:30am–8:30pm; Sun and holidays 9:30am–2:30pm. Metro: Serrano.

Museo Lázaro Galdiano   Madrid was the beneficiary of financier/author José Lázaro Galdiano's largesse, for when he died, he left the city his 30-room early-1900s mansion and a substantial private art collection. A multiyear renovation should be completed in 2004, giving the collection the space it deserves. There are paintings from Spain's Golden Age, including works by Spaniards

El Greco, Zurbarán, Murillo, and Goya; works by Renaissance Italians Tiepolo and Leonardo da Vinci; and canvases by Englishmen Gainsborough and Constable. However, the museum is most admired for its comprehensive array of enamels, ivories, and works in gold and silver, much of it created during the Middle Ages.

Serrano 122. Ⓒ 91-561-6084. www.flg.es/museo/museo.htm. Admission 3€ ($3.45) adults, 1.50€ ($1.75) students; free for seniors/children under 12, free for everyone Sat. Tues–Sun 10am–2pm Metro: Rubén Dario or Núñez de Balboa. Bus: 9, 16, 19, 51, or 89.

Real Academia de Bellas Artes de San Fernando (San Fernando Royal Fine Arts Academy) ✸ An easy stroll from the Puerta del Sol, this museum is located in the restored and remodeled 17th-century baroque palace of Juan de Goyeneche. The collection—more than 1,500 paintings and 570 sculptures, ranging from the 16th century to the present—was started in 1752 during the reign of Fernando VI (1746–59). It emphasizes works by Spanish, Flemish, and Italian artists. Masterpieces by El Greco, Rubens, Velázquez, Zurbarán, Ribera, Cano, Coello, Murillo, and Sorolla are here. The Goya collection in itself is worth a visit. Goya was a member of the academy from 1780, and the museum houses two of his self-portraits, along with a full-size portrait of the actress La Tirana, and a portrait of the royal favorite Manuel Godoy. Goya's carnival scene, *Burial of the Sardine,* and eight more of his oils are also on view.

Alcalá 13. Ⓒ 91-524-0864. rabasf.insde.es. Admission 2.40€ ($2.75) adults, 1.20€ ($1.40) students; free for seniors/children under 18. Tues–Fri 10am–2pm and 5–8pm; Sat–Mon and holidays 10am–2pm. Metro: Sol or Sevilla.

PARKS & GARDENS

Casa de Campo (Metro: Batán), the former royal hunting grounds, is composed of miles of parkland west of the Royal Palace across the Manzanares River. You can see the gate through which the kings rode out of the palace grounds—either on horseback or in carriages—on their way to the park. Casa de Campo has a zoo, many trees, and a lake that's usually filled with rowers. You can have refreshments around the lake or go swimming in a municipally operated pool. The park can be visited daily from 8am to 9pm.

Parque del Retiro ✸✸ (Metro: Retiro), originally a playground for the Spanish monarchs and their guests, is now a park of over 120 hectares (260 acres). The huge palaces that once stood here were destroyed in the early 19th century, and only the former dance hall, Casón del Buen Retiro (housing some of the Prado's modern works), remains. The park has many fountains and statues, plus a large lake in front of an extravagant monument to Alfonso XII. Along the promenade beside the lake are rows of tarot card readers, puppeteers, musicians, and other street performers. There are also two exposition centers: the Velázquez and the Crystal palaces. In summer, the rose gardens are worth a visit. The park is open daily 24 hours, but it's safest, as most public parks are, during daylight hours.

Immediately south of the Prado Museum is the **Real Jardín Botánico (Royal Botanical Garden),** Plaza de Murillo 2 (Ⓒ **91-420-3017;** Metro: Atocha). Founded in the 18th century, the garden contains more than 100 species of trees and 3,000 types of plants. The park is open daily from 10am to 9pm; admission is 1.50€ ($1.75) for adults, .75€ (85¢) for children, free for children 10 years old and under.

ORGANIZED TOURS

The best deals for organized bus tours of Madrid are the two companies whose buses follow set routes and allow you to hop off and reboard any of the subsequent buses at over a dozen museums, plazas, and other major stops. For the 9.60€ ($11) ticket, the distinctive **Madrid Vision Bus** (© **91-767-1743;** www.madridvision.es) lets riders get off and reboard as many times in a day as they want. The air-conditioned buses carry multilingual guides who provide commentary over earphones. Three routes make color-coded, 75-minute loops around themed sets of monuments and buildings: either Historic Madrid, Modern Madrid, or the length of the Gran Via. Convenient places to pick up the bus are at the Puerta de Alcalá and Puerta del Sol.

Pullmantur, Plaza de Oriente 8 (© **91-541-1807;** www.pullmantur-spain. com; Metro: Opera), is one of Spain's largest tour operators and offers several guided city tours, including a half-day tour of the Palacio Real and the Prado for 36€ ($41) and a 2-hour nighttime city tour leaving at 8:30 pm for 13€ ($14).

Pullmantur also offers full-day tours to Toledo, Avila, and Segovia. Similar out-of-town possibilities are supplied by **Juliá Tours,** Gran Vía 68 (© **91-559-9605;** Metro: Gran Vía), and **Trapsatur,** San Bernardo 23 (© **91-542-6666**). Expect full-day tours to Toledo or Avila and Segovia to cost around 60€ to 70€ ($69–$81) and half-day tours to run 40€ ($46) or so.

THE SHOPPING SCENE
THE MAIN SHOPPING AREAS

The sheer diversity of Madrid's shops is staggering. One of the greatest concentrations of stores lies immediately north of **Puerta del Sol,** along the pedestrian streets of Calle del Carmen, and Calle Preciados.

Conceived, designed, and built in the 1910s and 1920s as a showcase for the city's best shops, hotels, and restaurants, the **Gran Vía** has since been eclipsed by other shopping districts, although fragments of its Art Nouveau and Art Deco glamour still survive. The book and music shops along here are among the best in the city, as are the outlets for fashion, shoes, jewelry, and handcrafts from all regions of Spain.

The **Salamanca** district is the quintessential upscale shopping neighborhood. Here, you'll find exclusive furniture, fur, fashion, and jewelry stores, plus rug and art galleries. The main shopping streets here are Serrano and Velázquez. This district lies northeast of the center of Madrid, a few blocks north of Retiro Park. Its most central Metro stops are Serrano and Veláquez.

Tips **Spain's Biggest Flea Market**

Foremost among Madrid's flea markets is **El Rastro,** Plaza Cascorro and Ribera de Curtidores (Metro: La Latina; bus: 3 or 17), which occupies a roughly triangular area of streets and plazas that are a few minutes' walk south of Plaza Mayor. This market will delight anyone attracted to sometimes-intriguing kitsch. Goods are sold from open stalls arranged in front of stores selling antiques and paintings. Thieves are rampant here, so secure your purse and wallet, be alert, and proceed with caution. The market is open Saturday and Sunday only, from 9:30am to 1:30pm and (to a lesser extent) from 5 to 8pm.

SOME NOTEWORTHY SHOPS

El Corte Inglés, Preciados 3 (© **91-418-8800;** www.elcorteingles.es; Metro: Puerta del Sol), is Spain's number one department-store chain. The store sells Spanish handcrafts along with glamorous fashion articles, such as Pierre Balmain designs, often at lower prices than you'll find in most European capitals. Competition for El Corte Inglés has arrived just up the street in the form of **FNAC,** Preciados 28 (© **91-595-6100;** Metro: Sol), a chain of stores concentrating on photographic and audio equipment, video games, TVs, software, computers, and books. Predictably, El Corte Inglés has opened a mirror-image operation right next door. With a substantial stock of CDs in most musical genres, **Madrid Rock,** Gran Vía 25 (© **91-523-2652;** Metro: Gran Vía), also sells tickets to pop concerts. Near Madrid Rock is **La Casa del Libro,** Gran Vía 29 (© **91-521-2113;** Metro: Gran Vía), a large bookstore with a sizable English-language section.

For unique craft items, **El Arco de los Cuchilleros Artesiana de Hoy,** Plaza Mayor 9 (basement) (© **91-365-2680;** Metro: Sol or Opera), may be a mouthful of a name to remember, but it has an unparalleled array of pottery, leather, textiles, glassware, and jewelry produced by individual artisans throughout Spain. It's open daily 11am to 8pm, even during siesta.

Since 1846, **Loewe,** Gran Vía 8 (© **91-522-6815;** Metro: Gran Vía), has been Spain's most elegant leather store. Its designers keep abreast of changing tastes and styles, but the inventory retains a timeless chic. The store sells luggage, handbags, and jackets for men and women (in leather or suede). At **Casa de Diego,** Puerta del Sol 12 (© **91-522-6643;** Metro: Puerta del Sol), you'll find a wide inventory of fans, ranging from plain to fancy, from plastic to exotic hardwood, from cost-conscious to lavish.

MADRID AFTER DARK

From May through September, the municipal government sponsors a series of plays, concerts, and films, and the city has the atmosphere of a free arts festival. Pick up a copy of *Guía del Ocio* (available at most newsstands) for listings of these events. This guide also provides information about occasional discounts for commercial events, such as the concerts given in Madrid's parks. The guide is in Spanish, but it's not difficult to make out the times, locations, and prices for various events.

With some exceptions, flamenco in Madrid is geared primarily to tourists, and nightclubs are expensive. But since Madrid is a city of song and dance, you can often be entertained at very little cost—for the price of a glass of wine or beer, in fact—if you sit at a bar with live entertainment.

Tickets to dramatic and musical events can cost anywhere from 5€ ($5.75) to 120€ ($138), with discounts of up to 50% granted on certain days (usually Wed and early performances on Sun). In the event that your choice is sold out, you may be able to get tickets (with a reasonable markup) at **Localidades Galicia,** Plaza del Carmen 1 (© **91-531-2732;** www.eol.es/lgalicia; Metro: Puerta del Sol). It's open Tuesday through Sunday from 10am to 1pm and 4:30 to 7:30pm. Telephone ticket sales are also provided by the following agencies: **Caja de Cataluña** (© **90-210-1212**), **Servi-Caixa** (© **90-233-2211**), and **Entradas.com** (© **90-222-1622**).

THE PERFORMING ARTS

Ballet Nacional de España (© **91-517-4686;** http://balletnacional.mcu.es) is devoted exclusively to dances created by Spanish choreographers. Its performances are always well attended. Also look for performances by choreographer Nacho Duato's **Compañía Nacional de Danza** (② **91-354-5053;** http://cndanza. mcu.es).

World-renowned flamenco sensation António Canales and his troupe, **Ballet Flamenco António Canales** (② **91-531-2732**), offer high-energy, spirited performances. Productions are centered around Canales's impassioned *Torero*—his interpretation of the physical and emotional struggles of a bullfighter.

CLASSICAL MUSIC

Madrid's opera company is the **Teatro de la Opera,** and its symphony orchestra is the outstanding **Orquesta Sinfónica de Madrid** (at Teatro Real, see below).

Reopened in 1997 after a massive $157 million renovation, the **Teatro Real,** Plaza Isabel II (② **90-516-0660;** www.teatro-real.com; Metro: Opera), is one of the world's finest stage and acoustic settings for opera. Guided tours of the grand hall are available weekdays except Tuesdays and Saturday, Sunday, and holidays from 11am to 1:30pm at a cost of 4€ ($4.60). Today, the building is home to the Compañía del Teatro Real and the Teatro de la Opera, and is the major venue for classical music and opera. Tickets are 12€ ($14) to 102€ ($117).

Auditorio Nacional de Música, Príncipe de Vergara 146 (② **91-337-0139;** www.auditorionacional.mcu.es; Metro: Cruz del Rayo), is the ultramodern home of both the **National Orchestra of Spain,** which pays particular attention to the music of Spanish composers, and the **National Chorus of Spain.** Just north of Madrid's Salamanca district, the concert hall ranks as a major addition to the classical music circuit in Europe. Tickets are 9€ to 60€ ($10–$69).

FLAMENCO

At Madrid's flamenco *tablaos,* doors usually open at 9 or 9:30pm, and the show starts at about 10:45pm and ends at 12:30am or even later. To save money, go after dinner, when the still-hefty admission at least includes a drink. The later performances are usually better anyway, after the tour groups leave and the performers are warmed up. These stages feature large troupes with several dancers, two or three guitarists, and one or two singers, all in costume. Among the established *tablaos* are **Torres Bermejas,** Mesonero Romanos 11 (② **91-532-3322;** Metro: Callao); **Corral de la Morería,** Morería 17 (② **91-365-8446;** Metro: Opera); and **Café de Chinitas,** Torija 7 (② **91-559-5135;** Metro: Santa Domingo).

For a flamenco club that doesn't cater primarily to tourists, try **Casa Patas,** Cañizares 10 (② **91-369-0496;** www.casapatas.com; Metro: Antón Martín). In front, it's a restaurant, with a long bar, a high ceiling held up by cast-iron pillars, and three rows of tables with checked tablecloths. A pot-bellied stove in the middle provides heat, and photos of matadors and flamenco performers cover the walls. That's not where the shows are, though. Go to the closed door in back. Shortly before show time, a shuttered window opens, your money is taken, and you are allowed to enter. You are then seated at tiny tables around the open stage. The music will be powerful, the dancing fiery and gripping. Mondays through Thursdays, shows are at 10:30pm; Fridays and Saturdays, shows are at 9pm and midnight. Call ahead to reserve a table. The cover is 25€ ($29) per person, or 30€ ($35) on Fridays and Saturdays. It's worth the cost and effort, for this is modern flamenco at its best.

With the legendary **La Soleá** now closed, the place to go for *cante hondo* (deep song) is **Monteleón,** Monteleón 46 (② **91-445-6487;** Metro: San Bernardo). Monteleón observes the same format as the older club: One or two guitarists, a few singers, little or no dancing, and audience members occasionally getting caught up in the act. Things get started at 11pm, and the fun really starts around 1am or so. There's no cover, but performers expect tips. La Soleá wasn't too touristy, and Monteleón is even less so.

LIVE MUSIC

Off Plaza de Santa Ana, **Café Central,** Plaza del Angel 10 (© **91-369-4143;** www.cafecentralmadrid.com; Metro: Antón Martín), is *the* place for live jazz. Black bench seating, marble-topped tables, and glistening brass set the scene, and the place is usually packed with students, tourists, and Madrid's night beauties. Performances are usually at 10pm and midnight. While jazz is the main course, the cafe also hosts folkies, blues belters, and performers of related music. Calle de las Huertas runs through this plaza, so a visit to the cafe could be the start or the end of an extended pub-crawl. It's open daily 1:30pm to 2 or 3am, with a cover that varies from 10€ to 15€ ($11–$17).

Not far from the Central is **Café Jazz Populart,** Huertas 22 (© **91-429-8407;** Metro: Antón Martín), a showcase for American blues, Latin salsa, and Caribbean reggae as well as many varieties of jazz. The large space allows for a little elbowroom, and the atmosphere is laid-back. You can relax at the marble-topped bar or the tables ringing the stage. Admission is often free, but the drink prices tend to jump sharply when music is playing. Still, it's cheaper than Central. It's open daily 6pm to 3 or 4am, with shows at 11pm and 12:30am.

With dozens of small tables and a huge bar in its dark and smoky interior, **Clamores,** Albuquerque 14 (© **91-445-7938;** Metro: Bilbao), is the largest and one of the most popular jazz clubs in Madrid. It has thrived because of the noted American and Spanish jazz bands that appear here. Clamores is open daily from 7pm to 3am or so, but jazz is presented only from Tuesday to Saturday. From Tuesday to Thursday, performances are at 11pm and 1am; Saturday they're at 11:30pm and 1:30am. There are no live performances Sunday or Monday. Cover from Tuesday to Saturday is 4.80€ to 24€ ($5.50–$28), depending on the act.

DANCE CLUBS

Madrid's most popular dance clubs operate with a selective entrance policy, so dress stylishly and try to look as young, gorgeous, celebrated, and/or rich as possible. Admission, usually including a drink, can exceed 12€ ($14), and even a Coke can cost over 6€ ($6.90). The clubs are usually open nightly until 5am or later, with nothing much happening before 2am. (*Tip:* It's easier to get past the unsmiling gents at the door if you arrive before then.) Some clubs have a matinee, usually 7 to 9 or 10pm, attended primarily by teenagers. After closing for an hour or two to clear out the youngsters, they reopen to older patrons.

Two decades ago, an old Victorian-era theater was transformed into the popular disco **Joy Eslava,** Arenal 11 (© **91-366-3733;** www.joy-eslava.com; Metro: Sol or Opera). Laser shows, videos, and energetic performers keep things moving. The best nights are Friday and Saturday, and 20%-discount coupons are available around town. It's open daily from 11pm until 5:30am. Cover is 12€ ($14), or 15€ ($17) on Fridays and Saturdays; it includes the first drink. "Matinees" are Friday and Saturday 7pm to 10pm, for ages 14 to 18 only, with no alcohol or tobacco allowed (this may be a good way to send your teens for a few hours); cover is 7€ ($8.05).

The most multicultural, multifarious, and multimusical disco in Madrid, **Kapital,** Atocha 125 (© **91-420-2906;** Metro: Atocha), has seven floors, with the main dance floor at street level, a terrace up top, and more bars and dance floors (with different kinds of music) in between. Laser shows, karaoke, a movie room, and what used to be called go-go dancers are added attractions. Throngs of kids show up for the "afternoon" session from 6 to 11pm. Grown-ups arrive after midnight and stay until 6am. The cover is 12€ to 15€ ($14–$17). **Palacio Gaviria,** Arenal 9 (© **91-526-6069;** www.palaciogaviria.com; Metro: Sol), is a vintage mansion near Puerta del Sol that has been converted into a *multispacio* with several salons, each serving up expensive drinks, cabaret, and live or recorded dance music. Tuesday is salsa night, and Thursdays feature world music. It's open Monday to Thursday 10:30pm to 3am, Friday and Saturday 11pm to 5am, and Sunday 8:30pm to 2am. Cover is 15€ ($17), including the first drink.

PUBS & BARS

Hemingway and his journalist buddies suffered the Civil War siege of Madrid at **Chicote,** Gran Vía 12 (© **91-532-6737;** Metro: Gran Vía). Photos on the walls to the left and right of the entrance document the patronage of Coop, Ty, Orson, and Ava. A superior martini is still available, and they've added breakfast and light meals. **Cock,** Reina 12 (© **91-532-2826;** Metro: Gran Vía), a dark, cavernous room on a narrow street parallel to Gran Vía, is another old-timer, where Madrid's artistic and showbiz elite routinely assault their livers. It was given renewed cachet by the presence of internationally known film director Pedro Almodóvar.

If you want to witness a supremely assured professional mixologist in action, head up the same street a few doors. **Del Diego,** Reina 12 (© **91-523-3106;** Metro: Gran Vía), is a stylish contemporary watering hole that attracts exactly the upmarket crowd it seeks, including government ministers and upper-echelon executives. The maestro twirling the swizzle sticks is the eponymous head man, never losing his composure as he shakes and stirs everything from pure martinis to Long Island iced teas and Madrid's drink of the moment, the *mojito* (rum, lime juice, and mint). He's put in more than three decades at Chicote.

Pop in for at least a quick drink to admire the variety of pictorial ceramic tiles covering the walls of the five rooms of **Los Gabrieles,** Echegaray 17 (© **91-429-6261;** Metro: Sol or Sevilla), a century-old tavern. Live music, mostly flamenco, is presented Tuesday nights (no cover). Students and 20-something singles have given the 1890 tavern **Viva Madrid,** Manuel Fernández González 7 (© **91-429-3640;** Metro: Sol or Antón Martín), new life as a trendy meeting place. Both the facade and the interior are resplendent with intricately patterned tiles, and mythical creatures hold up carved ceilings. Light meals and tapas are served in the room behind the bar.

GAY & LESBIAN CLUBS & CAFES

The Plaza Chueca area is now Spain's number one hotspot for gays and bohemian straights, with more than 60 gay-friendly bars, cafes, and discos. Pick up a map of gay Madrid and a copy of the **Shanguide** pocket-size nightlife guide at the **Berkana** gay bookstore, Hortaleza 64 (© **91-522-5599**).

A small American-style drinking bar, **Rick's,** Clavel 9 (no phone; Metro: Chueca), brings together gays and straights. **D'Mystic,** Gravina 5 (no phone) and **Wy Not?,** San Bartolomé 6 (no phone), cater more exclusively to gay men.

Truco, Gravina 10 (© **91-532-8921;** Metro: Chueca), is a hub of Madrid's lesbian community; it's open nightly from 10pm. Ladies are also heavily represented at the **Escape** disco, Gravina 13 (no phone). Guys will find drag shows, male pole dancers, and even the inevitable Liza impersonator at **A Noite,** Hortaleza 43 (© **91-531-0715**). A less intimidating male crowd fills the cozy **La Lupe,** Torrecilla del Leal 12 (© **91-527-5019**), which plays "retro and happy music"; the 4€ ($4.60) mojitos are enough to make anyone happy.

DAY TRIPS FROM MADRID

TOLEDO ✶✶✶   Once the capital of Visigothic Spain, Toledo—69km (43 miles) southwest of Madrid—bristles with steeples and towers spread over an unlikely hill that's almost completely moated by the River Tajo. Toledo is undeniably a must-see, one of the most photogenic cities on the peninsula, its streets tilting and twisting past buildings representing over 1,500 years of construction. Here is history . . . deep, palpable, warming the stones. Those familiar with the painting of the city by El Greco, who lived most of his creative life here, will be struck by how closely his 16th-century canvas, *View of Toledo,* conforms to the present view, in overall impression if not in detail.

The streets are clogged all year with tour buses and their occupants and crammed with shops hung with Toledo cutlery, fake armor, Lladró figurines, and every kind of gaudy souvenir. If possible, stay overnight to get a less feverish picture of the city when it's briefly returned to its citizens.

Getting There   You can reach Toledo by **train** (six trips daily from Madrid's Atocha Station) or by **bus** (from Madrid's Estación Sur de Autobuses). The one-way trip takes about an hour and 15 minutes by either method. The train fare is 4.90€ ($5.65), while the bus (www.continental-auto.es) costs 3.90€ ($4.50). Taxis are available at the charming neo-Mudéjar train station in Toledo, but not in great numbers and not always when you want them. I really don't recommend driving to Toledo, but if you want to, take Route 401 for 69km (43 miles) south of Madrid.

Visitor Information   The **tourist office** is at Puerta de Bisagra (© **92-522-0843;** www.diputoledo.es), open Monday through Saturday from 9am to 7pm, and Sunday from 9am to 3pm.

Exploring Toledo   Although ranked among the greatest of Gothic structures, the **Cathedral** ✶✶✶, Arcos de Palacio (© **92-522-2241**), actually reflects a variety of styles because of the more than 2½ centuries that passed during its construction, from 1226 to 1493. Among its art treasures, the *transparente* stands out—a wall of marble and florid baroque alabaster sculpture overlooked for years because of the cathedral's poor lighting. The sculptor Narcisco Tomé cut a hole in the ceiling, much to the consternation of Toledans, and now light touches the high-rising angels, a *Last Supper* in alabaster, and a Virgin in ascension. The Treasure Room has a 225-kilogram (500-lb.) 15th-century gilded monstrance (receptacle of the Host)—allegedly made with gold brought back from the New World by Columbus—that's still carried through the streets of Toledo during the feast of Corpus Christi. Admission to the cathedral is free; admission to the Treasure Room is 3€ ($3.45). Both are open Monday through Saturday from 10:30am to 1:30pm and 3:30 to 7pm, and Sunday from 10:30am to 1:30pm and 4 to 7pm; there are shorter hours October through May.

The **Alcázar,** General Moscardó 4, near Plaza de Zocodover (© **92-522-3038**), at the eastern edge of the old city, dominates the Toledo skyline. It was damaged frequently over its centuries as a fortress and royal residence and leveled during a siege of the Spanish Civil War. The existing structure is essentially a replica but is built over the old cellars and foundations. Admission is 1.20€ ($1.40), and hours are daily from 9:30am to 2:30pm.

Queen Isabel had a hand in arranging the construction of the 16th-century building housing the **Museo Santa Cruz,** Cervantes 3 (© **92-522-1402**), with its impressive Plateresque facade. The paintings within are mostly from the 16th century and 17th century, with yet another by El Greco. Find the museum immediately east of Plaza de Zocodover. Admission is free. Hours are Monday to Saturday 10am to 6:30pm, and Sunday 10am to 2pm.

EL ESCORIAL PALACE ★★   The second-most important excursion from Madrid is a 55km (34-mile) trip to the Royal Monastery in the village of San Lorenzo de El Escorial. Felipe II commissioned Juan Bautista de Toledo and his assistant, Juan de Herrera, to build this gloomy Xanadu in the Sierra de Guadarrama, northwest of Madrid. Its purported intent was to commemorate an important victory over the French in Flanders, but the likely real reason was that the ascetic Felipe was unnerved by the stress of overseeing an empire bridging four continents and this retreat insulated him from the intrigues of the Madrid court. He ruled his troubled empire from the rooms here for the last 14 years of his life, and it was from here that he ordered his doomed "Invincible Armada" to set sail.

Getting There   More than two dozen **trains** depart daily from Madrid's Atocha and Chamartín stations (trip time: 60–80 min.), costing 2.45€ ($2.80) on weekdays and 2.65€ ($3.05) on weekends one-way. For schedules and information, contact **RENFE** (© **90-224-0202;** www.renfe.es).

Buses, however, are preferable. Use line nos. 661 and 664, run by **Empresa Herranz,** Isaac Peral 10, Moncloa (© **91-890-4122**), and which cost 2.85€ ($3.30) for the 55-minute trip one-way; they drop you closer to Felipe's royal retreat than do the trains. If you're **driving,** take N-IV northwest from Madrid; after about 48km (30 miles), exit south on M-505 about 10km (6¼ miles) to El Escorial.

VISITOR INFORMATION   The **tourist office** at Floridablanca 10 in El Escorial can be reached at © **91-890-1554** or on the Web at www.turismosan lorenzo.org.

Exploring the Monastery   The huge monastery/palace/mausoleum that is the **Real Monasterio de San Lorenzo de El Escorial** ★★★, San Lorenzo de El Escorial 1 (© **91-890-7818**), is typically praised for its massive, brooding simplicity. That impression is allayed inside, as the wealth of sumptuous detail, the hundreds of rooms, and the 24km (15 miles) of corridors are revealed. An extraordinary library reflects the scholarly king's intellectual interests, with tens of thousands of volumes and rare manuscripts in many languages, representative of the three primary religions that had existed in Spain. Also in the building is a sizable church with a frescoed dome over 90m (300 ft.) high. The main altar is four stories high with gold sculptures and paintings framed in jasper. Beneath the basilica is a royal pantheon with sarcophagi containing the remains of most of Spain's monarchs since Carlos V. Galleries and royal apartments contain canvases by El Greco, Titian, Ribera, Tintoretto, Rubens, and Velázquez, among others. Throughout the building, you'll see copies of a gridlike symbol that echoes the layout of the palace itself. These symbols represent St. Lawrence, who was roasted alive on a grill by the Romans. April to September, El Escorial is open Tuesday to Sunday and holidays 10am to 6pm (to 5pm in winter). An all-inclusive ticket is 8.50€ ($9.80) adults and 5€ ($5.75) seniors/students, and guided tours are 1€ ($1.15).

SEGOVIA ⭐⭐⭐ Less commercial than Toledo, Segovia, 87km (54 miles) northwest of Madrid, typifies the glory of Old Castile. Wherever you look, you'll see reminders of a golden era—whether it's the spectacular Alcázar or the well-preserved Roman aqueduct. Segovia lies on the slope of the Guadarrama Mountains, where the Eresma and Clamores rivers converge. Isabel was proclaimed queen of Castile here in 1474.

Getting There **Buses** are preferable to trains for price and speed, if not comfort. Between Madrid and Segovia, the bus takes 75 to 90 minutes and the train 2 hours. The unmarked bus station in Madrid is on Paseo de Florida, opposite the Estación del Norte and next to the Hotel Florida del Norte, right by the Príncipe Pío Metro station. Buses run by **La Sepulvedana** (www.lasepulvedana.es) depart every half-hour or so on weekdays from Madrid 6:30am to 10:30pm; on weekends, buses run pretty much hourly from 8am on. A same-day round-trip fare is 8.80€ ($10). Buses drop passengers off at the Estación Municipal de Autobuses at Paseo de Ezequile González 10. From the front of the terminal, turn left, cross the street, and walk down the largely pedestrian and arcaded Avenida Fernández Ladreda. This arrives in Plaza del Azoguejo, beneath the city's principal site. **Trains** depart from Madrid's Atocha, Nuevos Ministerios and Chamartín stations every 2 hours from 6am to 8pm, costing 5.10€ ($5.85) each way. The train station is a 20-minute walk from the town center, so I recommend taking local bus no. 3 instead; it leaves every 15 minutes for the Plaza Mayor. If you're **driving,** take NVI northwest out of Madrid; after about 98km (61 miles), exit north on Route 603. It's 55km (34 miles) from there to Segovia.

Visitor Information The **tourist office** is at Plaza Mayor 10 (© **92-146-0334**), open daily from 10am to 2pm and 5 to 7pm.

Exploring Segovia The town is quite walkable. Its narrow medieval streets suffer less from the ravages of mass tourism (except on weekends and holidays) than other destinations in Madrid's orbit and reveal much about what life must have been like here 500 years ago.

Located here is what might be the most recognizable structure in Spain—an intact **Roman Aqueduct** ⭐⭐, Plaza de Azoguejo. A spectacular engineering feat even if it were contemplated today, the double-tiered Roman aqueduct cuts across the city to the snow-fed waters of the nearby mountains. Almost 730m (2,400 ft.) long and nearly 30m (95 ft.) at its highest point at the east end of town, it contains over 160 arches fashioned of stone cut so precisely that no mortar was needed in the construction. Probably completed in the 2nd century A.D. (although some sources date it as many as 3 centuries earlier), it has survived war and partial dismantling by the Moors. Amazingly, it carried water until only a few decades ago.

Constructed between 1515 and 1558, the **Catedral de Segovia** ⭐⭐, Plaza de la Catedral, Marqués del Arco (© **92-146-2205**), was the last Gothic cathedral built in Spain. Fronting the Plaza Mayor, it stands on the spot where Isabel I was proclaimed queen of Castile. It contains numerous treasures, such as a chapel created by the flamboyant Churriguera, elaborately carved choir stalls, and 16th- and 17th-century paintings. More interesting, if only for historical reasons, is the attached 15th-century **cloister** ⭐. After rebels razed the earlier cathedral, its cloister was moved here stone by stone and reassembled. The cloister now contains a small museum. To reach the cathedral, walk west along Calle de Cervantes, which becomes Calle Bravo. Admission to the cathedral is free, but the cloister and museum cost 1.50€ ($1.70). The cathedral is open Tuesday to

Friday 10am to 2pm and 4 to 8pm, and weekends and the whole month of August from 10am to 2pm only.

Continue west on Calle de Daolz, where the prow of the old town rears above the confluence of the Clamores and Eresma rivers. The **Alcázar,** Daolz s/n (© **92-146-0759**), a fortified castle almost as familiar a symbol of Castilla (Castile) as the aqueduct, occupies this dramatic location. Though it satisfies our "castles in Spain" fantasies, at least from the outside, note that it's essentially a late-19th-century replica of the medieval fortress that stood here before a devastating fire in 1868. Admission is 3.10€ ($3.55) adults, 2.20€ ($2.55) seniors/students/children, and free for children under 6. From April to September, it's open daily from 10am to 7pm (to 6pm the rest of the year).

2 Barcelona ✶✶✶

With an unforgettable visual style, passionate life force, and continuous churn of old and new, the capital of the autonomous region of Catalonia (don't call it Spanish!) is easily Spain's most enjoyable city, a place where people play with gusto but still manage to get things done. Catalonians consider themselves a distinct nationality, speaking a language that owes as much to French as it does to Spanish. It says something that Catalonia's favorite sons have been four artists known for their brilliant eccentricity: Gaudí, Miró, Picasso, and Dalí.

Since the 19th century, the Catalan metropolis has always been at the forefront of modernity. Barcelona was the nation's first industrial center, expanding from its ancient settlement into the surrounding hills by the 1920s. The end of the 20th century brought another burst of expansion: first for the 1992 Olympics, and in 2004 for Expo 2004, a 6-month festival that gave rise to the construction of an entire new neighborhood on the waterfront.

A visual expression of Barcelona's quirky personality and willingness to take risks is some of Europe's most amazing architecture, from the Gothic cathedral to the parade of modernist masterpieces along the Passeig de Gràcia. The region has given birth to some of history's most visionary artists, among them the 21st-century chefs who have put themselves on the world map creating a brilliant, almost surrealist cuisine. Joyously joining the Europe of the new millennium, Barcelona has everything going for it—good looks, a sharp business sense, an appreciation for all forms of culture, and an unerring eye for style.

ESSENTIALS

GETTING THERE   By Plane   El Prat Airport (© **93-298-3838;** www.aena.es) lies 13km (8 miles) southwest of the city. A **train** runs between the airport and the Estació Sants rail station every 30 minutes from 6:13am to 11:40pm, continuing to the more central Plaça de Catalunya; it costs 2.20€ ($2.53). **Aerobuses** (© **93-415-6020**) run among the three terminals at the airport and to Plaça de Catalunya (with intermediate stops) Monday to Friday every 12 minutes 6:30am to midnight. The trip takes 25 to 40 minutes and costs 3.45€ ($4). A **taxi** into town is 20€ to 25€ ($23–$29), plus tip and supplements for luggage (about .85€/95¢ per piece).

By Train   National and international trains arrive at the **Estació Sants** or the **Estació de França,** both situated slightly outside the city center but linked to the municipal Metro network. Many trains also stop at the Metro station at **Plaça de Catalunya.** For schedules and prices, call **RENFE** (© **90/224-0202;** www.renfe.es) or **Rail Europe** (© **888/382-7245;** www.raileurope.com).

Barcelona

Plaça de
Francesc Macia

Carrer de Buenos Aires

Carrer de Londres

Carrer de Paris

Travessara de Gràcia

Via Augusta

Gran de Gràcia

Travessara de Gràcia

Av. de Sant Antoni Maria Claret

Avinguda Diagonal

Carrer de la Industria

Carrer de Còrsega

EIXAMPLE

Carrer de Provença

Carrer Enric Granados

Carrer de Balmes

Rambla de Catalunya

Passeig de Gràcia

Carrer de Pau Claris

Carrer de Rosselló

Avinguda Diagonal

Carrer de Roger de Flor

Plaça de la
Sagrada
Família

Carrer de Mallorca

Carrer de València

Carrer d'Aragó

Carrer de R. de Llúria

Carrer del Bruc

Carrer de Girona

Carrer de Bailèn

Passeig de Sant Joan

Carrer de Nápols

Carrer de Sicília

Carrer del Comte Borrell

Carrer del Comte d'Urgell

Carrer de Villarroel

Carrer de Casanova

Carrer de Muntaner

Carrer d'Aribau

Carrer del Consell de Cent

Carrer de la Diputació

Gran Via de les Corts Catalanes

Plaça de la
Universitat

Ronda Universitat

Plaça de
Tetuan

Carrer de Sardenya

Ronda de Sant Antoni

Carrer de Pelai

Plaça
Catalunya

Plaça
Urquinaona

Carrer de Casp

Carrer d'Ausias Marc

Carrer d'Ali Bei

Carrer de Ribes

Carrer de la Marina

RAVAL

La Rambla

Av. Portal
de l'Angel

Via Laietana

Ronda de Sant Pere

Carrer de Hospital

Palau de la
Música Catalana

**BARRI
GÒTIC**

Carrer de Sant Pau

Cathedral de
Barcelona

Gran Teatre
del Liceu

Carrer Nou de la Rambla

C. de

Ferran

C. de la Princesa

Passeig del Comerç

Passeig de
Lluís Companys

Passeig de Pujades

**PARC DE LA
CIUTADELLA**

Carrer de Wellington

LA RIBERA

Passeig de Picasso

Avda. de les Drassanes

La Rambla

Carrer Ample

Passeig de Colom

Pg. Isabel II

Moll de la Fusta

Plaça Portal
de la Pau

Moll d'Espanya

Port
Vell

Avinguda d'Icaria

**PARC
ZOOLOGIC**

Villa
Olímpica →

BARCELONETA

Passeig Marítim

Ronda Sant Pau

Carrer de Sant Antoni

(i) Information

927

By Bus The main bus terminal is the **Estació del Nord,** Ali-bei 80 (© **93-265-6508;** Metro: Arc de Triomf), near the Old Town. Some bus companies stop near the Estació Sants, which has a Metro station.

By Car From France, the major access route is at the eastern end of the Pyrenees, with the choice of the express highway (E-15) or the more scenic coastal road. From France, it's possible to approach Barcelona via Toulouse. Cross the border into Spain at Puigcerdá (frontier stations are there), near the principality of Andorra. From here, take N-152 to Barcelona. From Madrid, take N-2 to Zaragoza, then A-2 to El Vendrell, followed by A-7 to Barcelona.

VISITOR INFORMATION A conveniently located tourist office is the subterranean **Centre d'Informació,** at the southeast corner of Plaça Catalunya (© **93-368-9730;** Metro: Catalunya), open daily 9am to 9pm.

Websites A good place to start is **www.okspain.org**, where you can find up-to-date information and book hotels, restaurants, and tours. The excellent municipal website, **www.bcn.es**, features a terrific interactive map. Additional sources are **www.barcelonaturisme.com** and **www.bcn-guide.com**.

CITY LAYOUT Old Barcelona sits just north of the Mediterranean, bisected by the Rambla promenade. The **Barri Gótic,** the Gothic Quarter and the oldest part of town, lies east of the Rambla; south of the Barri Gótic is the **Ribera** district, also known as **El Born,** developed during the 13th and 14th centuries and home to the Picasso Museum.

The old-town areas west of the Rambla are grittier; the residential **Raval** district, home to many of Barcelona's Muslim residents, is currently balancing on the knife edge between marginally unsafe and breathtakingly hip. The **Barri Xinés,** south of Nou de la Rambla, is a once-rough area that's still best avoided at night.

Southeast of the Old City, right on the water, is **Barceloneta,** originally home to the city's fishermen and now known for its seafood restaurants. Farther east along the coast are the brand-new **Vila Olimpica** and **Diagonal Mar** neighborhoods, areas developed for the 1992 Olympics and 2004 Forum, respectively.

West of the Old City is the brooding **Montjuïc,** a towering hill that's home to the Miró Museum and a large park.

The **Plaça de Catalunya** marks the northern edge of the old city, leading out onto the **Passeig de Gràcia,** Barcelona's proudest boulevard. The Passeig de Gràcia cuts north across the **Eixample,** a grid of wide streets and modernist buildings that was the product of Barcelona's growing prosperity in the late 19th century. North of the Eixample are **Gràcia,** an area of small squares and lively bars and restaurants that's known as "Barcelona's Greenwich Village;" **Sarría,** a quiet residential area; and **Tibidabo,** Barcelona's tallest mountain.

GETTING AROUND

The best deal for getting around Barcelona is the T10 10-ride **Metro/bus pass,** which costs 5.80€ ($6.65) and can be shared by multiple people. If you're really going to be zipping around, a 1-day pass costs 4.40€ ($5.05), a 2-day pass costs 8€ ($9.20), and 3, 4, and 5-day versions are available as well. Passes are available at most Metro stations, tourist offices, many newsstands and lottery shops, and the office of the local transportation agency **TMB** (www.tmb.net; © **93-318-7074** for information).

BY METRO (SUBWAY) The Metro and integrated commuter train lines (called FGC) operate Monday to Thursday 5am to midnight; Friday and Saturday 5am to 2am, and Sunday and holidays 6am to midnight. The lines you'll

Barcelona Metro

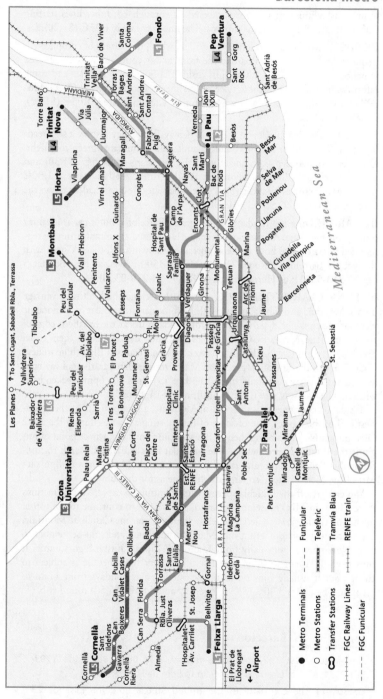

want to use within the city are numbered L1 through L8; other lines starting with L, R, and S serve various suburbs. The one-way fare is 1.05€ ($1.20).

BY BUS   TMB runs Barcelona's bus system, which has dozens of complicated, frequent, and useful lines. Board at the front to pay your fare, or get your pass punched in one of the machines just inside the bus. For schedules and route information, visit one of the service offices mentioned above, call ② **93-318-7074,** or visit TMB's website at **www.tmb.net**. The single fare is 1.05€ ($1.20), same as the Metro.

BY TAXI   Taxis are black and yellow. When available, they display a sign reading LIBRE (Spanish) or LLIURE (Catalan) and/or an illuminated green roof light. On weekdays between 6am and 10pm, the fare starts at 1.15€ ($1.30) and increases by .70€ (80¢) per kilometer; at other times, the fare starts at 1.30€ ($1.50) and increases by .90€ ($1.05) per kilometer. You can hail a taxi on the street or call one at ② **93-433-1020.**

BY CAR   Driving is a headache in congested Barcelona, but a car is ideal for touring the environs. All three of the major U.S.-based car-rental firms are represented in Barcelona, both at the airport and at downtown offices. Check with **Budget,** at Barcelona Airport 71 (② **93-298-3500**); **Avis,** at Rita Bonnat 5 (② **90-213-5531**); or **Hertz,** at Aragó 382 (② **93-270-0330**).

BY FUNICULAR & TELEFERIC   Two of Barcelona's high-altitude vantage points, Montjuïc and Tibidabo, accessible by funicular, are popular for panoramic views of the city. The departure point for Tibidabo lies at the northern edge of Barcelona. Take Metro FGC line L7 to Avinguda del Tibidabo, then a taxi (5€/$5.75), a bus (2€/$2.30), or, on weekends, the **Tramvía Blau** (blue trolley) (2€/$2.30) to the funicular. From late March to late October, the railway runs at least once every half-hour from 10:30am to 10pm (to 6pm weekends in winter). The one-way fare is 2€ ($2.30); round-trips are 3€ ($3.45).

Tibidabo's counterpart is the peak of Montjuïc, a hump of hill at the southwest end of the harbor. Site of some of the sporting activities during the 1992 Olympic games, it can be reached by the Montjuïc funicular, whose point of origin is the Parallel Metro station. The funicular runs daily: late March to mid-September 9am to 10pm and late September to early March 9am to 8pm. It's part of the Metro system, so fares are the same as for the subway.

You can get off the funicular partway up Montjuïc to explore the attractions there (the Joan Miró museum is nearby), and it's fun to continue to the top of the hill on the *teleféric,* an aerial cable car. It arrives near the Castell de Montjuïc, a 17th-century fortress. From mid-March to mid-June and mid-September to early November, it runs daily from 11am to 7:15pm. During high summer it runs from 11:15am to 9pm. The rest of the year the schedule is subject to change but it usually runs on Saturday, Sunday, and holidays from 11am to 7:15pm. The fare is 3.40€ ($3.90) one-way and 4.80€ ($5.50) round-trip.

FAST FACTS: Barcelona

American Express   The Amex office at Ramblas 74, 08002 Barcelona (② **93-301-3531**; Metro: Liceu), is open 9am to 9pm daily.

Consulates   The consulate of the **United States,** at Reina Elisenda 23 (② **93-280-2227**; Metro: Reina Elisenda), is open Monday through Friday from 9am to 12:30pm and 3 to 5pm. The consulate of **Canada,** Passeig de Gràcia 77 (© **93-215-0704;** Metro: Plaça Molina), is open Monday through Friday from 10am to noon. The consulate of the **United Kingdom,** Avinguda Diagonal 477 (© **93-366-6200;** Metro: Hospital Clínic), is open Monday through Friday from 9:30am to 1:30pm and 4 to 5pm. The consulate of **Australia** is at Gran Vía Carles III 98, 9th Floor (© **93-330-9494;** Metro: María Cristina), open Monday through Friday from 10am to noon.

Currency Exchange Most banks will exchange currency Monday through Friday from 8:30am to 2pm and Saturday from 8:30am to 1pm. *Oficinas de cambio* (exchange offices) are located in the airport and at the central rail station. Avoid the small exchange offices found in tourist areas that claim to charge no commission: They don't have to, because their rates are so much in their favor. ATMs are widely available; most machines provide directions in English. *You'll need a four-digit PIN,* so call your credit card company if you don't have one.

Dentists Call **Clinica Dental Beonadex,** Paseo Bona Nova 69, 3rd Floor (© **93-418-4433;** bus: 22), for an appointment. It's open Monday from 3 to 9pm and Tuesday through Friday from 8am to 3pm.

Drugstores After hours, various pharmacies take turns staying open at night. All pharmacies that are not open post the names and addresses of the pharmacies that are open all night in the area.

Emergencies In an emergency, © **112** is the central number for the municipal **police,** to report a **fire,** or to request an **ambulance.** To call the national **police,** the best choice if you are the victim of a crime, dial © **091.** To make a direct request for an **ambulance,** call © **061.**

Hospitals Barcelona has many hospitals and clinics, including **Hospital Clínic,** Casanova 143 (© **93-227-5400;** Metro: Hospital Clinic), and **Hospital de la Santa Creu i Sant Pau,** at the intersection of Carrer Cartagena and Carrer Sant Antoni Maria Claret (© **93-291-9000;** Metro: Hospital de Sant Pau).

Post Office The main post office is at Plaça d'Antoni López (© **93-318-3831;** Metro: Jaume I). It's open Monday through Friday from 8am to 9pm and Saturday from 8am to 2pm.

Safety Be particularly careful with cameras, purses, and wallets, all favorite targets of thieves and pickpockets in Barcelona—especially on La Rambla, in the Gothic Quarter, in the streets around the Picasso Museum, and in the parts of the old town near the waterfront. Avoid those sections at night or travel them by taxi. Muggings, increasingly violent, are reportedly on the upswing. New lighting on side streets is intended to alleviate the problem, but urban caution is still in order.

Telephone The **country code** for Spain is **34.** The **city code** for Barcelona is **93.** To make an **international call,** dial **07,** wait for the tone, and dial the country code, the area code, and the number. Note that an international call from a public phone booth requires stacks of coins. As an alternative, purchase a **phone card** from a tobacco shop *(estanco),* the post office, or other authorized dealer.

WHERE TO STAY
CIUTAT VELLA (OLD CITY)
Very Expensive
Le Meridien Barcelona ★★★   This is the finest hotel in the old town, thanks in large part to a major refurbishment over the last 3 years. A fave with CEOs and celebs—Madonna stayed here—it's far superior in both amenities and comfort to any competitor in the old town. It's a genteel retreat in the middle of the area's action. Have a cocktail in the calming piano bar after a long day of sightseeing. Rooms are spacious and comfortable, with double-glazed windows, extralarge beds, and bathrooms with heated floors.

La Rambla 111, 08002 Barcelona. ℂ 800/543-4300 in the U.S., or 93-318-6200. Fax 93-301-7776. www.lemeridien-barcelona.com. 212 units. 175€–400€ ($210–$460) double; from 500€ ($575) suite. AE, DC, MC, V. Parking 12€ ($14). Metro: Liceu or Plaça de Catalunya. **Amenities:** Restaurant; bar; access to a nearby health club; concierge; car-rental desk; business center; 24-hr. room service; babysitting; same-day laundry service and dry cleaning. *In room:* A/C, TV w/pay movies, dataport, minibar, hair dryer, safe.

Expensive
Colón ★★   This immensely popular hotel is blessed with one of the most dramatic locations in Barcelona, opposite the cathedral. Inside you'll find conservative and slightly old-fashioned public areas and a helpful staff. Rooms are filled with cushy furniture and (despite continuing renovations) an appealingly dowdy kind of charm. Though lacking views, those in back are quieter, especially when celebrations and rock concerts take place in front of the cathedral. Sixth-floor rooms have terraces overlooking the square, and are the most desirable and hardest to reserve. Some lower rooms are dark.

Av. de la Catedral 7, 08002 Barcelona. ℂ 800/845-0636 in the U.S., or 93-301-1404. Fax 93-317-2915. www.hotelcolon.es. 147 units. 220€–310€ ($253–$356) double; from 340€ ($390) suite. AE, DC, MC, V. Metro: Catalunya or Jaume I. **Amenities:** Restaurant; bar; concierge; 24-hr. room service; babysitting; same-day laundry service and dry cleaning. *In room:* A/C, TV, minibar, hair dryer, safe.

Moderate
Albinoni ★   Until recently, this was called the Allegro, and some confusion still remains, but it's worth the trouble of finding it. First, there is the beautiful building, a stately 1886 neoclassical mansion. Imagine the horse-drawn carriages wheeling into what is now the lobby, depositing their guests at the grand staircase, and continuing on to the stables beyond (there's a tented breakfast room back there now). Rooms are of decent dimensions, with 18 facing the courtyard and another 18 in front, over the street. All the street-side rooms have balconies, and they're the ones to request. It also rents bicycles, unusual for a center-city hotel.

Av. Portal de l'Angel 17 (south of Plaça de Catalunya), 08002 Barcelona. ℂ 93-318-4141. Fax 93-301-2631. www.hoteles-catalonia.es. 74 units. 167€ ($192) double. AE, DC, MC, V. Metro: Catalunya. **Amenities:** Bar; bike rental; limited room service; same-day laundry service and dry cleaning. *In room:* A/C, TV w/pay movies, minibar, hair dryer, safe.

Hotel Banys Orientals ★ *Value*   Possibly Barcelona's best economy choice, this spanking-new budget hotel is two notches above its price mates. Rooms are spare yet romantic, with modern four-poster beds and prints on the walls of Egyptian obelisks or Turkish harem scenes. All rooms have free high-speed Internet access, and everything, from bathtub to bedside table, is brand-new and sparkling clean. The hotel is three blocks from Barcelona's cathedral and on top of **Senyor Parellada,** a classy but inexpensive seafood restaurant.

Argenteria 37 (east of Via Laietana), 08003 Barcelona. ℂ 93-268-8460. Fax 93-268-8461. www.hotelbanysorientals.com. 43 units. 89€ ($102) double. AE, DC, MC, V. Metro: Jaume 1. *In room:* A/C, TV, minibar.

Duques de Bergara ★★   Here, guests can enjoy a striking 1898 mansion that underwent a recent expansion to triple the number of rooms. Some *modernista* details have been retained, including the magnificent carved wood and marble entry, although most everything else is sleekly contemporary. The halls were constructed to allow for relatively spacious rooms, many of which have separate seating and desk areas. The desk staff is multilingual.

Bergara 11 (off Plaça de Catalunya), 08002 Barcelona. ✆ 93-301-5151. Fax 93-317-3442. www.hoteles-catalonia.es. 148 units. 143€–242€ ($164–$278) double. AE, DC, MC, V. Metro: Universitat. **Amenities:** Restaurant; bar; small rooftop pool; business center; 24-hr. room service; same-day laundry service and dry cleaning; nonsmoking rooms. *In room:* A/C, TV w/pay movies, minibar, hair dryer, safe.

EIXAMPLE
Very Expensive

Claris ★★   An 1882 aristocratic residence was converted into one of only two officially designated *gran lujo* (grand luxury) hotels in the city center. The hotel opened in 1992, in time for the Olympics, and has a small pool and garden on its roof, as well as a gallery of Egyptian antiquities on its second floor. Rooms with clean-lined contemporary furnishings incorporate pieces of ancient Egyptian art, both real and copies, and all the high-end electronic accessories you could wish for.

Carrer de Pau Claris 150, 08009 Barcelona. ✆ 800/888-4747 in the U.S., or 93-487-6262. Fax 93-215-7970. www.derbyhotels.es. 124 units. 270€ ($310) double; from 439€ ($505) suite. AE, MC, V. Parking 14€ ($16). Metro: Passeig de Gràcia. **Amenities:** 2 restaurants; bar; outdoor pool; exercise room; sauna; concierge; 24-hr. room service; in-room massage; babysitting; same-day laundry service and dry cleaning. *In room:* A/C, TV, minibar, hair dryer, safe.

Ritz ★★★   Although it has competition now, this was the most prestigious hotel in Barcelona for decades. Built in 1919 in Belle Epoque style, its customer base has seen millionaires, celebrities, and bluebloods since its inception. After a period of perceptible decline and changes in ownership, it has returned to its former stature. The hotel's most jaw-dropping feature is the grand cream-and-gilt lobby, featuring marble floors and potted palms. Rooms are large, formal, and amply furnished, sometimes with Regency furniture; bathrooms are accented with mosaics and tubs inspired by those in ancient Rome. The concierges could give master classes to their less accomplished colleagues in the field.

Gran Vía de les Corts Catalanes 668, 08010 Barcelona. ✆ 93-510-1130. Fax 93-318-0148. www. ritzbcn.com. 125 units. 190€–505€ ($218–$580) double; from 300€ ($336) suite. AE, DC, MC, V. Parking 22€ ($25). Metro: Passeig de Gràcia. **Amenities:** Restaurant; bar; health club; concierge; salon; 24-hr. room service; in-room massage; babysitting; same-day laundry service and dry cleaning. *In room:* A/C, TV/VCR, dataport, minibar, hair dryer, safe.

Expensive

Condes de Barcelona ★   This fine old mansion on a corner of Barcelona's most glamorous avenue was stripped to the walls in 1988, and a postmodern minimalist interior was installed. Business was so good after the Olympic Games that the hotel opened a 74-room annex on the opposite corner. The annex lacks the style of the original but has better rooms. Some of the rooms in the original building are showing wear, but all have soundproof windows. The handsome marble bathrooms are well equipped with such extras as makeup mirrors, and some have whirlpool baths. There's a nonsmoking floor.

Passeig de Gràcia 73–75, 08008 Barcelona. ✆ 93-467-4786. Fax 93-467-4785. www.condesdebarcelona. com. 183 units. 187€–238€ ($215–$274) double; from 410€ ($470) suite. AE, DC, MC, V. Parking 16€ ($18). Metro: Passeig de Gràcia. **Amenities:** Restaurant; bar; outdoor pool; fitness center; concierge; limited room service; same-day laundry service and dry cleaning. *In room:* A/C, TV, minibar, dataport, hair dryer, safe.

Moderate/Expensive

Derby/Gran Derby These twin hotels are located in a peaceful neighborhood about 2 blocks south of the busy intersection of Avinguda Diagonal and Avinguda Sarría and the nightlife district around Plaça Francesc Macià. The Derby has 116 conventional rooms, and the Gran Derby (across the street) boasts 12 duplex suites among its 41 units, many of which have small balconies overlooking a flowered courtyard. Drinking and dining facilities are located in the Derby. Rooms and suites are outfitted with simple furniture in a variety of styles, and each is comfortable and quiet.

Loreto 21–25, and Loreto 28, 08029 Barcelona. ☎ 800/888-4747 in the U.S., or 93-322-3215. Fax 93-410-0862. www.derbyhotels.es. 141 units. 80€–236€ ($92–$270) double; from 115€ ($132) suite. AE, DC, MC, V. Parking 14€ ($16). Metro: Hospital Clínic. **Amenities:** 2 restaurants; bar; outdoor pool; concierge; limited room service; same-day laundry service and dry cleaning. *In room:* A/C, TV, dataport, minibar, hair dryer, safe.

Gallery Hotel ★★ Perched at the top of the Passeig de Gràcia, this super-stylish, ultramodern hotel is a perfect base for attacking the shops of both the Eixample and Grácia. The spare, spacious rooms have an almost Asian feel to them, with furnishings in red and black, firm beds, and big bathtubs. Service is impeccable.

Rosselló 249, 08008 Barcelona. ☎ 93-415-9911. Fax 93-415-9184. www.galleryhotel.com. 110 units. 118€–254€ ($136–$292) double. AE, DC, MC, V. Metro: Diagonal. **Amenities:** Restaurant; bar; gym; sauna; concierge; business center; limited room service; same-day laundry service and dry cleaning. *In room:* A/C, TV, dataport, minibar, hair dryer, safe.

Moderate

Astoria *Value* Another property from the growing Derby chain, the 1954 Astoria has a between-the-wars facade that makes it appear older than it is. The high ceilings, geometric designs, and brass-studded detailings in the gracious public areas hint of Moorish Andalusia. Rooms are soundproof and feature the warmth of exposed cedar as well as elegant modern accessories.

París 203, 08036 Barcelona. ☎ 800/888-4747 in the U.S., or 93-209-83-11. Fax 93-202-30-08. www.derbyhotels.es. 117 units. 85€–110€ ($98–$127) double. AE, DC, MC, V. Metro: Diagonal. **Amenities:** Cafe; bar; modest exercise room; sauna; concierge; limited room service; same-day laundry service and dry cleaning. *In room:* A/C, TV, minibar, hair dryer, safe.

NORTHERN NEIGHBORHOODS
Very Expensive

Gran Hotel La Florida ★★★ Perched on top of a mountain at the northern edge of town, this new hotel in a 1925 building is a surfeit of gorgeous views, perfect service, and unforgettable food. The restaurant, sun deck, and pool look out on the entire city of Barcelona, right down to the Mediterranean Sea. The spacious rooms are outfitted with cloudlike beds and plasma TVs. Service is impeccable, provided by a multinational staff who jump at the chance to make your trip more enjoyable.

The La Florida is on Tibidabo, best known for its amusement park. To get to the hotel from central Barcelona, hop on a complimentary car shuttle (available on demand), hail a taxi (10€/$11), or take an awkward bus-train combination—but any way you go the trip is worth it.

Vallvidrera 83–93, 08035 Barcelona. ☎ 93-259-3000. Fax 93-259-3001. www.hotellaflorida.com. 74 units. 310€–585€ ($356–$673) double; from 650€ ($748) suite. Breakfast 25€ ($29). AE, DC, MC, V. **Amenities:** Restaurant; 2 bars; nightclub; indoor/outdoor pool; gym; spa; business center; salon; 24-hr. room service; same-day laundry service and dry cleaning. *In room:* A/C, TV, minibar, hair dryer, safe.

Moderate

Hotel Silver ★ *Finds*   A little bit of adventurousness is rewarded here: Two subway stops from the Eixample, in an attractive neighborhood of hip bars and pubs, is this charming, affordable, family run hotel with kitchenettes in every room. The rooms vary widely, from cozy little nooks with older furnishings to shiny renovated units with blond wood furnishings, convection ovens, and spacious terraces. The back garden is a perfect place to sip your morning coffee. The staff bends over backward to help, and reservations manager Dafne Benedito speaks perfect English; she'll be happy to describe the rooms in detail for you.

Bretón de los Herreros 26, 08012 Barcelona. ☎ **93-218-9100.** Fax 93-416-1447. www.hotelsilver.com. 49 units. 72€–120€ ($83–$138) double. Breakfast 6.50€ ($7.45). Parking 11€ ($13). AE, DC, MC, V. Metro: Fontana. **Amenities:** Bar; limited room service; laundry service; free Internet access in lobby. *In room:* A/C, TV, kitchen, safe.

VILA OLIMPICA
Very Expensive

Arts ★★★   This deluxe hotel is the only lodging in Barcelona that gives the Ritz serious competition—which makes sense, because the Arts is a Ritz-Carlton hotel. The hotel occupies part of a postmodern tower marked by a huge Frank Gehry sculpture of a fish above the terrace facing the sea. The location is about 2.5km (1½ miles) east of Barcelona's historic core, adjacent to the sea and the Olympic Port. The decor is contemporary and elegant, and both the public and private areas are filled with contemporary art. Views from the rooms sweep the skyline and the Mediterranean. The multinozzle showers are a truly uplifting experience.

Marina 19–21, 08005 Barcelona. ☎ **800/241-3333** in the U.S., or 93-221-1000. Fax 93-221-1070. www. ritzcarlton.com. 482 units. 230€–630€ ($265–$725) double; from 590€ ($679) suite. AE, DC, MC, V. Parking 20€ ($23). Metro: Ciudadela–Vila Olímpica. **Amenities:** 4 restaurants; 2 bars; outdoor and indoor pools; health club and spa; concierge; business center; salon; 24-hr. room service; in-room massage; babysitting; same-day laundry service and dry cleaning. *In room:* A/C, TV, CD player, minibar, hair dryer, safe.

WHERE TO DINE
CIUTAT VELLA (OLD CITY)
Expensive

Casa Leopoldo ★ SEAFOOD   This surprisingly sophisticated restaurant in the somewhat seedy Barri Xínes has thrived since 1929. It offers some of the freshest seafood in town, and caters to a loyal clientele. Pictographic tiles and bullfighting paraphernalia constitute much of the traditional decor. There's a thriving tapas bar in front, plus two dining rooms, one slightly more formal than the other. Specialties include stuffed oxtail; roast *merluza* (hake) and *rape* (monkfish) with a *sofrito* of garlic and shrimp; and baby eels boiled in oil—a pricey delicacy. An enduring specialty is the enormous platter of fish and shellfish, prepared only for two.

Sant Rafael 24 (near Carrer de la Riereta). ☎ **93-441-3014.** Reservations advised. Main courses 11€–48€ ($13–$55); *menú del día* 37€ ($43) dinner. AE, DC, MC, V. Tues–Sat 1:30–4pm and 9–11pm; Sun 1:30–4pm. Closed Aug and Holy Week. Metro: Liceu.

Restaurant Hofmann ★ CATALAN/INTERNATIONAL   This restaurant is, in effect, a classroom of a demanding cooking school. The chefs, working under close professorial supervision, are all students. Don't take that to mean that the food is in any way amateurish. On the contrary, it is some of the most creative cuisine in Barcelona, full of twists and surprises. Trendy foams appear as garnish, and fish is fashionably underdone. Menus change every 2 months, with frequent daily specials. Expect such items as foie gras wrapped in puff pastry, ragout of crayfish with green risotto, and steak braised in Rioja wine and served with a confit of shallots and a gratin of potatoes. Celebrities have discovered the place—Mel Gibson, John Travolta, and Kevin Costner among them.

Argenteria 74–78 (at Plaça de Santa María). ✆ **93-319-5889**. www.hofmann-bcn.com. Reservations strongly advised. Main courses 9€–36€ ($10–$41); *menú del día* 30€ ($34) lunch. AE, DC, MC, V. Mon–Fri 1:30–3pm and 9–11pm. Metro: Jaume I.

Moderate

Agut ★★ SPANISH   If it weren't for Agut's location in a dark corner of the Gothic Quarter, you might not be able to get in at all. As it is, be there when the doors open to have a chance at a table if you don't have reservations. The chefs give all their attention to delicately balancing ingredients and allowing every flavor to take its bow. Their precision shows up even in salads, such as young basil and arugula leaves with toasted pine nuts and croutons on a bed of diced tomatoes, draped with slivers of smoked fish. The beef is superb—look for *filetitos de buey con salsa trufa* (beef filets with truffle sauce) with *trumpetas de la muerte* (black mushrooms). Around since 1924, the restaurant occupies several rooms on two floors with wooden wainscoting, marble floors, and early-1900s paintings.

Gignàs 16 (a block south of the main post office). ✆ **93-315-1709**. Reservations strongly advised. Main courses 17€–19€ ($20–$22). DC, MC, V. Tues–Sun 1:30–4pm; Tues–Sat 9pm–midnight. Metro: Barceloneta.

Can Culleretes CATALAN   Founded in 1786 as a pastry shop, Barcelona's oldest restaurant is located in the Gothic Quarter. The restaurant retains many original architectural features, with wooden beams overhead and a long bas-relief mural in wood depicting folkloric Catalunya. Every last dish on the menu is a Catalan standard, making this a good place to learn what the simple traditional form of this regional cuisine is all about. Just don't expect novelty. Rabbit with garlic mayo is typical, as is the sausage *butifarra* with beans. From October to January, game is featured, including *perdiz* (partridge).

Quintana 5 (between Fernando and Boquería). ✆ **93-317-6485**. Reservations suggested. Main courses 6€–16€ ($6.90–$18), *menú del día* 14€ ($16) lunch. DC, V. Tues–Sun 1:30–4pm; Tues–Sat 9–11pm. Closed 3 weeks in July. Metro: Liceu. Bus: 14 or 59.

El Gran Café SPANISH   The tobacco-brown ceiling of this restaurant is high enough to accommodate 4.5m (15-ft.) windows and a dining balcony over the service bar. The building is 19th century, and the restaurant has been given a Belle Epoque appearance. A piano player adds to the mood in the evening, when the crowd has a polished look. Fish and game dominate the menu, but specific ingredients are changed frequently, a sign that the chef follows the market. The fast-moving staff doesn't waste a step bringing the chef's creations to the table.

Avinyo 9 (a block south of Carrer Ferrán). ✆ **93-318-7986**. Main courses up to 10€–20€ ($12–$23); *menú del día* 11€ ($13). AE, DC, MC, V. Daily 1–4:30pm and 7:30pm–12:30am. Metro: Liceu or Jaume I.

Estrella de Plata ★★ SPANISH   For tapas elevated well beyond the traditional norm, it is next to impossible to equal, let alone surpass, this tony tavern near the harbor. Everything is wonderfully fresh, and much of it is made to order. Dishes are either upgraded versions of common recipes—*ensaladilla rusa* or *gambas* with aioli—or utterly new creations, such as the cylinder of barely poached shredded cod laid over salmon, tomatoes, and onions; or the artichoke heart baked with a soft quail egg inside and dusted with caviar. There is no menu; instead the specialties that are not displayed on the bar are described by a waiter or waitress, some of whom speak English. There's only one dessert, a tiny square of chocolate served on a bit of toast with a sauce tinged with olive oil and cocoa powder. Service could be faster.

Plaça del Palau 13 (north of Passeig d'Isabel II). ℂ 93-268-0635. Tapas and *raciónes* 7€–10€ ($8.05–$12). MC, V. Mon 8–11:30pm; Tues–Sat 1–4:30pm and 8–11:30pm. Closed last 2 weeks in Aug. Metro: Barceloneta.

Flo *Kids* FRENCH/CATALAN   The dining room is a sprawling, brightly lit, palm-filled replica of a Left Bank brasserie. Everyone is welcome, be they kids, tourists, execs, oldsters, or families visiting from the suburbs. The waitstaff is adroit and unflappable, even when a child gets whiny. Menu items are equally divided between specialties from the bistro traditions of France and those of Catalonia. French-derived items include fresh foie gras and large platters of Alsatian *choucroute* (sauerkraut). Catalan specialties include *mariscado* (shellfish stew) and *rissoto de calamares en su tinta* (squid served in its own ink). Keep this place in mind for dinner after a concert at the nearby Palau de la Música, or for Sunday, when most restaurants are closed.

Jonqueras 10 (near Laietana). ℂ **93-319-3102**. www.bcn-guide.com/flo. Main courses 11€–34€ ($13–$39); *menú del día* 16€ ($18) or 21€ ($24). AE, DC, MC, V. Sun–Thurs 1–4pm and 8:30pm–12:30am; Fri–Sat 1–4pm and 8:30pm–1am. Metro: Urquinaona.

Les Quinze Nits ☆ MEDITERRANEAN   As Barcelona restaurant prices have increased over the past few years, Les Quinze Nits has kept theirs down, making this a much better deal than in the past. A large front room overlooks an enclosed plaza, with tables out under the loggia most of the year. A smaller, quieter room in back suits couples who don't need to be seen. The earnest young staff swiftly brings fare like spinach-filled cannelloni under a blanket of melted cheese, and traditional Catalan *butifarra* sausage with white beans. Vegetarian dishes include a plate of grilled vegetables and a mushroom salad with cheese and grilled asparagus.

Plaça Reial 6 (east of La Rambla). ℂ 93-317-3075. Main courses 4.45€–9.95€ ($5–$11); *menú del día* 6.95€ ($8). AE, MC, V. Daily 1–3:30pm and 8:30–11:30pm. Metro: Liceu.

Pitarra ☆ SPANISH   Pitarra occupies the former home/watch shop of the prolific and much-honored 19th-century playwright/poet Frederic Soler Hubert (pseudonym: Pitarra). There are many antique clocks on display, some that hardly look like timepieces. Express interest in the surroundings, and Jaume, the partner who runs the front, may bring you a complimentary flute of Catalan cava, a sparkling wine (his brother Marc is the chef). The atmosphere is friendly, the service swift, and the food hearty. Look for game dishes in winter, like jugged wild boar in a sauce perfumed by bitter chocolate; or the most expensive item, woodcock with mushrooms.

Avinyo 56 (south of Carrer Ferrán). ℂ **93-301-1647**. Main courses 7€–22€ ($8.05–$25); *menú del día* 9€ ($10) (lunch only). MC, V. Mon–Sat 1–4pm and 8:30–11pm. Closed Aug. Metro: Liceu or Jaume I.

Taxidermista ☆ CATALAN/INTERNATIONAL   While it's named for the business of a previous tenant, you'll be the one stuffed. The creative kitchen provides worthy antidotes to usually vegetable-free Spanish meals. Ringing the couscous and lamb at the center of its plate, for example, are discreet portions of chickpeas, zucchini, carrots, and potatoes, with a small pitcher of broth and a spoonful of hot sauce on the side. A tasty little *aperitivo* (say, a pig's foot stuffed with duck confit) arrives with your drink order. The setting is an effective blend of 19th-century architecture and hand-hewn beams with postindustrial lighting.

Plaça Reial 8. ℂ **93-412-4536.** Main courses 8.30€–17€ ($9.60–$19). AE, DC, MC, V. Dining room Tues–Sun 1:30–4pm and 8:30pm–12:30am; tapas bar Tues–Sun noon–1am. Metro: Liceu.

Inexpensive

Biocenter VEGETARIAN This is Barcelona's largest and best-known vegetarian restaurant, a funky, countercultural sort of place on one of the better streets in the hip Raval. Meals are served in two ground-floor dining rooms. Take a tray and plate and fill up first at the self-service soup and salad bar. A waiter or waitress brings your choice of four main courses, which typically include a pasta, a rice dish, a vegetable tart, and something else. After eating, you pay at the cash register on the honor system.

Pintor Fortuny 25 (west of La Rambla). ℂ **93-301-4583.** Main courses 5€–7.25€ ($5.75–$8.35). No credit cards. Restaurant Mon–Sat 1–5pm. Bar Mon–Sat 9am–11pm. Metro: Plaça de Catalunya.

Irati TAPAS One of the latest food crazes to take hold of the city is a subcategory of tapas that hail from the Basque Country—*País Vasco*—in the north-central part of the country. Up there, they pin piles of delectable toppings to thick slices of bread with toothpicks and call them *pintxos,* not tapas. The possibilities are endless, from sardines to sweet peppers to sausages, and on and on. You simply ask for a plate and go down the bar to select as many toppings as you wish from the trays and platters arrayed there. Order a *copa* of the fizzy Basque wine and the staff will pour it from above their heads into a glass held .9m (3 ft.) below. To tote up your check, they count your toothpicks. (No fair throwing them away.)

Cardenal Casañas 17 (between La Rambla and Plaça de Pi). ℂ **93-302-3084.** Pintxos 1.10€ ($1.20). No credit cards. Daily noon–1am. Metro: Liceu.

La Dolça Hermína ✦ MEDITERRANEAN This stylish space doesn't *look* as if it qualifies as a budget choice, and the fashionable people lined up for tables might not seem likely patrons. But it's easy to walk away from lunch here with your wallet only $10 lighter. La Dolça Hermína offers simply sauced, handsome interpretations of Catalan classics like cannelloni and sausage with white beans; the food isn't too rich, and lights up with little bursts of flavors, like the bright sprinkling of cherry tomatoes in the ham-and-green-bean salad. The menu lists several vegetarian dishes, too. Given the high volume, the service is swift and understandably impersonal.

Magdalenes 27 (near the intersection of Vía Laietana and Carrer Comtal). ℂ **93-317-0676.** Main courses 4.45€–9.90€ ($5.10–$11). AE, DC, MC, V. Daily 1–3:45pm and 8:30–11:30pm. Metro: Urquinaona.

Senyor Parellada ✦ SPANISH Masonry arches in the dining room give this seafood-focused bistro next door to the Banys Orientales hotel (p. 932) a Middle Eastern feel, but the menu is Spanish through and through. Expect a wide range of seafood, such as baked monkfish with mustard and garlic sauce, and the occasional meat dish, such as roasted rack of lamb or stuffed cannelloni. Each menu item is labeled with the region of Spain where it's most popular, and the chefs turn out admirably precise renditions.

Argenteria 37 (east of Via Leitana). ℂ **93-310-5094.** Main courses 4.45€–14€ ($5.10–$16). AE, MC, V. Mon–Sat 1–4pm and 8:30pm–midnight. Reservations recommended. Metro: Jaume I.

DIAGONAL AND ABOVE
Very Expensive

Botafumeiro ★★ SEAFOOD   Widely regarded as Barcelona's best seafood restaurant, this is where the king of Spain comes for his fish. The menu is stacked with dozens of preparations of fish, mussels, clams, lobster, scallops, and other sea life. Whether grilled, fried, or served in paella, the fish is always fresh and often heartbreakingly simple, showcasing the beauty of Galician seafood. The *Mariscos Botafumeiro* specialty is a grand parade of all the shellfish owner Moncho Neira can get his hands on. Don't come here if you intend to eat anything other than fish, though a few meat dishes do lurk at the edges of the menu. White-jacketed waiters, always snapping to attention, make you feel like royalty. If the prices here are too high, Neira owns several other restaurants in town; grilled seafood is the specialty at **Moncho's Barcelona,** Traverssera de Grácia 44–46 (© **93-414-6622;** www.monchos.com).

Gran de Grácia 81. © **93-218-4230.** Reservations recommended. Main courses 21€–60€ ($24–$69). AE, DC, MC, V. Daily 1pm–1am. Metro: Fontana.

Drolma ★★ FRENCH/SPANISH   The setting here meets the high expectations fostered by the glowing reviews this trendsetter has garnered since the day it opened. The lamps are by Phillipe Starke, the china is Rosenthal, and the glasses are Baccarat. A squad of scrupulously trained male and female servers tends to your needs. They'll wheel over a cart of wines and offer any of them as an aperitif. Following that, they bring not one but two *aperitivos*—Spanish for *amuse-bouche*—an airy little dumpling, maybe, or a shot glass of crabmeat in basil oil. That's only a hint of what's to come. There's the salad with four quail eggs and four chunks of grilled foie gras, the potato soup with mushrooms and slivered truffles, the glazed goat, the lamb—some dishes even come with second helpings. The restaurant has a faint aura of corporate calm, but the bravura display of skill and largesse is not soon forgotten by serious diners.

In the Hotel Majestic, Passeig de Grácia 68. © **93-496-7710.** www.hotelmajestic.es/eng/res02.htm. Main courses 29€–43€ ($33–$49). AE, DC, MC, V. Mon–Sat 1–3:30pm and 8:30–11pm. Closed Aug. Metro: Passeig de Grácia.

Neichel ★★★ MEDITERRANEAN   Years ago, Alsatian-born Jean Louis Neichel came to Barcelona and melded French techniques with Catalan ingredients to create a cuisine all his own. Manipulating an array of ingredients that border on perfection, he employs a palette that features olive oil and distilled natural juices instead of the butter and cream of his homeland. Neichel displays a wizardry that manages to produce both pretty plates and supernal marriages of flavor and texture. With his artistry at the stove and his obsession with every detail of service, this is a high-wire act that is a privilege to witness. Nothing stays on the menu for long, so there isn't much point in listing dishes. Just put yourself in his hands. The *menú degustación* is the way to go. Save room for the memorable cheese tray.

Beltran i Rózpide 1 (off av. de Pedralbes). © **93-203-8408.** Reservations advised. Main courses 21€–39€ ($24–$45); *menú degustación* 65€ ($75) AE, DC, MC, V. Mon–Fri 1:30–3:30pm; Mon–Sat 8:30–11pm. Closed Aug and holidays. Metro: María Christina.

Expensive

La Dama ★★ CATALAN/INTERNATIONAL   Long possessed of a Michelin star, this stylish and adroitly managed place fully deserves the honor. A marvelously baroque elevator carries diners to the main floor of a splendid *modernista* building. Sinuously carved lines decorate the door panels, cornices, walls, and etched glass. Tables are set far enough apart for intimate conversation. If you arrive during the fall wild mushroom season, get a plate of the fungi, four or five kinds, sautéed lightly with garlic. Monkfish in an earthy sauce of thumb-size squid and black olives is another winner. An extra selling point is that La Dama is open for lunch and dinner every day of the week, unlike most in this high-echelon category.

Av. Diagonal 423 (at Eric Granados). (℃ **93-202-0686.** Reservations required. Main courses 24€–40€ ($28–$46); *menu degustación* 56€ ($64) and 73€ ($83). AE, DC, MC, V. Daily 1:30–3:30pm and 8:30–11pm. Metro: Provença.

Tragaluz ⊛ CREATIVE CATALAN Down an alley connecting Rambla de Catalunya and Passeig de Gràcia, this intelligently conceived enterprise broke rules and caused a stir when it opened back in the late 1980s. The overall design was startlingly new at the time. Downstairs, you'll find a bar and what amounts to a high-style fast-food emporium called Tragarrapid; upstairs is a more ambitious dining room with two tiers under an expansive skylight. You're not likely to be disappointed whichever level you choose—the light, casual, inexpensive meals downstairs, or the inventive, leisurely repasts upstairs. Consider hake with tomato sauce, or grilled sardines on sweet pepper couscous. Or try a selection from the menu of low-calorie dishes.

Passatage de la Concepció 5 (off Passeig de Gràcia). (℃ **93-487-0621.** www.grupotragaluz.com. Reservations advised for main dining room. Main courses 13€–22€ ($15–$25); *menu degustación* 49€ ($56). AE, DC, MC, V. Daily 1:30–4pm and 8:30pm–midnight (until 1am Thurs–Sat). Metro: Diagonal.

LA RIBERA & BARCELONETA
Moderate/Expensive

El Suquet de l'Almirall ⊛⊛ SEAFOOD The boulevard bordering the old fishermen's quarter is lined with seafood restaurants, most raucous and gaudy, often with sidewalk barkers trying to snare pedestrians. This retreat is the classiest of the strip, with tables on the terrace, where you can peer through palm trees at the boats in the harbor. The dishes served at the row of seafood restaurants aren't all that different in basic recipe, but the execution here is superior to that of most of the immediate neighbors, resulting in lighter, less oily food. Representative is the creamy fish chowder laced with *romescu,* a tangy Catalan sauce. For a memorable repast, leap for the *menú ciego,* composed of seven tapas and a final paella-like rice dish. If you head in that direction, you'll encounter red peppers draped with anchovies, puffy cod fritters, baby squid on potato slices, and a small piece of grilled tuna scattered with pine nuts (chopsticks provided, for some reason).

Passeig Joan de Borbó 65. (℃ **93-221-6233.** Reservations advised weekends. Main courses 11€–19€ ($13–$22); *menú ciego* 32€ ($37). DC, MC, V. Mon 8–11:30pm; Tues–Sat 1:30–4pm and 8:30–11:30pm. Closed holiday evenings. Metro: Barceloneta.

7 Portes CATALAN In business since 1836, these "Seven Doors" open into a food emporium that is a lunchtime favorite for businesspeople (the Stock Exchange is across the way) and an evening favorite for the anyone who enjoys the peachy glow of the hanging lamps and the ministrations of the piano player. Known for its paellas, changed daily, there are also regional dishes that include grilled rabbit, fresh herring with onions and potatoes, a wide selection of super-fresh fish and oysters, and an herb-laden stew of black beans with pork. Portions are enormous.

Passeig Isabel II 14. (℃ **93-319-3033.** www.setportes.com. Reservations required weekends. Main courses 9€–48€ ($10–$55). AE, DC, MC, V. Daily 1pm–1am. Metro: Barceloneta.

Inexpensive

Cal Pep SPANISH   This fine little tapas bar just south of the Picasso Museum is popular with both locals and tourists. There are 20 seats at the long marble bar and a tiny sit-down back room. While you'll probably get a seat if you arrive at 1:30pm during the week, expect a wait after 2pm and on weekends. (If it *is* full, there are two other cafes on the same square.) There's no menu—the manager will tell you what's available and use his lapel mike to relay your order to the kitchen when it gets busy. What comes forth from the kitchen doesn't stray far from the traditional repertoire, but it's so much better prepared. This is the way *pescados fritos* (fried fish), *almejas con jamón* (steamed clams with ham), and *pan con tomate* (Catalan tomato bread) rarely taste in less skilled hands. The bunch behind the bar joke and laugh with patrons and each other all the while.

Plaça de les Olles 8. ⓒ **93-310-7961.** Reservations required for dining room. Main courses and tapas 3.60€–13€ ($4–$14). *Menu del día* 15€ ($17). AE, DC, MC, V. Tues–Sat 1:15–4pm and 8–11:30pm; Mon 8–11:30pm. Closed Aug. Metro: Jaume I.

SEEING THE SIGHTS

Spain's second-largest city is also its most cosmopolitan. Barcelona is more European and internationalist than Madrid. The city is filled with landmark buildings and important museums, including Antoni Gaudí's Sagrada Família, Museu Picasso, the Gothic cathedral, and La Rambla, the famous tree-lined promenade cutting through the heart of the old city from Plaça de Catalunya to the harbor.

SIGHTSEEING SUGGESTIONS FOR FIRST-TIME VISITORS

If You Have 1 Day Spend the morning exploring the **Barri Gótic (Gothic Quarter).** In the afternoon visit the **Museu Picasso** in the Ribera quarter, which is filled with Renaissance mansions and is the site of the notable **Santa María del Mar church.** Return to the Plaça de Catalunya for a walk down **La Rambla.** To cap your day, take the funicular to the top of **Tibidabo** for a panoramic view of Barcelona and its harbor. Take the 10-minute walk to the **Gran Hotel La Florida** for a drink before heading back down.

If You Have 2 Days On day 2, see Antoni Gaudí's unfinished masterpiece, **La Sagrada Família.** Have a seafood lunch in **Barceloneta** and, in the afternoon, stroll up **Passeig de Gràcia** past the city's other masterpieces of modernist architecture. Explore **Montjuïc** and visit the **Museu d'Art de Catalunya** and the nearby **Poble Espanyol,** a village with replicas of regional architecture created for the 1929 World's Fair. End the day with a meal of paella at **Set Portes,** one of the oldest restaurants in the city.

If You Have 3 Days On day 3, take the train to the monastery of **Montserrat,** about 45 minutes outside of Barcelona, to see the venerated Black Virgin and the art museum, and to hear the famous 50-member boys' choir.

If You Have 4 or 5 Days On day 4, take a morning walk through the **Eixample** district, enjoying the upscale window-shopping and great 19th-century architecture. Have lunch at one of the tapas bars along the Passeig de Gràcia. After lunch, visit La Pedrera, Gaudí's signature apartment house. On day 5, take another excursion from the city. If you're interested in history, visit the former Roman city of **Tarragona** to the south. If you want to unwind on a beach, head south to **Sitges.**

THE TOP ATTRACTIONS

Catedral de Barcelona (La Seu) ☆☆   Begun in the late 13th century and completed in the mid–15th century (except for the main facade, which dates from the late 19th), this Gothic cathedral attests to the splendor of medieval Barcelona. Its main points of interest are the central choir, the 14th-century alabaster crypt of Santa Eulàlia, and the *Cristo de Lepanto,* whose twisted torso allegedly dodged a bullet during the naval battle of the same name. Do see the adjoining **cloister** ☆, with access down on the right from the front entrance. It encloses palm and magnolia trees, flowering medlars, a fountain erupting from a moss-covered rock, and a gaggle of live geese, said to be reminders of the Roman occupation (or of the Apostles or the virtuous St. Eulàlia, depending on the various convictions of writers and guides). On the steps at noon on Sunday, a band with ancient instruments plays the eerily haunting *sardana,* the music of the hallowed Catalan folk dance.

Plaça de la Seu. ☎ 93-315-3555. www.catedralbcn.org. Cathedral and cloister free admission; choir 1.50€ ($1.70); Museu de la Catedral 1€ ($1.15). Cathedral daily 9am–1:30pm and 4–7pm; museum daily 10am–1pm and 5–7pm. Metro: Jaume I. Bus: 17, 19, 40, or 45.

Fundació Joan Miró ☆☆   A tribute to the Catalan lyrical surrealist Joan Miró, this contemporary museum follows his work from 1914 to 1978 and includes many of his sculptures, paintings, and multimedia tapestries. Even the roof displays his whimsical sculptures as well as bestows impressive city vistas. There's also a gallery of "Miró's contemporaries"—"minor" artists like Henry Moore. Temporary exhibits of other contemporary artists are held on a regular basis. From the top of the Montjuïc funicular, turn left and walk down to the museum.

Parc de Montjuïc. ☎ 93-443-9470. www.bcn.fjmiro.es. Admission 7.20€ ($8.30) adults, 3.90€ ($4.50) students, free for children under 15. Temporary exhibitions 3.60€ ($4.15) adults, 1.80€ ($2.05) students. July–Sept Tues–Wed and Fri–Sat 10am–8pm, Thurs 10am–9:30pm, Sun and holidays 10am–2:30pm; Oct–June Tues–Sat 10am–7pm, Sun and holidays 10am–2:30pm. Funicular: Montjuïc. Bus: 50 from Plaça de Espanya.

La Sagrada Família ☆☆   If you see but one monument in Barcelona, this should be it. Looking like something halfway between a fever dream and a giant sandcastle, this *modernista* cathedral will be Europe's largest, with a 158m (525-ft.) central dome—*if* it's ever finished. In 1884, architect Antoni Gaudí i Cornet took over the then 2-year-old project and turned it into the ultimate statement of his flamboyant, surrealist vision. At the pinnacles of the completed towers, for example, are vivid mosaic sunbursts of gold and crimson, and much of the east facade appears to have melted under the blast of a giant blowtorch. Unfortunately, Gaudí died in 1926 after being run over by a tram and left no detailed plans. Construction has continued off and on, with different additions reflecting different eras, sometimes quite dissonantly (such as the aggressively Cubist sculptures on the west facade). As art critic Robert Hughes has written, Gaudí "is not someone with whom one can collaborate posthumously." One of the towers has an elevator that takes you up to a magnificent view. The crypt's **Museu del Temple** chronicles the cathedral's structural evolution.

Mallorca 401. ☎ 93-455-0247. www.sagradafamilia.org. Admission 8€ ($9.20) adults, 5€ ($5.75) students. Guided tour 3€ ($3.45) extra. Elevator 2€ ($2.30). Apr–Sept daily 9am–8pm; Oct–Mar daily 9am–6pm. Metro: Sagrada Família. Bus: 19, 33, 34, 43, 44, 50, or 51.

Museu Picasso ☆☆☆   Barcelona's most popular single attraction, this museum reveals much about the artist whose long, prolific career extended well beyond

Cubism. The paintings, drawings, engravings, and ceramics go all the way back to the artist's juvenilia, but the museum is light on his most famous later paintings—except for the series based on Velazquez' *Las Meninas,* on display here. The galleries in the original three Renaissance mansions have been expanded into two more adjoining palaces.

Montcada 15–23. ℂ 93-319-6310. www.museupicasso.bcn.es. Admission, permanent collection 5€ ($5.75) adults, 2.50€ ($2.90) seniors/students under 25, free for under 16; temporary exhibits up to 5€ ($5.75) extra. Free for everyone 1st Sun of every month. Tues–Sat and holidays 10am–8pm; Sun 10am–3pm. Metro: Jaume I.

MORE ATTRACTIONS

Casa Batlló ★★   As part of the 2002 citywide celebration of Gaudí, this, the architect's second-most important commission on the Passeig de Gràcia, was opened to public visits for the first time. Unlike La Pedrera (below), Gaudí didn't design this building from the ground up. Instead, he transformed an existing structure with a facade of shimmering tiles and a free-form roofline that evokes the scaly back of a dragon. The interior is just as striking. Inquire ahead to be certain it is still open.

Passeig de Gràcia 43 (corner of Aragó). ℂ 93-216-0306. www.casabatllo.es. Admission 10€ ($12). Mon–Sat 9am–2pm; Sun 9am–8pm. Metro: Passeig de Gràcia.

La Pedrera ★★   Formally the Casa Milà, the popular name of this apartment/office block means the "Stone Quarry." Antoni Gaudí didn't restrain himself here: the undulating exterior of carved stone gives the building the aspect of the lair of a mythical dragon, its balconies enclosed by freeform wrought iron. The top floor and an apartment are open to visitors. Don't miss the roof terrace, populated with highly sculptural chimneys and vents that might have been imagined by H. G. Wells.

Provença 261–265 (at the corner of Passeig de Gràcia). ℂ 90/240-0973. Admission to attic, terrace, and apartment, 7€ ($8.05). Daily 10am–8pm; guided tours daily at 4pm. Metro: Diagonal.

L'Aquàrium ★ *Kids*   This carefully conceived aquarium is one of the largest in Europe. It exhibits over 8,000 marine creatures of 450 species in 21 tanks. A highlight is the clear plastic tunnel where you glide on a moving walkway through a tank stocked with prowling sharks and gliding rays. The admission fee was recently boosted to truly fearsome levels.

On the Moll d'Espanya, in the harbor. ℂ 93-221-7474. www.aquariumbcn.com. Admission 14€ ($16) adults, 9.25€ ($11) seniors/children 4–12, free for children under 4. July–Aug daily 9:30am–11pm; June and Sept daily 9:30am–9:30pm; Oct–May daily 9:30am–9pm. Metro: Drassanes or Barceloneta. Bus: 14, 17, 19, 36, 38, 39, 40, 45, 57, 59, 64, 91, or 100.

Monument à Colom (Columbus Monument)   This waterfront landmark was erected in 1888 to commemorate Columbus's triumphant return after his first expedition to the New World. An 8m (25-ft.) bronze statue of the explorer surmounts the Victorian-era monument. Inside the iron column is a creaky elevator that ascends to a panoramic view.

Plaça Portal de la Pau. ℂ 93-302-5224. Admission 2€ ($2.30) adults, 1.30€ ($1.50) seniors/students 4–12, free for children under 4. June–Sept daily 9am–8:30pm; Oct–May daily 10am-6:30pm. Metro: Drassanes. Bus: 14, 36, 38, 57, 59, 64, or 91.

Poble Espanyol ★ *Kids*   This "village," executed for the 1929 World's Fair, houses examples of architectural styles found throughout Spain. After renovations and changes in operational philosophy, the once-stuffy open-air museum has become almost a village in its own right, with working artisans, dozens of crafts shops, restaurants, and assorted nightclubs and bars. Some visitors judge it a slightly kitschy theme park, but, in fact, the buildings are accurate full-size replicas of specific structures in the various regional styles of Spain. Nightclubs, discos, and restaurants take over in the evening; most stay open well into the early hours.

Marqués de Comillas, Montjuïc. © **93-508-6330.** www.poble-espanyol.com. Admission 5.95€ ($5.30) adults, 4.75€ ($4.25) students, 3.55€ ($3.15) seniors/students/children 7–14, free for children under 7. Mon 9am–8pm; Tues–Thurs 9am–2am; Fri–Sat 9am–4am; Sun 9am–midnight. Metro: Plaça de Espanya, then bus no. 61 or the free double-decker Poble Espanyol shuttle bus (on the half-hour).

MORE MUSEUMS

Fundació Antoni Tàpies ☆　Housed in a *modernista* building designed by Lluís Domènech i Muntaner and refurbished by his great-grandson in 1989, this museum continues the Barcelona tradition of honoring prominent native artists. Tàpies is thought by many to be the living heir to Miró and Picasso, and this exhibit space rotates examples of his work and that of younger Catalan artists. The tangle of tubing atop the building is a Tàpies sculpture that makes more sense when you realize it's called *Chair and Cloud.*

Aragó 255. © **93-487-0315.** www.fundaciotapies.org. Admission 4.20€ ($4.85) adults, 2.10€ ($2.40) seniors/students. Tues–Sun 10am–8pm. Metro: Passeig de Gràcia.

Museu Barbier-Mueller ☆　Dedicated by Queen Sofia in 1997, this collection contains 6,000 pieces of pre-Columbian sculpture. It contains religious, funerary, and ornamental objects of considerable variety, in stone and ceramics and, in some cases, jade. Richest are the exhibits relating to Mayan culture, originating in 1000 B.C. Descriptions are in English.

Montcada 12–14. © **93-310-4516.** Admission 3€ ($3.45) adults, 1.50€ ($1.75) seniors/students, free for under age 16. Free to all 1st Sat of the month 3–6pm. Tues–Sat 10am–6pm; Sun and holidays 10am–3pm. Metro: Jaume I. Bus: 17, 39, 40, 45, or 51.

Museu Frederic Marès　This repository of medieval sculpture is located just behind the cathedral, with a pleasant shaded courtyard in front. Housed in an ancient palace that's impressive in its own right, it displays hundreds of polychrome ecclesiastical sculptures.

Plaça de Santa Iú 5–6. © **93-310-5800.** www.museumares.bcn.es. Admission 3€ ($3.45) adults, 1.50€ ($1.75) students, free for children under 16. Free for all 1st Sun of month. Tues–Sat 10am–7pm; Sun 10am–3pm. Metro: Jaume I. Bus: 17, 19, or 45.

Museu d'Historia de la Ciutat (Museum of the History of the City) ☆　Housed in a 15th-century mansion that was moved here stone by stone from Carrer Mercaders, several blocks away, this museum features **excavations** ☆ of Roman and Visigothic remains below ground. On the upper floors are jumbled assortments of sculptures, weapons, ceramics, household implements, and more—a sort of municipal attic.

Plaça del Rei. © **93-315-1111.** www.museuhistoria.bcn.es. Admission 4€ ($4.60) adults, 2.50€ ($2.90) students/seniors, 2.75€ ($3.15) on nonholiday Wed; free for under 16. Free to all 1st Sat afternoon of the month. June–Sept Tues–Sat 10am–8pm; Sun and holidays 10am–3pm (the rest of the year closes 2–4pm). Metro: Jaume I.

Museu Marítim (Maritime Museum) ☆　Located in the Drassanes, the 14th-century Gothic royal shipyards, this museum's superb collection of maritime vessels and artifacts is distinguished by a full-size replica of Don Juan of

Austria's galleon. The baroque flagship of the Spanish and Italian fleet defeated a naval force of the Ottoman Empire in the 1571 Battle of Lepanto. There are also humbler fishing boats, intricate ship models, and a map owned by Amerigo Vespucci.

Av. de les Drassanes 1. (℡ 93-3301-1831. www.diba.es/mmaritim. Admission 5.40€ ($6.20) adults, 2.70€ ($3.10) seniors/students/children 7–16, free for children under 7. Free for all 1st Sat each month 3–6pm. Daily 10am–7pm. Metro: Drassanes.

Museu Nacional d'Art de Catalunya (MNAC) ✪ In this building—built for the 1929 World's Fair and redesigned inside by controversial Italian architect Gae Aulenti in the 1990s—is a collection of Catalan art from the Romanesque and Gothic periods as well as the 16th century to the 18th century, along with works by high-caliber non-Catalan artists like El Greco, Velázquez, Zurbarán, and Tintoretto. Pride of place goes to the sculptures and frescoes removed from the Romanesque churches strung across Catalunya's northern tier. The view of the city from the front steps is a bonus.

In the Palau Nacional, Parc de Montjuïc. (℡ 93-622-0375. www.mnac.es. Admission to permanent collection 4.80€ ($5.50) adults, 2.40€ ($2.75) seniors/students; extra fee for special exhibits. Free for everyone 1st Thurs of the month. Tues–Sat 10am–7pm; Sun and holidays 10am–2:30pm. Metro: Espanya.

Museu d'Art Contemporàni (MACBA) ✪ Much excitement attended the 1995 opening of this light-filled building by American architect Richard Meier. Standing in stark contrast to the 16th-century convent opposite and the surrounding tenements with laundry drying on their balconies, this museum has generated a renewal of the El Raval neighborhood. The permanent collection comprises about 1,300 paintings and sculptures from the late 1940s, including works by many Catalan and Spanish artists and a few by non-Spaniards like Calder and Dubuffet. To get here, walk 5 blocks west from the upper Rambla along Carrer Bonsucces, which changes to Elisabets.

Plaça de les Angels 1. (℡ 93-412-0810. www.macba.es. General admission 7€ ($8.05) adults, 5.50€ ($6.35) students, 3€ ($3.45) on nonholiday Wed. Mon-Fri 11am–7:30pm; Sat 10am–8pm; Sun and holidays 10am–3pm. Metro: Catalunya or Universitat.

Museu d'Art Modern del MNAC Despite its name, this museum focuses somewhat narrowly on the work of Catalan painters and sculptors during the *modernista* period (1880–1930), along with examples of furniture and decorative arts by craftspeople and designers of the time. Its importance has been markedly diminished by the Museu Nacional d'Art de Catalunya (see above), which has appropriated much of this museum's collection.

Plaça de les Armes, Parc de la Ciutadella. (℡ 93-319-5728. www.mnac.es. Admission 3€ ($3.45), 2.10€ ($2.40) seniors/students; free to all 1st Thurs of the month. Tues–Sat 10am–7pm; Sun and holidays 10am–2:30pm. Metro: Arc de Triomf.

PARKS & GARDENS

Parc Güell ✪, a fanciful park on the northern edge of Barcelona's inner core, is much more than green space. Begun by Antoni Gaudí as an upper-crust real-estate venture for his wealthy patron, Count Eusebi Güell, it was never completed. Only two houses were constructed, but Gaudí's whimsical creativity, seen in soaring columns that impersonate trees and splendid winding benches of broken mosaics, is on abundant display. The city took over the property in 1926 and turned it into a public park. Don't miss the ceramic mosaic lizard at the park's entrance stairway, the Hall of a Hundred Columns, and the panoramic views from the plaza above.

Tips **An Ancient Neighborhood to Explore**

The **Barri Gòtic** ✹✹ is Barcelona's old aristocratic quarter, parts of which have survived from the Middle Ages, and fragments of which have lasted from the Roman settlement here. To explore the Gothic Quarter's narrow streets and squares, start walking up Carrer del Carme, east of La Rambla. A nighttime stroll adds drama, but exercise caution. The buildings, for the most part, are austere and sober, and the cathedral is the crowning achievement. Roman ruins and the vestiges of 3rd-century walls add further interest. This area is packed full of details and attractions that are easy to miss, so take your time.

The **Parc de la Ciutadella** ✹ occupies the former site of a detested 18th-century citadel, some remnants of which remain. Here, you'll find the Museu d'Art Modern, the Museu de Zoología, the Museu de Geología, the regional Parliament, the zoo, and an ornate fountain that's in small part the work of the young Gaudí.

Another attraction, **Tibidabo** ✹, offers the best panoramic view of Barcelona. A funicular takes you up 490m (1,600 ft.) to the summit. A retro amusement park—with Ferris wheels and airplanes that spin over Barcelona—has been there since the thirties. There's also a church in this carnival-like setting called Santa Creu (Sacred Heart), plus bars and restaurants. Take the funicular uphill from Plaça John Kennedy.

ORGANIZED TOURS

Take advantage of the bargain **Bus Turístic** ✹ (www.tmb.net). A single ticket permits unlimited travel on these buses, many of them open-topped double-deckers. Originating at Plaça de Catalunya, the red bus makes two circular sweeps. Highlights of the northern route are the Parc Güell, La Sagrada Família, the base of Tibidabo, and the Monestir de Pedralbes. The southern circuit makes stops on Montjuïc, at the Port Olímpic, and in the Barri Gòtic. Together, they make 26 stops, and you can get off and reboard as often as you please. The buses run daily, about every 15 minutes in summer and every 30 minutes the rest of the year, 9am to 9:30pm. If you stay on the bus, without debarking, each tour takes about 2 hours. An all-day ticket is 15€ ($17), and a ticket good for 2 consecutive days is 19€ ($22), while one for children 4 to 12 years is 9€ ($10) for one day and 12€ ($14) for two. Admission is free for children under 4. You can buy tickets on the bus, and they come with a guidebook in six languages and vouchers providing discounts on entrance to attractions like the zoo and the Poble Espanyol. Multilingual guide/conductors announce stops and answer questions.

Children and adults enjoy **Las Golondrinas** (© **93-442-3106;** www.lasgolondrinas.com; Metro: Drassanes), the 30-minute round-trip boat ride from the Portal de la Pau, near the Monument à Colom, to the lighthouse on the harbor breakwater and back. The minivoyage offers close-up views of the maritime traffic and the skyline. While room has been made for pleasure craft, this is a working harbor, with tugs, cranes off-loading freighters, dry docks, and shipyards. The company also offers 2-hour cruises to the Forum 2004 area and back for 8.50€ ($9.75) adults, 6.10€ ($7) seniors and students, 3.70€ ($4.25) children 4 to 10, and free for children under 4. Departures are year-round at 11:30am and 1:30pm, with trips at 4:30, 6:30, and 8:30pm during warmer months.

THE SHOPPING SCENE
THE BEST SHOPPING STREETS

Barcelona's most beautiful shopping street is **Passeig de Gràcia.** Stroll this street from the Avinguda Diagonal (also called Avenida Diagonal) to the Plaça de Catalunya, and you'll pass some of Barcelona's most elegant boutiques. You'll also find interesting shops nearby in the Eixample on Avinguda Diagonal and Carrer de Balmes, and farther north in Gràcia on the Travessera de Gràcia and Carrer Verdi.

In the **old quarter,** the principal shopping streets are La Rambla, Carrer del Pi, Carrer de la Palla, and Avinguda Portal de l'Angel. Moving north in the Eixample are Passeig de Catalunya, Passeig de Gràcia, and Rambla de Catalunya.

THE BEST BUYS

El Corte Inglés is Spain's most prominent department store. Its main Barcelona emporium is at Plaça de Catalunya 14 (② 93-302-1212; www.elcorteingles.es; Metro: Catalunya), with a large new branch a block away on Portal de l'Angel. It stays open through the siesta period and has a full-size supermarket in the basement and a pleasant cafeteria/restaurant on the ninth floor. Up in the Eixample, the **Bulevard Rosa** (51–53 Passeig de Gràcia; www.bulevardrosa.com; no phone) is a floor-through mall of 110 shops, mostly midrange clothing boutiques.

For designer housewares and the best in Spanish contemporary furnishings, a good bet is **Vincón,** Passeig de Gràcia 96 (② 93-215-6050), housed in the former home of artist Ramón Casas. Various high-end shops on the Passeig de Gràcia and Avinguda Diagonalshowcase men's and women's fashions. Cutting-edge boutiques and nary a tourist are to be found on **Carrer Verdí** in the Grácia neighborhood, from the Plaça Revolució stretching about 6 blocks north and onto side streets. Pick up a shopping map from any of the Verdi boutiques.

In the city of Miró, Tàpies, and Picasso, art is a major business. There are dozens of galleries, especially in the Barri Gótic and around the Picasso Museum. In business since 1840, **Sala Parés,** Petritxol 5 (② 93-318-7020; www.salapares.com; Metro: Plaça de Catalunya), displays paintings in a two-story amphitheater; exhibitions change about once a month. **Galeria Maeght,** Montcada 25 (② 93-310-4245; www.maeght.com; Metro: Jaume I), occupies a mansion a few doors down from the Picasso Museum that's worth a visit for the architecture alone. Paintings, prints, and sculptures by Spanish and European artists are on view.

For antiques, drop by **El Bulevard des Antiquarius,** Passeig de Gràcia 55. This 70-unit complex, just off the city's most aristocratic avenues, has a huge collection of art and antiques assembled in a series of boutiques. Seekers after antiques should enjoy the open-air **Mercat Gòtic de Antigüedades** by the cathedral (Metro: Jaume I), held every Thursday from 9am to 8pm (except Aug), and more often during holiday periods.

Seeking out small specialty shops is a particular treat. A number of shops offer authentic ceramics from various regions of the country that are known for their pottery. Two worthwhile stops are **La Caixa de Frang,** Carrer Freneria (no phone; Metro: Jaume I), behind the cathedral; and **Itaca,** Carrer Ferrán (② 93-301-3044; Metro: Jaume I), near Plaça Sant Jaume.

ART Escudellers, Escudellers 5 (© **93-342-4164;** Metro: Drassanes), is a large space with individual stalls selling pottery and handicrafts of varying levels of aptitude. A potter demonstrates his work technique. **La Manual Alpargatera,** Avinyo 7 (© **93-301-0172;** Metro: Jaume I), is the best shop for the handmade espadrilles seen on dancers of the *sardana.* It offers many styles and also sells hats and folk art.

Angel Jobal, Princesa 38 (no phone; Metro: Jaume I), offers a variety of teas and spices, along with especially good prices on thread saffron, the world's costliest spice. Find it a block past the turn for the Picasso Museum. **La Boquería** just off the Rambla, officially the Mercat de Sant Josep, is Spain's most extensive, most fascinating market, purveying glistening-fresh produce, meats, cheeses, fish, and every imaginable edible daily. An open market of artisan food items, including cheeses, honey, vinegars, pâtés, fruit preserves, and quince pastes, is held on **Plaça del Pi** (Metro: Liceu) on Friday, Saturday, and Sunday.

BARCELONA AFTER DARK

Barcelona's nightlife runs from the campy burlesque of El Molino to the bizarre opulence of the Palau de la Música Catalana. For the latest information on concerts and other musical events, call the **Amics de la Música de Barcelona** at © **93-302-6870,** Monday through Friday from 10am to 1pm and 3 to 8pm. For information on the **Ballet Contemporáneo de Barcelona,** call © **93-322-1037.**

For a comprehensive list of evening activities, pick up a copy of the weekly *Guía del Ocio* or the entertainment guide offered with the Thursday edition of *El País.*

THE PERFORMING ARTS

The **Gran Teatre del Liceu,** La Rambla 51–59 (© **93-485-9913;** www.liceubarcelona.com; Metro: Liceu), is the traditional home to opera and ballet. It suffered a devastating fire in 1994 but has reopened after extensive renovations. The result is glorious, especially considering that only the walls were left standing after the fire. The decision was made to replicate the neobaroque interior, with lashings of gilt, intricate carvings, and swaths of brocade and velvet. Music lovers and ballet-goers will find more comfortable seats and better sightlines. The theater presents 8 to 12 operas every season and strives to make them accessible to a wide audience: Prices can be as low as 5.75€ ($6.60) for operas, concerts, ballets, and recitals. You can book tickets with credit cards from outside the country daily 10am to 10pm Barcelona time at © **93-274-6411.** In Barcelona, call © **90/253-3353** any time up to 3 hours before the performance desired.

A magnificent *modernista* concert hall, the **Palau de la Música Catalana,** Amadeu Vives 1 (© **93-295-7200;** www.palaumusica.org; Metro: Urquinaona), is the work of Catalan architect Lluís Domènech i Montaner, a rival of Antoni Gaudí. Its distinctive facade is a tour de force of brick, mosaic, and glass. Inside, the interplay of ceramic mosaics, stained glass, and a central skylight build to the stunning crescendo of massive carvings framing the stage. Many of the seats have limited sightlines, but this hall is devoted to music, not opera and dance, and even the cheapest corners enjoy superb sound. The Palau is home to the Orquestra Simfònica de Barcelona, one of whose directors is American Lawrence Foster, and hosts a variety of classical and jazz concerts and recitals. Tickets can cost anywhere from 5€ to over 70€ ($5.75–$81), depending on who's playing and how good your seat is. The box office is open Monday to Saturday 10am to 9pm.

Symphonic and chamber music has a new home at **L'Auditori,** Lepant 150 (© **93-247-9300;** www.auditori.org; Metro: Glories), with both large and small performance spaces. The Barcelona Symphony Orchestra, traveling groups, the Joven Orquestra de España (Young Orchestra of Spain), and string quartets all perform here. Tickets are 14€ to 43€ ($16–$49), half price for students. You can buy them outside the country with a credit card 24 hours a day at © **34/ 93-326-2946,** or inside Spain at 90/210-1212.

LIVE-MUSIC CLUBS

The clubs of the **Mas i Mas** group (www.masimas.com) are always a good bet for jazz, blues, or funk music, depending on the club and the date. Their most popular jazz club, **Jamboree,** Plaça Reial 17 (© **93-301-7564;** Metro: Liceu), is on a raucously diverse plaza off the lower Rambla. The cover charge can be anywhere from 3€ to 10€ ($3.45–$12), depending on who's playing; you descend to a vaulted brick cellar filled with young to middle-aged natives and tourists. Most shows start at 11pm. Arrive around 9:30pm and you'll probably get in free and might also catch the rehearsal.

Another Mas i Mas jazz outpost, **La Cova del Drac,** Vallmajor 33 (© **93-200-7032;** Metro: Muntaner or La Bonanova), is in a less intimidating neighborhood than most, with many other fun spots on nearby blocks. There's dancing here, too. It's open daily from 8pm to 3am, with a cover between 6€ and 12€ ($6.90–$14), including the first drink.

A popular old-timer is the **Harlem Jazz Club,** Comtessa de Sobradiel 8 (© **93-310-0755**), with live jazz nightly in all its permutations—flamenco fusion, Brazilian salsa, Afro-Caribbean, blues. Admission is free during the week, but costs 5€ ($5.75) on Friday, Saturday, and holidays.

Flamenco is best seen in Seville or Madrid, but if you aren't getting to those cities on your trip, **El Tablao de Carmen,** Arcs 9 in Poble Espanyol (© **93-325-6895;** www.tablaodecarmen.com), is the best place in Barcelona to see the passionate dance and music of Andalusia. Admission is 55€ ($63) for dinner and the first show or 29€ ($33) for the first show and a drink. Dinner begins at 9pm; the first show is at 9:30pm, the second at 11:55pm. Closed Monday.

DANCE CLUBS

In the basement of a shopping center, **Bikini,** Deu i Mata 105 (© **93-322-0005;** www.bikinibcn.com; Metro: Les Corts), covers the bases in a comprehensive entertainment compound that offers up multiple venues for dancing to music of every genre (including funk, rock, and oldies music). Rock and electronica groups perform concerts here nearly every night at 10pm; buy tickets in advance on Bikini's website. The dance club is open Tuesday through Sunday from midnight to 5am. Cover is 9€ to 18€ ($10–$21).

Up and Down, Numancia 179 (© **93-205-5194;** Metro: María Cristina), attracts the elite of Barcelona, spanning a couple of generations. The mature black-tie, postopera crowd heads for the upstairs section, leaving the downstairs to the thumping rock meant for their children. In business for many years, Up and Down continues to polish its reputation as the most cosmopolitan club in town. Technically, it is members only and you can be turned away at the door, so dress well and be nice to the doormen. The club is open Tuesday through Saturday from 12:30am to anytime between 5am and 6:30am, depending on business. Cover is 12€ to 17€ ($14–$20), including your first drink.

It's almost impossible to avoid ads for multilevel superclub **Otto Zutz,** Lincoln 15 (© **93-238-0722;** www.ottozutz.com; Metro: Plaça Molina). Go early to avoid the restrictive entrance policy, or pick up one of the little cards at shops around town that give you "guaranteed" entry. There are eight bars, there's dancing everywhere, and there's live rock on Wednesday night. The club is open Tuesday through Saturday from midnight to 4am or later, with a 15€ ($17) cover that includes a drink.

BARS & COCTELERIAS

Over in **Poble Nou,** near the Parc de la Ciutadella, the two skyscrapers marking the location of the former Olympic Port also point the way to the site of a frenetic bar scene. The artificial harbor that was the launch point for the Olympic sailing competition is now lined on three sides with over *200* bars and cafes that pound on till dawn. This is one of the safest nightlife districts.

Otherwise, you might start your evening at the **Bar Hivernacle,** Parc de la Ciutadella (© 932-95-4017; Metro: Arco del Triunfo), a wine tavern that lures a young, hip crowd to a setting of towering palms in a 19th-century greenhouse, just inside the gates of the city's most centrally located park. A restaurant adjoins it. The bar is open Monday through Saturday from 10am to midnight and Sunday from 10am to 4pm.

Located in a *modernista* building, chummy **Velvet,** Balmes 161 (© 93-217-6714; Metro: Diagonal), has a dance floor and two bars lined with buttocks-shaped stools. Don't miss the bathrooms. The music is mostly retro British and American rock, older than most of the patrons. It's open daily from 7pm to 5am, with no cover.

An exceptional retreat that eclipses all the rest for elegance and panache is the **Palau Dalmases,** Montcada 20 (© 93-310-0673; Metro: Jaume I), a 16th-century mansion a few doors down from the Picasso Museum. The multiple archways and ancient stone walls are hung with large copies of florid baroque paintings, and candles are lit on the marble-topped tables. Vivaldi and Bach provide the stereo underscore for murmured confidences and romantic intimacies. It's open Tuesday through Friday from 8pm to 2am and Saturday from 6 to 10pm; opera singers perform Thursday at 11pm. On those nights, the cover (including a drink) is 18€ ($21). No food is served.

GAY & LESBIAN BARS

Gays have a number of beguiling bars and dance clubs to choose from, but lesbians have relatively few. For the latest on the scene, log on to **www.gaybarcelona.net**. It's in Spanish, but it's not too difficult to decipher. Ads and listings in such weekly guides as *Guía del Ocio* referring to *el ambiente* nearly always mean places with a mostly or totally gay clientele.

Arena Sala Madre, Balmes 32 (© 93-487-8342; Metro: Universitat), is probably Barcelona's most popular mainstream gay club. Depending on the DJ, the music switches among techno, house, and classic disco. Admission changes by day and event. It's one corner of a triangle that includes **Arena Classic,** Diputació 233 (© 93-487-8342), which plays more retro tunes and has a ladies' night on Thursdays, and **Arena VIP,** Gran Vía 593 (© 93-487-8342), which plays disco and house.

Women should check in at **Cafe-Bar Aire,** Valencia 236 (© 93-451-8462; Metro: Passeig de Gràcia), the hub of the city's lesbian scene. Patrons and staff can offer advice on what else is happening in town.

DAY TRIPS FROM BARCELONA

SITGES ✦   The most frequented resort of the Costa Dorada, Sitges is packed in summer, mostly with affluent young northern Europeans, many of them gay.

For years, the resort, 40km (25 miles) south of Barcelona, was patronized largely by middle-class industrialists from Barcelona, but those rather staid days have gone. Sitges is as lively today as Benidorm and Torremolinos in the south, but it's nowhere near as tacky. By mid-October it goes into hibernation, but its scenic charms and museums may be motive enough for a winter visit. Things pick up with Carnaval in February, a riotously turbulent event with costumed revelers partying for days.

Long known as a city of culture, thanks in part to resident artist/playwright/ Bohemian mystic Santiago Rusinyol, this was the birthplace of the 19th-century *modernista* movement. The town remained a scene of artistic encounters and demonstrations long after *modernisme*, the Catalan form of Art Nouveau, waned. Salvador Dalí and the poet Federico García Lorca were regular visitors.

Getting There   RENFE's (© **90-224-0202;** www.renfe.es) Line C2 commuter trains run from Barcelona-Sants or Passeig de Gràcia to Sitges. From 5:45am to 10pm daily, there's a train at the rate of one every 10 to 15 minutes (trip time: 40 min.). A typical round-trip fare is 5.50€ ($6.25), with variations depending upon day of the week and other factors.

Sitges is a 45-minute drive from Barcelona along C-246, a coastal road. An express highway, A-7, is faster but less scenic.

Visitor Information   The **tourist information office** is at Carrer Sínis Morera 1 (© **93-894-4251;** www.sitges.org). It's open June through September 15, daily from 9am to 9pm; September 16 through May, Monday through Friday from 9am to 2pm and 4 to 6:30pm, and Saturday from 10am to 1pm.

Exploring Sitges   It's the **beaches** that attract most visitors. They have showers and changing facilities, and kiosks rent such items as motorboats and floating air cushions. Beaches on the eastern end and those inside the town center are the most peaceful, including **Aiguadoiç** and **Els Balomins. Playa San Sebastián, Fragata Beach,** and **"Beach of the Boats"** (under the church and next to the yacht club) are the area's family beaches. Most young people go to the **Playa de la Ribera,** in the west. The main gay beach is the **Playa del Mort.**

Beaches aside, Sitges has a couple of interesting museums. The **Museu Cau Ferrat,** Fonollar s/n (© **93-894-0364**), is the legacy of wealthy Catalan painter Santiago Rusinyol, a leading light of Belle Epoque Barcelona. His 19th-century house, fashioned of two 16th-century fishermen's homes, not only contains a collection of his works, but also several pieces by Picasso and El Greco, much ornate wrought iron (a Catalan specialty), folk art, and archaeological finds.

Next door is the **Museu Maricel de Mar,** Fonollar s/n (© **93-894-0364**), the legacy of Dr. Pérez Rosales, whose impressive accumulation of furniture, porcelain, and tapestries draws largely from the medieval, Renaissance, and baroque periods. Both museums are open Tuesday to Sunday between June 15 and September 30 from 10am to 2pm and 5 to 9pm. During the rest of the year, they're open Tuesday to Fri 10am to 1:30pm and 3 to 6:30pm, Saturdays from 10am to 7pm, and Sundays from 10am to 3pm. Admission to each is 3€ ($3.45).

MONTSERRAT ⚐ The vast **Montserrat Monastery** complex (www. abadiamontserrat.net), 52km (32 miles) northwest of Barcelona, contains a basilica with a venerated Black Virgin, an art museum, hotels, restaurants, and an excess of souvenir shops and food stalls. One of the most important pilgrimage spots in Spain, it's a good place to avoid on weekends.

Getting There   The least-expensive transport from Barcelona is the R5 train from Plaça de Espanya. It leaves hourly for the Aeri de Montserrat station, where a funicular carries you to the complex. If you're not in a screaming hurry, though, stay on to Monistrol de Montserrat (another 4 min.), and ride to the monastery on the newly restored rack railway (www.cremallerademontserrat. com), which offers the most spectacular views. "Trans Montserrat" tickets, available at any city FGC station, offer round-trip train, Metro, and rack railway use, and unlimited funicular and cable cars rides for 20.50€ ($24). "Tot Montserrat" tickets include admission to the museum and lunch at the cafeteria for a total of 35€ ($40). Call ✆ **93-205-1515** or try **www.fgc.es**.

Motorists can take N-2 southwest of Barcelona toward Tarragona, turning west at the junction with N-11. The signposts and exit to Montserrat will be on your right. From the main road, it's 14km (8¾ miles) to the monastery through dramatic scenery with eerie rock formations.

Visitor Information　The **tourist office** is at Plaça de la Creu (✆ **93-877-7777**), open daily from 10am to 6pm.

Exploring Montserrat　The monastery—a 19th-century structure that replaced a former monastery leveled by Napoleon's army in 1812—is 730m (2,400 ft.) up Montserrat. Its name, Montserrat, refers to the serrated peaks of the mountain, bulbous elongated formations that provided shelter for 11th-century Benedictine monks. One of the noted institutions of the monastery is the 50-voice **Boys' Choir** ✿, begun in the 13th century. The boys sing at 1 and 6:45pm. Their performances are thrilling to the faithful and curious alike and are the best reason for a visit. Admission is free.

Second on that list is the newly constituted subterranean **Museu de Montserrat** (✆ **93-877-7777**), near the entrance to the basilica. It brings together artworks that were once scattered around the complex, including gold and silver liturgical objects, archaeological artifacts from the Holy Land, and paintings from both the Renaissance and the 20th century. Numerous funiculars and paths lead to **hermitages** and **shrines** higher up the mountain.

Thousands travel here every year to see and touch the 12th-century statue of **La Moreneta (The Black Virgin),** the patron saint of Catalunya. To view the statue, enter the church through a side door to the right. The museum is open Monday through Friday from 9:30am to 6pm, Saturday and Sunday from 9:30am to 6:30pm. Admission is 3.60€ ($4.10) adults, 1.80€ ($2) children and students.

3 Andalusia & the Costa del Sol

Andalusia is the Spain of legend, where Moorish princes held court and veiled maidens danced flamenco under fragrant orange trees. The eight provinces of Spain's southernmost region were held, at least in part, by Muslim rulers for 700 years before Ferdinand and Isabella united Spain in 1492. They left a rich heritage of architectural treasures, including Seville's Giralda, Cordoba's Mezquita, and the unforgettable Alhambra in Granada.

This is also the land of the famed *pueblos blancos* ("white villages") and undulating olive groves that roll over tawny hillsides to the skirts of impressive mountain ranges. Give Andalusia a week and you'll still have only skimmed the surface of its many offerings.

Andalusia also embraces the Costa del Sol (Sun Coast), Spain's most noted and visited—inundated—strip of beach resorts. (Málaga, Marbella, and Torremolinos are covered here.) Go to the Costa del Sol for golf, tennis, watersports, after-dark partying, and relaxation, but save some days for the folklore, history, and architectural wonders of the major Andalusian cities.

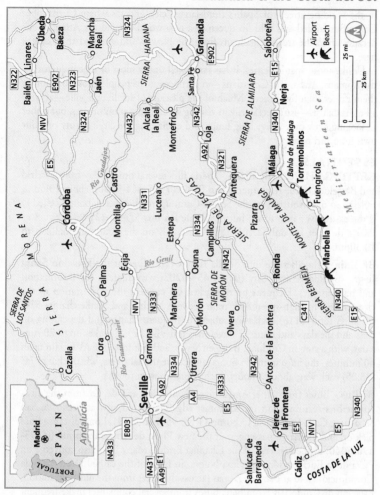

The mild winter climate and almost-guaranteed sunshine in summer have made the Costa del Sol a year-round attraction. It begins at the western frontier harbor city of Algeciras and stretches east to the port city of Almería. Sandwiched between these points is a rugged coastline backed by the Sierra Nevada. The beaches are no better than poor to fair, it should be said, but there are sandy coves, whitewashed houses, olive and almond trees, phalanxes of new apartment houses, fishing boats, a couple of dozen world-class golf courses, souvenir stands, fast-food outlets catering to the tastes of every national group, and widely varied flora and fauna—both human and vegetable. From June to October the coast is mobbed, so make sure that you've nailed down a reservation.

SEVILLE ✦✦✦

Seville, Andalusia's capital, is a city of operatic passion and romance. It is 550km (341 miles) southwest of Madrid and 217km (135 miles) northwest of Málaga. Mozart's Don Juan, Bizet's Carmen, and Rossini's Figaro all made their homes in the winding streets of Spain's third-largest city, and it's where Christopher Columbus landed and told his queen of a new world beyond the Atlantic. For decades after, the treasure galleons from the New World emptied their cargos here.

Unlike most Spanish cities, it has fared well under most of its conquerors—the Romans, Arabs, and Christians—in part because its people chose to embrace them rather than fight them. Much of the pleasure of strolling Seville—as with all of Andalusia—isn't necessarily in visiting specific museums or sites, but rather in kicking back over a *very* long lunch and embracing the city's beauty on your own time and pace.

ESSENTIALS

GETTING THERE   **By Plane**   **Iberia** flies several times a day from Madrid and Barcelona to the **Aeropuerto San Pablo** (© **95-444-9000**), about 13km (8 miles) east of downtown on the Seville-Carmona road. A **taxi** (about 12€/$11) is the easiest way into town, but the Route EA **bus** (© **90-221-0317**) goes to Puerta de Jerez for only 2.10€ ($2.40) roughly on the hour daily 6:30am to 10:30pm.

By Train   Train service into Sevilla is now centralized at the **Estación Santa Justa,** Avenida Kansas City (© **95-454-0202;** www.renfe.es for information and reservations). Frequent buses marked C1 connect the train station to the city center. The high-speed AVE train between Madrid and Seville charges 57€ to 103€ ($66–$118) each way, subject to frequent change and depending on class and the days and hours of travel (trip time: 2½ hr.). It makes up to 20 runs a day, with a stop in Córdoba. Between Seville and Córdoba, the AVE train takes 40 minutes, the *talgo* train 1½ hours, and conventional trains, which charge 7€ ($8.05) each way, about 2 hours, with many stops en route.

By Bus   Buses from other Andalusian towns arrive and depart from the city's largest **bus terminal,** on the southeast edge of the old city, at Prado de San Sebastián, Calle José María Osborne 11 (© **95-441-7111**). Long-distance lines pick up and discharge passengers at the new **Plaza de Armas terminal** (© **95-490-8040**) at the east end of the Chapina Bridge. Many lines also converge on Plaza de la Encarnación, on Plaza Nueva, in front of the cathedral on Avenida Constitución, and at Plaza de Armas (across the street from the old train station, Estación de Córdoba). From here, buses from several companies make frequent runs to and from Córdoba (trip time: 2½ hr.). One prominent bus company is **T. Alsina Graells Sur** (© **95-441-8811; www.continental-auto.es**).

VISITOR INFORMATION   The **Oficina de Información del Turismo,** at Av. de la Constitución 21B (© **95-422-1404**), is open Monday through Saturday from 9am to 7pm and Sunday and holidays from 10am to 2pm.

WHERE TO STAY

Seville hotels have three distinct pricing periods: lowest in winter, middling in summer, and highest during the adjacent celebratory weeks of Semana Santa (Holy Week) and the Fería de Abril (April Fair). During these last events, room rates are doubled or even tripled.

Very Expensive

Alfonso XIII ✦✦✦   At the southwestern corner of the gardens surrounding the Alcázar, this is a near-legendary hotel, Seville's *gran lujo* (grand luxury) address and one of Spain's most expensive lodgings. Now run by the U.S. chain

Seville

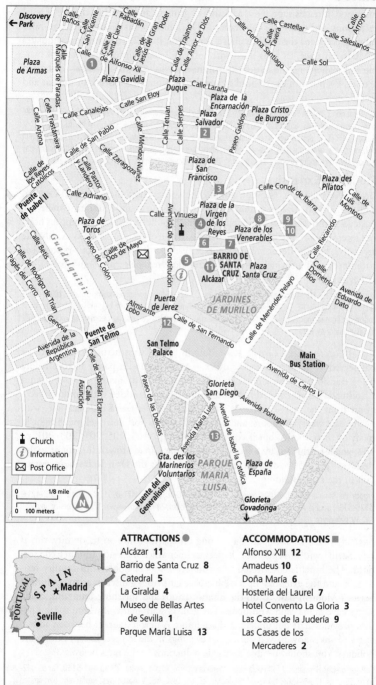

ATTRACTIONS ●
Alcázar **11**
Barrio de Santa Cruz **8**
Catedral **5**
La Giralda **4**
Museo de Bellas Artes
  de Sevilla **1**
Parque María Luisa **13**

ACCOMMODATIONS ■
Alfonso XIII **12**
Amadeus **10**
Doña María **6**
Hosteria del Laurel **7**
Hotel Convento La Gloria **3**
Las Casas de la Judería **9**
Las Casas de los
  Mercaderes **2**

Starwood, it reigns supreme as a bastion of glamour and privilege, the site of royal receptions and corporate celebrations. The lobby fountain is the cocktail-hour rallying point for the local Establishment. Built in 1929, the building simulates a Mudéjar palace, its halls lined with lustrous hand-painted tiles, acres of marble and mahogany, and antique furniture embellished with intricately embossed leather. Even if you can't afford to stay here, splurge for a drink in the bar and feel like a head of state.

San Fernando 2, 41004 Sevilla. ⓒ 800/221-2340 in the U.S. and Canada, or 95-491-7000. Fax 95-491-7099. www.westin.com. 147 units. 220€–335€ ($253–$385) double; from 585€ ($673) suite. AE, DC, MC, V. Parking 14€ ($16). **Amenities:** Restaurant; 2 bars (1 seasonal); heated outdoor pool; access to nearby health club; concierge; car-rental desk; business center; 24-hr. room service; in-room massage; babysitting; same-day laundry service and dry cleaning. *In room:* A/C, TV w/pay movies, dataport, minibar, hair dryer, safe.

Moderate/Expensive

Doña María ✿ Its location around the corner from the cathedral, Giralda, and the Alcázar creates a dramatic view from the rooftop terrace (where the postage-stamp-size pool is located). Originally built in 1969, this compact hotel has recently undergone needed upgrading. None of the rooms looks exactly like any other, but the decor favors elaborate headboards and some four-poster beds combined with provincial furniture and flowered patterns. Some rooms are rather small.

Don Remondo 19, 41004 Sevilla. ⓒ 95-422-4990. Fax 95-421-9546. www.hdmaria.com. 61 units. 100€–157€ ($115–$180) double. AE, DC, MC, V. Parking 12€ ($14). **Amenities:** Restaurant; bar; unheated rooftop pool; concierge; limited room service; babysitting; same-day laundry service and dry cleaning. *In room:* A/C, TV, minibar, hair dryer, safe.

Hotel Convento La Gloria ✿✿ Built in 1363, this structure at various times has served as Seville's first post office, a convent, and a pastry factory before being transformed into a hotel in 2003. Some of the rooms are even set around a cloister. Walls are covered in beautiful mosaics and studded with random pieces of art from the past 7 centuries. The sizable doubles feel a little cell-like, with nearly bare walls, tile floors, and comfortable beds. You don't get much light in many of these rooms, but if you stay in room no. 103, 105, 201, 203, 301, or 302, you'll be thrilled by a face-on view of the Giralda tower, floodlit at night. Residents get a 50% discount on the set menu at the **Don Raimundo** restaurant in the same building.

Argote de Molina 26–28, 41004 Sevilla. ⓒ 95-429-3670. Fax 95-421-8951. 43 units. 109€–121€ ($125–$138) double. AE, DC, MC, V. **Amenities:** Restaurant; bar; 24-hr. room service; laundry service. *In room:* A/C, TV, hair dryer.

Las Casas de la Judería ✿✿ Long on charm, short on modernity, this is Old Seville with a vengeance. Expect neither voice mail nor Internet connections. The hotel is constituted of a connected row of noble 16th-century residences, and the exteriors, up a cobblestone lane from a discreet archway, hint at Seville's Moorish past, as do the interior patios and splashing fountains. Some suites have saunas and whirlpools. The genteel staff, many of whom speak English, provides alert but understated attention. A new restaurant has been added, and a piano is now played during the evenings in the lounge. Except during the holidays, you should be able to haggle reductions in the rates below.

Callejón de Dos Hermanas 7 (off Plaza Santa María la Blanca), 41004 Sevilla. ⓒ 95-441-5150. Fax 95-442-2170. 56 units. 128€–156€ ($147–$179) double. AE, DC, DISC, MC, V. **Amenities:** Restaurant; bar; limited room service; laundry service; dry cleaning. *In room:* A/C, TV, minibar, hair dryer, safe.

Las Casas de los Mercaderes ★★ Under the same ownership as Las Casas de la Judería (above) and demonstrating a similar sensibility, this recently converted mansion has a far better location than its older sibling. It's right in the middle of things, with many of the best shops and department stores within 2 or 3 blocks and every major sight within walking distance. The grand lobby leads to an 18th-century inner court with a stained-glass skylight. Rooms are larger than usual, with carpeting, a small desk, and an easy chair or two.

Calle Alvarez Quintero 9–13 (1 block south of Plaza del Salvador), 41004 Sevilla. ℂ **95-422-5858.** Fax 95-422-9884. 47 units. 105€–128€ ($121–$147) double. AE, DC, MC, V. Free parking. **Amenities:** Cafe/bar; limited room service; laundry service; dry cleaning. *In room:* A/C, TV, minibar, hair dryer, safe.

Inexpensive

Amadeus ★★ *Finds* The former home of a family of music lovers is now a peaceful haven of high culture, run by that same family with warmth, grace, and cheer. Music is everywhere in this hotel, whether during the periodic concerts, on the stereo in the lobby, or in one of the soundproof practice rooms with pianos. As befits a former private home, rooms vary widely in terms of size and light. All are decorated with antiques and family pieces, and some have Jacuzzis.

Calle Farnesio 6 (1 block east of calle Mateos Gago), 41004 Sevilla. ℂ **95-450-1443.** Fax 95-450-0019. www.hotelamadeussevilla.com. 14 units. 76€–88€ ($87–$101) double. *In room:* A/C, TV, dataport, minibar, hair dryer, safe.

Hosteria del Laurel ★★ Touristy, yes; trashy, absolutely not. Sooner rather than later, every visitor comes upon this atmospheric restaurant in the Barrio's heart, with squat little tables beside the orange trees in the plaza. But most are unaware that there's also a spiffy little hotel behind the tavern. The rooms are immaculate, though they vary in size from tiny to ample and the marble floors amplify the noise of late-night comings and goings.

Plaza de los Venerables 5, 41004 Sevilla. ℂ **95-422-0295.** Fax 95-421-0450. www.hosteriadellaurel.com. 21 units. 70€–97€ ($81–$112) double. AE, DC, MC, V. **Amenities:** Restaurant; bar; 24-hr. room service; laundry service. *In room:* A/C, TV, hair dryer.

WHERE TO DINE
Moderate/Expensive

Casa Robles ★ REGIONAL With a row of outdoor tables, a busy bar, and a formal upstairs dining room, this restaurant covers most bases, in a setting that retains touches of old-fashioned formality. While the menu remains somewhat conservative, some surprisingly creative dishes are peppered throughout, most of them full of flavor and well prepared. Among these are *lubina con naranjas* (sea bass with Sevillana oranges); a suprême of hake garnished with clams, shrimp, and strips of Serrano ham; and filet of beef layered with foie gras. From time to time, you might even find *ortiguillas*—sea anemones.

Alvarez Quintero 58 (near the cathedral). ℂ **95-456-3272.** www.casa-robles.com. Main courses 12€–24€ ($14–$27). AE, DC, MC, V. Daily 1–4:30pm and 8:30pm–1am.

Enrique Becerra ★ REGIONAL Off Plaza Nueva near the cathedral, this restaurant has flourished since 1979 and just might provide one of your best meals in Seville. A popular tapas bar occupies the front, with a daily menu of over 25 possibilities, most of them notches above the usual renditions and only about 2€ ($2.30). The dining rooms upstairs and at the ground level are intimate settings made warmer by the friendly welcome. It's as good a place as any for your first taste of gazpacho and icy sangria. Specialties include roast lamb stuffed with spinach, honey, and pine nuts; rockfish cooked in Amontillado sherry; and oxtail braised in red wine. Many vegetarian dishes are also featured.

Gamazo 2 (2 blocks south of Plaza Nueva). ✆ **95-421-3049.** Main courses 14€–17€ ($15–$19). AE, DC, MC, V. Mon–Sat 1–5pm and 8pm–midnight.

La Albahaca BASQUE/SPANISH   On a corner of an attractive square in the Barrio de Santa Cruz, this elegant little manse dates from 1929 but looks much older. The high ceilings, many antiques and paintings, and extensive use of *azulejos* (decorative tiles) make it one of the most idyllic dining settings in Seville. In concert with the ministrations of the creative young Basque chef, this makes a most desirable place for a farewell dinner or an amorous proposal. The menu is adjusted seasonally, but look for such intriguing dishes as vegetables *escabeche* with oysters, or pork loin roasted with pear and vanilla sauce. The service is discreet. At the least, stop for a drink in the intimate snuggery.

Plaza de Santa Cruz 12. ✆ **95-422-0714.** www.andalunet.com/la-albahaca. Main courses 17€–21€ ($20–$24). AE, DC, MC, V. Mon–Sat 1–4pm and 8pm–midnight.

Taberna del Alabardero ✹✹ NEW SPANISH   The overachievers at the local hotel school marry Seville's most imaginative cuisine with one of its most charming small hotels in this restored 18th-century mansion. On the ground floor, a spacious coffee shop and tapas bar lets you kick back with free wireless Internet access. These are tapas with a difference—made to order, not scooped from a tray, and presented with panache. Even with four tapas, wine, and a wedge of cheese or cream tart, you should get out for well under 15€ ($17). In the back, chefs try ambitious new interpretations of Andalusian cuisine. Dinner for one runs about 40€ ($46) all-inclusive, but a lunchtime set menu costs only 15€ ($17). Too full to move? Head upstairs to one of the four rooms or three suites, with prices starting at 135€ ($155) for a double.

Zaragoza 20 (west of Plaza Nueva). ✆ **95-456-0637.** Tapas and *raciones* 2.20€–15€ ($2.55–$17). AE, DC, MC, V. *Cafetería* daily 8am–2am; dining room daily 1–4pm and 9pm–midnight.

EXPLORING SEVILLE

Alcázar ✹✹✹   This magnificent 14th-century Mudéjar palace was built by Pedro the Cruel after the reconquest of the city from the Moors. From the Dolls' Court to the Maidens' Court through the domed Ambassadors' Room, it contains some of the finest work of Sevillian artisans, most of them descendants of the former occupants of the palace. In many ways, it evokes the Alhambra at Granada. Isabel and Fernando, who at one time lived in the Alcázar, welcomed Columbus here on his return from America. On the top floor, the Oratory of the Catholic Monarchs has a fine altar in polychrome tiles made by Pisano in 1504.

Plaza del Triunfo. ✆ **95-450-2323.** Entrance is north of the cathedral. Admission 5€ ($5.75) adults, free for seniors, students, and children under 13. Apr–Sept Tues–Sat 9:30am–7pm, Sun 9:30am–1:30pm; Oct–Mar Tues–Sat 9:30am–5pm, Sun 9:30am–1:30pm.

Catedral ✹✹✹   Alleged to be the largest Gothic building in the world, Seville's cathedral was designed by builders with a stated goal—that "those who come after us will take us for madmen." Construction began in the late 1400s and took centuries to complete. Built on the site of an ancient mosque, the cathedral claims to contain the remains of Columbus, with his tomb mounted on four statues. That claim is in doubt, but it's fairly certain his son Fernando is buried here. Works of art abound, most immediately evident in the side chapels, the 75 stained-glass windows, and the elaborate choir stalls, and also including paintings by Murillo, Goya, and Zubarán. On the north side you'll find the fresh citrus scents and chirping birds of the Patio of Orange Trees, a relic of the original mosque, as is the Giralda (below).

Plaza del Triunfo, Av. de la Constitución. © 95-421-4971. Admission including La Giralda 6€ ($6.90) adults, 1.50€ ($1.75) seniors/students, free for children under 13. Free for all Sun. Mon–Sat 11am–5pm; Sun 2:30–6pm.

La Giralda ★★★ Just as Big Ben symbolizes London, La Giralda evokes Seville. This square-sided, 98m (322-ft.) bell tower, next to the cathedral, is the city's most famous monument. It began as a minaret for the mosque, progressing from the austere stonework of the fundamentalist Almohad Dynasty to the decorative brick patterns and pointed arches of their less rigid successors, and culminating in the florid Renaissance-influenced upper floors added by the Catholic bishops. Determined visitors can take the 35 ramps inside up to a

---

Moments Splendid Strolls

What was once a ghetto for Spanish Jews, who were forced out of Spain in the 15th century in the wake of the Inquisition, the **Barrio de Santa Cruz** ★★★ today is Seville's most colorful district. Near the old walls of the Alcázar, winding medieval streets with names like *Vida* (Life) and *Muerte* (Death) open onto pocket plazas. Balconies with draping bougainvillea and potted geraniums jut out over this labyrinth, and through numerous wrought-iron gates, you can glimpse tile-lined patios filled with fountains and plants. To enter the Barrio Santa Cruz, turn right after leaving the Patio de Banderas exit of the Alcázar. Turn right again at Plaza de la Alianza and go down Calle Rodrigo Caro to Plaza de Doña Elvira. Use caution when strolling through the area, particularly at night.

About a 7-minute walk northeast of the cathedral on the northern edge of the Barrio de Santa Cruz is the **Casa de Pilatos** ★, Plaza Pilatos 1 (© 95-422-5298). This 16th-century palace of the dukes of Medinaceli recaptures the splendors of the past, combining Gothic, Mudéjar, and Plateresque styles in its courtyards, fountains, and salons. Don't miss the two old carriages or the rooms filled with Greek and Roman statues. Admission to the museum upstairs is 5€ ($5.75). The museum and gardens are open daily from 9am to 7pm, until 6pm from October through February.

Parque María Luisa ★★, dedicated to María Luisa, sister of Isabel II, was once the grounds of the Palacio de San Telmo, Avenida de Roma. The former private royal park later became the site of the 1929 Ibero-Americana exposition, for which the vast Plaza de España was created. Running south along the Guadalquivir River, the park attracts those who want to take boat rides, walk along paths bordered by flowers, jog, or go bicycling. The most romantic way to traverse it is by rented horse and carriage, but this can be expensive, depending on your negotiation with the driver. Exercise caution while walking through this otherwise delightful park, as many muggings have been reported.

viewing platform ★★★ at the 70m (230-ft.) level. Make it to the top and you'll have an unsurpassed vista of the city.

Plaza Virgen de los Reyes. Entrance through the cathedral (admission is included with cathedral).

Museo de Bellas Artes de Sevilla ★★   A lovely old convent off Calle de Alfonso XII, this museum houses an important Spanish art collection. Some art experts claim that after the two leading art museums of Madrid, this is the most valuable and significant repository of art in Spain. A whole gallery is devoted to two paintings by El Greco, and works by Zurbarán are also exhibited; however, the devoutly religious paintings of the Seville-born Murillo outnumber all the others. An entire wing is given over to macabre paintings by the 17th-century artist Valdés-Leál. The top floor, which displays modern paintings, is less interesting.

Plaza del Museo 9. © **95-422-1829.** Admission 1.50€ ($1.75) adults, free for students. Tues 3–8pm; Wed–Sat 9am–8pm; Sun 9am–2pm.

SHOPPING

Seville's major shopping street is the pedestrianized **Calle Sierpes,** which runs from Plaza Magdalena Campaña to the top of Plaza San Francisco. For handmade ceramics, you should also prowl **Calle Alfareria** across the Isabel II bridge from the old town. On Sunday mornings, once the Saturday-night drunks have been cleared away, a huge flea market is held on the **Alameda de Hercules** plaza in the Macarena neighborhood. Close to Seville's town hall, **Ceramics Martian,** Sierpes 74 (© **95-421-3413**), sells a wide array of painted tiles and ceramics, all made in or near Seville. Many pieces reproduce traditional patterns of Andalusia. Along Alfareria, two ceramics merchants to seek out are **Ceramica R,** no. 45 (© **95-434-4370**), and **Azulejos Santa Isabel,** no. 12 (© **95-434-4608**). Their merchandise runs from simple tiles and dinner plates to elaborate coffee sets and garden fountains.

If Seville suggests lace fans to you, check out **Blasfor,** Calle de las Sierpes 33 (© **95-421-8449**). Past the north end of Sierpes, over to the left, is the local branch of the preeminent national department store, **El Corte Inglés,** Plaza del Duque 10 (© **95-422-1931**).

SEVILLE AFTER DARK

In the 1990s, Seville finally got its own opera house, **Teatro de la Maestranza,** Núñez de Balboa (© **95/422-65-73;** www.teatromaestranza.com), which quickly became a premier venue for world-class operatic performances. Jazz, classical music, and the quintessentially Spanish *zarzuelas* (operettas) are also performed here. The opera house can't be visited except during performances. The box office is open daily from 11am to 2pm and 5 to 8pm. Tickets vary in cost depending on the performance.

To hear some more informal singing and dancing, head for the Barrio de Santa Cruz to the flamboyant **El Tamboril,** Plaza de Santa Cruz 15 (© **95-456-1590**). In a room to the right of the eccentrically decorated bar, guitarists and singers assemble informally most nights, and patrons take to the dance floor to perform the *rumba* and *sevillanas,* a dance related to flamenco, as well as improvisations thereon. The doors open at 10pm and things start heating up by midnight. Get there well before midnight to have hope of a seat. There's no cover.

Sol Café Cantante, Sol 5 (© **95-422-5165**), in the Macarena neighborhood, claims to be a new kind of flamenco studio for a new generation. It specializes in young local performers and offers dance lessons (the two, obviously, are linked). This is theater, not a grass-roots participatory thing, but it's still got some of the city's freshest flamenco. Shows run at 9pm on Wednesdays through Saturdays, and admission costs 18 € ($21) for adults and 11€ ($13) for students, including the first drink. A signboard outside lists upcoming performances, so stroll by.

If you're under 35 (or just feel that way), join Seville's youth at the **Alameda de Hercules** just north of the city center, where more than a dozen bars and two dance clubs attract hundreds of college students and a smaller crowd of revelers in their 20s and 30s to chat, drink, flirt, and show off.

CORDOBA ★★★

Ten centuries ago, Córdoba was one of the world's greatest cities. The capital of Muslim Spain, it was Europe's largest city (with a reported population of 900,000) and a prominent cultural and intellectual center. This seat of the Western Caliphate flourished, constructing public baths, mosques, a great library, and palaces. But greedy hordes descended on the city, sacking ancient buildings and carting off art treasures. Despite these assaults, Córdoba retains traces of its former glory—enough to rival Seville and Granada in attraction.

A visit to Andalusia can easily begin in Córdoba, 418km (260 miles) southwest of Madrid. The city lies astride NIV (E-5) connecting Madrid with Seville and is one of the few stops made by the high-speed AVE train, only 1¾ hours out of Madrid. Today, this provincial capital is known chiefly for its great mosque, but it is filled with other artistic and architectural riches, especially its domestic dwellings. The old Arab and Jewish quarters are famous for their narrow streets lined with whitewashed homes and flower-filled patios and balconies; it's perfectly acceptable to walk along gazing into the courtyards.

ESSENTIALS
GETTING THERE   **By Train**   Córdoba is a railway junction for routes to the rest of Andalusia and Spain. The main rail station is on the town's northern periphery, at Avenida de América 130, near the corner of Avenida de Cervantes. For information about services in Córdoba, contact **RENFE** (© **95-740-0202;** www.renfe.es). There are about 22 *talgo* and AVE trains daily between Córdoba and Madrid (trip time: 1½–2 hr.). Other trains *(tranvías)* take 5 to 8 hours for the same trip. There are also 25 trains from Seville every day (45 min. by AVE).

By Bus   Several different bus companies maintain separate terminals. The town's most important bus terminal is at Calle Torrito 10, 1 block south of Avenida Medina Azahara 29 (© **95-740-4040**), on the western outskirts of town (just west of the gardens beside Paseo de la Victoria). There are at least 10 buses per day to Seville (trip time: 2 hr.).

VISITOR INFORMATION   The **Tourism Office** on the Plaza de las Tendillas (© **90-220-1774;** turismo@ayuncordoba.es) is open 7 days a week from 10am to 2pm and from 5 to 8:30pm.

WHERE TO STAY
Very Expensive
El Conquistador ★   Benefiting from one of the most evocative locations in Córdoba, this hotel lies just across a narrow street from one side of the Mezquita. It opened in 1986 within the renovated premises of a connected pair of 19th-century villas. The marble-and-granite lobby opens onto an interior

courtyard filled with seasonal flowers, a pair of splashing fountains, and a symmetrical stone arcade. The quality, size, and comfort of the rooms have earned the hotel four stars in the government rating system.

Magistral González Francés 15, 14003 Córdoba. © **95-748-1102.** Fax 95-747-4677. www.hotelconquistador cordoba.com. 103 units. 107€–155€ ($123–$178) double. AE, DC, MC, V. Garage parking 13€ ($15). Bus: 12. **Amenities:** Cafe; bar; sauna; car-rental desk; 24-hr. room service; babysitting; same-day laundry service and dry cleaning. *In room:* A/C, TV, minibar, hair dryer, safe.

Expensive

Parador de Cordoba ✸ About 4km (2½ miles) outside of town, in the suburb of El Brillante, this hotel from around 1960 (named after an Arab word meaning "palm grove") offers the conveniences and facilities of a resort hotel at reasonable rates. Built atop the foundations of a former caliphate palace, with panoramic views, the spacious rooms within have been furnished with fine dark-wood pieces; some have balconies.

Avenida de la Arruzafa s/n, 14012 Córdoba. © **95-727-5900.** Fax 95-728-0409. www.parador.es. 96 units. 113€ ($130) double. AE, DC, MC, V. Free parking. **Amenities:** Restaurant; bar; heated outdoor pool; tennis court; limited room service; babysitting; same-day laundry service and dry cleaning. *In room:* A/C, TV, data-port, minibar, hair dryer, safe.

Moderate/Inexpensive

González Located in the Judería, within easy walking distance of the Mezquita, this is among the more impressive of the city's inexpensive hotels. The converted 16th-century mansion is decorated in Andalusian style, with a dining courtyard. Rooms are plain and functional. Readers have praised the staff's attitude.

Manríquez 3, 14003 Córdoba. © **95-747-9819.** Fax 95-748-6187. 17 units. 52€–122€ ($60–$140) double. Rates include breakfast. MC, V. Parking 9€ ($10). **Amenities:** Restaurant; bar; same-day laundry service and dry cleaning. *In room:* A/C, TV, hair dryer.

Mezquita *(Finds)* The owners have incorporated ancient columns, arches, and genuinely old paintings for a downright grand effect. Many of the guest rooms carry through with that theme. Opposite the east entrance to the Mezquita, the intriguing parts of the Judería are a mere stroll away. Prices go up during Holy Week and the Feria de Abril.

Plaza Santa Catalina 1, 14003 Córdoba. © **95-747-5585.** Fax 95-747-6219. 21 units. 52€–108€ ($60–$124) double. AE, DC, MC, V. **Amenities:** Laundry service. *In room:* A/C, TV, hair dryer, safe.

WHERE TO DINE
Moderate

El Caballo Rojo ✸ SPANISH Córdoba's best-known restaurant is up an alley opposite the Mezquita's Puerta del Perdón. Hugely popular with both locals and tourists, the place has the noise level you'd expect, but the skilled waiters cope smoothly with all the demands. As soon as you order, they bring a dish of fritters and pour a complimentary aperitif. There are three floors, and enough room to get away from smokers if you wish. In addition to regional dishes, the chef offers centuries-old Sephardic and Mozarabic recipes, an example of the latter being monkfish with pine nuts, currants, carrots, and cream. *Rabo de toro* (oxtail stew) is among the favorites on the long menu.

Cardinal Herrero 28, Plaza de la Hoguera. © **95-747-5375.** Reservations required. Main courses 12€–27€ ($14–$31). AE, DC, MC, V. Daily 1–4:30pm and 8pm–midnight. Bus: 12.

La Almudaina ✸ SPANISH/FRENCH Fronting the river in the former Judería—the Jewish Quarter—La Almudaina is widely regarded as the city's top restaurant. That's a reach, in truth, but it's an attractive place, with dining in the central courtyard, with its stained-glass roof, or in one of the lace-curtained salons to the side. In cool weather, braziers under the table warm your feet. Specialties include salmon crepes, *merluza* (hake) with baby clams and shrimp, and spring lamb and pork loin in wine sauce. Meats are the best options, because fish is too often cooked to mushiness.

Plaza de los Santos Mártires 1. ℂ **95-747-4342.** www.restaurantealmudaina.com. Reservations required. Main courses 12€–18€ ($14–$21); *menu degustación* 31€ ($36). AE, DC, MC, V. Mon–Sat noon–4pm and 8:30pm–midnight; Sun noon–5pm. Closed Sun mid-June to Aug. Bus: 12.

EXPLORING CORDOBA

Alcázar de los Reyes Cristianos ✿   Commissioned in 1328 by Alfonso XI (the "Just"), the Alcázar de los Reyes Cristianos (Fortress of the Christian Kings) is a fine example of military architecture. Fernando and Isabel governed Castile from this fortress on the river as they prepared their assault on Granada, the last Moorish stronghold in Spain. Columbus journeyed here to fill Isabel's ears with his plans for exploration. Two blocks southwest of the mosque, this quadrangular building is notable for mighty walls and a trio of towers: the Tower of the Lions, the Tower of Allegiance, and the Tower of the River. The Tower of the Lions contains intricately decorated ogival ceilings that are the most notable example of Gothic architecture in Andalusia. The beautiful gardens (illuminated May–Sept Tues–Sat 10pm–1am) and the Moorish bathrooms are celebrated attractions. The Patio Morisco is a lovely spot, its pavement decorated with the arms of León and Castile.

Amador de los Ríos. ℂ **95-742-0151.** Admission 3€ ($3.45) adults, 1.50€ ($1.75) children. May–Sept Tues–Sat 10am–2pm and 6–8pm, Sun 10am–3pm; Oct–Apr Tues–Sat 9:30am–3pm and 4:30–6:30pm, Sun 9:30am–3pm. Bus: 3 or 12.

Mezquita-Catedral ★★★   Dating from the 8th century, this mosque was the crowning Muslim architectural achievement in the West, rivaled only by the architecture at Mecca. Córdoba's mosque boasts a fantastic labyrinth of red-and-white-striped pillars, over 850 of them, topped with double arches, some of them with scalloped edges. They are made from marble, onyx, granite, limestone, even wood. Of different heights and thickness, many were scavenged from Roman, Carthaginian, and Visigothic sites. They support a flat roof covering almost 3 hectares (8 acres).

Dropped into this graceful space is a Gothic-baroque cathedral that the bishops of the Church Triumphant ordered built after the reconquest of the city. While it squats awkwardly in the middle of the mosque, it would be impressive in its own right if it stood alone, somewhere else. The mosque's most interesting feature is the *mihrab*, a domed shrine lined with golden, glittering mosaics. The *mihrab* once housed a *Koran*. After exploring the interior, stroll through the Courtyard of the Orange Trees with its beautiful fountain.

Calle Cardenal Herrero. ℂ **95-747-0512.** Admission 6.50€ ($7.35) adults and students 14 and up, 3.25€ ($3.75) children 10–13, free for children 9 and under. May–Sept daily 10am–7pm; Oct–Apr daily 10am–6pm. Bus: 3 or 12.

Museo de Bellas Artes   Housed in an old hospital, the Fine Arts Museum contains medieval Andalusian paintings, examples of Spanish baroque art, and works by many of Spain's important 19th- and 20th-century painters, including Goya. The museum is east of the Mezquita, about a block south of the Church of St. Francis (San Francisco).

Plaza del Potro 1. ℂ **95-747-3345.** Admission 1.60€ ($1.85), free for children under 12. June 15–Sept 15 Tues 3–8pm; Wed–Sat 9am–8pm; Sun 9am–3pm (shorter hours during the rest of the year). Bus: 3 or 4.

Museo Municipal de Arte Taurino   Memorabilia of great bullfights are housed in this museum, a 16th-century building in the Jewish Quarter, inaugurated in 1983. Its galleries honor Córdoba's great bullfighters in their "suits of light," with pictures, trophies, posters, and the mounted heads of memorable bulls. You'll see Manolete in repose and the blood-smeared uniform of El Cordobés—both of these famous matadors came from Córdoba.

Plaza de las Bulas (also called Plaza Maimónides). ℭ **95-720-1056.** Admission 2.70€ ($3.20), free for children under 18 and to all on Tues. May–Sept Tues–Sat 10am–2pm and 5:30–7:30pm, Sun 9:30am–2:30pm; Oct–Apr Mon–Sat 10am–2pm and 4:30–6:30pm, Sun 9:30am–2:30pm. Bus: 3 or 12.

THE SHOPPING SCENE

The largest and most comprehensive association of craftspeople in Córdoba is **Arte Zoco,** Júdios s/n (no phone). Opened in the Jewish quarter as a business cooperative in the mid-1980s, it assembles the creative output of about a half dozen artisans, whose media include leather, wood, silver, crystal, terra cotta, and iron. Some of the artisans maintain on-premises studios, which you can visit to check out the techniques and tools they use to pursue their crafts. The center is open Monday through Friday from 9:30am to 7pm and Saturday and Sunday from 9:30am to 2pm. The workshops and studios of the various artisans open and close according to the whims of their occupants, but are usually open Monday through Friday from 10am to 2pm and 5:30 to 8pm.

At **Meryan,** Calleja de las Flores 2 (ℭ **95-747-5902**), artisans make leather objects in a 250-year-old building. Most items must be custom ordered, but there are some ready-made pieces for sale, including cigarette boxes, jewel cases, attaché cases, book and folio covers, and ottoman covers. Meryan is open Monday through Friday from 9am to 8pm and Saturday from 9am to 2pm.

GRANADA ✶✶

Granada, 122km (76 miles) northeast of Málaga, is 670m (2,200 ft.) above sea level. The last stronghold of Moorish Spain, it was finally captured in 1492 by the Catholic monarchs Ferdinand and Isabella. Granada is best known for the castle complex of the **Alhambra** ✶✶✶ (www.alhambra-patronato.es), one of the world's grandest and most elegant monuments, ranking up there with the Acropolis and the Taj Mahal. Author/diplomat Washington Irving lived in a former royal apartment on the grounds before he wrote his *Tales of the Alhambra.*

But Granada itself has much more to offer. The winding, hilly streets of the formerly Jewish Albayzín quarter and the gracious plazas of the 19th-century city below come together into a supremely civilized city, one that rewards wandering.

ESSENTIALS

GETTING THERE   By Plane   Iberia flies to Granada's small airport once or twice daily from both Barcelona and Madrid. Granada's airport (ℭ **95-824-5223**) is 16km (10 miles) west of the city center. Airline ticketing problems and information are more easily handled at the **Iberia ticketing office** in the city center, at Plaza Isabel la Católica 2 (ℭ **95-822-7592**). A shuttle bus makes runs several times a day between the airport and the city center, at hours that are timed to coincide with the arrivals and departures of flights. The buses meander through the city center before heading out to the airport, but the most convenient and central place to catch one is on the Gran Vía de Colón, immediately in front of the city's cathedral. It costs 3.40€ ($4) each way.

By Train Two trains daily connect Granada with Madrid's Atocha Station (trip time: 6–8 hr.), and there are four trains daily between Seville and Granada (3 hr.). Granada's railway station is on Calle Dr. Jaime García Royo (© **90-224-0202;** www.renfe.es), at the end of Avenida Andaluces.

By Bus Most buses pull into the station on the fringe of Granada at Carretera de Jaen s/n, the extension of Avenida de Madrid. **Alsina Graells** (© **95-818-5010;** www.continental-auto.es) is the most useful company here, offering seven buses per day from Córdoba (3 hr.), 10 per day from Madrid (5 hr.), 17 per day from Málaga (2 hr.), and 8 per day from Sevilla (3 hr.).

VISITOR INFORMATION The **tourist information office** is at Plaza de Mariana Pineda 10 (© **95-824-7128;** www.granadatur.com), open Monday through Saturday from 9am to 7pm and Sunday from 10am to 2pm.

WHERE TO STAY

Parador de San Francisco ★★★ The most famous hotel of Spain's "Parador" lodging chain (a distinguished chain of Spanish government-owned hotels, normally set in notable historical buildings) is housed in a 15th-century structure with a modern annex, set within the grounds of the Alhambra. A decidedly Andalusian ambience informs the decor, which is respectful of the rich history of its surroundings. Part of the building is a former convent founded by the Catholic monarchs immediately after they conquered the city in 1492. They were interred in one of its enclosed courts until the cathedral was built downtown. From the hotel's terrace, outside the dining room, there are views of the Alhambra gardens and Albayzín hill. Rooms are generally spacious and comfortable, if not extravagant. The hotel cannot begin to meet demand, though, and reservations must be made months in advance. (In the confusing manner of the Parador chain, this is also known as the "Parador de Granada.")

Alhambra, 18009 Granada. © 800/343-0020 in the U.S., or 95-822-1440. Fax 95-822-2264. www.parador.es. 214€ ($246) double. AE, DC, MC, V. Free parking. Bus: 31. **Amenities:** Restaurant; bar; limited room service; same-day laundry service and dry cleaning. *In room:* A/C, TV, minibar, hair dryer, safe.

Casa del Capitel Nazari ★ The least expensive of a quartet of historic Albayzin hotels brings together charm and affordability in a way no other Granada hotel quite pulls off. Built in 1503 by workers who remembered the last Moorish rulers of Granada, it was a private home for centuries before being converted to a hotel in 2001.

The 17 rooms, on three floors, cluster around an open-air patio. Yes, that means it rains *inside* the hotel sometimes; the patio has its own drainage system. Rooms are decorated with tapestries and old rugs, with tiny but sparkling bathrooms (shower only, no bathtub). Top-floor rooms have gorgeous wood-beam ceilings, and a few rooms have views of the Alhambra. The staff speaks a tiny bit of English.

Cuesta Aceituneros 6, 18010 Granada. © 95-821-5260. Fax 95-821-5806. www.hotelcasacapitel.com. 17 units. 85€ ($98) double; 499€ ($575) suite. AE, MC, V. **Amenities:** Breakfast room. *In room:* A/C, TV, minibar, hair dryer, safe.

Casa de los Migueletes ★★ *Finds* The newest of Granada's historic hotels was built in the 17th century as a slew of houses around a central courtyard; over the years, it became the headquarters for the local police and then a set of slum dwellings, before finally being left in ruins in 1995. It was renovated and reopened as a four-star hotel in 2003.

The Migueletes is full of high-tech conveniences, like a roll-back roof over the central courtyard and even an electrically heated courtyard floor. The varied rooms come with certifiably antique furniture and brand-new bathrooms; a few have views of the Alhambra. A 24-hour, ground-floor wine cellar serves as the world's largest minibar. Feel like having some fresh ham and a bottle of *vino tinto?* Just ask. The Migueletes's greatest asset, though, is its staff. All front-line staff speak fluent English and are tremendously helpful when it comes to recommending restaurants and attractions, providing the intangible smoothness that creates a luxury experience.

Benelua 11, 18010 Granada. ℂ **95-821-0700.** Fax 95-821-0702. www.casamigueletes.com. 25 units. 129€–199€ ($148–$230) double; 499€ ($575) suite. AE, MC, V. **Amenities:** Wine cellar; same-day laundry service and dry cleaning. *In room:* A/C, TV, dataport, minibar, hair dryer, safe.

WHERE TO DINE

Iberos y Patagonicos NEW SPANISH   Exciting, adventurous cuisine is crafted daily at this sophisticated bistro and served up by a small, friendly staff. At any given time, your plate may be adorned with cauliflower mousse, cumin foam, or cheese and cinnamon crisp, but there's also a focus on local ingredients that evoke classic Spanish dishes, like pork loin or chicken stewed in Granada beer. A dessert of stewed pears with ginger foam and lemon and vanilla gelatin was both fun to eat and refreshing. Portions are comfortable, not huge, except for the Alhambra-size salads.

Escudo de Carmen 36. ℂ **95-822-0772.** Reservations recommended. Main courses 11€–19€ ($13–$22). AE, MC, V. Mon–Sat 1:30–4pm and 8:30–11pm.

Pilar del Toro ✷ SPANISH   You'll find this former home of nobility partially hidden up a flight of stairs near the north end of the Plaza Nueva. You enter an atmospheric bar, cross into a large inner patio with an array of cushioned wicker chairs arranged around a bubbling fountain, and finally climb the stairs to one of the four dining rooms. Start with the *pimientos de piquillo*—small triangular sweet peppers stuffed with a cod brandade—a classic of the Basque kitchen. The veal *solomillo* (tenderloin) is butter-tender, served with a mustard and mushroom sauce.

Hospital de Santa Ana 12. ℂ **95-822-3847.** Main courses 9.15€–15€ ($10–$17). MC, V. Daily 1:30–4pm and 8:30–11pm.

Sevilla REGIONAL SPANISH   Attracting a mixed crowd of all ages, the Sevilla was the favorite restaurant of such hometown boys as García Lorca and Manuel de Falla—it's been around for over 70 years. Out front is one of the city's best tapas bars, and you can easily put together lunch or dinner there. For a more formal meal, there's a different take on standard rice dishes, including one with broad beans, green asparagus, and ham. For a main course, the "shepherd's style" lamb with pine nuts and raisins is a winner. You can dine in any of four attractively decorated rooms, or out on the terrace.

Oficios 12. ℂ **95-822-1223.** Reservations recommended. Main courses 9€–24€ ($10–$28). AE, DC, MC, V. Mon–Sat 1–4pm and 8–11pm; Sun 1–4pm.

EXPLORING GRANADA

Alhambra ✷✷✷   A fortress-palace of grand ambition, built over centuries for the governing caliphs during the long Moorish occupation, the Alhambra was a royal city surrounded by walls. The heart of the Alhambra, the **Palacios Nazaríes (Nasrid Palaces),** is a series of three connected palaces. Here, sultans and emirs conducted state business, concocted conspiracies, raised their families, and were entertained by their harems.

The first structure you'll enter is the **Casa Real,** built between 1335 and 1410. Signs direct visitors through rooms with reliefs of Arabic script and floral motifs carved in the plaster walls. This pathway leads into one of the Alhambra's most-photographed spaces, the **Patio de Comares (Court of the Myrtles),** a long, flat band of water bordered by rows of sculptured myrtle. At one end is the splendid **Salón de Embajadores (Hall of the Ambassadors),** one of the palace's loveliest rooms, with a high vaulted ceiling of carved cedar and walls of lustrous tiles and carved script. Exiting, you soon arrive in the **Patio de los Leones (Court of Lions),** named after its highly stylized fountain, a basin resting on the haunches of 12 stylized stone lions standing in a circle.

This was the heart of the palace, the most private section. Opening onto the court are the Hall of the Two Sisters, where the "favorite" of the moment was kept, and the Gossip Room, a factory of intrigue. In the dancing room in the Hall of Kings, entertainment was provided nightly to amuse the sultan's party. You can see the room where Washington Irving lived (in the chambers of Carlos V).

Carlos V may have been horrified when he saw the cathedral placed in the middle of the great mosque at Córdoba, but he's responsible for his own architectural meddling here, building a ponderous Renaissance palace in the middle of the Alhambra. Today, it houses the **Museo de la Bellas Artes en la Alhambra** (© **95-822-4883**), a site devoted to painting and sculpture from the 16th to the 19th centuries; and the **Museo de la Alhambra** (© **95-822-6279**), which focuses on the region's breathtaking traditions of Hispanic-Muslim art and architecture. Both museums are open Monday through Saturday from 9am to 2pm.

Note: The crowds here can be overwhelming during the summer months (though on a rainy Nov day, you may feel as if you have the Alhambra all to yourself). The latest experiment in crowd control restricts entry to the grounds to morning (8:30am–2pm), afternoon (2–6pm), or evening phases, and gives you a precise time when you're allowed to enter the Nasrid palaces. Once inside any area, you can stay as long as you want. To be safe, arrange for tickets in advance. Branches of the **Banco de Bilbao de Vizcaya** (© **91-537-9178**) across the country sell tickets; you can also book online at www.alhambratickets.com and pick up your ticket at the Alhambra ticket office; if you do, remember to print out and bring the confirmation number the site gives you. Hotel concierges in Granada can also arrange for tickets.

Palacio de Carlos V. © **95-822-8359.** Comprehensive ticket, including Alhambra and Generalife (below), 8€ ($9.20) adults, 6€ ($6.90) seniors, free for under age 8. Mar–Oct daily 8:30am–8pm, floodlit visits Tues–Sat 10–11:30pm; Nov–Feb daily 8:30am–6pm, floodlit visits Fri–Sat 8–9:30pm. Take bus no. 30 from the Plaza Nueva.

Generalife ✦ The sultans used to spend their summers in this palace (pronounced, roughly, hay-nay-rahl-*ee*-fay) with their wives, consorts, and extended families. Built in the 13th century to overlook the Alhambra, the Generalife's glory is in its gardens and courtyards. Don't expect an Alhambra in miniature: There are no major buildings—the Generalife is a place of fragrances and fountains, a retreat even from the splendors of the Alhambra.

Alhambra, Cerro de Sol. © **91-374-5420.** For tickets and hours, see the Alhambra, above.

Catedral & Capilla Real ✦ This Renaissance-baroque cathedral, with its spectacular altar, is one of the country's architectural highlights, acclaimed for its beautiful facade and gold-and-white decor. It was begun in 1521 and completed in 1714. Behind the cathedral (entered separately) is the Flamboyant Gothic **Capilla Real (Royal Chapel)** where the remains of Isabel and Fernando lie. It was their wish to be buried in recaptured Granada, not their home regions of Castile or Aragón. The coffins are remarkably tiny—a reminder of how short they must have been. Accenting the tombs is a wrought-iron grill masterpiece. In much larger tombs are the remains of their daughter, Joanna the Mad, and her husband, Philip the Handsome. The Capilla Real abuts the cathedral's eastern edge.

Plaza de la Lonja, Gran Vía de Colón 5. ℭ 95-822-2959. Admission to cathedral 2.50€ ($2.80). Mon–Sat 10:45am–1:30pm and 4–7pm; Sun and holidays 4–7pm.

ALBAYZIN ✦

This old Arab quarter (also spelled "Albaicín") occupies one of the two main hills of Granada, but it doesn't belong to the city of 19th-century buildings and wide boulevards beneath it. The district once flourished as the residential section of the Moors, even after the city's reconquest, but it fell into decline when the Christians eventually drove the Moors out. A labyrinth of steep, crooked streets, it escaped the fate of much of Granada, which was torn down in the name of progress. Fortunately, it has been preserved, as have its plazas, whitewashed houses, villas, and the decaying remnants of the old city gate. Here and there, you can catch a glimpse of a private patio filled with fountains and plants—these are home to a traditional and graceful way of life that flourishes today. Car traffic is only allowed 6 hours a day, so walk or take the no. 31 bus (.85€/95¢) from the Plaza Nueva deep into the quarter. Many bars and restaurants cluster around the Plaza Larga. You can always get out by walking downhill until you hit the Gran Vía or the river.

THE GYPSY CAVES OF SACROMONTE

Next to Albayzín are the Gypsy caves of Sacromonte. They are tawdry tourist traps, and wouldn't even be mentioned here if so many visitors didn't get conned into going, despite warnings. A few of the caves serve as troglodyte nightclubs. Strung with colored lights and furnished with stubby little tables and chairs, they function as flamenco *tablaos*. They aren't remotely romantic. With few exceptions, the performances of the singers, guitarists, and dancers are execrable. Patrons are hounded to buy vile sherry, shoddy trinkets, and cassettes, and to tip everyone in sight. You will be encouraged by leaflets scattered around the city and in every hotel lobby to join a "Granada By Night" tour. My heartfelt advice: *Don't!*

THE SHOPPING SCENE

The **Alcaicería,** once the Moorish silk market, is next to the cathedral in the lower city. The narrow streets of this rebuilt village of shops are filled with vendors selling the arts and crafts of the province. The Alcaicería offers you one of Spain's most diverse assortments of tiles, castanets, and wire figures of Don Quixote chasing windmills. The jewelry found here compares favorably with the finest Toledan work. For the window-shopper in particular, it makes a pleasant stroll.

MALAGA

Málaga is a bustling commercial and residential center whose economy doesn't depend exclusively on tourism. Its chief attraction is the mild off-season climate—summer can be sticky. Málaga's most famous native son is Pablo Picasso, born in 1881 at Plaza de la Merced, in the center of the city.

ESSENTIALS

GETTING THERE   **Iberia** (© 800/772-4642 in the U.S.) has flights every 2 hours into Málaga from Madrid. There are at least five trains a day from Madrid (trip time: 4½ hr.). For rail information in Málaga, contact **RENFE** (© 90-224-0202; www.renfe.es). Buses from all over Spain arrive at the terminal on Paseo de los Tilos, behind the RENFE office. Málaga is linked by bus to all the major cities of Spain. Call © 95-235-0061 in Málaga for **bus information** or go to **www.continental-auto.es**.

VISITOR INFORMATION   The **tourist information office** at Pasaje de Chinitas 4 (© **95-221-3445;** www.malagaturismo.com) is open Monday through Friday from 9am to 7pm and Saturday and Sunday from 9am to 2pm. Keeping longer hours is the municipal tourist information office at Av. Cervantes 1 (© **95-213-4734**), open Monday through Friday from 8:15am to 2:45pm and 4:30 to 7pm, Saturday from 9:30am to 1:30pm.

WHERE TO STAY

Parador de Málaga-Gibralfaro ✮   Originally established in 1948 and renovated in the 1990s, this member of the Parador chain is immediately adjacent to the foundations of a medieval castle. The lodging occupies the steep hill that dominates the city center, providing a vista that takes in the harbor, the bullring, mountains, and beaches. Rooms have sitting areas and wide glass doors opening onto terraces with garden furniture. They're tastefully decorated with modern furnishings and reproductions of Spanish antiques.

Monte Gibralfaro, 29016 Málaga. © 95-222-1902. Fax 95-222-1904. www.parador.es. 38 units. 123€ ($141) double. AE, DC, MC, V. Free parking. **Amenities:** Restaurant; bar; rooftop outdoor pool; concierge; limited room service; laundry service. *In room:* A/C, TV, minibar, hair dryer, safe.

WHERE TO DINE

Café de Paris ✮ FRENCH/SPANISH   Málaga's best restaurant is in La Malagueta, the district surrounding the Plaza de Toros (bullring). Much of the menu is French cuisine adapted to the Spanish palate, but classic Spanish recipes are also featured. Try crepes gratinées (filled with *angulas*—baby eels) or *lubina* or *dorada al sal*—fish baked in a hard crust of salt and cracked open at table; the fish proves to be exceptionally moist and not at all salty. Beef stroganoff is made here, but with *rabo de toro*—oxtail. Other specialties include artichokes stuffed with foie gras and a version of hake wrapped around pulverized shellfish and served with a tomato sauce.

Vélez Málaga 8. © 95-222-5043. Reservations required. Main courses 18€–26€ ($21–$30). *Menú del día* 45€ ($52). AE, DC, MC, V. Mon 1–4pm; Tues–Sat 1–4pm and 8:30pm–midnight. Closed Holy Week and last 2 weeks of July. Bus: 13.

EXPLORING MALAGA

The remains of the Moorish **Alcazaba** ✮, Plaza de la Aduana, Alcazabilla (© 95-222-5106; bus: 4, 18, 19, or 24), are within easy distance of the city center, off Paseo del Parque (plenty of signs point the way up the hill). The fortress was erected in the 10th or 11th century, though there have been later additions and reconstructions. Fernando and Isabel stayed here when they reconquered the city. The Alcazaba has extensive gardens and houses a small archaeological museum, with artifacts from cultures ranging from Greek to Phoenician to Carthaginian. Admission is 1.80€ ($2.05); it's open Tuesday to Sunday from 9:30am to 8pm in the summer and 8:30am to 7pm during the winter.

The 16th-century Renaissance **cathedral,** Plaza Obispo (© **95-221-5917;** bus: 14, 18, 19, or 24), in Málaga's center, was built on the site of a great mosque.

It suffered damage during the Civil War, but it remains vast and impressive, reflecting changing styles of interior architecture. Its most notable attributes are its richly ornamented choir stalls by Ortiz, Mena, and Michael. Admission is 3€ ($3.45). It's open weekdays from 10am to 6:45pm, to 5:45pm on Saturdays.

MARBELLA

Though packed with tourists, ranking just behind Torremolinos in numbers of visitors, Marbella is still the most exclusive resort along the Costa del Sol—with such bastions of posh as the Hotel Puente Romano. Despite the hordes, Marbella persists as a large, busy, but still mostly pleasant town at the foot of the Sierra Blanca, 80km (50 miles) east of Gibraltar and 76km (47 miles) east of Algeciras, or 600km (373 miles) south of Madrid.

Traces of the recent and distant past are found in Marbella's palatial town hall, its medieval ruins, and fragments of its Moorish walls. The most attractive area is the **old quarter,** with its narrow cobblestone streets and clustered houses, centering around Plaza de los Naranjos, which is planted with palms, trumpeteer vines, and orange trees. Seek out the Plaza de la Iglesia and the streets around it, with a church on one side and a rampart of an old fortress on the other.

The biggest attractions in Marbella are **El Fuerte** and **La Fontanilla,** the two main beaches. There are other, more secluded beaches, but you'll need your own transportation to get to them.

ESSENTIALS

GETTING THERE At least 18 buses run between Málaga and Marbella daily. Four buses come in from Madrid and another three come from Barcelona.

VISITOR INFORMATION The **tourist office,** on Glorieta de la Fontanilla (© 95-277-1442; www.pgb.es/marbella), is open April through October, Monday through Friday from 9:30am to 9pm and Saturday from 10am to 2pm. Another tourist office is on Plaza Naranjos (© 95-282-3550), keeping the same hours.

WHERE TO STAY

El Castillo This small 1960s *hostal* is at the foot of the castle in the narrow streets of the old town. The spartan rooms are scrubbed clean and look out onto a small, covered courtyard. No meals are served, but many cafes, suitable for breakfast, are nearby. A tiny bit of English is spoken.

Plaza San Bernabé 2, 29600 Marbella. © 95-277-1739. 26 units. 40€ ($46) double. MC, V. *In room:* No phone.

El Fuerte ⭐ This is the largest and most recommendable hotel in the center of Marbella. An underground tunnel leads beneath an all-pedestrian, traffic-free promenade to the sands of the beach. Built in 1957, it was last renovated in 1994. It caters to a sedate clientele of conservative northern Europeans. There's a palm-fringed pool across the street from a sheltered lagoon and a wide-open beach. The hotel offers a handful of terraces, some shaded by flowering arbors.

Av. del Fuerte, 29600 Marbella. © 800/448-8355 in the U.S., or 95-286-1500. Fax 95-282-4411. www. fuertehoteles.com. 263 units. 125€–227€ ($144–$261) double; from 221€ ($254) suite. AE, DC, MC, V. Free parking. **Amenities:** Restaurant; cafe; covered pool; heated outdoor pool; golf nearby; outdoor tennis courts lit for night play; fitness room; salon; nonsmoking rooms. *In room:* A/C, TV, minibar, hair dryer, safe.

Marbella Club ⭐⭐⭐ The first luxury hotel on the coast, this exclusive enclave was established in 1954 and has been renovated and refreshed many times since to keep up with newer competitors. It sprawls over a generously landscaped property that slopes from a roadside reception area down to the beach, incorporating small clusters of garden pavilions, bungalows, and small-scale annexes. Elegantly furnished rooms have private balconies or terraces. Golf can be arranged nearby, and tennis courts are within a 2-minute walk.

Bulevard Príncipe Alfonso von Hohenlohe, 29600 Marbella. © **800/448-8355** in the U.S., or 95-282-2211. Fax 95-282-9884. www.marbellaclub.com. 129 units. 250€–645€ ($287–$742) double; from 345€ ($397) suite. AE, DC, MC, V. Free parking. **Amenities:** Restaurant; bar; 3 pools; health club and spa; bike rental; concierge; business center; 24-hr. room service; babysitting; same-day laundry service and dry cleaning. *In room:* A/C, TV, minibar, hair dryer, safe.

Puente Romano ✯✯✯   This hotel began life as a condo annex of the older Marbella Club, down the road, but it soon surpassed its sibling in luxe and panache. There is no finer resort on the Costa. Like many of its fellows, the exterior style is mock Andalusian pueblo. A set of 27 small buildings encloses luxuriant gardens, with a brook spanned at one point by the Roman bridge that inspired the hotel's name. The always-stylish international clientele is afforded a beach club, twice-daily maid service, and reassuring security patrols. Rooms are vast and airy, with ground-floor units opening onto the gardens. Service excels: Order breakfast as you step into the shower and it arrives before you've reached for the towel.

Carretera de Cádiz, Km 177, 29600 Marbella. © **95-282-0900.** Fax 95-277-5766. www.puenteromano.com. 274 units. 370€–498€ ($425–$573) double; from 446€ ($513) suite. AE, DC, MC, V. Limited free parking. **Amenities:** 3 restaurants; bar; 2 large heated outdoor pools; golf nearby; 7 lighted tennis courts; state-of-the-art health club; watersports equipment; concierge; car-rental desk; secretarial services; 24-hr. room service; in-room massage; babysitting; same-day laundry service and dry cleaning. *In room:* A/C, TV, minibar, hair dryer, safe.

WHERE TO DINE

Altamirano SPANISH   Take the trouble to seek out this fine little tapas bar on a quiet square in the old town, up a narrow lane from Avenida de Nabeul. Conventional meals aren't the point. Put together a selection from the long list of traditional dishes available as *tapas* (small), *media raciones* (medium), and *raciones* (full plate). Beware the choices that list only their weight in grams— they're costly. *Almejas*—baby clams in garlicky wine sauce—are good starters. *Gambas pil-pil*—spicy shrimp—are another, and, if you're acclimated to calamari back home, discover a similar texture but new flavor in the *navajas*—grilled razor clams. It's smoky inside, so grab one of the tables outside if you're not a smoker.

Plaza Altamirano 3. © **95/282-4932.** Tapas and *raciones* 4.50€–9.25€ ($5.25–$11). MC, V. Thurs–Tues 1–4pm and 7:30pm–midnight.

Cipriano SPANISH   Puerto Banús, a satellite of Marbella centered on a large marina, has become a small city in the last 20 years. At the harbor, yachts have Mercedes in attendance to take their owners to dinner. This is one of their destinations, a crisply corporate enclave in a glass office building. With its burnished wood paneling, marble floors, and platoon of uniformed waiters, you'll not want to show up in shorts and T-shirts. Otherwise, everyone, even single diners, is made to feel special. Service is polished, balanced between warmth and professionalism, a pleasure to experience. Fish is your best bet, especially the classic *dorada a la sal,* sea bass baked in a hard salt shell. There are two main rooms and a terrace that seats over 200 diners.

Avenida Playas del Duque. © **95-281-1077.** Reservations suggested. Main courses 15€–23€ ($17–$26); *menú degustación* 55€ ($63). AE, DC, MC, V. Daily 1:30–4pm and 8–11pm. Closed mid-Jan to mid-Feb.

El Balcón de la Virgen SPANISH   Set in the historic core of old Marbella, this restaurant is named after a 200-year-old statue of the Virgin that adorns a wall niche. The ancient house is all but hidden under a blanket of flowering vines. You'll find it within a short walk of the Plaza de los Naranjos. Regardless of when you arrive, it's likely to be well patronized. The interior is as picturesque as anything, with amphorae and antique farm tools hanging on the white plaster walls. The menu is mostly Andalusian, which means lots of seafood, such as the mixed grill of three shrimp, three cuttlefish, and three fish filets. The food is unremarkable but prices are fair, the service attentive, and the setting entrancing. Note that it is open only for dinner.

Remedios 2. (✆) 95-277-6092. Reservations recommended. Main courses 7€–16€ ($8.05–$18). AE, MC, V. Daily 7pm–midnight. Closed Tues Nov–May.

La Hacienda ✦ MEDITERRANEAN   La Hacienda, 13km (8 miles) east of Marbella, has long enjoyed a reputation for serving some of the best food along the Costa del Sol. In cooler months, dine in the rustic tavern before an open fireplace; in fair weather, meals are served on a patio. The chef may offer foie gras with leeks, Serrano ham with green gazpacho, and saddle of hare with mushrooms and juniper, but the menu changes frequently. The expert kitchen knows how to heighten the flavors of the fresh ingredients, and the food presentation is stylish. Several items—guinea fowl, roast lamb, wild duck—are for two persons. Although the food is admirable, the service is sometimes lacking.

Urbanización Hacienda Las Chapas, Carretera de Cádiz, Km 193. (✆) 95-283-1267. Reservations recommended. Main courses 15€–42€ ($17–$48); *menu degustación* 50€ ($58). AE, DC, MC, V. Summer daily 8:30pm–midnight; winter Wed–Sun 1–3:30pm and 8:30–11:30pm. Closed Nov 15–Dec 20.

MARBELLA AFTER DARK

Near Puerto Banús, **Casino Nueva Andalucía Marbella,** Urbanización Nueva Andalucía ((✆) **95-281-4000;** www.casinomarbella.com), is on the lobby level of the Andalucía Plaza Hotel. It stands in an upscale development surrounded by foreign-owned condos and lush golf courses, 7km (4¼ miles) from Marbella's center beside the road leading to Cádiz. Gambling includes individual games such as French and American roulette, blackjack, punto y banco, craps, and chemin de fer. Entrance to the casino is 5€ ($5.75), and you'll have to present a valid passport. You can dine in the Casino Restaurant before or after gambling. The casino is open daily from 6pm to 4 or 5am.

TORREMOLINOS

This is the most famous—which isn't to say the finest—Mediterranean beach resort in Spain. It's a gathering place for international visitors, a stew of northern Europeans and North and South Americans. The once tranquil fishing village of Torremolinos has been engulfed in concrete-walled resort hotels. Some travelers relax here after whirlwind tours of Spain—the living is easy, the people are in a party mood, and there are no historic monuments to visit. Torremolinos is often a cacophonous refuge for people with nothing more elevated in mind than an all-over tan by Sunday. The sands along the beachfront tend to be gritty and grayish. The best beaches are **El Bajondillo** and **La Carihuela,** the latter bordering an old fishing village. All beaches here are public, but don't expect changing facilities. Many women go topless on the beaches. *Note:* If for some reason you find yourself here in December, January, or February, expect many restaurants, hotels, and casinos to be closed.

ESSENTIALS

GETTING THERE   Torremolinos is served by the nearby Málaga airport, 14km (8¾ miles) west. There are frequent rail departures from the terminal at Málaga; for information, contact **RENFE** ((✆) **90-224-0202;** www.renfe.es).

Buses run frequently between Málaga and Torremolinos; for information, call
€ 95-235-0061.

VISITOR INFORMATION   The **tourist information office** is at Plaza de las
Comunidades Autonomas (€ **95-221-3445**). It's open daily from 8am to 3pm
(Mon–Fri 9:30am–2:30pm in winter).

WHERE TO STAY

Meliá Costa del Sol   Admittedly nothing memorable, this massive chain
hotel provides most everything expected of it. The beach is just across the street
and the attached Centro de Talasoterapia purveys that non-tiring, nondietary
route to robust health so dear to Europeans—water therapy. The facility offers
massages, a mud bath, a whirlpool, a sauna, a pool, and a Turkish bath. Forgive
the management the stunningly unattractive sand-colored stucco exterior—it's
better inside.

Paseo Marítimo 11, 29620 Torremolinos. € **95-238-6677.** Fax 95-238-6417. www.meliacostadelsol.
solmelia.com. 540 units. 58€–146€ ($67–$168) double; from 125€ ($144) suite. AE, MC, V. **Amenities:**
2 restaurants; 2 bars; outdoor pool; health club and spa; concierge; car-rental desk; babysitting; same-day
laundry service and dry cleaning; nonsmoking rooms. In room: A/C, TV, hair dryer, safe.

Parador de Málaga Golf ⋆   Also known as the Parador de Torremolinos
and other variations thereof, this resort hotel was created by the Spanish government. The hacienda-style hotel is flanked by a golf course on one side and
the Mediterranean on another. It's 3km (1¾ miles) from the airport, 10km
(6¼ miles) from Málaga, and 4km (2½ miles) from Torremolinos. Rooms have
balconies with a view of the golfing greens, the circular pool, or the water; some
are equipped with Jacuzzis. Long tiled corridors lead to the air-conditioned
public areas and graciously furnished lounges.

Carretera de Málaga, Torremolinos, 29080 Apartado 324, Málaga. € **95-238-1255.** Fax 95-238-8963. www.
parador.es. 60 units. 113€ ($130) double. AE, DC, MC, V. Free parking. **Amenities:** Restaurant; bar; outdoor
pool; golf course; tennis court; limited room service; babysitting; same-day laundry service and dry cleaning.
In room: A/C, TV, minibar, hair dryer, safe.

Sol Aloha Puerto   Heralded as one of the most modern hotels along the
Costa del Sol when it was built in 1972, this now-aging hotel stands on the
seashore in the residential suburb of El Saltillo, on the southwestern edge of
Torremolinos. Away from the noise of the town center, it offers spacious rooms,
all facing the sea, the Benalmádena marina, or the beach. There's live entertainment most nights in a vast lounge with row after row of tub chairs. Drinks are
generously poured and cost under 5€ ($5.75). During the day, you can take part
in activities like darts, shuffleboard, archery, and Spanish classes.

Salvador Allende 45, 29620 Torremolinos. € **800/336-3542** in the U.S., or 95-238-7066. Fax 95-238-5701.
www.solalohapuerto.solmelia.com. 370 units. 63€–150€ ($72–$173) double. AE, DC, MC, V. **Amenities:**
2 restaurants; 4 bars; heated indoor and outdoor pools; tennis court; concierge; car-rental desk; limited room
service; same-day laundry service and dry cleaning. In room: A/C, TV, minibar, hair dryer, safe.

Sol Don Pablo ⋆   Despite its undistinguished exterior, this is one of the most
desirable resort hotels in Torremolinos, a minute from the beach and surrounded
by its own garden and playground. The surprise is the glamorous interior, which
borrows heavily from Moorish palaces and medieval castles. Splashing fountains
are found in the arched-tile arcades, and niches with life-size stone statues of
nude figures line the grand staircase. The comfortably furnished rooms have sea-
view terraces and private bathrooms. Live entertainment is staged inside and out
most days and nights, with dancing to a live band as well as a separate disco. A
variety of activities, including group games and fitness classes, are offered.

Paseo Marítimo, s/n, 29620 Torremolinos. ℂ **95-238-3888**. Fax 95-238-3783. 443 units. 75€–140€ ($86–$161) double. Free parking. AE, DC, MC, V. **Amenities:** Restaurant; bar; indoor pool with whirlpool; large circular outdoor pool; golf nearby; tennis court; children's program; limited room service; babysitting; same-day laundry service and dry cleaning. *In room:* A/C, TV, minibar, hair dryer.

WHERE TO DINE

Antonio ⭐ SPANISH   Facing the quiet west end of La Carihuela beach, across a paved promenade, the glass sides of this large room open wide in summer to accept the sea breezes. On the face, the menu looks indistinguishable from those of hundreds of others along the coast; but the execution and presentation here are decidedly superior to most. The *lenguado al champan,* for one, is a large filet of sole in a champagne sauce scattered with red peppercorns and mushroom bits—simple, pretty, tasty. While meat dishes are available, go for the seafood— that's the Mediterranean out there.

Plaza del Remo 6. ℂ **95-205-0735**. Reservations suggested. Main courses 8€–28€ ($9.20–$32). AE, DC, MC, V. Daily 1pm–2am. Closed Nov.

Casa Juan SEAFOOD   Nautical decor, such as boat models and brass-bordered windows, not to mention a lavish display of lobsters and company near the door, make clear the objectives of this restaurant. That in mind, you have some difficult choices to make. *Gazpachuelo,* a warm, creamy chowder crowded with fish and vegetables, is a splendid way to begin. Then, perhaps, the *fritura mixta*—lightly fried fish, squid, and other creatures—or paella, or *zarzuela,* a tomato-based fish stew. The restaurant is in a modern building in the old-fashioned satellite hamlet of La Carihuela, west of Torremolinos center. Whenever it gets busy (which is frequently), the staff is inclined to impatience. There are outdoor tables.

Calle Mar 14, La Carihuela. ℂ **95-237-3512**. Reservations recommended. Main courses 7.60€–42€ ($8.70–$48). AE, DC, MC, V. Tues–Sun 1–4:30pm and 7pm–midnight. Closed Dec.

El Gato Viudo SPANISH   Simple and amiable, this old-fashioned tavern with sidewalk seating occupies the street level and cellar of a building off Calle San Miguel. The menu lists platters of grilled fish, marinated hake, roasted pork and veal, calamari with spicy tomato sauce, grilled shrimp, and *zarzuela,* a Catalan fish stew similar to bouillabaisse.

La Nogalera 8. ℂ **95-238-51-29**. Main courses 7.40€–18€ ($8.30–$21). AE, DC, MC, V. Nov–Apr Thurs–Tues 1–3pm and 6–11:30pm; May–Oct daily 1–4pm and 6–11:30pm.

TORREMOLINOS AFTER DARK

One of the major casinos along the Costa del Sol, **Casino Torrequebrada,** Carretera de Cádiz 220, Benalmádena Costa (ℂ **95-244-6000;** www. casinotorrequebrada.net), is on the lobby level of the Hotel Torrequebrada. The Torrequebrada combines a nightclub/cabaret, a restaurant, and an array of tables devoted to blackjack, chemin de fer, punto y banco, and two kinds of roulette. The nightclub presents a flamenco show from Tuesday to Saturday at 10:30pm. Many visitors prefer to just attend the show, paying 32€ ($37), including the first drink. Dinner is served from Wednesday to Saturday at 9pm and costs 65€ ($75), which includes admission to the show. The casino is especially lively in midsummer. The casino, its facilities, and its gaming tables are open daily from 9pm to 4am. The entrance fee to the gaming rooms is 5€ ($5.75). You need a passport to enter.

17

Sweden

by Darwin Porter & Danforth Prince

Although it was founded 7 centuries ago, Stockholm didn't become Sweden's capital until the mid–17th century. Today it's the capital of a modern welfare state with a strong focus on leisure activities and access to nature only a few minutes away.

1 Stockholm & Environs

Stockholm is built on 14 islands in Lake Mälaren, marking the beginning of an archipelago of 24,000 islands, skerries, and islets that stretches all the way to the Baltic Sea. It's a city of bridges and islands, towers and steeples, cobblestone squares and broad boulevards, Renaissance splendor and steel-and-glass skyscrapers. The medieval walls of Gamla Stan (Old Town) no longer stand, but the winding streets have been preserved. You can even go fishing in downtown waterways, thanks to a long-ago decree from Queen Christina.

Once an ethnically homogeneous society, Stockholm has experienced a vast wave of immigration in the past several years. More than 10% of Sweden's residents are immigrants or children of immigrant parents, with most coming from other Scandinavian countries. Because of Sweden's strong stance on human rights, the country has also become a major destination for political and social refugees from Africa, the Middle East, and the former Yugoslavia as well.

An important aspect of Stockholm today is a growing interest in cultural activities. Over the past quarter of a century, attendance at live concerts has grown, book sales are up, and more and more people are visiting museums.

ESSENTIALS

GETTING THERE   By Plane   You'll arrive at **Stockholm Arlanda Airport** (© **08/797-60-00;** www.lfv.se), about 45km (27 miles) north of Stockholm on the E-4 highway. **SAS** (© **800/221-2350**) is the most common carrier. The fastest and cheapest way to go from the airport to the Central Station in Stockholm is on the **Arlanda Express** (www.arlandaexpress.com) train, which takes only 20 minutes and is covered by the Eurailpass. This high-speed link is the finest option for the rail traveler. Trains run every 15 minutes daily from 5am to midnight. If you don't have a rail pass, the cost of a one-way ticket is 180SEK ($23) for adults and 90SEK ($12) for seniors and students (those under 8 ride free). For more information, call © **020/22-22-24.** A **bus** (© **08/600-10-00**) outside the terminal building also goes to the City Terminal, Klarabergsviadukten, in the city center every 10 to 15 minutes (trip time: 40 min.), for 89SEK ($12). A taxi to or from the airport is expensive, costing 390SEK to 460SEK ($51–$60) or more. *Travelers beware:* Smaller taxi companies may charge up to 650SEK ($85) for the same ride. Be sure to ask in advance what the price is to your destination. For the name of a reputable company, see "Getting Around," below.

By Train   The first high-speed train between Stockholm and Oslo has reduced travel time to 4 hours and 50 minutes between these two once remotely linked Scandinavian capitals. Depending on the day, there are two to three trains daily in each direction. This high-speed train now competes directly with air travel. Trains arrive at Stockholm's **Centralstationen (Central Station)** on Vasagatan 14, in the city center ((*C* **020/95-75-75** in Sweden, or 08/696-75-09 from abroad). There you can make connections to Stockholm's subway, the T-bana. Follow the TUNNELBANA sign.

By Bus   Buses arrive at the **Centralstationen** on Vasagatan, and from here you can catch the T-bana (subway) to your Stockholm destination. For information in the Stockholm area, call (*C* **08/440-85-70.** Ticket-office hours are Monday through Friday and Sunday from 9am to 6pm; Saturday from 9am to 4pm.

By Car   Getting into Stockholm by car is relatively easy because the major national expressway from the south, E-4, joins with the national express highway, E-18, coming in from the west and leads right into the heart of the city. Stay on the highway until you see the turnoff for Central Stockholm or Centrum.

VISITOR INFORMATION   Tourist Offices   The **Tourist Centre** is at Sweden House, Hamngatan 27, off Kungsträdgården (Box 7542), S-103 93 Stockholm ((*C* **08/789-24-00** or 08/789-24-90; www.stockholm.com). It's open from May to September, Monday through Friday from 9am to 7pm, Saturday and Sunday from 9am to 3pm; from October to April, Monday through Friday from 9am to 6pm, Saturday and Sunday from 10am to 3pm. Maps and other free materials are available.

   Kulturhuset, Sergels Torg 3 ((*C* **08/508-314-00;** http://kulturhuset. stockholm.se), distributes information about cultural activities and organizations throughout Sweden and Europe. The largest organization of its kind in Sweden, it was built in 1974 by the city of Stockholm as a showcase for Swedish and international art and theater. There are no permanent exhibits; display spaces hold a changing array of paintings, sculpture, photographs, and live performance groups. Inside are a snack bar, a library (which has newspapers in several languages), a reading room, and a collection of recordings. Admission is 40SEK ($5.20) for adults, 20SEK ($2.60) for children 12 to 18, free for children under 12. It's open Tuesday through Thursday from 11am to 7pm, Friday from 11am to 6pm, Saturday from 11am to 5pm, and Sunday from 11am to 5pm.

Websites   Go to the Scandinavian Tourism Board website at **www.go scandinavia.com** for maps, sightseeing information, ferry schedules, and other advice. Other useful sites are **www.stockholmtown.com**, for updated events listings and advice on dining, lodging, and museums, and **www.visit-sweden.com**.

CITY LAYOUT   On the island of Norrmalm north of the Old Town are Stockholm's major streets, such as **Kungsgatan** (the main shopping street), **Birger Jarlsgatan,** and **Strandvägen** (leading to the Djurgården—home of many of the city's top sights). **Stureplan,** at the junction of the major avenues Kungsgatan and Birger Jarlsgatan, is the city's commercial hub.

   About 4 blocks west of the Stureplan rises **Hötorget City,** a landmark of modern urban planning. Its main traffic-free artery is the **Sergelgatan,** a 3-block shoppers' promenade that eventually leads to the modern sculptures in the center of the **Sergels Torg.** About 9 blocks south of the Stureplan, at **Gustav Adolfs Torg,** are the Royal Dramatic Theater and the Royal Opera House. A block east of the flaming torches of the Royal Opera House is the verdant north–south stretch of **Kungsträdgården,** part avenue, part public park, which serves as a

popular gathering place for students and as a resting perch for shoppers. Three blocks southeast, on a famous promontory, lie the landmark Grand Hotel and the National Museum.

Kungsholmen, King's Island, is across a narrow canal from the rest of the city, a short walk west of the Central Station. It's visited chiefly by those wanting to tour Stockholm's elegant Stadshuset (City Hall). South of the island where **Gamla Stan (Old Town)** is located—and separated from it by a narrow but much-navigated stretch of water—is **Södermalm,** the southern district of Stockholm. Quieter than its northern counterpart, it's an important residential area with a distinctive flavor of its own.

To the east of Gamla Stan, on a large and forested island completely surrounded by the complicated waterways of Stockholm, is **Djurgården (Deer Park).** The rustically unpopulated summer pleasure ground of Stockholm, it's the site of many of the city's most popular attractions: the open-air museums of Skansen, the *Vasa* man-of-war, Gröna Lund's Tivoli, the Waldemarsudde estate of the "painting prince" Eugen, and the Nordic Museum.

GETTING AROUND Walking is the best way to get to know the city. In any case, you have to explore Gamla Stan on foot, as cars are banned from most of the streets. Djurgården and Skeppsholmen are other popular haunts for strolling.

Value **The Stockholm Card**

Stockholmskortet (Stockholm Card) is a discount card that allows unlimited travel by bus (except airport buses), subway, and local trains throughout the city and county of Stockholm. Admission to 70 attractions is included in the package. You can also take a sightseeing tour with City Sightseeing, getting on and off as often as you please. Tours are available daily from mid-June to mid-August. The card is good for a 50% discount on a boat trip to the Royal Palace of Drottningholm.

You can buy the card at several places in the city, including the Tourist Centre in Sweden House, HotellCentralen, the Central Station, the tourist information desk in City Hall (summer only), the Kaknäs TV tower, SL-Center Sergels Torg (subway entrance level), and Pressbyrån newsstands. The cards are stamped with the date and time at the first use. A 24-hour card costs 220SEK ($29) for adults, 60SEK ($7.80) for children 7 to 17.

By Public Transportation   You can travel throughout Stockholm county by bus, local train, subway (T-bana), and tram, going from Singö in the north to Nynäshamn in the south. The routes are divided into zones, and one ticket is valid for all types of public transportation in the same zone within 1 hour of being stamped.

Regular Fares   The basic fare for public transportation (subway, tram, streetcar, or bus) is 20SEK ($2.60). Purchase a ticket for a tram or streetcar at the tollbooth on the subway platform. On buses you pay the driver. To travel in most of Stockholm, all the way to the borders of the inner city, requires two tickets. The maximum ride, to the outermost suburbs, requires five tickets. You can transfer free (or double back and return to your starting point) within 1 hour of your departure. Day passes can be purchased at the SL Center.

Special Discount Tickets   Your best transportation bet is a **tourist season ticket.** A 1-day card costs 80SEK ($10) and is valid for 24 hours of unlimited travel by T-bana (subway), bus, and commuter train within Stockholm. It also includes passage on the ferry to Djurgården. Most visitors will probably prefer the 3-day card for 150SEK ($20), valid for 72 hours in Stockholm and the adjacent county. The 3-day card is also valid for admission to the Skansen museum, the Kaknäs tower, and Gröna Lunds Tivoli. A card for a child 8 to 17 costs 45SEK to 90SEK ($5.85–$12); kids under 8 travel free with an adult. Tickets are available at tourist information offices, in subway stations, and from most news vendors. Call ℂ **08/689-10-00** for more information.

You can also opt for the **Stockholm Card;** see the box above for full details.

By T-bana (Subway)   Subway entrances are marked with a blue T on a white background. Tickets are bought on the platform. For information about schedules, routes, and fares, phone ℂ **08/600-10-00.**

By Bus   Where the subway line ends, the bus begins. If the subway doesn't reach an area, a bus will. Many visitors ride the bus to Djurgården (although you can walk), where the T-bana doesn't go. If you're staying long enough to warrant it, you can buy the *SL Stockholmskartan* booklet (220SEK/$29) at the Tourist Centre at Sweden House, Hamngatan 27, off Kungsträdgården (ℂ **08/789-24-95** for a list of bus routes).

By Ferry   Ferries from Skeppsbron on Gamla Stan (near the bridge to Södermalm) can take you to Djurgården if you don't want to walk or go by bus. They leave every 20 minutes Monday through Saturday, and about every 15 minutes on Sunday, from 9am to 6pm. The fare is 20SEK ($2.60) for adults, 15SEK ($1.95) for seniors and children 7 to 12. Free for children under 7.

By Taxi   Taxis in Stockholm are the most expensive in the world. The meter starts at 36SEK ($4.70), and a short ride can easily cost 80SEK ($10). You can hail those that display the sign LEDIG, or you can request one by phone. **Taxi Stockholm** (© 08/15-00-00 or 08/15-04-00) is a large, reputable company.

By Car   In general, you can park in marked spaces Monday through Friday from 8am to 6pm, but these spaces are hard to come by. Consider leaving your car in a parking garage—there are several in the city center and on the outskirts— and using public transportation. Parking exceptions or rules for specific areas are indicated on signs in the area. At Djurgården, parking is always prohibited, and from April to mid-September, it's closed to traffic Friday through Sunday.

Avis (© 08/797-99-70) and **Hertz** (© 08/797-99-00) maintain offices at Arlanda Airport. Hertz's downtown office is at Vasagatan 26 (© **08/454-62-50**); Avis's downtown office is at Vasagatan 10B (© **08/20-20-60**). Rentals at both organizations are usually cheaper if you reserve them by phone before leaving North America.

FAST FACTS: Stockholm

American Express   For local 24-hour customer service call © **08/429-58-00.**

Currency   You'll pay your way in Sweden with Swedish krone (singular, krona), or crowns, which is universally abbreviated SEK. These are divided into 100 øre. The exchange rate used throughout this chapter was US$1 = 7.5SEK (or 1SEK = 15¢). At press time, £1 = 12SEK (or 1SEK = 7 pence). Note that although Sweden is a member of the EU, in 2002 it opted not to adopt the euro as its national currency.

Dentists   In an emergency, go to **Sct. Eriks Hospital**, Fleminggatan 22 (© 08/545-51-20), open daily from 8am to 5pm.

Doctors   For 24-hour emergency medical care, check with **Medical Care Information** (© 08/672-10-00). There's also a private clinic, **City Akuten**, Apelberg Sq. 481, 4th Floor (© 08/412-29-61).

Drugstores   One 24-hour pharmacy is **C. W. Scheele**, Klarabergsgatan 64 (© **08/454-81-00**; T-bana: Centralen).

Embassies/Consulates   The embassy of the **United States** is at Daghammarskjölds väg 31, S-115 89 Stockholm (© 08/783-53-00; T-bana: Östermalmstorg); the embassy of the **United Kingdom** (© 08/671-30-00) is at Skarpügatan 6–8 (mailing address: P.O. Box 27819, S-115 93 Stockholm); the embassy of **Canada** is at Tegelbacken 4, S-103 23 Stockholm (© 08/453-30-00; T-bana: Centralen); the embassy of **Ireland** (© 08/661-80-05; T-bana: Östermalmstorg) is at Östermalmsgatan 97 (mailing address: P.O. Box 10326, S-100 55 Stockholm); the embassy of **Australia** (© 08/613-29-00; T-bana: Hötorget) is at Sergels Torg 12 (mailing address: P.O. Box 7003, S-103 86 Stockholm); the embassy of **South Africa** is at Linnégaten

76, S-115 00 Stockholm (℡ **08/24-39-50**; T-bana: Östermalmstorg), and the General Consulate of **New Zealand** at Stureplan 2, S-102 27 (℡ **08-611-2625**; T-bana: Östermalmstorg. Call for hours.

Emergencies Call ℡ **211** for the police, ambulance service, or the fire department.

Internet One of the most central places for receiving e-mail or checking messages is **Café Nine**, Odengatan 44 (℡ **08/673-67-97**; info@ninestudios.com; T-Bana: Odenplan). It charges only 1SEK (15¢) per minute, and is open daily from 9am to 1am.

Post Office The main post office is at Sveavagen 31 (℡ **08/411-61-17**), open Monday through Friday from 7am to 7pm and Saturday from 10am to 4pm.

Taxes Sweden imposes a "value-added tax," called *moms,* on most goods and services. Visitors from North America can beat the tax, however, by shopping in stores with the yellow-and-blue tax-free shopping sign. There are more than 15,000 of these stores in Sweden. To get a refund, your total purchase must cost a minimum of 200SEK ($26). Tax refunds range from 14% to 18%, depending on the amount purchased. *Moms* begins at 19% on food items, but is 25% for most goods and services. The tax is part of the purchase price, but you can get a tax-refund voucher before you leave the store. When you leave Sweden, take the voucher to a tax-free Customs desk at the airport or train station you're leaving from. They will give you your *moms* refund (minus a small service charge) before you wing off to your next non-Swedish destination. Two requirements: You cannot use your purchase in Sweden (it should be sealed in its original packaging), and it must be taken out of the country within 1 month after purchase. For more information, call **Global Refunds** at ℡ **0410/484-50.**

Telephone The **country code** for Sweden is **46.** The **city code** for Stockholm is **8;** use this code when you're calling from outside Sweden. If you're within Sweden but not in Stockholm, use **08.** If you're calling within Stockholm, simply leave off the code and dial the regular phone number.

Instructions in English are posted in **public phone boxes,** which can be found on street corners. Very few phones in Sweden are coin operated; most require the purchase of a phone card (called a **Telekort**). You can obtain phone cards at most newspaper stands and tobacco shops.

You can make international calls from the **TeleCenter Office** on the Central Station's ground floor (℡ **08/789-24-56**), open daily from 8am to 9pm, except major holidays. Long-distance rates are posted. To make a collect or calling-card call, dial one of the following access numbers to reach an American operator or an English-language voice prompt: **AT&T,** ℡ **800/CALL-ATT;** or **MCI,** ℡ **800/888-8000.**

For directory listings or other information for Stockholm or other parts of Sweden only, dial ℡ **118118;** for other parts of Europe, dial ℡ **118119.**

Tipping Hotels include a 15% service charge in your bill. Restaurants, depending on their class, add 13% to 15% to your tab. Taxi drivers are entitled to 8% of the fare, and cloakroom attendants usually get 6SEK (80¢).

WHERE TO STAY

By the standards of many U.S. and Canadian cities, hotels in Stockholm are very expensive. If the prices make you want to cancel your trip, read on. Dozens of hotels offer reduced rates on weekends all year and daily from around mid-June to mid-August. For further information, inquire at a travel agency or the tourist office (see "Visitor Information," above). In the summer, it's best to make reservations in advance just to be on the safe side.

Most medium-priced hotels are in Norrmalm, north of the Old Town, and many of the least expensive lodgings are near the Central Station. There are comparably priced inexpensive accommodations within 10 to 20 minutes of the city, easily reached by subway, streetcar, or bus. We'll suggest a few hotels in the Old Town, but they're limited and more expensive.

Note: In most cases a service charge ranging from 10% to 15% is added to the bill, plus the inevitable 21% *moms* (value-added tax). Unless otherwise indicated, all our recommended accommodations come with a private bathroom.

IN THE CITY CENTER
Very Expensive

Grand Hotel ★★★   Opposite the Royal Palace, this hotel—a bastion of elite hospitality since 1874 and a member of the Leading Hotels of the World—is the finest in Sweden. The most recent restoration was in 1996, but its old-world style has always been maintained. Guest rooms come in all shapes and sizes, all elegantly appointed with traditional styling. Some feature an air-cooling system. The bathrooms are decorated with Italian marble and tiles and have heated floors. The priciest rooms overlook the water. The hotel's ballroom is an exact copy of Louis XIV's Hall of Mirrors at Versailles.

Södra Blasieholmshamnen 8, S-103 27 Stockholm. ⓒ **800/223-5652** in the U.S. and Canada, or 08/679-35-00. Fax 08/611-86-86. www.grandhotel.se. 310 units. 3,400SEK–4,300SEK ($442–$559) double; from 5,300SEK ($689) suite. Rates include breakfast. AE, DC, MC, V. Parking 350SEK ($46). T-bana: Kungsträdgården. Bus: 46, 55, 62, or 76. **Amenities:** 2 restaurants; bar; fitness center; sauna; business center; 24-hr. room service; laundry service; dry cleaning; nonsmoking rooms; rooms for those with limited mobility. *In room:* TV, minibar, hair dryer, safe.

EXPENSIVE

Berns Hotel ★★   During its 19th-century heyday, this was the most elegant hotel in Sweden, with an ornate Gilded Age interior that was the setting for

---

Tips   Native Behavior

Although not as common as it once was, partaking in a Swedish smörgåsbord is the most typical of Swedish culinary delights. Some restaurants and hotels stage this lavish banquet. The secret of surviving it is to go gracefully to the table that's groaning with heaping platters of food and not overload your plate. You can always return for more of the *gravad lax* (thinly sliced salmon cured in dill) or Swedish Ping-Pong-shaped meatballs.

And when you've had too much smörgåsbord or other Swedish food delicacies, and joined in too many toasts fueled by the lethal aquavit, you can also always do as the Swedes do and retire to the nearest sauna bath to revitalize yourself for yet more revelry in the evening to come.

Stockholm

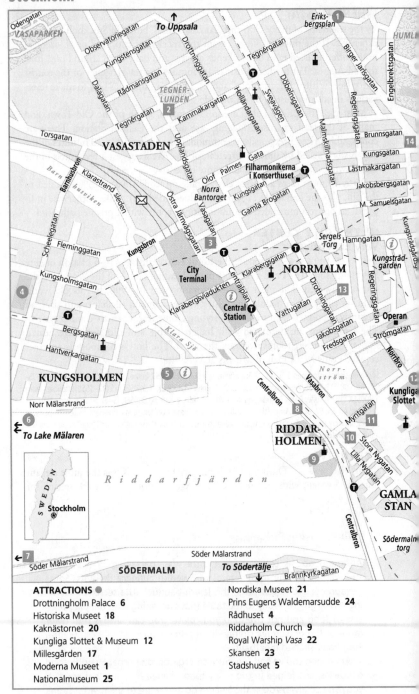

Odengatan
VASAPARKEN
Observatoriegatan
Kungstensgatan
Rådmansgatan
Dalagatan
Tegnérgatan
Torsgatan
TEGNÉR-LUNDEN **2**
Kammakargatan
Drottninggatan
↑ To Uppsala
Tegnérgatan
Hollándargatan
Sveavägen
Döbelnsgatan
Birger Jarlsgatan
Engelbrektsgatan
HUMLE
Eriks-bergsplan **1**
Regeringsgatan
Malmskillnadsgatan
Brunnsgatan **14**
Kungsgatan
Lästmakargatan
Jakobsbergsgatan
M. Samuelsgatan

VASASTADEN
Upplandsgatan
Olof Palmes Gata
Norra Bantorget
Vasagatan
Östra Järnvägsgatan
Filharmonikerna i Konserthuset
Kungsgatan
Gamla Brogatan
Barnhusbron
Klarastrand sleden
Barn busviken
Klarabergsgatan **3**
Sergels Torg
Hamngatan
Kungsträd-gården (i)
Regeringsgatan
Kungsträdgårdsg.
Scheelegatan
Flemminggatan
Kungsbron
City Terminal
Centralplan
NORRMALM
Drottninggatan
13
Vattugatan
Operan
Strömgatan
Kungsholmsgatan **4**
Klarabergsviadukten (i)
Central Station
Jakobsgatan
Fredsgatan
Norrbro
Bergsgatan
Hantverkargatan
Klara Sjö
Norr-ström
Vasabron
Kungliga Slottet **12**
11
KUNGSHOLMEN 5 (i)
Norr Mälarstrand
Centralbron
8
Myntgatan
Stora Nygatan
Lilla Nygatan
10
6
← To Lake Mälaren
SWEDEN
Stockholm ✵
Riddarfjärden
RIDDAR-HOLMEN 9
GAMLA STAN
Södermaln torg
7
Söder Mälarstrand
Söder Mälarstrand
SÖDERMALM
To Södertälje
Brännkyrkagatan
Centralbron

ATTRACTIONS ●

Drottningholm Palace **6**
Historiska Museet **18**
Kaknästornet **20**
Kungliga Slottet & Museum **12**
Millesgården **17**
Moderna Museet **1**
Nationalmuseum **25**

Nordiska Museet **21**
Prins Eugens Waldemarsudde **24**
Rådhuset **4**
Riddarholm Church **9**
Royal Warship *Vasa* **22**
Skansen **23**
Stadshuset **5**

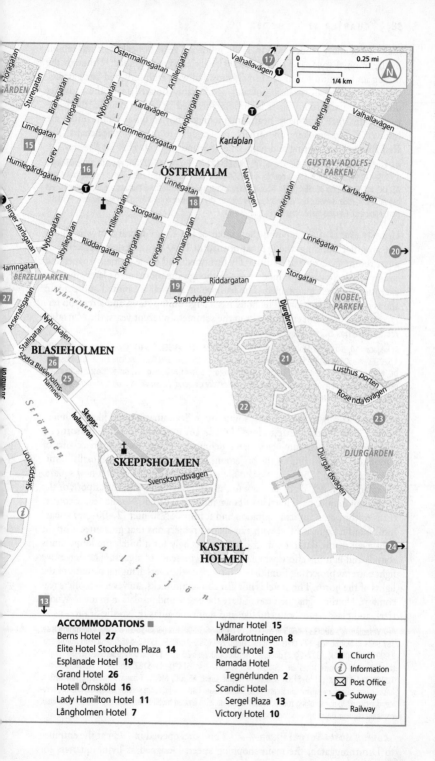

ACCOMMODATIONS ■

Berns Hotel **27**
Elite Hotel Stockholm Plaza **14**
Esplanade Hotel **19**
Grand Hotel **26**
Hotell Örnsköld **16**
Lady Hamilton Hotel **11**
Långholmen Hotel **7**

Lydmar Hotel **15**
Mälardrottningen **8**
Nordic Hotel **3**
Ramada Hotel
 Tegnérlunden **2**
Scandic Hotel
 Sergel Plaza **13**
Victory Hotel **10**

✝	Church
ⓘ	Information
✉	Post Office
- -ⓉⓉ-	Subway
——	Railway

many a legendary rendezvous. In 1989, following years of neglect, it was rebuilt in the original style, and the restaurant facilities were upgraded. Although the dining and drinking areas are usually crowded with club kids and bar patrons, the guest rooms are soundproof and comfortably isolated from the activities downstairs. Each room has a bathroom sheathed in Italian marble; the bathrooms are small but have neatly maintained shower units. Some units are reserved for nonsmokers, and others are accessible to those in wheelchairs. The **Red Room** is the setting and namesake of Strindberg's novel *Röda Rummet*.

Näckströmsgatan 8, S-111 47 Stockholm. (C) 08/566-322-00. Fax 08/566-322-01. www.berns.se. 65 units. 2,750SEK–3,900SEK ($358–$507) double; 4,600SEK–6,300SEK ($598–$819) suite. Rates include breakfast. AE, DC, MC, V. Parking 360SEK ($47). T-bana: Östermalmstorg. **Amenities:** Restaurant; 2 bars; sauna; fitness center; 24-hr. room service; babysitting; laundry service; dry cleaning; nonsmoking rooms. *In room:* TV, dataport, minibar, beverage maker, hair dryer, trouser press.

Lydmar Hotel Opposite the garden of the King's Library, in what looks like an office building, the Lydmar opened in 1930 (as the Eden Terrace). The guest rooms are cozy and traditionally furnished, and come in many shapes and sizes, each decorated with modern art. Although the rooms aren't large, they are exceptionally well maintained. The bathrooms are well appointed and contain shower-tub combinations. The hotel has a large dining room and a rooftop terrace where guests can enjoy drinks in the summer. In recent years, the **Matsalen** restaurant has become ever-so-chic.

Sturegatan 10, S-114 36 Stockholm. (C) 08/566-113-00. Fax 08/566-113-01. www.lydmar.se. 62 units. 1,520SEK–4,950SEK ($198–$644) double; 7,900SEK ($1,027) junior suite. Rates include buffet breakfast. AE, DC, MC, V. Parking 350SEK ($46). T-bana: Östermalmstorg. Bus: 41, 46, 56, or 91. **Amenities:** 2 restaurants; bar; limited room service; babysitting; laundry service; dry cleaning; nonsmoking rooms. *In room:* TV, dataport, minibar, hair dryer, iron.

Nordic Hotel *Finds* There's nothing in Scandinavia quite like this hotel, named "The World's Sexiest Hotel" by *Elle UK* magazine in 2004. It's sort of a split personality—its astrological sign is definitely Gemini. You're given a choice of a room of "watery calm" in the 367-room Nordic Sea or "post-minimalist luminescence" in the 175-room Nordic Light. Lying on either side of a new square, Vasaplan, the hotel stands adjacent to the express rail link with the airport, or the central rail station. Each hotel has its own individual design. Nordic Sea, of course, turns to the ocean for its inspiration and features a 530-liter (2,400-gal.) aquarium. Nordic Light is filled with sun-shaped projections that guarantee a bright light even in the darkest winter days. Surprisingly for a hotel, the lobby emits sounds and lighting effects when it senses the presence of a guest. The suggestive light patterns projecting from the walls re-create the ever-changing patterns of the lights of the north. This hotel is not just about gimmicks, however—it offers real comfort. Nordic Light guest rooms have the best sound insulation in town. Wood, steel, and glass create both clublike and maritime auras in Nordic Sea rooms.

4–7 Vasaplan. (C) 800/337-4685 in the U.S., or 08/50-56-30-00. Fax 08/50-56-30-60. www.nordichotels.se. 367 units in Nordic Sea, 175 units in Nordic Light. 2,400SEK–3,600SEK ($312–$468) double in Nordic Sea; 2,900SEK–3,600SEK ($377–$468) double in Nordic Light. June 20–Aug 17 and during selected Fri–Sun nights throughout the winter, rates are reduced to 1,100SEK–1,410SEK ($143–$183) double in Nordic Sea, and 1,310SEK–1,410SEK ($170–$183) double in Nordic Light. AE, DC, MC, V. T-bana: Centralen. **Amenities:** Restaurant; 2 bars; minigym; spa treatments; sauna; steam bath; 24-hr. room service; massage; laundry service; dry cleaning; nonsmoking rooms; rooms for those with limited mobility. *In room:* TV, dataport, minibar, coffeemaker, hair dryer, iron/ironing board, safe.

Scandic Hotel Sergel Plaza This hotel opened in 1984 at the entrance to Drottninggatan, the main shopping street. Designed as living quarters for parliament members, improvements have made it one of the city's leading hotels. The elegant decor includes 18th-century artwork and antiques. The beautifully decorated guest rooms are done in modern but traditional style. The average-size tiled bathrooms have shower-tub combinations. Maintenance is first-rate. A special executive floor offers enhanced luxuries and several electronic extras, such as dataports.

Brunkebergstorg 9, S-103 27 Stockholm. © **800/THE-OMNI** in the U.S., or 08/517-263-00. Fax 08/517-263-11. www.scandic-hotels.com/sergelplaza. 403 units. 1,490SEK–3,005SEK ($194–$391) double; from 4,600SEK ($598) suite. Rates include breakfast. AE, DC, MC, V. Parking 250SEK ($33). T-bana: Centralen. Bus: 46, 47, or 69. **Amenities:** Restaurant; bar; 24-hr. room service; laundry service; dry cleaning; nonsmoking rooms; rooms for those with limited mobility. *In room:* TV (teletext TV in superior rooms), minibar, hair dryer.

Moderate

Elite Hotel Stockholm Plaza ✦ Built on a triangular lot that might remind some visitors of New York's Flatiron Building, this first-class hotel is a well-run and inviting choice in the city center. From the time of its construction in 1903 until its renovation in 1984, the building had many uses—a run-down rooming house, private apartments, and offices. The light, fresh guest rooms have firm beds and tiled bathrooms with shower-tub combinations.

Birger Jarlsgatan 29, S-103 95 Stockholm. © **08/566-220-00.** Fax 08/566-220-20. www.elite.se. 151 units. 1,290SEK–2,395SEK ($168–$311) double; 2,790SEK–3,995SEK ($363–$519) suite. Rates include breakfast. AE, DC, MC, V. Parking 260SEK ($34). T-bana: Hötorget or Östermalmstorg. **Amenities:** Restaurant; bar; dance club; sauna; limited room service; laundry service; dry cleaning; rooms for those with limited mobility. *In room:* TV, dataport, minibar, hair dryer.

Esplanade Hotel ✦ This informal hotel, next to the more expensive Diplomat, attracts representatives from the nearby embassies and others who like its comfortable charm and traditional atmosphere. Constructed in 1910, it became a family-style hotel in 1954. Many of the rooms, furnished in old-fashioned style, have minibars. Single rooms are minuscule. Most doubles have double-glazed windows, extralong beds, and well-kept, decent-size tile bathrooms with shower-tub combinations. Four rooms have a water view, and the English lounge features a balcony with a view of Djurgården. Only breakfast is served.

Strandvägen 7A, S-114 56 Stockholm. © **08/663-07-40.** Fax 08/662-59-92. www.hotelesplanade.se. 34 units. Mon–Thurs 2,295SEK ($298) double; Fri–Sun 1,695SEK ($220) double. Rates include breakfast. AE, DC, MC, V. Parking nearby 250SEK ($33). T-bana: Östermalmstorg. Bus: 47 or 69. **Amenities:** Lounge; sauna; laundry service; dry cleaning. *In room:* TV, dataport, minibar, hair dryer.

Inexpensive

Hotell Örnsköld The five-story building that contains this hotel was built in 1910, and today the nearby Royal Dramatic Theater uses most of it for prop storage and staff housing. The hotel is situated on the second floor. High-ceilinged rooms have simple, contemporary furnishings, and more expensive units are big enough to hold extra beds if necessary. All units contain well-kept bathrooms with shower units. All rooms are nonsmoking.

Nybrogatan 6, S-114 34 Stockholm. © **08/667-02-85.** Fax 08/667-69-91. 27 units. 1,275SEK–1,975SEK ($166–$257) double. Rates include breakfast. AE, MC, V. Parking 250SEK ($33) in nearby public garage. T-bana: Östermalmstorg. **Amenities:** Lounge; laundry service; dry cleaning. *In room:* TV, dataport, minibar, hair dryer.

Ramada Hotel Tegnérlunden ✦ Ⓚids In a 19th-century building at the edge of a city park, this hotel has a few public rooms, a lobby, and a bar. The best feature is the tasteful, functionally furnished rooms, many suitable for families. They're blissfully quiet, especially those opening onto the rear. The rooms vary in size and shape, and those we inspected were well maintained. The hotel offers comfort but not a lot of style. The bathrooms equipped with shower units are small but beautifully kept.

Tegnérlunden 8, S-113 59 Stockholm. (②) **08/545-455-50.** Fax 08/545-455-51. www.hoteltegnerlunden.se. 103 units. 990SEK–1,560SEK ($129–$203) double; 1,395SEK–1,895SEK ($181–$246) junior suite. Rates include breakfast. AE, DC, MC, V. Parking 150SEK ($20) in nearby garage. Bus: 47, 53, or 69. **Amenities:** Bar; sauna; solarium; laundry service; dry cleaning; nonsmoking rooms; 1 room for those with limited mobility; wireless Internet access. *In room:* TV, hair dryer.

IN GAMLA STAN (OLD TOWN)
Expensive

Lady Hamilton Hotel ★ *(Finds)* This hotel, consisting of three connected buildings, stands on a quiet street surrounded by antiques shops and restaurants—a very desirable location indeed. Dozens of antiques are scattered among the well-furnished guest rooms. Most rooms have beamed ceilings. The beds (queen-size or double) are of high quality. Bathrooms are tiled but vary in size from spacious to cramped. All have heated towel racks, heated floors, and shower-tub combinations. Top-floor rooms have skylights and memorable views over the Old Town. Some rooms for nonsmokers are available. You'll get a sense of the 1470 origins of this hotel when you use the luxurious sauna, which encompasses the stone-rimmed well that formerly supplied the building's water. The ornate staircase wraps around a large model of a clipper ship suspended from the ceiling.

Storkyrkobrinken 5, S-111 28 Stockholm. (②) **08/506-401-00.** Fax 08/506-401-10. www.lady-hamilton.se. 34 units, some with shower only. 1,690SEK–2,390SEK ($220–$311) double with shower; 1,990SEK–2,690SEK ($259–$350) double with shower/tub. Rates include breakfast. AE, DC, MC, V. Parking: 295SEK ($38). T-bana: Gamla Stan. Bus: 48. **Amenities:** Bistro; sauna; limited room service; laundry service; dry cleaning; nonsmoking rooms. *In room:* TV, minibar, hair dryer.

Victory Hotel ★★ A small but stylish hotel, the Victory offers warm, inviting rooms, each named after a prominent sea captain. They sport a pleasing combination of exposed wood, antiques, and 19th-century memorabilia. Many rooms are smoke-free, and the beds are comfortable. The average-size bathrooms are tiled and have heated floors and shower units; only the suites have tubs. The hotel rests on the foundations of a 1382 fortified tower. In the 1700s the building's owners buried a massive silver treasure under the basement floor—you can see it in the Stockholm City Museum. From the stairs you'll see one of Sweden's largest collections of 18th-century nautical needlepoint, much of it created by the sailors during their long voyages.

Lilla Nygatan 3–5, S-111 28 Stockholm. (②) **08/506-400-00.** Fax 08/506-400-10. www.victory-hotel.se. 45 units, some with shower only (single and double rooms). 1,850SEK–3,590SEK ($241–$467) double; 2,750SEK–5,790SEK ($358–$753) suite. Rates include breakfast. AE, DC, MC, V. T-bana: Gamla Stan. Bus: 48. **Amenities:** Restaurant; bar; small pool; sauna; gift shop; 24-hr. room service; babysitting; laundry service; dry cleaning; nonsmoking rooms; rooms for those with limited mobility. *In room:* TV, dataport, minibar, hair dryer, safe.

Moderate

Mälardrottningen ★ *(Finds)* During its heyday, this was the most famous motor yacht in the world, the subject of gossip columns everywhere, thanks to the complicated friendships that developed among the passengers and, in some cases, the crew. Built in 1924 by millionaire C. K. G. Billings, it was the largest (72m/240 ft.) motor yacht in the world, and was later acquired by the Woolworth heiress, Barbara Hutton. The below-deck space originally contained only seven suites. The yacht was converted into a hotel in the early 1980s, and was permanently moored beside a satellite island of Stockholm's Old Town. The cabins are now cramped and somewhat claustrophobic. Most have bunk-style twin beds. Considering the hotel's conversation-piece status, and its location close to everything in the Old Town, it might be worth an overnight stay.

Riddarholmen, S-111 28 Stockholm. © 08/545-187-80. Fax 08/24-36-76. www.malardrottningen.se. 60 units. Sun–Thurs 1,220SEK–1,750SEK ($159–$228) double; Fri–Sat 1,030SEK–1,650SEK ($134–$215) double. Rates include breakfast. AE, DC, MC, V. Parking 17SEK ($2.20) per hour. T-bana: Gamla Stan. **Amenities:** Restaurant; bar; sauna; laundry service; dry cleaning. *In room:* TV, dataport, hair dryer.

ON LÅNGHOLMEN

Långholmen Hotel   Beginning in 1724, on the little island of Långholmen, this structure was a state penitentiary for women charged with "loose living." The last prisoner was released in 1972, and today it's a newly restored and reasonably priced accommodation that, in addition to comfortable but small rooms, also houses a museum of Sweden's prison history and one of the best restaurants in the country. Instead of a prison induction area, you get the hotel's reception area and a 24-hour snack bar. Accommodations were carved from some 200 cells, creating cramped but serviceable rooms equipped with small showers and toilets. Eighty-nine of the rooms are rented only to solo travelers, making this one of the best hotels in Stockholm for the single visitor on a budget. Just 13 rooms are large enough to accommodate two persons. All rooms are nonsmoking.

Långholm, S-102 72 Stockholm. © 08/668-05-00. Fax 08/720-85-75. www.langholmen.com. 102 units. Sun–Thurs 1,455SEK ($189) double; Fri–Sat 1,155SEK ($150) double. Extra bed 215SEK ($28) per person. Rates include breakfast. AE, DC, MC, V. T-bana: Hornstul. Bus: 4, 40, or 66. **Amenities:** Restaurant; bar; laundry service; dry cleaning; 10 rooms for those with limited mobility. *In room:* TV, dataport, hair dryer.

WHERE TO DINE
IN THE CITY CENTER
Very Expensive

Operakällaren (The Opera House) ★★★ FRENCH/SWEDISH   Opposite the Royal Palace, this is the most famous and unashamedly luxurious restaurant in Sweden. Its elegant decor and style are reminiscent of a royal court banquet. The service and house specialties are impeccable. Many come here for the elaborate fixed-price menus; others prefer the classic Swedish dishes or the modern French ones. A house specialty that's worth the trip is the platter of northern delicacies, with everything from smoked eel to smoked reindeer, along with Swedish red caviar. Salmon and game, including grouse from the northern forests, are prepared in various ways. There's a cigar room, too.

Operahuset, Kungsträdgården. © 08/676-58-00. www.operakallaren.se. Reservations required. Main courses 390SEK–420SEK ($51–$55); 4-course fixed-price menu 950SEK ($124); 7-course *menu dégustation* 1,150SEK ($152). AE, DC, MC, V. Daily 6–10pm. Closed July. T-bana: Kungsträdgården.

Paul & Norbert ★★★ CONTINENTAL   In a patrician residence dating from 1873, adjacent to the Hotell Diplomat, this is the finest and most innovative restaurant in Stockholm. Seating only 30 people, it has vaguely Art Deco decor, beamed ceilings, and dark paneling. Owner Norbert Lang worked in many top European restaurants before opening this establishment. To start, they prepare a tantalizing terrine of scallops in saffron sauce. The foie gras is the finest in town. Perfectly prepared main dishes include sautéed medallion of fjord salmon, scallops, and scampi in lobster sauce; crisp breast of duck with caramelized orange sauce; and juniper-stuffed noisettes of reindeer immersed in caraway sauce with portobello mushrooms.

Strandvägen 9. © 08/663-81-83. Reservations required. Main courses 250SEK–310SEK ($33–$40); 9-course *grand menu de frivolité* 1,300SEK ($169); 5-course meal 650SEK ($85). AE, DC, MC, V. Mid-Aug to June Tues–Fri noon–2pm, Mon–Sat 6–10pm; July to mid-Aug Mon–Sat 6–10pm. Closed Dec 24–Jan 6. T-bana: Östermalmstorg.

Expensive

Franska Matsalen (French Dining Room) ★★ FRENCH Widely acclaimed as one of the greatest restaurants in Stockholm, this elegant establishment is on the street level of the city's finest hotel. The dining room is appointed with polished mahogany, ormolu, and gilt accents under an ornate plaster ceiling. Tables on the enclosed veranda overlook the Royal Palace and the Old Town. Begin with a cannelloni of foie gras with cèpes, or perhaps mousseline of scallops with sevruga caviar. Main dishes include seared sweetbreads served with artichokes, *langoustines* (prawns) and frogs' legs with broad beans, and veal tartare with caviar. Fresh Swedish salmon is also featured. The chefs—highly trained professionals working with the finest ingredients—have pleased some of Europe's more demanding palates.

In the Grand Hotel, Södra Blasieholmshamnen 8. ☎ 08/679-35-84. Reservations required. Main courses 225SEK–575SEK ($29–$75); 7-course fixed-price menu 975SEK ($127); 8-course fixed-price menu 1,300SEK ($169). AE, DC, MC, V. Mon–Sat 6–11pm. T-bana: Kungsträdgården. Bus: 46, 55, 62, or 76.

Wedholms Fisk ★★★ SWEDISH/FRENCH This is one of the classic—and one of the best—restaurants in Stockholm. It has no curtains in the windows and no carpets, but the display of modern paintings by Swedish artists is riveting. You might begin with marinated herring with garlic and bleak roe, or tartare of salmon with salmon roe. The chef has reason to be proud of such dishes as perch poached with clams and saffron sauce, prawns marinated in herbs and served with Dijon hollandaise, and grilled filet of sole with Beaujolais sauce. The cuisine is both innovative and traditional—for example, chèvre mousse accompanies simple tomato salad. On the other hand, the menu features grandmother's favorite: cream-stewed potatoes.

Nybrokajen 17. ☎ 08/611-78-74. Reservations required. Main courses 65SEK–220SEK ($8.45–$29) lunch, 265SEK–535SEK ($34–$70) dinner. AE, DC, MC, V. Mon 11:30am–2pm and 6–11pm; Tues–Sat 11:30am–11pm. In July, only open for dinner. T-bana: Östermalmstorg.

Moderate

Bakfickan ★ *Finds* SWEDISH Tucked away behind the Operakällaren, the "Back Pocket" is a chic place to eat for a moderate price. It shares a kitchen with its glamorous neighbor Operakällaren (see above), but its prices are more bearable. Main dishes may include salmon in several varieties, including boiled with hollandaise and salmon roe. You might also try beef Rydberg (thinly sliced tenderloin). In season you can order reindeer and elk. In the summer, nothing's finer than the rich ice cream with a sauce of Arctic cloudberries. Many patrons like to dine at the horseshoe-shaped bar.

Jakobs Torg 12. ☎ 08/676-58-09. Reservations not accepted. Main courses 125SEK–209SEK ($16–$27). AE, DC, MC, V. Aug–June Mon–Sat noon–11:30pm. T-bana: Kungsträdgården.

Eriks Bakfica *Value* SWEDISH Although other restaurants in Stockholm bear the name Eriks, this one is relatively inexpensive and offers particularly good value. Established in 1979, it features a handful of Swedish dishes from the tradition of *husmanskost* (wholesome home cooking). A favorite opener is toast Skagen, with shrimp, dill-flavored mayonnaise, spices, and bleak roe. There's also a daily choice of herring appetizers. Try the tantalizing "archipelago stew," a ragout of fish prepared with tomatoes and served with garlic mayonnaise. Marinated salmon is served with hollandaise sauce. You might also try Eriks's cheeseburger with the special secret sauce, but you have to ask for it—the specialty is not on the menu.

Fredrikshovsgatan 4. ☎ 08/660-15-99. Reservations recommended. Main courses 165SEK–275SEK ($21–$36). AE, DC, MC, V. Mon–Fri 11:30am–11pm; Sat 5–11pm; Sun 5–10pm. Bus: 47.

KB Restaurant SWEDISH/CONTINENTAL   A traditional artists' ren-dezvous in the center of town, KB Restaurant features good Swedish food as well as Continental dishes. Fish dishes are especially recommended. You might begin with salmon trout roe and Russian caviar, followed by boiled turbot or lamb roast with stuffed zucchini in thyme-flavored bouillon. Dishes usually come with aromatic, freshly baked sourdough bread. Desserts include sorbets with fresh fruits and berries, and a heavenly lime soufflé with orange-blossom honey. There's also a relaxed and informal bar.

Smålandsgatan 7. © 08/679-60-32. Reservations recommended. Main courses 210SEK–300SEK ($27–$39). Fixed-price meals 270SEK–335SEK ($35–$44) lunch, 375SEK–470SEK ($49–$61) dinner. AE, DC, MC, V. Mon–Fri 11:30am–midnight; Sat 5–11:30pm. Closed June 23–Aug 7. T-bana: Östermalmstorg.

Lisa Elmquist ★ *Kids* SEAFOOD   Under a soaring roof, amid the food stalls of Stockholm's produce market (the Östermalms Saluhall), you'll find this lik-able cafe and oyster bar. Because of its good, affordable food, this is the most popular choice for Stockholm families visiting the market. It's owned by one of the city's largest fish distributors, so its menu varies with the catch. Some patrons come here for shrimp with bread and butter for 90SEK to 115SEK ($12–$15). Typical dishes include fish soup, salmon cutlets, and sautéed filet of lemon sole. It's not the most refined cuisine in town—it's an authentic "taste of Sweden," done exceedingly well.

Östermalms Saluhall, Nybrogatan 31. © 08/553-404-10. Reservations recommended. Main courses 86SEK–336SEK ($11–$44). AE, DC, MC, V. Mon–Thurs 10:30am–6pm; Fri 10am–6:30pm; Sat 10am–4pm. T-bana: Östermalmstorg.

Prinsens SWEDISH   A 2-minute walk from Stureplan, this artists' haunt has become increasingly popular with foreign visitors. It has been serving people since 1897. Seating is on two levels, and in summer some tables are outside. The fresh, flavorful cuisine is basically Swedish food prepared in a conservative French style. It includes such traditional Swedish dishes as veal patty with homemade lingonberry preserves, sautéed fjord salmon, and roulades of beef. For dessert, try the homemade vanilla ice cream. Later in the evening, the restau-rant becomes something of a drinking club.

Mäster Samuelsgatan 4. © 08/611-13-31. Reservations recommended. Main courses 129SEK–300SEK ($17–$39). AE, DC, MC, V. Mon–Fri 11:30am–10:30pm; Sat 1–10:30pm; Sun 5–9:30pm. T-bana: Östermalmstorg.

IN GAMLA STAN (OLD TOWN)
Very Expensive

Pontus in the Green House ★★ FRENCH/SWEDISH/ASIAN   Set within a building whose foundations date from the 16th century, this well-orchestrated and elegant restaurant attracts some of the most powerful figures in Stockholm. Your dining experience will begin with a drink or aperitif in the ground-floor bar and cocktail lounge, where a staff member will explain the menu. You'll then be ushered upstairs to a gold-and-green dining room with high arched windows and an undeniable sense of respect for the presentation of food. Chef Pontus Frithiof was inspired by two of the grand Francophile chefs of England, Marco Pierre White and Gordon Ramsay. Their influence is seen in dishes that include tender veal tongue with Jerusalem artichokes; steamed turbot with horseradish, prawns, and brown butter; and citrus-glazed *Challonais* duck breast served with foie gras, shiitake mushrooms, spring onions, and teriyaki sauce. In our view, the herring with vinegar-and-onion marmalade is the Old Town's tastiest. It's worth the trek across town to sample the creamy Roquefort made from the first milk produced by nursing cows. After tasting this cheese, you'll never go back—except with regret—to that store-bought stuff again.

Österlånggatan 17. ℭ 08/23-85-00. Reservations recommended. Main courses 385SEK–495SEK ($50–$64); 8-course fixed-price menu 965SEK ($125); 11-course fixed-price menu 1,200SEK ($156). AE, DC, MC, V. Mon–Fri 11:30am–3pm and 6–11pm; Sat 5:30–11pm. T-bana: Gamla Stan.

Expensive

Den Gyldene Freden ✯ SWEDISH "Golden Peace" is said to be Stockholm's oldest tavern. The restaurant opened in 1722 in a structure built the year before. The Swedish Academy owns the building, and members frequent the place every Thursday night. The cozy dining rooms are named for Swedish historical figures who were patrons. Today it's popular with artists, lawyers, and poets. You get good traditional Swedish cooking, especially fresh Baltic fish and game from the forests. Herring is a favorite appetizer. More imaginative appetizers include a creamy artichoke soup, Jerusalem artichokes with a dollop of caviar, and an especially intriguing consommé of oxtail with tiny ravioli stuffed with quail breast. Notable main courses are fried breast of wild duck in Calvados sauce, and roast of reindeer in juniper-berry sauce. A particular delight is homemade duck sausage with three kinds of mushrooms in black-pepper sauce. Want something different for dessert? How about warm rose-hip soup with vanilla ice cream? Of course, if you order that, you'd be denying yourself the "symphony" of lingonberries or the longtime favorite, Stockholm's best chocolate cake.

Österlånggatan 51. ℭ 08/24-97-60. Reservations recommended. Main courses 115SEK–445SEK ($15–$58). AE, DC, MC, V. Mon–Fri 5pm–midnight; Sat 1pm–midnight. Dec 1–21 Mon–Sat noon–3pm. Closed Dec 26–Jan 2. T-bana: Gamla Stan.

Inexpensive

Cattelin Restaurant *Value* SWEDISH This restaurant on a historic street opened in 1897 and continues to serve fish and meat in a boisterous, convivial setting. Don't expect genteel service—the clattering of china can sometimes be almost deafening, but few of the regular patrons seem to mind. First-rate menu choices include various preparations of beef, salmon, trout, veal, and chicken, which frequently make up the daily specials often preferred by lunch patrons. This restaurant has survived wars, disasters, and changing food tastes, so it must be doing something right. It remains a sentimental favorite—and not just for the memories. In a city where people have been known to faint when presented with their dining tabs, it has always been a good, reasonably priced choice. The fixed-price lunch is served only Monday through Friday from 11am to 3pm.

Storkyrkobrinken 9. ℭ 08/20-18-18. Reservations recommended. Main courses 90SEK–200SEK ($12–$26); *dagens* (daily) menu 62SEK ($8.05). AE, DC, MC, V. Mon–Fri 11am–10pm; Sat noon–3pm. T-bana: Gamla Stan.

ON DJURGÅRDEN

Ulla Winbladh ✯ SWEDISH Since it opened in 1994, this restaurant has enjoyed an explosion of publicity, which has impressed even the most jaded of Stockholm's restaurant aficionados. It's in a white stone structure, built as part of Stockholm's International Exposition of 1897. There's a large dining room decorated with works by Swedish artists, and a summer-only outdoor terrace laced with flowering plants. The menu focuses on conservative Swedish cuisine, all impeccably prepared. (Patrons who agree with this assessment include members of the Swedish royal family and a bevy of well-known TV, theater, and art-world personalities.) In 1996 the king presented a medal to chef Emel Ahalen for his proficiency in preparing Swedish cuisine. Menu choices include tender steak with artichokes, and a perfectly prepared rack of Swedish lamb flavored with bacon. Fish selections might be platters of herring (marinated and fried), whitefish, or pikeperch in white-wine sauce; divine turbot with saffron sauce; the inevitable salmon with dill sauce; and others that vary with the season.

Rosendalsvägen 8. (℡ 08/663-05-71. www.ullawinbladh.se/inenglish.html. Reservations required. Main courses 95SEK–295SEK ($12–$38). AE, DC, MC, V. Mon 11:30am–10pm; Tues–Fri 11:30am–11pm; Sat 1pm–1am; Sun 1–10pm. Bus: 47 or 69.

EXPLORING STOCKHOLM

Everything from the *Vasa* Ship Museum to the changing of the guard at the Royal Palace to the Gröna Tivoli amusement park will keep you intrigued. Even just window-shopping for well-designed Swedish crafts can be a great way to spend an afternoon.

SIGHTSEEING SUGGESTIONS FOR FIRST-TIME VISITORS

If You Have 1 Day Take a ferry to Djurgården to visit the **Royal Warship Vasa,** Stockholm's most famous attraction, and to explore the open-air **Skansen** folk museum. In the afternoon, walk through **Gamla Stan (Old Town)** and have dinner at one of its restaurants.

If You Have 2 Days On day 2, get up early and visit the **Kaknästornet** TV tower for a panoramic view of Stockholm, its many islands, and the archipelago. Go to the **Nordic Museum** for insight into 5 centuries of life in Sweden. After lunch, visit the **Millesgården** of Lidingü, the sculpture garden and former home of Carl Milles.

If You Have 3 Days Spend your third morning walking through the center of Stockholm and doing

some shopping. At noon (1pm on Sun), return to Gamla Stan to see the **changing of the guard at the Royal Palace.** View this French-inspired building that has been the residence of Swedish kings for more than 700 years. In the afternoon, see the attractions at the **National Museum.**

If You Have 4 or 5 Days On day 4, take one of the many tours of the **Stockholm archipelago.** Return to Stockholm and spend the evening at the **Gröna Tivoli** amusement park on Djurgården. On your last day, visit **Drottningholm Palace** and its 18th-century theater. In the afternoon, explore the university town of **Uppsala,** north of Stockholm, easily reached by public transportation.

THE TOP ATTRACTIONS
At Djurgården

Vasa Museum & the Royal Warship Vasa ✦✦✦   This 17th-century man-of-war is the number one attraction in Scandinavia—and for good reason. Housed in a museum specially constructed for it at Djurgården near Skansen, the *Vasa* is the world's oldest identified and complete ship. In 1628, on its maiden voyage and in front of thousands of horrified onlookers, the ship capsized and sank to the bottom of Stockholm harbor. When it was salvaged in 1961, more than 4,000 coins, carpenters' tools, and other items of archaeological interest were found on board. Best of all, 97% of the ship's 700 original sculptures were retrieved. Carefully restored and preserved, they're back aboard the ship, which looks stunning now that it once again carries grotesque faces, lion masks, fish-shaped bodies, and other carvings, some with their original paint and gilt.

> ### Moments   The Changing of the Royal Guard
>
> It may not have the pomp of a similar show in London, but the **Changing of the Royal Guard** in Stockholm at least provides a photo op. In summer you can watch the parade of the military guard daily. In winter it takes place on Wednesday and Sunday; on the other days there's no parade, but you can see the changing of the guard. For information on the time of the march, ask at the Tourist Centre in Sweden House. The changing of the guard takes place at noon Monday through Saturday and around 12:15pm on Sunday in front of the Royal Palace.

Galärvarvsvägen, Djurgården. ℂ **08/519-548-00.** www.vasamuseet.se/indexeng.html. Admission 70SEK ($9.10) adults, 40SEK ($5.20) seniors and students, 10SEK ($1.30) children 7–15, free for children under 7. June 10–Aug 20 daily 9:30am–7pm; Aug 21–June 9 Wed 10am–8pm, Thurs–Tues 10am–5pm. Closed Jan 1, May 1, Dec 23–25, and Dec 31. Bus: 44, 47, or 69. Ferry from Slussen year-round, from Nybroplan in summer only.

Skansen 🅐🅐🅐   Often called "Old Sweden in a Nutshell," this 35-hectare (75-acre) open-air museum and zoological park, near Gröna Lund's Tivoli, contains more than 150 dwellings, most from the 18th and 19th centuries. Exhibits range from a windmill to a manor house to a complete town quarter. Browsers can explore the old workshops and see where the early book publishers, silversmiths, and pharmacists plied their trade. Handcrafts (glass blowing, for example) are demonstrated here, along with peasant crafts like weaving and churning. Folk dancing and open-air symphonic concerts are also featured.

Djurgården 49–51. ℂ **08/442-80-00.** www.skansen.se. Depending on time of day, day of the week, and season, admission is 30SEK–70SEK ($3.90–$9.10) adults, 20SEK–30SEK ($2.60–$3.90) children 6–15, free for children 5 and under. Historic buildings May daily 10am–8pm; Oct–Apr daily 10am–4pm; June–Aug daily 10am–10pm; Sept daily 10am–5pm. Bus: 47 from central Stockholm. Ferry from Slussen.

Nordiska Museet 🅐🅐   This museum houses an impressive collection of implements, costumes, and furnishings of Swedish life from the 1500s to the present. The highlights are the period costumes ranging from matching garters and ties for men to purple flowerpot hats from the 1890s. In the basement is an extensive exhibit of the tools of the Swedish fishing trade, plus relics from nomadic Lapps.

Djurgårdsvägen 6–16, Djurgården. ℂ **08/519-560-00.** www.nordiskamuseet.se. Admission 70SEK ($9.10) adults, 50SEK ($6.50) seniors, free for children up to 18. June–Aug daily 10am–5pm; Sept–May daily 10am–4pm. Bus: 44, 47, or 69.

Prins Eugens Waldemarsudde 🅐🅐   This once-royal residence is today an art gallery and a memorial to one of the most famous royal artists in recent history, Prince Eugen (1865–1947). The youngest of King Oscar II's four children, he is credited with making innovative contributions to the techniques of Swedish landscape paintings, specializing in depictions of his favorite regions in central Sweden. Among his most visible works are the murals on the inner walls of the Stadshuset.

Prins Eugens Väg 6. ℂ **08/545-837-00.** www.waldemarsudde.com. Admission 75SEK ($9.75) adults, 55SEK ($7.15) seniors and students, free for children under 17. Tues–Wed and Fri–Sun 11am–5pm; Thurs 11am–4pm. Bus: 47 to the end of the line.

On Gamla Stan & Neighboring Islands

Kungliga Slottet (Royal Palace) & Museum 🅐🅐   Severely dignified, even cold looking on the outside, this palace has a lavish interior designed in the Italian baroque style. Kungliga Slottet is one of the few official residences of a European monarch that's open to the public. Although the Swedish king and queen prefer to live at Drottningholm, this massive 608-room showcase, built between 1691 and 1754, remains their official address. The most popular rooms are the **State Apartments** ★★; look for at least three magnificent baroque ceiling frescoes and fine tapestries. In the building's cellar is the **Stattkammaren (Treasury)** ★★, the repository for Sweden's crown jewels. Most intriguing to any student of war and warfare is the **Royal Armoury,** whose entrance is on the castle's rear side, at Slotts-backen 3. Gustavas III's collection of sculpture from the days of the Roman Empire can be viewed in the **Antikmuseum (Museum of Antiquities).**

Kungliga Husgerådskammaren. ⓒ **08/402-61-30** for Royal Apartments and Treasury, 08/402-61-30 for the Skattkammaren, 08/519-55-544 for Royal Armory, or 08/402-61-30 for Museum of Antiquities. Royal Apartments 70SEK ($9.10) adults, 35SEK ($4.55) students, free for children under 7; Royal Armory 65SEK ($8.45) adults, 50SEK ($6.50) seniors and students, free for children under 7; Museum of Antiquities 70SEK ($9.10) adults, 35SEK ($4.55) seniors and students, free for children under 7; Treasury 70SEK ($9.10) adults, 35SEK ($4.55) seniors and students, free for children under 7. Combination ticket to all parts of palace 110SEK ($14) adults, 65SEK ($8.45) students and children. Apartments and Treasury Sept–May 14 Tues–Sun noon–3pm; May 15–Aug daily 10am–4pm; closed during government receptions. Royal Armory Sept–May Tues–Sun 11am–4pm (closes at 8pm on Thurs); June–Aug daily 10am–5pm. Museum of Antiquities same hours as Apartments and Treasury. T-bana: Gamla Stan. Bus: 43, 46, 59, or 76.

Riddarholm Church ★ The second-oldest church in Stockholm is on the tiny island of Riddarholmen, next to Gamla Stan. It was founded in the 13th century as a Franciscan monastery. Almost all the royal heads of state are entombed here, except for Christina, who is buried in Rome. There are three principal royal chapels, including one, the Bernadotte wing, that belongs to the present ruling family. Guided tours are available daily at 2pm for 600SEK ($78).

Riddarholmen. ⓒ **08/402-61-30.** Admission 20SEK ($2.60) adults, 10SEK ($1.30) students and children. May 15–Aug 21 daily 10am–4pm; Sept Sat–Sun noon–3pm. Closed Oct–Apr. T-bana: Gamla Stan.

In the City Center

Historiska Museet (Museum of National Antiquities) ★★ If you're interested in Swedish history, especially the Viking era, here you'll find the nation's finest repository of relics left by those legendary conquerors who once terrorized Europe. Many relics have been unearthed from ancient burial sites. The collection of artifacts ranges from prehistoric to medieval times, including Viking stone inscriptions and 10th-century coins, silver and gold jewelry, large ornate charms, elaborate bracelet designs found nowhere else in the world, and a unique neck collar from Färjestaden.

Narvavägen 13–17. ⓒ **08/519-556-00.** Admission 60SEK ($7.80) adults, 50SEK ($6.50) seniors and stu-dents, free for children under 18. Tues–Wed and Fri–Sun 11am–5pm; Thurs 11am–8pm. T-bana: Karlaplan or Östermalmstorg. Bus: 44, 47, 69, or 76.

Nationalmuseum (National Museum of Art) ★★ At the tip of a penin-sula, a short walk from the Royal Opera House and the Grand Hotel, is Swe-den's state treasure house of paintings and sculpture, one of the oldest museums in the world. The first floor is devoted to applied arts (silverware, handcrafts, porcelain, furnishings), but first-time visitors may want to head directly to the second floor to the painting collection with works by Rembrandt and Rubens, Lucas Cranach's most amusing *Venus and Cupid,* and a rare collection of mid-16th-century Russian icons. The most important room in the gallery has one whole wall devoted to Rembrandt, and features his *Portrait of an Old Man, Por-trait of an Old Woman,* and *Kitchen Maid.*

Södra Blasieholmshamnen. © 08/519-543-00. www.nationalmuseum.se. Admission 75SEK ($9.75) adults, 60SEK ($7.80) seniors and students, free for children under 17. Tues and Thurs 11am–8pm; Wed and Fri–Sun 11am–5pm. T-bana: Kungsträdgården. Bus: 46, 62, 65, or 76.

Moderna Museet (Museum of Modern Art) ✸ Renovated in 2004, this museum focuses on contemporary works by Swedish and international artists, including kinetic sculptures. Highlights are a small but good collection of Cubist art by Picasso, Braque, and Léger; Matisse's *Apollo* decoupage; the famous *Enigma of William Tell* by Salvador Dalí; and works by Brancusi, Max Ernst, Giacometti, and Arp, among others.

Klaravergsviadukten 61. © 08/519-552-00. www.modernamuseet.se. Free admission. Tues–Thurs 10am–8pm; Fri–Sun 10am–6pm. T-bana: Kungsträdgården. Bus: 65.

Stadshuset (Stockholm City Hall) ✸✸ Built in what is called the "National Romantic Style," the Stockholm City Hall, on the island of Kungsholmen, is one of Europe's finest examples of modern architecture. Designed by Ragnar Ostberg, the redbrick structure is dominated by a lofty square tower, topped by three gilt crowns and the national coat of arms. The Nobel Prize banquet is held annually in the Blue Hall. About 18 million pieces of gold and colored mosaics made of special glass cover the walls, and the southern gallery contains murals by Prince Eugen, the painter prince.

Hantverksgatan 1. © 08/508-290-58. Admission 50SEK ($6.50) adults, free for children under 12. Tower additional 20SEK ($2.60). May–Sept daily 10am–4pm. City Hall tours (subject to change), June–Aug daily at 10am, 11am, noon, 2pm, and 3pm; Sept–Apr daily at 10am, noon, and 2pm; rest of the year 10am and 2pm. T-bana: Centralen or Rådhuset. Bus: 3 or 62.

JUST OUTSIDE STOCKHOLM

Drottningholm Palace ✸✸✸ Conceived as the centerpiece of Sweden's royal court, this regal complex of stately buildings sits on an island in Lake Mälaren. Dubbed the "Versailles of Sweden," Drottningholm (Queen's Island) lies about 11km (6¾ miles) west of Stockholm. The palace, loaded with courtly art and furnishings, sits amid fountains and parks, and still functions as one of the royal family's official residences.

On the grounds is one of the most perfectly preserved 18th-century theaters in the world, **Drottningholm Court Theater** (© **08/759-04-06**). Between June and August, 30 performances are staged. Devoted almost exclusively to 18th-century opera, it seats only 450 for one of the most unusual entertainment experiences in Sweden. Many performances sell out far in advance to season-ticket holders. The theater can be visited only as part of a guided tour, which focuses on the original sets and stage mechanisms.

For tickets to the evening performances, which cost 165SEK to 600SEK ($21–$78), call © **08/660-82-25.**

Ekerö, Drottningholm. © 08/402-62-80. Palace 60SEK ($7.80) adults, 30SEK ($3.90) students and persons under 26; theater guided tour 60SEK ($7.80) adults, 30SEK ($3.90) students and persons 7–26, free for children under 7. Palace Oct–Apr Sat–Sun noon–3:30pm; May–Aug daily 10am–4:30pm; Sept daily noon–3:30pm. Theater guided tours in English May Sat–Sun 11am, noon, 1pm, and 3pm; June–Aug daily 11am, noon, 1pm, and 3pm; Sept daily noon, and 2pm; Oct–Mar Sat–Sun noon, 1pm, and 2pm. T-bana: Brommaplan, then bus no. 301 or 323 to Drottningholm or 177 or 178. Ferry from the dock near City Hall.

Millesgården ✸✸ On the island of Lidingö, northeast of Stockholm, is Carl Milles's former villa and sculpture garden beside the sea, now a museum. Many of his best-known works are displayed here (some are copies), as are works of other artists. Milles (1875–1955), who relied heavily on mythological themes, was Sweden's most famous sculptor.

Carl Milles Väg 2, Lidingö. ✆ **08/446-75-90**. www.millesgarden.se. Admission 75SEK ($9.75) adults, 60SEK ($7.80) seniors and students, 20SEK ($2.60) children 7–16, free for children under 7. May–Sept daily 10am–5pm; Oct–Apr Tues–Fri noon–4pm, Sat-Sun 11am-5pm. T-bana: Ropsten, then bus to Torsviks Torg or train to Norsvik.

A VIEW ON HIGH

Kaknästornet (Kaknäs Television Tower) *Moments*   Situated in the northern district of Djurgården is the tallest constructed structure in Scandinavia—a radio and television tower that stands 155m (508 ft.) high. Two elevators take visitors to an observation platform, where you can see everything from the cobblestone streets of Gamla Stan (Old Town) to the city's modern concrete-and-glass structures and the archipelago beyond.

Mörkakroken. ✆ **08/789-24-35**. Admission 30SEK ($3.90) adults, 15SEK ($1.95) children 7–15, free for children under 7. May–Aug daily 9am–10pm; Sept–Apr daily 10am–9pm. Closed Dec 24–25. Bus: 69.

AN AMUSEMENT PARK

Gröna Lunds Tivoli *Kids*   For those who like Coney Island–type thrills, this is a good nighttime adventure. Unlike its Copenhagen namesake, this is an amusement park, not a fantasyland. You'll find everything here from the Tunnel of Love to the Hall of Mirrors (thin gets fat and other anatomical illusions). Bumper cars encourage reckless driving, and the Blue Train takes you on a classic horror trip. You get the idea.

Djurgården. ✆ **08/587-501-00**. Admission 60SEK ($7.80) adults, free for children under 7. Late Apr to Sept daily noon–midnight (hours subject to weekly variation). Bus: 44 or 47. Djurgården ferry from Nybroplan.

ORGANIZED TOURS

CITY TOURS   The quickest and most convenient way to see the highlights of Stockholm is to take one of the bus tours that leave from Karl XII Torg, near the Kungsträdgården.

City Sightseeing (✆ **08/587-140-30**) operates 90-minute and 3-hour bus tours of Stockholm; the tours leave from the Opera House. From mid-October to mid-April, the 90-minute "Panorama" tour departs at 10am and noon (also 11:30am Sat–Sun); from mid-April to mid-October, departure times are 10am, noon, and 2pm. The cost is 190SEK ($25) adults and half price for children 6 to 11. A 3-hour "Royal Stockholm" tour (300SEK/$39) departs daily at 10am; and the "Stockholm in a Nutshell" tour (280SEK/$36) combines 2 hours and 30 minutes of bus sightseeing with an hour-long boat ride around Djurgärden and the inner islands of the Stockholm archipelago; departure times are daily at 10am, noon, and 2pm.

Stockholm Sightseeing, Skeppsbron 22 (✆ **08/587-140-20**), offers a variety of tours, mostly in the summer. The most popular is the 1-hour "royal Canal Tour," for 110SEK ($14). It leaves daily year-round from the shady canal of Djurgården. "Under the Bridges" takes 2 hours and goes through two locks and two bodies of water. Departures are from Stromkajen (near the Grand Hotel), daily from mid-April to mid-September. The cost is 160SEK ($21). The 45-minute "Sightseeing Anno 1935" explores the Stockholm harbor in an open-topped wooden boat, with a captain in period uniform. The tour costs 100SEK ($13). Daily departures, from June 28 to mid-August, are from the statue of Gustavus III by the Royal Palace.

THE SHOPPING SCENE

A whopping 25% goods tax makes shopping in Sweden expensive, and you can get most items at home for less money. On the positive side, Swedish stores usually stock items of the highest quality. Swedish glass is world famous. The wooden items are outstanding, and many people love the functional furniture in blond pine or birch. Other items to look for include children's playsuits, silver necklaces, reindeer gloves, hand-woven neckties and skirts, sweaters and mittens in Nordic patterns, clogs, and colorful handicrafts from the provinces. The most famous souvenir is the Dala horse from Dalarna.

For full details on **tax rebates** on local goods, go to the "Fast Facts" section, earlier in this chapter.

For the best shopping and window-shopping, stroll along the streets of **Gamla Stan** (especially **Västerlånggatan**), filled with boutiques, art galleries, and jewelry stores. Attractive shops and galleries can also be found along the **Hornsgats-Puckeln** (the Hornsgatan-Hunchback, a reference to the shape of the street), on **Södermalm.** Other good browsing streets are **Hamngatan, Birger Jarlsgatan, Biblioteksgatan,** and **Kungsgatan,** all in **Norrmalm.**

In the center of Stockholm, the largest department store in Sweden is **Åhlsens City,** Klarabergsgatan 50 (© **08/676-60-00;** T-bana: T-Centralen), with a gift shop, a restaurant, and a famous food department. Also seek out the fine collection of home textiles and Orrefors and Kosta crystal ware. **Nordiska Kompanient (NK),** Hamngatan 18–20 (© **08/762-80-00;** T-bana: Kungsträdgården), is another high-quality department store. Most of the big names in Swedish glass are displayed at NK. Swedish handcrafted items are in the basement.

At **Loppmarknaden i Skärholmen (Skärholmen Shopping Center),** Skärholmsvagen, Skärholmen (© **08/710-00-60;** T-bana: 13 or 23 to Skärhol-men), the biggest flea market in northern Europe, you might find *anything.* Try to go on Saturday or Sunday (the earlier the better) when the market is at its peak. The location is 10km (6¼ miles) southwest of the center in the suburb of Skärholmen. Hours are Monday to Friday 11am to 6pm when admission is free; Saturday 9am to 3pm, costing 15SEK ($1.95), and Sunday, 10am to 3pm, with the entrance going for 10SEK ($1.30).

STOCKHOLM AFTER DARK

Pick up a copy of *Stockholm This Week,* distributed at the Tourist Centre in the Sweden House (see "Visitor Information," earlier in this chapter), to see what's on.

THE PERFORMING ARTS

All the major opera, theater, and concert seasons begin in autumn, except for special summer festival performances. Fortunately, most of the major opera and theatrical performances are funded by the state, which keeps the ticket price reasonable.

Founded by Gustavus III in 1766, the **Drottningholm Court Theater** (© **08/ 660-82-25;** T-bana: Brommaplan, then bus no. 301 or 323; boat from the City Hall in Stockholm), Drottningholm, is on an island in Lake Mälaren, 11km (6¾ miles) from Stockholm. It stages operas and ballets with full 18th-century regalia, period costumes, and wigs. Its machinery and 30 or more complete theater sets are intact and in use. The theater, a short walk from the royal residence, seats only 450, which makes it difficult to get tickets. Eighteenth-century music performed on antique instruments is a perennial favorite. The season is from May to Sep-tember. Most performances begin at 8pm and last 2½ to 4 hours. You can order tickets in advance by phone with an American Express card. Tickets cost 165SEK to 610SEK ($21–$79).

Filharmonikerna I Konserthuset (Concert Hall), Hötorget 8 (© **08/50-66-77-88**; T-bana: Hötorget), home of the **Stockholm Philharmonic Orchestra**, is the principal place to hear classical music in Sweden. (The Nobel Prizes are also awarded here.) Box office hours are Monday through Friday from noon to 6pm, Saturday from 11am to 3pm. Tickets are 70SEK to 420SEK ($9.10–$55).

Founded in 1773 by Gustavus III (who was later assassinated here at a masked ball), the **Operahuset (Royal Opera House)**, Gustav Adolfs Torg (© **08/24-82-40** or 08/791-43-00; T-bana: Kungsträdgården; www.operan.se), is the home of the Royal Swedish Opera and the Royal Swedish Ballet. The building dates from 1898. Performances are usually Monday through Saturday at 7:30pm (closed mid-June to Aug). The box office is open Monday through Friday from noon to 6pm (until 7:30pm on performance nights), Saturday from noon to 3pm;© **08/24-82-40.** Tickets cost from 100SEK to 450SEK ($13–$59); ask about the 10% to 30% senior and student discounts.

NIGHTCLUBS

Café Opera, Operahuset, Kungsträdgården (© **08/676-58-07**; T-bana: Kungsträdgården)—Swedish beaux arts at its best—functions as a brasserie-style restaurant during dinner hours and one of the most popular nightclubs in Stockholm late at night. Near the entrance of the cafe is a stairway leading to one of the Opera House's most beautiful corners, the clublike Operabaren (Opera Bar). Café Opera is open daily from 5pm to 3am. There's no cover before 11pm, 100SEK ($13) after.

Göta Källare, in the Medborgplatsen subway station, Södermalm (© **08/642-08-28**; T-bana: Medborgplatsen), is the largest and most successful supper-club-style dance hall in Stockholm. Large, echoing, and paneled with lots of wood in a *faux-Español* style, it has a large terrace that surrounds an enormous tree, and a restaurant. Expect a crowd of people ages 45 and older, and music from a live orchestra. The place is open every night from 8:30pm. Cover is 100SEK ($13) after 11pm only.

ROCK & JAZZ CLUBS

Some of Sweden's and the world's best-known jazz musicians regularly play **Fasching**, Kungsgatan 63 (© **08/534-829-64**; T-bana: T-Centralen). Small, cozy, and well known among jazz fans throughout Scandinavia, this is one of the most visible of the jazz clubs of Stockholm, with artists appearing from North America, Europe, and around the world. Cramped to point of claustrophobia, it gives you the feeling that you're very, very close to the men and women producing the music. The venue varies according to the night of the week and the availability of the artists performing, but after the end of most live acts, there's likely to be dancing to salsa, soul, and perhaps R&B. With many exceptions, varying with the acts being presented, the club is usually open every night from 7pm till at least 1am. Cover costs vary from 100SEK to 250SEK ($13–$33).

The Swedish branch of **Hard Rock Cafe**, Sveavägen 75 (© **08/545-494-00**; T-bana: Rådmansgaten), is fun and gregarious. Club sandwiches, hamburgers, T-bone steaks, and barbecued spareribs are available. It's open in summer, Monday through Thursday from 11:30am to 1am, Friday from 11:30am to 3am; Saturday 11am to 3am; Sunday 11am to 1am. There's no cover.

Pub Engelen and **Nightclub Kolingen**, Kornhamnstorg 59B (© **08/20-10-92**; T-bana: Gamla Stan), share a single address. The restaurant, which serves some of the best steaks in town, is open Sunday through Thursday from 5 to 11:30pm, Friday and Saturday from 5pm to 1:30am. Prices for platters of bar food run 120SEK to 195SEK ($16–$25). Live performances, usually soul, funk, and rock by Swedish groups, take over the pub daily from 8:30pm to midnight. The pub is open daily from 4pm to 3am. Beer begins at 42SEK ($5.45), and items on the bar menu cost 40SEK to 80SEK ($5.20–$10). The Nightclub Kolingen is a dance club nightly from 10pm to about 3am. It charges the same food and drink prices as the pub, and you must be at least 23 to enter. Cover runs from 60SEK to 80SEK ($7.80–$10) after 8pm.

BARS

One of the most talked-about bars in Stockholm, **Blue Moon Bar,** 18 Kungsgatan (© 08/24-47-00; T-bana: Östermalmstorg), attracts a bevy of supermodels and TV actors. The street level has black leather upholstery and an atmosphere of postmodern cool. The clean, modern decor of the basement-level bar draws an equally chic crowd. On both levels, everybody's favorite drink seems to be the Russian-inspired *caprinoshka,* concocted from vodka and limes. You might hear anything from recorded dance hits (Fri–Sat at midnight) to live salsa and merengue (Wed 9pm–5am). The place is open Thursday to Sunday from 7pm to 5am. Incidentally, no one will object if you light up a cigar. Cover is 80SEK ($10) Thursday, and 120SEK ($16) Friday, Saturday, and Sunday.

The **Cadier Bar,** Södra Blasieholmshamnen 8 (© 08/679-35-00; T-bana: Kungsträdgården), is one of the most sophisticated places in Stockholm. From the bar, which is situated in the Grand Hotel—one of the most famous hotels in Europe—you'll have a view of the harbor and the Royal Palace. Light meals—open-faced sandwiches and smoked salmon—are served all day in the extension overlooking the waterfront. Drinks run 96SEK to 120SEK ($12–$16); imported beer is 52SEK ($6.75). The bar is named for the hotel's builder. It's open Monday through Saturday from 11am to 2am, Sunday from 11am to 1am; a piano player performs Wednesday through Saturday from 9:30pm to 1:30am.

GAY & LESBIAN STOCKHOLM

Looking for a nonconfrontational bar peopled with regular guys who happen to be gay? Consider a round or two at **Sidetrack,** Wollmar Yxkullsgatan 7 (© 08/641-16-88; T-bana: Mariatorget). Small and committed to shunning trendiness, it's named after the founder's favorite gay bar in Chicago. It's open every night from 6pm to 1am. Tuesday here seems to be a gay Stockholm institution. Other nights are fine, too—Sidetrack is something like a Swedish version of a bar and lounge at the local bowling alley where everyone happens to be into same-sex encounters.

Many gays and lesbians gather at **Torget,** Mälartorget 13 (© 08/20-55-60; T-bana: Gamla Stan), a cozy, Victorian-era cafe and bar in the Old City (Gamla Stan) that's open for food every afternoon and for drinks around 5pm till around midnight. A gay place with a greater emphasis on food, but with a busy and crowded bar area and a particularly helpful and informative staff, is **Babs Kök n bar,** Birger Jarlsgatan 37 (© 08-23-61-01; T-bana Östermalmstorg). It's open Monday and Tuesday 5pm to midnight, Wednesday to Saturday 5pm to 1am, and Sunday 4 to 10pm. A well-recommended disco that attracts a fun-loving, hard-dancing clientele that's both gay and straight is **Tip-top,** Sveavagen 57 (© 08/32-98-00; T-bana: Rädmansgatan). It's open Monday to Saturday from around 7pm till between midnight and 3am, depending on business and the night ⌐f

For information on other aspects of gay and lesbian life in Stockholm, click on www.welcometogaystockholm.com. For an online version of the online gay and lesbian magazine *QX*, which is available in hard copy in newsstands, click on www.qx.se.

DAY TRIPS FROM STOCKHOLM

SKOKLOSTER CASTLE 🕏🕏   Skokloster, S-746 96 Skokloster (© 018/38-60-77), is a splendid 17th-century castle and one of the most interesting baroque museums in Europe. It's next to Lake Mälaren, 64km (40 miles) west of Stockholm and 40km (31 miles) south of Uppsala. Original interiors aside, the castle is noted for its rich collections of paintings, furniture, applied art, tapestries, arms, and books. Admission is 65SEK ($8.45) adults, 50SEK ($6.50) seniors, and 20SEK ($2.60) students and children. Guided tours are conducted from April to September daily every hour from 11am to 4pm. In September the guided tours are given from Monday to Friday at 1pm; Saturday and Sunday at 1, 2, and 3pm. The site is closed from October to April 24.

Skokloster Motor Museum (© 018/38-61-06), on the palace grounds, contains the largest collection of vintage automobiles and motorcycles in the country. One of the most notable cars is a 1905 eight-horsepower De Dion Bouton. It costs 50SEK ($6.50) adults, 20SEK ($2.60) children 7 to 14, free for children under 7. It's open from April to September 15, daily from noon to 4pm.

Getting There   From Stockholm take a **train** to the hamlet of Bålsta, which lies 19km (12 miles) from the castle. At the village train station, you can either take **bus** no. 894 directly to Skokloster, or call for a **taxi** from a direct telephone line that's prominently positioned just outside the railway station.

UPPSALA 🕏🕏   The major university city of Sweden, Uppsala, 68km (42 miles) northwest of Stockholm, is the most popular destination for day-trippers from Stockholm, and for good reason. Uppsala not only has a great university, but also a celebrated 15th-century cathedral. Even in the time of the Vikings, this was a religious center, the scene of animal and human sacrifices in honor of the old Norse gods. And it was once the center of royalty as well; Queen Christina occasionally held court here. The church is still the seat of the Swedish archbishop, and the first Swedish university was founded here in 1477.

Getting There   The **train** from Stockholm's Central Station takes about 45 minutes. Trains leave about every hour during peak daylight hours. Some visitors spend the day in Uppsala and return to Stockholm on the commuter train in the late afternoon. Eurailpass holders ride free. **Boats** between Uppsala and Skokloster depart Uppsala Tuesday through Sunday at 11:30am, returning to Uppsala at 5:15pm. Round-trip passage costs 135SEK ($18). For details, check with the tourist office in any of the towns.

Visitor Information   The **Tourist Information Office** is at Fyris Torg 8 (© 018/727-48-00), open Monday through Friday from 10am to 6pm and Saturday from 10am to 3pm.

Exploring Uppsala   At the end of Drottninggatan is the **Carolina Rediviva (University Library)** 🕏 (© 018/471-39-00; bus: 6, 7, or 22), with its more than five million volumes and 40,000 manuscripts, among them many rare works from the Middle Ages. But the manuscript that really draws visitors is the *Codex Argenteus* (Silver Bible), translated into the old Gothic language in the middle of the 3rd century and copied in about A.D. 525. It's the only book extant in the old Gothic script. Also worth seeing is the original woodblock engraving of the *Carta Marina,* the first printed map of the Nordic countries (1539), a fairly accurate rendering of Sweden and its neighboring countries. Admission is 20SEK ($2.60), free for children under 12. The library's exhibition room is open Monday through Friday from 8:30am to 9pm and Saturday 9am to 6pm.

Linnaeus Garden & Museum, Svartbäcksgatan 27 (© **018/10-94-90** for the museum, or 018/10-94-90 for the garden; walk straight from the rail station to Kungsgatan, and proceed for about 10 min. to Svartbäcksgatan), is the former home of Swedish botanist Carl von Linné, also known as Carolus Linnaeus, who developed a classification system for the world's plants and flowers. This museum is on the spot where he restored Uppsala University's botanical garden, which resembles a miniature baroque garden. His detailed sketches and descriptions of the garden have been faithfully followed. Admission to the museum is 25SEK ($3.25) adults, free for children. A donation is suggested for admission to the gardens. The museum is open from June to September 15, Tuesday through Sunday from noon to 4pm; closed from September 16 to May. The gardens are open from May to September daily from 9am to 9pm and September daily from 9am to 7pm; closed October through April.

The largest cathedral in Scandinavia at nearly 120m (400 ft.) tall, the twin-spired Gothic **Uppsala Domkyrka** ✵, Domkyrkoplan 5 (© **018/18-72-01;** bus: 1 or 2), was founded in the 13th century. It was severely damaged in 1702 in a disastrous fire that swept over Uppsala, then was restored near the turn of the last century. Among the regal figures buried in the crypt is Gustavus Vasa. The remains of St. Erik, patron saint of Sweden, are entombed in a silver shrine. Botanist Linnaeus and philosopher-theologian Emanuel Swedenborg are also buried here. A small museum displays ecclesiastical relics of Uppsala. Admission to the cathedral is free; museum admission is 30SEK ($3.90) adults, 15SEK ($1.95) seniors and students, and 10SEK ($1.30) children 7 to 15, free for children under 7. The cathedral is open daily from 8am to 6pm. The museum is open April through August, daily from 10am to 5pm; September through March, Tuesday through Saturday from 11am to 3pm, Sunday from 12:30 to 3pm.

GRIPSHOLM CASTLE ✵✵ On an island in Lake Mälaren, Gripsholm Castle (Gripsholm Slottsfervaltning), P.O. Box 14, 64721 Mariefred (© **0159/101-94**)—the fortress built by Gustavus Vasa in the late 1530s—is one of the best-preserved castles in Sweden. It lies near Mariefred, an idyllic small town known for its vintage narrow-gauge railroad.

Even though Gripsholm was last occupied by royalty (Charles XV) in 1864, it's still a royal castle. Its outstanding features include a large collection of portrait paintings depicting obscure branches of the Swedish monarchy, its brooding architecture, and its 18th-century theater built for the amusement of the 18th-century actor-king Gustavus III. It's open from May to August, daily from 10am to 4pm; in September, Tuesday through Sunday from 10am to 3pm; and from October to April, Saturday and Sunday from noon to 3pm. Admission is 60SEK ($7.80) adults, 30SEK ($3.90) children 7 to 15, free for ages 6 and under.

Getting There Gripsholm Castle is 68km (42 miles) southwest of Stockholm. By **car,** follow E20 south; you can drive directly to the castle parking lot. The Eskilstuna **bus** runs to the center of Mariefred, as do the boats. **Boats** leave from mid-May to September at 10am from Klara Mälarstrand Pier. The castle is a 10-minute walk from the center of Mariefred.

18

Switzerland

by Darwin Porter & Danforth Prince

Switzerland evokes images of towering peaks, mountain lakes, lofty pastures, and alpine villages, but it also offers a rich cultural life in cities such as sophisticated Geneva and perfectly preserved medieval Bern.

1 Geneva ★★★

Geneva is in the Rhône Valley at the southwestern corner of Lake Geneva (Lac Léman in French), between the Jura Mountains and the Alps. It's the capital of the canton of Geneva, the second-smallest canton in the Swiss confederation.

Switzerland's second-largest city is truly cosmopolitan. The setting is idyllic, on one of the biggest alpine lakes and within view of the glorious pinnacle of Mont Blanc. Filled with parks and promenades, the city becomes a virtual garden in summer. It's also one of the world's healthiest cities because the prevailing north wind blows away any pollution.

The yachts bobbing in the harbor and the Rolls-Royces cruising the promenades testify that Geneva is home to some of the richest people in the world. Its state religion is said to be banking—half of Switzerland's banks are located here.

Geneva has long held a position as a center of enlightenment and humane tolerance. Over the years it has offered a refuge to such controversial figures as Voltaire, Lenin, and native son Jean-Jacques Rousseau. Geneva also hosted religious reformers Knox and Calvin, and provided a safe haven for many artists. Today the headquarters of the International Red Cross and the World Health Organization are here, and they attract many other international organizations.

ESSENTIALS

GETTING THERE **By Plane** The **Geneva-Cointrin Airport** (© 022/717-71-11; www.gva.ch), though busy, is compact and easily negotiated. **Swissair** (© 877/359-7947) serves Geneva more frequently than any other airline. **Crossair** (© 0848/852-000) offers the best local connections, connecting Geneva with Lugano, Zurich, and Bern, plus flying in from several European capitals. Other international airlines flying into Geneva include **Air France** (© 022/827-87-87), with seven flights daily from Paris; and **British Airways** (© 022/710-61-00), with seven daily flights from London.

To get into the center of Geneva, there's a train station linked to the air terminal with trains leaving about every 8 to 20 minutes from 5:39am to 11:36pm (trip time: 7 min.); the one-way fare is 8.60SF ($5.60) first class and 5.20SF ($3.40) second class. A taxi into town costs 32SF ($21) and up, or you can take bus no. 10 for 12SF ($7.80).

By Train Geneva's busiest, most central, and most visible CFF (Chemins de Fer Fédéraux) rail station is **Gare Cornavin** (sometimes referred to as Genève-Cornavin), place Cornavin (© 0900/300-300). *Note:* When the Lausanne-Geneva railroad line was extended to Cointrin Airport, a second "main" railroad station was built here with both long-distance and intercity trains. To avoid having to make the trip back to the center from the airport, be sure you get off the train at the Cornavin station.

By Car From Lausanne, head southwest on N1 to the very "end of south-western Switzerland."

By Lake Steamer From late May to late September there are frequent daily arrivals by Swiss lake steamer from Montreaux, Vevey, and Lausanne (you can use your Eurailpass). If you're staying in the Left Bank (Old Town), get off at the Jardin Anglais stop in Geneva; Mont Blanc and Pâquis are the Right Bank stops. For more information, call ℂ **022/312-52-23.**

VISITOR INFORMATION   Tourist Office   The **Office du Tourisme de Genève,** 3 rue du Mont-Blanc (ℂ **022/909-70-00;** www.geneve-tourisme.ch), is at Gare Cornavin. The staff provides information and can arrange hotel reservations (in Geneva and throughout Switzerland) and excursion bookings, and can refer you to other establishments specializing in car and motorcycle rentals and excursion bookings. The office is open from June 15 to September 15, Monday to Friday from 9am to 6pm and Saturday and Sunday from 8am to 5pm; the rest of the year, Monday to Saturday from 10am to 6pm.

Websites   After visiting the Geneva tourist office website noted above, check the following. Not so much a destination in itself as a good launching pad to other websites, **www.switzerland.com** can point the way to museums, hotels, restaurants, and other attractions. Another good website, **www.myswitzerland. com**, has useful travel advice on hotels and travel packages and throws in current snow reports.

CITY LAYOUT   Geneva is divided by **Lake Geneva (Lac Léman)** and the **Rhône River** into two sections: the Right Bank and Left Bank. You may rent an audio-guided tour in English from the tourist office (see above) for 10SF ($6.50). This tour covers more than two dozen highlights in Old Town and comes with a cassette, player, and map. It lasts approximately 2 hours. A 50SF ($33) deposit is required.

Rive Gauche (Left Bank)   This compact and colorful area is the oldest section. Here you'll find Old Town, some major shopping streets, the famous Flower Clock, the university, and several important museums. **Grand Rue** is Old Town's well-preserved main street, flanked by many houses from the 15th and 18th centuries. The street winds uphill from the ponts de l'Ile; at place Bel-Air it becomes rue de la Cité, then Grand Rue, and finally rue Hôtel-de-Ville. Eventually it reaches **place du Bourg-de-Four**—one of Geneva's most historic squares (Rousseau was born in no. 40).

South of this street is **promenade des Bastions,** a greenbelt area with a monument to the Reformation; it overlooks the Arve River. Directly to the west, in the northern corner of promenade des Bastions, is **place Neuve,** Geneva's finest square. From place Neuve, you can take **rue de la Corraterie,** once surrounded by the city wall, to the Rhône and the **ponts de l'Ile.** On this bridge is the **Tour de l'Ile,** what's left of the 13th-century bishop's castle.

On the shore of Lake Geneva is the **Jardin Anglais (English Garden)** with its Flower Clock, and farther out are the **Parc La Grange** and **Parc des Eaux-Vives.**

Rive Droite (Right Bank)   You can cross to the other side of the Rhône on any of several bridges, including **pont du Mont-Blanc, pont de la Machine,**

pont des Bergues, and **ponts de l'Ile.** The Right Bank is home to **Gare Cornavin** (the train station), the major international organizations, and several attractive parks. **Place St-Gervais** is in the St-Gervais district; since the 18th century this has been an area for jewelers and watchmakers. Along the northern shore of Lake Geneva is **quai du Président-Wilson,** named for the U.S. president who helped found the League of Nations.

The Right Bank is surrounded by parks, from the tree-shaded promenades along the Rhône to the **Parc de la Perle du Lac, Parc Barton,** and **Parc Mon-Repos** on the outskirts.

GETTING AROUND   By Public Transportation   For the most part, all of Geneva's bus and tram lines begin at place Cornavin, in front of the rail station—running roughly from 5am to midnight daily. From here, you can take bus F or 8 to the Palais des Nations. Tickets for zone 10, the urban area, enveloping most of Geneva, are sold from automatic vending machines at each stop, operated by coins or magnetic cards (free cards are available from Geneva public transport agencies). Trips inside zone 10 cost 2.20SF ($1.45), with unlimited use of all zones costing 12SF ($7.80) for 1 day. Tickets for other zones, including Geneva's suburbs and France, are sold by drivers on the corresponding buses. These tickets and many other kinds, including combined bus/cable-car tickets to climb to the top of Mont Salève, are available from the Geneva public-transport systems agencies or from official dealers. For customer service and more information, call ✆ **022/308-34-34.**

By Taxi   Cab fares start at 6.30SF ($4.10), plus 2.70SF to 3.30SF ($1.75–$2.15) for each kilometer in the city. No tipping is required. For a taxi, call ✆ **022/ 331-41-33** or 022/320-20-20.

By Car   Driving isn't recommended—parking is too difficult and the many one-way streets make navigation complicated. However, should you wish to rent a car and tour Lake Geneva, you'll find many rental companies at the airport or in the city center. Major offices include **Avis,** 44 rue de Lausanne (✆ **022/731-90-00,**

Geneva

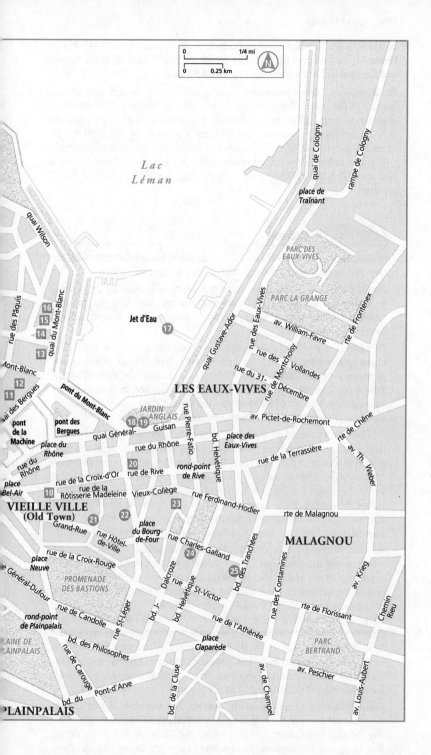

or 022/929-03-30 at the airport); **Budget,** at the airport (© **022/717-86-75**); **Hertz,** 60 rue de Berne (© **022/731-12-00,** or 022/798-22-02 at the airport); and **Europcar,** at the airport (© **022/909-69-90**).

By Bicycle or Motor Scooter Touring the city by bicycle isn't practical because of the steep cobblestone streets and general congestion. However, you might want to rent a bike to visit the nearby countryside. The major rental outlet is at the baggage *(bagages)* desk at **Gare Cornavin** (© **022/791-02-50**), where city bikes are 29SF ($19) per day and mountain bikes 40SF ($26) per day.

If you're interested in renting a motorbike, try **Horizon Motos,** 51 rue de Lausanne (© **022/732-29-90**), where rentals begin at 30SF to 80SF ($20–$52) per day.

FAST FACTS: Geneva

American Express The office at 7 rue du Mont-Blanc (© **022/731-76-00;** bus: 1) is open Monday through Friday from 8:30am to 6:45pm.

Business Hours Most **banks** are open Monday through Friday from 8:30am to 4:30pm (to 5:30pm on Wed). Most **offices** are open Monday through Friday from 8am to noon and 2 to 6pm, though this can vary. It's always best to call first.

Consulates If you lose your passport or have other business with your home government, go to your nation's consulate: **United States,** 7 rue Versonnex (© **022/840-51-61**); **Australia,** 2 chemin des Fins (© **022/799-91-00**); **Canada,** 5 av. de L'Areana (© **022/919-92-00**); **New Zealand,** 2 chemin des Fins (© **022/929-03-50**); the **United Kingdom,** 37–39 rue de Vermont (© **022/918-24-00**). Call for hours.

Currency Unlike most of the other nations of western Europe, Switzerland is not part of the euro zone. The country has opted to retain its allegiance to its national currency, the **Swiss franc (SF),** which is composed of 100 centimes. At press time, the rate of exchange for the dollar vs. the Swiss franc, and the rate used throughout this chapter, is $1 = 1.35SF. Stated differently, 1SF = approximately 74 U.S. cents. At press time, the approximate rate of exchange for the British pound is as follows: 1SF = approximately .46£; the rate of exchange for the euro was 1SF = .65€.

Currency Exchange In a city devoted to banking and the exchange of international currencies, you'll find dozens of places to exchange money in Geneva. Three of the most visible outlets, however, are run by **UBS-SA,** one of the country's largest banking conglomerates. You'll find a branch at the **Gare Cornavin,** 10 place Cornavin (© **022/375-33-60**), that's open daily from 8:30am to 8:30pm; a branch at the **Cointrin Airport** that's open daily from 6:30am to 9pm; and a downtown branch at 2 rue de la Confederation (© **022/375-75-75**) that's open Monday to Friday from 8:30am to 4:30pm. The branches in the airport and in the railway station also house "money-automats"—you receive an equivalent amount of Swiss francs for every $20, $50, and $100 bill you insert into the machine.

Dentists/Doctors English-speaking dentists are available at one of the *cliniques dentaires* at 5 rue Malombré (© **022/346-64-44;** tram: 12), Monday through Friday from 7:30am to 8pm and Saturday and Sunday from 8am to 6pm. If you become ill and want to consult a doctor, including one who will travel to your hotel, call ✆ **022/322-20-20;** or arrange an appointment with an English-speaking doctor at the **Hôpital Cantonal,** 24 rue Micheli-du-Crest (✆ **022/372-33-11;** tram: 12).

Drugstores Each night a different set of four drugstores stays open either till 9pm or 11pm. Call ✆ **144** or 111 to find out which drugstore will be open. One of the world's biggest drugstores, **Pharmacie Principale,** Confédération-Centre, rue de la Confédération (✆ **022/318-66-60;** bus: 12), offers everything from medicine to clothing, perfumes, optical equipment, cameras, and photo supplies. It's open Monday through Friday from 9am to 7pm and Saturday from 9am to 5pm.

Emergencies In an emergency, dial ✆ **117** for the police, ✆ **144** for an ambulance, and ✆ **118** to report a fire.

Hospitals You can go to the **Hôpital Cantonal,** 24 rue Micheli-du-Crest (✆ **022/372-33-11**).

Internet Access Try **Connections Net World,** 58 rue de Monthoux (✆ **022/715-38-28**), costing 3SF ($1.95) for every half-hour of use or 5SF ($3.25) per hour. It's open Monday to Saturday 9:30am to 2:30am and Sunday 1pm to 2am.

Post Office There's a limited **Office de Poste** at Gare Cornavin, 16 rue des Gares (✆ **022/739-21-11**), open Monday to Friday from 6am to 10:45pm, Saturday from 6am to 8pm, and Sunday from noon to 8pm. A better bet is the city's main post office, **Bureau de Poste Montbrillant,** rue des Gares (✆ **022/739-24-58**), which offers a full range of telephone, telegraph, and mail-related services Monday to Friday from 8am to 10:45pm, Saturday from 8am to 10pm, and Sunday from noon to 8pm.

Safety Geneva is one of the safest cities in the world, but that doesn't mean you shouldn't take the usual precautions when traveling anywhere. Protect your valuables. Car thefts have been on the rise. High-class prostitutes and confidence swindlers proliferate in Geneva to prey on the well heeled.

Taxes There is no special city tax, other than the 6.5% value-added tax (VAT) attached to all goods and services throughout Switzerland.

Telephones/Telex/Fax The **country code** for Switzerland is **41.** The **city code** for Geneva is **22;** use this code when you're calling from outside Switzerland. If you're within Switzerland but not in Geneva, use **022.** If you're calling within Geneva, simply leave off the code and dial the regular phone number.

Virtually every post office in Geneva maintains a handful of *tele-cabines* where you can pay cash for a phone call to anywhere in the world, but the densest concentration of these phones lies within the main railway station, **Gare Cornavin,** place Cornavin (open 24 hr.). Within less than a block, you'll find additional phones in the **Office de Poste Montbrillant** (Cornavin Dépôt), 16 rue des Gares, 1200 Geneve 2 (✆ **022/739-24-58**), which is open Monday to Friday from 7am to 10:45pm, and Sunday from noon to 8pm. Either site can send telegrams or faxes for you.

Tipping A 10% to 15% service charge is automatically included in most hotel and restaurant bills, although some people leave an additional tip for exceptional service. For taxis, a tip is usually included in the fare; look for the notice posted in the cab.

WHERE TO STAY
ON THE RIGHT BANK
Very Expensive

Hôtel Beau-Rivage ★★★ This landmark 1865 hotel receives our highest recommendation for its traditional Victorian charm and impeccable service. You will, however, pay dearly for them. The hotel underwent extensive renovations in 2001, combining several rooms into larger units and generally upgrading both the public and private areas. The "romantic" rooms are bigger than the "classical." Double-glazed windows cut down on street noise. Each unit has a roomy bathroom, with robes and deluxe toiletries. Units in front open onto views of the Right Bank. Its deluxe restaurant, **Le Chat-Botté,** is recommended below.

13 quai du Mont-Blanc, CH-1201 Genève. © 022/716-66-66. Fax 022/716-60-60. www.beau-rivage.ch. 97 units. 580SF–995SF ($377–$647) double; from 1,850SF ($1,203) suite. AE, DC, MC, V. Parking 40SF ($26). Bus: 1. **Amenities:** 2 restaurants; bar; 24-hr. room service; babysitting; laundry service; dry cleaning. *In room:* A/C, TV, dataport, minibar, hair dryer.

Hôtel des Bergues ★★★ After a recent massive renovation, this bastion of luxury looks fabulous. Even more dazzling than the Beau-Rivage, this is one of the world's grand hotels, the choice of any visiting monarch. It's grandly memorable from its central position at the edge of the Rhône. The staff is the most hospitable in Geneva. Rooms have Directoire and Louis-Philippe furnishings. Those ranked superior on the Bel Etage floor are the finest choices, although lake view rooms are more expensive. The hotel shelters two of the classiest dining rooms in Geneva: **Le Pavillon** and **L'Amphitryon.**

33 quai des Bergues, CH-1211 Genève. © 022/908-70-00. Fax 022/908-70-90. www.hoteldesbergues.com. 122 units. 725SF–1,025SF ($471–$666) double; from 3,475SF ($2,259) suite. AE, DC, MC, V. Parking 38SF ($25). Bus: 7. **Amenities:** 2 restaurants; bar; lounge; exercise room; sauna; 24-hr. room service; babysitting; laundry service; dry cleaning. *In room:* A/C, TV, dataport, minibar, hair dryer, safe.

Le Richemond ★★★ This regal palace is Geneva's greatest hotel and counts some of the world's most prominent people among its guests. Erected in 1875, the neoclassical building is near the lake. Nearly half of the units are suites. A large number are renovated every year but even those between rehabs look as good as new. This is true Grand Hotel living, with luxurious beds and spacious bathrooms with tub/shower combos. **Le Gentilhomme Bar** is among the finest dining rooms in Geneva.

Jardin Brunswick, CH-1211 Genève. © 022/715-70-00. Fax 022/715-70-01. www.richemond.ch. 98 units. 790SF–890SF ($514–$579) double; 1,400SF–2,000SF ($910–$1,300) suite. AE, DC, MC, V. Parking 55SF ($36). Bus: 1. **Amenities:** 2 restaurants; bar; lounge; health club; 24-hr. room service; babysitting; laundry service; dry cleaning. *In room:* A/C, TV, minibar, hair dryer.

Expensive

Hôtel de la Paix ★★ In terms of opulence it's a notch down from the Beau Rivage, but since its prices are less expensive and it's a lot less pretentious, many clients seek it out for those reasons. Although not in the ultra top tier, it's grand and glamorous, and after a complete overhaul, it's better than it's ever been. Royalty from Liechtenstein, Monaco, and the Netherlands, as well as international dignitaries and celebrities such as the guitarist Andrés Segovia, have stayed in this 1865 hotel directly on the lake. The main salon is a double-tiered arched extravaganza, with marble columns, elaborate Corinthian capitals, and a balustraded loggia overlooking a massive crystal chandelier. Rooms are traditionally furnished and often quite roomy, with antiques intermixed with well-chosen modern pieces. The marble-and-tile bathrooms are luxuriously equipped. This hotel is a member of the Leading Hotels of the World.

11 quai du Mont-Blanc, CH-1201 Genève. © **800/223-6800** in the U.S., or 022/909-60-00. Fax 022/909-60-01. www.hoteldelapaix.ch. 91 units. 450SF–650SF ($293–$423) double; 780SF–1,500SF ($507–$975) suite. AE, DC, MC, V. Parking 40SF ($26). Bus: 6, 8, 10, or 15. **Amenities:** Restaurant; bar; room service (6:30am–11pm); babysitting; laundry service; dry cleaning. *In room:* A/C, TV, dataport, minibar, hair dryer, safe.

Moderate

Best Western Strasbourg & Univers ⭐ It may have been constructed at the beginning of this past century, but 1999 renovations mean it's up to date and better than ever. For decades it has offered a safe haven for those arriving at the Geneva train station. The most spacious rooms tend to be those on the lower floors. The compact bathrooms are minimally equipped, each with a shower unit.

10 rue J-J-Pradier, CH-1201 Genève. © **800/528-1234** in the U.S., or 022/906-58-00. Fax 022/738-42-08. www.strasbourg-geneva.ch. 51 units. 250SF ($163) double; 400SF–500SF ($260–$325) suite. Rates include continental breakfast. AE, DC, MC, V. Bus: 1, 2, 3, 4, 8, 12, 13, or 44. **Amenities:** Lounge. *In room:* TV, minibar, hair dryer.

Hôtel du Midi On a tree-lined square near the center of Geneva, this hotel reminds most visitors of an apartment building. It's a comfortable place in spite of its plain appearance. The midsize rooms are well maintained, with double-glazed windows to keep out traffic noise. Bathrooms are a bit cramped but have adequate shelf space and warming racks for towels.

4 place Chevelu, CH-1211 Genève. © 022/544-15-00. Fax 022/544-15-20. www.hotel-du-midi.ch. 90 units. 250SF–400SF ($163–$260) double. AE, DC, MC, V. Parking 18SF ($12). Bus: 7. **Amenities:** Restaurant; bar; lounge; room service (7am–9:30pm); laundry service; dry cleaning. *In room:* A/C, TV, minibar, hair dryer, safe.

Inexpensive

Hôtel Bel-Espérance *(Value* This is an accommodation oddity, and a bit of a discovery. Once it was known as a *foyer pour dames* or boardinghouse for women. Right near the Old Town's place du Bourg-de-Four, it's owned by the Salvation Army, but don't fear that this is a rawboned joint. This little hotel of charm and grace has a panoramic terrace and bright midsize rooms; bathrooms have showers. It's also a choice for families, as some rooms are large enough for four beds. Try to get one with a balcony with a view of the Cathedrale St-Pierre.

1 rue de la Vallée, CH-1204 Genève. © **022/818-37-37**. Fax 022/818-37-73. www.hotel-bel-esperance.ch. 40 units. 140SF–180SF ($91–$117) double; 165SF–200SF ($107–$130) triple. Rates include breakfast. AE, DC, MC, V. Bus: 8. *In room:* TV.

Hôtel International & Terminus *(Kids* This hotel lies across from the main entrance of Geneva's railway station and has been run by three generations of the Cottier family. Built around 1900, it was radically upgraded in 2000, with pairs of smaller rooms reconfigured into larger units especially good for families. Don't expect grand style; the allure of this place is its exceedingly good value. Bathrooms seem to have been added as an afterthought in areas not designed for them, and are a bit cramped, each with a shower stall.

20 rue des Alpes, CH-1201 Genève. © **022/732-80-95**. Fax 022/732-18-43. 53 units. 150SF–180SF ($105–$126) double. Rates include continental breakfast. AE, DC, MC, V. Bus: 6, 10, or 33. **Amenities:** Restaurant; bar. *In room:* TV, minibar.

Hôtel Moderne This hotel is near the rail station and the lake. Public areas are modern. Rooms, with soundproof windows, are modern, clean, and sunny, though predictably furnished and a bit sterile. You'll probably wish the bathrooms had more room to spread out your stuff. The nearest parking is at the Cornavin rail station's underground garage.

1 rue de Berne, CH-1211 Genève. © **022/732-81-00.** Fax 022/738-26-58. www.hotelmoderne.ch. 55 units. 160SF–200SF ($104–$130) double. Rates include buffet breakfast. AE, DC, MC, V. Bus: 10. **Amenities:** Lounge; room service (7–11am); babysitting; laundry service; dry cleaning. *In room:* TV.

Hôtel St-Gervais *(Value* This good-value hotel lies in an old-fashioned, vaguely nondescript building within Geneva's medieval core, a 3-minute walk from Gare Cornavin. The old inn has the kind of quirky idiosyncrasies that appeal to architects and historic renovators. If you don't mind the lack of a bathroom, you'll find the midsize guest rooms tidily kept, tastefully furnished, and most comfortable. Most rooms have a sink, but the hall bathrooms are frequently tidied for the next guest's use.

20 rue des Corps-Saints, CH-1201 Genève. © and fax **022/732-45-72.** www.stgervais-geneva.ch. 26 units, 2 with bathroom. 105SF–110SF ($68–$72) double without bathroom; 98SF–105SF ($54–$58) double with bathroom. AE, DC, MC, V. Tram: 1, 3, 4, 5, or 6. **Amenities:** Bar; lounge; laundry service.

ON THE LEFT BANK
Expensive

Hôtel de la Cigogne ✦✦✦ Personalized and charming, this is our favorite Left Bank hotel, a chic, glamorous retreat for the discerning. This deluxe hotel was rebuilt after years of dilapidation and turned into an offbeat Relais & Châteaux that showcases designer and decorator talent. Combined with an adjoining building, the old hotel and its mate have the renovated facades of the original 18th- and 19th-century structures. With three sheltered courtyards overlooking a flowering plaza, this is one of the most tranquil hotels in Geneva. The bedrooms contain handmade mattresses, luxurious bathrooms, and bed linens embroidered with the hotel's coat of arms. Each bedroom is furnished differently, ranging from 1930s movie-mogul style to the "baron and baroness at their country place." Some units have working fireplaces.

17 place Longemalle, CH-1204 Genève. © **022/818-40-40.** Fax 022/818-40-50. www.cigogne.ch. 50 units. 445SF ($289) double; 780SF–890SF ($507–$579) suite. Rates include continental breakfast. AE, DC, MC, V. Parking 27SF ($18). Bus: 6 or 9. **Amenities:** Restaurant; 24-hr. room service; babysitting; laundry service; dry cleaning. *In room:* A/C, TV, dataport, minibar, hair dryer, safe.

Moderate

Edelweiss Manotel *(Finds* This is the most artfully folkloric hotel in Geneva, evoking the kind of cozy alpine decor that most Swiss people associate with isolated hamlets in the country's mountains. Although it was built in a seven-story boxy-looking design in 1967 and renovated in 1999, the interior—including each guest room—showcases the meticulous craftsmanship of another era. That's thanks to carefully finished pinewood paneling and country-baroque accessories that show off *gemütlich* Switzerland at its most charming. The hotel's social centerpiece is its restaurant.

2 place de la Navigation, CH-1201 Genève. © **022/544-51-51.** Fax 022/544-51-99. www.manotel.com. 42 units. 315SF ($205) double; 359SF ($233) triple. Rates include breakfast. AE, DC, MC, V. Bus: 1. **Amenities:** Restaurant; bar; concierge; room service (noon–11pm); massage; babysitting; laundry service; dry cleaning. *In room:* A/C, TV, dataport, minibar, safe.

Hôtel Tiffany ✦ *(Value* This little charmer of a Belle Epoque boutique hotel lies on a Left Bank street 3 blocks south of the river and about a 12-minute stroll from the center and the lake. Although it can hardly match the style and glamour of the lakeside palaces, it is attractive in its modest way. In its category, it offers some of the most reasonable prices in Geneva. Rooms are midsize with lots of extras, including soundproofing and spacious bathrooms with tub/shower combos. We like the rooms in the "attic," with their beams, rooftop vistas, and sloping walls.

1 rue des Marbriers, CH-1204 Genève. ✆ 022/708-1616. Fax 022/708-1617. www.hotel-tiffany.ch. 46 units. 320SF–360SF ($208–$234) double; from 470SF ($306) suite. Rates include buffet breakfast. AE, DC, MC, V. Bus: 1 or 4. **Amenities:** Restaurant; English bar; room service (7am–10:30pm); laundry service; dry cleaning. *In room:* A/C, TV, dataport, minibar, hair dryer, safe.

Inexpensive

Hotel Central *Value*   This Left Bank bargain has been completely rejuvenated. Since its reopening, it's been a success as word of its good value has spread to budget-minded travelers. On a shopping street, it has a warm and inviting Bali-inspired decor. The location is at the foot of the Old Town and only a 3-minute walk to the lake. The Gansted family is on hand to welcome you, and each of their rooms is personalized, containing comfortable beds and small but neat bathrooms with shower stalls. A few rooms have bunk beds suitable for families or friends traveling together. Some rooms are very large with two separate bathrooms.

2 rue de la Rôtisserie, CH-1204 Genève. ✆ 022/818-81-00. Fax 022/818-81-01. www.hotelcentral.ch. 30 units, 24 with private toilet. 80SF ($52) double without toilet; 130SF ($85) double with toilet; 200SF ($130) suite. Rates include breakfast. AE, DC, MC, V. Bus: 12. *In room:* TV, dataport.

WHERE TO DINE
ON THE RIGHT BANK
Very Expensive

Le Chat-Botté ★★★ FRENCH   "Puss in Boots" is in one of Geneva's grandest hotels. It's a close race between this deluxe dining room and the Hilton's Le Cygne (see below) as to which serves the best cuisine in Geneva. We'd give the honors to Le Chat Botté for French dishes, with Le Cygne winning for fresh seafood. In nice weather you can dine on the flower-decked terrace, overlooking the Jet d'Eau. The cuisine, though inspired by French classics, is definitely contemporary. The large selection includes carpaccio with black olives and Parmesan cheese, a divine lobster salad with eggplant "caviar," and oven-roasted Sisteron lamb with stuffed vegetables. Highly recommended is delicate perch filet from Lake Geneva, sautéed until it's golden.

In the Hôtel Beau-Rivage, 13 quai du Mont-Blanc. ✆ 022/716-69-20. Reservations required. Main courses 42SF–57SF ($27–$37). Fixed-price menus (Mon–Fri only) 60SF–115SF ($39–$75) at lunch, 118SF–150SF ($77–$98) at dinner. AE, DC, MC, V. Daily noon–2pm and 7–10pm. Bus: 6 or 33.

Le Cygne ★★★ FRENCH   This swank restaurant overlooks the harbor with the famous Jet d'Eau and, in the distance, the Alps. A refined cuisine is offered, with impeccable service. The menu may present such stellar choices as terrine of blackened chicken in crayfish- and anise-flavored aspic. Also worthy of an award are the smoked filet of sea bass with truffle-flavored vinaigrette and the roast lamb with coriander and tomatoes stuffed with moussaka. Five elaborate carts make one of the most spectacular arrays of desserts in Switzerland.

In the Noga Hilton International, 19 quai du Mont-Blanc. ✆ 022/908-90-85. Reservations required. Main courses 45SF–70SF ($29–$46); fixed-price meal 72SF–85SF ($47–$55) at lunch, 86SF–145SF ($56–$94) at dinner. AE, DC, MC, V. Daily noon–2pm and 7–10:30pm. Closed 1 week in Jan, 11 days at Easter, and 3 weeks in July. Bus: 1.

Le Neptune ★★★ SEAFOOD   At one of Geneva's finest seafood restaurant, the decor is intimate, intensely floral, and graced with an enormous fresco displaying an inside view of Neptune's kingdom. Though the kitchen closes on the weekend, during the week it entertains some of the most discerning palates in Geneva. You're likely to be offered such dishes as herbed vichyssoise with hazelnut oil and a dollop of foie gras; a perfect cassoulet of oysters seasoned with algae-flavored butter sauce; or a memorable Atlantic sea bass roasted in a salt crust with thyme. If you're not in the mood for fish, try rack of Scottish lamb in puff pastry with spices or partridge roasted en casserole with autumn herbs.

In the Hôtel Mandarin Oriental du Rhône, 1 quai Turrettini. ℂ 022/909-00-06. Reservations required. Main courses 34SF–41SF ($22–$27); fixed-price meal 72SF ($47) at lunch, 78SF–140SF ($51–$91) at dinner. AE, DC, MC, V. Mon–Fri noon–2pm and 7:30–10:30pm. Bus: 6, 8, 10, or 15.

Expensive

La Mère Royaume ✮ FRENCH Opened around the turn of the 20th century, this is one of the oldest restaurants in town. It's named after a heroine who in 1602 poured boiling stew over a Savoyard soldier's head and cracked his skull with the kettle. With an antecedent like that, you'd expect some of the heartiest fare in Geneva, but instead the kitchen offers perfectly cooked French specialties such as *omble chevalier*, a delicate Lake Geneva whitefish known as "the world's most divine trout." Less expensive meals are served in the brasserie.

9 rue des Corps-Saints. ℂ 022/732-70-08. Reservations required. Brasserie main courses 20SF–37SF ($13–$24); fixed-price menu 45SF–50SF ($29–$33). Restaurant main courses 32SF–55SF ($21–$36); fixed-price menu 57SF–108SF ($37–$70). AE, DC, MC, V. Mon–Fri noon–2pm and 7–10:30pm; Sat 7–10:30pm. Bus: 4, 6, or 7. Tram: 13.

Moderate

Chez Jacky ✮ *Finds* SWISS This provincial bistro is a delightful place for dining, attracting everyone from staid grandmothers to young skiers en route to Verbier. It's the domain of Jacky Gruber, an exceptional chef from Valais. You might begin with Chinese cabbage and mussels and continue with filet of turbot roasted with thyme or beautifully prepared pink duck on spinach with onion confit. Be prepared to wait for each course, as everything is prepared to order.

9–11 rue Necker. ℂ 022/732-86-80. Reservations recommended. Main courses 42SF–44SF ($27–$29); fixed-price meal 48SF ($31) at lunch, 60SF–90SF ($39–$59) at dinner. AE, DC, MC, V. Mon–Fri 11am–2pm and 6:30–11pm. Closed the 1st week of Jan and 3 weeks in Aug. Bus: 5, 10, or 44.

Le Boeuf Rouge LYONNAISE This brasserie serves Geneva's best cookery in the style of Lyons, the gastronomic capital of France. As such, you'll find authentic versions of such dishes as Lyonnais sausage with scalloped potatoes; chateaubriand in red-wine sauce; blood sausage; and quenelles of pikeperch, any of which might be preceded by a delectable version of onion soup or green salad with croutons and bacon. The decor is appealingly kitschy, complete with lots of Art Nouveau posters and late-19th-century ceramics. The staff here is brusque, but kind.

17 rue Alfred-Vincent (corner of the rue Paquis). ℂ 022/732-7537. Reservations recommended. Main courses 32SF–52SF ($21–$34); fixed-price meal 37SF ($24) at lunch, 48SF–55SF ($31–$36) at dinner. AE, DC, MC, V. Mon–Fri noon–2pm and 7–10:30pm; Sat 7–10pm. Bus: 1.

Inexpensive

Jeck's Place ✮ PAN-ASIAN Near the Cornavin rail station, this delightful place is like taking a culinary trip to southeast Asia, with stopovers in such places as China, Malaysia, Thailand, and India. The cuisine of Asian specialties provides temptation with every order. We often make a meal of the appetizers alone, including homemade steamed dumplings stuffed with a blend of pork and vegetables flavored with coriander. The house specialty, and our favorite dish, is

Jeck's chicken in green curry. Another exotic treat is a delicate whiting spread with spicy lemon-grass sauce and grilled on banana leaves.

14 rue de Neuchâtel. ✆ 022/731-3303. Reservations recommended. Main courses 21SF–33SF ($14–$21); special lunch platter 15SF ($9.75). AE, DC, MC, V. Mon–Fri 11:30am–2pm and 6:30–10pm; Sat–Sun 6:30–10pm. Bus: 4, 5, or 9.

ON THE LEFT BANK
Expensive

Le Béarn ★★★ FRENCH   This is the only deluxe restaurant on the Left Bank that matches the previously recommended three-star choices on the Right Bank. Jean-Paul Goddard and his excellent staff have created the best restaurant in Geneva's business center. With only 10 tables, everything is on a small scale, and the service is personal. The chef prepares dishes that appeal to the Rothschild palates, including such spectacular delights as tender morels stuffed with fresh asparagus tips. One of the world's most expensive birds, roasted Scottish thrush, might rest on your platter, or our all-time favorite concoction here, a platter called "three terrines of autumn" (rabbit, partridge, and thrush).

4 quai de la Poste. ✆ 022/321-00-28. Reservations required. Main courses 35SF–70SF ($23–$46); fixed-price meal 60SF–165SF ($39–$107) at lunch, 97SF–167SF ($63–$109) at dinner. AE, DC, MC, V. Mon–Fri noon–2pm and 7:15–10pm; Sat 7:15–10pm. Closed July 15–Aug 10 and Sat June–Sept. Bus: 2, 10, or 22.

Moderate

Brasserie de l'Hôtel de Ville ★ *Finds* SWISS   This is one of the most deliberately archaic-looking restaurants in Geneva, with a reputation that goes back to 1764 and a clientele who prefer that its old-fashioned decor and menu items absolutely not change. In spite of its look, it's rather fashionable among a growing number of arts-industry hipsters who appreciate the vintage charm and the increasingly sophisticated menu, including a fresh dandelion salad with medallions of sautéed duck liver; rack of lamb flavored with herbes de Provence; and the prized fish of Lake Geneva, *omble*, served in a butter sauce.

19 Grand Rue. ✆ 022/311-70-30. Reservations recommended. Main courses 37SF–52SF ($24–$34); fixed-price menus 60SF–109SF ($39–$71). AE, DC, MC, V. Daily 11:30am–11:30pm. Bus: 17.

Brasserie Lipp SWISS   This bustling place is named after the famous Parisian brasserie, and when you enter (especially at lunch), you'll think you've been transported to France. The impossibly long menu contains a sampling of the repertoire of bistro dishes, but, like its namesake, the Geneva Lipp specializes in several versions of charcuterie. You can also order three kinds of pot-au-feu and such classics as Toulousian cassoulet with *confit de canard* (duckling), available in autumn and winter. The fresh oysters are among the best in the city, and tables are placed outside in summer.

In Confédération-Centre, 8 rue de la Confédération. ✆ 022/311-10-11. Reservations recommended. Main courses 25SF–50SF ($16–$33); plats du jour 25SF ($16) lunch only; fixed-price menus 60SF–80SF ($39–$52). AE, DC, MC, V. Daily 11:45am–12:15am. Bus: 12.

La Coupole SWISS   This is a true brasserie, and far more elegant than its Parisian namesake. The place is most popular at noon, especially with shoppers and office workers. The menu is limited but well selected; the *cuisine du marché* (cooking based on market-fresh ingredients) is a delight, although many patrons stick to the standard old red-meat bistro specials such as the inevitable entrecôte.

116 rue du Rhône. ✆ 022/787-50-10. Main courses 36SF–42SF ($23–$27); fixed-price menus 40SF–45SF ($26–$29). AE, DC, MC, V. Mon–Sat 11:30am–2:30pm and 7:30pm–12:30am. Bus: 2, 9, or 22. Tram: 12.

La Favola ★ TUSCAN/ITALIAN This is the best Italian dining spot in Geneva, and its most devoted habitués go even further, hailing it as the best restaurant in Geneva. The menu is small and short but choice, varying with the availability of ingredients and the season. Look for such well-crafted dishes as carpaccio of beef; *vitello tonnato* (paper-thin veal with a tuna sauce); lobster salad; potato salad with cèpe mushrooms; and a highly pleasing ravioli made with either eggplant or mushrooms.

15 rue Jean-Calvin. ℂ 022/311-74-37. Reservations required. Main courses 45SF–60SF ($29–$39). AE, MC, V. Mon–Fri noon–2pm and 7:15–10pm. Closed 2 weeks in July–Aug and 1 week at Christmas. Tram: 12.

Inexpensive

Au Pied de Cochon ★ *Finds* LYONNAISE/SWISS Come here for hearty Lyonnaise fare if you don't mind smoke and noise. A lot of young people are attracted to this place, as well as lawyers from the Palais de Justice across the way, artists, and local workers. The cooking is like Grandma's—provided she came from Lyon. Naturally, the namesake *pieds de cochon* (pigs' feet) is included on the menu, along with tender alpine lamb, tripe, and grilled *andouillette* sausage.

4 place du Bourg-de-Four. ℂ 022/310-47-97. Reservations recommended. Main courses 32SF–42SF ($21–$27). AE, DC, MC, V. Daily 7:30am–2:30pm and 6:30pm–midnight (closed Sun June–Aug). Bus: 2 or 7. Tram: 12.

L'Aïoli *Finds* PROVENÇAL This popular neighborhood restaurant stands opposite Le Corbusier's Maison de Verre. Something of a local secret, it offers personalized service and the finest Provençal cooking in town. We recommend frogs' legs Provençal, lamb *gigot,* and scampi Provençal. The chefs also prepare a delectable lamb stew called *gardiane camarguaise.*

6 rue Adrien-Lachenal. ℂ 022/736-79-71. Reservations not required. Main courses 25SF–32SF ($16–$21); menu dégustation 79SF ($51). AE, DC, MC, V. Mon–Fri 11am–2:30pm and 7–10:30pm. Closed Aug. Bus: 1 or 6. Tram: 12.

Le Lyrique ★ SWISS This is a good place for a pre-theater dinner, with both a formal restaurant and a brasserie. The brasserie, which has a terrace, is open all day but serves hot meals only during the hours mentioned below. The restaurant is open only on weekdays, except for those weekends when there's a performance at the nearby Grand Théâtre de Genève. You can try such carefully prepared dishes as filet of sea wolf with grapefruit segments, a roulade of rabbit with pasta maison, and tagliatelle with scampi. In the brasserie, menu items include chicken suprême with ravioli and leeks, and an *assiette Lyrique,* a meal in itself that combines four vegetarian and fish dishes—tartare of salmon, tartare of vegetables, terrine of vegetables, and eggplant "caviar."

12 bd. du Théâtre. ℂ 022/328-00-95. Reservations recommended. Restaurant main courses 27SF–43SF ($18–$28); fixed-price meal 55SF–68SF ($36–$44). Brasserie main courses 25SF–35SF ($16–$23); fixed-price menu 42SF–54SF ($27–$35). AE, MC, V. Mon–Fri noon–2pm and 6:30–10pm. Bus: 2 or 22.

Les Armures ★ *Kids* SWISS/INTERNATIONAL In spite of the government-rated five-star elegance of the hotel that contains this restaurant, this is surprisingly unpretentious and affordable. Dining is possible on three different floors. The lower you go, the more animated the scene becomes. This stone building is located on a cobblestone street across from a medieval arsenal in one of the most colorful neighborhoods of the Old Town. The building was constructed in the 16th century, and this place has thrived as one of the most atmospheric restaurants since its founding in 1957. The three different fondues offered are the best in Geneva. Many Swiss children make an entire meal out of *rösti,* or Swiss-style hash browns. Other specialties include raclette and several pizza and pasta dishes, plus our favorite dishes here, duck liver terrine followed by seared scallops Provençal. The winter-only sauerkraut garni is also a savory meal—made with several types of sausage and pork. The staff still remembers the day in January 1994 when Bill Clinton dropped in to sample the sauerkraut during a break in political negotiations. Pastas and hamburgers round out the menu, which should make any child's palate happy.

1 rue des Puits-St-Pierre. ✆ **022/310-34-42.** Main courses 24SF–47SF ($16–$31); fixed-price menu 50SF ($33). AE, DC, MC, V. Mon–Fri 8am–midnight; Sat–Sun 11am–midnight. Bus: 3 or 5.

Nô Sushi *(Value)* JAPANESE Popular, hip, and mobbed every day at lunchtime, this is the only automated sushi bar in Switzerland and, as such, adds an eccentric and trend-conscious flair to a neighborhood that's better known for its relative conservatism. You'll pluck everything except the miso soup, which is carried to your seat by a waitress, directly from the moving conveyer belt. Hot foods remain hot thanks to a candle flickering beneath. Sushi (with rice) and sashimi (without rice) choices include mullet, calamari, octopus, salmon, and tuna. There's also teriyaki dishes, tempura, and a medley of rice and noodle dishes, any combinations of which make a full meal.

Confédération Centre, 8 rue de la Confédération. ✆ **022/810-39-73.** Reservations not necessary. Sushi, sashimi, rolls, and small platters 10SF–15SF ($6.50–$9.75). AE, MC, V. Mon–Thurs 11:30am–midnight; Fri–Sat 11:30am–1am. Closed Sun. Bus: 12.

Pizzeria da Paolo *(Value)* ITALIAN/PIZZAS Bustling, convivial, and completely unpretentious, this simple pizzeria offers a cozy, wood-sheathed setting from a position very close to the Jet d'Eau. More than 20 kinds of pizza are offered—the house specialty is a Pizza Paolo, made from fresh spinach and cheese. But if pizzas aren't your thing, there's a full complement of chicken parmigiana; stuffed and roasted turkey; fresh salads; ham dishes; and fresh fish. Don't expect glamour, just good value and some filling and very tasty Italian food.

3 rue du Lac. ✆ **022/736-3049.** Reservations recommended. Pizzas 18SF–25SF ($11–$16); main-course platters 25SF–50SF ($16–$33). AE, DC, MC, V. Daily 11:45am–2pm and 6:45–11pm. Tram: 12.

Taverne de la Madeleine *(Value)* SWISS Robust, unpretentious, and known for its no-nonsense approach to serving well-prepared, cost-conscious food, this restaurant is set against the old city wall beside the Eglise de la Madeleine. The brusquely efficient staff caters to a lunchtime business crowd, and the place is operated by a philanthropic organization that forbids the consumption of alcohol (alcohol-free beer is available). You can order a variety of well-prepared dishes or specials like four types of pasta, vegetarian sandwiches, and a big plate of osso buco (braised veal shank) with *pommes frites* (Belgian fries). The kitchen prides itself on its filet of lake perch meunière style (in butter sauce) or Vevey style with exotic mushrooms. Most dishes are at the lower end of the price scale.

20 rue Toutes-Ames. ✆ **022/310-60-70.** Reservations recommended. Main courses 18SF–30SF ($11–$19); plat du jour 17SF ($11). MC, V. Sept–June Mon–Fri 7:30am–6:30pm (last food order at 4pm), Sat 9am–4:30pm (last food order at 2:30pm); July–Aug Tues–Sat 7:30am–9pm. Bus: 2. Tram: 12.

SEEING THE SIGHTS

You can see most of Geneva on foot, which is the best way to familiarize yourself with the city.

THE TOP ATTRACTIONS

In addition to the sights below, Geneva's top attractions are the **Jet d'Eau,** the famous fountain that has virtually become the city's symbol; the **Flower Clock,** in the Jardin Anglais; and the **Old Town,** the oldest part of the city.

Baur Collections ✿ The collections, housed in a 19th-century mansion with a garden, constitute a private exhibit of artworks from 7th- to 20th-century China and 17th- to 20th-century Japan. The choice ceramics here are from the Tang Dynasty (618–908). On display are jade, ceramics, lacquer, ivories, and delicate sword fittings.

8 rue Munier-Romilly. ℂ 022/346-17-29. Admission 5SF ($3.25) adults, free for children. Tues–Sun 2–6pm. Bus: 1 or 8.

Cathédrale St-Pierre ✿ The old town, **Vieille Ville,** on the Left Bank, is dominated by the cathedral, built in the 12th and 13th centuries and partially reconstructed in the 15th century. In 1536, the people of Geneva gathered in the cloister of St-Pierre's and voted to make the cathedral Protestant. The church has a modern organ with 6,000 pipes. The northern tower was reconstructed at the end of the 19th century. If you don't mind the 145 steps, you can climb to the top of the north tower for a panoramic view.

To enter the St-Pierre archaeological site, called **Site Archéologique de St-Pierre,** go through the entrance in the Cour St-Pierre, at the right corner of the cathedral steps. The underground passage extends under the present cathedral and the High Gothic (early-15th-c.) **Chapelle des Macchabées,** which adjoins the church's southwestern corner. Excavations have revealed baptisteries, a crypt, the foundations of several cathedrals, the bishop's palace, 4th-century mosaics, sculptures, and geological strata.

Cour St-Pierre. ℂ 022/311-75-75. Admission: cathedral free admission (donations welcome); tower 3SF ($1.95) seniors and students; archaeological site 5SF ($3.25) adults, 3SF ($1.95) students and seniors. Cathedral and chapel open June–Sept daily 9am–7pm; Mar–May and Oct daily 9am–noon and 2–6pm; Jan–Feb and Nov–Dec daily 9am–noon and 2–3pm. Archaeological site open Tues–Sat 11am–1pm and 2–5pm. Bus: 3, 5, or 17. Tram: 12

Maison Tavel ✿ Built in 1303 and partially reconstructed after a fire in 1334, this is the city's oldest house and one of its newest museums. The museum exhibits historical collections from Geneva dating from the Middle Ages to the mid–19th century. The Magnin relief in the attic is outstanding, as is the copper-and-zinc model of 1850s Geneva. Objects of daily use are displayed in the old living quarters.

6 rue du Puits-St-Pierre. ℂ 022/418-37-00. Free admission. Tues–Sun 10am–5pm. Bus: 3, 5, or 17.

Musée Ariana ✿✿ This is one of the top porcelain, glass, and pottery museums of Europe. To the west of the Palais des Nations, this Italian Renaissance building was constructed by Gustave Revilliod, the 19th-century Genevese patron who began the collection. Here you'll see Sèvres, Delft faience, and Meissen porcelain, as well as pieces from Japan and China. It's also the headquarters of the International Academy of Ceramics.

10 av. de la Paix. ℂ 022/418-54-50. Admission: permanent collection free; temporary exhibitions 5SF ($3.25) adults, free children under 12. Wed–Mon 10am–5pm. Bus: 8 or F.

Musée d'Art et d'Histoire (Museum of Art and History) ✿✿ Geneva's most important museum is between boulevard Jacques-Dalcroze and boulevard Helvétique. It virtually presents the story of civilization from prehistoric times up to the present. Displays include prehistoric relics, Greek vases, medieval stained glass, 12th-century armor, Swiss timepieces, and Flemish and Italian paintings. The Etruscan pottery and medieval furniture are quite impressive. A 1444 altarpiece by Konrad Witz depicts the "miraculous" draught of fishes.

Many galleries also contain works by such artists as Rodin, Renoir, Le Corbusier, Picasso, Chagall, Corot, Monet, and Pissarro.

2 rue Charles-Galland. © **022/418-26-00.** Free admission; 4.50SF ($2.50) temporary exhibitions. Tues–Sun 10am–5pm. Bus: 2, 3, 5, 8, or 17.

Musée International de la Croix Rouge et du Croissant-Rouge (International Red Cross and Red Crescent Museum) ★ Here you can experience the legendary past of the Red Cross in the city where it started; it's across from the visitors' entrance to the European headquarters of the United Nations. The dramatic story from 1863 to the present is revealed through displays of rare documents and photographs, films, multiscreen slide shows, and cycloramas. You're taken from the battlefields of Europe to the plains of Africa to see the Red Cross in action.

17 av. de la Paix. © **022/748-95-25.** Admission 10SF ($6.50) adults; 5SF ($3.25) seniors, students, and children. Wed–Mon 10am–5pm. Bus: 8, F, V, or Z.

Palais des Nations ★★ Surrounded by ancient trees and modern monuments, these buildings comprise the second-largest complex in Europe after Versailles. Until 1936, the League of Nations met at the Palais Wilson, when the League's headquarters were transferred to the Palais des Nations. The international organization continued minor activities through the war years until it was dissolved in 1946, just as the newly created United Nations met in San Francisco. Today the Palais des Nations is the European headquarters of the United Nations, with a modern wing added in 1973.

Part of the interior is devoted to exhibitions showcasing the high-minded but ineffectual precursor of the United Nations, the League of Nations. Frequent tours, departing whenever the staff feels there are enough participants to justify conducting one, leave from the visitors' entrance at 14 av. de la Paix, opposite the Red Cross building. For information, contact the **Visitors' Service,** United Nations Office, 14 av. de la Paix (© **022/907-45-60**).

Parc de l'Ariana, 14 av. de la Paix. © **022/907-48-96.** Admission 8.50SF ($5.55) adults, 6.50SF ($4.25) students, 4SF ($2.60) for children 5 and under. July–Aug daily 9am–6pm; Sept–June daily 10am–noon and 2–4pm. Bus: 5, 8, 18, F, V, or Z.

ORGANIZED TOURS

If you're new in Geneva and want an easy-to-digest breakdown of the way the city is divided into various neighborhoods and districts, consider a tram tour. Departing from the south bank's Place du Rhône (May–Sept only), red-painted, open-sided trolley cars meander through neighborhoods that include the city's medieval center, the glossy shopping districts, and the hotel and museum-studded precincts of the river's north bank. Trams depart at 45-minute intervals every day between 10am and 6pm, last about an hour, and cost 8.90SF ($5.80) for adults and 5.90SF ($3.85) for children. For more information, contact **STT Trains Tours S.A.,** 36 bd. St-Georges (© **022/781-04-04**).

(**Fun Fact** The Red Cross Flag

When Henry Dunant founded the Red Cross in Geneva in 1863, he needed a recognizable symbol to suggest neutrality. The Swiss flag (a white cross on a red field), with the colors reversed, ended up providing the perfect symbol for one of the world's greatest humanitarian movements.

> *Moments* **Exploring Geneva's Parks & Gardens**
>
> If you walk along the quays, heading north as if to Lausanne, you'll come to some of the lushest parks in Geneva. **Parc Mon-Repos** ★★ is off avenue de France and **La Perle du Lac** lies off rue de Lausanne. Directly to the right is the **Jardin Botanique (Botanical Garden)**, opened in 1902. It has an alpine garden, a little zoo, greenhouses, and exhibitions. You can visit it free daily, October through March from 9:30am to 5pm and April through September from 8am to 7:30pm. From Cornavin Station, take bus no. 4.
>
> Back at the lakeside, you can take a boat to the other bank, getting off at quai Gustave-Ador. From here you can explore two more lakeside parks—**Parc la Grange,** which has the most extravagant rose garden in Switzerland (especially in June), and, next to it, **Parc des Eaux-Vives.**
>
> When you leave the Botanical Garden on the Left Bank, you can head west, along avenue de la Paix, about a mile north from pont du Mont-Blanc, to the Palais des Nations in **Parc de l'Ariana.**

A 2-hour City Tour is operated daily all year by **Key Tours S.A.,** 7 rue des Alpes, square du Mont-Blanc (℃ **022/731-41-40**). The tour starts from the Gare Routière, the bus station at place Dorcière, near the Key Tours office. From November to March the tour is offered only once a day at 2pm, but from April to October two tours leave daily, at 10am and 2pm.

A bus will drive you through the city to see the monuments, landmarks, and lake promenades. In the Old Town you can take a walk down to the Bastions Park to the Reformation Wall. After a tour through the International Center, where you'll be shown the headquarters of the International Red Cross, the bus returns to its starting place. Adults pay 39SF ($25) and children 4 to 12 accompanied by an adult are charged 18SF ($12), while children 3 and under go free.

THE SHOPPING SCENE

From boutiques to department stores, Geneva is a shopper's dream come true. The city, of course, is known for its watches and jewelry, but it's also a good place to buy embroidered blouses, music boxes from the Jura region, cuckoo clocks from German Switzerland, cigars from Havana (not allowed into the United States), chocolate, Swiss army knives, and many other items.

Geneva practically invented the wristwatch. In fact, watchmaking in the city dates from the 16th century. Be sure to avoid purchasing a Swiss watch in one of the souvenir stores. If jewelers are legitimate, they'll display a symbol of the Geneva Association of Watchmakers and Jewelers. Here, more than in any other Swiss city perhaps, you should be able to find all the best brands, including Vacheron & Constantin, Longines, Omega, and Blancpain, to name just a few. Sometimes there are discounts on such items as cameras. Most salespeople you'll encounter speak English and are very helpful.

A shopping spree might begin at **place du Molard.** Once this was the harbor of Geneva before the water receded. Merchants from all over Europe used to bring their wares to trade fairs here in the days before merchants immigrated to richer markets in Lyon.

If you walk along rue du Rhône and are put off by the prices, go 1 block south to rue du Marché, which in various sections becomes rue de la Croix-d'Or and rue de Rive, and is sometimes referred to by locals as "la rue du Tram" because of the many trolleys which run along its length. Don't be afraid to comparison-shop in Geneva—many stores jack up prices for visitors.

SELECT SHOPS   Virtually all the inventory at **Antiquorum,** 2 rue du Mont-Blanc (© **022/909-28-50;** bus: 1), consists of antique jewelry and antique watches—a sure attraction for a city that derives so much of its income from selling timepieces. The array includes some of the world's most historically important watches.

The aroma of chocolate from the **Confiserie Rohr,** 3 place du Molard (© **022/311-63-03;** bus: 9, 10, or 12), practically pulls you in off the street. You'll find chocolate-covered truffles, "gold" bars with hazelnuts, and *poubelles au chocolat* (chocolate "garbage pails"). There's another branch at 42 rue du Rhône (© **022/311-68-76;** bus: 2, 9, or 22).

Opposite pont du Mont-Blanc, the chrome-and-crystal **Bucherer,** 45 rue du Rhône (© **022/319-62-66;** bus: 2, 9, or 22), sells expensive watches and diamonds. The store offers such name brands as Rolex, Piaget, Baume & Mercier, Tissot, Rado, and Swatch. The third floor is filled with relatively inexpensive watches. You'll also find cuckoo clocks, music boxes, embroideries, souvenirs, porcelain pillboxes, and other gift items.

GENEVA AFTER DARK

For a preview of events at the time of your visit, pick up a copy of the monthly "List of Events" issued by the tourist office.

THE PERFORMING ARTS

Modeled on Paris's Opéra Garnier, the **Grand Théâtre de Genève,** place Neuve (© **022/418-31-30;** bus: 12), was opened in 1879, and is often included in lists of the world's 10 best opera houses. It burned down in 1951 and was subsequently rebuilt in the same style, except for the modern auditorium. From September to July, it presents eight operas and two ballets, as well as recitals and chamber-music concerts. Tickets are 30SF to 150SF ($20–$98) for opera, 24SF to 130SF ($16–$85) or more for ballet.

The 1,866-seat **Victoria Hall,** 14 rue du Général-Dufour, is home to the celebrated **Orchestre de la Suisse Romande** (© **022/418-35-00;** bus: 12). Tickets are 20SF to 60SF ($13–$39).

BARS

The fashionable **Le Francis Bar,** 8 bd. Helvétique (© **022/346-32-52**), is often a venue for *le tout Geneve* or the "cream of the crop" of Geneva. It becomes an attractive piano bar in the evening, when live music starts at 10pm.

Though this is technically the aperitif bar for the elegant Restaurant Le Gentilhomme, many visitors consider **Le Jardin,** in the Hôtel Richemond, Jardin Brunswick (© **022/715-77-20;** bus: 1 or 9), an attractive and stylish option in its own right. It attracts a chic crowd, ranging from U.S.-based beneficiaries of corporate mergers to Zurich bankers to glamorous women in $50,000 furs.

DAY TRIPS FROM GENEVA

MONT SALÈVE ✦   The limestone ridge of Mont Salève (House Mountain) is 6km (3¾ miles) south of Geneva in France, so you'll need your passport. Its peak is at 1,200m (4,000 ft.). If you have a car, you can take a road that goes up the mountain; it's also popular with rock climbers. Bus no. 8 will take you to Veyrier, on the French border, where there's a passport and Customs control. A 6-minute cable-car ride will carry you to a height of 1,125m (3,750 ft.) on Mont Salève. From the top you'll have a panoramic sweep of the Valley of the Arve, with Geneva and Mont Blanc in the background.

MONT BLANC & CHAMONIX ✦✦✦   We highly recommend a Mont Blanc excursion; an all-day trip to Chamonix, France, by bus; and a cable-car ride to the 3,850m (12,610-ft.) summit of the Aiguille du Midi. **Key Tours** (details below) leaves Geneva daily at 8:30am and returns at 6pm. Buses depart from Gare Routière, and you must take your passport with you.

Other climbs on this tour are to Vallée Blanche by télécabin, an extension of the Aiguille du Midi climb, from April to October; to Mer de Glâce via electric rack railway to the edge of the glacier, from where you may descend to the ice grotto (the climb isn't available in winter); and to Le Brevent, an ascent by cable car to a rocky belvedere at 2,400m (7,900 ft.), facing the Mont Blanc range.

An English-speaking guide will accompany your bus tour. Key Tours S.A., 7 rue des Alpes (place du Mont-Blanc), Case Postale 1745, CH-1211 Genève (✆ 022/731-41-40), requires a minimum of eight people per trip. Tours begin at 90SF ($59) adults and 50SF ($33) children.

LAKE GENEVA CRUISES ✦✦✦   Two companies offer cruises on Lake Geneva (Lac Léman). The smaller one, **Mouettes Genevoises Navigation,** 8 quai du Mont-Blanc (✆ 022/732-29-44), specializes in small-scale boats carrying only about 100 passengers. Each features some kind of guided (prerecorded) commentary, in French and English. An easy promenade that surveys the landscapes and bird life along the uppermost regions of the Rhône draining the lake is the company's "Tour du Rhône" (Rhône River Tour). The trip originates at a point adjacent to Geneva's ponts de l'Ile and travels downstream for about 14km (8¾ miles) to the Barrage de Verbois (Verbois Dam) and back. Between April and October, departures are daily at 2:15pm and also on Wednesday, Thursday, Saturday, and Sunday at 10am. It costs 15SF ($9.75) adults and 10SF ($6.50) children 4 to 12; free for children under 4. The same company also offers 1¼-hour tours (four times a day) and 2-hour tours (twice a day) out onto the lake. The longer tour includes a pre-recorded commentary on the celebrity residences and ecology of the lake. It's 12SF ($7.80) for the shorter tour and 22SF ($14) for the longer tour; no stops are made en route.

Bateaux de la Mouette's largest competitor, **CGN (Compagnie General de Navigation),** quai du Mont-Blanc (✆ 022/312-52-23; www.cgn.ch), offers roughly equivalent tours, May through September, that last an hour and depart four to six times a day from the company's piers along the quai du Mont-Blanc. Known as "Les Belles Rives Genevoises," they charge 12SF ($7.80) adults and 6SF ($3.90) children 6 to 16 (free for children under 6). Tours include prerecorded commentaries and are about as long in duration as many short-term visitors to the city really want.

2 Bern & the Berner Oberland

Dating from the 12th century, Bern is one of the oldest and loveliest cities in Europe. Since much of its medieval architecture has remained untouched, the United Nations declared it a World Cultural Landmark in 1983. As the capital of Switzerland, it's also an important city of diplomats and the site of many international organizations and meetings.

Bern is a convenient center for exploring the lakes and peaks of the Berner Oberland—a vast recreation area only minutes from the capital, sprawling between the Reuss River and Lake Geneva. It's an important center for winter sports, one of the best-equipped areas for downhill skiers, and a challenging place for hikers and mountain climbers. The 4,158m (13,642-ft.) Jungfrau and the 4,274m (14,022-ft.) Finsteraarhorn are the highest alpine peaks. The canton of Bern, encompassing most of the area, is Switzerland's second largest, and contains 260 sq. km (100 sq. miles) of glaciers.

The best center for exploring the Berner Oberland is Interlaken, a popular summer resort. Summer and winter playgrounds are Gstaad, Grindelwald, Kandersteg, and Mürren. You can ski in the mountains in winter, and surf, sail, and water-ski on Lake Thun in summer.

BERN

The modern mingles harmoniously with the old in this charming city. Contemporary buildings are designed to discreetly blend in with the historic environment. Bern stands on a thumb of land that's bordered on three sides by the Aare River, and several bridges connect the old city with the newer sections.

Market days in Bern are Tuesday and Saturday, when people from the outlying areas come to town to sell their produce and wares. If you're fortunate enough to arrive on the fourth Monday of November, you'll witness the centuries-old **Zwiebelmarkt (Onion Market),** the city's last big event before the onset of winter, as residents traditionally stock up on onions in anticipation of the first snows.

ESSENTIALS

GETTING THERE   By Plane   The **Bern-Belp Airport (℗ 031/960-21-11)** is 9.6km (6 miles) south of the city in Belpmoos. International flights arrive from Geneva, Zurich, and Lugano, but transatlantic jets are not able to land here. Fortunately, it's a short hop to Bern from the international airports in Zurich and Geneva.

Taxis are about 50SF ($33) from the airport to the city center, so it's better to take the shuttle bus that runs between the airport and the Bahnhof (train station), costing 15SF ($9.75) one-way.

By Train   Bern has direct connections to France, Italy, Germany, and the Benelux countries, even Scandinavia and Spain. The superfast TGV train connects Paris with Bern (trip time: 4½ hr.). Bern also lies on major Swiss rail links, particularly those connecting Geneva (90 min.) and Zurich (75 min.). For **information** about tickets and train schedules for the Swiss Federal Railways, call ℗ **0900/ 300-300.**

The **Bahnhof** rail station, on Bahnhofplatz, is in the center of town near all the major hotels. If your luggage is light, you can walk to your hotel; otherwise, take one of the taxis waiting outside the station.

VISITOR INFORMATION   Tourist Office   The **Bern Tourist Office,** in the Bahnhof, on Bahnhofplatz (℗ **031/328-12-12;** www.bernetourism.ch), is open June through September daily from 9am to 8:30pm; October through May, Monday through Saturday from 9am to 6:30pm and Sunday from 10am to 5pm. If you need help finding a hotel room, the tourist office can make a reservation for you in the price range you select.

Websites   Besides the Bern Tourist Office website noted above, check this guide under Geneva "Visitor Information" for other Swiss websites. Get the low-down on skiing the high country at **www.goski.com/switz.htm**. This website will help you find a resort, tell you the best time to go, and keep you posted about conditions.

GETTING AROUND   On Foot   This is the only practical means of exploring Altstadt and its many attractions. You can see what there is to see here in about 2½ hours.

By Bus & Tram   The public transportation system, the **Stadtische Verkehrsbetriebe (SVB),** is a reliable 77km (48-mile) network of buses and trams. Before you board, purchase a ticket from the self-service automatic machines at each stop (conductors don't sell tickets). If you're caught traveling without one, you'll be fined 60SF ($39). A short-range ticket (six stations) costs 1.70SF ($1.10). A regular ticket, valid for 45 minutes one-way only, is 2.60SF ($1.70).

By Taxi   You can catch a taxi at the public cab stands, or you can call a dispatcher. Try **Nova Taxi** at $\mathcal{C}$ **031/301-11-11** or **Bären Taxi** at $\mathcal{C}$ **031/371-11-11.**

By Car   Don't try to drive in the city; use your car for exploring the environs. Car-rental companies in Bern include **Hertz,** Casinoplatz at Kochergasse 1 ($\mathcal{C}$ **031/318-21-60;** www.hertz.ch); and **Avis,** Wabernstrasse 41 ($\mathcal{C}$ **031/378-15-15;** www.avis.ch).

By Bicycle   The Altstadt is compressed into such a small area that it's better to cover it on foot rather than on a bike. Bicycles aren't allowed on the many pedestrians-only streets anyway. However, in Greater Bern and its environs there are 400km (248 miles) of cycling paths. These are marked on a special cycling map available at the tourist office (see above). Bicycle lanes are indicated by yellow on parts of the road network. The point of departure for most official cycling routes is Bundesplatz (Parliament Square). Special red signs will guide you through a wide variety of landscapes. For 24SF to 29SF ($16–$19) per day, you can rent a bicycle at the **SBB Railway Station,** Bahnhofplatz ($\mathcal{C}$ 0**51/20-34-61**). Call the day in advance for a reservation.

WHERE TO STAY
Very Expensive

Bellevue Palace ★★★   All the grand allure of the Belle Epoque era lives on here in a hotel that respects tradition but is also completely modernized. This government-rated five-star hotel stands next to the Bundeshaus, the seat of the Swiss government, and is by far the most lavish hotel in town, although we prefer the antique charms of Hotel Schweizerhof (see below). Built in 1913 and restored in 2003 after massive renovations, the gray-stone building has carved Corinthian columns and ornate details, and one of its public salons is covered in stained glass. The opulent bedrooms are spacious and luxuriously furnished, many opening onto views of the Jungfrau and the Bernese Alps. Dining on the renowned Bellevue Terrace is one of the reasons to come to Bern. The market-fresh cuisine is among the most sophisticated in town.

Kochergasse 3–5, 3001 Bern. $\mathcal{C}$ **031/320-45-45.** Fax 031/311-47-43. www.bellevue-palace.ch. 130 units. 460SF–540SF ($299–$351) double; 650SF–950SF ($423–$618) suite. AE, DC, MC, V. Tram: 3, 9, or 12. **Amenities:** 2 restaurants; bar; 24-hr. room service; babysitting; laundry service; dry cleaning. *In room:* A/C, TV, dataport, minibar, hair dryer, safe.

Hotel Schweizerhof Bern ★★★   Built in 1859, this central hotel, owned by the prestigious Richmond Heritage Group, is popular with diplomats and remains one of the grandest hotels in the Swiss capital. It contains many antiques and

Bern

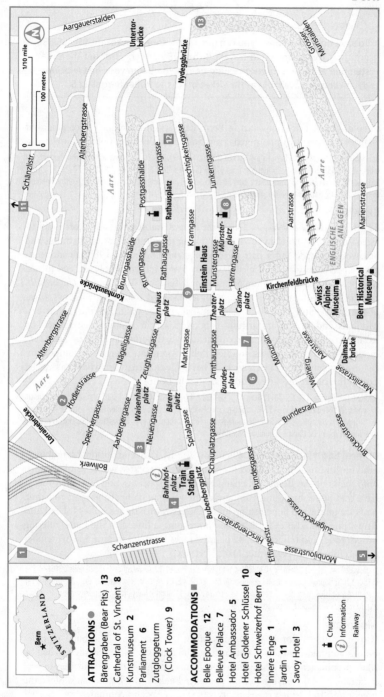

ATTRACTIONS ●
Bärengraben (Bear Pits) **13**
Cathedral of St. Vincent **8**
Kunstmuseum **2**
Parliament **6**
Zeitglockenturm
(Clock Tower) **9**

ACCOMMODATIONS ■
Belle Epoque **12**
Bellevue Palace **7**
Hotel Ambassador **5**
Hotel Goldener Schlüssel **10**
Hotel Schweizerhof Bern **4**
Innere Enge **1**
Jardin **11**
Savoy Hotel **3**

✝ Church
ⓘ Information
— Railway

⌒Value One-day Tickets

To save time and money, you can purchase a **tourist ticket** for 9SF ($5.85), entitling you to unlimited travel on the SVB network. Just get the ticket stamped at the automatic machine before you begin your first trip. One-day tickets are available at the **ticket offices** at Bubenbergplatz 5.

---

some of the best decorative art in Bern. Each room is uniquely decorated, but all offer comfortably upholstered chairs and sofas. The bathrooms are luxurious.

Bahnhofplatz 11, CH-3001 Bern. ⓒ 031/326-80-80. Fax 031/326-80-90. www.schweizerhof-bern.ch. 84 units. 365SF–455SF ($237–$296) double; from 625SF ($406) suite. AE, DC, MC, V. Parking 27SF ($18). Tram: 3, 9, or 12. **Amenities:** 2 restaurants; bar; 24-hr. room service; babysitting; laundry service/dry cleaning. *In room:* A/C, TV, dataport, minibar, hair dryer.

Expensive

Belle Epoque ✦✦✦ *Finds*　This is the hippest, most savvy, and most sophisticated small-scale hotel in town, with a countercultural slant, a charming and hardworking staff, and a flair for elegance and charm. In 1989, an interconnected pair of historic Bern medieval houses were gutted, renovated, and turned into this hotel, devoted to the promotion of Teutonic Art Nouveau *(Jugendstil).* Each of the bedrooms is outfitted with jewel-toned colors, big windows, turn-of-the-20th-century furniture, and unusual antique paintings and engravings. Minibars and closets are artfully concealed within trompe-l'oeil replicas of steamer trunks. Bathrooms are immaculately tiled (some have Jacuzzis) and very modern, with free condoms on offer. Public rooms are somewhat cramped but beautifully decorated and convivial. They include a cozy bar whose cafe tables extend out under the 17th-century arcades in front.

Gerechtigkeitsgasse 18, CH-3011 Bern. ⓒ 031/311-43-36. Fax 031/311-39-36. www.belle-epoque.ch. 17 units. 270SF–320SF ($176–$208) double; 330SF–450SF ($215–$293) suite. Rates include breakfast. AE, DC, MC, V. Bus: 12. **Amenities:** Restaurant; bar; limited room service; babysitting; laundry service; dry cleaning. *In room:* TV, dataport, minibar, hair dryer.

Innere Enge ✦✦✦ *Finds*　When you tire of Bern's impersonal bandboxes, head for this small, choice hotel just outside the city center, whose windows open onto views of the Berner Oberland. The light, spacious, and sun-filled rooms have traditional furnishings and are quite well maintained; the most romantic units are on the top floor, resting under the eaves with sloped ceilings. The Louis Armstrong Bar, also called **Marians Jazzroom,** is linked to the hotel, offering drinks, food, and traditional jazz performances February to June and September to December (see "Bern After Dark," below).

Engestrasse 54, CH-3012 Bern. ⓒ 031/309-61-11. Fax 301/309-61-12. www.zghotels.ch. 26 units. 230SF–320SF ($150–$208) double. Rates include continental breakfast. AE, DC, MC, V. Free parking. Bus: 21 from the rail station. **Amenities:** Restaurant; bar; room service (6:30am–11:30pm); babysitting; laundry service; dry cleaning. *In room:* TV, dataport, minibar, hair dryer.

Moderate

Hotel Ambassador ✦　This nine-story hotel in a neighborhood of older houses with red-tile roofs is not far from the train station and easily reached by tram. Rooms tend to be smallish and furnished impersonally, but they're well maintained; many have a view of the federal palace, the Bundeshaus. Since the hotel caters to business travelers, its rooms offer fax and computer hookups.

Seftigenstrasse 99, CH-3007 Bern. ⓒ 031/370-99-99. Fax 031/371-41-17. www.fhotels.ch. 97 units. 215SF–225SF ($140–$146) double. AE, DC, MC, V. Free parking. Tram: 9. **Amenities:** 2 restaurants; lounge;

pool; sauna; limited room service; babysitting; laundry service; dry cleaning. *In room:* TV, dataport, minibar, hair dryer, safe.

Savoy Hotel *Value* Close to the main rail depot and the commercial center, this is a traditional Bern hotel of some charm and grace, achieving a four-star rating from the government. This place is more welcoming than many straitlaced Bern hotels; you're even given a free welcome drink. Rooms are fairly standardized and plain but have recently been renovated and are quite comfortable, with mostly tub/shower combo bathrooms (15 with shower only). Soundproof windows keep the noise outside, and there is also individually adjustable ventilation.

Neuengasse 26, CH-3011 Bern. © 031/311-4405. Fax 031/312-1978. www.zghotels.ch. 56 units. 230SF–250SF ($150–$163) double; 270SF ($176) junior suite. AE, DC, MC, V. **Amenities:** Cafe-bar; limited room service; laundry service; dry cleaning. *In room:* TV, minibar, hair dryer.

Inexpensive

Hotel Goldener Schlüssel ★ In the heart of Altstadt, opening onto Rathausgasse, this cozy little inn dates from the 13th century, when it was used as a stable. Rooms are beautifully maintained, and some have wood-paneled walls. Immaculate linens on the beds and fresh tiles in the shower-only bathrooms reflect the good housekeeping. As it's fairly busy on the street outside, ask for a rear room if you want less noise. If you're a bargain hunter, request a room without a bathroom—the hallway plumbing is adequate.

Rathausgasse 72, CH-3011 Bern. © 031/311-02-16. Fax 031/311-56-88. www.goldener-schluessel.ch. 29 units, 21 with bathroom. 125SF ($81) double without bathroom; 155SF ($101) double with bathroom; 155SF ($101) triple without bathroom; 205SF ($133) triple with bathroom. Rates include continental breakfast. AE, MC, V. Free parking. Tram: 9. Bus: 12. **Amenities:** Restaurant; cafe; limited room service. *In room:* TV, hair dryer.

Jardin *Value* Set about .8km (½ mile) north of Bern's center, Jardin lies within a leafy residential suburb with lots of parking. This establishment functioned only as a restaurant and apartment building between the year it was built (ca. 1900) and 1985. Then, its apartments were transformed into modern, warmly appealing hotel rooms that are larger than virtually anything else within their price category. All rooms are equipped with private bathrooms. Your hosts are identical twins Andy and Daniel Balz. Joggers and nature enthusiasts appreciate the large verdant spaces (part of a military academy) across the street from this russet-brown, four-story hotel.

Militärstrasse 38, CH-3014 Bern. © 031/333-01-17. Fax 031/333-09-43. www.hotel-jardin.ch. 18 units. 145SF ($94) double; 205SF ($133) triple. Rates include breakfast. AE, DC, MC, V. Free parking. Tram: 9 to Breitenrainplatz. **Amenities:** Restaurant; lounge; laundry service; dry cleaning. *In room:* TV, hair dryer.

WHERE TO DINE
Expensive

Jack's Brasserie (Stadt Restaurant) ★★ FRENCH/CONTINENTAL Although this restaurant is the less formal eatery within the Schweizerhof, it's perfectly acceptable as the site for an important meal or even a celebratory dinner. Nostalgically outfitted in a style that evokes a Lyonnais bistro, it bustles in a way that's chic, convivial, and matter-of-fact, all at the same time. The best dishes on the menu include the kind of Wiener schnitzels that hang over the sides of the plate, succulent versions of sole meunière and sea bass, veal head vinaigrette for real regional flavor, and smaller platters piled high with salads, risottos, and succulent pastas.

In the Hotel Schweizerhof, Bahnhofplatz 11. © 031/326-80-80. Reservations recommended. Main courses 26SF–60SF ($17–$39); fixed-price menu 85SF ($55). AE, DC, MC, V. Daily 6am–11:30pm. Limited menu daily 1:45–6:15pm.

Wein & Sein ★★★ INTERNATIONAL   In terms of underground, word-of-mouth chic, this is the most hip restaurant in Bern today. Set within the cellar of a historic building in the city's medieval core, it's accessible via a steep staircase that leads you past the open kitchen. Chef and owner Beat Blum, a celebrity whose fame derives from his former administration of a more expensive restaurant near Lucerne, is the impresario who directs the show here. A set-price menu written on a blackboard allows little room for either variety or indecision—but you won't complain. On the night of our latest visit, it consisted of such heavenly concoctions as braised tuna and free-range chicken served with braised pepperoni in a sweet-and-sour sauce; terrine of melon; beef filet with a vegetable purée; and a quark (curd cheese) mousse served with pineapple and homemade ice cream.

Münstergasse 50. ℂ 031/311-98-44. Reservations required. Set-price menu 75SF ($49). MC, V. Tues–Sat 6–9pm. Closed 2 weeks in July–Aug. Bus: 12.

Moderate

Della Casa ★ CONTINENTAL   Entering the hotel, you'll find yourself immersed in what has been called Switzerland's "unofficial Parliament headquarters." The inner room, often filled with chattering diners, contains the day's newspapers. You'll find a quieter, more formal dining room upstairs. The menu features Continental and Italian dishes, such as *bollito misto* (a medley of mixed boiled meats) and rack of lamb. Two local favorites are the *ravioli maison* and the fried zucchini; a popular meat specialty is a filet mignon à la bordelaise with Creole rice. The cuisine is very authentic, very savory, and very satisfying.

Schauplatzgasse 16. ℂ 031/311-21-42. Reservations recommended. Main courses 20SF–40SF ($13–$26); fixed-price meal 25SF ($16). AE, DC, MC, V (downstairs only). Mon–Fri 11am–2pm and 6–9:30pm; Sat 9:30am–3pm. Upstairs level closed July. Tram: 3, 5, or 9.

Goldener Schlüssel ★ SWISS   You'll relish both the food and the bustling atmosphere at this very Swiss restaurant. Serving wholesome food in ample portions, the restaurant is on the street level of a budget-priced hotel of the same name (see "Where to Stay," above). Specialties include *mignon d'agneau au poivre vert* (tenderloin of lamb with green-pepper sauce and corn croquettes), *schweinbratwurst mit zwiebelsauce* (butter-fried sausage with onion sauce), and rösti.

Rathausgasse 72. ℂ 031/311-02-16. Reservations recommended. Main courses 23SF–32SF ($15–$21); fixed-price lunch 20SF–24SF ($13–$16). AE, MC, V. Sun–Thurs 7am–11:30pm; Fri–Sat 7am–12:30am. Tram: 9. Bus 12.

Räblus FRENCH/SWISS REGIONAL   A popular haunt, this 2-century-old restaurant lies near the landmark Clock Tower. It has a ground-floor bar where you can stop for an aperitif before proceeding up to the dining room. The kitchen prepares French cuisine with a definite Swiss/German influence. Try our favorites: saffron-flavored sole, a splendid potpourri of seafood flavored with Pernod, or citrus-flavored veal.

Zeughausgasse 3. ℂ 031/311-59-08. Reservations required. Main courses 22SF–39SF ($14–$25); 3-course fixed-price menus 35SF–60SF ($23–$39). AE, DC, MC, V. Mon–Wed 6pm–1:30am; Thurs 6pm–2:30am; Fri–Sat 6pm–3:30am. Tram: 3 or 9.

Restaurant Harmonie ★ SWISS/BERNESE   Located at the corner of Münstergasse a few blocks from Parliament, this Art Nouveau local favorite evokes 1890s Paris with its grimy overlay. It has been in the hands of the Gyger family since 1915. Service is efficient, and tables are spaced far enough apart to allow a feeling of privacy. There are two dining rooms and a handful of sidewalk tables set beneath ivy-clad trellises. You get the same regional specialties that Grandmother Gyger might have served between the wars: pork sausage with rösti, tripe with tomatoes, and cheese fondues. If you're not ravenously hungry, go for the simple platter of cooked ham with pickles, pickled onions, and sliced bread.

Hotelgasse 3. ℂ 031/313-11-41. Reservations recommended. Main courses 22SF–49SF ($14–$32). MC, V. Mon–Fri 8am–11:30pm. Closed mid-July to mid-Aug. Tram: 9.

Inexpensive

Ratskeller (Kids SWISS   There is no more typical Bernese restaurant than this local favorite, serving ample portions of good, rib-sticking food. Specialties include rack of lamb *à la diable* (peppery) for two, an omelet soufflé with fruit, and veal kidneys Robert. Your best bet is the *egli* (tiny filet of perch) with white sauce on a bed of spinach. Prized by gourmets, this tiny fish is native to the lakes around Bern.

Gerechtigkeitsgasse 81. ℂ 031/311-17-71. Reservations recommended. Main courses 20SF–51SF ($14–$36). AE, DC, MC, V. Daily 11:30am–2pm and 6–11pm. Tram: 9.

Restaurant Zimmermania ★ (Value FRENCH   This is a small and charming French bistro that's set on a quiet street of Bern's historic core. Inside, you'll find two dining rooms outfitted like something you might have expected in a small French town in the 1920s, a marble-topped service bar, and a menu that emphasizes many classic brasserie-style dishes from France. In addition to a short but well-chosen wine list, you can expect such well-prepared French classics as foie gras of duckling, carpaccio of beef, marinated herring with apple slices and sour cream, fresh oysters, veal kidneys in mustard sauce, rack of lamb with green beans, steak tartare, and guinea fowl roasted with rosemary.

Brunngasse 19. ℂ 031/311-15-42. Reservations recommended. Main courses 29SF–55SF ($19–$36); set-price lunch 24SF–41SF ($15–$26). Tues–Sat 12:30–2pm and 6–10pm. Closed July. Tram: 12.

SEEING THE SIGHTS

Zutgloggeturm (Clock Tower) ★, on Kramgasse, was built in the 12th century and restored in the 16th. Four minutes before every hour, crowds gather for the world's oldest (since 1530) and biggest horological puppet show: Mechanical bears, jesters, and emperors put on an animated performance. The tower marked the west gate of Bern until 1250.

Bärengraben (Bear Pits) ★, on the opposite side of the river, is a deep moon-shaped den where bears, Bern's mascots, have been kept since 1480. According

---

⌒Moments Taking a Cable-Train to Mont Gurten

The most panoramic attraction in the immediate vicinity is the **belvedere atop Mont Gurten** ★★, where there's also a children's fairyland and a walking area. The belvedere is connected to Bern by the Gurtenbahn cable-train, one of the fastest in all Europe. The train departs from a station beside the Monbijoustrasse, about 2.5km (1½ miles) from Bern's center. Round-trip passage on the cable-train is 9SF ($5.85). The train operates year-round, daily from 7:30am to sunset. For details, contact **Gurtenbahn Bern,** Eigerplatz 3 (ℂ 031/961-23-23). To reach the departure platform, take tram no. 9 to the Gurtenbahn station for 2.80SF ($1.80) each way. If you're driving, follow the road signs to Thun. There's a parking lot in the hamlet of Wabern, a short walk from the cable-train station.

to legend, when the duke of Zähringen established the town in 1191, he sent his hunters into the encircling woods, which were full of wild game. The duke promised to name the city after the first animal slain, which was a Bär (bear). Since then the town has been known as Bärn or Bern. Today, the bears are beloved, pampered, and fed by residents and visitors (carrots are most appreciated). The **Nydeggbrücke (Nydegg Bridge)** was built over one of the gorges of the Aare River; its central stone arch has a span of 55m (180 ft.) and affords a sweeping view of the city from its center. Below the Bear Pits, you can visit the **Rosengarten (Rose Gardens),** from which there's a much-photographed view of the medieval sector and the river.

Cathedral of St. Vincent ⚐   The Münster is one of Switzerland's newer Gothic churches; although dating from 1421, the belfry was completed only in 1893. The most exceptional feature of this three-aisle pillared basilica is the **tympanum** ⚐⚐ over the main portal, depicting the Last Judgment with more than 200 figures, some painted. Mammoth 15th-century stained-glass windows line the chancel. The 1523 choir stalls brought the Renaissance to Bern. In the Matter Chapel is a remarkable stained-glass window, the *Dance of Death,* created in the last year of World War I, but based on a much older design. The 90m (300-ft.) **belfry** ⚐⚐ offers a panoramic sweep, though you must climb 270 steps to get to the viewing platform. Outside the basilica on Münsterplatz is the 1545 Moses Fountain.

Münsterplatz. ✆ 031/312-04-62. Cathedral free admission; viewing platform 3SF ($1.95) adults, 1SF (65¢) children. Cathedral Easter Sun to Oct Tues–Sat 10am–5pm, Sun 11:30am–5pm; off season Tues–Fri 10am–noon and 2–4pm, Sat 10am–noon and 2–5pm, Sun 11:30am–2pm. Viewing platform closes half an hour before cathedral. Bus: 12.

Kunstmuseum (Fine Arts Museum) ⚐⚐   The world's largest collection of Swiss-born Paul Klee's works is the star attraction here. The Klee collection includes 40 oils and 2,000 drawings, gouaches, and watercolors. Other works emphasize the 19th and 20th centuries. The important 20th-century collection has works by Kandinsky, Modigliani, Matisse, Soutine, and Picasso, and by the Surrealist and Constructivist schools as well as contemporary Swiss artists. There's also a collection of Italian 14th-century primitives, notably Fra Angelico's *Virgin and Child,* and Swiss primitives, including the *Masters of the Carnation.*

Hodlerstrasse 12. ✆ 031/328-09-44. Permanent collection 7SF ($4.55) adults, 5SF ($3.25) seniors; special exhibitions 14SF–16SF ($9.10–$10) extra. Tues 10am–9pm; Wed–Sun 10am–5pm. Bus: 20.

ORGANIZED TOURS

Highly recommended is the 2-hour **bus tour** leaving from the tourist office at the Bahnhof, at Bahnhofplatz. An English-speaking guide will take you through the city's residential quarters, past museums, and down to the Aare River, which flows below the houses of Parliament. You'll see the Rose Gardens and the late Gothic cathedral and stroll under the arcades to the Clock Tower. After visiting the Bear Pits, you'll be led through medieval streets and back to the railroad station. Tours are offered from June through September daily at 2pm; April, May, and October, Monday through Saturday at 2pm; and November through March only on Saturday at 2pm. The cost is 27SF ($18) adults, 14SF ($9.10) children 6 to 16, and free for children under 6.

The tourist office also conducts **walking tours** of Bern from May through October. The daily meeting spot is either at the tourist office at 11am or at Zytglogge at 11:15am. The cost is 17SF ($11) adults, 9SF ($5.85) children 6 to 16, and free for children under 6.

BERN AFTER DARK

This Week in Bern, distributed free by the tourist office, keeps a current list of cultural events.

PERFORMING ARTS   The **Bern Symphony Orchestra,** one of Switzerland's finest, is directed by the widely acclaimed Russian-born Dmitrij Kitajenko; famous guest conductors also frequently appear. Performances are usually at the concert facilities in the **Bern Casino,** Herrengasse 25 (© **031/311-42-42**). Except for a summer vacation usually lasting from July until mid-August, the box office is open Monday through Friday from 12:30 to 3pm. Tickets range from 18SF to 55SF ($12–$36).

Major opera and ballet performances are usually staged in Bern's most beautiful theater, the century-old **Stadttheater,** Kornhausplatz 20 (© **031/329-51-51**). Plays and dance programs are presented in the **Theater am Käfigturm,** Spitalgasse 4 (© **031/311-61-00**). Plays are usually in German and, to a lesser degree, French. Contemporary German-language theater, usually very experimental, is featured in the **Kleintheater,** Kramgasse 6 (© **031/320-26-26**).

A WINE CELLAR   **Klötzlikeller,** 62 Gerechtigkeitsgasse (© **031/311-74-56**), the oldest wine tavern in Bern, is near the Gerechtigkeitsbrunnen (Fountain of Justice), the first fountain you see on your walk from the Bear Pits to the Clock Tower. Watch for the lantern outside an angled cellar door. The tavern, dating from 1635, is owned by the city and leased to an independent operator. Some 20 different wines are sold by the glass, with prices starting at 8.50SF ($5.55). The menu is changed every 6 weeks. The appetizing snacks are always traditional, including sliced cheese, with prices ranging from 12SF to 27SF ($7.80–$18). The traditional Bernese kitchen produces various dinner plates, reflecting regional specialties and costing 22SF to 45SF ($12–$25). It's open Tuesday through Saturday from 4pm to 12:30am.

A JAZZ CLUB   The Louis Armstrong Bar, site of **Marians Jazzroom** in the Innere Enge Hotel, Engerstrasse 54 (© **031/309-61-11**), has its own entrance separate from the hotel's. Unique in Bern, it's a setting for not only food and drink, but the finest traditional jazz performed live by top artists from around the world. From Tuesday through Thursday, hours are 7:30pm to 1am, Friday and Saturday 7:30pm to 2am. On Saturday, there is a Concert Apéro from 4 to 6:30pm, and on some Sundays a Jazz Brunch is offered from 10am to 1:30pm. Cover is 15SF to 47SF ($9.75–$31), depending on the act. The club is closed from June 6 to September 7.

GAY BARS   **Samurai Club,** Aarbergergasse 35 (© **031/311-88-03**), draws many people who work in the local embassies, Bern locals, and young men from the Bernese Oberland in for a night on the town. Women are also welcome. The club is open Sunday through Thursday from 8pm to 2:30am, Friday and Saturday from 8pm to 3:30am. **Bar aux Petits Fours,** Kramgasse 67 (© **031/312-73-74**), is a contender for the title of best gay bar in Bern, attracting a multilingual, attractive, and international group of gay people, mostly men. There's no dance floor and no restaurant, but what you get is a low-key bar, filled with regular clients, where a newcomer with a bit of effort can usually break the glacial freeze of Swiss reserve. The bar is open daily from 5pm to 12:30am.

CASINO ACTION   The only place in town to gamble is **Grand Casino Kursaal Bern,** Kornhausstrasse 3 (© **031/339-55-55**). Indeed, it's a great spot for novices to learn because serious money rarely changes hands here. It's open daily from noon to 3:30am, and admission is free. Drinks cost 10SF to 15SF ($6.50–$9.75). There are three restaurants and two bars, plus a dance hall that charges a 10SF ($6.50) cover. It's open Friday and Saturday from 9pm to 3:30am, and on Sunday from 3 to 10pm.

THE BERNER OBERLAND

The Berner Oberland is Valhalla for walkers, hikers, and skiers. Here nature's scenery satisfies both the most ambitious adventurer and the slowest stroller. It's one of the world's best-equipped regions for winter sports, and walking trails branch out from almost every junction. Most of these are paved and signposted, with distances and estimated walking times given. Most tourist offices, including those at Interlaken (see below), will provide guidance and suggested itineraries.

EXPLORING THE AREA BY TRAIN & BICYCLE   If you're not driving, you'll find that public transport is quite adequate for exploring the area. You can buy a **transportation pass** for the Bernese Oberland from the Swiss Rail System. The train ticket is valid for 7 days, and costs 195SF ($127) in second class and 233SF ($151) in first class. Another pass, valid for 15 days, costs 240SF ($156) in second class and 287SF ($187) in first class. With the 7-day pass, you'll travel free for 3 days and pay a reduced fare for the final 4 days. With a 15-day pass, you'll travel free for 5 days and pay reduced fares for the rest of the time. Children travel at half price. The pass is valid on most railroads; all mountain trains, cable cars, chairlifts, steamers on Lakes Thun and Brienz; and most postal-bus lines in the area. The ticket also qualifies you for a 25% reduction on the Kleine Scheidegg-Eigergletscher-Jungfraujoch railway, the Mürren-Schilthorn aerial cable line, and the bus to Grosse Scheidegg and Bussalp. You must purchase the pass at least 1 week before you arrive. For information about the pass, call © **800/794-7795.**

Cycling tours through the Berner Oberland often begin at Interlaken. Hundreds of miles of cycling paths cover the area. Separate from the network of hiking paths, the bicycle routes are signposted and marked on rental maps distributed at bike-rental agencies. Some 13 rail stations in the Berner Oberland offer bike-rental services, and rates are reasonable. For example, families can rent four bikes (two for adults, two for children 15 and under) for an all-inclusive price of 60SF ($39) per day or 420SF ($273) per week. Individual rentals cost 30SF ($20) per day or 210SF ($137) per week. You must make reservations in Interlaken at either of its rail stations, **Interlaken East** (© **033/828-73-19**) or **Interlaken West** (© **033/826-47-50**).

INTERLAKEN ✦✦✦

Interlaken is the Berner Oberland's tourist capital. Cableways and cog railways designed for steeply inclined hills and mountains connect it with most of the region's villages. A dazzling sight is the snowy heights of the Jungfrau, which rises a short distance to the south.

The "town between the lakes" (Thun and Brienz) has been a holiday resort for more than 300 years. Though it was once strictly a summer resort, it has developed into a year-round playground. Interlaken charges low-season prices in January and February, when smaller resorts at higher altitudes charge their highest rates. The most expensive time to visit is midsummer, when those same high-altitude ski resorts often charge their lowest rates.

ESSENTIALS

GETTING THERE   By Train   There are several trains daily between Zurich and Interlaken (trip time: 2 hr.) and between Bern and Interlaken (40 min.).

Frequent train service also connects Geneva and Interlaken (2½ hr.). For **rail information,** call © **0900/300-300.** *Note:* Although the town has two different railway stations, Interlaken East and Interlaken West, West is most convenient to the city's center.

By Car To reach Interlaken from Bern, drive south on N6 to Spiez, then continue east on N8 to Interlaken.

VISITOR INFORMATION The **Tourism Organization Interlaken** is at Höheweg 37 (© **033/826-53-00;** www.interlakentourism.ch), in the Hotel Metropole. It's open in July and August, Monday to Friday from 8am to noon and 1:30 to 6:30pm, Saturday from 8am to 5pm, and Sunday from 5 to 7pm; the rest of the year, Monday to Friday from 8am to noon and 2 to 6pm and Saturday from 8am to noon.

WHERE TO STAY
Very Expensive

Lindner Grand Hotel Beau-Rivage ★★★ This government-rated five-star and reconstructed Belle Epoque–styled hotel between Höheweg and the Aare River is one of Interlaken's grand hotels. Only Victoria-Jungfrau (see below) is better. The Beau-Rivage sells luxury on a smaller, more intimate scale than its competitors, and is located in a very tranquil spot, just a short distance from the Interlaken East rail station, which makes it a good center for excursions in all directions. The central tower has an ascending series of covered loggias decorated with carvings and flowers. The renovated rooms are conservatively modern with excellent beds and nicely kept bathrooms. The front rooms open onto the Jungfrau, and the rooms in the rear are not only quieter but front the river.

Höheweg 211, CH-3800 Interlaken. © 033/826-70-07. Fax 033/823-28-47. www.lindner.de. 101 units. 260SF–440SF ($169–$286) double; from 440SF ($286) suite. Rates include buffet breakfast. AE, DC, MC, V. Free parking outdoors. **Amenities:** Restaurant; bar; pool; health club; sauna; limited room service; babysitting; laundry service; dry cleaning. *In room:* TV, minibar, hair dryer, safe.

Victoria-Jungfrau Grand Hotel & Spa ★★★ *Kids*   Since 1865, this grand hotel has reigned as one of the most important resort properties in Switzerland. The owner of the Victoria Hotel, Edouard Ruchti, united it with the Jungfrau Hotel in 1895, and the landmark property has stood ever since. Through its corridors has passed everyone from the emperor of Brazil to the king of Siam to Mark Twain. Designed in a richly ornate Victorian style, it sits right in the town center at the foot of rigidly symmetrical gardens. The hotel boasts valuable antiques and one of the best-trained staffs in Interlaken. The most expensive rooms open onto views of the Jungfrau. The midsize to spacious accommodations are luxurious.

Höheweg 41, CH-3800 Interlaken. © 800/223-6800 in the U.S., or 033/828-28-28. Fax 033/828-28-80. www.victoria-jungfrau.ch. 212 units. Summer 640SF–720SF ($416–$468) double; winter 530SF–580SF ($345–$377) double; year-round from 770SF–850SF ($501–$553) junior suite, from 1,400SF ($910) suite. Half board 110SF ($72) per person extra. AE, DC, MC, V. Free parking outside, 22SF ($14) in garage. **Amenities:** 3 restaurants; 2 bars; pool; tennis courts; spa; Jacuzzi; sauna; kids' club; limited room service; massage; babysitting; laundry service/dry cleaning. *In room:* TV, dataport, minibar, hair dryer, safe.

Expensive

Hotel Interlaken ★   This is the resort's oldest hotel, receiving overnight guests since 1323, first as a hospital, later as a cloister and, beginning in the early 1400s, as a tavern and inn. Guests have included Byron and Felix Mendelssohn. The hotel, directly east of the casino, has been gutted and rebuilt since, with a salmon-colored facade sporting baroque touches. The most expensive rooms have a few 19th-century antiques; the rest have conservative, modern furnishings with excellent beds and well-maintained bathrooms.

Höheweg 74, CH-3800 Interlaken. © 033/826-68-68. Fax 033/826-68-69. www.interlakenhotel.ch. 60 units. 240SF–320SF ($156–$208) double. Rates include buffet breakfast. Half board 45SF ($29) per person extra. AE, DC, MC, V. Free parking. **Amenities:** Restaurant; bar; sauna; limited room service; laundry service; dry cleaning; nonsmoking rooms. *In room:* TV, dataport, minibar, hair dryer, safe.

Moderate

Park-Hotel Mattenhof ★   This large, old-fashioned hotel is in a secluded area at the edge of a forest south of the center; you can reach it by heading away from the center toward Wilderswil. Originally a simple 19th-century pension, it adopted a mock-medieval look after a massive 1908 enlargement. The Bühler family offers a calm retreat, with terraces, manicured lawns, and panoramic views of the Alps. The salons are warmly decorated and sunny, and some of the well-furnished but small bedrooms have a view of the Jungfrau and the Niederhorn.

Hauptstrasse, Matten, CH-3800 Interlaken. © 033/821-61-21. Fax 033/822-28-88. www.park-mattenhof.ch. 76 units. June–Sept and Dec 26–Jan 1 200SF–260SF ($130–$169) double; off season 140SF–170SF ($91–$111) double. Rates include buffet breakfast. AE, DC, MC, V. Free parking. Bus: 5. **Amenities:** 2 restaurants; 2 bars; pool; tennis court; health club; laundry service; dry cleaning. *In room:* TV, dataport, minibar, hair dryer.

Inexpensive

The Swiss Inn *Value*   This small-scale Edwardian inn with balconies and gables offers good value. Mrs. Vreny Müller Lohner rents tasteful, simply decorated one- to three-room apartments equipped with good beds and well-kept bathrooms with shower-tub combinations in one half, only showers in the others. They accommodate two to six guests, and children's beds or cots are available. The inn has a lounge, a sitting area with a fireplace, and a grill for barbecues in the garden.

Général Guisanstrasse 23, CH-3800 Interlaken. ℂ 033/822-36-26. Fax 033/823-23-03. www.swiss-inn.com. 9 units. 130SF–170SF ($85–$111) double; 160SF–200SF ($104–$130) apt for 2; 230SF–250SF ($150–$163) apt for 4. AE, MC, V. Free parking. **Amenities:** Lounge; laundry (self-service; coin-operated); dry cleaning. *In room:* TV.

WHERE TO DINE
Expensive
Il Bellini ★★ ITALIAN   This is one of the finest restaurants in the Bernese Oberland, offering fresh, good-tasting food. An assortment of antipasti from the buffet or a homemade minestrone is followed by such main courses as beefsteak Florentine, saltimbocca (veal with ham), or chicken breast grilled with tomatoes and mozzarella. The fish selections are well chosen, and can be grilled on request.

In the Hotel Metropole, Höheweg 37. ℂ 033/828-66-66. Reservations recommended Fri–Sun. Main courses 20SF–58SF ($13–$38); pastas 14SF–26SF ($9.10–$17). AE, DC, MC, V. Tues–Sat 11:30am–2pm and 6:30–10:30pm.

Moderate
Gasthof Hirschen *Value* SWISS   This hotel restaurant offers some of the best and most reasonably priced meals in town, and the menu is varied, with most dishes at the lower prices on the menu. The potato soup with mountain cheese is the finest we've ever tasted. For a main dish, try such standard but well-prepared fare as sautéed calves' liver, filet of beef bordelaise, broiled trout, or the resort's best chateaubriand. The Hirschen also operates its own farm, which supplies Bio-Angus beef, veal, cheese, fresh vegetables, and herbs. Fresh berries and honey are also brought in from the farm during summer.

Hauptstrasse 11, Matten. ℂ **033/822-15-45.** Reservations recommended. Main courses 20SF–60SF ($14–$42). AE, DC, MC, V. Wed 6:30–9:30pm; Thurs–Mon 11:30am–2pm and 6:30–9:30pm.

Inexpensive
Schuh SWISS/CONTINENTAL   This attractive restaurant and tearoom in the center of town has been known for its pastries since 1885. They are still the town's finest. The alpine building has a thick roof arched over fourth-floor windows and, in back, a sunny terrace with a view of the Jungfrau and a well-kept lawn. The dining room has big windows and a Viennese ambience. A pianist provides music.

Höheweg 56. ℂ **033/822-94-41.** Main courses 19SF–48SF ($12–$31); fixed-price meal 35SF–40SF ($23–$26). AE, DC, MC, V. Tues–Sun 8am–11pm. Closed Oct 25–Dec 9.

EXPLORING INTERLAKEN
What you do in Interlaken is walk. You can walk at random, as there are panoramic views in virtually all directions, or, if you'd like some guidance, go to the tourist office for a copy of "What to Do in Interlaken"; it maps out walks of all levels of difficulty.

The **Höheweg** ★★ covers 14 hectares (35 acres) in the middle of town, between the west and east train stations. Once the property of Augustinian monks, it was acquired in the mid–19th century by Interlaken's hotel keepers, who turned it into a park. As you stroll along **Höhenpromenade,** admire the famous view of the Jungfrau. Another beautiful sight is the **Flower Clock** at the Kursaal (casino), and you'll also see *fiacres* (horse-drawn cabs). The promenade is lined with hotels, cafes, and gardens.

Cross the Aare River to **Unterseen,** built in 1280 by Berthold von Eschenbach. Here you can visit the **parish church,** with its late Gothic tower from 1471. This is one of the most photographed sights in the Berner Oberland. The Mönch mountain appears on the left of the tower, the Jungfrau on the right.

Back in Interlaken, visit the **Touristik-Museum der Jungfrau-Region,** am Stadthausplatz, Obere Gasse 26 (*©* **033/822-98-39**), the country's first regional museum of tourism, showing the development of tourism over the past 2 centuries. It's open May through mid-October, Tuesday through Sunday from 2 to 5pm. Admission is 5SF ($3.25), or 3SF ($1.95) with a visitor's card. Children 12 and under pay 2SF ($1.30).

For a sightseeing *fiacre* (horse-drawn cab) ride, go to the Interlaken West train station. The half-hour round-trip is 39SF ($25) for one or two, plus 11SF

Moments **Glaciers in the Sky: A Trip to Jungfraujoch**

A trip to **Jungfraujoch** ★★★, at 3,454m (11,333 ft.), can be the highlight of your visit. Since the 1860s it's been the highest rail station in Europe. It's also one of the most expensive: A round-trip tour is 179SF ($116) first class or 167SF ($109) second. However, families can fill out a Family Card form, available at the rail station; it allows children 16 and under to ride free. Departures are usually daily at 8am from the east station in Interlaken; expect to return around 4pm. You'll get to see the mountain when it is most dazzlingly lit, and will have enough time for a leisurely lunch. To check times, contact the sales office of **Jungfrau Railways (Jungfrau Bahnen),** Höheweg 37 (*©* **033/828-71-11;** www.jungfraubahn.ch).

Once at the Jungfraujoch terminus, you may feel a little giddy until you get used to the air. You'll find much to do in this eerie world high up, Jungfrau. But take it slowly—your metabolism will be affected and you may tire quickly.

Within a 5-minute, well-marked walk from the Jungfraujoch railway terminus is an elevator that leads to the famed **Eispalast (Ice Palace)** ★. Here you'll be walking within what's called "eternal ice"—caverns hewn out of the slowest-moving section of the glacier. Cut 20m (65 ft.) below the glacier's surface, they were begun in 1934 by a Swiss guide and subsequently enlarged and embellished with additional sculptures. Everything in here is made of ice, including full-size replicas of vintage automobiles and local chaplains.

After returning to the station, you can take the **Sphinx Tunnel** to another elevator. This one takes you up 108m (356 ft.) to an observation deck called the **Sphinx Terraces,** overlooking the saddle between the Mönch and Jungfrau peaks. You can also see the **Aletsch Glacier,** a 23km (14-mile) river of ice—the longest in Europe. The snow melts into Lake Geneva and eventually flows into the Mediterranean.

There are five different **restaurants** from which to choose. The traditional choice is Jungfraujoch Glacier Restaurant. Top of Europe, opened in 1987, offers several different dining possibilities, and there's also a self-service cafeteria. As a final adventure, you can take a **sleigh ride,** pulled by stout huskies.

($7.15) for each extra person; children 7 to 16 are charged half fare, and those 6 and under ride free.

Other attractions include animal parks, afternoon concerts, and the luscious pastries sold in cafes. During summer, you can sit in covered grandstands and watch Schiller's version of the William Tell story. Steamers carry passengers across Lakes Brienz and Thun.

MÜRREN ★★

At 1,650m (5,414 ft.) above the Lauterbrunnen Valley, Mürren is the highest permanently inhabited village in the Berner Oberland. It's an exciting excursion from Interlaken in summer and a major ski resort in winter. Downhill skiing was developed and the slalom invented here in the 1920s, and Mürren is also the birthplace of modern alpine racing.

ESSENTIALS

GETTING THERE   By Train   Take the mountain railway from the Interlaken East rail station to Lauterbrunnen (trip time: 1 hr.). Once at Lauterbrunnen, you can take a cogwheel train the rest of the way to Mürren. Departures from Lauterbrunnen are every half-hour from 6:30am to 8:30pm daily, costing 9.80SF ($6.35) one-way.

By Bus & Car   A regular postal-bus service goes once an hour from Lauterbrunnen to Stechelberg; the rest of the way you must travel by cable car, costing 31SF ($20) round-trip. Departures are every half-hour, and the trip takes about 10 minutes. Mürren is not accessible to traffic. You can drive as far as Stechelberg, the last town on the Lauterbrunnen Valley road, and switch to the cable car discussed above.

VISITOR INFORMATION   The **Mürren Tourist Information Bureau** is at the Sportzentrum (© **033/856-86-86**). There is no street plan—follow the clearly indicated signs to the various hotels and commercial establishments. The office is open Monday to Friday 9am to noon and 2 to 7pm, Saturday to Sunday 2 to 6:30pm.

WHERE TO STAY

Hotel Alpenruh   In the most congested, yet still charming, section of the village, the Alpenruh offers a plusher interior than its chalet-style facade implies. The old building was upgraded to three-star status without sacrificing any of its small-scale charm. Rooms have pine paneling and a mix of antique and contemporary furniture; most have a view of the Jungfrau. The tidy bathrooms are small, compact, and efficiently organized, each with a shower stall.

CH-3825 Mürren. © 033/856-99-99. Fax 033/856-99-98. www.muerren.ch/palace. 44 units. Summer 140SF–180SF ($91–$117) double; winter 155SF–215SF ($101–$140) double. Rates include buffet breakfast and dinner. Half board 35SF–45SF ($23–$29) per person extra. AE, DC, MC, V. **Amenities:** 3 restaurants; 2 bars; pool; Jacuzzi; sauna; limited room service; babysitting; coin-operated laundry and laundry service; dry cleaning. *In room:* TV, dataport, minibar, hair dryer.

Hotel Blumental *(Value*   Centrally located and redecorated and remodeled, this is a small chalet-type hotel, with stone masonry and wood-paneled public areas. Run by the von Allmen family, it offers a cozy atmosphere inspired by the nearby mountains. Several rooms have private balconies.

CH-3825 Mürren. © 033/855-18-26. Fax 033/855-36-86. www.muerren.ch/blumental. 16 units. 150SF–200SF ($98–$130) double. Rates include buffet breakfast. Half board 25SF ($16) extra. AE, DC, MC, V. **Amenities:** Restaurant; lounge; free admission to nearby Sports Centre; limited room service; laundry service. *In room:* TV, hair dryer, minibar.

Hotel Eiger ⭐ Founded in the 1920s and last renovated in 1994, this chalet is the longest-established hotel in Mürren. The public areas are warmly decorated, and many of the windows have panoramic views. Rooms are small, cozy, comfortable, and decorated in a typical alpine style. The hotel, managed by Annelis Sähli-von Allmen and family, lies across the street from the terminus of the cable car from Lauterbrunne.

CH-3825 Mürren. ⓒ 033/856-54-54. Fax 033/856-54-56. www.hoteleiger.com. 44 units. Summer 260SF–360SF ($169–$234) double, 480SF–600SF ($312–$390) suite; winter 280SF–400SF ($182–$260) double, 460SF–680SF ($299–$442) suite. Rates include breakfast. AE, DC, MC, V. Closed Easter to early June and mid-Sept to Dec 19. **Amenities:** Restaurant; bar; pool; sauna; limited room service; babysitting; laundry service; dry cleaning. *In room:* TV, dataport, hair dryer.

WHERE TO DINE

Eigerstübli ⭐ SWISS Here you'll find Mürren's best food, served in a festive ambience. The cuisine includes fondue as well as an international range of hearty specialties well suited to the alpine heights and chill. Try, for example, roast lamb shoulder with lentils, roast breast of duck with orange sauce, or—our favorite—poached filet of trout with a sauce flavored with alpine herbs. All main dishes may be ordered with rösti.

In the Hotel Eiger. ⓒ 033/856-54-54. Reservations recommended. Main courses 21SF–50SF ($14–$33). AE, DC, MC, V. Daily 11:30am–2pm and 6–9pm. Closed Easter to mid-June and mid-Sept to mid-Dec.

HITTING THE SLOPES & OTHER ACTIVE ENDEAVORS

There are miles of downhill runs in the area. Mürren, one of the finest ski resorts of Switzerland, provides access to the Schilthorn at 2,923m (9,745 ft.), the start of a 15km (9¼-mile) run that drops all the way to Lauterbrunnen. It also has one funicular railway, seven lifts, and two cable cars. A 1-day ski pass that includes the area around Schilthorn costs 55SF ($36); a 7-day pass goes for 260SF ($169). For cross-country skiers there's a 12km (7½-mile) track in the Lauterbrunnen Valley, 10 minutes by railway from Mürren.

The alpine **Sportzentrum (Sports Center),** in the middle of Mürren (ⓒ **033/856-86-86**), is one of the finest in the Bernese Oberland. The modern building has an indoor pool, a lounge, a snack bar, an outdoor skating rink, a tourist information office, and a children's playroom and library. There are facilities for squash, tennis, and curling. Hotel owners subsidize the operation, tacking the charges onto your hotel bill. Supplemental charges include 20SF to 30SF ($13–$20) per hour for tennis, 16SF ($10) per 45-minute session for squash, 16SF ($10) per 2 hours use of the sauna. The facility is usually open Monday to Friday from 9am to noon and 1 to 6:45pm, and from Christmas through April and July to mid-September, also on Saturday from 1 to 6:30pm and Sunday from 1 to 5:30pm; but check locally as these times can vary.

NEARBY EXCURSIONS

The famous **Mürren-Allmendhubel Cableway** leaves from the northwestern edge of Mürren. From the destination, there's a panoramic view of the Lauterbrunnen Valley as far as Wengen and Kleine Scheidegg. Between mid-June and late August the alpine meadows are covered with wildflowers. A walk in this hilly region might be a highlight of your trip to Switzerland. The cable car operates daily throughout the year from 8am to 5pm. However, there are annual closings for maintenance in May and November. It costs 12SF ($7.80) per person round-trip. For information, call ⓒ **033/826-00-07.**

The most popular excursion from Mürren is a cable-car ride to the **Schilthorn** ⭐⭐⭐, famous for its 360-degree view. The panorama extends from the Jura to the Black Forest, including the Eiger, Mönch, and Jungfrau. The Schilthorn is also called "Piz Gloria" after the James Bond film *On Her Majesty's Secret Service* (the most dramatic scenes in the movie were filmed here). Today, Piz Gloria is the name of the revolving restaurant on-site. The summit is the start of the world's longest downhill ski race. The cable car to Schilthorn leaves every 30 minutes, and the round-trip costs 94SF ($61). The journey to the top takes 20 minutes. For details, call ✆ **033/826-00-07.**

WENGEN ★★★

The Mönch, Jungfrau, and Eiger loom above this sunny resort, built on a sheltered terrace high above the Lauterbrunnen Valley, at about 1,250m (4,160 ft.). Wengen (pronounced *Ven*-ghen) is one of the more chic and better-equipped ski and mountain resorts in the Berner Oberland. It has 30 hotels in all price categories, as well as 500 apartments and chalets for rent.

In the 1830s, the International Lauberhorn Ski Race was established here. At that time, Wengen was a farm community, but the Brits popularized the resort after World War I. Parts of the area retain their rural charm, but the main street is filled with cafes, shops, and restaurants. No cars are allowed in Wengen, but the streets still bustle with service vehicles and electric luggage carts.

ESSENTIALS

GETTING THERE   By Train   Take the train from Interlaken East to Wengen. Departures are every 45 minutes 6:30am to 11:30pm, costing 14SF ($9.10) one-way. After a stopover at Wengen, the train goes on to Kleine Scheidegg and Jungfraujoch. For **rail information,** call ✆ **0900/300-300.**

By Car   If you're driving, head south from Interlaken toward Wilderswil, following the minor signposted road to Lauterbrunnen, where you'll find garages and open-air spaces for parking. You cannot drive to Wengen but must take the train (see above). You can park in one of the garages at Lauterbrunnen for 12SF ($7.80) a day. Trains from Lauterbrunnen to Wengen leave at the rate of one every 15 minutes from 6am to midnight, costing 6.20SF ($4.05) one-way.

VISITOR INFORMATION   There are no street names; hotels, restaurants, and other major establishments are signposted with directional signs, which make them relatively easy to find. The **Wengen Tourist Information Office** (✆ **033/ 855-14-14**), in the center of the resort, is open mid-June to mid-September and mid-December to Easter, Monday to Saturday 9am to noon and 2 to 5pm.

WHERE TO STAY

Hotel Eiger ★   Rustic timbers cover the walls and ceilings of this attractive hotel behind the cog-railway station. Karl Fuchs and his family offer spacious, attractive rooms with balconies. A modern dining room has views of the Jungfrau massif and the Lauterbrunnen Valley. Rooms have cozy, alpine styling, but bathrooms are small and cramped, each with a shower stall. In the lobby is an inviting sitting area with a fireplace.

CH-3823 Wengen. ✆ **800/528-1234** in the U.S. and Canada, or 033/856-05-05. Fax 033/856-05-06. www. eiger-wengen.ch. 33 units. Summer 228SF ($148) double; winter 302SF ($196) double. Rates include buffet breakfast. Half board 25SF ($16) per person extra. AE, DC, MC, V. Closed mid-Apr to June 1 and Nov. **Amenities:** Restaurant; bar; laundry service. *In room:* TV, dataport.

Hotel Regina ★★   Wengen's most time-honored hotel lies in an embellished Victorian elephant of a building with balconies and lots of charm. Guido Meyer has been known to arrange unusual concerts for his guests (once, during our stay, a group of Oklahoma high school students gave a concert on the front lawn).

One of the public rooms has a baronial carved-stone fireplace. The midsize to spacious bedrooms are comfortable and cozy, each well furnished and immaculately maintained. All units contain tidily kept bathrooms. Maintenance is high, as is the level of service.

CH-3823 Wengen. ℂ 033/856-58-58. Fax 033/855-15-74. www.wengen.com/hotel/regina. 90 units. Summer 320SF ($208) double; winter 450SF ($293) double. For a suite add 20SF ($13) per person. Rates include half board. AE, DC, MC, V. Closed Oct 15–Dec 15. **Amenities:** 2 restaurants; bar; health club; sauna; limited room service; babysitting; laundry service. *In room:* TV, dataport, hair dryer, minibar.

WHERE TO DINE

Hotel Hirschen Restaurant *Finds* SWISS   An alpine flavor permeates this tranquil retreat at the foot of the slopes. The rear dining room is decorated with hunting trophies, pewter, and wine racks. Johannes Abplanalp and his family offer a dinner special called Galgenspiess—filet of beef, veal, and pork flambéed at your table. Other dishes include filet of breaded pork; rump steak Café de Paris; and fondue Bacchus (in white-wine sauce), bourguignon (hot oil), or chinoise (hot bouillon). A hearty lunch is *winzerrösti,* consisting of country ham, cheese, and a fried egg with homemade rösti.

CH-3823 Wengen. ℂ 033/855-15-44. Reservations recommended. Main courses 12SF–47SF ($7.80–$31); fixed-price menu 42SF–71SF ($27–$46). MC, V. Mon and Wed–Fri 5–11pm; Sat–Sun 11:30am–2:30pm and 5–11pm (closed Mon in summer and Tues all year). Closed mid-Apr to May and late Sept to Dec 15.

EXPLORING THE AREA

The **ski area** around Wengen is highly developed, with both straight and serpentine trails carved into the sides of such sloping geological formations as Männlichen, Kleine Scheidegg, Lauberhorn, and Eigergletscher. A triumph of alpine engineering, the town and its region contain three mountain railways, two aerial cableways, one gondola, 31 lifts, and 250km (155 miles) of downhill runs. You'll also find a branch of the Swiss Ski School, more than 11km (6¾ miles) of trails for cross-country skiing, an indoor and outdoor skating rink, a curling hall, an indoor swimming pool, and a day nursery.

In summer, the district attracts hill climbers from all over Europe. **Hiking trails** are well maintained and carefully marked, with dozens of unusual detours to hidden lakes and panoramas.

NEARBY ATTRACTIONS

From Wengen and Grindelwald (see below), there are a number of excursions up and down the Lauterbrunnen Valley. You can visit **Trümmelbach Falls** ★★★, which plunges in five powerful cascades through a gorge. You can take an elevator built through the rock to a series of galleries (bring a raincoat). The last stop is at a wall where the upper fall descends. The falls can be visited from the end of May through June and in September and October, daily from 9am to 5pm; in July and August, daily from 9am to 5:30pm. They're closed during other months. Admission is 10SF ($6.50) for adults, 4SF ($2.60) for children 6 to 16, and free for children 5 and under. It takes about 45 minutes to reach the falls on foot. For information, call ℂ 033/855-32-32. A postal bus from Lauterbrunnen (only 15 min. from Wengen by train) stops at Trümmelbach Falls. It costs only 3SF ($1.95) for adults, 2SF ($1.30) for children, and departs once an hour from Lauterbrunnen. For information, call ℂ 033/828-70-38.

You might also want to visit the base of the **Staubbach Waterfall** ★★, which plunges nearly 300m (1,000 ft.) in a sheer drop over a rock wall in the valley above Lauterbrunnen. Lord Byron compared this waterfall to the "tail of the pale horse ridden by Death in the Apocalypse." Staubbach can be reached from the resort village of Lauterbrunnen, which lies only 15 minutes from Wengen by train (see "Essentials," above).

GRINDELWALD ✦✦✦

The "glacier village" of Grindelwald, both a summer and a winter resort, is set against a backdrop of the Wetterhorn and the towering north face of the Eiger. Grindelwald is surrounded with folkloric hamlets, swift streams, and as much alpine beauty as you're likely to find anywhere in Switzerland. It's also easier to reach from Interlaken than either Wengen or Mürren. Though at first the hiking options and cable-car networks might seem baffling, the tourist office can provide helpful maps and clear up any confusion.

ESSENTIALS

GETTING THERE   By Train   The **Berner Oberland Railway (BOB)** leaves from the Interlaken East station (trip time: 35 min.). Call ℭ **0900/300-300** for information.

By Car   Unlike Wengen and Mürren, Grindelwald is the only major resort in the Jungfrau region that can be reached by car. Because of its accessibility, it's often crowded with visitors, many of whom come just for the day. Take the Wilderswil road south from Interlaken and follow the signs all the way to Grindelwald.

VISITOR INFORMATION   The tourist office is at the **Sportszentrum,** on Hauptstrasse, CH-3818 Grindelwald (ℭ **033/854-12-12**), open July and August, Monday to Friday 8am to 7pm, Saturday 8am to 5pm, Sunday 9 to 11am and 3 to 5pm; September to June, Monday to Friday 8am to noon and 2 to 6pm, Saturday 8am to noon and 2 to 5pm. *Note:* The resort doesn't use street names or numbers; instead of street names, hotel direction signs are used to locate places. If you're booked into a hotel or tourist home in Grindelwald, request a pass at your hotel that will entitle you to many discounts, especially on mountain rides.

WHERE TO STAY

Grand Hotel Regina ✦✦✦   Across from the Grindelwald train station, this turn-of-the-19th-century hotel is part rustic, part urban slick. The facade of the oldest part has an imposing set of turrets with red-tile roofs. The large bedrooms, done in various styles, are comfortable and contain well-maintained bathrooms. These elegantly furnished rooms are your finest choice for a vacation here in either summer or winter. Most bedrooms enjoy panoramic views.

CH-3818 Grindelwald. ℭ **800/223-6800** in the U.S., or 033/854-86-00. Fax 033/854-86-88. www.grandregina.ch. 90 units. 430SF–540SF ($280–$351) double; from 640SF–820SF ($416–$533) suite. AE, DC, MC, V. Free parking outside, 17SF ($11) in garage. Closed mid-Oct to Dec 18. **Amenities:** 2 restaurants; 2 bars; 2 pools; 2 tennis courts; health club; sauna; salon; limited room service; massage; babysitting; laundry service. *In room:* TV, dataport, minibar.

Hotel Eiger   This hotel appears to be a collection of interconnected balconies, each on a different plane, angled toward the alpine sunshine and built of contrasting shades of white stucco and natural wood. The interior is attractive and unpretentious, with lots of warmly tinted wood, hanging lamps, and contrasting lights. The small to midsize bedrooms are comfortable, well furnished, and alpine cozy. All are equipped with tidily kept bathrooms. Maintenance is high, and the hotel staff is extremely inviting and hospitable.

CH-3818 Grindelwald. ℭ 033/844-31-31. Fax 033/856-05-06. www.eiger-grindelwald.ch. 50 units. Summer 270SF–300SF ($176–$195) double; winter 290SF–320SF ($189–$208) double. Rates include buffet breakfast.

Half board 30SF ($20) per person extra. AE, DC, MC, V. Free parking outdoors, 6SF–12SF ($3.90–$7.80) in garage. **Amenities:** 2 restaurants; 2 bars; exercise room; sauna; salon; babysitting; laundry service. *In room:* TV, dataport, minibar.

Hotel Hirschen *Value* In the three-star Hirschen, the Bleuer family offers one of the resort's best values. Each room is comfortable and well furnished with good beds and equipped with neatly kept showers.

CH-3818 Grindelwald. ✆ **033/854-84-84.** Fax 033/854-84-80. www.hirschen-grindelwald.ch. 28 units. 180SF–220SF ($117–$143) double. Rates include continental breakfast. Half board 30SF ($20) extra. AE, DC, MC, V. Free parking outside, 8SF ($5.20) in garage. Closed Nov–Dec 19. **Amenities:** Restaurant; bar; limited room service; laundry service; bowling alley. *In room:* TV, dataport.

WHERE TO DINE

Il Mercato ITALIAN/SWISS The decor is elegant and alpine, with Italian touches you might expect in the Ticino. The dining room's visual centerpiece is a large window with a sweeping view over the mountains. During warm weather, tables are set out on a terrace dotted with flowers. Menu items include virtually everything from the Italian repertoire, with an emphasis on cold-weather dishes from the Val d'Aosta (northern Italy's milk and cheese district). There is a tempting array of salads, pizzas, pastas, risottos, and grilled veal, beef, and chicken dishes, always with fresh ingredients.

In the Hotel Spinne. ✆ **033/854-88-88.** Reservations recommended. Main courses 14SF–49SF ($9.10–$32). AE, DC, MC, V. Daily 11am–2pm and 6:30–11pm. Closed Oct to mid-Dec.

Restaurant Français ★★ INTERNATIONAL This is the best restaurant in Grindelwald. Special buffets are a feature of the restaurant. You might be served an appetizer of game terrine, Grindelwald air-dried meat, or thinly sliced lamb carpaccio. Fish dishes might include poached filet of turbot served on zucchini and potato rounds with a yellow-red pepper sauce or fried filet of salmon with a truffle butter sauce. Main dishes are likely to include lamb entrecôte in a coating of peppercorns or breast of guinea fowl with red wine and prunes. The cooks really know their stuff, and their wine list is among the finest in the area.

In the Hotel Belvedere. ✆ **033/854-54-54.** Reservations recommended. Main courses 28SF–50SF ($18–$33); fixed-price menu 56SF–70SF ($36–$46). AE, DC, MC, V. Daily noon–1pm and 6:45–9pm.

SEEING THE GLACIERS

Adjacent to the base of the **Lower Grindelwald Glacier (Untere Gletscher)** ★★ is a sheltered observation gallery offering a look at the rock-strewn ravine formed by the glacier and its annual snowmelt. The half-mile gallery stretches past deeply striated rocks, which include formations of colored marble worn smooth by the glacier's erosion. Don't expect a view of the glacier from this point, as you'll have go to a higher altitude, at least in summer, to see the actual ice. The gallery is easy to reach on foot or by car from the center of Grindelwald. Yellow-sided buses labeled GLETSCHERSCHLUCHT depart from a point in front of Grindelwald's rail station at least four times a day, year-round, for the lower glacier and points beyond. Passage to the lower glacier costs 12SF ($7.55) each way, but since the distance from the center of Grindelwald is about 4km (2½ miles), in nice weather many hardy souls opt to trek across well-marked hiking trails.

HIKING & MOUNTAIN CLIMBING

Grindelwald and environs offer dozens of challenging paths and mountain trails that are well marked and maintained. Outdoor adventures range from an exhilarating ramble across the gentle incline of an alpine valley to a dangerous trek with ropes and pitons along the north face of Mount Eiger. The choice depends on your inclination, degree of experience, and mountaineering skills. Maps showing the paths, trails, and their various elevations are available at the tourist office.

From Grindelwald, you can reach the high-altitude plateau known as **First Mountain** 🚠🚠 at 2,168m (7,113 ft.) after a 30-minute ride on a six-passenger gondola ("bubble car"). The round-trip transport is 48SF ($31). You can stop at such intermediate stations as Bort and Grindel (a site that some locals refer to as Scheckfeld) on your way to **First Mountain terminal and sun terrace.** From First, where there are dining facilities, you'll have many hiking possibilities into the neighboring Bussalp or Grosse Scheidegg area. Also, from First, an hour's brisk hike will take you to the still high-altitude waters of **Lake Bachalp.** Buses depart from Grindelwald from both Bussalp and Grosse Scheidegg if you opt not to walk all the way back.

Faulhorn 🚠🚠, at 2,681m (8,796 ft.), is a historic vantage point with a panorama of untouched alpine beauty. Near the summit is the **Faulhorn Hotel** (© 033/853-27-13), which has been here for more than 150 years. Faulhorn is a 7-hour hike from Grindelwald. For a shorter climb, take either the bus to Bussalp, the cable car to First, or the train to Schynige Platte. From any of these intermediate points, climbers can continue their treks on to Faulhorn. Hikes from Bussalp take 2¾ hours; from First, 2½ hours; and from Schynige Platte, 4 hours.

Grosse Scheidegg 🚠, at 1,960m (6,434 ft.), is a famous pass between the Grindelwald and Rosenlaui valleys. You can hike here in 3 hours from Grindelwald or can take a 40-minute bus ride from Grindelwald to Grosse Scheidegg and begin hill walking at a point that's far from the village traffic and crowds. Round-trip bus passage from Grindelwald to Grosse Scheidegg is 34SF ($22).

SKIING

In winter, Grindelwald is one of the major ski resorts of Europe, perfect as a base for skiing in the Jungfrau ski region. It has 22 lifts, eight funiculars, a trio of cable cars, and more than 160km (100 miles) of downhill runs. Snowboarders and novice skiers are also welcome. It's a ski circus for all ages and various skills.

In the winter, skiers take the cableway to **Männlichen,** at 2,200m (7,335 ft.), which opens onto a panoramic vista of the treacherous Eiger. From here there is no direct run back to Wengen; however, skiers can enjoy an uninterrupted ski trail stretching 7.2km (4½ miles) to Grindelwald. The cost of the Mannlichen cable car (Grindelwald-Grund to Mannlichen) is 33SF ($21) each way, or 48SF ($31) round-trip. For information, call the departure point for the **Mannlichen Bahn** in Grindelwald (© 033/854-80-80).

KANDERSTEG 🚠

Between Grindelwald and Gstaad, Kandersteg is a popular resort at one of the southern points of the Berner Oberland. It's a tranquil and lovely mountain village with rust- and orange-colored rooftops and green Swiss meadows. The summer and winter resort is spread over 4km (2½ miles), so nothing is crowded. The village itself is at the foot of the 3,660m (12,000-ft.) Blumlisalp chain and provides access to six remote alpine hamlets.

Kandersteg developed as a resting point on the road to the Gemmi Pass, which long ago linked the Valais with the Berner Oberland. The village still has many old farmhouses and a tiny church from the 16th century.

ESSENTIALS

GETTING THERE **By Train** Kandersteg is at the northern terminus of the 14km (8¾-mile) Lötschberg Tunnel, which, ever since the beginning of World War I, has linked Bern with the Rhône Valley. The railroad that runs through the tunnel can transport cars. Trains leave every 30 minutes; no reservations are necessary. The resort is also served by the Bern-Lötschberg-Simplon railway. Call © 0900/300-300 for information. The station is in the center of town.

By Car Kandersteg is 43km (27 miles) southwest of Interlaken. Take N8 west to where the Kandersteg road then heads south into the mountains. The journey from Spiez to Kandersteg along a well-built road takes only 20 minutes.

VISITOR INFORMATION The **Kandersteg Tourist Office,** Hauptstrasse CH-3718 Kandersteg (© 033/675-80-80; www.kandersteg.ch), is open Monday through Friday from 8am to noon and 2 to 6pm. *Note:* In lieu of street names, directional signs are used. All guests who have a room in Kandersteg are given a **visitor's card,** entitling them to certain price reductions, including a discount on the town's network of cable cars.

WHERE TO STAY & DINE

Chalet-Hotel Adler ★ An open fire crackling in the foyer sets the tone at this cozy inn, a wood-sided chalet on the main street near the town center that was rebuilt in 2002. The fourth-generation owner, Andreas Fetzer, and his Finnish-born wife, Eija, offer comfortable pinewood-paneled rooms, some with Jacuzzis, balconies, or fireplaces. The **Adler-Bar** is a popular après-ski hangout.

CH-3718 Kandersteg. © 033/675-80-10. Fax 033/675-80-11. www.chalethotel.ch/ . 24 units. Feb–Mar and July–Sept 180SF–210SF ($117–$137) double; off season 170SF ($111) double. Rates include buffet breakfast. Half board 30SF ($20) per person extra. AE, DC, MC, V. Free parking. Closed Nov 22–Dec 27. **Amenities:** 2 restaurants; bar; exercise room; sauna; limited room service; laundry service. *In room:* TV, dataport, minibar, hair dryer.

OUTDOOR ACTIVITIES

Around Kandersteg is an extensive network of level footpaths and strategically located benches; these paths are open year-round. In summer, qualified riders in proper clothes can rent horses at **Royal Park Hotel** (© 033/675-88-88; www.royalkandersteg.com). In winter, the resort attracts cross-country skiers and downhill novices (top-speed skiers go elsewhere). It has a cable car, two chair-lifts, and four ski tows; the National Nordic Ski Center offers a ski-jumping station. The 2.5km (1½-mile) cross-country ski trail is floodlit in the evening. Other facilities include indoor and outdoor ice rinks.

EXCURSIONS NEARBY

The most popular excursion from Kandersteg is to **Oeschinensee (Lake Oeschinen)** ★★★, high above the village. The lake is surrounded by the snow-covered peaks of the Blümlisalp, towering 1,830m (6,000 ft.) above the extremely clear water. You can walk to it from the Victoria Hotel, or you can take a chairlift, costing 17SF ($11) round-trip or 12SF ($7.50) one-way, to the Oeschinen station. If you opt to walk, allow about 1½ hours, or 2 hours if you'd like to stroll. Many visitors who take the chairlift decide to hike back to Kandersteg. Be aware, however, of the steep downhill grade.

Another popular excursion is to **Klus Gorge** ★★. Park your car at the cable station's lower platform at Stock and walk 3km (1¾ miles) to the gorge, which was formed by the abrasive action of the Kander River. The rushing water creates a romantic, even primeval, setting. There's a tunnel over the gorge, but in winter, the access route is dangerous and icebound.

GSTAAD ✦✦

Against a backdrop of glaciers and mountain lakes, Gstaad is a haven for the rich and famous. Built at the junction of four quiet valleys near the southern tip of the Berner Oberland, Gstaad was once only a place to change horses on the grueling trip by carriage through the Berner Oberland. As the rail lines developed, it grew into a resort for the wealthy who flocked to the Palace Hotel, which promised the ultimate in luxury.

The town retains much of its late-19th-century charm. Some first-time visitors, however, say that the resort is a bore if you can't afford to stay at the Gstaad Palace or mingle with the stars in their private chalets. Yet the town has many moderately priced hotels, taverns, and guesthouses, with an allure of their own.

ESSENTIALS

GETTING THERE   By Train   About a dozen trains come into Gstaad every day from Interlaken (trip time: 30 min.) and Montreux (1⅓ hr.). Call ✆ **0900/ 300-300** for rail information.

By Car   From Spiez, follow Route 11 southwest to Gstaad; from Bulle, head south and then east on Route 11.

VISITOR INFORMATION   The **Gstaad-Saanenland Tourist Association,** CH-3780 Gstaad (✆ **033/748-81-81;** www.gstaad.ch), can help you find hotels, restaurants, and attractions. It's open Monday through Friday from 8am to noon and 1:30 to 6pm, and Saturday from 9am to noon only. *Note:* Some streets have names; others are placed outside street plans, but there are directional signs to lead you to hotels and restaurants.

WHERE TO STAY

Hostellerie Alpenrose ✦✦✦   For those who like the charm of a small inn, this is the preferred choice, the only Relais & Châteaux listing within 50km (30 miles). Its owner, Michel von Siebenthal, is a memorable host, setting the fashionable tone of the chalet, which is famous for its cuisine. The pine-paneled public areas are exquisitely decorated with rustic furnishings. Rooms are tastefully appointed and have mountain views and well-maintained bathrooms.

Saanenmoserstrasse, CH-3778 Schönried-Gstaad. ✆ 033/744-67-67. Fax 033/744-67-12. www.relaischateaux. fr. 19 units. Summer 380SF–490SF ($247–$319) double; winter 480SF–710SF ($312–$462) double. Rates include buffet breakfast. Half board 50SF ($33) per person extra. AE, DC, MC, V. Free parking. Closed Nov. **Amenities:** 2 restaurants; 2 bars; lounge; whirlpool; sauna; limited room service. *In room:* TV, minibar.

Hotel Olden ✦✦   This is a low-key and gracefully unpretentious hotel, a sort of Victorian country inn set amid a sometimes chillingly glamorous landscape. The facade is painted with regional floral designs and pithy bits of folk wisdom. The folkloric alpine-style rooms are very cozy, and have modern bathrooms.

Hauptstrasse, CH-3780 Gstaad. ✆ 033/744-34-44. Fax 033/744-61-64. www.hotelolden.com. 16 units. 280SF–400SF ($182–$260) double. Rates include continental breakfast. AE, DC, MC, V. Parking 30SF ($20). Closed late Apr to late May. **Amenities:** Restaurant; bar; limited room service; laundry service; dry cleaning. *In room:* TV, minibar.

Palace Hotel Gstaad ✦✦✦   This landmark hotel is on a wooded hill overlooking the center of Gstaad. It's one of the most sought-after luxury hideaways in the world, attracting corporation heads, film stars, jet-setters, and the titled. The nerve center of this chic citadel is an elegantly paneled main salon, with an eternal flame burning in the baronial stone fireplace. Rooms (some large enough for Elizabeth Taylor and all her husbands) are country deluxe with regional artifacts, cheerful print wallpaper, and rustic pine furnishings. Bathrooms are exceedingly luxurious and beautifully maintained.

CH-3780 Gstaad. ✆ 800/223-6800 in the U.S., or 033/748-50-50. Fax 033/748-50-01. www.palace.ch. 104 units. Summer 490SF–800SF ($319–$520) double, from 1,720SF ($1,118) suite; winter 610SF–1,350SF ($397–$878) double, from 2,070SF–2,440SF ($1,346–$1,586) suite. AE, DC, MC, V. Free parking outside, 20SF ($13) in garage. Closed end of Mar to mid-June and late Sept to shortly before Christmas (dates vary). **Amenities:** 5 restaurants; 2 bars; nightclub; 2 pools; tennis courts; health club; sauna; salon; 24-hr. room service; massage; babysitting; laundry service/dry cleaning. *In room:* TV, dataport, minibar, hair dryer, safe.

WHERE TO DINE
Olden Restaurant ★★ MEDITERRANEAN/ITALIAN   Although there are grander restaurants in Gstaad, and dining rooms serving a more haute cuisine, the Olden remains our most satisfying choice year after year after countless visits. The service is formal and refined, the food as good as, or better than, anything in the area. The always tempting menu might include smoked salmon, fresh goose-liver terrine, shrimp bisque with green peppercorns, house-style tagliatelle, raclette, Scottish lamb, or sea bass with olives, potatoes, tomatoes, and onions.

In the Hotel Olden, Hauptstrasse. ✆ 033/744-34-44. Reservations recommended. Main courses 25SF–70SF ($16–$46). AE, DC, MC, V. Tues–Sun noon–2:30pm and 6:30–10:30pm. Closed mid-Apr to mid-May and 2 weeks in Nov.

Restaurant Chesery ★★★ FRENCH/SWISS   One of Switzerland's 10 best restaurants perches at an elevation of 1,100m (3,600 ft.). Natural stone floors and polished pine walls pair naturally with a menu that changes daily but is always based on the freshest of ingredients—grouse from Scotland, Charolais beef from France, truffles from Umbria. Taste the salt-crusted sea bass with wild rice or chicken Houban (a special breed from France), each a sensation. In the basement bar, **Casino,** a piano player entertains nightly; the bar is open from 6pm to around 3am, when the last ski bunny departs.

Lauenenstrasse. ✆ 033/744-24-51. Reservations required. Main courses 40SF–68SF ($26–$44); fixed-price lunch 52SF–65SF ($34–$42); fixed-price dinner 110SF–152SF ($72–$99). AE, DC, MC, V. Tues–Sun 11:30am–2:30pm and 7pm–midnight. Closed mid-Oct to mid-Dec, Easter to June 10, and in winter (Tues–Fri) for lunch.

SKIING & HIKING
The resort is rich in **sports facilities.** Many skiers stay in Gstaad and go to one of the nearby ski resorts in the daytime. Cable cars take passengers to altitudes of 1,500m and 3,000m (5,000 ft. and 10,000 ft.)—at the higher altitude there's skiing even in summer. Other facilities include tennis courts, heated indoor and outdoor pools, and some 320km (200 miles) of hiking trails. Many of these scenic trails are possible to walk or hike year-round (the tourist office will advise). The **Allianz Suisse Open** tennis tournament (http://swissopengstaad.ch), held in Gstaad the second week in July, is the most important tennis event in Switzerland.

Skiers setting off from Gstaad have access to 70 lifts, mountain railroads, and gondolas. The altitude of Gstaad's highest skiable mountain is 2,000m (6,550 ft.), with a vertical drop of 1,084m (3,555 ft.). Most beginner and intermediate runs are east of the village in **Eggli,** a sunny, south-facing ski area that's reached by cable car.

Wispellan-Sanetch is good for afternoon skiing, and has lots of runs down to the village. At the summit is the Glacier des Diablerets, at 3,000m (9,900 ft.). **Wasserngrat,** prized by skilled skiers for its powder skiing on steep slopes, is reached from the south side of the resort.

Index

Not just 4 anoraks

...but 3 duffel coats
59 gorgeous models
5 Tube simulators
4 dead man's handles
3 mucky miners
and 1 brilliant time had by all

... be *moved*

kidsgo**FREE**

 London's Transport Museum
Covent Garden Piazza

www.ltmuseum.co.uk

Great Trips Like Great Days Begin with a Plan

FranklinCovey and Frommer's Bring You *Frommer's Favorite Places*® Planner

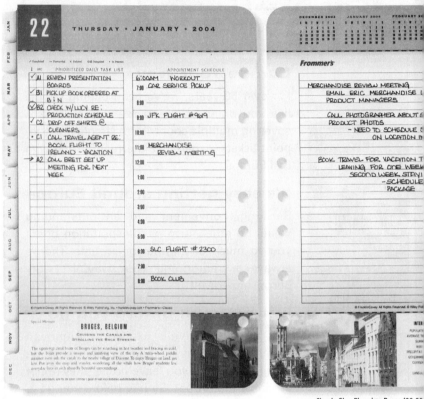

Classic Size Planning Pages $39.95

The planning experts at FranklinCovey have teamed up with the travel experts at Frommer's. The result is a full-year travel-themed planner filled with rich images and travel tips covering fifty-two of Frommer's Favorite Places.

- Each week will make you an expert about an intriguing corner of the world
- New facts and tips every day
- Beautiful, full-color photos of some of the most beautiful places on earth
- Proven planning tools from FranklinCovey for keeping track of tasks, appointments, notes, address/phone numbers, and more

Save 15%

when you purchase Frommer's Favorite Places travel-themed planner and a binder.

Order today before you next big trip.

www.franklincovey.com/frommers
Enter promo code 12252 at checkout for discount. Offer expires June 1, 2005.

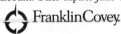

Frommer's is a trademark of Arthur Frommer.

FROMMER'S® COMPLETE TRAVEL GUIDES

Alaska
Alaska Cruises & Ports of Call
American Southwest
Amsterdam
Argentina & Chile
Arizona
Atlanta
Australia
Austria
Bahamas
Barcelona, Madrid & Seville
Beijing
Belgium, Holland & Luxembourg
Bermuda
Boston
Brazil
British Columbia & the Canadian
  Rockies
Brussels & Bruges
Budapest & the Best of Hungary
Calgary
California
Canada
Cancún, Cozumel & the Yucatán
Cape Cod, Nantucket & Martha's
  Vineyard
Caribbean
Caribbean Cruises & Ports of Call
Caribbean Ports of Call
Carolinas & Georgia
Chicago
China
Colorado
Costa Rica
Cuba
Denmark
Denver, Boulder & Colorado
  Springs
England
Europe
Europe by Rail
European Cruises & Ports of Call

Florence, Tuscany & Umbria
Florida
France
Germany
Great Britain
Greece
Greek Islands
Halifax
Hawaii
Hong Kong
Honolulu, Waikiki & Oahu
India
Ireland
Israel
Italy
Jamaica
Japan
Kauai
Las Vegas
London
Los Angeles
Maryland & Delaware
Maui
Mexico
Montana & Wyoming
Montréal & Québec City
Munich & the Bavarian Alps
Nashville & Memphis
Newfoundland & Labrador
New England
New Mexico
New Orleans
New York City
New York State
New Zealand
Northern Italy
Norway
Nova Scotia, New Brunswick &
  Prince Edward Island
Oregon
Ottawa
Paris

Peru
Philadelphia & the Amish
  Country
Portugal
Prague & the Best of the Czech
  Republic
Provence & the Riviera
Puerto Rico
Rome
San Antonio & Austin
San Diego
San Francisco
Santa Fe, Taos & Albuquerque
Scandinavia
Scotland
Seattle
Shanghai
Sicily
Singapore & Malaysia
South Africa
South America
South Florida
South Pacific
Southeast Asia
Spain
Sweden
Switzerland
Texas
Thailand
Tokyo
Toronto
USA
Utah
Vancouver & Victoria
Vermont, New Hampshire &
  Maine
Vienna & the Danube Valley
Virgin Islands
Virginia
Walt Disney World® & Orlando
Washington, D.C.
Washington State

FROMMER'S® DOLLAR-A-DAY GUIDES

Australia from $50 a Day
California from $70 a Day
England from $75 a Day
Europe from $70 a Day
Florida from $70 a Day
Hawaii from $80 a Day

Ireland from $80 a Day
Italy from $70 a Day
London from $90 a Day
New York from $90 a Day
Paris from $90 a Day
San Francisco from $70 a Day

Washington, D.C. from $80 a
  Day
Portable London from $90 a Day
Portable New York City from $90
  a Day
Portable Paris from $90 a Day

FROMMER'S® PORTABLE GUIDES

Acapulco, Ixtapa & Zihuatanejo
Amsterdam
Aruba
Australia's Great Barrier Reef
Bahamas
Berlin
Big Island of Hawaii
Boston
California Wine Country
Cancún
Cayman Islands
Charleston
Chicago
Disneyland®
Dominican Republic
Dublin

Florence
Frankfurt
Hong Kong
Las Vegas
Las Vegas for Non-Gamblers
London
Los Angeles
Los Cabos & Baja
Maine Coast
Maui
Miami
Nantucket & Martha's Vineyard
New Orleans
New York City
Paris

Phoenix & Scottsdale
Portland
Puerto Rico
Puerto Vallarta, Manzanillo &
  Guadalajara
Rio de Janeiro
San Diego
San Francisco
Savannah
Vancouver
Vancouver Island
Venice
Virgin Islands
Washington, D.C.
Whistler

FROMMER'S® NATIONAL PARK GUIDES

Algonquin Provincial Park
Banff & Jasper
Family Vacations in the National
   Parks

Grand Canyon
National Parks of the American
   West
Rocky Mountain

Yellowstone & Grand Teton
Yosemite & Sequoia/Kings
   Canyon
Zion & Bryce Canyon

FROMMER'S® MEMORABLE WALKS

Chicago
London

New York
Paris

San Francisco

FROMMER'S® WITH KIDS GUIDES

Chicago
Las Vegas
New York City

Ottawa
San Francisco
Toronto

Vancouver
Walt Disney World® & Orlando
Washington, D.C.

SUZY GERSHMAN'S BORN TO SHOP GUIDES

Born to Shop: France
Born to Shop: Hong Kong,
   Shanghai & Beijing

Born to Shop: Italy
Born to Shop: London

Born to Shop: New York
Born to Shop: Paris

FROMMER'S® IRREVERENT GUIDES

Amsterdam
Boston
Chicago
Las Vegas
London

Los Angeles
Manhattan
New Orleans
Paris
Rome

San Francisco
Seattle & Portland
Vancouver
Walt Disney World®
Washington, D.C.

FROMMER'S® BEST-LOVED DRIVING TOURS

Austria
Britain
California
France

Germany
Ireland
Italy
New England

Northern Italy
Scotland
Spain
Tuscany & Umbria

THE UNOFFICIAL GUIDES®

Beyond Disney
Central Italy
Chicago
Cruises
Disneyland®
England
Florida
Florida with Kids
Inside Disney

Hawaii
Las Vegas
London
Maui
Mexico's Best Beach Resorts
Mini Las Vegas
Mini-Mickey
New Orleans
New York City

Paris
San Francisco
Skiing & Snowboarding in the
   West
Walt Disney World®
Walt Disney World® for
   Grown-ups
Walt Disney World® with Kids
Washington, D.C.

SPECIAL-INTEREST TITLES

Athens Past & Present
Cities Ranked & Rated
Frommer's Best Day Trips from London
Frommer's Caribbean Hideaways
Frommer's China: The 50 Most Memorable Trips
Frommer's Exploring America by RV
Frommer's Gay & Lesbian Europe
Frommer's Best RV and Tent Campgrounds
   in the U.S.A.

Frommer's Road Atlas Europe
Frommer's Road Atlas France
Frommer's Road Atlas Ireland
Frommer's Wonderful Weekends from
   New York City
The New York Times' Guide to Unforgettable
   Weekends
Retirement Places Rated
Rome Past & Present

Travel Tip: He who finds the best hotel deal has more to spend on facials involving knobbly vegetables.

Hello, the Roaming Gnome here. I've been nabbed from the garden and taken round the world. The people who took me are so terribly clever. They find the best offerings on Travelocity. For very little cha-ching. And that means I get to be pampered and exfoliated till I'm pink as a bunny's doodah.

travelocity

1-888-TRAVELOCITY / travelocity.com / America Online Keyword: Travel

Travel Tip: Make sure there's customer service for any change of plans — involving friendly natives, for example.

One can plan and plan, but if you don't book with the right people you can't seize le moment and canoodle with the poodle named Pansy. I, for one, am all for fraternizing with the locals. Better yet, if I need to extend my stay and my gnome nappers are willing, it can all be arranged through the 800 number at, oh look, how convenient, the lovely company coat of arms.

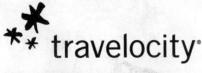